ECONOMICS

ECONOMICS

Eleventh edition

John Sloman

The Economics Network, University of Bristol

Visiting Professor, University of the West of England

Dean Garratt

Aston Business School

Aston University

Jon Guest

Aston Business School

Aston University

Harlow, England • London • New York • Boston • San Francisco • Toronto • Sydney
Dubai • Singapore • Hong Kong • Tokyo • Seoul • Taipei • New Delhi
Cape Town • São Paulo • Mexico City • Madrid • Amsterdam • Munich • Paris • Milan

PEARSON EDUCATION LIMITED
KAO Two
KAO Park
Harlow CM17 9NA
United Kingdom
Tel: +44 (0)1279 623623
Web: www.pearson.com/uk

Previously published 1991, 1994, 1995, 1997, 1998, 2000, 2003, 2006, 2009 (print); 2012, 2015, 2018 (print and electronic)
Eleventh edition published 2022 (print and electronic)

ISBN: 978-1-292-40533-9 (print)
978-1-292-40539-1 (PDF)
978-1-292-40540-7 (ePub)

British Library Cataloguing-in-Publication Data
A catalogue record for the print edition is available from the British Library

Library of Congress Cataloging-in-Publication Data
Names: Sloman, John, 1947- author. | Garratt, Dean, 1970- author. | Guest, Jon, author.
Title: Economics / John Sloman, The Economics Network, University of Bristol Visiting Professor, University of the West of England, Dean Garratt, Aston Business School, Aston University, Jon Guest, Aston Business School, Aston University,
Description: Eleventh edition. | New York, NY : Pearson Education, 2022. | Revised edition of Economics, [2017] | Includes bibliographical references and index. | Summary: "Now in its 10th edition, Economics by Sloman, Garratt & Guest is known and loved for its active learning, student-friendly approach and unrivalled lecturer and student support. Ithas been specially updated for 2020/21 to take into account the latest developments in the global economy, including the effects of the Covid-19pandemic"-- Provided by publisher.
Identifiers: LCCN 2021040149 (print) | LCCN 2021040150 (ebook) | ISBN 9781292405339 (paperback) | ISBN 9781292405407 (ebook) | ISBN 9781292405391 (adobe pdf)
Subjects: LCSH: Economics.
Classification: LCC HB171.5 .S635 2022 (print) | LCC HB171.5 (ebook) | DDC 330--dc23
LC record available at https://lccn.loc.gov/2021040149
LC ebook record available at https://lccn.loc.gov/2021040150

10 9 8 7 6 5 4 3 2 1
26 25 24 23 22

Cover design by Kelly Miller
Cover image © w3DProfi / Shutterstock

Print edition typeset in 8/12 pt Stone Serif ITC Pro by Straive
Printed in Slovakia by Neografia

NOTE THAT ANY PAGE CROSS REFERENCES REFER TO THE PRINT EDITION

About the Authors

John Sloman is Visiting Fellow at the University of Bristol and Associate of the Economics Network (www.economicsnetwork.ac.uk), a UK-wide organisation, where, until his retirement in 2012, he was Director. The Economics Network is based at the University of Bristol and provides a range of services designed to promote and share good practice in learning and teaching economics. The Network is supported by grants from the Royal Economic Society, the Scottish Economic Society and university economic departments and units from across the UK.

John is also Visiting Professor at the University of the West of England, Bristol, where, from 1992 to 1999, he was Head of School of Economics. He taught at UWE until 2007.

John has taught a range of courses, including economic principles on Economics, Social Science and Business Studies degrees, development economics, comparative economic systems, intermediate macroeconomics and managerial economics. He has also taught economics on various professional courses.

John is the co-author with Dean Garratt of *Essentials of Economics* (Pearson Education, 8th edition 2019); with Dean Garratt, Elizabeth Jones of the University of Warwick and Jon Guest of *Economics for Business* (Pearson Education, 8th edition 2019); and with Elizabeth Jones of *Essential Economics for Business* (Pearson Education, 6th edition 2020). Translations or editions of the various books are available for a number of different countries with the help of co-authors around the world.

John is very interested in promoting new methods of teaching economics, including group exercises, experiments, role playing, computer-aided learning and the use of audience response systems and podcasting in teaching. He has organised and spoken at conferences for both lecturers and students of economics throughout the UK and in many other countries.

As part of his work with the Economics Network he has contributed to its two sites for students and prospective students of economics: Studying Economics (www.studyingeconomics.ac.uk/) and Why Study Economics? (http://whystudyeconomics.ac.uk).

From March to June 1997, John was a visiting lecturer at the University of Western Australia. In July and August 2000, he was again a visiting lecturer at the University of Western Australia and also at Murdoch University in Perth.

In 2007, John received a Lifetime Achievement Award as 'outstanding teacher and ambassador of economics', presented jointly by the Higher Education Academy, the Government Economic Service and the Scottish Economic Society.

Dr Dean Garratt is a Senior Teaching Fellow at Aston Business School having previously been a Principal Lecturer at Nottingham Business School. Dean teaches economics at a variety of levels, including modules in macroeconomics and economic principles for business and management students.

He is passionate about encouraging students to communicate economics more intuitively, to deepen their interest in economics and to apply economics to a range of issues.

Earlier in his career Dean worked as an economic assistant at both HM Treasury and at the Council of Mortgage Lenders (now known as UK Finance). While at these institutions he was researching and briefing on a variety of issues relating to the household sector and to the housing and mortgage markets.

Dean is a Senior Fellow of the Higher Education Academy and an Associate of the Economics Network which aims to promote high-quality teaching practice. He has been involved in several projects promoting a problem-based learning (PBL) approach in the teaching of economics.

In 2006, Dean was awarded the Outstanding Teaching Prize by the Economics Network. The award recognises exemplary teaching practice that deepens and inspires interest in economics. In 2013, he won the student-nominated Nottingham Business School teacher of the year award.

Dean has worked as an academic assessor for the Government Economic Service (GES) helping to assess candidates at Economic Assessment Centres (EACs). He has also run sessions on HM Treasury's Graduate Development Programme (GDP) on principles in policy making and contemporary developments in macroeconomics.

Outside of work, Dean is an avid watcher of many sports. Having been born in Leicester, he is a season ticket holder at both Leicester City Football Club and Leicestershire County Cricket Club.

Jon Guest is a Senior Teaching Fellow at Aston Business School and a Teaching Associate at Warwick Business School. He joined Aston University in September 2017 having previously been a Senior Lecturer at Nottingham Business School, a Principal Teaching Fellow at Warwick Business School and a Senior Lecturer at Coventry University.

Jon has taught on a range of courses including Principles of Microeconomics, Intermediate Microeconomics, Economic Issues and Behavioural Economics. He has also taught economics on various professional courses for the Government Economic Service and HM Treasury.

Jon has worked on developing teaching methods that promote a more active learning environment in the classroom. In particular, he has published journal articles and carried out a number of funded research projects on the impact of games and experiments on student learning. These include an online version of the TV show *Deal or No Deal* and games that involve students acting as buyers and sellers in the classroom. He has recently included a series of short videos on economics topics and implemented elements of the flipped classroom into his teaching. Jon is also interested in innovative ways of providing students with feedback on their work.

Through his work as an Associate of the Economics Network, Jon has run sessions on innovative pedagogic practices at a number of universities and major national events. He is also an academic assessor for the Economics Assessment Centres run by the Government Economic Service. This involves interviewing candidates and evaluating their ability to apply economic reasoning to a range of policy issues. He has also acted as an External Examiner for a number of UK universities.

The quality of his teaching was formally recognised when he became the first Government Economic Service Approved Tutor in 2005 and won the student-nominated award from the Economics Network in the same year. Jon was awarded the prestigious National Teaching Fellowship by the Higher Education Academy in 2011.

Jon is a regular contributor and editor of the *Economic Review* and is a co-author of the 8th edition of the textbook *Economics for Business*. He has published chapters in books on the economics of sport and regularly writes cases for the 'Sloman in the News' website. He has also published research on the self-evaluation skills of undergraduate students.

Outside of work Jon is a keen runner and has completed the London Marathon. However, he now has to accept that he is slower than both of his teenage sons – Dan and Tom. He is also a long-suffering supporter of Portsmouth Football Club.

Brief Contents

Part E FOUNDATIONS OF MACROECONOMICS

Part F MACROECONOMIC MODELS, THEORIES AND POLICY

Part G THE WORLD ECONOMY

Contents

Part E FOUNDATIONS OF MACROECONOMICS

Part F MACROECONOMIC MODELS, THEORIES AND POLICY

Supporting Resources

Visit go.pearson.com/uk/sloman to find valuable online resources:

MyLab Economics

For students

- Study guide with exercises, quizzes and tests, arranged chapter by chapter
- Multiple-choice questions to test your learning
- Audio animations to illustrate key economic concepts and models
- Link to Sloman Economics News site
- Online textbook chapters
- Link to additional resources on the companion website (listed below)

For lecturers

- MyLab's gradebook, which automatically tracks student performance and progress
- Extensive test bank, allowing you to generate your own tests, assessments and homework assignment
- Access to a wealth of lecturer resources on the companion website (listed below)

Companion website

For students

- Answers to all in-chapter questions in the book
- Over 220 case studies with questions and activities, organised by chapter
- Over 130 audio animations explaining all the key models used in the book
- Regularly updated and searchable blog, featuring current news items with discussion of the issue, questions and links to articles and data
- Hotlinks to 284 sites relevant to the study of economics
- Maths case studies illustrating the key mathematical concepts used in the book

For lecturers

- Comprehensive range of PowerPoint slides, including figures and tables from the book, as well as animated slide shows for use in lectures, organised chapter by chapter. There are various versions of these slide shows, some including questions that can be used with 'clickers', phones or other smart devices
- Animated key models in PowerPoint
- Teaching and learning case studies, discussing ways of increasing student engagement and improving student learning
- 20 workshops in Word for use in large or small classes, plus a guide on ways of using the workshops. These can easily be customised to suit lecturers' needs. Answers are given to all the workshop questions
- Over 220 case studies with questions and student activities (as on student website). Answers to all questions in case studies
- Answers to all questions in the book (end-of-chapter questions, box questions and in-text questions) and to questions in maths case studies

Also: The companion website provides the following features:

- Search tool to help locate specific items of content
- Online help and support to assist with website usage and troubleshooting

For more information please contact your local Pearson Education sales representative or visit go.pearson.com/uk/sloman.

Preface

A NOTE TO THE STUDENT FROM THE AUTHORS

Economics affects all our lives. This has been dramatically brought home to us by the coronavirus pandemic. Governments imposed lockdowns and other restrictions. Many people lost their jobs or were put on furlough. Firms went out of business. Working lives changed and many switched to working online. Governments spent vast amounts of money, thereby increasing their debts. Later they tried to find ways of clawing down these debts, whether by raising taxes or cutting government expenditure.

We are all faced with economic questions and decisions. As consumers we try to make the best of our limited incomes. As workers – or future workers – we take our place in the job market. As citizens of a country our lives are affected by the decisions of our government and other policy makers: decisions over taxes, decisions over spending on health and education, decisions on interest rates, decisions that affect unemployment, inflation and growth. As dwellers on the planet Earth we are affected by the economic decisions of each other: the air we breathe, the water we drink and the environment we leave to our children are all affected by the economic decisions taken by the human race.

Economics thus deals with some of the most challenging issues we face. It is this that still excites us about economics after many years of teaching the subject. We hope that some of this excitement rubs off on you.

The first ten editions of *Economics* have been widely used in Britain and throughout the world. Like them, this eleventh edition is suitable for all students of economics at first-year degree level, A level or on various professional courses where a broad grounding in both principles and applications is required. It is structured to be easily understood by those of you who are new to the subject, with various sections and boxes that can be left out on first reading or on shorter courses; yet it also has sufficient depth to challenge those of you who have studied the subject before, with starred sections (appearing on a grey background) and starred case studies that will provide much that is new. There are also optional short mathematical sections for those of you studying a more quantitatively focused course.

The book gives a self-contained introduction to the world of economics and is thus ideal for those who will not study the subject beyond introductory level. But by carefully laying a comprehensive foundation and by the inclusion of certain materials in starred sections that bridge the gap between introductory and second-level economics, it provides the necessary coverage for those of you going on to specialise in economics.

The book looks at the world in the 2020s. Despite huge advances in technology and despite the comfortable lives led by many people in the industrialised world, we still suffer from unemployment, poverty and inequality, and in many countries (the UK included) the gap between rich and poor has grown much wider; our environment is polluted and the world is facing a climate emergency; our economy still goes through periodic recessions; conflict and disagreement often dominate over peace and harmony.

In today's world there are many challenges that face us, including:

- A growing interdependence of the economies of the world, with a seemingly inexorable process of 'globalisation', which links us all through a web of telecommunications and international trade into a world of Amazon, Facebook, Coca-Cola, Nike trainers, Google, Netflix and the English Premier League.
- Coping with the effects of the coronavirus (COVID-19) pandemic and its aftermath.
- New challenges for the UK now it has left the EU.
- A rise in populism as the lower paid and unemployed see their incomes stagnating while the wealthy get richer. This has led to many people calling for policies to protect their jobs and communities from cheap imports.
- Large-scale migration of people across and within continents placing pressures on resources, but also creating new economic opportunities.
- Evidence that economic problems spread like a contagion around the world, tying domestic economic growth to global events.
- The effects of financialisation, by which we mean the increasing economic importance of the financial sector,

and its impact on the financial health of people, businesses and governments as well as its potential to destabilise economies.

- The continuing hangover from the turmoil on international financial markets that culminated in the banking crisis of 2007–8, with many countries today still trying to tackle high levels of public and private debt, made worse by government spending to mitigate the effects of the COVID-19 pandemic.
- Rapid economic growth of some developing countries, such as India and China, which are increasingly influential in the global economy.
- A move away from the ideological simplicity of a 'free-market' solution to all economic problems.
- An EU struggling to reform its institutions and processes and to stimulate economic growth.
- An ever-deepening crisis for many of the poorest developing countries, often ravaged by disease, conflict and famines, and seemingly stuck in a cycle of poverty.
- A world struggling to tackle climate change and cope with its economic, social and ecological consequences.

Economists are called on to offer solutions to these and many other problems. We shall be seeing what solutions economists can offer as the book progresses.

But despite our changing environment, there are certain economic fundamentals that do not change. Although there are disagreements among economists – and there are plenty – there is a wide measure of agreement on how to analyse these fundamentals.

Critical thinking and employability

When you are approaching graduation and start applying for jobs, you will need to demonstrate to potential employers that you have the range of skills necessary for analysing and solving problems and for communicating ideas and solutions to colleagues and clients. This requires the ability to think critically and to apply core concepts and ideas to new situations. Universities recognise this and 'employability' is a key objective of courses nowadays.

Employability is a core focus of this book. Critical thinking is developed through questions positioned throughout the text to encourage you to reflect on what you have just read and thereby improve and deepen your learning. Answers to these questions are freely available on the website to enable you to check your progress. Critical thinking is also developed through the use of Boxes of case studies and applications occurring several times in each chapter. These apply the economics you're learning to a variety of real-world issues and data. There are many additional case studies with questions on the student website.

If your lecturer recommends the use of MyEconLab to accompany the text, you will find there large banks of additional questions and the ability to monitor your progress. These questions enable you to reflect on your learning and on where additional work is required.

Critical thinking is also encouraged through the use of 15 'threshold concepts'. These are core ideas and concepts that recur throughout economics. Understanding and being able to apply these core economic concepts helps you to 'think like an economist' and to relate the different parts of the subject to each other. An icon appears in the margin wherever the concept recurs so that you can easily recognise its use in a new context.

In addition there are 40 'key ideas' that encourage you to relate new material to a toolkit of ideas. Again, there are icons in the margin to help you identify the relevant idea.

The whole way through the book, you are encouraged to reflect on your learning, to apply it to the real world and to use real-world data to make sense of economic issues and problems.

In addition to the book, there is a news blog with news items added several times per month. Each blog post discusses economic issues in the news and relates these news items to key economic concepts and theories. Links are given to a range of articles, videos, podcasts, data and reports and each blog post finishes with a set of discussion questions. You can access the blog from the book's website at go.pearson.com/uk/sloman. Archived articles go back many months. You can also search the news articles by key word, chapter of this book or by month. Again, the use of real-world news topics, questions and data helps you apply the theories and ideas you will learn in this book and develop these all-important critical thinking skills that are so central to employability.

In terms of employability, employees who can think flexibly and apply concepts and theories in new and perhaps strange situations to analyse and solve problems will be much more valuable to their employer. This book helps you to develop these skills. What is more, the use of data in the book and in the blogs and other web resources, and the hyperlinks in the e-text to data sources and relevant articles, will allow you to gain experience in using evidence to support and assess arguments.

Employers value these problem-solving skills. Indeed, they like to employ graduates with an economics degree, or some element of economics in their degree, because of the skills you will develop. And it's not just for jobs as economists, but for a large number of professions where studying economics is seen to equip you with a valuable set of skills that are transferable to a range of non-economics situations.

We hope that this book will give you an enjoyable introduction to the economist's world and that it will equip you with the tools to understand and criticise the economic policies that others pursue.

Good luck and have fun.

John, Dean and Jon

TO LECTURERS AND TUTORS

In the light of the financial crisis and the struggle of many countries to tackle its aftermath, there has been much soul-searching amongst economists about the appropriateness of the models we use and what should be taught to our students. These concerns were debated at an international conference at the Bank of England in 2012. One outcome of this was the publication of a book, *What's the Use of Economics?*[1] This considers how undergraduate courses could be reformed to meet the needs of employers and how economic models and syllabuses could be revised to reflect the real world and to provide a foundation for devising effective economic policy. A second, follow-up conference, *Revisiting the State of Economics Education*, took place at the Bank of England in 2015 and the debate continues.[2]

We have attempted to address these concerns in the past three editions of this book and have gone further still in this new edition. In particular, we have incorporated recent developments in macroeconomics, including stressing the importance of balance sheets, credit cycles, financial instability and systemic risk, the increased use of the *DAD*/*DAS* framework and the integration of the expectations-augmented Phillips curve and the *IS*/*MP* model. But these have been treated at a level wholly suitable for first-year students.

We have also given further weight to behavioural economics in analysing the behaviour of both consumers, firms and workers. In particular, there is more detailed discussion of loss aversion and the endowment effect, present bias and self-control issues, reference points and biases when making decisions under conditions of uncertainty. Indeed, Chapter 5 on behavioural economics has been completely reworked for this edition. More weight is given to the importance of institutional structures and culture and we have also strengthened microeconomic analysis in several places, such as game theory and price discrimination.

We have also thoroughly revised the applied chapters and sections to reflect changes in policies. For example, we have included the implications of the Brexit vote and the UK's subsequent exit from the EU and also of the Trump and Biden administrations' policies in several parts of the book.

In addition, we show how many of the theories developed to explain the problems that existed at the time and how they have evolved to reflect today's issues. We have thus continued to emphasise the link between the history of economic thought and economic history.

1 Diane Coyle (ed.), *What's the Use of Economics?* London Publishing Partnership (2012).

2 Peter Day, 'Are economics degrees fit for purpose?', *BBC News* (5 February 2016).

This new edition also retains many of the popular features of the previous edition:

- A style that is direct and to the point, with the aim all the time to provide maximum clarity. There are numerous examples to aid comprehension.
- All economic terms highlighted in the text where they first appear and defined at the foot of that page. Each term is also highlighted in the index, so that the student can simply look up a given definition as required. By defining them on the page where they appear, the student can also see the terms used in context in the text.
- Key ideas highlighted and explained when they first appear. There are 40 of these ideas, which are fundamental to the study of economics. Students can see them recurring throughout the book, and an icon appears in the margin to refer back to the page where the idea first appears.
- Fifteen 'threshold concepts'. Understanding and being able to relate and apply these core economic concepts helps students to 'think like an economist' and to relate the different parts of the subject to each other. Again, an icon appears in the margin wherever the concept recurs.
- A wealth of applied material in boxes (172 in all), making learning more interesting for students and, by relating economics to the real world, bringing the subject alive. The boxes allow the book to be comprehensive without the text becoming daunting and allow more advanced material to be introduced where appropriate. Many of the boxes can be used as class exercises and virtually all have questions at the end.
- Extensive use of data, with links in the online version to general data sources and individual datasets, with many opportunities for students to explore data to help them reflect on policy choices.
- Full-page chapter introductions. These set the scene for the chapter by introducing the students to the topics covered and relating them to the everyday world. The introductions also include a 'chapter map'. This provides a detailed contents listing, helping students to see how the chapter is structured and how the various topics relate to each other.
- A consistent use of colour in graphs and diagrams, with explanations in panels where appropriate. These features make them easier to comprehend and more appealing.
- Starred sections and boxes for more advanced material (appearing with a grey background). These can be omitted without interrupting the flow of the argument. This allows the book to be used by students with different abilities and experience, and on courses of different levels of difficulty.
- 'Looking at the maths' sections. These short sections express a topic mathematically. Some use calculus; some

do not. They are designed to be used on more quantitatively focused courses and go further than other textbooks at introductory level in meeting the needs of students on such courses. Most refer students to worked examples in Maths Cases on the student website. Some of these use simultaneous equations; some use simple unconstrained optimisation techniques; others use constrained optimisation, using both substitution and Lagrange multipliers. The 'Looking at the maths' sections are short and can be omitted by students on non-mathematical courses without any loss of continuity.

- An open learning approach, with questions incorporated into the text so as to test and reinforce students' understanding as they progress. This makes learning a much more active process.
- End-of-chapter questions. These can be set as work for students to do in class or at home. Alternatively, students can simply use them to check their comprehension at the end of a topic.
- Summaries given at the end of each section, thus providing a point for reflection and checking on comprehension at reasonably frequent intervals.
- An even micro/macro split.
- The book is divided into seven parts. This makes the structure transparent and makes it easier for the student to navigate.

Despite retaining these popular features, there have been many changes to this eleventh edition.

Extensive revision

Economics (11th edition) uses a lot of applied material, both to illustrate theory and policy, and to bring the subject alive for students by relating it to contemporary issues. This has meant that, as with the previous edition, much of the book has had to be rewritten to reflect contemporary issues. Specifically this means that:

- Many new boxes have been included on topical and controversial issues, including the market for vaccines, the economics of two-sided markets, social media influencers, cash versus vouchers, evidence of Giffen behaviour in China, minimum unit pricing for alcohol, the secondary ticket market and takeovers, immigration and the labour market, minimum wage legislation, the roll out of Universal Credit in the UK, worker motivation and behavioural economics, the effects of consumer behaviour on firms' pricing, the dominance of Google and recent competition law cases, supermarket buying power, personalised pricing in digital markets, an analysis of the Dasgupta report on the economics of biodiversity, cap-and-trade and carbon emission taxes, measuring wellbeing, developments of HDI adjusted for inequality and planetary pressures, COVID-19 and public-sector spending, measuring fiscal impulses, labour productivity and measuring inflation bias. Existing boxes have been extensively revised.
- There are many new examples given in the text.
- Theoretical coverage has been strengthened at various points in the book to reflect developments in the subject. This includes:
  - further emphasis on the role of borrowing, debt, financial markets, balance sheets and risk at the government, corporate and household levels with reference in many places to the impact of the COVID-19 pandemic;
  - inclusion of the role of various amplifiers in macroeconomic models;
  - the further development of macroeconomic models, including the interaction between the *IS/MP* model, the *DAD/DAS* model and the expectations-augmented Phillips curve models;
  - reworking the Solow model in terms of output per worker;
  - increased emphasis on behavioural economics at the level of both the consumer and the firm, including extending the analysis of bounded rationality, framing, present bias, loss aversion, prospect theory, preferences for fairness and biases when making decisions in an uncertain environment;
  - a deepening of the exposition of game theory at various points in the book and more detailed analysis of price discrimination, externalities and public goods.
- The text provides extensive coverage of the recent developments in money and banking and their impact on the economy.
- All policy sections reflect the changes that have taken place since the last edition, including changes to the regulation of businesses and the protection of the environment, and the responses to the financial crisis and COVID-19 pandemic, which had implications for the scale and scope of interventions and the financial wellbeing of governments. The text enables students to see how they can apply fundamental economic concepts to gain a better understanding of these important issues. Hence, students will be in a better position to analyse the actual responses of policy makers as well as the alternatives that could perhaps have been pursued.
- For this eleventh edition, all tables and charts have been updated, as have factual references in the text.
- Most importantly, every single section and every single sentence of the book has been carefully considered, and if necessary redrafted, to ensure both maximum clarity and contemporary relevance. The result, we hope, is a text that your students will find exciting and relevant to today's world.

SUGGESTIONS FOR SHORTER OR LESS ADVANCED COURSES

The book is designed to be used on a number of different types of course. Because of its comprehensive nature, the inclusion of a lot of optional material and the self-contained nature of many of the chapters and sections, it can be used very flexibly.

It is suitable for one-year principles courses at first-year degree level, two-year economics courses on non-economics degrees, A level, HND and professional courses. It is also highly suitable for single-semester courses, either with a micro or a macro focus, or giving a broad outline of the subject.

The following suggests chapters which are appropriate to different types of course and gives some guidance on chapters that can be omitted while retaining continuity:

Alternative 1: Less advanced but comprehensive courses

Omit all starred sections, starred sub-sections and starred boxes.

Example of a comprehensive course, omitting some of these chapters: Chapters 1–8, 10, 12–14, 15, 17–22, 24–25.

Alternative 2: Economics for Business courses

Chapters 1–3, 5–9, 12–15, 18, 21, 23–6.

Example of an Economics for Business course, omitting some of these chapters: Chapters 1–3, 6–10, 14, 15, 18, 22, 24–25.

Alternative 3: Introduction to microeconomics

Chapters 1–14, 24. The level of difficulty can be varied by including or omitting starred sections and boxes from these chapters.

Example of an Introduction to Microeconomics course, omitting some of these chapters: Chapters 1–4, 6–8, 10, 12, 24.

Alternative 4: Introduction to macroeconomics

Chapters 1, 2, 15–26. The level of difficulty can be varied by including or omitting starred sections and boxes from these chapters.

Example of an Introduction to Macroeconomics course, omitting some of these chapters: Chapters 1, 2, (if microeconomics has not previously been covered) 15, 17–23, 25.

Alternative 5: Outline courses

Chapters 1, 2, 6, 7, 15, 17, 18, 22, 24, 25 (section 25.1). Omit boxes at will.

Alternative 6: Courses with a theory bias

Chapters 1, 2, 4–10, 12, 15–21, 23, 24, 25. The level of difficulty can be varied by including or omitting starred sections and boxes from these chapters.

Alternative 7: Courses with a policy bias (and only basic theory)

Chapters 1–3, 6, 7, 11–15, (17), 22–6.

COMPANION RESOURCES

MyEconLab (for students)

MyEconLab is a comprehensive set of online resources developed for the eleventh edition of *Economics*. The book is available with an access card, but if your book did not come with one, you can purchase access to the resources online at www.MyEconLab.com.

MyEconLab provides a variety of tools to enable students to assess their own learning, including exercises, quizzes and tests, arranged chapter by chapter. There are many new questions in this edition and each question has been carefully considered to reflect the learning objectives of the chapter. A personalised Study Plan identifies areas to concentrate on to improve grades, and specific tools are provided to each student to direct their studies in the most efficient way.

Student website

In addition to the materials on MyEconLab, there is an open-access companion website for students with a large range of other resources, including:

- Animations of key models with audio explanations. These can be watched online or downloaded to a computer, MP4 player, smart phone, etc.;
- Links to the Sloman Economics news blog with news items added several times each month by a small team of authors;
- 224 case studies with questions for self-study and a range of activities for individual students or groups. These case studies are ordered chapter by chapter and referred to in the text;

- Maths cases with exercises, related to the 'Looking at the Maths' sections in the book;
- Updated list of 284 hotlinks to sites of use for economics;
- Answers to all in-chapter questions.

Note that the companion website, news blog and hotlinks can also be accessed directly from **go.pearson.com/uk/sloman**.

See the Student Resources chart on page xxi.

MyEconLab (for lecturers)

You can register online at www.myeconlab.com to use MyEconLab, which is a complete virtual learning environment for your course or embedded into Blackboard, WebCT or Moodle. You can customise its look and feel and its availability to students. You can use it to provide support to your students in the following ways:

- MyEconLab's gradebook automatically records each student's time spent and performance on the tests and Study Plan. It also generates reports you can use to monitor your students' progress.
- You can use MyEconLab to build your own tests, quizzes and homework assignments from the question base provided to set for your students' assessment.
- Questions are generated algorithmically so that they use different values each time they are used.
- You can create your own exercises by using the econ exercise builder.

Additional resources for lecturers

There are also many additional resources for lecturers and tutors that can be downloaded from the lecturer section of MyEconLab or from the separate lecturer website. These have been thoroughly revised for this updated eleventh edition. These include:

- PowerPoint® slideshows in full colour for use with a data projector in lectures and classes. These can also be made available to students by loading them on to a local network. There are several types of these slideshows:
  - All figures from the book and most of the tables. Each figure is built up in a logical sequence, thereby allowing them to be shown in lectures in an animated form. They are also available in a simple version suitable for printing for handouts or display on an OHP or visualiser.
  - A range of models. There are 42 files, each containing one of the key models from the book, developed in an animated sequence of between 20 and 80 screens.
  - Customisable lecture slideshows. There is one for each chapter of the book. Each one can be easily edited, with points added, deleted or moved, so as to suit particular lectures. A consistent use of colour is made to show how the points tie together. It is not intended that all the material is covered in a single lecture; you can break at any point. It's just convenient to organise them by chapter. They come in various versions:
    - o Lecture slideshows with integrated diagrams. These include animated diagrams, charts and tables at the appropriate points.
    - o Lecture slideshows with integrated diagrams and questions. These include multiple-choice questions to allow lectures to become more interactive and can be used with or without an audience response system (ARS). An ARS version is available for TurningPoint® and is ready to use with the appropriate 'clickers' or on smartphones, tablets or laptops through the TurningPoint app (previously called ResponseWare®). The 'Show of Hands' version can easily be adapted for use with other ARS software.
    - o Lecture plans without the diagrams. These allow you to construct your own diagrams on the blackboard, whiteboard or visualiser.
- Answers to all questions in *Economics* (11th edition): i.e. questions embedded in the text, box questions and end-of-chapter questions. These can be edited as desired and distributed to students.
- Answers to the case studies and maths cases found on the student website.
- Case studies. These 224 cases, also available to students on the student website, can be reproduced and used for classroom exercises or for student assignments. Most cases have questions, to which answers are also provided (not available to students). Each case also has an activity for individual students or for groups, and most would be suitable for seminars.
- Maths cases. These 33 maths cases with exercises, also available to students on the student website, relate to the 'Looking at the Maths' sections in the book. Answers to the exercises are also provided (not available to students).
- Workshops. There are 20 of these (10 micro and 10 macro/international). They are in Word® and can be reproduced for use with large groups of students (up to 200). They can also be amended to suit your course. Suggestions for use are given in an accompanying file. Answers to all workshop questions are given in separate Word® files.
- Teaching/learning case studies. These 20 case studies examine various ways to improve student learning of introductory economics. They have been completely revised with new hyperlinks where appropriate.

The following two pages show in diagrammatic form all the student and lecturer resources.

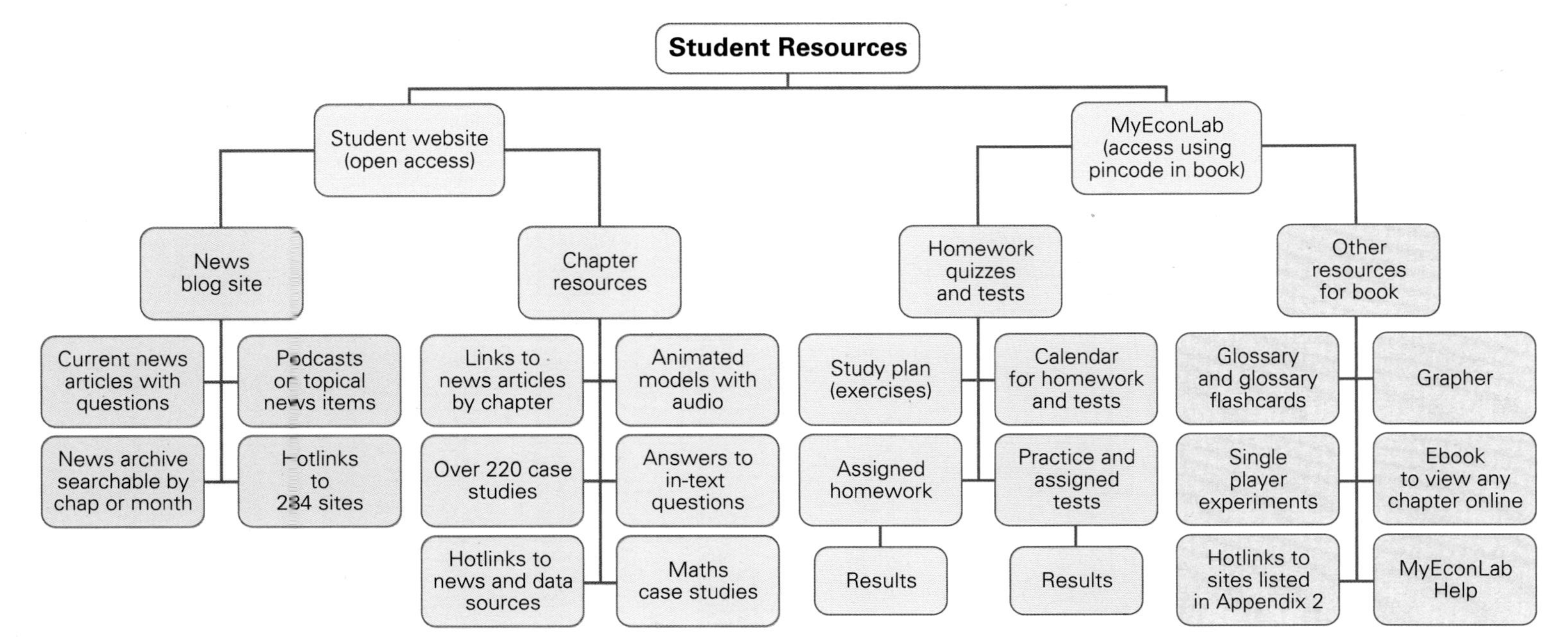
Student Resources
Student website (open access)
MyEconLab (access using pincode in book)
News blog site
Current news articles with questions
Podcasts or topical news items
News archive searchable by chap or month
Hotlinks to 234 sites
Chapter resources
Links to news articles by chapter
Animated models with audio
Over 220 case studies
Answers to in-text questions
Hotlinks to news and data sources
Maths case studies
Homework quizzes and tests
Study plan (exercises)
Calendar for homework and tests
Assigned homework
Practice and assigned tests
Results
Results
Other resources for book
Glossary and glossary flashcards
Grapher
Single player experiments
Ebook to view any chapter online
Hotlinks to sites listed in Appendix 2
MyEconLab Help

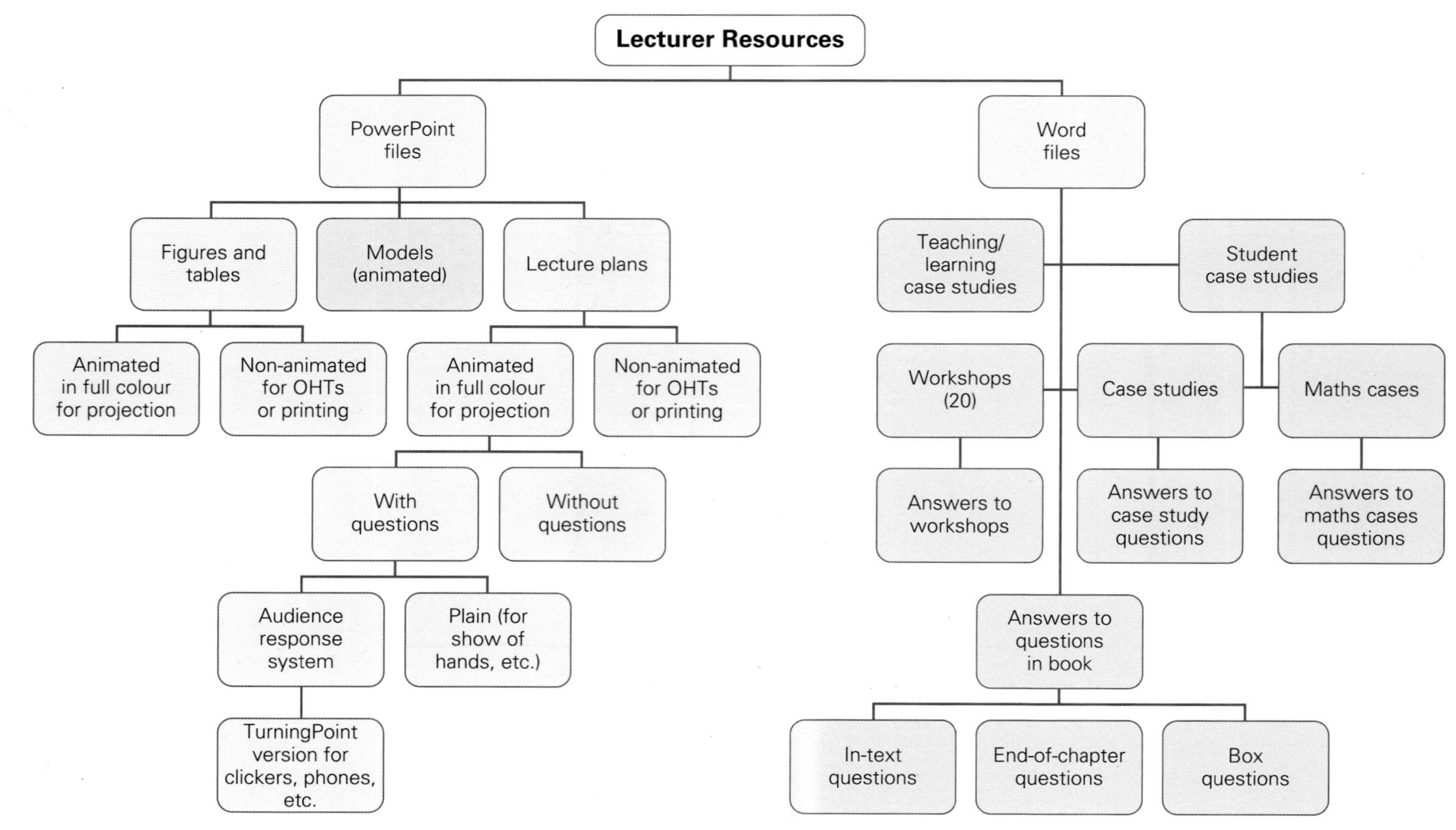
Lecturer Resources
PowerPoint files
Word files
Figures and tables
Models (animated)
Lecture plans
Animated in full colour for projection
Non-animated for OHTs or printing
Animated in full colour for projection
Non-animated for OHTs or printing
With questions
Without questions
Audience response system
Plain (for show of hands, etc.)
TurningPoint version for clickers, phones, etc.
Teaching/ learning case studies
Student case studies
Workshops (20)
Case studies
Maths cases
Answers to workshops
Answers to case study questions
Answers to maths cases questions
Answers to questions in book
In-text questions
End-of-chapter questions
Box questions

Acknowledgements

As with previous editions, we owe a debt to various people. The whole team from Pearson has, as always, been very helpful and supportive. Thanks in particular to Catherine Yates, the editor, and Melanie Carter, the production editor, who have offered great support throughout the long process of bringing the book to print. Thanks also to Kay Richardson who has worked long hours on building the online, interactive 'Revel' version of the book and to Jodie Mardell-Lines who has built the student and lecturer websites.

A huge thanks goes to Alison Wride from EML Learning who co-authored the 7th, 8th and 9th editions. Many of her ideas are still retained in this edition. And a special thanks, as previously, to Mark Sutcliffe from the Cardiff School of Management. He provided considerable help and support for the first few editions and it's still much appreciated.

Thanks too to colleagues and students from many universities who have been helpful and encouraging and, as in previous editions, have made useful suggestions for improvement. We have attempted to incorporate their ideas wherever possible. Please do write or email if you have any suggestions. Especially we should like to thank the following reviewers of the previous editions. Their analysis and comments have helped to shape this new edition.

Review of the 9th Edition:

Professor Francesco Feri, Royal Holloway, University of London, UK.

Helen Arce Salazar, The Hague University of Applied Sciences, Netherlands.

Dr Marie Wong, Middlesex University, UK.

Professor Peter Schmidt, Hochschule Bremen, City University of Applied Sciences, Germany.

Dr Sambit Bhattacharyya, University of Sussex, UK.

Review of the 10th Edition:

Dr Giorgio Motta, Lancaster University, UK.

Dr Eric Golson, University of Surrey, UK.

Dr Giancarlo Ianulardo, University of Exeter, UK.

A special thanks to Peter Smith from the University of Southampton who has again thoroughly revised and updated the MyEconLab online course. It's been great over the editions to have his input and ideas for improvements to the books and supplements.

Finally, our families have been remarkably tolerant and supportive throughout the writing of this new edition. A massive thanks to Alison, Pat and Helen, without whose encouragement the project would not have been completed.

Part A

Introduction

This opening part of the book introduces you to economics – what it is and why it is a great subject to study. Economics is not a set of facts or theories to be memorised; it is both more interesting and more useful than that. Studying economics enables you to think about the world in a different way; it helps you to make sense of the decisions people make: decisions about what to buy or what job to do; decisions governments make about how much to tax or what to spend those taxes on; decisions businesses make about what to produce, what prices to charge and what wages to pay. This makes economics relevant for everyone, not only those who are going on to further study.

And it is about some of the biggest issues that face society, such as poverty and inequality, health and wellbeing, the environment, biodiversity and sustainability, the relationships between nations and how we trade and how money gets moved around the world, economic recessions and unemployment, and how individuals and governments can help to tackle these issues.

By studying economics, you will gain a 'toolkit' of concepts, ideas and theories that will enable you to think about and analyse these issues. You will be able to apply this 'way of thinking' to your life both now and in the future. You will be able to think more analytically and to problem-solve more effectively; this helps explain why economics graduates are so highly valued by employers. Studying economics therefore opens up a variety of career opportunities.

Economics and Economies

CHAPTER MAP

We start by looking at two of the biggest issues of our time – the COVID-19 pandemic and global warming. These have had profound effects on societies around the world and, in the case of global warming, will do for decades to come. But they are not just issues studied by health and climate scientists. They are forcing us and our governments to make choices. Studying these choices is central to economics. Economists can analyse them and present us with policy alternatives. They can help us come to the best decisions in the light of the information presented by scientists.

Economics contains some core ideas. These ideas are simple, but can be applied to a wide range of economic problems. We start examining these ideas in this chapter. We begin on the journey to help you to 'think like an economist' – a journey that we hope you will find fascinating and will give you a sound foundation for many possible future careers.

In this chapter, we will attempt to answer the question, 'What is economics about?', and give you greater insight into the subject you are studying. We will see how the subject is divided up and distinguish between the two major branches of economics: microeconomics and macroeconomics.

We will also look at the ways in which different types of economy operate, from the centrally planned economies of the former communist countries to the more free-market economies of most of the world today. We will ask just how 'markets' work.

1.1 ECONOMICS AND GLOBAL ISSUES

Economists study very many of the issues we face, whether as individuals, families, firms and employees, local groups, societies, central and local government, and internationally through institutions and meetings of governments. Some of these issues are small everyday ones, such as what to buy in the supermarket or how much to save. Others are global in scale, requiring solutions at a whole range of levels from the international to actions by individuals.

Two of the greatest issues to confront society in recent times have been the coronavirus pandemic and the climate crisis.

As COVID-19 swept across the world in early 2020, it left a trail of deaths and lost livelihoods in its wake. Everyone had to adjust their way of living, faced with lockdowns, working from home, or jobs lost or furloughed. As scientists rushed to develop vaccines and health authorities rushed to distribute them, so governments were faced with the seeming dilemma of how much to prioritise saving lives versus how much to prioritise saving livelihoods through keeping the economy going. Or would prioritising saving lives and locking down allow the economy to bounce back more quickly later on with the virus sooner under control?

The other issue is the climate emergency, with scientific evidence becoming clearer of the devasting effect of global warming. Melting ice caps causing rising sea levels that devastate low-lying lands; a change in long-term rainfall totals, with some areas becoming drier and others wetter, affecting long-term crop yields and livelihoods and forcing people to migrate to survive; more frequent droughts, fires, floods and hurricanes causing death and destruction; a loss of biodiversity as species are wiped out and as humans take more desperate steps to survive, such as cutting down forests and farming more intensively – activities that compound environmental damage.

We examine each of these two issues and see how economists can contribute to understanding them and their consequences and what can be done about them. As we shall see, economists have played a major part and will continue to do so.

COVID-19 and the global health emergency

The COVID-19 pandemic dominated our lives during 2020 and 2021 and beyond. People and governments struggled to cope with illness and death, and the damage to lives and livelihoods. The impact on developing countries was particularly harsh. According to the World Bank, in 2020 alone the pandemic may have pushed around 100 million people into extreme poverty.[1]

Everyone was faced with choices and these affected behaviour. Most of these had an economic dimension. Indeed, economics studies the choices we make as individuals, firms, societies or governments.

Individual choices

People had to decide whether to follow the rules and advice about behaviour (e.g. whether to wear a face mask or socially distance). Some decided to follow lockdowns; others were ready to break or bend the rules. Economics studies people's behaviour – and how it impacts on economic decisions and the economy. We look at such behaviour in Chapters 2 to 5. For example, early on in the pandemic, many people stockpiled various items, such as hand sanitiser, toilet rolls and dried foods. This caused many shops to run out, which only further encouraged panic buying. Some shops responded by raising prices to increase their profit margins.

The lockdowns affected firms' profits. Some sectors were particularly hard hit, such as hospitality, leisure and tourism. Many suppliers found that their sales revenues had dried up as they were forced to close down, while others adjusted by trying to sell more online. Firms had to choose whether to give up or carry on.

On the plus side, some of their costs had fallen, such as heating and lighting and staff costs; we call these 'variable costs'. Other costs, however, such as rent, rates and interest charges generally did not fall; we call these 'fixed costs'.

Profits would have become losses if the government had not provided substantial support, which was still not enough to prevent many firms going out of business. Some managed to defer fixed costs, but these would have to be paid later – another difficult choice whether or not to give up.

And the pandemic hastened the move to online sales and away from the High Street, leading to the demise of many large chains of shops such as Arcadia, Laura Ashley and Debenhams. Others, such as John Lewis, closed a number of branches. Across the UK, some 17 500 chain-store outlets were permanently closed in 2020. In contrast, sales of online retailers such as Boohoo and Asos boomed.

We examine costs, revenues and profits in Chapters 6 to 9. We see how some firms are better protected against market forces than others, especially if they have a large market share and resulting market power.

As far as employees were concerned, some were easily able to work from home with a separate room to work in and a good Internet connection. They also saved money on commuting costs. Others with childcare responsibilities and shared working spaces and/or devices struggled to work efficiently from home. Some found their incomes constant or even rising; others saw a fall or had to rely on furlough money from the government. Most had little power in such a situation and had to accept the wages determined by the changing market environment.

Then vaccines began to be rolled out. Most people embraced getting jabbed to protect them and their loved ones. Others were suspicious for various reasons. But here was

1 Poverty and Shared Prosperity 2020: Reversals of Fortune, p. 11, World Bank (2020, revised 2021), https://openknowledge.worldbank.org/bitstream/handle/10986/34496/9781464816024.pdf

a classic problem in economics: what we do for ourselves often has spillover effects on others. If we are not protected, we are more likely to catch the disease and pass it on to others, even if we only get infected mildly or are largely asymptomatic. Many actions we take affect others – either beneficially or adversely. These can be as simple as whether to wear a face mask. So should the government constrain our actions? This is another key choice that has to be made and economists can help analyse these choices and identify their costs and benefits.

Government choices

The pandemic did not just affect individuals and firms; it had major effects on whole economies. With many firms being forced to shut down, even if only temporarily, and some sectors, such as public transport, facing a collapse in demand, economies around the world went into recession – economic growth was negative.

The UK was particularly badly hit at first, partly from the choice made by the government to delay locking down. National output (known as 'gross domestic product' or 'GDP') fell by nearly 10 per cent in 2020. Unemployment rose. The government responded by massively increasing spending by supporting individuals through the furlough scheme, whereby 80 per cent of the wages of those temporarily laid off were covered by the government and distributed through their employers. Other support was given to businesses and to the self-employed. This prevented unemployment from rising much further.

Other longer-term measures for recovery included large-scale spending on physical infrastructure, such as public transport, roads, green energy and broadband, and on public services, such as health and education. In the USA, President Biden introduced a $3 trillion programme of infrastructure spending to boost a green recovery. This followed a $1.9 trillion programme of support for vulnerable people and businesses to survive the pandemic.

We look at issues such as growth and unemployment in the second half of the book from Chapter 15 onwards.

But the massive support came at a cost. Government spending on support schemes plus a decline in tax revenues meant that government borrowing soared. In the UK, annual public-sector net borrowing rose from 2.6 per cent of GDP in 2019 to nearly 17 per cent in 2020, so adding to the total stock of public-sector debt, pushing it up from 84.4 per cent in 2019 to just over 100 per cent in 2020 – and forecast to rise to nearly 110 per cent by 2023 (see Figure 22.3 on page 697).

The government has to finance the borrowing through paying interest from taxes (or even more borrowing). So the government was faced with a choice about when to start raising taxes or cutting government spending to reduce the level of borrowing. This was a hard choice and the plan, announced in the 2021/22 Budget, was to raise taxes on business profits ('corporation tax') and to freeze income tax thresholds from April 2023. Similar dilemmas were faced by governments around the world. The general approach was to spend now and pay later – an easy choice at the time, but a difficult one later, especially for governments facing re-election. Policy choices such as these are examined in Chapter 22.

It was not just governments that were trying to keep their economies going. Central banks, such as the Federal Reserve in the USA, the European Central Bank for the eurozone and the Bank of England for the UK, were also playing their part. The general approach was to create more electronic money, through a process of 'quantitative easing'. If there was more money circulating through the banking system, people would borrow and spend more, helping to boost businesses.

But when you turn on the 'money tap' like this, you have to choose how much money to create and when to turn the tap off. Too little money and the recession may persist; too much money and prices may be pushed up by soaring spending. This 'inflation', as it is called, creates other problems for the economy, and central banks are keen not to let it go above 2 per cent per annum. The role of money in the economy is examined in Chapter 18 and subsequent chapters.

Give some other examples of choices that governments had to make during the pandemic. To what extent were they economic choices?

Getting all these economic choices right was a hard thing for individuals, businesses and governments. Economists had a crucial role in analysing the effects of these choices and advising on the best courses of action.

The environment and the global climate emergency

So can economists play a central role in addressing the climate emergency? The answer is 'yes' at many levels. Climate scientists can model the causes and effects of global warming. However, to address the problem and cut emissions to reach carbon neutrality and stop global warming – or at least limit it to 1.5°C above pre-industrial levels, which is the objective of the Intergovernmental Panel on Climate Change (IPCC) – then choices have to be made.

As we saw when looking at the coronavirus pandemic in the context of vaccination, people's actions affect others. Perhaps nowhere is this more crucial than with the environment. When people burn fossil fuels in their boilers or their cars, or buy goods which have travelled half way across the world on fossil-fuel hungry ships and planes, this affects others; not just themselves.

At an individual level, therefore, people need to think and behave 'green'. But what are the mechanisms for achieving this? Apart from education and developing greater social responsibility, pricing is key. If renewable energy were cheaper and fossil fuels were more expensive, then people would be more willing to switch to low-carbon consumption. Indeed, pricing is a central issue in economics. We look at pricing in Chapters 2 and 3 and later in Chapters 7 and 8.

But how can prices be altered? They can be reduced by government subsidies and raised by taxes. We look at green taxes and subsidies in Chapters 12 and 13. There are other methods too by which pricing can be used. One of these is emissions trading. This is where permits to emit CO_2 are allocated or auctioned to businesses, which can then trade them in markets. Low emitters will not have to pay so much, thereby giving them a cost advantage over high emitting companies, which will require more permits and hence have to pay more. Economists have played a key role in developing emissions trading in markets such as the EU Emissions Trading Scheme (EU ETS).

The issue of fairness

One of the key issues in economics is how to achieve a fair distribution of income and wealth, both today and over time. One area where this is vitally important is the environment. How can the world fairly share the costs and benefits of creating a low-carbon economy? If it fails, politicians will face a backlash from people who see their jobs and incomes under threat. Young people will blame the old for taking more than their fair share and degrading the environment in the process.

The problem is that change normally involves gainers and losers – a central dilemma in economics. Green investment may create jobs in alternative energy generation but result in jobs being lost in coal mining and heavy industry. And when there are groups of losers, populist politicians can use the resulting anger to drive wedges in society and turn people against tackling climate change – something that is easier if they can deny its existence.

International action

We live in an interdependent world. Actions in one part of the globe affect lives in others. If the rich countries are big carbon emitters, this affects people in poor countries too. Their lives may be more vulnerable to climate change and its impact on the weather and harvests. Economists play a large role in studying the trading between nations and how economic power affects patterns of trade and investment.

Multinational companies often drive intensive farming and mining in developing countries, and the effects on the environment in these countries can be devastating. Rainforests are cut down for mining, ranching or growing monocrops, such as palm oil plantations. And not only is the devastation confined to these countries: as well as hugely diminishing biodiversity, they contribute to global warming as the 'lungs of the world' are destroyed. From 2010 to 2019, in Brazil's Amazon basin 16.6 billion tonnes of CO_2 were released into the atmosphere from burning or destroying forest, or replacing it with plantations. Yet only 13.9 billion tonnes were drawn down through photosynthesis and new growth.[2]

Actions by the global community can help but very often there are international games being played, with countries often unwilling to commit to carbon-reducing measures unless they can be convinced that other countries are playing their part too. Economists study these types of 'games'. Indeed there is a major branch of economics called 'game theory', which looks at effective ways of incentivising people, firms and governments to behave in co-operative ways.

2 Xiangming Xiao et al., 'Carbon loss from forest degradation exceeds that from deforestation in the Brazilian Amazon', *Nature Climate Change* (29 April 2021), www.nature.com/articles/s41558-021-01026-5

BOX 1.1 WHAT'S THE LATEST ECONOMICS NEWS? CASE STUDIES AND APPLICATIONS

- The UK cannot retain the benefits of the EU's single market or customs union now it has left the EU.
- Researchers suggest that the long-term economic effects from the COVID-19 pandemic may be less serious than those from the financial crisis of 2007–8.
- Severe droughts cause crops to fail across sub-Saharan Africa: higher grain prices expected soon.
- There is concern that American trade policies will hurt both US consumers and producers, while reducing global growth.
- Unemployment falls and economic growth accelerates, leading to expectations of higher interest rates.
- The age at which UK workers can draw their state pension is raised further. Many predict that those currently under 30 will be working until at least the age of 70.
- Lack of training helps to explain low levels of productivity.
- Oil prices set to remain low for many years as more and more countries engage in fracking and as more investment takes place in green energy.
- The economy grows more rapidly and economists predict that interest rates will rise; house prices likely to stop rising.
- Government raises taxes to tackle soaring public-sector debt.

1. ***What is it that makes each one of the above news items an economics item (we explore this question in the next section)?***
2. ***In each case identify two different individuals or groups who might be affected by the news item.***

For what reasons may governments want other governments to stick to tough climate or emissions targets and yet be not willing to do so themselves?

Trade can make everyone better off. Countries can specialise in what they are good at and export these products, and then import products in which they are less efficient. But this only works if certain conditions hold, including recognition of the environmental impact of trade. Economists study these conditions and can advise governments on trade policy. This and other international issues are the subject of the final three chapters of the book.

All these economic issues stem from a core set of problems. It is to this core that we now turn.

1.2 THE CORE OF ECONOMICS

Many people think that economics is about *money*. Well, to some extent this is true. Economics has a lot to do with money: with how much money people earn; how much they spend; what various items cost; how much money firms make; the total amount of money there is in the economy. But, as we shall see later in the book, money is only important because of what it allows us to do; money is a tool and economics is more than just the study of money.

It is concerned with the following:

- The ***production*** of goods and services: how much an economy produces, both in total and of individual items; how much each firm or person produces; what techniques of production are used; how many people are employed.
- The ***consumption*** of goods and services: how much people spend (and how much they save); how much people buy of particular items; what individuals choose to buy; how consumption is affected by prices, advertising, fashion, people's incomes and other factors.

Could production and consumption take place without money? If you think they could, give some examples.

But we still have not got to the bottom of what economics is about. Is there one crucial ingredient that makes a problem an economic one? The answer is that there is a central problem faced by all individuals and all countries, no matter how rich. It is the problem of *scarcity* – an issue underlying all other economic problems. For an economist, scarcity has a very specific definition.

Before reading on, how would you define 'scarcity'? Must goods be at least temporarily unattainable to be scarce?

The problem of scarcity

Ask people if they would like more money, and the vast majority would answer 'Yes'. But they don't want more money for its own sake. Rather they want to be able to buy more goods and services, either today or in the future. These 'wants' will vary according to income levels and tastes. In a poor country 'wants' might include clean water, education and suitable housing. In richer nations 'wants' might involve a second car, longer holidays and more time with friends and family. As countries get richer, human wants may change but they don't disappear. Wants are virtually unlimited.

Yet the means of fulfilling wants are limited. At any point, the world can only produce a finite amount of goods and services because the world has a limited amount of *resources*. These resources, or ***factors of production*** as they are often called in economics, are of three broad types:

- Human resources: ***labour***. The labour force is limited in number, but also in skills. This limits the productivity of labour: i.e. the amount labour can produce.
- Natural resources: ***land and raw materials***. The world's land area is limited, as are its raw materials.
- Manufactured resources: ***capital***. Capital consists of all those inputs that have themselves had to be produced. The world has a limited stock of factories, machines, transportation and other equipment. The productivity of this capital is limited by the current state of technology.

Definitions

Production The transformation of inputs into outputs by firms in order to earn profit (or to meet some other objective).

Consumption The act of using goods and services to satisfy wants. This will normally involve purchasing the goods and services.

Factors of production (or resources) The inputs into the production of goods and services: labour, land and raw materials, and capital.

Labour All forms of human input, both physical and mental, into current production.

Land and raw materials Inputs into production that are provided by nature: e.g. unimproved land and mineral deposits in the ground.

Capital All inputs into production that have themselves been produced: e.g. factories, machines and tools.

Could each of these types of resources be increased in quantity or quality? Is there a time dimension to your answer?

So this is the fundamental economic problem: human wants are virtually unlimited, whereas the resources available to meet those wants are limited. We can thus define scarcity as follows:

Scarcity **is the excess of human wants over what can actually be produced. Because of scarcity, various choices have to be made between alternatives.**

If we would all like more money, why does the government not print a lot more? Could it not thereby solve the problem of scarcity 'at a stroke'?

Of course, we do not all face the problem of scarcity to the same degree. A poor family who may not be able to afford enough to eat, or a decent place to live, will hardly see it as a 'problem' that a rich family cannot afford a second skiing holiday. But economists do not claim that we all face an equal problem of scarcity. In fact this is one of the major issues economists study: how resources are distributed, whether between different individuals, different regions of a country or different countries of the world.

This economic problem – limited resources but limitless wants – makes people, both rich and poor, behave in certain ways. Economics studies that behaviour. It studies people at work, producing goods that people want. It studies people as consumers, buying the goods that they want. It studies governments influencing the level and pattern of production and consumption. It even studies why people get married and what determines the number of children they have! In short, it studies anything to do with the process of satisfying human wants.

Demand and supply

We have said that economics is concerned with consumption and production. Another way of looking at this is in terms of *demand* and *supply*. Demand and supply and the relationship between them lie at the very centre of economics. How does this relate to the problem of scarcity?

Demand is related to wants. If every good and service were free, people would simply demand whatever they wanted. In total, such wants are likely to be virtually boundless, perhaps only limited by people's imaginations. *Supply*, on the other hand, is limited. It is related to resources. The amount that firms can supply depends on the resources and technology available.

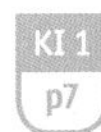

Given the problem of scarcity – that human wants exceed what can actually be produced – *potential* demands will exceed *potential* supplies. Society has to find some way of dealing with this problem, to try to match demand with supply. This applies at the level of the economy overall: total or '*aggregate*' demand needs to be balanced against total or *aggregate* supply. In other words, total spending in the economy should balance total production. It also applies at the level of individual goods and services. The demand and supply of cabbages should balance, and so should the demand and supply of cars, houses, tablets and holidays.

But if potential demand exceeds potential supply, how are *actual* demand and supply made equal? Either demand has to be reduced, or supply has to be increased, or a combination of the two. Economics studies this process. It studies how demand adjusts to available supplies, and how supply adjusts to consumer demands.

Dividing up the subject

Economics is traditionally divided into two main branches – *macroeconomics* and *microeconomics*, where 'macro' means big and 'micro' means small.

Macroeconomics is concerned with the economy as a whole. It is concerned with ***aggregate demand*** and ***aggregate supply***. By 'aggregate demand' we mean the total amount of spending in the economy, whether by consumers, by customers outside the country for our exports, by the government, or by firms when they buy capital equipment or stock up on raw materials. By 'aggregate supply' we mean the total national output of goods and services.

Microeconomics is concerned with the individual parts of the economy. It is concerned with the demand and supply of particular goods, services and resources such as cars, butter, clothes, haircuts, plumbers, accountants, blast furnaces, computers and oil.

Definitions

Scarcity The excess of human wants over what can actually be produced to fulfil these wants.

Macroeconomics The branch of economics that studies economic aggregates (grand totals): e.g. the overall level of prices, output and employment in the economy.

Aggregate demand The total level of spending in the economy.

Aggregate supply The total amount of output in the economy.

Microeconomics The branch of economics that studies individual units: e.g. households, firms and industries. It studies the interrelationships between these units in determining the pattern of production and distribution of goods and services.

Which of the following are macroeconomic issues, which are microeconomic ones and which could be either depending on the context?

(a) Inflation.
(b) Low wages in certain sectors.
(c) The rate of exchange between the pound and the euro.
(d) Why the prices of fresh fruit and vegetables fluctuate more than those of cars.
(e) The rate of economic growth this year compared with last year.
(f) The decline of traditional manufacturing industries.
(g) Immigration of workers.

Macroeconomics

KI 1 p7

Because scarcity exists, societies are concerned that their resources should be used *as fully as possible* and that over time their national output should grow.

Why should resources be used as fully as possible? If resources are 'saved' in one time period, surely they can be used in the next time period? The answer is that not all resources can be saved. For example, if a worker doesn't go to work one week then that resource is lost: labour can't be saved up for the future.

Why do societies want growth? To understand this, think back to the discussion of endless wants: if our output grows, then more of our wants can be satisfied. Individuals and society can be made better off.

The achievement of growth and the full use of resources are not easy. This is demonstrated by periods of high unemployment and stagnation that have occurred from time to time throughout the world (for example, in the recessions of the 1930s, the early 1980s and following the financial crisis of 2007–8 and COVID-19 pandemic of 2020). Furthermore, attempts by governments to stimulate growth and employment can result in inflation and rising imports. Economies have often experienced business cycles where periods of growth alternate with periods of recession, such periods varying from a few months to a few years.

Macroeconomic problems are closely related to the balance between aggregate demand and aggregate supply.

If aggregate demand is too *high* relative to aggregate supply, inflation and trade deficits are likely to result.

- ***Inflation*** refers to a general rise in the level of prices throughout the economy. If aggregate demand rises substantially, firms are likely to respond by raising their prices. If demand is high, they can probably still sell as much as before (if not more) even at the higher prices, and make higher profits. If firms in general put up their prices, inflation results. By comparing price levels between different periods we can measure the ***rate of inflation***. Typically, the rate of inflation reported is the *annual* rate of inflation: the percentage increase in prices over a 12-month period.
- ***Balance of trade*** deficits are the excess of imports over exports. If aggregate demand rises, people are likely to buy more imports. So part of the extra spending will go on goods from overseas, such as Japanese TVs, Chinese computers, German cars, etc. Also, if the rate of inflation is high, home-produced goods will become uncompetitive with foreign goods. We are likely to buy more foreign imports and people abroad are likely to buy fewer of our exports.

If aggregate demand is too low relative to aggregate supply, unemployment and recession may well result.

- ***Recession*** is where output in the economy declines for two successive quarters or longer. In other words, during this period growth becomes negative. Hence, not all periods during which the economy contracts are termed 'recessions'. It is the duration and persistence of the contraction that distinguishes a recession. Recessions are associated with low levels of consumer spending. If people spend less, shops are likely to find themselves with unsold stock. Then they will buy less from the manufacturers; they will cut down on production; and buy fewer capital goods such as machinery.
- ***Unemployment*** is likely to result from cutbacks in production. If firms are producing less, they will need to employ fewer people.

Macroeconomic policy, therefore, tends to focus on the balance of aggregate demand and aggregate supply. It can be ***demand-side policy***, which seeks to influence the level of spending in the economy. This in turn will affect the level of production, prices and employment. Or it can be ***supply-side policy***. This is designed to influence the level of production directly: for example, by trying to create more incentives for firms to innovate.

Definitions

Inflation A general rise in the level of prices throughout the economy.

(Annual) Rate of inflation The percentage increase in the level of prices over a 12-month period.

Balance of trade Exports of goods and services minus imports of goods and services. If exports exceed imports, there is a 'balance of trade surplus' (a positive figure). If imports exceed exports, there is a 'balance of trade deficit' (a negative figure).

Recession A period where national output falls for two or more successive quarters.

Unemployment The number of people of working age who are actively looking for work but are currently without a job. (Note that there is much debate as to who should officially be counted as unemployed.)

Demand-side policy Government policy designed to alter the level of aggregate demand, and thereby the level of output, employment and prices.

Supply-side policy Government policy that attempts to alter the level of aggregate supply directly.

BOX 1.2 **LOOKING AT MACROECONOMIC DATA** CASE STUDIES AND APPLICATIONS

Assessing different countries' macroeconomic performance

Rapid economic growth, low unemployment, low inflation and the avoidance of current account deficits[1] are major macroeconomic policy objectives of most governments around the world. To help them achieve these objectives they employ economic advisers. But when we look at the performance of various economies, the success of governments' macroeconomic policies seems decidedly 'mixed'.

The table shows data for the USA, Japan, Germany[2] and the UK from 1961 to 2022.

Macroeconomic performance of four industrialised economies (average annual figures)

	Unemployment (% of workforce)				Inflation (annual %)				Economic growth (annual %)				Balance on current account (% of national income)			
	USA	Japan	Germany	UK	USA	Japan	Germany	UK	USA	Japan	Germany	UK	USA	Japan	Germany	UK
1961–70	4.8	1.3	0.6	1.7	2.4	5.6	2.7	3.9	4.2	10.1	4.4	3.0	0.5	0.6	0.7	0.2
1971–80	6.4	1.8	2.2	3.8	7.0	8.8	5.1	13.2	3.2	4.4	2.8	2.0	0.9	0.5	1.1	−0.7
1981–90	2.5	2.5	6.0	9.6	4.5	2.2	2.5	6.2	3.2	3.9	2.3	2.6	−1.7	2.3	2.6	−1.4
1991–2000	3.3	3.3	7.9	7.9	2.2	0.4	2.3	3.3	3.3	1.5	1.9	2.4	−1.6	2.5	−0.7	−1.5
2001–07	5.3	4.6	9.2	5.2	2.8	−0.1	1.9	1.9	2.1	1.0	2.3	2.5	−4.8	3.3	3.8	−2.1
2008–11	8.4	4.7	7.0	7.3	2.1	−0.2	1.6	3.4	0.4	−0.6	0.8	−0.3	−3.2	2.9	5.9	−3.3
2012–19	5.5	3.3	4.3	5.5	1.6	0.7	1.3	1.8	2.4	1.1	1.4	1.9	−2.2	2.6	7.5	−4.3
2020	8.1	2.8	4.2	4.5	1.2	0.0	0.4	0.9	−3.5	−4.8	−4.9	−9.9	−3.1	3.3	7.1	−3.9
2021–22	5.0	2.6	4.1	6.1	2.3	0.4	1.7	1.7	5.0	2.9	3.5	5.2	−3.5	3.4	7.3	−3.9

Note: Years 2021 and 2022 are based on forecasts.
Sources: *Statistical Annex of the European Economy* (Commission of the European Communities, various tables and years) and *World Economic Outlook* (IMF, April 2021), www.imf.org/en/Publications/WEO/weo-database/2021/April

1. *Has the UK generally fared better or worse than the other three countries?*
2. *Was there a common pattern in the macroeconomic performance of each of the four countries over these 60 years?*

If the government does not have much success in managing the economy, it could be for the following reasons:

- Economists have incorrectly analysed the problems and hence have given the wrong advice.
- Economists disagree and hence have given conflicting advice.
- Economists have based their advice on inaccurate statistics or incorrect forecasts.
- Governments have not listened to the advice of economists. This could be for political reasons, such as the electoral cycle.
- There is little else that governments could have done: the problems were insoluble or could not have been predicted.

1 The current account balance is the trade balance plus any incomes earned from abroad minus any incomes paid abroad. These incomes could be wages, investment incomes or government revenues (see section 15.7 for details).
2 West Germany from 1961 to 1991.

Microeconomics

Microeconomics and choice

Because resources are scarce, choices have to be made. There are three main categories of choice that must be made in any society:

- *What* goods and services are going to be produced and in what quantities, since there are not enough resources to produce everything people want? How many electric cars, how much coffee, how much healthcare, how many smartphones, etc. will be produced?
- *How* are things going to be produced? What resources are going to be used and in what quantities? What techniques of production are going to be adopted? Will cars be produced by robots or by assembly-line workers? Will electricity be produced from coal, oil, gas, nuclear fission, renewable resources such as wind farms or a mixture of these?
- *For whom* are things going to be produced? In other words, how will the country's income be distributed? After all, the higher your income, the more you can consume of the total output. What will be the wages of shop workers, MPs, footballers and accountants? How much will pensioners receive? How much of the country's income will go to shareholders or landowners?

All societies have to make these choices, whether they are made by individuals, groups or the government. They can be seen as microeconomic choices, since they are concerned not with the total amount of national output, but with the individual goods and services that make it up: what they are, how they are made, and who gets to consume them.

Choice and opportunity cost

Choice involves sacrifice. The more food you choose to buy, the less money you will have to spend on other goods. The more food a nation produces, the fewer resources there will be for producing other goods. In other words, the production or consumption of one thing involves the sacrifice of alternatives. This sacrifice of alternatives in the production (or consumption) of a good is known as its ***opportunity cost***.

If the workers on a farm can produce either 1000 tonnes of wheat or 2000 tonnes of barley, then the opportunity cost of producing 1 tonne of wheat is the 2 tonnes of barley forgone. The opportunity cost of buying a textbook is the new pair of jeans that you have had to go without. The opportunity cost of saving for your old age is the consumption you sacrifice while younger.

Opportunity cost as the basis for choice is the first of our 'threshold concepts'. There are 15 of these threshold concepts, which we shall be exploring throughout the book. Once you have grasped these concepts and seen their significance, they will affect the way that you understand and analyse economic problems. They will help you to 'think like an economist'. TC 1 p10

KEY IDEA 2

The *opportunity cost* of any activity is the sacrifice made to do it. It is the best thing that could have been done as an alternative.

Definition

Opportunity cost The cost of any activity measured in terms of the best alternative forgone.

THRESHOLD CONCEPT 1 — CHOICE AND OPPORTUNITY COST — THINKING LIKE AN ECONOMIST

KI 1 p7

Scarcity, as we have seen, is at the heart of economics.

We all face scarcity. With a limited income we cannot buy everything we want. And even if we had the money, with only 24 hours in a day, we would not have time to enjoy all the things we would like to consume. The same applies at a national level. A country has limited resources and so cannot produce everything people would like. Of course, this is also true on a global scale: our planet has finite resources, and the technology and our abilities to exploit these resources are also limited.

With limited resources and endless wants, we have to make choices. In fact, virtually every time we do something, we are making a choice between alternatives. If you choose to watch television, you are choosing not to go out. If you buy a pair of trainers for £70, you are choosing not to spend that £70 on something else. Likewise, if a country devotes more of its resources to producing manufactured goods, there will be less to devote to the provision of services. If we devote more resources to producing a cleaner environment, we may have to produce less of the material goods that people want to consume.

What we give up in order to do something is known as its *opportunity cost*. Opportunity cost is the cost of doing something measured in terms of the best alternative forgone. It's what you would have chosen to do with your time or money if you had not made the choice you did. This is one of the most fundamental concepts in economics. It is a threshold concept: once you have seen its importance, it affects the way you look at economic problems. When you use the concept of opportunity cost, you are thinking like an economist. And this may be different from thinking like an accountant or from the way you thought before. It may sound deceptively simple, but in some cases working out the opportunity cost of an activity can be a tricky process. We will come across this concept many times throughout this book.

By looking at opportunity cost we are recognising that we face trade-offs. To do more of one thing involves doing less of something else. For example, we trade off work and leisure. The more we work, the less leisure time we will have. In other words, the opportunity cost of working is the leisure we have sacrificed. Nations trade off producing one good against others. The more a country spends on defence, the less it will have to spend on consumer goods and services. This has become known as the 'guns versus butter' trade-off. In other words, if a country decides to use more of its resources for defence, the opportunity cost is the consumer goods sacrificed. We examine such trade-offs at a national level on pages 14–16, when we look at the 'production possibility curve'.

We therefore have to make decisions between alternatives. To make sensible decisions we must weigh up the benefits of doing something against its opportunity cost. This is known in economics as 'rational decision making'. It is another of our threshold concepts (no. 8): see page 109.

1. *Think of three things you did last week. What was the opportunity cost of each one?*
2. *Assume that a supermarket has some fish that has reached its sell-by date. It was originally priced at £10, but yesterday was marked down to £5 'for quick sale'. It is now the end of the day and it still has not been sold. The supermarket is about to close and there is no one in the store who wants fish. What is the opportunity cost for the store of throwing the fish away?*

Rational choices

Economists often refer to ***rational choices***. This simply means that people are weighing up the *costs* and *benefits* of different activities and picking the option that allows them to maximise their objective. For consumers and workers this means making choices that maximise their happiness. For a firm it may mean choosing what and how much to produce to maximise profits.

Imagine you are doing your shopping in a supermarket and you want to buy a chicken. Do you spend a lot of money and buy a free-range organic chicken, or do you buy a cheap bird instead? To make a rational (i.e. sensible) decision, you will need to weigh up the costs and benefits of each alternative. The free-range chicken may taste better and it may meet your concerns about animal welfare, but it has a high opportunity cost: because it is expensive, you will need to sacrifice quite a lot of consumption of other goods if you decide to buy it. If you buy the intensively farmed chicken, however, although you will not enjoy it so much, you will have more money left over to buy other things: it has a lower opportunity cost.

Thus rational decision making, as far as consumers are concerned, involves choosing those items that give you the best value for money – i.e. the *greatest benefit relative to cost.*

The same principles apply to firms when deciding what to produce. For example, should a car firm open up another production line? A rational decision will again involve weighing up the benefits and costs. The benefits are the revenues the firm will earn from selling the extra cars. The costs will include the extra labour costs, raw material costs, costs of component parts, etc. It will be profitable to open up the new production line only if the revenues earned exceed the costs entailed: in other words, if it increases profits.

In the more complex situation of deciding which model of car to produce, or how many of each model, the firm must weigh up the relative benefits and costs of each – i.e. it will want to produce the most profitable product mix.

Assume that you are looking for a job and are offered two. One is more enjoyable, but pays less. How would you make a rational choice between the two jobs?

Marginal costs and benefits

In economics we argue that rational choices involve weighing up ***marginal costs*** and ***marginal benefits***. These are the costs and benefits of doing a little bit more or a little bit less of a specific activity. They can be contrasted with the total costs and benefits of the activity.

Take a familiar example. What time will you set your alarm to go off tomorrow morning? Let us say that you have to leave home at 8:30. Perhaps you will set the alarm for 7:00. That will give you plenty of time to get ready, but it will mean less sleep. Perhaps you will decide to set it for 8:00. That will give you a longer lie-in, but more of a rush in the morning to get ready.

So how do you make a rational decision about when the alarm should go off? What you have to do is to weigh up the costs and benefits of *additional* sleep. Each extra minute in bed gives you more sleep (the marginal benefit), but means you'll be more rushed when you get up (the marginal cost). The decision is therefore based on the costs and benefits of *extra* sleep, not on the total costs and benefits of a whole night's sleep.

This same principle applies to rational decisions made by consumers, workers and firms. For example, the car firm we were considering just now will weigh up the marginal costs and benefits of producing cars: in other words, it will compare the costs and revenue of producing *additional* cars. If additional cars add more to the firm's revenue than to its costs, it will be profitable to produce them.

Rational decision making, then, involves weighing up the marginal benefit and marginal cost of any activity. If the marginal benefit exceeds the marginal cost, it is rational to do the activity (or to do more of it). If the marginal cost exceeds the marginal benefit, it is rational not to do it (or to do less of it).

TC 8 p109

Rational decision making is Threshold Concept 8 and this is examined in Chapter 4, page 109.

How would the principle of weighing up marginal costs and benefits apply to a worker deciding how much overtime to work in a given week?

Microeconomic objectives

Microeconomics is concerned with the allocation of scarce resources: with the answering of the *what, how* and *for whom* questions. But how satisfactorily will these questions be answered? Clearly this depends on society's objectives. There are two major objectives that we can identify: *efficiency* and *equity*.

Efficiency. If altering what was produced or how it was produced could make us all better off (or at least make some of us

Definitions

Rational choices Choices that involve weighing up the benefit of any activity against its opportunity cost so that the decision maker successfully maximises their objective: i.e. happiness or profits.

Marginal costs The additional cost of doing a little bit more (or 1 unit more if a unit can be measured) of an activity.

Marginal benefits The additional benefits of doing a little bit more (or 1 unit more if a unit can be measured) of an activity.

Rational decision making Doing more of an activity if its marginal benefit exceeds its marginal cost and doing less if its marginal cost exceeds its marginal benefit.

better off without anyone losing), then it would be efficient to do so. For a society to achieve full ***economic efficiency***, three conditions must be met:

- Efficiency in production (***productive efficiency***). This is where production of each item is at minimum cost. Producing any other way would cost more.
- Efficiency in consumption. This is where consumers allocate their expenditures so as to get maximum satisfaction from their income. Any other pattern of consumption would make people feel worse off.
- Efficiency in specialisation and exchange. This is where firms specialise in producing goods for sale to consumers, and where individuals specialise in doing jobs in order to buy goods, so that everyone maximises the benefits they achieve relative to the costs of achieving them.

These last two are collectively known as ***allocative efficiency***. In any economic activity, allocative efficiency will be increased as long as doing more of that activity (and hence less of an alternative) involves a greater marginal benefit than marginal cost. Allocative efficiency will be achieved when all such improvements have been made.

Definitions

Economic efficiency A situation where each good is produced at the minimum cost and where individual people and firms get the maximum benefit from their resources.

Productive efficiency A situation where firms are producing the maximum output for a given amount of inputs, or producing a given output at the least cost.

Allocative efficiency A situation where the current combination of goods produced and sold gives the maximum satisfaction for each consumer at their current levels of income. Note that a redistribution of income would lead to a different combination of goods that was allocatively efficient.

BOX 1.3 THE OPPORTUNITY COSTS OF STUDYING

CASE STUDIES AND APPLICATIONS

What are you sacrificing?

You may not have realised it, but you probably consider opportunity costs many times a day. We are constantly making choices: what to buy, what to eat, what to wear, whether to go out, how much to study, and so on. Each time we make a choice to do something, we are in effect rejecting doing some alternative. This alternative forgone is the opportunity cost of the action we choose.

KI 2 p10

Sometimes the opportunity costs of our actions are the direct monetary costs we incur. Sometimes it is more complicated.

Take the opportunity costs of your choices as a student.

Buying a textbook costing £59.99

This choice does involve a direct money payment. What you have to consider are the alternatives you could have bought with the £59.99. You then have to weigh up the benefit from the best alternative against the benefit of the textbook.

1. *What might prevent you from making the best decision?*

Coming to lectures

Even though students now pay fees for their degrees in many countries, there is no extra (marginal) monetary cost in coming to classes once the fees have been paid. You will not get a refund by missing a lecture. The fees, once you've paid them, are what we call a 'sunk cost'.

So are the opportunity costs zero? No: by coming to a lecture you are not working in the library; you are not sleeping; you are not undertaking paid work during that time. If you are making a rational decision to come to classes, then you will consider such possible alternatives.

2. *If there are several other things you could have done, is the opportunity cost the sum of all of them?*
3. *What factors would make the opportunity cost of attending a class relatively high?*

Revising for an economics exam

Again, the opportunity cost is the best alternative to which you could have put your time. This might be revising for some other exam. You will probably want to divide your time sensibly between your subjects. A *sensible* decision is not to revise economics on any given occasion if you will gain a greater benefit from revising another subject. In such a case the (marginal) opportunity cost of revising economics exceeds the (marginal) benefit.

Choosing to study at university or college

What are the opportunity costs of being a student in higher education?

At first it might seem that the costs of higher education would include the following:

- Tuition fees.
- Books, stationery, etc.
- Accommodation, food, entertainment, travel and other living expenses.

But adding these up does not give the opportunity cost. The opportunity cost is the *sacrifice* entailed by going to university or college *rather than* doing something else. Let us assume that the alternative is to take a job that has been offered. The correct list of opportunity costs of higher education would include:

- Books, stationery, etc.
- Additional accommodation and travel expenses over what would have been incurred by taking the job.

- Wages that would have been earned in the job, less any income received as a student.
- The tuition fees paid by the student.

4. Why is the cost of food not included? Should the cost of clothing be included?

5. What impact would it have on the calculation of opportunity costs if you really disliked the nature of the work in the best alternative job?

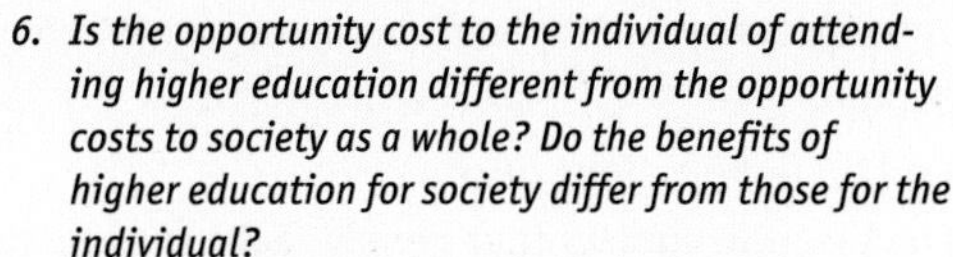

6. Is the opportunity cost to the individual of attending higher education different from the opportunity costs to society as a whole? Do the benefits of higher education for society differ from those for the individual?

Estimate your own cost of studying for a degree (or other qualification). For what reasons might you find it difficult to make such a calculation?

KEY IDEA 3

Economic efficiency **is achieved when each good is produced at the minimum cost and where individual people and firms get the maximum benefit from their resources.**

KEY IDEA 4

Equity **is where income is distributed in a way that is considered to be fair or just. Note that an equitable distribution is not the same as an equal distribution and that different people have different views on what is equitable.**

Equity. Even though the current levels of production and consumption might be efficient, they could be regarded as unfair, if some people are rich while others are poor. Another microeconomic goal, therefore, is that of ***equity***. Income distribution is regarded as equitable if it is considered to be fair or just. The problem with this objective, however, is that people have different notions of fairness. A rich person may well favour a much higher degree of inequality than will a poor person. Likewise, socialist governments will generally be in favour of a greater redistribution of income from the rich to the poor than will conservative governments. Equity is therefore described as a value judgement: notions of equity will depend on the values of individuals or society.

Definition

Equity A distribution of income that is considered to be fair or just. Note that an equitable distribution is not the same as an equal distribution and that different people have different views on what is equitable.

BOX 1.4 SCARCITY AND ABUNDANCE CASE STUDIES AND APPLICATIONS

Is lunch ever free?

KI 1 p7

The central economic problem is scarcity. But are *all* goods and services scarce? Is anything we desire truly abundant?

First, what do we mean by *abundance*? In the economic sense we mean something where supply exceeds demand at a *zero* price. In other words, even if it is free, there is no shortage. What is more, there must be no opportunity cost in supplying it. For example, if the government supplies health care free to the sick, it is still scarce in the economic sense because there is a cost to the government (and hence the taxpayer).

Two things that might seem to be abundant are air and water.

Air

In one sense air *is* abundant. There is no shortage of air to breathe for most people for most of the time. But if we define air as clean, unpolluted air, then in some parts of the world it is scarce. It costs money to clean polluted air. We may not pay directly – the cleaned-up air may be free to the 'consumer' – but the taxpayer or industry (and hence its customers) will have to pay.

Even if you live in a non-polluted part of the country, you may well have spent money moving there to escape the pollution. Again there is an opportunity cost to obtain the clean air.

Water

Whether water is abundant depends again on where you live. It also depends on what the water is used for.

Water for growing crops in a country with plentiful rain is abundant. In drier countries, resources have to be spent on irrigation. Water for drinking is not abundant. Reservoirs have to be built. The water has to be piped, purified and pumped.

1. There is a saying in economics, 'There is no such thing as a free lunch' (hence the subtitle for this box). What does this mean?

2. Are any other (desirable) goods or services truly abundant?

Can you think of any other (desirable) goods or services that are truly abundant? Discuss your ideas at a group level and see if you agree or disagree with any of the other suggestions.

Would it be desirable to have total equality in an economy, so that everyone receives the same share of resources?

The social implications of choice

In practice, the choices that people make may be neither efficient nor equitable. Firms may use inefficient techniques or be poorly managed; people often make wrong decisions about what to buy or what job to take; governments may be wasteful or inefficient in their use of tax revenues; there may be considerable inequality and injustice.

What is more, the effects of people's choices often spill over to other people. Take the case of pollution. It might be profitable for a firm to tip toxic waste into a river. But what is profitable for the firm will not necessarily be 'profitable' for society. Such an action may have serious environmental consequences.

Throughout the book we will be considering how well the economy meets various economic and social objectives, whether micro or macro. We will examine why problems occur and what can be done about them.

Illustrating economic issues: the production possibility curve

Economics books and articles frequently contain diagrams. The reason is that diagrams are very useful for illustrating economic relationships. Ideas and arguments that might take a long time to explain in words can often be expressed clearly and simply in a diagram.

Two of the most common types of diagram used in economics are graphs and flow diagrams. In this and the next section we will look at one example of each. These examples are chosen to illustrate the distinction between microeconomic and macroeconomic issues.

We start by having a look at a ***production possibility curve***. This diagram is a graph. Like many diagrams in economics it shows a simplified picture of reality – a picture stripped of all details that are unnecessary to illustrate the points being made. Of course, there are dangers in this.

In the attempt to make a diagram simple enough to understand, we run the risk of oversimplifying. If this is the case, the diagram may be misleading.

A production possibility curve is shown in Figure 1.1. The graph is based on the data shown in Table 1.1.

Assume that some imaginary nation devotes all its resources – land, labour and capital – to producing just two goods: food and clothing. Various possible combinations that could be produced over a given period of time (e.g. a year) are shown in the table. Thus the country, by devoting all its resources to producing food, could produce 8 million units of food but no clothing. Alternatively, by producing, say, 7 million units of food it could release enough resources – land, labour and capital – to produce 2.2 million units of clothing. At the other extreme, it could produce 7 million units of clothing with no resources at all being used to produce food.

Definition

Production possibility curve A curve showing all the possible combinations of two goods that a country can produce within a specified time period with all its resources fully and efficiently employed.

Figure 1.1 A production possibility curve

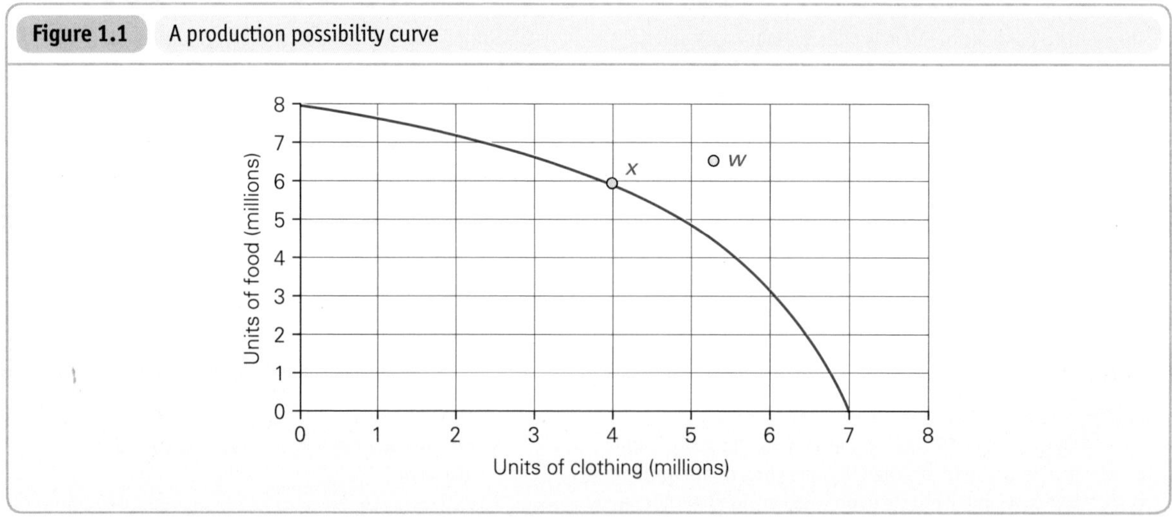

Table 1.1 Maximum possible combinations of food and clothing that can be produced in a given time period

Units of food (millions)	Units of clothing (millions)
8.0	0.0
7.0	2.2
6.0	4.0
5.0	5.0
4.0	5.6
3.0	6.0
2.0	6.4
1.0	6.7
0.0	7.0

The information in the table can be transferred to a graph (Figure 1.1). We measure units of food on one axis (in this case the vertical axis) and units of clothing on the other. The curve shows all the combinations of the two goods that can be produced with all the nation's resources fully and efficiently employed. For example, production could take place at point *x*, with 6 million units of food and 4 million units of clothing being produced. Production cannot take place beyond the curve. For example, production is not possible at point *w*: the nation does not have enough resources to do this.

Note that there are two simplifying assumptions in this diagram. First, it is assumed that there are just two types of good that can be produced. We have to assume this because we only have two axes on our graph. The other assumption is that there is only one type of food and one type of clothing. This is implied by measuring their output in particular units (e.g. tonnes). If food differed in type, it would be possible to produce a greater tonnage of food for a given amount of clothing simply by switching production from one foodstuff to another.

These two assumptions are obviously enormous simplifications when we consider the modern complex economies of the real world. But despite this, the diagram still allows important principles to be illustrated simply. In fact, this is one of the key advantages of using diagrams.

Microeconomics and the production possibility curve

A production possibility curve illustrates the microeconomic issues of choice and opportunity cost. KI 2 p10

If the country chose to produce more clothing, it would have to sacrifice the production of some food. This sacrifice of food is the opportunity cost of the extra clothing.

The fact that to produce more of one good involves producing less of the other is illustrated by the downward-sloping nature of the curve. For example, the country could move from point *x* to point *y* in Figure 1.2. In doing so it would be producing an extra 1 million units of clothing, but 1 million units less of food. Thus the opportunity cost of the 1 million extra units of clothing would be the 1 million units of food forgone.

It also illustrates the phenomenon of ***increasing opportunity costs***. By this we mean that as a country produces more of one good it has to sacrifice ever-increasing amounts of the other. The reason for this is that different factors of production have different properties. People have different skills; land varies across different parts of the country; raw materials differ one from another; and so on. Thus, as a country concentrates more on the production of one good, it has to start using resources that are less suitable – resources that would have been better suited to producing

Definition

Increasing opportunity costs of production When additional production of one good involves ever-increasing sacrifices of another.

Figure 1.2 Increasing opportunity costs

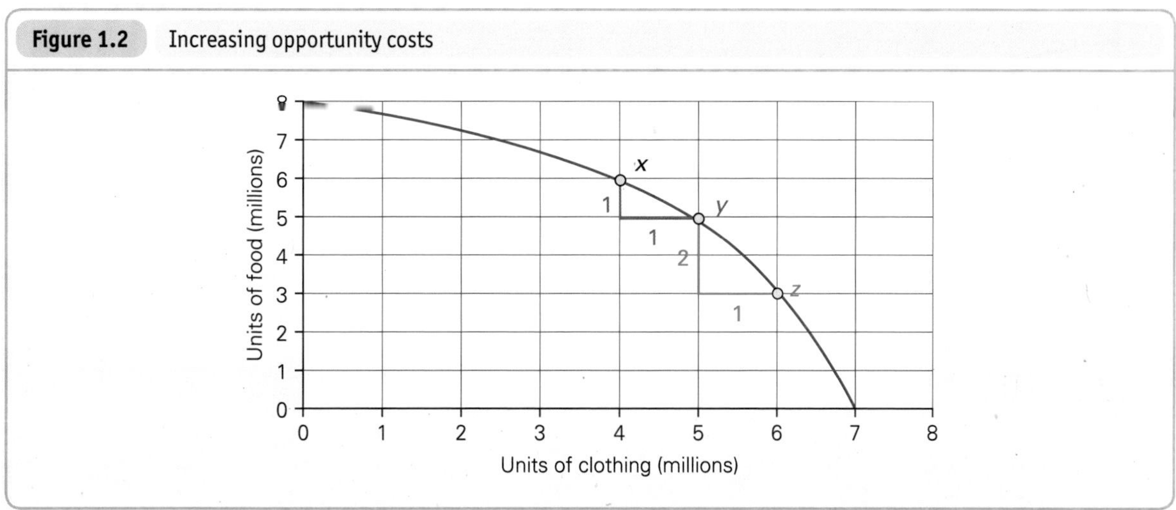

other goods. In our example, then, the production of more and more clothing will involve a growing *marginal cost*: ever-increasing amounts of food have to be sacrificed for each additional unit of clothing produced.

It is because opportunity costs increase that the production possibility curve is bowed outward rather than being a straight line. Thus in Figure 1.2, as production moves from point *x* to *y* to *z*, so the amount of food sacrificed rises for each additional unit of clothing produced. The opportunity cost of the fifth million units of clothing is 1 million units of food. The opportunity cost of the sixth million units of clothing is 2 million units of food.

1. *What is the opportunity cost of the seventh million units of clothing?*
2. *If the country moves upward along the curve and produces more food, does this also involve increasing opportunity costs?*
3. *Under what circumstances would the production possibility curve be (a) a straight line; (b) bowed in towards the origin? Are these circumstances ever likely?*

Macroeconomics and the production possibility curve

There is no guarantee that resources will be fully employed, or that they will be used in the most efficient way possible. The nation may thus be producing at a point inside the curve: for example, point *v* in Figure 1.3.

What we are saying here is that the economy is producing less of both goods than it is possible for it to produce, either because some resources are not being used (for example, workers may be unemployed), or because it is not using the most efficient methods of production possible, or a combination of the two. By using its resources to the full, the nation could move out onto the curve: to point *x* or *y*, for example. It could produce more clothing *and* more food.

Here we are concerned not with the combination of goods produced (a microeconomic issue), but with whether the total amount produced is as much as it could be (a macroeconomic issue).

Over time, the production possibilities of a nation are likely to increase. ***Investment*** in new plant and machinery will increase the stock of capital; new raw materials may be discovered; technological advances are likely to take place; through education and training, labour is likely to become more productive. This growth in potential output is illustrated by an outward shift in the production possibility curve. This will then allow actual output to increase: for example, from point *x* to point *x′* in Figure 1.4.

Will economic growth always involve a parallel outward shift of the production possibility curve?

Illustrating economic issues: the circular flow of goods and incomes

The process of satisfying human wants involves producers and consumers. The relationship between them is two-sided and can be represented in a flow diagram (see Figure 1.5).

The consumers of goods and services are labelled 'households'. Some members of households, of course, are also

Definition

Investment The production of items that are not for immediate consumption.

Figure 1.3 Making a fuller use of resources

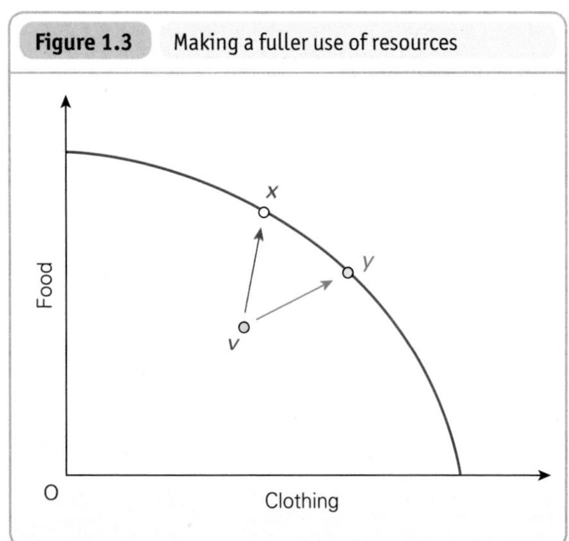

Figure 1.4 Growth in actual and potential output

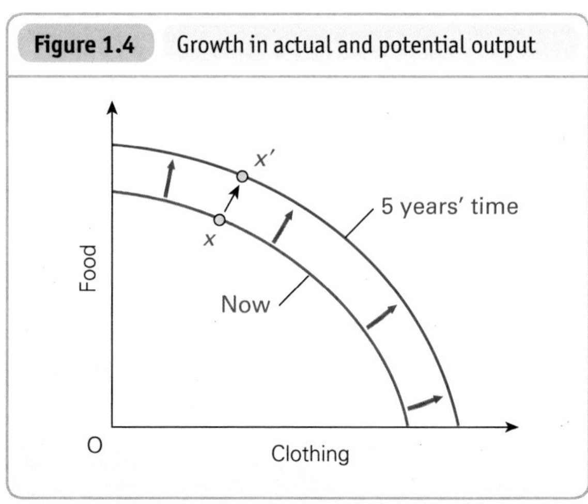

Figure 1.5 Circular flow of goods and incomes

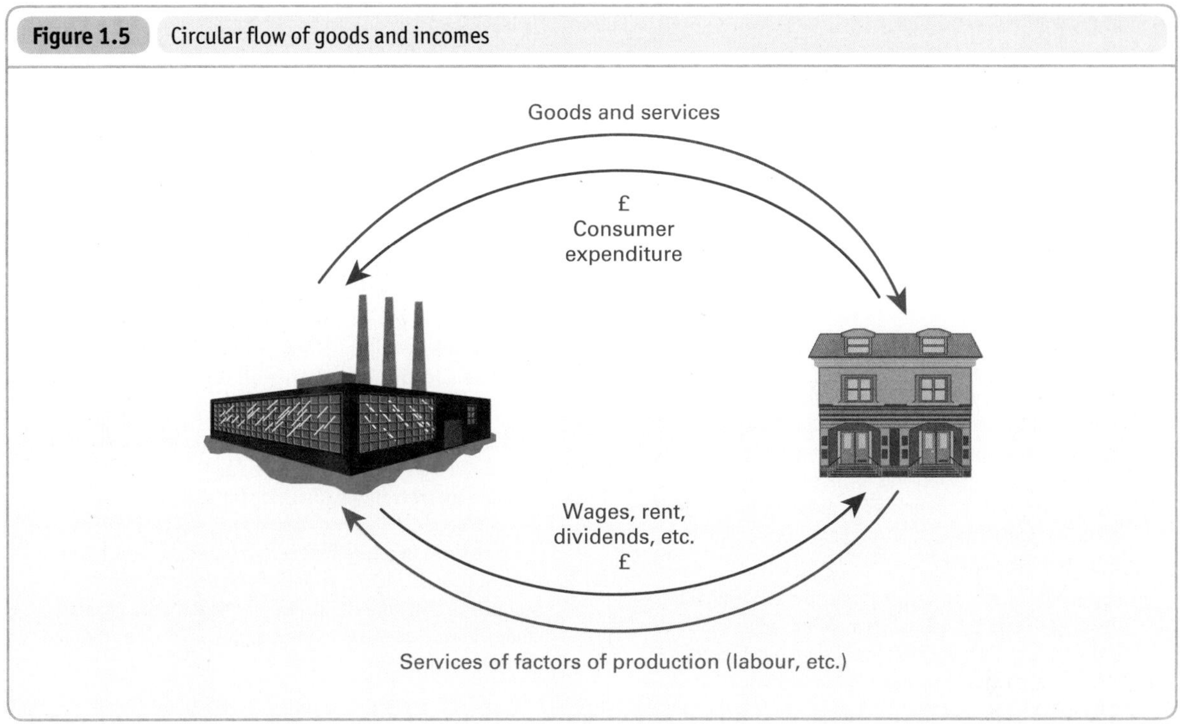

workers, and in some cases are the owners of other factors of production too, such as land. The producers of goods and services are labelled 'firms'.[3]

Firms and households are in a twin 'demand and supply' relationship with each other.

First, in the top part of the diagram, households demand goods and services, and firms supply goods and services. In the process, exchange takes place. In a money economy (as opposed to a ***barter economy***), firms exchange goods and services for money. In other words, money flows from households to firms in the form of consumer expenditure, while goods and services flow the other way – from firms to households.

This coming together of buyers and sellers is known as a ***market*** – it could be a street market, a shop or a website offering online shopping. Thus we talk about the market for apples, for oil, for houses, for televisions, and so on.

Second, firms and households come together in the market for factors of production. This is illustrated in the bottom half of Figure 1.5. This time the demand and supply roles are reversed. Firms demand the use of factors of production owned by households – labour, land and capital. Households supply them. Thus the services of labour and other factors flow from households to firms, and in exchange firms pay households money – namely, wages, rent, dividends and interest. Just as we referred to particular goods markets, so we can also refer to particular factor markets – the market for bricklayers, for footballers, for land, and so on.

So there is a circular flow of incomes. Households earn incomes from firms and firms earn incomes from households. The money circulates. There is also a circular flow of goods and services, but in the opposite direction. Households supply factor services to firms, which then use them to supply goods and services to households.

This flow diagram, like the production possibility curve, can help us to distinguish between microeconomics and macroeconomics.

Microeconomics is concerned with the composition of the circular flow: what combinations of goods make up the goods flow; how the various factors of production are combined to produce these goods; for whom the wages, dividends, rent and interest are paid out.

Macroeconomics is concerned with the total size of the flow and what causes it to expand and contract.

3 In practice, much of society's production takes place within the household for its members' own consumption. Examples include cooking, cleaning, growing vegetables, decorating and childcare. Also, firms buy from and sell to each other – whether it be raw materials, capital goods or semi-finished goods. Nevertheless, it is still useful to depict the flows of goods and services and money between households and firms when explaining the operation of markets.

Definitions

Barter economy An economy where people exchange goods and services directly with one another without any payment of money. Workers would be paid with bundles of goods.

Market The interaction between buyers and sellers.

Section summary

1. The central economic problem is that of scarcity. Given that there is a limited supply of factors of production (labour, land and capital), it is impossible to provide everybody with everything they want. Potential demands exceed potential supplies.
2. The subject of economics is usually divided into two main branches: macroeconomics and microeconomics.
3. Macroeconomics deals with aggregates such as the overall levels of unemployment, output, growth and prices in the economy.
4. Microeconomics deals with the activities of individual units within the economy: firms, industries, consumers, workers, etc. Because resources are scarce, people have to make choices. Society has to choose by some means or other *what* goods and services to produce, *how* to produce them and *for whom* to produce them. Microeconomics studies these choices.
5. Rational choices involve weighing up the marginal benefits of each activity against its marginal opportunity costs. If the marginal benefits exceed the marginal costs, it is rational to choose to do more of that activity.
6. The production possibility curve shows the possible combinations of two goods that a country can produce in a given period of time. Assuming that the country is already producing on the curve, the production of more of one good will involve producing less of the other. This opportunity cost is illustrated by the slope of the curve. If the economy is producing within the curve as a result of idle resources or inefficiency, it can produce more of both goods by taking up this slack. In the longer term, it can only produce more of both by shifting the curve outwards through investment, technological progress, etc.
7. The circular flow of goods and incomes shows the interrelationships between firms and households in a money economy. Firms and households come together in markets. In goods markets, firms supply goods and households demand goods. In the process, money flows from households to firms in return for the goods and services that the firms supply. In factor markets, firms demand factors of production and households supply them. In the process, money flows from firms to households as incomes for factor services.

1.3 DIFFERENT ECONOMIC SYSTEMS

The classification of economic systems

All societies face the problem of scarcity. They differ considerably, however, in the way they tackle the problem. One important difference between societies is in the degree of government control of the economy: the extent to which government decides 'what', 'how' and 'for whom' to produce.

At the one extreme lies the completely ***planned or command economy***, where all the economic decisions are taken by the government.

At the other extreme lies the completely ***free-market economy***. In this type of economy there is no government intervention at all. All decisions are taken by individuals and firms. Households decide how much labour and other factors to supply, and what goods to consume. Firms decide what goods to produce and what factors to employ. The pattern of production and consumption that results depends on the interactions of all these individual demand and supply decisions in free markets.

In practice, all economies are a mixture of the two; it is the *degree* of government intervention that distinguishes different economic systems. In China, the government plays a large role, whereas in the USA, the government plays a much smaller role.

It is still useful to analyse the extremes, in order to put the different ***mixed economies*** of the real world into perspective.

The mixture of government and the market can be shown by the use of a spectrum diagram such as Figure 1.6. It shows where particular economies of the real world *typically* lie along the spectrum between the two extremes.

The diagram is useful in that it provides a simple picture of the mixture of government and the market that exists in various economies. It can also be used to show changes in the mixture over time or from responses to crises.

The problem with this type of classification is that it is one-dimensional and oversimplified. Countries differ in the *type* of government intervention as well as the level. For example, governments can intervene through planning, public ownership, regulation, taxes and subsidies, partnership schemes with private industry, and so on. Two countries

Definitions

Centrally planned or command economy An economy where all economic decisions are taken by the central authorities.

Free-market economy An economy where all economic decisions are taken by individual households and firms and with no government intervention.

Mixed economy An economy where economic decisions are made partly by the government and partly through the market. In practice all economies are mixed.

Figure 1.6 Classifying economic systems

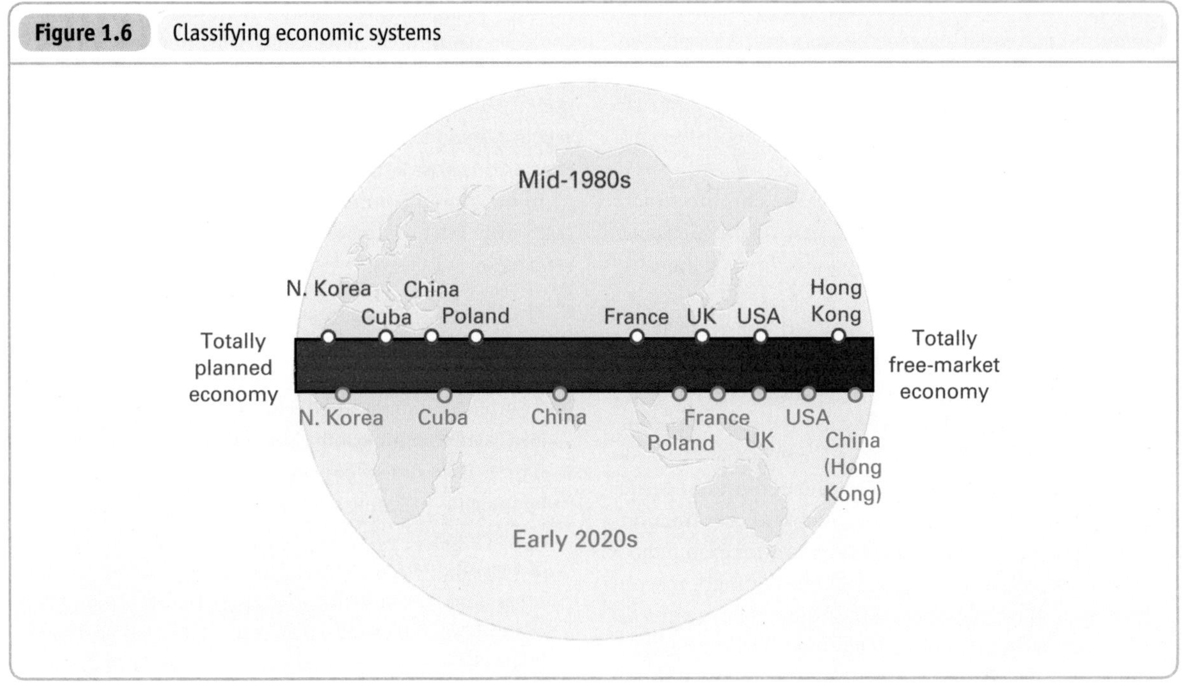

could be in a similar position along the spectrum but have very different types of government intervention.

Notice that there has been a general movement to the right along the spectrum since the 1980s. In former communist countries this has been a result of the abandonment of central planning and the adoption of private enterprise. In Western economies it has been a result of deregulation of private industry and privatisation (the selling of nationalised industries to the private sector).

How do you think the positions of these eight countries will change over the next decade?

The informal sector: a third dimension

In all societies, many economic decisions are made, whether individually or in groups, which involve neither the government nor the market. For example, many of the activities taking place in the home, such as cooking, cleaning, gardening and care for children or the elderly, can be seen as 'economic' activities. There is an output (such as a meal or a service provided) and there is an opportunity cost to the provider (in terms of alternative activities forgone). And yet no money changes hands. Similarly, many of the activities done in groups, such as clubs and charities, involve the provision of goods and/or services, but again, no money changes hands.

These activities are taking place in the ***informal sector***. The relative size of the informal sector varies from one country to another and over time. In rich countries, as more women continue to work after having children, and as working hours have increased, many people employ others to do the jobs, such as cleaning and childcare, that they once did themselves. What was once part of the informal sector is now part of the market sector.

In many developing countries, much of the economic activity in poorer areas involves ***subsistence production***. This is where people grow their own food, build their own shelter, etc. While some of the inputs (e.g. building materials) may have to be purchased through the market, much of this production is in the informal sector and involves no exchange of money. The importance of the informal sector, particularly to developing countries, should not be underestimated. This is an area of increasing interest to many economists, particularly those interested in the downsides of economic growth.

The command economy

The command economy is usually associated with a socialist or communist economic system, where land and capital are collectively owned. The state plans the allocation of resources at three levels:

- It plans the allocation of resources between current consumption and investment for the future. By sacrificing

Definitions

Informal sector The parts of the economy that involve production and/or exchange, but where there are no money payments.

Subsistence production Where people produce things for their own consumption.

some present consumption and diverting resources into investment, it could increase the economy's growth rate.

TC 1 p10 The amount of resources it chooses to devote to investment will depend on its broad macroeconomic strategy: the importance it attaches to growth as opposed to current consumption.

- At a microeconomic level, it plans the output of each industry and firm, the techniques that will be used, and the labour and other resources required by each industry and firm.

  In order to ensure that the required inputs are available, the state would probably conduct some form of ***input–output analysis***. All industries are seen as users of inputs from other industries and as producers of output for consumers or other industries. For example, the steel industry uses inputs from the coal and iron-ore industries and produces output for the vehicle and construction industries. Input–output analysis shows, for each industry, the sources of all its inputs and the destination of all its output. By using such analysis the state attempts to match up the inputs and outputs of each industry so that the planned demand for each industry's product is equal to its planned supply.
- It plans the distribution of output between consumers. This will depend on the government's aims. It may distribute goods according to its judgement of people's needs; or it may give more to those who produce more, thereby providing an incentive for people to work harder. It may distribute goods and services directly (for example, by a system of rationing); or it may decide the distribution of money incomes and allow individuals to decide how to spend them. If it does the latter, it may still seek to influence the pattern of expenditure by setting appropriate prices: low prices to encourage consumption, and high prices to discourage consumption.

Assessment of the command economy

With central planning, the government could take an overall view of the economy. It could direct the nation's resources in accordance with specific national goals.

High growth rates could be achieved if the government directed large amounts of resources into investment. Unemployment could be largely avoided if the government carefully planned the allocation of labour in accordance with production requirements and labour skills. National income could be distributed more equally or in accordance with needs. The social repercussions of production and consumption (e.g. the effects on the environment) could be taken into account, provided the government was able to predict these effects and chose to take them into account. 

In practice, a command economy could achieve these goals only at considerable social and economic cost. The reasons are as follows: KI 2 p10

- The larger and more complex the economy, the greater the task of collecting and analysing the information essential to planning, and the more complex the plan. Complicated plans are likely to be costly to administer and involve cumbersome bureaucracy.
- If there is no system of prices, or if prices are set arbitrarily by the state, planning is likely to involve the inefficient use of resources. It is difficult to assess the relative efficiency of two alternative techniques that use different inputs if there is no way in which the value of those inputs can be ascertained. For example, how can a rational decision be made between an oil-fired and a coal-fired furnace if the prices of oil and coal do not reflect their relative scarcity? KI 3 p13
- It is difficult to devise appropriate incentives to encourage workers and managers to be more productive without a reduction in quality. For example, if bonuses are given according to the quantity of output produced, a factory might produce shoddy goods, since it can probably produce a larger quantity of goods by cutting quality. To avoid this problem, a large number of officials may have to be employed to check quality.
- Complete state control over resource allocation would involve a considerable loss of individual liberty. Workers would have no choice where to work; consumers would have no choice what to buy.
- If production is planned, but consumers are free to spend money incomes as they wish, there will be a problem if the wishes of consumers change. Shortages will occur if consumers decide to buy more; surpluses will occur if they decide to buy less.

Most of these problems were experienced in the former Soviet Union and the other Eastern bloc countries, and were part of the reason for the overthrow of their communist regimes (see Box 1.5).

> **Definition**
>
> **Input–output analysis** This involves dividing the economy into sectors, where each sector is a user of inputs from and a supplier of outputs to other sectors. The technique examines how these inputs and outputs can be matched to the total resources available in the economy.

The free-market economy

Free decision making by individuals

In a free market, individuals are free to make their own economic decisions. Consumers are free to decide what to buy with their incomes: free to make demand decisions. Firms are free to choose what to sell and what production methods to use: free to make supply decisions. The demand and supply decisions of consumers and firms are transmitted to each other through their effect on prices: through the ***price mechanism***. The prices that result are the prices that firms and consumers have to accept.

The price mechanism

The price mechanism works as follows. Prices respond to shortages and surpluses. Shortages result in prices rising. Surpluses result in prices falling. Let us take each in turn.

If consumers want more of a good (or if producers decide to cut back supply), demand will exceed supply. The resulting shortage will cause the price of the good to rise. This will act as an incentive to producers to supply more, since production will now be more profitable. At the same time it will discourage consumers from buying so much. *The price will continue rising until the shortage has been eliminated.*

If, on the other hand, consumers decide they want less of a good (or if producers decide to produce more), then supply will exceed demand. The resulting surplus will cause the price of the good to fall. This will act as a disincentive to producers, who will supply less, since production will now be less profitable. It will encourage consumers to buy more. *The price will continue falling until the surplus has been eliminated.*

This price, where demand equals supply, is called the ***equilibrium price***. By ***equilibrium*** we mean a point of balance or a point of rest: in other words, a point towards which there is a tendency to move.

1. *Try using the same type of analysis in the labour market to show what will happen if there is an increase in demand for labour. What is the 'price' of labour?*
2. *Can you think of any examples where prices and wages do not adjust very rapidly to a shortage or surplus? For what reasons might they not do so?*

The response of demand and supply to changes in price illustrates a very important feature of how economies work: *people respond to incentives*. It is important, therefore, that incentives are appropriate and have the desired effect. This is the fifth of our 15 threshold concepts (see Chapter 2, page 48).

Definitions

Price mechanism The system in a market economy whereby changes in price in response to changes in demand and supply have the effect of making demand equal to supply.

Equilibrium price The price where the quantity demanded equals the quantity supplied: the price where there is no shortage or surplus.

Equilibrium A position of balance. A position from which there is no inherent tendency to move away.

The effect of changes in demand and supply

How will the price mechanism respond to changes in consumer demand or producer supply? Patterns of consumer demand will change over time: for example, people may decide they want more fixed gear bikes and fewer mountain bikes. Likewise the pattern of supply changes: for example, changes in technology may allow the mass production of microchips at lower cost, while the production of hand-built furniture becomes relatively expensive.

In all cases of changes in demand and supply, the resulting changes in price act as both signals and incentives.

A change in demand. A rise in demand is signalled by a rise in price, which then acts as an incentive for supply to rise. The high price of these goods relative to their costs of production signals that consumers are willing to see resources diverted from other uses. This is just what firms do. They divert resources from goods with lower prices relative to costs (and hence lower profits) to those goods that are more profitable.

A fall in demand is signalled by a fall in price. This then acts as an incentive for supply to fall. The goods are now less profitable to produce.

A change in supply. A rise in supply is signalled by a fall in price. This then acts as an incentive for demand to rise. A fall in supply is signalled by a rise in price. This then acts as an incentive for demand to fall.

The fact that markets adjust so as to equate demand and supply is our fourth 'Threshold Concept', which is discussed in Chapter 2, page 45.

Changes in demand or supply cause markets to adjust. **Whenever such changes occur, the resulting 'disequilibrium' will bring an automatic change in prices, thereby restoring equilibrium (i.e. a balance of demand and supply).**

1. *Why do the prices of fresh vegetables fall when they are in season? Could an individual farmer prevent the price falling?*
2. *If you were the manager of a supermarket, how would you set about deciding what prices to charge for food approaching its sell-by date?*
3. *Demand for streaming music has grown rapidly, yet the subscription prices have not increased. Why?*

BOX 1.5 COMMAND ECONOMIES

The rise and fall of planning

Russia

The Bolsheviks under the leadership of Lenin came to power in Russia with the October revolution of 1917. Communism was introduced and the market economy abolished. Industries were nationalised; workers were told what jobs to do; food was taken from peasants to feed the towns; workers were allocated goods from distribution depots.

With the ending of the civil war in 1921, the economy was in bad shape and Lenin embarked on the New Economic Policy. This involved a return to the use of markets. Smaller businesses were returned to private hands and peasants were able to sell their crops. The economy began to recover; however, Lenin died in 1924 and Stalin came to power.

The Russian economy underwent a radical transformation from 1928 onwards. The key features of the Stalinist approach were collectivisation, industrialisation and central planning. Peasant farms were abolished and replaced by large-scale collective farms where land was collectively owned and worked, and by state farms, owned by the state and run by managers. This caused disruption and famine, with peasants slaughtering their animals rather than giving them up. However, in the longer term more food was produced. Both collective and state farms were given quotas of output that they were supposed to deliver, for which the state would pay a fixed price.

Alongside the agricultural reforms a drive to industrialisation took place and a vast planning apparatus was developed. At the top was *Gosplan*, the central planning agency. This prepared five-year plans, which specified the general direction in which the economy was to move, and annual plans, which gave details of what was to be produced and with what resources for some 200 or so key products. The system operated without either the price mechanism or the profit motive, although incentives existed with bonuses paid to managers and workers if targets were achieved.

Stalin died in 1953, but the planning system remained largely unchanged throughout the Soviet Union until the late 1980s. Initially, high growth rates had been achieved, though at a cost of low efficiency. Poor flows of information led to inconsistencies in the plans. Targets were often unrealistic, and as a result there were frequent shortages and sometimes surpluses. There was little product innovation and goods were frequently of poor quality. A large 'underground economy' flourished in which goods were sold on the illegal market and in which people did second 'unofficial' jobs.

Moves to the market

By the time Gorbachev came to power in 1985 many people were pressing for economic reform. Gorbachev responded with his policy of perestroika (economic reconstruction), which involved managers preparing their own plans and managers and workers being rewarded for becoming more efficient. Under the new system, one-person businesses and larger co-operatives were allowed, while the price mechanism was reintroduced with the state raising prices if there were substantial shortages.

These reforms, however, did not halt the economic decline. Managers resented the extra responsibilities and people were unclear as to what to expect from the state. Queues lengthened in the shops and people became disillusioned with *perestroika*.

Communism fell apart in 1989 and both the Soviet Union and the system of central planning came to an end. Russia embarked upon a radical programme of market reforms in which competition and enterprise were intended to replace state central planning (see Case Studies 1.5, Free-market medicine in Russia; 14.9, Privatisation in transition economies; and 14.10, Forms of privatisation in transition countries, on the student website).

Initially, the disruption of the move to the market led to a sharp decline in the Russian economy. GDP fell by an average of 5.5 per cent per annum between 1993 and 1998. This was followed by a period of rapid economic growth, which averaged 7 per cent from 2000 to 2008. But the economy declined by nearly 8 per cent in the 2009 recession. Although this was followed by growth rates of 4.5 and 5.1 per cent in 2010 and 2011, since then growth has averaged only 1.4 per cent. Many commentators point to decades of underinvestment in industry and in road and rail infrastructure, corruption, disillusionment and continuing political uncertainty as root causes of this sluggish growth rate. From 2014, the economy was further dampened by Western economic sanctions in response to Russia's annexation of Crimea and the continuing conflict in Eastern Ukraine. Russia went into recession in 2015, but rebounded in 2017 and 2018 only to go back into recession with the onset of the coronavirus pandemic.

The interdependence of markets

The interdependence of goods and factor markets. A rise in demand for a good will raise its price and profitability. Firms will respond by supplying more. But to do this they will need more inputs. Thus the demand for the inputs (factors of production) will rise, which in turn will raise the price of the inputs. The suppliers of inputs will respond to this incentive by supplying more. This can be summarised as follows:

1. Goods market
   - Demand for the good rises.
   - This creates a shortage.
   - This causes the price of the good to rise.
   - This eliminates the shortage by reducing demand and encouraging firms to produce more.
2. Factor market
   - The increased supply of the good causes an increase in the demand for factors of production (i.e. inputs) used in making it.
   - This causes a shortage of those inputs.
   - This causes their prices to rise.
   - This eliminates their shortage by reducing demand and encouraging the suppliers of inputs to supply more.

CASE STUDIES AND APPLICATIONS

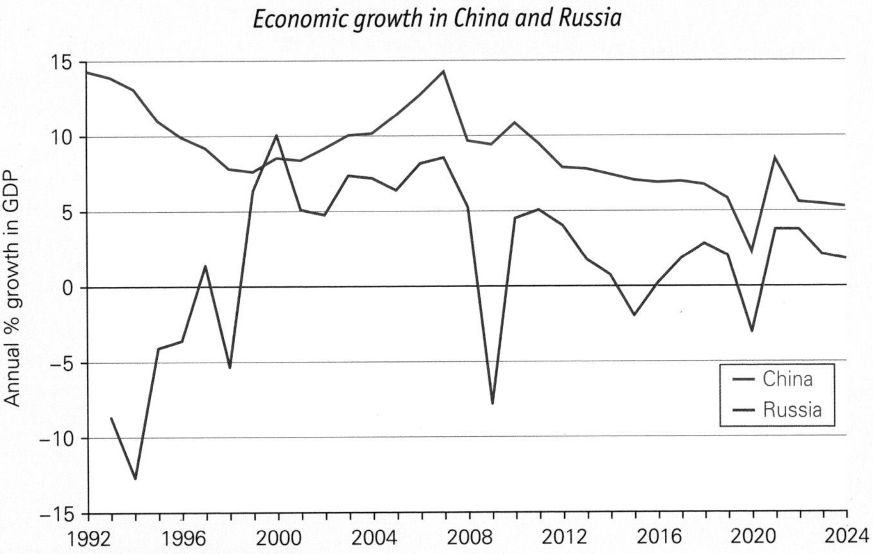

Note: Figures from 2021 based on forecasts

Source: Data drawn from *World Economic Outlook Database*, IMF (April 2021), www.imf.org/en/Publications/WEO/weo-database/2021/April

China

In contrast to the Soviet Union, China's move towards a more market-based economy has been carefully managed by the ruling Communist Party. From the 1940s to the 1970s central planning, combined with the removal of all property rights, resulted in low productivity, a creaking infrastructure and famine.

But after the death of Party Chairman Mao Zedong in 1976, a new breed of Chinese leaders came to power, and they were increasingly pragmatic. There was a focus on making use of aspects of capitalism alongside government control of the economy. Productivity was valued equally with political stability, while consumer welfare was considered as important as the elimination of unemployment. Economic zones were set up, where foreign investment was encouraged, and laws on patents and other intellectual property encouraged innovation. This approach was developed further over the following decades and from 1992 to 2010 China averaged growth of 10.5 per cent per annum – the highest in the world.

Today, China is the world's second largest economy and, although growth has slowed somewhat to around 6 per cent, is poised to overtake the USA by the mid-2020s, albeit with much lower output *per head*. Yet its human rights record remains a concern to many around the world; economic liberalisation and growth have not been accompanied by political freedom. Furthermore, it is experiencing some of the problems of capitalism: pollution, income inequality and potential instability of the financial system. It remains unclear how long the combination of capitalist economics alongside tight political control can continue to deliver.

Investigate some examples of market reforms in either China or Russia and discuss their likely effects.

So changes in goods markets will lead to changes in factor markets. Figure 1.7 summarises this sequence of events, where the subscripts 'g' and 'f' refer to the good and the factors used in making it respectively. (It is common in economics to summarise an argument like this by using symbols.)

Interdependence exists in the other direction too: factor markets affect goods markets. For example, the discovery of raw materials will lower their price. This will lower the costs of production of firms using these raw materials and will increase the supply of the finished goods. The resulting surplus will lower the price of the good, which will encourage consumers to buy more.

Summarise this last paragraph using symbols like those in Figure 1.7.

The interdependence of different goods markets. A rise in the price of one good will encourage consumers to buy alternatives. This will drive up the price of alternatives. This in turn will encourage producers to supply more of the alternatives.

Are different factor markets similarly interdependent? What would happen if the price of capital equipment rose?

Figure 1.7 The price mechanism: the effect of a rise in demand

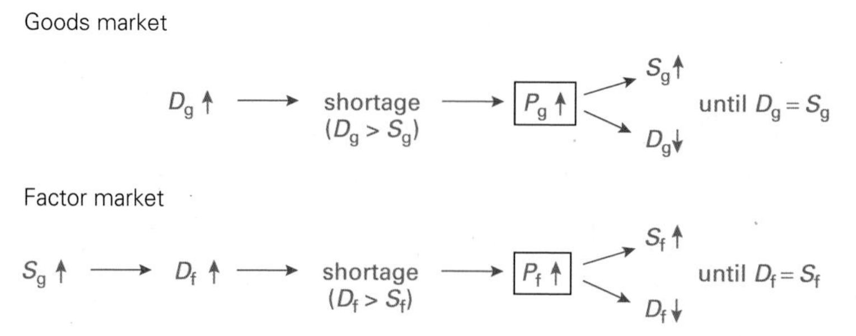

Goods market

$D_g \uparrow \longrightarrow$ shortage $(D_g > S_g) \longrightarrow$ $\boxed{P_g \uparrow}$ → $S_g \uparrow$ / $D_g \downarrow$ until $D_g = S_g$

Factor market

$S_g \uparrow \longrightarrow D_f \uparrow \longrightarrow$ shortage $(D_f > S_f) \longrightarrow$ $\boxed{P_f \uparrow}$ → $S_f \uparrow$ / $D_f \downarrow$ until $D_f = S_f$

Conclusion

Even though all individuals are merely looking to their own self-interest in the free-market economy, they are in fact being encouraged to respond to the wishes of others through the incentive of the price mechanism. (See Case Study 1.4, The interdependence of markets, on the student website; see also Box 1.6.)

Assessment of the free-market economy

The fact that a free-market economy functions automatically is one of its major advantages. There is no need for costly and complex bureaucracies to co-ordinate economic decisions. The economy can respond quickly to changing demand and supply conditions.

When markets are highly competitive, no one has great power. Competition between firms keeps prices down and acts as an incentive for efficiency. The more firms there are competing, the more responsive they will be to consumer wishes.

The more efficiently firms can combine their factors of production, the more profit they will make. The more efficiently workers work, the higher their wages are likely to be. The more carefully consumers decide what to buy, the greater the value for money they will receive.

Thus people pursuing their own self-interest through buying and selling in competitive markets helps to minimise the central economic problem of scarcity, by encouraging the efficient use of society's resources in line with consumer wishes. From this type of argument, the following conclusion is often drawn by defenders of the free market: 'The pursuit of private gain results in the social good.' This claim is the subject of much debate and has profound moral implications (see Threshold Concept 2).

BOX 1.6 **ADAM SMITH (1723–90)** EXPLORING ECONOMICS

The 'invisible hand' of the market

Many economists would argue that modern economics dates from 1776, the year in which Adam Smith's *An Inquiry into the Nature and Causes of the Wealth of Nations* was published – one of the most important books on economics ever written.

The work, in five books, is very wide-ranging, but the central argument is that market economies generally serve the public interest well. Markets guide production and consumption like an *invisible hand*. Even though everyone is looking after their own private self-interest, their interaction in the market will lead to the social good.

KI 5 p21

In book I, Chapter 2, Smith writes:

> Man has almost constant occasion for the help of his brethren and it is in vain for him to expect it from their benevolence only . . . It is not from the benevolence of the butcher, the brewer, or the baker that we expect our dinner, but from their regard to their own interest. We address ourselves, not to their humanity but to their self-love, and never talk to them of our own necessities, but of their advantages.

Later, in book IV, Chapter 2, he continues:

> Every individual is continually exerting himself to find out the most advantageous employment of whatever capital he can command. It is his own advantage, indeed, and not that of the society, which he has in view. But the study of his own advantage naturally, or rather necessarily, leads him to prefer that employment which is most advantageous to the society . . . he intends only his own gain, and he is in this, as in many other cases, led by an invisible hand to promote an end which was no part of his intention. Nor is it always the worse for the society that it was no part of it. By pursuing his own interest he frequently promotes that of society more effectually than when he really intends to promote it.

He argued, therefore, with one or two exceptions, that the state should not interfere with the functioning of the economy.

It should adopt a laissez-faire or 'hands-off' policy. It should allow free enterprise for firms and free trade between countries.

This praise of the free market has led many on the political right to regard him as the father of the 'libertarian movement' – the movement that advocates the absolute minimum amount of state intervention in the economy (see Box 12.7 on page 397). In fact, one of the most famous of the libertarian societies is called the Adam Smith Institute.

But Smith was not blind to the drawbacks of unregulated markets. In book I, Chapter 7, he looks at the problem of monopoly:

> A monopoly granted either to an individual or to a trading company has the same effect as a secret in trade or manufactures. The monopolists, by keeping the market constantly under-stocked, by never fully supplying the effectual demand, sell their commodities much above the natural price, and raise their emoluments, whether they consist in wages or profit, greatly above their natural rate.

Later on he looks at the dangers of firms getting together to pursue their mutual interest:

> People of the same trade seldom meet together, even for merriment or diversion, but the conversation ends in a conspiracy against the public or in some contrivance to raise prices.

Problems of the free market

In practice, however, markets do not achieve maximum efficiency in the allocation of scarce resources, and governments therefore feel it necessary to intervene to rectify this and other problems of the free market. The problems of a free market include:

- Power and property may be unequally distributed. Those who have power and/or property (e.g. big business, unions and landlords) will gain at the expense of those without power and property.
- Competition between firms is often limited. A few firms may dominate an industry, charging high prices and making large profits.
- Consumers and firms may not have full information about the costs and benefits associated with different goods and factor inputs and may thus make the wrong decisions.
- Rather than responding to consumer wishes, firms may attempt to persuade consumers by advertising.
- Lack of competition and high profits may remove the incentive for firms to be efficient.
- The practices of some firms may be socially undesirable. For example, a chemical works may pollute the environment.
- Some socially desirable goods would simply not be produced by private enterprise. Who would carry out counter-terrorism activities if this were not funded by governments?
- A free-market economy may lead to macroeconomic instability. There may be periods of recession with high unemployment and falling output, and other periods of rising prices.
- Finally, there is the ethical objection, that a free-market economy, by rewarding self-interested behaviour, may encourage selfishness, greed, materialism and the acquisition of power.

The fact that free markets may fail to meet various social objectives is Threshold Concept 3.

The mixed economy

Because of the problems of both free-market and command economies, all real-world economies are a mixture of the two systems.

In ***mixed market economies***, the government may control the following:

- ***Relative prices*** of goods and inputs, by taxing or subsidising them or by direct price controls.
- Relative incomes, by the use of income taxes, welfare payments or direct controls over wages, profits, rents, etc.
- The pattern of production and consumption, by the use of legislation (e.g. making it illegal to produce unsafe goods), by direct provision of goods and services (e.g. education and defence) or by taxes and subsidies.
- The macroeconomic problems of unemployment, inflation, lack of growth, balance of trade deficits and exchange rate fluctuations, by the use of taxes and government expenditure, the control of bank lending and interest rates, the direct control of prices and the control of foreign exchange rates.

The fact that government intervention can be used to rectify various failings of the market is Threshold Concept 7 (see Chapter 3, page 79). It is important to realise, however, that government actions may bring adverse as well as beneficial consequences. For more on government intervention in the mixed economy see Chapters 11 to 14.

TC 7
p79

Definitions

Mixed market economy A market economy where there is some government intervention.

Relative price The price of one good compared with another (e.g. good X is twice the price of good Y).

THRESHOLD CONCEPT 2 PEOPLE GAIN FROM VOLUNTARY ECONOMIC INTERACTION

THINKING LIKE AN ECONOMIST

Economic interaction between people can take a number of different forms. Sometimes it takes place in markets. For example, when goods are exchanged, there is interaction between the consumer and the shop. When someone is employed, there is interaction between the employer and the employee. When a firm buys raw materials, there is interaction between the purchasing firm and the selling firm.

In each case there is expected to be a mutual gain. If there wasn't, the interaction would not take place. If you go on a holiday costing £400, then assuming the holiday turns out as you expected, you will have gained. You would rather have the holiday than spend the £400 on something else. The marginal benefit to you exceeds the marginal cost. The travel agent and tour operator also gain. They make a profit on selling you the holiday. It is a 'win–win situation'. This is sometimes called a *positive sum game*: an interaction where there is a positive net gain.

Another example is international trade (the subject of Chapter 24). If two countries trade with each other, there will be a net gain to both of them. If there wasn't, they would not trade. Both countries will end up consuming a greater value of products than they could without trade. The reason is that each country can specialise in the products it is relatively good at producing (compared to the other country) and export them, and import from the other country the goods it is relatively poor at producing.

That there is a net gain from voluntary interaction is a *threshold concept* because realising this tends to change the way we look at economic activity. Often it is important to identify what these overall gains are so that we can compare them with alternative forms of interaction. For example, even though both workers and their employer respectively gain from the wages currently paid and the output currently produced, it might still be possible to reorganise the workforce in a way that increases production. This could allow the employer to pay higher wages and still gain an increase in profits. Both sides could thus gain from constructive negotiation about wages and new work practices.

Sometimes it may appear that voluntary interaction results in one side gaining and the other losing. For example, a firm may raise its price. It gains and the consumer loses. But is this strictly true? Consumers are certainly worse off than before, but as long as they are still prepared to buy the product, they must consider that they are still gaining more by buying it than by not. There is still a gain to both sides: it's just that the firm is gaining more and the consumer is gaining less.

1. *Would you ever swap things with friends if both of you did not gain? Explain your answer.*
2. *Give one or two examples of involuntary (i.e. compulsory) economic interaction, where one side gains but the other loses.*

THRESHOLD CONCEPT 3 MARKETS MAY FAIL TO MEET SOCIAL OBJECTIVES

THINKING LIKE AN ECONOMIST

We have seen that market forces can automatically equate demand and supply. The outcomes of the process may be desirable, but they are by no means always so. Unrestrained market forces can result in severe problems for individuals, society and the environment.

Markets tend to reflect the combined actions of individual consumers and firms. But when consumers and firms make their decisions, they may act selfishly and fail to take account of the broader effects of their actions. If people want to buy guns, market forces will make their supply profitable. If people want to drive fuel-hungry cars, then this will create the market for firms to supply them. Market forces are not kind and caring. They mechanically reflect human behaviour.

And it's not just selfish behaviour that markets reflect, but ignorance too. You may be unaware that a toy you buy for a child is dangerous, but by buying it, you encourage unscrupulous firms to supply them. A firm may not realise that a piece of machinery it uses is dangerous until an accident happens. In the meantime, it continues using it because it is profitable to do so.

If wages are determined purely by demand and supply, then some people, such as footballers and bankers, may be very well paid. Others, such as cleaners and shop workers, may be very poorly paid. If the resulting inequality is seen as unfair, then market forces alone will not be enough to achieve a fair society.

Recognising the limitations and failings of markets is a *threshold concept*. It helps us to understand how laws or taxes or subsidies could be framed to counteract such failings. It helps us to relate the mechanical operation of demand and supply to a whole range of social objectives and ask whether the market system is the best way of meeting such objectives.

But to recognise market failures is only part of the way to finding a solution. Can the government put things right, and if so, how? Or do the limitations of government mean that the solution is sometimes worse than the problem? We examine these issues in many parts of the book. We set the scene in Threshold Concept 7 on page 79.

1. *If global warming affects all of us adversely, why in a purely market economy would individuals and firms continue with activities that contribute towards global warming?*
2. *In what ways do your own consumption patterns adversely affect other people?*

Section summary

1. The economic systems of different countries vary according to the extent to which they rely on the market or the government to allocate resources.
2. At the one extreme, in a command economy, the state makes all the economic decisions. It plans amounts of resources to allocate for present consumption and amounts for investment for future output. It plans the output of each industry, the methods of production it will use and the amount of resources it will be allocated. It plans the distribution of output between consumers.
3. A command economy has the advantage of being able to address directly various national economic goals, such as rapid growth and the avoidance of unemployment and inequality. A command economy, however, is likely to be inefficient and bureaucratic; prices and the choice of production methods are likely to be arbitrary; incentives may be inappropriate; shortages and surpluses may result.
4. At the other extreme is the free-market economy. In this economy, decisions are made by the interaction of demand and supply. Price changes act as the mechanism whereby demand and supply are balanced. If there is a shortage, price will rise until the shortage is eliminated. If there is a surplus, price will fall until that is eliminated.
5. A free-market economy functions automatically and if there is plenty of competition between producers this can help to protect consumers' interests. In practice, however, competition may be limited; there may be great inequality; there may be adverse social and environmental consequences; there may be macroeconomic instability.
6. In practice, all economies are some mixture of the market and government intervention. It is the degree and form of government intervention that distinguishes one type of economy from another.

1.4 THE NATURE OF ECONOMIC REASONING

Economics is one of the social sciences. So in what sense is it a *science*? Is it like the natural sciences such as physics and astronomy? What is the significance of the word 'social' in social science? What can economists do, and what is their role in helping governments devise economic policy?

Economics as a science

The methodology employed by economists has a lot in common with that employed by natural scientists. Both attempt to construct theories or ***models*** which are then used to *explain* and *predict*. An astronomer, for example, constructs models of planetary movements to *explain* why planets are in the position they are and to *predict* their position in the future.

Models in economics

In order to explain and predict, the economist constructs models which show simplified relationships between various economic phenomena. The simplification is deliberate – economists know their models look nothing like the real world they hope to explain. It is referred to as abstraction. An example of a model is one showing the relationships between demand, supply and price of a product. Although most models can be described verbally, they can normally be represented more precisely in graphical or mathematical form.

Building models

Models are constructed by making general hypotheses about the causes of economic phenomena: for example, that consumer demand will rise when consumer incomes rise. These hypotheses will often be based on observations. This process of making general statements from particular observations is known as ***induction***.

Using models

Explanation. Models explain by showing how things are caused: what the causes of inflation are, why workers in some industries earn more than others, and so on. A model is constructed to help explain a particular relationship or set of phenomena. An economic model might be really useful for one purpose but not very useful for another.

Prediction. Models are sometimes used to make simple forecasts: for example, inflation will be below 5 per cent next year. Usually, however, predictions are of the 'If . . . then . . .' variety: for example, if demand for good x rises, its price will rise. This process of drawing conclusions from models is known as ***deduction***.

When making such deductions it has to be assumed that nothing else that can influence the outcome has changed in the meantime. For example, if demand for

Definitions

Economic model A formal presentation of an economic theory.

Induction Constructing general theories on the basis of specific observations.

Deduction Using a theory to draw conclusions about specific circumstances.

good *x* rises, its price will rise *assuming* the cost of producing good *x* has not fallen. This is known as the ***ceteris paribus*** assumption. *Ceteris paribus* is Latin for 'other things being equal'.

Assessing models

Models can be judged according to how successful they are in explaining and predicting. They are not judged by how closely they resemble the real world.

If the predictions are wrong, the first thing to do is to check whether the deductions were correctly made. If they were, the model must be either adapted or abandoned in favour of an alternative model with better predictive ability. But in economics, as with many other disciplines, academics are often unwilling to abandon their models. Instead they prefer the minimum adaptation necessary. This can lead to lively debates between different 'schools of thought', each claiming that their models paint a more accurate picture of the economy.

There has been a great deal of debate in recent years about why economic models failed to forecast the financial crisis of 2007–8. In September 2010, Ben Bernanke, the then Federal Reserve Board Chairman, said the failure of the economic models did not mean that they were irrelevant or significantly flawed. Rather than throwing out the models, more work was needed to capture how the financial system impacts on growth and stability. Some people argued that the models were simply misused: i.e. used for a purpose they were not designed for. John Kay argued it was like using a London Underground map to work out the best walking route![4]

Others disagreed. They claimed that many of the main models that had failed to predict the crisis were fundamentally flawed and needed replacing with other models – perhaps amended versions of older ones; perhaps new ones.

We look at these debates in Parts E and F of the book.

4 John Kay, *Obliquity* (Profile Books, 2010).

Economists as detectives

Because of a lack of conclusive evidence about just how many parts of the economy function, economists also need the skills of detectives. This involves a third type of reasoning (in addition to induction and deduction), known as ***abduction***. This involves making informed guesses or estimates from limited evidence. It is using the scraps of evidence as clues to what might be really going on. It is how many initial hypotheses are formed. Then the researcher (or detective) will use the clues to search for more evidence that can be used for induction that will yield a more robust theory. The clues may lead to a false trail, but sometimes they may allow the researcher to develop a new theory or amend an existing one. A good researcher will be alert to clues; to seeing patterns in details that might previously have been dismissed or gone unnoticed.

Before the banking crisis of 2007–8 and the subsequent credit crunch and recession in the developed world, many economists were picking up clues and trying to use them to develop a theory of systemic risk in financial markets. They were using the skills of an economic detective to try to discover not only what was currently going on but also what might be the consequences for the future. Some used abductive reasoning successfully to predict the impending crisis; most did not.

Definitions

Ceteris paribus Latin for 'other things being equal'. This assumption has to be made when making deductions from theories.

Abduction Using pieces of evidence to develop a plausible explanation. This can then be tested by gathering more evidence.

BOX 1.7 *CETERIS PARIBUS*

CASE STUDIES AND APPLICATIONS

Because of the complexities of the real world, economic models have to make various simplifying assumptions. Sometimes, however, economists are criticised for making unrealistic assumptions, assumptions that make their models irrelevant. The following joke illustrates the point.

There were three people cast away on a desert island: a chemist, an engineer and an economist. There was no food on the island and their plight seemed desperate.

Then they discovered a crate of canned food that had been washed up on the island. When they realised that they had no means of opening the cans, they decided that each of them should use their expertise to find a solution.

The chemist searched around for various minerals that could be heated up to produce a compound that would burn through the lids of the cans.

The engineer hunted around for rocks and then worked out what height of tree they would have to be dropped from in order to smash open the cans.

Meanwhile the economist sat down and thought 'Assuming we had a can opener . . . '.

Economics as a social science

Economics concerns human behaviour. One problem here is that individuals often behave in very different ways. People have different tastes and different attitudes. This problem, however, is not as serious as it may seem at first sight. The reason is that people *on average* are likely to behave more predictably. For example, if the price of a product goes up by 5 per cent, we might be able to predict, *ceteris paribus*, that the quantity demanded will fall by approximately 10 per cent. This does not mean that every single individual's demand will fall by 10 per cent, only that *total* demand will. Some people may demand a lot less; others may demand the same as before.

Even so, there are still things about human behaviour that are very difficult to predict, even when we are talking about whole groups of people. How, for example, will firms react to a rise in interest rates when making their investment decisions? This will depend on things such as the state of business confidence, something that is notoriously difficult to predict. How will a business respond to price changes by its rivals? This will often depend on how it thinks its rivals themselves will react to its own response. How will people respond to a crisis, such as the global banking and credit crisis of 2007–8? This depends very much on the mood of financial and other companies and individuals. A mood of pessimism (or optimism for that matter) can quickly spread, but not to a degree that is easily predictable.

For these reasons there is plenty of scope for competing models in economics, each making different assumptions and leading to different policy conclusions. As a result, economics can often be highly controversial. As we shall see later on in the book, different political parties may adhere to different schools of economic thought. Thus the political left may adhere to a model which implies that governments must intervene if unemployment is to be cured, whereas the political right may adhere to a model which implies that unemployment will be reduced if the government intervenes less and relies more on the free market.

One branch of economics that has seen considerable growth in recent years is behavioural economics, which adds elements of psychology to traditional models in an attempt to gain a better understanding of decision making by investors, consumers and other economic participants. Much of the early evidence in support of behavioural economics came from laboratory experiments where people made decisions in simulated environments – normally a computer room. More recent evidence has come from field experiments, where people make decisions in a more natural environment and do not know their behaviour is being observed. For more on behavioural economics see Chapters 4, 5, 9, 10, 13 and 14.

The fact that there are different economic theories does not mean that economists always disagree. Despite the popular belief that 'if you laid all the economists of the world end to end they would still not reach a conclusion', there is in fact a large measure of agreement between economists about how to analyse the world and what conclusions to draw.

Economics and policy

Economists play a major role in helping governments to devise economic policy. In order to understand this role, it is necessary to distinguish between 'positive' and 'normative' statements.

A ***positive statement*** is a statement of fact. It may be right or wrong, but its accuracy can be tested by appealing to the facts. 'Unemployment is rising', 'Inflation will be over 6 per cent by next year' and 'If the government cuts taxes, imports will rise' are all examples of positive statements.

A ***normative statement*** is a statement of value: a statement about what ought or ought not to be, about whether something is good or bad, desirable or undesirable. 'It is right to tax the rich more than the poor', 'The government ought to reduce inflation' and 'State pensions ought to be increased' are all examples of normative statements. They cannot be proved or disproved by a simple appeal to the facts.

Economists can only contribute to questions of policy in a positive way. That is, they can analyse the consequences of following certain policies. They can say which of two policies is more likely to achieve a given aim, but they should not, as economists, say whether the aims of the policy are desirable. For example, economists may argue that a policy of increasing government expenditure will reduce unemployment and raise inflation, but they cannot, as economists, decide whether such a policy is desirable. TC 1 p10

KEY IDEA 6

The importance of the positive/normative distinction. **Economics can only contribute to policy issues in a positive way. Economists, as scientists, should not make normative judgements. They can make them only as individual people, with no more moral right than any other individual.**

Which of the following are positive statements and which are normative?

(a) Cutting the higher rates of income tax will redistribute incomes from the poor to the rich.
(b) It is wrong that inflation should be targeted if the consequence is higher unemployment.
(c) It is incorrect to state that putting up interest rates will reduce inflation.
(d) The government should introduce road pricing to address the issue of congestion.
(e) Current government policies should be aimed at reducing the deficit rather than stimulating growth.

Definitions

Positive statement A value-free statement which can be tested by an appeal to the facts.

Normative statement A value judgement.

Section summary

1. The methodology used by economists is similar to that used by natural scientists. Economists construct models, which they use to explain and predict economic phenomena. These models can be tested by appealing to facts and seeing how successfully they have been predicted or explained by the model. Unsuccessful models can be either abandoned or amended.
2. Being a social science, economics is concerned with human actions. Making accurate predictions in economics is very difficult given that economics has to deal with a constantly changing environment.
3. Economists can help governments to devise policy by examining the consequences of alternative courses of action. In doing this, it is important to separate positive questions about what the effects of the policies are from normative ones as to what the goals of policy should be. Economists in their role as economists have no superior right to make normative judgements. They do, however, play a major role in assessing whether a policy meets the political objectives of government (or opposition).

END OF CHAPTER QUESTIONS

1. Imagine that a country can produce just two things: goods and services. Assume that over a given period it could produce any of the following combinations:

Units of goods										
0	10	20	30	40	50	60	70	80	90	100
Units of services										
80	79	77	74	70	65	58	48	35	19	0

(a) Draw the country's production possibility curve.

(b) Assuming that the country is currently producing 40 units of goods and 70 units of services, what is the opportunity cost of producing another 10 units of goods?

(c) Explain how the figures illustrate the principle of increasing opportunity cost.

(d) Now assume that technical progress leads to a 10 per cent increase in the output of goods for any given amount of resources. Draw the new production possibility curve. How has the opportunity cost of producing extra units of services altered?

2. Imagine that you won millions of pounds on the National Lottery. Would your 'economic problem' be solved?

3. Assume that in a household one parent currently works full-time and the other stays at home to look after the family. How would you set about identifying and calculating the opportunity costs of the second parent now taking a full-time job? How would such calculations be relevant in deciding whether it is worth taking that job?

4. When you made the decision to study economics, was it a 'rational' decision (albeit based on the limited information you had available at the time)? What additional information would you like to have had in order to ensure that your decision was the right one?

5. In what way does specialisation reduce the problem of scarcity?

6. Would redistributing incomes from the rich to the poor reduce the overall problem of scarcity?

7. Assume that fracking becomes common across the UK. The result is that supplies of shale gas and oil increase sharply. Trace through the effects of this on the market for oil, gas and the market for other fuels.

8. Give two examples of positive statements about the economy, and two examples of normative ones. Now give two examples that are seemingly positive, but which have normative implications or undertones.

Online resources

Additional case studies on the student website

1.1 **Buddhist economics.** A different perspective on economic problems and economic activity.

1.2 **Green economics.** This examines some of the environmental costs that society faces today. It also looks at the role of economics in analysing these costs and how the problems can be tackled.

1.3 **Global economics.** This examines how macroeconomics and microeconomics apply at the global level and identifies some key issues.

1.4 **The interdependence of markets.** A case study in the operation of markets, examining the effects on a local economy of the discovery of a large coal deposit.

1.5 **Free-market medicine in Russia.** This examines the operating of the fledgling market economy in Russia and the successes and difficulties in moving from a planned to a market economy.

1.6 **Alternative measures of well-being.** This case study takes a preliminary look at how we measure the well-being of society. Should we use output (GDP) per head or some other measure?

Websites relevant to this chapter

Numbers and sections refer to websites listed in the Web Appendix and hotlinked from this book's website at **go.pearson.com/uk/sloman**.

- For news articles relevant to this chapter, see the *Sloman Economics News* site link from MyEconLab or the *Economics News* section on the student website.
- For general economics news sources, see websites in section A of the Web Appendix at the end of the book, and particularly A1–9, 24, 25, 35, 36. See also A39–44 for links to newspapers worldwide.
- For sources of economic data, see sites in section B and particularly B1–5, 21, 33, 34, 38, 47.
- For general sites for students of economics, see sites in section C and particularly C1–10.
- For sites giving links to relevant economics websites, organised by topic, see sites I2, 3, 7, 12, 13, 14, 16.
- For news on the Russian economy (Box 1.5 and Case Study 1.5 on the student website), see sites A14, 15.
- For an excellent site giving details of the lives, works and theories of famous economists from the history of economic thought (including Adam Smith from Box 1.6), see C18.

Part B

Foundations of Microeconomics

In the first half of the book, we focus on microeconomics. Despite being 'small economics' – in other words, the economics of the individual parts of the economy, rather than the economy as a whole – it is still concerned with many of the big issues of today. To understand how the economy works at this micro level, we must understand how markets work. This involves an understanding of demand and supply.

In Chapter 2, we look at how demand and supply interact to determine prices (and so allocate resources) in a free-market economy. We will also see just how responsive they are to changing circumstances.

Markets, however, are not always free: governments frequently intervene in markets. In Chapter 3, we look at some of the reasons why governments may choose to reject the free market and examine the methods they use to influence prices, output and allocation.

We look at markets, their efficiency and government intervention in more detail in Parts C and D.

Supply and Demand

CHAPTER MAP

As we saw in Chapter 1, in a free-market economy prices play a key role in transmitting information from buyers to sellers and from sellers to buyers. This chapter examines this 'price mechanism' in more detail.

We examine what determines demand, what determines supply and what the relationship is between demand, supply and price. We see how the price mechanism transmits information both from consumers to producers, and from producers to consumers; and how prices act as incentives – for example, if consumers want more European city breaks, how this increased demand leads to an increase in their price and hence to an incentive for firms to increase their production.

What we will see is the mechanism whereby the free market responds to changes in demand or supply – and responds in a way that balances demand and supply at a position of 'equilibrium'.

But we will also need to see just how much prices and output respond to changes in demand and supply. How much will the demand for music downloads go up if their price comes down? How much will the supply of new houses go up if the price of houses rises? In section 2.4 we develop the concept of elasticity of demand and supply to examine this responsiveness.

Finally, we look at how quickly markets adjust and also examine how people's expectations of price changes affect what actually happens to prices. In particular, we look at speculation – people attempting to gain from anticipated price changes.

The markets we will be examining are highly competitive ones, with many firms competing against each other. In economics we call this ***perfect competition***. This is where consumers and producers are too numerous to have any control over prices: they are ***price takers.***

In the case of consumers, this means that they have to accept the prices as given for the things that they buy. On most occasions this is true; when you get to the supermarket checkout you cannot start haggling with the checkout operator over the price of a can of beans or a tub of ice cream.

In the case of firms, perfect competition means that producers are small and face too much competition from other firms to be able to raise prices. Take the case of foreign exchange traders selling euros. They have to sell the currency at the current market price. If individually they try to sell at a higher price, no one will buy, since purchasers of currency can get all the euros they want at the market price.

Of course, many firms *do* have the power to choose their prices. This does not mean that they can simply charge whatever they like. They will still have to take account of overall consumer demand and their competitors' prices. Apple, when setting the price of its iPhones, will have to ensure that they remain competitive with those produced by Samsung, Huawei, etc. Nevertheless, most firms have some flexibility in setting their prices: they have a degree of 'market power'.

If this is the case, then why do we study *perfect* markets, where firms are price takers? One reason is that they provide a useful approximation to the real world and give us many insights into how a market economy works. Many markets, such as those in agriculture and finance, do function very similarly to those we shall be describing.

Another is that perfect markets provide an ideal against which to compare the real world, since in perfect markets we see resources being used and allocated efficiently. Economists can therefore use them as a benchmark when comparing the prices, output, profit, etc. in different types of market. For example, will the consumer end up paying higher prices in a market dominated by just a few firms than in one operating under perfect competition? Will Netflix respond to an increase in the demand for streaming services in the same way as a farmer does to an increase in the demand for cauliflowers?

Markets with powerful firms are examined in Chapters 7 and 8. For now we concentrate on price takers.

2.1 DEMAND

The relationship between demand and price

The headlines announce, 'Major crop failures in Brazil and Vietnam: coffee prices soar'. Shortly afterwards you find that coffee prices have increased sharply in the shops. What do you do? You will probably cut back on the amount of coffee you drink. Perhaps you will reduce it from, say, six cups per day to four. Perhaps you will give up drinking coffee altogether.

This is simply an illustration of the general relationship between price and consumption: *when the price of a good rises, the quantity demanded will fall.* This relationship is known as the ***law of demand***. There are two reasons for this law:

- People will feel poorer. They will not be able to afford to buy as much of the good with their money. The purchasing power of their income (their *real income*) has fallen. This is called the ***income effect*** of a price rise.
- The good will now cost more than alternative or 'substitute' goods, and people will switch to these. This is called the ***substitution effect*** of a price rise.

Similarly, when the price of a good falls, the quantity demanded will rise. People can afford to buy more (the income effect), and they will switch away from consuming alternative goods (the substitution effect).

Therefore, returning to our example of the increase in the price of coffee, we will not be able to afford to buy as much as before, and we will probably drink more tea, cola, fruit juices or even water instead.

Definitions

Perfect competition (preliminary definition) A situation where the consumers and producers of a product are price takers. (There are other features of a perfectly competitive market; these are examined in Chapter 7.)

Price taker A person or firm with no power to be able to influence the market price.

Law of demand The quantity of a good demanded per period of time will fall as price rises and will rise as price falls, other things being equal (*ceteris paribus*).

Income effect The effect of a change in price on quantity demanded arising from the consumer becoming better or worse off as a result of the price change.

Substitution effect The effect of a change in price on quantity demanded arising from the consumer switching to or from alternative (substitute) products.

The income and substitution effects are useful concepts as they help to explain why people react to a price rise by buying less. The size of these effects depends on a range of factors. These factors determine the shape of the demand curve.

A word of warning: be careful about the meaning of the words ***quantity demanded***. They refer to the amount that consumers are willing and able to purchase at a given price over a given period (e.g. a week, or a month, or a year). They do not refer to what people would simply *like* to consume. You might like to own a luxury yacht, but your demand for luxury yachts will almost certainly be zero at the current price. Quantity demanded may also be different from the quantity actually purchased. A consumer may be willing and able to purchase the good but cannot find a supplier willing to sell at that price.

The demand curve

Consider the hypothetical data in Table 2.1, which shows how many kilograms of potatoes per month would be purchased at various prices.

Columns (2) and (3) show the ***demand schedules*** for two individuals, Kate and Simon. Column (4) shows the total ***market demand schedule***. This is the total demand by all consumers. To obtain the market demand schedule for potatoes, we simply add up the quantities demanded at each price by all consumers: i.e. Kate, Simon and everyone else who demands potatoes. Notice that we are talking about demand *over a period of time* (not at a *point* in time). Thus we could talk about daily demand or weekly demand or annual demand.

Assume that there are 200 consumers in the market. Of these, 100 have schedules like Kate's and 100 have schedules like Simon's. What would be the total market demand schedule for potatoes now?

The demand schedule can be represented graphically as a ***demand curve***. Figure 2.1 shows the market demand curve for potatoes corresponding to the schedule in Table 2.1. The price of potatoes is plotted on the vertical axis. The quantity demanded is plotted on the horizontal axis.

Point *E* shows that at a price of 100p per kilo, 100 000 tonnes of potatoes are demanded each month. When the price falls to 80p we move down the curve to point *D*. This shows that the quantity demanded has now risen to 200 000 tonnes per month. Similarly, if the price falls to 60p we move down the curve again to point *C*: 350 000 tonnes are now demanded. The five points on the graph (*A*–*E*) correspond to the figures in columns (1) and (4) of Table 2.1. The graph also enables us to read off the likely quantities demanded at prices other than those in the table.

1. *How much would be demanded at a price of 30p per kilogram?*
2. *Assuming that demand does not change from month to month, plot the annual market demand for potatoes.*

Table 2.1 The demand for potatoes (monthly)

	Price (pence per kg) (1)	Kate's demand (kg) (2)	Simon's demand (kg) (3)	Total market demand (tonnes: 000s) (4)
A	20	28	16	700
B	40	15	11	500
C	60	5	9	350
D	80	1	7	200
E	100	0	6	100

Definitions

Quantity demanded The amount of a good that a consumer is willing and able to buy at a given price over a given period of time.

Demand schedule for an individual A table showing the different quantities of a good that a person is willing and able to buy at various prices over a given period of time.

Market demand schedule A table showing the different total quantities of a good that consumers are willing and able to buy at various prices over a given period of time.

Demand curve A graph showing the relationship between the price of a good and the quantity of the good demanded over a given time period. Price is measured on the vertical axis; quantity demanded is measured on the horizontal axis. A demand curve can be for an individual consumer or group of consumers, or more usually for the whole market.

Figure 2.1 Market demand curve for potatoes (monthly)

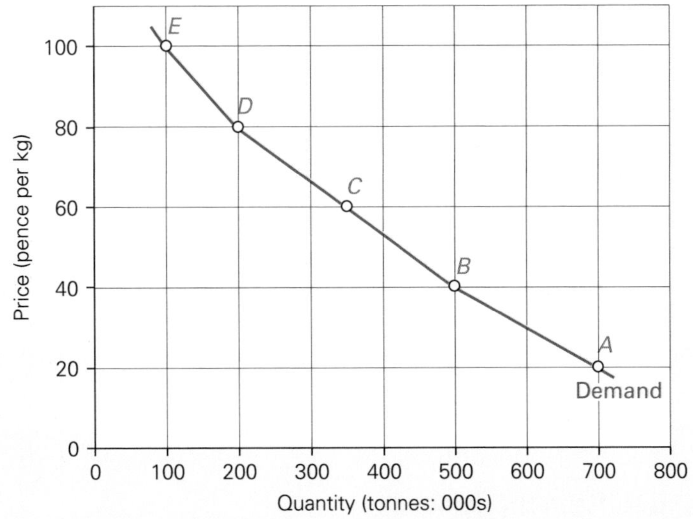

A demand curve could also be drawn for an individual consumer. Like market demand curves, individuals' demand curves generally slope downwards from left to right: they have negative slope. The lower the price of the product, the more a person is likely to buy.

1. *Draw Kate's and Simon's demand curves for potatoes on one diagram. Note that you will use the same vertical scale as in Figure 2.1, but you will need a quite different horizontal scale.*
2. *At what price is their demand the same?*
3. *What explanations could there be for the quite different shapes of their two demand curves? (This question is explored in section 3.1 below.)*
4. *Assume that Kate and Simon are the only two consumers in the market. Show how it is possible to derive a market demand curve from their individual demand curves.*

Two points should be noted at this stage:

- In textbooks, demand curves (and other curves too) are only occasionally used to plot specific data. More frequently they are used to illustrate general theoretical arguments. In such cases the axes will simply be price and quantity, with the units unspecified.
- The term 'curve' is used even when the graph is a straight line. In fact when using demand curves to illustrate arguments we frequently draw them as straight lines – it's easier.

Other determinants of demand

Price is not the only factor that determines how much of a good people will buy. Demand is also affected by the following.

Tastes. The more desirable people find the good, the more they will demand. Tastes are affected by advertising, by trends and fashion, by observing other consumers, by considerations of health and by the experience of consuming the good on previous occasions. For example, during the lockdowns in 2020 roller-skating became very popular with the impact of influencers such as Oumi Janta. Big increases in the demand for roller skates caused a world-wide shortage.

TC 1 p10

The number and price of substitute goods (i.e. competitive goods). The higher the price of ***substitute goods***, the higher will be the demand for this good as people switch from the substitutes. For example, the price of cigarettes will influence the demand for e-cigarettes. If the price of cigarettes increases, the demand for e-cigarettes will rise.

The number and price of complementary goods. ***Complementary goods*** are those that are consumed together; cars and petrol, paper and ink cartridges, fish and chips. The higher the price of complementary goods, the fewer of them will be bought and hence the less will be the demand for the good under consideration. For example, the demand for games will depend on the price of games consoles, such as the Sony

Definitions

Substitute goods A pair of goods which are considered by consumers to be alternatives to each other. As the price of one goes up, the demand for the other rises.

Complementary goods A pair of goods consumed together. As the price of one goes up, the demand for both goods will fall.

PlayStation® and Microsoft box®. If the price of games consoles comes down, so that more are purchased, the demand for games will rise.

Income. As people's incomes rise, their demand for most goods will rise. Such goods are called ***normal goods***. There are exceptions to this general rule, however. As people get richer, they spend less on ***inferior goods***, such as supermarket 'value' ranges, and switch to better quality goods.

Distribution of income. If national income were redistributed from the poor to the rich, the demand for luxury goods would rise. At the same time, as the poor got poorer they might have to buy more inferior goods; demand for these would rise too.

Expectations of future price changes. If people think that prices are going to rise in the future, they are likely to buy more now before the price does go up.

Figure 2.2 An increase in demand

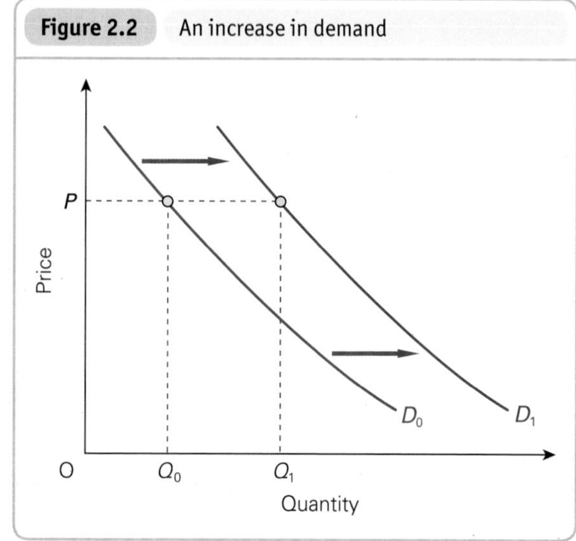

Movements along and shifts in the demand curve

A demand curve is constructed on the assumption that 'other things remain equal' (*ceteris paribus*). In other words, it is assumed that none of the determinants of demand, other than price, changes. The effect of a change in price is then simply illustrated by a movement along the demand curve: for example, from point *B* to point *D* in Figure 2.1 when the price of potatoes rises from 40p to 80p per kilo.

What happens, then, when one of these other determinants does change? The answer is that we have to construct a whole new demand curve: the curve shifts. If a change in one of the other determinants causes demand to rise – say, income rises – the whole curve will shift to the right. This shows that at each price more will be demanded than before. Thus, in Figure 2.2, at a price of *P*, a quantity of Q_0 was originally demanded. But now, after the increase in demand, Q_1 is demanded. (Note that D_1 is not necessarily parallel to D_0.)

If a change in a determinant other than price causes demand to fall, the whole curve will shift to the left.

To distinguish between shifts in and movements along demand curves, it is usual to distinguish between a change in *demand* and a change in the *quantity demanded*. A shift in the demand curve is referred to as a ***change in demand***, whereas a movement along the demand curve as a result of a change in price is referred to as a ***change in the quantity demanded***.

1. *Assume that in Table 2.1 the total market demand for potatoes increases by 20 per cent at each price – due, say, to substantial increases in the prices of bread and rice. Plot the old and the new demand curves for potatoes. Is the new curve parallel to the old one?*
2. *The price of strawberries rises and yet the sales of strawberries increase. Does this mean that the demand curve for strawberries is upward sloping? Explain.*

Definitions

Normal good A good whose demand rises as people's incomes rise.

Inferior good A good whose demand falls as people's incomes rise.

Change in demand The term used for a shift in the demand curve. It occurs when a determinant of demand other than price changes.

Change in the quantity demanded The term used for a movement along the demand curve to a new point. It occurs when there is a change in price.

*LOOKING AT THE MATHS

We can represent the relationship between the market demand for a good and the determinants of demand in the form of an equation. This is called a ***demand function***. It can be expressed either in general terms or with specific values attached to the determinants.

Simple demand functions

Demand equations are often used to relate quantity demanded to just one determinant. Thus an equation relating quantity demanded to price could be in the form

$$Q_d = a - bP \qquad (1)$$

For example, the actual equation might be:

$$Q_d = 10\,000 - 200P \qquad (2)$$

From this can be calculated a complete demand schedule or demand curve, as shown in the table and diagram. As price (P) changes, the equation tells us how much the quantity demanded (Q_d) changes.

Demand schedule for equation (2)

P	Q_d
5	9000
10	8000
15	7000
20	6000
25	5000

Demand curve for equation (2)

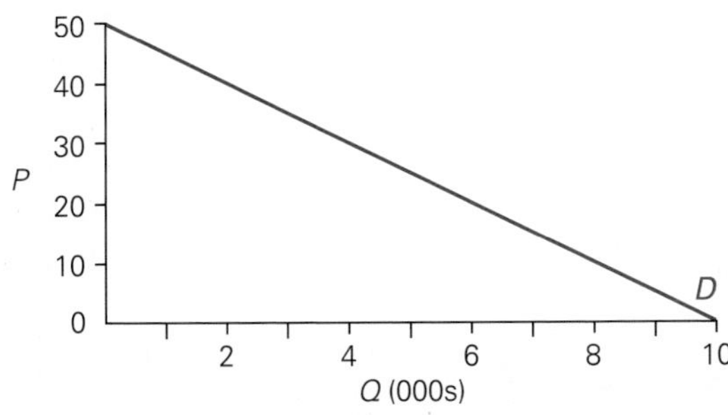

1. ***Complete the demand schedule in the table up to a price of 50.***
2. ***What is it about equation (2) that makes the demand curve (a) downward sloping; (b) a straight line?***

Definitions

Demand function An equation which shows the mathematical relationship between the quantity demanded of a good and the values of the various determinants of demand.

Regression analysis A statistical technique which allows a functional relationship between two or more variables to be estimated.

Econometrics The science of applying statistical techniques to economic data in order to identify and test economic relationships.

This equation is based on a *ceteris paribus* assumption: it is assumed that all the other determinants of demand remain constant. If one of these other determinants changed, the equation itself would change. There would be a shift in the curve: a change in demand. If the a term alone changed, there would be a parallel shift in the curve. If the b term changed, the slope of the curve would change.

Simple equations can be used to relate demand to other determinants too. For example, an equation relating quantity demanded to income would be in the form

$$Q_d = a + bY \qquad (3)$$

1. ***Referring to equation (3), if the term 'a' has a value of −50 000 and the term 'b' a value of 0.001, construct a demand schedule with respect to total income (Y). Do this for incomes between £100 million and £300 million at £50 million intervals.***
2. ***Now use this schedule to plot a demand curve with respect to income. Comment on its shape.***

More complex demand functions

In a similar way, we can relate the quantity demanded to two or more determinants. For example, a demand function could be of the form:

$$Q_d = a - bP + cY + dP_s - eP_c \qquad (4)$$

This equation says that the quantity demanded (Q_d) will fall as the price of the good (P) rises, will rise as the level of consumer incomes (Y) rises, will rise as the price of a particular substitute (P_s) rises and will fall as the price of a particular complement (P_c) rises, by amounts b, c, d and e respectively.

Estimated demand equations

Surveys can be conducted to show how demand depends on each one of a number of determinants, while the rest are held constant. Using statistical techniques called ***regression analysis***, a demand equation can be estimated.

For example, assume that it was observed that the demand for butter (measured in 250g units) depended on its price (P_b), the price of margarine (P_m) and total annual consumer incomes (Y). The estimated weekly demand equation may then be something like

$$Q_d = 2\,000\,000 - 50\,000P_b + 20\,000P_m + 0.01Y \qquad (5)$$

Thus if the price of butter were 50p, the price of margarine were 35p and consumer incomes were £200 million, and if P_b and P_m were measured in pence and Y was measured in pounds, then the demand for butter would be 2 200 000 units. This is calculated as follows:

$$\begin{aligned} Q_d &= 2\,000\,000 - (50\,000 \times 50) + (20\,000 \times 35) \\ &\quad + (0.01 \times 200\,000\,000) \\ &= 2\,000\,000 - 2\,500\,000 + 700\,000 + 2\,000\,000 \\ &= 2\,200\,000 \end{aligned}$$

The branch of economics that applies statistical techniques to economic data is known as ***econometrics***. Econometrics is beyond the scope of this book. It is worth noting, however, that econometrics, like other branches of statistics, cannot produce equations and graphs that allow totally reliable predictions to be made. The data on which the equations are based are often incomplete or unreliable, and the underlying relationships on which they are based (often ones of human behaviour) may well change over time.

Section summary

1. When the price of a good rises, the quantity demanded per period of time will fall. This is known as the 'law of demand'. It applies both to individuals' demand and to the whole market demand.
2. The law of demand is explained by the income and substitution effects of a price change.
3. The relationship between price and quantity demanded per period of time can be shown in a table (or 'schedule') or as a graph. On the graph, price is plotted on the vertical axis and quantity demanded per period of time on the horizontal axis. The resulting demand curve is downward sloping (negatively sloped).
4. Other determinants of demand include tastes, the number and price of substitute goods, the number and price of complementary goods, income, distribution of income and expectations of future price changes.
5. If price changes, the effect is shown by a movement along the demand curve. We call this effect 'a change in the quantity demanded'.
6. If any other determinant of demand changes, the whole curve will shift. We call this effect 'a change in demand'. A rightward shift represents an increase in demand; a leftward shift represents a decrease in demand.

*7. The relationship between the quantity demanded and the various determinants of demand (including price) can be expressed as an equation.

2.2 SUPPLY

Supply and price

Imagine you are a farmer deciding what to do with your land. Part of your land is in a fertile valley, while part is on a hillside where the soil is poor. Perhaps, then, you will consider growing vegetables in the valley and keeping sheep on the hillside.

Your decision will depend to a large extent on the price that various vegetables will fetch in the market and the price you can expect to get for meat and wool. As far as the valley is concerned, you will plant the vegetables that give the best return. If, for example, the price of potatoes is high, you might use a lot of the valley for growing potatoes. If the price gets higher, you may well use the whole of the valley. If the price is very high indeed, you may even consider growing potatoes on the hillside, even though the yield per acre is much lower there.

In other words, the higher the price of a particular farm output, the more land will be devoted to it. This illustrates the general relationship between supply and price: *when the price of a good rises, the quantity supplied will also rise.* There are three reasons for this:

- As firms supply more, they are likely to find that beyond a certain level of output, costs rise more and more rapidly. In the case of the farm just considered, if more and more potatoes are grown, then the land which is less suitable for potato cultivation has to be used. This raises the cost of producing extra potatoes. It is the same for manufacturers. Beyond a certain level of output, costs are likely to rise rapidly as workers have to be paid overtime and as machines approach capacity working. If higher output involves higher costs of producing each unit, producers will need to get a higher price if they are to be persuaded to produce extra output.
- The higher the price of the good, the more profitable it becomes to produce. Firms will thus be encouraged to produce more of it by switching from producing less profitable goods.
- Given time, if the price of a good remains high, new producers will be encouraged to enter the industry. Total market supply thus rises.

The first two determinants affect supply in the short run. The third affects supply in the long run. We distinguish between short-run and long-run supply in section 2.5 on page 69.

The supply curve

The amount that producers would like to supply at various prices can be shown in a ***supply schedule***. Table 2.2 shows a monthly supply schedule for potatoes, both for an individual farmer (farmer X) and for all farmers together (the whole market). (Note, however, that the amount they supply at a given price may not be the same as the amount they actually sell. Some supply may remain unsold.)

Definition

Supply schedule A table showing the different quantities of a good that producers are willing and able to supply at various prices over a given time period. A supply schedule can be for an individual producer or group of producers, or for all producers (the market supply schedule).

Table 2.2 The supply of potatoes (monthly)

	Price of potatoes (pence per kg)	Farmer X's supply (tonnes)	Total market supply (tonnes: 000s)
a	20	50	100
b	40	70	200
c	60	100	350
d	80	120	530
e	100	130	700

The supply schedule can be represented graphically as a ***supply curve***. A supply curve may be an individual firm's supply curve or a market curve (i.e. that of the whole industry).

Figure 2.3 shows the *market* supply curve of potatoes. As with demand curves, price is plotted on the vertical axis and quantity on the horizontal axis. Each of the points *a–e* corresponds to a figure in Table 2.2. Thus, for example, a price rise from 60p per kilogram to 80p per kilogram will cause a movement along the supply curve from point *c* to point *d*: total market supply will rise from 350 000 tonnes per month to 530 000 tonnes per month.

1. *How much would be supplied at a price of 70p per kilo?*
2. *Draw a supply curve for farmer X. Are the axes drawn to the same scale as in Figure 2.3?*

Not all supply curves will be upward sloping (positively sloped). Sometimes they will be vertical, or horizontal or even downward sloping. This will depend largely on the time period over which firms' response to price changes is considered. This question is examined in the section on the elasticity of supply (see section 2.4 below) and in more detail in Chapters 6 and 7.

Other determinants of supply

Like demand, supply is not simply determined by price. The other determinants of supply are as follows.

The costs of production. The higher the costs of production, the less profit will be made at any price. As costs rise, firms will cut back on production, probably switching to alternative products whose costs have not risen so much.

The main reasons for a change in costs are as follows:

- Change in input prices: costs of production will rise if wages, raw material prices, rents, interest rates or any other input prices rise.
- Change in technology: technological advances can fundamentally alter the costs of production. Consider, for example, how the microchip revolution has changed production methods and information handling in virtually every industry in the world.
- Organisational changes: various cost savings can be made in many firms by reorganising production.
- Government policy: costs will be lowered by government subsidies and raised by various taxes. Government regulation may also increase costs; examples include minimum wages and obligations for employers to provide and contribute to employee pensions.

Definition

Supply curve A graph showing the relationship between the price of a good and the quantity of the good supplied over a given period of time.

Figure 2.3 Market supply curve of potatoes (monthly)

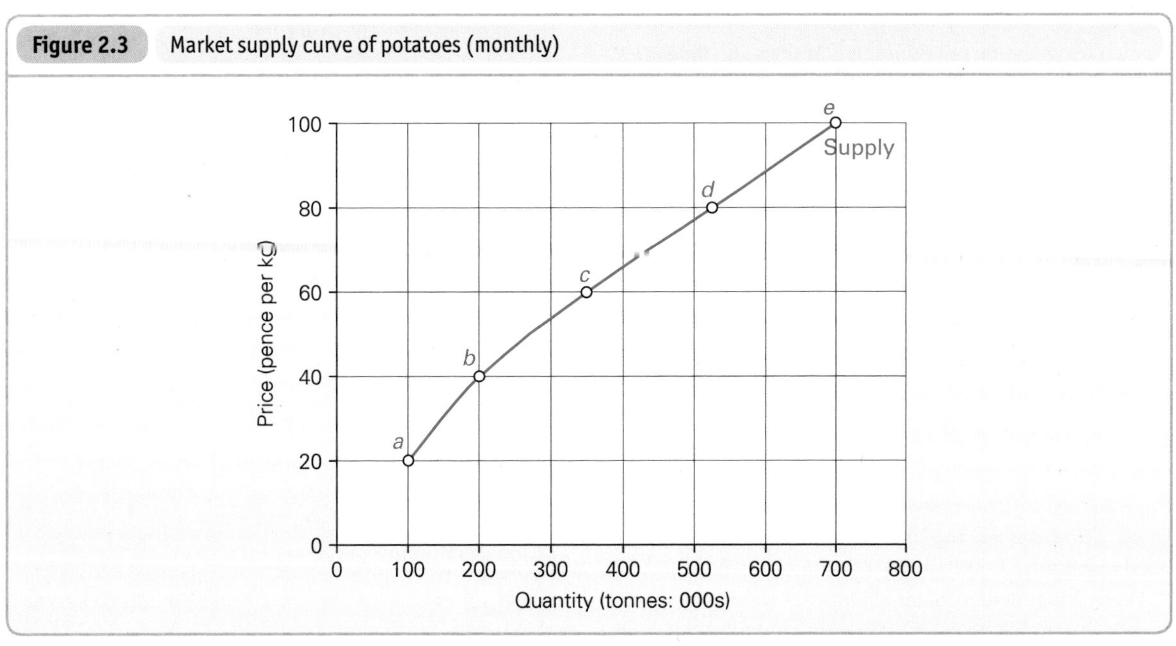

The profitability of alternative products (substitutes in supply). If a product which is a ***substitute in supply*** becomes more profitable to supply than before, producers are likely to switch from the first good to this alternative. Supply of the first good falls. Other goods are likely to become more profitable if their prices rise and/or their costs of production fall. For example, during 2020 many gin distilleries switched to producing hand sanitiser.

The profitability of goods in joint supply. Sometimes when one good is produced, another good is also produced at the same time. These are said to be ***goods in joint supply***. An example is the refining of crude oil to produce petrol. Other grade fuels will be produced as well, such as diesel and paraffin. If more petrol is produced due to a rise in demand and hence its price, then the supply of these other fuels will rise too.

Nature, 'random shocks' and other unpredictable events. In this category we would include the weather and diseases affecting farm output, wars affecting the supply of imported raw materials, the breakdown of machinery, industrial disputes, earthquakes, floods and fire, etc. Research suggest that one third of the variation in the annual harvests of maize wheat and rice is caused by changes in the weather (temperature and rainfall). In one specific example, unexpected frosts in Brazil in July 2019 put upward pressure on coffee prices over fears it would have a negative impact on harvests.

The aims of producers. A profit-maximising firm will supply a different quantity from a firm that has a different aim, such as maximising sales. For most of the time we shall assume that firms are profit maximisers. In Chapter 9, however, we consider alternative aims.

Expectations of future price changes. If suppliers believe that the prices of the goods they produce will rise in the future, they may temporarily reduce the amount they sell today. They may build up their stocks and only release them on to the market when the price does rise. At the same time, they may install new machines or take on more labour, so that they can be ready to supply more when the price has risen.

The number of suppliers. If new firms enter the market, supply is likely to increase.

By referring to each of the above determinants of supply, identify what would cause (a) the supply of potatoes to fall and (b) the supply of leather to rise.

Movements along and shifts in the supply curve

The principle here is the same as with demand curves. The effect of a change in price is illustrated by a movement along the supply curve: for example, from point *d* to point *e* in Figure 2.3 when price rises from 80p to 100p. Quantity supplied rises from 530 000 to 700 000 tonnes per month.

If any other determinant of supply changes, the whole supply curve will shift. A rightward shift illustrates an increase in supply. A leftward shift illustrates a decrease in supply. Thus in Figure 2.4, if the original curve is S_0, the curve S_1 represents an increase in supply (more is supplied at each price), whereas the curve S_2 represents a decrease in supply (less is supplied at each price).

Figure 2.4 Shifts in the supply curve

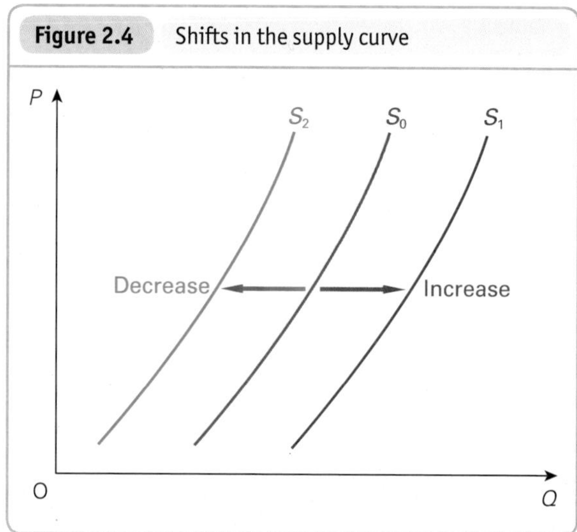

A movement along a supply curve is often referred to as a ***change in the quantity supplied***, whereas a shift in the supply curve is simply referred to as a ***change in supply***.

This question is concerned with the supply of oil for central heating. In each case consider whether there is a movement along the supply curve (and in which direction) or a shift in it (and whether left or right).

(a) New oil fields start up in production.
(b) The demand for central heating rises.
(c) The price of gas falls.
(d) Oil companies anticipate an upsurge in demand for central-heating oil.
(e) The demand for petrol rises.
(f) New technology decreases the costs of oil refining.
(g) All oil products become more expensive.

Definitions

Substitutes in supply These are two goods where an increased production of one means diverting resources away from producing the other.

Joint supply goods These are two goods where the production of more of one leads to the production of more of the other.

Change in the quantity supplied The term used for a movement along the supply curve to a new point. It occurs when there is a change in price.

Change in supply The term used for a shift in the supply curve. It occurs when a determinant other than price changes.

*LOOKING AT THE MATHS

Using survey data and regression analysis, equations can be estimated relating supply to some of its determinants. Note that not all determinants can be easily quantified (e.g. nature and the aims of firms), and they may thus be left out of the equation.

The simplest form of supply equation relates supply to just one determinant. Thus a function relating supply to price would be of the form

$$Q_s = c + dP \quad (1)$$

Using regression analysis, values can be estimated for *c* and *d*. Thus an actual supply equation might be something like

$$Q_s = 500 + 1000P \quad (2)$$

1. ***If P was originally measured in pounds, what would happen to the value of the d term in equation (2) if P were now measured in pence?***
2. ***Draw the schedule (table) and graph for equation (2) for prices from £1 to £10. What is it in the equation that determines the slope of the supply 'curve'?***

If any determinant other than price changed, a new equation would result. For example, if costs of production fell, the equation might then be

$$Q_s = 1000 + 1500P \quad (3)$$

More complex supply equations would relate supply to more than one determinant. For example:

$$Q_s = 200 + 80P - 20a_1 - 15a_2 + 30j \quad (4)$$

where P is the price of the good, a_1 and a_2 are the profitabilities of two alternative goods that could be supplied instead, and j is the profitability of a good in joint supply.

Explain why the P and j terms have a positive sign, whereas the a_1 and a_2 terms have a negative sign.

Section summary

1. When the price of a good rises, the quantity supplied per period of time will usually also rise. This applies both to individual producers' supply and to the whole market supply.
2. There are two reasons in the short run why a higher price encourages producers to supply more: (a) they are now willing to incur the higher costs per unit associated with producing more; (b) they will switch to producing this product and away from products that are now less profitable. In the long run, there is a third reason: new producers will be attracted into the market.
3. The relationship between price and quantity supplied per period of time can be shown in a table (or schedule) or as a graph. As with a demand curve, price is plotted on the vertical axis and quantity per period of time on the horizontal axis. The resulting supply curve is upward sloping (positively sloped).
4. Other determinants of supply include the costs of production, the profitability of alternative products, the profitability of goods in joint supply, random shocks and expectations of future price changes.
5. If price changes, the effect is shown by a movement along the supply curve. We call this effect 'a change in the quantity supplied'.
6. If any determinant *other* than price changes, the effect is shown by a shift in the whole supply curve. We call this effect 'a change in supply'. A rightward shift represents an increase in supply; a leftward shift represents a decrease in supply.

*7. The relationship between the quantity supplied and the various determinants of supply can be expressed in the form of an equation.

2.3 PRICE AND OUTPUT DETERMINATION

Equilibrium price and output

We can now combine our analysis of demand and supply. This will show how the actual price of a product and the actual quantity bought and sold are determined in a free and competitive market.

Let us return to the example of the market demand and market supply of potatoes, and use the data from Tables 2.1 and 2.2. These figures are given again in Table 2.3.

What will be the actual price and output? If the price started at 20p per kilogram, demand would exceed supply by 600 000 tonnes ($A - a$). Consumers would be unable to obtain all they wanted and would thus be willing to pay a higher price. Producers, unable or unwilling to supply enough to meet the demand, will be only too happy to accept a higher price. The effect of the shortage, then, will be to drive up the price. The same would happen at a price of 40p per kilogram. There would still be a shortage; price would still rise. But as the price rises, the quantity demanded falls and the quantity supplied rises. The shortage is progressively eliminated.

Table 2.3 The market demand and supply of potatoes (monthly)

Price of potatoes (pence per kg)	Total market demand (tonnes: 000s)	Total market supply (tonnes: 000s)
20	700 (A)	100 (a)
40	500 (B)	200 (b)
60	350 (C)	350 (c)
80	200 (D)	530 (d)
100	100 (E)	700 (e)

?

Explain the process by which the price of houses would rise if there were a shortage.

What would happen if the price of potatoes started at a much higher level: say, at 100p per kilogram? In this case supply would exceed demand by 600 000 tonnes $(e - E)$. The effect of this surplus would be to drive the price down as farmers competed against each other to sell their excess supplies. The same would happen at a price of 80p per kilogram. There would still be a surplus; price would still fall.

In fact, only one price is sustainable – the price where demand equals supply: namely, 60p per kilogram, where both demand and supply are 350 000 tonnes. When supply matches demand the market is said to ***clear***. There is no shortage and no surplus.

TC 4 p45

As we have already seen in section 1.2, the price where demand equals supply is called the *equilibrium price* and we return to this in more detail in Threshold Concept 4. In Table 2.3, if the price starts at anything other than 60p per kilogram, it will tend to move towards 60p. The equilibrium price is the only price at which producers' and consumers' wishes are mutually reconciled: where the producers' plans to supply exactly match the consumers' plans to buy.

KEY IDEA 8

Equilibrium is the point where conflicting interests are balanced. **Only at this point is the amount that demanders are willing to purchase the same as the amount that suppliers are willing to supply. It is a point that will be automatically reached in a free market through the operation of the price mechanism.**

Demand and supply curves

The determination of equilibrium price and output can be shown using demand and supply curves. Equilibrium is where the two curves intersect.

Figure 2.5 shows the demand and supply curves of potatoes corresponding to the data in Table 2.3. Equilibrium price is P_e (60p) and equilibrium quantity is Q_e (350 000 tonnes).

At any price above 60p, there would be a surplus. Thus at 80p there is a surplus of 330 000 tonnes $(d - D)$. More is supplied than consumers are willing and able to purchase at that price. Thus a price of 80p fails to clear the market. Price will fall to the equilibrium price of 60p. As it does so, there will be a movement along the demand curve from point *D* to point *C*, and a movement along the supply curve from point *d* to point *c*.

At any price below 60p, there would be a shortage. Thus at 40p there is a shortage of 300 000 tonnes $(B - b)$.

Definition

Market clearing A market clears when supply matches demand, leaving no shortage or surplus.

Figure 2.5 The determination of market equilibrium (potatoes: monthly)

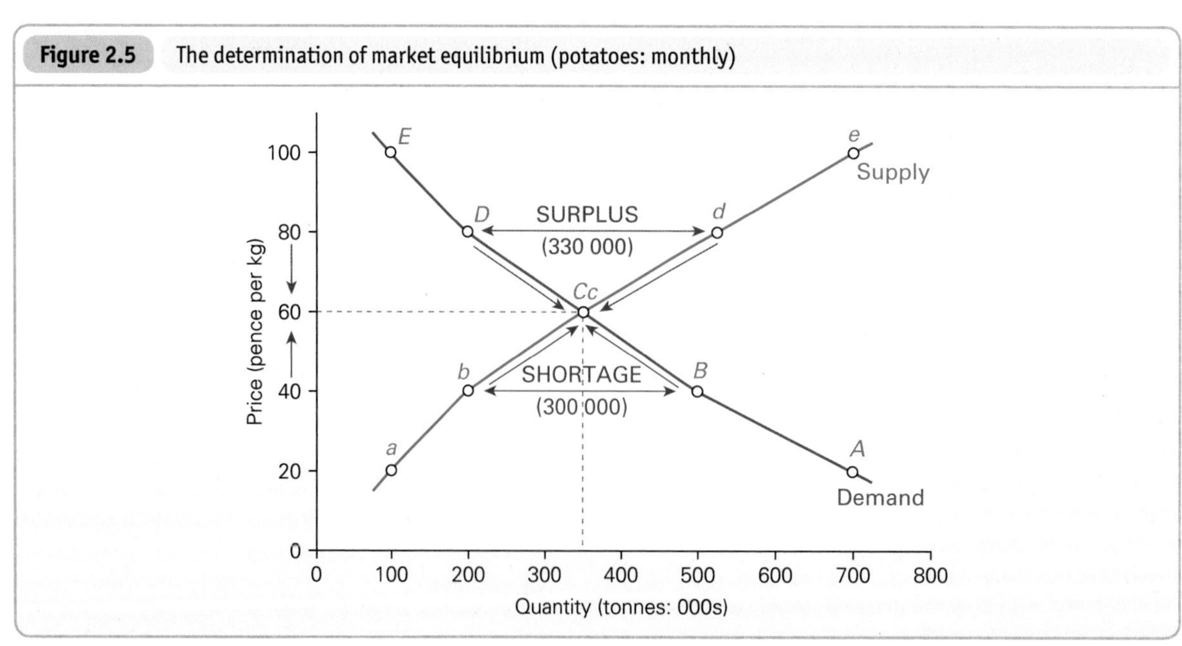

Price will rise to 60p. This will cause a movement along the supply curve from point *b* to point *c* and along the demand curve from point *B* to point *C*.

Point *Cc* is the equilibrium: where demand equals supply.

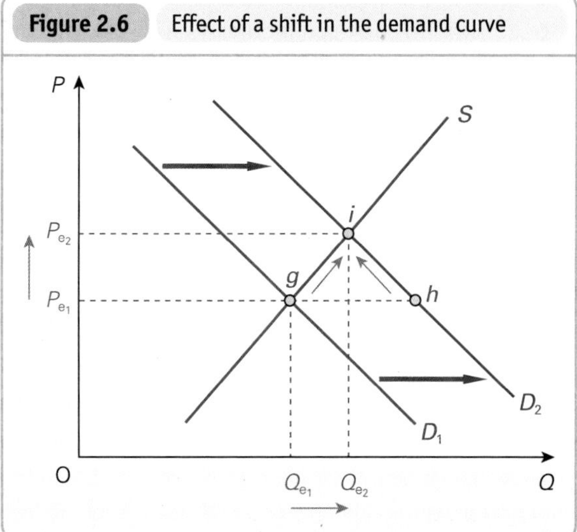

Figure 2.6 Effect of a shift in the demand curve

Movement to a new equilibrium

KI 5 p21 The equilibrium price will remain unchanged only so long as the demand and supply curves remain unchanged. If either of the curves shifts, a new equilibrium will be formed.

A change in demand

If one of the determinants of demand changes (other than price), the whole demand curve will shift. This will lead to a movement *along* the *supply* curve to the new intersection point.

For example, in Figure 2.6, if a rise in consumer incomes led to the demand curve shifting to D_2, there would be a

THRESHOLD CONCEPT 4 MARKETS EQUATE DEMAND AND SUPPLY

THINKING LIKE AN ECONOMIST

'Let the market decide.' 'Market forces will dictate.' 'You can't buck the market.'

These sayings about the market emphasise the power of market forces and how they affect our lives. Markets affect the prices of the things we buy and the incomes we earn. Even governments find it difficult to control many key markets. Governments might not like it when stock market prices plummet or when oil prices soar, but there is little they can do about it.

In many ways a market is like a democracy. People, by choosing to buy goods, are voting for them to be produced. Firms finding 'a market' for their products are happy to oblige and produce them. The way it works is simple. If people want more of a product, they buy more and thereby 'cast their votes' (i.e. their money) in favour of more being produced. The resulting shortage drives up the price, which gives firms the incentive to produce more of the product. In other words, firms are doing what consumers want – not because of any 'love' for consumers, or because they are being told to produce more by the government, but because it is in their own self-interest. They supply more because the higher price has made it profitable to do so.

This is a *threshold concept* because to understand market forces – the forces of demand and supply – is to go straight to the heart of a market economy. And in this process, prices are the key. It is changes in price that balance demand and supply. If demand exceeds supply, price will rise. This will choke off some of the demand and encourage more supply until demand equals supply – until an equilibrium has been reached. If supply exceeds demand, price will fall. This will discourage firms from supplying so much and encourage consumers to buy more, until, once more, an equilibrium has been reached.

In this process, markets act like an 'invisible hand' – a term coined by the famous economist Adam Smith (see Box 1.6 on page 24). Market prices guide both producers to respond to consumer demand and consumers to respond to changes in producer supply.

In many circumstances, markets bring outcomes that people want. As we have seen, if consumers want more, then market forces will lead to more being produced. Sometimes, however, market forces can bring adverse effects. We explore these in various parts of the book. It is important, at this stage, however, to recognise that markets are rarely perfect. Market failures, from pollution to the domination of our lives by big business, are very real. Understanding this brings us to Threshold Concept 7 (see page 79).

Partial equilibrium

The type of equilibrium we will be examining for the next few chapters is known as 'partial equilibrium'. It is partial because what we are doing is examining just one tiny bit of the economy at a time: just one market (e.g. that for eggs). It is even partial within the market for eggs because we are assuming that price is the *only* thing that changes to balance demand and supply: that nothing else changes. In other words, when we refer to equilibrium price and quantity, we are assuming that all the other determinants of both demand and supply are held constant.

If another determinant of demand or supply *does* change, there would then be a new partial equilibrium as price adjusts and both demanders and suppliers respond. For example, if a health scare connected with egg consumption causes the demand for eggs to fall, the resulting surplus will lead to a fall in the equilibrium price and quantity.

1. *If there is a shortage of certain skilled workers in the economy, how will market forces lead to an elimination of the skills shortage?*
2. *If consumers want more of a product, is it always desirable that market forces result in more being produced?*

shortage of h–g at the original price P_{e_1}. This would cause price to rise to the new equilibrium P_{e_2}. As it did so, there would be a movement along the supply curve from point g to point i, and along the new demand curve (D_2) from point h to point i. Equilibrium quantity would rise from Q_{e_1} to Q_{e_2}.

The effect of the shift in demand, therefore, has been a movement *along* the supply curve from the old equilibrium to the new: from point g to point i.

What would happen to price and quantity if the demand curve shifted to the left? Draw a diagram to illustrate your answer.

A change in supply

Likewise, if one of the determinants of supply changes (other than price), the whole supply curve will shift. This will lead to a movement *along* the *demand* curve to the new intersection point.

For example, in Figure 2.7, if costs of production rose, the supply curve would shift to the left: to S_2. There would be a shortage of $g - j$ at the old price of P_{e_1}. Price would rise from P_{e_1} to P_{e_3}. Quantity would fall from Q_{e_1} to Q_{e_3}. In other words, there would be a movement along the demand curve from point g to point k, and along the new supply curve (S_2) from point j to point k.

To summarise: a shift in one curve leads to a movement along the other curve to the new intersection point.

Sometimes a number of determinants might change. This might lead to a shift in *both* curves. When this happens, equilibrium simply moves from the point where the old curves intersected to the point where the new ones intersect.

What will happen to the equilibrium price and quantity of butter in each of the following cases? You should state whether demand or supply (or both) have shifted and in which direction. (In each case assume ceteris paribus.*)*

(a) A rise in the price of non-dairy spread.
(b) A rise in the demand for cream.
(c) A rise in the price of bread.
(d) A rise in the demand for bread.
(e) An expected rise in the price of butter in the near future.
(f) A tax on butter production.
(g) The invention of a new, but expensive, process for removing all saturated fat from butter, alongside the passing of a law which states that all butter producers must use this process.

Figure 2.7 Effect of a shift in the supply curve

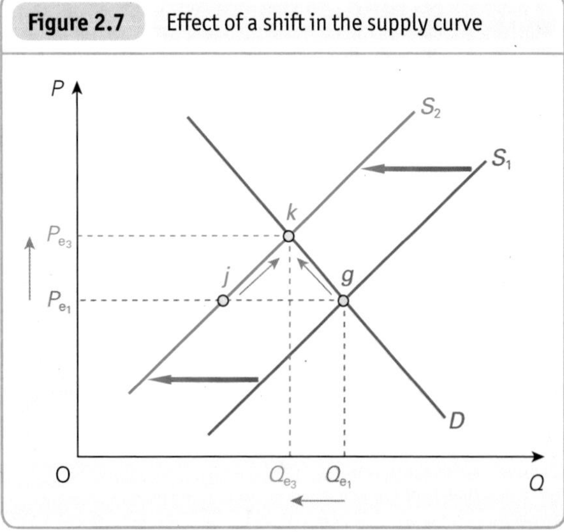

Incentives in markets

Throughout this chapter we have seen that people and firms respond to incentives. In all cases of changes in demand and supply, the resulting changes in price act as both signals and incentives. This is Threshold Concept 5.

*LOOKING AT THE MATHS

We saw on pages 39 and 43 how demand and supply curves can be represented by equations. Assume that the equations for the supply and demand curves in a particular market are as follows:

$$Q_d = a - bP \quad (1)$$

$$Q_s = c + dP \quad (2)$$

We can find the market equilibrium price by setting the two equations equal to each other, since, in equilibrium, the quantity supplied (Q_S) equals the quantity demanded (Q_D). Thus:

$$c + dP = a - bP$$

Subtracting c from and adding bP to both sides gives:

$$dP + bP = a - c$$
$$\therefore (d + b)P = a - c$$
$$\therefore P = \frac{a - c}{d + b} \quad (3)$$

We can then solve for equilibrium quantity (Q_e) by substituting equation (3) in either equation (1) or (2) (since $Q_D = Q_S$). Thus, from equation (1):

$$Q_e = a - b\left(\frac{a - c}{d + b}\right)$$
$$= \frac{a(d + b) - b(a - c)}{d + b}$$
$$= \frac{ad + ab - ba + bc}{d + b} = \frac{ad + bc}{d + b} \quad (4)$$

or, from equation (2):

$$Q_e = c + d\left(\frac{a - c}{d + b}\right)$$
$$= \frac{cd + cb + da - dc}{d + b} = \frac{cb + da}{d + b} \quad (5)$$

Thus:

$$Q_e = \frac{ad + bc}{d + b} \text{(equation (4))} = \frac{cb + da}{d + b} \text{(equation(5))}$$

A worked example is given in Maths Case 2.1 on the student website.

*Identifying the position of demand and supply curves

Both demand and supply depend on price, and yet their interaction determines price. For this reason it is difficult to identify just what is going on when price and quantity change, and to identify just what the demand and supply curves look like.

Let us say that we want to identify the demand curve for good X. We observe that when the price was 20p, 1000 units were purchased. At a later date the price has risen to 30p and 800 units are now purchased. What can we conclude from this about the demand curve? The answer is that without further information we can conclude very little. Consider Figures 2.8 and 2.9. Both are consistent with the facts.

In Figure 2.8 the demand curve has not shifted. The rise in price and the fall in sales are due entirely to a shift in the supply curve. The movement from point *a* to point *b* is thus a movement along the demand curve. If we can be certain that the demand curve has not shifted, then the evidence allows us to identify its position (or, at least, two points on it).

In Figure 2.9, however, not only has the supply curve shifted, but so also has the demand curve. Let us assume that people's tastes for the product have increased. In this case a movement from *a* to *b* does *not* trace out the demand curve. We cannot derive the demand curve(s) from the evidence of price and quantity alone.

The problem is that when the supply curve shifts, we often cannot know whether or not the demand curve has shifted, and if so by how much. How would we know, for example, just how much people's tastes have changed?

The problem works the other way round too. It is difficult to identify a supply curve when the demand curve shifts. Is the change in price and quantity entirely due to the shift in the demand curve, or has the supply curve shifted too?

This is known as the ***identification problem***. It is difficult to identify just what is causing the change in price and quantity.

Definition

Identification problem The problem of identifying the relationship between two variables (e.g. price and quantity demanded) from the evidence when it is not known whether or how the variables have been affected by other determinants. For example, it is difficult to identify the shape of a demand curve simply by observing price and quantity when it is not known whether changes in other determinants have shifted the demand curve.

Figure 2.8 Problems in identifying the position and shape of the demand curve: shift in supply curve alone

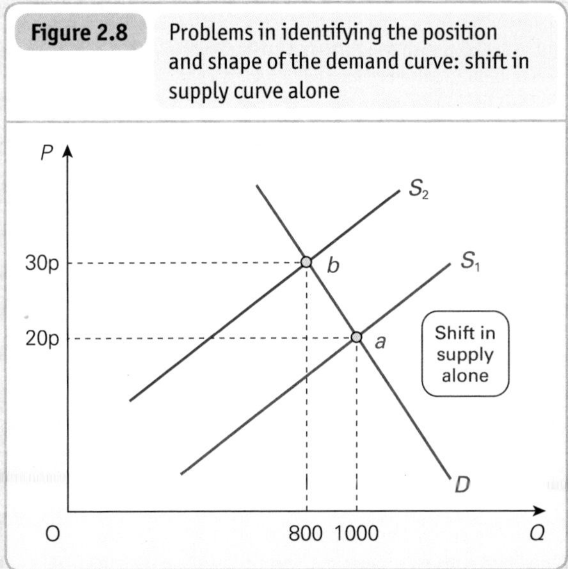

Figure 2.9 Problems in identifying the position and shape of the demand curve: shift in supply *and* demand curves

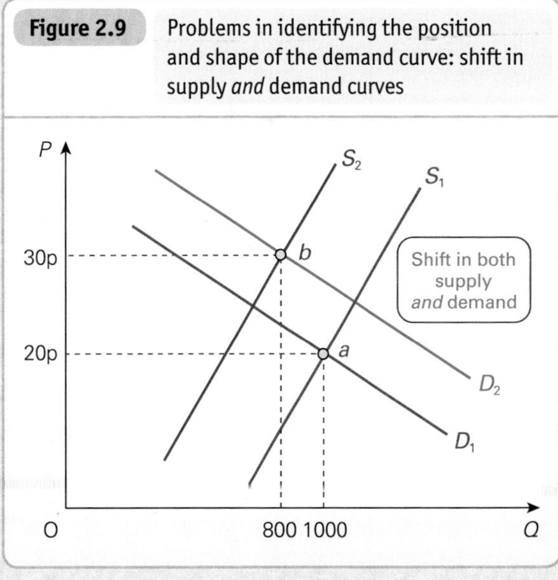

THRESHOLD CONCEPT 5 PEOPLE RESPOND TO INCENTIVES

So it's important to get them right

What gets you out of bed and into an economics lecture on time? What helps decide whether you wear a cycle helmet when out for a bike ride? What motivates a firm to invest in extra training for its workforce? Incentives drive the way individuals and businesses behave – even when we don't see that the incentive exists.

Financial and non-financial incentives

When there is a shortage of a good, its market price will rise, the opportunity cost goes up and there is an incentive for us to consume less. Similarly there is an incentive for firms to produce more. After all, the good is now more profitable to produce. This is an example of a financial incentive, for both buyers and producers. Other financial incentives include wages (i.e. being paid to work), bursaries for students and tax relief on investment for businesses.

But when we look at what motivates people making decisions, we see that non-financial incentives also play an important role. When we give to charity, support a football team, buy presents for our family or decide to run across a busy road rather than use a crossing, we are reacting to non-financial incentives.

Do incentives lead to desirable outcomes?

Let us return to the example of a shortage of a good, leading to a price rise. The resulting incentives could be seen as desirable, the shortage is eliminated and consumers are able to buy more of a good where demand initially exceeds supply.

However, there are plenty of instances where incentives may be 'perverse'. In other words, they could have undesirable effects. For example, if a particular course or module on your degree is assessed by two pieces of coursework, this may act as an incentive for you to concentrate solely on these two pieces and do little work on the rest of the syllabus.

There are plenty of other examples where incentives can be perverse. Making cars safer may encourage people to drive faster. Increasing top rates of income tax may encourage high earners to work less or to evade paying taxes by not declaring income – tax revenues may end up falling.

If an economic system is to work well, it is important, therefore, that the incentives are appropriate and do not bring about undesirable

BOX 2.1 UK HOUSE PRICES

The housing market is very important to consumers, firms and government in the UK. Households spend more on housing as a proportion of their income than any other good or service. Higher house prices tend to increase consumer confidence, leading to higher levels of spending and economic growth. Banks may also feel more confident about lending money to both consumers and firms. If house prices fall, the opposite is true. It is therefore not surprising that so many people take such a keen interest in both house prices and the outlook for the market.

The chart shows what happened to house prices in the period 1984 to the first quarter of 2021.[1] It clearly illustrates the volatility of the market. For example, in the late 1980s there was a boom, with prices doubling between 1984 and 1989. By the end of 1988, prices were rising at an astonishing annual rate of 34 per cent.

The boom came to an end in late 1989 and between 1990 and 1995, house prices fell by 12.2 per cent, causing many households to move into 'negative equity'. This is where the size of a household's mortgage is greater than the value of their house, meaning that if they sold their house, they would still owe money. Many people during this period, therefore, found that they were unable to move house.

In the latter part of the 1990s the housing market started to recover. This then turned into another boom, with house prices rising at an annual rate of 26 per cent at the peak (in the 12 months to January 2003). This boom came to an abrupt end in 2007–8 with the financial crisis. In 2009, prices fell by 19 per cent and then remained flat for several years, mirroring the lack of growth in the economy.

Prices started to rise again in late 2013 and by the first quarter of 2016, annual house price inflation had reached 10 per cent.

The result of the EU Referendum led to slower growth in prices until the decisive general election result in 2019. This resulted in house price growth accelerating for a couple of months before the impact of the COVID-19 pandemic. Quarterly house prices fell between March and April 2020 following the first national lockdown as people were advised not to move house during this period. With the easing of lockdown restrictions, prices rose more sharply in the second half of 2020 and reached an annual growth rate of 7.6 per cent in November.

The determinants of house prices

Changes in demand and supply determine house prices. If demand rises (i.e. shifts to the right) or if supply falls (i.e. shifts to the left), the equilibrium price of houses will rise. Similarly, if demand falls or supply rises, the equilibrium price will fall. Demand tends to determine price volatility in the short term while supply has a greater impact in the long run.

So what factors in the demand function for housing caused prices to rise so rapidly in periods such as the 1980s, 1997–2007, 2013–16 and the latter half of 2020 and into 2021? Why did they fall in the early 1990s and again from 2008 to 2013? What are the longer-run trends in demand?

1 There are four widely quoted measures of house prices – Nationwide, Halifax, Rightmove and the official House Price Index (HPI).

THINKING LIKE AN ECONOMIST

side effects. This is a *threshold concept* because virtually every action taken by households or firms is influenced by incentives. We need to understand just what the incentives are, what their effects are likely to be, and how the incentives could be improved.

We can see the outcome of inappropriate incentives, when we look at what happened in the former Soviet Union in the days of central planning. The targets given to factory managers (see Box 1.5 on pages 22–3) were often inappropriate. For example, if targets were specified in tonnes, the incentive was to produce heavy products. Soviet furniture and cooking utensils tended to be very heavy! If targets were set in area (e.g. sheet glass), then the incentive was to produce thin products. If targets were set simply in terms of number of units, then the incentive was to produce shoddy products.

Despite the lessons that should have been learnt from the failures of Soviet planning, we still see a lack of real understanding of incentives and the role they can play. If banks are told to increase the amount of financial capital they hold, they may cut down on lending to small businesses. If a university's quality is measured by how many first- and upper second-class degrees it awards, then there is an incentive to make it easier for students to get high marks.

We will examine the role of incentives in more detail later in the book, particularly when we look at behavioural economics. One crucial incentive is that of profit. In a competitive environment, firms striving for increased profit may result in better products and a lower price for consumers as firms seek to undercut each other. In other cases, however, firms may be able to make bigger profits by controlling the market and keeping competitors out or by colluding with them. Here the profit incentive has a perverse effect: it leads to higher prices for consumers and less choice.

1. *Give two other examples of perverse incentives. How could the incentives be improved?*
2. *Suppose that the kitchen is very untidy – what are the incentives for you to address this? What incentives could you use to get someone else to do it for you?*
3. *Many students undertake voluntary work while at university. What do think the incentives are for this? Identify any perverse incentives associated with volunteering and how they could be addressed.*

CASE STUDIES AND APPLICATIONS

UK house price inflation (annual %, adjusted quarterly)

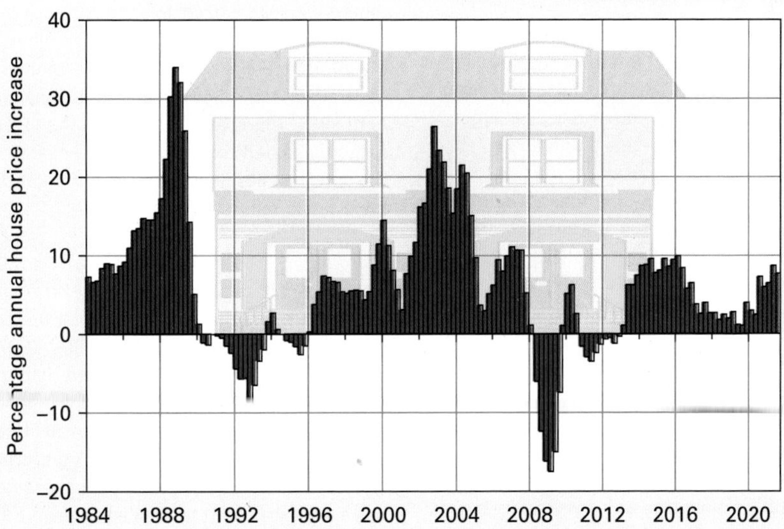

Source: Based on data in *Halifax House Price Index*, Lloyds Banking Group, www.halifax.co.uk/assets/pdf/sep-2021-halifax-house-price-index.pdf

Incomes (actual and anticipated). The second half of the 1980s, 1996–2007 and 2013–16 were periods of rising incomes. Many people wanted to spend much of their extra income on housing – either as first-time buyers or moving to a better property. They were confident their incomes would continue to grow and were prepared to borrow as much as they could against their current incomes, assuming that their mortgage payments would become more affordable over time.

The early 1990s and late 2000s, by contrast, were periods of recession or low growth, with rising unemployment

(continued)

and flat or falling incomes. People were less confident about their ability to afford large mortgages. With faster growth in incomes from 2013, house prices rose. However, as income growth stalled in 2017 and with uncertainty about the terms of Brexit, so house price inflation slowed between 2017 and 2019.

With falling incomes and rising unemployment during the COVID-19 crisis, many people expected house prices to fall throughout 2020. However, whereas national income fell by 15 per cent in the second quarter of 2020, there was only a 3.3 per cent fall in household disposable income. The impact of the Coronavirus Job Retention Scheme and the Self-Employment Income Support Scheme helps to explain this difference. There were also sharp falls in household consumption expenditure, such as on commuting, restaurants and hotels. This freed up income that people could choose to spend on housing. The impact of the pandemic on people's economic prospects also varied significantly. Poorer families were far more likely to experience falls in income and savings than middle- and high-income households.

The number of households. Social and demographic changes have resulted in a sharp increase in the number of households over the past 40 years. This has had a longer-run impact on the demand for housing. For example, in 1981, there were 20.2 million households in Great Britain; by 2020 this had increased to 27.8 million. Reasons include more lone parents, increased life expectancy and flows of workers from abroad.

The cost of mortgages. During the second half of the 1980s, mortgage interest rates were generally falling. Although they were still high compared with rates today, in real terms they were negative. In other words, they were lower than the rate of house price inflation.

In 1989, however, this trend went into reverse. Mortgage interest rates started rising. Many people found it difficult to maintain their existing payments, let alone take on a larger mortgage. From 1996 to 2003 mortgage rates generally fell, once more fuelling the demand for houses. Even with gently rising interest rates from 2003 to 2007, mortgages were still relatively affordable. Between 2009 and 2021, interest rates remained at an all-time low because of the uncertainty caused by (a) the slow recovery from the financial crisis, (b) the impact of the EU referendum result and (c) the COVID-19 crisis.

The availability of mortgages. In the late 1980s, mortgages became more readily available for two reasons. First, banks and building societies were prepared to offer an increasing number of high loan-to-value (LTV) mortgages. For example, a 95 per cent LTV mortgage is one where the buyer only has to make a 5 per cent deposit. Secondly, lenders were more willing to grant mortgages of up to 3.5 times a person's annual income (compared with 2.5 times in the early 1980s).

With the recession in the early 1990s, banks and building societies became much more cautious. The number of high LTV mortgages fell because of concerns that falling house prices, rising unemployment and negative equity would lead to more borrowers defaulting on payments.

With the recovery of the economy in the mid-1990s and with increased competition between lenders, mortgages became more readily available and for even greater amounts relative to people's incomes. This helped to push up prices. The belief that prices would continue to rise led lenders to relax their requirements even further. By the mid-2000s, many were allowing borrowers to self-certificate their income and were increasingly willing to lend to those with a poor credit history. This was known as the 'sub-prime' market. The ratio of average house prices to average earnings increased from 3.4 in 2002 to 5.74 in 2007. Problems in the mortgage market were a key contributing factor to the financial crises of 2007–8.

From late 2007 to 2012 the willingness of lenders to issue mortgages changed dramatically. The credit crunch in 2008–9 meant that the banks had less money to lend. Falling house prices and rising unemployment also made them much more wary. The number of 95 percent LTV mortgages available in the market collapsed from over 700 products in 2008 to virtually none in 2009. The highest LTV mortgages available were typically 75 per cent.

With support from the government-backed 'Help to buy' scheme, the number of 95 per cent LTV products recovered to around 400 in early 2020. This contributed to increasing house prices. However, the COVID-19 crisis had a similar impact on lenders as earlier recessions. The number of 95 per cent LTV products collapsed again. Research by the Bank of England in December 2020 found that around 75 per cent of renters were more likely to be constrained by a lack of sufficient savings to meet deposit requirements, rather than by the affordability of repayments. In response to this issue, the government introduced the Mortgage Guarantee Scheme in April 2021. This gives lenders who offer 95 per cent LTV mortgages the opportunity to purchase a guarantee that means the government will compensate a proportion of any losses in the event of repossession.

Speculation. A belief that house prices will continue to move in a particular direction can exacerbate house price movements. In other words, speculation tends to increase house price movements. In the 1980s, 1997–2007 and 2013–16, people generally believed that house prices would continue rising. This encouraged them to buy before prices went up any further. There was also an effect on supply. Those with houses to sell held back until the last possible moment in the hope of getting a higher price. The net effect was a rightward shift in the demand curve for houses and a leftward shift in the supply curve. The effect of this speculation, therefore, was to help bring about the very effect that people were predicting (for more on the impact of speculation see section 2.5).

In the early 1990s and late 2000s, the opposite occurred. Potential house buyers held back, hoping to get a better deal when prices had fallen. People with houses to sell tried to sell as quickly as possible before prices fell any further. Again, the effect of this speculation was to reinforce the changes – this time a fall in prices.

The impact of speculation has also been compounded by the growth in the 'buy-to-let' industry, with mortgage lenders entering this market in large numbers and a huge amount of media attention focused on the possibilities for individuals to make very high returns.

Taxation. Stamp duty is a transaction tax that buyers of property and land have to pay in England and Northern Ireland if the price is above a certain level. Governments sometimes make temporary changes to the thresholds and/or the rates of this tax in response to large downturns in the housing market. For example, in September 2008 the government temporarily increased the threshold from £125 000 to £175 000 and this helped to boost prices. When the thresholds returned to their pre-crisis levels in January 2010, the number of house sales fell considerably.

The government responded in a similar manner during the COVID-19 crisis by increasing the stamp duty threshold to £500 000 in July 2020.[2] This appears to be one of the key driving factors behind the increase in prices in the second half of 2020. Originally, the government planned to return the thresholds back to their pre-crisis levels in April 2021. However, in the March 2021 Budget, the Chancellor announced that the temporary £500 000 threshold would be extended until July 2021. It would then fall to £250 000 before returning to pre-crisis levels in October 2021.

Supply. Over the longer term, rising real incomes and the number of households have increased the demand for housing. How has supply responded?

In the 30 years from 1959 to 1988, 7 449 160 houses were built in England with the annual figure peaking at 352 540 in 1968. Just over 42 per cent of these (149 220) were built by not-for-profit organisations, such as local authorities or housing associations. In the 30 years from 1989 to 2018, 3 328 850 houses were built in England with an annual figure of just 125 000 in 2012–13. There were 220 600 new build completions in 2019–20[3] with less than 20 per cent financed by not-for-profit organisations.

Over the longer term, demand has exceeded the supply of houses and this has put upward pressure on prices.

What of the future?

The affordability of housing remains an important concern. In April 2020, the average house in England and Wales cost 7.8 times more than average annual earnings from work.[4] In 1997, the corresponding figure was 3.6. Housing is the least affordable it has ever been.

The supply of housing remains an issue. Estimates suggest that between 300 000 and 340 000 new homes need to be built per annum in England to make up for the lack of house building over the previous 40 years and the forecast growth in the number of households. Although there has been an increase in house building in recent years, it is still lower than the estimated number required. Local opposition, planning rules and building on the 'Green Belt' remain contentious issues.

The long-run impact of the COVID-19 crisis on the housing market is still very uncertain but it could lead to permanent changes in consumer preferences. For example, the increase in working from home means that a desk in the corner of a spare room is no longer sufficient for many people. Instead, they want dedicated workspaces and this increases the demand for bigger properties with more space. In the second half of 2020, the prices of detached houses in England and Wales grew faster than other property types. People may also not value proximity to offices in city centres as much as they did pre-crisis. Data show that house price growth in rural areas converged with urban areas in 2020, having been lower in previous years.[5] In May 2020, a survey found that 19 per cent of first-time buyers were more inclined to relocate to rural areas.

It will be interesting to see if these are temporary effects or whether they reflect permanent changes in people's preferences.

1. ***Draw supply and demand diagrams to illustrate and explain what was happening to house prices (a) in the period from 1997 to 2007; (b) from 2008 to 2012; (c) in 2020.***
2. ***What determines the supply of housing? How will factors on the supply side influence house prices?***
3. ***What is the role of the prices of 'other goods' in determining the demand for housing?***
4. ***There are four widely quoted measures of house prices – Nationwide, Halifax, Rightmove and the official House Price Index (HPI). Explain the strengths and weaknesses of these different measures. To what extent do they show the same movement in house prices?***

Find out what forecasters are predicting for house prices over the next year and attempt to explain their views.

2 Prior to the crisis, the rate of stamp duty for former owner occupiers was 2 per cent on the value of properties between £125 000 and £250 000 and then 5 per cent for values over £250 000. First-time buyers did not pay stamp duty until the value of the property exceeded £300 000.

3 'Tackling the under-supply of housing in England', *House of Commons Research Briefing*, UK Parliament (January 2021), https://commonslibrary.parliament.uk/research-briefings/cbp-7671/

4 *Housing affordability in England and Wales: 2020*, ONS (March 2021), www.ons.gov.uk/peoplepopulationandcommunity/housing/bulletins/housingaffordabilityinenglandandwales/2020

5 *Recent trends in the housing market: January 2021*, ONS (February 2021), www.ons.gov.uk/economy/inflationandpriceindices/articles/priceseconomicanalysisquarterly/january2021

BOX 2.2 STOCK MARKET PRICES

A business can transition from a private to a public company by selling shares to the public and becoming listed on the stock market. This is called an initial public offering (IPO). Firms that have already had an IPO can raise money by issuing new shares to the public. These are referred to as follow-on public offers (FPOs). In both cases the shares are sold on the 'primary stock market' and the owners of the shares receive 'dividend' payments, normally six-monthly. The size of the dividend will depend on the profitability of the company.

People or institutions that buy shares may not wish to hold on to them. They have the option to sell them in the 'secondary stock market' where existing shares are bought and sold. There are stock markets, primary and secondary, in all the major countries of the world.

There are 1988 companies (as of March 2021) whose shares and other securities are listed on the London Stock Exchange and trading in them takes place each weekday. The prices of shares depend on demand and supply. For example, if the demand for Vodafone shares at any one time exceeds the supply on offer, the price will rise until demand and supply are equal. Share prices fluctuate throughout the trading day and sometimes price changes can be substantial.

To give an overall impression of share price movements, stock exchanges publish share price indices. The most famous one in the UK is the FTSE ('footsie') 100, which stands for the 'Financial Times Stock Exchange' index of the 100 largest companies' shares. The index represents an average price of these 100 shares.

The chart shows movements in the FTSE 100 from 1995 to March 2021. The index was first calculated on 3 January 1984 with a base level of 1000 points. It reached a peak of 6930 points on 30 December 1999 and fell to 3287 on 12 March 2003, before rising again to a high of 6730 on 12 October 2007. However, with the financial crisis, the index fell to a low of 3512 on 3 March 2009. During the latter part of 2009, the index began to recover and then started on an upward trend. It reached its highest ever closing level of 7877 on 22 May 2018. Concerns about the impact of a trade war between China and the USA, and uncertainty over Brexit, put downward pressure on share prices and the index fell to 6728 in December 2018. It then recovered and reached 7457 on 19 February 2020.

Worries about the impact of the COVID-19 pandemic then began to have an impact on investor sentiment. The FTSE 100 fell by 32 per cent in just over a month and dropped below 5000 on 23 March 2020. With the ending of the first lockdown it climbed to over 6000 in May 2020. The development and successful rollout of the vaccine programme had a positive impact on investor confidence and the index climbed back over 7000 in April 2021.

What causes share prices to change? The answer lies in the determinants of the demand and supply of shares.

Demand

There are five main factors that affect the demand for shares.

Financial Times Stock Exchange Index (FTSE 100) (3/1/1984 = 1000)

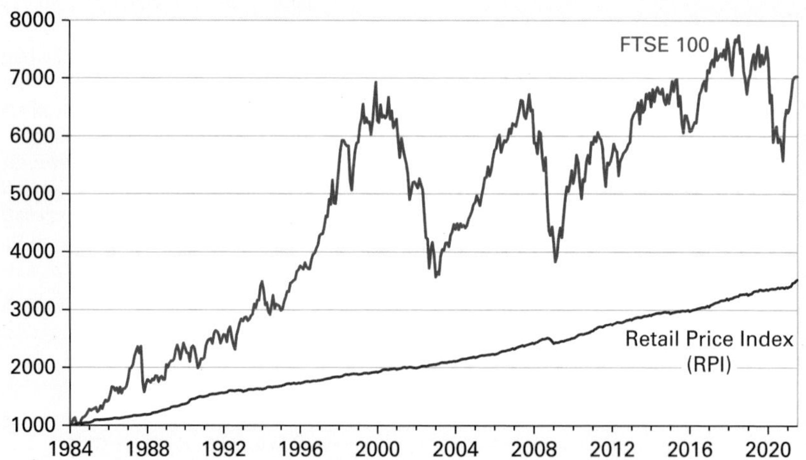

Note: FTSE figures based on end-of-month values.

Sources: Based on data from *RPI All Items Index*, ONS, www.ons.gov.uk/economy/inflationandpriceindices/timeseries/chaw/mm23; and various (2021).

The dividend yield. This is the dividend on a share as a percentage of its price. The higher the dividend yields on shares the more attractive they are as a form of saving. One of the main explanations of rising stock market prices from 2003 to 2007 was high profits and resulting high dividends. The financial crisis and slowdown in the world economy explains the falling profits and dividends of companies from 2007 and the subsequent recovery in the global economy caused them to increase once again.

The price of and/or return on substitutes. The main substitutes for shares in specific companies are other shares. If in comparison with other shares, Vodafone shares are expected to pay high dividends relative to the share price, people will buy Vodafone shares. As far as shares in general are concerned, the main substitutes are other forms of saving. If the interest rate on savings accounts in banks and building societies fell, people with such accounts would be tempted to withdraw their money and buy shares instead.

Another major substitute is property. If house prices rise rapidly, this will reduce the demand for shares as many people switch to buying property in anticipation of even higher prices. If house prices level off, as they did in 2018–19, this makes shares relatively more attractive as an investment and can boost the demand for them. If both house and share prices fall, investors may look for other, lower-risk substitutes, such as gold and government bonds.

Incomes. If the economy is growing rapidly and people's incomes are rising rapidly, they are likely to save some of their extra income and therefore buy more shares. Thus from 2003 to 2007, when UK average real incomes were rising, share prices rose rapidly (see chart). When real incomes fell following the financial crisis in 2007–8, so did share prices. Average real incomes hardly grew after the financial crisis, and then fell in 2020 because of the COVID-19 crisis.

Wealth. 'Wealth' is people's accumulated savings and property. Wealth rose rapidly from the mid-1990s to mid-2000s with rising property prices and many people used their increased wealth to buy shares.

Expectations. From 2003 to 2007, people expected share prices to go on rising. There was optimism about continued growth in the economy and in certain sectors, such as leisure and high-tech industries. As people bought shares, it put more upward pressure on share prices, thereby fuelling further speculation that they would go on rising and encouraging further buying.

With both the financial crisis and the COVID-19 pandemic, there were dramatic falls in share prices as investor confidence fell. As people anticipated further price falls, they held back from buying, thereby reducing demand and pushing prices lower. The success of the vaccine programme in the UK made investors increasingly confident about the chances of an economic recovery. So share prices began to rise consistently once more. Speculation is examined in more detail in section 2.5.

Supply

The factors affecting supply are largely the same as those affecting demand, but in the opposite direction.

If the return on alternative forms of saving falls, people with shares are likely to hold on to them, as they represent a better form of saving. The supply of shares to the market will fall. If incomes or wealth rise, people again are likely to want to hold on to their shares.

As far as expectations are concerned, if people believe that share prices will rise, they will hold on to the shares they have. Supply to the market will fall, thereby pushing up prices. If, however, they believe that prices will fall, as they did in 2008, they will sell their shares now before prices do fall. Supply will increase, driving down the price. Another clear example of this was the coronavirus pandemic. Fears over its negative impact on the economy led the FTSE index to fall dramatically between February and March 2020.

Share prices and business

Changes in share prices can crucially affect businesses. If a company's share price falls, it is a sign that 'the market' is losing confidence. Given the negative impact of the COVID-19 pandemic on air travel, the two companies that experienced the largest falls in their share price in 2020 were International Consolidated Airline Group (IAG) (British Airways, Iberia, Aer Lingus) and Rolls Royce Holdings (the second largest global producer of aircraft engines).

A falling share price makes it more difficult for a business to raise finance, not only by issuing additional shares in the primary market, but also from banks. It will also make the company more vulnerable to a takeover bid. This is where one company seeks to acquire another by offering to buy all its shares. A takeover will succeed if the owners of more than half of the company's shares vote to accept the price offer. Shareholders are more likely to accept the price offer if they have been disappointed by the recent performance of the company's shares.

1. ***If the rate of economic growth in the economy is 3 per cent in a particular year, why are share prices likely to rise by more than 3 per cent that year?***
2. ***Why would you expect the return on shares to be greater than that offered by a bank savings account?***

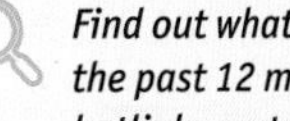

Find out what has happened to the FTSE 100 index over the past 12 months and explain why (see site B27 on the hotlinks part of the website).

Section summary

1. If the demand for a good exceeds the supply, there will be a shortage. This will lead to a rise in the price of the good.
2. If the supply of a good exceeds the demand, there will be a surplus. This will lead to a fall in the price.
3. Price will settle at the equilibrium. The equilibrium price is the one that clears the market: the price where demand equals supply.
4. If the demand or supply curve shifts, this will lead either to a shortage or to a surplus. Price will therefore either rise or fall until a new equilibrium is reached at the position where the supply and demand curves now intersect.
5. It is difficult to identify the position of a real-world supply (or demand) curve simply by looking at the relationship between price and quantity at different points in time. The problem is that the other curve may have shifted (by an unknown amount).

2.4 ELASTICITY

Price elasticity of demand

When the price of a good rises, the quantity demanded will fall. But in most cases we will want to know more than this. We will want to know by just *how much* the quantity demanded will fall. In other words, we will want to know how *responsive* demand is to a rise in price.

Take the case of two products: oil and cabbages. In the case of oil, a rise in price is likely to result in a relatively small fall in the quantity demanded. If people want to continue driving, they have to pay the higher prices for fuel. A few may turn to riding bicycles, and some people may make fewer journeys, but for most people, a rise in the price of petrol and diesel will make little difference in the short term to how much they use their cars.

Figure 2.10 Market supply and demand

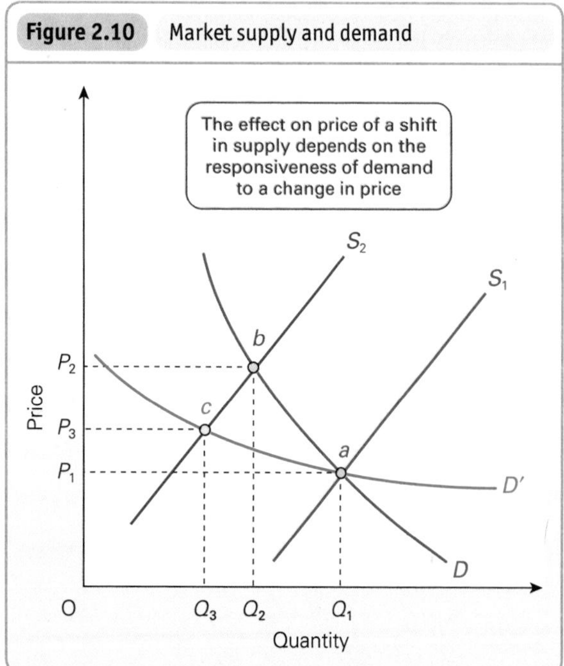

In the case of cabbages, however, a rise in price may lead to a substantial fall in the quantity demanded. The reason is that there are alternative vegetables that people can buy. Many people, when buying vegetables, will buy whatever is reasonably priced.

We call the responsiveness of demand to a change in price the ***price elasticity of demand***, and it is one of the most important concepts in economics. For example, if we know the price elasticity of demand for a product, we can predict the effect on price and quantity of a shift in the *supply* curve for that product.

Figure 2.10 shows the effect of a shift in supply with two quite different demand curves (D and D'). Curve D' is more elastic than curve D over any given price range. In other words, for any given change in price, there will be a larger change in quantity demanded along curve D' than along curve D.

Assume that initially the supply curve is S_1, and that it intersects with both demand curves at point *a*, at a price of P_1 and a quantity of Q_1. Now supply shifts to S_2. What will happen to price and quantity? In the case of the less elastic demand curve D, there is a relatively large rise in price (to P_2) and a relatively small fall in quantity (to Q_2): equilibrium is at point *b*. In the case of the more elastic demand curve D', however, there is only a relatively small rise in price (to P_3), but a relatively large fall in quantity (to Q_3): equilibrium is at point *c*.

Measuring the price elasticity of demand

What we want to compare is the size of the change in quantity demanded with the size of the change in price. But since

Definition

Price elasticity of demand The responsiveness of quantity demanded to a change in price.

price and quantity are measured in different units, the only sensible way we can do this is to use percentage or proportionate changes. This gives us the following ***formula for the price elasticity of demand*** (P_{ϵ_D}) for a product: percentage (or proportionate) change in quantity demanded divided by the percentage (or proportionate) change in price. Putting this in symbols gives:

$$P\epsilon_D = \frac{\%\Delta Q_D}{\%\Delta P}$$

where ϵ (the Greek epsilon) is the symbol we use for elasticity, and Δ (the capital Greek delta) is the symbol we use for a 'change in'.

Thus if a 40 per cent rise in the price of oil caused the quantity demanded to fall by a mere 10 per cent, the price elasticity of oil over this range will be

$$\frac{-10\%}{40\%} = -0.25$$

whereas if a 5 per cent fall in the price of cabbages caused a 15 per cent rise in the quantity demanded, the price elasticity of demand for cabbages over this range would be

$$\frac{15\%}{-5\%} = -3$$

Cabbages have a more elastic demand than oil, and this is shown by the figures. But just what do these two figures show? What is the significance of minus 0.25 and minus 3?

Interpreting the figure for elasticity

The use of proportionate or percentage measures

Elasticity is measured in proportionate or percentage terms for the following reasons:

- It allows comparison of changes in two qualitatively different things, which are thus measured in two different types of unit: i.e. it allows comparison of *quantity* changes with *monetary* changes.
- It is the only sensible way of deciding *how big* a change in price or quantity is. Take a simple example. An item goes up in price by £1. Is this a big increase or a small increase? We can answer this only if we know what the original price was. If a can of beans goes up in price by £1 that is a huge price increase. If, however, the price of a house goes up by £1 that is a tiny price increase. In other words, it is the percentage or proportionate increase in price that determines how big a price rise is.

The sign (positive or negative)

Demand curves are generally downward sloping. This means that price and quantity change in opposite directions. A *rise* in price (a positive figure) will cause a *fall* in the quantity demanded (a negative figure). Similarly a *fall* in price will cause a *rise* in the quantity demanded. Thus when working out price elasticity of demand, we either divide a negative figure by a positive figure, or a positive figure by a negative. Either way, we end up with a negative figure.

The value (greater or less than 1)

If we now ignore the negative sign and just concentrate on the value of the figure, this tells us whether demand is ***elastic*** or ***inelastic***.

Elastic ($\epsilon > 1$). This is where a change in price causes a proportionately larger change in the quantity demanded. In this case, the value of elasticity will be greater than 1, since we are dividing a larger figure by a smaller figure. Hence, if the elasticity figure is -2.5 it tells us that if prices were increased by 1 per cent, demand would fall by 2.5 per cent. Customers are very sensitive to a change in the price.

Inelastic ($\epsilon < 1$). This is where a change in price causes a proportionately smaller change in the quantity demanded. In this case, elasticity will be less than 1, since we are dividing a smaller figure by a larger figure. Hence, if the elasticity figure is -0.3 it tells us that if prices were increased by 1 per cent, demand would fall by 0.3 per cent. Customers are relatively insensitive to a change in the price.

Unit elastic ($\epsilon = 1$). ***Unit elasticity of demand*** occurs where price and quantity demanded change by the same proportion. This will give an elasticity equal to 1 since we are dividing a figure by itself. An increase in price by 1 per cent leads to a fall in demand by 1 per cent.

Determinants of price elasticity of demand

The price elasticity of demand varies enormously from one product to another. For example, the demand for a holiday in any given resort typically has a price elasticity greater than 5, whereas the demand for electricity has a price elasticity less than 0.5 (ignoring the negative signs). But why do some products have a highly elastic demand, whereas others have a highly *in*elastic demand? What determines price elasticity of demand? KI 9 p64

The number and closeness of substitute goods. This is the most important determinant. The more substitutes there are and the closer they are to the good, the more people will switch

Definitions

Formula for price elasticity of demand ($P\epsilon_D$) The percentage (or proportionate) change in quantity demanded divided by the percentage (or proportionate) change in price: $\%\Delta Q_D \div \%\Delta P$.

Elastic demand Where quantity demanded changes by a larger percentage than price. Ignoring the negative sign, it will have a value greater than 1.

Inelastic demand Where quantity demanded changes by a smaller percentage than price. Ignoring the negative sign, it will have a value less than 1.

Unit elasticity of demand Where quantity demanded changes by the same percentage as price. Ignoring the negative sign, it will have a value equal to 1.

to these alternatives when the price of the good rises: the greater, therefore, will be the price elasticity of demand. The number of substitutes is strongly influenced by how broadly a market is defined.

A broadly defined market, such as alcohol, has very few substitutes. Customers tend to be relatively insensitive to the price. Using data from the *UK Expenditure and Food Survey* and its successor the *Living Costs and Food Survey*, Pryce, Hollingsworth and Walker[1] estimated an elasticity figure of −0.41 for alcohol sold on trade (in pubs and restaurants) in the UK, and −0.66 for alcohol sold off trade (in supermarkets and licensed shops). A more narrowly defined market, such as beer, is likely to have more substitutes (i.e. wine, spirits and cider) and so demand will tend to be less price inelastic. A figure of −0.81 has been estimated for off-trade beer and −0.99 for off-trade cider.[2] The elasticity of demand for a good produced by a single firm (i.e. a particular brand of whisky or beer) is likely to be even more price sensitive. Consumers can switch to another supplier of the same product.

Why will the price elasticity of demand for holidays in Crete be greater than that for holidays in general? Is this difference the result of a difference in the size of the income effect or the substitution effect? Is there anything the suppliers of holidays in Crete can do to reduce this higher price elasticity?

The proportion of income spent on the good. The higher the proportion of our income we spend on a good, the more we will be forced to cut consumption when its price rises: the bigger will be the income effect and the more elastic will be the demand.

Thus salt has a very low price elasticity of demand. Part of the reason is that there is no close substitute. But part is that we spend such a tiny fraction of our income on salt that we would find little difficulty in paying a relatively large percentage increase in its price: the income effect of a price rise would be very small. By contrast, there will be a much bigger income effect when a major item of expenditure rises in price. For example, if mortgage interest rates rise (the 'price' of loans for house purchase), people may have to cut down substantially on their demand for housing – being forced to buy somewhere much smaller and cheaper, or to live in rented accommodation.

Will a general item of expenditure such as food or clothing have a price-elastic or inelastic demand? (Consider both the determinants we have considered so far.)

1 Robert Pryce, Bruce Hollingsworth and Ian Walker, 'Alcohol quantity and quality price elasticities', *The European Journal of Health Economics*, Vol 20 (October 2018), https://pubmed.ncbi.nlm.nih.gov/30276497/

2 David Whitaker, 'Modelling UK alcohol and tobacco demand using the Living Costs and Food Survey', *Deloitte Media* (June 2019), https://ukdataservice.ac.uk/media/622477/whitaker.pdf

The time period. When price rises, people may take time to adjust their consumption patterns and find alternatives. The longer the time period after a price change the more elastic the demand is likely to be.

To illustrate this, let us return to our example of oil. The Office for Budget Responsibility estimates that the price elasticity of demand for fuel is −0.07 in the short run and −0.13 in the medium term. Other studies have estimated a long-run figure of approximately −0.583.[3] Why is the figure for fuel so much more inelastic in the short run than the long run? If fuel prices rise, people will find it difficult to reduce their consumption by a significant amount in the short run. If public transport options are limited, they still have to drive their cars to work and for leisure purposes. Although the number of journeys they make may remain unchanged, some people may be able to reduce their fuel consumption slightly by driving more economically. Firms still have to use fuel to transport their goods and oil may be a major source of energy in a production process that cannot easily be changed.

Over time, people can find other ways to respond, such as purchasing new fuel-efficient vehicles, car sharing or moving closer to their work. Firms can also change their production methods and the way they transport their goods.

Demand for oil might be relatively elastic over the longer term, and yet it could still be observed that over time people consume more oil (or only very slightly less) despite rising oil prices. How can this apparent contradiction be explained?

Price elasticity of demand and consumer expenditure

One of the most important applications of price elasticity of demand concerns its relationship with the total amount of money consumers spend on a product. ***Total consumer expenditure (TE)*** is simply price multiplied by quantity purchased.

$$TE = P \times Q$$

For example, if consumers buy 3 million units (*Q*) at a price of £2 per unit (*P*), they will spend a total of £6 million (*TE*).

Total consumer expenditure will be the same as the ***total revenue*** (*TR*) received by firms from the sale of the product (before any taxes or other deductions).

Definitions

Total consumer expenditure on a product (*TE*) (per period of time) The price of the product multiplied by the quantity purchased: $TE = P \times Q$.

Total revenue (*TR*) (per period of time) The total amount received by firms from the sale of a product, before the deduction of taxes or any other costs. The price multiplied by the quantity sold: $TR = P \times Q$.

3 *Analysis of the Dynamic Effects of Fuel Duty Reductions* (HM Treasury, April 2014), www.gov.uk/government/publications/analysis-of-the-dynamic-effects-of-fuel-duty-reductions

What will happen to consumer expenditure (and hence firms' revenue) if there is a change in price? The answer depends on the price elasticity of demand.

Elastic demand

As price rises, so quantity demanded falls and vice versa. When demand is elastic, quantity demanded changes proportionately more than price. Thus the change in quantity has a bigger effect on total consumer expenditure than does the change in price. For example, when the price rises, there will be such a large fall in consumer demand that *less* will be spent than before. This can be summarised as follows:

- *P* rises; *Q* falls proportionately more; thus *TE* falls.
- *P* falls; *Q* rises proportionately more; thus *TE* rises.

In other words, total expenditure changes in the same direction as *quantity*.

This is illustrated in Figure 2.11. The areas of the rectangles in the diagram represent total expenditure. Why? The area of a rectangle is its height multiplied by its length. In this case, this is price multiplied by quantity bought, which is total expenditure. Demand is elastic between points *a* and *b*. A rise in price from £4 to £5 causes a proportionately larger fall in quantity demanded: from 20 million to 10 million. Total expenditure *falls* from £80 million (the striped area) to £50 million (the pink area).

When demand is elastic, then, a rise in price will cause a fall in total consumer expenditure and thus a fall in the total revenue that firms selling the product receive. A reduction in price, however, will result in consumers spending more, and hence firms earning more.

Inelastic demand

When demand is ***inelastic,*** it is the other way around. Price changes proportionately more than quantity. Thus the change in price has a bigger effect on total consumer expenditure than does the change in quantity. To summarise the effects:

- *P* rises; *Q* falls proportionately less; *TE* rises.
- *P* falls; *Q* rises proportionately less; *TE* falls.

In other words, total consumer expenditure changes in the same direction as *price*.

This is illustrated in Figure 2.12. Demand is inelastic between points *a* and *c*. A rise in price from £4 to £8 causes a proportionately smaller fall in quantity demanded: from 20 million to 15 million. Total expenditure *rises* from £80 million (the striped area) to £120 million (the pink area).

In this case, firms' revenue will increase if there is a rise in price and fall if there is a fall in price.

Assume that demand for a product is inelastic. Will consumer expenditure go on increasing as price rises? Would there be any limit?

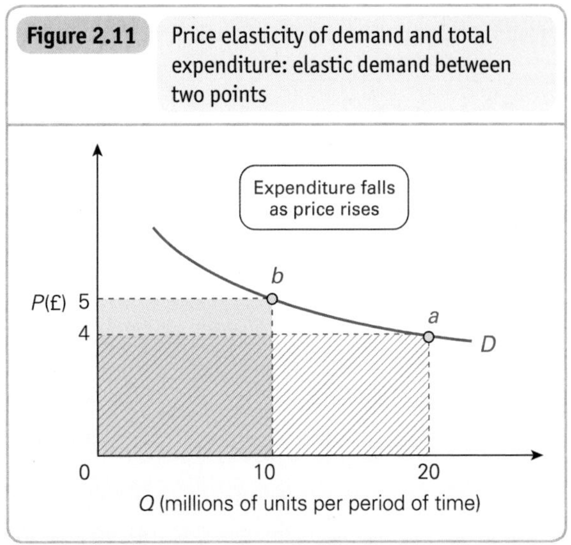

Figure 2.11 Price elasticity of demand and total expenditure: elastic demand between two points

Special cases

Figure 2.13 shows three special cases: (a) a totally inelastic demand ($P\epsilon_D = 0$), (b) an infinitely elastic demand ($P\epsilon_D = \infty$) and (c) a unit elastic demand ($P\epsilon_D = -1$).

Totally inelastic demand. This is shown by a vertical straight line. No matter what happens to price, quantity demanded remains the same. It is obvious that the more the price rises, the bigger will be the level of consumer expenditure. Thus in Figure 2.13(a), consumer expenditure will be higher at P_2 than at P_1.

Can you think of any examples of goods which have a totally inelastic demand (a) at all prices; (b) over a particular price range?

Infinitely elastic demand. This is shown by a horizontal straight line. At any price above P_1 in Figure 2.13(b), demand is zero. But at P_1 (or any price below) demand is 'infinitely' large.

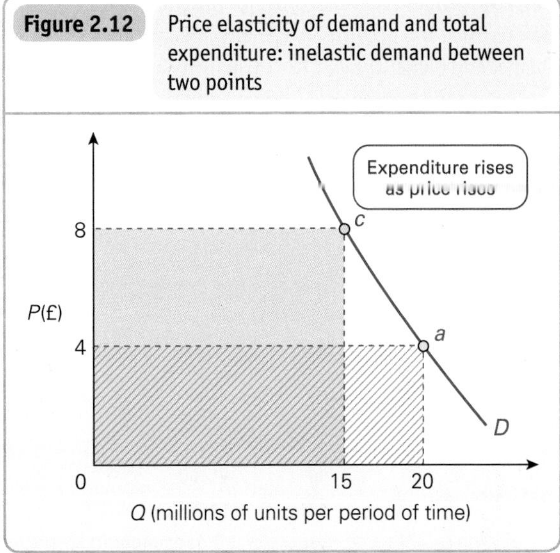

Figure 2.12 Price elasticity of demand and total expenditure: inelastic demand between two points

Figure 2.13 Price elasticity of demand: special cases

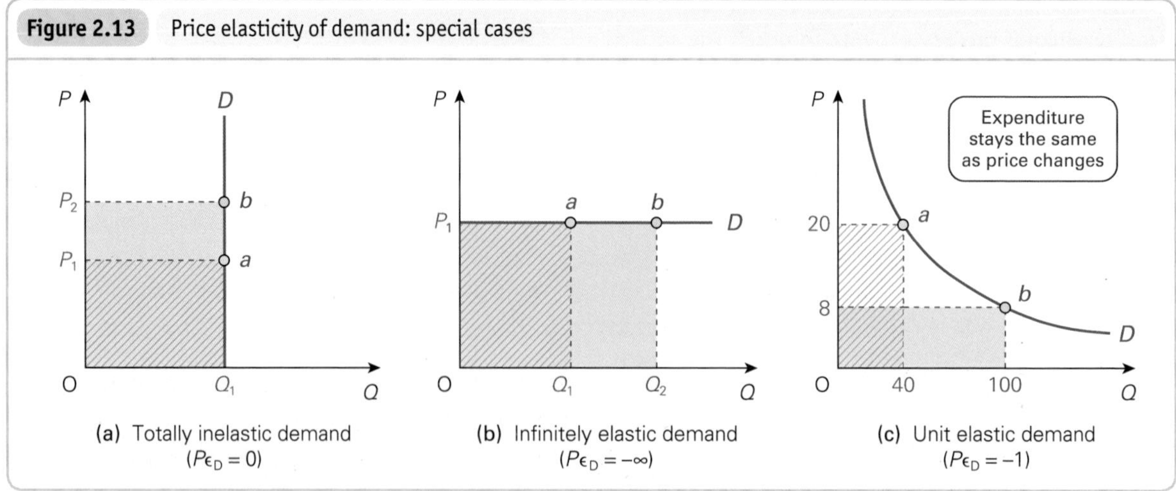

(a) Totally inelastic demand ($P\epsilon_D = 0$)

(b) Infinitely elastic demand ($P\epsilon_D = -\infty$)

(c) Unit elastic demand ($P\epsilon_D = -1$)

This seemingly unlikely demand curve is in fact relatively common for an *individual producer.* In a perfect market, as we have seen, firms are small relative to the whole market (like the small-scale grain farmer). They have to accept the price as given by supply and demand in the *whole market,* but at that price they can sell as much as they produce. (Demand is not *literally* infinite, but as far as the firm is concerned it is.) In this case, the more the individual firm produces, the more revenue will be earned. In Figure 2.13(b), more revenue is earned at Q_2 than at Q_1.

Unit elastic demand. This is where price and quantity change in exactly the same proportion. Any rise in price will be exactly offset by a fall in quantity, leaving total consumer expenditure unchanged. In Figure 2.13(c), the striped area is exactly equal to the pink area: in both cases, total expenditure is £800.

You might have thought that a demand curve with unit elasticity would be a straight line at 45° to the axes. Instead it is a curve called a *rectangular hyperbola.* The reason for its shape is that the proportionate *rise* in quantity must equal the proportionate *fall* in price (and vice versa). As we move down the demand curve, in order for the *proportionate* change in both price and quantity to remain constant there must be a bigger and bigger *absolute* rise in quantity and a smaller and smaller absolute fall in price. For example, a rise in quantity from 200 to 400 is the same proportionate change as a rise from 100 to 200, but its absolute size is double. A fall in price from £5 to £2.50 is the same percentage as a fall from £10 to £5, but its absolute size is only half.

To illustrate these figures, draw the demand curve corresponding to the following table.

P	Q	TE
£2.50	400	£1000
£5.00	200	£1000
£10.00	100	£1000
£20.00	50	£1000
£40.00	25	£1000

If the curve had an elasticity of −1 throughout its length, what would be the quantity demanded (a) at a price of £1; (b) at a price of 10p; (c) if the good were free?

The measurement of elasticity: arc elasticity

We have defined price elasticity as the percentage or proportionate change in quantity demanded divided by the percentage or proportionate change in price. But how, in practice, do we measure these changes for a specific demand curve? We shall examine two methods. The first is called the *arc method.* The second (in an optional section) is called the *point method.*

A common mistake that students make is to think that you can talk about the elasticity of a *whole curve.* In fact in most cases the elasticity will vary along the length of the curve.

Take the case of the demand curve illustrated in Figure 2.14. Between points *a* and *b,* total expenditure rises ($P_2Q_2 > P_1Q_1$): demand is thus elastic between these two points. Between points *b* and *c,* however, total expenditure falls ($P_3Q_3 < P_2Q_2$). Demand here is inelastic.

Normally, then, we can only refer to the elasticity of a *portion* of the demand curve, not of the *whole* curve. There are, however, two exceptions to this rule.

Figure 2.14 Different elasticities along different portions of a demand curve

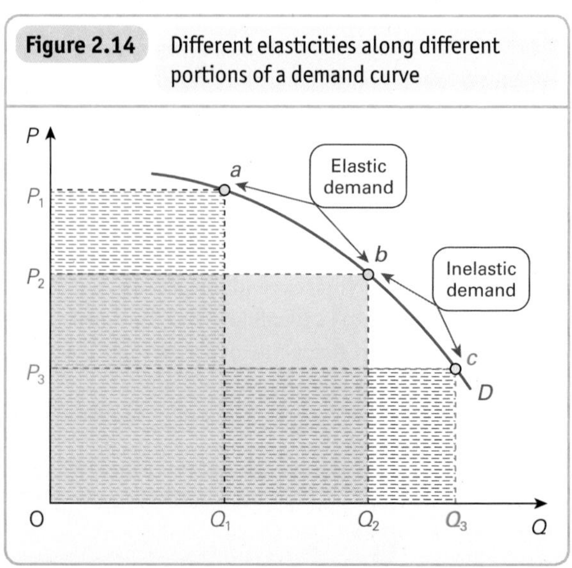

BOX 2.3 **SOCIAL MEDIA INFLUENCERS AND THEIR EFFECT ON DEMAND CURVES** EXPLORING ECONOMICS

How to increase sales and price

When we are told that a product will make us more attractive, enrich our lives, make our clothes smell great or allow us to save the planet, just what are the social media influencers up to? 'Trying to sell the product', you may reply.

In fact there is a bit more to it than this. Social media influencers are trying to do two things:

- Shift the product's demand curve to the right.
- Make it less price elastic.

This is illustrated in the diagram.

Effect of advertising on the demand curve

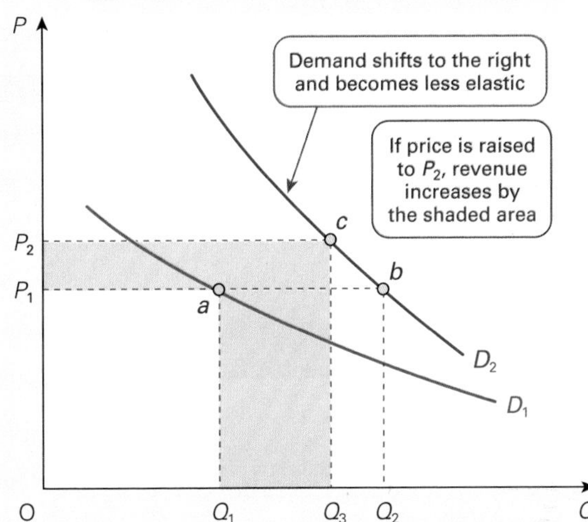

D_1 shows the original demand curve with price at P_1 and sales at Q_1. D_2 shows the curve after an endorsement by a social media influencer. The rightward shift allows an increased quantity (Q_2) to be sold at the original price. If the demand is also made highly inelastic, the firm can raise its price and still have a substantial increase in sales. Thus, in the diagram, price can be raised to P_2 and sales will be Q_3 – still substantially above Q_1. The total gain in revenue is shown by the shaded area.

How can endorsements bring about this new demand curve?

Shifting the demand curve to the right

This can occur in two ways. First, if the social media influencer brings the product to more people's attention, then the market for the good grows and the demand curve shifts to the right. Second, if the social influencer increases people's desire for the product, they will be prepared to pay a higher price for each unit purchased.

Making the demand curve less elastic

This will occur if the social influencer creates greater brand loyalty. People must be led to believe (rightly or wrongly) that competitors' brands are inferior. This can be done directly by comparing the brand being endorsed with a competitor's product. Alternatively, the endorsement may concentrate on making the product seem so special that it implies that no other product can compete. These approaches will allow the firm to raise its price above that of its rivals with no significant fall in sales. The substitution effect will have been lessened because consumers have been led to believe that there are no close substitutes.

1. *Think of some social media endorsements or advertisements that deliberately seek to make demand less elastic.*
2. *Imagine that a social influencer endorses a particular brand of gym wear. In particular, they state that the light breathable material keeps moisture away from your body during exercise, leaving you feeling dry and more comfortable. What do you think would happen to the demand curve for another brand of gym wear? Consider both the direction of the shift and the effect on elasticity. How will this affect the pricing policy and sales of this other brand?*
3. *Research a recent advertising or social media campaign. Identify what characteristics or attributes the campaign is attempting to highlight and what perceptions it is trying to influence. Where possible, examine the impact of the campaign so far.*

The first is when the elasticity just so happens to be the same all the way along a curve, as in the three special cases illustrated in Figure 2.13. The second is where two curves are drawn on the same diagram, as in Figure 2.10. Here we can say that demand curve *D* is less elastic than demand curve *D'* at any given price. Note, however, that each of these two curves will still have different elasticities along its length.

Although we cannot normally talk about the elasticity of a whole curve, we can nevertheless talk about the elasticity between any two points on it. This is known as ***arc elasticity***. In fact, the formula for price elasticity of demand that we have used so far is the formula for arc elasticity. Let us examine it more closely. Remember the formula we used was:

$$\frac{\text{Proportionate } \Delta Q}{\text{Proportionate } \Delta P} \text{(where } \Delta \text{ means 'change in')}$$

The way we measure a proportionate change in quantity is to divide that change by the level of *Q*: $\Delta Q/Q$. Similarly, we measure a proportionate change in price by dividing that change by the level of *P*: $\Delta P/P$. Price elasticity of demand can thus now be rewritten as

$$\frac{\Delta Q}{Q} \div \frac{\Delta P}{P}$$

Definition

Arc elasticity The measurement of elasticity between two points on a curve.

Figure 2.15 Measuring elasticity

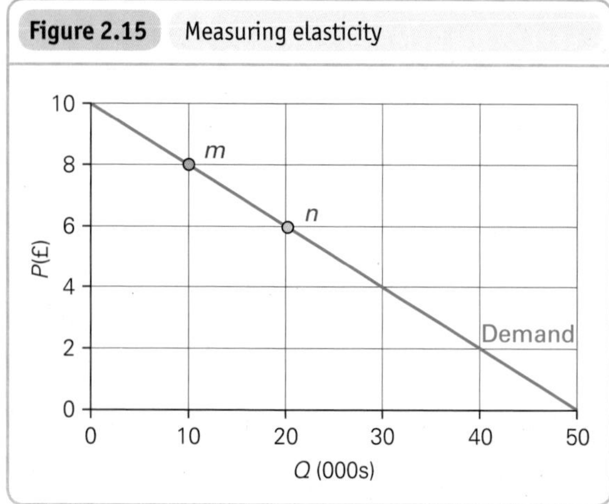

But just what value do we give to P and Q? Consider the demand curve in Figure 2.15. What is the elasticity of demand between points m and n? Price has fallen by £2 (from £8 to £6), but what is the proportionate change? Is it $-^2/_8$ or $-^2/_6$? The convention is to express the change as a proportion of the average of the two prices, £8 and £6: in other words, to take the midpoint price, £7. Thus the proportionate change is $-^2/_7$.

Similarly, the proportionate change in quantity between points m and n is $^{10}/_{15}$, since 15 is midway between 10 and 20.

Thus using the ***average (or 'midpoint') formula***, arc elasticity between m and n is given by:

$$\frac{\Delta Q}{\text{average } Q} \div \frac{\Delta P}{\text{average } P} = \frac{10}{15} \div \frac{-2}{7} = -2.33$$

Since, ignoring the negative sign, 2.33 is greater than 1, demand is elastic between m and n.

Referring to Figure 2.15, use the midpoint formula to calculate the price elasticity of demand between (a) P = 6 and P = 4; (b) P = 4 and P = 2. What do you conclude about the elasticity of a straight-line demand curve as you move down it?

Definition

Average (or 'midpoint') formula for price elasticity of demand ΔQ_D/average Q_D ÷ ΔP/average P.

BOX 2.4 **ANY MORE FARES?** CASE STUDIES AND APPLICATIONS

Pricing on the buses

Imagine that a local bus company is faced with increased costs and fears that it will make a loss. What should it do?

The most likely response of the company will be to raise its fares. But this may be the wrong policy, especially if existing services are underutilised. To help it decide what to do, it commissions a survey to estimate passenger demand at three different fares: the current fare of 50p per mile, a higher fare of 60p and a lower fare of 40p. The results of the survey are shown in the first two columns of the table.

Demand turns out to be elastic. This is because of the existence of alternative means of transport. As a result of the elastic demand, total revenue can be increased by reducing the fare from the current 50p to 40p. Revenue would rise from £2m to £2.4m per annum.

But what will happen to the company's profits? Its profit is the difference between the total revenue from passengers and its total costs of operating the service. If buses are currently underutilised, it is likely that the extra passengers can be carried without the need for extra buses, and hence at no extra cost.

At a fare of 50p, the old profit was £0.2m (£2.0m − £1.8m). After the increase in costs, a 50p fare now gives a loss of £0.2m (£2.0m − £2.2m).

By raising the fare to 60p, the loss is increased to £0.4m. But by lowering the fare to 40p, a profit of £0.2m can again be made.

1. *Estimate the price elasticity of demand between 40p and 50p and between 50p and 60p.*
2. *Was the 50p fare the best fare originally?*
3. *The company considers lowering the fare to 30p, and estimates that demand will be 8.5 million passenger miles. It will have to put on extra buses, however. How should it decide?*

Investigate ticket pricing on a local bus service near you. Assess whether the pricing policy is in (a) the company's interests; (b) the passengers'.

Fare (£ per mile)	*Estimated demand (passenger miles per year: millions)*	*Total revenue (£ millions per year)*	*Old total cost (£ millions per year)*	*New total cost (£ millions per year)*
(1)	(2)	(3)	(4)	(5)
0.40	6	2.4	1.8	2.2
0.50	4	2.0	1.8	2.2
0.60	3	1.8	1.8	2.2

*The measurement of elasticity: point elasticity

Rather than measuring elasticity between two points on a demand curve, we may want to measure it at a single point: for example, point *r* in Figure 2.16. In order to measure ***point elasticity*** we must first rearrange the terms in the formula $\Delta Q/Q \div \Delta P/P$. By doing so we can rewrite the formula for price elasticity of demand as:

$$\frac{\Delta Q}{\Delta P} \times \frac{P}{Q}$$

Since we want to measure price elasticity at a *point* on the demand curve, rather than between two points, it is necessary to know how quantity demanded would react to an *infinitesimally small* change in price. In the case of point *r* in Figure 2.16, we want to know how the quantity demanded would react to an infinitesimally small change from a price of 30.

An infinitesimally small change is signified by the letter *d*. The formula for price elasticity of demand thus becomes

$$\frac{dQ}{dP} \times \frac{P}{Q}$$

where dQ/dP is the differential calculus term for the rate of change of quantity with respect to a change in price (see Appendix 1). And conversely, dP/dQ is the rate of change of price with respect to a change in quantity demanded. At any given point on the demand curve, dP/dQ is given by the *slope* of the curve (its rate of change). The slope is found by drawing a tangent to the curve at that point and finding the slope of the tangent.

The tangent to the demand curve at point *r* is shown in Figure 2.16. Its slope is $-50/100$. Thus, dP/dQ is $-50/100$ and dQ/dP is the inverse of this, $-100/50 = -2$.

Figure 2.16 Measuring elasticity at a point

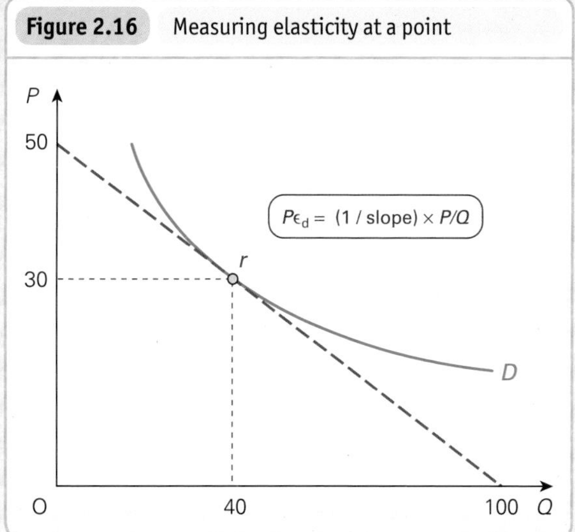

Returning to the formula $dQ/dP \times P/Q$, elasticity at point *r* equals

$$-2 \times \frac{30}{40} = -1.5$$

Rather than having to draw the graph and measure the slope of the tangent, the technique of differentiation can be used to work out point elasticity as long as the equation for the demand curve is known. An example of the use of this technique is given in Box 2.5 (on page 62).

Definition

Point elasticity The measurement of elasticity at a point on a curve. The formula for price elasticity of demand using the point elasticity method is $dQ/dP \times P/Q$, where dQ/dP is the inverse of the slope of the tangent to the demand curve at the point in question.

*LOOKING AT THE MATHS

Elasticity of a straight-line demand curve

A straight-line demand curve has a different elasticity at each point on it. The only exceptions are a vertical demand curve ($P\epsilon_D = 0$) and a horizontal demand curve ($P\epsilon_D = \infty$). The reason for this differing elasticity can be demonstrated using the equation for a straight-line demand curve:

$$Q = a - bP$$

The term '$-b$' would give the slope of the demand curve if we were to plot *Q* on the vertical axis and *P* on the horizontal. Since we plot them the other way around,[1] the term '*b*' gives the inverse of the slope as plotted. The slope of the curve as plotted is given by dP/dQ; the inverse of the slope is given by $dQ/dP = -b$).

The formula for price elasticity of demand (using the point elasticity method) is

$$P\epsilon_D = \frac{dQ}{dP} \cdot \frac{P}{Q}$$

Different elasticities along a straight-line demand curve

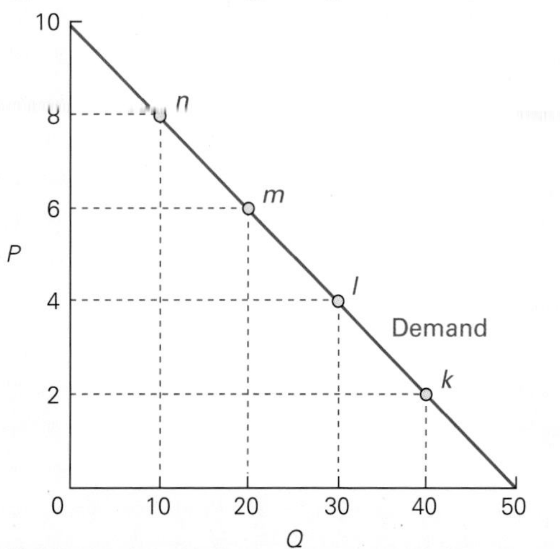

This can thus be rewritten as

$$P\epsilon_D = -b\frac{P}{Q}$$

This is illustrated in the diagram, which plots the following demand curve:

$$Q = 50 - 5P$$

The slope of the demand curve (dP/dQ) is constant (i.e. $-10/50$ or -0.2). The inverse of the slope (dQ/dP) is thus -5, where 5 is the 'b' term in the equation. In this example, therefore, price elasticity of demand is given by

$$P\epsilon_D = -5\frac{P}{Q}$$

The value of P/Q, however, differs along the length of the demand curve. At point n, $P/Q = 8/10$. Thus

$$P\epsilon_D = -5(8/10) = -4$$

At point m, however, $P/Q = 6/20$. Thus

$$P\epsilon_D = -5(6/20) = -1.5$$

These questions refer to the diagram.

1. *What is the price elasticity of demand at points l and k?*
2. *What is the price elasticity of demand at the point (a) where the demand curve crosses the vertical axis; (b) where it crosses the horizontal axis?*
3. *As you move down a straight-line demand curve, what happens to elasticity? Why?*
4. *Calculate price elasticity of demand between points n and l using the arc method. Does this give the same answer as the point method? Would it if the demand curve were actually curved?*

1 It is contrary to normal convention to plot the independent variable (P) on the vertical axis and the dependent variable (Q) on the horizontal axis. The reason why we do this is because there are many other diagrams in economics where Q is the *independent* variable. Such diagrams include cost curves and revenue curves, which we will consider in Chapter 6. As you will see, it is much easier if we *always* plot Q on the horizontal axis even when, as in the case of demand curves, Q is the dependent variable.

*BOX 2.5 USING CALCULUS TO CALCULATE THE PRICE ELASTICITY OF DEMAND

EXPLORING ECONOMICS

(A knowledge of the rules of differentiation is necessary to understand this box. See Appendix 1.)

The following is an example of an equation for a demand curve:

$$Q_d = 60 - 15P + P^2$$

(where Q_d is measured in thousands of units). From this the following table and the graph can be constructed.

P	60	$-15P$	$+P^2$	=	Q_d (000s)
0	60	−0	+0	=	60
1	60	−15	+1	=	46
2	60	−30	+4	=	34
3	60	−45	+9	=	24
4	60	−60	+16	=	16
5	60	−75	+25	=	10
6	60	−90	+36	=	6

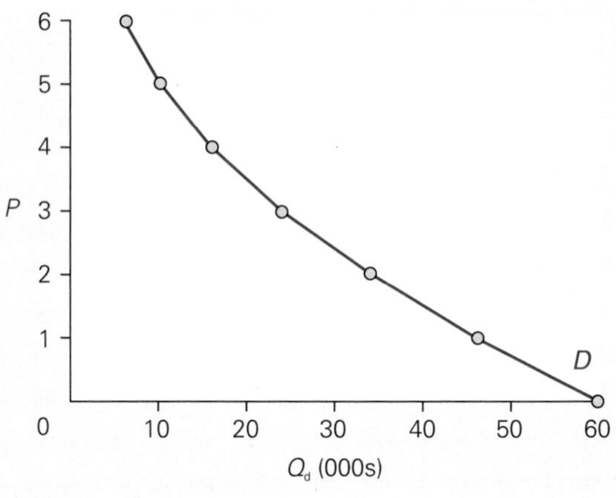

Point elasticity can be easily calculated from such a demand equation using calculus. To do this you will need to know the rules of differentiation (see pages A:9–13). Remember the formula for point elasticity:

$$P\epsilon_D = dQ/dP \times P/Q$$

The term dQ/dP can be calculated by differentiating the demand equation:

Given $Q_d = 60 - 15P + P^2$
then $dQ/dP = -15 + 2P$

Thus at a price of 3, for example,

$$dQ/dP = -15 + (2 \times 3) = -9$$

Thus price elasticity of demand at a price of 3

$$= -9 \times P/Q$$
$$= -9 \times 3/24$$
$$= -9/8 \text{(which is elastic)}$$

Calculate the price elasticity of demand on this demand curve at a price of (a) 5; (b) 2; (c) 0.

Price elasticity of supply ($P\epsilon_S$)

When price changes, there will be not only a change in the quantity demanded, but also a change in the quantity supplied. Frequently we will want to know just how responsive quantity supplied is to a change in price. The measure we use is the ***price elasticity of supply***.

Figure 2.17 shows two supply curves. Curve S_2 is more elastic between any two prices than curve S_1. Thus, when price rises from P_0 to P_1 there is a larger increase in quantity supplied with S_2 (namely, Q_0 to Q_2) than there is with S_1 (namely, Q_0 to Q_1). For any shift in the demand curve there will be a larger change in quantity supplied and a smaller change in price with curve S_2 than with curve S_1. Thus the effect on price and quantity of a shift in the demand curve will depend on the price elasticity of supply.

The ***formula for the price elasticity of supply*** (P_{ϵ_S}) is: the percentage (or proportionate) change in quantity supplied divided by the percentage (or proportionate) change in price. Putting this in symbols gives

$$P\epsilon_S = \frac{\%\Delta Q_S}{\%\Delta P}$$

In other words, the formula is identical to that for the price elasticity of demand, except that quantity in this case is quantity *supplied.* Thus if a 10 per cent rise in price caused a 25 per cent rise in the quantity supplied, the price elasticity of supply would be

$$25\%/10\% = 2.5$$

and if a 10 per cent rise in price caused only a 5 per cent rise in the quantity, the price elasticity of supply would be

$$5\%/10\% = 0.5$$

In the first case, supply is elastic ($P\epsilon_S > 1$); in the second it is inelastic ($P\epsilon_S < 1$). Notice that, unlike the price elasticity of demand, the figure is positive. This is because price and quantity supplied change in the *same* direction.

Determinants of price elasticity of supply

The amount that costs rise as output rises. The less the additional costs of producing additional output, the more firms will be encouraged to produce for a given price rise; the more elastic will supply be.

Supply is thus likely to be elastic if firms have plenty of spare capacity, if they can readily get extra supplies of raw materials, if they can easily switch away from producing alternative products and if they can avoid having to introduce overtime working, at higher rates of pay. The less these conditions apply, the less elastic will supply be.

Time period

- Immediate time period. Firms are unlikely to be able to increase supply by much immediately. Supply is virtually fixed, or can only vary according to available stocks. Supply is highly inelastic.

Figure 2.17 Supply curves with different price elasticity of supply

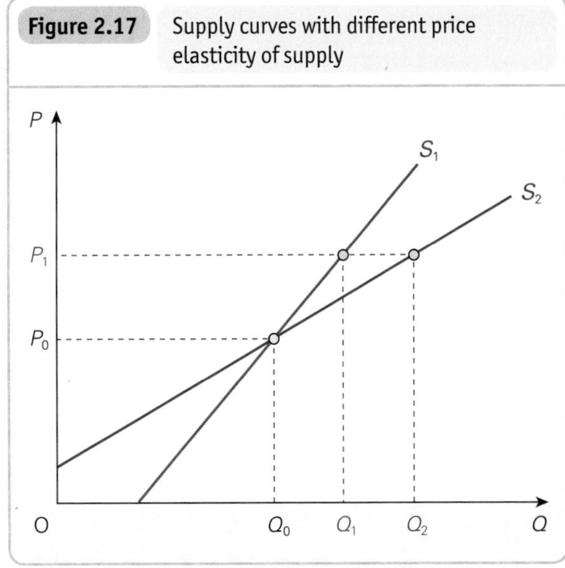

- Short run. If a slightly longer period of time is allowed to elapse, some inputs can be increased (e.g. raw materials) while others will remain fixed (e.g. heavy machinery). Supply can increase somewhat.
- Long run. In the long run, there will be sufficient time for all inputs to be increased and for new firms to enter the industry. Supply, therefore, is likely to be highly elastic in many cases. In some circumstances the long-run supply curve may even slope downwards. (See the section on economies of scale in Chapter 6, pages 167–8.)

The measurement of price elasticity of supply

A vertical supply has zero elasticity. It is totally unresponsive to a change in price. A horizontal supply curve has infinite elasticity. There is no limit to the amount supplied at the price where the curve crosses the vertical axis.

When two supply curves cross, the steeper one will have the lower price elasticity of supply (e.g. curve S_1 in Figure 2.17). Any straight-line supply curve starting at the origin, however, will have an elasticity equal to 1 throughout its length, *irrespective of its slope.* This perhaps rather surprising result is illustrated in Figure 2.18. This shows three supply curves, each with a different slope, but each starting from the origin. On each curve two points are marked. In each case there is the *same* proportionate rise in Q as in P. For example, with curve S_1 a doubling in price from £3 to £6 leads to a doubling of output from 1 unit to 2 units.

Definitions

Price elasticity of supply The responsiveness of quantity supplied to a change in price.

Formula for price elasticity of supply ($P\epsilon_S$) The percentage (or proportionate) change in quantity supplied divided by the percentage (or proportionate) change in price: $\%\Delta Q_S \div \%\Delta P$. Using the arc formula, this is calculated as ΔQ_S/average $Q_S \div \Delta P$/average P.

Figure 2.18 Unit elastic supply curves

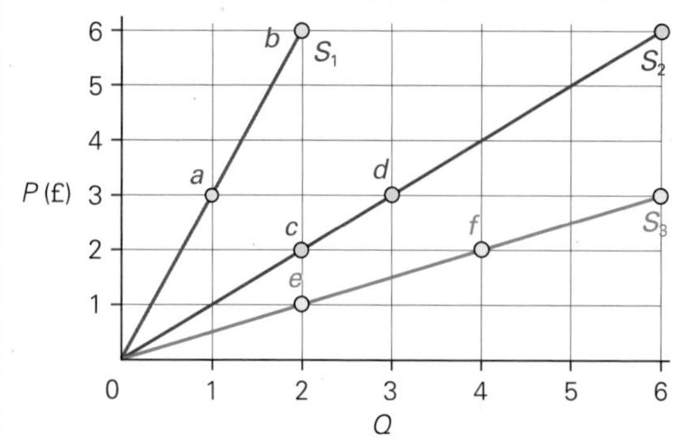

This demonstrates nicely that it is not the *slope* of a curve that determines its elasticity, but its proportionate change.

Other supply curves' elasticities will vary along their length. In such cases we have to refer to the elasticity either between two points on the curve, or at a specific point. Calculating elasticity between two points will involve the ***arc method***. Calculating elasticity at a point will involve the point method. These two methods are just the same for supply curves as for demand curves: the formulae are the same, only the term Q now refers to quantity supplied rather than quantity demanded.

Income elasticity of demand

So far, we have looked at the responsiveness of demand and supply to a change in price. But price is just one of the determinants of demand and supply. In theory, we could look at the responsiveness of demand or supply to a change in *any* one of their determinants. We could have a whole range of different types of elasticity of demand and supply.

KEY IDEA 9

Elasticity. The responsiveness of one variable (e.g. demand) to a change in another (e.g. price). This concept is fundamental to understanding how markets work. The more elastic variables are, the more responsive is the market to changing circumstances.

In practice, there are just two other elasticities that are particularly useful to us, and both are demand elasticities.

The first is the ***income elasticity of demand*** (Y_{ϵ_D}). This measures the responsiveness of demand to a change in consumer incomes (Y). It enables us to predict how much the demand curve will shift for a given change in income. The ***formula for the income elasticity of demand*** is: the percentage (or proportionate) change in demand divided by the percentage (or proportionate) change in income. Putting this in symbols gives

$$Y\epsilon_D = \frac{\%\Delta Q_D}{\%\Delta Y}$$

*LOOKING AT THE MATHS

We can use a supply equation to demonstrate why a straight-line supply curve through the origin has an elasticity equal to 1. Assume that the supply equation is

$$Q_s = a + bP \qquad (1)$$

If the supply curve passes through the origin, the value of $a = 0$. Thus:

$$Q_s = bP \qquad (2)$$

The point elasticity formula for price elasticity of supply is similar to that for price elasticity of demand (see pages 61–2) and is given by

$$P\epsilon_s = \frac{dQ_s}{dP} \cdot \frac{P}{Q_s} \qquad (3)$$

But

$$b = \frac{dQ_s}{dP} \qquad (4)$$

since this is the slope of the equation (the inverse of the slope of the curve). Substituting equation (4) in equation (3) gives

$$P\epsilon_s = b \cdot \frac{P}{Q_s} \qquad (5)$$

Substituting equation (2) in equation (5) gives:

$$P\epsilon_s = b \cdot \frac{P}{bP} = \frac{bP}{bP} = 1$$

Given the following supply schedule:

P	*2*	*4*	*6*	*8*	*10*
Q	*0*	*10*	*20*	*30*	*40*

(a) Draw the supply curve.
(b) Using the arc method, calculate price elasticity of supply (i) between P = 2 and P = 4; (ii) between P = 8 and P = 10.
*(c) *Using the point method, calculate price elasticity of supply at P = 6.*
(d) Does the elasticity of the supply curve increase or decrease as P and Q increase? Why?
(e) What would be the answer to (d) if the supply curve were a straight line but intersecting the horizontal axis to the right of the origin?

Definitions

Formula for price elasticity of supply (arc method) ΔQ_s/average $Q_s \div \Delta P$/average P.

Income elasticity of demand The responsiveness of demand to a change in consumer incomes.

Formula for income elasticity of demand ($Y\epsilon_D$) The percentage (or proportionate) change in demand divided by the percentage (or proportionate) change in income: $\%\Delta Q_D \div \%\Delta Y$.

In other words, the formula is identical to that for the price elasticity of demand, except that we are dividing the change in demand by the change in income that caused it rather than by a change in price. Thus if a 2 per cent rise in income caused an 8 per cent rise in a product's demand, then its income elasticity of demand would be:

$$8\%/2\% = 4$$

The major determinant of income elasticity of demand is the degree of 'necessity' of the good. In a developed country, the demand for luxury goods expands rapidly as people's incomes rise, whereas the demand for basic goods rises only a little. Thus items such as designer handbags and foreign holidays have a high income elasticity of demand, whereas items such as vegetables and socks have a low income elasticity of demand.

If income elasticity of demand is positive and greater than 1 then this tells us that the share of consumers' income spent on the good increases as their income rises. If the figure is positive but less than 1 then this tells us that the share of consumers' income spend on the good falls as income rises. In both of these cases people demand more of the good as incomes rise. However, the demand for some goods actually *decreases* as people's incomes rise beyond a certain level. These are inferior goods such as supermarkets' 'value lines' and bus journeys. As people earn more, so they switch to better quality products. Unlike ***normal goods***, which have a positive income elasticity of demand, ***inferior goods*** have a negative income elasticity of demand.

Look ahead to Table 3.1 (page 95). It shows the income elasticity of demand for various foodstuffs. Explain the difference in the figures for milk, fish and fruit juice.

Income elasticity of demand is an important concept to firms considering the future size of the market for their product. If the product has a high income elasticity of demand, sales are likely to expand rapidly as national income rises, but may also fall significantly if the economy moves into recession. (See Case Study 2.6, Income elasticity of demand and the balance of payments, on the student website. This shows how the concept of income elasticity of demand can help us understand why so many developing countries have chronic balance of payments problems.)

Cross-price elasticity of demand ($C\epsilon_{D_{AB}}$)

This is often known by its less cumbersome title of ***cross elasticity of demand***. It is a measure of the responsiveness of demand for one product to a change in the price of another (either a substitute or a complement). It enables us to predict how much the demand curve for the first product will shift when the price of the second product changes.

The ***formula for the cross-price elasticity of demand*** (**$C\epsilon_{D_{AB}}$**) is: the percentage (or proportionate) change in demand for good A divided by the percentage (or proportionate) change in price of good B. Putting this in symbols gives

$$C\epsilon_{D_{AB}} = \frac{\%\Delta Q_{D_A}}{\%\Delta P_B}$$

If good B is a *substitute* for good A, A's demand will *rise* as B's price rises. In this case, cross elasticity will be a positive figure. For example, if the demand for butter rose by 2 per cent when the price of margarine (a substitute) rose by 8 per cent, then the cross elasticity of demand for butter with respect to margarine would be

$$2\%/8\% = 0.25$$

If good B is *complementary* to good A, however, A's demand will *fall* as B's price rises and thus as the quantity of B demanded falls. In this case, cross elasticity of demand will be a negative figure. For example, if a 4 per cent rise in the price of bread led to a 3 per cent fall in demand for butter, the cross elasticity of demand for butter with respect to bread would be

$$-3\%/4\% = -0.75$$

The major determinant of cross elasticity of demand is the closeness of the substitute or complement. The closer it is, the bigger will be the effect on the first good of a change in the price of the substitute or complement, and hence the greater the cross elasticity – either positive or negative. For example, a figure of 1.169 has been estimated for the cross-price elasticity of demand for on-trade spirits (i.e. whisky, vodka, etc.) with respect to the price of on-trade beer. This suggests they are moderately close substitutes in consumption.

Firms need to know the cross elasticity of demand for their product when considering the effect on the demand

Definitions

Normal goods Goods whose demand increases as consumer incomes increase. They have a positive income elasticity of demand. Luxury goods will have a higher income elasticity of demand than more basic goods.

Inferior goods Goods whose demand decreases as consumer incomes increase. Such goods have a negative income elasticity of demand.

Cross-price elasticity of demand The responsiveness of demand for one good to a change in the price of another.

Formula for cross-price elasticity of demand ($C\epsilon_{D_{AB}}$) The percentage (or proportionate) change in demand for good A divided by the percentage (or proportionate) change in price of good B: $\%\Delta Q_{D_A} \div \%\Delta P_B$.

for their product of a change in the price of a rival's product or of a complementary product. These are vital pieces of information for firms when making their production plans.

Another application of the concept of cross elasticity of demand is in the field of international trade and the balance of payments. How does a change in the price of domestic goods affect the demand for imports? If there is a high cross elasticity of demand for imports (because they are close substitutes for home-produced goods), and if prices at home rise due to inflation, the demand for imports will rise substantially, thus worsening the balance of trade.

Which are likely to have the highest cross elasticity of demand: two brands of coffee, or coffee and tea?

THRESHOLD CONCEPT 6 **ELASTICITY: OF A VARIABLE TO A CHANGE IN A DETERMINANT** **THINKING LIKE AN ECONOMIST**

As we have seen in the case of price elasticity of demand, elasticity measures the responsiveness of one variable (e.g. quantity demanded) to change in another (e.g. price). This concept is fundamental to understanding how markets work. The more elastic variables are, the more responsive is the market to changing circumstances.

Elasticity is more than just a technical term. It's not difficult to learn the formula

$$P\epsilon_D = \frac{\%\Delta Q_D}{\%\Delta P}$$

in the case of price elasticity of demand, and then to interpret this as

$$P\epsilon_D = \frac{\Delta Q_D}{\text{average } Q_D} \div \frac{\Delta P}{\text{average } P}$$

using the arc elasticity method, or as

$$P\epsilon_D = \frac{dQ_D}{dP} \times \frac{P}{Q}$$

using the point elasticity method.

We can also very simply state the general formula for any elasticity as

$$\epsilon_{XY} = \frac{\%\Delta X}{\%\Delta Y}$$

where the formula refers to the responsiveness of variable X to a change in variable Y (where X could be quantity supplied or demanded, and Y could be price, income, the price of substitutes, or any other determinant of demand or supply). Again, we could use the arc or point elasticity methods. Although students often find it hard at first to use the formulae, it's largely a question of practice in mastering them.

What makes elasticity a *threshold concept* is that it lies at the heart of how economic systems operate. In a market economy, prices act as signals that demand or supply has changed. They also act as an incentive for people to respond to the new circumstances. The greater the elasticity of demand, the bigger will be the response to a change in supply; the greater the elasticity of supply, the bigger will be the response to a change in demand.

Understanding elasticity and what determines its magnitude helps us understand how an economy is likely to respond to the ever-changing circumstances of the real world.

In a perfect market economy, firms face an infinitely elastic (horizontal) demand curve: they are price takers (see page 35 and Figure 2.13(b)). What this means is that they have no power to affect prices: they are highly dependent on market forces.

By contrast, big businesses (and some small ones too) are in a very different position. If there are only one or two firms in a market, each is likely to face a relatively inelastic demand. This gives them the power to raise prices and make more profit. As we have seen, if demand is price inelastic, then raising price will increase the firm's revenue (see Figure 2.13(b)). Even if demand is elastic (but still downward sloping) the firm could still increase profit by raising prices, provided that the fall in revenue was less than the reduction in costs from producing less. The general point here is that the less elastic is the firm's demand curve, the greater will be its power to raise prices and make a bigger profit.

It's not just price elasticity of demand that helps us understand how market economies operate. In a perfect market, market supply is likely to be highly elastic, especially in the long run after firms have had time to enter the industry. Thus, if a new lower-cost technique is discovered, which increases profits in an industry, new firms will enter the market, attracted by the higher profits. This increased supply will then have the effect of driving prices down and hence profit rates will fall back. What this means is that in highly competitive industries firms are very responsive to changing economic circumstances. If they are not, they are likely to be forced out of business; it's a question of survival of the fittest. We explore this process in more detail in section 7.2.

If there is less competition, firms have an easier life. But what is good for them may be bad for us as consumers. We may end up paying higher prices and having poorer quality goods – although not necessarily. We explore this in sections 7.3 and 7.4 and in Chapter 8.

So, getting to grips with elasticity is not just about doing calculations. It's about understanding the very essence of how economies operate.

1. ***What would you understand by the 'wage elasticity of demand for labour'? How would the magnitude of this elasticity affect the working of the market for (a) plumbers and (b) footballers?***
2. ***How can income elasticity of demand help explain how the structure of economies changes over the years?***

*LOOKING AT THE MATHS

Calculating income and cross-price elasticities from a demand equation

The following demand equation relates quantity demanded (Q_A) for good A to its own price (P_A), consumer income (Y) and the price of a substitute good B (P_B).

$$Q_A = a - bP_A + cY + eP_B$$

Note that this is a 'linear' equation because it has no power terms, such as P^2 or Y^2. The formula[1] for income elasticity of demand for good A will be

$$Y\epsilon_D = \frac{\partial Q_A}{\partial Y} \cdot \frac{Y}{Q_A}$$

But since the term $\partial Q_A/\partial Y$ represents the amount that Q_A will change for a given change in Y (i.e. the value of c), then

$$Y\epsilon_D = c\frac{Y}{Q_A}$$

Similarly, the formula for cross-price elasticity of demand for good A with respect to good B will be

$$C\epsilon_{D_{AB}} = \frac{\partial Q_A}{\partial P_B} \cdot \frac{P_B}{Q_A} = e\frac{P_B}{Q_A}$$

A worked example of these two formulae is given in Maths Case 2.2 on the student website. We can also use calculus to work out the two elasticities for both linear and non-linear demand equations. A worked example of this is given in Maths Case 2.3 on the student website.

1 Note that in this case we use the symbol '∂' rather than 'd' to represent an infinitely small change. This is the convention when the equation contains more than one independent variable (in this case P_A, Y and P_B). The term $\partial Q_A/\partial Y$ is the 'partial derivative' (see pages A:12–13) and refers to the rate of change of Q_A to just one of the three variables (in this case Y).

BOX 2.6 DIGITAL PLATFORMS

EXPLORING ECONOMICS

The economics of two-sided markets

When we study markets, we tend to think of suppliers selling a good or service to one side of that market. For example, manufacturers selling to wholesalers, wholesalers selling to retailers or retailers selling to final customers. For many markets to work effectively, appropriate institutions and procedures are sometimes required to help facilitate the exchange of goods. Some businesses compete by offering these services. For example, they:

- help to put buyers and sellers of goods into contact with one another in a cost-effective manner
- supply impartial information about the quality of the goods/services on offer
- supply information about the reliability of consumers (i.e. do they pay promptly?) and the sellers (i.e. do they supply the good in a timely fashion?)
- offer payment systems to enable exchange to take place as smoothly as possible.

Therefore, these businesses act as intermediaries and sell their services to both sides of a market – both consumers and sellers. In other words, they operate in two-sided markets.

Institutions and organisations that offer these services date back over many hundreds of years. Good examples which date back hundreds of years are the market squares and market days in many European towns. Modern examples are shopping centres such as the *'Metrocentre'* in Gateshead, *'Meadowhall'* in Sheffield and *'Merry Hill'* in the West Midlands. The private businesses that own these shopping centres, such as Intu, Hammerson and British Land, help to facilitate exchange by bringing customers and retailers together.

The number and relative importance of businesses offering these services has increased significantly with the growth in digital markets. Out of the ten most valuable companies in the world measured by market capitalisation (i.e. the number of shares issued multiplied by the value of each share), seven (Apple, Microsoft, Amazon, Alphabet, Facebook, Tencent, Alibaba) are online market platforms. Some other examples are:

- Uber (taxi drivers and riders)
- Airbnb (hosts and guests)
- JustEat (takeaway food outlets and customers)
- Sony PlayStation, Microsoft Xbox, Nintendo Switch (games players and games developers)
- Viagogo (ticker buyers and ticket resellers)
- Checkatrade (tradespeople and customers).

In some cases, users on one side of the market do not always value the interaction the platform provides with users on another side of the market. Social media users often dislike advertisers and their intrusive adverts.

Network effects

An important factor that helps to determine the success of two-sided platforms is network effects. Direct network effects exist where the value or benefit a person experiences from using a platform increases with the number of other users on the same side of the market. For example, the more people that use a particular social media website, the more valuable it becomes to other users.

However, indirect/cross network effects are even more important. These exist where the value of, and hence willingness to pay for, the services of people on one side of the market increases with the number of users on the other side of the market. This creates a chicken-and-egg problem for the platform businesses. Having large numbers of buyers will attract more sellers, but to attract the buyers, the platform initially needs more sellers.

(continued)

Pricing

How should the firm set prices? Should they charge users on one side of the market far more than those on the other? In traditional one-sided markets, price elasticity of demand plays a key role in determining an effective strategy: i.e. charging lower prices to more price-sensitive consumers. Indirect network effects in two-sided markets can further reinforce this effect.

For example, assume a platform business has two different types of users – buyers and sellers. Assume the buyers are more price sensitive than the sellers, so the platform reduces prices to this group of users. The initial benefit to the business is the increase in the number of buyers now using the platform in response to the lower prices. However, there are additional benefits. The indirect network effects mean that sellers will now value the platform more highly and so will be willing to pay higher fees for its services. More sellers will also start using the platform, which may in turn attract more buyers.

The whole process sets off a virtuous circle – more buyers leads to more sellers, which leads to more buyers and so on. Reducing prices even further for buyers may lower the profits the platform makes from that side of the market but this may be more than offset by the extra profits it makes from sellers. Therefore, optimal pricing strategies in two-sided markets may be very different from those in one-sided markets.

Some key questions affect the size of these indirect network effects. These include:

- To what extent do sellers value the platform's services more than the buyers?
- How much more price insensitive are the sellers than the buyers?
- How responsive is the willingness to pay of the sellers to the number of buyers who use the platform?
- How responsive are the numbers of sellers to the numbers of buyers that use the platform and *vice versa*?

In some circumstances, the indirect network effects are so strong that the platform subsidises one group of users so they can access the services free of charge, for example search engines and social media websites.

Compatibility

Another issue for platform businesses is the extent to which they are compatible with other rival platforms. In other words, can a consumer on one platform connect with a seller on a different platform and *vice versa*? Platform businesses may be tempted to make them incompatible so consumers are locked into using their services. However, users can overcome this problem by joining more than one platform, known as 'multihoming'. For example, people can use eBay and Amazon, while the developers of popular applications usually make them available on both Android and iOS operating systems.

1. *When we draw demand curves, we usually assume that the number of other customers has no impact on the value a consumer places on a product. How would the diagram change if there were network effects?*
2. *What factors determine the extent of multihoming in platform markets?*

Investigate one or two other real-world examples where a firm operates in both single- and two-sided markets simultaneously. Examine their network effects and pricing policies.

Section summary

1. Elasticity is a measure of the responsiveness of demand (or supply) to a change in one of the determinants.
2. It is defined as the proportionate change in quantity demanded (or supplied) divided by the proportionate change in the determinant.
3. If quantity changes proportionately more than the determinant, the figure for elasticity will be greater than 1 (ignoring the sign): it is elastic. If the quantity changes proportionately less than the determinant, the figure for elasticity will be less than 1: it is inelastic. If they change by the same proportion, the elasticity has a value of 1: it is unit elastic.
4. Price elasticity of demand measures the responsiveness of demand to a change in price. Given that demand curves are downward sloping, price elasticity of demand will have a negative value. Demand will be more elastic the greater the number and closeness of substitute goods, the higher the proportion of income spent on the good and the longer the time period that elapses after the change in price.
5. When demand is price elastic, a rise in price will lead to a reduction in total expenditure on the good and hence a reduction in the total revenue of producers.
6. Demand curves normally have different elasticities along their length. We can thus normally refer only to the specific value for elasticity between two points on the curve or at a single point.
7. Elasticity measured between two points is known as arc elasticity. When applied to price elasticity of demand the formula is

$$\frac{\Delta Q_d}{\text{average } Q_d} \div \frac{\Delta P}{\text{average } P}$$

*8. Elasticity measured at a point is known as point elasticity. When applied to price elasticity of demand the formula is

$$\frac{dQ}{dP} \times \frac{P}{Q}$$

where dQ/dP is the inverse of the slope of the tangent to the demand curve at the point in question.

9. Price elasticity of supply measures the responsiveness of supply to a change in price. It has a positive value. Supply will be more elastic the less costs per unit rise as output rises and the longer the time period.

10. Income elasticity of demand measures the responsiveness of demand to a change in income. For normal goods it has a positive value. Demand will be more income elastic the more luxurious the good and the less rapidly demand is satisfied as consumption increases. For inferior goods, income elasticity has a negative value.

11. Cross-price elasticity of demand measures the responsiveness of demand for one good to a change in the price of another. For substitute goods the value will be positive; for complements it will be negative. The cross-price elasticity will be higher the closer the two goods are as substitutes or complements.

2.5 THE TIME DIMENSION

The full adjustment of price, demand and supply to a situation of disequilibrium will not be instantaneous. It is necessary, therefore, to analyse the time path which supply takes in responding to changes in demand, and which demand takes in responding to changes in supply.

Short-run and long-run adjustment

As we saw in the previous section, elasticity varies with the time period under consideration. The reason is that producers and consumers take time to respond to a change in price. The longer the time period, the bigger the response, and thus the greater the elasticity of supply and demand.

TC 6 p66

This is illustrated in Figures 2.19 and 2.20. In both cases, as equilibrium moves from points *a* to *b* to *c*, there is a large short-run price change (P_1 to P_2) and a small short-run quantity change (Q_1 to Q_2), but a small long-run price change (P_1 to P_3) and a large long-run quantity change (Q_1 to Q_3).

Price expectations and speculation

In a world of shifting demand and supply curves, prices do not stay the same. Sometimes they go up; sometimes they come down.

If people think prices are likely to change in the foreseeable future, this will affect the behaviour of buyers and sellers *now*. If, for example, it is now December and you are thinking of buying a new television, you might decide to wait until the January sales, and in the meantime make do with your set. If, on the other hand, in December you see a summer holiday advertised that you like, you might well book it then and not wait until nearer the summer for fear that the price will have gone up by then. Thus a belief that prices will go up will cause people to buy now; a belief that prices will come down will cause them to wait.

The reverse applies to sellers. If you are thinking of selling your house and prices are falling, you will want to sell it as quickly as possible. If, on the other hand, prices are rising

Figure 2.19 Response of supply to an increase in demand

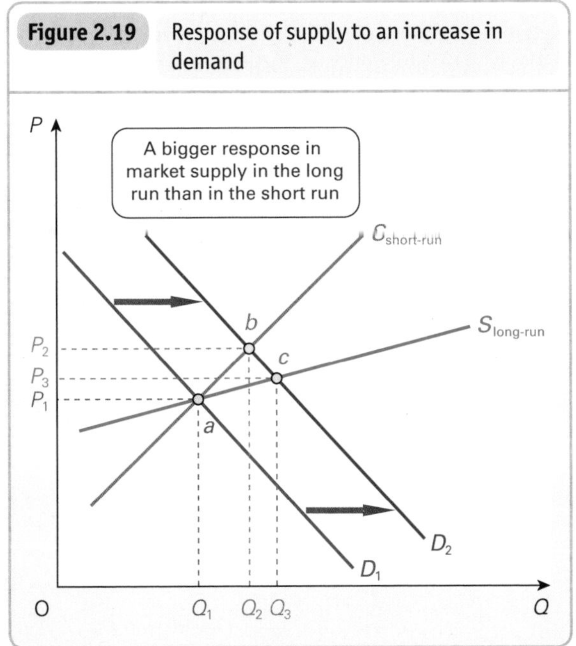

Figure 2.20 Response of demand to an increase in supply

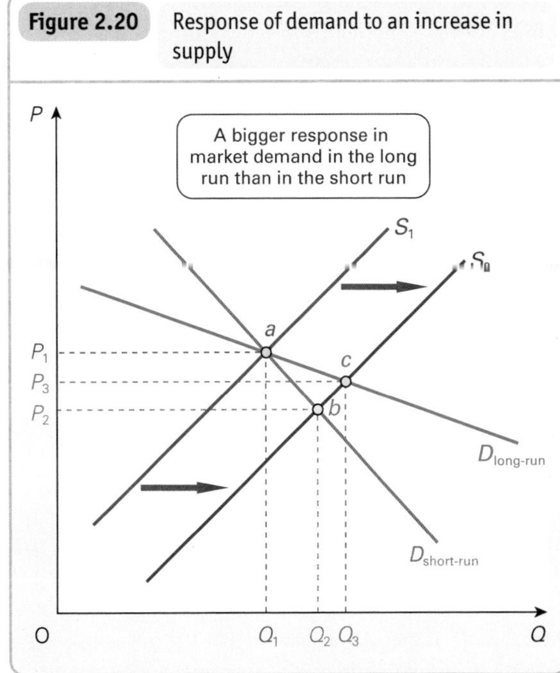

sharply, you will wait as long as possible so as to get the highest price. Thus a belief that prices will come down will cause people to sell now; a belief that prices will go up will cause them to wait.

People's actions are influenced by their expectations. **People respond not just to what is happening now (such as a change in price), but to what they anticipate will happen in the future.**

This behaviour of looking into the future and making buying and selling decisions based on your predictions is called ***speculation***. Speculation is often based on current trends in prices. If prices are currently rising, people may try to decide whether they are about to peak and go back down again, or whether they are likely to go on rising. Having made their prediction, they will then act on it. Their actions will then affect demand and supply, which in turn will affect price. Speculation is commonplace in many markets: the stock exchange, the foreign exchange market and the housing market are three examples.

Sometimes people will take advantage of expected price rises purely to make money and have no intention of keeping the item they have bought. For example, if shares in a particular company are expected to rise in price, people may buy them now while they are cheap and sell them later when the price has risen, thereby making a profit from the difference in price.

Similarly, people will sometimes take advantage of expected price reductions by selling something now only to buy it back later. For example, if you own shares and expect their price to fall, you may sell them now and buy them back later when their price has fallen. Again, you make a profit from the difference in price.

Sometimes the term *speculation* is used in this narrower sense of buying (or selling) commodities or financial assets simply to make money from later selling them (or buying them back) again at a higher (or lower) price. The term ***speculators*** usually refers to people engaged in such activities.

In the extreme case, speculators need not part with any money. If they buy an item and sell it back fairly soon at a higher price, they may be able to use the money from the sale to pay the original seller: just pocketing the difference. Alternatively, speculators may sell an item they do not even possess, as long as they can buy it back in time (at a lower price) to hand it over to the original purchaser. Again, they simply pocket the difference in price.

It may sound as if speculators are on to a good thing, and often they are, but speculation does carry risks: the predictions of individual speculators may turn out to be wrong, and then they could make losses rather than profits.

Nevertheless, speculators on average tend to gain rather than lose. The reason is that speculation tends to be ***self-fulfilling***. In other words, the actions of speculators tend to bring about the very effect on prices that they had anticipated. For example, if speculators believe that the price of Barclays shares is about to rise, they will buy some. But by doing this they will contribute to an increase in demand and ensure that the price *will* rise; the prophecy has become self-fulfilling.

Speculation can either help to reduce price fluctuations or aggravate them: it can be stabilising or destabilising.

Stabilising speculation

Speculation will tend to have a ***stabilising*** effect on price fluctuations when suppliers and/or demanders believe that a change in price is only *temporary*.

An initial fall in price. In Figure 2.21 demand has shifted from D_1 to D_2; equilibrium has moved from point *a* to point *b*, and price has fallen to P_2. How do people react to this fall in price?

Given that they believe this fall in price to be only temporary, suppliers *hold back*, expecting prices to rise again: supply shifts from S_1 to S_2. After all, why supply now when, by waiting, they could get a higher price?

Buyers *increase* their purchases, to take advantage of the temporary fall in price. Demand shifts from D_2 to D_3.

The equilibrium moves to point *c*, with price rising back towards P_1.

An initial rise in price. In Figure 2.22 demand has shifted from D_1 to D_2. Price has risen from P_1 to P_2.

Suppliers bring their goods to market now, before price falls again. Supply shifts from S_1 to S_2. Demanders, however, hold

Definitions

Speculation Where people make buying or selling decisions based on their anticipations of future prices.

Speculators People who buy (or sell) commodities or financial assets with the intention of profiting by selling them (or buying them back) at a later date at a higher (lower) price.

Self-fulfilling speculation The actions of speculators tend to cause the very effect that they had anticipated.

Stabilising speculation Where the actions of speculators tend to reduce price fluctuations.

Figure 2.21 Stabilising speculation: initial price fall

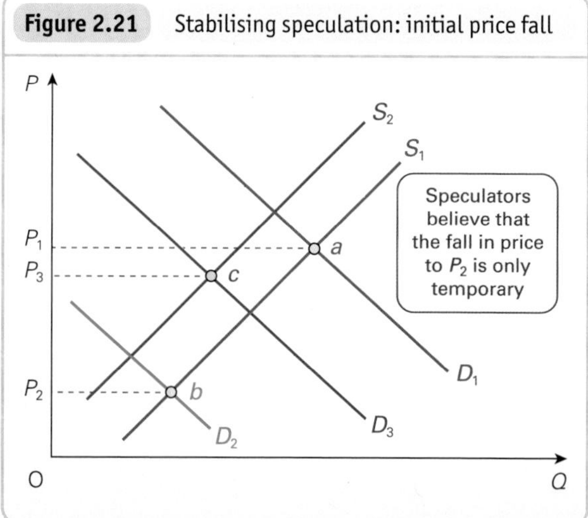

Figure 2.22 Stabilising speculation: initial price rise

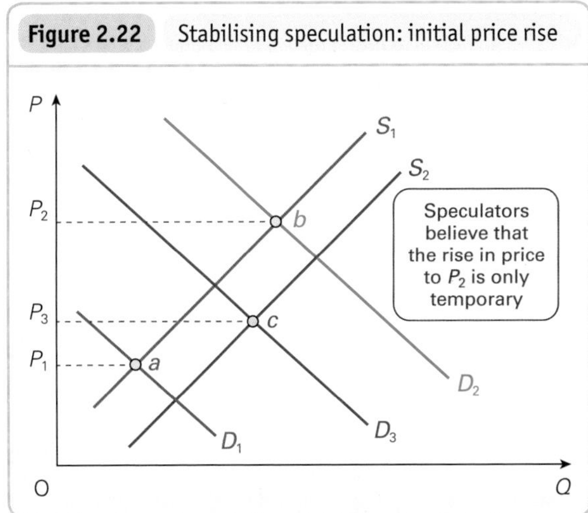

back until price falls. Demand shifts from D_2 to D_3. The equilibrium moves to point *c*, with price falling back towards P_1.

An example. A good example of stabilising speculation is that which occurs in agricultural commodity markets. Take the case of wheat. When it is harvested in the autumn, there will be a plentiful supply. If all this wheat were to be put on the market, the price would fall to a very low level. Later in the year, when most of the wheat would have been sold, the price would then rise to a very high level. This is all easily predictable.

So what do farmers do? The answer is that they speculate. When the wheat is harvested, they know price will tend to fall, and so instead of bringing it all to market they put some into store. The more the price falls, the more they will put into store *anticipating that the price will later rise.* But this holding back of supplies prevents prices from falling. In other words, it stabilises prices.

Later in the year, when the price begins to rise, they will gradually release grain onto the market from the stores. The more the price rises, the more they will release on to the market *anticipating that the price will fall again by the time of the next harvest.* But this releasing of supplies will again stabilise prices by preventing them from rising so much.

Rather than the farmers doing the speculation, it could be done by grain merchants. When there is a glut of wheat in the autumn, and prices are relatively low, they buy wheat on the grain market and put it into store. When there is a shortage in the spring and summer, they sell wheat from their stores. In this way they stabilise prices just as the farmers did when they were the ones who operated the stores.

In Figures 2.21 and 2.22, the initial change in price was caused by a shift in the demand curve. Redraw these two diagrams to illustrate the situation where the initial change in price was caused by a shift in the supply curve (as would be the case in the wheat market that we have just considered).

Destabilising speculation

Speculation will tend to have a ***destabilising*** effect on price fluctuations when suppliers and/or buyers believe that a change in price heralds similar changes to come.

Figure 2.23 Destabilising speculation: initial price fall

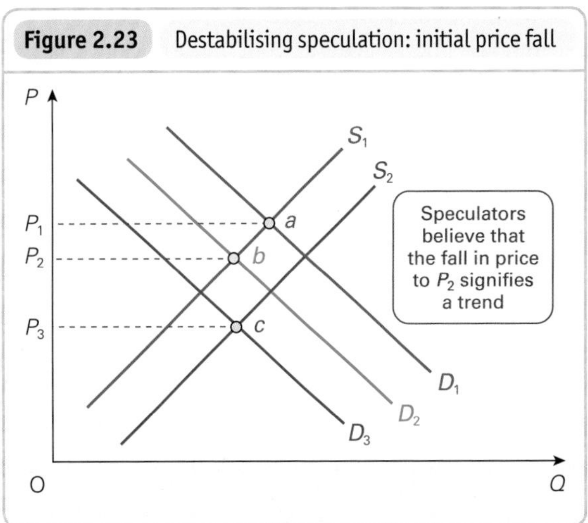

An initial fall in price. In Figure 2.23 demand has shifted from D_1 to D_2 and price has fallen from P_1 to P_2. This time, believing that the fall in price heralds further falls in price to come, suppliers sell now before the price does fall. Supply shifts from S_1 to S_2. And demanders wait: they wait until price does fall further. Demand shifts from D_2 to D_3.

Their actions ensure that price does fall further: to P_3.

An initial rise in price. In Figure 2.24 a price rise from P_1 to P_2 is caused by a rise in demand from D_1 to D_2. Suppliers wait until price rises further. Supply shifts from S_1 to S_2. Demanders buy now before any further rise in price. Demand shifts from D_2 to D_3. As a result, price continues to rise: to P_3.

In section 2.3 we examined the housing market (see Box 2.1). In this market, speculation is frequently destabilising. Assume that people see house prices beginning to move upwards. This might be the result of increased demand brought about by a cut in mortgage interest rates or by

Figure 2.24 Destabilising speculation: initial price rise

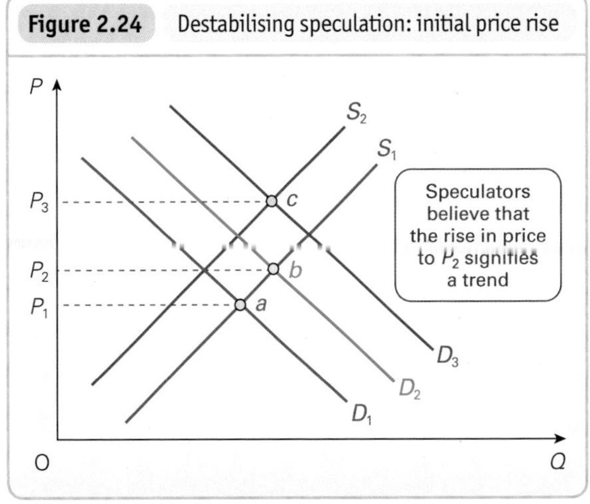

Definition

Destabilising speculation Where the actions of speculators tend to make price movements larger.

growth in the economy. People may well believe that the rise in house prices signals a boom in the housing market: that prices will go on rising. Potential buyers will thus try to buy as soon as possible before prices rise any further. This will increase demand (as in Figure 2.24) and will thus lead to even bigger price rises. This is precisely what happened in the UK housing market in 1999–2007 and from mid-2013 (see chart in Box 2.1 on page 48). Conversely, in early 2008 prices started to fall; potential buyers believed that they would fall further and thus held off entering the market, leading to even bigger price falls.

Estate agents consistently 'talk up' the housing market, often predicting price rises when other commentators are more cautious. Explain why they might have a vested interest in doing so.

Conclusion

In some circumstances, then, the action of speculators can help to keep price fluctuations to a minimum (stabilising speculation). This is most likely when markets are relatively stable in the first place, with only moderate underlying shifts in demand and supply.

In other circumstances, however, speculation can make price fluctuations much worse. This is most likely in times of uncertainty, when there are significant changes in the determinants of demand and supply. Given this uncertainty, people may see price changes as signifying some trend. They then 'jump on the bandwagon' and do what the rest are doing, further fuelling the rise or fall in price.

Redraw Figures 2.23 and 2.24 assuming, as in the first question on page 71, that the initial change in price was caused by a shift in the supply curve.

Dealing with uncertainty and risk

When price changes are likely to occur, buyers and sellers will try to anticipate them. Unfortunately, on many occasions no one can be certain just what these price changes will be. Take the case of stocks and shares. If you anticipate that the price of, say, Marks & Spencer shares is likely to go up substantially in the near future, you may well decide to buy some now and then sell them later after the price has risen. But you cannot be certain that they will go up in price: they may fall instead. If you buy the shares, therefore, you will be taking a gamble.

Now, gambles can be of two types. The first is where you know the odds. Let us take the simplest case of a gamble on the toss of a coin. Heads you win; tails you lose. You know that the odds of winning are precisely 50 per cent. If you bet on the toss of a coin, you are said to be operating under conditions of ***risk***. *Risk is when the probability of an outcome is known.* Risk itself is a measure of the *variability* of an outcome. For example, if you bet £1 on the toss of a coin, such that heads you win £1 and tails you lose £1, then the variability is −£1 to £1.

The second form of gamble is the more usual. This is where the odds are not known or are known only roughly. Gambling on the stock exchange is like this. You may have a good idea that a share will go up in price, but is it a 90 per cent chance, an 80 per cent chance or what? You are not certain. Gambling under this sort of condition is known as operating under ***uncertainty***. *This is when the probability of an outcome is not known.*

You may well disapprove of gambling and want to dismiss people who engage in it as foolish or morally wrong. But 'gambling' is not just confined to horses, cards, roulette and the like. Risk and uncertainty pervade the whole of economic life, and decisions are constantly having to be made whose outcome cannot be known for certain. Even the most morally upright person will still have to decide which career to go into, whether and when to buy a house, or even something as trivial as whether or not to take an umbrella when going out. Each of these decisions and thousands of others are made under conditions of uncertainty (or occasionally risk).

People's actions are influenced by their attitudes towards risk. **Many decisions are taken under conditions of risk or uncertainty. Generally, the lower the probability of (or the more uncertain) the desired outcome of an action, the less likely people will be to undertake the action.**

Give some examples of decisions you have taken recently that were made under conditions of uncertainty. With hindsight do you think you made the right decisions?

We shall be examining how risk and uncertainty affect economic decisions on several occasions throughout the book. For example, in Chapter 5 we will see how it affects people's attitudes and actions as consumers and how taking out insurance can help to reduce their uncertainty. At this point, however, let us focus on firms' attitudes when supplying goods.

Stock holding as a way of reducing the problem of uncertainty

A simple way that suppliers can reduce the problem of uncertainty is by holding stocks. Take the case of the wheat farmers we saw in the previous section. At the time when

Definitions

Risk When a (desirable) outcome of an action may or may not occur, but the probability of its occurring is known. The lower the probability, the greater the risk involved in taking the action.

Uncertainty When an outcome may or may not occur and its probability of occurring is not known.

they are planting the wheat in the spring, they are uncertain as to what the price of wheat will be when they bring it to market. If they keep no stores of wheat, they will just have to accept whatever the market price happens to be at harvest time. If, however, they have storage facilities, they can put the wheat into store if the price is low and then wait until the price goes up. Alternatively, if the price of wheat is high at harvest time, they can sell the wheat straight away. In other words, they can choose the time to sell.

BOX 2.7 **SHORT SELLING** EXPLORING ECONOMICS

Gambling on a fall in share prices

A form of speculation that can be very damaging to stock markets is the practice of ***short selling***. This is where people take advantage of anticipated falls in share prices by selling shares they do not possess. How does this work?

Assume that a share price is currently £10 per share and traders on the stock market believe that the price is about to fall. They want to take advantage of this but don't possess any. What they do is borrow shares from dealers who do own some and agree to return them on a specified date. They pay a fee for doing this. In the meantime they sell the shares on the market at the current price of £10 and wait for it to fall. They are now 'short' of the shares (i.e. they don't possess them but still owe them).

Assume that just before the agreed time comes for returning the shares the price has fallen to £8. The trader then buys the shares, returns them to the dealer who had lent them and pockets the difference of £2 (minus the fee).

Although anyone can short sell shares, it is largely traders from various financial institutions who engage in this practice. Huge bonuses can be earned from their employers if the short selling is profitable. This encourages an atmosphere of risk-taking and looking to short-term gains rather than providing long-term capital to firms.

Short selling in the banking crisis of 2008

The practice of short selling had become rife and added to the instability of markets, driving share prices down that were anticipated to fall. This was a particular problem in 2008, when worries about bad debts and losses in the banking sector led many traders to short sell the shares of banks and other financial institutions felt to be most at risk.

The short selling of Halifax Bank of Scotland (HBOS) shares in September 2008 was a major contributing factor to the collapse in its share price. HBOS, the UK's largest mortgage lender, had been suffering losses as a result of falling house prices and difficulties of many house owners in keeping up with their monthly mortgage payments. The share price plummeted by over 70 per cent in the space of a few days. The fall was driven on by speculation, much of it short selling. On 17 September it was announced that HBOS would be taken over by Lloyds TSB.

Concerns about the practice of short selling driving instability in financial markets led a number of governments – or agencies acting on their behalf – to introduce temporary bans on the practice. In September 2008, the Financial Services Authority, the UK industry's regulator at the time, announced a four-month ban on the practice. At the same time, the US financial regulator, the Securities and Exchange Commission, announced a similar move. Both these bans were imposed for a matter of months, whereas Denmark held a similar policy for more than two years.

In May 2012, the EU passed a law giving the European Securities and Markets Authority (ESMA) the power to ban short selling in emergency situations: i.e. where it threatens the stability of the EU financial system. The UK government opposed the legislation but the EU Court of Justice rejected the challenge in 2014.

Is short selling always profitable?

Short selling, as with other forms of speculation, is a type of gambling. If you gamble on a price fall and the price does fall, your gamble pays off and you make a profit. If you get it wrong, however, and the price rises, you will make a loss. In the case of short selling, you would have to buy the shares (to give back to the lender) at a higher price than you sold them for.

This is just what happened in September 2008. With central banks around the world supporting markets, with the US government announcing that it would take over the bad debts of banks and with future short selling temporarily banned, share prices rapidly increased. The FTSE rose by a record 8.8 per cent on 19 September. Those with 'short positions' – i.e. those who had sold shares they had borrowed – then had to buy them back at a much higher price. Losses of hundreds of millions of pounds were made by short sellers. But they gained little sympathy from the general public, who blamed their 'greed' for much of the falls in share prices of the previous weeks.

1. *Why would owners of shares, such as pension funds, lend them to short sellers rather than selling the shares themselves and then buying them back later?*
2. *What are the potential benefits of short selling for the economy?*
3. *'Naked' short selling has been banned in many countries. What exactly is naked short selling?*

Undertake desktop research on the positions taken by different countries in relation to short selling. Summarise your findings.

Definition

Short selling (or shorting) Where investors borrow an asset, such as shares, oil contracts or foreign currency; sell the asset, hoping the price will soon fall; then buy it back later and return it to the lender. Assuming the price has fallen, the short seller will make a profit of the difference (minus any fees). There is always the danger, however, that the price may have risen, in which case the short seller will make a loss.

BOX 2.8 DEALING IN FUTURES MARKETS

EXPLORING ECONOMICS

A way of reducing uncertainty

One way of reducing or even eliminating uncertainty is by dealing in ***futures or forward markets***. Let us examine first the activities of sellers and then those of buyers.

Sellers

Suppose you are a farmer and want to store grain to sell at some time in the future, expecting to get a better price then than now. The trouble is that there is a chance that the price will go down. Given this uncertainty, you may be unwilling to take a gamble.

An answer to your problem is provided by the *commodity futures market*. This is a market where prices are agreed between sellers and buyers today for delivery at some specified date in the future.

For example, if it is 20 October today, you could be quoted a price today for delivery in six months' time (i.e. on 20 April). This is known as the six-month ***future price***. Assume that the six-month future price is £160 per tonne. If you agree to this price and make a six-month forward contract, you are agreeing to sell a specified amount of wheat at £160 on 20 April. No matter what happens to the ***spot price*** (i.e. the current market price) in the meantime, your selling price has been agreed. The spot price could have fallen to £140 (or risen to £180) by April, but your selling price when 20 April arrives is fixed at £160. There is thus *no risk to you whatsoever of the price going down*. You will, of course, have lost out if the spot price is *more* than £160 in April.

Buyers

Now suppose that you are a flour miller. In order to plan your expenditures, you would like to know the price you will have to pay for wheat, not just today, but also at various future dates. In other words, if you want to take delivery of wheat at some time in the future, you would like a price quoted *now*. You would like the risks removed of prices going *up*.

Let us assume that today (20 October) you want to *buy* the same amount of wheat on 20 April that a farmer wishes to sell on that same date. If you agree to the £160 future price, a future contract can be made with the farmer. You are then guaranteed that purchase price, no matter what happens to the spot price in the meantime. There is thus *no risk to you whatsoever of the price going up*. You will, of course, have lost out if the spot price is *less* than £160 in April.

The determination of the future price

Prices in the futures market are determined in the same way as in other markets: by demand and supply. For example, the six-month wheat price or the three-month coffee price will be that which equates the demand for those futures with the supply. If the five-month sugar price is currently £220 per tonne and people expect by then, because of an anticipated good beet harvest, that the spot price for sugar will be £170 per tonne, there will be few who want to buy the futures at £220 (and many who want to sell). This excess of supply of futures over demand will push the price down.

Speculators

Many people operate in the futures market who never actually handle the commodities themselves. They are neither producers nor users of the commodities. They merely speculate. Such speculators may be individuals, but they are more likely to be financial institutions.

Let us take a simple example. Suppose that the six-month (April) coffee price is £1300 per tonne and that you, as a speculator, believe that the spot price of coffee is likely to rise above that level between now (October) and six months' time. You thus decide to buy 20 tonnes of April coffee futures now.

But you have no intention of taking delivery. After four months, let us say, true to your prediction, the spot price (February) has risen and as a result the April price (and other future prices) have risen too. You thus decide to *sell* 20 tonnes of April (two-month) coffee futures, whose price, let us say, is £1500. You are now 'covered'.

When April comes, what happens? You have agreed to buy 20 tonnes of coffee at £1300 per tonne and to sell 20 tonnes of coffee at £1500 per tonne. All you do is to hand the futures contract to buy to the person to whom you agreed to sell. They sort out delivery between them and you make £200 per tonne profit.

If, however, your prediction had been wrong and the price had *fallen*, you would have made a loss. You would have been forced to sell coffee contracts at a lower price than you bought them.

Speculators in the futures market thus incur risks, unlike the sellers and buyers of the commodities, for whom the futures market eliminates risk. Financial institutions offering futures contracts will charge for the service: for taking on the risks.

If speculators believed that the price of cocoa in six months was going to be below the six-month future price quoted today, how would they act?

Choose three commodities and find out their spot price and their future prices for three different dates. Explain the difference in prices.

Definitions

Futures or forward market A market in which contracts are made to buy or sell at some future date at a price agreed today.

Future price A price agreed today at which an item (e.g. commodities) will be exchanged at some set date in the future.

Spot price The current market price.

Section summary

1. A complete understanding of markets must take into account the time dimension.
2. Given that producers and consumers take a time to respond fully to price changes, we can identify different equilibria after the lapse of different lengths of time. Generally, short-run supply and demand tend to be less price elastic than long-run supply and demand. As a result, any shifts in *D* or *S* curves tend to have a relatively bigger effect on price in the short run and a relatively bigger effect on quantity in the long run.
3. People often anticipate price changes and this will affect the amount they demand or supply. This speculation will tend to stabilise price fluctuations if people believe that the price changes are only temporary. However, speculation will tend to destabilise these fluctuations (i.e. make them more severe) if people believe that prices are likely to continue to move in the same direction as at present (at least for some time).
4. Many economic decisions are taken under conditions of risk or uncertainty. Uncertainty over future prices can be tackled by holding stocks. When prices are low, the stocks can be built up. When they are high, stocks can be sold.

END OF CHAPTER QUESTIONS

1. The weekly demand and supply schedules for T-shirts (in millions) in a free market are as follows:

Price (£)	**8**	**7**	**6**	**5**	**4**	**3**	**2**	**1**
Quantity demanded	6	8	10	12	14	16	18	20
Quantity supplied	18	16	14	12	10	8	6	4

   (a) What are the equilibrium price and quantity?

   (b) Assume that changes in fashion cause the demand for T-shirts to rise by 4 million at each price. What will be the new equilibrium price and quantity? Has equilibrium quantity risen as much as the rise in demand? Explain why or why not.

   (c) Now plot the data in the table and mark the equilibrium. Also plot the new data corresponding to (b).

2. On separate demand and supply diagrams for bread, sketch the effects of the following: (a) a rise in the price of wheat; (b) a rise in the price of butter and margarine; (c) a rise in the price of rice, pasta and potatoes. In each case, state your assumptions.
3. For what reasons might the price of overseas holidays rise? In each case, identify whether these are reasons affecting demand, supply, or both.
4. If both demand and supply change, and if we know which direction they have shifted but not how much, why are we able to predict the direction in which *either* price *or* quantity will change, but not both? (Clue: consider the four possible combinations and sketch them if necessary: (a) *D* left, *S* left; (b) *D* right, *S* right; (c) *D* left, *S* right; (d) *D* right, *S* left.)
5. If you were the owner of a clothes shop, how would you set about deciding what prices to charge for each garment at the end-of-season sale?
6. Is there any truth in the saying that the price of a good is a reflection of its quality?
7. Assume that oil begins to run out and that extraction becomes more expensive. Trace through the effects of this on the market for oil and the market for other fuels.
8. Why are both the price elasticity of demand and the price elasticity of supply likely to be greater in the long run?
9. Which of the following will have positive signs and which will have negative ones: (a) price elasticity of demand; (b) income elasticity of demand (normal good); (c) income elasticity of demand (inferior good); (d) cross elasticity of demand (with respect to changes in price of a substitute good); (e) cross elasticity of demand (with respect to changes in price of a complementary good); (f) price elasticity of supply?
10. What are the advantages and disadvantages of speculation from the point of view of (a) the consumer; (b) firms?

Online resources

Additional case studies on the student website

2.1 **The demand for lamb.** An investigation of a real-world demand function.

2.2 **Adjusting to oil price shocks.** A case study showing how demand and supply analysis can be used to examine the price changes in the oil market since 1973.

2.3 **Coffee prices.** An examination of the coffee market and the implications of fluctuations in the coffee harvest for growers and coffee drinkers.

2.4 **Shall we put up our price?** This uses the concept of price elasticity of demand to explain why prices are higher where firms face little or no competition.

2.5 **Response to changes in petrol and ethanol prices in Brazil.** This case examines how drivers with 'flex-fuel' cars responded to changes in the relative price of two fuels: petrol and ethanol (made from sugar cane).

2.6 **Income elasticity of demand and the balance of payments.** This examines how a low income elasticity of demand for the exports of many developing countries can help to explain their chronic balance of payments problems.

2.7 **The role of the speculator.** This assesses whether the activities of speculators are beneficial or harmful to the rest of society.

Maths Case 2.1 Finding equilibrium price and quantity using algebra. This gives an example of solving equilibrium price and quantity from a demand and a supply equation using the method of simultaneous equations.

Maths Case 2.2 Calculating income and cross-price elasticities from a demand equation: a worked example (Part 1: not using calculus). This gives an example of working out cross and income elasticities from a particular demand function.

Maths Case 2.3 Calculating income and cross-price elasticities from a demand equation: a worked example (Part 2: using calculus). This shows how simple differentiation can be used to work out elasticity values. It gives an example of working out cross and income elasticities from a particular demand function.

Websites relevant to this chapter

Numbers and sections refer to websites listed in the Web Appendix and hotlinked from this book's website at **go.pearson.com/uk/sloman.**

- For news articles relevant to this chapter, see the *Economics News* section on the student website.
- For general news on markets, see websites in section A, and particularly A1–9, 23–6, 35, 36. See also links to newspapers worldwide in A38, 39, 43 and 44, and the news search feature in Google at A41.
- For links to sites on markets, see the relevant sections of I7, 13 and 14.
- For data on the housing market (Box 2.1), see sites B7–11.
- For sites favouring the free market, see C17 and E34.
- For student resources relevant to this chapter, see sites C1–10, 19, 28.
- For a range of classroom games and simulations of markets, see sites C23, 24 and 27 (computer-based) and C20 (non-computer-based).

Government and the Market

CHAPTER MAP

In the previous chapter we looked at free markets: markets where there is no government intervention. However, as we saw in Chapter 1 the real world is one of mixed economies. Indeed, the government intervenes in many markets, even highly competitive ones. This intervention can take a number of forms:

- Fixing prices, either above or below the free-market equilibrium.
- Taxing the production or sale of various goods, such as petrol.
- Subsidising the production or sale of various goods, such as public transport.
- Producing goods or services directly (e.g. defence and health care).
- Regulation. Various laws could be passed to regulate the behaviour of firms. For example, some activities, such as the dumping of toxic waste, could be made illegal; or licences or official permission might have to be obtained to produce certain goods; or a regulatory body could supervise the activities of various firms and prevent any that it felt to be against the public interest (e.g. the production of unsafe toys).

Supply and demand analysis is a useful tool for examining the effects of government intervention. First, in section 3.1, we examine what could happen if a government fixes prices, either above or below the equilibrium. Then, in the following section, we look at the effects of government taxes on products. We see the impact on prices and output and how this depends on the price elasticity of demand and supply.

In section 3.3 we examine what happens if the government seeks to do away with a market system of allocation altogether, either by providing things free to consumers, or by banning certain harmful activities.

Finally, we look at the impact of government intervention in agriculture – a sector that has received massive government support in many countries of the world. We look at the economic arguments for such intervention and then examine some specific measures that governments have taken.

The role of government in the economy is examined further in Chapters 11 to 14.

3.1 THE CONTROL OF PRICES

TC 3 p26
TC 7 p79

At the equilibrium price, there will be no shortage or surplus. The equilibrium price, however, may not be the most desirable price. The government, therefore, may prefer to keep prices above or below the market clearing level.

If the government sets a ***minimum price*** above the equilibrium (a price floor), there will be a surplus. This is illustrated in Figure 3.1. With curves *S* and *D*, the surplus is $Q_s - Q_d$ $(b - a)$. Legislation prevents the price from falling to eliminate this surplus.

The size of the surplus at any given minimum price will depend on the price elasticity of demand and supply. For example, if supply and demand are less elastic (S_1 and D_1 instead of *S* and *D*) the same minimum price will create a smaller surplus: $Q_{s_1} - Q_{d_1}$ $(d - c)$. Given the impact of time on elasticity, the surplus will tend to be larger in the long run.

If the government sets a ***maximum price*** below the equilibrium (a price ceiling), there will be a shortage. This is illustrated in Figure 3.2. With curves *S* and *D* the shortage is $Q_d - Q_s$ $(b - a)$. Legislation prevents the price from rising to eliminate this shortage.

Definitions

Minimum price A price floor set by the government or some other agency. The price is not allowed to fall below this level (although it is allowed to rise above it).

Maximum price A price ceiling set by the government or some other agency. The price is not allowed to rise above this level (although it is allowed to fall below it).

Figure 3.1 Minimum price: price floor

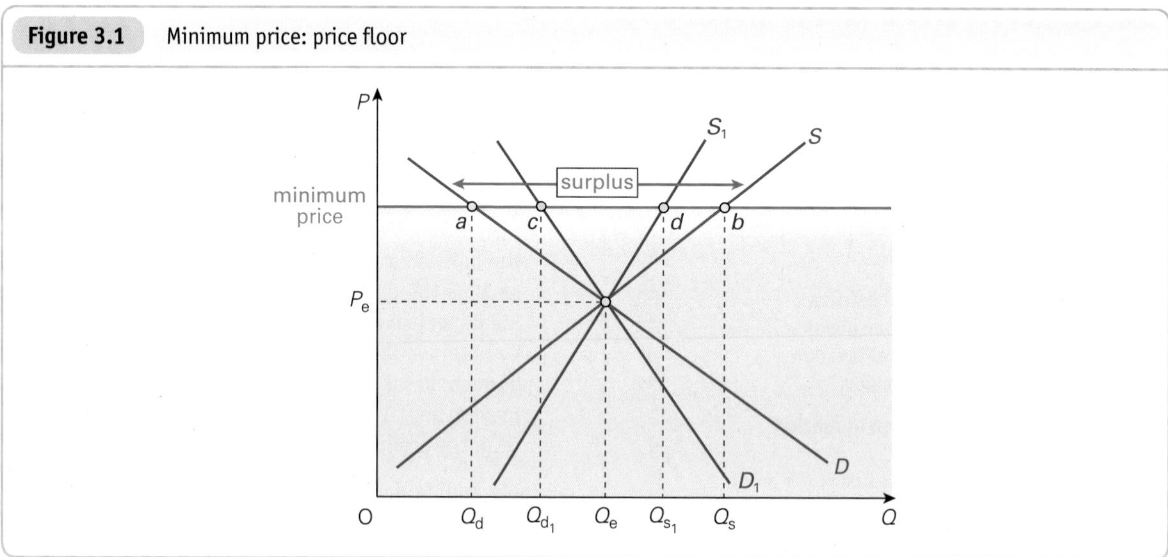

Figure 3.2 Maximum price: price ceiling

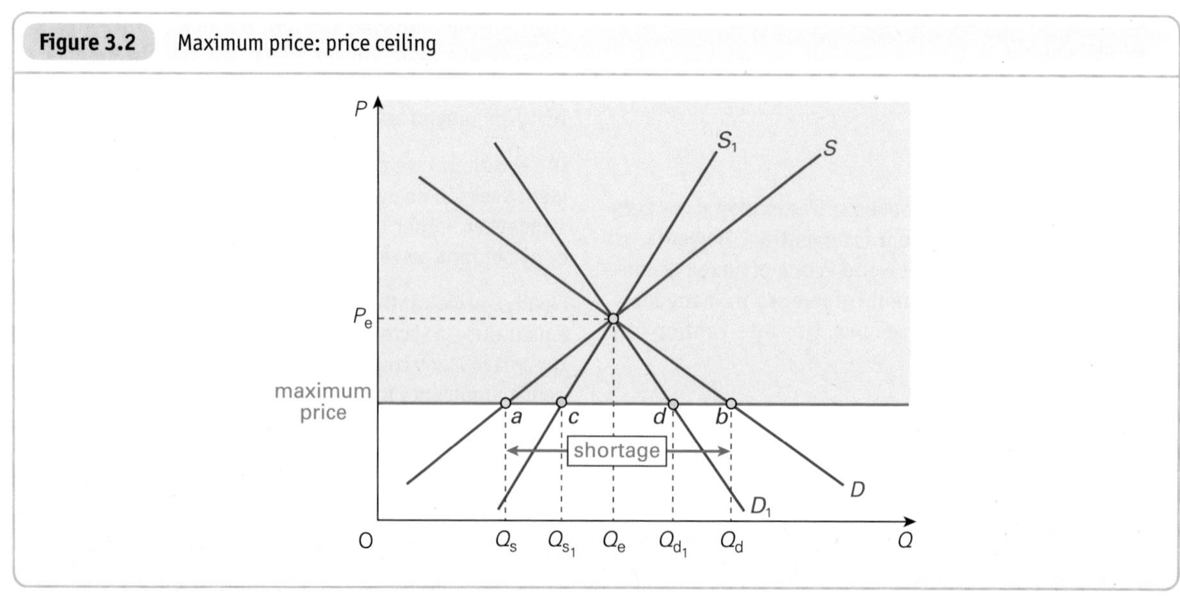

THRESHOLD CONCEPT 7 **GOVERNMENTS CAN SOMETIMES IMPROVE MARKET OUTCOMES** THINKING LIKE AN ECONOMIST

Threshold Concept 3 was that markets may fail to meet social objectives; this implies that there may be a need for government intervention. Governments have a number of policy instruments that they can use, either to influence markets or to replace them altogether. These policy instruments include taxation, benefits and subsidies, laws and regulations, licences and permits, and direct provision by government departments or agencies (such as the National Health Service in the UK).

The threshold concept here is not merely that governments intervene, but that they can correct, or at least lessen, market failures. Once we have understood the nature of a market failure, we can then set about designing a policy to correct it. For example, if we could identify that the cost to society of producing a product in a way which created pollution was £20 per unit more than the benefit that society gained from the product, then the government could tax the producer £20 per unit.

In Chapters 11 to 14 we consider a number of these policy instruments and seek to identify the *optimum* level of government intervention to meet social objectives. In this chapter we have a preliminary look at some of these instruments.

Governments themselves, however, are imperfect organisations with a number of different motivations. For an economic adviser to recommend a particular policy as the best means of correcting a market failure does not mean that the government will carry it out efficiently or, indeed, carry it out at all. In fact sometimes intervention can make things worse rather than better.

1. *What market failures could be corrected by the use of welfare benefits? Does the payment of such benefits create any problems for society?*
2. *Assume that the government sees litter as a market failure that requires government action. Give some examples of policies it could adopt to reduce litter.*

The size of the shortage at any given maximum price will again depend on the price elasticity of demand and supply. For example, if demand is less elastic (D_1 instead of D) the same maximum price will create a smaller shortage: $Q_{d_1} - Q_{s_1}$ $(d - c)$.

Setting a minimum (high) price

The government sets minimum prices to prevent them from falling below a certain level. It may do this for various reasons:

- To protect producers' incomes. If the industry is subject to supply fluctuations (e.g. fluctuations in weather affecting crops), prices are likely to fluctuate severely. Minimum prices will prevent the fall in producers' incomes that would accompany periods of low prices. (This is examined further in section 3.4 in the context of agricultural intervention.)
- To create a surplus (e.g. of grains) – particularly in times of plenty – which can be stored in preparation for possible future shortages.
- To deter the consumption of particular goods. Some people may consume more of a good than is in their own self-interest because they do not fully appreciate the future costs to their health. They may also act irrationally because of self-control and addiction issues. See Chapter 5 for more detail.
- In the case of wages (the price of labour), minimum wage legislation can be used to prevent workers' wage rates from falling below a certain level. This may form part of a government policy on poverty and inequality (see Box 11.2).

Draw a supply and demand diagram with the price of labour (the wage rate) on the vertical axis and the quantity of labour (the number of workers) on the horizontal axis. What will happen to employment if the government raises wages from the equilibrium to some minimum wage above the equilibrium?

The government can use various methods to deal with the surpluses associated with minimum prices.

- The government could buy the surplus and store it, destroy it or sell it abroad in other markets. This is illustrated in Figure 3.3, where the government purchases the unsold surplus of $b - a$ (i.e. $Q_s - Q_d$). The cost to the government of buying this surplus is the shaded area (abQ_sQ_d). This is what happened in the EU's Common Agricultural Policy where 'Intervention Boards' bought up surpluses and, in most cases, (e.g. grains, milk, powder and beef) put them in storage. The expense of storage would have to be added to the shaded area in Figure 3.3 to obtain the full cost to the government of the policy. These costs would be lower if the government could sell surpluses on the world market.
- Supply could be artificially lowered by restricting producers to particular quotas. For example, in Figure 3.1, supply could be reduced to Q_d (or Q_{d_1} in the case of D_1).

Figure 3.3 The cost to the government of a minimum price

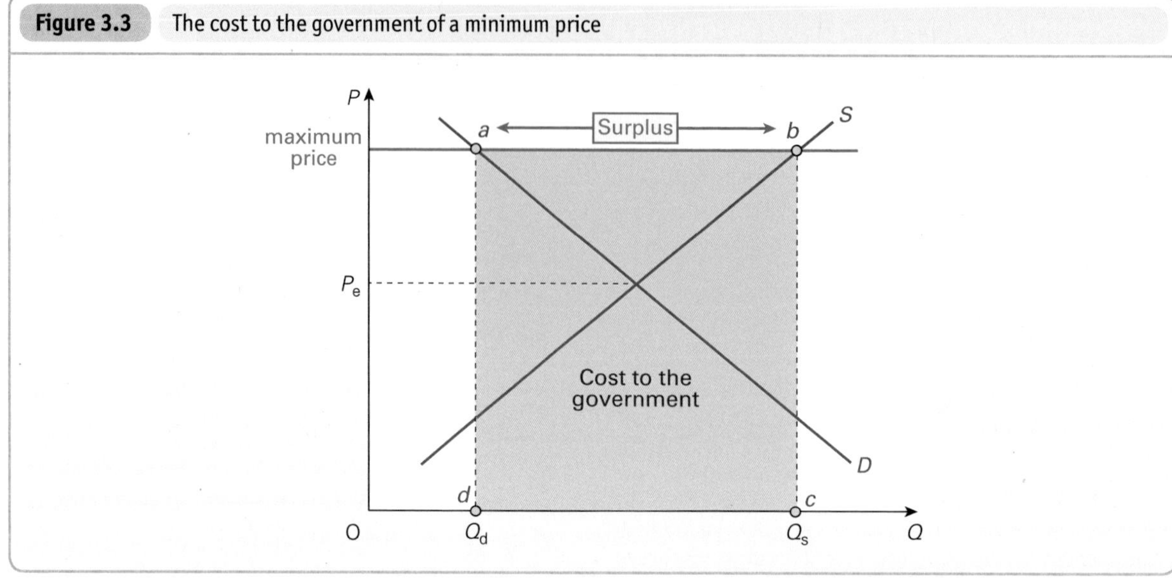

This would reduce the costs to the government of having to purchase the surplus, but it might be a difficult policy to enforce.

- Demand could be raised by advertising, by finding alternative uses for the good, or by reducing consumption of substitute goods (e.g. by imposing taxes or quotas on substitutes, such as imports).

TC 5 p48

One of the problems with minimum prices is that firms with surpluses on their hands may try to evade the price control and cut their prices.

Another problem is that high prices may cushion inefficiency. Firms may feel less need to find more efficient methods of production and to cut their costs if their profits are being protected by the high price. Also, the high price may discourage firms from producing alternative goods which they could produce more efficiently or which are in higher demand, but which nevertheless have a lower (free-market) price.

TC 5 p48

Setting a maximum (low) price

TC 7 p79 KI 4 p13

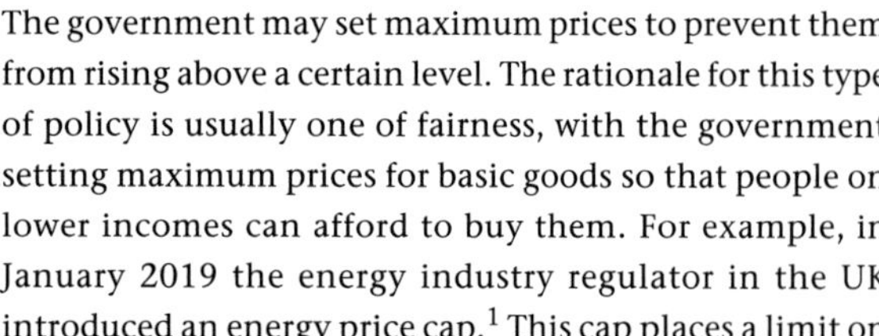

The government may set maximum prices to prevent them from rising above a certain level. The rationale for this type of policy is usually one of fairness, with the government setting maximum prices for basic goods so that people on lower incomes can afford to buy them. For example, in January 2019 the energy industry regulator in the UK introduced an energy price cap.[1] This cap places a limit on the price energy suppliers can charge for each unit of energy (kWh). Price controls may be used in times of crises, emergencies or natural disasters where supply is disrupted and/or demand rises rapidly. See Box 3.2 for more detail.

The resulting shortages, however, create further problems. If the government merely sets prices and does not intervene further, the shortages will lead to sellers having to allocate the good amongst its potential customers in one or more of the following ways:

- *'First-come, first-served' basis.* This is likely to lead to queues developing outside shops, or websites crashing if people try to purchase the good online. To try to deal with these issues firms may have to adopt waiting lists. Queues have been a common feature of life in Venezuela and Argentina where the governments have kept the prices of many basic goods below the level necessary to equate demand and supply.
- *Random ballot.* The seller puts the name of every customer willing to pay the maximum price into a random draw. Only those who are lucky enough to have their name drawn receive the good.
- *Favoured customers.* This could be the seller's friends, family and/or regular customers.
- *A measure of merit.* For example, the number of students who want a place on a particular course at a university and are willing to pay the tuition fee may exceed the number of places available. In this instance, the university may allocate places to those who achieve the highest grades.

1 About the energy price cap, Ofgem, www.ofgem.gov.uk/energy-price-caps/about-energy-price-cap

- *A rule or regulation.* State schools facing excess demand often allocate places based on the distance children live from the school (in this case the maximum price is zero). Preference is also given to applicants who have an older sibling already at the school.

KI 4 p13 None of the above may be considered fair, however, since some people in need may be forced to go without. Therefore, the government may adopt a system of ***rationing***. People could be issued with a set number of coupons for each item rationed. Sometimes suppliers may place restrictions on the amounts consumers can purchase. For example, during the COVID-19 pandemic supermarkets in the UK placed limits on the sales of certain essential goods: e.g. three multipacks of toilet rolls per customer.

A major problem with maximum prices is likely to be the emergence of ***illegal markets*** (sometimes called ***underground*** or ***shadow markets***), where customers, unable to buy enough in legal markets, may well be prepared to pay very high prices: prices above P_e in Figure 3.2 (see Case Study 3.3 on the student website, which examines the imposition of maximum prices (charges) in the payday loan market).

Definitions

Rationing Where the government restricts the amount of a good that people are allowed to buy.

Illegal or underground or shadow markets Where people ignore the government's price and/or quantity controls and sell illegally at whatever price equates illegal demand and supply.

Another problem is that the maximum prices reduce the quantity produced of an already scarce commodity. For example, artificially low prices in a famine are likely to reduce food supplies: if not immediately, then at the next harvest, because of less being sown. In many developing countries, governments control the price of basic foodstuffs in order to help the urban poor. The effect, however, is to reduce incomes for farmers, who are then encouraged to leave the land and flock into the ever-growing towns and cities.

To minimise these types of problems the government may attempt to reduce the shortage by encouraging supply: by drawing on stores, by direct government production, or by giving subsidies or tax relief to firms. Alternatively, it may attempt to reduce demand: by the production of more alternative goods (e.g. home-grown vegetables in times of war) or by controlling people's incomes.

Another example of maximum prices is where the government imposes rent controls in an attempt to make rented accommodation more affordable. Here the 'price' is the rent people are charged. The danger of this policy is that it will create a shortage of rental property. The policy is examined in Case Study 3.3 on the student website.

Every year the number of people who want to run the London Marathon far exceeds the number of places available. For example, 457 861 applicants were willing to pay £39 to enter the 2020 event. Unfortunately, there were only 17 500 places for these applicants and so the majority ended up very disappointed. Find out the different methods used by the organisers to allocate all 40 000 places and consider their advantages and disadvantages.

Section summary

1. There are several ways in which the government intervenes in the operation of markets. It can fix prices, tax or subsidise products, regulate production, or produce goods directly itself.
2. The government may fix minimum or maximum prices. If a minimum price is set above the equilibrium, a surplus will result. If a maximum price is set below the equilibrium price, a shortage will result. The size of the surplus or shortage will depend on the price elasticity of demand and supply.
3. Minimum prices are set as a means of protecting the incomes of suppliers or creating a surplus for storage in case of future reductions in supply. If the government is not deliberately trying to create a surplus, it must decide what to do with it.
4. Maximum prices are set as a means of keeping prices down for the consumer. The resulting shortages will lead to sellers of the good having to allocate the good among its potential customers in a number of ways including: first-come, first-served; random ballot; favoured customers; measures of merit; rules/regulations. Alternatively, the government could introduce a system of rationing. With maximum prices, underground markets are likely to arise. This is where goods are sold illegally above the maximum price.

BOX 3.1 A MINIMUM UNIT PRICE FOR ALCOHOL

A way of reducing alcohol consumption?

An economic justification for intervening in the market for alcohol is the wider costs its consumption can sometimes impose on society. For example, in 2018/19 there were almost 1.3 million alcohol-related hospital admissions in England.[1] In 2017, approximately 8600 people were either killed or injured in an accident where at least one driver was over the drink-drive limit. In the Crime Survey for England and Wales for the year ending March 2018,[2] 561 000 victims (39 per cent) of violent crime believed the perpetrator was under the influence of alcohol. Estimates of the total societal costs of alcohol consumption in the UK are in the range of £20 to £50 billion.[3]

Minimum unit pricing in the UK

One policy that has been extensively discussed to help address these issues is the use of minimum pricing. In early 2010, the UK House of Commons Health Select Committee[4] proposed the introduction of a particular form of minimum pricing. Known as a 'minimum unit price' (MUP), the price floor is set according to the alcoholic content of the drink rather than the volume of liquid. The alcoholic content of a drink is measured by the amount of pure alcohol it contains, with ten millilitres of pure alcohol counting as one unit.

In March 2012, the UK government announced its intention to introduce an MUP following a period of consultation with industry stakeholders. The Scottish government went further and passed legislation for the introduction of a 50p MUP in June 2012.

After the consultation period, the UK government announced that it was not going ahead with its proposed MUP policy. In July 2013, the then Home Secretary, Theresa May, stated:

> Consultation has been extremely useful. But it has not provided evidence that conclusively demonstrates that Minimum Unit Pricing will actually do what it is meant to do.[5]

It decided instead to introduce a minimum price at a much lower level. In May 2014, it became illegal for firms to sell alcoholic drinks at prices below the amount of duty and VAT levied on them. In 2018, this was £9.66 for a standard bottle of whisky and £2.60 for a standard bottle of wine.

In Scotland, the Scottish Whisky Association (SWA) challenged the 2012 Act in the European and Scottish Courts claiming it would penalise responsible drinkers and was in breach of EU law. After a lengthy six-year legal battle, the SWA lost its case and a 50p MUP came into force in May 2018. In March 2020, the devolved Welsh government also introduced a 50p MUP.

Effects of a 50p MUP on prices

How does a 50p MUP affect the price of alcoholic drinks? The standard way of displaying information to the public on the alcoholic content of a drink is *alcohol by volume* (ABV). This indicates the proportion of the liquid that is pure alcohol. For example, a 250ml glass of wine with a 12.5% ABV contains 31.25ml of pure alcohol or 3.125 units. The calculation for beer is more complicated as it is often sold in pints. A pint of beer (568.26ml) with a 5% ABV contains 28.413ml of pure alcohol or 2.84 units. In these cases, a 50p MUP means that the glass of wine cannot be sold for less than £1.56, while the pint of beer cannot be sold for less than £1.42. The table shows more examples across a range of drinks.

Effect of a 50p MUP on the price of various alcoholic drinks

Product	Volume	Strength (% ABV)	Units of alcohol	Minimum price
Cider	1 litre	5.0	5.0	£2.50
Whisky	70cl	40.0	28.00	£14.00
Alcopop	70ml	4.0	2.80	£1.40
Lager (4 pack)	440ml × 4	5.0	2.20	£4.40
Wine (white)	750ml	12.0	9.00	£4.50

Minimum unit pricing versus higher taxes

Evidence suggests that the great majority of the societal costs of consuming alcohol are caused by heavier drinkers. Therefore, an ideal policy would reduce the consumption of these heavier drinkers while having little impact on the consumption of moderate drinkers whose actions do not impose any costs on society.

Heavier drinkers tend to consume beverages, such as spirits and strong cider, that contain large amounts of alcohol at a relatively low per-unit price. Research[6] found that harmful drinkers with liver disease paid a median price of 33p per unit of alcohol, whereas moderate drinkers paid a median price of £1.10 per unit. Therefore, a 50p MUP would seem to be an effective way of targeting heavier drinkers. A number of economic simulations carried out by researchers at Sheffield University[7] before the introduction of the MUP in Scotland produced results that supported this view.

One potential disadvantage of a minimum unit price is the negative impact on price competition. This could lead to significant increases in company revenues. A major advantage of using higher taxes is that the revenue goes to the government instead of increasing the profits of the alcohol suppliers. Based on its research the Institute for Fiscal Studies (IFS)[8] forecast that the introduction of a 50p MUP across the whole of the UK would increase alcohol industry revenues by more than £175 million per year and decrease tax revenues by £390 million per year.

The current system of taxation in the UK is complex, with the same alcohol content in various drinks being taxed at different rates. For example, the tax/duty rate per unit of alcohol for cider with an ABV of 7.5% is just 5p whereas for beer with the same ABV it is 18p. An alternative policy, then, would be to increase the average rate of this tax per unit and apply this same rate across all drinks. This would be effective if every unit of alcohol consumed generated the same cost to society. However, as previously discussed, this is not the case.

The impact of the 50p MUP in Scotland

What has been the impact of the 50p MUP in Scotland? A study by the IFS analysed data on 32 480 households living in Scotland and England. The research found that between May 2016 and May 2018 (i.e. the period before the MUP was introduced in Scotland) the movement in both per-unit prices and quantities purchased was very similar in the two countries.

After the introduction of the MUP in Scotland, the average price per unit of alcohol (after controlling for differences in the types of beverages purchased) increased by 5 per cent compared to England. The average quantity of units purchased per adult per week fell by 11 per cent compared to England. The study also found that the policy was having a larger impact on heavier drinkers. In households that previously consumed 30 units per week, the average reduction was 12 per cent per adult, whereas in households that previously consumed 5 units, the reduction was 6 per cent.

Conclusions

As previously discussed, one major limitation with MUP is the loss of tax revenue. The IFS research suggests that by *combining* changes to the tax system (i.e. one single rate per unit of alcohol in beer/cider/wine and another higher rate for spirits) with an MUP, the policy remains well targeted but results in a smaller loss of tax revenue.

In March 2020, a minister announced that:

> There are no plans for the introduction of MUP in England. The Government will continue to monitor the progress of MUP in Scotland and will consider available evidence of its impact, including the report by NHS Scotland.[9]

The impact of an MUP or higher taxes will ultimately depend on how responsive alcohol consumption is to higher prices. In particular, how the price elasticity of demand varies between heavy and moderate drinkers.

1. ***Draw a diagram to illustrate the likely impact of setting a minimum price based on duty and VAT levels.***
2. ***Explain how price elasticity of demand determines the impact of a 50p MUP on the consumption of alcohol.***
3. ***In his 2017 Budget, the UK Chancellor introduced plans to introduce a minimum excise tax on cigarettes. Explain how this effectively imposes a price floor.***

Undertake desktop research to compare taxation on alcohol across different countries. In summarising your findings distinguish between different types of taxation and different rates of taxation.

1 *Statistics on Alcohol, England 2020*, NHS Digital (4 February 2020), https://digital.nhs.uk/data-and-information/publications/statistical/statistics-on-alcohol/2020

2 'The nature of violent crime in England and Wales: year ending March 2018', *Crime Survey of England and Wales*, ONS, (7 February 2019), www.ons.gov.uk/peoplepopulationandcommunity/crimeandjustice/articles/thenatureofviolentcrimeinenglandandwales/yearendingmarch2018

3 *The Public Health Burden of Alcohol and the Effectiveness and Cost-Effectiveness of Alcohol Control: Policies An evidence review*, Public Health England (2016), https://assets.publishing.service.gov.uk/government/uploads/system/uploads/attachment_data/file/733108/alcohol_public_health_burden_evidence_review_update_2018.pdf

4 *Alcohol: First Report of Session 2009-10*, House of Commons Health Committee (April 2010), https://publications.parliament.uk/pa/cm200910/cmselect/cmhealth/151/151i.pdf

5 *Next steps following the consultation on delivering the government's alcohol strategy*, p. 3, Home Office (July 2013), https://assets.publishing.service.gov.uk/government/uploads/system/uploads/attachment_data/file/223773/Alcohol_consultation_response_report_v3.pdf

6 N. Sheron, F. Chilcott, L. Matthews, B. Challoner and M. Thomas, 'Impact of minimum price per unit of alcohol on patients with liver disease in the UK', *Clinical Medicine*, vol. 14 (August 2014), https://www.ncbi.nlm.nih.gov/pmc/articles/PMC4952834/

7 'Minimum pricing for alcohol effectively targets high risk drinkers, with negligible effects on moderate drinkers with low incomes', *The University of Sheffield News* (February 2014), www.sheffield.ac.uk/news/nr/moderate-effects-on-high-risk-drinkers-1.347743

8 R. Griffith, M. O'Connell, K. Smith, 'Price floors and externality correction', *IFS Working Paper 20/37* (November 2020), https://ifs.org.uk/uploads/WP202037-Price-floors-and-externality-correction_2.pdf

9 *Written questions, answers and statements*, UK Parliament (24 February 2020), https://questions-statements.parliament.uk/written-questions/detail/2020-02-24/HL1749

BOX 3.2 THE IMPACT ON PRICES OF NATURAL DISASTERS/HEALTH CRISES

Price gouging and price controls

Natural disasters such as hurricanes, earthquakes and flooding can have a sudden and dramatic impact on the market for some goods.

Supply. The destruction of buildings/infrastructure can devastate existing stocks. For example, in 2005, Hurricane Katrina damaged drinking water and sewage treatment plants in New Orleans. Flooding caused by Hurricane Harvey in 2017 damaged oil and gas production refineries in Texas. Supply may also fall if it becomes logistically difficult, if not impossible, to transport goods into the disaster area. Even if transportation is possible, retail outlets/shops may be unable to open due to physical damage or staff being unable to travel to work.

Demand. The disaster/emergency may increase the demand for a particular good/service, such as power tools to clear fallen trees. If consumers become anxious or uncertain about the future availability of some essential goods, they may engage in stock-piling/panic buying – in other words, purchasing more than they require whenever the items are available in shops. For example, the week before Hurricane Irma in Florida, there were significant increases in demand for bottled water, oil and foods. If some goods become unavailable, then the demand for alternatives can also surge.

Public outrage can follow natural disasters if consumers observe some suppliers raising the prices of essential goods. For example, during Hurricane Irma, the authorities in Florida received over 14 000 complaints about excessive prices. Examples included cases of bottled water that normally cost around $5 being priced at over $30 and petrol that normally costs $2.65 a gallon being advertised for $3.30 a gallon.

Significant price rises during a crisis are often referred to as ***price gouging***. The practice invokes very negative responses from many consumers who consider the actions as unethical. A number of states in the USA have responded to this anger by introducing legislation that limits the ability of suppliers to increase the price of some essential goods during an emergency. If suppliers break these rules, they face large fines and possible prison sentences.

One issue for policy makers is that price gouging lacks a precise and widely agreed definition. The approach taken by a number of US states is shown in the table. Some try to quantify the size of a price rise for it to qualify as an example of price gouging, while others use less precise definitions such as 'exorbitant' or 'excessive'.

Definition

Price gouging Where sellers raise their prices by an amount considered to be excessive, to take advantage of a crisis such as a war, natural disaster or pandemic.

(a) Price gouging definitions and penalties in selected US states

State	What is considered to be price gouging	Products/ services where the law applies	Penalty
California	Price increase ≥ 10 per cent	All major necessities	Up to $10 000 and/or one year jail term
Georgia	Price increases that do not accurately reflect an increase in the cost to make or transport an item	Goods/services necessary to preserve, protect or sustain life	$2 000 – $15 000 per violation
Kansas	Price increase ≥ 25 per cent	Necessary property or service	Up to $10 000 per violation
Maine	Price increase ≥ 25 per cent	Necessities	Up to $10 000 per violation
Texas	Exorbitant or excessive price increase	Necessities	Up to $10 000 per violation

The impact of price controls

What impact do price controls have on a competitive market during a crisis? The diagram illustrates a competitive market for bottled water. The market is initially in equilibrium at point *a*. The market-clearing price and quantity are P_{e_1} and Q_{e_1}, respectively.

The impact of price controls after a crisis

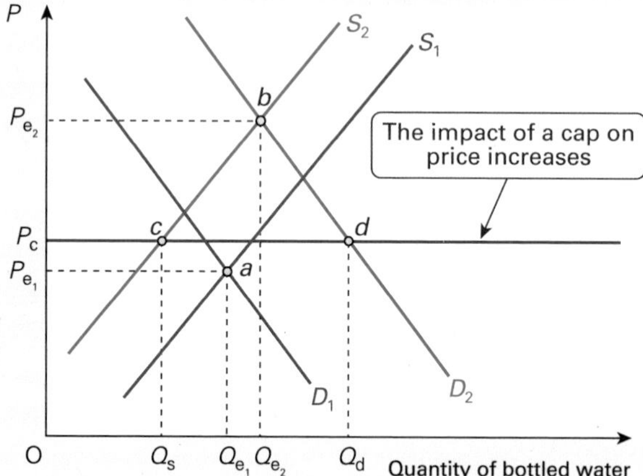

Following a hurricane, the demand for bottled water increases from D_1 to D_2, while supply falls from S_1 to S_2 as it becomes difficult to transport goods into the disaster area. In the absence of price regulation, the market equilibrium moves to point *b* with a new market-clearing price and quantity of P_{e_2} and Q_{e_2}.

If, instead, the authorities impose a price cap of P_c, the simple demand and supply model predicts a fall in the quantity of bottled water supplied from Q_{e_1} to Q_s, while the quantity demanded increases from Q_{e_1} to Q_d. The supply side of the market dominates, so the quantity of bottled water bought and sold falls to Q_s at point *c*. There is a shortage of $Q_d - Q_s$ $(d - c)$. The crisis causes an initial shortage of bottled water and the demand/supply model predicts that temporary price caps actually make the problem worse.

CASE STUDIES AND APPLICATIONS

This is certainly the view of some famous economists. A number of years ago, two influential economists, Gary Becker and Richard Posner, wrote a blog[1] that strongly opposed the use of temporary price controls in response to natural disasters. They suggested that people who are in favour of these caps demonstrate a *sheer ignorance of basic economics*. In May 2020, a panel of 43 expert economists were asked whether they agreed or not with the following statement.[2]

> Laws to prevent high prices for essential goods in short supply in a crisis would raise social welfare.

Only 10 agreed, while 11 disagreed, 14 were uncertain and 8 failed to provide an answer.

The impact of COVID-19 – a health crisis

To what extent did the COVID-19 pandemic follow the pattern of other emergencies? The health crisis did cause sudden and dramatic increases in demand for particular goods, such as hand sanitisers and face masks. There were also numerous examples of stock-piling and panic buying. This was most apparent in the UK in the run-up to the first national lockdown on 21 March 2020.

Research[3] shows that spending on staple foods, such as canned goods, pasta and rice, increased rapidly at the end of February 2020. On 14 March, expenditure peaked at just over 80 per cent above the average in January and February. Spending on non-food household supplies, such as soap, cold treatments and toilet tissue, followed a similar pattern. On 14 March, demand peaked at just over 70 per cent above the average in the previous two months. When comparing the four-week period ending 22 March in 2020 with the same period in 2019, the four products that experienced the biggest increases in demand were soap, soup, facial tissues and cold treatments.

Did suppliers respond to this sudden increase in demand by significantly raising their prices? On 20 March 2020, the competition authority in the UK – the Competition and Markets Authority (CMA) – launched its COVID-19 taskforce[4] to identify, monitor and respond to competition and consumer problems caused by the pandemic.

Between March and June, the taskforce received over 7000 complaints about excessive price increases. The most complained about product was meat, followed by hand sanitiser, toilet paper and rice. In early April 2020, the CMA asked complainants to specify the usual price for the product and the new higher price. The average increase across all goods was 160 per cent. The largest reported increase for a particular product was hand sanitiser, which had a median reported price rise of just under 400 per cent.[5]

In May 2020, the chief executive of the CMA argued that consumer and competition laws in the UK were not really designed for emergencies. The authority lobbied the government to introduce 'emergency time-limited legislation' that would give it more power to sanction price gouging.

In June 2020, the consumer group, *Which*, argued that the reaction of the UK government was too slow and trailing behind that of other countries.[6] In March 2020, the French government used emergency legislation to impose temporary limits on the price of face masks and alcohol-based hand sanitiser. Spain's Ministry of Health introduced similar measures in April – see table (b).

(b) Price caps in France and Spain

	Hand sanitiser (50ml)	Hand sanitiser (100ml)	Hand sanitiser (300ml)	Face masks
France	€2.00	€3.00	€5.00	€0.95
Spain	€1.05	€2.10	€4.50	€0.96

On 18 June 2020, the CMA announced that it was investigating four pharmacy and convenience stores which were suspected of charging excessive and unfair prices for hand sanitiser products during the COVID-19 pandemic. By 3 September 2020, all the cases had been closed as the CMA judged it to be unlikely that the prices infringed existing competition law in the UK.[7]

1. ***Using a demand and supply diagram, explain why the price of some essential goods, such as hand sanitiser and face masks, increased so dramatically in the early months of the pandemic. Illustrate the impact of the price controls introduced in countries such as France and Spain.***
2. ***Explain the reasoning that makes so many economists oppose the introduction of temporary price controls in response to a natural disaster or health crisis.***
3. ***Discuss some of the economic arguments for introducing temporary price controls in response to a health crisis such as the COVID-19 pandemic.***

Discuss with your fellow students what would constitute a 'fair' price increase at a time of shortage. If the price is not allowed to rise to its equilibrium level, consider what system of rationing should be used.

1 G. Becker and R. Posner, 'Should price gouging in the aftermath of catastrophes be punished?', *The Becker-Posner Blog* (23 October 2005), www.becker-posner-blog.com/2005/10/should-price-gouging-in-the-aftermath-of-catastrophes-be-punished—posner.html

2 'Prices of medical supplies', *IGM Forum* (26 May 2020), www.igmchicago.org/surveys/prices-of-medical-supplies-2/

3 A. de Paula, M. O'Connell and K. Smith, *Preparing for a pandemic: Spending dynamics and panic buying during the COVID-19 first wave*, Centre for Economic Policy Research, Discussion Paper 15371 (October 2020), https://cepr.org/active/publications/discussion_papers/dp.php?dpno=15371

4 *CMA launches COVID-19 taskforce*, CMA (20 March 2020), www.gov.uk/government/news/cma-launches-covid-19-taskforce

5 *Protecting consumers during the coronavirus (COVID-19) pandemic: update on the work of the CMA's Taskforce*, CMA (21 May 2020), www.gov.uk/government/publications/cma-coronavirus-taskforce-update-21-may-2020/protecting-consumers-during-the-coronavirus-covid-19-pandemic-update-on-the-work-of-the-cmas-taskforce

6 'UK lagging behind on laws to protect against price gouging', *Which* (June 2020), www.which.co.uk/news/2020/06/uk-lagging-behind-on-laws-to-protect-against-price-gouging/

7 *Statement regarding the CMA's decision to close an investigation into suspected charging of excessive and unfair prices for hand sanitiser products during the coronavirus (COVID-19) pandemic*, CMA (3 September 2020), https://assets.publishing.service.gov.uk/media/5f50df3f8fa8f535b650435c/3_September_2020_case_closure_statement.pdf

BOX 3.3 HOW CAN TICKET TOUTS MAKE SO MUCH MONEY?

Some pricing issues in the market for tickets

Some organisations set prices below market clearing levels. Take the example of the ticketing industry.

Tickets for live music, theatre, comedy and sporting events are sold by event organisers or authorised ticketing websites such as Ticketmaster®. This is the 'primary market' where the organiser or promoter sets the prices. There is evidence that ticket prices in the primary market are consistently below market clearing levels. For example, research by Media Insight Consulting found that, on average, fans were willing to pay £181 to see Adele in concert in the Spring 2016 tour, whereas the tickets cost £65.

Why do organisers/promoters often set ticket prices below the market clearing level? Two major reasons are:

- The sale of tickets typically takes place months/years in advance of the live event, making it difficult to predict levels of demand (i.e. how many people are willing to buy tickets at different prices). Consumers may even be uncertain about their own demand. For example, either positive or negative comments on social media about previous shows may influence consumers' willingness to pay as the date of the live event approaches. Given this uncertainty over levels of demand and the importance to the performers of a full venue, event organisers may choose to play it safe and price below rather than above the expected market clearing level.
- Bands/solo artists may be very conscious about making tickets available for a price that 'regular fans' can afford. Setting high prices could result in negative comments on social media that reduce the future popularity of the band.

One consequence of setting prices in the primary market below the market clearing level is that it enables people to make large amounts of money in the secondary market.

The 'secondary market' is where someone resells a ticket they previously purchased in the primary market. The event organiser has no control over prices in this sector. One type of seller in the secondary market is someone who, because of changes in their circumstances, is no longer able to attend the event. Such people are simply trying to get their money back. However, another type of seller purchases tickets deliberately to resell them at a mark-up in the secondary market. This type of seller is sometimes called a 'ticket tout' or 'scalper' and the potential returns are considerable. The worldwide value of the secondary ticketing market has been estimated at around $8 billion.

The scope for profit by ticket touts

Why can ticket touts sell for such large profits? The diagram helps to explain how it is possible. The supply curve is perfectly inelastic in the short run as the capacity of the venue holding the event (stadium, concert hall, theatre, etc.) is fixed at Q_c. The market-clearing price is P_e where the quantity of tickets demanded is equal to the quantity supplied. The price in the primary market is P_p. So there is a shortage of tickets: i.e. $Q_d > Q_c$.

Suppose that ticket touts are able to purchase half of the tickets on sale in the primary market (Q_t) using computer

How ticket touts make money

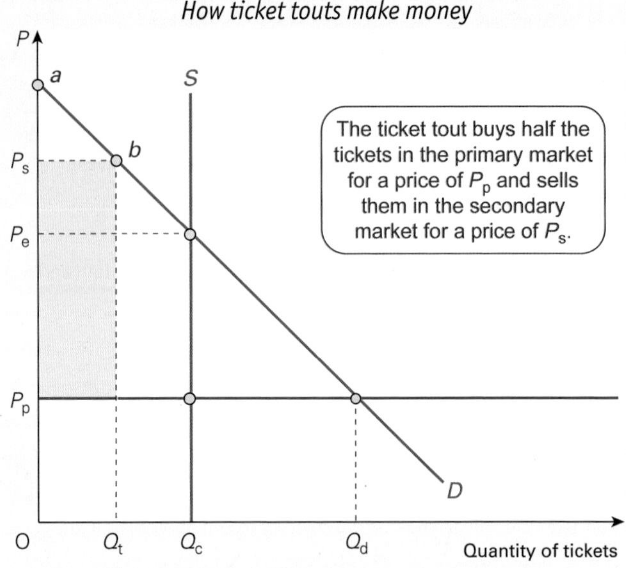

programs called bots. These automated pieces of software enable the user to make multiple transactions at the same time.

Assuming that none of the people with the highest willingness to pay (represented by points *a* to *b* on the demand curve) purchase the tickets in the primary market, the ticket touts will be able to resell all of their tickets for a price of P_s. The shaded area represents the potential profit.

The secondary ticketing market

For a number of years, media reports highlighted cases where tickets in the primary market would sell out in less than an hour. They would then start reappearing for prices far in excess of their face value on one of the four websites that once dominated the secondary ticket market: Viagogo (based in Switzerland), StubHub (owned by eBay), Seatwave and GetMeIn (both owned by Ticketmaster). For example, £140 tickets for the West End show *Harry Potter and the Cursed Child* have appeared on Viagogo for nearly £5000 while a £75 ticket to see Ed Sheeran was advertised for £7000. Ticket touts were suspected of purchasing large numbers using bots.

Attempts to regulate the secondary ticketing market in the UK

Consumer Rights Act In response to these concerns, the government introduced the Consumer Rights Act (CRA) in 2015. This came into force in May 2015 and placed the following requirements on people offering tickets for resale in the secondary market:

- The face value of the ticket, the seat location (i.e. its block, row and seat number) and any usage restrictions must be prominently displayed.

- Any relationship between the seller and the event organiser or official website must be clearly shown.
- Tickets purchased in the secondary market cannot be cancelled by the event organiser unless this condition has been made very clear in the original terms of sale.

The Waterson Review. The Act also stipulated that a review of the secondary ticketing market should take place within 12 months of the new legislation coming into force. In October 2015, the government commissioned the review and announced that its chair would be an economist, Professor Michael Waterson. Final recommendations were published in May 2016[1] and included the following:

- Secondary ticketing websites should make sure that sellers using their sites adhere to the conditions stipulated in the CRA 2015.
- The sale of tickets in the primary market should be made much more transparent. For example, event organisers should clearly indicate the proportion of tickets already sold before they go on general sale.
- More actions should be taken to make sure that consumers understand the difference between the primary and secondary market.

Professor Waterson opposed an outright ban of the secondary market as he thought it would (a) drive sellers into the illegal sector, so increasing the chances of fraud; (b) reduce consumer welfare, as evidence for the review indicated that prices were often below their face value. He also opposed a cap on resale prices as he argued that sellers respond to this type of regulation by finding innovative ways of circumventing the rules. He also questioned whether the cost of the resources required to enforce a price cap would exceed the benefits the regulation would provide.

The government stated in March 2017 that it fully accepted all of the report's recommendations and announced it would introduce a new Act of Parliament. The resulting Digital Economy Act 2017 included the following provisions:

- It criminalised the use of bots to purchase large amounts of tickets.
- It required resellers to provide ticket numbers that may help buyers identify the precise seat or standing area in the stadium.

CMA review. In June 2016, the Competition and Markets Authority (CMA) began a completely separate review of secondary ticketing websites. In November 2017, it began enforcement action against the four leading websites over the way sales information was presented.[3] Three of the four websites responded promptly and made the necessary changes. Viagogo only complied in September 2019 after the threat of legal action from the CMA.[4]

ASA ruling. In March 2018, the Advertising Standards Authority ruled that the four largest operators in the secondary ticketing market had also used misleading pricing information on their websites.

Changes in the primary and secondary market. Following all the negative publicity, Ticketmaster announced in August 2018 that it was closing down its secondary ticket websites – Seatwave and GetMeIn. Consumers can now resell tickets via Ticketmaster's website. However, the maximum price they can now charge is the original ticket price plus any booking fees. Some other websites, such as Twickets and TicketSwap, had already limited the resale price in a similar manner. In February 2020, Viagogo completed a $4 billion deal to purchase StubHub from eBay. However, in February 2021 the Competition and Markets Authority announced that Viagogo must sell all of StubHub's business outside North America – see Box 14.3 in Chapter 14 for more detail.

A number of organisers, bands and solo artists have recently gone to great lengths to reduce the activity of tickets touts. For example in July 2016, a number of prominent managers in the music industry financed a new initiative called FanFair. This body provides guidance for managers, artists and consumers on how to limit the mass reselling of tickets. One popular approach is to send a confirmation email when someone purchases the ticket. When attending the event, customers then have to take a copy of this email, the debit/credit card used to make the booking and photo ID in order to gain entry.

Ed Sheeran's management team took this a step further for his 18-date stadium tour in 2018. They managed to get Seatwave, GetMeIn and StubHub to agree not to sell any tickets on their websites, while any listed on Viagogo were invalidated. They also employed a team of people to go through all the transactions in the primary market and cancel any tickets purchased by known large-scale resellers. This did cause unhappiness among some fans who, when arriving at the event, found out that their ticket was invalid.

The secondary ticketing market is a controversial area and its workings continue to be scrutinised by both the media and the government.

1. ***Why might it be so important for bands/artists that all the tickets for a live event are sold?***
2. ***To what extent is it in the interests of society to allow people to resell tickets at a price far in excess of their face value? What is the impact on allocative efficiency?***

Identify two popular concerts/events and examine the system for selling tickets in the primary and secondary markets. Discuss the prices in these markets and whether the fans are being well served.

1 'Independent review of consumer protection measures concerning online secondary ticketing facilities', *Waterson Review*, May 2016.
2 'Secondary ticket platforms compliance review', CMA, July 2016.
3 'CMA to take enforcement action on secondary ticketing sites', *CMA press release*, November 2017.
4 'Viagogo fixes concerns in face of further CMA legal action', *CMA press release*, September 2019.

3.2 INDIRECT TAXES AND SUBSIDIES

The effect of imposing taxes on goods

We now turn to another example of government intervention – the imposition of taxes on goods. These ***indirect taxes***, as they are called, include taxes such as value added tax (VAT) and excise duties on cigarettes, petrol and alcoholic drinks.

TC 7 p79

These taxes can be a fixed amount per unit sold – a ***specific tax***. An example is the tax per litre of petrol. Alternatively, they can be a percentage of the price or value added at each stage of production – an ***ad valorem tax***. An example is VAT.

When a tax is levied on a good, this has the effect of shifting the supply curve upwards by the amount of the tax (see Figure 3.4). In the case of a specific tax, it will be a parallel shift since the amount of the tax is the same at all prices. In the case of an *ad valorem* tax, the curve will *swing* upwards. At a zero price there would be no tax and hence no shift in the supply curve. As price rises, so the gap between the original and new supply curves will widen, since a given *percentage* tax will be a larger *absolute* amount the higher the price.

But why does the supply curve shift upwards by the amount of the tax? This is illustrated in Figure 3.5. To be persuaded to produce the same quantity as before the imposition of the tax (i.e. Q_1), firms must now receive a price which allows them fully to recoup the tax they have to pay (i.e. P_1 + tax).

The effect of the tax is to raise price and reduce quantity. Price will not rise by the full amount of the tax, however, because the demand curve is downward sloping. In Figure 3.5, price rises only to P_2. Thus the burden or ***incidence*** of such taxes is distributed between consumers and producers. Consumers pay to the extent that price rises. Producers pay to the extent that this rise in price is not sufficient to cover the tax.

KI 5 p21

Definitions

Indirect tax A tax on the expenditure on goods. Indirect taxes include value added tax (VAT) and duties on tobacco, alcoholic drinks and petrol. These taxes are not paid directly by the consumer, but indirectly via the sellers of the good. Indirect taxes contrast with direct taxes (such as income tax) which are paid directly out of people's incomes.

Specific tax An indirect tax of a fixed sum per unit sold.

***Ad valorem* tax** An indirect tax of a certain percentage of the price of the good.

Incidence of tax The distribution of the burden of tax between sellers and buyers.

*LOOKING AT THE MATHS

Assume that a specific tax per unit of t is imposed on producers of a good. This is then added to the pre-tax price of P_1. The price paid by consumers is thus $P_1 + t$.

Assuming linear demand and supply equations (see page 46), these can be written as:

$$Q_D = a - b(P_1 + t) \quad (1)$$

$$Q_S = c + dP_1 \quad (2)$$

In equilibrium, $Q_D = Q_S$. Thus:

$$a - b(P_1 + t) = c + dP_1$$

We can rearrange this equation to give:

$$bP_1 + dP_1 = a - c - bt$$

Thus:

$$P_1 = \frac{a - c - bt}{b + d} \quad (3)$$

Take the following example. If the demand and supply equations were

$$Q_D = 120 - 10(P_1 + t) \quad (4)$$

and

$$Q_S = 10 + 5P_1 \quad (5)$$

and $t = 2$, then from equation (3):

$$P_1 = \frac{120 - 10 - (10 \times 2)}{10 + 5} = 6$$

and from equations (4) and (5):

$$Q_D = 120 - 80 = Q_S = 10 + 30 = 40$$

The market price will be

$$P_1 + t = 6 + 2 = 8$$

Assuming that the pre-tax equations were

$$Q_D = 120 - 10P$$

and

$$Q_S = 10 + 5P$$

what is (a) the consumer share of the tax and (b) the producer share?

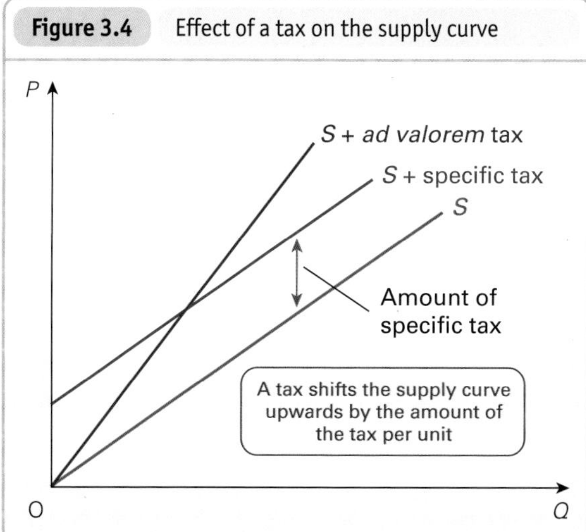

Figure 3.4 Effect of a tax on the supply curve

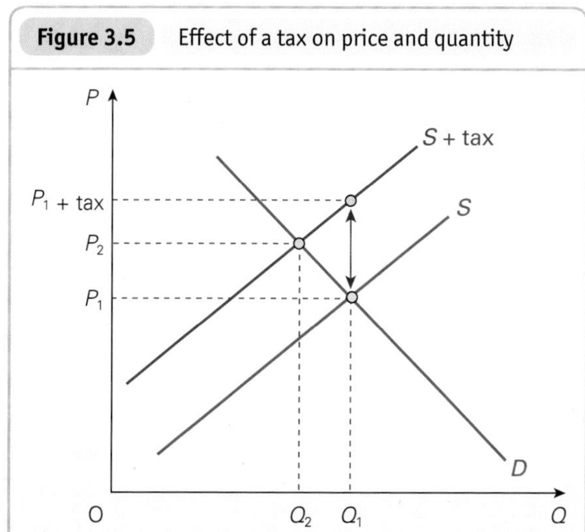

Figure 3.5 Effect of a tax on price and quantity

Elasticity and the incidence of taxation

TC 6 p66

The incidence of indirect taxes depends on the elasticity of demand and supply of the commodity in question.

Consider cases (1)–(4) in Figure 3.6. In each of the diagrams (which are all drawn to the same scale), the size of the tax is the same: the supply curve shifts upwards by the same amount. Price rises to P_2 in each case and quantity falls to Q_2; but, as you can see, the size of this increase in price and decrease in quantity differs in each case, depending on the price elasticity of demand and supply.

The total tax revenue is given by the amount of tax per unit (the vertical difference between the two supply curves) multiplied by the new amount sold (Q_2). This is shown as the total shaded area in each case in Figure 3.6.

The rise in price from P_1 to P_2 multiplied by the number of goods sold (Q_2) (the pink area) is the amount of the tax passed on to consumers and thus represents the ***consumers' share*** of the tax. The remainder (the green area) is the ***producers' share***. This is the amount by which the producers' net price ($P_2 - t$) is below the original price (P_1) multiplied by Q_2.

The following conclusions can be drawn:

- Quantity will fall less, and hence tax revenue for the government will be greater, the less elastic are demand and supply (cases (1) and (3)).

Definitions

Consumers' share of a tax on a good The proportion of the revenue from a tax on a good that arises from an increase in the price of the good.

Producers' share of a tax on a good The proportion of the revenue from a tax on a good that arises from a reduction in the price to the producer (after the payment of the tax).

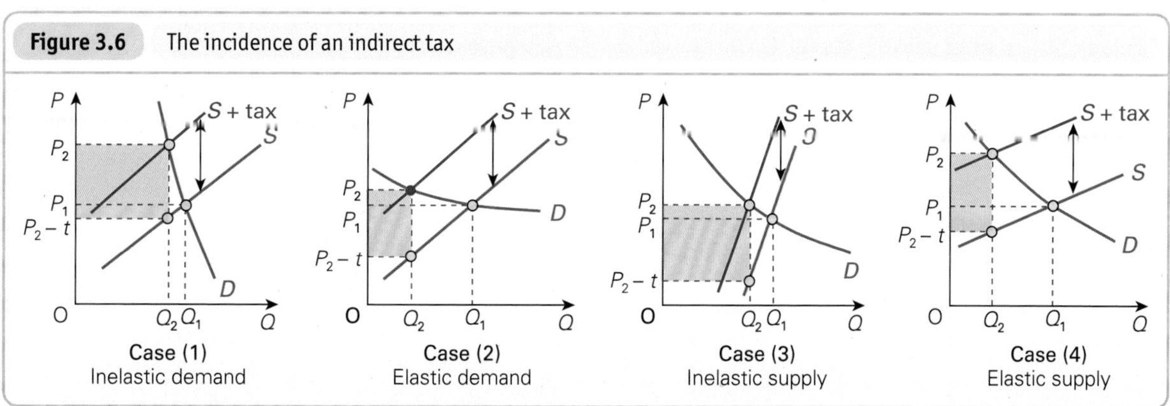

Figure 3.6 The incidence of an indirect tax

- Price will rise more, and hence the consumers' share of the tax will be larger, the less elastic is demand and the more elastic is supply (cases (1) and (4)).
- Price will rise less, and hence the producers' share will be larger, the more elastic is demand and the less elastic is supply (cases (2) and (3)).

Cigarettes, petrol and alcohol have been major targets for indirect taxes. Demand for each of them is high and fairly inelastic. Thus the tax will not curb demand greatly. They are good sources, therefore, of tax revenue to the government (see Box 3.4).

Supply tends to be more elastic in the long run than in the short run. Assume that a tax is imposed on a good that was previously untaxed. How will the incidence of this tax change as time passes? How will the incidence be affected if demand too becomes more elastic over time?

BOX 3.4 ASHES TO ASHES?

A moral dilemma of tobacco taxes

Revenue from tobacco taxes

In the UK, 6.9 million people aged 18 and over (14.1 per cent) smoked cigarettes in 2019.[1] How responsive are these smokers to changes in the price?

Many studies have tried to estimate the price elasticity of demand for cigarettes and found demand was relatively price inelastic at current prices. For example, Reed, Arnott and Langley (2013)[2] reported estimates of between −0.35 and −0.75. Therefore, taxing tobacco might be an effective means for the government to generate revenue. In 2019/20 tobacco duty in the UK raised approximately £8.8 billion. This figure excludes significant additional revenue raised through VAT. For example, over 60 per cent of the price of 20 cigarettes is tobacco duty but once VAT is included, this figure rises to over 80 per cent.

Clearly, tobacco duty is a major source of revenue for the government. The fewer people who respond to higher taxes by either quitting or smoking less, the greater the increase in revenue from any tax increase. If the government encouraged people to smoke, it would raise more money still! However, this creates an interesting dilemma, as a strong pressure exists on governments around the world to discourage people from smoking: the more successful they are, the lower will be their tax revenue.

The costs of smoking

What is the impact on the UK economy of fewer people smoking? Tax revenues would clearly fall, but there would also be less spending on smoking-related health care.

A study by the Department of Health[3] estimated that the total cost of smoking to the UK economy in 2015/16 was over £11 billion. This was broken down into three categories – cost to the NHS, cost to employers and wider cost to society.

The table below shows the total figures for each category. The cost to the NHS includes extra GP visits (£794 million), extra hospital admissions (£851 million) and extra outpatient visits (£696 million). The cost to employers includes an average of 2.7 extra days of absenteeism per worker (£1.7 billion) and lost output from smoking breaks (£3.6 billion). The wider costs to society include higher levels of unemployment/economic inactivity caused by smoking-related ill health (£1 billion) and loss of potential lifetime earnings (£3.1 billion).

■ Cost to the NHS	£2.5 billion
■ Cost to employers	£5.3 billion
■ Wider costs to society	£4.1 billion

Although some people have questioned the accuracy of these data, they do help to illustrate the wide range of potential costs.

There is also the human cost from suffering and deaths. Tobacco is still the single biggest cause of preventable deaths. Data from the Office of National Statistics for 2019/20 indicate that 74 600 deaths in the UK were attributable to smoking – 15 per cent of all deaths. In 2019/20, 506 100 admissions to hospitals in England were due to smoking.

However, the NHS may acquire some financial benefits from smokers. These stem from the fact that smokers die younger. The NHS gains from avoiding many of the high-cost treatments required by elderly patients, and the state gains from having to pay out less in pensions and other benefits.

The effects of raising tobacco taxes

So perhaps raising tobacco taxes would be doubly beneficial. Not only would it raise revenue, but it could also help people to quit smoking, thereby reducing the cost to the NHS, employers and society. The tax revenue could also be used to support other anti-smoking measures. Current UK policy includes a tobacco duty escalator – tobacco duty rises by 2 per cent above the rate of inflation each year. There are, however, three problems with this policy.

The first concerns smuggling and tobacco-related crime. Higher differentials between tax rates in the UK and abroad encourage criminality. HM Revenue and Customs (HMRC) estimates that 2.5 billion illegal cigarettes and 3500 tonnes of illegal hand rolling tobacco were consumed in the UK in 2018/19.[4] This meant that the government lost an estimated £1.9 billion in tax revenue. In the 2020 Spring Budget, the government announced new measures to support tobacco duty enforcement, including a £1 million grant for National Trading Standards anti-illicit tobacco projects.

Another issue concerns the disproportionate impact on poorer members of society. In 2019, 26.8 per cent of the unemployed were smokers compared to 14.5 per cent of people who had a job. The proportion of graduates that smoke (7.3 per cent) is approximately a quarter of the proportion of those with no qualifications (29.1 per cent). Among the employed, workers

The effect of subsidising products

A subsidy is a payment by the government to a producer or consumer and so is the opposite of a tax. For example, in 2018/19 the train operating company Northern received 29.5p from the government per passenger kilometre travelled. This provided a total subsidy of £763.3 million. Investment in renewable energy such as wind farms has also received considerable government support.

When a government pays a subsidy per unit of a product to the producer it has the effect of shifting the market supply curve downwards by the amount of the subsidy. Why is this? Take the example of a fixed subsidy per unit sold (a specific subsidy) illustrated in Figure 3.7.

The market is initially in equilibrium at point *a* where the quantity demanded equals the quantity supplied. Price and quantity are P_0 and Q_0, respectively. Now assume the government introduces a subsidy per unit of an amount $a - b$.

CASE STUDIES AND APPLICATIONS

in routine/manual occupations (e.g. labourers, bar staff, lorry drivers and receptionists) were 2.5 times more likely to smoke than people in managerial and professional occupations (e.g. lawyers, architects and teachers). In 2017/18, 1.2 per cent of the total household expenditure by the poorest 10 per cent of the population was on cigarettes. The figure for the richest 10 per cent was just 0.3 per cent.[5] Therefore, the higher the tax on tobacco, the more it redistributes incomes from the poor to the rich.

A third problem is that raising tobacco taxes may no longer be an effective way for the government to raise more money. Price elasticity of demand estimates for cigarettes from a recent study[6] are between −1.1 and −1.3 (i.e. price elastic). According to the author, raising tobacco taxes may even reduce tax revenue. In many ways, this is a success story – more people now respond to higher tax rates by quitting smoking. The problem for the government is the need to find alternative sources of revenue to help finance public services in the future.

The use of alternative policies

Other policies have been introduced to deter smoking. In 2006 and 2007, legislation came into force in the UK banning smoking in workplaces and public places such as shops, bars and restaurants. In October 2015, it also became illegal in England and Wales to smoke in a vehicle carrying children.

Other measures are targeted at the promotion and advertising of tobacco. For example, large shops selling cigarettes have to keep them hidden from public view. A law on the plain packaging of cigarettes came into full effect in May 2017. This includes the following restrictions:

- Picture and text health warnings must cover at least 65 per cent of the front and back of the packet.
- The only advertising allowed on the packet are the product name and brand variant in a standard font size and colour.
- Packets must be cuboid in shape and contain a minimum of 20 cigarettes.

All of these measures, including the increases in taxation, appear to have had some impact. The percentage of adults in Great Britain who are smokers has fallen consistently over the past 50 years, with figures of 45 per cent, 30 per cent, 20 per cent and 14.1 per cent for the years 1974, 1990, 2011 and 2019, respectively.

What are the possible alternatives as a replacement source of tax revenue? A number of countries are investigating the possibility of introducing new duties on e-cigarettes to make up for some of the shortfall. In 2019, almost 3 million adults in the UK (5.7 per cent) were e-cigarette users. This was slightly down on the previous year but triple the number in 2012.

1. *What has been the likely impact on businesses and individuals of the ban on smoking in public places?*
2. *Discuss the arguments for introducing a tax on e-cigarettes.*
3. *Many people think that if tobacco were to be discovered today it would be an illegal substance, as is the case with cannabis. What problems would a government face if it tried to ban smoking completely (see section 3.3)?*

Put yourself in the position of an advisor to a government Treasury minister. Prepare a briefing note in favour of maximising the revenue from cigarette taxation and how this might be achieved.

1 *Adult smoking habits in the UK: 2019*, ONS (7 July 2020), www.ons.gov.uk/peoplepopulationandcommunity/healthandsocialcare/healthandlifeexpectancies/bulletins/adultsmokinghabitsingreatbritain/2019
2 H. Reed, D. Arnott and T. Langley, 'The price elasticity of demand for cigarettes in the UK, 2001-2011', *European Journal of Public Health*, vol. 23 (October 2013), https://academic.oup.com/eurpub/article/23/suppl_1/ckt123.012/2837531
3 *Towards a smoke free generation: A tobacco control plan for England*, Department of Health, 2017), www.gov.uk/government/publications/towards-a-smoke-free-generation-tobacco-control-plan-for-england
4 *Sanctions to tackle tobacco duty evasion*, HM Revenue & Customs, (1 December 2020), https://www.gov.uk/government/consultations/sanctions-to-tackle-tobacco-duty-evasion
5 *Detailed household expenditure as a percentage of total expenditure by disposable income decile group, UK*, Table 3.2, ONS (2019)
6 D. Whitaker, *Sin tax analysis: Tobacco*, Deloitte LLP (August 2019), deloitte.com/content/dam/Deloitte/uk/Documents/tax/deloitte-uk-tax-2019-sin-tax-reports-tobacco.pdf

Figure 3.7 Effect of a subsidy on price and quantity

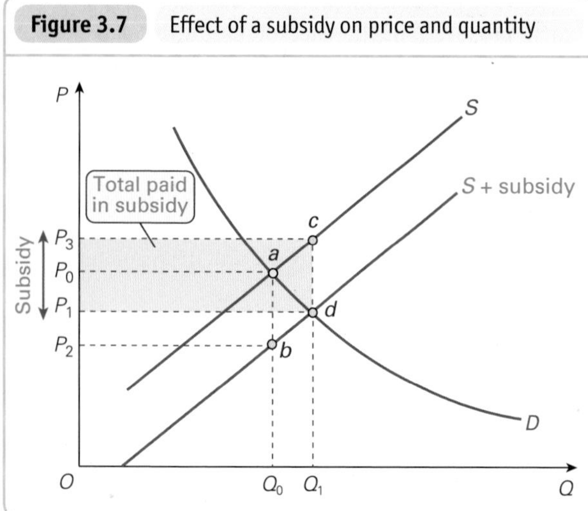

Firms are now willing to supply the same quantity (Q_0) for a lower market price (P_2) because the government is paying the difference ($P_0 - P_2$) via the subsidy. This willingness to supply at lower market prices is true for all quantities of output and so the whole market supply curve shifts downwards by the amount of the subsidy to S + subsidy. As the amount of the subsidy paid by the government is the same at all prices the shift is a parallel one.

The subsidy reduces the equilibrium price from P_0 to P_1 and increases the equilibrium quantity from Q_0 to Q_1. However, as you can see, the price does not fall by the full amount of the subsidy. As with the analysis of tax, the extent to which the subsidy is passed on to the consumer depends on the price elasticity of demand and supply. The consumer's share of the subsidy will be greater (i.e. the price fall will be greater), the less elastic the demand and the more elastic the supply.

Demonstrate with a supply and demand diagram the incidence of a subsidy when demand is price elastic and supply is price inelastic.

How much does the subsidy cost the taxpayer? This will depend on two things – the size of the per-unit subsidy and the quantity sold after it has been introduced. This is illustrated by the shaded area in Figure 3.7: i.e. the per-unit subsidy ($P_3 - P_1$) multiplied by the quantity produced (Q_1).

Section summary

1. If the government imposes a tax on a good, this will cause its price to rise to the consumers, but it will also cause the revenue to producers (after the tax has been paid) to fall.
2. The 'incidence of tax' will depend on the price elasticity of demand and supply of the good.
3. The consumers' burden will be higher and the producers' burden correspondingly lower, the less elastic the demand and the more elastic the supply of the good. The total tax revenue for the government will be higher the less elastic are both demand and supply.
4. A subsidy is a payment by the government to a producer or consumer. It will cause the equilibrium price to fall and quantity to increase.
5. The cost of a specific subsidy for the government will depend on the size of the per-unit payment and the equilibrium quantity after it has been introduced.

3.3 GOVERNMENT REJECTION OF MARKET ALLOCATION

TC 7 p79

Sometimes the government may consider that certain products or services are best not allocated through the market at all.

This section examines two extreme cases. The first is goods or services that are provided free at the point of delivery, such as treatment in National Health Service hospitals and education in state schools. The second is goods and services whose sale is banned, such as certain drugs, weapons and pornography.

Providing goods and services free at the point of delivery: the case of hospital treatment

KI 4 p13

When the government provides goods and services free to consumers, this often reflects the public's view that they have a *right* to such things. Most people believe that it would be wrong to charge parents for their children's schooling or for having treatment in a hospital, certainly emergency treatment. However, there are also economic reasons that lie behind the provision: for example, educating children brings a benefit to *all* society.

But what are the consequences of not charging for a service such as health? The analysis is similar to that of a maximum price, only here the maximum price is zero. Figure 3.8 illustrates the situation. It shows a demand and a supply curve for a specific type of treatment in a given hospital.

The demand curve is assumed to be downward sloping. If people had to pay, the amount of treatment demanded would fall as the price went up – partly because some people would feel that they could not afford it (the income effect), and partly because people would turn to alternative treatments, such as prescription drugs. The fewer the alternatives,

Figure 3.8 The demand for and supply of hospital treatment

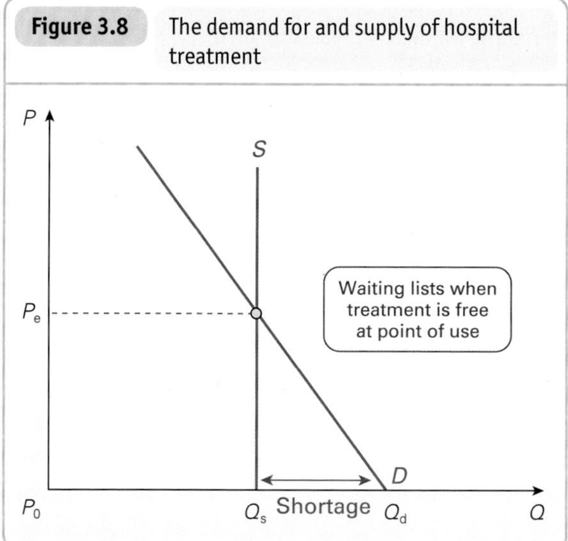

and the less close they are to hospital treatment, the less elastic would be the demand curve.

The supply curve is assumed to be totally inelastic, at least in the short run, given current space and equipment. In the longer run, the supply curve may be upward sloping, but only if any charges made could be used to employ extra staff and buy more equipment, and even build extra wards and theatres, rather than the money simply going to the government.

At a price of zero, there is a shortage of $Q_d - Q_s$. Only at the equilibrium price of P_e will demand equal supply.

The shortage will have to be dealt with and some form of rationing will be required. One way to ration health care is to have a waiting list system. Most hospitals in the UK have waiting lists for non-emergency treatments. The trouble with this 'solution', however, is that waiting lists will continue to lengthen unless the shortage is reduced. There is also the problem that some people on the waiting list may require urgent treatment; these cases will get faster treatment than non-urgent cases. A consequence is that people waiting for non-urgent treatments, such as hip replacements or the treatment of varicose veins, may have to wait a very long time. Public health care systems that do not make any charges for treatment are sometimes criticised for being unresponsive to the needs of patients.

Changes in demand and supply

One of the problems for the provision of health care is that the demand has grown more rapidly than people's incomes. Unless an increasing proportion of a nation's income is devoted to health care, shortages are likely to get worse. The demand curve in Figure 3.8 will shift to the right faster than the supply curve.

But why has demand grown so rapidly? There are two main reasons. The first has to do with demography. People in developed countries are living longer and the average age of the population is rising. But elderly people require a larger amount of medical treatment than younger people. The second has to do with advances in medical science and technology. More and more medical conditions are now treatable, so there is now a demand for such treatment where none existed before.

What is the solution? The answer for most people would be to increase supply, while keeping treatment free. Partly this can be done by increases in efficiency, and, indeed, various initiatives have been taken by government and health managers to try to reduce costs and increase the amount of treatment offered. Often, however, such measures are highly controversial; examples include reducing the length of time people are allowed to stay in hospital after an operation, or moving patients to hospitals, often at a distance, where operations can be done more cheaply.

The only other way of increasing supply is to allocate more funds to health care, and this means either increasing taxes or diverting resources from other forms of public expenditure, such as education or social security. But then, as we know, scarcity involves choices! Between 2000 and 2010, spending on the National Health Service in the UK increased from 4.9 per cent of GDP to 7.6 per cent.[2] It then gradually fell back to 7.25 per cent in 2015 and has remained fairly constant at this level. This has placed increasing pressure on the resources, given the ageing population and rapidly rising treatment costs. However, attention has increasingly been focused on improving outcomes and reducing administrative costs.

Schooling is free in state schools in most countries. If parents are given a choice of schools for their children, there will be a shortage of places at popular schools (the analysis will be the same as in Figure 3.8, with the number of places in a given school measured on the horizontal axis). What methods could be used for dealing with this shortage? What are their relative merits?

Prohibiting the sale of certain goods and services: the case of illegal drugs

It is illegal to sell certain goods and services, and yet many of these goods have flourishing markets. Billions of pounds change hands worldwide in the illegal drugs, arms and pornography trades. What, then, is the impact of making certain products illegal? How would the effect compare with other policies, such as taxing these products? TC 1 p10

Note that as economists we can examine the effects of such policies and hence help to inform public debate: we cannot, however, *as economists* make judgements as to whether such policies are *morally* right or wrong (see page 29 on the distinction between positive and normative statements).

2 *NHS spending as a percentage of GDP*, Nuffield Trust, www.nuffieldtrust.org.uk/chart/nhs-spending-as-a-percentage-of-gdp-1950-2020

Figure 3.9 The market for an illegal drug

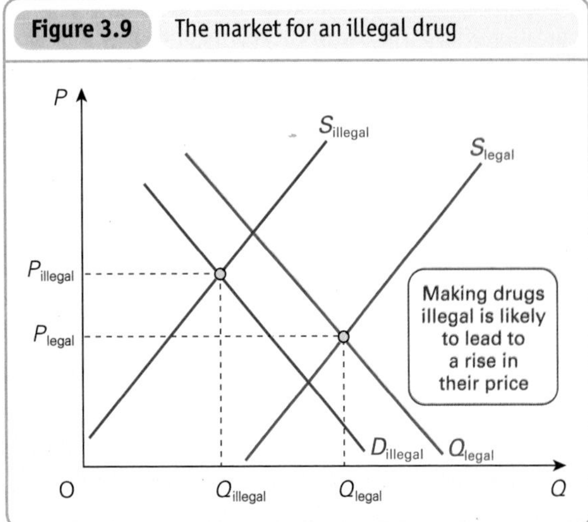

The market for illegal products

Figure 3.9 illustrates the market for a product such as a drug. If it were not illegal, the demand and supply curves would look something like D_{legal} and S_{legal}. The equilibrium price and quantity would be P_{legal} and Q_{legal}.

Now assume that the drug is made illegal. The effect will be to reduce supply and demand (i.e. shift both curves to the left), as both suppliers and users of the drug fear being caught and paying the penalty (fines or imprisonment). Also, some people will stop supplying or using the drug simply because it is illegal and irrespective of any penalty. The harsher the penalties for supplier or user, and the more likely they are to get caught, and also the more law-abiding people are, the bigger will be the leftward shift in the respective supply or demand curve.

In Figure 3.9, the supply curve shifts to $S_{illegal}$ and the demand curve shifts to $D_{illegal}$. The quantity sold will fall to $Q_{illegal}$ and the price will rise to $P_{illegal}$. It is assumed that there will be a bigger shift in the supply curve (and hence a rise in price) as the penalties for supplying drugs are usually higher than those for merely possessing them.

Under what circumstances would making a product illegal (a) cause a fall in its price; (b) cause the quantity sold to fall to zero?

A comparison of prohibition with taxing the product

Cocaine is illegal. Other drugs, such as tobacco and alcohol, are taxed. But the effect in both cases is to reduce consumption. So are there any differences in the results of using taxation and prohibition?

A *tax* on a product, like making a product illegal, will have the effect of shifting the supply curve upwards to the left (as we saw in Figure 3.5 on page 89). Unlike making the product illegal, however, a tax will not shift the demand curve. A bigger shift in the supply curve would therefore be needed than in Figure 3.9 for a tax to have the same effect as prohibition on the level of consumption. It would also result in a higher price for any given level of consumption.

So why not simply use taxes rather than making goods illegal? Those in favour of legalising various drugs argue that this would avoid the associated criminal activity that goes with illegal products (such as drugs gangs, violence and money laundering) and the resulting costs of law enforcement. It would also bring in tax revenue for the government.

The reason given by governments for keeping drugs illegal is that it sends out important messages to society and reflects what the majority wants. Taxing something, by contrast, implies that the product is acceptable. Also, if taxes were to be set high enough to reduce legal consumption to a politically acceptable level, there would then develop a large illegal market in the drugs as people sought to evade the tax.

What are the arguments for and against making the sale of alcoholic drinks illegal? To what extent can an economist help to resolve the issue?

Section summary

1. Sometimes the government will want to avoid allocation by the market for a particular good or service. Examples include things provided free at the point of use and products that are prohibited by the government.
2. If products are provided free to consumers, demand is likely to exceed supply. This is a particular problem in the case of health care, where demand is growing rapidly.
3. If products such as drugs are prohibited, an illegal market is likely to develop. Demand and supply would be less than in a free market. The price could be either higher or lower, depending on who faces the harshest penalties and the greatest likelihood of being caught – suppliers or users.
4. A similar reduction in consumption could be achieved by using taxation. Other effects, however, such as on the price, on allied crime and on public perceptions of the acceptability of the product, will be different.

3.4 AGRICULTURE AND AGRICULTURAL POLICY

TC 4 p45

If markets for agricultural products were free from government intervention, they would be about as close as one could get to perfect competition in the real world. There are thousands of farmers, each insignificantly small relative to the total market. As a result, farmers are price takers.

Yet despite this high degree of competition, there is more government intervention in agriculture throughout the world than in virtually any other industry. For example, nearly half of the EU budget is spent on agricultural support. Agricultural markets therefore pose something of a paradox. If they are so perfect, why is there so much government intervention?

Why intervene?

TC 7 p79

The following are the most commonly cited problems of a free market in agricultural products.

Agricultural prices are subject to considerable fluctuations. This has a number of effects:

- Fluctuating prices cause fluctuating farm incomes. In some years, farm incomes may be very low.
- In other years, the consumer will suffer by having to pay very high prices.
- Fluctuating prices make the prediction of future prices very difficult. This in turn makes rational economic decision making very difficult. How is a farmer to choose which of two or more crops to plant if their prices cannot be predicted? KI 10 p70

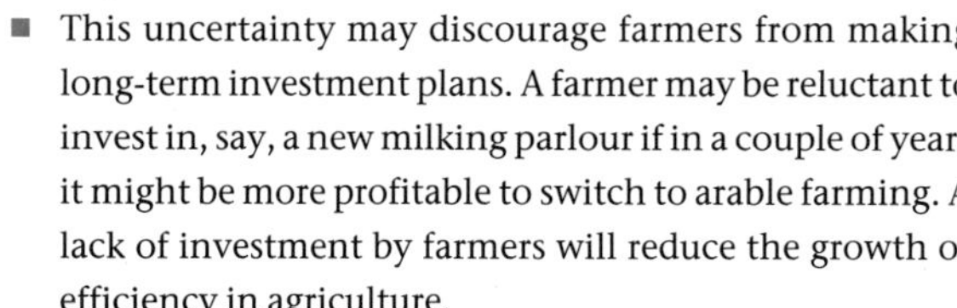

- This uncertainty may discourage farmers from making long-term investment plans. A farmer may be reluctant to invest in, say, a new milking parlour if in a couple of years it might be more profitable to switch to arable farming. A lack of investment by farmers will reduce the growth of efficiency in agriculture.

Low incomes for those in farming. Over the years, farm incomes have tended to decline relative to those in other sectors of the economy. What is more, farmers have very little market power. A particular complaint of farmers is that they have to buy their inputs (tractors, fertilisers, etc.) from non-competitive suppliers who charge high prices. Then they often have to sell their produce at very low prices to food processors, packers, distributors and supermarkets. Farmers thus feel squeezed from both directions.

Traditional rural ways of life may be destroyed. The pressure on farm incomes may cause unemployment and bankruptcies; smaller farms may be taken over by larger ones; village life may be threatened – with the break-up of communities and the closure of schools, shops and other amenities.

Competition from abroad. Farming may well be threatened by cheap food imports from abroad. This may drive farmers out of business.

Against all these arguments must be set the argument that intervention involves economic costs. These may be costs to the taxpayer in providing financial support to farmers, or costs to the consumer in higher prices of foodstuffs, or costs to the economy as a whole by keeping resources locked into agriculture that could have been more efficiently used elsewhere.

Then there is the question of recent trends in food prices. With the rise in demand for food from rapidly growing countries, such as China and India, and with the increased use of land for growing biofuels rather than food crops, world food prices have risen. Farming in many parts of the world is becoming more profitable.

Causes of short-term price fluctuations

Supply problems. A field is not like a machine. It cannot produce a precisely predictable amount of output according to the inputs fed in. The harvest is affected by a number of unpredictable factors such as the weather, pests and diseases. Fluctuating harvests mean that farmers' incomes will fluctuate.

Demand problems. Food, being a basic necessity of life, has no substitute. If the price of food in general goes up, people cannot switch to an alternative: they have either to pay the higher price or to consume less food. They might consume a bit less, but not much. The price elasticity for food in general, therefore, is very low, as Table 3.1 shows. KI 9 p64

It is not quite so low for individual foodstuffs because if the price of one goes up, people can always switch to an alternative. If beef goes up in price, people can buy pork or lamb instead. Nevertheless, certain foodstuffs still have a

Table 3.1 Price and income elasticities of demand in the UK for various foodstuffs

Foodstuff	Price elasticity of demand (average 2001–9)	Income elasticity of demand (1998–2000)
Milk	−0.70	−0.17
Cheese	−0.60	0.23
Poultry	−0.94	0.16
Lamb	−0.59	0.15
Pork	−0.77	0.13
Fish	−0.36	0.27
Eggs	−0.57	−0.01
Fresh vegetables	−1.00	0.22
Potatoes	−0.51	0.09
Fresh fruit	−0.99	0.30
Bananas	−0.62	0.12
Canned and dried fruit	−0.78	0.37
Fruit juice	−0.79	0.45
All foods	−0.07	0.20

Sources: Price elasticity data: based on and averaged from multiple tables by JS in Richard Tiffin, Kelvin Balcombe, Matthew Salois and Ariane Kehlbacher *Estimating Food and Drink Elasticities*, University of Reading (2011); Income elasticity data: *National Food Survey 2000*, National Statistics (2001), extracted by JS from Tables 6.3 and 6.5.

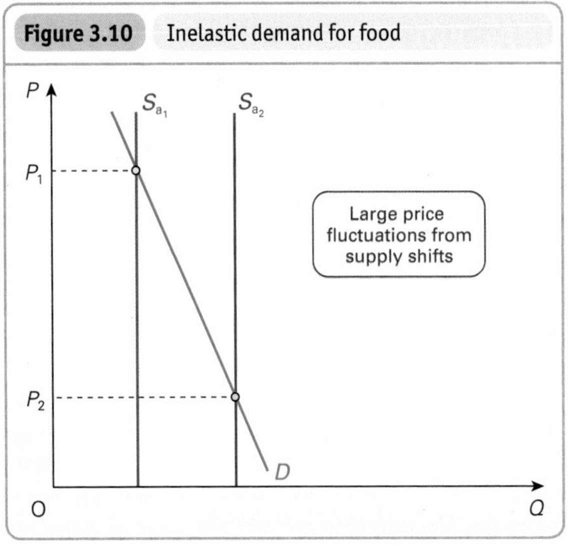

Figure 3.10 Inelastic demand for food

low price elasticity, especially if they are considered to be basic foods rather than luxuries, there are no close substitutes, or they account for a relatively small portion of consumers' income.

With an inelastic demand curve, any fluctuations in supply will cause large fluctuations in price. This is illustrated in Figure 3.10.

Why is the supply curve drawn as a vertical straight line in Figure 3.10?

Causes of declining farm incomes

Demand problems. There is a limit to the amount people wish to eat. As people get richer, they might buy better cuts of meat, or more convenience foods, but they will spend very little extra on basic foodstuffs. Their income elasticity of demand for basic foods is very low (see Table 3.1).

BOX 3.5 THE FALLACY OF COMPOSITION

EXPLORING ECONOMICS

Or when good is bad

Ask farmers whether they would like a good crop of potatoes this year, or whether they would rather their fields be ravaged by pests and disease, and the answer is obvious. After all, who would wish disaster upon themselves!

And yet what applies to an individual farmer does not apply to farmers as a whole. Disaster for all may turn out not to be disaster at all.

Why should this be? The answer has to do with price elasticity. The demand for food is highly price inelastic. A fall in supply, due to a poor harvest, will therefore cause a proportionately larger rise in price. Farmers' incomes will thus rise, not fall.

Look at diagram (a). Farmer Giles is a price taker. If he alone has a bad harvest, price will not change. He simply sells less (Q_2) and thus earns less. His revenue falls by the amount of the shaded area. But if all farmers have a bad harvest the picture is quite different, as shown in diagram (b). Supply falls from Q_1 to Q_2, and consequently price rises from P_1 to P_2. Revenue thus rises from areas (1 + 2) to areas (1 + 3).

(a) *Farmer Giles*

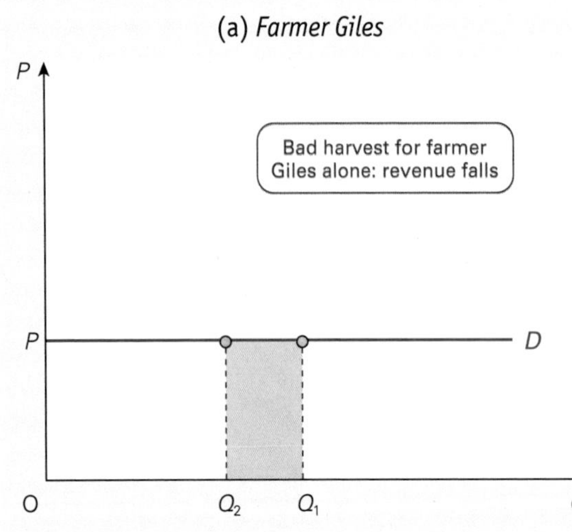

(b) *All farmers*

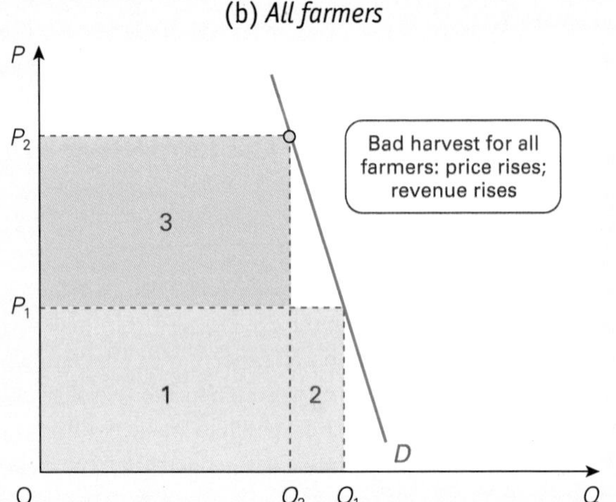

And so what applies to a single farmer in isolation (a fall in revenue) does not apply to farmers in general. This is known as the 'fallacy of composition'.

The fallacy of composition. **What applies in one case will not necessarily apply when repeated in all cases.**

1. *Can you think of any other (non-farming) examples of the fallacy of composition?*
2. *Would the above arguments apply in the case of foodstuffs that can be imported as well as being produced at home?*

Take two examples of the fallacy of composition and in each case describe why it is a problem. In your two examples, consider ways in which a government or other agency could tackle the problem. Why might difficulties be encountered in trying to find and implement a solution? This activity could be undertaken individually or in pairs. The findings could then be compared and discussed at group level.

Why don't farmers benefit from a high income elasticity of demand for convenience foods?

This very low income elasticity of demand has a crucial effect on farm incomes. It means that a rise in national income of 1 per cent leads to a rise in food consumption of considerably less than 1 per cent. As a result, total farm incomes will grow much more slowly than the incomes of other sectors, farmers' incomes will grow less rapidly than those of the owners of other businesses, and farm workers' wages will grow less rapidly than those of other workers.

Supply problems. Farming productivity has grown dramatically over the years as farmers have invested in new technology and improved farming methods. But, given the price-inelastic demand for food, increased supply will have the effect of driving down agricultural prices, thus largely offsetting any reduction in costs. And given the income-inelastic demand for food, the long-term rise in demand will be less than the long-term rise in supply.

Figure 3.11 shows a basic foodstuff like potatoes or other vegetables. Rising productivity leads to an increase in supply from S_1 to S_2. But given that demand is price inelastic and shifts only slightly to the right over time, from D_1 to D_2, price falls from P_1 to P_2.

As we saw above, this national effect of low price and income elasticities of demand and rising supply has been offset in recent years by growing *world* demand for food and problems with world supply, such as poor harvests, rising input costs (such as diesel and fertilisers) and the diversion of land to growing biofuels – in 2013, some 35 per cent of the US maize (corn) crop was being used for ethanol production. The effect of all this is a substantial increase in the prices of many foodstuffs, and in particular wheat, rice, maize and soya.

Figure 3.11 Decline in food prices over time

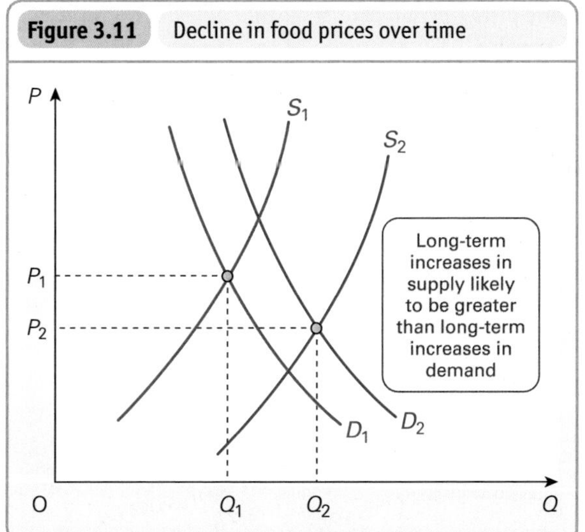

Government intervention

There are five main types of government intervention that can be used to ease the problems for farmers.

Buffer stocks

Buffer stocks involve the government buying food and placing it in store when harvests are good, and then releasing the food back on to the market when harvests are bad. They can thus only be used with food that can be stored: i.e. non-perishable foods, such as grain; or food that can be put into frozen storage, such as butter. The idea of buffer stocks is a very ancient one, as Case Study 3.4 on the student website demonstrates.

What the government does is to fix a price. Assume that this is P_g in Figure 3.12. At this price demand is Q_{d_1}. If there is a good harvest (S_{a_1}), the government buys up the surplus, $Q_{s_1} - Q_d$, and puts it into store. If there is a bad harvest (S_{a_2}), it releases $Q_d - Q_{s_2}$ from the store on to the market.

This system clearly stabilises price, at P_g. At this price, though, farm incomes will still fluctuate with the size of the harvest. It is possible, however, to have a buffer stock system that stabilises *incomes*. Such a system is examined in Case Study 3.5 on the student website.

To prevent stores mounting over time, the government price will have to be the one that balances demand and supply over the years. Surpluses in good years will have to match shortages in bad years. Buffer stocks, therefore, can only *stabilise* prices or incomes; they do not *increase* farm incomes over the long term.

Definition

Buffer stocks Stocks of a product used to stabilise its price. In years of abundance, the stocks are built up. In years of low supply, stocks are released on to the market.

Figure 3.12 Buffer stocks to stabilise prices

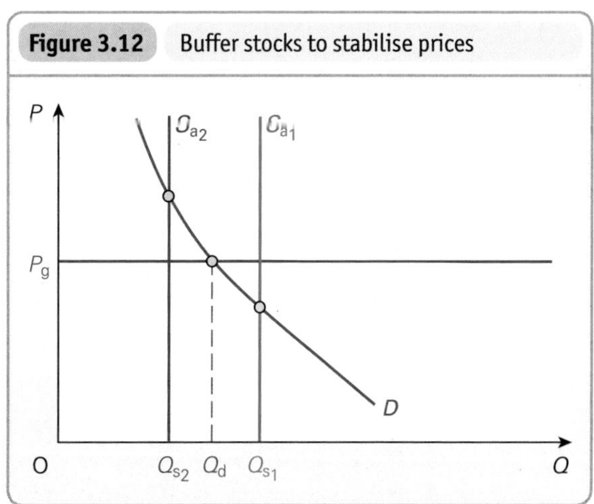

Subsidies

The government can pay subsidies or grant tax relief to farmers to compensate for low market prices. Subsidies can be used to increase farm incomes as well as to stabilise them. The simplest form of subsidy is one known as ***direct income support*** or ***direct aid***. Here farmers are paid a fixed sum of money irrespective of output. Given that such subsidies are unrelated to output, they do not provide an incentive to produce more.

An alternative system is to pay a subsidy *per unit of output,* which we examined in section 3.2. Figure 3.7 on page 92 illustrates the impact of a specific subsidy on an agricultural product in which the country is self-sufficient – farmers have an incentive to produce more, and the market price falls.

When some of the product is imported, the effect is slightly different. Let us assume, for simplicity, that a country is a price taker in world markets. It will face a horizontal world supply curve of the product at the world price. In other words, consumers can buy all they want at the world price. In Figure 3.13 the world price is P_w. Without a subsidy, domestic supply is Q_{s_1}. Domestic demand is Q_d. Imports are therefore the difference: $Q_d - Q_{s_1}$.

Assume now that the government wants farmers to receive a price of P_g. At that price, domestic supply increases to Q_{s_2}, but the price paid by the consumer does not fall. It remains at P_w. The subsidy paid per unit is $P_g - P_w$. The cost to the taxpayer is again shown by the shaded area.

A problem with subsidies of a fixed amount per unit is that the price the farmer receives will fluctuate along with the market price. An alternative, therefore, would be to let the size of the subsidy vary with the market price. The lower the price, the bigger the subsidy.

An advantage of subsidies is that they result in lower prices for the consumer. On the other hand, they have to be paid from tax revenues and therefore result in higher taxes.

Figure 3.13 Effect of subsidies on agricultural products which are partly imported

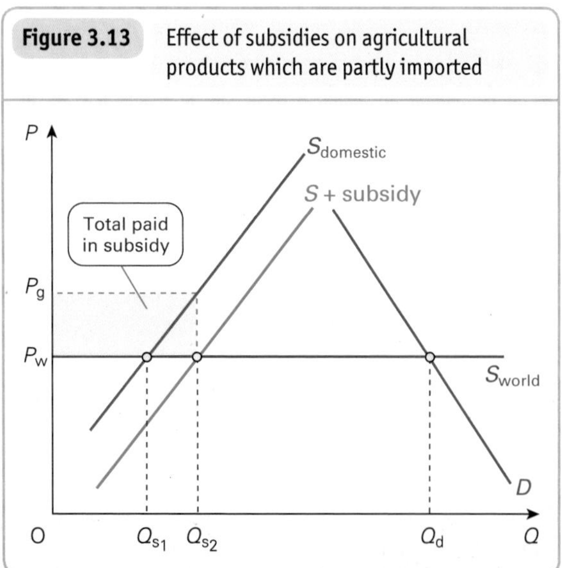

Figure 3.14 Minimum price where some of the product is imported

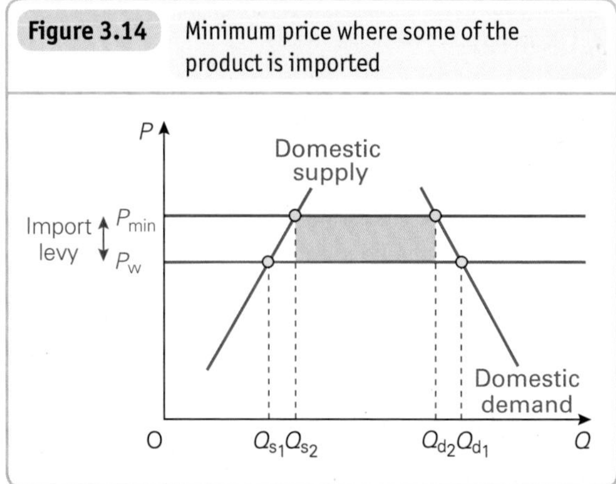

High minimum prices

If the government considers agricultural prices to be too low, it can set a minimum price for each product above the free-market level as we discussed in section 3.1. This was the traditional approach adopted in the EU under its Common Agricultural Policy (CAP) (see Case Study 3.8 on the student website). In recent years, however, forms of intervention under the CAP have become more diverse.

Once again, the effect of high minimum prices will vary between products, depending on whether the country is a net importer or self-sufficient. If the country is self-sufficient, Figure 3.3 on page 80 would illustrate its impact.

How would Figure 3.3 change if the government were able to sell the surplus food on the world market?

Agricultural products where the country is a net importer. Assuming that the minimum price is above the world price, the government will need to impose customs duties (known alternatively as ***tariffs or import levies***) on imported products to bring them up to the required price. Given that the world price will fluctuate, these import levies would need to be variable.

The effects of this system are illustrated in Figure 3.14. If trade took place freely at the world price P_w, Q_{d_1} would be demanded and Q_{s_1} supplied domestically. The difference ($Q_{d_1} - Q_{s_1}$) would be imported.

Definitions

Direct income support or direct aid A fixed grant to farmers that does not vary with current output. It may be based on acreage, number of livestock or past output.

Tariffs or import levies Taxes on imported products: i.e. customs duties.

If a minimum price P_{min} is now set and a levy imposed on imports to raise their price to P_{min}, domestic prices will also rise to this level. Demand will fall to Q_{d_2}. Domestic supply will rise to Q_{s_2}. Imports will fall to $Q_{d_2} - Q_{s_2}$. The amount paid in import levies is shown by the shaded area.

What would be the amount paid in Figure 3.14 if instead of the government buying the surpluses, export subsidies were given to farmers so as to guarantee them a price (plus subsidy) of P_{min}?

Reductions in supply

An alternative approach would be to find some way of reducing supply. This would lead to a higher market price and could avoid the cost to the taxpayer of buying surpluses or paying subsidies.

In open markets, however, a reduction in domestic supply could simply lead to an increase in imports, with the result that the price would not rise to the desired level. In such a case, a combination of a reduction in domestic supply and import levies (or other import restrictions) would be required.

But how could supply be reduced? The simplest way would be to give farmers a quota specifying how much each was allowed to produce. Milk quotas, which have been in force in the EU since 1984, are an example of this system.

Alternatively, farmers could be required to limit the amount of *land* they use for a particular product. The problem with this is that supply, and hence price, would still vary according to the yield. Another alternative would be to require farmers to withdraw a certain percentage of their land from agricultural use. This would shift supply curves for food to the left generally, but they would still be upward sloping because farmers could still switch from one product to another on their remaining land, according to which products gave the best price.

Compare the relative merits of (a) quotas on output, (b) limits to the amount of land used for a particular product and (c) farmers being required to take land out of food production.

The impact of the UK leaving the EU

The largest subsidy available to farmers under the CAP is the 'Basic Payment Scheme' (BPS).[3] This replaced previous schemes where grants were based on output levels. The main objective of the BPS is to provide farmers with basic income support, while giving them greater freedom over what to produce. The grant is based upon the amount of agricultural land managed and is approximately £233 per hectare.

This subsidy has been heavily criticised for disproportionately benefiting wealthy landowners, making it difficult for potential younger farmers to enter the sector, putting upward pressure on land prices, and incentivising the farming of relatively unproductive land that could have been developed into wildlife habitat.

The UKs decision to leave the EU gives it greater freedom to support the farming sector in different ways. In November 2020, the government announced a seven-year transition plan to replace the BPS with a series of different subsidies.[4] Starting in 2021, grants to farmers under the BPS will gradually be reduced, with the money released being used to fund a range of new schemes. The objective of these new schemes will be to incentivise (a) sustainable farming practices, (b) the creation of habitats for wildlife and (c) the planting of new woodland to help tackle climate change.

3 *Basic payments explained*, The European Commission, https://ec.europa.eu/info/food-farming-fisheries/key-policies/common-agricultural-policy/income-support/basic-payment_en

4 *Government unveils path to sustainable farming from 2021*, Department for Environment, Food & Rural Affairs (30 November 2020), www.gov.uk/government/news/government-unveils-path-to-sustainable-farming-from-2021

Section summary

1. Despite the fact that a free market in agricultural produce would be highly competitive, there is large-scale government intervention in agriculture throughout the world. The aims of intervention include preventing or reducing price fluctuations, encouraging greater national self-sufficiency, increasing farm incomes, encouraging farm investment, and protecting traditional rural ways of life and the rural environment generally.
2. Price fluctuations are the result of fluctuating supply combined with a price-inelastic demand. The supply fluctuations are due to fluctuations in the harvest.
3. The demand for food is generally income inelastic and thus grows only slowly over time. Supply, on the other hand, has generally grown rapidly as a result of new technology and new farm methods. This puts downward pressure on prices – a problem made worse for farmers by the price inelasticity of demand for food.
4. Government intervention can be in the form of buffer stocks, subsidies, price support, quotas and other ways of reducing supply, and structural policies.
5. Buffer stocks can be used to stabilise prices. They cannot be used to increase farm incomes over time.
6. Subsidies will increase farm incomes but will lower consumer prices to the world price level (or to the point where the market clears).
7. Minimum (high) prices will create surpluses, which must be bought by the government and possibly resold on international markets. In the case of partly imported foodstuffs, the high price is achieved by imposing variable import levies.
8. Supply can be reduced by the imposition of quotas on output or restricting the amount of land that can be used.

END OF CHAPTER QUESTIONS

1. Assume that the (weekly) market demand and supply of tomatoes are given by the following figures:

Price (£ per kilo)	4.00	3.50	3.00	2.50	2.00	1.50	1.00
Q_d (000 *kilos*)	30	35	40	45	50	55	60
Q_s (000 *kilos*)	80	68	62	55	50	45	38

   (a) What are the equilibrium price and quantity?

   (b) What will be the effect of the government fixing a *minimum* price of (i) £3 per kilo; (ii) £1.50 per kilo?

   (c) Suppose that the government paid tomato producers a subsidy of £1 per kilo.
      (i) Give the new supply schedule.
      (ii) What will be the new equilibrium price?
      (iii) How much will this cost the government?

   (d) Alternatively, suppose that the government guaranteed tomato producers a price of £2.50 per kilo.
      (i) How many tomatoes would it have to buy in order to ensure that all the tomatoes produced were sold?
      (ii) How much would this cost the government?

   (e) Alternatively, suppose it bought *all* the tomatoes produced at £2.50.
      (i) At what single price would it have to sell them in order to dispose of the lot?
      (ii) What would be the net cost of this action?

2. Think of two things that are provided free of charge. In each case, identify whether and in what form a shortage might occur. In what ways are/could these shortages be dealt with? Are they the best solution to the shortages?
3. Discuss the relative merits of the different methods used by the All England Lawn Tennis Club to allocate tickets for Wimbledon each year.
4. If the government increases the tax on a litre of petrol by 5p, what will determine the amount by which the price of petrol will go up as a result of this tax increase?
5. Illustrate on four separate diagrams (as in Figure 3.6) the effect of different elasticities of demand and supply on the incidence of a subsidy.
6. The UK government introduced The Soft Drinks Industry Levy in April 2018. Explain how this tax works and discuss its impact on both soft drinks companies and consumer behaviour.
7. Why are agricultural prices subject to greater fluctuations than those of manufactured products?
8. Compare the relative benefits of subsidies and high minimum prices to (a) the consumer; (b) the producer.

Online resources

Additional case studies on the student website

3.1 Rationing. A case study in the use of rationing as an alternative to the price mechanism. In particular, it looks at the use of rationing in the UK during the Second World War.

3.2 Underground (or shadow) markets How underground markets can develop when prices are fixed below the equilibrium.

3.3 Maximum price for payday loans. The reasons for and effects of maximum pricing in the payday loans market.

3.4 Rent control. The effect of government control of rents on the market for rental property

3.5 Seven years of plenty and seven years of famine. This looks at how buffer stocks were used by Joseph in biblical Egypt.

3.6 Buffer stocks to stabilise farm incomes. This theoretical case shows how the careful use of buffer stocks combined with changes in set prices can be used to stabilise farm incomes.

3.7 Agricultural subsidies. This considers who gains and who loses from the use of subsidies on the production of agricultural products.

3.8 The CAP and the environment. This case shows how the system of high intervention prices had damaging environmental effects. It also examines the more recent measures the EU has adopted to reverse the effects.

3.9 The Common Agricultural Policy of the EU. This case study looks at the various forms of intervention in agriculture that have been used in the EU. It looks at successes and problems and at various reforms that have been introduced.

Websites relevant to this chapter

Numbers and sections refer to websites listed in the Web Appendix and hotlinked from this book's website at **go.pearson.com/uk/sloman.**

- For news articles relevant to this chapter, see the *Economics News* section on the student website.

- For general news on markets and market intervention, see websites in section A, and particularly A1–9, 23–26, 35, 36. See also A38, 39, 42, 43 and 44 for links to newspapers worldwide; and A40 and 41 for links to economics news articles from newspapers worldwide.
- For information on taxes in the UK, see sites E25, 30 and 36.
- For information on agriculture and the Common Agricultural Policy, see sites E14 and G9.
- For sites favouring the free market, see C17 and E34.
- For student resources relevant to this chapter, see sites C1–10, 19, 28.
- For a range of classroom games and simulations of markets and market intervention, see sites C23, 24 and 27 (computer-based) and C20 (non-computer-based).

Part C

Microeconomic Theory

We now examine in more detail how economies function at a micro level. In doing so, we look at some of the big questions of our time. How do consumers choose between different goods? Why do some firms make such large profits? Why is there such a gap between the rich and the poor?

Chapters 4 and 5 examine demand and supply in more detail. Then in Chapters 6 to 9 we look at how the degree of competition a firm faces affects its prices and profits. Finally, in Chapter 10 we look at the distribution of income: why some people are rich while others are poor.

Background to Demand: the Rational Consumer

CHAPTER MAP

In this chapter we take a more detailed look at consumer demand. If we had unlimited income and time we would not have to be careful with our money. In the real world, however, given limited incomes and the problem of scarcity, we have to make choices about what to buy. You may have to choose between buying textbooks and going to a festival, between a new pair of jeans and a meal out, between saving for a car and having more money to spend on everyday items.

We start by assuming in this chapter that consumers behave 'rationally'. Remember in Chapter 1 we defined rational choices, those that involve weighing up the costs and benefits of our actions. As far as consumption is concerned, rational action involves considering the relative costs and benefits to us of the alternatives we could spend our money on. We do this in order to gain the maximum satisfaction possible from our limited incomes.

Of course, this does not mean that you look at every item on the supermarket shelf and weigh up the satisfaction you think you would get from it against the price on the label. Nevertheless, you have probably learned over time the sort of things you like and what they cost and can make out a 'rational' shopping list quite quickly.

There are two main approaches to analysing consumer behaviour: the marginal utility approach and the indifference approach. We examine both of them in this chapter.

We also look at the problem of making rational choices when benefits occur over a period of time, as is the case with durable goods, or later, as is the case with goods where there is a waiting list or where orders take some time to deliver.

As we start by examining the ***rational consumer***, it is important to understand what we mean by the term. Economists use it to refer to a person who attempts to get the best value for money from their purchases, given a limited income. Thus the rational consumer tries to ensure that the benefits of a purchase are worth the expense.

TC 1 p10

Sometimes we may act 'irrationally'. We may buy goods impetuously or out of habit. In general, however, economists believe it is reasonable to assume that people behave rationally.

Do you ever purchase things irrationally? If so, what are they and why is your behaviour irrational?

Two words of warning before we go on. First, don't confuse irrationality and ignorance. In this chapter we assume that consumers behave rationally (something we query in the next chapter), but that does not mean they have perfect information. Have you ever been disappointed after buying something? Perhaps it was not as good as you had expected from an advert? Or perhaps you found later that you could have bought an alternative more cheaply? Perhaps a holiday may not turn out to be as good as the website led you to believe. This is a problem of ignorance rather than irrationality.

Second, the term 'rational' does not imply any approval of the decision involved. It is simply referring to behaviour that is consistent with your own particular goals: behaviour directed at getting the most out of your limited income. People may disapprove of the things that others buy – their clothes, junk food, lottery tickets – but as economists we should not make judgements about people's goals. We can, however, look at the implications of people behaving rationally in pursuit of those goals. This is what we are doing when we examine rational consumer behaviour: we are looking at its implications for consumer demand.

KI 6 p29

4.1 MARGINAL UTILITY THEORY

Total and marginal utility

People buy goods and services because they get satisfaction from them. Economists call this satisfaction 'utility'.

An important distinction must be made between *total utility* and *marginal utility*.

Total utility (*TU*) is the total satisfaction a person gains from all those units of a commodity consumed within a given time period. If Lucy drinks 10 cups of tea a day, her daily total utility from tea is the satisfaction derived from those 10 cups.

Marginal utility (*MU*) is the additional satisfaction gained from consuming one *extra* unit within a given period of time. Thus we might refer to the marginal utility that Lucy gains from her third cup of tea of the day or her eleventh cup.

A difficulty arises with the utility approach to explaining demand: how do you measure utility? Utility is subjective. There is no way of knowing what another person's experiences are really like. How satisfying does Nick find his first cup of tea in the morning? How does his utility compare with Lucy's?

For the moment, we will assume that a person's utility *can be measured*. We use an imaginary measure called utils, where a ***util*** is one unit of satisfaction.

Diminishing marginal utility

Up to a point, the more of a commodity you consume, the greater will be your total utility. However, as you become more satisfied, each extra unit that you consume will probably give you less additional utility than previous units. In other words, your marginal utility falls, the more you consume. This is known as the ***principle of diminishing marginal utility***.

KEY IDEA 13

The principle of diminishing marginal utility. **The more of a product a person consumes, the less will be the additional utility gained from one more unit.**

For example, the second cup of tea in the morning gives you less additional satisfaction than the first cup. The third cup gives less satisfaction still.

At some level of consumption, your total utility will be at a maximum. No extra satisfaction can be gained by the consumption of further units within that period of time. Thus marginal utility will be zero. Your desire for tea may be fully satisfied at seven cups per day. An eighth cup will yield no extra utility. It may even give you displeasure (i.e. negative marginal utility).

Definitions

Rational consumer A person who weighs up the costs and benefits to them of each additional unit of a good purchased.

Total utility The total satisfaction a consumer gets from the consumption of all the units of a good consumed within a given time period.

Marginal utility The extra satisfaction gained from consuming one extra unit of a good within a given time period.

Util An imaginary unit of satisfaction from the consumption of a good.

Principle of diminishing marginal utility As more units of a good are consumed, additional units will provide less additional satisfaction than previous units.

Are there any goods or services where consumers do not experience diminishing marginal utility?

Total and marginal utility curves

If we could measure utility, we could construct a table showing how much total and marginal utility a person would gain at different levels of consumption of a particular commodity. This information could then be transferred to a graph. Table 4.1 and Figure 4.1 do just this. They show the imaginary utility that Ollie gets from consuming packets of crisps.

Referring first to the table, if Ollie consumes no crisps, he obviously gets no satisfaction from crisps: his total utility is zero. If he now consumes one packet a day, he gets 7 utils of satisfaction. (Sorry if this sounds silly, but we will tackle this question of measurement later.) His total utility is 7, and his marginal utility is also 7. They must be equal if only one unit is consumed.

Table 4.1 Ollie's utility from consuming crisps (daily)

Packets of crisps consumed	*TU* in utils	*MU* in utils
0	0	–
1	7	7
2	11	4
3	13	2
4	14	1
5	14	0
6	13	−1

If he now consumes a second packet, he gains an extra 4 utils (*MU*), giving him a total utility of 11 utils (i.e. 7 + 4). His marginal utility has fallen because, having already eaten one packet, he has less craving for a second. A third packet gives him less extra utility still: marginal utility has fallen to 2 utils, giving a total utility of 13 utils (i.e. 11 + 2).

By the time he has eaten five packets, he would rather not eat any more. A sixth actually reduces his utility (from 14 utils to 13): its marginal utility is negative.

The information in Table 4.1 is plotted in Figure 4.1. Notice the following points about the two curves:

- The *MU* curve slopes downwards. This is simply illustrating the principle of diminishing marginal utility.
- The *TU* curve starts at the origin. Zero consumption yields zero utility.
- The *TU* curve reaches a peak when marginal utility is zero. When marginal utility is zero (at five packets of crisps), there is no addition to total utility. Total utility must be at the maximum – the peak of the curve.
- Marginal utility can be derived from the *TU* curve. It is the slope of the line joining two adjacent quantities on the curve. For example, the marginal utility of the third packet of crisps is the slope of the line joining points *a* and *b*. The slope of such a line is given by the formula

$$\frac{\Delta TU}{\Delta Q}(= MU)$$

In our example $\Delta TU = 2$ (total utility has risen from 11 to 13 utils), and $\Delta Q = 1$ (one more packet of crisps has been consumed). Thus $MU = 2$.

Figure 4.1 Ollie's utility from consuming crisps (daily)

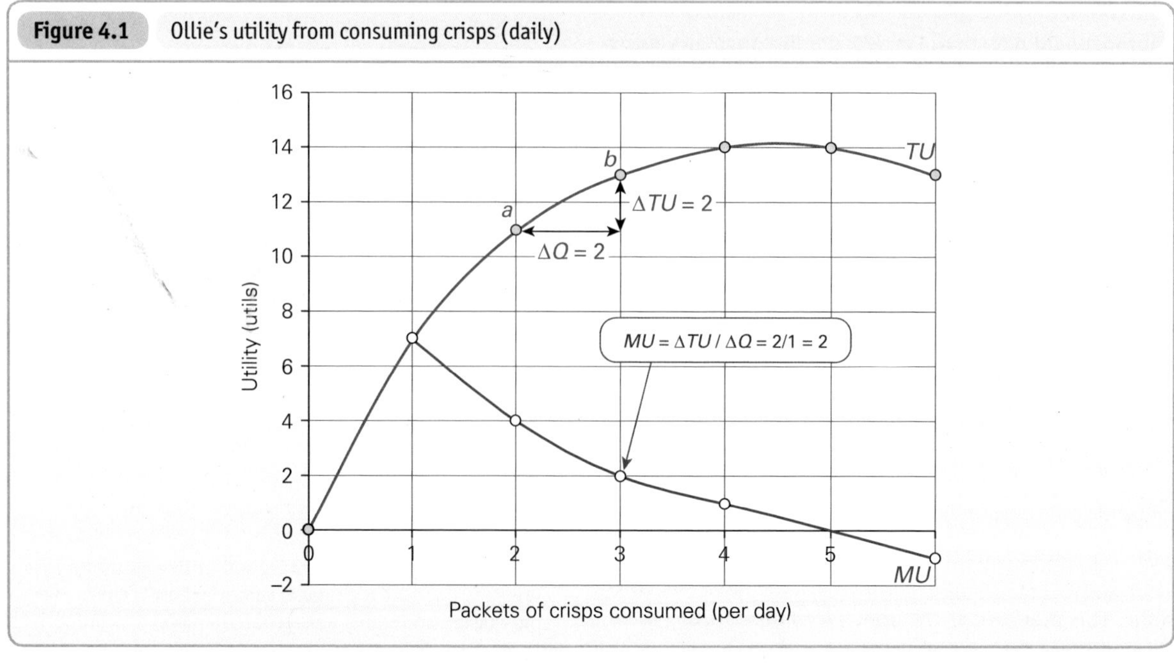

*BOX 4.1 USING CALCULUS TO DERIVE A MARGINAL UTILITY FUNCTION

EXPLORING ECONOMICS

The relationship between total utility and marginal utility can be shown using calculus. If you are not familiar with the rules of calculus, ignore this box (or see Appendix 1, pages A:9–13).

A consumer's typical utility function for a good might be of the form

$$TU = 600Q - 4Q^2$$

where Q is the quantity of the good consumed. This would give the figures shown in the following table.

Q	60Q	$-4Q^2$	=	TU
1	60	−4	=	56
2	120	−16	=	104
3	180	−36	=	144
4	240	−64	=	176

1. Complete this table to the level of consumption at which TU is at a maximum.

Marginal utility is the first derivative of total utility. In other words, it is the rate of change of total utility. Differentiating the *TU* function gives

$$MU = \frac{dTU}{dQ} = 600 - 8Q$$

This gives the figures shown in the following table.

Q	60Q	− 8Q	=	MU
1	60	−8	=	52
2	60	−16	=	44
3	60	−24	=	36
4	60	−32	=	28

Note that the marginal utility diminishes.

The *MU* function we have derived is a straight-line function. If, however, the *TU* function contained a cubed term (Q^3), the *MU* function would be a curve.

2. Derive the MU function from the following TU function:

$$TU = 200Q - 25Q^2 + Q^3$$

From this MU function, draw a table (like the one above) up to the level of Q where MU becomes negative. Graph these figures.

If Ollie were to consume more and more crisps, would his total utility ever (a) fall to zero; (b) become negative? Explain.

The ceteris paribus assumption

The table and graph we have drawn are based on the assumption that other things do not change.

In practice, other things *do* change – and frequently. The utility that Ollie gets from crisps depends on what else he eats. If on Saturday he has a lot to eat he will get little satisfaction from crisps. If on Monday, however, he is too busy to eat proper meals, he would probably welcome one or more packets of crisps.

Each time the consumption of *other* goods changed – whether substitutes or complements – a new utility schedule would have to be drawn up. The curves would shift. Remember, utility is not a property of the goods themselves. Utility is in the mind of the consumer, and consumers change their minds. Their tastes change; their circumstances change; their consumption patterns change.

The optimum level of consumption: the simplest case – one commodity

Just how much of a good should people consume if they are to make the best use of their limited income? To answer this question we must tackle the problem of how to measure utility, given that in practice we cannot measure 'utils'.

One solution to the problem is to measure utility with money. In this case, utility becomes the value that people place on their consumption. Marginal utility thus becomes the amount of money a person would be prepared to pay to obtain one more unit: in other words, what that extra unit is worth to that person. If Ollie is prepared to pay 60p to obtain an extra packet of crisps, then we can say that packet yields him 60p worth of utility: $MU = 60p$.

So how many packets should he consume if he is to act rationally? To answer this we need to introduce the concept of ***consumer surplus***.

Marginal consumer surplus

Marginal consumer surplus (*MCS*) is the difference between what you are willing to pay for one more unit of a good and what you are actually charged. If Ollie were willing to pay 45p for another packet of crisps which in fact only cost him 40p, he would be getting a marginal consumer surplus of 5p.

$$MCS = MU - P$$

Definitions

Consumer surplus The excess of what a person would have been prepared to pay for a good (i.e. the utility) over what that person actually pays.

Marginal consumer surplus The excess of utility from the consumption of one more unit of a good (*MU*) over the price paid: $MCS = MU - P$.

Total consumer surplus

Total consumer surplus (*TCS*) is the sum of all the marginal consumer surpluses that you have obtained from all the units of a good you have consumed. It is the difference between the total utility from all the units and your expenditure on them. If Ollie consumes four packets of crisps, and if he would have been prepared to spend £2.60 on them and only had to spend £2.20, then his total consumer surplus is 40p.

$$TCS = TU - TE$$

where *TE* is the total expenditure on a good: i.e. $P \times Q$.

Let us define ***rational consumer behaviour*** as the attempt to maximise consumer surplus. How do people set about doing this?

People will go on purchasing additional units as long as they gain additional consumer surplus: in other words, as long as the price they are prepared to pay exceeds the price they are charged ($MU > P$). But as more is purchased, so they will experience diminishing marginal utility. They will be prepared to pay less for each additional unit.

Their marginal utility will go on falling until $MU = P$: i.e. until no further consumer surplus can be gained. At that point, they will stop purchasing additional units. Their optimum level of consumption has been reached: consumer surplus has been maximised. If they continue to purchase beyond this point, *MU* would be less than *P*, and thus they would be paying more for the last units than they were worth to them.

The process of maximising consumer surplus can be shown graphically. Let us take the case of Tanya's annual purchases of petrol. Tanya has her own car, but as an alternative she can use public transport or walk. To keep the analysis simple, let us assume that Tanya's parents bought her the car and pay the licence duty, and that Tanya does not have the option of selling the car. She does, however, have to buy the petrol. The current price is £1.30 per litre. Figure 4.2 shows her consumer surplus.

If she were to use just a few litres per year, she would use them for very important journeys for which no convenient alternative exists. For such trips she may be prepared to pay up to £1.60 per litre. For the first few litres, then, she is getting a marginal utility of around £1.60 per litre, and hence a marginal consumer surplus of around 30p (i.e. £1.60 – £1.30).

By the time her annual purchase is around 200 litres, she would be prepared to pay only around £1.50 for additional litres. The additional journeys, although still important, would be less vital. Perhaps these are journeys where she could have taken public transport, albeit at some inconvenience. Her marginal consumer surplus at 200 litres is 20p (i.e. £1.50 – £1.30).

Gradually, additional litres give less and less additional utility as less important journeys are undertaken. The 500th litre yields £1.40 worth of extra utility. Marginal consumer surplus is now 10p (i.e. £1.40 – £1.30). KI 13 p105

By the time she gets to the 900th litre, Tanya's marginal utility has fallen to £1.30. There is no additional consumer surplus to be gained. Her total consumer surplus is at a maximum. She thus buys 900 litres, where $P = MU$.

Figure 4.2 Tanya's consumer surplus from petrol

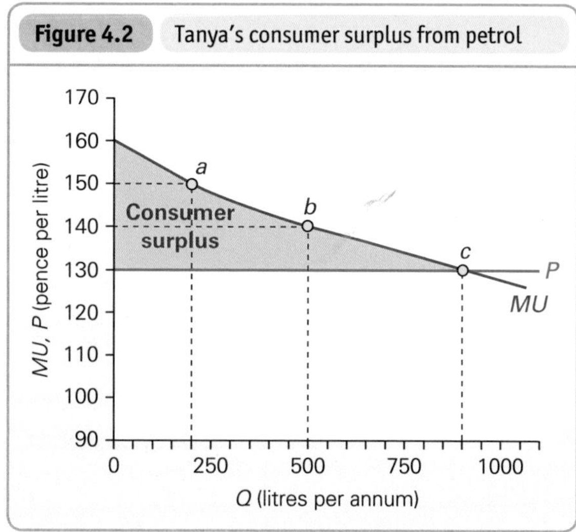

Her total consumer surplus is the sum of all the marginal consumer surpluses: the sum of all the 900 vertical lines between the price and the *MU* curve. This is shown by the total *area* between *P* and *MU* up to 900 litres (i.e. the pink shaded area in Figure 4.2).

This analysis can be expressed in general terms. In Figure 4.3, if the price of a commodity is P_1, the consumer will consume Q_1. The person's total expenditure (*TE*) is P_1Q_1,

Figure 4.3 Consumer surplus

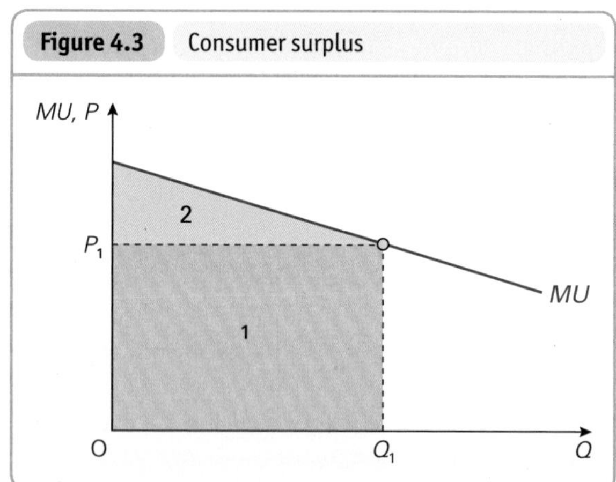

Definitions

Total consumer surplus The excess of a person's total utility from the consumption of a good (*TU*) over the total amount that person spends on it (*TE*):

$$TCS = TU - TE.$$

Rational consumer behaviour The attempt to maximise total consumer surplus.

THRESHOLD CONCEPT 8

RATIONAL DECISION MAKING INVOLVES CHOICES AT THE MARGIN

THINKING LIKE AN ECONOMIST

Rational decision making involves weighing up the marginal benefit and marginal cost of any activity. If the marginal benefit exceeds the marginal cost, it is rational to do the activity (or to do more of it). If the marginal cost exceeds the marginal benefit, it is rational not to do it (or to do less of it).

Let's take the case of when you go to the supermarket to do shopping for the week. Assume that you have £50 to spend. Clearly, you will want to spend it wisely. With each item you consider buying, you should ask yourself what its marginal benefit is to you: in other words, how much you would be prepared to spend on it. This will depend on the prices and benefits of alternatives. Thus if you were considering spending £3 from the £50 on wholemeal bread, you should ask yourself whether the £3 would be better spent on some alternative, such as white bread, rolls or crackers. The *best* alternative (which might be a combination of products) is the marginal opportunity cost. If the answer is that you feel you are getting better value for money by spending it on the wholemeal bread, then you are saying that the marginal benefit exceeds the marginal opportunity cost. It is an efficient use of your money to buy the wholemeal bread and forgo the alternatives.

Most decisions are more complex than this, as they involve buying a whole range of products. In fact, that is what you are doing in the supermarket. But the principle is still the same. In each case, a rational decision involves weighing up marginal benefits and marginal costs.

This is another example of a *threshold concept* because it is a way of thinking about economic problems. It is a general principle that can be applied in a whole host of contexts: whether it is individuals deciding what to buy, how much to work, what job to apply for, or whether to study for a degree or take a job; or firms deciding how much to produce, whether to invest in new capacity or new products, or what type of people to employ and how many; or governments deciding how much to spend on various projects, such as roads, hospitals and schools, or what rates of tax to impose on companies that pollute the environment.

In each case, better decisions will be made by weighing up marginal costs and marginal benefits.

1. *Assume that a firm is selling 1000 units of a product at £20 each and that each unit on average costs £15 to produce. Assume also that to produce additional units will cost the firm £19 each and that the price will remain at £20. To produce additional products will therefore reduce the average profit per unit. Should the firm expand production? Explain.*
2. *Assume that a ferry has capacity for 500 passengers. Its operator predicts that it will typically have only 200 passengers on each of its midweek sailings over the winter. Assume also that each sailing costs the company £10 000. This means that midweek winter sailings cost the company an average of £10 000/200 = £50 per passenger. Currently tickets cost £60.*

   Should the company consider selling stand-by tickets during the winter for (a) less than £60; (b) less than £50? (Clue: think about the marginal cost of taking additional passengers.)

shown by area 1. Total utility (*TU*) is the area under the marginal utility curve: i.e. areas 1 + 2. Total consumer surplus ((*TU* – *TE*)) is shown by area 2.

If a good were free, why would total consumer surplus equal total utility? What would be the level of marginal utility at the equilibrium level of consumption?

Marginal utility and the demand curve for a good

An individual's demand curve

Individual people's demand curve for any good will be the same as their marginal utility curve for that good, where utility is measured in money.

This is demonstrated in Figure 4.4, which shows the marginal utility curve for a particular person and a particular good. If the price of the good were P_1, the person would consume Q_1, where $MU = P_1$. Thus point *a* would be one point on that person's demand curve. If the price fell to P_2, consumption would rise to Q_2, since this is where $MU = P_2$. Thus point *b* is a second point on the demand curve. Likewise if price fell to P_3, Q_3 would be consumed. Point *c* is a third point on the demand curve.

Figure 4.4 An individual person's demand curve

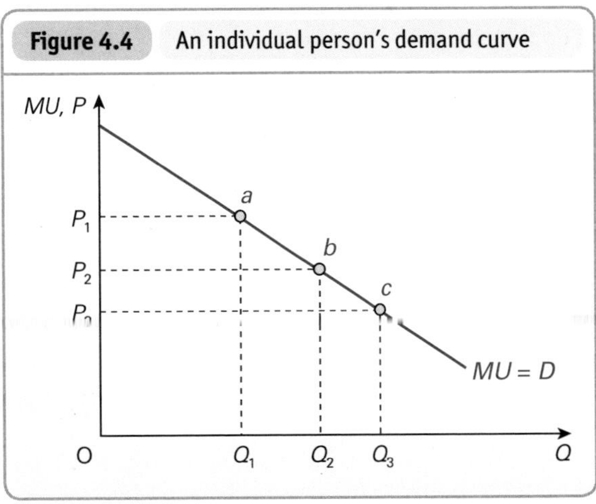

Thus as long as individuals seek to maximise consumer surplus and hence consume where $P = MU$, their demand curve will be along the same line as their marginal utility curve.

The market demand curve

The market demand curve will simply be the (horizontal) sum of all individuals' demand curves and hence *MU* curves.

The shape of the demand curve. The price elasticity of demand will reflect the rate at which *MU* diminishes. If there are close substitutes for a good, it is likely to have an elastic demand, and its *MU* will diminish slowly as consumption increases. The reason is that increased consumption of this product will be accompanied by decreased consumption of the alternative product(s). Since total consumption of this product plus the alternatives has increased only slightly (if at all), the marginal utility will fall only slowly.

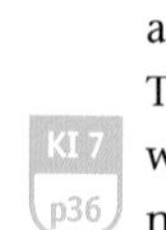

For example, the demand for a certain brand of petrol is likely to have a fairly high price elasticity, since other brands are close substitutes. If there is a cut in the price of Texaco petrol (assuming the prices of other brands stay constant), then consumption of Texaco petrol will increase a lot. The *MU* of Texaco petrol will fall slowly, since people consume less of other brands. Petrol consumption *in total* may be only slightly greater, and hence the *MU* of petrol only slightly lower.

Why do we get less total consumer surplus from goods where our demand is relatively elastic?

Shifts in the demand curve. How do shifts in demand relate to marginal utility? For example, how would the marginal utility of (and hence demand for) tea be affected by a rise in the price of coffee? The higher price of coffee would cause less coffee to be consumed. This would increase the marginal utility of tea since if people are drinking less coffee, their desire for tea is higher. The *MU* curve (and hence the demand curve) for tea thus shifts to the right.

How would marginal utility and market demand be affected by a rise in the price of a complementary good?

Weaknesses of the one-commodity version of marginal utility theory

A change in the consumption of one good will affect the marginal utility of substitute and complementary goods. It will also affect the amount of income left over to be spent on other goods. Thus, a more satisfactory explanation of demand would involve an analysis of choices between goods, rather than looking at one good in isolation.

What is more, deriving a demand curve from a marginal utility curve measured in money assumes that money itself has a constant marginal utility. The trouble is that it does not. If people have a rise in income, they will consume more. Other things being equal, the marginal utility of the goods that they consume will diminish. Thus an extra £1 of consumption will bring less satisfaction than previously. In other words, it is likely that the *marginal utility of money diminishes as income rises.*

Unless a good occupies only a tiny fraction of people's expenditure, a fall in its price will mean that their real income has increased: i.e. they can afford to purchase more goods in general. As they do so, the marginal utility of their money will fall. We cannot, therefore, legitimately use money to measure utility in an absolute sense. We can, however, still talk about the relative utility that we get from various goods for a given increase in expenditure.

The following sections thus look at the choice between goods, and how it relates to marginal utility.

The optimum combination of goods consumed

We can use marginal utility analysis to show how a rational person decides what combination of goods to buy. Given that we have limited incomes, we have to make choices. It is not just a question of choosing between two obvious substitutes, like a holiday in Greece and one in Spain, but about allocating our incomes between all the goods and services we might like to consume. If you have, say, an income of £20 000 per year, what is the optimum 'bundle' of goods and services for you to spend it on?

The rule for rational consumer behaviour is known as the ***equi-marginal principle***. This states that a consumer will get the highest utility from a given level of income when the ratio of the marginal utilities is equal to the ratio of the prices. Algebraically, this is when, for any pair of goods, A and B, that are consumed:

$$\frac{MU_A}{MU_B} = \frac{P_A}{P_B} \qquad (1)$$

To understand this, suppose that the last unit of good A you consumed gave three times as much utility as the last unit of B. Yet good A only cost twice as much as good B. You would obviously gain by increasing your consumption of A and cutting your purchases of B. But as you switched from B to A, the marginal utility of A would fall due to diminishing marginal utility, and conversely the marginal utility of B would rise.

KI 13 p105

To maximise utility you would continue this substitution of A for B until the ratios of the marginal utilities (MU_A/MU_B) equalled the ratio of the prices of the two goods (P_A/P_A). At this point, no further gain can be made by switching from one good to another. This is the optimum combination of goods to consume.

Equation (1) is a specific example of the general equi-marginal principle in economics, which applies to all

Definition

Equi-marginal principle (in consumption) Consumers will maximise total utility from their incomes by consuming that combination of goods where

$$\frac{MU_A}{MU_B} = \frac{P_A}{P_B}$$

BOX 4.2 **THE MARGINAL UTILITY REVOLUTION: JEVONS, MENGER, WALRAS** EXPLORING ECONOMICS

Solving the diamonds–water paradox

What determines the market value of a good? We already know the answer: demand and supply. So if we find out what determines the position of the demand and supply curves, we will at the same time be finding out what determines a good's market value.

This might seem obvious. Yet for years economists puzzled over just what determines a good's value.

Some economists like Karl Marx and David Ricardo concentrated on the supply side. For them, value depended on the amount of resources used in producing a good. This could be further reduced to the amount of labour time embodied in the good. Thus, according to the labour theory of value, the more labour that was directly involved in producing the good, or indirectly in producing the capital equipment used to make the good, the more valuable would the good be.

Other economists looked at the demand side. But here they came across a paradox.

Adam Smith in the 1760s gave the example of water and diamonds. 'How is it', he asked, 'that water, which is so essential to human life, and thus has such a high "value-in-use", has such a low market value (or "value-in-exchange")? And how is it that diamonds which are relatively so trivial have such a high market value?' The answer to this paradox had to wait over a hundred years until the marginal utility revolution of the 1870s. William Stanley Jevons (1835–82) in England, Carl Menger (1840–1921) in Austria and Léon Walras (1834–1910) in Switzerland all independently claimed that the source of the market value of a good was its marginal utility, not its total utility.

This was the solution to the diamonds–water paradox. Water, being so essential, has a high total utility: a high 'value in use'. But for most of us, given that we consume so much already, it has a very low marginal utility. Do you leave the cold tap running when you clean your teeth? If you do, it shows just how trivial water is to you at the margin. Diamonds, on the other hand, although they have a much lower total utility, have a much higher marginal utility. There are so few diamonds in the world, and thus people have so few of them, that they are very valuable at the margin. If, however, a new technique were to be discovered of producing diamonds cheaply from coal, their market value would fall rapidly. As people had more of them, so their marginal utility would rapidly diminish. Marginal utility still only gives the demand side of the story. The reason why the marginal utility of water is so low is that supply is so plentiful. Water is very expensive in Saudi Arabia! In other words, the full explanation of value must take into account both demand and supply.

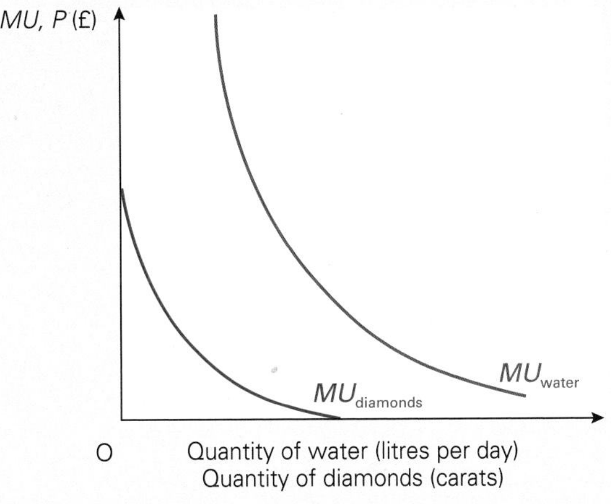

The diagram illustrates a person's MU curves of water and diamonds. Assume that diamonds are more expensive than water. Show how the MU of diamonds will be greater than the MU of water. Show also how the TU of diamonds will be less than the TU of water. (Remember: TU is the area under the MU curve.)

Identify two other products that have a high total utility to you and yet are cheap (or even free). Explain why this is the case.

rational choices between two alternatives, whether in production, consumption, employment or whatever.

The multi-commodity version of marginal utility and the demand curve

How can we derive a demand curve from the above analysis?

Let us simply reinterpret equation (1) so that it relates the *MU* and *P* of good A to the *MU* and *P* of *any* other good.

KEY IDEA 14

The equi-marginal principle. **The optimum amount of two alternatives consumed (or produced) will be where the marginal benefit ratios of the two alternatives are equal to their marginal cost ratios:**

$$\frac{MU_A}{MU_B} = \frac{P_A}{P_B}$$

In other words, the equation would be the same for goods B, C, D, E and any other good. For any given income, and given prices for good A and all other goods, the quantity a person will demand of good A will be that which satisfies equation (1). One point on the individual's demand curve for good A has been determined.

If the price of good A now falls, such that

$$\frac{MU_A}{MU_B} > \frac{P_A}{P_B} \text{ (and similarly for goods C, D, E, etc.)}$$

the person would buy more of good A and less of all other goods (B, C, D, E, etc.), until equation (1) is once more satisfied. A second point on the individual's demand curve for good A has been determined.

Further changes in the price of good A would bring further changes in the quantity demanded, in order to satisfy equation (1). Further points on the individual's demand curve would thereby be derived.

If the price of *another* good changed, or if the marginal utility of any good changed (including good A), then again the quantity demanded of good A (and other goods) would change, until again equation (1) were satisfied. These changes in demand will be represented by a *shift* in the demand curve for good A.

BOX 4.3 TAKING ACCOUNT OF TIME

CASE STUDIES AND APPLICATIONS

Do you take a taxi or go by bus? How long do you spend soaking in the bath? Do you cook a meal from scratch, or will you get a take-away?

We have argued that if decisions are to be rational, they should involve weighing up the relative marginal utilities of these activities against their relative marginal costs. As economists, of course we are interested in considering all costs, including time. One of the opportunity costs of doing any activity is the sacrifice of time.

A take-away meal may be more expensive than one cooked at home, but it saves you time. Part of the cost of the home-cooked meal, therefore, is the sacrifice of time involved. The full cost is therefore not just the cost of the ingredients and the fuel used, but also the opportunity cost of the alternative activities you have sacrificed while you were cooking.

Given the busy lives many people lead in affluent countries, they often put a high value on time. Increased sales of ready meals and the employment of home cleaners are consequences of this valuation.

Of course, leisure activities also involve a time cost. The longer you spend doing pleasurable activity 'a', the less time you will have for doing pleasurable activity 'b'. The longer you laze in the bath, the less TV you will be able to watch (unless you have a TV in the bathroom).

1. *We have identified that consumers face limits on their income and time. Can you think of any other constraints that we face when making consumption decisions?*
2. *Give some examples of business opportunities that could arise as a consequence of people being 'cash-rich, but time-poor'.*
3. *If someone hires a cleaner, does this imply that they are 'cash-rich, but time-poor'? How about hiring a personal trainer?*

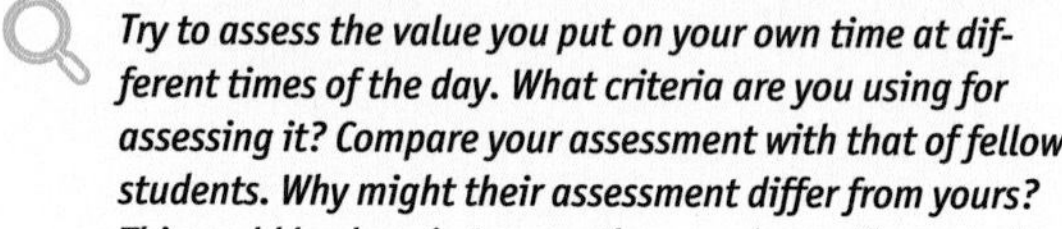

Try to assess the value you put on your own time at different times of the day. What criteria are you using for assessing it? Compare your assessment with that of fellow students. Why might their assessment differ from yours? This could be done in twos or threes or in small groups in a seminar or in the whole seminar.

Section summary

1. The satisfaction people get from consuming a good is called 'utility'. Total utility is the satisfaction gained from the total consumption of a particular good over a given period of time. Marginal utility is the extra satisfaction gained from consuming one more unit of the good.
2. The marginal utility tends to fall the more that people consume. This is known as the 'principle of diminishing marginal utility'.
3. The utility that people get from consuming a good will depend on the amount of other goods they consume. A change in the amount of other goods consumed, whether substitutes or complements, will shift the total and marginal utility curves.
4. 'Rational' consumers will attempt to maximise their consumer surplus. Consumer surplus is the excess of people's utility (measured in money terms) over their expenditure on the good. This will be maximised by purchasing at the point where the *MU* of a good is equal to its price.
5. In the simple case where the price and consumption of other goods is held constant, a person's *MU* curve will lie along the same line as that person's demand curve.
6. The market demand curve is merely the horizontal sum of the demand curves of all the individual consumers. The elasticity of the market demand curve will depend on the rate at which marginal utility diminishes as more is consumed. This in turn depends on the number and closeness of substitute goods. If there are close substitutes, people will readily switch to this good if its price falls, and thus marginal utility will fall only slowly. The demand will be elastic.
7. Measuring the marginal utility of a good in money avoids the problem of using some imaginary unit such as utils, but it assumes that money has a constant utility. In reality, the marginal utility of money is likely to decrease as income rises.
8. A more satisfactory way of analysing the demand for goods is to look at people's choices between goods. A consumer will maximise utility from a given income by consuming according to the 'equi-marginal principle'. This states that goods should be consumed in that combination which equates the *MU*/*P* ratio for each good.

4.2 THE TIMING OF COSTS AND BENEFITS

The timing of the costs incurred and the benefits received varies between different types of consumption. This has implications for the way the rational choice model is applied. In some cases, all the costs and benefits of a decision are virtually instantaneous with only a very small delay between them. For example, if you purchase a coffee the cost is immediate (unless you use a credit card) and the total pleasure from consuming the drink occurs shortly afterwards.

However, for a whole range of other consumption decisions all the costs and benefits are not instantaneous and occur over a more prolonged period of time. There may also be significant delays between the point in time the costs are incurred and the benefits received. This is called intertemporal choice.

Take the example of buying a consumer durable, such as a mobile phone, dishwasher or car. The major cost of purchasing many of these products is often immediate, or virtually so (unless paying by instalments), while the stream of benefits they provide occurs for months or years after the initial costs are paid. In other cases, all the benefits from consumption are instantaneous, while some of the costs occur in the future. For example, the consumption benefits and monetary costs of purchasing cigarettes are fairly immediate, while the health costs occur in the future. The same would be true about decisions to purchase alcohol and unhealthy food.

Optimum consumption with intertemporal choice

How can the rational choice model be extended to analyse and explain these types of intertemporal choices?

The standard economic theory of consumer choice assumes that most people are impatient most of the time. They would prefer to consume the things they like immediately rather than having to wait until a later date. They would also prefer to delay any costs until later: e.g. paying for goods using a credit card.

This impatience can be illustrated by the following simple example. Imagine that it is 10:00am on Monday morning and you are given the choice between receiving a payment of £500 immediately or having to wait until 10:00am on Tuesday morning. When asked this type of question most people prefer to have the £500 immediately.

The key to understanding this impatience is to think about the point in time the person makes the decision. If they prefer to receive £500 on Monday rather than having to wait until Tuesday, then the following must be true.

$$U^{\text{Monday}}:u(£500_{\text{Monday}}) > u(£500_{\text{Tuesday}})$$

This is simply stating that from the person's point of view on Monday (U^{Monday}), the utility from receiving the money on Monday ($u(£500_{\text{Monday}})$) is greater than the utility of having to wait until Tuesday ($u(£500_{\text{Tuesday}})$).

This does not mean that receiving the money on Tuesday gives them less pleasure. In other words:

$$U^{\text{Monday}}:u(£500_{\text{Monday}}) = U^{\text{Tuesday}}:u(£500_{\text{Tuesday}})$$

From the person's point of view on Tuesday (U^{Tuesday}), £500 received on Tuesday provides the same utility as receiving the £500 on Monday from their point of view on Monday. Impatience in this example means that judging the decision from Monday's perspective, receiving £500 immediately would give the person more pleasure than having to wait 24 hours.

What is the minimum amount by which the pay-off of £500 would have to increase in order for you personally to agree to wait for another 24 hours before receiving it?

Discounting: measuring impatience

From Monday's perspective, how much more utility does receiving £500 immediately provide rather than having to wait until Tuesday? To capture this impatience, standard economic theory uses a method of weighting future costs and benefits. It is called ***exponential discounting*** and multiplies any costs and benefits that occur in the future by a fraction of less than one to adjust them to what they are worth to the person immediately: i.e. their ***present value***. This fraction is called the ***discount factor***.

To illustrate this idea, assume a person is considering a consumption decision when all the costs occur immediately, while all the benefits occur in the future. To keep the example as simple as possible, assume the benefits all occur at one point in time in the future rather than being spread out over a number of days, weeks or months. The good costs £10, which is payable immediately, and provides £20 of utility in exactly one month's time (perhaps there is a month's delay before it can be delivered). As all the costs are immediate, they are weighted at 100 per cent of their value. However, impatience means that the future benefits have to be

Definitions

Exponential discounting A method of reducing future benefits and costs to a present value. The discount rate depends on the level of impatience and remains constant in exponential discounting.

Present value (in consumption) The value a person places today on a good that will not be consumed until some point in the future.

Discount factor The value today of deciding to consume a good one period in the future as a proportion of the value when it is actually consumed.

weighted by a fraction of less than one to adjust them to what they are worth to the person immediately.

If the person's impatience could be captured by a monthly discount factor of, say, 0.9 then £20 of pleasure in a month would be worth £18 (0.9 × £20) to that person today. The present value of the benefits from consuming the good (£18) would still be greater than the immediate cost (£10); so a rational person would purchase the product and be prepared to wait for delivery.

Levels of impatience will vary from one individual to another. The more impatient people are, the lower their discount factor and the less they will value benefits and costs that occur at some point in the future. For example, imagine that in the previous example a person's greater level of impatience could be captured by a discount factor of 0.4. This makes £20 of benefits received in a month's time worth only £8 to that person now. As the immediate cost of £10 is now greater than the discounted value of the future benefits, this more impatient individual would not purchase the good.

The further into the future any costs and benefits occur, the greater their values have to be reduced to adjust them to what they are worth to an individual today. If the benefits from consuming the product all occur in two months' time the discount factor will be less than 0.9.

How is the discount factor for a two-month delay calculated using exponential discounting? The per-period discount factor is the amount by which each discount factor in one period has to be multiplied in order to work out the discount factor for the following period. Assuming the size of the delay between each period remains the same (i.e. in this case it is always a month), the per-period discount factor remains constant. Therefore, the discount factor of 0.9 for a one-month delay would have to be multiplied by 0.9 to calculate the discount factor for a two-month delay. It would equal 0.81. A benefit of £20 in two months has a present value of 0.81 × £20 or £16.20.

The standard exponential approach to discounting assumes that the discount factor declines at a *constant* rate over time. This approach does have one major limitation – it assumes the consumer's degree of impatience remains constant with the passage of time. This implies that people will stick to their plans unless they learn new information about the relative size of any costs or benefits of the decision.

Alternatives to exponential discounting are discussed in section 5.2 (pages 146–8). Section 10.3 (pages 310–12) examines discounting in the context of capital investment.

1. (a) *What discount factor is used to weight benefits that occur in three months' time for a person with a per-monthly discount factor of 0.9?*
   (b) *What does this make the present value of £20 of benefits received in three months' time?*
2. *Assume that the good costs £10, which has to be paid today. How long would the maximum delay in months before receiving the £20 of benefits have to be before a person with a monthly discount of 0.9 would no longer purchase the good?*

*LOOKING AT THE MATHS

How do we calculate the present value of the purchase of a product whose utility occurs over a period of time? Let us assume that a person's discount factor is 0.8. In other words, a good yielding £100 of benefits one period in the future would be valued at only 0.8 × £100 = £80 today.

But what about a product that yields utility in several future periods? The formula we use for calculating its present value (i.e. its utility over its lifetime expressed in a value today) is:

$$U = \sum_{t=0}^{t=n} \delta^t U_t \tag{1}$$

where U is the total present utility value of a good consumed over various time periods, $t = 0$ to $t = n$; δ is the discount factor applied for each time period t and U_t is the utility gained in each specific time period t.

Let us assume that a good has a life of three years and yields £100 of utility at the end of year 1, £300 at the end of year 2 and £200 at the end of year 3. Its total present utility is not the simple sum of the three utilities that will be experienced; it is not £100 + £300 + £200 = £600. Instead it is found by applying the above formula. Again, let us assume that the discount factor is 0.8. Substituting the figures for the three years in equation (1) gives:

$$\begin{aligned} U &= (0.8 \times £100) + (0.8^2 \times £300) + (0.8^3 \times £200) \\ &= (0.8 \times £100) + (0.64 \times £300) + (0.512 \times £200) \\ &= £80 + £192 + £102.40 \\ &= £374.40 \end{aligned}$$

What is the present value (utility) of a good which yields £50 of utility at the end of year 1, £60 at the end of year 2, £100 at the end of year 3 and £50 at the end of year 4, assuming a discount factor of 0.9? Would it be worth the consumer paying £200 for it today?

Section summary

1. The benefits, and sometimes the costs, of some consumer goods occur over a period of time rather than instantaneously. Consumers are thus faced with making intertemporal choices.
2. Because consumers would generally rather have goods now than later, benefits (and costs) that occur in the future have to be discounted to give them a present value.
3. The higher the discount factor, the lower will be the present value for any given future benefit or cost.
4. Exponential discounting assumes the degree of impatience remains constant with the passage of time: i.e. people stick to their plans.

*4.3 INDIFFERENCE ANALYSIS

The limitations of the marginal utility approach to demand

Even though the multi-commodity version of marginal utility theory is useful in demonstrating the underlying logic of consumer choice, it still has a major weakness. Utility cannot be measured in any absolute sense. We cannot really say, therefore, by how much the marginal utility of one good exceeds another.

An alternative approach to rational choice theory is to use *indifference analysis*. This does not involve measuring the *amount* of utility a person gains, but merely *ranking* various combinations of goods in order of preference. In other words, it assumes that consumers can decide whether they prefer one combination of goods to another. For example, if you were asked to choose between two baskets of fruit, one containing four oranges and three pears and the other containing two oranges and five pears, you could say which you prefer or whether you are indifferent between them. It does not assume that you can decide just *how much* you prefer one basket to another or just how much you like either.

The aim of indifference analysis, then, is to analyse, *without having to measure utility*, how a rational consumer chooses between two goods. As we shall see, it can be used to show the effect on this choice of (a) a change in the consumer's income and (b) a change in the price of one or both goods. It can also be used to analyse the income and substitution effects of a change in price.

Indifference analysis involves the use of *indifference curves* and *budget lines*.

Indifference curves

An ***indifference curve*** shows all the various combinations of two goods that give an equal amount of satisfaction or utility to a consumer.

To show how one can be constructed, consider the following example. Imagine that a supermarket is conducting a survey about the preferences of its customers for different types of fruit. One of the respondents is Ali, a student who likes a healthy diet and regularly buys fresh fruit. He is asked his views about various combinations of oranges and pears. Starting with the combination of 10 pears and 13 oranges, he is asked what other combinations he would like the same amount as this one. From his answers a table is constructed (Table 4.2). What we are saying here is that Ali would be equally happy to have any one of the combinations shown in the table.

This table is known as an ***indifference set***. It shows alternative combinations of two goods that yield the same level of satisfaction. From this we can plot an indifference curve. We measure units of one good on one axis and units of the other good on the other axis. Thus in Figure 4.5, which is based on Table 4.2, pears and oranges are measured on the two axes. The curve shows that Ali is indifferent as to whether he consumes 30 pears and 6 oranges (point *a*) or 24 pears and 7 oranges (point *b*) or any other combination of pears and oranges along the curve.

Table 4.2 Combinations of pears and oranges that Ali likes the same amount as 10 pears and 13 oranges

Pears	Oranges	Point in Figure 4.5
30	6	a
24	7	b
20	8	c
14	10	d
10	13	e
8	15	f
6	20	g

Notice that we are not saying *how much* Ali likes pears and oranges; merely that he likes all the combinations along the indifference curve the same amount. All the combinations thus yield the same (unspecified) utility.

The shape of the indifference curve

As you can see, the indifference curve we have drawn is not a straight line. It is bowed in towards the origin. In other words, its slope gets shallower as we move down the curve. Indifference curves are normally drawn this shape. But why?

Let us see what the slope of the curve shows us. It shows the rate at which the consumer is willing to exchange one good for the other, holding their level of satisfaction the same. For example, consider the move from point *a* to point *b* in Figure 4.5. Ali gives up 6 units of pears and requires 1 orange to compensate for the loss. The slope of the indifference curve is thus $-6/1 = -6$. Ignoring the negative sign, the slope of the indifference curve (that is, the rate at which the consumer is willing to substitute one good for the other) is known as the ***marginal rate of substitution*** (*MRS*). In this case, therefore, the $MRS = 6$.

Definitions

Indifference curve A line showing all those combinations of two goods between which a consumer is indifferent: i.e. those combinations that give the same level of utility.

Indifference set A table showing the same information as an indifference curve.

Marginal rate of substitution (between two goods in consumption) The amount of one good (Y) that a consumer is prepared to give up in order to obtain one extra unit of another good (X): i.e. $\Delta Y/\Delta X$.

Figure 4.5 An indifference curve

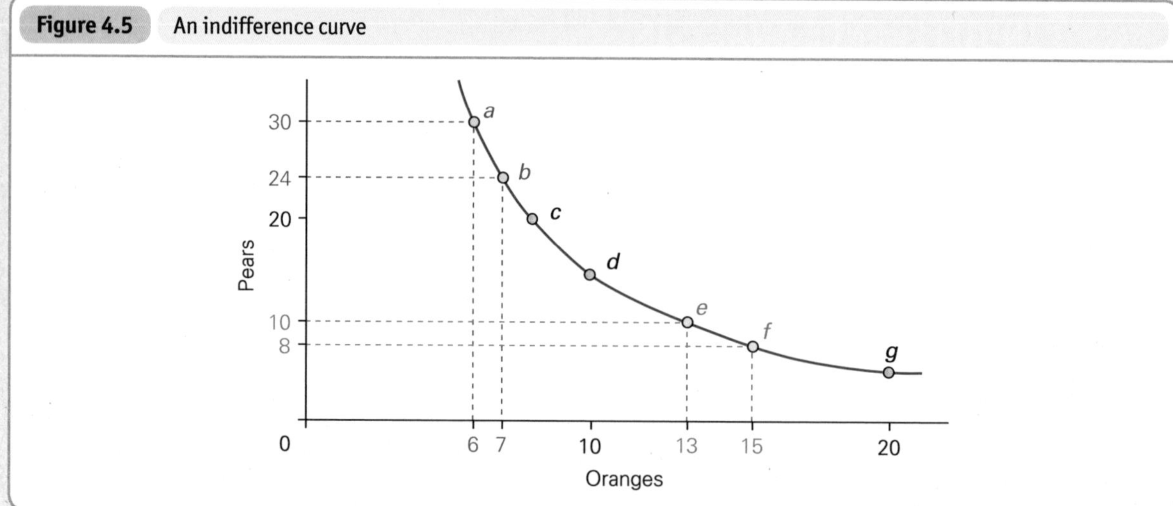

Note that as we move down the curve, the marginal rate of substitution diminishes as the slope of the curve gets less. For example, look at the move from point *e* to point *f*. Here the consumer gives up 2 pears and requires 2 oranges to compensate. Thus, along this section of the curve, the slope is $-2/2 = -1$ (and hence the $MRS = 1$).

The reason for a ***diminishing marginal rate of substitution*** is related to the *principle of diminishing marginal utility* that we looked at in section 4.1. This stated that individuals will gain less and less additional satisfaction the more of a good that they consume. This principle, however, is based on the assumption that the consumption of other goods is held *constant*. In the case of an indifference curve, this is not true. As we move down the curve, more of one good is consumed but *less* of the other. Nevertheless the effect on consumer satisfaction is similar. As Ali consumes more pears and fewer oranges, his marginal utility from pears will diminish, while that from oranges will increase. He will thus be prepared to give up fewer and fewer pears for each additional orange. *MRS* diminishes.

The relationship between the marginal rate of substitution and marginal utility

In Figure 4.5, consumption at point *a* yields equal satisfaction with consumption at point *b*. Thus the utility sacrificed by giving up six pears must be equal to the utility gained by consuming one more orange. In other words, the marginal utility of an orange must be six times as great as that of a pear. Therefore, $MU_{\text{oranges}}/MU_{\text{pears}} = 6$. But this is the same as the marginal rate of substitution. With *X* measured on the horizontal axis and *Y* on the vertical axis, then

$$MRS = \frac{MU_X}{MU_Y} = \text{slope of indifference curve (ignoring negative sign)}$$

Although indifference curves will normally be bowed in towards the origin, on odd occasions they might not be. Which of the following diagrams correspond to which of the following? Explain the shape of each curve.

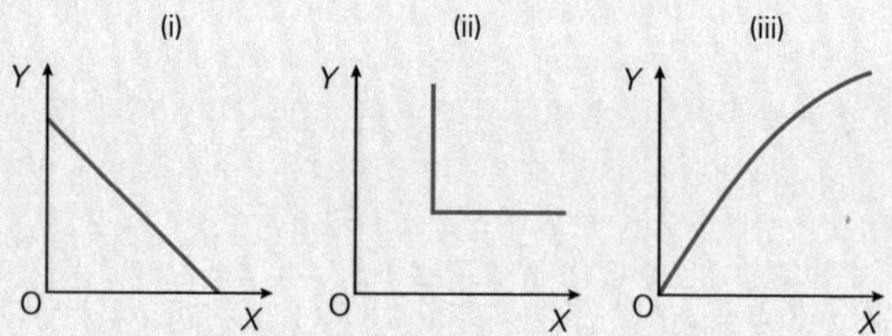

(a) X and Y are left shoes and right shoes.
(b) X and Y are two brands of the same product, and the consumer cannot tell them apart.
(c) X is a good but Y is a 'bad' – like household refuse.

The curvature and slope of indifference curves

Although indifference curves for two goods are normally bowed in towards the origin, the slope and curvature can vary. This provides some information about consumer preferences. For example, if the indifference curve is relatively steep, then the *MRS* remains large along the whole length of the line. The consumer has a stronger preference for the good on the horizontal axis over the good on the vertical axis. If the indifference curve is relatively flat, the reverse is true.

The more curved or bow-shaped the curve, the more complementary the two goods are in consumption. The lower the curvature (i.e. closer it is to being a straight line) the more substitutable the two goods are in consumption.

An indifference map

More than one indifference curve can be drawn. For example, referring back to Table 4.2, Ali could give another set of combinations of pears and oranges that all give him a higher (but equal) level of utility than the set shown in the table. This could then be plotted in Figure 4.5 as another indifference curve.

Definition

Diminishing marginal rate of substitution The more a person consumes of good X and the less of good Y, the less additional Y will that person be prepared to give up in order to obtain an extra unit of X: i.e. $\Delta Y/\Delta X$ diminishes.

Although the actual amount of utility corresponding to each curve is not specified, indifference curves further out to the right would show combinations of the two goods that yield a higher utility, and curves further in to the left would show combinations yielding a lower utility.

In fact, a whole ***indifference map*** can be drawn, with each successive indifference curve showing a higher level of utility. Combinations of goods along I_2 in Figure 4.6 give a higher utility to the consumer than those along I_1. Those along I_3 give a higher utility than those along I_2 and so on. The term 'map' is appropriate here, because the indifference curves are rather like contours on a real map. Just as a contour joins all those points of a particular height, so an indifference curve shows all those combinations yielding a particular level of utility.

Draw another two indifference curves on Figure 4.5, one outward from and one inward from the original curve. Read off various combinations of pears and oranges along these two new curves and enter them on a table like Table 4.2.

The budget line

We turn now to the ***budget line***. This is the other important element in the analysis of consumer behaviour. Whereas indifference maps illustrate people's preferences, the actual choices they make will depend on their incomes and the prices of the goods. The budget line shows what combinations of two goods you are able to buy, given (a) your income available to spend on them and (b) their prices.

Just as we did with an indifference curve, we can construct a budget line from a table. The first two columns of Table 4.3 show various combinations of two goods X and Y that can be purchased assuming that (a) the price of X is £2 and the price of Y is £1 and (b) the consumer has a budget of £30 to be divided between the two goods.

In Figure 4.7, then, if you are limited to a budget of £30, you can consume any combination of X and Y along the line (or inside it). You cannot, however, afford to buy combinations that lie outside it: i.e. in the darker shaded area. This area is known as the *infeasible region* for the given budget.

Table 4.3 Consumption possibilities for budgets of £30 and £40

Budget of £30			Budget of £40	
Units of good X	Units of good Y	Point on budget line in Figure 4.7	Units of good X	Units of good Y
0	30	a	0	40
5	20	b	5	30
10	10	c	10	20
15	0	d	15	10
			20	0

Note: It is assumed that $P_X = £2$, $P_Y = £1$.

We have said that the amount people can afford to buy will depend on (a) their budget and (b) the prices of the two goods. We can show how a change in either of these two determinants will affect the budget line.

A change in income

If the consumer's income (and hence budget) increases, the budget line will shift outwards, parallel to the old one. This is illustrated in the last two columns of Table 4.3 and in Figure 4.8, which show the effect of a rise in the consumer's

Definitions

Indifference map A graph showing a whole set of indifference curves. The further away a particular curve is from the origin, the higher the level of satisfaction it represents.

Budget line A graph showing all the possible combinations of two goods that can be purchased at given prices and for a given budget.

Figure 4.6 An indifference map

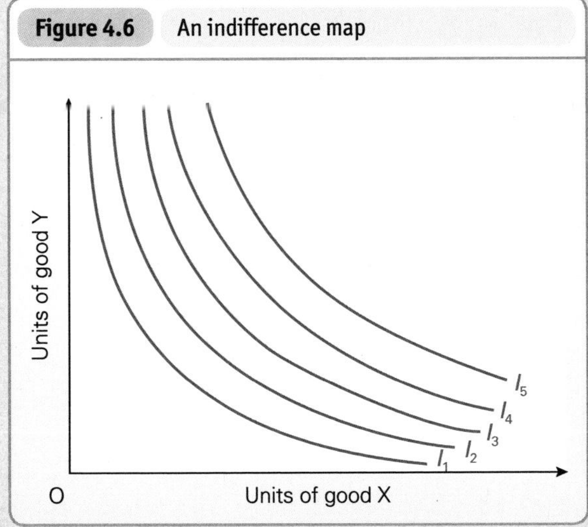

Figure 4.7 A budget line

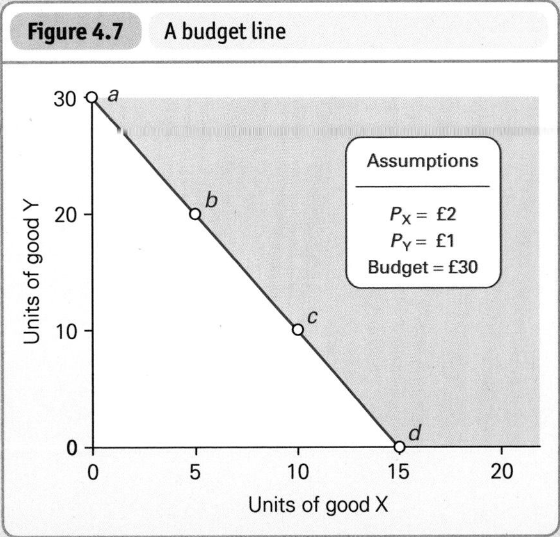

Figure 4.8 Effect of an increase in income on the budget line

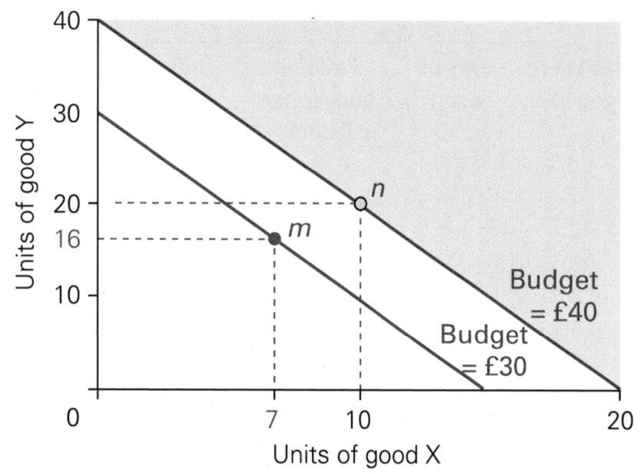

budget from £30 to £40. (Note that there is no change in the prices of X and Y, which remain at £2 and £1 respectively.)

More can now be purchased. For example, if the consumer was originally purchasing 7 units of X and 16 units of Y (point *m*), this could be increased with the new budget of £40, to 10 units of X and 20 units of Y (point *n*) or any other combination of X and Y along the new higher budget line.

A change in price

The relative prices of the two goods are given by the slope of the budget line. The slope of the budget line in Figure 4.7 is 30/15 = 2. (We are ignoring the negative sign: strictly speaking, the slope should be −2.) Similarly, the slope of the new higher budget line in Figure 4.8 is 40/20 = 2. But in each case, this is simply the ratio of the price of X (£2) to the price of Y (£1).

Thus the slope of the budget line equals

$$\frac{P_X}{P_Y}$$

If the price of either good changes, the slope of the budget line will change. This is illustrated in Figure 4.9 which, like Figure 4.7, assumes a budget of £30 and an initial price of X of £2 and a price of Y of £1. The initial budget line is B_1.

Figure 4.9 Effect on the budget line of a fall in the price of good X

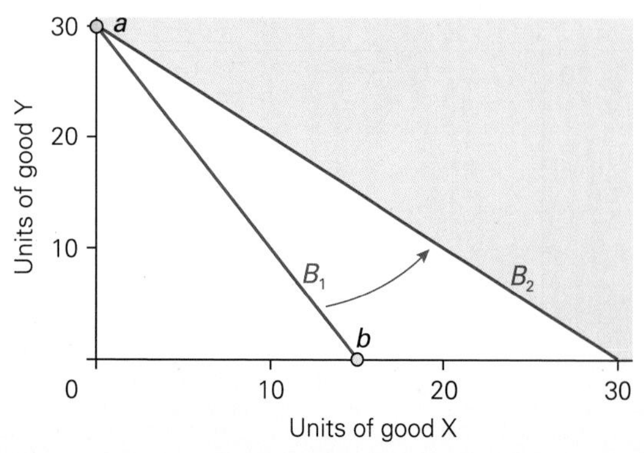

Now let us assume that the price of X falls to £1 but that the price of Y remains the same (£1). The new budget line will join 30 on the Y axis with 30 on the X axis. In other words, the line pivots outwards on point *a*. If, instead, the price of Y changed, the line would pivot on point *b*.

1. *Assume that the budget remains at £30 and the price of X stays at £2, but that Y rises in price to £3. Draw the new budget line.*
2. *What will happen to the budget line if the consumer's income doubles and the prices of both X and Y double?*

The optimum consumption point

We are now in a position to put the two elements of the analysis together: the indifference map and a budget line. This will enable us to show how much of each of the two goods the 'rational' consumer will buy from a given budget. Let us examine Figure 4.10.

The consumer would like to consume along the highest possible indifference curve. This is curve I_3 at point *t*. Higher indifference curves, such as I_4 and I_5, although representing higher utility than curve I_3, are in the infeasible region: they represent combinations of X and Y that the consumer cannot afford with the current budget. The consumer *could* consume along curves I_1 and I_2, between points *r* and *v*, and *s* and *u* respectively, but they give a lower level of utility than consuming at point *t*.

The optimum consumption point for the consumer, then, is where the budget line touches (is 'tangential to') the highest possible indifference curve.

If the budget line is tangential to an indifference curve, they will have the same slope. (The slope of a curve is the slope of the tangent to it at the point in question.) But as we have seen, the slope of the budget line is TC 8 p109

$$\frac{P_X}{P_Y}$$

and the slope of the indifference curve is

$$MRS = \frac{MU_X}{MU_Y}$$

Figure 4.10 The optimum consumption point

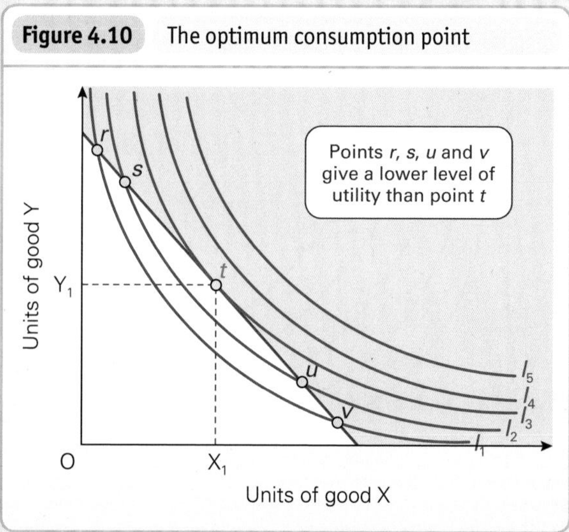

Therefore, at the optimum consumption point

$$\frac{P_X}{P_Y} = \frac{MU_X}{MU_Y}$$

But this is the *equi-marginal principle* that we established in the first part of this chapter: only this time, using the indifference curve approach, there has been no need to measure utility. All we have needed to do is to observe, for any two combinations of goods, whether the consumer preferred one to the other or was indifferent between them.

KI 14 p111

*LOOKING AT THE MATHS

We can express the optimum consumption point algebraically. With a limited budget of B, the objective is to maximise utility subject to this budget constraint. This can be expressed as

$$\text{Max}\,TU(X, Y) \qquad (1)$$

subject to the budget constraint that

$$P_X X + P_Y Y = B \qquad (2)$$

Equation (1) is known as the 'objective function' and says that the objective is to maximise utility, which depends on the consumption of two goods, X and Y. For example, assume that the utility function is

$$TU = X^{3/4}Y^{1/4}$$

This is known as a 'Cobb–Douglas utility function' and will give smooth convex indifference curves. Assume also that the price of X is 4, the price of Y is 2 and the budget is 64. Thus:

$$4X + 2Y = 64$$

Rearranging this constraint to express X in terms of Y gives

$$X = 16 - \frac{Y}{2}$$

By first substituting this value of X into the utility function (so that it is expressed purely in terms of Y) and then differentiating the resulting equation and setting it equal to zero, we can solve for the value of Y and then X that yields the maximum utility for the given budget. The answer is:

$$X = 12 \text{ and } Y = 8$$

The workings of this are given in Maths Case 4.1 on the student website.

An alternative method, which is slightly longer but is likely to involve simpler calculations, involves the use of 'Lagrangian multipliers'. This method is explained, along with a worked example, in Maths Case 4.2.

The effect of changes in income

As we have seen, an increase in income is represented by a parallel shift outward of the budget line (assuming no change in the price of X and Y). This will then lead to a new optimum consumption point on a higher indifference curve. A different consumption point will be found for each different level of income.

In Figure 4.11, a series of budget lines is drawn representing different levels of consumer income. The corresponding optimum consumption points (r, s, t, u) are shown. Each point is where the new higher budget line just touches (i.e. is tangential to) the highest possible indifference curve.[1] The line joining these points is known as the ***income–consumption curve***.

If your money income goes up and the price of goods does not change, we say that your ***real income*** has risen. In other words, you can buy more than you did before. But your real income can also rise even if you do not earn any more money. This will happen if prices fall. For the same amount of money, you can buy more goods than previously. We analyse the effect of a rise in real income caused by a fall in prices in just the same way as we did when money income rose and prices stayed the same. Provided the *relative* prices of the two goods stay the same (i.e. provided they fall by the same percentage), the budget line will shift outwards parallel to the old one.

Income elasticity of demand and the income–consumption curve

The income–consumption curve in Figure 4.11 shows that the demand for both goods rises as income rises. Thus both goods have a positive income elasticity of demand: they are both normal goods.

KI 9 p64

Now let us focus just on good X. If the income–consumption curve became flatter at higher levels of income,

Definitions

Income–consumption curve A line showing how a person's optimum level of consumption of two goods changes as income changes (assuming the prices of the goods remain constant).

Real income Income measured in terms of how much it can buy. If your *money* income rises by 10 per cent, but prices rise by 8 per cent, you can buy only 2 per cent more goods than before. Your *real* income has risen by 2 per cent.

Figure 4.11 Effect on consumption of a change in income

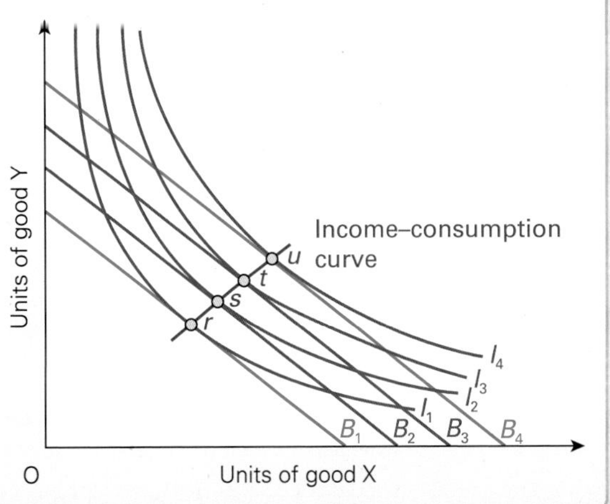

1 We can always draw in an indifference curve that will be tangential to a given budget line. Just because we only draw a few indifference curves on a diagram, it does not mean that there are only a few possible ones. We could draw as many as we liked. Again, it is rather like the contours on a real map. They may be drawn at, say, 10 metre intervals. We could, however, if we liked, draw them at 1 metre or even 1cm intervals, or at whatever height was suitable to our purpose. For example, if the maximum height of a lake were 32.45 metres above sea level, it might be useful to draw a contour at that height to show what land might be liable to flooding.

it would show an increasing proportion of income being spent on X. The flatter it became, the higher would be the income elasticity of demand for X.

If, by contrast, X were an inferior good, such as value own-label supermarket brands, its demand would fall as income rose; its income elasticity of demand would be negative. This is illustrated in Figure 4.12. Point *b* is to the left of point *a*, showing that at the higher income B_2, the demand for good X falls from Q_{X_1} to Q_{X_2}. Good Y is a normal good as demand increases from Q_{X_1} to Q_{X_2}.

*BOX 4.4 CASH VERSUS VOUCHERS

An application of indifference curve analysis

Governments use a range of different polices to reduce inequality and redistribute income from rich to poor households. For example, various payments financed by tax revenue are made to those on lower incomes (for more detail see Chapter 11, section 11.2). Many of these transfers are in the form of unconditional cash payments – they place no restrictions on how the recipients spend the money. Examples in the UK include Universal Credit, Jobseeker's Allowance, Employment and Support Allowance and Working Tax Credit.

Governments sometimes choose to make these transfers in kind. In-kind transfers constrain choice as they tie payments to the consumption of particular goods or services. One type of in-kind transfer is a voucher: i.e. a conditional payment that recipients can only spend on a limited number of specified goods. A good example in the UK is the Healthy Start programme.

This scheme provides pregnant women and low-income families with food vouchers. To be eligible, the household must (a) be receiving specified government benefits; (b) have children under the age of four and/or a woman who is at least 10 weeks pregnant. The vouchers can only be spent on the following items at registered retailers.

- Milk
- Fresh, frozen and tinned fruit and vegetables
- Fresh, dried and tinned pulses
- Infant formula milk.

From April 2021, the value of each voucher rose to £4.25. Families receive them for each eligible member of the household – one per week for each child aged one to three, one per week for a pregnant woman and two per week for each child in their first year. Therefore, a pregnant woman with two children, one aged six months and one aged three, receives 4 vouchers per week worth a total of £17.

During 2020, another voucher made news headlines – school meal vouchers. The closure of schools for the majority of pupils in the first COVID-19 national lockdown (March to June 2020) meant that children who qualified for free school meals were unable to obtain them in the usual way. To address this issue, the government provided eligible families with either an electronic voucher or a gift card worth £15 per week per pupil that they could spend at all the major supermarkets.

The initial advice from the Department for Education stated that:

> Families are free to select the most appropriate food and drink for their child . . . The vouchers should not be redeemed for any age-restricted items, such as alcohol, cigarettes or lottery tickets.[1]

After some controversial stories in the media over how they were being spent,[2] supermarkets started to tighten the rules by providing restricted item lists: i.e. products the vouchers could not be used to purchase. Initially, the government planned to operate the payments in term-time only. However, after a successful campaign by the footballer Marcus Rashford, the scheme was continued in the school holidays.

In April 2020, the Director of the Child Poverty Action Group[3] argued that:

> Cash payments are the most effective way to protect and support most families, giving parents the greatest choice and agency to meet their family's needs . . . They are a dignified response that avoid the stigma and lack of choice too often associated with vouchers.[4]

Using indifference analysis to compare the use of cash and vouchers to provide support

What are the predictions of the standard economic model of consumer choice? Should the government make greater use of unconditional cash payments as the statement from the Child Poverty Action Group suggests?

The diagram opposite illustrates a low-income individual, Robert, who has £400 per month to spend on healthy food and all other goods. His indifference curves are relatively flat. That indicates he strongly prefers all other goods over healthy food (the $MRS_{h,c}$ is low).

Initially his optimum consumption point is *f*. He spends £20 on healthy food (Q_{h1}) and £380 on all other goods. If Robert spent all of his income on healthy food the maximum quantity he could purchase per month is £400 divided by the price of healthy food ($400/P_h$) (point *b*).

Assume now that Robert receives £100 per month of healthy food vouchers. What impact does this have on his budget constraint?

The intercept on the vertical axis will remain the same, as Robert cannot use the vouchers to purchase other goods. The maximum amount he can spend on all other goods does not change. He can use the vouchers to purchase healthy food while still leaving himself £400 to spend on all other goods. This makes part of the budget constraint a horizontal line (*a–g*). The total quantity of healthy food Robert can purchase per month with the vouchers is £100 divided by the price of healthy food: i.e. $100/P_h$.

Once the vouchers are all spent, if he wants to buy additional healthy food, he will have to start using some of his £400 income. Hence, the budget line is kinked at this point and starts to slope downwards with the same gradient as the original budget constraint. If Robert spent all his income and the vouchers on the healthy food, the maximum amount he can purchase is $500/P_h$ (point *c*).

Given the impact on the budget constraint, his optimum consumption point moves from point *f* to point

1. *The income–consumption curve in Figure 4.12 is drawn as positively sloped at low levels of income. Why?*
2. *Show the effect of a rise in income on the demand for X and Y where, this time, Y is the inferior good and X is the normal good. Is the income–consumption curve positively or negatively sloped?*

The effect of changes in price

If either X or Y changes in price, the budget line will 'pivot'. Take the case of a reduction in the price of X (but no change in the price of Y). If this happens, the budget line will swing outwards. We saw this effect in Figure 4.9 (on page 118).

CASE STUDIES AND APPLICATIONS

Cash versus vouchers

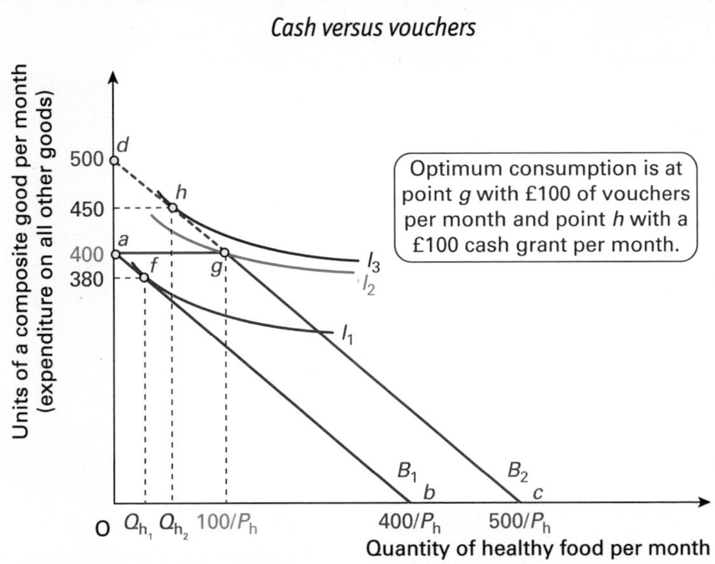

g. Indifference curve I_2 is the highest that can be achieved. Receiving the transfers makes him happier: I_2 is higher than I_1.

What does the standard theory predict if he receives £100 per month in cash instead of the vouchers? This causes the budget constraint to shift from B_1 to B_2, which is now a straight line, continuing up the dashed section to point *d*. He now has greater freedom to spend the money on other goods as well as healthy foods. His optimum consumption point moves from point *f* to point *h*.

Even though the size of the payment is £100 in each case, the cash increases his utility by more than the voucher. Given the freedom, Robert would rather increase his spending on (a) healthy food by £30 (Q_{h_1} to Q_{h_2}) and (b) all other goods by £70 (£380 to £450). The theory appears to support the views of the Child Poverty Action Group.

However, when making policy decisions, the government has to take into account the welfare of society as a whole and not just the happiness of the recipients. What about the preferences of taxpayers who vote and finance the scheme but are not eligible for the transfers? They may prefer the use of vouchers that force the recipients to spend the money in a specified way: e.g. on healthy food.

1 https://dfemedia.blog.gov.uk/2020/04/17/free-school-meals-covid-19-faq/
2 'Parents trying to buy beer with school meal vouchers', *Daily Mirror* (13 May 2020), www.mirror.co.uk/money/parents-trying-buy-beer-school-22021673
3 https://cpag.org.uk/
4 'Coronavirus: Call for cash to replace school meal vouchers', *BBC News* (14 April 2020), www.bbc.co.uk/news/uk-scotland-52286500

1. *Assume Robert has very different preferences and is initially spending more than £100 on healthy food per month. Using an indifference curve diagram, compare the impact of the following on his utility: (a) £100 cash per month and (b) £100 healthy food vouchers per month.*
2. *Discuss some other potential advantages and disadvantages of using vouchers.*
3. *Another type of conditional cash payment is a price subsidy. Here the government pays a proportion of the price for each unit of the good a recipient purchases. Using an indifference curve diagram, compare the impact of a price subsidy and an unconditional cash payment on the utility of the recipient.*

During the coronavirus pandemic, UK families that would normally qualify for free school meals were given food vouchers and then later food parcels, about which there were many complaints as to their standard. Using newspaper articles from the time (early 2021) compare the relative benefits of food vouchers, food parcels and cash (all of the same monetary value).

Figure 4.12 Effect of a rise in income on the demand for an inferior good

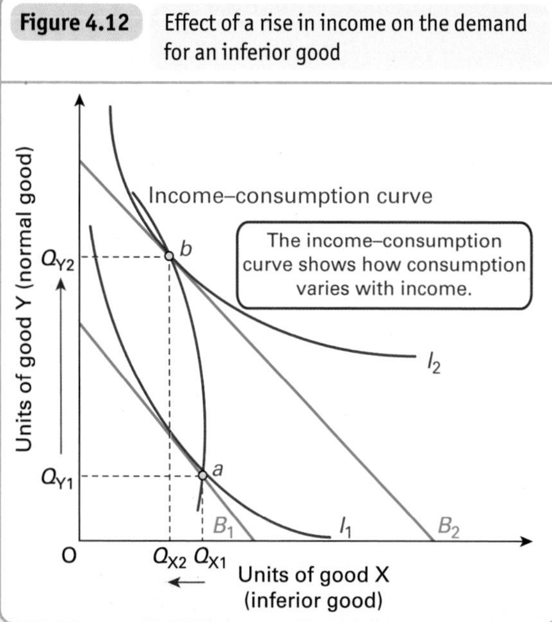

These same budget lines are reproduced in Figure 4.13, but this time we have added indifference curves.

The original optimum consumption point is at *j* where the consumer purchases 7 units of good X and 13 units of good Y. After the reduction in the price of good X, a new optimum consumption point is at *k* where the consumer now purchases 13 units of good X and 17 units of good Y.

Illustrate on an indifference diagram the effects of the following:
(a) A rise in the price of good X (assuming no change in the price of Y).
(b) A fall in the price of good Y (assuming no change in the price of X).

A series of budget lines could be drawn, all pivoting round point *a* in Figure 4.13. Each one represents a different price of good X, but with money income and the price of Y held constant. The flatter the curve, the lower the price of X. At each price, there will be an optimum consumption point. The line that connects these points is known as the **price–consumption curve**.

The slope of the price–consumption curve indicates the relationship between the two goods in consumption. In Figure 4.13, the curve is upward sloping. When the price of good X falls, the demand for *both* goods increases. X increases from 7 to 13 units and Y from 13 to 17 units. They are complements.[2] If the price–consumption curve is downward sloping then the goods are substitutes in consumption.

Figure 4.13 Effect of a fall in the price of good X

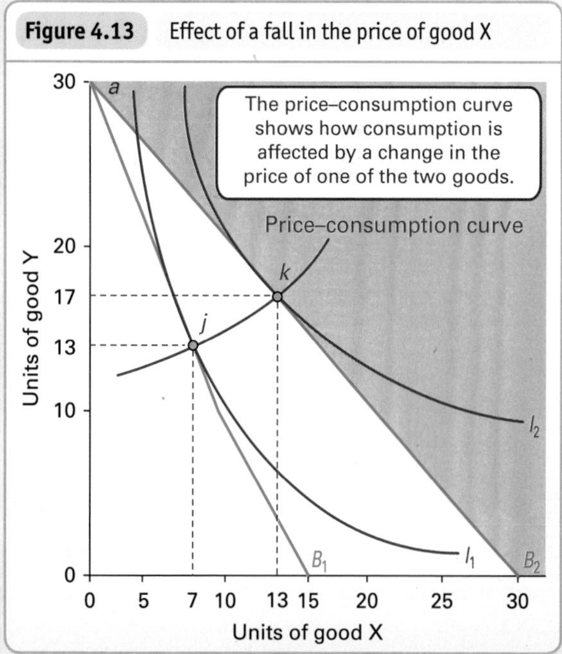

Composite goods – extending the analysis to more than two goods

One limitation of indifference curve analysis so far is that it has only been possible to examine choices between two goods. In reality, consumers choose between many goods. How can we extend the diagrammatic analysis to examine these situations while keeping the two-dimensional diagrams that make it easier to visualise the theory?

The answer is to consider the consumer's choice between one particular good and a combination of *all other goods.* This combination is called a composite good. Therefore, in the diagrams, we measure units of good X on the horizontal axis and units of the composite good on the vertical axis.

A unit of the combined or composite good is defined so that the price is £1 per unit. This might seem a little strange but it means that the vertical axis not only measures units of the composite good, it now also measures the consumer's expenditure on *all other goods*. For example, if the consumer purchases 10 units of the composite good, they must also be spending £10 on *all other goods.*

Another useful implication of drawing the diagram this way is that the vertical axis can illustrate both the consumer's budget/income and their expenditure on good X. For example, in Figure 4.14, the intercept of the budget line on the vertical axis shows the total expenditure on *all other goods* when the consumer does not purchase any of good X (i.e. £100). Remember, we assume that the consumer spends all of their income – they do not save. Therefore, the intercept also shows that the consumer's total income/budget is £100.

At the optimum point *a*, in Figure 4.14, the consumer purchases 75 units of the composite good and Q_{X_1} units of good X. Unless the price of X is £1, the horizontal axis does not illustrate the expenditure on good X. However, if

Definition

Price–consumption curve A line showing how a person's optimum level of consumption of two goods changes as the price of one of the two goods changes (assuming that income and the price of the other good changes as income changes (assuming the prices of the good remain constant).

2 Strictly speaking, they are *gross* substitutes and complements as utility changes: i.e. consumers move onto a higher indifference curve. *Net* complements and substitutes occur where utility is held constant.

Figure 4.14 A composite good

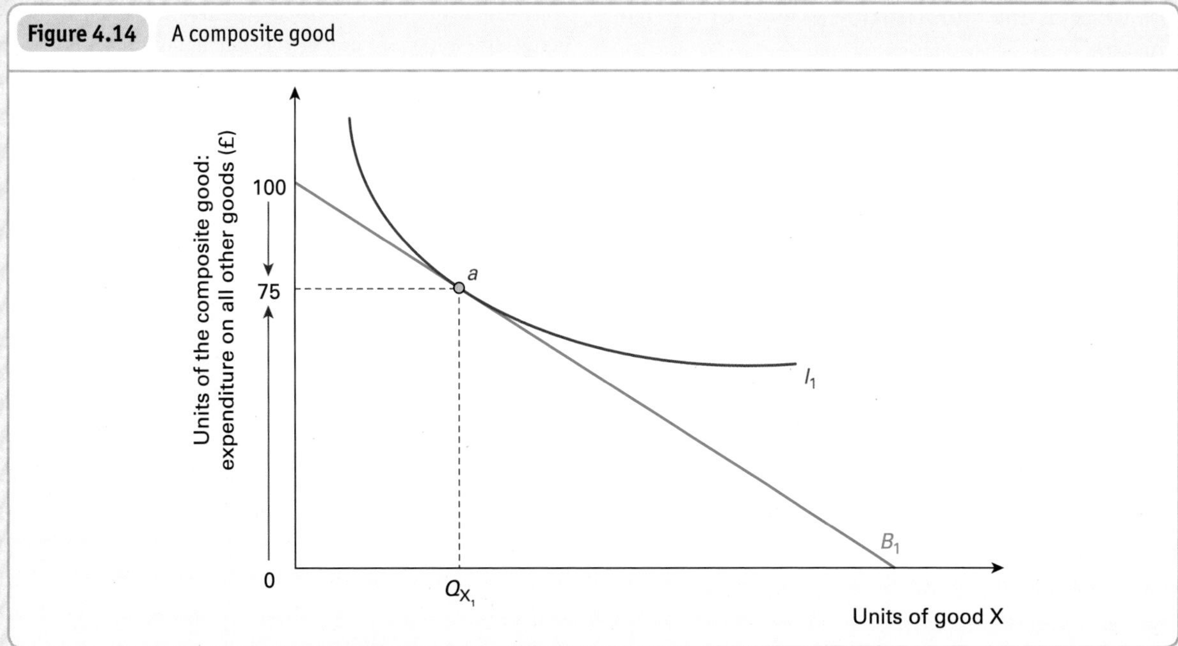

the consumer is spending £75 on *all other goods*, they must be spending £25 on good X. Travelling downwards along the vertical axis from the intercept tells us the consumer's expenditure on the good X.

Deriving the individual's demand curve

One useful application of a composite good is that it makes it possible to derive an individual consumer's demand curve from an indifference curve diagram.

Let us assume that we want to derive a person's demand curve for good X. We need to show the effect on the consumption of X of a change in the price of X assuming the prices of all other goods, tastes and money income remain constant. Plotting the quantity of the composite good and hence expenditure on all other goods on the vertical axis makes this possible. This is demonstrated in Figure 4.15.

We illustrate the changes in the price of X by pivoting the budget line at the point where it intersects the vertical axis. By pivoting the budget line at this point we are holding money income and the price of all other goods (the composite good) constant. It is then possible, by drawing a price–consumption line, to show the amount of X demanded at different prices of X, all other things equal. It is then a simple matter of transferring these price–quantity relationships on to a demand curve. In Figure 4.15, each of the points *a, b, c* and *d* on the demand curve in the lower part of the diagram corresponds to one of the four points on the price–consumption curve. P_1 is the price of good X along budget line B_1, P_2 is the price of good X along budget line B_2 and so on. (Note that P_2 is half of P_1, P_3 is one-third of P_1 and P_4 is one-quarter of P_1.)

Figure 4.15 Deriving the demand curve for good X from a price–consumption curve

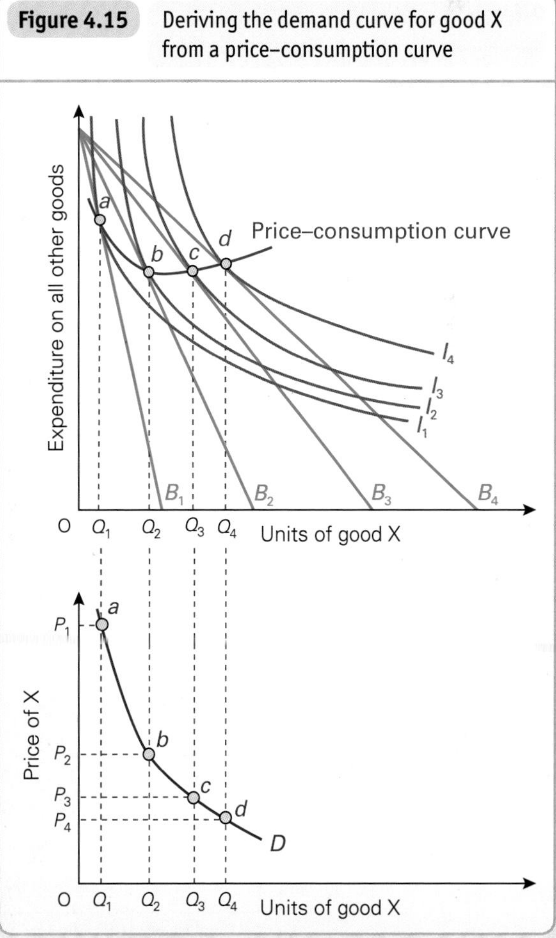

As quantity demanded increases from Q_1 *to* Q_2 *in Figure 4.15, the expenditure on all other goods decreases. (Point b is lower than point a.) This means, therefore, that the person's total expenditure on X has correspondingly increased. What, then, can we say about the person's price elasticity of demand for X between points a and b? What can we say about the price elasticity of demand between points b and c, and between points c and d?*

The income and substitution effects of a price change

In Chapter 2 we argued that when the price of a good rises, consumers will purchase less of it for two reasons:

KI 7 p36

- They cannot afford to buy so much. This is the ***income effect***.
- The good is now more expensive relative to other goods. Therefore consumers substitute alternatives for it. This is the ***substitution effect***.

We can extend our arguments from Chapter 2 by demonstrating the income and substitution effects with the use of indifference analysis. Let us start with the case of a normal good and show what happens when its price changes.

A normal good

In Figure 4.16 the price of ***normal good*** X has risen and the budget line has pivoted inwards from B_1 to B_2. The consumption point has moved from point *f* to point *h*. Part of this shift in consumption is due to the substitution effect and part is due to the income effect.

The substitution effect. To separate these two effects a new budget line is drawn, parallel to B_2 but tangential to the original indifference curve I_1. This is the line B_{1a}. Being parallel to B_2, it represents the new price ratio (i.e. the higher price of X). Being tangential to I_1, however, it enables the consumer to obtain the same utility as before: in other words, there is no loss in real income to the consumer. By focusing, then, on B_{1a}, which represents no change in real income, we have excluded the income effect. The movement from point *f* to point *g* is due purely to a change in the relative prices of X and Y. The movement from Q_{X_1} to Q_{X_2} is the negative substitution effect on good X. Note the substitution effect of the higher price of good X on the demand for good Y is positive – it increases from Q_{Y_1} to Q_{Y_2}. Good Y is now relatively cheaper.

The income effect. In reality, the budget line has shifted to B_2 and the consumer's optimum point (point *h*) is on a lower indifference curve I_2: real income has fallen. Thus, the movement from Q_{X_2} to Q_{X3} is the income effect on good X of the price increase.

In the case of a normal good, therefore, the income and substitution effects of a price change reinforce each other. They are both negative: they *both* involve a *reduction* in the quantity demanded as price *rises* (and vice versa).[3] The bigger the income and substitution effects, the higher will be the price elasticity of demand for good X.

3 It is important not to confuse the income effect of a price change with the simple effect on demand of an increase in income. In the latter case, a rise in income will cause a rise in demand for a normal good – a positive effect (and hence there will be a positive income elasticity of demand). In the case of a price reduction, although for a normal good the resulting rise in real income will still cause a rise in demand, it is in the opposite direction from the change in price – a negative effect with respect to price (and hence there will be a negative price elasticity of demand).

Definitions

Income effect of a price change That portion of the change in quantity demanded that results from the change in real income holding relative prices constant.

Substitution effect of a price change That portion of the change in quantity demanded that results from the change in the relative price of the good holding real income constant.

Normal good A good whose demand increases as income increases.

Figure 4.16 The income and substitution effects of a rise in the price of good X if X is a normal good

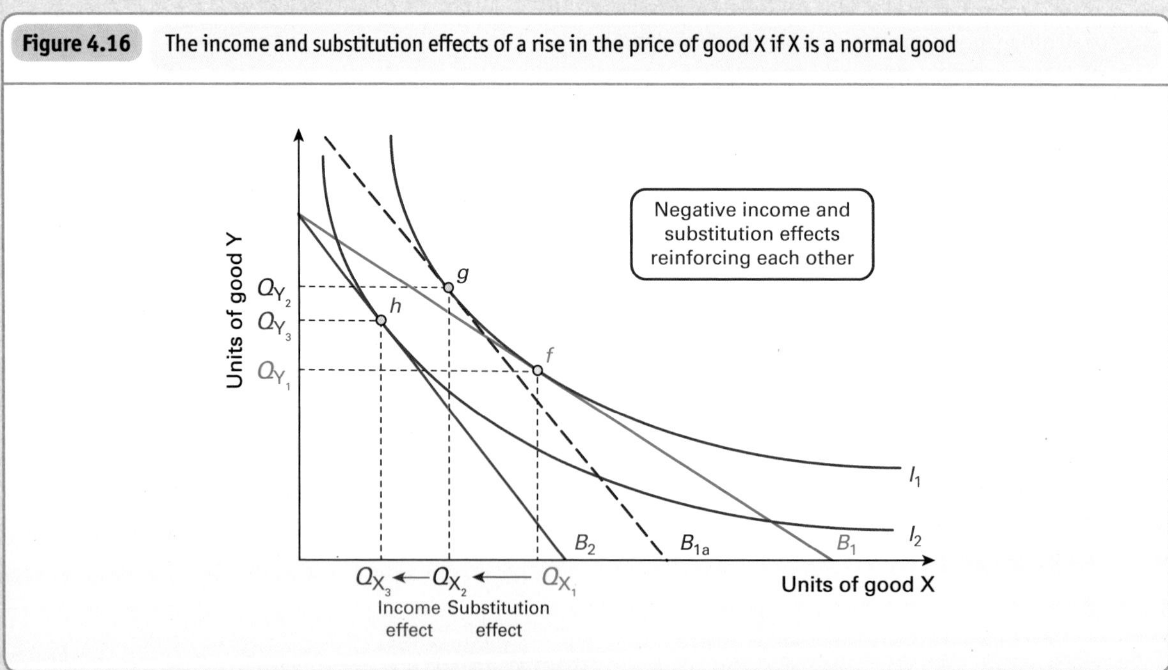

Note that good Y is also a normal good. Even though demand rises from Q_{Y_1} to Q_{Y_3} as people substitute Y for X, the fall in real income from the rise in the price of X leads to demand for Y not rising as far as Q_{Y_2} – an effective fall from Q_{Y_2} to Q_{Y_3}.

Illustrate on two separate indifference diagrams the income and substitution effects of the following:
(a) A decrease in the price of good X (and no change in the price of good Y).
(b) An increase in the price of good Y (and no change in the price of good X).

An inferior good

As we saw above, when people's incomes rise, they will buy less of ***inferior goods*** (e.g. value own-label supermarket brands), since they will now be able to afford better-quality goods instead (e.g. a premium own-label brands). Conversely, when their income falls, they will have to reduce their living standards: their consumption of inferior goods will thus rise.

The substitution effect. If the price of an inferior good (good X) rises, the substitution effect will be in the same direction as for a normal good: i.e. it will be negative. People will consume less X relative to Y, since X is now more expensive relative to Y. For example, if the price of inferior-quality margarine (good X) went up, people would tend to use better-quality margarine or butter (good Y) instead. This is illustrated in Figure 4.17 by a movement along the original indifference curve (I_1) from point *f* to point *g*. The quantity of X demanded falls from Q_{X_1} to Q_{X_2}.

The income effect. The income effect of the price rise of good X on the demand for X, however, will be the opposite of that for a normal good: it will be positive. The reduction in real income from the rise in the price of X will tend to *increase* the consumption of X, since with a fall in real income more inferior goods will now be purchased – including more X. Thus point *h* is to the right of point *g*: the income effect increases quantity back from Q_{X_2} to Q_{X_3} but does not outweigh the substitution effect.

Note that the income effect of the price rise of good X on the demand for good Y is negative. The demand for Y decreases from Q_{Y_2} to Q_{Y_3}, hence unlike X, good Y is a normal good. The income effect on Y outweighs the substitution effect, so, as the price of X increases, the demand for Y falls: i.e. they are complements.

A Giffen good: a particular type of inferior good

If the inferior good were to account for a very large proportion of a consumer's expenditure, a change in its price would have a significant effect on the consumer's real income, resulting in a large income effect. It is conceivable, therefore, that this large abnormal income effect could outweigh the normal substitution effect. In such a case, a rise in the price of X would lead to more X being consumed!

This is illustrated in Figure 4.18, where point *h* is to the *right* of point *f*. In other words, the fall in consumption (Q_{X_1} to Q_{X_2} as a result of the substitution effect is more than offset by the rise in consumption (Q_{X_2} to Q_{X_3}) as a result of the large positive income effect.

Definition

Inferior good A good whose demand decreases as income increases.

Figure 4.17 The income and substitution effects of a rise in the price of good X if X is an inferior (non-Giffen) good

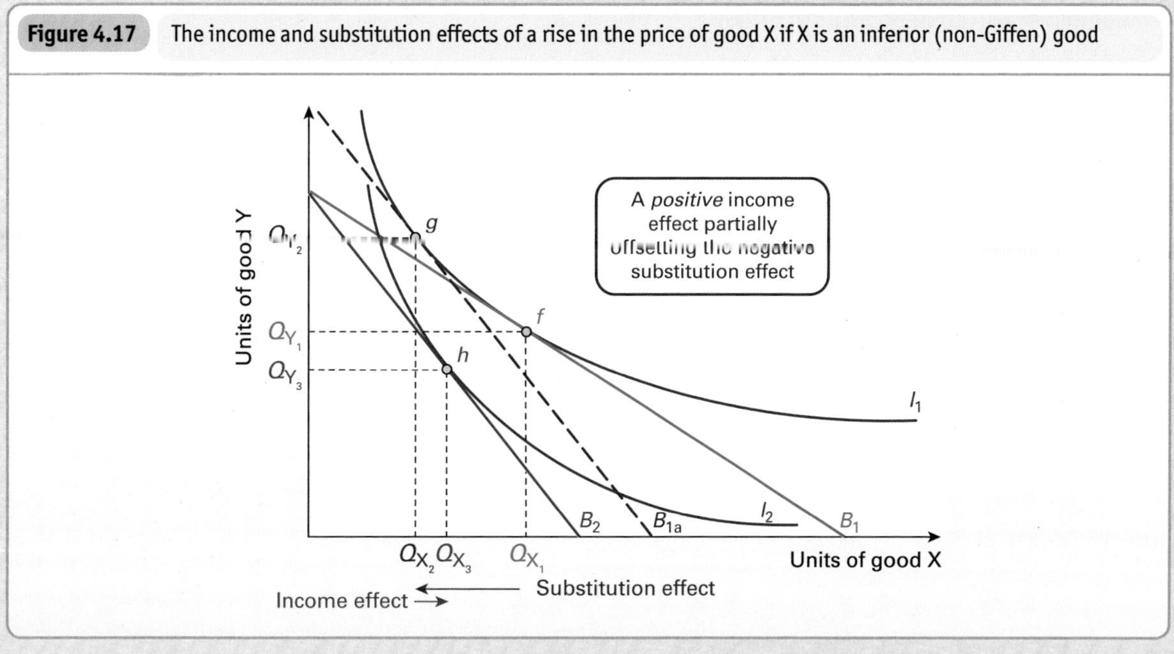

Figure 4.18 The income and substitution effects of a rise in the price of good X if X is a Giffen good

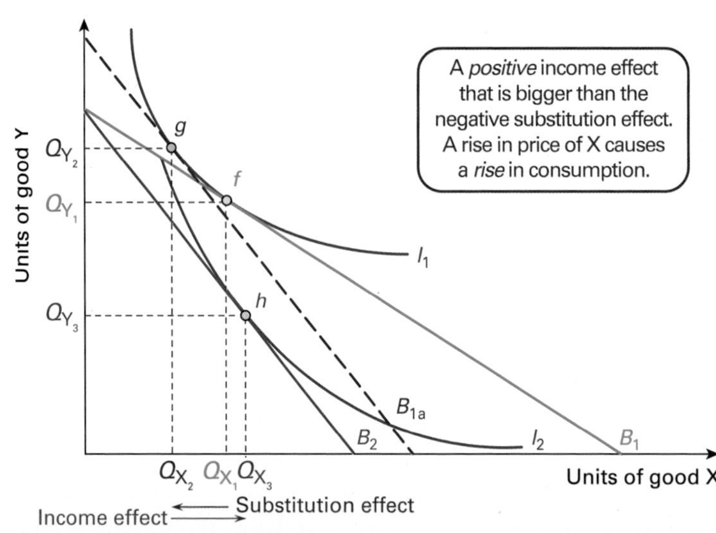

Such a good is known as a ***Giffen good***, after Sir Robert Giffen (1837–1910), who is alleged to have claimed that the consumption of bread by the poor rose when its price rose. Bread formed such a large proportion of poor people's consumption that, if its price went up, the poor could not afford to buy so much meat, vegetables, etc., and had to buy more bread instead. It is possible that in countries in Africa today with very low incomes, staple foods such as manioc (cassava) and maize are Giffen goods. (Box 4.5 discusses a possible example in China.) Naturally, such cases must be very rare indeed and some economists remain unconvinced of their existence, except as a theoretical possibility.

Definition

Giffen good An inferior good whose demand increases as its price increases as a result of a positive income effect larger than the normal negative substitution effect.

***BOX 4.5 GIFFEN GOODS VERSUS GIFFEN BEHAVIOUR** CASE STUDIES AND APPLICATIONS

Evidence of Giffen behaviour in China

A product where the positive income effect of a price rise is greater than the negative substitution effect is an example of a Giffen good. For this to occur for a staple food such as rice, bread or potatoes, consumers must:

- spend a large share of their income on the staple food: i.e. they are highly dependent on the staple food for their nutritional needs
- not be able to switch from consuming one staple food item to another, such as substituting bread for potatoes
- purchase other food items that are a more expensive source of calories.

This last point is important. If people do not consume a more expensive source of calories, they have nothing to switch away from if the price of the staple food rises.

Jensen and Miller (2008)[1] argue that the majority of people who consume staple food items in poorer countries are unlikely to meet all of these conditions. Therefore, the market demand curve will be downward sloping. However, they may be relevant for a subgroup of consumers in the market. Hence, rather than a Giffen good it is more appropriate to talk about the possibility of Giffen behaviour amongst a group of consumers of a particular good.

Case study from China

To test for evidence of Giffen behaviour, the researchers carried out a field experiment in Hunan, a province in the south of China. The households in the study completed a 'food recall' survey, where they had to list the different foods they had eaten in the previous 24 hours.

The responses indicated that most households were poor, as their diets were simple, comprising a few basic foods. In particular, average per capita consumption of rice made up 64 per cent of their daily calorie intake. This compared with just

8 per cent from wheat, 7 per cent from meat, 5 per cent from fruit/vegetables and 2 per cent from pulses. The evidence clearly shows that these households are highly dependent on rice for their nutritional needs.

As part of the research, randomly selected households received vouchers for a five-month period. These vouchers reduced the price of rice by a substantial amount – between 8 and 25 per cent. The authors could then estimate the price elasticity of demand for this staple food by comparing the demand for rice in the treatment groups with a control group where the households did not receive any vouchers.

Rather than just one overall price elasticity of demand figure, the researchers estimated figures for different subgroups. These subgroups were based upon the household's 'initial staple calorie share' (ISCS). This is the share of total calorie intake obtained from the consumption of rice. The results are shown in the table below.

	Subgroup 1 $0.6 \leq \text{ISCS} \leq 0.8$	Subgroup 2 $\text{ISCS} > 0.8$
Price elasticity of demand for rice	+0.640	−0.585

For those households who consume more than 80 per cent of their total calories from rice, the price elasticity of demand for rice is negative. In other words, when the price of rice increases their demand falls. For them, rice is thus a normal good and they are not exhibiting Giffen behaviour. These people are so poor that they effectively only consume rice and do not have enough income to purchase more expensive sources of calories such as meat. When the price of rice increases, all other things equal, they have no choice but to purchase less.

However, for those households who consume between 60 and 80 per cent of their calories from rice, the price elasticity of demand for rice is *positive*. When the price of rice increases, these households purchase more; they exhibit Giffen behaviour. These people are poor but can initially afford to purchase other food items, such as meat or cheese, that are a more expensive source of calories. When the price of rice increases, it considerably reduces their purchasing power. This means they can no longer afford to buy the more expensive food items and are left with no option but to consume more calories from rice.

Could you conceive of any circumstances in which one or more items of your expenditure could become an example of Giffen behaviour? Apply the same analysis to an elderly couple on a state pension.

1 Robert T Jensen and Nolan H Miller, 'Giffen behaviour and subsistence consumption', *American Economic Review*, Vol. 98, No. 4 (2008), pp. 1553–77.

Drawing an indifference curve diagram that illustrates Giffen behaviour can be difficult. Given that the substitution effect of the price change must be relatively small, how do you draw the indifference curves: i.e. how bowed in towards the origin should they be?

The usefulness of indifference analysis

Indifference analysis has made it possible to demonstrate the logic of 'rational' consumer choice, the derivation of the individual's demand curve, and the income and substitution effects of a price change. All this has been done without having to measure utility.

Nevertheless there are limitations to the usefulness of indifference analysis:

- In practice, it is virtually impossible to derive indifference curves, since it would involve a consumer having to imagine a whole series of different combinations of goods and deciding in each case whether a given combination gave more, equal or less satisfaction than other combinations.
- Consumers may not behave 'rationally', and hence may not give careful consideration to the satisfaction they believe they will gain from consuming goods. They may behave impetuously.
- Indifference curves are based on the satisfaction that consumers believe they will gain from a good. This belief may well be influenced by advertising. Consumers may be disappointed or pleasantly surprised, however, when they actually consume the good. In other words, consumers are not perfectly knowledgeable. Thus the 'optimum consumption' point may not in practice give consumers maximum satisfaction for their money.

- Certain goods are purchased only now and again, and then only one at a time. Examples would include consumer durables such as cars, televisions and washing machines. Indifference curves are based on the assumption that marginal increases in one good can be traded off against marginal decreases in another. This will not be the case with consumer durables.

*BOX 4.6 CONSUMER THEORY: A FURTHER APPROACH

EXPLORING ECONOMICS

Characteristics theory

Characteristics theory was developed in the mid-1960s by Kelvin Lancaster. He argued that people demand goods not for their own sake, but for the characteristics they possess.

Take cars, for example. When choosing between the different makes, consumers do not just consider their relative prices, they also consider their attributes: comfort, style, performance, durability, reliability, fuel consumption, etc. It is these characteristics that give rise to utility.

Characteristics theory, then, is based on four crucial assumptions:

- All goods possess various characteristics.
- Different brands possess them in different proportions.
- The characteristics are measurable: they are 'objective'.
- The characteristics (along with price and income) determine consumer choice.

Let us assume that you are choosing between three different goods or brands of a good (e.g. a foodstuff). Each one has a different combination of two characteristics (e.g. protein and calories). Your choices can be shown graphically.

The choice between brands of a product: each brand has different characteristics

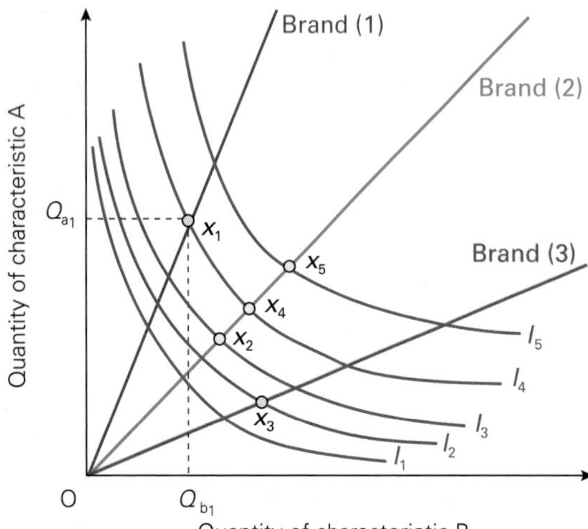

The levels of two characteristics are shown on the two axes. An indifference map can be constructed, showing the different combinations of the two characteristics that yield given levels of utility. Thus any combination of the two characteristics along indifference curve I_4 in the diagram gives a higher level of utility than those along I_3, and so on. The shape of the indifference curves (bowed in) illustrates a diminishing marginal rate of substitution between the two characteristics.

The amounts of the two characteristics given by the three brands are shown by the three rays. The more that is consumed of each brand, the further up the respective ray will the consumer be. Thus at x_1, the consumer is gaining Q_{a1} of characteristic A and Q_{b1} of characteristic B.

Assume that, for the same money, the consumer could consume at x_1 with brand (1), x_2 with brand (2) and x_3 with brand (3). The consumer will consume brand (1): x_1 is on a higher indifference curve than x_2 or x_3.

Now assume that the price of brand (2) falls. For a given expenditure, the consumer can now move up the brand (2) ray. But not until the price has fallen enough to allow consumption at point x_4 will the consumer consider switching from brand (1). If price falls enough for consumption to be at point x_5, clearly the consumer will switch.

The characteristics approach has a number of advantages over conventional indifference curve analysis in explaining consumer behaviour.

- It helps to explain brand loyalty. When price changes, people will not necessarily gradually move from one brand to another. Rather they will stick with a brand until a critical price is reached. Then they will switch brands all at once.
- It allows the choice between several goods to be shown on the same diagram. Each good or brand has its own ray.
- It helps to explain the nature of substitute goods. The closer substitutes are, the more similar will be their characteristics and hence the closer will be their rays. The closer the rays, the more likely it is that there will be a shift in consumption to one good when the price of the other good changes.
- A change in the quality of a good can be shown by rotating its ray.

There are weaknesses with the approach, however:

- Some characteristics cannot be measured. Such characteristics as beauty, taste and entertainment value are subjective: they are in the mind of the consumer.
- Only two characteristics can be plotted. Most goods have several characteristics.

1. *Make a list of the characteristics of shoes. Which are 'objective' and which are 'subjective'?*
2. *If two houses had identical characteristics, except that one was near a noisy airport and the other was in a quiet location, and if the market price of the first house were £280 000 and that of the second £300 000, how would that help us to put a value on the characteristic of peace and quiet?*

Choose three different products that you purchase. What characteristics of these products enable you to choose between different brands? How might your preferences be used by manufacturers in designing new versions of these products? Compare your answers with those of other members of your class or group.

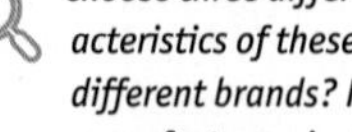

Characteristics theory is examined in more detail in Case Study 4.7 on the student website.

Section summary

1. The indifference approach to analysing consumer demand avoids having to measure utility.
2. An indifference curve shows all those combinations of two goods that give an equal amount of satisfaction to a consumer. An indifference map can be drawn with indifference curves further to the north-east representing higher (but still unspecified) levels of satisfaction.
3. Indifference curves are usually drawn convex to the origin. This is because of a diminishing marginal rate of substitution between the two goods. As more of one good is purchased, the consumer is willing to give up less and less of the other for each additional unit of the first. The marginal rate of substitution is given by the slope of the indifference curve, which equals MU_X/MU_Y.
4. A budget line can be drawn on an indifference diagram. A budget line shows all those combinations of the two goods that can be purchased for a given amount of money, assuming a constant price of the two goods. The slope of the budget line depends on the relative price of the two goods. The slope is equal to P_X/P_Y.
5. The consumer will achieve the maximum level of satisfaction for a given income (budget) by consuming at the point where the budget line just touches the highest possible indifference curve. At this point of tangency, the budget line and the indifference curve have the same slope. Thus $MU_X/MU_Y = P_X/P_Y$, which is the 'equi-marginal principle' for maximising utility from a given income that was established in section 4.1.
6. If the consumer's real income (and hence budget) rises, there will be a parallel outward shift of the budget line. The 'rational' consumer will move to the point of tangency of this new budget line with the highest indifference curve. The line that traces out these optimum positions for different levels of income is known as the 'income–consumption curve'.
7. If the price of one of the two goods changes, the budget line will pivot on the axis of the other good. An outward pivot represents a fall in price; an inward pivot represents an increase in price. The line that traces the tangency points of these budget lines with the appropriate indifference curves is called a 'price–consumption curve'.
8. By measuring the expenditure on all other goods on the vertical axis and by holding their price constant and money income constant, a demand curve can be derived for the good measured on the horizontal axis. Changes in its price can be represented by pivoting the budget line. The effect on the quantity demanded can be found from the resulting price–consumption curve.
9. The effect of a change in price on quantity demanded can be divided into an income and a substitution effect. The substitution effect is the result of a change in relative prices alone. The income effect is the result of the change in real income alone.
10. For a normal good, the income and substitution effects of a price rise will both be negative and will reinforce each other. With an inferior good, the substitution effect will still be negative but the income effect will be positive and thus will to some extent offset the substitution effect. If the good is 'very' inferior and the (positive) income effect is bigger than the (negative) substitution effect, it is called a Giffen good. A rise in the price of a Giffen good will thus cause a rise in the quantity demanded.
11. Indifference analysis, although avoiding having to measure utility, nevertheless has limitations. Indifference curves are difficult to derive in practice; consumers may not behave rationally; the 'optimum' consumption point may not be optimum if the consumer lacks knowledge of the good; indifference curves will not be smooth for items where single units each account for a large proportion of income.

END OF CHAPTER QUESTIONS

1. Imagine that you had £10 per month to allocate between two goods, A and B. Imagine that good A cost £2 per unit and good B cost £1 per unit. Imagine also that the utilities of the two goods are those set out in the table below. (Note that the two goods are not substitutes for each other, so that the consumption of one does not affect the utility gained from the other.)
   (a) What would be the marginal utility ratio (MU_A/MU_B) for the following combinations of the two goods: (i) 1A, 8B; (ii) 2A, 6B; (iii) 3A, 4B; (iv) 4A, 2B? (Each combination would cost £10.)
   (b) Show that where the marginal utility ratio (MU_A/MU_B) equals the price ratio (P_A/P_B), total utility is maximised.
   (c) If the two goods were substitutes for each other, why would it not be possible to construct a table like the one given here?

The utility gained by a person from various quantities of two goods: A and B

Good A			Good B		
Units per month	*MU* (utils)	*TU* (utils)	Units per month	*MU* (utils)	*TU* (utils)
0	–	0.0	0	–	0.0
1	11.0	11.0	1	8.0	8.0
2	8.0	19.0	2	7.0	15.0
3	6.0	25.0	3	6.5	21.5
4	4.5	29.5	4	5.0	26.5
5	3.0	32.5	5	4.5	31.0
			6	4.0	35.0
			7	3.5	38.5
			8	3.0	41.5
			9	2.6	44.1
			10	2.3	46.4

(continued)

2. Is it reasonable to assume that people seek to equate the marginal utility/price ratios of the goods that they purchase, if (a) they have never heard of 'utility', let alone 'marginal utility'; (b) marginal utility cannot be measured in any absolute way?
3. Consider situations where you might think about swapping items with someone. Why are such situations relatively rare? Can you think of circumstances in which this might be more common?
4. Explain why the price of a good is no reflection of the total value that consumers put on it.
*5. Sketch a person's indifference map for two goods X and Y. Mark the optimum consumption point. Now illustrate the following (you might need to draw a separate diagram for each):
   (a) A rise in the price of good X, but no change in the price of good Y.
   (b) A shift in the person's tastes from good Y to good X.
   (c) A fall in the person's income and a fall in the price of good Y, with the result that the consumption of Y remains constant (but that of X falls).
*6. Distinguish between a normal good, an inferior good and a Giffen good. Use indifference curves to illustrate your answer.
*7. Assume that commuters regard bus journeys as an inferior good and car journeys as a normal good. Using indifference curves, show how (a) a rise in incomes and (b) a fall in bus fares will affect the use of these two modes of transport. How could people's tastes be altered so that bus journeys were no longer regarded as an inferior good? If tastes were altered in this way, what effect would it have on the indifference curves?

Online resources

Additional case studies on the student website

4.1 Bentham and the philosophy of utilitarianism. This looks at the historical and philosophical underpinning of the ideas of utility maximisation.

4.2 Utility under attack. This looks at the birth of indifference analysis, which was seen as a means of overcoming the shortcomings of marginal utility analysis.

4.3 Applying indifference curve analysis to taxes on goods. Assume that the government wants to raise extra revenue from an expenditure tax. Should it put a relatively small extra tax on all goods, or a relatively large one on just certain selected goods?

4.4 Love and caring. An illustration of how rational choice behaviour can be extended to family behaviour.

4.5 Income and substitution effects: the Slutsky approach. This looks at an alternative way of using indifference analysis to analyse income and substitution effects.

4.6 Deriving an Engel curve. Income elasticity of demand and the income–consumption curve.

4.7 The characteristics approach to analysing consumer demand. This is an extension of the analysis of Box 4.6.

Maths Case 4.1 Finding the optimum consumption point: Part 1. This case looks at how the utility maximisation point can be discovered with a Cobb–Douglas utility function with given prices and a given budget constraint.

Maths Case 4.2 Finding the optimum consumption point: Part 2. This case uses the Lagrange method to solve the same problem as in Maths Case 4.1.

Websites relevant to this chapter

See sites listed at the end of Chapter 5 on page 152.

3 for 2 on longer lasting

Chapter 5

Consumer Behaviour in an Uncertain World

CHAPTER MAP

In this chapter, we extend the rational choice model to examine situations where consumers are uncertain about the size of the costs and benefits of their choices. We then examine the possibility that they make systematic mistakes and fail to make decisions that maximise their own self-interest.

When we buy goods or services there is often the risk that the benefits will not turn out as we had expected. The quality may be poorer or the good may not last as long as we had anticipated. In section 5.1 we look at consumption decisions when consumers are faced with uncertainty. We also look at how rational consumers may take out insurance to safeguard against uncertainty and at how the firms providing insurance may behave.

In section 5.2 we examine the possibility that consumers may lack both the time and processing ability to deal effectively with all the relevant information. In these situations, consumers may revert to using mental short-cuts, often referred to as 'heuristics'. Although these sometimes prove to be an effective method of dealing with complex problems, their use can also result in people making systematic errors. Consumers may also code potential benefits and costs as either separate gains or losses, rather than assessing their effect on their overall income/wealth. There is evidence that the outcomes coded as losses appear to cause far greater levels of discomfort than the pleasure associated with an equivalent sized gain. People also seem to overweight the immediate costs/benefits of a decision.

5.1 DEMAND UNDER CONDITIONS OF RISK AND UNCERTAINTY

The problem of imperfect information

In the previous chapter, we assumed that when we buy a good or service, we know the price and how much value we put on it. In many cases this is a reasonable assumption. When you buy a bar of chocolate, you know how much you are paying for it and have a good idea how much you will like it. But what about a mobile phone, or a car, or a laptop, or any other ***consumer durable***? In each of these cases you are buying something that will last you a long time, and the further into the future you look, the less certain you can be of its costs and benefits to you.

Take the example of purchasing a tablet computer that costs £300. If you pay cash, your immediate outlay involves no uncertainty: it is £300. But the computer can break down. In 12 months' time you could face a repair bill of £100. This is impossible to predict and yet it is a price you will have to pay, just like the original £300. In other words, when you buy the tablet computer, you are uncertain as to the full 'price' you will have to pay over its lifetime.

KEY IDEA 15

Good decision making requires good information. **Where information is poor, decisions and their outcomes are also likely to be poor.**

If the costs of the tablet computer are uncertain, so too are the benefits. You might have been attracted in the first place by the description in an online advert or at a shop. Once you have used the tablet for a while, however, you might discover things you had not anticipated. Perhaps it takes longer than you had anticipated to boot up, or to connect to the Internet or to run various types of software/games.

Buying consumer durables thus involves uncertainty. So too does the purchase of assets, whether a physical asset such as a house or financial assets such as shares. In the case of assets, the uncertainty is over their future *price*. If you buy shares in a company, what will happen to the price? Will it shoot up, thus enabling you to sell them at a large profit, or will it fall? You cannot know for certain.

The problems surrounding making decisions today based on expectations of the future are explored in Threshold Concept 9.

Definition

Consumer durable A consumer good that lasts a period of time, during which the consumer can continue gaining utility from it.

THRESHOLD CONCEPT 9 PEOPLE'S ACTIONS DEPEND ON THEIR EXPECTATIONS

THINKING LIKE AN ECONOMIST

Many, if not most, economic actions are taken before the benefits are enjoyed. You work first and get paid at the end of the month; you buy something in a shop today, and consume it later. In the case of a bar of chocolate, you may consume it fairly soon and pretty well all at once, in the case of many 'consumer durables', such as electrical goods, you will enjoy them over a much longer period.

It is the same with firms. What they produce today will be sold at some point in the future. In other words, firms typically incur costs first and receive revenues later. In the case of investing in new buildings or equipment, it may be a very long time before the firm starts seeing profits from the investment.

In each of these cases, then, the decision is made to do something now in anticipation of what will happen in the future. The threshold concept here is that decision making is only as good as the information on which it is based. If your expectations turn out to be wrong, a seemingly good decision may turn out disastrously. Part of what we do as economists is to examine how people get information and on what basis they form their expectations; part of what we do is to forecast the future.

When information about the future is imperfect, as it nearly always will be, there are risks involved in basing decisions on such information. Businesses constantly have to live with risk: risk that market prices will decline, that costs will rise, that machinery will break down, that competitors will launch new products, and so on. But in our everyday lives, we too face risks because of poor information about the future. Do you spend money on a holiday in this country and risk having a wet week? Do you go to the cinema to see a film, only to find out that you don't enjoy it?

Sometimes you lack information simply because you have not taken the time or paid the money to acquire it. This could apply to the specifications of a product. A little research could give you the information you require. Sometimes, however, the information is simply not available – at least not in the form that will give you certainty. A firm may do market research to find out what consumers want, but until a product is launched, it will not be certain how much will be sold. A market analyst may give you a forecast of what will happen to stock market prices or to the dollar/euro exchange rate, but analysts frequently get it wrong.

1. *What risks are involved in buying the latest version of the iPhone? Compare these with the risks of buying a house.*
2. *Give some examples of ways in which it is possible to buy better information. Your answer should suggest that there is profitable business to be made in supplying information.*
3. *Is there a role for government intervention in the provision of information? (We return to this in Chapter 12).*

Attitudes towards risk and uncertainty

So how will uncertainty affect people's behaviour? The answer is that it depends on their attitudes towards taking a gamble. To examine these attitudes let us assume that people do at least know the chances involved when taking a gamble (i.e. they know the exact *probabilities* of different outcomes occurring). In other words, they operate under conditions of risk rather than uncertainty.

KI 11 p72

Explain the difference between 'risk' and 'uncertainty' (see Chapter 2, page 72).

Consider the following example. Imagine that as a student you only have £105 left to spend out of your student loan and have no other income or savings. You are thinking of buying an instant lottery ticket/scratch card. The lottery ticket costs £5 and there is a 1 in 10 or 10 per cent chance that it will be a winning ticket. A winning ticket pays a prize of £50. Would you buy the lottery ticket? This will depend on your attitude towards risk.

In order to explain people's attitude towards risk it is important to understand the concept of expected value. The ***expected value*** of a gamble is the amount the person would earn on average if the gamble was repeated on many occasions. To calculate the expected value of a gamble you simply multiply each possible outcome by the probability that outcome will occur. You then simply add these values together.

In our example, the gamble has only two possible outcomes – you purchase a winning ticket or a losing ticket. There is a 10 per cent chance it is a winning ticket, which will give you a total of £150 to spend (£100 left out of your loan after you have purchased the ticket plus a £50 prize). There is a 90 per cent chance it is a losing ticket, in which case you will only have £100 left to spend out of your student loan. Therefore, the expected value of this gamble is:

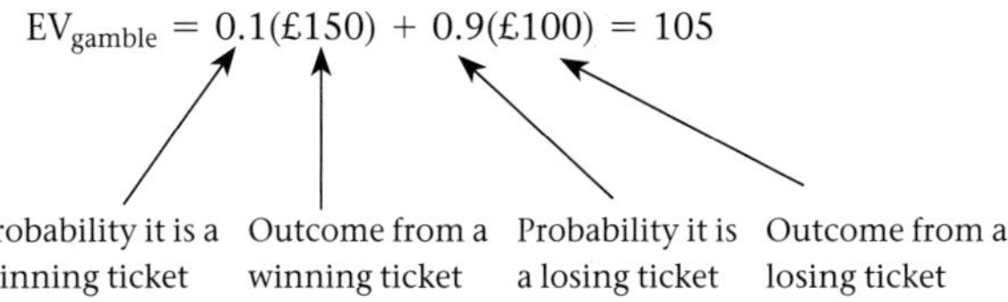

If you do not purchase the ticket, you will have £105 to spend for sure.

$$EV_{no\ gamble} = 1(105) = 105$$

There are three possible categories of attitude towards risk.

Risk neutral. If people are risk neutral, they will always choose the option with the highest expected value. Therefore, in this example, a student who is risk neutral would be indifferent between buying or not buying the instant lottery ticket, as each outcome has the same expected value of £105.

Risk averse. If people are risk averse, they will never choose a gamble if it has the same expected value as a certain pay-off. Therefore, a student who is risk averse would definitely not buy the instant lottery ticket.

It is too simplistic, however, to say that a risk-averse person will never take risks. Such a person may choose a gamble if it has a greater expected value than a certain pay-off. If the probability of purchasing a winning instant lottery ticket in the previous example was 20 per cent instead of 10 per cent, then a risk-averse student might buy the ticket, as the expected value of the gamble (£110) is greater than the certain pay-off (£105).

Whether or not risk-averse people do take gambles depends on the strength of their aversion to risk, which will vary from one individual to another. The greater people's level of risk aversion, the greater the expected value of a gamble they are willing to give up in order to obtain a certain pay-off.

The certain amount of money that gives a person the same utility as the gamble is known as the gamble's ***certainty equivalent***. The more risk averse people are, the lower their certainty equivalent of a gamble. The expected value of a gamble minus a person's certainty equivalent of that gamble is called the ***risk premium***. The more risk averse people are, the greater their positive risk premium.

Risk loving. If people are risk loving they would always choose a gamble if it had the same expected value as the pay-off from not taking the gamble. Therefore, a risk-loving student would definitely purchase the lottery ticket.

Once again, it is too simplistic to say that risk-loving people will always choose a gamble. They may choose a certain-pay-off if it has a higher expected value than the gamble. For a risk-loving person the certainty equivalent of a gamble is greater than its expected value. For example, if the probability of purchasing a winning instant lottery ticket in the previous example was 1 per cent instead of 10 per cent, then even a risk-loving student might choose not to buy the ticket. It would depend on the extent to which that person enjoyed taking risks. The more risk loving people are, the greater the return from a certain pay-off they are willing to sacrifice in order to take a gamble. Because the certainty equivalent of a gamble is greater than its expected value the risk premium is negative.

1. *What is the expected value of the above lottery ticket gamble if the chances of purchasing a winning ticket with a prize of £50 are 30 per cent? How much of the expected value of the gamble are risk-averse*

Definitions

Expected value The long-run average value of a random variable. It is calculated by taking the sum of each possible value of the random variable multiplied by the probability it will occur.

Certainty equivalent The guaranteed amount of money that an individual would view as equally desirable as the expected value of a gamble. Where a person is risk averse, the certainty equivalent is less than the expected value.

Risk premium The expected value of a gamble minus a person's certainty equivalent.

people willing to sacrifice if they decide against purchasing the ticket? If they were indifferent between purchasing and not purchasing the ticket, what is their certainty equivalent and risk premium of the gamble?

2. *What is the expected value of the lottery ticket gamble if the chances of purchasing a winning ticket are 1 per cent? How much of the certain pay-off are risk-loving people willing to sacrifice if they decide to purchase the lottery ticket? If they were indifferent between purchasing and not purchasing the ticket what is their certainty equivalent and risk premium of the gamble?*

Diminishing marginal utility of income and attitudes towards risk taking

Avid gamblers may be risk lovers. People who spend lots of money on various online betting websites or at the race track may enjoy the thrill of taking a risk, knowing that there is always the chance that they might win. On average, however, such people will lose. After all, the bookmakers have to take their cut and thus the odds they offer are generally unfavourable.

Most people, however, are risk averse most of the time. We prefer to avoid insecurity. But is there a simple reason for this? Economists use marginal utility analysis to explain why.

They argue that the gain in utility to people from an extra £100 is less than the loss of utility from forgoing £100. Imagine your own position. You have probably adjusted your standard of living to your income, or are trying to do so. If you unexpectedly gained £100 that would be very nice: you could buy some new clothes or have a meal out. But if you lost £100, you might have serious difficulties in making ends meet. Thus if you were offered the gamble of a 50:50 chance of winning or losing £100, you might well decline the gamble.

Which gamble would you be more likely to accept, a 60:40 chance of gaining or losing £10 000, or a 50:50 chance of gaining or losing £1? Explain why.

This risk-averse behaviour accords with the principle of *diminishing marginal utility*. In the previous chapter we focused on the utility from the consumption of individual goods: Lucy and her cups of tea; Ollie and his packets of crisps. In the case of each individual good, the more we consume, the less satisfaction we gain from each additional unit: the marginal utility falls. But the same principle applies if we look at our *total* consumption. The higher our level of total consumption, the less additional satisfaction will be gained from each additional £1 spent.

What we are saying here is that there is a ***diminishing marginal utility of income***. The more you earn, the lower will be the utility gained from each *extra* £1. If a person on £15 000 per year earned an extra £1000, they will feel much happier: their marginal utility from that income will be relatively very high. If people already earning £500 000 per year earned an extra £1000, however, their gain in utility will be far less.

Do you think that this provides a moral argument for redistributing income from the rich to the poor? Does it prove that income should be so redistributed?

Why, then, does a diminishing marginal utility of income make us risk averse? The answer is illustrated in Figure 5.1, which shows the *total* utility you get from your income.

The slope of this curve gives the *marginal* utility of your income. As the marginal utility of income diminishes, so the curve gets flatter. Assume that you experiences 70 units or utils of pleasure from spending £5000 on the goods you like. This is shown at point *a* on Figure 5.1.

If your income now rises from £5000 to £10 000 your total utility increases by 30 utils, from 70 to 100 utils. This is shown as the movement along the total utility curve from point *a* to point *b*. A similar rise in income from £10 000 to £15 000 leads to a move from point *b* to point *c*. This time, however, total utility has increased by only 16 utils, from 100 to 116 utils. Marginal utility has diminished.

Now assume that your income is £10 000 and you are offered the following gamble: a 50:50 chance of gaining an extra £5000 or losing £5000. Effectively, then, you have an equal chance of your income rising to £15 000 or falling to £5000. The expected value of the gamble is £10 000 – the same as the pay-off from not taking the gamble.

At an income of £10 000, your total utility is 100. If your gamble pays off and increases your income to £15 000, your total utility will rise to 116: i.e. an increase of 16. If it does not pay off, you will be left with only £5000 and a utility of 70 utils: i.e. a decrease of 30. Therefore, you have a 50:50 chance of experiencing either 116 or 70 utils of pleasure. Your *average* or expected utility will be $(116 + 70)/2 = 93$ utils – less than the 100 utils from not taking the gamble.

This point can be illustrated on Figure 5.1 by drawing a straight line or chord between points *a* and *c*. Points along this chord represent all the possible weighted averages of the utility at point *a* and point *c*. In this example, because the probability is 50:50, expected utility is represented half-way along the chord at point *e*. As you can see from the *TU* curve, the expected utility from the gamble is the same as the utility experienced from receiving £8000 for certain (point *d*). This is the certainty equivalent of the gamble.

The risk premium is £2000: i.e. the expected value of £10 000 minus the certainty equivalent of £8000. In other words, £10 000 for certain provides greater utility than the gamble. In the case illustrated in Figure 5.1, you always prefer a certain pay-off as long as it is greater than £8000. Hence risk aversion is part of rational utility-maximising behaviour.

Definition

Diminishing marginal utility of income Where each additional pound earned yields less additional utility than the previous pound.

Figure 5.1 The total utility of income

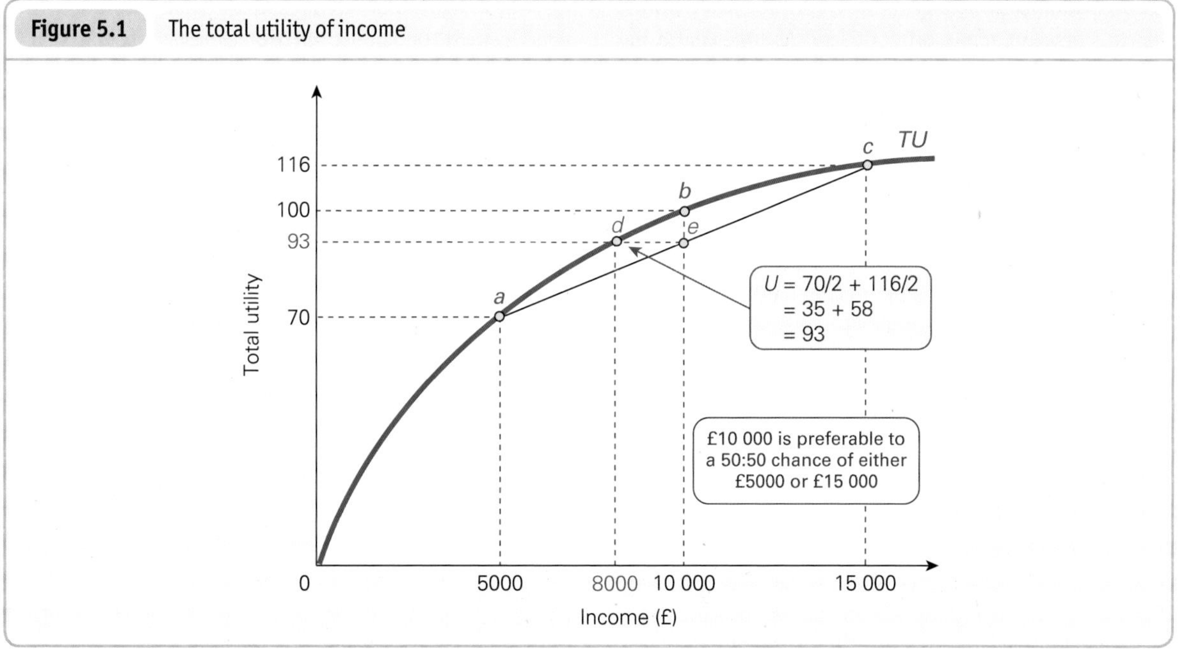

If people are generally risk averse, why do so many around the world take part in national lotteries?

Most of the time we do not know the exact chances involved of taking a gamble. In other words, we operate under conditions of *uncertainty*. We often have to make judgements about what we think are the different likelihoods of various outcomes occurring. There is evidence that in some circumstances people are not very good at making probabilistic judgements and are prone to making systematic errors. This is discussed in more detail in section 5.2 (see pages 141–4).

Insurance: a way of removing risks

Insurance is the opposite of gambling. It removes the risk. For example, every day you take the risk that you will either lose your mobile phone or drop and break it. In either case you will have to incur the cost of purchasing a new handset to replace it. Alternatively, you can remove the risk by taking out an appropriate insurance policy that pays out the cost of a new handset if the original one gets lost or broken.

Given that many people are risk averse, they may be prepared to pay a premium for an insurance policy even though it will leave them with less than the expected value of not buying the insurance and taking the gamble. The total premiums paid to the insurance companies, and hence the revenue generated, will be *more* than the amount the insurance companies pay out: that is, after all, how such companies make a profit.

But does this mean that the insurance companies are less risk averse than their customers? Why is it that the insurance companies are prepared to shoulder the risks that their customers were not? The answer is that the insurance company is able to ***spread its risks***.

The spreading of risks

Take the following simple example. Assume you have £100 000 worth of assets (i.e. savings, car, property, etc.). You drive your car to school/university every day and there is a 1 in 20 (or 5 per cent) chance that at some point during the year you will be responsible for an accident that results in your car being a write-off. Assume the market value of the car is currently £20 000 and remains unchanged for the following 12 months. The expected value of taking the gamble for the year (i.e. not purchasing comprehensive car insurance) is 0.95(100 000) + 0.05(80 000) = £99 000.

If you are risk averse you would be willing to pay more than an additional £1000 to purchase a fully comprehensive car insurance policy that covers you for a year. For example, you may be willing to pay £1100 (over and above a simple third-party insurance) for an annual policy that pays out the full £20 000 if you have the accident and are responsible for it. Having paid the extra £1100 out of your total assets of £100 000, you would be left with £98 900 for sure. If you are risk averse, this may give you a higher level of utility than not purchasing the insurance and taking the gamble that you do not have an accident where your car is a write-off and you are responsible.

Definition

Spreading risks (for an insurance company) The more policies an insurance company issues and the more independent the risks of claims from these policies are, the more predictable will be the number of claims.

The insurance company, however, is not just insuring you. It is insuring many other drivers. Assume that it has many customers with exactly the same assets as you and facing the same 5 per cent risk every year of causing an accident that results in their car being a write-off. As the number of its customers increases, the outcome each year will become much closer to its expected or average value. Therefore, the insurance company can predict with increasing confidence that, on average, 5 out of every 100 of its customers will cause an accident every year and make a claim on their own insurance for £20 000, while the other 95 out of every 100 will not cause an accident and so not make a claim on their insurance for their own car.

This means that the insurance company will pay out £100 000 in such claims for every 100 of its customers. This works out as an average pay-out of £1000 per customer. If each customer is willing to pay £1100 extra for such a policy, by charging that amount the insurance company will generate more in revenue from its customers than it is paying out in claims. Assuming that the administrative costs of providing each policy per customer is less than £100, the insurance company can make a profit.

This is an application of the ***law of large numbers***. What is unpredictable for an individual becomes highly predictable in the mass. The more people the insurance company insures, the more predictable the final outcome becomes. In other words, an insurance company will be able to convert your *uncertainty* into their *risk*.

In reality, people taking out insurance will not all have the same income and the same chances of having an accident. However, using statistical data the insurance company will be able to work out the average chances of an event occurring for people in similar situations. Basing premiums on average chances can, however, create some problems for the insurance company, which will be discussed later in the chapter.

The independence of risks

The spreading of risks does not just require that there should be a large number of policies. It also requires the risks to be ***independent***. This means that if one person makes a claim it does not increase the chances of another person making a claim too. If the risks are independent in the previous example, then if one person has a car accident the chances of another person having a car accident remain unchanged at 5 per cent.

Now imagine a different example. If an insurance company insured 1000 houses *all in the same neighbourhood*, and then there were a major fire in the area, the claims would be enormous. The risks of fire would *not* be independent – if one house catches fire, it increases the chances of the surrounding houses catching fire. If, however, a company provided fire insurance for houses scattered all over the country, the risks *would be* independent.

1. *Why are insurance companies unwilling to provide insurance against losses arising from war or 'civil insurrection'?*
2. *Name some other events where it would be impossible to obtain insurance.*
3. *Explain why an insurance company could not pool the risk of flooding in a particular part of a country. Does your answer imply that insurance against flooding is unobtainable?*

Another way in which insurance companies can spread their risks is by ***diversification***. The more types of insurance a company offers (car, house, life, health, etc.), the greater the likelihood the risks would be independent.

Problems for unwary insurance companies

A major issue for insurance companies is that they operate in a market where there is significant ***asymmetric information***. Asymmetric information exists in a market if one party has some information that is relevant to the value of that transaction that the other party does not have. In the insurance market, buyers often have private information about themselves (e.g. their attitudes towards risk) that the insurance company does not have access to.

Asymmetric information is often split into two different types – unobservable characteristics and unobservable actions. Each separate type of asymmetric information can potentially generate a different problem. Unobservable characteristics could generate the problem of *adverse selection*; unobservable actions could generate the problem of *moral hazard*. We consider each in turn.

Potential problems caused by unobservable characteristics – adverse selection

Different potential consumers of insurance will have different characteristics. Take the case of car insurance: some drivers may be very skilful and careful, while others may be

Definitions

Law of large numbers The larger the number of events of a particular type, the more predictable will be their average outcome.

Independent risks Where two risky events are unconnected. The occurrence of one will not affect the likelihood of the occurrence of the other.

Diversification Where a firm expands into new types of business.

Asymmetric information Where one party in an economic relationship has information that the other does not have. This may give them an advantage in any transactions with the other party.

less able and enjoy the thrill of speeding. Or take the case of life assurance: some people may lead a very healthy lifestyle by eating a well-balanced diet and exercising regularly; others may eat large quantities of fast food and do little or no exercise.

In each of these cases, the customer is likely to know more about their own characteristics than the insurance company. These characteristics will also influence the cost to the firm of providing insurance. For example, less able drivers are more likely to be involved in an accident and make a claim on their insurance than more able drivers. The problems this might cause can best be explained with a simple numerical example.

In the previous car insurance example, we assumed that all the customers had the same characteristics: i.e. they all had a 5 per cent chance per year of being responsible for a car accident where damage to their own car costs, on average, £20 000. In reality, because of their different characteristics, the chances of having a car accident will vary from one customer to another. To keep the example simple, we will assume that an insurance company has only two types of potential customer. One half of them are very skilful drivers and have a 1 per cent chance per year of causing a car accident, while the other half are less able drivers who each have a 9 per cent chance per year of causing an accident. The problem for the insurance company is that when a customer purchases the insurance it does not know if they are a skilful or a less able driver.

When faced with this situation the insurance company might set the same profit-making risk premium for all drivers on the assumption that half will be highly competent drivers, while the other half will have relatively poor driving skills. Using the law of large numbers, the firm can predict that 5 per cent of its customers will make a claim and so the average pay-out would be £1000 per customer (i.e. £20 000/20). Once again, assuming administration costs of less than £100 per customer, the insurance company could potentially make a profit by charging each customer £1100.

The problem is that the skilful drivers might find this premium very unattractive. For them, the expected value of the gamble (i.e. not taking out the insurance) is 0.99(100 000) + 0.01(8000) = £99 800. Taking out the extra insurance would leave them with £98 900: i.e. their initial wealth of £100 000 minus the premium of £1100. Unless they were very risk averse, the maximum amount they would be willing to pay is likely to be far lower than £1100.

On the other hand, the less skilful drivers might find the offer from the insurance company very attractive. Their expected value from taking the gamble is 0.91(100 000) + 0.09(80 000) = £98 200. Their maximum willingness to pay is likely to be greater than £1100. In fact, if they were all risk averse, they would all purchase the policy if it cost £1800, as this would leave them with £98 200 – the same as the expected value of the gamble.

The insurance company could end up with only the less able drivers purchasing the insurance. If this happens, then nine out of every 100 customers would make a claim of £20 000 each. The average pay-out per customer would be £1800. Therefore the firm would be paying out far more in claims than it would be generating from the premiums.

If, however, the insurer *knew* a potential customer was a skilful driver, then it could offer the insurance policy at a much lower price: one that the risk-averse skilful driver would be willing to pay. If all the customers purchasing the policy were skilful drivers, then 1 in 100 would make a claim for £20 000. The average claim per customer would only be £200. All the skilful and risk-averse customers would be willing to pay more than £200 for the insurance policy.

But if the insurance company does not know who is careful and who is not, this asymmetric information will block mutually beneficial trade from taking place.

This example has illustrated the problem of ***adverse selection*** in insurance markets. This is where customers with the least desirable characteristics from the sellers' point of view (i.e. those with the greatest chance of making a claim) are more likely to take out the insurance policy at a price based on the average risk of *all* the potential customers. This can result in the insurance market for low-risk individuals collapsing even though mutually beneficial trade would be possible if symmetric information were present.

The potential problem of adverse selection is not unique to the insurance market. Unobservable characteristics are present in many other markets and may relate to the buyer, the seller or the product that is being traded. A well-known example is that of a second-hand car dealer who sells a 'lemon' (a car with faults) to an unsuspecting buyer who does not have the technical knowledge to check on the car. Another is a shop buying second-hand items paying a low price for a valuable antique from a seller who does not know its value. Table 5.1 provides some other examples.

We can define adverse selection more generally as follows. It is Key Idea 16.

Adverse selection **A market process whereby buyers, sellers or products with certain unobservable characteristics (e.g. high risk or low quality) are more likely to enter the market at the current market price. This process can have a negative impact on economic efficiency and cause some potentially profitable markets to collapse.**

Definition

Adverse selection in the insurance market Where customers with the least desirable characteristics from the sellers' point of view are more likely to purchase an insurance policy at a price based on the average risk of all the potential customers.

Table 5.1 Adverse selection in various markets

Market	Hidden characteristic	Informed party	Uninformed party
The labour market	Innate ability of the worker/ preference for working hard	The potential employee: i.e. the seller of labour services	The employer: i.e. the buyer of labour services
The credit market	Ability of people to manage their money effectively	The customer applying for credit	The firm lending the money
A street market with haggling	How much the person is willing to pay	The customer	The seller of the product
The electronic market: e.g. eBay	The quality/condition of the product	The seller of the product	The buyer of the product

Tackling the problem of adverse selection. Are there any ways that the potential problems caused by adverse selection can be overcome? One way would be for the party who is uninformed about the relevant characteristics of the other parties to ask them for information. For example, an insurance company may require people to fill out a questionnaire giving details about their lifestyle and family history, or undergo a medical, so that the company can assess the particular risk and set an appropriate premium. There may need to be legal penalties for people caught lying! This process of the uninformed trying to get the information from the informed is called 'screening'.

An alternative would be for the person or party who is informed about the relevant characteristics to reveal it to the uninformed person or party. This is called 'signalling'. For example, a potentially hardworking and intelligent employee could signal this fact to potential employers by obtaining a good grade in an economics degree or working for a period of time as an unpaid intern.

What actions can either the buyers or sellers take in each of the examples in Table 5.1 to help overcome some of the potential problems caused by the unobservable characteristics?

Potential problems caused by unobservable actions – moral hazard

Imagine in the previous example if the different characteristics of the drivers were perfectly observable to the insurance company: i.e. the insurance company could identify which drivers were more able or careful and could charge them a lower premium than those who were less able or careful. The company might still face problems caused by *unobservable actions* – again, a problem of asymmetric information.

Once drivers have purchased comprehensive insurance their driving behaviour may change. All types of driver now have an incentive to take less care when they are driving. If they are involved in an accident, all the costs will be covered by the insurance policy and so the marginal benefit from taking greater care will have fallen. This will result in the chances of the skilful driver having an accident rising above 1 per cent and of the less skilful driver rising above 9 per cent.

The problem for the insurer is that these changes in driving behaviour are difficult to observe. The companies may end up in a position where the amount of money claimed by both the skilful and less skilful drivers increases above the revenue that they are collecting in premiums based on the risk before the insurance was taken out.

This is called ***moral hazard*** and can more generally be defined as where the actions/behaviour of one party to a transaction change in a way that reduces the pay-off to the other party. It is caused by a change in incentives once a deal has been reached. It can only exist if there are unobservable actions.

Moral hazard **Following a deal, the actions/behaviour of one party to a transaction may change in a way that reduces the pay-off to the other party. In the context of insurance, it refers to customers taking more risks when they have insurance than when they do not have insurance.**

The problem of moral hazard may occur in many different markets and different situations.

- Once a person has a permanent contract of employment they might not work as hard as the employer would have expected.
- If someone else is willing to pay your debts (e.g. your parents) it is likely to make you less careful in your spending! A similar type of argument has been used for not cancelling the debts of poor countries.
- If a bank knows that it will be bailed out by the government and not allowed to fail, it may undertake more risky lending strategies.

Definition

Moral hazard Where one party to a transaction has an incentive to behave in a way which reduces the pay-off to the other party.

- If you hire a car, you may be rough with the clutch or gears, knowing that you will not bear the cost of the extra wear and tear on the car.
- When working in teams, some people may slack, knowing that more diligent members of the team will cover for them (giving them a 'free ride').

Tackling moral hazard. What are the most effective ways of reducing moral hazard? One approach would be for the uninformed party to devote more resources to *monitoring* the actions and behaviour of the informed party – in other words, to reduce the asymmetry of information. Examples include: insurance companies employing loss adjusters to assess the legitimacy of claims; lecturers using plagiarism detection software to discourage students from attempting to pass off other people's work as their own. However, monitoring may often be difficult and expensive.

An alternative is to change the terms of the deal so that the party with the unobservable actions has an incentive to behave in ways which are in the interests of the uninformed party. Examples include: employees who take sick leave being required to produce a medical certificate to prevent people taking 'sickies'; students doing group project work being assessed on their own contribution to the project rather than being given the same mark as everyone else in the group, thereby discouraging free riding.

How will the following reduce the moral hazard problem?
(a) A no-claims bonus in an insurance policy.
(b) Having to pay the first so many pounds of any insurance claim (an 'excess').
(c) The use of performance-related pay.

Section summary

1. When people buy consumer durables, they may be uncertain of their benefits and any future costs. When they buy financial assets, they may be uncertain of what will happen to their price in the future. Buying under these conditions of imperfect knowledge is therefore a form of gambling.
2. The expected value of a gamble is the amount the person would earn on average if the gamble were repeated on many occasions. If we know the expected value of such gambles, we are said to be operating under conditions of risk. If we do not know the expected value, we are said to be operating under conditions of uncertainty.
3. People can be divided into risk lovers, those who are risk averse and those who are risk neutral. Because of the diminishing marginal utility of income, it is rational for people to be risk averse (unless gambling is itself pleasurable).
4. Insurance is a way of eliminating risks for policy holders. If people are risk averse, they will be prepared to pay premiums in order to obtain insurance. Insurance companies, on the other hand, are prepared to take on these risks because they can pool risk by selling a large number of policies. According to the law of large numbers, what is unpredictable for a single policy holder becomes highly predictable for a large number of them provided that their risks are independent of each other.
5. Insurance markets arise as an institutional response to risk aversion. Their existence potentially makes society 'better off' as they can increase individual utility. Insurance market failure may arise as a result of asymmetric information, through either adverse selection or moral hazard. Adverse selection is where customers with the least desirable characteristics from the sellers' point of view are more likely to purchase an insurance policy at a price based on the average risk of all the potential customers. Moral hazard occurs when insured people have an incentive to take more risks.
6. Both adverse selection and moral hazard are likely to occur in a range of economic relationships whenever there is a problem of asymmetric information. They can both be reduced by tackling asymmetry of information. Better information can be provided by screening, signalling or monitoring, or there can be incentives for providing more accurate information.

5.2 BEHAVIOURAL ECONOMICS

The field of behavioural economics has developed rapidly over the past 25 years and, in October 2017, Richard Thaler was awarded the Nobel Prize in Economics[1] for his work in the area. In this chapter, the focus is on the contribution behavioural economics can make in helping to improve our understanding of consumer behaviour. In Chapter 9, we look at the contribution behavioural economics can make in helping to explain the behaviour of firms.

What is behavioural economics?

Behavioural economics integrates some simple insights from psychology into standard economic theory in an attempt to improve its ability to explain and predict behaviour. It is important to understand that the development of modern

1 www.nobelprize.org/prizes/economic-sciences/2017/thaler/facts/

behavioural economics is not an attempt to replace mainstream economic theory. It aims, instead, to complement and enhance existing models.

Standard economic theory

To understand what behavioural economics is, it is useful to think back to an important assumption underpinning many standard economic theories. This is that people successfully attempt to maximise their own self-interest. In other words, they make 'rational choices'. They do this by accurately assessing all the costs and benefits involved when making both simple and complicated decisions. They then successfully make choices that maximise their own happiness. In most standard theories it is assumed that people's happiness depends only on the pay-offs to themselves. They are not interested in the welfare of others.

TC 8 p109

However, this does not mean that economists actually believe that everyone in the real world behaves like this. They accept that real human beings make mistakes and often care about the pay-offs to others. What economists assume is that the people in their theoretical models behave in a rational and selfish manner.

But why assume that people in theories, such as consumer choice, behave differently from people in the real world? This is an example of *abstraction*. If theories built upon this simplified view of human behaviour can effectively explain and predict real-world behaviour, then it is a useful assumption to make.

The alternative would be to assume that people in theories are as complicated as their real-word counterparts. This would introduce much greater complexity into the analysis and make it much more difficult to understand and apply. If the simpler model is doing a good job at explaining and predicting real-world behaviour, why make it any more complicated than it needs to be?

To what extent does conventional economic theory successfully explain and predict real-world behaviour? In many instances, it does a pretty good job, which explains why this textbook and many others are full of economic theories built on these assumptions. But sometimes people's behaviour seems to run counter to traditional theory. We examine such occasions in this section and in Chapter 9.

Why might the predictions of the rational choice model generally approximate human behaviour in many situations?

Evidence on human behaviour and the challenge to standard theory

Results from a number of *laboratory experiments* inspired a growing interest in behavioural economics. Some studies found that people really dislike losses and are sometimes

BOX 5.1 EXPERIMENTAL ECONOMICS EXPLORING ECONOMICS

A way of understanding human behaviour

In Chapter 1 (see page 29) we explained that economics is a social science, with methodologies in common with the natural sciences; both construct models which can be used to explain and predict.

In the natural sciences, it is common to use experiments to test models or to determine their design features. This, however, was generally not the case with economics. But with the rise of behavioural economics, the use of experiments has become increasingly popular, both for research and teaching purposes.

Initially, the most common type of experiments in economics were *laboratory experiments*. These typically take place in a specially designed computer room in a university. The participants are usually students, who make decisions in simple online environments that attempt to simulate a particular economic model or scenario. They are often paid for taking part and receive additional payments depending on the choices they make during the experiment. This provides incentives for the participants to take the decisions seriously. The researcher observes and records behaviour for later analysis.

An advantage of laboratory experiments is that they allow economists to control the decision-making environment. One factor can be changed at a time and the response of the participants observed while holding all other things equal. The biggest disadvantage is that the participants take decisions in a very artificial environment and people may behave differently when faced with the same incentives in a real-world setting.

To address this issue, an increasing number of economists have started using *field experiments*. A field experiment differs from a laboratory experiment in two main ways. It takes place in the real-world environment where decisions are usually taken (i.e. not a computer room in a university) and the participants are unaware their behaviour is being observed and recorded by the researcher.

Both laboratory and field experiments can help to understand why individuals behave the way they do and how changing incentives will affect this behaviour.

What are the limitations of using laboratory experiments and games to understand consumer behaviour?

Individually or in pairs, devise an experiment to determine people's price elasticity of demand for a particular everyday item that people purchase frequently. Then in a group (e.g. a seminar group) discuss each of these experiments and choose one that the group will run with its members. After running the experiment, the group should consider the results and what difficulties there may be in drawing conclusions from the experiment.

willing to reduce their own earnings to avoid outcomes they perceive as unfair – see Box 5.4 for more detail.

Economists also now make much greater use of *field experiments* to study a wide range of behaviours, including charitable donations, the educational performance of children, customers tipping taxi drivers, and apologies by companies. Results from a number of these field experiments are also inconsistent with mainstream theory.

Box 5.1 discusses the use of experiments in more detail.

Data generated from some naturally occurring events also contradict the predictions of the rational choice model in a number of areas, including (a) gym membership; (b) the housing market; (c) trading in financial markets; (d) the labour supply decisions of taxi drivers.

Behavioural economists have developed a number of theories, therefore, that are more consistent with these research findings. We will discuss some of the most influential in the remainder of this section.

A lack of processing ability: bounded rationality

Consumers might try to maximise utility but may face limits on their ability to both find and process the relevant information in order to make the best decision. This is sometimes referred to as ***bounded rationality***. Finding and processing information requires time and mental effort, and busy individuals may decide it is simply not worth it.

KI 15 p132

For example, in some circumstances it may be difficult to compare the price and quality of all the different versions of a good or service offered by different suppliers. This is likely to become more of a problem as the range of alternatives increases.

With many consumption decisions, there is also an element of uncertainty about the exact size and nature of the cost and benefits. This is particularly true for consumer durables such as laptop computers, mobile phones and TVs. For example, when purchasing a laptop, a customer may be unsure about (a) how well it will perform, (b) how useful it will be and (c) the chances it will break down. Considerable uncertainty may also exist when booking a hotel or holiday.

In these circumstances, the consumer will have to make a judgement about the likelihood of different events occurring. For example, what are the chances that a holiday resort/hotel is not as pleasant as it appears on the website or that the weather will be worse than expected? There is evidence that people often find it very difficult to make these types of probability assessments.

Heuristics

To simplify choice problems, consumers often revert to using mental short-cuts that save on time and effort. Research by Anesbury et al.[2] studied of the online shopping behaviour of 40 customers. One key finding was that the modal time taken to select an item was just 7 seconds. The results for in-store shopping are similar, with mean selection times varying between 9 and 17 seconds. To make these decisions so quickly, people typically use very simple rules of thumb. These are called ***heuristics***.

For example, when deciding what make or brand to buy, consumers may revert to using the so-called 'halo heuristic'. This simple rule is to assume that because a person or business is good at doing one thing, they will also be good at doing something else that may be completely unrelated. Therefore, if a consumer is happy with their experience of consuming a particular brand of a product, they may choose the same brand when deciding to purchase a different product they have never tried before. For example, if you are happy with your Samsung TV, then you may choose another Samsung product when buying a laptop computer or smartphone for the first time. The halo heuristic generates brand loyalty and is something that companies recognise and strive to develop in their customers.

The experience of friends or relatives may heavily influence consumers when making a choice. This is an example of the 'availability heuristic' and is explained in more detail in the next section.

Using heuristics can often help consumers make the best choices while also reducing the time and effort costs of carefully comparing each option. However, their use can sometimes lead to decisions that differ from rational choices in systematic and predictable ways.

KI 15 p132

Behavioural economics attempts to identify these heuristics and the systematic errors they sometimes cause. Understanding these mental short-cuts is important for policy makers in business, government or other organisations who want to influence people's behaviour.

Types of heuristic

There are several different types of heuristic that people use. These include the following:

Choice overload or the paradox of choice. When faced with numerous different choices consumers may respond by using a very simple rule of thumb – avoid making a decision altogether. This results in two possible outcomes:

- Those consumers who have no prior experience of consuming the good fail to make any purchases even though it would increase their utility.

Definitions

Bounded rationality When the ability to make rational decisions is limited by lack of information or the time necessary to obtain such information or by a lack of understanding of complex situations.

Heuristic A mental short-cut or rule of thumb that people use when trying to make complicated choices. They reduce the computational and/or research effort required but sometimes lead to systematic errors.

2 Zachary W. Anesbury et al., 'How do shoppers behave on-line? An observational study of online grocery shopping', *Journal of Consumer Behaviour*, vol. 15, no. 3 (2015).

- Those consumers who have previously consumed the good continue buying the same brand without attempting to search for other options that are better value for money. This leads to purchases with a lower consumer surplus than the alternatives.

A well-known experiment to test this idea of choice overload was conducted by Sheena Iyengar and Mark Lepper[3] who set up a jam tasting stall in a grocery store. People were more likely to buy a jam when there were only six varieties available than when there were 24. This and other evidence on choice overload is discussed in more detail in Case Study 5.1 on the student website.

The herding heuristic. Some consumers may use a quick decision rule of copying and imitating the actions of others. In other words, they are strongly influenced by what other people purchase. A fashion might catch on; people might grab an item in a sale because other people seem to be grabbing it as well; people might buy a particular share on the stock market because other people are buying it.

In some circumstances, the herding heuristic may be an effective decision rule as other people have better information about the quality of the good or service. However, in some situations other consumers may not have superior information. They start buying the good because many other people have. Sales soar and prices may be driven well above a level that reflects the utility people end up gaining.

The anchoring heuristic. This is a tendency for consumers to be overly influenced by the first piece of information they see, even if it is unrelated to the decision. In one famous piece of research by Tversky and Kahneman[4] the participants in an experiment first spun a wheel that randomly generated a number between 0 and 100. They were then asked how many African countries were in the UN. The participants seemed to be influenced by this irrelevant random number. For example, those whose spin resulted in a bigger number answered with a larger number of countries than those whose spin produced a lower number.

Another example of anchoring is partial computation. Assume two different groups of people are given 5 seconds to find the product of eight numbers. The calculation is presented to the first group in ascending order ($1 \times 2 \times 3 \times 4 \times 5 \times 6 \times 7 \times 8$) and to the second group in descending order ($8 \times 7 \times 6 \times 5 \times 4 \times 3 \times 2 \times 1$). Which group do you think will give the most accurate answers? Explain your reasoning.

The availability heuristic. When assessing the likely size of any uncertain benefits or costs, consumers disproportionately weight single events that are easy to imagine or retrieve from memory. One example of the availability heuristic is the tendency for people to overweight the single experience of a friend or relative and underweight the experience of a large number of customers they have never met. For example, assume that you are thinking of buying a particular tablet computer and are trying to determine its reliability. A friend has recently purchased the same model and has had to send it back to the manufacturer for costly repairs. This may lead you to underestimate the reliability of this particular model and overestimate the chances of it breaking down. When making the probability assessment you underweight the information from a survey based on the experience of 10 000 users of the same tablet computer.

Gamblers and hot-hand fallacy. With the 'gambler's fallacy', people believe the likelihood the next outcome will be different from the previous outcome is greater than it actually is. For example, assume a coin is tossed on four consecutive occasions and comes up heads each time. Many people mistakenly believe that a tail is more likely on the next toss.

KI 10 p70

With the 'hot-hand fallacy', people believe the likelihood the next outcome will be the same as the previous outcome is greater than it actually is. For example, many people think that sports stars have so-called 'hot hands' when they score on repeated occasions. This leads them to believe that the likelihood of them scoring again is greater than it really is. Fans tend to overestimate the impact of skill and underestimate the impact of luck.

How good are you at making probabilistic judgements? Here is an interesting example. Suppose that one out of every hundred people in the population has a genetic medical condition. There is a test for this medical condition that is 99 per cent accurate. This means that if a person has the condition, the test returns a positive result with a 99 per cent probability; and if a person does not have the condition, it returns a negative result with 99 per cent probability. If a person's test comes back positive (and you know nothing else about that person), what is the probability that s/he has the medical condition?

Reference dependent preferences – coding outcomes as losses and gains

In standard economic theory, we assume that people make choices by incorporating the benefits and costs of a decision into their *total* income or wealth and then assessing the final outcomes.[5] For example, imagine that your assets and income give you total current wealth of £100 000. You now have an offer of taking a 50:50 gamble of gaining £11 or losing £10. Standard economic theory predicts that you will assess the situation as a 50:50 gamble of having £100 011 or £99 990 of total wealth. When judged in this way, we would expect many people to accept moderate stake gambles such as these.

3 Sheena S. Iyengar and Mark R. Lepper, 'When choice is demotivating: can one desire too much of a good thing?', *Journal of Personality and Social Psychology*, vol. 79, no. 6 (American Psychological Association, 2000).

4 A. Tversky and D. Kahneman, 'Judgment under uncertainty: heuristics and biases', *Science*, vol. 185 (1974), pp. 1124–31.

5 Rational consumers should incorporate any costs and benefits into their total expected lifetime wealth. If, for example, a consumer expected to inherit a large amount of money in the future, we would expect it to influence that person's decisions today.

Reference dependent preferences suggest that people judge decisions in a different way. Instead of incorporating any benefits and costs into their total wealth, they assess them according to some reference point.

A simple example of a reference point is a person's *current* income and wealth. When applied to the previous example, you would code the gamble as a 50:50 chance of gaining £11 or losing £10. The pay-offs would not be incorporated into your total wealth. This is known as *decision isolation* or *narrow framing*.

A number of factors other than current wealth/income can influence the reference point used by people to judge an outcome as a gain or a loss. For example:

- *Their expectations.* Imagine that Ellie and Haroon are both students on an economics course. They have both exerted the same level of effort writing an assessed essay and each receives a mark of 60 per cent. Will they both be equally happy? If Ellie expected to get 70 per cent, then this might be her reference point. She might 'code' the result as a 10 percentage point loss and feel very unhappy. If Haroon, on the other hand, expected to get a mark of 50 per cent, he might code the result as a gain of 10 percentage points and feel much happier. A similar argument could be made
KI 10 p70
if a worker was expecting to receive a real wage increase of 3 per cent but only received one of 2 per cent.
- *By making comparisons with others.* If customers obtain a 10 per cent discount on a product they purchase, they may initially feel happy and code the outcome as a gain. However, if they subsequently find out that other customers obtained a 20 per cent discount on the same product, this might change their reference point and they might begin to code the outcome as a loss.
- *Adjusting slowly to a changed income/asset position.* Contestants on the game show *Who Wants to be a Millionaire?* who have already won £16 000 may still take a 50:50 gamble of winning another £16 000 (i.e. having a total prize of £32 000) or losing £15 000 (i.e. having a total prize of £1000). When asked why they took the gamble, participants are likely to explain that even if they lose they will still have £1000 more than before they played the game. Comments such as these suggest that the contestants' reference point while playing the game remains at their income level before playing the game: i.e. every pay-off is coded as a gain. However, as they play the game, their income/asset position is changing. When they take the gamble, they have already won £16 000. If their perception of their income position had fully adjusted, the reference income level would include the £16 000 and the chances of losing would be coded as a £15 000 loss.

Loss aversion

The theory of reference dependent preferences leads to another important result: that of ***reference dependent loss aversion***. Outcomes coded as losses are disliked far more than the pleasure received from an equivalent sized gain.

We saw in section 5.1 how the standard economic theory of diminishing marginal utility of income predicts that people dislike losses more than gains. However, if an individual codes an outcome as a loss in relation to a reference point, the dislike of this loss seems to be even greater than that predicted by standard theory. Some estimates suggest that the dislike of a financial loss is at least twice as big as the pleasure associated with an equivalent gain. This would produce a discrete kink or change in the slope of the utility function at the reference point.

KI 13 p105

The theory of loss aversion is a potential explanation for the ***endowment effect***, sometimes known as ***divestiture aversion***. This is where people ascribe more value to things when they own them than when they are merely considering purchasing or acquiring them. One explanation for this difference is that ownership of a good influences a person's reference point. If a good is not already owned, its purchase by the consumer is coded as a gain. Once purchased, its ownership is included in the consumer's reference point. Selling the good would now be coded as a loss. Box 5.2 examines the endowment effect in more detail.

Decision isolation and loss aversion may also help to explain why consumers seem to be so risk averse for small-stake gambles. In particular, they appear to be willing to buy very highly priced insurance policies for products they have purchased, such as mobile handsets.

According to rational choice theory, the money you've already spent – known as 'sunk costs' (see page 161) – should be excluded from decision making. However, there is considerable evidence that it does affect consumer behaviour. Using loss aversion, explain why this might be the case.

Prospect theory

Two famous behavioural economists, Kahneman and Tversky,[6] used the concepts of reference dependent preferences and loss aversion to develop an alternative theory of decision

Definitions

Reference dependent preferences Where people value (or 'code') outcomes as either gains or losses in relation to a reference point.

Reference dependent loss aversion Where a loss is disliked far more than the pleasure associated from an equivalent sized gain. This dislike of losses is far greater than that predicted by standard economic theory.

Endowment effect (or divestiture aversion) The hypothesis that people ascribe more value to things when they own them than when they are merely considering purchasing or acquiring them – in other words, when the reference point is one of ownership rather than non-ownership.

6 D. Kahneman and A. Tversky, 'Prospect theory: an analysis of decision making under risk', *Econometrica*, vol. 47, no. 2, (1979), pp. 263–91.

making under conditions of risk and uncertainty – 'prospect theory'. This theory also includes two other important ideas.

Diminishing marginal sensitivity to gains and losses. In a similar manner to diminishing marginal utility of income, each additional £1 coded as a gain gives less extra pleasure than the previous £1. The same is also true for losses. Each additional £1 coded as a loss gives less extra discomfort than the previous £1.

KI 13 p105

The probability weighting function. People assign their own subjective decision weights to the objective probabilities associated with a risky choice. They tend to overweight low probabilities and underweight high probabilities. For example, if someone believed that an outcome had a probability of occurring of only 1 per cent, they might treat it as if it were 10 per cent. Whereas, if they believed that an outcome had a probability of occurring of 99 per cent, they might treat it as if it were only 90 per cent.

This is illustrated in Figure 5.2. The blue line gives an example of how a person might treat a given probability of an outcome. For example, at point *a*, the actual probability of the outcome occurring is 10 per cent. The person overweights this and treats it as if it were 20 per cent. At point *b*, the actual probability of the outcome occurring is 90 per cent. In this case, the person underweights the probability and treats it as if it were only 76 per cent.

Prospect theory predicts that consumers will have a fourfold pattern of risk preferences. They will be (a) risk loving when faced with a small chance of a relatively large gain, (b) risk averse when faced with a small chance of a relatively large loss, (c) risk averse when faced with a high chance of a relatively small gain, (d) risk loving when faced with a high chance of a relatively small loss.

Framing

Traditional economic theory predicts that different ways of presenting or framing the same choice to consumers should have no impact on the decisions they make. However, because of the use of heuristics and the impact of loss aversion there is lots of evidence that it does.

Policymakers can take advantage of this by presenting choices in ways that encourage more socially desirable behaviour. For example, disposable single use coffee cups have a plastic lining that helps to keep the liquid in the cup. This makes them difficult to recycle. To encourage people to take re-usable cups to a coffee shop it is possible to present the same monetary incentive in two different ways.

- The price of a standard coffee is £2.50. If you have a re-usable cup instead of a disposable cup, you get a 25p discount: i.e. the coffee costs £2.25.
- The price of a standard coffee is £2.25. If you have a disposable cup instead of a re-usable cup, you have to pay an additional 25p charge: i.e. the coffee costs £2.50.

Definition

Framing Consumption decisions are influenced by the way the costs and benefits are presented to the individual.

Figure 5.2 Probability weighting function in prospect theory

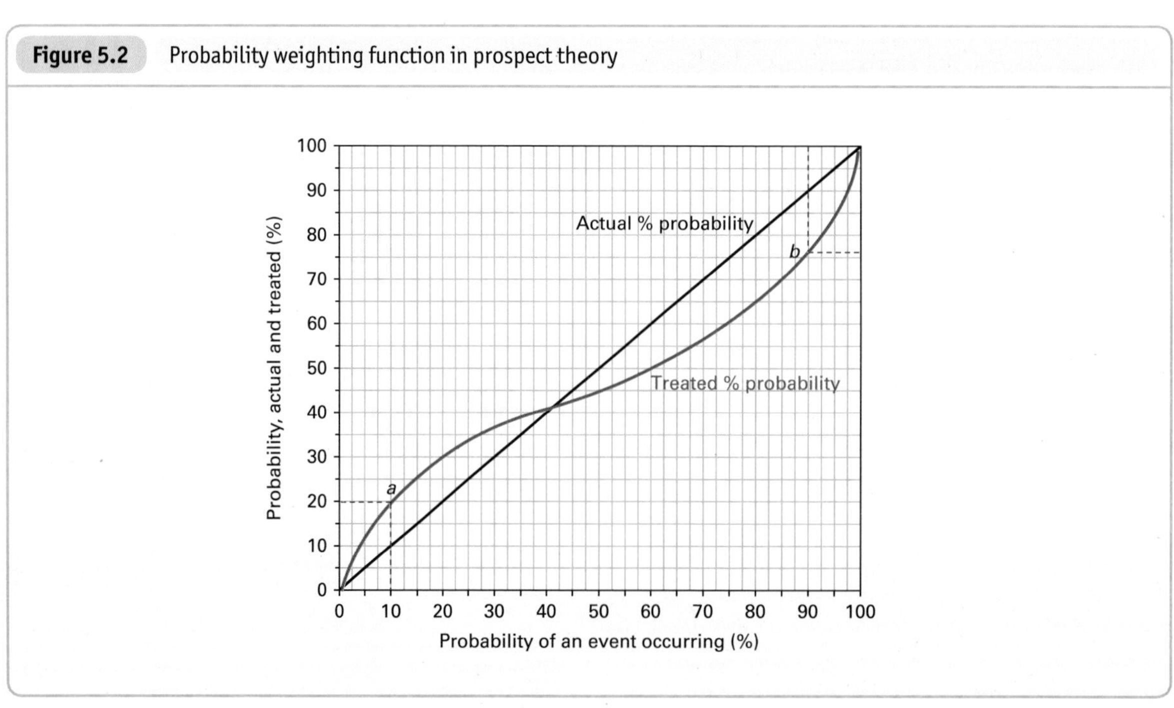

The first presentation makes £2.50 the reference point. A lower price is a gain. Therefore, the decision to use a disposable cup may be coded as a forgone gain: i.e. the consumer misses out on the 25p discount. The second presentation makes £2.25 the reference point. A higher price is a loss. Therefore, the decision to use a disposable cup may be coded as a loss: i.e. the consumer has to pay an additional 25p charge. If consumers are loss averse, they may react more strongly to the second presentation. A study for Zero Waste Scotland[7] found that when four cafés switched from using a re-usable cup discount to a disposable cup charge, the proportion of people using reusable cups rose by 50 per cent.

Firms may also be able to take advantage of framing effects when pricing their products. One example is *partitioned* or *drip pricing*. This is a strategy where, instead of presenting one total combined price for a product, the seller splits the price into two or more components. For example, an airline might have a headline fare, but then add additional charges for luggage or the positions of the seat: i.e. enabling people to sit together. There is evidence that consumers anchor their decision to the headline price and fail to take full account of and adjust to the other additional charges, which causes them to underestimate the product's total price. This is discussed in more detail in Box 9.2 in Chapter 9.

7 Michael Lenaghan, William Clark and Thomas Middlemass, *Cups Sold Separately* (Zero Waste Scotland, 2019), www.zerowastescotland.org.uk/research-evaluation/cups-sold-separately

*BOX 5.2 THE ENDOWMENT EFFECT

EXPLORING ECONOMICS

An example of loss aversion

Consider the following two slightly different situations for the same person, Clare: (a) she is thinking of buying a good such as a coffee mug; (b) she has already purchased it and now owns it. In each case we can think of a way of measuring her valuation of that good.

In the first case it could be measured as the maximum amount she is willing to pay for the mug. This is known as her willingness to pay (WTP). In the second case it could be measured as the minimum amount she needs to be offered in order for her to be willing to sell it to someone else. This is known as her willingness to accept (WTA).

Apart from a few exceptions, traditional economic theory predicts that ownership of a product should have no impact on peoples' valuation of that product. Therefore, their WTP for the product should be equal to their WTA for the same product.

This means that utility functions and indifference curves should be unaffected by people purchasing and owning a product. For example, the diagram illustrates Clare's total utility from coffee mugs. If she purchases one mug, her utility increases from 0 to U_1: i.e. she moves from point *a* to point *b* along her utility function. If she were then to sell this mug, her total utility would decrease from U_1 to 0: i.e. she would move back along the same utility function from point *b* to point *a*, merely giving up the utility from owning the mug. In other words, her utility function is reversible. As the gain in utility from buying the mug is the same as the loss in utility from selling the same mug, WTP should equal WTA.

The endowment effect: when WTA is greater than WTP

In a famous study, Kahneman, Knetch and Thaler[1] carried out a series of experiments with students on a Law and Economics degree at Cornell University. They were randomly divided into two equal-sized groups. Students in one group were each given a coffee mug and told that they could sell it if they wished. They were asked for their WTA. Students in the other group could each examine the mugs and make an offer to buy one. They were asked their WTP. The authors found that the median WTA of the students who were given the mugs was $5.25 whereas the median WTP in the other group was only $2.25.

Impact of the endowment effect

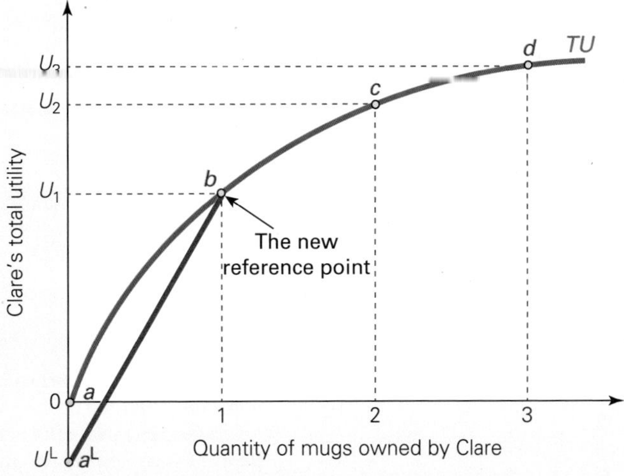

(continued)

As the students had been randomly allocated into the two groups, standard theory predicts that WTP should be equal to WTA. However, the evidence suggests that those who were given ownership of the mugs at the start of the experiment valued them far more than those who were not.

A similar exercise was carried out with pens. In this experiment the median WTP remained constant at $1.25, while the median WTA varied between $1.75 and $2.50. Once again, ownership seemed to have an impact on valuation.

After purchase, ownership becomes the new reference point

One explanation for these results is that ownership of a good influences a person's reference point. Those who do not already own the good perceive (or 'code') its purchase as a *gain* in utility and would move from point *a* to *b* in the diagram. However, once they have purchased a good its ownership is included in their reference point. Selling the good would be coded as a *loss*.

If people are loss averse then the sale of the good has a much bigger negative impact on their utility than the gain in utility from purchasing the product. This creates a discrete kink in the utility function at point *b*; the utility function is no longer reversible. Sale of the good would cause a movement from *b* to a_L. The negative impact on utility of selling the good (U_1 to U_L) is greater than the gain in utility from purchasing the good (0 to U_1). This discrete kink in the utility function helps to illustrate people's WTA being greater than their WTP.

1. *What explanations other than the endowment effect could help to explain any differences between a buyer's WTP and a seller's WTA?*

*2. *Illustrate the impact of the endowment effect on indifference curves.*

Devise and run an experiment similar to those conducted by Kahneman, Knetch and Thaler that can be conducted with a group of friends. How do the WTA and WTP differ? Explain the differences (or lack of them) that you observe.

1 D. Kahneman, J. L. Knetch and R. H. Thaler, 'Experimental tests of the endowment effect and the Coase theorem', *Journal of Political Economy*, vol. 98, no. 6 (1990), pp. 1352–75.

Present bias and self-control issues

The costs and benefits of making some choices occur in different time-periods. If people choose to:

- study for exams instead of watching videos on YouTube, the effort costs of studying are immediate, whereas the benefits (better grades/higher paid job) occur in the future;
- buy a chocolate muffin instead of a same-priced piece of fruit, the nicer flavour from eating the muffin is immediate, whereas the negative health impacts occur in the future;
- exercise at the gym rather than playing a computer game, the effort costs of exercising are immediate, whereas the health benefits occur in the future.

Economists refer to these as intertemporal choices – see section 4.2 for more detail. Evidence suggests that the majority of people tend to be impatient most of the time. Standard economic theory uses *exponential discounting* (see 113–14) to model and explain this impatience. This approach assumes that a person's degree of impatience remains constant with the passage of time. This implies that people will stick to their plans unless they learn new information.

For example, if a consumer plans to shop around for a new energy supplier or a new mobile phone contract when their current deal expires, they indeed do so. If they plan to start a diet tomorrow, they do so when tomorrow arrives. This is referred as ***time consistency***.

The only reason people with time-consistent preferences would change their mind is if new information became known about the size of the costs and benefits related to the decision. For example, you plan to shop around for a new energy supplier when your current deal expires but when it does expire the current supplier offers a much better deal than you anticipated. This is still time consistent behaviour, as the only reason you changed your mind is that the information changed. The opportunity cost of not switching supplier is much smaller than you anticipated before the current deal expired. KI 15 p132

Time consistency seems to predict and explain behaviour reasonably well when all the costs and benefits of a decision occur in the future. A consumer's plan of action often remains the same with the passage of time as long as none of the cost and benefits occur immediately. For example, at 9:00am today you may plan to eat a healthy lunch tomorrow: i.e. you plan to eat a piece of fruit instead of a chocolate muffin. The plan remains the same throughout today and tomorrow morning.

However, when lunchtime finally arrives you do not stick to the plan and eat the chocolate muffin instead. What has changed? When lunchtime finally arrives, the costs of not eating the chocolate muffin are now immediate – missing out on the greater enjoyment – but the health benefits are still in the future. Once the time arrives to experience the costs or benefits of a decision, many people have a tendency to change their minds. They act in a time inconsistent manner and suffer from self-control problems. Behavioural economists refer to this as ***present bias*** (see Box 5.3).

Definitions

Time consistency Where a person's preferences remain the same over time. If they plan to do something in the future such as change energy supplier, they do so when the time arrives.

Present bias Where the relative weight people place on immediate costs and benefits versus those that occur in the future is far greater than predicted by the standard theory of exponential discounting. This can lead to time inconsistent behaviour.

BOX 5.3 **THE BEST MADE PLANS** EXPLORING ECONOMICS

Present bias

Standard economic theory predicts that consumers will behave in a time consistent manner. However, in the real world we often observe people behaving in a time *inconsistent* way. They plan to do things such as changing their energy supplier, bank account, mobile phone contract and car insurance. They also plan to drink less alcohol, eat more healthily and quit smoking. Unfortunately, they never seem to get around to doing most of these things. When the moment arrives, they often procrastinate and decide to put it off until later.

Take the example of exercise. On Sunday night, Dean is considering whether to go down the gym after work on Monday evening. Although the costs (the exertion of exercising on Monday) occur sooner than the benefits (long-term improvements to his health) he still plans to go. The key point is that, from his point of view on Sunday, all of these costs and benefits are in the future.

The problem occurs for Dean when Monday evening finally arrives. The costs of going to the gym are now immediate. If he suffers from present bias, he will now weight these immediate costs far more heavily than the future benefits. He changes his mind and watches football on the TV while planning to go to the gym on Tuesday evening instead. From his point of view on Monday evening, all the costs and benefits of going on Tuesday are once again in the future.

Unfortunately, when Tuesday arrives the same thing happens again. As soon as the costs become immediate, he weights them much more heavily and decides once more to stay in and watch TV while planning to go on Wednesday evening instead. This process continues with Dean continually planning to go to the gym but never quite making it.

This inability to make accurate predictions about their future behaviour means that present-biased consumers may choose gym membership contracts that do not maximise their utility. To investigate this possibility, DellaVigna and Malmendier[1] analysed data from three health clubs in the USA where consumers could choose between a \$70 monthly fee with no payment per visit or \$10 per visit with no monthly fee. Those consumers who opted for the monthly fee went on average 4.3 times per month. This works out to a price of around \$17 per visit. They could have saved around \$30 per month by opting for the pay-as-you-go option. The authors found that 80 per cent of those who chose the monthly membership option ended up paying more per visit.

Why did so many consumers make such a poor choice? When asked how often they would visit the gym, on average consumers forecast they would go 9.5 times per month. If they stuck to their plans, the monthly membership would have been the best option. Unfortunately, because of present bias, consumers have problems anticipating their future behaviour.

The impact of automatic renewal

The tendency to procrastinate because of present bias means that automatic renewal of a deal can have a significant impact on consumer choice. Many insurance policies, mobile phone contracts, TV/Internet contracts and energy supply policies are automatically renewed when an existing deal expires. What happens if the new terms are significantly worse than the initial deal? Do consumers plan to search around for an alternative supplier but never get around to it? In this case, automatic renewal could be an effective way for firms to increase their profits by charging longstanding customers higher prices than newer customers – the so-called loyalty penalty.

In September 2018, Citizens Advice made a super-complaint[2] to the Competition and Markets Authority (CMA) about the loyalty penalty in five markets – mobile phone contracts, broadband, cash savings, home insurance and mortgages. In response to this complaint, the CMA carried out an initial investigation[3] that found evidence of firms using auto-renewal policies to exploit consumers – taking advantage of their present bias to make them pay more than they intended. Particular examples of harmful practices include:

- requiring customers to sign up for auto-renewal when they buy a product
- rolling customers onto new contracts without sufficient warning
- imposing large price increases on auto-renewal
- making it more difficult for customers to leave than sign up for a contract.

Following its initial report, the CMA decided to launch further investigations into two sectors: online game consoles and anti-virus software. The video games market had changed dramatically over the previous five years, with more customers using online services to play with people in different households. In order to use this service, people have to pay a monthly or yearly subscription fee. In April 2019,[4] the CMA opened cases on Nintendo Switch, PlayStation and Xbox to determine whether the automatic renewal of these subscription services is unfairly taking advantage of users. Similar cases were opened in December 2018,[5] on firms in the anti-virus software sector.

In April 2017, the Financial Conduct Authority in the UK issued new regulations[6] on how the details in insurance renewal notices had to be presented to customers to increase the likelihood of them shopping around.

Interestingly, in the study conducted by DellaVigna and Malmendier, the monthly gym contract was automatically renewed unless customers informed the management of their intention to cancel the membership. The researchers found that, on average, the gap between the last date a person attended the gym and when they cancelled the contract was 2.31 full months! This meant that people wasted over \$180 paying for a service they did not use. Twenty per cent delayed by at least four months!

(continued)

1. *Outline the new regulations issued by the Financial Conduct Authority. To what extent will they encourage customers to shop around for insurance?*
2. *Assume you have present bias but are fully aware of the time inconsistent nature of your preferences. What actions could you take to make sure you carry out your planned decisions?*

Search for two or three motivational apps and consider the extent to which they are likely to tackle the problem of present bias.

1 Stefano DellaVigna and Ulrike Malmendier, 'Paying not to go to the gym', *American Economic Review*, vol. 96, no. 3 (June 2006), pp. 694–719, www.aeaweb.org/articles?id=10.1257/aer.96.3.694

2 A super-complaint is a complaint submitted by a designated consumer body that 'any feature, or combination of features, of a market in the UK for goods or services is or appears to be significantly harming the interests of consumers'. See www.citizensadvice.org.uk/about-us/our-work/our-campaigns/all-our-current-campaigns/citizens-advice-super-complaint-on-the-loyalty-penalty/

3 *Tackling the loyalty penalty*, Competition and Markets Authority (19 December 2018), https://assets.publishing.service.gov.uk/media/5c194665e5274a4685bfbafa/response_to_super_complaint_pdf.pdf

4 www.gov.uk/cma-cases/online-console-video-gaming

5 www.gov.uk/cma-cases/anti-virus-software

6 *Transparency in insurance renewals*, Financial Conduct Authority (8 March 2017), www.fca.org.uk/firms/transparency-insurance-renewals

If people are impatient, they weight costs and benefits that occur sooner more heavily than those that occur later. However, present bias is different from the impatience implied by exponential discounting. The theory predicts that once any costs or benefits are immediate, the relative weighting people place upon them changes dramatically – it becomes much larger. In other words, they become magnified in people's minds. Therefore, a person's degree of impatience does not remain constant with the passage of time. This is referred to as ***hyperbolic discounting***.

In the previous example, the costs of not eating the chocolate muffin appear to be much greater when it is in front of a consumer – the degree of impatience suddenly increases! This theory predicts that a consumer can appear both patient when making a decision when all the costs and benefits occur in the future (e.g. planning to eat healthily) and very impatient when making the same decision when the benefits occur now but the costs are still in the future (e.g. eating unhealthily now).

Present bias helps explain why many people have difficulty in sticking to commitments. Think of how many people make and then quickly break New Year's resolutions.[8] Indeed, some behavioural economists have actually created a website called stickK,[9] which enables people to make their own commitment contracts to help them stick to their plans.

Give some other examples of decisions where people often change their mind with the passage of time once the costs or benefits become immediate.

Caring about the pay-offs to others

In many standard economic theories, it is assumed that people are motivated only by pay-offs to themselves. They do not value any pay-offs to others. However, casual observation and evidence from experiments suggest that this is not true. People tip waiters, give to charity and undertake voluntary work. Participants in laboratory experiments reward those that are perceived to have acted fairly while punishing those who have not – see Box 5.4 for more detail. Many consumers have what behavioural economists call *other regarding preferences* and this has significant economic consequences in market transactions.

KI 4 p13

Altruism, envy and reciprocity

Behavioural economists have tried to develop utility functions that capture the idea that consumers care about the pay-offs to other people as well as themselves.

Having ***altruistic*** preferences in economics means that you positively value the pay-offs to others as well as to yourself. If this relative weighting of the welfare of others is strong enough, then you may be willing to increase their income at personal cost to yourself, for example by making donations to charity. Altruism is a type of unconditional kindness as people do not have to be nice to you for you to value their welfare.

Having ***spiteful*** or ***envious*** preferences is the opposite of having altruistic preferences. You now value the pay-offs to others negatively and might be willing to take costly actions to *reduce* their income.

Evidence from experiments suggests that individuals can display both altruistic and spiteful behaviour. They are often willing to increase the pay-offs to others at a personal cost to themselves in some situations, while reducing the pay-offs to others at a personal cost to themselves in other situations.

To capture these ideas, behavioural economists have developed a number of models of ***reciprocity***. Some of these

8 www.lifehack.org/articles/communication/50-new-years-resolution-ideas-and-how-achieve-each-them.html

9 www.stickk.com/

Definitions

Hyperbolic discounting The discount factor falls more quickly when comparing immediate pay-offs with those that occur at some point in the future than it does when comparing the same pay-offs but which all occur in the future.

Altruism (in economics) Positively valuing the pay-offs to others.

Spite or envy (in economics) Negatively valuing the pay-offs to others.

Reciprocity (in economics) Where people's behaviour is influenced by the effects it will have on others.

*BOX 5.4 A SIMPLE EXPERIMENT TO TEST FOR SOCIAL PREFERENCES

CASE STUDIES AND APPLICATIONS

Responding to fair and unfair offers: the ultimatum game

Imagine taking part in the following laboratory experiment, known as the ***ultimatum game***.

You are randomly assigned as a proposer. This is the initial decision maker in the game. You are matched with a responder – a participant who must respond to the decision you make. Your identity and that of the responder remain anonymous; you will never know who each other is.

The person in charge of the experiment (the 'experimenter') gives you £20 and asks you to suggest a way of dividing this sum of money between yourself and the responder. Your proposal is communicated by the experimenter (usually online) to the responder.

The responder then has one simple decision to make – either accept or reject the offer. If the responder accepts the offer, the money is divided in the way you propose. If the responder rejects the offer, then you both earn zero and the £20 is returned to the experimenter. A proposer only plays with the same responder on one occasion. There is no opportunity for reputation building by the responder, such as rejecting offers in the hope of influencing future behaviour.

What share of the £20 would you offer to the responder? Would you suggest a 50:50 split or an offer where you keep a larger or smaller share of the money? You could make an offer of 1p and if accepted you would make £19.99.

Now imagine that you are randomly assigned to be the responder in the game. Would you accept or reject an offer of 1p, £1, £5, or £10? What is the minimum-sized offer you would accept?

The predictions of standard theory

What does standard economic theory predict will happen in the game? If the proposer (a) only cares about their own monetary pay-off and (b) knows the responder feels the same, then they should offer 1p. The responder will accept the offer, as 1p is better than nothing and the proposer gets to keep £19.99.

The results of experiments: demonstrating altruism and spite

This game has been played on numerous occasions in many different countries and for different amounts of money. The results are consistent and are completely at odds with the predictions of standard theory. The majority of proposers offer between 40 and 50 per cent of the money.

Responders often reject lower offers. For example, they decline around half of the offers that are below 20 per cent.

How can these results be explained? It seems that many responders consider offers of less than 40 per cent as unfair. They decline these offers in order to punish the proposers. The key point about this punishment is that it is costly to the responder. If they decline an offer of 20 per cent in the above game, they are effectively sacrificing £4 of potential earnings. As the responder only plays the game with the same proposer on one occasion, the punishment cannot be used to create a reputation and enhance the responders' future earnings. Therefore, they appear to be demonstrating social preferences.

A COVID-19 lockdown example

Do lower levels of social interaction have an impact on preferences for fairness? Buso et al. (2020)[1] ran this same experiment with participants who were experiencing a lockdown during the COVID-19 pandemic. There were three key findings. The first was that proposer participants who had experienced lockdown for more than six weeks made responders lower offers. The second was that proposers living on their own during lockdown made lower offers than those living with housemates. The third was that proposers living away from their hometown made lower offers than those living in their hometown. This evidence suggests that social isolation reduces the preference for fairness.

1. *In what circumstances would a proposer who only cares about their own monetary pay-offs make an offer of £10 in the above game?*
2. *What are the limitations of using the results from the game to help explain real-world behaviour?*

Devise another game to demonstrate a person's degree of altruism (or spite).

Definition

The ultimatum game A two-player, single round game where the first player (the proposer) proposes how to divide a sum of money with the second player (the responder). If the second player rejects this division, neither gets anything. The proposal is, in effect, an ultimatum by the first player: 'accept my offer, or you get nothing.'

1 Irene M. Buso et al., 'The effects of COVID-19 lockdown on fairness and cooperation: evidence from a lablike experiment', *Economics Letters*, vol. 196 (2020), pp. 1553–77, www.ncbi.nlm.nih.gov/pmc/articles/PMC7500343/

suggest that people may experience an increase in their own utility by taking costly actions to (a) increase the income of those who have acted fairly and (b) reduce the incomes of those who have acted unfairly. This is different from tit-for-tat strategies in standard economic theory (see page 245) where people or firms are willing to reward or punish people in a repeated setting in an attempt to increase their own personal pay-off in the long run.

Consumers may have particular fairness concerns about the supply conditions of the goods and services they purchase. They may be willing to pay more for a good that is produced in an environmentally friendly manner and/or where the workers are well treated. An increasing number of firms now engage in corporate social responsibility (CSR) activities.

Reciprocity can also have implications for firms' pricing strategies. For example, emergencies, crises or natural disasters (e.g. the COVID-19 pandemic) often cause sudden increases in demand for essential goods (e.g. hand sanitisers and face masks). If firms respond by substantially raising their prices for these products, angry consumers may accuse them of profiteering and seek to punish them by shopping elsewhere. This will be discussed in more detail in Box 9.2.

Implications for economic policy

Governments, in designing policy, will normally attempt to change people's behaviour. They might want to encourage people to save more, recycle rubbish, use their cars less, exercise more, eat more healthily, and so on. If the policy is to be successful, it is vital that it contains appropriate incentives: whether it be a tax rise, a grant or subsidy, a new law or regulation, an advertising campaign or direct help.

TC 5 p48

Traditional approaches to policy making (i.e. tax, subsidy and regulation) are based on the assumption that people respond to incentives as rational maximisers. Behavioural economics identifies a number of areas where this might not be true and where people appear to make systematic mistakes. In these circumstances, the response to the policy will not be what the government expected.

Behavioural economists suggest an alternative approach. If people are making poor decisions for themselves because of the impact of systematic biases, they can be ***nudged*** into making better decisions by making use of information about these biases to inform the way the choice is presented. Evidence suggests that some small changes to the framing of decisions can have a significant impact on the choices people make even when the monetary pay-offs remain the same. The use of nudges by policy makers is examined in Box 5.5.

An effective nudge will help some people make much better decisions for themselves, while imposing little or no cost on those who are already making choices in their own best interests. An effective nudge will not reduce choice and is far less intrusive than traditional regulation: i.e. where governments prohibit some actions or make other actions compulsory.

Remember the question we asked at the beginning of Chapter 4 (page 105): 'Do you ever purchase things irrationally? If so, what are they and why is your behaviour irrational?' Can you better explain this behaviour in the light of behavioural economics?

Definition

Nudge theory Small changes in the way the same policy is presented can help some people make much better decisions for themselves while imposing very little or no cost on those who are already making choices that are in their own interests.

BOX 5.5 NUDGING PEOPLE

EXPLORING ECONOMICS

How to change behaviour without taking away choice

One observation of behavioural economists is that people make many decisions out of habit. They use simple rules such as the halo and herding heuristics. People may also continually delay decisions (status quo bias) because they are loss averse and/or present biased. These systematic biases may prevent people from acting in their own self-interest.

Are there 'nudges' which will encourage people to act in their own self-interest, such as taking more exercise or eating more healthily? ***Nudges*** are small changes to the way the same choice is presented that help some people make better decisions for themselves while imposing very little or no cost on those who are already making choices that are in their own interests. Governments will be interested in effective nudges as it improves policy making. Firms too will want to know how to manipulate consumers so they purchase more of their products. In this case, rather than a 'nudge', the policy is referred to as 'sludge'[1] because it might reduce the welfare of consumers.

TC 5 p48

An example of a nudge – changing the default

When a person starts a new job, they often have to decide whether to contribute to the company's pension scheme. The default option is typically for employees not to contribute. They have to do something actively, such as filling in a form, to opt in to the scheme. In many cases, people intend to complete the form but never quite get around to doing so. In other words, they are present biased and find reasons to put it off.

An alternative is to change the default option so that employees *automatically* contribute to the pension scheme. They now have to do something if they wish to opt out of it.

Changing the default should have no impact on people who behave in ways that are consistent with the rational choice model in economics. It is simply a small change in the way the same decision is presented. However, research by Madrian and Shea (2001)[2] found that it had a big effect. When employees had to opt in, 49 per cent enrolled in a company pension. When they had to opt out, the figure increased to 86 per cent enrolment. Under UK pension arrangements introduced in 2012, firms automatically deduct pension contributions from employees' wages unless they opt out of the scheme.

Nudging people in this way is called 'soft paternalism'. It can improve the welfare of those who suffer from present bias, while imposing very limited harm on those who act in a time-consistent manner.

One policy area where the choice of default has been a topical issue is organ donation. In 2017, over 400 people died in the UK because it was impossible to find an appropriate donor. The scheme in England required people to sign up to the organ donor register: i.e. they had to opt in. Although 80 per cent of the public support organ donation, less than 50 per cent ever got around to signing this register.

In May 2020, the default position changed. Now people are automatically signed up for organ donation. If they do not want to donate their organs, they have to opt out of the register. It will be interesting to see the impact this scheme has on organ donation.

The Behavioural Insights Team

The UK Coalition government (2010–15) established the Behavioural Insights Team (BIT) (also unofficially known as the Nudge Unit) in the Cabinet Office in 2010. A major objective of this team is to use ideas from behavioural science to design policies that enable people to make better choices for themselves. Some of this work involves the use of behavioural economics.

BIT was partially privatised in 2014 and is now equally owned by the UK government, the innovation charity Nesta and the Team's employees. Case Study 5.3 on the student website looks at some examples of the work of BIT.

1. *Explain the difference between a nudge and a traditional type of government regulation such as banning the use of hand-held phones when driving.*
2. *How could the government nudge people to stop dropping litter?*
3. *Instead of changing defaults, an alternative nudge is to promote 'active/forced choice'. What is active choice? Is it more or less paternalistic than changing defaults?*

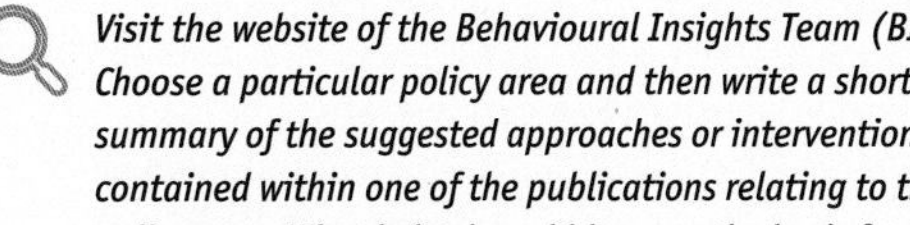

Visit the website of the Behavioural Insights Team (BIT). Choose a particular policy area and then write a short summary of the suggested approaches or interventions contained within one of the publications relating to that policy area. What behavioural ideas are the basis for the team's recommendations?

1 Richard Thaler, 'Nudge, not sludge', *Science*, vol. 361, issue 6401 (August 2018).

2 Brigitte C. Madrian and Dennis F. Shea, 'The power of suggestion: inertia in 401(k) Participation and Savings Behavior', *The Quarterly Journal of Economics*, vol. 116, no. 4 (Nov 2001), pp. 1149–87.

Section summary

1. Traditional economics is based on the premise that consumers act rationally, weighing up the costs and benefits of the choices open to them. Behavioural economics acknowledges that real-world decisions do not always appear rational; it seeks to understand and explain what economic agents actually do.
2. Evidence for behavioural economics can come from laboratory experiments, field experiments and naturally occurring data.
3. People's ability to make rational decisions is bounded by limited information and time. Thus people resort to using heuristics – rules of thumb. Types of heuristics include: avoiding making decisions when faced with too much choice, copying and imitating the actions of others, basing the likelihood of events on information that is vivid/easy to imagine, believing that past outcomes have a larger impact on current outcomes than they actually do.
4. Seemingly irrational behaviour may arise from decision isolation and the choice of a reference point for decision taking. The reference point used by people to judge an outcome as a gain or a loss can be influenced by a range of factors, including their expectations, comparisons with others and adjusting slowly to new information.
5. People generally seem to put a greater weight on the loss of £x than on the gain of £x. This reference dependent loss aversion is greater than that implied by diminishing marginal utility of income.
6. People who are loss averse may value things more highly when they own them than when they are considering buying them (the endowment effect).
7. Prospect theory is based upon decision isolation, reference dependent preferences, loss aversion, diminishing marginal sensitivity of gains/losses and the probability weighting function. It predicts that people will have a fourfold pattern of risk preferences.
8. The way choices are presented/framed can influence the choices people make. The careful framing of a policy or promotion can influence consumers' reference points and hence how they code the outcome.
9. People may give additional weight to immediate costs and benefits. This is called 'present bias' and can lead to time-inconsistent behaviour, with people changing their minds and not acting in accordance with previous plans.
10. Apparently irrational behaviour may also be the result of people taking other people's interests into account: i.e. positively or negatively valuing the pay-offs to others.
11. Governments, in devising policy, are increasingly looking at ways to influence people's behaviour. One way is by using nudges. These are small changes to the way the policy is presented that helps some people make much better decisions for themselves while imposing little or no cost on those who are already making choices in their own best interests.
12. An example of a nudge is moving from an opting in to an opting out system for schemes such as pensions and organ donation.

END OF CHAPTER QUESTIONS

1. A country's central bank (e.g. the Bank of England or the US Federal Reserve Bank) has a key role in ensuring the stability of the banking system. In many countries the central bank is prepared to bail banks out which find themselves in financial difficulties. Although this has the benefit of reducing the chance of banks going bankrupt and depositors losing their money, it can create a moral hazard. Explain why.
2. Discuss the EU ruling that gender may not be used to differentiate insurance premiums. Which insurance markets would be affected by outlawing age 'discrimination' in a similar manner? What would be the impact?
3. The European New Car Assessment Programme (Euro NCAP) carries out crash tests on new cars in order to assess the extent to which they are safer than the minimum required standard. The cars are given a percentage score in four different categories, including adult occupant protection and child occupant protection. An overall safety rating is then awarded. Based on the test results in 2020, the Volkswagen ID.3 was judged to be the safest car on the market. If you observed that these cars were *more* likely to be involved in traffic accidents, could this be an example of adverse selection or moral hazard? Explain.
4. How does economics predict rational consumers will treat spending on credit cards compared with spending cash? Do you think that there are likely to be differences in the way people spend by each? If so, can you explain why?
5. How does behavioural economics differ from standard economics?
6. Give some examples of mental short-cuts/heuristics that you use. Why do you use them?
7. What is the representativeness heuristic? Explain how gamblers and hot-hand fallacies are examples of the representativeness heuristic.
8. Using the availability heuristic, explain hindsight bias.
9. Outline the so-called 'disposition effect'. Provide an explanation of why it might occur.
10. Dean supports Leicester City football club and has paid £80 for a ticket to watch them play in a cup final. The maximum amount he is willing to pay for the ticket is £200. Another Leicester City supporter offers him £400 for the ticket. Even though there are no restrictions on the resale of the tickets, Dean decides not to sell. Is his decision consistent with the predictions of rational decision making in standard economic theory? Explain your answer.
11. Draw a utility/value function that illustrates the concepts of reference dependent preferences, loss aversion and diminishing marginal sensitivity to gains/losses.
12. Using the theory of present bias, provide an economic rationale for government regulation of the payday loan market.
13. Give some examples of how governments try to nudge people to help them make better decisions.

Online Resources

Additional case studies on the student website

5.1 Choice overload. Is more choice always a good thing for consumers?

5.2 Modelling present bias. A case study of gym attendance.

5.3 Work of the UK Behavioural Insights Team. Nudge theory in practice.

5.4 Is economics the study of selfish behaviour? Is what's best for the individual best for others?

Websites relevant to Chapters 4 and 5

Numbers and sections refer to websites listed in the Web Appendix and hotlinked from this book's website at **go.pearson.com/uk/sloman.**

- For news articles relevant to this chapter, see the *Economics News* section on the student website.
- For general news on demand and consumers, see websites in section A, and particularly A1–4, 8, 9, 11, 12, 21–5, 36. See also site A41 for links to economics news articles on particular search topics (e.g. consumer demand and advertising).
- For data, information and sites on products and marketing, see sites B1, 3, 11, 13, 17, 39, 48.
- For student resources relevant to Part C, see sites C1–10, 19.
- For more on behavioural economics, see sites C1, 6, 7, 23.
- For material on consumer behaviour see the consumer behaviour section in site D3.
- For experiments and games examining consumer behaviour see D13, 14, 17–20.

Background to Supply

CHAPTER MAP

So far we have assumed that supply curves are upward sloping: that a higher price will encourage firms to supply more. But just how much will firms choose to supply at each price? It depends largely on the amount of profit they will make. If a firm can increase its profits by producing more, it will normally do so.

Profit is made by firms earning more from the sale of goods than they cost to produce. A firm's total profit ($T\Pi$) is thus the difference between its total sales revenue (TR) and its total costs of production (TC):

$$T\Pi = TR - TC$$

In order then to discover how a firm can maximise its profit or even get a sufficient level of profit, we must first consider what determines costs and revenue.

The first four sections build up a theory of short-run and long-run costs. They show how output depends on the inputs used, and how costs depend on the amount of output produced. Section 6.5 then looks at revenue. Finally, in section 6.6, we bring cost and revenue together to see how profit is determined. In particular, we shall see how profit varies with output and how the point of maximum profit is found.

Chapter 4 went behind the demand curve. It saw how the 'rational' consumer weighs up the *benefits* (utility) of consuming various amounts of goods or combinations of goods against their *costs* (their price).

We now need to go behind the supply curve and find out just how the ***rational producer*** (or 'firm' as we call all producers) will behave.

In this case, we shall be looking at the benefits and costs to the firm of producing various quantities of goods and using various alternative methods of production. We shall be asking:

- How much will be produced?
- What combination of inputs will be used?
- How much profit will be made?

Profit and the aims of a firm

The traditional theory of supply, or ***theory of the firm***, assumes that firms aim to *maximise profit*; this is a realistic assumption in many cases. The traditional profit-maximising theory of the firm is examined in this and the following two chapters. First, we examine the general principles that govern how much a firm supplies. Then, in Chapters 7 and 8, we look at how supply is affected by the amount of competition a firm faces.

In some circumstances, however, firms may not seek to maximise profits. Instead they may seek to maximise sales, or the rate of growth of sales. Alternatively, they may have no *single* aim, but rather a series of potentially conflicting aims held by different managers in different departments of the firm. Sometimes there may be a conflict between the owners of the firm and those running it. Not surprisingly, a firm's behaviour will be influenced by what its objectives are: i.e. what it is trying to achieve. Chapter 9 looks at the implications of firms having different aims and objectives. It also considers some ideas from behavioural economics.

6.1 THE SHORT-RUN THEORY OF PRODUCTION

The cost of producing any level of output will depend on the amount of inputs (or 'factors of production') used and the price the firm must pay for them. Let us first focus on the quantity of factors used.

Output depends on the amount of resources and how they are used. **Different amounts and combinations of inputs will lead to different amounts of output. If output is to be produced efficiently, then inputs should be combined in the optimum proportions.**

Short- and long-run changes in production

If a firm wants to increase production, it will take time to acquire a greater quantity of certain inputs. For example, a manufacturer can use more electricity by turning on switches, but it might take a while to obtain and install more machines, and longer still to build a bigger, or a second, factory.

If the firm wants to increase output relatively quickly, it will only be able to increase the quantity of certain inputs. It can use more raw materials and more fuel. It may be able to use more labour by offering overtime to its existing workforce, or by recruiting extra workers if they are available. But it will have to make do with its existing buildings and most of its machinery.

The distinction we are making here is between ***fixed factors*** and ***variable factors***. A *fixed* factor is an input that cannot be increased within a given time period (e.g. buildings). A *variable* factor is one that can.

The distinction between fixed and variable factors allows us to distinguish between the ***short run*** and the ***long run***.

The short run is a time period during which at least one factor of production is fixed. Output can be increased only by using more variable factors. For example, if a coffee bar became more successful it could serve more customers per day in its existing shops, if there was space. It could increase the quantity of milk and coffee beans it purchases. It may be able to hire more staff, depending on conditions in the local labour market, and purchase additional coffee machines if

Definitions

Rational producer behaviour When a firm weighs up the costs and benefits of alternative courses of action and then seeks to maximise its net benefit.

Theory of the firm The analysis of pricing and output decisions of the firm under various market conditions, assuming that the firm wishes to maximise profit.

Fixed factor An input that cannot be increased in supply within a given time period.

Variable factor An input that can be increased in supply within a given time period.

Short run The period of time over which at least one factor is fixed.

Long run The period of time long enough for *all* factors to be varied.

there was space to install them. However, in the short run it could not extend its existing shops or have new ones built. This would take more time.

The long run is a time period long enough for all inputs to be varied. Given enough time, a firm can build additional factories and install new plant and equipment; a coffee shop can have new shops built.

The actual length of the short run will differ from firm to firm and industry to industry. It is not a fixed period of time. It might take a farmer a year to obtain new land, buildings and equipment; if so, the short run is any time period up to a year and the long run is any time period longer than a year. If it takes a mobile phone handset manufacturer two years to get a new factory built, the short run is any period up to two years and the long run is any period longer than two years.

1. *How will the length of the short run for an airline depend on the state of the aircraft industry?*
2. *Up to roughly how long is the short run in the following cases?*
   (a) A firm supplying DJs for clubs and parties.
   (b) Nuclear power generation.
   (c) A street food wagon.
   (d) 'Superstore Hypermarkets Ltd'.
   In each case specify your assumptions.

For the remainder of this section we will concentrate on short-run production.

The law of diminishing returns

Production in the short run is subject to ***diminishing returns***. You may well have heard of 'the law of diminishing returns': it is one of the most famous of all 'laws' of economics. To illustrate how this law underlies short-run production let us take the simplest possible case where there are just two factors: one fixed and one variable.

Take the case of a farm. Assume the fixed factor is land and the variable factor is labour. Since the land is fixed in supply, output per period of time can be increased only by increasing the amount of workers employed. But imagine what would happen as more and more workers crowd on to a fixed area of land. The land cannot go on yielding more and more output indefinitely. After a point the additions to output from each extra worker will begin to diminish.

We can now state the law of diminishing (marginal) returns.

KEY IDEA 19

The law of diminishing marginal returns states that when increasing amounts of a variable factor are used with a given amount of a fixed factor, there will come a point when each extra unit of the variable factor will produce less extra output than the previous unit.

A good example of the law of diminishing returns is given in Case Study 6.1 on the student website. It looks at diminishing returns to the application of nitrogen fertiliser on farmland.

The short-run production function: total physical product

Let us now see how the law of diminishing returns affects the total output of a firm in the short run. When a variable factor is added to a fixed factor the total output that results is often called ***total physical product*** (*TPP*).

The relationship between inputs and output is shown in a ***production function***. In the simple case of the farm with only two factors – namely, a fixed supply of land ($\bar{Ln}$) and a variable supply of farm workers (*Lb*) – the short-run production function would be

$$TPP = f(\bar{Ln}, Lb)$$

This states that total physical product (i.e. the output of the farm) over a given period of time is a function of (i.e. depends on) the quantity of land and labour employed. The total physical output illustrated by the short-run production function shows the maximum output that can be produced by adding more of a variable input to a fixed input: i.e. it shows points that are all ***technically efficient***. Technical efficiency is where the maximum output is achieved from a given set of inputs. It is about things such as cutting out waste, or motivating people better, or making sure equipment is properly serviced or that controls of machines are correctly set.

In reality, total output from any given combination of inputs may be lower than the production function indicates because of inefficient management and methods of production. This issue is discussed in more detail in Box 7.5 in the next chapter. The level of technology is also assumed to be constant. (If there is technological progress, the whole production function would change.)

We could express the production function using an equation (an example is given in Box 6.4).

Alternatively, the production function could be expressed in the form of a table or a graph. Table 6.1 and Figure 6.1

Definitions

Law of diminishing (marginal) returns When one or more factors are held fixed, there will come a point beyond which the extra output from additional units of the variable factor will diminish.

Total physical product The total output of a product per period of time that is obtained from a given amount of inputs.

Production function The mathematical relationship between the output of a good and the inputs used to produce it. It shows how output will be affected by changes in the quantity of one or more of the inputs used in production holding the level of technology constant.

Technical efficiency The firm is producing as much output as is technologically possible given the quantity of factor inputs it is using.

BOX 6.1 **MALTHUS AND THE DISMAL SCIENCE OF ECONOMICS** EXPLORING ECONOMICS

Population growth + diminishing returns = starvation

The law of diminishing returns has potentially cataclysmic implications for the future populations of the world.

If the population of the world grows rapidly, then food output may not keep pace with it. There could be diminishing returns to labour as more and more people crowd on to the limited amount of land available.

This is already a problem in some of the poorest countries of the world, especially in sub-Saharan Africa. The land is barely able to support current population levels. Only one or two bad harvests are needed to cause mass starvation – witness the appalling famines in recent years in Ethiopia and Sudan.

The relationship between population and food output was analysed as long ago as 1798 by the Reverend Thomas Robert Malthus (1766–1834) in his *Essay on the Principle of Population*. This book was a bestseller and made Robert Malthus perhaps the best known of all social scientists of his day.

Malthus argued as follows:

> I say that the power of population is indefinitely greater than the power in the earth to produce subsistence for man.
>
> Population when unchecked, increases in a geometrical ratio. Subsistence increases only in an arithmetical ratio. A slight acquaintance with numbers will show the immensity of the first power in comparison with the second.[1]

What Malthus was saying is that world population tends to double about every 25 years or so if unchecked. It grows geometrically, like the series 1, 2, 4, 8, 16, 32, 64, etc. But food output, because of diminishing returns, cannot keep pace with this. It is likely to grow at only an arithmetical rate, like the series 1, 2, 3, 4, 5, 6, 7, etc. It is clear that population, if unchecked, will soon outstrip food supply.

So what is the check on population growth? According to Malthus, it is starvation. As population grows, so food output per head will fall until, with more and more people starving, the death rate will rise. Only then will population growth stabilise at the rate of growth of food output.

Have Malthus' predictions been borne out by events? Two factors have mitigated the forces that Malthus described:

- The rate of population growth tends to slow down as countries become more developed. Although improved health prolongs life, this tends to be more than offset by a decline in the birth rate as people choose to have smaller families. This is illustrated in the table below. Population growth peaked in the 1960s, has fallen substantially since then and is projected to fall further in future decades.
- Technological improvements in farming have greatly increased food output per hectare. These include better fertilisers and the development of genetically modified crops. (See Case Study 6.1 on the student website for an example.)

The growth in food output has thus exceeded the rate of population growth in developed countries and in some developing countries too. Nevertheless, the Malthusian spectre is very real for some of the poorest developing countries, which are simply unable to feed their populations satisfactorily. It is these poorest countries of the world which have some of the highest rates of population growth – around 3 per cent per annum in many African countries.

A further cause for concern arises from the move in Asia towards a westernised diet, with meat and dairy products playing a larger part. This further increases pressure on the land, since cattle require considerably more grain to produce meat than would be needed to feed humans a vegetarian diet.

A third factor is cited by some commentators, who remain unconvinced of the strength of Malthus' gloomy prognostication for the world. They believe that he seriously underestimated humankind's capacity to innovate; perhaps human ingenuity is one resource that doesn't suffer from diminishing returns.

1. *Why might it be possible for there to be a zero marginal productivity of labour on many family farms in poor countries and yet just enough food for all the members of the family to survive? (Illustrate using MPP and APP curves.)*
2. *The figures in the following table are based on the assumption that birth rates will fall faster than death rates. Under what circumstances might these forecasts underestimate the rate of growth of world population?*

Construct two charts using data from World Population Prospects (United Nations, Department of Economic and Social Affairs). The first should show the level of the world population since 1950 with forecasts to 2100, and the second the annual rate of growth over the same period. Write a short summary describing what the charts show.

World population levels and growth: actual and projected

Year	World population (billions)	Average annual rate of increase (%)		
		World	More developed regions	Less developed regions
1950	2.5			
1960	3.0	1.8	1.2	2.1
1970	3.7	2.0	1.0	2.4
1980	4.5	1.9	0.7	2.3
1990	5.3	1.8	0.6	2.1
2000	6.1	1.4	0.4	1.7
2010	7.0	1.2	0.4	1.4
2020	7.8	1.1	0.3	1.3
2030	8.5	0.9	0.1	1.1
2040	9.2	0.7	0.0	0.9
2050	9.7	0.6	−0.1	0.7
2060	10.2	0.4	−0.1	0.5

Source: World Population Prospects: The 2019 Revision (United Nations, Department of Economic and Social Affairs), https://population.un.org/wpp/ (Medium variant for predictions)

1 T. R. Malthus, *First Essay on Population* (Macmillan, 1926), pp. 13–14.

Table 6.1 Wheat production per year from a particular farm

	Number of workers (*Lb*)	*TPP*	*APP* (= *TPP*/*Lb*)	*MPP* (= Δ*TPP*/Δ*Lb*)
a	0	0	–	
	1	3	3	3
	2	10	5	7
b	3	24	8	14
c	4	36	9	12
	5	40	8	4
	6	42	7	2
d	7	42	6	0
	8	40	5	−2

show a hypothetical short-run production function for a farm producing wheat. The first two columns of Table 6.1 and the top diagram in Figure 6.1 show how total wheat output per year varies as extra workers are employed on a fixed amount of land.

With nobody working on the land, output will be zero (point *a*). As the first farm workers are taken on, wheat output initially rises more and more rapidly. The assumption behind this is that with only one or two workers productivity is low, since the workers are spread too thinly. With more workers, however, they can work together – each, perhaps, doing some specialist job – and thus they can use the land more productively. In Table 6.1, output rises more and more rapidly up to the employment of the third worker (point *b*). In Figure 6.1 the *TPP* curve gets steeper up to point *b*.

After point *b*, however, diminishing marginal returns set in: output rises less and less rapidly, and the *TPP* curve correspondingly becomes less steeply sloped.

When point *d* is reached, wheat output is at a maximum: the land is yielding as much as it can. Any more workers employed after that are likely to get in each other's way. Thus beyond point *d* output is likely to fall again: eight workers actually produce less than seven workers.

All the points along the total physical product are technically efficient. Any point below it is technically inefficient. For example, if production were at point *e* with five workers producing 30 tonnes, it would be technically possible for those five workers to produce 40 tonnes at point *f*.

What would happen to the TPP curve if the quantity of the fixed factor used in production were to increase to a new higher fixed level?

Figure 6.1 Wheat production per year (tonnes)

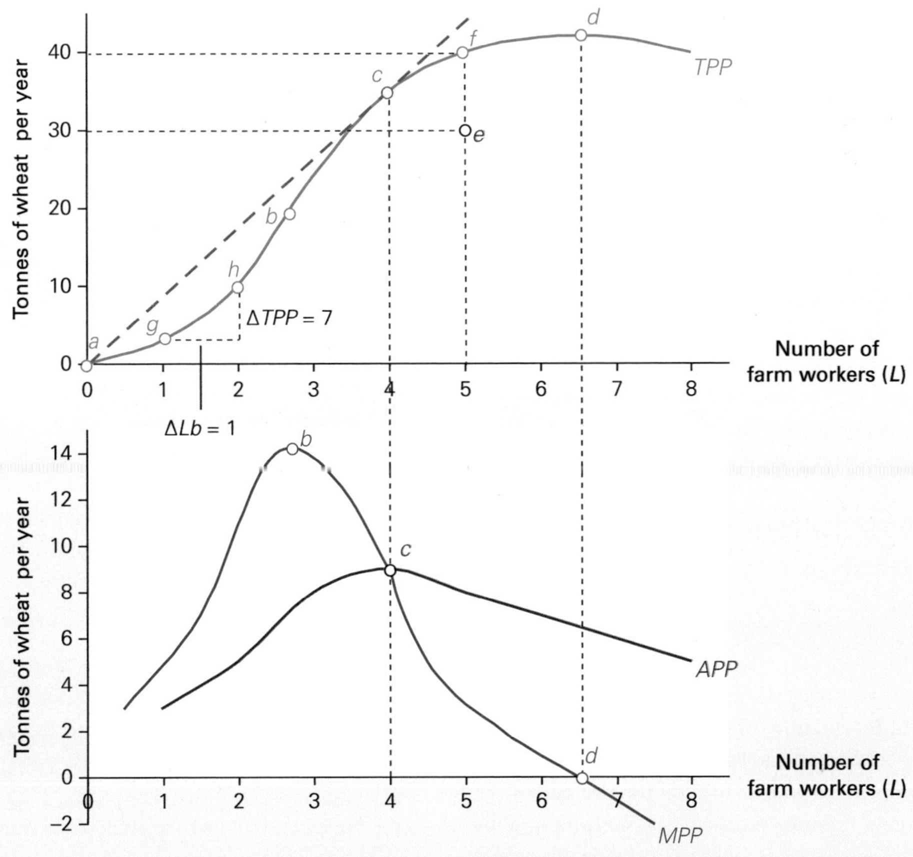

BOX 6.2 **DIMINISHING RETURNS IN THE BREAD SHOP** CASE STUDIES AND APPLICATIONS

Is the baker using his loaf?

Just up the road from where John lives is a bread shop. Like many others, he buys his bread there on a Saturday morning. Not surprisingly, Saturday morning is the busiest time of the week for the shop and as a result it takes on extra assistants.

During the week only one assistant serves the customers, but on a Saturday morning there used to be five serving. But could they serve five times as many customers? No, they could not. There were diminishing returns to labour.

The trouble is that certain factors of production in the shop are fixed:

- The shop is a fixed size. It gets very crowded on Saturday morning. Assistants sometimes had to wait while customers squeezed past each other to get to the counter, and with five serving, the assistants themselves used to get in each other's way.
- There is only one cash till. Assistants frequently had to wait while other assistants used it.
- There is only one pile of tissue paper for wrapping the bread. Again the assistants often had to wait.

The fifth and maybe even the fourth assistant ended up serving very few extra customers.

John is still going to the same bread shop and they still have only one till and one pile of tissue paper. But now only three assistants are employed on a Saturday! The shop, however, is just as busy. People still have to queue at busy times – although during the coronavirus pandemic, they queued outside, rather than in the shop.

How would you advise the baker as to whether he should (a) employ four assistants on a Saturday; (b) extend his shop, thereby allowing more customers to be served on a Saturday morning; (c) extend his opening hours on a Saturday?

Investigate a department store or other large shop. Identify any cases of diminishing returns. Consider what the shop could do to reduce these diminishing returns. Is it necessarily desirable for the shop to do so? Do online retailers experience the same types of diminishing returns and with what implications?

The short-run production function: average and marginal product

In addition to total physical product, two other important concepts are illustrated by a production function: namely, ***average physical product*** (***APP***) and ***marginal physical product*** (***MPP***).

Average physical product

This is output (*TPP*) per unit of the variable factor (Q_v). In the case of the farm, it is the output of wheat per worker.

$$APP = TPP/Q_v$$

Thus in Table 6.1 the average physical product of labour when four workers are employed is $36/4 = 9$ tonnes per year.

Marginal physical product

This is the *extra* output (ΔTPP) produced by employing *one more* unit of the variable factor.

Thus in Table 6.1 the marginal physical product of the fourth worker is 12 tonnes. The reason is that by employing the fourth worker, wheat output has risen from 24 tonnes to 36 tonnes: a rise of 12 tonnes.

In symbols, marginal physical product is given by

$$MPP = \Delta TPP/\Delta Q_v$$

Thus in our example:

$$MPP = 12/1 = 12$$

The reason why we divide the increase in output (ΔTPP) by the increase in the quantity of the variable factor (ΔQ_v) is that some variable factors can be increased only in multiple units. For example, if we wanted to know the *MPP* of fertiliser and we found out how much extra wheat was produced by using an extra 20kg bag, we would have to divide this output by 20 (ΔQ_v) to find the *MPP* of *one* more kilogram.

Note that in Table 6.1 the figures for *MPP* are entered in the spaces between the other figures. The reason is that *MPP* can be seen as the *difference* in output *between* one level of input and another. Thus in the table the difference in output between five and six workers is 2 tonnes.

The figures for *APP* and *MPP* are plotted in the lower diagram of Figure 6.1. We can draw a number of conclusions from these diagrams:

- The *MPP* between two points is equal to the slope of the *TPP* curve between those two points. For example, when the number of workers increases from 1 to 2 ($\Delta Lb = 1$), *TPP* rises from 3 to 10 tonnes ($\Delta TPP = 7$) *MPP* is thus 7: the slope of the line between points *g* and *h*.
- *MPP* rises at first: the slope of the *TPP* curve gets steeper.
- *MPP* reaches a maximum at point *b*. At that point the slope of the *TPP* curve is at its steepest.
- After point *b*, diminishing returns set in. *MPP* falls. *TPP* becomes less steep.  KI 19 p155
- *APP* rises at first. It continues rising as long as the addition to output from the last worker (*MPP*) is greater than the average output (*APP*): the *MPP* pulls the *APP* up (see Box 6.3). This continues beyond point *b*. Even though *MPP* is now falling, the *APP goes on* rising as long as the *MPP* is still above the *APP*. Thus *APP* goes on rising to point *c*.

Definitions

Average physical product Total output (*TPP*) per unit of the variable factor in question: $APP = TPP/Q_v$.

Marginal physical product The extra output gained by the employment of one more unit of the variable factor: $MPP = \Delta TPP/\Delta Q_v$.

- Beyond point *c*, *MPP* is below *APP*. New workers add less to output than the average. This pulls the average down: *APP* falls.
- As long as *MPP* is greater than zero, *TPP* will go on rising: new workers add to total output.
- At point *d*, *TPP* is at a maximum (its slope is zero). An additional worker will add nothing to output: *MPP* is zero.
- Beyond point *d*, *TPP* falls; *MPP* is negative.

1. *What is the significance of the slope of the line a–c in the top part of Figure 6.1?*
2. *Given that there is a fixed supply of land in the world, what implications can you draw from Figure 6.1 about the effects of an increase in world population for food output per head? (See Box 6.1.)*

BOX 6.3 THE RELATIONSHIP BETWEEN AVERAGES AND MARGINALS

EXPLORING ECONOMICS

In this chapter we have just examined the concepts of *average* and *marginal* physical product. We shall be coming across several other average and marginal concepts later on. It is useful at this stage to examine the general relationship between averages and marginals. In all cases there are three simple rules that relate them.

To illustrate these rules, consider the following example.

Imagine a room with 10 people in it. Assume that the *average* age of those present is 20.

Now if a 20-year-old enters the room (the *marginal* age), this will not affect the average age. It will remain at 20. If a 56-year-old now comes in, the average age will rise: not to 56, of course, but to 23. This is found by dividing the sum of everyone's ages (276) by the number of people (12). If then a child of 10 were to enter the room, this would pull the average age down.

From this example we can derive the three universal rules about averages and marginals:

- If the marginal equals the average, the average will not change.
- If the marginal is above the average, the average will rise.
- If the marginal is below the average, the average will fall.

Suppose a course you are studying has five equally weighted pieces of coursework. Assume each one is marked out of 100 and your results are shown in the table below.

Coursework	1	2	3	4	5
Mark	60	60	70	70	20

Each number in the second row of the table is the marginal mark from each piece of coursework. Calculate your total and average number of marks after each piece of coursework. Show how your average and marginal marks illustrate the three rules above.

See if you can find another activity (sporting or otherwise) and calculate the total, average and marginal variables. Do the numbers you have found still illustrate the rules that explain the relationship between averages and marginals?

*BOX 6.4 THE RELATIONSHIP BETWEEN *TPP*, *MPP* AND *APP*

EXPLORING ECONOMICS

Using calculus again

The total physical product of a variable factor (e.g. fertiliser) can be expressed as an equation. For example:

$$TPP = 100 + 32Q_f + 10Q_f^2 - Q_f^3 \quad (1)$$

where *TPP* is the output of grain in tonnes per hectare, and Q_f is the quantity of fertiliser applied in kilograms per hectare.

From this we can derive the *APP* function. *APP* is simply TPP/Q_f: i.e. output per kilogram of fertiliser. Thus:

$$APP = \frac{100}{Q_f} + 32 + 10Q_f - Q_f^2 \quad (2)$$

We can also derive the *MPP* function. *MPP* is the rate of increase in *TPP* as additional fertiliser is applied. It is thus the first derivative of *TPP*: $dTPP/dQ_f$ Thus:

$$MPP = 32 + 20Q_f - 3Q_f^2 \quad (3)$$

From these three equations we can derive the table shown.

Check out some figures by substituting values of Q_f into each of the three equations.

Maximum output (484 tonnes) is achieved with 8kg of fertiliser per hectare. At that level, *MPP* is zero: no additional output can be gained.

Q_f	*TPP*	*APP*	*MPP*
1	141	141	49
2	196	98	60
3	259	86	65
4	324	81	64
5	385	77	57
6	436	72	44
7	471	67	25
8	484	60	0
9	469	52	−31

This maximum level of *TPP* can be discovered from the equations by using a simple technique. If *MPP* is zero at this level, then simply find the value of Q_f where

$$MPP = 32 + 20Q_f - 3Q_f^2 = 0 \quad (4)$$

Solving this equation[1] gives $Q_f = 8$

1 By applying the second derivative test (see Appendix 1) you can verify that $Q_f = 8$ gives the *maximum TPP* rather than the *minimum*. (Both the maximum *and* the minimum point of a curve have a slope equal to zero.)

Section summary

1. A production function shows the relationship between the amount of inputs used and the amount of output produced from them (per period of time). It assumes technical efficiency in production.
2. In the short run it is assumed that one or more factors (inputs) are fixed in supply. The actual length of the short run will vary from industry to industry.
3. Production in the short run is subject to diminishing returns. As greater quantities of the variable factor(s) are used, so each additional unit of the variable factor will add less to output than previous units: marginal physical product will diminish and total physical product will rise less and less rapidly.
4. As long as marginal physical product is above average physical product, average physical product will rise. Once *MPP* has fallen below *APP*, however, *APP* will fall.

6.2 COSTS IN THE SHORT RUN

We have seen how output changes as inputs are varied in the short run. We now use this information to show how costs vary with the amount a firm produces. Obviously, before deciding how much to produce, it has to know the precise level of costs for each level of output.

But first we must be clear on just what we mean by the word 'costs'. The term is used differently by economists and accountants.

Measuring costs of production

When measuring costs, economists always use the concept of ***opportunity cost***. Remember from Chapter 1 how we defined opportunity cost. It is the cost of any activity measured in terms of the *sacrifice* made in doing it: in other words, the cost measured in terms of the value of the best alternative forgone.

How do we apply this principle of opportunity cost to a firm? First we must discover what factors of production it is using. Then we must measure the sacrifice involved. To do this it is useful to put factors into two categories.

Factors not owned by the firm: explicit costs

The opportunity cost of using factors not already owned by the firm is simply the price that the firm has to pay for them. Thus if the firm uses £100 worth of electricity, the opportunity cost is £100. The firm has sacrificed £100, which could have been spent on something else. The same would be true for machinery or buildings (factories/shops/units) that have been rented from other organisations. These costs are called ***explicit costs*** because they involve direct payment of money by firms.

Factors already owned by the firm: implicit costs

When the firm already owns factors (e.g. machinery), it does not as a rule have to pay out money to use them. Their opportunity costs are thus ***implicit costs***. They are equal to what the factors could earn for the firm in some alternative use, either within the firm or hired out to some other firm. Implicit costs do not involve actual cash outlays. They are less visible than explicit costs but just as important in decision making.

Here are some examples of implicit costs:

- A firm owns some buildings. The opportunity cost of using them in production for a year is the highest rent that could have been earned by letting them out to another firm over the same period.
- A firm draws £100 000 from the bank out of its savings in order to invest in new plant and equipment. The opportunity cost of this investment is not just the £100 000 (an explicit cost), but also the interest it thereby forgoes (an implicit cost).
- The owner of the firm could have earned £40 000 per annum by working for someone else. This £40 000 is then the opportunity cost of the owner's time running the business over the same period.

The opportunity costs of any decision in production are the implicit and explicit costs that are relevant to that

Definitions

Opportunity cost Cost measured in terms of the value of the best alternative forgone.

Explicit costs Costs where an actual transfer of money takes place between parties.

Implicit costs Costs that do not involve a direct payment of money to a third party, but which nevertheless involve a sacrifice of some alternative.

particular decision. By relevant we mean the costs that are incurred if the firm chose one particular course of action: e.g. expand output or stay in business. If a different decision is taken these costs would be avoided.

What implicit and explicit costs would a firm avoid if it decided not to expand production?

Some costs may remain unaffected by whatever decision a firm makes. These are not opportunity costs and so are irrelevant. They are called ***sunk costs*** and should be completely disregarded.

A sunk cost often exists when a firm has paid for a factor of production in the past and that factor of production no longer has value in any alternative uses. For example, a firm may have previously purchased a piece of machinery that is highly specialised and tailored to its own production process. If this machinery is of no value to any other firms and has no scrap value, the opportunity cost of using it is *zero*. No matter what decisions the firm makes in the future, the money used to purchase the machinery – its ***historic cost*** – is irrelevant. Not using the machine will not bring that money back – it cannot be recovered. In such a case, if the output from the machinery is worth more than the cost of all the *other* inputs involved, the firm might as well use the machine rather than let it stand idle.

It is important to remember that the cost of the machine was not always a sunk cost. Before its purchase, the opportunity cost of buying the machine was the money paid for it. It was only after its purchase that it became a sunk cost and had an opportunity cost of zero. The timing of a decision is crucial when deciding whether a cost is relevant or sunk.

KEY IDEA 20

The 'bygones' principle **states that sunk costs should be ignored when deciding whether to produce or sell more or less of a product. Only those costs that can be avoided should be taken into account.**

Costs and inputs

A firm's costs of production will depend on the factors of production it uses. The more factors it uses, the greater will its costs be. More precisely, this relationship depends on two elements:

- The productivity of the factors. The greater their physical productivity, the smaller will be the quantity of them required to produce a given level of output, and hence the lower will be the cost of that output. In other words, there is a direct link between *TPP, APP* and *MPP* and the costs of production.
- The price of the factors. The higher their price, the higher will be the costs of production.

In the short run, some factors are fixed in supply. Their total costs, therefore, are fixed, in the sense that they do not

Definitions

Sunk costs Costs that cannot be recouped (e.g. by transferring assets to other uses). Examples include specialised machinery or the costs of an advertising campaign.

Historic costs The original amount the firm paid for factors it now owns.

BOX 6.5 THE FALLACY OF USING HISTORIC COSTS

EXPLORING ECONOMICS

Or there's no point crying over spilt milk

If you fall over and break your leg, there is little point in saying 'If only I hadn't done that, I could have gone on that skiing holiday; I could have done so many other things [sigh].' Wishing things were different won't change history. You have to manage as well as you can with your broken leg.

It is the same for a firm. Once it has purchased some inputs, it is no good then wishing it hadn't. It has to accept that it has now got them, and make the best decisions about what to do with them.

Take a simple example. The local greengrocer decides in early December to buy 100 Christmas trees for £10 each. At the time of purchase, this represents an opportunity cost of £10 each, since the £10 could have been spent on something else. The greengrocer estimates that there is enough local demand to sell all 100 trees at £20 each, thereby making a reasonable profit.

But the estimate turns out to be wrong. On 23 December there are still 50 trees unsold. What should be done? At this stage the £10 that was paid for the trees is irrelevant. It is an historic cost. It cannot be recouped: the trees cannot be sold back to the wholesaler, nor can they be kept for next year. KI 20 p161

In fact, the opportunity cost is now zero. It might even be negative if the greengrocer has to pay to dispose of any unsold trees. It might, therefore, be worth selling the trees at £10, £5 or even £1. Last thing on Christmas Eve it might even be worth giving away any unsold trees.

1. *Why is the correct price to charge (for the unsold trees) the one at which the price elasticity of demand equals −1? (Assume no disposal costs.)*
2. *Supermarkets have to pay for the rubbish they produce to be disposed of. Given this, what should they do with food that is approaching the sell-by date?*

Visit your nearest supermarket towards the end of the day and look for items marked at a reduced price because they are near their sell-by date. In each case try to decide what the optimum reduced price is and why. Would observing customers' behaviour help you to make this decision?

BOX 6.6 **ARE FIXED COSTS ALWAYS THE SAME AS SUNK COSTS?** EXPLORING ECONOMICS

All sunk costs are fixed costs, but not all fixed costs are sunk costs

Within a given time period (i.e. the economic short run) some costs of production are completely insensitive to the quantity of output a firm produces. They remain the same whether the firm produces zero or a million units of output. These are called fixed costs. Other costs are responsive to the amount the firm produces. If it expands production, these costs will increase and if it reduces output they will fall. These are known as variable costs.

A variable cost can never be an example of a sunk cost as its size depends on the decision taken by a firm. A variable cost is always an opportunity cost. What about fixed costs? Is a fixed cost always a sunk cost? Could they be different in some circumstances?

Consider the following examples of costs that are likely to remain fixed for a number of different firms across a range of different sectors.

- Developing a new product – this could involve R&D.
- Advertising campaign to launch a new product.
- Physical capital:
  - machinery;
  - business premises.
- Human capital:
  - recruitment/training.
- Heating and lighting the business premises.
- Complying with government regulation.

If a firm temporarily shuts down then some of these costs cannot be avoided. For example, the costs of (a) developing a new product, (b) an advertising campaign and (c) complying with government regulation can never be recovered. These categories of fixed cost are also examples of sunk costs. They remain the same no matter what the firm decides to do. KI 20 p161

What about the cost of heating and lighting the business premises? Although these are fixed costs of production it is highly likely that they could be avoided if the firm temporarily shut down: i.e. with no staff in the building, the heating and lighting could simply be turned off. This is an example of a fixed cost that is *not* a sunk cost.

It may be possible for the firm to avoid some of the fixed costs associated with physical capital. If the firm temporarily shuts down, it might be able to rent the business premises and machinery to other firms. The higher the rental value of these assets, the greater the proportion of the fixed cost that is not a sunk cost.

The chances of a firm being able to rent out its physical capital to other businesses will depend on how much it has been tailored to its own particular use. Is the physical capital very specialised or is it more generic (such as a lorry) and so of value to a large number of other firms?

You need to think very carefully before deciding whether a fixed cost is also a sunk cost.

A firm currently rents a piece of machinery for £500 per month. The rental contract stipulates that this fee must be paid for the next 12 months. If the firm temporarily shut down it could rent the machinery to another business for £300 per month. To what extent is this fixed cost also a sunk cost?

vary with output. Rent on land is a ***fixed cost***. It is the same whether the firm produces a lot or a little.

The total cost of using variable factors, however, does vary with output. The cost of raw materials is a ***variable cost***. The more that is produced, the more raw materials are used and therefore the higher is their total cost.

The following are some costs incurred by a sports footwear manufacturer. Assume the manufacturer wants to increase output over a relatively short time period: i.e. in the economic short run. Decide whether each one of the following is a fixed or a variable cost of expanding production in the short run or has some element of both. Clearly explain any assumptions you have made.

(a) The cost of synthetic leather and mesh materials.
(b) The fee paid to an advertising agency.
(c) Wear and tear on machinery.
(d) Business rates on the factory.
(e) Electricity for heating and lighting.
(f) Electricity for running the machines.
(g) Basic minimum wages agreed with the union.
(h) Overtime pay.
(i) Depreciation of machines as a result purely of their age (irrespective of their condition).

Total cost

The ***total cost*** (*TC*) of production is the sum of the *total variable costs* (*TVC*) and the *total fixed costs* (*TFC*) of production:

$$TC = TVC + TFC$$

Consider Table 6.2 and Figure 6.2. They show the total costs for firm X of producing different levels of output (Q). Let us examine each of the three cost curves in turn.

Total fixed cost (TFC)

In our example, total fixed cost is assumed to be £12. Since this does not vary with output, it is shown by a horizontal straight line.

Definitions

Fixed costs Total costs that do not vary with the amount of output produced.

Variable costs Total costs that do vary with the amount of output produced.

Total cost The sum of total fixed costs and total variable costs: $TC = TFC + TVC$.

Table 6.2 Total costs for firm X

Output (*Q*)	*TFC* (£)	*TVC* (£)	*TC* (£)
0	12	0	12
1	12	10	22
2	12	16	28
3	12	21	33
4	12	28	40
5	12	40	52
6	12	60	72
7	12	91	103
.	.	.	.

Total variable cost (TVC)

With a zero output, no variable factors will be used. Thus *TVC* = 0. The *TVC* curve, therefore, starts from the origin.

KI 19 p155 The shape of the *TVC* curve follows from the law of diminishing returns. Initially, *before* diminishing returns set in, *TVC* rises less and less rapidly as more variable factors are added. Take the case of a factory with a fixed supply of machinery: initially as more workers are taken on the workers can do increasingly specialist tasks and make a fuller use of the capital equipment. This corresponds to the portion of the *TPP* curve that rises more rapidly (up to point *b* in Figure 6.1 on page 157).

As output is increased beyond point *m* in Figure 6.2, diminishing returns set in. Since extra workers (the extra variable factors) are producing less and less extra output, the extra units of output they do produce will cost more and more in terms of wage costs. Thus *TVC* rises more and more rapidly. The *TVC* curve gets steeper. This corresponds to the portion of the *TPP* curve that rises less rapidly (between points *b* and *d* in Figure 6.1).

Total cost (TC)

Since *TC* = *TVC* + *TFC*, the *TC* curve is simply the *TVC* curve shifted vertically upwards by £12.

Average and marginal costs

Average cost (*AC*) is cost per unit of production:

$$AC = TC/Q$$

Thus if it cost a firm £2000 to produce 100 units of a product, the average cost would be £20 for each unit (£2000/100).

Like total cost, average cost can be divided into the two components, fixed and variable. In other words, average cost equals ***average fixed cost*** (*AFC* = *TFC*/*Q*) plus ***average variable cost*** (*AVC* = *TVC*/*Q*):

$$AC = AFC + AVC$$

Definitions

Average (total) cost Total cost (fixed plus variable) per unit of output: *AC* = *TC*/*Q* = *AFC* + *AVC*.

Average fixed cost Total fixed cost per unit of output: *AFC* = *TFC*/*Q*.

Average variable cost Total variable cost per unit of output: *AVC* = *TVC*/*Q*.

Figure 6.2 Total costs for firm X

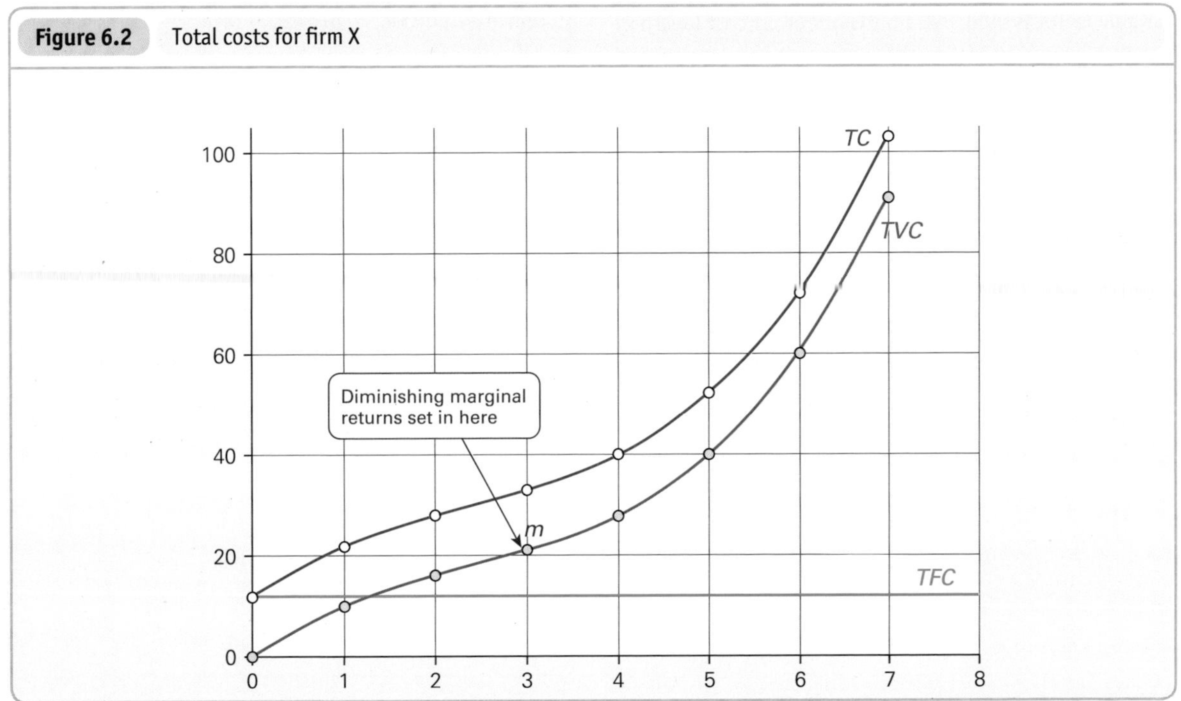

Marginal cost (*MC*) is the *extra* cost of producing *one more unit*: i.e. the rise in total cost per one unit rise in output:

$$MC = \frac{\Delta TC}{\Delta Q}$$

For example, assume that a firm is currently producing 1000 000 boxes of matches a month. It now increases output by 1000 boxes (another batch): $\Delta Q = 1000$. As a result, its total costs rise by £30: $\Delta TC = £30$. What is the cost of producing one more box of matches? It is

$$\frac{\Delta TC}{\Delta Q} = \frac{£30}{1000} = 3\text{p}$$

(Note that all marginal costs are variable, since, by definition, there can be no extra fixed costs as output rises.)

Given the *TFC, TVC* and *TC* for each output, it is possible to derive the *AFC, AVC, AC* and *MC* for each output using the above definitions.

For example, using the data of Table 6.2, Table 6.3 can be constructed.

Fill in the missing figures in Table 6.3. (Note that the figures for MC come in the spaces between each level of output.)

What will be the shapes of the *MC, AFC, AVC* and *AC* curves? These follow from the nature of the *MPP* and *APP* curves that we looked at in section 6.1 above. You may recall that the typical shapes of the *APP* and *MPP* curves are like those illustrated in Figure 6.3.

Figure 6.3 Average and marginal physical product

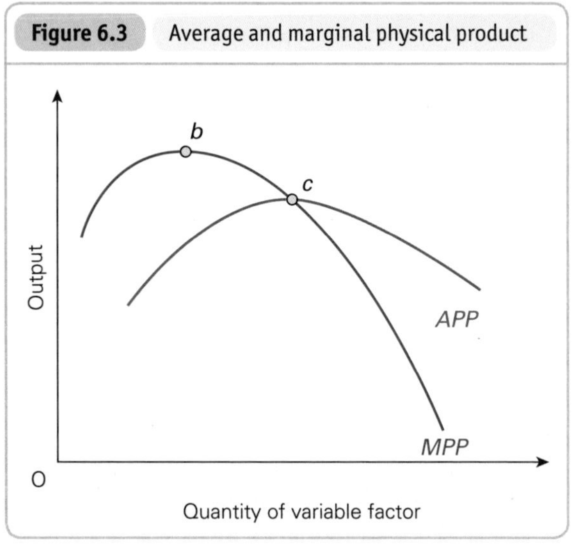

Marginal cost (MC)

The shape of the *MC* curve follows directly from the law of diminishing returns. Initially, in Figure 6.4, as more of the variable factor is used, extra units of output cost less than previous units. *MC* falls. This corresponds to the rising portion of the *MPP* curve in Figure 6.3 and the portion of the *TVC* curve in Figure 6.2 to the left of point *m*.

Beyond a certain level of output, diminishing returns set in. This is shown as point *x* in Figure 6.4 and corresponds to point *b* in Figure 6.3 (and point *m* in Figure 6.2). Thereafter *MC* rises as *MPP* falls. Additional units of output cost more and more to produce, since they require ever-increasing amounts of the variable factor.

Average fixed cost (AFC)

This falls continuously as output rises, since *total* fixed costs are being spread over a greater and greater output.

Definition

Marginal cost The extra cost of producing one more unit of output: $MC = \Delta TC/\Delta Q$.

Table 6.3 Total, average and marginal costs for firm X

Output (*Q*) (units)	*TFC* (£)	*AFC (TFC/Q)* (£)	*TVC* (£)	*AVC (TVC/Q)* (£)	*TC (TFC + TVC)* (£)	*AC (TC/Q)* (£)	*MC* ($\Delta TC/\Delta Q$) (£)
0	12	–	0	–	12	–	
							10
1	12	12	10	10	22	22	
							...
2	12	6	16	...	28	14	
							5
3	...	...	21	7	...	...	
							7
4	...	3	28	...	40	...	
							12
5	...	2.4	...	8	52	10.4	
							...
6	...	...	...	10	...	12	
							31
7	...	1.7	91	13	103	14.7	

Figure 6.4 Average and marginal costs

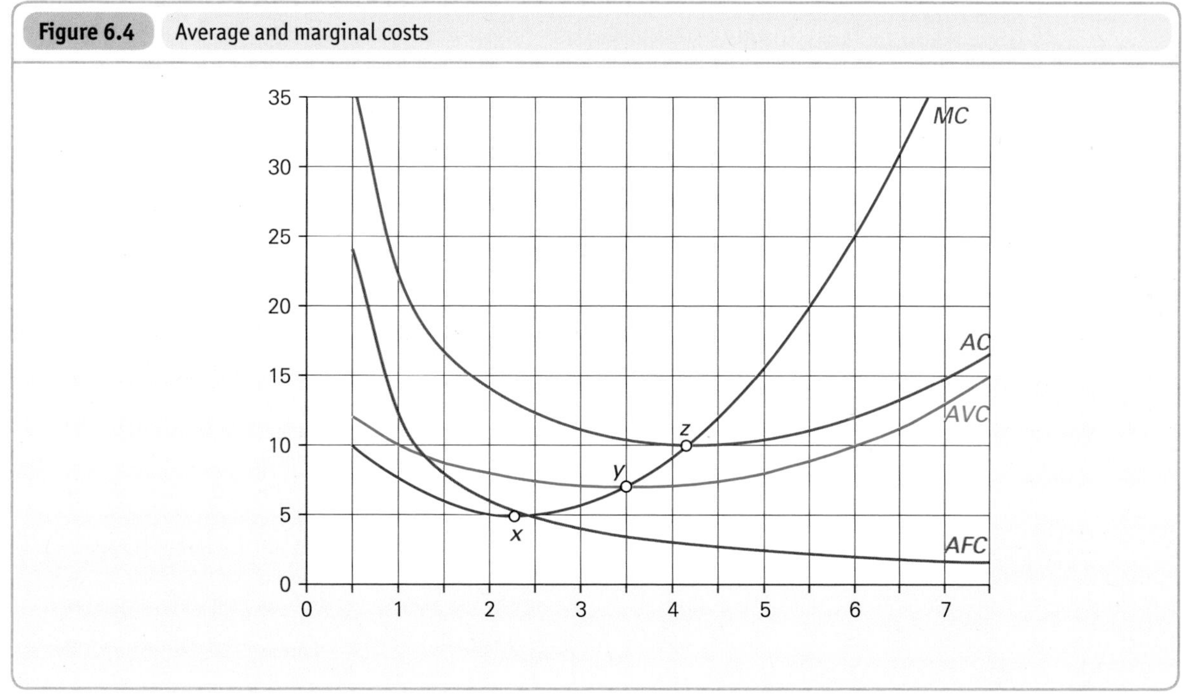

Average variable cost (AVC)

The shape of the *AVC* curve depends on the shape of the *APP* curve. As the average product of workers rises (up to point *c* in Figure 6.3), the average labour cost per unit of output (the *AVC*) falls: as far as point *y* in Figure 6.4. Thereafter, as *APP* falls, *AVC* must rise.

Average (total) cost (AC)

This is simply the vertical sum of the *AFC* and *AVC* curves. Note that as *AFC* gets less, the gap between *AVC* and *AC* narrows.

The relationship between average cost and marginal cost

This is simply another illustration of the relationship that applies between *all* averages and marginals (see Box 6.3).

As long as new units of output cost less than the average, their production must pull the average cost down: i.e. if *MC* is less than *AC*, *AC* must be falling. Likewise, if new units cost more than the average, their production must drive the average up: i.e. if *MC* is greater than *AC*, *AC* must be rising. Therefore, the *MC* crosses the *AC* at its minimum point (point *z* in Figure 6.4).

Since all marginal costs are variable, the same relationship holds between *MC* and *AVC*.

Why is the minimum point of the AVC curve at a lower level of output than the minimum point of the AC curve?

*LOOKING AT THE MATHS

The total, average and marginal cost functions can be expressed algebraically as follows:

$$TFC = a \qquad (1)$$

$$TVC = bQ - cQ^2 + dQ^3 \qquad (2)$$

$$TC = a + bQ - cQ^2 + dQ^3 \qquad (3)$$

where a is the constant term representing fixed costs, and the signs of the terms in the *TVC* equation have been chosen to give *TVC* and *TC* curves shaped like those in Figure 6.2. Dividing each of the above by Q gives:

$$AFC = \frac{a}{Q} \qquad (4)$$

$$AVC = b - cQ + dQ^2 \qquad (5)$$

$$AC = \frac{a}{Q} + b - cQ + dQ^2 \qquad (6)$$

Differentiating equation (3) or (2) gives:

$$MC = b - 2cQ + 3dQ^2 \qquad (7)$$

A worked example of each of these is given in Maths Case 6.1 on the student website.

BOX 6.7 COST CURVES IN PRACTICE

EXPLORING ECONOMICS

When fixed factors are divisible

Are cost curves always the shape depicted in this chapter? The answer is no. Sometimes, rather than being U-shaped, the *AVC* and *MC* curves are flat-bottomed, like the curves in the diagram below. Indeed, they may be constant (and equal to each other) over a substantial range of output.

The reason for this is that fixed factors may sometimes not have to be in full use all the time. Take the case of a firm with 100 identical machines, each one requiring one person to operate it. Although the firm cannot use more than the 100 machines, it could use fewer: in other words, some of the machines could be left idle. Assume, for example, that instead of using 100 machines, the firm uses only 90. It would need only 90 operatives and 90 per cent of the raw materials.

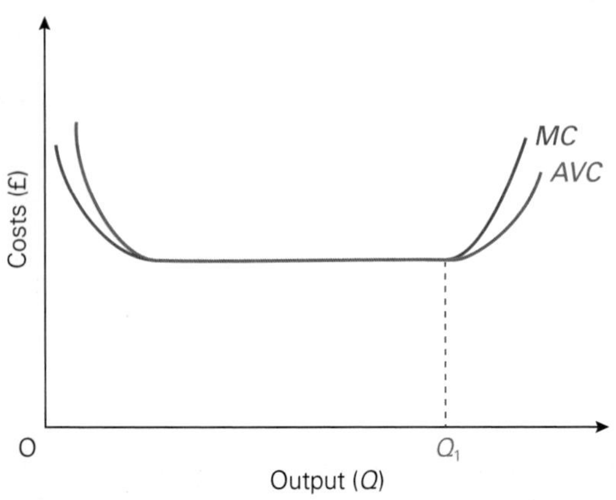

Similarly, if it used only 20 machines, its total variable costs (labour and raw materials) would be only 20 per cent. What we are saying here is that average variable cost remains constant – and over a very large range of output, using anything from 1 machine to 100 machines.

The reason for the constant *AVC* (and *MC*) is that by varying the amount of fixed capital used, the proportions used of capital, labour and raw materials can be kept the same and hence the average and marginal productivity of labour and raw materials will remain constant.

Only when all machines are in use (at Q_1) will *AVC* start to rise if output is further expanded. Machines may then have to work beyond their optimal speed, using more raw materials per unit of output (diminishing returns to raw materials), or workers may have to work longer shifts with higher (overtime) pay.

1. *Assume that a firm has five identical machines, each operating independently. Assume that with all five machines operating normally, 100 units of output are produced each day. Below what level of output will AVC and MC rise?*
2. *Manufacturing firms like the one we have been describing will have other fixed costs (such as rent and managerial overheads). Does the existence of these affect the argument that the AVC curve will be flat-bottomed?*

Investigate a particular firm and establish whether it is likely to experience flat-bottomed AVC and MC curves.

Section summary

1. When measuring costs of production, we should be careful to use the concept of opportunity cost. In the case of factors not owned by the firm, the opportunity cost is simply the explicit cost of purchasing or hiring them. It is the price paid for them. In the case of factors already owned by the firm, it is the implicit cost of what the factor could have earned for the firm in its next best alternative use.
2. In the short run, some factors are fixed in supply. Their total costs are thus fixed with respect to output. In the case of variable factors, their total cost will increase as more output is produced and hence as more of the variable factor is used.
3. Total cost can be divided into total fixed and total variable costs. Total variable cost will tend to increase less rapidly at first as more is produced, but then, when diminishing returns set in, it will increase more and more rapidly.
4. Marginal cost is the cost of producing one more unit of output. It will probably fall at first (corresponding to the part of the TVC curve where the slope is getting shallower), but will start to rise as soon as diminishing returns set in.
5. Average cost, like total cost, can be divided into fixed and variable costs. Average fixed cost will decline as more output is produced since total fixed cost is being spread over a greater and greater number of units of output. Average variable cost will tend to decline at first, but once the marginal cost has risen above it, it must then rise.

6.3 THE LONG-RUN THEORY OF PRODUCTION

KI 18 p154

In the long run, *all* factors of production are variable. There is time for the firm to build a new factory, to install new machines, to use different production techniques and to combine its inputs in whatever proportion and in whatever quantities it chooses.

In the long run, then, there are several decisions that a firm has to make: decisions about the scale and location of its operations and what techniques of production it should use. These decisions affect the costs of production. It is important, therefore, to get them right.

Table 6.4 Illustrating figures derived from a production function

		Number of machines				
		1	2	3	4	5
Number of workers	1	4	7	13	13	12
	2	11	16	19	20	21
	3	16	21	24	25	26
	4	19	24	27	29	30
	5	21	25	28	30	32

The distinction between long-run and short-run production is illustrated in Table 6.4. The numbers in the table show the maximum output (the technically efficient output) that can be produced by employing different combinations of capital and labour. The impact of increasing the quantity of labour can be seen by working down each column. For example, if one worker is employed with one machine the maximum output that can be produced is 4. If a second worker is employed with one machine the total output is 11 and so on. The impact of increasing the amount of capital – i.e. the number of machines – can be seen by working across each row.

The scale of production

If a firm were to double all of its inputs – something it could do in the long run – would it double its output? Or will output more than double or less than double? We can distinguish three possible situations:

Increasing returns to scale. This is where a given percentage increase in inputs leads to a *larger* percentage increase in output. For example, look what happens in Table 6.4 if the number of workers and machines used in production are both doubled from 1 to 2. Total output increases from 4 to 16 (look diagonally downwards). In this case a 100 per cent increase in the inputs used in production leads to a 300 per cent increase in output. Production exhibits increasing returns to scale.

Constant returns to scale. This is where a given percentage increase in inputs leads to the *same* percentage increase in output. This is illustrated in Table 6.4 when the number of workers and machines are both increased from 2 to 3. This 50 per cent increase in inputs leads to a 50 per cent increase in output: i.e. total output increases from 16 to 24.

Decreasing returns to scale. This is where a given percentage increase in inputs leads to a *smaller* percentage increase in output. If, in the table, both the number of workers and machines are increased from 3 to 4 (a 33.3 per cent increase) then output increases from 24 to only 29 (a 20.8 per cent increase).

Notice the terminology here. The words 'to scale' mean that *all* inputs increase by the same proportion. Increasing and decreasing returns *to scale* are therefore quite different from increasing and diminishing returns to a variable factor (where only the *variable* factor increases). Returns to a variable factor is a characteristic of *short-run* production and can be illustrated in Table 6.4 by working down each of the columns – assuming labour is the variable factor and capital is the fixed factor.

Table 6.4 illustrates five different short-run productions functions: i.e. where the number of machines remains constant at one, two, three, four or five. In each case explain if there are diminishing or increasing marginal returns.

Economies of scale

The concept of increasing returns to scale is closely linked to that of ***economies of scale***. Whereas returns to scale focuses on how output changes in proportion to the quantity of inputs used in production, economies of scale looks at how costs change in proportion to the output produced. A firm experiences economies of scale if costs per unit of output fall as the scale of production increases: i.e. the proportionate increase in total costs is lower than the proportionate increase in output. Clearly, if a firm is getting increasing returns to scale from its factors of production, then as it produces more it will be using smaller and smaller amounts of factors per unit of output. Other things being equal, this means that it will be producing at a lower unit cost.

However, unlike returns to scale, economies of scale does not impose the restriction that *inputs* increase by the same proportionate amount. The increase in output can come from increasing inputs by different proportionate amounts, such as changing labour by 5 per cent and capital by 10 per cent.

There are several reasons why firms are likely to experience economies of scale. Some are due to increasing returns to scale; some are not.

Specialisation and division of labour. In large-scale plants workers can often do simple, repetitive jobs. With this ***specialisation and division of labour*** less training is needed; workers can become highly efficient in their particular job, especially with long production runs; there is less time lost in workers switching from one operation to another; and supervision is easier. Workers and managers can be employed who have specific skills in specific areas.

Indivisible/lumpy inputs. The quantity of some factor inputs increases continuously or in small increments as production rises. For example, if a factory expands output, its use of electricity and raw materials tends to rise roughly in proportion to this increase in production. If a coffee shop sells more coffee, its use of coffee beans/milk constantly rises. These are examples of divisible or non-lumpy inputs.

Other inputs are indivisible or lumpy. They can only be purchased in large discrete units and cannot be divided into

Definitions

Economies of scale When increasing the scale of production leads to a lower cost per unit of output.

Specialisation and division of labour Where production is broken down into a number of simpler, more specialised tasks, thus allowing workers to acquire a high degree of efficiency.

smaller sizes. Many machines, such as a blast furnace or a combine harvester exhibit such ***indivisibility***. Also, once built, a factory or an assembly line cannot easily be increased or decreased in size by small increments.

At low levels of output, an indivisible input may not be fully utilised. As it is impossible to split the input into smaller units, this increases the firm's average cost of production. As the firm expands output, the input can be utilised more fully and closer to its full capacity. This will reduce the firm's average cost and is a key benefit of increasing production.

Capital-intensive methods of production will tend to use a larger proportion of indivisible inputs and so may benefit significantly from these economies of scale.

The 'container principle'. Any capital equipment that contains things (blast furnaces, oil tankers, pipes, vats, etc.) tends to cost less per unit of output the larger its size. The reason has to do with the relationship between a container's volume and its *surface area*. A container's cost depends largely on the materials used to build it and hence roughly on its surface area. Its output depends largely on its *volume*. Large containers have a bigger volume relative to surface area than do small containers.

For example, a container with a bottom, top and four sides, with each side measuring 1 metre, has a volume of 1 cubic metre and a surface area of 6 square metres (six surfaces of 1 square metre each). If each side were now to be doubled in length to 2 metres, the volume would be 8 cubic metres and the surface area 24 square metres (six surfaces of 4 square metres each). Thus an eightfold increase in capacity has been gained at only a fourfold increase in the container's surface area, and hence an approximate fourfold increase in cost.

Greater efficiency of large machines. Large machines may be more efficient in the sense that more output can be gained for a given amount of inputs. For example, only one worker may be required to operate a machine whether it be large or small. Also, a large machine may make more efficient use of raw materials.

By-products. With production on a large scale, there may be sufficient waste products to enable some by-product or by-products to be made.

Multi-stage production. A large factory may be able to take a product through several stages in its manufacture. This saves time and cost in moving the semi-finished product from one firm or factory to another. For example, a large cardboard-manufacturing firm may be able to convert trees or waste paper into cardboard and then into cardboard boxes in a continuous sequence.

All the above are examples of ***plant economies of scale***. They are due to an individual factory or workplace or machine being large. There are other economies of scale, however, that are associated with the *firm* being large – perhaps with many factories.

Organisational economies. With a large firm, individual plants can specialise in particular functions. There can also be centralised administration of the firm; for example, one human resources department could administer all the wages. Often, after a merger between two firms, savings can be made by ***rationalising*** their activities in this way.

Spreading overheads. Some expenditures are economic only when the *firm* is large: for example, research and development – only a large firm can afford to set up a research laboratory. This is another example of indivisibilities, only this time at the level of the firm rather than the plant. The greater the firm's output, the more these ***overhead*** costs are spread.

Financial economies. Large firms are often able to obtain finance at lower interest rates than small firms, since they are seen by banks to be lower risk. They may be able to obtain certain inputs cheaper by buying in bulk.

Economies of scope. These are cost savings when a firm produces two or more products together rather than different firms producing them separately. More formally, for two goods (X and Y) they occur where:

$$TC(Q_X, Q_Y) < TC(Q_X, 0) + TC(0, Q_Y)$$

Economies of scope arise where factor inputs used in the production and/or sale of one good can also be used in the production and/or sale of other goods. By using such factors more intensively, the average costs of producing each good falls. One example is where the administrative systems in a company's head office can be used to support the production of more than one good. Another example is where a firm extends the use of a popular brand into different products/markets: e.g. Apple producing mobile phones, tablets, computers and smart watches. Discounts from suppliers can be achieved, common distribution networks can be used and certain marketing costs can be spread over a larger number of units.

1. *Which of the economies of scale we have considered are due to increasing returns to scale and which are due to other factors?*
2. *What economies of scale is a large department store likely to experience?*

Definitions

Indivisibility The impossibility of dividing a factor into smaller units.

Plant economies of scale Economies of scale that arise because of the large size of a factory.

Rationalisation The reorganising of production (often after a merger) so as to cut out waste and duplication and generally to reduce costs.

Overheads Costs arising from the general running of an organisation, and only indirectly related to the level of output.

Economies of scope When increasing the range of products produced by a firm reduces the cost of producing each one.

Diseconomies of scale

When firms get beyond a certain size, costs per unit of output may start to increase. There are several reasons for such ***diseconomies of scale***:

- Management problems of co-ordination may increase as the firm becomes larger and more complex, and as lines of communication get longer. There may be a lack of personal involvement by management.
- Workers may feel 'alienated' if their jobs are boring and repetitive, and if they feel that they are an insignificantly small part of a large organisation. Small to medium-sized companies often report that workers feel they 'make a difference'; this may be lost in a large firm and as a consequence lower motivation may lead to shoddy work.
- Industrial relations may deteriorate as a result of these factors and also as a result of the more complex interrelationships between different categories of worker. More levels of 'people management' may therefore be required.
- Production-line processes and the complex interdependencies of mass production can lead to great disruption if there are hold-ups in any one part of the firm.

Whether firms experience economies or diseconomies of scale will depend on the conditions applying in each individual firm.

Why are firms likely to experience economies of scale up to a certain size and then diseconomies of scale after some point beyond that?

Location

In the long run, a firm can move to a different location. The location will affect the cost of production since locations differ in terms of the availability and cost of raw materials, suitable land and power supply, the qualifications, skills and experience of the labour force, wage rates, transport and communications networks, the cost of local services, and banking and financial facilities. In short, locations differ in terms of the availability, suitability and cost of the factors of production.

Transport costs will be an important influence on a firm's location. Ideally, a firm will wish to be as near as possible to both its raw materials and the market for its finished product. When market and raw materials are in different locations, the firm will minimise its transport costs by locating somewhere between the two.

In general, if the raw materials are more expensive to transport than the finished product, the firm should be located as near as possible to the raw materials. Thus heavy industry, which uses large quantities of coal and various ores, tends to be concentrated near the coal fields or near the ports. If, on the other hand, the finished product is more expensive to transport (e.g. bread and beer), the firm will probably be located as near as possible to its market.

When raw materials or markets are in many different locations, transport costs will be minimised at the 'centre of gravity'. This location will be nearer to those raw materials and markets whose transport costs are greater per mile.

How has the opening up of trade and investment between eastern and western Europe likely to have affected the location of industries within Europe that have (a) substantial economies of scale; (b) little or no economies of scale?

The size of the whole industry

As an *industry* grows in size, this can lead to ***external economies of scale*** for its member firms. This is where a firm, whatever its own individual size, benefits from the *whole industry* being large. For example, the firm may benefit from having access to specialist raw material or component suppliers, labour with specific skills, firms that specialise in marketing the finished product, and banks and other financial institutions with experience of the industry's requirements. What we are referring to here is the ***industry's infrastructure***: the facilities, support services, skills and experience that can be shared by its members.

1. *Name some industries where external economies of scale are gained. What are the specific external economies in each case?*
2. *Would you expect external economies to be associated with the concentration of an industry in a particular region?*

The member firms of a particular industry might experience ***external diseconomies of scale***. For example, as an industry grows larger, this may create a growing shortage of specific raw materials or skilled labour. This will push up their prices, and hence the firms' costs.

The optimum combination of factors: the marginal product approach

In the long run, all factors can be varied. The firm can thus choose what techniques of production to use: what design of factory to build, what types of machine to buy, how to organise the factory, whether to use highly automated processes or more labour-intensive techniques. It must be very careful in making these decisions. After all, once it has built a factory and installed machinery, these then become fixed factors of production, and the subsequent 'short-run' time period may in practice last a very long time.

Definitions

Diseconomies of scale Where costs per unit of output increase as the scale of production increases.

External economies of scale Where a firm's costs per unit of output decrease as the size of the whole industry grows.

Industry's infrastructure The network of supply agents, communications, skills, training facilities, distribution channels, specialised financial services, etc. that supports a particular industry.

External diseconomies of scale Where a firm's costs per unit of output increase as the size of the whole industry increases.

For any given scale, how should the firm decide what technique to use? How should it decide the optimum 'mix' of factors of production?

The profit-maximising firm will obviously want to use the least costly combination of factors to produce any given output. It will therefore substitute factors, if by so doing it can reduce the cost of a given output. What then is the optimum combination of factors?

The simple two-factor case

TC 8 p109

Take first the simplest case where a firm uses just two factors: labour (L) and capital (K). The least-cost combination of the two will be where

$$\frac{MPP_L}{P_L} = \frac{MPP_K}{P_K}$$

In other words, where the extra product (MPP) from the last pound spent on each factor is equal. But why should this be so? The easiest way to answer this is to consider what would happen if they were not equal.

If they were not equal, it would be possible to reduce cost per unit of output by using a different combination of labour and capital. For example, if

$$\frac{MPP_L}{P_L} > \frac{MPP_K}{P_K}$$

more labour should be used relative to capital, since the firm is getting a greater physical return for its money from extra workers than from extra capital. As more labour is used per unit of capital, however, diminishing returns to labour set in. Thus MPP_L will fall. Likewise, as less capital is used per unit of labour, MPP_K will rise. This will continue until

KI 19 p155

$$\frac{MPP_L}{P_L} = \frac{MPP_K}{P_K}$$

At this point, the firm will stop substituting labour for capital.

Since no further gain can be made by substituting one factor for another, this combination of factors or 'choice of technique' can be said to be the most efficient. It is the least-cost way of combining factors for any given output or the maximum output for a given cost of production. Efficiency in this sense of using the optimum factor proportions is known as ***productive efficiency***.

KI 3 p13

The multi-factor case

Where a firm uses many different factors, the least-cost combination of factors will be where

$$\frac{MPP_a}{P_a} = \frac{MPP_b}{P_b} = \frac{MPP_c}{P_c} \cdots = \frac{MPP_n}{P_n}$$

where a . . . *n* are different factors. This is a variant of the equi-marginal principle that we examined on page 110.

The reasons are the same as in the two-factor case. If any inequality exists between the MPP/P ratios, a firm will be able to reduce its costs by using more of those factors with a high MPP/P ratio and less of those with a low MPP/P ratio until they all become equal.

A major problem for a firm in choosing the least-cost technique is in predicting future factor price changes.

If the price of a factor were to change, the MPP/P ratios would cease to be equal. The firm, to minimise costs, would then like to alter its factor combinations until the MPP/P ratios once more became equal. The trouble is that, once it has committed itself to a particular technique, it may be several years before it can switch to an alternative one. Thus if a firm invests in labour-intensive methods of production and is then faced with an unexpected wage rise, it may regret not having chosen a more capital-intensive technique. While there is no simple solution to this issue, there are a number of companies that have made a business of predicting trends across different sectors to assist firms in their decision making.

If factor X costs twice as much as factor Y ($P_X/P_Y = 2$), what can be said about the relationship between the MPPs of the two factors if the optimum combination of factors is used?

*LOOKING AT THE MATHS

We can express the long-run production function algebraically. In the simple two-factor model, where capital (K) and labour (L) are the two factors, the production function is

$$TPP = f(K,L)$$

A simple and widely used production function is the ***Cobb–Douglas production function***. This takes the form

$$TPP = AK^{\alpha}L^{\beta}$$

Box 6.8 demonstrates that where $\alpha + \beta = 1$, there are constant returns to scale; where $\alpha + \beta > 1$, there are increasing returns to scale; and where $\alpha + \beta < 1$, there are decreasing returns to scale.

A multiple-factor Cobb–Douglas production function would take the form

$$TPP = AF_1^{\alpha}F_2^{\beta}F_3^{\gamma} \cdots F_n^{\omega}$$

where $F_1, F_2, F_3 \ldots F_n$ are all the factors. For example, if there were six factors, *n* would be factor 6. Again, it can be shown that where $\alpha + \beta + \gamma + \ldots \omega = 1$, there are constant returns to scale; where $\alpha + \beta + \gamma + \ldots \omega > 1$, there are increasing returns to scale; and where $\alpha + \beta + \gamma + \ldots \omega < 1$, there are decreasing returns to scale.

Definitions

Productive efficiency The least-cost combination of factors for a given output or the maximum output for a given cost of production.

Cobb–Douglas production function Like other production functions, this shows how output (TPP) varies with inputs of various factors (F_1, F_2, F_3, etc.). In the simple two-factor case it takes the following form:

$$TPP = f(F_1,F_2) = AF_1^{\alpha}F_2^{\beta}$$

If $\alpha + \beta = 1$, there are constant returns to scale; if $\alpha + \beta > 1$, there are increasing returns to scale; if $\alpha + \beta < 1$, there are decreasing returns to scale.

*BOX 6.8 THE COBB–DOUGLAS PRODUCTION FUNCTION | EXPLORING ECONOMICS

Exploring its properties

Let us take the simple Cobb–Douglas production function (see 'Looking at the Maths' box on page 170):

$$TPP = AK^{\alpha}L^{\beta} \quad (1)$$

Returns to scale and the Cobb–Douglas production function

What would happen if you were to double the amount of both K and L used (in other words, the scale of production doubles)? If output doubles, there are constant returns to scale. If output more than doubles, there are increasing returns to scale; if it less than doubles, there are decreasing returns to scale. Let us see what happens when we double the amount of K and L in equation (1).

$$\begin{aligned} TPP &= A(2K)^{\alpha}(2L)^{\beta} \\ &= A2^{\alpha}K^{\alpha}2^{\beta}L^{\beta} \\ &= A2^{\alpha+\beta}K^{\alpha}L^{\beta} \end{aligned}$$

If $\alpha + \beta = 1$, then $2^{\alpha+\beta} = 2$. Thus

$$TPP = 2AK^{\alpha}L^{\beta}$$

In other words, doubling the amount of K and L used has doubled output: there are constant returns to scale.

If $\alpha + \beta > 1$, then $2^{\alpha+\beta} > 2$. In this case, doubling inputs will more than double output: there are increasing returns to scale. Similarly, if $\alpha + \beta > 1$, then $2^{\alpha+\beta} < 2$ and there are decreasing returns to scale.

Finding the marginal physical products of labour and capital

The marginal physical product (*MPP*) of a factor is the additional output obtained by employing one more unit of that factor, while holding other factors constant. The *MPP* of either factor in the above Cobb–Douglas production function can be found by differentiating the function with respect to that factor (see pages A:12–13 for the rules of partial differentiation). Thus

$$MPP_K = \frac{\partial(TPP)}{\partial K} = \alpha AK^{\alpha-1}L^{\beta} \quad (2)$$

and

$$MPP_L = \frac{\partial(TPP)}{\partial L} = \beta AK^{\alpha}L^{\beta-1} \quad (3)$$

For example, if the production function were

$$TPP = 4K^{3/4}L^{1/2} \quad (4)$$

and if $K = 81$ and $L = 36$, then, from equations (2) and (4),

$$\begin{aligned} MPP_K &= \alpha AK^{\alpha-1}L^{\beta} \\ &= \frac{3}{4} \times 4(81^{-1/4})(36^{1/2}) \\ &= 3 \times \frac{1}{3} \times 6 = 6 \end{aligned}$$

$$\begin{aligned} \text{and } MPP_L &= \beta AK^{\alpha}L^{\beta-1} \\ &= \frac{1}{2} \times 4(81^{3/4})(36^{-1/2}) \\ &= 2 \times 27 \times \frac{1}{6} = 9 \end{aligned}$$

In other words, an additional unit of capital will produce an extra 6 units of output and an additional unit of labour will produce an extra 9 units of output.

Assume that the production function is given by

$$TPP = 36K^{1/3}L^{1/2}R^{1/4}$$

where R is the quantity of a particular raw material used.

(a) Are there constant, increasing or decreasing returns to scale?

(b) What is the marginal productivity of the raw material if $K = 8$, $L = 16$ and $R = 81$?

*The optimum combination of factors: the isoquant/isocost approach

This section is optional. You can skip straight to page 175 without loss of continuity.

A firm's choice of optimum technique can be shown graphically. This graphical analysis takes the simplest case of just two variable factors – for example, labour and capital. The amount of labour used is measured on one axis and the amount of capital used is measured on the other.

The graph involves the construction of *isoquants* and *isocosts*.

Isoquants

Imagine that a firm wants to produce a certain level of output: say, 5000 units per year. Let us assume that it estimates all the possible combinations of labour and capital that could produce that level of output. Once again this is assuming technical efficiency in production. Some of these estimates are shown in Table 6.5.

Technique *a* is a capital-intensive technique, using 40 units of capital and only 5 workers. As we move towards technique *e*, labour is substituted for capital. The techniques become more labour intensive.

These alternative techniques for producing a given level of output can be plotted on a graph. The points are joined to form an ***isoquant***. Figure 6.5 shows the 5000 unit isoquant corresponding to Table 6.5.

Definition

Isoquant A line showing all the alternative combinations of two factors that can produce a given level of output.

Table 6.5 Various capital and labour combinations to produce 5000 units of output per year

	a	*b*	*c*	*d*	*e*
Units of capital (*K*)	40	20	10	6	4
Number of workers (*L*)	5	12	20	30	50

The isoquant shows the whole *range* of alternative ways of producing a given output. Thus Figure 6.5 shows not only points *a* to *e* from the table, but all the intermediate points too.

KI 18 p154

Like an indifference curve, an isoquant is rather like a contour on a map. As with contours and indifference curves, a whole series of isoquants can be drawn, each one representing a different level of output (*TPP*). The higher the output, the further out to the right will the isoquant be. Thus in Figure 6.6, isoquant I_5 represents a higher level of output than I_4, and I_4 a higher output than I_3, and so on.

1. Could isoquants ever cross?
2. Could they ever slope upwards to the right?
Explain your answers.

The shape of the isoquant. Why is the isoquant 'bowed in' towards the origin? This illustrates a diminishing ***marginal rate of factor substitution*** (*MRS*). This, as we shall see very soon, is due to the law of diminishing returns.

KI 19 p155

The *MRS*[1] is the amount of one factor (e.g. *K*) that can be replaced by a 1 unit increase in the other factor (e.g. *L*), if output is to be held constant. So if 2 units of capital ($\Delta K = 2$) could be replaced by 1 unit of labour ($\Delta L = 1$) the *MRS* would be 2. Thus:

$$MRS = \frac{\Delta K}{\Delta L} = \frac{2}{1} = 2$$

The *MRS* between two points on the isoquant will equal the slope of the line joining those two points. Thus in Figure 6.7, the *MRS* between points *g* and *h* is 2($\Delta K/\Delta L = 2/1$). But this is merely the slope of the line joining points *g* and *h* (ignoring the negative sign).

When the isoquant is bowed in towards the origin, the slope of the isoquant will diminish as one moves down the curve, and so too, therefore, will the *MRS* diminish. Referring again to Figure 6.7, between points *g* and *h* the *MRS* = 2. Lower down the curve between points *j* and *k*, it has fallen to 1.

Calculate the MRS moving up the curve in Figure 6.5 between each pair of points: e–d, d–c, c–b and b–a. Does the MRS diminish moving in this direction?

The relationship between MRS and MPP. As one moves down the isoquant, total output, by definition, will remain the same. Thus the loss in output due to less capital being used (i.e. $MPP_K \times \Delta K$) must be exactly offset by the gain in output due to more labour being used (i.e. $MPP_L \times \Delta L$). Thus:

$$MPP_L \times \Delta L = MPP_K \times \Delta K$$

Definition

Marginal rate of factor substitution The rate at which one factor can be substituted by another while holding the level of output constant:

$$MRS = \Delta F_1/\Delta F_2 = MPP_{F_2}/MPP_{F_1}$$

1 Note that we use the same letters *MRS* to refer to the marginal rate of factor substitution as we did in the previous chapter to refer to the marginal rate of substitution in consumption. Sometimes we use the same words too – just 'marginal rate of substitution' rather than the longer title. In this case we must rely on the context in order to tell which is being referred to.

Figure 6.5 An isoquant

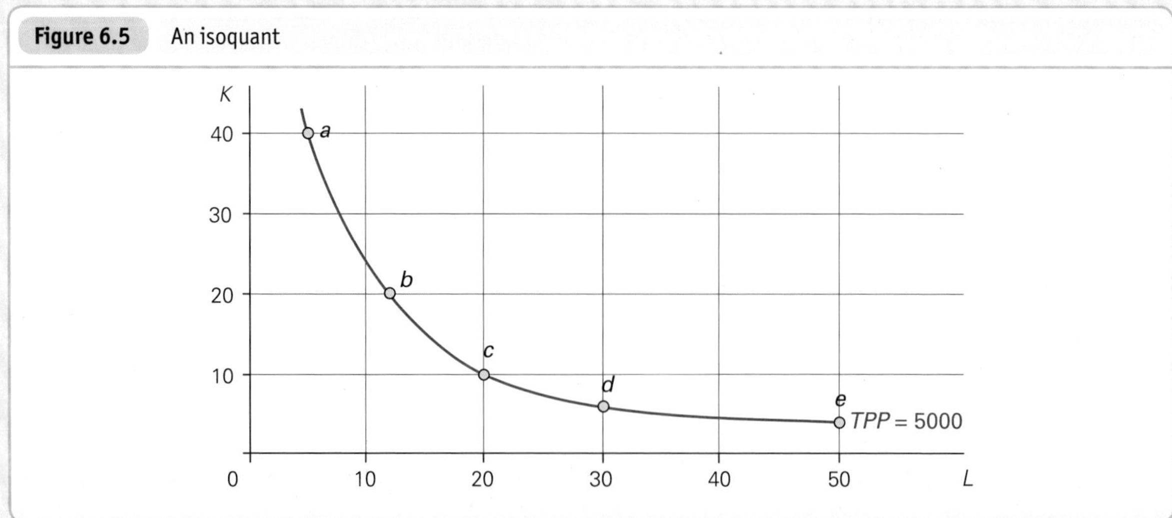

Figure 6.6 An isoquant map

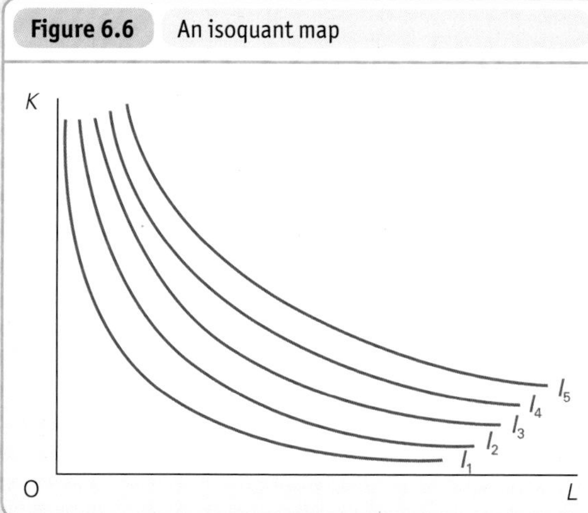

This equation can be rearranged as follows:

$$\frac{MPP_L}{MPP_K} = \frac{\Delta K}{\Delta L}(= MRS)$$

Thus the *MRS* is equal to the inverse of the marginal productivity ratios of the two factors.

Diminishing MRS and the law of diminishing returns. The principle of diminishing *MRS* is related to the law of diminishing returns. As one moves down the isoquant, increasing amounts of labour are being used relative to capital. This, given diminishing returns, would lead the *MPP* of labour to fall relative to the *MPP* of capital. But since $MRS = MPP_L/MPP_K$, if MPP_L/MPP_K diminishes, then, by definition, so must *MRS*.

The less substitutable factors are for each other, the faster *MRS* will diminish, and therefore the more bowed in will be the isoquant.

Isocosts

We have seen how factors combine to produce different levels of output, but how do we choose the level of output? This will involve taking costs into account.

Figure 6.7 Diminishing marginal rate of factor substitution

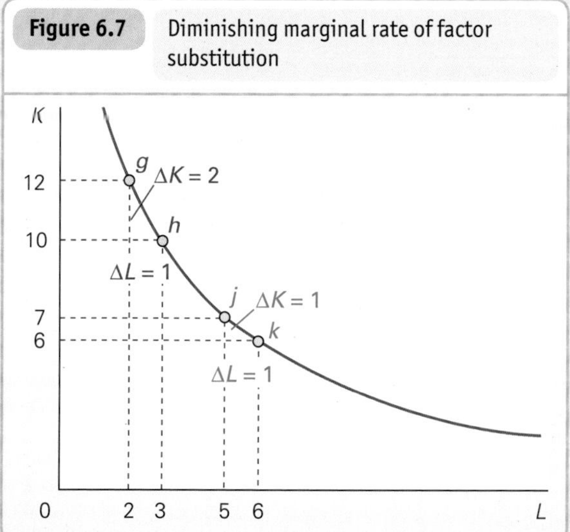

Table 6.6 Combinations of capital and labour costing the firm £300 000 per year

Units of capital (at £20 000 per unit)	0	5	10	15
No. of workers (at a wage of £10 000)	30	20	10	0

Assume that factor prices are fixed. A table can be constructed showing the various combinations of factors that a firm can use for a particular sum of money.

For example, assuming that P_K is £20 000 per unit per year and P_L is £10 000 per worker per year, Table 6.6 shows various combinations of capital and labour that would cost the firm £300 000 per year.

These figures are plotted in Figure 6.8. The line joining the points is called an ***isocost***. It shows all the combinations of labour and capital that cost £300 000.

As with isoquants, a series of isocosts can be drawn. Each one represents a particular cost to the firm. The higher the cost, the further out to the right will the isocost be.

1. *What will happen to an isocost if the prices of both factors rise by the same percentage?*
2. *What will happen to the isocost in Figure 6.8 if the wage rate rises to £15 000?*

The slope of the isocost equals

$$\frac{P_L}{P_K}$$

This can be shown in the above example. The slope of the isocost in Figure 6.8 is $15/30 = {}^1/_2$. But this is P_L/P_K (i.e. £10 000/£20 000).

Isoquants and isocosts can now be put on the same diagram. The diagram can be used to answer either of two questions: (a) What is the least-cost way of producing a particular level of output? (b) What is the highest output that can be achieved for a given cost of production?

These two questions are examined in turn.

The least-cost combination of factors to produce a given level of output

First the isoquant is drawn for the level of output in question: for example, the 5000 unit isoquant in Figure 6.5. This is reproduced in Figure 6.9.

Then a series of isocosts are drawn representing different levels of total cost. The higher the level of total cost, the further out will be the isocosts.

The least-cost combination of labour and capital is shown at point *r*, where $TC = £400\,000$. This is where the isoquant just touches the lowest possible isocost. Any other point on the isoquant (e.g. *s* or *t*) would be on a higher isocost.

Definition

Isocost A line showing all the combinations of two factors that cost the same to employ.

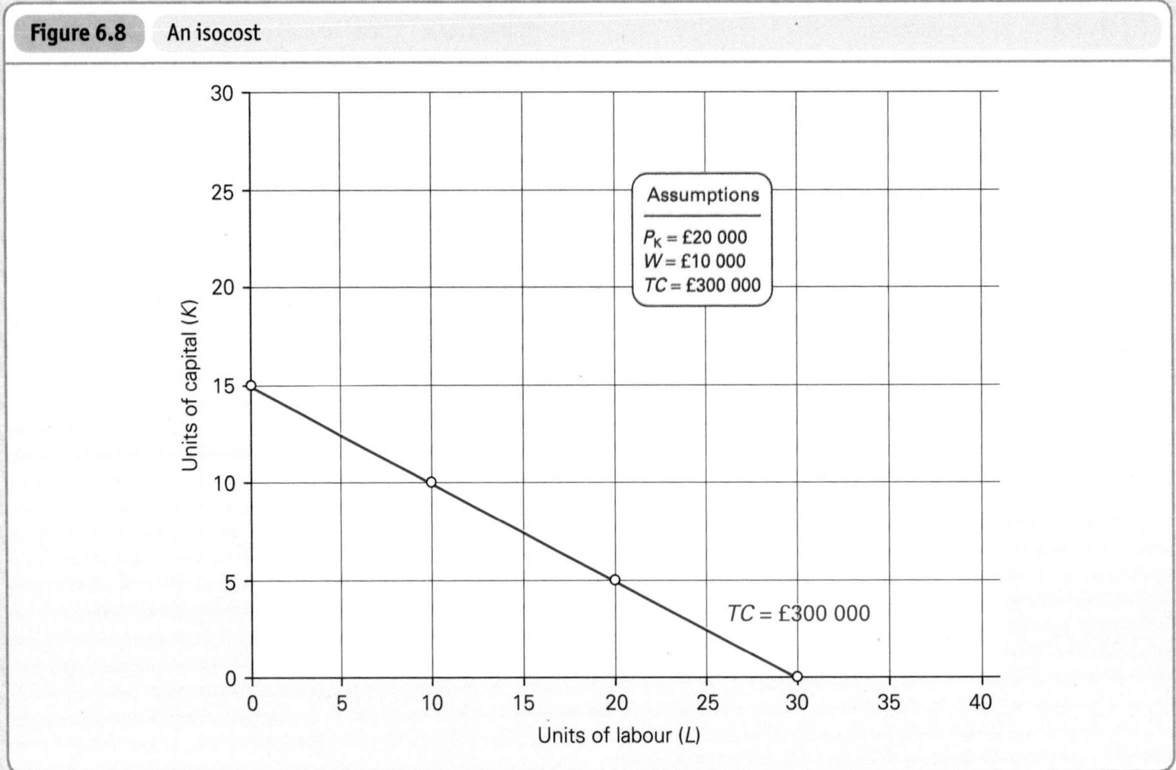

Figure 6.8 An isocost

TC 8 p109

Comparison with the marginal productivity approach. We showed earlier that the least-cost combination of labour and capital was where

$$\frac{MPP_L}{P_L} = \frac{MPP_K}{P_K}$$

In this section it has just been shown that the least-cost combination is where the isoquant is tangential to an isocost (i.e. point *r* in Figure 6.9). Thus their slope is the same. The slope of the isoquant equals *MRS*, which equals MPP_L/MPP_K; and the slope of the isocost equals P_L/P_K.

$$\therefore \frac{MPP_L}{MPP_K} = \frac{P_L}{P_K}$$

$$\therefore \frac{MPP_L}{P_L} = \frac{MPP_K}{P_K}$$

KI 14 p111

Thus, as one would expect, the two approaches yield the same result.

Highest output for a given cost of production

An isocost can be drawn for the particular level of total cost outlay in question. Then a series of isoquants can be drawn, representing different levels of output (*TPP*). This is shown in Figure 6.10. The higher the level of output, the further

Figure 6.9 The least-cost method of production

TC = £200 000
TC = £300 000
TC = £400 000
TC = £500 000
TPP = 5000 units
s
r
t
K
L
0
10
20
30
40
50

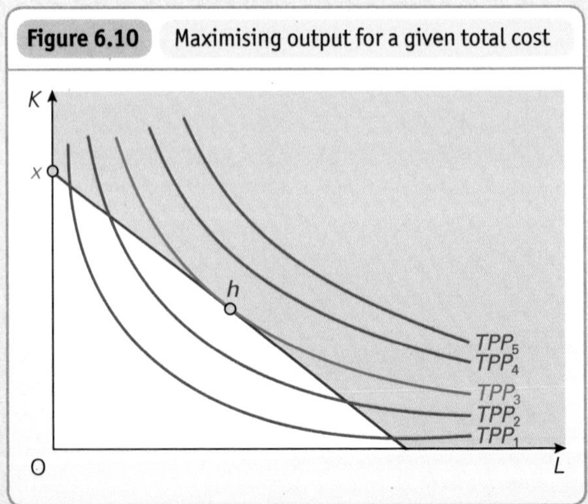

Figure 6.10 Maximising output for a given total cost

out will lie the corresponding isoquant. The point at which the isocost touches the highest isoquant will give the factor combination yielding the highest output for that level of cost. This will be at point *h* in Figure 6.10. Again this will be where the slopes of the isocost and isoquant are the same: where $P_L/P_K = MRS$.

The tangency points in both Figure 6.9 and 6.10 represent a point of productive efficiency (see pages 12 and 170).

If the prices of factors change, new isocosts will have to be drawn. Thus in Figure 6.10, if the wage rate goes up, less labour can be used for a given sum of money. The isocost will swing inwards round point *x*. The isocost will get steeper. Less labour will now be used relative to capital.

*LOOKING AT THE MATHS

We can express the optimum production point algebraically. This can be done in either of two ways, corresponding to Figures 6.9 or 6.10. The method is similar to that used for finding the optimum consumption point that we examined on page 118.

(a) Corresponding to Figure 6.9

The first way involves finding the least-cost method of producing a given output (Q). This can be expressed as

$$\text{Min } P_K K + P_L L \quad (1)$$

subject to the output constraint that

$$Q = Q(K,L) \quad (2)$$

In other words, the objective is to find the lowest isocost (equation 1) to produce on a given isoquant (equation 2).

(b) Corresponding to Figure 6.10

The second involves finding the highest output that can be produced for a given cost. This can be expressed as

$$\text{Max } Q(K,L) \quad (3)$$

subject to the cost constraint that

$$P_K K + P_L L = C \quad (4)$$

In other words, the objective is to find the highest isoquant (equation 3) that can be reached along a given isocost (equation 4).

There are two methods of solving (a) and (b) for any given value of P_K, P_L and either Q (in the case of (a)) or C (in the case of (b)). The first involves substituting the constraint equation into the objective function (to express K in terms of L) and then finding the value of L and then K that minimises the objective function in the case of (a) or maximises it in the case of (b). This involves differentiating the objective function and setting it equal to zero. A worked example of this method is given in Maths Case 6.2 on the student website.

The second method, which is slightly longer but is likely to involve simpler calculations, involves the use of 'Lagrangian multipliers'. This method is explained, along with a worked example, in Maths Case 6.3. It is the same method as we used in Maths Case 4.2 when finding the optimal level of consumption of two products.

Postscript: decision making in different time periods

We have distinguished between the short run and the long run. Let us introduce two more time periods to complete the picture. The complete list then reads as follows.

Very short run (immediate run). All factors are fixed. Output is fixed. The supply curve is vertical. On a day-to-day basis, a firm may not be able to vary output at all. For example, a flower seller, once the day's flowers have been purchased from the wholesaler, cannot alter the amount of flowers available for sale on that day. In the very short run, all that may remain for a producer to do is to sell an already produced good.

Why are Christmas trees and fresh foods often sold cheaply on Christmas Eve? (See Box 6.5 on page 161.)

Short run. At least one factor is fixed in supply. More can be produced, but the firm will come up against the law of diminishing returns as it tries to do so.

Long run. All factors are variable. The firm may experience constant, increasing or decreasing returns to scale. But although all factors can be increased or decreased, they are of a fixed *quality*.

Very long run. All factors are variable, *and* their quality and hence productivity can change. Labour productivity can increase as a result of education, training, experience and social factors. The productivity of capital can increase as a result of new inventions (new discoveries) and innovation (putting inventions into practice).

Improvements in factor quality will increase the output they produce: *TPP*, *APP* and *MPP* will rise. These curves will shift vertically upwards.

Just how long the 'very long run' is will vary from firm to firm. It will depend on how long it takes to develop new techniques, new skills or new work practices.

It is important to realise that decisions *for* all four time periods can be made *at* the same time. Firms do not make short-run decisions *in* the short-run and long-run decisions *in* the long run. They can make both short-run and long-run decisions today. For example, assume that a firm experiences an increase in consumer demand and anticipates that it will continue into the foreseeable future. It thus wants to increase output. Consequently, it makes the following four decisions *today*:

- (*Very short run*) It accepts that for a few days it will not be able to increase output. It informs its customers that they will have to wait. In some markets the firm may temporarily raise prices to choke off some of the demand.
- (*Short run*) It negotiates with labour to introduce overtime working as soon as possible, to tide it over the next few weeks. It orders extra raw materials from its suppliers. It launches a recruitment drive for new labour so as to avoid paying overtime longer than is necessary.
- (*Long run*) It starts proceedings to build a new factory. What would this involve? In some cases the firm may talk to the bank directly about finance and start investigating sites. A different approach might be to discuss requirements with a firm of consultants.
- (*Very long run*) It institutes a programme of research and development and/or training in an attempt to increase productivity.

1. *Could the long run and and the very long run ever be the same length of time?*
2. *What will the long-run and very-long-run market supply curves for a product look like? How will the shape of the long-run curve depend on returns to scale?*

*3. *In the very long run, new isoquants will have to be drawn as factor productivity changes. An increase in productivity will shift the isoquants inwards towards the origin: less capital and labour will be required to produce any given level of output. Will this be a parallel inward shift of the isoquants? Explain.*

Although we distinguish these four time periods, it is the middle two we are primarily concerned with. The reason for this is that there is very little the firm can do in the *very* short run. And concerning the *very* long run, although the firm will obviously want to increase the productivity of its inputs, it will not be in a position to make precise calculations of how to do it. It will not know precisely what inventions will be made, or just what will be the results of its own research and development.

Section summary

1. In the long run, a firm is able to vary the quantity it uses of all factors of production. There are no fixed factors.
2. If it increases all factors by the same proportion, it may experience constant, increasing or decreasing returns to scale.
3. Economies of scale occur when costs per unit of output fall as the scale of production increases. This can be due to a number of factors, some of which result directly from increasing (physical) returns to scale. These include the benefits of specialisation and division of labour, the use of larger and more efficient machines, and the ability to have a more integrated system of production. Other economies of scale arise from the financial and administrative benefits of large-scale organisations.
4. Long-run costs are also influenced by a firm's location. The firm will have to balance the needs to be as near as possible both to the supply of its raw materials and to its market. The optimum balance will depend on the relative costs of transporting the inputs and the finished product.
5. To minimise costs per unit of output, a firm should choose that combination of factors which gives an equal marginal product for each factor relative to its price: i.e. $MPP_a/P_a = MPP_b/P_b = MPP_c/P_c$, etc. (where *a*, *b* and *c* are different factors). If the *MPP*/*P* ratio for one factor is greater than for another, more of the first should be used relative to the second.

*6. An isoquant shows the various combinations of two factors to produce a given output. A whole map of such isoquants can be drawn with each isoquant representing a different level of output. The slope of the isoquant ($\Delta K/\Delta L$) gives the marginal rate of factor substitution (MPP_L/MPP_K). The bowed-in shape of isoquants illustrates a diminishing marginal rate of factor substitution, which in turn arises because of diminishing marginal returns.

*7. An isocost shows the various combinations of two factors that cost a given amount to employ. It will be a straight line. Its slope is equal to the price ratio of the two factors (P_L/P_K).

*8. The tangency point of an isocost with an isoquant represents the optimum factor combination. It is the point where MPP_L/MPP_K (the slope of the isoquant) $= P_L/P_K$ (the slope of the isocost). By drawing a single isoquant touching the lowest possible isocost, we can show the least-cost combination of factors for producing a given output. By drawing a single isocost touching the highest possible isoquant, we can show the highest output obtainable for a given cost of production.

9. Four distinct time periods can be distinguished. In addition to the short- and long-run periods, we can also distinguish the very-short- and very-long-run periods. The very short run is when all factors are fixed. The very long run is where not only the quantity of factors but also their quality is variable (as a result of changing technology, etc.).

6.4 COSTS IN THE LONG RUN

We turn now to *long-run* cost curves. Since there are no fixed factors in the long run, there are no long-run fixed costs. For example, the firm may rent more land in order to expand its operations. Its rent bill therefore goes up as it expands its output. In the long run, then, all costs are variable costs.

KEY IDEA 21

Fixed costs and the time period. **Fixed costs occur only in the short run, since in the long run all inputs can be varied.**

Long-run average costs

Long-run average cost (LRAC) curves can take various shapes, but a typical one is shown in Figure 6.11.

It is often assumed that as a firm expands, it will initially experience economies of scale and thus face a downward-sloping *LRAC* curve. After a point, however, all such economies will have been achieved and thus the curve will flatten out. Then (possibly after a period of constant *LRAC*) the firm will get so large that it will start experiencing diseconomies of scale and thus a rising *LRAC*. At this stage, production and financial economies will begin to be offset by the managerial problems of running a giant organisation.

Given the LRAC curve in Figure 6.11, what would the firm's long-run total cost curve look like?

Assumptions behind the long-run average cost curve

We make three key assumptions when constructing long-run average cost curves.

Factor prices are given. At each level of output, it is assumed that a firm will be faced with a given set of factor prices. If factor prices *change*, therefore, both short- and long-run cost curves will shift. Thus an increase in nationally negotiated wage rates would shift the curves upwards.

However, factor prices might be different at *different* levels of output. For example, one of the economies of scale that many firms enjoy is the ability to obtain bulk discount on raw materials and other supplies. In such cases, the curve does *not* shift. The different factor prices are merely experienced at different points along the curve, and are reflected in the shape of the curve. Factor prices are still given for any particular level of output.

The state of technology and factor quality are given. These are assumed to change only in the *very* long run. If a firm gains economies of scale, it is because it is able to exploit *existing* technologies and make better use of the existing availability of factors of production.

Firms choose the least-cost combination of factors for each output. The assumption here is that firms operate efficiently: that they choose the cheapest possible way of producing any level of output. In other words, at every point along the *LRAC* curve, the firm will adhere to the cost-minimising formula (see pages 169–70):

$$\frac{MPP_a}{P_a} = \frac{MPP_b}{P_b} = \frac{MPP_c}{P_c} = \dots = \frac{MPP_n}{P_n}$$

where $a \dots n$ are the various factors the firm uses.

If the firm did not choose the optimum factor combination, it would be producing at a point above the *LRAC* curve.

Definition

Long-run average cost curve A curve that shows how average cost varies with output on the assumption that *all* factors are variable. (It is assumed that the least-cost method of production will be chosen for each output.)

Figure 6.11 A typical long-run average cost curve

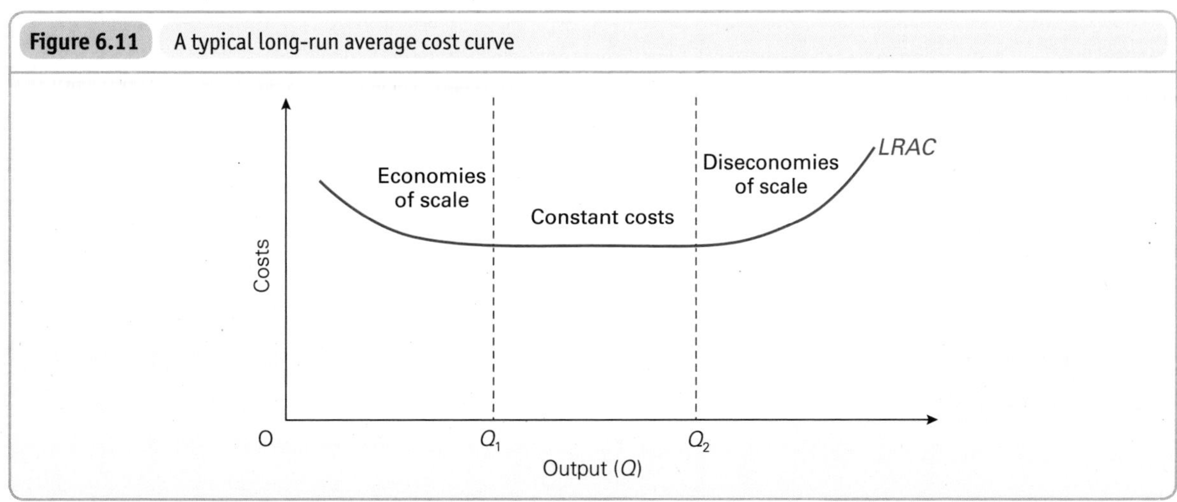

Long-run marginal costs

The relationship between long-run average and ***long-run marginal cost*** curves is just like that between any other averages and marginals (see Box 6.3). This is illustrated in Figure 6.12.

If there are economies of scale (diagram (a)), additional units of output will add less to costs than the average. The *LRMC* curve must be below the *LRAC* curve and thus pulling the average down as output increases. If there are diseconomies of scale (diagram (b)), additional units of output will cost more than the average. The *LRMC* curve must be above the *LRAC* curve, pulling it up. If there are no economies or diseconomies of scale, so that the *LRAC* curve is horizontal, any additional units of output will cost the same as the average and thus leave the average unaffected (diagram (c)).

> **Definition**
>
> **Long-run marginal cost** The extra cost of producing one more unit of output assuming that all factors are variable. (It is assumed that the least-cost method of production will be chosen for this extra output.)

1. *Explain the shape of the LRMC curve in diagram (d) in Figure 6.12.*
2. *What would the LRMC curve look like if the LRAC curve were 'flat-bottomed', as in Figure 6.11?*

The relationship between long-run and short-run average cost curves

Take the case of a firm which has just one factory and faces a short-run average cost curve illustrated by $SRAC_1$ in Figure 6.13.

In the long run, it can build more factories. If it thereby experiences economies of scale (due, say, to savings on administration), each successive factory will allow it to produce with a new lower *SRAC* curve. Thus with two factories it will face $SRAC_2$, with three factories $SRAC_3$, and so on. Each *SRAC* curve corresponds to a particular amount of the factor

Figure 6.12 The relationship between long-run average and marginal costs

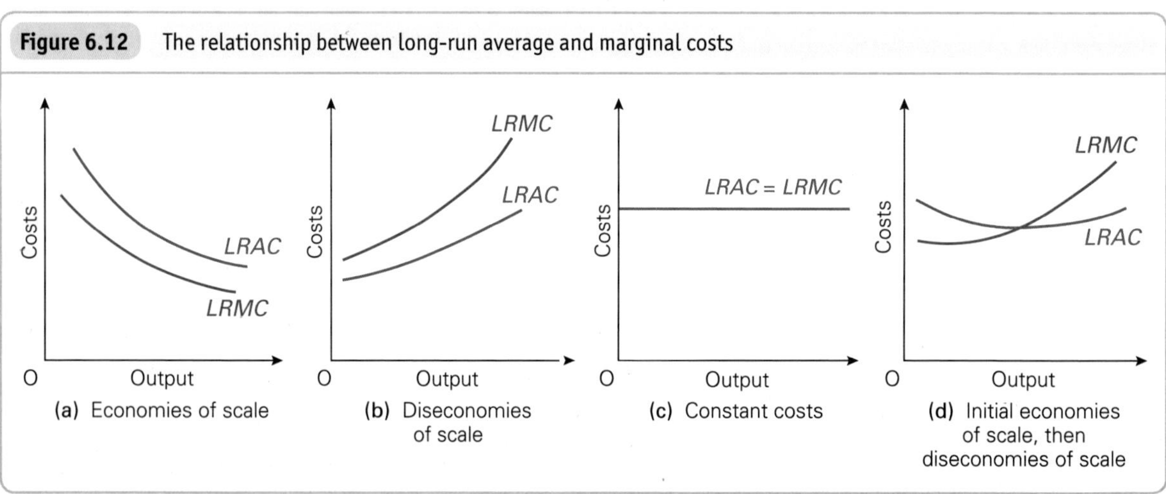

Figure 6.13 Constructing long-run average cost curves from short-run average cost curves

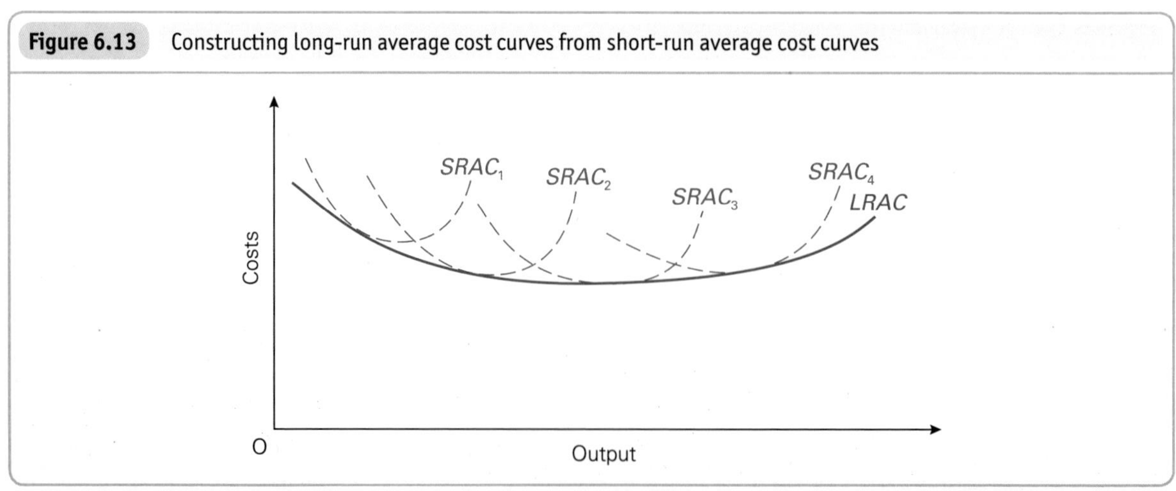

that is fixed in the short run: in this case, the factory. (There are many more *SRAC* curves that could be drawn between the ones shown, since factories of different sizes could be built or existing ones could be expanded.)

From this succession of short-run average cost curves we can construct a long-run average cost curve, as shown in Figure 6.13. This is known as the ***envelope curve***, since it envelopes the short-run curves.

Definition

Envelope curve A long-run average cost curve drawn as the tangency points of a series of short-run average cost curves.

Will the envelope curve be tangential to the bottom of each of the short-run average cost curves? Explain why it should or should not be.

Long-run cost curves in practice

Firms do experience economies of scale. Some experience continuously falling *LRAC* curves, as in Figure 6.12(a). Others experience economies of scale up to a certain output and thereafter constant returns to scale.

Evidence is inconclusive on the question of diseconomies of scale. There is little evidence to suggest the existence of *technical* diseconomies, but the possibility of diseconomies due to managerial and industrial relations problems cannot be ruled out.

Some evidence on economies of scale in the UK is considered in Box 6.9.

BOX 6.9 MINIMUM EFFICIENT SCALE — CASE STUDIES AND APPLICATIONS

The extent of economies of scale in practice

Two of the most important studies of economies of scale are those by C. F. Pratten[1] in the late 1980s and by a group advising the European Commission[2] in 1997. Both studies found strong evidence that many firms, especially in manufacturing, experienced substantial economies of scale.

In a few cases, long-run average costs fell continuously as output increased. For most firms, however, they fell up to a certain level of output and then remained constant.

The extent of economies of scale can be measured by looking at a firm's *minimum efficient scale* (*MES*). The *MES* is the size beyond which no significant additional economies of scale can be achieved: in other words, the point where the *LRAC* curve flattens off. In Pratten's studies, he defined this level as the minimum scale above which any possible doubling in scale would reduce average costs by less than 5 per cent (i.e. virtually the bottom of the *LRAC* curve). In the diagram, *MES* is shown at point *a*.

The *MES* can be expressed in terms either of an individual factory or of the whole firm. Where it refers to the minimum efficient scale of an individual factory, the *MES* is known as the *minimum efficient plant size* (*MEPS*).

The *MES* can then be expressed as a percentage of the total size of the market or of total domestic production. Table (a), based on the Pratten study, shows *MES* for plants and firms in various industries. The first column shows *MES* as a percentage of total UK production. The second column shows *MES* as a percentage of total EU production. Table (b), based on the 1997 study, shows *MES* for various plants.

Expressing *MES* as a percentage of total output gives an indication of how competitive the industry could be. In some industries (such as footwear and carpets), economies of scale were exhausted (i.e. *MES* was reached) with plants or firms that were still small relative to total UK production and even smaller relative to total EU production. In such industries,

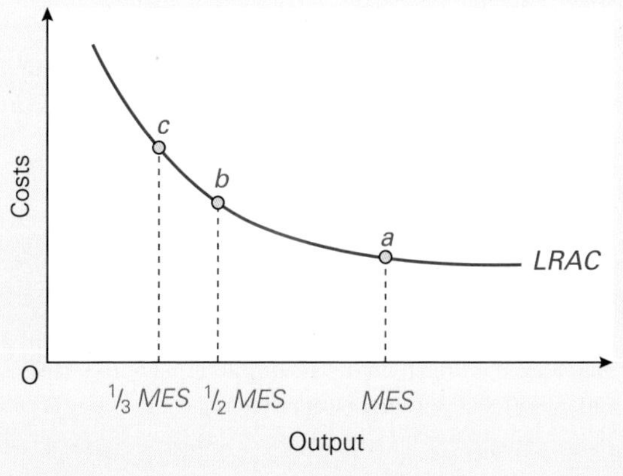

Table (a)

Product	MES as % of production: UK	MES as % of production: EU	% additional cost at ½ MES
Individual plants			
Cellulose fibres	125	16	3
Rolled aluminium semi-manufactures	114	15	15
Refrigerators	85	11	4
Steel	72	10	6
Electric motors	60	6	15
TV sets	40	9	9
Cigarettes	24	6	1.4
Ball-bearings	20	2	6
Beer	12	3	7
Nylon	4	1	12
Bricks	1	0.2	25
Carpets	0.3	0.04	10
Footwear	0.3	0.03	1
Firms			
Cars	200	20	9
Lorries	104	21	7.5
Mainframe computers	>100	n.a.	5
Aircraft	100	n.a.	5
Tractors	98	19	6

Source: See footnote 1 below.

(continued)

Table (b)

Plants	MES as % of total EU production
Aerospace	12.19
Agricultural machinery	6.57
Electric lighting	3.76
Steel tubes	2.42
Shipbuilding	1.63
Rubber	1.06
Radio and TV	0.69
Footwear	0.08
Carpets	0.03

Source: See footnote 2 below.

there would be room for many firms and thus scope for considerable competition.

In other industries, however, even if a single plant or firm were large enough to produce the whole output of the industry in the UK, it would still not be large enough to experience the full potential economies of scale: the *MES* is greater than 100 per cent. Examples from Table (a) include factories producing cellulose fibres, and car manufacturers. In these industries, there is no possibility of competition from within the country. In fact, as long as the *MES* exceeds 50 per cent, there will not be room for more than one firm large enough to gain full economies of scale (unless they export). In this case, the industry is said to be a natural monopoly.

As we shall see in the next few chapters, when competition is lacking, consumers may suffer by firms charging prices considerably above costs.

A second way of measuring the extent of economies of scale is to see how much costs would increase if production were reduced to a certain fraction of *MES*. The normal fractions used are $\frac{1}{2}$ or $\frac{1}{3}$ *MES*. This is illustrated in the diagram.

Point *b* corresponds to $\frac{1}{2}$ *MES*; point *c* to $\frac{1}{3}$ *MES*. The greater the percentage by which *LRAC* at point *b* or *c* is higher than at point *a*, the greater will be the economies of scale to be gained by producing at *MES* rather than at $\frac{1}{2}$ *MES* or $\frac{1}{3}$ *MES*. For example, in Table (a) there are greater economies of scale to be gained from moving from $\frac{1}{2}$ *MES* to *MES* in the production of electric motors than in cigarettes.

The main purpose of the studies was to determine whether the single EU market is big enough to allow both economies of scale and competition. The tables suggest that in all cases, other things being equal, the EU market is indeed large enough for this to occur. The second study also found that 47 of the 53 manufacturing sectors analysed had scope for further exploitation of economies of scale.

In the 2007–13 research framework the European Commission agreed to fund a number of research projects, to conduct further investigations of *MES* across different industries and to consider the impact of the expansion of the EU.

1. ***Why might a firm operating with one plant achieve MEPS and yet not be large enough to achieve MES? (Clue: are all economies of scale achieved at plant level?)***
2. ***Why might a firm producing bricks have an MES which is only 0.2 per cent of total EU production and yet face little effective competition from other EU countries?***

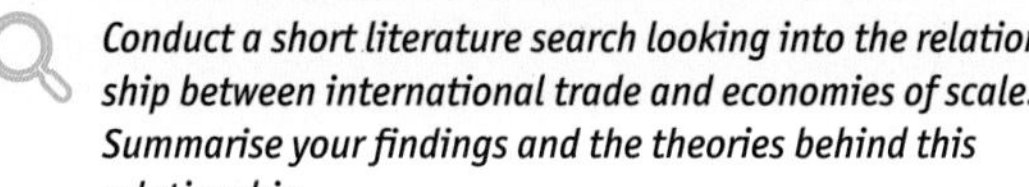

Conduct a short literature search looking into the relationship between international trade and economies of scale. Summarise your findings and the theories behind this relationship.

1 C. F. Pratten, 'A survey of the economies of scale', in *Research into the 'Costs of Non-Europe'*, Volume 2 (Commission of the European Communities, Luxembourg, 1988).

2 European Commission/Economists Advisory Group Ltd, 'Economies of scale', *The Single Market Review*, Sub-series V, Volume 4 (Commission of the European Communities, Luxembourg, 1997).

*Derivation of long-run costs from an isoquant map[2]

Cost curves are drawn on the assumption that, for any output, the least-cost combination of factors is used: that is, that production will take place at the tangency point of the isoquant and an isocost, where $MPP_L/MPP_K = P_L/P_K$: i.e. where $MPP_L/P_L = MPP_K/P_K$. By drawing a series of isoquants and isocosts, long-run costs can be derived for each output.

In Figure 6.14, isoquants are drawn for a hypothetical firm at 100 unit intervals. Up to 400 units of output, the isoquants are getting closer together. Thereafter, the gap between the isoquants widens again.

The line from *a* to *g* is known as the ***expansion path***. It traces the tangency points of the isoquants and isocosts, and thus shows the minimum-cost combinations of labour and capital to produce each output: the (long-run) total cost being given by the isocost.

Up to point *d*, less and less *extra* capital (*K*) and labour (*L*) are required to produce each extra 100 units of output. Thus

Definition

Expansion path The line on an isoquant map that traces the minimum-cost combinations of two factors as output increases. It is drawn on the assumption that both factors can be varied. It is thus a long-run path.

2 This optional section is based on the material in the optional section on pages 171–5.

Figure 6.14 Deriving an *LRAC* curve from an isoquant map

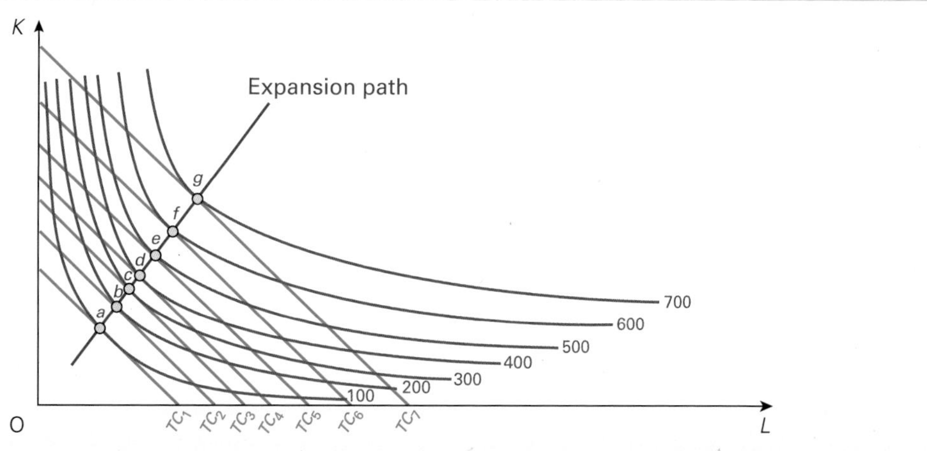

long-run marginal cost is falling. Above point *d*, more and more extra *K* and *L* are required and thus *LRMC* rises.

Thus the isoquant map of Figure 6.14 gives an *LRMC* curve that is -shaped. The *LRAC* curve will therefore also be -shaped (only shallower) with the *LRMC* coming up through the bottom of the *LRAC*.

What would the isoquant map look like if there were
(a) continuously increasing returns to scale;
(b) continuously decreasing returns to scale?

Section summary

1. In the long run, all factors are variable. There are thus no long-run fixed costs.
2. When constructing long-run cost curves, it is assumed that factor prices are given, that the state of technology is given and that firms will choose the least-cost combination of factors for each given output.
3. The *LRAC* curve can be downward sloping, upward sloping or horizontal, depending in turn on whether there are economies of scale, diseconomies of scale or neither. Typically, *LRAC* curves are drawn saucer-shaped or -shaped. As output expands, initially there are economies of scale. When these are exhausted, the curve will become flat. When the firm becomes very large, it may begin to experience diseconomies of scale. If this happens, the *LRAC* curve will begin to slope upwards again.
4. The long-run marginal cost curve will be below the *LRAC* curve when *LRAC* is falling, above it when *LRAC* is rising and equal to it when *LRAC* is neither rising nor falling.
5. An envelope curve can be drawn which shows the relationship between short-run and long-run average cost curves. The *LRAC* curve envelops the short-run *LRAC* curves: it is tangential to them.
6. *Costs can be derived from an isoquant map. Long-run total costs are found from the expansion path, which shows the least-cost combination of factors to produce any given output. It traces out the tangency points of the isocosts and isoquants.

6.5 REVENUE

Remember that we defined a firm's total profit as its total revenue minus its total costs of production. So far in this chapter we have examined costs. We now turn to revenue.

As with costs, we distinguish between three revenue concepts: total revenue (*TR*), average revenue (*AR*) and marginal revenue (*MR*).

Total, average and marginal revenue

Total revenue (TR)

Total revenue is the firm's total earnings per period of time from the sale of a particular amount of output (*Q*). For example, if a firm sells 1000 units (*Q*) per month at a price of £5 each (*P*), then its monthly total revenue will be £5000: in other words, £5 × 1000 (*P* × *Q*). Thus

$$TR = P \times Q$$

Average revenue (AR)

Average revenue is the amount the firm earns per unit sold. Thus

$$AR = TR/Q$$

So if the firm earns £5000 (*TR*) from selling 1000 units (*Q*), it will earn £5 per unit. But this is simply the price! Thus

$$AR = P$$

(The only exception to this is when the firm is selling its products at different prices to different consumers. In this case, *AR* is simply the (weighted) average price.)

Marginal revenue (MR)

Marginal revenue is the extra total revenue gained by selling one more unit (per time period). So if a firm sells an extra 20 units this month compared with what it expected to sell, and in the process earns an extra £100, then it is getting an extra £5 for each extra unit sold: *MR* = £5. Thus

$$MR = \Delta TR/\Delta Q$$

We now need to see how each of these three revenue concepts (*TR, AR* and *MR*) varies with output. We can show this graphically in the same way as we did with costs.

The relationships will depend on the market conditions under which a firm operates. A firm that is too small to be able to affect market price will have different-shaped revenue curves from a firm that is able to choose the price it charges. Let us examine each of these two situations in turn.

Revenue curves when price is not affected by the firm's output

Average revenue

If a firm is very small relative to the whole market, it is likely to be a ***price taker***. That is, it has to accept the price given by the intersection of demand and supply in the whole market. But, being so small, it can sell as much as it is capable of producing at that price. This is illustrated in Figure 6.15.

The left-hand part of the diagram shows market demand and supply. Equilibrium price is £5. The right-hand part of the diagram looks at the demand for an individual firm that is tiny relative to the whole market. (Look at the differences in the scale of the horizontal axes in the two parts of the diagram.)

Being so small, any change in its output will be too insignificant to affect the market price. It thus faces a horizontal demand 'curve' at the price. It can sell 200 units, 600 units, 1200 units or whatever without affecting this £5 price.

Average revenue is thus constant at £5. The firm's average revenue curve must therefore lie along exactly the same line as its demand curve.

Definitions

Total revenue A firm's total earnings from a specified level of sales within a specified period: *TR* = *P* × *Q*.

Average revenue Total revenue per unit of output. When all output is sold at the same price, average revenue will be the same as price: *AR* = *TR*/*Q* = *P*.

Marginal revenue The extra revenue gained by selling one more unit per period of time: *MR* = Δ*TR*/Δ*Q*.

Price taker A firm that is too small to be able to influence the market price.

Figure 6.15 Deriving a firm's *AR* and *MR*: price-taking firm

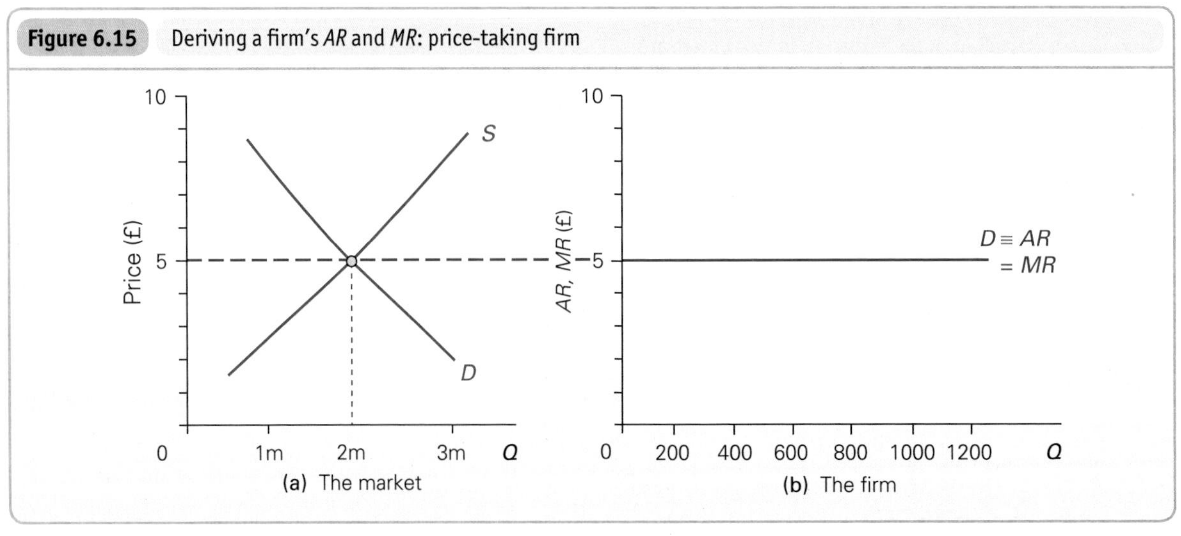

Table 6.7 Deriving total revenue for a price-taking firm

Quantity (units)	Price = *AR* = *MR* (£)	*TR* (£)
0	5	0
200	5	1000
400	5	2000
600	5	3000
800	5	4000
1000	5	5000
1200	5	6000
.	.	.

Table 6.8 Revenues for a firm facing a downward-sloping demand curve

Q (units)	*P* = *AR* (£)	*TR* (£)	*MR* (£)
1	8	8	
2	7	14	6
3	6	18	4
4	5	20	2
5	4	20	0
6	3	18	−2
7	2	14	−4
.	.	.	.

Figure 6.16 Total revenue for a price-taking firm

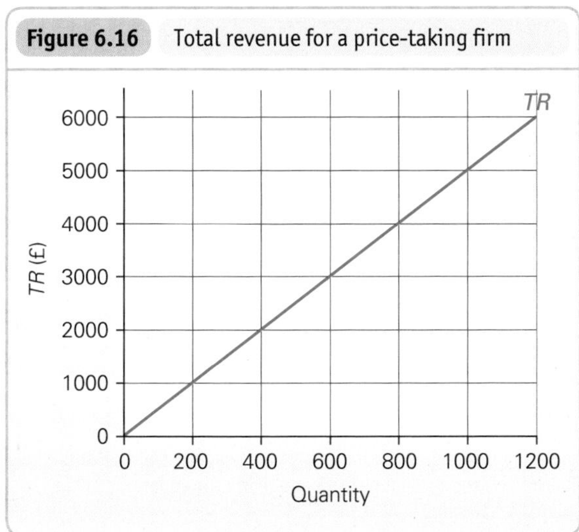

Marginal revenue

In the case of a horizontal demand curve, the marginal revenue curve will be the same as the average revenue curve, since selling one more unit at a constant price (*AR*) merely adds that amount to total revenue. If an extra unit is sold at a constant price of £5, an extra £5 is earned.

Total revenue

Table 6.7 shows the effect on total revenue of different levels of sales with a constant price of £5 per unit. As price is constant, total revenue will rise at a constant rate as more is sold. The *TR* 'curve' will therefore be a straight line through the origin, as in Figure 6.16.

What would happen to the TR curve if the market price rose to £10? Try drawing it.

Revenue curves when price varies with output

The three curves (*TR*, *AR* and *MR*) look quite different when price does vary with the firm's output. If a firm has a relatively large share of the market, it will face a downward-sloping demand curve. This means that if it is to sell more, it must lower the price. It could also choose to raise its price. If it does so, however, it will have to accept a fall in sales.

Average revenue

Remember that average revenue equals price. If, therefore, price has to be lowered to sell more output, average revenue will fall as output increases.

Table 6.8 gives an example of a firm facing a downward-sloping demand curve. The demand curve (which shows how much is sold at each price) is given by the first two columns.

Note that, as in the case of a price-taking firm, the demand curve and the *AR* curve lie along exactly the same line. The reason for this is simple: $AR = P$, and thus the curve relating price to quantity (the demand curve) must be the same as that relating average revenue to quantity (the *AR* curve).

Marginal revenue

When a firm faces a downward-sloping demand curve, marginal revenue will be less than average revenue, and may even be negative. But why?

If a firm is to sell more per time period, it must lower its price (assuming it does not advertise). This will mean lowering the price not just for the extra units it hopes to sell, but also for those units it would have sold had it not lowered the price.

Thus the marginal revenue is the price at which it sells the last unit, minus the loss in revenue it has incurred by reducing the price on those units it could otherwise have sold at the higher price. This can be illustrated with Table 6.8.

Assume that the price is currently £7. Two units are thus sold. The firm now wishes to sell an extra unit. It lowers the price to £6. It thus gains £6 from the sale of the third unit, but loses £2 by having to reduce the price by £1 on the two units it could otherwise have sold at £7. Its net gain is therefore £6 − £2 = £4. This is the marginal revenue: it is the extra revenue gained by the firm from selling one more unit. (Notice that in Table 6.8 the figures for *MR* are entered in the spaces between the figures for the other three columns.)

There is a simple relationship between marginal revenue and *price elasticity of demand*. Remember from Chapter 2 (pages 56–7) that if demand is price elastic, a *decrease* in price

will lead to a proportionately larger increase in the quantity demanded and hence an *increase* in revenue. Marginal revenue will thus be positive. If, however, demand is inelastic, a decrease in price will lead to a proportionately smaller increase in sales. In this case, the price reduction will more than offset the increase in sales and as a result revenue will fall. Marginal revenue will be negative.

If, then, at a particular quantity sold marginal revenue is a positive figure (i.e. if sales per time period are 4 units or less in Figure 6.17), the demand curve will be elastic at that quantity, since a rise in quantity sold (as a result of a reduction in price) would lead to a rise in total revenue. If, on the other hand, marginal revenue is negative (i.e. at a level of sales of 5 or more units in Figure 6.17), the demand curve will be inelastic at that quantity, since a rise in quantity sold would lead to a *fall* in total revenue.

Figure 6.17 *AR* and *MR* curves for a firm facing a downward-sloping demand curve

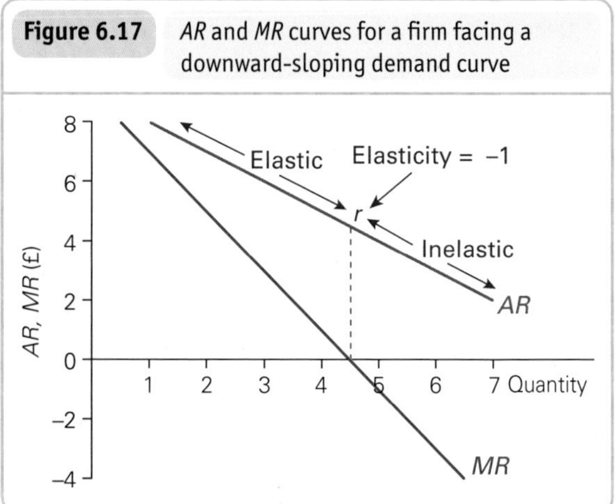

*LOOKING AT THE MATHS

As with cost curves (see page 165), we can express revenue curves algebraically.

Price-taking firms

Let us take *TR*, *AR* and *MR* in turn. They will take the following forms:

$$TR = bQ \quad (1)$$

This equation will give an upward-sloping straight-line *TR* 'curve', with a slope of b. Note that the absence of a constant (a) term means that the line passes through the origin. This is obviously the case, given that if sales (Q) are zero, total revenue will be zero.

$$AR = \frac{TR}{Q} = b \quad (2)$$

This will give a horizontal *AR* curve at an *AR* (i.e. price) of b.

$$MR = \frac{d(TR)}{dQ} = b \quad (3)$$

Differentiating the *TR* function gives a value of b. As we have seen, $AR = MR$ when the firm is a price taker and faces a horizontal demand curve (at the market price).

Price-making firms: a straight-line demand 'curve'

'Price makers' face a downward-sloping demand curve. If this is a straight-line demand curve, the revenue equations will be as follows:

$$TR = bQ - cQ^2 \quad (4)$$

The negative cQ^2 term will give a revenue curve whose slope gets less until a peak is reached (see Figure 6.18). Thereafter, as the cQ^2 term becomes bigger than the bQ term, *TR* will fall.

$$AR = \frac{TR}{Q} = b - cQ \quad (5)$$

This gives a straight-line downward-sloping *AR* curve (demand curve) with a slope of $-c$, which crosses the horizontal axis when cQ becomes bigger than b.

$$MR = \frac{d(TR)}{dQ} = b - 2cQ \quad (6)$$

This again gives a straight downward-sloping line, this time with a slope of $2-c$. Note that this means that the slope of the *MR* curve is twice that of the *AR* curve.

But what if the demand curve is actually curved? What will the three revenue equations be then? We explore this in Maths Case 6.4 on the student website and relate the equations to the relevant diagrams.

The relationship between marginal revenue and price elasticity of demand

You can see from Figure 6.17 how price elasticity of demand and marginal revenue are related. We can express this relationship algebraically as follows:

$$MR = P(1 + (1/P\epsilon_D)) \quad (7)$$

or

$$P = \frac{MR}{1 + (1/P\epsilon_D)}$$

Proof of this relationship is given in Maths Case 6.2 on the student website, but for now we can see how equation (7) relates to Figure 6.17. The P term must be positive. If demand is elastic, then $P\epsilon_D$ must have a value less than -1 (i.e. the figure for elasticity, ignoring the negative sign, must be greater than 1). Thus the term $1/P\epsilon_D$ must have a negative value between 0 and -1. This means, therefore, that the term $(1 + (1/P\epsilon_D))$ must be positive, and hence *MR* must be positive.

If, however, demand is inelastic, then $P\epsilon_D$ must have a value between -1 and zero. Thus the term $1/P\epsilon_D$ must have a negative value less than -1 (i.e. an absolute value, ignoring the negative sign, that is greater than 1). This means, therefore, that the term $(1 + (1/P\epsilon_D))$ must be negative, and hence *MR* must be negative.

Finally, if demand is unit elastic, then the term $1/P\epsilon_D$ must have a value of -1 and hence the term $(1 + (1/P\epsilon_D))$ must have a value of zero. *MR* must be zero.

Figure 6.18 Total revenue for a firm facing a downward-sloping demand curve

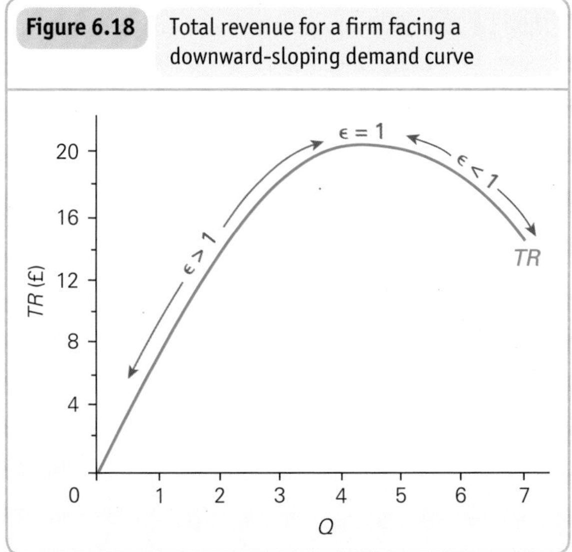

Thus the demand (*AR*) curve in Figure 6.17 is elastic to the left of point *r* and inelastic to the right.

Total revenue

Total revenue equals price times quantity. This is illustrated in Table 6.8. The *TR* column from Table 6.8 is plotted in Figure 6.18.

Unlike the case of a price-taking firm, the *TR* curve is not a straight line. It is a curve that rises at first and then falls. But why? As long as marginal revenue is positive (and hence demand is price elastic), a rise in output will raise total revenue. However, once marginal revenue becomes negative (and hence demand is inelastic), total revenue will fall. The peak of the *TR* curve will be where $MR = 0$. At this point, the price elasticity of demand will be equal to 1.

Shifts in revenue curves

We saw in Chapter 2 that a change in *price* will cause a movement along a demand curve. It is similar with revenue curves, except that here the causal connection is in the other direction. Here we ask what happens to revenue when there is a change in the firm's *output*. Again the effect is shown by a movement along the curves.

A change in any *other* determinant of demand, such as tastes, income or the price of other goods, will shift the demand curve. By affecting the price at which each level of output can be sold, there will be a shift in all three revenue curves. An increase in revenue is shown by a shift upwards; a decrease by a shift downwards.

Copy Figures 6.17 and 6.18 (which are based on Table 6.8). Now assume that incomes have risen and that, as a result, two more units per time period can be sold at each price. Draw a new table and plot the resulting new AR, MR and TR curves on your diagrams. Are the new curves parallel to the old ones? Explain.

Section summary

1. Total revenue (*TR*) is the total amount a firm earns from its sales in a given time period. It is simply price times quantity: $TR = P \times Q$.
2. Average revenue (*AR*) is total revenue per unit: $AR = TR/Q$. In other words, $AR = P$.
3. Marginal revenue is the extra revenue earned from the sale of one more unit per time period.
4. The *AR* curve will be the same as the demand curve for the firm's product. In the case of a price taker, the demand curve and hence the *AR* curve will be a horizontal straight line and will also be the same as the *MR* curve. The *TR* curve will be an upward-sloping straight line from the origin.
5. A firm that faces a downward-sloping demand curve must obviously also face the same downward-sloping *AR* curve. The *MR* curve will also slope downwards, but will be below the *AR* curve and steeper than it. The *TR* curve will be an arch shape starting from the origin.
6. When demand is price elastic, marginal revenue will be positive and the *TR* curve will be upward sloping. When demand is price inelastic, marginal revenue will be negative and the *TR* curve will be downward sloping.
7. A change in output is represented by a movement along the revenue curves. A change in any other determinant of revenue will shift the curves up or down.

6.6 PROFIT MAXIMISATION

We are now in a position to put costs and revenue together to find the output at which profit is maximised, and also to find out how much that profit will be.

There are two ways of doing this. The first and simpler method is to use total cost and total revenue curves. The second method is to use marginal and average cost and marginal and average revenue curves. Although this method is a little more complicated (but only a little!), it is more useful when we come to compare profit maximising under different market conditions.

We will look at each method in turn. In both cases, we will concentrate on the short run: namely, that period in which one or more factors are fixed in supply. In both cases, we take the instance of a firm facing a downward-sloping demand curve.

Table 6.9 Total revenue, total cost and total profit

Q (units)	*TR* (£)	*TC* (£)	*TΠ* (£)
0	0	6	−6
1	8	10	−2
2	14	12	2
3	18	14	4
4	20	18	2
5	20	25	−5
6	18	36	−18
7	14	56	−42
.	.	.	.

Figure 6.19 Finding maximum profit using totals curves

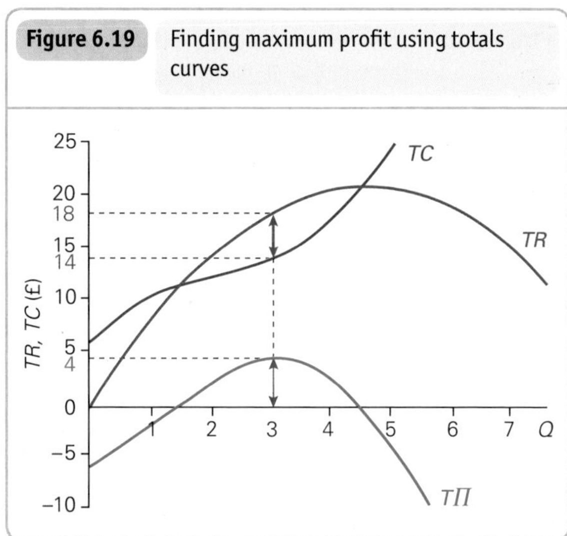

Short-run profit maximisation: using total curves

Table 6.9 shows the total revenue figures from Table 6.8. It also shows figures for total cost. These figures have been chosen so as to produce a *TC* curve of a typical shape.

Total profit (*TΠ*) is found by subtracting *TC* from *TR*. Check this out by examining the table. Where *TΠ* is negative, the firm is making a loss. Total profit is maximised at an output of 3 units, where there is the greatest gap between total revenue and total costs. At this output, total profit is £4 (£18 − £14).

The *TR*, *TC* and *TΠ* curves are plotted in Figure 6.19. The size of the maximum profit is shown by the arrows.

What can we say about the slope of the TR and TC curves at the maximum profit point? What does this tell us about marginal revenue and marginal cost?

Short-run profit maximisation: using average and marginal curves

Table 6.10 is based on the figures in Table 6.9.

1. *Fill in the missing figures (without referring to Table 6.8 or 6.9).*
2. *Why are the figures for MR and MC entered in the spaces between the lines in Table 6.10?*

Finding the maximum profit that a firm can make is a two-stage process. The first stage is to find the profit-maximising output. To do this we use the *MC* and *MR* curves. The second stage is to find out just how much profit is at this output. To do this we use the *AR* and *AC* curves.

Stage 1: Using marginal curves to arrive at the profit-maximising output

There is a very simple ***profit-maximising rule***: if profits are to be maximised, *MR must equal MC*. From Table 6.10 it can be seen that it *MR* = *MC* at an output of 3. This is shown as point *e* in Figure 6.20.

But why are profits maximised when *MR* = *MC*? The simplest way of answering this is to see what the position would be if *MR* did not equal *MC*.

Definition

Profit-maximising rule Profit is maximised where marginal revenue equals marginal cost.

Table 6.10 Revenue, cost and profit

Q(units)	*P* = *AR* (£)	*TR* (£)	*MR*(£)	*TC*(£)	*AC* (£)	*MC*(£)	*TΠ* (£)	*AΠ* (£)
0	9	0		6	–		−6	–
			8			4		
1	8	8		10	10		. . .	−2
			. . .			2		
2	7	14		12	. . .		2	1
			4			2		
3	6	18		14	$4^2/_3$		4	$1^1/_3$
			2			4		
4	5	20		18	$4^1/_2$		2	$^1/_2$
			0			7		
5	4	20		25	5		−5	−1
			−2			. . .		
6	3	18		36	. . .		. . .	. . .
			. . .			20		
7	2	14		56	8		−42	−6
			.			.		
.	.	.		.	.		.	.

Figure 6.20 Finding the profit-maximising output using marginal curves

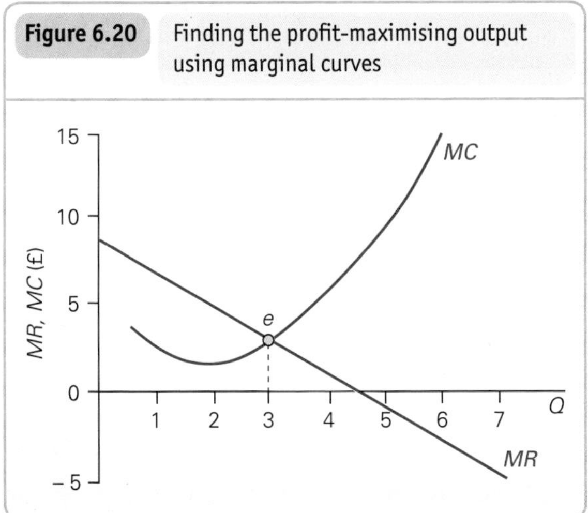

Figure 6.21 Measuring the maximum profit using average curves

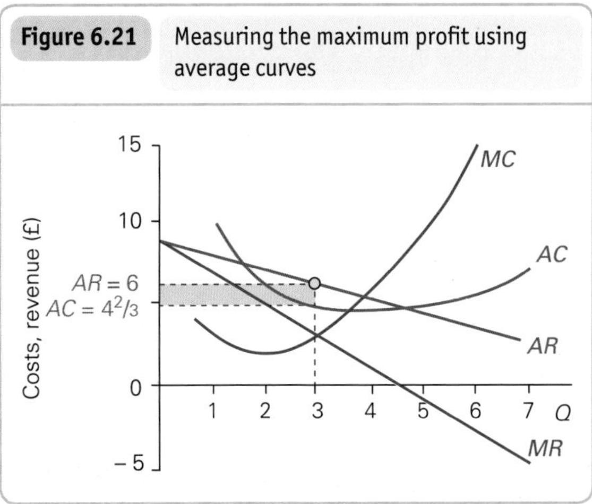

Referring to Figure 6.20, at a level of output below 3, *MR* exceeds *MC*. This means that by producing more units there will be a bigger addition to revenue (*MR*) than to cost (*MC*). Total profit will *increase. As long as MR exceeds MC, profit can be increased by increasing production.*

At a level of output above 3, *MC* exceeds *MR*. All levels of output above 3 thus add more to cost than to revenue and hence *reduce* profit. *As long as MC exceeds MR, profit can be increased by cutting back on production.*

Profits are thus maximised where *MC* = *MR*: at an output of 3. This can be confirmed by reference to the *TΠ* column in Table 6.10.

Students worry sometimes about the argument that profits are maximised when *MR* = *MC*. Surely, they say, if the last unit is making no profit, how can profit be at a *maximum*? The answer is very simple. If you cannot *add* anything more to a total, the total must be at the maximum. Take the simple analogy of going up a hill. When you cannot go any higher, you must be at the top.

Stage 2: Using average curves to measure the size of the profit

Once the profit-maximising output has been discovered, we use the average curves to measure the *amount* of profit at the maximum. Both marginal and average curves corresponding to the data in Table 6.10 are plotted in Figure 6.21.

First, average profit (*AΠ*) is found. This is simply *AR* – *AC*. At the profit-maximising output of 3, this gives a figure for *AΠ* of £6 – £4²/₃ = £1¹/₃. Then total profit is obtained by multiplying average profit by output:

$$T\Pi = A\Pi \times Q$$

This is shown as the shaded area. It equals £1¹/₃ × 3 = £4. This can again be confirmed by reference to the *TΠ* column in Table 6.10.

*LOOKING AT THE MATHS

As we have seen, the rule for profit maximisation is that firms should produce where *MC* = *MR*. This can be derived algebraically as follows. Profit is defined as

$$T\Pi = TR - TC \qquad (1)$$

Profit is maximised at the point where an additional unit of output will add no more to profit – that is, where

$$\frac{\Delta T\Pi}{\Delta Q} = M\Pi = 0 \qquad (2)$$

or, from (1), where

$$\frac{\Delta TR}{\Delta Q} - \frac{\Delta TC}{\Delta Q} = 0 \qquad (3)$$

or

$$\frac{\Delta TR}{\Delta Q} = \frac{\Delta TC}{\Delta Q} \qquad (4)$$

that is, where *MR* = *MC*.

Equation (2) can be related to Figure 6.19. Profits are maximised at the highest point of the *TΠ* curve. At the top of any curve (or bottom for that matter), its slope is zero. Thus $\Delta T\Pi/Q = M\Pi = 0$. Put another way, the tangent to the top of the *TΠ* curve is horizontal.

From the information for a firm given in the table below, construct a table like 6.10.

Q	0	1	2	3	4	5	6	7
P	12	11	10	9	8	7	6	5
TC	2	6	9	12	16	21	28	38

Use your table to draw diagrams like Figures 6.19 and 6.21. Use these two diagrams to show the profit-maximising output and the level of maximum profit. Confirm your findings by reference to the table you have constructed.

*BOX 6.10 USING CALCULUS TO FIND THE MAXIMUM PROFIT OUTPUT

EXPLORING ECONOMICS

Imagine that a firm's total revenue and total cost functions were

$TR = 48Q - Q^2$
$TC = 12 + 16Q + 3Q^2$

From these two equations the following table can be derived.

Q	TR	TC	$T\Pi (= TR - TC)$
0	0	12	−12
1	47	31	16
2	92	56	36
3	135	87	48
4	176	124	52
5	215	167	48
6	252	216	36
7	287	271	16
.	.	.	.

1. *How much is total fixed cost?*
2. *Continue the table for $Q = 8$ and $Q = 9$*
3. *Plot TR, TC and $T\Pi$ on a diagram like Figure 6.19.*

It can clearly be seen from the table that profit is maximised at an output of 4, where $T\Pi = 52$.

This profit-maximising output and the level of profit can be calculated without drawing up a table. The calculation involves calculus. There are two methods that can be used.

Finding where $MR = MC$

Marginal revenue can be found by differentiating the total revenue function.

$$MR = dTR/dQ$$

The reason is that marginal revenue is the rate of change of total revenue. Differentiating a function gives its rate of change.

Similarly, marginal cost can be found by differentiating the total cost function:

$$MC = dTC/dQ$$

Differentiating TR and TC gives

$$dTR/dQ = 48 - 2Q = MR$$

and

$$dTC/dQ = 16 + 6Q = MC$$

Profit is maximised where $MR = MC$: in other words, where

$$48 - 2Q = 16 + 6Q$$

Solving this for Q gives

$$32 = 80$$
$$\therefore Q = 4$$

The equation for total profit $T\Pi$ is

$$T\Pi = TR - TC$$
$$= 48Q - Q^2 - (12 + 16Q + 3Q^2)$$
$$= -12 + 32Q - 4Q^2$$

Substituting $Q = 4$ into this equation gives

$$T\Pi = -12 + (32 \times 4) - (4 \times 4^2)$$
$$\therefore T\Pi = 52$$

These figures can be confirmed from the table.

Maximising the total profit equation

To maximise an equation we want to find the point where the slope of the curve derived from it is zero. In other words, we want to find the top of the $T\Pi$ curve.

The slope of a curve gives its rate of change and is found by differentiating the curve's equation. Thus to find maximum $T\Pi$ we differentiate it (to find the slope) and set it equal to zero (to find the top).

$$T\Pi = -12 + 32Q - 4Q^2 \text{(see above)}$$
$$\therefore dT\Pi/dQ = 32 - 8Q$$

Setting this equal to zero gives

$$32 - 8Q = 0$$
$$\therefore 8Q = 32$$
$$\therefore Q = 4$$

This is the same result as was found by the first method. Again $Q = 4$ can be substituted into the $T\Pi$ equation to give

$$T\Pi = 52$$

Given the following equations:

$TR = 72Q - 2Q^2$; $TC = 10 + 12Q + 4Q^2$

calculate the maximum profit output and the amount of profit at that output using both methods.

Some qualifications

Long-run profit maximisation

Assuming that the *AR* and *MR* curves are the same in the long run as in the short run, long-run profits will be maximised at the output where *MR* equals the *long-run MC*. The reasoning is the same as with the short-run case.

The meaning of 'profit'

KI 2 p10 One element of cost is the opportunity cost to the owners of the firm of being in business. This is the minimum return the owners must make on their capital in order to prevent them from eventually deciding to close down and perhaps move into some alternative business. It is a *cost* because, just as with wages, rent, etc., it has to be covered if the firm is to continue producing. This opportunity cost to the owners is sometimes known as ***normal profit***, and is *included in the cost curves*.

What determines this normal rate of profit? It has two components. First, someone setting up in business invests capital in it. There is thus an opportunity cost. This is the interest that could have been earned by lending it in some riskless form (e.g. by putting it in a savings account in a bank). Nobody would set up a business unless they expected to earn at least this rate of profit. Running a business is far from riskless, however, and hence a second element is a return to compensate for risk. Thus:

normal profit (%) = rate of interest on a riskless loan
+ a risk premium

The risk premium varies according to the line of business. In those with fairly predictable patterns, such as food retailing, it is relatively low. Where outcomes are very uncertain, such as mineral exploration or the manufacture of fashion garments, it is relatively high.

Thus if owners of a business earn normal profit, they will (just) be content to remain in that industry. If they earn more than normal profit, they will also (obviously) prefer to stay in this business. If they earn less than normal profit, then after a time they will consider leaving and using their capital for some other purpose. We will see in Chapter 7 that the level of profits that a firm can make plays a pivotal role in the way markets are structured.

? *How will the size of 'normal profit' vary with the general state of the economy?*

Given that normal profits are included in costs, any profit that is shown diagrammatically (e.g. the shaded area in Figure 6.21) must therefore be over and above normal profit. It is known by several alternative names: ***supernormal profit***, ***pure profit***, ***economic profit*** or sometimes simply ***profit***. They all mean the same thing: the excess of total profit over normal profit.

Figure 6.22 Loss-minimising output

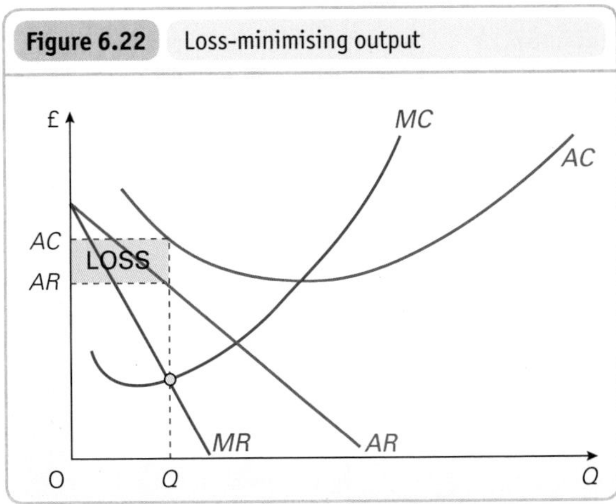

Loss minimising

It may be that there is no output at which the firm can make a profit. Such a situation is illustrated in Figure 6.22: the *AC* curve is above the *AR* curve at all levels of output.

In this case, the output where $MR = MC$ will be the loss-minimising output. The amount of loss at the point where $MR = MC$ is shown by the shaded area in Figure 6.22. Even though the firm is making losses, there is no 'better' level of output at this point.

Whether or not to produce at all

The short run. Fixed costs have to be paid even if the firm is producing nothing at all. Rent and business rates have to be paid, etc. It was explained in Box 6.6 how some of these could sometimes be avoided if the firm temporarily shut down. However, to keep the following discussion as simple as possible it is assumed that all fixed costs are also sunk costs. This means that providing the firm is able to cover its *variable* costs, it is no worse off than it would be if it temporarily shut down. Therefore it should continue to produce because, if it shut down, its losses would be greater. Of course, if the firm's revenues are more than its variable costs, then it is able to go some way to covering the fixed costs and again it will continue to produce. KI 20 p161

Definitions

Normal profit The opportunity cost of being in business: the profit that could have been earned in the next best alternative business. It is counted as a cost of production.

Supernormal profit (also known as pure profit, economic profit or simply profit) The excess of total profit above normal profit.

Figure 6.23 The short-run shut-down point

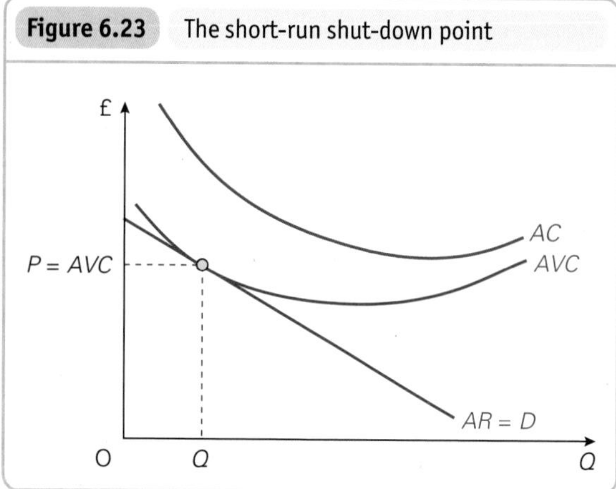

What happens if the firm's revenue is not enough to cover its variable costs: that is, if the *AVC* curve is above, or the *AR* curve below, the position illustrated in Figure 6.23? In that case the firm is worse off than if it only has fixed costs and it will shut down production. This situation is known as the ***short-run shut-down point***.

The long run. All costs are variable in the long run. If, therefore, the firm cannot cover its long-run average costs (which include normal profit), it will close down. The ***long-run shut-down point*** will be where the *AR* curve is tangential to the *LRAC* curve.

Definitions

Short-run shut-down point Where the *AR* curve is tangential to the *AVC* curve. The firm can only just cover its variable costs. Any fall in revenue below this level will cause a profit-maximising firm to shut down immediately.

Long-run shut-down point Where the *AR* curve is tangential to the *LRAC* curve. The firm can just make normal profits. Any fall in revenue below this level will cause a profit-maximising firm to shut down once all costs have become variable.

BOX 6.11 THE LOGIC OF LOGISTICS

CASE STUDIES AND APPLICATIONS

Driving up profits

One key to a company's success is the logistics of its operations. 'Logistics' refers to the management of the inflow of resources to a company and the outflow of finished goods from it; in other words, it refers to 'supply-chain management'. This includes the purchasing of raw materials, transporting them, production sequencing, stock control, delivery to wholesalers or retailers, and so on.

Logistics depends on the provision of high-quality and timely information. As IT systems have become increasingly sophisticated, they have enabled modern developments in logistics to transform the operation of many industries.

Driving down costs

With the widespread use of containerisation and development of giant distribution companies, such as DPD, UPS, DHL and Wincanton, transporting materials and goods around the world has become much faster and much cheaper. These specialist firms can take advantage of the considerable economies of scale in developing larger logistics networks. This means that instead of having to make parts in-house, companies can now use the logistics industry to obtain them at lower cost elsewhere, often from the other side of the world.

With improved systems for ordering materials, and deliveries becoming more and more reliable, firms no longer need to keep large stocks of parts; they simply buy them as they need them. The same opportunity to save costs lies with the finished product: a company can keep lower levels of stocks when its own delivery mechanisms are more efficient.

The globalisation of logistics, with increasing use of the Internet, has resulted in a hugely complex logistics industry. Firms that were once solely concerned with delivery are now employed to manage companies' supply chains and achieve substantial cost savings for them. The whole industry can now be split into three broad and overlapping sectors – logistics service providers (LSP), carriers (trucking, rail freight, sea freight and air freight companies) and courier/express/parcel companies (CEP). CEP is the smallest but fastest growing segment of the market.

Driving up revenues

Efficient logistics has not just resulted in lower costs. The flexibility it has given firms has allowed many to increase their sales.

Carrying lower levels of stocks and switching from supplier to supplier, with the process often being managed by a logistics company, can allow companies to change the products they offer more rapidly. They can be more responsive to consumer demand and thereby increase their sales.

A well-known example of a company benefiting from this approach is Primark. This low-cost fashion retailer focuses much more on buying, logistics and supply-chain management than on branding or advertising.

The impact of Brexit and the COVID-19 pandemic

The UK's exit from the EU Single Market has had a negative impact on the industry as it has increased some of the administrative costs of transporting goods between the UK and EU. In a November 2020 survey by Barclays and BDO of logistics companies,[1] 26 per cent believed that the single most important issue facing their business in 2021 was the impact of Brexit, with the increased paperwork, customs delays and other administrative burdens.

The impact of the COVID-19 pandemic has had a positive impact on part of the industry. As more people switched to online shopping, the demand for large warehouses and last-mile delivery facilities increased dramatically. Estimates suggest that every increase in £1 billion spent online requires an additional 900 000 square feet of logistic space.[2] Investment in distribution warehouses in the UK was £4.7 billion in 2020, an increase of 25 per cent on the previous year.

1. *What dangers are there in keeping stocks to a minimum and relying on complex supply chains?*
2. *Which industries do you think would benefit most from reduced transport times for their finished products? Think of an industry, other than low-cost fashion, which would benefit from the ability to switch rapidly the products offered.*

Identify some industries that would particularly benefit from reduced transport times for their finished products. How might they reorganise their supply chains in order to reduce transport costs?

1 'Survey: Brexit and driver shortages the main challenges for UK logistics operators', *trans.INFO* (25 November 2020), https://trans.info/en/survey-brexit-and-driver-shortages-the-main-challenges-for-uk-logistics-operators-210640

2 'Investors "back with a vengeance" as warehouse demand surges', *Financial Times* (12 August 2020), www.ft.com/content/919fc491-b6e4-4ab8-a523-8f19a9c59bb9

*LOOKING AT THE MATHS

We can state the short- and long-run shut-down points algebraically. Remember that total profit ($T\Pi$) is defined as

$$T\Pi = TR - TC = TR - (TFC + TVC) \qquad (1)$$

A negative value for $T\Pi$ means that the firm makes a loss. This will occur when

$$TR - (TFC + TVC) < 0$$

or

$$TR < (TFC + TVC)$$

But when should the firm shut down?

Short-run shut-down point

If the firm shuts down, TR and TVC will be zero, but in the short run it will still incur total fixed costs (TFC) and thus

$$T\Pi = -TFC \qquad (2)$$

In other words, it will make a loss equal to total fixed costs. From this it can be seen that the firm should close in the short run only if

$$T\Pi < -TFC$$

i.e.

$$(TR - TFC - TVC) < -TFC \qquad (3)$$

In other words, the loss should not exceed fixed costs. Put another way (i.e. by rearranging (3)), it should continue in production as long as

$$TR \geq TVC$$

or, dividing both sides of (4) by quantity, where

$$AR \geq AVC \qquad (4)$$

The firm, therefore, should shut down if

$$AR < AVC$$

This is shown in Figure 6.23.

Long-run shut-down point

In the long run, there are no fixed costs. Thus

$$T\Pi = TR - TVC = TR - TC \qquad (5)$$

If the firm shuts down, it will earn no revenue, but incur no costs. Thus

$$T\Pi = TR - TC = 0 - 0 = 0$$

The firm should therefore continue in production as long as

$$(TR - TC) \geq 0$$

i.e.

$$TR \geq TC$$

or, dividing both sides by quantity, as long as

$$AR \geq AC$$

where AC in this case is long-run average cost. The firm, therefore, should shut down if

$$AR < AC$$

Section summary

1. Total profit equals total revenue minus total cost. By definition, then, a firm's profits will be maximised at the point where there is the greatest gap between total revenue and total cost.
2. Another way of finding the maximum profit point is to find the output where marginal revenue equals marginal cost. Having found this output, the level of maximum profit can be found by finding the average profit ($AR - AC$) and then multiplying it by the level of output.
3. Normal profit is the minimum profit that must be made to persuade a firm to stay in business in the long run. It is counted as part of the firm's costs. Supernormal profit is any profit over and above normal profit.
4. For a firm that cannot make a profit at any level of output, the point where $MR = MC$ represents the loss-minimising output.
5. In the short run, a firm will close down if it cannot cover its variable costs. In the long run, it will close down if it cannot make normal profits.

END OF CHAPTER QUESTIONS

1. The following table shows the average cost and average revenue (price) for a firm at each level of output.

Output	**1**	**2**	**3**	**4**	**5**	**6**	**7**	**8**	**9**	**10**
AC (£)	7.00	5.00	4.00	3.30	3.00	3.10	3.50	4.20	5.00	6.00
AR (£)	10.00	9.50	9.00	8.50	8.00	7.50	7.00	6.50	6.00	5.50

   (a) Construct a table to show *TC, MC, TR* and *MR* at each level of output (put the figures for *MC* and *MR* mid-way between the output figures).
   (b) Using *MC* and *MR* figures, find the profit-maximising output.
   (c) Using *TC* and *TR* figures, check your answer to (b).
   (d) Plot the *AC, MC, AR* and *MR* figures on a graph.
   (e) Mark the profit-maximising output and the *AR* and *AC* at this output.
   (f) Shade in an area to represent the level of profits at this output.

*2. Draw the isoquant corresponding to the following table, which shows the alternative combinations of labour and capital required to produce 100 units of output per day of good X.

K	16	20	$26\frac{2}{3}$	40	60	80	100
L	200	160	120	80	$53\frac{1}{3}$	40	32

   (a) Assuming that capital costs are £20 per day and the wage rate is £10 per day, what is the least-cost method of producing 100 units? What will the daily total cost be? (Draw in a series of isocosts.)
   (b) Now assume that the wage rate rises to £20 per day. Draw a new set of isocosts. What will be the least-cost method of producing 100 units now? How much labour and capital will be used?

3. Choose two industries that you believe are very different. Identify factors used in those industries that in the short run are (a) fixed; (b) variable.
4. Taking the same industries, identify as many economies of scale as you can.
5. 'Both short-run and long-run average cost curves may be ⌣-shaped, but the explanations for their respective shapes are quite different.' Explain this statement.
6. Why do marginal cost curves intersect both the average variable cost curve and the average cost curve at their lowest point?
7. Draw a diagram like that in Figure 6.21. Now illustrate the effect of a rise in demand for the product. Mark the new profit-maximising price and output. Will the profit-maximising output, price, average cost and profit necessarily be higher than before?
8. Why might it make sense for a firm which cannot sell its output at a profit to continue in production for the time being? For how long should the firm continue to produce at a loss?

Online resources

Additional case studies on the student website

6.1 Diminishing returns to nitrogen fertiliser. This case study provides a good illustration of diminishing returns in practice by showing the effects on grass yields of the application of increasing amounts of nitrogen fertiliser.

6.2 Deriving cost curves from total physical product information. This shows how total, average and marginal costs can be derived from total product information and the price of inputs.

6.3 Division of labour in a pin factory. This is the famous example of division of labour given by Adam Smith in his *Wealth of Nations* (1776).

6.4 Followers of fashion. This case study examines the effects of costs on prices of fashion-sensitive goods.

6.5 Putting on a duplicate. This examines the effects on marginal costs of additional passengers on a coach journey.

6.6 Comparing the behaviour of long-run and short-run costs. This is an application of isoquant analysis.

Maths Case 6.1 Total, average and marginal cost. Looking at the mathematical functions for these curves and deriving specific types of cost from a total cost equation.

Maths Case 6.2 Finding the optimum production point: Part 1. Examples using the method of substituting the constraint equation into the objective function.

Maths Case 6.3 Finding the optimum production point: Part 2. The same examples as in Maths Case 6.2, but this time using the Lagrangian methods.

Maths Case 6.4 Total, average and marginal revenue. Looking at the mathematical functions for these curves for both price-taking and price-making firms and relating them to revenue curves.

Websites relevant to this chapter

Numbers and sections refer to websites listed in the Web Appendix and hotlinked from this book's website at **go.pearson.com/uk/sloman.**

- For news articles relevant to this chapter, see the *Economics News* section on the student website.
- For student resources relevant to this chapter, see sites C1–7, 9, 10, 14, 19, 20 and 28.
- For a case study examining costs, see site D2.
- For sites that look at companies, their scale of operation and market share, see E4, 9, 10; G7, 8.
- For links to sites on various aspects of production and costs, see sites I7 and 14.

Profit Maximising under Perfect Competition and Monopoly

CHAPTER MAP

As we saw in Chapter 6, a firm's profits are maximised where its marginal cost equals its marginal revenue: $MC = MR$. But we will want to know more than this.

- What determines the amount of profit that a firm will make? Will profits be large, or just enough for the firm to survive, or so low that it will be forced out of business?
- Will the firm produce a high level of output or a low level?
- Will it be producing efficiently, making best use of resources?
- Will the price charged to the consumer be high or low?
- More generally, will the consumer and society as a whole benefit from the decisions a firm makes? This is, of course, a normative question (see section 1.3). Nevertheless, economists can still identify and analyse the wider effects of these decisions.

The answers to these questions largely depend on the amount of competition that a firm faces. A firm in a highly competitive environment will behave quite differently from a firm facing little or no competition. In particular, a firm facing competition from many other firms will be forced to keep its prices down and be as efficient as possible, simply to survive. If, however, the firm faces little or no competition (like a local water company or a major pharmaceutical company), it may have considerable power over prices, and we may end up paying considerably more as a result.

In this chapter and the next, we consider different types of market structure. Here we focus on the extremes: perfect competition (very many firms competing) and monopoly (only one firm in the industry).

7.1 ALTERNATIVE MARKET STRUCTURES

It is traditional to divide industries into categories according to the degree of competition that exists between the firms within the industry. There are four such categories.

At one extreme is ***perfect competition***, where there are very many firms competing. Each firm is so small relative to the whole industry that it has no power to influence price. It is a price taker. At the other extreme is ***monopoly***, where there is just one firm in the industry, and hence no competition from within the industry. In the middle come ***monopolistic competition***, which involves quite a lot of firms competing and where there is freedom for new firms to enter the industry, and ***oligopoly***, which involves only a few firms and where entry of new firms is restricted.

To distinguish more precisely between these four categories, the following must be considered:

- How freely firms can enter the industry. Is entry free or restricted? If it is restricted, just how great are the barriers to the entry of new firms?
- The nature of the product. Do all firms produce an identical product, or do firms produce their own particular brand or model or variety?
- The firm's degree of control over price. Is the firm a price taker or can it choose its price, and if so, how will changing its price affect its profits? What we are talking about here is the nature of the demand curve it faces. How elastic is it? If the firm puts up its price, will it lose (a) all its sales (a horizontal demand curve), or (b) a large proportion of its sales (a relatively elastic demand curve), or (c) just a small proportion of its sales (a relatively inelastic demand curve)?

KI 9 p64

KEY IDEA 22

Market power. When firms have market power over prices, they can use this to raise prices and profits above the perfectly competitive level. Other things being equal, the firm will gain at the expense of the consumer. Similarly, if consumers or workers have market power, they can use this to their own benefit.

Table 7.1 shows the differences between the four categories.

1. *Give two more examples in each category.*
2. *Would you expect builders and restaurateurs to have the same degree of control over price?*

TC 5 p48

The market structure under which a firm operates will determine its behaviour. Firms under perfect competition will behave quite differently from firms which are monopolists, which will behave differently again from firms under oligopoly or monopolistic competition.

This behaviour (or 'conduct') will in turn affect the firm's performance: its prices, profits, efficiency, etc. In many cases, it will also affect other firms' performance: *their* prices, profits, efficiency, etc. The collective conduct of all the firms in the industry will affect the whole industry's performance.

Economists thus see a causal chain running from market structure to the performance of that industry.

Structure → Conduct → Performance

However, it is important to remember that feedback loops are possible, where the conduct of firms has an impact on structure.

First, we shall look at the two extreme market structures: perfect competition and monopoly. Then in Chapter 8 we shall look at the two intermediate cases of monopolistic competition and oligopoly.

The two intermediate cases are sometimes referred to collectively as ***imperfect competition***. The vast majority of firms in the real world operate under imperfect competition. It is still worth studying the two extreme cases, however, because they provide a framework within which to understand the real world. Some industries tend more to the competitive extreme, and thus the behaviour and performance of firms with these industries corresponds more closely to the predictions of perfect competition. Other industries tend more to the other extreme: for example, when there is one dominant firm and a few much smaller firms. In such cases, the behaviour and performance of firms corresponds more closely to the predictions of monopoly.

Chapters 7 and 8 assume that firms, under whatever market structure, are attempting to maximise profits. Chapter 9 questions this assumption. It looks at alternative theories of the firm: theories based on assumptions *other* than profit maximising.

Definitions

Perfect competition A market structure where there are many firms, none of which is large; where there is freedom of entry into the industry; where all firms produce an identical product; and where all firms are price takers.

Monopoly A market structure where there is only one firm in the industry. (Note that this is the economic definition of a pure monopoly. In UK competition law, the part that applies to the abuse of monopoly power covers firms that are in a position of 'market dominance'. Such firms will have a large share, but not necessarily a 100 per cent share of the market. See Chapter 14 for more on this.)

Monopolistic competition A market structure where, as with perfect competition, there are many firms and freedom of entry into the industry, but where each firm produces a differentiated product and thus has some control over its price.

Oligopoly A market structure where there are few enough firms to enable barriers to be erected against the entry of new firms.

Imperfect competition The collective name for monopolistic competition and oligopoly.

Table 7.1 Features of the four market structures

Type of market	Number of firms	Freedom of entry	Nature of product	Examples	Implication for demand curve for firm
Perfect competition	Very many	Unrestricted	Homogeneous (undifferentiated)	Cabbages, carrots, foreign exchange (these approximate to perfect competition)	Horizontal. The firm is a price taker
Monopolistic competition	Many/several	Unrestricted	Differentiated	Builders, restaurants, hairdressers, garage mechanics	Downward sloping, but relatively elastic. The firm has some control over price
Oligopoly	Few	Restricted	1. Undifferentiated 2. Differentiated	1. Petrol, cement 2. Cars, electrical appliances, supermarkets, retail banking	Downward sloping, relatively inelastic but depends on reactions of rivals to a price change
Monopoly	One	Restricted or completely blocked	Unique	Prescription drugs produced under a patent, local water companies	Downward sloping, more inelastic than oligopoly. The firm has considerable control over price

BOX 7.1 **CONCENTRATION RATIOS** EXPLORING ECONOMICS

Measuring the degree of competition

We can get some indication of how competitive a market is by observing the number of firms: the greater the number of firms, the more competitive the market would seem to be. However, this does not tell us anything about how *concentrated* the market might be. There may be *many* firms (suggesting a situation of perfect competition or monopolistic competition), but the largest two firms might produce 95 per cent of total output. This would make these two firms behave more like oligopolists.

Thus, even though a large number of producers may make the market *seem* highly competitive, this could be deceiving. Another approach, therefore, to measuring the degree of competition is to focus on the level of concentration in the market.

Five-firm concentration ratios for various sub-sectors (by revenue)

Sector	2003–04	2015–16
Manufacture of cocoa and chocolate confectionery	94	94
Retail sales of mobile phones	77	89
Milk and cream production	79	89
Gambling and betting activities	68	85
Publishing of computer games	39	84
Manufacture of prepared meals	68	84
Distilling and blending spirits	77	81
Manufacture of cars	65	78
Butter and cheese production	54	60
Film, TV and theatrical casting	71	52
Accounting and auditing activities	40	42
Pubs and bars	22	29
Funeral services	26	26
Advertising agencies	14	15
Maintenance and repair of cars	9	13
Sale of used cars	6	11
Take-away food shops	8	10
Hairdressing and beauty treatments	10	3

Source: Based on data in *Is everybody concentrating?* Resolution Foundation

The simplest measure of industrial concentration involves adding together the market share of the largest so many firms: e.g. the largest 3, 5 or 15. This would give what is known as the '3-firm', '5-firm' or '15-firm' 'concentration ratio'. There are different ways of estimating market share: by revenue, by output, by profit, etc.

The table shows the 5-firm concentration ratios of selected sub-sectors in the UK by revenue. As you can see, there is an enormous variation in the degree of concentration from one sector to another but the majority of sectors (55 per cent) have become more concentrated over time.

One of the main reasons for these differences is the percentage of total industry output at which economies of scale are exhausted. If this occurs at a low level of output, there will be room for several firms in the sector which can all benefit from the maximum economies of scale.

The degree of concentration will also depend on the barriers to entry of other firms into the sector (see pages 207–10) and on various factors such as transport costs and historical accident. It will also depend on how varied the products/services are within any one sector. For example, in the take-away food sector there is room for many firms, each producing a specialised range of dishes.

Other measures of competitiveness

So is the degree of concentration a good guide to the degree of competitiveness of the industry? The answer is that it is *some* guide, but on its own it can be misleading. In particular, it ignores the degree of competition from abroad. For example, research by the Competition and Markets Authority (CMA) found that levels of concentration in manufacturing had increased over time, but so had the relative share of imports.[1]

Other possible indicators of competitiveness include:

- The rate of entry and exit of firms into and from the market. In a competitive market, we would expect less efficient firms to exit the market and be replaced by newer and more dynamic enterprises.
- The average age of larger firms. If the same group of large firms dominates the market from one year to the next, then this average age will increase.
- The extent to which the ranking of the largest firms remains the same or changes over time.
- The level of business profitability and the mark-up of price over marginal costs.
- The extent to which the most profitable businesses remain the same over time.

1. ***What are the advantages and disadvantages of using a 5-firm concentration ratio rather than a 15-firm, a 3-firm or even a 1-firm ratio?***
2. ***Why are some industries, such as bread baking and brewing, relatively concentrated, in that a few firms produce a large proportion of total output (see Box 8.2 and Case Studies 8.5 and 8.6 on the student website), and yet there are also many small producers?***

Research a particular industry and attempt to establish its 5-firm concentration ratio. What does this tell you about the degree of competition in the industry? How important is it to define the 'market' when trying to establish the intensity of competition?

1 'The state of UK competition', CMA (November 2020), www.gov.uk/government/publications/state-of-uk-competition-report-2020

7.2 PERFECT COMPETITION

Assumptions of perfect competition

The model of perfect competition is built on four assumptions:

- Firms are *price takers*. There are so many firms in the industry that each one produces an insignificantly small portion of total industry supply, and therefore has no power whatsoever to affect the price of the product. It faces a horizontal demand 'curve' at the market price: the price determined by the interaction of demand and supply in the whole market.
- There is complete *freedom of entry* into the industry for new firms. Existing firms are unable to stop new firms setting up in business. Setting up a business takes time, however. Freedom of entry, therefore, applies in the long run.
- All firms produce an *identical product*. (The product is 'homogeneous'.) There is therefore no branding and no advertising, since there would be no point in the firm incurring this cost.
- 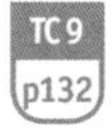 TC 9 p132 Producers and consumers have *perfect knowledge* of the market. Producers have access to the same technology, input prices and market opportunities and are fully aware of these. Consumers are fully aware of the price, quality and availability of the product.

These assumptions are very strict. Few, if any, industries in the real world meet these conditions. Certain agricultural markets are perhaps closest to perfect competition. The market for fresh vegetables is an example.

Nevertheless, despite the lack of real-world cases, the model of perfect competition plays a very important role in economic analysis and policy. It acts as a benchmark that helps us to understand the impact on markets of a number of factors, such as product differentiation and barriers to entry.

Sometimes it is held up as an 'ideal type' for society. Many argue that achieving perfect competition would bring a number of important advantages, such as keeping prices down to marginal cost and preventing firms from making supernormal profit over the long run. The model can thus be used as a standard against which to judge the shortcomings of real-world industries. However, we will also see that it has disadvantages, when compared with other market structures.

1. *It is sometimes claimed that the market for various stocks and shares is perfectly competitive, or nearly so. Take the case of the market for shares in a large company like Apple. Go through each of the four assumptions above and see if they apply in this case. (Don't be misled by the first assumption. The 'firm' in this case is not Apple itself.)*
2. *Is the market for gold perfectly competitive?*

The short run and the long run

Before we can examine what price, output and profits will be, we must first distinguish between the short run and the long run as they apply to perfect competition.

In the ***short run***, the number of firms is fixed. Depending on its costs and revenue, a firm might be making large profits, small profits, no profits or a loss; and in the short run, it may continue to do so.

In the ***long run***, however, the level of profits affects entry and exit from the industry. If supernormal profits are made (see page 189), new firms will be attracted into the industry, whereas if losses are being made, firms will leave.

Note that although we shall be talking about the *level* of profit (since that makes our analysis of pricing and output decisions simpler to understand), in practice it is usually the *rate* of profit that determines whether a firm stays in the industry or leaves. The ***rate of profit*** (r) is the level of profit ($T\Pi$) as *a proportion of the level of capital (K) employed*: $r = T\Pi/K$. If $T\Pi$ is measured as profit before tax and interest payments, r is referred to as the return on capital employed (ROCE). As you would expect, larger firms will need to make a larger *total* profit to persuade them to stay in an industry. Total normal profit is thus larger for them than for a small firm. The *rate* of normal profit, however, will probably be similar.

1. *Why do economists treat normal profit as a cost of production?*
2. *What determines (a) the level and (b) the rate of normal profit for a particular firm?*

Thus whether the industry expands or contracts in the long run will depend on the rate of profit. Naturally, since the time a firm takes to set up in business varies from industry to industry, the length of time before the long run is reached also varies from industry to industry.

The short-run equilibrium of the firm

TC4 p45

The determination of price, output and profit in the short run under perfect competition can best be shown in a diagram.

Figure 7.1 shows a short-run equilibrium for both an industry and a firm under perfect competition. Both parts of the diagram have the same scale for the vertical axis. The horizontal axes have totally different scales, however. For example, if the horizontal axis for the firm were measured in, say, thousands of units, the horizontal axis for the whole industry might be measured in millions or tens of millions of units, depending on the number of firms in the industry.

Let us examine the determination of price, output and profit in turn.

Price. The price is determined in the industry by the intersection of demand and supply. The firm faces a horizontal demand (or average revenue) 'curve' at this price. It can sell

Definitions

Short run under perfect competition The period during which there is insufficient time for new firms to enter the industry.

Long run under perfect competition The period of time that is long enough for new firms to enter the industry.

Rate of profit Total profit ($T\Pi$) as a proportion of the capital employed (K): $r = T\Pi/K$. Often measured by using ROCE in the real world.

BOX 7.2 IS PERFECT BEST?

EXPLORING ECONOMICS

Be careful of the word 'perfect'.

'Perfect competition' refers to competition that is complete. Perhaps 'complete competition' would be a better term. There is a complete absence of power, a complete absence of entry barriers, a complete absence of product differentiation between producers, and complete information for producers and consumers on the market. It is thus useful for understanding the effects of power, barriers, product differentiation and lack of information.

Perfect does not mean 'best', however.

Just because it is at the extreme end of the competition spectrum, it does not follow that perfect competition is desirable. After all, you could have a perfect killer virus – i.e. one that is totally immune to drugs, and against which humans have no natural protection at all. Such a thing, though perfect, is hardly desirable.

KI 6 p29

To say that perfect competition is desirable and that it is a goal towards which government policy should be directed are normative statements. Economists, in their role as economists, cannot make such statements.

This does not mean, of course, that economists cannot identify the effects of perfect competition, but whether these effects are *desirable* or not is an ethical question.

The danger is that by using perfect competition as a yardstick, and by using the word 'perfect' rather than 'complete', economists may be surreptitiously persuading their audience that perfect competition is a goal we *ought* to be striving to achieve.

Give some other examples of 'perfect' things that may not be desirable. Discuss these in groups to establish what criteria are being used to decide whether each example is perfect (or near perfect).

Figure 7.1 Short-run equilibrium of an industry and a firm under perfect competition

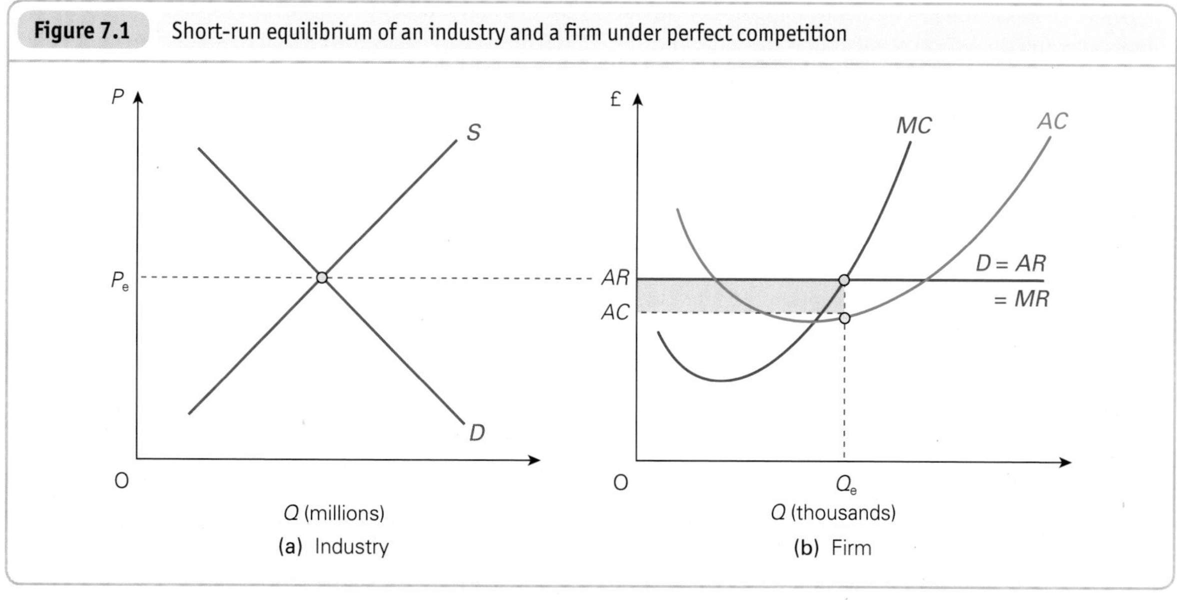

all it can produce at the market price (P_e), but nothing at a price above P_e.

Output. The firm will maximise profit where marginal cost equals marginal revenue ($MR = MC$), at at an output of Q_e. Note that, since the price is not affected by the firm's output, marginal revenue will equal price (see pages 182–3 and Figure 6.15).

Profit. If the average cost (AC) curve (which includes normal profit) dips below the average revenue (AR) 'curve', the firm will earn supernormal profit. Supernormal profit per unit at Q_e is the vertical difference between AR and AC at Q_e. Total supernormal profit is the shaded rectangle in Figure 7.1.

What happens if the firm cannot make a profit at *any* level of output? This situation would occur if the AC curve were above the AR curve at all points. This is illustrated in Figure 7.2, where the market price is P_1. In this case, the point where $MC = MR$ represents the *loss-minimising* point (where loss is defined as anything less than normal profit). The amount of the loss is represented by the shaded rectangle.

As we saw in section 6.6, whether the firm is prepared to continue making a loss in the short run or whether it will close down immediately depends on whether it can cover its *variable* costs – assuming all fixed costs are also sunk costs.

Provided price is above average variable cost (AVC), the firm will still continue producing in the short run: it can pay its variable costs and go some way to paying its fixed costs. It will shut down in the short run only if the market price falls below P_2 in Figure 7.2.

The firm's short-run supply curve

The *firm's* short-run supply curve will be a section of its (short-run) marginal cost curve.

A supply curve shows how much will be supplied at each price: it relates quantity to price. The marginal cost curve relates quantity to marginal cost. But under perfect competition,

Figure 7.2 Loss minimising under perfect competition

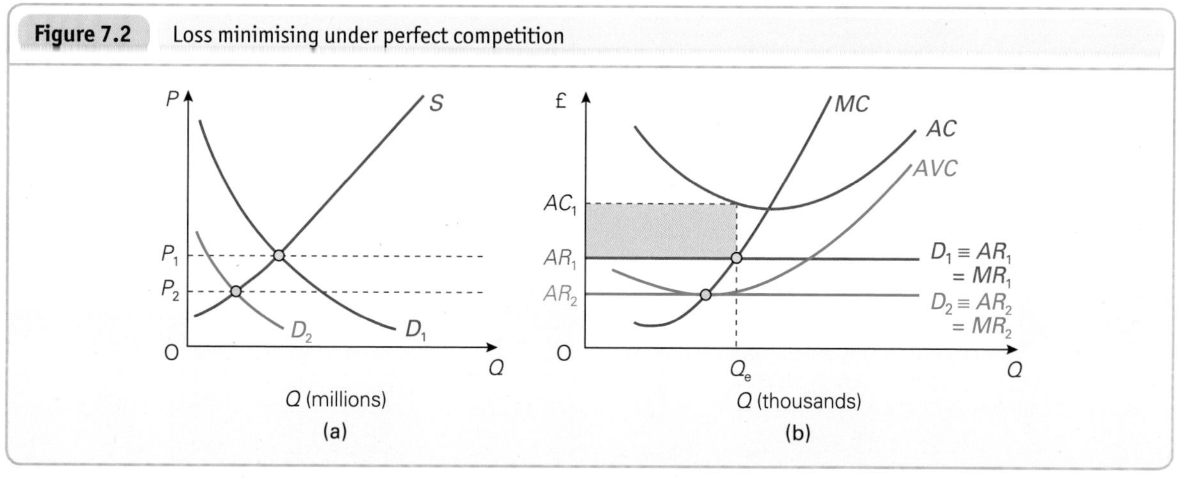

given that $P = MR$, and $MR = MC$, P must equal MC. Thus the supply curve and the MC curve will follow the same line.

For example, in Figure 7.3(b), if price were P_1, profits would be maximised at Q_1 where $P_1 = MC$. Thus point *a* is one point on the supply curve. At a price of P_2, Q_2 would be produced. Thus point *b* is another point on the supply curve, and so on.

So, under perfect competition, the firm's supply curve is entirely dependent on costs of production. This demonstrates why the firm's supply curve is upward sloping. Given that marginal costs rise as output rises (due to diminishing marginal returns), a higher price will be necessary to induce the firm to increase its output.

Note that, assuming all fixed costs are also sunk costs, the firm will not produce at a price below AVC. Thus the supply curve is only that portion of the MC curve above point *e*.

The short-run industry supply curve

What is the short-run supply curve of the whole *industry?* This shows the total quantity supplied by all the firms already in the industry at each possible price. It does not include the output produced by any new entrants as this would only apply in the long run. To calculate short-run industry supply at any price we simply add up how much each individual firm wants to supply at that price. For example, if there were 100 firms in the market which all wanted to supply 10 units at a price of £5, then the market supply at £5 would be 1000. To derive the industry supply curve, therefore, we simply sum the short-run supply curves (and hence MC curves) of all the firms already in the industry. Graphically this will be a *horizontal* sum, since it is only the *quantities* that are added at each price.

Will the industry supply be zero below a price of P_5 in Figure 7.3?

The long-run equilibrium of the firm

In the long run, if typical firms are making supernormal profits, new firms will be attracted into the industry. Likewise, if established firms can make supernormal profits by increasing the scale of their operations, they will do so, since all factors of production are variable in the long run.

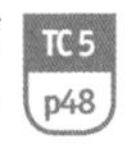

TC 5 p48

The effect of the entry of new firms and/or the expansion of existing firms is to increase industry supply. This is illustrated in Figure 7.4. At a price of P_1 supernormal profits are earned. This causes industry supply to expand (the short-run industry supply curve shifts to the right). This in turn leads

Figure 7.3 Deriving the short-run supply curve

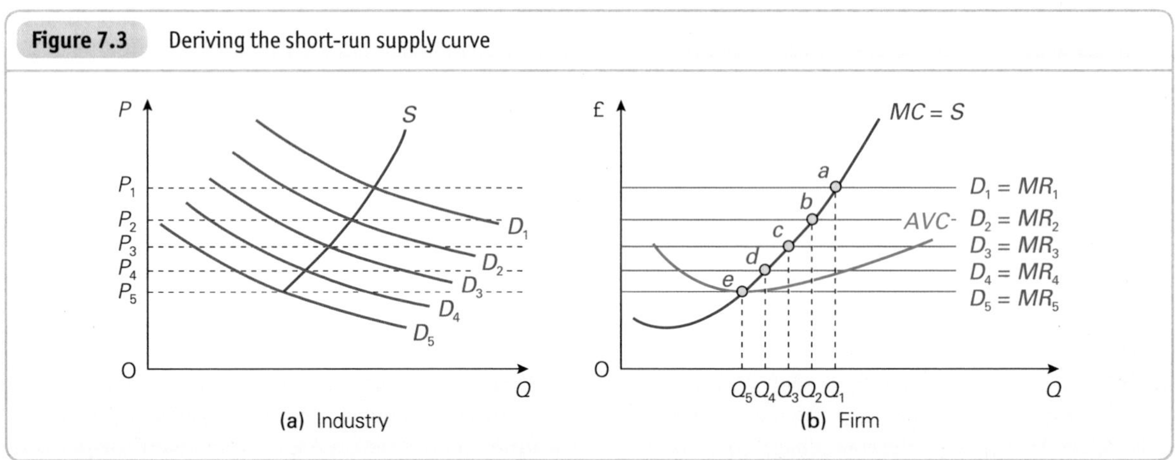

Figure 7.4 Long-run equilibrium under perfect competition

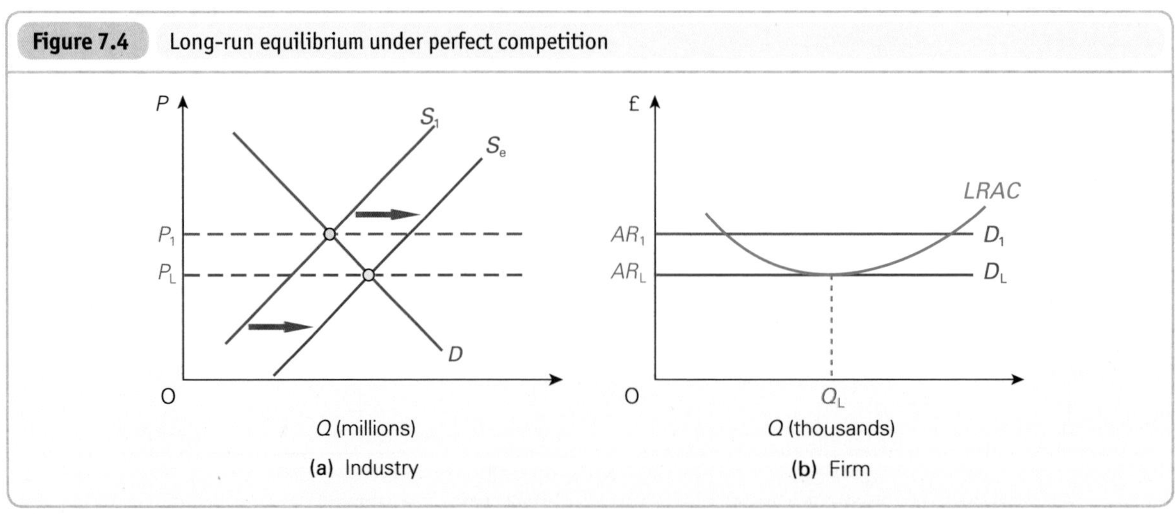

Figure 7.5 Long-run equilibrium of the firm under perfect competition

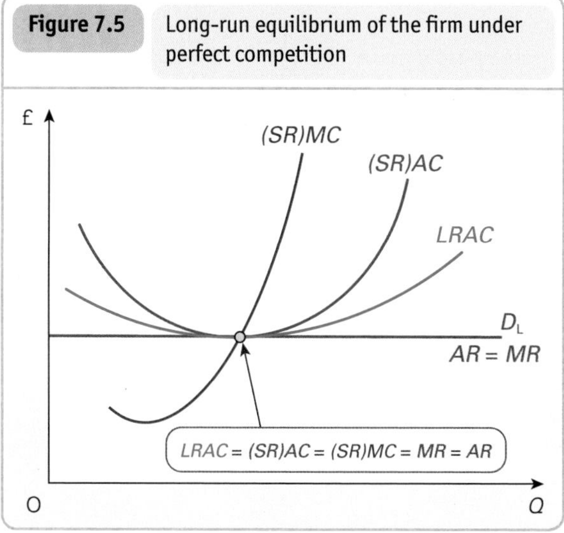

to a fall in price. Supply will go on increasing and price falling until firms are making only normal profits. This will be when price has fallen to the point where the demand 'curve' for the firm just touches the bottom of its long-run average cost curve. Q_L is thus the long-run equilibrium output of the firm, with P_L the long-run equilibrium price.

KI 5 p21

Illustrate on a diagram similar to Figure 7.4 what would happen in the long run if price were initially below P_L.

Since the *LRAC* curve is tangential to all possible short-run *AC* curves (see section 6.4), the full long-run equilibrium will be as shown in Figure 7.5 where

$$LRAC = AC = MC = MR = AR$$

*LOOKING AT THE MATHS

As we have seen, the long-run equilibrium output is where long-run average cost is minimised. If we know the equation for *LRAC*, we can simply use the techniques of minimisation (see pages A:10–12) to find the equilibrium output. Assume that the long-run average cost function is

$$LRAC = a - bQ + cQ^2$$

The technique is to differentiate this function and set it equal to zero, i.e.

$$\frac{d(LRAC)}{dQ} = -b + 2cQ = 0 \quad (1)$$

Solving equation (1) for Q gives the long-run equilibrium output. Once we have found the value of Q, we can substitute it back into equation (1) to find the value of *LRAC* and hence the equilibrium price (since $P = LRAC$).

We can then use the second derivative test (see page A:12) to check that this indeed does represent a minimum, not a maximum, *LRAC*. An example of this is given in Maths Case 7.1 on the student website.

The firm's long-run supply curve

The firm's long-run supply curve is derived in a very similar way to the firm's short-run supply curve. The major difference is that, in the long run, the firm can adjust all of its inputs. This means that all of its costs are now variable and hence the long-run average cost curve is the same as long-run average variable cost curve. Therefore, the firm's long-run supply curve is the portion of its long-run marginal cost curve above the point where it is cut by the average cost curve. At prices below this level it would be loss minimising for the firm to produce zero.

The long-run industry supply curve

The long-run industry supply curve cannot be derived in the same way as the short-run industry supply curve: i.e. by horizontally summing all the individual firms' supply curves. This is because, in the long run, the number of firms in the industry is no longer fixed and account has to be taken of the output produced by any new firms entering the industry. This has to be added to the quantity produced by existing firms.

The long-run industry supply curve can be derived by analysing the impact of an increase in demand on a market that is initially in long-run equilibrium. This initial equilibrium is shown at point *a* in Figure 7.6(a), where market demand (D_{M1}) is equal to both long-run and short-run market supply (LRS_M and SRS_{M1}). The market price and output are P_1 and Q_{M1}, respectively.

Given this market price, the representative firm maximises profit at point *x* in Figure 7.6(b), where $MC = MR$. It produces Q_{F1} and, with $P_1 = AC_1$, makes normal profit.

Assume now that the market demand curve increases from D_{M1} to D_{M2}. Firms in the market respond to the higher prices by increasing production. The market equilibrium in the short run moves from point *a* to point *b* – a movement up along the short-run market supply curve (SRS_{M1}). The market price and quantity increase to P_2 and Q_{M2}.

Given this new higher market price of P_2 the profit-maximising response of the representative firm is to move upwards along its supply or *MC* curve from point *x* to point *y*. Its output increases from Q_{F1} to Q_{F2} and, as the price is now greater than the firm's average cost, it makes supernormal profit.

In the long run, this supernormal profit will act as a signal to entrepreneurs and new firms will enter the market. The arrival of new entrants will cause the short-run market supply curve to shift to the right (to SRS_{M2}), putting downward pressure on the market price.

Not only will the new entrants affect the market for the final product, they will also have an impact on the various markets for different factors of production. For example, the demand for raw materials required to produce the good will increase as new entrants and existing firms try to purchase them. This might put upward pressure on the prices of various input prices, such as raw materials, energy, labour and physical capital. If the price of factor inputs does rise, this will cause the firm's *AC* and *MC* curves in Figure 7.6(b) to shift upwards: e.g. from AC_1 to AC_2 and MC_1 to MC_2.

Figure 7.6 Long-run industry supply curve (increasing cost industry)

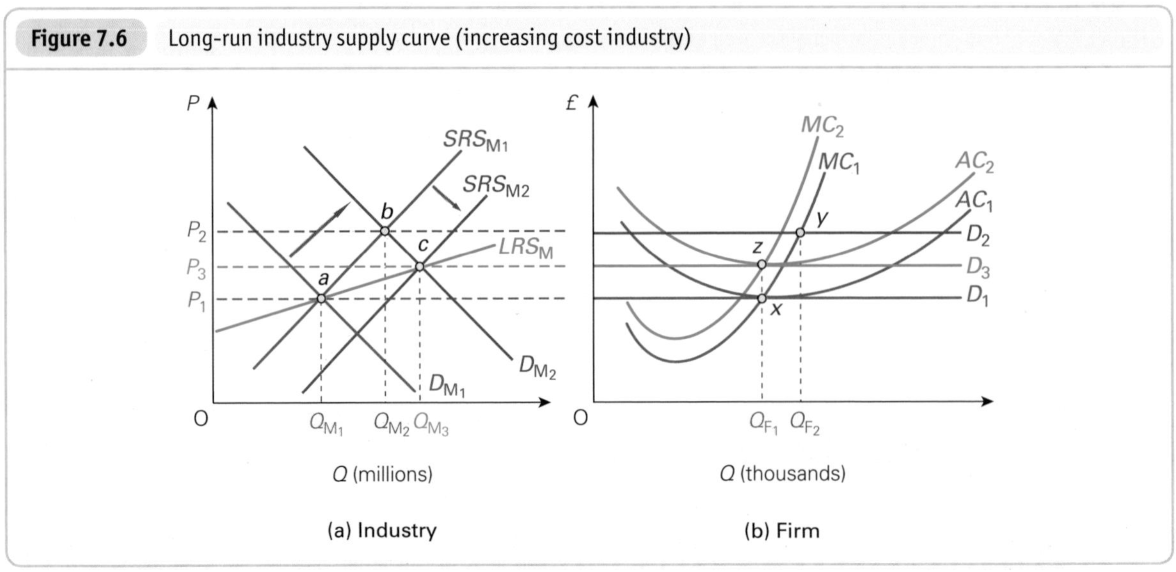

Given this rise in the costs of production, new firms will stop entering the industry once the short-run industry supply curve has shifted to SRS_{M2}. The new long-run market equilibrium is at point *c* with the price falling back to P_3 and industry output increasing to Q_{M3}. At the new lower market price of P_3 the firm will maximise profits at point *z*. The market price is now equal to the firm's new higher *AC* curve (AC_2) – profits have returned to the normal level. There is thus no longer any incentive for other firms to enter the industry.

The long-run market supply curve (LRS_M) goes through points *a* and *c*: i.e. the two positions of long-run equilibrium.

Increasing cost industry – upward-sloping long-run supply curve. In the example in Figure 7.6, the long-run industry supply curve is upward sloping because the extra demand for factor inputs generated by new entrants puts upward pressure on their prices. This is referred to as an ***increasing-cost industry*** (i.e. where there are external diseconomies of scale – see page 169). It is likely to occur when the demand for factor inputs from firms within one industry make up a relatively large proportion of the total demand for those inputs. This is more likely when most of the factor inputs are industry specific: i.e. specialist capital equipment tailored to the production of a particular good. In these circumstances, any increase in demand from new entrants will have a significant impact on the total demand for the inputs, making an increase in their price more probable.

Constant-cost industry – horizontal long-run supply curve. In some industries the majority of factor inputs will be far less specialised. Take the example of an input such as electricity. The demand for electricity from firms in a particular industry will be small relative to the total demand for electricity across the whole economy. If the demand from new entrants in one industry increased, it is unlikely to affect the market price of electricity. If this were true for all factor inputs used by firms then it would be a ***constant-cost industry***. As new firms entered, the average total cost curve of the individual firms would remain unchanged. A constant-cost industry would have a horizontal long-run industry supply curve.

Decreasing-cost industry – downward-sloping long-run supply curve. Another possibility is that increasing demand from new entrants within the industry causes the price of factor inputs to decrease. This is called a ***decreasing-cost industry***. It can occur when the increased demand for inputs enables the suppliers of these inputs to exploit internal economies of scale. It can also occur when firms in the industry share common transport, training or other infrastructure. These external economies of scale (see page 169) cause the cost curves in Figure 7.6(b) to shift downwards. A decreasing-cost industry will therefore have a downward-sloping long-run industry supply curve.

Use a diagram similar to Figure 7.6 to derive a long-run market supply curve for (a) a constant-cost industry; (b) a decreasing-cost industry.

The incompatibility of perfect competition and substantial economies of scale

Why is perfect competition so rare in the real world – if it even exists at all? One important reason for this has to do with economies of scale.

Definitions

Increasing-cost industry An industry where average costs increase as the size of the industry expands.

Constant-cost industry An industry where average costs stay constant as the size of the industry expands.

Decreasing-cost industry An industry where average costs decrease as the size of the industry expands.

In many industries, firms may have to be quite large if they are to experience the full potential economies of scale. But perfect competition requires there to be *many* firms and that each one is a price taker. Firms must therefore be small under perfect competition: too small in most cases for economies of scale.

Once a firm expands sufficiently to achieve economies of scale, it will usually gain market power. It will be able to undercut the prices of smaller firms, which will thus be driven out of business. Perfect competition is destroyed.

Perfect competition could only exist in any industry, therefore, if there were no (or virtually no) economies of scale.

1. *What other reasons can you think of why perfect competition is so rare?*
2. *Why does the market for fresh vegetables approximate to perfect competition, whereas that for aircraft does not?*

Perfect competition and the public interest

Benefits of perfect competition

There are a number of features of perfect competition which, it could be argued, benefit society:

- Price equals marginal cost. As we shall see in Chapter 12, this has important implications for the allocation of resources between alternative products. Given that price equals marginal utility (see Chapter 4), marginal utility will equal marginal cost. This is argued to be an optimal position as it represents allocative efficiency in consumption (see page 12).

  To demonstrate why, consider what would happen if they were not equal. If price were greater than marginal cost, this would mean that consumers were putting a higher value ($P = MU$) on the production of extra units than they cost to produce (MC). Therefore more ought to be produced. If price were less than marginal cost, consumers would be putting a lower value on extra units than they cost to produce. Therefore less ought to be produced. When they are equal, therefore, production levels are just right. But, as we shall see later, it is only under perfect competition that $MC = P$.

KI 3 p13

- Long-run equilibrium is at the bottom of the firm's long-run AC curve. That is, for any given technology, the firm, in the long run, will produce at the least-cost output.
- Perfect competition is a case of 'survival of the fittest'. Inefficient firms will be driven out of business, since they will not be able to make even normal profits. This encourages firms to be as efficient as possible.
- The combination of (long-run) production being at minimum average cost and the firm making only normal profit keeps prices at a minimum.
- If consumer tastes change, the resulting price change will lead firms to respond (purely out of self-interest). An increased consumer demand will result in extra supply with only a short-run increase in profit.

Because of these last two points, perfect competition is said to lead to ***consumer sovereignty***. Consumers, through the market, determine what and how much is to be produced. Firms have no power to manipulate the market. They cannot control price. The only thing they can do to increase profit is to become more efficient, and that benefits the consumer too.

Possible disadvantages of perfect competition

Even under perfect competition, however, the free market has various limitations. For example, there is no guarantee that the goods produced will be distributed to the members of society in the *fairest* proportions. There may be considerable inequality of income. (We examine this issue in Chapter 10.) What is more, a redistribution of income would lead to a different pattern of consumption and hence production. Thus there is no guarantee that perfect competition will lead to the optimum combination of goods being produced when society's views on equity are taken into account.

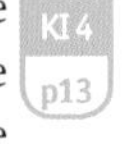

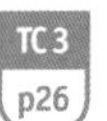

Another limitation is that the production of certain goods may lead to various undesirable side effects, such as pollution. Perfect competition cannot safeguard against this either.

What is more, perfect competition may be less desirable than other market structures such as monopoly.

- Even though firms under perfect competition may seem to have an incentive to develop new technology (in order to gain supernormal profits, albeit temporarily), the long-run normal profits they make may not be sufficient to fund the necessary research and development. Also, with complete information available, if they did develop new, more efficient methods of production, their rivals would merely copy them, in which case the investment would have been a waste of money.
- Perfectly competitive industries produce undifferentiated products. This lack of variety might be seen as a disadvantage to the consumer. Under monopolistic competition and oligopoly there is often intense competition over the quality and design of the product. This can lead to innovation and improvements that would not exist under perfect competition. The issue of the efficiency or otherwise of perfect markets and the various failings of real-world markets is examined in more detail in Chapters 12–14.

> **Definition**
>
> **Consumer sovereignty** A situation where firms respond to changes in consumer demand without being in a position in the long run to charge a price above average cost.

BOX 7.3 E-COMMERCE AND MARKET STRUCTURE

Has technology shifted market power?

In this case study, we will consider the impact of *e-commerce* on the competitive environment. Does it undermine the dominance of large existing firms or does it create new powerful businesses with significant market power?

What do we mean by e-commerce?

E-commerce or e-shopping is a shorthand term for buying and selling products through the Internet. The chart shows the rise in online retail sales as a proportion of all retail sales in the UK between 2010 and 2021. This grew steadily from 8 per cent in 2010 to 19 per cent in 2019.

However, it is important to note that the data may underestimate the true extent of this growth, as it predominately includes spending by consumers on physical goods. It does not include spending on services such as holidays and music downloads: i.e. sectors that have experienced significant increases in online spending over recent years. For the 2010–19 period, it also illustrates how the proportion of Internet sales rises each year in the run-up to Christmas as many people buy gifts online.

The chart clearly demonstrates the dramatic impact of the lockdowns on consumer behaviour during the COVID-19 pandemic. The share of online retail sales shot up in April/May 2020 from 19 per cent to just under 33 per cent. As non-essential stores then began to re-open in the summer of 2020, the share fell, but remained well above the pre-pandemic level.

It then increased again to over 36 per cent during both the second and third lockdowns in November 2020 and January 2021, respectively. The largest year-on-year growth was for food – 126.4 per cent. However, it remains the sector with by far the lowest proportion of online sales – 11 per cent in December 2020. The figures for 'department stores', 'textile clothing and footwear stores', 'other stores' (pharmacies, technology, books, sports, etc) and 'household goods stores' were 35.4 per cent, 31.9 per cent, 22.2 per cent, 20.9 per cent respectively.[1]

Unsurprisingly, 16–34-year-olds are the most likely to shop online. In 2019, 97 per cent of this age group in the UK had used the Internet to shop in the previous 12 months, compared to 54 per cent of over 65s. However, the over 65s had the fastest growth over the previous decade.[2] Data from the EU[3] also illustrates the impact of differing levels of education. The number of Internet users with higher levels of education who purchase goods online was 33 percentage points above the figure for those with a lower level of education.

Moving markets back towards perfect competition?

In an article published in the *Economist*[4] in 2000, it was stated that 'the Internet cuts costs, increases competition and improves the functioning of the price mechanism. It thus moves the economy closer to the textbook model of perfect competition, which assumes abundant information, zero transaction costs and no barriers to entry'.

To see if this is true, let us look at the assumptions of this market structure.

Large numbers of buyers and sellers. The growth of e-commerce has led to many new firms starting up in business. The majority of these are small companies that often sell directly to consumers via their own websites or use online marketplaces such as eBay or Amazon. In the

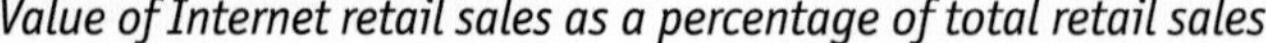
Value of Internet retail sales as a percentage of total retail sales

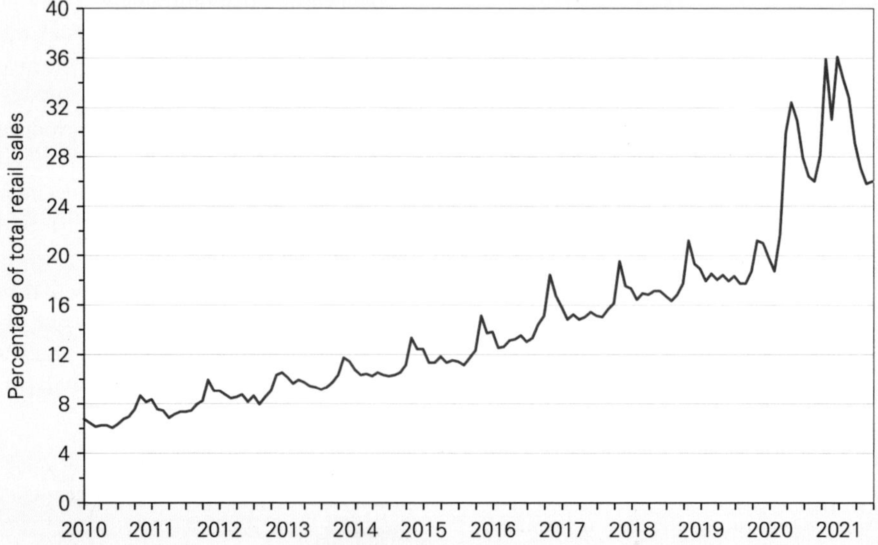

Source: Based on series J4MC from *Time Series Data* (National Statistics), www.ons.gov.uk/businessindustryandtrade/retailindustry/timeseries/j4mc/drsi

fourth quarter of 2020, eBay had approximately 185 million active buyers and 19 million active sellers worldwide and 1.6 billion listings. Amazon had over 2.5 million active sellers, and over 150 million mobile users accessed the Amazon app, while 55 per cent of the units shipped by Amazon during this period were goods sold by third-party sellers. The majority of these third-party sellers are small suppliers; data from 2018 shows that 75 per cent had between just one and five employees.

Perfect knowledge. The Internet has significantly reduced some of the transaction costs of using a market. Consumers can easily compare the prices and other features of the goods they are interested in purchasing by using price comparison websites, such as Google Shopping, BizRate, NexTag, CamelCamelCamel, Pronto and Shopping.com. Indeed, it is common to see people in shops (physical shops in this case) browsing competitors' prices on their mobile phones.

This places the High Street retailer under intense competitive pressure. In the final quarter of 2020, both Debenhams and Arcadia went into administration. Boohoo, the online fashion retailer, purchased the Debenhams brand in January 2021 but not the department stores. Another online retailer, Asos, purchased the Topshop, Topman, Miss Selfridge and HIIT brand names from Arcadia in February 2021. Once again, the deal did not include the stores.

Although the competitive pressures seem to have increased in 'B2C' (business-to-consumers) e-commerce the impact may be even greater in 'B2B' (business-to-business) e-commerce. Many firms are constantly searching for cheaper sources of supply, and the Internet provides a cheap and easy means of conducting such searches.

Freedom of entry. Internet companies often have lower start-up costs than their conventional rivals. Their premises are generally much smaller, with no 'shop-front' costs and lower levels of stockholding; in fact, many of these businesses are initially operated from their owners' homes and garages with little more required than a computer and good Wi-Fi connection. An e-commerce website for the business can be set up in a matter of hours. Marketing costs will also be lower if consumers can quickly locate the new entrant's website using a search engine.

Internet companies are often smaller and more specialist, relying on Internet 'outsourcing' (buying parts, equipment and other supplies through the Internet), rather than making everything themselves. They are also more likely to use delivery firms rather than having their own transport fleet. All this can make it relatively cheap for new firms to set up and begin trading over the Internet.

Not only do these factors make markets more price competitive, they can also bring other benefits. Costs might be driven down as firms economise on stockholding, rely more on outsourcing and develop more efficient relationships with suppliers.

What are the limits to e-commerce?

The coronavirus pandemic has accelerated the trend to online shopping but will the only shopping malls eventually be virtual ones? Although e-commerce is revolutionising markets, a number of factors still constrain its growth.

When asked to explain why they did not buy goods or services over the Internet, respondents to a survey in 2019[5] gave the following responses:

- Prefer to shop in person, like to see the product, force of habit (83%)
- Payment security or privacy concerns (43%)
- Uncertainty around how to shop online (31%)
- Concerns about receiving or returning goods (25%)
- Concerns about delivery of items (14%)
- Delivery takes too long/too logistically difficult (14%)
- Do not have a payment card (11%)

The most important reason people continue to shop in physical stores is they get to see, touch and possibly try the good before making a purchase. They can also take instant possession. Although it is possible to order things online and often get next-day delivery, it may not provide the same pleasure as immediate ownership.

Furthermore, shopping can be an enjoyable experience. Many people like wandering round the shops, meeting friends, trying on clothes, etc. 'Retail therapy' can be a pleasurable leisure activity and one that some people are willing to pay for in the form of higher prices. However, one of the most common reasons given in the survey for shopping in physical stores was 'force of habit'. Given the impact of the pandemic on shopping behaviour, people may get out of the habit of shopping in physical stores and into the habit of shopping online.

Concerns about payment security and privacy concerns is another factor that deters many people. Between September and December 2019, Action Fraud, the UK's national reporting centre for fraud and cybercrime, received 22 455 complaints about online shopping and online auctions. A report published in May 2020,[6] found that the most important issue for consumers when selecting an online payment method was concerns about fraud. Approximately one third of consumers in the survey reported being more concerned about protection against financial losses and security of their financial data since the beginning of the COVID-19 pandemic.

Fears about delivery issues also discourage many consumers. Between March and November 2020, Citizens Advice received three times as many complaints about delivery issues as in the same period the previous year.[7]

A final constraint on the spread of online shopping is that access to a credit or debit card is often required to make a purchase. This option might not be available to everyone, particularly younger consumers and those on lower incomes.

Always treating traditional and online shopping as substitute experiences may also be too simplistic. In many

(continued)

situations, they are complementary. Large numbers of people go onto the High Street, try on clothes and try out electronic appliances before going home to order them on the Internet. This enables them to get the best possible prices, while also having more certainty about the characteristics of the product they are purchasing.

Increasing market power

There are some concerns that the rise of e-commerce could actually reduce competition and result in the growth of more firms with substantial market power. Greater price transparency could actually result in *less* competition. For example, sellers may have previously reduced their prices in the belief that they could make extra sales before their competitors responded. However, the greater price transparency provided by the Internet means that rivals are able to spot price changes and respond more quickly. This reduces the incentive for some firms to reduce their prices in the first place.

If firms can more easily monitor their rivals' pricing behaviour, it might also increase the likelihood of price-fixing agreements. The topic of collusion is discussed in more detail in Chapter 8.

We previously explained how the marketing costs for start-ups in e-commerce might be lower than in traditional retailing. However, simply creating a website is not enough to make online businesses successful – potential customers also have to visit them. New firms might have to spend considerable amounts of money on marketing to increase consumers' awareness of their brands and websites. The majority of this expenditure could be a sunk cost and so would act as a significant barrier to entry. One way of reducing promotion costs is if the new entrant's website appears on a search engine's results page. However, customers are most likely to visit the links that appear towards the top of the results page. These will be those with the greatest number of hits, which are likely to be the more established firms.

Although comparison websites increase price transparency, they could also result in consumers paying higher prices. Many of these websites make considerable profits. They earn revenue by charging a fee every time a customer is referred to a listed firm's website via the price comparison website. These fees add to costs and could result in firms charging higher prices. One important issue is the size of the fee. If consumers only use one price comparison website it would have considerable market power and the ability to charge listed firms high fees.

If users build up a familiarity and knowledge of using a particular website it might create switching costs. Consumers are then less likely to visit other rival websites and so this reduces competition.

There may also be significant economies of scale in logistics: i.e. the storage, packaging and shipping of the products to the consumer. Amazon has invested heavily in automating its distribution centres using Kiva robots. This type of indivisible capital investment will only reduce a firm's average costs if it sells a large volume of products. Interestingly, the Head of Amazon UK stated in 2004 that 'one of the greatest myths in the 1990s was there are no barriers to entry in e-commerce'.

There is no doubt that e-commerce is here to stay in all sectors. Many large companies recognise that their retail outlets have effectively become display space for their online activities. It will be interesting to see if the continued growth of e-commerce results in either increasing competition or more market power.

1. ***Why may the Internet work better for replacement buys than for new purchases?***
2. ***Give three examples of products that are particularly suitable for selling over the Internet and three that are not. Explain your answer.***
3. ***As Amazon has grown in size it has acquired substantial monopoly power. What are the barriers to entry for other companies wishing to act as a marketplace for B2C and B2B business?***

Using the Eurostat database, construct a time series chart showing the trend in the percentage of individuals who have made an online purchase in the past two years in the UK, France, Germany, Ireland and Spain. Write a short summary of your findings.

1 *Retail sales, Great Britain: December 2020*, ONS (22 January 2021), www.ons.gov.uk/businessindustryandtrade/retailindustry/bulletins/retailsales/december2020
2 *How our internet activity has influenced the way we shop: October 2019*, ONS (November 2019), www.ons.gov.uk/businessindustryandtrade/retailindustry/articles/howourinternetactivityhasinfluencedthewayweshop/october2019
3 *E-commerce statistics for individuals*, Eurostat (2019), https://ec.europa.eu/eurostat/statistics-explained/index.php/E-commerce_statistics_for_individuals
4 'A thinkers' guide', *The Economist* (30 March 2000), www.economist.com/business-special/2000/03/30/a-thinkers-guide
5 *How our internet activity has influenced the way we shop: October 2019*, ONS (November 2019), www.ons.gov.uk/businessindustryandtrade/retailindustry/articles/howourinternetactivityhasinfluencedthewayweshop/october2019
6 *How COVID-19 is impacting consumer preferences*, Paysafe (4 May 2020), www.paysafe.com/en/blog/how-covid-19-is-impacting-consumer-payment-preferences/
7 Miles Brignall, 'Parcel delivery complaints treble amid UK's Covid online shopping boom', *The Guardian* (16 November 2020), www.theguardian.com/business/2020/nov/16/parcel-delivery-complaints-treble-amid-uks-covid-online-shopping-boom

Section summary

1. The assumptions of perfect competition are: a very large number of firms, complete freedom of entry, a homogeneous product and perfect knowledge of the good and its market on the part of both producers and consumers.
2. In the short run, there is not time for new firms to enter the market, and thus supernormal profits can persist. In the long run, however, any supernormal profits will be competed away by the entry of new firms.
3. The short-run equilibrium for the firm will be where the price, as determined by demand and supply in the market, is equal to marginal cost. At this output, the firm will be maximising profit. The firm's short-run supply curve is the same as its marginal cost curve (that portion of it above the *AVC* curve).
4. The long-run equilibrium will be where the market price is just equal to firms' long-run average cost. The long-run industry supply curve will thus depend on what happens to firms' *LRAC* curves as industry output expands. If their *LRAC* curves shift upwards due to increasing industry costs (external diseconomies of scale), the long-run industry supply curve will slope upwards. If their *LRAC* curves shift downwards due to decreasing industry costs (external economies of scale), the long-run industry supply curve will slope downwards.
5. There are no substantial (internal) economies of scale to be gained by perfectly competitive firms. If there were, the industry would cease to be perfectly competitive as the large, low-cost firms drove the small, high-cost ones out of business.
6. Under perfect competition, production will be at the point where $P = MC$. This can be argued to be optimal. Perfect competition can act as a spur to efficiency and bring benefits to the consumer in terms of low costs and low prices.
7. On the other hand, perfectly competitive firms may be unwilling to invest in research and development or may have insufficient funds to do so. They may also produce a lack of variety of goods. Finally, perfect competition does not necessarily lead to a fair distribution of income or guarantee an absence of harmful side effects of production.

7.3 MONOPOLY

What is a monopoly?

This may seem a strange question because the answer seems obvious. A monopoly exists when there is only one firm in the industry.

But whether an industry can be classed as a monopoly is not always clear. It depends how narrowly the industry is defined. For example, a confectionary company may have a monopoly on certain chocolate bars, but it does not have a monopoly on chocolate in general. A pharmaceutical company may have a monopoly of a certain drug, but there may be alternative drugs for treating a particular illness.

To some extent, the boundaries of an industry are arbitrary. What is more important for a firm is the amount of monopoly *power* it has, and that depends on the closeness of substitutes produced by rival industries. A train company may have a monopoly over railway journeys between two towns, but it faces competition in transport from cars, coaches and sometimes planes.

As an illustration of the difficulty in identifying monopolies, try to decide which of the following are monopolies: BT; a local evening newspaper; food sold in a university outlet; a village post office; Interflora®; the London Underground; ice creams in the cinema; Guinness; the board game 'Monopoly'. (As you will quickly realise in each case, it depends how you define the industry.)

Barriers to entry

For a firm to maintain its monopoly position, there must be ***barriers to entry*** that make it difficult for new firms to enter the market. Barriers also exist under oligopoly, but in the case of monopoly they must be high enough to block the entry of all new firms.

Economists sometimes distinguish between *structural* and *strategic* barriers.

- Structural or natural barriers exist because of the characteristics of the industry. The firm is not deliberately seeking to construct such barriers. Rather, they are a side effect of attempts by the monopoly to run its business more efficiently.
- Strategic barriers, on the other hand, are the result of actions by the firm for the sole purpose of deterring potential entrants.

In reality, this distinction between structural and strategic barriers is often blurred. Firms might take advantage of the

Definition

Barrier to entry Anything that prevents or impedes the entry of firms into an industry and thereby limits the amount of competition faced by existing firms.

Figure 7.7 Natural monopoly

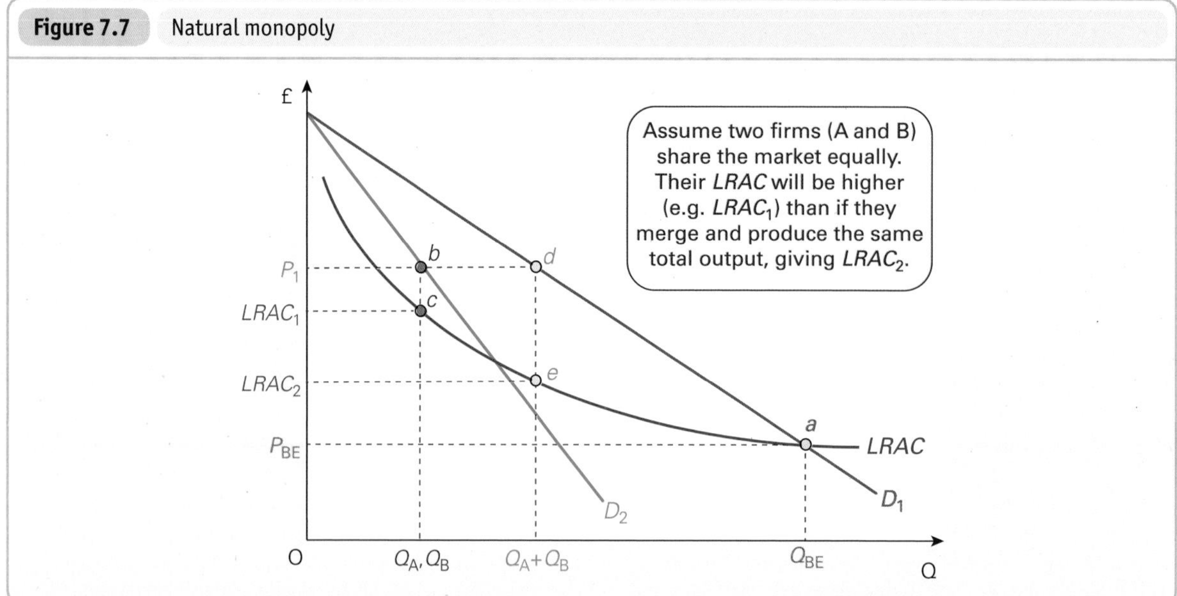

underlying characteristics of the industry to increase the size of any barriers that occur naturally.

Barriers can exist for a number of different reasons.

Economies of scale. If an industry experiences substantial economies of scale, it may have lower long-run average costs of production when one firm supplies the entire output of the industry. This is illustrated in Figure 7.7. D_1 represents the industry demand curve, and hence the demand curve for the monopoly. P_{BE} and Q_{BE} represent the break-even price and output of the industry. The profit-maximising level of output will be below this level (not illustrated on this diagram).

The long-run average costs of producing any level of output up to Q_{BE} are lower if one firm supplies the whole market. This can be illustrated by imagining a situation where two firms (A and B) compete against one another and share the market with each producing half of the total industry output. The demand curve for each firm would, in effect, be D_2. Assuming that both firms have equal access to the same technology and factor inputs at the same prices, they would have identical long-run average cost curves, as shown by *LRAC*.

If each firm produced an output of Q_A and Q_B respectively, total industry output would be $Q_A + Q_B$ and the market price would be P_1, given by point *e* on the market demand curve. Both firms have a long-run average cost of $LRAC_1$ of producing Q_A and Q_B respectively and make long-run average supernormal profits of $b - c$. However, if the firms merged and the new unified business produced the same total output of $Q_A + Q_B$, its long-run average costs would be lower: i.e. $LRAC_2$ (point *e*).

This is an example of a ***natural monopoly*** where long-run average costs are lower if one firm supplies the entire market.

In some extreme cases of natural monopoly it might be impossible for two or more firms to charge any price that would enable them to cover their long-run average costs. This would be true in Figure 7.7 if the *LRAC* curve was above the demand curve for the individual firms (D_2) for its entire length.

A natural monopoly is most likely to occur if the market is relatively small and/or the industry has relatively high capital/infrastructure costs (i.e. fixed costs) and relatively low marginal costs. One real-world example is the network of pipelines that supply gas to homes and businesses. If two competing firms each built a national network of pipes it might be difficult for them both to make a profit as they would share the customers but each have the same infrastructure costs. A monopoly that supplies all customers could make a profit as it would have much lower average total costs from supplying the whole market. Electricity transmission via a national grid is another example of a natural monopoly.

BT Openreach is responsible for providing and maintaining the fixed-line network connections to customers in the UK. This includes the huge system of telegraph poles and cable ducts (small underground tunnels) that carry telecom lines between BT exchanges and houses/business premises. To what extent do you think this is a natural monopoly?

An industry may not be a natural monopoly, but significant economies of scale might still act as a barrier to entry. For example, potential new businesses might be deterred from trying to enter a market in the knowledge that they would have to sell large volumes of output before they could

Definition

Natural monopoly A situation where long-run average costs would be lower if an industry were under monopoly than if it were shared between two or more competitors.

compete. The monopolist already experiencing economies of scale could charge a price below the cost of the new entrant and drive it out of business. There are, however, some circumstances where a new entrant may be able to survive this competition – if, for example, it is a firm already established in another industry. For example, Virgin Money entered the UK retail banking market in 2010 when it purchased Church House Trust, and Amazon entered the UK online grocery market in 2016.

Absolute cost advantages. If a monopolist has an absolute cost advantage, its average cost curve will be below that of any potential entrants at all levels of output. What might give a monopolist such a cost advantage?

- *More favourable access or control over key inputs.* In some markets the monopolist might be able to obtain access to important factor inputs on more favourable terms for a certain period of time. For example, if there was a supplier that provided a much higher quality of a factor input than its rivals, the monopoly could either sign a long-term exclusive contract with this firm or take ownership via a merger. For example, in 2012 Amazon purchased Kiva Systems. This company was the leading supplier of robotics for a number of warehouse operators and retailers. After the takeover, Kiva only supplied Amazon and was renamed Amazon Robotics in 2015. In more extreme cases the monopolist may be able to gain complete control if there is only one supplier of that input. For many years, the De Beers company owned both the majority of the world's diamond mines and the major distribution system.
- *Superior technology.* The monopolist may have access to superior technology that is difficult for rival firms either to copy or to imitate. For many years, Google's search ranking algorithm helped it to provide a results page that many people found more useful than those of its rivals.
- *More efficient production methods.* Through years of experience of running the business an established monopoly might have learnt the most efficient way of organising the production of its good or service. Much of this knowledge is tacit. It is developed and refined through a process of trial and error and cannot be written down in a way which could be easily understood by others. The new entrant would have to go through the same learning experience over a number of years before it could operate on the same cost curve as the monopolist.
- *Economies of scope.* A firm that produces a range of products is also likely to experience a lower average cost of production. For example, a large pharmaceutical company producing a range of drugs and toiletries can use shared research, marketing, storage and transport facilities across its range of products. These lower costs make it difficult for a new single-product entrant to the market, since the large firm could undercut its price to drive it out of the market.

Under what circumstances might a new entrant succeed in the market for a product, despite existing firms benefiting from economies of scale?

Switching costs for consumers. Sometimes, if customers are considering whether or not to buy a product from a different firm, they may decide against it because of the additional costs involved. These are called ***switching costs*** and some examples include: TC 1 p10

- *Searching costs.* How easy is it for the consumer to find and compare the price and quality of goods/services offered by alternative suppliers? The more time and effort it takes, the greater the switching costs. Some firms have been accused of deliberately making it more difficult for consumers to make these comparisons. For example, a report into the retail banking market by the Competition and Markets Authority in 2016[1] found low switching rates amongst current account holders, because they found it almost impossible to compare 'prices'. The price in this case is a combination of the account fees, overdraft charges and forgone interest.
- *Contractual costs.* In some markets customers have to sign a contract which stipulates that they purchase the good or service from the same supplier for a certain period of time: e.g. energy, mobile phones, broadband. A termination fee has to be paid if the customer wants to switch to a different supplier before the end of the contract period. Some firms also provide incentives for repeat purchases: e.g. loyalty cards, frequent flyer programmes.
- *Learning costs.* These may occur if the consumer invests time and effort in learning how to use a product or service. The switching costs increase as this knowledge becomes more specific to the brand/product supplied by a particular firm. For example, a consumer might have spent a considerable amount of time learning how to use applications with the iOS operating system on an iPhone®. This may deter them from switching to a smartphone that uses Google's Android operating system.
- *Product uncertainty costs.* Consumers might not fully discover either the quality or how much they like a good until after they have purchased and used it for some time. This might make them reluctant to change supplier once they have found and experienced a particular brand or product they like. KI 15 p132
- *Compatibility costs.* Some products have two elements to them. One part is more durable, while the other needs replacing more regularly. Once customers have purchased the more durable element from a supplier, they are 'locked in' to purchasing the non-durable part from the same supplier for compatibility reasons. Examples

Definition

Switching costs The costs to a consumer of switching to an alternative supplier.

1 *Retail Banking Market Investigation: Final Report*, Competition and Markets Authority (9 August 2016), see section 14.

include razor handles and razor blades, coffee machines and coffee pods, printers and ink cartridges.

Some goods or services have very large switching costs because of the existence of network externalities. A ***network externality*** exists when consumers' valuation of a good is influenced by the number of other people who also use the same product. For example, the benefits of having a mobile phone increase with the number of other people who also have one. In some cases, a consumer's valuation will depend on the extent to which other people use one particular brand. For a specific social media website, such as Facebook, its success depends on lots of people using the same website. Buyers and sellers are willing to pay higher fees to use Amazon and eBay as an online marketplace because so many other buyers and sellers use the same websites.

When a good or service has significant network externalities it makes it difficult for a new entrant. Even if it produces a far superior and/or cheaper version of a product, it is difficult to get people to switch because they are unwilling to give up the network benefits associated with their current supplier. Other examples of products with network externalities include Microsoft's Windows (see Case Study 7.4 on the student website), Adobe's Acrobat (for PDF files) and airlines operating interconnecting routes (see Box 7.7).

Product differentiation and brand loyalty. If a firm produces a clearly differentiated product, where the consumer associates the product with the brand, it will be very difficult for a new firm to break into that market.

In 1908, James Spengler invented, and patented, the electric vacuum cleaner. Later that year he sold the patent to his cousin's husband, William Hoover, who set about putting mass production in place. Decades after their legal monopoly (see below) ran out, people still associate vacuum-cleaning with Hoover and many of us would say that we are going to 'Hoover the carpet', despite using a Dyson, or other machine. When looking for some information by using an Internet search engine people often say they 'Googled it'.

Other examples of strong brand image include Guinness®, Kellogg's® Cornflakes, Coca-Cola®, Nescafé® and Sellotape®. In many cases, strong brand presence would not be enough to *block* entry, but it might well reinforce other barriers.

More favourable or complete control over access to customers. If a firm can gain more favourable access or control over the best outlets through which the product is sold, this can hinder the ability of new entrants to gain access to potential customers. For example, approximately 50 per cent of public houses (pubs) in the UK operate on tenancy contracts known as the 'tied lease model'. This is effectively an exclusive supply contract which means that landlords of such pubs have to purchase almost all of their beverages from the pub company (e.g. Stonegate, Punch Pubs and J. D. Wetherspoon) that owns the pub.

> **Definition**
>
> **Network externalities or network economies** The benefits a consumer obtains from consuming a good/service increase with the number of other people who use the same good/service.

Legal protection. The firm's monopoly position may be protected by patents on essential processes, by copyright, by various forms of licensing (allowing, say, only one firm to operate in a particular area) and by tariffs (i.e. customs duties) and other trade restrictions to keep out foreign competitors. Examples of monopolies protected by patents include most new medicines developed by pharmaceutical companies, Microsoft's Windows operating systems and agrochemical companies, such as Monsanto, with various genetically modified plant varieties and pesticides.

Mergers and takeovers. The monopolist can put in a takeover bid for any new entrant. The mere threat of takeovers may discourage new entrants.

Aggressive tactics. An established monopolist can probably sustain losses for longer than a new entrant. Thus it can start a price war, mount massive advertising campaigns, offer an attractive after-sales service, introduce new brands to compete with new entrants, and so on.

Intimidation. The monopolist may resort to various forms of harassment, legal or illegal, to drive a new entrant out of business.

Equilibrium price and output

Since there is, by definition, only one firm in the industry, the firm's demand curve is also the industry demand curve.

Compared with other market structures, demand under monopoly will be relatively inelastic at each price. The monopolist can raise its price and consumers have no alternative firm in the industry to turn to. They either pay the higher price or go without the good altogether.

Unlike the firm under perfect competition, the monopoly firm is a 'price maker'. It can choose what price to charge. Nevertheless, it is still constrained by its demand curve. A rise in price will lower the quantity demanded. Be careful not to fall into the trap of thinking that a monopoly can control both price *and* output simultaneously.

As with firms in other market structures, a monopolist will maximise profit where $MR = MC$. In Figure 7.8, profit is maximised at Q_m. The supernormal profit obtained is shown by the shaded area.

These profits will tend to be larger the less elastic is the demand curve (and hence the steeper is the *MR* curve), and thus the bigger is the gap between *MR* and price (*AR*). The actual elasticity will depend on whether reasonably close substitutes are available in *other* industries. The demand for a rail service will be much less elastic (and the potential for profit greater) if there is no bus service to the same destination.

Figure 7.8 Profit maximising under monopoly

Since there are barriers to the entry of new firms, these supernormal profits will not be competed away in the long run. The only difference, therefore, between short-run and long-run equilibrium is that in the long run the firm will produce where $MR = long\text{-}run\ MC$.

Try this brain teaser. A monopoly would be expected to face an inelastic demand. After all, there are no direct substitutes. And yet, if it produces where MR = MC, MR must be positive and demand must therefore be elastic. Therefore, the monopolist must face an elastic demand! Can you solve this conundrum?

Limit pricing

If the barriers to the entry of new firms are not total, and if the monopolist is making very large supernormal profits, there may be a danger in the long run of potential rivals breaking into the industry. In such cases, the monopolist may keep its price down and thereby deliberately restrict the size of its profits in the short run so as not to attract new entrants. This practice is known as ***limit pricing***.

In Figure 7.9, three AC curves are drawn: one for the monopolist (firm M), one for a potential entrant (firm A)

*LOOKING AT THE MATHS

From Figure 7.8, it can be seen that the less elastic the demand at the output where $MC = MR$, the greater will be the gap between AR and MR, and hence the further above MR will the price be. The relationship between price, MR (or MC) and price elasticity of demand ($P\epsilon_D$) is given by the following formula:

$$P = \frac{MR}{1 + (1/P\epsilon_D)}$$

Thus if $MR = MC = £12$ and $P\epsilon_D = -4$, the profit-maximising price would be

$$\frac{£12}{1 + (1/-4)} = \frac{£12}{1-1/4} = \frac{£12}{0.75} = £16$$

Proof of this rule is given in Maths Case 7.2 on the student website. You can see simply by examining the formula, however, that the lower the elasticity, the greater will be the price relative to MR or MC.[1]

What is the profit-maximising price if $MR = MC = £12$ and $P\epsilon_D = -2$?

1 Note that this formula works only if demand is elastic, as it must be if MR is positive (which it will be, since MC must be positive).

Definition

Limit pricing Where a monopolist (or oligopolist) charges a price below the short-run profit-maximising level in order to deter new entrants.

Figure 7.9 Limit pricing

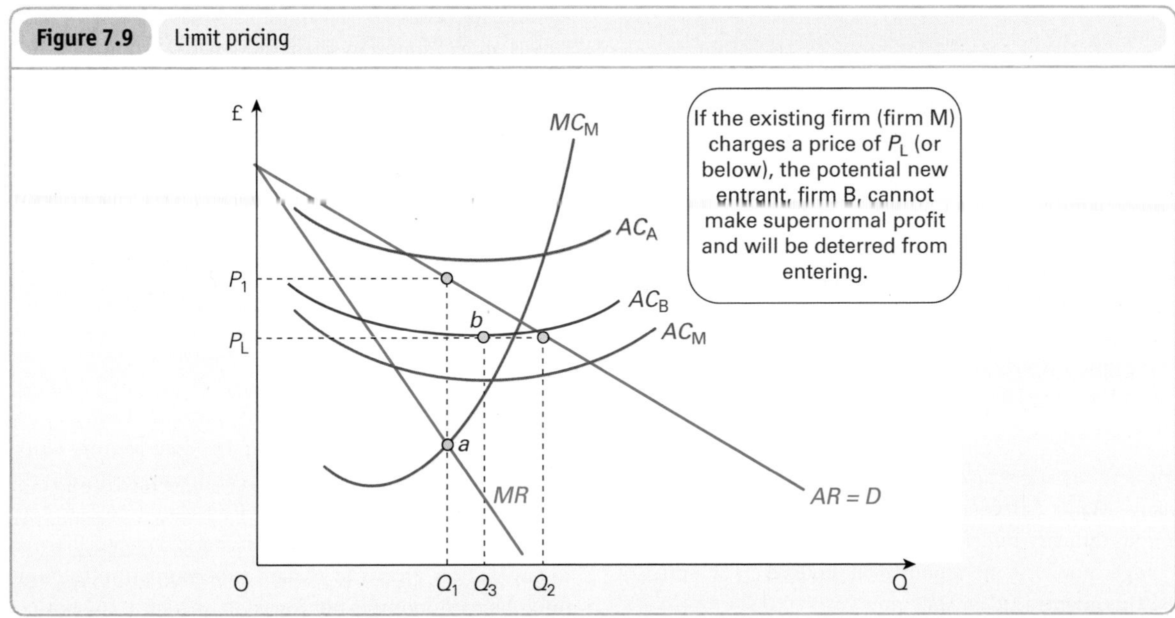

and one for another potential entrant (firm B). It is assumed that the monopolist has an absolute cost advantage over both potential entrants (e.g. more favourable access to factor inputs) so it has a lower *AC* curve over all levels of output. Any potential new entrant, if it is to compete successfully with the monopolist, must charge the same price or a lower one (assuming no product differentiation).

The short-run profit-maximising position for the monopolist is to produce where $MC = MR$. This is illustrated at point *a* in Figure 7.9. The firm will produce an output of Q_1 and charge a price of P_1. If it faces potential competition from a new entrant such as firm A, it can charge this price without any fear of entry. Firm A's average costs are above this profit-maximising price and so it would not be profitable to enter the market at this price or any level below it. The barriers to entry for firm A are total.

However, if a potential new entrant, such as firm B, had average costs below P_1, it could make supernormal profits by entering at that price. In such a case, it is in the monopolist's interests to charge the lower price of P_L, and produce Q_2, to deter firm B from entering the market. At a price of P_L, the best firm B could do would be to make just normal profit by producing Q_3 (point *b*). However, if it did enter the market and the monopolist continued to produce Q_2, the market price would fall below P_L and the new entrant would make a loss at any output. Thus, P_L can be seen as a *limit price* – a price ceiling, at or below which potential new entrants will be deterred from entering the industry.

P_L may be below the monopolist's short-run profit-maximising price, but it may prefer to limit its price to P_L to protect its long-run profits from the damage caused by competition.

Fear of government intervention to curb the monopolist's practices may have a similar restraining effect on the price that the monopolist charges. In the UK, the Competition and Markets Authority may undertake an investigation: see section 14.1 for more on this.

1. *What does this analysis assume about the price elasticity of demand for the new entrant (a) above P_L; (b) below P_L?*
2. *Can you think of any limitations with the limit price model?*

Monopoly and the public interest

Disadvantages of monopoly

There are several reasons why monopolies may be against the public interest. As we shall see in Chapter 14, these have given rise to legislation to regulate monopoly power and/or behaviour.

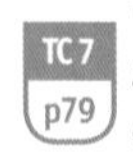

Higher price and lower output than under perfect competition (short run). Figure 7.10 compares the profit-maximising position for an industry under monopoly with that under perfect competition. The monopolist will produce Q_1 at a price of P_1. This is where $MC = MR$.

KI 22 p195

Figure 7.10 Equilibrium of the industry under perfect competition and monopoly: with the same *MC* curve

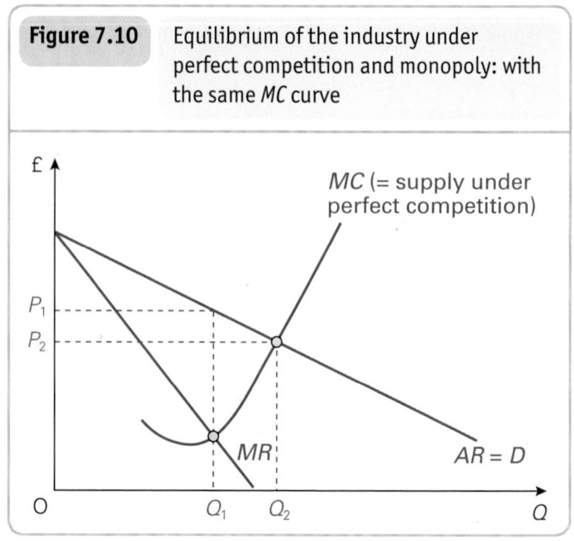

If the same industry operated under perfect competition, however, it would produce at Q_2 and P_2 – a higher output and a lower price. This is where industry supply under perfect competition equals industry demand. (Remember, we showed in section 7.2 that the firm's supply curve under perfect competition is its *MC* curve and thus the industry's supply curve is simply the *industry MC* curve: the *MC* curve shown in Figure 7.10.)

This analysis assumes that the industry has the *same AC* and *MC* curves whether under perfect competition or run as a monopoly. For example, suppose some potato farmers initially operate under perfect competition. The market price is P_2 in Figure 7.10. Then they set up a marketing agency through which they all sell their potatoes. The agency therefore acts as a monopoly supplier to the market and charges a price of P_1. Since it is the same farmers before and after, production costs are unlikely to have changed much. But as we shall see below, even if an industry has *lower AC* and *MC* curves under monopoly than under perfect competition, it is still likely to charge a higher price and produce a lower output.

When we were looking at the advantages of perfect competition, we said that the level where $P = MC$ could be argued to be the *optimum* level of production. Clearly, if a monopolist is producing below this level (e.g. at Q_1 in Figure 7.10 – where $P > MC$), the monopolist can be argued to be producing at *less* than optimal output. Consumers would be prepared to pay more for additional units than they cost to produce.

Higher price and lower output than under perfect competition (long run). Under perfect competition, freedom of entry eliminates supernormal profit and forces firms to produce at the bottom of their *LRAC* curve. The effect, therefore, is to keep long-run prices down. Under monopoly, however, barriers to entry allow profits to remain supernormal in the long run. The monopolist is not forced to operate at the bottom of the AC curve. Thus, other things being equal, long-run prices will tend to be higher, and hence output lower, under monopoly.

Possibility of higher cost curves due to lack of competition. The sheer survival of a firm in the long run under perfect competition requires that it uses the most efficient known technique, and develops new techniques wherever possible. The monopolist, however, sheltered by barriers to entry, can still make large profits even if it is not using the most efficient technique. It has less incentive, therefore, to be efficient (see Box 7.5).

On the other hand, if it can lower its costs by using and developing more efficient techniques, it can gain extra supernormal profits which will not be competed away.

KI 4 p13

Unequal distribution of income. The high profits of monopolists may be considered as unfair, especially by competitive firms, or anyone on low incomes for that matter. The scale of this problem obviously depends on the size of the monopoly and the degree of its power. The monopoly profits of the village store may seem of little consequence when compared to the profits of a giant national or international company.

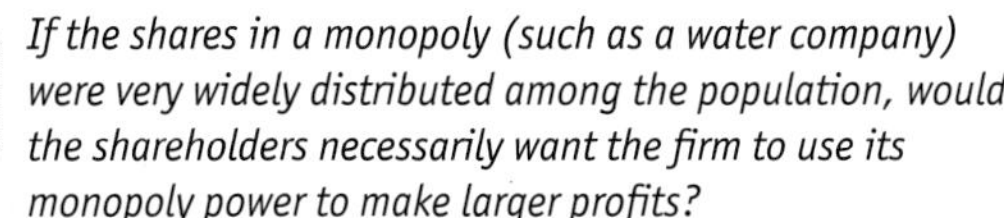

If the shares in a monopoly (such as a water company) were very widely distributed among the population, would the shareholders necessarily want the firm to use its monopoly power to make larger profits?

TC 5 p48

In addition to these problems, monopolies may lack the incentive to introduce new product varieties, and large monopolies may be able to exert political pressure and thereby get favourable treatment from governments.

Advantages of monopoly

Despite these arguments, monopolies can have some advantages.

Economies of scale. The monopoly may be able to achieve substantial economies of scale due to larger plant, centralised administration and the avoidance of unnecessary duplication (e.g. a monopoly water company would eliminate the need for several sets of rival water mains under each street). If this results in an MC curve substantially below that of the same industry under perfect competition, the monopoly will produce a *higher* output at a *lower* price. In Figure 7.11, the monopoly produces Q_1 at a price of P_1, whereas the perfectly competitive industry produces Q_2 at the higher price P_2.

Note that this result follows only if the monopoly MC curve is below point x in Figure 7.11. Note also that since an industry cannot exist under perfect competition if substantial economies of scale can be gained, it is somewhat hypothetical to make the comparison between a monopoly and an alternative situation that could not exist. What is more, were the monopolist to follow the $P = MC$ rule observed by perfectly competitive firms, it would charge an even lower price (P_3) and produce an even higher output (Q_3).

Figure 7.11 Equilibrium of the industry under perfect competition and monopoly: with different *MC* curves

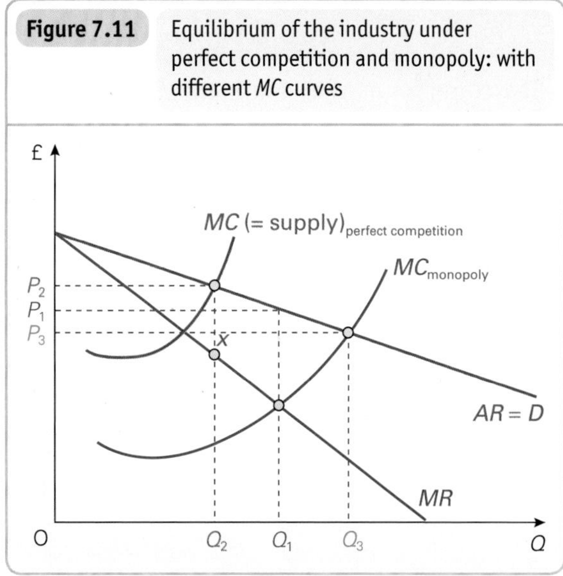

Possibility of lower cost curves due to more research and development and more investment. Although the monopolist's sheer survival does not depend on its finding ever more efficient methods of production, it can use part of its supernormal profits for research and development and investment. It thus has a greater ability to become efficient than has the small firm with limited funds. KI 3 p13

Competition for corporate control. Although a monopoly faces no competition in the goods market, it may face an alternative form of competition in financial markets. A monopoly, with potentially low costs, which is currently run inefficiently, is likely to be subject to a takeover bid from another company. This ***competition for corporate control*** may thus force the monopoly to be efficient in order to avoid being taken over. KI 3 p13

Innovation and new products. The promise of supernormal profits, protected perhaps by patents, may encourage the development of new (monopoly) industries producing new products.

TC 5 p48 KI 10 p70

Monopoly and price discrimination

One further characteristic of monopoly is that it allows firms to price discriminate: to charge different prices either to all customers or to different groups of customers. Firms undertake this as a way of further increasing profits. The ability to price discriminate rests on the firm having some monopoly power, although this need not be a complete monopoly. Price discrimination is discussed in more detail in section 8.4, pages 248–55.

Definition

Competition for corporate control The competition for the control of companies through takeovers.

BOX 7.4 GOOGLE – A MONOPOLY ABUSING ITS MARKET POWER?

Searching for market dominance?

The early days of search engines and the rise of Google

Google is in a dominant position in the general Internet search engine market. In July 2021, it had an 86.78 per cent share of the global desktop search engine market and a 94.53 per cent share of the global mobile search engine market.

However, this has not always been the case. When the company began in 1997 it was a new entrant, doing battle with other established firms that dominated this new dynamic and growing market.

In 1994, Lycos® and Webcrawler® were the first businesses to introduce modern search engine services, where a user could input a general query and obtain a results page. AltaVista® entered the market in 1995 and soon became the dominant player as it provided a results page that users found the most useful.

Other companies such as Inktomi and HotBot entered the market successfully but Google began to rise to prominence at the turn of the century. Its global market share grew dramatically from less than 5 per cent at the beginning of 2000 to over 50 per cent by 2003. By 2007, it had reached the dominant position it has today.

Google appears to have obtained a dominant position in the market by using superior technology to search the Web. Its initial success is largely credited to its providing a results page that its users found far more useful than those of its rivals. It has now remained in a dominant position for over 15 years.

Google's barriers to entry

Is there any evidence that Google has engaged in business activities whose sole purpose is to prevent or limit competition? Has it created any strategic barriers to entry?

Some switching costs may exist because of *network externalities*. As more people use the same search engine it enables the provider to collect more data about users' search behaviour. This information helps the firm to improve its search-engine results page making it more difficult for a new entrant to compete with a much smaller user base. This is an example of a structural barrier to entry because it is a result of the underlying characteristics of the industry. The size of these network externalities are smaller, however, than in other digital industries, such social media and office software (see Case Study 7.4 on the student website for an analysis of Microsoft's Windows and Office software).

Other switching costs appear to be trivial. It is possible to use different search engines irrespective of the device (desktop or mobile), the operating system or the web browser being used. The service is free and so there are no contractual switching costs. The search costs are minimal – a search engine can be used to find its rivals. The learning costs are also small: i.e. customers could quickly become accustomed to the results page display with a different search engine.

It is hard to see how Google does anything to 'lock-in' its users. For example, it cannot strategically increase switching costs to such a level that consumers are prevented from switching to other search engines they would find more useful. If Google introduced a small fee for its search services, the majority of users would probably switch to one of its rivals.

European Commission investigation – the case of Google Shopping

After an investigation that began in 2010, the European Commission (EC) accused Google of using its dominant position in the general search engine market to suppress competition in another market where it faces much greater competition – the comparison shopping market.

Comparison shopping websites collect product information together from participating retailers and display them on a single results page in response to a shopper's search enquiry. The EC argued that Google had systematically favoured its own comparison shopping service – Google Shopping. The shopping service appears as a very prominent box of images and links at

BOX 7.5 X INEFFICIENCY

The cost of a quiet life

The major criticism of monopoly has traditionally been that of the monopoly's power in selling the good. The firm charges a price above *MC* (see Figure 7.10). This is seen as *allocatively inefficient* because at the margin consumers are willing to pay more than it is costing to produce ($P > MC$); and yet the monopolist is deliberately holding back, so as to keep its profits up. Allocative inefficiency is examined in detail in section 12.1.

KI 3 p13

But monopolies may also be inefficient for another reason: they may have higher costs. Why is this?

Higher costs may be the result of ***X inefficiency***[1] (an example of *technical inefficiency*: see page 156). Without competitive pressure on profit margins, cost control may become lax. The firm may employ too many staff and spend on prestigious buildings and equipment. There may be less effort to keep technologically up to date, to research new products, or to develop new domestic and export markets.

The more comfortable the situation, the less may be the effort which is expended to improve it. The effect of this X inefficiency is to make the *AC* and *MC* curves higher than they would otherwise be. The outcome is that consumers pay higher prices and the firm moves even further away from the efficient, competitive, outcome.

Following the financial crisis in 2007/8 and subsequent recession, there were significant reductions in X inefficiency in many countries. To cope with falling sales, and a fall in both sales and profits, many firms embarked on cost-cutting programmes. Much out-of-date plant was closed down, and employment was reduced. Those firms that survived the recession (and many did not) tended to emerge both more competitive and more efficient.

CASE STUDIES AND APPLICATIONS

the top of the general search results page. By doing this, Google is accused of potentially preventing consumers from seeing comparison shopping websites they would find more useful.

The EC noted that 'Google Shopping' grew very quickly after changes to the search page display results were first introduced. It argued that these changes significantly weakened its rivals in the comparison shopping market and deterred potential new entrants.

Google responded to the EC's concerns by arguing that general search engines, comparison shopping sites, supplier websites and merchant platforms, such as Amazon and eBay, are all effectively in competition with each other and so are in the *same* market. It referred to studies in the USA that found only 28 per cent of customers start their online shopping with a search engine, whereas 55 per cent go directly to Amazon and 16 per cent to the individual supplier's website.

In its report, the EC argued that they are *separate* markets, as companies such as Amazon pay comparison shopping service websites for referrals. Google's response was that it is quite possible for companies simultaneously to compete and co-operate with one another.

In June 2017, the EC imposed a fine of €2.4 billion[1] on Google for abusing its dominant market position and gave the company 90 days to change the search page display. Google responded by operating Google Shopping as a separate business unit in Europe. At the same time, it introduced an auction system whereby other comparison websites can bid to place advertisements alongside those of Google Shopping. The company also appealed against the EC's decision at a three-day hearing in the General Court in February 2020. It will be interesting to see how this legal battle develops over the next few years. At the time of writing, the five-judge panel was yet to deliver its final verdict.

Other European Commission investigations into Google's conduct

In July 2018, the EC imposed a fine of €4.34 billion on Google for using its dominance in the market for smart mobile operating systems (Android) to help maintain its dominant position in the general Internet search market.[2] The Commission objected to Google (a) insisting that manufacturers had to pre-install the Google Search app and browser app, as a condition for licensing the Google Play Store and (b) making payments to certain large manufacturers and mobile network operators on condition that they exclusively pre-installed the Google Search app on their devices.

In March 2019, the EC imposed a fine of €1.49 billion on Google for abusing its dominant position and stifling competition in the market for online search adverts.[3] In particular, the business was found guilty of breaking competition law by imposing anti-competitive clauses in its *AdSense* contracts with third-party websites. These exclusivity clauses prevented any of Google's rivals from placing search adverts on these websites. In June 2019, Google launched an appeal against the decision.

1. ***Explain why network externalities are much smaller in the general Internet search market than they are for social media.***
2. ***Provide a critique of Google's responses to the European Commission in the comparison shopping case.***

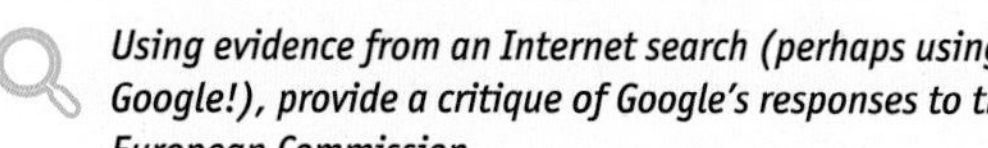

Using evidence from an Internet search (perhaps using Google!), provide a critique of Google's responses to the European Commission.

1 'Antitrust: Commission fines Google €2.42 billion for abusing dominance as search engine by giving illegal advantage to own comparison shopping service', *EC press release*, European Commission (27 June 2017), https://ec.europa.eu/commission/presscorner/detail/en/IP_17_1784

2 'Antitrust: Commission fines Google €4.34 billion for illegal practices regarding Android mobile devices to strengthen dominance of Google's search engine', *EC press release*, European Commission (18 July 2018), https://ec.europa.eu/commission/presscorner/detail/en/IP_18_4581

3 'Antitrust: Commission fines Google €1.49 billion for abusive practices in online advertising', European Commission', *EC press release*, European Commission (20 March 2019), https://ec.europa.eu/commission/presscorner/detail/en/IP_19_1770

EXPLORING ECONOMICS

A further factor in the reduction in X inefficiency has been the growth in international competition. Even if a firm has monopoly power at home, the growth in global markets and e-commerce (see Box 7.3), and reductions in customs duties and other barriers to trade (see section 24.2), provide fiercer competition from abroad.

1. ***How might you measure X inefficiency?***
2. ***Another type of inefficiency is productive inefficiency. What do you think this is? (Clue: it has to do with the proportions in which factors are used.)***
3. ***Explain why X inefficiency might be more common in state monopolies than those owned by shareholders.***

Individually or in pairs, select a company that has been in operation for a few decades. How do you think it has performed in terms of X efficiency? You might want to look at its costs of production and whether any cost-cutting practices have been put in place. Did the firm's strategy change at all during the COVID-19 pandemic? As a group exercise, the findings of individual students or pairs could be compared to see if similar trends can be identified in the various companies.

1 This term was coined by Harvey Leibenstein, 'Allocative efficiency or X efficiency', *American Economic Review* (June 1966).

Definition

X inefficiency When a firm fails to be technically efficient because of a lack of competitive pressures to cut costs.

BOX 7.6 CUT-THROAT COMPETITION

CASE STUDIES AND APPLICATIONS

The UK razor market

The market for wet razors and their blades is worth approximately £400 million in the UK. For many years it was dominated by just two producers, Gillette® and Procter & Gamble (P&G), with more than two thirds of sales between them. When they merged in 2007, the result was a new unified firm with substantial monopoly power. The Wilkinson Sword brand, owned by Edgewell Personal Care, was the next largest manufacturer in the UK, with around 18 per cent of sales. These two businesses also dominate the $3 billion US market.

The industry displays many of the characteristics we would expect of a market dominated by one large firm – very high levels of advertising and strong branding that make it difficult for new entrants. There is also evidence of ongoing innovation: where once the twin-blade razor was a novelty, now five blades are the norm.

New entrants: the US market

Yet, despite all the potential barriers to entry, some new firms have successfully entered the market in recent years and changed the way that many customers purchase their razors. One of the most successful of all these businesses is the Dollar Shave Club. Founded in California in 2011, this company has had a significant impact on the US market. It introduced an innovative subscription service: customers sign up via the company's website for a year's supply of 60 standard twin-blade razor cartridges, which the firm delivers to their homes for $1 per month.

Perhaps the most novel aspect of this business was its marketing strategy. As a new start-up, it did not have the multimillion-dollar advertising budget to compete with Gillette and Wilkinson Sword in traditional methods of marketing. It decided, instead, to launch its products using humorous YouTube videos featuring the company's CEO, Michael Dublin. Its first video cost $4500 and included advertising messages such as 'Do you think your razor needs a vibrating handle, a flashlight, a back scratcher and 10 blades? . . . So stop paying for shave tech you don't need.'

The focus of the business is clearly on price rather than product differentiation.

Within two hours of posting its first video the company's website crashed and within six hours it had completely sold out of stock. The video has been viewed over 20 million times and has proved to be a very successful marketing tool. Sales increased from $4 million in 2012 to $200 million in 2016. Its impact on consumer behaviour has been dramatic. Online sales in the USA increased rapidly and now account for 8 per cent of the razor market.

Other new start-ups, such as Harry's, Razor Co and Shave Mob, also entered the growing online market. Gillette tried to block these entrants by taking out patent infringement cases but they ultimately proved unsuccessful.

One of the biggest threats to P&G's dominant global position came in July 2016 when Unilever entered the razor market by purchasing the Dollar Shave Club for $1 billion. With the financial backing of the third largest consumer goods company in the world, this new entrant could pose serious competition. By 2018, Harry's and the Dollar Shave Club had a combined market share of 12 per cent.

In May 2019, one of P&G's other leading rivals, Edgewell Personal Care, announced a $1.37 billion deal to acquire Harry's. However, in February 2020 the US Federal Trade Commission announced that it would take legal action to prevent the deal because of competition concerns. Edgewell responded to this decision by pulling out of the deal, citing concerns over a lengthy and uncertain legal battle.

New entrants: the UK market

Similar changes have also occurred in the UK. During 2015–16, a number of domestic businesses, such as King of Shaves, Cornerstone and Bearded Colonel, entered the market with online subscription services. The large existing companies responded in 2017 by launching their own subscription services. In May, Gillette introduced a scheme whereby customers can text or subscribe for deliveries of razors, and BIC introduced its own Shave Club in November. In the same year, US companies, Harry's and the Dollar Shave Club, launched in the UK market.

Lockdowns during the COVID-19 pandemic had a negative impact on the demand for razors in the UK, with sales volumes falling by 16.6 per cent in the 12 weeks to 14 June 2020. Men who were either furloughed or working from home did not feel the need to shave as frequently as they once did. The switch to online shopping did help some of the new entrants. For example, the sale of Harry's razors increased by 18.2 per cent during the same 12-week period, whereas Gillette's fell by 21.1 per cent.

It will be interesting to see what impact long-term trends in working from home and changing shopping habits have on the market for razors.

1. *What are the characteristics of the razor market that present barriers to entry for new firms? How have companies, such as the Dollar Shave Club, sought to overcome these barriers?*
2. *High levels of innovation have been a key characteristic of the market for wet razors for many years. Do these always benefit the consumer?*
3. *It has been estimated that Gillette makes a profit of 3000 per cent on each razor blade sold. Explain how this figure might have arisen.*

Research the market for razors in an EU country. Which are the main competitors and what sort of market share do they have? Based on this, what type of market structure do you think there is in your chosen country? How do the firms behave in terms of their pricing?

1 'The lockdown look', *The Grocer* (18 July 2020), www.thegrocer.co.uk/category-reports/the-lockdown-look-male-grooming-category-report-2020/646562.article

Section summary

1. A monopoly is where there is only one firm in an industry. In practice, it is difficult to determine that a monopoly exists because it depends on how narrowly an industry is defined.
2. Barriers to the entry of new firms are usually necessary to protect a monopoly from competition. They may be either structural or strategic barriers.
3. Such barriers include cost advantages: these include economies of scale – perhaps with the firm being a natural monopoly – and absolute cost advantages, such as more favourable access or control over key inputs, the use of superior technology, more efficient production methods or economies of scope.
4. Barriers also include switching costs for customers, more favourable or complete control over access to customers, product differentiation, patents or copyright and tactics to eliminate competition (such as takeovers or aggressive advertising).
5. Profits for the monopolist (as for other firms) will be maximised where $MC = MR$. In the case of monopoly, this will probably be at a higher price relative to marginal cost than for other firms, due to the less elastic nature of its demand at any given price.
6. Monopolies may be against the public interest to the extent that they charge a higher price relative to cost than do competitive firms; if they cause a less desirable distribution of income; if a lack of competition removes the incentive to be efficient and innovative; and if they exert undesirable political pressures on governments.
7. On the other hand, any economies of scale will in part be passed on to consumers in lower prices, and the monopolist's high profits may be used for research and development and investment, which in turn may lead to better products at possibly lower prices.

7.4 THE THEORY OF CONTESTABLE MARKETS

Potential competition or monopoly?

In recent years, economists have developed the theory of contestable markets. This theory argues that what is crucial in determining price and output is not whether an industry is *actually* a monopoly or competitive, but whether there is the real *threat* of competition.

If a monopoly is protected by high barriers to entry – for example, it controls the supply of the key raw materials – then it will be able to make supernormal profits with no fear of competition.

If, however, another firm *could* potentially take away all of its customers with little difficulty, it will behave much more like a competitive firm. The threat of competition has a similar effect to actual competition.

As an example, consider a catering company engaged by a university to run its cafés and coffee bars. The catering company has a monopoly over the supply of food to the students at the university assuming there are no other eating places nearby. If, however, it starts charging high prices or providing a poor service, the university could offer the running of the cafés to an alternative catering company. This threat may force the original catering company to charge 'reasonable' prices and offer a good service.

Perfectly contestable markets

A market is ***perfectly contestable*** when potential rivals (a) face no costs of entry and exit, and (b) can rapidly enter the market before the monopolist has time to respond. In such cases, the instant it becomes possible to earn supernormal profits, new firms will quickly enter the market and charge a price below the monopolist's price.

If the monopolist is unable to respond immediately, the new entrant sells to all of the customers in the market and makes supernormal profit. When the monopolist finally does respond by cutting its own prices, profits are driven back down towards their normal level. At that stage, the new entrant is able to exit the market costlessly. This is known as ***'hit and run'***.

The sheer threat of this happening, so the theory goes, will ensure that the firm already in the market will (a) keep its prices down, so that it just makes normal profits, and (b) produce as efficiently as possible, taking advantage of any economies of scale and any new technology. If it did not do this, rivals would enter, and potential competition would become actual competition.

This is illustrated in Figure 7.12. Assume that there is only one firm in the industry, which faces a long-run average cost curve given by *LRAC*. Assume that profits are maximised at a price of P_1, with supernormal profits being shown by the shaded area. If entry and exit costs are high, the price will remain at this level. If entry and exit costs are low, however, rival firms may be tempted to enter, charge a slightly lower price than the monopoly and take all of its customers.

Definitions

Perfectly contestable market A market where there is free and costless entry and exit and the monopolist cannot immediately respond to entry.

Hit and run A strategy whereby a firm is willing to enter a market and make short-run profits and then leave again when the existing firm(s) cut prices. Costless exit makes hit-and-run behaviour more likely.

Figure 7.12 A contestable monopoly

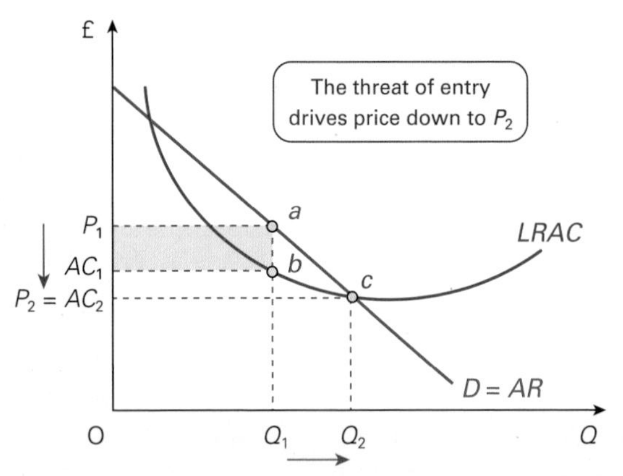

To avert this, the existing firm will have to lower its price. In the case of zero entry and exit costs, the monopolist will have to lower its price to P_2, where price equals *LRAC*, and where, therefore, profits are normal and would not attract rival firms to enter. At the same time, the monopolist will have to ensure that its *LRAC* curve is as low as possible (i.e. that it avoids any X inefficiency (see Box 7.5)).

Contestable markets and natural monopolies

So why in such cases are the markets not *actually* perfectly competitive? Why do they remain monopolies?

The most likely reason has to do with economies of scale and the size of the market. To operate close to its minimum efficient scale, the firm may have to be so large relative to the market that there is only room for one such firm in the industry. If a new firm does come into the market, then one or other of the two firms will not survive the competition. The market is simply not big enough for both of them. This is the case in Figure 7.12. The industry is a natural monopoly, given that the *LRAC* curve is downward sloping even at output *c*.

If, however, there are no entry or exit costs, new firms will be perfectly willing to enter even though there is only room for one firm – either because they believe that they are more efficient than the established firm or because they are willing to engage in hit-and-run competition. The established firm, knowing this, will be forced to produce as efficiently as possible and with only normal profit.

The importance of costless exit

There is always an element of risk whenever a firm is thinking of entering an industry. It is often difficult to forecast its costs and future demand accurately and there is no guarantee these forecasts will prove to be correct. For example, there could be an unanticipated fall in demand for the product caused by a negative shock such as a recession; the technology used by the entrant might quickly become obsolete, especially if it is entering an industry with high levels of innovation; the established firm may respond far more quickly to the new firm's entry than anticipated, leaving it unable to make any supernormal profit.

But does this risk matter? Cannot a new entrant engage in hit-and-run competition and quickly leave a market? This depends on the costs of exit – on the extent of *sunk costs* (see page 161). Setting up in a new business often involves large expenditures on physical capital (plant and machinery), advertising and complying with government regulations. Once this money is spent, it may not be possible to recover. For example, the losing firm may be left with capital equipment that it cannot use or sell. The firm may therefore be put off entering in the first place. The market is not perfectly contestable; the established firm can make supernormal profit.

If, however, the capital equipment does generate the same return in *alternative* uses, the exit costs will be zero (or at least very low), and new firms will be more willing to make the necessary investment and take the risks of entry. KI 11 p72 For example, a rival coach company may open up a service on a route previously operated by only one company, and where there is still only room for one operator. If the new firm loses the resulting battle, it can still use the coaches it has purchased. It simply uses them for a different route. The cost of the coaches is not a sunk cost.

Costless exit, therefore, encourages firms to enter an industry, knowing that, if unsuccessful, they can always transfer their capital elsewhere.

The lower the exit costs, the more contestable the market. This implies that firms already established in other similar markets may provide more effective competition against monopolists, since they can simply transfer capital from one market to another. For example, studies of airlines in the USA show that entry to a particular route may be much easier for an established airline, which can simply transfer planes from one route to another (see Box 7.7).

In which of the following industries are exit costs likely to be low: (a) steel production; (b) market gardening; (c) nuclear power generation; (d) specialist financial advisory services; (e) production of a new drug; (f) street food; (g) car ferry operators? Do these exit costs depend on how narrowly the industry is defined?

Assessment of the theory

The theory of contestable markets is an improvement on simple monopoly theory, which merely focuses on the existing structure of the industry and makes no allowance for potential competition.

Perfectly contestable markets may exist only rarely. But, like perfect competition, they provide an *ideal type* against which to judge the real world. It can be argued that they provide a more useful ideal type than perfect competition, since they provide a better means of predicting firms' price and output behaviour than does the simple portion of the market currently supplied by the existing firm.

BOX 7.7 AIRLINE DEREGULATION IN THE USA AND EUROPE

CASE STUDIES AND APPLICATIONS

A case study of contestable markets

If a market is highly contestable, the mere threat of competition may successfully keep prices and profits down to near-competitive levels. Of course, established firms would be keen to erect barriers to entry and to make exit more costly for any firm that did enter.

Governments around the world are generally in favour of increased competition and frown on the erection of entry barriers (see section 14.1). This means that they generally prefer not to intervene if markets are competitive or highly contestable, but may attempt to regulate the prices, profits or behaviour of firms where competition or contestability is limited. Conversely, if markets have been regulated and yet are potentially competitive, many governments have then deregulated them (i.e. removed regulations).

A good case study of deregulation and contestability (or lack of it) is the airline industry. Here the reduction of regulations over decades has allowed low-cost airlines to build market share and challenge the large network carriers.

The USA

The airline industry in the United States was deregulated in 1978. Prior to that, air routes were allocated by the government, with the result that many airlines operated as monopolies or shared the route with just one other airline. Now there exists a policy of 'open skies'.

Initially the consequences were dramatic, with lower fares and, over many routes, a greater choice of airlines. The Brookings Institute calculated that, in the first 10 years of deregulation, the lower fares saved consumers some $100 billion. One consequence of the increased competition was that many long-established US airlines went out of business.

Even where routes continued to be operated by just one or two airlines, fares still fell if the route was *contestable*: if the entry and exit costs remained low. In 1992, despite the bankruptcies, 23 new carriers were established in North America, and many routes were taken over by existing carriers.

But deregulation did not make all routes more contestable. In some cases the reverse happened. In a situation of rising costs and falling revenues, there were mergers and takeovers of the vulnerable airlines. By 2000, just 7 airlines accounted for over 90 per cent of American domestic air travel, compared with 15 in 1984. With this move towards greater monopolisation, some airlines managed to make their routes *less* contestable. The result was that air fares over the 1990s rose faster than prices in general.

A key ingredient in making routes less contestable was the development of a system of air routes radiating out from about 30 key or 'hub' airports. With waves of flights scheduled to arrive and depart within a short space of time, passengers can make easy connections at these hub airports.

The problem is that several of these hub airports became dominated by single airlines which, through economies of scale and the ownership or control of various airport facilities, such as boarding gates or check-in areas, could effectively keep out potential entrants. By 2002, at 15 of the hub airports, including some of the busiest, the dominant airline had a market share in excess of 70 per cent.

The airlines also used measures to increase contractual switching costs and thereby make entry barriers higher. These measures include frequent flyer rewards, deals with travel agents and code sharing with 'partner' airlines.

The rise of the low-cost airlines In the 2000s, however, the domestic US airlines market became more competitive again, thanks to the growth of low-cost carriers (LCCs), the largest being Southwest Airlines. These accounted for just 7 per cent of US domestic passengers in 1990; by 2009 this had risen to 34 per cent and in 2013, for the first time, LCCs had a greater market share than the network carriers. The response of the major airlines was to create their own low-cost carriers, such as Delta's 'Song' in 2004 and United's 'Ted' in 2004.

This created the danger that the big airlines might use their LCCs to undercut the prices of small new entrants to drive them out of the market. Such 'predatory pricing' (see pages 254 and 429) is illegal, and the Department of Justice investigated several cases. However, predatory pricing is very difficult to distinguish from price competition between firms. Thus cases have been consistently dismissed by juries, who have concluded that there was insufficient proof that the big airlines were breaking the law. This issue re-emerged in 2011, when Delta Airlines was criticised for adopting predatory practices in order to maintain a monopoly position at Minneapolis St Paul Airport.

With the rise in fuel prices in 2006–8 and lower passenger numbers from 2007, resulting from the global recession, some of these new LCCs went out of business. Delta shut its Song division in 2006 and United shut Ted in 2008.

The whole industry has gone through a period of major consolidation with five big mergers reducing the number of large airlines from nine to four. For example, in 2011 Southwest acquired AirTran, another major low-cost carrier. This deal enabled it to remove one of its leading rivals. In 2020, American, United, Delta, and Southwest controlled 65 per cent of the US market and some observers have expressed concerns about the lack of competition on prices. At 93 of the largest 100 US airports, one or two airlines now have the majority of the market.

The US airline market is more competitive than it was before the industry deregulated in 1978. However, the level of competition has fallen dramatically in the past 10 years. It will be interesting to see if the threat of potential competition constrains the pricing behaviour of the four big airlines in the future.

Europe

Until the early 1990s, the European air transport industry was highly regulated, with governments controlling routes. National routes were often licensed to the national airline and international routes to the two respective national airlines. Since 1993, the industry has been progressively deregulated and competition has increased, with a growing availability of discount fares. Now, within the EU, airlines are free to set prices, and any EU airline can fly on any route it wants, providing it can get slots at the airports.

(continued)

As in the USA, however, whilst increased competition has benefited passengers, many of the airlines have tried to make their routes less contestable by erecting entry barriers. Predatory pricing occurred, as the established airlines tried to drive out new competitors. The proliferation of fare categories made it hard for consumers to compare prices, and established carriers' highly publicised fares often had many restrictions, with most people having to pay considerably higher fares. As in the USA, code sharing and airline alliances have reduced competition. Finally, at busy airports, such as Heathrow, the shortage of check-in and boarding gates, runways and airspace provided a major barrier to new entrants.

Nevertheless, new low-cost airlines, such as EasyJet and Ryanair, provided effective competition for the established national and short-haul international carriers. They were able to enter the market by using smaller regional airports such as Stansted and Luton. Many passengers showed themselves willing to travel further at the beginning and end of their journey if the overall cost remained much lower. The established carriers were forced to cut fares on routes where they faced greater competition.

Lower costs

How do the LCCs compete? The airline industry does not on the face of it seem to be a highly contestable one. Apart from anything else, aircraft would appear to be a high-cost input.

The answer lies in a variety of cost-saving opportunities. The LCCs are able to lease planes rather than buy them; even when they own their own planes, the aircraft are generally older and more basic, offering a standard accommodation rather than different classes. The result is reduced exit costs, increasing contestability. In addition, by charging extra for each item of luggage, they reduce the amount they carry, thus saving fuel.

There is also evidence of lower staff costs. Initially, LCCs paid less than the traditional airlines; however, this is no longer the case. Today, however, salaries and benefits for LCC employees are similar to those available to employees of the larger carriers. Yet productivity is measurably higher, with 15 per cent more available seat miles per employee, given faster turnaround at airports and more passengers on any given aircraft type.

The large hub-and-spoke carriers have also found that the very nature of their operations constricts their ability to compete with the LCCs on city-to-city routes. Not only are the hubs themselves expensive, but the movement of passengers in and out of the terminals takes longer than with smaller airports. Thus the LCCs, with operating costs some 25 to 50 per cent lower than the traditional carriers, have become a highly effective competitive force on these routes between various city pairs and have forced down prices.

The impact of the COVID-19 pandemic

The pandemic and subsequent travel restrictions had a dramatic impact on both LCCs and traditional carriers. For example, International Airline Group (owners of BA) announced record losses of £5.1 billion for the first nine months of 2020. Between April and June, their passenger numbers fell by 98 per cent. EasyJet made its first ever annual loss in 2020, while Wizz Air, the low-cost Hungarian carrier, reported losses before tax of €237 million for the six months to September.

A number of factors make it highly likely the LCCs will outperform the traditional carriers as the economy recovers and travel restrictions ease. Every airline had to respond to the collapse in demand by reducing their costs. However, the LCCs made the largest reductions, hence further increasing their cost advantage over the traditional carriers. This will enable these businesses to make profits on routes where they sell a smaller percentage of tickets (i.e. a lower load factor). They will also be able to offer better deals to customers who become more price sensitive following the pandemic.

The demand for short-haul leisure trips is likely to recover far more quickly than long-haul business flights: i.e. the area of the market where the LCCs have already been very successful. The demand for long-haul business flights is unlikely to recover to previous levels as businesses (a) focus on cutting costs, (b) are increasingly concerned about their environmental image and (c) continue to make greater use of video conferencing following their positive experience during lockdown.

The greater flexibility of the LCCs means they can respond more rapidly to any increases in demand. The chief executives of Ryanair, EasyJet and Wizz Air have all stated that they see the recovery after the pandemic as a great opportunity to gain market share at the expense of the traditional carriers. The leasing approach means they can expand the number of aircraft very quickly.

One issue that might constrain the future growth of LCCs is the waiver of the '80/20 use-it-or-lose-it' rules for slots at airports. The rules meant that carriers which used less than 80 per cent of their allocated slots risked losing them to competitors. The temporary suspension of this rule was designed to discourage 'ghost flights' of empty planes by carriers fearful of losing their slots, with the associated environmental costs as well as private costs. But it did prevent entry of competitors.

1. *Make a list of those factors that determine the contestability of a particular air route.*
2. *In the UK, train operators compete for franchises to run services on a particular route. The franchises are normally for 7, 10, 12 or 15 years. The franchise specifies prices and minimum levels of services (frequency, timing and quality). Would this be a good system to adopt in the airline market over particular routes? How is the airline market similar to/different from the rail market in this regard?*
3. *In a period of rising fuel prices, and thus higher airfares, do you think that the low-cost carriers are more or less vulnerable than the traditional carriers in the short term? Would your answer differ when we look at the longer-term decisions of passengers?*

Find out what has happened to the 80/20 rule in various jurisdictions such as the EU, the USA and the UK since the onset of the pandemic and consider the impact on competition between airlines.

One criticism of the theory, however, is that it does not take sufficient account of the possible reactions of the established firm. There could be a contestable market, with no barriers to entry or exit, but the established firm may signal very clearly that it will respond immediately if any firm dares to enter its market. The threat of facing an immediate price war might deter any potential entrant, allowing the established firm to continue charging high prices and making supernormal profits.

Perhaps the most important contribution of the theory is to help us focus on the importance of sunk costs when determining the threat of entry and performance of a market. Many of the factors that create barriers to entry, such as economics of scale and product differentiation/advertising, may only actually create a barrier to a new entrant if they involve expenditures that cannot be recovered if it later exits the market.

Contestable markets and the public interest

If a monopoly operates in a perfectly contestable market, it might bring the 'best of both worlds'. Not only will it be able to achieve low costs through economies of scale, but also the potential competition will keep profits and hence prices down.

For this reason, the theory has been seized on by politicians on the political right to justify a policy of laissez-faire (non-intervention) and deregulation (e.g. coach and air routes). They argue that the theory vindicates the free market. There are two points in reply to this:

- Few markets are perfectly contestable. If entry and exit are not costless, a monopoly can still make supernormal profits in the long run.
- There are other possible failings of the market beside monopoly power (e.g. inequality, pollution). These failings are examined in Chapters 11 and 12.

Nevertheless, the theory of contestable markets has highlighted the importance of sunk costs in determining monopoly behaviour. Monopolists may deliberately spend large amounts of money on advertising as they realise it increases the sunk costs of entry and hence deters new firms from entering its market. Many policy makers now focus on sunk costs when considering anti-monopoly policy.

Section summary

1. Potential competition may be as important as actual competition in determining a firm's price and output strategy.
2. The threat of this competition increases as entry and exit costs to and from the industry diminish. If the entry and exit costs are zero, the market is said to be perfectly contestable. Under such circumstances, an existing monopolist will be forced to keep its profits down to the normal level if it is to resist entry by new firms. Exit costs will be lower, the lower are the sunk costs of the firm.
3. The theory of contestable markets provides a more realistic analysis of firms' behaviour than theories based simply on the existing number of firms in the industry.

END OF CHAPTER QUESTIONS

1. A perfectly competitive firm faces a price of £14 per unit. It has the following short-run cost schedule:

Output	0	1	2	3	4	5	6	7	8
TC (£)	10	18	24	30	38	50	66	91	120

   (a) Copy the table and put in additional rows for average cost and marginal cost at each level of output. (Enter the figures for marginal cost in the space between each column.)
   (b) Plot *AC*, *MC* and *MR* on a diagram.
   (c) Mark the profit-maximising output.
   (d) How much (supernormal) profit is made at this output?
   (e) What would happen to the price in the long run if this firm were typical of others in the industry? Why would we need to know information about long-run average cost in order to give a precise answer to this question?
2. If the industry under perfect competition faces a downward-sloping demand curve, why does an individual firm face a horizontal demand curve?
3. If supernormal profits are competed away under perfect competition, why will firms have an incentive to become more efficient?
4. Is it a valid criticism of perfect competition to argue that it is incompatible with economies of scale?
5. On a diagram similar to Figure 7.4, show the long-run equilibrium for both firm and industry under perfect competition. Now assume that the demand for the product falls. Show the short-run and long-run effects.
6. Why is the profit-maximising price under monopoly greater than marginal cost? In what way can this be seen as inefficient?
7. On three diagrams like Figure 7.8, illustrate the effect on price, quantity and profit of each of the following: (a) a rise in demand; (b) a rise in fixed costs; (c) a rise in variable costs. In each case, show only the *AR*, *MR*, *AC* and *MC* curves.
8. Think of three examples of monopolies (local or national) and consider how contestable their markets are.

Online resources

Additional case studies on the student website

7.1 B2B electronic marketplaces. This case study examines the growth of firms trading with each other (business-to-business or 'B2B') over the Internet and considers the effects on competition.

7.2 Measuring monopoly power. This case study examines how the degree of monopoly power possessed by a firm can be measured.

7.3 Competition in the pipeline? This examines monopoly in the supply of gas.

7.4 Windows cleaning. This discusses the examination of Microsoft's market dominance by the US Justice Department and the European Commission.

Maths Case 7.1 **Long-run equilibrium under perfect competition.** Using calculus to find equilibrium output and price.

Maths Case 7.2 **Price elasticity of demand and the profit-maximising price.** A proof of the profit-maximising rule relating price elasticity of demand, price and marginal revenue.

Websites relevant to this chapter

See sites listed at the end of Chapter 8 on page 256.

Profit Maximising under Imperfect Competition

CHAPTER MAP

Very few markets in practice can be classified as perfectly competitive or as a pure monopoly. The vast majority of firms do compete with other firms, often quite aggressively, and yet they are not price takers: they do have some degree of market power. Most markets, therefore, lie between the two extremes of monopoly and perfect competition, in the realm of 'imperfect competition'.

There are two types of imperfect competition: monopolistic competition and oligopoly.

Under monopolistic competition, there will normally be quite a large number of relatively small firms. Think of the number of car repair garages, builders, hairdressers, restaurants and other small traders that you get in any large town or city. They are in fierce competition with each other, and yet competition is not perfect. They are all trying to produce a product that is different from their rivals' product.

Under oligopoly, there will be only a few firms competing. Most of the best-known companies, such as Ford, Coca-Cola, Nike, BP and Apple, are oligopolists. Sometimes oligopolists will attempt to collude with each other to keep prices up. On other occasions, competition will be intense, with rival firms trying to undercut each other's prices, or developing new or better products in order to gain a larger share of the market. We will examine both collusion and competition between oligopolists and show when each is more likely to occur.

8.1 MONOPOLISTIC COMPETITION

We will start by looking at monopolistic competition. This was a theory developed in the 1930s by the American economist Edward Chamberlin. Monopolistic competition is nearer to the competitive end of the spectrum. It can best be understood as a situation where there are a lot of firms competing, but where each firm does nevertheless have some degree of market power (hence the term 'monopolistic' competition): each firm has some choice over what price to charge for its products.

Assumptions of monopolistic competition

- There are *quite a large number of firms*. As a result, each firm has an insignificantly small share of the market, and therefore its actions are unlikely to affect its rivals to any great extent. This means that when each firm makes its decisions it does not have to worry how its rivals will react. It assumes that what its rivals choose to do will *not* be influenced by what it does.

  This is known as the assumption of ***independence***. (As we shall see later, this is not the case under oligopoly. There we assume that firms believe that their decisions *do* affect their rivals, and that their rivals' decisions will affect them. Under oligopoly, we assume that firms are *inter*dependent.)
- There is *freedom of entry* of new firms into the industry. If any firm wants to set up in business in this market, it is free to do so.

  In these two respects, therefore, monopolistic competition is like perfect competition.
- The situation differs from perfect competition, however, in that each firm produces a product or provides a service in some way different from those of its rivals. As a result, it can raise its price without losing all its customers. Thus its demand curve is downward sloping, although it will be relatively elastic given the large number of competitors to which customers can turn. This is known as the assumption of ***product differentiation***.

Restaurants, hairdressers and builders are all examples of monopolistic competition.

Give some other examples of monopolistic competition. (Try looking at www.yell.com if you are stuck.)

Definitions

Independence (of firms in a market) Where the decisions of one firm in a market will not have any significant effect on the demand curves of its rivals.

Product differentiation Where one firm's product is sufficiently different from that of its rivals to allow it to raise the price of the product without customers all switching to the rivals' products. A situation where a firm faces a downward-sloping demand curve.

Equilibrium of the firm

Short run

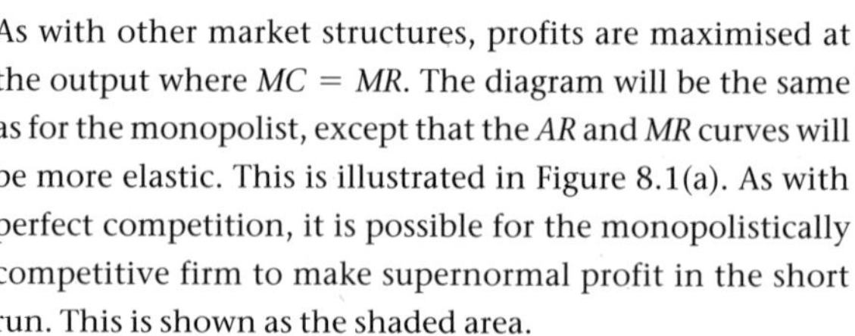

TC 8 p109

As with other market structures, profits are maximised at the output where $MC = MR$. The diagram will be the same as for the monopolist, except that the AR and MR curves will be more elastic. This is illustrated in Figure 8.1(a). As with perfect competition, it is possible for the monopolistically competitive firm to make supernormal profit in the short run. This is shown as the shaded area.

Just how much profit the firm will make in the short run depends on the strength of demand: the position and elasticity of the demand curve. The further to the right the demand curve is relative to the average cost curve, and the less elastic the demand curve is, the greater will be the firm's short-run profit. Thus a firm facing little competition and whose product is considerably differentiated from that of its rivals may be able to earn considerable short-run profits.

KI 9 p64

1. *Why may a food shop charge higher prices than supermarkets for 'essential items' and yet very similar prices for delicatessen items?*
2. *Which of these two items is a petrol station more likely to sell at a discount: (a) oil; (b) sweets? Why?*

Long run

If typical firms are earning supernormal profit, new firms will enter the industry in the long run. As they do, they will take some of the customers away from established firms. The demand for the established firms will therefore fall. Their demand (AR) curve will shift to the left, and will continue doing so as long as supernormal profits remain and thus new firms continue entering.

Long-run equilibrium is reached when only normal profits remain: when there is no further incentive for new firms to enter. This is illustrated in Figure 8.1(b). The firm's demand curve settles at D_L, where it is tangential to the firm's $LRAC$ curve. Output will be Q_L: where $AR_L = LRAC$. (At any other output, $LRAC$ is greater than AR and thus less than normal profit would be made.)

1. *Why does the* LRMC *curve cross the* MR_L *curve directly below the tangency point of the* LRAC *and* AR_L *curves?*
2. *Assuming that supernormal profits can be made in the short run, will there be any difference in the long-run and short-run elasticity of demand? Explain.*

Limitations of the model

There are various problems in applying the model of monopolistic competition to the real world:

- Information may be imperfect. Firms will not enter an industry if they are unaware of what supernormal profits are being made, or if they underestimate the demand for the particular product they are considering selling.

Figure 8.1 Equilibrium of the firm under monopolistic competition

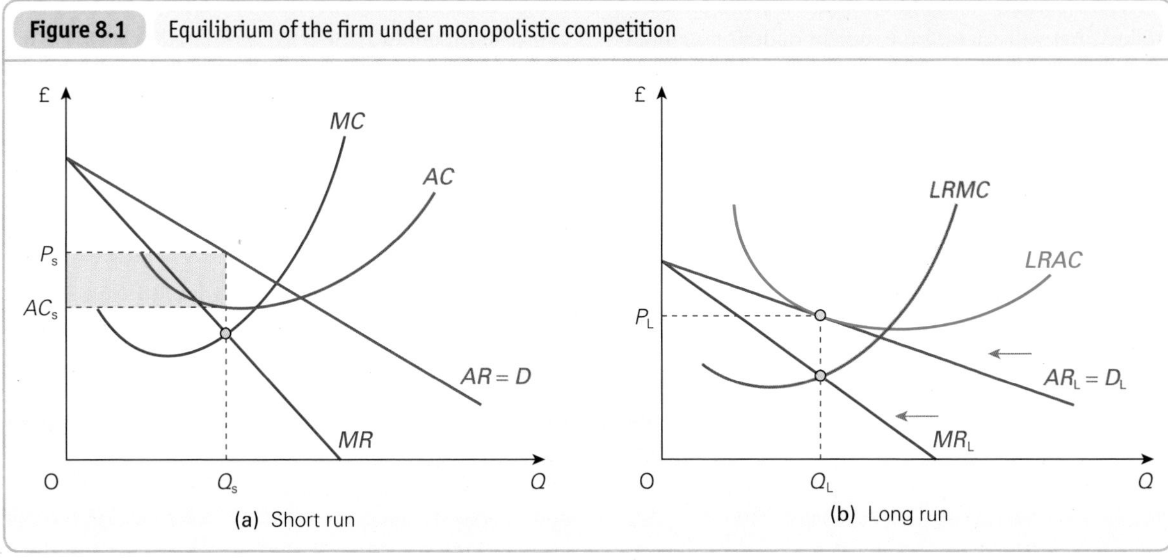

- Given that the firms in the industry produce different products, it is difficult if not impossible to derive a demand curve for the industry as a whole. Thus the analysis has to be confined to the level of the firm.
- Firms are likely to differ from each other not only in the product they produce or the service they offer, but also in their size and cost structure. What is more, entry may not be *completely* unrestricted. Two petrol stations could not set up in exactly the same place – on a busy crossroads, say. Thus although the typical or 'representative' firm may earn only normal profit in the long run, other firms may be able to earn long-run supernormal profit. They may have some cost advantage or produce something that is impossible to duplicate perfectly.
- One of the biggest problems with the simple model shown in Figure 8.1 is that it concentrates on price and output decisions. In practice, the profit-maximising firm under monopolistic competition also has to decide the exact variety of product to produce and how much to spend on advertising it. This will lead the firm to take part in non-price competition.

Non-price competition

Non-price competition involves two major elements: product development and advertising.

Definition

Non-price competition Competition in terms of product promotion (advertising, packaging, etc.) or product development.

BOX 8.1 SELLING ICE CREAM AS A STUDENT — CASE STUDIES AND APPLICATIONS

John's experience of monopolistic competition

When I was a student, my parents lived in Exeter in Devon, and at that time the city's bypass became completely jammed on a summer Saturday as holidaymakers made their way to the coast. Traffic queues were several miles long.

For a summer job, I drove a small ice-cream van. Early on, I had the idea of selling ice cream from a tray to the people queuing in their cars. I made more money on a Saturday than the rest of the week put together. I thought I was on to a good thing.

But news of this lucrative market soon spread, and each week new ice-cream sellers appeared – each one reducing my earnings! By the middle of August there were over 30 ice-cream sellers from five different ice-cream companies. Most tried to get to the beginning of the queue, to get ahead of their rivals.

Imagine the scene. A family driving to the coast rounds a bend and is suddenly met by a traffic jam and several ice-cream sellers all jostling to sell them an ice cream. It was quite surreal. Not surprisingly, many of the potential customers refused to buy, feeling somewhat intimidated by the spectacle. It was not long before most of us realised that it was best to disperse and find a section of the road where there were no other sellers.

But with so many ice-cream sellers, no one made much money. My supernormal earnings had been reduced to a normal level. I made about the same on Saturday to people stuck in queues as I would have done if I had driven my van around the streets.

1. *Was there totally free entry to this market?*
2. *What forms of product differentiation were there?*

Investigate a case of your choosing of monopolistic competition. How closely does it adhere to the assumptions of the model? How responsive are firms to changing market conditions?

The major aims of *product development* are to produce a product that will sell well (i.e. one in high or potentially high demand) and that is different from rivals' products (i.e. has a relatively inelastic demand due to lack of close substitutes). For shops or other firms providing a service, 'product development' takes the form of attempting to provide a service which is better than, or at least different from, that of rivals: personal service, late opening, certain lines stocked, and so on.

The major aim of *advertising* is to sell the product. This can be achieved not only by informing the consumer of the product's existence and availability, but also by deliberately trying to persuade consumers to purchase the good. Like product development, successful advertising will not only increase demand, but also make the firm's demand curve less elastic since it stresses the specific qualities of this firm's product over its rivals' (see Box 2.3 on page 59).

Product development and advertising not only increase a firm's demand and hence revenue, they also involve increased costs. So how much should a firm advertise to maximise profits?

For any given price and product, the optimal amount of advertising is where the revenue from *additional* advertising (MR_A) is equal to its cost (MC_A). As long as $MR_A > MC_A$, additional advertising will add to profit. But extra amounts spent on advertising are likely to lead to smaller and smaller increases in sales. Thus MR_A falls, until $MR_A = MC_A$. At that point, no further profit can be made. It is at a maximum.

Why will additional advertising lead to smaller and smaller increases in sales?

Two problems arise with this analysis:

- The effect of product development and advertising on demand will be difficult for a firm to forecast.
- Product development and advertising are likely to have different effects at different prices. Profit maximisation, therefore, will involve the more complex choice of the optimum combination of price, type of product, and level and variety of advertising.

Monopolistic competition and the public interest

Comparison with perfect competition

It is often argued that monopolistic competition leads to a less efficient allocation of resources than perfect competition.

Figure 8.2 compares the long-run equilibrium positions for two firms. One firm is under perfect competition and thus faces a horizontal demand curve. It will produce an output of Q_1 at a price of P_1. The other is under monopolistic competition and thus faces a downward-sloping demand curve. It will produce the lower output of Q_2 at the higher price of P_2. A crucial assumption here is that a firm would have the *same* long-run average cost (*LRAC*) curve in both cases. Given this assumption, monopolistic competition has the following disadvantages:

- Less will be sold and at a higher price.
- Firms will not be producing at the least-cost point.

By producing more, firms would move to a lower point on their *LRAC* curve. Thus firms under monopolistic competition are said to have ***excess capacity***. In Figure 8.2 this excess capacity is shown as $Q_1 - Q_2$. In other words, monopolistic competition is typified by quite a large number of firms (e.g. petrol stations), all operating at an output less than that necessary to achieve minimum cost, and thus being forced to charge a price above that which they could charge if they had a bigger turnover. How often have you been to a petrol station and had to queue for the pumps?

Does this imply that if, say, half of the petrol stations were closed down, the consumer would benefit? (Clue: what would happen to the demand curves of the remaining stations?)

On the other hand, it is often argued that these wastes of monopolistic competition may be insignificant. In the

Definition

Excess capacity (under monopolistic competition) In the long run, firms under monopolistic competition will produce at an output below their minimum-cost point.

Figure 8.2 Long-run equilibrium of the firm under perfect and monopolistic competition

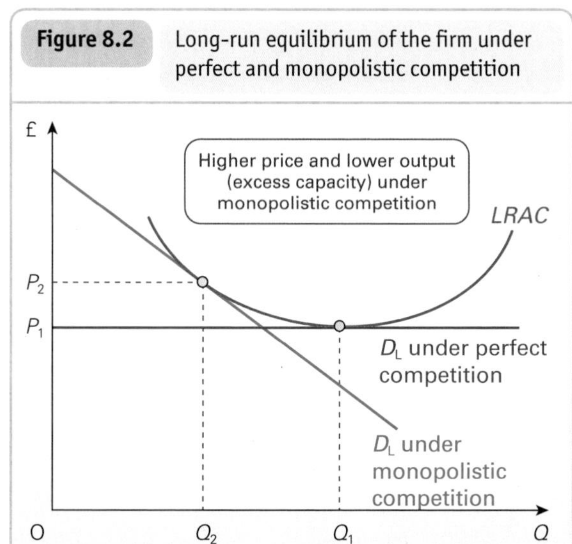

TC 6 p66

first place, although the firm's demand curve is downward sloping, it is still likely to be highly elastic due to the large number of substitutes. In the second place, although the firm under monopolistic competition will not be operating quite at the bottom of its *LRAC* curve, the nature of the industry may allow some economies of scale to be gained. The *LRAC* curve would thus be lower than in the case of the larger number of smaller firms that would be necessary to keep the industry perfectly competitive. The size of the economies of scale, if any, will obviously vary from industry to industry.

Perhaps more importantly, consumers are likely to benefit from monopolistic competition by having a greater variety of products to choose from. Given that we all have individual tastes and preferences, our utility will be higher with choice.

Which would you rather have: five restaurants to choose from, each with very different menus and each having spare tables so that you could always guarantee getting one; or just two restaurants to choose from, charging less but with less choice and making it necessary to book well in advance?

Comparison with monopoly

The arguments here are very similar to those comparing perfect competition and monopoly.

On the one hand, freedom of entry for new firms and hence the lack of long-run supernormal profits under monopolistic competition are likely to help keep prices down for the consumer and encourage cost saving. On the other hand, monopolies are likely to achieve greater economies of scale and have more funds for investment and research and development.

Section summary

1. Monopolistic competition occurs where there is free entry to the industry and quite a large number of firms operating independently of each other, but where each firm has some market power as a result of producing differentiated products or services.
2. In the short run, firms can make supernormal profits. In the long run, however, freedom of entry will drive profits down to the normal level. The long-run equilibrium of the firm is where the (downward-sloping) demand curve is tangential to the long-run average cost curve.
3. The long-run equilibrium is one of excess capacity. Given that the demand curve is downward sloping, its tangency point with the *LRAC* curve will not be at the bottom of the *LRAC* curve. Increased production would thus be possible at *lower* average cost.
4. In practice, supernormal profits may persist into the long run: firms have imperfect information; entry may not be completely unrestricted; firms may use non-price competition to maintain an advantage over their rivals.
5. Non-price competition may take the form of product development or product promotion (advertising, etc.).
6. Monopolistically competitive firms, because of excess capacity, may have higher costs than perfectly competitive firms, but consumers may gain from a greater diversity of products.
7. Monopolistically competitive firms may have fewer economies of scale than monopolies and conduct less research and development, but the competition may keep prices lower than under monopoly.

8.2 OLIGOPOLY

Oligopoly occurs when just a few firms between them share a large proportion of the industry.

There are, however, significant differences in the structure of industries under oligopoly and similarly significant differences in the behaviour of firms. The firms may produce a virtually identical product (e.g. metals, chemicals, sugar, petrol). Most oligopolists, however, produce differentiated products (e.g. cars, soap powder, soft drinks, electrical appliances). Much of the competition between such oligopolists is in terms of the marketing of their particular brand. Marketing practices may differ considerably from one industry to another.

The two key features of oligopoly

Despite the differences between oligopolies, two crucial features distinguish oligopoly from other market structures.

Barriers to entry

In contrast to the situation under monopolistic competition, there are various barriers to the entry of new firms. These are similar to those under monopoly (see pages 207–10). The size of the barriers, however, varies from industry to industry. In some cases entry is relatively easy, whereas in others it is virtually impossible.

Interdependence of the firms

Because there are only a few firms under oligopoly, each has to take account of the others. This means that they are mutually dependent: they are ***interdependent***. Each firm is affected by its rivals' actions. If a firm changes the price or specification of its product, for example, or the amount of its advertising, the sales of its rivals will be affected. The rivals may then respond by changing their price, specification or advertising. No firm can afford to ignore the actions and reactions of other firms in the industry.

It is impossible, therefore, to predict the effect on a firm's sales of, say, a change in its price without first making some assumption about the reactions of other firms. Different assumptions yield different predictions. For this reason there is no one single theory of oligopoly. Firms may react differently and unpredictably.

Definition

Interdependence (under oligopoly) One of the two key features of oligopoly. Each firm will be affected by its rivals' decisions. Likewise its decisions will affect its rivals. Firms recognise this interdependence. This recognition will affect their decisions.

People often think and behave strategically. **How you think others will respond to your actions is likely to influence your own behaviour. Firms, for example, when considering a price or product change will often take into account the likely reactions of their rivals.**

BOX 8.2 DECLINING LEVELS OF COMPETITION CASE STUDIES AND APPLICATIONS

Evidence from the UK

We have identified barriers to entry under oligopoly as a factor that limits the number of firms. But why does market power grow in some oligopolies, with the number of firms decreasing? Possible answers include mergers and acquisitions, tough economic conditions and increasing brand loyalty, all of which can reduce competition.

As we saw in Box 7.1, one of the simplest ways of assessing the extent of market power is to look at concentration ratios – the market share of the leading firms. The table below provides some more data.

5-firm concentration ratios for various sectors in 2018 (by turnover)

Sector	5-firm ratio
Electricity distribution	90
Mining and quarrying	60
Banking	50
Software and games	40
Motor vehicle/cycle repair	15
Professional services	10

Source: *The State of UK Competition, November 2020*, Competition and Markets Authority (30 November 2020)

1. *Can you identify the largest firms in the computer games publishing sector?*
2. *What characteristics of the motor vehicle/cycle repair sector make it so 'unconcentrated'?*

Unsurprisingly, the sectors with the highest concentration ratios display a number of varying characteristics. They often have a relatively high share of fixed/capital costs, allowing firms to benefit from economies of scale: e.g. electricity distribution.

In sectors with differentiated products, such as computer software and games, there are high levels of sunk costs in branding and advertising. On the other hand, the sectors with the lowest ratios tend to have a relatively small share of fixed costs and lower costs of entry (e.g. professional services). In many cases their advertising spend is likely to be local, if it exists at all: e.g. motor vehicle/cycle repairs (see Case Study 8.2 on the student website).

Recent trends in the UK

Concentration ratios. Recent research by the Competition and Markets Authority (CMA)[1] shows an overall rise in seller concentration over the past 20 years. The average combined market share (by turnover) of the largest 10 businesses in each sector of the UK economy (CR10) remained relatively stable from 1998 to 2007. Following the impact of the financial crisis, the figure then increased from around 47 per cent in 2009 to 54 per cent in 2011. From 2014 to 2018, the figure declined to 50 per cent – still 3 percentage points above its level in 1998.

There were some dramatic differences between sectors. For example, CR10 for plumbing: heat and air installation fell from 55 per cent in 2008 to just 5 per cent in 2018, whereas CR10 for the manufacture of non-domestic cooling and ventilation equipment increased from 28 per cent to 86 per cent over the same period. However, most sectors did experience increases in CR5, CR10 and CR15.

Other indicators. As we discussed in Box 7.1, concentration ratios are only one indicator of the degree of competition. If concentration in a market rises, it does not necessarily mean that the level of competition is declining. Therefore, it is important to consider other factors such as rank persistence and the mark-up of price over marginal costs.

Rank persistence is the extent to which the largest firms in a sector remain the same over time. In a competitive market, we would expect to see low levels of persistence as dynamic newer firms replace poorly performing businesses. To measure this, the CMA compared the largest ten firms in a sector in a particular year with the largest ten three years earlier. The evidence shows an overall increase in this measure over time. Some sectors such as wholesale and retail trade, and information and communication had a rank persistence of nine in a number of years.

The mark-up of price over the marginal cost of producing a good is another useful indicator of the strength of competition. A mark-up of 1.2 means that prices are 20 per cent higher than marginal costs. In a highly competitive market, economic theory predicts this ratio should be close to 1, with firms making normal profits. Research by the Bank of England[2] found that the average mark-up of UK listed firms (i.e. those with shares traded on the stock exchange) increased from 1.2 in 1987 to 1.6 in 2017. Using data on both listed and private companies, the CMA reported an increase from 1.22 in 2000 to 1.31 in 2018.

Both studies found that for the majority of businesses (75 per cent) the figure remained the same. The rise in the average figure was caused by large increases among a relatively small number of companies that already had the highest mark-ups: i.e. those that were already the most profitable. Other research[3] also found that the greatest increase occurred among firms in more digitally intensive sectors.

Although not conclusive, a number of indicators suggest that the level of competition in the UK economy has fallen in recent years. There are concerns that the difficult economic conditions caused by the COVID-19 pandemic could further reduce the degree of rivalry as some firms are forced to close.

1. *Explain why increases in the levels of (a) concentration and (b) mark-ups of price over marginal cost do not necessarily mean that levels of competition are falling.*
2. *Identify some other indicators that you could use to judge the strength and intensity of competition in a market.*
3. *Do small independent burger companies have any market advantages over global firms such as McDonald's and Burger King?*

Using the CMA report (endnote 1 below), write a summary of changes in sector-level concentration in the UK from 1998 to 2018.

1 *The State of UK Competition Report 2020*, CMA (30 November 2020), www.gov.uk/government/news/cma-reports-on-the-state-of-competition-in-the-uk

2 Tommaso Aquilante et al., 'Market power and monetary policy', *Staff Working Paper*, No. 798, Bank of England (3 May 2019), www.bankofengland.co.uk/working-paper/2019/market-power-and-monetary-policy

3 Sara Calligarisi, Chiara Criscuoloi and Luca Marcolini, 'Mark-ups in the digital era', *OECD Science, Technology and Industry Working Papers*, OECD (25 April 2018), www.oecd-ilibrary.org/industry-and-services/mark-ups-in-the-digital-era_4efe2d25-en

Competition and collusion

The interdependence of firms in an oligopolistic market pulls them in two very different directions:

- Each firm, by carefully studying the market and its rivals' strategy may believe that, by competing, it can gain a greater share of industry profits.
- On the other hand, firms may conclude that competition will be destructive and lead to lower profits: i.e. through retaliatory price-cutting. So instead, they may prefer to collude with each other by making agreements about price, output, product design, etc. By acting together as if they were a monopoly, the firms could take actions that jointly maximise industry profits and share these profits between them.

These two policies are incompatible. The more fiercely firms compete to gain a bigger share of industry profits, the smaller these industry profits will become. For example, price competition will drive down the average industry price, while competition through advertising will raise industry costs. Either way, industry profits will fall.

Sometimes firms collude, sometimes not. The following sections examine first ***collusive oligopoly*** (both open and tacit), and then ***non-collusive oligopoly***.

Industry equilibrium under collusive oligopoly

When firms under oligopoly engage in collusion, they may agree on output, prices, market share, advertising expenditure, etc. Such collusion reduces the uncertainty they face. It reduces the fear of engaging in competitive price cutting or retaliatory advertising, both of which could reduce total industry profits.

A formal collusive agreement is called a ***cartel***. The cartel will maximise profits if it acts like a monopoly: if the members behave as if they were a single firm. This is illustrated in Figure 8.3.

Definitions

Collusive oligopoly Where oligopolists agree (formally or informally) to limit competition between themselves. They may set output quotas, fix prices, limit product promotion or development, or agree not to 'poach' each other's markets.

Non-collusive oligopoly Where oligopolists have no agreement between themselves, formal, informal or tacit.

Cartel A formal collusive agreement.

Figure 8.3 Profit-maximising cartel

£
Industry profit maximised at Q_1 and P_1
Industry *MC*
P_1
Members must agree to restrict total output to Q_1
Industry *D* = *AR*
Industry *MR*
O
Q_1
Q

The total market demand curve is shown with the corresponding market *MR* curve. The cartel's *MC* curve is the *horizontal* sum of the *MC* curves of its members (since we are adding the *output* of each of the cartel members at each level of marginal cost). Profits are maximised at Q_1 where $MC = MR$. The cartel must therefore set a price of P_1 (at which Q_1 will be demanded).

TC 8 p109

KI 22 p195

Having agreed on the cartel price, the members may then compete against each other using *non-price competition,* to gain as big a share of resulting sales (Q_1) as they can.

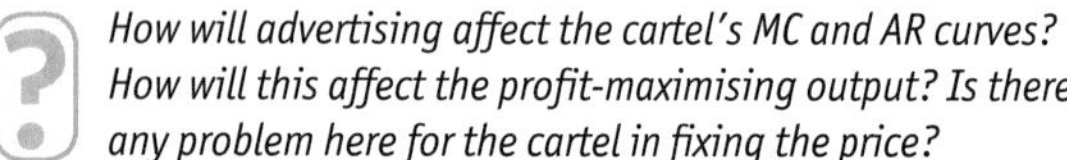

How will advertising affect the cartel's MC and AR curves? How will this affect the profit-maximising output? Is there any problem here for the cartel in fixing the price?

Alternatively, the cartel members may somehow agree to divide the market between them. Each member would be given a ***quota***. The sum of all the quotas must add up to Q_1. If the quotas exceeded Q_1, either there would be output unsold if price remained fixed at P_1, or the price would fall.

But if quotas are to be set by the cartel, how will it decide the level of each individual member's quota? The most likely method is for the cartel to divide the market between the members according to their current market share. This is the solution most likely to be accepted as 'fair'.

If this 'fair' solution were adopted, what effect would it have on the industry MC curve in Figure 8.3?

In many countries, cartels are illegal – being seen by the government as a means of driving up prices and profits, and thereby as being against the public interest (see section 14.1). Where open collusion is illegal, however, firms may simply break the law, or get round it. Alternatively, firms may stay within the law, but still *tacitly* collude by watching each other's prices and keeping theirs similar. Firms may tacitly 'agree' to avoid price wars or aggressive advertising campaigns.

Tacit collusion: price leadership

One form of ***tacit collusion*** is where firms keep to the price set by an established leader. The leader may be the largest firm: the one dominating the industry. This is known as ***dominant firm price leadership***. Alternatively, the price leader may simply be the one that has proved to be the most reliable one to follow: the one that is the best barometer of market conditions. This is known as ***barometric firm price leadership***. Let us examine each of these two types of price leadership in turn.

Dominant firm price leadership

How in theory does the leader set the price? The leader will maximise profits where its marginal revenue is equal to its marginal cost. Figure 8.4(a) shows the total market demand curve and the supply curve of all followers. These firms, like perfectly competitive firms, accept the price as given, only in this case it is the price set by the leader, and thus their joint supply curve is simply the sum of their *MC* curves – the same as under perfect competition.

The leader's demand curve can be seen as that portion of market demand unfilled by the other firms. In other words, it is market demand minus other firms' supply. At P_1 the whole of market demand is satisfied by the other firms, and so the demand for the leader is zero (point *a*). At P_2 the other firms' supply is zero, and so the leader faces the full market demand (point *b*). The leader's demand curve thus connects points *a* and *b*.

The leader's profit will be maximised where its marginal cost equals its marginal revenue. This is shown in Figure 8.4(b). The diagram is the same as Figure 8.4(a) but with the addition of *MC* and *MR* curves for the leader. The leader's marginal cost equals its marginal revenue at an output of Q_L (giving a point *l* on its demand curve). The leader thus sets a price of P_L, which the other firms then duly follow. They supply Q_F (i.e. at point *f* on their supply curve). Total market demand at P_L is Q_T

Definitions

Quota (set by a cartel) The output that a given member of a cartel is allowed to produce (production quota) or sell (sales quota).

Tacit collusion Where oligopolists take care not to engage in price cutting, excessive advertising or other forms of competition. There may be unwritten 'rules' of collusive behaviour such as price leadership.

Dominant firm price leadership Where firms (the followers) choose the same price as that set by a dominant firm in the industry (the leader).

Barometric firm price leadership Where the price leader is the one whose prices are believed to reflect market conditions in the most satisfactory way.

Figure 8.4 Dominant firm price leadership

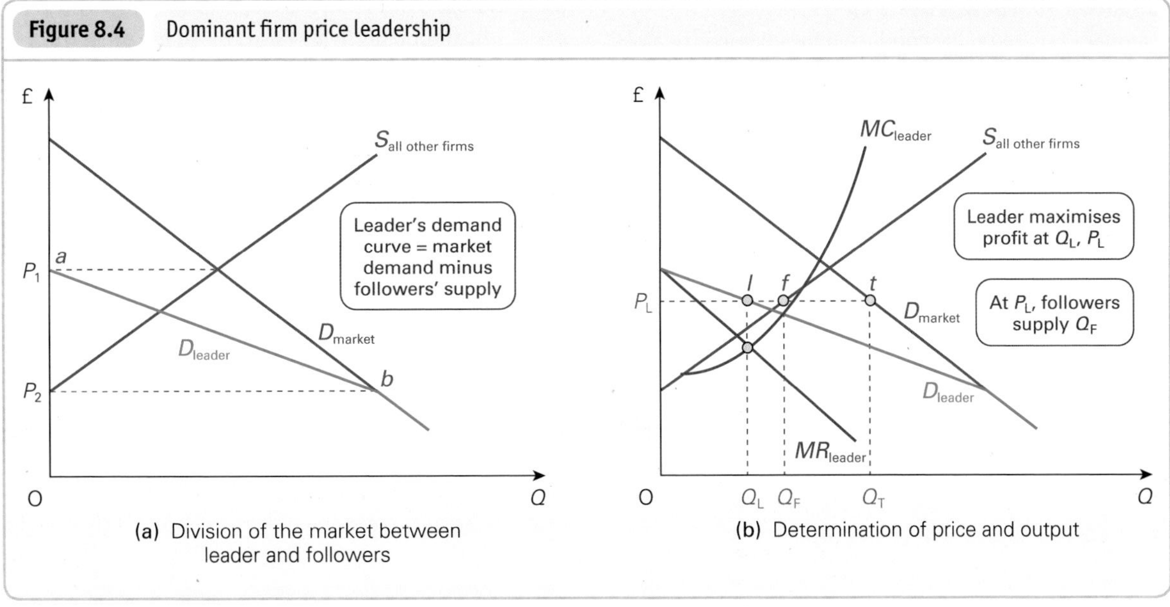

(a) Division of the market between leader and followers

(b) Determination of price and output

(i.e. point *t* on the market demand curve), which must add up to the output of both leader and followers (i.e. $Q_L + Q_F$).

Draw a pair of diagrams like those in Figure 8.4. Illustrate what would happen if market demand rose but the costs of neither leader nor followers rose. Would there be an equal percentage increase in the output of both leader and followers?

In practice, however, it is very difficult for the leader to apply this theory. The leader's demand and *MR* curves depend on the followers' supply curve – something the leader will find virtually impossible to estimate with any degree of accuracy. The leader will thus have to make a rough estimate of what its profit-maximising price and output will be, and simply choose that. That is the best it can do. TC 9 p132

A simpler model is where the leader assumes that it will maintain a constant *market share* (say, 50 per cent). It makes this assumption because it also assumes that all other firms will follow its price up and down. This is illustrated in Figure 8.5. It knows its current position on its demand curve (say, point *a*). It then estimates how responsive its demand will be to industry-wide price changes and thus constructs its demand and *MR* curves accordingly. It then chooses to produce Q_L at a price of P_L: at point *l* on its demand curve (where $MC = MR$). Other firms then follow that price. Total market demand will be Q_T, with followers supplying that portion of the market not supplied by the leader, namely $Q_T - Q_L$.

There is one problem with this model: the assumption that the followers will want to maintain a constant market share. If the leader raises its price, the followers may want to supply more, given that the new price (= *MR* for a price-taking follower) may well be above their marginal cost. On the other hand, the followers may decide merely to maintain their market share for fear of retaliation from the leader, in the form of price cuts or an aggressive advertising campaign.

Figure 8.5 Price leader aiming to maximise profits for a given market share

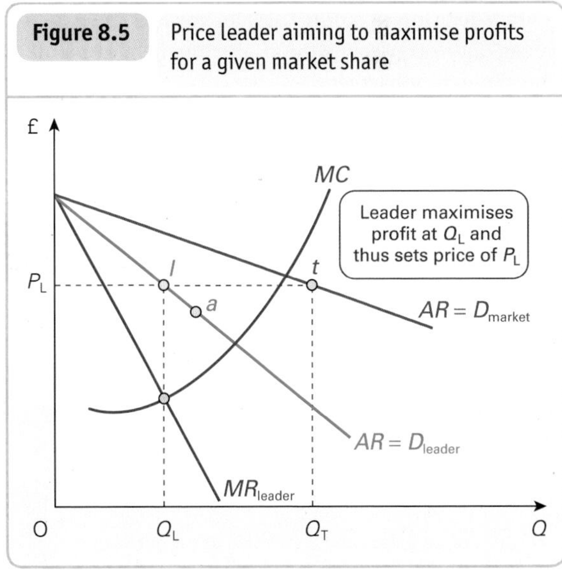

*LOOKING AT THE MATHS

In Figure 8.4, the various curves can be represented by equations and this would allow us to solve for P_L, Q_L, Q_F and Q_T. An example of this is given in Maths Case 8.1 on the student website.

Note that we derived all the curves in Figure 8.4 from just three: the market demand curve, the followers' supply curve and the leader's *MC* curve. It follows that, if we know the functions for these three curves, we can derive the functions for the remainder.

Barometric firm price leadership

A similar exercise can be conducted by a barometric firm. Although such a firm does not dominate the industry, its price will be followed by the others. It merely tries to estimate its demand and *MR* curves – assuming, again, a constant market share – and then produces where $MR = MC$ and sets price accordingly.

In practice, which firm is taken as the barometer may frequently change. Whether we are talking about oil companies, car producers or banks, any firm may take the initiative in raising prices. Then, if the other firms are merely waiting for someone to take the lead – say, because costs have risen – they will all quickly follow suit. For example, if one of the banks raises its mortgage rates by 1 per cent, then this is likely to stimulate the others to follow suit.

Tacit collusion: rules of thumb

An alternative to following an established leader is to follow an established set of simple 'rules of thumb'. These rules do not involve setting *MC* equal to *MR*, and thus may involve an immediate loss of profit. They do, however, help to prevent an outbreak of competition, and thus help to maintain profits into the longer term.

One example of a rule of thumb is ***average cost pricing***. Here, producers simply add a certain percentage for profit on top of average costs. Thus, if average costs rise by 10 per cent, prices will automatically be raised by 10 per cent. This is a particularly useful rule of thumb in times of inflation, when all firms will be experiencing similar cost increases.

If a firm has a typically shaped average cost curve and sets prices 10 per cent above average cost, what will its supply curve look like?

Another rule of thumb is to have certain ***price benchmarks***. Thus clothes may sell for £19.95, £24.95 or £49.95 (but not £18.31 or £36.42). If costs rise, then firms simply raise their price to the next benchmark, knowing that other firms will do the same.

Rules of thumb can also be applied to advertising (e.g. you do not criticise other firms' products, only praise your own); or to the design of the product (e.g. lighting manufacturers tacitly agreeing not to bring out an everlasting light bulb).

Definitions

Average cost pricing Where a firm sets its price by adding a certain percentage for (average) profit on top of average cost.

Price benchmark A price that is typically used. Firms, when raising a price, will usually raise it from one benchmark to another.

BOX 8.3 OPEC — CASE STUDIES AND APPLICATIONS

The history of the world's most famous cartel

OPEC, the Organization of the Petroleum Exporting Countries, is probably the best known of all cartels. It was set up in 1960 by the five major oil-exporting countries: Saudi Arabia, Iran, Iraq, Kuwait and Venezuela. Today it has 13 members, including Nigeria, Angola, Libya and Ecuador. Its stated objectives were as follows:

- The co-ordination and unification of the petroleum policies of member countries.
- The organisation of means to ensure the stabilisation of prices, eliminating harmful and unnecessary fluctuations.

The years leading up to 1960 had seen the oil-producing countries increasingly in conflict with the international oil companies, which extracted oil under 'concessionary agreement'. The oil-producing countries had little say over output and price levels.

The early years

Despite the formation of OPEC in 1960, it was not until 1973 that control of oil production was effectively transferred from the oil companies to the oil countries, with OPEC making the decisions on how much oil to produce and thereby influencing price and oil revenue.

In October 1973, OPEC decided to reduce exports to those countries who provided military support to Israel during the Yom Kippur War. In December 1973, this became a full oil embargo. OPEC had 56 per cent of the oil market at the time so did not have full monopoly power, but the embargo still had a dramatic impact as countries scrambled to get oil supplies from other nations. Eventually the price of oil quadrupled from \$3 to \$12 per barrel.

The second big shock to supply occurred in 1979 with the Iranian Revolution. Protesting oil workers in Iran virtually halted production – a loss of production of around 2.5 million barrels per day. Lower output levels caused prices to rise from around \$15 to \$40 per barrel.

Illustrate what was happening here on a demand and supply diagram. Remember that demand was highly inelastic and was increasing over time.

Despite the impact of the Iran–Iraq war, demand and prices fell after 1980. This was largely due to (a) the recession of the early 1980s and (b) countries switching to coal, natural gas and nuclear power in an attempt to become less reliant on oil.

The use of quotas

Faced by declining demand, OPEC after 1982 agreed to limit output and allocate production quotas in an attempt to maintain prices. However, the cartel was having problems with some of its members exceeding their quota limits, and growing output from non-OPEC members. With a glut of oil,

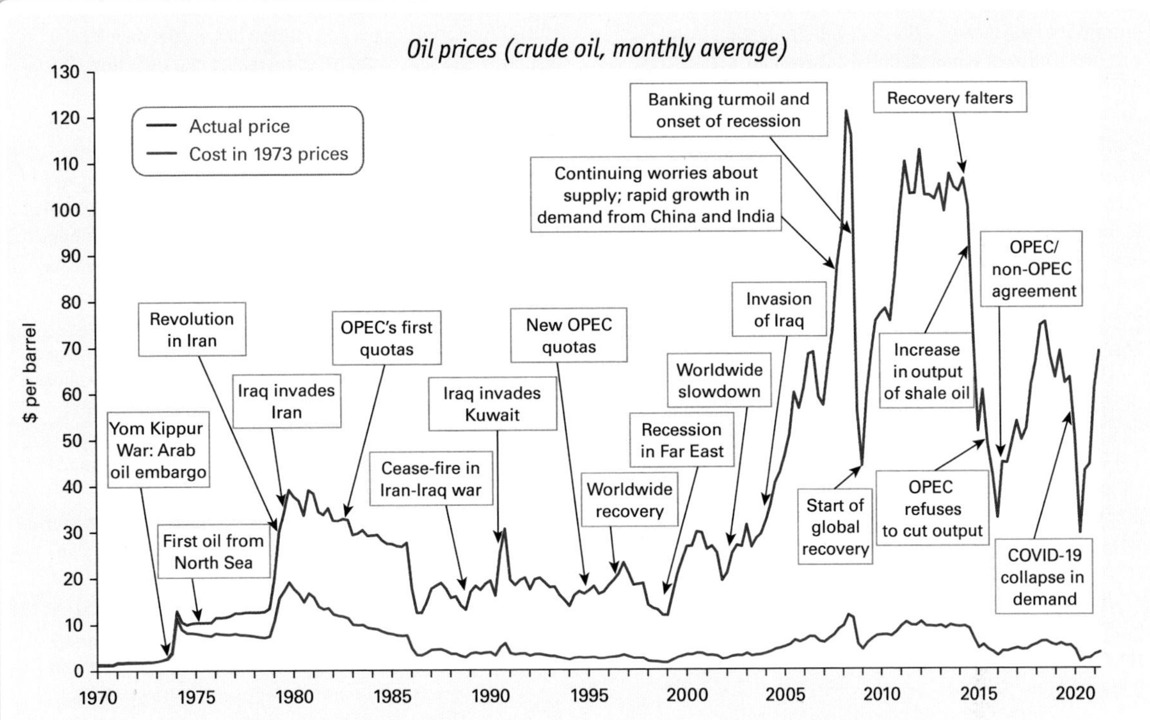

Sources: Nominal oil price data from *World Commodity Price Data (The Pink Sheet)*, *Commodity Markets* (World Bank), www.worldbank.org/en/research/commodity-markets; Price Index from *Data Extracts* (OECD).

OPEC could no longer maintain the price. As the chart shows, the oil price continued to fall.

The trend of lower prices was reversed in the late 1980s with a booming world economy increasing the demand for oil. Then in 1990, Iraq invaded Kuwait and the first Gulf War ensued. With disrupted supplies, the supply of oil fell and there was a sharp rise in its price.

The ending of the war and the recession of the early 1990s led to prices falling rapidly again and they only recovered slowly as the world economy started expanding once more.

On the demand side, the development of energy-saving technology plus increases in fuel taxes led to a relatively slow growth in consumption. On the supply side, the growing proportion of output supplied by non-OPEC members, plus the adoption of a relatively high OPEC production ceiling, meant that supply more than kept pace with demand.

The situation for OPEC deteriorated further in the late 1990s, following the recession in the Far East. By early 1999, the price had fallen to around $10 per barrel – a mere $2.70 in 1973 prices! In response, OPEC members agreed to cut production by 4.3 million barrels per day in an attempt to push the price back up to around $18–20 per barrel.

With the world generally experiencing more rapid economic growth, the price rose rapidly and soon overshot the $20 mark. By early 2000, it had reached $30: a tripling in price in just 12 months. However, a period of slower growth led to prices falling to $18 in November 2001.

In late 2001 five of the major oil producing countries outside the cartel formed an alliance with OPEC and all parties agreed to reduce output in an attempt to push up prices.

The price surge of 2003–8

The Iraq war in 2003 led to supply problems that resulted in prices rising to over $50 per barrel. From 2006, oil prices increased more sharply than ever before, with the real price exceeding the level in the 1970s. The major cause was very substantial increases in demand, particularly from India and China, coupled with continuing concerns about supply. The implications of the sharp price increases were substantial: inflationary pressures built up across the world, while the income of the OPEC nations doubled in the first half of 2008.

. . . and then a fall but rise again

The financial crisis pushed oil prices down dramatically: falling from a high of $147 per barrel in July 2008 to a low of $34 in December of that year. While this was good news for the consumer, it was potentially damaging for investment in both oil exploration/development and alternative energy supplies.

OPEC responded to the falling price by announcing cuts in production between August 2008 and January 2009. But with OPEC producing less than a third of global oil output, this represented less than 5 per cent of global production and thus had little effect on the price.

A new threat to OPEC

Prices rose again as global demand recovered. Between mid-2011 and mid-2014 they remained relatively stable at around $100 to $120 per barrel. However, OPEC was beginning to face increased competition from a big new

(continued)

entrant into the market – US shale oil. Production from this new source of supply doubled between 2011 and 2014, contributing to a fall in the oil price from $112 a barrel in June 2014 to just $30 a barrel in February 2016.

OPEC responded to the fall in prices by announcing that it would retain output at existing levels in an attempt to drive this new competitor out of business in the medium to long term. Shale oil wells have high start-up costs and low marginal costs but supplies only last a few years. OPEC members hoped that the lower oil price would deter people from investing in the high start-up costs of new wells once the existing ones had exhausted their reserves.

However, with revenues from oil falling so dramatically, OPEC and ten non-OPEC producers, including Russia, reached an agreement in December 2016 to cut production. Known as the *OPEC+ Alliance*, the group accounts for approximately 55 per cent of global output. It was the first time oil-producing nations had reached this type of agreement since 2001 and the oil price started to increase as countries adhered to their agreed quotas.

The higher oil prices made more US shale oil producers profitable once again. A number of rigs that had temporarily shut down became operational and production reached record levels of over 9.1 million barrels a day in early 2020. The OPEC + Alliance responded by extending its quota agreements. In December 2019, the group agreed to future production cuts of 2.1 million barrels per day.

The impact of COVID-19

The pandemic had a dramatic impact on the oil market. Lockdowns across the world led to global demand falling by over 30 per cent. To counter the downward pressure on prices, Saudi Arabia wanted the *OPEC+ Alliance* to implement larger and more prolonged cuts in production. However, at a meeting on 6 March 2020 an agreement could not be reached as Russia opposed any cuts as it would help to keep US oil producers in business.

Saudi Arabia responded by initiating a price war. It announced daily increases in output from just under 10 million barrels to over 13 million barrels per day. Russia responded by also announcing increases in production. This joint demand and supply shock had a dramatic impact on prices – they fell from over $50 per barrel on 5 March to under $32 per barrel on 9 March.

After a month-long price war, the *OPEC+ Alliance* agreed to record cuts in production of 9.7 million barrels a day in May and June 2020 – approximately 10 per cent of global supply.

As lockdowns eased, the price gradually recovered to over $40 per barrel. The group responded by agreeing to ease the cuts to 7.7 million barrels per day in August 2020 and 5.8 million per day in January 2021. However, with increases in the spread of the virus and further lockdowns in November/ December 2020, there were disagreements about whether to implement the plans in January 2021. The group finally agreed to ease the cuts to just 7.2 million barrels per day.

Given the increasing uncertainty over the future demand for oil, it will be interesting to see what influence OPEC has on the price of oil in the future.

1. *What conditions facilitate the formation of a cartel? Which of these conditions were to be found in the oil market in (a) the early 1970s; (b) the mid-1980s; (c) the mid-2000s; (d) 2016?*
2. *Could OPEC have done anything to prevent the long-term decline in real oil prices seen from 1981 to 2002?*
3. *Does the increased demand seen from China and India imply that the era of cheap energy is over? What impact could technology have in the long run on (a) demand; (b) supply?*
4. *Investigate and explain the effects of the coronavirus pandemic on the price of oil.*

Download monthly price data on commodity markets from the World Bank (www.worldbank.org/en/research/commodity-markets) for the period since 2020 and create a chart showing the annual rate of oil price inflation. Write a short commentary explaining the price movements.

Factors favouring collusion

Collusion between firms, whether formal or tacit, is more likely when firms can clearly identify with each other or some leader and when they trust each other not to break agreements. It will be easier for firms to collude if the following conditions apply:

- There are only very few firms all well known to each other.
- They are not secretive with each other about costs and production methods.
- They have similar production methods and average costs, and are thus likely to want to change prices at the same time and by the same percentage.
- They produce similar products and can thus more easily reach agreements on price.
- There is a dominant firm.
- There are significant barriers to entry and therefore little fear of disruption by new firms.
- The market is stable. If industry demand or production costs fluctuate wildly, it will be difficult to make agreements, partly due to difficulties in predicting and partly because agreements may frequently have to be amended. There is a particular problem in a declining market where firms may be tempted to undercut each other's prices in order to maintain their sales.
- There are no government measures to curb collusion.

In which of the following industries is collusion likely to occur: bricks, beer, margarine, cement, crisps, washing powder, blank DVDs, carpets?

Non-collusive oligopoly: the breakdown of collusion

In some oligopolies, there may only be a few (if any) factors favouring collusion. In such cases, the likelihood of price competition is greater.

Even if there is collusion, there will always be the temptation for individual oligopolists to 'cheat', by cutting prices or by selling more than their allotted quota.

Let us take the case of a cartel consisting of five equal-sized firms. The whole cartel is illustrated in Figure 8.6(a). Assume that the cartel sets the industry profit-maximising price of £10. This will give an industry output of 1000 units, which the cartel divides equally between its five members: i.e. each member is assigned a quota of 200 units.

Now consider Figure 8.6(b). This shows the position for one of the members of the cartel, firm A. Provided the cartel's price remains fixed at £10, then £10 would also be the marginal revenue for the individual firm. This will create an incentive for cartel members to cheat: to sell more than their allotted quota. Firm A would maximise its own profits by selling 600 units, where $MC = P(= MR)$, provided it could do this by taking market share off the other members, and thus leaving total industry output (and hence price) unaffected.

Alternatively, individual members might be tempted to undercut the cartel's price. Again, provided the rest of the cartel maintained its price at £10, firm A would face a relatively elastic demand curve (shown by *AR* in Figure 8.6(b)). A modest cut in its price would attract considerable custom away from the other members of the cartel. Firm A would maximise its profit by cutting its price to £8 and thereby increasing its sales to 400 units.

The danger, of course, with either selling above quota or cutting price is that this would invite retaliation from the other members of the cartel, with a resulting price war. Price would then fall and the cartel could well break up in disarray.

Non-collusive oligopoly: assumptions about rivals' behaviour

Even though oligopolists might not collude, they will still need to take account of rivals' likely behaviour when deciding their own strategy. In doing so, they will probably look at rivals' past behaviour and make assumptions based on it. There are three well-known models, each based on a different set of assumptions.

The Cournot model: firms choose quantity and the market determines the price

One of the earliest models of oligopoly was developed by the French economist Augustin Cournot in 1838. The simplest version of the ***Cournot model*** has the following assumptions.

- Each firm has to choose an output level for a given period without knowing its rivals' production plans (although, except in the case of new firms, they will know how much their rivals have produced in the past). In other words, firms have to make decisions about production simultaneously.
- Production has long lead times and is relatively inflexible. For example, imagine a business investing in a factory or unit that has a specific production capacity. Once the building work begins and the specialised machinery has been ordered and installed, it is difficult for the firm to alter its planned output.

Definition

Cournot model A model of duopoly where each firm makes its price and output decisions on the assumption that its rival will produce a particular quantity.

Figure 8.6 The incentive for a firm to produce more than its quota, or undercut the cartel's price

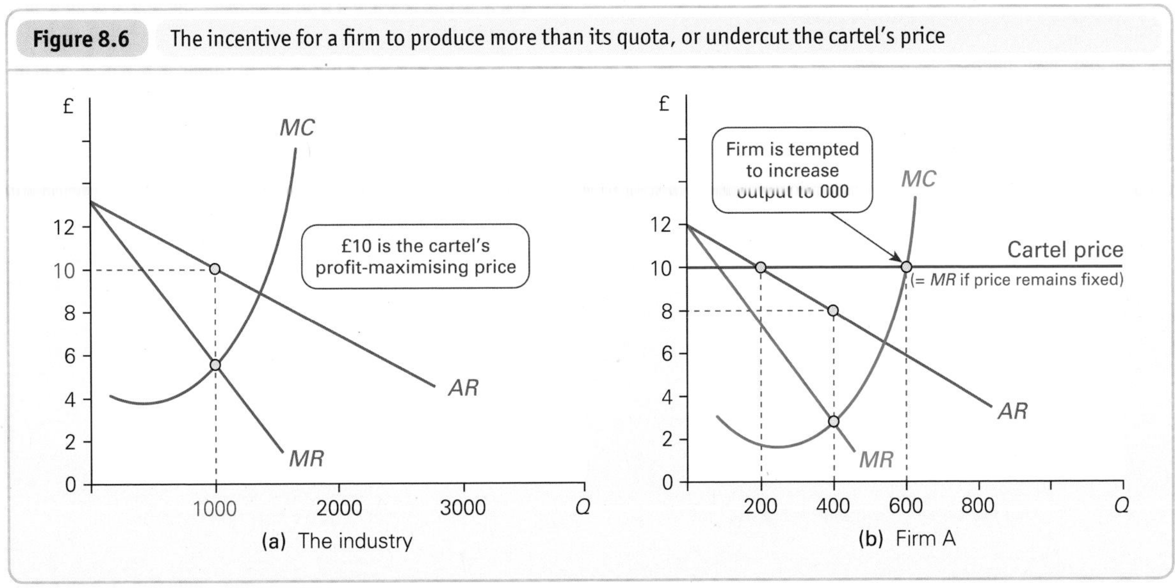

- Whereas output has long lead times, the market price adjusts instantly so that each firm is able to sell all the output it produces.
- The good is homogenous and each firm has the same costs. This means that all the firms in the market sell their output for the same price.

This combination of flexible prices and inflexible output creates an interesting strategic environment. The price the firm receives for its output, in any given period, depends on the production decisions of other firms as well as its own. To calculate its profit-maximising output it has to estimate the most likely output its rivals will produce. The Cournot model assumes that each firm expects its rival(s) to produce the same amount in the current period as it did in the previous period.

To make the analysis as simple as possible we will assume that the industry is a ***duopoly*** and that the two firms, A and B, each have the same costs.

Figure 8.7(a) illustrates the profit-maximising price and output for firm A. The total market demand curve is shown as D_M. Assume that firm B produced Q_{B1} units last year. Firm A, according to the model's assumption, therefore believes that firm B will continue to produce Q_{B1} units this year.

To calculate firm A's profit-maximising output we need to identify its ***residual demand curve***: i.e. the curve showing how much of the total demand is left for firm A, after B has supplied the market with its output. With firm B's output assumed to be Q_{B1}, firm A perceives its own residual demand curve to be D_{A1}. This is the market demand curve, D_M, minus Q_{B1} units: i.e. the horizontal gap between D_M and D_{A1} in Figure 8.7(a).

The marginal revenue curve corresponding to D_{A_1} is MR_{A_1} and the profit-maximising output is Q_{A_1}, where $MR_{A_1} = MC_A$. The market will adjust instantly so that firm A can sell Q_{A_1} units and firm B can sell Q_{B_1} units of this homogenous product for a price of P_1.

If firm A believed that firm B would produce *more* than Q_{B_1}, its residual demand and *MR* curves would be further to the left and the profit-maximising quantity and price would both be lower. This illustrates that the outputs are strategic substitutes – as firm A believes that firm B will produce more, its best response is to produce less. TC 8 p109

One limitation of the analysis so far is that it only illustrates firm A's profit-maximising best response to one predicted level of output: i.e. that firm B will produce Q_{B_1} units. Firm A's ***reaction function***, illustrated by curve R_A in Figure 8.7(b), shows its profit-maximising best responses to *all* the different outputs its rival could produce. It has a negative slope because outputs are strategic substitutes: the more firm B produces, the less will firm A produce. Thus if it perceived that firm B would produce Q_{B_2} units, it would produce Q_{A_2} units (point *y*).

Figure 8.7(b) also illustrates firm B's reaction function, assuming that firm B behaves similarly to firm A and assumes

Definitions

Duopoly An oligopoly where there are just two firms in the market.

Residual demand curve A firm's residual demand curve illustrates the relationship between the output it produces and the market price for the product, holding constant the output produced by other firms.

Reaction function (or curve) This shows how a firm's optimal output varies according to the output chosen by its rival (or rivals).

Figure 8.7 The Cournot model of duopoly

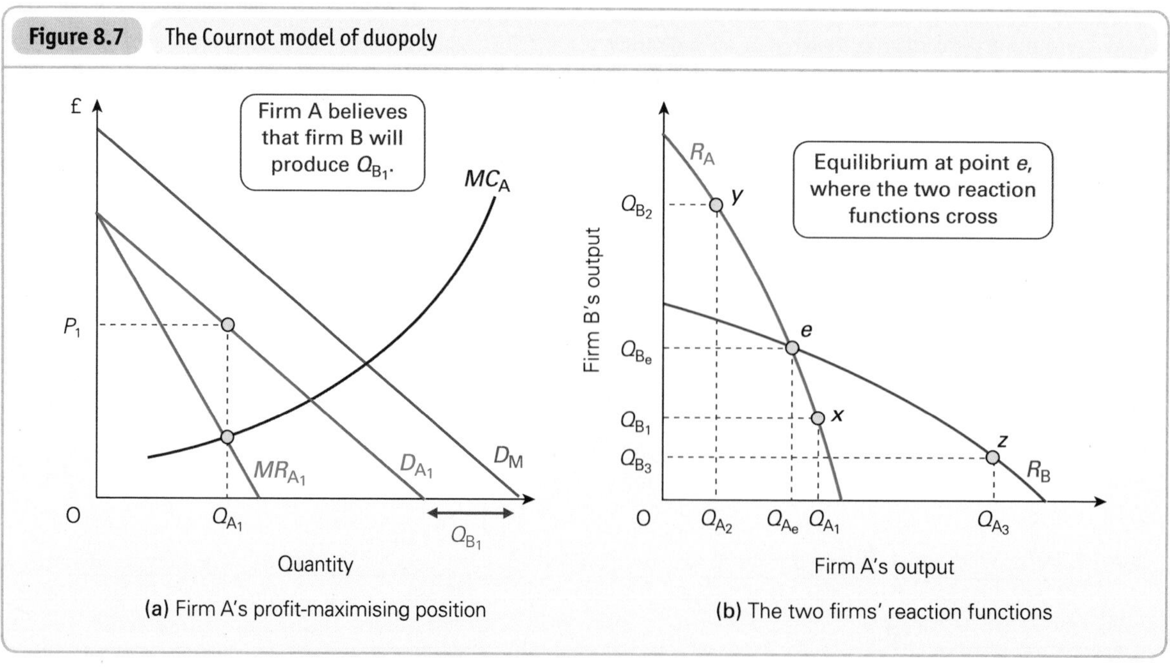

(a) Firm A's profit-maximising position

(b) The two firms' reaction functions

that its rival will produce a particular level of output. Firm B's reaction function is given by the curve R_B. Thus if firm B perceived that A would produce Q_{A_3} units, firm B would produce Q_{B_3} units (point *z*).

What is the ***Cournot equilibrium***? This will occur at point *e* in Figure 8.7(b). Only at this point will neither firm choose to adjust its output once it has discovered the production level of its rival. How is this point reached if neither firm currently produces that level of output?

Assume that production is at point *x*. Firm A predicts that firm B will produce Q_{B_1}. Although firm A is on its reaction curve, firm B is not. If firm B predicts that firm A will produce Q_{A_1} its best move is *not* to produce Q_{B_1}. It will instead produce at a point on its reaction curve vertically above this (i.e. an output *greater* than Q_{B_1}). Firm A will discover that firm B has produced a greater output than it predicted. It will respond by reducing its own production level – it will move up along its reaction curve. This process will continue until point *e* is reached. Only at this point will the levels of production chosen by each firm (in the light of what the other one chooses) add up to the total amount demanded.

Profits in the Cournot model. Industry profits will be *less* than under a monopoly or a cartel. The reason is that price will be lower than the monopoly price. This can be seen from Figure 8.7(a). If this were a monopoly, then to find the profit-maximising output, we would need to construct an *MR* curve corresponding to the market demand curve (D_M). This would intersect with the *MC* curve at a higher output than Q_{A_1} and a *higher* price (given by D_M).

Nevertheless, profits in the Cournot model will be higher than under perfect competition, since price is still above marginal cost. However, as the number of firms in the industry increases the price would move closer to the level in a competitive market and industry profits would fall.

Maths Case 8.2 on the student website shows how the Cournot equilibrium can be derived algebraically from the market demand function and the cost functions of the two firms.

The Bertrand model: firms set prices and the market determines the quantity sold

Another famous model of oligopoly was developed by the French economist Joseph Bertrand in 1883. He criticised the Cournot model as he argued that firms are more likely to set prices and let the market determine the quantity sold. Bertrand again took the simple case of a duopoly where both firms have the same costs of production. However, the conclusions of the model apply equally to oligopolies with three or more firms. It is based on the following assumptions:

- Each firm has to choose its price without knowing the price set by the other firm. It assumes its rival will charge the same price in the current period as it did in the previous period.
- Firms have to set prices in advance and decisions cannot be easily changed: i.e. prices are inflexible.
- The good is homogenous – the only thing that customers care about when they purchase the product is its price.
- Each firm can adjust its output instantly and has no capacity constraints. Therefore, if a firm charges a lower price than its rival it can immediately supply the entire market.

The model predicts that each firm will keep reducing its price until all supernormal profits are competed away. The reason for this result is simple. If firm A assumes that its rival, firm B, will hold price constant, then firm A predicts that by undercutting this price by a small amount it will gain the whole market, which it can instantly supply. By following the same line of reasoning firm B will be forced to respond by cutting its price. The model, therefore, predicts a price war with prices being reduced until they equal average total cost, with only normal profits remaining.

This outcome is very different from the one predicted by the Cournot model. It is referred to as the *Bertrand Paradox* because the result seems counterintuitive: i.e. a duopoly results in an outcome very similar to that of perfect competition. The prediction changes significantly if product differentiation and/or limits in the ability of the firm to supply the entire market (i.e. capacity constraints) are introduced into the model. Firms may also seek to collude long before profits have been reduced to a normal level. Alternatively, firms may put in a ***takeover bid*** for their rival(s).

Nash equilibrium. The equilibrium outcome in either the Cournot or Bertrand models is not in the *joint* interests of the firms. In each case, total profits are less than under a monopoly or cartel. But, in the absence of collusion, the outcome is the result of each firm doing the best it can, given the assumptions it makes about what its rivals are doing. The resulting equilibrium is known as a ***Nash equilibrium***, after John Nash, a US mathematician (and subject of the film *A Beautiful Mind*) who introduced the concept in 1951. This concept will be discussed in more detail in section 8.3.

Definitions

Cournot equilibrium Where each of two firm's actual output is the same as what the other firm predicted it would produce: where the two firms' reaction curves cross.

Takeover bid Where one firm attempts to purchase another by offering to buy the shares of that company from its shareholders.

Nash equilibrium The position resulting from everyone making their optimal decision based on their assumptions about their rivals' decisions. Without collusion, there is no incentive for any firm to move from this position.

Can you think of any reasons why the predictions of the Cournot and Bertrand models of oligopoly are so different?

The kinked demand curve assumption

In 1939, a theory of non-collusive oligopoly was developed simultaneously on both sides of the Atlantic: in the USA by Paul Sweezy and in Britain by R. L. Hall and C. J. Hitch. This ***kinked demand theory*** has since become perhaps the most famous of all theories of oligopoly. The model seeks to explain how it is that, even when there is no collusion at all between oligopolists, prices can nevertheless remain stable.

The theory is based on two asymmetrical assumptions:

- If an oligopolist cuts its price, its rivals will feel forced to follow suit and cut theirs, to prevent losing customers to the first firm.
- If an oligopolist raises its price, however, its rivals will *not* follow suit since, by keeping their prices the same, they will gain customers from the first firm.

The logic that follows from these assumptions is that each oligopolist will face a demand curve that is *kinked* at the current price and output (see Figure 8.8). A rise in price will lead to a large fall in sales as customers switch to the now relatively lower-priced rivals. The firm will thus be reluctant to raise its price. Demand is relatively elastic above the kink. On the other hand, a fall in price will bring only a modest increase in sales, since rivals lower their prices too and therefore customers do not switch. The firm will thus also be reluctant to lower its price. Demand is relatively inelastic below the kink. Therefore oligopolists will be reluctant to change prices at all.

This price stability can be shown formally by drawing in the firm's marginal revenue curve, as in Figure 8.9.

To see how this is done, imagine dividing the diagram into two parts, one on either side of Q_1. At quantities less than Q_1 (the left-hand part of the diagram), the *MR* curve will correspond to the shallow part of the *AR* curve. At quantities greater than Q_1 (the right-hand part), the *MR* curve will correspond to the steep part of the *AR* curve. To see how this part of the *MR* curve is constructed, imagine extending the steep part of the *AR* curve back to the vertical axis. This and the corresponding *MR* curve are shown by the dotted lines in Figure 8.9.

As you can see, there will be a gap between points *a* and *b*. In other words, there is a vertical section of the *MR* curve between these two points.

Profits are maximised where $MC = MR$. Thus, if the *MC* curve lies anywhere between MC_1 and MC_2 (i.e. between points *a* and *b*), the profit-maximising price and output will be P_1 and Q_1. Thus prices will remain stable *even with a considerable change in costs.*

Despite its simple demonstration of the real-world phenomenon of price stability, the model does have two major limitations:

- Price stability may be due to *other* factors. Firms may not want to change prices too frequently as this involves modifying price lists, working out new revenue predictions and revaluing stocks of finished goods, and it may upset customers. Price stability, therefore, is not proof of the accuracy of the model.
- Although the model can help to explain price stability, it does not explain how prices are set in the first place. To do this, some other model would be required. This is a

Definition

Kinked demand theory The theory that oligopolists face a demand curve that is kinked at the current price, demand being significantly more elastic above the current price than below. The effect of this is to create a situation of price stability.

Figure 8.8 Kinked demand for a firm under oligopoly

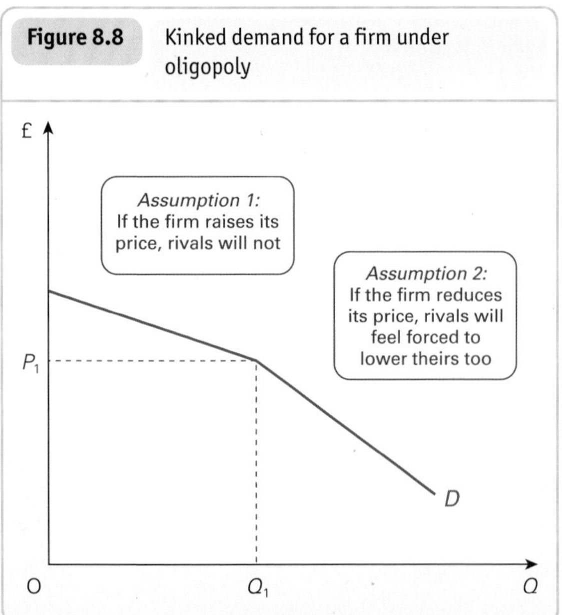

Figure 8.9 Stable price under conditions of a kinked demand curve

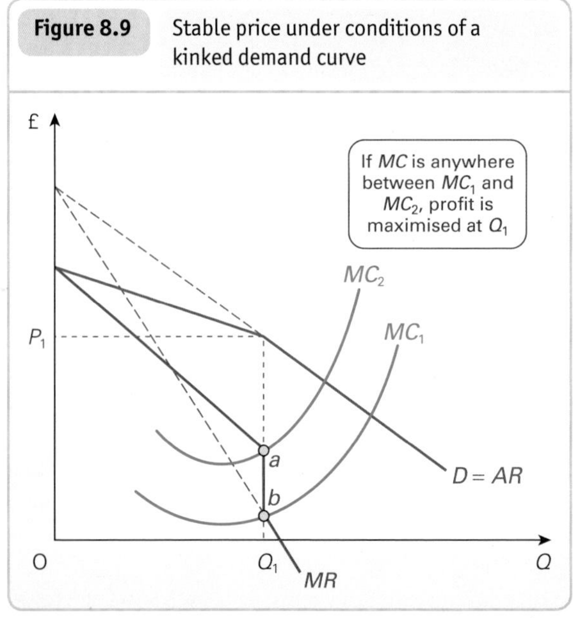

serious limitation in times of inflation, when oligopolists, like other firms, raise prices in response to higher costs and higher demand. What the model does predict, however, is that the price will be raised only after marginal cost has risen above MC_2 in Figure 8.9, and that once it has been raised, a new kink will form at that price. Price will then remain fixed at that level until higher costs once more force a further price rise.

Oligopoly and the public interest

KI 22 p195

If oligopolists act collusively and jointly maximise industry profits, they will in effect be acting together as a monopoly. In such cases, the disadvantages to society experienced under monopoly will also be experienced under oligopoly (see section 7.3).

TC 3 p26

Furthermore, in two respects, oligopoly may be more disadvantageous than monopoly:

- Depending on the size of the individual oligopolists, there may be less scope for economies of scale to mitigate the effects of market power.
- Oligopolists are likely to engage in much more extensive advertising than a monopolist (see Case Study 8.10 on the student website).

These problems will be less, however, if oligopolists do not collude, if there is some degree of price competition and if barriers to entry are weak.

Also, the power of oligopolists in certain markets may to some extent be offset if they sell their product to other powerful firms. Thus oligopolistic producers of baked beans sell a large proportion of their output to giant supermarket chains, which can use their market power to keep down the price at which they purchase the beans. This phenomenon is known as ***countervailing power***.

Which of the following are examples of effective countervailing power?

(a) Tour operators purchasing seats on charter flights.
(b) A large office hiring a photocopier from Xerox®.
(c) Marks & Spencer buying clothes from a garment manufacturer.
(d) A small village store (but the only one for miles around) buying food from a wholesaler.

Definition

Countervailing power Where the power of a monopolistic/oligopolistic seller is offset by powerful buyers who can prevent the price from being pushed up.

BOX 8.4 BUYING POWER CASE STUDIES AND APPLICATIONS

The UK grocery sector

Concerns about the business conduct of large supermarket chains in the UK have led to a number of investigations by the competition authorities. One of the largest took place from 2006 to 2008 and focused on concerns about possible anti-competitive practices, such as price collusion and rival chains agreeing not to build stores in the same town. (For more on government competition policy, see Chapter 14, pages 429–39).

The final report[1] concluded that there was intense competition in product markets at the national level but some measures were needed to improve competition at the local level. In 2015, the consumer group *Which* raised concerns about pricing and promotional practices. The resulting investigation by the authorities did not find a systematic problem in the grocery market but did identify some areas of concern.[2] The proposed merger of Sainsbury's and Asda was also blocked in 2019[3] because of fears it would lead to a substantial weakening of competition in the sector.

What the 2008 report did uncover was far more evidence of supermarkets abusing their excessive market power as *buyers*. If a small supplier, such as a craft distiller of gin, wants to reach a wider customer base, it will need to deal with the eight largest supermarket chains. In August 2021, these eight businesses controlled over 92 per cent of the market. A market where there are a few large purchasers of goods and services is known as an ***oligopsony***. (A single large buyer of goods, services or factors of production is known as a *monopsony* and we look at this in Chapter 10, pages 293–4.)

Abusing market power?

The competition authorities found evidence of supermarkets engaging in a number of unfair practices with their suppliers. This included retrospectively changing contracts, delaying payments and demanding payments towards the promotional costs of a product.

In response to these findings, a stronger Grocery Supplies Code of Practice (GSCP) was introduced in 2009. This code regulates a number of aspects of any supply agreement that a firm enters into with a *designated retailer*. Originally, there were ten designated retailers (Asda Stores Limited, Co-operative Group Limited, Marks & Spencer PLC, Wm Morrison Supermarkets PLC, J Sainsbury PLC, Tesco PLC, Waitrose Limited, Aldi Stores Limited, Iceland Foods Limited, and Lidl UK GmbH). In November 2018, Ocado and B&M Homestores were added to the list as their annual turnover exceeded £1 billion. TJ Morris (Home Bargains) became the thirteenth designated retailer in September 2019.

In January 2013, the government appointed a 'Groceries Code Adjudicator' (GCA) to make sure the designated retailers

Definition

Oligopsony A goods market with just a few buyers (or employers in the case of labour markets).

(continued)

were complying with the GSCP. Since January 2015, the regulator has had the power to fine retailers up to 1 per cent of their UK turnover.

In 2020, the GCA's annual survey[4] found that 36 per cent of suppliers had experienced code-related issues with a retailer in the previous 12 months. This was down from 79 per cent in 2014. The most important code-related issues identified by suppliers in the survey were:

- lack of compensation for extra costs incurred because of inaccurate demand/order forecasts by retailers for their product (13 per cent)
- de-listing (retailer no longer stocking the supplier's product) without reasonable notice (12 per cent)
- delay in payments (later than the terms agreed with the retailer) (12 per cent)
- demands to finance promotional costs that vary from those agreed (10 per cent).

In a high profile case, the GCA concluded in March 2019 that the Co-operative Group had breached the code in two ways. The retailer had (a) failed to provide reasonable notice to suppliers when it was de-listing products and (b) varied supply agreements unilaterally and without reasonable notice. It was ordered to pay a fine of £1.3 million.[5]

Who benefits?

Overall, the evidence suggests that intense price competition in product markets holds down the cost of food bills in the UK. The supermarkets also stock a variety of goods and offer very convenient shopping for many people. Regulation by the GCA appears to have reduced the abuse of market power with suppliers. However, survey evidence suggests that the buying power of the supermarkets needs to be continually monitored. Perhaps the biggest shock to the sector moving forward will be the growth in online shopping.

1. *Explain why manufacturers of food products continue to supply supermarkets, despite concerns that they are not always treated fairly.*
2. *Is the supermarket sector an oligopoly or monopolistically competitive, in your opinion? Justify your answer.*

Search the CMA, GCA and newspaper websites to find recent cases of potential abuse by supermarkets of their buying power. Summarise and discuss your findings.

1 'Groceries market investigation – final report', *press release*, CMA (30 April 2008), https://assets.publishing.service.gov.uk/media/55194b9c40f0b61404000330/14-08.pdf
2 'Groceries promotions to be clearer for shoppers', *press release*, CMA (27 April 2016), www.gov.uk/government/news/groceries-promotions-to-be-clearer-for-shoppers
3 'CMA blocks merger between Sainsbury's and Asda', *press release*, CMA (25 April 2019), www.gov.uk/government/news/cma-blocks-merger-between-sainsburys-and-asda
4 *GCA annual survey 2020*, Groceries Code Adjudicator, https://assets.publishing.service.gov.uk/government/uploads/system/uploads/attachment_data/file/886761/GCA_YouGov_2020_Presentation.pdf
5 'Co-op breached code finds Groceries Code Adjudicator', *press release*, GCA (25 March 2019), www.gov.uk/government/news/co-op-breached-code-finds-groceries-code-adjudicator

The power of oligopolists will also be reduced if the market in which they operate is contestable (see section 7.4). The lower the entry and exit costs for new firms, the more difficult it will be for oligopolists to collude and make supernormal profits.

Which of the following markets do you think are contestable: (a) credit cards; (b) brewing; (c) petrol retailing; (d) insurance services; (e) compact discs?

In some respects, oligopoly may have *advantages* to society over other market structures:

- Oligopolists, like monopolists, can use part of their supernormal profit for research and development. Unlike monopolists, however, oligopolists will have a considerable *incentive* to do so. If the product design is improved, this may allow the firm to capture a larger share of the market, and it may be some time before rivals can respond with a similarly improved product. If, in addition, costs are lowered by technological improvement, the resulting higher profits will improve the firm's capacity to withstand any price war.
- Non-price competition through product differentiation may result in greater choice for the consumer. Take the case of stereo equipment. Non-price competition has led to a huge range of different products of many different specifications, each meeting the specific requirements of different consumers.

It is difficult, however, to draw any general conclusions, since oligopolies differ so much in their performance.

Section summary

1. An oligopoly is where there are just a few firms in the industry with barriers to the entry of new firms. Firms recognise their mutual dependence.
2. Oligopolists will want to maximise their joint profits. This will tend to make them collude to keep prices high. On the other hand, they will want the biggest share of industry profits for themselves. This will tend to make them compete.
3. They are more likely to collude if there are few of them; if they are open with each other; if they have similar products

and cost structures; if there is a dominant firm; if there are significant entry barriers; if the market is stable; and if there is no government legislation to prevent collusion.

4. Collusion can be open or tacit.
5. A formal collusive agreement is called a 'cartel'. A cartel aims to act as a monopoly. It can set price and leave the members to compete for market share, or it can assign quotas. There is always a temptation for cartel members to 'cheat' by undercutting the cartel price if they think they can get away with it and not trigger a price war.
6. Tacit collusion can take the form of price leadership. This is where firms follow the price set by either a dominant firm in the industry or a firm seen as a reliable 'barometer' of market conditions. Alternatively, tacit collusion can simply involve following various rules of thumb, such as average cost pricing and benchmark pricing.
7. Even when firms do not collude, they will still have to take into account their rivals' behaviour. In the Cournot model, firms assume that their rivals' output is given and then choose the profit-maximising price and output in the light of this assumption. The resulting price and profit are lower than under monopoly, but still higher than under perfect competition.
8. In the Bertrand model, firms assume that their rivals' price is given. This will result in prices being competed down until only normal profits remain.
9. In the kinked demand curve model, firms are likely to keep their prices stable unless there is a large shift in costs or demand.
10. Whether oligopoly behaviour is in the public interest depends on the particular oligopoly and how competitive it is; whether there is any countervailing power; whether the firms engage in extensive advertising and of what type; whether product differentiation results in a wide range of choice for the consumer; how much of the profits are ploughed back into research and development; and how contestable the market is. Since these conditions vary substantially from oligopoly to oligopoly, it is impossible to state just how well or how badly oligopoly in general serves the public interest.

8.3 GAME THEORY

When firms operate in a competitive environment and recognise their interdependence, what is the most probable outcome? If each firm aims to maximise its profits it needs to think strategically: it needs to work out its optimal response to the actual or most likely actions of its rivals.

At first sight, this might seem like an almost impossible task given the complexity of the reasoning involved. However, economists have developed ***game theory*** as a useful framework and set of tools for thinking about these situations. By helping to identify the best strategy that each firm can adopt for each assumption about its rivals' behaviour, game theory can help economists to predict the most likely outcome in markets with strategic interdependence.

This section will show how game theory can provide useful insights into firms' behaviour in oligopolistic markets. It is important to remember that it can also be applied to a broad range of issues, including the negotiations over the UK's exit from the European Union. For some types of games, however, game theory offers few insights. For example, where the outcomes are determined purely by chance: e.g. lotteries, bingo, etc.; or where there is only one player: e.g. solitaire. Nevertheless, there are many economic situations where game theory can provide considerable insights.

Simultaneous single-move games

As we have seen, the firm's profit-maximising strategy in a competitive oligopoly market depends, in part, on how it thinks its rivals will react to its decisions on prices, output, product development, advertising, etc. If this competition is a one-off event (such as firms competing for a specific contract) then it can be modelled as a ***simultaneous single-move game***. This type of game is also called a single-period or one-shot game.

A 'complete-information' simultaneous single-move game has the following characteristics. Each firm:

- is aware of all the choices available to its rival: i.e. all the decisions it could possibly make about pricing, output, advertising, product development, etc.
- is able to calculate the impact of each of these potential decisions on its own profits;
- makes its own decision without knowing the choice of its rival.

These assumptions are very similar to those found in the Bertrand and Cournot models of oligopoly discussed in section 8.2. Economists have actually reinterpreted both of these models as examples of simultaneous single-move games.

Definitions

Game theory A mathematical method of decision making in which alternative strategies are analysed to determine the optimal course of action for the interested party, depending on assumptions about rivals' behaviour. Widely used in economics, game theory is also used as a tool in biology, psychology and politics.

Simultaneous single-move game A game where each player has just one move, where each player plays at the same time and acts without knowledge of the actions chosen by other players.

Another example is the Rock–Paper–Scissors game. Each player knows the three choices available to both participants and has to decide without knowing the choice made by the other player. A sealed bid auction is another example, where each bidder submits a price without knowing any of the bids submitted by their competitors.

This type of environment poses a significant challenge for a firm. As a first step it can work out the impact of each of its rivals' actions on its own profit. However, to determine its best response it would usually need to know which of these actions its rival has actually taken. In a simultaneous single-move game it does not have this information. How can a firm work out its best response to a rival's decision that it cannot observe?

TC 9 p132

Simultaneous single-move games with dominant strategies

In some strategic environments the firm does not have to worry about trying to work out the most likely actions of its rivals. Its best response remains the same, no matter what assumptions it makes about its rivals' behaviour. In the terminology of game theory, the firm has a ***dominant strategy***.

One of the best ways of illustrating this idea is to represent the strategic environment facing the firms as a ***normal-form game***. A normal (or strategic) representation of a game is presented as a matrix. This matrix illustrates the pay-offs (e.g. profits) from each of the different available decisions. A simple example of a pay-off is shown in Table 8.1.

This example illustrates the various profits two firms (X and Y) could earn from charging two different prices – £2 and £1.80. To keep the example simple, we assume the firms have identical costs, products and demand and can only choose one or other of the two prices.

Let us initially consider firm Y's position. Should it set its price at £2 or £1.80? Which decision would make it the most profit? To answer this question we need to look at the impact of firm X's different pricing decisions on the profits of firm Y and work out its best response. If firm Y assumes that firm X chooses a price of £2, it needs to focus on the left-hand column of the pay-off matrix. Firm Y's best response is clearly to charge £1.80, earning it £12 million in profits, as illustrated in cell C. If firm Y sets its price at £2, it makes a lower profit of £10 million, as illustrated in cell A.

What happens if firm Y now assumes that firm X chooses a price of £1.80? All the relevant information is now in the right-hand column of the pay-off matrix. Firm Y's best response once again is to charge £1.80, earning it profits of £8 million, as illustrated in cell D. If firm Y sets its price at £2, it makes a lower profit of £5 million, as illustrated in cell B.

Therefore, no matter which of the two prices firm Y assumes that firm X will charge, firm Y's best response is always to charge £1.80 as this will yield the highest possible profits. Charging £1.80 is a dominant strategy for firm Y.

If we now look at the game from firm X's viewpoint, we get exactly the same result. No matter what price firm X assumes that firm Y will charge, its best response is always to charge £1.80. Therefore charging £1.80 is also a dominant strategy for firm X.

Because both firms have a dominant strategy, the outcome of the game is easy to predict. Both firms charge £1.80 and earn £8 million in profit, as illustrated in cell D. This is the dominant strategy equilibrium of the game.

This game is an example of the ***prisoners' dilemma***. The original scenario with two prisoners is discussed in more detail in Box 8.5. What exactly is the dilemma in the game above? By pursuing a strategy to maximise its own individual profit, each firm makes less money than it could have if it had acted collectively. If they both co-operated with one another (i.e. colluded) and agreed to charge the higher price of £2 they would each have made a profit of £10 million (cell A) instead of £8 million (cell D). The game clearly illustrates the incentive each firm has to cheat on a collusive arrangement in the absence of any binding agreements.

Is the incentive structure in the single-move prisoners' dilemma game in the interests of society?

More complex simultaneous single-move games

In many instances, one or both firms will not have a dominant strategy. In these cases, a firm's best response will vary depending on what it thinks its rival will do. Take the example shown in Table 8.2. This is very similar to the example in Table 8.1, but has a different profit structure.

Let us once again consider firm Y's position. If firm Y assumes that firm X chooses a price of £2, its best response is

Table 8.1 Profits for firms X and Y at different prices

		X's price	
		£2.00	£1.80
Y's price	£2.00	A £10m, £10m	B £5m, £12m
	£1.80	C £12m, £5m	D £8m, £8m

Definitions

Dominant-strategy game Where the firm's optimal strategy remains the same, irrespective of what it assumes its rivals are going to do.

Normal-form game Where the possible pay-offs from different strategies or decisions are presented as a matrix.

Prisoners' dilemma Where two or more firms (or people), by attempting independently to choose the best strategy, think about what their rivals are likely to do, but end up in a worse position than if they had co-operated in the first place.

to charge £1.80, earning £20 million in profits as shown in cell C. However, if it assumes that firm X chooses a price of £1.80, its best response is to charge £2, earning £15 million in profits as shown in cell B. Hence, its best response changes depending on what price it thinks firm X will charge.

Accurately predicting firm X's decision is important for firm Y if it wants to maximise its profits. If its belief turns out to be wrong, it will make less profit. What is the most effective way of anticipating what your rival will do? The answer is for firm Y to try to examine the decision from the perspective of firm X. Can it successfully put itself in its rival's shoes and analyse the competition from their viewpoint?

Table 8.2 A more complicated game

		X's price	
		£2.00	**£1.80**
Y's price	**£2.00**	**A** £18m, £5m	**B** £15m, £6m
	£1.80	**C** £20m, £3m	**D** £12m, £4m

BOX 8.5 THE PRISONERS' DILEMMA

EXPLORING ECONOMICS

Game theory is not just relevant to economics. A famous non-economic example is the prisoners' dilemma.

Nigel and Amanda have been arrested for a joint crime of serious fraud. Each is interviewed separately and given the following alternatives:

- First, if they say nothing, the court has enough evidence to sentence both to a year's imprisonment.
- Second, if either Nigel or Amanda *alone* confesses, he or she is likely to get only a three-month sentence but the partner could get up to ten years.
- Third, if both confess, they are likely to get three years each.

What should Nigel and Amanda do?

		Amanda's alternatives	
		Not confess	Confess
Nigel's alternatives	Not confess	**A** Each gets 1 year	**C** Nigel gets 10 years; Amanda gets 3 months
	Confess	**B** Nigel gets 3 months; Amanda gets 10 years	**D** Each gets 3 years

Let us consider Nigel's dilemma. Should he confess in order to get the short sentence? This is better than the year he would get for not confessing. There is, however, an even better reason for confessing. Suppose Nigel doesn't confess but, unknown to him, Amanda does confess. Then Nigel ends up with the long sentence. Better than this is to confess and to get no more than three years. Nigel's best response is always to confess.

Amanda is in exactly the same dilemma, so the result is simple. When both prisoners act in their own self-interest by confessing, they both end up with relatively long prison terms. Only when they collude will they end up with relatively short prison terms, the best combined solution.

Of course, the police know this and will do their best to prevent any collusion. They will keep Nigel and Amanda in separate prison cells and try to persuade each of them that the other is bound to confess.

Thus the choice of strategy depends on:

- Nigel's and Amanda's risk attitudes: i.e. are they 'risk lovers' or 'risk averse'?
- Nigel's and Amanda's estimates of how likely the other is to own up.

1. *Why is this a dominant-strategy 'game'?*
2. *How would Nigel's choice of strategy be affected if he had instead been involved in a joint crime with Rikki, Kate, Amrita and Dave, and they had all been caught?*

The prisoners' dilemma is a good illustration of *the fallacy of composition* that we examined in Box 3.5 (see page 96). What applies at the level of the individual does not apply to the group as a whole. It might be in the individual's interests to confess. It is clearly not in the interests of both, however, for both to confess.

Let us now look at two real-world examples of the prisoners' dilemma.

Standing at football

When people go to some public event, such as a football match, they often stand in order to get a better view. But once people start standing, everyone is likely to do so: after all, if they stayed sitting, they would not see at all. If everyone stands, no one has an incentive to sit down, since they would then see nothing. In this Nash equilibrium, most people are worse off, since, except for tall people, their view is likely to be worse and they lose the comfort of sitting down.

Too much advertising

Why do firms spend so much on advertising? If they are aggressive, they do so to get ahead of their rivals. If they are cautious, they do so in case their rivals increase their advertising. Although in both cases it may be in the individual firm's best interests to increase advertising, the resulting Nash equilibrium is likely to be one of excessive advertising: the total spent on advertising (by all firms) is not recouped in additional sales.

Can collusion by firms overcome the prisoners' dilemma?

Give some other non-economic examples of the prisoners' dilemma. Are there any solutions for the people caught in the dilemma?

If firm Y looks at the pricing decision from firm X's point of view it will see that firm X actually has a dominant strategy. If firm Y charges £2 it can see that firm X's best response is to charge £1.80 (making a profit of £6 million rather than £5 million). If firm Y charges £1.80, firm X's best response is also to charge £1.80 (making a profit of £4 million rather than £3 million). Therefore, firm Y can predict with a high level of certainty that firm X will charge £1.80 – its dominant strategy. Firm Y's best response, therefore, is to charge £2.00 and make a profit of £15 million rather than £12 million. This combination of prices in cell B is the equilibrium in the game.

Some games can be much more complicated than the one shown in Table 8.2. For example, neither firm could have a dominant strategy; there could be more than two firms and more than two choices. How can we predict the most likely outcome in these circumstances? At what point will every firm have no incentive to change its strategy?

Nash equilibrium and expected behaviour

In section 8.2 (page 237), we looked at the concept of the Nash equilibrium. This is the position that results from everyone making their optimal decision based on their assumptions about their rivals' decisions. The dominant strategy equilibrium in the prisoners' dilemma and the equilibrium in Table 8.2 are both examples of a Nash equilibrium. In each case, neither firm has an incentive to change its decision as it is choosing its best price in response to the price chosen by its rival.

In fact, all dominant strategy equilibria (i.e. where both firms have a dominant strategy) are examples of Nash equilibria. Identifying any dominant strategies, if they exist, makes it easier to find the Nash equilibrium.

In many games, there is more than one Nash equilibrium. In these cases, it is more difficult to predict the most likely outcome.

If a firm's actual behaviour was *different* from its expected behaviour, then the decisions of its rivals do not represent a Nash equilibrium. In these circumstances, what the firm perceives to be its best response, based on the expected behaviour of its rival, proves not to be the case when the actual behaviour of the other firm is observed. The firm will have an incentive to change its behaviour.

Repeated simultaneous-move games

The previous analysis of simultaneous single-move games gives some useful insights but instances of one-off interactions are relatively unusual. In most real-world settings, firms in oligopolistic markets compete against one another on a repeated basis. Decisions about pricing, advertising, product development, etc., are made continually over the months and years that firms are in business. For example, Apple and Samsung launch new versions of their smartphone handsets on an annual basis. Do the predicted outcomes of single-move games remain the same when the game is repeated?

We previously examined a single-move prisoners' dilemma game in which the most likely outcome was for both firms to charge the lower price of £1.80 (see Table 8.1 on page 242). There was a strong incentive for both firms to cheat on any collusive agreement to fix prices at £2.00. Does repeated interaction between the same firms change the predicted outcome of the game? For example, if firms X and Y make the same simultaneous pricing decisions repeatedly, could their optimal strategy change so that they both start charging £2.00?

The big difference between a single-move game and a repeated game is that each firm can now see what its rivals did in previous periods. This creates the possibility that whatever firms choose to do in one period might have an impact on the behaviour of their rivals, and hence their own profits, in later periods. In particular, decisions that generate higher profits today could lead to lower profits in the future. The potential impact of this trade-off can be illustrated by using the prisoners' dilemma example in Table 8.1.

Assume that firm X and Y have an agreement to charge £2.00 (or simply follow each other's lead in doing so). Each firm will thus continue charging £2 as long as the other firm does too. If, however, firm Y ever cut its price to £1.80 in one period, then firm X would do the same in all future periods. Once this has happened, no matter what firm Y then does, firm X is unlikely to charge a price of £2 ever again. In game theory, this new strategy employed by firm Y is known as the ***trigger strategy***.

The profit profile for firm Y of following two different pricing strategies is illustrated in Figure 8.10. By following the same dominant strategy as in the single-move game and charging a price of £1.80 (i.e. breaking the agreement), firm Y can increase its profit in the first period from £10 million

Definition

Trigger strategy Once a firm observes that its rival has broken some agreed behaviour it will never co-operate with them ever again.

Figure 8.10 Profits for firm Y in a repeated game

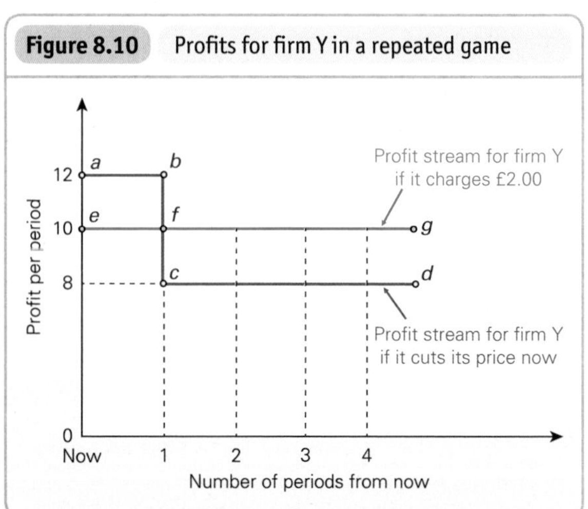

to £12 million. The downside of this strategy is that its profits in all future periods will fall to £8 million as firm X responds by also charging £1.80. This is illustrated by the profit profile of $a \rightarrow b \rightarrow c \rightarrow d$ in Figure 8.10.

Alternatively, firm Y could stick to the agreement and charge £2.00 in the first period. Its profit of £10 million is £2 million lower than it would have earned by charging £1.80. However, as long as it maintains its price at this level, firm X will also charge £2.00. Firm Y's profits in all future period will thus be £10 million as opposed to £8 million. This is shown by the profit profile $e \rightarrow f \rightarrow g$.

After a while, both Y and X will realise that the Nash equilibrium (£1.80) is not to the advantage of either. This may persuade them to set up a stronger collusive agreement to restore prices to £2. This outcome is most likely to occur when:

- firms value future profits quite highly;
- firms compete against each other very frequently – there are more future time periods to benefit from the higher profits of charging £2 and area *fgdc* is larger;
- the higher profits from charging £1.80 in the first period are relatively small. This reduces the size of area *abfe*;
- a firm can quickly observe that its rival is charging the lower price. This reduces the length of time over which a firm will benefit from the higher profits of charging £1.80, again reducing the size of area *abfe*;
- both firms adopt the trigger strategy, putting them in a similar position.

Backwards induction and movement to the Nash equilibrium. Another issue is whether both firms know just how long the current product designs and costs will last – in other words, when the current round of repeated price settings will end. If they do, then the chances of the firm co-operating and charging higher prices is much lower. The most likely outcome is the same as for a single-move game, with the dominant strategy being to cut price.

To understand why this is the case both firms need to think about the most likely outcome in the last period of competition (i.e. the last time prices are set before any changes in product design, costs, etc.) and then work backwards to think about the most likely outcome in earlier periods. This is called ***backwards induction***.

The incentive for each firm to charge £2 in any period is to influence the behaviour of its rivals in future periods. However, in the last period of competition there is no future to affect, as the firms will never compete against one another again with the same product. Therefore, the last period is effectively the same as a simultaneous single-move game and both firms are highly likely to follow their dominant strategies of charging £1.80.

If both firms realise in the last-but-one period of competition that they cannot influence what their rival will do in the last period of competition then their best strategy is also to charge £1.80. If they keep following the same line of reasoning, they will both charge £1.80 in every period of competition.

Therefore, the chances of the firms charging a higher price is much greater when they both believe that competition between them will carry on indefinitely: i.e. neither of them knows the precise date when the current type of interaction between them will come to an end.

Another type of strategy firms can follow in a repeated game is the 'tit-for-tat' strategy. What is the 'tit-for-tat' strategy? What impact will it have on the most likely outcome in a repeated game?

Sequential-move games

So far, we have looked at simultaneous games: where firms take decisions at the same time without seeing the decision of the other firm(s). However, in many real-world competitive environments, one firm (the first mover) makes and implements a decision (i.e. it produces a certain output, sets a particular price or introduces a new product) *before* its rivals (the second movers). The second movers are then able to observe the actions of the first mover before deciding on their best response. These strategic environments can be studied by using ***sequential-move games***.

Take the case of a new generation of large passenger aircraft that can fly further without refuelling. Assume that there is a market for a 500-seater version of this type of aircraft and a 400-seater version, but that the market for each size of aircraft is not big enough for the two manufacturers, Boeing and Airbus, to share it profitably. Let us also assume that the 400-seater market would give an annual profit of £50 million to a single manufacturer and the 500-seater would give an annual profit of £30 million, but that if both manufacturers produced the same version, they would each make an annual loss of £10 million.

Assume that Boeing is the first mover and announces which plane it will build: the 400-seater or the 500-seater. Airbus then has to respond to the decision and decide which plane it will build.

This scenario can be illustrated as a sequential-move game and is shown in Figure 8.11. Sequential-move games are typically illustrated in 'extensive form' by use of a ***decision tree***,

Definitions

Backwards induction A process by which firms think through the most likely outcome in the last period of competition and then work backwards step by step thinking through the most likely outcomes in earlier periods of competition.

Sequential-move game One firm (the first mover) makes and implements a decision. Rival firms (second movers) can observe the actions taken by the first mover before making their own decisions.

Decision tree (or game tree) A diagram showing the sequence of possible decisions by competitor firms and the outcome of each combination of decisions.

Figure 8.11 A decision tree

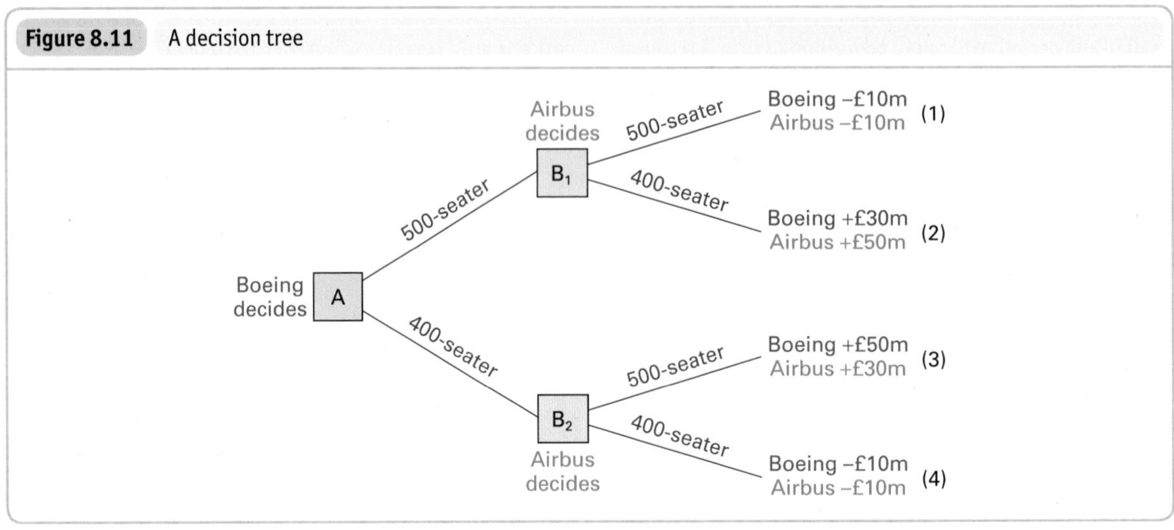

which identifies the possible sequence of events. The small square on the left of the decision tree shown in Figure 8.11 is Boeing's decision point (point A). If it decides to build the 500-seater plane, we move up the top branch. Airbus would now have to make a decision (point B_1). If it too decides to build the 500-seater plane, we would move to outcome 1: a loss of £10 million for both manufacturers.

Clearly, with Boeing building a 500-seater plane, the best response for Airbus would be to choose the 400-seater plane: we would move to outcome 2, with Boeing making a profit of £30 million and Airbus a profit of £50 million. Airbus would be very pleased!

Boeing's best strategy at point A, however, would be to build the 400-seater plane. We would then move to Airbus's decision point B_2. In this case, Airbus's best response is to build the 500-seater plane. Its profit would be only £30 million (outcome 3), but this is better than a £10 million loss if it too built the 400-seater plane (outcome 4). With Boeing deciding first, the Nash equilibrium will thus be outcome 3.

There is clearly a ***first-mover advantage*** here. Once Boeing has decided to build the more profitable version of the plane, the best response for Airbus is to build the less profitable one. Naturally, Airbus would like to build the more profitable one and be the first mover. Which company succeeds in going first depends on how advanced they are in their research and development and in their production capacity.

The importance of threats and promises

In a sequential-move game, a second mover could threaten or promise to behave in a certain way in an attempt to influence the behaviour of the first mover. For example, in the above game Airbus could announce that it was going to build a 400-seater plane irrespective of what Boeing decides to do. Why would Airbus do this? If Boeing believed Airbus' announcement then its best move is to build a 500-seater plane, making a profit of £30 million as opposed to a loss of £10 million. Hence, the announcement influences Boeing's behaviour in a manner that is favourable to Airbus – it earns greater profits.

However, there is a problem with Airbus' announcement – Boeing will probably not believe it! If Boeing actually built a 400-seater plane, Airbus' best move would be to build a 500-seater plane. Boeing can clearly see that it is not in Airbus' own self-interest to do what it said it was going to do. Therefore the strategy is not ***credible*** and Boeing will build the 400-seater plane.

Could Airbus take some irreversible actions so it is committed in advance to building the 400-seater plane? The key to the success of this policy is that Boeing must believe it: it must be credible. If this were possible, then by limiting its own options, Airbus could actually make greater profits. In some circumstances, inflexibility can actually improve the competitive position of the firm by altering its rivals' expectations about how it will behave. TC 9 p132

More complex sequential-move games

The aircraft example is the simplest version of a sequential-move game, with just two companies and each one making only one key decision. In many business situations, much more complex trees could be constructed. The 'game' would be more like one of chess, with many moves and several options on each move. If there were more than two companies, the decision tree would be more complex still.

Definitions

First-mover advantage When a firm gains from being the first one to take action.

Credible threat (or promise) One that is believable to rivals because it is in the threatener's interests to carry it out.

Assessing the simple theory of games

Game theory provides a very useful framework for helping us to think about competitive environments where there is strategic interdependence. It highlights the importance of each firm trying to think through situations from their rival's viewpoint in order to work out their own profit-maximising decision.

In this section, we have considered a number of quite simple games, with just two firms having to choose between just two different options. In reality, many oligopolistic markets will consist of a number of firms that each have to choose from multiple options on pricing, product design, advertising, etc. Therefore it would be very difficult if not impossible for them to obtain precise information on (a) the pay-offs to all their rivals from all the possible actions they could take and (b) the impact of all the possible actions of their rivals on their own pay-offs. The approach is useful, therefore, only in relatively simple cases, and even then, the estimates of profit from each outcome may amount to no more than a rough guess.

Even if we assume that both firms have full information on all the relevant pay-offs, the outcome of real-world competition may still be different from that predicted by standard game theory. At a Nash equilibrium each firm assumes that its rivals behave in a rational manner: that they can consider all the pay-offs and successfully make decisions that maximise their own profits.

Decision making under uncertainty. In reality, decision makers may make systematic errors, especially when faced with complicated problems. How sure can a firm be when working out its best response that its rival is in fact behaving in a rational manner? Could it mistakenly choose a suboptimal strategy?

If firms believe there is a strong chance that their rivals will behave in an irrational manner, then the outcome of competition is much harder to predict. In response to this uncertainty they might play it safe by choosing the strategy that minimises their losses from the worst-case scenario from the unpredictable behaviour of their rival. Such a strategy is known as ***maximin***. Alternatively, if they were more risk loving, they could gamble and choose the outcome that maximises their pay-off from the best-case scenario. Such a strategy is known as ***maximax***.

Changing behaviour patterns over time. Behaviour may also change over time as firms learn about the consequences of their actions and the competitive environment changes. For example, firms may compete hard for a time (in price or non-price terms) and then realise that it is making them all worse off. Firms may then start to collude and jointly raise prices and reduce advertising. Later, after a period of tacit collusion, competition may break out again. This may be sparked off by the entry of a new firm, by the development of a new product design, by a change in market demand, or simply by one or more firms no longer being able to resist the temptation to 'cheat'. In short, the behaviour of particular oligopolists may change quite radically over time as they find out new information.

The objectives of firms. Finally, we have been assuming that firms behave selfishly – that they make decisions with the sole purpose of maximising profits. In reality, people's actions are likely to be influenced by their moral values. Businesspeople may be unwilling to behave ruthlessly or dishonestly, or to undertake profitable activities that they regard as unfair. In Chapter 9, we examine some of the consequences of pursuing goals other than ruthless profit maximisation.

Given the lack of perfect information, uncertainty about the rationality of rivals and varying objectives of firms, simple game theory cannot predict with any accuracy what price, output and level of advertising firms will choose in the real world.

Definitions

Maximin The strategy of choosing the policy whose worst possible outcome is the least bad. Maximin is usually a low-risk strategy.

Maximax The strategy of choosing the policy that has the best possible outcome. Maximax is usually a high-risk strategy.

Section summary

1. Game theory is a way of modelling behaviour in strategic situations where the outcome for an individual or firm depends on the choices made by others. Thus game theory examines various strategies that firms can adopt when the outcome of each is not certain.
2. One of the simplest types of 'game' is a simultaneous single-move or single-period game. They are often presented in normal form: i.e. as a pay-off matrix. Some simultaneous single-move games have predictable outcomes, no matter what assumptions each firm makes about its rivals' behaviour. Such games are known as dominant-strategy games. Many other simultaneous games are more complicated and either one or both firms do not have a dominant strategy. The Nash equilibrium is a useful way to predict the most likely outcome in any of these games.
3. If a simultaneous game is repeated, the equilibrium can change. The final result depends on a number of factors such as whether the end date of the game is known.
4. In sequential-move games play passes from one 'player' to the other sequentially. Firms will respond not only to what firms do, but what they say they will do. To this end, a firm's threats or promises must be credible if they are to influence rivals' decisions.
5. A firm may gain a strategic advantage over its rivals by being the first one to take action (e.g. to launch a new product). The second mover may gain an advantage if it can commit in advance to behave in a certain manner. A decision tree can be constructed to show the possible sequence of moves in a multiple-move game.

8.4 PRICE DISCRIMINATION

Up until this point in the chapter, we have assumed that a firm sells each unit of its output for the same price. This is called *uniform pricing* and may result in the firm foregoing an opportunity to make greater profits. Why? Because some customers value a product more highly and thus have a greater willingness to pay. They would still purchase the good if the price were higher.

To exploit this situation, the firm might increase prices in an attempt to capture some of this consumer surplus and convert it into profit. However, it faces a trade-off. A higher price will increase the profit *per transaction*, but some customers will no longer buy the product: i.e. the ones who do not value it so highly. It is possible for the firm to avoid this trade-off by charging a higher price to those customers with a higher valuation for the product, and a lower price to those consumers with a lower valuation for the product. Businesses can do this by implementing a strategy of ***price discrimination***.

Care needs to be taken when explaining the precise meaning of this concept, as vague definitions can sometimes lead to it being incorrectly applied.

If the cost to the firm of supplying different customers does not vary, then price discrimination is defined as the practice of selling the same or similar products to different customers for different prices.

If the cost of supplying different customers *does* vary, then the definition is slightly more complicated. It is defined as the practice of selling the same or a similar product at different prices and the difference in price cannot be fully accounted for by any difference in the cost of supply. If any difference in the cost of supplying each customer can fully explain the variation in prices, then it is not an example of price discrimination.

If customers were all charged the same price for a product could this ever be classed as an example of price discrimination? Explain your answer.

Economists traditionally distinguish between three different types of price discrimination.

First-degree price discrimination is also referred to as 'perfect price discrimination'. It is where the seller charges each consumer the maximum price they are willing to pay (WTP) for each unit of the good. In other words, each consumer pays a different price based on their own personal valuation of the product.

In reality, only the buyer truly knows their WTP for each unit of the product. The difficulties involved for the firm in overcoming this asymmetric information mean that first-degree price discrimination is more of a theoretical benchmark than a viable business strategy. Firms may not be able to set prices precisely equal to WTP, but in some circumstances, they may be able to charge consumers different prices for the same product that are *related* to their WTP. This is called *personalised* or *person-specific pricing* and is a strategy that can approach one of first-degree price discrimination. The potential for personalised pricing in digital markets is discussed in Box 8.7.

Second-degree price discrimination is where a firm offers consumers a range of different pricing options for the same or similar product. Consumers are then free to choose whichever option they wish but the lower prices are conditional on factors such as:

- The quantity of the product purchased. In order to obtain the good at a lower price the customer has to purchase a certain minimum quantity of the good or service.
- The use of coupons/vouchers. To be eligible to purchase the product for a lower price, customers have to produce a voucher or coupon that they have collected: e.g. from a flyer inside a local newspaper or from the Internet. For this approach to work, consumers must have to exert some time and effort in collecting the vouchers/coupons. In this way, only the more price-sensitive customers should find it worth their while.
- When the product is purchased. For example, some goods are priced at a higher level when they are first released onto the market. Rail fares are higher at peak times than at off-peak times.
- The version of the product purchased. Firms can produce different versions of the same core product that have different levels of actual or perceived quality: e.g. value ranges of own-label products sold in supermarkets. This is called 'versioning'. One example of versioning is the 'damaged goods strategy', where a firm creates a lower-quality version of its good by deliberately damaging the product. It does this by removing some features or reducing its performance characteristics. Note that versioning is not *pure* price discrimination because the product is slightly different.

Definitions

Price discrimination Where a firm sells the same product at different prices.

First-degree price discrimination Where the seller of the product charges each consumer the maximum price they are prepared to pay for each unit.

Second-degree price discrimination Where a firm offers consumers a range of different pricing options for the same or similar product. Consumers are then free to choose whichever option they wish, but the price is often dependent on some factor such as the quantity purchased.

Table 8.3 Examples of third-degree price discrimination

Characteristic	Example
Age	16–25 or senior rail card; half-price children's tickets in the cinema.
Nationality	In several countries, foreign visitors are charged higher entrance fees than locals to various tourist sites.
Location	Pharmaceutical companies often charge different prices for the same medicine/drug in different countries. Consumers in the USA are often charged more than those from other countries.
Occupation	Apple, Microsoft and Orange™ provide price discounts to employees of educational institutions.
Business or individual	Publishers of academic journals charge much lower subscription rates to individuals than university libraries.
Past buying behaviour	Firms often charge new customers a lower price than existing customers for the same product or service as an 'introductory offer'.

Third-degree price discrimination is where a firm divides consumers into different groups based on some characteristic that is (a) relatively easy to observe; (b) informative about consumers' willingness to pay; (c) legal; and (d) acceptable to the consumer. The firm then charges a different price to consumers in different groups, but the same price to all consumers in the same group. Some examples include charging different prices based on age, occupation, geographical location and past buying behaviour. See Table 8.3 for some specific examples.

Definition

Third-degree price discrimination Where a firm divides consumers into different groups based on some characteristic that is relatively easy to observe and informative about how much consumers are willing to pay. The firm then charges a different price to consumers in different groups, but the same price to all the consumers within a group.

BOX 8.6 WHAT'S THE TRAIN FARE TO LONDON? CASE STUDIES AND APPLICATIONS

Price discrimination on the trains

Ask the question 'What's the fare to London?' at ticket enquiries, and you may receive any of the following replies:

- Do you want 1st or standard class?
- Do you want single or return?
- How old are you?
- Do you have a railcard (Family & Friends, 16–25, Disabled Person, Senior, Two Together)?
- Will you be travelling on a weekday?
- Will you be travelling out before 9:30am?
- Will you be leaving London between 4pm and 6:30pm?
- Are you able to book your ticket in advance?
- Do you need to be flexible about the time and date of your journeys, or are you willing to pre-commit to a specific train?

1. *Look at each of the above questions. In each case, decide whether price discrimination is being practised. If it is, is it sensible for train operators to practise it? How are the train operators able to identify travellers with different price elasticities of demand?*
2. *Are these various forms of price discrimination in the traveller's interest?*

Choose a journey on the National Rail website at www.nationalrail.co.uk. Compare the different prices available at different times of the day and different periods and for different types of traveller with various railcards and without any card. How might the different prices be justified?

Conditions necessary for price discrimination to operate

Given that firms can generate greater revenue and profits by using a strategy of price discrimination, why don't they all implement the policy? Unfortunately for some firms, it might not be possible for a number of reasons. The following are the conditions necessary for price discrimination to work successfully:

- The firm must have some market power. In other words, it must face a downward sloping demand curve and hence set its price. Thus, price discrimination will be impossible in a perfectly competitive market where firms are price takers.
- Re-sale of the product between consumers must be difficult/impossible. A potentially profitable strategy of price discrimination will fail if consumers in the low-price market are able to resell the good to those consumers who are in the high-price market.
- Demand elasticity must vary between consumers at any given price. The firm will charge the higher price in the market where demand is less elastic, and thus less sensitive to a price rise.

KI 9 p64

BOX 8.7 **PERSONALISED PRICING IN DIGITAL MARKETS** EXPLORING ECONOMICS

Is it widespread and do customers think it is fair?

It is impossible for firms to gather enough information to implement a policy of perfect price discrimination: i.e. charging each customer the maximum price they are willing to pay (WTP). However, some businesses may still be able to charge each person a different price based on certain characteristics and behaviours that are relatively easy to observe. This is called ***personalised pricing***.

Personalised pricing is sometimes confused with *price steering*. This is where the ordering of online search results differs between consumers. For example in 2012, the travel website Orbitz was showing Mac users more expensive hotels than people browsing with a Windows PC. However, the business stated that it never presented different users with the same hotel room for different prices.

Personalised pricing is also not the same as *dynamic pricing*. This is where prices adjust in response to changing demand and supply conditions. These adjustments can happen on a weekly, daily or even hourly basis. For example, research has found that some third-party sellers on Amazon alter prices over 100 times per day in response to changing market conditions.

The difficulties of implementing personalised pricing in traditional retailing

Personalised pricing is a difficult strategy to implement in traditional *bricks and mortar* retailing. The clothes people wear, the cars they drive, the houses they live in and their ethnicity/nationality might enable an experienced salesperson to make an informed guess about their likely income. This information can prove very useful if they haggle with buyers in an attempt to push prices closer to their WTP.

However, there are limits to the information on both the characteristics and behaviour of consumers that sellers can collect in this manner. Negotiation is a time-consuming process, especially for firms selling large volumes of goods. Just imagine how long it would take to shop at a supermarket if every customer had to haggle with a member of staff over each item in their trolley! There is also the problem of designing compensation contracts that provide sales staff with appropriate incentives to negotiate in the interests of their employer. The extra administrative costs of dealing with thousands of personalised prices for the same product may also be considerable.

For all of these reasons, the incremental costs of personalised pricing in traditional bricks and mortar retailing often outweigh the benefits to the firm. In many cases, the firm's best strategy is to post the same price for all consumers, who either accept or reject the purchase.

The impact of digital markets

The recent growth of digital markets has opened up new possibilities for personalised pricing. It gives organisations the opportunity to collect and process detailed data about both the characteristics and online behaviour of consumers in a cost-effective manner. This is 'digital big data'.

Capturing customers' characteristics. For example, the browsing behaviour of buyers enables sellers to access Internet protocol (IP) addresses and/or cookies. This allows firms to capture data on the following characteristics of a user and their smart device:

- geographical location (high- vs low-income area)
- Internet service provider (e.g. BT vs TalkTalk)
- type and speed of Internet connection (mobile vs fixed, copper vs fibre)
- browser (e.g. Chrome vs Firefox)
- type of device (laptop vs tablet vs mobile phone)
- make of device (e.g. Apple vs Huawei)
- battery level of the device (high vs low).

All of this information helps sellers to build detailed profiles of their customers and provides useful indicators of their different WTP. Importantly, it is possible without the need for any time-consuming negotiation by a salesperson.

Tracking browsing behaviour. Some businesses also specialise in collecting data by tracking the browsing behaviour of people across a number of different websites. This can give them:

- details of different purchases from different online stores;
- the number of other websites visited (i.e. how much a customer searches and shops around before making a purchase);
- the type of website visited (discount vs luxury stores);
- 'likes' on social media.

Businesses process this information and sell it to other firms as it helps to tailor advertising and perhaps pricing in a more personalised manner.

The use of sophisticated pricing algorithms also makes it easier to set thousands of personalised prices for the same product. It enables sellers to communicate prices to consumers on an individual basis, making it less likely that those with a higher WTP will find out that the seller offers the same good to other consumers for a lower price.

Although digital markets enable sellers to collect more information about the characteristics and behaviour of their customers, any estimates of WTP will never be perfectly accurate. They will always be approximations, as firms cannot read people's minds. The fear of overestimating WTP and so potentially losing sales will tend to make firms cautious. They are likely to include some margin for error. For example, they could charge each customer a certain percentage of their estimated WTP (e.g. 80 per cent).

Evidence of personalised pricing

To what extent are firms in the UK currently personalising their prices? Recent research carried out for Citizens Advice[1] found little evidence of it happening in essential markets such as water, energy and telecoms. The Competition and Markets Authority (CMA) carried out a small experiment where multiple users looked at three products on the websites of ten leading online suppliers – Opodo, Booking.com, Expedia, Ryanair, Amazon, Asda, Tesco, Apple, Zara and Staples.[2] The different users accessed the webpages at exactly the same time to control for dynamic pricing. However, the browsing behaviour varied by (a) the operating system – Windows vs MacOS (b) how they arrived at the website – general search vs a comparison website and (c) logging into the site vs general search.

The research found very little evidence of personalised pricing but did find evidence of price steering. For example, when searching for hotels on Opodo, users who logged into the site were listed more expensive rooms than those who accessed the website via a general search.

Constraints on the use of personalised pricing

Why are firms so reluctant to implement a strategy that could be so profitable? One potential constraint is the attitude and perceptions of the public. Research carried out by Citizens Advice found that 84 per cent of people were uncomfortable about the use of personalised pricing in markets for essential services and 75 per cent would not trust a seller who used this pricing strategy. In focus groups carried out for Ofcom, the majority of participants thought the practice was unfair.[3]

Given this evidence on its unpopularity, firms who use personalised pricing are likely to receive negative comments on social media. Concerns about the potential damage to a business's reputation and fears of a consumer boycott may deter managers from implementing the policy in the first place.

Another potential constraint is legislation. For example, the EU's General Data Protection Regulation (GDPR) stipulates that businesses must get explicit, informed and unambiguous consent from the consumer for the use of their data. Recent research[4] found that only 11.8 per cent of the consent pop-ups that appear on websites met the minimum requirements of GDPR.

1. *Draw a diagram to illustrate a firm with market power implementing a strategy of personalised pricing. Assume the firm sets prices equal to 80 per cent of the estimated WTP of its consumers.*
2. *To what extent is personalised pricing in the interests of consumers?*

Read the August 2018 Citizens Advice Report (see below). Summarise the findings and assess whether the practice of personalised pricing has any benefits for the consumer.

1 Morgan Wild and Marini Thorne, *A price of one's own: An investigation into personalised pricing in essential markets*, Citizens Advice (August 2018), www.citizensadvice.org.uk/a-price-of-ones-own-an-investigation-into-personalised-pricing-in-essential-markets/

2 'Pricing algorithms: economic working paper on the use of algorithms to facilitate collusion and personalised pricing' *CMA Working Papers*, No.94 (8 October 2018), https://assets.publishing.service.gov.uk/government/uploads/system/uploads/attachment_data/file/746353/Algorithms_econ_report.pdf

3 *Personalised pricing for communications: Making data work for consumers*, Ofcom (4 August 2020), www.ofcom.org.uk/phones-telecoms-and-internet/information-for-industry/personalised-pricing-for-communications

4 Midas Nouwens et al., 'Dark patterns after the GDPR: scraping consent pop-ups and demonstrating their influence', in *CHI '20: Proceedings of the 2020 CHI Conference on Human Factors in Computing Systems*. Association for Computing Machinery (25–30 April 2020), https://arxiv.org/pdf/2001.02479.pdf

Definition

Personalised pricing Where firms use information obtained on consumers (e.g. from browsing or purchasing history) to enable them to charge people a price specific to them and as close as possible to their willingness to pay (WTP).

Advantages to the firm

Price discrimination allows the firm to earn a higher revenue from any given level of sales. Let us examine the case of third-degree price discrimination.

Figure 8.12 represents a firm's demand curve. If it is to sell 200 units without price discrimination, it must charge a price of P_1. The total revenue it earns is shown by the green area. If, however, it can practise third-degree price discrimination by selling 150 of those 200 units at the higher price of P_2, it will gain the pink area in addition to the green area in Figure 8.12.

Figure 8.12 Third-degree price discrimination

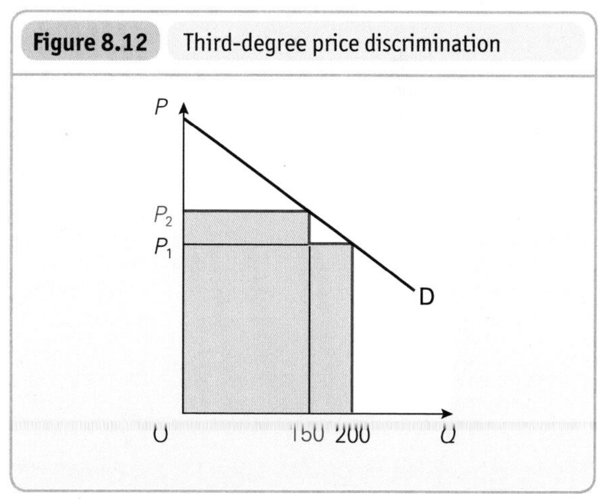

Explain why, if the firm can practise first-degree price discrimination by selling every unit at the maximum price each consumer is prepared to pay, its revenue from selling 200 units will be the green area plus the pink area in Figure 8.13.

Another advantage to the firm of price discrimination is that it may be able to use it to drive competitors out of business. If a firm has a monopoly in one market (e.g. the home market), it may be able to charge a high price due to relatively inelastic demand, and thus make high profits. If it is under oligopoly in another market (e.g. the export market), it may use the high profits in the first market to subsidise a very low price in the oligopolistic market, thus forcing its competitors out of business.

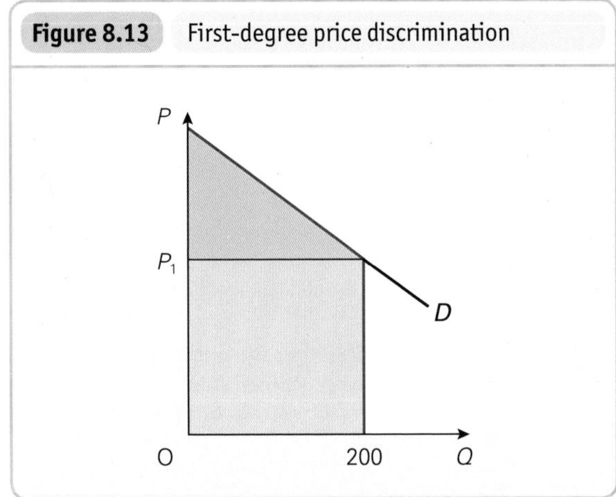

Figure 8.13 First-degree price discrimination

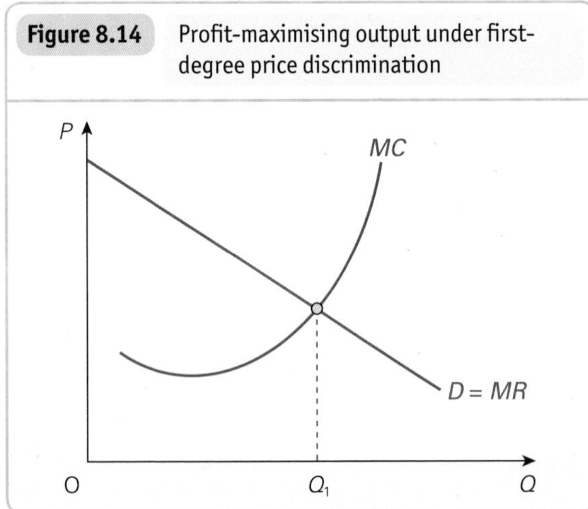

Figure 8.14 Profit-maximising output under first-degree price discrimination

Profit-maximising prices and output

Assuming that the firm wishes to maximise profits, what discriminatory prices should it charge and how much should it produce? Let us first consider the case of first-degree price discrimination.

First-degree price discrimination

Since an increase in sales does not involve lowering the price for any unit save the *extra* one sold, the extra revenue gained from the last unit (*MR*) will be its price. Thus profit is maximised at Q_1 in Figure 8.14, where $MC = MR$ ($= P$ of the *last* unit).

Third-degree price discrimination

Assume that a firm sells a given product (such as window cleaning services) and can split its customers into two groups, based on location, where people in market H have a higher average income than people in market L. This is illustrated in Figure 8.15.

It is highly probable that most consumers with the higher incomes would be willing to pay more for the product than those on low incomes. Panel (a) in Figure 8.15 illustrates the demand curve for the firm's product in the high-income market, market H, while panel (b) illustrates the demand curve for those in the low-income market, market L.

Equilibrium for a single-price firm. If the firm were unable to split its customers into these two groups, then a market demand curve could be derived. This is illustrated in panel (c) and is obtained by horizontally aggregating the demand curves in panel (a) and (b). The market demand curve between points *g* and *h* is the same as the demand curve in market H between points *a* and *b*. This is because no consumer in market L is willing to pay a price above *d*. As the price falls below *d*, consumers

Figure 8.15 Profit-maximising output under third-degree price discrimination

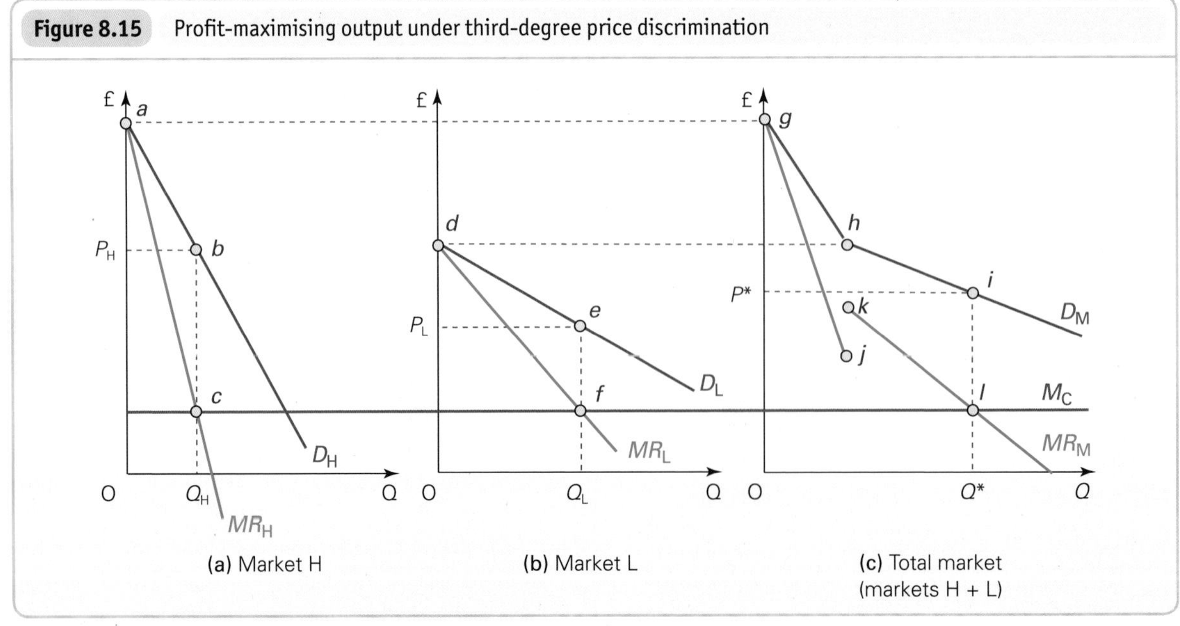

in both market H and market L are willing to buy the good, so horizontal aggregation of both demand curves must take place from this point onwards. This creates a kink in the market demand curve at point *h*. This kink also creates a discontinuity in the *MR* curve between points *j* and *k*. To simplify the explanation it is also assumed that the firm's marginal cost is constant and it has no fixed costs. Thus $AC = MC$.

To understand how a firm would behave if it could only set one price for all of its customers, we need to focus on the market demand curve in panel (c). If it were a profit-maximising firm then it would produce where the market *MR* (i.e. MR_M) $= MC$. This occurs at point *l* in panel (c) of Figure 8.15. It would therefore produce an output of Q^* and sell all of this output at the same price of P^*.

Equilibrium under third-degree price discrimination. What happens if the firm could now charge a different price to the customers in market H from those in market L? At the single price of P^* the price elasticity of demand in market H is lower than it is in market L. (Note that demand is nevertheless elastic in both markets at this price as *MR* is positive.) Therefore the firm could increase its profits by charging a price above P^* in market H and below P^* in market L. Once again this can be illustrated in Figure 8.15.

In market H the profit-maximising firm should produce where $MR_H = MC$ at point c. Therefore it should sell an output of Q_H for a price of P_H.

In market L the profit-maximising firm should produce where $MR_L = MC$ at point *f*. Therefore it should sell an output of Q_L for a price of P_L.

Note that P_L is below P^*, while P_H is above P^*. Also, because the demand curves are linear, the total output sold is the same under third-degree price discrimination as it is under uniform pricing: i.e. $Q^* = Q_H + Q_L$. We will see later in the chapter that this is a key point when considering whether or not price discrimination is in the public interest.

How easy do you think it would be for a firm to split customers into different groups based on their incomes?

*LOOKING AT THE MATHS

We can use calculus to work out the profit-maximising prices and outputs in each of the two markets *H* and *L* in Figure 8.15. If we know the demand functions in each of the two markets, *H* and *L*, we can derive the total revenue functions in each market (TR_H and TR_L) and hence in the two markets together ($TR = TR_H + TR_L$). Total profit is given by

$$T\Pi = TR_H + TR_L - TC$$

To find the maximum-profit output in each market, we (partially) differentiate the total profit equation with respect to output in each of *H* and *L* and set each equal to zero and solve for Q_H and Q_L (see pages A:10–12 for how calculus is used to find a maximum value). We can then substitute these values of Q_H and Q_L in the respective demand functions to work out P_H and P_L.

Maths Case 8.3 in MyEconLab and on the student website shows how this is done by using a worked example.

Price discrimination and the public interest

The word 'discrimination' carries with it negative connotations, so people often assume that the pricing strategy must not be in the public interest. It is also tempting to think that anything that increases firms' profits must be at the expense of consumers' welfare. However, this is not necessarily the case and no clear-cut decision can be made over the social desirability of price discrimination. Some people benefit from it; others lose. This can be illustrated by considering the effects of price discrimination on the following aspects of the market.

Distribution effects on those customers who previously purchased the good at a uniform price

Those paying the higher price will probably feel that price discrimination is unfair to them. Price has risen for them and their consumer surplus is lower. On the other hand, those who previously purchased the good but are now paying a lower price will feel better off. Their consumer surplus will be higher. Judgements could be made about whether the gains were more socially desirable than the losses.

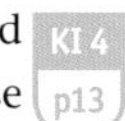

The impact of any extra sales

In Figure 8.15, the quantity of sales under price discrimination remained the same as under uniform pricing. However, in some circumstances the quantity of sales may increase. There may be some consumers, such as pensioners, who previously could not afford to buy the good when the firm used uniform pricing. The lower price, made possible by price discrimination, now enables them to purchase the good. These extra sales will have a positive impact on the welfare of society. They will increase both consumer surplus and profit.

Misallocation effects

Price discrimination may cause a negative allocation effect. Under uniform pricing the product is allocated through the price mechanism to those consumers who value it the most, given their incomes. The implementation of third-degree price discrimination could result in some units of the product being reallocated away from those consumers with a higher willingness to pay to those with a lower willingness to pay.

Without any restrictions, mutually beneficial trade might be able to take place between the buyers. Those consumers with a higher valuation of the good could, under some circumstances, purchase it from those with a lower valuation at a price that would improve the welfare of both parties. However, the seller blocks this resale from taking place and in the process reduces society's welfare.

Competition

As explained above, a firm may use price discrimination to drive competitors out of business. This is known as

predatory pricing. For example, in many towns, large bus companies have used profits they make in *other* towns where they have a monopoly to subsidise their bus fares and thereby drive competitors out of business, only then to raise prices above those that the competitors had been charging. On the other hand, a firm might use the profits from its high-priced market to break into another market and withstand a possible price war. Competition is thereby increased.

Definition

Predatory pricing Where a firm temporarily charges a price below its short-run profit-maximising price in order to drive one or more competitors out of the market. This would normally involve setting a price below the average variable cost of a competitor.

Profits

Price discrimination raises a firm's profits. This could be seen as an undesirable redistribution of income in society, especially if the average price of the product is raised. On the other hand, the higher profits may be reinvested and lead to innovation or lower costs in the future.

BOX 8.8 JUST THE TICKET? CASE STUDIES AND APPLICATIONS

Price discrimination in the cinema

One of the commonest forms of price discrimination is where children are charged a lower price than adults, whether on public transport or for public entertainment. Take the case of cinema tickets. In most cinemas, children pay less than adults during the day. In the evening, however, many cinemas charge both adults and children the same price.

But why do cinemas charge children less during the day? After all, the child is seeing the same film as the adult and occupying a whole seat. In other words, there is no difference in the 'product' that they are 'consuming'. And why are children charged the higher price in the evenings, given that the seat and the film are the same as during the day?

The answer has to do with revenue maximisation and the price elasticity of demand. Once a cinema has decided to show a film, the marginal costs of an additional customer are zero. There are no additional staffing, film-hire, electricity or other costs. With marginal costs equal to zero, profits will be maximised where marginal revenue is also equal to zero: in other words, where total revenue is maximised.

Take the case of a cinema with 500 seats. This is illustrated in the diagrams, which show the demand and marginal revenue curves for both adults and children. It is assumed that the elasticity of demand for children's tickets is greater than that for adults' tickets. Diagram (a) shows demand during the late afternoon (i.e. after school). Here the demand by children is relatively high compared with adults, but the overall demand is low. Diagram (b) shows demand during the evening. Here there is a higher overall level of demand, especially by adults, many of whom work during the day.

For the afternoon screening (diagram (a)), revenue is maximised from children by charging them a price of £8.00: i.e. at the point on the demand curve where $MR = 0$. At this price, 200 child tickets will be sold.

Assuming that the same adult price is charged in both the afternoon and the evening, we need to look at the *total* demand for full-priced tickets (i.e. for both afternoon and evening screenings) in order to ascertain the revenue-maximising price. This will be a price of £14.00, where total adult $MR = 0$ (see diagram (b)). This will lead to 100 adult tickets being sold in the afternoon and 500 in the evening.

But why are reduced-price tickets not available for children in the evening? In diagram (b), the sale of low-priced

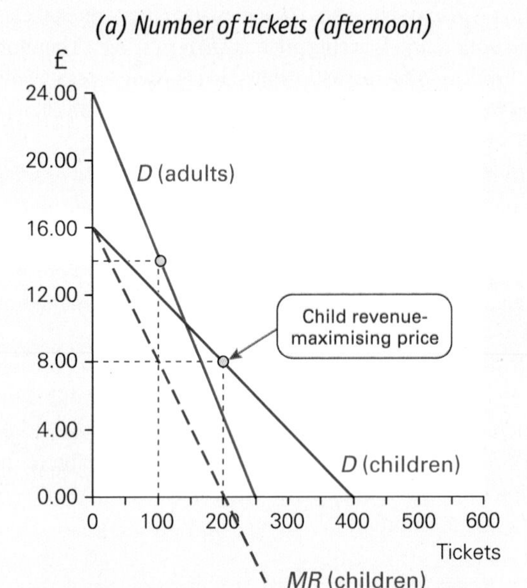

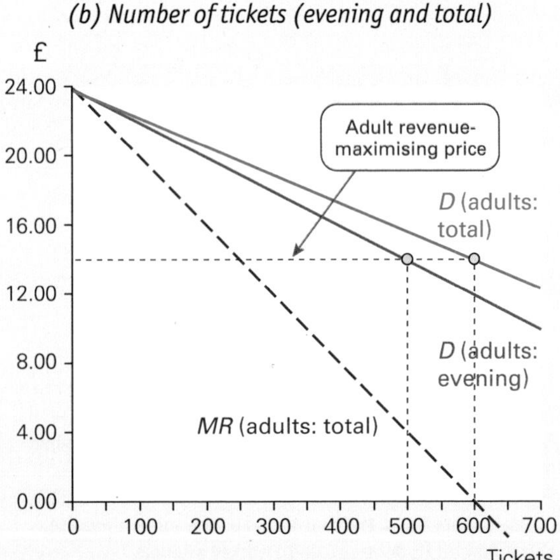

tickets for children would lead to demand exceeding the 500-seat capacity of the cinema. Each time an adult was turned away because the seat had already been sold to a child, the cinema would lose.

1. *Which type of price discrimination is the cinema pursuing: first, second or third degree? Could it pursue either of the other two types?*
2. *If all cinema seats could be sold to adults in the evenings at the end of the week, but only a few on Mondays and Tuesdays, what price discrimination policy would you recommend to the cinema in order for it to maximise its weekly revenue?*
3. *Would the cinema make more profit if it could charge adults a different price in the afternoon and the evenings?*

Investigate pricing in a cinema near you. Find out the extent to which it is using price discrimination. Provide a short briefing paper for the management of the cinema on ways in which it could increase revenue and profit by adopting different prices for different groups of people at different times of the day/week.

Section summary

1. If the costs to the firm of supplying different customers do not vary, then price discrimination is the practice of selling the same or similar products to different customers for different prices. If the costs of supplying different customers *do* vary, then price discrimination is the practice of selling the same or similar product at different prices where the difference in price cannot be fully accounted for by the difference in the cost of supply.
2. Price discrimination allows the firm to earn a higher revenue from a given level of sales.
3. First-degree price discrimination is where the consumer is charged the maximum he or she is prepared to pay. Second-degree price discrimination is where the consumer is offered a range of different prices for the same or similar product. They are free to choose whichever option they wish but the lower prices are conditional on some features of the purchase. Third-degree price discrimination is where consumers are divided into groups and the groups with the lower price elasticity of demand are charged the higher prices.
4. Whether price discrimination is in the consumer's interest or not is uncertain. Some individuals will gain and some will lose.

END OF CHAPTER QUESTIONS

1. Assume there are just two firms (X and Y) and they are considering which of two alternative prices to charge. The decisions are made simultaneously: i.e. without either firm knowing the choice of its rival. The various profits are illustrated in the following pay-off matrix.

Table 8.4 Profits for firms X and Y at different prices

		X's price	
		£25	£19
Y's price	£20	A £6m, £6m	B £2m, £5m
	£15	C £4m, £3m	D £4m, £4m

   (a) What is firm Y's best response to each of the different prices Firm X could charge? Does firm Y have a dominant strategy?
   (b) What is firm X's best response to each of the different prices firm Y could charge? Does firm X have a dominant strategy?
   (c) What is/are the Nash equilibrium/equilibria? What is the most likely outcome of this game? Explain your answer.
2. Assume that a monopolistically competitive industry is in long-run equilibrium. On a diagram like Figure 8.1(b), show the effect of a fall in demand on a firm's price and profit in (a) the short run and (b) the long run.
3. In what ways is a monopolistically competitive firm likely to be less efficient than one under perfect competition?
4. Are there any shops in your area that stay open later than others? If so, does this affect the prices they charge? Why do you think this is?
5. Give three examples of oligopolistic industries. In what ways do the firms in each of these industries compete? Why do they choose to compete in the way that they do?
6. Why, under oligopoly, might a particular industry be collusive at one time and yet highly price competitive at another?
7. What is meant by the prisoners' dilemma game when applied to the behaviour of oligopolists? Discuss some factors that will determine the outcome of the game.
8. What three characteristics must a strategic move have if it is to be successful in altering the behaviour of a competitor later in the game?
9. Give two examples of price discrimination. Which category of price discrimination are they? In what ways do the consumers gain or lose? What information would you need to be certain in your answer?
10. Explain why the rise in e-commerce might increase the number of firms engaging in person-specific pricing.
11. For a firm to be able to implement a strategy of price discrimination it must be able to prevent resale amongst its customers. What factors would make it more difficult for a consumer to resell a good?

Online resources

Additional case studies on the student website

8.1 Edward Chamberlin and Joan Robinson. A portrait of the two economists who developed the model of monopolistic competition.

8.2 The motor vehicle repair and servicing industry. A case study of monopolistic competition.

8.3 The corner shop and the hypermarket. A case study in non-price competition: how the corner shop can survive competition from the big supermarkets.

8.4 Curry wars. Monopolistic competition in the take-away food market.

8.5 Bakeries: oligopoly or monopolistic competition. A case study on the bread industry, showing that small-scale local bakeries can exist alongside giant national bakeries.

8.6 Is beer becoming more concentrated? A study of oligopoly in the brewing industry. There have been mergers between large brewers, but a rise in small breweries.

8.7 'Rip-off Britain'. This examines the practice of charging higher prices to loyal customers in various markets.

8.8 Fair wars in the skies? The effect of the entry of low-cost airlines on air fares.

8.9 A product's life cycle. How market conditions vary at different stages in a product's life.

8.10 Advertising and the public interest. Does the consumer benefit from advertising?

8.11 Peak-load pricing An example of price discrimination: charging more when it costs more to produce.

Maths Case 8.1 Calculating the profit-maximising price of a price leader. Using equations for demand, revenue and cost curves.

Maths Case 8.2 Deriving the Cournot equilibrium. An algebraic example.

Maths Case 8.3 Calculating the profit-maximising prices under third-degree price discrimination. Using calculus to find the profit-maximising output and price in each market and to compare the profit with and without price discrimination.

Websites relevant to Chapters 7 and 8

Numbers and sections refer to websites listed in the Web Appendix and hotlinked from this book's website at **go.pearson.com/uk/sloman.**

- For news articles relevant to this and the previous chapter, see the *Economics News* section on the student website.
- For general news on companies and markets, see websites in section A, and particularly A1–9, 23–6, 35, 36. See also A38, 39, 42, 43 and 44 for links to newspapers worldwide; and A40 and 41 for links to economics news articles from newspapers worldwide.
- For sites that look at competition and market power, see sites E4, 10, 15, 16, 19, 20, 22; G7, 8. See also links in I7 and 14.
- For information on OPEC (Box 8.3), see site H6.
- For sites with resources on game theory, see C20, 23, 24, 25; D4, 20.
- For a site that contains a number of open-access computer-based games on oligopoly and game theory that can be played between students, see sites D13–20.
- For models and simulations on pricing and price discrimination use the search feature in site D3.

The Behaviour of Firms

CHAPTER MAP

The traditional theories of the firm that we have been looking at in the previous three chapters assume that firms aim to maximise profits. Although this is an accurate assumption for many firms, for many others it is not.

Some firms would *like* to maximise profits but have insufficient information to enable them to do so. Others do not even want to maximise profits, if that means sacrificing some other aim, such as rapid growth or increased market share.

In this chapter, we focus on the behaviour of decision makers in firms. We look at various aims they might pursue as an alternative to maximum profits: aims such as maximum sales revenue or maximum growth. We also examine the implications of pursuing alternative aims for the profitability of the firm and for the prices paid by the consumer.

Many firms, especially larger ones, are complex organisations, with different individuals and departments pursuing their own agenda. What happens when these various goals come into conflict? How does conflict get resolved? What are the implications for consumers and other 'stakeholders'? We examine these issues in section 9.5.

Finally, we ask how prices are determined in practice. If firms do not use marginal revenue and marginal cost concepts in setting their prices, or if they are not aiming to achieve maximum profits, how do they choose the price to charge? As we shall see, firms often base their prices on average cost.

9.1 PROBLEMS WITH TRADITIONAL THEORY

The traditional profit-maximising theories of the firm have been criticised for being unrealistic. The criticisms are mainly of two sorts: (a) that firms wish to maximise profits but for some reason are unable to do so; or (b) that firms have aims other than profit maximisation. Let us examine each in turn.

Difficulties in maximising profit

One criticism of traditional theory is that firms do not use *MR* and *MC* concepts. This may well be true, but firms could still arrive at maximum profit by trial and error adjustments of price, or by finding the output where *TR* and *TC* are furthest apart. Provided they end up maximising profits, they will be equating *MC* and *MR*, even if they did not adopt that as a strategy. In this case, traditional models will still be useful in predicting price and output.

Lack of information

KI 15 p132

The main difficulty in trying to maximise profits is a *lack of information.*

Firms may well use accountants' cost concepts not based on opportunity cost. If it were thereby impossible to measure true profit, a firm would not be able to maximise profit except by chance.

> ? *What cost concepts are there other than those based on opportunity cost? Would the use of these concepts be likely to lead to an output greater or less than the profit-maximising one?*

More importantly, firms are unlikely to know even approximately their demand curves and hence their *MR* curves. Even though they will know how much they are selling, this only gives them one point on their demand curve and no point at all on their *MR* curve. In order to make an informed guess of marginal revenue, they would need an idea of how responsive demand will be to a change in price. But how are they to estimate this price elasticity? Market research may help. But this may be unreliable.

KI 9 p64

The biggest problem in estimating the firm's demand curve is in estimating the actions and reactions of *other* firms and their effects. Even under collusion there will still be a considerable uncertainty.

TC 9 p132

As we saw in Chapter 8, game theory may help a firm decide its price and output strategy. But for this to be accurate, it requires that a firm knows the consequences for its profits of each of the possible reactions of its rivals. In reality, no firm will have this information, because it will not know for sure how consumers will respond to each of its rivals' alternative strategies.

KI 23 p228

Time period

Finally, there is the problem of deciding the time period over which the firm should be seeking to maximise profits. Firms operate in a changing environment. Demand curves shift; supply curves shift. Some of these shifts occur as a result of factors outside the firm's control, such as changes in competitors' prices and products. Some, however, change as a direct result of a firm's policies, such as an advertising campaign or the installation of new equipment. The firm, therefore, does not face static costs and revenue curves from which it can read off its profit-maximising price and output. Instead, it faces a changing and unpredictable set of curves. If it chooses a price and output that maximises profits this year, it may be entirely the wrong decision months, or even weeks, later.

Take a simple example. The firm may be considering whether to invest in new equipment. If it does, its costs will rise in the short run and thus short-run profits will fall. On the other hand, if the quality of the product thereby increases, demand is likely to increase over the longer run. Also, variable costs will decrease if the new equipment is more efficient. In other words, long-run profit is likely to increase, but probably by an uncertain amount.

Given these problems in trying to work out complex strategies to maximise profits, managers may fall back on simple rules of thumb or mental shortcuts for pricing and output decisions (see page 232).

Alternative aims

An even more fundamental attack on traditional theory is that firms do not even *aim* to maximise profits (even if they could).

The traditional theory of the firm assumes that it is the *owners* of the firm who make price and output decisions. It is reasonable to assume that many owners *will* want to maximise profits. The question is, however, whether the owners do in fact make the decisions.

In ***public limited companies*** the shareholders are the owners. Many economic theories assume that shareholders want the firm to maximise profits as this increases their dividends and the value of their shares. (It is interesting to note that many investors are now showing a growing interest in the environmental, social and governance (ESG) record of businesses). Shareholders elect directors. Directors in turn employ professional managers who are often given considerable discretion in making decisions. There is therefore a *separation between the ownership and control* of a firm. (See Case Study 9.1 on the student website for an examination of the legal structure of firms.)

> **Definition**
>
> **Public limited company** A company owned by its shareholders. Shareholders' liability is limited to the value of their shares. Shares may be bought and sold publicly – on the stock market.

So what are the objectives of managers? Will *they* want to maximise profits? Or will they have some other aim?

We can assume that they want to *maximise their own utility*. They may pursue higher salaries, greater power, a more prestigious company car or a project in which they have a personal interest. Different managers in the same firm may well pursue different aims. These aims may conflict with profit maximisation.

Managers will still have to ensure that *sufficient* profits are made to keep shareholders happy, but that may be very different from *maximising* profits.

Alternative theories of the firm to those of profit maximisation, therefore, tend to assume that large firms are ***profit satisficers***. That is, managers strive hard for a minimum target level of profit, but are less interested in profits above this level.

Such theories fall into two categories: first, those theories that assume that firms attempt to maximise some other aim, provided that sufficient profits are achieved (these are examined in section 9.3); and second, those theories that assume that firms pursue a number of potentially conflicting aims, of which sufficient profit is merely one (these are examined in section 9.5).

The nature of institutions and organisations is likely to influence behaviour. **There are various forces influencing people's decisions in complex organisations. Assumptions that an organisation will follow one simple objective (e.g. short-run profit maximisation) are thus too simplistic in many cases.**

Make a list of six possible aims that a manager of a high street department store might have. Identify some conflicts that might arise between these aims.

Definition

Profit satisficing Where decision makers in a firm aim for a target level of profit rather than the absolute maximum level.

BOX 9.1 WHAT DO YOU MAXIMISE?

EXPLORING ECONOMICS

Managers are only human too

You are a student studying economics. So what do you maximise?

Do you attempt to maximise marks in assessed work? If so, you will probably have to spend most of each week studying. Obviously, you will have to have breaks for food and sleep, and you will need some recreation, but you will need to spend most of your time studying.

What is more likely is that you will, in some rather vaguely defined way, try to maximise your happiness. Getting good marks in your exams is just one element contributing to this aim, and you will have to weigh it against the opportunity cost of studying – namely, time not spent out with friends, playing sport, working for money, etc.

To argue that managers seek to maximise profits to the exclusion of everything else is rather like arguing that you seek to maximise your assessment marks. Managers' happiness (or utility) will depend on many factors, including their salaries, the pleasantness of their job, their power and the friendship of their colleagues.

Achieving profits may be an important aim (after all, it does contribute to a manager's utility), but the effort required to make additional profits will involve an opportunity cost to the manager – having, say, to work longer hours or firing a close colleague.

1. *When are increased profits in the manager's personal interest?*
2. *Does the way you allocate your time between study and leisure vary at different times of the year? If so, why?*

Section summary

1. There are two major types of criticism of the traditional profit-maximising theory: (a) firms may not have the information to maximise profits; (b) they may not even want to maximise profits.
2. Lack of information on demand and costs and on the actions and reactions of rivals, and a lack of use of opportunity cost concepts, may mean that firms adopt simple 'rules of thumb' for pricing.
3. In large companies, there is likely to be a separation between ownership and control. The shareholders (the owners) may want maximum profits, but it is the managers who make the decisions, and managers are likely to aim to maximise their own utility rather than that of the shareholders. This leads to profit 'satisficing'.

9.2 BEHAVIOURAL ECONOMICS OF THE FIRM

Is firm behaviour consistent with the rational choice model?

Section 5.2 in Chapter 5 introduced behavioural economics, the field of study that integrates some simple insights from psychology into standard economic theory. We saw how ideas such as heuristics, loss aversion, present bias and reciprocity sometimes predict human behaviour more effectively than the traditional approach.

The focus in Chapter 5 was on consumer behaviour. In this chapter, we consider how to apply behavioural economics to the theory of the firm. For example, in what ways might managerial decision making deviate from that predicted by rationality? How might managers' concerns for fairness have an impact on firm's actions? How might firms respond to the fairness preferences of their consumers and employees? How might they react if they think that their rivals are behaving unfairly?

Some potential heuristics

Firms operate in complex environments, dealing with imperfect information and uncertainty about both the present and the future. Trying to work out and implement a profit-maximising strategy in these situations is a cognitively demanding task that places great strain on a manager's computational capacity. Rather like consumers, managers may respond by using heuristics (rules of thumb/mental shortcuts) to simplify things. Some heuristics might include the following:

Copying the strategy of the most profitable businesses in the market. This is only possible if a firm can observe the actions and profits made by its rivals. If some firms follow a strategy of imitation in an oligopolistic market, it might lead to more intense competition, with lower prices and higher output. Some research found that firms which simply imitate do at least as well as those that successfully calculate their own profit-maximising strategy.

Focusing on relative rather than absolute profits. It is easier to see if a firm is making more profit than its rivals, than if it is making the maximum profit possible. Therefore, managers may judge their success by comparing their firm's performance with that of its competitors. There may also be financial incentives to behave in this way as many firms base bonuses on relative, as opposed to absolute, profits.

This type of behaviour may lead to firms implementing strategies that reduce their own profits (e.g. an aggressive price war) if it reduces the profits of their rivals by a greater amount. Section 9.5 discusses how having multiple goals may also lead to managers focusing on their relative performance.

Making a satisfactory/target level of profit. Instead of constantly looking for new opportunities to maximise profits in a dynamic market, managers may instead only change a firm's strategy when its profits fall below some target level.

The most influential early exponents of this approach were Richard Cyert and James March[1] (see section 9.5 for more detail).

Which is easier – for managers to make decisions that maximise profits or for consumers to make decisions that maximise their utility? Discuss some of the arguments in favour of each case.

Managerial preferences for fairness

As we saw in Chapter 8, the behaviour of a firm in an oligopoly depends on how it thinks its rivals will react to its actions. In collusive oligopoly firms agree to limit competition in order to maximise joint profits. Game theory allows us to examine these strategic decisions in more depth. A consistent assumption is that firms are attempting to maximise profits and believe that their rivals will always behave in a rational and selfish manner (i.e. try to maximise their own profits). But is this always a reasonable assumption?

Rather than being rational profit maximisers, some managers may have a strong preference for fairness. In particular, they may care about the equitable distribution of profits between firms in their industry. If a rival takes actions that enable it to obtain a larger share of industry profits, firms with managers who have a strong preference for fairness might be willing to take costly actions to punish it. By costly, we mean actions that reduce the firm's own profits as well as those of its rivals. Many research experiments have found that people are sometimes willing to reduce their own earnings to punish other 'players' for what they consider to be unfair behaviour.

Preferences for fairness may increase the chances of collusive oligopoly by reducing the likelihood of cheating. Take the following example. Imagine an industry dominated by two large firms (firm A and firm B). These two firms make a collusive agreement to charge prices above the competitive level for an indefinite time period. If they both stick to the deal, they split the higher level of industry profits between them. We explained in Chapter 8 how the chances of both firms sticking to the deal depends on a number of factors, including the expected size of any punishment for cheating. What impact do fairness preferences have on the size of expected punishment?

Assume the sole objective of the managers at firm A is to maximise profits, while those at firm B have a strong preference for fairness. If they both stick to the terms of the collusive agreement, the managers at firm B will think the outcome is fair.

If firm A knows that firm B has this strong preference for fairness, this will have an impact on its expected costs of cheating. It knows that firm B will be willing to take further actions

1 Richard Cyert and James March, *A Behavioural Theory of the Firm* (Blackwell, 1963).

that reduce its own profits as long as it reduces the profits of firm A by a greater amount. This helps to equalise the profits between the two businesses, something firm B values, even though they both end up with lower profits. If firm A anticipates this more aggressive response from the fairness-minded firm B, this will deter it from cheating in the first place. What about firm B? If firm A sticks to the agreement, firm B will not cheat because it believes the outcome to be fair.

In reality, the outcome of these examples of strategic interdependence will depend on a number of factors, including (a) the knowledge each firm has about the preferences of its rivals and (b) the strength of its own fairness preferences compared with its desire to make more profit.

Some potential biases

Economists have long identified over-optimism as a trait seen in many people. Adam Smith commented that 'the chance of gain is by every man, more or less over-valued, and the chance of loss is by most men under-valued.'[2] A number of factors may make over-optimism even greater among managers than the population as a whole.

Why might it present problems for a firm if managers are over-confident? Can you think of any reason why CEOs might be more inclined to optimism than the population average?

There is also survey evidence that managers include sunk costs as well as avoidable costs, when making pricing decisions.[3] This can lead to different prices from those set by a profit-maximising firm (we examine cost-based pricing in section 9.6).

2 See: Adam Smith, *An Inquiry into the Nature and Causes of the Wealth of Nations*, Book 1, Chapter 10, para. 29.

3 See for example: Steve Buchheit and Nick Feltovich, 'Experimental evidence of a sunk-cost paradox: a study of pricing behavior in Bertrand–Edgeworth duopoly', *University of Aberdeen Discussion Paper, 2008-4* (April 2008).

Why may managers choose to set prices that cover all costs, including sunk costs?

Can firms make use of behavioural economics?

Firms might be able to make use of behavioural economics if they are rational but their customers use heuristics or make systematic mistakes. Indeed, there is evidence that firms have been making use of some key insights from behavioural economics for many years. For example, they develop marketing strategies that do not concentrate solely on price, but are tailored to consumers' (sometimes irrational) preferences.

In 2015, the consumer group *Which* made a formal complaint to the competition authorities about the way supermarkets present prices to consumers – in particular, the misleading use of special offers that make extensive use of reference prices and volume offers such as 'buy one, get one free'. In Box 9.2 we look at another example, *drip pricing*, in more detail.

Consumer preferences for fairness may also constrain the pricing behaviour of many businesses. We discuss this issue in more detail in Box 9.3.

Behavioural economics is also relevant to firms as employers. Since, for most firms, labour is a major input, it will be important to account for the motivation of employees – to ensure that they work hard and that their actions align with the interests of the firm. Mechanisms of reward (and possibly punishment) may be most effective when the firm fully understands the behaviour of workers and their preference for fairness. This is considered in more detail in Chapter 10.

Are there other points in the supply chain/production process where firms could make use of a better understanding of behavioural economics?

BOX 9.2 HOW FIRMS INCREASE PROFITS BY UNDERSTANDING 'IRRATIONAL' CONSUMERS — EXPLORING ECONOMICS

In section 5.2 we looked at how behavioural economics can help our understanding of consumer behaviour. We examined in some detail the reasons why people's actions may be inconsistent with the predictions of traditional economic theory.

How firms present prices

The insights of behavioural economics suggest that businesses may be able to increase profits by taking advantage of consumer 'irrationality'. One potential application is the way companies present prices to consumers.

According to the predictions of standard economic theory, different ways of presenting the same price should have no impact on consumer behaviour. However, there is evidence that it does and firms can take advantage of these biases to boost their profits.

Partitioned or drip pricing. One example is 'partitioned' or 'drip pricing'. This is a strategy where, instead of presenting one total combined price for a product, the seller splits the price into one or more components. This usually includes a base price and then additional fees for factors such as handling, administration, processing, credit/debit card, tax, postage and packaging.

If the seller displays all the different elements of the total price simultaneously, it is called *partitioned pricing*.

Drip pricing is where only part of the price is advertised before the seller gradually includes additional fees as the consumer proceeds through the buying process. This

(continued)

approach is widely used in online markets where supplements to the total price appear after customers have worked their way through a series of web pages.

For example, in 2013, the consumer group *Which* carried out a mystery shopping investigation[1] into ticket prices for music, comedy and theatre events. In 76 out of 78 cases additional booking charges and delivery fees were added towards the end of the transaction. In some instances, these were up to a third of the advertised ticket price.

Evidence on the impact

Is there any evidence that partitioned or drip pricing has an impact on consumer behaviour?

Morwitz, Greenleaf and Johnson (1998)[2] carried out an auction experiment and found that when a 15 per cent surcharge was separated from the base price, the participants were willing to pay more.

Hossain and Morgan (2006)[3] conducted a field experiment on auctions for CDs and Xbox games on eBay. They found that the sales price in auctions was always greater when a low reserve price was displayed with high shipping/handling costs, as opposed to a high reserve price with low shipping/handling costs.

In a laboratory experiment, Huck and Wallace (2015) found that drip pricing reduced consumer surplus by 22 per cent.[4]

What behavioural biases can help to explain these results?

Anchoring. Consumers anchor to the advertised or headline price as they believe this to be the most important and relevant piece of information. They fail to take full account of and adjust to the other elements of the price (delivery, costs, etc.), which causes them to underestimate the product's total price.

Loss aversion/the endowment effect. Consumers may decide that they want to purchase the product once they see the initial advertised price. This makes them feel like they already own the good and so their reference point changes and they begin to value it more highly. This is the endowment effect (see pages 143–6). Loss aversion means they are willing to pay the additional elements to avoid having to give up the purchase.

Some other examples of company pricing strategies that possibly exploit biases in consumers' decision making include:

- *Reference pricing.* The price of the product is displayed next to another price: e.g. a price the seller claims is more typical, such as one previously charged by the same supplier.
- *Complex pricing.* The information is displayed in such a way that the consumer has to exert some cognitive effort to work out the price per unit: e.g. buy three for the price of two.
- *Time-limited pricing.* The customer is informed that the same offer will not be available at some point in the future. Therefore, if they delay, they will miss out on the deal.

1. *Is 'Black Friday' an example of any of the pricing strategies discussed in the box?*
2. *What behavioural biases are reference pricing, time-limited pricing and complex pricing trying to exploit?*

Find some real-world examples of these types of pricing strategies. Are they more likely to occur in some sectors than others?

1 'Play fair on ticket fees', *Which press release* (17 December 2013), https://press.which.co.uk/whichpressreleases/play-fair-on-ticket-fees/

2 V. G. Morwitz, E. A. Greenleaf andE. J. Johnson, 'Divide and prosper: consumers' reactions to partitioned prices', *Journal of Marketing Research*, vol. 35, pp. 453–63 (1998), www.jstor.org/stable/3152164

3 Tanjim Hossain and John Morgan, 'Plus shipping and handling: revenue (non) equivalence in field experiment on eBay', *Advances in Economic Analysis and Policy*, vol. 6, pp. 1–26 (2006), https://citeseerx.ist.psu.edu/viewdoc/download?doi=10.1.1.520.4216&rep=rep1&type=pdf

4 Steffan Huck and Brian Wallace, 'The impact of price frames on decision making: experimental evidence', *UCL Working Paper* (October 2015), www.ucl.ac.uk/~uctpbwa/papers/price-framing.pdf

BOX 9.3 CONSTRAINTS ON FIRMS' PRICING — CASE STUDIES AND APPLICATIONS

The fairness preferences of consumers

In Box 3.2, we discussed some examples of price gouging in the UK during the first national lockdown. For example, in the seven-week period between 26 March and 15 May 2020, the competition authorities received consumer complaints about 4779 different retail premises charging excessive prices.[1] However, this is less than 1 per cent of the estimated 587 022 retail premises in the UK. Just 264 traders were responsible for over 3100 of these complaints. The authorities concluded that, although a small minority of firms tried to exploit the situation, the vast majority behaved responsibly and fairly.

Were some types of retailers more likely to increase prices?

Fung and Roberts (2021)[2] analysed pricing data on eight of the most complained about products – toilet rolls, eggs, flour, pasta, rice, disinfectant, paracetamol and hand sanitiser – during the first UK national lockdown. The researchers found very different patterns of pricing. For example, whereas the price of 50ml of hand sanitiser remained stable at around £1 per bottle in national grocery and chemist chains, they increased rapidly in some independent chemists, peaking at around £5 per bottle.

The study found similar results for the other products – large price rises in some local convenience/symbol stores[3] compared to stable or small price rises in national supermarket/pharmacy chains. Rather than increasing prices, many national supermarket/pharmacy chains placed limits on the quantity each customer could purchase.

Responding to consumers' concepts of fairness

Why did the pricing behaviour of different retailers vary so much? One possible explanation is the behavioural economics theory of *reciprocity*. As discussed in Chapter 5 (pages 148–50), this is the idea that some people may experience an increase in their own utility by taking costly actions to reduce the incomes of those who they judge to have acted unfairly. Reciprocity can have implications for firms' pricing strategies. For example, building upon research by Kahneman, Knetch and Thaler (1986),[4] Piron and Fernandez (1995)[5] carried out a survey where they asked people to judge the fairness of a number of different market scenarios. For example:

> A local hardware store located conveniently for your shopping has been selling snow shovels for $15. The morning after a large snowstorm, the store raises the price to $25. You need a snow shovel to clear your driveway and the nearest store with snow shovels in stock is 10 minutes travel time away. This store is charging $20. The next closest store is so far away that it is irrelevant to your decision.

Just under 75 per cent of the respondents thought the store's actions were unfair. In a follow-up question, the participants were asked to choose between five different actions: (a) buy the shovel at the store; (b) buy the shovel at the store but complain to the manager; (c) buy the shovel at the store but shop elsewhere in the future; (d) buy the shovel at the other store; (e) do without the shovel.

Out of the people who believed the price increase was unfair, 35.7 per cent chose option (c), 28.6 per cent chose option (e) and 5.7 per cent chose option (d). In others words, 70 per cent of the respondents said they would punish the supplier at personal cost to themselves.

The previous evidence suggests that many people believe it is neither fair nor socially acceptable for firms to raise prices in response to surges in demand.

This potential damage to business reputation may be greater for larger national chains than for local stores. For example, following increases in the price of bottled water that occurred in some of the eastern states of the USA following the impact of Hurricane Sandy, Cowen[6] commented that:

> The reluctance to raise prices is especially strong for nationally branded stores. A local merchant may not care much if people in Iowa are upset at his prices, but major companies will fear damage to their national reputations. The short-term return from selling the water at a higher price is dwarfed by the risk to their business prospects.

Firms who have been trading for longer may also have more to lose from negative consumer perceptions of fairness. To test this idea, Cabral and Xu (2021)[7] analysed the prices of hand sanitiser and face masks on Amazon during the early months of the pandemic. They found that when Amazon itself was out of stock, third-party sellers increased their prices. However, continuing third-party sellers (i.e. those businesses/individuals who sold the items on Amazon prior to the pandemic) tended to raise prices significantly less than new third-party sellers.

Kahneman, Knetch and Thaler (1986) conclude that:

> Even in the absence of government intervention, the actions of firms that wish to avoid a reputation for unfairness will depart in significant ways from the standard model of economic behaviour.

Kahneman, Knetch and Thaler (1986) asked people to judge the fairness of the following market scenario: 'Suppose that, due to a transportation mix up, there is a local shortage of lettuce and the wholesale price has increased. A local grocer has bought the usual quantity of lettuce at a price that is 30 cents per head higher than normal. The grocer raises the price of lettuce to customers by 30 cents per head.' Only 21 per cent of the respondents thought the store's actions were unfair. Explain why this result is so different from the snow shovel example.

Devise and conduct a small-scale survey of friends and/or fellow students to discover their attitudes to cases of retailers raising prices during the pandemic. What lessons would you draw for firms seeking to maximise profits over the long run?

1 *Protecting consumers during the coronavirus pandemic: Update on the work of the CMA's Taskforce*, CMA (21 May 2020), www.gov.uk/government/publications/cma-coronavirus-taskforce-update-21-may-2020

2 San Sau Fung and Simon Roberts, 'The economics of potential price gouging during Covid-19 and the applications to complaints received by the CMA', *Working paper 21-02*, UEA Centre for Competition Policy (13 January 2021), https://www.researchgate.net/publication/348522040_The_economics_of_potential_price_gouging_during_Covid-19_and_the_application_to_complaints_received_by_the_CMA

3 A symbol store is run by an independent retailer who enters into a franchise agreement with a symbol group such as Spar and Costcutter.

4 Daniel Kahneman, Jack L. Knetch and Richard Thaler, 'Fairness as a constraint of profit seeking: entitlement in the market'. *American Economic Review*, vol. 76, no. 4 (September 1986), www.jstor.org/stable/1806070

5 Robert Piron and Luis Fernandez, 'Are fairness constraints on profit seeking important?' *Journal of Economic Psychology*, vol. 16 (March 1995), pp. 73–96, www.sciencedirect.com/science/article/abs/pii/016748709400037B

6 Tyler Cowen, 'Price gouging can be a type of hurricane aid', *Bloomberg Opinion* (5 September 2017), www.bloomberg.com/opinion/articles/2017-09-05/price-gouging-can-be-a-type-of-hurricane-aid

7 Luis Cabral and Lei Xu, 'Seller reputation and price gouging: evidence from the COVID-19 pandemic', *Economic Inquiry* (7 March 2021), https://onlinelibrary.wiley.com/doi/10.1111/ecin.12993

Section summary

1. Behavioural economics is relevant for understanding why and how the aims and strategies of firms deviate from traditional profit maximisation. This deviation is in part explained by managers using various mental shortcuts or heuristics to simplify complex decisions made in conditions of uncertainty. Some examples include imitation and focusing on performance.
2. Since firms are managed by individuals, who are motivated by a number of possible factors such as fairness, we should not be surprised if companies do not always appear to adopt 'selfish' strategies. The strength and awareness of any preferences for fairness will help to determine the equilibrium outcome in the market.
3. Firms can make use of the principles identified in behavioural economics to increase profits. Opportunities may arise in the relationship with consumers, particularly when looking at marketing and pricing. Consumer preferences for fairness may also constrain pricing decisions. There may also be examples where greater understanding of behaviour can be used to inform contracts with employees or with suppliers.
4. Levels of optimism and attitudes to risk will vary among owners and managers. If a firm is unwilling to make bold decisions it may increase its chances of survival, but it may pay for this with lower profits. Over-cautious strategies may also leave a firm vulnerable if its competitors are able to gain market share by being bold.

9.3 ALTERNATIVE MAXIMISING THEORIES

Long-run profit maximisation

The traditional economic theory of the firm assumes *short-run* profit maximisation. Many actions by firms may appear to diverge from this aim and yet could be consistent with ***long-run profit maximisation***. For example, policies to increase either the size of the firm or its market share may involve heavy advertising or low prices to the detriment of short-run profits. But if this results in a larger market share, the resulting economic power may enable the firm to make larger profits in the long run. For example, Amazon first sold shares to the public in May 1997 but did not make a profit until the fourth quarter of 2001. Its profits remained relatively modest until the fourth quarter of 2017, when they shot up to $1.86 billion. In the third quarter of 2020, the company reported a net income of $6.3 billion.

At first sight, a theory of long-run profit maximisation would seem to be a realistic alternative to the traditional short-run profit-maximisation theory. In practice, however, the theory is not a very useful predictor of firms' behaviour and is very difficult to test.

A claim by managers that they were attempting to maximise long-run profits could be an excuse for virtually any policy. When challenged as to why the firms had, say, undertaken expensive research or high-cost investment, or had engaged in a damaging price war, the managers could reply, 'Ah, yes, but in the long run it will pay off.' This is very difficult for shareholders to refute (until it is too late!).

Definition

Long-run profit maximisation An alternative theory which assumes that managers aim to shift cost and revenue curves so as to maximise profits over some longer time period.

Even if long-run profit maximisation *is* the prime aim, the means of achieving it are extremely complex. The firm will need a plan of action for prices, output, investment, etc., stretching from now into the future. But today's pricing and marketing decisions affect tomorrow's demand. Therefore, future demand curves cannot be taken as given. Today's investment decisions will affect tomorrow's costs. Therefore, future cost curves cannot be taken as given either. These shifts in demand and cost curves will be very difficult to estimate with any precision.

Quite apart from this, the actions of competitors, suppliers, unions, the future state of the economy, etc., are difficult to predict. Thus the picture of firms making precise calculations of long-run profit-maximising prices and outputs is an unrealistic one.

It may be useful, however, simply to observe that firms, when making current price, output and investment decisions, try to judge the approximate effect on new entrants, consumer demand, future costs, etc., and try to avoid decisions that would appear to conflict with long-run profits. Often this will involve steering clear of a decision (e.g. cutting price) that may stimulate an unfavourable result from rivals (e.g. rivals cutting their price).

Managerial utility maximisation

One of the most influential alternative theories of the firm was developed by O. E. Williamson[4] in the 1960s. Williamson argued that, provided satisfactory levels of profit are achieved, managers often have the discretion to choose what policies to pursue. In other words, they are free to pursue their *own* interests: i.e. to maximise their own utility.

4 O. E. Williamson, *The Economics of Discretionary Behaviour* (Prentice Hall, 1964), p. 3.

BOX 9.4 WHEN IS A THEORY NOT A THEORY?

EXPLORING ECONOMICS

Have you heard the joke about the man sitting in a railway carriage who was throwing pieces of paper out of the window? A fellow traveller was curious and asked him why he kept doing this.

'It keeps the elephants down', was the reply.

'But', said the other man, 'there are no elephants around here.'

'I know', said the first man. 'Effective, isn't it?'

Let's reformulate this joke.

Once upon a time there was this boss of a company who kept doing strange things. First, he would spend a massive amount of money on advertising, and then stop. Then he would pay a huge wage increase 'to keep his workforce happy'. Then he would close the factory for two months to give everyone a break. Then he would move the business, lock, stock and barrel, to a new location.

One day he was talking to an accountant friend, who asked, 'Why do you keep doing these strange things?'

'I have to do them to make the business profitable', was the reply.

'But your business is profitable', said the accountant.

'I know. It just goes to show how effective my policies are.'

1. *Why might it be difficult to refute a theory of long-run profit maximisation?*
2. *If a theory cannot in principle be refuted, is it a useful theory?*

Try inventing a business strategy that could be effective and then try justifying it using the spurious logic of this case study.

Williamson identified a number of factors that affect a manager's utility. The four main ones were salary, job security, dominance (including status, power and prestige) and professional excellence.

Of these, only salary is *directly* measurable. The rest have to be measured indirectly. One way of doing this is to examine managers' expenditure on various items, and in particular on *staff*, on *perks* (such as a company car) and on *discretionary investment*. The greater is the level of expenditure by managers on these items, the greater is likely to be their status, power, prestige, professional excellence and job security, and hence utility.

Having identified the factors that influence a manager's utility, Williamson developed several models in which managers seek to maximise their utility. He used these to predict managerial behaviour under various conditions and argued that they performed better than traditional profit-maximising theory.

One important conclusion was that average costs are likely to be higher when managers have the discretion to pursue their own utility. For example, perks and unnecessarily high staffing levels add to costs.

On the other hand, the resulting 'slack' allows managers to rein in these costs in times of low demand (see page 276). This enables them to maintain their profit levels. To support these claims he conducted a number of case studies. These did indeed show that staff and perks were cut during recessions and expanded during booms, and that new managers were frequently able to cut staff without influencing the productivity of firms.

Sales revenue maximisation (short-run)

Perhaps the most famous of all alternative theories of the firm is that developed by William Baumol in the late 1950s. This is the theory of ***sales revenue maximisation***. Unlike the theories of long-run profit maximisation and managerial utility maximisation, it is easy to identify the price and output that meet this aim – at least in the short run.

So why would managers want to maximise their firm's sales revenue? The answer is that the success of managers, and in particular sales managers, may be judged according to the level of the firm's sales. Sales figures are an obvious barometer of the firm's health and cannot be as easily manipulated as measures of profit. Managers' salaries, power and prestige may depend directly on sales revenue. The firm's sales representatives may be paid commission on their sales. Thus sales revenue maximisation may be a more dominant aim in the firm than profit maximisation, particularly if it has a dominant sales department. KI 24 p259

Sales revenue will be maximised at the top of the *TR* curve at output Q_1 in Figure 9.1. Profits, by contrast, would be maximised at Q_2. Thus, for given total revenue and total cost curves, sales revenue maximisation will tend to lead to a higher output and a lower price than profit maximisation.

Draw a diagram with MC and MR curves. Mark the output (a) at which profits are maximised; (b) at which sales revenue is maximised.

The firm will still have to make sufficient profits, however, to keep the shareholders happy. Thus firms can be seen to be operating with a profit constraint. They are *profit satisficers*.

The effect of this profit constraint is illustrated in Figure 9.2. The diagram shows a total profit (*TΠ*) curve. (This is found by simply taking the difference between *TR* and *TC* at each output.) Assume that the minimum acceptable profit

Definition

Sales revenue maximisation An alternative theory which assumes that managers aim to maximise the firm's short-run total revenue.

Figure 9.1 Sales-revenue-maximising output

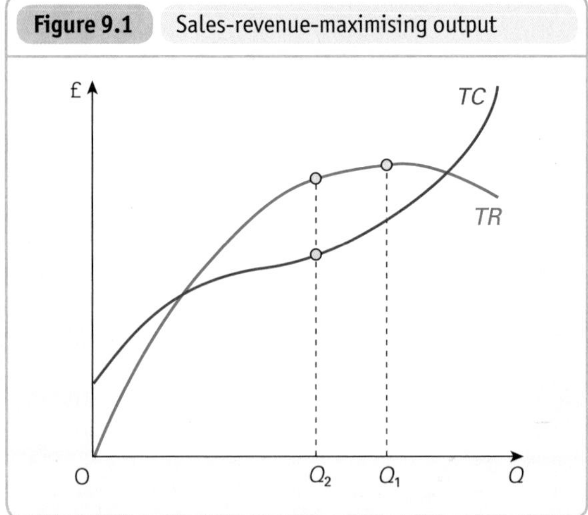

Figure 9.2 Sales revenue maximising with a profit constraint

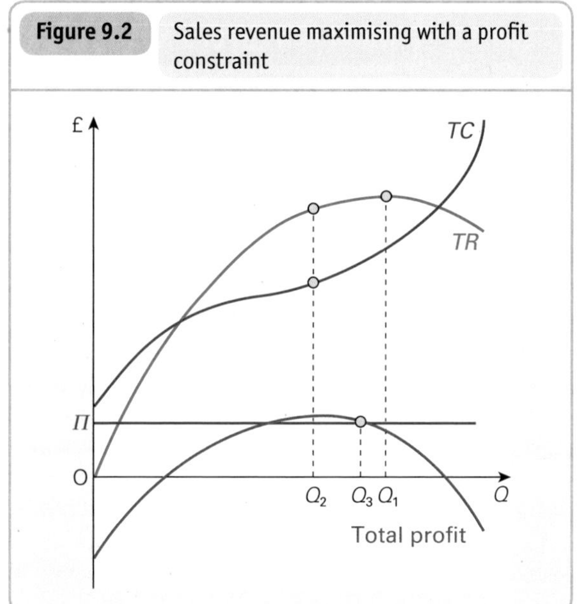

is Π (whatever the output). Any output greater than Q_3 will give a profit less than Π. Thus the sales revenue maximiser that is also a profit satisficer will produce Q_3, not Q_1. Note, however, that this output is still greater than the profit-maximising output Q_2.

If the firm could maximise sales revenue and still make more than the minimum acceptable profit, it would probably spend this surplus profit on advertising to increase revenue further. This would have the effect of shifting upwards the *TR* curve and also the *TC* curve (since advertising costs money).

Sales revenue maximisation will tend to involve more advertising than profit maximisation. The profit-maximising firm will advertise up to the point where the marginal revenue of advertising equals the marginal cost of advertising (assuming diminishing returns to advertising). The firm aiming to maximise sales revenue will go beyond this, since further advertising, although costing more than it earns the firm, will still add to total revenue. The firm will continue advertising until surplus profits above the minimum have been used up.

Since advertising increases a firm's costs, will prices necessarily be lower with sales revenue maximisation than with profit maximisation?

*LOOKING AT THE MATHS

We can express sales revenue maximisation algebraically. We start with the situation with no profit constraint.

Unconstrained sales revenue maximisation

Assume that the total revenue function is given by

$$TR = bQ - cQ^2 \quad \textbf{(1)}$$

This will give a straight-line *MR* function given by

$$MR = \frac{dTR}{dQ} = b - 2cQ$$

Total revenue is maximised where $MR = 0$, since, when total revenue is maximised, any increase in output will give a zero rise in total revenue. In other words, at the top of the total revenue curve in Figures 9.1 and 9.2, the slope of the curve is zero (the tangent to the curve is horizontal). Thus:

$$MR = b - 2cQ = 0$$

i.e.

$$2cQ = b$$

i.e.

$$Q = \frac{b}{2c} \quad \textbf{(2)}$$

Thus, if the total revenue function were

$$TR = 120 - 3Q^2$$

then, from equation (2), total revenue would be maximised at an output (Q), where

$$Q = \frac{b}{2c} = \frac{120}{2 \times 3} = 20$$

Constrained sales revenue maximisation

If there is a profit constraint, we can write the objective function as Max *TR*, subject to $(TR - TC) \geq T\Pi^*$ where $T\Pi^*$ is the minimum profit that must be achieved. Assume that the *TR* and *TC* functions are given by

$$TR = bQ - cQ^2$$

and

$$TC = a + dQ - eQ^2 + gQ^3$$

Note that these two equations match the shapes of the *TR* and *TC* curves in Figures 9.1 and 9.2. The constraint can now be written:

$$TR - TC = -a + (b - d)Q + (e - c)Q^2 - gQ^3 \geq T\Pi^*$$

We can use this to solve for Q. An example of this is given in Maths Case 9.1 on the student website.

Growth maximisation

Rather than aiming to maximise *short-run* revenue, managers may take a longer-term perspective and aim for ***growth maximisation*** in the size of the firm. They may directly gain utility from being part of a rapidly growing 'dynamic' organisation; promotion prospects are greater in an expanding organisation since new posts tend to be created; larger firms may pay higher salaries; managers may obtain greater power in a larger firm.

Growth is probably best measured in terms of a growth in sales revenue, since sales revenue (or 'turnover') is the simplest way of measuring the size of a business. An alternative would be to measure the capital value of a firm, but this will depend on the ups and downs of the stock market and is thus a rather unreliable method.

If a firm is to maximise growth, it needs to be clear about the time period over which it is setting itself this objective. For example, maximum growth over the next two or three years might be obtained by running factories to absolute maximum capacity, cramming in as many machines and workers as possible, and backing this up with massive advertising campaigns and price cuts. Such policies, however, may not be sustainable in the longer run. The firm may simply not be able to finance them. A longer-term perspective (say, five to ten years) may require the firm to 'pace' itself, and perhaps to direct resources away from current production and sales into the development of new products that have a potentially high and growing long-term demand.

Growth may be achieved either by internal expansion or by merger.

Growth by internal expansion

Internal growth requires an increase in sales, which requires an increase in the firm's productive capacity. In order to increase its *sales,* the firm is likely to engage in extensive product promotion and to try to launch new products. In order to increase *productive capacity,* the firm will require new investment. Both product promotion and investment will require finance.

TC 1 p10

In the short run, the firm can finance growth by borrowing, by retaining profits or by a new issue of shares. What limits the amount of finance that a firm can acquire, and hence the rate at which it can grow? If the firm *borrows* too much, the interest payments it incurs will make it difficult to maintain the level of dividends to shareholders. Similarly, if the firm *retains* too much *profit,* there will be less available to pay out in dividends. If it attempts to raise capital by a *new issue of shares,* the distributed profits will have to be divided between a larger number of shares. Whichever way it finances investment, therefore, the more it invests, the more the dividends on shares in the short run will probably fall.

This could lead shareholders to sell their shares, unless they are confident that *long-run* profits and hence dividends will rise again, thus causing the share price to remain high in the long run. If shareholders do sell their shares, this will cause share prices to fall. If they fall too far, the firm runs the risk of being taken over and of certain managers losing their jobs. The ***takeover constraint*** therefore requires that the growth-maximising firm distribute sufficient profits to avoid being taken over.

In the long run, a rapidly growing firm may find its profits increasing, especially if it can achieve economies of scale and a bigger share of the market. These profits can then be used to finance further growth.

Growth through vertical integration

If market conditions make growth through increased sales difficult, then a firm may choose to grow through vertical integration. This has a number of advantages.

Economies of scale. These can occur by the business performing complementary stages of production within a single business unit. The classic example of this is the steel manufacturer combining the furnacing and milling stages of production, saving the costs that would have been required to reheat the iron had such operations been undertaken by independent businesses. Clearly, for most firms, the performing of more than one stage on a single site is likely to reduce transport costs, as semi-finished products no longer have to be moved from one plant to another.

Reduced uncertainty. A business that is not vertically integrated may find itself subject to various uncertainties in the marketplace. Examples include uncertainty over future price movements, over supply reliability or over access to markets.

Barriers to entry. Vertical integration may give the firm greater power in the market by enabling it to erect entry barriers to potential competitors. For example, a firm that undertakes backward vertical integration and acquires a key input resource may effectively close the market to potential new entrants, either by simply refusing to supply a competitor, or by charging a very high price for the input, such that new firms face an absolute cost disadvantage.

See if you can identify two companies that are vertically integrated and what advantages they gain from such integration.

The major problem with vertical integration is that it may reduce the firm's ability to respond to changing market demands. A business that integrates may find itself tied to its own supply source. If, by contrast, it were free to choose

KI 24 p259

Definitions

Growth maximisation An alternative theory which assumes that managers seek to maximise the growth in sales revenue (or the capital value of the firm) over time.

Takeover constraint The effect that the fear of being taken over has on a firm's willingness to undertake projects that reduce distributed profits.

between suppliers, inputs might be obtained at a lower price than the firm could achieve by supplying itself.

Many firms are finding that it is better *not* to be vertically integrated but to focus on their core business and to outsource their supplies, their marketing and many other functions. That way they put alternative suppliers and distributors in competition with each other.

Growth through diversification

An alternative internal growth strategy to vertical integration is that of diversification. A good example of a highly diversified company is Virgin. Its interests include planes, trains, finance, music, mobile phones, holidays, hotels, wine, cinemas, broadband, health care, publishing, balloon flights and even space travel.

If the current market is saturated or in decline, diversification might be the only avenue open to the business if it wishes to maintain a high growth performance. In other words, it is not only the level of profits that may be limited in the current market, but also the growth of sales.

Diversification also has the advantage of spreading risks. If a business produces a single product in a single market, it is vulnerable to changes in that market's conditions. If a farmer produces nothing but potatoes and the potato harvest fails, the farmer is ruined. If, however, the farmer produces a whole range of vegetables, or even diversifies into livestock, then they are less subject to the forces of nature and the unpredictability of the market.

Growth by merger

A merger may be the result of the mutual agreement of two firms to come together. Alternatively, one firm may put in a takeover bid for another. This involves the first firm offering to buy the shares of the second for cash, to swap them for shares in the acquiring company, or to issue fixed-interest securities (debentures). The shareholders of the second firm then vote on whether to accept the offer. (Technically this is an 'acquisition' or 'takeover' rather than a merger, but the term 'merger' is generally used to include both mutual agreements and acquisitions.)

There are three types of merger:

- A ***horizontal merger*** is where firms in the same industry and at the same stage of production merge. For example, in June 2020, Just Eat Takeaway (the biggest takeaway food ordering and delivery platform in Europe) announced a $7.3 billion takeover of the US business Grubhub. This created the largest food delivery company in the world outside of China.
- A ***vertical merger*** is where firms in the same industry but at different stages in the production of a good merge. For example, in 2018, AT&T (a large owner of satellite and cable TV in the USA) acquired Time Warner (producer of TV content and owner of HBO, CNN and DC Comics) in a $85 billion deal.
- A ***conglomerate merger*** is where firms in different industries merge. For example, Google has acquired approximately 200 firms across a range of different sectors including robotics, video broadcasting, education and smoke alarms; in January 2021, Google completed the $2.1 billion purchase of Fitbit, the smartwatch producer.

Motives for merger

Economists have identified a number of possible motives for mergers.

Merger for growth. Mergers provide a much quicker means to growth than internal expansion. Not only does the firm acquire new capacity, it also acquires additional consumer demand. However, there is a danger that growth-maximising firms will make relatively low profits and have a low stock market value, making them attractive to takeover by other firms.

Merger for economies of scale. Once the merger has taken place, the constituent parts can be reorganised through a process of 'rationalisation'. This can result in some lumpy/indivisible inputs being utilised more fully and closer to their full capacity. For example, it is possible to spread the administrative costs of one head office over a larger level of output, hence reducing average costs. Evidence, however, suggests that many takeovers result in few if any cost savings. The newly merged businesses often struggle to exploit the potential economies of scale, and diseconomies can result from the disruptions of reorganisation. New managers installed by the parent company can often appear unsympathetic, and staff morale may go down.

Merger for monopoly power. Here the motive is to reduce competition and thereby gain greater market power and larger profits. With less competition, the firm will face a less elastic demand and will be able to charge a higher percentage above marginal cost. This obviously fits well with the traditional theory of the firm.

KI 22 p195

Which of the three types of merger (horizontal, vertical and conglomerate) are most likely to lead to (a) reductions in average costs; (b) increased market power?

Merger for increased market valuation. A merger can benefit shareholders of *both* firms by leading to a potential increase in the stock market valuation of the merged firm. If both sets of shareholders believe that they will make a capital gain, then they are more likely to approve the merger. In practice,

Definitions

Horizontal merger Where two firms in the same industry at the same stage in the production process merge.

Vertical merger Where two firms in the same industry at different stages in the production process merge.

Conglomerate merger Where two firms in different industries merge.

however, there is little evidence to suggest that mergers lead to long-run increases in market valuation.

Merger to reduce uncertainty. There are two major sources of uncertainty for firms. The first is the behaviour of rivals. Mergers, by reducing the number of rivals, can correspondingly reduce uncertainty. At the same time, they can reduce the costs of competition (e.g. by reducing advertising). The second source of uncertainty is the economic environment. In a period of rapid change, such as often accompanies a boom or recession, firms may seek to protect themselves by merging with others.

Merger due to opportunity. Sometimes mergers occur as a consequence of opportunities that suddenly and unexpectedly arise. Such mergers are largely unplanned and thus virtually impossible to predict. Dynamic business organisations are constantly on the lookout for such opportunities.

Other motives. Other motives for mergers include:

- Getting bigger so as to make the firm less likely to be taken over itself.
- Merging with another firm to prevent it being taken over by an unwanted predator (the 'White Knight' strategy).
- Asset stripping. This is where a firm buys another and then breaks it up, selling off the profitable bits and probably closing down the remainder.
- Empire building. This is where owners or managers like the power or prestige of owning or controlling several (preferably well-known) companies.
- Broadening the geographical base of the company by merging with a firm in a different part of the country or the world.
- Reducing levels of taxation. A takeover may enable a firm to change its tax domicile to a country with a lower rate of corporation tax.

These theories, alongside the general area of mergers and acquisitions, are the subject of ongoing research, but most are in need of greater empirical investigation and support.

1. *Which of the above theories overlap and in what way?*
2. *Why do you think it is difficult to find adequate empirical support for any of them?*

Mergers and the relationship between growth and profit

In order for a firm to be successful in a takeover bid, it must be sufficiently profitable to finance the takeover. Thus the faster it tries to grow and the more takeovers it attempts, the higher must be its profitability.

In addition to being an obvious means to the growth of the firm, mergers may be a means of increasing profits since mergers can lead to both lower average costs through economies of scale and higher average revenue through increased market power over prices. These profits in turn may be seen as a means of financing further growth.

It can therefore be seen that, whichever way it is financed, growth is closely linked to profits. High profits can help a firm grow. Rapid growth can lead to a rapid growth in profits.

These are not inevitable links, however. For example, long-run profits may not increase if a firm invests in risky projects or projects with a low rate of return. Expansion alone is no guarantee of profits. Also, high profits will not necessarily lead to growth if a large proportion is distributed to shareholders and only a small proportion is reinvested. High profits may help growth, but they do not guarantee it.

BOX 9.5 MERGER ACTIVITY — CASE STUDIES AND APPLICATIONS

A worldwide perspective

What have been the trends, patterns and driving factors in mergers and acquisitions[1] (M&As) around the world over the past 30 years? An overview is given in chart (a).

The 1990s

The early 1990s saw relatively low M&A activity as the world was in recession, but as world economic growth picked up, so worldwide M&A activity increased. Economic growth was particularly rapid in the USA, which became a major target for many acquisitions.

There was also an acceleration in the process of 'globalisation'. With the dismantling of trade barriers around the world and increasing financial deregulation, international competition increased. Companies felt the need to become bigger in order to compete more effectively.

In Europe, M&A activity was boosted by the development of the Single Market, which came into being in January 1993. Companies took advantage of the abolition of trade barriers in the EU, which made it easier for them to operate on an EU-wide basis. Strong economic growth experienced throughout the EU, combined with the arrival of the euro, led to a booming M&A market in the late 1990s.

By the 2000s, the number of annual worldwide M&As was three times the level in 1990. Very large deals included a €29.4 billion marriage of pharmaceutical companies Zeneca of the UK and Astra of Sweden in 1998, a €205 billion takeover of telecoms giant Mannesmann of Germany by Vodafone of the UK in 1999 and a €50.8 billion takeover of Orange™ of the UK by France Telecom in 2000.

Other sectors in which merger activity was high included financial services and the privatised utilities sector. In the UK, in particular, most of the privatised water and electricity companies were taken over by French and US buyers, attracted by the sector's monopoly profits.

The 2000s

The number of cross-border deals peaked at 6 497 in 2000 and had a combined total value of $960 billion. However, a worldwide economic slowdown after 2000 led to a fall in both the number and value of mergers throughout most

(continued)

of the world. The value of cross-border M&As in 2003 was $165 billion – a fall of 83 per cent from the peak of three years earlier. Activity began to increase again after 2003 as economic growth in the world economy began to accelerate. Two major target regions were (a) the 10 countries that joined the EU in 2004 plus Russia and (b) Asian countries, especially India and China.

In 2007, the number of cross-border mergers reached a new peak of 7 582 with a combined market value of over $1000 billion. However, the Great Recession of 2008–9 led to both the number and value of cross-border deals falling dramatically. Recession is a difficult time for deal making and the number of withdrawn mergers – that is, where two firms agree in principle to merge but later pull out of the deal – increased. As diagram (a) shows, the value of cross-border M&As in 2009 was $288 billion – a fall of 72 per cent from the record high in 2007.

The 2010s

A faltering economic recovery in 2010 meant there was a small increase in global M&A. However, the eurozone crisis and fears about the state of the public finances in the USA had a negative impact on the number of deals in 2012 and 2013.

Economic growth and growing business confidence saw global M&A activity grow quickly from 2014 to 2018 with over 6000 deals per annum throughout this period. The combined market value of deals was over $800 billion in 2018. The total value of all M&As was $3.9 trillion in 2019 – the fourth highest figure on record. Historically low interest rates, slow rates of internal growth, large cash reserves and defensive moves against the threat of entry from 'tech giants' were important drivers behind this increase.

Some analysts believe that the US–China trade war, slower growth of China's economy and greater political uncertainty will all have a negative impact on future global M&A activity.

The worldwide pattern of cross-border M&A activity has also changed between the mid-1990s and the mid-2010s. Diagram (b) illustrates three trends.

- First, North America saw a rise in its average global share of cross-border M&As from 21.2 per cent in the mid-1990s to 25.5 per cent in the mid-2010s. Its share measured by value also increased from 32.1 per cent to 34.9 per cent. Between 2015 and 2017 M&A activity in the USA was at historically high levels.
- Second, Asian countries (excluding Japan) saw an increase in their share of the number of cross-border M&As from 8.6 per cent in the mid-1990s to 12.8 per cent in the mid-2010s. Their share of the value increased from 5 per cent to 10.6 per cent. India has experienced rapid growth in the value of M&As in recent years, with deals rising from $7.96 billion in 2016 to $33.18 billion in 2018. China experienced rapid growth in 2013 and 2014 but M&A activity has declined significantly in recent years.
- Third, EU countries saw a reduction in their share of the number of cross-border M&As from 49.7 per cent in the mid-1990s to 42.1 per cent in the mid-2010s, and a fall in their share of the value of M&As from 42.4 per cent to 37.6 per cent.

The impact of COVID-19

The pandemic and associated national lockdowns led to the number and value of deals falling dramatically in the second quarter of 2020. However, the market then grew very rapidly in the second half of the year. The value of all deals (both domestic and cross border) exceeded $1 trillion in both the third and fourth quarters – the first time this has occurred since 2008. Technology was the sector with the highest value and volume of takeovers. Big increases in the number of people working from home had a dramatic impact on demand in the markets for video conferencing, collaboration software

(a) Cross-border mergers and acquisitions by target

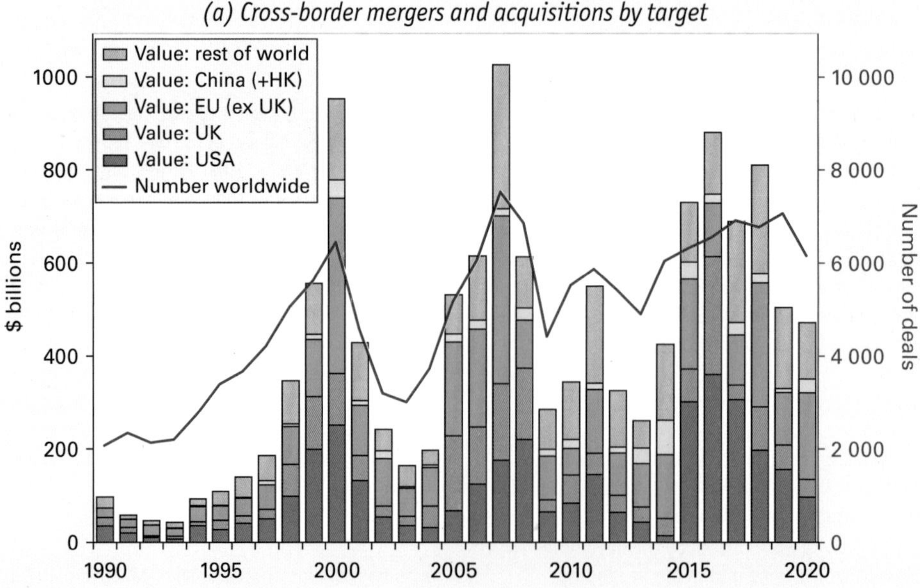

Note: The data cover only those deals that involve an acquisition of an equity of more than 10%; China excludes Hong Kong.
Source: 'Cross Border Mergers & Acquisitions', *World Investment Report* Annex Tables (UNCTAD, June 2021), Tables 5 and 7, https://worldinvestmentreport.unctad.org/annex-tables/

(b) Cross-border mergers and acquisitions by target region (% of total number and value)

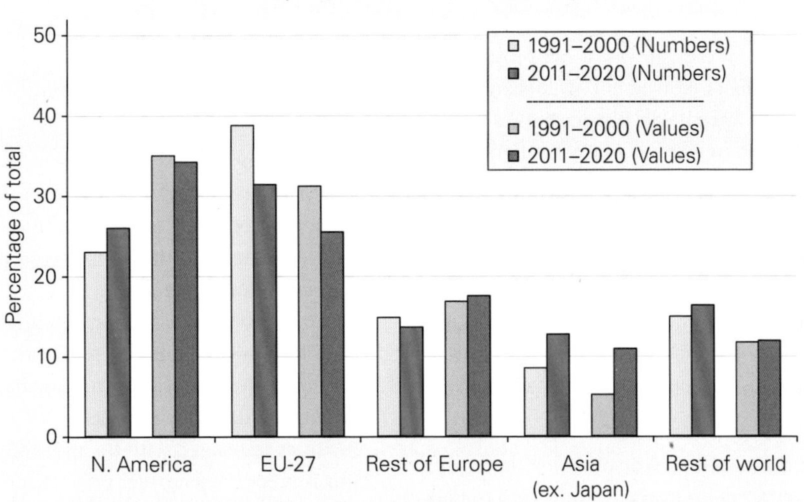

Source: 'Cross Border Mergers & Acquisitions', *World Investment Report* Annex Tables (UNCTAD, June 2021), Tables 7 and 5, https://worldinvestmentreport.unctad.org/annex-tables/

and cyber security. Many firms saw this as a chance to expand in a growing market.

Different types and consequences of M&A activity

When viewed in terms of long-run trends, cross-border M&As have become more common as globalisation has gathered pace. In the mid-1990s they accounted for about 16 per cent of all deals, whereas now they account for over 40 per cent.

Between 2016 and 2020 the total value of M&As where a foreign company purchased a UK company was £375.8 billion compared with £91.1 billion for domestic deals.[2]

Cross-border M&As can be an effective strategy for firms that want to gain large-scale entry into an overseas market. One motivating factor for Just Eat Takeaway's $7.3 billion takeover of Grubhub was to gain access to the lucrative food delivery market in the US.

Horizontal cross-border mergers

These are the most common type of merger. A horizontal merger or acquisition of a domestic firm by an overseas firm may not alter the number of firms competing in the sector if the foreign firm merely replaces an existing firm. Its presence may generate greater competition and innovation in the industry if the new owners bring with them fresh ideas.

If the foreign firm is already present in the domestic economy and it then takes over a rival, the number of firms in the industry is reduced. This could lead to less competition and higher prices. Alternatively, the newly merged firm may benefit from lower costs that it can pass on to its customers in the form of lower prices.

Vertical cross-border mergers

Vertical and conglomerate cross-border M&As are less common than their horizontal counterparts, but also come with potential costs as well as benefits. For example, a backward vertical M&A can help a firm compete globally by reducing its supply costs, but it can impose harsh terms on suppliers in the domestic economy where it operates in order to achieve this. Forward vertical M&A into the retail sector can help a foreign firm secure a domestic market and offer customers a better service. However, they may now move away from supplying rival retailers on comparable terms so that customer choice is reduced.

Conglomerate cross-border mergers

There was a wave of these mergers in the 1960s as firms tried to diversify, but they are now far less popular. The tendency instead has been for many companies to try to become more focused, by selling off parts of the business that are not seen as 'core activities'. For example, in October 2012, the conglomerate Kraft Foods split its business into a global snacks business, named Mondelez International, and a food business, named Kraft Foods Group. In 2015, Kraft Foods Group merged with Heinz to become Kraft Heinz.

There is no doubt that many M&As have been good for society and are a sign of a healthy capital market. However, evidence suggests that approximately two-thirds of deals fail to achieve the anticipated gains.

Are the motives for merger likely to be different in a recession from those in a period of rapid economic growth? What would you predict about the pattern of mergers over the next few years, given the current state of the economy?

Use newspaper and other resources to identify the anticipated benefits (extra revenue and lower costs) of a recent cross-border merger. Do you think they are realistic?

1 By 'acquisitions' we mean takeovers or the acquiring of at least 5 per cent of a company's shares.

2 'Mergers and acquisitions involving UK companies: Oct to Dec 2020', *Statistical Bulletin* (ONS), www.ons.gov.uk/businessindustryandtrade/changestobusiness/

Growth through strategic alliances

KI 23 p228

One means of achieving growth is through the formation of ***strategic alliances*** with other firms. They are a means whereby business operations can be expanded relatively quickly and at relatively low cost, and are a common way in which firms can deepen their involvement in global markets.

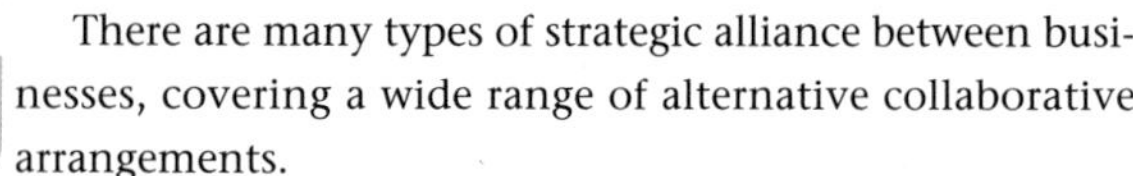

KI 24 p259

There are many types of strategic alliance between businesses, covering a wide range of alternative collaborative arrangements.

Joint ventures. A ***joint venture*** is where two or more firms decide to create, and jointly own, a new independent organisation. Hulu, the television on demand and streaming business, was originally a joint venture between the Walt Disney Company, 21st Century Fox, Comcast and Time Warner. Disney gained full control with its acquisition of 21st Century Fox in 2019.

Consortia. Some of the largest logistic operators in Europe formed the Customs Clearance Consortium (CCC) to help deal with the increase in custom checks following Brexit. A ***consortium*** is usually created for a very specific project or contract. For example, a consortium led by Fujitsu won a two-year government contract in 2020 to help firms with customs checks for goods entering into Northern Ireland from the rest of the UK. Other members of the consortium include McKinsey, the Institute of Export & International Trade and CCC.

Franchising. A less formal strategic alliance is where a business agrees to ***franchise*** its operations to third parties. McDonald's, Costa and Coca-Cola are good examples of businesses that use a franchise network. In such a relationship, the franchisee is responsible for manufacturing and/or selling, and the franchiser retains responsibility for branding and marketing.

Subcontracting. Like franchising, ***subcontracting*** is a less formal source of strategic alliance, where companies maintain their independence. When a business subcontracts, it employs an independent business to manufacture or supply some service rather than conduct the activity itself. Car manufacturers are major subcontractors. Given the multitude and complexity of components that are required to manufacture a car, the use of subcontractors to supply specialist items, such as brakes and lights, seems a logical way to organise the business.

Networks. ***Networks*** are less formal than any of the above alliances. A network is where two or more businesses work collaboratively but without any formal relationship binding one to the other. Such a form of collaboration is highly prevalent in Japan. Rather than a formal contract regulating the behaviour of the partners to the agreement, their relationship is based upon an understanding of trust and loyalty.

Why form strategic alliances?

As a business expands, possibly internationally, it may well be advantageous to join with an existing player in the market. Such a business would have local knowledge and an established network of suppliers and distributors.

KI 11 p72

In addition, strategic alliances allow firms to share risk. The Channel Tunnel and the consortium of firms that built it is one such example. The construction of the Channel Tunnel was a massive undertaking and far too risky for any single firm to embark upon. With the creation of a consortium, risk was spread and the various consortium members were able to specialise in their areas of expertise.

Projects that might have prohibitively high start-up costs, or running costs, may become feasible if firms co-operate and pool their capital. In addition, an alliance of firms, with their combined assets and credibility, may find it easier to generate finance, whether from investors in the stock market or from the banking sector.

The past 30 years have seen a flourishing of strategic alliances. They have become a key growth strategy for business both domestically and internationally. They are seen as a way of expanding business operations quickly without the difficulties associated with the more aggressive approach of acquisition or the lengthier process of merger.

Growth through going global

In many respects, a firm's global strategy is simply an extension of its strategy within its own domestic market. However, opening up to global markets can provide an obvious means for a business to expand its markets and spread its risks. It is also a means of reducing costs, whether through economies of scale or from accessing cheap sources of supply or low-wage production facilities.

A firm's global growth strategy may involve simply exporting or opening up factories abroad, or it may involve merging with businesses abroad or forming strategic alliances. As barriers to trade and to the international flow of capital have reduced, so more and more businesses have sought to become multinational. The result is that the global business environment has tended to become more and more competitive.

Definitions

Strategic alliance Where two firms work together, formally or informally, to achieve a mutually desirable goal.

Joint venture Where two or more firms set up and jointly own a new independent firm.

Consortium Where two or more firms work together on a specific project and create a separate company to run the project.

Franchise A formal agreement whereby a company uses another company to produce or sell some or all of its product.

Subcontracting Where a firm employs another firm to produce part of its output or some of its input(s).

Network An informal arrangement between businesses to work together towards some common goal.

Equilibrium for a growth-maximising firm

What will a growth-maximising firm's price and output be? Unfortunately there is no simple formula for predicting this.

In the short run, the firm may choose the profit-maximising price and output – so as to provide the greatest funds for investment. On the other hand, it may be prepared to sacrifice some short-term profits in order to mount an advertising campaign. It all depends on the strategy it considers most suitable to achieve growth.

In the long run, prediction is more difficult still. The policies that a firm adopts will depend crucially on the assessments of market opportunities made by managers. But this involves judgement, not fine calculation. Different managers will judge a situation differently.

TC 9 p132

One prediction can be made: growth-maximising firms are likely to diversify into different products, especially as they approach the limits to expansion in existing markets.

Alternative maximising theories and the public interest

TC 3 p26

It is difficult to draw firm conclusions about the public interest.

In the case of sales revenue maximisation, a higher output will be produced than under profit maximisation, but the consumers will not necessarily benefit from lower prices, since more will be spent on advertising – costs that will be reflected in a higher price.

In the case of growth and long-run profit maximisation, there are many possible policies that a firm could pursue. To the extent that a concern for the long run encourages firms to look to improved products, new products and new techniques, the consumer may benefit from such a concern. To the extent, however, that growth encourages a greater level of industrial concentration through merger, the consumer may lose from the resulting greater level of monopoly power.

As with the traditional theory of the firm, the degree of competition a firm faces is a crucial factor in determining just how responsive it will be to the wishes of the consumer.

How will competition between growth-maximising firms benefit the consumer?

Section summary

1. Rather than seeking to maximise short-run profits, a firm may take a longer-term perspective. It is very difficult, however, to predict the behaviour of a long-run profit-maximising firm, since (a) different managers are likely to make different judgements about how to achieve maximum profits and (b) demand and cost curves may shift unpredictably both in response to the firm's own policies and as a result of external factors.
2. Managers may seek to maximise their own utility, which, in turn, will depend on factors such as salary, job security and power within the organisation. However, given that managerial utility depends on a range of variables, it is difficult to use the theory to make general predictions of firms' behaviour.
3. Managers may gain utility from maximising sales revenue. They will, however, still have to ensure that a satisfactory level of profit is achieved. The output of a firm which seeks to maximise sales revenue will be higher than that for a profit-maximising firm. Its level of advertising will also tend to be higher. Whether price will be higher or lower depends on the relative effects on demand and cost of the additional advertising.
4. Many managers aim for maximum growth of their organisation, believing that this will help their salaries, power, prestige, etc.
5. Growth may be by internal expansion. This can be financed by ploughing back profits, by share issue, or by borrowing. Whichever method a firm uses, it will require sufficient profits to avoid becoming vulnerable to a takeover.
6. Vertical integration can reduce a firm's costs through various economies of scale. It can also help to reduce uncertainty, as the vertically integrated business could secure supply routes and/or retail outlets.
7. Growth may be by merger. Mergers can be horizontal, vertical or conglomerate. Merger activity tends to occur in waves. Various motives have been suggested for mergers, including growth, economies of scale, market power, increased share values, reduction in uncertainty, and simply taking advantage of opportunities as they occur.
8. One means of achieving growth is through the formation of strategic alliances with other firms. They have the advantage of allowing easier access to new markets, risk sharing and capital pooling. Many firms' growth strategy includes expansion abroad.
9. As with long-run profit-maximising theories, it is difficult to predict the price and output strategies of a growth-maximising firm. Much depends on the judgements of particular managers about growth opportunities.
10. Alternative aims will benefit the consumer to the extent that they encourage firms to develop new products and to find more efficient methods of production. They may be against the consumer's interest to the extent that they lead firms to engage in extensive advertising or to merge with a resulting increased concentration of market power.

9.4 ASYMMETRIC INFORMATION AND THE PRINCIPAL–AGENT PROBLEM

Principals and agents

A useful way to think about alternative maximisation theories is as examples of the *principal–agent problem*. Let us examine this problem.

One of the features of a complex modern economy is that people (principals) have to employ others (agents) to carry out their wishes. If you want to sell a house, it is more convenient to go to an estate agent than to do it yourself. These agents have specialist knowledge and can save you, the principal, a great deal of time and effort. It is an example of the benefits of the specialisation and division of labour.

It is the same with firms. They employ people with specialist knowledge and skills to carry out specific tasks. Companies frequently employ consultants to give them advice, or engage the services of specialist firms such as an advertising agency. Even employees of a company can be seen as 'agents' of their employer. In the case of workers, they can be seen as the agents of management. Junior managers are the agents of senior management. Senior managers are the agents of the directors, who are themselves agents of the shareholders. Thus in large firms there is often a complex chain of principal–agent relationships.

Asymmetric information

But these relationships have an inherent danger for the principal: there is ***asymmetric information*** between the two sides.

The agent knows more about the situation than the principal – of course, this is part of the reason why the principal employs the agent in the first place. The danger is that the agent may well not act in the principal's best interests, and may be able to get away with it because of the principal's imperfect knowledge. The estate agent may try to convince the vendor that it is necessary to accept a lower price, while the real reason is to save the agent time, effort and expense.

In firms, too, agents may not act in the best interests of their principals. For example, workers may be able to get away with not working very hard, preferring instead an easy life. Similarly, given the divorce between the ownership and control of a company, managers (agents) may pursue goals different from those of shareholders (principals). Thus *X inefficiency* is likely to occur (see Box 7.5).

So asymmetric information creates a problem for principals – known as the ***principal–agent problem***:

The principal–agent problem. **Where people (principals), as a result of a lack of knowledge, cannot ensure that their best interests are served by their agents. Agents may take advantage of this situation to the disadvantage of the principals.**

So how can principals tackle the problem? There are two elements in the solution:

- The principals must have some way of *monitoring* the performance of their agents. For example, a company might employ efficiency experts to examine the operation of its management. 
- Second, there must be *incentives* for agents to behave in the principals' interests. For example, managers' salaries could be closely linked to the firm's profitability. 

Alternative theories of the firm therefore place considerable emphasis on incentive mechanisms in explaining the behaviour of managers and the resulting performance of their companies.

In a competitive market, managers' and shareholders' interests are more likely to coincide. Managers have to ensure that the company remains efficient or it may not survive the competition and they might lose their jobs. In monopolies and oligopolies, however, where supernormal profits can often be relatively easily earned, the interests of shareholders and managers are likely to diverge. Here it will be in shareholders' interests to institute incentive mechanisms that ensure that their agents, the managers, are motivated to strive for profitability.

Definitions

Asymmetric information Where one party in an economic relationship (e.g. an agent) has more information than another (e.g. the principal).

Principal–agent problem Where people (principals), as a result of lack of knowledge, cannot ensure that their best interests are served by their agents.

The adverse impact of asymmetric information

If effective monitoring and incentive systems cannot be found, then asymmetric information might prevent firms from achieving the most efficient outcomes. Consider the example of a small business seeking finance for investment purposes. Banks and financial institutions are unlikely to have full access to information about the business or the individuals who own it. Since investment opportunities often also involve some uncertainty about the future, the likely outcome is a lower level of lending than is desirable.

Explain why the existence of asymmetric information may be damaging for both parties in an economic exchange, not only for the one who has incomplete information.

Firms also face asymmetric information about the quality of supplies and the ability of customers to pay; the latter may be a particular issue for transactions that take place between firms and where credit is extended. If firms recognise these issues when writing contracts, they may be able to address the problem and achieve better outcomes. But often the problem only becomes apparent when it is too late.

On occasion the impact of asymmetric information can be so serious that the consequences are devastating, not only for the individual market, but also for the wider economy. One example of this is the US sub-prime housing market, where poor information in the mid-2000s led to house prices soaring, only later to collapse, trigging the 2007–8 financial crisis. This is examined in Case Study 9.9 on the student website.

Section summary

1. The problem of managers not pursuing the same goals as the owners is an example of the *principal–agent problem*. Agents (in this case, the managers) may not always carry out the wishes of their principals (in this case, the owners).
2. Possible solutions for owners are to (a) monitor the performance of managers, and (b) create incentives for managers to behave in the owners' interests. If they are ineffective then asymmetric information may prevent firms from achieving their most efficient outcomes.

9.5 MULTIPLE AIMS

Satisficing and the setting of targets

Large firms are often complex institutions with many departments (sales, production, design, purchasing, personnel, finance, etc.). Each department is likely to have its own specific set of aims and objectives, which may come into conflict with those of other departments. These aims in turn will be constrained by the interests of shareholders, workers, customers and creditors (collectively known as ***stakeholders***), who will need to be kept sufficiently happy.

KI 24 p259

In many firms, targets are set for production, sales, profit, stockholding, etc. If, in practice, target levels are not achieved, a 'search' procedure will be started to find out what went wrong and how to rectify it. If the problem cannot be rectified, managers will probably adjust the target downwards. If, on the other hand, targets are easily achieved, managers may adjust them upwards. Thus the targets to which managers aspire depend to a large extent on the success in achieving *previous* targets.

Targets are also influenced by expectations of demand and costs, by the achievements of competitors and by expectations of competitors' future behaviour. For example, if it is expected that the economy is likely to move into recession, sales and profit targets may be adjusted downwards.

If targets conflict, the conflict could be settled by a bargaining process between managers. In this case, the outcome of the bargaining will depend on the power and ability of the individual managers concerned and the governance structure in which they operate. Thus a similar set of conflicting targets may be resolved differently in different firms.

Definition

Stakeholders (in a company) People who are affected by a company's activities and/or performance (customers, employees, owners, creditors, people living in the neighbourhood, etc.). They may or may not be in a position to take decisions, or influence decision taking, in the firm.

BOX 9.6 **STAKEHOLDER POWER?** EXPLORING ECONOMICS

Who governs the firm?

The concept of the 'stakeholder economy' became fashionable in the late 1990s. Rather than the economy being governed by big business, and rather than businesses being governed in the interests of shareholders (many of whom are big institutions, such as insurance companies and pension funds), the economy should serve the interests of everyone. But what does this mean for the governance of firms?

The stakeholders of a firm include customers, employees (from senior managers to the lowest-paid workers), shareholders, suppliers, lenders and the local and national communities.

The supporters of a stakeholding economy argue that *all* these interest groups ought to have a say in the decisions of the firm. Trade unions or workers' councils ought to be included in decisions affecting the workforce, or indeed all company decisions. They could be represented on decision-making bodies and perhaps have seats on the board of directors. Alternatively, the workforce might be given the power to elect managers.

Banks or other institutions lending to firms ought to be included in investment decisions. In Germany, where banks finance a large proportion of investment, banks are represented on the boards of most large companies.

Local communities ought to have a say in any projects (such as new buildings or the discharge of effluent) that affect the local environment. Customers ought to have more say in the quality of products being produced: for example, by being given legal protection against the production of shoddy or unsafe goods.

Where interest groups cannot be directly represented in decision making, companies ought to be regulated by the government in order to protect the interests of the various groups. For example, if farmers and other suppliers to supermarkets are paid very low prices, then the purchasing behaviour of the supermarkets could be regulated by some government agency.

But is this vision of a stakeholder economy likely to become reality? Trends in the international economy suggest that the opposite might be occurring. The growth of multinational corporations, with their ability to move finance and production to wherever it is most profitable, has weakened the power of employees, local interest groups and even national governments.

Employees in one part of the multinational may have little in the way of common interests with employees in another. In fact, they may vie with each other: for example, over which plant should be expanded or closed down. With new 'flexible labour markets', firms are making more use of casual, part-time, temporary or agency workers. These employees are generally 'outsiders' to decision making within the firm (see Box 10.8).

However, many firms in recent years have started to publish reports that outline their progress towards a broader set of societal goals, such as reducing CO_2 emissions, increasing the use of energy from renewable sources, treating employees in a fair/ethical manner and donating money to charity/local community projects. This is widely referred to as 'corporate social responsibility' (CSR).

CSR requires costly investments by firms whose managers may have a genuine commitment to the interests of society. An alternative interpretation is that firms see it as a way of making greater profits from reciprocity – see Box 9.3. If consumers perceive the investments as fair or socially desirable, they may be willing to reward the company by paying higher prices for their brands. CSR and business ethics are explored in Case Study 9.4 on the student website.

Are customers' interests best served by profit-maximising firms, answerable primarily to shareholders, or by firms where various stakeholder groups are represented in decision taking?

Investigate two well-known companies and find out to what extent they take account of stakeholders' interests. Do they have formal mechanisms in place to do so and, if so, how effective are they likely to be?

Organisational slack

Since changing targets often involves search procedures and bargaining processes and is therefore time-consuming, and since many managers prefer to avoid conflict, targets tend to be changed fairly infrequently. Business conditions, however, often change rapidly. To avoid the need to change targets, therefore, managers will tend to be fairly conservative in their aspirations. This leads to the phenomenon known as ***organisational slack*** – a term coined by Cyert and March (see above, page 260).

When the firm does better than expected, it will allow slack to develop. This slack can then be taken up if the firm does worse than expected. For example, if the firm produces more than it planned, it will build stocks of finished goods and draw on them if subsequently production falls. It would not, in the meantime, increase its sales target or reduce its production target. If it did, and production then fell below target, the production department might not be able to supply the sales department with its full requirement.

Thus keeping targets fairly low and allowing slack to develop allows all targets to be met with minimum conflict.

Organisational slack, however, adds to a firm's costs. If firms are operating in a competitive environment, they may be forced to cut slack in order to survive. In the 1970s, many

Definition

Organisational slack Where managers allow spare capacity to exist, thereby enabling them to respond more easily to changed circumstances.

Japanese firms succeeded in cutting slack by using ***just-in-time*** methods of production. These involve keeping stocks to a minimum and ensuring that inputs are delivered as required. Clearly, this requires that production is tightly controlled and that suppliers are reliable. Many firms today have successfully cut their warehouse costs by using such methods. These methods are examined in Box 10.8.

Multiple goals: predictions of behaviour

Conservatism

Some firms may be wary of change, seeing it as risky. They may prefer to stick with current practices. This could apply to pricing policies, marketing techniques, product design and range, internal organisation of the firm, etc. This is simple heuristics: if it works, stick with it.

If something does not work, managers will probably change it, but again they may be cautious: perhaps imitating successful competitors.

This safe, satisficing approach makes prediction of any given firm's behaviour relatively straightforward. You simply examine its past behaviour. Making generalisations about all such cautious firms, however, is more difficult. Different firms will have established different rules of behaviour depending on their experiences of their own particular market.

Comparison with other firms

Managers may judge their success by comparing their firm's performance with that of rivals. For example, growing market share may be seen as a more important indicator of 'success' than simple growth in sales. Similarly, they may compare their profits, their product design, their technology or their industrial relations with those of rivals. To many managers it is *relative* performance that matters, rather than absolute performance.

What predictions can be made if this is how managers behave? The answer is that it depends on the nature of competition in the industry. The more profitable, innovative and efficient are the competitors, the more profitable, innovative and efficient will managers try to make their particular firm.

The further ahead of their rivals that firms try to stay, the more likely it is that there will be a 'snowballing' effect, with each firm trying to outdo the other.

Will this type of behaviour tend to lead to profit maximisation?

Satisficing and the public interest

Firms with multiple goals will be satisficers. The greater the number of goals of the different managers, the greater is the chance of conflict, and the more likely it is that organisational slack will develop. Satisficing firms are therefore likely to be less responsive to changes in consumer demand and changes in costs than profit-maximising firms. They may thus be less efficient.

On the other hand, such firms may be less eager to exploit their economic power by charging high prices, or to use aggressive advertising, or to pay low wages.

The extent to which satisficing firms do act in the public interest will, as in the case of other types of firm, depend to a large extent on the amount and type of competition they face, and their attitudes towards this competition. Firms that compare their performance with that of their rivals are more likely to be responsive to consumer wishes than firms that prefer to stick to well-established practices. On the other hand, they may be more concerned to 'manipulate' consumer tastes than the more traditional firm.

Are satisficing firms more likely to suffer from X inefficiency (see Box 7.5) than firms which seek to maximise profit or sales revenue?

Definition

Just-in-time methods Where a firm purchases supplies and produces both components and finished products as they are required. This minimises stockholding and its associated costs. It does, however, put pressure on the supply chain and increases the probability that on occasion firms may not be able to meet demand – for example in times of bad weather.

Section summary

1. In large firms, decisions are taken by or influenced by a number of different people, including various managers, shareholders, workers, customers, suppliers and creditors. If these different people have different aims, a conflict between them is likely to arise. A firm cannot maximise more than one of these conflicting aims. The alternative is to seek to achieve a satisfactory target level of a number of aims.
2. If targets were easily achieved last year, they are likely to be made more ambitious next year. If they were not achieved, a search procedure will be conducted to identify how to rectify the problem. This may mean adjusting targets downwards, in which case there will be some form of bargaining process between managers.
3. Life is made easier for managers if conflict can be avoided. This will be possible if slack is allowed to develop in various parts of the firm. If targets are not being met, the slack can then be taken up without requiring adjustments in other targets.
4. Satisficing firms may be less innovative, less aggressive and less willing to initiate change. If they do change, it is more likely to be in response to changes made by their competitors. Managers may judge their performance by comparing it with that of rivals.
5. Satisficing firms may be less aggressive in exploiting a position of market power. On the other hand, they may suffer from greater X inefficiency.

9.6 PRICING IN PRACTICE

What is the typical procedure by which firms set prices? Do they construct marginal cost and marginal revenue curves (or equations) and find the output where they are equal? Do they then use an average revenue curve (or equation) to work out the price at that output?

As we saw in section 9.1, firms often do not have the information to do so, even if they wanted to. In practice, firms look for rules of pricing that are relatively simple to apply.

KI 15 p132

Cost-based pricing

One approach is ***average cost*** or ***mark-up pricing***. Here producers work out the price by simply adding a certain percentage (mark-up) for profit on top of average costs (average fixed costs plus average variable costs). It is a very straightforward heuristic.

$$P = AFC + AVC + \text{profit mark-up}$$

Choosing the mark-up

The level of profit mark-up on top of average cost will depend on the firm's aims: whether it is aiming for high or even maximum profits, or merely a target based on previous

Definition

Average cost or mark-up pricing Where firms set the price by adding a profit mark-up to average cost.

BOX 9.7 HOW DO COMPANIES SET PRICES?

In 2012, the Bank of England published a survey of price-setting behaviour in UK companies.[1] The 693 respondents were representative of firms pricing to maximise profits – organisations in the public sector and/or subject to regulatory controls were excluded from the sample. The survey asked companies how they determine prices. The results are shown in Table (a).

(a) *How are prices determined?*

	Not important	Slightly important	Important	Very important
Price is primarily determined by your competitors' price	4.9	16.3	35.6	32.6
Price is based on direct cost per unit plus a percentage mark-up that varies	8.9	14.9	25.2	32.9
Price is based on direct cost per unit plus a fixed percentage mark-up	15.9	19.3	19.0	24.7
Price is primarily specified by your principal customer	22.5	20.5	17.7	9.5
Price is primarily determined in other ways	15.6	3.0	4.3	12.6

Source: Jennifer Greenslade and Miles Parker, 'New insights into price-setting behaviour in the UK: introduction and survey results', *The Economic Journal*, vol. 122, issue 558 (February 2012), https://onlinelibrary.wiley.com/doi/abs/10.1111/j.1468-0297.2011.02492.x

On average, competitors' prices appears to be the most important factor in determining a firm's pricing strategy, with 68.2 per cent of companies considering it to be either important or very important. Both variable mark-up (58.1 per cent) and fixed mark-up (43.7 per cent) pricing also play an important role. Further analysis found that firms who thought competition was very important in their sector were more likely to set prices based on competitors' prices. Larger firms were also more likely to use variable mark-up pricing.

The survey also sought to establish if those factors that cause prices to rise differ from those that cause prices to fall. Companies were asked about the importance of a range of possible reasons (see Table (b)).

The results show significant differences. Cost increases, especially labour and raw materials, are the most important reasons given by companies for raising prices. Lower demand and competitors' prices are the most important reasons given for reducing prices. Interestingly, companies appear to be less likely to respond to competitors increasing their prices than they are to respond to competitors reducing their prices. Price reductions by overseas rivals also have a much weaker effect than those of domestic rivals.

profit. It will also depend on the likely actions of rivals and their responses to changes in this firm's price and how these responses will affect demand.

If a firm could estimate its demand curve, it could then set its output and profit mark-up at levels that will avoid a shortage or surplus. Thus in Figure 9.3 it could choose a lower output (Q_1) with a higher mark-up (*fg*) or a higher output (Q_2) with a lower mark-up (*hj*), depending on its aims. If the firm could not estimate its demand curve, it could adjust its mark-up and output over time by a process of trial and error, according to its success in meeting profit and sales aims.

Figure 9.3 Choosing output and profit mark-up

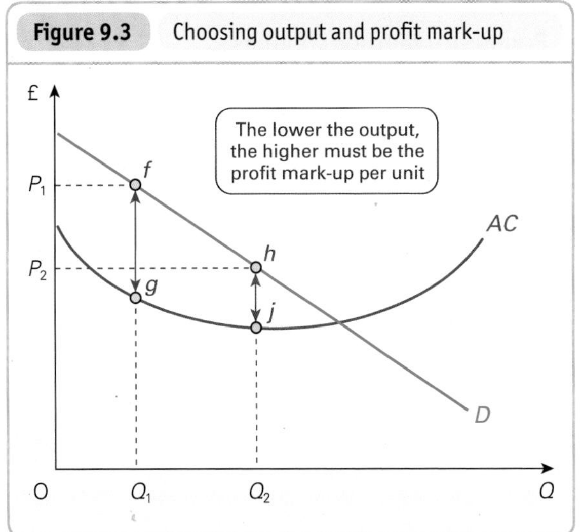

The equilibrium price and output

Is it possible to identify an equilibrium price and output for the firm that sets its prices by adding a mark-up to average cost? To answer this we can identify a supply curve for the firm.

CASE STUDIES AND APPLICATIONS

(b) *Factors leading to a rise or fall in price*

Rise	%[a]	Fall	%[a]
Increase in cost of labour	67.5	Actual decline in demand	67.5
Increase in the prices of fuel, raw materials or other inputs	62.9	Actual price reduction by domestic rivals	62.9
Actual rise in demand	54.4	Expected decline in demand	55.9
Increasing costs arising out of regulation	45.1	Significant reduction in market share	50.7
Actual price increase by domestic competitor(s)	44.9	Expected price reduction by domestic competitor(s)	45.6
Expected rise in demand	42.7	Decrease in the price of fuel, raw materials or other inputs	44.1
Increase in financing cost	30.4	Decrease in the cost of labour	29.9
Expected price increase by domestic competitor(s)	28.9	Decreasing cost arising out of regulation	22.1
Significant increase in market share	26.8	Actual price reduction by overseas competitor(s)	20.7

[a] The percentage of firms which judged the factor as important or very important.
Source: Jennifer Greenslade and Miles Parker, 'New insights into price-setting behaviour in the UK: introduction and survey results', *The Economic Journal*, vol. 122, issue 558 (February 2012), https://onlinelibrary.wiley.com/doi/abs/10.1111/j.1468-0297.2011.02492.x

More recent surveys

In 2019, the European Central Bank (ECB) reported results from a survey of 58 leading non-financial businesses that operate across the eurozone.[2] Companies were given a list of factors and asked to judge their importance when setting prices (see Table (c)).

The findings broadly support those of the Bank of England survey. Competitors' prices appear to be the most important factor that firms take into account when setting prices. Cost-based pricing is also very important.

(c) *Information that firms consider when setting prices*

Factor	Rank	Price reduction	Rank
Competitors' prices/market shares	1	Product-specific forecasts	5
Raw materials and other supply costs	2	General economic environment	6
Demand for the product or service	3	General economic forecasts	7
Labour costs	4	Financial costs	8

Source: Richard Morris and Rupert de Vincent-Humphreys, 'Price-setting behaviour: insights from a survey of large firms', *European Central Bank Economic Bulletin Boxes* (November 2019), www.ecb.europa.eu/pub/economic-bulletin/focus/2019/html/ecb.ebbox201907_04~1d48c6bf77.en.html

(continued)

Frequency of price changes

The Bank of England survey also considered the issue of price flexibility. Just under 20 per cent of respondents changed prices at least monthly, whereas 33.7 per cent did so annually.

However, there were large variations by sector. Just over 45 per cent of companies in the retail sector changed prices at least monthly, whereas the figure for businesses in manufacturing was 10.5 per cent. Just over 10 per cent of retail companies actually changed their prices on a daily basis, whereas 43.8 per cent of manufacturing companies change theirs on an annual basis. Larger firms, and those facing stronger competition, also tended to change their prices more frequently.

The ECB survey found similar results, with approximately 18 per cent of respondents changing prices at least monthly. The majority of retail firms reviewed their prices on a daily, weekly or monthly basis, whereas in manufacturing price reviews were more likely to be carried out on a monthly basis.

Another interesting question is whether the regularity of price changes has increased over time. The Bank of England survey asked respondents if the frequency of price adjustments had changed in the past decade. Just under 40 per cent of companies reported that they did change prices more frequently, whereas just 6 per cent reported that the frequency had fallen. The use of algorithms by online retailers makes it possible for some suppliers to change prices hundreds of times a day.

Sticky prices

Evidence suggests that prices are sticky – they do not always adjust in response to changes in cost and demand conditions.

Respondents to the Bank of England survey stated that the most important reasons for not increasing prices were:

- Co-ordination failure (i.e. the risk competitors would not change prices).
- The existence of an explicit contract (i.e. specifying that prices can only be changed when the contract is renegotiated).
- An implicit contract (i.e. not wanting to damage long-term relationships with customers).
- Concerns it would antagonise customers more generally.

An important reason given for not reducing prices is the fear it would start a price war. Menu costs (i.e. the time and effort cost of changing prices) were not found to be an important factor.

The ECB survey found very similar results with co-ordination failure, explicit contracts and implicit contracts given as important reasons for sticky prices.

1. *Which of the following is more likely to be consistent with the aim of maximising profits: pricing on the basis of (a) cost per unit plus a variable percentage mark-up; (b) cost per unit plus a fixed percentage mark-up?*
2. *Explain the differences between the importance attached to the different factors leading to price increases and those leading to price reductions.*
3. *Why do you think percentage price changes are bigger than the rate of inflation?*

Do a search for pricing strategies of companies. Are the results of your search consistent with the findings of the surveys reported in this Box?

1 See source for Tables (a) and (b).
2 See source for Table (c).

If a firm is aiming for a particular profit *per unit* of output and does not adjust this target, the firm's supply curve is derived by adding the mark-up to the *AC* curve. This is shown by curve S_1 in Figure 9.4. If, however, a firm is aiming for a particular level of *total* profit, and does not adjust this target, its supply curve will be like curve S_2. The greater the output, the less the profit per unit needs to be (and hence the less the mark-up) to give a particular level of total profit.

In either case, price and quantity can be derived from the intersection of demand and supply. Price and output will change if the demand or cost (and hence supply) curve shifts.

The main problem here is in predicting the demand curve, since it depends not only on consumer tastes but on the prices and behaviour of competitors. In practice, firms will usually base their assumptions about future sales on current figures, add a certain percentage to allow for growth in demand and then finally adjust this up or down if they decide to change the mark-up.

Figure 9.4 A firm's supply curve based on average cost

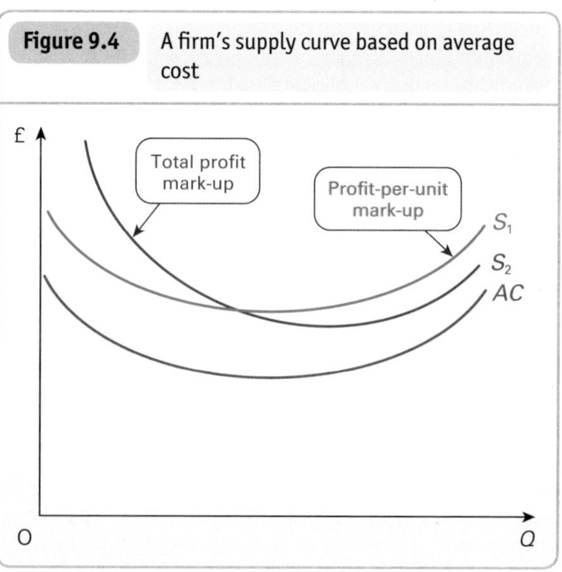

Variations in the mark-up

In most firms, the mark-up is not rigid. In expanding markets, or markets where firms have monopoly/oligopoly power, the size of the mark-up is likely to be greater. In contracting markets, or under conditions of rising costs and constant demand, a firm may well be forced to accept lower profits and thus reduce the mark-up.

Multi-product firms often have different mark-ups for their different products depending on their various market conditions. Such firms will often distribute their overhead costs unequally between their products. The potentially most profitable products, often those with the least elastic demands, will probably be required to make the greatest contribution to overheads.

The firm is likely to take account of the actions and possible reactions of its competitors. It may well be unwilling to change prices when costs or demand change, for fear of the reactions of competitors (see the discussion of kinked demand curve theory on pages 238–9). If prices are kept constant but costs change, either due to a movement along the AC curve in response to a change in demand, or due to a shift in the AC curve, the firm must necessarily change the size of the mark-up.

All this suggests that, whereas the mark-up may well be based on a target profit, firms are often prepared to change their target and hence their mark-up, according to market conditions.

1. *If the firm adjusts the size of its mark-up according to changes in demand and the actions of competitors, could its actions approximate to setting price and output where $MC = MR$?*
2. *Some firms set their prices by adding a mark-up to average variable cost (the mark-up would be larger to include an element to cover fixed cost). Why might this make pricing easier for the firm? (See Box 6.7.)*

*LOOKING AT THE MATHS

Using a mark-up approach to find the profit-maximising price

Could the firm use a mark-up approach to set the *profit-maximising* price? It could, provided it bases its mark-up on marginal cost (MC), rather than average cost, and provided it knows the price elasticity of demand ($P\varepsilon_D$) for its product. The rule is:

$$P = \frac{MC}{1 + (1/P\varepsilon_D)}$$

This is simply the formula for profit-maximising price that we derived in section 6.3 (see page 184), except that we have used MC rather than MR (where profits are maximised, $MC = MR$). Proof of this formula is given in Maths Case 6.2 on the student website.

Thus if $MC =$ £10 and $P\varepsilon_D = -5$, the firm should charge a price of

$$\frac{£10}{1 + (1/-5)} = \frac{£10}{1 - 1/5} = \frac{£10}{0.8} = £12.50$$

The weakness of this pricing rule is that it applies only at the profit-maximising output. If the firm is currently a long way from that output, MC and ($P\varepsilon_D$) may diverge considerably from the values that the firm should use in its calculation. If, however, the firm is producing relatively near to its profit-maximising output, the rule can give a price that is a close approximation to the profit-maximising price.

Section summary

1. Many firms set prices by adding a profit mark-up to average cost. This cost-plus pricing is most likely when firms are profit satisficers or when they do not have the information to find the price that will equate marginal cost and marginal revenue.
2. The mark-up could be based on achieving a target level of either *total* profit or profit per unit. In either case, a supply curve can be derived by adding the corresponding mark-up to the average cost curve.
3. For firms keen to increase profit, the size of the mark-up can be varied as market conditions permit the target profit to be increased.

END OF CHAPTER QUESTIONS

1. Assume that a firm faces a downward-sloping demand curve. Draw a diagram showing the firm's AR, MR, AC and MC curves. (Draw them in such a way that the firm can make supernormal profits.) Mark the following on the diagram:
   (a) The firm's profit-maximising output and price.
   (b) Its sales-revenue-maximising output and price.
   (c) Its sales-maximising output and price (subject to earning at least normal profit).

   Could the answer to (a) and (b) ever be the same?

   Could the answer to (b) and (c) ever be the same?
2. Would it be possible for firms to calculate their maximum-profit output if they did not use marginal cost and marginal revenue concepts?

(continued)

3. What is meant by the principal–agent problem? Give two examples of this problem that you have come across in your own experience.
4. 'A firm will always prefer to make more profit rather than less.' Do you agree with this statement? Is it compatible with alternatives to the profit-maximising theory of the firm?
5. A firm under monopoly or oligopoly that aims to maximise sales revenue will tend to produce more than a firm that aims to maximise profits. Does this conclusion also apply under (a) perfect competition and (b) monopolistic competition, given that there is freedom of entry?
6. What are the potential costs and benefits of mergers to (a) shareholders; (b) managers; (c) customers?
7. Why is it difficult to test the assumption that firms seek to maximise *long-run* profits?
8. Do behavioural theories of the firm allow us to make any predictions about firms' prices and output?
9. Are 'special offers' likely to benefit consumers?

Online resources

Additional case studies on the student website

9.1 **The legal structure of firms.** A study of the different types of legal identity that a firm can take – from the sole proprietor to the partnership to the limited company.

9.2 **Inside the firm.** An examination of alternative organisation structures of firms.

9.3 **The Body Shop.** A case study of 'alternative business values'.

9.4 **Corporate social responsibility.** An examination of social responsibility as a goal of firms and its effect on business performance.

9.5 **The global information economy and strategic alliances.** The way forward for companies such as America Online?

9.6 **Downsizing and business organisation.** The case of IBM.

9.7 **Vouchers and discounts.** This case examines the rise of Groupon and looks at its business practices.

9.8 **J. K. Galbraith.** A portrait of this pioneer of alternative theories of the firm and critic of traditional neoclassical analysis and free-market capitalism.

9.9 **The US sub-prime housing market.** How asymmetric information led to poor decision making by house purchasers in the USA and was a key factor in the 2007–8 global financial crisis.

Maths Case 9.1 Sales revenue maximising with a profit constraint: Part 1. Using simple algebra to find the sales-revenue-maximising output.

Maths Case 9.2 Sales revenue maximising with a profit constraint: Part 2. Using the Lagrangian approach.

Websites relevant to this chapter

Numbers and sections refer to websites listed in the Web Appendix and hotlinked from this book's website at **go.pearson.com/uk/sloman**.

- For news articles relevant to this chapter, see the *Economics News* section on the student website.
- For general news relevant to alternative strategies, see websites in section A, and particularly A2, 3, 8, 21, 23, 25, 26, 35, 36. See also A38, 39, 42, 43 and 44 for links to newspapers worldwide, and A40 and 41 for links to economics news articles on particular search topics from newspapers worldwide.
- For student resources relevant to this chapter, see sites C1–10, 14, 19.
- For information on mergers, see sites B3, 43; E4, 10, 18, 20; G1 and 8.
- For data on small and medium-sized enterprises, see the database in B3 or E10.
- For information on pricing, see site E10 and the sites of the regulators of the privatised industries: E15, 16, 19, 22.
- For sites with games and experiments examining the behaviour of firms see D13, 14, 16–20.

The Theory of Distribution of Income

CHAPTER MAP

Why do film stars, footballers and investment bankers earn such large incomes? Why, on the other hand, do cleaners, hospital porters and workers in clothing factories earn very low incomes? These are the types of question that the theory of distribution seeks to answer. It attempts to explain why some people are rich and others poor.

The explanation for differences in wages lies in the working of labour markets. In sections 10.1 and 10.2, we will consider how labour markets operate. In particular, we will focus on the determination of wage rates in different types of market: ones where employers are wage takers, ones where they can choose the wage rate, and ones where wage rates are determined by a process of collective bargaining. In the final two sections, we turn to capital and land and ask what determines the rewards that their owners receive.

This chapter examines the theory of income distribution by showing how the rewards to factors of production (labour, capital and land) depend on market conditions. Chapter 11, on the other hand, looks at income distribution in practice. It looks at inequality and poverty and at government policies to tackle the problem

10.1 WAGE DETERMINATION UNDER PERFECT COMPETITION

Perfect labour markets

When looking at the market for labour, it is useful to distinguish between perfect and imperfect markets. Although in practice few labour markets are totally perfect, many are at least approximately so.

The assumptions of perfect labour markets are similar to those of perfect goods markets. For example, everyone is a ***wage taker***. In other words, neither employers nor employees have any economic power to affect wage rates. This situation is not uncommon. Small employers are likely to have to pay the 'going wage rate' to their employees, especially when the employee is of a clearly defined type, such as an electrician, a bar worker, a data analyst or a porter. As far as employees are concerned, being a wage taker means competing with other identical (or very similar) workers. It also means not being a member of a union and therefore not being able to use collective bargaining to push up the wage rate.

The other assumptions of a perfect labour market are as follows:

Freedom of entry. There are no restrictions on the movement of labour. Workers are free to move to different jobs or to areas of the country where wages are higher. There are no barriers erected by, say, unions, professional associations or the government. Of course, it takes time for workers to change jobs and maybe to retrain. This assumption therefore applies only in the long run.

Perfect knowledge. Workers are fully aware of what jobs are available at what wages and with what conditions of employment. Likewise, employers know what labour is available and how productive that labour is.

Homogeneous labour. Workers of a given category are identical in terms of productivity. For example, in a perfect labour market for bricklayers we assume they are all equally skilled and motivated.

Definition

Wage taker An employer or employee who has no power to influence the market wage rate.

Which of the above assumptions do you think would be correct in each of the following cases?
(a) Supermarket checkout operators.
(b) Agricultural workers.
(c) Crane operators.
(d) Economics teachers.
(e) Call-centre workers.
(f) Professional footballers.
(g) Bar workers.

Wage rates and employment under perfect competition are determined by the interaction of the market demand and supply of labour. This is illustrated in Figure 10.1(a).

TC 4 p45

Generally, we would expect the supply and demand curves to have the same positive and negative slopes as in goods markets. The higher the wage paid, the more workers will want to do that job and the more hours each will be willing to work. This gives an upward-sloping supply curve of labour. On the other hand, the higher the wage that employers have to pay, the less labour they will employ. They may produce less, or they may substitute other factors of production, like machinery, for labour. Thus the demand curve for labour slopes downwards.

Figure 10.1(b) shows how an individual employer has to accept this wage. The supply of labour to that employer is infinitely elastic. In other words, at the market wage W_m, there is no limit to the number of workers available to that employer (but no workers at all will be available below it: they will all be working elsewhere). At the market wage W_m, the employer will employ Q_1 hours of labour.

Figure 10.1 A perfectly competitive labour market

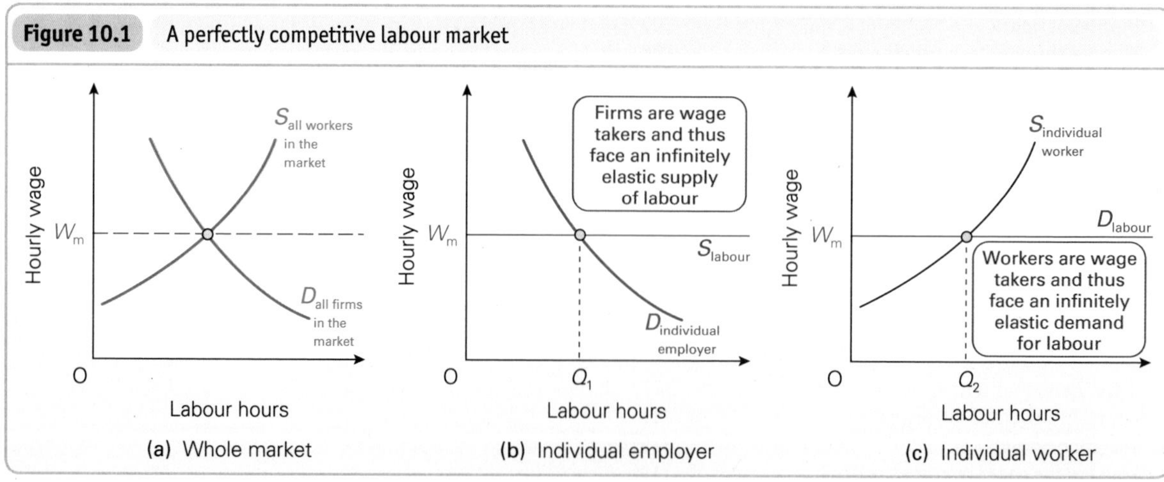

BOX 10.1 LABOUR AS A FACTOR OF PRODUCTION

EXPLORING ECONOMICS

Is this any way to treat a worker?

The theory that wages depend on demand and supply is often referred to as the 'neoclassical' theory of wages. Treated as pure theory, it is value free and does not involve moral judgements. It does not say, for example, whether the resulting distribution of income is fair or just.

In practice, however, neoclassical theory is often used in such a way as to imply moral judgements. It is a theory that tends to be associated with the political right and centre: those who are generally in favour of markets and the capitalist system. Many on the political left are critical of its implied morality. They make the following points:

- By treating labour as a 'factor of production', it demeans labour. Labour is not the same as a piece of land or a machine.
- It legitimises the capitalist system, where some people own land and capital while others have only their own labour. It implies that people have a right to income from their property even if that property is unequally distributed among the population.
- It implies that labour has no rights to the goods that it produces. These goods are entirely the property of the employer, even though it is the workers who made them.

Karl Marx (1818–83) was highly critical of these values and the way that the capitalist system led to extremes of wealth and poverty. He argued that labour was the only true source of value as it is labour that (i) makes machines, (ii) works the land, (iii) mines coal and other natural resources. Property, he argued, is therefore a form of theft. When capitalists extract profits from their enterprises, he continued, they are stealing part of the value produced by labour.

Neoclassical economists defend their position against the Marxist 'labour theory of value' by arguing the following:

- They are merely describing the world. If people want to draw pro-capitalist conclusions from their theory, then that is up to them.
- If the labour theory of value is used in any practical way to evaluate costs and output, it will lead to a misallocation of resources. Labour is not the only scarce resource. Land, for example, is also scarce and needs to be included in calculations of costs, otherwise it will be used wastefully.

Assume that it is agreed by everyone that it is morally wrong to treat labour as a mere 'factor of production', with no rights over the goods produced. Does this make the neoclassical theory wrong?

Conduct a small survey to establish what people think ought to be the basis of a person's hourly pay. What general conclusions do you draw from the survey and what would be the implications for pay and the economy if the findings were put into practice by employers?

Figure 10.1(c) shows how an individual worker also has to accept this wage. In this case it is the demand curve for that worker that is infinitely elastic. In other words, there is as much work as the worker chooses to do at this wage, but none at all above it.

We now turn to look at the supply and demand for labour in more detail.

The supply of labour

We can look at the supply of labour at three levels: the supply of hours by an individual worker, the supply of workers to an individual employer, and the total market supply of a given category of labour. Let us examine each in turn.

The supply of hours by an individual worker

Work involves two major costs (or 'disutilities') to the worker:

- When people work they sacrifice leisure.
- The work itself may be unpleasant or tedious.

Each extra hour worked will involve additional disutility. This ***marginal disutility of work*** (*MDU*) will tend to *increase* as people work more hours. There are two reasons for this. First, the less leisure they have left, the greater is the disutility they experience in sacrificing a further hour of leisure. Second, any unpleasantness they experience in doing the job tends to increase due to boredom, tiredness, or frustration.

Re-word the explanation of marginal disutility of work in terms of the marginal utility of leisure.

This increasing marginal disutility (see Figure 10.2(a)) will tend to give an upward-sloping supply curve of hours by an individual worker (see Figure 10.2(b)). The reason is that, in order to persuade people to work more hours, a higher hourly wage must be paid to compensate for the higher marginal disutility incurred. This helps to explain why overtime rates are higher than standard rates.

TC 8 p109

Under certain circumstances, however, the supply of hours curve might bend backwards (see Figure 10.3). The reason is that when wage rates go up, two opposing forces operate on the individual's labour supply.

On one hand, with higher wage rates people tend to work more hours, since time taken in leisure now involves a greater sacrifice of income and hence consumption.

Definition

Marginal disutility of work The extra sacrifice/hardship to a worker of working an extra unit of time in any given time period (e.g. an extra hour per day).

Figure 10.2 Marginal disutility of work and an individual's supply of labour

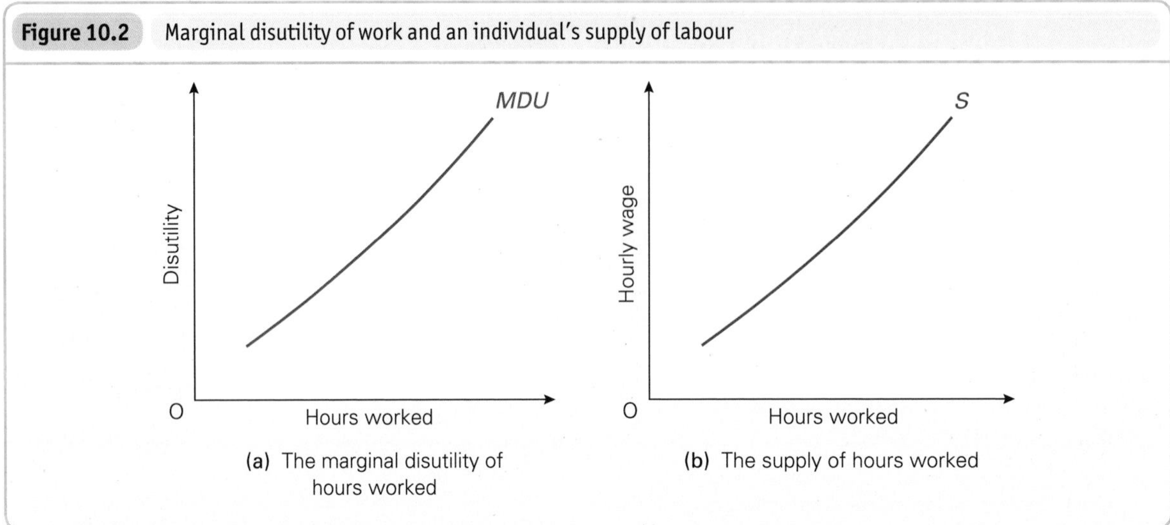

Figure 10.3 Backward-bending supply curve of labour

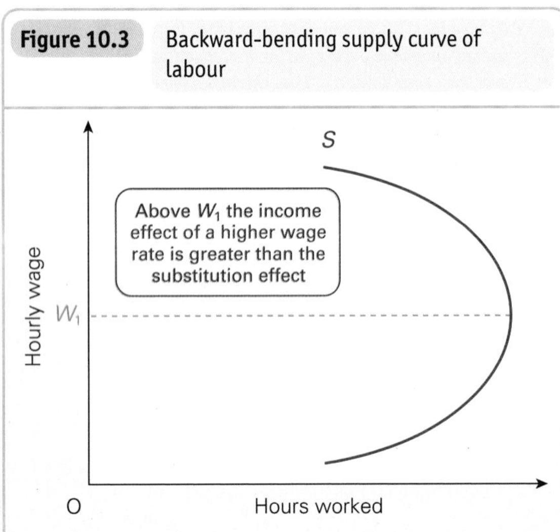

They thus substitute income (i.e. work) for leisure. This is called the ***substitution effect*** of the increase in wage rates.

On the other hand, people may feel that with higher wage rates they can afford to work less and have more leisure. This is called the ***income effect***. It reflects the fact that leisure is a *normal good,* one which is consumed in greater quantities as incomes rise.

With two effects working in opposite directions, the relative size of the effects determines the slope of the individual's supply curve. At lower wage rates, it is generally assumed that the substitution effect outweighs the income effect. A rise in the wage rate acts as an incentive and encourages a person to work more hours. At higher wage rates, however, the income effect might outweigh the substitution effect. As wages rise, people may feel they can afford to give up some consumption in exchange for more leisure time.

If the wage rate becomes high enough for the income effect to outweigh the substitution effect, the supply curve will begin to slope backwards. This occurs above a wage rate of W_1 in Figure 10.3.

These considerations are particularly important for a government when thinking about policies on income tax. Conservative governments have often argued that cuts in income taxes are the equivalent of giving people a pay rise, and that they provide an incentive for people to work harder. This analysis is only correct, however, if the substitution effect dominates. If the income effect dominates, people will work *less* after the tax cut. These questions are examined in Chapter 11.

The supply of labour to an individual employer

Under perfect competition, the supply of labour to a particular firm will be perfectly elastic, as in Figure 10.1(b). The firm is a 'wage taker' and thus has no power to influence wages. Take the case of a small firm that wishes to employ a temporary receptionist via an agency. It has to pay the 'going rate', and presumably will be able to employ as many receptionists as it likes (within reason) at that wage rate.

The market supply of a given type of labour

This will typically be upward sloping, as in Figure 10.1(a). The higher the wage rate offered in a particular type of job, the more people will want to do that job.

Definitions

Substitution effect of a rise in wage rates Workers will tend to substitute income for leisure as leisure now has a higher opportunity cost. This effect leads to *more* hours being worked as wage rates rise.

Income effect of a rise in wage rates Workers get a higher income for a given number of hours worked and may thus feel they need to work *fewer* hours as wage rates rise.

*BOX 10.2 USING INDIFFERENCE CURVE ANALYSIS TO DERIVE THE INDIVIDUAL'S SUPPLY CURVE OF LABOUR

EXPLORING ECONOMICS

Indifference curve analysis (see section 4.3) can be used to derive the individual's supply curve of labour. The analysis can show why the supply curve may be backward bending.

Assume that an individual can choose the number of hours to work and has 12 hours a day to divide between work and leisure (the remaining 12 being for sleep, shopping, travelling, etc.). In the diagram, with an hourly wage rate of £10, budget line B_1 shows all the possible combinations of daily income and leisure hours. For example, at point *x* the individual has an income of £80 by working eight hours and having four hours of leisure.

TC 1 p10

At an hourly wage of £20, the budget line becomes B_2, and at an hourly wage of £25 it becomes B_3.

The choice of hours worked at different wage rates

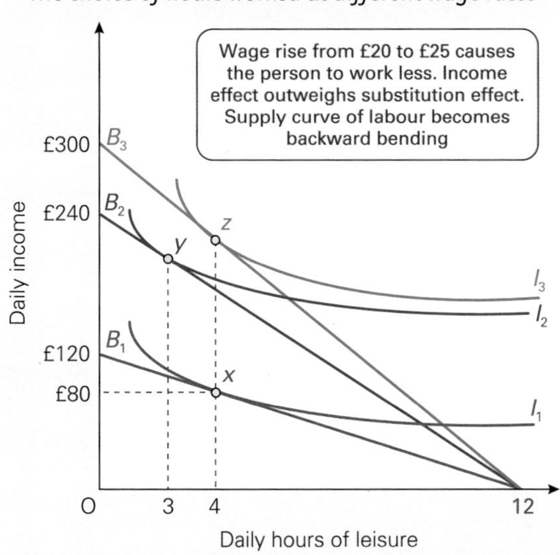

The diagram also shows three indifference curves. Each indifference curve shows all those combinations of income and leisure that give the individual a particular level of utility. The curves are bowed in towards the origin, showing that increasingly higher incomes are necessary to compensate for each hour of leisure sacrificed. Curve I_3 shows a higher level of utility than I_2, and I_2 a higher level than I_1.

At a wage rate of £10 per hour, the individual can move along budget line B_1. Point *x* shows the highest level of utility that can be achieved. The individual thus supplies eight hours of labour (and has four hours of leisure).

At the higher wage rate of £20 per hour, the individual is now on budget line B_2 and maximises utility at point *y* by working nine hours. Thus the higher wage has encouraged the individual to work one more hour. So far, then, the individual's supply curve would be upward sloping: a higher wage rate leads to more labour hours supplied.

At the still higher wage rate of £25 per hour, the individual is on budget line B_3, and now maximises utility at point *z*. But this means that only eight hours are now worked. The supply curve has begun to bend backwards. In other words, the individual is now in a position to be able to afford to take more time off in leisure. The income effect has begun to offset the substitution effect.

KI 7 p36

1. *Using the analysis developed in Chapter 4, try to show the size of the income and substitution effects when moving from point x to point y and from point y to point z.*
2. *Illustrate on an indifference diagram the effect on the hours a person works of (a) a cut in the rate of income tax; (b) the introduction of a weekly tax credit, worth £30 to all adults irrespective of income.*

The *position* of the market supply curve of labour depends on the number of people willing and able to do the job at each given wage rate. This depends on three things:

- The number of qualified people. Of course, if the job is unskilled then a large number of people will be 'qualified'.
- The non-wage benefits or costs of the job, such as the pleasantness of the working environment, job satisfaction or dissatisfaction, status, the degree of job security, pensions and other fringe benefits.
- The wages and non-wage benefits in alternative jobs.

TC 1 p10

A change in the wage rate will cause a movement along the supply curve. A change in any of these other three determinants will shift the whole curve.

Which way will the supply curve shift if the wage rates in alternative jobs rise?

The elasticity of the market supply of labour

How responsive will the supply of labour be to a change in the wage rate? If the market wage rate goes up, will a lot more labour become available or only a little? We looked at elasticity of demand and supply in Chapter 3; a similar analysis is used for the labour market. Thus the responsiveness (elasticity) depends on (a) the difficulties and costs of changing jobs and (b) the time period under consideration.

TC 6 p66

Another way of looking at the elasticity of supply of labour is in terms of the ***mobility of labour***: the willingness and ability of labour to move to another job, whether in a different location (geographical mobility) or in a different

Definition

Mobility of labour The willingness and ability of labour to move to another job.

industry (occupational mobility). The mobility of labour (and hence the elasticity of supply of labour) will be higher when there are alternative jobs in the same location, when alternative jobs require similar skills, and when people have good information about these jobs. It is also much higher in the long run, when people have the time to move or to acquire new skills and when the education system has time to adapt to the changing demands of industry.

1. *Assume that there is a growing demand for computer programmers. As a result more people train to become programmers. Does this represent a rightward shift in the supply curve of programmers, or merely the supply curve becoming more elastic in the long run, or both? Explain.*
2. *Which is likely to be more elastic, the supply of coal miners or the supply of shop assistants? Explain.*

If the demand for a particular category of worker increases, the wage rate will rise. The more inelastic the supply of labour, the higher the rise will be. Workers already employed in that industry will get the benefit of that rise, even though they are doing the same job as before. They are now earning a premium above the wage that was necessary to attract them into the industry in the first place. This premium is called ***economic rent***. Case Study 10.1 on the student website explores this concept and its relationship with the elasticity of supply of labour.

The demand for labour: the marginal productivity theory

In the traditional 'neoclassical' theory of the firm, which we examined in Chapters 8 and 9, it is assumed that firms aim to maximise profits. The same assumption is made in the neoclassical theory of labour demand. This theory is generally known as ***marginal productivity theory***.

The profit-maximising approach

How many workers will a profit-maximising firm want to employ? The firm will answer this question by weighing up the costs of employing extra labour against the benefits. It will use exactly the same principles as in deciding how much output to produce.

TC 8 p109

Definitions

Economic rent The excess that a factor of production is paid over the amount necessary to keep it in its current employment.

Marginal productivity theory The theory that the demand for a factor depends on its marginal revenue product.

BOX 10.3 IMMIGRATION AND THE UK LABOUR MARKET

Free movement of people and the single European market

One reason for the result in the UK referendum on membership of the European Union (EU) was the desire of many voters for lower levels of immigration.

The free movement of people is one of the four key principles that underpins the EU's single market (the others being free movement of goods, services and capital). The full implications of this rule for migration became clear when the so-called EU8 countries (Czech Republic, Estonia, Hungary, Latvia, Lithuania, Poland, Slovakia and Slovenia) joined the EU in 2004.

When new countries gain EU membership, existing countries have an option to introduce transitional arrangements. This typically involves some restrictions on the free movement of citizens from new member states for a period of up to seven years. Most existing members of the EU decided to use this option following the accession of the EU8 countries. Without controls, they feared that their labour markets would become overwhelmed by a large inflow of new economic migrants. However, the UK, Sweden and Ireland decided to allow immediate free movement.

The impact of this decision on the volume of immigration was quite dramatic. The number of EU8 nationals living in the UK increased from 125 000 in 2004 to over a million in 2012. Immigration from the EU as a proportion of total immigration into the UK increased from around 10 per cent in 1990 to 44 per cent in 2016.

Impact of EU immigration on the UK economy

What impact did this big increase in immigration have on the UK labour market? The predictions of economic theory are inconclusive. If immigrants have the same skills as UK-born workers (i.e. they are perfect substitutes) economic theory predicts an increase both in labour supply and in the elasticity of supply. This effect on its own will put downward pressure on wages and rates of employment for UK-born workers. However, if immigrants have complementary skills, this will lead to increases in productivity and wages for all workers. As well as expanding labour supply, migrant workers will also buy goods and services that will increase the demand for labour and so create new jobs.

In order to see which effects are stronger, a number of economists have analysed UK labour market data.

This research finds no evidence that immigration has had a negative impact on the *employment outcomes* of (i) existing UK residents in general or (ii) specific groups such as the young and unskilled workers.[1] There is more variation in the findings on *wages,* with studies reporting either small or no impact. For example, Nickell and Saleheen (2015) conclude that a 10-percentage point increase in the share of immigrants leads to a 1.5 per cent reduction in the wages of UK-born workers in the semi/unskilled service sector.[2] This implies that immigration since 2004 reduced annual pay increases of UK-born workers in this sector by a penny an hour.

In 2016, a study by the Centre for Economic Performance[3] found that UK-born workers in those parts of the country that had the highest levels of EU immigration did not experience bigger falls in wages than the rest of the country. It also found little impact on the pay of low-skilled workers.

Ottaviano et al. (2018) focus on the impact on productivity and report that a 1 per cent increase in immigrants in local

In the goods market, the firm will maximise profits where the marginal cost of an extra unit of *goods* produced equals the marginal revenue from selling it: $MC = MR$.

In the labour market, the firm will maximise profits where the marginal cost of employing an extra *worker* equals the marginal revenue that the worker's output earns for the firm: *MC* of labour = *MR* of labour. The reasoning is simple. If an extra worker adds more to a firm's revenue than to its costs, the firm's profits will increase. It will be worth employing that worker. But as more workers are employed, diminishing returns to labour will set in (see pages 155–8). Each extra worker will produce less than the previous one, and thus bring in less revenue for the firm.

KI 19 p155

Eventually, the marginal revenue from extra workers will fall to the level of their marginal cost. At that point, the firm will stop employing extra workers. There are no additional profits to be gained from employing further workers. Profits are at a maximum.

Measuring the marginal cost and revenue of labour

Marginal cost of labour (MC_L). This is the extra cost of employing one more worker. Under perfect competition, the firm is too small to affect the market wage. It faces a horizontal supply curve (see Figure 10.1(b) on page 284). Thus the additional cost of employing one more person will simply be the wage: $MC_L = W$.

Marginal revenue of labour (MRP_L). The marginal revenue that the firm gains from employing one more worker is called the ***marginal revenue product*** of labour. The MRP_L is found by multiplying two elements – the *marginal physical product* of labour (MPP_L) and the marginal revenue gained by selling one more unit of output (*MR*):

$$MRP_L = MPP_L \times MR$$

The MPP_L is the extra output produced by the last worker. Thus if the last worker produces 100 tonnes of output per week (MPP_L), and if the firm earns an extra £4 for each additional tonne sold (*MR*), then the worker's *MRP* is £400. This extra worker is adding £400 to the firm's revenue.

The profit-maximising level of employment for a firm

The *MPP* curve was illustrated in Figure 6.3 (see page 164). As more workers are employed, there will come a point when diminishing returns set in (point *b*). The MPP_L curve thus

> **Definition**
>
> **Marginal revenue product (of a factor)** The extra revenue that a firm earns from employing one more unit of a variable factor: $MRP_{\text{factor}} = MPP_{\text{factor}} \times MR_{\text{good}}$

CASE STUDIES AND APPLICATIONS

labour markets increases labour productivity by around 3 per cent.[4]

Immigration remains a controversial issue with commonly held views that are seemingly at odds with the available evidence.

The ending of free movement

Freedom of movement between the UK and EU eventually ended on 31 December 2020 and the government introduced a new points-based system for immigration.[5] The scheme treats EU and non-EU citizens in the same way, with all applicants needing a minimum of 70 points to work in the UK. The authorities award points if the applicant or job meets certain criteria. Some examples include: 20 points if the job is at an appropriate skill level; 10 points if the applicant speaks English at the required level; 20 points if the job has a salary of £25 600 or above.

It will be interesting to see the impact of the new points-based scheme on (a) future patterns of immigration and (b) the UK economy. Economists will be analysing the data to assess the effects.

Immigration from the EU to the UK fell significantly after the EU referendum. For example, net migration from EU8 countries fell from 80 000 in the year ending December 2015 to around zero for the year ending June 2019. Draw a diagram illustrating the impact of this fall in immigration on UK labour markets. Show the situation both before and after the change. Consider both the position and slope of the labour supply curve and the impact on the number employed and on wages. Would you expect there to be any movement in the demand for labour?

Research examples of other countries using a points-based system for immigration and assess the impact on their economies.

1 Ciaran Devlin, Olivia Bolt, Dhiren Patel, David Harding and Ishtiaq Hussain. *Impacts of migration on UK native employment: An analytical review of the evidence*, Home Office and Department for Business, Innovation and Skills (March 2014), https://assets.publishing.service.gov.uk/government/uploads/system/uploads/attachment_data/file/287287/occ109.pdf

2 Stephen Nickell and Jumana Saleheen, 'The impact of EU and Non-EU immigration on British wages', *IZA Journal of Development and Migration*, vol. no. 7, 15 (October 2017), https://izajodm.springeropen.com/articles/10.1186/s40176-017-0096-0

3 Jonathan Wadsworth, Swati Dhingra, Gianmarco Ottaviano and John Van Reenen, *Brexit and the Impact of Immigration on the UK*, Centre for Economic Performance (May 2016), https://cep.lse.ac.uk/pubs/download/brexit05.pdf

4 Gianmarco Ottaviano, Giovanni Peri and Greg Wright, 'Immigration, trade and productivity in services: evidence from U.K. firms', *Journal of International Economics*, vol. 112 (May 2018), www.sciencedirect.com/science/article/pii/S0022199618300254?

5 *UK points-based immigration system: Employer information*, HM Government (January 2021), www.gov.uk/government/publications/uk-points-based-immigration-system-employer-information

Figure 10.4 The profit-maximising level of employment

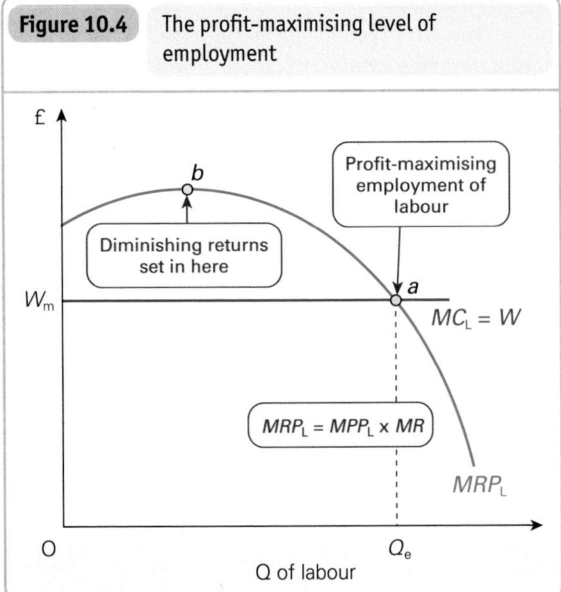

slopes down after this point. The MRP_L curve will be a similar shape to the MPP_L curve, since it is merely being multiplied by a constant figure, *MR*. (Under perfect competition *MR* equals *P* and does not vary with output.) The MRP_L curve is illustrated in Figure 10.4, along with the MC_L 'curve'.

Why is the MC_L curve horizontal?

Profits will be maximised at an employment level of Q_e, where MC_L (i.e. *W*) $= MRP_L$. Why? At levels of employment below Q_e, MRP_L exceeds MC_L. The firm will increase profits by employing more labour. At levels of employment above Q_e, MC_L exceeds MRP_L. In this case, the firm will increase profits by reducing employment.

TC 8 p109

*LOOKING AT THE MATHS

The marginal product of labour can be expressed using calculus. It is the rate of increase in output of good *X* with respect to changes in the quantity of labour:

$$MPP_L = \frac{\partial X}{\partial L}$$

The marginal revenue product of labour is thus given by

$$MRP_L = MR\frac{\partial X}{\partial L}$$

Profits are maximised at the level of employment (*L*) where $W = MRP_L$: i.e. where

$$W = MR\frac{\partial X}{\partial L} \qquad (1)$$

We can easily move from this to the level of profit-maximising *output* of good *X* (where $MC = MR$). Rearranging equation (1), we get

$$\frac{W}{\partial X/\partial L} = MR \qquad (2)$$

But, assuming that labour is the only variable factor, the marginal cost (of output) is the extra cost of employing labour (the only extra cost) *per unit of output*. In other words:

$$MC = \frac{W}{\partial X/\partial L} \qquad (3)$$

i.e.

$$MC = MR$$

Thus, not surprisingly, the profit-maximising employment of labour (where $W = MRP_L$) will yield the profit-maximising output (where $MC = MR$).

Derivation of the firm's demand curve for labour

No matter what the wage rate, the quantity of labour demanded will be found from the intersection of *W* and MRP_L (see Figure 10.5). At a wage rate of W_1, Q_1 labour is demanded; at W_2, Q_2 is demanded; at W_3, Q_3 is demanded.

Thus the MRP_L curve will show the quantity of labour employed at each wage rate. But this is just what the demand curve for labour shows. Thus the MRP_L curve is the demand curve for labour.

There are three determinants of the demand for labour:

- The wage rate. This determines the position *on* the demand curve, i.e. the quantity demanded.
- The productivity of labour (MPP_L). This determines the position *of* the demand curve.
- The demand for the good being produced. The higher the demand for the good, the higher its price, and hence the higher will be the *MR*, and the MRP_L. This too determines the position of the demand curve. It shows how the demand for labour (and other factors)

Figure 10.5 Deriving the firm's demand curve for labour

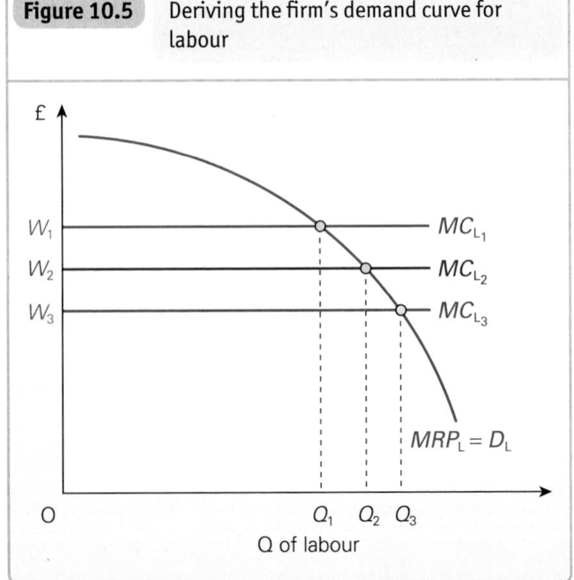

is a ***derived demand***: i.e. one derived from the demand for the good. For example, the higher the demand for houses, and hence the higher their price, the higher will be the demand for bricklayers.

A change in the wage rate is represented by a movement *along* the demand curve for labour. A change in the productivity of labour or the demand for the good *shifts* the curve.

Derivation of the industry demand curve for labour

This is not simply the sum of the demand curves of the individual firms. The firm's demand curve is based on a constant *P* and *MR*, no matter how many workers the firm employs (this is one of the assumptions of perfect competition). In Figure 10.6, when the wage rate falls from W_1 to W_2 the firm will employ more labour by moving from *a* to *b* along its demand curve MRP_1.

The trouble with this analysis is that when the wage rate falls, it will affect *all* employers. They will all want to employ more labour. But when they do, the total industry output will increase, and hence *P* (and *MR*) will be pushed down. This will shift the firm's *MRP* curve to the left and lead to a lower level of employment at point *c*. Therefore, when we allow for the effect of lower wages on the market price of the good, the firm's demand curve for labour will be the *green* line passing through points *a* and *c*.

Thus the *industry* demand curve for labour is the (horizontal) sum of the *green* lines for each firm and is therefore less elastic than the firm's *MRP* curve.

What will determine the elasticity of this curve?

The elasticity of demand for labour

KI 9 p64

The elasticity of demand for labour (with respect to changes in the wage rate) will be greater:

- The greater the price elasticity of demand for the good. A fall in *W* leads to higher employment and more output. This will drive *P* down. If the market demand for the good is elastic, this fall in *P* will lead to a lot more being sold and hence to a lot more people being employed.
- The easier it is to substitute labour for other factors and vice versa. If labour can be readily substituted for other factors, then a reduction in *W* will lead to a large increase in labour used to replace these other factors.
- The greater the elasticity of supply of complementary factors. If the wage rate falls, a lot more labour will be demanded if plenty of complementary factors can be obtained at little increase in their price.

KI 7 p36

Definition

Derived demand Demand for a factor of production that depends on the demand for the good that uses it.

Figure 10.6 Using the firm's demand curves for labour to derive the industry demand curves for labour

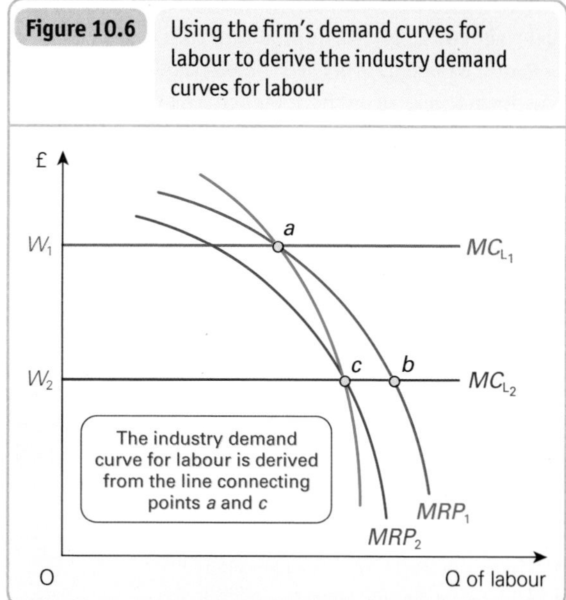

- The greater the elasticity of supply of substitute factors. If the wage rate falls and more labour is used, less substitute factors will be demanded and their price will fall. If their supply is elastic, a lot less will be supplied and therefore a lot more labour will be used instead.
- The greater the wage cost as a proportion of total costs. If wages are a large proportion of total costs and the wage rate falls, total costs will fall significantly; therefore production will increase significantly, and so too will the demand for labour.
- The longer the time period. Given sufficient time, firms can respond to a fall in wage rates by reorganising their production processes to make use of the now relatively cheap labour.

For each of the following jobs, check through the above list of determinants (excluding the last), and try to decide whether demand would be relatively elastic or inelastic: fire-fighters; telesales operators; app developers; bus drivers; accountants; farm workers; car workers.

Wages and profits under perfect competition

The wage rate (*W*) is determined by the interaction of demand and supply in the labour market. It will be equal to the value of the output that the last person produces (MRP_L).

Profits to the individual firm arise from the fact that the MRP_L curve slopes downwards (diminishing returns). Thus the last worker adds less to the revenue of firms than was added previously by workers already employed.

If *all* workers in the firm receive a wage equal to the *MRP* of the *last* worker, everyone but the last worker will receive a wage less than their *MRP*. This excess of MRP_L over *W* of previous workers provides a surplus to the firm over its wages bill (see Figure 10.7). Part of this will be required for paying non-wage costs; part will be profits for the firm.

Perfect competition between firms ensures that profits are kept down to *normal* profits. If the surplus over wages is such that *supernormal* profits are made, new firms will enter the industry. The price of the good (and hence MRP_L) will fall, and the wage rate will be bid up, until only normal profits remain.

Equality and inequality under perfect competition

The mythical world of perfect wage equality

Under certain very strict assumptions, a perfectly competitive market will lead to perfect equality of wage rates. All workers will earn exactly the same. These strict assumptions are as follows:

- All workers have identical abilities.
- There is perfect mobility of labour.
- All jobs are equally attractive to all workers.
- All workers and employers have perfect knowledge.
- Wages are determined entirely by demand and supply.

Given these assumptions, if consumer demand rose in any industry, the demand for labour would rise. As a result, wage rates would begin to rise. Immediately workers would flood into this industry, attracted by the higher wages. Very quickly, then, wage rates would be competed back down to the level in the rest of the economy. Likewise if wage rates began to fall in any industry, workers would leave, thereby eliminating any labour surplus and preventing the fall in wage rates.

Under these conditions, therefore, not only would the labour supply curve to a *firm* be infinitely elastic, but so too would the labour supply curve to each *industry* at the universal wage rate. TC 6 p66

Of course, in the real world these conditions do not hold and we do not see perfectly competitive labour markets.

Figure 10.7 Wages and profits

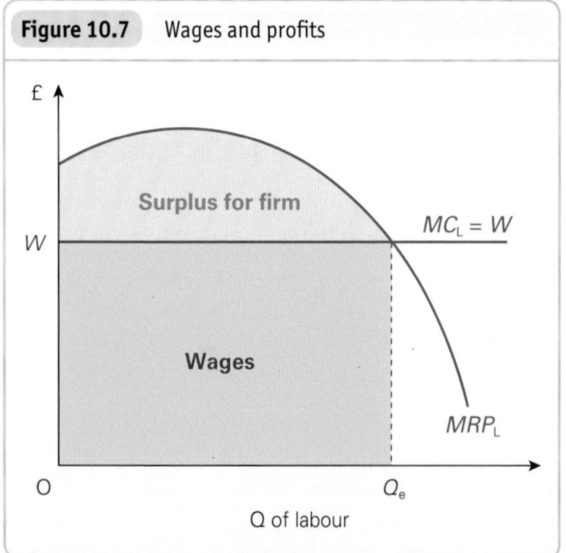

Huge inequalities of wages exist. But even if markets *were* perfect, inequality would be expected to persist.

Causes of inequality under perfect competition

In the short run, inequality will exist under perfect competition because it takes time for changes in demand and supply conditions to bring new long-run equilibria. Thus expanding industries will tend to pay higher wage rates than contracting industries. KI 4 p13

But even after enough time has elapsed for all adjustments to be made to changes in demand and supply, long-run wage differentials will still exist for the following reasons:

- Workers do not have identical abilities.
- Workers are not perfectly mobile, even in the long run. People have different preferences about where they want to live and the jobs they like to do. They may not have access to training or may be unable to afford to retrain. Workers may not have the innate talent to do particular jobs, even if they did retrain.
- Jobs differ enormously in terms of the skills they require and in terms of their pleasantness or unpleasantness.

What is more, since demand and supply conditions are constantly changing, long-run general equilibrium throughout the economy will never be reached.

Who are the poor? Who are the rich?

The lowest paid will be those whose labour is in low demand or high supply. Low demand will be due to low demand for the good or low labour productivity. High supply will be due to low mobility out of industries in decline or to a surplus of people with the same skills or qualifications. Thus, for example, workers who possess few skills, are working in contracting industries, do not want to move from the area and will not or cannot retrain will be low paid. KI 4 p13

The highly paid will be those whose labour is in high demand or low supply. Thus workers who possess skills or talents that are in short supply, especially if those skills take a long time for others to acquire, and those who are working in expanding industries, will tend to earn high wages.

Although the movement of labour from low-paid to high-paid jobs will tend to reduce wage differentials, considerable inequality will persist even under perfect competition. It is, therefore, not possible to eliminate poverty and inequality by 'freeing up' markets and encouraging workers to 'stand on their own feet' or 'get on their bikes'.

Furthermore, in the real world there exist many market imperfections, which tend to make inequality greater. These imperfections are examined in the next section. TC 3 

Finally, income inequality under capitalism will also arise from the unequal distribution of the ownership of land and capital. Even under perfect competition, considerable inequality will therefore exist if wealth is concentrated in the hands of the few.

Section summary

1. Wages in a perfect market are determined by supply and demand.
2. The supply curve of hours by an individual worker reflects the increasing marginal disutility of work. Its shape depends on the relative sizes of the substitution and income effects of a wage change. The substitution effect is positive: higher wages encourage people to work more by substituting wages for leisure. The income effect, however, is negative: higher wages make people feel that they can afford to enjoy more leisure. If the income effect is bigger than the substitution effect, the supply curve for labour hours will bend backwards.
3. The supply of labour to a particular employer under perfect competition is infinitely elastic.
4. The market supply is typically upward sloping. Its elasticity depends on labour mobility.
5. The demand for labour depends on a worker's marginal revenue product. This is the extra revenue that a firm will gain from the output of an extra worker. The profit-maximising firm will continue taking on extra workers until MRP_L is equal to MC_L (= W under perfect competition).
6. The elasticity of demand for labour depends on the elasticity of demand for the good being produced, the ease of substituting labour for other factors and vice versa, the elasticity of supply of substitute and complementary factors, wages as a proportion of total costs, and the time period involved.
7. Although market forces will tend to lead to the elimination of differentials as workers move from low-paid to high-paid jobs, nevertheless inequality can persist even under perfect competition. People have different abilities and skills; people are not perfectly mobile; and jobs differ in their labour requirements.
8. Inequality is also caused by market imperfections and by unequal ownership of land and capital.

10.2 WAGE DETERMINATION IN IMPERFECT MARKETS

In the real world, firms and/or workers are likely to have the power to influence wage rates: they are not wage takers. This is one of the major types of labour market imperfection.

TC 3 p26

When a firm is the only employer of a certain type of labour, this situation is called a ***monopsony***. A monopsony may arise in a market for particular types of labour; Royal Mail is a monopsony employer of postal workers. Alternatively, and more commonly, it may arise in a local market. Thus a factory may be the only employer of certain types of labour in that district. When there are just a few employers, this is called ***oligopsony***. Oligopsony is much more common than monopsony, just as in goods markets oligopoly is much more common than monopoly.

In monopsonistic or oligopsonistic labour markets the employers have market power. Workers too may have market power as members of unions. When a single union bargains on behalf of a certain type of labour, it is acting as a monopolist. When there is more than one union, they are oligopolists.

When a monopsonist employer faces a monopolist union, the situation is called ***bilateral monopoly***.

Definitions

Monopsony A market with a single buyer or employer.

Oligopsony A market with just a few buyers or employers.

Bilateral monopoly Where a monopsony buyer faces a monopoly seller.

Firms with market power in employing labour (monopsony, etc.)

Monopsonists (and oligopsonists too) are 'wage setters', not 'wage takers'. A large employer in a small town, for example, may have considerable power to resist wage increases or even to force wage rates down. The National Health Service has considerable power in setting wages for health workers in the UK.

KI 22 p195

Such firms face an upward-sloping supply curve of labour. This is illustrated in Figure 10.8. If the firm wants to take on more labour, it will have to pay a higher wage rate to

Figure 10.8 Monopsony

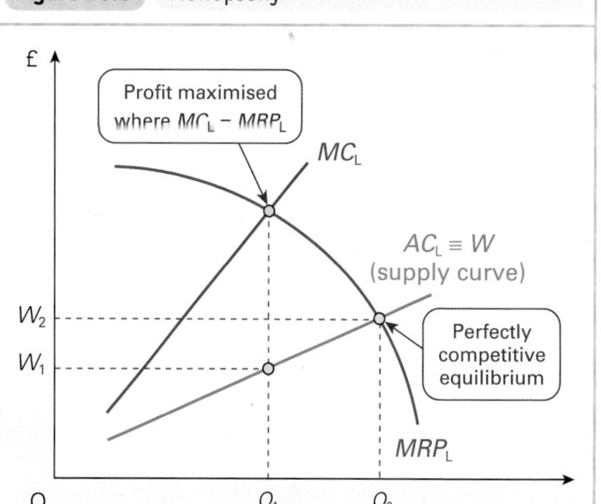

attract workers away from other industries. But conversely, when employing less labour it will be able to pay a lower wage rate.

The supply curve shows the wage rate that must be paid to attract a given quantity of labour. The wage it pays is the *average cost* to the firm of employing labour (AC_L). The supply curve is also therefore the AC_L curve.

The *marginal cost* of employing one more worker (MC_L) will be above the wage (AC_L). The reason is that the wage rate has to be raised to attract extra workers. The MC_L will thus be the new higher wage paid to the new employee *plus* the small rise in the total wages bill for existing employees: after all, they will have to be paid the higher wage too.

The profit-maximising employment of labour would be at Q_1, where $MC_L = MRP_L$. The wage paid would thus be W_1.

If this had been a perfectly competitive labour market, equilibrium employment would have been at the higher level Q_2, with the wage rate at the higher level W_2, where $W = MRP_L$. The monopsonist is therefore forcing the wage rate down by restricting the number of workers employed.

1. *The following table shows data for a monopsonist employer. Fill in the missing figures. How many workers should the firm employ if it wishes to maximise profits?*

Number of workers	Wage rate (£)	Total cost of labour (£)	Marginal cost of labour (£)	Marginal revenue product (£)
1	100	100	110	230
2	105	210	120	240
3	110	330	...	240
4	115	...	...	230
5	120	...	...	210
6	125	...	...	190
7	130	...	...	170
8	135	...	...	150
9	140	...	...	

2. *Will a monopsony typically also be a monopoly? Give examples of monopsonists that are not monopolists, and monopolists that are not monopsonists.*

Labour with market power (union monopoly or oligopoly)

The extent to which unions will succeed in pushing up wage rates depends on their power and willingness to take action. It also depends on the power of firms to resist and on their ability to pay higher wages. In particular, the scope for unions to gain a better deal for their members depends on the sort of market in which the employers are producing.

If the employers are producing under perfect or monopolistic competition, wage rates will only rise at the expense of employment. Firms are earning only normal profit. Thus if unions force up wage rates, the marginal firms will make losses and eventually leave the industry. Fewer workers will be employed. The fall in output will lead to higher prices. This will enable the remaining firms to pay a higher wage rate.

Figure 10.9 illustrates these effects. If unions succeed in raising the wage from W_1 to W_2, employment will fall from Q_1 to Q_2. There will be a surplus of people ($Q_3 - Q_2$) wishing to work in this industry for whom no jobs are available.

The union faces a second effect. Not only will jobs be lost as a result of the higher wage rate, but there is also a danger that those who are unemployed as a result might undercut the union wage.

In a competitive goods market, wage rates can only be increased without a reduction in the level of employment if, as part of the bargain, the productivity of labour is increased. This is called a ***productivity deal***. The *MRP*

Definition

Productivity deal Where a union agrees to changes in working practices that will increase output per worker. This may be in return for a rise in the wage rate.

BOX 10.4 LIFE AT THE MILL — CASE STUDIES AND APPLICATIONS

Monopsony in Victorian times

A dramatic illustration of the effects of extreme monopsony power is that of the textile mill in nineteenth-century England. When a mill was the only employer in a small town, or when factory owners colluded as oligopsonists, things could be very bad for the worker. Very low pay would be combined with often appalling working conditions.

Friedrich Engels described the life of the textile factory worker as follows:

> The factory worker is condemned to allow his physical and mental powers to become atrophied. From the age of eight he enters an occupation which bores him all day long. And there is no respite from this boredom. The machine works ceaselessly. Its wheels, belts and spindles hum and rattle ceaselessly in his ears, and if he thinks of taking even a moment's rest, the overlooker is always there to punish him with a fine. It is nothing less than torture of the severest kind to which the workers are subjected by being condemned to a life-sentence in the factory, in the service of a machine which never stops.[1]

1. ***Why did competition between employers not force up wages and improve working conditions?***
2. ***Were the workers making a 'rational economic decision' when they chose to work in such factories?***

Investigate whether garment workshops in parts of the world today, including the UK, have similar economic circumstances to that described by Engels in Victorian England.

1 F. Engels, *The Condition of the Working Class in England*, translated by W. O. Henderson and W. H. Chaloner (Basil Blackwell, 1971), pp. 199–200.

Figure 10.9 Monopoly union facing producers under perfect competition

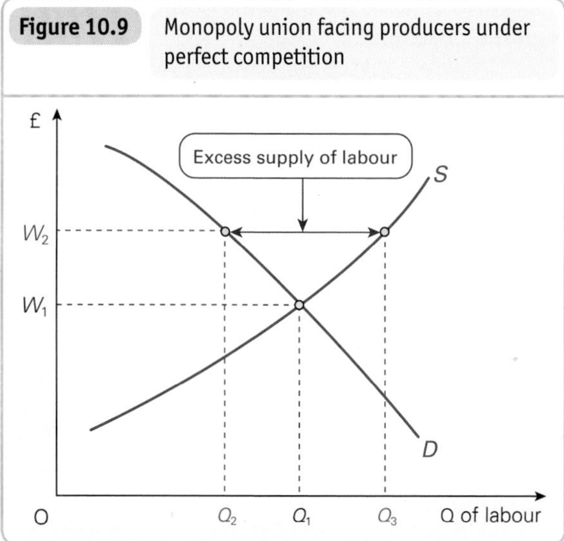

curve, and hence the demand curve in Figure 10.9, shifts to the right.

Which of the following unions find themselves in a weak bargaining position for the above reasons?
(a) The shopworkers' union (USDAW).
(b) The tube and train drivers' union (ASLEF).
(c) The farm workers' union (part of Unite).

In a competitive market, then, the union faces the choice between wages and jobs. Its actions will thus depend on its objectives.

If it wants to *maximise employment,* it will have to content itself with a wage of W_1 in Figure 10.9, unless productivity deals can be negotiated. At W_1, Q_1 workers will be employed. Above W_1 fewer than Q_1 workers will be *demanded.* Below W_1 fewer than Q_1 workers will be *supplied.*

If the union is more concerned with securing higher wages, it may be prepared to push for a wage rate above W_1 and accept some reduction in employment. This is more likely if the reduction can be achieved through ***natural wastage.*** This is where people retire, or take voluntary redundancy, or simply leave for another job.

Firms and labour with market power (bilateral monopoly)

It is common to find the strongest unions where there is a monopsonistic labour market. In these circumstances we can think of the union monopoly as a counterweight to the power of a monopsony employer. What will the wage rate be under these circumstances? What will the level of employment be? Unfortunately, economic theory cannot give a precise answer. There is no 'equilibrium' level as such. Ultimately, the wage rate and the level of employment will depend on the relative bargaining strengths and skills of unions and management.

Strange as it may seem, unions may be in a stronger position to make substantial gains for their members when they are facing a powerful employer. There is often considerable scope for them to increase wage rates *without* this leading to a reduction in employment, or even for them to increase both the wage rate *and* employment. Figure 10.10 shows how this can be so.

Assume first that there is no union. The monopsonist will maximise profits by employing Q_1 workers at a wage rate of W_1. (Q_1 is where $MRP_L = MC_L$.)

What happens when a union is introduced into this situation? Wage rates will now result from negotiation between unions and management. Once a wage rate has been agreed, the employer can no longer drive the wage rate down by employing fewer workers. If it tries to pay less than the agreed wage, it may well be faced by a strike, and thus have a zero supply of labour.

Similarly, if the employer decides to take on *more* workers, it will not have to *increase* the wage rate, as long as the negotiated wage is above the free-market wage: as long as the wage rate is above that given by the supply curve S_1.

The effect of this is to give a new supply curve that is horizontal up to the point where it meets the original supply curve. Assume that the union succeeds in negotiating a wage rate of W_2 in Figure 10.10. The supply curve will be horizontal at this level to the left of point *x*. To the right of this point it will follow the original supply curve S_1, since to acquire

Definition

Natural wastage Where a firm wishing to reduce its workforce does so by not replacing those who leave or retire.

Figure 10.10 Bilateral monopoly

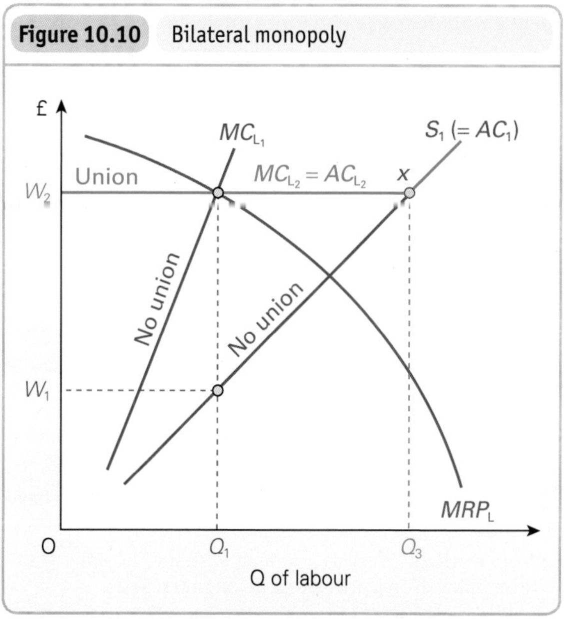

more than Q_3 workers the employer would have to raise the wage rate above W_2.

If the supply curve is horizontal to the left of point x at a level of W_2, so too will be the MC_L curve. The reason is simply that the extra cost to the employer of taking on an extra worker (up to Q_3) is merely the wage rate: no rise has to be given to existing employees. If MC_L is equal to the wage, the profit-maximising level of employment ($MC_L = MRP_L$) will now be where $W = MRP_L$. At a negotiated wage rate of W_2, the firm will therefore choose to employ Q_1 workers.

What this means is that the union can push the wage rate right up from W_1 to W_2 and the firm will still *want* to employ Q_1. In other words, a wage rise can be obtained *without* a reduction in employment.

If the negotiated wage rate were somewhere between W_1 and W_2, what would happen to employment?

The union could go further still. By threatening industrial action, it may be able to push the wage rate above W_2 and still insist that Q_1 workers are employed (i.e. no redundancies). The firm may be prepared to see profits drop right down to normal level rather than face a strike and risk losses. The absolute upper limit to wages will be that at which the firm is forced to close down.

Collective bargaining

Sometimes when unions and management negotiate, *both* sides can gain from the resulting agreement. For example, the introduction of new technology may allow higher wages, improved working conditions and higher profits. Usually, however, one side's gain is the other's loss. Higher wages mean lower profits.

In collective bargaining, there are various threats or promises that either side can make. Union *threats* might include strike action, ***picketing***, ***working to rule*** or refusing to co-operate with management: for example, in the introduction of new technology. Alternatively, in return for higher wages or better working conditions, unions might *offer* no-strike agreements, increased productivity or long-term deals over pay.

In turn, employers might *threaten* employees with redundancies or reduced benefits. Alternatively, they might *offer*, in return for lower wage increases, better rewards such as productivity bonuses, profit-sharing schemes, more holiday or greater job security.

The outcome of negotiations. The success of a union in achieving its demands depends on its financial strength, the determination of its members and the level of support from the public in general. It also depends on the willingness of the firm to make concessions and on its profitability. Firms earning substantial profits are in a much better position to pay wage increases than firms operating in a highly competitive environment.

The wage settlement may be higher if the union represents only ***core workers***. It may be able to secure a higher wage rate at the expense of non-members, who might lose their jobs or be replaced by part-time or temporary workers. The core workers can be seen as ***insiders***. Their union(s) can prevent the unemployed – the ***outsiders*** – from competing wages down.

Industrial action imposes costs on both unions and firms. Union members lose pay. Firms lose revenue. It is usually in both sides' interests, therefore, to settle by negotiation. Nevertheless, to gain the maximum advantage, each side must persuade the other that it will carry out its threats if pushed.

The approach described so far has essentially been one of confrontation. The alternative is for both sides to concentrate on increasing the total net income of the firm by co-operating on ways to increase efficiency or the quality of the product. This approach is more likely when unions and management have built up an atmosphere of trust over time.

Recall the various strategies that rival oligopolists can adopt. What parallels are there in union and management strategies?

The role of government in collective bargaining

The government can influence the outcome of collective bargaining in a number of ways. One is to try to set an example. It may take a tough line in resisting wage demands by public-sector workers, hoping thereby to persuade employers in the private sector to do likewise.

Additionally, it could set up mechanisms to assist in arbitration or conciliation. For example, in the UK, the Advisory, Conciliation and Arbitration Service (ACAS) is largely funded by the Department for Business, Energy & Industrial Strategy (BEIS) and conciliates in over 1000 disputes each year.

Definitions

Picketing Where people on strike gather at the entrance to the firm and attempt to dissuade workers or delivery vehicles from entering.

Working to rule Workers do the bare minimum they have to, as set out in their job descriptions.

Core workers Workers, normally with specific skills, who are employed on a permanent or long-term basis.

Insiders Those in employment who can use their privileged position (either as members of unions or because of specific skills) to secure pay rises.

Outsiders Those out of work or employed on a casual, part-time or short-term basis, who have little or no power to influence wages or employment.

Another approach is to use legislation. The government could pass laws that restrict the behaviour of employers or unions; that set a minimum wage rate (see Box 11.2); that prevent discrimination against workers on various grounds. The UK Conservative governments between 1979 and 1997 put considerable emphasis on reducing the power of trade unions and making labour markets more 'flexible'. Several Acts of Parliament were passed. These effectively ended ***closed-shop*** agreements, made secret ballots mandatory and outlawed political strikes and ***secondary action***. It was also made unlawful for employers to deny employment on the grounds that an applicant does not belong to a union, or indeed to penalise them for joining a union.

The effect of these measures was considerably to weaken the power of trade unions in the UK.

The efficiency wage hypothesis

We have seen that a union may be able to force an employer to pay a wage above the market-clearing rate. But it may well be in firms' interests to pay higher wage rates, even in non-unionised sectors.

One explanation for this is the ***efficiency wage hypothesis***. This states that the productivity of workers rises as the wage rate rises. As a result, employers may be willing to offer wage rates above the market-clearing level, attempting to balance increased wage costs against gains in productivity. But why might higher wage rates lead to higher productivity? There are three main explanations.

TC 5 p48

Less 'shirking'

In many jobs it is difficult to monitor the effort individuals put into their work. Workers may thus get away with shirking or careless behaviour. This is an example of the principal–agent problem (see section 9.4 and Box 10.9). The worker, as an agent of the employer (the principal), is not necessarily going to act in the principal's interest.

KI 25 p274

The business could attempt to reduce shirking by imposing a series of sanctions, the most serious of which would be dismissal. The higher the wage rate, the greater will be the cost to the individual of dismissal, and the less likely it is, therefore, that workers will shirk. The business will benefit not only from the additional output but also from a reduction in the costs of having to monitor workers' performance. As a consequence the ***efficiency wage rate*** for the business will lie above the market-determined wage rate.

Reduced labour turnover

If workers receive on-the-job training or retraining, then to lose a worker once the training has been completed is a significant cost to the business. Labour turnover, and hence its associated costs, can be reduced by paying a wage above the market-clearing rate. By paying such a wage rate the business is seeking a degree of loyalty from its employees.

Morale

A simple reason for offering wage rates above the market-clearing level is to motivate the workforce – to create the feeling that the firm is a 'good' employer that cares about its employees. As a consequence, workers might be more industrious and more willing to accept the introduction of new technology (with the reorganisation and retraining that it involves).

TC 5 p48

The paying of efficiency wages above the market-clearing wage will depend upon the type of work involved. Workers who occupy skilled positions, especially where the business has invested time in their training (thus making them costly to replace) are likely to receive efficiency wages considerably above the market wage. By contrast, workers in unskilled positions, where shirking can be easily monitored, where little training takes place and where workers can be easily replaced, are unlikely to command an 'efficiency wage premium'. In such situations, rather than keeping wage rates high, the business will probably try to pay as little as possible.

Other labour market imperfections

The possession of power by unions and/or firms is not the only way in which real-world labour markets diverge from the perfectly competitive model.

- Workers or employers may have imperfect information.
- Wages may respond very slowly to changes in demand and supply, causing disequilibrium in labour markets to persist.
- Firms may not be profit maximisers. Likewise workers may not seek to maximise their 'worker surplus' – the excess of benefits from working (i.e. wages) over the disutility of working (displeasure in doing the job and lost leisure).

Some of the forms and effects of these three imperfections are examined in Case Study 10.3 on the student website.

Definitions

Closed shop Where a firm agrees to employ only union members.

Secondary action Industrial action taken against a company not directly involved in a dispute (e.g. a supplier of raw materials to a firm whose employees are on strike).

Efficiency wage hypothesis The hypothesis that the productivity of workers is affected by the wage rate that they receive.

Efficiency wage rate The profit-maximising wage rate for the firm after taking into account the effects of wage rates on worker motivation, turnover and recruitment.

BOX 10.5 THE RISE AND DECLINE OF THE LABOUR MOVEMENT IN THE UK

Modern trade unionism had its birth with the industrial revolution of the eighteenth and nineteenth centuries. Unions were seen as a means of improving the lot of industrial workers, most of whom suffered low pay and poor working conditions. But, with great hostility from employers, membership grew slowly. By the end of the nineteenth century, only just over 10 per cent of manual workers were in an effective union.

The big change came after the First World War, when returning troops demanded that the sacrifices made should be rewarded. Membership of trade unions increased sharply as workers sought to improve wages and working conditions. By 1920, 45 per cent of the total labour force (8.3 million workers) were in trade unions.

But it was after the Second World War that the trade union movement in the UK really became established as a substantial economic and political force. This can be explained by three crucial trends:

- The growth in the public sector meant that government was itself becoming increasingly responsible for determining wages and conditions of service for many workers.
- In their attempt to control inflation in the 1960s and 1970s, governments sought to impose an 'incomes policy' constraining wage increases. To be successful, this required acceptance by the trade union movement.
- The philosophy of many post-war governments was to govern by consent. Social contracts and discussions between government, employers and unions gave the union movement considerable influence over economic decision making.

Union power grew steadily during the 1950s and 1960s, so much so that successive governments tried to curb its influence. However, such moves attracted fierce and widespread opposition, and legislation was in many cases abandoned. The trade union movement had become very powerful by the late 1970s with over 13 million members. The number of working days lost because of labour disputes peaked at 29 974 in 1979.

The election of the Conservative government in 1979 ushered in a new wave of trade union reform, eroding and removing many rights and privileges acquired by unions over the years.

Trade union membership stood at just below 6.44 million in 2019, the third consecutive year of relatively small rises. However, the long-term trend since 1979 has been downwards – membership is around half of that seen in the late 1970s. This is due to a number of factors: the shift to a service-based economy; continued privatisation and the introduction of private-sector management practices, such as local pay bargaining; and contracted-out services in many of the remaining parts of the public sector. More women working and more part-time and casual work, with many people having no guaranteed hours (so-called 'zero-hour contracts'), are also contributory factors, as are the attitudes of many firms to union recognition.

In many cases, an aggressive management style and a highly competitive environment have made it virtually impossible for unions to gain bargaining rights in the private sector. The proportion of private-sector workers who are union members (membership density) was just 13.3 per cent in 2019.

Union membership among public-sector employees increased by 74 000 in 2019, while membership density fell slightly from 52.5 per cent to 52.3 per cent. The two industries with the highest membership density are education (48.7 per cent) and public administration and defence (44.2%). But even in these areas there is little doubt that union power has declined.

In the light of these changes, many unions have adopted a 'new realism', accepting single-union agreements and

BOX 10.6 HOW USEFUL IS MARGINAL PRODUCTIVITY THEORY?

Reality or the fantasy world of economists?

The marginal productivity theory of income distribution has come in for a lot of criticism. Is this justified?

To start with, marginal productivity theory has been criticised for assuming perfect competition. It doesn't! Rather, it merely states that to maximise profits an employer will employ workers up to the point where the worker's marginal cost equals the extra revenue added by that worker: $MC_L = MRP_L$. This applies equally under perfect competition, monopsony and oligopsony.

What it does say is that, if there is perfect competition, then the worker's wage will equal MRP_L. It certainly does not say that $W = MRP_L$ in other market structures.

A second criticism is that employers do not behave in this 'marginal way', weighing up each additional worker's costs and revenues for the firm. There are three possible reasons for this.

Ignorance of the theory of profit maximisation. The employer may use some rule of thumb, but nevertheless is attempting to maximise profits.

This is a criticism of the theory only if the theory is supposed to describe how employers actually behave. It does not. It merely states that, if firms are attempting to maximise profits, they will in fact be equating MC_L and MRP_L, whether they realise it or not!

A worker's marginal productivity cannot be calculated. When workers are part of a team, it is not usually possible to separate out the contribution to output of each individual. What is the marginal productivity of a cleaner, a porter or even a member of a production line? Similarly, it may not be possible to separate the contribution of workers from that of their tools. A lathe operator is useless without a lathe, as is a lathe without a lathe operator.

This is a more fundamental criticism. Nevertheless it is possible to amend the theory to take this into account. First, an employer can look at the composition of the team, or the partnership of worker and tools, and decide whether any reorganisations or alternative production methods will

CASE STUDIES AND APPLICATIONS

supporting flexible working practices and individualised pay packets based on performance (see Box 10.8).

However, unions have not lost all of their power. In December 2020, the Communication Workers Union agreed the following deal with Royal Mail after a two-year dispute: its members would receive a 2.7 per cent pay increase, effective from April 2020, and a one-hour reduction in the working week in return for agreeing to flexible methods of working.

In January 2021, staff at Centrica (Owners of British Gas) who were members of the GMB union went on strike over planned changes to their contracts of employment. The changes mean that standard working hours will increase from 37 to 40 hours per week. The union argues that this will result in a 10 per cent reduction in real pay.

Critics argue that strikes cause inconvenience to customers and other workers. However, others cite it as an example of the benefits of a strong union, protecting its members from the monopsony power of employers.

What factors, other than the ones identified above, could account for the long-run decline in union membership?

Source: Based on *Trade union statistics 2019*, Table 1.2b (BEIS and ONS), www.gov.uk/government/statistics/trade-union-statistics-2019

EXPLORING ECONOMICS

increase the firm's profitability (i.e. increase revenue more than costs). Second, the employer can decide whether to expand or contract the overall size of the team, or the number of workers plus machines. Here the whole team or the worker plus machine is the 'factor of production' whose marginal productivity must be weighed against its costs.

Firms are not always profit maximisers. This is a criticism only if the theory states that firms are. As long as the theory is merely used to describe what would happen if firms maximised profits, there is no problem.

This criticism, then, is really one of how the theory is used. And even if it is used to predict what will actually happen in the real world, it is still relatively accurate in the large number of cases where firms' behaviour diverges only slightly from profit maximising. It is clearly wrong in other cases.

Moral issues. A final criticism is the moral one. If economists focus their attention exclusively on how to maximise profits, it might be concluded that they are putting their seal of approval on this sort of behaviour. Of course, economists will respond by saying that they are doing no such thing: they are confining themselves to positive economics. Nevertheless, the criticism has some force. What an economist chooses to study is in part a normative decision.

Do any of the following contradict marginal productivity theory: (a) wage scales related to length of service (incremental scales); (b) nationally negotiated wage rates; (c) discrimination; (d) firms taking the lead from other firms in determining this year's pay increase?

In pairs, consider a range of occupations (pick some traditional ones and also some more obscure ones!). How would you measure the productivity of a worker in each case? How would the firm then decide whether or not it is worth taking on one extra worker? In which occupations is it easiest to calculate a worker's marginal product?

BOX 10.7 THE PERSISTENT GENDER PAY GAP?

(a) Average hourly pay (mean), excluding overtime, for full-time UK employees, aged 18 and over, 1970–2019 (£ per hour)

	1970	1974	1978	1982	1990	1994	1998	2002	2004	2008	2012	2016	2019
Men	0.67	1.05	2.00	3.55	6.89	8.65	10.65	12.92	13.73	15.53	16.52	17.38	19.01
Women	0.42	0.71	1.48	2.62	5.28	6.88	8.39	10.32	11.21	12.92	14.07	14.96	16.52
Women's pay as a % of men's	63.1	67.4	73.9	73.9	76.6	79.5	78.8	79.9	81.6	83.2	85.2	86.1	86.9
Gender pay gap	36.9	32.6	26.1	26.1	23.4	20.5	21.2	20.1	18.4	16.8	14.8	13.9	13.1

Source: Table 1.6a: Annual Survey of Hours and Earnings (National Statistics, 2019).

(b) Average hourly pay (median), excluding overtime, for selected occupations, full-time UK employees on adult rates, 2019 (£ per hour)

Occupation	Men	Women	Women's pay as a % of men's	Gender pay gap
Call centre workers	9.14	9.77	107.0	−6.9
Bar staff	8.58	8.50	99.1	0.9
Human resource managers/directors	25.35	24.74	97.6	2.4
Social workers	19.43	18.83	96.9	3.1
Police officers (sergeant and below)	19.39	18.77	96.8	3.2
Economists and statisticians	22.99	22.14	96.3	3.7
Chefs	10.20	9.81	96.2	3.8
Secondary school teachers	24.06	23.12	96.1	3.9
Sales and retail assistants	9.46	9.04	95.6	4.4
Nurses	18.75	17.87	95.3	4.7
Laboratory technicians	11.38	10.81	95.0	5.0
Hairdressers, barbers	9.35	8.52	91.1	8.9
Chief executives and senior officials	46.57	40.33	86.6	13.4
Librarians	15.23	12.93	84.9	15.1
Solicitors	25.20	20.81	82.6	17.4
Assemblers and routine operatives	11.40	9.38	82.3	17.7
Medical practitioners	31.89	25.60	80.3	19.7
All occupations	15.34	13.97	91.1	8.9
Average *gross weekly* pay (incl. overtime)	581.83	505.90	86.9	13.1
Average weekly paid hours (incl. overtime)	38.5	37.4		
Average weekly overtime	4.3	2.8		

Source: Table 1.3a, 1.9a, 1.11a and 14.6a: *Annual Survey of Hours and Earnings* (ONS, 2019).

The gender pay gap is usually calculated as the difference between the average hourly earnings (excluding overtime) of men and women as a proportion of average hourly earnings (excluding overtime) of men. Using mean values for full-time employees, Table (a) shows how the figure has fallen from just under 37 per cent in 1970 to just over 13 per cent in 2019.[1]

Using median values for full-time employees, Table (b) shows how the figure varies between some different occupations. The Office for National Statistics has recently created a Gender Pay Gap Explorer. This is an interactive on-line tool where you can search for the gender pay gap for different jobs.

The size of the gender pay gap depends on how earnings are measured. For example, based on median values, the full-time hourly earnings of women are 8.9 per cent less than men. When weekly pay is used instead of hourly pay, the figure increases to 13.1 per cent. The gender pay gap for all employees (full-time and part-time) was 17.3 per cent in 2019.

The average gender pay gap for all employees across the EU-27 countries[2] is similar to that of the UK and stood at 14.1 per cent in 2019. However, it varies considerably. For example, in Estonia the figure for all workers was 21.7 per cent, whereas in Luxembourg it was just 1.3 per cent. For *full-time* workers it varied from −0.2 per cent in Belgium to 24.1 per cent in Latvia.

It is important not to confuse the gender pay gap with unequal pay. Unequal pay refers to situations where men and women receive different rates of pay even though they are doing exactly the same job. This is illegal under the 2010 Equality Act. It probably still exists in some workplaces but it is very difficult to tell how significant it is in the economy as a whole.

1. *If we were to look at weekly rather than hourly pay and included the effects of overtime, what do you think would happen to the pay differentials in Table (a)?*
2. *In Table (b), which of the occupations have a largely female workforce?*

Unequal pay provides one possible explanation for the gender pay gap but there are a number of other reasons. For example, the existence of occupational segregation is a contributing factor. Women are far more likely to be employed in poorly-paid occupations. However, there must be other explanations as quite substantial pay gaps persist within particular occupations – see Table (b).

CASE STUDIES AND APPLICATIONS

So why has the pay gap persisted? Reasons include:

- The marginal productivity of labour in typically female occupations may be lower because women tend to work in more labour-intensive occupations. With less capital equipment per female worker than there is per male worker, we would expect the marginal product of a woman to be less than a man. Evidence from the EU as a whole suggests that occupational segregation is a significant factor in explaining pay differences.
- Many women take career breaks to have children. For this reason, employers are sometimes more willing to invest money in training men (thereby increasing their marginal productivity) and more willing to promote men. A study by the Institute for Fiscal Studies (IFS)[3] estimated that for every year a woman takes away from work her earnings fall by 2 per cent below those who remain in work.
- Women tend to be less geographically mobile. If social norms are such that the man's job is seen as somehow more 'important' than the woman's, then a couple will often move for the man to get promotion. The woman, however, will have to settle for whatever job she can get in the same locality as her partner. A study by IFS[4] found that women tend to work in less productive firms and this was potentially because of their lack of geographical mobility caused by childcare responsibilities.
- A smaller proportion of women workers are members of unions than men. Even when they are members of unions, these are often in jobs where unions are weak (e.g. clothing industry workers and shop assistants).
- Part-time workers (mainly women) have less bargaining power, less influence and less chance of obtaining promotion. The IFS study found that when women switch from full-time to part-time work their hourly wage does not fall immediately. However, over time their growth in earnings falls behind those of people working full-time.
- Custom and practice. Many jobs done wholly or mainly by women continue to be low-paid, irrespective of productivity.

Why has the gender pay gap narrowed in the past 20 years? The IFS research suggests that the main reason is the increasing proportion of women who are now educated to A level and degree standard. However, the same study also found that the gender wage gap for the highly educated has not really changed over the same period. The difference in pay between male and female graduates is approximately the same is it was in the late 1990s.

One reason for this is the possibility that in many jobs women are discriminated against when it comes to promotion, especially to senior positions – the so-called 'glass ceiling'. This may be an example of *people appointing in their own image*: i.e. men favouring male applicants.

The UK government has introduced a number of initiatives to try to close the gender pay gap, including:

- Shared parental leave. This was introduced in April 2015 and enables parents to share up to 50 weeks of leave, of which 37 is paid. At present, the take-up of the scheme has been low – approximately 5 per cent.
- Mandatory gender pay gap reporting. Companies employing more than 250 people now have to publish information about their gender pay gap as of 5 April each year. The median pay gap of the 10 428 employers who submitted data in April 2019 was 11.9 per cent – virtually unchanged from the 11.8 per cent figure reported in 2018.[5] Some critics argue that it should also be mandatory for firms to publish details of how they plan to close the gap.
- Women in Finance Charter. This is a pledge for greater balance in the financial services.

The impact of COVID-19

The lockdowns during the COVID-19 pandemic had a larger impact on female employment. For example, a survey carried out by the IFS[6] found that of those who were in paid work prior to the first national lockdown, mothers were 47 per cent more likely than fathers to have permanently lost or quit their job. Out of those mothers who remained in paid work, average hours worked per week fell from 6.3 to 4.9 hours. This was proportionately more than fathers, whose average hours fell from 8.6 to 7.2 hours. One potential reason for this difference was the impact of closing schools, crèches and day-care centres. Evidence shows that women took on more of the childcare and home-schooling responsibilities.

The long-run impact of these changes on the gender pay gap are uncertain but previous research shows that career breaks due to maternity leave have an adverse impact on female earnings.

3. *If employers were forced to give genuinely equal pay for equal work, how would this affect the employment of women and men? What would determine the magnitude of these effects?*
4. *How could family policy ensure that parents are able to work, while reducing pay differentials?*
5. *What measures could a government introduce to increase the number of women getting higher-paid jobs?*

Access data from the gender pay gap statistics section of the Eurostat site. Using the latest available data, create a chart showing the variation in the size of the gender pay gap across a selection of EU member countries along with the gap for the UK.

1 The 2020 data have not been included because of the temporary impact of the furlough scheme on reported earnings.
2 *Gender Pay Gap Statistics*, Eurostat (February 2021), https://ec.europa.eu/eurostat/statistics-explained/index.php?title=Gender_pay_gap_statistics
3 *The Gender Wage Gap*, Institute for Fiscal Studies (August 2016), www.ifs.org.uk/uploads/publications/bns/bn186.pdf
4 *The gender pay gap: women work for lower paying firms than men*, Institute for Fiscal Studies (April 2019), www.ifs.org.uk/publications/14032
5 The deadline for firms to report their 2020 data was delayed until October 2021 because of the impact of COVID-19.
6 *How are mothers and fathers balancing work and family under lockdown?*, Institute for Fiscal Studies (May 2020), www.ifs.org.uk/uploads/BN290-Mothers-and-fathers-balancing-work-and-life-under-lockdown.pdf

BOX 10.8 FLEXIBLE LABOUR MARKETS AND THE FLEXIBLE FIRM

New work practices for old?

KI 24 p259

The past 35 years have seen sweeping changes in the ways that firms organise their workforces. Global recessions combined with rapid changes in technology led many firms to question the wisdom of appointing workers on a permanent basis to specific jobs. Instead, they want the flexibility to respond to changing situations. If demand falls, they want to be able to reduce labour without facing large redundancy costs. If demand rises, they want rapid access to additional labour. If technology changes they want to have the flexibility to move workers around, or to take on new workers in some areas and lose some in others.

What many firms seek, therefore, is flexibility in employing and allocating labour. Many countries are experiencing an increasingly flexible labour market, as workers and employment agencies respond to the new 'flexible firm'.

There are three main types of flexibility in the use of labour:

- ***Functional flexibility***. This is where an employer is able to transfer labour between different tasks within the production process. It contrasts with traditional forms of organisation where people are employed to do specific tasks. A functionally flexible labour force will tend to be multi-skilled and relatively highly trained.
- ***Numerical flexibility***. This is where the firm is able to adjust the size and composition of its workforce according to changing market conditions. To achieve this, the firm is likely to employ a proportion of its labour on a part-time or casual basis, or even subcontract specialist requirements. An increasingly common practice is for workers to be on 'zero-hour contracts', where the employee has no guaranteed hours and they can vary on a weekly basis. Data for the UK shows that 978 000 workers were on zero-hour contracts in the final quarter of 2020. This accounts for 3 per cent of people in employment.[1]
- ***Financial flexibility***. This is where the firm has flexibility in its wage costs that is largely the result of functional and numerical flexibility. It is possible to achieve financial flexibility by rewarding individual effort and productivity rather than paying a given rate for a particular job. This results in growing occupational and regional pay differentials.

The diagram shows how these three forms of flexibility are reflected in the organisation of a ***flexible firm***, an organisation quite different from that of the traditional firm. The most significant difference is the segmentation of the labour force. The core group, drawn from the ***primary labour market***, will be composed of functionally flexible workers, who are generally on secure full-time permanent contracts. Such workers will be relatively well paid and receive wages reflecting their scarce skills.

The periphery, drawn from the ***secondary labour market***, is more fragmented than the core, and can be subdivided into a first and a second peripheral group. The first peripheral group is composed of workers with lower levels of skill than those in the core, skills that tend to be general rather than firm-specific. Thus workers in this group can be drawn from the external labour market, often through agencies. Such workers may be employed on full-time contracts, but they will generally face less secure employment than core workers.

The gig economy

One type of flexible working that has grown rapidly in recent years is the so-called 'gig economy'. An online survey found that the number of people working in this sector at least once a week had doubled from 4.7 per cent of the adult population in 2016 to 9.6 per cent in 2019.[2] For the majority of people (71.5 per cent) it represents less than half of their income and is a way of topping up other earnings.

What exactly is the gig economy? Unfortunately, there is no single agreed definition. In its 2017 report, the Department for Business, Energy and Industrial Strategy developed the following working definition.[3]

The flexible firm

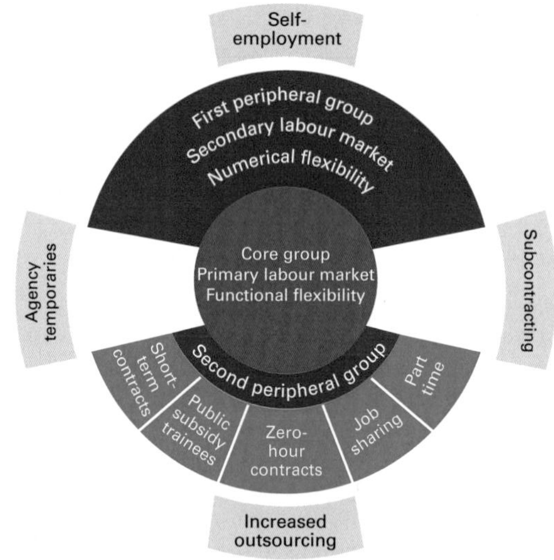

Definitions

Functional flexibility Where employers can switch workers from job to job as requirements change.

Numerical flexibility Where employers can change the size of their workforce as their labour requirements change.

Financial flexibility Where employers can vary their wage costs by changing the composition of their workforce or the terms on which workers are employed.

Flexible firm A firm that has the flexibility to respond to changing market conditions by changing the composition of its workforce.

Primary labour market The market for permanent full-time core workers.

Secondary labour market The market for peripheral workers, usually employed on a temporary or part-time basis, or a less secure 'permanent' basis.

CASE STUDIES AND APPLICATIONS

The exchange of labour for money between individuals or companies via digital platforms that actively facilitate the matching between providers and customers, on a short-term and payment by task basis.

Some important characteristics follow from this definition.

First, the exchange of labour services between the worker and customer is typically for a task of very short duration (i.e. one food delivery or one taxi ride). This differs from more traditional agency work where the job/project typically takes weeks/months.

The gig economy also differs from zero-hour contracts because earnings depend on the number of tasks (i.e. gigs) completed. With zero-hour contracts, pay depends on time in the workplace rather than tasks completed. For example, a bartender's earnings do not vary with the amount of drinks they serve, whereas a delivery rider's earnings vary with the number of deliveries they make.

One of the biggest areas of controversy has been the nature of the working relationship between the individual and the digital platform. The platforms (e.g. Deliveroo and Uber) argue that people are free to choose (a) when they want to start work (i.e. by logging into the platform) and (b) when they want to finish work (i.e. by logging out of the platform). They claim, therefore, that they should be classed as self-employed independent contractors and so not entitled to any rights of employment, such as redundancy pay, notice periods and protection against unfair dismissal.

Clearly, people do not have a traditional contract of service with the platforms so do not qualify as employees. However, this does not necessarily mean they are self-employed. Those people who are not in business for themselves but provide labour services come under the category of '*limb (b) workers*' in employment law. This means they qualify for some employment rights such as the national minimum wage, holiday pay and workplace pension. One of the recommendations of the Taylor Review[4] of flexible working practices was to rename *limb (b) workers* as '*dependent contractors*'.

In 2016, some taxi drivers took Uber to an employment tribunal claiming they were workers rather than self-employed. After a long legal battle, the Supreme Court delivered its final judgment in February 2021.[5] It ruled that the drivers were not self-employed, as Uber:

- unilaterally sets the fares;
- sets the contract terms for drivers;
- can penalise drivers if they reject too many fares;
- monitors a driver's service and can terminate the relationship if, after repeated warnings, it does not improve.

In March 2021, the company announced that its UK drivers would now receive holiday pay, a minimum earnings guarantee and a workplace pension. It will be interesting to see what impact the Supreme Court ruling has on other parts of the gig economy.

1. *Is a flexible firm more likely or less likely to employ workers up to the point where their MRP = MC_L?*
2. *Would you expect the advent of flexible firms to alter the gender balance of employment and unemployment?*
3. *If a firm is trying to achieve flexibility in its use of labour, do you think this would be harder or easier in a period of recession? Explain why.*
4. *Assume workers in a firm are allowed to choose between a 20 per cent reduction in pay or 20 per cent of the workforce being laid off. What factors would influence the workers' choice?*

Individually or in pairs, look through job adverts in employment agencies, in newspapers or online. Classify the types of jobs according to the flexible firm diagram above. In each case, consider how the degree of flexibility benefits the firm and whether or not it benefits the potential employee. The findings of the individuals or pairs could then be compared at group level to gain a fuller picture of the nature and impact of flexibility in employment.

1 *Data EMP17: People in employment on zero hours contracts*, ONS (February 2021), www.ons.gov.uk/employmentandlabourmarket/peopleinwork/employmentandemployeetypes/datasets/emp17peopleinemploymentonzerohourscontracts
2 *Platform Work in the UK 2016–2019, Statistical Services and Consultancy Unit (SSCU)*, University of Hertfordshire and Hertfordshire Business School (HBS) (26 June 2019), www.feps-europe.eu/attachments/publications/platform work in the uk 2016-2019 v3-converted.pdf
3 *The characteristics of those in the gig economy*, Department for Business, Energy & Industrial Strategy (February 2018), https://www.gov.uk/government/publications/gig-economy-research
4 *Good work: the Taylor review of modern working practices*, Department for Business, Energy & Industrial Strategy, (11 July 2017), www.gov.uk/government/publications/good-work-the-taylor-review-of-modern-working-practices
5 Uber BV and others (Appellants) v Aslam and others (Respondents) [2021] UKSC 5 On appeal from: [2018] EWCA Civ 2748, *Press Summary*, The Supreme Court (19 February 2021), www.supremecourt.uk/press-summary/uksc-2019-0029.html

Discrimination

Discrimination can be another major factor in determining wages. It can take many forms: it can be by race, gender, sexual orientation, age, class, religion, etc.; it can occur in many different aspects of society. This section is concerned with ***economic discrimination***, where workers of identical ability receive different pay for doing the same job, or are given different chances of employment or promotion.

Take the case of racial discrimination by employers. Figure 10.11 illustrates the wages and employment of black and white workers by a firm with monopsony power which practises racial discrimination against black workers. Let us assume that there is no difference in the productivity of black and white workers. Let us also assume for simplicity that

Definition

Economic discrimination Where workers of identical *ability* are paid different wages or are otherwise discriminated against because of race, age, sex, etc.

there is an equal number of black workers and white workers available at any given wage rate. Finally, let us assume that there are no laws to prevent the firm discriminating in terms of either wages or employment.

Figure 10.11(a) shows the *MC* and *MRP* curves for black workers. If there were no discrimination, employment of black workers would be at Q_{B_1}, where $MRP_B = MC_B$. The wage rate paid to black workers would be W_{B_1}.

Figure 10.11(b) shows the position for white workers. Again, if there were no discrimination, Q_{W_1} white workers would be employed at a wage of W_{W_1}: the same wage as that of black workers. (Note that in each case the *MRP* curve

BOX 10.9 BEHAVIOUR AT WORK

EXPLORING ECONOMICS

What motivates employees?

Effort in the workplace is difficult to observe. Unless it falls below some minimum level, employers will find it difficult to monitor how hard their employees are working. What can organisations do to motivate their workers to exert more than minimal levels of effort? What ideas can economists contribute?

Standard economic theory

Models in standard economic theory assume that employees are motivated by material self-interest. Therefore, they predict that to motivate greater effort, organisations should link pay more closely with measured employee performance.[1] Some research evidence finds that many workers respond to continuous output incentives (i.e. piece rates) in ways that are consistent with this prediction. For example, when:

- a glass company in the US changed its compensation scheme for its windscreen fitters from an hourly rate of pay to a piece rate scheme (i.e. per windscreen fitted) productivity increased by 44 per cent;[2]
- tree planters in British Columbia switched from a fixed wage to piece rates, average output per worker increased by 21 per cent;[3]
- field managers on a fruit farm in the UK started receiving bonuses half-way through the picking season, overall productivity increased by 25 per cent. It was possible for the field managers to have a direct impact on the productivity of fruit pickers by clearing crates faster and assigning workers more efficiently.[4]

In these three examples, it is relatively straightforward to measure workers' output and monitor its quality.

In many jobs, however, the 'output' workers produce is more complex and multidimensional. It involves employees allocating effort levels across a number of different tasks. The output from some of these tasks is likely to be far easier to measure than from others. If employers link monetary rewards/bonuses only to those measurable dimensions, then there is a danger of distortion. This is where employees focus their effort on tasks that have monetary rewards rather than balancing their time across different dimensions of the job in a way that maximises value for the firm. This is called the multi-tasking problem. A classic example is where incentives are based on the quantity of a product produced rather than its quality. Employees may then neglect quality in their effort to produce more.

In these situations, rather than linking pay to current performance, organisations can use the long-term nature of the employment contract to link future pay to more holistic measures of current performance. This typically involves some element of subjective performance evaluation. Promotion is a widely used policy that takes this approach. Employees may be willing to work hard today in order to increase their chances of gaining promotion to better positions in the organisation in the future.

Behavioural economics – the impact of reciprocal fairness

Theories in behavioural economics predict that some people have preferences for fairness. Box 9.2 discusses evidence about consumer preferences for fairness and the influence this has on shopping intentions and willingness to pay. Do some people have the same preferences for fairness when they are employees in the workplace? Do their perceptions about how employers treat them (i.e. fairly or unfairly) have an impact on the effort they exert?

A number of field experiments have tested this proposition. The researchers hire people to carry out a one-time clerical task (e.g. entering the details of books into a library system or putting material into envelopes) at an advertised rate of pay. When the recruits arrive on the day, they are split into groups that sit in completely separate rooms. Some groups are informed that the wage rate differs from the one advertised with no reason given for the change. These studies are examples of 'gift exchange' experiments. The gift from the employer is the higher rate of pay, and some employees may reciprocate by exerting higher effort levels.

In one of these experiments, Kube, Maréchal and Puppe (2012)[5] hired people at an advertised rate of €36 to complete some clerical work. The researchers then split the workers into three groups – a baseline group paid the advertised rate, a second group paid €43 and a final group paid €36 plus a €7 Nalgene water bottle. Productivity in the €43 group was not significantly higher than in the baseline group, whereas productivity in the €36-plus-bottle group was 25 per cent higher. Adding a €7 price tag to the bottle made very little difference to the results.

Why does the gift of an item worth $x appear to have a much stronger effect on effort than a wage rise of $x? One explanation is that non-monetary gifts send a stronger signal that the employer cares about their workers.

Extrinsic rewards and intrinsic motivation

Some research has found evidence of monetary rewards having a negative impact on productivity. For example, Fryer (2013)[6] found that offering bonuses to teachers in the USA actually had a negative impact on some measures of student attainment. Gneezy and Rustichini (2000)[7] examined the impact of offering monetary incentives to students collecting donations for charity. The average amount collected was greater in the groups that did not receive any monetary incentives.

Why might some monetary incentives have a negative impact on productivity? Some researchers argue that it can have a negative impact on intrinsic motivation. Intrinsic motivation is the pleasure that comes from within a person when they undertake an activity. For example, employees may simply enjoy the work or get a personal sense of pleasure or fulfilment from completing a difficult/demanding task.

Piece rates and bonuses are examples of extrinsic rewards – they come from external sources. The motivation/reward does not come from within, but instead comes from a separate party. Some people argue that the use of extrinsic rewards can sometimes damage or crowd out intrinsic motivation. If this effect is strong enough, it may explain why monetary incentives can sometimes lead to lower productivity in the workplace.

Motivating workers is a complex problem for most organisations. The best approach will depend on the type of job and the preferences of the worker.

1. *Many incentives schemes, such as promotion, use relative performance evaluation: i.e. employers judge/compare the performance of workers against their peers. Discuss some of the strengths and weaknesses of using relative performance evaluation.*
2. *Explain how a monetary incentive could have a negative impact on a non-monetary extrinsic reward and so lead to lower productivity.*

Investigate the incentive systems used in a particular company of your choice and assess how appropriate they are for motivating employees doing complex tasks.

1 Employee performance depends on both effort and random factors. Therefore, performance pay introduces greater levels of risk into employee compensation. Performance pay will only increase a firm's profits if the value of the extra output is greater than the compensating wage for this extra risk.
2 Edward Lazear, 'Performance pay and productivity', *American Economic Review,* vol. 90, no. 5 (December 2000), pp. 1346–61, www.aeaweb.org/articles?id=10.1257/aer.90.5.1346
3 Bruce Shearer, 'Piece rates, fixed wages and incentives: evidence from a field experiment' *Review of Economic Studies,* vol. 71, no. 2 (April 2004), pp. 513–34, www.jstor.org/stable/3700636
4 Oriana Bandiera, Iwan Barankay and Imran Raul, 'Incentives for managers and inequality amongst workers: evidence from a firm level experiment', *Quarterly Journal of Economics*, vol. 122, no. 2 (May 2007), pp. 729–73, https://academic.oup.com/qje/article/122/2/729/1942123
5 Sebastian Kube, Michel André Maréchal, and Clemens Puppe, 'The currency of reciprocity: gift exchange in the workplace', *American Economic Review,* vol. 102, no. 4 (June 2012), pp. 1644–62, www.aeaweb.org/articles?id=10.1257/aer.102.4.1644
6 Roland Fryer, 'Teacher incentives and student achievement: evidence from New York City public schools', *Journal of Labour Economics,* vol 31, no. 2 (April 2013), pp. 373–407, https://www.journals.uchicago.edu/doi/10.1086/667757
7 Uri Gneezy and Aldo Rustichini, 'Pay enough or don't pay at all', *The Quarterly Journal of Economics,* vol. 115, no. 3 (August 2000), pp. 791–810, www.jstor.org/stable/2586896

is drawn on the assumption that the number of workers employed from the other ethnic group is constant.)

If the firm now discriminates against black workers, it will employ workers along a lower curve, $MRP_B - x$ (where x can be seen as the discriminatory factor). Employment of black workers will thus be at the lower level of Q_{B_2} and the wage they receive will be at the lower level of W_{B_2}.

How will discrimination against black workers affect wages and employment of white workers? Let us consider two cases.

In the first case, assume that the employer practises economic discrimination purely in the negative sense: i.e. it discriminates against black workers but employs white workers on profit-maximising principles. Thus white workers would be employed up to that point where their *MC* equals their *MRP*. But the fact that fewer black workers are now being employed will mean that for any given quantity of white workers there will be fewer workers employed in total, and therefore the *MRP* of white workers will have increased. In Figure 10.11(b), the white workers' *MRP* curve

Figure 10.11 The effect of racial discrimination by a monopsonist employer

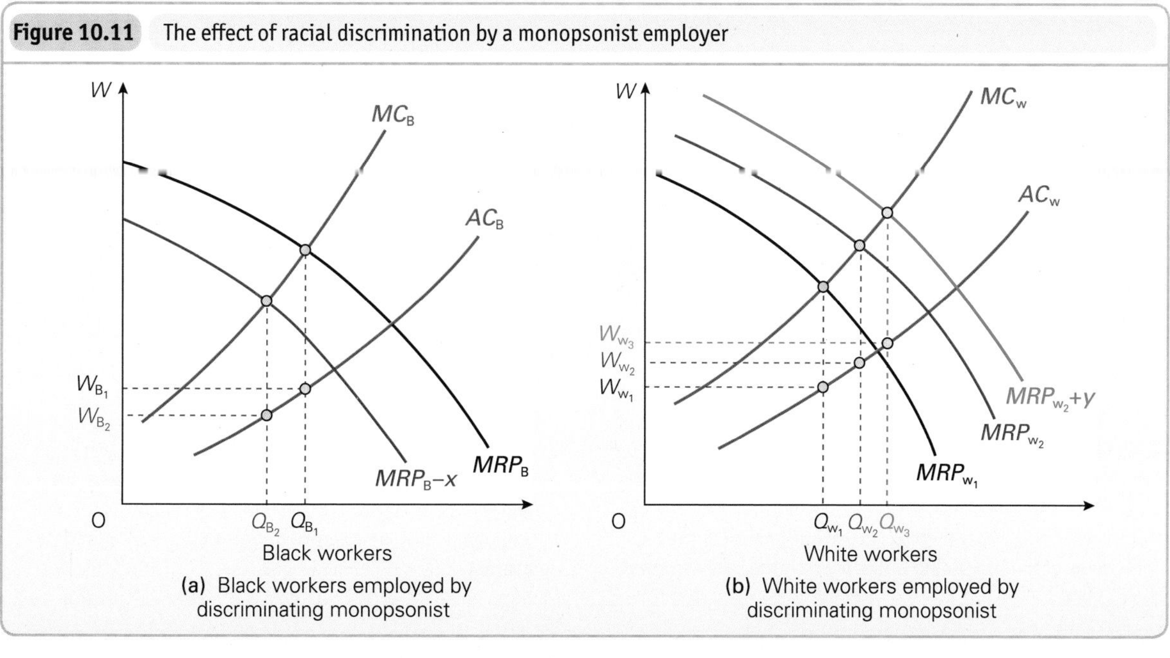

(a) Black workers employed by discriminating monopsonist

(b) White workers employed by discriminating monopsonist

has shifted to MRP_{W_2}. This has the effect of raising employment of white workers to Q_{W_2} and the wage rate to W_{W_2}.

Firms may, however, also practise economic discrimination *in favour* of certain groups. Figure 10.11(b) also illustrates this second case, where the employer practises economic discrimination in favour of white workers. Here the firm will employ workers along a higher curve, $MRP_{W_2} + y$, where y is the discriminatory factor. The effect is further to increase the wage rate and level of employment of white workers, to W_{W_3} and Q_{W_3} respectively.

What effect will the discrimination by the firm have on the wages and employment of black workers in other firms in the area if (a) these other firms discriminate against black workers; (b) they do not discriminate?

If the government now legislates for equal pay for equal work, then employers that discriminate will respond by further cutting back on black workers. The answer to *this* problem would seem to be for the government to pass laws that insist not only that black workers be paid the same as white workers for doing the same job, but also that they be treated equally when applying for jobs.

The type of discrimination considered so far can be seen as 'irrational' if the firm wants to maximise profits. After all, to produce a given amount of output, it would be paying out more in wages to employ white workers than black workers. In a competitive market environment, such firms may be forced to end discrimination simply to survive the competition from non-discriminating rivals. If, however, the firm has market power, it will probably be making sufficient profits to allow it to continue discriminating. The main pressure to end discrimination is then likely to come from unions, customers, shareholders or race relations organisations.

Other examples of non-economic discrimination stem from unequal educational opportunities. If the educational system discriminates against black children, they are likely to end up with poorer qualifications. They have less ***human capital*** invested in them. Under these circumstances, employers, preferring to employ the best-qualified applicants, are likely to choose white people. This is particularly so in the more highly paid jobs that require a higher level of educational attainment. Tackling this problem at source means tackling weaknesses early on in the education system and breaking what has come to be known as the cycle of deprivation.

Who are the poor? Who are the rich?

To the list we made at the end of section 10.1 we can now add the following factors that will tend to make people poor:

- Lack of economic power, not belonging to a union or belonging to a union with only weak bargaining power.
- Ignorance of better job opportunities.
- Lack of will or ability to search for a better job.
- Discrimination against them by employers or fellow workers.

Thus before the advent of the minimum wage many people of Asian origin, especially women, working in the garment industry in back-street 'sweatshops' earned pitifully low wages. Conversely, belonging to a powerful union, working for a profitable employer which nevertheless is not a ruthless profit maximiser, being aware of new job opportunities and having the 'get up and go' to apply for better jobs, and being white, male and middle-class are all factors that help to contribute to people earning high wages. KI 4 p13

Definition

Human capital The qualifications, skills and expertise that contribute to a worker's productivity.

Section summary

1. If a firm is a monopsony employer, it will employ workers to the point where $MRP_L = MC_L$. Since the wage is below MC_L, the monopsonist, other things being equal, will employ fewer workers at a lower wage than would be employed in a perfectly competitive labour market.
2. If a union has monopoly power, its power to raise wage rates will be limited if the employer operates under perfect or monopolistic competition in the goods market. A rise in wage rates will force the employer to cut back on employment.
3. In a situation of bilateral monopoly (where a monopoly union faces a monopsony employer), the union may have considerable scope to raise the wage rate above the monopsony level, without the employer wishing to reduce the level of employment. There is no unique equilibrium wage. The wage will depend on the outcome of a process of collective bargaining between union and management.
4. Each side can make various threats or promises. The outcome of the bargaining will depend on the relative power, attitudes and bargaining skills of both sides, the firm's profitability and the information each side has about the other. The outcome also depends on the legal framework within which the negotiations take place.
5. Power is not the only factor that makes actual wage determination different from the perfectly competitive model. Firms and workers may have imperfect knowledge of the labour market; disequilibrium in labour markets may persist; firms may not be profit maximisers (see Case Study 10.3 on the student website).
6. Firms may exercise discrimination (by race, sex, age, etc.) in their employment policy. By discriminating against a particular group, an employer with market power can drive down the wages of the members of that group. Unless firms are forced not to discriminate, equal pay legislation may well lead to a reduction in the employment of members of groups that are discriminated against.

10.3 CAPITAL AND PROFIT

The non-human factors of production

In the final two sections of the chapter, we consider the market for *other* factors of production. These can be divided into two broad groups.

Land. This includes all those productive resources supplied by nature: in other words, not only land itself, but also all natural resources. (We examine land in section 10.4.)

Capital. This includes all manufactured products that are used to produce goods and services. Thus capital includes such diverse items as a blast furnace, a bus, a computer, a factory building and a screwdriver.

The capital goods described above are physical assets and are known as *physical* capital. The word 'capital' is also used to refer to various *paper* assets, such as shares and bonds. These are the means by which firms raise finance to purchase physical capital, and are known as *financial* capital. Being merely paper assets, however, they do not count as factors of production. Nevertheless, financial markets have an important role in determining the level of investment in physical capital, and we shall be examining these markets on pages 313–6.

Factor prices versus the price of factor services

A feature of most non-human factors is that they last a period of time. A machine may last 10 years; an oil well may last 50 years before it is exhausted; farmland will last forever if properly looked after. We must therefore distinguish between the income the owner will get from *selling* the factor and that which the owner will get from *using* it or *hiring* it out.

- The income from selling the factor is the factor's *price.* Thus a machine might sell for £20 000, or a hectare of farming land for £15 000.
- The income gained from using a factor is its *return,* and the income gained from hiring a factor out is its *rental.* This income represents the value or price of the factor's *services,* expressed per period of time. Thus a machine might earn a firm £1000 per year. A hectare of land might earn a landowner £600 rent per year.

Obviously, the price of a factor will be linked to the value of its services. The price that a hectare of land will fetch if sold will depend on the return or rent that can be earned on that land. If it is highly productive farmland, it will sell for a higher price than a piece of scrubby moorland.

When we were looking at wage rates, were we talking about the price of labour or the price of labour services? Is this distinction between the price of a factor and the price of factor services a useful one in the case of labour? Was it in Roman times?

The profit-maximising employment of land and capital

On the demand side, the same rules apply for land and capital as for labour, if a firm wishes to maximise profits. Namely, it should demand factors up to the point where the marginal cost of the factor equals its marginal revenue product: $MC_f = MRP_f$. This same rule applies whether the firm is buying the factor outright, or merely renting it.

Figure 10.12 illustrates the two cases of perfect competition and monopsony. In both cases the *MRP* curve slopes downwards. This is another illustration of the law of diminishing returns, but this time applied to land or capital. For example, if a farmer increases the amount of land farmed while *holding other factors constant,* diminishing returns to land will occur. If the same number of farm workers and the same amount of agricultural machinery and fertilisers are used but on a larger area, then returns per hectare will fall.

In Figure 10.12(a) the firm is a price taker. The factor price is given at P_{f1}. Profits are maximised at Q_{f1} where $MRP_f = P_f$ (since $P_f = MC_f$).

Figure 10.12 Profit-maximising employment of a factor

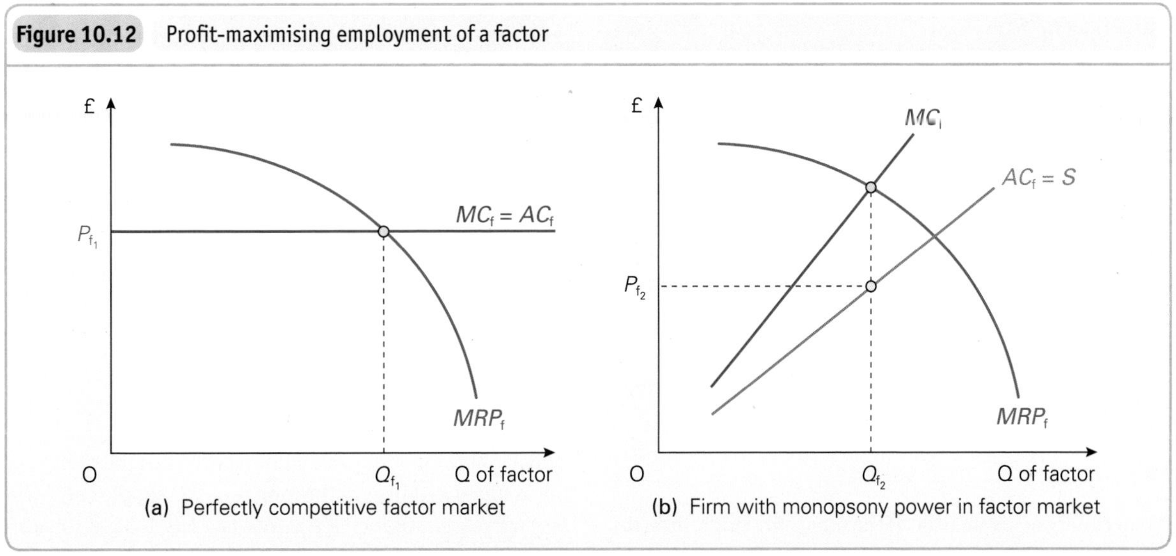

In Figure 10.12(b) the firm has monopsony power. The factor price will vary, therefore, with the amount that the firm uses. The firm will again use factors to the point where $MRP_f = MC_f$. In this case, it will mean using Q_{f2} at a price of P_{f2}.

What is the difference between buying a factor and renting it? Although the $MRP_f = MC_f$ rule remains the same, there are differences. As far as buying the factors is concerned, the MC_f is the extra outlay for the firm in *purchasing* one more unit of the factor; and the MRP_f is all the revenue produced by that factor over its *whole life* (but measured in terms of what this is worth when purchased: see pages 310–12). In the case of renting, MC_f is the extra outlay for the firm in rent *per period,* while *MRP* is the extra revenue earned from it *per period.*

The demand for capital services

What we are talking about in this section is the hiring of capital equipment for a period of time (as opposed to buying it outright). The analysis is virtually identical to that of the demand for labour. As with labour, we can distinguish between an individual firm's demand and the whole market demand.

Individual firm's demand

Take the case of a small painting and decorating firm thinking of hiring some scaffolding in order to complete a job. It could use ladders, which it already owns, but the job would take longer to complete. If it hires the scaffolding for one day, it can perhaps shorten the job by, say, two or three days. If it hires it for a second day, it can perhaps save another one or two days. Hiring it for additional days may save extra still. But diminishing returns are occurring: the longer the scaffolding is up, the less intensively it will be used, and the less additional time it will save. Perhaps for some of the time it will be used when ladders could have been used equally easily.

The time saved allows the firm to take on extra work. Thus each extra day the scaffolding is hired gives the firm extra revenue. This is the scaffolding's marginal revenue product of capital (MRP_K). Diminishing returns mean that it has the normal downward-sloping shape (see Figure 10.12).

Market demand

The market demand for capital services is derived in exactly the same way as the market demand for labour (see Figure 10.6 on page 291). It is the horizontal sum of the MRP_K curves of the individual firms, corrected for the fact that increased use of capital will increase output, drive down the price of the good and hence reduce *MRP*. This means that the market demand curve for capital is steeper than the horizontal sum of the demand curves (MRP_K) of all the firms in the market.

Under what circumstances would the market demand for renting a type of capital equipment be (a) elastic; (b) inelastic? (Clue: turn back to page 291 and see what determines the elasticity of demand for labour.)

The supply of capital services

It is necessary to distinguish (a) the supply *to* a single firm, (b) the supply *by* a single firm and (c) the market supply.

Supply to a single firm

This is illustrated in Figure 10.13(a). The small firm renting capital equipment is probably a price taker. If so, it faces a horizontal supply curve at the going rental rate (R_e). If, however, it has monopsony power, it will face an upward-sloping supply curve as in Figure 10.12(b).

Supply by a single firm

This is illustrated in Figure 10.13(b). On the demand side, the firm is likely to be a price taker. It has to accept the going rental rate (R_e) established in the market. If it tries to charge more, then customers are likely to turn to rival suppliers.

But what will the individual supplier's *supply* curve look like? The theory here has a lot in common with perfect competition in the goods market (see pages 197–200): the supply curve is the firm's *MC* curve, only here the *MC* is the extra cost of supplying one more unit of capital equipment for rent over a given time period.

The problem with working out the marginal cost of renting out capital equipment is that the equipment probably cost a lot to buy in the first place, but lasts a long time. How then are these large costs to be apportioned to each new rental? The answer is that it depends on the time period under consideration.

The short run. In the short run, the hire company is not buying any new equipment: it is simply hiring out its existing stock of equipment. In the case of the scaffolding hire firm, the marginal costs of doing this will be as follows:

- Depreciation. Scaffolding has second-hand value. Each time the scaffolding is hired out it deteriorates, and thus its second-hand value falls. This loss in value is called 'depreciation'.
- Maintenance and handling. Hiring out equipment involves labour time (e.g. in the office) and possibly transport costs; the equipment may need servicing after being hired out.

These marginal costs are likely to rise relatively slowly. For each extra day a piece of equipment is hired out, the company will incur the same or only slightly higher additional costs. This gives a relatively flat supply curve of capital services in Figure 10.13(b) up to the hire company's maximum capacity. Once the scaffolding firm is hiring out all its scaffolding, the supply curve becomes vertical.

Assume now that the firm has monopoly power in hiring out equipment, and thus faces a downward-sloping demand curve. Draw in two such demand curves on a diagram like Figure 10.13(b), one crossing the MC curve in the horizontal section, and one in the vertical section. How much will the firm supply in each case and at what price? (You will need to draw in MR curves too.) Is the MC curve still the supply curve?

The long run. In the long run, the hire company will consider purchasing additional equipment. It can therefore supply as much as it likes in the long run. The supply curve will be relatively elastic, or if it is a price taker itself (i.e. if the scaffolding firm simply buys scaffolding at the market price), the

Figure 10.13 Long-run equilibrium rental rate for the services of a particular type of capital

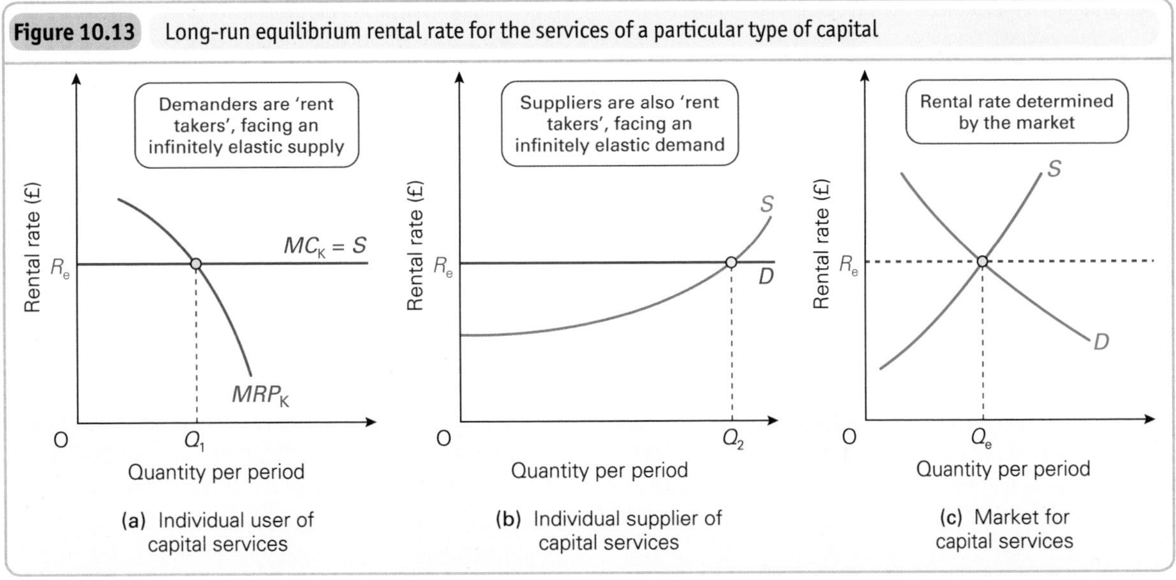

supply curve will be horizontal. This long-run supply curve will be vertically higher than the short-run curve, since the long-run *MC* includes the cost of purchasing each additional piece of equipment.

Maths Case 10.1 on the student website shows how this marginal cost can be calculated.

Market supply

This is illustrated in Figure 10.13(c). The market supply curve of a particular type of capital service is the sum of the quantities supplied by all the individual firms.

In the short run, the market supply will be relatively inelastic, given that it takes time to manufacture new equipment and that stocks of equipment currently held by manufacturers are likely to be relatively small. Also, capital is *heterogeneous*: i.e. one piece of capital equipment is not the same as another. If there is a shortage of scaffolding, you cannot use a cement mixer instead: people would fall off! Finally, hire companies may be unwilling to purchase (expensive) new equipment immediately there is a rise in demand: after all, the upsurge in demand may turn out to be short-lived.

BOX 10.10 STOCKS AND FLOWS

EXPLORING ECONOMICS

The discussion of the rewards to capital and land leads to a very important distinction: that between stocks and flows.

A stock is a quantity of something held. A landowner may own 200 hectares. A farmer may have a barn with 500 tonnes of grain. You may have £1000 in a savings account. These are all stocks: they are all quantities held at a given point in time.

A flow is an increase or decrease in quantity over a specified period. The landowner may buy another 10 hectares during the year. The farmer may use 10 tonnes of grain from the barn each week as animal feed. You may save £10 per month.

Wages, rent and interest are all rewards to flows. Wages are the amount paid for the services of a person's labour for a week or month. Rent is the amount paid per period of time to use the services of land. Likewise, interest is the reward paid to people per year for the use of their money.

If an asset is sold, its value is the value of the stock. It is a simple payment at a single point in time for the transfer of a whole asset. Thus the price of land and the price of capital are stock concepts.

An important example of stocks and flows arises with capital and investment. If a firm has 100 machines, that is a stock of capital. It may choose to build up its stock by investing. Investment is a flow concept. The firm may choose to invest in 10 new machines each year. This may not add 10 to the stock of machines, however, as some may be wearing out (a negative flow).

KEY IDEA 26

Stocks and flows. **A stock is a quantity of something at a given point in time. A flow is an increase or decrease in something over a specified period of time. This is an important distinction and a common cause of confusion.**

Which of the following are stocks and which are flows?
(a) Unemployment.
(b) Redundancies.
(c) Profits.
(d) A firm's stock market valuation.
(e) The value of property after a period of inflation.

Divide into pairs and see if you can agree on other examples of stocks and flows of relevance to business. Which do you think a firm will be more concerned about? Does your answer change if you consider different companies?

If supply is totally inelastic, what determines the rental value of capital equipment in the short run?

In the *long run*, the supply curve of capital services will be more elastic because extra capital equipment can be produced. It will not be horizontal, however, but upward sloping. Its elasticity will depend on the elasticity of supply of capital equipment to the hire companies.

Determination of the price of capital services

KI 8 p44

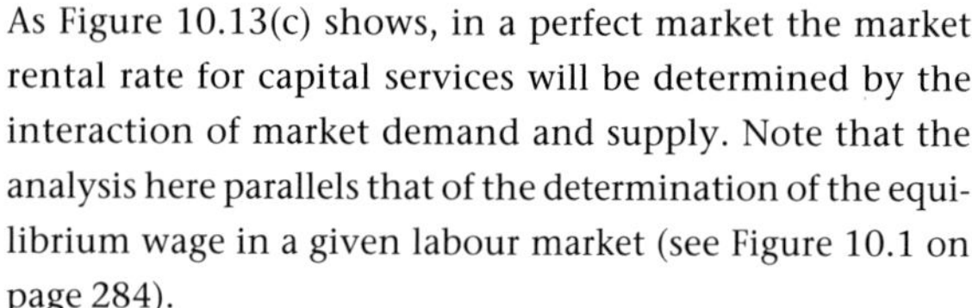

As Figure 10.13(c) shows, in a perfect market the market rental rate for capital services will be determined by the interaction of market demand and supply. Note that the analysis here parallels that of the determination of the equilibrium wage in a given labour market (see Figure 10.1 on page 284).

What will happen to the demand for capital services and the equilibrium rental if the price of some other factor, say labour, changes? Assume that wage rates fall. Trace through the effects on a three-section diagram like Figure 10.13. (Clue: a fall in wages will reduce costs and hence the price of the product, so that more will be sold; and it will make labour cheaper relative to capital.)

If there is monopsony power on the part of the users of hired capital, this will have the effect of depressing the rental rate below the MRP_K (see Figure 10.12(b)). If, on the other hand, there is monopoly power on the part of hire companies, the analysis is similar to that of monopoly in the goods market (see Figure 7.8 on page 211). The firm, by reducing the supply of capital for hire, can drive up the rental rate. It will maximise profit where the marginal revenue from hiring out the equipment is equal to the marginal cost of so doing: at a rental rate (price) *above* the marginal cost.

*Demand for and supply of capital for purchase

The alternative to hiring capital is to buy it outright. This section examines the demand and supply of capital for purchase.

The demand for capital: investment

How many computers will an engineering firm want to buy? Should a steelworks install another blast furnace? Should a removal firm buy another furniture lorry? These are all ***investment*** decisions. Investment involves purchasing of additional capital.

The demand for capital, or 'investment demand', by a profit-maximising firm is based on exactly the same principles as the demand for labour or the demand for capital services. The firm must weigh up the marginal revenue product of that investment (i.e. the money it will earn for the firm) against its marginal cost.

TC 8 p109

The problem is that capital is durable. It goes on producing goods, and hence yielding revenue for the firm, for a considerable period of time. Calculating these benefits therefore involves taking account of their timing.

There are two ways of approaching the problem: the *present value* approach and the *rate of return* approach. In both cases, the firm is comparing the marginal benefits with the marginal costs of the investment.

Present value approach. To work out the benefit of an investment (its *MRP*), the firm must estimate all the future earnings it will bring and then convert them to a ***present value***. It can then compare this with the cost of the investment. Let us take a simple example.

Assume that a firm is considering buying a machine. It will produce £1000 per year (net of operating costs) for four years and then wear out and sell for £1000 as scrap. What is the benefit of this machine to the firm? At first sight the answer would seem to be £5000. This, after all, is the total income earned from the machine. Unfortunately, it is not as simple as this. The reason is that money earned in the future is less beneficial to the firm than having the same amount of money today: if the firm has the money today, it can earn interest on it by putting it in the bank or reinvesting it in some other project.

To illustrate this, assume that you have £100 today and can earn 10 per cent interest by putting it in a bank. In one year's time that £100 will have grown to £110, in two years' time to £121, in three years' time to £133.10 and so on. This process is known as ***compounding***.

KEY IDEA 27

The principle of discounting. **People generally prefer to have benefits today rather than in the future. Thus future benefits have to be reduced (discounted) to give them a present value.**

Definitions

Investment The purchase by the firm of equipment or materials that will add to its stock of capital.

Present value approach to appraising investment This involves estimating the value *now* of a flow of future benefits (or costs).

Compounding The process of adding interest each year to an initial capital sum.

It follows that if someone offered to give you £121 in two years' time, that would be no better than giving you £100 today, since, with interest, £100 would grow to £121 in two years. What we say, then, is that, with a 10 per cent interest rate, £121 in two years' time has a *present value* of £100.

The procedure of reducing future value back to a present value is known as ***discounting***.

When we do discounting, the rate we use is called the ***rate of discount***: in this case, 10 per cent. The formula for discounting is as follows:

$$PV = \sum \frac{R_t}{(1 + r)^t}$$

where PV is the present value, R_t is the revenue from the investment in year t, r is the rate of discount (expressed as a decimal: e.g. 10% = 0.1) and $\sum$ is the sum of each of the years' discounted earnings.

So what is the present value of the investment in the machine that produced £1000 for four years and then is sold as scrap for £1000 at the end of the four years? According to the formula it is:

$$\begin{aligned} &\quad\ \text{Year 1} \qquad \text{Year 2} \qquad \text{Year 3} \qquad \text{Year 4} \\ &= \frac{£1000}{1.1} + \frac{£1000}{(1.1)^2} + \frac{£1000}{(1.1)^3} + \frac{£2000}{(1.1)^4} \\ &= £909 + £829 + £751 + £1366 \\ &= £3852 \end{aligned}$$

Thus the present value of the investment (i.e. its *MRP*) is £3852, *not* £5000 as it might seem at first sight. In other words, if the firm had £3852 today and deposited it in a bank at a 10 per cent interest rate, the firm would earn exactly the same as it would by investing in the machine.

So is the investment worthwhile? It is now simply a question of comparing the £3852 benefit with the cost of buying the machine. If the machine costs less than £3852, it will be worth buying. If it costs more, the firm would be better off keeping its money in the bank.

The difference between the present value of the benefits (PV_b) of the investment and its cost (C) is known as the ***net present value*** (NPV).

$$NPV = PV_b - C$$

If the NPV is positive, the investment is worthwhile.

What is the present value of a machine that lasts three years, earns £100 in year 1, £200 in year 2 and £200 in year 3, and then has a scrap value of £100? Assume that the rate of discount is 5 per cent. If the machine costs £500, is the investment worthwhile? Would it be worthwhile if the rate of discount were 10 per cent?

Rate of return approach. The alternative approach when estimating whether an investment is worthwhile is to calculate the investment's *rate of return*. This rate of return is known as the firm's ***marginal efficiency of capital*** (MEC) or ***internal rate of return*** (IRR).

We use the same formula as for calculating present value:

$$PV = \sum \frac{R_t}{(1 + r)^t}$$

and then calculate what value of r would make the PV equal to the cost of investment: in other words, the rate of discount that would make the investment just break even. Say this worked out at 20 per cent. What we would be saying is that the investment would just cover its costs if the current rate of interest (rate of discount) were 20 per cent. In other words, this investment is equivalent to receiving 20 per cent interest: it has a 20 per cent rate of return (MEC).

Details of how to calculate the internal rate of return, along with a worked example, are given in Maths Case 10.2 on the student website.

So should the investment go ahead? Yes, if the actual rate of interest (i) is less than 20 per cent. The firm is better off investing its money in this project than keeping it in the bank: i.e. if $MEC > i$ the investment should proceed. KI 27 p310 TC 8 p109

This is just one more application of the general rule that if $MRP_f > MC_f$ then more of the factor should be used: only in this case, MRP is expressed as a rate of return (MEC), and MC is expressed as a rate of interest (i).

The profit-maximising position is illustrated in Figure 10.14. As the firm invests more, and thus builds up its stock of capital, so MEC will fall due to diminishing returns. As long as MEC is greater than i, the firm should invest more. It should stop when the stock of capital has reached Q_1. Thereafter it should cut investment to a level just sufficient to replace worn-out machines, and thus keep the capital stock at Q_1.

The risks of investment. One of the problems with investment is that the future is uncertain. The return on an investment will depend on the value of the goods it produces, which will depend on the goods market. But future markets depend on consumer tastes, the actions of rivals and the whole state of the economy, none of which can be known with certainty. Investment is thus risky.

Definitions

Discounting The process of reducing the value of future flows to give them a present valuation.

Rate of discount The rate that is used to reduce future values to present values.

Net present value of an investment The discounted benefits of an investment minus the cost of the investment.

Marginal efficiency of capital or internal rate of return The rate of return of an investment: the discount rate that makes the net present value of an investment equal to zero.

Figure 10.14 The profit-maximising stock of capital

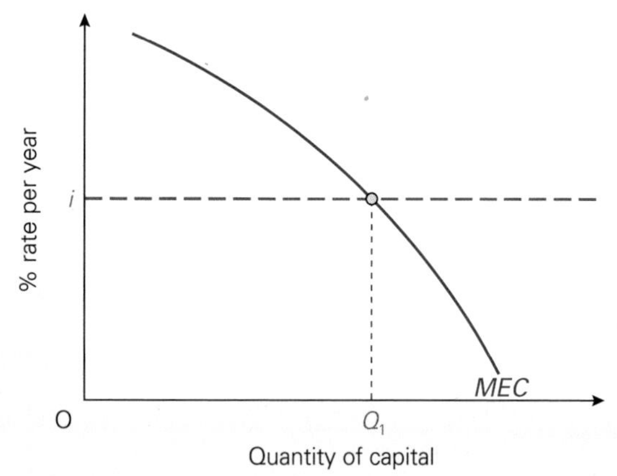

Risk may also be incurred in terms of the output from an investment. Take the case of prospecting for oil. An oil company may have a major strike, but it may simply drill dry well after dry well. If it does get a major strike, and hence earn a large return on its investment, these profits will not be competed away by competitors prospecting in other fields, because they too still run the risk of drilling dry holes.

How is this risk accounted for when calculating the benefits of an investment? The answer is to use a higher rate of discount. The higher the risk, the bigger the risk premium that must be added to the rate.

The supply of capital

It is necessary to distinguish the supply of *physical* capital from the supply of *finance* to be used by firms for the purchase of capital.

Supply of physical capital. The principles here are just the same as those in the goods market. It does not matter whether a firm is supplying lorries (capital) or cars (a consumer good): it will still produce up to the point where $MC = MR$ if it wishes to maximise profits.

Supply of finance. An economy will have a stock of financial capital (or 'loanable funds') held in banks and other financial institutions. These funds can be borrowed by firms for investment in new physical capital.

When people save, this will build up the stock of loanable funds. This flow of saving represents the resources released when people refrain from consumption. Among other things, saving depends on the rate of interest. This is illustrated in Figure 10.15. A rise in the interest rate will encourage people to save more, thereby increasing the supply (i.e. the stock) of loanable funds (a movement up along the supply curve).

This supply curve will be relatively inelastic in the short run, since the flow of saving over a short time period (say, a month) will have only a relatively small effect on the total stock of funds. Over a year, however, the effect would be 12 times bigger. The longer the time period, therefore, the more elastic the supply curve.

Saving also depends on the level of people's incomes, their expectations of future price changes, and their willingness to sacrifice present consumption in order to be able to have more in the future. A change in any of these other determinants will shift the supply curve.

*Determination of the rate of interest

The rate of interest is determined by the interaction of supply and demand in the market for loanable funds. This is illustrated in Figure 10.15. As we have seen, supply represents accumulated savings.

The demand curve includes the demand by households for credit and the demand by firms for funds to finance their investment. The curve slopes downwards for two reasons. First, households will borrow more at lower rates of interest. It effectively makes goods cheaper for them to buy. Second, it reflects the falling rate of return on investment as investment increases. This is simply due to diminishing returns to investment. As rates of interest fall, it will become profitable for firms to invest in projects that have a lower rate of return: the quantity of loanable funds demanded thus rises.

Equilibrium will be achieved where demand equals supply at an interest rate of i_e and a quantity of loanable funds £$_e$.

How will this market adjust to a change in demand or supply? Assume that there is a rise in demand for capital equipment, due, say, to an improvement in technology that increases the productivity of capital. There is thus an increase in demand for loanable funds. The demand curve shifts to the right in Figure 10.15. The equilibrium rate of interest will rise and this will encourage more savings. The end result is that more money will be spent on capital equipment.

Figure 10.15 The market for loanable funds

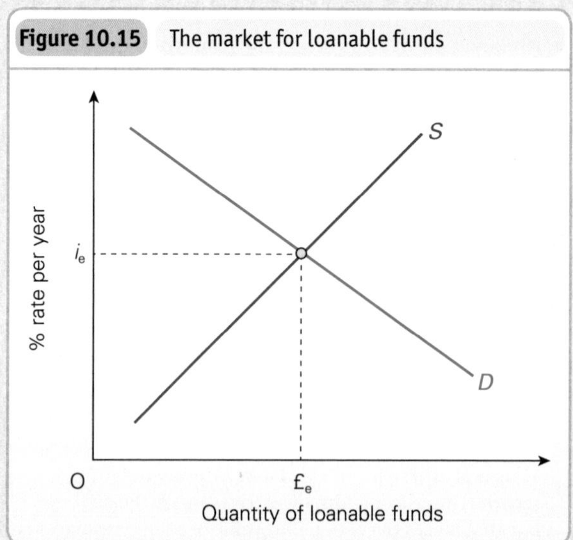

Capital and profit

What does the analysis so far tell us about the amount of profit that firms will earn? After all, profit is the reward that the owners of firms get from owning and using capital.

Remember from Chapter 7 the distinction between normal and supernormal profit. In a perfectly competitive world, all supernormal profits will be competed away in the long run.

Another way of putting this is that a perfectly competitive firm in the long run will earn only a ***normal rate of return*** on capital. This means that the return on capital (after taking risk into account) will be the same as if the owners of capital had simply deposited their money in a bank instead. If a firm's capital yields a higher rate of return than this normal level (i.e. supernormal returns), other firms will be attracted to invest in similar capital. The resulting increased level of capital will increase the supply of goods. This, in turn, will lower the price of the goods and hence lower the rate of return on capital until it has fallen back to the normal level.

Can a perfectly competitive firm earn a supernormal rate of return on capital if it continuously innovates?

If, however, capital owners have monopoly/oligopoly power and can thus restrict the entry of new firms or the copying of innovations – for example, by having a patent on a particular process – they can continue to get a supernormal return on their capital.

Financing investment

Sources of business finance

A firm can finance capital investment in one of three major ways:

- Internal funds (i.e. retained profits).
- Borrowing from the banking sector.
- Issuing new shares (equities) or debentures (fixed-interest loan stock).

The largest source of finance for investment in the UK is firms' own internal funds (i.e. ploughed-back profits). Given, however, that business profitability depends in large part on the general state of the economy, internal funds as a source of business finance are likely to vary considerably across the business cycle. When profits are squeezed in a recession, this source of investment will decline.

Other sources of finance, which include borrowing and the issue of shares and debentures, are known as 'external funds'. These are then categorised as short-term, medium-term or long-term sources of finance.

Short-term finance. This is usually in the form of a short-term bank loan or overdraft facility, and is used by a business as a form of working capital to aid it in its day-to-day business operations.

Medium-term finance. This again is provided largely by banks, usually in the form of a loan with set repayment targets. It is common for such loans to be made at a fixed rate of interest, with repayments being designed to fit in with the business's expected cash flow. Bank lending has been the most volatile source of business finance, and has been particularly sensitive to the state of the economy. While part of the reason is the lower demand for loans during a recession, a further part of the reason is the caution of banks in granting loans if prospects for the economy are poor. In 2008, there was a reduction in the willingness of banks to grant loans to businesses following the credit crunch. This is examined in more detail in sections 18.2 and 22.3.

Long-term finance. Long-term finance, especially in the UK, tends to be acquired through the stock market. It will usually be in the form of ***shares*** (or ***equities***). This is where members of the public or institutions (such as pension funds) buy a part-ownership in the company and, as a result, receive dividends on those shares. The dividends depend on the amount of profit the company makes and distributes to shareholders. The proportion of business financing from this source clearly depends on the state of the stock market.

In the late 1990s, with a buoyant stock market, the proportion of funds obtained through share issue increased. Then with a decline in stock market prices from 2000 to 2003, this proportion fell. In 2008, there were very substantial falls in the values of shares, further reducing the ability of firms to raise finance. The recovery in share prices seen in 2013 gave rise to hope that firms would be able to fund the investment needed to increase growth back to pre-recession levels.

Alternatively, firms can issue ***debentures*** (or ***company bonds***). These securities are fixed-interest loans to firms. Debenture holders have a prior claim on company shares. Their interest must be paid in full before shareholders can receive any dividends.

Definitions

Normal rate of return The rate of return (after taking risks into account) that could be earned elsewhere.

Shares (equities) A part-ownership of a company. Companies' distributed profits are paid to shareholders in the form of dividends according to the number of shares held.

Debentures (company bonds) Fixed-interest loans to firms. These assets can be traded on the stock market and their market price is determined by demand and supply.

Despite the traditional reliance on the stock market for external long-term sources of finance, there has been a growing involvement of banks in recent years. Prior to the credit crunch in 2008, banks had become more willing to provide finance for business start-ups and for diversification. This has been less apparent since and there is a concern that banks are inherently cautious. This risk aversion results in a problem of 'short-termism', with bankers often demanding a quick return on their money or charging high interest rates, and being less concerned to finance long-term investment.

Comparison of the UK with other European countries. In other European countries, notably Germany and France, the attitude towards business funding is quite different from that in the UK. In these countries banks provide a significant amount of long-term, fixed-rate finance (see Case Study 18.6 on the student website). This provides a much more stable source of finance and creates an environment where banks are much more committed to the long-run health of companies.

The role of the stock market

The London Stock Exchange operates as both a primary and secondary market in capital.

*As a **primary market**.* The primary market is where public limited companies (see Case Study 9.1 on the student website) can raise finance by issuing new shares (equities) or fixed interest securities, whether to new shareholders or to existing ones. To raise finance on the Stock Exchange a business must be 'listed'. The Listing Agreement involves directors agreeing to abide by a strict set of rules governing behaviour and levels of reporting to shareholders. Companies must have at least three years' trading experience and make at least 25 per cent of their shares available to the public. In December 2019, there were 928 UK and 215 international companies on the Official List.

As well as those on the Official List, there are over 800 companies on what is known as the Alternative Investment Market (AIM). Companies listed here tend to be young but with growth potential, and do not have to meet the strict criteria or pay such high costs as companies on the Official List.

In 2019, nearly £17 billion's worth of new equity capital was raised through 50 main market issues and £334 billion's worth of fixed interest securities through 1636 issues. In addition, £3.8 billion's worth of capital was raised on the AIM.

*As a **secondary market**.* The Stock Exchange enables investors to sell *existing* shares and debentures to one another. In 2019 on an average day £4.7 billion's worth of trading in equities and other securities took place.

The advantages and disadvantages of using the stock market to raise capital

As a market for raising capital, the stock market has a number of advantages:

- It brings together those that wish to invest and companies that seek investment, and does so in a relatively low-cost way. It thus represents a way that savings can be mobilised to generate output.
- Firms that are listed on the Stock Exchange are subject to strict regulations. This is likely to stimulate investor confidence, making it easier for business to raise finance.
- The process of merger and acquisition is facilitated by having a share system, which in turn increases competition for corporate control (see page 213).

The main weaknesses of the stock market for raising capital are:

- The cost to a business of getting listed can be immense, not only in a financial sense, but also in being open to public scrutiny. Directors' and senior managers' decisions will often be driven by how the market is likely to react, rather than by what they perceive to be in the business's best interests. They always have to think about the reactions of those large shareholders in the City that control a large proportion of their shares.
- In the UK, it is often claimed that the market suffers from ***short-termism***. Investors on the Stock Exchange are mainly concerned with a company's short-term performance and its share value. In responding to this, the business might neglect its long-term performance and potential.

Is the stock market efficient?

One of the arguments made in favour of the stock market is that it acts as an arena within which share values can be accurately or efficiently priced. If new information comes onto the market concerning a business and its performance, this will be quickly and rationally transferred into the business's share value. This is known as the ***efficient market hypothesis***. For example, if an investment analyst found that, in terms of its actual and expected dividends, a particular share was

Definitions

Primary market in capital Where shares are sold by the issuer of the shares (i.e. the firm) and where, therefore, finance is channelled directly from the purchasers (i.e. the shareholders) to the firm.

Secondary market in capital Where shareholders sell shares to others. This is thus a market in 'second-hand' shares.

Short-termism Where firms and investors take decisions based on the likely short-term performance of a company, rather than on its long-term prospects. Firms may thus sacrifice long-term profits and growth for the sake of a quick return.

Efficient (capital) market hypothesis The hypothesis that new information about a company's current or future performance will be quickly and accurately reflected in its share price.

underpriced and thus represented a 'bargain', the analyst would advise investors to buy. As people then bought the shares, their price would rise, pushing their value up to their full worth. So by attempting to gain from inefficiently priced securities, investors will encourage the market to become more efficient.

How efficient, then, is the stock market in pricing securities? Is information rationally and quickly conveyed into the share's price? Or are investors able to prosper from the stock market's inefficiencies?

We can identify three levels of efficiency.

The weak form of efficiency. Share prices often move in cycles that do not reflect the underlying performance of the firm. If information is imperfect, those with a better understanding of such cycles gain from buying shares at the trough and selling them at the peak of the cycles. They are taking advantage of the market's inefficiency.

Increasing numbers of investment analysts are using technical models to track share cycles. As they do so and knowledge becomes more perfect, so the market will become more efficient and the cycles will tend to disappear. But why?

As more people buy a company's shares as the price falls towards its trough, extra demand will prevent the price falling so far. Similarly, as people sell as the price rises towards its peak, so this extra supply will prevent the price rising so far. This is an example of stabilising speculation (see pages 70–1). As more and more people react in this way, so the cycle all but disappears. When this happens, ***weak efficiency*** has been achieved.

The semi-strong form of efficiency. ***Semi-strong efficiency*** is when share prices adjust fully to publicly available information. In practice, not all investors will interpret such information correctly: their knowledge is imperfect. But increasingly more advice is available to shareholders (through stockbrokers, newspapers, online commentators, published accounts, etc.), and more shares are purchased by professional fund managers. The result is that the interpretation of public information becomes more perfect and the market becomes more efficient in the semi-strong sense.

If the market were efficient in the semi-strong sense, then no gain could be made from studying a company's performance and prospects, as this information would *already* be included in the current share price. In selecting shares, you would do just as well by pinning the financial pages of a newspaper on the wall, throwing darts at them, and buying the shares the darts hit!

The strong form of efficiency. If the stock market showed the ***strong form of efficiency***, then share prices would fully reflect *all* available information – whether public or not. For this to be so, all 'inside' information would have to be reflected in the share price the moment the information became available.

If the market is *not* efficient at this level, then people who have access to privileged information will be able to make large returns from their investments by acting on such information. For example, directors of a company would know if the company was soon to announce better-than-expected profits. In the meantime, they could gain by buying shares in the company, knowing that the share price would rise when the information about the profits became public. Gains made from such 'insider dealing' are illegal. However, proving whether individuals are engaging in it is very difficult. By the time of its replacement by the Financial Conduct Authority in April 2013, the Financial Services Authority had secured just 23 convictions for insider dealing, prompting criticism that it was toothless.

TC 3 p26

Given the penalties for insider dealing and the amount of private information that firms possess, it is unlikely that all such information will be reflected in share prices. Thus the strong form of stock market efficiency is unlikely to hold.

Would the stock market be more efficient if insider dealing were made legal?

If stock markets were fully efficient, the expected returns from every share would be the same. The return is referred to as the ***yield***: this is measured as the dividends paid on the share as a percentage of the share's market price. For example, if you hold shares whose market price is £1 per share and you receive an annual dividend of 3p per share, then the yield on the shares is 3 per cent. But why should the expected returns on shares be the same? If any share was expected to yield a higher-than-average return, people would buy it; its price would rise and its yield would correspondingly fall.

Definitions

Weak efficiency (of share markets) Where share dealing prevents cyclical movements in shares.

Semi-strong efficiency (of share markets) Where share prices adjust quickly, fully and accurately to publicly available information.

Strong efficiency (of share markets) Where share prices adjust quickly, fully and accurately to all available information, both public and that only available to insiders.

Yield on a share The dividend received per share expressed as a percentage of the current market price of the share.

It would only be unanticipated information, therefore, that would cause share prices to deviate from that which reflected expected average yields. Such information must, by its nature, be random, and as such would cause share prices to deviate randomly from their expected price, or follow what we call a ***random walk***. Evidence suggests that share prices do tend to follow random patterns.

Challenging the efficient market hypothesis

The efficient markets hypothesis has been challenged by critics who laid the blame for the financial crisis in 2007–8 on unfounded belief in rational markets. They argued that regulators failed to understand the role that exuberance plays in financial markets. If investors are 'caught up' in the belief that share prices (or property values) will continue to increase in value, regardless of underlying information, then the result will be a bubble – a situation where assets are traded above their fundamental value.

According to behavioural economists, bubbles can be explained by a number of psychological factors. Among these are paying too little attention to the past, over-confidence, over-optimism and herding. In short, people pay too much for assets because they remember recent returns more than historical averages, because they take more notice of economic good news than bad and because everyone else is doing it. Asset bubbles are vulnerable to breaking on the basis of changes in beliefs, as we saw in the collapse of the US housing market from 2006 and the subsequent stock market crash.

What does this imply for policy makers? The argument might be made that an asset bubble is simply a magnification of any market, with both losers and winners; this does not suggest a need for intervention. However, this ignores the macroeconomic consequences of the bubble, consequences which were clearly seen from 2007 on. Behaviourists therefore believe that effective financial regulation must take account of irrationality.

Definition

Random walk Where fluctuations in the value of a share away from its 'correct' value are random, i.e. have no systematic pattern. When charted over time, these share price movements would appear like a 'random walk': like the path of someone staggering along drunk!

Section summary

1. It is necessary to distinguish between buying the services of land (by renting) or capital (by hiring) and buying them outright.
2. The profit-maximising employment of land and capital services will be where the factor's *MRP* is equal to its price (under perfect competition) or its *MC* (where firms have monopsony power).
3. The demand for capital services will be equal to MRP_K. Due to diminishing returns, this will decline as more capital is used.
4. The supply of capital services to a firm will be horizontal or upward sloping depending on whether the firm is perfectly competitive or has monopsony power. The supply of capital services by a firm in the short run is likely to be relatively elastic up to its maximum use, and then totally inelastic. In the long run, the supplying firm can purchase additional capital equipment for hiring out. The long-run supply curve will therefore be very elastic, but at a higher rental rate than in the short run, given that the cost of purchasing the equipment must be taken into account in the rental rate.
5. The market supply of capital services is likely to be highly inelastic in the short run, given that capital equipment tends to have very specific uses and cannot normally be transferred from one use to another. In the long run, it will be more elastic.
6. The price of capital services is determined by the interaction of demand and supply.
7. The demand for capital for purchase will depend on the return it earns for the firm. To calculate this return, all future earnings from the investment have to be reduced to a present value by discounting at a market rate of interest (discount). If the present value exceeds the cost of the investment, the investment is worthwhile. Alternatively, a rate of return from the investment can be calculated and then this can be compared with the return that the firm could have earned by investing elsewhere.
8. The supply of finance for investment depends on the supply of loanable funds, which in turn depends on the rate of interest, on the general level of thriftiness and on expectations about future price levels and incomes.
9. The rate of interest will be determined by the demand and supply of loanable funds. When deciding whether to make an investment, a firm will use this rate for discounting purposes. If, however, an investment involves risks, the firm will require a higher rate of return on the investment than current market interest rates.
10. Business finance can come from internal sources (ploughed-back profits) or from external ones. External sources of finance include borrowing and the issue of shares.
11. The stock market operates as both a primary and a secondary market in capital. As a primary market it channels finance to companies as people purchase new shares and debentures. It is also a market for existing shares and debentures.
12. The stock market helps to stimulate growth and investment by bringing together companies and people

who want to invest in them. By regulating firms and by keeping transaction costs of investment low, it helps to ensure that investment is efficient.

13. The stock market does impose costs on firms, however. It is expensive for firms to be listed and the public exposure may make them too keen to 'please' the market. It can also foster short-termism.

14. The stock market is relatively efficient. It achieves weak efficiency by reducing cyclical movements in share prices. It achieves semi-strong efficiency by allowing share prices to respond quickly and fully to publicly available information. Whether it achieves strong efficiency by adjusting quickly and fully to all information (both public or insider), however, is more doubtful.

10.4 LAND AND RENT

Rent: the reward to landowners

We turn now to land. The income it earns for landowners is the *rent* charged to the users of the land. This rent, like the rewards to other factors, is determined by demand and supply.

What makes land different from other factors of production is that it has an inelastic supply. In one sense, this is obvious. The total supply of land in any area is fixed.

In another sense, supply is not *totally* inelastic. Land can be improved. It can be cleared, levelled, drained, fertilised, etc. Thus the supply of a certain type of land can be increased by expending human effort on improving it. The question is whether *land* has thereby increased, or whether the improvements constitute *capital* invested in land, and if so whether the higher rents that such land can earn really amount to a return on the capital invested in it.

To keep the analysis simple, let us assume that land *is* fixed. Let us take the case of an area of 10 000 hectares surrounding the village of Oakleigh. This is shown as a vertical supply 'curve' in Figure 10.16. The demand curve for that land will be like the demand curve for other factors of production. It is the *MRP* curve and slopes down due to diminishing returns from land. The equilibrium rent is r_e, where demand and supply intersect.

Figure 10.16 Determination of rent

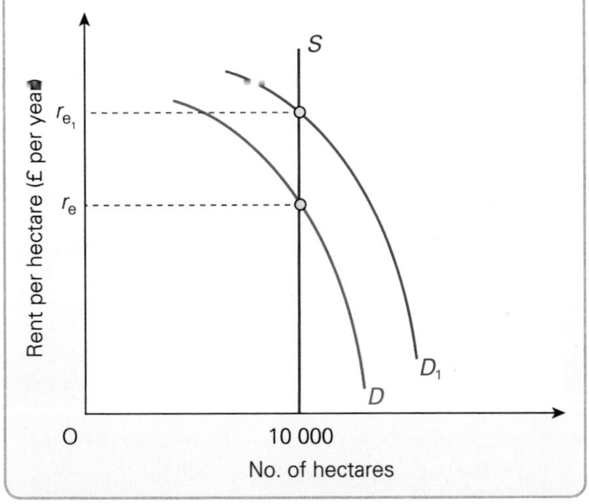

Notice that the level of this rent depends entirely on *demand*. If a new housing development takes place in Oakleigh, due perhaps to a growth in employment in a nearby town, the demand curve will shift to D_1 and the equilibrium rent will rise to r_{e_1}. But the supply of land remains fixed at 10 000 hectares. Landowners will earn more rent, but they themselves have done nothing: the higher rent is a pure windfall gain.

So why are rents in the centre of London many times higher per hectare than they are in the north of Scotland? The answer is that demand is very much higher in London.

Demand for land depends on its marginal revenue product. Thus it is differences in the *MRP* of land that explain the differences in rent from one area to another. There are two reasons for differences in *MRP*. Remember that $MRP = MPP$ (marginal physical product of the factor) $\times$ MR (marginal revenue of the good produced by that factor).

Differences in MPP. Land differs in productivity. Fertile land will produce a higher output than deserts or moorland. Similarly, land near centres of population will be of much more use to industry than land in the middle of nowhere.

What other factors will determine the MPP of land for industry?

Differences in MR. The higher the demand for a particular good, the higher its price and marginal revenue, and hence the higher the demand and rent for the land on which that good is produced. Thus if the demand for housing rises relative to the demand for food, the rent on land suitable for house building will rise relative to the rent on agricultural land.

To summarise: rents will be high on land that is physically productive (high *MPP*) and produces goods in high demand (high *MR*).

1. *We defined the factor of production 'land' to include raw materials. Does the analysis of rent that we have just been looking at apply to raw materials?*
2. *The supply of land in a particular area may be totally inelastic, but the supply of land in that area for a*

specific purpose (e.g. growing wheat) will be upward sloping: the higher the price of wheat and thus the higher the rent that wheat producers are prepared to pay, the more will be made available for wheat production. What will determine the elasticity of supply of land for any particular purpose?

The price of land

Not all land is rented: much of it is bought and sold outright. Its price will depend on what the purchaser is prepared to pay, and this will depend on the land's rental value.

Let us say that a piece of land can earn £1000 per year. What would a person be prepared to pay for it? There is a simple formula for working this out:

$$P = \frac{R}{i} \quad (1)$$

where P is the price of the land, R is the rent per year and i is the market rate of interest.

Let us assume that the market rate of interest is 10 per cent (i.e. 0.1). Then according to the formula, a purchaser would be prepared to pay

$$\frac{£1000}{0.1} = £10\,000$$

Why should this be so? If a person deposits £10 000 in the bank, with an interest rate of 10 per cent this will earn that person £1000 per year. Assuming our piece of land is guaranteed to earn a rent of £1000 per year, then provided it costs less than £10 000 to buy, it is a better investment than putting money in the bank. The competition between people to buy this land will drive its price up until it reaches £10 000.

This is just another example of equilibrium being where marginal cost equals marginal benefit. This can be demonstrated by rearranging equation (1) to give

$$Pi = R$$

Remember that the equilibrium price of the land (P) is £10 000 and that the rate of interest (i) is 0.1. If you borrow the £10 000 to buy the land, it will cost you £1000 per year in interest payments (i.e. Pi). This is your annual marginal cost. The annual marginal benefit will be the rent (R) you will earn from the land.

1. *What price would the same piece of land sell for if it still earned £1000 rent per year, but if the rate of interest were now (a) 5 per cent; (b) 20 per cent?*
2. *What does this tell us about the relationship between the price of an asset (like land) and the rate of interest?*

BOX 10.11 THE ECONOMICS OF NON-RENEWABLE RESOURCES

What happens as stocks diminish?

As world population rises, so the demands on resources continue to grow. Some of these resources are renewable. Water resources are replenished by rain. The soil, if properly managed, can continue to grow crops. Felled forests can be replanted. Of course, if we use these resources more rapidly than they are replenished, stocks will run down. We are all aware of the problems of seas that are overfished, or rainforests that are cleared, or reservoirs that are inadequate to meet our growing demand for water.

But whereas these resources can be replenished, others cannot. These are known as non-renewable resources. What determines the price of such resources and their rate of depletion? Will we eventually run out of resources such as oil, coal, gas and various minerals? To answer these questions, we need to distinguish between the available stock of such resources, and their use (a flow). The greater their use, the faster the stocks will run down.

KI 26 p309

Price increases over time

As stocks run down, so the price of the resources will tend to increase. Thus we can all expect to pay more for fossil fuels as remaining reserves are depleted. Owners of the reserves (e.g. mine owners and owners of oil wells) will thus find the value of their assets increasing. But how quickly will prices rise? In a perfect market, they will rise at the market rate of return on other assets (of equivalent risk). This is known as the Hotelling rule, named after Harold Hotelling who developed the argument in the early 1930s.

To understand why this is so, consider what would happen if the price of oil rose more slowly than the rate of return on other assets. People who owned oil wells would find that the value of their oil reserves was increasing less rapidly than the value of other assets. They might as well sell more oil now and invest the money in other assets, thereby getting a higher return. The extra oil coming to the market would depress the current oil price, but also reduce reserves, thereby creating a bigger shortage for the future and hence a higher future price. This would cause oil prices to rise more quickly over time (from the new lower base). Once the rate of price increase has risen to equal the rate of return on other assets, equilibrium has occurred. There will no longer be an incentive for the oil to be extracted faster.

The current price

But what determines the current price level (as opposed to its rate of increase)? This will be determined by supply and demand for the extracted resource (its flow).

In the case of a resource used by households, demand will depend on consumer tastes, the price of other goods, income, etc. Thus the greater the desire for using private cars, the greater the demand for petrol. In the case of minerals used by firms, demand will depend on the marginal revenue product of the resources. In either case, a rise in demand will cause a rise in the resource's price.

Supply will depend on three things:

- The rate of interest on other assets. As we have seen, the higher the rate of interest, the faster will the resource

Who are the poor? Who are the rich?

We have been building up an answer to these questions as this chapter has progressed. The final part of the answer concerns the ownership of land and capital. Many people own no land or capital at all. These people will therefore earn no profit, rent or interest.

For those who are fortunate enough to own productive assets, their income from them will depend on (a) the quantity they own and (b) their rental value.

The quantity of assets owned

This will depend on the following:

- Inheritance. Some people have rich parents who leave them substantial amounts of land and capital.
- Past income and savings. If people have high incomes and save a large proportion of them, this helps them to build up a stock of assets.
- Skill in investment (entrepreneurial skill). The more skilful people are in investing and in organising production, the more rapidly will their stock of assets grow.
- Luck. When people open up a business, there are usually substantial risks. The business might flourish or fail.

The rental value

This is the income earned per unit of land and capital. It will depend on the following:

- The level of demand for the factor. This depends on the factor's *MRP*, which in turn depends on its physical productivity (*MPP*) and the demand for the good it produces and hence the good's *MR*.
- The elasticity of demand for the good. The greater the monopoly power that capital owners have in the goods market, the less elastic will be the demand for the product and the greater will be the supernormal returns they can earn on their capital.
- The elasticity of supply of the factor. The less elastic its supply, the more factor owners can gain from a high demand. The high demand will simply push up the level of economic rent that the factor will earn.

- The total factor supply by other factor owners. The further to the left the total factor supply curve, the higher the level of economic rent that each unit of the factor can earn for any given level of demand.

Thus if you are lucky enough to have rich parents who leave you a lot of money when you are relatively young; if you are a skilful investor and save and reinvest a large

EXPLORING ECONOMICS

be extracted, in order that the mine owners (or well owners) can reinvest their profits at these higher rates of interest.

- The stock of known reserves. As new reserves are discovered, this will push down the price.
- The costs of extraction. The lower the costs, the greater will be the amount extracted, and hence the lower will be the market price of the resource.

Are we extracting non-renewable resources at the optimum rate?

If there are limited reserves of fossil fuels and other minerals, are we in danger that they will soon run out? Should we be more concerned with conservation?

In fact, the market provides an incentive to conserve such resources. As reserves run down, so the price of non-renewable resources will rise. This will create an incentive to discover alternatives. For example, as fossil fuels become more expensive, so renewable sources of energy, such as solar power, wind power and wave power, will become more economical. There will also be a greater incentive to discover new techniques of power generation and to conserve energy.

Markets, however, are imperfect. As we shall see in Chapter 12, when we consume natural resources, we do not take into account the full costs. For example, the burning of fossil fuels creates harmful environmental effects in the form of acid rain and the greenhouse effect, but these 'external' costs are not included in the price we pay.

Then there is the question of the distribution of income between present and future generations. If non-renewable resources are going to be expensive in the future, should we not be conserving these resources today in order to help our descendants? The problem is that consumers may well act totally selfishly, saying, 'Why should we conserve resources? By the time they run out, we will be dead.' We almost certainly do care about the welfare of our children and grandchildren, but what about our great-great-grandchildren, whom we will never meet?

1. *Will the market provide incentives for firms to research into energy-conserving techniques, if energy prices at present are not high enough to make the use of such techniques profitable?*
2. *How will the existence of monopoly power in the supply of resources influence their rate of depletion?*
3. *If the current generation wants to consume all non-renewable resources, is there any market solution to prevent this happening? (We will return to this in Chapter 13.)*

Debate the following proposition: 'Thanks to the market, the switch from fossil fuels to renewable sources of energy will take place without need for government intervention.' This could be debated informally in groups, with each group divided into two sub-groups. Or it could be a formal debate with two people speaking on each side and with questions from the floor. There could be a vote at the beginning and at the end to see if the audience's views have been swayed by the debate.

proportion of your earnings; if you own assets that few other people own, and which produce goods in high demand: then you may end up very rich.

If you have no assets, you will have no property income at all. If at the same time you are on a low wage or are unemployed, then you may be very poor indeed.

Section summary

1. Rent on land, like the price of other factor services, is determined by the interaction of demand and supply. Its supply is totally inelastic (or nearly so). Its demand curve is downward sloping and will equal the *MRP* of land.
2. The price of land depends on its potential rental value (its marginal benefit) and the repayment costs of borrowing to pay for the land (its marginal cost). Equilibrium is where the two are equal.
3. People's income depends not only on their wages but on whether they own any land or capital, and, if they do, the rental value of these assets. This is the final element in determining the distribution of income in the economy.

END OF CHAPTER QUESTIONS

1. The wage rate that a firm has to pay and the output it can produce vary with the number of workers as follows (all figures are hourly):

Number of workers	1	2	3	4	5	6	7	8
Wage rate (AC_L) (£)	3	4	5	6	7	8	9	10
Total output (TPP_L)	10	22	32	40	46	50	52	52

   Assume that output sells at £2 per unit.
   (a) Copy the table and add additional rows for TC_L, MC_L, TRP_L and MRP_L. Put the figures for MC_L and MRP_L in the spaces between the columns.
   (b) How many workers will the firm employ in order to maximise profits?
   (c) What will be its hourly wage bill at this level of employment?
   (d) How much hourly revenue will it earn at this level of employment?
   (e) Assuming that the firm faces other (fixed) costs of £30 per hour, how much hourly profit will it make?
   (f) Assume that the workers now formed a union and that the firm agreed to pay the negotiated wage rate to all employees. What is the maximum to which the hourly wage rate could rise without causing the firm to try to reduce employment below the level of (b) above? (See Figure 10.10.)
   (g) What would be the firm's hourly profit now?
2. If a firm faces a shortage of workers with very specific skills, it may decide to undertake the necessary training itself. If, on the other hand, it faces a shortage of unskilled workers, it may well offer a small wage increase in order to obtain the extra labour. In the first case, it is responding to an increase in demand for labour by attempting to shift the supply curve. In the second case, it is merely allowing a movement along the supply curve. Use a demand and supply diagram to illustrate each case. Given that elasticity of supply is different in each case, do you think that these are the best policies for the firm to follow? What would happen to wages and economic rent if it used the second policy in the first case?
3. Why do the world's top footballers earn millions of pounds per year, while the top lacrosse players are paid less than the equivalent of £30 000?
4. For what reasons is the median hourly wage rate of women some 16 per cent lower than that of men in the UK, and the average gross weekly pay, including overtime, more than 21 per cent less?
5. Given the analysis of bilateral monopoly, if the passing of minimum wage legislation forces employers to pay higher wage rates to low-paid employees, will this necessarily cause a reduction in employment?
6. Using a diagram like Figure 10.13, demonstrate what will happen under perfect competition when there is an increase in the productivity of a particular type of capital. Consider the effects on the demand, price (rental rate) and quantity supplied of the services of this type of capital.
7. What factors could cause a rise in the market rate of interest?
8. How is the market price of land related to its productivity?
9. In recent years there have been a number of changes in planning laws to make it easier for commercial properties to be converted to housing. What would be the impact on property values?

Online resources

Additional case studies on the student website

10.1 **Economic rent and transfer earnings.** This examines a way of classifying the earnings of a factor of production and shows how these earnings depend on the elasticity of supply of the factor.

10.2 **Telecommuters.** This case study looks at the rise of telecommuting, whereby people are able to work from home utilising modern technology.

10.3 **Other labour market imperfections.** This looks at the three imperfections identified on page 297: namely, imperfect information, persistent disequilibria in labour markets and non-maximising behaviour by firms or workers.

10.4 **Profit sharing.** An examination of the case for and against profit sharing as a means of rewarding workers.

10.5 **Holidays: good for workers; bad for employers?** An examination of holiday entitlements in the USA and Europe and their effects on workers and business.

Maths Case 10.1 **Calculating the long-run cost of supplying additional equipment for rent.** A worked example.

Maths Case 10.2 **Calculating the internal rate of return.** A worked example.

Websites relevant to this chapter

See sites listed at the end of Chapter 11 on page 354.

Microeconomic Policy

We now turn to the application of microeconomics and its role in government policy. In Part C we looked at how market economies function at a micro level. In Part D we examine the various policies that can be adopted to deal with shortcomings of the market system.

There are various questions that governments will ask. How much monopoly power is too much? How equal do we want the distribution of income to be? How can we make markets more efficient? How can we protect the environment and prevent the depletion of resources? How can we prevent climate change?

In Chapter 11 we look at policies that address the distribution of income. In Chapter 12 we examine the issue of market failure and consider the potential for government intervention. Finally in Chapters 13 and 14 we turn to government policies with respect to the environment and business.

Inequality, Poverty and Policies to Redistribute Income

CHAPTER MAP

In Chapter 10 we saw that there are considerable differences in wage rates, and that these depend on market conditions. Similarly, we saw that differences in rewards to owners of capital and land also depend on their respective markets.

But differences in factor rewards are only part of the explanation of inequality. In this chapter, we open out the analysis. We take a more general look at why some people are rich while others are poor, and consider the overall degree of inequality in our society: a society that includes the super-rich, with their luxury yachts, and people living in slum conditions, with not enough to feed themselves or their children. We will see how the gap between rich and poor has tended to widen over time.

We will show how inequality can be measured so that we can make comparisons over time and between countries. We will also look at how incomes are distributed between particular groups, whether by occupation, age, sex, household composition or geographical area.

The second part of the chapter considers what can be done to reduce inequality. Is the solution to tax the rich heavily, so that the money can be redistributed to the poor? Or might this discourage people from working so hard? Would it be better, then, to focus on benefits and increase the support for the poor? Or might this discourage people from taking on work for fear of losing their benefits? We look at the attitudes of governments and at some of the debates taking place today over how to reduce inequality without discouraging effort or initiative.

11.1 INEQUALITY AND POVERTY

Inequality is one of the most contentious issues in the world of economics and politics. Some people have incomes far in excess of what they need to enjoy a luxurious lifestyle, while others struggle to purchase even necessities.

The need for some redistribution from rich to poor is broadly accepted across the political spectrum. Thus the government taxes the rich (and those who most would agree are not rich) and transfers some of the proceeds to the poor, either as cash benefits or as benefits in kind. Nevertheless, there is considerable disagreement as to the appropriate *amount* of redistribution.

KI 6 p29

Whether the current distribution of income is desirable or not is a normative question. Economists therefore should not specify how much the government should redistribute incomes. However, economists do have a role to play in the analysis of inequality and in assessing the impact of policies. They can do the following:

- Identify the extent of inequality and analyse how it has changed over time.
- Explain why a particular level of income distribution occurs and what causes inequality to grow or to lessen.
- Examine the relationship between equality and other economic objectives such as efficiency.
- Identify various government policies to deal with problems of inequality and poverty.
- Examine the effects of these policies, both on inequality itself and on other questions such as efficiency, inflation and unemployment.
- Examine the effect of other policies, such as the reduction of the budget deficit, on inequality and poverty.

Types of inequality

There are a number of different ways of looking at the distribution of income and wealth.

The distribution of income

There are three broad ways of examining the distribution of income. First, we can look at how evenly incomes are distributed among the population. This is known as the ***size distribution of income***. It can be expressed between *households*, or between *individual earners*, or between *all individuals*. It can be expressed either *before* or *after* the deduction of taxes and the receipt of benefits. For example, we might want to know the proportion of pre-tax national income going to the richest 10 per cent of households.

Then there is distribution between different *factors of production*, known as the ***functional distribution of income***. At the *broader* level, we could look at the distribution between the general factor categories: labour, land and capital. At a *narrower* level, we could look at distribution within the factor categories. Why are some jobs well paid while others are badly paid? Why are rents higher in some areas than in others? We looked at this distribution in Chapter 10.

Finally, there is the question of the ***distribution of income by class of recipient***. This can be by *class of person*: women, men, single people, married people, people within a particular age group or ethnic group, and so on. Alternatively, it can be by *geographical area*. Typically, this is expressed in terms of differences in incomes between officially defined regions within a country.

The distribution of wealth

Income is a *flow*. It measures the receipt of money per period of time (e.g. £25 000 per year). Wealth, by contrast, is a stock (see Box 10.10). It measures the value of a person's assets at a particular point in time. The distribution of wealth can be measured as a size distribution (how evenly it is distributed among the population); as a functional distribution (the proportion of wealth held in various forms, such as dwellings, land, company shares, bank deposits, etc.); or according to the holders of wealth, classified by age, sex, geographical area, etc. KI 26 p309

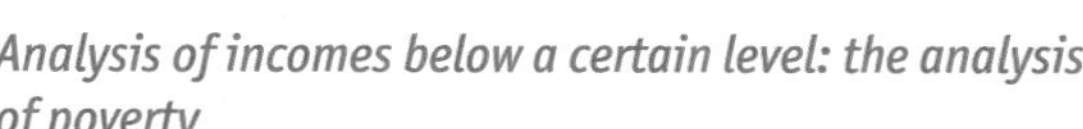

Analysis of incomes below a certain level: the analysis of poverty

A major problem here is in defining just what is meant by poverty. The dividing line between who is poor and who is not is necessarily arbitrary. Someone who is classed as poor in the UK may seem rich to an Ethiopian.

The extent and nature of poverty can be analysed in a number of ways:

- The number or proportion of people or households falling into the category.
- The occupational distribution of poverty.
- The geographical distribution of poverty.
- The distribution of poverty according to age, sex, ethnic origin, marital status, educational attainment, etc.

Definitions

Size distribution of income Measurement of the distribution of income according to the levels of income received by individuals (irrespective of source).

Functional distribution of income Measurement of the distribution of income according to the source of income (e.g. from employment, from profit, from rent, etc.).

Distribution of income by class of recipient Measurement of the distribution of income between the classes of person who receive it (e.g. homeowners and non-homeowners or those in the north and those in the south).

It is not possible in this chapter to look at all aspects of inequality in the UK. Nevertheless some of the more important facts are considered, along with questions of their measurement and interpretation.

The size distribution of income in the UK

Figure 11.1 shows the size distribution of income in the UK. It covers income from all sources. In each chart, households are grouped into five equal-sized groups or ***quintiles***, from the poorest 20 per cent of households up to the richest 20 per cent. (The general term for division into equal-sized groups is ***quantiles***.) The following points can be drawn from these statistics:

- In the financial year ending 2020, the richest 20 per cent of households earned 50.7 per cent of national income, and even after the deduction of taxes this was still 42.4 per cent.
- The poorest 20 per cent, by contrast, earned a mere 4.0 per cent of national income, and even after the receipt of cash benefits this had risen to only 6.8 per cent.

Inequality grew dramatically in the 1980s and did not begin to fall again until 2000, and then only very slightly.

> **Definitions**
>
> **Quintiles** Divisions of the population into five equal-sized groups (an example of a quantile).
>
> **Quantiles** Divisions of the population into equal-sized groups.

Between 1977 and 2019/20 the post-tax-and-benefits share of national income ('disposable income') of the bottom 40 per cent of households fell from 23 per cent to 19 per cent, while the share of the top 20 per cent grew from 37.0 per cent to 42.4 per cent.

Income inequality began to increase again between 2016/17 and 2019/20. The median disposable real income of the poorest fifth of the population (i.e. the lowest quintile) fell by an average of 3.8 per cent per year over this period, while that of the highest quintile grew by an average of 1.0 per cent per year. The ratio of the 90th to the 10th percentile of income increased from 3.9 to 4.5.

The impact of the COVID-19 crisis is likely to increase most measures of inequality. Excluding key workers, most people in the bottom decile of the earnings distribution are in sectors that were forced to shut down.

Effects of taxes and benefits. As we shall see in section 11.2, by taxing the rich proportionately more than the poor, taxes can be used as a means of reducing inequality. In the UK, however, indirect taxes (e.g. on tobacco and alcohol) are paid proportionately more by the poor and so have the opposite effect. In the financial year ending 2020, the lowest-earning quintile of households paid 17.2 per cent of their gross income (original income plus cash benefits) in direct taxes (e.g. income tax, national insurance), while the highest-earning quintile paid 29.7 per cent.[1] When we look at indirect taxes, however, we see that in the financial year ending 2019 the poorest quintile paid 23.8 per cent of their gross income in such taxes, while the richest quintile paid

1 *The Effects of Taxes and Benefits on Household Income, 2019/20, disposable income estimate*, Table 13, National Statistics (January 2021), www.ons.gov.uk/peoplepopulationandcommunity/personalandhouseholdfinances/incomeandwealth/datasets/householddisposableincomeandinequality

Figure 11.1 Size distribution of UK income by quintile group of households: financial year ending 2020

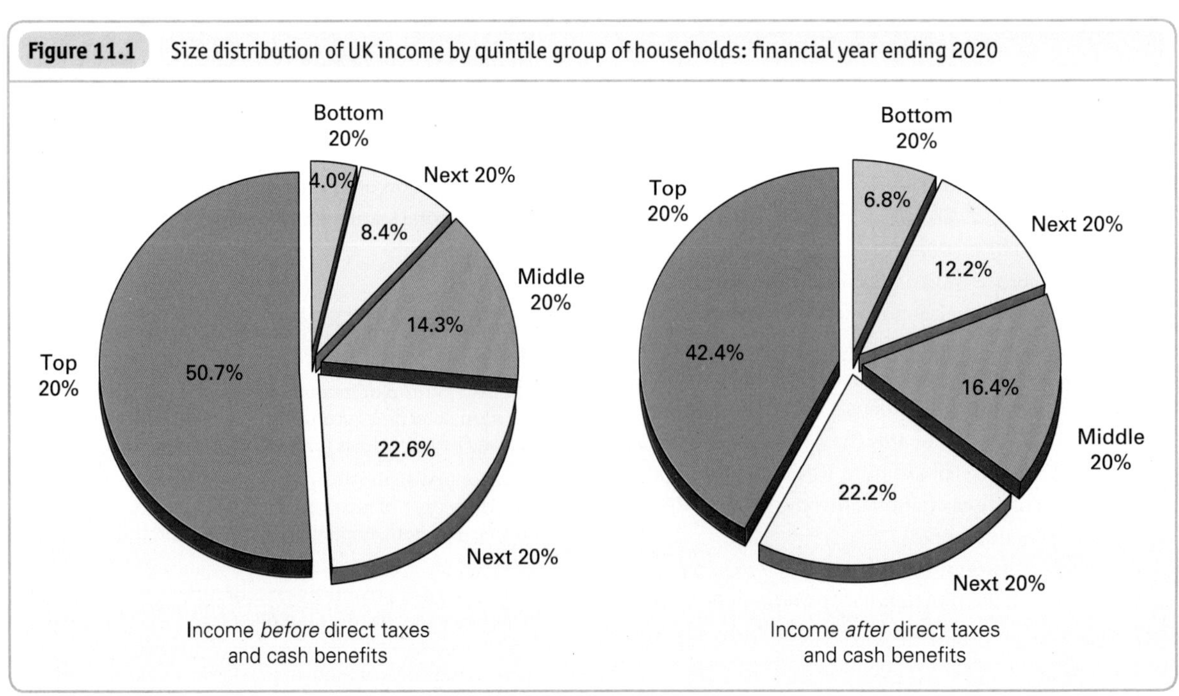

Source: Based on data from *Household Disposable Income and Inequality, UK, 2019/20* – Reference Tables, Table 12, ONS (January 2021), www.ons.gov.uk/peoplepopulationandcommunity/personalandhouseholdfinances/incomeandwealth/datasets/householddisposableincomeandinequality

only 9 per cent. This nearly offset the redistributive effect from direct tax being paid proportionately more by the rich. The top quintile paid 39.7 per cent of their gross income in tax, while the bottom quintile paid 35 per cent.

Redistribution of income in the UK, therefore, is achieved mainly through the benefits system.

Measuring the size distribution of income

Apart from tables and charts, two of the most widely used methods for measuring inequality are the *Lorenz curve* and the *Gini coefficient.*

Lorenz curve

Figure 11.2 shows the ***Lorenz curve*** for a country based on pre-tax (but post-benefit) incomes.

The horizontal axis measures percentages of the population from the poorest to the richest. Thus the 40 per cent point represents the poorest 40 per cent of the population. The vertical axis measures the percentage of national income they receive.

The curve starts at the origin: zero people earn zero incomes. If income were distributed totally equally, the Lorenz curve would be a straight 45° line. The 'poorest' 20 per cent of the population would earn 20 per cent of national income; the 'poorest' 60 per cent would earn 60 per cent, and so on. The curve ends up at the top right-hand corner, with 100 per cent of the population earning 100 per cent of national income.

In practice, the Lorenz curve will 'hang below' the 45° line. Point *x*, for example, shows a country where the poorest 50 per cent of households receive only 24 per cent of national income. The further the curve drops below the 45° line, the greater will be the level of inequality.

The Lorenz curve is quite useful for showing the change in income distribution over time. From 1949 to 1979 the curve for the UK moved inwards towards the 45° line, suggesting a lessening of inequality. Then from 1979 to 1990 it moved downwards away from the 45° line, suggesting a deepening of inequality. Since 1990 it has remained approximately the same.

The problem with simply comparing Lorenz curves by eye is that it is imprecise. This problem is overcome by using Gini coefficients.

Gini coefficient

The ***Gini coefficient*** is a precise way of measuring the position of the Lorenz curve. It is the ratio of the area between the Lorenz curve and the 45° line to the whole area below the 45° line. In Figure 11.2 this is the ratio of the shaded area A to the whole area $(A + B)$, sometimes expressed as a percentage.

If income is equally distributed so that the Lorenz curve follows the 45° line, area A disappears and the Gini coefficient is zero. As inequality increases, so does area A, and the Gini coefficient rises. In the extreme case of total inequality, where one person earns the whole of national income, area B would disappear and the Gini coefficient would be 1. Thus the Gini coefficient will be between 0 and 1. The higher the figure, the greater is the measure of inequality.

Figure 11.2 Lorenz curve

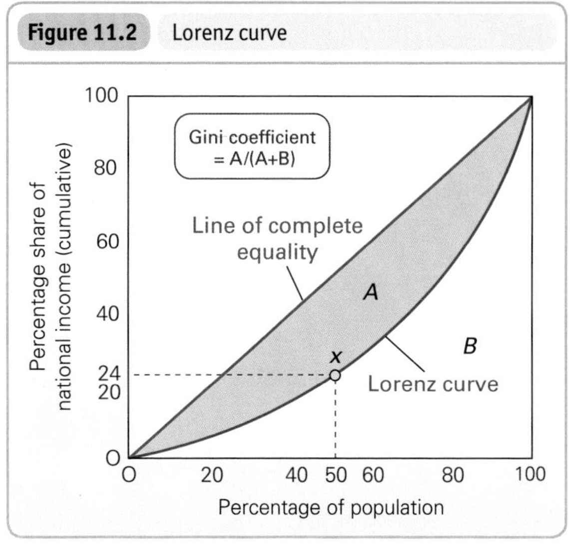

In 1979, the *gross income* (original income plus cash benefits) Gini coefficient in the UK was 0.276 (see Figure 11.3). With the growth in inequality during the 1980s, the coefficient steadily increased and stood at 0.366 in 1990. Since then it has edged up to stand at 0.408 in 2019/20. *The disposable income* coefficient (gross income minus direct taxes) also rose dramatically – from 0.254 in 1979 to 0.349 in 1990. It was 0.363 in 2019/20, having been as high as 0.386 in 2007/8. In terms of *post-tax income* (disposable income minus indirect taxes), a similar pattern emerged, but by including indirect taxes, which, as we have seen, are paid proportionately more by the poor, the Gini coefficient was higher in all years.

Figure 11.4 shows the Gini coefficients for a selection of countries for the latest year available from 2013 to 2019. These are based on *disposable income*: that is, income after the deduction of taxes and the receipt of cash benefits (transfers). They also include the value of goods produced for own consumption as an element of self-employed income. As you can see, Slovakia had the lowest Gini coefficient (0.236) and hence was the most equal. Scandinavian countries were also relatively equal. The most unequal country in the sample was South Africa (0.620), followed by Brazil (0.539). The average of the 38 developed countries that form the Organisation for Economic Co-operation and Development (OECD) was 0.317, more equal than both the USA (0.390) and the UK (0.366).

Gini coefficients have the advantage of being relatively simple to understand and use. They provide a clear way of comparing income distribution either in the same country at different times, or between different countries.

Definitions

Lorenz curve A curve showing the proportion of national income earned by any given percentage of the population (measured from the poorest upwards).

Gini coefficient The area between the Lorenz curve and the 45° line divided by the total area under the 45° line.

Figure 11.3 UK Gini coefficients: 1977 to 2019/20

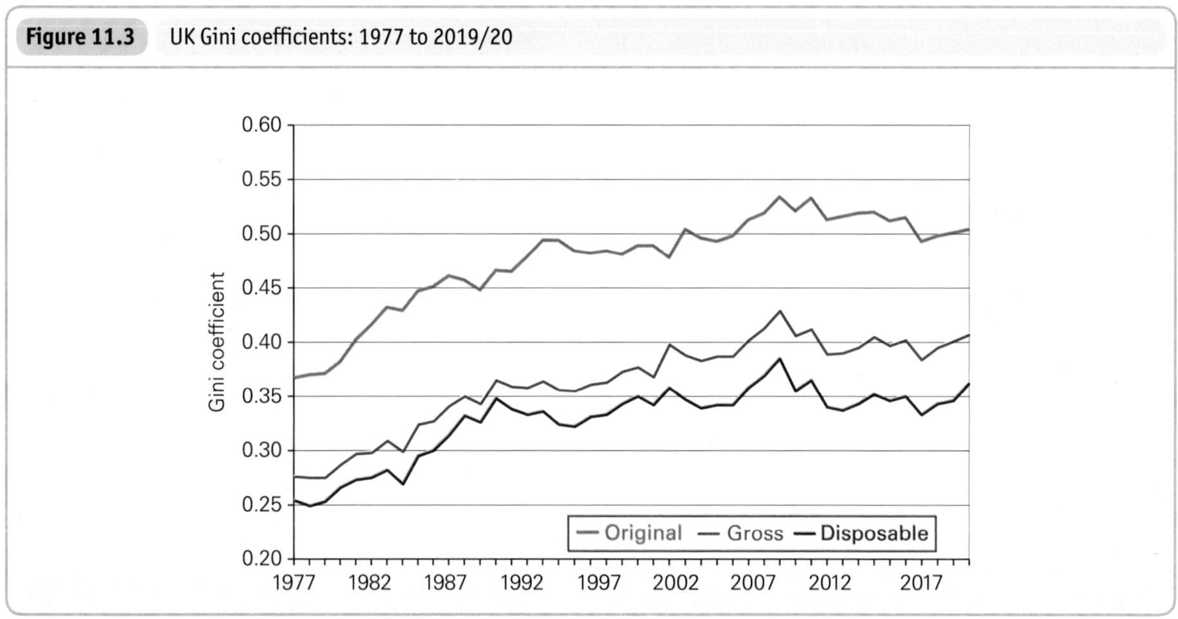

Note: From 1994/5 the figures refer to financial years ending in the year shown.
Source: Based on data from *The Effects of Taxes and Benefits on UK Household Income*, Table 6a (ONS, 2021).

Figure 11.4 Gini coefficients for selected countries, based on disposable income: latest year, 2013–19

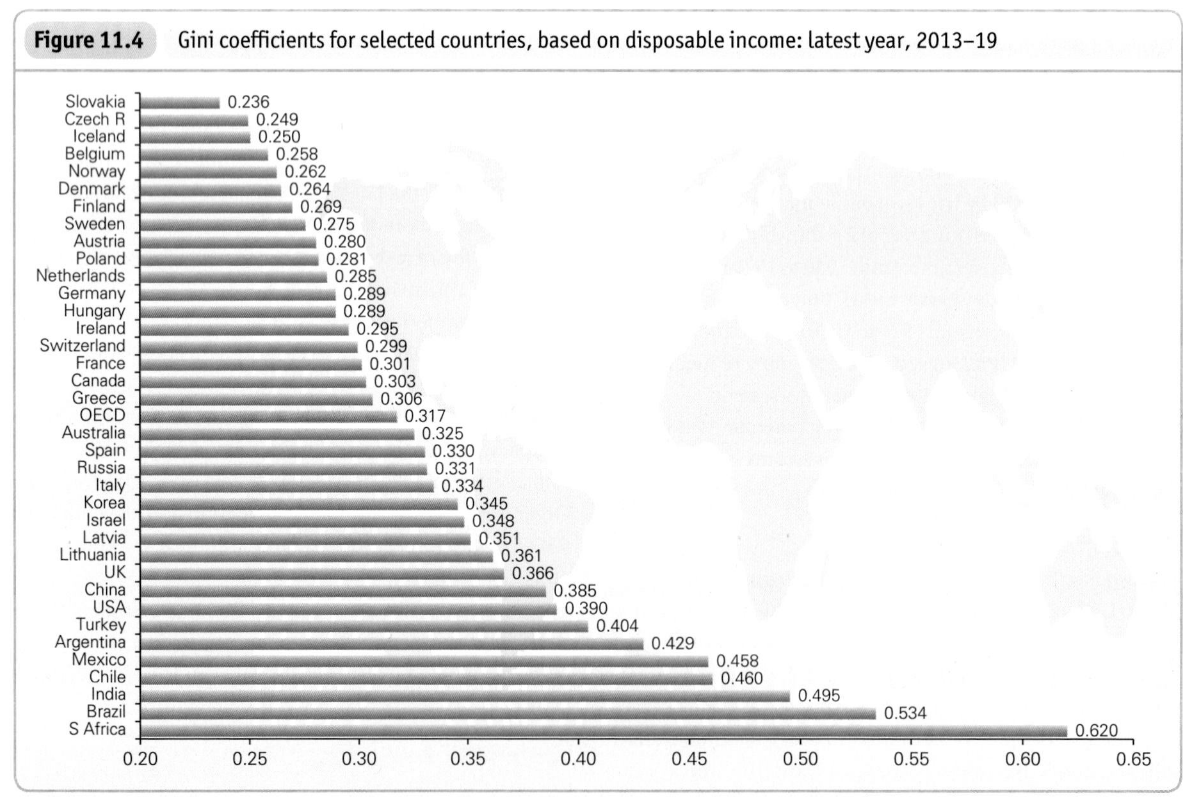

Note: India figure 2011
Source: Based on data in *Income Inequality*, OECD dataset (accessed 21 April 2021), https://data.oecd.org/inequality/income-inequality.htm; and the *World Bank Gini Index* (2021), https://data.worldbank.org/indicator/SI.POV.GINI

Figure 11.5 Lorenz curves for two countries with the same Gini coefficients

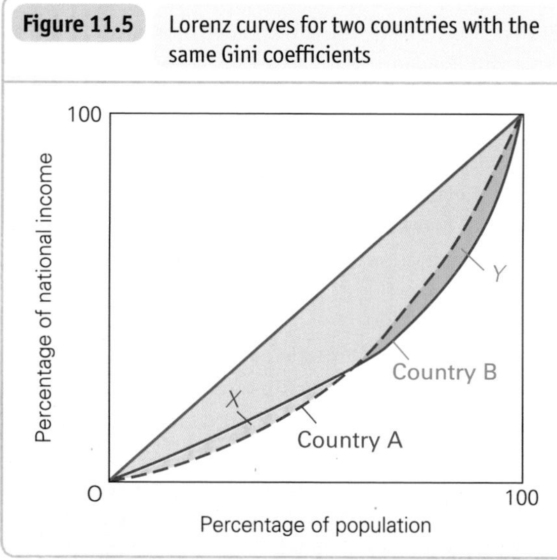

However, they cannot take into account all the features of inequality. Take the case of the two countries illustrated in Figure 11.5. If area X is equal to area Y, they will have the same Gini coefficient, and yet the pattern of their income distribution is quite different.

Also, it is important to note what statistics are used in the calculation. Are they pre-tax or post-tax; do they include benefits; do they include non-monetary incomes (such as food grown for own consumption: a major item in many developing countries); are they based on individuals, households or tax units?

In which country in Figure 11.5 would you expect to find the highest number of poor people? Describe how income is distributed in the two cases.

Ratios of the shares in national income of two quantile groups

This is a very simple method of measuring income distribution. A ratio quite commonly used is that of the share of national income of the *bottom 40 per cent* of the population to that of the *top 20 per cent*. Thus if the bottom 40 per cent earned 15 per cent of national income and the top 20 per cent earned 50 per cent of national income, the ratio would be 15/50 = 0.3. The lower the ratio, therefore, the greater the inequality. Some figures are shown in Table 11.1.

As can be seen from the table, South Africa is the most unequal country with a ratio of just 0.11 (its Gini coefficient in 2015 was 0.62). Zambia and Brazil also have high levels of inequality. Some of the former communist countries such as Hungary and Slovenia have greater levels of equality. Generally, advanced countries are more equal than developing countries. Western European countries typically have a ratio of between 0.4 and 0.65. For example, the UK has a ratio of 0.45 and Denmark of 0.60. The USA, however, is less equal, with a ratio of 0.33.

1. *Why do you think that the ratios for developing countries are lower than those for developed countries?*
2. *Make a list of reasons why the ratios of the bottom 40 per cent to the top 20 per cent may not give an accurate account of relative levels of inequality between countries.*
3. *What would the ratio be if national income were absolutely equally distributed?*

Do earnings statistics give a true representation of inequality?

Although the size distribution of income gives a good first indication of inequality, there are various factors that need to be taken into account when interpreting the statistics.

The first is the diminishing marginal utility of income. If a rich person spends twice as much as a poor person, does that mean that they get twice as much utility? The answer is probably no. The more you earn and spend, the less additional utility you will get for each extra amount spent (see page 134). Part of the reason is that you buy more luxurious versions of products. The argument here is that a car costing £40 000 will not give you four times as much utility as one costing £10 000.

The second factor concerns the interpretation of changes in inequality over time. The past 30 years have seen income increases skewed towards the rich, with the top 10 per cent of income earners getting a lot richer, while the incomes of the poor have risen very little. From 1979 to 2019/20 the Gini coefficient of post-tax income in the UK rose from 0.25 to 0.36.

Although it appears from these figures that inequality has grown rapidly, there may have been factors that mitigate against this. As people earn more, they spend proportionately more on services, such as childcare and personal trainers, and on luxury goods such as designer clothing and fast cars, and proportionately less on items such as basic foodstuffs and clothing. The argument here is that if the prices of these more luxurious goods and services rise faster than

Table 11.1 National income share of the poorest 40 per cent of the population as a proportion of the share of the richest 20 per cent

Country	Quantile ratio
South Africa	0.11
Zambia	0.15
Brazil	0.18
USA	0.33
India	0.45
UK	0.45
Hungary	0.55
Denmark	0.60
Slovenia	0.72

Source: World Development Indicators: Distribution of income or consumption, Table 1.3, The World Bank (various years), http://wdi.worldbank.org/tables

those of more basic goods, the poor will experience a lower inflation rate than the rich. This is what happened over the period 1990–2005, meaning that inequality did not rise as fast as the simple statistics would suggest.

More recently, however, the inflation rate of the poor has overtaken that of the rich. Prices of food and energy have risen faster than those of luxury goods. This would suggest that more recent statistics may have *understated* the growth in inequality.

The third factor that needs to be taken into account when assessing inequality is the distribution of *wealth*. We consider this below (pages 333–4).

The functional distribution of income in the UK

Distribution of income by source

Figure 11.6 shows the sources of household incomes in 1977 and 2019/20. Wages and salaries constitute by far the largest element. However, their share fell from 73 per cent to 67 per cent of national income between 1977 and 2019/20. Conversely, the share coming from pensions rose from 3 per cent to 6 per cent, reflecting the growing proportion of the population past retirement age. The share coming from cash benefits fell from 13 per cent to 10 per cent, reflecting less generous welfare benefits and the stage of the economic cycle.

In contrast to wages and salaries, investment income (dividends, interest and rent) accounts for a relatively small percentage of household income – a mere 5 per cent in 2019/20. Nevertheless, some groups, typically elderly people, rely on savings interest as a key source of income. Nominal interest rates have remained at historically low levels and for much of the 2009–21 period they have been below inflation. This has meant that for most savers real interest rates have been negative. Conversely, those with large mortgages linked to the Bank of England's Bank Rate ('tracker mortgages'), have found themselves with much smaller payments each month. There has thus been a major redistributive effect away from net savers to net borrowers. KI 40 pA:0

With the growth of small businesses and the increased numbers of people being 'employed' on a freelance basis, the proportion of incomes coming from self-employment has grown. It rose from 7 per cent in 1977 to 10 per cent in 2019/20.

The overall shares illustrated in Figure 11.6 hide the fact that the sources of income differ quite markedly between different income groups. These differences are shown in Table 11.2.

Column (1) shows that higher-income groups (save the top group) get a larger proportion of their income from wages and salaries than do lower-income groups. This can be largely explained by examining column (5). As would be expected, the poor tend to get a larger proportion of their incomes in cash benefits from the government than do people further up the income scale.

One feature to note is that the proportion of income coming from profits, rent and interest (column (3)) varies little between the lower four income groups. In fact only for those people in the top 1 or 2 per cent is it significantly higher. The conclusion from this, plus the fact that investment incomes account for only 5.3 per cent of household incomes in total, is that incomes from capital and land are of only relatively minor significance in explaining income inequality.

The major cause of differences in incomes between individuals in employment is the differences in wages and salaries between different occupations.

Figure 11.6 Sources of UK household income as a percentage of gross household income

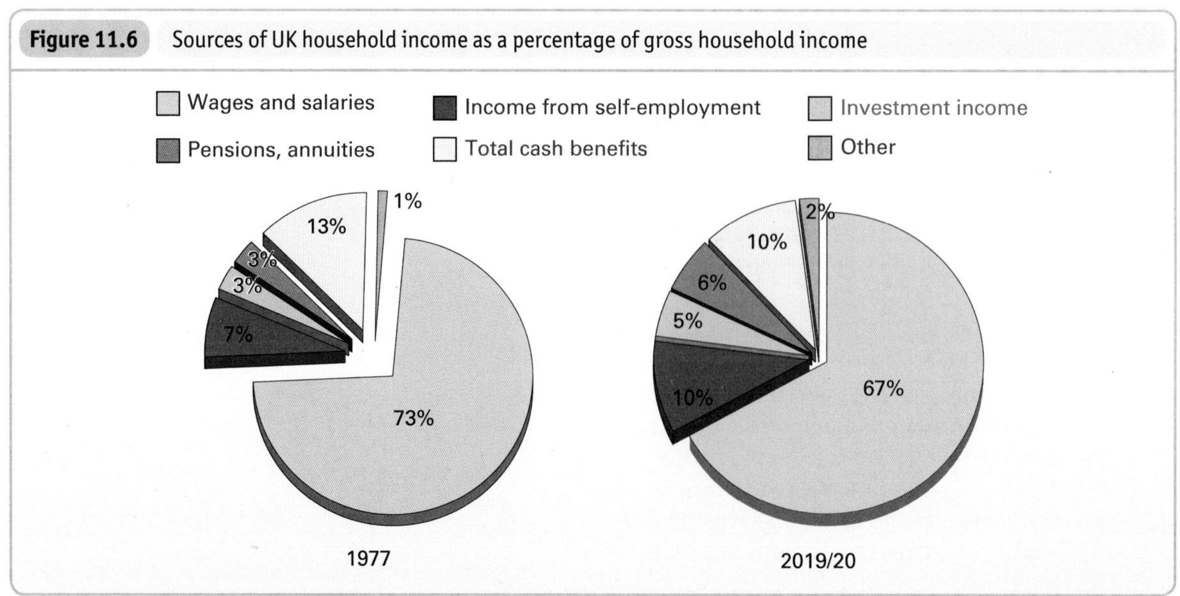

Source: Based on data from *Household Disposable Income and Inequality, UK, 2019/20 – Reference Tables*, Table 28, ONS (January 2021), www.ons.gov.uk/peoplepopulationandcommunity/personalandhouseholdfinances/incomeandwealth/datasets/householddisposableincomeandinequality

Table 11.2 Sources of UK household income as a percentage of total gross household income by quintile groups: 2019/20

Gross household weekly incomes (quintiles)	Wages and salaries (1)	Income from self-employment (2)	Income from investments (3)	Pensions and annuities (4)	Total cash benefits (5)	Other (6)	Total (7)
Lowest 20%	41.9	9.8	1.7	4.0	40.0	2.6	100
Next 20%	55.1	8.5	1.1	5.5	27.6	2.3	100
Middle 20%	68.6	7.7	1.1	6.5	14.1	1.9	100
Next 20%	75.5	7.3	2.1	7.2	6.0	1.8	100
Highest 20%	68.6	12.7	9.8	5.3	1.9	1.8	100
All households	66.9	10.1	5.3	5.8	9.9	1.9	100

Source: *The effects of taxes and benefits on household income, disposable income estimate: 2020*, Table 13, ONS (January 2021), www.ons.gov.uk/peoplepopulationandcommunity/personalandhouseholdfinances/incomeandwealth/datasets/householddisposableincomeandinequality

Distribution of wages and salaries by occupation

Differences in full-time wages and salaries are illustrated in Figure 11.7. This shows the average gross weekly pay of full-time adult workers in selected occupations in 2020. As you can see, there are considerable differences in pay between different occupations. The causes of differences in wage rates from one occupation to another were examined in Chapter 10.

If fringe benefits (such as long holidays, company cars and health insurance) were included, do you think the level of inequality would increase or decrease? Explain why.

Since the late 1970s, wage differentials have widened. Part of the explanation lies in a shift in the demand for labour. Many firms have adopted new techniques which require a more highly educated workforce. Wage rates in some of these skilled occupations have increased substantially.

At the same time, there has been a decline in the number of unskilled jobs in industry and, along with it, a decline in the power of unions to represent such people. Where low-skilled jobs remain, there will be pressure on employers to reduce wage costs if they are competing with companies based in developing countries, where wage rates are much lower.

Figure 11.7 Mean gross weekly earnings (excluding overtime) of UK full-time adult employees (£): 2020

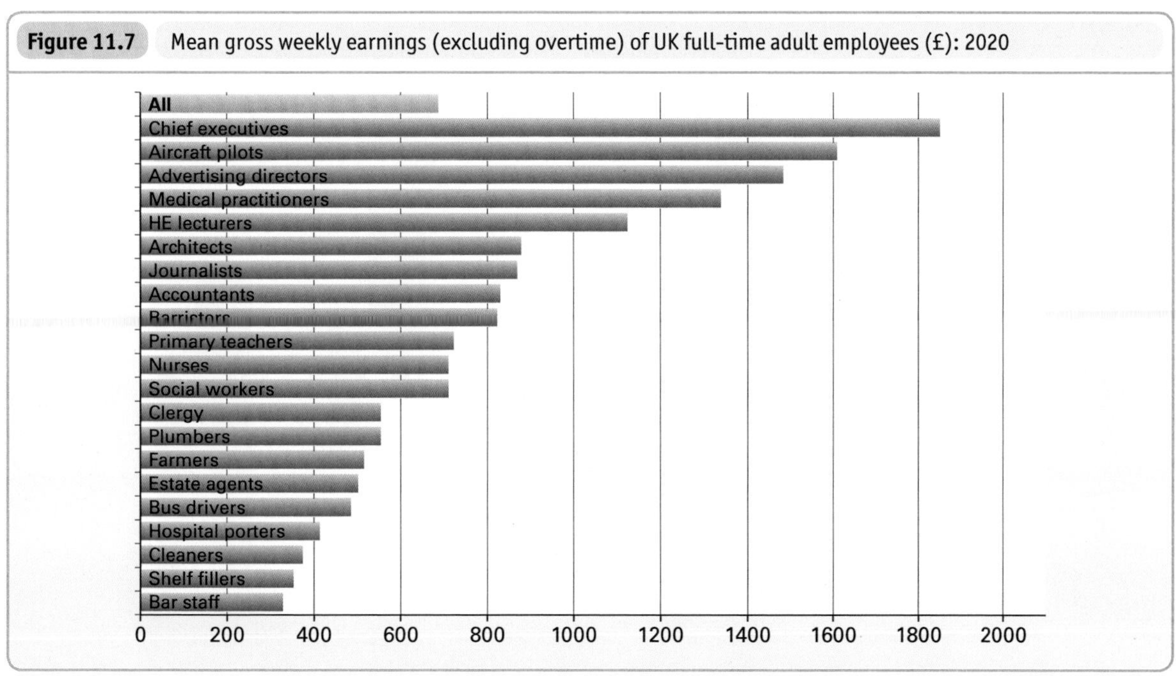

Source: Based on data in the *Annual Survey of Hours and Earnings*, Table 14.2a, National Statistics (October 2020), www.ons.gov.uk/employmentandlabourmarket/peopleinwork/earningsandworkinghours/datasets/occupation4digitsoc2010ashetable14

As prospects for unskilled people decline in industry, so people with few qualifications increasingly compete for low-paid, service-sector jobs (e.g. in supermarkets and fast-food outlets). The growth in people seeking part-time work has also kept wage rates down in this sector.

Other determinants of income inequality

Differences in household composition

KI 4 p13

Other things being equal, the more dependants there are in a household, the lower the income will be *per member* of that household. Figure 11.8 gives an extreme example of this. It shows the average household income in the UK both before taxes and benefits ('original income') and after all taxes and benefits ('final income') in the financial year ending 2020 of five different categories of household.

Households containing two adults and three children had considerably less original income than households with two adults and no children. Households with just one adult and one or more children had even less income. This means that they had an even lower income *per member* of the household. This, however, was offset somewhat by the tax and benefits system, with a smaller gap between final incomes of the households with three or more children and those with two adults and no children. Final income was actually greater for households with three or more children than those with just one adult. Final income *per member* of the household, however, was still considerably less.

There is a twin problem for many large households. Not only may there be relatively more children and elderly dependants, but also the total household income will be reduced if one of the adults stays at home to look after the family or works only part-time.

Differences by gender

Box 10.7 on pages 300–1 looked at some of the aspects of income inequality between the sexes. In 2020, the median gross weekly pay for full-time female employees was £535.30. For male employees it was £597.93. There are three important factors to note:

- Women are paid less than men in the same occupations. You will see this if you compare some of the occupations in Table (b) in Box 10.7.
- Women tend to be employed in lower-paid occupations than men.
- Women do less overtime than men (the median is 2.8 hours for women and 4.3 for men).

List the reasons for each of the three factors above. (Re-read section 10.2 and Box 10.7 if you need help.)

Differences in the geographical distribution of income

Figure 11.9 shows the gross yearly household incomes in different regions of the UK in the financial year ending 2020. Differences in incomes between the regions reflect regional differences in industrial structure, unemployment and the cost of living. As can be seen from the figure, average incomes are significantly lower in Northern Ireland, Wales and the East Midlands than in the South East of England and in London.

Figure 11.8 Yearly income for different types of non-retired UK households (£): financial year ending 2020

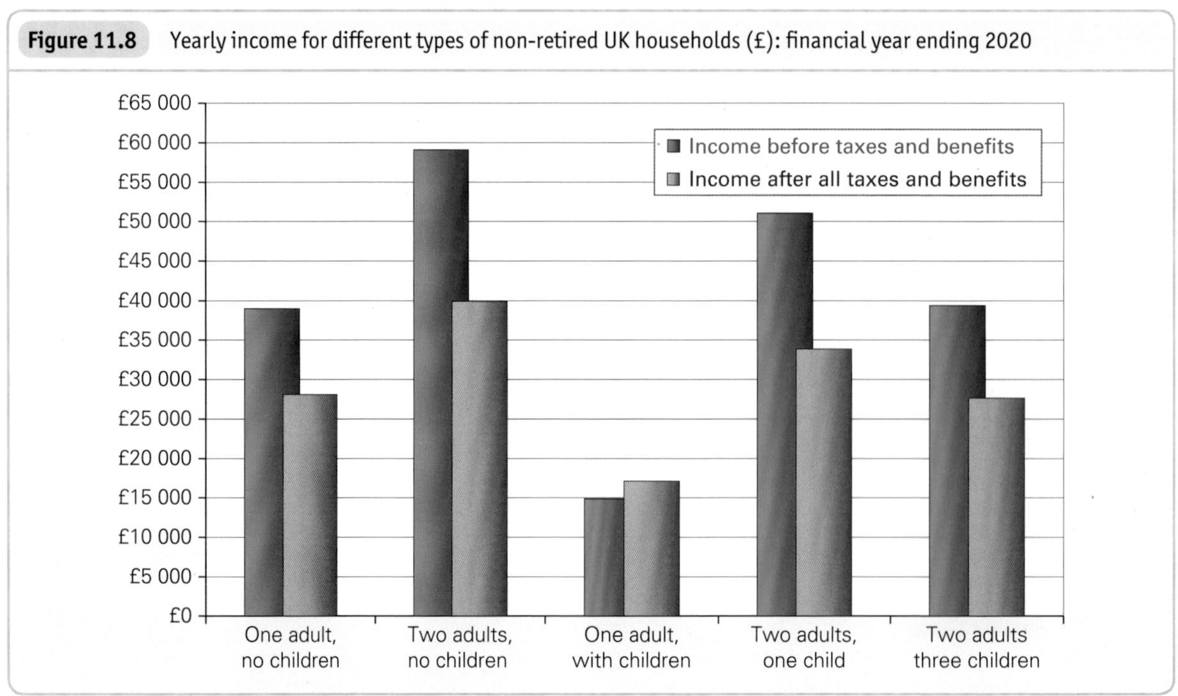

Source: Based on data in *The Effects of Taxes and Benefits on UK Household Income,* Tables 12a and 12b (2021).

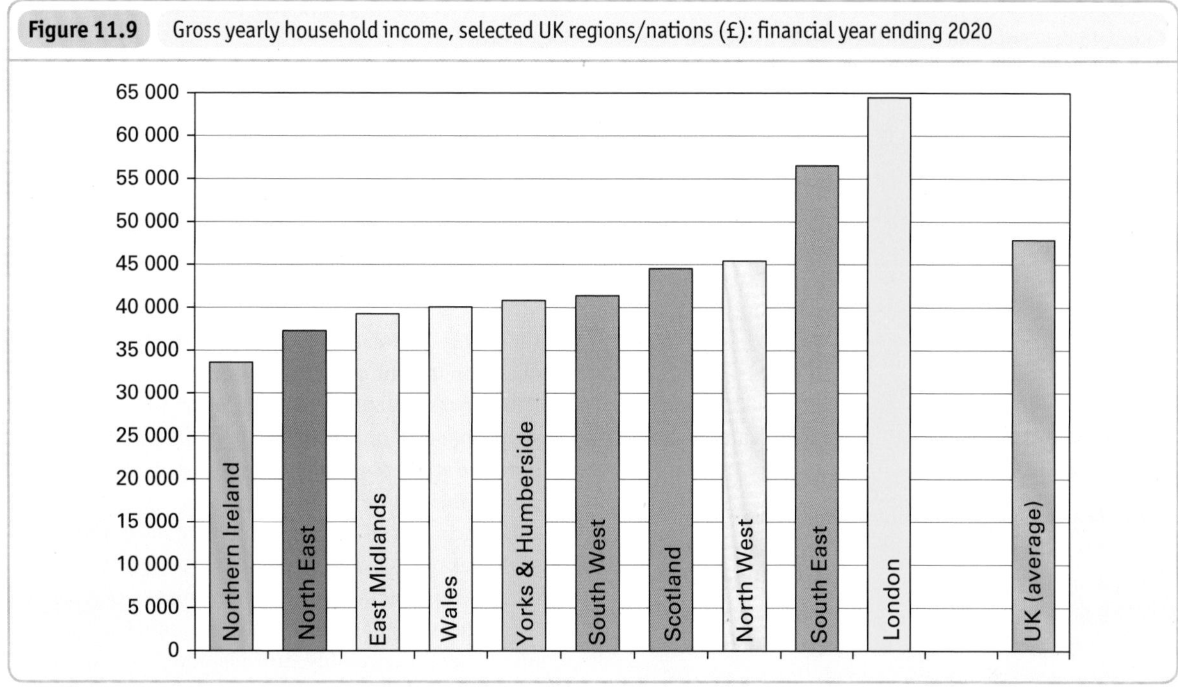

Figure 11.9 Gross yearly household income, selected UK regions/nations (£): financial year ending 2020

Note: Based on 2019/20 prices.
Source: Based on data in *The Effects of Taxes and Benefits on UK Household Income*, Table 17, ONS (2021).

On a more local level, there are considerable differences in incomes between affluent areas and deprived areas. It is at this level that some of the most extreme examples of inequality can be observed, with 'leafy' affluent suburbs only a mile or two away from run-down estates. Regional inequality and local inequality are explored in Case Study 23.14 on the student website.

The distribution of wealth

Wealth is difficult to measure. Being a *stock* of assets (such as a house, land, furniture, personal possessions and investments), it has an easily measurable value only when it is sold. What is more, individuals are not required to keep any record of their assets. Only when people die and their assets are assessed for inheritance tax does a record become available. One set of data, therefore, is based on HMRC records of the assets of those who have died that year.

Another dataset is based on the ONS *Wealth and Assets Survey* (WAS) for Great Britain, which is conducted every two years. This partly relies on the self-valuation estimates of the respondents. According to the 2016–18 WAS, the median wealth of households was £286 600. Figure 11.10 shows the composition of wealth from this survey split into four categories. Private pension wealth (occupational/personal pensions) is the largest component, followed by net property wealth (value of property owned less any mortgages) and then net financial wealth (savings/financial investments less any loans/arrears). Physical wealth (value of household contents, possessions, valuables and vehicles) is the smallest component.

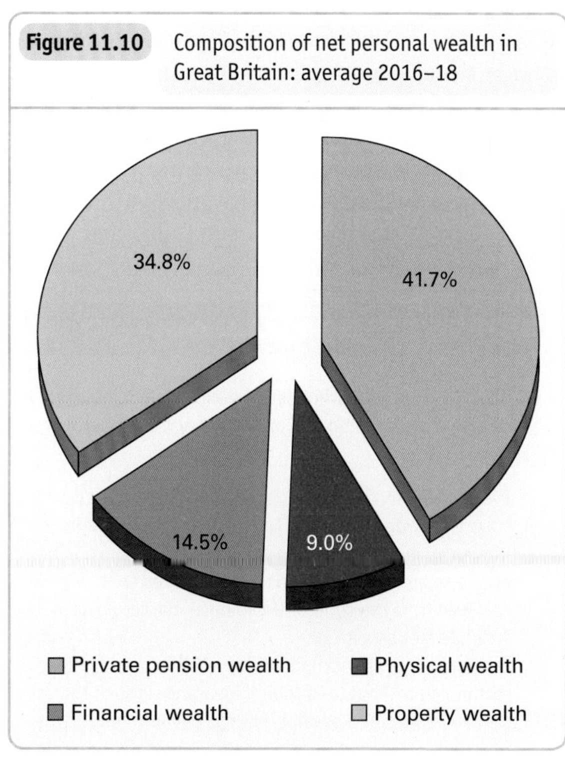

Figure 11.10 Composition of net personal wealth in Great Britain: average 2016–18

Source: Based on *Total Wealth: Wealth in Great Britain: April 2016 to March 2018*, National Statistics (5 December 2019).

Inequality of wealth is far greater than inequality of income. Many people have virtually no wealth and many more have net debts. By contrast, the richest 10 per cent own around 45 per cent of all identifiable wealth and the richest 20 per cent own around 64 per cent.

The four major causes of inequality in the distribution of wealth are as follows:

- Inheritance. This allows inequality to be perpetuated from one generation to another.
- Income inequality. People with higher incomes can save more.
- Different propensities to save. People who save a larger proportion of their income will build up a bigger stock of wealth.
- Entrepreneurial and investment talent/luck. Some people are successful in investing their wealth and making it grow rapidly.

Even though wealth is highly concentrated, there was a significant reduction in inequality of wealth up to the early 1990s. From 1971 to 1991 the Gini coefficient of wealth fell a full 16 percentage points from 0.80 to 0.64. A major reason for this was the increased taxation of inherited wealth. Since 1991, however, this reduction in inequality has been reversed. This can be explained by lower levels of inheritance tax and substantial rises in property prices and share values. The Gini coefficient is largest for net financial wealth (0.91) and lowest for physical wealth (0.47).

During the pandemic, wealth inequality grew further. Between February 2020 and May 2021, the wealthiest 10 per cent saw their wealth increase by just under 5 per cent, driven by asset price increases (housing, private pensions and shares), while the poorest 20 per cent saw their wealth rise by only 1 per cent. Nevertheless, the fourth and fifth deciles saw their wealth rise by around 7 per cent, driven by the rise in house prices and increased saving during lockdown.[1]

Causes of inequality

We turn now to identify the major causes of inequality. The problem has many dimensions and there are many factors that determine the pattern and depth of inequality. It is thus wrong to try to look for a single cause, or even the major one. The following are possible determinants of inequality:

- Inequality of wealth. People with wealth are able to obtain an income other than from their own labour.
- Differences in ability. People differ in intelligence, strength, etc. Some of these differences are innate and some are acquired through the process of 'socialisation' – education, home environment, etc.
- Differences in attitude. Some people are adventurous, willing to take risks, willing to move for better jobs, keen to push themselves forward. Others are much more cautious. KI 11 p72
- Differences in qualifications. These are reflections of a number of things: ability, attitudes towards study, access to good education, income of parents, etc.
- Differences in hours worked. Some people do a full-time job plus overtime, or a second job; others work only part-time.
- Differences in job utility/disutility. Other things being equal, unpleasant or dangerous jobs will need to pay higher wages.
- Differences in power. Monopoly power in the supply of factors or goods, and monopsony power in the demand for factors, is unequally distributed in the economy.

1 See Jack Leslie and Krishan Shah, *(Wealth) gap year: the impact of the coronavirus crisis on UK household wealth*, Resolution Foundation (July 2021).

BOX 11.1 POVERTY IN THE PAST

CASE STUDIES AND APPLICATIONS

Consider from the following passage whether it is reasonable or even possible to compare poverty today with poverty in the 1800s.

> Every great city has one or more slums, where the working class is crowded together. True, poverty often dwells in hidden alleys close to the palaces of the rich; but, in general, a separate territory has been assigned to it, where, removed from the sight of the happier classes, it may struggle along as it can.
>
> The houses are occupied from cellar to garret, filthy within and without, and their appearance is such that no human being could possibly wish to live in them . . . the filth and tottering ruin surpass all description. Scarcely a whole window-pane can be found, the walls are crumbling, doorposts and window-frames loose and broken, doors of old boards nailed together, or altogether wanting in this thieves' quarter, where no doors are needed, there being nothing to steal. Heaps of garbage and ashes lie in all directions, and the foul liquids emptied before the doors gather in stinking pools. Here live the poorest of the poor, the worst-paid workers with thieves and the victims of prostitution indiscriminately huddled together . . . and those who have not yet sunk in the whirlpool of moral ruin which surrounds them, sinking daily deeper, losing daily more and more of their power to resist the demoralising influence of want, filth, and evil surroundings.[1]

1. *If we were to measure poverty today and in the nineteenth century in absolute terms, in which would there be the greater number of poor?*
2. *If we measure poverty in relative terms, must a society inevitably have a problem of poverty, however rich it is?*

Identify some other concepts where we talk about them in absolute terms and in relative terms. In each case, do you think that the relative or the absolute term is more useful? Why? Compare your answers with those of other students.

1 F. Engels, *The Condition of the Working Class in England*, Progress Publishers (1973), pp. 166–7.

- Differences in the demand for goods. Factors employed in expanding industries will tend to have a higher marginal revenue product because their output has a higher market value.
- Differences in household composition. The greater the number of dependants relative to income earners, the poorer the average household member will be (other things being equal).
- Discrimination by race, sex, age, social background, etc.
- Degree of government support. The greater the support for the poor, the less will be the level of inequality in the economy.
- Unemployment. When unemployment levels are high, this is one of the major causes of poverty.

Which of the above causes are reflected in differences in the marginal revenue product of factors?

Government attitudes towards inequality

Attitudes of the right. The political right sees inequality as having an important economic function. Factor price differences are an essential part of a dynamic market economy. They are the price signals that encourage resources to move to sectors of the economy where demand is growing, and away from sectors where demand is declining. If the government interferes with this process by taxing high incomes and subsidising low incomes, working people will not have the same incentive to gain better qualifications, to seek promotion, to do overtime, or to move for better jobs. Similarly, owners of capital will not have the same incentive to invest.

If inequality is to be reduced, claims the political right, it is better done by encouraging greater factor mobility. If factor supply curves are more elastic (greater mobility), then any shifts in demand will cause smaller changes in factor prices and thus less inequality. But how is greater mobility to be encouraged? The answer, they say, is to create a culture of self-help: where people are not too reliant on state support; where they will look for higher incomes of their own volition. At the same time, they argue that the monopoly power of unions to interfere in labour markets should be curtailed. The net effect of these policies, they claim, would be to create a more competitive labour market which would help to reduce inequality as well as promoting economic growth and efficiency.

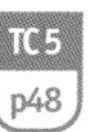

State support, say those on the right, should be confined to the relief of 'genuine' poverty. Benefits should be simply a minimum safety net for those who cannot work (e.g. the sick or disabled), or on a temporary basis for those who, through no fault of their own, have lost their jobs. Even at this basic level, however, the right argues that state support can discourage people from making more effort.

Attitudes of the centre and left. Although many in the political centre and on the left accept that there is a trade-off between equality and efficiency, they tend to see it as a far less serious problem. They claim that questions of efficiency and growth are best dealt with by encouraging investment. They argue that this can be achieved by creating an environment of industrial democracy where workers participate in investment decisions. This common purpose is in turn best achieved in a more equal and less individualistically competitive society. The left also sees a major role for government in providing support for investment: for example, through government-sponsored research, by investment grants or by encouraging firms to get together and plan a co-ordinated strategy.

KI 3 p13

These policies to achieve growth and efficiency, claims the left, will leave the government freer to pursue a much more active policy on redistribution.

Section summary

1. Inequality can be examined by looking at the size distribution of income, the functional distribution of income, the distribution of income by recipient, the distribution of wealth, or the extent and nature of poverty.
2. An analysis of the size distribution of income in the UK shows that inequality has grown over the past 30 to 40 years.
3. The size distribution of income can be illustrated by means of a Lorenz curve. The greater the inequality, the more bowed the curve will be towards the bottom right-hand corner.
4. Size distribution can also be measured by a Gini coefficient. This will give a figure between 0 (total equality) and 1 (total inequality). Income distribution can also be measured as the ratio of the share of national income of a given lower income quantile to that of a higher income quantile.
5. Wages and salaries constitute by far the largest source of income, and thus inequality can be explained mainly in terms of differences in wages and salaries. Nevertheless, state benefits are an important moderating influence on inequality and constitute the largest source of income for the poorest 20 per cent of households. Investment earnings are only a minor determinant of income except for the richest 1 or 2 per cent.
6. Other determinants of income inequality include differences in household composition, gender and where people live.
7. The distribution of wealth is less equal than the distribution of income.
8. Attitudes towards government redistribution of income vary among political parties. The political right stresses the danger that redistributive policies may destroy incentives. The best approach to inequality, according to the right, is to 'free up' markets so as to encourage greater mobility. The left, by contrast, sees fewer dangers in reducing incentives and stresses the moral and social importance of redistribution from rich to poor.

11.2 TAXES, BENEFITS AND THE REDISTRIBUTION OF INCOME

In this section, we will look at policies to redistribute incomes more equally, and in particular we will focus on the use of government expenditure and taxation. Redistribution is just one of three major roles for government expenditure and taxation. The second is to compensate for the failure of the market to allocate resources efficiently. We examine this role in the following three chapters. The third is to influence the overall level of activity in the economy. Adjusting government expenditure and/or taxation for this purpose is known as *fiscal policy* and is examined in Chapter 22.

The use of taxation and government expenditure to redistribute income

Taxation. If the rich are taxed proportionately more than the poor, the post-tax distribution of income will be more equal than the pre-tax distribution.

Subsidies. Subsidies are of two broad types. First, *cash benefits* can be seen as subsidies to people's incomes. They include such things as child benefit and old-age pensions. Second, *benefits in kind* provide subsidised goods and services, which may be provided free (e.g. education or bus travel) or at a reduced price (e.g. NHS dental treatment). Subsidies will lessen inequality if they account for a larger proportion of a poor person's income than a rich person's.

Although we shall focus mainly on the use of taxes and benefits, there are two other types of redistributive policy.

Legislation. Examples include minimum wage legislation (see Box 11.2) and anti-discrimination legislation.

Structural policies. These are policies where the government tries to alter those institutions and attitudes of society that increase or at least perpetuate inequalities. Examples of such policies include removing privileges, encouraging widening participation in higher education, promoting worker share ownership, encouraging industries to move to areas of high unemployment and encouraging the provision of crèche facilities at work.

Before we turn to look at the use of taxation and government expenditure to redistribute incomes, we must first look at what taxes are available to a government and what are the requirements of a good tax system.

The requirements of a good tax system

Whatever the purpose of taxation, when it comes to devising and administering particular taxes there are various principles that many people argue should be observed.

Horizontal equity. According to the principle of ***horizontal equity***, people in the *same circumstances* should be taxed equally. In other words, taxes should be levied impartially. For example, people earning the same level of income and with the same personal circumstances (e.g. number and type of dependants, size of mortgage, etc.) should pay the same level of income tax.

KI 4 p13

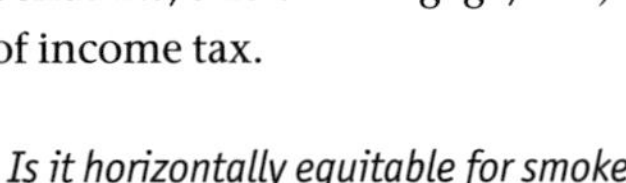

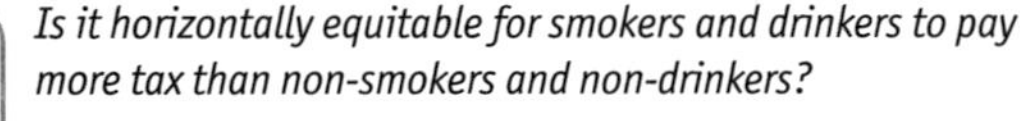

Is it horizontally equitable for smokers and drinkers to pay more tax than non-smokers and non-drinkers?

Vertical equity. According to the principle of ***vertical equity***, taxes should be 'fairly' apportioned between rich and poor. What constitutes fairness here is highly subjective. No one likes paying taxes and thus a rich person's concept of a fair tax is unlikely to be the same as a poor person's. This whole question of using taxes as a means of redistributing incomes will be examined in detail below.

Equity between recipients of benefits. Under the ***benefit principle***, it is argued that those who receive the most benefits from government expenditure ought to pay the most in taxes. For example, it can be argued that roads should be paid for from fuel tax. That way those who use the roads the most will pay the most towards their construction and maintenance.

1. *Does the benefit principle conflict with either vertical or horizontal equity?*
2. *Would this be a good principle to apply in the case of health care?*

In most cases, the benefits principle would be difficult to put into practice. There are two reasons why. First, a specific tax would have to be devised for each particular good and service provided by the state. Second, in the case of many goods and services provided by the state, it would be difficult to identify the amount of benefit received by each individual. Just how much benefit (in money terms) do you derive from street lighting, from the police, from clean air, etc.?

Cheapness of collection. Taxes cost money to collect. These costs should be kept to a minimum relative to the revenue they yield.

Definitions

Horizontal equity The equal treatment of people in the same situation.

Vertical equity The redistribution from the better off to the worse off. In the case of taxes, this means the rich paying proportionately more taxes than the poor.

Benefit principle of taxation The principle that people ought to pay taxes in proportion to the amount that they use government services.

Difficulty of evasion. If it is desirable to have a given tax, people should not be able to escape paying. A distinction is made between ***tax evasion*** and ***tax avoidance***:

- Tax evasion is illegal. This is where, for example, people do not declare income to the tax authorities.
- Tax avoidance is legal, albeit from the government's point of view undesirable. This is where people try to find ways of managing their affairs so as to reduce their tax liability.

Measuring the extent of evasion and avoidance is inherently tricky, but every year HMRC publishes a figure for the 'tax gap'. In 2018/19 this was estimated at £31 billion or 4.7 per cent of tax liabilities.

Tax avoidance is more likely to be practised by the rich than the poor – in part because they stand to gain more; in part because they can afford to pay for the specialist advice required. In a period of public-sector cuts, a great deal of attention has been focused on tax avoidance by large companies such as Amazon, Google and Facebook.

Non-distortion. Taxes alter market signals: taxes on goods and services alter market prices; taxes on income alter wages. They should not do this in an undesirable direction.

If prices are not distorted in the first place, it is best to use taxes that have the same percentage effect on prices of all goods and services. That way *relative* prices remain the same. For example, VAT in the UK is levied on most goods and services at a single rate of 20 per cent. If goods were taxed at different rates, this would create distortions, switching consumption and production from goods with high taxes to goods with low taxes.

If, however, the government feels that market prices *are* distorted in the first place, taxes can be used to alter price signals in the desired direction.

How can the market distortions argument be used to justify putting excise duties on specific goods such as petrol, alcohol and tobacco? Is this the only reason why excise duties are put on these particular products?

Convenience to the taxpayer. Taxes should be certain and clearly understood by taxpayers so that they can calculate their tax liabilities. The method of payment should be straightforward.

Convenience to the government. Governments use tax changes as an instrument for managing the economy. Tax rates should thus be simple to adjust. Also, the government will need to be able to calculate as accurately as possible the effects of tax changes, both on the total tax yield and on the distribution of the burden between taxpayers.

Minimal disincentive effects. Taxes may discourage people from working longer or harder, from saving, from investing or from taking initiative. For example, a high rate of income tax may discourage people from seeking promotion or from doing overtime. 'What is the point', they may say, 'if a large proportion of my extra income is taken away in taxes?' It is desirable that these disincentives should be kept to a minimum.

TC5 p48

Of course, not all these requirements can be met at the same time. There is no perfect tax. The government thus has to seek a compromise when there is a conflict between any of the requirements. One of the most serious conflicts is between vertical equity and the need to keep disincentives to a minimum. The more steeply the rich are taxed, it is argued, the more serious are the disincentive effects on them likely to be. This particular conflict is examined below.

Types of tax

Taxes can be divided into two broad categories. ***Direct taxes*** are paid directly by the taxpayer to the tax authorities. Such taxes include personal income tax, tax on companies' income and tax on capital and wealth. ***Indirect taxes***, on the other hand, are paid via a middle person. For example, value added tax (VAT) is designed to be a tax on consumption. But you the consumer do not pay it to the authorities: it is paid by firms, which then pass it on to consumers in higher prices (see section 3.2). You are thus taxed indirectly when you buy goods and services.

Direct taxes

Personal income tax. All types of income are included – wages, salaries, interest, dividends and rent. In most countries, people can earn a certain amount of income free of tax: this is known as their personal ***tax allowance***. In many countries, employees' income tax is paid directly on their behalf by their employers. In the UK this is known as the pay-as-you-earn scheme (PAYE).

Definitions

Tax evasion The illegal non-payment of taxes (e.g. by not declaring income earned).

Tax avoidance The rearrangement of one's affairs so as to reduce one's tax liability.

Direct taxes Taxes on income and wealth. Paid directly to the tax authorities on that income or wealth.

Indirect taxes Taxes on expenditure. Paid to the tax authorities not by the consumer, but indirectly by the suppliers of the goods or services.

Tax allowance An amount of income that can be earned tax-free. Tax allowances vary according to a person's circumstances.

BOX 11.2 MINIMUM WAGE LEGISLATION

A way of helping the poor?

Calls for a minimum wage in the UK grew during the 1990s with the increasing number of low-paid jobs. With the abolition of the 'wages councils' in 1993, there was no longer any legally enforceable minimum hourly rate. Falls in the demand for unskilled labour, growing rates of part-time employment, and weaker labour laws were all putting downward pressure on the pay of those at the lower end of the earnings distribution.

In response to these calls, the Labour government introduced a statutory UK national minimum wage (NMW) in April 1999. Two different rates were set – £3.60 per hour for those aged 22 and over, and £3.00 for those between 18 and 21. Rates for 16–17-year-olds and apprentices were added in 2004 and 2010 respectively. In 2015, the government announced that a new statutory 'national living wage' (NLW) would be introduced in April 2016. This was effectively a new higher minimum wage for those workers aged 25 and above. It was extended to 23- and 24-year-olds in April 2021.

The government sets rates on an annual basis, after taking advice from the Low Pay Commission (LPC).[1] The LPC assesses any possible negative consequences for the economy before making its recommendations.

The recommended rates for 2021/22 that were implemented by the government are as follows.

- 23 and over £8.91
- 21 to 22 £8.36
- 18 to 20 £6.56
- Under 18 £4.62
- Apprentice £4.30

A number of other countries also have minimum wages and the OECD publishes a comparison.[2] After adjusting for differences in the cost of living, rates are calculated in US$. In 2019, Australia had the highest rate ($12.60), the UK was eighth on the list ($10.50) while Mexico had the lowest rate ($1.20).

The scope of the UK national minimum wage

How many workers receive wages that are directly affected by the NMW? The LPC measures this by reporting data on the number of jobs paying no more than 5p above the different minimum wage rates – so called *'minimum wage jobs'*. Estimates show that there were initially 835 000 *minimum wage jobs* in 1999, with the figure gradually rising to just under 1.5 million in 2015.[3] There was a sudden increase to approximately 2 million in 2016 with the introduction of the NLW. The figure remained relatively stable between 2016 and 2021 and accounts for around 7 per cent of all employee jobs. Nearly 50 per cent of these workers are in just three occupational groups – retail, hospitality, cleaning & maintenance.

A second key issue is the extent to which the NMW raises the earnings of low-paid workers. This is known as the policy's 'bite'. One way to measure 'bite' is to look at the level of the NMW relative to median earnings.

This ratio increased gradually from 45.3 per cent in 1999 to 52.6 per cent in 2015. It then increased rapidly by another 7.5 percentage points in just five years because of two key policy decisions. The government (a) introduced the NLW and (b) set the LPC a target of increasing NLW rates so they were 60 per cent of median earnings by 2020. This target was reached in April 2020. The government then set the LPC a new target of increasing rates so they are two-thirds of median earnings by 2024.

Both the number of workers covered by the NMW and its bite are considerable. They have increased significantly since 2016.

Impact of the minimum wage on the economy

The national minimum wage can affect the economy in a number of different ways.

Wage inequality. Does the NMW actually reduce wage inequality? It can have both a direct effect on those whose pay was previously below the rate (as long as employers comply with the law) and a spillover or ripple effect on those paid just above the new minimum. There is potential for considerable spillover effects if employers worry that reductions in pay differentials may have a negative impact on the morale/productivity of those workers who already earn just above the NMW.

Avram and Harkness (2019)[4] found that increases in the NMW did lead to pay growing more quickly at the lower end of the earnings distribution. This includes evidence of both direct and spillover effects for workers up to the 30th percentile of earnings. The direct effects on pay were larger than

The marginal rate of income tax is the rate that people pay on additional income. In most countries, the marginal rate increases in bands as people earn more. In many countries, there is a main marginal rate of tax that most people pay. This is known as the standard or ***basic rate of tax***.

Definition

Basic rate of tax The main marginal rate of tax, applying to most people's incomes.

The *average* rate is a person's total income tax as a fraction of total income. This will always be less than the marginal rate, since part of a person's income will be tax-free; and for higher tax rate payers, part will be taxed at lower rates.

Individuals' social security contributions. In the UK these are known as national insurance contributions (NICs). These are like income taxes in that they are generally charged as a percentage of a person's income, the marginal rate varying with income. Unlike other taxes, which are paid into a common fund to finance government expenditure, they are used to finance *specific* expenditure: namely, pensions and social the spillover effects so the net impact was to reduce wage inequality in the lower half of the earnings distribution.

Employment. One of the principal arguments against imposing a NMW are concerns over its impact on the demand for labour and employment. Higher costs may lead to lower levels of output (the scale effect), while rising wages may incentivise firms to replace labour with capital in production (the substitution effect). Both the scale and substitution effects have a negative impact on the demand for labour and employment. However, if firms have monopsony power, then, as we saw in Figure 10.10 (on page 295), higher wages can lead to higher employment.

Research in the UK has found very little evidence of actual declines in employment and hours worked by those in receipt of the NMW, just lower rates of increase. For example, Baily, Popov and Wilson (2020)[5] report that between 2015 and 2018, growth in employment in firms directly affected by the NLW was 2 to 3 percentage points lower than in a control group. The effects were particularly strong in retail and food service chains. However, the researchers found this same lower growth rate in the data before the introduction of the NLW. They conclude that this long-term trend is the result of firms automating routine processes in the workplace (e.g. self-service checkouts) rather than a response to the NLW.

Prices. How responsive are prices to changes in the NMW? Researchers estimate an elasticity figure for affected firms of between 0.023 and 0.11. Hence, a 10 per cent increase in the NMW leads to a maximum increase of 1.1 per cent in prices. Given that this only has an impact on the prices of goods in affected firms, the effect on inflation as a whole is trivial.

Limitations

The policy has two major limitations. Setting the same minimum wage rate across the whole country takes no account of different living costs. For example, the percentage of employee jobs covered by the NMW in 2019 was just 1.1 per cent in the City of London, whereas the figure was 10 per cent in the North East.[6] The policy also only affects the employed, yet one of the major causes of poverty is unemployment.

It is clear that a NMW on its own cannot address the issue of poverty and needs to be combined with reforms to the benefit system.

1. ***If an increase in wage rates for low-paid workers leads to their being more motivated, how would this affect the marginal revenue product and the demand for such workers? What implications does your answer have for the effect on employment in such cases? (See page 297 on the efficiency wage hypothesis.)***
2. ***If a rise in the minimum wage encourages employers to substitute machines for workers, will this necessarily lead to higher long-term unemployment in (a) that industry and (b) the economy in general?***

Research minimum wage legislation in a developed country of your choice (other than the UK). How have the rates and their percentage of median or mean pay changed over time and with what effect on income distribution and the economy?

1 The Low Pay Commission: About us, www.gov.uk/government/organisations/low-pay-commission/about
2 *Real minimum wages*, OECD Stat, https://stats.oecd.org/viewhtml.aspx?datasetcode=RMW&lang=en
3 *Low Pay Commission 2020 report* (December 2020), www.gov.uk/government/publications/low-pay-commission-report-2020
4 Silvia Avram and Susan Harkness, 'The impact of minimum wage upratings on wage growth and the wage distribution,' *Research Report for the Low Pay Commission* (November 2019).
5 Thomas Baily, Danail Popov and Cavin Wilson, *Estimating the Impact of the National Living Wage on businesses*, Research Report for the Low Pay Commission (December 2020), www.gov.uk/government/publications/low-pay-commission-research-2020
6 Brigid Francis-Devine, 'National Minimum Wage Statistics', *House of Commons Briefing Paper 7735*, UK Parliament (15 February 2021), https://commonslibrary.parliament.uk/research-briefings/cbp-7735/

security. Although they do not officially count as 'taxes', to all intents and purposes they are so.

Table 11.3 and Figure 11.11 show the marginal and average rates of income tax and social security contributions in England, Wales and Northern Ireland in 2021/22. Notice that above £100 000, the personal allowance is reduced by £1 for each £2 earned. This is equivalent to an extra 20 per cent for the next £25 140 (i.e. £12 570 × 2).

Employers' social security contributions. Employers also have to pay social security contributions on behalf of their employees. These are paid per employee. In some countries, small firms pay reduced rates.

Tax on corporate income. In the UK this is known as corporation tax. It is a tax on the profits of limited companies. In most countries, there are lower rates for small companies. Profits can usually be offset against capital expenditure and interest payments when working out the tax liability. This effectively means that profits that are reinvested are not taxed.

Tax on capital gains. This is a tax payable when a person sells assets, such as property or shares. It is payable on the gain in value of these assets since a set date in the past, or since they were purchased if this was after the set date.

Taxes on wealth. These are taxes on assets held or acquired by individuals. One form of wealth tax in most countries is that

Table 11.3 UK[1] marginal income tax and national insurance rates: 2021/22[2]

Income per annum (£)	Marginal income tax rate (%)	Marginal NIC rate (%)	Marginal income tax plus NIC rate (%)
0–9568	0	0	0
9569–12 570	0	12	12
12 571–50 270	20	12	32
50 271–100 000	40	2	42
100 001–125 140	40 + 20	2	62
125 141–150 000	40	2	42
Above 150 000	45	2	47

1 The structure is very similar in Scotland, but the Scottish Government used its devolved powers to have a starting rate of income tax of 19% (£12 571); then rates of 20% (£14 668) and 21% (£25 297); then a higher rate of 41% (£43 663) and a top rate of 46% (£150 001).

2 In September 2021, the government announced that in 2022/23 it would be raising national insurance rates by 1.25 percentage points for all bands in order to provide extra funding for the NHS and social care.

on inherited assets or assets transferred before a person's death. Another is taxes based on the value of a person's property. This is a particularly common form of local taxation (the others being local income tax, local business tax and local sales tax).

Poll taxes. These are fixed-sum charges per head of the population, irrespective of the person's income. Very few countries use such taxes as they are regarded as unfair. A poll tax (or 'community charge') was introduced in Scotland in 1989 and in England and Wales in 1990 as the new form of local tax, replacing the property tax called 'rates', which was based on property values. But it was massively unpopular with the electorate, leading to demonstrations and riots, and was replaced by 'council tax' (again based on property values) in 1993.

Indirect taxes

There are three main types of indirect tax, all of which are taxes on *expenditure.*

General expenditure taxes. An example of this is ***value added tax (VAT)***. This is the main indirect tax throughout the EU. VAT is paid on the value that firms add to goods and services at each stage of their production and distribution. For example, if a firm purchases supplies costing £10 000 and with them produces goods that it sells for £15 000 (before VAT), it is liable to pay VAT on the £15 000 minus £10 000: in other words, on the £5000 value it has added. Suppliers must provide invoices to show that the VAT has already been paid on all the inputs.

The example in Table 11.4 can be used to show how the tax eventually gets passed on to the consumer. For simplicity's sake, assume that the rate of VAT is 20 per cent and that each firm uses only one supplier.

The value added at each stage plus VAT adds up to the total amount paid by the consumer: £48 000 in this case. The total VAT paid, therefore, amounts to a tax on the consumer.

Definition

Value added tax (VAT) A tax on goods and services, charged at each stage of production as a percentage of the value added at that stage.

Figure 11.11 UK[3] marginal and average rates of income tax plus national insurance contributions, 2021/22

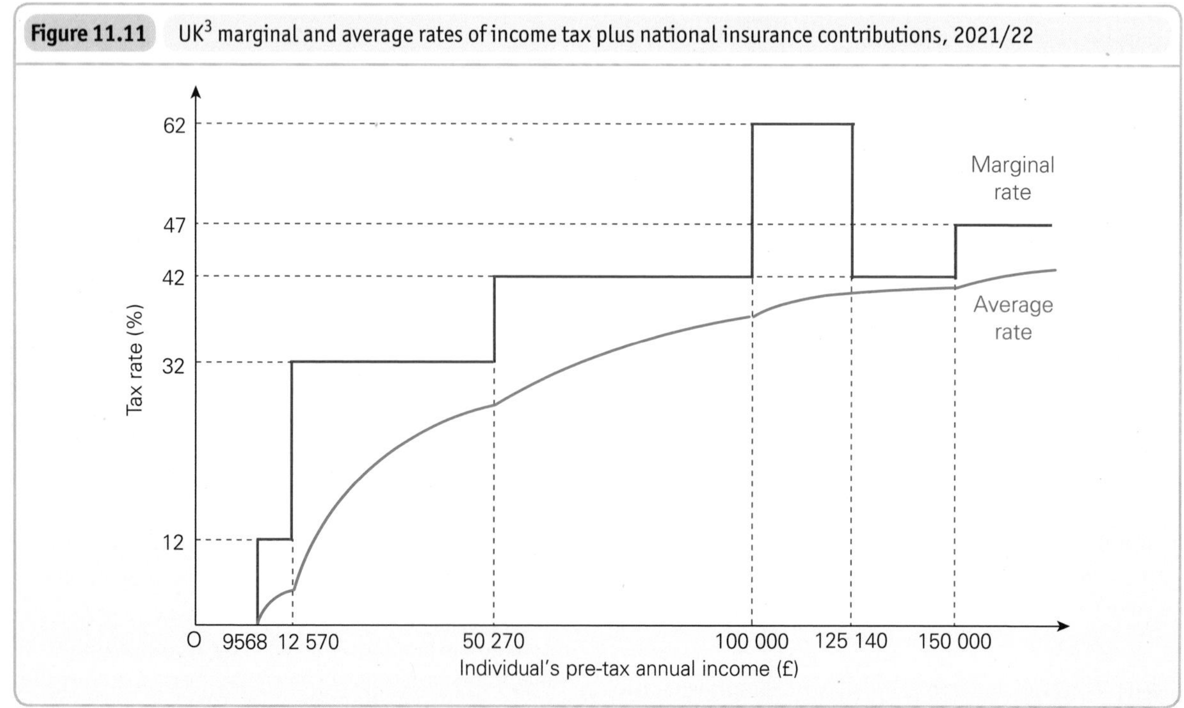

3 Income Tax rates and thresholds are slightly different in Scotland, with the rate rising in stages from 19% to 20% to 21% and then to 41% above £43 662 and 46% above £150 000.

4 In 2022/23 rates rose by 1.25 percentage points for all bands given a rise in national insurance rates of that much.

Table 11.4 Calculating VAT: an example where the rate of VAT is 20%

	Value added (1)		VAT (2)		Value added plus VAT (3)	Price sold to next stage (4)
Firm A sells raw materials to firm B for £12 000	£10 000		£2000		£12 000	£12 000
Firm B processes them and sells them to a manufacturer, firm C, for £21 600	£8 000		£1600		£9 600	£21 600
Firm C sells the manufactured goods to a wholesaler, firm D, for £30 000	£7 000		£1400		£8 400	£30 000
Firm D sells them to a retailer, firm E, for £36 000	£5 000		£1000		£6 000	£36 000
Firm E sells them to consumers for £48 000	£10 000		£2000		£12 000	£48 000
	£40 000	+	**£8000**	=	**£48 000**	

In the example, the £8000 VAT is 20 per cent of the (pre-tax) consumer price of £40 000.

The rates of VAT in the various EU countries are considered in Box 24.10. Each country has a standard rate and up to two lower rates for basic goods and services. Standard rates vary between 15 and 27 per cent, but are typically between 20 and 25 per cent.

Many other countries levy general expenditure taxes at a *single* stage (either wholesale or retail). These taxes are called *purchase taxes* and will normally be a percentage of the price of the good at that stage.

Excise duties. These are taxes on particular goods and services: for example, petrol and diesel, alcoholic drinks, tobacco products and gambling. They are a single-stage tax levied on the manufacturer. For example, duty on beer in the UK depends on its alcoholic strength measured as alcohol by volume (ABV). If the ABV of the beer is between 2.8 per cent and 7.5 per cent then the rate of duty in 2021/22 is 19.08 pence per litre for each 1 per cent of ABV. This means that the duty paid on a 5 per cent ABV pint of beer would be 54p. Duty is paid in addition to VAT.

VAT is an ***ad valorem tax***. This means that the tax is levied at a *percentage* of the value of the good. The higher the value of the good, the higher the tax paid. Excise duties, by contrast, are a ***specific tax***. This means that they are levied at a *fixed amount,* irrespective of the value of the good. Thus the duty on a litre of unleaded petrol is the same for a cut-price filling station as for a full-price one.

Customs duties. Economists normally refer to these as ***tariffs***. They are duties on goods imported from outside the country.

To what extent do (a) income tax, (b) VAT and (c) a poll tax meet the various requirements for a good tax system on pages 336–7 above? (Some of the answers to this question are given below.)

Details of tax rates in the UK are given in Case Study 11.3 on the student website. This case study also examines how progressive or regressive the various types of tax are.

The balance of taxation

Table 11.5 shows the balance of the different types of tax in selected countries. Some striking differences can be seen between the countries. In France, income and capital gains taxes account for only 21.1 per cent of tax revenue, whereas

Definitions

***Ad valorem* tax** A tax on a good levied as a percentage of its value. It can be a single-stage tax or a multi-stage tax (as with VAT).

Specific tax A tax on a good levied at a fixed amount per unit of the good, irrespective of the price of that unit.

Tariff A tax on imported goods.

Table 11.5 Balance of taxation in selected countries (2019)

Types of tax as percentage of GDP	France	Germany	Japan	Sweden	UK	USA
Personal income tax and capital gains tax	9.6	10.6	6.1	12.2	9.1	10.1
Social security contributions	14.9	14.7	12.9[1]	9.2	6.4	6.1
Corporate taxes	2.2	2.0	4.2	2.9	2.5	1.0
Payroll taxes	1.8	0.0	0.0	5.3	0.1	0.0
Taxes on property and wealth	4.0	1.1	2.6	1.0	4.1	3.0
Taxes on goods and services	12.3	10.4	6.5	12.1	10.7	4.3
Other taxes	0.6	0.3	0.0	0.2	0.1	0.0
Total taxes	**45.4**	**38.8**	**32.0[1]**	**42.9**	**33.0**	**24.5**

1 2018

Source: Extracted from revenue statistics tables in *StatExtracts*, OECD, https://data.oecd.org/tax/tax-revenue.htm#indicator-chart

in the USA they account for 41.2 per cent. In the UK, social security contributions (national insurance) are a lower percentage of total taxes than in other countries, whereas taxes on property (mainly the council tax) are a higher percentage of total taxes.

In terms of total taxes, again there are large differences between countries. In France 45.4 per cent of GDP is paid in tax whereas in the USA the figure is only 24.5 per cent.

Taxes as a means of redistributing income

If taxes are to be used as a means of achieving greater equality, the rich must be taxed proportionately more than the poor. The degree of redistribution will depend on the degree of 'progressiveness' of the tax. In this context, taxes may be classified as follows:

- ***Progressive tax***. As people's income (Y) rises, the percentage of their income paid in the tax (T) rises. In other words, the *average* rate of tax (T/Y) rises.
- ***Regressive tax***. As people's income rises, the percentage of their income paid in the tax falls: T/Y falls.
- ***Proportional tax***. As people's income rises, the percentage of their income paid in the tax stays the same: T/Y is constant.

In other words, progressiveness is defined in terms of what happens to the average rate of tax as incomes rise. (Note that it is not defined in terms of the *marginal* rate of tax.)

1. *If a person earning £10 000 per year pays £1000 in a given tax and a person earning £20 000 per year pays £1600, is the tax progressive or regressive?*
2. *A proportional tax will leave the distribution of income unaffected. Why should this be so, given that a rich person will pay a larger absolute amount than a poor person?*

An extreme form of regressive tax is a lump-sum tax (e.g. a poll tax). This is levied at a fixed *amount* (not rate) irrespective of income.

Figure 11.12 illustrates these different categories of tax. Diagram (a) shows the total amount of tax that a person pays. With a progressive tax, the curve gets progressively steeper, showing that the average rate of tax (T/Y) rises. The marginal rate of tax ($\Delta T/\Delta Y$) is given by the slope. Thus between points x and y the marginal tax rate is 40 per cent.

Diagram (b) shows the average rates. With a proportional tax, a person pays the same amount of tax on each pound earned. With a progressive tax, a larger proportion is paid by a rich person than by a poor person, and vice versa with a regressive tax.

The more steeply upward sloping the average tax curve, the more progressive is the tax, and the more equal will be the post-tax incomes of the population.

Definitions

Progressive tax A tax whose average rate with respect to income rises as income rises.

Regressive tax A tax whose average rate with respect to income falls as income rises.

Proportional tax A tax whose average rate with respect to income stays the same as income rises.

Figure 11.12 Different categories of tax

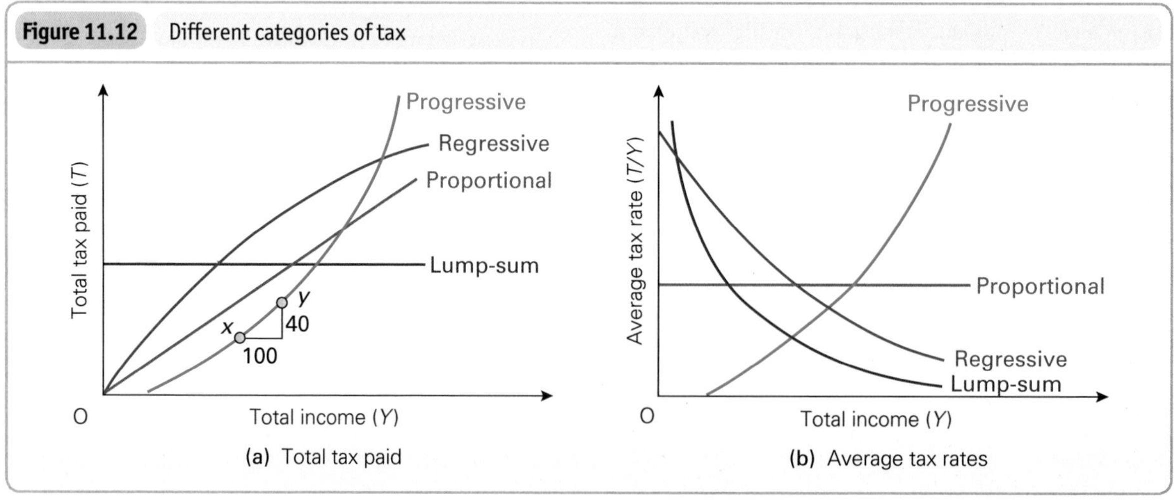

Problems with using taxes to redistribute incomes

How successfully can taxes redistribute income, and at what economic cost?

Problems in achieving redistribution

How to help the very poor. Taxation takes away income. It can thus reduce the incomes of the rich. But no taxes, however progressive, can *increase* the incomes of the poor. This will require subsidies (i.e. benefits).

But what about tax cuts? Can bigger tax cuts not be given to the poor? This is possible only if the poor are already paying taxes in the first place. Take the two cases of income tax and taxes on goods and services.

- *Income tax.* If the government cuts income tax, then anyone currently paying it will benefit. A cut in tax *rates* will give proportionately more to the rich, since they have a larger proportion of taxable income relative to total income. An increase in personal *allowances,* on the other hand, will give the same *absolute* amounts to everyone above the new tax threshold. This will therefore represent a smaller proportionate gain to the rich. In either case, however, there will be no gain at all to those people below the tax threshold. They paid no income tax in the first place and gain nothing at all from income tax cuts.
- *Taxes on goods and services.* Since these taxes are generally regressive, any cut in their rate will benefit the poor proportionately more than the rich. A more dramatic effect would be obtained by cutting the rate most on those goods consumed relatively more by the poor.

The government may not wish to cut the overall level of taxation, given its expenditure commitments. In this case, it can switch the burden from regressive to progressive taxes, if it wishes to benefit the very poor.

TC 5 p48

Tax evasion and tax avoidance. The higher the rates of tax, the more likely are people to try to escape paying some of their taxes.

People who are subject to higher rates of income tax will be more tempted not to declare all their income. This tax *evasion* will be much easier for people not paying all their taxes through a pay-as-you-earn (PAYE) scheme. This will include the self-employed and people doing casual work on top of their normal job ('moonlighting'). Furthermore, richer people can often reduce their tax liability – engage in *tax avoidance* – by a careful use of various legal devices such as trusts and tax loopholes such as being allowed to offset 'business expenses' against income.

Part of the government's justification for abolishing income tax rates above 40 per cent in 1988 was that many people escaped paying these higher taxes. Nevertheless, in 2009 the Labour Chancellor, Alistair Darling, announced that a new top rate of 50 per cent would be introduced in 2010/11. He forecast that this would bring an extra £3 billion per year in tax revenues. However, in 2011, the Office for Budget Responsibility suggested that the overall increases were likely to be much lower than this and HMRC figures suggested that £100 million a year would be lost in avoidance.

In 2013, the Conservative/Liberal Democrat Coalition government reduced the top rate to 45 per cent. It is difficult, if not impossible, to calculate the exact effect of these marginal changes.

Why may a steeply progressive income tax which is designed to achieve greater vertical equity lead to a reduction in horizontal equity?

Undesired incidence of tax. High rates of income tax on high wage earners may simply encourage employers to pay them higher wages. At the other end of the scale, tax cuts for low-paid workers may simply allow employers to cut wages. In other words, part of the incidence of income taxes will be borne by the employer and only part by the employee. Thus attempting to make taxes more 'progressive' will fail if employers simply adjust wages to compensate.

KI 9 p64

The incidence of income tax is determined by the elasticity of supply and demand for labour. In Figure 11.13, the initial supply and demand curves for labour (before the imposition of the tax) intersect at point (1), giving Q_1 labour employed at a wage of W_1. Now an income tax is imposed. This shifts the labour supply curve vertically upwards by the amount of the tax, giving the new labour supply curve, S + tax. The new equilibrium is reached at point (2) with Q_2 labour employed at a (gross) wage of W_2.

The incidence of the tax is as follows:

- The total tax revenue for the government is shown by the total shaded area.
- Workers' take-home pay is cut from W_1 to W_2 – tax. Their share of the tax is thus area *A*.
- Employers have to pay workers a rise of $W_2 - W_1$. They pay area *B*.

If the supply curve of labour of well-paid workers is relatively elastic, as shown in Figure 11.13, there will only be a

Figure 11.13 The incidence of an income tax: elastic supply of labour

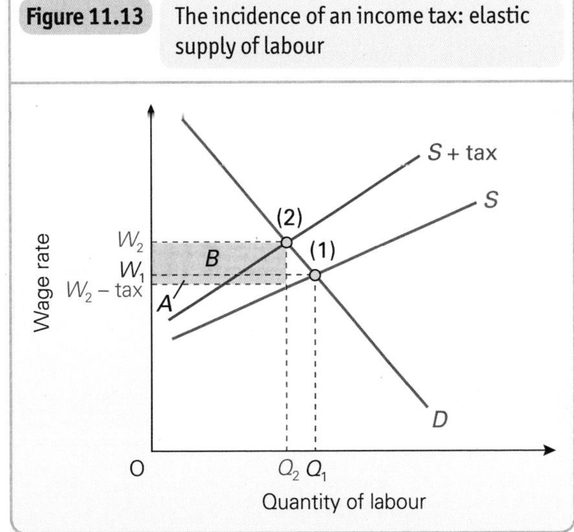

relatively slight fall in take-home pay (the workers' share of the tax is relatively small). The tax will, therefore, have only a relatively slight redistributive effect away from this group of workers.

1. *Do poor people gain more from a cut in income tax with an elastic or an inelastic supply of labour? Is the supply of unskilled workers likely to be elastic or inelastic?*
2. *Draw two diagrams like Figure 11.13, one with a steep demand curve and one with a shallow demand curve. How does the elasticity of demand affect the incidence of the income tax?*

Of course, income taxes are not imposed on workers in one industry alone. People therefore cannot move to another industry to avoid paying taxes. This fact will cause a relatively inelastic supply response to any rise in income tax, since the only alternative to paying the income tax is to work less. The less elastic this response, the more will the burden of the tax fall on the taxpayer and the more effectively can income taxes be used to redistribute incomes.

The economic costs of redistribution

KI 3 p13

If redistribution is to be achieved through *indirect* taxes, this can lead to market distortions.

Take first the case of an indirect tax applied to one good only. Assume for simplicity that there is universal perfect competition. Raising the price of this good relative to other goods will introduce a market distortion. Consumption will shift away from this good towards other goods that people preferred less at the original prices. What is more, the loss to consumers and producers (other things being equal) will be greater than the gain to the community from the tax revenue. This is illustrated in Figure 11.14.

With no tax, price will be at P_1 and output at Q_1, where demand equals supply. By imposing a tax on the good, the supply curve shifts upwards to S + tax. Price rises to P_2 and output falls to Q_2. Producers are left with P_2 – tax. What are the various losses and gains?

Figure 11.14 Indirect tax applied to good X

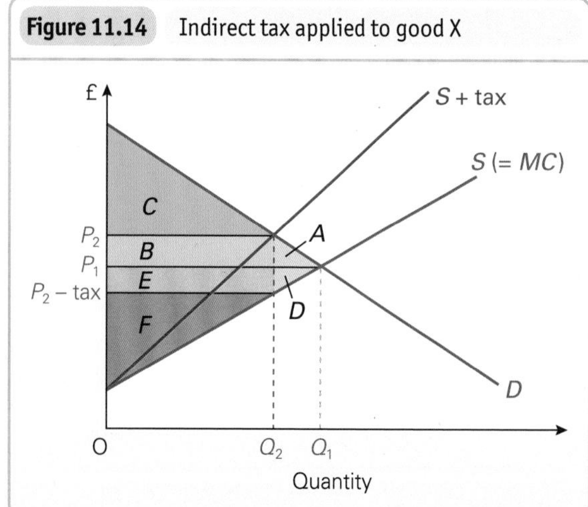

Consumers, by having to pay a higher price, lose consumer surplus (see section 4.1). Originally their consumer surplus was areas $A + B + C$. With the price now at P_2, the consumer surplus falls to area C alone. The loss to consumers is areas $A + B$.

Producers, by receiving a lower price after tax and selling fewer units, lose profits. In the simple case where there are no fixed costs of production, total profits are simply the sum of all the marginal profits (P (= MR) − MC) on each of the units sold. Thus before the tax is imposed, firms receive total profits of areas $D + E + F$. After the tax is imposed, they receive a profit of area F alone. The loss in profits to producers is therefore areas $D + E$.

The total loss to consumers and producers is areas $A + B + D + E$. The gain to the government in tax revenue is areas $B + E$: the tax rate times the number of units sold (Q_2). There is thus a net loss to the community of areas $A + D$. This is known as the ***deadweight loss of the tax***.

However, if the money raised from the tax is redistributed to the poor, their gain in welfare is likely to exceed the loss in welfare from the higher tax. The reason is that a pound sacrificed by the average consumer is probably of less value to them than a pound gained by a poor person.

What is more, if the tax is applied at a uniform rate to *all* goods, there is no distortion resulting from reallocation between goods. This is one of the major justifications for having a single rate of VAT.

Of course, in the real world, markets are highly imperfect and there is no reason why taxes will necessarily make these imperfections worse. In fact, it might be desirable on efficiency grounds to tax certain goods and services, such as cigarettes, alcohol, petrol and gambling, at higher rates than other goods and services. We will examine these arguments in the next chapter.

Although there are costs of redistribution, there are also benefits extending beyond those to whom income is redistributed. If redistribution to the poor reduces crime, vandalism and urban squalor, then it is not just the poor who gain: it is everyone, both financially in terms of reduced policing and social work costs, and more generally in terms of living in a happier and less divided society.

Taxation and incentives

Another possible economic cost of high tax rates is that they may act as a disincentive to work, thereby reducing national output and consumption. This whole question of incentives is highly charged politically. According to the political right,

TC 5 p48

Definition

Deadweight loss of an indirect tax The net loss of consumer plus producer surplus (after adding in the tax revenue) from the imposition of an indirect tax.

there is a trade-off between output and equity. High and progressive income taxes can lead to a more equal distribution of income, but a smaller national output. Alternatively, if taxes are cut there will be a bigger national output, but less equally divided. If many on the left are correct, however, we can have both a more equal society *and* a bigger national output: there is no trade-off.

KI 7 p36

The key to analysing these arguments is to distinguish between the *income effect* and the *substitution effect* of a tax rise. Raising taxes does two things:

- It reduces incomes. People may therefore work *more* in an attempt to maintain their consumption of goods and services. This is the ***income effect***.
- It reduces the opportunity cost of leisure. An extra hour taken in leisure now involves a smaller sacrifice in consumption, since each hour less worked involves less sacrifice in after-tax income. Thus people may substitute leisure for consumption, and work *less*. This is the ***substitution effect***.

The relative size of the income and substitution effects is likely to differ for different types of people and different types of tax change.

Different types of people

The *income* effect is likely to dominate for people with long-term commitments: for example, those with families, or those with mortgages and other debts. They may feel forced to work *more* to maintain their disposable income. Clearly for such people, higher taxes are *not* a disincentive to work. The income effect is also likely to be relatively large for people on higher incomes, for whom an increase in tax rates represents a substantial cut in income.

The *substitution* effect is likely to dominate for those with few commitments: those whose families have left home, the single- and second-income earners in families where that second income is not relied on for 'essential' consumption. A rise in tax rates for these people is likely to encourage them to work less.

Definitions

Income effect of a tax rise Tax increases reduce people's incomes and thus encourage people to work more.

Substitution effect of a tax rise Tax increases reduce the opportunity cost of leisure and thus encourage people to work less.

BOX 11.3 THE LAFFER CURVE

EXPLORING ECONOMICS

Having your cake and eating it

TC 5 p48

Professor Art Laffer was one of President Reagan's advisers during his first administration (1981–4). He was a strong advocate of income tax cuts, arguing that substantial increases in output would result.

He went further than this. He argued that tax cuts would actually increase the amount of tax revenue that the government earned.

If tax cuts cause income to rise (due to incentives) proportionately more than the tax rate has fallen, then tax revenues will increase. These effects are illustrated by the now famous 'Laffer' curve.

If the average tax rate were zero, no revenue would be raised. As the tax rate is raised above zero, tax revenues will increase. The curve will be upward sloping. Eventually, however, the curve will peak (at tax rate t_1). Thereafter tax rates become so high that the resulting fall in output more than offsets the rise in tax rate. When the tax rate reaches 100 per cent, the revenue will once more fall to zero, since no one will bother to work.

The curve may not be symmetrical. It may peak at a 40 per cent, 50 per cent, 60 per cent or even 90 per cent rate. Nevertheless, Laffer and others on the political right argued that tax rates were above t_1. In fact, most evidence suggests that tax rates in most countries were well below t_1 in the 1980s and certainly are now, given the cuts in income tax rates that have been made around the world over the past 20 years.

1 *What is the elasticity of supply of output with respect to changes in tax rates at a tax rate of t_1? What is it below t_1? What is it above t_1?*

2. *If the substitution effect of a tax cut outweighs the income effect, does this necessarily mean that the economy is to the right of point t_1?*

Identify the rate of corporation tax/profit tax in four countries and produce a PowerPoint slide with a chart showing the countries' rates over the past 10 years. Also search for articles considering worldwide cuts in profit tax and consider whether countries have attempted to cut rates below that of their competitors. If countries have pursued this strategy, what is the Nash equilibrium? What should countries do to avoid this Nash equilibrium? What approach has the Biden Administration adopted to encourage countries to increase profit taxes and stop large multinationals avoiding such taxes?

Total tax revenue

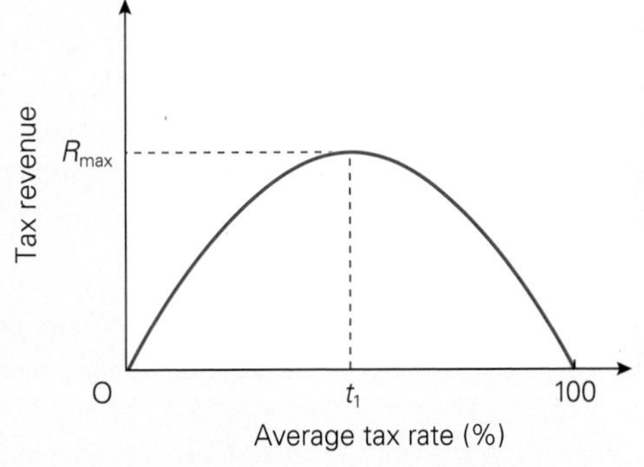

Although high income earners may work more when there is a tax *rise*, they may still be discouraged by a steeply progressive tax *structure*. If they have to pay very high marginal rates of tax, it may simply not be worth their while seeking promotion or working harder (see Boxes 11.3 and 11.4).

1. *Who is likely to work harder as a result of a cut in income tax rates, a rich person or a poor person? Why? Would your answer be different if personal allowances were zero?*
2. *How will tax cuts affect the willingness of women to return to employment after having brought up a family?*

Different types of tax change A government may wish to raise income taxes in order to redistribute incomes through higher benefits. There are three main ways it can do so: raising the higher rates of tax; raising the basic rate; and reducing tax allowances.

Raising the higher rates of tax. This may seem the most effective way of redistributing incomes: after all, it is only the rich who will suffer. There are, however, serious problems:

- The income effect will be relatively small, since it is only that part of incomes subject to the higher rates that will be affected. The substitution effect, however, could be relatively high. Rich people are likely to put a higher premium on leisure, and may well feel that it is not worth working so hard if a larger proportion of any increase in income is taken in taxes.
- It may discourage risk-taking by businesspeople.
- The rich may be more mobile internationally, so there may be a 'brain drain'. This criticism was made by the then Mayor of London, Boris Johnson, when discussing the effect of a 50 per cent tax rate on the financial sector.

KI 11 p72

Raising the basic rate of tax. As we have seen, the income effect is likely to be relatively large for those with higher incomes, especially if they have substantial commitments like a large mortgage. For such people, a rise in tax rates is likely to act as an incentive.

For those just above the tax threshold, there will be very little extra to pay on *existing* income, since most of it is tax-free. However, each *extra* pound earned will be taxed at the new higher rate. The substitution effect, therefore, is likely to outweigh the income effect. For these people, a rise in tax rates will act as a disincentive.

For those below the tax threshold, the marginal rate remains at zero. A rise in the basic rate might nevertheless deter them from undertaking training in order to get a better wage.

For those people who are not employed, a rise in tax rates may make them feel that it is no longer worth looking for a job.

Reducing tax allowances. For all those above the old tax threshold, there is no *substitution* effect at all. The rate of tax has not changed. However, there is an *income* effect. The effect is like a lump-sum tax. Everyone's take-home pay is cut by a fixed sum, and people will need to work harder to make up some of the shortfall. This type of tax change, however, is highly regressive. If everyone pays the same *amount* of extra tax, this represents a bigger percentage for poorer people than richer people. In other words, there may be no negative incentive effects, but it is not suitable as part of a policy to redistribute incomes more equally!

The conclusion from the theoretical arguments is that tax changes will have very different effects depending on (a) whom they affect and (b) the nature of the change.

1. *A key policy of the UK Coalition government, achieved in April 2014, was to raise the personal income tax allowance to £10 000. This was accompanied by the gradual removal of the same allowance from those earning over £100 000 (see Table 11.3 on page 340). Evaluate these policies.*
2. *What would the effects be of cuts in (i) the basic rate of tax (ii) the top rate of tax?*
3. *What tax changes (whether up or down) will have a positive incentive effect and also redistribute incomes more equally?*

One final point should be stressed. For many people, there is no choice in the amount they work. The job they do dictates the number of hours worked, irrespective of changes in taxation.

Evidence

All the available evidence suggests that the effects of tax changes on output are relatively small. Labour supply curves seem highly inelastic to tax changes.

Benefits

Benefits can be either cash benefits or benefits in kind.

Cash benefits

Means-tested benefits. ***Means-tested benefits*** are available only to those whose income (and savings in some instances) fall below a certain level. To obtain such benefits, therefore, people must apply for them and declare their personal circumstances to the authorities. Examples include housing benefit and income support, the safety net that exists for all in the UK.

The benefits could be given as grants or merely as loans. They could be provided as general income support or for the meeting of specific needs, such as rents, fuel bills and household items.

Universal benefits. ***Universal benefits*** are those that everyone is entitled to, irrespective of their income, if they fall into a

Definitions

Means-tested benefits Benefits whose amount depends on the recipient's income or assets.

Universal benefits Benefits paid to everyone in a certain category irrespective of their income or assets.

*BOX 11.4 TAX CUTS AND INCENTIVES

EXPLORING ECONOMICS

An application of indifference curve analysis[1]

Will tax cuts provide an incentive for people to work more? This question can be analysed using indifference curves (see section 4.3). The analysis is similar to that developed in Box 10.2. It is assumed that individuals can choose how many hours a day to work.

The position with no income tax

Diagram (a) shows the situation without income tax.

(a) Without income tax

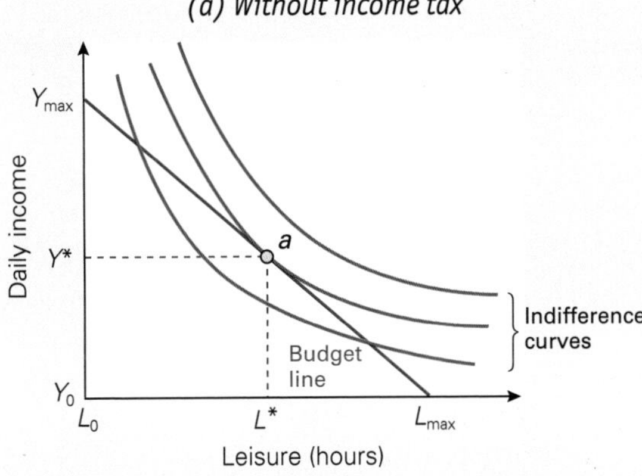

The budget line shows the various combinations of leisure and income open to an individual at a given wage rate.

Why is the budget line straight? What would it look like if overtime were paid at higher rates per hour?

The indifference curves show all the combinations of income and leisure that give the person equal satisfaction. The optimum combination of income and leisure is at Y^* and L^* where the individual is on the highest possible indifference curve: point *a*.

The position with income tax

Now let us introduce a system of income taxes. This is illustrated in diagram (b).

(b) With income tax

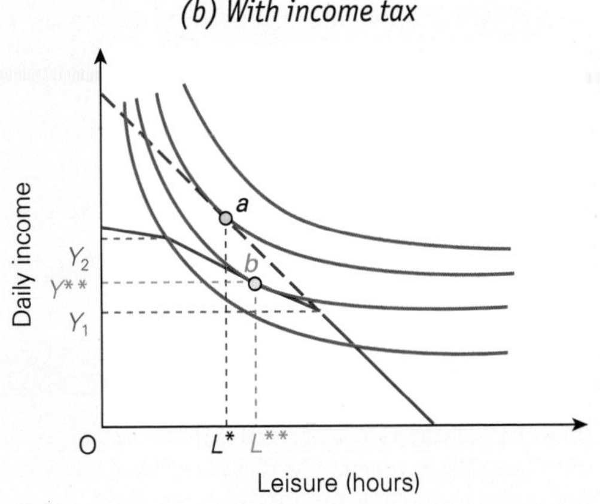

Assume that the tax has the following features:

- Up to an income of Y_1 no tax is paid: Y_1 is the individual's personal allowance.
- From Y_1 to Y_2 the basic rate of tax is paid. The budget line is flatter, since less extra income is earned for each extra hour of leisure sacrificed.
- Above Y_2 the higher rate of tax is paid. The budget line becomes flatter still.

The individual illustrated in the diagram will now choose to earn a take-home pay of Y^{**} and have L^{**} hours of leisure: point *b*. Note that this is more leisure than in the no-tax situation (point *a*). In this diagram, then, the tax has acted as a disincentive. The substitution effect has outweighed the income effect.

Redraw diagram (b), but in such a way that the income effect outweighs the substitution effect.

A cut in the basic tax rate

We can now analyse the effects of tax cuts. A cut in the basic rate is shown in diagram (c).

The tax cut makes the budget line steeper above point *q* (the tax threshold).

(c) Cut in the basic rate of tax

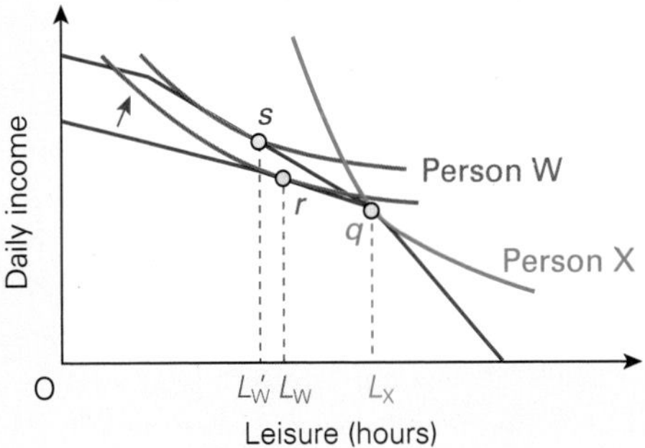

For people on the tax threshold – like person X – the cut in the basic rate makes no difference. Person X was originally taking L_X hours of leisure (point *q*) and will continue to do so.

For people above the tax threshold – like person W – the tax cut will enable them to move to a higher indifference curve. Person W will move from point *r* to point *s*. The way this diagram is drawn, point *s* is to the left of point *r*. This means that person W will work more: the substitution effect is greater than the income effect.

Try drawing two or three diagrams like diagram (c), with the tangency point at different points along the budget line to the left of q. You will find that the further to the left you move, the less likely is the substitution effect to outweigh the income effect: i.e. the more likely are people to work less when given a tax cut.

1 This box is based on D. Ulph, 'Tax cuts: will they work?', *Economic Review* (March 1987).

(continued)

A rise in the tax threshold

Diagram (d) shows a rise in personal allowances while the tax rates stay the same.

(d) Increase in the tax threshold

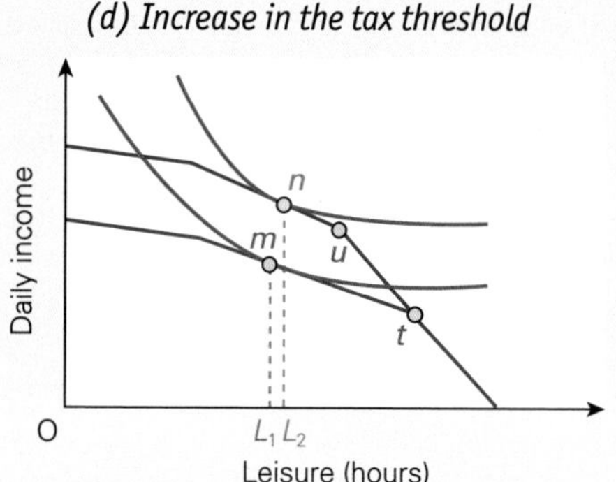

The point at which people start paying taxes rises from point *t* to point *u*. The slope of the budget line remains the same, however, since the tax rates have not changed.

For people paying taxes, the increase in allowances represents a lump-sum increase in income: there will thus be an income effect. But since tax rates have not changed, there is no substitution effect. People therefore work less. The person in the diagram moves from point *m* to point *n*, taking L_2 rather than L_1 hours in leisure.

Will people actually on the old tax threshold (i.e. those whose indifference curve/budget line tangency point is at t) work more or less? Try drawing it.

A cut in the higher rate of tax

It is likely that the income effect of this will be quite small except for those on very high incomes. The substitution effect is therefore likely to outweigh the income effect, causing people to work more.

All the above analysis assumes that taxes will not affect people's gross wage rates. If part of the incidence of taxes is borne by the employer, so that gross wages fall, after-tax wages will fall less. There will therefore be a smaller shift in the budget line. How will this affect the argument for tax cuts?

certain category or fulfil certain conditions (these conditions might include a contributions record). Examples include state pensions, and certain unemployment, sickness and invalidity benefits.

Benefits in kind

Individuals receive other forms of benefit from the state, not as direct monetary payments, but in the form of the provision of free or subsidised goods or services. These are known as ***benefits in kind***. The two largest items in most countries are health care and education. They are distributed very unevenly, however, largely due to the age factor. Old people use a large proportion of health services, but virtually no education services.

Benefits in kind tend to be consumed roughly equally by the different income groups. Nevertheless they still have some equalising effect, since they represent a much larger proportion of poor people's income than rich people's. They still have a far smaller redistributive effect, however, than cash benefits.

Figure 11.15 shows the expenditure on social protection benefits in selected European countries. These include unemployment, sickness, invalidity, maternity, family, survivors' and housing benefits and state pensions. They are mainly cash benefits, but do include some benefits in kind. They exclude health and education.

As you can see, the benefits vary significantly from one country to another. Part of the reason for this is that countries differ in their rates of unemployment and in the age structure of their population. Thus Ireland has a very low percentage of people over 65, compared with other countries in the EU and the smallest share of benefits devoted to pensions. Despite this, however, the generosity and coverage of benefits varies considerably from country to country, reflecting, in part, the level of income per head.

Also, you will see from chart (b) that benefits were generally greater in 2017 than in 1990. This is largely a reflection of the higher rates of unemployment in 2017, and hence more people in receipt of unemployment benefits.

The system of benefits in the UK and their redistributive effects are examined in Case Study 11.5 on the student website.

Benefits and the redistribution of income

It might seem that means-tested benefits are a much more efficient system for redistributing income from the rich to the poor: the money is directed to those most in need. With universal benefits, by contrast, many people may receive them who have little need for them. Do families with very high incomes need child benefit? Would it not be better for the government to redirect the money to those who are genuinely in need? In the UK, from 2012, families with at least one higher-rate taxpayer have no longer been eligible for child benefit (see Box 11.5 for more on this).

Definition

Benefits in kind Goods or services that the state provides directly to the recipient at no charge or at a subsidised price. Alternatively, the state can subsidise the private sector to provide them.

Figure 11.15 Social protection benefits in various European countries

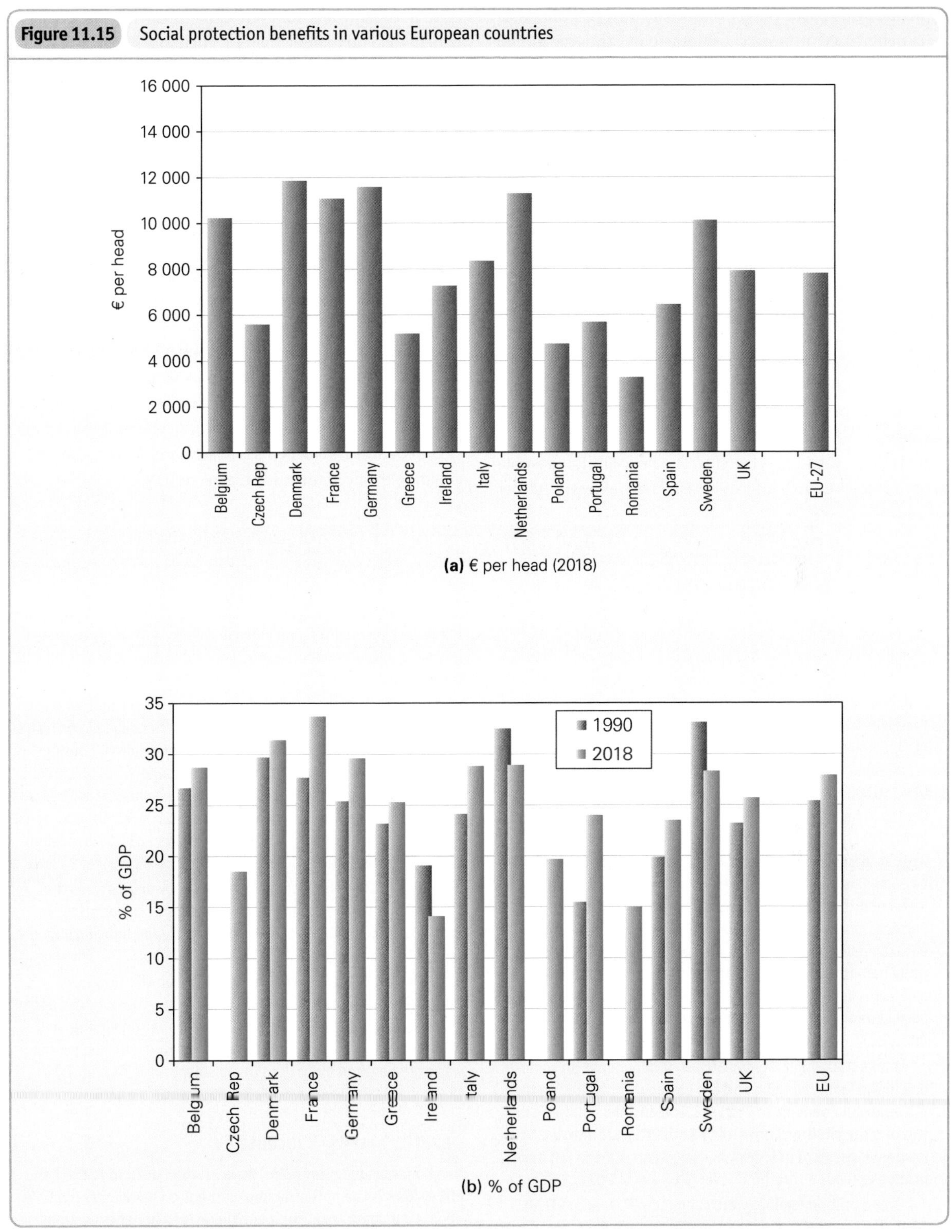

Source: Based on data in *Social Protection* tables, Eurostat (2021), https://ec.europa.eu/eurostat/databrowser/view/tps00098/default/table?lang=en

There are, however, serious problems in attempting to redistribute incomes by the use of means-tested benefits:

- Not everyone entitled to means-tested benefits applies for them, whether from ignorance of what is available, from the complexities of claiming or from reluctance to reveal personal circumstances or from a feeling that it is demeaning to claim. Thus some of the poorest families receive no support. This is a particular issue with pensioners living in poverty.
- The level of income above which people become ineligible for benefits may be set too low. Even if it were raised, there will always be some people just above the level who will still find difficulties.

- Means tests based purely on *income* (or even universal benefits based on broad categories) ignore the very special needs of many poor people. A person earning £120 a week and living in a small, well-appointed flat with a low rent and an allotment to grow vegetables will have less need of assistance than another person who also earns £120 per week but lives in a cold, draughty and damp house with large bills to meet and no means of growing their own food. If means tests are to be really fair, *all* of a person's circumstances would need to be taken into account.

The tax/benefit system and the problem of disincentives: the poverty trap

TC5 p48

When means-tested benefits are combined with a progressive income tax system, there can be a serious problem of disincentives. As poor people earn more money, not only will they start paying income taxes and national insurance, but also they will begin losing means-tested benefits. Theoretically, it is possible to have a marginal tax-plus-lost-benefit rate in excess of 100 per cent. In other words, for every extra £1 earned, taxes and lost benefits add up to more than £1. High marginal tax-plus-lost-benefit rates obviously act as a serious disincentive. What is the point of getting a job or trying to earn more money if you end up earning little more or even losing money?

This situation is known as the ***poverty trap***. People are trapped on low incomes with no realistic means of bettering their position.

The problem of the poverty trap could be overcome by switching to a system of universal benefits unrelated to income. For example, *everyone* could receive a flat payment from the state fixed at a sufficiently high level to cover their basic needs. There would still be *some* disincentive, but this would be confined to an income effect: people would not have the same need to work if the state provided a basic income. But there would no longer be the disincentive to work caused by a resulting *loss* of benefits (a substitution effect). In addition, a system of universal benefits is relatively cheap to administer, avoiding the need for costly means-testing.

BOX 11.5 REPLACING TAX CREDITS WITH UNIVERSAL CREDIT

An escape from the poverty trap?

Tax credits[1] (which share characteristics with negative income taxes) were first introduced in the UK in 1999 as a way of topping up the earnings of working people on low incomes[2] and supporting the costs of childcare. Along with a number of other benefits, they are gradually being replaced by Universal Credit (UC).

Working Tax Credit (WTC) and Child Tax Credit (CTC) were first introduced in 2003 and replaced Working Families Tax Credit. To be eligible for the basic amount of WTC (£2005 in 2021/22) claimants without children must be over 25 and work at least 30 hours a week, while those with children must be 16 and over and work at least 16 hours per week. Eligibility for additional payments (called 'elements') depend on personal circumstances. For example, couples and lone parents can receive an additional element (£2060 in 2021/22), while parents can claim support for 70 per cent of eligible childcare costs up to a weekly limit. WTC payments start to fall once earnings exceed an income threshold level (£6656 in 2021/22).

Unlike WTC, eligibility for CTC is not dependent on someone in the family working and the payment is in addition to WTC and child benefit. In 2021/22, low-income families with two or more children born after 5 April 2017 are entitled to a maximum payment of £5690. CTC payments start to fall once income exceeds a threshold level (£16 480 in 2021/22).

Over 6 million families were claiming WTC and/or CTC in 2010. This figure fell to just under 2 million in December 2020 with the roll out of Universal Credit.

Universal Credit

Universal Credit (UC) is a means-tested payment that is replacing WTC/CTC and four other benefits: Housing Benefit, Income Support, income-based Jobseeker's Allowance (JSA) and income-related Employment and Support Allowance (ESA). The six previous benefits are collectively referred to as the legacy system. By replacing this legacy system, the single UC payment supports people (a) in work (b) out of work and (c) with disabilities.

The policy initially sets the claimant's maximum entitlement. This includes a standard allowance (which varies depending on age/circumstances) and additional allowances for children, housing costs, childcare costs and disabilities. For example, in 2021/22 the monthly standard allowance for a person aged under 25 is £257.33[3] whereas for a couple both aged over 25 it is £509.91. The additional allowance for a child born after 6 April 2017 is £237.08 and people can claim up to £646.35 per month for childcare costs.

The next stage is calculating a *work allowance*. This is the amount that can be earned before payments are deducted. In 2021/22 this was £293 if the UC claim included housing support and £515 if it did not.

By March 2020, 3 million people were on UC. However, because of the impact of the COVID-19 crisis, the numbers began to increase dramatically. In the four-week period ending on 9 April 2020, 1.2 million people started making a UC claim. This was over a million more than the usual monthly figures. By November 2020, there were 5.8 million people on UC.

Benefits and work incentives

One major problem for policy makers when designing the benefit system is the potential impact it has on work incentives. As people's incomes rise, their entitlement to benefits declines and this may discourage them from working – the so-called 'poverty trap'. TC5 p48

Two key issues are the income thresholds at which entitlement begins to fall and the rate at which it declines – the taper rate. A taper rate of 50 per cent means that for every pound earned above the threshold, entitlement to the benefit falls by 50p. A lower taper rate increases work incentives for people on lower incomes – they lose less benefit by working. However, withdrawing benefits at a slower rate means that families on higher incomes

The big drawback with universal benefits, however, is their cost. If they were given to everyone and were large enough to help the poor, their cost would be enormous. Thus, although the benefits themselves would not create much disincentive effect, the necessary taxation to fund them probably would.

There is no ideal solution to this conundrum. On the one hand, the more narrowly benefits are targeted on the poor, the greater is the problem of the poverty trap. On the other hand, the more widely they are spread, the greater is the cost of providing any given level of support to individuals. One compromise proposal is that of a ***negative income tax***. This is examined in Case Study 11.6 on the student website. Box 11.5 examines the use of tax credits – which have similarities with a negative income tax – in the UK.

Conclusions

Redistribution is not costless. Whether it takes place through taxes or benefits or both, it can pose a problem of disincentives. The size of the disincentive problem varies from one tax to another and from one benefit to another, and in some cases there may even be an incentive effect: for example, when the income effect of a tax outweighs the substitution effect. It is therefore important to estimate the particular effects of each type of proposal not only on income distribution itself, but also on economic efficiency.

TC5 p48

Ultimately, the questions of how much income should be redistributed, and whether the costs are worth bearing,

Definitions

Poverty trap Where poor people are discouraged from working or getting a better job because any extra income they earn will be largely or entirely taken away in taxes and lost benefits.

Negative income tax A combined system of tax and benefits. As people earn more, they gradually lose their benefits until beyond a certain level they begin paying taxes.

CASE STUDIES AND APPLICATIONS

will become eligible to receive payments and this in turn may reduce their work incentives. For example, it may be deter a household member from working more hours and/or applying for a better job if the resulting increase in family income reduces the entitlement to benefits. A lower taper rate will also increase the cost of the policy to the government and hence the need for higher tax rates elsewhere to finance the scheme.

One problem with the legacy system is that different benefits have different income thresholds and different taper rates. For example, although WTC and CTC have the same taper rate (41 per cent), the thresholds at which entitlement declines vary. In 2021/22 this was £6656 for WTC and £16 480 for CTC. Housing Benefit has a 65 per cent taper for any earnings that exceed the amount received in non-work benefits. This system is complex and difficult for people to understand. It could significantly weaken the work incentives for some individuals if their eligibility for two or more different benefits fell simultaneously as their earnings increased.

UC tries to address this issue by reducing claimants' total benefit payments at a rate of 63 per cent once their income exceeds the *worker allowance*. This single taper system may also make it easier for people to see the potential financial advantages of working.

Other arguments for Universal Credit

- By removing eligibility based on the number of hours worked (i.e. 16 and 30 hours with WTCs), it eradicates a needless distortion from the legacy system.
- It simplifies the process of claiming benefits for applicants who no longer have to make multiple applications to different government departments. It also reduces the administration costs for government: only one government department (Department for Work and Pensions) manages the process, and uses online systems to do so.
- By combining in-work and out-of-work benefits into one system, it makes the administrative process much simpler for claimants who move between unemployment and work.

Criticisms of Universal Credit

- The roll out has been beset by technical issues and delays. According to the original timetable, all 8 million claimants on the legacy system were supposed to have moved over to UC by October 2017. In reality, the figure was just 540 000. After another series of delays, a new target date was set for September 2024.
- The design of the benefit system was supposed to be similar to a working environment, where employees receive pay on a monthly basis and in arrears (i.e. after they have worked for a month). This means that new UC applicants have to wait five weeks after their initial application before receiving any payments. Many claimants struggle financially during this five-week period. Applicants can apply for monetary advances but these have to be repaid via reductions in subsequent UC payments.
- The assessment for UC payments is made on a monthly basis. This can cause issues if in-work claimants receive pay on a weekly basis: they may have four paydays in some months and five in others. This can cause significant fluctuations in monthly benefits payments that make it difficult for people to manage their finances.
- UC payments are made with certain conditionality requirements, which include work search activities and/or attending regular interviews at job centres. If claimants do not meet these conditionality requirements, then benefit payments can be reduced. Some people[4] have argued that the current system is overly harsh.
- The persistently poor (defined as those with average incomes in the lowest decile over an 8-year period) lose on average 1.1 per cent (£100) per annum.[5]

(continued)

1. ***Economists sometimes refer to an 'unemployment trap'. People are discouraged from taking work in the first place. Explain how such a 'trap' arises. Does Universal Credit create an unemployment trap? What are the best ways of eliminating, or at least reducing, the unemployment trap?***
2. ***Universal Credit involves a single monthly payment direct to the claimant's bank account. This replaces fortnightly payments, some in the form of cashable cheques, and rent payments direct to landlords. What additional support might claimants need under this system?***

Conduct desktop research to investigate how a sample of other European economies provide support for families on low incomes. What are the key similarities or differences of these systems?

1 The term 'tax credit' is a little misleading as people do not need to be paying tax in order to receive the benefit. It is not the same thing as tax relief.
2 Policies to support the incomes of poorer working families date back to 1971 with the introduction of the Family Income Supplement.
3 This excludes the temporary £20 per week uplift to Universal Credit until September 2021.
4 *Universal Credit isn't working: proposals for reform*, House of Lords Economic Affairs Committee (July 2020), https://publications.parliament.uk/pa/ld5801/ldselect/ldeconaf/105/105.pdf
5 Universal Credit and its impact on household incomes: the long and the short of it', *IFS Briefing Note BN248*, Institute for Fiscal Studies (April 2019), https://ifs.org.uk/publications/14083

are normative questions, and ones that an economist cannot answer. They are moral and political questions. Unfortunately there is no mechanism for measuring the 'utility' gained by the poor and lost by the rich so that any net gain from redistribution can be weighed up against lost output. For example, the benefit that a person receives from a cooker or an electric fire cannot be measured in 'utils' or any other 'psychic unit'. What people are prepared to pay for the items is no guide either, since a poor person obviously cannot afford to pay nearly as much as a rich person, and yet will probably get the same if not more personal benefit from them.

Section summary

1. Government intervention in the economy through taxation and government expenditure has a number of purposes including redistribution, the correction of market distortions and macroeconomic stabilisation.
2. There are various requirements of a good tax system, including horizontal and vertical equity; payment according to the amount of benefit received; being cheap to collect, difficult to evade, non-distortionary and convenient to the taxpayer and the government; and having the minimum disincentive effects.
3. Taxes can be divided into those paid directly to the authorities (direct taxes: e.g. income tax) and those paid via a middle person (indirect taxes: e.g. VAT).
4. Taxes can be categorised as progressive, regressive or proportional. Progressive taxes have the effect of reducing inequality. The more steeply progressive they are, the bigger is the reduction in inequality.
5. There are various limitations to using taxes to redistribute incomes. First, they cannot on their own increase the incomes of the poor. (Cutting taxes, however, can help the poor if the cuts are carefully targeted.) Second, high taxes on the rich may encourage evasion or avoidance. Third, higher income taxes on the rich will probably lead to their employers paying higher (gross) wages.
6. Using indirect taxes to redistribute incomes involves costs of resource reallocation.
7. Raising taxes has two effects on the amount that people wish to work. On the one hand, people will be encouraged to work more in order to maintain their incomes. This is the income effect. On the other hand, they will be encouraged to substitute leisure for income (i.e. to work less), since an hour's leisure now costs less in forgone income. This is the substitution effect. The relative size of the income and substitution effects will depend on the nature of the tax change. The substitution effect of a tax rise is more likely to outweigh the income effect for those with few commitments, for people just above the tax threshold and in cases where the highest rates of tax are increased.
8. Benefits can be cash benefits or benefits in kind. Means-tested cash benefits include support for poor families and for low-paid people. Universal benefits include state pensions and child benefit. Benefits in kind include health care, education and free school meals.
9. Means-tested benefits can be specifically targeted to those in need and are thus more 'cost effective'. However, there can be serious problems with such benefits, including limited take-up, some relatively needy people falling just outside the qualifying limit, and inadequate account being taken of all relevant circumstances affecting a person's needs.
10. The poverty trap occurs when the combination of increased taxes and reduced benefits removes the incentive for poor people to earn more. The more steeply progressive this combined system is at low incomes, the bigger is the disincentive effect.

BOX 11.6 WHAT THE FUTURE HOLDS

CASE STUDIES AND APPLICATIONS

The relative income of pensioners in the UK

For many years, the average income of pensioners fell relative to that of the working-age population. The value of the basic state pension as a percentage of average full-time earnings fell from a peak of 26 per cent in 1979 to 16 per cent in 2000. This was due to the decision in 1980 to abolish the link between pensions and average earnings.

There was particular public outrage in 1999 when the government announced a 1.1 per cent increase in the state pension at a time when average earnings were rising by 4.6 per cent. In 2001/2, weekly incomes in average pensioner households were £70 below those in average households of people of working age. Nearly 3 million pensioners were living in poverty. The government responded by introducing more generous means-tested benefits for pensioners as well as a number of universal benefits, such as free bus travel and winter fuel allowances.

The situation began to change in the mid-2000s when average pensioner incomes began to rise more rapidly than those of working-age families. After adjusting income for differences in housing costs, a report[1] found that median pensioner income was actually higher than the equivalent figure for people of working age between 2011 and 2015.

Intergenerational equity

These recent trends lead to a greater focus on questions of equity between different generations. To what extent should companies and wage earners be the key beneficiaries of economic growth? Is it socially more desirable to spread the gains across all age groups?

Some factors in the past 20 years have had varying effects on the different generations. For example, low and negative real interest rates after 2008 had an adverse impact on the living standards of many pensioners who rely on income from savings and personal pensions. At the same time, many younger people with mortgages and other debts had their living standards boosted by this approach to monetary policy.

However, many pensioners benefited from generous final salary pension schemes and rising house prices. This helped them to build up substantial levels of wealth and so have comfortable retirements. Younger generations, in contrast, have to pay university tuition fees, face much higher house prices and have seen the closure of many of the most generous final salary pension schemes.

Another negative impact on people of working age has been the long-run effect of the 2008 recession on the growth in earnings. In April 2019, real median weekly earnings were still 2 per cent below their level in April 2008. Prior to 2007, real average earnings grew at between 1.5 and 2 per cent per year. If this growth had continued post 2008 then median earnings in 2021 would have been £28 000 as opposed to the actual figure of £24 000.

The impact of changes to the tax and benefit system

Changes to the tax and benefit system introduced between 2010 and 2019[2] led to working-age families with children experiencing the largest proportional losses in income. The impact was particularly strong on lower income groups. At the same time, the government introduced the so-called 'triple lock' on state pensions in 2010. This policy means that the state pension increases by whichever one of the following is greatest – the increase in average earnings, the increase in the consumer price index, or 2.5 per cent.

When the 'triple lock' was first introduced, the expectation was that in most years the increase in average earnings would be the largest of the three figures. However, because of the historically low increases in pay after 2009, this was only the case on three occasions between 2011/12 and 2021/22. The increase in the basic state pension over this period was 10.3 per cent higher than it would have been if it had risen in line with average earnings. This faster growth means that, as a percentage of full-time earnings, the state pension has increased from 17 to 19 per cent. However, the benefit cost taxpayers £7.9 billion (8 per cent) more in 2021/22 than if it had risen in line with average earnings.

In 2021/22, the basic state pension was £137.60. However, many pensioners receive income from other sources. For example, in 2018/19, 61 per cent of pensioners received investment income, while 60 per cent received earnings from an occupational pension scheme. The average income of all pensioners was £320, whereas for pensioner couples it was £474. In 1994/95, 38 per cent of pensioners were in the top half of the overall income distribution. This increased to 50 per cent in 2018/19.[3]

The impact of COVID-19

The impact of COVID-19 on the labour market has brought the issue of intergenerational equity into even greater focus. By March 2021, 11.4 million jobs had been furloughed through the government's Job Retention Scheme, with younger people aged 25–34 the group most affected. Also, those under the age of 25 were much more likely to lose their jobs than other groups. At the same time, with average earnings falling by 1 per cent in the three months to July 2020 and a CPI figure of 0.5 per cent, the state pension increased by 2.5 per cent in 2021/22.

1. *What polices has the UK government introduced to encourage people of working age to save more for their future retirement?*
2. *Previous UK governments have used universal benefits, such as winter fuel allowances and free bus travel, as part of their approach to eliminating pensioner poverty. What are the advantages (and disadvantages) of this approach?*
3. *If you could find out, with some associated probability, when you might die, would you choose to find out? How might the answer affect the way you live today?*

1 Adam Corlett, *As Time Goes By: Shifting incomes and inequality between and within generations*, Resolution Foundation and Intergenerational Commission (February 2017), www.resolutionfoundation.org/app/uploads/2017/02/IC-intra-gen.pdf

2 Pascale Bourquin, Agnes Norris Keiller and Tom Waters, 'The distributional impact of personal tax and benefit reforms, 2010 to 2019', *IFS Briefing Note BN270*, Institute for Fiscal Studies (December 2019), www.ifs.org.uk/uploads/BN270-The-distributional-impact-of-personal-tax-and-benefit-reforms-v2.pdf

3 *'Pensioners' Incomes Series: An analysis of trends in Pensioner Incomes: 1994/95 to 2018/19*, DWP (March 2020), https://www.gov.uk/government/statistics/pensioners-incomes-series-financial-year-2018-to-2019

END OF CHAPTER QUESTIONS

1. Using the data shown on the pie charts in Figure 11.1, construct two Lorenz curves (on the same diagram), corresponding to the before- and after-tax income figures. Interpret and comment on the diagram you have drawn.
2. Can taxes be used to relieve poverty?
3. In what ways might the views of different politicians on what constitutes a 'good' tax system conflict?
4. Distinguish between proportional, progressive and regressive taxation. Could a progressive tax have a constant marginal rate?
5. Consider the cases for and against a poll tax.
6. Under what circumstances would a rise in income tax act as (a) a disincentive and (b) an incentive to effort?
7. What is meant by the poverty trap? What design of benefit system would offer the best solution to the problem of the poverty trap?
8. How would you go about deciding whether person A or person B gets more personal benefit from each of the following: (a) an electric fire; (b) a clothing allowance of £x; (c) free higher education; (d) child benefit? Do your answers help you in deciding how best to allocate benefits?
9. Just under 2 million pensioners were identified as living in poverty in the UK in 2020. In the same year it was estimated that the total property wealth of pensioner households had grown to a record high of £1.133 trillion. What does this imply about inequality and poverty?

Online resources

Additional case studies on the student website

11.1 How can we define poverty? This examines different definitions of poverty and, in particular, distinguishes between absolute and relative measures of poverty.

11.2 Adam Smith's maxims of taxation. This looks at the principles of a good tax system as identified by Adam Smith.

11.3 Taxation in the UK. This case study looks at the various types of tax in the UK. It gives the current tax rates and considers how progressive the system is.

11.4 The poll tax. This case charts the introduction of the infamous poll tax (or 'community charge') in the UK and its subsequent demise.

11.5 The system of benefits in the UK. A description of the various benefits used in the UK and their redistributive effects.

11.6 Negative income tax and redistribution. How effectively can a negative income tax redistribute income without causing adverse incentive effects?

11.7 The squeezed middle. What have been the effects on people on 'middle incomes' of attempts by successive governments to support poor families?

11.8 Increased life expectancy. This examines the likely future impact on individuals and economies of people living longer.

Websites relevant to Chapters 10 and 11

Numbers and section refer to websites listed in the Web Appendix and hotlinked from this book's website at **go.pearson.com/uk/sloman.**

- For news articles relevant to this and the previous chapter, see the *Economics News* section on the student website.
- For general news on labour markets, see websites in section A, and particularly A1, 2, 4, 5 and 7. See also 40 and 41 for links to economics news articles from newspapers worldwide.
- For data on labour markets, see links in B1, especially to the National Statistics site. Also see B18, B19 and H3. For international data on labour markets, see the ILO datasets in the ESDS International site (B35) (you will need to log in, available free to all students in UK higher education).
- For information on international labour standards and employment rights, see site H3.
- Links to the TUC and Confederation of British Industry sites can be found at E32 and 33.
- For information on poverty and the redistribution of income, see B18; E9, 13, 30, 31, 36; G5, 13; H3.
- For student resources relevant to these two chapters, see sites C1–10, 19, 28.
- For simulations and for information and various articles on the labour market see site D3.

Markets, Efficiency and the Public Interest

CHAPTER MAP

In Chapter 11 we examined the problem of inequality. In this chapter we turn to examine another major area of concern. This is the question of the efficiency (or inefficiency) of markets in allocating resources.

First we show how a perfect market economy could under certain conditions lead to 'social efficiency'. In section 12.2 we examine the real world and show how real-world markets fail to meet social goals. These failures provide the major arguments in favour of government intervention in a market economy. We then turn to discuss the alternative ways in which a government can intervene to correct these various market failings.

If the government is to replace the market and provide goods and services directly, it will need some way of establishing their costs and benefits. Section 12.4 looks at 'cost–benefit analysis'. This is a means of establishing the desirability of a public project such as a new motorway or a new hospital. Finally, in section 12.5, we look at the case for restricting government intervention. We examine the advantages of real-world markets and the drawbacks of government intervention.

12.1 EFFICIENCY UNDER PERFECT COMPETITION

Perfect competition has been used by many economists and policy makers as an ideal against which to compare the benefits and shortcomings of real-world markets.

As was shown in Chapter 7, perfect competition has various advantages for society. Under perfect competition, firms' supernormal profits are competed away in the long run by the entry of new competitors. As a result, firms are forced to produce at the bottom of their average cost curves. What is more, the fear of being driven out of business by the entry of new firms forces existing firms to try to find lower-cost methods of production, thus shifting their *AC* curves downwards.

Perhaps the most wide-reaching claim for perfect competition is that under certain conditions it will lead to a *socially efficient* use of a nation's resources.

Social efficiency: 'Pareto optimality'

If it were possible to make changes in the economy – changes in the combination of goods produced or consumed, or changes in the combination of inputs used – and if these changes benefited some people without anyone else being made worse off, economists would describe this as an *improvement in social efficiency*, or a ***Pareto improvement***, after Vilfredo Pareto, the Italian social scientist (see Case Study 12.1 on the student website).

Do you agree that, if some people gain and if no one loses, then this constitutes an 'improvement' in the well-being of society? Does it depend who gains? Would it be possible to improve the well-being of society without a Pareto improvement?

When all Pareto improvements have been made – in other words, when any additional changes in the economy would benefit some people only by making others worse off – the economy is said to be ***socially efficient***, or Pareto optimal. What we shall show is that under certain conditions a perfect market will lead to ***Pareto optimality***.

But a word of caution. Just because social efficiency is achieved in a particular market environment, it does not necessarily make that environment *ideal*. It may be a *necessary* condition for an ideal allocation of resources that all Pareto improvements are made. It is not *sufficient*, however. If, for example, the government redistributed income from the rich to the poor, there would be no Pareto improvement, since the rich would lose. Thus both an equal and a highly unequal distribution of income could be Pareto optimal, and yet it could be argued that a more equal distribution is socially more desirable. For the moment, however, we will ignore questions of fairness and just focus on social efficiency.

So why may a perfect market lead to social efficiency? The following sections explain.

The simple analysis of social efficiency: marginal benefit and marginal cost

Remember how we defined 'rational' choices. A rational person will choose to do an activity if the gain from so doing exceeds any sacrifice involved. In other words, whether as a producer, a consumer or a worker, a person will gain by expanding any activity whose marginal benefit (*MB*) exceeds its marginal cost (*MC*) and by contracting any activity whose marginal cost exceeds its marginal benefit. Remember that when economists use the term 'cost', they are referring to 'opportunity cost': in other words, the *sacrifice* of alternatives. Thus when we say that the marginal benefit of an activity is greater than its marginal cost, we mean that the additional benefit gained exceeds any sacrifice in terms of alternatives forgone.

Thus the economist's rule for ***rational economic behaviour*** is that a person should expand or contract the level of any activity until its marginal benefit is equal to its marginal cost. At that point, the person will be acting efficiently in his or her own private interest. Only when $MB = MC$ can no further gain be made. This is known as a situation of ***private efficiency***.

By analogy, *social* efficiency will be achieved where, for any activity, the marginal benefit to *society* (*MSB*) is equal to the marginal (opportunity) cost to *society* (*MSC*).

$$MSB = MSC$$

Allocative efficiency (simple formulation) **in any activity is achieved where marginal benefit equals marginal cost. Private efficiency is achieved where marginal private benefit equals marginal private cost ($MB = MC$). Social efficiency is achieved where marginal social benefit equals marginal social cost ($MSB = MSC$).**

Definitions

Pareto improvement Where changes in production or consumption can make at least one person better off without making anyone worse off.

Social efficiency A situation of Pareto optimality. A situation of allocative efficiency after taking into account all externalities.

Pareto optimality Where all possible Pareto improvements have been made: where, therefore, it is impossible to make anyone better off without making someone else worse off.

Rational economic behaviour Doing more of those activities whose marginal benefit exceeds their marginal cost and doing less of those activities whose marginal cost exceeds their marginal benefit.

Private efficiency Where a person's marginal benefit from a given activity equals the marginal cost.

But why is social efficiency (i.e. Pareto optimality) achieved at this point? If *MSB* were greater than *MSC*, there would be a Pareto improvement if there were an increase in the activity. For example, if the benefits to consumers from additional production of a good exceed the cost to producers, the consumers could fully meet the cost of production in the price they pay, and so no producer loses, and yet there would still be a net gain to consumers. Thus society has gained. Likewise if *MSC* were greater than *MSB*, society would gain from a decrease in production.

Economists argue that under certain circumstances the achievement of *private* efficiency will result in *social* efficiency also. Two major conditions have to be fulfilled, however:

- There must be *perfect competition* throughout the economy. This is examined in the following sections.
- There must be ***no externalities***. Externalities are additional costs or benefits of production or consumption experienced by people other than the producers and consumers directly involved in the transaction. They are sometimes referred to as spillover or third-party costs or benefits. Pollution is an example. It is a cost that society experiences from production, but it is not a cost that the individual producer has to pay. In the *absence* of externalities, the only costs or benefits to society are the ones that the individual producer or consumer experiences: i.e. marginal social benefit (*MSB*) is the same as marginal private benefit (*MB*), and marginal social cost (*MSC*) is the same as marginal private cost (*MC*).

To understand just how social efficiency is achieved, we must look at how people maximise their interests through the market.

Achieving social efficiency through the market

Consumption: MU = P

The marginal benefit to a consumer from the consumption of any good is its marginal utility. The marginal cost is the price the consumer has to pay.

As demonstrated in section 4.1, the 'rational' consumer will maximise consumer surplus where $MU = P$: in other words, where the marginal benefit from consumption is equal to the marginal cost of consumption. Do you remember the case of Tanya and her purchases of petrol? (See page 108.) She goes on making additional journeys and hence buying extra petrol as long as she feels that the journeys are worth the money she has to spend: in other words, as long as the marginal benefit she gets from buying extra petrol (its marginal utility to her) exceeds its marginal cost (its price). She will stop buying extra petrol when its marginal utility has fallen (the law of diminishing marginal utility) to equal its price. At that point, her consumer surplus is maximised: she has an 'efficient' level of consumption.

KI 13 p105

Figure 12.1 Maximum total surplus under perfect competition

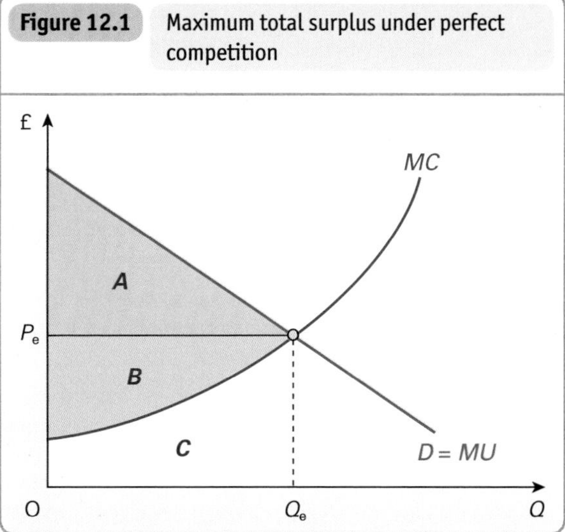

Assume that the price of a good falls. How will an 'efficient' level of consumption be restored?

As we have seen, an individual's consumer surplus is maximised at the output where $MU = P$. With all consumers doing this, and all facing the same market price, their collective consumer surplus will be maximised. This is illustrated in Figure 12.1. Consumers' total utility is given by the area under the demand (*MU*) curve (areas $A + B + C$). Consumers' total expenditure is $P \times Q$ (areas $B + C$). Consumer surplus is the difference between total utility and total expenditure: in other words, the area between the price and the demand curve (area *A*).

Production: P=MC

The marginal benefit to a producer from the production of any good is its marginal revenue (which under perfect competition will be the same as the price of the good). As demonstrated in section 6.6, the 'rational' firm will maximise its profit where its marginal revenue (i.e. the price under conditions of perfect competition) is equal to its marginal cost of production. This is the same thing as saying that it will produce where the marginal benefit from production is equal to the marginal cost from production.

Profit is the excess of total revenue over total costs. A related concept is that of ***total producer surplus (TPS)***.

Definitions

Externalities Costs or benefits of production or consumption experienced by people *other* than the producers and consumers directly involved in the transaction. They are sometimes referred to as 'spillover' or 'third-party' costs or benefits.

Total producer surplus Total revenue minus total variable costs ($TR - TVC$): in other words, total profit plus total fixed costs ($T\Pi + TFC$).

THRESHOLD CONCEPT 10 **GENERAL EQUILIBRIUM** THINKING LIKE AN ECONOMIST

When all markets are in balance

In previous chapters we have been looking at individual markets: goods markets and factor markets. But any change in one market is likely to have repercussions in other markets. And changes in these other markets will probably affect other markets, and so on.

The point about a market economy is that it is like an interconnected web. Understanding these connections helps us understand the concept of an 'economy'.

If we started with an economy where all markets were in equilibrium, we would have a state of ***general equilibrium***. Then let's assume that a change occurs in just one market – say a rise in oil prices resulting from increased demand from China and other rapidly growing newly industrialised countries. This will have knock-on effects throughout the economy. Costs, and hence prices, will rise in oil-consuming industries. Consumption will fall for the products of these industries and rise for substitute products which do not use oil, or use less of it. Some motorists will be encouraged to use public transport or cycle. This could have knock-on effects on the demand for houses, with people choosing to live nearer to their work. This could then have effects on the various parts of the construction industry. You can work out some of these effects for yourself.

You will quickly see that a single change in one industry can set off a chain reaction throughout the economy. If there is just the one initial change, things will settle to a new general equilibrium where all markets are back in balance with demand equal to supply. In practice, of course, economic 'shocks' are occurring all the time and thus the economy is in a constant state of flux with no stable general equilibrium.

The concept of general equilibrium is a *threshold concept* because it gives us an insight into how market forces apply to a *whole* economy, and not just to its individual parts. It is about seeing how the whole jigsaw fits together and how changes ripple throughout the economy.

Many other subjects use the concept of general equilibrium. Take meteorology. We could study a single weather system, such as a low pressure area or a cold front. But, to make sense of the development and movement of such systems, we need to see them as part of a bigger picture: as part of the whole world's weather system, which at any time is moving towards a general equilibrium in response to various changes.

For instance, in the short term, we can see how weather systems respond to the changing seasons: for example, how pressure systems move northwards in the northern hemisphere summer. In the longer term, we could model how world weather systems will respond to climate change. Will the resulting general equilibrium be one where sea levels rise; where the Gulf Stream is turned off, with much of north-western Europe becoming colder; where the deserts of north Africa spread to southern Europe; and so on?

But in economics, understanding general equilibrium is not just about understanding and predicting the output of the various industries that make up the economy. It can help us make value judgements and formulate policy. As we shall see in Threshold Concept 11 (see page 361), under certain conditions, general equilibrium can be seen as *socially efficient*. These conditions are (a) perfect competition and (b) an absence of externalities.

If social efficiency is seen as desirable, then one policy implication might be to try to make markets as perfect as possible and to 'internalise' externalities. In this chapter we examine whether such policies should be adopted and, if so, what form should they take?

1. *If general equilibrium is achieved when all markets have responded to a change and its knock-on effects, and if such changes are constantly occurring, will general equilibrium actually be achieved? Does your answer have any implications for policy?*
2. *If social efficiency is seen as desirable (a normative issue), should policy always be geared to achieving this?*

Definition

General equilibrium Where all the millions of markets throughout the economy are in a simultaneous state of equilibrium.

This is the excess of total revenue over total *variable* costs: $TPS = TR - TVC$. In other words, total producer surplus is total profit plus fixed costs: $TPS = T\Pi + TFC$. But since there are no marginal fixed costs (by definition), both producer surplus and profit will be maximised at the same output.

Total producer surplus for all firms in the market is shown in Figure 12.1. Total revenue (i.e. total expenditure) is $P \times Q$ (areas $B + C$). Total variable cost is the area under the MC curve (area C): i.e. it is the sum of all the marginal costs of each unit produced. Producer surplus is thus the area between the price and the MC curve (area B).

Private efficiency in the market: MU = MC

In Figure 12.1, both consumer surplus and producer surplus are maximised at output Q_e. This is the equilibrium output under perfect competition. Thus, under perfect competition, the market will ensure that ***total surplus*** (areas $A + B$),

Definition

Total (private) surplus Total consumer surplus ($TU - TE$) plus total producer surplus ($TR - TVC$).

sometimes called ***total private surplus***, is maximised. At this output, $MU = P = MC$.

At any output other than Q_e total surplus will be less. If output were below Q_e, then MU would be above MC: total surplus would be increased by producing more. If output were above Q_e, then MU would be below MC: total surplus would be increased by producing less.

Social efficiency in the market: MSB = MSC

KI 28 p356

Provided the two conditions of (a) perfect competition and (b) the absence of externalities are fulfilled, Pareto optimality (i.e. social efficiency) will be achieved. Let us take each condition in turn.

Perfect competition. Perfect competition will ensure that private efficiency is achieved:

$$MU = MC \text{ (for all producers and all consumers)}$$

No externalities. In the absence of externalities, $MSB = MU$ (i.e. the benefits of consumption within society are confined to the direct consumers) and $MSC = MC$ (i.e. the costs of production to society are simply the costs paid by the producers). Thus

$$MSB = MU = P = MC = MSC$$

i.e.

$$MSB = MSC$$

With no externalities, the total surplus shown in Figure 12.1 will represent ***total social surplus***.

Inefficiency would arise if (a) competition were not perfect and so marginal revenue were *not* equal to price and as a result marginal cost were not equal to price; or (b) there were externalities and hence either marginal social benefit were different from marginal utility (i.e. marginal *private* benefit) or marginal social cost were different from marginal (private) cost. We examine such 'market failures' in section 12.2.

1. *If monopoly power existed in an industry, would production be above or below the socially efficient level (assuming no externalities)? Which would be greater, MSB or P?*
2. *Assuming perfect competition and no externalities, social efficiency will also be achieved in factor markets. Demonstrate that this will be where*

$$MSB_f = MRP_f = P_f = MDU_f = MSC_f$$

(where MRP is the marginal revenue product of a factor, MDU is the marginal disutility of supplying it, and f is any factor – see section 10.1).

3. *Why will marginal social benefit not equal marginal social costs in the labour market if there exists (a) union monopoly power and/or (b) firms with monopsony power?*

Definition

Total social surplus Total benefits to society from consuming a good minus total costs to society from producing it. In the absence of externalities, total social surplus is the same as total (private) surplus.

Interdependence, efficiency and the 'invisible hand': the simple analysis of general equilibrium

If there is perfect competition and an absence of externalities throughout the economy, then the whole economy, when in equilibrium, will be socially efficient. A state of general Pareto optimality will exist.

No economy, however, is static. Conditions of demand and supply are constantly changing. Tastes change, technology changes and so on. Thus old patterns of consumption and production will cease to be Pareto optimal. Nevertheless, provided there is perfect competition and no externalities, forces will come into play to restore Pareto optimality.

In this perfect market economy, Pareto optimality is restored not by government action, but rather by the individual actions of producers, consumers and factor owners all seeking their own self-interest. It is as if an 'invisible hand' were working to guide the economy towards social efficiency (see Box 1.5).

KI 5 p21

The economic system will respond to any change in demand or supply by a whole series of subsequent changes in various interdependent markets. Social efficiency will thereby be restored. The whole process can be illustrated with a diagram showing the circular flow of income (see Figure 12.2).

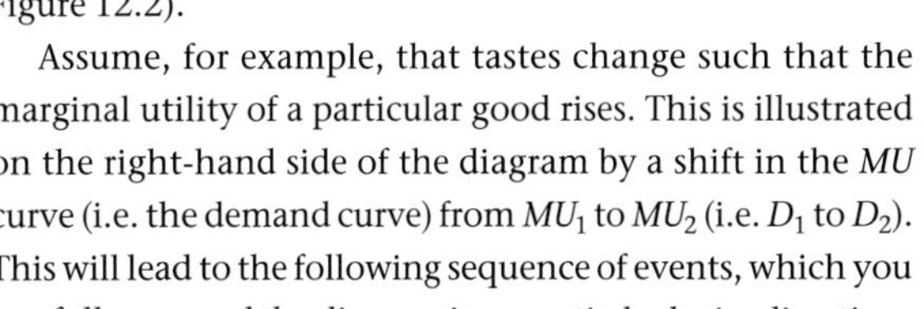

Assume, for example, that tastes change such that the marginal utility of a particular good rises. This is illustrated on the right-hand side of the diagram by a shift in the MU curve (i.e. the demand curve) from MU_1 to MU_2 (i.e. D_1 to D_2). This will lead to the following sequence of events, which you can follow round the diagram in an anti-clockwise direction.

Consumer demand

The rise in marginal utility (i.e. the rise in marginal social benefit of the good, MSB_g) leads to increased consumption. The resulting shortage will drive up the market price.

Producer supply

The rise in the market price will mean that price is now above the marginal (social) cost of production. It will thus be profitable for firms to increase their production. This in turn will lead to an increase in marginal cost (a movement up along the marginal cost curve) due to diminishing returns. There is a movement up along the supply curve from point *a*. Price will continue to rise until equilibrium is reached at P_2Q_2 (point *b*), where $MSB_{g_2} = MSC_g$.

Factor demand

The rise in the price of the good will lead to an increase in the marginal revenue product of factors that are employed in producing the good. The reason for this is that the marginal *revenue* product of a factor is its marginal *physical* product

Figure 12.2 The interdependence of goods and factor markets

(3) Factor demand
£
Factor services
(2) Producer supply
£
Goods
P
$S = MDU_f = MSC_f$
P_{f_2}
P_{f_1}
d
c
$D_2 = MRP_{f_2} = MSB_{f_2}$
$D_1 = MRP_{f_1} = MSB_{f_1}$
O Q_{f_1} Q_{f_2} Q
P
$S = MC = MSC_g$
P_2
P_1
b
a
$D_2 = MU_2 = MSB_g$
$D_1 = MU_1 = MSB_{g_1}$
O Q_1 Q_2 Q
Factor services
£
(4) Factor supply
Goods
£
(1) Consumer demand

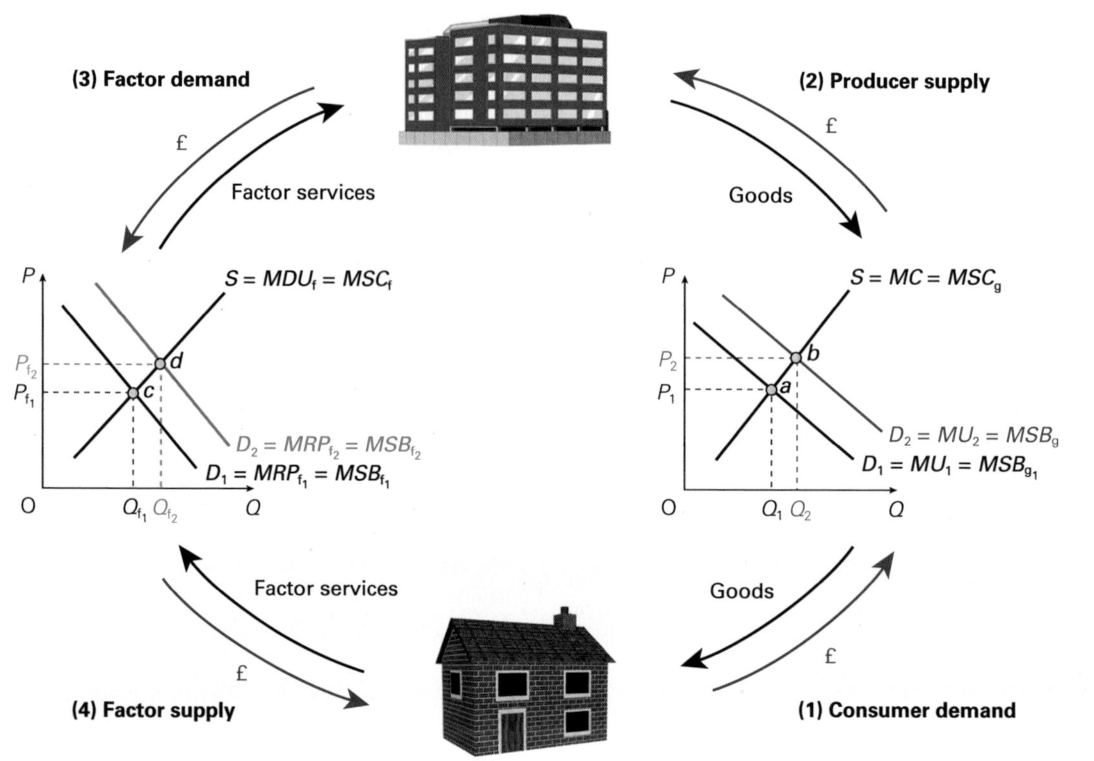

multiplied by the *price* of the good (see section 10.1). The marginal physical product is unchanged, but since the price of the good has now gone up, the output of factors will be worth correspondingly more. The following takes just one factor (f) as an example.

A rise in the value of the factor's output (due to the higher price of the good) will make its marginal revenue product higher than its marginal cost to the firm. This will increase the demand for the factor. Factor demand shifts to D_2 ($= MRP_{f_2} = MSB_{f_2}$). This in turn will drive up the price of the factor.

Factor supply

The rise in the price of the factor will raise the marginal benefit of supplying it (and hence the marginal social benefit). This will mean that the marginal benefit now exceeds the marginal cost (the marginal disutility, MDU_f) of supplying the factor. There is thus a movement up along the factor supply curve from point *c* as more units of the factor are supplied. The price of the factor will continue to rise until equilibrium is reached at $P_{f_2}Q_{f_2}$ (point *d*), where $MSB_{f_2} = MSC_f$.

The process of adjustment does not end here. If supernormal profits are made, new firms will enter. Similarly, if factor rewards are supernormal, new factors will be attracted from other industries. This in turn will affect prices and hence quantities in *other* industries in both goods and factor markets.

In other words, a single change in tastes will create a ripple effect throughout the economy, through a whole series of interdependent markets. Eventually, long-run equilibrium will be restored with $MSB = MSC$ in all markets. The economy has returned to a position of Pareto optimality. And all this has taken place with no government intervention. It is the 'invisible hand' of the market that has achieved this state of social efficiency.

These arguments form a central part of the neoclassical case for laissez-faire: the philosophy of non-intervention by the government. Under ideal conditions, it is argued, the free pursuit of individual self-interest will lead to the social good. Since intervention is always associated with costs, the neoclassical case says that the optimal approach is to allow this move to the social good to take place, unimpeded.

1. *Trace through the effects in both factor and goods markets of the following: (a) an increase in the productivity of a particular type of labour; (b) an increase in the supply of a particular factor.*
2. *Show in each case how social efficiency will initially be destroyed and then how market adjustments will restore social efficiency.*

The following pages examine social efficiency in more detail. You may omit these and skip straight to section 12.2 (page 364) if you want to.

THRESHOLD CONCEPT 11 ALLOCATIVE EFFICIENCY: PRIVATE AND SOCIAL

THINKING LIKE AN ECONOMIST

Economics is concerned with the allocation of scarce resources. Whenever choices are made, whether by consumers, firms, the government or any other agency, a choice is being made about the allocation of resources.

When you buy a T-shirt costing £10, you are choosing to allocate £10 of your money to the purchase – £10 that could have been spent on something else. But have you allocated your money in the best way?

Similarly, when a firm chooses to produce one product rather than another, or to use technique A rather than some alternative technique, it is choosing to allocate its resources in particular ways. But are these the best ways?

The question is whether the resources have been allocated *efficiently*. We define an efficient allocation of resources as one which brings the maximum benefit for that level of costs. In other words, no gain would be made by reallocating resources in some alternative way. Thus your decision to spend £10 on a T-shirt is an efficient allocation of your resources, if it brings you more benefit (i.e. utility) for the £10 than could any other purchase. The firm's decision to use technique A is an efficient one if it leads to a higher rate of profit: if the marginal benefit (i.e. marginal revenue) relative to the marginal cost is greater than for any other technique.

KI 14 p111

What we are talking about here is 'allocative efficiency'. It is a *threshold concept* because to understand it is to understand how to make the most of scarce resources: and scarcity is the core problem of economics for all of us. It is obvious that poor people on very limited incomes will want to spend their money as efficiently as possible. But even exceedingly rich people, who can buy anything they want, are still likely to have limited time or opportunities.

Allocative efficiency is a threshold concept for another reason. We need to see how it relates to *social* objectives. If people all individually achieve their own *private efficiency*, does this mean that society will have an efficient allocation of resources? The answer is no. The reason is that our decisions often have consequences for *other* people: our actions have external costs and/or benefits. These externalities mean that private efficiency and *social efficiency* diverge. We need to understand how and why, and how social efficiency can be achieved.

Then there is the question of equity. Just because everyone is allocating their resources in the best possible way for them, and even if there were no externalities, it does not follow that the allocation of resources is *fair*. However efficiently rich people spend their money, most people would still argue that it is socially desirable to redistribute part of rich people's income to the poor through the tax and benefit system.

KI 4 p13

1. *Why might consumers not always make efficient consumption decisions?*
2. *Explain the meaning of social efficiency using the concept of Pareto improvements.*

*The intermediate analysis of social efficiency: marginal benefit and marginal cost ratios

In practice, consumers do not consider just one good in isolation. They make choices between goods. Likewise, firms make choices as to which goods to produce and which factors to employ. A more satisfactory analysis of social efficiency, therefore, considers the choices that firms and households make.

Whether as a producer, consumer or worker, a person will gain by expanding activity X relative to activity Y if

$$\frac{MB_X}{MB_Y} > \frac{MC_X}{MC_Y}$$

The reason is straightforward. Activity X is giving a greater benefit relative to its cost than is activity Y. Only when

$$\frac{MB_X}{MB_Y} = \frac{MC_X}{MC_Y}$$

can no further gain be made by switching from the one activity to the other. At this point, people will be acting efficiently in their own private interest.

By analogy, social efficiency is achieved where the social marginal benefit ratio of two goods is equal to the social marginal cost ratio.

Social efficiency (equi-marginal formulation) **is achieved where the marginal social benefit ratios are equal to the marginal social cost ratios for any two alternatives. In the case of two alternatives X and Y, this will be where**

$$\frac{MSB_X}{MSB_Y} = \frac{MSC_X}{MSC_Y}$$

As with the simple analysis of social efficiency, it can be shown that, provided there is perfect competition and no externalities, the achievement of private efficiency will result in social efficiency also. This will be demonstrated in the following sections.

*Efficiency in the goods market (intermediate analysis)

Private efficiency under perfect competition

Consumption. The optimum combination of two goods X and Y consumed for any consumer is where

$$\frac{MU_X}{MU_Y} \text{ (i.e. } MRS) = \frac{P_X}{P_Y}$$

The *marginal rate of substitution in consumption (MRS)* (see page 115) is the amount of good Y that a consumer would be willing to sacrifice for an increase in consumption of good X (i.e. $\Delta Y/\Delta X$). $MRS = MU_X/MU_Y$ since, if X gave twice the marginal utility of Y, the consumer would be prepared to give up two of Y to obtain one of X (i.e. $MRS = 2/1$).

If MU_X/MU_Y were greater than P_X/P_Y, how would consumers behave? What would bring consumption back to equilibrium where $MU_X/MU_Y = P_X/P_Y$?

Production. The optimum combination of two goods X and Y produced for any producer is where

$$\frac{MC_X}{MC_Y} \text{ (i.e. } MRT) = \frac{P_X}{P_Y}$$

The *marginal rate of transformation in production (MRT)* is the amount of good Y that the producer will have to give up producing for an increase in production of good X (i.e. $\Delta Y/\Delta X$) if total costs of production are to remain unchanged. $MRT = MC_X/MC_Y$ since, if the marginal cost of good X were twice that of Y, the firm's costs would remain constant if it gave up producing two of Y in order to produce an extra X (i.e. $MRT = 2/1$).

If MC_X/MC_Y were greater than P_X/P_Y, how would firms behave? What would bring production back into equilibrium where $MC_X/MC_Y = P_X/P_Y$?

Social efficiency under perfect competition

In each of the following three cases, it will be assumed that there are no externalities.

Social efficiency between consumers. If MU_X/MU_Y for person a is greater than MU_X/MU_Y for person b, *both* people would gain if person a gave person b some of good Y in exchange for some of good X. There would be a Pareto improvement. The Pareto optimal distribution of consumption will therefore be where

$$\frac{MU_X}{MU_Y}\text{person a} = \frac{MU_X}{MU_Y}\text{person b} = \frac{MU_X}{MU_Y}\text{person c}\ldots$$

i.e. *MRS* is the same for all consumers.

But this will be achieved *automatically* under perfect competition, since each consumer will consume that combination of goods where $MU_X/MU_Y = P_X/P_Y$ and all consumers face the *same* (market) prices and hence the *same* P_X/P_Y.

Social efficiency between producers. If MC_X/MC_Y for producer g is greater than MC_X/MC_Y for producer h, then if producer g produced relatively more Y and producer h produced relatively more X, the same output could be produced at a lower total cost (i.e. with less resources). There would be a Pareto improvement. The Pareto optimal distribution of production between firms is therefore where

KI 29 p361

$$\frac{MC_X}{MC_Y}\text{producer g} = \frac{MC_X}{MC_Y}\text{producer h} = \frac{MC_X}{MC_Y}\text{producer i}\ldots$$

i.e. *MRT* is the same for all producers.

This too will be achieved *automatically* under perfect competition, since each producer will maximise profits where $MC_X/MC_Y = P_X/P_Y$ and all producers face the *same* (market) prices and hence the *same* P_X/P_Y.

Social efficiency in exchange. If MU_X/MU_Y (i.e. *MRS*) for all consumers is greater than MC_X/MC_Y (i.e. *MRT*) for all producers, then there would be a Pareto improvement if resources were reallocated to produce relatively more X and less Y.

Assume the *MRS* (i.e. $\Delta Y/\Delta X$) = 3/1 and the *MRT* (i.e. $\Delta Y/\Delta X$) = 2/1. Consumers will be prepared to give up three units of Y to obtain one unit of X, and yet producers only have to sacrifice producing two units of Y to produce one unit of X. Thus consumers can pay producers in full for extra units of X they produce and there will still be a net gain to consumers. There has been a Pareto improvement.

The Pareto optimal allocation of resources is where

$$\textit{Social MRS (SMRS)} = \textit{Social MRT (SMRT)}$$

Assuming no externalities, this will be achieved automatically under perfect competition, since (a) with no externalities, social and private marginal rates of substitution will be the same, and similarly social and private marginal rates of transformation will be the same, and (b) P_X/P_Y is the same for all producers and consumers. In other words:

$$SMRS = MRS_{\text{all consumers}} = \frac{MU_X}{MU_Y}\text{all consumers} = \frac{P_X}{P_Y}$$

and

$$SMRT = MRT_{\text{all producers}} = \frac{MC_X}{MC_Y}\text{all producers} = \frac{P_X}{P_Y}$$

i.e.

KI 29 p361

$$SMRS = SMRT$$

Thus the pursuit of private gain, it is argued, has led to the achieving of social efficiency. This is an important conclusion. It is clearly very attractive to people (and to many politicians) to think that, simply by looking after their own interests, social efficiency will thereby be achieved!

This is illustrated graphically in Figure 12.3. A production possibility curve (the red line) shows the various combinations of two goods X and Y that can be produced (see pages 14–16). Its slope is given by $\Delta Y/\Delta X$ and shows how much Y must be given up to produce 1 more of X. Its slope, therefore, is the marginal rate of transformation (*MRT*).

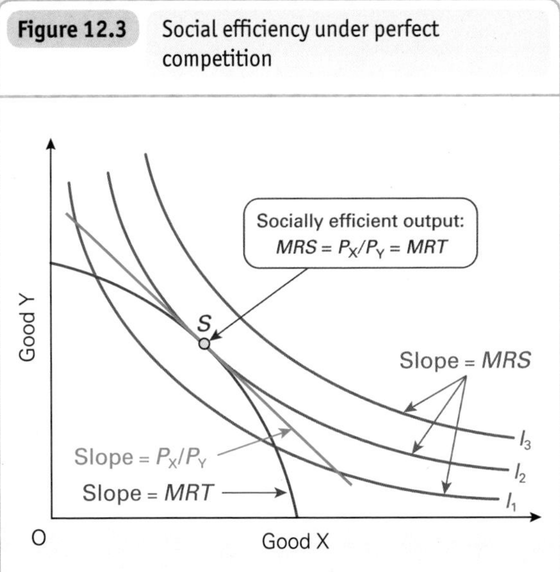

Figure 12.3 Social efficiency under perfect competition

Social indifference curves can be drawn showing the various combinations of X and Y that give particular levels of satisfaction to consumers as a whole. Their slope is given by $\Delta Y/\Delta X$ and shows how much Y consumers are prepared to give up to obtain one more unit of X. Their slope, therefore, is the marginal rate of substitution in consumption (*MRS*).

The Pareto optimal combination of goods is at point *S*, where the production possibility curve is tangential to the highest possible indifference curve. At any other point on the production possibility curve, a lower level of consumer satisfaction is achieved. The slope of the tangent at *S* is equal to both *MRT* and *MRS*, and hence also to P_X/P_Y.

If production were at a point on the production possibility curve below point S, describe the process whereby market forces would return the economy to point S.

*Efficiency in the factor market (intermediate analysis)

A similar analysis can be applied to factor markets, showing that perfect competition and the absence of externalities will lead to efficiency in the use of factors between firms. Assume that there are two factors: labour (*L*) and capital (*K*).

If MPP_L/MPP_K for firm g is greater than MPP_L/MPP_K for firm h, then if firm g were to use relatively more labour and firm h relatively more capital, more could be produced for the same total input. There would be a Pareto improvement.

The Pareto optimum distribution of factors between firms will therefore be where

$$\frac{MPP_l}{MPP_K}\text{firm g} = \frac{MPP_l}{MPP_K}\text{firm h} = \frac{MPP_l}{MPP_K}\text{firm i} \ldots$$

But this will be achieved automatically under perfect competition since, as we saw in section 6.3, each producer will be producing where $MPP_L/MPP_K = P_L/P_K$ and each producer will face the same factor prices and hence P_L/P_K.

Provided there are no externalities, the marginal private benefit of labour to a firm (MPP_L) will equal the marginal social benefit of labour (MSB_L). The same applies to capital. Thus $MPP_L/MPP_K = MSB_L/MSB_K = P_L/P_K$. Similarly on the cost side, if there are no externalities, then $MC_L/MC_K = MSC_L/MSC_K = P_L/P_K$. Therefore:

$$\frac{MSB_L}{MSB_K} = \frac{MSC_L}{MSC_K}$$

KI 29 p361

*The intermediate analysis of general equilibrium

General equilibrium is where equilibrium exists in all markets. Under perfect competition and in the absence of externalities, general equilibrium will give Pareto optimality.

If any change in the conditions of demand or supply occurs, this disequilibrium will automatically create a whole series of interdependent reactions in various markets.

Assume, for example, that tastes change such that MU_X rises and MU_Y falls. This will lead to the following sequence of events in the goods market.

MU_X/MU_Y will now be greater than P_X/P_Y. Thus consumers buy more X relative to Y. This causes MU_X/MU_Y to fall (due to diminishing marginal utility) and P_X/P_Y to rise (due to a relative shortage of X and a surplus of Y), helping to restore equilibrium where $MU_X/MU_Y = P_X/P_Y$. The rise in P_X/P_Y causes P_X/P_Y to be greater than MC_X/MC_Y. Thus firms produce more X relative to Y. This causes MC_X/MC_Y to rise (due to diminishing returns), helping to restore equilibrium where $P_X/P_Y = MC_X/MC_Y$. This process of price and quantity adjustment thus continues until once more

$$\frac{MU_X}{MU_Y} = \frac{P_X}{P_Y} = \frac{MC_X}{MC_Y}$$

Similar adjustments will take place in the factor market. The price of those factors used in producing good X will be bid up and those used in producing Y will be bid down. This will encourage factors to move from industry Y and into industry X. The whole process of adjustment continues until equilibrium and Pareto optimality are restored in all goods and factor markets.

Section summary

1. Social efficiency (Pareto optimality) will be achieved when it is not possible to make anyone better off without making someone else worse off. This will be achieved if people behave 'rationally' under perfect competition providing there are no externalities.
2. Rational behaviour involves doing more of any activity whose marginal benefit (MB) exceeds its marginal cost (MC) and less of any activity whose marginal cost exceeds its marginal benefit. The optimum level of consumption or production for the individual consumer or firm will be where $MB = MC$. This is called a situation of 'private efficiency'.
3. In a perfectly competitive goods market, the consumer will achieve private efficiency where $MU = P$, and the producer where $P = MC$. Thus $MU = MC$. In the absence of externalities, private benefits and costs will equal social benefits and costs. Thus $MU = MSB$ and $MC = MSC$. Thus $MSB = MSC$: a situation of social efficiency (Pareto optimality).
4. Given perfect competition and an absence of externalities, if the equality of marginal benefit and marginal cost is destroyed in any market (by shifts in demand or supply), price adjustments will take place until general equilibrium is restored where $MSB = MSC$ in all markets: a situation of general Pareto optimality.

*5. The rational producer or consumer will choose the combination of any two pairs of goods where their marginal benefit ratio is equal to their marginal cost ratio. Consumers will achieve private efficiency where

$$\frac{MU_X}{MU_Y} \text{ (i.e. } MRS) = \frac{P_X}{P_Y}$$

Producers will achieve private efficiency where

$$\frac{P_X}{P_Y} = \frac{MC_X}{MC_Y} \text{ (i.e. } MRT)$$

Thus:

$$\frac{MU_X}{MU_Y} = \frac{MC_X}{MC_Y}$$

In the absence of externalities, this will give a situation of social efficiency where

$$\frac{MSB_X}{MSB_Y} = \frac{MSC_X}{MSC_Y}$$

*6. Similarly, in factor markets, social efficiency will be achieved if there is perfect competition and an absence of externalities. This will be where the MSB ratio for any two factors is equal to their MSC ratio.

*7. Again assuming perfect competition and an absence of externalities, general equilibrium will be achieved where there is a socially efficient level of production, consumption and exchange in all markets: where the MSB ratio for any pair of goods or factors is equal to the MSC ratio.

12.2 THE CASE FOR GOVERNMENT INTERVENTION

The discussion above considered what happens 'under ideal conditions', but in the real world, markets fail to achieve social efficiency. Part of the problem is the existence of externalities, part is a lack of perfect competition. Even if those were not considerations, we are also faced with markets that may take a long time to adjust to any disequilibrium given short-run immobility of factors. What is more, social efficiency (i.e. Pareto optimality) is not the only economic goal of society. Markets may also fail to the extent that they fail to achieve other objectives such as greater equality and faster growth. In this section we explore the various categories of market failure.

TC3 p26

KEY IDEA 30

Markets generally fail to achieve social efficiency. **There are various types of market failure. Market failures provide one of the major justifications for government intervention in the economy.**

Externalities

Markets tend to work more effectively when either (a) all the benefits and costs are experienced/incurred by the consumers and producers directly involved in the transaction or (b) any impact on third parties happens through the price mechanism. If third parties are affected other than through the market, these effects are known as ***externalities*** and constitute a market failure.

KEY IDEA 31

Externalities are spillover costs or benefits. **Where these exist, even an otherwise perfect market will fail to achieve social efficiency.**

To illustrate (b) above, take the following example. If Apple reduces the price of iPhones, this will reduce the profits of Samsung. A third party (Samsung) not directly involved in the transaction between Apple and its consumers is affected. However, this is not an example of an externality as the impact on Samsung happens indirectly through the price mechanism and Samsung can respond through the market by altering its price or bringing out a new model.

If, however, Apple starts manufacturing iPhones in areas popular with tourists and the production process generates pollution, then this will have a negative impact on businesses in the tourist sector. This negative impact is more

Figure 12.4 Negative externality in production

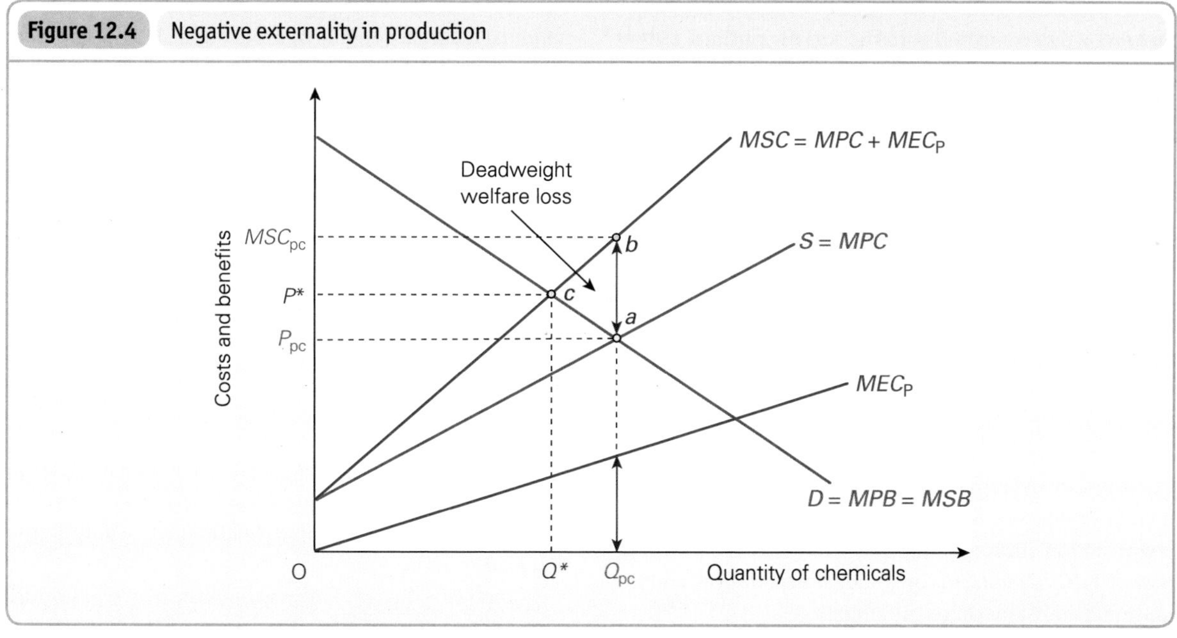

direct and does not happen through the price mechanism. Therefore, it is an example of an externality.[1]

If the direct impact on third parties (i.e. those not directly involved in the transaction) is beneficial, there are said to be ***external benefits***. If the direct impact on third parties is unfavourable, there are said to be ***external costs***.

The full cost to society (the ***social cost***) of the production of any good is the private cost faced by firms plus any externalities of production. Likewise the full benefit to society (the ***social benefit***) from the consumption of any good is the private benefit enjoyed by consumers plus any externalities of consumption.

In the following section, we will consider four different types of externality. (In each case, we will assume that the market is in other respects perfect.)

External costs of production ($MSC > MPC$) with no external costs/benefits of consumption

When a chemical firm dumps waste in a river or pollutes the air, the community bears additional costs to those borne by the firm. There are marginal external costs MEC_P of chemical production. This is illustrated in Figure 12.4. In this example we assume that the external costs begin with the first unit of production and increase at a constant rate.

The marginal *social* cost (*MSC*) of chemical production equals the marginal private costs (*MPC*) plus the MEC_P. This means that the *MSC* curve is above the *MPC* curve. The vertical distance between them is equal to the MEC_P. It is also assumed that there are no externalities in consumption, which means that the marginal social benefit (*MSB*) curve is the same as the marginal private benefit (*MPB*) curve.

Competitive market forces, with producers and consumers responding only to private costs and benefits, will result in a market equilibrium at point *a* in Figure 12.4: i.e. where demand equals supply. The market equilibrium price is P_{pc} while the market equilibrium quantity is Q_{pc}.

At P_{pc}, *MPB* is equal to *MSB*. The market price reflects both the private and social benefits from the last unit consumed. However, the presence of external costs in production means that $MSC > MPC$.

The ***socially optimal output*** would be Q^*, where $P = MSB = MSC$, achieved at the socially optimal price of P^*. This is illustrated at point *c* and clearly shows how external costs of production in a perfectly competitive market result in overproduction: i.e. $Q_{pc} > Q^*$. From society's point of view too much waste is being dumped in rivers.

1 Spillover effects on third parties that take place through the price mechanism are sometimes referred to as 'pecuniary externalities', whereas those that are more direct are called 'technical externalities'. However, we are adopting the more usual definition and not defining these pecuniary effects as externalities.

Definitions

External benefits Benefits from production (or consumption) experienced by people *other* than the producer (or consumer) directly involved in the transaction.

External costs Costs of production (or consumption) borne by people *other* than the producer (or consumer) directly involved in the transaction.

Social cost Private cost plus externalities in production.

Social benefit Private benefit plus externalities in consumption.

Socially optimal or socially efficient output The output where $MSC = MSB$: the output where total social surplus is maximised.

At the market equilibrium (Q_{pc}) there is a ***deadweight welfare loss*** when compared with the socially optimal output (Q^*). In this context, deadweight welfare loss represents the excess of social costs over social benefits at all outputs above Q^*. At Q_{pc}, this is given by the shaded area, *abc*. Put another way, moving from Q_{pc} to Q^* would represent a *gain* in ***social surplus*** of the area *abc*.

One of the reasons why external costs cause problems in a free-market economy is because no one has legal ownership of factors such as the air or rivers., Therefore, nobody has the ability either to prevent or to charge for their use as a dumping ground for waste. Such a 'market' is *missing*. Control must, therefore, be left to the government, local authorities or regulators.

Other examples of external costs of production include extensive use of pesticides in agriculture that damage water quality, global warming caused by CO_2 emissions from power stations/factories, transportation of goods by diesel-powered HGVs adding to congestion and pollution, and the noise and emissions caused by aircraft.

External benefits of production (MSC < MPC) with no external costs/benefits of consumption

If companies in the forestry industry plant new woodlands, there is a benefit not only to the companies themselves, but also to the world through a reduction of CO_2 in the atmosphere (forests are a carbon sink). In this case there are marginal external benefits of production (MEB_P). These are shown in Figure 12.5. We assumed that they begin with the first tree planted but that the marginal benefit declines with each additional tree. In other words, the MEB_P is a downward sloping line.

Why are marginal external benefits typically likely to decline as output increases? Why in some cases might marginal external benefits be constant at all levels of output or even increase as more is produced?

Given these positive externalities, the marginal *social* cost (MSC) of providing timber is less than the marginal private cost: $MSC = MPC - MEB_P$. This means that the MSC curve is *below* the MPC curve. The vertical distance between the curves is equal to the MEB_P. Once again it is assumed that there are no externalities in consumption so that $MSB = MPB$.

Competitive market forces will result in an equilibrium output of Q_{pc} where market demand ($= MPB$) equals market supply ($= MPC$) (point *a*). The socially efficient level of output, however, is Q^* and the socially efficient price is P^*: i.e. where $MSB = MSC$ (point *c*). The external benefits of production thus result in a level of output *below* the socially efficient level. From society's point of view not enough trees are being planted. The deadweight welfare loss caused by this under-production is illustrated by the area *abc*. Output is not being produced between Q_{pc} and Q^* even though $MSB > MSC$.

Another example of external benefits in production is that of research and development. An interesting recent example has been the development of touchscreen technology for tablets and mobile phones. If other firms have access to the results of the research, then clearly the benefits extend beyond the firm which finances it. Since the firm

Definitions

Deadweight welfare loss from externalities The loss of social surplus at the competitive market equilibrium compared with the social optimum where $MSC = MSB$.

Social surplus Total social benefits minus total social costs.

Figure 12.5 Positive eternality in production

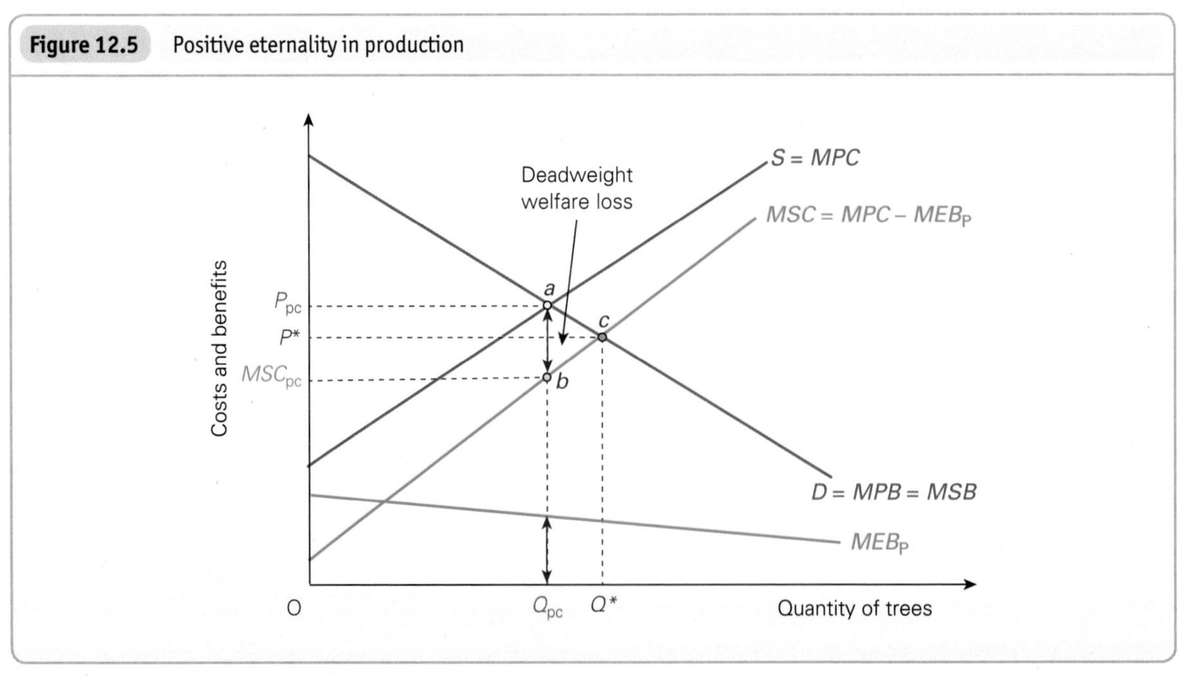

Figure 12.6 Negative externality in consumption

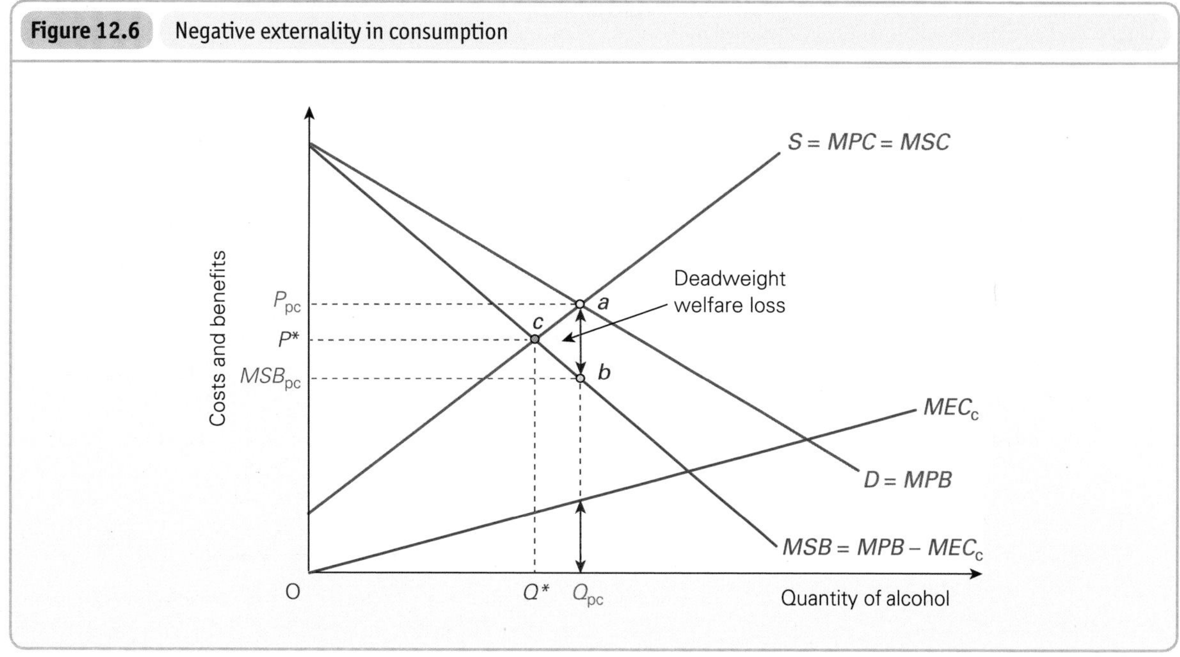

only receives the private benefits, it may conduct a less than optimal amount of research. In turn, this may reduce the pace of innovation and so negatively affect economic growth over the longer term.

External costs of consumption ($MSB < MPB$) with no external costs/benefits of production ($MSC = MPC$)

Excessive drinking of alcohol often leads to marginal external costs of consumption. For example, there are the extra nightly policing costs to deal with the increased chance of social disorder. Public health costs may also be greater as a direct consequence of peoples' drinking behaviour: e.g. through an increase in hospitalisations. It may also lead to a number of alcohol-related road accidents. These marginal external costs of consumption (MEC_C) result in the marginal social benefit of alcohol consumption being lower than the marginal private benefit: i.e. $MSB = MPB - MEC_C$.

This is illustrated in Figure 12.6 where the *MSB* curve is below the *MPB* curve. In this example, it is assumed that there are no externalities in production so that $MSC = MPC$.

Competitive market forces will result in an equilibrium output of Q_{pc} (point *a*), whereas the socially efficient level of output is Q^* and the socially efficient price is P^*: i.e. where $MSB = MSC$ (point *c*). The external costs of consumption result in a level of output *above* the socially efficient level: i.e. $Q_{pc} > Q^*$. From society's point of view too much alcohol is being produced and consumed. The deadweight welfare loss caused by this overconsumption is illustrated by the area *abc*.

Other possible examples of negative externalities of consumption include mobile phone usage while driving, speeding, smoking in-doors, the use of cars for leisure purposes such as shopping, playing loud music and dropping litter – especially chewing gum.

External benefits of consumption ($MSB > MPB$) with no external costs/benefits of production ($MSC = MPC$)

How do people travel to a city centre to go shopping on a Saturday? How do they travel to a football match? If they use the train then other people benefit, as there is less congestion and exhaust fumes and fewer accidents on the roads. These marginal external benefits of consumption (MEB_C) result in the marginal social benefit of rail travel being *greater* than the marginal private benefit (i.e. $MSB = MPB + MEB_C$).

This is illustrated in Figure 12.7 where the *MSB* curve is above the *MPB* curve. The vertical distance between the curves is equal to the MEB_C. Once again it is assumed that there are no externalities in production so that $MSC = MPC$.

External benefits of consumption result in a level of output below the socially efficient level: i.e. $Q_{pc} < Q^*$. From society's point of view not enough journeys are being made on the train. The deadweight welfare loss caused by this underconsumption is illustrated by the area *abc*.

Other examples of external benefits of consumption include the beneficial effects for other people from someone using a deodorant, parents getting their children vaccinated, and people planting flowers in their front garden.

To summarise: whenever there are external benefits, there will be too little produced or consumed. Whenever there are external costs, there will be too much produced or consumed. The market will not equate *MSB* and *MSC*.

The above arguments have been developed in the context of perfect competition with prices determined by

Figure 12.7 Positive externality in consumption

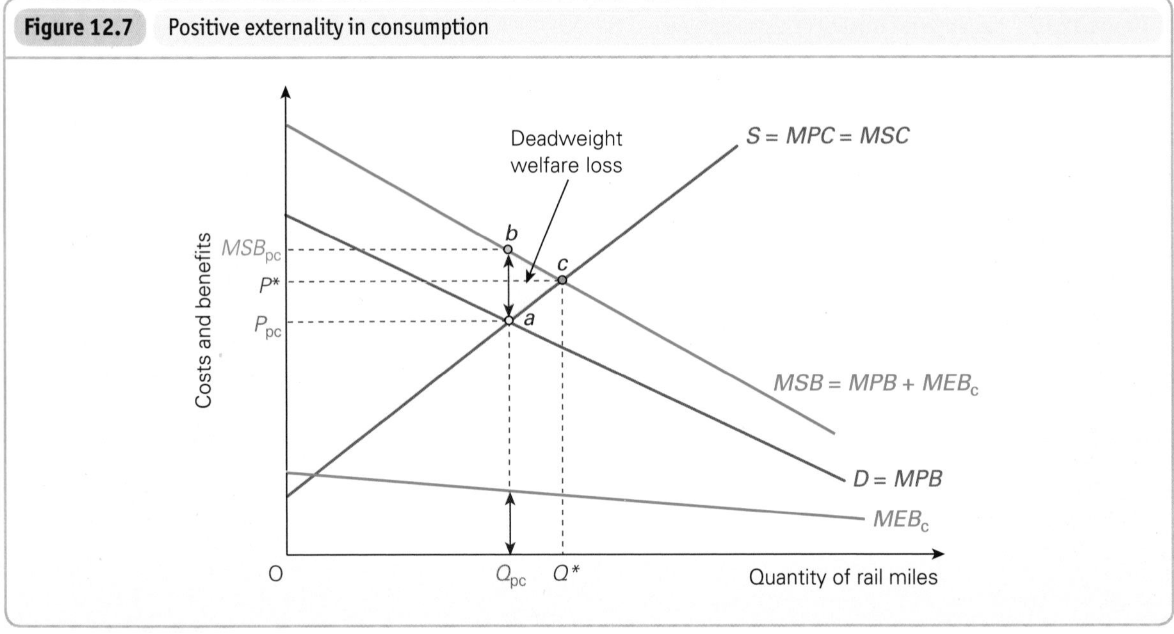

demand and supply. Externalities can also occur in all other types of market.

1. *Give other examples of each of the four types of externality.*
2. *Redraw Figure 12.4, only this time assume there is only one producer that is a monopoly. How does the existence of market power affect the relationship between the private and the social optimum positions?*
3. *Redraw Figure 12.4, only this time assume that at low levels of production the good generates no external costs. Only once a certain output is reached (Q*) does the production of additional units generate rising marginal external costs.*

BOX 12.1 THE MARKET FOR VACCINES CASE STUDIES AND APPLICATIONS

The double externality problem

In section 12.2 of the chapter, we have been outlining how four categories of externality can occur in different markets. However, it is possible to have two different types of externality in the same market. Vaccines provide a good example where there are external benefits in both consumption and production.

Consumption externalities – having a vaccine

Consider the decision of whether to have a flu jab at a local pharmacy. What are the personal costs and benefits?

Two key factors determine the size of the benefits. First, how unpleasant is the illness and what are the mortality risks? Second, by how much does the vaccine reduce the chances of catching the disease? The greater the risk of death from the illness and the more effective the vaccine, the greater the benefits.

The costs include the price (if the person is not eligible for a free jab) and a number of non-monetary costs. These non-monetary factors include the inconvenience/time of making an appointment, the discomfort from having a jab and concerns about potential side effects/impacts on health. Data for Great Britain[1] show that the most commonly reported reason for not getting a COVID-19 vaccine were: worries about the long-term effects on health (43 per cent); not thinking it is safe (31 per cent); wanting to see how well the vaccine works (30 per cent); and feeling worried about side effects (29 per cent).

Rational choice theory in economics predicts that if the personal benefits are lower than the personal costs, then the individual will not have the vaccination.

However, the decision to have the jab affects other people not directly involved in the transaction between the consumer and pharmacy. Their chances of becoming ill decline, as the disease is less likely to spread – the herd immunity effect. Importantly, these external benefits are direct and do not occur through the price mechanism. Therefore, this is an example of a positive externality in consumption.

The total benefit to society from an individual having a vaccine jab are the private benefits plus these external benefits. If the external benefits of consumption do not enter into an individual's own cost/benefit calculation when deciding whether to have a vaccine, then the market will produce an economically inefficient outcome. Some vaccinations will not take place even though the benefits to society are greater than the costs. The larger the external benefits, the bigger the problem, as individuals do not have strong enough incentives to get a jab.

Similar arguments apply to (a) wearing facemasks, (b) social distancing and (c) isolating after a positive COVID-19 test. If people only consider private benefits, socially desirable outcomes will not occur.

How large are the external consumption benefits from vaccines? A recent study in the USA[2] tried to estimate the social benefits of influenza vaccinations. It found that a 1-percentage point increase in the vaccination rate would lead to (a) 795 fewer deaths per year and (b) 14.5 million fewer hours of absence from work per year due to illness. In monetary term, this means that each influenza vaccine generates at least $63 in social benefits due to fewer deaths and $87 due to lower absences from work. The research also found that the majority of these returns come from the external as opposed to the private benefits.

Given how COVID-19 spreads more easily than influenza and has higher mortality rates, the externalities are likely to be larger. Some initial research[3] estimates that, if no one in the population has immunity, then the personal benefit from a COVID-19 vaccination is $26 000, whereas the social benefit is $430 000 – nearly 17 times larger.

Production externalities

Developing new vaccines is a research-intensive and expensive business. It costs anywhere between several hundred million and a couple of billion dollars per vaccine. It is also a very risky investment. Only 10 per cent of vaccines that enter a phase one trial (tested on 20–80 volunteers) and 50–70 per cent that enter a phase three trial (tested on thousands of volunteers) actually receive regulatory approval.

If, after all of this expense, a pharmaceutical business successfully develops a vaccine, other firms can benefit from the costly innovation. They can either copy or learn from the new knowledge (i.e. Messenger RNA technology) without having to incur the same outlay on research and development (R&D). As these external benefits do not take place through the price mechanism, they are an example of a positive externality in production.

Given that R&D expenditure makes up by far the largest proportion of the costs of developing a vaccine, these external benefits are considerable. Once regulatory approval has taken place, the manufacture of the doses is relatively inexpensive. Therefore, the investment by the innovating firm significantly reduces the costs of all the other potential vaccine producers. The marginal private costs are significantly greater than the marginal social cost and so the market does not provide firms with strong enough incentives to produce the socially desirable number of vaccines. There is clearly an economic rationale for government intervention, such as the use of patents to give the developer the sole right to produce the vaccine or the right to charge other companies a royalty.

However, even with the use of patents the regulated market may still face incentive issues. In 2019, worldwide revenue in the pharmaceutical market was $1.3 trillion but only $33 billion (2.5 per cent) came from vaccines. Why is this share so small? One potential answer is that vaccines are likely to be far less profitable than the development of a therapeutic drug that treats people who already have an illness/disease. Health organisations/patients will typically have to purchase therapeutic drugs repeatedly, whereas a vaccine has much longer-lasting effects, meaning fewer sales.

Between 2014 to 2018, the Food and Drug Administration in the USA approved 213 new therapeutic drugs and just 9 vaccines. It will be interesting to see if COVID-19 has a long-term impact on the market for vaccines.

1. ***Draw a diagram to illustrate the double externality problem in the market for vaccines.***
2. ***Explain why vaccines are likely to provide greater external benefits than therapeutic drugs.***
3. ***Why were so many businesses willing to invest in the development of new vaccines for COVID-19?***

Write a short briefing paper to a minister, making the economic case for paying people to have a COVID-19 vaccine. Also supply likely criticisms of the argument by opponents of paying people.

1 *Coronavirus and the social impacts on Great Britain*, ONS (19 March 2021), www.ons.gov.uk/peoplepopulationandcommunity/healthandsocialcare/healthandwellbeing/bulletins/coronavirusandthesocialimpactsongreatbritain/19march2021
2 Cory White, 'Measuring the social and externality benefits of influenza vaccination', *Journal of Human Resources*, (September 2019), http://jhr.uwpress.org/content/early/2019/09/10/jhr.56.3.1118-9893R2
3 Zachary A. Bethune and Anton Korinek, 'Covid-19 infection externalities: trading off lives vs. livelihoods', *NBER Working Papers 27009* (April 2020),www.nber.org/papers/w27009

Public goods

There is a category of goods where the positive externalities are so great that the free market, whether perfect or imperfect, may not produce at all. They are called ***public goods***. In order to understand exactly what a public good is it is important to discuss two of its key characteristics – ***non-rivalry*** and ***non-excludability***. Before looking specifically at public goods, let us explore the concepts of rivalry and excludability in more detail.

KI 30 p364

Definitions

Public good A good or service that has the features of non-rivalry and non-excludability and as a result would not be provided by the free market.

Non-rivalry Where the consumption of a good or service by one person will not prevent others from enjoying it.

Non-excludability Where it is not possible to provide a good or service to one person without it thereby being available free for others to enjoy.

The degree of rivalry

Rivalry occurs when one person's consumption of a good reduces the amount of it that is available for other consumers. Goods can vary in their degree of rivalry.

Perfectly rivalrous goods. At one extreme are goods that are *perfectly* rivalrous. A good has this characteristic if, as one or more people increase their consumption of the product, it prevents all other or 'rival' consumers from enjoying it. This is typical with non-durable goods such as food, alcohol and fuel. For example, imagine that you have purchased a bar of chocolate for your own consumption. Each chunk of the chocolate bar that you eat means that there is less available for other or 'rival' consumers to enjoy. They cannot eat the same piece that you have eaten! The good gets 'used up' when it is consumed.

Many durable goods such as mobile phones also have the property of being rivalrous. For example, if you use your mobile phone it usually prevents other people from using it. Although the mobile phone does not get 'used up', only one person can usually consume the benefits it provides at a time: e.g. sending a text or calling someone.

Perfectly non-rivalrous goods. At the other extreme are goods that have the property of being perfectly non-rivalrous. A good has this characteristic if as one or more people increase their consumption of the product it has no impact on the ability of other, or 'rival', consumers to enjoy the good. For example, imagine that you turn on either your television or tablet to watch a live football match or an episode of your favourite TV programme. Your decision to watch the programme has no impact on the ability of other people to enjoy watching the same programme on a different device. The television set may be rivalrous but the broadcast is not.

Goods with a degree of rivalry and non-rivalry. In reality, many goods and services will be neither perfectly rival nor non-rival. For example, it may be possible for more than one person to enjoy watching a video clip on a mobile phone. However, a 'crowding effect' will soon occur. As additional people try watching the video it will prevent others from seeing it on the same phone.

There are a number of goods and services that may have the characteristic of being relatively non-rival with low numbers of consumers, before becoming more rivalrous at high levels of consumption. For example, some goods cover a comparatively small geographic area. Here overcrowding, and hence rivalry, will become an issue with relatively few consumers. Viewing a carnival procession, for example, may be non-rivalrous with just a few observers, but quickly any location along the route will become crowded and a good view becomes rivalrous. Another example is enjoying open spaces sitting on a beach: space becomes more rivalrous as the beach fills up with people. In other cases, such as access to the Internet, rivalry might only set in beyond very high levels of usage, when global demand is exceptionally high.

Rather than trying to categorise many goods as either rivalrous or non-rivalrous it makes more sense to think of them as having different *degrees* of rivalry. They could be placed on a scale of rivalry as illustrated along the horizontal axis in Figure 12.8.

How rivalrous in consumption are each of the following: (a) a can of drink; (b) public transport; (c) a radio broadcast; (d) the sight of flowers in a public park?

Figure 12.8 Classifying goods according to the degree of rivalry and ease of excludability

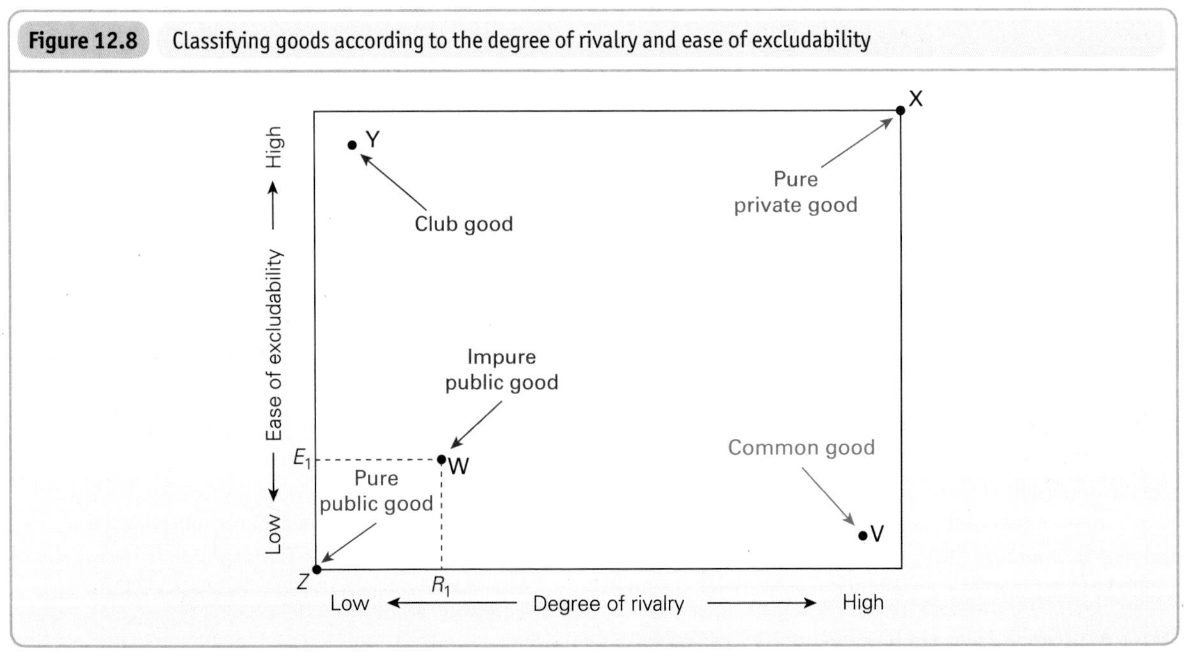

The ease of excludability

Excludability occurs when the supplier of a good can restrict who consumes it. This is the case for goods sold in the market. Suppliers allow only those consumers who are prepared to pay for the good to have it. Just as with rivalry, goods vary in their ease of excludability.

Easily excludable goods. At one extreme, some goods have the property of being very easily excludable. In this case a relatively low-cost and effective system can be implemented which guarantees that only those people who have paid for the good are able to enjoy the benefits it provides. The system must also prevent anyone who does not pay from obtaining any of the benefits that consuming the good provides. For example, although television broadcasts have a high degree of non-rivalry, a relatively straightforward and reasonably effective system of encryption could be implemented to exclude non-payers from watching the programmes. If this were not possible then pay television channels and pay-per-view broadcasting could not exist. YouTube has also introduced a number of subscription channels.

Advances in technology may also change the ease of excludability for any given good or service over time.

Perfectly non-excludable goods. At the other extreme there may be some goods for which excludability is impossible: i.e. they have the property of being non-excludable. A good has this characteristic if it is too costly or simply not feasible to implement a system that would effectively prevent those people who have not paid from enjoying the benefits it provides.

In some circumstances it may be theoretically possible to exclude non-payers, but in reality the transaction costs involved are too great. For example, it may be very difficult to prevent anyone from fishing in the open ocean or enjoying the benefits of walking in a country park.

Once again, many goods will be neither perfectly excludable nor non-excludable. In these cases it makes more sense to think about the differing levels of ease with which non-payers can be excluded from consuming the good. This is also illustrated in Figure 12.8, this time up the vertical axis.

Pure private goods

Good X in Figure 12.8 is a pure private good. It is very easy to exclude any non-payers from the consuming the product, which is perfectly rivalrous. A pure private good is one where the benefits can be enjoyed only by the consumer who owns (or rents) it.

In reality, many goods will be close to point X and have significant degrees of rivalry and ease of excludability. Products that fall into this category can normally be provided by the market mechanism.

Pure public goods

Good Z in Figure 12.8, by contrast, has the characteristics of being perfectly non-rival and completely non-excludable. This is a known as a ***pure public good***. Once a given quantity of a pure public good is produced, everyone can obtain the same level of benefits it provides. Therefore, the marginal cost of supplying another customer with a given quantity of a public good is zero. However, this should not be confused with the marginal cost of producing another unit of the good. This would involve using additional resources; so the marginal cost of producing another unit would be positive.

Another way to think about the characteristics of pure public goods is that they cannot be sold in separate units to different customers. For example, it is impossible for you to consume five units of a pure public good while somebody else consumes an additional two units of the good. Once five units are produced for one person's consumption, those same five units are freely available for everyone else to consume.

There is some debate as to whether pure public goods actually exist or whether they are merely a theoretical idea. Perhaps one of the closest real-world examples is that of national defence. Once a given investment in national defence has been made, additional people can often benefit from the protection it provides at no additional cost. It would also be very difficult to exclude anyone within a country from obtaining the benefits from the increase in security.

To what extent is national defence a pure public good? Can it ever be rivalrous or excludable in consumption?

Impure public goods

Good W in Figure 12.8 is an example of an ***impure public good***. It has a low level of rivalry, without being perfectly rivalrous, and it is difficult, but not impossible, to exclude non-payers. In reality, many public goods will fall into this category, with some being more impure than others. We will see later that as the degree of rivalry and ease of excludability fall it becomes increasingly difficult for the good to be provided by the market mechanism.

Club goods. Good Y has a low degree of rivalry but exclusion is relatively easy. This is called a ***club good***. Wireless Internet connection on a train or in a café are examples of a club good if a password is required; other examples include subscription TV services, such as Netflix or Amazon Prime.

Common good or resource. Good V has a high degree of rivalry but the exclusion of non-payers is very difficult. This is

Definitions

Pure public good A good or service that has the characteristics of being perfectly non-rival and completely non-excludable and, as a result, would not be provided by the free market.

Impure public good A good that is partially non-rivalrous and non-excludable.

Club good A good which has a low degree of rivalry but is easily excludable.

called a ***common good or resource***. The high degree of rivalry means that the quantity or quality of the common resource available to one person is negatively affected by the number of other people who consume or make use of the same resource. Because it is difficult to exclude non-payers, a common resource is also potentially available to everyone, free of charge.

Fishing in the open ocean is an example. In the absence of intervention, fishing boats can catch as many fish as is possible. There is no 'owner' of either the fish or the sea to stop them. As one fishing boat catches more fish, it means there is less available for other fishing boats: fish are *rivalrous*. Other examples include the felling of trees in the rainforests and the use of the atmosphere as a common 'dump' for emissions.

If producers/consumers only consider the costs and benefits to themselves, then it is inevitable that common resources will be overused. As the good is free, a rational self-interested individual will keep consuming or using it until the marginal private benefit is zero, even though they are reducing the quantity or quality available for others; they are consuming past the point where $MSC = MSB$. This is the extreme case of a negative externality where the cost of the resource to the user is zero.

The inevitability of the outcome is known as the ***tragedy of the commons***. Depleted fish stocks, disappearing rainforests and a heavily polluted atmosphere all provide evidence to support the tragedy of the commons.

However, is it inevitable that all common resources will be overused? The Nobel Prize winning economist Elinor Ostrom discovered many real-world common resources that were consumed in a sustainable manner. Her work is discussed in more detail in Case Study 12.2 on the student website.

1. *To what extent can the following be regarded as common resources: (a) rainforests; (b) children's playgrounds in public parks; (c) silence in a library; (d) the Internet?*
2. *Where would you place each of the following in Figure 12.8: (a) an inner city road at 3:00am; (b) an inner city road at 8:00am; (c) a toll motorway at 3:00am; (d) a toll motorway at 8:00am?*

The efficient level of output for a pure public good

The socially efficient level of output is the quantity at which the marginal social benefit is equal to the marginal social cost. In a competitive market without externalities the marginal social benefit curve is the same as the market demand curve.

The market demand curve for a private good illustrates the sum of all the quantities demanded by all consumers at each possible price. Different consumers will each want to purchase varying amounts at each price. These different individual demands at each price are simply added together in order to derive the market demand curve for a private good. This is known as horizontal aggregation or summation of individual demand curves.

The market demand curve for a pure public good cannot be derived in the same way, because consumers are unable to purchase and consume different quantities of the good. Once a given amount of a pure public good is produced for one customer, every other customer can consume that same amount at no additional cost.

Therefore, instead of thinking about how much people are willing to buy at each different price, we have to work out how much people are willing to pay *in total* for each possible level of output. In other words, we have to add together the maximum amount each consumer is willing to pay for each possible level of output. This is illustrated in Figure 12.9.

To keep the example simple it is assumed that there are just two consumers of the public good – Dean and Jon. In most real-world examples there would be many more. The maximum amount Dean would be willing to pay to consume the 10th unit of the good is illustrated at point *a* on his demand curve (D_D) and is £30. The maximum amount Jon would be willing to pay for the 10th unit of the good is illustrated at point *b* on his demand curve (D_J) and is £50.

Therefore, if we simply add these willingness-to-pay figures together we obtain the marginal benefit to society from producing the tenth unit of the public good. This is illustrated at point *c* and is £80. This provides us with one point on the marginal social benefit curve. If we continue this exercise for each different level of output, the marginal social benefit (*MSB*) can be derived as illustrated in Figure 12.9. The curve has been derived in this example by vertically aggregating Dean's and Jon's individual demand curves: $MSB = D_D + D_J$.

Producing a public good would normally have the same characteristics as producing a private good. Costs would vary with output in a very similar manner. Therefore the marginal cost (*MC*) for the market as a whole would be derived in the same way as it would be for a private good: i.e. by adding together the quantities that each firm would want to supply at each price – the horizontal summation of all the individual firms' marginal cost curves. Hence it is drawn as an upward-sloping line.

Assuming there are no externalities in production, the private marginal cost curve is the same as the social marginal cost curve ($MC = MSC$). The socially efficient quantity can be found where $MSC = MSB$, which is at point *f* at an output level of 16.

Definitions

Common good or resource A good or resource that has a high degree of rivalry but the exclusion of non-payers is difficult.

Tragedy of the commons When resources are commonly available at no charge, people are likely to overexploit them.

Figure 12.9 The efficient output of a pure public good

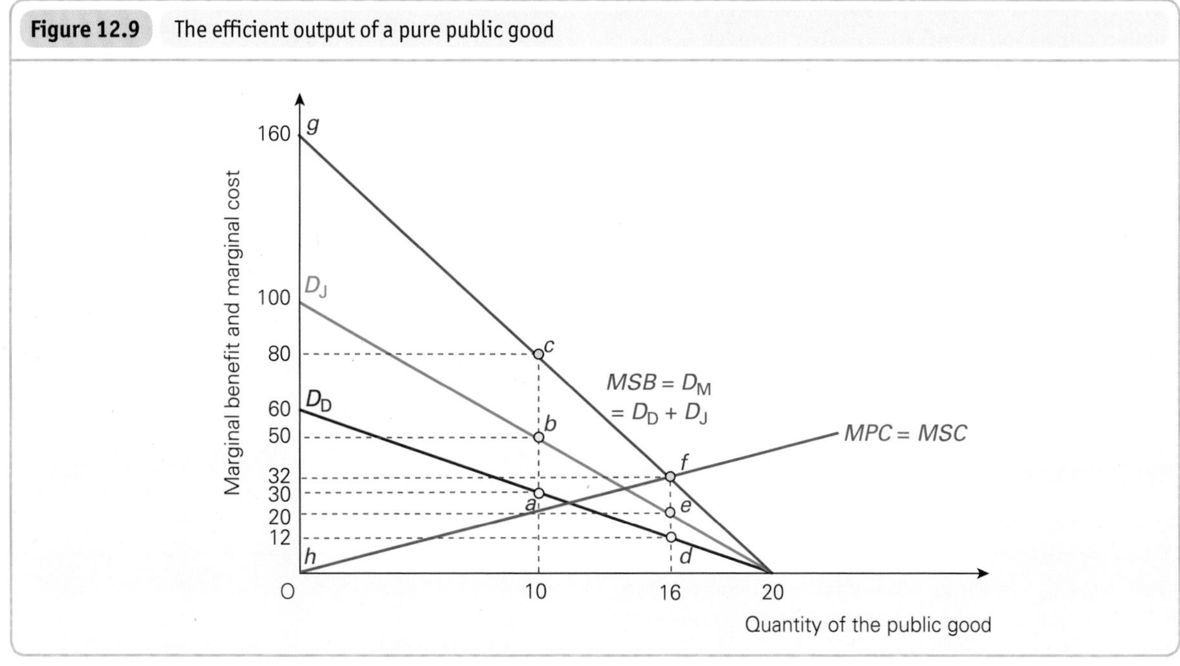

Provision of pure public goods and the free-rider problem

Assume a private firm produced 16 units of the good and charged Jon a price of £20 per unit (point *e*) and Dean £12 per unit (point *d*). These prices would equal their maximum willingness to pay for 16 units. If Jon acts in a perfectly rational and selfish manner we can predict that he will not pay for the good. Why? Because once the 16 units are produced, he can consume them whether he has paid for them or not. He can act as a ***free-rider*** by enjoying the benefits of a good which have been paid for by Dean.

***The free-rider problem*. People are often unwilling to pay for things if they can make use of things other people have bought. This problem can lead to people not purchasing things that would be to the benefit of them and other members of society to have.**

Unfortunately for Jon, if Dean thinks the same way, then he will not pay for the good either. If neither of them pays for the good then the firm will not generate any revenue and quickly go out of business. As a result, both Dean and Jon will be worse off. Because of the free-riding problem, firms cannot produce the good and make a profit in a private market; so the output will be zero. The social inefficiency this creates can be illustrated by the area of deadweight welfare loss in Figure 12.9: i.e. the shaded area *fgh*.

With just two people it may be possible for the consumers to agree on contribution levels. However, as the number of people who benefit from the public good gets larger, free-riding becomes more likely. This will make it increasingly difficult for private firms to produce public goods in an unregulated market without any government support. If they charge a price they are, in effect, asking for a voluntary contribution from each customer who can consume the good, whether they have paid or not. If no voluntary contributions are forthcoming, then the good will not be provided. Some newspapers, such as *The Guardian*, provide a website that is freely accessible without a password. They do, however, ask for contributions from readers to help fund the site. (This is not a pure public good, however, as newspaper sites sell advertising space, which is both rivalrous and excludable.)

The more closely an impure public good resembles a pure public good, the more likely the free-riding problem becomes. It is then increasingly unlikely that the market mechanism will produce the socially efficient level of the good. In these circumstances the good may have to be provided by the government or by the government subsidising private firms.

Note that not all goods and services produced by the public sector come into the category of public goods and

Definition

Free-rider problem When it is not possible to exclude other people from consuming a good that someone has bought.

services. Thus education and health are publicly provided, but they *can* be, and indeed are, privately provided as well.

1. *Give some other examples of public goods. Does the provider of these goods (the government or local authority) charge for their use? If so, is the method of charging based on the amount of the good that people use? Is it a good method of charging? Could you suggest a better method?*
2. *Name some goods or services provided by the government or local authorities that are not public goods.*
3. *Are there ways in which we could overcome the free-rider problem? Start by thinking about the provision of a public good amongst a group of friends or neighbours.*

Market power

Lack of Pareto optimality

KI 22 p195

Whenever markets are imperfect, whether as pure monopoly or monopsony or as some form of imperfect competition, the market will fail to equate *MSB* and *MSC*. Pareto optimality will not be achieved.

This is illustrated in Figure 12.10, which shows revenue and cost curves for a monopolist. It assumes no externalities. The socially efficient (Pareto optimal) output is Q_2, where $MSB = MSC$. The monopolist, however, produces the lower output Q_1, where $MR = MC$.

Figure 12.10 The monopolist producing less than the Pareto optimum

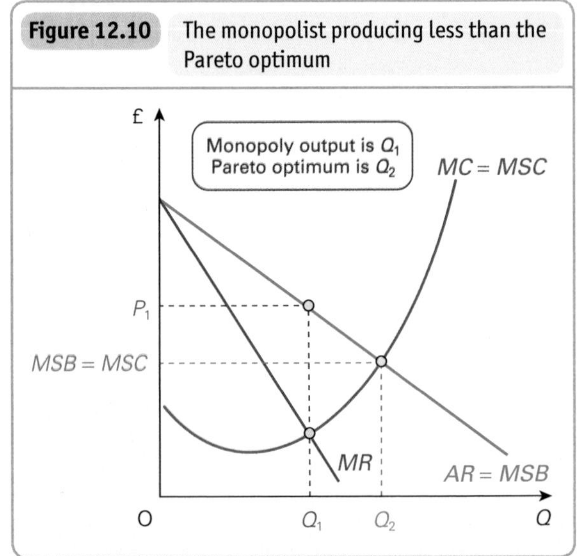

Referring back to Figure 10.8 on page 293, and assuming that the MRP_L curve represents the marginal social benefit from the employment of a factor, and that the price of the factor represents its marginal social cost (i.e. assuming no externalities), show that a monopsony will employ less than the Pareto optimal amount of factors.

BOX 12.2 THE POLICE AS A PUBLIC SERVICE

Could some aspects of policing be provided privately?

A good example of a good or service that has public-good properties is policing. Police officers provide a general service to the community by deterring and detecting crime.

The cost to individuals of privately employing their own police officers would be considerable. For most people this cost would far outweigh the benefits. However, the impact of having police officers on the beat would benefit many individuals in a community.

Voluntary contributions from local residents for local policing

Perhaps local residents could all privately contribute a relatively small amount towards the costs of employing the police officers and collectively enjoy the benefits.

This idea might seem rather strange, but this is exactly what the residents of Woodford in London have done, where 139 people pay £50 per month to the company My Local Bobby (MLB) for a number of services. These include regular patrols of the neighbourhood by security staff in hi-vis clothing, mobile contact numbers for fast response to incidents and the ability to track the whereabouts of the security staff via an app.

The company, established by two former Metropolitan Police detectives, already operates similar services in the districts of Belgravia, Mayfair and Kensington in London. It has plans to expand into other areas. In another example, around 60 residents in an area of Sutton Coldfield paid a private security firm to patrol the streets.

Why is it unlikely that everyone will contribute? Employing security staff to deter crime in a whole town or suburb has public-good properties. If one member of the community benefits from the lower chance of a crime being committed, it does not prevent other members of the community from enjoying the same benefits. The deterrence effect is not 'used up' in consumption and so has a very low degree of rivalry.

It would also be very difficult to prevent someone in the local community from benefiting, even if they had not paid towards the costs of the scheme.

The combination of a low degree of rivalry with the difficulty of excluding non-payers gives a strong incentive for people to free-ride. This provides an economic rationale for the police to be funded by the government and paid for from taxation. The services offered by MLB are very unusual and it will be interesting to see if enough people continue to make voluntary contributions so that the business can remain viable.

Deadweight loss under monopoly

Once again, the welfare loss can be illustrated by using the concepts of *consumer* and *producer surplus*. The two concepts are illustrated in Figure 12.11, which is similar to Figure 12.10. The diagram shows an industry that is initially under perfect competition and then becomes a monopoly (but faces the same revenue and cost curves).

Under *perfect competition* the industry will produce an output of Q_{pc} at a price of P_{pc}, where $MC (= S) = P (= AR)$: i.e. at point *a*. Consumer surplus is shown by areas 1 + 2 + 3, and producer surplus by areas 4 + 5. Total surplus (i.e. consumer plus producer surplus) is maximised at this output (see Figure 12.1 on page 357).

What happens when the industry is under *monopoly*? The firm will produce where $MC = MR$, at an output of Q_m and a price of P_m (at point *b* on the demand curve). Total revenue is $P_m \times Q_m$ (areas 2 + 4 + 6). Total cost is the area under the *MC* curve (area 6). Thus the producer surplus is areas 2 + 4. This is clearly a *larger* surplus than under perfect competition (since area 2 is larger than area 5). The consumer surplus, however, will fall dramatically. With consumption at Q_m, total utility is given by areas 1 + 2 + 4 + 6, whereas consumer expenditure is given by areas 2 + 4 + 6. Consumer surplus, then, is simply area 1. (Note that area 2 has been transformed from consumer surplus to producer surplus.)

Total surplus under monopoly is therefore areas 1 + 2 + 4: a smaller surplus than under perfect competition. 'Monopolisation' of the industry has resulted in a loss of total surplus of areas 3 + 5. The producers' gain has been more than offset by the consumers' loss. This loss of surplus is known as the ***deadweight welfare loss of monopoly***. KI 30 p364

Figure 12.11 Deadweight loss under monopoly

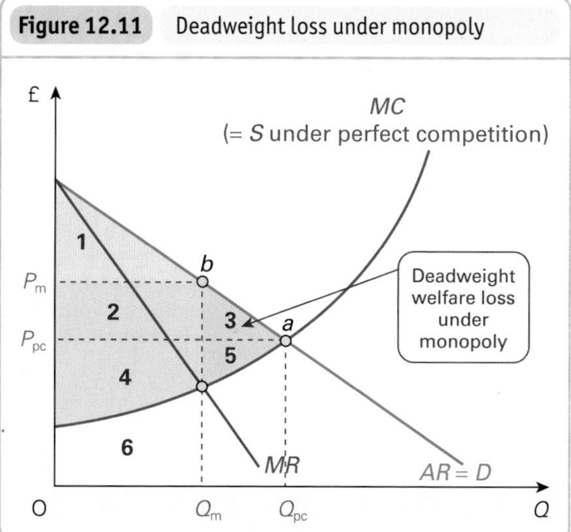

Definition

Deadweight welfare loss of monopoly The loss of consumer plus producer surplus in monopoly or other imperfect markets (when compared with perfect competition).

CASE STUDIES AND APPLICATIONS

Policing where there is no free-rider problem

But do all aspects of policing have a free-rider problem? The answer is no. When there is a *specific* task of guarding specific property, policing can be provided by the market. This is in fact done by security firms. Organisations such as banks and shops employ security guards to prevent theft or criminal damage to their property. In these cases, the private benefits are perceived to exceed the private costs.

Should such security services be provided privately or are they better provided by the police? Since the *private* benefits in such cases are large, there is a strong argument for charging the recipient. But why should the service be provided by private security firms? Could the police not charge firms for specific guard duties? A potential problem might arise if private security firms were not allowed to operate, as the police would have monopoly power and could charge very high prices unless they were regulated by the government. Also, the quality of the service might be poorer than that provided by private security companies which were competing against each other for business.

On the other hand, the police are likely to bring greater expertise to the job. There are also economies of scale to be gained: for example, the police may have knowledge of criminal activities in other parts of the area which may pose a threat to the particular property in question. Finally, there is the problem that private security guards may not show the same level of courtesy as the police in dealing with the public (or criminals for that matter).

1. *The police charge football clubs for policing inside football grounds, but make no charge for policing outside the ground. Explain this approach.*
2. *Could other aspects of policing make use of market forces? Examine the case for charging to investigate the theft of a bicycle. Would your conclusion differ if the crime involved an attack on an individual rather than property?*

Investigate what other aspects of policing could make use of charging. In each case consider (a) the practicality of charging; (b) whether charging would be desirable, even if practical; (c) who should pay the charge (e.g. individuals or organisations); and (d) the basis on which to charge – here you should consider the question of who gains or loses and what is considered to be (i) fair and (ii) efficient.

*LOOKING AT THE MATHS

Total consumer surplus (*TCS*) equals total utility minus total expenditure (i.e. total revenue). Total producer surplus (*TPS*) equals total revenue minus total variable cost. Thus total surplus (*TS*) is given by:

$$TS = TCS + TPS = (TU - TR) + (TR - TVC) = TU - TVC$$

Assuming that the demand curve traces out the marginal utility curve (see pages 109–10), this allows us to derive the total utility function. To do this, you would need to use the technique of integration. Assuming that the total utility function is

$$TU = bQ - cQ^2$$

and that the total variable cost function is

$$TVC = jQ - kQ^2 + lQ^3$$

this will give a total surplus function of

$$TS = (bQ - cQ^2) - (jQ - kQ^2 + lQ^3) \quad \textbf{(1)}$$

To find the level of deadweight welfare loss, we would then subtract total surplus under perfect competition from that under monopoly. To do this, we would solve equation (1) first for Q_{pc} and then for Q_m and then subtract the second from the first. A worked example of this is given in Maths Case 12.1 on the student website.

Conclusions

The firm with market power uses fewer factors and produces less output than the Pareto optimum. It also causes deadweight welfare loss. To the extent, however, that the firm seeks aims *other* than profit maximisation and thus may produce more than the profit-maximising output, so these criticisms must be relaxed.

As was shown in Chapter 7, there are possible social *advantages* from powerful firms: advantages such as economies of scale and more research and development. These advantages may outweigh the lack of Pareto optimality. It can be argued that an ideal situation would be where firms are large enough to gain economies of scale and yet are somehow persuaded or compelled to produce where $P = MC$ (assuming no externalities).

With oligopoly and monopolistic competition, further wastes may occur because of possibly substantial resources involved in non-price competition. Advertising is the major example. It is difficult to predict just how much oligopolists will diverge from the Pareto optimum, since their pricing and output depends on their interpretation of the activities of their rivals.

Why will Pareto optimality not be achieved in markets where there are substantial economies of scale in production?

Other market failures

Imperfect information

Perfect competition assumes that consumers, firms and factor suppliers have perfect knowledge of costs and benefits. In the real world, there is often a great deal of ignorance and uncertainty. Thus people are unable to equate marginal benefit with marginal cost.

Consumers purchase many goods infrequently. Cars, washing machines and other consumer durables fall into this category, as do houses. Consumers may not be aware of the quality of such goods until they have purchased them, by which time it is too late. Advertising may contribute to people's ignorance by misleading them as to the benefits of a good.

Firms are often ignorant of market opportunities, prices, costs, the productivity of factors (especially white-collar workers), the activity of rivals, etc.

Many economic decisions are based on expected future conditions. Since the future can never be known for certain, many decisions may turn out to be wrong.

In some cases, it may be possible to obtain the information through the market. There may be an agency that will sell you the information or a newspaper or magazine that contains the information. In this case, you will have to decide whether the cost to you of buying the information is worth the benefit it will provide you. A problem here is that you may not have sufficient information to judge how reliable the information is that you are buying!

1. *Assume that you wanted the following information. In which cases might you (i) buy perfect information, (ii) buy imperfect information, (iii) be able to obtain information without paying for it, (iv) not be able to obtain information?*
   (a) Which washing machine is the most reliable?
   (b) Which of two vacant jobs is more satisfying?
   (c) Which builder will repair my roof most cheaply?
   (d) Which builder is the best value for money?
   (e) How big a mortgage would it be wise for me to take out?
   (f) Should I take a degree or get a full-time job?
   (g) What brand of washing powder washes whiter?
   (h) Will a house need any work done on it over the next few years?
2. *Make a list of pieces of information that a firm might want to know, and consider whether it could buy the information and how reliable that information might be.*
3. *What has been the impact of the Internet on the provision of information?*

Asymmetric information. One form of imperfect information occurs when different sides in an economic relationship have different amounts of information. This, as we saw on page 274, is known as 'asymmetric information' and is at the heart of the principal–agent problem.

Take the case of a firm (the principal) using the services of a bank (the agent) to finance its investments. The bank is likely to have a much better knowledge of its range of products and of the current state of financial markets and may mis-sell products to the firm in order to earn a larger profit for the bank. For example, it could provide loans at fixed rates of interest, knowing that rates were likely to fall. The firm would end up being locked into paying a higher rate of interest than if it had taken out a variable rate loan and the bank would consequently make more profit. This practice came to light in 2012, with banks accused of mis-selling such products to some 28 000 small and medium-sized enterprises (SMEs).

Immobility of factors and time lags in response

Even under conditions of perfect competition, factors may be very slow to respond to changes in demand or supply. Labour, for example, may be highly immobile both occupationally and geographically. This can lead to large price changes and hence to large supernormal profits and high wages for those in the sectors of rising demand or falling costs. The long run may be a very long time coming!

The problem of time lags. **Many economic actions can take a long time to take effect. This can cause problems of instability and an inability of the economy to achieve social efficiency.**

In the meantime, there will be further changes in the conditions of demand and supply. Thus the economy is in a constant state of disequilibrium and the long run never comes. As firms and consumers respond to market signals and move towards equilibrium, so the equilibrium position moves and the social optimum is never achieved.

Whenever monopoly/monopsony power exists, the problem is made worse if firms or unions put up barriers to the entry of new firms or factors of production.

Protecting people's interests

Dependants. People do not always make their own economic decisions. They are often dependent on decisions made by others. Parents make decisions on behalf of their children; partners on each other's behalf; younger adults on behalf of old people; managers on behalf of shareholders; etc. This, again, is an example of the principal–agent issue.

KI 25 p274

A free market will respond to these decisions, however good or bad they may be, and whether or not they are in the interests of the dependant. Thus the government may feel it necessary to protect dependants.

Give examples of how the government intervenes to protect the interests of dependants from bad economic decisions taken on their behalf.

Poor economic decision making by individuals on their own behalf. The government may feel that people need protecting from poor economic decisions that they make on their own behalf. As we discussed in Chapter 5, this may be a particular problem when the benefits from consuming a good are immediate while the cost happens at some point in the future. People may place too much weight on the immediate benefits and too little weight on the long-run costs of their decisions. Products where this might be an issue include tobacco, alcohol and fast/unhealthy food.

On the other hand, the government may feel that people consume too little of things that are good for them: things such as education, preventative health care and sports facilities. Such goods are known as ***merit goods***. The government could either provide them free or subsidise their production; it could also make their consumption compulsory (e.g. as with fluoride added to water in many areas).

How do merit goods differ from public goods?

Other objectives

As we saw in Chapter 11, one of the major criticisms of the free market is the problem of *inequality*. The Pareto criterion gives no guidance, however, as to the most desirable distribution of income. A redistribution of income will benefit some and make others worse off. Thus Pareto optimality can be achieved for *any* distribution of income. Pareto optimality merely represents the efficient allocation of resources for any *given* distribution of income.

In addition to social efficiency and greater equality, we can identify other social goals: goals such as moral behaviour (however defined), enlightenment, social consciousness, co-operation, the development of culture, fulfilment, freedom from exploitation, and freedom to own, purchase and inherit property. The unfettered free market may not be very successful in achieving social efficiency. It may be even less successful in achieving many other social goals.

Finally, the free market is unlikely to achieve simultaneously the *macroeconomic objectives* of rapid economic growth, full employment, stable prices and a balance of international payments. These problems, and methods of government intervention that may be used to deal with them, are examined in later chapters.

Conclusions

It is not the role of economists to make judgements as to the relative importance of social goals. Economics can only consider the means to achieving stated goals. First, therefore, the goals have to be clearly stated by the policy makers. Second, they have to be quantifiable so that the

Definition

Merit goods Goods that the government feels people will underconsume and which therefore ought to be subsidised or provided free.

effectiveness of different policies can be compared. Certain goals, such as growth in national income, changes in the distribution of income and greater efficiency, are relatively easy to quantify. Others, such as enlightenment, are virtually impossible to quantify. For this reason, economics tends to concentrate on the means to achieving a relatively narrow range of goals. The danger is that, by concentrating on a limited number of goals, economists may well influence policy makers into doing the same, and thus into neglecting other social goals.

Different objectives are likely to conflict. For example, economic growth may conflict with greater equality. In the case of such 'trade-offs', all the economist can do is to demonstrate the effects of a given policy, and leave the policy makers to decide whether the benefits in terms of one goal outweigh the costs in terms of another goal. TC 1 p10

How do the economic policies of the major political parties differ? How far can an economist go in assessing these policies?

Section summary

1. Real-world markets will fail to achieve Pareto optimality. What is more, there are objectives other than social efficiency, and real-world markets may fail to achieve these too.
2. Externalities are costs and benefits of consumption experienced by people other than those directly involved in the transaction and not through the price mechanism. Whenever there are external costs, the market will (other things being equal) lead to a level of production and consumption *above* the socially efficient level. Whenever there are external benefits, the market will (other things being equal) lead to a level of production and consumption *below* the socially efficient level.
3. Public goods have the characteristics of being non-rival and non-excludable. Once a given quantity of a pure public good is produced, everyone can obtain the same level of benefit it provides. They will tend to be underprovided by the market. Without government intervention it would not be possible to prevent people having a 'free ride' and thereby escaping any contributions to their cost of production.
4. Common resources are likely to be overused – a problem known as the 'tragedy of the commons'. This is because people are unlikely to take into account the effect of their use of such resources on other people.
5. Monopoly power will (other things being equal) lead to a level of output below the socially efficient level. It will lead to a deadweight welfare loss: a loss of consumer plus producer surplus.
6. Imperfect information may prevent people from consuming or producing at the levels they would otherwise choose. There may be an asymmetry of information between buyers and sellers, which can result in a principal–agent problem. Information, however, may sometimes be provided (at a price) by the market.
7. Markets may respond sluggishly to changes in demand and supply. The time lags in adjustment can lead to a permanent state of disequilibrium and to problems of instability.
8. In a free market there may be inadequate provision for dependants and an inadequate output of merit goods; there are likely to be macroeconomic problems and problems of inequality and poverty; finally, there may be a whole series of social, moral, attitudinal and aesthetic problems arising from a market system.
9. These being normative questions, the economist cannot make ultimate pronouncements on the rights and wrongs of the market. The economist can, however, point out the consequences of the market and of various government policies, and also the trade-offs that exist between different objectives.

12.3 FORMS OF GOVERNMENT INTERVENTION

Faced with all the problems of the free market, what is a government to do?

There are several policy instruments that a government can use. At one extreme, it can totally replace the market by providing goods and services itself. At the other extreme, it can merely seek to persuade producers, consumers or workers to act differently. Between the two extremes, the government has a number of instruments that it can use to change the way markets operate. These include taxes, subsidies, laws and regulatory bodies.

Before looking at different forms of government intervention and their relative merits, it is first necessary to look at a general problem concerned with all forms of intervention. This is known as the ***problem of the second best***.

Definition

Problem of the second best The difficulty of working out the best way of correcting a specific market distortion if distortions in other parts of the market continue to exist.

In an ideal free market, where there are no market failures of any sort (the 'first-best' world), there would be no need for government intervention at all. If in this world there did then arise just one failure, in theory its correction would be simple. Say a monopoly arose, or some externality (e.g. pollution) was produced by a particular firm, with the result that the marginal social cost was no longer equal to the marginal social benefit. In theory, the government should simply intervene to restore production to the point where $MSC = MSB$. This is known as the ***first-best solution***.

Of course, the real world is not like this. It is full of imperfections. What this means is that, if one imperfection is 'corrected' (i.e. by making $MSB = MSC$), it might aggravate problems elsewhere. For example, if a local authority introduces residents-only parking in an inner city area to prevent commuters parking there, they may simply park just outside the area, thus imposing additional costs on people living there.

Give some examples of how correcting problems in one part of the economy will create problems elsewhere.

As the first-best solution of a perfectly efficient, distortion-free world is obviously not possible, the ***second-best solution*** needs to be adopted. Essentially this involves seeking the best compromises. This means attempting to minimise the *overall* distortionary effects of the policy measure. Some second-best *rules* can be applied in certain cases. We will examine these in the following sections as we look at specific policy measures.

Definitions

First-best solution The solution of correcting a specific market distortion by ensuring that the whole economy operates under conditions of social efficiency (Pareto optimality).

Second-best solution The solution to a specific market distortion that recognises distortions elsewhere and seeks to minimise the overall distortionary effects to the economy of tackling this specific distortion.

BOX 12.3 SHOULD HEALTH-CARE PROVISION BE LEFT TO THE MARKET? CASE STUDIES AND APPLICATIONS

A case of multiple market failures

In the UK, the National Health Service provides free hospital treatment, a free general practitioner service, and free prescriptions for certain categories of people. Their marginal cost to the patient is thus zero. Of course, these services use resources and they thus have to be paid for out of taxes.

TC 3 p26

But why are these services not sold directly to the patient, thereby saving the taxpayer money? There are, in fact, a number of reasons why the market would fail to provide the optimum amount of health care.

The issue of equity

This is a problem connected with the distribution of income. Because income is unequally distributed, some people will be able to afford better treatment than others, and the poorest people may not be able to afford treatment at all. On grounds of equity, therefore, it is argued that health care should be provided free – at least for those on low incomes.

KI 4 p13

The concept of equity that is usually applied to health care is that individuals should be able to access treatment according to their medical need rather than according to their ability to pay. This was brought into sharp relief with the COVID-19 pandemic. It was generally believed that access to NHS resources should depend solely on clinical need.

1. *Does this argument also apply to food and housing?*

Difficulty of predicting future medical needs

If you were suddenly taken ill and required a major operation, it could be very expensive if you had to pay. On the other hand, you may go through life requiring very little if any medical treatment. In other words, there is great uncertainty about your future medical needs. As a result it would be very difficult to plan your finances and budget for possible future medical expenses if you had to pay for treatment.

Medical insurance could provide a solution to this problem if the probability of requiring different treatments (a) can be estimated and (b) is independent across different individuals. There would also have to be no serious problems of adverse selection or moral hazard. Even if an effective market for medical insurance could be established there would still remain a problem of equity. Would the chronically sick or very old be able to obtain cover and, if so, would they be able to afford the premiums? This issue of 'gaps' in an insurance-based system means that some form of intervention on grounds of equity may be needed, even if most provision is private.

KI 16 p137

KI 17 p138

2. *Give some examples of adverse selection and moral hazard that might occur with medical insurance (see section 5.1, pages 136–9).*

Externalities

Health care generates a number of benefits *external* to the patient. If you are cured of an infectious disease, for example,

(continued)

KI 31 p364

it is not just you who benefits but also others, since you will not infect them. In addition, if you have a job you will be able to get back to work, thus reducing the disruption there. These external benefits of health care could be quite large.

If sick people have to pay the cost of their treatment, they may decide not to be treated – especially if they are poor. They will consider the costs and benefits they might experience, but will probably not take into account the effect that their illness has on other people. The market, by equating *private* benefits and costs, would produce too little health care.

Information problems and patient ignorance

Markets only function well to allocate resources efficiently if the consumer has the knowledge to make informed decisions. For many products we purchase, there is reasonably good information and so we can judge which products/services we will like the most.

In the case of health care the situation is different. Much of the information is complex and difficult to understand without specialist knowledge. The one-off nature of many treatments also means that patients are unable to learn from repeat purchases.

In some circumstances the demand for health care might be urgent. In these cases people do not have the time to shop around and may be unable to make rational decisions because of heightened emotional distress. For these reasons a patient has to rely on the professional advice of others. They have to enter an agency relationship with a doctor or health-care provider.

KI 25 p274

For example, if you have a pain in your chest, it may be simple muscular strain, or it may be a symptom of heart disease. You rely on the doctor (the *supplier* of the treatment) to give you the information: to diagnose your condition. The key issue is whether the incentives of the doctor and the patient are aligned.

If health care was provided through the market, unscrupulous doctors might advise more expensive treatment than is necessary; they might even have an agreement with certain drugs companies that they will try to persuade you to buy an expensive branded product rather than an identical cheaper version. This problem will also exist in an insurance-based system, where the doctor may be even more inclined to oversupply if the patient has sufficient cover.

KI 25 p274

If people had to pay, those suffering from the early stages of a serious disease might not consult their doctor until the symptoms become very acute, by which time it might be too late to treat the disease, or very expensive to do so. With a health service that is free at the point of use, however, a person is more likely to receive an earlier diagnosis of serious conditions.

Oligopoly

If doctors and hospitals operated in the free market as profit maximisers, it is unlikely that competition would drive down their prices. Instead they might collude to fix standard prices for treatment, so as to protect their incomes. Even if doctors did compete openly, it is unlikely that consumers would have enough information to enable them to 'shop around' for the best value.

We have to be careful: to argue that the market system will fail to provide an optimal allocation of health-care resources does not in itself prove that *free provision* will result in optimal provision. For example, with no charge for GP appointments it is likely that some patients will consult their doctors over trivial complaints. The result will be consumption beyond the socially efficient point.

In the USA there is much more reliance on *private medical insurance*. Alternatively, the government may simply *subsidise* health care, so as to make it cheaper rather than free. This is the case with prescriptions and dental treatment in the UK, where many people only have to pay part of the cost of treatment. Also, the government can *regulate* the behaviour of the providers of health care, to prevent exploitation of the patient. Thus only people with certain qualifications are allowed to operate as doctors, nurses, pharmacists, etc.

3. ***If health care is provided free at the point of consumption, the demand is likely to be high. How is this high demand likely to be dealt with? Is this a good way of dealing with the issue?***
4. ***Go through each of the market failings identified in this box. In each case, consider what alternative policies are open to a government to tackle them. What are the advantages and disadvantages of these alternatives?***
5. ***Does the provision of free health care mean that it needs to be publicly produced? What would be the advantages, and disadvantages, of private provision?***

Go through each of the market failings identified in this box. In each case, write a short summary of the alternative policies open to a government to tackle them and discuss their advantages and disadvantages.

Taxes and subsidies

A policy instrument particularly favoured by many economists is that of taxes and subsidies. They can be used for two main microeconomic purposes: (a) to promote greater social efficiency by altering the composition of production and consumption: and (b) to redistribute incomes. We examined their use for the second purpose in Chapter 11. Here we examine their use to achieve greater social efficiency.

When there are imperfections in the market (such as externalities or monopoly power), Pareto optimality will not be achieved. Taxes and subsidies can be used to correct these imperfections. Essentially the approach is to tax those goods or activities where the market produces too much, and subsidise those where the market produces too little.

Figure 12.12 Using taxes to correct a market distortion: an individual firm

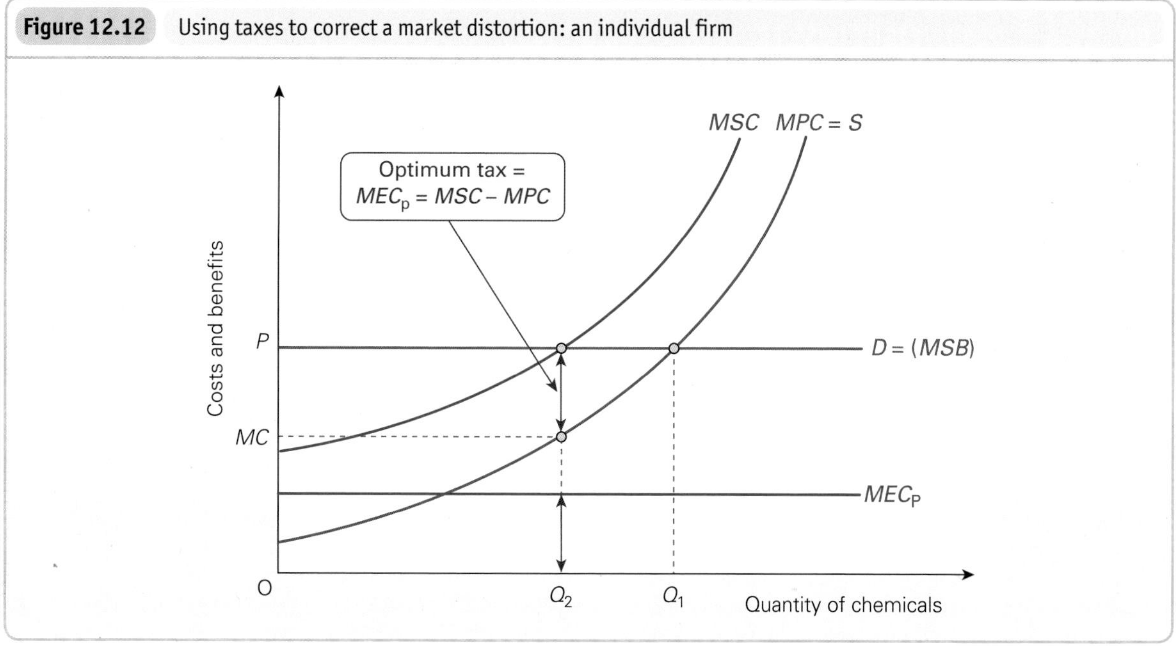

Taxes and subsidies to correct externalities

The first-best solution. The *first-best solution* when there is only one market imperfection is simple: the government should impose a tax equal to the marginal external cost (or grant a subsidy equal to the marginal external benefit). This is known as a ***Pigouvian tax*** (or ***Pigouvian subsidy***).

Previously, we examined the impact of external costs of pollution created by the chemical industry as a whole. We will now focus on one firm in that industry, which otherwise is perfectly competitive. Assume that this particular chemical company emits smoke from a chimney and thus pollutes the atmosphere. This creates external costs for the people who breathe in the smoke. The marginal social cost of producing the chemicals thus exceeds the marginal private cost to the firm: $MSC > MPC$. This is illustrated in Figure 12.12.

KI 31 p364

In this example, it is assumed the external pollution cost begins with the first unit of production but remains constant. Hence the MEC_P is drawn as a horizontal line. The vertical distance between the MPC and MSC curves is equal to the MEC_P. The firm produces Q_1 where $P = MPC$ (its profit-maximising output), but in doing so takes no account of the external pollution costs it imposes on society.

Definition

Pigouvian tax (or subsidy) A tax (or subsidy) designed to 'internalise' an externality. The marginal rate of a Pigouvian tax (or subsidy) should be equal to the marginal external cost (or benefit).

If the government now imposes a tax on production equal to the marginal pollution cost, it will effectively 'internalise' the externality. The firm will have to pay an amount equal to the external cost it creates. It will therefore now maximise profits at Q_2, which is the socially optimal output where $MSB = MSC$.

By analogy, if a firm produced an external benefit, then in the first-best world it ought to be given a subsidy equal to that marginal external benefit.

Note that a tax or subsidy ought to be directed as closely as possible to the source of the externality. For example, if a firm trains labour, and that creates a benefit to society, then ideally it ought to be given a subsidy for each person trained, rather than a general output subsidy. After all, an output subsidy not only encourages the firm to train more people (the desired effect), but also encourages it to use more capital and raw materials (an undesired side effect). This is a general maxim of welfare economics: *a distortion should be corrected at source if side-effect problems are to be avoided.*

Second-best tax and subsidy policies. In reality, the government must tackle imperfections in a world that has many other imperfections. Figure 12.13 shows a firm that both produces an external cost ($MSC > MPC$) and *also* has monopoly power. It will maximise profits at Q_1 where $MPC = MR$ (point x).

The socially efficient level of output in this case is Q_2, where MSB equals MSC. Note that in this case, the welfare loss from a monopoly is actually less than if the market were perfectly competitive: i.e. the extent of overproduction is lower. The perfectly competitive equilibrium would be at point c, with price P_{pc} and output Q_{pc}.

To provide an incentive for the monopolist to produce Q_2, a tax of $a - b$ must be imposed (since at point a,

BOX 12.4 **DEADWEIGHT LOSS FROM TAXES ON GOODS AND SERVICES** EXPLORING ECONOMICS

The excess burden of taxes

Taxation can be used to correct market failures, but taxes can have adverse effects themselves. One such effect is the deadweight loss that results when taxes are imposed on goods and services (see page 344).

The diagram shows the demand and supply of a particular good. Equilibrium is initially at a price of P_1 and a level of sales of Q_1 (i.e. where $D = S$).

Now an excise tax is imposed on the good. The supply curve shifts upwards by the amount of the tax, to S + tax. Equilibrium price rises to P_2 and equilibrium quantity falls to Q_2. Producers receive an after-tax price of P_2 – tax.

Consumer surplus falls from areas 1 + 2 + 3, to area 1 (the green area). Producer surplus falls from areas 4 + 5 + 6 to area 6 (the blue area). Does this mean, therefore, that total surplus falls by areas 2 + 3 + 4 + 5? The answer is no, because there is a gain to the government from the tax revenue (and hence a gain to the population from the resulting government expenditure). The revenue from the tax is known as the ***government surplus***. It is given by areas 2 + 4 (the pink area).

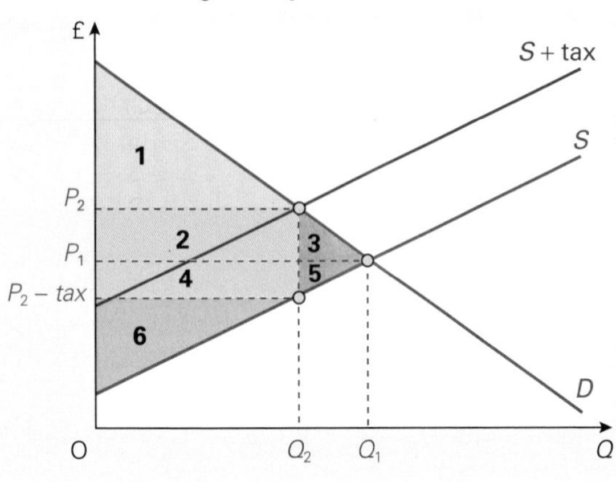

But even after including government surplus, there is still a fall in total surplus of areas 3 + 5. This is the deadweight loss of the tax. It is sometimes known as the ***excess burden***.

Does this loss of total surplus from taxation imply that taxes on goods are always a 'bad thing'? The answer is no. This conclusion would follow only in a 'first-best' world where there were no market failures: where competition was perfect, where there were no externalities and where income distribution was optimum. In such a world, the loss of surplus from imposing a tax on a good would represent a reduction in welfare.

In the real world of imperfect markets and inequality, taxes can do more good than harm. As we have shown in this section, they can help to correct for externalities; and as we showed in the previous chapter, they can be used as a means of redistributing incomes. Nevertheless, the excess burden of taxes is something that ideally ought to be considered when weighing up the desirability of imposing taxes on goods and services, or of increasing their rate.

1. *How far can an economist contribute to this normative debate over the desirability of an excise tax?*
2. *What is the excess burden of a lump-sum tax? (For a clue, see Figure 12.14.)*

Research the use of at least two taxes in each of two developed countries that are used solely or partly to correct for external costs. Consider how well they tackle the problem.

Definitions

Government surplus (from a tax on a good) The total tax revenue earned by the government from sales of a good.

Excess burden (of a tax on a good) The amount by which the loss in consumer plus producer surplus exceeds the government surplus.

$MR = MPC$ + tax). This tax is *less* than the full amount of the externality because of the monopoly power. Were the monopolist to be charged a tax *equal* to the externality (so that its MPC + tax curve was equal to the MSC curve), it would maximise profits at point y, at a price of P_3 and an output of Q_3. This would not be socially efficient, since MSB would now be *above MSC*.

Taxes to correct for monopoly

So far, we have considered the use of taxes to correct for externalities. Taxes can also be used to regulate the behaviour of monopolies and oligopolies.

If the government wishes to tackle the problem of excessive monopoly profits, it can impose a *lump-sum* tax on the monopolist. An example of such a tax was the 'windfall tax', imposed by the UK government in 1997. This was on the profits of various privatised utilities. In 2005, another tax was imposed on the 'excess' profits of oil companies operating in the North Sea. There were also numerous calls in 2008 to impose a windfall tax on energy companies, but this was never implemented. The use of a lump-sum tax is illustrated in Figure 12.14.

Being of a fixed amount, a lump-sum tax is a fixed cost to the firm. It does not affect the firm's marginal cost. It shifts the AC curve upwards.

Profits continue to be maximised where $MC = MR$, at an output of Q_1 and a price of P_1. But profits are reduced from areas 1 + 2 to area 1 alone. Area 2 now represents the

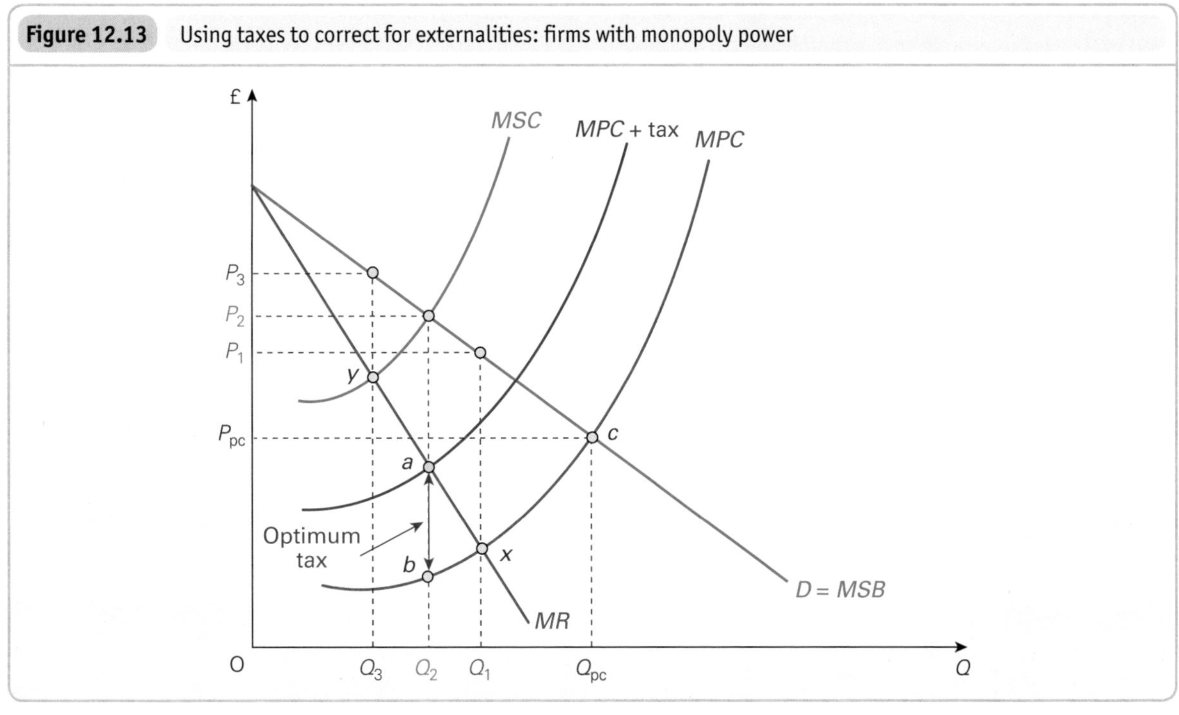

Figure 12.13 Using taxes to correct for externalities: firms with monopoly power

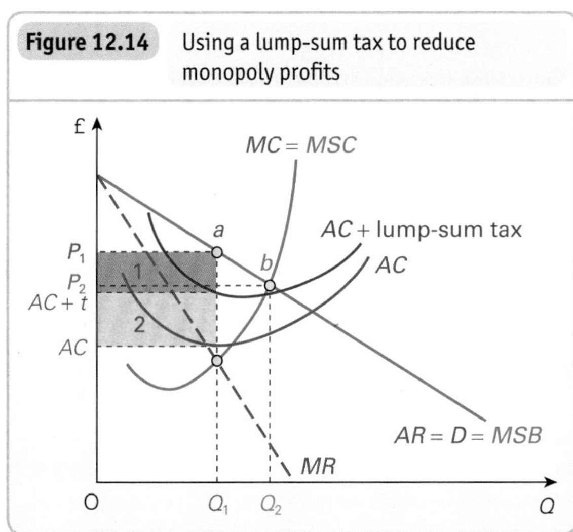

Figure 12.14 Using a lump-sum tax to reduce monopoly profits

amount of tax paid to the government. If the lump-sum tax were large enough to make the *AC* + lump-sum tax curve cross the demand curve at point *a*, *all* the supernormal profits would be taken as tax.

If the government also wants to increase the monopolist's output to the socially efficient level of Q_2, and wants it to charge a price of P_2, it could do this with a careful combination of a per-unit subsidy (which will shift both the *AC* and the *MC* curves downwards) and a lump-sum tax. The required level of subsidy will be that which shifts the *MC* curve downwards to the point where it intersects *MR* at output Q_2. Then a lump-sum tax would be imposed that would be big enough to shift the *AC* curve back up again so that it crosses the demand curve at point *b*.

What could we say about the necessary subsidy if the MR curve crossed the horizontal axis to the left of point b?

Advantages of taxes and subsidies

Many economists favour the tax/subsidy solution to market imperfections (especially the problem of externalities) because it still allows the market to operate. It forces firms to take on board the full social costs and benefits of their actions; as we have seen, this is often described as *internalising the externality*. Furthermore, once the policy is in place, taxes and subsidies can be adjusted according to the magnitude of the problem.

Moreover, if firms are taxed for polluting, they are encouraged to find cleaner ways of producing. The tax acts as an incentive over the longer run to reduce pollution. Likewise, by subsidising *good* practices, firms are given the incentive to adopt more good practices.

The most suitable situation for imposing a pollution tax is when there is a clearly measurable emission, like a particular chemical waste. The government can then impose a tax per litre or per tonne of that waste.

Disadvantages of taxes and subsidies

Infeasibility of using different tax and subsidy rates. Each firm produces different levels and types of externality and operates under different degrees of imperfect competition. It would be administratively very difficult and expensive to charge every offending firm its own particular tax rate (or grant every relevant firm its own particular rate of subsidy). Even in the case of pollution where it is possible to measure a firm's emissions, there would still have to be a different tax rate for each pollutant and even for each environment, depending on its ability to absorb the pollutant.

Lack of knowledge. Even if a government did decide to charge a tax equal to each offending firm's marginal external costs, it would still have the problem of measuring those costs and apportioning blame. The damage to lakes and forests from acid rain has been a major concern since the beginning of the 1980s. But just how serious is that damage? What is its current monetary cost? How long lasting is the damage? Just what and who are to blame? These questions cannot be answered precisely. It is thus impossible to fix the 'correct' pollution tax on, say, a particular coal-fired power station. KI 15 p132

1. *Why is it easier to use taxes and subsidies to tackle the problem of car exhaust pollution than to tackle the problem of peak-time traffic congestion in cities?*
2. *CFCs in fridges were known to cause environmental damage and their use has been banned in most countries. Why has this approach been adopted rather than the tax solution?*

Changes in property rights

One cause of market failure is the limited nature of property rights. If someone dumps a load of rubble in your garden, you can insist that it is removed. If, however, someone dumps a load of rubble in their *own* garden, which is next door to yours, what can you do? You can still see it from your window. It is still an eyesore. But you have no property rights over the next-door garden.

Property rights define who owns property, to what uses it can be put, the rights other people have over it and how it may be transferred. By *extending* these rights, individuals may be able to prevent other people from imposing costs on them or charge them for doing so.

KI 28 p356 The socially efficient level of charge would be one that was equal to the marginal external cost (and would have the same effect as the government charging a tax on the firm of that amount: see Figure 12.12). The ***Coase theorem***[2] states that when there are well-defined property rights and there are no bargaining or negotiation costs, then the socially efficient charge *will* be levied. But why?

Let us take the case of river pollution by a chemical works that imposes a cost on people fishing in the river. If property rights to the river were now given to the fishing community, they could impose a charge on the chemical works per unit of output. If they charged *less* than the marginal external cost, they would suffer more from the last unit (in terms of lost fish) than they were being compensated. If they charged *more*, and thereby caused the firm to cut back its output below the socially efficient level, they would be sacrificing receiving charges that would be greater than the marginal suffering. It will be in the sufferers' best interests, therefore, to charge an amount *equal* to the marginal externality. KI 31 p364

Alternatively, the property rights to the river could be awarded to the chemical works. In this situation the fishing community could offer payments to the firm on condition that it did not pollute the river.

One interesting result is that the efficient solution to the problem caused by the externality does not depend on which party is assigned the property rights: i.e. the fishing community or the chemical works. All that matters is that the property rights are fully assigned to either one or the other and that there are no bargaining costs.

If the sufferers had no property rights, show how it would still be in their interests to 'bribe' the firm to produce the socially efficient level of output.

In most instances, however, this type of solution is totally impractical. It is impractical when *many* people are *slightly* inconvenienced, especially if there are many culprits imposing the costs. For example, if I were disturbed by noisy lorries passing by my house, it would not be practical to negotiate with every haulage company involved. What if I wanted to ban the lorries from the street but my next-door neighbour wanted to charge them 10p per journey? Who gets their way?

The extension of private property rights becomes more practical where the parties involved are few in number, are easily identifiable and where the costs are clearly defined. Thus a noise abatement Act could be passed which allowed me to prevent my neighbours from playing noisy radios, having noisy parties or otherwise disturbing the peace in my home. The onus would be on me to report them. Or I could agree not to report them if they paid me adequate compensation.

But even in cases where only a few people are involved, there may still be the problem of litigation. I may have to incur the time and expense of taking people to court. Justice may not be free, and thus there may be concerns about equity. The rich can afford 'better' justice. They can employ top lawyers. Even if I have a right to sue a large company for dumping toxic waste near me, I may not have the legal muscle to win.

Finally, there is the broader question of equity. Although the socially efficient outcome does not depend on who has

Definition

Coase theorem When there are well-defined property rights and zero bargaining costs, then negotiations between the party creating the externality and the party affected by the externality can bring about the socially efficient market quantity.

2 Named after Ronald Coase, who developed the theory. See his 'The problem of social cost', *Journal of Law and Economics*, vol. 3 (1960).

the property rights, the equity of the outcome will. Extending the rights of property owners may favour the rich, who tend to have more property, at the expense of the poor. Ramblers may get great pleasure from strolling across a great country estate, along public rights of way. If the owner's property rights were now extended to exclude the ramblers, would this be a social gain?

Of course, equity considerations can also be dealt with by altering property rights, but in a different way. *Public* property, like parks, open spaces, libraries and historic buildings, could be extended. Also, the property of the rich could be redistributed to the poor. Here it is less a question of the rights that ownership confers, and more a question of altering the ownership itself.

1. *To what extent could property rights (either public or private) be successfully extended and invoked to curb the problem of industrial pollution (a) of the atmosphere; (b) of rivers; (c) by the dumping of toxic waste; (d) by the erection of ugly buildings; (e) by the creation of high levels of noise?*
2. *What protection do private property rights in the real world give to sufferers of noise (a) from neighbours; (b) from traffic; (c) from mobile phones on public transport?*

Laws prohibiting or regulating undesirable structures or behaviour

Laws are frequently used to correct market imperfections. This section examines three of the most common cases.

Laws prohibiting or regulating behaviour that imposes external costs

Laws can be applied both to individuals and to firms. In the case of individuals, it is illegal to drive when drunk. Drunk driving imposes costs on others in the form of accidents and death. Other examples include the banning of (a) smoking in public places (b) using mobile phones while driving.

In the case of firms, various polluting activities could be banned or restricted; safety standards could be imposed in the place of work; building houses or factories could be prohibited in green-belt areas.

In the case of common resources, restrictions could be placed on their use. For example, in the case of fishing grounds, governments could limit the size of fleets, impose quotas on catches or specify the types of net to be used. In extreme cases, they could ban fishing altogether for a period of time to allow fish stocks to recover. In order to be able to enforce restrictions, many governments have extended their 'territorial waters' to 200 miles from their coast.

Advantages of legal restrictions

- They are simple and clear to understand and are often relatively easy to administer. Inspectors or the police can conduct spot checks to see that the law is being obeyed.
- When the danger is very great, it might be much safer to ban various practices altogether rather than to rely on taxes or on individuals attempting to assert their property rights through the civil courts.
- When a decision needs to be taken quickly, it might be possible to invoke emergency action. For example, in a city it would be simpler to ban or restrict the use of private cars during a chemical smog emergency than to tax their use (see Case Study 13.5 on the student website).

Disadvantages of legal restrictions. The main problem is that legal restrictions tend to be a rather blunt weapon. If, for example, a firm were required to reduce the effluent of a toxic chemical to 20 tonnes per week, it would have no incentive to reduce it further. With a tax on the effluent, however, the more the firm reduced the effluent, the less tax it would pay. Thus with a system of taxes there is a *continuing* incentive to cut pollution.

Laws to prevent or regulate monopolies and oligopolies

Governments often introduce laws that prohibit various types of collusive activities, the misuse of market power by a dominant firm and mergers or takeovers that would result in a substantial lessening of competition. These will be examined in detail in Chapter 14.

How suitable are legal restrictions in the following cases? (a) Ensuring adequate vehicle safety; (b) reducing traffic congestion; (c) preventing the abuse of monopoly power; (d) ensuring that mergers are in the public interest; (e) ensuring that firms charge a price equal to marginal cost.

Laws to prevent firms from exploiting people's ignorance

Given that consumers have imperfect information, consumer protection laws can make it illegal for firms to sell shoddy or dangerous goods, or to make false or misleading claims about their products.

The problem is that the firms most likely to exploit the consumer are often the ones that are most elusive when it comes to prosecuting them.

Regulatory bodies

A more subtle approach than banning or restricting various activities involves the use of regulatory bodies.

Having identified possible cases where action might be required (e.g. potential cases of pollution or the abuse of monopoly power), the regulatory body would probably conduct an investigation and then prepare a report containing its findings and recommendations. It might also have the power to enforce its decisions, or this might be up to some higher authority.

An example of such a body is the UK's Competition and Markets Authority, the work of which is examined in section 14.1. Other examples are the bodies set up to regulate the privatised utilities: e.g. Ofwat (the Water Services Regulation Authority). These are examined in section 14.2.

The advantage of this approach is that a case-by-case method can be used and, as a result, the most appropriate solution adopted. However, investigations may be expensive and time-consuming, only a few cases may be examined and offending firms may make various promises of good behaviour which, if not followed up by the regulatory body, may not in fact be carried out.

What other forms of intervention are likely to be necessary to back up the work of regulatory bodies?

Price controls

Price controls could be used to prevent a monopoly or oligopoly from charging excessive prices. Currently, sections of various privatised industries, such as water and rail industries, are restricted in their ability to raise their prices (see section 14.2).

Price controls could also be used with the objective of redistributing incomes. Prices could be fixed either above or below equilibrium. Thus (high) minimum farm prices can be used to protect the incomes of farmers, and minimum wage legislation can help those on low incomes. On the consumption side, (low) maximum rents might be put in place with the intention of helping those on low incomes afford housing, and price ceilings on food or other essentials during a war or other emergency can ensure everyone can afford such items. However, as was argued in section 3.1, the problem with price controls is that they cause shortages (in the case of low prices) or surpluses (high prices).

Provision of information

KI 15 p132 When imperfect information is a reason for market failure, the direct provision of information by the government or one of its agencies may help to correct that failure. An example is the information on jobs provided by job centres to those looking for work. This will speed up the 'matching process' between the unemployed and employers. It helps the labour market to work better and increases the elasticity of supply of labour.

Another example is the provision of consumer information – for example, on the effects of smoking, or of the benefits of eating vegetables. Another is the provision of government statistics on prices, costs, employment, sales trends, etc. This enables firms to plan with greater certainty.

In what way is the provision of information a public good? Do all the examples above come into the category of public goods? Give some other examples of information that is a public good. (Clue: refer back to the characteristics of public goods in section 12.2 and do not confuse a public good with something merely provided by the government which could also be provided by the private sector.)

The direct provision of goods and services

In the case of public goods and services, such as streets, pavements, seaside illumination and national defence, the market may completely fail to provide the socially efficient amount because of free-riding. Government may have to finance the optimal provision of the public good by requiring compulsory payments from members of society. One way of obtaining the compulsory payments is through the central/local tax system.

Before collecting the money the government needs to try to work out the socially efficient amount of the public good to finance. How could the real-world equivalent of point *f* in Figure 12.9 be identified in practice? The solution is to identify all the costs and benefits to society and to weight them appropriately. This is where cost–benefit analysis comes in – the subject of section 12.4.

Once the compulsory payments have been collected, the central government, local government or some other government agency could then manage the production of the goods or services directly. Alternatively, they could pay private firms to do so.

The government could also provide goods and services directly which are *not* public goods. Examples include health and education. There are four reasons why such things are provided free or well below cost.

Social justice. Society may feel that these things should not be provided according to ability to pay. Rather, as *merit goods*, they should be provided according to need.

Large positive externalities. People other than the consumer may benefit substantially. If a person decides to get treatment for an infectious disease, other people benefit by not being infected. A free health service thus helps to combat the spread of disease.

Dependants. If education were not free, and if the quality of education depended on the amount spent, and if parents could choose how much or how little to buy, then the quality of children's education would depend not just on their parents' income, but also on how much they cared. A government may choose to provide such things free in order to protect children from 'bad' or 'foolish' parents. A similar argument is used for providing free prescriptions and dental treatment for all children.

Imperfect information. Consumers may not realise how much they will benefit. If they had to pay, they might choose (unwisely) to go without. Providing health care free may persuade people to consult their doctors before a complaint becomes serious.

Public ownership

This is different from direct provision, in that the goods and services produced by publicly owned (nationalised) industries are sold in the market. The costs and benefits of public ownership are examined in detail in section 14.2.

Section summary

1. If there were a distortion in just one part of the economy, the 'first-best' solution would be possible. This would be to correct that one distortion. In the real world, where there are many distortions, the first-best solution will not be possible. The second-best solution will be to seek the best compromise that minimises the *relative* distortions between the industry in question and other parts of the economy.
2. Taxes and subsidies are one means of correcting market distortions. In the first-best world, externalities can be corrected by imposing tax rates equal to the size of marginal external costs, and granting rates of subsidy equal to marginal external benefits. In the second-best world, taxes and subsidies can be used to correct externalities that create *relative* distortions between this industry and others, or externalities that exist along with other distortions within this industry.
3. Taxes and subsidies can also be used to affect monopoly price, output and profit. Subsidies can be used to persuade a monopolist to increase output to the competitive level. Lump-sum taxes can be used to reduce monopoly profits without affecting price or output.
4. Taxes and subsidies have the advantages of 'internalising' externalities and of providing incentives to reduce external costs. On the other hand, they may be impractical to use when different rates are required for each case, or when it is impossible to know the full effects of the activities that the taxes or subsidies are being used to correct.
5. An extension of property rights may allow individuals to prevent others from imposing costs on them. This is not practical, however, when many people are affected to a small degree, or where several people are affected but differ in their attitudes towards what they want doing about the 'problem'.
6. Laws can be used to tackle various market failures. Legal controls are often simpler and easier to operate than taxes, and are safer when the danger is potentially great. However, they tend to be rather a blunt weapon.
7. Regulatory bodies can be set up to monitor and control activities that are against the public interest (e.g. anti-competitive behaviour of oligopolists).
8. The government may provide information in cases where the private sector fails to provide an adequate level. It may also provide goods and services directly. These could be either public goods or other goods where the government feels that provision by the market is inadequate.

*12.4 COST-BENEFIT ANALYSIS

Cost-benefit analysis (CBA) is a technique used to help governments decide whether to go ahead with various projects such as a new motorway, a bypass, an underground line, a hospital, a health-care programme, a dam, and so on. The analysis seeks to establish whether the benefits to society from the project outweigh the costs, in which case the project should go ahead; or whether the costs outweigh the benefits, in which case it should not.

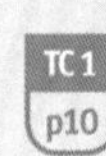

CBAs are usually commissioned either by a government department or by a local authority. Unlike the techniques of project evaluation used by private firms, which take into account only *private monetary* costs and benefits, CBA takes into account *externalities* and private *non-monetary* costs and benefits as well. Thus a cost-benefit study of a proposed new road might attempt to assess the external costs of noise to local residents and destruction of wildlife as well as the direct costs and benefits to motorists.

The procedure

The procedure at first sight seems fairly straightforward.

- All costs and benefits are identified. These include all private monetary and non-monetary costs and benefits and all externalities.
- A monetary value is assigned to each cost and benefit. This is essential if costs and benefits are to be added up: a common unit of measurement must be used. As might be expected, assigning monetary values to externalities like noise, pollution and the quality of life is fraught with difficulties and may involve subjective decisions.

KI 31 p364

- Account is taken of the likelihood of a cost or benefit occurring. The simplest way of doing this is to multiply the monetary value of a cost or benefit by the probability of its occurrence. This is called the ***expected value***. So if there were a 60 per cent chance of a cost of £100 occurring, it would be valued at £60.
- Account is taken of the timing of the costs and benefits. Thus £100 of benefits received today would be regarded as more desirable than having to wait, say, 10 years to receive the £100. Likewise it is a greater sacrifice to pay

Definitions

Cost-benefit analysis The identification, measurement and weighing up of the costs and benefits of a project in order to decide whether or not it should go ahead.

Expected value The value of a possible outcome multiplied by the probability of its occurrence.

£100 today than to have to pay it within 10 years. Thus future costs and benefits must be reduced in value to take this into account. Discounting techniques (similar to those we examined in section 10.3: see pages 310–12) are used for this purpose.

KI 27 p310

- Some account may also be taken of the distribution of the costs and benefits. Is it considered fair that, although some people will gain from the project, others will lose? Will the losers be compensated in any way?
- A recommendation is then made by weighing up the costs and benefits. In the simplest terms, if the benefits exceed the costs, it will be recommended that the project goes ahead.

Each of these stages involves a number of difficulties. These are examined in the following sections.

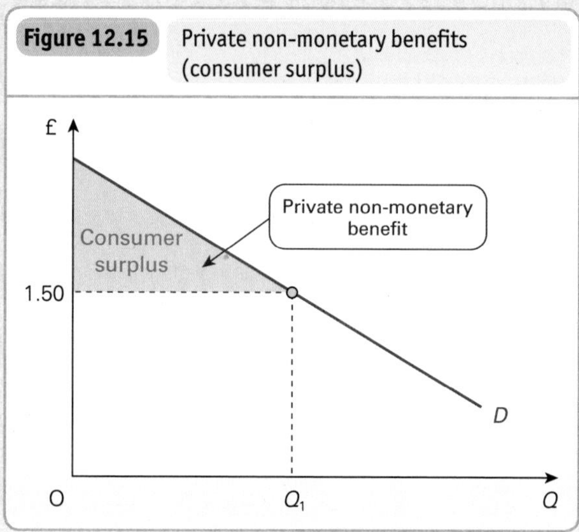

Figure 12.15 Private non-monetary benefits (consumer surplus)

Identifying the costs and benefits

Identifying costs and benefits is relatively easy, although there are some problems in predicting what types of external effect are likely to occur.

Costs

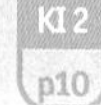

Direct (private) monetary costs. These include all the construction costs and the operating and maintenance costs.

External costs. These fall into two categories:

- *Pecuniary external costs*, such as the loss of profits to ferry operators if a tunnel is constructed under a large river. As we saw on page 365, they are not normally included in the definition of externalities as they are internalised (i.e. taken account of) by the market. Pecuniary external costs are thus not normally included in CBA when considering the efficiency implications of the project: i.e. they do not lead to deadweight welfare loss – though they may become relevant when assessing its distributional implications. Pecuniary costs *may* be included, however, when they are borne by the general public, such as money spent on sound insulation to block out the noise from traffic on a new road, or by non-competitor firms, such as those in the tourism industry affected by pollution.
- *Technical external costs*, such as pollution, spoiling the landscape, noise and various other forms of inconvenience to local residents. In some projects, such as a tunnel, these costs will be confined largely to the construction phase. With other projects, however, such as a new airport, there may be considerable externalities resulting from its operation (e.g. noise). These technical externalities are usually the most difficult costs to identify and measure.

Benefits

Direct (private) monetary benefits. These are also easy to identify. They consist of the revenues received from the users of the project. The direct monetary benefits of a toll bridge, for example, are the tolls paid.

Private non-monetary benefits. These are the benefits to consumers over and above what they actually pay: in other words, the consumer surplus. For example, if a bridge had a toll of £1.50, and yet a person was prepared to pay £3 if necessary to avoid the long trip round the estuary, then the person's consumer surplus is £1.50. Total consumer surplus is thus the area between the demand curve (which shows what people are willing to pay) and the price charged. This is illustrated in Figure 12.15.

Technical external benefits. These are the benefits to the non-users of the project. For example, the Victoria Underground line CBA identified external benefits to road users in central London. The roads would become less congested as people used the new Underground line.

Measuring the costs and benefits

Identifying costs and benefits may be relatively easy: measuring them is another matter. Difficulties in measurement depend on the type of cost and benefit. There are four types.

Direct private monetary costs and benefits

These would seem to be the simplest to measure. Normally the simple financial costs and revenues are used. In the case of a new Underground line, for example, such costs would include excavation, construction and capital costs (such as new rolling stock) and the operating costs (such as labour, electricity and maintenance). Revenues would be the fares paid by travellers. There are two problems, nevertheless:

- What *will* these financial costs and revenues be? It is all very well using current prices, but prices rise over time, and at different and unpredictable rates. Also, it is difficult to forecast demand and hence revenues. There is thus a large element of *uncertainty*.
- The prices will often be distorted by the existence of monopoly power. Should this be taken into account? In an otherwise perfect world (the first-best situation), the

answer would be yes. But in the real world, where price distortions exist throughout the economy, actual prices should normally be used. In the case of a proposed Underground line, for example, it makes sense to use market prices, given that market prices are paid by car drivers and by users of taxis and buses (the alternatives to using the Underground). Thus the second-best solution is to use actual market prices *unless* there is a price distortion that applies *only* to the specific project.

What price should be used when there is such a distortion?

Non-monetary private benefits: consumer surplus

Consumer surplus is a private benefit – it accrues to the users of the project – but is not part of the money earned from the project. There are two ways of estimating it.

The first way is to estimate the demand curve and then estimate the shaded area in Figure 12.15. Estimating demand is very difficult, since it depends on the price and availability of substitutes. The demand for the Channel Tunnel depends on the price, frequency and convenience of ferry crossings. It also depends on the overall level of activity in the economy and perhaps the world generally. Thus estimates of air traffic (essential information when deciding whether to build a new airport) have often been proved wrong as the world economy has grown more rapidly or less rapidly than previously forecast.

Another problem is that the consumer surplus gained from the project (e.g. the Channel Tunnel) may replace some of the albeit smaller consumer surplus from a competing service (e.g. cross-Channel ferries). In this case, the non-monetary private benefit is merely the *additional* consumer surplus of those who switch, but still the *full* consumer surplus of those who would not otherwise have crossed the Channel. This makes calculation less straightforward.

An alternative approach is to focus on specific non-monetary benefits to consumers. This approach is more useful when the service is to be provided free and thus no estimate of a demand curve can be made. Assume that a new motorway saves 20 000 hours of travelling time per week. (This, of course, will first have to be estimated, and again a prediction will have to be made of the number of people using the motorway.) How is this 20 000 hours to be evaluated? In the case of businesspeople and lorry drivers, the average hourly wage rate will be used to estimate the value of each labour hour saved. In the case of leisure time, there is less agreement on how to value an hour saved. Usually it is simply assumed to be some fraction of the average hourly wage. This method is somewhat arbitrary, however, and a better approach, though probably impractical, would be to attempt to measure how the travellers themselves evaluate their time.

Another way of measuring time saved would be to see how much money people would be prepared to spend to save travelling time. For example, how much extra would people be prepared to pay for a taxi that saved, say, 10 minutes over the bus journey? This method, however, has to take account of the fact that taxis may be more desirable for other reasons too, such as comfort.

How would you attempt to value time that you yourself save (a) getting to work; (b) going on holiday; (c) going out in the evening?

Pecuniary external costs and benefits

These would normally be counted at face value. Thus, the pecuniary external costs of a new Underground line would include the loss of profits to taxi and bus companies. The external monetary benefits of a new motorway would include the profits to be made by the owners of the motorway service stations. As they are internalised by the market, they would not be included in the CBA, except in any distributional analysis of the scheme. However, they would be counted when borne by non-competitors or non-collaborators and would include the loss (or increase) in profits of such firms: e.g. the loss in profits of a hotel from the construction of a new motorway flyover close to it.

KI 31 p364

Technical externalities

These are likely to be the hardest to measure. The general principle employed is to try to find out how much people would be prepared to pay to obtain the benefits or avoid the costs, if they were able to do so. There are two approaches here.

Ask people (questionnaires). Take the case of noise from an airport or motorway. People could be asked how much they would need to be compensated. There are two problems with this:

- *Ignorance*. People will not know just how much they will suffer *until* the airport or motorway is built.
- *Dishonesty*. People will tend to exaggerate the compensation they would need. After all, if compensation is actually going to be paid, people will want to get as much as possible. But even if it is not, the more people exaggerate the costs to themselves, the more likely it is that they can get the project stopped.

These problems can be lessened if people are questioned who have already experienced a similar project elsewhere. They have less to gain from being dishonest.

Make inferences from people's behaviour. Take the case of noise again. In similar projects elsewhere, how have people actually reacted? How much have they spent on double glazing or other noise insulation? How much financial loss have they been prepared to suffer to move somewhere quieter?

What needs to be measured, however, is not just the financial cost, but also the loss of consumer surplus. The Roskill Commission in 1968 examined the siting of a third London airport. It attempted to evaluate noise costs, and looked at the difference in value of house prices round Gatwick compared with elsewhere. A problem with this approach is in finding cases elsewhere that are directly comparable. Were the four potential sites for the third London airport directly comparable with Gatwick?

Another example of externalities would be a reduction in accidents from a safer road. How is this to be measured? Obviously there are the monetary benefits from reduced medical expenditures. But how would you value a life saved? This question is examined in Box 12.5.

How would you evaluate (a) the external effects of building a reservoir in an area of outstanding natural beauty; (b) the external effects of acid rain pollution from a power station?

Risk and uncertainty

Taking account of *risk* is relatively straightforward. The value of a cost or benefit is simply multiplied by the probability of its occurrence. KI 11 p72

The problem is that *risk* is less frequent than *uncertainty*. As was explained in section 4.3, in the case of uncertainty all that is known is that an outcome *might* occur. The likelihood of its occurring, however, is uncertain.

How then can uncertainty be taken into account? The best approach is to use ***sensitivity analysis***. Let us consider two cases.

Definition

Sensitivity analysis Where a range of possible values of uncertain costs and benefits are given to see whether the project's desirability is sensitive to these different values.

*BOX 12.5 WHAT PRICE A HUMAN LIFE?

EXPLORING ECONOMICS

A difficult question for cost–benefit analysis

Many projects involve saving lives, whether it is a new hospital or transport system. This is obviously a major benefit, but how can you place a value on life?

Some people argue: 'You can't put a price on a human life: life is priceless.' But just what are they saying here? Are they saying that life has an *infinite* value? If so, the project must be carried out *whatever* the costs, and even if other benefits are zero! Clearly, when evaluating lives saved from the project, a value less than infinity must be given.

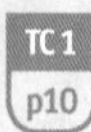

TC 1 p10

Other people might argue that human life cannot be treated like other costs and benefits and put into mathematical calculations. But what are these people saying? That the question of lives saved should be excluded from the cost–benefit study? If so, the implication is that life has a *zero* value! Again this is clearly not the case.

So if a value somewhere between zero and infinity should be used, what should it be?

Some economists have suggested that a life be valued in terms of a person's future earning potential. But this implies that the only value of a person is as a factor of production. Would the life of a disabled person who is unable to work and draws state benefit, be given a *negative* value? Again this is clearly not the solution. It would also value the life of a banker considerably higher than that of most other workers; an approach that would be hard to justify!

Can any inferences be drawn from people's behaviour?

How much are people prepared to spend on safety: on making their car roadworthy, on buying crash helmets, etc.? This approach too has serious drawbacks. People are wishful thinkers and tend to underestimate the chances they will be killed in an accident.

Then again, there are the problems of estimating the effects on other people: on family and friends. Can the amount that people are willing to spend on life insurance be a guide here? Again, people are optimists and, in any case, may be cash-constrained. Also, it is not the family and friends who buy the insurance; it is the victim, who may not take the effect on others fully into account.

The UK Department for Transport[1] puts a value of £2 029 237 on a life saved from a road safety project (in 2019 prices). The majority of this estimate comprises the (discounted) value of individuals' lost output for the rest of their lives (£670 000) and the human costs[2] (£1.32 million) if the life had not been saved. These human costs include (a) the victim's and their friends'/relatives' willingness to pay to avoid the grief and suffering and (b) the intrinsic loss of enjoyment of life as a result of a fatal accident. Other smaller factors include police costs (£20 000), damage to property (£12 000) and emergency services/hospital costs (£6500).

The US Department of Transportation uses a much higher average valuation of $9.4 million per person (in 2015 prices).

1. *Can you think of any other ways of getting a more 'rational' evaluation of human life? Would the person's age make any difference?*
2. *If you had to decide whether more money from a hospital's budget were to be spent on hip replacements (which do not save lives, but do dramatically improve the quality of the patient's life), or on heart transplants (which do save lives, but are expensive), how would you set about making a rational decision?*
3. *If different values are used in different countries, does this have implications for policy makers? Does your answer change if different departments within a government use varying valuations?*

1 *Accident and casualty costs*, Tables RAS60001 and RA60003, Department for Transport (2020), www.gov.uk/government/statistical-data-sets/ras60-average-value-of-preventing-road-accidents

2 *A valuation of road accidents and casualties in Great Britain: Methodology note*, Department for Transport (2013), https://assets.publishing.service.gov.uk/government/uploads/system/uploads/attachment_data/file/254720/rrcgb-valuation-methodology.pdf

Individual uncertain outcomes

A range of possible values can be given to an uncertain item in the CBA: for example, damage from pollution. Table 12.1 illustrates two possible cases.

The lowest estimate for pollution damage is £10 million; the highest is £50 million. In case A, given a very high margin of benefits over *other* costs, the project's desirability is *not* sensitive to different values for pollution damage. Even with the highest value (£50 million), the project still yields a net benefit.

In case B, however, the project's desirability *is* sensitive to pollution damage. If the damage exceeds £20 million, the project becomes undesirable. In this case, the government will have to decide whether it is prepared to take the gamble.

Table 12.1 Effect of different estimates of the costs of production on the viability of a project

	Total costs other than pollution (£m)	Total pollution cost (£m)	Total benefits (£m)	Net benefits (total benefits – total costs) (£m)
	100	10	200	90
Case A	100	20	200	80
	100	50	200	50
	140	10	160	10
Case B	140	20	160	0
	140	50	160	−30

*BOX 12.6 HS2: IS IT REALLY WORTH IT?

CASE STUDIES AND APPLICATIONS

The case for (and against) High Speed Rail in the UK

In January 2009, the Department for Transport published a report[1] into various options for a new high speed rail network in the UK. It concluded that an initial route between London and the West Midlands would be the best way forward. The government set up a company, High Speed Two Limited (HS2 Ltd), tasked with further investigating the proposals and providing advice on factors such as connectivity with the existing network and further extensions of the line to cities in the north of England and in Scotland.

In 2011, it was confirmed that the first section of the route would run from London Euston to Birmingham Curzon Street. After three years of parliamentary scrutiny, legislation was finally passed in February 2017. This meant work on construction of the line could finally begin. A completion date for phase 1 was set for December 2026. This has since been delayed until 2028.

HS2 Ltd also made an economic case for the 'V'-shaped second phase of the project. The two routes will take services from Birmingham Curzon Street to Manchester Piccadilly and to Leeds. The finalised route from Birmingham to Manchester was announced in November 2016, while Birmingham to Leeds remains under discussion.

HS2 Ltd also examined the possibility of further extending the service to Scotland. In May 2015, it announced that there was 'no business case' for this extension.

The rationale for HS2

HS2 Ltd published a detailed analysis of the potential benefits of this infrastructure project in February 2011. The report focused on both phases of the project and stated that:

> The economic appraisal of a transport scheme seeks to cover the full economic costs and full economic benefits of a scheme and to quantify these in monetary terms. . . . we look at some of the wider economic impacts on the UK economy, using Department for Transport guidance to quantify and value these impacts. The appraisal of quantified benefits provides a numerical result, a 'benefit–cost ratio' or BCR. This ratio represents the level of benefit per pound (£) spent by Government (e.g. if a scheme generates £2 of benefit for every £1 spent this is presented as a BCR of 2.0).[2]

There was considerable public debate about the estimated costs and benefits published in the initial report. Following criticism of its approach, HS2 Ltd has extended and updated its initial analysis on a number of occasions. The latest estimates, published in April 2020,[3] are summarised in the table.

Quantified benefits and costs (£ billions) of the Y network (2015 PV/prices) and the resulting benefit-cost ratio (BCR)

(1) Transport user benefits	£77.5bn
(2) Other quantifiable benefits	£0.8bn
(3) Loss to government of indirect taxes	−£4.1 bn
(4) Net transport benefits = (1) + (2) + (3)	**£74.2bn**
(5) Wider economic impacts (WEIs)	£20.5bn
(6) Net benefits including WEIs = (4) + (5)	**£94.7bn**
(7) Capital costs	£78.2bn
(8) Renewals	£5.4bn
(9) Operating costs	£25.2bn
(10) Total costs = (7) + (8) + (9)	**£108.9bn**
(11) Revenues	£45.4bn
(12) Net costs to government = (10) − (11)	**£63.5bn**
(13) BCR without WEIs (ratio) = (4)/(12)	**1.2**
(14) BCR with WEIs (ratio) = (6)/(12)	**1.5**

Source: Full Business Case: High Speed Two, Table 2.9, Department for Transport (April 2020)

Transport user benefits

The estimated transport user benefits include:

- Reductions in train journey times (£39.1 billion)
- Reductions in crowding (£13.5 billion)
- Greater reliability (£11.9 billion)
- Reductions in waiting times (£8.9 billion)
- Improvements in interchange (£2.8 billion)

(continued)

The two largest transport user benefits help to illustrate the complexity of the economic assessment, and the sensitivity of results to any assumptions used in the analysis.

Reductions in train journey times

The £39.1 billion figure involves valuing the time saved by business, commuter and leisure travellers from faster train journeys. For example, HS2 is forecast to reduce the travel time between Birmingham and London from 1 hour 21 minutes to 49 minutes. How much do travellers value this extra 32 minutes?

One approach is to ask people how much they are willing to pay for shorter journey times. Using results from a 1994 survey of motorists that asks these types of questions, the study put a value of £6.04 for each hour of leisure travel time saved per person.

With no survey results of this kind available for business travellers, a different approach is required to value commuters' time. The cost-savings method assumes that none of the time spent on business travel is productive. Therefore, shorter journeys free up time that can be put to productive use in the workplace. To estimate the value of this extra work time, the research uses the gross wage of those people who use the train for business purposes. Taking this approach, the analysis puts a value of £31.96 for each hour of business travel time saved per person.

There is considerable uncertainty and debate about the use of these figures. In reality, improvements in WiFi availability mean business travellers are increasingly able to use their travel time productively: i.e. checking/responding to emails, writing reports, etc. If further research finds that people can work just as effectively on a train as they can in their normal place of work then the benefits of HS2 will be considerably lower than current estimates suggest. Also, big increases in the number of people working from home would significantly reduce the size of this benefit.

Reductions in crowding

The £13.5 billion figure assumes that the capacity of the rail network is beginning to reach its limit. Two critical reports by the House of Lords Economic Affairs Committee[4,5] questioned this assumption. Evidence in these publications shows that long-distance trains that serve the cities that will be on the HS2 line were the least crowded on the network. The £13.5 billion figure also assumes that the recent growth in passenger numbers will continue at similar rates in the future: i.e. that the impact of GDP and population growth on the demand for rail travel remains the same. Forecasting GDP and population changes over many years involves high levels of uncertainty.

Even if it were possible to forecast GDP and population changes accurately, the COVID-19 pandemic has increased the level of uncertainty about the future relationship between economic activity and demand for rail travel. If the shift to homeworking during the crisis becomes more of a permanent trend rather than a temporary phenomenon, then this relationship could change dramatically. In response to a question at a House of Commons Public Accounts Committee in October 2020, the Permanent Secretary at the Department for Transport stated: 'Much as I wish it were otherwise, we do not actually know what demand will be like in six months or six years.'[6]

Sensitivity analysis carried out by the Department for Transport, found that if demand for rail travel is 16 per cent lower than forecast levels before the pandemic, then the benefit–cost ratio (BCR) with wider economic impacts (WEIs) falls from 1.5 to 1.1.

Other quantifiable benefits

These tend to be smaller and include

- Reductions in the number of car accidents (£550 million)
- Reductions in CO_2 emissions (£280 million)
- Reductions in car noise (£40 million)

The reduction in CO_2 emissions and the impact on the environment continues to be an area of controversy, with protesters tunnelling under London's Euston station. Some argue that the extra emissions from the construction work will outweigh any future reductions from fewer people driving. Others have expressed concerns about the damage caused by construction work to wildlife sites and ancient woodlands. A recent report commissioned by HS2,[7] however, concluded that the project will have a positive impact on biodiversity. In particular, it will help to join together existing pockets of wildlife.

Wider economic impacts (WEIs)

These include:

- Agglomeration (£13.7 billion)
- Imperfect competition (£6 billion)
- Increased labour participation (£0.8 billion)

Agglomeration effects are the largest of the WEIs. These refer to the benefits of greater connectivity between firms,

A number of uncertain outcomes

When there are several uncertain outcomes the typical approach is to do three cost–benefit calculations: the most optimistic (where all the best possible outcomes are estimated), the most pessimistic (where all the worst possible outcomes are estimated) and the most likely (where all the middle-of-the-range outcomes are estimated). This approach can give a good guide to just how 'borderline' the project is.

Discounting future costs and benefits

As we saw in section 10.3, discounting is a procedure for giving a present value to costs and benefits that will not occur until some time in the future.

KI 27 p310

which opens up more opportunities for closer integration and trade. It may also enable cities to develop greater specialisms.

Imperfect competition refers to the value of extra output that results because of the lower transport costs.

Increased labour participation occurs as shorter journey times encourage more people to look for work and become economically active.

The benefit–cost ratio (BCR)

The estimated BCR with WEIs is 1.5 – classing the project as low-to-medium value for money. This figure has fallen from earlier estimates of 2.5 in 2012 and 2.3 in 2017. This can partly be explained by the higher than anticipated costs. For example, the forecast net economic cost, in 2015 prices, has increased from just under £40 billion to over £60 billion.[8]

The actual BCR may be higher as it is impossible to quantify some of the potential wider economic benefits in the analysis. This is because the techniques to estimate their value require further development. This includes one of the major justifications for the scheme – economic rebalancing: i.e. increasing the relative wealth of cities and regions in the Midlands and the North of the country.

Other potential benefits that have not been quantified include increases in the clustering of firms that enhances knowledge sharing, the possibility of workers moving to more productive jobs and higher foreign investment due to better connectivity.

If the appraisal period is extended from 60 to 100 years, it also increases the BCR with WEIs to 2.1, making the project high value for money.

The 2020 report concludes by stating that the 'Benefits of the scheme continue to outweigh the costs, providing long-term value for the taxpayer.'

The future

The impact of COVID-19 has introduced greater uncertainty into the cost–benefit analysis since the Department for Transport published its report in April 2020. In response to questioning at a House of Commons Public Accounts Committee, the Permanent Secretary at the Department for Transport stated that:

> It is a project that we expect to be still delivering for passengers in 100 years and 150 years. The conscious decision was taken to continue because it is a very long-term project and it is a long-term investment in future infrastructure and future economic activity. That is the driving factor. You could not ever build any long-term project if you were constantly being driven by shorter-term fluctuations in demand.

It will take decades before we find out whose views are correct.

1. *Why is this type of cost–benefit analysis so complex?*
2. *'The "losers" will be compensated, so there is no reason for them to protest.' Assess this statement with reference to HS2.*
3. *Explain why companies in London might benefit as much from HS2 as those in Manchester.*

Choose another cost–benefit analysis of a major project. Prepare a short briefing for a non-specialist audience on the background to the CBA and the methodology used and whether any challenges have been made to the methodology, assumptions, measurements or conclusions.

1 *Britain's Transport Infrastructure - High Speed Two*, Department for Transport (January 2009), https://www.railwaysarchive.co.uk/docsummary.php?docID=3150
2 *Economic Case for HS2 - the Y Network and London-West Midlands*, Department for Transport (February 2011).
3 *Full Business Case: High Speed 2 Phase One*, Department for Transport (15 April 2020), www.gov.uk/government/publications/hs2-phase-one-full-business-case
4 *The Economics of High Speed 2*, House of Lords (March 2015), https://publications.parliament.uk/pa/ld201415/ldselect/ldeconaf/134/13404.htm
5 *Rethinking High Speed 2*, House of Lords (16 May 2019), https://publications.parliament.uk/pa/ld201719/ldselect/ldeconaf/359/359.pdf
6 'Public Accounts Committee oral evidence: Department for Transport recall', *Public Accounts Committee*, House of Commons (15 October 2020), https://committees.parliament.uk/oralevidence/1038/default/
7 *High Speed Rail and Nature Networks*, High Speed Rail Group (15 January 2021), https://www.rail-leaders.com/publications/high-speed-rail-and-nature-networks/
8 *Oakervee Review of HS2*, Department for Transport (11 February 2020), www.gov.uk/government/publications/oakervee-review-of-hs2

Discounting in CBA

The procedure is as follows:

- Work out the costs and benefits for each year of the life of the project.
- Subtract the costs from the benefits for each year, to give a net benefit for each year.
- Discount each year's net benefit to give it a present value.
- Add up all of these present values. This gives a *net present value (NPV)*.
- If the *NPV* is greater than zero, the benefits exceed the costs: the project is worthwhile.

Maths Case 12.2 on the student website gives a worked example.

Choosing the discount rate

Apart from the problems of measuring the costs and benefits, there is the problem of choosing the rate of interest/discount.

If it were a private-sector project, the firm would probably choose the market rate of interest as its rate of discount. This is the rate that it would have to pay to borrow money to finance the project.

In the case of CBA, however, it is argued that the government ought to use a ***social rate of discount***. This rate should reflect society's preference for present benefits over future benefits. But just what is this rate? If a high rate is chosen, then future net benefits will be discounted more, and projects with a long life will appear less attractive than projects yielding a quick return. Since the government has a responsibility to future generations and not just to the present one, it is argued that a relatively low discount rate should be chosen.

Imagine that a specific public project yields a return of 13 per cent (after taking into account all social costs and benefits), whereas a 15 per cent private return could typically be earned by projects in the private sector. How would you justify diverting resources from the private sector to this project?

Inevitably, the choice of discount rate is arbitrary. As a result, the analysis will normally be conducted using two or three alternative discount rates to see whether the outcome is sensitive to the choice of discount rate. If it is, then again the project will be seen as borderline.

CBA and the distribution of costs and benefits

Virtually all projects involve gainers and losers. For example, the majority may gain from the construction of a new motorway, but not those whose homes lie alongside it. So how is the distribution of costs and benefits to be taken into account? KI 4 p13

The strict Pareto criterion

According to the strict Pareto criterion, a project is unequivocally desirable only if there are some gains and *no one* is made worse off. But are there likely to be any projects that fulfil this criterion? If there are always losers then let us think about a situation where the losers are compensated. Thus we can now state that a project would be accepted only if the gainers *fully* compensated the losers, with the gainers still being better off after doing so.

Definition

Social rate of discount A rate of discount that reflects society's preferences for present benefits over future ones.

In practice, this never happens. Often compensation is simply not paid. Even when it is, the recipients rarely feel as well off as before, and there will still be many who do not get compensation. Also, the compensation is usually paid not by the project users, but by the general taxpayer (who will thus be *worse* off).

The Hicks–Kaldor criterion

To get round this problem, J. R. Hicks and N. Kaldor suggested an alternative criterion. This states that a project is desirable if it leads to a *potential* Pareto improvement: in other words, if the gainers could *in principle* fully compensate the losers and still have a net gain, even though in practice they do not pay any compensation at all.

This criterion is what lies behind conventional CBA. If the benefits of a project are greater than the costs, then in principle the losers could be fully compensated with some net benefits left over.

But what is the justification for using this test? The losers, after all, will still lose. Its advocates argue that questions of *efficiency* should be kept separate from questions of *equity*. Projects, they argue, should be judged on efficiency grounds. They are efficient if their benefits exceed their costs. Questions of fairness in distribution, on the other hand, should be dealt with through the general system of taxation and welfare. KI 4 p13

This is a 'useful' argument because it lets the proponents of the project off the hook. Nevertheless, the problem still remains that some people will lose. People do not like living near a new motorway, airport or power station. These people cannot expect to receive special welfare benefits from general taxation.

Thus other economists have argued that more specific account should be taken of distributional effects when *measuring* costs and benefits.

Taking specific account of distributional consequences

One way this could be done would be to give a higher weighting to the costs of individual, as opposed to corporate, losers. The justification is simple. The pain for one person of losing £10 000 is greater than the collective pain of 10 000 people losing just £1 each. Just how much higher this weighting should be, however, is a matter of judgement, not of precise calculation.

Another way distribution can be taken into account is to give a higher weighting to the costs incurred by poor people than to those incurred by rich people. For example, assume that a new airport is built. As a result, house prices nearby fall by 10 per cent. A rich person's house price falls from £2 000 000 to £1 800 000 – a loss of £200 000. A poor person's house price falls from £200 000 to £180 000 – a loss of £20 000. Is the loss to the rich person eight times as painful as that to the poor person? Probably not. It is argued, therefore, that the poorer people are, the higher the weighting that should be given to each £1 lost. Just what this weighting should be, however, is controversial.

Section summary

1. Cost–benefit analysis (CBA) can help a government decide whether or not to go ahead with a particular public project, or which of alternative projects to choose. CBA involves a number of stages.
2. All costs and benefits must be identified. These include the direct costs of constructing and operating the project, the direct monetary benefits to the operators and the consumer surplus of the users. They also include external costs and benefits to non-users.
3. Direct monetary costs and benefits are relatively easy to measure. Nevertheless there is still uncertainty about their *future* values. Also, there is a problem if prices are distorted.
4. Non-monetary private benefit (consumer surplus) is difficult to estimate because of the difficulty of estimating the shape and position of the demand curve. The alternative approach is to focus on specific non-monetary benefits, such as journey time saved, and then to evaluate how much people would be prepared to pay for them if they could.
5. Monetary external costs would not normally be counted if they were borne by competitors or collaborators. Otherwise they would typically be counted at face value. Non-monetary (technical) externalities are much more difficult to estimate. The approach is to try to estimate the value that consumers would put on them in a market environment. Questionnaire techniques could be used, or inferences could be drawn from people's actual behaviour elsewhere.
6. Figures would then have to be adjusted for risk and uncertainty.
7. Discounting techniques would then have to be used to reduce future benefits and costs to a present value.
8. The study may also take distributional questions into account. The Hicks–Kaldor criterion suggests a compensation test for deciding whether a project is desirable. But given that in practice full compensation would be unlikely, the distributional questions may need to be taken into account more specifically.
9. Having adjusted the costs and benefits for risk and uncertainty, timing and distributional effects, a recommendation to go ahead with the project will probably be given if its net present value (NPV) is positive: in other words, if the discounted social benefits exceed the discounted social costs.

12.5 GOVERNMENT FAILURE AND THE CASE FOR THE MARKET

Government intervention in the market can itself lead to problems. The case for non-intervention (laissez-faire) or very limited intervention is not that the market is the *perfect* means of achieving given social goals, but rather that the problems created by intervention are greater than the problems overcome by that intervention.

TC 7 p109

Drawbacks of government intervention

Shortages and surpluses. If the government intervenes by fixing prices at levels other than the equilibrium, this will create either shortages or surpluses (see section 3.1).

If the price is fixed *below* the equilibrium, there will be a shortage. For example, if the rent of social housing is fixed below the equilibrium in order to provide affordable housing for low-income households, demand will exceed supply. In the case of such shortages the government will have to adopt a system of waiting lists, or rationing, or giving certain people preferential treatment. Alternatively it will have to allow allocation to be on a first-come, first-served basis or allow queues to develop. Underground markets are also likely to develop (see page 81 and Case Study 3.2 on the book's website).

If the price is fixed *above* the equilibrium price, there will be a surplus. Such surpluses are wasteful, and high prices may protect inefficient producers. (The problem of food surpluses in the EU was examined in section 3.4.)

What are the possible arguments in favour of fixing prices (a) below and (b) above the equilibrium? Are there any means of achieving the same social goals without fixing prices?

Poor information. The government may not know the full costs and benefits of its policies. It may genuinely wish to pursue the interests of consumers or any other group, and yet may be unaware of people's wishes or misinterpret their behaviour.

Bureaucracy and inefficiency. Government intervention involves administrative costs. The more wide-reaching and detailed the intervention, the greater the number of people and material resources that will be involved. These resources may be used wastefully and the effect on welfare may not be an improvement on the free-market situation. Think back to the problem of scarcity we discussed in Chapter 1; if we 'use up' resources on managing intervention, we need to be sure that the outcome is markedly better than without intervention.

Lack of market incentives. If government intervention removes market forces or reduces their effect (by the use of subsidies, welfare provisions, minimum wages, etc.), it may remove certain useful incentives. Subsidies may allow inefficient firms to survive. Welfare payments may discourage people from working. The market may be imperfect, but it does tend to encourage efficiency by allowing the efficient to receive greater rewards. TC 5 p48

Shifts in government policy. Industrial performance may suffer if government intervention changes too frequently. It makes it difficult for firms to plan if they cannot predict tax rates, subsidies, wage controls, etc. Shifts in policy are also likely to involve costs for both business and public-sector providers. This may result in wasted resources.

Lack of freedom for the individual. Government intervention may involve a loss of freedom for individuals to make economic choices. The argument is not just that the pursuit of individual gain is seen to lead to the social good, but that it is desirable in itself that individuals should be as free as possible to pursue their own interests with the minimum of government interference, and with that minimum being largely confined to the maintenance of laws consistent with the protection of life, liberty and property.

Go through the above arguments and give a reply to the criticisms made of government intervention.

Advantages of the free market

Although markets in the real world are not perfect, even imperfect markets can be argued to have positive advantages over government provision or even government regulation.

Automatic adjustments. Government intervention requires administration. A free-market economy, on the other hand, leads to the automatic, albeit imperfect, adjustment to demand and supply changes. TC 4 p45

Even under oligopoly, it is claimed, the competition between firms will be enough to encourage firms to produce goods that are desirable to consumers and at not excessively high prices, and will encourage more efficient production methods. Cases of pure monopoly with total barriers to entry are extremely rare.

Dynamic advantages of the free market. The chances of making high monopoly/oligopoly profits will encourage capitalists to invest in new products and new techniques. Prices may be high initially, but new firms will sooner or later break into the market and competition will ensue. If the government tries to correct the misallocation of resources under monopoly/oligopoly, either by regulating monopoly power or by nationalisation, any resulting benefits could be outweighed by a loss in innovation and growth. This is one of the major arguments put forward by the neo-Austrian libertarian school – a school that passionately advocates the free market (see Box 12.7).

Are there any features of free-market capitalism that would discourage innovation?

A high degree of competition even under monopoly/oligopoly. Even though an industry at first sight may seem to be highly monopolistic, competitive forces may still work for the following reasons.

- A fear that excessively high profits might encourage firms to attempt to break into the industry (assuming that the market is contestable).
- Competition from closely related industries (e.g. coach services for rail services, or electricity for gas).
- The threat of foreign competition. Additional competition was one of the main purposes behind the Single European Act which led to the abolition of trade barriers within the EU in 1993 (see section 26.2).
- Countervailing powers. Large, powerful producers often sell to large, powerful buyers. For example, the power of detergent manufacturers to drive up the price of washing powder is countered by the power of supermarket chains to drive down the price at which they purchase it. Thus power is to some extent neutralised.
- The competition for corporate control (see page 213).

Should there be more or less intervention in the market?

No firm conclusions can be drawn in the debate between those who favour more and those who favour less government intervention, for the following reasons:

- The debate involves normative issues that cannot be settled by economic analysis. For example, it could be argued that freedom to set up in business and freedom from government regulation are desirable *for their own sake*. As a fundamental ethical point of view, this can be disputed, but not disproved. 
- In principle, the issue of whether a government ought to intervene in any situation could be settled by weighing up the costs and benefits of that intervention. Such costs and benefits, however, even if they could be identified, are extremely difficult, if not impossible, to measure, especially when the costs are borne by different people from those who receive the benefits and when externalities are involved.
- Often the effect of more or less intervention simply cannot be predicted: there are too many uncertainties.

Nevertheless, economists can make a considerable contribution to analysing problems of the market and the effects of government intervention. Chapters 13 and 14 illustrate this by examining specific problem areas.

BOX 12.7 **MISES, HAYEK AND THE MONT PELERIN SOCIETY** EXPLORING ECONOMICS

The birth of post-war libertarianism

After the Second World War, governments in the Western world were anxious to avoid a return to the high levels of unemployment and poverty experienced in the 1930s. The free market was seen to have failed. Governments, it was therefore argued, should take on the responsibility for correcting or counteracting these failings. This would involve various measures such as planning, nationalisation, the restriction of monopoly power, controls on prices, the macroeconomic management of the economy and the provision of a welfare state.

But this new spirit of intervention deeply troubled a group of economists and other social scientists who saw it leading to an erosion of freedom. In 1947, this group met in a hotel in the Swiss Alps. There they formed the Mont Pelerin Society: a society pledged to warn against the dangers of socialism and to advocate the freedom for individuals to make their own economic choices.

Two of the most influential figures in the society were the Austrians Ludwig von Mises (1881–1973) and Friedrich von Hayek (1899–1992). They were the intellectual descendants of the nineteenth-century 'Austrian school'. Carl Menger, the originator of the school, had (along with Jevons and Walras (see Box 4.2)) emphasised the importance of individuals' marginal utility as the basis of demand. The Austrian school of economists was famous for its stress on individual choice as the basis for rational economic calculation and also for its advocacy of the free market.

Mises and Hayek (the 'neo-Austrians' as they became known) provided both a critique of socialism and an advocacy of the free market. There were two main strands to their arguments.

The impossibility of rational calculation under socialism

In his famous book *Socialism* (1922), Mises argued that centrally planned socialism was logically incapable of achieving a rational allocation of resources. Given that scarcity is the fundamental economic problem, all societies, whether capitalist or socialist, will have to make choices. But rational choices must involve weighing up the costs and benefits of alternatives. Mises argued that this cannot be done in a centrally planned economy. The reason is that costs and benefits can be measured only in terms of money prices, prices which reflect demand and supply. But such prices can be established only in a market economy.

TC 8 p109

KI 15 p132

In a centrally planned economy, prices will be set by the state and no state will have sufficient information on demand and supply to set rational prices. Prices under centrally planned socialism will thus inevitably be arbitrary. Also, with no market for land or capital these factors may not be given a price at all. The use of land and capital, therefore, may be highly wasteful.

Many democratic socialists criticised Mises' arguments that rational prices *logically* cannot be established under socialism. In a centrally planned economy, the state can in theory, if it chooses, set prices so as to balance supply and demand. It can, if it chooses, set an interest rate for capital and a rent for land, even if capital and land are owned by the state. And certainly in a mixed-market socialist economy, prices will merely reflect the forces of demand and supply that have been modified by the state in accordance with its various social goals.

Hayek modified Mises' arguments somewhat. He conceded that some imperfect form of pricing system could be established under socialism, even under centrally planned socialism. Hayek's point was that such a system would inevitably be inferior to capitalism. The problem was one of imperfect information under socialism.

KI 15 p132

Calculation of costs and benefits requires knowledge. But that knowledge is dispersed amongst the millions of consumers and producers throughout the economy. Each consumer possesses unique information about his or her own tastes; each manager or worker possesses unique information about his or her own job. No government could hope to have this knowledge. Planning will inevitably, therefore, be based on highly imperfect information.

The market, by contrast, is a way of co-ordinating this dispersed information: it co-ordinates all the individual decisions of suppliers and demanders, decisions based on individuals' own information. And it does it all without the need for an army of bureaucrats.

> The economic problem of society is thus not merely a problem of how to allocate 'given' resources – if 'given' is taken to mean given to a single mind which deliberately solves the problem set by these 'data'. It is rather a problem of how to secure the best use of resources known to any of the members of society, for ends whose relative importance only these individuals know. Or, to put it briefly, it is a problem of the utilization of knowledge not given to anyone in its totality.[1]

Lack of dynamic incentives under socialism

A planned socialist economy will, according to Mises and Hayek, lack the incentives for people to take risks. Even a 'market socialist' society, where prices are set so as to equate demand and supply, will still lack the crucial motivating force of the possibility of large personal economic gains. Under capitalism, by contrast, a firm that becomes more efficient or launches a new or improved product can gain huge profits. The prospect of such profits is a powerful motivator.

> Without the striving of entrepreneurs (including the shareholders) for profit, of the landlords for rent, of the capitalists for interest and the labourers for wages, the successful functioning of the whole mechanism is not to be thought of. It is only the prospect of profit which directs production into those channels in which the demands of the consumer are best satisfied at least cost. If the prospect of profit disappears the mechanism of the market loses its mainspring, for it is only this prospect which sets it in motion and maintains it in operation. The market is thus the focal point of the capitalist order of society; it is the essence of capitalism. Only under capitalism, therefore, is it possible; it cannot be 'artificially' imitated under socialism.[2]

(continued)

In addition to these economic criticisms of socialism, Mises and Hayek saw government intervention as leading down the road towards totalitarianism. The more governments intervened to correct the 'failings' of the market, the more this tended to erode people's liberties. But the more people saw the government intervening to help one group of people, the more help they would demand from the government for themselves. Thus inexorably the role of the state would grow and grow, and with it the size of the state bureaucracy.

In the early years after the war, the Mont Pelerin Society had little influence on government policy. Government intervention and the welfare state were politically popular.

In the late 1970s, however, the society, along with other similar libertarian groups, gained increasing influence as a new breed of politicians emerged who were wedded to the free market and were looking for an intellectual backing for their beliefs.

Libertarian thinkers such as Hayek and Milton Friedman (see Case Study 16.8 on the student website) had a profound effect on many right-wing politicians, and considerably influenced the economic programmes of the Thatcher, Reagan, Bush (Snr and Jnr) and Trump administrations.

Do the arguments of Mises and Hayek necessarily imply that a free market is the most desirable alternative to centrally planned socialism?

Imagine you are advising a centre-left government, which is keen to rebuff the arguments of the right that intervention in the market will destroy its dynamism and the progress that comes from it. What arguments would you advise the government to use?

1 F. von Hayek, 'The use of knowledge in society', *American Economic Review* (September 1945), p. 519, www.econlib.org/library/Essays/hykKnw.html

2 L. von Mises, *Socialism: An Economic and Sociological Analysis* (Jonathan Cape, 1936), p. 138, https://mises.org/library/socialism-economic-and-sociological-analysis

Section summary

1. Government intervention in the market may lead to shortages or surpluses; it may be based on poor information; it may be costly in terms of administration; it may stifle incentives; it may be disruptive if government policies change too frequently; it may remove certain liberties.
2. By contrast, a free market leads to automatic adjustments to changes in economic conditions; the prospect of monopoly/oligopoly profits may stimulate risk taking and hence research and development and innovation; there may still be a high degree of actual or potential competition under monopoly and oligopoly.
3. It is impossible to draw firm conclusions about the 'optimum' level of government intervention. This is partly due to the normative nature of the question, partly due to the difficulties of measuring costs and benefits of intervention/non-intervention, and partly due to the difficulties of predicting the effects of government policies, especially over the longer term.

END OF CHAPTER QUESTIONS

1. Assume that a firm discharges waste into a river. As a result, the marginal social costs *(MSC)* are greater than the firm's marginal private costs *(MPC)*. The following table shows how *MPC, MSC, AR* and *MR* vary with output.

Output	1	2	3	4	5	6	7	8
MPC (£)	23	21	23	25	27	30	35	42
MSC (£)	35	34	38	42	46	52	60	72
TR (£)	60	102	138	168	195	219	238	252
AR (£)	60	51	46	42	39	36.5	34	31.5
MR (£)	60	42	36	30	27	24	19	14

   (a) How much will the firm produce if it seeks to maximise profits?
   (b) What is the socially efficient level of output (assuming no externalities on the demand side)?
   (c) How much is the marginal external cost at this level of output?
   (d) What size tax would be necessary for the firm to reduce its output to the socially efficient level?
   (e) Why is the tax less than the marginal externality?
   (f) Why might it be equitable to impose a lump-sum tax on this firm?
   (g) Why will a lump-sum tax not affect the firm's output (assuming that in the long run the firm can still make at least normal profit)?

2. Why might it be argued that a redistribution of consumption, while not involving a Pareto improvement, could still be desirable?
3. Assume that a country had no state education at all. For what reasons might the private education system not provide the optimal allocation of resources to and within education?
4. Why might it be better to ban certain activities that cause environmental damage rather than to tax them?
5. Distinguish between publicly provided goods, public goods and merit goods.

6. Consider the advantages and disadvantages of extending property rights so that everyone would have the right to prevent people imposing any costs on them whatsoever (or charging them to do so).
7. The food industry provides a great deal of information about its products. Why, despite this, does the government run various campaigns about healthy eating?
8. Should all investment be subject to a social cost–benefit appraisal?
9. Make out a case for (a) increasing and (b) decreasing the role of the government in the allocation of resources.

Online resources

Additional case studies on the student website

12.1 Vilfredo Pareto (1843–1923). A profile of a key figure in the development of welfare economics.

12.2 A commons solution. Changing social attitudes towards common resources.

12.3 Can the market provide adequate protection for the environment? This explains why markets generally fail to take into account environmental externalities.

12.4 Catastrophic risk. This examines how a cost–benefit study could put a monetary value on a remote chance of a catastrophe happening (such as an explosion at a nuclear power station).

12.5 Evaluating the cost of aircraft noise. This case study looks at the method used by the Roskill Commission, which in the 1960s investigated the siting of a third major London airport.

12.6 CBA of the Glasgow canal project. A cost–benefit study carried out in the late 1980s on the restoration of the Glasgow canal system.

12.7 Meeting the Kyoto Protocol. This examines the options open to the EU in meeting the targets set under international climate change agreements. It illustrates the use of cost–benefit analysis.

12.8 Public choice theory. This examines how economists have attempted to extend their analysis of markets to the field of political decision making.

Maths Case 12.1 Calculating deadweight welfare loss. A worked example.

Maths Case 12.2 Calculating net present value. The use of discounting techniques in CBA.

Websites relevant to this chapter

See sites listed at the end of Chapter 14 on pages 448–9.

Environmental Policy

CHAPTER MAP

Just how far should things be left to the market in practice? Just how much should a government intervene? These are clearly normative questions, and the answers to them may depend on a person's politics. Politicians on the right tend to favour a lesser degree of intervention while those on the left generally prefer more intervention.

In the final two chapters of Part D we examine some topics that illustrate well the possible strengths and weaknesses of both the market and government intervention. In Chapter 13 we look closely at the environment, an area where the existence of externalities results in substantial market failure. We start by considering the broader environmental issues and then turn to alternative policies for dealing with pollution and urban traffic congestion.

As we shall see, the economist's approach is to focus on both the costs and the benefits of various policies and how these costs and benefits can be weighed up. Scientists are the ones who need to assess whether global warming is a real phenomenon and to determine the physical consequences of our actions, such as the degree of warming that might result from a particular level of CO_2 emissions. But it is economists who must assess the implications for various policies to deal with the problems.

13.1 ECONOMICS OF THE ENVIRONMENT

Scarcely a day goes by without some environmental issue featuring in the news: another warning about global warming, a company fined for illegally dumping waste, a drought or flood blamed on pollution, poor air quality in our major cities. Attempts by policy makers to improve the environment also cause controversy and hit the headlines: for example, the impact of government climate change policies on the size of customers' energy bills.

Nearly everyone would like a cleaner, more attractive environment but there are deep disagreements about how much people should pay for it. Environmental improvement normally comes at a cost: whether in cleaning up waste or pollution, or in terms of the higher price we might need to pay for 'green' products, such as organic foods, low-emission cars and electricity from renewable sources.

Economists are concerned with choices, and rational choices involve weighing up costs and benefits. Increasingly, people are recognising that such costs and benefits ought to include the effects on the environment: the effects on the planet we share with each other and with future generations.

The environmental problem

Why is the environment used in such a suboptimal way? Why are policies that try to address these environmental issues always so controversial? To answer these questions we have to understand the nature of the economic relationship between humans and the natural world.

We all benefit from the environment in three ways:

- as an amenity to be enjoyed;
- as a source of primary products (food, raw materials and other resources);
- as a place where we can dump waste.

The relationship between these uses and the rest of the economy is illustrated in Figure 13.1. Unfortunately, having more of one of these benefits usually means having less of another.

TC 1 p10

The use of the environment as a productive resource reduces its amenity value. Intensive agriculture, with hedges and woods removed, spoils the beauty of the countryside and can lead to a decline in animal and plant species. Mines and quarries are ugly. Commercial forestry is often at the expense of traditional broad-leaved forests.

Similarly, the use of the environment as a dump for waste reduces its amenity value. The environment becomes dirtier and uglier. The burning of fossil fuels dumps CO_2 into the atmosphere and contributes towards global warming.

Using examples, discuss the conflicts between using the environment as a productive resource and as a dump.

These conflicts have always existed, but are they getting worse? Let us examine the arguments.

Figure 13.1 The economy and the environment

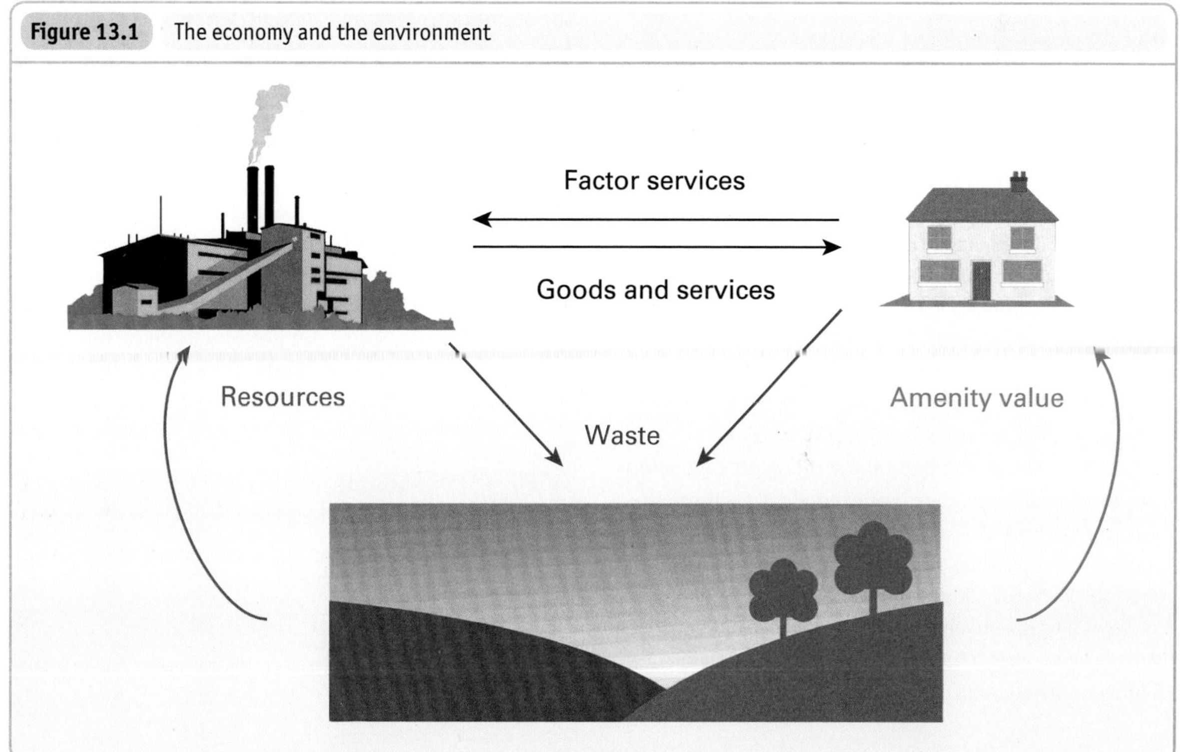

Population pressures and limited resources

As we saw in Box 6.1, as more people crowd on to the fixed supply of world land, so diminishing returns to labour will occur. If food output per head is to remain constant, let alone increase, land must be made to yield more and more. One answer has been to use increasing amounts of fertiliser and pesticides. Likewise, if the increasing world population is to have higher levels of material consumption, this will generate increased demands for natural resources, many of which are non-renewable and generate pollution. With the rapid growth of countries such as China and India, the pressures on the environment are already growing sharply.

The environment is able to absorb most types of waste up to certain levels of emission. Beyond such levels, however, environmental damage is likely to accelerate. Other things being equal, as population and waste grow, so environmental degradation is likely to grow at a faster rate.

Cause for optimism?

Despite population pressures, there are various factors that are helping to reduce environmental degradation.

Technological developments. Many newer industrial processes are cleaner and make a more efficient use of resources, leading to less waste and a slowdown in the rate of extraction of various minerals and fossil fuels. For example, World Bank data indicate that the amount of CO_2 emitted per $ of GDP fell from 0.439kg in 1990 to 0.288kg in 2016 (at 2017 prices). What is more, the production of less waste, or the recycling of waste, is often in the commercial interests of firms: it allows them to cut costs.

Increased price of non-renewable resources. As we saw in Box 10.11 (see Pages 318–19), as resources become scarcer, so their prices rise. This encourages people to use less of them, either by using more efficient technology or by switching to renewable alternatives as they become available.

TC 5 p48

Public opinion. As knowledge about environmental damage has grown, so too has pressure from public opinion to do something about it. Many firms see the opportunity to gain commercially from having a 'green image' and to publicise their positive attitude towards corporate social responsibility. In addition, governments see electoral advantage in policies to create a cleaner, greener environment.

Despite these developments, however, many aspects of environmental degradation continue to worsen.

Data from the World Bank show that global emissions have continued to increase. For example, CO_2 tonnes per capita rose from 2.986 in 1961 to 4.555 in 2016. The variation between countries is also significant. The figures for Qatar, the USA, the UK and Somalia in 2016 are 37.3, 15.5, 5.6 and 0.09 respectively. A UN Environment Report published in November 2019 concluded that by 2030 emissions would have to fall by 25 per cent from 2018 levels in order to limit the growth in global warming to 2°C and by 55 per cent to limit it to 1.5°C,[1] goals set in the international Paris Climate Change Agreement in December 2015.

An optimum use of the environment

If the current levels of pollution and environmental degradation are too high, then can we identify an optimum use of the environment? To do this, we have to go back to first principles of efficiency and also look at our attitudes towards ***sustainability***.

Different approaches to sustainability

We can identify four different approaches to the environment and sustainability.

The free-market approach. At the one extreme, we could regard the world as there purely for ourselves: a resource that belongs to individual property owners to do with as they choose, or a 'common asset', such as the air and seas, for individuals to use for their own benefit. In this view of the world, we are entitled simply to weigh up the marginal costs and benefits to ourselves of any activity. Sustainability is achieved in this free-market world only to the extent that resource prices rise as they become scarce and to the extent that environmentally friendly technologies are in firms' (or consumers') private interests.

The social efficiency approach. A somewhat less extreme version of this view is one that takes the social costs and benefits of using the environment into account: i.e. the costs and benefits not only to the direct producer or consumer, but to people in general. Here we would apply the standard rules for social efficiency: use resources to provide goods/services until the marginal social benefit equals the marginal social cost. Even though this approach does take into account environmental externalities (such as pollution), it is only to the extent that they adversely affect *human beings*.

Within this general approach, however, more explicit account can be taken of sustainability, by including the costs of our use of the environment today to *future* generations. For example, we could take into account the effects of climate change not just on ourselves, but on our children and their descendants. Depending on people's

> **Definition**
>
> **Sustainability** The ability of the environment to survive its use for economic activity.

1 *Emissions Gap Report 2019*, UN Environment Programme (29 November 2019), www.unep.org/resources/emissions-gap-report-2019

views on 'intergenerational' equity, a higher or lower weighting could be given to future (as opposed to present) costs and benefits (see page 394 on the choice of a social discount rate).

KI 27 p310

The conservationist approach. Many environmentalists argue that our responsibilities should not be limited to each other, or even to future generations, but should include the environment for its own sake. Such a view would involve downplaying the relative importance of material consumption and economic growth, and putting greater emphasis on the maintenance of ecosystems. Growth in consumption would be ethically acceptable only if it led to no (or only very minor) environmental degradation. Maintenance of the environment is thus seen as an ethical *constraint* on human activity.

The Gaia approach. The strongest approach to sustainability involves a fundamentally different ethical standpoint. Here the Earth itself, and its various natural species of animals and plants, have moral rights. According to this ***Gaia philosophy***, people are seen as mere custodians of the planet: the planet does not belong to them, any more than a dog belongs to the fleas on its back! This view of the environment is similar to that held by some indigenous peoples living in marginal areas, such as the Aborigines in Australia and the San (Bushmen) of the Kalahari, and to various other 'hunter-gatherer' peoples in developing countries. Their ethic is that the land they leave their descendants should be as good as, if not better than, the land they inherited from their ancestors. Conservation is a 'prime directive'. This approach to the environment has been dubbed the 'deep green' approach.

Making optimum decisions concerning the environment

Choice between these four approaches is essentially normative, and therefore we cannot as economists stand in judgment between them.

KI 6 p29

Nevertheless, economists can help in identifying optimum decisions *within* a given set of values. Most environmental economists adopt an approach that is consistent with the social efficiency view, which can be easily modified to fit the conservationist view. The main area for disagreement is over the *value* to be placed on specific environmental costs and benefits.

Let us take the case of the production of a good by a firm in a perfectly competitive market that yields benefits to consumers, but which involves pollution to the environment. What is the optimum level of output of the good? The choices are illustrated in Figure 13.2.

The line $MEC_{pollution}$ shows the external costs of pollution from each additional unit of the good produced by the firm. This diagram is very similar to Figure 12.12 on page 381. However, we now assume that up to Q_1 there are no external costs: the environment can cope with the waste generated.

> **Definition**
>
> **Gaia philosophy** The respect for the rights of the environment to remain unharmed by human activity. Humans should live in harmony with the planet and other species. We have a duty to be stewards of the natural environment, so that it can continue to be a self-maintaining and self-regulating system.

Figure 13.2 Optimum level of an activity that involves pollution

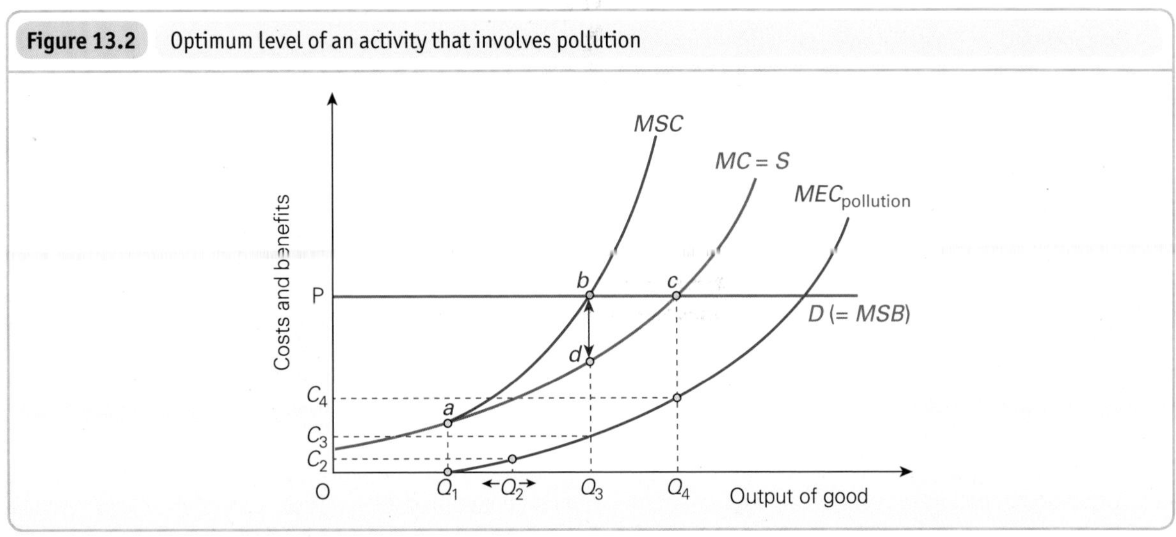

BOX 13.1 THE ECONOMICS OF BIODIVERSITY

Economists and environmental policy

In 2006, Lord Nicholas Stern, the then Head of the Government Economic Service and former chief economist at the World Bank, led an independent review on the Economics of Climate Change.[1] The policy recommendations focused on altering incentives, such as taxing CO_2 emissions and subsidising green technology. Details of the Stern Review are given in Case Study 13.1 on the student website.

In March 2019, the Chancellor of the Exchequer announced a new independent global review on the economics of biodiversity. Sir Partha Dasgupta, Professor of Economics at the University of Cambridge and winner of the Blue Planet Prize for Environmental Research, led the review. The final report was published on 21 February 2021.[2]

The Dasgupta Review

The report emphasises that a successful economy in the future is dependent on the biosphere, the part of the Earth occupied by living organisms. The biosphere provides the following essential services:

- Provisioning services – the goods and services that people harvest and extract, including food, fibres, timber and medicines.
- Cultural services – the parks, beauty spots, woods and coastline people visit for pleasure. There is increasing evidence that visiting these places has positive effects on mental as well as physical health.
- Regulating services – the processes that help to maintain and regenerate the environment. In particular, key elements in the biosphere enable it to absorb and assimilate waste and so make the environment habitable for humans. For example, trees, plants and soil remove carbon dioxide from the atmosphere; ecosystems such as wetlands filter effluents and decompose waste through the biological activity of bacteria; soil organisms purify water. Other processes that help to maintain the quality of the biosphere include biological processes such as nitrogen fixation that helps to maintain soil fertility, pollination by insects and tree roots that prevent soil erosion.

Biodiversity, the diversity of life in all of its forms, is extremely important for the biosphere and for the quality of these three services. Rather like the advantages of having diversity in a portfolio of financial assets, it reduces risk and helps the system deal with shocks.

What has been happening to the biosphere?

Between 1950 and 2019, measured economic activity grew at a much faster rate than ever before. The world's output of final goods and services increased from around \$9 trillion to above \$120 trillion (in 2011 prices). The proportion of the world's population living in absolute poverty fell from 60 per cent in 1950 to under 10 per cent in 2019.

However, this rapid growth in measured economic activity has led to serious declines in biodiversity, which in turn, has reduced the quality of the services provided by the biosphere. For example, current extinction rates of species are between 100 to 1000 times greater than the average rate over the past 10 million years. Current forecasts suggest these rates will grow rapidly in the future.

The report also assesses the impact of this economic growth on the portfolio of assets. It does this by splitting these assets into three categories.

- Produced capital – buildings, machines and infrastructure
- Human capital – education, aptitude and skills
- Natural capital – plants, water, soils, air and minerals

Research suggests that between 1992 and 2014, the value of the stock of (a) produced capital per capita increased by 100 per cent (b) human capital per capita increased by 13 per cent, while (c) natural capital per capita declined by 40 per cent. In other words, growth in measured economic activity has led to the accumulation of produced and human capital at the expense of natural capital. The portfolio of assets has become very unbalanced.

Why is the current demand for biosphere services so much greater than supply?

One important factor is the characteristics of the services provided by the biosphere. Many, especially regulating and maintenance services, are mobile, invisible and silent. We cannot see or hear bacteria decomposing waste, plants

We also assume that the curve gets steeper as output increases because the environment is increasingly unable to cope with the waste. The marginal external costs of pollution therefore accelerate.

A profit-maximising firm will produce Q_4 units of output, with external pollution costs of C_4. The *socially* efficient level of output (where $MSB = MSC$), however, is Q_3, with the lower external costs of pollution, C_3. (We are assuming that there are no other externalities.) Identifying this socially efficient level of output is not easy in practice, since it requires us to *measure* pollution costs, and that is fraught with problems. These problems were considered in section 12.4. KI 28 p356

A more conservationist approach could be to set a maximum pollution cost of, say, C_2. This would reduce the optimum output to Q_2. A Gaian approach would be to restrict output to Q_1 in order to prevent any pollution. Of course, as we move towards 'greener' approaches, so it becomes more

CASE STUDIES AND APPLICATIONS

removing carbon dioxide or natural processes in the soil purifying water. Most people are completely unaware it is happening. This makes it impractical to assign and enforce property rights. For example, it is impossible to measure (a) the extent to which production makes use of these services and (b) the impact this use has on the service's future productivity. If it is not possible to assign property rights, then anyone can use the services without having to pay – they are non-excludable. The services also have a high degree of rivalry – use by one person depletes the quantity and/or quality available to others. In other words, they are natural resources with large negative externalities.

This creates an incentive structure that often results in consumption levels that exceed socially desirable levels. It is an example of the tragedy of the commons (see pages 371–2). When a resource is free, it is likely to be overused. In the case of the biosphere, governments often make matters worse by paying suppliers for their use of the environment. Many governments subsidise agriculture, fossil fuels, energy, fertilisers, etc. Estimates suggest that the size of direct subsidies that harm biodiversity are approximately $500 billion per year (see Case Study 13.2 on the student website). Therefore, the services of the biosphere suffer from both market and institutional failure.

Policy recommendations

Dasgupta outlines four broad mechanisms to deal with the problem. These are (i) reducing per capita global consumption, (ii) lowering the global population, (iii) increasing the efficiency with which the biosphere's supply of goods are converted into global output and converted into waste, and (iv) increasing the stock of nature and its regenerative rate. More specific polices include:

- Improving women's access to information, education and community-based family planning to influence fertility choices and hence reduce population growth.
- Payments for ecosystem services (PES). This involves the creation of supra-national institutions to help organise payments for ecosystems that exist both within and outside national boundaries – for example, payments to a country for the maintenance of tropical rainforests that exist within its borders. Charges or rents could also be applied to the use of ecosystems such as oceans that are outside national boundaries.
- Changes to measures of economic success. This would involve amending GDP to include environmental degradation (−ve) and improvement (+ve). (See Section 15.2 and the Appendix to Chapter 15 for an explanation of how GDP is measured.) Measures of national wealth should also include all natural assets, such as biodiversity and the quality of land, air, sea and water.
- The implementation of education initiatives that help pupils to gain a better understanding of the three key services the biosphere provides. These should begin in the early years of primary education and be reinforced in later years in secondary education.
- Developing local community management of geographically confined ecosystems (common pool resources) where mutual enforcement replaces external enforcement of rules by governments.

1. ***Working out how much today's society should invest in trying to limit the impact of damage to the environment in the future requires the use of social discount rates. How is the social discount rate calculated and why is it so important?***
2. ***In his review, Dasgupta refers to 'the fundamental inequality at the core of the economics of biodiversity'. Outline and explain what this means.***

Investigate some policies being pursued by the government in a country of your choice that are designed to achieve economic growth while protecting or even improving the biosphere. Assess how successful such policies are likely to be.

1 *Stern Review of the Economics of Climate Change*, HM Treasury (2006), https://webarchive.nationalarchives.gov.uk/20100407172811/http:/www.hm-treasury.gov.uk/stern_review_report.htm

2 *The Economics of Biodiversity: The Dasgupta Review*, HM Treasury (2021), www.gov.uk/government/publications/final-report-the-economics-of-biodiversity-the-dasgupta-review

important to look for less polluting methods for producing this good (causing the $MEC_{pollution}$ curve to shift downwards), and for alternative goods that involve less pollution (thus reducing the need to consume this good).

Market failures

What is clear from all the attitudes towards sustainability, other than the free-market one, is that the market system will fail to provide adequate protection for the environment. In fact, the market fails for various reasons.

Externalities. We saw above (Figure 13.2) how pollution could be classified as a 'negative externality' of production or consumption. In the case of production, there are marginal external costs (*MEC*), which means that the marginal social costs (*MSC*) are greater than the marginal private costs (*MC*) to the polluter. The failure of the market system to equate *MSC* and marginal social benefit (*MSB*) is due to either consumers or firms lacking the appropriate property rights.

KI 30 p364

The environment as a common resource. The air, the seas and many other parts of the environment are not privately owned. It is argued that they are a global 'commons'. As such, it is extremely difficult to exclude non-payers from consuming the benefits they provide. Because of this property of 'non-excludability', it is often possible to consume the benefits of the environment at a zero price. If the price of any good or service to the user is zero, there is no incentive to economise on its use.

KI 1 p7

Many parts of the environment, however, are *scarce*: there is *rivalry* in their use. As people increase their use of the environment, it may prevent other or rival consumers from enjoying it. This could lead to the *tragedy of the commons* (see page 372).

Ignorance. There have been many cases of people causing environmental damage without realising it, especially when the effects build up over a long time. Take the case of aerosols. It was not until the 1980s that scientists connected their use to ozone depletion. Even when scientists discover problems, consumers may not appreciate the full environmental costs of their actions. So even if people would like to be more 'environmentally friendly' in their activities, they might not have the knowledge to be so.

Intergenerational problems. The environmentally harmful effects of many activities are long term, whereas the benefits are immediate. Thus consumers and firms are frequently prepared to continue with various practices and leave future generations to worry about their environmental consequences. The problem, then, is a reflection of the importance that people attach to the present relative to the future.

Look through the categories of possible market failings in section 12.2. Are there any others, in addition to the four we have just identified, that will result in a socially inefficient use of the environment?

Section summary

1. The environment benefits humans in three ways: as an amenity, as a source of primary products and as a dump for waste.
2. Given the increasing population pressures and the demands for economic growth, the pressures on the environment are likely to grow. These pressures can be lessened, however, with the use of cleaner technology, a more efficient use of natural resources and 'greener' behaviour of consumers, firms and governments.
3. The concept of an 'optimum' use of the environment depends on people's attitudes towards sustainability. These attitudes vary from regarding the environment simply as a resource for human use at the one extreme to seeing the environment as having moral rights at the other.
4. Under the social efficiency approach to sustainability, the optimum output of a good is where the marginal external environmental cost is equal to the marginal net benefit to users (assuming no other externalities).
5. The market fails to achieve a socially efficient use of the environment because large parts of the environment are a common resource, because production or consumption often generates environmental externalities, because of ignorance of the environmental effects of our actions, and because of a lack of concern for future generations.

13.2 POLICIES TO TACKLE POLLUTION AND ITS EFFECTS

Environmental policy can take many forms. It is useful to split these policies into three broad categories: (a) those that attempt to work through the market by changing property rights or by changing market signals (e.g. through the use of charges, taxes or subsidies); (b) those that involve the use of laws, regulations and controls (e.g. legal limits on the volume of sulphur dioxide emissions); (c) those that attempt to combine the approaches (e.g. 'cap and trade'). The following sections will examine each of these three categories in more detail.

Market-based policies

The policies that a government adopts to reduce pollution will depend on its attitudes towards sustainability: on how 'green' it is.

If governments adopt a social efficiency approach to sustainability, environmental problems are viewed as the result of prices not reflecting marginal social costs and benefits. In this section, we look at ways in which governments can adjust market incentives so that they do achieve social efficiency.

Extending private property rights

If those suffering from pollution, or causing it, are granted property rights, then charges can be introduced for the right to pollute. According to the Coase theorem (see page 384), this would result in the socially efficient level of output being achieved.

We can use Figure 13.2 to illustrate the Coase theorem. If output is initially less than Q_3, the marginal profit to the polluter will exceed the external costs the pollution imposes on the sufferers. In this case, if the sufferers impose a charge on the polluter that is greater than the sufferers' marginal pollution cost but less than the polluter's marginal profit, both sides will benefit from more of the good being produced. Such a situation can continue up to Q_3. Beyond Q_3, the marginal pollution cost exceeds the marginal profit. There is no charge that would compensate for the victim's suffering and leave enough over for the polluter to make a profit. Equilibrium output is therefore at Q_3, the socially efficient output.

TC 2 p26

Similarly, if the polluting *firm* is given the right to pollute, victims could offer a payment to persuade it not to pollute. The victims would be prepared to pay only up to the cost to them of the pollution. The firm would cut back production only provided the payment was at least as great as the loss in profit. This would be the case at levels of output above Q_3. Once output falls below Q_3, the maximum payment that the victim would be prepared to pay would be less than the minimum that the firm would be prepared to accept. Again, equilibrium would be at Q_3.

Extending private property rights in this way is normally impractical whenever there are many polluters and many victims. But the principle of the victims paying polluters to reduce pollution is sometimes followed by governments. Thus, one element of the 2015 Paris Agreement on tackling climate change is for the developed countries to provide $100 billion of financial assistance to the developing countries to help them reduce greenhouse gas emissions (see Box 13.3 for more details).

In addition, there are sometimes direct environmental gains to be made from extending private property rights to individuals. In many developing countries, tenant farmers or squatters in urban slums have no incentive to invest in the land where they work or live. Give such people secure property rights, however, and they are more likely to take care of the property. For example, farmers are much more likely to plant trees if they know they have the right to the wood or fruit several years later.

Introducing charges for use of the environment

We previously discussed how the environment can be thought of as a common or natural resource where the user pays no price. For example, the emissions created by a coal burning power station can be spewed into the atmosphere at no cost to the firm even though it imposes costs on society. A firm could also use resources from the environment in its production process at a zero price. For example, it could extract water, cut down trees for timber or extract minerals out of the ground (assuming it owned or rented the land). With a zero price, these resources will tend to be depleted at rate that is not optimal for society: i.e. too quickly.

To overcome these problems, the government could introduce ***environmental charges*** for the use of resources that would otherwise be free to the user: for example, the extraction of a primary product such as timber or the use of the environment to dump waste. The latter approach involves a charge per unit of pollution. For example, *emissions charges* could be levied on firms discharging waste e.g. wastewater effluent charges. In order to be a direct charge on environmental use this involves measuring the pollutants contained in the wastewater. If a social efficiency approach to sustainability is taken, the optimum level of environmental use would be where the marginal social benefits and costs of that use were equal. This is illustrated in Figure 13.3, which shows the emission of toxic waste into a river by a chemical plant.

It is assumed that all the benefits from emitting the waste into the river accrue to the firm (i.e. there are no external benefits). Marginal private and marginal social benefits are thus the same ($MB = MSB$). The curve slopes downwards because, with a downward-sloping demand for the good, higher output results in lower marginal benefit, and so too will the waste associated with it.

But what about the marginal costs? Without charges, the marginal private cost of using the river for emitting the waste is zero. The pollution of the river, however, imposes an external cost on those using it for fishing or water supply. The marginal external cost rises as the river becomes less and less able to cope with increased levels of emission. As there

> **Definition**
>
> **Environmental charges** Charges for using natural resources (e.g. water or national parks), or for using the environment as a dump for waste (e.g. factory emissions or sewage).

Figure 13.3 An emissions charge

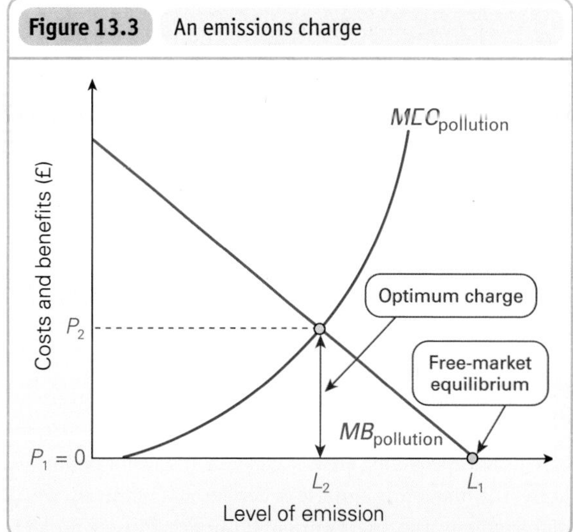

is no private cost, the marginal social cost is the same as the marginal external cost.

Without a charge, the firm will emit L_1, since this is where its private marginal cost (= 0) equals its private marginal benefit. The socially efficient level of emission is L_2 and the socially efficient level of emission charge, therefore, is P_2.

If these charges are to achieve a reduction in pollution, they must be a charge *per unit* of emissions or resource use (as in Figure 13.3). *Fixed total* charges, by contrast, such as water rates or council tax, will *not* encourage households to cut back on water use or reduce domestic refuse, since this will not save them any money: such charges have a *marginal* rate of zero. If the firm in Figure 13.3 were charged a fixed total pollution fee, it would still choose to emit L_1 waste.

Environmental ('green') taxes and subsidies

In reality, it may often be difficult to measure actual emissions and so charge for environmental use. An alternative is to tax an easier-to-measure activity, such as the output or consumption of a *good* that generates external environmental costs. Such taxes are known as ***green taxes***. In this case, the good already has a market price but this price is below the marginal cost to society. The tax has the effect of increasing the price, thereby pushing it closer to the *MSC*.

To achieve a socially efficient output, the rate of tax should be equal to the marginal external cost (i.e. distance *b–d* in Figure 13.2 on page 403) and so make the price equal to *MSC*. As such, it should fully internalise the costs of the externality.

An alternative is to subsidise activities that reduce pollution (such as the installation of loft insulation). Here the rate of subsidy should be equal to the marginal external benefit.

Although green taxes and subsidies are theoretically a means of achieving social efficiency, they do have serious limitations (see Box 13.2).

Draw a diagram like Figure 13.2, only this time assume that the activity has the effect of reducing pollution, with the result that there are marginal external benefits. Identify the socially optimal level of the activity. What would be the level of subsidy required to achieve this level of activity?

Non-market-based policies

Command-and-control systems (laws and regulations)

One way of tackling pollution has been to set maximum permitted levels of emission or resource use, or minimum acceptable levels of environmental quality, and then to fine firms contravening these limits. Measures of this type are known as ***command-and-control (CAC) systems***. Clearly, there have to be inspectors to monitor the amount of pollution, and the fines have to be large enough to deter firms from exceeding the limit.

Virtually all countries have environmental regulations of one sort or another. For example, the EU has over 230 items of legislation covering areas such as air and water pollution, noise, the marketing and use of dangerous chemicals, waste management, the environmental impacts of new projects (such as power stations, roads and quarries), recycling, depletion of the ozone layer and global warming.

Typically, there are three approaches to devising CAC systems.[2]

- ***Technology-based standards***. The focus could be on the amount of pollution generated, irrespective of its environmental impact. As technology for reducing pollutants improves, so tougher standards could be imposed, based on the 'best available technology' (as long as the cost were not excessive). For example, the European Union introduced a directive in 1992, called Euro 1, which set permitted levels of harmful emissions from new petrol and diesel cars in the European Economic Area for the following – Nitrogen Oxide (NOx), Carbon Monoxide (CO), Hydrocarbons (HC) and Particulate Matter (PM). In September 2015, the sixth version of the directive, Euro 6, came into effect. For new diesel cars, it imposed the following restrictions – CO: 0.5g/km; NOx: 0.08g/km; PM: 0.005g/km. Companies, such as Volkswagen, breaking these rules led to the so-called *dieselgate scandal*.
- ***Ambient-based standards***. Here the focus is on the environmental impact. For example, standards could be set for air or water purity. Depending on the location and the number of polluters in that area, a given standard would be achieved with different levels of discharge. If the object is a cleaner environment, this approach is more efficient than technology-based standards.
- ***Social-impact standards***. Here the focus is on the effect on people. Thus tougher standards would be imposed in densely populated areas. Whether this approach is more efficient than that of ambient-based standards depends on the approach to sustainability. If the objective is to

Definitions

Green tax A tax on output or consumption designed to charge for the adverse effects of production or consumption on the environment. The socially efficient level of a green tax is equal to the marginal environmental cost of production or consumption.

Command-and-control (CAC) systems The use of laws or regulations backed up by inspections and penalties (such as fines) for non-compliance.

Technology-based standards Pollution control that requires firms' emissions to reflect the levels that could be achieved from using the best available pollution control technology.

Ambient-based standards Pollution control that requires firms to meet minimum standards for the environment (e.g. air or water quality).

Social-impact standards Pollution control that focuses on the effects on people (e.g. on health or happiness).

2 See R. K. Turner, D. Pearce and I. Bateman, *Environmental Economics*, Harvester Wheatsheaf (1994), p. 198.

achieve social efficiency, human-impact standards are preferable. If the objective is to protect the environment for its own sake (a deeper green approach), ambient standards would be preferable.

Assessing CAC systems. Given the uncertainty over the environmental impacts of pollutants, especially over the longer term, it is often better to play safe and set tough emissions or ambient standards. These could always be relaxed at a later stage if the effects turn out not to be so damaging, but it might be too late to reverse damage if the effects turn out to be more serious. Taxes may be a more sophisticated means of reaching a socially efficient output, but CAC methods are usually more straightforward to devise, easier to understand by firms and easier to implement.

Voluntary agreements

Rather than imposing laws and regulations, the government can seek to enter into voluntary agreements (VAs) with firms for them to cut pollution. For example, the UK government operates a system of climate change agreements (CCAs). These are voluntary agreements by firms to reduce energy use and carbon dioxide (CO_2) emissions in return for a reduction in the Climate Change Levy (a tax on fuel bills).

VAs may involve a formal contract, and hence be legally binding, or they may be looser commitments by firms. VAs will be helped if (a) companies believe that this will improve their image with customers and hence improve sales; (b) there is an underlying threat by the government of introducing laws and regulations should voluntary agreements fail; (c) there are financial incentives (as with CCAs).

Firms often prefer VAs to regulations, because they can negotiate such agreements to suit their own particular circumstances and build them into their planning. The result is that the firms may be able to meet environmental objectives at lower cost. This clearly helps their competitive position.

Education

People's attitudes are very important in determining the environmental consequences of their actions. Fortunately for the environment, people are not always out simply to maximise their own narrow self-interest. They are sometimes willing to pay higher prices for 'green products' and keen to recycle products wherever possible. There is evidence that peoples' attitudes have changed markedly over the past few decades. Partly this is due to education and better environmental information.

Tradable permits

A policy measure that has grown in popularity in recent years is that of ***tradable permits***, also known as a 'cap-and-trade' system. This is a combination of command-and-control and market-based systems.

Capping pollution

Initially, some criteria have to be set in order to determine which factories, power plants and installations the scheme will cover. Policy makers then have to set a limit or 'cap' on the total volume of pollution these organisations will collectively be allowed to produce before any financial penalties are incurred.

Once an aggregate cap is set, pollution permits, known as allowances, are either issued or sold to the firms. Each allowance held by a firm gives it the right to produce a given volume of pollution. The total volume of all the allowances should be equal to the size of the aggregate cap set by the authorities. The quantity of allowances awarded in subsequent years to each firm is reduced by a certain percentage – the cap is tightened – to give firms an incentive to invest in more environmentally friendly technology.

The most common way to determine the number of permits to allocate to individual plants, factories or installations at the beginning of the scheme is by their current levels of pollution. This approach is known as ***grandfathering***. A major criticism of this method is that it seems unfair on those firms that have already invested in cleaner technology. Why should they be required to make the same reductions in the future as firms currently using older polluting technology? As a solution to this problem, it is increasingly common to auction allowances – see Box 13.4.

All firms covered by the scheme must monitor and report the levels of pollution from their production. At the end of the year, they must submit enough allowances to the authorities to match the level of pollution they have caused. It is only possible to use an allowance once. If a firm fails to submit enough allowances then it is subject to heavy fines.

The EU ETS scheme. The biggest cap-and-trade system in the world is the European Union's Emissions Trading Scheme (EU ETS) – for more details see Box 13.4. It covers energy-intensive installations in four broad sectors that have emissions above certain threshold levels. The four sectors are

Definitions

Tradable permits Firms are issued or sold permits by the authorities that give them the right to produce a given level of pollution. Firms that do not have sufficient permits to match their pollution levels can purchase additional permits to cover the difference, while those that reduce their pollution levels can sell any surplus permits for a profit.

Grandfathering Where the number of emission permits allocated to a firm is based on its current levels of emission (e.g. permitted levels for all firms could be 80 per cent of their current levels).

BOX 13.2 GREEN TAXES

Are they the perfect answer to the problem of pollution?

Countries are increasingly making use of 'green' taxes to discourage pollution. The Office for National Statistics estimated that environmental taxes raised £52.620 billion of revenue for the UK government in 2019 (7.1 per cent of total taxes and national insurance) and that households paid an average of £760 in green taxes in 2018. The table shows some of the more important environmental taxes that have been used in the UK. Taxes on hydrocarbon oils (i.e. duty and VAT on petrol and diesel) are by far the most significant and account for 53 per cent of total revenue from all environmental taxes.

Environmental taxes and charges in the UK

Tax	Revenue £ millions (2019)[a]
Tax on hydrocarbon oils (i.e. petrol and diesel)	27 795
Climate Change Levy	2 091
Renewable Energy Obligations	6 118
Contracts for Difference	1 471
Emissions Trading Scheme (EU-ETS)	1 255
CRC Energy Efficiency Scheme	298
Air Passenger Duty	3 810
Rail Franchise Premia	1 258
Motor vehicle duties	
Households	4 998
Businesses	2 007
Landfill Tax	784
Aggregates Levy	396
Other	339
Total	52 620

[a] The 2019 figures have been used as the 2020 data were significantly affected by the national lockdowns. The 2019 figures are more typical.

Source: *Environmental Taxes*, Table 1 (ONS, 3 June 2021), https://www.ons.gov.uk/search?q=Environmental+taxes

Environmental tax revenue in the UK as a percentage of GDP has remained broadly stable over the past 20 years at between 2 to 3 per cent. The chart shows how the UK compares with other countries. Note that the figures shown are for 2019. The 2020 figures were substantially lower because of the pandemic and are unlikely to be typical of future revenues.

As can be seen, they are higher than average in Denmark and the Netherlands, reflecting the strength of their environmental concerns. They are lowest in the USA and Canada.

There are various problems, however, with using taxes to tackle pollution.

Problems with environmental taxes

Identifying the socially efficient tax rate. It will be difficult to identify the $MEC_{pollution}$ curve for each firm (see Figure 13.2), given that each one is likely to produce different amounts of pollutants for any given level of output. Even if two firms produce identical amounts of pollutants, the environmental damage might be quite different, because the ability of the environment to cope with it will differ between the two locations. Also, the human impact will vary. We can add to these issues the fact that harmful effects are likely to build up over time, and predicting this is fraught with difficulty.

One issue in the UK is the variation in rates of tax on CO_2 emissions by sector. Research by Catapult Energy Systems[1] found that people pay £109 in tax per tonne of CO_2 emissions when they drive their cars as opposed to just £7 if they heat their homes with oil. Gas central heating and air travel have effective subsidies through lower VAT rates of £14 and £26 per tonne respectively.

Problems of demand inelasticity. The less elastic the demand for the product, the less effective will a tax be in cutting production and hence in cutting pollution. Thus taxes on petrol (where we know demand is inelastic) would have to be very high to make significant reductions in the exhaust gases that contribute towards global warming and acid rain.

Problems with international trade. If a country imposes pollution taxes on its industries, its products will become less competitive in world trade. To compensate for this, it may be necessary to give the industries tax rebates for exports. Also, taxes would have to be imposed on imports of competitors' products from countries where there is no equivalent green tax.

Effects on employment. Reduced output in the industries affected by green taxes will lead to a reduction in employment. If, however, the effect was to encourage investment in new cleaner technology, employment might not fall. Furthermore, employment opportunities could be generated elsewhere, if the extra revenues from the green taxes were spent on alternative products (e.g. buses and trains rather than cars).

Redistributive effects. Many green taxes are regressive. The poor spend a higher proportion of their income on domestic

energy (electricity, oil, coal), ferrous metals (iron, steel), minerals (cement, glass, ceramics) and wood pulp (paper and card). The EU set a total cap on the aggregate CO_2 emissions produced by organisations in these sectors of 2 084 301 856 tonnes for 2013. This cap then declined between 2014 and 2020 at an annual rate of 1.74 per cent of the average total quantity of allowances issued between 2008 and 2012. This works out at a fall of 38 264 246 allowances per year over the period.

CASE STUDIES AND APPLICATIONS

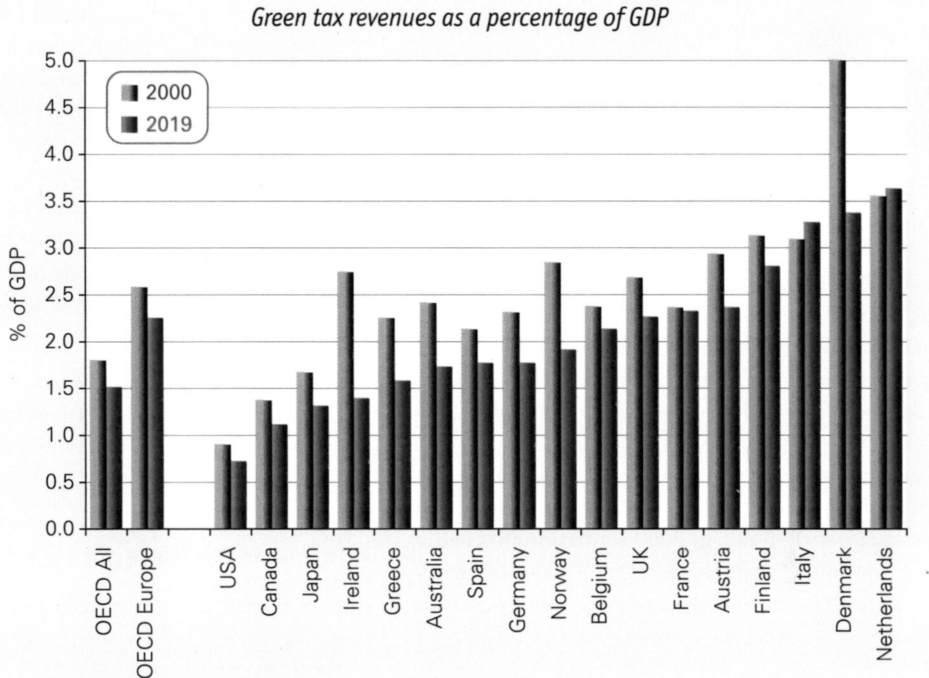

Source: Based on data in *Environmental Taxation* (OECD, 2021), www.oecd.org/environment/tools-evaluation/environmentaltaxation.htm

fuel than the rich. A 'carbon tax' on such fuel therefore has the effect of redistributing incomes away from the poor. The poor also spend a larger proportion of their income on food than the rich do. Taxes on agriculture, designed to reduce the intensive use of fertilisers and pesticides, also tend to hit the poor proportionately more than the rich.

Not all green taxes, however, are regressive. The rich spend a higher proportion of their income on motoring than the poor (see Figure 13.4 on page 419). Thus petrol and other motoring taxes could have a progressive effect.

Despite these problems, such taxes can still move output closer to the socially efficient level. What is more, they do have the major advantage of providing a continuing incentive to firms to find cleaner methods of production and thereby save more on their tax bills.

1. ***Is it a good idea to use the revenues from green taxes to subsidise green alternatives (e.g. using petrol taxes for subsidising rail transport)? Consider the implications for wider tax policy in your answer.***
2. ***If a green tax is highly regressive, does this mean that a government concerned with inequality should avoid implementing it? Consider the long-term impact of climate change on welfare, in your answer.***

Choose two countries and compare their use of taxes and subsidies to tackle environmental issues. If this is done as a group exercise, individual members of the group could each choose different countries. The group could then compare the findings.

1 George Day and Danial Sturge, 'Rethinking carbonisation incentives', Catapult Energy Systems (June 2019), https://esc-non-prod.s3.eu-west-2.amazonaws.com/2019/07/Rethinking-Decarbonisation-Incentives-Future-Carbon-Policy-for-Clean-Growth.pdf

Trading under a cap-and-trade system

The 'trade' part of the scheme refers to the ability of firms to buy and sell allowances in a secondary market once they have been allocated by the authorities. However, in what circumstances would a firm wish either to buy or to sell an allowance?

Take the example of an organisation that estimates it will not have enough permits at the end of the year to match its forecast level of pollution. If it cannot reduce its pollution, say by installing new equipment, or if it is too costly to do so, then it can purchase extra permits.

In order to buy permits (allowances) in the secondary market there must be other firms that have excess permits and hence are willing to sell. These may be firms which have recently made large investments in a more energy-efficient production process.

The price that firms pay to buy, or receive from selling, the allowances in the secondary market will depend on the levels of demand and supply. These will be heavily influenced by the initial number of permits allocated by the authorities, the state of the economy and developments in technology.

The principle of tradable permits can be used as the basis of international agreements on pollution reduction – see Box 13.3 for more details.

Assessing the system of tradable permits

It is argued that one major advantage of the cap-and-trade system over most command-and-control methods is that it can reduce pollution at a much lower cost to society. This can be illustrated by using the following simple example.

Assume there are just two firms that each own one plant that pollutes the environment. Firm A and B's production processes currently result in 2000 tonnes of CO_2 being emitted into the atmosphere each year – 1000 tonnes by each firm. Decreasing emissions of CO_2 would cost firm A £100 per tonne, whereas it would cost firm B £200 per tonne.

Assume that the government wishes to reduce emissions from 2000 to 1600 tonnes. It could do this by setting an emissions cap on both firms of 800 tonnes of CO_2. Each would be given permits for that amount. Without the possibility of trading the permits, firm A would have to spend £20 000 to comply with the cap (200 tonnes × £100), while firm B would have to spend £40 000 (200 tonnes × £200). Thus the cost to society of reducing total emissions from 2000 to 1600 tonnes is £60 000.

With trading, however, the cost can be reduced below £60 000. If the two firms traded permits at a price somewhere between £100 and £200 per tonne, say £150, both could gain. Firm A would have an incentive to reduce its emissions to 600 tonnes, costing £40 000 (400 × £100). It could then sell the unused permits (200 tonnes) to firm B for £30 000 (200 × £150), which could then maintain emissions at 1000 tonnes. The net cost to firm A is now only £10 000 (£40 000 − £30 000), rather than the £20 000 from reducing its production to 800 without trade. The cost to Firm B is £30 000, rather than the £40 000 from reducing its production to 800.

Society will have achieved the same total reduction in pollution (i.e. from 2000 tonnes to 1600 tonnes) but at a much lower cost: i.e. £40 000 instead of £60 000. The smaller increase in costs means that price increases in the sector for consumers will be lower than they would otherwise have been.

One potential drawback of using tradable permits is that it could result in pollution being concentrated in certain geographic areas. Some other problems are discussed in Box 13.3.

Comparison with CAC systems. In theory, the same outcome could be obtained in a CAC system if the policy makers knew the compliance costs of the different firms. In this case, an emission standard of 600 tonnes could be placed on firm A and 1000 tonnes on firm B. However, this would require the authorities collecting enormous amounts of detailed information on plant-specific costs in order to calculate the appropriate emissions standard for each business. The cap-and-trade system allows policy makers to achieve the same outcome without the need to collect such large amounts of detailed information.

Comparison with green taxes/charges. An interesting comparison can also be made between tradable permits and green taxes or charges. This is discussed in more detail in Box 13.3.

How much can we rely on governments?

If governments are to be relied upon to set the optimum green taxes or regulations, several conditions must be met.

First, they must have the will to protect the environment. But governments are accountable to their electorates and must often appease various pressure groups, such as representatives of big business. In the USA, for example, there has been great resistance to cuts in greenhouse gases from the automobile, power and various other industries, many of which have powerful representation in Congress. So there must be the political will in a country if significant environmental improvements are to be made. One of the problems here is that many of the environmental effects of our actions today will be on future generations; but governments are elected by today's generation, and today's generation may not be prepared to make the necessary sacrifices. This brings us back to the importance of education.

Second, it must be possible to identify just what the optimum is. This requires a clear set of objectives concerning sustainability and any conflicts between human and ecological objectives. It also requires a knowledge of just what are the environmental effects of various activities, such as the emission of CO_2 into the atmosphere, and that is something on which scientists disagree.

Finally, there is the problem that many environmental issues are global and not just local or national. Many require concerted action by governments around the world. The history of international agreements on environmental issues, however, is one plagued with difficulties between countries, which seem more concerned with their own national interests. To understand the difficulties of reaching international agreements, we can draw on game theory (see section 8.3).

Game theory and international agreements

Assume that the world would benefit from a reduction in greenhouse gases and that these benefits would exceed the costs of having to cut back on activities (such as motoring or the generation of electricity) that release such gases into the atmosphere. What would be in the interests of an *individual* country, such as the USA? Its optimum solution would be for *other* countries to cut their emissions, while maintaining its own levels. This approach would yield most of the benefits to the USA and none of the costs. However, when *all* countries refuse to cut emissions, no one gains! This is an example of the *prisoners' dilemma* (see Box 8.5, page 243), and is illustrated in Table 13.1.

Table 13.1 Outcomes for countries from strategies of pollution reduction

		Other countries' strategy		
		All cut pollution	Some cut pollution	None cut pollution
USA's strategy	Cut pollution	A Moderate net gain for all	B Small loss for USA; gain for countries not cutting pollution	C Large loss for USA; slight gain for other countries
	Don't cut pollution	D High gain for USA; small gain for other countries	E Fairly high gain for USA; loss for other countries	F No gain for any country

Assume that there is an international agreement (as at the Kyoto summit in December 1997: see Box 13.4) to cut emissions. If all countries stick to the agreement, the outcome is cell A: a moderate gain to all. What should Congress do? Whatever other countries do (all stick to the agreement, some stick to it, none stick to it), it will be in the USA's interests *not* to stick to it: this is the dominant strategy. Cell D is preferable to Cell A; E is preferable to B; F is preferable to C. But when *all* countries reason like this, the world ends up in Cell F, with no cut in pollution. Cell F is worse for all countries than Cell A.

Only if countries believe that the other countries will (a) ratify the agreement and (b) stick to the approved terms, is the agreement likely to succeed. This requires trust on all sides as well as the ability to monitor the outcomes.

The other major problem area concerns equity. Most countries will feel that they are being asked to do too much and that others are being asked to do too little. Developed countries will want to adopt a grandfathering approach. The starting point with this approach would be current levels of pollution. Every country would then be required to make the same percentage cut. Developing countries, on the other hand, will want the bulk of the cuts, if not all of them, to be made by the developed countries. After all, the rich countries produce much higher levels of pollutants per capita than do the poor countries, and curbing growth in developing countries would have a far more serious impact on levels of absolute poverty.

How does an international negotiation 'game' differ from the prisoners' dilemma game?

Section summary

1. One approach to protecting the environment is to use the market. This can be done by extending private property rights. In many cases, however, this approach is impractical. Another approach is to impose charges for using the environment or taxes per unit of output. The problem with these methods is in identifying the appropriate charges or tax rates, since these will vary according to the environmental impact.
2. Another approach is to use command-and-control systems, such as making certain practices illegal or putting limits on discharges. This is a less sophisticated alternative to taxes or charges, but it is safer when the environmental costs of certain actions are unknown. Other alternatives to market-based approaches include voluntary agreements and education.
3. Tradable permits are a mix of command-and-control and market-based systems. Firms are given permits to emit a certain level of pollution and then these can be traded. A firm that can relatively cheaply reduce its pollution below its permitted level can sell this credit to another firm that finds it more costly to do so. The system is an efficient and administratively cheap way of limiting pollution to a designated level. It can, however, lead to pollution being concentrated in certain areas and can reduce the pressure on firms to find cleaner methods of production.
4. Although governments can make a major contribution to reducing pollution, government action is unlikely to lead to the perfect outcome (however defined). Governments may be more concerned with short-run political considerations and will not have perfect information. What is more, given that many environmental effects spill over national borders, governments may 'play games' internationally to try to reduce the costs to their country of any international action to protect the environment.

BOX 13.3 PLACING A PRICE ON CO_2 EMISSIONS

Cap-and-trade and carbon emission taxes

Cap-and-trade systems and carbon taxes now apply to approximately one-fifth of the world's emissions. The initiatives are similar as they place a price on CO_2 emissions in order to discourage pollution. They also both differ from regulation as they use market forces in an attempt to reduce emissions in the least-cost manner.

However, there are important differences. With cap-and-trade schemes, the authorities impose direct limits on the total level of emissions (the cap) and let market forces determine the resulting price of carbon (the trade). This means there is more certainty over the quantity of emissions but more uncertainty over the price. With carbon taxes, the authorities directly determine the price of carbon, while market forces determine the resulting level of emissions. This means there is more certainty over the price of carbon but more uncertainty over the quantity of emissions.

Cap-and trade schemes – some real-world examples

Some real-world examples of this type of policy include the California Cap and Trade scheme, the US Regional Greenhouse Gas Initiative (RGGI) (an agreement of eastern US states), and the New Zealand Emission Trading Scheme (NZ ETS).

The world's first and still the largest example is the European Union Emissions Trading Scheme (EU ETS). Established in 2005, it was the key policy response to the environmental targets set by the international treaty, the Kyoto Protocol (see Box 13.4). It currently applies to approximately 11 000 industrial plants that are heavy users of energy (power stations/industrial plants) and airlines that operate flights within the European Economic Area. In total, the businesses covered by the scheme are responsible for around 40 per cent of the EU's greenhouse gas emissions.

The authorities that run the schemes typically implement annual reductions in the size of the cap. In the case of the EU ETS, the planned reduction is approximately 48 million tonnes per year from 2021 to 2030. As with all cap-and-trade schemes, organisations covered by the EU ETS have to monitor, report and verify their emissions. Firms are either allocated emission allowances by the authorities and/or have to purchase them via auctions. Each allowance provides the right to emit one tonne of CO_2 and organisations are obliged to hand over enough allowances to the authorities to match their emissions on an annual basis. Failure to do so results in a financial penalty.

Carbon emissions taxes – some real-world examples

Some real-world examples of carbon emission taxes (CETs) include those in Sweden, Finland, Denmark and Norway. Sweden introduced its emission tax in 1991 and it applies to motor and heating fuels. The size of the tax depends on the estimated CO_2 emissions when fossil fuels are burning. Therefore, no measurement of actual emissions is necessary. The tax rate has increased over time from \$26 per tonne in 1991 to \$126 per tonne in 2020. This is one of the highest rates in the world. Some sectors are exempt from the tax, such as those already covered by the EU ETS.

Options for the UK

The UK was part of the EU ETS scheme until the end of the Brexit transition period in December 2020. In the run-up to its final departure from the European Union, the government considered a number of alternative policy options.[1] These included (i) a new stand-alone UK ETS scheme, (ii) a new UK ETS scheme linked to the EU ETS, and (iii) a new carbon emissions tax. It finally opted for a stand-alone UK ETS scheme to operate from 1 January 2021. There is some uncertainty at the time of writing about possible links with the EU ETS. For example, it is unclear whether it will be possible to have *'one way'* links (i.e. UK firms can use EU ETS allowances) or *'two way'* links (i.e. EU and UK allowances can be used in both systems).

What are the relative merits of the different schemes?

The impact of uncertainty. There will always be some uncertainty about the size of the benefits and costs of reducing emissions. For example, if CO_2 emissions decline by 10 per cent, what will be the precise benefit to the environment? By how much will business costs rise as organisations have to change production methods and invest in greener technologies to achieve this reduction (the abatement costs)? This is important as higher business costs will result in (a) higher prices for consumers (b) smaller wage rises for workers and (c) smaller dividend payments for shareholders.

The relative sensitivity of these two effects helps to determine the more effective policy. If improvements to the environment are more sensitive, the greater certainty over the impact on the quantity of emissions makes cap-and-trade the more desirable policy. If business costs are more sensitive, the greater certainty over the price of carbon makes the tax a more desirable policy.

Other advantages/disadvantages will depend on the precise design of the scheme.

Revenue. A CET raises revenue that governments can use to compensate low-income families through higher benefits or lower payroll taxes. Free allocation of emission allowances in a cap-and-trade scheme means the revenue goes to organisations rather than the government. If instead, the authorities auction the allowances, it could raise the same revenue as a CET.

In the early years of the EU ETS (phases I and II)[2] the majority of the allowances were freely allocated to the plants and factories covered by the scheme using the grandfathering method (see page 409). The two arguments for taking this approach are that firms may need time to adjust to the new scheme and there may be an issue with carbon leakage – companies transferring production to countries with weaker climate change policies in order to lower their costs. However, a number of observers were very critical about the free distribution. Some estimates suggest that between 2008 and 2014, it enabled businesses to make £24 billion in windfall profits.[3] In response to this criticism, auctioning replaced free provision as the default option in 2013. However, free allocation still occurs in sectors where the authorities consider the risk of carbon leakage to be significant. A CET could also be designed to deal with fears about carbon leakage by exempting the relevant sectors from the tax.

Free provision will continue in the UK ETS and the methods used to determine the allocation will be similar to those currently used in the EU ETS. To deal with carbon leakage in the future, the EU is considering the implementation of a carbon border tax. The *carbon border adjustment mechanism* (CBAM) would impose charges on raw materials imported from countries with weaker environmental policies/ regulations. There is some uncertainty about whether current international trading rules permit this type of policy.

Carbon price volatility. With a CET there is no short-term price volatility. Governments can change tax rates on an annual basis but prices remain constant over shorter periods. As market forces determine prices in cap-and trade schemes they can change on a daily basis. This short-term price volatility may deter firms from making long-term investments in greener technologies.

Price volatility has certainly been a feature of the EU ETS. Volatility within one day (intra-day price volatility) has been over €1 per allowance while quarterly/half-yearly volatility has also been considerable. Between 2 November 2020 and 1 April 2021, the price increased from €23.67 to €42.37 – nearly 80 per cent.

Different design features in a cap-and-trade scheme can reduce this volatility. For example, a Market Stability Reserve (MSR) was introduced into the EU ETS in January 2019. This initiative attempts to deal with imbalances between demand and supply by controlling the volume of allowances auctioned at any point in time. If the number of surplus allowances in circulation exceeds 833 million (putting downward pressure on prices), the authorities reduce the quantity auctioned by 24 per cent of this total. If the number in circulation it too low (putting upward pressure on prices) allowances are released from the MSR.

The UK ETS also has a number of design features to reduce price volatility. The authorities have set an initial Auction Reserve Price (ARP) of £22. Any bids below this price will be unsuccessful. The scheme also has a Cost Containment Mechanism (CCM). This makes it possible to (a) redistribute allowances between auctions in the same year, (b) bring forward auctioned allowances from future years to the current year and (c) draw allowances from a market stability mechanism account.

Difficulties setting the size of the cap/tax rates. Setting the appropriate size of both the overall cap and the tax rate is difficult. Businesses may lobby governments and exaggerate the negative impacts of both policies. For example, people criticised the early years of the EU ETS for setting a cap that was far too large. Initially, each member state developed a National Allocation Plan that set out a total cap on its emissions. This gave each country an incentive to game the system by exaggerating its volume of emissions in order to keep costs down for its domestic firms. This in turn would help to maintain its national economic competitiveness. The EU ETS now uses a more centralised method for setting the cap.

It is also difficult to set the appropriate level for the tax and rates per tonne of CO_2 vary widely. For example, in Europe the rates in Sweden, Finland, Denmark and the Ukraine are €108.81, €62.18, €23.77 and €0.37 respectively.

Administrative costs for the authorities. A number of the administrative costs of both schemes are similar. For example, the authorities have to measure emissions and impose penalties if firms do not (a) have enough allowances or (b) pay the required taxes. Cap-and-trade schemes do have the additional costs of having to allocate allowances. This would make it very expensive to extend the scheme to emissions from motoring and residential heating.

Transaction costs for firms. Having to buy and sell allowances in a market will generate higher transaction costs than simply paying a tax.

Corruption/market manipulation/tax evasion. Firms might try to manipulate prices in the market for allowances. There is also the risk of cyber theft with the electronic systems used in most cap-and-trade schemes. With a CET, the authorities have to deal with potential tax evasion.

Relationships with other policies. CETs may work more effectively with other domestic environmental policies. However, it may be easier to link cap-and-trade systems across different countries. This enables emissions to be reduced in the most cost effective way.

Some people have argued that the exact design of CETs and cap-and-trade systems is more important than the choice between the two different policies when governments are trying to tackle climate change.

CO_2 emissions are a stock externality. Their impact depends on the amount that has accumulated in the atmosphere over time as opposed to emissions at a particular point in time. What implications does this have for the choice of policies for climate change. I.e. cap-and-trade vs a carbon emissions tax?

Investigate the design of either a CET or a cap-and-trade system used in a particular country or group of countries. Assess how it might be improved to make it more effective in achieving its goals. To what extent might political pressures influence the design of such a policy?

1 *Carbon Emissions Tax: Summary of responses to the consultation*, HM Treasury (March 2021), https://assets.publishing.service.gov.uk/government/uploads/system/uploads/attachment_data/file/971509/201202_CET_Summary_of_Responses_2021.pdf

2 Phase I ran from January 2005 to December 2007, Phase II ran from January 2008 to December 2012, Phase III ran from January 2013 to December 2020, while Phase IV runs from January 2021 to December 2029.

3 *Industry windfall profits from Europe's carbon market*, Carbon Market Watch Policy Briefing (March 2016), https://carbonmarketwatch.org/wp-content/uploads/2016/03/Policy-brief_Industry-windfall-profits-from-Europe%E2%80%99s_web_final-1.pdf

BOX 13.4 INTERNATIONAL CO-ORDINATION ON CLIMATE CHANGE

From the Kyoto Protocol to the Paris Agreement

In 1992, governments from around the world met at Rio de Janeiro and established the United Nations Framework Convention on Climate Change (UNFCC). The aim of the UNFCC is to limit the concentration of greenhouses gas in the atmosphere to avoid climate change. Representatives from the countries involved in the UNFCC have met annually since 2005 at 'Conferences of the Parties of UNFCC' or, more simply, 'COP'.

The third meeting, COP3, took place in Kyoto in Japan in 1997, where a draft accord was agreed to reduce greenhouse gas emissions by 5.2 per cent (based on 1990 levels) by the year 2012.

To become a legally binding treaty, the Kyoto Protocol had to be signed and ratified by nations accounting for at least 55 per cent of greenhouse gas emissions. In March 2001, the US government announced that it would not ratify the accord, so it took until October 2004 before reaching the 55 per cent threshold. The protocol officially came into force on 6 February 2005.

Market-based systems

Although not originally envisaged in this way, the agreement turned climate change into a market, where it is possible to buy and sell the right to pollute through a system of emissions credits. These credits can be earned by reducing emission levels below those agreed or by creating conditions that help to minimise the impact of greenhouse gases on global warming: for example, by planting forests (which absorb carbon).

Within the Kyoto Protocol there are three distinct market-based mechanisms:

- Emissions trading;
- Joint implementation (JI);
- Clean Development Mechanism (CDM).

Emissions trading. Rights to emit six greenhouse gases could be traded amongst the countries that ratified the Kyoto Protocol. If a country reduces emissions below its agreed limit, it can sell the additional reduction as a credit. If a country is finding it difficult to cut emissions, it can buy these credits within a type of marketplace. (Box 13.3 explains how CO_2 emissions trading began within the EU in January 2005.)

Joint implementation. An industrialised country can earn credits by investing in projects that reduce emissions in other industrialised countries. These credits, called 'emission reduction units' (ERUs) then reduce the country's own requirement to cut emissions.

Clean Development Mechanism. This is similar to JI, but involves a country or company from the industrialised world earning credits, called 'certified emissions reductions' (CERs), by investing in emission reduction schemes in *developing* countries. A typical CDM or JI project might involve installing solar panels, planting forests, or investing in a factory producing energy-efficient light bulbs.

Assessing the Kyoto Protocol

The Kyoto Protocol was criticised on a number of grounds. For example:

- Many commentators argued that the 5.2 per cent target was too low. The Intergovernmental Panel on Climate Change estimated that a 60 to 80 per cent cut in greenhouse gas emissions from 1990 levels is required to avert serious climate disruption.
- Some of the reduction in emissions that did take place would have happened anyway due to recessions.
- A relatively small number of developed countries agreed to set emission targets at a national level. Many, such as China, India, Brazil and Mexico, were under no obligation to reduce emissions, although they did have to monitor and report the levels. Rapid economic growth in these countries over the past 20 years means that they are responsible for an increasing share of global emissions.
- The US government, under the George W. Bush presidency, significantly weakened the effectiveness of the treaty by opting out of the protocol. It introduced its own Clear Skies and Global Climate Change Initiatives in February 2002. This provided tax incentives to encourage renewable energy schemes and fuel efficiency schemes, but businesses were not obliged to meet any CO_2 targets.

13.3 THE ECONOMICS OF TRAFFIC CONGESTION

Traffic congestion is a problem faced by many countries, especially in large cities and at certain peak times. This problem has grown at an alarming rate as people have become increasingly reliant on their cars. Vehicles stuck in traffic jams impose huge costs on countries.

It is not only the motorist that suffers. Congested streets make life less pleasant for the pedestrian, and increased traffic leads to increased accidents and significant problems of pollution.

Between 1960 and 2019 the number of vehicle kilometres travelled on UK roads in Great Britain increased from 241 billion to 781 billion (224 per cent). The length of public roads over the same period increased from 312 502 kilometres to 398 359 (27.5 per cent), although some roads

CASE STUDIES AND APPLICATIONS

From Kyoto to Paris

Countries made very little progress from COP13 to COP20. Some, such as Canada, withdrew from the Kyoto Accord arguing that it was ineffective for a number of reasons. In particular, both China and the USA were not part of the scheme and a number of countries were not meeting their emission targets.

The situation changed in December 2015, when COP21 took place in Paris. After two weeks of intense haggling, the Paris Climate Accord was agreed. This was the first new global climate deal in 18 years.

All parties agreed to the following:

- All countries need to take action to reduce emissions so that global temperatures rise by less than 2°C above their pre-industrial levels. Further efforts should also be made to limit this increase to 1.5°C.
- They recognise that the pledges made by all countries before the conference would only limit the increase in global temperatures to 2.7°C in the best-case scenario.
- Countries need to take actions so that at some point between 2050 and 2100 a net zero target is reached. This means global emissions are equal to the amount that can be absorbed by natural sinks (i.e. trees, soil, etc.) and carbon-capturing technology.
- By 2020, $100 billion should be raised by richer developed countries to assist poorer developing countries with the cost of switching to renewable energy.

All of these objectives were aspirational goals rather than legally binding commitments. However, unlike the Kyoto Protocol, all the signatories, rather than just the richer nations, have made one important legal obligation.

Each country now has to submit its individual climate action plans, known as Nationally Determined Contributions (NDCs), every five years. The expectation is that each NDC should be more ambitious than the previous one. The authorities are also trying to develop a common standard of reporting NDCs so it becomes far easier to observe (a) how much pollution a country produces; (b) what policies it is using or plans to introduce to reduce its emissions; (c) how well these policies are working.

By October 2016, enough countries had ratified the Paris Climate Accord for it to come into force. However, in November 2020, under the Trump presidency, the USA became the first country to withdraw. However, with a change in administration, the USA re-joined the agreement in February 2021.

At the time of writing, a number of people have described the delayed COP26 in November 2021 as the most important meeting on climate change since COP21. Unfortunately, the parties were unable to make much progress at the previous COP24 and COP25 meetings in Katowice and Madrid. A key objective for COP26 in Glasgow is for countries to outline specific plans about how they intend to reach the targets set in Paris. In particular, it is a chance to revisit the first set of NDCs and see how ambitious countries have been with their second submissions. These were due by the end of 2020, but by September 2021 only 85 countries had submitted new targets, 5 had proposed new targets and 74 countries had not updated their targets.

Other important issues that need to be resolved at COP26 are (i) what kinds of financing count towards the $100 billion aid target for developing countries and (ii) carbon offsetting under Article 6 of the agreement. This latter issue has proved particularly difficult. Article 6 is similar to the Clean Development Mechanism (CDM) in the Kyoto Protocol. One important area of disagreement is the extent to which it is possible to use old CDM credits as part of the Paris Accord.

During the past 30 years of intergovernmental climate change conferences, global emissions have continued to rise. It will be interesting to see what concrete actions countries take following the COP26 in Glasgow.

Explain who are likely to be the 'winners' and 'losers' as a result of talks on carbon dioxide emissions. Use the concepts of game theory to illustrate your argument.

Assess the success of the Glasgow COP26 climate change talks.

were widened. Most passenger and freight transport travels by road. In 2019, 89.5 per cent of passenger kilometres (see Table 13.2) and 79 per cent of freight tonnage kilometres in Great Britain were by road, whereas rail accounted for just 9.5 per cent of passenger traffic and 8 per cent of freight tonnage. The total percentage of passenger kilometres by road peaked at 94 per cent in the mid-1990s before falling to its current figure.

With the lockdowns imposed during the coronavirus pandemic and restrictions on the use of public transport, car usage fell somewhat and rail and bus usage fell dramatically, whereas bicycle usage rose. It will be interesting to see if they return to previous levels with the passing of the pandemic.

Average weekly household expenditure on transport in the financial year 2019/20 was £81.60, equating to 13.9 per cent of total expenditure. Out of this total figure on transport, households spent £22.30 (27.3 per cent) on fuel, £6.20 (7.6 per cent) on repairs and services, £26.30 (32.2 per cent) on purchase of vehicles, £6.10 (7.5 per cent) on train and bus fares and £15.0 (18.4 per cent) on air and other travel.

Should the government do anything about the problem? Is traffic congestion a price worth paying for the benefits we

Table 13.2 Passenger transport in Great Britain: percentage of passenger kilometres

Year	Cars, vans and taxis	Motorcycles	Buses and coaches	Bicycles	Rail	Air (UK)
1952	26.6	3.2	42.2	10.5	17.4	0.1
1962	56.5	3.3	24.5	3.1	12.2	0.4
1972	75.9	0.9	13.9	0.9	7.9	0.5
1982	80.5	2.0	9.5	1.3	6.1	0.6
1992	86.0	0.7	6.3	0.7	5.6	0.7
2002	85.6	0.7	6.0	0.6	6.1	1.1
2012	83.6	0.6	5.3	0.6	8.7	1.1
2019	84.5	0.6	3.7	0.6	9.5	1.1

Source: Based on data from Table TSGB0101, *Transport Statistics of Great Britain Database 2020* (Department for Transport, December 2020), www.gov.uk/government/statistical-data-sets/tsgb01-modal-comparisons

gain from using cars? Are there things that can be done to ease the problem without generally inconveniencing the traveller?

We will look later in this section at various schemes and at their relative costs and benefits. But first it is necessary to examine the existing system of allocating road space to see the extent to which it meets or fails to meet society's transport objectives.

The existing system of allocating road space

The allocation of road space depends on both demand and supply. Demand is by individuals who base their decisions on largely private considerations. Supply, by contrast, is usually by central government or local authorities. Let us examine each in turn.

Demand for road space (by car users)

The demand for road space can be seen largely as a *derived* demand. What people want is not the car journey for its own sake, but to get to their destination. The greater the benefit they gain at their destination, the greater the benefit they gain from using their car to get there.

The demand for road space, like the demand for other goods and services, has a number of determinants. If congestion is to be reduced, it is important to know how responsive demand is to a change in any of these: it is important to consider the various elasticities of demand.

Price. This is the *marginal cost* to the motorist of a journey. It includes petrol, oil, maintenance, depreciation and any toll charges.

Are there any costs associated with motoring that would not be included as marginal costs? Explain why.

The price elasticity of demand for motoring tends to be relatively low. There can be a substantial rise in the price of petrol, for example, and there will be only a modest fall in traffic.

KI 9 p64

Estimates of the short-run price elasticity of demand for road fuel in industrialised countries typically range from −0.1 to −0.5. Long-run elasticities are somewhat higher, but are still generally inelastic.[3]

TC 6 p66

The low price elasticity of demand suggests that schemes to tackle traffic congestion that merely involve raising the costs of motoring will have only limited success.

In addition to monetary costs, there are also the time costs of travel. Data from the Department for Transport show that in 2019 the average time spent travelling to work by car in Great Britain was 27 minutes with a figure of 53 minutes for those working in central London. The opportunity cost of sitting in your car is the best alternative activity you could have been pursuing – relaxing, working, sleeping or whatever. Congestion, by increasing the duration of the journey, increases the opportunity cost.

KI 2 p10

Income. As incomes rise, car ownership and usage increase substantially. Demand for road space is elastic with respect to income.

Figure 13.4 shows motoring costs as a percentage of UK household expenditure by quintile groups of household income. The higher the household income, the higher the percentage of income spent on motoring. Indeed, the richest quintile's expenditure on motoring is double that of the poorest as a percentage of household expenditure. Clearly, the income elasticity of demand is significantly greater than 1.

This is also reflected in international statistics of car ownership. Figure 13.5 shows the growth of car ownership between 1980 and 2018 in selected European countries. As national incomes have risen, so has the proportion of car ownership. People see car transport as a 'luxury good' compared with alternatives such as public transport, walking or cycling. Also, the growth of suburbs has meant that many people travel longer distances to work.

The implication of this is that, if countries continue to experience economic growth, car ownership and usage are likely to increase substantially: a conclusion in line with most forecasts.

3 See: *Road Traffic Demand Elasticities* (Department for Transport, 2015).

Figure 13.4 Motoring costs as % of UK household expenditure: 2019/20

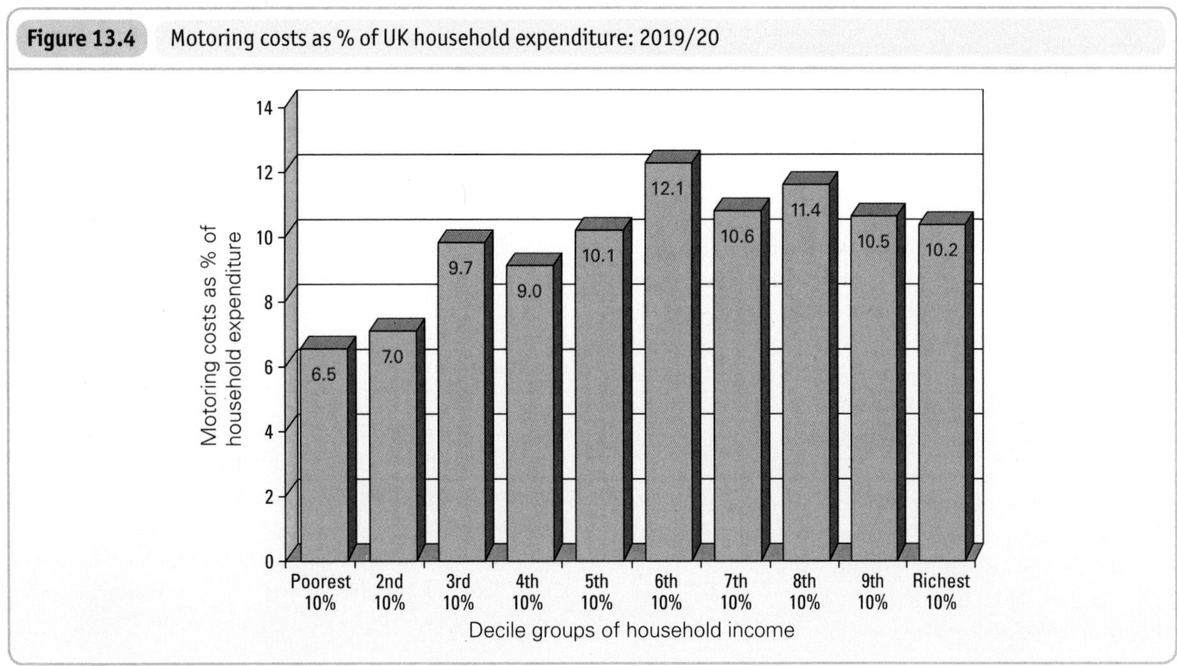

Source: Based on data in *Family spending workbook 1: detailed expenditure and trends* (National Statistics, March 2021), www.ons.gov.uk/peoplepopulationandcommunity/personalandhouseholdfinances/expenditure/datasets/familyspendingworkbook1detailedexpenditureandtrends

KI 9 p64

Price of substitutes. If bus and train fares came down, people might switch from travelling by car. The cross-price elasticity, however, is likely to be relatively low, given that most people regard these alternatives as a poor substitute for travelling in their own car. Cars are seen as more comfortable and convenient.

The 'price' of substitutes also includes the time taken to travel by these alternatives. The quicker a train journey is compared with a car journey, the lower will be its time cost to the traveller and thus the more people will switch from car to rail.

Price of complements. Demand for road space will depend on the price of cars. The higher the price of cars, the fewer people will own cars and thus the fewer cars there will be on the road.

Is the cross-price elasticity of demand for road space with respect to the price of cars likely to be high or low?

Demand will also depend on the price of complementary services, such as parking. A rise in car parking charges will reduce the demand for car journeys. But here again the

Figure 13.5 Increase in car ownership in various European countries

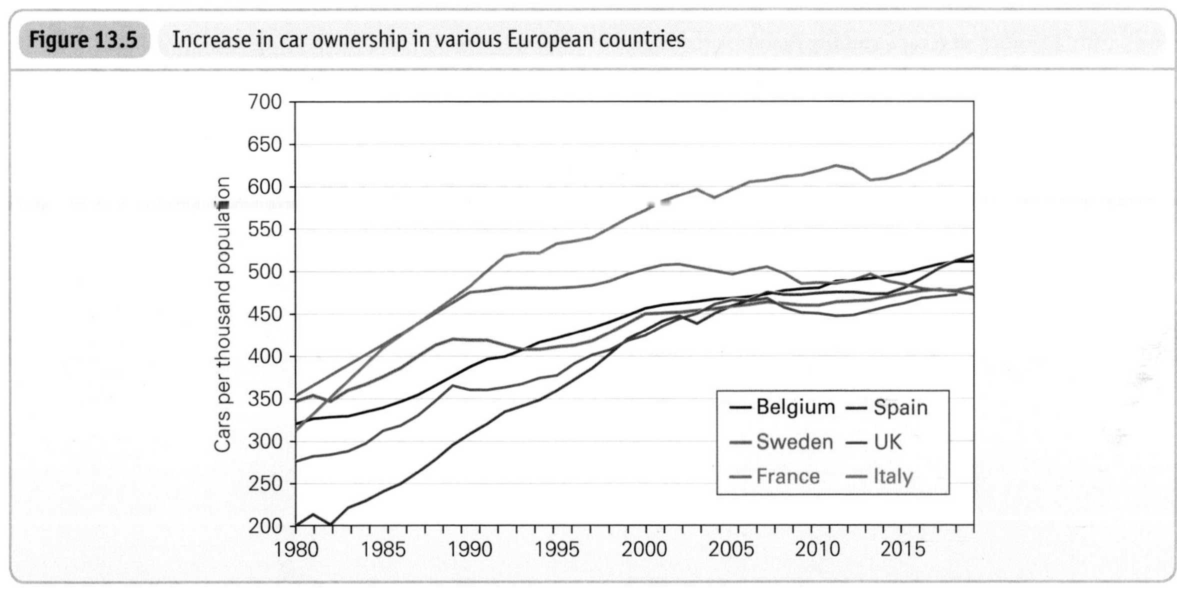

Source: *Passenger cars per 1000 inhabitants* (Eurostat, 2021), https://ec.europa.eu/eurostat/web/products-datasets/-/ROAD_EQS_CARHAB

cross elasticity is likely to be relatively low. In most cases, the motorist will either pay the higher charge or park elsewhere, such as in side streets.

Go through each of the determinants we have identified so far and show how the respective elasticity of demand makes the problem of traffic congestion difficult to tackle.

Tastes/utility. Another factor explaining the preference of many people for travelling by car is the pleasure they gain from it compared with alternative modes of transport. Car ownership is regarded by many people as highly desirable, and once accustomed to travelling in their own car most people are highly reluctant to give it up.

One important feature of the demand for road space is that it fluctuates. There will be periods of peak demand, such as during the rush hour or at holiday weekends. At such times, roads can get totally jammed. At other times, however, the same roads may be virtually empty.

Supply of road space

The supply of road space can be examined in two contexts: the short run and the long run.

The short run. In the short run, as we have seen, the supply of road space is constant. When there is no congestion, supply is more than enough to satisfy demand. There is spare road capacity. At times of congestion, there is pressure on this fixed supply. Maximum supply for any given road is reached at the point where there is the maximum flow of vehicles per minute along the road.

The long run. In the long run, the authorities can build new roads or improve existing ones. This will require an assessment of the costs and benefits of such schemes.

Identifying a socially efficient level of road usage (short run)

The existing system of *government* provision of roads and *private* ownership of cars is unlikely to lead to an optimum allocation of road space. So how do we set about identifying just what the social optimum is?

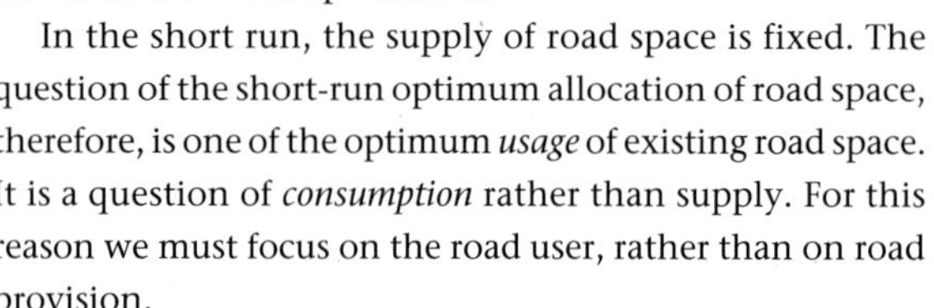

TC 11 p361

In the short run, the supply of road space is fixed. The question of the short-run optimum allocation of road space, therefore, is one of the optimum *usage* of existing road space. It is a question of *consumption* rather than supply. For this reason we must focus on the road user, rather than on road provision.

A socially efficient level of consumption occurs where the marginal social benefit of consumption equals its marginal social cost ($MSB = MSC$). So what are the marginal social benefits and costs of using a car?

KI 28 p356

Marginal social benefit of road usage

Marginal social benefit equals marginal private benefit plus marginal external benefit. Marginal private benefit is the direct benefit to the car user and is reflected in the demand for car journeys, the determinants of which we examined above. External benefits are few. The one major exception occurs when drivers give lifts to other people.

KI 31 p364

Marginal social cost of road usage

Marginal social cost equals marginal private cost plus marginal external cost. Marginal private costs to the motorist include the costs of petrol, wear and tear, tolls, etc. They also include the time costs of travel. There may also be substantial external costs. These include the following.

KI 31 p364

Congestion costs: time. When a person uses a car on a congested road, it will add to the congestion. This will therefore slow down the traffic even more and increase the journey time of other car users.

This is illustrated in Table 13.3 (which uses some imaginary figures).

Column (1) shows the number of cars travelling along a given road per minute. Column (2) shows the time taken for each car and thus can be seen as the marginal time cost to a motorist of making this journey. It is thus the *private* marginal time cost. With up to three cars per minute there is no congestion and therefore the traffic flows freely, each car taking

Table 13.3 Time taken to travel between two points along a given road

Traffic density (cars entering road per minute) (1)	Journey time per car (marginal private time cost: in minutes) (2)	Total journey time for all cars (total time cost: in minutes) (3) = (1) × (2)	Extra total journey time as traffic increases by one more car (marginal social time cost: in minutes) (4) = Δ (3)	Additional time cost imposed on other road users by one more car (marginal external time cost: in minutes) (5) = (4) − (2)
1	5	5	5	0
2	5	10	5	0
3	5	15	5	0
4	6	24	9	3
5	8	40	16	8
6	11	66	26	15
7	16	112	46	30

5 minutes to complete the journey. As traffic increases beyond this, however, the road becomes progressively more congested, and thus journey times increase. It is not just the additional cars that are forced to travel more slowly, but *all* the cars on the road. The extra cars thus impose a congestion cost on existing users of the road. By the time seven cars per minute are entering the road, journey time has increased to 16 minutes.

Column (3) shows the sum of the journey times of all the motorists on the road. For example, with six cars on the road, each taking 11 minutes, total journey time for all six is 66 minutes. Column (4) shows the increase in total journey time as one more car enters the road. Thus when the seventh car enters the road, total journey time increases from 66 to 112 minutes: an increase of 46 minutes. This is the additional cost to *all* road users: in other words, the marginal *social* cost. But of these 46 minutes, 16 are the private marginal costs incurred by the extra motorist. Only the remaining 30 minutes are *external* costs imposed on other road users. These external costs are shown in column (5).

Complete Table 13.3 up to 9 cars per minute, assuming that the journey time increases to 24 minutes for the eighth car and 35 minutes for the ninth car.

Time costs can be converted into money costs if we know the value of people's time. If time were valued at 10p per minute, the congestion costs (external costs) imposed by the seventh car would be £3 (i.e. 30 minutes × 10p per minute). Case Study 13.6 on the student website examines the method used in the UK for estimating the value of time (in the context of evaluating new road schemes).

Congestion costs: monetary. Congestion increases fuel consumption, and the stopping and starting increases the costs of wear and tear. When a motorist adds to congestion, therefore, there will be additional monetary costs imposed on other motorists. A table similar to Table 13.3 could be drawn to illustrate this.

Environmental costs. When motorists use a road, they reduce the quality of the environment for others. Cars emit fumes and create noise. This is bad enough for pedestrians and other car users, but can be particularly distressing for people living along the road. Driving can cause accidents, a problem that increases as drivers become more impatient as a result of delays. Also, as we saw in section 13.1, exhaust gases contribute to global warming and acid rain.

Research[4] suggests that the marginal external costs per kilometre of motoring in Great Britain in 2015 were as follows: congestion 13.2p, accidents 2.2p, greenhouse gases 0.9p, local air quality 0.3p, noise 0.1p. However, these are average external costs. The marginal external cost on London A roads is 80.6p per kilometre and just 10 per cent of total kilometres travelled account for over 60 per cent of the external costs.

Figure 13.6 Actual and optimum road usage

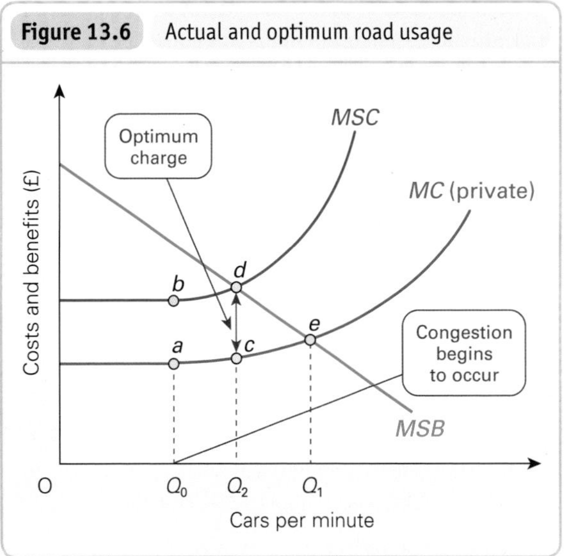

The socially efficient level of road usage

KI 28 p356

The point where the marginal social benefit of car use is equal to the marginal social cost can be illustrated on a diagram. In Figure 13.6, costs and benefits are shown on the vertical axis and are measured in money terms. Thus any non-monetary costs or benefits (such as time costs) must be given a monetary value. The horizontal axis measures road usage in terms of cars per minute passing a specified point on the road.

For simplicity it is assumed that there are no external benefits from car use and that therefore marginal private and marginal social benefits are the same. The *MSB* curve is shown as downward sloping. The reason for this is that different road users put a different value on this particular journey. If the marginal (private) cost of making the journey were high, only those for whom the journey had a high marginal benefit would travel along the road. If the marginal cost of making the journey fell, more people would make the journey: people choosing to make the journey at the point at which the marginal cost of using their car had fallen to the level of their marginal benefit. Thus the greater the number of cars in any given time period, the lower the marginal benefit.

The marginal (private) cost curve (*MC*) is likely to be constant up to the level of traffic flow at which congestion begins to occur. This is shown as point *a* in Figure 13.6. Beyond this point, marginal cost is likely to rise as time costs increase and as fuel consumption rises.

The marginal *social* cost curve (*MSC*) is drawn above the marginal private cost curve. The vertical difference between the two represents the external costs. Up to point *b*, external costs are simply the environmental costs. Beyond point *b*, there are also external congestion costs, since additional road users slow down the journey of *other* road users. These external costs get progressively greater as the volume of traffic increases (as column (5) of Table 13.3 illustrated).

4 Stuart Adam and Rebekah Stroud, 'A road map for motoring taxation', *IFS Green Budget*, Chapter 9 (October 2019), www.ifs.org.uk/uploads/GB2019-Chapter-9-A-road-map-for-motoring-taxation.pdf

The actual level of traffic flow will be at Q_1, where marginal private costs and benefits are equal (point *e*). The socially efficient level of traffic flow, however, will be at the lower level of Q_2, where marginal social costs and benefits are equal (point *d*). In other words, the existing system of allocating road space is likely to lead to an excessive level of road usage.

Identifying a socially optimum level of road space (long run)

In the long run, the supply of road space is not fixed. The authorities must therefore assess what new road schemes (if any) to adopt. This will involve the use of some form of *cost–benefit analysis* (see section 12.4).

The socially efficient level of construction will be where the marginal social benefit from construction is equal to the marginal social cost. This means that schemes should be adopted as long as their marginal social benefit exceeds their marginal social cost.

But how are these costs and benefits assessed in practice? Case Study 13.5 on the student website examines the procedure used in the UK.

Section summary

1. Increased car ownership and car usage have led to a growing problem of traffic congestion.
2. The allocation of road space depends on demand and supply. Demand depends on the price to motorists of using their cars, incomes, the cost of alternative means of transport, the price of cars and complementary services (such as parking), and the comfort and convenience of car transport. The price and cross-price elasticities of demand for car usage tend to be low: many people are unwilling to switch to alternative modes of transport. The income elasticity, on the other hand, is high. The demand for cars and car usage grows rapidly as incomes grow.
3. The short-run supply of road space is fixed. The long-run supply depends on government road construction programmes.
4. The existing system of government provision of roads and private ownership of cars is unlikely to lead to the optimum allocation of road space.
5. In the short run, with road space fixed, allocation depends on the private decisions of motorists. The problem is that motorists create two types of external cost: pollution costs and congestion costs. Thus $MSC > MC$. Because of these externalities, the actual use of road space (where $MB = MC$) is likely to be greater than the optimum (where $MSB = MSC$).
6. In the long run, the socially efficient amount of road space will be where $LRMSB = LRMSC$. New road schemes should be adopted as long as their $LRMSB > LRMSC$. Governments must therefore conduct some form of cost–benefit analysis in order to estimate these costs and benefits.

13.4 URBAN TRANSPORT POLICIES

We now turn to look at different solutions to traffic congestion. These can be grouped into three broad types: direct provision, regulation and legislation, and changing market signals.

Direct provision (supply-side solutions)

The road solution

One obvious solution to traffic congestion is to build more roads. There are, however, serious problems with this approach.

The objective of equity. The first problem concerns *equity*. After all, social efficiency is not the only possible economic objective. For example, when an urban motorway is built, those living beside it will suffer from noise and fumes. Motorway users gain, but the local residents lose. The question is whether this is fair.

KI 4 p13

The more the government tries to appeal to the car user by building more and better roads, the fewer people will use public transport, and thus the more will public transport decline. Those without cars lose, and these tend to be from the most vulnerable groups – poor, elderly and disabled people, and children.

Building more roads may lead to a *potential* Pareto improvement: in other words, if the gainers had fully to compensate the losers (e.g. through taxes or tolls), they would still have a net gain. The problem is that such compensation is rarely if ever paid. There is thus no actual Pareto improvement.

Congestion may not be solved. Increasing the amount of road space may encourage more people to use cars.

A good example is the London orbital motorway, the M25. In planning the motorway, not only did the government underestimate the general rate of traffic growth, but it also underestimated the direct effect it would have in encouraging people to use the motorway rather than using some alternative route, or some alternative means of transport, or even not making the journey at all. It also underestimated the effect it would have in encouraging people to live further from their place of

TC 5 p48

work and to commute along the motorway. The result is that there is now serious congestion on the motorway and many sections have been widened from the original dual three-lane model to dual four, five and, in some parts, six lanes.

Thus new roads may simply generate extra traffic, with little overall effect on congestion in the long term.

The environmental impact of new roads. New roads lead to the loss of agricultural land, the destruction of many natural habitats, noise, the splitting of communities and disruption to local residents. To the extent that they encourage a growth in traffic, they add to atmospheric pollution and a depletion of oil reserves. It is thus important to take account of these costs when assessing new road schemes. The problem, however, is that these environmental costs are frequently ignored, or only considered as an afterthought and not taken seriously. Part of the problem is that they are difficult to assess, and part is that there is often a strong road lobby which persuades politicians to ignore or play down environmental considerations.

Government or local authority provision of public transport

An alternative supply-side solution is to increase the provision of public transport. If, for example, a local authority ran a local bus service and decided to invest in additional buses, open up new routes and operate a low-fare policy, these services might encourage people to switch from using their cars.

To be effective, this would have to be an attractive alternative. Many people would switch only if the buses were frequent, cheap, comfortable and reliable, and if there were enough routes to take people close to where they wanted to go.

What other types of transport could be directly provided by the government or a local authority?

A policy that has proved popular with many local authorities is to adopt park-and-ride schemes. Here the authority provides free or cheap out-of-town parking and cheap bus services from the car park to the town centre. These schemes are likely to be most effective when used in combination with charges for private cars entering the inner city.

Regulation and legislation

An alternative strategy is to restrict car use by various forms of regulation and legislation.

Restricting car access

One approach involves reducing car access to areas that are subject to high levels of congestion. The following measures are widely used: bus and cycle lanes, 'high occupancy vehicle lanes' (confined to cars with two or more occupants), pedestrian-only areas and no entry to side streets from main roads.

There is a serious problem, with these measures, however. They tend not to solve the problem of congestion, but merely to divert it. Bus lanes tend to make the car lanes more congested; no entry to side streets tends to make the main roads more congested; and pedestrian-only areas often make the roads round these areas more congested, with drivers adopting side streets as 'rat-runs'.

Parking restrictions

An alternative to restricting road access is to restrict parking. Prohibiting cars from parking along congested streets will improve the traffic flow. Also, if parking is difficult, this will discourage people from using their cars to come into city centres.

Apart from being unpopular with people who want to park, there are some serious drawbacks with parking restrictions:

- People may well 'park in orbit', driving round and round looking for a parking space, and in the meantime adding to congestion.
- People may park illegally. This may add to rather than reduce congestion, and may create a safety hazard.
- People may feel forced to park down side streets in residential areas, thereby causing a nuisance for residents.

Changing market signals

The solution favoured by many economists is to use the price mechanism. As we have seen, one of the causes of traffic congestion is that road users do not pay the full marginal social costs of using the roads. If they could be forced to do so, a social optimum usage of road space could be achieved.

In Figure 13.6 (page 421) this would involve imposing a charge on motorists of *d–c*. By 'internalising' the congestion and environmental externalities in this way, traffic flow will be reduced to the social optimum of Q_2.

So how can these external costs be charged to the motorist? There are several possible ways.

Extending existing taxes

Three major types of tax are levied on the motorist: fuel tax (duty per litre plus VAT), taxes on new cars and car licences. Could increasing these taxes lead to the optimum level of road use being achieved?

Increasing the rates of new car tax and car licences may have *some* effect on reducing the total level of car ownership, but will probably have little effect on car use. The problem is that these taxes do not increase the *marginal* cost of car use and so do not discourage you from using your car.

Unlike the other two, fuel taxes are a marginal cost of car use. The more you use your car, the more fuel you use and the more fuel tax you pay. They are also mildly related to the level of congestion, since fuel consumption tends to increase as congestion increases. Nevertheless, they are not ideal. The problem is that *all* motorists would pay an increase in fuel tax, even those travelling on uncongested roads. To have a significant effect on congestion, there would have to be a very large increase in fuel taxes and this would be very unfair on those who are not causing congestion, especially those who have to travel long distances. Also, as the fuel protests in recent years have shown, increasing fuel taxes could make the government very unpopular.

Would a tax on car tyres be a good way of restricting car usage?

Introducing new taxes

An alternative to extending existing taxes is to introduce new ones. One that has received much attention in recent times has been the taxing of car parking spaces, particularly those provided by businesses for their employees. The problem with taxing car parking, however, is similar to that of restricting car parking places: people may simply try to park on neighbouring streets (a negative externality imposed on residents), and may spend longer driving around trying to find a space (thereby adding to congestion in the process).

Road pricing

Taxes are inevitably an indirect means of tackling congestion. Charging people for using roads, on the other hand, where the size of the charge reflects the marginal social cost, is a direct means of achieving an efficient use of road space. The higher the congestion, the higher should be the charge. This would encourage people not only to look for alternative means of transport, but also to travel, wherever possible, at off-peak times.

TC 5 p48

Variable tolls. Tolls are used in many countries, and could be adapted to reflect marginal social costs.

One obvious problem, however, is that, even with automatic tolls, there can be considerable tailbacks at peak times. Another problem is that they may simply encourage people to use minor roads into cities, thereby causing congestion on these roads. Cities have networks of streets and thus in most cases it is not difficult to avoid the tolls. Finally, if the tolls are charged to people *entering* the city, they will not affect *local* commuters. But it is these short-distance commuters *within* the city who are most likely to be able to find some alternative means of transport and who thus could make a substantial contribution to reducing congestion.

Area charges. One simple and practical means of charging people to use congested streets is the area charge. People would have to pay (normally by the day) for using their car in a city centre. Earlier versions of this scheme involved people having to purchase and display a ticket on their car, rather like a 'pay-and-display' parking system.

More recently, electronic versions have been developed. The introduction of the London Congestion Charge in February 2003 is an example. Car drivers must pay a standard charge of £15.00 per day to enter the inner London area (or 'congestion zone') any time between 7:00 and 22:00, every day of the week. Payment can be made by monthly auto deduction from a debit or credit card or by direct debit, or motorists can pay online on the day or in advance or, for an extra £2.50, up to three days later online or by phone.

Cars entering the congestion zone have their number plate recorded by camera and a computer check then leads to a penalty charge of £160 being sent to those who have not paid.

A report by Transport for London estimated that traffic levels had fallen by 10 per cent in the first 10 years of the London Congestion Charge, although average traffic speeds have also fallen. One unanticipated benefit of the scheme is that it appears to have reduced the number of traffic accidents by 40 per cent.

The London Congestion Charge is not a marginal one in the sense that it does not vary with the degree of congestion or the amount of time spent or distance travelled by a motorist within the zone. This is an intrinsic problem of area charges. Nevertheless, their simplicity makes the system easy to understand and relatively cheap to operate.

Other charges have been introduced in London to address the issue of pollution more directly. The Cleaner Vehicle Discount (CVD) was introduced in April 2019 and replaces a similar scheme – the Ultra Low Emission Discount. With the CVD, vehicles that emit 75g/km of CO_2 or less and meet the Euro VI standard for air quality are eligible for a 100 per cent discount. Since October 2021, only electric cars have qualified for the discount.

Increasing concerns over air pollution led to the introduction of the toxicity charge (T-charge) in October 2017. This was replaced by the Ultra Low Emission Zone (ULEZ) in April 2019. ULEZ applies 24 hours per day, 7 days per week. Under this scheme, any vehicle that enters the congestion zone and fails to meet the Euro 3 standard for motorbikes, the Euro 4 standard for petrol cars, the Euro 6 standard for diesel cars and the Euro VI standard for lorries and other heavy vehicles has to pay an additional charge of £12.50 for cars, motorbikes and vans, and £100 for lorries, buses and coaches.

There does appear to be a growing commitment by the London authorities to use charges to deal with the external costs of both congestion and emissions.

Variable electronic road pricing. The scheme most favoured by many economists and traffic planners is that of variable electronic road pricing. It is the approach that can most directly relate the price that the motorist is charged to the specific level of marginal social cost. The greater the congestion, the greater the charge imposed on the motorist. Ideally, the charge would be equal to the marginal congestion cost plus any marginal environmental costs additional to those created on non-charged roads.

Various systems have been adopted in various parts of the world, or are under consideration. One involves devices in the road which record the number plates of cars as they pass. Alternatively, cars may be required to be fitted with sensors. Charges are registered to cars on a central computer and owners are billed. Several cities around the world, including Barcelona, Dallas, Orlando, Lisbon, Oklahoma City and Oslo, are already operating such schemes.

Another system involves having a device installed in the car into which a 'smart card' is inserted. Beacons or overhead gantries automatically charge the cards at times of congestion. Such a system was introduced in 1997 on Stockholm's ring road, and in 1998 in Singapore (see Box 13.5).

BOX 13.5 ROAD PRICING IN SINGAPORE

CASE STUDIES AND APPLICATIONS

Part of an integrated transport policy

Singapore has some 280 vehicles per kilometre of road (this compares with 271 in Hong Kong, 222 in Japan, 77 in the UK, 75 in Germany and 37 in the USA). The average car in Singapore is driven some 17 500 kilometres per year, but with low car ownership (see below), this translates into a relatively low figure for kilometres travelled by car per person. Part of the reason is that Singapore has an integrated transport policy. This includes the following:

- A 230-kilometre long rapid transit (RTS) rail system with six main lines (mass rail transport (MRT)) and three light rail lines (LRT) connecting to the MRT, 163 stations and subsidised fares. Trains are comfortable, clean and frequent. Stations are air-conditioned.
- A programme of building new estates near MRT stations.
- Cheap, frequent buses, serving all parts of the island.
- A modest expansion of expressways.

But it is in respect to road usage that the Singaporean authorities have been most innovative.

Area licences

The first innovation came in 1975 when the Area Licensing Scheme (ALS) was introduced. The city centre was made a restricted zone. Motorists who wished to enter this zone had to buy a ticket (an 'area licence') at any one of 33 entry points. Police were stationed at these entry points to check that cars had paid and displayed. This scheme was extended to the major expressways in 1995 with the introduction of the Road Pricing Scheme (RPS).

The Vehicle Quota System

In 1990, the government also introduced restrictions on the number of new cars, known as the Vehicle Quota System. In order to register and drive a new vehicle in Singapore, the owner has to purchase a Certificate of Entitlement (COE) which is valid for 10 years. The quantity of COEs issued by the government is limited and the number available each year is announced in April. The COEs are then sold to the public via monthly auctions which operate in a similar manner to those on eBay. Buyers specify a maximum price and bids are automatically revised upwards until that maximum price is reached. The price of COEs increases until the quantity demanded is just equal to the number of certificates on offer.

Partly as a result of the quota system, there are only 114 private cars per 1000 population. As you can see from Figure 13.5 on page 419, this is only a fraction of the figure for European countries.

A problem with the licences is that they are a once-and-for-all payment, which does not vary with the amount people use their car. In other words, their marginal cost (for additional miles driven) is zero. Many people feel that, having paid such a high price for their licence, they ought to use their car as much as possible in order to get value for money!

Electronic road pricing

With traffic congestion steadily worsening, it was recognised that something more had to be done. In 1998, a new Electronic Road Pricing Scheme (ERP) replaced the Area Licensing Scheme for restricted areas and the Road Pricing Scheme for expressways. This alternative not only saves on police labour costs, but enables charge rates to be varied according to levels of congestion, times of the day and locality. How does it work?

All vehicles in Singapore are fitted with an in-vehicle unit (IU). Every journey made requires the driver to insert a smart card into the IU. On specified roads, overhead gantries read the IU and deduct the appropriate charge from the card. If a car does not have sufficient funds on its smart card, the car's details are relayed to a control centre and a fine is imposed. The system has the benefit of operating on three-lane highways and does not require traffic to slow down.

The ERP system operates on roads subject to congestion and charges can vary every 5, 20 or 30 minutes according to predicted traffic flows. Rates are published in advance for a three-month period: e.g. from February to April 2021. A review of traffic conditions takes place every quarter and the results can lead to rates being adjusted in future periods. The system is thus very flexible to allow traffic to be kept at the desired level.

One potential problem with charging different rates at different times is that some drivers may substantially speed up or slow down as they approach the gantries to avoid paying higher ERP charges. To try to overcome this problem the ERP rates are adjusted gradually for the first five minutes of a time slot with either new higher or lower charges.

The authorities in Singapore will begin installing a new Global Navigation Satellite System in 2021 with an expected completion date of mid-2023. This removes the need for large overhead gantries, although slimmer gantries will still be used to indicate the charges. Initial plans to charge drivers based on how far they travel have been temporarily suspended. New on-board units will also need to be fitted in all vehicles to replace the existing in-vehicle units.

The ERP system was expensive to set up, however. Cheaper schemes have been adopted elsewhere, such as Norway and parts of the USA. These operate by funnelling traffic into a single lane in order to register the car, but they have the disadvantage of slowing the traffic down.

One message is clear from the Singapore solution. Road pricing alone is not enough. Unless there are fast, comfortable and affordable public transport alternatives, the demand for cars will be highly price inelastic. People have to get to work!

Explain how, by varying the charge debited from the smart card according to the time of day or level of congestion, a socially optimal level of road use can be achieved.

Referring to a town or city with which you are familiar, consider what would be the most appropriate mix of policies to deal with its traffic congestion problems.

With both these systems, the rate can easily be varied electronically according to the level of congestion (and pollution). The rates could be in bands and the current bands displayed by the roadside and/or broadcast on local radio so that motorists knew what they were being charged.

The most sophisticated scheme would involve equipping all vehicles with a receiver. Their position is located by satellites, which then send this information to a dashboard unit, which deducts charges according to location, distance travelled, time of day and type of vehicle. The charges can operate through either smart cards or central computerised billing. It is likely that such schemes would initially be confined to lorries.

Despite the enthusiasm for such schemes amongst economists, there are nevertheless various problems associated with them:

- Estimates of the level of external costs are difficult to make.
- Motorists have to be informed in advance what the charges will be, so that they can plan the timing of their journeys.
- There may be political resistance. Politicians may therefore be reluctant to introduce road pricing for fear of losing popular support.
- If demand is relatively inelastic, the charges might have to be very high to have a significant effect on congestion.
- The costs of installing road-pricing equipment could be very high.
- If road pricing were introduced only in certain areas, shoppers and businesses would tend to move to areas without the charge.
- A new industry in electronic evasion may spring up!

Subsidising alternative means of transport

An alternative to charging for the use of cars is to subsidise the price of alternatives, such as buses and trains. But cheaper fares alone may not be enough. The government may also have to invest directly in or subsidise an *improved* public transport service: more frequent services, more routes, more comfortable buses and trains.

Subsidising public transport need not be seen as an alternative to road pricing: it can be seen as complementary. If road pricing is to persuade people not to travel by car, the alternatives must be attractive. Unless public transport is seen by the traveller as a close substitute for cars, the elasticity of demand for car use is likely to remain low. This problem is recognised by the UK government, which encourages local authorities to use various forms of road pricing and charges on businesses for employee car parking spaces on condition that the revenues generated are ploughed back into improved public transport. All local authorities have to produce five-year Local Transport Plans covering all forms of transport. These include targets for traffic reduction and increases in the use of public transport.

Subsidising public transport can also be justified on grounds of equity, since it is used most by low-income groups.

Which is preferable: general subsidies for public transport, or cheap fare policies for specific groups (such as children, students and pensioners)?

Conclusions

It is unlikely that any one policy can provide the complete solution. Certain policies or mixes of policies are better suited to some situations than others. It is important for governments to learn from experiences both within their own country and in others, in order to find the optimum solution to each specific problem.

Section summary

1. There are various types of solution to traffic congestion. These include direct provision by the government or local authorities (of additional road space or better public transport); regulation and legislation (such as restricting car access – by the use of bus and cycle lanes, or pedestrian-only areas – and various forms of parking restrictions); changing market signals (by the use of taxes, by road pricing, and by subsidising alternative means of transport).
2. Problems associated with building additional roads include the decline of public transport, attracting additional traffic onto the roads, and environmental costs.
3. The main problem with restricting car access is that it tends merely to divert congestion elsewhere. The main problem with parking restrictions is that they may actually increase congestion.
4. Increasing taxes is effective in reducing congestion only if it increases the marginal cost of motoring. Even when it does, as in the case of additional fuel tax, the additional cost is only indirectly related to congestion costs, since it applies to all motorists and not just those causing congestion.
5. Road pricing is the preferred solution of many economists. By the use of electronic devices, motorists can be charged whenever they add to congestion. This should encourage less essential road users to travel at off-peak times or to use alternative modes of transport, while those who gain a high utility from car transport can still use their cars, but at a price. Variable tolls and area charges are alternative forms of congestion pricing, but are generally less effective than the use of variable electronic road pricing.
6. If road pricing is to be effective, there must be attractive substitutes available. A comprehensive policy, therefore, should include subsidising efficient public transport. The revenues required for this could be obtained from road pricing.

END OF CHAPTER QUESTIONS

1. Assume that as traffic density increases along a given stretch of road, there comes a point when traffic begins to slow down. The following table gives the times taken for a car to travel the stretch of road (in minutes) according to the number of cars entering the road per minute.

Cars entering the road	5	6	7	8	9	10	11
Journey time	10	10	11	13	16	22	30

   (a) Copy out the table and add the following rows: (i) total journey time for all cars; (ii) extra journey time as traffic increases by one more car (marginal social time cost); (iii) additional time cost imposed on other road users for each additional car entering the road (marginal external time cost). (See Table 13.3.)

   (b) Assume that time is valued at 10p per minute. On a graph, plot the marginal private time cost (journey time) and the marginal social time cost.

   (c) Assume that electronic road pricing is introduced. What charge should be levied when traffic density reaches (i) 6 cars per minute; (ii) 8 cars per minute; (iii) 11 cars per minute?

   (d) What additional information would you need in order to work out the socially efficient traffic density on this particular stretch of road?

2. Assume that there are several chemical firms in an industry, each one producing different levels of an effluent, whose damage to the environment depends on the location of the firm. Compare the relative merits of using green taxes, tradable permits and controls as means of achieving the socially optimum levels of effluent from these firms.

3. Make out a case from a deep green perspective for rejecting the 'social efficiency' approach to the environment.

4. Why might efforts to address the issue of global warming be hampered by a lack of understanding of probability amongst the general public?

5. In 2007, China overtook the USA as the world's largest emitter of CO_2. Yet USA per capita emissions are three times those of China. What issues arise from this in the formulation of a global policy to reduce CO_2 emissions?

6. Make out a case for adopting a policy of individual tradable carbon permits, allocated to all citizens within a country. Could such a policy be extended globally?

7. Compare the relative merits of increased road fuel taxes, electronic road pricing and tolls as means of reducing urban traffic congestion.

8. Why is the price inelasticity of demand for private car transport a problem when formulating a policy for the reduction of traffic congestion? What could be done to change the price elasticity of demand in a desirable direction?

9. How would you set about measuring the external costs of road transport?

10. Many London councils now have residents' street parking permits, with charges that vary according to the carbon emissions of the registered vehicle. Explain the thinking behind this policy.

11. Since 2008, the UK government has provided free off-peak bus travel for the over-60s in England and Wales. What do you think the impact of this policy has been on car usage? Is there a case for extending the policy to (a) bus travel for pensioners at all times of the day, as is the case in Scotland; (b) bus travel for all?

12. In 2010, the number of air passengers using UK airports fell by 3.4 per cent compared with 2009. In 2015, passengers were 5.5 per cent up compared with 2014. Can we deduce anything about people's attitude to the environment and their behaviour from these data?

Online resources

Additional case studies on the student website

13.1 A Stern warning. This looks at the 2006 independent review on climate change and the economy led by Sir Nicholas Stern.

13.2 Perverse subsidies. An examination of the use of subsidies around the world that are harmful to the environment.

13.3 Selling the environment. This looks at the proposals made at international climate conferences to use market-based solutions to global warming.

13.4 Environmental auditing. Are businesses becoming greener? A growing number of firms are subjecting themselves to an 'environmental audit' to judge just how 'green' they are.

13.5 Green growth. Is economic growth consistent with protection of the environment?

13.6 Evaluating new road schemes. The system used in the UK of assessing the costs and benefits of proposed new roads.

13.7 Restricting car access to Athens. A case study that examines how the Greeks have attempted to reduce local atmospheric pollution from road traffic.

Websites relevant to this chapter

See sites listed at the end of Chapter 14 on pages 448–9.

Government Policy towards Business

CHAPTER MAP

In this chapter we continue our examination of government policy to tackle market imperfections. The focus here is on the problem of market power. We examine various policies the government or its agencies can use to prevent firms abusing a monopolistic or oligopolistic position.

In section 14.1 we examine 'competition policy'. We will see that the targets of such policy include the abuse of monopoly power, the problem of oligopolistic collusion, and mergers that will result in the firm having a dominant position in the market.

Then in section 14.2, we look at privatisation and the extent to which privatised industries should be regulated to prevent them abusing their market power. We also consider whether it is possible to introduce enough competition into these industries to make regulation unnecessary.

The relationship between government and business is always likely to be complex. Governments face the twin pressures of having to ensure consumer protection while needing a dynamic and profitable business environment that will ensure high levels of employment, output and growth. In this chapter we see the conflicts that can arise as a consequence.

14.1 COMPETITION POLICY

Competition, monopoly and the public interest

Most markets in the real world are imperfect, with firms having varying degrees of market power. But will this power be against the public interest? This question has been addressed by successive governments in framing legislation to deal with monopolies and oligopolies.

KI 22 p195

It is tempting to think that market power is always 'a bad thing', certainly as far as the consumer is concerned. After all, it enables firms to make supernormal profit, which implies they may be 'exploiting' the consumer. The greater the firm's power, the higher will prices be relative to the costs of production. In addition, a lack of competition removes the incentive to become more efficient.

But market power is not necessarily a bad thing. Firms may choose not to fully exploit their position of power – perhaps thinking that very high profits would encourage other firms to overcome entry barriers, or perhaps because they are not aggressive profit maximisers. Even if they do make large supernormal profits, they may still charge lower prices than firms in more competitive sectors of the industry because of their economies of scale. Finally, they may use profits for research and development and for capital investment. The consumer might then benefit from new or improved products at lower prices.

Competition policy could seek to ban various structures. For example, there could be restrictions on any mergers that lead to newly combined firms having market shares above a certain level. Most countries, however, focus on whether the *practices* of particular monopolists or oligopolists are anti-competitive. The authorities may make some of these practices illegal, such as price fixing between oligopolists, while assessing others on a case-by-case basis. Such an approach does not presume that the existence of power is against the public interest, but rather that certain uses of that power may be.

Try to formulate a definition of 'the public interest'.

The three broad areas of competition policy

There are three broad areas of competition policy.

Abuse of the existing power of monopolies and oligopolies: monopoly policy

Monopoly policy seeks to prevent firms from abusing a dominant market position: i.e. misusing their economic power. Although it is referred to as 'monopoly' policy, it also applies to large oligopolists facing very limited competition. Once a position of dominance has been identified, the competition agencies usually weigh up the gains and losses to the public of the firm's behaviour.

As we saw in Figure 7.8 (on page 211), faced with the same cost curves as an industry under perfect competition, a profit-maximising monopoly will charge a higher price, produce a lower output and make a larger profit. This is called an ***exploitative abuse*** – a business practice that directly harms the customer. Other examples include reductions in product quality, limited product ranges and poor levels of customer service. However, a monopolist may achieve substantial economies of scale, with lower costs and a price below the competitive price (see Figure 7.11 on page 213). It may also retain profits for investment and research and development (R&D). This may result in better products and/or lower prices.

However, governments (or regulatory authorities) have tended to avoid investigating allegations of exploitative abuses because of the challenges involved with correctly identifying and addressing this type of behaviour. For example, measuring differences between price and costs is very difficult in reality and requires the processing of large amounts of complex information supplied by the firm involved. Regulating prices is also a complicated process. Therefore, price regulation tends to be left to cases of natural monopoly (i.e. the privatised utilities) which have specific regulators – see 14.2 for more details. For these reasons, competition agencies tend to focus on investigating allegations of ***exclusionary abuses***.

Exclusionary abuses. These are business practices that limit or prevent effective competition from either actual or potential rivals. Exclusionary abuses may be a necessary condition before firms can implement the more direct exploitative abuses. A business that successfully limits or prevents competition today, may be able to charge higher prices in the future.

Some of the more frequently cited examples of exclusionary abuses in competition cases include:

- *Predatory pricing.* Prices are set by a dominant firm below average variable costs with the sole intent of driving its competitor(s) out of business. It then raises prices.
- *Exclusivity rebates/discounts.* Customers are offered special deals if they agree to make 'all or most' of their purchases of the product from the dominant firm. See Box 14.2 for some interesting examples in the market for computer chips.

> **Definitions**
>
> **Exploitative abuses** Business practices that directly harm the customer. Examples include high prices and poor quality.
>
> **Exclusionary abuses** Business practices that limit or prevent effective competition from either actual or potential rivals.

- ***Tying.*** This is where a firm controlling the supply of a first product (the tying product), insists that its customers buy a second product (the tied product) from it rather than from its rivals. One of the most famous cases of tying was Microsoft's decision to include its media player and web browser (Internet Explorer) with the sale of its Windows operating system. In 2004, the European Union competition authority judged that this was an abuse of a dominant market position.
- *Refusal to supply and margin squeeze.* This occurs where a vertically integrated firm has a dominant position in an upstream market (e.g. components) but faces competition in later stages of the production process (e.g. assembly). If competitors in the downstream market are completely reliant on the supply of some input from the dominant firm in the upstream market, then the dominant firm could *refuse to supply* them. Its aim would be to drive them out of business, thereby giving it a dominant position in the downstream market. A more subtle approach for the dominant firm would be to charge high prices for the input so that its rivals in the downstream market are unable to cover their costs and therefore go out of business. This is called ***margin squeeze.***
- *Price discrimination.* This would be an abuse if the lower prices are used to drive competitors out of business.
- ***Vertical restraints.*** This is where a supplying firm imposes conditions on a purchasing firm (or *vice versa*). For example, in 2020 a number of musical instrument makers (Casio, Fender, Roland and Korg) insisted that online retailers sold their products at or above certain minimum prices. This is called ***resale price maintenance.***

The growth of power through mergers and acquisitions: merger policy

Competition authorities typically have powers to control merger and acquisition (M&A) activity. In many cases, M&As are beneficial for consumers and the economy as a whole, as the newly combined firms may be able to rationalise and reduce costs. For example, central services such as finance and human resources can be consolidated. Greater financial strength may allow the merged firm to drive down the prices charged by its suppliers and the combined profits may allow larger-scale investment and R&D.

However, in some cases M&As result in significant reductions in competition. This may lead to the newly combined firm abusing its dominant position in the market. Also, by reducing the number of firms, M&As may increase the chances of collusion.

Most competition authorities carry out a relatively quick initial review of M&As and clear the majority of cases where the impact on competition is judged to be negligible. When the potential impact on competition is more serious, the authorities carry out a more detailed investigation to see whether the potential benefits of the merger outweigh the costs. In only a minority of cases is the M&A actually prohibited.

What are the possible disadvantages of vertical mergers?

In deciding how tough to be with mergers, the government must consider how this will affect firms' behaviour. If the government adopts a liberal policy, this may actually encourage firms to be more efficient. The threat of a takeover may incentivise managers to control costs and make difficult decisions so shareholders perceive performance to be better than under alternative ownership. This competition for corporate control (see page 213) may benefit the consumer. However, it could also make it easier for firms to obtain a dominant market position through the takeover of rival businesses. TC 5 p48

Government policy towards corporate control will need to ensure that potential mergers encourage competition rather than reduce it.

Oligopolistic collusion: restrictive practice policy

In most countries, the approach towards oligopolistic collusion, known as ***restrictive practices***, tends to be more prohibitive than for mergers and monopoly power. This is because it is far less likely that agreements to restrict, limit or prevent competition will ever be in the interests of society. The most likely outcome is higher joint profits for the firms and higher prices for the customer.

Examples of restrictive practices commonly cited in competition cases include:

- *Horizontal price fixing.* These are direct or indirect agreements between rival firms to fix prices above competitive levels. Some different ways that firms can make price agreements include:
  - Setting a minimum level below which they agree not to reduce prices.
  - Adhering to a published price list.
  - Increasing prices by a fixed absolute or percentage amount.
  - Charging customers the same amount for delivery.
  - Passing on all additional costs in higher prices.

Definitions

Tying Where a firm is only prepared to sell a first product (the tying good) on the condition that its consumers buy a second product from it (the tied good).

Margin squeeze Where a vertically integrated firm with a dominant position in an upstream market deliberately charges high prices for an input required by firms in a downstream market to drive them out of business.

Vertical restraints Conditions imposed by one firm on another which is either its supplier or its customer.

Resale price maintenance Where a supplier insists that firms selling its products do not charge below a certain price.

Restrictive practices Where two or more firms agree to adopt common practices to restrict competition.

- *Market sharing.* These are agreements on how to distribute markets or customers between the firms. This could be done by geographical area, type of product or type of customer. For example, two or more supermarket chains could agree to open only one supermarket in each district.
- *Limit production.* Firms agree quotas on how much each should produce.
- ***Bid rigging.*** In response to a call for tenders, firms agree to discuss bids with one another rather than submitting them independently. They could agree on high-priced bids, with one of the firms (agreed in turn, possibly) submitting a slightly lower price. Or one or more of them may agree not to submit a bid, withdraw a bid, or submit a bid at an artificially high price.
- *Information sharing.* Firms share sensitive information with one another, such as future plans on pricing, product design and output.

Are all such agreements necessarily against the interests of consumers?

Banning formal cartels is relatively easy. Preventing tacit collusion is another matter. It may be very difficult to prove that firms are making informal agreements behind closed doors.

Competition policy in the European Union

Relevant EU legislation is contained in Articles 101 and 102 of the 2009 Treaty of the Functioning of the European Union (TFEU). Additional regulations covering mergers came into force in 1990 and were amended in 2004. Further minor amendments have since been introduced, and many of these focus on specific market regulation.

Article 101 is concerned with restrictive practices and Article 102 with the abuse of market power. The Articles focus on firms trading between EU members and do not cover monopolies or oligopolies operating solely within a member country. They are implemented by the European Commission (EC), which monitors compliance, investigates behaviour and imposes fines where unlawful conduct is identified.

Firms can appeal against EC judgments to the *General Court* – formerly known as the *Court of First Instance.* The General Court has the power to overturn decisions made by the EC and is able to amend the size of any fines. The EC and/or the firms involved in the case can appeal against decisions made by the *General Court* to the *European Court of Justice.* However, appeals to the *European Court of Justice* can only be made on points of law. See Box 14.2 for an example.

Definition

Bid rigging Where two or more firms secretly agree on the prices they will tender for a contract. These prices will be above those that would have been submitted under a genuinely competitive tendering process.

EU restrictive practices policy

Article 101 covers agreements between firms, joint decisions and concerted practices that prevent, restrict or distort competition. In other words, it covers all types of oligopolistic collusion that are against the interests of consumers.

The legislation is designed to prevent collusive *behaviour* not oligopolistic *structures* (i.e. the simple existence of co-operation between firms). For example, agreements between oligopolists are permissible under Article 101(3). This states that they must meet all of the following conditions: (a) they directly enhance the quality of the good/service for the customer; (b) they are the only way to do so; (c) they do not eliminate competition; (d) consumers receive a fair share of the resulting benefits.

If the authorities find companies guilty of undertaking any anti-competitive practices that are in contravention of Article 101, they are ordered to cease the activity with immediate effect and are subject to financial penalties.

Fines. Table 14.1 illustrates the largest fines imposed by the EC on individual companies involved in cartel activity.

Five of the largest eight fines relate to just one case. The EC ruled in July 2016 and September 2017 that the truck producers MAN, Volvo/Renault, Daimler, Iveco, DAF and Scania were guilty of operating a cartel.[1] In particular, they colluded over (a) the factory price of trucks (b) the speed at which they would introduce new emission technologies and (c) how the compliance costs of stricter emissions rules would be passed on to their customers.

What determines the size of these fines? (See Box 14.1 for an interesting real-world example.) The size of the initial fine imposed on an organisation depends on a number of factors including:

- the size of its annual sales affected by the anti-competitive activities – referred to as the 'relevant sales';
- its market share/the combined market of all the participating firms and the geographical area of the affected sales;

Table 14.1 Highest EC cartel fines per firm

Year	Firm	Case	Amount in €
2016	Daimler	Trucks	1 008 766 000
2017	Scania	Trucks	880 523 000
2016	DAF	Trucks	752 679 000
2008	Saint-Gobain	Car glass	715 000 000
2012	Philips	TV/computer monitor tubes	705 296 000
2012	LG Electronics	TV/computer monitor tubes	687 537 000
2016	Volvo/Renault	Trucks	670 448 000
2016	Iveco	Trucks	494 606 000

Source: Cartel Statistics, Competition DG, European Commission (December 2020), https://ec.europa.eu/competition/cartels/statistics/statistics.pdf

1'Commission fines truck producers €2.93 billion for participating in a cartel', *press release* (European Commission, 19 July 2016), https://ec.europa.eu/commission/presscorner/detail/en/IP_16_2582

BOX 14.1 FIXING PRICES AT MINI-GOLF MEETINGS?

The EU approach to cartels

In September 2010, the European Commission began an investigation into the market for both standardised and customised paper envelopes in the EU. In December 2014, the Commission found Bong (of Sweden), GPV and Hamelin (of France), Mayer-Kuvert (of Germany) and Tompla (of Spain) guilty of participating in activities that restricted competition in this market. The meetings at which the details of the cartel arrangements were discussed were referred to by the participating firms as 'golf' or 'mini-golf' meetings!

The cartel arrangements directly affected the market for envelopes in Denmark, France, Germany, Norway, Sweden and the UK. The authorities found evidence of the firms engaging in the following restrictive practices that were in violation of Article 101:

- allocating customers amongst members of the cartel: i.e. agreeing not to target customers that 'belonged' to other firms;
- agreeing on price increases;
- co-ordinating responses to tenders initiated by major European customers;
- exchanging commercially sensitive information on customers and sales volumes.

Details of the sales of the companies and the fines imposed are given in the table.

The proportion of the value of sales used to calculate the size of the fine was set at 15 per cent in this case (see row 2 of the table). Four out of the five firms began taking part in the cartel on 8 October 2003 and their involvement in anti-competitive activities lasted until 22 April 2008. Therefore, for these firms the duration multiplier (row 3) was set at 4.5. Hamelin was judged to have entered the cartel a month later than the other participants so the multiplier in its case was set at 4.416. A percentage rate of 15 per cent was also

	Bong	GPV group	Hamelin	Mayer-Kuvert	Tompla
1. Value of relevant sales (€)	140 000 000	125 086 629	185 521 000	70 023 181	143 316 000
2. Percentage (15%) of the value of relevant sales (€)	21 000 000	18 762 994	27 828 15	10 503 477	21 497 00
3. Duration multiplier	4.5	4.5	4.416	4.5	4.5
4. Duration multiplier × 15% sales (€)	94 500 000	84 433 475	122 889 110	47 265 646	96 738 300
5. Plus the entry fee (€) (= row 2)	21 000 000	18 762 994	27 828 150	10 503 477	21 497 400
6. Basic fine (€) (= rows 4 + 5)	115 500 000	103 196 000	150 717 260	57 769 000	118 235 000
7. Final fine	3 118 000	1 651 000	4 996 000	4 991 000	4 729 000

- the length of time the firm has engaged in the anti-competitive activities;
- whether it has been found guilty of engaging in anti-competitive practices in the past;
- whether it initiated the formation of the cartel: i.e. acted as the ringleader.

Fines are also capped and cannot be greater than 10 per cent of a firm's annual turnover.

Reducing fines through co-operation with the Commission. The size of the initial or basic fine can be reduced if members of a cartel provide information that helps the Commission with its investigations. Such firms would be granted a 'Leniency Notice'. To qualify, they have to provide information about cartel meetings and details of how anti-competitive practices operated. The first company to supply this type of information can be granted full immunity (Type 1A leniency) if its co-operation brings the case to the Commission's attention. If an investigation has already begun, the first company to provide detailed information could *possibly* receive full immunity at the discretion of the Commission (Type 1B leniency). In the truck manufacturing case, MAN was awarded full immunity under Type 1A leniency as it had revealed the existence of the cartel to the Commission and so did not have to pay a fine.

Other companies supplying information can be given reduced fines (Type 2 leniency). The second company to come forward with this type of information can receive a reduction of up to 50 per cent, the third of up to 30 per cent and any firm after this of up to 20 per cent. In the truck case, Volvo/Renault, Daimler and Iveco were granted reductions of 40, 30 and 10 per cent respectively under Leniency Notices.

Firms can receive a further 10 per cent reduction if they accept the Commission's decision and the size of any financial penalties imposed on them. This is referred to as a Settlement. By speeding up the final decision process, these agreements can reduce the administrative costs to the parties involved and avoid the legal costs of any possible appeals.

The aim of all these further reductions is to encourage firms to co-operate with the authorities. Volvo/Renault, Daimler, Iveco and DAF were all granted 10 per cent reductions. However, Scania maintained its innocence and opted not to reach a Settlement agreement. This meant that the investigation into its behaviour took another 14 months to conclude. Finally, in September 2017 the EC announced that it had found the business guilty of colluding with the other five truck producers and imposed a fine of €880 million. Given its lack of co-operation, Scania was not entitled to a 10 per cent reduction in the size of the fine.

CASE STUDIES AND APPLICATIONS

used to calculate the entry fee (row 5). The final figures for the basic amounts of the fine are illustrated in row 7 of the table, which the Commission rounded down to the nearest €1000.

It was considered to be an exceptional case as the sales of envelopes affected by the cartel activities made up a large fraction of each firm's total turnover. Therefore, the unadjusted basic fines would exceed the 10 per cent cap on turnover set by the authorities. The fines were reduced in a way that took account of (a) the value of affected sales for each firm as a proportion of their turnover and (b) the level of involvement in the restrictive practices. Unfortunately, the size of each firm's basic fine, after these adjustments, are not published in the non-confidential report.

Under the Commission's 2006 Leniency Notice we do know that Tompla received a 50 per cent reduction in the size of its adjusted basic fine, Hamelin received a reduction of 25 per cent and Mayer-Kuvert received a reduction of 10 per cent. All five firms obtained an additional 10 per cent reduction for agreeing to the Settlements and not taking their cases to court. Two firms also claimed that they were unable to pay the fine without getting into serious final difficulties and were granted a further reduction.

The final sizes of the fines paid by the companies are illustrated in the final row of the table.

Commissioner Margrethe Vestager in charge of competition policy said:

> Everybody uses envelopes. When cartelists raise the prices of everyday household objects they do so at the expense of millions of Europeans. The Commission's fight against cartels penalises such behaviour and also acts as a deterrent, protecting consumers from harm. On this case we have closed the envelope, sealed it and returned it to the sender with a clear message: don't cheat your customers, don't cartelise.[1]

Why might global cartels be harder to identify and eradicate than cartels solely located within the domestic economy? What problems does this raise for competition policy?

Examine data on cartel investigations by the European Commission and identify the ten cases that had the highest total fines. Choose two of these cases and find out why the EC imposed such large fines in each case. If this is done as a group exercise, individual members of the group could each choose a different cartel and then compare the findings.

1 'Antitrust: Commission on fines five envelope producers over 19.4 million in cartel settlement', *press release* (European Commission, 11 December 2014), https://ec.europa.eu/commission/presscorner/api/files/document/print/en/ip_14_2583/IP_14_2583_EN.pdf

EU monopoly policy

Article 102 relates to the abuse of a dominant market position and has also been extended to cover mergers. The implementation of the policy follows a two-stage process.

First, the EC has to define the relevant market: i.e. identify which products and suppliers are close substitutes for one another. Then it has to decide if the firm has a dominant position in this market. To do so it will look at factors such as market shares, the position of competitors, the bargaining strength of customers, measures of profitability and the existence of any significant barriers to entry – see the case in Box 14.2 for an example.

Second, if the evidence confirms that the firm does have a dominant position, the EC will then assess whether the firm is using its market power to restrict competition. As previously discussed, the focus tends to be on exclusionary as opposed to exploitative abuses of power.

If the authorities find a business guilty of engaging in exclusionary abuses that contravene Article 102, such as those discussed on pages 429–30, they are ordered to cease the activities with immediate effect and are subject to financial penalties.

The fines for any infringements of Article 102 are calculated in a very similar manner to those for infringements of Article 101. There is also some guidance on how a dominant firm can defend its behaviour on efficiency grounds. The business has to prove that its conduct meets all four of the following conditions:

- Any efficiencies are the direct result of the exclusionary conduct.
- The same efficiencies could not be achieved by the firm engaging in different behaviour that is less anti-competitive.
- The efficiencies produced by the exclusionary conduct outweigh any of its negative effects.
- The conduct does not result in the removal of all or most of the competition in the market.

EU merger policy

Under current regulations (2004), M&As are prohibited if they *significantly impede effective competition* in the EU (the 'SIEC' test). This could occur through individual dominance (the M&A leads to a strengthening in the market power of one firm) or through collective dominance (the reduction in the number of firms following the M&A makes collusion more likely).

Therefore, the EU investigates 'large' M&As that have an 'EU dimension'. A merger or acquisition is judged as having an 'EU dimension' when no more than two-thirds of each firm's EU-wide business is conducted in a single member state. If a firm does conduct more than two-thirds of its business in

BOX 14.2 **EXPENSIVE CHIPS?** CASE STUDIES AND APPLICATIONS

The biggest fine in EU monopoly policy history

In May 2004, the European Commission (EC) launched a formal investigation into the business conduct of Intel following complaints submitted by Advanced Micro Devices (AMD) in October 2000 and November 2003. These complaints focused on the behaviour of Intel in the market for microprocessors. These computer chips, also known as Central Processing Units (CPUs), are the most important hardware component in the manufacture of computers. AMD argued that Intel was using its dominance in this market to act in ways that contravened Article 102 of the Treaty on the Functioning of the European Union (TFEU).

EU monopoly policy follows a two-stage process and is similar to the approach adopted by most national competition agencies such as the Competition and Markets Authority in the UK.

Stage 1

The first element in stage 1 of the policy is the identification of the relevant market. After its analysis, the EC concluded that the relevant geographical market was global while the relevant product market was x86 CPUs.

Data indicated that Intel's share of the x86 CPU market was approximately 70 per cent or more over the whole six-year period investigated from October 2002 to December 2007. The EC typically treats market shares of over 50 per cent as one important indicator of market power. The competition authorities also found evidence of substantial barriers to entry. In particular, the production of CPUs requires considerable sunk investments in R&D, manufacturing facilities and branding. They noted that no new businesses had entered the market in the previous 10 years, while a number had exited. This left Intel with only one significant rival – AMD. All of this evidence led the EC to conclude that Intel did have a dominant position in the market for x86 CPUs.

Having a dominant position is not in itself unlawful under Article 102. However, the legislation does state that firms in a dominant position have a special responsibility not to abuse their market power by restricting competition either in the market in which they are dominant or in adjacent markets.

Stage 2

In stage 2 of the investigation, the authorities focus on the behaviour of the firm. Final judgements are made about business practices that are potential examples of market abuse. Intel was found guilty of engaging in the following two activities that were seen as examples of exclusionary abuses.

- Discounts were given to four major computer manufacturers (Dell, Lenovo™, HP and NEC) and to the retailer Media-Saturn on the condition that these businesses purchased all or most of their x86 CPUs from Intel.
- Direct payments were made to HP, Acer® and Lenovo on the condition that they postponed or cancelled the launch of products containing x86 CPUs manufactured by AMD.

The fine

In 2009, the EC imposed a record fine of €1.06 billion.[1] The size of the penalty reflected the fact that Intel's unlawful behaviour affected the sales of x86 CPUs in the whole of the European Economic Area (EEA). It was also less than 10 per cent of Intel's annual turnover.

The Commission can reduce the size of any fine if the firm co-operates by more than the minimum that is legally required and ceases the abusive conduct as soon as the authorities intervene. Neither of these factors were relevant in the Intel case, so no reductions were applicable.

The appeal process

Intel challenged the decision by appealing to the General Court, which in June 2014 announced that it was upholding the EC's decision.[2] Intel then lodged an appeal against the judgment of the General Court with the European Court of Justice (ECJ). The General Court agreed with the EC that loyalty rebates, by their very nature, were clear examples of abuse of a dominant market position. Intel argued that each case needed to be examined in detail, as rebates do not necessarily restrict competition. In September 2017, the ECJ upheld Intel's argument and referred the case back to the General Court.[3] At the time of writing (17 years after the investigation began), the General Court has yet to publish a final decision.

Qualcomm – a similar case

Qualcomm is the world's largest supplier of LTE baseband chipsets for smart phones and tablets. These chipsets enable the devices to connect to mobile networks. In 2011, Qualcomm agreed to make significant payments to Apple on the condition that only Qualcomm chipsets were used in all iPhones and iPads. If Apple launched a device with a chipset from another supplier, such as Intel, the payments would cease.

In January 2018, the EC ruled that this conduct was an abuse of market dominance by Qualcomm as it prevented rival chipset manufacturers from effectively competing in the market. The firm was ordered to pay a fine of €997 million.[4]

In July 2019, the EC fined Qualcomm a further €242 million[5] for selling 3G baseband chipsets below cost in an attempt to drive its competitor, Icera, out of the market.

1. ***What methods are commonly used by competition authorities to define the relevant market?***
2. ***Why might a firm involved in a monopoly case, such as Intel, try to convince the competition authorities to define the relevant market as broadly as possible?***
3. ***Using some examples, explain the difference between exploitative and exclusionary abuse.***

1 'Commission imposes fine of €1.06 bn on Intel', *press release* (European Commission, 13 May 2009), https://ec.europa.eu/commission/presscorner/detail/en/IP_09_745

2 'Commission welcomes General Court judgment upholding its decision', *press release* (European Commission, 12 June 2014), https://ec.europa.eu/commission/presscorner/detail/en/MEMO_14_416

3 'The Court of Justice sets aside the judgment of the General Court', *press release* (Court of Justice of the European Union, 6 September 2017), https://curia.europa.eu/jcms/upload/docs/application/pdf/2017-09/cp170090en.pdf

4 'Commission fines Qualcomm €997 million for abuse of a dominant market position', *press release* (European Commission, 24 January 2018), https://ec.europa.eu/commission/presscorner/detail/en/IP_18_421

5 'Commission fines US chipmaker Qualcomm €242 million for engaging in predatory pricing', *press release* (European Commission, 18 July 2019), https://ec.europa.eu/commission/presscorner/detail/en/ip_19_4350

one country, then investigation of the merger would be the responsibility of that member state's competition authority.

Thresholds. M&As are deemed 'large' if they exceed one or other of two turnover thresholds.

The first threshold is exceeded if (a) the firms involved have combined worldwide sales greater than €5 billion and (b) at least two of the firms individually have sales of more than €250 million within the EU.

The second threshold is exceeded if (a) the firms involved have combined worldwide sales of more than €2.5 billion; (b) in each of at least three member states, combined sales of all firms involved are greater than €100 million; (c) in each of the three member states, at least two of the firms each have domestic sales greater than €25 million; and (d) EU-wide sales of each of at least two firms is greater than €100 million.

If the intended M&A exceeds either of these thresholds, it is judged to have an EU dimension, and formal notification of the intention has to be made by the firms to the European Commission. There were 361 notifications in 2020 and the figure has been around 300 per year since 1999.

Investigations. Once a notification is made, the Commission must carry out a preliminary investigation (Phase 1), which is normally completed within 25 working days. At the end of Phase 1 the majority of cases (over 90 per cent) are usually settled and the merger is either allowed to proceed unconditionally or subject to certain conditions being met. These conditions usually relate to the sale of some of the assets of the newly formed business.

In a small number of cases, competition concerns are raised at the end of Phase 1 and a decision is made to refer the proposed merger to a formal, in-depth investigation (Phase 2). In 2020, eight of the 361 notifications made to the EC proceeded to Phase 2. These investigations must normally be completed within 90 working days or 110 in complex cases.

At the end of Phase 2 there are three possibilities: (a) the merger is allowed to proceed with no conditions attached; (b) the merger is allowed to proceed subject to certain conditions being met; (c) the merger is prohibited.

Assessment of the process. The process of EU merger control is thus very rapid and administratively inexpensive. The regulations are also potentially quite tough but also flexible since they recognise that M&As *may* be in the interests of consumers if they result in cost reductions. In such cases they are permitted.

This flexibility has led to criticism that the Commission has been too easily persuaded by firms, allowing mergers to go ahead with few, if any restrictions. Indeed, since the current M&A control measures were put in place in 1990 over 8000 M&As have been notified but, as of March 2021, only 279 had been referred to Phase 2 of the process and, of these, only 30 had been prohibited.

None of the Phase 2 investigations resulted in a prohibited merger in 2020, while three were prohibited in 2019. For example, in February 2019 the Commission blocked the acquisition of Alstrom by Siemens. These businesses are two of the largest suppliers of railway and metro signalling systems and the Commission judged that the merger would significantly impede effective competition.

The small number of prohibited mergers highlights a problem for EU policy makers: there is a trade-off between encouraging competition within the EU and supporting European companies to become world leaders. The ability to compete in *world* markets normally requires companies to be large, which may well lead to them having monopoly power within the EU.

To what extent is Article 102 consistent with both these points of view?

The EC appears to be taking a tougher stance towards M&A activity under the competition Commissioner, Margrethe Vestager. For example, deals are increasingly being scrutinised for their impact on innovation as opposed to just price and product choice.

UK competition policy

There have been substantial changes to UK competition policy since the first legislation was introduced in 1948. The current approach is based on the 1998 Competition Act and the 2002 Enterprise Act, together with Part 3 of the 2013 Enterprise and Regulatory Reform Act.

The Competition Act brought UK policy in line with EU policy, detailed above. The Act has two key sets (or 'chapters') of prohibitions. Chapter I prohibits various restrictive practices, and mirrors EU Article 101. Chapter II prohibits various abuses of monopoly power, and mirrors Article 102. The Enterprise Act strengthened the Competition Act and introduced new measures for the control of mergers.

The 2013 Enterprise and Regulatory Reform Act set up of a new body, the Competition and Markets Authority (CMA), to carry out investigations into particular markets suspected of not working in the best interests of consumers and being in breach of one or more of the Acts. It can make rulings, as we shall see below. Firms affected by a CMA ruling have the right of appeal to the independent Competition Appeal Tribunal (CAT), which can uphold or overturn the ruling.

UK restrictive practices policy

The 1998 Competition Act brought UK restrictive practices policy into line with the EU. In particular, the calculation of fines for anti-competitive behaviour was made comparable to the approach used by the European Commission. A leniency programme was developed with Type 'A' and 'B' immunity corresponding to EC Type 1A and 1B immunity (see page 432) and Type C immunity corresponding to EC Type 2 immunity.

In a recent example, the CMA ruled that two of the largest suppliers of rolled lead, Associated Lead Mills Ltd, and H. J. Enthoven Ltd, had broken Chapter I of the Competition Act. Rolled lead is an important product in the construction industry, mainly used for roofing. The CMA found that between October 2015 and April 2017 these two firms were guilty of (a) sharing the market, by arranging not to target certain customers, (b) colluding on prices, (c) exchanging commercially sensitive information on prices and (d) arranging not to supply a new business that risked disrupting the firms' existing customer relationships. Both firms entered into Settlement agreements (i.e. admitting their involvement in cartel activities) and so received reduced fines of £1.5 million and £8 million in November 2020.[2] In March 2021, three managers involved in the anti-competitive practices were disqualified from acting as company directors for between 3 and 6.5 years.

The 2002 Enterprise Act did introduce one big difference between UK and EU policy. It made it a *criminal* offence for individuals to implement arrangements that enabled price fixing, market sharing, restrictions in production and bid rigging irrespective of whether there are appreciable effects on competition. Convicted offenders can receive a prison sentence of up to five years and/or an unlimited fine.

Assessing the policy. When the 2002 Act was introduced, people expected it to result in 6–10 prosecutions per year. In reality, the authorities found the policy more difficult to implement and only four cases were prosecuted between 2002 and 2020, with just two successful outcomes.

In order to address some of the issues, the 2013 Act included a number of legal amendments to try to make it easier for the CMA to bring successful prosecutions against executives involved in cartel behaviour.

UK monopoly policy

The Chapter II prohibition of the 1998 Competition Act closely mirrors Article 102 of the TFEU. Investigations by the CMA follow the same two-stage process to establish whether the firm (a) has a dominant position and, if so, (b) is using its dominant position to carry out either exploitative or exclusionary abuses. Fines are calculated in a very similar manner to the EC and can be up to 10 per cent of worldwide turnover. One difference between UK and EU policy is that the CMA has the power to ban senior managers from serving as a director of a UK company for up to 15 years.

One potential example of an exploitative abuse case occurred in the pharmaceutical sector. The CMA judged that the pharmaceutical business, Advanz Pharma, had breached competition law between January 2009 and July 2017 by charging excessive and unfair prices for Liothyronine tablets. Liothyronine is an essential thyroid drug and during this period, Advanz Pharma, was the sole supplier. The price paid by the NHS had increased from £15.15 to £258.19, a rise of 1605 per cent.[3]

In common with other competition authorities, UK agencies tend to focus on behaviour that might excluded competitors from the market. For example, in February 2016, GlaxoSmithKline (GSK), the manufacturer of the anti-depressant drug Paroxetine, was fined over £37 million by the CMA for making payments to suppliers of non-branded versions of this same drug in return for these businesses delaying their entry into the market. GSK and the generic manufacturers all appealed the CMA decision to the Competition Appeal Tribunal (CAT) in April 2016. After referring some issues about the case to the Court of Justice of the European Union, the CAT finally upheld the CMA's original infringement decision in May 2021.[4]

UK merger policy

The framework for merger and acquisition (M&A) policy is set out in the 2002 Enterprise Act. The CMA will investigate a merger or acquisition if the resulting company meets one of two conditions: (a) it has a UK turnover that exceeds £70 million or (b) it has a market share of 25 per cent or above. The CMA makes its assessment solely on competition issues. More specifically, M&As can be prevented if they are likely to result in a substantial lessening of competition (SLC). This could lead to a unilateral effect (the elimination of competitors enables the merged entity to raise prices) or a co-ordinated effect (it increases the likelihood of collusion).

The CMA makes the final judgment, apart from in a few exceptional circumstances when a minister can intervene – where the proposed merger or acquisition would have an impact on national security, media plurality or the stability of the financial system. For example, in April 2021 the government issued an intervention notice on national security grounds for the proposed $40 billion acquisition of Arm, a British chip designer, by Nvidia, a US company. This means the CMA must start a Phase 1 investigation that looks at both competition and national security issues. The government has only made around 20 of these interventions since 2002, but they are becoming more common with over 10 in the four years to 2021.

One unusual aspect of UK policy is the lack of any obligation on the participating firms to pre-notify the authorities about a merger that meets either of the two thresholds. They can make a voluntary notice or the CMA can initiate an investigation following information received from third parties. The CMA instigates around 30 to 40 per cent of merger investigations as the firms fail to notify the authorities.

It is also possible for firms to complete a merger before it has been officially cleared by the CMA. If the CMA then decides to prevent it, the firms face the costs of having to split the business back into two separate entities. The 2013 Act increased the CMA's power to force companies to reverse integration activities undertaken prior to an investigation.

The investigation. In other respects, UK policy is similar to EU policy. The CMA conducts a preliminary or Phase 1 investigation to see whether there are any potential competition issues. The 2013 Act introduced a statutory deadline of 40 working days to complete Phase 1 of the process.

At the end of this period, the CMA has to decide whether there is a significant chance that the merger would result in

2 'CMA issues fines of over £9m for roofing lead cartel', *CMA press release* (4 November 2020), www.gov.uk/government/news/cma-issues-fines-of-over-9m-for-roofing-lead-cartel

3 'Liothyronine tablets: suspected excessive and unfair pricing', CMA (25 October 2016), www.gov.uk/cma-cases/pharmaceutical-sector-anti-competitive-conduct

4 'CAT upholds infringement decision for pay for delay pharma deals', *CMA press release* (10 May 2021), https://www.gov.uk/government/news/cat-upholds-infringement-decision-for-pay-for-delay-pharma-deals

a substantial lessening of competition. Sometimes the firms involved will offer to take certain actions to help address any competition concerns. These are known as Undertakings in Lieu (UILs) and usually involve commitments to sell some of the assets of the newly formed business.

If substantial lessening of competition (SLC) issues still remain, the CMA begins Phase 2 of the process, which is a much more in-depth assessment. At the end of this process if no SLC issues are raised, or if they are addressed by any UILs, the merger is allowed to go ahead.

In 2020/21 only 9 out of the 38 Phase 1 cases were referred for a Phase 2 investigation; 18 cases were cleared unconditionally; six were cleared after UILs were accepted; three were cleared on 'de minimis' grounds (the affected market is sufficiently low as not to justify the cost of a Phase 2 inquiry); one case was judged not to qualify; one was abandoned. An example of where the CMA cleared a takeover was the acquisition of the pub chain business Ei Group by Stonegate in February 2020, following a Phase 1 investigation. Stonegate made a UIL to sell 42 pubs to address concerns that the merger would significantly reduce competition in 51 areas.

There is a 24-week statutory time limit for Phase 2 decisions. This can be extended in special circumstances by up to eight weeks. The membership of the team that carries out Phase 2 of the process differs from the one that carries out Phase 1. It is thought to be useful to get 'fresh eyes' to look at a case. If the investigations get to the end of Phase 2 the CMA makes one of the following decisions:

- *Unconditional clearance of the merger.* In 2020/21 this happened in one out of the 11 cases. In August 2020, Amazon's investment in Deliveroo was cleared after a Phase 2 investigation concluded that it would not lead to a substantial lessening of competition.
- *Conditional clearance subject to the firms taking certain actions that are legally binding.* These are referred to as 'remedies' and typically involve commitments to sell certain parts of the newly merged business. See Box 14.3 for an example.
- *Prohibition of the merger.* In the 17 years between 2004/5 and 2020/21 only 17 mergers were prohibited out of 175 Phase 2 investigations. In November 2020, the CMA ordered FNZ to sell GBST. FNZ, a global platform service business, had previously acquired GBST, a provider of financial services technology without seeking clearance from the authorities. The CMA concluded that the merger raised a number of competition concerns.

If anti-monopoly legislation is effective enough, is there ever any need to prevent mergers from going ahead?

Assessment of competition policy

Most commentators favour the way monopoly policy in both the EU and UK concentrates on anti-competitive practices and their effects rather than simply on the existence of market dominance. Economic power is a problem only when it is abused. If, by contrast, it enables firms to achieve economies of scale, or more finance for investment, the result can be of benefit to consumers.

The stricter and more prohibitive approach taken towards restrictive practices also gains widespread approval. The policing and penalties for infringements of Article 101 and Chapter I have become more severe in recent years. For example, the fines imposed by the EC for the period 1990–94 totalled just under €350 million. For the period 2015–19 the figure was just over €8.2 billion. The Leniency Notice is also seen as a good way of trying to deal with the problem of uncovering instances of collusion.

The approach towards M&As remains the most controversial area of competition policy, with criticisms that it is far too lenient. Specific areas of contention with UK policy are whether: (a) firms should be forced to notify the authorities of proposed mergers and be prevented from undertaking any integration activities until the merger is cleared; (b) there should be a return to a broad public interest test rather than judging mergers purely by their impact on competition.

More recently, the CMA has started to examine online platforms and digital advertising markets. Some people have criticised the competition authorities for being too lenient in their approach to companies such as Google and Facebook. Following a year-long study, the CMA published its final market report in July 2020.[5] One of its key conclusions is that the existing set of laws and regulations are not an effective way to regulate digital advertising markets. To help address this issue, one of the recommendations was for the government to establish a Digital Markets Unit within the CMA. The government accepted this proposal and a new Digital Markets Unit was launched on 7 April 2021.[6]

The impact of the UK's departure from the EU

The UK's departure from the European Union has had an impact on the way competition policy operates. Prior to January 2021, it was necessary for the CMA and UK courts to make sure there was no inconsistency between their decisions and those taken at a European level.

It is now possible for the regulations to diverge and the UK could use this greater freedom to take a tougher approach. However, different standards could result in more uncertainty for businesses. For example, what is considered an abuse of a dominant market position may begin to vary.

Businesses operating in the UK and EU may also face parallel investigations by the two different competition authorities. This could result in additional costs, delays and complexity. For example, businesses will have to start making two different leniency applications in restrictive practices

5 'New regime needed to take on tech giants', *CMA press release* (1 July 2020), www.gov.uk/government/news/new-regime-needed-to-take-on-tech-giants

6 'New watchdog to boost online competition launches', *CMA press release* (7 April 2021), www.gov.uk/government/news/new-watchdog-to-boost-online-competition-launches--3

BOX 14.3 TICKETING TAKEOVERS

CASE STUDIES AND APPLICATIONS

The merger between two of the largest secondary ticketing platforms in the world

In November 2019, Viagogo, one of the largest and most controversial secondary ticketing platforms in the world, announced a $4.05 billion deal to purchase its rival, StubHub. eBay had previously acquired StubHub for $310 million in January 2007. Viagogo was by far the largest secondary ticketing platform in the UK and StubHub was its biggest rival. On 13 February 2020, the acquisition was officially completed.

On 14 April 2020, the Competition and Markets Authority (CMA) issued a commencement notice instructing the firms that it was launching a Phase 1 investigation into the merger. On 11 June, the CMA announced that the merger did raise competition concerns and invited the businesses to offer some remedial Undertakings in Lieu (UIL).[1] In response, Viagogo offered to sell parts of StubHub's global business as a potential remedy. However, the CMA doubted whether the proposal would effectively address its competition concerns and so referred the merger for a Phase 2 investigation.

The definition of the market

As with all monopoly and merger cases, one key issue for competition authorities is to identify the relevant market. As the CMA states in the Phase 1 report: 'Market definition provides a framework for assessing the competitive effects of a merger and involves an element of judgement.'[2]

Ticketing platforms, such as StubHub and Viagogo, are examples of two-sided markets. They offer services to both ticket buyers (i.e. the fans) and ticket resellers. There are a number of different segments in this market.

Primary ticketing platforms. Event organisers (promotors, artist management teams, etc.) sell tickets to consumers using these platforms. Some of the larger primary ticketing platforms include Ticketmaster, See Tickets, Eventim, AXS and SeatGeek.

Uncapped secondary ticketing platforms. These are platforms where people can resell tickets they previously purchased via a primary platform. In the uncapped market, the secondary platforms do not place any restrictions on prices. Examples include Viagogo, StubHub and Gigsberg.

Capped secondary ticketing platforms. In the capped market, the platforms do place restrictions on reseller prices. Some websites are stand-alone organisations such as Twickets and TicketSwap. Other websites operate as part of a primary market platform such as Ticketmaster Ticket Exchange, See Tickets Fan-to-Fan, Eventim fanSALE and AXS Official Resale.

Other online channels. These include classified advertising websites (e.g. Gumtree), social networks (e.g. Facebook), specialised online platforms for a specific team, venue or sport (e.g. Chelsea FC Ticket Exchange) and professional reseller websites.

Unsurprisingly, Viagogo/StubHub wanted the definition of the market to be as broad as possible and claimed that all of these segments are close substitutes.

The CMA did not accept these arguments for a number of reasons. For example, classified advertising websites/ social networks do not provide services such as guarantees about the authenticity of tickets, while it is not possible for people to resell tickets via a primary platform. Therefore, in the Phase 1 report, the CMA considered the secondary ticket platform services as the relevant market. Based upon this definition, the market shares in 2019 were as follows:

Platform	Market share (%)
Viagogo	50–60
StubHub	30–40
Ticketmaster Ticket Exchange	5–10
AXS Official Resale	0–5
Eventim fanSALE	0–5
Gigantic Fan-to-Fan	0–5
Gigsberg	0–5
See Tickets Fan-to-Fan	0–5
TicketSwap	0–5
Twickets	0–5

As the merger significantly increases Viagogo's already high market share and removes its only significant competitor, it raises competition concerns. In the Phase 2 report,[3] the CMA narrowed the definition of the relevant market further to include just the uncapped secondary ticketing platform services. Based on this definition, the newly merged firm would have a 90–100 percent share of the market.

The level of competition between the firms

Another important part of an investigation is for the authorities to assess the level of competition between the businesses that plan to merge. For example, the CMA states that horizontal unilateral effects are more likely when the merging parties are close competitors.[4]

The CMA found evidence that prior to the merger, Viagogo and StubHub did compete strongly to attract both buyers and sellers to their platforms. For example, the research found instances of the platforms altering both their fees and payment terms in response to competition from each other. The vast majority of resellers who responded to a CMA survey also listed the two companies as close substitutes and sold tickets on both platforms.

The potential for competition from existing firms and new entrants

Timely entry by new firms into the secondary ticketing platform market, or expansion by existing firms, could help to limit any negative effects of the merger on competition. Given the combined market share of the newly merged firm, the CMA concluded that indirect network effects are likely to act as a significant barrier to both entry and expansion. Large online advertising and marketing costs also make it difficult for rival firms.

Recommendations

In the final report of the Phase 2 investigation, the CMA concluded that the completed acquisition would result in a substantial lessening of competition in the UK market for uncapped secondary ticketing platform services. In particular, it could lead to customers having to pay higher fees and/or receiving a lower quality of service.

The final remedy proposed by the CMA is for Viagogo to sell off those parts of StubHub's business that are outside of North America: i.e. a partial divestiture. This is subject to approval of the identity of the purchaser and the terms of the deal. On 8 April 2021, the CMA announced that an agreement had been reached with the businesses about the details of the sale.[5]

1. *Compare and contrast the merger notification systems used in the European Union and the UK.*
2. *Outline the difference between unilateral and co-ordinated effects of a merger. Discuss the circumstances that make unilateral effects of a merger more likely.*
3. *Explain why indirect network effects might act as a barrier to entry and expansion.*

Find out what Viagogo's detailed arguments were to justify the merger. Is there any merit in these arguments?

1 'Merger of Viagogo and StubHub raises competition concerns', *CMA news story* (11 June 2020), www.gov.uk/government/news/merger-of-viagogo-and-stubhub-raises-competition-concerns

2 'Decision on relevant merger situation and substantial lessening of competition', *Phase 1 full text decision*, CMA (17 July 2020), https://assets.publishing.service.gov.uk/media/5f11717ed3bf7f5bb2fd2752/VSH_Decision_on_SLC.pdf

3 *Summary of Phase 2 final report*, CMA (2 February 2021), https://assets.publishing.service.gov.uk/media/6018393e8fa8f53fbdc27dab/Summary_V-SH.pdf

4 *Merger Assessment Guidelines*, CMA (November 2020), https://assets.publishing.service.gov.uk/government/uploads/system/uploads/attachment_data/file/935593/Revised_MAGs_Nov_2020.pdf

5 *Notice of acceptance of final undertakings*, CMA (9 April 2021), https://assets.publishing.service.gov.uk/media/60702d848fa8f57362ca4922/Final_undertakings_acceptance_letter.pdf

cases. They may be unsure if the protection from fines and prosecution in one application will be the same as another.

With M&As, the European Union operates the 'one-stop shop' principle. This means that once a merger meets the criteria for investigation by the European Commission, a parallel inquiry does not take place in a member state. The one-stop shop no longer applies to the UK. Therefore, it is now possible for both the UK and EU to review the same case, for example the proposed acquisition of ARM by Nvidia. This will significantly increase the CMA's workload and raises the possibility that the same M&A could receive different rulings – prohibited by one authority and cleared by the other.

If two or more firms were charging similar prices, what types of evidence would you look for to prove that this was collusion rather than coincidence?

Section summary

1. Competition policy in most countries recognises that monopolies, mergers and restrictive practices can bring both costs and benefits to the consumer. Generally, though, restrictive practices tend to be more damaging to consumers' interests than simple monopoly power or mergers.
2. European Union legislation applies to firms trading between EU countries. Article 101 applies to restrictive practices. Article 102 applies to dominant firms. There are also separate merger control provisions.
3. UK legislation is covered largely by the 1998 Competition Act, the 2002 Enterprise Act and the 2013 Enterprise and Regulatory Reform Act. The Chapter I prohibition of the 1998 Act applies to restrictive practices and is similar to EU Article 101. The Chapter II prohibition applies to dominant firms and is similar to Article 102. Under the 2002 Act, certain cartel agreements became a criminal offence, and mergers over a certain size must be investigated by the Competition and Markets Authority (CMA).
4. The focus of both EU and UK legislation is on anti-competitive practices rather than on the simple existence of agreements between firms or market dominance. Practices that are found, after investigation, to be detrimental to competition are prohibited and heavy fines can be imposed, even for a first offence.

14.2 PRIVATISATION AND REGULATION

Nationalisation and privatisation

One possible solution to market failure, advocated by some on the political left, is nationalisation. If industries are not being run in the public interest by the private sector, then bring them into public ownership. This way, so the argument goes, the market failures can be corrected. Problems of monopoly power, externalities, inequality, etc. can be dealt with directly if these industries are run in the public interest rather than for private gain.

Most nationalisation in the UK took place under the Labour government of 1945–51, when coal, railways, gas and steel were nationalised. The Labour Party at the time saw nationalisation not just as a means of correcting market failures, but as something that was morally desirable. It was seen to be much fairer and less divisive to have a society based on common ownership of the means of production than one where people were divided into separate classes: workers and capitalists.

By the mid-1970s, however, it became increasingly clear that the nationalised industries were inefficient and also a source of much industrial unrest. A change of policy was introduced from the early 1980s, when successive Conservative governments engaged in an extensive programme of 'privatisation', returning virtually all of the ***nationalised industries*** to the private sector. These included telecommunications, gas, water, steel, electricity and the railways.

By 1997, the year the Conservatives left office, with the exception of the rail industry in Northern Ireland and the water industry in Northern Ireland and Scotland, the only nationalised industry remaining in the UK was the Post Office (including post offices and mail). The Post Office and Royal Mail were split in 2012 and Royal Mail was privatised in October 2013. Post Office Ltd remains state owned but, under the 2011 Postal Services Act, there is the option for it to become a mutual organisation in the future.

Other countries have followed similar programmes of privatisation in what has become a worldwide phenomenon. Many politicians view it as a way of both revitalising inefficient industries and raising revenues to ease budgetary problems.

In the 2019 general election, however, the Labour party stated that, if elected, it would renationalise the train operating companies, the water industry, the energy industries, Royal Mail and fibre broadband provision. A national opinion poll carried out by YouGov in December 2019 found that 63 per cent, 64 per cent and 53 per cent of respondents respectively were in favour of nationalising the water industry, the train operating companies and the energy industries.

How desirable is privatisation?

Arguments for privatisation

Market forces. The first argument is that privatisation will expose these industries to market forces, from which will flow the benefits of greater efficiency, faster growth and greater responsiveness to the wishes of the consumer. There are three parts to this argument.

- Greater competition in the market. If privatisation involves splitting an industry into competing parts (for example, separate power stations competing to sell electricity to different electricity distribution companies), the resulting competition may drive costs and prices down.
- Greater competition for finance. After privatisation a company has to finance investment through the market: it must issue shares or borrow from financial institutions. In doing so, it will be competing for funds with other companies, and thus must be seen as capable of using these funds profitably.
- Accountability to shareholders. Shareholders want a good return on their shares and this puts pressure on the privatised company to perform well. If the company does not make sufficient profits, shareholders will sell their shares. The share price will fall and the company will be at greater risk of a takeover. The market for corporate control (see page 213) thus provides incentives for private firms to be efficient. There has been considerable takeover activity in the water and electricity industries, with most of the regional electricity companies and several of the water companies acquired by non-UK companies.

Reduced government interference. In nationalised industries, managers may frequently be required to adjust their targets for political reasons. At one time they may have to keep prices low as part of a government drive against inflation. At another they may have to increase their prices substantially in order to raise extra revenue for the government and help finance tax cuts. At another they may find their investment programmes cut as part of a government economy drive.

Privatisation frees the company from these constraints and allows it to make better economic decisions and plan future investments with greater certainty.

Financing tax cuts. The privatisation issue of shares earns money directly for the government and thus reduces the amount it needs to borrow. Effectively, then, the government can use the proceeds of privatisation to finance tax cuts.

There is a danger here, however, that in order to raise the maximum revenue the government will want to make the industries as potentially profitable as possible. This may involve selling them as monopolies. But this, of course, would probably be against the interests of the consumer.

Potential problems with privatisation

The markets in which privatised industries operate are unlikely to be perfect. What is more, the process of privatisation itself can create problems.

Natural monopolies. The market forces argument for privatisation largely breaks down if a public monopoly is simply replaced by a private monopoly, as in the case of the water

Definition

Nationalised industries State-owned industries that produce goods or services that are sold in the market.

KI 22 p195

companies. Critics of privatisation argue that at least a public-sector monopoly is not out to maximise profits and thereby exploit the consumer.

Some industries have such great economies of scale that there is only room for one firm in the industry. They are natural monopolies. The best examples of natural monopolies are the various grids that exist in the privatised utilities: the national electricity grid, the national gas pipe network, the network of railway lines. These grids account for a relatively high proportion of the total costs of these industries.

In Figure 14.1, assume that the total industry output is Q_1. With just one company in the industry, long-run average cost is therefore $LRAC_1$. Now assume that the industry is split into two equal-sized companies, each with its own grid. If total output remains at Q_1, the two firms will produce Q_2 each at the higher long-run average cost of $LRAC_2$.

It is potentially more efficient, therefore, to have a single monopoly supplier whenever there is a natural monopoly. It avoids wasteful duplication.

The problem is that the monopoly producer in a free market could use its power to drive up prices. The long-run profit-maximising position is illustrated in Figure 14.2. The monopolist produces Q_m at a price P_m and at a cost of $LRAC_m$.

If, however, the industry remained nationalised, or if it was privatised but regulated, it could be run as a monopoly and thus achieve the full economies of scale. And yet it could be directed to set a price that just covered costs (including normal profits), and thus make no more profit than a highly competitive industry. In Figure 14.2, it would produce Q_n at a price of P_n. We examine regulation later in this section.

Planning and the co-ordination of industry. Road use and road construction affect the demand for railways and vice versa. Decisions in the coal, electricity, gas and oil industries (and to a large extent in the steel industry) all affect each other. If these industries were nationalised, it should make their decisions easier to co-ordinate in the public interest and could help the sensible planning of the nation's infrastructure. If these industries were under private enterprise, however, either there would be little co-ordination, or alternatively co-ordination might degenerate into oligopolistic collusion, with the consumer losing out. In the extreme case, the same company may have a monopoly in more than one industry. For example, in some regions of the UK, one company runs both buses and trains.

Figure 14.1 Natural monopoly

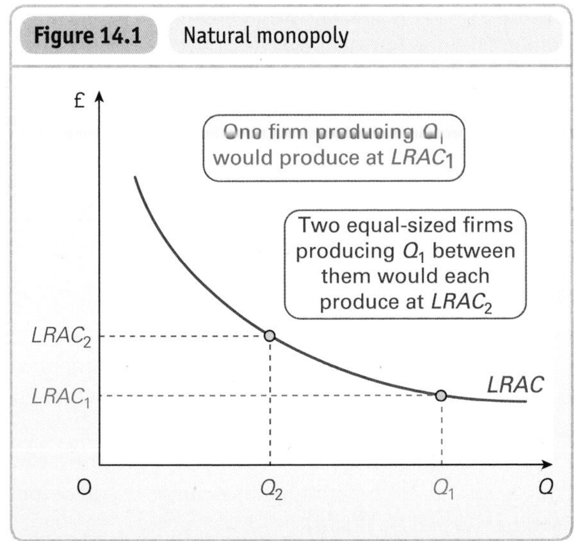

Figure 14.2 Profit-maximising natural monopoly

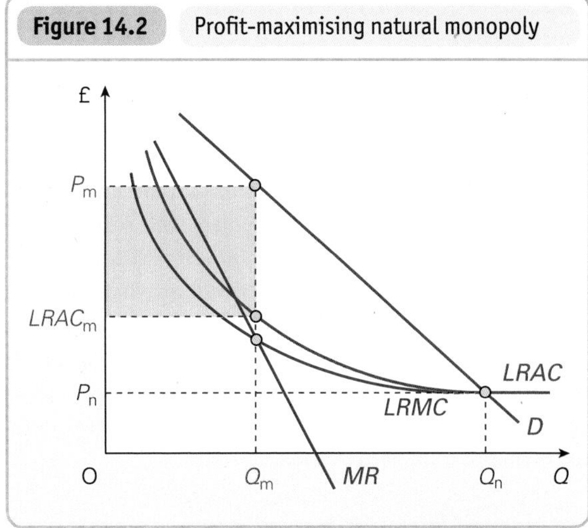

KI 31 p364

Problems of externalities and inequality. Various industries may create substantial external benefits and yet may be privately unprofitable. A railway or an underground line, for example, may considerably ease congestion on the roads, thus benefiting road as well as rail users. Other industries may cause substantial external costs. Nuclear power stations may produce nuclear waste that is costly to dispose of safely, and/or provides hazards for future generations. Coal-fired power stations emit CO_2 and cause acid rain.

KI 4 p13

For reasons of equity, it can be argued that various transport services should be subsidised in order to keep them going and/or to keep their prices down. For instance, it can be argued that rural bus services should be kept operating at subsidised prices and that certain people (e.g. pensioners) should be charged lower prices.

Will such externalities and issues of equity be ignored under privatisation? The advocates of privatisation argue that externalities can be dealt with by appropriate taxes, subsidies and regulations even if the industry is privatised. Likewise, questions of fairness and social justice can be dealt with by subsidies or regulations. It is possible to subsidise a loss-making bus service so that it can be run profitably by a private bus company.

Critics argue that externalities are widespread and need to be taken into account by the industry itself and not just by an occasionally intervening government.

In assessing these arguments, a lot depends on the effectiveness of government legislation and regulation.

To what extent can the problems with privatisation be seen as arguments in favour of nationalisation?

Regulation: identifying the optimum price and output

Privatised industries, if left free to operate in the market, will have monopoly power; they will create externalities; and they will be unlikely to take into account questions of fairness. An answer to these problems is for the government or some independent agency to regulate their behaviour so that they produce at the socially optimum price and output.

Exactly what this optimum is depends on what problems need to be taken into account. Take three cases. In the first, the privatised industry is a monopoly (perhaps it is a natural monopoly), but there are no other problems. In the second case, there are also externalities to be considered, and in the third, questions of fairness too.

The privatised industry is a monopoly

The 'first-best' situation: $P = MC$. Assume that all other firms in the economy are operating under perfect competition, and thus producing where $P = MC$. This is the imaginary 'first-best' situation. If this were so, the privatised company should be required to follow the same pricing rule: $P = MC$. As we saw in section 12.1, this will give the Pareto optimal output, where total consumer plus producer surplus is maximised (see pages 356–8).

KI 28 p356

The theory of the 'second best': $P = MC + Z$. Now let us drop the assumption that the rest of the economy operates under perfect competition. If other industries on average are charging a price, say, 10 per cent above *MC*, then the theory of the second best suggests that the privatised company should also charge a price 10 per cent above *MC*. At least that way it will not cause a diversion of consumption away from relatively low-cost industries (at the margin) to a relatively high-cost one. The second-best rule is therefore to set $P = MC + Z$, where *Z* in this case is 10 per cent.

The privatised industry produces externalities

In the first-best situation the privatised industry should produce where price equals marginal social (not private) cost: $P = MSC$. The second-best solution is to produce where $P = MSC + Z$ (where *Z* is the average of other industries' price above their *MSC*).

KI 31 p364

The difficulty for the regulator in applying these rules in practice is to identify and measure the externalities: not an easy task! (See section 12.4.)

The behaviour of the privatised industry involves questions of fairness

If the government wishes the regulator to insist on a price below *MC* because it wishes to help certain groups (e.g. pensioners, children, rural dwellers, those below certain incomes), what should this price be?

In practice, one of two simple rules could be followed. Either the industry could be required to charge uniform prices, despite higher costs for supplying certain categories of people (this could apply, for example, to rural customers of a privatised postal service); or a simple formula could be used (e.g. half price for pensioners and children). These are often the only practical solutions given the impossibility of identifying the specific needs of individual consumers.

Two further questions arise:

- Should the lower price be subsidised by central or local government, or by the privatised company and hence by other users of the service (i.e. by them paying higher prices)? Justice would suggest that support should come from the community as a whole – the taxpayer – and not just from other users of the service.
- If people require help, should they not be given general tax relief or benefits, rather than specifically subsidised services? For example, should pensioners not be paid better pensions, rather than be charged reduced fares on buses?

1. *In the case of buses, subsidies are often paid by local authorities to support various loss-making routes. Is this the best way of supporting these services?*
2. *In the case of postal services, profitable parts of the service cross-subsidise the unprofitable parts. Should this continue if the industry is privatised?*

The long run

In the short run, certain factors of production are fixed in supply. For example, electricity output can be increased by using existing power stations more fully, but the number of power stations is fixed. There will thus be a limit to the amount of electricity that can be generated in the short run. As that limit is approached, the marginal cost of electricity is likely to rise rapidly. For example, oil-fired power stations, which are more costly to operate, will have to be brought online.

In the long run, all factors are variable. New power stations can be built. The long-run marginal costs therefore will probably not rise as more is produced. In fact, they may even fall due to economies of scale.

Long-run marginal costs, however, unlike short-run marginal costs, will include the extra capital costs of increasing output. The long-run marginal cost of electricity will thus be all the extra costs of producing one more unit: namely, the extra operating costs (fuel, labour, etc.) plus the extra capital costs (power stations, pylons, etc.).

The rule for the optimum long-run price and output is simple. The regulator should require the industry to produce where price equals long-run marginal social cost (*LRMSC*). This is illustrated in Figure 14.3.

In the short run, optimum price and output are P_S and Q_S where $P =$ (short-run) *MSC*. This might mean that production is at quite a high cost: existing capital equipment is being stretched and diminishing returns have become serious.

In the long run, then, it will be desirable to increase capacity if $LRMSC < MSC$. Optimum long-run price and output are thus at P_L and Q_L where $P = LRMSC$.

Figure 14.3 Short-run and long-run marginal cost pricing

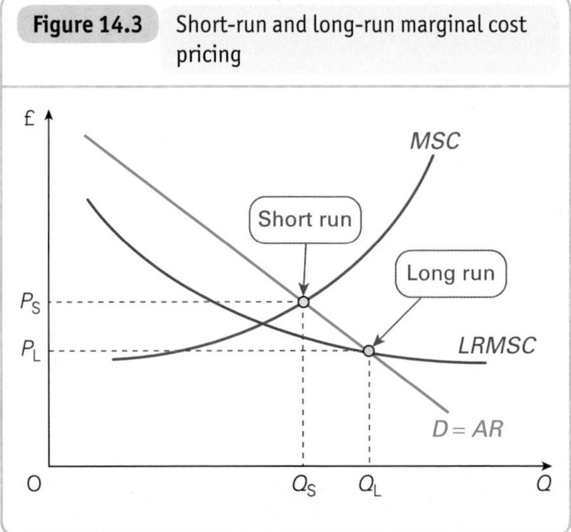

This is the rule for the first-best situation. In the second-best situation, the industry should produce where $P = LRMSC + Z$ (where Z is the average of other industries' price above their *LRMSC*).

If the regulator imposed such rules, would they cause the firm to make a loss if it faced a downward-sloping LRMSC curve? (Clues: Where would the LRAC curve be relative to the LRMC curve? What would be the effect of externalities and the addition of the Z factor on the price?)

Regulation in the UK

To some extent the behaviour of privatised industries may be governed by general monopoly and restrictive practice legislation. For example, in the UK, following a two-year investigation into the energy industry in 2016, the Competition & Markets Authority (CMA) published a report with various recommendations (see Box 14.4).

In addition to the CMA, there are regulatory offices to oversee the structure and behaviour of each of the privatised utilities. These regulators are as follows: the Office for Gas and Electricity Markets (Ofgem), the Office of Communications (Ofcom) (for telecommunications and broadcasting), the Office of Rail and Road (ORR) and the Office of Water Services (Ofwat).

The regulators set terms under which the industries have to operate. For example, the ORR sets the terms under which rail companies have access to the track and stations. The terms set by the regulator can be reviewed by negotiation between the regulator and the industry. If agreement cannot be reached, the CMA acts as an appeal court and its decisions are binding.

The regulator for each industry also sets limits to the prices that certain parts of the industry can charge (see Case Study 14.6 on the student website). These parts are those where there is little or no competition: for example, the charges made to electricity and gas retailers by National Grid, the owner of the electricity grid and major gas pipelines.

For many years after privatisation, the price-setting formulae were largely of the 'RPI minus X' variety (although other factors, including competition and excessive profits, were also taken into account). This type of regulation allowed industries to raise their prices by the rate of increase in the retail price index (RPI) (i.e. by the rate of inflation) *minus* a certain percentage (X) to take account of expected increases in efficiency. Thus if the rate of inflation were 3 per cent, and if the regulator considered that the industry (or firm) could be expected to reduce its costs by 2 per cent (X = 2%), then price rises would be capped at 1 per cent. The RPI − X system is thus an example of ***price-cap regulation***. The argument for this system of regulation is that it will force the industry to pass cost savings on to the consumer.

In March 2008, Ofgem began a two-year review of regulation in the energy industry called *RPI–X@20*. In 2010 it announced plans for a new system of price regulation called RIIO (Revenue = Incentives + Innovation + Outputs) to be introduced in 2013. Under this system, firms' prices and hence permitted revenue (R) should not only depend on costs, but also have an element for incentives (I), innovation (I), and the quality of output (Q).

The RIIO approach is similar to RPI−X but places much greater weight on the quality of the output supplied and allows the climate change agenda to be addressed as part of the price control system.

Why might it equally result in average cost pricing?

Assessing the system of regulation in the UK

The system that has evolved in the UK has various advantages over that employed in the USA and elsewhere, where regulation often focuses on the level of profits (see Case Study 14.7 on the student website).

- It is a discretionary system, with the regulator able to judge individual examples of the behaviour of the industry on their own merits. The regulator has a detailed knowledge of the industry which would not be available to government ministers or other bodies such as the CMA. The regulator could thus be argued to be the best body to decide on whether the industry is acting in the public interest.
- The system is flexible, since it allows for the licence and price formulae to be changed as circumstances change.

Definition

Price-cap regulation Where the regulator puts a ceiling on the amount by which a firm can raise its price.

BOX 14.4 SELLING POWER TO THE PEOPLE

The impact of privatisation and competition in the electricity industry

Competition is generally seen as better than regulation as a means of protecting consumers' interests, but there is evidence that this requires a strong regulatory framework to be retained. The electricity industry provides a good case study on the impact of the introduction of competition into a privatised industry.

The industry before privatisation

Under nationalisation, the industry in England and Wales was organised as a monopoly with the Central Electricity Generating Board (CEGB) supplying 99 per cent of all electricity. It operated the power stations and transmitted the electricity round the country via the national grid. However, the CEGB did not sell electricity directly to the consumer; rather it sold it to 12 regional boards, which in turn supplied it to the consumer.

Privatisation of the industry

Non-nuclear generation in England and Wales was privatised in 1990 as two companies: National Power (with just over 50 per cent of capacity) and PowerGen (with nearly 30 per cent). Nuclear power stations were privatised in 1996.

The 12 regional boards were privatised in 1991 as separate regional electricity companies (RECs), which were responsible for local distribution and supply to consumers. They were also permitted to build their own power stations if they chose. The RECs jointly owned the national grid, but it was run independently. It was eventually sold as a separate company in 1996. The national grid is now managed and operated by National Grid Electricity Transmission plc, a subsidiary of the multinational business National Grid.

The diagram shows the structure of the industry. Electricity is produced by the *generators* (the power stations). The electricity is *transmitted* along the power lines of the national grid to different parts of the country. It is then transmitted locally by the *distributors*. There are currently six licensed distribution network operators (DNOs) covering 14 different regions in Britain. They are responsible for the distribution of electricity from the high voltage transmission grid to businesses and households.

At the time of privatisation an Office of Electricity Regulation (OFFER) was set up to control prices in parts of the industry where there was no competition. OFFER was later merged with the gas regulator to become the Office of Gas and Electricity Markets (Ofgem). Initially prices were controlled using the RPI – X approach (see page 443). For example, the charges paid by the generators and the suppliers to the National Grid Electricity Transmission company were regulated in this way, as this part of the business is considered to be a natural monopoly. The same is true for the DNOs, as each has a natural monopoly in the region for which it is responsible. In 2013, Ofgem replaced the RPI – X price controls with Revenue = Incentives + Innovation + Outputs (RIIO). As the name suggests, these set targets to encourage innovation.

The rationale behind introducing the new structure was to increase competition, thereby making regulation increasingly unnecessary. But given the natural monopoly market structure in both transmission and distribution, where was the competition supposed to come from?

It was hoped that competition would be possible at two levels: at the *wholesale* level, with generators competing with each other to sell to suppliers; and at the *retail* level, with suppliers competing to sell to customers. Let us examine each of these markets in turn.

The electricity industry in England and Wales

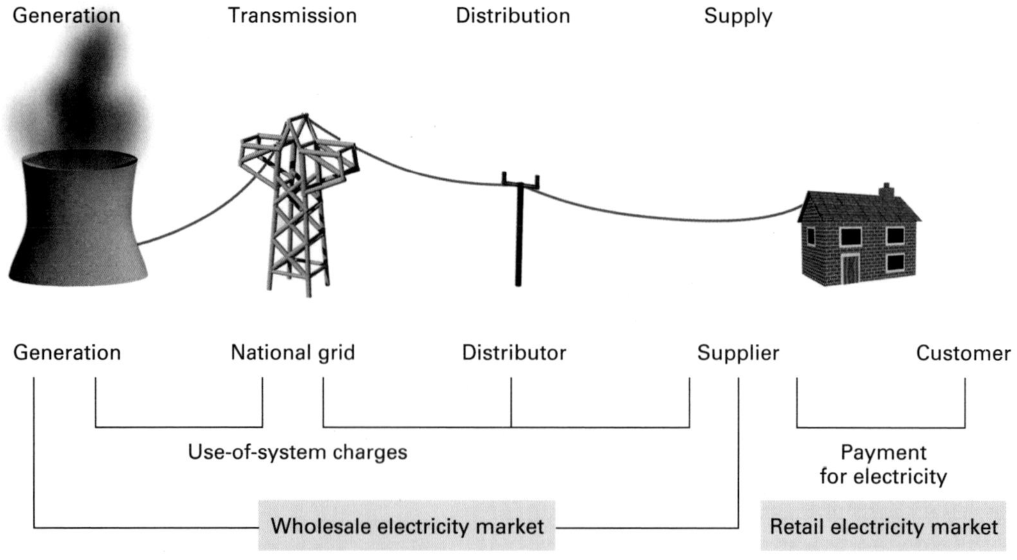

CASE STUDIES AND APPLICATIONS

Competition in the wholesale market for electricity

In its latest 'State of the Market' report, Ofgem described the wholesale electricity market as being moderately concentrated. The four largest companies (EDF, RWE, SSE and Drax) have a combined market share of 53 per cent. The degree of vertical integration has remained relatively stable over the past few years and Ofgem has found no evidence that it is detrimental to market competition.

One measure of potential market power is *pivotality* analysis – the extent to which power stations owned by a particular company are essential to meet demand at any given time. Although there is evidence this has increased, it still only occurs for relatively short periods. The profit margins for the larger generation businesses have also fallen.

Liquidity,[1] as measured by the 'churn ratio', has remained relatively stable over recent years and is similar to other European power markets. The churn ratio is the total volume of electricity traded divided by the total demand. It shows how often a unit of electricity is traded before it is delivered to end consumers. A high churn ratio reflects a large number of buyers and sellers and the ease of entry to the market.

Competition in the retail market for electricity

Since 1999 all customers, whether domestic or business, have been able to choose their supplier. Over that period there have been several new entrants into the market, including various gas companies diversifying into electricity supply.

By 2001, 38 per cent of customers had switched suppliers at least once and the former regional monopoly suppliers' market share had fallen to 70 per cent. In the light of this, Ofgem announced that competition was sufficiently developed to allow all regulation of the retail market to be removed by April 2002.

However, the rise of the Big Six (British Gas, EDF, E.ON, npower, Scottish Power and SSE), which resulted from M&As in the industry, meant that by 2004 they had a collective market share of 99 per cent of the retail market. There were increasing concerns that competition was not working effectively as the real price of electricity rose significantly.

Ofgem investigations

Ofgem published the results from its first investigation into the market in 2009. The Energy Supply Probe[2] concluded that there was no evidence of collusion in the retail market but proposed a number of remedies to help the market work more effectively. This included improvements in the way information on bills was presented to customers.

In late 2010 Ofgem launched its Retail Market Review (RMR).[3] This report recognised that some improvements had been made but that energy bills were still too complex, making it difficult for consumers to find the best deals. For example, there were over 300 different tariffs available to domestic users! The review recommended that tariffs should be calculated on simple per-unit pricing and energy suppliers limited to offering only four different deals – 'the four-tariff rule'.

After carrying out these reviews, Ofgem concluded that its powers as a market regulator were insufficient to determine whether barriers were blocking effective competition. In June 2014, it referred the energy market to the CMA for a full investigation.

The CMA inquiry

In 2014, the CMA launched the most comprehensive and wide-ranging review of the energy market since privatisation. The inquiry took two years to complete and the final report was published in June 2016.[4] Some of its key findings were:

- The wholesale market for electricity was working effectively with no evidence of firms exploiting any market power.
- Vertical integration between the suppliers and generators was not having any negative impact on consumers. Independent electricity generators were able to compete effectively with those that were vertically integrated with the energy suppliers.
- A number of new firms had successfully entered the retail market and had increased their market shares.
- A significant number of customers did not actively engage in the market by shopping around for the best deals. For example, in a survey of 7000 domestic customers carried out as part of the inquiry, 34 per cent of respondents stated that they had never considered switching energy supplier.
- Approximately 70 per cent of the customers of the Big Six were on a standard variable tariff (SVT): i.e. the default pricing scheme when people do not shop around.
- The tariffs available to those people who did shop around closely followed changes in industry costs. However, the gap between SVT and industry costs had increased significantly in recent years.
- The majority of customers using prepayment meters were on SVTs because of low levels of competition. This was partly due to the limitations of non-smart meters.
- The restriction on the number of tariffs imposed by Ofgem following its 2010 review had had a negative impact on competition. It forced some firms to withdraw pricing schemes that had previously benefited many customers.
- A large number of small businesses (those employing fewer than 10 people) were on expensive default schemes. The tariffs available to these businesses were not published by the energy suppliers but were instead the outcome of individual-level negotiation.

In response to these findings, the CMA made the following recommendations:

- The creation of a database that includes the details of customers who have been on the SVT for three years or more. Energy suppliers would have access to this database to offer better deals for these customers. The aim of this reform was to reduce switching costs.
- The 'four-tariff' rule on energy suppliers should be scrapped.
- Energy companies supplying businesses employing fewer than 10 people should publish the different available tariffs to increase transparency and make it easier for these small businesses to choose the best deal.
- A temporary price cap (2017–20) should be introduced for those customers using prepayment meters.

Four of the five panel members opposed the introduction of a price cap on SVTs for all customers, as they believed it would undermine competition.

(continued)

The outcome

Ofgem agreed to implement the CMA's recommendations and in April 2017, a temporary price cap was introduced for customers using prepayment meters. In February 2018, the price cap was extended to consumers who were eligible for the Warm Home Discount Scheme – a benefit for people on low incomes. This extension meant that 5 million households had energy bills covered by price controls.

Political pressure continued for the introduction of a price cap for all customers on SVTs. In response, Parliament passed the Domestic Gas and Electricity (Tariff Cap) Act in July 2018 imposing a temporary cap on unit prices for all SVTs. This became effective from January 2019 and covered 11 million households. The initial cap was set at £1137 for an average household paying dual fuel bills by direct debit. However, energy bills can be greater than this level if a household consumes more than the average amount of energy as the cap is set per unit of energy. Ofgem reviews the size of the cap every six months to reflect any changes in the underlying cost of supplying energy.

It will be interesting to see how competition and regulation in the electricity industry continue to evolve over the next few years. One development has been the declining market share of the Big Six (now the Big Five with the merger of E.ON and npower in 2019) – down to 72 per cent in 2020 from 91 per cent in 2015 and almost 100 per cent in 2010.

1. ***Wholesale and retail energy markets are expected to deliver on a number of targets including competitive pricing, environmental objectives and equity. Explain why this may present problems.***
2. ***Why do you think switching rates have been so low in the retail energy market?***
3. ***Assess some of the arguments for and against the use of price caps for all customers on SVTs.***

Investigate how the wholesale market for electricity has changed in recent years and whether these changes have benefited end consumers – households and businesses.

1 Ofgem defines liquidity as the ability to buy or sell a desired commodity or financial instrument quickly without causing a significant change in its price and without incurring significant transaction costs. An important feature of a liquid market, it says, is that it has a large number of buyers and sellers willing to transact at all times. A high level of liquidity is seen as being good because it enables new players to enter the market and reduces the ability of incumbents to manipulate it (*Utility Week*, 3 September 2009).

2 'Energy supply probe', *Market Review and Reform*, Ofgem (2009), https://www.ofgem.gov.uk/publications/energy-supply-probe-proposed-retail-market-remedies

3 'Retail market review', *Market Review and Reform*, Ofgem (2010), https://www.ofgem.gov.uk/energy-policy-and-regulation/policy-and-regulatory-programmes/retail-market-review

4 'Energy market investigation: overview', CMA (24 June 2016), www.gov.uk/cma-cases/energy-market-investigation

- Both the RPI minus X and the RIIO formulae provide incentives for privatised firms to be as efficient as possible. If they can lower their costs, then, in theory, they should, make larger profits that they can retain. If, on the other hand, they do not succeed in reducing costs sufficiently, they will make a loss. (In other countries where profits rather than prices are regulated, there is little incentive to increase efficiency, since any cost reductions must be passed on to the consumer in lower prices, and do not, therefore, result in higher profits.)

There were, however, some inherent problems with the RPI−X system that were identified in the RPI-X@20 review:

- It motivated organisations to reduce their costs but did not provide strong enough incentives for them to deliver a high-quality service to their customers.
- Where some aspects of the quality of service were taken into account, they were different from those most highly valued by the network's customers.
- There was a tendency to focus on reforming certain parts of the regulatory structure rather than thinking about the impact of the framework as a whole.
- It often underestimated the scope for cost reductions, so enabling firms to make excessive profits. For example, Ofgem reported that during the final period of RPI - X regulation, all the gas distribution and network companies made greater than expected profits.
- The five-year duration of each price regulation was too short and deterred long-run investment. Indeed, not enough attention was given to longer-run and more dynamic elements of competition such as innovation.

In response to these limitations, Ofgem decided that the terms of the new RIIO system would apply for eight (not five years). What is more, the new approach tries to incentivise the network companies to deliver more clearly defined outputs. Their ability to raise prices is conditional on their performance in the following areas – levels of customer satisfaction, reliability, the conditions for connection, the environmental impact, social obligations and safety. One challenge for the regulator, however, is to find effective performance measures for each of these different attributes of the network companies' output.

Some more general problems with regulation include:

- A tendency for the whole process to become increasingly complex. This makes it difficult for the firms to plan and may lead to a growth of 'short-termism' as firms are subjected to short-term changes in regulation or government intervention. It is also likely to result in resources being wasted as the industry spends time and energy trying to outwit the regulator. 
- There is the danger of ***regulatory capture***. As regulators become more and more involved in their industry and get to know the senior managers at a personal level, so they are increasingly likely to see the managers' point of view and will thus become less objective. KI 24 p259

Definition

Regulatory capture Where the regulator is persuaded to operate in the industry's interests rather than those of the consumer.

- The regulators could, instead, be 'captured' by the government. Rather than being totally independent, there to serve the interests of the consumer, they might bend to pressures from the government to do things that might help the government win the next election or serve the interests of friends of the governing party.

One alternative to ineffective or over-intrusive regulation is to replace it with competition wherever this is possible. Indeed, one of the major concerns of the regulators has been to do just this. (See Box 14.4 for ways in which competition has been increased in the electricity industry.)

Increasing competition in the privatised industries

Where natural monopoly exists, competition is not desirable in a free market. The industry could be broken up by the government, with firms prohibited from owning more than a certain percentage of the industry. However, this would lead to higher costs of production with firms operating at a higher point on their long-run average cost curve. In such cases, therefore, regulation is an appropriate way of curbing excessive profits.

But many parts of the privatised industries are not natural monopolies. In such cases, competition can be an appropriate way of keeping prices down. For example, in the UK, competition was introduced into the retail market for gas and electricity in the late 1990s. In January 2021, there were 55 active energy suppliers. These businesses purchase gas and electricity from companies that produce energy (e.g. power stations that generate electricity) and/or import energy (e.g. natural gas transported through pipelines connecting the UK with mainland Europe).

The energy purchased by the suppliers needs to be transported to the final customer through the transmission and distribution network. The huge infrastructure costs of building and maintaining these networks makes them natural monopolies. The same is true for the infrastructure of the water industry and the network of rail track. As competition is not feasible in these parts of the market, the monopoly suppliers are subject to price regulation as discussed in the previous section.

In some parts of the industry where there is a natural monopoly, some attempts have been made to introduce the threat of potential competition by creating contestable monopolies. One way of doing this is by granting operators a licence for a specific length of time. This is known as ***franchising*** and the approach has been used for the railways (see Case Study 14.8 on the student website). Once a company has been granted a franchise, it has the monopoly of passenger rail services over specific routes. But the awarding of the franchise can be highly competitive, with rival companies putting in competitive bids, in terms of both price (or, in the case of many of the train operating companies, the level of government subsidy required) and the quality of service.

As competition was introduced into the retail market of many of the privatised industries, the system of price regulation in those sectors was gradually eliminated. For example, in 2002 Ofgem removed all price controls on energy suppliers, with its chief executive stating that, 'The evidence is overwhelming that competition is effective across all social groups and all methods of payment.' However, 16 years later price controls were re-introduced. See Box 14.4 for more detail.

> **Definition**
>
> **Franchising** Where a firm is granted the licence to operate a given part of an industry for a specified length of time.

Section summary

1. From around 1983 the Conservative government in the UK embarked on a large programme of privatisation. Many other countries have followed suit.
2. The economic arguments for privatisation include: greater competition, not only in the goods market but in the market for finance and for corporate control; reduced government interference; and raising revenue to finance tax cuts.
3. The economic arguments against privatisation of utilities include the following: the firms are likely to have monopoly power because their grids are natural monopolies; it makes overall planning and co-ordination of the transport and power sectors more difficult; and the industries produce substantial externalities and raise questions of fairness in distribution.
4. Regulators could require firms to charge the socially efficient price. In the first-best world, this will be where price equals marginal social cost. In the real world, this is not the case given that prices elsewhere are not equal to marginal social costs. Ideally, prices should still *reflect* marginal social costs, but there are difficulties in identifying and measuring social costs.
5. In the long run, the optimum price and output will be where price equals long-run marginal social cost. If $LRMSC < MSC$, it will be desirable to invest in additional capacity.
6. Regulation in the UK has involved setting up regulatory offices for the major privatised utilities. These use negotiation and bargaining to persuade the industries to behave in the public interest and set the terms under which firms can operate (e.g. access rights to the respective grid).
7. As far as prices are concerned, the industries have generally been required to abide by an '*RPI* minus *X*' formula, or some variant of it, in all sectors where there is a lack of competition. This means that potential cost

(continued)

reductions are passed on to the consumer while allowing them to retain any additional profits gained from cost reductions greater than *X*. This has provided them with an incentive to achieve even greater increases in efficiency, but may not have incentivised innovation.

8. Many parts of the privatised industries are not natural monopolies. In these parts, competition has been seen as a more effective means of pursuing the public interest. Various attempts have been made to make the privatised industries more competitive, often at the instigation of the regulator. Nevertheless, considerable market power remains in the hands of many privatised firms, and thus regulators need to be able to retain the ability to prevent the abuse of monopoly power.

END OF CHAPTER QUESTIONS

1. Should governments or regulators always attempt to eliminate the supernormal profits of monopolists/oligopolists?
2. Compare the relative merits of banning certain types of market *structure* with banning certain types of market *behaviour*.
3. Consider the argument that whether an industry is in the public sector or private sector has far less bearing on its performance than the degree of competition it faces.
4. If two or more firms are charging similar prices, does this imply that collusion is taking place? What evidence would you need to determine the existence of collusion?
5. There exists a view that the UK is too small an economy to benefit from competition in many industries, with firms failing to reach minimum efficient scale. What does this imply for competition policy?
6. Should regulators of utilities that have been privatised into several separate companies allow (a) horizontal mergers (within the industry); (b) vertical mergers; (c) mergers with firms in other industries?
7. Summarise the relative benefits to consumers of (a) privatising a nationalised industry, (b) keeping it in the public sector but introducing competition.
8. If an industry regulator adopts an $RPI - X$ formula for price regulation, is it desirable that the value of X should be adjusted as soon as cost conditions change?
9. Examine the case for public ownership of an industry where a natural monopoly exists.
10. If price regulation results in lower profits, will this always imply lower investment? How might a government incentivise innovation in a regulated industry?
11. Price-cap regulation was abandoned in the gas and electricity industries because the regulator (Ofgem) felt that there was sufficient competition. Consider whether this was a wise decision.

Online resources

Additional case studies on the student website

14.1 **Cartels set in concrete, steel and cardboard.** This examines some of the best-known Europe-wide cartels of recent years.
14.2 **Taking your vitamins – at a price.** An examination of a global vitamins cartel and the action taken against it by the EU.
14.3 **A lift to profits?** The EC imposes a record fine on four companies operating a lift and escalator cartel.
14.4 **Misleading advertising.** Do firms intentionally mislead consumers and, if so, what can government do?
14.5 **Payday loans.** This case examines the rise of payday loans and looks at attempts to control their harsh terms and sky-high interest rates in order to protect the poor and vulnerable.
14.6 **Price-cap regulation in the UK.** How $RPI - X$ regulation has been applied to the various privatised industries.
14.7 **Regulation US-style.** This examines rate-of-return regulation: an alternative to price-cap regulation.
14.8 **The right track to reform?** How successful has rail privatisation been in the UK?
14.9 **Privatisation in transition economies.** This extended case study examines state ownership under former communist countries of the USSR and how the transition of these countries to market economies involved a process of privatisation.
14.10 **Forms of privatisation in transition countries.** This focuses on how different types of privatisation are likely to affect the way industries are run.

Websites relevant to Chapters 12–14

Numbers and sections refer to websites listed in the Web Appendix and hotlinked from this book's website at **go.pearson.com/uk/sloman**.

- For news articles relevant to this and the previous chapter, see the *Economics News* section on the student website.
- For general news on market failures and government intervention, see websites in section A, and particularly A1–12, 18, 19, 21, 24, 26, 31, 35. See also links to newspapers worldwide in A38, 39, 43 and 44; and see A40 and 41 for links to economics news articles from newspapers worldwide.

- UK and EU departments relevant to competition policy can be found at sites E4 and 10; G7, 8.
- UK regulatory bodies can be found at sites E4, 11, 15, 16, 18, 19, 22, 29.
- For information on taxes and subsidies, see E25, 30, 36; G13. For use of green taxes (Box 13.2), see E2, 14, 30; G11; H5.
- For information on health and the economics of health care (Box 12.3), see E8; H8. See also discussions in I11.
- For sites favouring the free market, see C17; E34. See also C18 for the development of ideas on the market and government intervention.
- For policy on the environment and transport, see E2, 7,11, 14, 21, 29; G10, 11, 19. See also H11.
- For student resources relevant to these three chapters, see sites C1–10, 19.

Foundations of Macroeconomics

Why do economies sometimes grow rapidly, while at other times they suffer from recession? Why, if people want to work, do they sometimes find themselves unemployed? Why do economies experience inflation (rising prices), and does it matter if they do? Why do exchange rates change and what will be the impact of such changes on imports and exports? Why do individuals, firms and governments borrow and what are the implications of borrowing and debt for the economic health of countries? These macroeconomic issues affect all countries, and economists are called on to try to find explanations and solutions.

In the next two chapters we will be looking at these issues and giving you a preliminary insight into the causes of these problems and what governments can do to tackle them. In the second of these chapters (Chapter 16) we shall see how macroeconomics has developed over the years as economists have sought to explain the macroeconomic problems of the time – right up to the financial crisis and recession of 2007–10 and the macroeconomic effects of the COVID-19 pandemic and the response of governments to it.

An Introduction to Macroeconomic Issues and Ideas

CHAPTER MAP

We turn now to macroeconomics. This will be the subject of the second half of this book. As we have already seen, microeconomics focuses on individual markets. It studies the demand for and supply of, for example, oranges, music downloads, petrol and haircuts; bricklayers, doctors, office accommodation and computers. It examines the choices people make between goods, and what determines their relative prices and the relative quantities produced.

In macroeconomics we take a much broader view. We examine the economy as a whole. We still examine demand and supply, but now it is the total level of spending in the economy and the total level of production. In other words, we examine aggregate demand and aggregate supply.

We still examine output, employment and prices, but now it is national output and its rate of growth, national employment and unemployment, and the general level of prices and their rate of increase (i.e. the rate of inflation).

In this chapter, we identify the major macroeconomic issues facing society. Among these is the volatility of the economy. This volatility is perhaps most evident in the fluctuations we see in the economy's output, but we observe it too in other macroeconomic variables, such as unemployment and inflation.

By providing an overview of macroeconomics, this chapter provides the platform necessary to analyse in subsequent chapters some of the key debates of our time.

15.1 AN OVERVIEW OF KEY MACROECONOMIC ISSUES

Macroeconomics examines various issues affecting whole economies. Many of these are the big issues on which elections are won or lost.

Is the economy growing and, if so, how rapidly? How can we avoid, or get out of, recessions? What causes unemployment and how can the rate be got down? Why is inflation sometimes a problem and what can be done to keep rates of inflation at modest levels? Conversely, why do prices sometimes fall, and does this itself create a problem? What will happen to interest rates? How big a problem is government debt? Are financial institutions lending too much or too little? What affects a country's balance of trade in goods and services? How attractive is the country as a destination for investment by foreign businesses?

Major macroeconomic issues

The questions we have just identified give you a flavour of the macroeconomic issues that we will be studying in the following chapters. For simplicity, we will group them under the following headings: economic growth, unemployment, inflation, economic relationships with the rest of the world, the financial well-being of individuals, businesses and government and the relationship between the financial system and the economy. While we will be studying other issues too, such as consumer behaviour and taxation, these still link to these major macroeconomic issues and, more generally, to how economies function.

The purpose of this section is to provide you with some background on these key issues and to look at some key macroeconomic data. This allows us to put these issues into context before later considering them in more depth.

Economic growth and the business cycle

One of the most basic concerns for macroeconomists is understanding what affects the level of an economy's output and, in turn, what causes it to rise or fall. *Economic growth* is the term economists use to describe the change in the level of an economy's output from period to period. The rate of economic growth measures the percentage change in output. This is usually measured over short periods, such as 12 or 3 months. If we measure the ***rate of growth*** over a 12-month period we are measuring the economy's annual rate of growth, while if we measure it over a 3-month period we are measuring the quarterly rate of growth.

One of the most important observations to make about economic growth is its *volatility*. This is evident from Figure 15.1, which plots the annual rates of growth of a selection of economies. 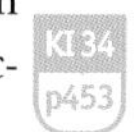

KI34 p453

KEY IDEA 34

Economies suffer from inherent instability. **As a result, economic growth and other macroeconomic indicators tend to fluctuate.**

Definition

Rate of economic growth The percentage increase in national output, normally expressed over a 12-month or 3-month period.

Figure 15.1 Growth rates in selected developed economies

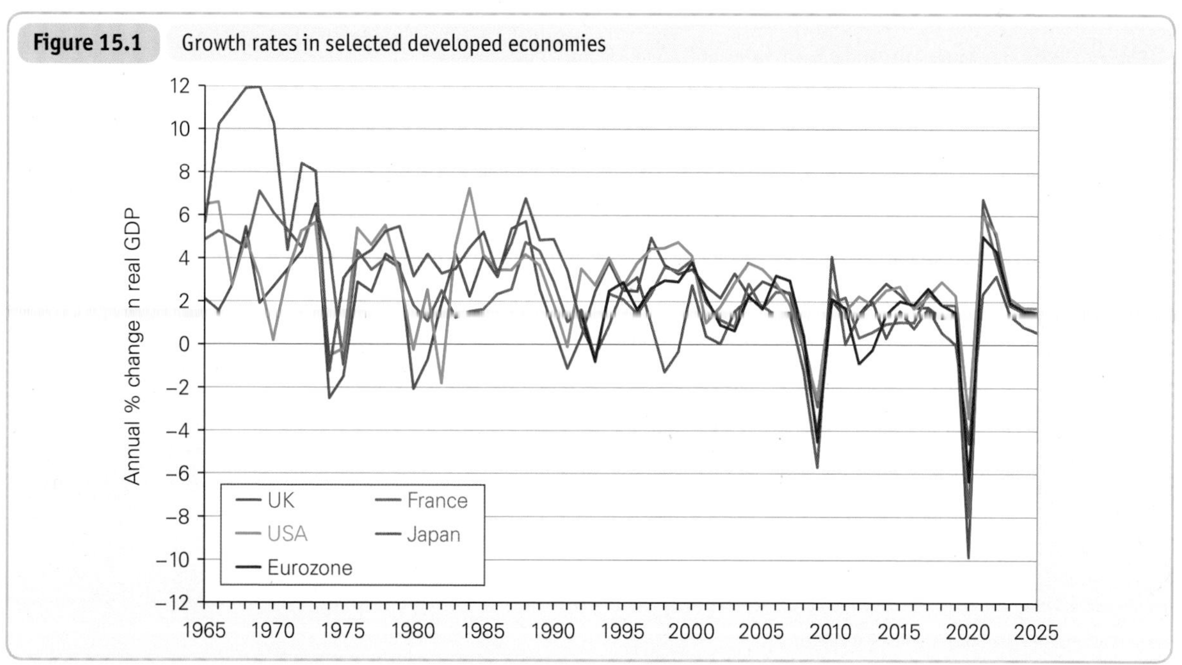

Notes: Data from 2021 based on forecasts; Eurozone = 19 countries using the euro (as of 2021).
Source: Based on data in data in *AMECO Database*, European Commission, https://ec.europa.eu/info/business-economy-euro/indicators-statistics/economic-databases/macro-economic-database-ameco/ameco-database_en; and *World Economic Outlook*, IMF (October 2021), www.imf.org/en/Publications/SPROLLS/world-economic-outlook-databases

Countries rarely experience stable economic growth; instead, growth rates tend to fluctuate. Understanding the volatility of economic growth and its effects is the focus of much analysis by macroeconomists. After all, fluctuating activity levels are likely to affect the behaviour and well-being of many of us.

Sometimes these effects are extraordinarily large. In recent years, the world has experienced two 'once-in-a-lifetime' shocks: the financial crisis and the COVID-19 pandemic. These events help to show the importance of the economy to everyday lives and the impact that economic volatility, even when less extreme, can have.

TC 12 p455 The significance of the volatility of short-term economic growth makes it our next threshold concept. It is the volatility of growth that gives rise to the well-known phenomenon of the ***business cycle***. The business cycle refers to the fluctuations we observe in the path traced out from period to period in an economy's output level. Because rates of economic growth affect an economy's output path, the more growth rates vary, the more marked are the fluctuations in this path.

To illustrate the effect of fluctuating growth rates on an economy's output path, consider Figure 15.2. This shows the volume of output and the annual rate of economic growth in three advanced economies, France, the UK and the USA, since 1990.

The fluctuating nature of economic growth is most starkly illustrated in the late 2000s and again in the early 2020s. For example, in 2009 the volume of output shrank by 2.5 per cent in the USA and 2.9 per cent in France compared with the year before and by 4.2 per cent in the UK. Compare this, for example, with growth rates in the period 1998–2000, when output rose by over 3 per cent per year in all three countries.

The key point here is that if the rate of growth from year to year were constant, then the bars would be the same height and the output level lines would be smoothly upward sloping.[1] Clearly, this is not the case and it is the fluctuations in short-term growth rates, including periods when economic growth is very weak or even negative, that gives rise to the business cycle. In other words, economies experience neither constant growth nor continued expansion.

We will refer frequently to the volatility of economies in this second half of the book. But, given its central importance to much of the subsequent analysis, we will provide an overview of economists' thinking on this important issue in section 15.3.

Definition

Business cycle or trade cycle The periodic fluctuations of national output. Periods of rapid growth are followed by periods of low growth or even decline in national output.

1 With the index plotted on the vertical axis, a constant growth rate would be shown by a line whose slope gradually increased, as a constant percentage increase would give a steeper line, the higher the index. For example, a 5 per cent annual growth rate from an index of 100 in year 1, would give an index of 105 in year 2, whereas a 5 per cent annual growth rate from an index of 200 in, say, year 10 would give an index of 210 in year 11. Thus the slope between years 10 to 11 would be twice that between years 1 and 2 and yet the growth rate would be identical. If the vertical axis were measured in a *log scale*, then a constant growth rate would be shown as a straight line.

Figure 15.2 Output paths and growth rates of France, UK and USA

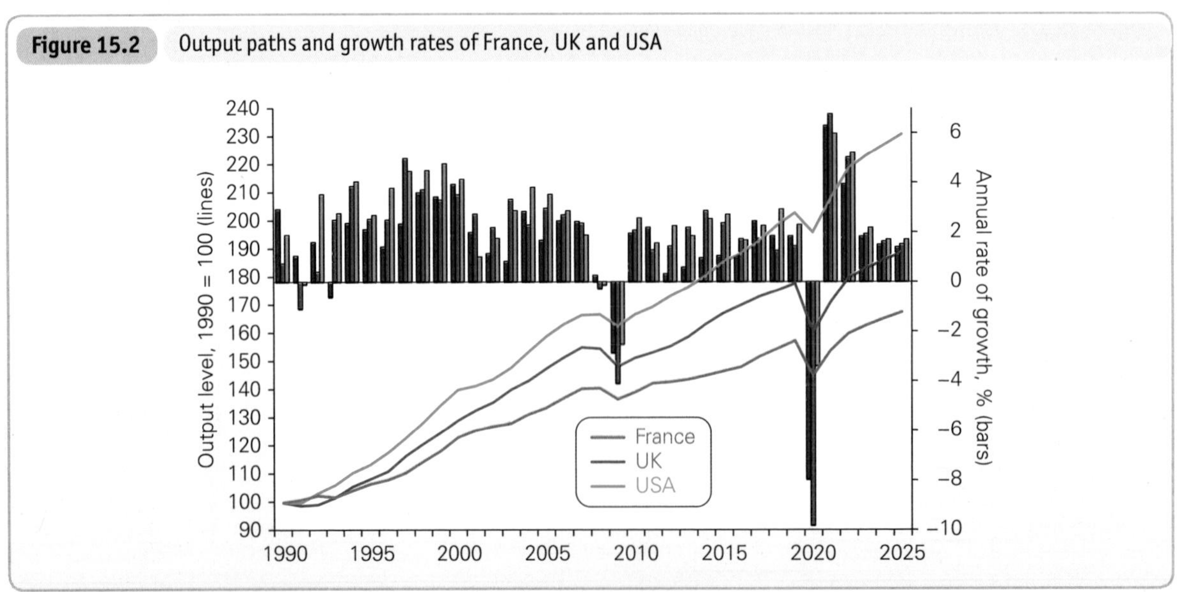

Note: Data for 2020 onwards are based on forecasts.
Source: Based on data in *World Economic Outlook*, IMF (October 2021), www.imf.org/en/Publications/SPROLLS/world-economic-outlook-databases

THRESHOLD CONCEPT 12

SHORT-TERM GROWTH IN A COUNTRY'S OUTPUT TENDS TO FLUCTUATE

THINKING LIKE AN ECONOMIST

Countries rarely experience stable economic growth. Instead they experience *business cycles*. Periods of rapid economic growth can be followed by periods of low growth or even negative growth (falling output).

Explaining volatility

Sometimes volatility can arise from extreme events, as was the case with the COVID-19 pandemic. On other occasions, rising or falling output can be explained by the deliberate actions of governments or central banks (such as the Bank of England). For example, a rise in government spending, a reduction in taxes or a reduction in interest rates may stimulate the economy and raise the rate of economic growth.

But fluctuations in economic growth can often be explained by the working of the market system.

Some economists see the problem as rooted in fluctuations in *aggregate demand*: in other words, in the total demand for the economy's goods and services, whether by individuals or firms (see page 470). What is more, changes in the demands of individuals and firms may interact with each other, affecting the character of the business cycle. For example, a rise in consumer expenditure could stimulate firms to invest in order to build up capacity to meet the extra demand. This, in turn, generates more employment, additional national income and so more consumption. A similar effect could occur if banks felt able to lend more in response to the growing economy, which would further stimulate the economy as these funds are spent.

Other economists see the problem as rooted in fluctuations in *aggregate supply*: in other words, in the total amount of goods and services firms plan to supply at a given level of prices (see page 471). These 'real-business-cycle' economists argue that changes in aggregate supply occur if the price, availability or effectiveness of the inputs in firms' production processes are in some way affected. One example could be technological changes that boost output and employment. Often such changes come in waves, which would contribute to the observed volatility of output.

But whatever the cause, it is vital to recognise the fundamental instability of market economies. This is what makes the volatility in short-term growth rates a threshold concept.

1. *If people believe that the economy's output level is about to fall, how may their actions aggravate the problem?*
2. *Why will some people suffer more than others from a downturn in economic activity?*

Longer-term economic growth

Although growth rates fluctuate, most economies experience positive growth over the longer term. In other words, most economies have output paths that trend upwards over time. We can see this in Figure 15.2, for example. Therefore, we need to distinguish between short-run and long-run economic growth.

While an analysis of short-run growth involves understanding the determinants of the business cycle, analysing long-run economic growth involves understanding what affects a country's capacity to produce. This is because, for growth to be sustained over the longer term, the economy's capacity must increase.

Table 15.1 shows the average annual growth in output by decade since the 1960s for selected countries. As you can see, the differences between countries are quite marked. There are also big differences between the growth rates of individual countries in different periods. Look, for example, at the figures for Japan. From being an 'economic miracle' in the 1960s, by the 1990s Japan had become a laggard, with growth rates well below the OECD average.

The final column of the table takes an even longer-term perspective by focusing on the average annual rate of economic growth from 1960 to 2022. We still observe differences in growth rates, even when averaged over many years.

Table 15.1 Economic growth rates (average % per annum)

	1960s	1970s	1980s	1990s	2000s	2010s	1960–2022
Ireland	4.4	4.7	3.1	6.9	3.7	6.3	4.7
Japan	10.1	5.2	4.4	1.6	0.5	1.3	3.5
Australia	5.4	3.0	3.4	3.3	3.0	2.5	3.3
Spain	7.7	3.9	2.7	2.7	2.6	1.1	3.2
Canada	5.4	4.1	2.9	2.4	2.1	2.2	3.0
USA	4.7	3.2	3.1	3.2	1.9	2.3	2.9
France	5.7	4.1	2.4	2.0	1.5	1.4	2.6
Germany	4.4	3.3	2.0	2.2	0.8	1.9	2.3
Italy	6.5	3.8	2.3	1.5	0.5	0.3	2.2
UK	3.1	2.6	2.7	2.3	1.8	1.8	2.2
OECD[a]	5.4	3.8	3.0	2.7	1.8	2.1	3.0

[a] The Organisation for Economic Co-operation and Development (OECD) is an organisation of 38 major industrialised countries (as of May 2021).
Note: Figures from 2020 are forecasts.
Sources: *AMECO database*, European Commission, DGECFIN; and OECD data, OECD.

While some of the differences may not appear particularly large, it is important to bear in mind is that even small differences in the figures have potentially significant implications for economic development and the well-being of nations when you consider that these differences are being compounded year after year.

How have growth rates varied over the decades? Does the answer vary by country?

Unemployment

The inherent instability of economies has implications for the number of people in work and so for the number unable to find work. Higher levels of economic activity will tend to decrease unemployment numbers; reduced economic activity will tend to increase them.

In addition, many countries have seen significant effects on the labour market of rapid industrial change, technological advance and globalisation. Hence, labour markets need to be able to adapt to the dynamic environment in which they operate, not only for the sake of those who are made unemployed, but also because it represents a waste of human resources and because unemployment benefits are a drain on
KI 1 p0 government revenues.

Unemployment can be expressed either as a number (e.g. 1.5 million) or as a percentage (e.g. 5 per cent). The most usual definition that economists use for the ***number unemployed*** is: *those of working age who are without work, but who are available for work at current wage rates*. If the figure is to be expressed as a percentage, then it is a percentage of the total ***labour force***. The labour force is defined as *those in employment plus those unemployed*. Thus if 30 million people were employed and 2 million people were unemployed, the ***unemployment rate*** would be:

$$\frac{2}{30 + 2} \times 100 = 6.25\%$$

When comparing unemployment across countries it is sensible to compare *rates* of unemployment. Table 15.2 shows average unemployment rates across a sample of countries since the 1960s. It shows how in the 1980s and early 1990s unemployment rates were significantly higher than in the 1960s and 1970s. Then, in the late 1990s and early 2000s, it fell in some countries, such as the UK and USA. In others, such as Germany and France, it remained stubbornly high. The global financial crisis of the late 2000s caused unemployment rates to rise. They then eased, before rising significantly in response to the COVID-19 pandemic.

We take a preliminary look at the nature and causes of unemployment in section 15.5.

Have unemployment rates generally risen or fallen over the decades or is there no discernible pattern? Does the answer vary by country?

Inflation

By inflation we mean a general rise in prices throughout the economy. Government policy here is to keep inflation both low and stable. One of the most important reasons for this is that it will aid the process of economic decision making. For example, businesses will be able to set prices and wage rates, and make investment decisions with far more confidence.

The ***rate of inflation*** measures the annual percentage increase in prices. Typically, when we hear about inflation

Definitions

Number unemployed (economist's definition) Those of working age who are without work, but who are available for work at current wage rates.

Labour force The number employed plus the number unemployed.

Unemployment rate The number unemployed expressed as a percentage of the labour force.

Rate of inflation The percentage increase in prices over a 12-month period.

Table 15.2 Average unemployment rates (%)

	1960s	1970s	1980s	1990s	2000s	2010s	1960–2022
Japan	1.3	1.7	2.5	3.1	4.7	3.6	2.8
Germany	0.6	2.0	5.8	7.8	9.1	4.7	5.0
UK	1.6	3.5	9.5	8.2	5.4	6.0	5.8
USA	4.7	6.2	7.3	5.8	5.5	6.2	6.0
Australia	2.4	5.0	9.4	9.5	7.0	6.8	6.8
France	1.7	4.4	8.6	9.7	8.4	9.6	7.3
Canada	4.8	6.7	9.4	9.5	7.0	6.9	7.5
Italy	4.7	5.9	8.4	10.5	8.1	10.8	8.3
Ireland	5.3	7.5	14.2	12.1	5.7	10.7	9.2
Spain	2.5	4.5	16.4	19.5	11.4	20.5	12.9
OECD[a]	3.2	4.2	6.7	6.8	6.8	7.0	5.8

[a] The Organisation for Economic Co-operation and Development (OECD) is an organisation of 38 major industrialised countries (as of May 2021).
Note: Figures from 2020 are forecasts.
Sources: *AMECO database*, European Commission, DGECFIN; and OECD data, OECD.

it is in relation to *consumer* prices. The UK government publishes a consumer prices index (CPI) each month, and the rate of inflation is the percentage increase in that index over the previous 12 months. This index is used throughout the EU, where it generally goes under its full title of the harmonised index of consumer prices (HICP). The HICP covers virtually 100 per cent of consumer spending (including cross-border spending) and uses sophisticated weights for each item (see Appendix 1, page A:7 for an analysis of weighting in indices).

KI 40 pA:6

In most developed countries, governments now have a target for the rate of consumer price inflation. This is frequently around 2 per cent, as is the case in the UK, USA and eurozone. Central banks, such as the Bank of England, the US Federal Reserve Bank (the Fed) and the European Central Bank, then adjust interest rates to try to keep inflation on target (we see how this works in Chapter 22). The advent of inflation-rate targeting has tended to narrow differences in inflation rates between countries, as have the increasing economic ties between countries.

Table 15.3 shows that in the 1970s and 1980s average price inflation in many developed countries was in double figures. In the UK, it reached 24 per cent in 1975.

Today inflation rates are significantly lower, typically between 0 and 3 per cent, and some countries have experienced periods of negative inflation rates or what is sometimes called 'deflation'.

We will take a preliminary look at the factors affecting rates of inflation in section 15.6.

Would it matter if all prices rose by 20 per cent, but everyone's income also rose by 20 per cent? (We consider this issue in section 15.6.)

Foreign trade and global economic relationships

A county's macroeconomic environment is shaped not only by domestic conditions but also by its economic relationships with other countries. These relationships evolve as the global economy develops and the world order changes. Take, for example, the rapid economic growth observed over the past couple of decades or more in newly industrialised economies like China and India.

International economic relationships also evolve as countries or groups of countries come together to shape their economic relationships with other economies. With the EU–UK Trade and Cooperation Agreement, which took effect on 31 December 2020, a new set of economic relationships between the UK, the EU 27 and other foreign partners was to develop.

One way of viewing the economic relationship between a country and other economies is through its ***balance of payments account***. This records all transactions between the residents of that country and the rest of the world. These transactions enter as either debit items or credit items. The debit items include all payments *to* other countries: these include the country's purchases of imports, the investments it makes abroad and the interest and dividends paid to people abroad who have invested in the country. The credit items include all receipts *from* other countries: these include the sales of exports, inflows of investment into the country and earnings of interest and dividends from abroad.

Definition

Balance of payments account A record of the country's transactions with the rest of the world. It shows the country's payments to or deposits in other countries (debits) and its receipts or deposits from other countries (credits). It also shows the balance between these debits and credits under various headings.

Table 15.3 Average consumer price inflation rates (%)

	1960s	1970s	1980s	1990s	2000s	2010s	1960–2022
Germany	2.5	4.9	2.9	2.5	1.6	1.3	2.5
Japan	5.5	9.1	2.5	1.2	−0.3	0.5	2.9
USA	2.4	7.1	5.6	3.0	2.6	1.8	3.6
Canada	2.7	7.4	6.5	2.2	2.1	1.7	3.7
France	4.0	8.8	7.4	1.9	1.7	1.1	4.0
Australia	2.3	9.8	8.4	2.5	3.2	2.1	4.6
UK	3.8	12.6	7.2	3.6	1.9	2.1	5.1
Ireland	4.4	12.8	9.3	2.3	3.2	0.6	5.2
Italy	3.8	12.4	11.2	4.2	2.3	1.2	5.6
Spain	6.1	14.4	10.3	4.2	3.0	1.2	6.2
OECD[a]		8.6	11.2	6.2	2.6	1.9	

[a] The Organisation for Economic Co-operation and Development (OECD) is an organisation of 38 major industrialised countries (as of May 2021).
Note: Figures from 2020 are forecasts; OECD average inflation rate since 1970 is 5.9 per cent.
Sources: *AMECO database*, European Commission, DGECFIN; and OECD data, OECD.

The sale of exports and any other receipts earn foreign currency. The purchase of imports or any other payments abroad require foreign currency. If a country starts to spend more foreign currency than it earns, then its balance of payments will go into deficit. If the government does nothing to correct the balance of payments deficit, the ***exchange rate*** of the country's currency must fall. The exchange rate is the rate at which one currency exchanges for another. For example, the exchange rate of the pound into the dollar might be £1 = $1.40.

A falling exchange rate (e.g. from $1.40 to $1.20) is a problem because it pushes up the price of imports and so reduces people's purchasing power. It can also fuel inflation. This was the situation facing the UK in the aftermath of the vote to leave the European Union, when the pound fell sharply. Exchange-rate fluctuations can also be problematic because they can cause great uncertainty for traders and can damage international trade and economic growth.

What are the underlying causes of balance of payments problems? How do the balance of payments and the exchange rate relate to the other macroeconomic issues? What are the best policies for governments to adopt? We take an initial look at these questions in section 15.7 and then examine them in more detail in Chapters 25 and 26.

Financial well-being

The financial system is an integral part of most economies. Financial markets, financial institutions and ***financial instruments*** have become increasingly important in determining the financial well-being of nations, organisations, government and people. The increasing importance of the financial system to economies is known as ***financialisation***.

The most immediate evidence of financialisation is the extent to which many of us interact with financial institutions and our use of financial instruments. Financialisation is most frequently associated with the level of indebtedness of ***economic agents***, such as households and firms, to banks. In the UK, for example, by the end of 2020 households had debt outstanding borrowed from banks and building societies in excess of £1.4 trillion.

The importance of financial stability and the problem of financial distress. It is important for policy makers to ensure the stability of the financial system and the general financial well-being of economic agents: i.e. households, firms and government. This importance was most starkly demonstrated by the events surrounding the financial crisis of 2007–9, when many banks looked as if they might become bankrupt. The financial distress of banks and other financial institutions resulted in global economic turmoil. Because of the global interconnectedness of financial institutions and markets, these problems spread globally like a contagion.

And it was not just financial institutions that were distressed in the late 2000s; we also witnessed financially distressed households and businesses, many of which were burdened by unsustainable levels of debt.

Subsequently, the financial distress affected government too, especially in advanced economies. Governments were burdened by growing levels of debt as they spent more to offset rapidly weakening private-sector spending. At the same time, tax revenues fell because of lower or even negative economic growth. The consequence was a prolonged period during which many governments felt it necessary to tighten their budgets – dubbed 'austerity policies'. And this constraint on government spending was a brake on economic growth.

With governments once more forced to support their economies during the COVID-19 pandemic, the issue again arose of whether and how much governments would feel it necessary to tighten spending and/or raise taxes as the pandemic waned.

Financial accounts. In thinking about financial well-being or distress, three key accounts can be considered. These are compiled for the main sectors of the economy: the household, corporate and government sectors, and the whole economy.

First, there is the *income account* which records the various *flows* of income (a credit) alongside the amounts either spent or saved (debits). Economic growth refers to the annual real growth in a country's income flows (i.e. after taking inflation into account).

KI 26 p309

Next, there is the *financial account*. There are two elements here. First, we can record financial *flows*, which determine the net acquisition of financial wealth by each sector. These flows comprise new saving, borrowing or repayments. Reductions in the flows of borrowing, in countries like the UK and USA, were very important in explaining the credit crunch and subsequent deep recession of the late 2000s/early 2010s.

Definitions

Exchange rate The rate at which one national currency exchanges for another. The rate is expressed as the amount of one currency that is necessary to purchase *one unit* of another currency (e.g. e.g. €1.10 = £1).

Financial instruments Tradable financial assets, such as shares ('equities'), bonds, foreign currency and bank account deposits.

Financialisation A term used to describe the process by which financial markets, institutions and instruments becoming increasingly significant in economies.

Economic agents People or institutions making economic decisions. These could be individuals as consumers, workers, borrowers or savers, or firms, governments or other public institutions.

The other element of the financial account is its ***balance sheet***. A balance sheet is a record of *stocks* of ***assets*** and ***liabilities*** of individuals or institutions. An asset is something owned by or owed to you. A liability is a debt: i.e. something you owe to someone else. In the case of the financial account, we have a complete record of the stocks of financial assets (arising from saving) and financial liabilities (arising from borrowing) of a sector, and include things such as currency, bank deposits, loans, bonds and shares. The flows of borrowing during the 2000s meant that many individuals and organisations experienced a significant increase in stocks of financial liabilities.

Finally, there is the *capital account*, which looks at flows and stocks of *physical* assets and liabilities. Again, there are two elements. The first records the capital *flows* of the various sectors, which occur when acquiring or disposing of physical assets, such as property and machinery. The second records the *stock* of physical wealth held by the various sectors.

The national balance sheet. This is a measure of the wealth of a country (i.e. the nation's financial and physical stock of net assets). It shows the *composition* of a country's wealth and the contribution of each of the main *sectors* of the economy.

The balance of a sector's or country's stock of financial and non-financial assets over its financial liabilities is referred to as its ***net worth***. An *increase* in the net worth of the sectors or the whole country implies greater financial well-being. However, during the 2000s many sectors experienced increases in net worth as asset values rose, despite the rising stock of financial liabilities. For example, rising house prices were financed by rising mortgage debt. Subsequently, the increase in the stock of liabilities was not financially sustainable and asset prices fell, causing financial distress for many households and firms as their assets became worth less than their borrowing.

These various accounts are part of an interconnected story detailing the financial well-being of a country's households, companies and government. To illustrate how, consider what would happen if, over a period of time, you were to spend more than the income you receive. This would result in your income account deteriorating. To finance your excess spending you could perhaps draw on any financial wealth that you have accumulated through saving. Alternatively, you might fund some of your spending through a loan from a financial institution, such as a bank. Either way,

Societies face trade-offs between economic objectives. **For example, the goal of faster growth may conflict with that of greater equality; the goal of lower unemployment may conflict with that of lower inflation (at least in the short run). This is an example of opportunity cost: the cost of achieving one objective may be achieving less of another. The existence of trade-offs means that policy makers must make choices.**

Balance sheets affect people's behaviour. **The size and structure of governments', institutions' and individuals' liabilities (and assets too) affect economic well-being and can have significant effects on behaviour and economic activity.**

your financial balance sheet will deteriorate. Or you may dispose of some physical assets, such as property. However your excess spending is financed, your capital balance will deteriorate: your net worth declines.

The importance of balance-sheet effects is now widely recognised since the financial crisis of 2007–9. Understanding these effects and their consequences is crucial in devising the most appropriate macroeconomic policies.

Government macroeconomic policy

From the above issues we can identify a series of macroeconomic policy objectives that governments might typically pursue:

- High and stable economic growth.
- Low unemployment.
- Low rates of inflation.
- The avoidance of balance of payments deficits and excessive exchange rate fluctuations.
- A stable financial system and the avoidance of excessively financially distressed sectors of the economy, including government itself.

Unfortunately, these policy objectives may conflict, which presents government with awkward policy choices. For example, a policy designed to reduce the rate of unemployment may result in a higher rate of inflation, a balance of payments deficit and excessive lending. The possibility of a trade-off between inflation and unemployment was investigated by Bill Phillips whose name is associated with the ***Phillips curve*** (see Box 15.6). The ability of governments to exploit such a trade-off will be a theme we will return to frequently in subsequent chapters.

Definitions

Balance sheet A record of the stock of assets and liabilities of an individual or institution.

Asset Possessions of an individual or institution, or claims held on others.

Liability Claims by others on an individual or institution; debts of that individual or institution.

Net worth A sector's or country's stock of financial and non-financial assets minus its financial liabilities.

Phillips curve A curve showing the relationship between (price) inflation and unemployment. The original Phillips curve plotted wage inflation against unemployment for the years 1861–1957.

Section summary

1. Macroeconomics, like microeconomics, looks at issues such as output, employment and prices; but it looks at them in the context of the whole economy.
2. Economies are inherently volatile, as evidenced by fluctuations in short-term economic growth rates. These fluctuations cause an economy's output path to fluctuate, generating what economists call the business cycle.
3. Among the macroeconomic goals that are generally of most concern to governments are: economic growth, reducing unemployment, reducing inflation, avoiding balance of payments and exchange rate problems, a stable financial system and the avoidance of excessively financially distressed economic agents.
4. Unfortunately, these goals are likely to conflict. Governments may thus be faced with difficult policy choices.

15.2 MEASURING NATIONAL INCOME AND OUTPUT

A constant theme of section 15.1 was the inherent volatility of economies. One of the principal ways in which we observe this is through the volatility of national income or output. But just how do we measure national income or output? The measure we use is called ***gross domestic product (GDP)***.

This section focuses on how GDP is calculated. It also looks at difficulties in interpreting GDP statistics. Can the figures be meaningfully used to compare one country's standard of living with another? The appendix to this chapter goes into more detail on the precise ways in which the statistics for GDP are derived.

The three ways of measuring GDP

GDP can be calculated in three different ways, which should all result in the same figure. These three methods can be understood in the context of the *circular flow of income model*, which we introduced in Chapter 1 (see pages 16–17). This model allows us to trace the resources and, as its name suggests, the income flows that pass between the major groups in the economy.

A simplified version of the model is shown in Figure 15.3. In the diagram, the economy is divided into two major groups: *firms* and *households*. Each group has two roles. Firms are producers of goods and services; they are also the employers of labour and other factors of production. Households (which include all individuals) are the consumers of goods and services; they are also the suppliers of labour and various other factors of production.

Figure 15.3 The circular flow of income

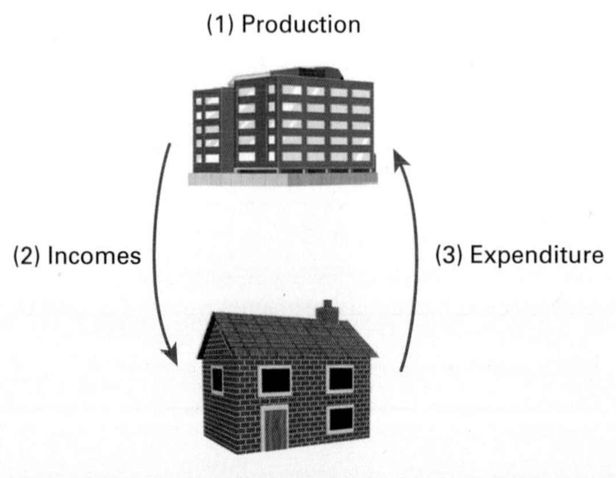

The first method of measuring GDP is to add up the value of all the goods and services produced in the country, industry by industry. In other words, we focus on firms and add up all their production. This first method is known as the *product method*.

The production of goods and services generates incomes for households in the form of wages and salaries, profits, rent and interest. The second method of measuring GDP, therefore, is to add up all these incomes. This is known as the *income method*.

The third method focuses on the expenditures necessary to purchase the nation's production. In this simple model of the circular flow of income, whatever is produced is sold. The value of what is sold must therefore be the value of what is produced. The *expenditure method* measures this sales value.

Because of the way the calculations are made, the three methods of calculating GDP *must* yield the same result. In other words,

national product = national income
= national expenditure

In the appendix to this chapter, we look at each of the three methods in turn, and examine the various factors that have to be taken into account to ensure that the figures are accurate.

Taking account of inflation

If we are to make a sensible comparison of one year's national income with another, we must take inflation into account. For example, if this year national income is 10 per cent higher than last year, but at the same time prices are also 10 per cent higher, then the average person will be no better off at all. There has been no *real* increase in income (see discussion in Appendix 1 at the end of the book on page A:6).

Definition

Gross domestic product (GDP) The value of output produced within the country over a 12-month period.

Figure 15.4 UK GDP since 1960

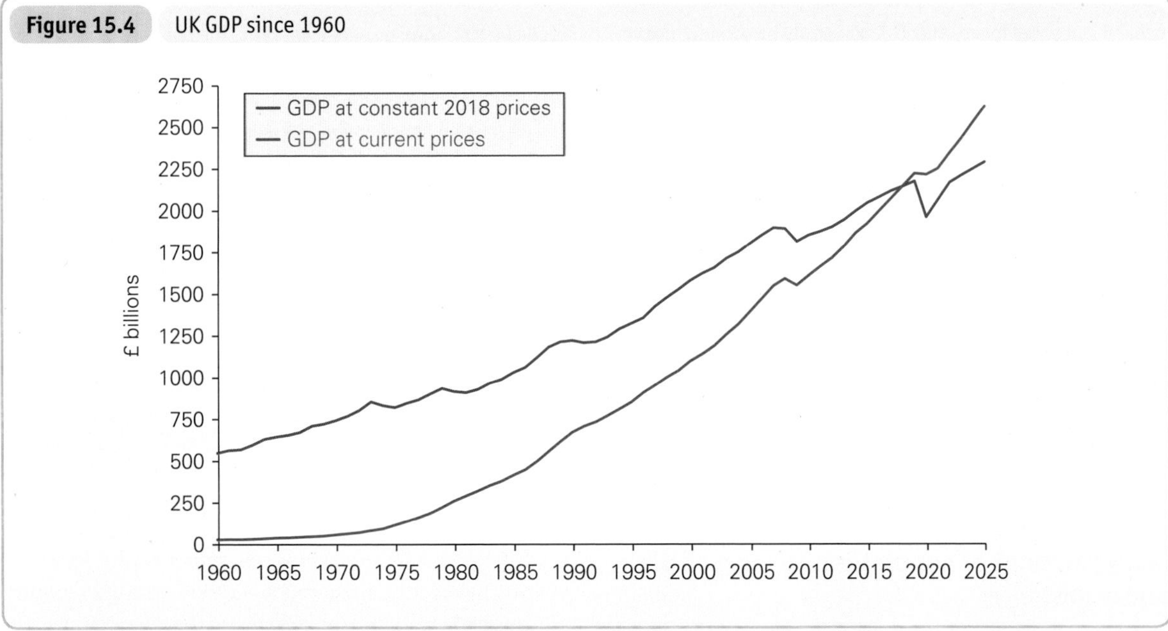

Note: Data from 2021 based on forecasts.
Source: Based on *Time Series Data*, series YBHA and ABMI, Office for National Statistics, www.ons.gov.uk/economy/grossdomesticproductgdp/; and *World Economic Outlook Database*, IMF (April 2021), www.imf.org/en/Publications/SPROLLS/world-economic-outlook-databases

TC 13 p461

An important distinction here is between ***nominal GDP*** and ***real GDP***. *Nominal* (or 'money') GDP, sometimes called 'GDP at current prices', measures GDP in the prices that were ruling and hence current at the time. When comparing nominal GDP from one year to another no account of inflation is taken.

Real GDP, sometimes called 'GDP at constant prices', measures GDP in the prices that ruled in some particular year – the *base year*. Thus we could measure each year's GDP in, say, 2000 prices. This would enable us to see how much *real* GDP had changed from one year to another. In other words, it would eliminate increases in nominal GDP that were due merely to an increase in prices.

The official statistics give both nominal and real figures. (Case Study 15.1 on the student website shows in more detail how real GDP figures are calculated.) Figure 15.4 shows UK GDP at current and constant 2018 prices since 1960. If we had mistakenly used the nominal GDP figures to compare the size of output forecast for 2025 with output in 1960 we would have thought that the economy would be over 90 times larger. In fact, the real figures show the UK economy would be only around 4 times larger.

As well as revealing the extent of long-term economic growth, the real figures also show the *variability* of economic growth from year to year. We can see falls in output in the mid-1970s, early 1980s and early 1990s that are not directly observable from nominal GDP. Instead, nominal GDP continued to increase because of rising price levels. However, in 2009 when output fell by over 4 per cent and then in 2020 when it fell by almost 10 per cent, nominal GDP fell too (by 2.5 and 4.8 per cent respectively). In other words, price rises were not enough to offset a substantial decline in the volume of output.

Definitions

Nominal GDP GDP measured at current prices.

Real GDP GDP after allowing for inflation: i.e. GDP measured in *constant* prices, in other words in terms of the prices ruling in some base year.

THRESHOLD CONCEPT 13 THE DISTINCTION BETWEEN REAL AND NOMINAL VALUES

THINKING LIKE AN ECONOMIST

Which would you rather have: (a) a pay rise of 5 per cent when inflation is 2 per cent, or (b) a pay rise of 10 per cent when inflation is 9 per cent? Which debt would you rather have: (a) one where the interest rate is 10 per cent and inflation is 8 per cent, or (b) one where the interest rate is 5 per cent and the inflation rate is 1 per cent?

To answer these questions, you need to distinguish between real and nominal values. *Nominal values* are measured in current prices and take no account of inflation. Thus in the questions above, the nominal pay rises are (a) 5 per cent and (b) 10 per cent; the nominal interest rates are (a) 10 per cent and (b) 5 per cent. In each case it might seem that you are better off with alternative (b).

(continued)

But if you opted for answers (b), you would be wrong. Once you take inflation into account, you would be better off in each case with alternative (a). What we need to do is to use real values. Real values take account of inflation. Thus in the first question, although the nominal pay rise in alternative (a) is 5 per cent, the real pay rise is only 3 per cent, since 2 of the 5 per cent is absorbed by higher prices. You are only 3 per cent better off in terms of what you can buy. In alternative (b) the real pay rise is only 1 per cent, since 9 of the 10 per cent is absorbed by higher prices. Thus in real terms, alternative (a) is better.

In the second question, although in alternative (a) you are paying 10 per cent in nominal terms, your debt is being reduced in real terms by 8 per cent and thus you are paying a real rate of interest of only 2 per cent. In alternative (b), although the nominal rate of interest is only 5 per cent, your debt is being eroded by inflation by only 1 per cent. The real rate of interest is thus 4 per cent. Again, in real terms, you are better off with alternative (a).

The distinction between real and nominal values is a threshold concept, as understanding the distinction is fundamental to assessing statistics about the economy.

It's easy to make the mistake of using nominal figures when we should really be using real ones. This is known as 'money illusion': the belief that a rise in money terms represents a real rise.

When comparing two countries' GDP growth rates, does it matter if we use nominal figures, provided we use them for both countries?

Taking account of population: the use of per capita measures

The figures we have been looking at up to now are *total* GDP figures. Although they are useful for showing how big the total output or income of one country is compared with another, we are often more interested in output or income *per head*. Luxembourg obviously has a much lower total national income than the UK, but it has a higher GDP per head. In 2009 China overtook Japan to become the second largest economy in the world, and some estimate that it will become the biggest economy during the 2020s. But these are total figures. Despite China's rapid growth, it is estimated that by 2025 GDP per capita in China will still be only around one-fifth of that of the USA.

Other per capita measures are sometimes useful. For example, measuring GDP per head of the *employed* population allows us to compare how much the average worker produces. A country may have a relatively high GDP per head of population, but also have a large proportion of people at work. Its output per worker will therefore not be so high.

By what would we need to divide GDP in order to get a measure of labour productivity per hour?

Taking account of exchange rates: the use of PPP measures

There is a big problem with comparing GDP figures of different countries. They are measured in the local currency and thus have to be converted into a common currency (e.g. dollars or euros) at the current exchange rate. But the exchange rate may be a poor indicator of the purchasing power of the currency at home. For example, £1 may exchange for, say, 140 yen. But will £1 in the UK buy the same amount of goods as ¥140 in Japan? The answer is almost certainly no.

To compensate for this, GDP can be converted into a common currency at a ***purchasing-power parity rate***. This is a rate of exchange that would allow a given amount of money in one country to buy the same amount of goods in another country after exchanging it into the currency of the other country. For example, the OECD publishes PPP rates against the US dollar for all OECD currencies. Using such rates to measure GDP gives the ***purchasing-power standard (PPS) GDP***.

Box 15.1 compares GDP with PPS GDP for various countries.

Do GDP statistics give a good indication of a country's standard of living?

If we take into account both inflation and the size of the population, and use figures for *real* per capita PPS GDP, will this give us a good indication of a country's standard of living? The figures *do* give quite a good indication of the level of production of goods and the incomes generated from it, provided we are clear about the distinctions between the different measures.

But when we come to ask the more general question of whether the figures give a good indication of the welfare or happiness of the country's citizens, then there are serious problems in relying exclusively on GDP statistics.

Problems of measuring national output

The main problem here is that the output of some goods and services goes unrecorded and thus the GDP figures will understate the nation's output. There are two reasons why items are not recorded.

Definitions

Purchasing-power parity (PPP) exchange rate An exchange rate corrected to take into account the purchasing power of a currency. $1 would buy the same in each country after conversion into its currency at the PPP rate.

Purchasing-power standard (PPS) GDP GDP measured at a country's PPP exchange rate.

BOX 15.1 WHICH COUNTRY IS BETTER OFF? CASE STUDIES AND APPLICATIONS

Comparing national income statistics

Using PPS GDP figures can give a quite different picture of the relative incomes in different countries than using simple GDP figures. The table shows the GDP per head and PPS GDP per head in various countries. The figures are expressed as a percentage of the average of the eurozone countries (i.e. the 19 countries using the euro as of 2020).

Thus in 2020, GDP per head in Switzerland was estimated to be 127 per cent higher than the average in the eurozone. But, because of higher Swiss prices, the average person in Switzerland could buy only 55 per cent more goods and services. By contrast, GDP per head in the Czech Republic (Czechia) was only 60 per cent of the eurozone average but, because of lower prices in Czechia, the average person there could buy 89 per cent as much as the average citizen of the eurozone.

Referring to the figures in the table, which countries' actual exchange rates would seem to understate the purchasing power of their currency?

GDP per head as a percentage of the eurozone average, 2020

	GDP per head	GDP (PPS) per head
Poland	41.0	72.6
Greece	47.2	62.0
Portugal	58.8	73.2
Czechia	59.5	88.7
Spain	71.2	81.4
Italy	82.9	88.0
France	102.3	98.1
Japan	104.7	90.5
UK	106.4	95.8
Germany	122.9	117.3
Netherlands	137.3	123.7
Sweden	138.9	118.7
Australia	143.6	117.6
Denmark	158.8	127.3
USA	169.2	137.3
Ireland	215.4	194.1
Switzerland	226.8	154.5
Luxembourg	292.8	250.6

Note: Eurozone = the 19 countries using the euro as of January 2015.
Source: *AMECO database*, Table 6.2, European Commission, DGECFIN.

Using data from the IMF World Economic Outlook Database, download GDP per capita figures for Australia, France, Germany, Japan, the UK and the USA in US dollars both at market and PPP rates. Prepare a short PowerPoint presentation. Begin by explaining the concept of Purchasing Power Parity. Next, plot two line charts: one showing relative living standards (GDP per capital) in Australia, France, Germany, Japan and the USA compared to the UK at market exchange rates and the other at PPP exchange rates. Finally, summarise the key findings of your charts.

Non-marketed items. If you employ a decorator to paint your living room, this will be recorded in the GDP statistics. If, however, you paint the room yourself, it will not. Similarly, if a nanny is employed by parents to look after their children, this childcare will form part of GDP. If, however, a parent stays at home to look after the children, it will not. The exclusion of these 'do it yourself' and other home based activities means that the GDP statistics understate the true level of production in the economy.

If over time there is an *increase* in the amount of do-it-yourself activities that people perform, the figures will also understate the *rate of growth* of national output. On the other hand, if in more and more families both partners go out to work and employ people to look after their children, this will overstate the rate of growth in output. The childcare that was previously unrecorded now enters into the GDP statistics.

If we were trying to get a 'true' measure of national production, which of the following activities would you include: (a) washing-up; (b) planting flowers in the garden; (c) playing an educational game with children in the family; (d) playing any game with children in the family; (e) cooking your own supper; (f) cooking supper for the whole family; (g) reading a novel for pleasure; (h) reading a textbook as part of studying; (i) studying holiday brochures? Is there a measurement problem if you get pleasure from the do-it-yourself activity itself as well as from its outcome?

The 'underground' or 'shadow' economy. The underground economy consists of illegal and hence undeclared transactions. These could be transactions where the goods or services are themselves illegal, as with drugs, guns and prostitution. Alternatively, they could be transactions that are illegal only in that they are not declared for tax purposes. For example, to avoid paying VAT, a garage may be prepared to repair your car slightly more cheaply if you pay cash. Another example is that of 'moonlighting', where people do extra work outside their normal job and do not declare the income for tax purposes. For example, an electrician employed by a building contractor during the day may rewire people's houses in the evenings, again for cash. Unemployed people may do casual jobs that they do not declare, to avoid losing benefits.

Problems of using GDP statistics to measure welfare

GDP is essentially an indicator of a nation's *production*. But production may be a poor indicator of society's well-being for the following reasons.

Production does not equal consumption. Production is desirable only to the extent that it enables us to *consume* more. If GDP rises as a result of a rise in *investment*, this will not lead to an increase in *current* living standards. It will, of course, help to raise *future* consumption.

The same applies if GDP rises as a result of an increase in exports. Unless there is a resulting increase in imports, it will be consumers abroad that benefit, not domestic consumers.

Production has human costs. If production increases, this may be due to technological advance. If, however, it increases as a result of people having to work harder or longer hours, its net benefit will be less. Leisure is a desirable good, and so too are pleasant working conditions, but these items are not included in the GDP figures.

KI 2 p10

GDP ignores externalities. The rapid growth in industrial society is recorded in GDP statistics. What the statistics do not record are the environmental side effects: the polluted air and rivers, the ozone depletion, the problem of global warming. If these external costs were taken into account, the *net* benefits of industrial production would be much less.

KI 31 p364

Name some external benefits that are not included in GDP statistics.

The production of certain 'bads' leads to an increase in GDP. Some of the undesirable effects of growth may in fact *increase* GDP! Take the examples of crime, stress-related illness and environmental damage. Faster growth may lead to more of all three. But increased crime leads to more expenditure on security; increased stress leads to more expenditure on health care; and increased environmental damage leads to more expenditure on environmental clean-up. These expenditures *add* to GDP. Thus, rather than reducing GDP, crime, stress and environmental damage actually increase it.

Total GDP figures ignore the distribution of income. If some people gain and others lose, we cannot say that there has been an unambiguous increase in welfare. A typical feature of many rapidly growing countries is that some people grow very rich while others are left behind. The result is a growing inequality. If this is seen as undesirable, then clearly total GDP statistics are an inadequate measure of welfare.

KI 4 p14

Conclusions

If a country's citizens put a high priority on a clean environment, a relaxed way of life, greater self-sufficiency, a less materialistic outlook, more giving rather than selling, and greater equality, then such a country will probably have a lower GDP than a similarly endowed country where the pursuit of wealth is given high priority. Clearly, we cannot conclude that the first country will have a lower level of well-being.

However, this does not mean that we should reject GDP statistics as a means of judging economic performance. While GDP statistics are not a good measure of economic welfare, they are an effective measure of *output* or *income*, and should be seen in that context.

BOX 15.2 CAN GDP MEASURE NATIONAL HAPPINESS? EXPLORING ECONOMICS

An alternative perspective on well-being

The domains of national well-being

GDP is not a complete measure of economic welfare; nor is it meant to be. Consequently, there is considerable interest in alternative methods of establishing the level of human well-being and happiness.

In 2010 the UK's Office for National Statistics launched its *Measuring National Well-being (MNW) programme*.[1] The principal aim was to develop a set of national statistics which would both help people to gain a better understanding of well-being and allow well-being to be monitored. The data, for instance, would enable policy makers to make more informed policy decisions by better understanding the impact of their choices across society.

The MNW programme has identified a series of 'domains' with associated measures. There are 10 domains: personal well-being, our relationships, health, what we do, education and skills, where we live, personal finance, the economy, governance and the natural environment. These 10 domains produce a series of indicators – 43 as of 2021.

The October 2019 National Well-being Dashboard published by the ONS showed that of the 38 indicators for which there were data, 25 had shown a long-term improvement (generally taken to be a five-year period), 12 showed no overall change and 1 had deteriorated.

Domains such as 'personal finance' and 'where we live' included several indicators showing improvement. For example, real median disposable income rose, the number of people reporting financial hardship fell and the number accessing the natural environment weekly rose.

The one indicator that had fallen was in the domain of 'our relationships'. Fewer people than before tended to feel that they had a family member or friend that they could rely on a lot if they had a serious problem. How this will change after people have responded to the coronavirus pandemic remains to be seen.

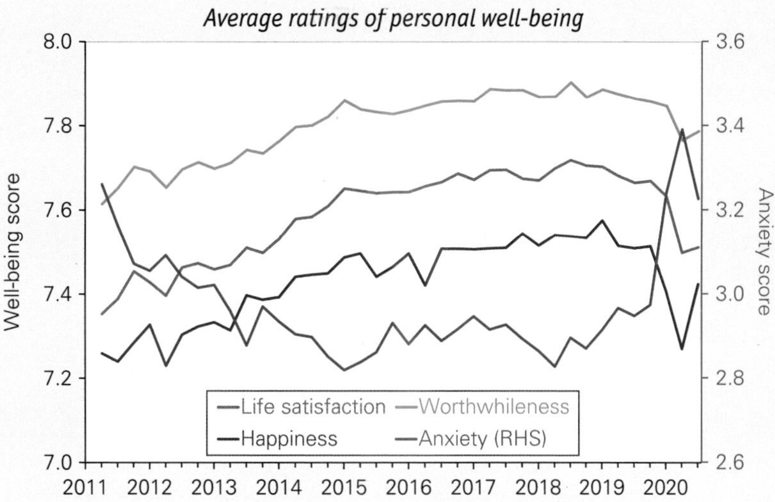

Note: Data are mean averages and seasonally adjusted.
Source: *Personal well-being in the UK, quarterly: April 2011 to September 2020*, Office for National Statistics (February 2021), www.ons.gov.uk/peoplepopulationandcommunity/wellbeing/bulletins/personalwellbeingintheukquarterly/april2011toseptember2020

Personal well-being and the pandemic

Since 2011, adults in the UK over 16 have been asked the following four questions in an attempt to monitor individual well-being:

- Overall, how satisfied are you with your life nowadays?
- Overall, to what extent do you feel the things you do in your life are worthwhile?
- Overall, how happy did you feel yesterday?
- Overall, how anxious did you feel yesterday?

Respondents give their answers using a scale of 0 to 10 where 0 is 'not at all' and 10 is 'completely'.

As the chart illustrates, the impact of the COVID-19 pandemic on personal well-being was stark. All four personal well-being measures fell back significantly in the second quarter of 2020. This followed the announcement of the first national lockdown across the UK on 23 March. While some easing of measures occurred through May and June, most national lockdown measures remained in place until July.

The anxiety score, for example, saw an increase of 4.5 per cent between the first and second quarter of 2020 from 3.24 to 3.39. The proportion of people rating anxiety as 'high' (an anxiety score of 6–10) rose from 21 to 24.8 per cent.

Although the anxiety and happiness scores improved in the third quarter of 2020, there was little improvement in the average scores for life satisfaction and the feeling that things done in life are worthwhile.

The impact on personal well-being was to become one of the defining features of the pandemic. It was an important reminder that individual and national well-being are multi-faceted. Identifying and gaining a better understanding of these various dimensions is therefore important for a more complete analysis of policy choices.

1. *Is well-being the same as happiness or utility?*
2. *For what reasons might a person have a high income but a poor level of well-being?*

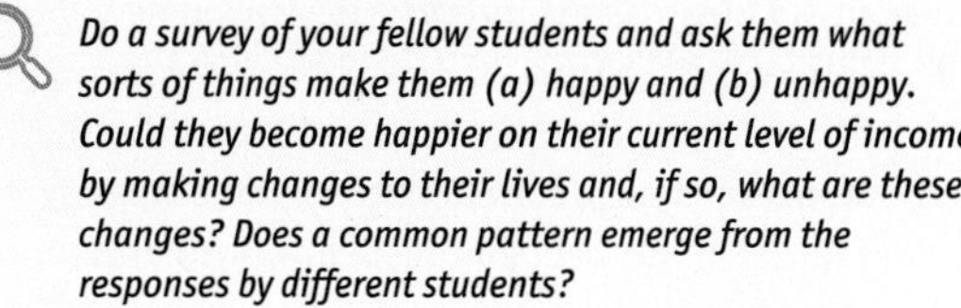

Do a survey of your fellow students and ask them what sorts of things make them (a) happy and (b) unhappy. Could they become happier on their current level of income by making changes to their lives and, if so, what are these changes? Does a common pattern emerge from the responses by different students?

1 *Measuring National Well-being in the UK, Domains and Measures: September 2016* (Office for National Statistics, September 2016).

Section summary

1. National income is usually expressed in terms of gross domestic product. This is simply the value of domestic production over the course of the year. It can be measured by the product, expenditure or income methods.
2. Real national income takes account of inflation by being expressed in the prices of some base year.
3. In order to compare living standards of different countries, national income has to be expressed per capita and at purchasing-power parity exchange rates.
4. Even if it is, there are still problems in using national income statistics for comparative purposes. Certain items will not be included: items such as non-marketed products, services in the family and activities in the underground economy. Moreover, the statistics include certain 'bads' and ignore externalities, and they also ignore questions of the distribution of income.

15.3 THE BUSINESS CYCLE

The distinction between actual and potential growth

As we have seen, economies experience business cycles. These are alternating periods of rapid growth and periods of slowdown or even contraction. Sometimes periods of contraction can be brought about by an economic shock and, in these circumstances, can be steep, resulting in a severe recession. This happened in the aftermath of the financial crisis in 2009 and following the onset of the coronavirus pandemic in 2020.

The published statistics on growth show ***actual growth***: the percentage change in national output over a period of time. As we saw in section 15.1, this is commonly measured over a year (12 months) or a quarter (3 months). It is fluctuations in actual growth that we see in business cycles.

However, we should be careful to distinguish between actual growth and potential growth. ***Potential growth*** is the speed at which the economy *could* grow. It is the percentage annual increase in the economy's *capacity* to produce: the rate of growth in *potential output*.

Potential output (i.e. potential GDP) is the level of output when the economy is operating at 'normal capacity utilisation'. This allows for firms having a planned degree of spare capacity to meet unexpected demand or for hold-ups in supply. It also allows for some unemployment as people move from job to job. Because potential output is normal-capacity output, it is somewhat below full-capacity output, which is the absolute maximum that could be produced with firms working flat out.

The output gap. The difference between actual and potential output is known as the ***output gap***. Thus if actual output exceeds potential output, the output gap is positive: the economy is operating above normal capacity utilisation. If actual output is below potential output, the output gap is negative: the economy is operating below normal capacity utilisation. Box 15.3 looks at the output gap since 1965 for five major industrial economies.

Assume that the actual growth rate is less than the potential growth rate. This will lead to an increase in spare capacity and probably an increase in unemployment. In turn, the output gap will become less positive or perhaps more negative, depending on the economy's starting point.

In contrast, if the actual growth rate were to exceed the potential growth rate, there would be a reduction in spare capacity and the output gap would become less negative or more positive. However, periods when actual growth exceeds potential growth can only be temporary. In the long run, the actual growth rate will be limited to the potential growth rate.

Definitions

Actual growth The percentage increase in national output actually produced.

Potential growth The percentage increase in the capacity of the economy to produce.

Potential output The sustainable level of output that could be produced in the economy: i.e. one that involves a 'normal' level of capacity utilisation and does not result in rising inflation.

Output gap The difference between actual and potential output. When actual output exceeds potential output, the gap is positive. When actual output is less than potential output, the gap is negative.

Factors affecting potential output and potential growth

Although our focus in section 15.3 is on short-term volatility and hence on actual growth, it is worth briefly considering the principal factors that contribute to potential economic growth. We look at this in much more depth in Chapter 23.

Explanations tend to focus on the role of the economy's resources. This is the fourteenth of our threshold concepts, which states that long-term growth in a country's output depends on a growth in the quantity and/or productivity of its resources.

First, there is the issue of quantity. An increase in resources, whether they are natural resources, labour or capital, enables the economy's potential output to increase.

Second, there is the issue of the effectiveness or productivity of resources. An increase in the effectiveness of the resources used, perhaps through advances in technology, improved labour skills or improved organisation, also enables growth in potential output.

Although the growth in potential output varies to some extent over the years – depending on the rate of advance of technology, the level of investment and the discovery of new raw materials – it nevertheless tends to be much steadier than the growth in actual output.

How might the volatility of an economy affect the growth of potential output?

The hypothetical business cycle

As we saw above, actual growth tends to fluctuate. In some years, countries will experience high rates of economic growth: the country experiences a boom. In other years, economic growth is low or even negative: the country

BOX 15.3 OUTPUT GAPS

EXPLORING ECONOMICS

A measure of excess or deficient demand

If the economy grows, how fast and for how long can it grow before it runs into inflationary problems? On the other hand, what minimum rate must be achieved to avoid rising unemployment?

To answer these questions, economists have developed the concept of 'output gaps'.[1] The output gap is the difference between actual output and potential output (i.e. normal-capacity output).

If actual output is below potential output (the gap is negative), there will be a higher than normal level of unemployment as firms are operating below their normal level of capacity utilisation. There will, however, be a downward pressure on inflation, resulting from a lower than normal level of demand for labour and other resources.

If actual output is above potential output (the gap is positive), there will be excess demand and a rise in inflation.

Generally, the gap will be negative in a recession and positive in a boom. In other words, output gaps follow the course of the business cycle.

Measuring the output gap

But how do we measure the output gap? There are two principal statistical techniques.

De-trending techniques. This approach is a purely mechanical exercise which involves smoothing the actual GDP figures. In doing this, it attempts to fit a trend growth path. This is illustrated by the dashed line in Figure 15.5. The main disadvantage of this approach is that it is not grounded in economic theory and therefore does not account for those factors likely to determine normal-capacity output.

Production function approach. Many institutions, such as the European Union, use an approach which borrows ideas from economic theory. Specifically, this uses the idea of a production function, which relates output to a set of inputs. Estimates of potential output are generated by using statistics on the size of a country's capital stock (see Box 23.1), the potential available labour input and, finally, the productivity or effectiveness of these inputs in producing output.

In addition to these statistical approaches, use could be made of *business surveys*. These involve asking businesses directly about normal capacity working and current levels of output. However, survey-based evidence can provide only a broad guide to rates of capacity utilisation and whether there is deficient or excess demand.

International evidence

The chart shows output gaps for five countries from 1965 estimated using a production function approach. What is apparent from the chart is that all the countries have experienced significant output gaps, both positive and negative. This is consistent with a core theme of this chapter and one to which we will return repeatedly throughout the second half of the book: economies are inherently volatile. In other words, countries experience business cycles.

The chart shows that the characteristics of countries' business cycles can differ, particularly in terms of depth and duration. However, we also see evidence of an international business cycle (see pages 469–70), which results from national cycles appearing to share characteristics. The increased global interconnectedness of economies from financial and trading

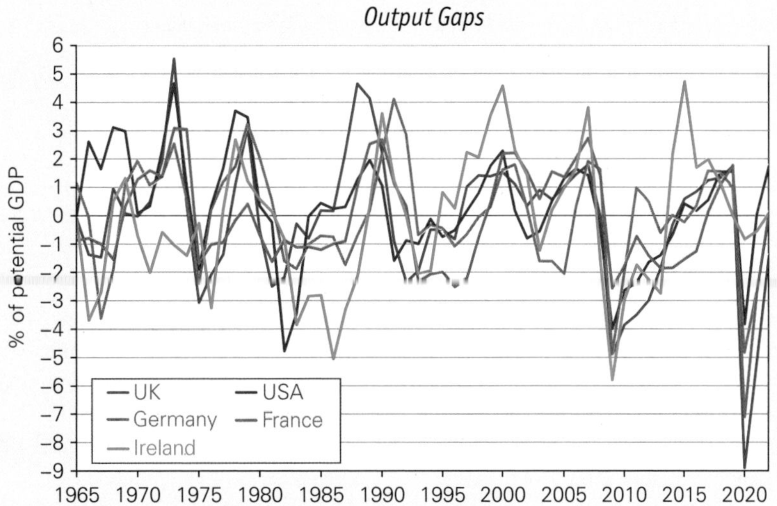

Note: Figures for Germany based on West Germany prior to 1992; figures from 2020 based on forecasts.
Source: Based on data from *AMECO database*, European Commission, DGECFIN (May 2021) and various forecasts, http://ec.europa.eu/economy_finance/ameco/user/serie/SelectSerie.cfm

(continued)

links is likely to have increased the importance of the global component to many countries' business cycles.

However the internationalisation of the business cycle is most stark from the late 2000s. First, there was the impact on national economies from the global financial crisis. Then, in the early 2020s, there was the impact of the global health emergency that arose from the COVID-19 pandemic.

Yet while countries experience volatility and the size of their output gaps vary from year to year, over the longer term, output gaps tend towards zero. In other words, the longer-term rate of economic growth is determined by the growth in an economy's potential output.

Under what circumstances would potential output (i.e. a zero output gap) move further away from the full-capacity output ceiling shown in Figure 15.5? (See page 469 opposite.)

Using the AMECO database, section 6.5, calculate the average output gap for the period 2020–21 for each of the following countries: France, Germany, Ireland, the UK and the USA. Using these values, construct a column chart. Briefly discuss your findings.

1 See C. Giorno et al., 'Potential output, output gaps and structural budget balances', *OECD Economic Studies*, no. 24 (1995), p. 1.

THRESHOLD CONCEPT 14 LONG-TERM GROWTH IN A COUNTRY'S OUTPUT DEPENDS ON A GROWTH IN THE QUANTITY AND/OR PRODUCTIVITY OF ITS RESOURCES

THINKING LIKE AN ECONOMIST

In the short term, economic growth is likely to be influenced by changes in aggregate demand. If the economy is in recession, an expansion in aggregate demand will help to bring the economy out of recession and move it closer to full employment.

Actual output, however, cannot continue growing faster than potential output over the longer term. Firms will start reaching capacity and actual growth will then have to slow. The rate of potential growth thus places a limit to the rate of actual growth over the longer term.

What then determines the rate of growth in potential output? The answer lies predominantly on the supply side. It depends on the rate of growth of factors of production. There are two key elements here. The first is growth in the *quantity* of factors: growth in the size of the workforce, of the available land and raw materials, and of the stock of capital. The second is productivity growth. This involves elements such as growth in the educational attainments and skills of the workforce, growth in technology, and growth in the efficiency with which resources are used.

To recognise the importance of resources and their productivity in determining long-term growth is a threshold concept. It helps in understanding the importance of designing appropriate supply-side policies: policies that focus on increasing aggregate supply rather than managing aggregate demand. It is easy to worry too much about the short term.

This is not to say that the short term should be neglected. The famous economist John Maynard Keynes argued that it was fundamentally important to focus on aggregate demand and the short term to avoid severe economic fluctuations, with the twin problems of high unemployment in recessions and high inflation in periods of unsustainably high growth. He used the famous phrase, 'In the long term we're all dead.'

Furthermore, the longer-term growth of the economy reflects the actions of the present. If significant fluctuations in actual output affect the growth of aggregate supply, then it may be appropriate for policy makers to focus on managing aggregate demand. Indeed during the COVID-19 pandemic there was much agreement that governments needed to pursue expansionary economic policies, not only to mitigate the immediate impact on output and employment, but also to lessen the harmful 'scarring effects' on longer-term growth from a collapse in investment and the deskilling of workers made redundant.

1. ***Give some examples of supply-side policy (see Chapter 23 for some ideas if you are stuck).***
2. ***If there is an increase in aggregate supply, will this result in an increase in potential growth?***

experiences a slowdown or recession.[2] This cycle of expansion and slowdown causes fluctuations in the path of output.

Figure 15.5 illustrates a hypothetical business cycle. While it is a stylised representation of the business cycle, it is useful for illustrating four identifiable 'phases' of the cycle.

1. *The upturn.* In this phase, a contracting or stagnant economy begins to recover, and growth in actual output resumes, or begins to accelerate.
2. *The expansion.* During this phase, there is rapid economic growth: the economy is booming. A fuller use is made of resources, and the gap between actual and potential output narrows.
3. *The peaking out.* During this phase, growth slows down or even ceases.
4. *The slowdown, recession or slump.* During this phase, there is little or no growth or even a decline in output. Increasing slack develops in the economy. The economy is operating with a negative output gap.

A word of caution: do not confuse a high *level* of output with a high rate of *growth* in output. The level of output is

2 In official statistics, a recession is defined as when an economy experiences falling real GDP (negative growth) for two or more successive quarters.

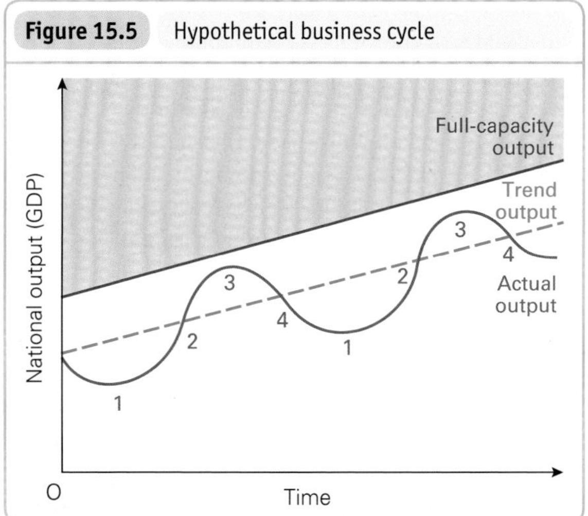

highest in phase 3. The rate of growth in output is highest in phase 2 (i.e. where the curve is steepest).

Figure 15.5 shows a decline in actual output in recession. Redraw the diagram, only this time show a mere slowing down of growth in phase 4.

Long-term output trend

A line can be drawn showing the trend of national output over time (i.e. ignoring the cyclical fluctuations around the trend). This is shown as the dashed line in Figure 15.5. If, over time, firms on average operate with a 'normal' degree of capacity utilisation (a zero output gap), the trend output line will be the same as the potential output line. Also, if the average level of capacity that is unutilised stays constant from one cycle to another, the trend line will have the same slope as the full-capacity output line.

If, however, the level of unutilised capacity changes from one cycle to another, then the trend line will have a different slope from the full-capacity output line. For example, if unemployment and unused industrial capacity *rise* from one peak to another, or from one trough to another, the trend line will move further away from the full-capacity output line (i.e. it will be less steep).

If the average percentage (as opposed to the average level) of capacity that was unutilised remained constant, would the trend line have the same slope as the potential output line?

The business cycle in practice

The hypothetical business cycle illustrated in Figure 15.5 is nice and smooth and regular. Drawing it this way allows us to make a clear distinction between each of the four phases. In practice, however, business cycles are highly irregular. They are irregular in two important ways:

- *The length of the phases.* Some booms are short-lived, lasting only a few months or so. Others are much longer, lasting perhaps several years. Likewise some recessions are short while others are long.
- *The magnitude of the phases.* Sometimes in phase 2 there is a very high rate of economic growth, perhaps 4 per cent per annum or more. On other occasions in phase 2 growth is much gentler. Sometimes in phase 4 there is a recession, with an actual decline in output, as occurred in 2008–9 and 2020. On other occasions, phase 4 is merely a 'pause', with growth simply being low.

An international business cycle

All countries tend to experience business cycles. Typically the timing is similar from one country to another. In other words, there is an international business cycle. Figure 15.6 shows the annual rate of growth in real GDP in the global economy alongside that in Germany, the UK and USA.

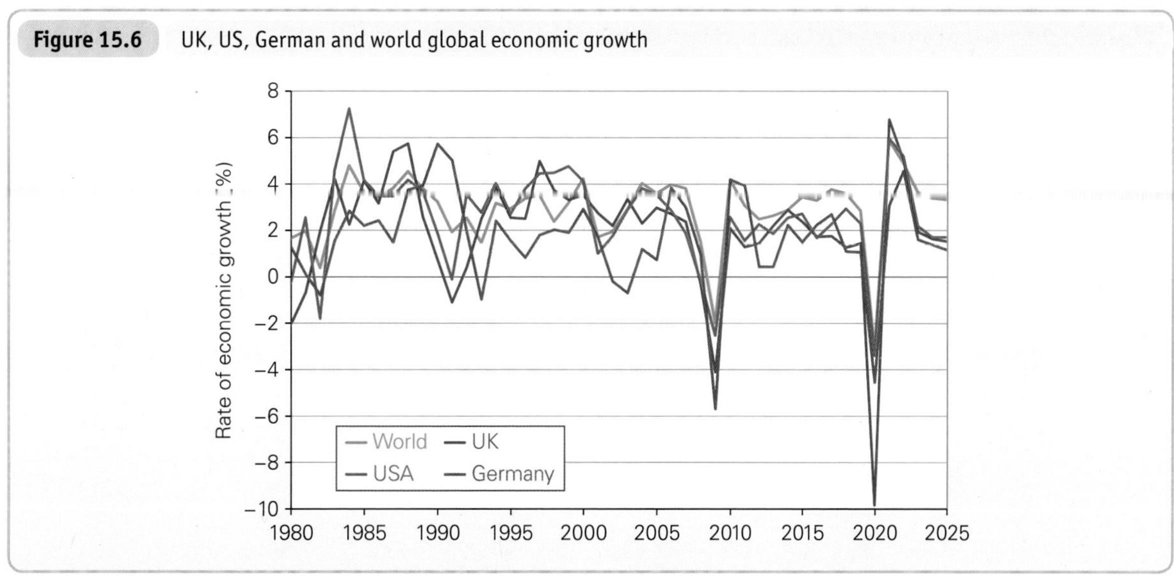

Note: Data for 2021 onwards are based on forecasts; German figures are West Germany up to 1991.
Source: Based on data in *World Economic Outlook Database*, IMF (October 2021), www.imf.org/external/ns/cs.aspx?id=28

Global growth rates fluctuated significantly during recent global crises from +3¾ per cent in 2007 to −2% in 2009 and from +2½ per cent in 2019 to −3½ per cent in 2020.

Figure 15.6 illustrates how global economic volatility is mirrored, at least in part, by the economic volatility in Germany, the UK and USA. More generally, this suggests that countries' business cycles have both a national and a global component. With increased global economic ties, many countries have seen the global component increase in its relative importance.

Aggregate demand and the business cycle

The focus of much of the analysis of business cycles is on fluctuations in ***aggregate demand*** (*AD*). This is the total spending on goods and services made within the country ('domestically produced goods and services'). It consists of spending by four groups of people: consumers on goods and services (*C*), firms on investment (*I*), the government on goods, services and investment (such as education, health and new roads) (*G*) and people abroad on this country's exports (*X*). From these four we have to subtract any imports (*M*) since aggregate demand refers only to spending on *domestic* firms. Thus

$$AD = C + I + G + X - M$$

Periods of rapid growth are associated with periods of rapid expansion of aggregate demand. Periods of recession are associated with a decline in aggregate demand.

Definition

Aggregate demand Total spending on goods and services produced in the economy. It consists of four elements, consumer expenditure (*C*), investment (*I*), government expenditure (*G*) and the expenditure on exports (*X*), less any expenditure on foreign goods and services (*M*). Thus $AD = C + I + G + X - M$.

Fluctuations in private-sector expenditure

When analysing the sources of economic volatility, it makes sense to begin by looking at consumer spending. This is because, by value, it is the largest expenditure component of aggregate demand. In the UK, for example, it frequently accounts for over 60 per cent of national income. This means that even small fluctuations in consumer expenditure can be significant for aggregate demand. As Figure 15.7 shows, annual rates of economic growth mirror fairly closely those in real household consumption.

Yet this still leaves many important questions to be addressed. What factors affect consumption? Which are most important? How do changes in consumption then affect the macroeconomic environment? Are the effects always the same? These are questions we will examine in section 17.1.

Another component of aggregate demand is investment. If we look again at Figure 15.7, we can see that fluctuations in the annual rate of growth of real investment spending are considerably greater than those in output (real GDP).

It appears then that the volatility of investment is one of the factors contributing to the ups and downs of the business cycle. However, this does not mean that fluctuations in investment are the primary *cause* of the economy's short-term volatility. They can be, but, as we will discuss in Chapter 17, some economists emphasise more the role that investment plays in *amplifying* the impact of economic shocks and therefore the peaks and troughs of the business cycle. The argument here is that investment decisions are affected by the growth in national income. Rising national income may encourage firms to invest to meet increasing demand. But this also has the effect of increasing aggregate demand, which further boosts national income. In contrast, an economy experiencing weak growth, or one where national income is contracting, might see investment levels fall, perhaps very sharply. This, of course, weakens aggregate demand, further amplifying already weak or negative economic growth.

Figure 15.7 Annual growth of UK consumption, investment and GDP

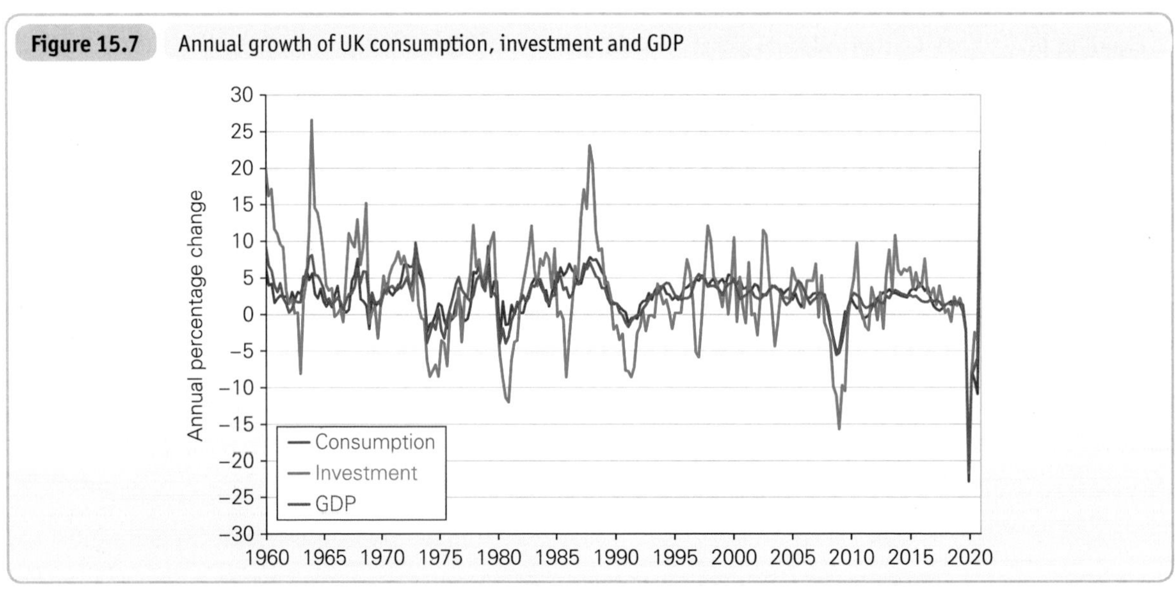

Note: Growth rates are calculated using constant-price data; investment growth is the growth in gross fixed capital formation.
Source: Based on data in *Quarterly National Accounts*, series KGZ7, KG7T and IHYR, ONS, www.ons.gov.uk/economy/grossdomesticproductgdp/

The role of the financial sector

The financial sector plays a crucial role in affecting economic activity. While we will focus in detail on the markets, institutions and products and services which comprise the financial sector in Chapter 18, the economic significance of the sector means that it will be referred to frequently in subsequent chapters.

With the financial crisis of the late 2000s, there was a surge in interest in how the financial sector affects the business cycle. Some economists argue that the financial sector is a major *source* of economic volatility. Some go as far as to say that the behaviour of financial institutions, through their lending and investments, generates unsustainable economic growth, which inevitably ends with an economic downturn.

Other economists argue that the financial sector *amplifies* economic shocks. The argument here is not that financial institutions are the source of fluctuations in economic growth but rather that they magnify the shocks that affect the economy. They can do this by boosting lending when growth is strong or by reducing lending when growth is weak.

Aggregate supply and the business cycle

While much of the economic analysis of business cycles stresses the importance of fluctuations in aggregate demand, economists recognise that fluctuations in ***aggregate supply*** can also cause fluctuations in output. Sudden sharp changes to input prices, such as in the price of oil, can be one such cause. Meanwhile, the COVID-19 pandemic of the early 2020s saw governments around the world implement health intervention measures, such as lockdowns, that resulted in negative shocks to both the demand- *and* the supply-side of their economies.

Some economists go further and argue that shifts in aggregate supply are the *primary* source of economic volatility. They argue that these aggregate supply shocks affect the economy's potential output. Consequently, the business cycle is the result of fluctuations in potential output, which in turn affect actual output.

They argue that economies are frequently affected by supply shocks, many of which might be described as 'technological shocks'. As well as changes to input prices, these could include changes to production methods, the regulatory climate or the political environment. These shocks affect production processes and levels of productivity. Some of these changes affect potential output positively, some negatively.

Definition

Aggregate supply The total amount of output in the economy.

Section summary

1. Actual growth must be distinguished from potential growth. The actual growth rate is the percentage annual increase in the output that is actually produced, whereas potential growth is the percentage annual increase in the capacity of the economy to produce (whether or not this capacity is utilised).
2. Actual growth will fluctuate with the course of the business cycle. The hypothetical business cycle can be broken down into four phases: the upturn, the expansion, the peaking out, and the slowdown or recession. In practice, the length and magnitude of these phases will vary: the cycle is thus irregular.
3. Countries' business cycles may have both national and international components. The international component has tended to increase over time as countries have become increasingly interconnected, for example through trade and growing financial ties.
4. Explanations of the business cycle tend to focus on fluctuations originating in aggregate demand. This requires a deeper understanding of the behaviour of the components of aggregate demand, including that of private-sector behaviour.
5. However, fluctuations in aggregate supply can also result in economic instability. Some economists go further and argue that business cycles can result from fluctuations in potential output caused by frequent technology shocks.

15.4 THE CIRCULAR FLOW OF INCOME

As we have seen, the economic choices of people, businesses and organisations can have profound effects for the macroeconomy. One model which allows us to develop an understanding of the impact of these choices for economic growth and which does so by focusing on aggregate demand is the *circular flow of income model.*

We encountered the circular flow model in section 15.2 when looking at how we measure GDP. Consider Figure 15.8. As before, the economy is divided into two major groups: *firms* and *households*. Each group has two roles. Firms are producers of goods and services; they are also the employers of labour and other factors of production. Households (which

Figure 15.8 The circular flow of national income and expenditure

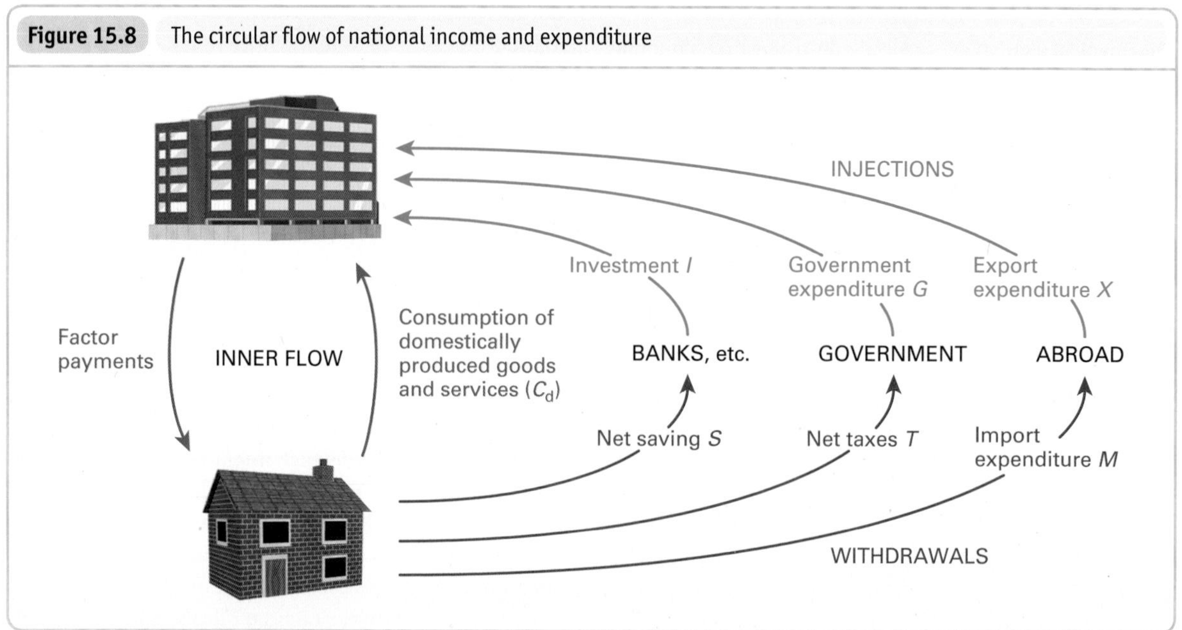

include all individuals) are the consumers of goods and services; they are also the suppliers of labour and various other factors of production. In the diagram there is an inner flow and various outer flows of incomes between these two groups.

Before we look at the various parts of the diagram, a word of warning. Do not confuse *money* and *income*. Money is a *stock* concept. At any given time, there is a certain quantity of money in the economy (e.g. £1 trillion). But that does not tell us the level of national *income*. Income is a *flow* concept (as is expenditure). It is measured as so much *per period of time*. The relationship between money and income depends on how rapidly the money *circulates*: its 'velocity of circulation'. (We will examine this concept in detail later on: see pages 504 and 600.) If there is £1 trillion of money in the economy and each £1 on average is paid out as income twice per year, then annual national income will be £2 trillion.

KI 26 p309

The inner flow, withdrawals and injections

The inner flow

Firms pay money to households in the form of wages and salaries, dividends on shares, interest and rent. These payments are in return for the services of the factors of production – labour, capital and land – that are supplied by households. Thus on the left-hand side of the diagram, money flows directly from firms to households as 'factor payments'.

Households, in turn, pay money to domestic firms when they consume domestically produced goods and services (C_d). This is shown on the right-hand side of the inner flow. There is thus a circular flow of payments from firms to households to firms and so on.

If households spend *all* their incomes on buying domestic goods and services, and if firms pay out *all* this income they receive as factor payments to domestic households, and if the velocity of circulation does not change, the flow will continue at the same level indefinitely. The money just goes round and round at the same speed and incomes remain unchanged.

Would this argument still hold if prices rose?

In the real world, of course, it is not as simple as this. Not all income gets passed on round the inner flow; some is *withdrawn*. At the same time, incomes are injected into the flow from outside. Let us examine these withdrawals and injections.

Withdrawals (W)

Only part of the incomes received by households will be spent on the goods and services of domestic firms. The remainder will be withdrawn from the inner flow. Likewise, only part of the incomes generated by firms will be paid to UK households. The remainder of this will also be withdrawn. There are three forms of ***withdrawals*** (or ***'leakages'*** as they are sometimes called).

Net saving (S). Saving is income that households choose not to spend but to put aside for the future. Savings are normally deposited in financial institutions such as banks and building societies. This is shown in the bottom centre of the diagram. Money flows from households to 'banks, etc.'. What we are seeking to measure here, however, is the net flow from households to the banking sector. We therefore have to subtract from saving any borrowing or drawing on past savings

Definition

Withdrawals (*W*) (or leakages) Incomes of households or firms that are not passed on round the inner flow. Withdrawals equal net saving (*S*) plus net taxes (*T*) plus import expenditure (*M*): $W = S + T + M$.

by households to arrive at the *net* saving flow. Of course, if household borrowing exceeded saving, the net flow would be in the other direction: it would be negative.

Net taxes (T). When people pay taxes (to either central or local government), this represents a withdrawal of money from the inner flow in much the same way as saving; only, in this case, people have no choice. Some taxes, such as income tax and employees' national insurance contributions (called social contributions in some countries), are paid out of household incomes. Others, such as VAT and excise duties, are paid out of consumer expenditure. Others, such as corporation tax, are paid out of firms' incomes before being received by households as dividends on shares. For simplicity, however, taxes are shown in Figure 15.8 as leaving the circular flow at just one point.

When, however, people receive *benefits* from the government, such as unemployment benefits, child benefit and pensions, the money flows the other way. Benefits are thus equivalent to a 'negative tax'. These benefits are known as ***transfer payments***. They transfer money from one group of people (taxpayers) to others (the recipients).

In the model, 'net taxes' (T) represents the *net* flow to the government (central and local) from households and firms. It consists of total taxes minus benefits.

Import expenditure (M). Not all consumption is of totally home-produced goods. Households spend some of their incomes on imported goods and services, or on goods and services using imported components. Although the money that consumers spend on such goods initially flows to domestic retailers, it will eventually find its way abroad, either when the retailers or wholesalers themselves import them, or when domestic manufacturers purchase imported inputs to make their products. This expenditure on imports constitutes the third withdrawal from the inner flow. This money flows abroad.

Total withdrawals are simply the sum of net saving, net taxes and the expenditure on imports:

$$W = S + T + M$$

Injections (J)

Only part of the demand for firms' output arises from consumers' expenditure. The remainder comes from other sources outside the inner flow. These additional components of aggregate demand are known as ***injections (J)***. This important insight means that we can write aggregate demand as:[3]

$$AD = C_d + J$$

There are three types of injection.

Investment (I). This is the money that firms spend after obtaining it from various financial institutions – either past savings or loans, or through a new issue of shares. They may invest in plant and equipment or may simply spend the money on building up stocks of inputs, semi-finished or finished goods.

Government purchases (G). When the government spends money on goods and services produced by firms, this counts as an injection. Examples of such government expenditure include spending on roads, hospitals and schools. (Note that government expenditure in this model does not include state benefits, hence, the use of the term 'government purchases'. Benefits are transfer payments, as we saw above. They are the equivalent of negative taxes and have the effect of reducing the T component of withdrawals.)

Export expenditure (X). Money flows into the circular flow from abroad when residents abroad buy our exports of goods and services.

Total injections are thus the sum of investment, government expenditure and exports:[4]

$$J = I + G + X$$

The relationship between withdrawals and injections

There are indirect links between saving and investment, taxation and government expenditure, and imports and exports, via financial institutions, the government (central and local) and foreign countries respectively. If more money is saved, there will be more available for banks and other financial institutions to lend out. If tax receipts are higher, the government may be keener to increase its expenditure. Finally, if imports increase, incomes of people abroad will increase, which will enable them to purchase more of our exports.

These links, however, do not guarantee that $S = I$ or $G = T$ or $M = X$. Firms may wish to invest (I) more or less than people wish to save (S); governments can spend (G) more than they receive in taxes (T) or vice versa; and exports (X) can exceed imports (M) or vice versa.

> **Definitions**
>
> **Transfer payments** Moneys transferred from one person or group to another (e.g. from the government to individuals) without production taking place.
>
> **Injections (J)** Expenditure on the production of domestic firms coming from outside the inner flow of the circular flow of income. Injections equal investment (I) plus government purchases (G) plus expenditure on exports (X).

3 Note that this definition of aggregate demand ($AD = Cd + J$) is equivalent to the one we gave on page 470, i.e. $AD = C + I + G + X - M$, since both the terms C_d and J exclude expenditure on imports.

4 We assume, for simplicity, in this equation that all investment, government expenditure and export expenditure is on domestic products. Where any part of these three is on imports, we need to subtract this imported element to arrive at I, G or X.

A major point here is that the decisions to save and invest are made by different people, and thus they plan to save and invest different amounts. Likewise the demand for imports may not equal the demand for exports. As far as the government is concerned, it may choose not to make $T = G$. It may choose not to spend all its tax revenues: to run a 'budget surplus' ($T > G$). Or it may choose to spend more than it receives in taxes – to run a budget deficit ($G > T$) – by borrowing or printing money to make up the difference.

Thus planned injections (J) may not equal planned withdrawals (W).

In terms of the UK economy, are the following net injections, net withdrawals or either? If there is uncertainty, explain your assumptions.

(a) Firms are forced to take a cut in profits in order to give a pay rise.
(b) Firms spend money on research.
(c) The government increases personal tax allowances.
(d) The general public invests more money in banks and building societies.
(e) UK investors earn higher dividends on overseas investments.
(f) The UK government purchases US military aircraft.
(g) People draw on their savings to finance holidays abroad.
(h) People draw on their savings to finance holidays in the UK.
(i) The government runs a budget deficit (spends more than it receives in tax revenues) and finances it by borrowing from the general public.
(j) The government runs a budget deficit and finances it through new money created by the central bank.

Equilibrium in the circular flow

We saw earlier in the chapter how fluctuations in aggregate demand cause short-term growth rates to fluctuate. The circular flow of income model helps us understand the process.

If planned injections do not equal planned withdrawals, aggregate demand will change and so too will national income. Take the case where injections exceed withdrawals. Perhaps there has been a rise in business confidence so that investment has risen. Or perhaps there has been a tax cut so that withdrawals have fallen. As we have seen, the excess of injections over withdrawals will lead to a rise in national income.

But as national income rises, so households will not only spend more on domestic goods (C_d), but also save more (S), pay more taxes (T) and buy more imports (M). In other words, withdrawals will rise too. This will continue until they have risen to equal injections. At that point, national income will stop rising, and so will withdrawals. Equilibrium has been reached. Thus equilibrium is where:

$$W = J$$

Similarly, if withdrawals exceed injections, the resulting fall in national income will lead to a fall in withdrawals. Again, this will continue until $W = J$.

Section summary

1. The circular flow of income model depicts the flows of money round the economy. The inner flow shows the direct flows between firms and households. Money flows from firms to households in the form of factor payments, and back again as consumer expenditure on domestically produced goods and services.
2. Not all incomes get passed on directly round the inner flow. Some is withdrawn in the form of net saving, some is paid in net taxes, and some goes abroad as expenditure on imports.
3. Likewise, not all expenditure on domestic firms is by domestic consumers. Some is injected from outside the inner flow in the form of investment expenditure, government purchases and expenditure on the country's exports.
4. Planned injections and withdrawals are unlikely to be the same.
5. If injections exceed withdrawals, national income will rise and the economy grows. The reverse will happen if withdrawals exceed injections.
6. If injections exceed withdrawals, the resulting rise in national income will lead to a rise in withdrawals. This will continue until $W = J$. At this point, the circular flow will be in equilibrium.

15.5 UNEMPLOYMENT

Understandably one of the most emotive of all macroeconomic issues is that of unemployment, not least because of the very personal costs to those affected. Box 15.4 considers in more detail these and the broader costs to the economy of unemployment.

In this section, we look briefly at the potential causes of unemployment. What does the volatility of economies mean for unemployment? Is unemployment merely the result of the business cycle? If not, what other factors might be important? Before addressing these questions, we do two things.

First, we look at how we measure unemployment. Second, we look at evidence on the composition of unemployment and the duration that people are unemployed.

Claimant unemployment and standardised unemployment

Two common measures of unemployment are used in official statistics. The first is ***claimant unemployment***. This is simply a measure of all those in receipt of unemployment-related benefits. Claimant statistics have the advantage of being very easy to collect. However, they exclude all those of working age who are available for work at current wage rates, but who are *not* eligible for benefits. The net effect is that the claimant statistics tend to understate the true level of unemployment. They are also sensitive to government changes in the eligibility conditions for unemployment-related benefits.

Because of the weaknesses of claimant statistics many governments use the ***standardised unemployment rate*** as the main measure of unemployment. In this measure, the unemployed are defined as people of working age who are without work, available to start work within two weeks and *actively seeking employment* or waiting to take up an appointment.

This is the measure used by the International Labour Organization (ILO) and the Organisation for Economic Co-operation and Development (OECD), two international organisations that publish unemployment statistics for many countries. The figures are compiled from the results of national labour force *surveys*. A representative cross-section of the population is asked whether they are employed, unemployed (using the above definition) or economically inactive. From their replies, national rates of unemployment can be extrapolated. In the UK, the Labour Force Survey is conducted quarterly.

As we have seen, the standardised rate is likely to be higher than the claimant rate to the extent that it includes people seeking work who are nevertheless not entitled to claim benefits. However, it will be lower to the extent that it excludes those who are claiming benefits and yet who are not actively seeking work.

Generally, the standardised rate is significantly higher than the claimant rate. Over the five-year period from 2015 to 2019, for example, the average claimant count rate in the UK was 2.5 per cent, while the average standardised unemployment rate (for all aged 16 and over) was 4.5 per cent.

How does the ILO/OECD definition differ from the economist's definition given on page 456? What is the significance of the phrase 'available for work at current wage rates' in the economist's definition?

The composition of unemployment

Unemployment rates can vary enormously between countries and between different groups within countries. In part, this is likely to reflect structural factors. Countries and regions within countries can, for example, have very different labour markets. Countries often have very different policies on unemployment, training schemes, redundancy, etc., and demonstrate very different attitudes of firms towards their workers.

Table 15.4 highlights differences between European countries, age groups and men and women in the 2010s.

Definitions

Claimant unemployment Those in receipt of unemployment-related benefits.

Standardised unemployment rate The measure of the unemployment rate used by the ILO and the OECD. The unemployed are defined as persons of working age who are without work, are available to start work within two weeks and either have actively looked for work in the last four weeks or are waiting to take up an appointment.

Table 15.4 Standardised European unemployment rates by age and gender, average 2010–19

	Less than 25 years			25 to 74 years			15 to 74 years		
	Male	Female	Total	Male	Female	Total	Male	Female	Total
Norway	10.7	8.1	9.5	3.1	2.6	2.9	4.1	3.3	3.7
Switzerland	8.5	8.2	8.3	3.9	4.5	4.2	4.5	4.9	4.7
Germany	8.2	6.6	7.5	4.7	4.1	4.4	5.1	4.4	4.7
Austria	10.1	9.4	9.7	4.7	4.3	4.5	5.4	5.0	5.2
Netherlands	10.7	10.0	10.4	4.3	5.0	4.7	5.3	5.9	5.6
UK	18.1	14.1	16.2	4.4	4.2	4.3	6.3	5.6	6.0
Poland	19.2	21.6	20.2	5.9	6.7	6.3	7.1	7.8	7.5
Sweden	22.3	20.2	21.2	5.6	5.4	5.5	7.6	7.3	7.5
Belgium	20.8	18.9	19.9	6.5	6.2	6.4	7.7	7.2	7.5
France	23.5	22.6	23.1	8.1	8.3	8.2	9.7	9.6	9.6
Eurozone	21.3	20.2	20.8	8.7	9.3	9.0	9.9	10.3	10.1
Ireland	25.4	17.5	21.6	9.9	8.1	9.1	11.8	9.3	10.7
Italy	33.5	37.1	34.9	8.4	10.2	9.2	10.0	11.9	10.8
Portugal	27.3	30.1	28.6	10.0	10.6	10.3	11.3	12.0	11.7
Spain	45.3	44.1	44.7	17.5	19.9	18.6	19.5	21.6	20.5
Greece	41.4	51.2	46.0	17.0	23.9	20.0	18.4	25.7	21.6

Note: Eurozone = 19 countries using the euro as of January 2015.
Source: Based on data from *Eurostat Database*, Eurostat, European Commission.

BOX 15.4 **THE COSTS OF UNEMPLOYMENT** EXPLORING ECONOMICS

Who loses and by how much?

The most obvious cost of unemployment is to the unemployed themselves. There is the direct financial cost of the loss in their earnings. Then there are the personal costs of being unemployed. The longer people are unemployed, the more dispirited they may become. Their self-esteem is likely to fall, and they are more likely to succumb to stress-related illness.

Beyond the unemployed themselves, there are the costs to their family and friends. Personal relations can become strained, and there may be an increase in domestic violence and the number of families splitting up.

Then there are the broader costs to the economy. Unemployment represents a loss of output. In other words, actual output is below potential output. Apart from the loss of disposable income to the unemployed themselves, this underutilisation of resources leads to lower incomes for other people too:

- The government loses tax revenues, since the unemployed pay no income tax and national insurance and, given that the unemployed spend less, they pay less VAT and excise duties. The government also incurs administrative costs associated with the running of benefit offices. It may also have to spend extra on health care, the social services and the police.
- Firms lose the profits that could have been made if there had been full employment.
- Other workers lose any additional wages they could have earned from higher national output.

What is more, the longer people remain unemployed, the more deskilled they tend to become. This scarring effect reduces potential as well as actual income.

Why have the costs to the government of unemployment benefits not been included as a cost to the economy?

Finally, there is some evidence that higher unemployment leads to increased crime and vandalism. This obviously imposes a cost on the sufferers.

The costs of unemployment are to some extent offset by benefits. If workers voluntarily quit their jobs to look for better ones, then they must reckon that the benefits of a better job more than compensate for their temporary loss of income. From the nation's point of view, a workforce that is prepared to quit jobs and spend a short time unemployed will be a more adaptable, more mobile workforce – one that is responsive to changing economic circumstances. Such a workforce will lead to greater allocative efficiency in the short run and more rapid economic growth over the longer run.

Long-term involuntary unemployment is quite another matter. The costs clearly outweigh any benefits, both for the individuals involved and for the economy as a whole. A demotivated, deskilled pool of long-term unemployed is a serious economic and social problem.

Which of the above costs would be recorded as a reduction in GDP?

Conduct a literature search on the concept of unemployment scarring (also known as labour market scarring). Briefly summarise your findings in a short paper aimed at a newly appointed government minister with responsibility for employment.

In many countries, female unemployment has traditionally been higher than male unemployment. Causes have included differences in education and training, discrimination by employers, more casual or seasonally related employment among women and other social factors. In many countries, as highlighted by Table 15.4, the position has changed in recent years. One important reason has been the decline in many of the older industries, such as coal and steel, which employed mainly men.

Many traditional shops have closed in recent years as more people have shopped online – a trend hastened by the forced closure of non-essential shops in the lockdowns during the COVID-19 pandemic. How is this likely to have affected the balance of employment and unemployment of women and men?

Table 15.4 does, however, show some stark differences in unemployment rates across different age groups. Rates in the under-25 age group are higher than the average, and substantially so in many countries. Higher youth unemployment rates can be explained by the suitability (or unsuitability) of the qualifications of school leavers, the attitudes of employers to young people, and the greater willingness of young people to spend time unemployed looking for a better job or waiting to start a further or higher education course. The difference in rates is less in Germany, which has a well-established apprenticeship system.

The duration of unemployment

A few of the unemployed may never have had a job and maybe never will. For most, however, unemployment lasts only a certain period. For some it may be just a few days while they are between jobs. For others it may be a few months. For others – the long-term unemployed – it could be several years. Figure 15.9 shows the composition of standardised unemployment in the UK for all aged 16 and over by duration.

What determines the average duration of unemployment? There are three important factors here.

The number unemployed (the size of the stock of unemployment). Unemployment is a 'stock' concept (see Box 10.10). It measures a *quantity* (i.e. the number unemployed) at a particular *point in time*. The higher the stock of unemployment, the longer will tend to be the duration of unemployment. There will be more people competing for vacant jobs.

The rate of inflow and outflow from the stock of unemployment. The people making up the unemployment total are constantly changing. Each week some people are made redundant or quit their jobs. They represent an inflow to the stock of unemployment. Other people find jobs and thus represent an outflow from the stock of unemployment. The various inflows and outflows are shown in Figure 15.10. KI 26 p309

Unemployment is often referred to as 'the pool of unemployment'. This is quite a good analogy. If the water flowing into a pool exceeds the water flowing out, the level of water in the pool will rise. Similarly, if the inflow of people into

Figure 15.9 UK standardised unemployment by duration

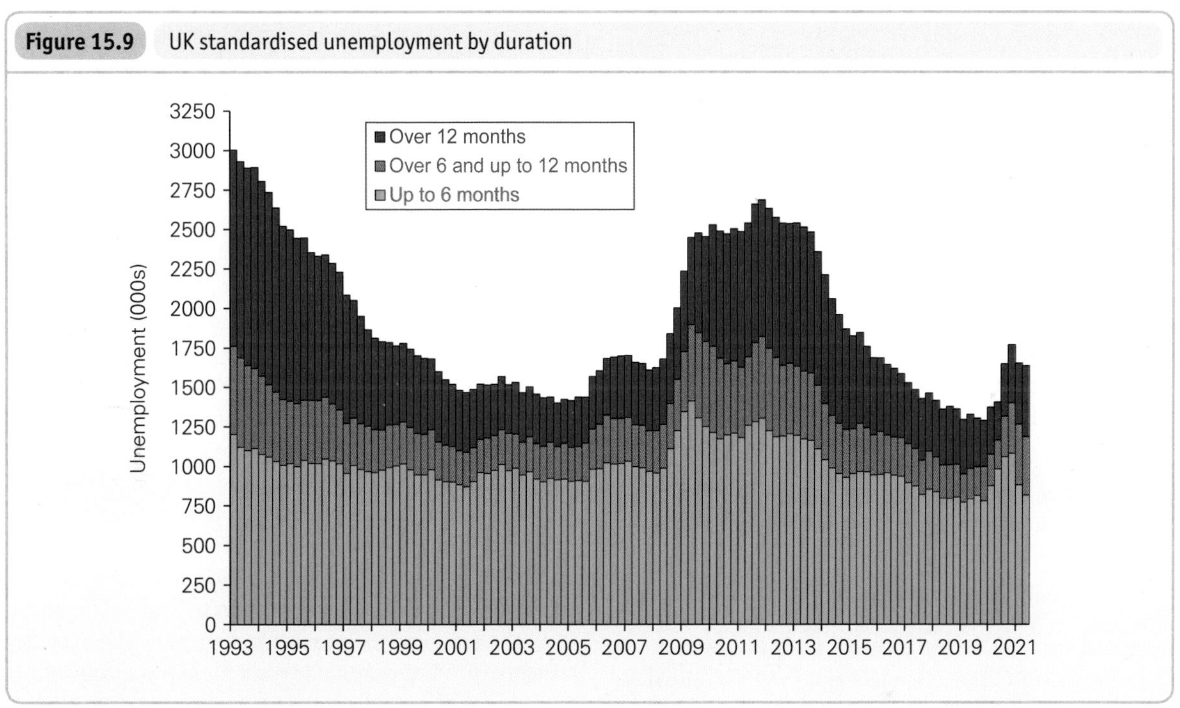

Source: Based on data *in Labour Force Survey*, series YBWF, YBWG and YBWH, National Statistics, www.ons.gov.uk/employmentandlabourmarket/peoplenotinwork/unemployment/

Figure 15.10 Flows into and out of unemployment

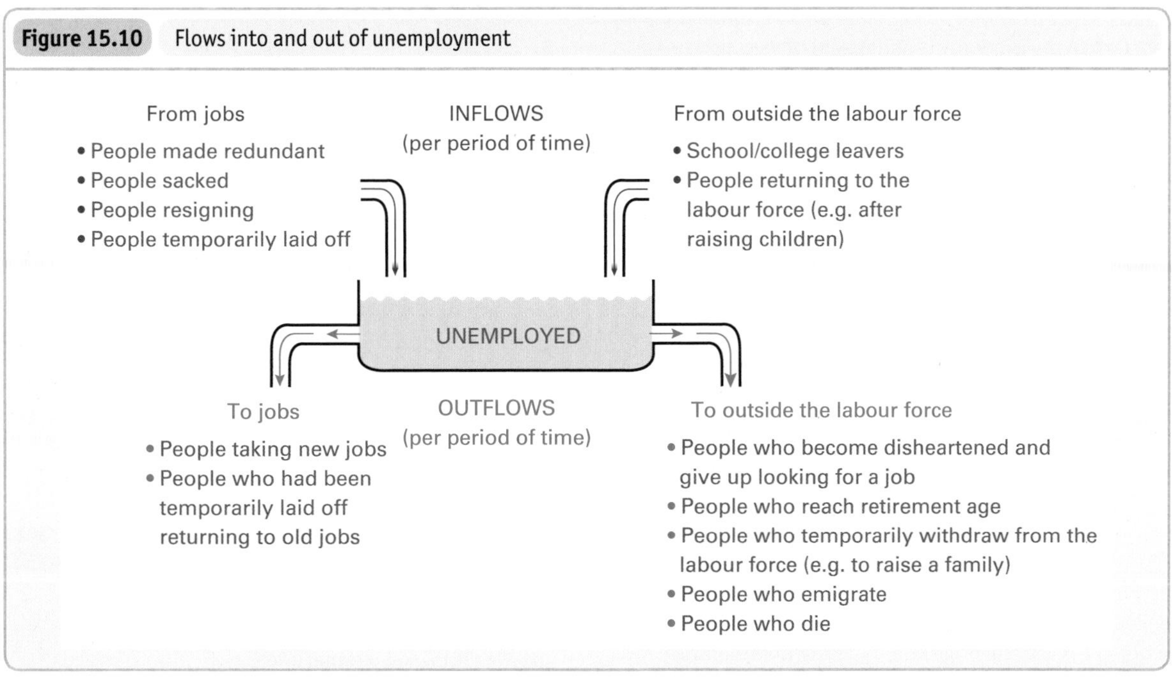

*LOOKING AT THE MATHS

The average duration of unemployment (D_U) will equal the stock of unemployment (U) as a proportion of the outflow (F) from unemployment.

$$D_U = \frac{U}{F}$$

Thus the bigger the stock of unemployment relative to the outflow from it, the longer will unemployment last. Taking the UK figures for 2015, where the number unemployed (U) was 1.78 million and the total outflow from unemployment (F) was 3.44 million:

$$D_U = \frac{1.781}{3.344} = 0.533$$

Thus the average duration of unemployment was 0.533 years or 195 days. By contrast, in 2012, the average duration was 2.572/3.945 = 0.652 years or 239 days.

unemployment exceeds the outflow, the level of unemployment will rise.

The duration of unemployment will depend on the *rate* of inflow and outflow. The rate is expressed as the number of people per period of time. The bigger the flows are relative to the total number unemployed, the less will be the average duration of unemployment. This is because people move into and out of the pool more quickly, and hence their average stay will be shorter.

1. *If the number unemployed exceeded the total annual outflow, what could we conclude about the average duration of unemployment?*
2. *Make a list of the various inflows to and outflows from employment from and to (a) unemployment; (b) outside the workforce.*

The phase of the business cycle. The duration of unemployment also depends on the phase of the business cycle. At the onset of a recession, unemployment will rise, but as yet the average length of unemployment is likely to have been relatively short. Once a recession has lasted for a period of time, however, people will on average have been out of work longer, and this long-term unemployment is likely to persist even when the economy is pulling out of recession.

Causes of unemployment

There are various possible causes of unemployment. It is important when thinking about policies to tackle unemployment to understand its determinants. The following are among those most commonly identified by economists.

Real wage rates

Nominal wage rates are the actual value of wage rates paid to workers. The real wage rate is the wage rate expressed in terms of its purchasing power to workers and the purchasing cost to employers. In other words, the real wage is the nominal wage corrected for inflation.

$$W_r = \frac{W_n}{P}$$

where W_r is the real wage rate; W_n is the nominal wage rate; and P is the price index (e.g. the CPI).

Real-wage unemployment occurs when trade unions use their monopoly power to drive wages *above* the market-clearing level. It could also be caused by the government setting the national minimum wage too high.

A rise in real wage rates increases the effective cost to firms of employing workers. This is because the wage rates paid by firms have increased *relative* to the prices of their goods and services. Excessive real wage rates were blamed by the UK Conservative governments under Thatcher and Major for the high unemployment of the 1980s and 1990s. The possibility of higher real-wage unemployment was also one of the reasons for their rejection of a national minimum wage.

One effect of high real wage rates, however, may help to reduce real-wage unemployment. The extra wages paid to those who are still employed could lead to extra *consumer* expenditure. Higher real wage rates increase the purchasing power of workers. This addition to aggregate demand could, in turn, lead to firms demanding more labour, as they attempt to increase output to meet the extra demand.

If the higher consumer expenditure and higher wages subsequently led to higher prices, what would happen to (a) real wages; (b) unemployment (assuming no further response from unions)?

The phase of the business cycle

We have seen throughout this chapter how volatile economies are. Changes in output associated with the business cycle will result in changes in employment and unemployment. In a recession, unemployment is likely to rise, whereas in a boom, it is likely to fall.

Demand-deficient is the name we give to unemployment associated with falling aggregate demand. As aggregate demand falls, firms find that they are unable to sell their current level of output. For a time they may be prepared to build up stocks of unsold goods, but sooner or later they will start to cut back on production and cut back on the amount of labour they employ.

Definition

Real-wage unemployment Disequilibrium unemployment caused by real wages being driven up above the market-clearing level.

As aggregate demand begins to grow again and firms increase output, so demand-deficient unemployment will start to fall again. Because demand-deficient unemployment fluctuates with the business cycle, it is sometimes referred to as ***cyclical unemployment***. Figure 15.11 shows the fluctuations in unemployment in industrialised economies. If you compare this figure with Figure 15.1 on page 453, you can see how unemployment tends to rise in recessions and fall in booms.

Demand-deficient unemployment is also referred to as 'Keynesian unemployment', after John Maynard Keynes (see pages 501 and 507 below and Case Study 16.6 on the student website for a profile of the great economist), who saw a deficiency of aggregate demand as the cause of the high unemployment between the two world wars. Today, many economists are known as 'Keynesian'. Although there are many strands of Keynesian thinking, these economists all see aggregate demand as important in determining a nation's output and employment.

The more that aggregate demand fluctuates, the more significant the cyclical component of unemployment becomes. But what affects the amount that unemployment rises following a fall in aggregate demand?

One consideration is the magnitude and persistence of the fall in aggregate demand. This will affect the aggregate demand for labour. A large or enduring downturn could result in a large rise in unemployment as the aggregate demand for labour falls. On the other hand, a small or transitory downturn is more likely to have a smaller impact on unemployment.

Another consideration is the extent to which, if at all, the *real* average wage rate falls. A fall in real wage rates reduces the effective cost to firms of employing workers and thus helps to offset some of the fall in employment that arises from the general reduction in firms' demand for labour. The UK has a relatively 'flexible' labour market, with many people on zero-hour, part-time or 'self-employed' contracts and having no union representation. In the recession that followed the financial crisis in the late 2000s, many workers faced cuts in real wages, but unemployment rose less than in some other countries with less flexible labour markets.

Is it in the interest only of workers (i.e. and not employers) to resist falls in real wage rates?

For some Keynesian economists, however, the problem is much more fundamental than a downward stickiness in real wages. For them, the problem is that the low level of aggregate demand causes an *equilibrium* in the *goods* market at an output that is too low to generate full employment. Firms' supply is low (below the full-employment level of supply) because aggregate demand is low.

This low-level equilibrium in the goods market, and the corresponding disequilibrium in the labour market, may *persist*. This can be exacerbated by a lack of confidence on the part of firms and consumers. After all, why should firms produce more and take on more workers if they believe that the recession will persist and that they will therefore not sell any more? And if consumers are fearful that the recession will persist, they will be more cautious in their spending.

Definition

Demand-deficient or cyclical unemployment
Disequilibrium unemployment caused by a fall in aggregate demand with no corresponding fall in the real wage rate.

Figure 15.11 Standardised unemployment rates in selected industrialised economies

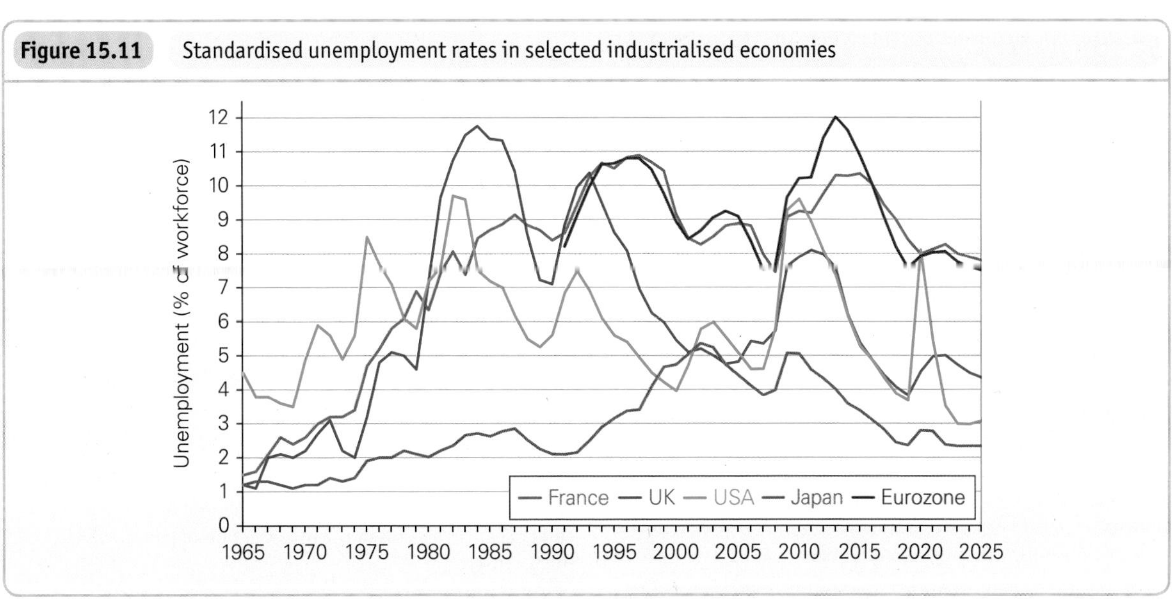

Notes: Data from 2021 based on forecasts; Eurozone = 19 countries using the euro (as of October 2021).
Source: Based on data in *AMECO Database*, European Commission (to 1980), https://ec.europa.eu/info/business-economy-euro/indicators-statistics/economic-databases/macro-economic-database-ameco/ameco-database_en; and *World Economic Outlook*, IMF (October 2021), www.imf.org/en/Publications/SPROLLs/world-economic-outlook-databases

The economy can, therefore, remain trapped in a low-output equilibrium. In such cases, a fall in real wages would not cure the unemployment. In fact, it might even make the problem worse.

If this analysis is correct, namely that a reduction in wages will reduce the aggregate demand for goods, what assumption must we make about the relative proportions of wages and profits that are spent (given that a reduction in real wage rates will lead to a corresponding increase in rates of profit)?

Information

Frictional (search) unemployment occurs when people leave their jobs, either voluntarily or because they are sacked or made redundant, and are unemployed for a period of time while they are looking for a new job. They may not get the first job they apply for, despite a vacancy existing and despite their being suitably qualified.

KI 15 p132 The problem is that information is imperfect. Employers are not fully informed about what labour is available; workers are not fully informed about what jobs are available and what they entail. Both employers and workers, therefore, have to search: employers searching for the right labour and workers searching for the right jobs.

One obvious remedy for frictional unemployment is to provide better job information through government job centres, private employment agencies or the media. Another much more controversial remedy is for the government to reduce the level of unemployment benefit. This will make the unemployed more desperate to get a job and thus prepared to accept a lower wage. It may, of course, make them more dispirited and more likely to give up in their search.

Structural change

Structural unemployment occurs where the structure of the economy changes. Many countries have witnessed rapid structural change over recent years. This has seen employment in some industries expand while in others it has contracted. There are two main reasons for this.

A change in the pattern of demand. Some industries experience declining demand. This may be due to a change in consumer tastes as certain goods go out of fashion; or it may be due to competition from other industries or from competition overseas. For example, consumer demand may shift away from fossil fuels to green energy. This will lead to structural unemployment in mining areas.

A change in the methods of production (technological unemployment). New techniques of production often allow the same level of output to be produced or the same level of demand to be met with fewer workers (see Case Study 15.9 on the student website). This is known as 'labour-saving technical progress'. Unless output expands sufficiently to absorb the surplus labour, people will be made redundant. This creates ***technological unemployment***. Examples include the loss of jobs in the retail sector caused by the rise of e-retail and in banking by the increased use of electronic payments and online banking services – trends that have been accentuated by the COVID-19 pandemic.

Structural unemployment often occurs in particular regions of the country when industries located in those regions decline or introduce labour-saving technology. When it does, it is referred to as ***regional unemployment***.

The level of structural unemployment depends on three factors:

- The degree of *regional concentration* of industry. The more that industries are concentrated in particular regions, the greater will be the level of structural unemployment if particular industries decline. For example, the collapse in the South Wales coal-mining industry in the 1980s and 1990s led to high unemployment in the Welsh valleys.
- The *speed of change* of demand and supply in the economy. The more rapid the rate of technological change or the shift in consumer tastes, the more rapid will be the rate of redundancies.
- The *immobility of labour*. The less able or willing workers are to move to a new job, the higher will be the level of structural unemployment. In Chapter 10 we made the distinction between geographical and occupational immobility (see pages 287–8). Geographical immobility is a particular problem with regional unemployment. Occupational immobility is a particular problem with technological unemployment where old skills are no longer required.

Definitions

Frictional (search) unemployment Equilibrium unemployment that occurs as a result of imperfect information in the labour market. It often takes time for workers to find jobs (even though there are vacancies) and in the meantime they are unemployed.

Structural unemployment Equilibrium unemployment that arises from changes in the pattern of demand or supply in the economy. People made redundant in one part of the economy cannot immediately take up jobs in other parts (even though there are vacancies).

Technological unemployment Structural unemployment that occurs as a result of the introduction of labour-saving technology.

Regional unemployment Structural unemployment occurring in specific regions of the country.

There are two broad approaches to tackling structural unemployment: *market-orientated* and *interventionist*.

A market-orientated approach involves encouraging people to look more actively for jobs, if necessary in other parts of the country. It involves encouraging people to adopt a more willing attitude towards retraining and, if necessary, to accept some reduction in wages.

An interventionist approach involves direct government action to match jobs to the unemployed. Two examples are providing grants to firms to set up in areas of high unemployment (regional policy), and government-funded training schemes.

Policies to tackle structural unemployment are examined in detail in sections 23.5 and 23.6.

Seasonal factors

Seasonal unemployment occurs when the demand for certain types of labour fluctuates with the seasons of the year. This problem is particularly severe in holiday areas, such as Cornwall, where unemployment can reach very high levels in the winter months. Policies for tackling seasonal unemployment are similar to those for structural unemployment.

Definition

Seasonal unemployment Unemployment associated with industries or regions where the demand for labour is lower at certain times of the year.

Section summary

1. Who should be counted as 'unemployed' is a matter for some disagreement. The two most common measures of unemployment are claimant unemployment (those claiming unemployment-related benefits) and ILO/OECD standardised unemployment (those available for work and actively seeking work or waiting to take up an appointment). Standardised unemployment measures are based on labour force surveys.
2. The 'stock' of unemployment will grow if the inflow of people into unemployment exceeds the outflow (to jobs or out of the labour market altogether). The more rapid these flows, the shorter the average duration of unemployment.
3. In most countries, unemployment is unevenly distributed across geographical regions, between women and men, between age groups and between different ethnic groups.
4. The costs of unemployment include the financial and other personal costs to the unemployed person, the costs to relatives and friends, and the costs to society at large in terms of lost tax revenues, lost profits and lost wages to other workers, and in terms of social disruption.
5. When thinking about possible policies to tackle unemployment it is important to understand its causes.
6. Possible causes include excessive real wages (real-wage unemployment), deficient aggregate demand (demand-deficient or cyclical unemployment), poor information in the labour market and hence a time lag before people find suitable jobs (frictional unemployment), structural change in the economy (structural unemployment – specific types being technological and regional unemployment), or seasonal fluctuations in the demand for labour (seasonal unemployment).

15.6 INFLATION

The rate of inflation refers to the annual percentage increase in price levels. By this is meant the percentage increase in a specific price index.

Different inflation rate measures

As we saw in section 15.1, the term 'rate of inflation' is typically used to refer to the annual percentage change in *consumer* prices. The index that is normally used is the consumer prices index (CPI), which is used throughout the EU. Sometimes in the UK an older measure is used, the retail price index (RPI). Unlike CPI, RPI includes housing costs. The CPI is seen as more sophisticated as it is based on a geometric mean of the basket of goods making up the index, whereas the RPI is based on an arithmetic mean. The effect is to make the RPI typically around 1.25 percentage points higher than the CPI. People whose incomes are increased in line with inflation will thus fare better if this is based on the RPI rather than the CPI.[5]

A broader measure of inflation relates to the rate at which the prices of all domestically produced goods and services are changing. The price index used in this case is known as the

***LOOKING AT THE MATHS**

The inflation rate (π) is calculated from the following formula:

$$\pi_t = \frac{P_t - P_{t-1}}{P_{t-1}} \times 100$$

where P_t is the price index for year t and P_{t-1} is the price index for the previous year. Thus if the price index for year 1 is 140.0 and that for year 2 is 149.1, then inflation in year 2 is

$$\pi = \frac{149.1 - 140.0}{140.0} \times 100 = 6.5\%$$

5 See Julian Champkin, 'RPI versus CPI: what's the difference? Why does it matter? Will it make you poorer or richer?', *Significance* (RSS/ASA, 10 January 2013).

GDP deflator (see Case Study 15.1 on the student website). Figure 15.12 shows inflation rates for selected industrialised countries using the GDP deflator. It helps to reinforce the evidence from Table 15.3 (see page 457) that inflation rates in many countries have been significantly lower since the 1990s than those experienced in the 1970s and the early 1980s.

It is also possible to give the rates of inflation for other prices. For example, indices are published for commodity prices, for food prices, for house prices, for import prices, for prices after taking taxes into account, and so on. Their respective rates of inflation are simply their annual percentage increases. Likewise it is possible to give the rate of inflation of earnings.

Figure 15.13 shows earnings and consumer price inflation rates for the UK from 2001. These rates have implications for the purchasing power of workers. We can see, for example, a marked erosion of purchasing power from 2009 following the financial crisis, which was to persist through much of the first half of the 2010s, and again, to some degree, during 2017 and 2020.

Before we proceed, a word of caution: be careful not to confuse a rise or fall in *inflation* with a rise or fall in *prices*. A rise in inflation means a *faster* increase in prices. A fall in inflation means a *slower* increase in prices (but still an increase as long as inflation is positive). (See Box A1.1 on page A:11.)

Make a list of those who are most likely to gain and those who are most likely to lose from inflation.

Causes of inflation

Demand-pull inflation

Demand-pull inflation is caused by continuing rises in aggregate demand. Firms will respond to a rise in demand partly by raising prices and partly by increasing output. Just how much they raise prices depends on how much their costs rise as a result of increasing output. The closer actual output gets to potential output, and the less slack there is in the economy, the more will firms respond to a rise in demand by raising their prices. On the other hand, the greater the spare capacity, the more will firms respond by raising output and the less by raising prices.

Sometimes there may be a *single* increase in demand (or a 'demand shock'). This could be due, for example, to an increased level of government expenditure. The effect is to give a *single* rise in the price level. Although this causes inflation in the short run, once the effect has taken place,

Definitions

GDP deflator The price index of all final domestically produced goods and services: i.e. all those items that contribute towards GDP.

Demand-pull inflation Inflation caused by persistent rises in aggregate demand.

Figure 15.12 Inflation rates in selected developed economies

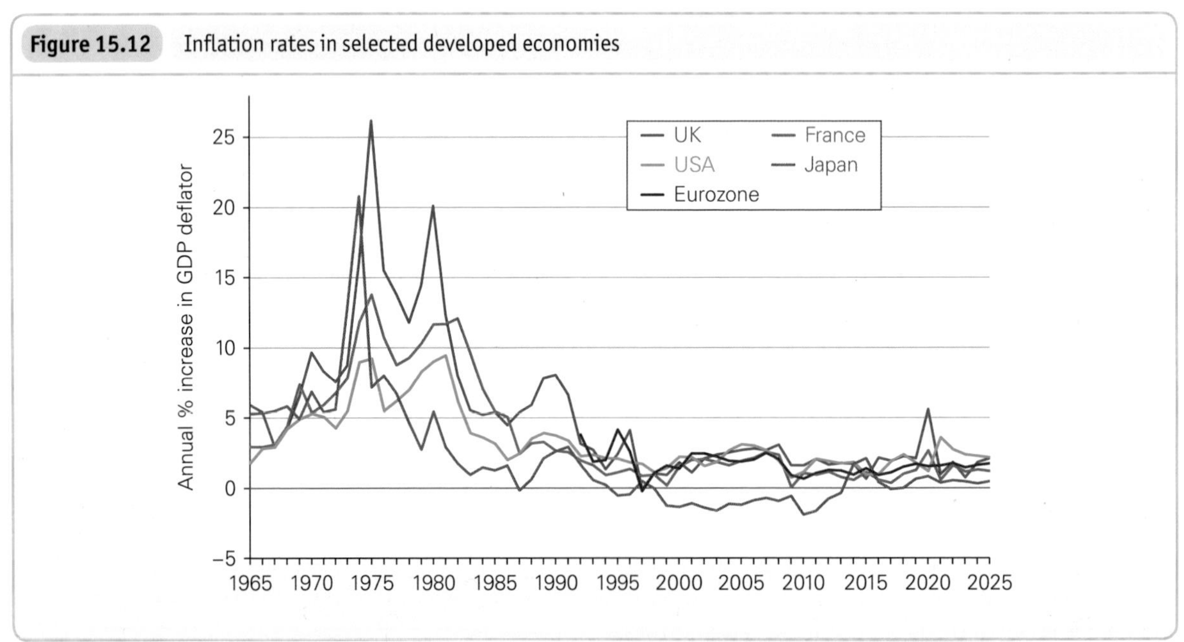

Notes: Data from 2021 based on forecasts; Eurozone = 19 countries using the euro (as of 2021).
Source: Based on data in *AMECO Database*, European Commission (to 1980), https://ec.europa.eu/info/business-economy-euro/indicators-statistics/economic-databases/macro-economic-database-ameco/ameco-database_en; *World Economic Outlook*, IMF (October 2021), www.imf.org/en/Publications/SPROLLS/world-economic-outlook-databases; and various forecasts.

Figure 15.13 UK inflation rates: consumer prices and average earnings

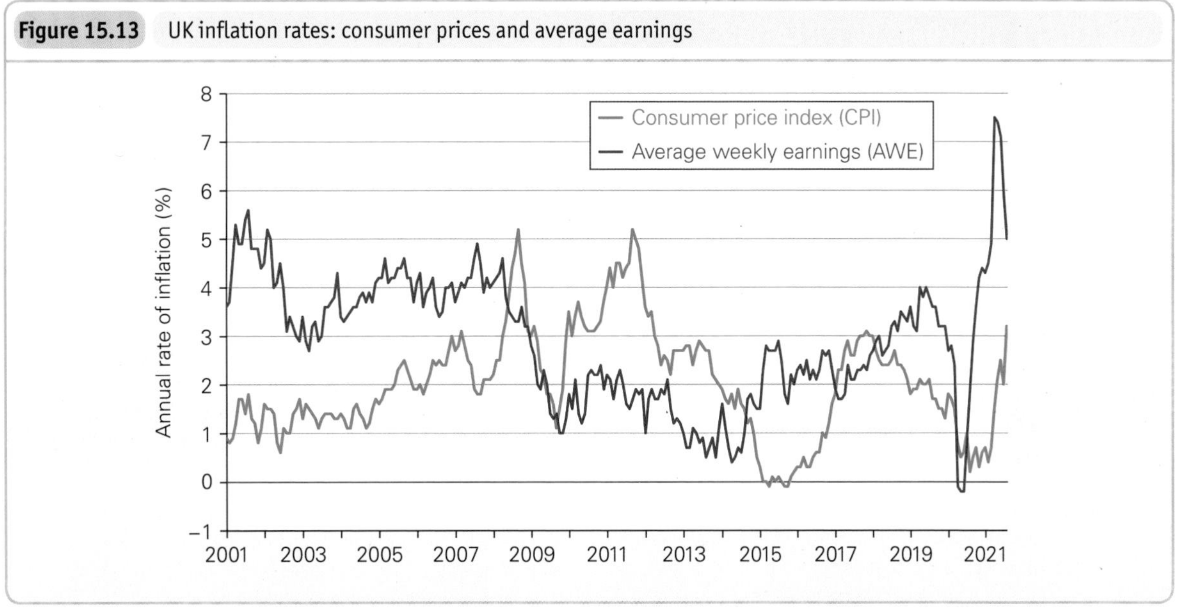

Note: Earnings inflation is the annual percentage change in the monthly-average weekly regular pay (excluding bonuses and arrears).
Source: Based on *Time Series Data*, series D7G7 and KAI8, ONS, www.ons.gov.uk/economy/inflationandpriceindices/

inflation will fall back again. For inflation to persist, there must be *continuing* increases in aggregate demand and thus continuing rises in the price level. If inflation is to rise, the rate of increase in aggregate demand must also rise.

Demand-pull inflation is typically associated with a booming economy. Many economists therefore argue that it is the counterpart of demand-deficient unemployment. When the economy is in recession, demand-deficient unemployment is high, but demand-pull inflation is low. When, on the other hand, the economy is near the peak of the business cycle, demand-pull inflation is high, but demand-deficient unemployment is low.

Cost-push inflation

Cost-push inflation is associated with continuing rises in costs which occur *independently* of aggregate demand.

If firms face a rise in costs, they will respond partly by raising prices and passing the costs on to the consumer, and partly by cutting back on production. Just how much firms raise prices and cut back on production depends on the impact of price changes on aggregate demand. The less responsive is aggregate demand to price changes, the less will sales fall as a result of any price rise. This allows firms to pass on more of the rise in their costs to consumers as higher prices. On the other hand, the more sensitive aggregate demand is to price changes, the less able are firms to pass on their higher costs to consumers: hence prices rise by less.

Note that the effect on output and employment is the opposite of demand-pull inflation. With demand-pull inflation, output and hence employment tend to rise. With cost-push inflation, however, output and employment tend to fall.

As with demand-pull inflation, we must distinguish between *one-off* increases in cost (a 'supply shock') from *continuing* increases. If there is a one-off increase in costs, there will be a one-off rise in the price level. For example, if the government raises the excise duty on petrol and diesel, there will be a single rise in fuel prices and hence in firms' fuel costs. This will cause *temporary* inflation while the price rise is passed on through the economy. Once this has occurred, prices will stabilise at the new level and the rate of inflation will fall back again. If cost-push inflation is to continue over a number of years, therefore, then costs must *continually* increase. If cost-push inflation is to *rise*, the rate of increase in costs must also rise.

Sources of cost-push inflation. Rises in costs may originate from a number of different sources, such as increases in international commodity prices, trade unions pushing up wages, or firms with monopoly power raising prices in order to increase their profits. With the process of globalisation and increased international competition, cost-push pressures have tended to decrease in recent years. One major exception has been the oil shocks that have occurred from time to time. For example, the near tripling of oil prices from $51 per barrel in January 2007 to $147 per barrel in July 2008, and again from $41 a barrel in January 2009 to $126 a barrel in April 2011, put upward pressure on costs and prices around the world.

Definition

Cost-push inflation Inflation caused by persistent rises in costs of production (independently of demand).

BOX 15.5 **THE COSTS OF INFLATION** EXPLORING ECONOMICS

Who loses and by how much?

A lack of growth is obviously a problem if people want higher living standards. Unemployment is obviously a problem, both for the unemployed themselves and also for society, which suffers a loss in output and has to support the unemployed. But why is inflation a problem? If prices go up by 10 per cent, does it really matter? Provided your wages kept up with prices, you would have no cut in your living standards.

If people could correctly anticipate the rate of inflation and fully adjust prices and incomes to take account of it, then the costs of inflation would indeed be relatively small. For us as consumers, they would simply be the relatively minor inconvenience of having to adjust our notions of what a 'fair' price is for each item when we go shopping. For firms, they would again be the relatively minor costs of having to change price labels, or prices in catalogues or on menus, or adjust slot machines. These are known as ***menu costs***.

In reality, people frequently make mistakes when predicting the rate of inflation and are not able to adapt fully to it. This leads to the following problems, which are likely to be more serious the higher the rate of inflation becomes and the more the rate fluctuates.

Redistribution. Inflation redistributes income away from those on fixed incomes and those in a weak bargaining position, to those who can use their economic power to gain large pay, rent or profit increases. It redistributes wealth to those with assets (e.g. property) that rise in value particularly rapidly during periods of inflation, and away from those with types of savings that pay rates of interest below the rate of inflation and hence whose value is eroded by inflation. Elderly people who rely on the interest from their savings may be particularly badly hit by rapid inflation.

Uncertainty and lack of investment. Inflation tends to cause uncertainty among the business community, especially when the rate of inflation fluctuates. (Generally, the higher the rate of inflation, the more it fluctuates.) If it is difficult for firms to predict their costs and revenues, they may be discouraged from investing. This will reduce the rate of economic growth. On the other hand, as will be explained below, policies to reduce the rate of inflation may themselves reduce the rate of economic growth, especially in the short run. This may then provide the government with a policy dilemma.

Balance of payments. Inflation is likely to worsen the balance of trade. If a country suffers from relatively high inflation, its exports will become less competitive in world markets. At the same time, imports will become relatively cheaper than home-produced goods. Thus exports will fall and imports will rise. This is known an international substitution effect. As a result, the balance of trade will deteriorate and/or the exchange rate will fall. Both of these effects can cause problems.

Resources. Extra resources are likely to be used to cope with the effects of inflation. Accountants and other financial experts may have to be employed by companies to help them cope with the uncertainties caused by inflation.

The costs of inflation may be relatively mild if inflation is kept to single figures. They can be very serious, however, if inflation gets out of hand. If inflation develops into 'hyperinflation', with prices rising perhaps by several hundred per cent or even thousands per cent per year, the whole basis of the market economy will be undermined. Firms constantly raise prices in an attempt to cover their soaring costs. Workers demand huge pay increases in an attempt to stay ahead of the rocketing cost of living. Thus prices and wages chase each other in an ever-rising inflationary spiral. People will no longer want to save money. Instead they will spend it as quickly as possible before its value falls any further. People may even resort to barter in an attempt to avoid using money altogether. (Case Study 15.12 on the student website looks at historical cases of hyperinflation in Germany in the 1920s, Serbia in the 1990s and Zimbabwe in the 2000s.)

Do you personally gain or lose from inflation? Why?

Draw up a list of those who are most likely to gain and those who are most likely to lose from inflation.

Definition

Menu costs of inflation The costs associated with having to adjust price lists or labels.

Temporary supply shocks can come from bad harvests, major labour disputes or an infectious disease, such as the COVID-19 pandemic. Longer-term supply-side problems can come from the depletion of natural resources, such as the gradual running down of North Sea oil, pollution of the seas and hence a decline in incomes for nations with large fishing industries, and, perhaps the most devastating of all, the effects of global warming, including the problem of 'desertification' in sub-Saharan Africa, rising sea levels and more frequent floods, droughts and wildfires.

The interaction of demand-pull and cost-push inflation

Demand-pull and cost-push inflation can occur together, since wage and price rises can be caused both by increases in aggregate demand and by independent causes pushing up costs. Even when an inflationary process *starts* as either

BOX 15.6 THE PHILLIPS CURVE

EXPLORING ECONOMICS

Is higher inflation the price for lower unemployment?

If inflation tends to be higher when the economy is booming and if unemployment tends to be higher in recessions, does this mean that there is a 'trade-off' between inflation and unemployment: that lower unemployment tends to be associated with higher inflation, and lower inflation with higher unemployment? Such a trade-off was observed by the New Zealand economist Bill Phillips (see Case Study 15.13 on the student website), and was illustrated by the famous ***Phillips curve***.

The original Phillips curve

In 1958, Phillips showed the statistical relationship between wage inflation and unemployment in the UK from 1861 to 1957. With wage inflation (ω) on the vertical axis and the unemployment rate (U) on the horizontal axis, a scatter of points was obtained. Each point represented the observation for a particular year. The curve that best fitted the scatter has become known as the 'Phillips curve'. It is illustrated in Figure (a) and shows an inverse relationship between inflation and unemployment.[1]

Given that wage increases over the period were approximately 2 per cent above price increases (made possible because of increases in labour productivity), a similar-shaped, but lower curve could be plotted showing the relationship between *price* inflation and unemployment.

The curve has often been used to illustrate the effects of changes in aggregate demand. When aggregate demand rose (relative to potential output), inflation rose and unemployment fell: there was an upward movement along the curve. When aggregate demand fell, there was a downward movement along the curve.

There was also a second reason given for the inverse relationship. If wages rose, the unemployed might have believed that the higher wages they were offered represented a *real* wage increase. That is, they might not have realised that the higher wages would be 'eaten up' by price increases: they might have suffered from ***money illusion***. They would thus have accepted jobs more readily. The average duration of unemployment therefore fell. This is a reduction in *frictional* unemployment.

TC 13 p461

(a) *The original Phillips curve*

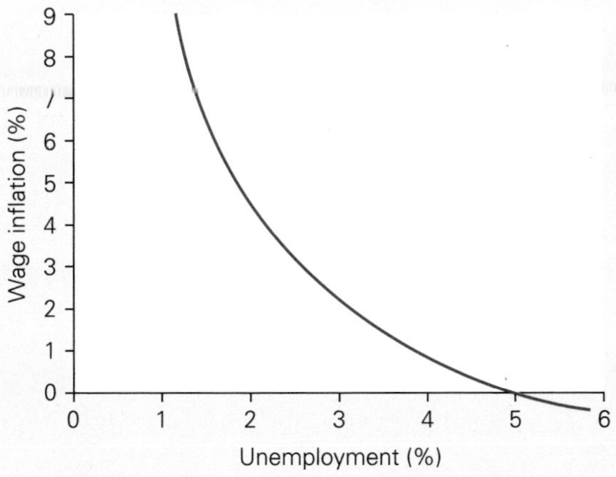

The Phillips curve was bowed in to the origin. The usual explanation for this is that, as aggregate demand expanded, at first there would be plenty of surplus labour, which could meet the extra demand without the need to raise wages very much. But as labour became increasingly scarce, firms would find they had to offer increasingly higher wages to obtain the labour they required, and the position of trade unions would be increasingly strengthened.

The *position* of the Phillips curve depended on *non-*demand factors causing inflation and unemployment: frictional and structural unemployment; and cost-push, structural and expectations-generated inflation. If any of these non-demand factors changed so as to raise inflation or unemployment, the curve would shift outwards to the right. The relative stability of the curve over the hundred years or so observed by Phillips suggested that these non-demand factors had changed little.

The Phillips curve seemed to present governments with a simple policy choice. They could trade off inflation against unemployment. Lower unemployment could be bought at the cost of higher inflation, and vice versa. Unfortunately, the experience since the late 1960s has suggested that no such simple relationship exists beyond the short run.

KI 36 p459

The breakdown of the Phillips curve

From about 1967 the Phillips curve relationship seemed to break down. The UK, and many other countries in the Western world too, began to experience growing unemployment *and* higher rates of inflation.

Figure (b) shows price inflation (π) and (standardised) unemployment in the UK from 1960. From 1960 to 1967 a curve similar to the Phillips curve can be fitted through the data (the red line). From 1968 to the early 1990s, however, no simple picture emerges. Certainly the original Phillips curve could no longer fit the data; but whether the curve shifted to the right and then back again somewhat (the broken lines), or whether the relationship broke down completely, or whether there was some quite different relationship between inflation and unemployment, is not clear by simply looking at the data.

Since 1997, the Bank of England has been targeting inflation (see section 22.3). For much of this period the

Definitions

Phillips curve A curve showing the relationship between (price) inflation and unemployment. The original Phillips curve plotted wage inflation against unemployment for the years 1861–1957.

Money illusion When people believe that a money wage or price increase represents a real increase: in other words, they ignore or underestimate inflation.

(continued)

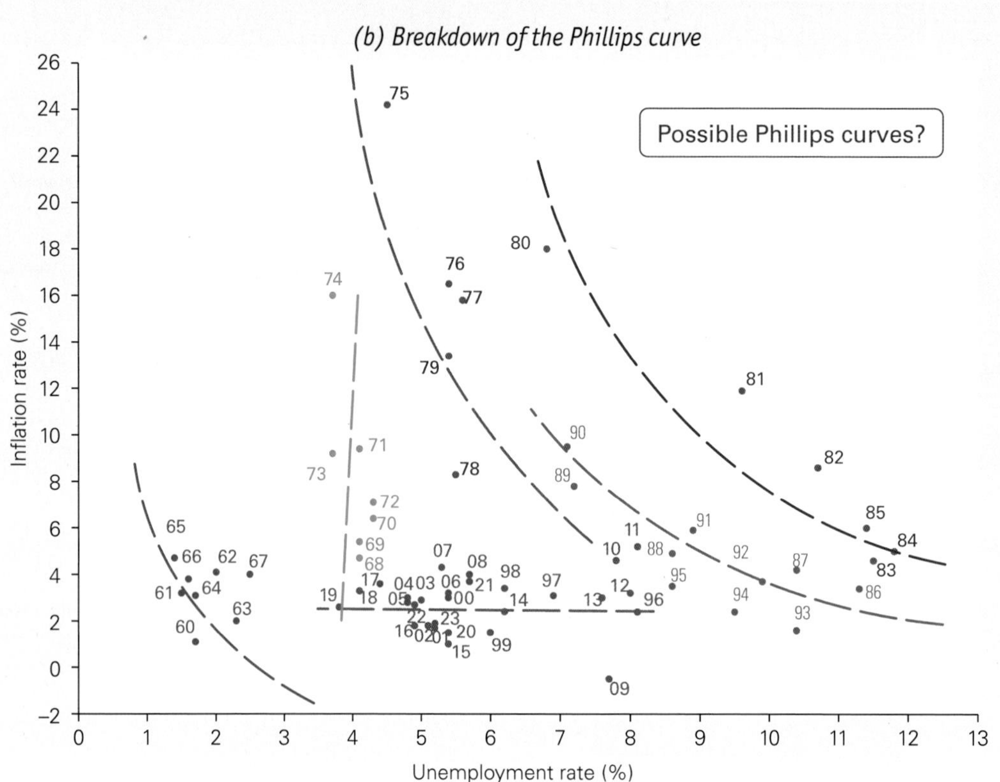

Source: Based on data from the Office for National Statistics; forecasts based on data from *World Economic Outlook Database* (IMF), www.imf.org/external/ns/cs.aspx?id=28

'curve' would seem to have become a virtually horizontal straight line. However, from the late 2000s, against a backdrop of significant economic volatility and uncertainty, the range of inflation rates increased despite inflation rate targeting. A contributory factor to this was the volatility experienced in commodity prices. This is because central bank adjustments to interest rates work principally by affecting aggregate demand and so rates of demand-pull inflation. Fluctuations in *cost-push* inflation can therefore cause inflation rates to diverge from its target level.

Over the years, there has been much debate among economists about the relationship between inflation and unemployment. One particular contribution has been to examine the effect of inflationary expectations on the Phillips curve. Changes in inflationary expectations, it is argued, can affect the vertical position of the short-run relationship between inflation and unemployment. This gave rise to the idea of an ***expectations-augmented Phillips curve*** whose vertical position is higher the higher are people's expectations of inflation. We will discuss this further in later chapters and particularly in Chapter 21. One thing does seem clear, however: the relationship is different in the short run and the long run.

Definition

Expectations-augmented Phillips curve A (short-run) Phillips curve whose position depends on the expected rate of inflation.

Assume that there is a trade-off between unemployment and inflation, traced out by a 'Phillips curve'. What could cause a leftward shift in this curve?

Find data on unemployment and price inflation since 1980 for a developed country other than the UK. Plot the figures on a diagram similar to the one in this box. Are there similar patterns between inflation and unemployment to those in the UK?

1 Phillips' estimated equation was $\omega = -0.9 + 9.638U^{-1.394}$.

demand-pull or cost-push, it is often difficult to separate the two. An initial cost-push inflation may encourage the government to expand aggregate demand to offset rises in unemployment. Alternatively, an initial demand-pull inflation may strengthen the power of certain groups, which then use this power to drive up costs.

Expectations and inflation

Workers and firms take account of the *expected* rate of inflation when making decisions.

TC9 p132

Imagine that a union and an employer are negotiating a wage increase. Let us assume that both sides expect a rate of inflation of 5 per cent. The union will be happy to receive a wage rise somewhat above 5 per cent. That way the members would be getting a *real* rise in incomes. The employers will be happy to pay a wage rise somewhat below 5 per cent. After all, they can put their price up by 5 per cent, knowing that their rivals will do approximately the same. The actual wage rise that the two sides agree on will thus be somewhere around 5 per cent.

Now let us assume that the expected rate of inflation is 10 per cent. Both sides will now negotiate around this benchmark, with the outcome being somewhere round about 10 per cent. Thus the higher the expected rate of inflation, the higher will be the level of pay settlements and price rises, and hence the higher will be the resulting *actual* rate of inflation.

Just how expectations impact on inflation depends on how they are formed. We examine this in Chapter 21.

Section summary

1. Demand-pull inflation occurs as a result of increases in aggregate demand. This can be due to monetary or non-monetary causes.
2. Cost-push inflation occurs when there are increases in the costs of production independent of rises in aggregate demand. If there is a single supply-side shock, the inflation will peter out. For cost-push inflation to persist, there must be continuous increases in costs.
3. Cost-push and demand-pull inflation can interact to form spiralling inflation.
4. Expectations play a crucial role in determining the rate of inflation. The higher people expect inflation to be, the higher it will be.

15.7 THE OPEN ECONOMY

All countries trade with and have financial dealings with the rest of the world. In other words, all countries are ***open economies.*** Indeed, over time the economies of nations have become ever more intimately linked. Key drivers of this global interconnectedness of economies are globalisation, financialisation and improved communications.

Global interconnectedness means economic events in one part of the world, such as changes in interest rates or a downturn in economic growth, can have myriad knock-on effects for the international community at large – from the international investor, to the foreign exchange dealer, to the domestic policy maker, to the business which exports or imports, or which has subsidiaries abroad. Consequently, the international component of countries' business cycles has tended to become ever more important.

The balance of payments account

The flows of money between residents of a country and the rest of the world are recorded in the country's ***balance of payments account.***

Receipts of money from abroad are regarded as *credits* and are entered in the accounts with a positive sign. *Outflows* of money from the country are regarded as *debits* and are entered with a negative sign.

There are three main parts of the balance of payments account: the *current account*, the *capital account* and the *financial account*. Each part is then subdivided. We shall look at each part in turn, and take the UK as an example. Table 15.5 gives a summary of the UK balance of payments for 2019, while also providing an historical perspective.

The current account

The ***current account*** records payments for imports and exports of goods and services, plus incomes flowing into and out of the country, plus net transfers of money into and out of the country. It is normally split into four subdivisions.

The trade in goods account. This records imports and exports of physical goods (previously known as 'visibles'). Exports result in an inflow of money and are therefore a credit item. Imports result in an outflow of money and are therefore a debit item. The balance of these is called the ***balance on trade in goods*** or ***balance of visible trade*** or ***merchandise balance.*** A *surplus* is when exports exceed imports. A *deficit* is when imports exceed exports.

Definitions

Open economy One that trades with and has financial dealings with other countries.

Balance of payments account The record of all the economic transactions between the residents of a specific country with the rest of the world for a specific time period, typically a year or a quarter. It records all the inflows and outflows of money under various headings. Inflows are recorded as credits; outflows are recorded as debits.

Current account of the balance of payments The record of a country's imports and exports of goods and services, plus incomes and transfers of money to and from abroad.

Balance on trade in goods or **balance of visible trade** or **merchandise balance** Exports of goods minus imports of goods.

Table 15.5 UK balance of payments

	2020		Average 1987–2020 as % of GDP
	£m	% of GDP	
CURRENT ACCOUNT			
Balance on trade in goods	-114 956	−5.4	−4.3
Balance on trade in services	107 399	5.1	2.9
Balance of trade	**−7 557**	**−0.4**	**−1.4**
Income balance	−38 159	−1.8	−0.4
Net current transfers	−28 215	−1.3	−0.9
Current account balance	**−73 931**	**−3.5**	**−2.7**
CAPITAL ACCOUNT			
Capital account balance	**−1 811**	**−0.1**	**0.0**
FINANCIAL ACCOUNT			
Net direct investment	41 444	2.0	−0.4
Portfolio investment balance	−11 490	−0.5	3.0
Other investment balance	92 519	4.4	0.4
Balance of financial derivatives	−29 539	−1.4	−0.1
Reserve assets	2 582	0.1	−0.2
Financial account balance	**95 516**	**4.5**	**2.7**
Net errors and omissions	**−19 774**	**−0.9**	**0.0**
Balance	*0.0*	*0.0*	*0.0*

Source: Based on data from Office for National Statistics.

The trade in services account. This records imports and exports of services (such as transport, tourism and insurance). Thus the purchase of a foreign holiday would be a debit, since it represents an outflow of money, whereas the purchase by an overseas resident of a UK insurance policy would be a credit to the UK services account. The balance of these is called the *services balance*.

The balance of both the goods and services accounts together is known as the ***balance on trade in goods and services*** or simply the ***balance of trade***.

Income flows. These consist of wages, interest and profits flowing into and out of the country. For example, dividends earned by a foreign resident from shares in a UK company would be an outflow of money (a debit item).

Current transfers of money. These include government contributions to and receipts from the EU and international organisations, and international transfers of money by private individuals and firms for the purpose of *consumption*. Transfers out of the country are debits. Transfers into the country (e.g. money sent from Greece to a Greek student studying in the UK) would be a credit item.

The ***current account balance*** is the overall balance of all the above four subdivisions. A *current account surplus* is where credits exceed debits. A *current account deficit* is where debits exceed credits. Figure 15.14 shows the current account balances of a selection of countries as a proportion of their GDP since 1965. The chart shows how global imbalances on the current account have tended to increase over time, particularly since the 1980s. In conjunction with Table 15.5 we can also see that the UK has consistently run a current account deficit over the past three decades or so. This has been driven by a large trade deficit in goods.

Why are the US and UK current balances approximately a 'mirror image' of the Japanese and German current balances?

The capital account

The ***capital account*** records the flows of funds, into the country (credits) and out of the country (debits), associated with the acquisition or disposal of fixed assets (e.g. land or intangibles, such as patents and trademarks), the transfer of

Definitions

Balance on trade in goods and services or **balance of trade** Exports of goods and services minus imports of goods and services.

Balance of payments on current account The balance on trade in goods and services plus net investment incomes and current transfers.

Capital account of the balance of payments The record of the transfers of capital to and from abroad.

Figure 15.14 Current account balance as percentage of GDP in selected industrial countries

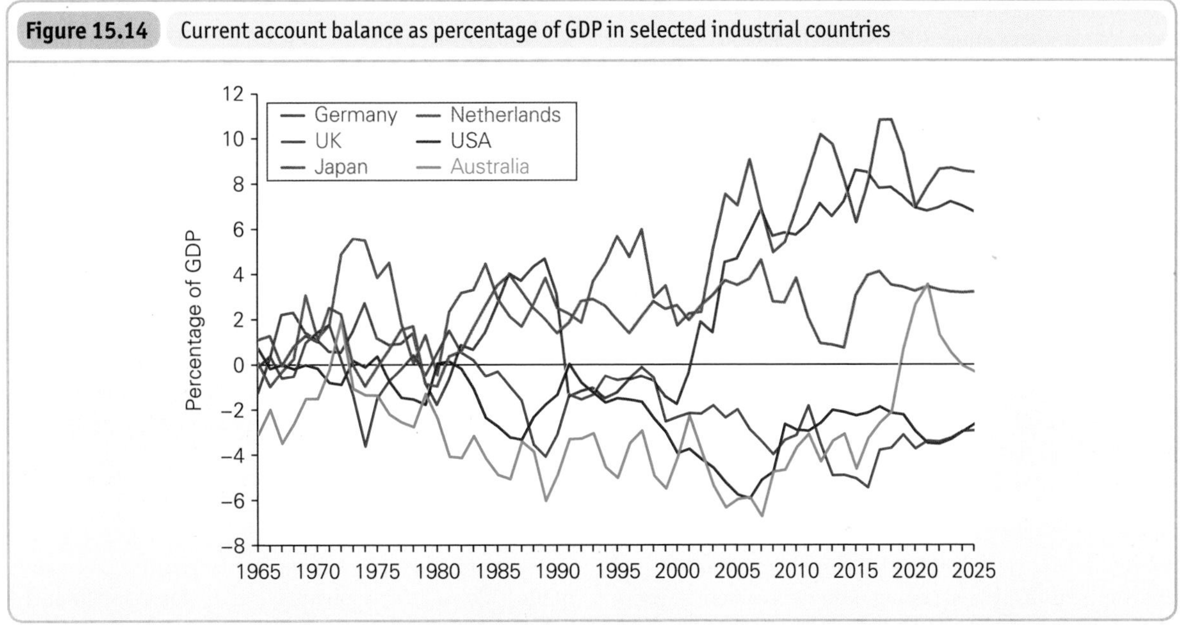

Notes: Figures from 2021 based on forecasts; German figures are West Germany up to 1991.
Source: Based on data in data in *AMECO Database*, European Commission (to 1980), https://ec.europa.eu/info/business-economy-euro/indicators-statistics/economic-databases/macro-economic-database-ameco/ameco-database_en; and *World Economic Outlook*, IMF (October 2021), www.imf.org/en/Publications/SPROLLS/world-economic-outlook-databases

funds by migrants, the payment of grants by the government for overseas projects, debt forgiveness by the government and the receipt of money for capital projects (e.g. from the EU's Agricultural Guidance Fund).

As Table 15.5 shows, the balance on the capital account is small in comparison to that on the current and financial accounts.

The financial account

The ***financial account*** of the balance of payments records cross-border changes in the holding of shares, property, bank deposits and loans, government securities, etc. In other words, unlike the current account, which is concerned with money *incomes*, the financial account is concerned with the purchase and sale of *assets*. Case Study 15.14 on the student website considers some of the statistics behind the UK's financial account.

Investment (direct and portfolio). This account covers primarily long-term investment.

- *Direct investment.* This involves a significant and lasting interest in a business in another country. If a foreign company invests money from abroad in one of its branches or associated companies in the UK, this represents an inflow of money when the investment is made and is thus a credit item. (Any subsequent profit from this investment that flows abroad will be recorded as an *investment income outflow* on the current account.) Investment abroad by UK companies represents an outflow of money when the investment is made. It is thus a debit item.

  Note that what we are talking about here is the acquisition or sale of assets: e.g. a factory or farm, or the takeover of a whole firm, not the imports or exports of equipment.
- *Portfolio investment.* This relates to transactions in debt and equity securities which do not result in the investor having any significant influence on the operations of a particular business. If a UK resident buys shares (equity securities) in an overseas company, this is an outflow of funds and is hence a debit item.

> **Definition**
>
> **Financial account of the balance of payments** The record of the flows of money into and out of the country for the purposes of investment or as deposits in banks and other financial institutions.

Other financial flows. These consist primarily of various types of short-term monetary movement between the UK and the rest of the world. Deposits by overseas residents in banks in the UK and loans to the UK from abroad are credit items since they represent an inflow of money. Deposits by UK residents in overseas banks and loans by UK banks to overseas residents are debit items. They represent an outflow of money.

Short-term monetary flows are common between international financial centres to take advantage of differences in countries' interest rates and changes in exchange rates.

1. *Why may inflows of short-term deposits create a problem?*
2. *Where would interest payments on short-term foreign deposits in UK banks be entered on the balance of payments account?*

Note that in the financial account, credits and debits are recorded *net*. For example, UK investment abroad consists of the net acquisition of assets abroad (i.e. the purchase *less* the sale of assets abroad). Similarly, foreign investment in the UK consists of the purchase *less* the sale of UK assets by foreign residents. Note that in either case the flow could be in the opposite direction. For example, if UK residents purchased fewer assets abroad than they sold, this item would be a net credit, not a debit (there would be a net return of money to the UK).

By recording financial account items as net figures, the flows seem misleadingly modest. For example, if UK residents deposited an extra £100 billion in banks abroad but drew out £99 billion, this would be recorded as a mere £1 billion net outflow on the other financial flows account. In fact, *total* financial account flows vastly exceed current plus capital account flows.

Flows to and from the reserves. The UK, like all other countries, holds reserves of gold and foreign currencies. From time to time the Bank of England (acting as the government's agent) will sell some of these reserves to purchase sterling on the foreign exchange market. It does this normally as a means of supporting the rate of exchange (see below). Drawing on reserves represents a *credit* item in the balance of payments accounts: money drawn from the reserves represents an *inflow* to the balance of payments (albeit an outflow from the reserves account). The reserves can thus be used to support a deficit elsewhere in the balance of payments.

Conversely, if there is a surplus elsewhere in the balance of payments, the Bank of England can use it to build up the reserves. Building up the reserves counts as a debit item in the balance of payments, since it represents an outflow from it (to the reserves).

When all the components of the balance of payments account are taken together, the balance of payments should exactly balance: credits should equal debits. As we shall see below, if they were not equal, the rate of exchange would have to adjust until they were, or the government would have to intervene to make them equal.

When the statistics are compiled, however, a number of errors are likely to occur. As a result, there will not be a balance. To 'correct' for this, a *net errors and omissions* item is included in the accounts. This ensures that there will be an exact balance. The main reason for the errors is that the statistics are obtained from a number of sources, and there are often delays before items are recorded and sometimes omissions too.

With reference to the above, provide an assessment of the UK balance of payments in 2020.

Figure 15.15 graphically summarises the main accounts of the UK's balance payments: current, capital and financial accounts. It presents each as a percentage of national income (see also right-hand column of Table 15.5). In conjunction with the net errors and omissions item, which averages close to zero over the long run, we can see how the accounts combine to give a zero overall balance. For much of the period since the late 1980s, current account deficits have been offset by surpluses on the financial account.

What causes deficits to occur on the various parts of the balance of payments? The answer has to do with the demand for and supply of sterling on the foreign exchange market. Thus before we can answer the question, we must examine this market and in particular the role of the rate of exchange.

Figure 15.15 UK balance of payments as a percentage of GDP

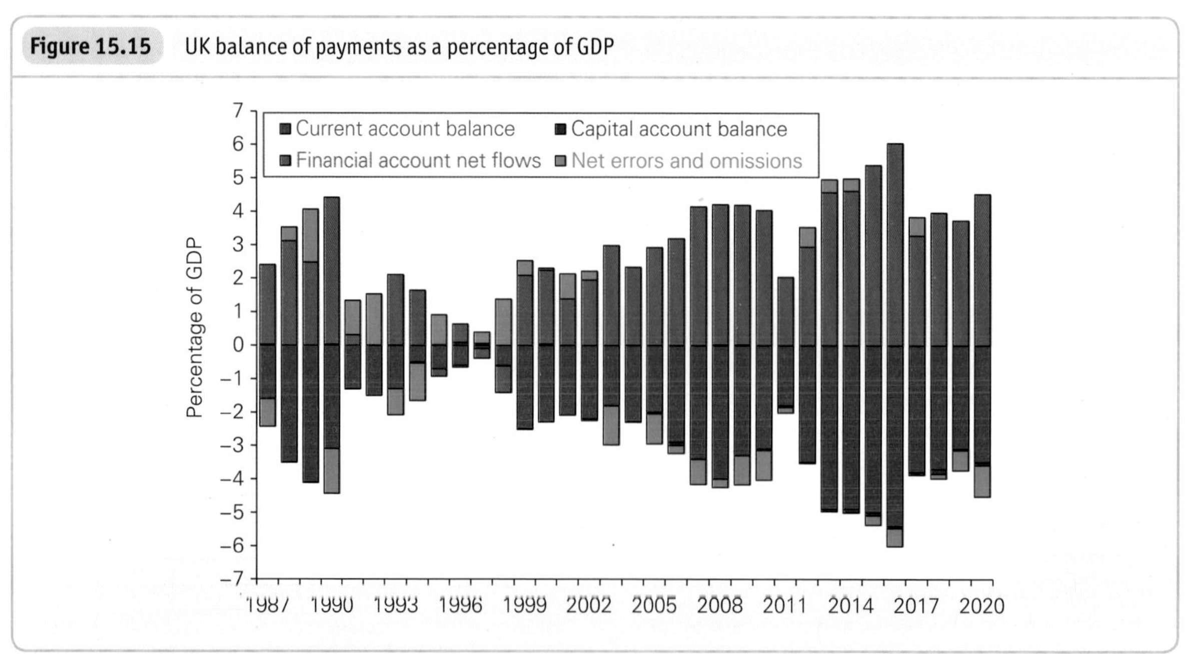

Source: Based on data from Balance of Payments time series and series YBHA, ONS, www.ons.gov.uk/economy/nationalaccounts/balanceofpayments/datasets/balanceofpayments; www.ons.gov.uk/economy/grossdomesticproductgdp/timeseries/ybha/ukea

Exchange rates

An exchange rate is the rate at which one currency trades for another on the foreign exchange market.

If you live in the UK and go abroad, you will need to exchange your pounds into euros, dollars, Swiss francs or whatever. You will get the money at the exchange rate in operation at the time you draw it from a cash machine abroad or from a bank: for example, €1.15 to the pound, or $1.25 to the pound.

It is similar for firms. If an importer wants to buy, say, some machinery from Japan, it will require yen to pay the Japanese supplier. It will thus ask the foreign exchange section of a bank to quote it a rate of exchange of the pound into yen. Similarly, if you want to buy some foreign stocks and shares, or if companies based in the UK want to invest abroad, sterling will have to be exchanged into the appropriate foreign currency.

Likewise, if Americans want to come on holiday to the UK or to buy UK assets, or US firms want to import UK goods or to invest in the UK, they will require sterling. They will get it at an exchange rate such as £1 = $1.25. This means that they will have to pay $1.25 to obtain £1 worth of UK goods or assets.

Exchange rates are quoted between each of the major currencies of the world. These exchange rates are constantly changing. Minute by minute, dealers in the foreign exchange dealing rooms of the banks are adjusting the rates of exchange. They charge commission when they exchange currencies. It is important for them, therefore, to ensure that they are not left with a large amount of any currency unsold. What they need to do is to balance the supply and demand of each currency: to balance the amount they purchase to the amount they sell. To do this, they will need to adjust the price of each currency, namely the exchange rate, in line with changes in supply and demand.

Not only are there day-to-day fluctuations in exchange rates, but also there are long-term changes in them. Figure 15.16 shows the average quarterly exchange rates between the pound and various currencies since 1980.

One of the problems in assessing what is happening to a particular currency is that its rate of exchange may rise against some currencies (weak currencies) and fall against others (strong currencies). In order to gain an overall picture of its fluctuations, therefore, it is best to look at a weighted average exchange rate against all other currencies. This is known as the ***exchange rate index***. The weight given to each currency in the index depends on the percentage of UK trade in goods and services done with countries using that currency. The weights are revised annually. Figure 15.16 also shows the sterling exchange rate index based on 2005 = 100.

From looking at Figure 15.16, how has the pound 'fared' compared with the US dollar and the yen from 1980? What conclusions can be drawn about the relative movements between these currencies?

Note that all the exchange rates must be consistent with each other. For example, if £1 exchanged for $1.50 or 150 yen, then $1.50 would have to exchange for 150 yen directly (i.e. $1 = 100 yen), otherwise people could make money by moving around in a circle between the three currencies in a process known as ***arbitrage***.

Definitions

Exchange rate index A weighted average exchange rate expressed as an index, where the value of the index is 100 in a given base year. The weights of the different currencies in the index add up to 1.

Arbitrage Buying an asset in a market where it has a lower price and selling it again in another market where it has a higher price and thereby making a profit.

Figure 15.16 Sterling exchange rates against selected currencies

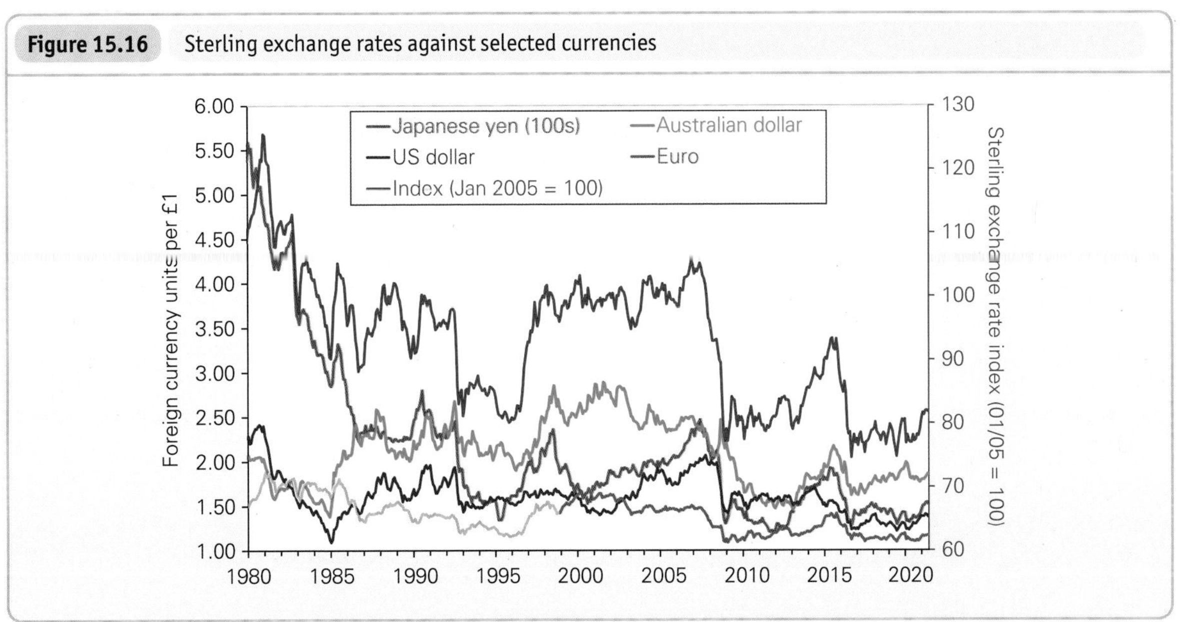

Note: The euro was introduced in 1999, with notes and coins circulating from 2001. The euro figures prior to 1999 (in grey) are projections backwards in time based on the average exchange rates of the currencies that made up the euro.

Source: Based on data in *Statistical Interactive Database*, Bank of England, www.bankofengland.co.uk/boeapps/iadb/

The determination of the rate of exchange in a free market

TC4 p45

In a free foreign exchange market, the rate of exchange is determined by demand and supply. This is known as a ***floating exchange rate***, and is illustrated in Figure 15.17.

For simplicity, assume that there are just two countries: the UK and the USA. When UK importers wish to buy goods from the USA, or when UK residents wish to invest in the USA, they will *supply* pounds on the foreign exchange market in order to obtain dollars. The higher the exchange rate, the more dollars they will obtain for their pounds. This will effectively make US goods cheaper to buy, and investment more profitable. Thus the *higher* the exchange rate, the *more* pounds will be supplied. The supply curve of pounds, therefore, typically slopes upwards.

When US residents wish to purchase UK goods or to invest in the UK, they will require pounds. They *demand* pounds by selling dollars on the foreign exchange market. The lower the dollar price of the pound (the exchange rate), the cheaper it will be for them to obtain UK goods and assets, and hence the more pounds they are likely to demand. The demand curve for pounds, therefore, typically slopes downwards.

The equilibrium exchange rate is where the demand for pounds equals the supply. In Figure 15.17 this is at an exchange rate of £1 = $1.30. But what is the mechanism that equates demand and supply?

KI8 p44

If the current exchange rate were above the equilibrium, the supply of pounds being offered to the banks would exceed the demand. For example, in Figure 15.17, if the exchange rate were $1.40, there would be an excess supply of pounds of $a - b$. The banks, wishing to make money by *exchanging* currency, would have to lower the exchange rate in order to encourage a greater demand for pounds and reduce the excessive supply. They would continue lowering the rate until demand equalled supply.

Similarly, if the rate were below the equilibrium, say at $1.20, there would be a shortage of pounds of $c - d$. The banks would find themselves with too few pounds to meet all the demand. At the same time, they would have an excess supply of dollars. The banks would thus raise the exchange rate until demand equalled supply.

In practice, the process of reaching equilibrium is extremely rapid. The foreign exchange dealers in the banks are continually adjusting the rate as new customers make new demands for currencies. What is more, the banks have to watch each other closely since they are constantly in competition with each other and thus have to keep their rates in line. The dealers receive minute-by-minute updates on their computer screens of the rates being offered around the world.

Definition

Floating exchange rate When the government does not intervene in the foreign exchange markets, but simply allows the exchange rate to be freely determined by demand and supply.

Shifts in the currency demand and supply curves

Any shift in the demand or supply curves will cause the exchange rate to change. This is illustrated in Figure 15.18, which shows the euro/sterling exchange rate. If the demand and supply curves shift from D_1 and S_1 to D_2 and S_2 respectively, the exchange rate will fall from €1.40 to €1.20. A fall

KI5 p21

Figure 15.17 Determination of the rate of exchange

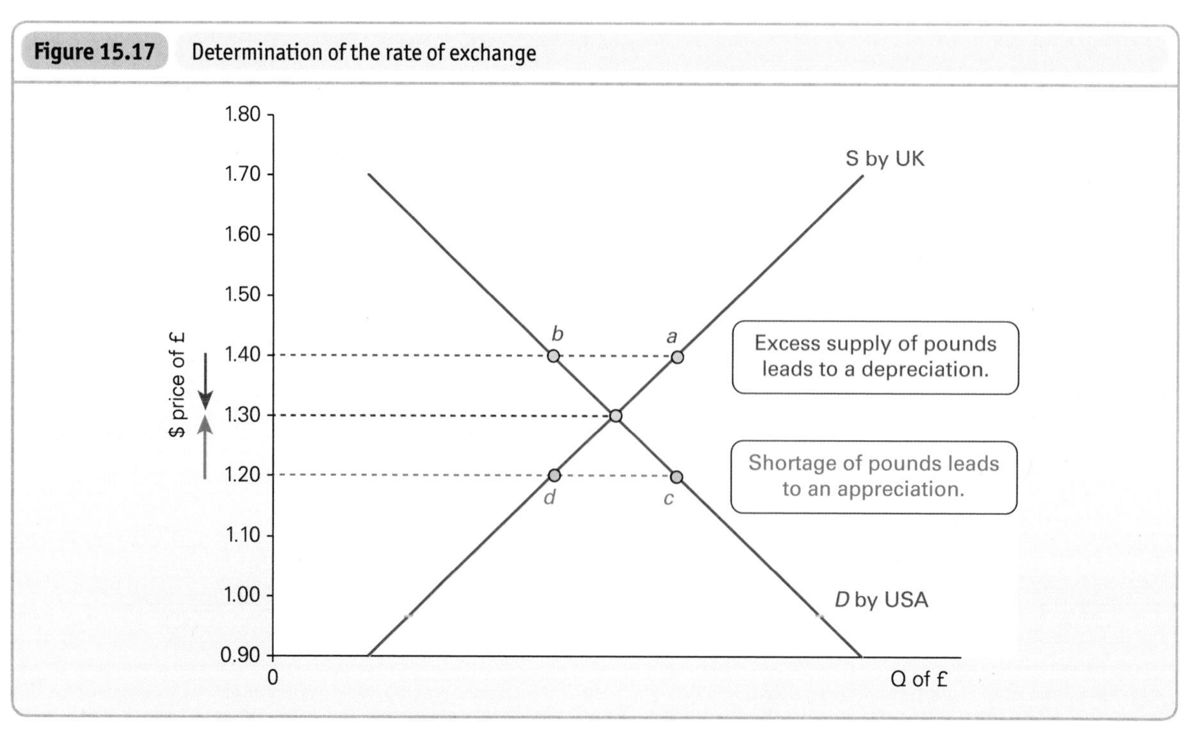

Figure 15.18 Floating exchange rates: movement to a new equilibrium

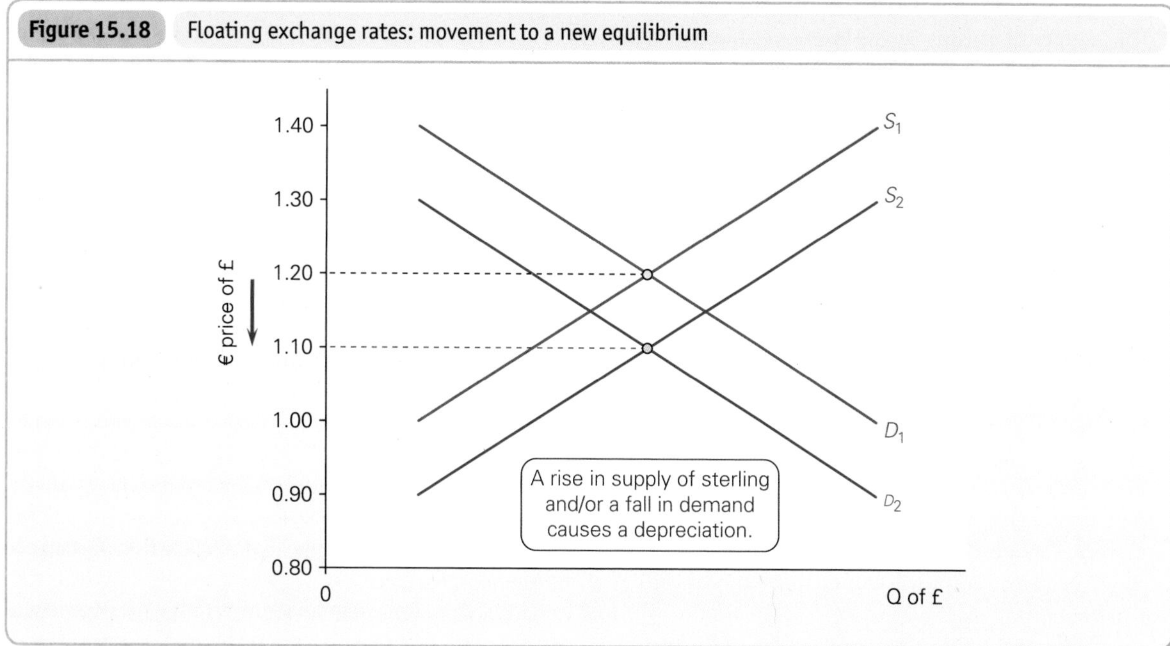

in the exchange rate is called a ***depreciation***. A rise in the exchange rate is called an ***appreciation***.

But why should the demand and supply curves shift? The following are the major possible causes of a depreciation of sterling (similar causes apply to other currencies):

- *A fall in domestic interest rates.* UK rates would now be less competitive for savers and other depositors. More UK

Definitions

Depreciation A fall in the free-market exchange rate of the domestic currency with foreign currencies.

Appreciation A rise in the free-market exchange rate of the domestic currency with foreign currencies.

BOX 15.7 DEALING IN FOREIGN EXCHANGE

EXPLORING ECONOMICS

A daily juggling act

Imagine that a large car importer in the UK wants to import 5000 cars from Japan costing ¥15 billion. What does it do?

It will probably contact a number of banks' foreign exchange dealing rooms in London and ask them for exchange rate quotes. It thus puts all the banks in competition with each other. Each bank will want to get the business and thereby obtain the commission on the deal. To do this it must offer a higher rate than the other banks, since the higher the ¥/£ exchange rate, the more yen the firm will get for its money. (For an importer a rate of, say, ¥160 to £1 is better than a rate of, say, ¥140.)

Now it is highly unlikely that any of the banks will have a spare ¥15 billion. But a bank cannot say to the importer, 'Sorry, you will have to wait before we can agree to sell them to you.' Instead the bank will offer a deal and then, if the firm agrees, the bank will have to set about obtaining the ¥15 billion. To do this, it must offer to obtain pounds for Japanese who are *supplying* yen at a sufficiently *low* ¥/£ exchange rate. (The lower the ¥/£ exchange rate, the fewer yen the Japanese will have to pay to obtain pounds.)

The banks' dealers thus find themselves in the delicate position of wanting to offer a *high* enough exchange rate to the car importer in order to gain its business, but a *low* enough exchange rate in order to obtain the required amount of yen. The dealers are thus constantly having to adjust the rates of exchange in order to balance the demand and supply of each currency.

KI 8 p44

In general, the more of any foreign currency that dealers are asked to supply (by being offered sterling), the lower will be the exchange rate they will offer. In other words, a higher supply of sterling pushes down the foreign currency price of sterling (see Figure 15.18).

Assume that a firm based in the USA wants to import Scotch whisky from the UK. Describe how foreign exchange dealers will respond.

Choose a currency and investigate the buying and selling rates against sterling and how they change over the short term. Also investigate the differences in the gap between the buying and selling rates depending on where you buy or sell the currency. Also establish whether there is any commission charged. What might explain the size of the difference between the buying and selling rates and the size of the commission (if any)?

residents would be likely to deposit their money abroad (the supply of sterling would rise), and fewer people abroad would deposit their money in the UK (the demand for sterling would fall).

- *Higher inflation in the domestic economy than abroad.* UK exports will become less competitive. The demand for sterling will fall. At the same time, imports will become relatively cheaper for UK consumers. The supply of sterling will rise.
- *A rise in domestic incomes relative to incomes abroad.* If UK incomes rise, the demand for imports, and hence the supply of sterling, will rise. If incomes in other countries fall, the demand for UK exports, and hence the demand for sterling, will fall.
- *Relative investment prospects improving abroad.* If investment prospects become brighter abroad than in the UK, perhaps because of better incentives abroad, or because of worries about an impending recession in the UK, again the demand for sterling will fall and the supply of sterling will rise.
- *Speculation that the exchange rate will fall.* If businesses involved in importing and exporting, and also banks and other foreign exchange dealers, think that the exchange rate is about to fall, they will sell pounds *now* before the rate does fall. The supply of sterling will thus rise. People thinking of buying pounds will wait until the rate does fall and hence, in the meantime, the demand for sterling will fall. Speculation thus helps to bring about the very effect people had anticipated (see pages 69–72).
- *Longer-term changes in international trading patterns.* Over time the pattern of imports and exports is likely to change as (a) consumer tastes change, (b) the nature and quality of goods change, (c) the costs of production change and (d) trading restrictions between countries change (e.g. the effects of Brexit). If, as a result, UK goods become less competitive than, say, German or Japanese goods, the demand for sterling will fall and the supply will rise. These shifts, except in the case of new trading agreements, are gradual, taking place over many years.

KI 10 p70

Go through each of the above reasons for shifts in the demand for and supply of sterling and consider what would cause an appreciation of the pound.

Exchange rates and the balance of payments

KI 5 p21

In a free foreign exchange market, the balance of payments will *automatically* balance. But why?

The credit side of the balance of payments constitutes the demand for sterling. For example, when people abroad buy UK exports or assets, they will demand sterling in order to pay for them. The debit side constitutes the supply of sterling. For example, when UK residents buy foreign goods or assets, the importers of them will require foreign currency to pay for them. They will thus supply pounds. A floating exchange rate ensures that the demand for pounds always equals the supply. It thus also ensures that the credits on the balance of payments are equal to the debits: that the balance of payments balances.

This does not mean that each part of the balance of payments account will separately balance, but simply that any current account deficit must be matched by a capital plus financial account surplus and vice versa.

For example, suppose initially that each part of the balance of payments *did* separately balance. Then let us assume that interest rates rise. This will encourage larger short-term financial inflows as people abroad are attracted to deposit money in the UK: the demand for sterling would shift to the right (e.g. from D_2 to D_1 in Figure 15.18). It will also cause smaller short-term financial outflows as UK residents keep more of their money in the country: the supply of sterling shifts to the left (e.g. from S_2 to S_1 in Figure 15.18). The financial account will go into surplus. The exchange rate will appreciate.

As the exchange rate rises, this will cause imports to be cheaper and exports to be more expensive. The current account will move into deficit. There is a movement up along the new demand and supply curves until a new equilibrium is reached. At this point, any financial account surplus is matched by an equal current (plus capital) account deficit.

Section summary

1. The balance of payments account records all payments to and receipts from foreign countries. The current account records payments for imports and exports, plus incomes and transfers of money to and from abroad. The capital account records all transfers of capital to and from abroad. The financial account records inflows and outflows of money for investment and as deposits in banks and other financial institutions; it also includes dealings in the country's foreign exchange reserves.
2. The whole account must balance, but surpluses or deficits can be recorded on any specific part of the account.
3. The rate of exchange is the rate at which one currency exchanges for another. Rates of exchange are determined by demand and supply in the foreign exchange market. Demand for the domestic currency consists of all the credit items in the balance of payments account. Supply consists of all the debit items.
4. The exchange rate will depreciate (fall) if the demand for the domestic currency falls and/or the supply increases. These shifts can be caused by increases in domestic prices or incomes relative to foreign ones, reductions in domestic interest rates relative to foreign ones, worsening investment prospects at home compared with abroad, or the belief by speculators that the exchange rate will fall. The opposite in each case would cause an appreciation (rise).

APPENDIX: CALCULATING GDP

As explained in section 15.2, there are three ways of estimating GDP. In this appendix, we discuss each method in more detail. We also look at some alternative measures of national income.

The product method of measuring GDP

This approach simply involves adding up the value of everything produced in the country during the year: the output of cars, timber, lollipops, shirts, etc.; and all the myriad of services, such as football matches, haircuts, bus rides and insurance services. In the national accounts these figures are grouped together into broad categories such as manufacturing, construction and distribution. The figures for the UK economy for 2019 are shown in Figure 15.19.

Figure 15.19 UK GVA (product-based measure): 2019

	Percentage of GVA
Agriculture, forestry and fishing £12 951m	0.7
Mining and quarrying £20 276m	1.0
Manufacturing £191 672m	9.7
Electricity, gas, steam and air conditioning supply £27 919m	1.4
Water supply, sewerage, waste management £24 532m	1.2
Construction £129 271m	6.5
Total distribution, transport, hotels and restaurants £345 091m	17.5
Total information and communications £136 887m	6.9
Financial and insurance £125 929m	6.4
Real estate activities £264 263m	13.4
Professional and support services £257 374m	13.0
Total government, health and education £361 716m	18.3
Other services and miscellaneous £79 215m	4.0
Gross value added (GVA) at basic prices £1 977 096m	**100.0**
plus VAT and other taxes on products £250 351m	
less Subsidies on products –£13 085m	
Total GDP (at market prices) £2 214 362m	

Source: *UK National Accounts, The Blue Book: 2020*, ONS.

When we add up the output of various firms, we must be careful to avoid *double counting*. For example, if a manufacturer sells a television to a retailer for £600 and the retailer sells it to the consumer for £800, how much has this television contributed to GDP? The answer is *not* £1400. We do not add the £600 received by the manufacturer to the £800 received by the retailer: that would be double counting. Instead we either just count the final value (£800) or the *value added* at each stage (£600 by the manufacturer + £200 by the retailer).

The sum of all the values added at each of the stages of production by all the various industries in the economy is known as ***gross value added (GVA) at basic prices***.

Some qualifications

Stocks (or inventories). We must be careful only to include the values added in the *particular year in question*. A problem here is that some goods start being produced *before* the year begins. Thus when we come to work out GDP, we must ignore the values that had previously been added to stocks of raw materials and goods. Similarly, other goods are only sold to the consumer *after* the end of the year. Nevertheless we must still count the values that have been added during *this* year to these stocks of partially finished goods.

A final problem concerned with stocks is that they may increase in value simply due to increased prices. This is known as ***stock (or inventory) appreciation***. Since there has been no real increase in output, stock appreciation must be deducted from value added.

Government services. The output of private industry is sold on the market and can thus be easily valued. This is not the case with most of the services provided by the government. Such services (e.g. health and education) should be valued in terms of what they cost to provide.

Ownership of dwellings. When a landlord rents out a flat, this service is valued as the rent that the tenant pays. But owner-occupiers living in their own property do not pay rent and yet they are 'consuming' a similar 'service'. Here a rental value for owner-occupation is 'imputed'. In other words, a figure corresponding to a rent is included in the GDP statistics under the heading 'letting of property' in the real estate activities category.

Definitions

Gross value added (GVA) at basic prices The sum of all the values added by all industries in the economy over a year. The figures exclude taxes on products (such as VAT) and subsidies on products.

Stock (or inventory) appreciation The increase in monetary value of stocks due to increased prices. Since this does not represent increased output, it is not included in GDP.

Taxes and subsidies on products. Taxes paid on goods and services (such as VAT) and any subsidies on products are *excluded* from gross value added (GVA), since they are not part of the value added in production. Nevertheless the way GDP is measured throughout the EU and most other countries of the world is at *market prices*: i.e. at the prices actually paid at each stage of production. Thus ***GDP at market prices*** (sometimes referred to simply as GDP) is GVA *plus* taxes on products *minus* subsidies on products.

The income method of measuring GDP

The second approach focuses on the incomes generated from the production of goods and services. This must be the same as the sum of all values added, since value added is simply the difference between a firm's revenue from sales and the costs of its purchases from other firms. This difference is made up of wages and salaries, rent, interest and profit: the incomes earned by those involved in the production process.

Since GDP is the sum of all values added, it must also be the sum of all incomes generated: the sum of wages and salaries, rent, interest and profit.

If a retailer buys a product from a wholesaler for £80 and sells it to a consumer for £100, then the £20 of value that has been added will go partly in wages, partly in rent and partly in profits. Thus £20 of income has been generated at the retail stage. But the good actually contributes a total of £100 to GDP. Where, then, is the remaining £80 worth of income recorded?

Figure 15.20 shows how these incomes are grouped together in the official statistics. By far the largest category is 'compensation of employees': in other words, wages and salaries. As you can see, the total in Figure 15.20 is the same as in Figure 15.19, although the components are quite different. In other words, GDP is the same whether calculated by the product or the income method.

Figure 15.20 UK GVA (by category of income): 2019

Category	Percentage of GVA
Compensation of employees (wages and salaries) £1 096 110m	55.4
Operating surplus (gross profit, rent and interest of firms government and other institutions) £460 269m	23.3
Mixed incomes £393 368m	19.9
Tax less subsidies on production (other than those on products) plus statistical discrepancy £27 349m	1.4
Gross value added (GVA) at basic prices £1 977 096	**100.0**
plus VAT and other taxes on products £250 351m	
less Subsidies on products –£13 085m	
Total GDP (at market prices) £2 214 362m	

Source: UK National Accounts, The Blue Book: 2020, ONS.

Some qualifications

Stock (inventory) appreciation. As in the case of the product approach, any gain in profits from inventory appreciation must be deducted, since they do not arise from a real increase in output.

Transfer payments. GDP includes only those incomes that arise from the production of goods and services. We do not, therefore, include *transfer payments* such as social security benefits, pensions and gifts.

Direct taxes. We count people's income *before* the payment of income and corporation taxes, since it is this *gross* (pre-tax) income that arises from the production of goods and services.

Definition

GDP (at market prices) The value of output (or income or expenditure) in terms of the prices actually paid. GDP = GVA + taxes on products − subsidies on products.

Taxes and subsidies on products. As with the product approach, if we are working out GVA, we measure incomes before the payment of taxes on products or the receipt of subsidies on products, since it is these pre-tax-and-subsidy incomes that arise from the value added by production. When working out GDP, however, we add in these taxes and subtract these subsidies to arrive at a *market price* valuation.

The expenditure method of measuring GDP

The final approach to calculating GDP is to add up all expenditure on final output (which will be at market prices). This will include the following:

- *Consumer expenditure* (*C*). This includes all expenditure on goods and services by households and by non-profit institutions serving households (NPISH) (e.g. clubs and societies).
- *Government expenditure* (*G*). This includes central and local government expenditure on final goods and services. Note that it includes non-marketed services (such as health and education), but excludes transfer payments, such as pensions and social security payments.

- *Investment expenditure* (I). This includes investment in capital, such as buildings and machinery. It also includes the value of any increase (+) or decrease (−) in inventories, whether of raw materials, semi-finished goods or finished goods.
- *Exports of goods and services* (X).

We then have to *subtract* imports of goods and services (M) from the total in order to leave just the expenditure on *domestic* product. In other words, we subtract the part of consumer expenditure, government expenditure and investment that goes on imports. We also subtract the imported component (e.g. raw materials) from exports.

$$\text{GDP (at market prices)} = C + I + G + X + M$$

Table 15.6 shows the calculation of the 2019 UK GDP by the expenditure approach.

From GDP to national income

Gross national income

Some of the incomes earned in this country will go abroad. These include wages, interest, profit and rent earned in this country by foreign residents and remitted abroad, and taxes on production paid to foreign governments and institutions. On the other hand, some of the incomes earned by domestic residents will come from abroad. Again, these can be in the form of wages, interest, profit or rent, or in the form of subsidies received from governments or institutions abroad. Gross *domestic* product, however, is concerned only with incomes generated *within* the country, irrespective of ownership. If, then, we are to take 'net income from abroad' into account (i.e. these inflows minus outflows), we need a new measure. This is ***gross national income (GNY)***.[6] It is defined as follows:

$$\text{GNY at market prices} = \text{GDP at market prices} + \text{Net income from abroad}$$

Thus GDP focuses on the value of domestic production, whereas GNY focuses on the value of incomes earned by domestic residents.

Net national income

The measures we have used so far ignore the fact that each year some of the country's capital equipment wears out or becomes obsolete: in other words, they ignore capital depreciation. If we subtract from gross national income an allowance for ***depreciation*** (or 'capital consumption' as it is called in the official statistics), we get ***net national income (NNY)***.

$$\text{NNY at market prices} = \text{GNY at market prices} - \text{Depreciation}$$

Table 15.7 shows the 2019 GDP, GNY and NNY figures for the UK.

Although NNY gives a truer picture of a nation's income than GNY, economists tend to use the gross figures because depreciation is hard to estimate accurately.

Households' disposable income

Finally, we come to a measure that is useful for analysing consumer behaviour. This is called ***households' disposable income***. It measures the income that people have available

Definitions

Gross national income (GNY) GDP plus net income from abroad.

Depreciation The decline in value of capital equipment due to age, or wear and tear.

Net national income (NNY) GNY minus depreciation.

Households' disposable income The income available for households to spend: i.e. personal incomes after deducting taxes on incomes and adding benefits.

Table 15.6 UK GDP at market prices by category of expenditure, 2019

	£ million	% of GDP
Consumption expenditure of households and NPISH (C)	1 416 877	65.5
Government final consumption (G)	423 121	18.5
Gross capital formation (I)	405 449	17.3
Exports of goods and services (X)	690 823	30.0
Imports of goods and services (M)	−721 325	−31.8
Statistical discrepancy	−583	0.5
GDP at market prices	**2 214 362**	**100.0**

Source: UK National Accounts, The Blue Book: 2020, ONS.

Table 15.7 UK GDP, GNY, NNY at market prices and household disposable income, 2019

	£ million
Gross domestic product (GDP)	**2 214 362**
Plus net income from abroad	−37 313
Gross national income (GNY)	**2 177 049**
Less capital consumption (depreciation)	327 897
Net national income (NNY)	**1 849 152**
Disposable income of households and NPISHs	***1 486 720***

Source: UK National Accounts, The Blue Book: 2020, ONS.

6 In the official statistics, this is referred to as GNI. We use Y to stand for income, however, to avoid confusion with investment.

for spending (or saving): i.e. after any deductions for income tax, national insurance, etc. have been made. It is the best measure to use if we want to see how changes in household income affect consumption.

How do we get from GNY at market prices to households' disposable income? As GNY measures the incomes that firms receive from production[7] (plus net income from abroad), we must deduct that part of their income that is *not* distributed to households. This means that we must deduct taxes that firms pay – taxes on goods and services (such as VAT), taxes on profits (such as corporation tax) and any other taxes – and add in any subsidies they receive. We must then subtract allowances for depreciation and any undistributed profits.

7 We also include income from any public-sector production of goods or services (e.g. health and education) and production by non-profit institutions serving households.

This gives us the gross income that households receive from firms in the form of wages, salaries, rent, interest and distributed profits.

To get from this to what is available for households to spend, we must subtract the money that households pay in income taxes and national insurance contributions, but add all benefits to households, such as pensions and child benefit: in other words, we must *include* transfer payments.

Households' disposable income = GNY at market prices
− Taxes paid by firms + Subsidies received by firms
− Depreciation − Undistributed profits − Personal taxes
+ Benefits

As Table 15.7 shows, UK disposable income of households and NPISHs in 2019 was £1 486 720 million (lower than NNY).

Section summary

1. The product method measures the values added in all parts of the economy. Care must be taken in the evaluation of stocks, government services and the ownership of dwellings.
2. The income method measures all the incomes generated from domestic production: wages and salaries, rent, interest and profit. Transfer payments are not included, nor is stock appreciation.
3. The expenditure method adds up all the categories of expenditure: consumer expenditure, government expenditure, investment and exports. We then have to deduct the element of each that goes on imports in order to arrive at expenditure on domestic products. Thus GDP $= C+G+I+X-M$.
4. GDP at market prices measures what consumers pay for output (including taxes and subsidies on what they buy). Gross value added (GVA) measures what factors of production actually receive. GVA, therefore, is GDP at market prices minus taxes on products plus subsidies on products.
5. Gross national income (GNY) takes account of incomes earned from abroad (+) and incomes earned by people abroad from this country (−). Thus GNY = GDP plus net income from abroad.
6. Net national income (NNY) takes account of depreciation of capital. Thus NNY = GNY − depreciation.
7. Personal disposable income is a measure of household income after the deduction of income taxes and the addition of benefits.

END OF CHAPTER QUESTIONS

1. In 1974, the UK economy shrank by 2.5 per cent before shrinking by a further 1.5 per cent in 1975. However, actual GDP rose by 13 per cent in 1974 and by 24 per cent in 1975. What explains these apparently contradictory results?
2. Economists sometimes refer to the 'twin characteristics of economic growth'. What are these characteristics?
3. (i) What do you understand by the term financialisation? (ii) How might we assess the financial well-being of households?
4. Explain how the financial sector could amplify the effects of shocks to the economy, such as those from the COVID-19 pandemic.
5. Explain how equilibrium would be restored in the circular flow of income if there were a fall in investment.
6. Explain the circumstances under which an increase in pensions and child benefit would (a) increase national income; (b) leave national income unaffected; (c) decrease national income.
7. For what reasons might GDP be a poor indicator of (i) the level of development of a country; (ii) its rate of economic development?
8. (i) Will the rate of actual growth have any effect on the rate of potential growth? (ii) For what possible reasons may one country experience a persistently faster rate of economic growth than another?
9. Why will investment affect both actual (short-term) growth and the long-term growth in potential output? What will be the implications if these two effects differ in magnitude?
10. At what phase of the business cycle is the average duration of unemployment likely to be the highest? Explain.
11. Consider the most appropriate policy for tackling each of the different types of unemployment.

12. Do any groups of people gain from inflation?

13. If everyone's incomes rose in line with inflation, would it matter if inflation were 100 per cent or even 1000 per cent per annum?

14. Imagine that you had to determine whether a particular period of inflation was demand-pull, or cost-push, or a combination of the two. What information would you require in order to conduct your analysis?

15. What do you understand by people's expectations of inflation becoming 'anchored'? Why might this be important for actual rates of inflation?

16. Explain how the current account of the balance of payments is likely to vary with the course of the business cycle.

17. The overall balance of payments must always balance. If this is the case, why might a deficit on one part of the balance of payments be seen as a problem?

18. List some factors that could cause an increase in the credit items of the balance of payments and a decrease in the debit items. What would be the effect on the exchange rate (assuming that it is freely floating)? What effect would these exchange rate movements have on the balance of payments?

19. Explain how you would derive a figure for households' disposable income if you were starting from a figure for GDP.

Online resources

Additional case studies on the student website

15.1 **The GDP deflator.** An examination of how GDP figures are corrected to take inflation into account.

15.2 **Taking into account the redistributive effects of growth.** This case study shows how figures for economic growth can be adjusted to allow for the fact that poor people's income growth would otherwise count for far less than rich people's.

15.3 **Simon Kuznets and the system of national income accounting.** This looks at the work of Simon Kuznets, who devised the system of national income accounting that is used around the world. It describes some of the patterns of economic growth that he identified.

15.4 **Is stability always desirable?** Should firms sometimes be a given short, sharp shock?

15.5 **Theories of growth.** From dismal economics to the economics of optimism.

15.6 **The costs of economic growth.** Is more necessarily better?

15.7 **How big is the underground economy?** This case study looks at the factors that determine the size of the underground economy.

15.8 **The use of ISEW.** This looks at an alternative measure of economic well-being popular among environment groups: the Index of Sustainable Economic Welfare.

15.9 **Technology and employment.** Does technological progress create or destroy jobs?

15.10 **Cost-push illusion.** When rising costs are not a case of cost-push inflation.

15.11 **Disinflation.** The experience of Europe and Japan.

15.12 **Hyperinflation.** This looks at the extraordinarily high rates of inflation experienced in Germany in the early 1920s, Serbia and Montenegro in the 1990s and more recently in Zimbabwe.

15.13 **A. W. Phillips (1914–75).** A portrait of the discoverer of the Phillips curve, the New Zealand economist Bill Phillips.

15.14 **Making sense of the financial balances on the balance of payments.** An examination of the three main components of the financial account.

Websites relevant to this chapter

Numbers and sections refer to websites listed in the Web Appendix and hotlinked from this book's website at **go.pearson.com/uk/sloman.**

- For news articles relevant to this chapter, see the *Economics News Articles* link from the book's website.
- For general news on macroeconomic issues, both national and international, see websites in section A, and particularly A1–5, 7–9, 20–25, 31. See also links to newspapers worldwide in A38, 39, 42, 43 and 44, and the news search feature in Google at A41.
- For macroeconomic data, see links in B1; also see B4 and 12. For UK data, see B2, 3 and 34. For EU data, see B38 and 47. For US data, see B15, 17 and 25. For international data, see B15, 21, 24, 31, and 35. For links to datasets, see I7, 13, 14 and 18.
- For UK data on specific topics, such as unemployment or GDP, search site B3.
- For international data on balance of payments and exchange rates, see *World Economic Outlook* in B31 and *OECD Economic Outlook* in B21 (also in section B of B1).
- For UK data on balance of payments, search 'Pink Book' on site B3.
- For exchange rates, see A1, 3; B34, 45; F2.

The Development of Macroeconomic Thinking: a Historical Perspective

CHAPTER MAP

In this second and final chapter of Part E we provide an overview of how macroeconomics has developed over the past 100 years or so. In reading this chapter you will see how macroeconomic debates and theories have been shaped by real-world events, such as the Great Depression of the 1930s, the rapid inflation of the 1970s, the global economic and financial crisis of the late 2000s and the COVID-19 pandemic of the early 2020s. You will also see how the development of economic ideas has affected actual policy, such as the granting of independence to central banks and the pursuit of inflation targets.

The unfolding of the 'macroeconomic story' allows us to see how different theories and approaches have developed. It also helps us to understand where there is greatest agreement among economists and where controversies remain. The chapter helps put macroeconomics into historical context, though, if your lecturer recommends it, you may move directly to Chapter 17.

16.1 THE MACROECONOMIC ENVIRONMENT AND DEBATES

In the previous chapter we identified some key macroeconomic issues: growth, unemployment, inflation, our interconnectedness with foreign economies, the financial well-being of economic agents and the stability of the financial system. While these issues are interconnected, we tend to find that the focus of macroeconomic debates at any moment in time reflects the macroeconomic environment of the time.

Events often dictate the focus of macroeconomic analysis and policy. This is demonstrated by the significant effects of the financial crisis and COVID-19 pandemic. Both required extraordinary policy measures: responses that would have been seen previously as unimaginable. In the case of the financial crisis, it led macroeconomists to consider how the subject was developing and how better to model the relationship between the economy and the financial system. It would also affect the curriculum of students of economics as, understandably, their curiosity was aroused by the financial crisis of the late 2000s.

Many of the debates and advancement of ideas, therefore, arise because existing theories appear unable to explain fully the prevailing macroeconomic conditions. Sometimes this has resulted in relatively small incremental changes to theory and to policy, but on other occasions very different views of how economies work have come to the fore and consequently policy has been radically reshaped.

Figure 16.1 plots the path of a selection of macroeconomic indicators since 1900. It helps to set the scene for some of the key macroeconomic debates over the past 100 years or so.

Macroeconomics as a separate branch of economics had its birth with the mass unemployment experienced in the 1920s and 1930s. The old 'classical theories' of the time, which essentially said that free markets would provide a healthy economy with full employment, could not provide solutions to the problem. Their analysis seemed totally at odds with the facts.

A new analysis of the economy – one that *did* offer solutions to mass unemployment – was put forward by the economist John Maynard Keynes. His book *The General Theory of Employment, Interest and Money*,[1] published in 1936, saw the dawn of 'Keynesian economics'. Keynes advocated active intervention by governments, in particular through changes to government expenditures and taxation to affect aggregate demand. By carefully managing aggregate demand, the government could prevent mass unemployment on the one hand, or an 'overheated' economy with unsustainable growth and high inflation on the other.

After the Second World War, governments around the world adopted Keynesian demand-management policies;

1 www.marxists.org/reference/subject/economics/keynes/general-theory/

Figure 16.1 UK macroeconomic indicators

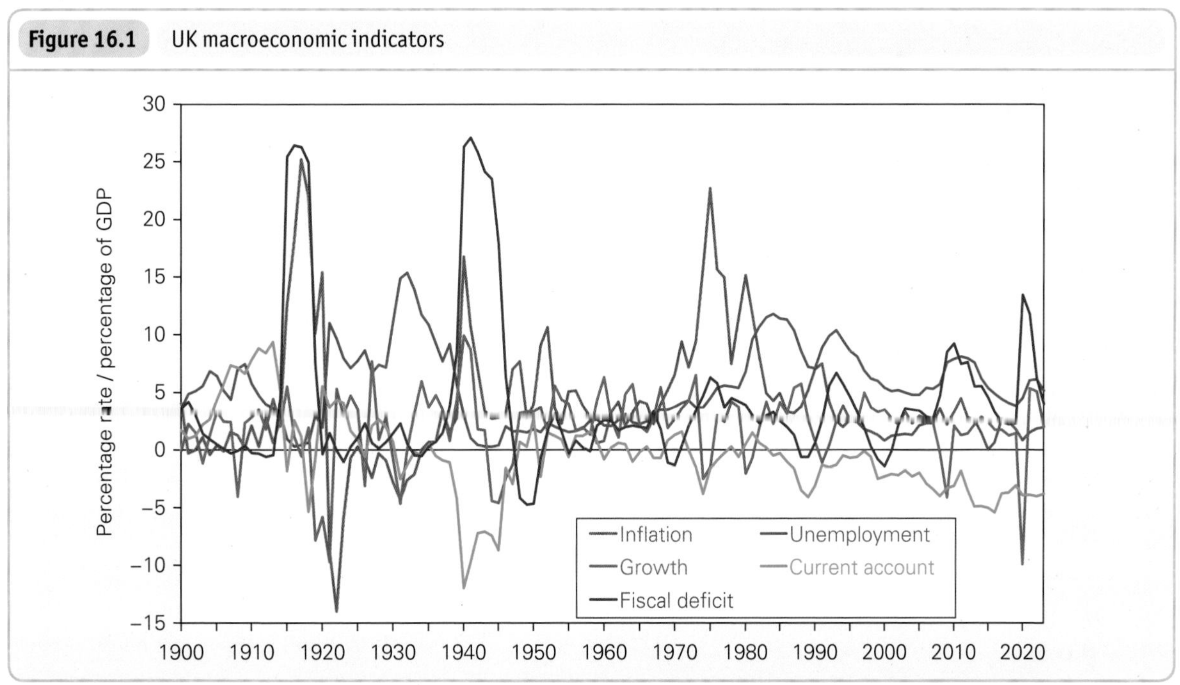

Notes: (i) Inflation is the annual rate of consumer price inflation; (ii) Unemployment rate is the standardised unemployment rate as % of UK workforce; (iii) Growth is the annual growth in constant-price GDP; (iv) Current account is the sum of net exports (balance of trade) and net payments of income and current transfers (net primary and secondary balance) as % of GDP; (v) Fiscal deficit is public sector net borrowing as a % of GDP.

Source: Based on data from *Millennium of Macroeconomic Data*, Bank of England, www.bankofengland.co.uk/statistics/research-datasets; *ONS time series explorer*, ONS), www.ons.gov.uk/timeseriestool; and *World Economic Outlook Database*, IMF (April 2021), www.imf.org/en/Publications/SPROLLS/world-economic-outlook-databases. Data from 2021 based on forecasts.

and they seemed to be successful. The 1950s and 1960s were a period of low inflation, low unemployment and relatively high economic growth. Macroeconomists were largely concerned with refining Keynesian economics.

In the 1970s, however, the macroeconomic consensus broke down. As we can see from Figure 16.1, both inflation and unemployment rose and growth slowed. Macroeconomics was characterised by strong debates. Different 'schools of thought' had their own explanations of what was going wrong, and each had its own solutions to the problems.

Then, as the macroeconomic environment generally improved in the 1990s, increasingly common ground was found and a *new consensus* emerged. At the heart of the new consensus was a view that markets tend to adjust relatively quickly to the random shocks that frequently hit the economy. Nonetheless, market imperfections do affect adjustment processes and the characteristics of an economy's equilibrium.

While some economists were highly sceptical of the new consensus, it was the financial crisis of the late 2000s and the subsequent global economic downturn that re-energised long-standing debates and differences amongst macroeconomists. These differences were mirrored by the debates amongst politicians and policy makers and were significantly greater than they had been for many years.

In some ways, the debates that followed the financial crisis and later the COVID-19 pandemic were a microcosm of much of the preceding 100 years. Many familiar questions were again being asked, not least concerning the role of governments and the size of their budgets. However, other questions emerged concerning the way that macroeconomic analysis and macroeconomic models had developed during the new orthodoxy.

The new consensus had largely sought to model the effect of economic shocks on key macroeconomic variables, such as the growth of real GDP or the rate of inflation, by building models based on aggregating the behaviour of representative rational, forward-looking economic agents. Elaborately technical models began to characterise macroeconomics. However, in light of the general failure of macroeconomists to foresee the financial crisis, economists began to ask whether the models of the new orthodoxy had taken a wrong turn. New models began to be developed which put more emphasis on the role of the financial sector, balance sheets and speculative behaviour.

Some disagreement between economists is inevitable. Nonetheless, there exist some areas of broad agreement between many macroeconomists over the causes of macroeconomic problems and the appropriate policies to deal with them. Therefore, in this chapter we will be identifying areas not only where disagreement remains, but areas where there is more agreement.

The focus of the remainder of the chapter is to provide an understanding of key developments in macroeconomic thinking. To do so, we introduce some of the principal 'schools of macroeconomic thought'. Essentially, these schools are a means of understanding different views on the determinants of key macroeconomic variables, such as growth, unemployment and inflation. We shall see how these schools have evolved as time has passed. An important reason for this is that the macroeconomic environment that economists try to understand changes and different issues become more or less important.

16.2 CLASSICAL MACROECONOMICS

We begin our story in the earlier twentieth century. Classical economists had over the previous century or so advocated a policy of laissez-faire (non-intervention) and free trade. Britain had experienced rapid industrialisation and growth and seen a massive expansion of its overseas trade. This had, if anything, strengthened their advocacy of laissez-faire. Consequently, in the early years of the twentieth century, most economists, most politicians and virtually all bankers and businesspeople were relatively confident in the power of the free market to provide growing output and low unemployment.

The main role for the government was to provide 'sound finance' (i.e. not to print too much money), so as to maintain stable prices.

The classical analysis of output and employment

The classical theory predicted that, in the long run, equilibrium in the economy would be at virtually full employment. In the long run, any unemployment would be merely *frictional* unemployment: namely, people in the process of changing jobs.

There were two important elements in the classical theory.

The free-market economy works to equate demand and supply in all markets

This element of classical theory assumes flexible prices: of goods and services, of labour (i.e. wage rates) and of money (i.e. the rate of interest).

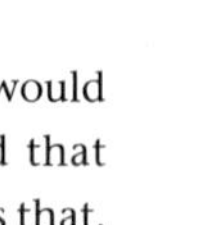

The classical economists argued that flexible prices would ensure that saving equalled investment ($S = I$) and that imports equalled exports ($M = X$). From this it follows that, if the government were to 'balance its budget' and make taxation equal to government expenditure ($T = G$), then total withdrawals would equal total injections ($W = J$).[2]

But why should flexible prices ensure that $S = I$ and $M = X$? The reasoning of the classical economists was as follows.

2 The classical economists did not use the terms 'withdrawals' and 'injections': these are modern terms. Nevertheless, their analysis implied an automatic equation of W and J if markets cleared and the government balanced its budget.

$S = I$. This would be brought about by flexible rates of interest in the ***market for loanable funds***. When firms want to invest in new plant and equipment, they will require finance. Investment demand, therefore, represents a demand for loanable funds from financial institutions (an outflow). Meanwhile, saving represents a supply of loanable funds (an inflow). The supply of savings represents the deposits by people in financial institutions.

The relevant interest rate for loanable funds is the *real* rate of interest (r). This is the nominal rate (i) minus the rate of inflation (π) The higher the real rate of interest, the more expensive will borrowing be, and hence the less will be the demand for investment. On the other hand, the higher the real rate of interest, the more people will be attracted to save: that is, the more they will deposit in financial institutions.

KI 8 p44

The equilibrium real interest rate is that where $S = I$. If the rate of interest were above this, financial institutions would be accumulating funds. They would have to lower the rate of interest to attract sufficient borrowers. If the rate of interest were below this, financial institutions would find their funds reducing. They would have to raise the rate of interest to attract sufficient savers.

Illustrate equilibrium in the market for loanable funds using a demand and supply diagram.

$M = X$. This would be brought about by flexible prices and wages. At the start of the twentieth century many countries, including the UK, Russia, Japan and the USA, operated some form of ***gold standard***. This was a *fixed* exchange rate system in which each participating country's currency was valued at a certain fixed amount of gold.

If a country had a balance of trade deficit ($M > X$), this had to be paid for in gold from its reserves (unless there was a compensating net inflow of finance on the financial account from, say, deposits in domestic banks or the purchase of domestic shares). A country was then supposed to respond to this outflow of gold by reducing the amount of money in the economy and hence reducing total expenditure. This would create surpluses in the goods and labour markets, which would, in turn, lead to a fall in prices and wages.

This fall in the prices of domestic goods would increase the sale of exports and reduce the consumption of the now relatively expensive imports. This whole process would continue until the balance of payments trade was eliminated: until $M = X$.[3]

3 Note that, under a system of freely floating exchange rates, it is the flexibility in exchange rates, rather than the prices of goods and factors, that ensures that the balance of payments balances.

What would have happened if countries in deficit had not responded to an outflow of gold by reducing total expenditure?

Provided governments balanced their budgets ($T = G$), therefore, flexibility in the various markets would ensure that withdrawals equalled injections.

Say's law

Jean-Baptiste Say was a French economist of the early nineteenth century. ***Say's law*** states that *supply creates its own demand.* What this means is that the production of goods and services will generate expenditures sufficient to ensure that they are sold. There will be no deficiency of demand and no need to lay off workers. There will be full employment. The justification for the law is as follows.

When firms produce goods, they pay out money either directly to other firms, or as factor payments to households. The income that households receive is then partly paid back to firms in the form of consumption expenditure (C_d): the inner flow of the circular flow of income.

But any withdrawals by firms or households are also fully paid back to firms in the form of injections, since $S = I, M = X$ and $T = G$. Thus, all the incomes generated by firms' supply will be transformed into demand for their products, either directly in the form of consumption, or indirectly via withdrawals and then injections. There will thus be no deficiency of demand.

Of course, although aggregate demand might equal aggregate supply, consumers may shift their demand away from some industries in favour of others. Consequently, structural unemployment may then occur (see section 15.5). But then wages would fall in the declining industries and rise in the expanding industries. This would help to eliminate the structural unemployment.

The reduction in structural unemployment will be quicker (a) the more flexible are wages and (b) the more willing and able are workers to move to industries and towns where jobs are available (labour mobility). In other words, the better markets work, the lower will be the level of structural unemployment (and frictional unemployment too).

Definitions

Market for loanable funds The market for loans from and deposits into the banking system.

Gold standard The system whereby countries' exchange rates were fixed in terms of a certain amount of gold and whereby balance of payments deficits were paid in gold.

Say's law Supply creates its own demand. In other words, the production of goods will generate sufficient demand to ensure that they are sold.

The classical analysis of prices and inflation

The classical economists based their analysis of inflation on the ***quantity theory of money***. In its simplest form, it states that the general level of prices (P) in the economy depends on the supply of money (M):[4]

$$P = f(M)$$

The greater the quantity of money, the higher the level of prices. Under this theory, inflation is simply caused by a rise in money supply. (We examine the role of money in the economy in Chapters 18 and 19.)

To understand the reasoning behind the quantity theory of money, we need to examine the ***equation of exchange***. This comes in various versions (see Case Study 16.1 on the student website), but the one most useful for our purposes is the simple identity between national expenditure and national income. This identity may be expressed as follows:

$$MV = PY$$

M, as we have already seen, is the supply of money in the economy. V is the ***velocity of circulation***. This is the number of times per year a unit of currency (e.g. £1) is spent on buying goods and services that make up GDP. Suppose that each pound's worth of money is typically spent eight times per year on such goods and services, and that money supply is £250 billion. This would mean that total expenditure on GDP ($M \times V$) is £2 trillion (£2000 billion).

P, again as we have already seen, is the general level of prices. Let us define it more precisely as the price index based on some specific year (e.g. 2015), where the index in the base year is assumed to be 1.00 (not 100) (see pages A:6–7). Y is the real value of national income (i.e. GDP expressed in the prices of the base year). $P \times Y$, therefore, is simply the 'nominal' value of GDP (i.e. GDP expressed in *current* prices, rather than those of the base year). Thus if GDP in real terms (Y) (i.e. measured in base-year prices) were £1 trillion and if the current price index (P) were 2, then nominal GDP ($P \times Y$) would be £2 trillion.

Thus both MV and PY are equal to GDP and must, therefore, by definition be equal to each other.

The classical economists argued that both V and Y were determined independently of the money supply: i.e. a change in the money supply would *not* be expected to lead to a change in V or Y. The velocity of circulation (V), they claimed, was determined by the frequency with which people were paid (e.g. weekly or monthly), the nature of the banking system and other institutional arrangements for holding money. As far as Y was concerned, Say's law would ensure that the real value of output (Y) was maintained at the full-employment level.

With V and Y as 'constants' with respect to M, therefore, the quantity theory must hold:

$$P = f(M)$$

Increases in money supply simply lead to inflation. This is consistent with the principle known as the ***neutrality of money***. Classical economists argued that changes in the money supply would not affect real variables such as real output or real consumption. Changes in the money supply would merely affect nominal variables through their impact on prices.

Assuming that Y rises each year as a result of increases in productivity, can money supply rise without causing inflation? Would this destroy the validity of the quantity theory?

The classical response to the Great Depression

As Figure 16.1 (see page 501) helps to show, the period between the First and Second World War (1919–38) saw Britain experience bouts of prolonged recession of unparalleled severity. To help put this period into perspective, the size of Britain's real GDP in 1934 was roughly that of 1913.

Throughout Britain's prolonged 'Great Depression' unemployment was very much higher than before the war. By 1933 there were 3.4 million people unemployed, equivalent to almost 16 per cent of the working population. However, the depression eliminated inflation. In every year from 1921 to 1934 prices either were constant or fell. During this period, the annual rate of inflation averaged −3.2 per cent and the unemployment rate 10 per cent.

The events of the 1920s and early 1930s appeared to contradict the predictions of classical economists. After all, they had predicted that there would be virtually full employment.

Definitions

Quantity theory of money The price level (P) is directly related to the quantity of money in the economy (M).

Equation of exchange $MV = PY$ The total level of spending on GDP (MV) equals the total value of goods and services produced (PY) that go to make up GDP.

Velocity of circulation The average number of times annually that money is spent on goods and services that make up GDP.

Neutrality of money The principle that changes in the money supply affect only nominal variables and have no effect on real variables.

4 In the quantity theory of money the letter M is used to refer to money supply, whereas in the circular flow of income it is used to refer to the expenditure on imports. Naturally, this is potentially confusing, but unfortunately it is normal practice to use the letter M in both ways. To avoid any such confusion we will always specify which is being referred to. Elsewhere, however, you will just have to judge from the context! (There is the same problem with the letter P, which can refer either to price or to product.)

Any unemployment would simply be the frictional and structural unemployment of people being 'between jobs'.

Part of the cause of the Depression was the decision in 1925 by Winston Churchill, the Chancellor of the Exchequer, to return to the gold standard following the UK's withdrawal from it in 1914 at the outbreak of the First World War. The decision was made to return at the pre-war rate of £1 = $4.86. But with many export markets lost in the war and a rapid rise in imports for rebuilding the economy, the balance of payments was in severe deficit. The UK's trade deficit had risen to 5 per cent by 1925.

To correct the UK's trade position required severely deflationary policies. The aim was to drive wage rates down, reduce costs and restore the competitiveness of exports. The result, however, was a severe recession: the UK economy contracted by an estimated 3.1 per cent in 1926.

But while in Britain output slumped and unemployment soared, most of the rest of the industrialised world initially experienced a boom. But in 1929, after a decade of rapid growth and a huge rise in share values, Wall Street crashed. This sent the US economy plunging into deep recession, with the rest of the world following suit. As the world economy slumped, so did international trade. With a collapse of its exports, Britain dived even deeper into depression. 1931 saw the UK economy contract by 4.6 per cent.

Eventually, in 1932, Britain was forced to leave the gold standard and allow the pound to depreciate. (Case Study 16.4 on the student website looks at the bitter experience of the return to the gold standard in 1925 and its aftermath.)

The deflationary policies of the 1920s seemed to be directly responsible for increasing unemployment. Many critics argued that the government ought deliberately to *expand* aggregate demand. However, the Treasury and other classical economists rejected the analysis that unemployment was caused by a lack of demand; they also rejected policies of reflation (e.g. increased government expenditure).

The classical Treasury view on unemployment

Would deflation of demand not lead to unemployment? According to the Treasury view, unemployment would occur only if labour markets *failed to clear*: if real wage costs did not fall sufficiently.

The Treasury concluded that people should be encouraged to take wage cuts. This would also help to reduce prices and restore export demand, thus correcting the balance of payments. People should also be encouraged to save. This would, via flexible interest rates, lead to more investment and hence a growth in output and demand for labour.

The classical Treasury view on public works

In the 1920s and 1930s, some politicians and economists argued that unemployment could be reduced if the government pursued a programme of public works: building roads, hospitals, houses, etc. The Treasury view was that this would not work and could have costly side effects.

A programme of public works could be funded in three ways: from extra taxation, from extra government borrowing or by printing extra money. *None* of these three ways would, according to the classical Treasury view, solve the unemployment problem.

- *Extra taxation* would merely have the effect of reducing the money that consumers would spend on private industry. Extra public-sector demand would thus be offset by a fall in private-sector demand.
- If the government *borrowed more*, it would have to offer higher interest rates in order to persuade people to buy the additional government securities. The private sector

---

BOX 16.1 BALANCE THE BUDGET AT ALL COSTS — CASE STUDIES AND APPLICATIONS

Fiscal policy in the early 1930s

The budget must be balanced. All government expenditure should be financed from taxation. This was orthodox opinion in the 1920s.

But as unemployment increased during the Great Depression (see Figure 16.1), spending on unemployment benefits (the most rapidly growing item of government expenditure) threatened the balanced budget principle. Other spending had to be cut to restore balance. The result was more unemployment, and hence the payment of more unemployment benefits.

Treasury officials and classical economists called for cuts in unemployment benefits. The May Committee, set up to investigate the budgetary problem, recommended a 20 per cent reduction. Even the Labour government, elected on a mandate to tackle the unemployment problem, proposed a 10 per cent reduction in 1931. This contributed to its subsequent collapse.

Philip Snowden, Labour's Chancellor of the Exchequer, remarked in 1931 how pensioners had returned their pension books and children sent in their savings to help the nation balance its budget. And yet, as Keynes argued, it was not saving that was necessary to cure the unemployment, but spending. Government deficits were *desirable*. Attempts to balance the budget merely deflated the economy further and deepened the problem of unemployment.

Conduct an online search to find out opinions about restoring a balanced budget in 2010. Did the arguments mirror those of the early 1930s?

BOX 16.2 **THE CROWDING-OUT EFFECT** EXPLORING ECONOMICS

When public expenditure replaces private

Critics of the use of government expenditure to stimulate output and employment often refer to the problem of *crowding out*. In its starkest form, the argument goes like this.

There is no point in the government embarking on a programme of public works to bring the economy out of recession. If it attempts to spend more, it can do so only by reducing private expenditure. The effect on total spending will be zero. This crowding out can take two main forms.

Resource crowding out

This is when the government uses resources such as labour and raw materials that would otherwise be used by the private sector. If the economy is operating near full capacity, then if resources are used by the government, they cannot at the same time be used by private companies.

The argument is far less convincing, however, if there is slack in the economy. If the government merely mobilises otherwise *idle* resources, there need be no reduction in private-sector output. In fact, if private-sector firms have spare capacity, they will respond to the higher demand by producing more themselves: aggregate demand will stimulate extra production.

Financial crowding out

This occurs when extra government spending diverts *funds* from private-sector firms and thus deprives them of the finance necessary for investment.

If the government spends more (without raising taxes or printing more money), it will have to borrow more and will therefore have to offer higher rates of interest. Private companies will then have to offer higher rates of interest themselves in order to attract funds. Alternatively, if they borrow from banks, and banks have less funds, the banks will charge them higher interest rates. Higher interest rates will discourage firms from borrowing and hence discourage investment.

The weakness with this argument is that it assumes that the supply of money is fixed. If the government spends more but *increases* the amount of money in the economy, it need not deprive the private sector of finance. Interest rates will not be bid up.

But would that not be inflationary? Not if there are idle resources and hence the extra money can be spent on extra output. Only if *resource* crowding out takes place would it be inflationary.

1. *Could resource crowding out take place at less than full employment?*
2. *What is the connection between financial crowding out and resource crowding out?*

The aim of this activity is to assess whether a more expansionary fiscal policy in the UK since 2010 would have resulted in crowding out or whether it would have stimulated increased output (both actual and potential). In your analysis you should examine alternative specific fiscal measures that could have been taken and assess whether they would have had different outcomes from each other.

The activity could be taken individually, or you could discuss it in small groups and prepare a group report, which could then be presented to the other students in the seminar or class.

Many articles have been written on the topic and it should be easy to conduct an Internet search to find articles from newspapers, magazines (such as The Economist, http://pearsonblog.campaignserver.co.uk/the-economist/) and journals. Try searching the Sloman Economic News site (http://pearsonblog.campaignserver.co.uk/).

would then have to offer higher interest rates, to compete for funds. As interest rates went up, private borrowing would go down. Thus public investment would ***crowd out*** private investment (see Box 16.2). This debate was to be revisited many years later when, following the financial crisis and subsequent economic downturn of the late 2000s, government borrowing rose sharply (see Figure 16.1).

- According to the quantity theory of money, printing extra money would simply lead to inflation. The argument here is that a rise in aggregate demand would simply lead to a rise in the price level with no increase in national output and, hence, employment. A re-emergence of inflation, which had been eliminated in the early 1920s, would further erode the competitiveness of British goods, jeopardising the return to the gold standard at the pre-war exchange rate.

Treasury orthodoxy insisted, therefore, that the government should attempt to balance its budget, even if this meant cutting welfare benefits to the rising numbers of unemployed (see Box 16.1). The governments of the 1920s and early 1930s followed these classical recommendations. They attempted to balance their budgets and rejected policies of reflation. Yet mass unemployment persisted.

It is interesting to note that the policy of reducing deficits through cuts in government expenditure, even at a time of recession, was a central part of the UK Coalition government's policy in the early 2010s.

Definition

Crowding out Where increased public expenditure diverts money or resources away from the private sector.

Section summary

1. The classical analysis of output and employment assumes that markets clear. More specifically, it assumes that there are flexible wages, flexible prices and flexible rates of interest. The result will be that demand and supply are equated in the labour market, in the goods market and in the market for loanable funds.
2. Given that markets will clear, Say's law will operate. This law states that supply creates its own demand. In other words, the production of goods and services will generate incomes for households, which in turn will generate consumption expenditure, ensuring that the goods are sold. If any incomes are not directly spent on domestic goods, flexible prices will help to ensure that any money withdrawn is reinjected. Flexible interest rates will ensure that investment equals saving, and flexible prices and wages will ensure that exports equal imports. Provided the government balances its budget, withdrawals will equal injections and Say's law will hold.
3. The classical economists based their analysis of prices on the quantity theory of money. This states that the level of prices is directly related to the quantity of money (M) in the economy. Their position can be demonstrated using the equation of exchange:

   $$MV = PY$$

   where V is the velocity of circulation, P is the price index and Y is real national income expressed in the prices of the base year. The classical economists assumed that V and Y were not affected by changes in the money supply and could thus be regarded as 'constants'. From this it follows that

   $$P = f(M)$$

   Increases in the money supply simply lead to inflation.
4. In 1925, Britain returned to the gold standard system of fixed exchange rates at the pre-war rate. But given the massive balance of payments deficit at this rate, it had to pursue tough deflationary policies. The result was mass unemployment.
5. The classical economists saw the remedy to the problem as lying in reductions in wages and prices. According to the classical theory, this would allow Say's law to operate and full employment to be restored. They rejected public works as the solution, arguing that it would lead to crowding out if financed by borrowing, and to inflation if financed by printing money.

16.3 THE KEYNESIAN REVOLUTION

Keynes' rejection of classical macroeconomics

The main critic of classical macroeconomics was John Maynard Keynes. In his major work, *The General Theory of Employment, Interest and Money* (1936), he rejected the classical assumption that markets would clear. Disequilibrium could persist and mass unemployment could continue. There are two crucial markets in which disequilibrium could persist.

The labour market

Workers would resist wage cuts. Wages were thus 'sticky' downwards. In a recession, when the demand for labour is low, wages might not fall far or fast enough to clear the labour market. Consequently, there would exist demand-deficient unemployment (see section 15.5).

But even if wage cuts could be introduced, as advocated by classical economists, Keynes rejected that as the solution to demand deficiency. Workers are also consumers. A cut in workers' wages would mean less consumer spending. Firms would respond to this by further reducing their demand for labour, which would more than offset the reduction in wages. Wage rates would not fall fast enough to clear the market. Disequilibrium would worsen. The recession would deepen.

Employers might well find that labour was cheaper to employ, but if demand for their product were falling, they would hardly be likely to take on more labour.

The market for loanable funds

Keynes also rejected the classical solution of increased saving as a means of stimulating investment and growth. Again the problem was one of market disequilibrium.

An increase in saving will cause a disequilibrium in the market for loanable funds. An increase in the supply of loanable funds will lead to the real rate of interest for loanable funds falling. But an increase in saving also means a fall in consumption. Consequently, firms will sell less and will thus be discouraged from investing. This results in a fall in the demand for loanable funds. The rate of interest would have to fall further to clear the market, perhaps considerably so.

The demand for investment, according to Keynes, depends very much on business confidence in the future. A slide into recession could shatter such confidence. The resulting fall in investment would deepen the recession.

The problem of disequilibrium in the market for loanable funds is made worse, according to Keynes, because neither saving nor investment is very responsive to changes in interest rates, and thus very large changes in interest rates would be necessary if equilibrium were ever to be restored after any change in the supply of loanable funds (saving) or demand for loanable funds (investment).

Keynes also rejected the simple quantity theory of money. Increases in money supply will not necessarily lead merely to rises in prices. If there is a lot of slack in the economy,

BOX 16.3 **WILL WAGE CUTS CURE UNEMPLOYMENT?** EXPLORING ECONOMICS

Keynes' dismissal of the classical remedy

In *The General Theory of Employment, Interest and Money,* Keynes rejects the classical argument that unemployment is due to excessive wages. In Chapter 2 he argues:

> [T]he contention that the unemployment which characterises a depression is due to a refusal by labour to accept a reduction of money wages is not clearly supported by the facts. It is not very plausible to assert that unemployment in the United States in 1932 was due either to labour obstinately refusing to accept a reduction of money wages or to its obstinately demanding a real wage beyond what the productivity of the economic machine was capable of furnishing. Wide variations are experienced in the volume of employment without any apparent change either in the minimum real demands of labour or in its productivity. Labour is not more truculent in the depression than in the boom – far from it. Nor is its physical productivity less. These facts from experience are a *prima facie* ground for questioning the classical analysis.[1]

Conduct an online search to find cases of politicians in recent years calling for wage restraint as a way of helping increase employment. Do their arguments mirror those of classical economists?

1 J. M. Keynes, *The General Theory of Employment, Interest and Money,* Macmillan (1967), p. 9.

with high unemployment, idle machines and idle resources, an increased spending of money may lead to substantial increases in real income (Y) and leave prices (P) little affected.

If the government were to cut money supply in an attempt to reduce prices, the major effect might be to reduce output and employment instead. In terms of the quantity equation, a reduction in M may lead to a reduction in output and hence real income Y rather than a reduction in P.

All these arguments meant a rejection of Say's law. Far from supply creating demand and thus ensuring full employment, Keynes argued that it was *demand that created supply.* If aggregate demand rose, firms would respond to the extra demand by producing more and employing more people. But a fall in demand would lead to less output and rising unemployment.

Keynes' central point was that an unregulated market economy *could not ensure sufficient demand.* Governments should therefore abandon laissez-faire and should intervene to *control* aggregate demand.

Keynes' analysis of employment and inflation

Keynes' analysis of unemployment can be explained most simply in terms of the circular flow of income (see Figure 16.2). Keynes himself did not use this exact model, but it clearly explains the essence of his argument.

If injections (J) do not equal withdrawals (W), a state of disequilibrium exists. What will bring them back into equilibrium, however, is not a change in prices (of labour or of loanable funds), but rather a change in *national income* and *employment.*

Start with a state of equilibrium, where injections equal withdrawals, but with substantial unemployed resources (as was the case in the Great Depression). If there is now a rise in injections – for example, a rise in government expenditure – aggregate demand ($C_d + J$) will be higher. Firms will respond to this increased demand by using more labour and other resources and thus paying out more incomes (Y) to households. Household consumption will rise and so firms will sell more.

Firms will respond by producing more, and thus using more labour and other resources. Household incomes will rise again. Consumption and hence production will rise again, and so on. There will thus be a multiplied rise in incomes and employment. This is known as the ***multiplier effect*** and is an example of the 'principle of cumulative causation'. ***Cumulative causation*** refers to where an initial event can cause an ultimate effect that is much larger. It is our final threshold concept and we examine it in detail in Chapter 17 (see pages 542–3). TC 15 p543

Cumulative causation arises from self-reinforcing processes, like the multiplier, that trigger further changes and provide additional momentum to the initial impulse or shock. These processes are examples of ***propagation mechanisms*** that

Definitions

Multiplier effect An initial increase in aggregate demand of £xm leads to an eventual rise in national income that is greater than £xm.

Cumulative causation An initial change which causes an eventual change that is larger, often much larger.

Propagation mechanisms The means by which economic shocks are transmitted through the economy.

Figure 16.2 The circular flow of income

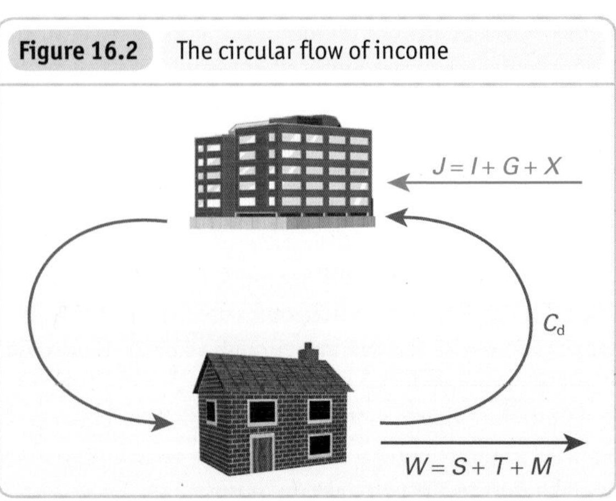

cause economic shocks to be transmitted through the economy. They are important because they can *amplify* the effects of impulses, such as a change in injections or withdrawals, and potentially result in lasting effects on the economy.

In this case, changes in production that occur in response to changes in aggregate demand trigger further changes in aggregate demand. The multiplier process, however, does not go on forever. Each time household incomes rise, households save more, pay more taxes and buy more imports. In other words, withdrawals rise. When withdrawals have risen to match the increased injections, equilibrium will be restored and national income and employment will stop rising. The process can be summarised as follows:

$$J > W \rightarrow Y\uparrow \rightarrow W\uparrow \text{until } J = W$$

Similarly, an initial fall in injections (or rise in withdrawals) will lead to a multiplied fall in national income and employment:

$$J < W \rightarrow Y\downarrow \rightarrow W\downarrow \text{ until } J = W$$

Thus equilibrium in the circular flow of income can be at *any* level of output and employment.

If aggregate demand is too low, there will be a recession and high unemployment. The equilibrium output level would be considerably below that consistent with the full employment of the economy's resources. In this case, argued Keynes, governments should intervene to boost aggregate demand. There are two policy instruments that they can use.

Fiscal policy

Fiscal policy is where the government alters the balance between government expenditure (G) and taxation (T). By engaging in fiscal policy, government can alter the balance between injections and withdrawals. In this way, it controls aggregate demand. Faced with a recession, it should raise G and/or lower T. In other words, the government should run a budget deficit rather than a balanced budget. There will then be a multiplier effect:

$$G\uparrow \text{or} T\downarrow \rightarrow J > W \rightarrow Y\uparrow \rightarrow W\uparrow \text{until} J = W$$

The larger the multiplier effect the larger the eventual increase in output following the initial increase in aggregate demand.

Monetary policy

Monetary policy is where the central bank alters the supply of money in the economy and/or manipulates interest rates. If it were to raise money supply, there would be more available in the economy for spending, interest rates would fall and aggregate demand would rise. Keynes argued that this was a less reliable policy than fiscal policy, since some of the extra money could be used for speculating in paper assets rather than spending on real goods and services. The details of how the central bank controls money supply and interest rates and the effects of such actions on the economy are examined in later chapters.

It is most effective if both fiscal and monetary policies are used simultaneously. For example, if the government undertook a programme of public works (fiscal policy) and financed it through increases in money supply (monetary policy), there would be no crowding out. There would be a significant rise in output and employment.

What would be the classical economists' criticisms of this argument?

If aggregate demand rises too much, however, inflation becomes a problem. (This was the case during the Second World War, with the high expenditure on the war effort.) As the economy's full-capacity output is approached, with more and more firms reaching their full capacity and with fewer and fewer idle resources, so additional increases in aggregate demand lead more and more to higher prices rather than higher output. The aggregate level of employment therefore becomes unresponsive to an increase in the effective demand for output. Thus, the level of output when this situation arises is sometimes referred as to the 'full-employment output level'.

If a rise in aggregate demand were to encourage firms to invest more, how would this influence the size of the rise in real GDP?

Governments faced with the resulting demand-pull inflation should, according to Keynes, use *contractionary* fiscal and monetary policies to reduce demand. Contractionary fiscal policy would involve reducing government expenditure and/or raising taxes. Contractionary monetary policy would involve reducing the rate of growth of money supply and/or raising interest rates. Keynes argued that here too fiscal policy was the more reliable, but again that the best solution was to combine both policies.

The Keynesian policies of the 1950s and 1960s

By the end of the Second World War, the economic consensus had changed and this was to have a direct impact on economic policy making in many countries. The dominance of classical economics was to be replaced by Keynesian ideas. From 1945 up to the mid-1970s, many governments around the world, including Conservative and Labour governments in the UK, pursued Keynesian ***demand-management policies*** in an attempt to stabilise the economy and avoid excess or deficient demand. KI 34 p453

Definitions

Monetary policy Where the central bank alters the supply of money in the economy and/or manipulates interest rates.

Demand-management policies Demand-side policies (fiscal and/or monetary) designed to smooth out the fluctuations in the business cycle.

When the economy began to grow too fast, with rising inflation and balance of trade deficits, the government adopted *deflationary* (contractionary) fiscal and monetary policies. When inflation and the balance of payments were sufficiently improved, but probably with recession looming, threatening rising unemployment and little or no growth, governments adopted *reflationary* (expansionary) fiscal and monetary policies. This succession of deflationary and reflationary policies to counteract the effect of the business cycle became known as ***stop-go policies*** (see Case Study 16.7 on the student website for an account of 'fine-tuning' in the UK).

As Figure 16.1 shows (see page 501), during the 1950s and 1960s, inflation in the UK averaged 4 per cent and unemployment a mere 1.7 per cent. Low rates of inflation and unemployment were experienced in other industrialised countries too.

Nevertheless, from the mid-1960s onwards there was increasing criticism of short-term demand-management policies. Criticisms included the following:

- *Economic fluctuations still existed.* The policies had mixed success in stabilising economies. The business cycle remained. Some economists even claimed that demand-management policies made fluctuations worse. The main reason given was the time it took for policies to be adopted and to work. If time lags are long enough, a deflationary policy may begin to work only when the economy has already turned down into recession. Likewise, a reflationary policy may begin to work only when the economy is already booming, thus further fuelling inflation.
- *Neglect of structural problems.* Some economists argued that an over-concentration on short-term policies of stabilisation meant that underlying structural problems in economies were neglected. This was particularly significant in the UK since its post-war growth rate of around $2^3/_4$ per cent per annum was appreciably lower than that of other industrialised countries.
- *Balance of payments problems.* Countries like the UK and the USA had persistent balance of trade deficits. At the time, with virtually fixed rates of exchange (something we shall examine in Chapter 25), a depreciation of the exchange rate was not an option for correcting balance of payments deficits. This meant that Keynesian reflationary policies were not always possible in recessions. The reason was that deflationary policies had to be pursued instead to bring prices down to boost exports and dampen demand to reduce imports.
- *Breakdown of the simple Phillips curve.* The simple Phillips curve relationship between inflation and unemployment was breaking down (see Box 15.6 on page 485). If reflationary policies were the cure for unemployment and deflationary policies were the cure for inflation, what policies should be pursued when both inflation and unemployment were rising?
- *Focus on aggregate demand.* Perhaps the most fundamental criticism of all came from a group of economists called 'monetarists'. They rejected Keynesianism as a whole, with its concentration on demand. They returned to the earlier classical analysis, with its concentration on supply, and extended it to take account of the increasingly important role of price expectations in explaining 'stagflation' – the problem of slow growth and rising unemployment (i.e. stagnation) combined with rising inflation (see the next section).

From the mid-1970s onwards, the Keynesian/monetarist split between economists was often reflected in countries' political systems. For example, in the UK the Conservative leadership embraced monetarism, whereas the other political parties continued to embrace variants of Keynesianism.

Definition

Stop-go policies Alternate deflationary and reflationary policies to tackle the currently most pressing of the four problems that fluctuate with the business cycle.

Section summary

1. Keynes rejected the classical assumption that all markets would clear. Disequilibrium could persist in the labour market. A fall in aggregate demand would not simply lead to a fall in wages and prices and a restoration of the full-employment equilibrium. Instead there would be demand-deficient unemployment: as demand fell, there would be less demand for labour.
2. Disequilibrium could also persist in the market for loanable funds. As aggregate demand fell and, with it, business confidence, so the demand for loanable funds for investment would shrink. Reductions in interest rates would be insufficient to clear the market for loanable funds.
3. Keynes also rejected the simple quantity theory. If there is slack in the economy, an expansion of the money supply can lead to an increase in *output* rather than an increase in prices.
4. Keynes argued that there would be a multiplier effect from changes in injections or withdrawals. A rise in investment, for example, would cause a multiplied rise in national income, as additional expenditures flowed round and round the circular flow, stimulating more and more production and thus generating more and more real income.

5. If the economy is operating below full employment, the government can use fiscal and/or monetary policies to boost aggregate demand and thereby take up the slack in the economy. Excessive aggregate demand, however, causes inflation. Deflationary fiscal and monetary policies can be used to remove this excess demand.
6. Keynesianism became the orthodoxy of the 1950s and 1960s. Governments used fiscal (and to a lesser extent monetary) policies to manage the level of aggregate demand.
7. After the mid-1960s, however, there was growing criticism of Keynesian demand management. Economies still fluctuated and the various macroeconomic problems seemed to be getting worse.

16.4 THE RISE OF THE MONETARIST AND NEW CLASSICAL SCHOOLS

Sowing the seeds of a new orthodoxy

As we saw in section 16.3, the Keynesian orthodoxy began to break down during the 1960s. This breakdown can be seen in the context of a more volatile macroeconomic environment (see Figure 16.1 on page 501). The high inflation rates and low growth of the 1970s stimulated macroeconomic debates. As we shall see, some of the resulting developments were to have a significant impact on macroeconomics, helping to shape a new orthodoxy.

In charting the path to a new orthodoxy, we begin by considering the rise of the monetarist and new classical schools. A feature that distinguished both schools from the Keynesian orthodoxy was the belief that the market economy can deliver macroeconomic stability. Government intervention, they argued, can be a contributory factor to macroeconomic *instability*.

The monetarist counter-revolution

The chief advocate of monetarism was Milton Friedman, Professor of Economics at Chicago University and recipient of the Nobel Memorial Prize in Economics in 1976 (see Case Study 16.8 on the student website). Monetarists returned to the old classical theory as the basis for their analysis and extended it to take account of the growing problem of ***stagflation*** – low growth accompanied by high inflation.

At the heart of monetarism is the *quantity theory of money*, which, as we saw earlier, was central to the classical analysis of inflation (see section 16.2). Friedman examined the historical relationship between money supply and prices and concluded that inflation was 'always and everywhere a monetary phenomenon'. If money supply over the long run rises faster than the potential output of the economy, inflation will be the inevitable result.

Monetarists argued that over the long run, in the equation $MV = PY$, *both* V and Y are independently determined and are not, therefore, affected by changes in M. Any change in money supply (M), therefore, will only affect prices (P). In other words, the *neutrality of money* (see section 16.2) holds in the long run.

Monetarists drew two important conclusions from their analysis.

- The rising inflation from the mid-1960s onwards was entirely due to the growth in money supply increasingly outstripping the growth in output. If money supply rises, they argued, then the resulting rise in aggregate demand will lead to higher output and employment only in the short run. But soon people's expectations will adjust. Workers and firms come to expect higher wages and prices. Their actions then ensure that wages and prices *are* higher. Thus after a short period, perhaps one or two years, the extra demand is fully taken up in inflation, and so output and employment fall back again. Then governments are tempted to raise money supply and aggregate demand again in a further attempt to get unemployment down. The effect of this over several years is for the inflation rate to get higher and higher. 
- Reducing the rate of growth of money supply will reduce inflation without leading to long-run increases in unemployment. It *will* lead to temporary increases in unemployment, they argued, as the demand for goods and labour fall. But as price and wage inflation adjust down to this new level of demand, unemployment will fall. This process will be hindered and high unemployment is likely to persist if workers continue demanding excessive wage increases, or if firms and workers continue to expect high inflation rates.

Monetarists argued that inflation is damaging to the economy. Inflation creates uncertainty for businesspeople and so

Definition

Stagflation A term used to refer to the combination of stagnation (low growth and high unemployment) and high inflation.

reduces investment while also reducing a country's competitiveness in international trade. They saw it as essential, therefore, for governments to keep a tight control over money supply and advocated the setting of money supply *targets*. Modest and well-publicised targets should help to reduce the *expected* rate of inflation. Targets for the growth of the money supply were central to the 'medium-term financial strategy' from the late 1970s to the mid-1980s of the UK governments of Margaret Thatcher.

TC 9 p132

The natural rate hypothesis

Monetarist analysis implied that the long-run Phillips curve is vertical at the equilibrium rate of unemployment. The equilibrium rate is frequently referred to as the ***natural rate of unemployment*** by monetarists. This is illustrated in Figure 16.3. It is the rate of unemployment consistent with the economy being at its potential or 'long-run' output level. It is therefore argued to be determined principally by structural factors. Though not directly measurable, it can be thought of as capturing structural and frictional unemployment (see section 15.5).

In the *short run,* higher aggregate demand will cause output to rise above its potential level and hence reduce the unemployment rate below the natural rate. This is because there is a *real* increase in aggregate demand. This is captured by a move upwards along a *short-run* Phillips curve (*EAPC* – see below for an explanation of the terminology). But in the long run an increase in aggregate demand is fully absorbed by higher inflation. Therefore, a monetary expansion will increase output and employment in the short run, but not so in the long run, when money neutrality holds. The idea that unemployment will return to a natural rate in the long-run is known as the ***natural rate hypothesis***. The key to understanding why is the role of expectations.

Friedman argued that, in forming expectations of inflation, people learn from experience. If, for example, in the previous period, they under-predicted the rate of inflation, then this period they will adapt: they will revise their expectations of inflation upwards. This type of behaviour is thus known as ***adaptive expectations***.

Short-run deviations in unemployment and output could be explained by people's misperceptions of price changes: firms or workers wrongly misperceiving *general* price changes as *relative* price changes. In other words, people see changes in particular prices or wages as specific to those goods or labour markets rather than merely reflecting the general rate of inflation. This is an application of what has become known as ***misperceptions theory***. Friedman referred to a 'fooling model', whereby workers misperceive changes in *nominal* wages as *real* changes. For example, if workers are given a pay rise of 4 per cent, but inflation is 3 per cent, then although they may be fooled into seeing this as a rise of 4 per cent, it is a real rise of only 1 per cent.

Assume that the economy is in equilibrium with unemployment at its natural rate (U_n) and the rate of inflation at zero. This is represented by point *a* in Figure 16.3. Now assume that the authorities engage in a monetary expansion. This increases aggregate demand, resulting in an excess demand for goods and labour. The effect of this is to cause prices and nominal wages to rise.

If workers misperceive the rise in nominal wages as a rise in *real* wages they can be 'fooled' into supplying more labour than they would if they knew the 'true' real wage. In fact, prices sometimes rise more quickly than nominal wages, resulting in a *fall* in real wages. Consequently, firms increase their demand for labour; output expands above its potential level and the unemployment rate falls below its natural rate. This is captured by the move from point *a* to point *b* on our short-run Phillips curve ($EAPC_0$).

Gradually workers recognise that their real wages have fallen following the monetary expansion. They revise upwards their expectations of the rate of inflation. This puts further upward pressure on money wages as wage demands increase to reflect the now higher expectations of the rate of inflation. Importantly this causes the short-run Phillips curve to move vertically upwards: each rate of unemployment is now associated with a higher rate of inflation. In Figure 16.3 the short-run Phillips curve shifts upwards to $EAPC_1$. Because

Figure 16.3 Phillips curves and the natural rate hypothesis

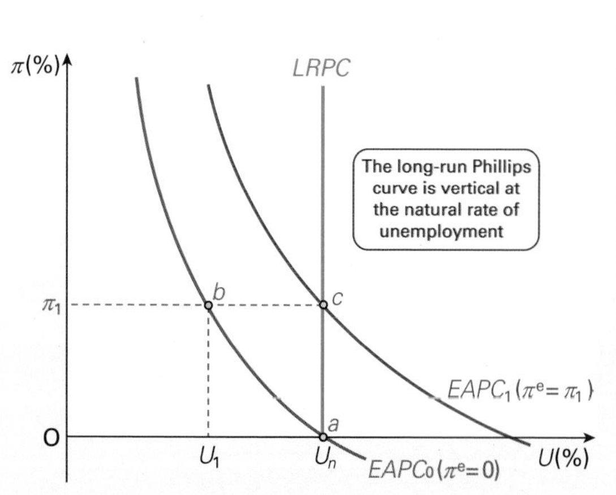

Definitions

Natural rate of unemployment The rate of unemployment consistent with market clearing in the labour market. It is the rate of unemployment at which the vertical long-run Phillips curve cuts the horizontal axis.

Natural rate hypothesis The theory that, following fluctuations in aggregate demand, unemployment will return to a natural rate. This rate is determined by supply-side factors, such as labour mobility.

Adaptive expectations hypothesis The theory that people base their expectations of inflation on past inflation rates.

Misperceptions theory The theory that changes in economic activity are caused by people confusing changes in *general* prices with changes in *relative* prices.

of the importance of inflationary expectations to the short-run trade-off between inflation and unemployment, our short-run Phillips curves are also referred to as 'expectations-augmented Phillips curves' or *EAPCs* (see Box 15.6).

In the long run, as expectations of inflation converge on actual inflation, all the extra demand is absorbed in higher inflation. Output falls to its potential level and unemployment rises back to the natural rate. This is captured by point *c* in Figure 16.3.

If unemployment is to be reduced in the long run, therefore, this vertical Phillips curve must be shifted to the left. This will be achieved by a reduction in the natural (equilibrium) rate of unemployment (U_n), *not* by an increase in demand. To reduce the natural rate, argued the monetarists, ***supply-side policies*** would be needed. These are policies that focus on increasing *potential* output by increasing the quantity and/or productivity of factors of production.

Give some examples of supply-side policies that would help to reduce the natural rate of unemployment.

The new classical school

The ***new classical school*** took on increasing significance during the 1970s and 1980s. The monetarist view was that markets adjust relatively quickly, but that there may be disequilibrium in the short run.

In contrast, new classical economists believed that markets clear continuously. The implication of ***continuous market clearing*** for the labour market is that there is no demand-deficient unemployment: wage flexibility equates the demand and supply of labour. The only unemployment is 'voluntary' unemployment, where unemployed people choose not to take jobs on offer, preferring, perhaps, to spend time looking for better-paid employment.

Is voluntary unemployment the same as frictional unemployment?

TC 9 p132

Another key assumption of the new classical school is ***rational expectations***. This means that economic agents use all available information and predict inflation, or any other macroeconomic variable, as well as they can. The important point here is that, unlike with adaptive expectations, economic agents avoid making the same error repeatedly. Therefore, errors are random. This means that, on average, economic agents' expectations of inflation are correct.

The combined assumptions of continuous market clearing and rational expectations have another important implication: the distinction between the short run and long run breaks down. This means that a change in aggregate demand will simply cause a change in prices, not a change in output and employment, even in the short run. This applies equally to both a rise and a fall in aggregate demand. If we therefore refer back to Figure 16.3, an increase in aggregate demand from point *a* will be followed by a rapid and perhaps instantaneous adjustment of the economy to point *c*.

But, with continuous market clearing and rational expectations, how did new classical models explain the fluctuations in output and unemployment associated with the business cycle?

Monetary surprises

The first strand of new classical models focused on how imperfect information could generate unexpected inflation. This is a further application of misperceptions theory. The work was led by Professor Robert Lucas, who, like Friedman, spent much of his career at the University of Chicago. Lucas was a recipient of the Nobel Memorial Prize in Economics in 1995 (see Box 21.3 on page 670). KI 15 p132

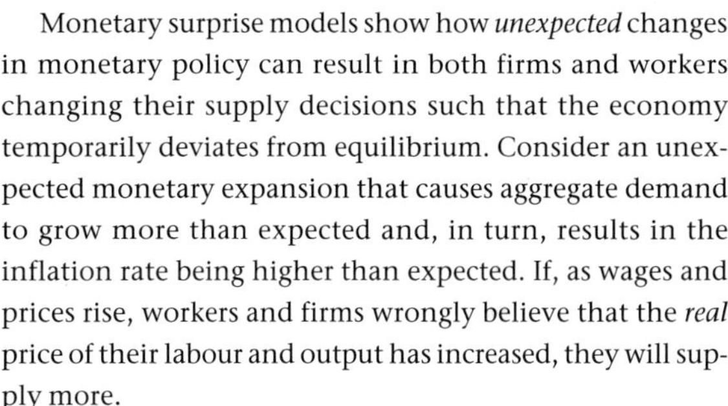

Monetary surprise models show how *unexpected* changes in monetary policy can result in both firms and workers changing their supply decisions such that the economy temporarily deviates from equilibrium. Consider an unexpected monetary expansion that causes aggregate demand to grow more than expected and, in turn, results in the inflation rate being higher than expected. If, as wages and prices rise, workers and firms wrongly believe that the *real* price of their labour and output has increased, they will supply more.

Conversely, an unexpected monetary contraction would see labour supply and output fall. This time, workers and firms wrongly believe that a fall in wages and prices represents a real fall in the price of labour and output.

Why are monetary surprises less likely with independent central banks pursuing an inflation target? Would monetary surprises still be possible in such circumstances?

Definitions

Supply-side policies Policies to increase *potential* output or reduce the equilibrium rate of unemployment. Such policies focus on increasing the quantity and/or productivity of resources.

New classical school A body of economists who believe that markets are highly competitive and clear very rapidly; any expansion of demand will feed through virtually instantaneously into higher prices, giving a vertical short-run as well as a vertical long-run Phillips curve.

Continuous market clearing The assumption that all markets in the economy continuously clear so that the economy is permanently in equilibrium.

Rational expectations Expectations based on the *current* situation. These expectations are based on the information people have to hand. While this information may be imperfect and therefore people will make errors, these errors will be random.

KI 15 p132

The key to economic fluctuations in monetary surprise models is the errors in expected inflation that arise from imperfect information. These errors allow for movements along an expectations-augmented Phillips curve. Once economic agents recognise these errors, output and employment return to their equilibrium levels. In the presence of continuous market clearing and rational expectations, *anticipated* changes in economic policy have no effect on output and employment, which remain at their equilibrium levels. The Phillips curve is then vertical even in the short run. This prediction is known as the ***policy ineffectiveness proposition***.

TC 9 p132

The monetary surprise models and the policy ineffectiveness proposition are highly contentious. Two principal objections have been raised.

The first objection is the assumption of *continuous market clearing*. As we shall see in the next section, a key Keynesian response has been to explore why, instead, prices might adjust only *slowly* in clearing product and labour markets. If prices do adjust slowly then economic policy can have real effects on output and employment, even in the presence of rational expectations.

The second objection is the conclusion of *money neutrality*, whereby expected changes in monetary policy do not affect output. Could the business cycle be explained only by monetary *surprises*? It was this second concern that some new classical economists attempted to address with the development of 'real business cycle models'.

Real business cycles

Like the monetary surprise models, ***real business cycle theories*** also assume continuous market clearing and rational expectations. However, real business cycle theories challenge the traditional understanding of the business cycle as fluctuations in real GDP around potential (natural) output (see section 15.3). Instead, it is argued, the business cycle is created by movements in potential output itself.

TC 12 p455

Real business cycle (RBC) theories focus on supply-side shocks or impulses that permanently affect the path of the economy's output over time. They argue that the economy is buffeted regularly by supply-side shocks, and, in particular, by technology shocks. Technology shocks can, in theory, refer to anything that affects production processes and levels of productivity. For example, a technological breakthrough in telecommunications could positively affect potential output, while a decline in energy sources could negatively affect potential output.

Definitions

Policy ineffectiveness proposition The conclusion drawn from new classical models that when economic agents anticipate changes in economic policy, output and employment remain at their equilibrium (or natural) levels

Real business cycle theories The new classical theory which explains fluctuations in real GDP in terms of economic shocks, especially technology shocks, and which have persistent effects on potential output.

Would an intensification of government regulation constitute a positive or negative economic shock in RBC models?

Real business cycle theory challenges the traditional view that technology is important largely when explaining the *long-term* rate of economic growth and development. Instead, frequent technology shocks are also seen as an important explanation of business cycles. Therefore, real business cycle theories dispense with the distinction between the business cycle and long-term economic growth; supply-side shocks are important both in the short run and in the long run.

The economic effects of shocks to the economy are assumed to reflect the optimal decisions of economic agents (firms, households, government, etc.). In making consumption and production choices, economic agents consider the impact of their choices not only in the current period, but in all future periods too.

This means that an expansion in the economy's output (e.g. from a technological breakthrough) reflects purposeful decisions by firms to increase output and workers to increase their labour supply. On the other hand, declining output (e.g. from a less business-friendly regulatory climate) reflects decisions by firms to reduce output and workers to reduce labour supply.

The role of representative agents. Real business cycle models use representative agents (i.e. a typical person or firm) to analyse and illustrate the impact of economic shocks. They are assumed to allocate their time between work and leisure so as to maximise their lifetime satisfaction.

Consider the effect of a positive technology shock and the propagation mechanisms by which the shock is transmitted through the economy. Again, this could be a technological breakthrough. This enables people to produce and earn more now. If they believe that the benefits of this positive shock will be relatively short-lived, the incentive to work and earn more now is especially strong. Therefore, following positive economic shocks people actively choose to work more. In doing so, output rises. Some of the increased income from the additional production is invested, increasing levels of investment. This further increases the economy's potential output, so raising possible future output levels.

When economic shocks are negative, such as from a decline in energy sources, people choose to work less. Such shocks reduce current output levels and reduce levels of investment. The effect is to reduce possible future output levels.

Assume that there is a positive economic shock and the economy expands. Why may it continue to expand for some time? Why may the expansion eventually cease and be followed by a recession?

Government policies

Governments up to the late 1970s responded to rising unemployment by boosting aggregate demand (the balance of payments permitting). This, however, as monetarists and new classical economists predicted, led only to more inflation, fuelled by rising expectations of inflation (see Figure 16.1 on page 501). When governments eventually did curb the growth in aggregate demand, it took time for expectations to adjust downwards.

TC 9 p132

As we saw earlier, to help bring inflationary expectations down, the UK government from the late 1970s to the mid-1980s set targets for the growth of money supply. This was largely consistent with monetarist principles. In the short term, however, the effect was a rise in unemployment. As can be seen in Figure 16.1, the standardised UK unemployment rate rose to as high as 12 per cent by 1984.

Nevertheless, the pursuit of these policies did, according to monetarists, lead to a dramatic fall in the rate of inflation. Inflationary expectations fell and wage rises moderated. In 1980, the inflation rate was 15 per cent; by 1986, it had fallen to 3 per cent. Eventually the rise in unemployment was to be reversed too.

The rise of monetarist and new classical macroeconomics was to be reflected in economic policy during the 1980s in many countries, though particularly so in the USA and the UK. The result was that governments were again to place a greater reliance on the market. The UK saw policies of privatisation and deregulation pursued; union power curbed; and tax rates cut. Controls over the financial system were reduced, with banks given much more freedom to expand their activities (we examine this in Chapter 18). This 'supply-side' revolution was designed to increase incentives to work, invest and innovate. We explore these market-orientated supply-side policies in section 23.5.

Section summary

1. Monetarists argued that there is a close correlation between the rate of growth of the money supply and the rate of inflation. Increases in money supply cause increases in aggregate demand, which in turn cause inflation. Along with the classical economists, they argued that output and employment are determined independently of money supply (at least in the long run). This means that a deflationary policy to cure inflation will *not* in the long run cause a fall in output or a rise in unemployment.
2. Monetarists thus argued that the long-run Phillips curve is vertical. Its position along the horizontal axis will depend on the level of equilibrium or 'natural' unemployment. However, because people may form adaptive expectations of the rate of inflation, there can exist a short-run trade-off between the rates of inflation and unemployment. This trade-off is captured by expectations-augmented Phillips curves (*EAPCs*).
3. Building on monetarist ideas, early new classical macroeconomic models focused on how monetary surprises induce short-term deviations in unemployment from its natural rate. However, under the assumptions of continuous market clearing and rational expectations, unemployment does not deviate from its natural rate if monetary policy is anticipated.
4. Real business cycle theorists argue that the business cycle is the result of frequent economic shocks, such as technology shocks, which affect the path of potential output. Economic outcomes, including the path of real GDP, are the result of optimal choices made by rational economic agents under continuous market clearing.

16.5 THE KEYNESIAN RESPONSE

Market imperfections

Monetarist and new classical ideas reshaped macroeconomics radically during the 1970s and 1980s. These ideas affected policy making with increasing emphasis placed on the supply side of the economy. Governments began to place less emphasis on using its discretion over monetary and fiscal policy to fine-tune the economy.

Many Keynesians could agree with monetarists and new classical economists on one point. If demand is expanded too fast and for too long, inflation will result – and there will be a certain amount of unemployment of labour (and other resources too) that cannot be eliminated simply by expanding aggregate demand. However, they rejected the notion that the policy ineffectiveness proposition always holds. Because of the behaviour of markets, they argued, governments could intervene through policies designed to affect aggregate demand and make a positive difference.

A large number of academic Keynesians began a research agenda focused on gaining a better understanding of *aggregate supply*. The motivation was to develop stronger theoretical explanations of why markets may be slow to adjust. Consequently, a large amount of work was undertaken into market imperfections and the frictions which cause prices to be 'sticky'. Much of the focus was to establish stronger *microeconomic* foundations. The group of Keynesians who have taken this approach have been subsequently labelled ***new Keynesians***.

Menu costs and nominal price rigidity

The assumption of continuous market clearing is seen by many Keynesians as the most controversial of the new classical assumptions. New Keynesians have focused on the *frictions* that may cause prices to adjust only slowly following economic shocks, especially to aggregate demand.

New Keynesians argue that firms are often operating in imperfectly competitive markets (see Chapter 8). Therefore, firms are price-makers rather than price-takers as portrayed in the perfectly competitive model (see Chapter 7). In other words, firms set not just quantity but also price.

However, a firm's product price may exhibit *stickiness* in the presence of demand shocks because of the *menu costs* of price changes (see Box 15.5, page 484). Menu costs include both the physical costs to firms in updating price lists and the costs incurred in determining and negotiating prices with customers and suppliers.

If the menu costs to an individual firm are larger than the profit lost from not adjusting prices, then the rational firm will not change its prices. When price rigidity is commonplace throughout the economy, any change in aggregate demand can have a significant effect on national *output*. Price behaviour is therefore a key propagation mechanism affecting the size and persistence of changes in output resulting from demand shocks.

Consider a decrease in demand for a representative profit-maximising firm with power to affect both price and output. Intuitively, we would expect the firm to reduce both output and prices. The extent of both would ordinarily be determined by the rule for the profit-maximising level of output: marginal revenue (MR) equals marginal cost (MC) (see section 6.6). However, if frictions, such as those arising from menu costs, result in price stickiness, then output will fall further. The stickiness in prices causes the quantity demanded to fall more than it otherwise would do following the initial decline in demand. Box 16.4 analyses menu costs more formally.

Illustrate the effect of a fall in demand for an imperfectly competitive firm (a) in the presence of menu costs and (b) in the absence of menu costs.

The significance of price rigidities is that changes in aggregate demand can have significant effects on an economy's actual output. Therefore, in the presence of such frictions to market adjustment, governments may need to intervene to affect the level of aggregate demand.

Such frictions are also important because they mean that changes in the money supply can affect the economy's output. In other words, money ceases to be neutral as predicted by real business cycle theory: it can have real effects on the economy.

What technological developments are likely to have reduced menu costs in recent years?

Sources of other frictions and imperfections

The extensive new Keynesian literature that has developed since the 1980s has identified a series of other market imperfections. These imperfections can help to reinforce the nominal rigidity in product prices arising from menu costs and so amplify fluctuations in real GDP. Imperfections include the following:

- *Price inelasticity of demand.* Where competition is limited, demand will be less elastic. Under such circumstances a firm will be under less pressure to reduce prices if demand falls. In an economic downturn, therefore, firms may prefer to reduce output than cut prices. KI 22 p195 TC 6 p66
- *Anticipating other firms' pricing strategy.* If firms' products are close substitutes for one another, they are likely to be very wary of cutting prices for fear of retaliation from their rivals. They may prefer to reduce output during a downturn rather than risk a price war.
- *Sticky nominal wages.* Wage rates are largely determined through negotiation between workers and employers. The presence of contracts allows both sides to avoid the costs incurred in frequent wage negotiations and provide both with a degree of certainty. Even in the absence of contracts, workers are likely to be resistant to cuts in their money wages. They may prefer a reduction in hours, or the non-replacement of workers who leave, rather than take a cut in wages. Indeed, the flexibility of hours, often with 'zero hours contracts', where workers have no guaranteed hours, but simply are allocated hours on a weekly or monthly basis, means that employers are more likely to adjust hours than wage rates.
- *Real wage rigidity.* New Keynesians argue that equilibrium real wage rates may be above market clearing levels. The result can be involuntary unemployment. As we saw in section 10.2 (page 297), the ***efficiency wage hypothesis*** maintains that firms may pay wage rates above market levels in order to provide an incentive for workers. The implication that new Keynesians draw is that, in a downturn, a firm may be reluctant to cut real wages for fear of lowering morale and thereby reducing productivity. TC 5 p48

Insider–outsider theories emphasise the power of employees in resisting real wage cuts. Those currently employed (the ***insiders***, see page 296) may, through their unions or close

Definitions

New Keynesians Economists who seek to explain how market imperfections and frictions can result in fluctuations in real GDP and the persistence of unemployment.

Efficiency wage hypothesis The hypothesis that the productivity of workers is affected by the wage rate that they receive.

Insiders Those in employment who can use their privileged position (either as members of unions or because of specific skills) to secure pay rises, or resist wage cuts, despite an excess supply of labour (unemployment).

relationships with their employers, or because of the possession of specific skills, be able to prevent the unemployed (the ***outsiders***) from competing wages down.

- *Sources of finance.* During a downturn, both internal and external sources of finance for investment may diminish. The decline in demand will reduce profit and hence internal sources. What is more, banks may be less willing to lend, seeing risks rising in a downturn. The result is a decline in investment. During a boom, by contrast, sources of funds for investment are likely to increase. These 'pro-cyclical' changes in the availability of finance are thus likely to amplify existing fluctuations in real GDP.
- *Attitudes towards debt.* In a boom, consumer and business confidence is likely to encourage borrowing. Debts are likely to rise. In a recession, however, with people more anxious about the future, consumers and firms may seek to reduce their debts by curbing spending. These effects could be reinforced by risk-averse financial institutions which reduce lending, seeing it as riskier when firms are more likely to go out of business or individuals more likely to lose their jobs. Again, this means that bank lending tends to be pro-cyclical and amplifies existing fluctuations in real GDP.

KI 11 p72

Definition

Outsiders Those out of work or employed on a casual, part-time or short-term basis, who have little or no power to influence wages or employment.

Hysteresis

In the early 1980s there was a recession, or slowdown, throughout the industrialised world. Unemployment rose to unprecedented levels. But as the world began to recover, unemployment remained stubbornly high. This focused minds on the extent to which current rates of unemployment

BOX 16.4 MENU COSTS EXPLORING ECONOMICS

How sticky prices amplify fluctuations in output

Menu costs are any costs incurred by firms when changing prices. These include not only costs to firms of updating price lists, such as the costs of printing new menus in restaurants from which the name of the concept is derived, but also costs in developing new price strategies, in negotiating new contracts and in the very processing of the information around the new price structure that customers will need to undertake.

Menu costs, it is argued, may create a stickiness or rigidity in firms' prices because they are reluctant to change prices even when faced with a change in demand. In other words, menu costs create a friction to the adjustment of nominal (actual) product prices to economic shocks. The more widespread is such price rigidity the more significant can be the effect of a change in aggregate demand on national output.

To illustrate the effect of price rigidity on output, consider the diagram of a monopolistically competitive firm. The firm's demand curve (D_1) is downward sloping, the elasticity depending on how close its competitors' products are as substitutes to its own. The marginal revenue (MR_1) curve lies below the demand curve (average revenue curve) because, in reducing price to sell more units, all units attract the lower price (see Chapter 7, pages 210–11). For simplicity, we assume that marginal cost (MC) is constant across all output levels.

The firm experiences a decrease in demand for its product because of a decrease in aggregate demand in the economy. Before the decrease in aggregate demand, the firm is producing at output level Q_1, where marginal cost (MC) equals marginal revenue (MR_1), and selling its output at price P_1. Its profit is represented by the area CP_1DE.

The decrease in demand results in a leftward movement in both the demand curve (D_1 to D_2) and the marginal revenue curve (MR_1 to MR_2). In the absence of frictions, our price setting firm will reduce price from P_1 to P_2 and output from Q_1 to Q_2. Profit falls to CP_2FG.

Price frictions and the monopolistically competitive firm

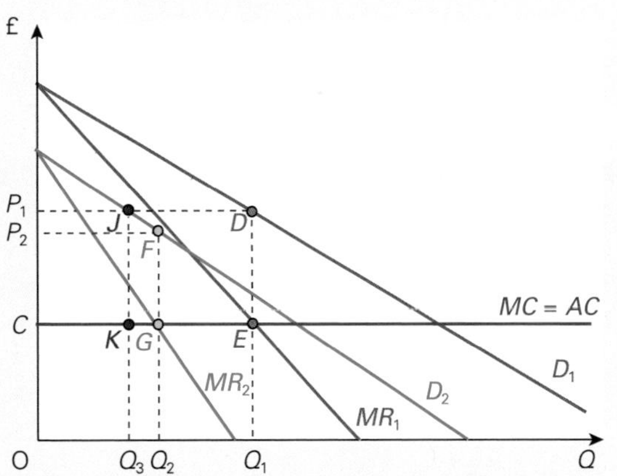

However, if frictions, such as those arising from menu costs, result in price stickiness, then output will fall further. If price remains at P_1 then output falls to Q_3. Hence, output has fallen by the additional amount equivalent to $Q_2 - Q_3$. Profits fall to CP_1JK. But, the key point is that firms will be willing to incur this forsaken profit, $CP_2FG - CP_1JK$, if the menu costs incurred in reducing prices are greater.

Illustrate the effect of nominal price rigidities on output if the firm's demand increases because of a rise in aggregate demand.

affect the future path of unemployment. Could there be a persistence or inertia in unemployment rates? And, if so why?

Keynesians argued that the rise in unemployment, though largely caused by a lack of demand, could not simply be reversed by a *rise* in demand. The recession had itself *caused* higher rates of unemployment to become embedded in the economy. The reason is that during a recession, many people become deskilled and/or demoralised and firms become more cautious about taking on workers, preferring to manage with a smaller, more efficient workforce. What is more, as we saw above, people who remain employed (the *insiders*) are often able to secure wage increases for themselves, and prevent the unemployed (the *outsiders*) from competing wages down. Many of the unemployed thus remain unemployed.

This persistence of high unemployment that characterised many developed economies through the 1980s and into the 1990s and once more in the late 2000s and into the 2010s is an example of ***hysteresis***. This term, used in physics, refers to the lagging or persistence of an effect, even when the initial cause has been removed. In the context of the labour market, it refers to the persistence of unemployment even when the initial demand deficiency no longer exists.

Past rates of aggregate demand and unemployment were thus affecting the *natural rate of unemployment,* or what some Keynesians refer to as the ***non-accelerating-inflation rate of unemployment (NAIRU)***.

Although the natural rate and the NAIRU are theoretically different, the concepts are often used interchangeably. The natural rate of unemployment is the unemployment rate consistent with market clearing in the labour market. It depends on structural factors affecting labour demand and supply. On the other hand, the NAIRU is the rate of unemployment in a world characterised by market imperfections and frictions at which the inflation rate is steady in the short term, say the next 12 months or so.

It is not only the labour market that can be affected by hysteresis effects. The global financial crisis of the late 2000s and later the COVID-19 pandemic fuelled concerns about a range of ***scarring effects*** on the economy. These include effects on the growth of labour productivity and potential output, which are fundamental to a country's future wellbeing (see Chapter 23). We discuss the issue of hysteresis and scarring effects further in section 16.7 when analysing the impact of these two global crises on economic policy and theory.

What is the connection between the concepts of 'hysteresis' and 'propagation mechanisms'?

Government intervention

Targeted government intervention may be needed to help smooth the path of aggregate demand. A substantial increase in demand may be necessary if the economy is in danger of falling into deep recession, as was the case in 2008–9 and in 2020–21. The debate then concerns the form that this intervention should take.

One approach is for the government to increase its expenditure on public works such as roads, school building and housing. The advantages of such infrastructural projects is that they can directly impact on the economy's potential output and, because they have a relatively low import content, increased expenditure on such projects does not lead to balance of payments problems.

Thereafter, the government should maintain a high and stable demand by appropriate demand-management policies. This should keep unemployment down and set the environment for long-term investment and growth.

Definitions

Hysteresis The persistence of an effect even when the initial cause has ceased to operate. In economics, it refers typically to the persistence of effects on macroeconomic variables, such as unemployment, even when the economic event that caused them no longer exists.

Non-accelerating-inflation rate of unemployment (NAIRU) The rate of unemployment consistent with steady inflation in the near term, say, over the next 12 months.

Scarring effects Long-lasting damage to the economy and to the economic situations of individuals and firms that can result from an economic downturn.

Section summary

1. A group of Keynesian economists sometimes referred to as 'new Keynesians' responded to the monetarist/new classical challenge by building models highlighting market imperfections, including frictions that affect the adjustment of markets to shocks. These imperfections were argued to provide a rationale for government intervention.
2. Keynesians argued that unemployment caused initially by a recession (a deficiency of demand) may persist even when the economy is recovering. Labour market hysteresis can arise from effects such as the deskilling of labour or firms being cautious about taking on extra labour when the recovery does come. Other macroeconomic variables may also be affected, notably the growth in labour productivity and potential output.
3. Whereas monetarist and new classical macroeconomists generally favoured policies of freeing up markets, Keynesians generally favoured a rather more interventionist approach by the government. Through appropriately targeted fiscal measures, governments can help to smooth the business cycle and limit the adverse effects on the economy's future potential output.

16.6 AN EMERGING CONSENSUS UP TO THE CRISIS OF 2008

The Great Moderation and a new mainstream consensus

The period from the early 1990s up to the financial crisis of the late 2000s was to be known as the 'Great Moderation'. The period was characterised in many developed countries by low and stable inflation and continuous economic growth. As Figure 16.1 shows (see page 501), the UK was no exception. From 1994 to 2007 annual UK growth averaged 3.1 per cent while the annual rate of consumer price inflation averaged 1.7 per cent.

The period of the Great Moderation also saw the emergence of a new mainstream macroeconomic consensus. The new consensus built on elements from the new classical and new Keynesian schools of thought. In particular, it combined the idea from real business cycle theory of the economy being hit by frequent random shocks, particularly supply shocks, with the new Keynesian idea of market imperfections that then affect the adjustment process of the economy to the shocks.

The new consensus macroeconomics argued that there is no long-run trade-off between inflation and unemployment, with the natural rate of unemployment and the economy's potential output being determined by supply-side or structural factors. The new Keynesian market imperfections, therefore, explain the deviations of output from its potential or long-run level.

DSGE models – the new consensus macro model

The new consensus has been identified with the development of elaborately technical models of the economy. One particularly well-known group of models are known as ***dynamic stochastic general equilibrium models*** or ***DSGE models*** for short.

The dynamic nature of DSGE models. DSGE models of the economy are a fusion of new Keynesian and new classical ideas. In these models, forward-looking rational economic agents (individuals and firms) make choices to maximise their welfare. They attempt to achieve the best outcomes in any given set of circumstances. These choices are affected by future uncertain outcomes and so evolve as events unfold and changes occur in agents' rational expectations. Hence, the models are *dynamic*.

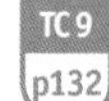

The stochastic element in DSGE models. The economy is hit by frequent random (stochastic) 'shocks'. These ***stochastic shocks*** generate uncertainty for economic agents. Crucially, it is these shocks and hence the uncertainty that they generate that result in the economy's output deviating from what would otherwise be a predictable growth path. These deviations or disturbances also affect the economy's future growth path. In other words, their impact can persist, perhaps because of hysteresis effects. This means that new consensus models combine an analysis of both short-term and long-term economic growth.

Give some examples of stochastic shocks.

The types of shock considered by new consensus economists are quite broad. On the supply side, shocks include, for instance, changes in the price mark-up (over marginal cost) of imperfectly competitive firms, changes in the cost to firms of external finance relative to internal finance, or productivity shocks. On the demand side, shocks include changes to the 'impatience' of economic agents and therefore their preference for spending now relative to the future, and changes in expected future consumption, in government spending or in interest rates.

General equilibrium. DSGE models seek to understand macroeconomic aggregates, such as real GDP, by analysing the interaction of economic agents in markets. They take a 'bottom-up approach' by analysing the macroeconomy through the interaction of representative agents in different markets which all tend to equilibrium. This explains why DSGE models are *general equilibrium* models.

KI 22 p195

Market imperfections and frictions. DSGE models typically assume monopolistically competitive firms and monopolistically competitive labour markets. Furthermore, they incorporate a number of frictions to price adjustment drawn from new Keynesian developments. The exact nature of competition in product and labour markets and the frictions applied in the models can vary. This allows economists and policy makers to analyse how these imperfections affect the way in which economic shocks impact on the economy.

Constrained policy discretion

In the UK, as in many other industrialised countries, the Great Moderation was a period when policy makers

Definitions

Dynamic stochastic general equilibrium (DSGE) models Models that seek to explain macroeconomic phenomena by examining the microeconomic behaviour of rational forward-looking individual economic agents acting in a variety of market conditions. The microeconomic equilibria are subject to random shocks, such as technological change, political events or changes in the supply of natural resources.

Stochastic shocks Shocks that are random and hence unpredictable, or predicable only as occurring within a range of values.

frequently spoke about the importance of policies that help to foster a stable economic environment and that are conducive to long-term economic growth and prosperity. This led to the birth of what economists call ***constrained discretion***: a set of rules or principles providing a framework for economic policy.

Constrained discretion typically involves the use of targets, such as an inflation target or a public-sector deficit target or a debt ceiling. The key is to affect the *expectations* of the public, for example in relation to inflation.

TC 9 p132

Does the use of public-sector deficit targets rule out the use of fiscal policy to reduce economic fluctuations associated with the business cycle?

In many countries, governments handed over the operation of monetary policy to central banks. In the UK, in 1997 the Bank of England was granted independence to determine interest rates to meet an inflation rate target.

The new classical models of the late 1970s and early 1980s played an important role in developing the theoretical foundations for central bank independence. If a short-term trade-off between inflation and unemployment only arises because of *unanticipated* changes in monetary policy then, new classical economists argued, it makes sense to remove the temptation for governments to use expansionary monetary policy unexpectedly.

In the longer term, in the absence of central bank independence or transparent inflation-rate targeting, the result is likely to be higher inflationary expectations and higher actual inflation. However, output and unemployment will be at their natural levels. This is because the general public is only too aware of governments' incentive to want to induce faster growth by loosening monetary policy and creating 'surprise' inflation. Economic agents therefore push up the inflation rate by revising their inflationary expectation upwards, so choking off any increase in output and employment. This excessive inflation is known as ***inflation bias***.

The elimination of inflation bias is commonly identified as a key economic benefit of central bank independence. By sticking to an inflation target, a central bank can create the stable environment necessary for the market to flourish: expectations will adjust to the target rate of inflation (assuming central banks are successful in achieving the target) and firms will be able to plan with more confidence. Investment is thereby encouraged and this, in turn, encourages a growth in potential output. In other words, sticking to the targets creates the best environment for the expansion of aggregate *supply*.

From the mid-1990s to 2007/8, these policies seemed to be successful. But then things went horribly wrong!

Definitions

Constrained discretion A set of principles or rules within which economic policy operates. These can be informal or enshrined in law.

Inflation bias Excessive inflation that results from people raising their expectations of the inflation rate following expansionary demand management policy, encouraging government to loosen policy even further.

Section summary

1. During the 1990s a new mainstream consensus began to develop. It drew ideas principally from the new classical and new Keynesian schools. Central to most new consensus models are representative forward-looking economic agents who form rational expectations.
2. Dynamic stochastic general equilibrium (DSGE) models became the standard model of the economy. These allowed economists to model the impact of frequent economic shocks under certain assumptions about competition in product and labour markets and the speed with which these markets adjust to equilibrium.
3. Government policy moved to one of constrained discretion, with fiscal and monetary targets. This, it was argued, would provide the stable environment for the mixed market system to flourish and for firms and consumers to take a longer-term perspective.

16.7 THE FINANCIAL CRISIS AND THE COVID-19 PANDEMIC

Two global crises

The period following the Great Moderation was to see two global crises: a global financial crisis and global health emergency (COVID-19 pandemic).

The financial crisis. An unsustainable extension of credit by financial institutions during the 1990s and 2000s was to result in substantial pressures on the financial system. In 2007, several smaller banks were in difficulties and some had to be bailed out. Then, in 2008, Lehman Brothers in the USA collapsed and was liquidated. With many of the world's major banks being seen as having too little capital, there was a real danger that many more would collapse. Lending between banks dried up and several banks had to be bailed out by their governments.

KI 11 p72

There followed a sharp reduction in banks' lending to customers which markedly dampened aggregate demand. This was exacerbated by the financial distress of the private sector as their balance sheets deteriorated. The liabilities of the private sector became increasingly exposed as asset prices fell sharply. This, in turn, led people and businesses to attempt to pay down debts or increase precautionary saving. The economic slowdown has therefore been described as a ***balance sheet recession***. The term is associated with economist Richard Koo who used it to explain the persistence of low growth following the collapse of the residential and commercial property markets in Japan in the early 1990s.

KI 35 p459

As Figure 16.4 shows, the financial crisis saw global growth close to zero in 2009, while the economies of Japan, the UK and USA shrank by 5.4 per cent, 4.2 per cent and 2.5 per cent, respectively.

The 2020/21 coronavirus pandemic. A little over a decade later and economies were experiencing a second 'once-in-a-lifetime' shock. The health intervention measures implemented during the COVID-19 pandemic included lockdowns and the forced closure of many firms in the retail and leisure sectors. This dramatically affected both the volume of production and consumption activities and the ways in which they could take place. In other words, the pandemic was to affect the ability and willingness of producers to produce and consumers to consume.

The pandemic saw global output in 2020 fall by over 3 per cent, with output in advanced economies falling by an average of 4¾ per cent and by almost 10 per cent in the UK.

Although different, both crises raised some common issues. Not least, how should policy makers respond, and would the crises result in enduring effects that could affect future economic activity and levels of wellbeing.

Policy responses

Financial crisis

Despite disagreements about the causes of the financial crisis, the immediate priorities of policy makers were to ensure the stability of the financial system and to mitigate the effects on aggregate demand of the limited levels of credit now available for households and firms. There was initially a general consensus on the medicine to be applied: vast amounts of liquidity were supplied to the banking sector, interest rates were slashed, and fiscal stimulus packages were adopted. In other words, the consensus was that central banks and governments needed to act.

This consensus was to be relatively short-lived, however, as many countries saw a marked deterioration in the state of their public finances. Governments began running relatively large fiscal deficits which needed financing. These deficits were worsened by governments having to bail out banks and by the recession which saw tax revenues fall and the number claiming benefits rising.

Cutting the deficit became the new priority of many governments, including the UK's Coalition government from 2010 to 2015. Meanwhile, in the eurozone the ***sovereign debt crisis*** became so serious that Greece, Portugal, Ireland and

Definitions

Balance sheet recession A recession or economic slowdown caused by a collapse in aggregate demand arising from the actions of financially distressed people and businesses.

Sovereign debt crisis The financial and economic problems caused by excessive public-sector debt and by the fear that governments will be unable to raise sufficient finance to repay maturing debt.

Figure 16.4 Growth rate in selected economies

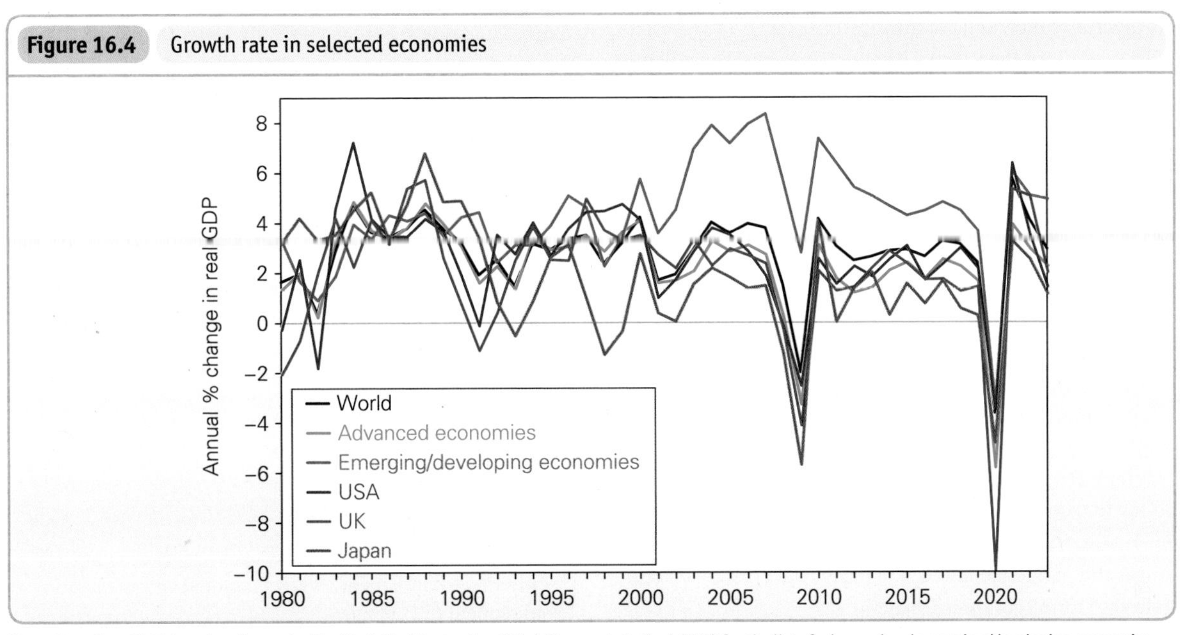

Notes: Data from 2020 based on forecasts. See Statistical Appendix of *World Economic Outlook* (IMF) for the list of advanced and emerging/developing economies.
Source: *World Economic Outlook Database*, IMF (April 2021) www.imf.org/en/Publications/SPROLLS/world-economic-outlook-databases; data from 2021 based on forecasts.

later Cyprus had to receive bailouts from European funds and the IMF. In return they were obliged to agree to severe fiscal austerity measures.

Debates over policy. In some ways the 2010s were reminiscent of 1920s and 1930s, with debates over the economic costs of fiscal deficits and of public expenditure crowding out private expenditure.

Those on the political left took a more Keynesian line, believing that cutting the deficit too quickly would endanger the economic recovery, with private-sector demand unable to offset the cuts to public expenditure.

Those on the political right argued in favour of rapid deficit reduction. Without this, they claimed, there would be upward pressure on interest rates as confidence in the government's finances was undermined and as the public sector competed with the private sector for scarce resources. This was the line taken in the UK by the Coalition government, although, in practice, their measures (and those of the Conservative government that succeeded it in 2015) were not as deflationary as their targets for deficit reduction.

COVID-19 pandemic

As with the response to the financial crisis, governments and central banks around the world adopted extraordinary fiscal and monetary measures. With the scope for interest-rate cuts more limited, since rates were still historically low in many countries following the financial crisis, monetary easing would involve vast amounts of liquidity once more injected into the financial system.

TC 7 p79

Yet the crisis is likely to be remembered for, among other things, the scale and scope of the fiscal interventions. In many countries, including the UK, these interventions would include policies designed to mitigate the impact on the income streams of people and businesses, including the payment of some or all of the wages of staff put on furlough, tax deferrals and grants for business.

As a result of the various interventions and the collapse in national output, public-sector spending in the UK in 2020/21 rose to 56 per cent of national income, while public-sector net borrowing rose to 20 per cent of national income – double that in 2009/10 following the global financial crisis. Both figures were their highest since the Second World War.

Scarring effects

Because of the significant decline in economic activity experienced during both crises, concerns grew that their economic impact would be felt well into the future. During the pandemic in particular, the concept of scarring effects would be referred to regularly. This was not only by economists and policy makers but also more widely by the general public. For many, this was no longer some abstract concept: the longer the pandemic lasted, the more concerns grew about its longer-term economic impact.

The prospect of scarring effects had a significant effect on the fiscal choices of many governments. Interventions to protect jobs and limit the disruption of businesses, such as the Job Retention Scheme (www.gov.uk/government/collections/coronavirus-job-retention-scheme) and the Business Interruption Loans Scheme (www.british-business-bank.co.uk/ourpartners/coronavirus-business-interruption-loan-scheme-cbils-2/) in the UK, were designed, in part, with the aim of enabling economic activity to resume more seamlessly when the pandemic subsided. Alongside these interventions were measures to provide training or job placements to prevent the risk of deskilling and long-term unemployment.

The consensus was that governments needed to act. The concern was that negative hysteresis effects would affect not only the labour market but also the growth of potential output. The channels through which this might occur included a reduction in the accumulation of knowledge and innovation and in the accumulation of physical capital. This would reflect lower rates of investment, R&D expenditure and reduced opportunities for learning by doing.

Some economists raised the possibility of ***super-hysteresis*** – a more extreme form of hysteresis. To help understand this distinction consider Figure 16.5. Assume that the economy's actual output (the dark green line) fluctuates around an initial trend growth path captured by the dashed line g_1. Then at time T_1, the economy experiences a significant negative shock, such as the pandemic. Actual output then falls sharply. In the absence of negative hysteresis effects, the loss in national output is recovered across subsequent cycles and the economy's trend growth path is unaffected: the economy continues to fluctuate around path g_1.

Now consider the impact of hysteresis effects on actual output and the trend growth path. If the loss of national output is not fully recovered across future cycles, but the trend growth rate is unaffected, then the economy will fluctuate around a growth path such as g_2. This is the hysteresis scenario. The growth path is vertically lower than growth path g_1, which is consistent with national output being permanently lower, but has the same gradient. The extent to which it is vertically lower will depend on how much, if any, of the national output is ever recovered.

If national output is permanently lower *and* the trend rate of growth is lower too, then national output will fluctuate around a lower and flatter growth path such as g_3. This is the super-hysteresis scenario and has significant implications for future wellbeing.

What are the potential implications for future aggregate living standards of 'super-hysteresis' compared with 'hysteresis' following the COVID-19 pandemic?

Definition

Super-hysteresis The situation where a recession not only affects subsequent levels of national output but also subsequent rates of growth.

Figure 16.5 Hysteresis effects and an economy's output path

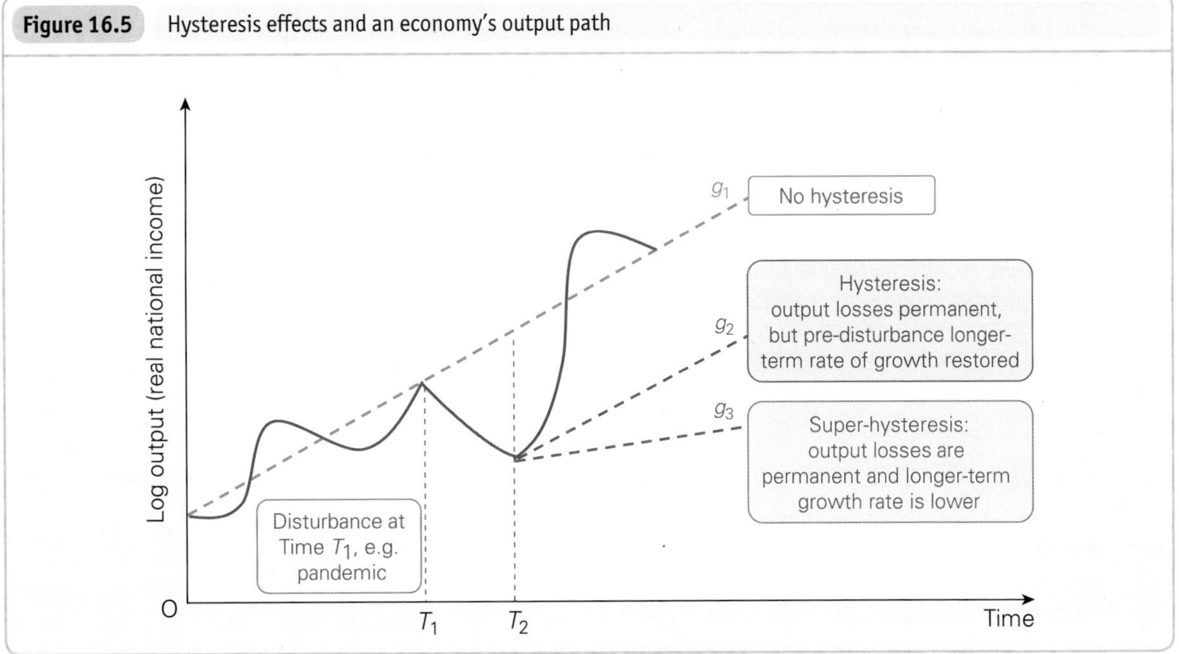

Source: Adapted from G. Dosi, M. C. Pereira, A. Roventini and M. E. Virgillito, 'Causes and consequences of hysteresis: aggregate demand, productivity, and employment', *Industrial and Corporate Change*, vol. 27, issue 6 (December 2018), pp. 1015–44, https://doi.org/10.1093/icc/dty010

Debates about the state of macroeconomics

A common theme of this chapter has been how macroeconomic debates and developments have often been fuelled by periods of turbulence and crisis. The period following the financial crises saw the new mainstream consensus that had developed in the 1990s and early 2000s come under considerable scrutiny.

However, it is important to recognise that the views of macroeconomists in relation to key issues, particularly the flexibility of prices, the role of expectations, the impact of changes in aggregate demand on economic activity and the role of government policy (see section 16.2), tend to fall along a spectrum, rather than being in some very specific camp.

At one end of the *spectrum of views* are those who see the free market as working well and who generally blame macroeconomic problems on excessive government intervention. At the other are those who see the free market as fundamentally flawed.

Then there are economists who were never party to the consensus. In particular, objections were raised by a group of Keynesians who have become known as ***post-Keynesians***. They highlight some of the key features of Keynes' *General Theory* to explain why economies are not self-correcting. In particular, they stress the importance of what Keynes called 'animal spirits', or what is today known as sentiment or confidence. Changes in confidence can have fundamental effects on the behaviour of economic agents. For instance, the mood of the country's business community can be crucial in determining firms' investment and output decisions. Without appropriate demand-management policy, this mood can remain depressed into the long term.

Post-Keynesians and other ***heterodox economists*** also challenge most of the microeconomic assumptions on which other more 'mainstream' macroeconomic theories are based. Firms, for example, are not cold, rational profit maximisers, making calm calculations based on marginal analysis. Instead, firms make output decisions largely in response to anticipated demand, again based on their *confidence* in

Definitions

Post-Keynesians Economists who stress the importance of institutional and behavioural factors, and the role of confidence in explaining the state of the economy. They argue that firms are more likely to respond to changes in demand by changing output rather than prices.

Heterodox economists Economists who reject the assumptions of neoclassical economics, in particular the assumptions of rational optimising behaviour. They highlight the importance of institutional behaviour and factors influencing human behaviour.

their market. The result is that anticipated demand changes are likely to lead to *output* and *employment* changes, not price changes.

KI 24 p259

Post-Keynesians tend to focus on a country's *institutions* and *culture* to explain how firms and consumers respond to economic stimuli. In other words, they try to base their explanations and policies on real-world institutional and behavioural information rather than on abstract models.

Two economists disagree over what would have been the best way of tackling the problem of unemployment arising from the credit crunch and recession. For what reasons might they disagree? Are these reasons positive or normative?

Emergence of a new consensus?

While some groups, including post-Keynesians, consistently voiced their concerns about the new consensus, a more broad-based debate began to develop in the aftermath of the financial crisis. The debate extended to the macroeconomics curriculum being taught in universities – a debate that continues to this day. Conferences and working parties have considered both what should be taught and how it should be taught.

Problems with relying on micro foundations

One concern is the extent to which the new consensus had focused too heavily on developing microeconomic foundations and thereby applying a 'bottom-up' approach to analysing macroeconomic aggregates. In the process, often very technical and mathematical models emerged. These models would often be built around representative agents with rational expectations, which some economists point out spells out RARE! This is a reminder of the importance of the behavioural assumptions we attach to economic agents in our economic models.

KI 12 p96

Another issue with a purely 'bottom-up' approach to macroeconomic analysis is the fallacy of composition. We first came across this in Chapter 3 (see page 96) in the context of poor harvests. When one farmer alone has a poor harvest their own revenue falls, but if all farmers have poor harvests total revenue may well rise. More generally, what applies in one case does not necessarily apply when repeated in all cases. This is important in macroeconomics because we are analysing aggregates. For this reason, the fallacy of composition is also known as the *paradox of aggregates*.

The paradox of thrift. The most commonly cited paradox of aggregates is the paradox of thrift (see Box 16.5). If just a few individuals increase their propensity to save, their saving increases and they can consume more in the future. However, if this is repeated across all individuals, it can lead to a fall in aggregate saving because the fall in consumption causes firms to produce less, which reduces national income.

The example of the paradox of thrift illustrates the importance, when building macroeconomic models, of taking into account not only how individuals behave but how they *interact*. Consequently, it also illustrates how aggregate or group behaviour impacts on individual behaviour and well-being.

A contemporary example of the paradox of thrift is the attempt by economic agents to improve their financial well-being following the financial crisis. To reduce their debts many people cut back on their spending. The general effect of this was a decline in sales, output and jobs and therefore, as we saw at the start of this section, a balance sheet recession. Additionally, people sought to sell assets, such as property and shares. However, because large numbers of people looked to do likewise, the value of property, shares and other assets fell. Therefore, rather than individuals seeing their net worth increase as they sold assets, group behaviour resulted in the aggregate net worth of economic agents actually falling. For this reason it is known as the ***paradox of debt***.

The paradox of thrift and the paradox of debt are illustrations of what, in this context, is known as ***downward causation***: group behaviour affects individual behaviour and well-being.

TC 15 p543

The importance of the financial sector

The financial crisis led economists to reflect further on the assumptions they make about the financial system in their models. Financial frictions and imperfections have therefore been incorporated in new consensus models, albeit to varying degrees. The financial crisis illustrated the importance of incorporating financial institutions and markets both fully and appropriately in macroeconomic models. As the financial crisis showed, the behaviour of financial institutions can be acutely destabilising.

Definitions

Paradox of debt (or paradox of deleveraging) The paradox that one individual can increase their net worth by selling assets, but if this is undertaken by a large number of people aggregate net worth declines because asset prices fall.

Downward causation The name given to the impact on individual behaviour or well-being of aggregate or group effects. This is an example of cumulative causation (Threshold Concept 15, page 543).

BOX 16.5 THE PARADOX OF THRIFT

EXPLORING ECONOMICS

When prudence is folly

The classical economists argued that saving was a national virtue. More saving would lead via lower interest rates to more investment and faster growth. Keynes was at pains to show the opposite. Saving, far from being a national virtue, could be a national vice.

Remember the fallacy of composition (see Box 3.5 on page 96). Just because something is good for an individual, it does not follow that it is good for society as a whole. This fallacy applies to saving. If individuals save more, they will increase their consumption possibilities in the future. If society saves more, however, this may *reduce* its future income and consumption. As people save more, they will spend less. Firms will thus produce less. There will thus be a multiplied *fall* in income. The phenomenon of higher saving leading to *lower* national income is known as 'the paradox of thrift'.

But this is not all. Far from the extra saving encouraging more investment, the lower consumption will *discourage* firms from investing. There will then be a further multiplied fall in national income.

The paradox of thrift had in fact been recognised before Keynes, and Keynes himself referred to various complaints about 'underconsumption' that had been made back in the sixteenth and seventeenth centuries:

> In 1598 Laffemas . . . denounced the objectors to the use of French silks on the grounds that all purchasers of French luxury goods created a livelihood for the poor, whereas the miser caused them to die in distress. In 1662 Petty justified 'entertainments, magnificent shews, triumphal arches, etc.', on the ground that their costs flowed back into the pockets of brewers, bakers, tailors, shoemakers and so forth . . . In 1695 Cary argued that if everybody spent more, all would obtain larger incomes 'and might then live more plentifully'.[1]

But despite these early recognitions of the danger of underconsumption, the belief that saving would increase the prosperity of the nation was central to classical economic thought.

When is an increase in saving desirable?

Conduct a brief survey of students who are not economists. Your questions should establish their views on the effects of an increase in saving for themselves and for the economy as a whole if everyone saved more. Write a brief report on people's views and whether they accord with economic theory.

1 J. M. Keynes, *The General Theory of Employment, Interest and Money*, Macmillan (1967), pp. 358–9.

Areas of general agreement?

The global financial crisis and global health emergency have helped to re-energise long-standing macroeconomic debates, while also fuelling important debates about the current state of macroeconomics. Nonetheless, we can attempt to identify some *general* points of agreement that have emerged in recent years, at least among the majority of economists.

- In the short run, changes in aggregate demand can have a significant effect on output and employment. If there is a collapse in demand, as in 2008 and 2020, governments and/or central banks should intervene through expansionary fiscal and/or monetary policies. Only a few extreme new classical economists would disagree with this proposition.
- In the long run, changes in aggregate demand will have much less effect on output and employment and much more effect on prices. In fact, many economists say that there will be no effect at all on output and employment, and that the whole effect will be on prices. There is still a substantial body of Keynesians, however, especially post-Keynesians, who argue that changes in aggregate demand will have substantial effects on long-term output and employment via changes in investment and hence in potential output – and in the case of a fall in aggregate demand via hysteresis or even super-hysteresis.
- There is no simple long-run trade-off between inflation and unemployment. There is still disagreement, however, as to whether there is no relationship between them at all (i.e. the long-run Phillips curve is vertical), or whether they are connected indirectly via the long-term effects of changes in aggregate demand, for example, on investment, innovation or the overall skillset of a country's workforce.
- Expectations have an important effect on the economy. There is still disagreement, however, as to whether it is people's expectations of price changes or of output changes that are more important. Also, it is difficult to model people's expectations when these can so easily be affected by random shocks; and where optimism can sometimes build in a burst of 'irrational exuberance' or pessimism descend in a cloud of despondency, while at other times optimism or pessimism can quickly fade.
- Excessive growth in the money supply will lead to inflation. Some economists argue that the quantity theory of money holds in the long run (i.e. that inflation is entirely due to increases in the money supply). Others argue that the relationship is more general. Nevertheless, the consensus is that governments should avoid allowing the money supply to grow too rapidly.
- Controlling inflation through control of the money supply, however, is difficult since money supply itself

KI 10 p70

is not easy to control. Even if it were possible to control money supply accurately, there is a time lag between changes in money supply and the resulting changes in inflation. This makes a precise control of inflation by this means very difficult. Most economists, therefore, argue that it is easier to control inflation by controlling interest rates, since this directly affects aggregate demand. Most central banks around the world today therefore use interest rate changes to achieve a target rate of inflation.

- If the economy is in deep recession, most economists agree that it may be necessary to expand the money supply, rather than relying on cuts in interest rates. However, monetary expansion (known as 'quantitative easing') does not directly affect spending. Banks have to be willing to lend the extra money and individuals and firms have to be willing to borrow and spend it.
- Macroeconomic policy should not focus exclusively on the demand side. Long-term growth depends primarily on changes in supply (i.e. in potential output). It is important, therefore, for governments to develop an effective supply-side policy if they want to achieve faster economic growth. There is still disagreement, however, over the forms that supply-side policy should take: should it focus on freeing up the market, or should it focus on various forms of government intervention to compensate for market deficiencies?

- Governments' ability to control their country's macroeconomic destiny is being increasingly eroded by the process of globalisation. As countries have become more interdependent, and as capital moves freely around the globe, so there is a need for co-ordinated policies between governments to tackle problems of global recessions or excessive exchange rate fluctuations. This lesson was brought home in 2008, when it became obvious that most countries were experiencing a collapse in aggregate demand following the banking crisis and the credit crunch. Leaders discussed common policy approaches at several international summits, including both bank rescue packages and expansionary fiscal and monetary policies.

The future directions of macroeconomic research, teaching and policy cannot be known with certainty. But each will reflect in some way the impact of recent major events, which include the global financial crisis, the rise in populism and protectionism and the COVID-19 pandemic. This means that we can expect the debates around macroeconomics to be particularly passionate and lively for some time to come.

As the book progresses, we will be looking at the various areas of agreement and disagreement in more detail. One thing is certain: these are incredibly fascinating times to be studying macroeconomics.

Section summary

1. There are many shades of opinion among economists, from extreme new classical economists, who advocate almost complete laissez-faire, to post-Keynesian and heterodox economists, who focus much more on individual and institutional behaviour and who see markets as having many failings. In between comes a whole spectrum of opinions and theories about the relative effectiveness of markets and the government in achieving the various macroeconomic goals.
2. The period after the great moderation reignited long-standing debates about policy, while also fuelling debates about the state of macroeconomics. Key concerns included the significance of scarring effects from large shocks to the economy, the importance that had been placed on developing models with microeconomic foundations, the appropriateness of the behavioural assumptions of economic agents, and the assumptions made around the role of the financial system.
3. Despite these disagreements, most economists would agree on the following points:
   - changes in aggregate demand have a direct effect on output and employment in the short run, but either no effect or a far less certain effect in the long run;
   - there is no simple long-run trade-off between inflation and unemployment;
   - expectations have an important effect on the economy, but can be affected in ways that are not easy to predict;
   - excessive growth in the money supply causes inflation;
   - it is easier to achieve inflation targets by controlling interest rates than by controlling money supply;
   - monetary expansion is an important policy tool in tackling recession;
   - changes on the supply side of the economy are the major determinant of long-term growth;
   - globalisation has reduced individual countries' ability to control their economies.

END OF CHAPTER QUESTIONS

1. In a given economy, the supply of money is £10 billion; the velocity of circulation of money (spent on final goods and services) is 3; and the price index is 2.00.
   (a) What is the level of real national income?
   (b) How much have prices risen (in percentage terms) since the base year?
   (c) Assume that money supply increases by 10 per cent and that the velocity of circulation remains constant. By what percentage will prices rise if
      (i) there is no increase in real national income;
      (ii) real national income increases by 10 per cent;
      (iii) real national income increases by 5 per cent?
2. In what way will the nature of aggregate supply influence the effect of a change in aggregate demand on prices and real national income?
3. Criticise the classical theory that higher government spending will necessarily crowd out private spending.
4. Criticise the use of increasing government expenditure as a means of reducing unemployment.
5. In what way may short-term demand-management policies help to stabilise the economy? What problems occur in the use of such policies?
6. What explanations can you give for the increase in *both* unemployment and inflation in the 1970s?
7. What do you understand by the policy ineffectiveness proposition? On what assumptions is the proposition based?
8. How is the distinction between nominal and real variables relevant to misperceptions theory?
9. Identify a series of possible frictions which could affect the speed with which markets adjust or which affect the nature of market equilibria.
10. What is meant by *hysteresis* when applied to unemployment? How do you account for this phenomenon in the 1980s?
11. What is meant by *super-hysteresis*? Why might this phenomenon occur?
12. What will cause people to expect higher rates of inflation? How will expectations of inflation affect the actual rate of inflation?
13. Explain how pro-cyclical lending criteria applied by financial institutions could amplify fluctuations in real GDP.
14. What is meant by the paradox of aggregates? Of what importance might they be for how we analyse macroeconomic problems?
15. What policy prescriptions could be recommended for an economy experiencing a balance sheet recession?

Online resources

Additional case studies on the student website

16.1 The equation of exchange. This examines two more versions that are commonly used: the Fisher version and the Cambridge version.

16.2 Money and inflation in ancient Rome. A very early case study of the quantity theory of money: how the minting of extra coins by the Romans caused prices to rise.

16.3 Thomas Malthus, David Ricardo and Jean-Baptiste Say. A look at the work of three of the most famous classical economists and their degree of optimism or pessimism about the working of the free market.

16.4 The Great Depression and the return to the gold standard. A time of great hardship and sacrifice.

16.5 Classical 'remedies' for unemployment. How the policies advocated by the classical economists to cure unemployment would, according to Keynes, make the problem worse.

16.6 John Maynard Keynes (1883–1946). A profile of the great economist.

16.7 A little bit less of this and a little bit more of that. Fine-tuning in 1959 and 1960.

16.8 Milton Friedman (1912–2006). A profile of the most influential of the monetarist economists.

16.9 Spectrum of views. An overview of the different schools of macroeconomic thought.

Websites relevant to this chapter

See sites listed at the end of Chapter 17 on page 560.

Macroeconomic Models, Theories and Policy

We now build on the foundations of Part E. We will see why economies grow over the longer term but fluctuate in the short term and what governments can do to prevent these fluctuations.

In the following three chapters, we look at what determines the level of national income and the role that money plays in the process. Then, in Chapters 20 and 21 we look at the relationship between inflation and unemployment. In Chapter 22, we look at government policy to stabilise the economy. Finally, in Chapter 23, we turn to the long run and ask how economies can sustain faster growth.

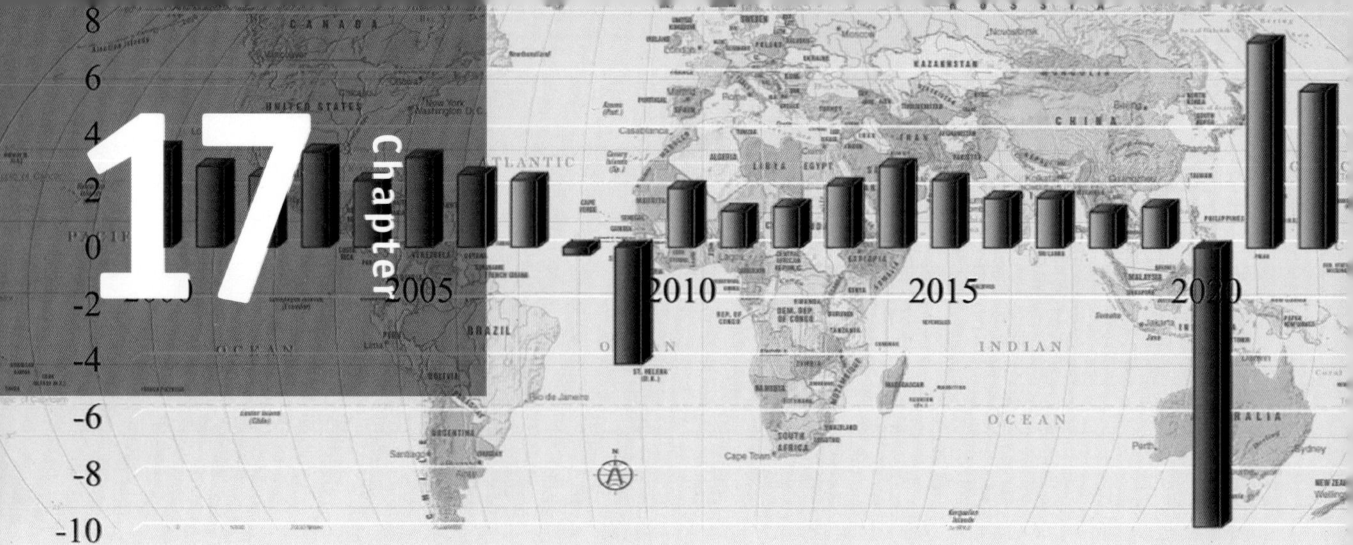

Short-run Macroeconomic Equilibrium

CHAPTER MAP

In this chapter we look at the determination of national income, employment and inflation in the short run: i.e. over a period of up to around two years. The analysis is based on the model developed by Keynesians. Although many economists argue that this is not appropriate for analysing the performance of the macroeconomy over the longer term, most agree that the analysis is essentially true over the short term.

The model assumes that aggregate demand determines the level of economic activity in the economy. In other words, the nation's production and employment depend on the amount of spending. Too little spending will lead to unemployment. More spending will stimulate firms to produce more and employ more people. Too much spending, however, will cause inflation. This chapter examines this relationship between aggregate demand and national income (GDP), employment and inflation.

One important simplifying assumption is made: the rate of interest is fixed. This allows us for the time being to ignore what is happening to the amount of money in the economy. A fixed interest rate effectively means that the supply of money will passively rise or fall as aggregate demand rises or falls. In other words, if spending rises and hence the demand for money from the banking system also rises, there will be a corresponding increase in the amount of money made available and hence no need for interest rates to rise. In subsequent chapters, we will drop this assumption and take specific account of the role of money in the economy.

17.1 BACKGROUND TO THE THEORY

The relationship between aggregate demand and national income

This chapter explains what determines the level of national income (GDP) in the short run. It is based on the model developed by John Maynard Keynes, back in the 1930s (see Case Study 16.6 on the student website).

The basic explanation is quite simple: the level of production in the economy depends on the level of aggregate demand. If people buy more, firms will produce more in response to this, providing they have spare capacity. If people buy less, firms will cut down their production and lay off workers. But just *how much* will national income rise or fall as aggregate demand changes? We will answer this as the chapter progresses.

TC 12 p455

First, let us return to the circular flow of income that we looked at in Chapter 15. This is illustrated in Figure 17.1. Looking at the bottom of the diagram, the consumption of domestically produced goods (C_d) and the three withdrawals (W) – net saving (S), net taxes (T) and spending on imports (M) – all depend on the level of national income (Y). In fact, in the model, national income must always equal consumption of domestic goods plus withdrawals: there is nothing else people can do with their incomes!

$$Y = C_d + W$$

Moving now to the top part of Figure 17.1, total spending in the economy on the goods and services of domestic firms is what we have already defined as aggregate demand (AD). In the Keynesian model that we are examining in this chapter, it is normally referred to as ***aggregate expenditure (E)***. Aggregate expenditure consists of C_d plus the three injections (J): investment in the domestic economy (I), government purchases in the domestic economy (G) and expenditure from abroad on the country's exports (X).

$$AD = E = C_d + J$$

Figure 17.1 A simplified circular flow of income model

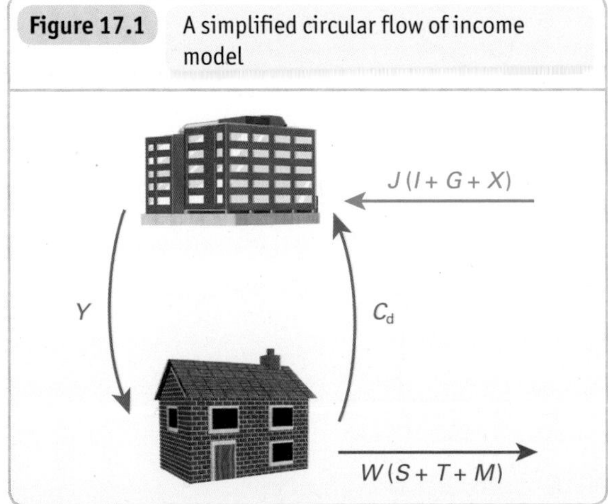

In equilibrium, withdrawals equal injections. (We demonstrated this in Chapter 15.) Since national income (Y) is simply withdrawals plus C_d, and aggregate expenditure (E) is simply injections plus C_d, it follows that in equilibrium national income must equal aggregate expenditure. To summarise:

$$W = J$$
$$\therefore C_d + W = C_d + J$$
$$\therefore Y = E\,(= AD)$$

Whenever aggregate expenditure ($C_d + J$) exceeds national income ($C_d + W$), injections will exceed withdrawals. Firms will respond to the extra demand by producing more and hence employing more factors of production. National income will thus rise. But as national income rises, so too will saving, imports and the amount paid in taxes: in other words, withdrawals will rise. Withdrawals will go on rising until they equal injections: until a new equilibrium has been reached. To summarise:

$$J > W \rightarrow Y\uparrow \rightarrow W\uparrow \text{ until } W = J$$

But *how much* will national income (GDP) rise when aggregate demand (expenditure) rises? What will the new equilibrium level of national income be? To answer this question we must examine the relationship between national income and the component parts of the circular flow of income: consumption, withdrawals and injections. This relationship is shown in the Keynesian '45° line diagram', also known as the 'Keynesian cross diagram'.

Introducing the Keynesian 45° line diagram

In this model, it is assumed that the levels of consumption and withdrawals are determined by the level of national income. Since national income is part of the model, we say that consumption and withdrawals are ***endogenous***. This means that they vary with one of the other components of the model (i.e. income). Injections, however, are assumed to be ***exogenous***: they are determined independently of what is going on in the model; they do *not* depend on the level of national income.

Definitions

Aggregate expenditure (E) Aggregate demand in the Keynesian model: i.e. $C_d + J$.

Endogenous variable A variable whose value is determined by the model of which it is part.

Exogenous variable A variable whose value is determined independently of the model of which it is part.

We will justify these assumptions later. First, we must look at how the diagram is constructed, and at the significance of the 45° line, which is shown in Figure 17.2. We plot real national income (i.e. national income matched by *output*) on the horizontal axis, and the various component parts of the circular flow (C_d, W and J) on the vertical axis. If the two axes are plotted to the same scale, then at every point on the 45° line the items on each axis are equal.

But what items on the vertical axis will always equal national income (Y), which is plotted on the horizontal axis? The answer is $C_d + W$, since, by definition, $Y = C_d + W$. For example, if Y were £100 billion, then $C_d + W$ must also be £100 billion (see Figure 17.2).

We turn now to look at each of the components of the circular flow and see how they fit into the 45° line diagram.

Figure 17.2 The 45° line

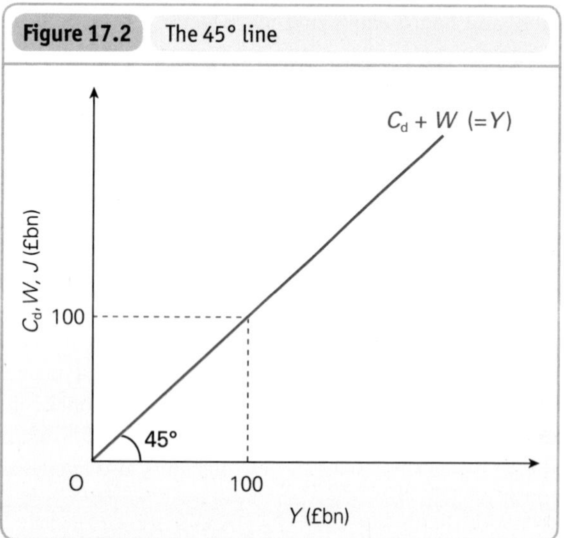

Consumption

We will need to distinguish total consumption (C) from that part of consumption that goes purely on the output of domestically produced goods (C_d). C_d excludes expenditure taxes (e.g. VAT) and expenditure on imports.

We start by looking at *total* consumption.

The consumption function

As national income increases, so does consumption. The reason is simple: if people earn more, they can afford to spend more. The relationship between consumption and income is expressed by the ***consumption function***:

$$C = f(Y)$$

It can be shown graphically on the 45° line diagram (see Figure 17.3 which is based on Table 17.1). The consumption function slopes upwards. This illustrates that, as national income rises, so does consumption. To keep the analysis simple, the consumption function is drawn as a straight line.

At very low levels of income, the consumption function will lie above the 45° line. When a nation is very poor, most people may be forced to spend more than they earn merely to survive. They usually do this by borrowing or drawing on savings. Above a certain level of income, however (£500 billion in Figure 17.3), the consumption function will lie

Definition

Consumption function The relationship between consumption and national income. It can be expressed algebraically or graphically.

Figure 17.3 The consumption function

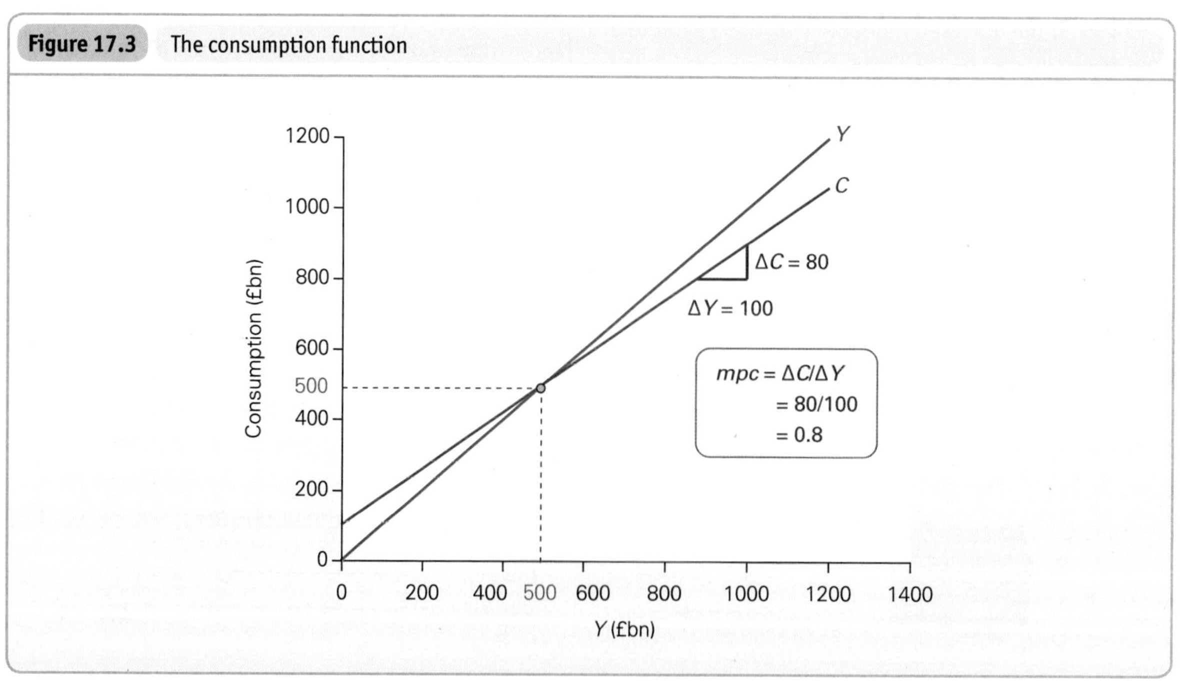

Table 17.1 $C = f(Y)$

National income (£bn)	Consumption (£bn)
0	100
100	180
200	260
300	340
400	420
500	500
600	580
700	660
800	740
900	820
1000	900
1100	980

below the 45° line. People will spend less than they earn. The remainder will go on saving and taxes.

The higher the level of national income, the smaller the proportion that will be consumed: people can afford to save proportionately more, and will have to pay proportionately more in taxes. It follows that the slope of the consumption function is less than that of the 45° line.

The marginal propensity to consume. The slope of the consumption function is given by the ***marginal propensity to consume***. This is the proportion of any increase in national income that goes on consumption.[1] In Table 17.1, for each £100 billion rise in national income there is an £80 billion rise in consumption. Thus the marginal propensity to consume is £80 billion/£100 billion = 80/100 or 4/5 or 0.8. The formula is

$$mpc = \Delta C/\Delta Y$$

In Figure 17.3, the consumption function is a straight line: it has a *constant* slope, and hence the *mpc* is also constant.

It is possible that as people get richer, they will spend a smaller and smaller fraction of each rise in income (and save a larger fraction). Why might this be so? What effect will it have on the shape of the consumption function?

The other determinants of consumption

Of course, people's incomes are not the only determinants of the amount they consume. There are several other determinants.

Taxation. The higher the level of income taxes, the less will people have left to spend out of their gross income: consumption depends on ***disposable income***.

Expected future incomes. Many people take into account both current and expected future incomes when planning their current and future consumption. You might have a relatively low income when you graduate but can expect to earn much more in the future. You are thus willing to take on more debts now in order to support your current consumption, anticipating that you will be able to pay back these loans later. KI 10 p70

The financial system (such as banks and building societies) plays an important part in facilitating this ***smoothing of consumption*** by households. You can look to borrow or draw on accumulated savings from the past when your current income is low. The hope is that you can then pay back the loans or replenish your savings later on when your income is higher.

The financial system can provide households with greater flexibility over when to spend their expected future incomes. The preference of households for a more constant flow of consumption across time is consistent with the idea that people experience diminishing marginal utilities of consumption and income (see section 5.1, page 134). This is explored further in Case Study 17.5 on the student website.

The financial system and attitudes of lenders. The financial sector provides households not only with longer-term loans but also short-term credit. This short-term credit enables transactions to take place by bridging short-term gaps between income and expenditure. This helps to explain why short-term rates of change in household spending, say from one quarter of the year to the next, are often less variable than those in disposable income.

But financial institutions can affect the growth in consumption if their ability and willingness to lend changes. The global financial crises of the late 2000s saw credit criteria tighten dramatically. A tightening of credit practices, such as reducing overdraft facilities and the size of loans, weakens consumption growth. The growth of consumption becomes more dependent on the growth of *current* incomes and there is an increase in the number of ***credit-constrained households***.

In contrast, a relaxation of lending practices, as seen in many countries during the 1980s, can strengthen consumption growth. This allows households more readily to borrow against future incomes: there are fewer credit-constrained households.

Definitions

Marginal propensity to consume The proportion of a rise in national income that goes on consumption: $mpc = \Delta C/\Delta Y$.

Disposable income Household income after the deduction of taxes and the addition of benefits.

Consumption smoothing The act by households of smoothing their levels of consumption over time despite facing volatile incomes.

Credit-constrained households Households which are limited in their ability to borrow against expected future incomes.

1 The *mpc* is normally defined as the proportion of a rise in *disposable* national income that goes on consumption, where disposable income is income *after taxes*. By defining it the way we have done (i.e. as the proportion of *gross* income that goes in consumption), the analysis is simpler. The conclusions remain the same.

Changes in interest rates affect household spending by affecting how expensive loans are to 'service'. ***Debt-servicing costs*** are the costs incurred in repaying loans and the interest payments on them. Where the rate of interest on debt is variable, any changes in interest rates affect the cost of servicing the debt. This can be especially important for mortgages. In the UK, where a large proportion of mortgage-payers are on a variable mortgage rate, changes in mortgage rates can have a sizeable impact on their debt-servicing costs. This then has significant implications for the proportion of income households need to set aside to pay the mortgage.

KI 26 p309

Wealth and household sector balance sheets. By borrowing and saving, households accumulate financial liabilities (debts), financial assets (savings) and physical assets (mainly property). The household sector's *financial* balance sheet details the sector's holding of financial assets and liabilities, while its *capital* balance sheet details its physical assets. Its balance of financial assets over liabilities is the household sector's net *financial wealth*. The household sector's *net worth*, as recorded in the capital balance sheet, is the sum of its net financial wealth and its physical wealth.

KI 35 p459

Changes on the household sector's balance sheets affect the sector's financial wellbeing. Such changes can significantly affect short-term prospects for household spending. For instance, a declining net worth to income ratio is an indicator of greater financial distress. This could be induced by falling house prices or falling share prices. In response, households may attempt to restore their financial wellbeing through saving or the repayment of debt.

Worsening household balance sheets may, therefore, dampen spending, while improvements on the balance sheets may strengthen the growth of consumption. Balance sheets are discussed in Box 17.6.

Consumer confidence. This relates to consumers' perceptions of the health of the economy and to their disposition or state of mind. The greater the confidence of consumers, the more willing they are to spend. Surveys of consumer confidence are therefore closely followed by policy makers (see Box 17.2) as an indicator of the level of future spending.

Uncertainty. Expectations of variables such as income and employment prospects affect current spending decisions. The greater the perceived *range* of possible outcomes for these variables, the more uncertain is the economic environment. Uncertainty is likely to make households more prudent and want to increase their buffer-stocks of wealth. By doing so, for example by increasing their saving, they will have greater insurance against unexpected events such as the loss of income. The idea of ***buffer-stock saving*** is considered further in Case Study 17.6 on the student website.

Expectations of future prices. If people expect prices to rise, they tend to buy durable goods such as furniture and cars before this happens.

The distribution of income. The poor have a higher *mpc* than the rich, with very little left over to save. A redistribution of national income from the poor to the rich will therefore tend to reduce the total level of consumption in the economy.

Impatience, tastes and attitudes. If people have a 'buy now, pay later' mentality, or a craving for consumer goods, they are likely to have a higher level of consumption than if their tastes are more frugal. The more 'consumerist', materialistic or impatient people become, facilitated by the financial system, the higher will their consumption be for any given level of income.

The age of durables. If people's cars, carpets, clothes, etc., are getting old, they will tend to have a high level of 'replacement' consumption, particularly after a recession when they had cut back on their consumption of durables. Conversely, as the economy reaches the peak of the boom, people are likely to spend less on durables as they have probably already bought the items they want.

Movements along and shifts in the consumption function

The effect on consumption of a change in national income is shown by a movement *along* the consumption function. A change in any of the other determinants is shown by a *shift* in the consumption function and/or a change in its shape.

What effect will the following have on the mpc: (a) the rate of income tax rises; (b) the economy begins to recover from recession; (c) people anticipate that the rate of inflation is about to rise; (d) the government redistributes income from the rich to the poor? In each case sketch what would happen to the consumption function.

Long-run and short-run consumption functions

The long-run consumption function is likely to be steeper than the short-run one (see Figure 17.4).

In the short run, people may be slow to respond to a rise in income. Perhaps they are cautious about whether their higher income will last, or are slow to change their consumption habits. In the short run, then, people may have a relatively low *mpc*. In the long run, however, people have time to adjust their consumption patterns.

Assuming that national income rises over time, the long-run consumption function will be intersected by a series of short-run ones. Each year's short-run function will be above the previous year's.

Which is likely to show the greater variation from one person to another at any given level of income: the short-run mpc or the long-run mpc?

Definitions

Debt-servicing costs The costs incurred when repaying debt, including debt interest payments.

Buffer-stock saving The idea that people engage in saving partly to self-insure against unexpected events, such as the loss of income.

Figure 17.4 Long-run and short-run consumption functions

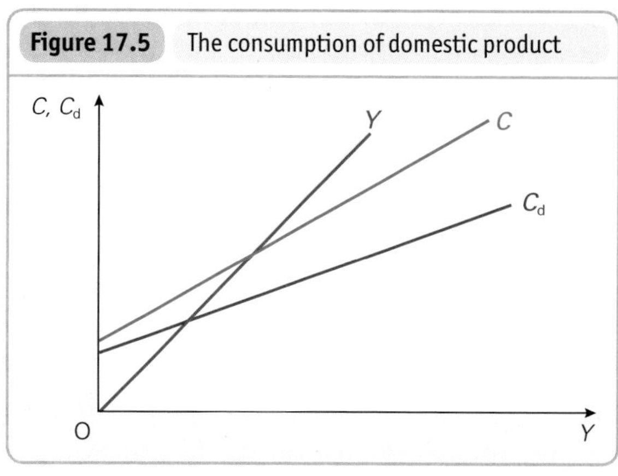

Figure 17.5 The consumption of domestic product

Consumption of domestically produced goods (C_d)

The parts of consumption that go on imports and indirect taxes constitute withdrawals from the circular flow of income and thus do not contribute to aggregate demand. We shall concentrate on the part of consumption that *does*: namely, the consumption of domestic product (C_d). The C_d function lies below the *C* function, as in Figure 17.5. The gap between them constitutes imports of consumer goods and indirect taxes.

Withdrawals

All three withdrawals – net saving, net taxes and import expenditure – depend on the level of national income. They are thus all *endogenously* determined within the model.

Net saving

As with consumption, the major determinant of net saving (i.e. saving minus consumer borrowing and drawing on past savings) is income. As income increases, and a decreasing fraction of it goes on consumption, so an increasing fraction

*BOX 17.1 USING CALCULUS TO DERIVE THE *MPC*

EXPLORING ECONOMICS

The consumption function can be expressed as an equation. For example, the consumption function of Table 17.1 and Figure 17.3 is given by the equation:

$$C = 100 + 0.8Y \qquad (1)$$

Try using this equation to derive the figures in Table 17.1.

From this equation we can derive an equation for *mpc*. It is found by differentiating the consumption function. Remember from previous calculus boxes what it is we are doing when we differentiate an equation. We are finding its rate of change. Thus by differentiating the consumption function, we are finding the rate of change of consumption with respect to income. But this is what we mean by the *mpc*.

The difference between using differentiation and the formula $\Delta C/\Delta Y$ is that with the former we are looking at the *mpc* at a single point on the consumption function. With the $\Delta C/\Delta Y$ formula we were looking at the *mpc* between two points.

Differentiating equation (1) gives

$$mpc = dC/dY = 0.8 \qquad (2)$$

Note that, since the consumption function is a straight line in this case, the *mpc* (which measures the slope of the consumption function) is constant.

What would we do to find the *mpc* of a non-linear (curved) consumption function? The procedure is the same.

Assume that the consumption function is given by the following equation:

$$C = 250 + 0.9Y - 0.0001Y^2 \qquad (3)$$

The *mpc* is given by dC/dY:

$$mpc = 0.9 - 0.0002Y$$

1. *First of all, try constructing a table like Table 17.1 and then graph the consumption function that it gives. What is it about equation (3) that gives the graph its particular shape?*
2. *What are the values of mpc at incomes of (a) 200; (b) 1000?*
3. *What happens to the value of mpc as national income increases? Is this what you would expect by examining the shape of the consumption function?*

KI 26 p309

of it will be saved. The rich can afford to save a larger proportion of their income than the poor.

The proportion of an increase in national income that is saved is given by the ***marginal propensity to save*** (*mps*).

$$mps = \Delta S/\Delta Y$$

Other determinants of saving. To a large extent these are the same as the other determinants of consumption, since most things that encourage people to spend more will thereby encourage them to save less.

*LOOKING AT THE MATHS

Let us examine the relationship between C and C_d a bit more closely. When people make consumption decisions, this is largely based on their *disposable* income (Y_{dis}), where disposable income is income after the payment of income taxes and the receipt of benefits. We use the term 'net income taxes (T_Y)' to refer to income taxes minus benefits. Thus

$$Y_{dis} = Y - T_Y$$

Also, people tend not to distinguish between domestic goods and imports when they make consumption decisions. Let us then focus on total consumption (C), not just the consumption of domestic products (C_d).

To get a better understanding of people's consumption behaviour, we could express the marginal propensity to consume *all products* (domestic and imported) relative to *disposable* income. Let us call this term mpc' (rather than mpc or mpc_d) where

$$mpc' = \frac{\Delta C}{\Delta Y_{dis}} = \frac{\Delta C}{\Delta Y - \Delta T_Y} \quad (1)$$

To get from C to C_d, we would have to subtract the amount spent on imports (M) and the part of consumer expenditure paid in indirect taxes, such as VAT and excise duties, (T_E). Thus

$$C_d = C - M - T_E \text{ or } C = C_d + M + T_E$$

Thus

$$\Delta C = \Delta C_d + \Delta M + \Delta T_E \quad (2)$$

Substituting equation (2) in equation (1) gives

$$mpc' = \frac{\Delta C_d + \Delta T_E + \Delta M}{\Delta Y - \Delta T_Y} \quad (3)$$

Contrast this with the mpc_d, where

$$mpc_d = \frac{\Delta C_d}{\Delta Y} \quad (4)$$

It might be easy to get the impression that saving is merely what is left over after consumption has taken place. In fact, for many people the decision to save is a purposeful one. For example, they might be saving up for something they are eager to buy but cannot afford at the moment, or they may be saving for retirement. Or, as we saw above (page 534), they may undertake precautionary or buffer stock saving to insure themselves against the possibility of future income loss, such as from unemployment or theft. Indeed, people may be encouraged to save *more* by various factors, such as changes in pension provisions, new government-sponsored saving schemes or uncertainty about the macroeconomic environment.

Go through each of the determinants of consumption that were listed in the previous section and consider how they will affect saving. Are there any determinants of consumption that will not cause saving to rise if consumption is caused to fall?

Net taxes

As national income increases, so the amount paid in tax will also increase. The ***marginal tax propensity*** (*mpt*) is the proportion of an increase in national income paid in taxes:[2]

$$mpt = \Delta T/\Delta Y$$

The *mpt* depends on tax rates. In a simple world where there was only one type of tax, which was charged at a constant rate – for example, an income tax of 20 per cent – the *mpt* would be given directly by the tax rate. In this example, for each extra pound earned, 20p would be paid in income tax. The $mpt = \Delta T/\Delta Y = 20/100 = 0.20$. In practice, of course, there are many types of tax charged at many different rates, and thus working out the *mpt* is more complicated.

In most countries, the *mpt* rises as national income rises. This is because income tax is progressive. At higher incomes, people pay a higher marginal rate of income tax. In the UK and many other countries, however, income tax became much less progressive in the 1980s and 1990s, but the *mpt* remained roughly the same because of rises in indirect taxes.

Imports

The higher the level of national income, the higher will be the amount spent on imports. The ***marginal propensity to import*** (*mpm*) is the proportion of a rise in national income that goes on imports:

$$mpm = \Delta M/\Delta Y$$

Note that we only count that part of the expenditure on imports that actually goes abroad. Amounts retained by the retailer, the wholesaler and the importer, and amounts paid in indirect taxes, are excluded.

Definitions

Marginal propensity to save The proportion of an increase in national income saved: $= \Delta S/\Delta Y$.

Marginal tax propensity The proportion of an increase in national income paid in tax: $mpt = \Delta T/\Delta Y$.

Marginal propensity to import The proportion of an increase in national income that is spent on imports: $mpm = \Delta M/\Delta Y$.

2 We have defined net taxes as taxes minus benefits (i.e. the net flow from the household sector to the government). For our purposes, then, the *mpt* is the proportion of any rise in income going in taxes and reduced benefits.

Figure 17.6 The W and C_d functions

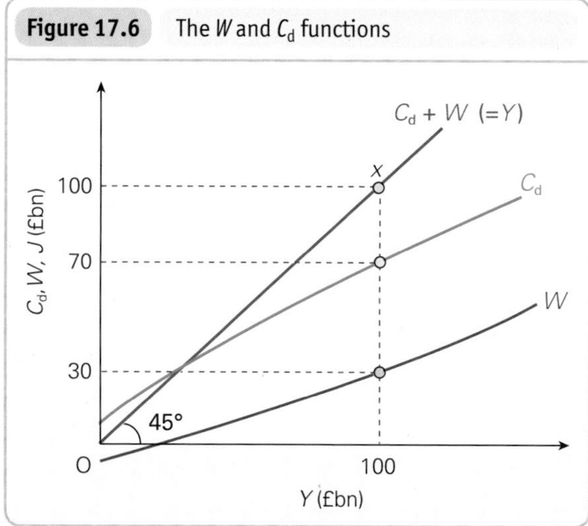

Whether the *mpm* rises or falls as national income rises depends on the nature of a country's imports. If a country imports predominantly basic goods, which have a relatively low income elasticity of demand, the rate of increase in their consumption would tail off rapidly as incomes increase. The *mpm* for such a country would thus also rapidly decrease.

If, however, a country's imports were mainly of luxury goods, they would account for an increasing proportion of any rise in national income: the *mpm* would rise.

If a country imports a whole range of goods whose average income elasticity of demand is the same as for home-produced goods, will the mpm rise or fall as national income rises?

The determinants of the level of imports. Apart from national income, there are a number of other determinants of the level of imports:

- *Relative prices.* If the prices of home-produced goods go up relative to the prices of imports, the level of imports will rise. The rate of exchange is a major influence here. The higher the rate of exchange, the cheaper will imports be and hence the more will be spent on them.
- *Tastes.* If consumer tastes shift towards foreign goods and services, imports will rise. For example, it might become more popular to go abroad for your holidays.
- *Relative quality.* If the quality of foreign goods and services increases relative to that of domestic goods and services, imports will rise.
- *The determinants of consumption.* Since imports of goods and services are part of *total* consumption (as opposed to C_d), the various determinants of consumption that we looked at on pages 532–4 will also be determinants of imports.

The total withdrawals function

Remember that withdrawals consist of the three elements: net saving, net taxes and imports, all of which rise as national income rises. A withdrawals function along with the corresponding consumption of domestic goods function is shown in Figure 17.6.

Note the relationship between the C_d and W curves. The steeper the slope of the one, the flatter the slope of the other. The reason for this is that C_d and W add up to total national income (Y):

$$Y = C_d + W$$

Since the 45° line measures $C_d + W$, the distance between the C_d function and the 45° line must equal withdrawals. Thus at point *x*, where national income is £100 billion and C_d is £70 billion, W must be £30 billion – the gap between C_d and the 45° line. Note that at zero national income, there is negative saving (and hence a negative W) as people will draw on saving, or borrow, to pay for basic consumption.

The marginal propensity to withdraw

The formula for the ***marginal propensity to withdraw*** (*mpw*) is as we would expect:

$$mpw = \Delta W / \Delta Y$$

The *mpw* is the slope of the withdrawals function. Note that, since $W = S + T + M$, *mpw* must equal $mps + mpt + mpm$. For example, if for any rise in national income, 1/10 were saved, 2/10 paid in net taxes, and 2/10 spent on imports, then 5/10 must be withdrawn.

Note also that, since $C_d + W = Y$, $mpc_d + mpw$ must add up to 1. For example, if the country spends, say, 3/5 of any rise in income on domestically produced goods, the remaining 2/5 must go on withdrawals.

If the slope of the C_d function is 3/4, what is the slope of the W function?

Injections

In simple Keynesian theory, injections are assumed not to depend on the level of national income: they are *exogenously* determined. This means that the injections function is drawn as a horizontal straight line. Injections will be at a given level irrespective of the level of national income. The injections function is the vertical addition of the investment, government expenditure and export functions, each of which is a horizontal straight line.

The assumption that injections are independent of national income makes the theory simpler. (It is possible to drop this assumption, however, without destroying the theory.) But is the assumption sufficiently realistic? Let us examine each of the injections in turn.

Definition

Marginal propensity to withdraw The proportion of an increase in national income that is withdrawn from the circular flow: $mpw = \Delta W / \Delta Y$, where $mpw = mps + mpt + mpm$.

Investment

There are several determinants of investment.

Increased consumer demand. Investment is to provide extra capacity. This will only be necessary, therefore, if consumer demand increases. The bigger the increase in consumer demand, the more investment will be needed.

You might think that, since consumer demand depends on the level of national income, investment must too, and that therefore our assumption that investment is independent of national income is wrong. But we are not saying that investment depends on the *level* of consumer demand; rather, it depends on *how much it has risen*. If income and consumer demand are high but *constant*, there will be no point in firms expanding their capacity: no point in investing.

The relationship between investment and *increased* consumer demand is examined by the 'accelerator theory'. We look at this theory in section 17.4.

Expectations. Since investment is made in order to produce output for the future, investment must depend on firms' expectations about future market conditions.

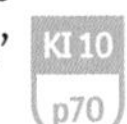

The cost and efficiency of capital equipment. If the cost of capital equipment goes down or machines become more efficient, the return on investment will increase. Firms will invest more. Technological progress is an important determinant here.

The rate of interest. The higher the rate of interest, the more expensive it will be for firms to finance investment, and hence the less profitable will the investment be. Just how responsive

BOX 17.2 CONFIDENCE AND SPENDING

Does confidence help forecast spending?

Keynesian economists identify confidence as an important influence on expenditure decisions. Consumer or business optimism affects the willingness to spend.

Measuring confidence

Each month, on behalf of the European Commission, consumers and firms across Europe are asked a series of questions, the answers to which are used to compile indicators of confidence. For instance, consumers are asked about how they expect both their own financial position and the general economic situation to change over the coming 12 months. For each question, they are offered various options, such as 'get a lot better, 'get a lot worse', and balances are then calculated based on the number of positive and negative replies.[1]

Chart (a) plots the confidence indicators for consumers, the construction industry and industry as a whole in the eurozone since 1996. The chart shows the volatility of confidence. This is generally greater among businesses than consumers and especially so in the construction sector. However, confidence fell dramatically across all groups during the global financial crisis and the COVID-19 pandemic.

Confidence and spending

Now compare the volatility of confidence in Chart (a) with the annual rates of growth in household consumption and investment, shown in Chart (b). You can see that the volatility of confidence is reflected in both consumer and investment spending, although investment is significantly more volatile.

What is less clear is the extent to which changes in confidence *lead* to changes in spending. In fact, a likely scenario is that spending and confidence interact. High rates of spending growth may result in high confidence through economic growth, which in turn leads to more spending. The reverse is the case when economic growth is subdued: low

(a) *Confidence indicators in the eurozone*

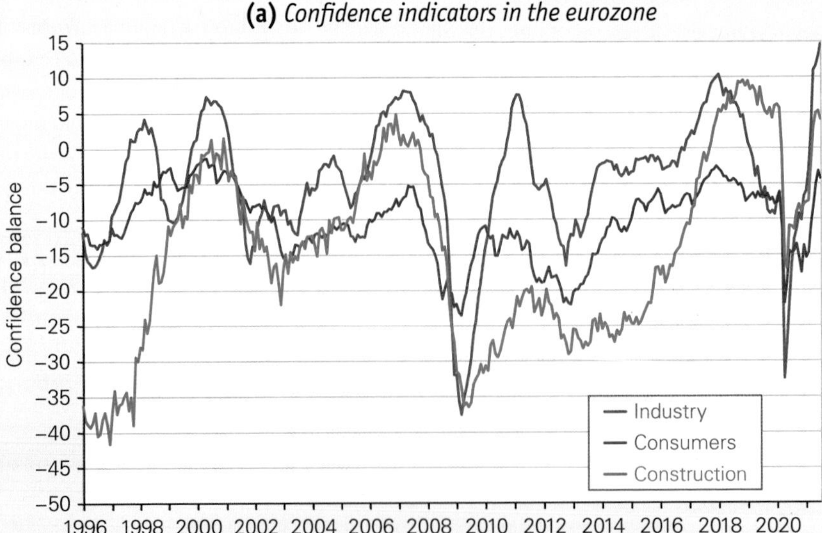

Source: Based on data from *Business and Consumer Surveys*, European Commission, DGECFIN, http://ec.europa.eu/economy_finance/db_indicators/surveys/time_series/index_en.htm

total investment in the economy is to changes in interest rates is a highly controversial issue and we will return to it later.

Availability of finance. Investment requires financing. Retained earnings provide one possible source. Alternatively, firms could seek finance from banks, or perhaps issue debt instruments, such as bonds, or issue new shares. Therefore, difficulties in raising finance, such as seen following the global financial crisis, can limit investment.

Uncertainty. Capital expenditure can be 'lumpy' and costly and its effects may be irreversible. Therefore greater uncertainty can make firms more cautious about undertaking investment, preferring to 'wait and see'.

So if these are the main determinants of investment, does it mean that investment is totally independent of the level of national income? Not quite. Replacement of worn-out or outdated equipment *will* depend on the level of national income. The higher the current level of national income, the greater will be the stock of capital and therefore the more will need replacing each year. It is also possible that, if the level of national income is high and firms' profits are high, they will be able to *afford* more investment. However, it is not a gross distortion of reality to assume that investment and the level of national income are independent, at least in the short run.

CASE STUDIES AND APPLICATIONS

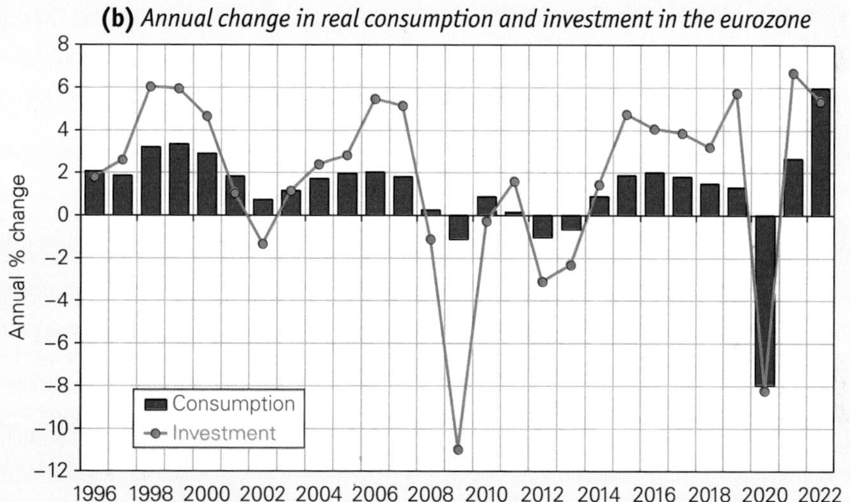

Notes: Figures from 2021 based on forecasts; eurozone figures are the weighted average of the 19 countries using the euro as of January 2015; Investment is Gross Fixed Capital Formation.
Source: Based on data in *AMECO Database*, European Commission, DGECFIN (May 2021), http://ec.europa.eu/economy_finance/ameco/user/serie/SelectSerie.cfm

spending growth leads to a lack of confidence, which results in low spending growth and so low rates of economic growth.

Therefore, while confidence may be a source of volatility it is also an important *propagation mechanism* by which shocks are transmitted through the economy. Consequently, it may amplify the peaks and troughs of the business cycle and contribute to the persistence of booms and recessions.

TC 15 p543

What makes measures of confidence particularly useful is their timeliness: they are released monthly with a delay of only a few days and reflect actions that consumers and investors are likely to take. Although technological progress has facilitated monthly measures of GDP and spending, there remains a time lag of several weeks. Therefore, measures of confidence are extremely timely for policy makers and provide them with very useful information about the likely path of spending and output growth.

What factors are likely to influence the confidence of (i) consumers; and (ii) businesses? Could the trends in the economic sentiment indicators for consumers and businesses diverge?

Using time series data from the European Commission based on business and consumer survey data (https://ec.europa.eu/info/business-economy-euro/indicators-statistics/economic-databases/business-and-consumer-surveys_en), plot a line chart to show the path of consumer confidence for any two countries of your choice. Describe the patterns you observe, noting any similarities or differences between the consumer confidence profile of the two countries.

1 More information on the EU programme of business and consumer surveys can be found at http://ec.europa.eu/economy_finance/db_indicators/surveys/index_en.htm

Government purchases

Government spending on goods and services in any year is independent of the level of national income. In the months preceding the Budget each year, spending departments make submissions about their needs in the coming year. These are discussed with the Treasury and a sum is allocated to each department. That then (excepting any unforeseen events) fixes government expenditure on goods and services for the following financial year.

Thus, again, for our purposes we can take government purchases as independent of national income in the short term. Even if tax revenues turn out to be more or less than expected, this will not influence that year's government spending. The government can end up running either a budget surplus ($T > G$) or a budget deficit ($G > T$).

Over the longer term, however, government purchases *will* depend on national income. The higher the level of national income, the higher is the amount of tax revenue that the government receives, and hence the more it can afford to spend. The governments of richer nations clearly spend much more than those of developing countries.

Exports

Exports are sold to people abroad, and thus depend largely on *their* incomes, not on incomes at home. Nevertheless, there are two indirect links between a country's national income and its exports:

- Via other countries' circular flows of income. If domestic incomes rise, more will be spent on imports. But this will cause a rise in other countries' incomes and lead them to buy more imports, part of which will be this country's exports.
- Via the exchange rate. A rise in domestic incomes will lead to a rise in imports. Other things being equal, this will lead to a depreciation in the exchange rate. This will make it cheaper for people in other countries to buy this country's exports. Export sales will rise.

However, it is useful in simple Keynesian models to assume that exports are determined independently of domestic national income.

Note that, although the injections function is assumed to be constant with respect to income and is drawn as a horizontal straight line, this does not mean that it will be constant *over time*. Investment can suddenly rise or virtually collapse as the confidence of businesspeople changes. Exports can change too with shifts in the exchange rate or with speculation. The injections line, then, is constantly shifting up and down.

Section summary

1. In the simple Keynesian model, equilibrium national income is where withdrawals equal injections, and where national income equals the total expenditure on domestic products: where $W = J$ and where $Y = E$.
2. The relationships between national income and the various components of the circular flow of income can be shown on a 45° line diagram. In such a diagram, C, C_d and W are endogenous variables. Each one rises as income rises. The relationships can also be expressed in terms of marginal propensities. The marginal propensity is given by $\Delta V/\Delta Y$ (where V is the variable in question).
3. Apart from being determined by national income, consumption is determined by other variables including taxation, wealth, credit conditions, expectations, the distribution of income, impatience and uncertainty. Consumption of domestic product (C_d) is total consumption minus imports of goods and services and minus indirect taxes and plus subsidies on goods and services.
4. Like consumption, withdrawals (S, T and M) vary with national income. Net saving is also determined by the various factors that determine consumption: if these factors cause consumption to rise, then, except in the case of a cut in income taxes, they will cause saving to fall and vice versa. Net tax revenues, apart from being dependent on incomes, depend on the rates of tax and benefits that the government sets and how progressive or regressive they are. Imports depend on the relative prices and quality of domestic and foreign goods, total consumption and tastes.
5. In the simple Keynesian model, injections are assumed to be exogenous variables. They are therefore drawn as a horizontal straight line in the 45° line diagram. In practice, there will be *some* relationship between injections and national income. Replacement investment depends to some extent on the level of output; government purchases depend to some extent on the level of tax revenues; and exports depend on exchange rates and foreign incomes, both of which will depend on the level of imports. Nevertheless, in the short run it is reasonable to assume that injections are independent of national income.
6. The determinants of investment include the size of increases in consumer demand, the cost and efficiency of capital equipment, expectations, uncertainty and finance.

17.2 THE DETERMINATION OF NATIONAL INCOME

Equilibrium national income

We can now put the various functions together on one diagram. This is done in Figure 17.7. Note that there is a new line on the diagram that we have not looked at so far. This is the aggregate expenditure (i.e. the aggregate demand) function. We defined aggregate expenditure as $C_d + J$. Graphically, then, the E function is simply the C_d function shifted upwards by the amount of J.

Equilibrium national income can be found in either of two ways.

$W = J$

Withdrawals equal injections at point x in Figure 17.7. Equilibrium national income is thus Y_e. If national income were below this level, say at Y_1, injections would exceed withdrawals (by an amount $a - b$). This additional net expenditure injected into the economy would encourage firms to produce more and hence cause national income to rise. But as people's incomes rose, so they would save more, pay more taxes and buy more imports. In other words, withdrawals would rise. There would be a movement up along the W function. This process would continue until $W = J$ at point x.

If, on the other hand, national income were at Y_2, withdrawals would exceed injections (by an amount $c - d$). This deficiency of demand would cause production and hence national income to fall. As it did so, there would be a movement down along the W function until again point x was reached.

$Y = E$

If $W = J$, then $C_d + W = C_d + J$. In other words, another way of describing equilibrium is where national income ($Y \equiv C_d + W$) equals aggregate expenditure ($E \equiv C_d + J$). This is shown at point z in Figure 17.7. This is where the expenditure function ($C_d + J$) crosses the 45° line ($C_d + W$).

Figure 17.7 Equilibrium national income

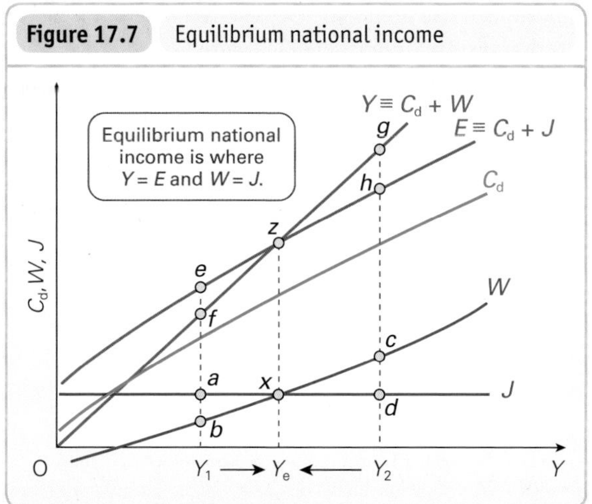

If aggregate expenditure exceeded national income, say at Y_1, there would be excess demand in the economy (of $e - f$). In other words, people would be buying more than was currently being produced. Firms would find their stocks dwindling and would therefore increase their level of production. In doing so, they would employ more factors of production. National income would thus rise. As it did so, consumption and hence aggregate expenditure would rise. There would be a movement up along the expenditure function. But because not all the extra income would be consumed (i.e. some would be withdrawn), expenditure would rise less quickly than income (the E line is flatter than the Y line). As income rises towards Y_e, the gap between Y and E gets smaller. Once point z is reached, $Y = E$. There is then no further tendency for income to rise.

If national income exceeded national expenditure, at say Y_2, there would be insufficient demand for the goods and services currently being produced. Firms would find their stocks of unsold goods building up. They would thus respond by producing less and employing fewer factors of production. National income would thus fall and go on falling until Y_e was reached.

Why is it the case that $a - b = e - f$, and $c - d = g - h$?

The multiplier: the withdrawals and injections approach

When injections rise (and continue at the higher level), this will cause national income to rise. But by how much?

In fact, national income will rise by *more* than injections: Y rises by a *multiple* of the rise in J.

$$\Delta Y > \Delta J$$

The number of times that the increase in income (ΔY) is greater than the increase in injections (ΔJ) is known as the ***multiplier*** (k).

$$k = \Delta Y / \Delta J$$

Thus if a £10 billion rise in injections caused a £30 billion rise in national income, the multiplier would be 3.

What causes the multiplier effect? The answer is that, when extra spending is injected into the economy, it will then stimulate further spending, which in turn will stimulate yet more spending and so on. For example, if firms decide to invest more its effect is 'propagated', since more people

Definition

(Injections) multiplier The number of times by which a rise in income exceeds the rise in injections that caused it: $k = \Delta Y / \Delta J$.

are employed and hence more income is paid to households. Households will then spend part of this increased income on domestically produced goods (the remainder will be withdrawn). This increased consumption will encourage firms to produce more goods to meet the demand. Firms will thus employ more people and other factors of production. This leads to even more incomes being paid out to households. Consumption will thus increase yet again. And so the process continues.

The multiplier is an example of an important principle in economics: that of ***cumulative causation***. This is the last of our 15 threshold concepts, which we first came across in Chapter 16 (see page 508).

TC 15 p543

Note that in this simple Keynesian theory we are assuming that prices are constant (i.e. that there is no inflation) and hence that any increase in income is a *real* increase in income matched by extra production. So when we talk about extra injections into the economy causing extra spending, it is the extra *output* that this spending generates that we are concerned with. If the multiplier were 3, for example, this would mean that an injection of £1 of expenditure into the economy would lead to an increase in *output* of £3.

TC 13 p461

But even if there were limitless resources, an increase in injections would not cause national income to go on rising for ever: the multiplier is not infinite. Each time people receive extra income, they will save some of it, pay some of it in taxes and spend some of it on imports: in other words, withdrawals will rise. Eventually, as income goes on rising, all the extra injections will have leaked away into the three withdrawals. At that point, the multiplier process will have ceased; a new equilibrium will have been reached.

What determines the size of the multiplier? This can be shown graphically using either withdrawals and injections or income and expenditure. The income/expenditure approach will be examined shortly. For now we will use the withdrawals/injections approach. This is illustrated in Figure 17.8.

Assume that injections rise from J_1 to J_2. Equilibrium will move from point *a* to point *b*. Income will thus rise from Y_{e1} to Y_{e2}. The multiplier is therefore

$$\frac{Y_{e_2} - Y_{e_1}}{J_2 - J_1}\left[\text{i.e. } \frac{\Delta Y}{\Delta J}\right]$$

It can be seen that the size of the multiplier depends on the slope of the *W* function. Remember that the slope of the *W* function is given by the marginal propensity to withdraw ($\Delta W/\Delta Y$). The less steep the line (and hence the lower the *mpw*), the bigger will be the rise in national income: the bigger will be the multiplier.

Try this simple test of the above argument. Draw a series of W lines of different slopes, all crossing the J line at the same point. Now draw a second J line above the first. Mark the original equilibrium and all the new ones corresponding to each of the W lines. It should be quite obvious that the flatter the W line is, the more Y will have increased.

Figure 17.8 The multiplier: a shift in injections

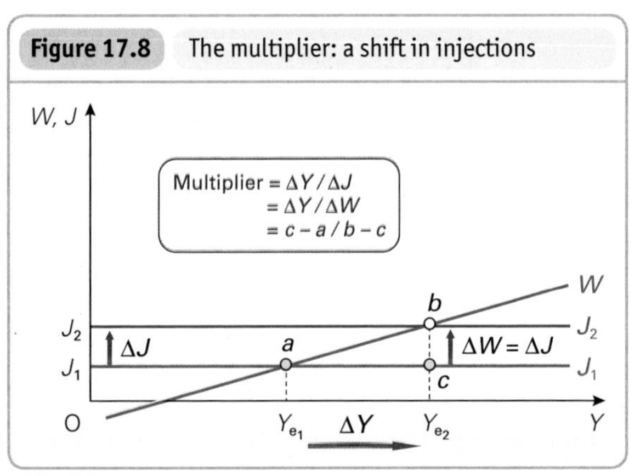

The point here is that the less is withdrawn each time extra income is generated, the more will be recirculated and hence the bigger will be the rise in national income. The size of the multiplier thus varies inversely with the size of the *mpw*. The bigger the *mpw*, the smaller the multiplier; the smaller the *mpw*, the bigger the multiplier. In fact, the ***multiplier formula*** simply gives the multiplier as the inverse of the *mpw*:

$$k = 1/mpw$$

or alternatively, since $mpw + mpc_d = 1$ and thus $mpw = 1 - mpc_d$,

$$k = 1/(1 - mpc_d)$$

Thus if the *mpw* were $^1/_4$ (and hence the mpc_d were $^3/_4$), the multiplier would be 4. So if *J* increased by £10 billion, *Y* would increase by £40 billion.

But why is the multiplier given by the formula $1/mpw$? This can be illustrated by referring to Figure 17.8. The *mpw* is the slope of the *W* line. In the diagram, this is given by the amount $(b - c)/(c - a)$. The multiplier is defined as $\Delta Y/\Delta J$. In the diagram, this is the amount $(c - a)/(b - c)$. But this is merely the inverse of the *mpw*. Thus the multiplier equals $1/mpw$.[3]

A shift in withdrawals

A multiplied rise in income can also be caused by a fall in withdrawals. This is illustrated in Figure 17.9.

Definitions

Principle of cumulative causation An initial event can cause an ultimate effect that is much larger.

(Injections) multiplier formula The formula for the multiplier: $K = 1/mpw$ or $1/(1 - mpc_d)$.

3 In some elementary textbooks, the formula for the multiplier is given as $1/mps$. The reason for this is that it is assumed (for simplicity) that there is only one withdrawal, namely saving, and only one injection, namely investment. As soon as this assumption is dropped, $1/mps$ becomes the wrong formula.

THRESHOLD CONCEPT 15 CUMULATIVE CAUSATION

THINKING LIKE AN ECONOMIST

Economic effects can snowball

Once an economy starts to expand, growth is likely to gather pace. Once it starts slowing down, this can gather pace too and end up in a recession. There are many other examples in economics of things getting 'onto a roll'. A rising stock market is likely to breed confidence in investors and encourage them to buy. This 'destabilising speculation' (see pages 71–2) will then lead to further rises in share prices. A fall in stock market prices can lead to panic selling of shares. The booming stock market of the late 1990s and 2003–8, and the falls in the early 2000s and 2008–9 are good examples of this (see chart in Box 2.2 on page 52).

This phenomenon of things building on themselves is known as 'cumulative causation' and occurs throughout market economies. It is a *threshold concept* because it helps us to understand the built-in instability in many parts of the economy and in many economic situations.

Central to explaining cumulative causation is people's psychology. Good news creates confidence and this optimism causes people to behave in ways that build on the good news. Bad news creates pessimism and this leads to people behaving cautiously, which tends to reinforce the bad news.

Take two regions of an economy: an expanding region and a declining region. The expansion of the first region encourages workers to move there in search of jobs. The optimism in the area causes long-term investment as firms have confidence in an expanding market. This encourages house building and other forms of investment in infrastructure and services. And so the region thrives. Meanwhile, the declining region suffers from deprivation as unemployment rises. This encourages people to move away and businesses to close. There is a further decline in jobs and further migration from the region.

Cumulative causation does not just occur at a macro level. If a company is successful, it is likely to find raising extra finance easier; it may be able to use its power more effectively to out-compete rivals. Giant companies, such as Microsoft, can gain all sorts of economies of scale, including network economies (see Case Study 7.4 on the student website), all of which help the process of building their power base. Success breeds success.

1. ***How might cumulative causation work at the level of an individual firm that is losing market share?***
2. ***Are there any market forces that work against cumulative causation? For instance, how might markets help to arrest the decline of a depressed region of the economy and slow down the expansion of a booming region?***

*LOOKING AT THE MATHS

The multiplier can be expressed as the first derivative of national income with respect to injections.

$$k = \frac{dY}{dJ}$$

Since in equilibrium $J = W$, it is also the first derivative of income with respect to withdrawals. Thus

$$k = \frac{dY}{dW}$$

The marginal propensity to withdraw (i.e. the slope of the withdrawals curve) is found by differentiating the withdrawals function:

$$mpw = \frac{dW}{dY} = \frac{1}{k}$$

Thus

$$k = \frac{1}{mpw}$$

The analysis of Box 17.3 is similar to that here but avoids the use of calculus. The algebra of the multiplier is explored in Maths Case 17.1 on the student website, which does not use calculus, and Maths Case 17.2, which does.

The withdrawals function shifts from W_1 to W_2. This means that, at the old equilibrium of Y_{e1}, injections now exceed withdrawals by an amount $a - b$. This will cause national income to rise until a new equilibrium is reached at Y_{e2} where $J = W_2$. Thus a downward shift of the withdrawals function of $a - b(\Delta W)$ causes a rise in national income of $c - a(\Delta Y)$. The multiplier in this case is given by $\Delta Y/\Delta W$: in other words, $(c - a)/(a - b)$. Note that the multiplier is based on the *initial* fall in withdrawals. Once the multiplier effect

Figure 17.9 The multiplier: a shift in withdrawals

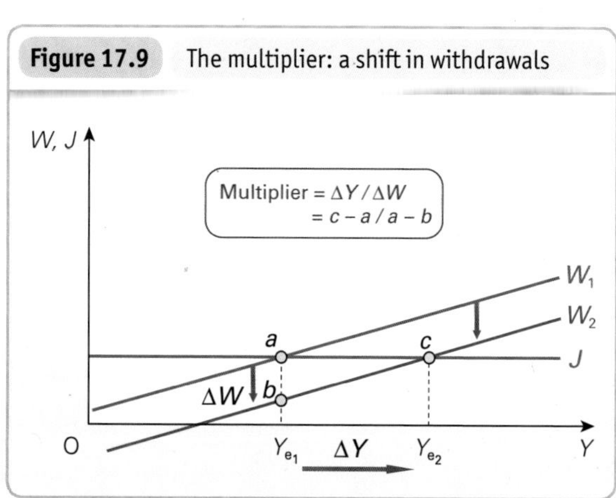

has worked through, withdrawals will have risen back to equal injections at point *c*.

Why is the 'withdrawals multiplier' strictly speaking a negative figure?

The multiplier: the income and expenditure approach

The multiplier can also be demonstrated using the income/expenditure approach. Assume in Figure 17.10 that the aggregate expenditure function shifts to E_2. This could be due either to a rise in one or more of the three injections or to a rise in the consumption of domestically produced goods TC 15 p543 (and hence a fall in withdrawals). Equilibrium national income will rise from Y_{e_1} to Y_{e_2}.

What is the size of the multiplier? The initial rise in expenditure was $b - a$. The resulting rise in income is $c - a$. The multiplier is thus $(c - a)/(b - a)$.

The effect is illustrated in Table 17.2. Consumption of domestic product (C_d) is shown in column 2 for various levels of national income (Y). For every £100 billion rise in Y, C_d rises by £80 billion. Thus the $mpc_d = 0.8$. Assume initially that injections equal £100 billion at all levels of national income. Aggregate expenditure (column 4) equals $C_d + J$.

Figure 17.10 The multiplier: a shift in the expenditure function

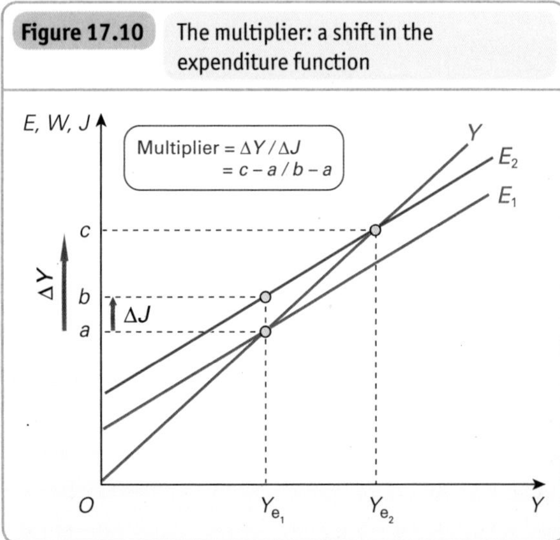

Equilibrium national income is £700 billion. This is where $Y = E$.

Now assume that injections rise by £20 billion to £120 billion. Aggregate expenditure is now shown in the final column and is £20 billion higher than before at each level of national income (Y). At the original equilibrium national income (£700 billion), aggregate expenditure is now £720 billion. This excess of E over Y of £20 billion will generate extra incomes and continue doing so as long as E remains above Y. Equilibrium is reached at £800 billion, where once more $Y = E$. The initial rise in aggregate expenditure of £20 billion (from £700 billion to £720 billion) has led to an eventual rise in both national income and aggregate expenditure of £100 billion. The multiplier is thus 5 (i.e. £100 billion/£20 billion). But this is equal to $1/(1 - 0.8)$ or $1/(1 - mpc_d)$.

1. *What determines the slope of the E function?*
2. *How does the slope of the E function affect the size of the multiplier? (Try drawing diagrams with E functions of different slopes and see what happens when they shift.)*

The multiplier: a numerical illustration

The multiplier effect does not work instantaneously: transmission takes time. When there is an increase in injections, whether investment, government expenditure or exports, it takes time before this brings about the full multiplied rise in national income.

Consider the following example. Let us assume for simplicity that the mpw is $^1/_2$. This will give an mpc_d of $^1/_2$ also. Let us also assume that investment (an injection) rises by £160 million and stays at the new higher level. Table 17.3 shows what will happen.

As firms purchase more machines and construct more factories, the incomes of those who produce machines and those who work in the construction industry will increase by £160 million. When this extra income is received by households, whether as wages or profits, half will be withdrawn ($mpw = 1/2$) and half will be spent on the goods and services of domestic firms. This increase in consumption thus generates additional incomes for firms of £80 million over and above the initial £160 million (which is still being generated in each time period). When this additional £80 million of incomes is received by households (round 2), again half will be withdrawn and half will go on consumption of domestic

Table 17.2 The effect of an increase in aggregate expenditure (£ billions)

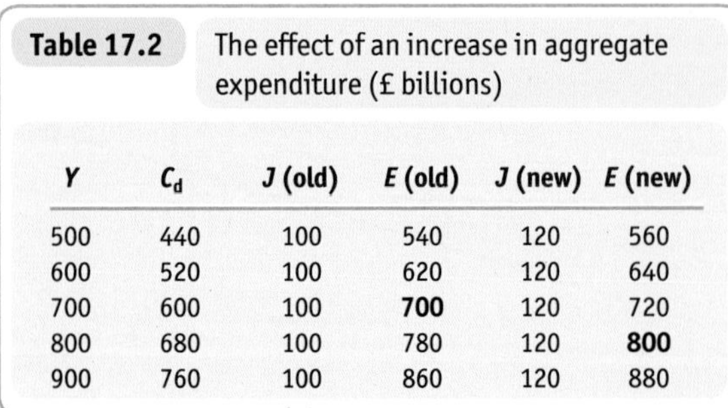

Y	C_d	J (old)	E (old)	J (new)	E (new)
500	440	100	540	120	560
600	520	100	620	120	640
700	600	100	**700**	120	720
800	680	100	780	120	**800**
900	760	100	860	120	880

Table 17.3 The multiplier 'round'

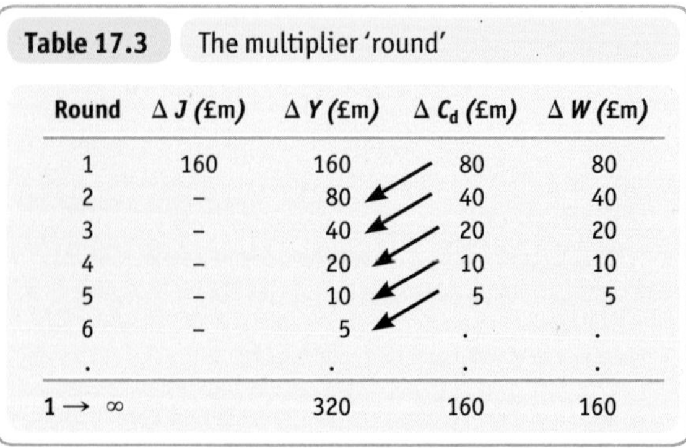

Round	Δ J (£m)	Δ Y (£m)	Δ C_d (£m)	Δ W (£m)
1	160	160	80	80
2	–	80	40	40
3	–	40	20	20
4	–	20	10	10
5	–	10	5	5
6	–	5	.	.
.		.	.	.
1 → ∞		320	160	160

BOX 17.3 DERIVING THE MULTIPLIER FORMULA

EXPLORING ECONOMICS

An algebraic proof

The formula for the multiplier can be derived using simple algebra. First of all, remember how we defined the multiplier:

$$k \equiv \Delta Y/\Delta J \quad (1)$$

and the marginal propensity to withdraw:

$$mpw \equiv \Delta W/\Delta Y \quad (2)$$

If we now take the inverse of equation (2), we get

$$1/mpw \equiv \Delta Y/\Delta W \quad (3)$$

But in equilibrium we know that $W = J$. Hence any change in injections must be matched by a change in withdrawals and vice versa, to ensure that withdrawals and injections remain equal. Thus

$$\Delta W = \Delta J \quad (4)$$

Substituting equation (4) in equation (3) gives

$$1/mpw = \Delta Y/\Delta J \ (= k)$$

i.e. the multiplier equals $1/mpw$.

product. This increases national income by a further £40 million (round 3). And so each time we go around the circular flow of income, national income increases, but by only half as much as the previous time ($mpc_d = 1/2$).

If we add up the additional income generated in each round (assuming the process goes on indefinitely), the total will be £320 million: twice the rise in injections. The multiplier is 2.

The bigger the mpc_d (and hence the smaller the mpw), the more will expenditure rise each time national income rises, and hence the bigger will be the multiplier.

*The multiplier: some qualifications

(This section examines the multiplier formula in more detail. You may omit it without affecting the flow of the argument.)

Some possible errors can easily be made in calculating the value of the multiplier. These often arise from a confusion over the meaning of terms.

The marginal propensity to consume domestic product

Remember the formula for the multiplier:

$$k = 1/(1 - mpc_d)$$

It is important to realise just what is meant by the mpc_d. It is the proportion of a rise in households' gross (i.e. pre-tax-and-benefit) income that actually accrues to domestic firms. It thus excludes that part of consumption that is spent on imports and that part which is paid to the government in VAT and other indirect taxes.

Up to now we have also been basing the *mpc* on gross income. As Case Study 17.2 on the student website shows, however, the *mpc* is often based on *disposable* (i.e. post-tax-and-benefit) income. After all, when consumers decide how much to spend, it is their disposable income rather than their gross income that they will consider. So how do we derive the mpc_d (based on gross income) from the *mpc* based on disposable income (mpc')? To do this, we must use the following formula:

$$mpc_d = mpc'(1 - t_E)(1 - t_Y) - mpm$$

where t_Y is the marginal rate of income tax, and t_E is the marginal rate of expenditure tax.

To illustrate this formula consider the following effects of an increase in national income of £100 million. It is assumed that $t_Y = 20$ per cent, $t_E = 10$ per cent and $mpc = 7/8$. It is also assumed that the *mps* (from gross income) = 1/10 and the *mpm* (from gross income) = 13/100. Table 17.4 sets out the figures.

Gross income rises by £100 million. Of this, £20 million is taken in income tax ($t_Y = 20$ per cent). This leaves a rise in disposable income of £80 million. Of this, £10 million is saved ($mps = 1/10$) and £70 million is spent. Of this, £7 million goes in expenditure taxes ($t_E = 10$ per cent) and £13 million leaks abroad ($mpm = 13/100$). This leaves £50 million that goes on the consumption of domestic product ($mpc_d = 50/100 = 1/2$). Substituting these figures in the above formula gives:

$$mpc_d = mpc(1 - t_E)(1 - t_Y) - mpm$$

$$= \frac{7}{8}\left(1 - \frac{1}{10}\right)\left(1 - \frac{2}{10}\right) - \frac{13}{100}$$

$$= \left(\frac{7}{8} \times \frac{9}{10} \times \frac{8}{10}\right) - \frac{13}{100}$$

$$= \frac{63}{100} - \frac{13}{100} = \frac{50}{100} = \frac{1}{2}$$

Table 17.4 Calculating the mpc_d

	ΔY	–	ΔT_Y	=	ΔY_{dis}		
(£m)	100		20		80		
	ΔY_{dis}	–	ΔS	=	ΔC		
(£m)	80		10		70		
	ΔC	–	ΔT_E	–	ΔM	=	ΔC_d
(£m)	70		7		13		50

Note that the mpc_d, *mps*, *mpm* and *mpt* are all based on the rise in *gross* income, not disposable income. They are 50/100, 10/100, 13/100 and 27/100 respectively.

Maths Case 17.3 on the student website derives the multiplier formula when the propensities to consume, save and import are all based on *disposable* as opposed to gross income.

Assume that the rate of income tax is 15 per cent, the rate of expenditure tax is 12.5 per cent, the mps is 1/20, the mpm is 1/8 and the mpc (from disposable income) is 16/17. What is the mpc_d? Construct a table like Table 17.4, assuming again that national income rises by £100 million.

The effects of changes in injections and withdrawals on other injections and withdrawals

In order to work out the size of a multiplied rise or fall in income, it is necessary to know first the size of the initial *total* change in injections and/or withdrawals. The trouble is that a change in one injection or withdrawal can affect others. For example, a rise in income taxes will reduce not only consumption, but also saving, imports and the revenue from indirect taxes. Thus the total rise in withdrawals will be *less* than the rise in income taxes.

Give some other examples of changes in one injection or withdrawal that can affect others.

Section summary

1. Equilibrium national income can be shown on the 45° line diagram at the point where $W = J$ and $Y = E$.
2. If there is an increase in injections (or a reduction in withdrawals), there will be a multiplied rise in national income. The multiplier is defined as $\Delta Y/\Delta J$.
3. The size of the multiplier depends on the marginal propensity to withdraw (*mpw*). The smaller the *mpw*, the less will be withdrawn each time incomes are generated round the circular flow, and thus the more will go round again as *additional* demand for domestic product. The multiplier formula is $k = 1/mpw$ or $1/(1 - mpc_d)$.
4. When working out the size of the multiplier, you must be careful to identify clearly the mpc_d (which is based on *gross* income and only includes expenditure that actually accrues to domestic firms) and not to confuse it with the *mpc* based on *disposable* income (which includes consumption of imports and the payment of indirect taxes). It is also necessary to identify the *full* changes in injections and withdrawals on which any multiplier effect is based.

17.3 THE SIMPLE KEYNESIAN ANALYSIS OF UNEMPLOYMENT AND INFLATION

'Full-employment' national income

The simple Keynesian theory assumes that there is a maximum level of national output, and hence real income, which can be obtained at any one time. If the equilibrium level of income is at this level, there will be no deficiency of aggregate demand. This level of income is referred to as the ***full-employment level of national income***. In practice, there would still be some unemployment at this level because of structural, frictional and seasonal unemployment (see section 15.5).

From the 1950s to the early 1970s, governments aimed to achieve this full-employment income (Y_F), if inflation and the balance of payments permitted. To do this, they attempted to manipulate the level of aggregate demand.

Many countries around the world in response to the global financial crisis of 2007–8 and the COVID-19 pandemic used fiscal and monetary policies to stimulate aggregate demand in an attempt to combat a deepening recession.

The deflationary gap

If the equilibrium level of national income (Y_e) is *below* the full-employment level (Y_F), there will be excess capacity in the economy and hence demand-deficient unemployment.

There will be what is known as a ***deflationary*** or ***recessionary gap***. This is illustrated in Figure 17.11.

The full-employment level of national income (Y_F) is represented by the vertical line. The equilibrium level of

Definitions

Full-employment level of national income The level of national income at which there is no deficiency of demand.

Deflationary or recessionary gap The shortfall of national expenditure below national income (and injections).

Figure 17.11 The deflationary (recessionary) gap

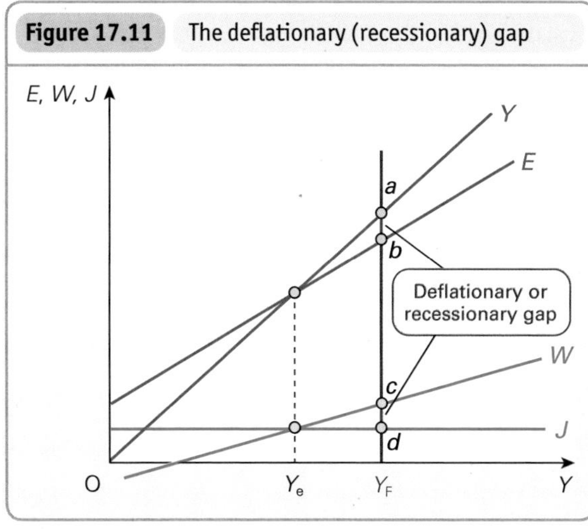

Figure 17.12 The inflationary gap

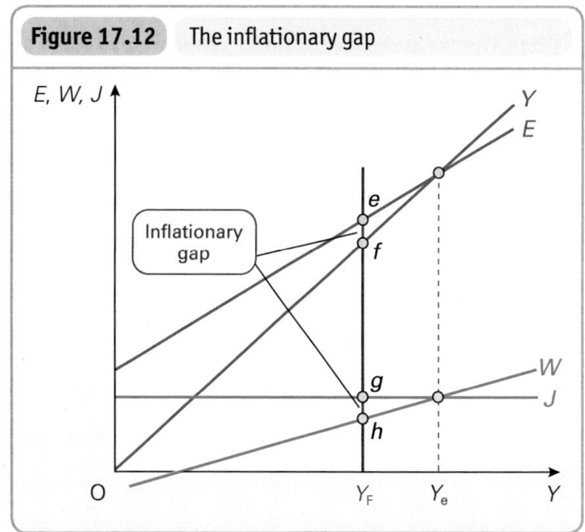

national income is Y_e, where $W = J$ and $Y = E$. The deflationary gap is $a - b$: namely, the amount that the E line is below the 45° line at the full-employment level of income (Y_F). It is also $c - d$: the amount that injections fall short of withdrawals at the full-employment level of income.

Note that the size of the deflationary gap is *less* than the amount by which Y_e falls short of Y_F. This provides another TC 15 p543 illustration of the multiplier. If injections were raised by $c - d$, income would rise by $Y_F - Y_e$. The multiplier is thus given by

$$\frac{Y_F - Y_e}{c - d}$$

In this simple Keynesian model, then, the cure for demand-deficient unemployment is to close the deflationary gap. An increase in aggregate expenditure is needed. This could be achieved by an expansionary *fiscal* policy of increasing government expenditure and/or lowering taxes, or by an expansionary *monetary* policy of reducing interest rates and increasing the amount of money in the economy, thereby encouraging extra consumption and investment. Either way, if the deflationary gap is successfully closed, there will be a multiplied rise in income of $Y_F - Y_e$. Equilibrium national income will be restored to the full-employment level.

The inflationary gap

If, at the full-employment level of (real) income, aggregate expenditure exceeds national income, there will be a problem of *excess* demand. Y_e will be above Y_F. The problem is that Y_F represents a real ceiling to output. In the short run, real national  TC 13 p461 income *cannot* expand beyond this point.[4] Y_e cannot be reached. The result will therefore be demand-pull inflation.[5]

4 Note that the horizontal axis in the 45° line diagram represents *real* national income. If incomes were to rise by, say, 10 per cent but prices also rose by 10 per cent, real income would not have risen at all. People could not buy any more than before. In such a case, there will have been no rightward movement along the horizontal axis.

5 Except with increased overtime working. In this simple model, we assume that this is not possible.

This situation involves an ***inflationary gap***. This is the amount by which aggregate expenditure exceeds national income or injections exceed withdrawals at the full-employment level of national income. This is illustrated by the gaps $e - f$ and $g - h$ in Figure 17.12.

To eliminate this inflation, the inflationary gap must be closed by either raising withdrawals or lowering injections, or some combination of the two, until Y_e equals Y_F. A reduction in aggregate expenditure could be achieved through a deliberate government policy of deflation. This could be either a contractionary *fiscal* policy of lowering government expenditure and/or raising taxes, or a contractionary *monetary* policy of raising interest rates and reducing the amount of money in the economy.

Even if the government does not actively pursue a deflationary policy, the inflationary gap may still close *automatically*, though this may take some time. The mechanisms by which this could occur would move the E line down and the J line up and/or the W line up. These include the following:

- Higher domestic prices will lead to fewer exports being sold and more imports being bought in preference to the now dearer home-produced goods. The precise effect will depend on what happens to exchange rates – a subject we explore in Chapter 25.
- Higher prices increase the demand for money. The average amount of money that people and firms would need to hold for spending purposes is greater. In the absence of an increase in the money supply, the shortage of money drives up interest rates. This reduces investment and encourages saving.

Definition

Inflationary gap The excess of national expenditure over income (and injections over withdrawals) at the full-employment level of national income.

- Higher prices reduce the real value of people's savings. They may therefore save more to compensate for this.
- As money (nominal) incomes go up, people will tend to find themselves paying higher rates of tax (unless the government increases tax bands and allowances in line with inflation). Hence, higher money incomes lead to increased taxes.
- If the rich are better able than the poor to defend themselves against inflation, there will be a redistribution from the poor to the rich. But the rich tend to have a higher marginal propensity to save (*mps*) than the poor. Thus saving will rise and consumption will fall.

The present level of a country's exports is £12 billion; investment is £2 billion; government expenditure is £4 billion; total consumer spending (not C_d) is £36 billion; imports are £12 billion; and expenditure taxes are £2 billion. The economy is currently in equilibrium. It is estimated that an income of £50 billion is necessary to generate full employment. The mps is 0.1, the mpt is 0.05 and the mpm is 0.1.

(a) Is there an inflationary or deflationary gap in this situation?

(b) What is the size of the gap? (Don't confuse this with the difference between Y_e and Y_F.)

(c) What would be the appropriate government policies to close this gap?

The multiplier and the full-employment level of national income

The simple analysis of the preceding pages implies that up to the full-employment level of national income (Y_F), output and employment can increase with no rise in prices at all. There is no inflation because the economy's deflationary gap is being closed. Hence, increases in aggregate expenditure set in motion the multiplier process resulting in a multiplied increase in real national income.

At Y_F no further rises in output are possible. Any further rise in aggregate demand is entirely reflected in higher prices. An inflationary gap opens. Hence, the additional demand no longer generates an increase in output. There is no increase in real national income because the real value of expenditure has not increased. Additional sums of spending on domestically produced goods and service are purely *nominal* reflecting only higher prices. The volume of purchases and, hence, the level of output is unchanged.

In this simple model, therefore, resource constraints become effective at the full-employment national income level. Up to this point, additional demand generates increases in output without inflation. At the full-employment national income level any further increases in aggregate demand generate only inflation. The multiplier process ceases to operate. We can use the 45° line diagram to illustrate these ideas as shown in Figure 17.13.

Assume that the economy is initially at Y_{e1} where E_1 crosses the 45° line. Now let us assume that there is a rise in aggregate demand. The E line shifts to E_2 resulting in a full multiplied rise in real income. Therefore, equilibrium national income rises to Y_F.

Figure 17.13 Allowing for inflation in the 45° line

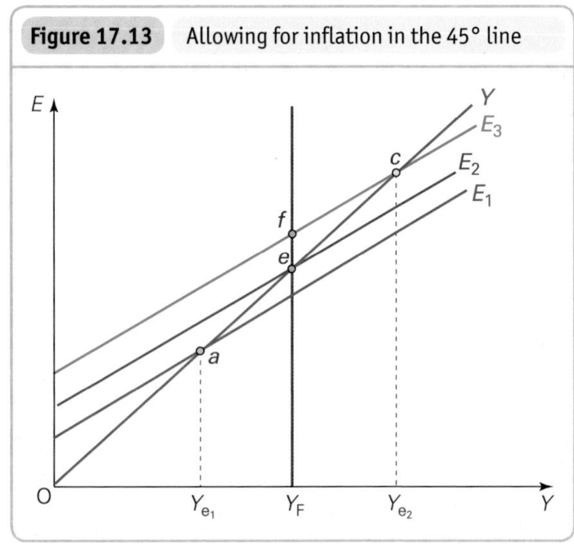

Consider now a further rise in aggregate demand which causes the E line to shift to E_3. An inflationary gap opens up, illustrated by the gap $e - f$. This time the increase in demand will be reflected only in higher prices with no increase in output. Equilibrium real income will be unchanged. If there is no compensating increase in money supply, the E line will fall back to E_2. The means by which this happens are those we identified above as the automatic mechanisms that tend to close an inflationary gap.

Unemployment and inflation at the same time

Our simple model implies that either inflation *or* unemployment can occur, but not both simultaneously. Two important qualifications need to be made to this analysis to explain the occurrence of both unemployment *and* inflation at the same time.

First, there are *other* types of inflation and unemployment not caused by an excess or deficiency of aggregate demand: for example, cost-push and expectations-generated inflation; frictional and structural unemployment.

Thus, even if a government could manipulate national income so that the equilibrium income level, Y_e, and full-employment income level, Y_F, coincided, this would not eliminate all inflation and unemployment – only demand-pull inflation and demand-deficient unemployment. Keynesians argue, therefore, that governments should use a whole package of policies, each tailored to the specific type of problem. But certainly one of the most important of these policies will be the management of aggregate demand.

Second, not all firms operate with the same degree of slack. Thus a rise in aggregate demand can lead to *both* a reduction in unemployment *and* a rise in prices: some firms responding to the rise in demand by taking up slack and hence increasing output; other firms, having little or no slack, responding by raising prices; others doing both. Similarly, labour markets have different degrees of slack and therefore the rise in demand will lead to various mixes of higher wages and lower unemployment.

How does the above argument about firms' responses to a rise in demand relate to the shape of their marginal cost curves?

These types of argument were used to justify a belief in a downward-sloping Phillips curve (see Box 15.6) by the majority of economists and politicians in the 1960s and into the 1970s. A modified version of these arguments is still used today by Keynesian economists. This is examined in more detail in Chapter 21.

KI 36 p459

The problem is that if there is a trade-off between unemployment and inflation, demand management policies used to make one of the objectives better will succeed only in making the other one worse. It then becomes a matter of political judgement which of the objectives is the right one to direct demand management policies towards. Is *inflation* public enemy number one, or is it *unemployment*?

The multiplier and inflation

We saw earlier how the multiplier process is affected by the constraint posed by the full-employment national income level. We have now introduced the argument that inflation can begin to occur *before* the full-employment level of income is reached. This means that increases in aggregate demand no longer increase real national income by the full extent of the multiplier even before the full-employment output level is reached.

We might expect inflationary pressures to become more significant, and the size of the multiplier to become smaller, the closer the economy is to the full-employment national income level. This is because an increasingly large part of the increase in demand is being reflected in higher prices and a smaller part in higher output.

BOX 17.4 ALLOWING FOR INFLATION IN THE 45° LINE DIAGRAM — EXPLORING ECONOMICS

The relationship between the *AD/AS* framework and the Keynesian cross

In this box we consider more formally how we can extend the simple Keynesian model to *allow* for inflation. In other words, the price level is no longer assumed to be constant. Here we introduce a new model: the aggregate demand (*AD*) and aggregate supply (*AS*) model. This is a model we develop later (in Chapter 20) and just the bare bones of the model are considered here.

The *AD/AS* framework enables us to incorporate prices within the context of aggregate demand and aggregate supply. In this box we show the relationship between this framework and the 45° line diagram, known as the 'Keynesian Cross'.

The *AD/AS* model

Consider the top half of the diagram, part (a). AD_1 and *AS* are representative aggregate demand and aggregate supply curves. They show how aggregate demand and supply vary with the overall level of prices in the economy (*P*). The *AD* curve is downward sloping while the *AS* curve is upward sloping. But what is the economics behind these curves?

The aggregate demand curve (AD). The downward-sloping *AD* curve captures the idea that economic agents will demand fewer domestically produced goods and services as the economy's general price level rises (a movement upwards along the curve). Reasons for this include:

- people switching from domestic products to now relatively cheaper imported products;
- an increase in the demand for money (to pay the higher prices), which pushes up interest rates and reduces spending;
- a decrease in the real value of people's savings, which increases the incentive to save;
- people perhaps finding that they are paying a larger proportion of their incomes in taxes as money incomes rise.

Allowing for inflation in the 45° line and AD/AS diagrams

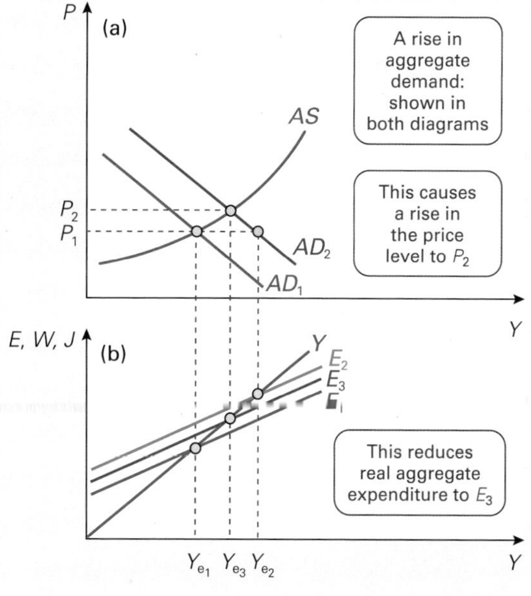

A *shift* in the *AD* curve will occur if, for any given price level, there is a change in any of the components of aggregate demand. For an example, an increase in consumer confidence may encourage increased consumer spending (*C*) and so the *AD* curve shifts to the right.

(continued)

The aggregate supply curve (AS). The upward-sloping *AS* curve shows firms supplying more as the economy's general price level rises. The curve is drawn on the assumption that various things remain constant. These include wage rates and other input prices, technology and the total supply of factors of production. Because we are holding wages and other input prices constant, as the prices of firms' products rise it becomes profitable for them to expand their output.

The aggregate supply curve will shift if any of the variables that are held constant when we draw the curve now change. For example, a rise in wage rates throughout the economy reduces the amount that firms wish to produce at any level of prices. The *AS* curve shifts to the left.

The Keynesian cross model

The bottom half of the diagram, part (b), is the 45° line diagram – the Keynesian cross model. Alongside the 45° line ($Y = C_d + W$) are three aggregate expenditure lines (E_1, E_2 and E_3), which show aggregate demand (E) dependent on the level of national income.

Combining *AD/AS* and the 45° line models

We are now in a position to combine our two models. Assume initially that the economy is in equilibrium at national income level Y_{e1}, where aggregate demand (AD_1) equals aggregate supply (AS) and where the aggregate expenditure line (E_1) crosses the 45° line.

Now assume that there is a rise in aggregate demand caused, say, by an increase in consumer confidence that results in a rise in consumption. In part (a) of the diagram the *AD* curve shifts rightwards from AD_1 to AD_2. Meanwhile in part (b), the *E* line shifts to E_2.

TC 13 p461

If this rise in demand were to lead to a full multiplied rise in real income, equilibrium income would rise to Y_{e2}. For this to happen we would require the *AS* curve in part (a) to be a flat horizontal line, with no general price rises resulting from the increase in the aggregate demand. If, as is more likely, prices do rise, giving an upward-sloping *AS* curve, the increase in aggregate demand from AD_1 to AD_2 results in the price level rising to P_2.

Hence, part of the increase in demand is reflected in higher prices and only *part* is reflected in higher output. Equilibrium real income therefore rises only to Y_{e3} and not Y_{e2}. In other words, it does not rise by the full extent of the multiplier.

In part (b) of the diagram, the effect of the higher prices is to reduce the real value of expenditure (E). In other words, a given amount of money buys fewer goods. If there is no compensating increase in money supply (which would shift the *AD* curve further to the right in diagram (a)), the *E* line must fall to the point where it intersects the 45° line at a real income of Y_{e3}: the *E* line must fall to E_3.

1. ***What impact would a greater flexibility of wages have on the government purchases multiplier?***
2. ***Assume that the AS curve is flat up to the full-employment national income level, Y_F, after which it becomes vertical. Combining the AD/AS and 45° line models, illustrate the effect on the multiplier of an increase in AD at output levels below Y_F and at Y_F.***

Conduct an Internet search to find examples of governments in the past using expansionary fiscal policy to boost economic growth, only to find that much of the increase in (nominal) demand resulted merely in higher prices. What were the governments' responses to the higher prices?

Section summary

1. If equilibrium national income (Y_e) is below the full-employment level of national income (Y_F), there will be a deflationary (recessionary) gap. This gap is equal to $Y - E$ or $W - J$ at Y_F. at Y_F. This gap can be closed by expansionary fiscal or monetary policy, which will then cause a multiplied rise in national income (up to a level of Y_F) and will eliminate demand-deficient unemployment.
2. If equilibrium national income exceeds the full-employment level of income, the inability of output to expand to meet this excess demand will lead to demand-pull inflation. This excess demand gives an inflationary gap, which is equal to $E - Y$ or $J - W$ at Y_F. This gap can be closed by deflationary policies.
3. This simple analysis tends to imply that aggregate demand can expand up to Y_F without generating inflation. In practice, inflationary pressures are likely to emerge at lower levels of national income, but become more significant as national income approaches its full-employment level. As it does so, resource constraints and bottlenecks are increasingly likely to occur.
4. An initial rise in aggregate demand (and an upward shift in the *E* curve) will be eroded to the extent that inflation reduces the real value of this demand: the *E* curve will shift back downwards again somewhat, unless there is a further boost to demand.

17.4 THE KEYNESIAN ANALYSIS OF THE BUSINESS CYCLE

Volatility of aggregate demand

In the previous sections of the chapter we developed the simple Keynesian model. The model shows how fluctuations in aggregate demand can have multiplied effects on output and employment. This is an important insight because we know that economies are inherently volatile. Therefore, Keynesian analysis of the business cycle focuses on fluctuations in aggregate demand.

TC 12 p455

The instability of aggregate demand, Keynesians argue, is central to explaining the business cycle. In the upturn (phase 1), aggregate demand starts to rise. It rises rapidly in the expansionary phase (phase 2). It then slows down and may start to fall in the peaking-out phase (phase 3). It then falls or remains relatively stagnant in the recession (phase 4) (see Figure 15.5 on page 469).

Keynesians also argue that market imperfections or frictions can magnify the impact of the instability on aggregate demand. For instance, the reluctance of firms to change prices because of menu costs (the costs incurred in adjusting prices) could see them change output levels substantially in response to fluctuations in demand (see section 16.5). When there are frictions to prices adjusting then changes in aggregate demand will tend to have larger effects on output and employment levels: the multiplier effect is larger.

KI 34 p453

The volatility of aggregate demand must reflect the volatility of the expenditure components: *C, I, G, X* and *M*. However, Keynesians argue that central to the volatility of aggregate demand is the volatility of private-sector spending. Hence, this volatility will often require the authorities to devise appropriate stabilisation policies to iron out the fluctuations in economic activity that result. A more stable economy, they argue, provides a better climate for investment. With more investment, *potential* output grows more rapidly. This, given appropriate demand management policy, then allows a faster growth in actual output to be maintained. We examine demand management policies (fiscal and monetary) in Chapter 22.

Instability of investment: the accelerator

Of the expenditure components that comprise aggregate demand the most volatile is investment (*I*). To illustrate this volatility consider Figure 17.14, which shows the annual rate of growth in investment for a sample of industrialised countries.

When an economy begins to recover from a recession, investment can rise very rapidly. When the growth of the economy slows down, however, investment can fall dramatically, and during a recession it can all but disappear. Since investment is an injection into the circular flow of income, these changes in investment will cause multiplied changes in income and thus heighten a boom or deepen a recession.

The theory that relates investment to *changes* in national income is called the ***accelerator theory***. The term 'accelerator'

> **Definition**
>
> **Accelerator theory** The level of investment depends on the rate of change of national income, and as a result tends to be subject to substantial fluctuations.

Figure 17.14 Annual growth in investment in selected countries

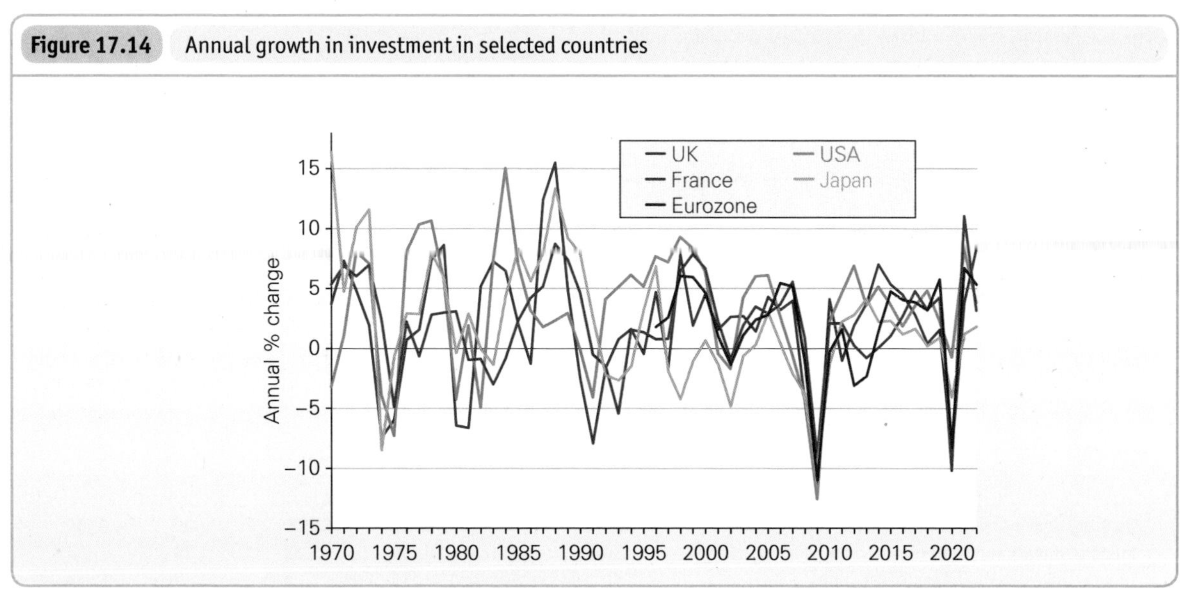

Note: Investment growth is the growth in gross fixed capital formation; *eurozone* = 19 countries using the euro as of 1 January 2015.
Source: Based on data in *AMECO Database*, European Commission, DGECFIN (May 2021), http://ec.europa.eu/economy_finance/db_indicators/ameco/index_en.htm; figures from 2021 based on forecasts.

is used because a relatively modest rise in national income can cause a much larger percentage rise in investment.

When there is no change in income and hence no change in consumption, the only investment needed is a relatively small amount of replacement investment for machines that are wearing out or have become obsolete. When income and consumption increase, however, there will have to be *new* investment in order to increase production capacity. This is called ***induced investment*** (I_i). Once this has taken place, investment will fall back to mere replacement investment (I_r) unless there is a further rise in income and consumption.

Thus induced investment depends on *changes* in national income (ΔY):

$$I_i = \alpha \Delta Y$$

where α is the amount by which induced investment depends on changes in national income, and is known as the ***accelerator coefficient***. Thus if a £1 million *rise* in national income caused the *level* of induced investment to be £2 million, the accelerator coefficient would be 2.

The size of α depends on the economy's ***marginal capital/output ratio*** ($\Delta K/\Delta Y$). If an increase in the country's capital stock of £2 million (i.e. an investment of £2 million) is required to produce £1 million extra national output, the marginal capital/output ratio would be 2. Other things being equal, the accelerator coefficient and the marginal capital/output ratio will therefore be the same.

How is it that the cost of an investment to a firm will exceed the value of the output that the investment will yield? Surely, that would make the investment unprofitable. (Clue: the increase in output refers to output over a specific time period, usually a year.)

The example in Table 17.5 illustrates some important features of the accelerator. It looks at the investment decisions made by a firm in response to changes in the demand for its product. The firm is taken as representative of firms throughout the economy. The example is based on various assumptions:

- The firm's machines last exactly 10 years and then need replacing.
- At the start of the example, the firm has ten machines in place, one 10 years old, one 9 years old, one 8 years old, one 7, one 6 and so on. Thus one machine needs replacing each year.
- Machines produce exactly 100 units of output per year. This figure cannot be varied.
- The firm always adjusts its output and its stock of machinery to match consumer demand.

The example shows what happens to the firm's investment over a six-year period when there is first a substantial rise in consumer demand, then a levelling off and then a slight fall. It illustrates the following features of the accelerator.

- *Investment will rise when the growth of national income (and hence consumer demand) is rising* ($\Delta Y_{t+1} > \Delta Y_t$). Years 1 to 2 illustrate this (see Table 17.5). The rise in consumer demand is zero in year 1 and 1000 units in year 2. Investment rises from 1 to 11 machines. The growth in investment may be considerably greater than the growth in consumer demand, giving a large accelerator effect. Between years 1 and 2, consumer demand doubles but investment goes up by a massive *11* times!
- *Investment will be constant even when national income is growing, if the increase in income this year is the same as last year* ($\Delta Y_{t+1} = \Delta Y_t$). In years 2 to 3, consumer demand continues to rise by 1000 units, but investment is constant at 11 machines.
- *Investment will fall even if national income is still growing, if the rate of growth is slowing down* ($\Delta Y_{t+1} < \Delta Y_t$). In years 3 to 4, consumer demand rises by 500 units (rather than 1000 units as in the previous year). Investment falls from 11 to 6 machines.
- *If national income is constant, investment will be confined to replacement investment only*. In years 4 to 5, investment falls to the one machine requiring replacement.

Definitions

Induced investment Investment that firms make to enable them to meet extra consumer demand.

Accelerator coefficient The level of induced investment as a proportion of a rise in national income: $\alpha = I_i/\Delta Y$.

Marginal capital/output ratio The amount of extra capital (in money terms) required to produce a £1 increase in national output. Since $I_i = \Delta K$, the marginal capital/output ratio $\Delta K/\Delta Y$ equals the accelerator coefficient (α).

Table 17.5 The accelerator effect

	Year						
	0	1	2	3	4	5	6
Quantity demanded by consumers (sales)	1000	1000	2000	3000	3500	3500	3400
Number of machines required	10	10	20	30	35	35	34
Induced investment (I_i) (extra machines)		0	10	10	5	0	0
Replacement investment (I_r)		1	1	1	1	1	0
Total investment ($I_i + I_r$)		1	11	11	6	1	0

- *If national income falls, even if only slightly, investment can be wiped out altogether.* In years 5 to 6, even though demand has fallen by only 1/35, investment will fall to zero. Not even the machine that is wearing out will be replaced.

In practice, the accelerator will not be as dramatic and clear-cut as this. The effect will be extremely difficult to predict for the following reasons:

- Many firms may have spare capacity and/or carry stocks. This will enable them to meet extra demand without having to invest.
- The willingness of firms to invest will depend on their confidence in *future* demand (see Box 17.2 on page 538). Firms are not going to rush out and spend large amounts of money on machines that will last many years if it is quite likely that demand will fall back again the following year.
- Firms may make their investment plans a long time in advance and may be unable to change them quickly.
- Even if firms do decide to invest more, the producer goods industries may not have the capacity to meet a sudden surge in demand for machines.
- Machines do not as a rule suddenly wear out. A firm could thus delay replacing machines and keep the old ones for a bit longer if it was uncertain about its future level of demand.

TC 9 p132

KI 33 p377

All these points tend to reduce the magnitude of the accelerator and make it very difficult to predict. Nevertheless, the effect still exists. Firms still take note of changes in consumer demand when deciding how much to invest.

Box 17.5 looks at how fluctuations in investment in the UK specifically have typically been far more severe than fluctuations in national income. However, similar findings can be observed in many countries (see also Figure (b) in Box 17.2 on page 539). This tends to support the idea that significant accelerator effects contribute towards the instability of economies.

The multiplier/accelerator interaction

If there is an initial change in injections or withdrawals, then theoretically this will set off a chain reaction between the multiplier and the accelerator. In other words, these two propagation mechanisms *interact*, affecting how economic shocks are transmitted through the economy.

TC 15 p543

Consider a rise in government expenditure. This will lead to a multiplied rise in national income. But this *rise* in national income will set off an accelerator effect: firms will respond to the rise in income and the resulting rise in consumer demand by investing more. But this rise in investment constitutes a further rise in injections and thus will lead to a second multiplied rise in income. If this rise in income is larger than the first, there will then be a second rise in investment (the accelerator), which in turn will cause a third rise in income (the multiplier). And so the process continues indefinitely.

But does this lead to an exploding rise in national income? Will a single rise in injections cause national income to go on rising for ever? The answer is no, for two reasons. The first is that national income, in real terms, cannot go on rising faster than the growth in potential output. It will bump up against the ceiling of full employment, whether of labour or of other resources.

A second reason is that, if investment is to go on rising, it is not enough that national income should merely go on *rising*: instead, national income must *rise faster and faster*. Once the growth in national income slows down, investment will begin to fall, and then the whole process will be reversed. A fall in investment will lead to a fall in national income, which will lead to a massive fall in investment. The multiplier/accelerator interaction is shown more formally in Table 17.6. A numerical example is given in Case Study 17.9 on the student website.

Fluctuations in stocks

Firms hold stocks (inventories) of finished goods. These stocks tend to fluctuate with the course of the business cycle, and these fluctuations in stocks themselves contribute to fluctuations in output.

KI 34 p453

Imagine an economy that is recovering from a recession. At first, firms may be cautious about increasing production. Doing so may involve taking on more labour or making additional investment. Firms may not want to make these commitments if the recovery could soon peter out. They may, therefore, run down their stocks rather than increase output. Initially the recovery from recession will be slow.

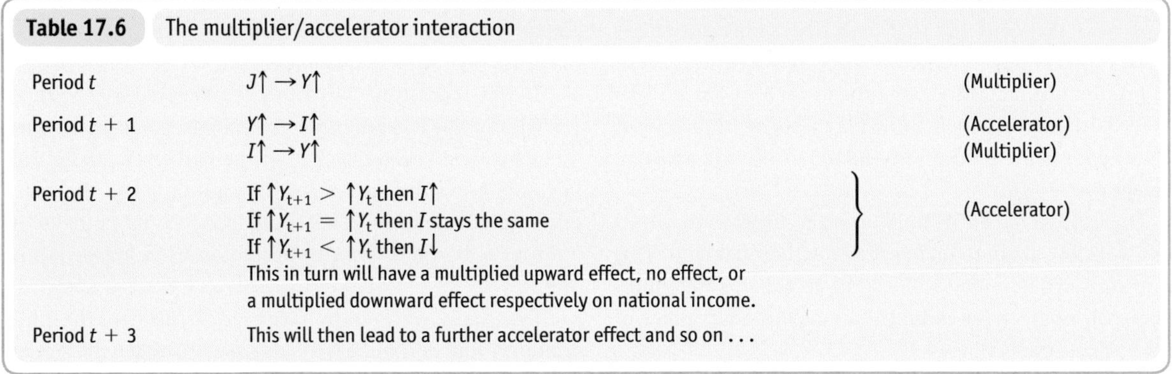

Table 17.6 The multiplier/accelerator interaction

Period t	$J\uparrow \rightarrow Y\uparrow$	(Multiplier)
Period $t + 1$	$Y\uparrow \rightarrow I\uparrow$	(Accelerator)
	$I\uparrow \rightarrow Y\uparrow$	(Multiplier)
Period $t + 2$	If $\uparrow Y_{t+1} > \uparrow Y_t$ then $I\uparrow$ If $\uparrow Y_{t+1} = \uparrow Y_t$ then I stays the same If $\uparrow Y_{t+1} < \uparrow Y_t$ then $I\downarrow$	(Accelerator)
	This in turn will have a multiplied upward effect, no effect, or a multiplied downward effect respectively on national income.	
Period $t + 3$	This will then lead to a further accelerator effect and so on . . .	

BOX 17.5 HAS THERE BEEN AN ACCELERATOR EFFECT IN THE UK? CASE STUDIES AND APPLICATIONS

The volatility of investment

KI 34 p453

If we look at the period from 1960 to 2020, the average annual rate of increase in GDP was 2.3 per cent, while that for investment was only slightly higher at 2.7 per cent. But the key point is that investment is highly volatile. Economic growth has fluctuated with the business cycle; but investment has typically been subject to far more violent swings.

If we look at the chart, we can see that, outside of the pandemic, the fastest annual rate of increase in GDP was 9.7 per cent (Q1 1973), while the sharpest rate of decline was 5.7 per cent (Q1 2009). By contrast, the fastest annual rate of increase in investment was 26.5 per cent (Q1 1964), while the sharpest rate of decline was 15.8 per cent (Q2 2009).

These figures are consistent with the accelerator theory, which argues that the *level* of investment depends on the *rate of change* of national income. A relatively small percentage change in national income can induce a much bigger percentage change in investment.

The ups and downs in GDP and investment do not completely match because there are additional factors that determine investment other than simply changes in national income. These factors include interest rates, the availability of finance, exchange rates and businesses' expectations of future demand.

1. ***Can you identify any time lags in the graph? Why might there be time lags?***
2. ***Why does investment in the construction and producer goods industries tend to fluctuate more than investment in retailing and the service industries?***

Conduct a literature search to further your understanding of the determinants of the aggregate level of investment in an economy. Summarise your findings in a short technical report aimed at economists.

Fluctuations in UK real GDP and investment

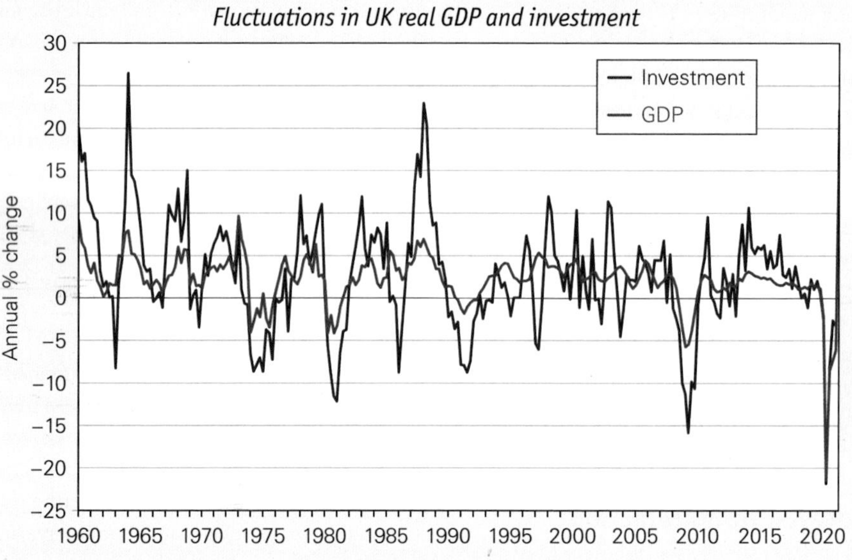

Note: Investment growth is the growth in gross fixed capital formation.
Source: Based on data in *Quarterly National Accounts*, series IHYR and KG7T, ONS, www.ons.gov.uk/economy/grossdomesticproductgdp/

If the recovery does continue, however, firms will start to gain more confidence and will increase production. Also, they will find that their stocks have got rather low and will need building up. This gives a further boost to production, and for a time the growth in output will exceed the growth in demand. This extra growth in output will then, via the multiplier, lead to a further increase in demand.

Once stocks have been built up again, the growth in output will slow down to match the growth in demand. This slowing down in output will, via the accelerator and multiplier, contribute to the ending of the expansionary phase of the business cycle.

As the economy slows down, firms will find their stocks building up. Unless they cut back on production immediately, this increase in stocks cushions the effect of falling demand on output and employment.

If the recession continues, however, firms will be unwilling to go on building up stocks. But as firms attempt to reduce their stocks back to the desired level, production will fall *below* the level of sales, despite the fact that sales themselves are lower. This could lead to a dramatic fall in output and, via the multiplier, to an even bigger fall in sales.

Eventually, once stocks have been run down to the minimum, production will have to rise again to match the level of sales. This will contribute to a recovery and the whole cycle will start again.

Fluctuations in borrowing and debt

During an upswing, when confidence is high, businesses will be more willing to borrow to invest and consumers will be more willing to borrow to spend. At the same time, banks will be more willing to lend, being confident in people's ability to repay. The extra borrowing and lending fuel the expansion. Private debt as a percentage of GDP thus tends to rise.

During a recession, banks are less willing to lend and both firms and consumers are less willing to borrow, fearing their ability to repay. Indeed, many people will seek to reduce their debts by increasing repayments. The reduction in borrowing and debt will push the economy deeper into recession.

Box 17.6 discusses the importance of borrowing and debt for the household sector's balance sheets and the relationship between financial wellbeing and the business cycle.

BOX 17.6 **BALANCE SHEETS AND THE BUSINESS CYCLE** CASE STUDIES AND APPLICATIONS

Financial wellbeing and macroeconomic effects

KI 35 p459

Balance sheets allow us to analyse the financial wellbeing of different sectors of the economy. They detail the *stocks* of financial liabilities, financial assets, and non-financial assets of different sectors, such as the corporate and household sectors.

The importance of the balance sheets for the macroeconomy was demonstrated starkly by the financial crisis. It showed how financial distress can spread like a contagion across the interconnected balance sheets of different sectors, both at home and abroad. This importance was further intensified by the twin processes of financialisation and globalisation.

Household-sector balance sheet

Before considering some of the mechanisms by which balance sheets can affect economic activity and the course of the business cycle, we look at the summary balance sheet of the household sector. Case Study 17.10 on the student website looks at the balance sheets of the financial and non-financial corporate sectors.

The household sector's net worth is the sum of its *net financial wealth* and *non-financial assets*.

- Net financial wealth is the stock of financial assets minus the stock of financial liabilities. Financial assets include wealth held in savings accounts, shares and pension funds. Financial liabilities include debts secured against property, largely residential mortgages, and unsecured debts, such as overdrafts and unpaid balances on credit cards.
- The stock of non-financial assets largely comprises the sector's residential housing wealth. Therefore, this is affected by changes in house prices.

The table summarises the net worth of the UK household sector. By the end of 2020, the sector had a stock of net worth estimated at £11.39 trillion compared with £2.68 trillion at the end of 1995 – an increase of 325 per cent. This, of course, is a nominal increase, not a real increase, as part of it merely reflects the rise in asset prices.

TC 13 p461

To put the size of net worth and its components into context, we can express them relative to annual disposable income or GDP. This shows that the household sector's net worth in 2020 was equivalent to 7.9 times the flow of household disposable income in that year, or 5.4 times GDP. In 1995 it was 4.7 times and 3.2 times, respectively.

The ratio of the sector's net worth to disposable income has typically increased year on year as can be seen in the chart. An important factor behind this long-term rise has been the rise of non-financial assets (mainly land and dwellings). Although falling following the financial crisis, this has increased from £1.15 trillion (204 per cent of disposable income) in 1995 to £5.97 trillion (413 per cent of disposable income) in 2020.

In contrast, net financial wealth to disposable income has been even more volatile, without the marked upward trend seen in non-financial assets. The ratio of net financial wealth to disposable income in 2020, for example, was the same as its 2005 value. However, the absolute value of net financial wealth increased by 254 per cent from 1995 to 2020, though considerably less than the 419 per cent by which non-financial assets rose. Net worth rose by 325 per cent.

Summary of household-sector balance sheets, 31 December 1995 and 2020

	1995			2020		
	£ billions	**% of disposable income**	**% of GDP**	**£ billions**	**% of disposable income**	**% of GDP**
Financial assets	2 063.2	365.3	242.7	7 372.9	509.8	349.1
Financial liabilities	533.9	94.5	62.8	1 957.0	135.3	92.7
Net financial wealth	**1 529.4**	**270.8**	**179.9**	**5 416.0**	**374.5**	**256.4**
Non-financial assets	1 150.5	203.7	135.3	5 974.7	413.1	282.9
Net worth	**2 679.8**	**474.5**	**315.2**	**11 390.6**	**787.5**	**539.3**

Source: Based on data from *National Balance Sheet* and series YBHA and HABN, National Statistics, www.ons.gov.uk/economy/nationalaccounts/uksectoraccounts/datasets/thenationalbalancesheetestimates; www.ons.gov.uk/economy/grossdomesticproductgdp/

(continued)

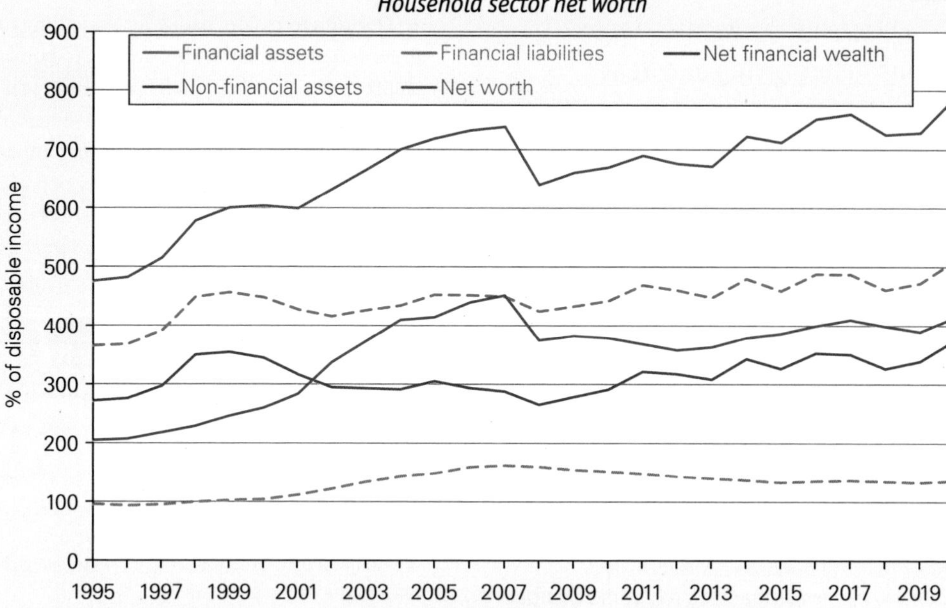

Source: Based on data from *Preliminary UK National Balance Sheet Estimates* and series HABN, National Statistics, www.ons.gov.uk/economy/nationalaccounts/uksectoraccounts/datasets/preliminaryuknationalbalancesheetestimates; www.ons.gov.uk/economy/grossdomesticproductgdp/timeseries/habn/ukea

KI 35 p459

The balance sheets of different sectors, such as the household sector, allow us to analyse their financial wellbeing. This is important for two reasons.

First, the balance sheets can affect how economic shocks, ranging from monetary policy changes to the COVID-19 pandemic, *transmit* through the economy. Here the balance sheets act as a *propagation mechanism*.

Second, changes on the balance sheets, such as their size and composition, can themselves be an important *source* of economic volatility. The rate of debt accumulation that preceded the global financial crisis is one such example.

Balance sheet congestion

A deterioration of the balance sheets may arise from increased levels of indebtedness, a build-up of debt-servicing obligations, an increased risk of default on loans, a decline in liquidity or falls in asset prices.

A deterioration of the balance sheets can lead to the phenomenon of ***balance sheet congestion*** whereby the balance sheets constrain people or businesses from obtaining finance. This can happen for two principal reasons.

Credit constraints. Existing liabilities can impose a credit constraint if a debt ceiling is reached, or if the costs of servicing these debts are relatively large compared to the income streams used to service them.

Collateral value effects. Collateral (i.e. assets) can be used to secure borrowing. Fluctuating asset prices, such as residential and commercial property prices or share prices, therefore affect the value of collateral available to secure lending.

Definition

Balance sheet congestion A deterioration of the financial wellbeing of economic agents that constrains their ability to obtain finance.

Determinants of the course of the business cycle

We are now in a position to paint a more complete Keynesian picture of the business cycle. We need to answer two key questions: (a) why do booms and recessions last for several months or even years, and (b) why do they eventually come to an end – what determines their turning points? Let us examine each in turn.

TC 12 p455

Why do booms and recessions persist?

Time lags. Propagation mechanisms, such as the multiplier, take time to transmit the impact of economic shocks. Therefore it takes time for fluctuations in injections and withdrawals to be fully reflected in changes in national income, output and employment. Moreover, consumers, firms and government may not all respond immediately to new situations.

KI 33 p377

Falling asset prices tend to tighten credit limits and/or raise the cost of borrowing.

Where people and businesses are looking to borrow in anticipation of higher *future* income streams, such borrowing may be constrained by *current* income streams or by restrictions on borrowing. On the supply side, if there is less business investment, this may reduce the growth of the economy's potential output.

Debt-servicing effects

Levels of indebtedness and their associated debt servicing costs have implications for the interest-rate responsiveness of aggregate demand and for propagation mechanisms, such as the multiplier and the accelerator.

Interest-rate responsiveness of spending. Consumption and investment are likely to be more sensitive to interest rate shocks the greater are the flows of income needed to service the stock of liabilities. Therefore, a high level of liabilities may cause a significant cash-flow constraint when interest rates rise. In the case of consumers, increases in interest rates can place a substantially larger burden on households if they are faced with high levels of debt, including mortgage debt. This will dampen aggregate demand as households feel under pressure to curb their expenditures.

KI 26 p309

Multiplier and the accelerator. These two propagation mechanisms are *flow*-based mechanisms. Changes in flows of borrowing affect economic activity through their impact on flows of income and spending. For example, these mechanisms mean that an increase in borrowing, perhaps because of an increase in confidence, will result in an amplified increase in national income.

But this ignores the impact of borrowing on the *stock* of debt. As debt stocks accumulate, more income is needed to service these debts. A stock–flow process develops, whereby higher debt has a negative effect on demand, and hence on national income. This offsets some of the positive effects from borrowing on national income associated with the multiplier and accelerator.

The extent to which these stock effects blunt the impact of the multiplier and accelerator will depend on the amount of debt that has previously been accumulated. This can be understood in terms of a so-called 'predator–prey relationship'. The larger the existing stock of liabilities, the 'hungrier' is the predator (lenders), and the more income that serves as its prey.

Uncertainty and financial buffers

Sector balance sheets are important in the context of *macroeconomic uncertainty*. In the face of greater uncertainty, and hence a greater range of possible future macroeconomic outcomes, risk-averse individuals are likely to want a larger stock of wealth (net worth). This is because it acts as a buffer against unexpected shocks and can be drawn on should lower-than-expected future income streams occur. In the face of greater uncertainty, consumers may reduce current consumption, while businesses may postpone investment.

KI 11 p72

Since uncertainty often increases following negative economic shocks, as observed with the onset of the global financial crisis and then the COVID-19 pandemic, the wellbeing of the balance sheets at the time is likely be an important determinant of the subsequent transmission and persistence of the shocks.

The financial crisis led to a significant deterioration of the balance sheets. With the heightened uncertainty that followed, there was a prolonged period in many countries during which the private sector attempted to rebuild balance sheets. A similar experience occurred in Japan in the early 1990s following the dramatic falls in commercial and residential property prices.

The dramatic slowdown in aggregate demand that results from attempts to rebuild wealth stocks is known as a *balance sheet recession* (see section 16.7). The balance sheets had a persistent dampening effect on economic activity.

A series of policy interventions, including the furlough scheme and business disruption loans, helped support the private sector's net worth during the pandemic. However, as these measures were withdrawn the longer-term impact of the pandemic on the financial wellbeing of all sectors was less clear.

Draw up a list of the various factors that could affect the household sector's net worth and then consider how these could impact on consumer spending.

Using the latest ONS National Balance Sheet estimates for the UK, construct a briefing note on the summary balance sheet for the UK general government (central and local government).

'Bandwagon' effects. Once the economy starts expanding, expectations become buoyant. People think ahead and adjust their expenditure behaviour: they consume and invest more now. Likewise in a recession, a mood of pessimism may set in. The effect is cumulative. The multiplier and accelerator interact: they feed on each other.

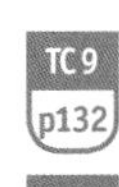

Group behaviour. Individual consumers and businesses may take their lead from others and so mimic their behaviour. This helps to reinforce bandwagon effects, thereby amplifying economic upturns and downturns.

For example, during the 2000s many financial institutions loosened their lending criteria. This helped to fuel unsustainable property booms in several countries, including the UK, Ireland and the USA. They engaged in a competitive race, offering ever more favourable terms for borrowers. Often the borrowers could only repay if their assets (e.g. property) appreciated in value, as they tend to do in a boom – but not in a recession.

This rush to lend meant that many banks over-extended themselves and operated with too little capital. This made them much more vulnerable to financial crises and much more likely to cut back lending dramatically in a downturn – as indeed they did from 2008.

Why do booms and recessions come to an end?

Ceilings and floors. Actual output can go on growing more rapidly than potential output only as long as there is slack in the economy. As full employment is approached and as more and more firms reach full capacity, so a ceiling to output will be reached.

At the other extreme, there is a basic minimum level of consumption that people tend to maintain. During a recession, people may not buy many luxury and durable goods, but they will continue to buy food and other basic goods. There is thus a floor to consumption.

The industries supplying these basic goods will need to maintain their level of replacement investment. Also, there will always be some minimum investment demand as firms feel the need to install the latest equipment. There is thus a floor to investment too.

Echo effects. Durable consumer goods and capital equipment may last several years, but eventually they will need replacing. The replacement of goods and capital purchased in a previous boom may help to bring a recession to an end.

The accelerator. For investment to continue rising, consumer demand must rise at a faster and faster rate. If this does not happen, investment will fall back and the boom will break.

Sentiment and expectations. A change of sentiment and a sense that current rates of growth will not be sustained can lead people to adjust their spending behaviour, so contributing to the very slowdown that was expected. The impact of this will be amplified by bandwagon effects and group behaviour.

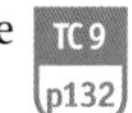
TC 9 p132

Random shocks. National or international political, social, institutional or natural events can affect the mood and attitudes of firms, governments and consumers, or the conditions under which they operate, and thus affect aggregate demand. Changes in world oil prices, a war, an election or a banking crisis are all examples.

Changes in government policy. In a boom, a government may become most worried by inflation, balance of payments deficits and rising levels of private debt, and thus pursue contractionary policies. In a recession, it may become most worried by unemployment and lack of growth and thus pursue expansionary policies. These government policies, if successful, will bring about a turning point in the cycle.

Keynesians argue that governments should attempt to reduce cyclical fluctuations by using active stabilisation policies. A more stable economy will encourage investment and allow a faster growth in output to be maintained. The policy traditionally favoured by Keynesians is *fiscal policy*. This is the subject of Chapter 22.

An analysis of the factors contributing to each of the four phases of the business cycle is given in Case Study 17.13 on the student website.

Section summary

1. Keynesians explain cyclical fluctuations in the economy by examining the causes of fluctuations in the level of aggregate demand.
2. A major part of the Keynesian explanation of the business cycle is the instability of private-sector expenditure. Investment is the most volatile component of aggregate demand. The accelerator theory explains this volatility. It relates the level of investment to changes in national income and consumer demand. An initial increase in consumer demand can result in a very large percentage increase in investment; but as soon as the rise in consumer demand begins to level off, investment will fall; and even a slight fall in consumer demand can reduce investment to virtually zero.
3. The accelerator effect will be dampened by the carrying of stocks, the cautiousness of firms, forward planning by firms and the inability of producer goods industries to supply the capital equipment.
4. The interaction of the multiplier and accelerator will cause cycles.
5. Fluctuations in stocks and in levels of borrowing and debt are also major contributors to the business cycle.
6. Keynesians identify other causes of cyclical fluctuations, such as time lags, 'bandwagon' effects, ceilings and floors to output, echo effects, swings in government policy and random shocks.

END OF CHAPTER QUESTIONS

1. An economy is currently in equilibrium. The following figures refer to elements in its national income accounts.

	£ billions
Consumption(total)	60
Investment	5
Government expenditure	8
Imports	10
Exports	7

   (a) What is the current equilibrium level of national income?
   (b) What is the level of injections?
   (c) What is the level of withdrawals?
   (d) Assuming that tax revenues are £7 billion, how much is the level of saving?
   (e) If national income now rose to £80 billion and, as a result, the consumption of domestically produced goods rose to £58 billion, what is the mpc_d?
   (f) What is the value of the multiplier?
   (g) Given an initial level of national income of £80 billion, now assume that spending on exports rises by £4 billion, spending on investment rises by £1 billion, whilst government expenditure falls by £2 billion. By how much will national income change?
   (h) Given this new level of national income, assume that full employment is achieved at a national income of £100 billion. Is there an inflationary or a deflationary gap?
   (i) What is the size of this gap?

2. What is the relationship between the *mpc*, the mpc_d and the *mpw*?
3. Why will the short-run consumption function be different from the long-run consumption function?
4. Construct a table similar to Table 17.3 (on page 544), only this time assume that the mpc_d is $^3/_4$. Show that national income will increase by £640 million.
5. Assume that the multiplier has a value of 3. Now assume that the government decides to increase aggregate demand in an attempt to reduce unemployment. It raises government expenditure by £100 million with no increase in taxes. Firms, anticipating a rise in their sales, increase investment by £200 million, of which £50 million consists of purchases of foreign machinery. How much will national income rise? (Assume *ceteris paribus*.)
6. What factors could explain why some countries have a higher multiplier than others?
7. How can the interaction of the multiplier and the accelerator explain cyclical fluctuations in national income?
8. Why is it difficult to predict the size of the accelerator?
9. What is meant by 'consumption smoothing' and of what significance might it be for the relationship between spending and income?
10. How might uncertainty propagate the impact of shocks, such as the COVID-19 pandemic, on the macroeconomy?

Online resources

Additional case studies on the student website

17.1 How does consumption behave? The case looks at evidence on the relationship between consumption and disposable income from the 1950s to the current day.

17.2 Keynes' views on the consumption function. An analysis of how the assumptions made by Keynes affect the shape of the consumption function.

17.3 Consumption and saving in practice. An international comparison of consumption and saving rates over time.

17.4 The relationship between income and consumption. This examines three different theories of the consumption function – the absolute income hypothesis, the relative income hypothesis and the permanent income hypothesis. Each one is based on different assumptions about consumer behaviour.

17.5 Consumption smoothing and the diminishing marginal utility of consumption. This explains why people who experience a diminishing marginal utility of consumption or income will prefer to smooth their spending across time.

17.6 Buffer-stock saving. An analysis of buffer-stock saving as a form of self-insurance against unexpected events or income loss and its relationship with the diminishing marginal utility of income.

17.7 An international comparison of household wealth and indebtedness. An examination of households' financial assets and liabilities relative to disposable income in seven developed countries (the G7).

17.8 Business expectations and their effects on investment. An examination of business surveys in Europe and the effects of business sentiment on investment.

17.9 The multiplier/accelerator interaction. A numerical example showing how the interaction of the multiplier and accelerator can cause cycles in economic activity.

17.10 The corporate balance sheets. An overview of the balance sheets of the financial and non-financial sectors.

17.11 Trends in housing equity withdrawal (HEW). An analysis of the patterns in HEW and consumer spending.

(continued)

17.12 Heavenly cycles. An examination of the claim by Jevons in the late nineteenth century that the business cycle depends on the sunspot cycle!

17.13 The phases of the business cycle. A demand-side analysis of the factors contributing to each of the four phases.

Maths Case 17.1 Calculating the value of the multiplier. Examining the algebra.

Maths Case 17.2 Calculating the value of the multiplier. Using calculus.

Maths Case 17.3 Calculating the value of the multiplier with marginal propensities based on disposable income. Examining the algebra.

Websites relevant to this Chapters 16 and 17

Numbers and sections refer to websites listed in the Web Appendix and hotlinked from this book's website at **go.pearson.com/uk/sloman.**

- For news articles relevant to this and the previous chapter, see the *Economics News* section on the student website.
- For general news on national economies and the international economy, see websites in section A, and particularly A1–5, 7–9, 13, 20–26, 31, 33, 35, 36. See also links to newspapers worldwide in A38, 39, 42, 43 and 44, and the news search feature in Google at A41.
- For information on the development of ideas, see C12, 18.
- For data on economic growth, employment and the business cycle, see links in B1; also see B4 and 12. For UK data, see B3, 5 and 34. For EU data, see B38 and 47. For US data, see B15 and the *Data* section of B17. For international data, see B15, 21, 24, 31, 33, 35, 37, 40, 43 and 46.
- For a model of the economy (based on the Treasury model), see *The Virtual Chancellor* (site D1). The model allows you to devise your own Budget.
- For student resources relevant to this chapter, see sites C1–10, 19, 28.

Chapter 18

Banking, Money and Interest Rates

CHAPTER MAP

In this chapter and the next, we are going to look at the role that money and financial institutions play in an economy. The financial crisis that developed during the late 2000s demonstrated the importance of the financial system to modern-day economies. It is generally recognised that changes in the amount of money can have a powerful effect on all the major macroeconomic indicators, such as inflation, unemployment, economic growth, interest rates, exchange rates and the balance of payments. But the financial crisis did more than this: it demonstrated the systemic importance of financial institutions.

There continues to be a vibrant debate about how, if at all, we can avoid a repeat of the recent financial crisis. Governments and regulators worldwide are grappling with many very important questions. For instance, are some financial institutions simply *too big to fail*? How can we ensure that banks operate with adequate loss-absorbing capacity? Can we prevent financial institutions from contributing to excessive cycles in the credit extended to households and firms? Can we better align the incentives of banks with those of the wider community? These and other questions about financial institutions are considered here.

The chapter begins by defining what is meant by money and examining its functions. Then in sections 18.2 and 18.3 we look at the operation of the financial sector of the economy and its role in determining the supply of money. It is here where we consider the possible causes of the financial crisis, its impact on financial institutions themselves and some of the responses by central banks to the problems faced by financial institutions and, as a result, the economy.

In section 18.4 we turn to look at the demand for money. What we are asking is: how much of people's assets do they want to hold in the form of money? Finally, in section 18.5 we put supply and demand together to see how free-market interest rates – which have a crucial impact on aggregate demand – are determined.

18.1 THE MEANING AND FUNCTIONS OF MONEY

Before going any further, we must define precisely what we mean by 'money' – not as easy a task as it sounds. Money is more than just notes and coin. In fact the main component of a country's money supply is not cash, but deposits in banks and other financial institutions. Only a very small proportion of these deposits is kept by the banks in their safes or tills in the form of cash. The bulk of the deposits appear merely as bookkeeping entries in the banks' accounts.

This may sound very worrying. Will a bank have enough cash to meet its customers' demands? The answer in the vast majority of cases is yes. Only a small fraction of a bank's total deposits will be withdrawn at any one time, and banks always seek to ensure that they have the ability to meet their customers' demands. The chances of banks running out of cash are very low indeed. The only circumstance where this could become possible is if people lost confidence in a bank and started to withdraw money in what is known as a 'run on the bank'. This happened with the Northern Rock bank in 2008. But in these circumstances the central bank or government would intervene to protect people's deposits by making more cash available to the bank or, in the last resort, by nationalising the bank (as happened with Northern Rock).

What is more, the bulk of all but very small transactions are not conducted in cash at all. By the use of cheques, credit cards and debit cards, most money is simply transferred from the purchaser's to the seller's bank account without the need for first withdrawing it in cash.

What items should be included in the definition of money? To answer this we need to identify the functions of money.

The functions of money

The main purpose of money is for buying and selling goods, services and assets: i.e. as a 'medium of exchange'. It also has three other important functions. Let us examine each in turn.

A medium of exchange

In a subsistence economy, where individuals make their own clothes, grow their own food, provide their own entertainments, etc., people do not need money. If people want to exchange any goods, they will do so by barter. In other words, they will do swaps with other people.

The complexities of a modern developed economy, however, make barter totally impractical for most purposes (see Case Study 18.1 on the student website). What is necessary is a ***medium of exchange*** that is generally acceptable as a means of payment for goods and services and as a means of payment for labour and other factor services. 'Money' is any such medium.

To be a suitable physical means of exchange, money must be light enough to carry around, must come in a number of denominations, large and small, and must not be easy to forge (the attributes of money are explored in Case Study 18.2 on the student website). Alternatively, money must be in a form that enables it to be transferred indirectly through some acceptable mechanism. For example, money in the form of bookkeeping entries in bank accounts can be transferred from one account to another by the use of such mechanisms as debit cards and direct debits.

A means of storing wealth

People need a means whereby the fruits of today's labour can be used to purchase goods and services in the future. People need to be able to store their wealth: they want a means of

> **Definition**
>
> **Medium of exchange** Something that is acceptable in exchange for goods and service.

BOX 18.1 MONEY SUPPLY, NATIONAL INCOME AND NATIONAL WEALTH

EXPLORING ECONOMICS

Don't confuse the supply of money with the money value of national income. National income is a *flow* concept. It measures the value of the nation's output per year. Money supply, by contrast, is a *stock* concept. At any one point in time, there is a given amount of money in the economy.

But what if the money supply increases? Will the national income increase by that amount? No, because the extra money will usually be spent more than once per year on final goods and services. The rise in national income would thus be greater than the rise in money supply. On the other hand, some of the extra spending may simply result in higher prices. *Real* national income will rise by less than national income measured at current prices.

So if money supply is not the same as national *income,* is it the same as national *wealth?* After all, wealth is a stock concept. Again the answer is no. The nation's wealth consists of its *real* assets: land, buildings, capital equipment, works of art, etc. People may well hold part of their wealth in the form of money, it is true, but this is not wealth as far as the nation is concerned: if it were, the government could make us all wealthier by simply printing more money! Money represents wealth to the individual only to the extent that it represents a claim on *real* goods and services. It has nothing to do with national wealth.

saving. Money is one such medium in which to hold wealth. It can be saved.

A means of evaluation

Money allows the value of goods, services or assets to be compared. The value of goods is expressed in terms of prices, and prices are expressed in money terms. Money also allows dissimilar things, such as a person's wealth or a company's assets, to be added up. Similarly, a country's GDP is expressed in money terms. Money thus serves as a 'unit of account'.

Why may money prices give a poor indication of the value of goods and services?

A means of establishing the value of future claims and payments

People often want to agree today the price of some future payment. For example, workers and managers will want to agree the wage rate for the coming year. Firms will want to sign contracts with their suppliers specifying the price of raw materials and other supplies. Money prices are the most convenient means of measuring future claims.

What should count as money?

What items, then, should be included in the definition of money? Unfortunately, there is no sharp borderline between money and non-money.

Cash (notes and coin) obviously counts as money. It readily meets all the functions of money. Goods (fridges, cars and cabbages) do not count as money. But what about various financial assets, such as bank accounts, building society accounts and stocks and shares? Do they count as money? The answer is: it depends on how narrowly money is defined. The narrowest definition of money includes just cash (i.e. notes and coins). Broader definitions include various types of bank account, and broader definitions still include various financial assets as well. We examine the different definitions in the UK and the eurozone in Box 18.4.

In terms of the broad definition of money, would a deposit account passbook count as money?

In order to understand the significance of different measures of the money supply and the ways in which money supply can be controlled, it is first necessary to look at the various types of account in which money can be held and at the various financial institutions involved.

Section summary

1. Money's main function is as a medium of exchange. In addition, it is a means of storing wealth, a means of evaluation and a means of establishing the value of future claims and payments.
2. What counts as money depends on how narrowly it is defined. All definitions include cash, but they vary according to what other financial assets are included.

18.2 THE FINANCIAL SYSTEM

The role of the financial sector

Banks and other financial institutions are known as ***financial intermediaries***. They provide a link between those who wish to lend and those who wish to borrow. In other words, they act as the mechanism whereby the supply of funds is matched to the demand for funds. In this process, they provide five important services.

KI 24 p259

Expert advice

Financial intermediaries can advise their customers on financial matters: on the best way of investing their funds and on alternative ways of obtaining finance. This should help to encourage the flow of savings and the efficient use of them.

Expertise in channelling funds

Financial intermediaries have the specialist knowledge to be able to channel funds to those areas that yield the highest return. They also have the expertise to assess risks and to refuse loans for projects considered too risky or to charge a risk premium to others. This all encourages the flow of saving as it gives savers the confidence that their savings will earn a good rate of interest. Financial inter-mediaries also help to ensure that projects that are potentially profitable will be able to obtain finance. They help to increase allocative efficiency.

TC 11 p361

Definition

Financial intermediaries The general name for financial institutions (banks, building societies, etc.) which act as a means of channelling funds from depositors to borrowers.

Maturity transformation

Many people and firms want to borrow money for long periods of time, and yet many depositors want to be able to withdraw their deposits on demand or at short notice. If people had to rely on borrowing directly from other people, there would be a problem here: the lenders would not be prepared to lend for a long enough period. If you had £100 000 of savings, would you be prepared to lend it to a friend to buy a house if the friend were going to take 25 years to pay it back? Even if there was no risk whatsoever of your friend defaulting, most people would be totally unwilling to tie up their savings for so long.

This is where a bank or building society comes in. It borrows money from a vast number of small savers, who are able to withdraw their money on demand or at short notice. It then lends the money to house purchasers for a long period of time by granting mortgages, which are typically paid back over 20 to 30 years. This process whereby financial intermediaries lend for longer periods of time than they borrow is known as ***maturity transformation***. They are able to do this because with a large number of depositors it is highly unlikely that they would all want to withdraw their deposits at the same time. On any one day, although some people will be withdrawing money, others will be making new deposits.

This does not mean that maturity transformation is without risks for financial institutions. Maturity transformation implies a maturity mismatch between the liabilities and assets on institutions' balance sheets. This needs managing. Box 18.2 considers the potential risks of maturity transformation for financial institutions and the wider economy.

What dangers are there in maturity transformation for (a) financial institutions; (b) society generally?

Risk transformation

KI 11 p72

You may be unwilling to lend money directly to another person in case they do not pay up. You are unwilling to take the risk. Financial intermediaries, however, by lending to large numbers of people, are willing to risk the odd case of default. They can absorb the loss because of the interest they earn on all the other loans. This spreading of risks is known as ***risk transformation***. What is more, financial intermediaries may have the expertise to be able to assess just how risky a loan is.

Which of the above are examples of economies of scale?

Transmission of funds

In addition to channelling funds from depositors to borrowers, certain financial institutions have another important function. This is to provide a means of transmitting payments. Thus by the use of debit cards, credit cards, the Internet and telephone banking, cheques, direct debits, etc., money can be transferred from one person or institution to another without having to rely on cash.

The banking system

Types of bank

By far the largest element of money supply is bank deposits. It is not surprising, then, that banks play an absolutely crucial role in the monetary system. Banking can be divided into two main types: retail banking and wholesale banking. Most banks today conduct both types of business and are thus known as 'universal banks'.

Retail banking. ***Retail banking*** is the business conducted by the familiar high street banks, such as Barclays, Lloyds, HSBC, Royal Bank of Scotland, NatWest (part of the RBS group) and Santander. They operate bank accounts for individuals and businesses, attracting deposits and granting loans at published rates of interest.

Wholesale banking. The other major type of banking is ***wholesale banking***. This involves receiving large deposits from and making large loans to companies or other banks and financial institutions; these are known as ***wholesale deposits and loans***.

As far as companies are concerned, these may be for short periods of time to account for the non-matching of a firm's payments and receipts from its business, or they may be for longer periods of time, for various investment purposes. As these wholesale deposits and loans are very large sums of money, banks compete against each other for them and negotiate individual terms with the firm to suit the firm's particular requirements.

In the past, there were many independent wholesale banks, known as *investment banks*. These included famous names such as Morgan Stanley, Rothschild, S G Hambros and Goldman Sachs. With the worldwide financial crisis of the

Definitions

Maturity transformation The transformation of deposits into loans of a longer maturity.

Risk transformation The process whereby banks can spread the risks of lending by having a large number of borrowers.

Retail banking Branch, telephone, postal and Internet banking for individuals and businesses at published rates of interest and charges. Retail banking involves the operation of extensive branch networks.

Wholesale banking Where banks deal in large-scale deposits and loans, mainly with companies and other banks and financial institutions. Interest rates and charges may be negotiable.

Wholesale deposits and loans Large-scale deposits and loans made by and to firms at negotiated interest rates.

late 2000s, however, most of the independent investment banks merged with universal banks which conduct both retail and wholesale activities.

Functional separation of retail and wholesale banking. One particular concern of the rise of large universal banks is that the core activities of retail banks need isolating from risky wholesale banking activities. Otherwise there is the danger that losses from wholesale activities may impact on the retail division. One way of achieving this is through the ***functional separation*** of retail and wholesale banking, such as by enforcing a ringfence between the different divisions of a financial institution.

KI 11 p72

The ring-fencing of UK banking groups with more than £25 billion of core retail deposits became effective from January 2019. This followed the passing of the Financial Services (Banking Reform) Act in December 2013. Banks which are functionally separated from the rest of their groups are known as ring-fenced banks or RFBs.

Building societies

These UK institutions specialise in granting loans (mortgages) for house purchase. They compete for the savings of the general public through a network of high street branches. Unlike banks, they are not public limited companies, their 'shares' being the deposits made by their investors. In recent years, many of the building societies have converted to banks (including all the really large building societies except the Nationwide).

In the past, there was a clear distinction between banks and building societies. Today, however, they have become much more similar, with building societies now offering current account facilities and cash machines, and retail banks granting mortgages. As with the merging of retail and wholesale banks, this is all part of a trend away from the narrow specialisation of the past and towards the offering of a wider and wider range of services. This was helped by a process of ***financial deregulation***.

In fact, banks and building societies are both examples of what are called ***monetary financial institutions (MFIs)***. This term is used to describe all deposit-taking institutions, including central banks (e.g. the Bank of England).

MFIs also lend and borrow wholesale funds to and from each other, and deposit with and borrow from the central bank. Up to the financial crisis of 2008/9, there had been a marked growth in wholesale funding. In many countries, including the UK, this contributed to the growth in the size of banks' balance sheets. Wholesale funds can be distributed amongst banks by means of a series of financial instruments. These instruments are typically short term and acquired in markets known as ***money markets***.

During the financial crisis many forms of inter-bank lending virtually dried up in many countries. MFIs became increasingly fearful of other MFIs defaulting on loans. In response to the crisis, the Bank of England and other central banks, such as the Federal Reserve Bank in the USA, supplied extra money to MFIs to ensure the security of these institutions and the stability of the financial system. It did this by purchasing various assets from them with money it had, in effect, created (see Box 18.4).

Deposit taking and lending

Balance sheets

Banks and building societies provide a range of ***financial instruments***. These are financial claims, either by customers on the bank (e.g. deposits) or by the bank on its customers (e.g. loans). They are best understood by analysing the balance sheets of financial institutions, which itemise their liabilities and assets.

A financial institution's liabilities are those financial instruments involving a financial claim on the financial institution itself. As we shall see, these are largely ***deposits*** by customers, such as current and savings accounts. Its assets are financial instruments involving a financial claim on a third party: these are *loans,* such as personal and business loans and mortgages.

The total liabilities and assets for UK MFIs are set out in a balance sheet in Table 18.1. The aggregate size of the balance sheet in the first quarter of 2021 was roughly 4 times the UK's annual GDP. This is perhaps the simplest indicator of the significance of banks in modern economies, like the UK.

Both the *size* and *composition* of banks' balance sheets have become the focus of the international community's effort to ensure the stability of countries' financial systems. The growth of the aggregate balance sheet in the UK is considered in Box 18.2. But it is to the composition of the balance sheet that we now turn. To do this, we focus on banks' liabilities and assets.

Definitions

Functional separation (banking) The separation of investment and retailing banking designed to insulate core financial activities from other riskier activities.

Financial deregulation The removal of or reduction in legal rules and regulations governing the activities of financial institutions.

Monetary financial institutions (MFIs) Deposit-taking institutions including banks, building societies and the Bank of England.

Money market The market for short-term debt instruments, such as government bills (Treasury bills), in which financial institutions are active participants.

Financial instruments Financial products resulting in a financial claim by one party over another.

Table 18.1 Balance sheet of UK banks and building societies: February 2021

Sterling liabilities	£bn	%	Sterling assets	£bn	%
Sight deposits		51.8	Notes and coin	9.6	0.2
UK banks, etc.	92.3		Balances with B of E		18.1
UK public sector	21.6		Reserve balances	760.8	
UK private sector	1833.0		Cash ratio deposits	11.2	
Non-residents	210.1		Market loans		6.6
Time deposits		24.9	UK banks, etc.	188.0	
UK banks, etc.	212.5		UK banks' CDs, etc.	1.4	
UK public sector	11.4		Non-residents	93.0	
UK private sector	656.3		Bills of exchange	4.2	0.1
Non-residents	157.8		Reverse repos	406.7	9.6
Certificates of deposit & bonds	186.3	4.5	Investments	426.7	10.0
Repos	300.8	7.2	Advances	2271.9	53.4
Sterling capital & other funds	448.5	10.8	Items in suspense & collection	37.5	0.9
Other liabilities	31.3	0.8	Other assets	43.9	1.0
Total sterling liabilities	4161.9	100.0	**Total sterling assets**	4254.9	100.0
Liabilities in other currencies	4460.8		Assets in other currencies	4367.8	
Total liabilities	**8622.7**		**Total assets**	**8622.7**	

Source: Based on data in *Bankstats*, Table B1.4, Bank of England (29 March 2021), www.bankofengland.co.uk/statistics/tables

Liabilities

Customers' deposits in banks (and other deposit-taking institutions such as building societies) are ***liabilities*** to these institutions. This means simply that the customers have the claim on these deposits and thus the institutions are liable to meet the claims.

There are five major types of liability: sight deposits, time deposits, certificates of deposit (CDs), 'repos' and capital.

Sight deposits. ***Sight deposits*** are any deposits that can be withdrawn on demand by the depositor without penalty. In the past, sight accounts did not pay interest. Today, however, there are many sight accounts that do. In fact, there is quite aggressive competition nowadays between banks to offer apparently very attractive interest rates on such accounts, although these are often on balances up to a relatively small amount.

The most familiar form of sight deposits are current accounts at banks. Depositors are issued with chequebooks and/or debit cards (e.g. Visa debit or MasterCard's Maestro) that enable them to spend the money directly without first having to go to the bank and draw the money out in cash. In the case of debit cards, the person's account is electronically debited when the purchase is made. This process is known as EFTPOS (electronic funds transfer at point of sale). Money can also be transferred between individuals and businesses through direct debits, standing orders and Internet banking transfers.

An important feature of current accounts is that banks often allow customers to be overdrawn. That is, they can draw on their account and make payments to other people in excess of the amount of money they have deposited.

Time deposits. ***Time deposits*** require notice of withdrawal. However, they normally pay a higher rate of interest than sight accounts. With some types of account, a depositor can withdraw a certain amount of money on demand, but there will be a penalty of so many days' lost interest. They are not chequebook or debit-card accounts, although some allow customers to use cash cards. The most familiar form of time deposits are the deposit and savings accounts in banks and the various savings accounts in building societies. No overdraft facilities exist with time deposits.

A substantial proportion of time deposits are from the banking sector. Inter-bank lending grew over the years as money markets were deregulated and as deposits were moved from one currency to another to take advantage of different rates of interest between different countries. A large proportion of overseas deposits are from foreign banks.

Certificates of deposit. ***Certificates of deposit*** are certificates issued by banks to customers (usually firms) for large deposits of a fixed term (e.g. £100 000 for 18 months). They can be sold by one customer to another, and thus provide a means whereby the holders can get money quickly if they need it

Definitions

Liabilities All legal claims for payment that outsiders have on an institution.

Sight deposits Deposits that can be withdrawn on demand without penalty.

Time deposits Deposits that require notice of withdrawal or where a penalty is charged for withdrawals on demand.

Certificates of deposit (CDs) Certificates issued by banks for fixed-term interest-bearing deposits. They can be resold by the owner to another party.

without the banks that have issued the CDs having to supply the money. (This makes them relatively 'liquid' to the depositor but 'illiquid' to the bank: we examine this below.) The use of CDs has grown rapidly over the past two decades. Their use by firms has meant that, at a wholesale level, sight accounts have become less popular.

Sale and repurchase agreements (repos). If banks have a temporary shortage of funds, they can sell some of their financial assets to other banks or to the central bank – the Bank of England in the UK and the European Central Bank in the eurozone (see below) – and later repurchase them on some agreed date, typically a fortnight later. These ***sale and repurchase agreements (repos)*** are in effect a form of loan – the bank borrowing for a period of time using some of its financial assets as the security for the loan. One of the major assets to use in this way are government bonds (issued when the government borrows), normally called 'gilt-edged securities' or simply 'gilts' (see below). Sale and repurchase agreements involving gilts are known as gilt repos. Gilt repos play a vital role in the operation of monetary policy (see section 22.3).

Capital and other funds. This consists largely of the share capital in banks. Since shareholders cannot take their money out of banks (although they can sell them to other investors on the stock market), share capital provides a source of funding to meet sudden increases in withdrawals from depositors and to cover bad debts.

It is vital that banks have sufficient capital. As we shall see, an important part of the response to the financial crisis has been to require banks to hold relatively larger amounts of capital. In the first quarter of 2021, the aggregate amount of sterling capital held by banks based in the UK was equivalent to 11 per cent of their sterling liabilities.

Assets

A bank's financial ***assets*** are its claims on others. There are three main categories of assets.

Cash and reserve balances in the central bank (Bank of England in the UK, ECB in the eurozone). Banks need to hold a certain amount of their assets as cash. This is largely used to meet the day-to-day demands of customers. They also keep 'reserve balances' in the central bank. In the UK these earn interest at the Bank of England's repo rate (or 'Bank Rate' as it is called), These are like the banks' own current accounts and are used for clearing purposes (i.e. for settling the day-to-day payments between banks). They can be withdrawn in cash on demand. With inter-bank lending being seen as too risky during the crisis of the late 2000s, many banks resorted to depositing surplus cash in the Bank of England, even though Bank Rate was lower than inter-bank interest rates (see Box 18.3).

In the UK, banks and building societies are also required to deposit a small fraction of their assets as 'cash ratio deposits' with the Bank of England. These cannot be drawn on demand and earn no interest.

As you can see from Table 18.1, cash and balances in the Bank of England account for a very small proportion of banks' assets. The vast majority of banks' assets are in the form of various types of loan – to individuals and firms, to other financial institutions and to the government. These are 'assets' because they represent claims that the banks have on other people. Loans can be grouped into two types: short and long term.

Short-term loans. These are in the form of market loans, bills of exchange or reverse repos. The market for these various types of loan is known as the money market.

- ***Market loans*** are made primarily to other financial institutions. This inter-bank lending consists of (a) money lent 'at call' (i.e. reclaimable on demand or at 24 hours' notice); (b) money lent for periods up to one year, but typically a few weeks; (c) CDs (i.e. certificates of deposits made in other banks or building societies).
- ***Bills of exchange*** are loans either to companies (***commercial bills***) or to the government (***Treasury bills***). These are, in effect, an IOU, with the company issuing them (in the case of commercial bills), or the government (in the case of Treasury bills), promising to pay the holder a specified sum on a particular date (the 'maturity date'), typically three months later. Since bills do not pay interest, they are sold below their face value, i.e. at a 'discount', but redeemed on maturity at face value. This enables the purchaser, in this case the bank, to earn a return. The market for new or existing bills is therefore known as the ***discount market***.

The price paid for bills will depend on demand and supply. For example, the more Treasury bills that are offered for sale (i.e. the higher the supply), the lower will be their equilibrium price, and hence the higher will be their rate of return (i.e. their rate of interest, or 'rate of discount').

Definitions

Sale and repurchase agreements (repos) An agreement between two financial institutions whereby one in effect borrows from another by selling its assets, agreeing to buy them back (repurchase them) at a fixed price and on a fixed date.

Assets Possessions or claims on others.

Market loans Short-term loans (e.g. money at call and short notice).

Bills of exchange Certificates promising to repay a stated amount on a certain date, typically three months from the issue of the bill. Bills pay no interest as such, but are sold at a discount and redeemed at face value, thereby earning a rate of discount for the purchaser.

Commercial bills Bills of exchange issued by firms.

Treasury bills Bills of exchange issued by the Bank of England on behalf of the government. They are a means whereby the government raises short-term finance.

Discount market An example of a money market in which new or existing bills, such as Treasury bills or Commercial bills, are bought and sold at a discount below their face value: i.e. the value at which they will be redeemed on maturity.

BOX 18.2 THE GROWTH OF BANKS' BALANCE SHEETS

The rise of wholesale funding

Banks' traditional funding model relied heavily on deposits as the source of funds for loans. However, new ways for financial institutions to access funds to generate new loans evolved. These reflected the deregulation of financial markets and the rapid pace of financial innovation.

Seeds of the crisis

Increasingly, financial institutions made greater use of *wholesale funds*. These are funds from other financial institutions. This coincided with the growth in a process known as securitisation. This involves the conversion of non-marketable banks' assets, such as residential mortgages, which have regular income streams (e.g. from payments of interest and capital) into securities, which can be bought and sold on financial markets. These provide lenders who originate the loans with a source of funds for further loans. The growth of securitisation is discussed in more detail in Box 18.3.

KI 26 p309

With an increasing use of money markets by financial institutions, vast sums of funds became available for lending. One consequence of this, as illustrated in the chart, was an expansion of the aggregate balance sheet of banks. The balance sheet grew from £2.6 trillion ($2\frac{3}{4}$ times GDP) at the start of 1998 to £8.5 trillion ($5\frac{1}{2}$ times GDP) at the start of 2010.

The growth in banks' balance sheets was accompanied by a change in their composition. First, the profile of banks' assets became less liquid as they extended more long-term credit to households and firms. Assets generally became riskier too, as banks increasingly granted mortgages of 100 per cent or more of the value of houses – a problem for banks if house prices fell and they were forced to repossess.

Second, there was a general increase in the use of fixed-interest bonds as opposed to ordinary shares (equities) for raising capital. The ratio of bonds to shares is known as the ***gearing*** (or ***leverage***) ratio. The increase in leverage meant that, prior to the financial crisis, banks were operating with lower and lower levels of loss-absorbing capital, such as ordinary shares. If banks run at a loss, dividends on shares can be suspended; payments to bond holders cannot. This meant that as the crisis unfolded, policy makers were facing a liquidity problem, not among one or two financial institutions, but across the financial system generally.

The market failure we are describing is a form of ***co-ordination failure*** and is an example of the *fallacy of composition*. When one bank pursues increased earnings by borrowing from and lending to other financial institutions, this is not necessarily a problem. But, if many institutions expand their balance sheets by borrowing from and lending to *each other*, then it becomes a problem for the whole financial system. The apparent increase in liquidity for individual banks, on which they base credit, is not an overall increase in liquidity for the financial system as a whole. The effect is to create a credit bubble.

The dangers of the bubble for the financial system and beyond were magnified by the increasingly tangled web of interdependencies between financial institutions, both nationally and globally. There was a danger that this complexity was masking fundamental weaknesses of many financial institutions and too little overall liquidity.

Financial crisis

Things came to a head in 2007 and 2008. Once one or two financial institutions failed, such as Northern Rock in the UK in August 2007 and Lehman Brothers in the USA in September 2008, the worry was that failures would spread like a contagion. Banks could no longer rely on each other as their main source of liquidity.

The problems arising from the balance sheet expansion, increased leverage and a heightened level of maturity mismatch meant that central banks around the world, including the Bank of England, were faced with addressing a liquidity problem of huge proportions. They had to step in to supply central bank money to prevent a collapse of the banking system.

Subsequently, the Basel Committee on Banking Supervision (see pages 574–6) agreed a set of measures, to

Normally, a bank will buy commercial bills only if they have been first 'accepted' by another financial institution (typically an investment bank). This means that the investment bank will redeem the bill (i.e. pay up) on the maturity date, if the firm issuing the bill defaults on payment. Of course the investment bank charges for this insurance (or 'underwriting'). Bills that have been accepted in this way are known as ***bank bills***.

- ***Reverse repos***. When a sale and repurchase agreement is made, the financial institution purchasing the assets

Definitions

Gearing or leverage (US term) The ratio of debt capital to equity capital: in other words, the ratio of borrowed capital (e.g. bonds) to shares.

Co-ordination failure When a group of firms (e.g. banks) acting independently could have achieved a more desirable outcome if they had co-ordinated their decision making.

Bank bills Bills that have been accepted by another financial institution and hence insured against default.

Reverse repos Gilts or other assets that are purchased under a sale and repurchase agreement. They become an asset to the purchaser.

CASE STUDIES AND APPLICATIONS

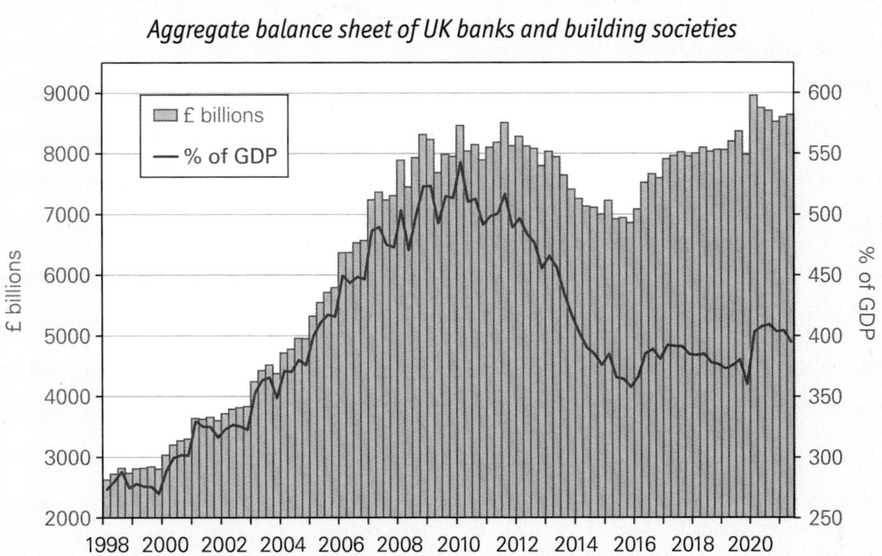

Note: Since 2010 all loans securitised by MFIs are recorded on MFI balance sheets.
Sources: (i) Data showing liabilities of banks and building societies based on series LPMALOA and RPMTBJF (up to the end of 2009) and RPMB3UQ (from 2010) from *Statistical Interactive Database*, Bank of England (data published 29 July 2021, not seasonally adjusted), www.bankofengland.co.uk/boeapps/iadb/
(ii) GDP data from *Quarterly National Accounts* series YBHA, Office for National Statistics (GDP figures are the sum of the latest four quarters), www.ons.gov.uk/economy/grossdomesticproductgdp/timeseries/ybha/qna

be applied globally, designed to ensure the greater financial resilience of banks and banking systems. The chart shows that during the 2010s there was a decline in the size of the aggregate balance sheet of banks resident in the UK from around $5\frac{1}{2}$ times to $3\frac{1}{2}$ times GDP.

1. ***What are the potential costs and benefits for financial institutions, lenders and borrowers and for the wider economy arising from maturity transformation?***

2. ***Are these dangers an inherent and unavoidable consequence of maturity transformation?***

Using the Bank of England Statistical Interactive Database (www.bankofengland.co.uk/boeapps/iadb/NewInterMed.asp?Travel=), download monthly data on MFI total sterling assets (RPMB3XP). Construct a bar chart showing the series across time. Briefly summarise your findings.

(e.g. gilts) is, in effect, giving a short-term loan. The other party agrees to buy back the assets (i.e. pay back the loan) on a set date. The assets temporarily held by the bank making the loan are known as 'reverse repos'. Reverse repos are typically for one week, but can be for as little as overnight or as long as one year.

Longer-term loans. These consist primarily of loans to customers, both personal customers and businesses. These loans, also known as advances, are of four main types: fixed-term (repayable in instalments over a set number of years – typically, six months to five years), overdrafts (often for an unspecified term), outstanding balances on credit card accounts, and mortgages (typically for 25 years).

Banks also make investments. These are partly in government bonds (gilts), which are effectively loans to the government. The government sells bonds, which then pay a fixed sum each year as interest. Once issued, they can then be bought and sold on the stock exchange. Banks are normally only prepared to buy bonds that have less than five years to maturity (the date when the government redeems the bonds). Banks also invest in various subsidiary financial institutions and in building societies.

Taxing the banks

Bank levy. In January 2011, the UK introduced the bank levy: a tax on the *liabilities* of banks and building societies operating in the UK. For banking groups with their headquarters in the UK the levy initially applied to their global balance sheet; for subsidiaries of non-UK banks it applies just to their UK activities. The tax was founded on two key principles. First, the revenues raised should be able to meet the full fiscal costs of any future support for financial institutions. Second, it should provide banks with incentives to reduce risk-taking behaviour and so reduce the likelihood of future financial crises.

The UK bank levy has two rates: a full rate on taxable liabilities with a maturity of less than one year and a half rate on taxable liabilities with a maturity of more than one year. This differential is intended to discourage excessive short-term borrowing by the banks in their use of wholesale funding.

Not all liabilities are subject to the levy. First, it is not imposed on the first £20 billion of liabilities. This is to encourage small banks (note that the largest UK banks, such as HSBC, Barclays and RBS, each have liabilities of over £2 trillion). Second, various liabilities are excluded. These are: (a) gilt repos; (b) retail deposits insured by public schemes such as the UK's Financial Services Compensation Scheme, which guarantees customers' deposits of up to £85 000; (c) a large part of a bank's capital known as Tier 1 capital (see below) – the argument here is that it is important for banks to maintain sufficient funds to meet the demands of its depositors.

Banks are also able to offset against their taxable liabilities holdings of highly liquid assets, such as Treasury bills and cash reserves at the Bank of England. These exclusions and deductions are designed to encourage banks to engage in less risky lending.

The levy rates were initially set at 0.075 and 0.0375 per cent with the intention that the levy raise at least £2.5 billion each year. As the aggregate balance sheets of banks began to shrink, the rates were increased several times. Then in the 2015 Budget it was announced that the levy rates, which at time were 0.21 and 0.105 per cent, were to be gradually reduced until in 2021 they would be 0.1 and 0.05 per cent. From 2021, with concerns about the effect of the levy on the international competitiveness of UK-headquartered banks, the levy was to apply only to the UK liabilities of UK banks, as was already the case with non-UK banks.

Bank corporation tax surcharge. The 2015 Budget also saw the announcement of a new 8 per cent corporation tax surcharge on banks. This marked a shift in the tax base from banks' balance sheets to their profits. The 8 per cent bank surcharge was introduced in January 2016 for all banks with annual profits over £25 million. When the main corporation tax rate fell from 20 to 19 per cent in April 2017, the surcharge on banks meant that their effective corporation tax rate was 27 per cent. However, with the announcement in March 2021 that the main corporation tax rate would rise to 25 per cent, the government announced a review of the surcharge. Again the concern was that UK-headquartered banks were being put at a disadvantage. Changes were to be announced later in 2021.

Receipts from the bank levy peaked in 2015/16 at £3.4 billion before easing to £1.9 billion by 2020/21. However, this fall was largely offset by the introduction of the bank surcharge which in 2020/21 raised £1.1 billion.

Liquidity, profitability and capital adequacy

As we have seen, banks keep a range of liabilities and assets. The balance of items in this range is influenced by three important considerations: profitability, liquidity and capital adequacy.

Profitability

Profits are made by lending money out at a higher rate of interest than that paid to depositors. The average interest rate received by banks on their assets is greater than that paid by them on their liabilities.

Liquidity

The ***liquidity*** of an asset is the ease with which it can be converted into cash without loss. Cash itself, by definition, is perfectly liquid.

Some assets, such as money lent at call to other financial institutions, are highly liquid. Although not actually cash, these assets can be converted into cash virtually on demand with no financial penalty. Other short-term inter-bank lending is also very liquid (at least to individual banks: see Box 18.2). The only issue here is one of confidence that the money will actually be repaid. This was a worry in the financial crisis of 2008/9 when many banks stopped lending to each other on the inter-bank market for fear that the borrowing bank might become insolvent.

Other assets, such as gilts, can be converted into cash straight away by selling them on the Stock Exchange, but with the possibility of some financial loss, given that their market price fluctuates. Such assets, therefore, are not as liquid as money at call.

Other assets are much less liquid. Personal loans to the general public or mortgages for house purchase can be redeemed by the bank only as each instalment is paid. Other advances for fixed periods are repaid only at the end of that period.

Banks must always be able to meet the demands of their customers for withdrawals of money. To do this, they must hold sufficient cash or other assets that can be readily turned into cash. In other words, banks must maintain sufficient liquidity.

Definition

Liquidity The ease with which an asset can be converted into cash without loss.

1. *If a bank buys a £500 000 Treasury bill at the start of its 91-day life for £480 000, at roughly what price could it sell it to another financial institution after 45 days? Why is it not possible to predict the precise price when the bill is first purchased?*
2. *Suppose there were a sudden surge in demand for cash from the general public. Would the existence of inter-bank market loans help to meet the demand in any way?*

The balance between profitability and liquidity

Profitability is the major aim of banks and most other financial institutions. However, the aims of profitability and liquidity tend to conflict. In general, the more liquid an asset, the less profitable it is, and vice versa. Personal and business loans to customers are profitable to banks, but highly illiquid. Cash is totally liquid, but earns no profit. Thus financial institutions like to hold a range of assets with varying degrees of liquidity and profitability.

For reasons of profitability, the banks will want to 'borrow short' (at low rates of interest, as are generally paid on current accounts) and 'lend long' (at higher rates of interest, as are normal on personal loans). The difference in the average maturity of loans and deposits is known as the ***maturity gap***. In general terms, the larger the maturity gap between loans and deposits, the greater the profitability. For reasons of liquidity, however, banks will want a relatively small gap: if there is a sudden withdrawal of deposits, banks will need to be able to call in enough loans.

The ratio of an institution's liquid assets to total assets is known as its ***liquidity ratio***. For example, if a bank had £100 million of assets, of which £10 million were liquid and £90 million were illiquid, the bank would have a 10 per cent liquidity ratio. If a financial institution's liquidity ratio is too high, it will make too little profit. If the ratio is too low, there will be the risk that customers' demands may not be able to be met: this would cause a crisis of confidence and possible closure. Institutions thus have to make a judgement as to what liquidity ratio is best – one that is neither too high nor too low.

Balances in the central bank, short-term loans (i.e. those listed above) and government bonds with less than 12 months to maturity would normally be regarded as liquid assets.

Why are government bonds that still have 11 months to run regarded as liquid, whereas overdrafts granted for a few weeks are not?

KI 11 p72

As Box 18.2 explains, over the years, banks had reduced their liquidity ratios (i.e. the ratio of liquid assets to total assets). This was not a problem as long as banks could always finance lending to customers by borrowing on the inter-bank market. In the late 2000s, however, banks became increasingly worried about bad debt. They thus felt the need to increase their liquidity ratios and hence cut back on lending and chose to keep a higher proportion of deposits in liquid form. In the UK, for example, banks substantially increased their reserve accounts at the Bank of England.

Secondary marketing and securitisation

As we have seen, one way of reconciling the two conflicting aims of liquidity and profitability is for financial institutions to hold a mixture of liquid and illiquid assets. Another way is through the ***secondary marketing*** of assets. This is where holders of assets sell them to someone else before the maturity date. This allows banks to close the maturity gap for liquidity purposes, but maintain the gap for profitability purposes.

Certificates of deposit (CDs) are a good example of secondary marketing. CDs are issued for fixed-period deposits in a bank (e.g. one year) at an agreed interest rate. The bank does not have to repay the deposit until the year is up. CDs are thus illiquid liabilities for the bank, and they allow it to increase the proportion of illiquid assets without having a dangerously high maturity gap. But the holder of the CD in the meantime can sell it to someone else (through a broker). It is thus liquid to the holder. Because CDs are liquid to the holder, they can be issued at a relatively low rate of interest and thus allow the bank to increase its profitability.

Another example of secondary marketing is when a financial institution sells some of its assets to another financial institution. The advantage to the first institution is that it gains liquidity. The advantage to the second one is that it gains profitable assets. The most common method for the sale of assets has been through a process known as ***securitisation***.

Securitisation occurs when a financial institution pools some of its assets, such as residential mortgages, and sells them to an intermediary known as a ***special purpose vehicle (SPV)***. SPVs are legal entities created by the financial institution. In turn, the SPV funds its purchase of the assets by

Definitions

Maturity gap The difference in the average maturity of loans and deposits.

Liquidity ratio The proportion of a bank's total assets held in liquid form.

Secondary marketing Where assets are sold before maturity to another institution or individual. The possibility of secondary marketing encourages people or institutions to buy assets/grant loans in the primary market, knowing that they can sell them if necessary in the secondary market. The sale of existing shares and bonds on the stock market is an example of secondary marketing.

Securitisation Where future cash flows (e.g. from interest rate or mortgage payments) are turned into marketable securities, such as bonds. The sellers (e.g. banks) get cash immediately rather than having to wait and can use it to fund loans to customers. The buyers make a profit by buying below the discounted value of the future income. Such bonds can be very risky, however, as the future cash flows may be less than anticipated.

Special purpose vehicle (SPV) Legal entity created by financial institutions for conducting specific financial functions, such as bundling assets together into fixed-interest bonds and selling them.

BOX 18.3 THE RISE OF SECURITISATION

Spreading the risk or securing a crisis?

The conflict between profitability and liquidity may have sown the seeds for the credit crunch that affected economies across the globe in the second half of the 2000s.

To understand this, consider the size of the 'advances' item in the banking sector's balance sheet – just over half of the value of sterling assets (see Table 18.1). The vast majority of these are to households. Advances secured against property have, in recent times, accounted for around 80 per cent by value of all household advances. Residential mortgages involve institutions lending long.

Securitisation of debt

One way in which individual institutions can achieve the necessary liquidity to expand the size of their mortgage lending (illiquid assets) is through *securitisation*. Securitisation grew especially rapidly in the UK and USA. In the UK this was particularly true amongst banks; building societies have historically made greater use of retail deposits to fund advances.

Securitisation is a form of financial engineering. It provides banks (originator-lenders) with liquidity and enables them to engage in further lending opportunities. It provides the special purpose vehicles with the opportunity to issue profitable securities.

In the period up to 2010 most securitisations in the UK saw the original loans moving off the balance sheet of MFIs and onto the balance sheet of the special purpose vehicle (SPV) issuing the collateralised debt obligations (CDOs). From 2010, however, all securitisations are detailed on the balance sheets of MFIs, including previous securitisations which, as a result, have been brought back on to the balance sheets of MFIs.

The chart shows the rapid growth in the flows of securitised secured loans from an estimated £8 billion in 2000 to over £100 billion by 2008. This increase in securitisation reflects the strong demand amongst investors for CDOs. The attraction of these fixed-income products for the noteholders was the potential for higher returns than on (what were) similarly rated products. However, investors have no recourse should people with mortgages fall into arrears or, worse still, default on their mortgages.

Risk and the sub-prime market

The securitisation of assets is not without risks for all those in the securitisation chain and consequently for the financial system as a whole.

The pooling of advances in itself *reduces* the cash-flow risk facing investors. However, there is a ***moral hazard*** problem here (see pages 138–9). The pooling of the risks may encourage originator-lenders to lower their credit criteria by offering higher income multiples (advances relative to annual household incomes) or higher loan-to-value ratios (advances relative to the price of housing).

Towards the end of 2006, the USA witnessed an increase in the number of defaults by households on residential mortgages. This was a particular problem in the sub-prime market – higher-risk households with poor credit ratings. Similarly, the number falling behind with their payments rose. This was on the back of rising interest rates.

These problems in the US sub-prime market were the catalyst for the liquidity problem that beset financial systems in 2007 and 2008. Where these assets were securitised, investors, largely other financial institutions, suffered from the contagion arising from arrears and defaults.

Securitisation also spread the contagion across the world. Investors are global, so that advances, such as an American family's residential mortgage, supporting CDOs are effectively travelling across national borders. This resulted in institutions having to write off debts, a deterioration of their balance sheets, the collapse in the demand for securitised assets and the drying up of liquidity.

issuing bonds to investors (noteholders). These bonds are known as ***collateralised debt obligations*** (CDOs). The sellers (e.g. banks) get cash now rather than having to wait and can use it to fund loans to customers. The buyers make a profit if the income yielded by the CDOs are as expected. Such bonds can be very risky, however, as the future cash flows may be *less* than anticipated.

The securitisation chain is illustrated in Figure 18.1. The financial institution looking to sell its assets is referred to as the 'originator' or the 'originator-lender'. Working from left to right, we see that the originator-lender sells its assets to another financial institution, the SPV, which then bundles assets together into CDOs and sells them to investors (e.g. banks or pension funds) as bonds. Now working from right to left, we see that by purchasing the bonds issued by the SPV, the investors provide the funds for the SPV's purchase of the lender's assets. The SPV is then able to use the proceeds from the bond sales (CDO proceeds) to provide the originator-lender with liquidity.

Definitions

Moral hazard The temptation to take more risks when you know that someone else will cover the risks if you get into difficulties. In the case of banks taking risks, the 'someone else' may be another bank, the central bank or the government.

Collateralised debt obligations (CDOs) These are a type of security consisting of a bundle of fixed-income assets, such as corporate bonds, mortgage debt and credit card debt.

CASE STUDIES AND APPLICATIONS

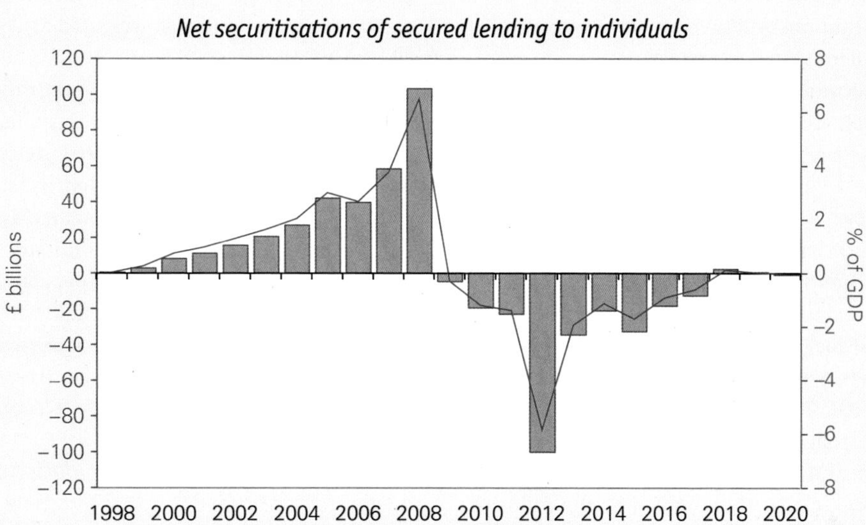

Note: Data up to 2010 relate to changes in other specialist lenders' sterling net securitisations of secured lending to individuals and housing associations. From 2010 data relate to changes in resident MFI sterling securitised loans secured on dwellings to individuals.
Sources: Based on data from *Statistical Interactive Database*, Bank of England series LPMVUJD (up to 2010) and LPMB8G0 (data published 29 March 2021), www.bankofengland.co.uk/boeapps/iadb/; and series YBHA, National Statistics, www.ons.gov.uk/economy/grossdomesticproductgdp/timeseries/ybha/

The chart shows that during the 2010s, banks resident in the UK were *buying back* CDOs from SPVs (negative net securitisations). A similar pattern was observed in many countries. This, therefore, contributed to an easing in the growth of the aggregate balance sheet of banks (see Box 18.2).

Does securitisation necessarily involve a moral hazard problem?

Using the Bank of England Statistical Interactive Database (www.bankofengland.co.uk/boeapps/iadb/), download monthly data on the stocks of securitised loans secured on dwellings (LPMB7GT) and of other securitised loans (LPMB7GU). Construct a stacked column chart showing the size and composition of the securitised debt stock of MFIs resident in the UK.

The effect of secondary marketing is to reduce the liquidity ratio that banks feel they need to keep. It has the effect of increasing their maturity gap.

Dangers of secondary marketing. There are dangers to the banking system, however, from secondary marketing. To the extent that banks individually feel that they can operate with a lower liquidity ratio, so this will lead to a lower national liquidity ratio. This may lead to an excessive expansion of credit (illiquid assets) in times of economic boom.

KI 11 p72

Also, there is an increased danger of banking collapse. If one bank fails, this will have a knock-on effect on those banks which have purchased its assets. In the specific case of securitisation, the strength of the chain is potentially

Figure 18.1 Securitisation chain

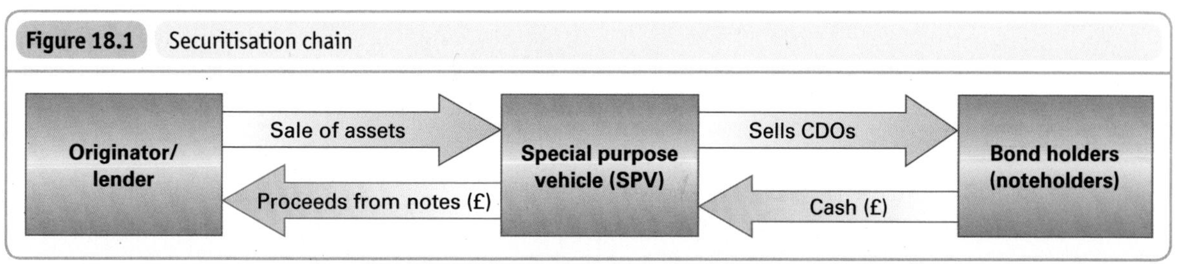

weakened if individual financial institutions move into riskier market segments, such as ***sub-prime*** residential mortgage markets. Should the income streams of the originator's assets dry up – for instance, if individuals default on their loans – then the impact is felt by the whole of the chain. In other words, institutions and investors are exposed to the risks of the originator's lending strategy.

The issue of securitisation and its impact on the liquidity of the financial system during the 2000s is considered in Box 18.3.

KI 11 p72

Capital adequacy

In addition to sufficient liquidity, banks must have sufficient capital (i.e. funds) to allow them to meet all demands from depositors and to cover losses if borrowers default on payment. Capital adequacy is a measure of a bank's capital relative to its assets, where the assets are weighted according to the degree of risk. The riskier the assets, the greater the amount of capital that will be required.

A measure of capital adequacy is given by the ***capital adequacy ratio (CAR)***. This is given by the following formula:

$$\text{CAR} = \frac{\text{Common Equity Tier 1 capital} + \text{Additional Tier 1 capital} + \text{Tier 2 capital}}{\text{Risk-weighted assets}}$$

Common equity Tier 1 capital includes bank reserves (from retained profits) and ordinary share capital (equities), where dividends to shareholders vary with the amount of profit the bank makes. Such capital thus places no burden on banks in times of losses as no dividend need be paid. What is more, unlike depositors, shareholders cannot ask for their money back.

Additional Tier 1 (AT1) capital consists largely of preference shares. These pay a fixed dividend (like company bonds). But although preference shareholders have a prior claim over ordinary shareholders on company profits, dividends need not be paid in times of loss.

Tier 2 capital is 'subordinated debt' with a maturity greater than five years. Subordinated debt holders only have a claim on a failing company after the claims of all other bondholders have been met.

Risk-weighted assets are the value of assets, where each type of asset is multiplied by a risk factor. Under the internationally agreed Basel II accord, cash and government bonds have a risk factor of zero and are thus not included. Inter-bank lending between the major banks has a risk factor of 0.2 and is thus included at only 20 per cent of its value; residential mortgages have a risk factor of 0.35; personal loans, credit card debt and overdrafts have a risk factor of 1; loans to companies carry a risk factor of 0.2, 0.5, 1 or 1.5, depending on the credit rating of the company. Thus the greater the average risk factor of a bank's assets, the greater will be the value of its risk-weighted assets, and the lower will be its CAR.

The greater the CAR, the greater the capital adequacy of a bank. Under Basel II, banks were required to have a CAR of at least 8 per cent (i.e. 0.08). They were also required to meet two supplementary CARs. First, banks needed to hold a ratio of Tier 1 capital to risk-weighted assets of at least 4 per cent and, second, a ratio of ordinary share capital to risk-weighted assets of at least 2 per cent. It was felt that these three ratios would provide banks with sufficient capital to meet the demands from depositors and to cover losses if borrowers defaulted. The financial crisis, however, meant a rethink.

Strengthening international regulation of capital adequacy and liquidity

Capital adequacy. In the light of the financial crisis of 2008/9, international capital adequacy requirements were strengthened by the *Basel Committee on Banking Supervision*, with a final agreement in December 2017. The 'Basel III' capital requirements, as they are called, were to be phased in with the 'new' minimum capital adequacy ratios to apply from 2019. They are summarised in Figure 18.2.

From 2013 banks continued to need a CAR of at least 8 per cent (i.e. 0.08), but, by 2015 were required to operate with a ratio of CET1 to risk-weighted assets of at least 4.5 per cent. From 2016 began a phased introduction of a *capital conservation buffer* raising the CET1 ratio to no less than 7 per cent from 2019. This increases the overall CAR to at least 10.5 per cent. If a bank breaches the capital conservation buffer, then automatic limitations to dividend and bonus payments apply.

Definitions

Sub-prime debt Debt where there is a high risk of default by the borrower (e.g. mortgage holders who are on low incomes facing higher interest rates and falling house prices).

Capital adequacy ratio (CAR) The ratio of a bank's capital (reserves and shares) to its risk-weighted assets.

Figure 18.2 Basel III minimum capital requirements

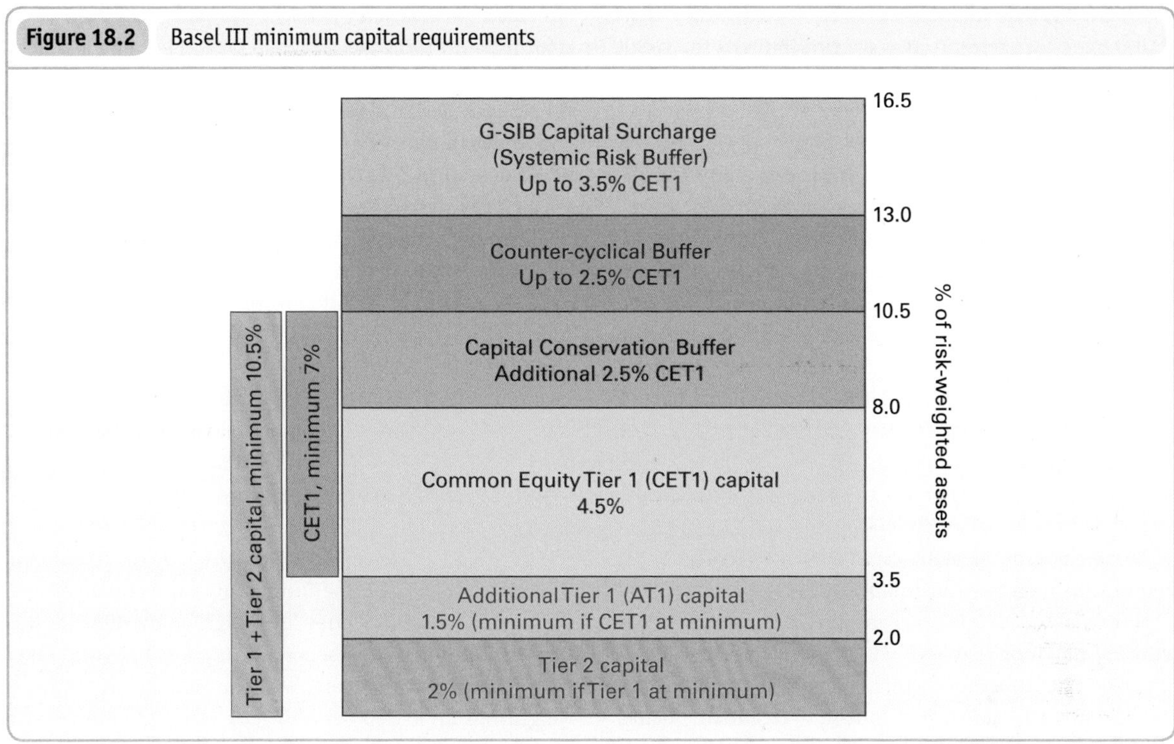

On top of this, national regulators are required to assess the financial resilience across all financial institutions under its jurisdiction, particularly in light of economic conditions. This is ***macro-prudential regulation***. If necessary, regulators will then apply a *counter-cyclical buffer* (CCyB) to all banks, so increasing the CET1 ratio by up to a further 2.5 per cent. This will allow financial institutions to build up a capital buffer in boom times to allow it to be drawn on in times of recession or financial difficulty. It should also help to reduce the likelihood of financial institutions destabilising the economy by amplifying the business cycle through the generation of pro-cyclical credit cycles (see section 19.4).

In the UK it is the Bank of England's Financial Policy Committee (FPC), which monitors the systemic risks to financial stability, that determines the level of the counter-cyclical buffer. In March 2020, the FPC reduced the CCyB from 1 per cent to zero. The hope was that, by reducing the buffer, banks could use their additional funds to lend to households and business. Therefore banks could help to absorb rather than amplify the shock.

KI 24 p259

Large global banks, known as ***global systemically important banks*** (G-SIBs), will be required to operate with a CET1 ratio of up to 3.5 per cent higher than other banks. The global and systemic importance of these institutions is scored against a series of indicators which determine the magnitude of their additional capital requirements. These indicators include their size and the extent of cross-border activity. The reason for this extra capital requirement, known as a *G-SIB systemic risk buffer*, is that the failure of such an institution could trigger a global financial crisis. This means that the overall CAR for very large financial institutions can be as high as 16.5 per cent (see Figure 18.2).

What are the economic arguments for larger 'systemically important banks' (SIBs) having an additional capital requirement?

In the UK it was decided that individual ring-fenced banks (RFBs), as well as large building societies which hold more than £25 billion in deposits, would be required to hold an additional capital buffer in excess of the Basel III requirements. These financial institutions have been identified as domestic systemically important banks (and building societies) (D-SIBs). Hence, this buffer is also referred as the *D-SIB systemic risk buffer*.

Definitions

Macro-prudential regulation Regulation which focuses not on a single financial institution but on the financial system as a whole and which monitors its impact on the wider economy.

Global systemically important banks (SIBs) Banks identified by a series of indicators as being significant players in the global financial system.

UK bank groups identified as G-SIBs containing a ring-fenced bank are subject to two systemic buffers: the G-SIB systemic risk buffer at the group level and the D-SIB systemic risk buffer at the level of the ring-fenced bank.

The UK's domestic systemic risk buffer depends on the size of risk-weighted assets, with the initial plan for additional capital requirement of up to 3 per cent of these assets. However, depending on the judgement of the Financial Policy Committee, the asset bands and the systemic risk buffer rates applied can be reviewed and adjusted if necessary.

To supplement the risk-based capital requirements, the Basel III framework introduced from 2018 a *non-risk-based leverage ratio*. Described by regulators as a complementary to the risk-based framework, this requires financial institutions to operate with a Tier 1 capital-to-asset ratio of 3 per cent. In contrast to the risk-based ratios, the assets in the denominator in this ratio are *not* weighted by risk factors.

To conclude: the Basel III's capital adequacy requirements significantly increased the capital cushions of many banks.

Nonetheless, discussions continued around the calculation of risk-weighted assets. Because of the complexity of banks' asset structures, which tend to vary significantly from country to country, it is difficult to ensure that banks are meeting the Basel III requirements. It was therefore proposed that banks would have to compare their own calculations with a 'standardised' model. Their own calculations of risk-based assets would then not be allowed to fall below a set percentage, known as 'the output floor', of the standardised approach.

The argument then centred on how high the output floor should be set. Too low and it could undermine confidence in the toughness of the regulatory framework; too high and it could penalise countries where defaults are rare. For example, Germany argued that mortgage defaults have been rare and thus German mortgage debt should be given a lower weighting than US mortgage debt, where defaults have been more common. If all assets were assessed according to the output floor, several banks, especially in Europe, would be judged to be undercapitalised.

In December 2017 the Basel Committee finally agreed that the output floor for the risk weighting of assets would be set at 72.5 per cent, meaning that individual countries could not set the risk of an asset, such as a mortgage, at less than 72.5 per cent of the level set by international regulators in their standardised models. This will, however, be phased in, with an output floor of 50 per cent from 2023, increasing each year until reaching 72.5 per cent in 2028.

Liquidity. The financial crisis highlighted the need for banks not only to hold adequate levels of capital but also to manage their liquidity better. The Basel III framework includes a *liquidity coverage ratio* (LCR). This requires that financial institutions have high-quality liquid assets (HQLAs) to cover the expected net cash flow over the next 30 days. From 2019, the minimum LCR ratio (HQLAs relative to the expected 30-day net cash flow) became 100 per cent.

Net stable funding ratio (NSFR). As part of the Basel III reforms, a *net stable funding ratio* (NSFR) became a regulatory standard from 2018. This takes a longer-term view of the funding profile of banks by focusing on the reliability of liabilities as a source of funds, particularly in circumstances of extreme stress. The NSFR is the ratio of stable liabilities to assets likely to require funding (i.e. assets where there is a likelihood of default).

On the liabilities side, these are weighted by their expected reliability – in other words, by the stability of these funds. This weighting reflects the maturity of the liabilities and the propensity of lenders to withdraw their funds. For example, Tier 1 and 2 capital have a weighting of 100 per cent; term deposits with less than one year to maturity have a weighting of 50 per cent; and unsecured wholesale funding has a weighting of 0 per cent. The result of these weightings is a measure of *stable funding.*

On the assets side, these are weighted by the likelihood that they will have to be funded over the course of one year. This means that they are weighted by their liquidity, with more liquid assets requiring less funding. Thus cash has a zero weighting, while more risky assets have weightings up to 100 per cent. The result is a measure of *required funding.*

Banks will need to hold a stable liabilities-to-required-funding ratio (NSFR) of at least 100 per cent.

The central bank

The Bank of England is the UK's ***central bank***. The European Central Bank (ECB) is the central bank for the countries using the euro. The Federal Reserve Bank of America (the Fed) is the USA's central bank. All countries with their own currency have a central bank. They fulfil two vital roles in the economy.

The first is to oversee the whole monetary system and ensure that banks and other financial institutions operate as stably and as efficiently as possible.

The second is to act as the government's agent, both as its banker and in carrying out monetary policy.

The Bank of England traditionally worked in very close liaison with the Treasury, and there used to be regular meetings between the Governor of the Bank of England and the Chancellor of the Exchequer. Although the Bank may have disagreed with Treasury policy, it always carried it out. In 1997, however, the Bank of England was given independence to decide the course of monetary policy. In particular,

Definition

Central bank Banker to the banks and the government. It oversees the banking system, implements monetary policy and issues currency.

this meant that the Bank of England and not the government would now decide interest rates.

Another example of an independent central bank is the European Central Bank (ECB), which operates the monetary policy for the eurozone countries. Similarly, the Fed is independent of both the President and Congress, and its chair is generally regarded as having great power in determining the country's economic policy. Although the degree of independence of central banks from government varies considerably around the world, there has been a general move in recent years to make central banks more independent.

Within their two broad roles, central banks typically have a number of different functions. Although we will consider the case of the Bank of England, the same principles apply to other central banks, such as the ECB and the Fed.

It issues notes

The Bank of England is the sole issuer of banknotes in England and Wales. (In Scotland and Northern Ireland, retail banks issue notes.) The issue of notes is done through the Issue Department, which organises their printing. This is one of two departments of the Bank of England. The other is the Banking Department, through which it deals with banks.

Table 18.2 shows the consolidated balance sheet across the two departments of the Bank of England for the end of March 2020. As we shall discuss shortly, the balance sheet of the Bank of England was to expand markedly following the financial crisis. This was the case for many central banks across the world.

On the balance sheet we see the outstanding value of the banknote issue (notes in circulation). The amount of banknotes issued by the Bank of England depends largely on the demand for notes from the general public. If people draw more cash from their bank accounts, the banks will have to draw more cash from their balances in the Bank of England. These balances are held in the Banking Department. The Banking Department will thus have to acquire more notes from the Issue Department, which will simply print more in exchange for extra government or other securities supplied by the Banking Department.

It acts as a bank

To the government. It keeps the two major government accounts: the 'Exchequer' and the 'National Loans Fund'. Taxation and government spending pass through the Exchequer. Government borrowing and lending pass through the National Loans Fund. The government tends to keep its deposits in the Bank of England (the public deposits item in the balance sheet) to a minimum. If the deposits begin to build up (from taxation), the government will probably spend them on paying back government debt. If, on the other hand, it runs short of money, it will simply borrow more.

To banks. Banks' deposits in the Bank of England consist of reserve balances and cash ratio deposits (see Table 18.2). The reserve balances are used for clearing purposes between the banks but are also a means by which banks can manage their liquidity risk. Therefore, the reserve balances provide banks with an important buffer stock of liquid assets.

To overseas central banks. These are deposits of sterling (or euros in the case of the ECB) made by overseas authorities as part of their official reserves and/or for purposes of intervening in the foreign exchange market in order to influence the exchange rate of their currency.

It operates the government's monetary policy

The Bank of England's Monetary Policy Committee (MPC) sets Bank Rate at its regular meetings. This nine-member committee consists of four experts appointed by the Chancellor of the Exchequer and four senior members of the Bank of England, plus the Governor in the chair.

By careful management of the liquidity of the financial system the Bank of England aims to keep interest rates in

Table 18.2 Consolidated balance sheet of the Bank of England: 31 March 2020

Liabilities	£bn	%	Assets	£bn	%
Notes in circulation	74.9	11.4	Ways and means advance to National Loans Fund	0.4	0.1
Reserves balances	507.5	77.4	Short-term open market operations	0.0	0.0
Short-term open market operations	0.0	0.0	Long-term open market operations	32.9	5.0
Cash ratio deposits	8.8	1.3	Sterling denominated bond holdings	13.6	2.1
Other sterling liabilities	17.5	2.7	Loans to Asset Purchase Facility	454.0	69.2
Capital and reserves (equity)	4.7	0.7	Loans to COVID Corporate Finance Facility	1.9	0.3
Foreign currency public securities issued	3.3	0.5	Term Funding Scheme loan	107.2	16.3
Other foreign currency liabilities	39.2	6.0	Other sterling assets	0.8	0.1
			Foreign currency reserve assets	5.8	0.9
			Other foreign currency assets	39.3	6.0
Total	**655.9**	**100.0**	**Total**	**655.9**	**100.0**

Note: The Bank of England publishes its balance sheet with a five-quarter delay. Hence the end-March 2020 figures in this table were first made available in July 2021.
Source: *Bankstats* Table B1.1.3, Bank of England (7 July 2021), www.bankofengland.co.uk/statistics/tables

line with the level decided by the MPC. It is able to do this through operations in the money markets. These are known as ***open-market operations (OMOs)***. If shortages of liquidity are driving up short-term interest rates above the desired level, the Bank of England purchases securities (gilts and/or Treasury bills) on the open market: e.g. through reverse repos (a repo to the banks). This releases liquidity into the financial system and puts downward pressure on interest rates. Conversely, if excess liquidity is driving down interest rates, the Bank of England will sell more securities. When these are purchased, this will reduce banks' reserves and thereby put upward pressure on interest rates.

In normal times the Bank of England manages the aggregate amount of reserves through weekly auctions of 1-week repos. It also agrees with commercial banks an *average* amount of overnight reserve balances they would hold over the period between MPC meetings. Individual banks are then able to deposit or borrow reserves using the Bank of England's ***operational standing facilities.*** Banks deposit reserves at the deposit facility rate if they have an excess of reserves or borrow reserves from the Bank of England if they are short of reserves through overnight repo operations priced at the lending facility rate. The deposit rate is set below the Bank Rate, while the borrowing rate is set above the Bank Rate. This process is known as ***reserve averaging***.

The operational standing facilities are designed to provide banks with excess or surplus reserves an incentive to trade them with other banks. Banks would prefer to borrow reserves at a lower interest rate or deposit reserves at a higher interest rate than they can through the operational standing facilities. By managing the aggregate amount of reserves, agreeing an average overnight holding of reserves and providing operational standing facilities, the Bank of England aims to establish a 'corridor' for inter-bank rates between its lending and deposit rates.

From its inception in March 2006 up until the middle of 2007 the corridor system kept short-term money market rates close to Bank Rate. But then, with growing concerns about the solvency of banks, the inter-bank market ceased to operate effectively, and banks were forced to make greater use of the more costly operational standing facilities and draw reserves from the Bank. In other words, banks could no longer trade reserves with each other (in order to meet their average reserve target) at a lower cost than by using the Bank's standing facilities.

As the financial crisis unfolded it became increasingly difficult for the Bank to meet its monetary policy objectives while maintaining financial stability. New policies were thus adopted. October 2008 also saw the Bank of England stop short-term open-market operations. The key priority was now ensuring sufficient liquidity and so the focus switched to longer-term OMOs.

The advent of quantitative easing. March 2009 saw the Bank begin its programme of ***quantitative easing (QE)*** (see Box 22.7). The aim is to increase the amount of money in the financial system and thereby stimulate bank lending and hence aggregate demand. QE involves the Bank creating electronic money and using it to purchase assets, mainly government bonds, predominantly from non-deposit-taking financial institutions, such as unit trusts, insurance companies and pension funds. These institutions then deposit the money in banks, which can lend it to businesses and consumers for purposes of spending.

Given this large quantity of 'new money' being supplied to the banking system it was decided to end the practice of banks voluntarily setting their own reserve targets between meetings of the MPC. Instead, *all* reserves were now to be remunerated at the official Bank Rate. The effect of remunerating all reserves was to replace the 'corridor system' with a 'floor system' since no commercial bank would be willing to lend surplus reserves at any rate lower than the Bank Rate (see Box 22.5). Therefore, the inter-bank rate would not fall below the Bank Rate.

The Bank of England's programme of asset purchases are conducted by a subsidiary of the Bank of England, known as the Asset Purchase Facility (APF). We can see the effect of these asset purchases in the Bank of England's balance sheet in Table 18.2: by far the largest item on the assets side is 'Loans to Asset Purchase Facility'. Another way of seeing their effect is through the increase in the Bank of England's sterling reserves balances (see Figure 18.3). These are the monies held by commercial banks in their accounts with the central bank, either for purposes of settling accounts with other commercial banks or for managing their liquidity.

The Bank argues that, in normal times, the reserves averaging framework remains an effective framework for implementing monetary policy. But with further quantitative easing undertaken in response to the COVID-19 pandemic, its reintroduction was to be further delayed.

Definitions

Open-market operations (OMOs) The sale (or purchase) by the authorities of government securities in the open market in order to reduce (or increase) money supply and thereby affect interest rates.

Operational standing facilities Central bank facilities by which individual banks can deposit reserves or borrow reserves.

Reserve averaging The process whereby individual banks manage their average level of overnight reserves between MPC meetings using the Bank of England's operational standing facilities and/or the inter-bank market.

Quantitative easing (QE) A deliberate attempt by the central bank to increase the money supply by buying large quantities of securities through open-market operations. These securities could be securitised mortgage and other private-sector debt or government bonds.

Figure 18.3 Bank of England sterling reserves balances

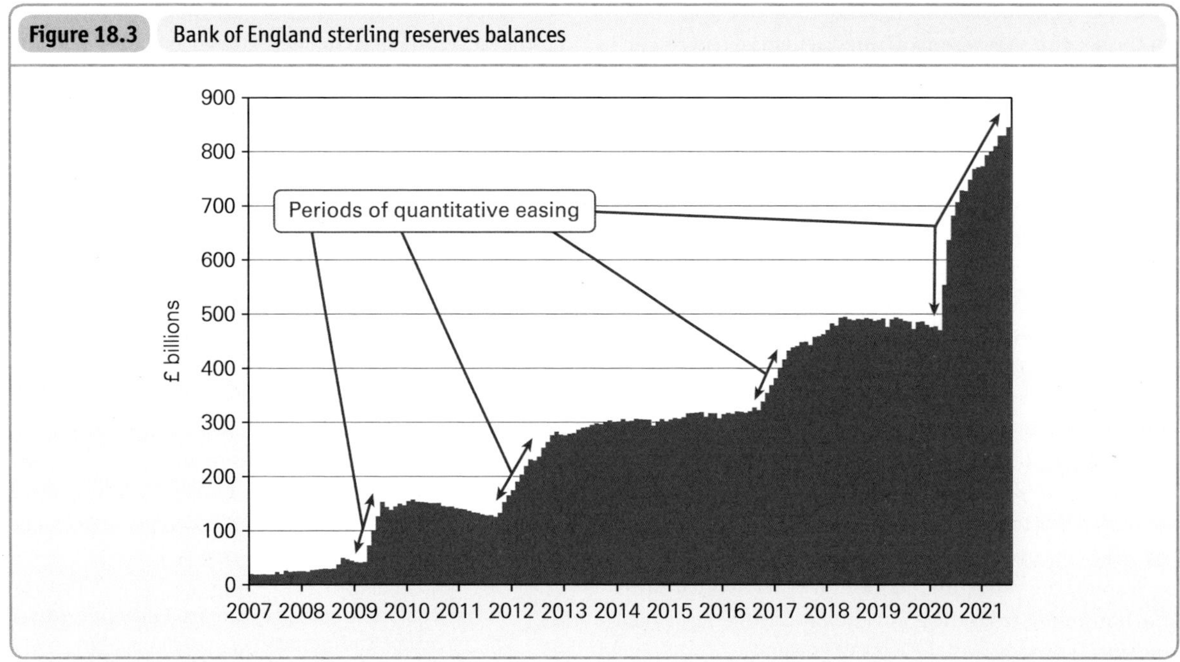

Source: Based on data from *Statistical Interactive Database*, series LPMBL22, Bank of England (9 April 2021), www.bankofengland.co.uk/boeapps/iadb/

It provides liquidity, as necessary, to banks

Financial institutions engage in maturity transformation. While most customer deposits can be withdrawn instantly, financial institutions will have a variety of lending commitments, some of which span many years. Hence, the Bank of England acts as a 'liquidity backstop' for the banking system. It attempts to ensure that there is always an adequate supply of liquidity to meet the legitimate demands of depositors in banks.

Banks' reserve balances provide them with some liquidity insurance. However, the Bank of England needs other means by which to provide both individual banks and the banking system with sufficient liquidity. The financial crisis, for instance, saw incredible pressure on the aggregate liquidity of financial system. The result is that the UK currently has three principal insurance facilities:

Index long-term repos (ILTRS). These are the basis of the Bank's regular liquidity operations, whereby it provides MFIs with reserves for a six-month period secured against collateral and indexed against the Bank Rate. Financial institutions can borrow reserves against different levels of collateral. These levels reflect the quality and liquidity of the collateral. The reserves are distributed through an auction where financial institutions indicate, for their particular level of collateral, the number of basis points over the Bank Rate (the 'spread') they are prepared to pay. Successful bidders pay a uniform price: this is the clearing price at which the Bank of England's preparedness to lend reserves has been met. The Bank of England will provide a greater quantity of reserves if, from the bids, it observes a greater demand for it to provide liquidity insurance.

Discount window facility (DWF). This on-demand facility allows financial institutions to borrow government bonds (gilts) for 30 days against different classes of collateral. They pay a fee to do so. The size of the fee is determined by both the level of collateral and the size of the collateral being traded. Gilts are long-term government debt instruments used by government as a means of financing its borrowing. Gilts can be used in repo operations as a means of securing liquidity. In this way, financial institutions are performing a liquidity upgrade of their collateral. However, the Bank may agree to lend cash rather than gilts if gilt repo markets cease to provide the necessary amount of liquidity, perhaps because the cost of doing so becomes prohibitively high. Financial institutions can look to roll over the funds obtained from the DWF beyond the normal 30 days.

Contingent term repo facility (CTRP). This is a facility which the Bank of England can activate in exceptional circumstances, such as it did in March 2020 in response to the disruption to financial markets resulting from the COVID-19 pandemic. As with the ILTRS, financial institutions can obtain liquidity secured against different levels of collateral through an auction. However, the terms, including the maturity of the funds, are intended to be more flexible.

It oversees the activities of banks and other financial institutions

The Bank of England requires all recognised banks to maintain adequate liquidity: this is called ***prudential control***.

Definition

Prudential control The insistence by the Bank of England that recognised banks maintain adequate liquidity.

In May 1997, the Bank of England ceased to be responsible for the detailed supervision of banks' activities. This responsibility passed to the Financial Services Authority (FSA). But the financial crisis of the late 2000s raised concerns about whether the FSA, the Bank of England and HM Treasury where sufficiently watchful of banks' liquidity and the risks of liquidity shortage. Some commentators argued that a much tighter form of prudential control needed to be imposed.

In 2013, a new regulatory framework came into force, with an enhanced role for the Bank of England.

First, the Bank's *Financial Policy Committee* became responsible for ***macro-prudential regulation***. This type of regulation takes a broader view of the financial system. It considers, for instance, its health or resilience to possible shocks and its propensity to create macroeconomic instability through credit creation. As we saw earlier, it sets the countercyclical buffer (CCyB) and can, should it wish, review and adjust the operation of the domestic systemic risk buffer.

Second, the prudential regulation of individual firms was transferred from the FSA to the *Prudential Regulation Authority*, a subsidiary of the Bank of England.

Third, the *Financial Conduct Authority (FCA)* took responsibility for consumer protection and the regulation of markets for financial services. The FCA is an independent body accountable to HM Treasury. The FSA was wound up.

1. ***Would it be possible for an economy to function without a central bank?***
2. ***What effect would a substantial increase in the sale of government bonds and Treasury bills have on interest rates?***

It operates the government's exchange rate policy

The Bank of England manages the country's gold and foreign currency reserves on behalf of the Treasury. This is done through the ***exchange equalisation account***. The Treasury sets the Bank an annual remit for the management of the account (for example, setting a limit on changes in the level of reserves).

By buying and selling foreign currencies on the foreign exchange market, the Bank of England can affect the exchange rate. For example, if there were a sudden selling of sterling (due, say, to bad trade figures and a resulting fear that the pound would depreciate), the Bank of England could help to prevent the pound from falling by using reserves to buy up pounds on the foreign exchange market. Intervention in the foreign exchange market is examined in detail in Chapter 25.

The money markets

We now turn to the money markets where participants, including financial institutions, are able to lend and borrow to and from each other. In these markets debts typically have maturities of less than one year.

It has been traditional to distinguish money markets from another set of financial markets known as ***capital markets***. In capital markets borrowing typically takes place over a longer duration. Capital markets include the market for ordinary shares and longer-term government debt instruments, known in the UK as gilts, which pay periodic fixed payments (known as 'coupons'). However, as we shall see, the boundaries in practice between these markets are rather difficult to pinpoint.

Central banks are also important participants in money markets. It is through the money markets that a central bank exercises control over interest rates. As we have seen throughout this chapter, the financial system has evolved rapidly and the money markets are no exception. This has widened the lending and borrowing opportunities for financial institutions.

We take the case of the London money market, which is normally divided into the 'discount' and 'repo' markets and the 'parallel' or 'complementary' markets.

How might the development of new financial instruments affect a central bank's conduct of monetary policy?

The discount and repo markets

The discount market. The discount market is the market for commercial or government bills. In the UK, government bills are known as Treasury bills and operations are conducted by the Debt Management Office, usually on a weekly basis. Treasury Bills involve short-term lending, say for one or three months, which, in conjunction with their low default risk, make them highly liquid assets.

These markets are examples of ***discount markets*** because the instruments being traded are issued at a discount. In other words, the redemption price of the bills is greater than the issue price. The redemption price is fixed, but the issue price depends on demand and supply in the discount market. The rate of discount on bills can be calculated by the size of the discount relative to the redemption value and is usually expressed as an annual rate.

Definitions

Macro-prudential regulation Regulation that focuses on the overall stability of the financial system and its resilience to shocks.

Exchange equalisation account The gold and foreign exchange reserves account in the Bank of England.

Capital market A financial market where longer-term debt instruments, like government bonds (gilts), can be bought and sold.

Discount market The market for corporate bills and Treasury bills whose initial price is below the redemption value.

The discount market is also known as the 'traditional market' because it was the market in which many central banks traditionally used to supply central bank money to financial institutions. For instance, if the Bank of England wanted to increase liquidity in the banking system it could purchase from the banks Treasury bills which had yet to reach maturity. This process is known as ***rediscounting***. The Bank of England would pay a price below the face value, thus effectively charging interest to the banks. The price could be set so that the 'rediscount rate' reflected the Bank Rate.

The repo market The emergence of the repo market is a more recent development dating back in the UK to the 1990s. As we saw earlier, repos have become an important source of wholesale funding for financial institutions. But they have also become an important means by which central banks can affect the liquidity of the financial system both to implement monetary policy and to ensure financial stability.

By entering into a repo agreement the Bank of England can buy securities, such as gilts, from the banks (thereby supplying them with money) on the condition that the banks buy them back at a fixed price and on a fixed date. The repurchase price will be above the sale price. The difference is the equivalent of the interest that the banks are being charged for having what amounts to a loan from the Bank of England. The repurchase price (and hence the 'repo rate') is set by the Bank of England to reflect the Bank Rate chosen by the MPC.

The Bank of England first began using repo operations to manage the liquidity of the financial system in 1997 when it undertook daily operations, with the repurchases of securities usually occurring two weeks after the initial sale. This system was refined so that in 2006 operations became weekly and the repurchase period typically shortened to one week.

However, the financial crisis caused the Bank to modify its repo operations to manage liquidity both for purposes of monetary policy and to ensure financial stability. These changes included a widening of the securities eligible as collateral for loans, a move to longer-term repo operations and a suspension of short-term repo operations.

So central banks, like the Bank of England, are prepared to provide central bank money through the creation of bank reserves. Central banks are thus the ultimate guarantor of sufficient liquidity in the monetary system and, for this reason, are known as the ***lender of last resort***.

The parallel money markets

Like repo markets, complementary or parallel money markets have grown rapidly in recent years. In part, this reflects the opening up of markets to international dealing, the deregulation of banking and money market dealing and the desire of banks to keep funds in a form that can be readily switched from one form of deposit to another, or from one currency to another.

Examples of parallel markets include the markets for *certificates of deposit* (CDs), *foreign currencies markets* (dealings in foreign currencies deposited short term in the country) and *the inter-bank market*.

The inter-bank market. The inter-bank market involves wholesale loans from one bank to another over periods from one day to up to several months. Banks with surplus liquidity lend to other banks, which then use this as the basis for loans to individuals and companies.

In the UK, the inter-bank rate has traditionally been measured by the LIBOR (the London inter-bank offered rate), varying by the length of loan. (In the eurozone the inter-bank rate is known as the Euribor, with the weighted average of all overnight rates known as Eonia). However, in 2012 there were allegations of false reporting by financial institutions of LIBOR rates. Because LIBOR was a reference rate for other financial products, this had potentially serious implications for the interest rates being charged.

From April 2016 the Bank of England took over the administration of an alternative inter-bank benchmark rate. Known as SONIA, the Sterling Overnight Index Average is the rate of interest paid on sterling unsecured loans for one business day. SONIA has become the new benchmark determining commercial interest rates. Figure 18.4 shows how closely SONIA typically tracks the Bank Rate. The exception was during the financial crisis of the late 2000s when financial markets were in turmoil and the Bank of England loosened monetary policy aggressively.

Why should Bank of England determination of the rate of interest in the discount and repo markets also influence rates of interest in the parallel markets?

Definitions

Rediscounting bills of exchange Buying bills before they reach maturity.

Lender of last resort The role of the Bank of England as the guarantor of sufficient liquidity in the monetary system.

Figure 18.4 SONIA and Bank Rate (monthly averages)

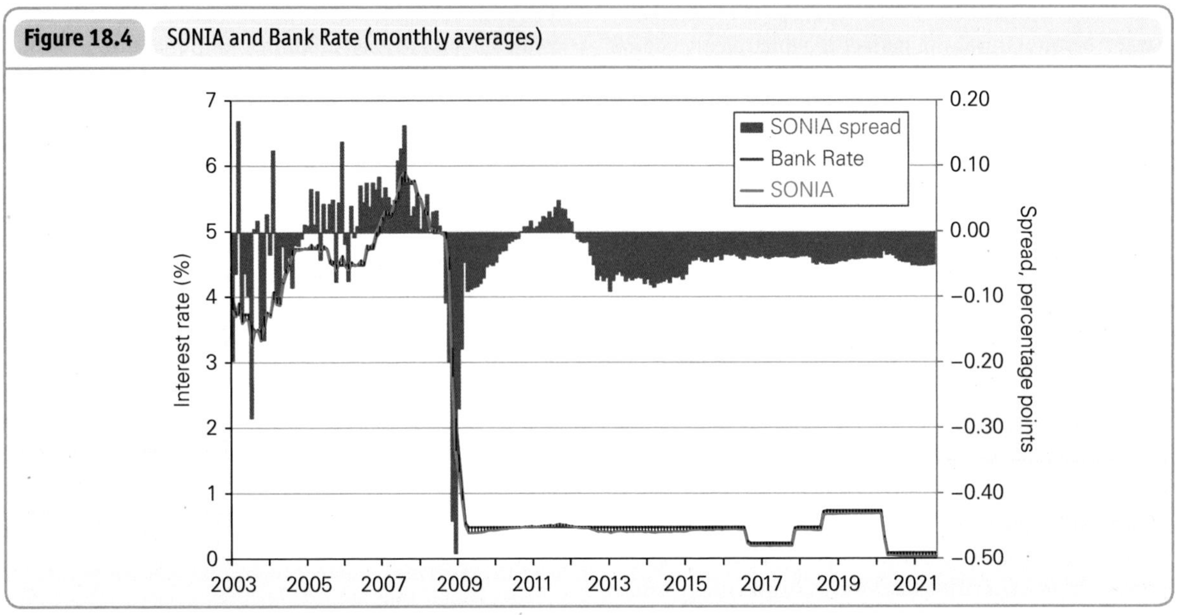

Note: The Sterling Overnight Index Average reflects the average interest rate that banks pay to borrow sterling overnight from other financial institutions
Source: Based on data from *Statistical Interactive Database*, series IUMABEDR and IUMASOIA, Bank of England (9 April 2021), www.bankofengland.co.uk/boeapps/iadb/

Section summary

1. Central to the financial system are the retail and wholesale arms of banks. Between them they provide the following important functions: giving expert advice, channelling capital to areas of highest return, maturity transformation, risk transformation and the transmission of payments. During the financial crisis the systemic importance of some of these banks meant they had to be rescued by governments. They were seen as too important or too big to fail (TBF).
2. Banks' liabilities include both sight and time deposits. They also include certificates of deposit and repos. Their assets include: notes and coin, balances with the Bank of England, market loans, bills of exchange (Treasury bills and commercial bills), reverse repos, advances to customers (the biggest item – including overdrafts, personal loans, credit card debt and mortgages) and investments (government bonds and inter-bank investments). In the years up to 2008 they had increasingly included securitised assets.
3. Banks aim to make profits, but they must also have a sufficient capital base and maintain sufficient liquidity. Liquid assets, however, tend to be relatively unprofitable and profitable assets tend to be relatively illiquid. Banks therefore need to keep a balance of profitability and liquidity in their range of assets.
4. The Bank of England is the UK's central bank. It issues notes; it acts as banker to the government, to banks and to various overseas central banks; it ensures sufficient liquidity for the financial sector; it operates the country's monetary and exchange rate policy.
5. The money market is the market in short-term deposits and loans. It consists of the discount and repo markets and the parallel money markets.
6. Through repos the Bank of England can provide liquidity to the banks at the rate of interest chosen by the Monetary Policy Committee (Bank Rate). It is always prepared to lend in this way in order to ensure adequate liquidity in the economy. The financial crisis saw the Bank adapt its operations in the money market and introduce new mechanisms for providing liquidity insurance, including the Discount Window Facility and longer-term repos.
7. The parallel money markets consist of various markets in short-term finance between various financial institutions.

18.3 THE SUPPLY OF MONEY

Definitions of the money supply

If money supply is to be monitored and possibly controlled, it is obviously necessary to measure it. But what should be included in the measure? Here we need to distinguish between the monetary base and broad money.

The ***monetary base*** (or 'high-powered money') consists of cash (notes and coin) in circulation outside the central bank. Thus, in the eurozone, the monetary base is given by cash (euros) in circulation outside the ECB.[1] In 1970, the stock of notes and coins in circulation in the UK was around £4 billion, equivalent to 7 per cent of annual GDP. By 2021 this had grown to around £95 billion, but equivalent to just 4 per cent of annual GDP.

But the monetary base gives us a very poor indication of the effective money supply, since it excludes the most important source of liquidity for spending: namely, bank deposits. The problem is which deposits to include. We need to answer three questions:

- Should we include just sight deposits, or time deposits as well?
- Should we include just retail deposits, or wholesale deposits as well?
- Should we include just bank deposits, or building society (savings institution) deposits as well?

In the past there has been a whole range of measures, each including different combinations of these accounts. However, financial deregulation, the abolition of foreign exchange controls and the development of computer technology have led to huge changes in the financial sector throughout the world. This has led to a blurring of the distinctions between different types of account. It has also made it very easy to switch deposits from one type of account to another. For these reasons, the most usual measure that countries use for money supply is ***broad money***, which in most cases includes both time and sight deposits, retail and wholesale deposits, and bank and building society (savings institution) deposits.

In the UK, this measure of broad money is known as M4. In most other European countries and the USA it is known as M3. There are, however, minor differences between countries in what is included. (Official UK and eurozone measures of money supply are given in Box 18.4.)

In 1970, the stock of M4 in the UK was around £25 billion, equivalent to 48 per cent of annual GDP. By 2021 this had grown to around £3 trillion, equivalent to about 130 per cent of annual GDP.

As we have seen, bank deposits of one form or another constitute by far the largest component of (broad) money supply. To understand how money supply expands and contracts, and how it can be controlled, it is thus necessary to understand what determines the size of bank deposits. Banks can themselves expand the amount of bank deposits, and hence the money supply, by a process known as 'credit creation'.

The creation of credit: the simplest case

To illustrate this process in its simplest form, assume that banks have just one type of liability – deposits – and two types of asset – balances with the central bank (to achieve liquidity) and advances to customers (to earn profit).

Banks want to achieve profitability while maintaining sufficient liquidity. Assume that they believe that sufficient liquidity will be achieved if 10 per cent of their assets are held as balances with the central bank. The remaining 90 per cent will then be in advances to customers. In other words, the banks operate a 10 per cent liquidity ratio.

Assume initially that the combined balance sheet of the banks is as shown in Table 18.3. Total deposits are £100 billion, of which £10 billion (10 per cent) are kept in balances with the central bank. The remaining £90 billion (90 per cent) are lent to customers.

Now assume that the government spends more money – £10 billion, say, on roads or hospitals. It pays for this with cheques drawn on its account with the central bank. The people receiving the cheques deposit them in their banks. Banks return these cheques to the central bank and their balances correspondingly increase by £10 billion. The combined banks' balance sheet now is shown in Table 18.4.

Table 18.3 Banks' original balance sheet

Liabilities	£bn	Assets	£bn
Deposits	100	Balances with the central bank	10
		Advances	90
Total	100	Total	100

Definitions

Monetary base Notes and coin outside the central bank.

Broad money Cash in circulation plus retail and wholesale bank and building society deposits.

1 Before 2006, there used to be a measure of narrow money called 'M0' in the UK. This included cash in circulation outside the Bank of England and banks' non-interest-bearing 'operational balances' in the Bank of England, with these balances accounting for a tiny proportion of the whole. Since 2006, the Bank of England has allowed banks to hold interest-bearing reserve accounts, which are much larger than the former operational balances. The Bank of England thus decided to discontinue M0 as a measure and focus on cash in circulation as its measure of the monetary base.

BOX 18.4 **UK AND EUROZONE MONETARY AGGREGATES** CASE STUDIES AND APPLICATIONS

How long is a piece of string?

UK measures

There are two main measures of the money supply in the UK: cash in circulation (i.e. outside the Bank of England) and M4. Cash in circulation is referred to as the 'monetary base' or 'narrow money' and M4 is referred to as 'broad money' or simply as 'the money supply'. In addition, there is a measure called 'Retail deposits and cash in M4' (previously known as M2). This measure excludes wholesale deposits.

The definitions are as follows:

- *Cash in circulation.* This is all cash held outside the Bank of England: in other words by individuals, firms, banks and the public sector.
- *Retail deposits and cash in M4.* Cash in circulation with the public (but not cash in banks and building societies) + private-sector *retail* sterling deposits in banks and building societies.
- *M4.* Retail deposits and cash in M4 + private-sector wholesale sterling deposits (including repos) in banks and building societies + private-sector holdings of sterling certificates of deposit, commercial paper and other short-term paper issued by MFIs.

Table (a) gives the figures for these aggregates at the end of February 2021.

(a) *UK monetary aggregates, end February 2021 (not seasonally adjusted)*

		£ billion
	Cash in circulation (i.e. outside the Bank of England)[a]	91.85
−	Cash in banks and cash held outside the UK[a, b]	−15.94
+	Private-sector retail bank and building society deposits	2021.43
=	**Retail deposits and cash in M4**	**2097.34**
+	Private-sector wholesale bank and building society deposits + CDs	746.84
=	**M4**	**2844.18**

[a] Cash in circulation is calculated mid-month and thus the figure slightly understates the end-month value.
[b] Row 4 minus rows 3 and 1.
Source: Based on data in *Bankstats*, Tables A1.1.1 and A2.2.1, Bank of England (29 March 2021), www.bankofengland.co.uk/statistics/tables

Why is cash in banks and building societies not included in M4?

Eurozone measures

Although the ECB uses three measures of the money supply, they are different from those used by the Bank of England. The narrowest definition (M1) includes overnight deposits (i.e. call money) as well as cash, and is thus much broader than the UK's narrow money measure. The broadest eurozone measure (M3) is again broader than the UK's broadest measure (M4), since the eurozone measure includes various other moderately liquid assets. The definitions of the three eurozone aggregates are:

- *M1.* Cash in circulation with the public + overnight deposits.
- *M2.* M1 + deposits with agreed maturity up to two years + deposits redeemable up to three months' notice.
- *M3.* M2 + repos + money-market funds and paper + debt securities with residual maturity up to two years.

Table (b) gives the figures for UK money supply for each of these three ECB measures – again at the end of February 2021.

(b) *UK money supply using ECB measures: end February 2021 (not seasonally adjusted)*

		£ billion
	Currency in circulation	85.61
+	Overnight deposits	2106.37
=	**M1**	**2191.98**
+	Deposits with agreed maturity up to 2 years	140.34
+	Deposits redeemable up to 3 months' notice	480.52
=	**M2**	**2812.84**
+	Repos	323.67
+	Money market funds and paper	131.53
=	**M3**	**3268.04**

Note: M1, M2 and M3 estimates relate to non-MFI residents, excluding central government and contain deposits in all currencies.
Source: Based on data in *Bankstats*, Table A2.3, Bank of England (29 March 2021), www.bankofengland.co.uk/statistics/tables

What are the benefits of including these additional items in the broad measure of money supply?

Using the Bank of England Statistical Interactive Database, download series LPMVQUU and LPMVQJW. Then construct a time-series chart showing the annual growth rates of notes and coins (cash in circulation) and of M4 (broad money) since 2000. Briefly summarise the main findings from your chart.

But this is not the end of the story. Banks now have surplus liquidity. With their balances in the central bank having increased to £20 billion, they now have a liquidity ratio of 20/110, or 18.2 per cent. If they are to return to a 10 per cent liquidity ratio, they need only retain £11 billion as balances at the central bank. The remaining £9 billion they can lend to customers.

Table 18.4 The initial effect of an additional deposit of £10 billion

Liabilities	£bn	Assets	£bn
Deposits (old)	100	Balances with the central bank (old)	10
Deposits (new)	10	Balances with the central bank (new)	10
		Advances	90
Total	110	Total	110

Table 18.5 The full effect of an additional deposit of £10 billion

Liabilities	£bn	Assets	£bn
Deposits (old)	100	Balances with the central bank (old)	10
Deposits (new: initial)	10	Balances with the central bank (new)	10
(new: subsequent)	90	Advances (old)	90
		Advances (new)	90
Total	200	Total	200

Assume now that customers spend this £9 billion in shops and the shopkeepers deposit the cheques in their bank accounts. When the cheques are cleared, the balances in the central bank of the *customers'* banks will duly be debited by £9 billion, but the balances in the central bank of the shopkeepers' banks will be credited by £9 billion, leaving overall balances in the central bank unaltered. There is still a surplus of £9 billion over what is required to maintain the 10 per cent liquidity ratio. The new deposits of £9 billion in the shopkeepers' banks, backed by balances in the central bank, can thus be used as the basis for further loans. Ten per cent (i.e. £0.9 billion) must be kept back in the central bank, but the remaining 90 per cent (i.e. £8.1 billion) can be lent out again.

When the money is spent and the cheques are cleared, this £8.1 billion will still remain as surplus balances in the central bank and can therefore be used as the basis for yet more loans. Again, 10 per cent must be retained and the remaining 90 per cent can be lent out. This process goes on and on until eventually the position is as shown in Table 18.5.

The initial increase in balances with the central bank of £10 billion has allowed banks to create new advances (and hence deposits) of £90 billion, making a total increase in money supply of £100 billion.

TC 15 p543

This effect is known as the ***bank deposits multiplier***. In this simple example with a liquidity ratio of 1/10 (i.e. 10 per cent), the bank deposits multiplier is 10. An initial increase in deposits of £10 billion allowed total deposits to rise by £100 billion. In this simple world, therefore, the bank deposits multiplier is the inverse of the liquidity ratio (l).

Bank deposits multiplier $= 1/l$

If banks choose to operate a 20 per cent liquidity ratio and receive extra cash deposits of £10 million,

(a) How much credit will ultimately be created?

(b) By how much will total deposits have expanded?

(c) What is the size of the bank deposits multiplier?

Definition

Bank deposits multiplier The number of times greater the expansion of bank deposits is than the additional liquidity in banks that causes it: $1/l$ (the inverse of the liquidity ratio).

*LOOKING AT THE MATHS

The process of credit creation can be expressed mathematically as the sum of an infinite series. If a is the proportion of any deposit that is lent by banks, where $a = 1 - l$, then total deposits will expand by

$$D_r = D_0(1 + a + a^2 + a^3 + \dots)$$
$$= D_0(1/1 - a)$$
$$= D_0(1/l) \qquad (1)$$

Thus if there were an initial additional deposit (D_0) of £100 and if $a = 0.8$, giving a liquidity ratio (l) of 0.2, total deposits would expand by £100 × 1/0.2 = £500. The bank deposits multiplier is 5.

Proof of equation (1) is given in Maths Case 18.1 on the student website.

Note that the maths of the bank deposits multiplier is very similar to that of the Keynesian expenditure multiplier of section 17.2 (see Maths Case 17.1 on the student website). The economics, however, is quite different. The Keynesian multiplier is concerned with the effects of increased demand on real national output. The bank deposits multiplier is simply concerned with money creation.

TC 15 p543

The creation of credit: the real world

In practice, the creation of credit is not as simple as this. There are three major complications.

Banks' liquidity ratio may vary

Banks may choose a different liquidity ratio. At certain times, banks may decide that it is prudent to hold a bigger proportion of liquid assets. For example, if banks are worried about increased risks of default on loans, they may choose to hold a higher liquidity ratio to ensure that they have enough to meet customers' needs. This was the case in the late 2000s when many banks became less willing to lend to other banks for fear of the other banks' assets containing sub-prime debt. Banks, as a result, hoarded cash and became more cautious about granting loans.

On the other hand, there may be an upsurge in consumer demand for credit. Banks may be very keen to grant additional loans and thus make more profits, even though they have acquired no additional assets. They may simply go ahead and expand credit, and accept a lower liquidity ratio.

Customers may not want to take up the credit on offer. Banks may wish to make additional loans, but customers may not want to borrow. There may be insufficient demand. But will the banks not then lower their interest rates, thus encouraging people to borrow? Possibly; but if they lower the rate they charge to borrowers, they must also lower the rate they pay to depositors. But then depositors may switch to other institutions such as building societies.

How will an increased mobility of savings and other capital between institutions affect this argument?

Banks may not operate a simple liquidity ratio

The fact that banks hold a number of fairly liquid assets, such as short-term loans to other banks on the inter-bank market, bills of exchange and certificates of deposit, makes it difficult to identify a simple liquidity ratio. For example, if banks use £1 million in cash to purchase £1 million of bills, can we assume that the liquidity ratio has remained exactly the same? In other words, can we assume that ***near money*** assets, such as bills, are just as liquid as cash? If we assume that they are not, then has the liquidity ratio fallen? If so, by how much?

Banks do not see a clear-cut dividing line between liquid and non-liquid assets. They try to maintain a rough balance across the liquidity range, but the precise composition of assets will vary as interest rates on the various assets vary, and as the demands for liquidity vary.

In practice, therefore, the size of the bank deposits multiplier will vary and is thus difficult to predict in advance.

Is the following statement true: 'The greater the number of types of asset that are counted as being liquid, the smaller will be the bank deposits multiplier'?

Some of the extra cash may be withdrawn by the public

If extra cash comes into the banking system, and as a result extra deposits are created, part of them may be held by households and non-bank firms (known in this context as the ***non-bank private sector***) as cash outside the banks. In other words, some of the extra cash leaks out of the banking system. This will result in an overall multiplier effect that is smaller than the full bank deposits multiplier. This overall multiplier is known as the ***money multiplier***. It is defined as the rise in total money supply expressed as a proportion of the rise in the monetary base that caused it: $\Delta M_s/\Delta M_b$ (where M_s is total broad money supply and M_b is the monetary base). Box 18.5 shows how the money multiplier is calculated.

The broad money multiplier in the UK

In the UK, the principal money multiplier measure is the broad money multiplier. This is given by $\Delta M4/\Delta M_b$, where M_b in this case is defined as cash in circulation with the public

Definitions

Near money Highly liquid assets (other than cash).

Non-bank private sector Households and non-bank firms. In other words, everyone in the country other than banks and the government (central and local).

Money multiplier The number of times greater the expansion of money supply is than the expansion of the monetary base that caused it: $\Delta M_s/\Delta M_b$.

Figure 18.5 UK broad money multiplier

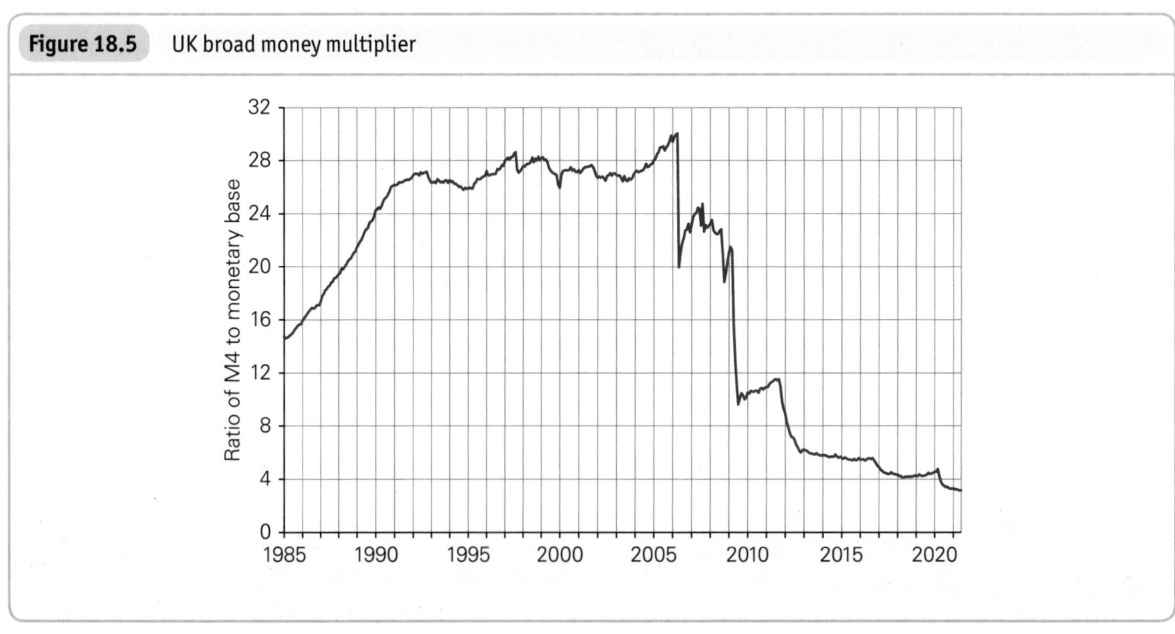

Source: Based on series LPMBL22 (reserves), LPMAVAB (notes and coin) and LPMAUYN (M4) from *Statistical Interactive Database*, Bank of England (29 July 2021, seasonally adjusted except for reserves), www.bankofengland.co.uk/boeapps/iadb/

*BOX 18.5 CALCULATING THE MONEY MULTIPLIER

EXPLORING ECONOMICS

The money multiplier (m) is the rise in total money supply (ΔM_s) divided by the rise in the monetary base (ΔM_b):

$$m = \Delta M_s / \Delta M_b \quad (1)$$

The total money supply (M_s) consists of deposits in banks and building societies (D) plus cash held by the public (C). Thus a rise in money supply would be given by

$$\Delta M_s = \Delta D + \Delta C \quad (2)$$

The monetary base (M_b) consists of bank and building society reserves (R) plus cash held by the public (C). Thus a rise in the monetary base would be given by

$$\Delta M_b = \Delta R + \Delta C \quad (3)$$

Thus, by substituting equations (2) and (3) into equation (1), the money multiplier is given by

$$m = \frac{\Delta D + \Delta C}{\Delta R + \Delta C} \quad (4)$$

Assume now that banks wish to hold a given fraction (r) of any rise in deposits in the form of reserves, i.e.

$$r = \Delta R / \Delta D \quad (5)$$

and that the public wishes to hold a given fraction (c) of any rise in its deposits as cash, i.e.

$$c = \Delta C / \Delta D \quad (6)$$

If we now divide the top and bottom of equation (4) by ΔD, we get

$$m = \frac{\Delta D/\Delta D + \Delta C/\Delta D}{\Delta R/\Delta D + \Delta C/\Delta D} = \frac{1 + c}{r + c} \quad (7)$$

Thus if c were 0.2 and r were 0.1, the money multiplier would be

$$(1 + 0.2)/(0.1 + 0.2) = 1.2/0.3 = 4$$

i.e.

$$\Delta M_s = 4 \times \Delta M_b$$

1. *If c were 0.1 and r were 0.01, by how much would money supply expand if the monetary base rose by £1 million?*
2. *Money supply (M4) includes wholesale as well as retail deposits. Given that firms will wish to keep only a very small fraction of a rise in wholesale deposits in cash (if any at all), how will a change in the balance of wholesale and retail deposits affect the value of c and hence of the money multiplier?*

plus banks' interest-bearing deposits (reserve accounts) at the Bank of England.

Another indicator of the broad money multiplier is simply the ratio of the *level* of (as opposed to the change in) M4 relative to the *level* of cash in circulation with the public and banks' reserves accounts at the central bank. This 'levels' relationship is shown in Figure 18.5 and helps us to analyse the longer-term relationship between the stocks of broad money and the monetary base.

From Figure 18.5 we can see how broad money grew rapidly relative to the monetary base during the late 1980s and into the early 1990s. From the early 1990s to the mid-2000s, the level of M4 relative to the monetary base fluctuated in a narrow range.

From May 2006 the Bank of England began remunerating banks' reserve accounts at the official Bank Rate. This encouraged banks to increase their reserve accounts at the Bank of England and led to a sharp fall in the broad money multiplier. It then decreased further during 2009. The significant decline in the ratio of broad to narrow money in 2009 and 2011/12, coincided with the Bank of England's programme of asset purchases (quantitative easing) in response to the financial crisis. This led to a large increase in banks' reserves. However this increase in the monetary base did not lead to the same percentage increase in broad money, as banks were more cautious about lending and chose to keep higher reserves.

Further asset purchases were made by the Bank of England in 2016, following the result of the EU referendum vote in the UK, and, like many other central banks, in 2020–21 in response to the COVID-19 pandemic. Again the broad money multiplier fell, albeit less dramatically than following the earlier rounds of asset purchases. The policy of quantitative easing is discussed more in Chapter 22.

In the next section we focus on those factors which help to explain movements in the money multiplier and changes in the money supply.

Which would you expect to fluctuate more, the money multiplier (ΔM4/Δcash), or the simple ratio, M4/cash, illustrated in Figure 18.4?

What causes money supply to rise?

Money supply can change for a number of reasons. We consider five sets of circumstances which can cause the money supply to *rise.*

Central bank action

The central bank may decide that the stock of money is too low and that this is keeping up interest rates and restraining spending in the economy. In such circumstances, it may choose to create additional money.

As we saw above, this was the case following the financial crisis of the late 2000s and the COVID-19 pandemic of the early 2020s, when central banks around the world embarked on programmes of quantitative easing (QE). QE involves the central bank creating electronic (narrow) money, which is used to purchase assets, mainly government bonds. When the recipients of this money (mainly non-bank financial institutions) deposit it in banks, the banks can then lend it to businesses and consumers for spending and, through the bank deposits multiplier, broad money would increase. (We examine quantitative easing in the UK in Box 22.7.)

As we can see from Figure 18.6, however, this was not enough to prevent UK broad money supply falling during much of the first half of the 2010s.

An inflow of funds from abroad

When sterling is used to pay for UK exports and is deposited in UK banks by the exporters, credit can be created on the basis of it. This leads to a multiplied increase in the domestic money supply.

The money supply will also expand if depositors of sterling in banks overseas then switch these deposits to banks in the UK. This is a direct increase in the money supply. In an open economy like the UK, movements of sterling and other currencies into and out of the country can be very large, leading to large fluctuations in the money supply.

A public-sector deficit

A public-sector deficit is the difference between public-sector expenditure and public-sector receipts. To finance a public-sector deficit, the government has to borrow money by selling interest-bearing securities (Treasury bills and gilts). The precise amount of money the public sector requires to borrow in any one year is known in the UK as the ***public-sector net cash requirement (PSNCR)***. In general, the bigger the deficit, the greater will be the growth in the money supply. Just how the money supply will be affected, however, depends on who buys the securities.

Consider first the case where government securities are purchased by the non-bank private sector. When people or firms buy the bonds or bills, they will draw money from their banks. When the government spends the money, it will be re-deposited in banks. There is no increase in money supply. It is just a case of existing money changing hands.

This is not the case when the securities are purchased by monetary financial institutions, including the central bank. Consider the purchase of Treasury bills by commercial banks: there will be a multiplied expansion of the money supply. The reason is that, although banks' balances at the central bank will go down when the banks purchase the bills, they will go up again when the government spends the money. In addition, the banks will now have additional liquid assets (bills), which can be used as the basis for credit creation. This effect could be partly mitigated if the government is able to issue debt instruments of longer maturity (gilts) since these are less liquid.

If there is a public-sector *surplus* this will either reduce the money supply or have no effect, depending on what the government does with the surplus. The fact that there is a surplus means that the public sector is spending less than it

Definition

Public-sector net cash requirement (PSNCR) The (annual) deficit of the public sector, and thus the amount that the public sector must borrow.

Figure 18.6 Annual rate of growth of M4

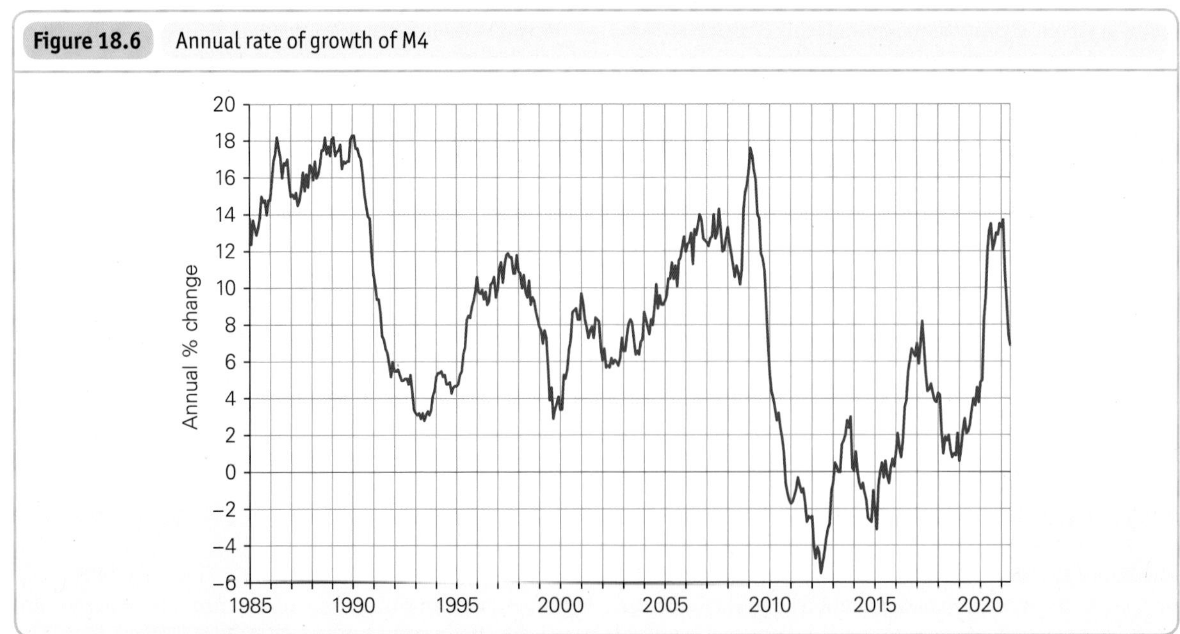

Source: Statistical Interactive Database, Series LPMVQJW, Bank of England (29 July 2021, seasonally adjusted), www.bankofengland.co.uk/boeapps/iadb/

receives in taxes, etc. The initial effect, therefore, is to reduce the money in the economy: it is being 'retired' in the central bank.

If, however, the government then uses this money to buy back securities from the non-bank private sector, the money will merely return to the economy, and there will be no net effect on money supply.

If the government borrows but does not spend the proceeds, what effect will this have on the money supply if it borrows from:
(a) the banking sector;
(b) the non-bank private sector?

These first three reasons for an expansion of broad money supply (M4) are reasons why the monetary base itself might expand.

The final two reasons focus on how more credit is being created for a *given* monetary base. These reasons would therefore see a rise in the money multiplier. As Figure 18.5 showed, the money multiplier rose substantially in the UK in the late 1980s/early 1990s and then again in the first half of the 2000s.

Banks choose to hold a lower liquidity ratio

If banks collectively choose to hold a lower liquidity ratio, they will have surplus liquidity. The banks have tended to choose a lower liquidity ratio over time because of the increasing use of direct debits and debit card and credit card transactions.

Surplus liquidity can be used to expand advances, which will lead to a multiplied rise in broad money supply (e.g. M4).

An important trend up to the late 2000s was the growth of the use of wholesale funds by financial institutions. Table 18.1 showed that short-term loans to other banks (including overseas banks) are now the largest element in banks' liquid assets. These assets may be used by a bank as the basis for expanding loans and thereby starting a chain of credit creation.

But although these assets are liquid to an individual bank, they do not add to the liquidity of the banking system as a whole. By using them for credit creation, the banking system is operating with a lower *overall* liquidity ratio.

This was a major element in the banking crisis of 2008. By operating with a collectively low liquidity ratio, banks were vulnerable to people defaulting on debt, such as mortgages. The problem was compounded by the holding of sub-prime debt in the form of securitised assets. Realising the vulnerability of other banks, banks became increasingly unwilling to lend to each other. The resulting decline in inter-bank lending reduced the amount of credit created, thereby depressing the money supply (see Figure 18.6).

What effects do debit cards and cash machines (ATMs) have on (a) banks' prudent liquidity ratios; (b) the size of the bank deposits multiplier?

The non-bank private sector chooses to hold less cash

Households and firms may choose to hold less cash. Again, the reason may be a greater use of cards, direct debits, etc. This means that a greater proportion of the cash base will be held as deposits in banks rather than in people's wallets, purses or safes outside banks. The extra cash deposits allow banks to create more credit.

The flow-of-funds equation

All these effects on money supply can be summarised using a ***flow-of-funds equation***. This shows the components of a change in money supply (ΔM_s). The following flow-of-funds equation is the one most commonly used in the UK, that for M4. It consists of four items (or 'counterparts' as they are known):

ΔM4	*equals*	The public-sector net cash requirement (PSNCR), i.e. amount the public sector needs to borrow	(Item 1)
	minus	Sales of public-sector debt to (or plus purchases of public-sector debt from) the non-bank private sector	(Item 2)
	plus	Banks' and building societies' sterling net lending to the UK private sector	(Item 3)
	plus	External effect	(Item 4)

Public-sector borrowing (item 1) will lead to a direct increase in the money supply, but not if it is funded by selling bonds and bills to the non-bank private sector. Such sales (item 2) have therefore to be subtracted from the public-sector net cash requirement (PSNCR). But conversely, if the government buys back old bonds from the non-bank private sector, this will further increase the money supply.

The initial increase in liquidity from the sale of government securities to the banking sector is given by item 1. This increase in their liquidity will enable banks to create credit. To the extent that this extra lending is to the UK private sector (item 3), money supply will increase, and by a multiple of the initial increase in liquidity (item 1). Bank lending may also increase (item 3) even if there is no increase in liquidity or even a reduction in liquidity (item 1 is zero or negative), if banks respond to increases in the demand for loans by accepting a lower liquidity ratio, or if, through securitisation and other forms of secondary marketing, individual banks gain extra liquidity from each other, even though there is no total increase in liquidity in the banking system. Item 3 will be reduced if banks choose to hold more capital.

Finally, if there is a net inflow of funds from abroad (item 4), this too will increase the money supply.

Definition

Flow-of-funds equation The various items making up an increase (or decrease) in money supply.

Figure 18.7 Counterparts to changes in M4

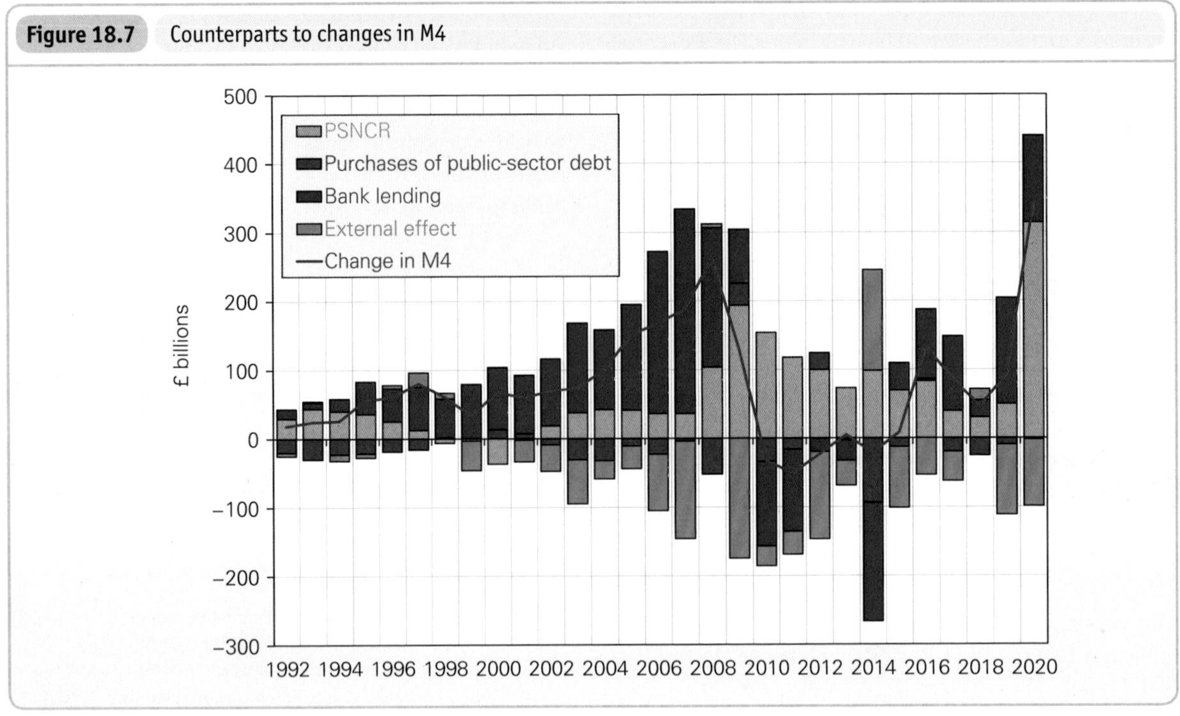

Source: Based on data in *Bankstats*, Table A3.2, Bank of England (29 March 2021)

Figure 18.7 shows the components of changes in broad money (M4) in the UK since 1992. It illustrates the contribution from bank lending to the strong growth of the money supply during the 2000s, up to the financial crisis. However, the curbing of lending by banks following the financial crisis, and then the requirement to hold larger capital buffers as part of the new Basel framework (see pages 574–6), dampened monetary growth. This helped to offset the otherwise expansionary impact on the money supply of the large public-sector deficits in the first half of the 2010s.

In the second half of the 2010s, a resurgence in lending along with still large public-sector deficits helped to boost the growth in broad money. Then, in 2020, the fiscal measures in response to the COVID-19 pandemic led to a historically large budget deficit and therefore to a significant expansion of M4.

The relationship between money supply and the rate of interest

Simple monetary theory often assumes that the supply of money is totally independent of interest rates. This is illustrated in Figure 18.8. The money supply is ***exogenous***. It is assumed to be determined by the government or central bank ('the authorities'): what the authorities choose it to be, or what they allow it to be by their choice of the level and method of financing the public-sector deficit.

In practice, however, even if narrow money were to be tightly controlled by the central bank (which it is not), it would be very hard to have a precise control of broad money. More complex models, therefore, and especially Keynesian models, assume that money supply is ***endogenous***: that it depends on the demand for money. The argument is that

Figure 18.8 The supply of money curve: exogenous money supply

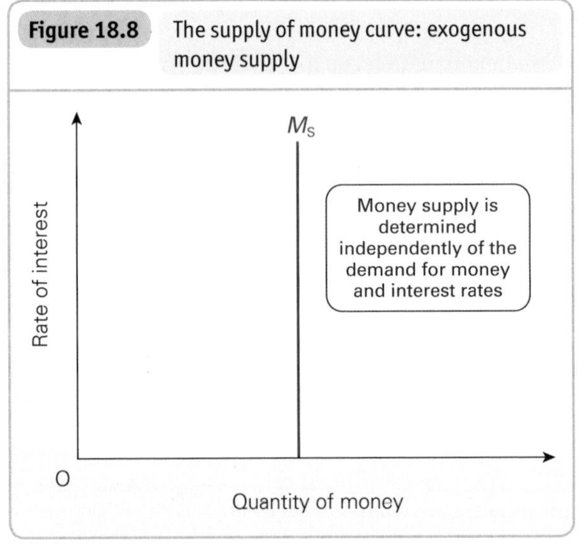

Definitions

Exogenous money supply Money supply that does not depend on the demand for money but is set by the authorities.

Endogenous money supply Money supply that is determined (at least in part) by the demand for money.

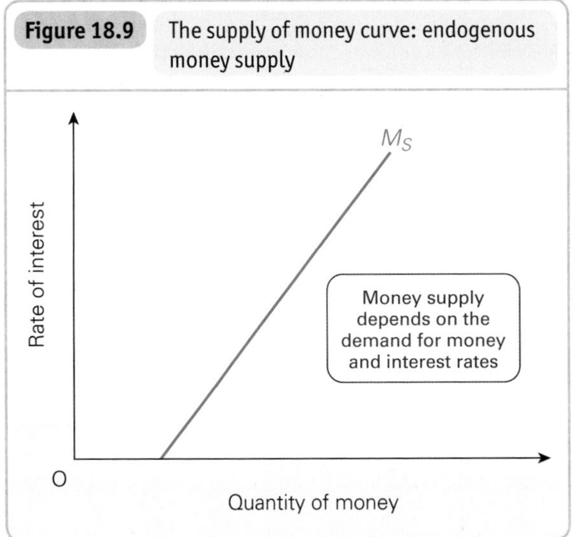

Figure 18.9 The supply of money curve: endogenous money supply

higher money demand will result in higher interest rates and in higher levels of money supplied. The result is an upward-sloping money supply curve, as in Figure 18.9. The reasons for this are as follows:

- *Banks accommodating an increase in the demand for credit.* Increases in money supply may occur as a result of banks expanding credit in response to the demand for credit. This assumes that banks have surplus liquidity in the first place, or are happy to operate with lower liquidity, or can increase liquidity through secondary marketing of otherwise illiquid assets, or can obtain liquidity from the central bank through repos. Higher demand for credit will drive up interest rates, making it more profitable for banks to supply more credit.
- *Depositors switch to less liquid deposits.* Higher interest rates may encourage depositors to switch their deposits from sight accounts (earning little or no interest) to time accounts. Since money is less likely to be withdrawn quickly from time accounts, banks may feel the need to hold less liquidity, and therefore may decide to increase credit, thus expanding the money supply.
- *Inflow of funds from abroad.* Higher interest rates attract deposits from overseas. This increases the money supply to the extent that the Bank of England does not allow the exchange rate to appreciate in response.

To summarise: an increase in demand for money raises interest rates, which in turn increases the quantity of money supplied (see sections 18.4 and 18.5): a movement along an upward-sloping money supply curve.

Some economists go further still. They argue that not only is money supply endogenous, but the 'curve' is effectively horizontal; money supply expands passively to match the demand for money. In practice, the shape varies with the confidence of MFIs. In periods of optimism, banks may be willing to expand credit to meet the demand from customers. In periods of pessimism, such as that following the financial crisis, banks may be very unwilling to grant credit when customers seek it.

Section summary

1. Money supply can be defined in a number of different ways, depending on what items are included. A useful distinction is between narrow money and broad money. Narrow money includes just cash, and possibly banks' balances at the central bank. Broad money also includes deposits in banks and possibly various other short-term deposits in the money market. In the UK, M4 is the preferred measure of broad money. In the eurozone it is M3.
2. Bank deposits are a major proportion of broad money supply. The expansion of bank deposits is the major element in the expansion of the money supply.
3. Bank deposits expand through a process of credit creation. If banks' liquid assets increase, they can be used as a base for increasing loans. When the loans are redeposited in banks, they form the base for yet more loans, and thus a process of multiple credit expansion takes place. The ratio of the increase of deposits to an expansion of banks' liquidity base is called the 'bank deposits multiplier'. It is the inverse of the liquidity ratio.
4. In practice, it is difficult to predict the precise amount by which money supply will expand if there is an increase in cash. The reasons are that banks may choose to hold a different liquidity ratio; customers may not take up all the credit on offer; there may be no simple liquidity ratio given the range of near money assets; and some of the extra cash may leak away into extra cash holdings by the public.
5. Money supply will rise if (a) banks choose to hold a lower liquidity ratio and thus create more credit for an existing amount of liquidity; (b) people choose to hold less cash outside the banks; (c) there is a net inflow of funds from abroad; (d) the government runs a public-sector deficit and finances it by borrowing from the banking sector or from abroad.
6. The flow-of-funds equation shows the components of any change in money supply. A rise in money supply equals the public-sector net cash requirement (PSNCR) *minus* sales of public-sector debt to the non-bank private sector, *plus* banks' lending to the private sector (less increases in banks' capital), *plus* inflows of money from abroad.
7. Simple monetary theory assumes that the supply of money is independent of interest rates. In practice, a rise in interest rates (in response to a higher demand for money) will often lead to an increase in money supply.

18.4 THE DEMAND FOR MONEY

The motives for holding money

The demand for money refers to the desire to hold money: to keep your wealth in the form of money, rather than spending it on goods and services or using it to purchase financial assets such as bonds or shares. It is usual to distinguish three reasons why people want to hold their assets in the form of money. Note that we are talking here about broad money: M4 in the UK.

The transactions motive

Since money is a medium of exchange, it is required for conducting transactions. But since people receive money only at intervals (e.g. weekly or monthly) and not continuously, they require to hold balances of money in cash or in current accounts.

The precautionary motive

Unforeseen circumstances can arise, such as a car breakdown. Thus individuals often hold some additional money as a precaution. Firms too keep precautionary balances because of uncertainties about the timing of their receipts and payments. If a large customer is late in making payment, a firm may be unable to pay its suppliers unless it has spare liquidity.

TC 9 p132

The speculative or assets motive

Certain firms and individuals who wish to purchase financial assets, such as bonds, shares or other securities, may prefer to wait if they feel that their price is likely to fall. In the meantime, they will hold money balances instead. This speculative demand can be quite high when the price of securities is considered certain to fall. Money when used for this purpose is a means of temporarily storing wealth.

Similarly, people who will require foreign currency at some time in the future (people such as importers, holidaymakers, or those thinking of investing abroad or in foreign securities) may prefer to wait before exchanging pounds into the relevant foreign currencies if they believe that the sterling price of these currencies is likely to fall (the pound is likely to appreciate).

The transactions plus precautionary demand for money: L_1

The transactions plus precautionary demand for money is termed L_1. 'L' stands for ***liquidity preference***: that is, the desire to hold assets in liquid form. Money balances held for these two purposes are called ***active balances***: money to be used as a medium of exchange. What determines the size of L_1?

The major determinant of L_1 is nominal national income (i.e. national income at current prices). The higher people's money income, the greater their (nominal) expenditure and the bigger their demand for active balances. The frequency with which people are paid also affects L_1. The less frequently they are paid, the greater the level of money balances they will require to tide them over until the next payment.

Will students in receipt of a loan, grant or an allowance who receive the money once per term have a high or a low transactions demand for money relative to their income?

KI 9 p64

The rate of interest has some effect on L_1, albeit rather small (see Figure 18.9). At high rates of interest, people may choose to spend less and save more of their income, e.g. by buying shares. The effect is likely to be bigger on the precautionary demand: a higher interest rate may encourage people to risk tying up their money. Firms' active balances are more likely to be sensitive to changes in r than those of individuals.

Other determinants of L_1 include the season of the year: people require more money balances at Christmas, for example. Also, any other factors that affect consumption will affect L_1.

The increased use of credit cards in recent years has reduced both the transactions and precautionary demands. Paying once a month for goods requires less money on average than paying separately for each item purchased. Moreover, the possession of a credit card reduces or even eliminates the need to hold precautionary balances for many people. On the other hand, the increased availability of cash machines, the convenience of debit cards and the ability to earn interest on current accounts have all encouraged people to hold more money in bank accounts. The net effect has been an increase in the demand for (broad) money.

The speculative (or assets) demand for money: L_2

The speculative demand for money balances is termed L_2. Money balances held for this purpose are called ***idle balances***.

People who possess wealth, whether they are wealthy or simply small savers, have to decide the best form in which to hold that wealth. Do they keep it in cash in a piggy bank, or in a current account in a real bank; or do they put it in some interest-bearing time account; or do they buy stocks and shares or government bonds; or do they buy some physical asset such as a car or property?

Definitions

Liquidity preference The demand for holding assets in the form of money.

Active balances Money held for transactions and precautionary purposes.

Idle balances Money held for speculative purposes: money held in anticipation of a fall in asset prices.

In making these decisions, people will have to weigh up the relative advantages and disadvantages of the various alternative assets. Assets can be compared according to two criteria: liquidity and the possibility of earning income.

Just as we saw in the case of a bank's assets, these two criteria tend to conflict. The more liquid an asset is, the lower is likely to be the income earned from holding it. Thus cash is totally liquid to the holder: it can be used to buy other assets (or spent on goods) instantly, but it earns no interest. Shares, on the other hand, are not very liquid since they cannot be sold instantly at a guaranteed price. (They can be sold pretty well instantly, but if share prices are depressed, a considerable loss may be incurred in so doing. In other words, they are a risky means of holding wealth.) But shares have the potential of earning quite a high income for the holder, not only in terms of the dividends paid out of the firms' profits, but also in terms of the capital gain from any increase in the shares' prices.

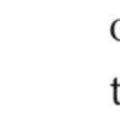

Buying something like a car is at the other end of the spectrum from holding cash. A car is highly illiquid, but yields a high return to the owner. In what form is this 'return'?

There are three major determinants of the speculative demand for money. Let us examine each in turn.

The rate of interest (or rate of return) on assets

In terms of the operation of money markets, this is the most important determinant. The higher the rate of return on assets, such as shares and bonds, the greater the opportunity cost of holding money and therefore the lower the speculative demand for money.

The rate of return on assets varies inversely with their price. Take the case of a government bond (which pays a fixed sum of money throughout its life). Assume that the government issued a £100 bond at a time when interest rates were 10 per cent. Thus the bond must pay £10 per year. Although the government will not redeem bonds until their maturity date, which could well be 20 years from when they were issued, holders can sell bonds at any time on the bond market. Their market price will reflect (nominal) market rates of interest. Assume, for example, that interest rates fall to 5 per cent. What will happen to the market price of the bond paying £10 per year? It will be driven up to £200. At that price, the £10 per year is worth the current market rate of 5 per cent. Thus the market price of bonds varies inversely with the rate of interest.

If the market price of securities is high, the rate of interest (i.e. the rate of return) on these securities will be low. Potential purchasers of these securities will probably wait until their prices fall and the rate of interest rises. Similarly, existing holders of securities will probably sell them while the price is high, hoping to buy them back again when the price falls, thus making a capital gain. In the meantime, therefore, large speculative balances of money will be held. L_2 is high.

If, on the other hand, the rate of interest is high, then L_2 is likely to be low. To take advantage of the high rate of return on securities, people buy them now instead of holding on to their money.

Would the demand for securities be low if their price was high, but was expected to go on rising?

The relationship between L_2 and the rate of interest is again shown in Figure 18.10. The inverse relationship between the rate of interest and L_2 gives a downward-sloping curve.

Expectations of changes in the prices of securities and other assets

If people believe that share prices are about to rise rapidly on the stock market, they will buy shares and hold smaller speculative balances of money. If they think that share prices will fall, they will sell them and hold money instead. Some clever (or lucky) individuals anticipated the 2007–8 stock market decline (see figure in Box 2.2 on page 52). They sold shares and 'went liquid'.

Speculative demand and the exchange rate

In an open economy like the UK where large-scale movements of currencies across the foreign exchanges take place, expectations about changes in the exchange rate are a major determinant of the speculative demand for money.

If people believe that the pound is likely to appreciate, they will want to hold sterling until it does appreciate. For example, if the current exchange rate is £1 = \$1.25 and speculators believe that it will shortly rise to £1 = \$1.50, then if they are correct, they will make a 25¢ per £1 profit by holding sterling. The more quickly is the exchange rate expected to rise, the more will people want to hold sterling (as money). If, however, people believe that it will be a slow rise over time, they will want to buy sterling assets (such as UK government bonds) rather than money, since such assets will also earn the holder a rate of interest.

Conversely, if people believe that the exchange rate is likely to fall in the near future, they will economise on their holdings of sterling, preferring to hold their liquid assets in some other currency – the one most likely to appreciate against other currencies.

Graphically, changes in expectations about the exchange rate will have the effect of shifting the L_2 curve in Figure 18.10.

There is a further complication here. Expectations about changes in the exchange rate will themselves be influenced by the interest rate (relative to overseas interest rates). If the UK rate of interest goes up, people will want to deposit their money in the UK. This will increase the demand for sterling on the foreign exchange market: there will be a short-term financial inflow into the UK (the financial account of the balance of payments will go into surplus). The effect will be to drive up the exchange rate. Thus if people believe that the UK rate of interest will rise, they will also believe that the rate

Figure 18.10 The demand for money

Rate of interest
$L (= L_1 + L_2)$
L_2
L_1
O
Total money balances

of exchange will appreciate, and they will want to hold larger speculative balances of sterling.

KI 9 p64

The introduction of the 'foreign exchange dimension' into our analysis will have two effects on the L_2 curve. First, the curve will become more *elastic*. If the rate of interest is low and is thought likely to rise, the speculative demand is likely to be very high. Not only will people hold money in anticipation of a fall in security prices, but they will also hold money (sterling) in anticipation of an appreciation of the exchange rate.

Second, the curve will become more *unstable*. Expectations of changes in the exchange rate do not just depend on current domestic interest rates. They depend on the current and anticipated future state of the balance of trade, the rate of inflation, the current and anticipated levels of interest rates in other major trading countries, the price of oil, and so on. If any of these cause people to expect a lower exchange rate, the speculative demand for money will fall: L_2 will shift to the left.

Which way is the L_2 curve likely to shift in the following cases?

(a) The balance of trade moves into deficit.
(b) People anticipate that foreign interest rates are likely to rise substantially relative to domestic ones.
(c) The domestic rate of inflation falls below that of other major trading countries.
(d) People believe that the pound is about to depreciate.

The total demand for money: $L_1 + L_2$

Figure 18.10 also shows the total demand for money balances (L). This is found by the horizontal addition of curves L_1 and L_2. This curve is known as the 'liquidity preference curve' or simply the demand for money curve.

Any factor, other than a change in interest rates, that causes the demand for money to rise will shift the L curve to the right. For example, a rise in national income will cause L_1 to increase, and thus L will shift to the right.

Additional effects of expectations

KI 10 p70

We have talked about expectations and their importance in determining the speculative demand for money. In particular, we have looked at (a) the effect of interest rates on people's anticipations of future security prices and (b) the effect of expectations about exchange rate movements. There are two other ways in which expectations can influence the demand for money, and make it more unstable.

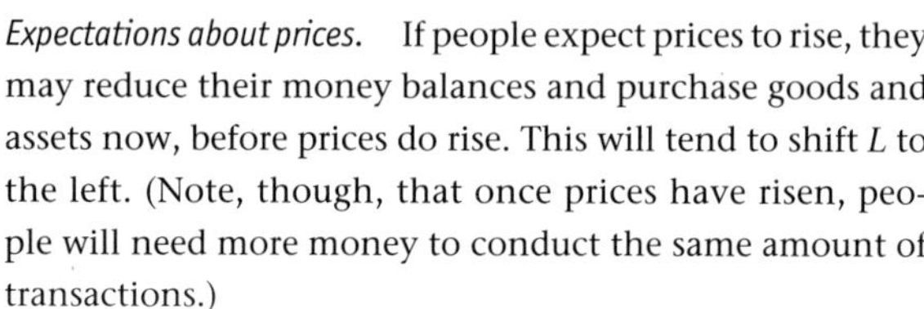

Expectations about prices. If people expect prices to rise, they may reduce their money balances and purchase goods and assets now, before prices do rise. This will tend to shift L to the left. (Note, though, that once prices have risen, people will need more money to conduct the same amount of transactions.)

Expectations of interest rate levels over the longer term. If people come to expect that interest rates will normally be higher than they used to be, then any given interest rate will seem lower relative to the 'normal' rate than it used to be. People will be more inclined to hold speculative balances of money in anticipation of a rise in interest rates. This will tend to shift L upwards.

In an era of uncertainty about inflation, interest rates and exchange rates, people's expectations will be hard to predict. They will be volatile and susceptible to rumours and political events. In such circumstances, the L curve itself will be hard to predict and will be subject to considerable shifts. Generally, it is likely that the greater the uncertainty, the greater will be the preference for liquidity, and the greater the risk of tying wealth up in illiquid assets.

*LOOKING AT THE MATHS

The demand for money (L) can be expressed by the following function:

$$\begin{aligned} L &= L_1 + L_2 \\ &= l_1(PY, f, i) + l_2(i, er^e) \\ &= l_1(PY, f, (r + \pi^e) + l_2((r + \pi^e), er^e) \end{aligned} \tag{1}$$

This states that L_1 is a function l_1 of nominal national income (i.e. real national income (Y) multiplied by the price index (P)), the frequency with which people are paid (f) and the nominal rate of interest (i), which equals the real rate of interest (r) on alternative assets to money plus the expected rate of inflation (π^e). L_2 is a function of the nominal rate of interest (i) and the expected value of the exchange rate er^e.

The advantage of specifying a relationship in this way is that it gives a simple way of representing a situation where something depends on a number of determinants. It is a convenient shorthand. Indeed, a more complex function could easily be specified where the demand for money depends on a longer list of variables. The one above, however, identifies the main determinants. By putting plus and minus signs under each of the terms, we could also identify whether the relationship with each of the determinants is a positive or negative one (i.e. whether the respective partial derivative is positive or negative). Equation (1) could thus be written

$$L = l_1(\underset{+}{PY}, \underset{-}{f}, \underset{-}{i}) + l_2(\underset{-}{i}, \underset{+}{er^e}) \tag{2}$$

This merely states that the demand for money will rise as PY and er^e rise and f and i fall.

Section summary

1. The three motives for holding money are the transactions, precautionary and speculative (or assets) motives.
2. The transactions-plus-precautionary demand for money (L_1) depends primarily on the level of nominal national income, the frequency with which people are paid and institutional arrangements (such as the use of credit or debit cards). It also depends to some degree on the rate of interest.
3. The speculative demand for money (L_2) depends on the rate of return on assets and on anticipations about future movements in security prices (and hence their rate of return) and future movements in exchange rates. If security prices are anticipated to fall or the exchange rate to rise, people will hold more money balances.
4. The demand for money is also influenced by expectations of price changes and the levels of interest rates over the longer term.

18.5 EQUILIBRIUM

Equilibrium in the money market

Equilibrium in the money market is where the demand for money (L) is equal to the supply of money (M_s). This equilibrium is achieved through changes in the *nominal* rate of interest (i). To make the analysis more straightforward, we assume there is no inflation (π). Hence, the nominal rate of interest (i) is the same as the real rate of interest (r) (we drop this assumption in later chapters).

In Figure 18.11, equilibrium is achieved with a nominal rate of interest i_e and a quantity of money M_e. If the rate of interest were above i_e, people would have money balances surplus to their needs. They would use these to buy shares, bonds and other assets. This would drive up the price of these assets and drive down the rate of interest.

As the rate of interest fell, so there would be a contraction of the money supply (a movement down along the M_s curve) and an increase in the demand for money balances, especially speculative balances (a movement down along the liquidity preference curve). The interest rate would go on falling until it reached i_e. Equilibrium would then be achieved.

Similarly, if the rate of interest were below i_e, people would have insufficient money balances. They would sell securities, thus lowering their prices and raising the rate of interest until it reached i_e.

A shift in either the M_s or the L curve will lead to a new equilibrium quantity of money and rate of interest at the new intersection of the curves. For example, a rise in the supply of money will cause the rate of interest to fall.

In practice, there is no one single rate of interest. Equilibrium in the money markets, therefore, will be where demand and supply of each type of financial asset separately balance. If, for example, there were excess demand for short-term loans (such as one-month inter-bank lending) and excess supply of money to invest in long-term assets (such as bonds), short-term rates of interest would rise relative to long-term rates. Generally, however, different interest rates tend to move roughly together as the overall demand for money and other liquid assets (or their supply) changes. Thus interest rates may generally rise or generally fall.

Figure 18.11 Equilibrium in the money market

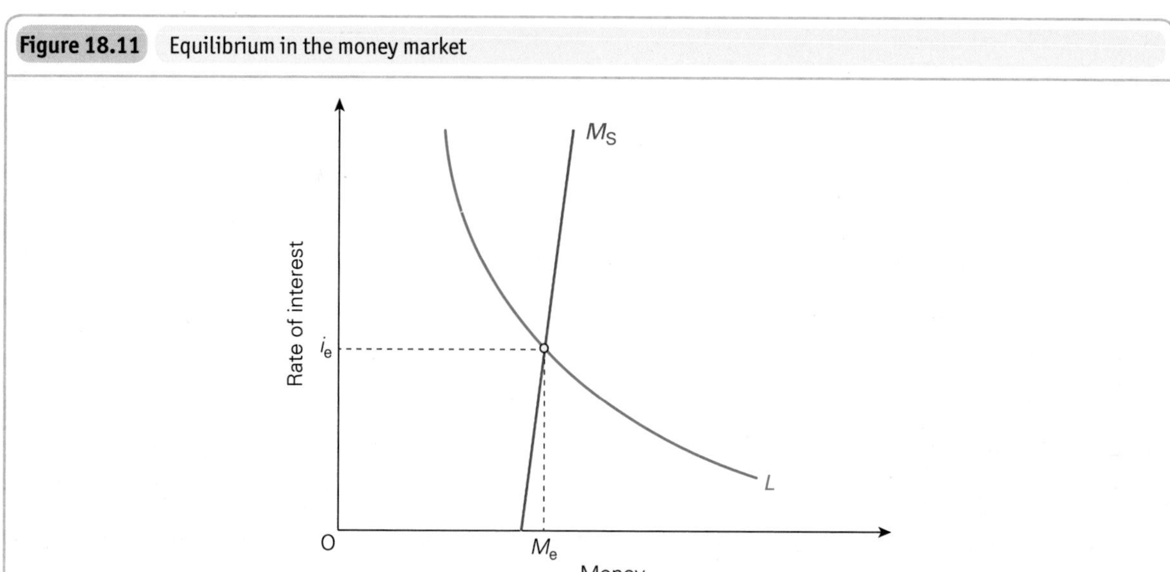

Figure 18.12 Selected interest rates (monthly averages)

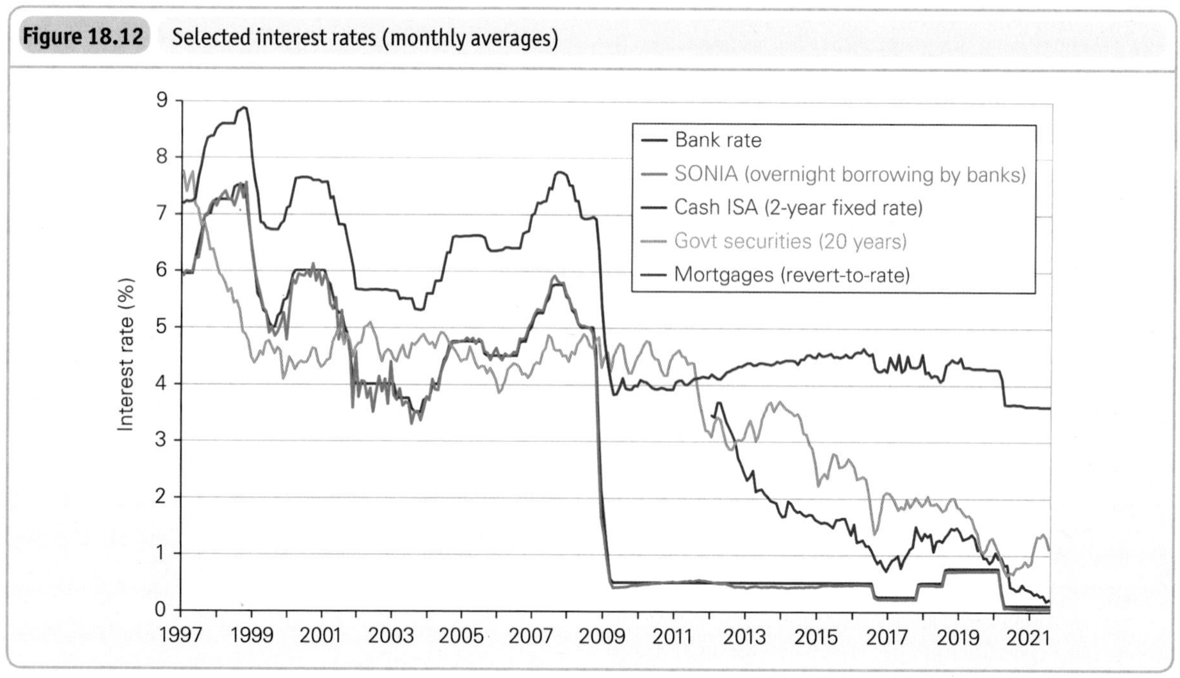

Note: Government securities: zero coupon, 20-year nominal yields.
Source: Based on data from *Statistical Interactive Database*, series IUMABEDR, IUMASOIA, IUMZID2, IUMALNZC, IUMTLMV, Bank of England (6 August 2021), www.bankofengland.co.uk/boeapps/iadb/

Figure 18.12 gives some examples of the rates of interest on various financial instruments in the UK. It shows how they move together. As we saw in section 18.2, the Bank of England conducts open-market operations to affect the general structure of the economy's interest rates and, in turn, the inflation rate. We can see how significant reductions to the policy rate were mirrored by falls in other interest rates. A similar pattern occurred following the historic cut to the Bank Rate to 0.1 percent in March 2020 in response to the COVID-19 pandemic.

What patterns in interest rates emerged following the global financial crisis?

Equilibrium in the foreign exchange market

Changes in the money supply also affect the foreign exchange market. In a free foreign exchange market, equilibrium will be achieved by changes in the exchange rate. Assume that the money supply increases. This has three direct effects:

- Part of the excess money balances will be used to purchase foreign assets. This will therefore lead to an increase in the supply of domestic currency coming on to the foreign exchange markets.
- The excess supply of money in the domestic money market will push down interest rates. This will reduce the return on domestic assets below that on foreign assets. This, like the first effect, will lead to an increased demand for foreign assets and thus an increased supply of the domestic currency on the foreign exchange market. It will also reduce the demand for domestic assets by those outside the country, and thus reduce the demand for the domestic currency.
- Speculators will anticipate that the higher supply of the domestic currency will cause the exchange rate to depreciate. They will therefore sell domestic currency and buy foreign currencies before the expected depreciation takes place.

The effect of all three is to cause the exchange rate to depreciate.

Trace through the effects on the foreign exchange market of a fall in the money supply.

*LOOKING AT THE MATHS

Equilibrium in the money market is where demand and supply of money are equal. From Box 18.5, the money supply (M_s) equals the monetary base (M_b) multiplied by the money multiplier:

$$M_s = M_b\left(\frac{1 + c}{rs + c}\right)$$

Note that this is the more complex version of the money multiplier that we examined in Box 18.5, not the simple bank deposits multiplier developed in the text.

From the 'Looking at the Maths' panel on page 595, the demand for money (L) is given by

$$L = l_1(PY, f, (r + \pi^e) + l_2((r + \pi^e), er^e)$$

Thus, in equilibrium,

$$M_s = L$$

that is

$$M_b\left(\frac{1 + c}{rs + c}\right) = l_1(PY, f, (r + \pi^e) + l_2((r + \pi^e), er^e) \quad \textbf{(1)}$$

At first sight, this equation looks quite daunting, but what we have done is to bring together money supply and demand, each of which has been separately derived in a set of simple stages. In one single equation (equation (1)) we have completed a jigsaw made up of several simple parts.

Section summary

1. Equilibrium in the money market is where the supply of money is equal to the demand. Equilibrium will be achieved through changes in the nominal rate of interest.
2. A rise in money supply causes money supply to exceed money demand. This causes interest rates to fall and a movement down along both the supply of money curve and the demand for money curve until money supply is equal to money demand.
3. Equilibrium in the foreign exchange market is where the demand and supply of a currency are equal. A rise in money supply causes interest rates to fall. The rise in money supply plus the fall in interest rates causes an increased supply of domestic currency to come on to the foreign exchange market and a reduced demand for the domestic currency. This causes the exchange rate to depreciate.

END OF CHAPTER QUESTIONS

1. Imagine that the banking system receives additional deposits of £100 million and that all the individual banks wish to retain their current liquidity ratio of 20 per cent.
   (a) How much will banks choose to lend out initially?
   (b) What will happen to banks' liabilities when the money that is lent out is spent and the recipients of it deposit it in their bank accounts?
   (c) How much of these latest deposits will be lent out by the banks?
   (d) By how much will *total* deposits (liabilities) eventually have risen, assuming that none of the additional liquidity is held outside the banking sector?
   (e) How much of these are matched by (i) liquid assets; (ii) illiquid assets?
   (f) What is the size of the bank deposits multiplier?
   (g) If one-half of any additional liquidity is held *outside* the banking sector, by how much less will deposits have risen compared with (d) above?
2. What is meant by the terms *narrow money* and *broad money*? Does broad money fulfil all the functions of money?

(continued)

3. How does money aid the specialisation and division of labour?
4. What enables banks safely to engage in both maturity transformation and risk transformation?
5. Why do banks hold a range of assets of varying degrees of liquidity and profitability?
6. What is meant by the securitisation of assets? How might this be (a) beneficial and (b) harmful to banks and the economy?
7. What were the causes of the credit crunch and the banking crisis of the late 2000s?
8. If the government reduces the size of its borrowing, why might the money supply nevertheless increase more rapidly?
9. Why might the relationship between the demand for money and the rate of interest be an unstable one?
10. What effects will the following have on the equilibrium rate of interest? (You should consider which way the demand and/or supply curves of money shift.)
    (a) Banks find that they have a higher liquidity ratio than they need.
    (b) A rise in incomes.
    (c) A growing belief that interest rates will rise from their current level.

Online resources

Additional case studies on the student website

18.1 **Barter: its use in Russia in the 1990s.** When barter was used as an alternative to money.

18.2 **The attributes of money.** What distinguishes it from other assets?

18.3 **From coins to bank deposit money.** This case traces the evolution of modern money.

18.4 **Gresham's law.** This examines the famous law that 'bad money drives good money out of circulation'.

18.5 **German banking.** This case compares the tradition of German banks with that of UK retail banks. Although the banks have become more similar in recent years, German banks have a much closer relationship with industry.

18.6 **Residential mortgages and securitisation.** Was the bundling of residential mortgage debt into securitised assets the cause of the 2008 credit crunch?

18.7 **Bailing out the banks.** An overview of the concerted efforts made to rescue the banking system in the crisis of 2007–9.

18.8 **Changes in the banking industry.** This looks at ringfencing and other ways of reducing risks in retail banking.

18.9 **Making money grow.** A light-hearted illustration of the process of credit creation.

18.10 **Consolidated MFI balance sheet** A look at the *consolidated* balance sheet of UK monetary and financial institutions, including the Bank of England.

18.11 **Parallel money markets.** A description of the variety of short-term financial instruments available in the parallel money markets.

18.12 **Are the days of cash numbered?** Are credit and debit cards and direct money transfers replacing cash transactions?

Maths Case 18.1 Calculating the value of the bank multiplier. Looking at the algebra.

Websites relevant to this chapter

See sites listed at the end of Chapter 19 on page 634.

The Relationship between the Money and Goods Markets

CHAPTER MAP

In Chapter 17 we saw how equilibrium national output was determined. In other words, we looked at macro-economic equilibrium in goods markets. In Chapter 18 we saw how equilibrium was determined in the money market. In this chapter we combine the analysis of the two chapters.

In section 19.1 we examine how changes in money supply affect real national income. In other words, we see how changes in money markets are transmitted through to goods markets: how monetary changes affect real output. Then, in section 19.2, we look at things the other way round. We examine the effects on money markets and interest rates of changes in the goods market. For example, if aggregate demand increases and firms start to produce extra goods, to what extent will money markets act as a constraint on this process?

In the remaining sections we look at the interplay of goods and money markets. In doing so, we introduce models which allow us to study how these markets interact. In section 19.3 the interaction is analysed in the contemporary context of central banks setting interest rates to target the rate of inflation. In doing so, we introduce a relatively new model: the *IS/MP* model. In the Appendix to the chapter we introduce the more traditional model: the *IS/LM* model. This helps us to see how the two markets interact when interest rates adjust to bring about equilibrium in the money market.

19.1 THE EFFECTS OF MONETARY CHANGES ON NATIONAL INCOME

In this section we examine the impact on the economy of changes in money supply and interest rates: how they affect aggregate demand and how this, in turn, affects national income and prices. A simple way of understanding the issues is in terms of the *quantity theory of money*.

The quantity theory of money

In section 16.2 (page 504), we looked at the following version of the quantity equation:

$$MV = PY$$

In case you did not study Chapter 16, let us state the theory again. First a definition of the terms: *M* is the supply of money; *V* is the income velocity of circulation (the number of times money is spent per year on national output (GDP)); *P* is the price index (where the index = 1 in the base year); and *Y* is the real value of national income (= national output) for the year in question (i.e. GDP measured in base-year prices).

MV is the total spending on national output. For example, if total money supply (*M*) was £1 trillion and each pound was spent on average twice per year (*V*) on national output, then total spending on national output (*MV*) would equal £2 trillion for that year. *MV* is thus simply (nominal) aggregate demand, since total spending on national output consists of the four elements of aggregate demand: consumer spending (*C*), investment expenditure (*I*), government purchases
TC 13 p461 (*G*), and expenditure on exports less expenditure on imports (*X* − *M*), all measured in current prices.

PY is the money value of national output: in other words, GDP measured at *current* prices. For example, if real national income (*Y*) (i.e. in base-year prices) were £1 trillion, and the price index (*P*) were 2 (in other words, prices were twice as high as in the base year), then the value of national output in current prices would be £2 trillion.

Because of the way we have defined the terms, *MV* must equal *PY*. A simple way of looking at this is that *MV* and *PY* are both ways of measuring GDP. *MV* measures it in terms of national *expenditure*. *PY* measures it in terms of the value of what is *produced*.

The effect of a change in money supply

If money supply (*M*) changes, how will it affect the other three elements of the quantity equation? Will a rise in money supply simply lead to a rise in prices (*P*), or will there be a rise in real national income (*Y*): i.e. a rise in real GDP? What will happen to the velocity of circulation (*V*)? Can we assume that it will remain constant, or will it change?

Clearly the relationship between money supply and prices depends on what happens to *V* and *Y*. What happens to them has been the subject of considerable debate between economists over the years. Keynesians have generally had different views from monetarists and new classical economists.

Essentially there are two issues. In this chapter we look at the first one: the variability of *V*. If *V* is constant, a change in money supply (*M*) will directly affect nominal aggregate demand (*MV*) and hence nominal national income (*PY*). If, however, *V* varies, a change in *M* may have a much less predictable effect on *PY*.

The second issue is examined in Chapter 20. This concerns the variability of *Y*. Will a rise in aggregate demand lead to increased employment and output (*Y*), or will it simply lead to higher prices (*P*), or some combination of the two?

1. *If V is constant, will (a) a £10 million rise in M give a £10 million rise in MV; (b) a 10 per cent rise in M give a 10 per cent rise in MV?*
2. *If both V and Y are constant, will (a) a £10 million rise in M lead to a £10 million rise in P; (b) a 10 per cent rise in M lead to a 10 per cent rise in P?*

Two principal means by which a rise in money supply can cause a rise in aggregate demand are the ***interest rate transmission mechanism*** and the ***exchange rate transmission mechanism***. These are illustrated in Figure 19.1. We start with the interest rate transmission mechanism.

The interest rate transmission mechanism

The interest rate transmission mechanism is summarised in the top part of Figure 19.1. It shows the process by which changes in interest rates, following a change in the money supply, can affect aggregate demand.

When analysing expenditure decisions, it is typically *real* interest rates that are important. Consumers and producers are interested in the additional future volumes of consumption and production respectively that their investment, borrowing or saving today will enable them to enjoy.

The *realised* ('*ex post*') real rate of interest (*r*) received on savings or paid on borrowing is the nominal (actual) interest rate (*i*) *less* the rate of inflation (π). However, for savers and borrowers it is the future rate of inflation that is relevant in their decision making. Of course, future inflation rates

Definitions

Interest rate transmission mechanism How a change in money supply affects aggregate demand via a change in interest rates.

Exchange rate transmission mechanism How a change in money supply affects aggregate demand via a change in exchange rates.

Figure 19.1 Monetary transmission mechanisms

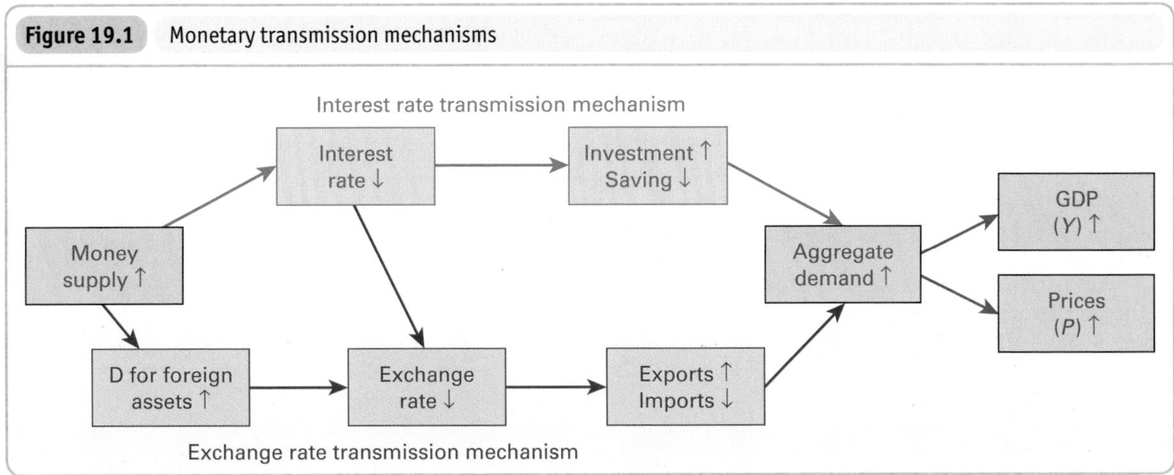

cannot be known with certainty and, instead, people must form *expectations* of inflation. Hence, the perceived real interest rate when the decision is made ('*ex ante*') is the nominal interest rate (i) *less* the *expected* rate of inflation (π^e).

We assume in the following analysis of the short term that prices are constant and that the expected rate of inflation is zero. Therefore, a change in real interest rates is equivalent to that in nominal interest rates.

KI 5 p21 Figure 19.2 allows us to analyse the interest rate transmission mechanism in more detail. It is a three-stage process.

Money market and interest rates (stage 1). Figure 19.2(a) shows the money market. The horizontal axis shows real money balances (the real purchasing power of money); the vertical axis shows the real interest rate (r). With the economy's price level held constant, an increase in nominal money supply increases the supply of real balances (M): e.g. from M to M'. This, in turn, leads to a surplus of real money balances at the initial equilibrium real interest rate r_1 and hence a fall in the real rate of interest from r_1 to r_2.

What is the opportunity cost of holding money? Is it the real or the nominal rate of interest? Explain.

Interest rates and investment (stage 2). Figure 19.2(b) shows the relationship between real investment levels (I) and the real rate of interest. A fall in the real rate of interest from r_1 to r_2 leads to a rise in investment (and any other interest-sensitive expenditures) from I_1 to I_2. Note that it also encourages consumers to spend, since borrowing through credit cards and personal loans is now cheaper. At the same time, it discourages saving.

Investment and national income (stage 3). Figure 19.2(c) is the Keynesian withdrawals and injections diagram we discussed in Chapter 17. With no change in the economy's price level, a rise in investment leads to a full multiplied rise in real national income from Y_1 to Y_2. If there was also a fall in saving, there would also be a downward shift in the W line, which would further amplify the effects on real national income and national output from the fall in the real rate of interest.

However, the increase in real income to Y_2 shown in Figure 19.2(c) does not take into account the likelihood that any rise in real income will lead to a rise in the demand for real balances from the rise in the transactions demand

Figure 19.2 Effect of a rise in money supply: the interest rate transmission mechanism

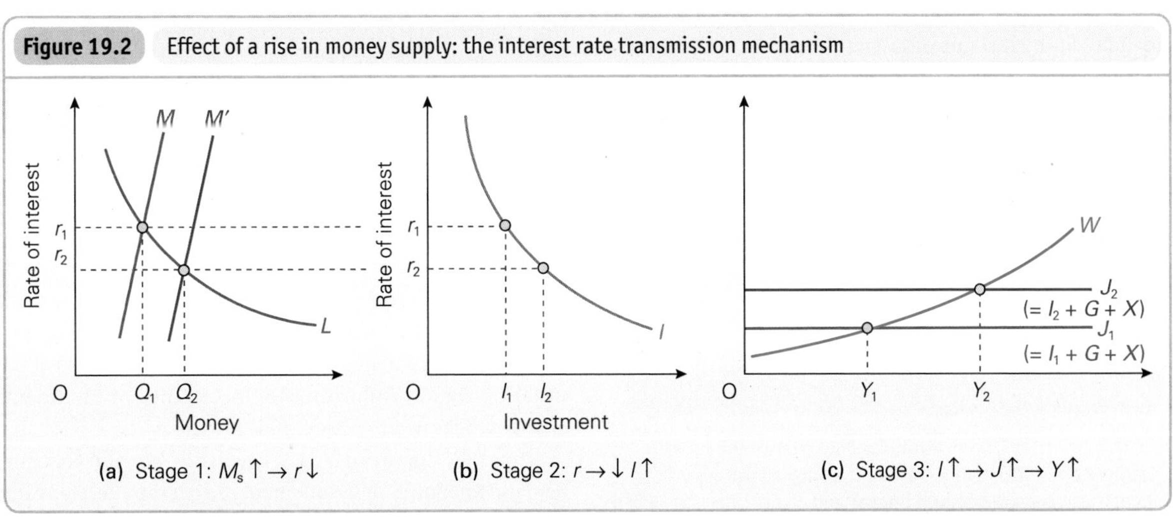

(a) Stage 1: $M_s \uparrow \rightarrow r \downarrow$

(b) Stage 2: $r \rightarrow \downarrow I \uparrow$

(c) Stage 3: $I \uparrow \rightarrow J \uparrow \rightarrow Y \uparrow$

for money, L_1. In other words, L will shift to the right in Figure 19.2(a), and thus r will not fall as much as illustrated. Thus investment (Figure 19.2(b)) and real national income (Figure 19.2(c)) will not rise as much as illustrated either.

TC 6 p66

The overall effect of a change in money supply on national income will depend on the size of the effect in each of the three stages. This will depend on the shapes of the curves in each of the three diagrams and whether they are likely to shift. The effect will be bigger:

- the less elastic the liquidity preference curve (L): this will cause a bigger change in the rate of interest;
- the more interest-elastic the investment curve (I): this will cause a bigger change in investment;
- the lower the marginal propensity to withdraw (*mpw*), and hence the flatter the withdrawals function: this will cause a bigger multiplied change in national income and aggregate demand.

The problem is that stages 1 and 2 may be both weak and unreliable, especially in the short run. This problem is stressed by Keynesians.

Problems with stage 1: the money–interest link

An interest-elastic demand for money. According to Keynesians, the speculative demand for money is highly responsive to changes in interest rates. If people believe that the rate of interest will rise, and thus the price of bonds and other securities will fall, few people will want to buy them now. Instead there will be a very high demand for money and near money as people prefer to hold their assets in liquid form. The demand for money will therefore be very elastic in response to changes in interest rates.

If the demand for money is interest elastic, the demand-for-money curve (the liquidity preference curve, L) will be relatively flat and may even be infinitely elastic at some minimum interest rate. This is the point where everyone believes interest rates cannot go any lower and sooner or later will rise, and therefore no one wants to buy bonds.

With a very gently sloping L curve (as in Figure 19.3), a rise in (real) money supply from M to M' will lead to only a small fall in the real rate of interest from r_1 to r_2. Once people believe that the rate of interest will not go any lower, any further rise in money supply will have no effect on r. The additional money will be lost in what Keynes called the ***liquidity trap***. People simply hold the additional money as idle balances.

Keynes himself saw the liquidity trap as merely a special case: the case where the economy is in deep recession.

Definition

Liquidity trap The absorption of any additional money supply into idle balances at very low rates of interest, leaving aggregate demand unchanged.

Figure 19.3 An elastic liquidity preference curve

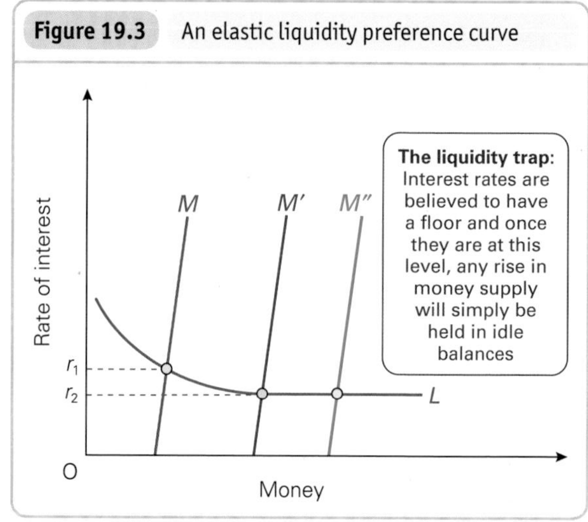

In normal times, an expansion of money supply would be likely to have *some* effect on interest rates. But in a deep recession an expansion of money supply may have no effect on the economy.

The possibility that additional real money balances might simply find themselves lost in a liquidity trap, with individuals and firms unwilling to spend it, was of concern to policy makers after the financial crisis of 2007–8. Central banks responded to the recession which followed by increasing the money supply – a policy known as 'quantitative easing' (see Box 22.10). But, with interest rates at historical lows, the extra money supply was spent largely on assets, such as property and shares, with little extra spending on national output. There was a liquidity trap and V fell.

Similarly, there was concern that increases in money supply by central banks around the world in response to the COVID-19 pandemic might have limited effects on expanding aggregate demand, especially, in this case, with parts of countries' economies forced to close and people thus finding they were saving more.

How might we go about assessing whether quantitative easing actually worked?

An unstable demand for money. Another problem is that the liquidity preference curve (L) is unstable. People hold speculative balances when they anticipate that interest rates will rise (security prices will fall). But it is not just the current interest rate that affects people's expectations of the future direction of interest rates. Many factors could affect such expectations. These could include, for instance, economic policy announcements from government or newly released inflation figures indicating the possibility of imminent changes to monetary policy.

Thus the L curve can be highly volatile. With an unstable demand for money, it is difficult to predict the effect on various interest rates of a change in money supply.

A policy of *targeting* money supply (whether nominal or real) can be criticised for similar reasons. A volatile demand for money can cause severe fluctuations in interest rates if the supply of money is kept constant (see Figure 19.4). These fluctuations will cause further uncertainty and further shifts in the speculative demand for money. Targeting the money supply can therefore add to the volatility of the velocity of circulation (V).

Problems with stage 2: the interest rate–investment link

An interest-inelastic investment demand. In the 1950s and 1960s, many Keynesians argued that investment was unresponsive to interest rate changes: that the I curve in Figure 19.2(b) was steep (as in Figure 19.5). In these circumstances, a very large change in real interest rates would be necessary to have any significant effect on investment and aggregate demand.

KI 9 p64

Figure 19.4 The effect on interest rates of a fluctuating demand for money

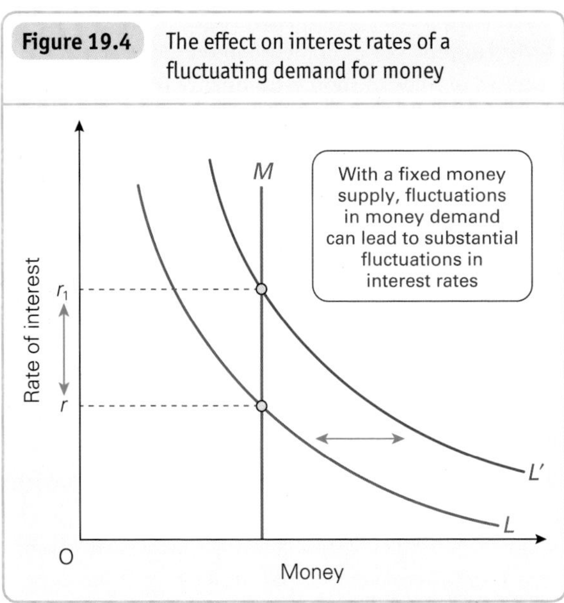

Figure 19.5 Does a fall in interest rates cause only a small rise in investment?

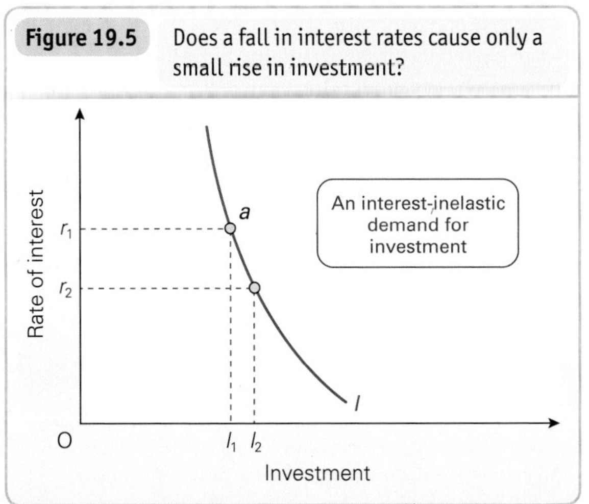

Investment, it was argued, depends on confidence in future markets. If confidence is high, firms will continue to invest even if interest rates are high. They can always pass the higher costs on to the consumer. If confidence is low, firms will not invest even if interest rates are low and borrowing is cheap. Evidence seemed to confirm the interest inelasticity of investment demand.

TC 9 p132

Few Keynesians hold this extreme position today. The evidence for an inelastic investment demand has been challenged. Just because investment was not significantly higher on occasions when interest rates were low, it does not follow that investment is unresponsive to interest rate changes. There may have been changes in *other* factors that helped to *curb* investment: in other words, the I curve shifted to the left. For example, a fall in consumer demand would both cause the low interest rate *and* discourage investment.

Figure 19.5 shows a steep investment demand curve. If the real rate of interest falls from r_1 to r_2 there is only a small rise in investment from I_1 to I_2. Now draw a much more elastic I curve passing through point a. Assume that this is the true I curve. Show how the rate of interest could still fall to r_2 and investment still only rise to I_2 if this curve were to shift.

Even if fixed investment in plant and machinery is not very interest sensitive, other components of aggregate demand may well be: for example, investment in stocks, consumer demand financed through credit cards, bank loans or hire purchase, and the demand for houses financed through mortgages.

The process of financialisation (see section 15.1), some economists argue, may have made aggregate demand more interest-rate sensitive. Increased levels of indebtedness to financial institutions, for example, means that the real expenditure of people and firms is potentially more sensitive to interest rate changes than in the past. This is because debt-servicing costs have a more significant effect on the income they have to spend.

Interest rate changes can generate sizeable *cash flow effects* for highly indebted people and firms. For example, when interest rates fall, the interest payments on those debts subject to variable interest rates fall too, giving people/firms more money to spend. However, it does reduce the interest receipts on savings. The net effect on aggregate demand will depend on which of these two counteracting effects is stronger. Evidence tends to suggest that it is debtors who have the higher marginal propensity to consume. Therefore, the overall effect of a fall in interest rates would be to generate a positive cash flow. This helps to boost aggregate expenditure and so reinforce the interest rate mechanism.

An unstable investment demand. Investment is notoriously volatile (see section 17.5). It is sensitive to a multitude of factors other than the rate of interest, which means that the investment curve in Figure 19.5 can shift erratically. These factors include, for example, business optimism, credit conditions and the availability of finance.

KI 34 p453

Figure 19.6 The effects of interest rate changes, given an unstable investment demand curve

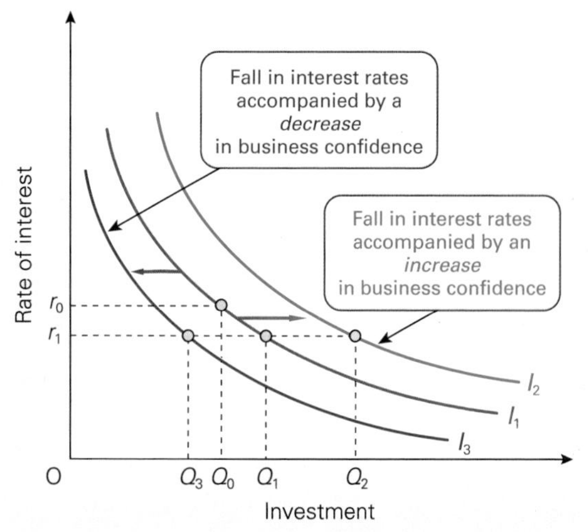

To analyse the effect of interest rate changes given an unstable investment curve consider Figure 19.6. Assume that the initial investment demand curve is given by I_1. Now assume that the central bank reduces interest rates from r_0 to r_1. Other things being equal, the level of investment will rise from Q_0 to Q_1.

However, the fall in real interest rates might be accompanied by other changes that affect investment too. For example, if firms believe that the economy will now pull out of recession, their confidence will increase. Firms may also believe that this growth will help to improve their balance sheets and hence their financial well-being, while financial institutions might be more confident to provide finance. The investment curve will shift to I_2 and investment will increase quite markedly to Q_2.

KI 10 p70

KI 35 p459

If, on the other hand, firms become more pessimistic about the business environment in which they operate, their confidence may well decrease. Again, this could affect credit conditions, with financial institutions now less confident to provide finance. The investment curve will shift to I_3 and the level of investment will actually fall to Q_3.

What we have seen here is that the effectiveness of monetary (and fiscal policy) is dependent on how people respond. Its effectiveness is therefore dependent on a range of factors, many of which are peculiar to that moment in time. Nonetheless, monetary policy is likely to be more effective if people have confidence in its effectiveness. This *psychological* effect can be quite powerful. This helps to explain the co-ordinated responses of central bankers to the financial crisis of 2007–8 and the concerted attempts to inject extra liquidity into the banking system. By doing so they were trying to reassure individuals and firms that the measures would work.

Central banks can also attempt to reinforce the effects of policy through ***forward guidance***. This is where they announce the likely path of policy into the future. In doing so, they hope to influence the decisions of households and businesses. For example, a cut in interest rates could be accompanied by guidance that interest rates are likely to stay low, perhaps until the rate of unemployment falls to some particular level. The hope is that such guidance will provide the confidence that people need to increase their borrowing and spending.

The exchange rate transmission mechanism

A second transmission mechanism is the *exchange rate transmission mechanism*. This is illustrated in the bottom half of Figure 19.1 on page 601 and graphed in Figure 19.7. This mechanism backs up the interest rate mechanism. It includes the exchange rate as an intermediate variable between changes in the money supply and changes in aggregate demand.

Figure 19.7 shows that there are four stages in this exchange rate transmission mechanism. We continue to assume that the economy's price level is constant in the short term and that the expected rate of inflation is 'anchored' at zero.

Money market and interest rates (stage 1). In Figure 19.7(a), a rise in money supply causes a fall in domestic interest rates from to r_1 to r_2.

Interest rates and foreign exchange market (stage 2). In Figure 19.7(b), the fall in domestic interest rates leads to an increased outflow of short-term finance from the country as people demand more foreign assets instead. There will also be a reduced inflow, as depositors seek to take advantage of relatively higher interest rates abroad. The supply of the domestic currency on the foreign exchange market rises from S_1 to S_2 and the demand falls from D_1 to D_2. This causes a depreciation of the exchange rate from er_1 to er_2 (assuming the authorities allow it). In addition, part of the increased money supply will be used to buy foreign assets directly, further contributing to the rightward shift in the supply curve. What is more, the depreciation in the exchange rate may be speeded up or amplified by speculation.

Exchange rates and net exports (stage 3). In Figure 19.7(c), the depreciation of the exchange rate causes a rise in demand for exports (X), since they are now cheaper for people abroad to buy (there is a movement down along the X curve). It also causes a fall in demand for imports (M), since they are now more expensive (there is a movement down along the M curve). Note that the rise in exports and fall in imports gives a current account balance of payments surplus (assuming a previous balance). This is matched by the financial account deficit resulting from the lower interest rate encouraging people to buy foreign assets and people abroad buying fewer of this country's assets. We examine these balance of payments effects in more detail in Chapter 25.

Net exports and national income (stage 4). In Figure 19.7(d), the rise in exports (an injection) and a fall in imports (a withdrawal)

Definition

Forward guidance Announcements from central banks about the likely path of policy which are designed to influence the decisions of households and businesses.

Figure 19.7 The exchange rate transmission mechanism

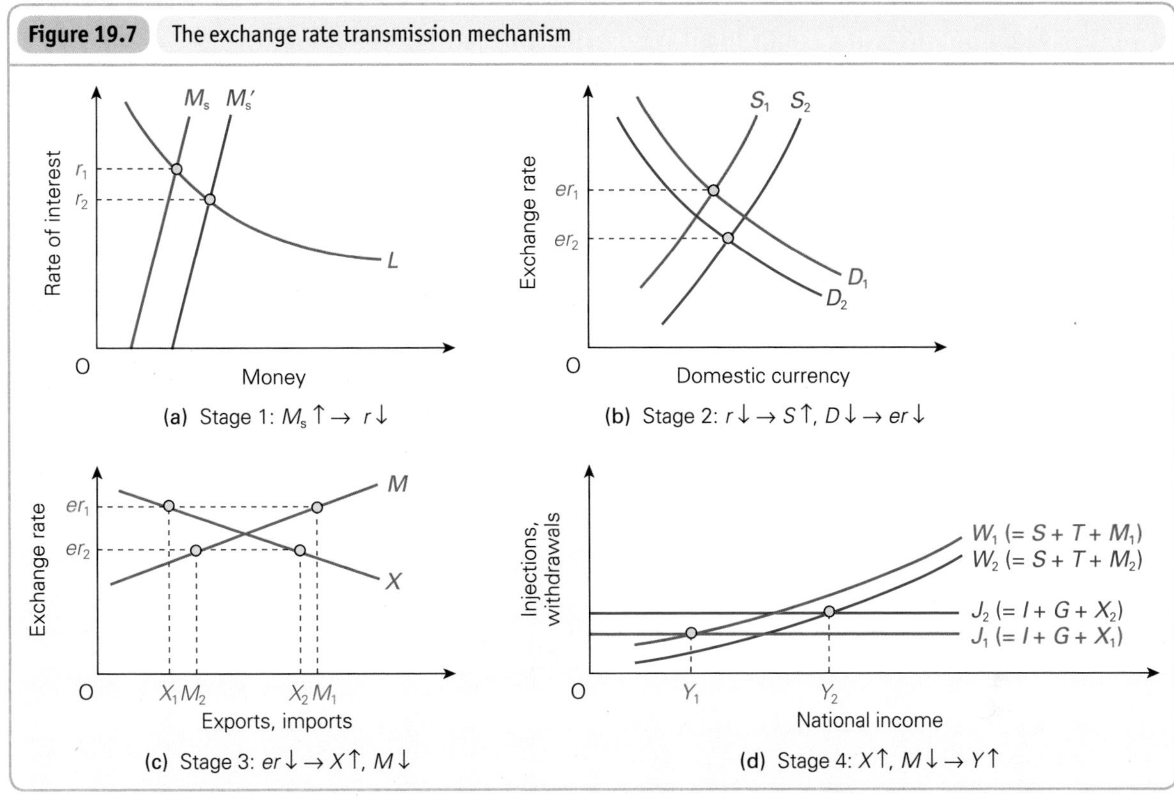

(a) Stage 1: $M_s \uparrow \rightarrow r \downarrow$

(b) Stage 2: $r \downarrow \rightarrow S \uparrow, D \downarrow \rightarrow er \downarrow$

(c) Stage 3: $er \downarrow \rightarrow X \uparrow, M \downarrow$

(d) Stage 4: $X \uparrow, M \downarrow \rightarrow Y \uparrow$

will cause a multiplied rise in national income. The equilibrium level of real national income rises from Y_1 to Y_2.

Stage 1 will tend to be more powerful in a more open economy. The liquidity preference curve will tend to be less elastic because, as interest rates fall, people may fear a depreciation of the domestic currency and switch to holding other currencies. Just how strong stage 1 will be depends on *how much* people think the exchange rate will depreciate.

Stage 2 is likely to be very strong indeed. Given the openness of international financial markets, international financial flows can be enormous in response to interest rate changes. Only a relatively small change in interest rates is necessary to cause a relatively large financial flow. Monetarists and new classical economists stress the importance of this effect. Any fall in interest rates, they argue, will have such a strong effect on international financial flows and the exchange rate that the rise in money supply will be relatively quickly and fully transmitted through to aggregate demand.

Stage 3 may be rather limited in the short run, as the demand and supply of both imports and exports may be relatively inelastic in the short run. Given time, however, consumers and firms may be more responsive and the effects on imports and exports correspondingly larger. However, the size of the effect depends on people's expectations of exchange rate movements. If people think that the exchange rate will fall further, importers will buy *now* before the rate does fall. Exporters, on the other hand, will hold back as long as possible before shipping their exports. These actions will tend to push the exchange rate down. But such speculation is very difficult to predict as it depends on often highly volatile expectations.

KI 10 p70

If importers and exporters believe that the exchange rate has 'bottomed out', what will they do?

Stage 4 is the familiar multiplier, only this time triggered by a change in imports and exports.

Again, as with the interest rate transmission mechanism, the full effect is unlikely to be as large as that illustrated. This is because the increased real national income (Y) will cause an increased *transactions* demand for money. This will shift the L curve to the right in Figure 19.7(a), and thus lead to a smaller fall in the rate of interest than that illustrated.

The overall effect via the exchange rate transmission mechanism can still be quite strong, but the precise magnitude is usually highly unpredictable.

The effects of changes in money supply will also depend on just how free the exchange rate is. If the government intervenes to 'peg' (i.e. fix) the exchange rate or to prevent excessive fluctuations, the transmission mechanism will not work in the way described. Alternative exchange rate systems (or 'regimes', as they are called) are examined in Chapter 25.

The portfolio balance effect

Money can also impact on the economy through a process of 'portfolio adjustment': a mechanism that was stressed by monetarists. If money supply increases, people will have more money than they need to hold. They will spend this

BOX 19.1 CHOOSING THE EXCHANGE RATE OR THE MONEY SUPPLY EXPLORING ECONOMICS

You can't choose both

If the government expands the money supply, then interest rates will fall and aggregate demand will tend to rise. With a floating exchange rate, this will cause the currency to depreciate.

But what if the government attempts to maintain a fixed exchange rate? To do this it must keep interest rates comparable with world rates. This means that it is no longer free to choose the level of money supply. The money supply has become endogenous.

The government can't have it both ways. It can choose the level of the money supply (providing it has the techniques to do so) and let interest rates and the exchange rate be what they will. Or it can choose the exchange rate, but this will then determine the necessary rate of interest and hence the supply of money. These issues are explored in Chapter 25.

Can the government choose both the exchange rate and the money supply if it is prepared to use the reserves to support the exchange rate?

surplus. Much of this spending will go on goods and services, thereby directly increasing aggregate demand:

$$M_s\uparrow \rightarrow M_s > M_d \rightarrow AD\uparrow$$

The theoretical underpinning for this is given by the *theory of **portfolio balance***. People have a number of ways of holding their wealth: as money, or as financial assets such as bills, bonds and shares, or as physical assets such as houses, cars and televisions. In other words, people hold a whole portfolio of assets of varying degrees of liquidity – from cash to property.

If money supply expands, people may find themselves holding more money than they require: their portfolios are unnecessarily liquid. Some of this money will be used to purchase financial assets, and some to purchase *goods and services*. As more assets are purchased, this will drive up their price. This will effectively reduce their 'yield'. For bonds and other financial assets, this means a reduction in their rate of interest. For goods and services, this means a reduction in their marginal utility/price ratio: a higher level of consumption will reduce their marginal utility and drive up their price. The process will stop when a balance has been restored in people's portfolios. In the meantime, there will have been extra consumption and hence a rise in aggregate demand.

Definition

Portfolio balance The balance of assets, according to their liquidity, that people choose to hold in their portfolios.

Do you think that this is an accurate description of how people behave when they acquire extra money?

Many Keynesian economists, however, argue that this mechanism may be weak and unreliable. What is more, a rise in money supply may itself come about as a result of a direct change in one of the components of aggregate demand, making it difficult to identify how much of any effect is due solely to the change in money supply.

Consider an increase in government expenditure financed by purchases of Treasury bills by the banking system. Will any impact on output and prices come primarily from the extra liquidity in the balance sheets of households and firms, or will it come directly from the higher government expenditure?

Even if there is a direct increase in liquidity (e.g. through quantitative easing) without any accompanying change in government expenditure or taxation, the effect of this additional liquidity will depend on the extent to which banks use it to extend new credit. This, in turn, will depend on the *demand* for credit, which in a recession may fall as people try to rein in their spending.

The question then is the extent to which any extra money will be passed on around the economy. Box 19.2 looks at this process.

Portfolio balance and the interest rate mechanism

The holding of a range of assets in people's portfolios can strengthen the interest rate transmission mechanism by making the liquidity preference curve less elastic (curve L in Figure 19.2(a) on page 601 is relatively steep). The reason is TC 6 p66 that speculative balances of money may now have a much smaller role. But why?

A reduction in the rate of interest (r) following an increase in the money supply may well make bond holding less attractive, but this does not mean that the extra money will be mainly held in idle balances. Again, it can be used to purchase other assets such as property. Idle balances may expand only slightly.

Redraw the three diagrams of Figure 19.2 with a steeper L curve. Show how an increase in money supply will have a larger effect on national income.

How stable is the velocity of circulation?

Short-run variability of V

Most economists agree that there is some variability of the velocity of circulation (V) in the short run if the money supply is changed. To the extent that interest rates and yields do fall with an expansion of the money supply, people may well hold somewhat larger money balances: after all, the interest sacrificed by not holding bonds, etc., has been reduced. If people hold relatively more money, the velocity of circulation is thereby reduced, thus reducing the effect on aggregate demand. Furthermore, the direct mechanism (i.e. the portfolio balance mechanism) may take time to operate. In the meantime, V will fall.

KI 33 p377

TC 9 p132

Also, the demand for money can shift unpredictably in the short run with changing expectations of prices, interest rates and exchange rates. Thus V is unpredictable in the short run, and so is the effect of monetary policy on aggregate demand. For these reasons, changing the money supply may not be an effective means of short-run demand management.

Long-run stability of V

The main claim of monetarists is that the velocity of circulation (V) is relatively stable over the longer run, and any changes that do occur are the predictable outcome of institutional changes, such as the increased use of credit cards (see Box 19.3).

One explanation of why V remains relatively stable in the long run, despite an increase in money supply, is that sufficient time has elapsed for the direct mechanism to have worked fully through.

Another explanation is the effect on inflation and consequently on interest rates. This works as follows.

Assume an initial increase in money supply. Interest rates fall. V falls. But if money supply goes on rising and hence expenditure goes on rising, inflation will rise. This will drive up *nominal* interest rates (even though *real* interest rates will stay low). But in choosing whether to hold money or to buy assets, it is the nominal rate of interest that people look at, since that is the opportunity cost of holding money. Thus people economise on money balances and V rises back again.

In extreme cases, V will even rise to levels higher than before. This is likely if people start speculating that prices will rise further. People will rush to buy goods and assets before their prices rise further. This action will help to push the prices up even more. This form of destabilising speculation took place in the hyperinflation of Germany in the 1920s and in Zimbabwe in the years up to 2008, as people spent their money as quickly as possible (see Case Study 15.12 on the student website).

With a predictable V in the longer run, monetarists have claimed that monetary policy is the essential means of controlling long-term aggregate demand. For this reason, they have favoured a longer-term approach to monetary policy, including targets for the growth of the money supply (see page 511).

Most governments adopt a policy of setting a target for the rate of inflation. This involves the central bank controlling aggregate demand by choosing an appropriate rate of interest. In these circumstances, the money supply must be *passively* adjusted to ensure that the chosen rate of interest is the equilibrium rate. This means expanding the money supply in line with the increase in real national income (Y) and the targeted increase in the price level (P).

These rules can, however, be relaxed. Central banks around the world aggressively loosened monetary policy in response to the global financial crisis of the late 2000s and COVID-19 pandemic of the early 2020s. Huge amounts of extra money were created through programmes of quantitative easing. Mitigating the damage to economic activity became more important than strictly adhering to a (short-run) inflation target. Nevertheless, central banks were still keen to ensure that these policies were consistent with meeting their inflation target over the medium term. Indeed, with inflation rates generally well below the target during these periods, expansionary monetary policy was consistent with meeting the inflation target.

We explore inflation targeting and its effects in section 19.4. We explore the operation of monetary policy in section 22.3.

BOX 19.2 **PARTY GAMES AND THE VELOCITY OF MONEY**

Are you ready for a game of pass-the-parcel?

What will be the effect of an increase in money supply on spending, output and prices? To address this we need to understand how money supply interacts with money demand. This requires an analysis of the velocity of circulation of money (V).

An interesting way of thinking about V and what it might mean for the economy is to consider changes in money in the context of a game of pass-the-parcel!

Assume there has been an increase in money supply and that this causes individuals and firms to have *excess* money balances. In response, they can look to pass the excess on to somebody else and, of course, if that individual or firm also has excess money balances, they too will look to pass it on. The consequence is a game of pass-the-parcel, where the parcel is money and the passing occurs through spending. The quicker the 'parcel' is passed, the higher will V be. If the extra spending is not matched by extra output (Y), then we would expect prices (P) to rise too.

But what if the increase in money occurred at a time when people are wanting to increase their money holdings? This time, there will be little impact on spending (and, in turn, output and prices) as people hold on tightly to the parcel and refuse to play the game. In this case, the velocity of circulation would fall.

The growth in money and spending

One way of assessing the extent to which the non-bank private sector might be holding excess money balances is to compare the annual growth in broad money with the annual growth in nominal spending (nominal GDP). Chart (a) is an indicator of the *excess nominal money balances* of the UK's non-bank private sector.

Positive values show excess money holdings: the velocity of circulation has slowed. This was the situation through the second half of the 1980s and much of the 2000s. To restore the balance of their portfolios, individuals and firms would be expected to pass the parcel more quickly, so causing the velocity of circulation to increase again. In turn, this increased spending would be expected to result in increasing economic activity, but perhaps in inflationary pressures too.

On the other hand, negative values indicate a deficit of liquid funds: the velocity of circulation has increased. This was the situation for much of the 2010s. To restore balance in this case, individuals and firms would be expected to increase money balances and so pass the parcel more slowly. The reduction in spending would act to constrain economic activity and limit any potential inflationary pressures.

Money balances in different sectors

The non-bank private sector comprises households, non-financial corporations (firms) and other financial corporations (e.g. insurance companies, pension funds and unit trusts). The implications for spending, economic activity and prices will depend in part on which of these groups is experiencing excess or deficit money balances since the adjustment of their portfolios is likely to have different economic effects. Excess money holdings by households, for example, may lead to more consumption; that by firms to more investment;

(a) *Annual money growth less nominal spending growth*

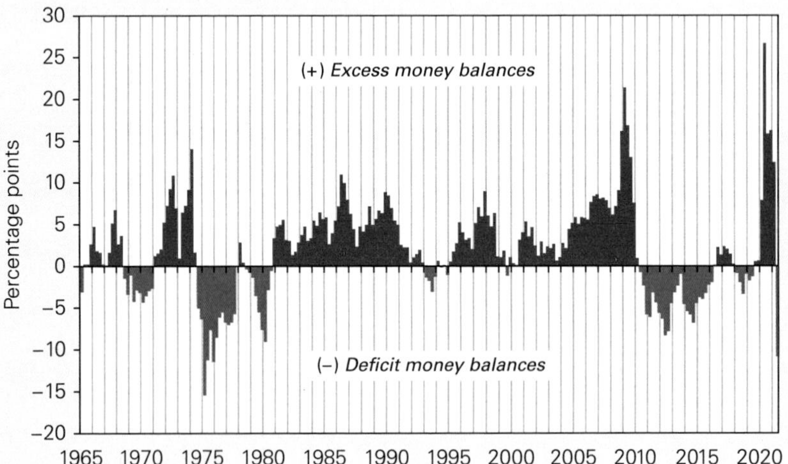

Sources: (i) *Statistical Interactive Database*, series LPQVQJW, Bank of England (29 July 2021), www.bankofengland.co.uk/boeapps/database/; and (ii) *Quarterly National Accounts*, series IHYO, Office for National Statistics, www.ons.gov.uk/economy/grossdomesticproductgdp/timeseries/ihyo/pn2

EXPLORING ECONOMICS

and that by other financial corporations to changes in asset purchases.

Chart (b) shows, alongside the annual rate of growth of M4 and nominal GDP, the growth in the stock of M4 across the non-bank private sector since 2000.

It captures the dramatic slowdown from 2008 in the growth of broad money holdings of households and non-financial corporations. This reflected a substantial contraction in lending and so of credit creation by financial institutions.

As if the negative impact of this on spending growth was not enough, households and firms were also looking to rebuild their balance sheets and reduce their debt exposure. An important element of this was their increased demand for money balances. In what were incredibly uncertain times, and with the markets for shares and housing depressed, households and firms sought to increase the liquidity of their portfolios. It was almost as if the music for our game of pass-the-parcel had stopped. Inevitably, the growth in nominal spending fell sharply, economic activity floundered and the economy entered into recession.

By contrast, broad money holdings of other financial corporations (OFCs) grew rapidly in the late 2000s. This was largely the result of quantitative easing with OFCs exchanging gilts for money from the Bank of England. While this growth would wane for a time, the additional quantitative easing in 2016, following the outcome of the UK referendum on EU membership, and again during the COVID-19 pandemic, would mean further substantial increases in the liquidity of OFCs' balance sheets.

Excessive money holdings by OFCs can be passed on by purchasing other assets. In doing so, asset prices tend to rise and their yields fall. Therefore, it was hoped that among the positive effects of passing-the-parcel would be lower borrowing costs, a boost to the wealth of asset holders and increased economic activity.

What can we infer from charts (a) and (b) about the stability of the velocity of circulation in the short run? What can we learn from chart (b) about the association between the growth of money holdings and that in nominal GDP?

Create a time series chart since the early 1990s showing the annual rate of growth of broad money (series LPQVQJW available from the Bank of England Statistical Interactive database: www.bankofengland.co.uk/boeapps/database/) alongside the annual rate of consumer price inflation (series D7G7 available from the ONS; https://www.ons.gov.uk/economy/inflationandpriceindices/). Write a short summary of your findings.

(b) *Annual growth of spending and broad money by sector*

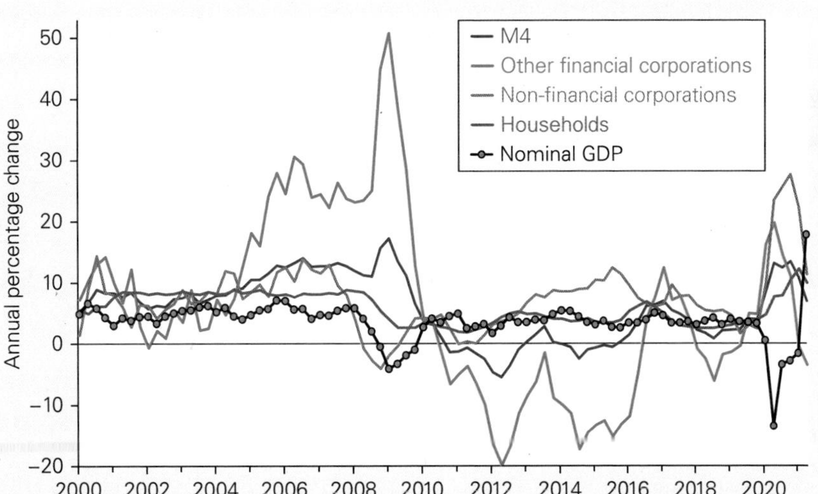

Sources: (i) *Statistical Interactive Database*, series LPQVVHK, LPQVVHQ, LPQVVHW and LPQVQJW, Bank of England, (29 July 2021), www.bankofengland.co.uk/boeapps/database/; and (ii) *Quarterly National Accounts*, series IHYO, Office for National Statistics, www.ons.gov.uk/economy/grossdomesticproductgdp/

BOX 19.3 THE STABILITY OF THE VELOCITY OF CIRCULATION

What is the evidence?

How stable is the velocity of circulation (*V*) in practice? Does the evidence support the monetarist case that it is relatively stable or the Keynesian case that it fluctuates unpredictably, at least in the short run? Unfortunately, the facts do not unequivocally support either side.

The evidence

How has *V* behaved over time? To answer this we need to measure *V*. A simple way of doing this is to use the formula $V = PY/M$ (rearranging the terms in the quantity equation $MV = PY$). Thus we need to measure *PY* and *M*. *PY* is simply the money value of national output: in other words, GDP at current prices. The value of *M* (and hence *V*) will depend on which measure of the money supply we use.

The diagram shows how the velocities of circulation in the UK of both broad money (M4) and narrow money (notes and coin) have changed over the years.

Broad money

Long-term increases in the velocity of broad money from 1973 to 1979 are explained by the increase in money substitutes and credit cards, and thus smaller holdings of money balances.

The decrease after 1980 reflects falling inflation and nominal interest rates, with people being increasingly prepared to hold money in sight accounts; the growth in wholesale deposits (which earn interest); and people putting a larger proportion of their savings into bank and building society accounts, attracted by higher real interest rates and new types of high-interest instant-access accounts. As the pace of these changes slowed, so the fall in velocity became gentler after 1990.

However, in the second half of the 2000s the velocity of broad money once again fell sharply. The financial and economic upheaval of this period is likely to have increased the demand for liquid assets.

After the effects of the financial crisis waned, and spending began to grow again, so the velocity of circulation increased. The size of people's desired money balances gradually decreased as confidence slowly grew.

But the COVID-19 pandemic of the early 2020s necessitated measures to curb social interaction and restrict

Velocities of circulation of narrow and broad money

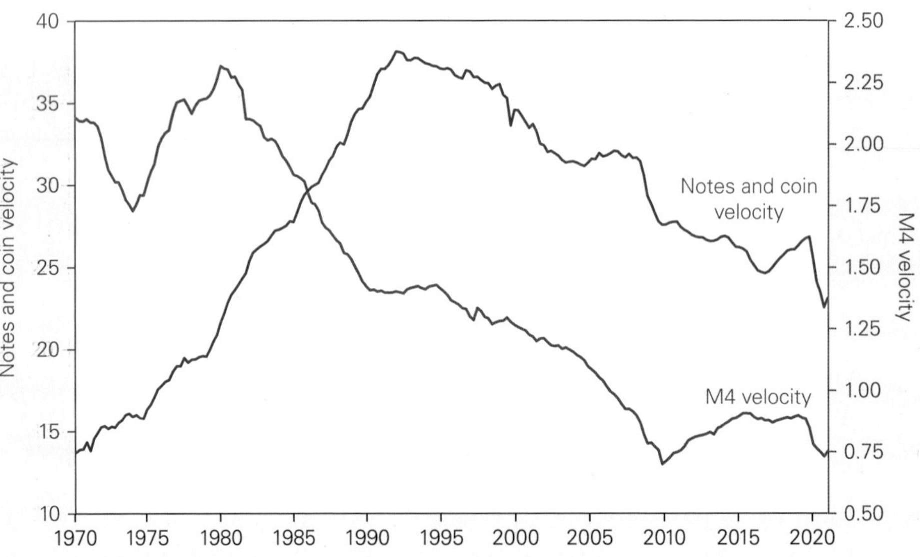

Sources: (i) *Statistical Interactive Database*, series LPMAVAB and LPQAUYN, Bank of England (4 August 2021), www.bankofengland.co.uk/boeapps/database/; and (ii) *Quarterly National Accounts*, series YBHA, Office for National Statistics, www.ons.gov.uk/economy/grossdomesticproductgdp/

economic activity. While policies were introduced to try to limit the effect on employment and incomes, the nominal value of household spending in the second quarter of 2020 was down 14 per cent on the same quarter a year earlier. With the marked fall in spending and the expansion of the money supply (see below) the velocity of broad money fell back to financial crisis levels.

Narrow money

The velocity of narrow money more than doubled between 1974 and 1993. One reason for this was the increased use of credit and debit cards, which reduced the amount of cash people needed to hold. The growth of cash machines also reduced the need to hold so much cash, given that many people could easily obtain more at any time. The relatively smaller amount of cash thus circulated faster. But, as with broad money, these changes in the velocity of narrow money ceased in the early 1990s.

Then, during the 2000s, the velocity of narrow money fell back sharply. Low inflation rates, by reducing the opportunity cost of holding cash, contributed to the fall during the first half of 2000s. As with broad money, the impact of the economic and financial crisis contributed to a further fall in the velocity of narrow money during the second half of the 2000s.

But, unlike broad money velocity, narrow money velocity continued to fall through much of the 2010s. Part of the reason had to do with the continuing rapid growth of purchases with cards. This was fuelled by the growth in online sales and by the use of contactless card payments. At the same time, with continuing record low interest rates, the opportunity cost of holding narrow money was very low.

These factors were then exacerbated by the COVID-19 pandemic. The health intervention measures restricted the use of notes and coin and boosted contactless card payments and e-commerce. The result was the velocity of narrow money was at its lowest in nearly 40 years.

The point however made by monetarists is that in more normal times many of the changes referred to here are predictable and gradual and do not, therefore, undermine the close relationship between M and PY.

Velocity and active monetary policy

Evidence shows periods when the velocity of circulation has been relatively stable in the short run, especially during the 1990s. However, this is largely because changes in money supply were not used to manipulate aggregate demand and hence national income.

This is not the case in periods when active monetary policy is used. In response to the financial crisis of the late 2000s and the COVID-19 pandemic of 2020, the Bank of England embarked on a policy of quantitative easing to increase the money supply. As we discussed in Box 19.2 its success depends on the responses of individuals and firms and so the extent to which V would fluctuate. A fall in the velocity of circulation makes quantitative easing less successful.

The direction of causality

Monetary and real changes often work together – especially in the long run. An expansionary fiscal policy over a number of years will increase public-sector borrowing, which, in turn, will lead to an increase in money supply (M). If the fiscal policy increases nominal national income (PY), V may well as a result remain constant. But it does not follow from this that it was the growth in M that *caused* the growth in PY. On the few occasions when fiscal and monetary policy work in opposite directions, the evidence is unclear as to which has the bigger effect – especially as the time period is rarely long enough for the full effects to be identified.

What we are concerned about here is the direction of causality. Changes in aggregate demand may go together with changes in money supply. But is it higher money supply causing higher aggregate demand, or the other way round, or the two simply occurring simultaneously?

Monetarists argue that increases in money supply cause (nominal) aggregate demand to expand (with a lag of perhaps a few months). For them money supply is exogenous: determined independently by the central bank. Keynesians, by contrast, argue that higher aggregate demand causes an increased demand for bank loans, and banks are only too happy to create the necessary credit, thus expanding the money supply. For them, money supply is endogenous.

Why might it be difficult to establish the direction of causality from the evidence?

Create a time series chart since the early 1980s comparing the annual rates of growth of notes and coin (series LPMB8H3) and broad money (series LPQVQJW) available from the Bank of England Statistical Interactive database (www.bankofengland.co.uk/boeapps/database/). Write a short summary of your findings.

Section summary

1. The quantity equation $MV = PY$ can be used to analyse the possible relationship between money and prices. Whether and how much increases in money supply (M) affect the price level (P) depends on whether the velocity of circulation (V) and the level of real national income (Y) are independent of money supply (M).
2. The interest rate transmission mechanism works as follows: (a) a rise in money supply causes money supply to exceed money demand; assuming that expected inflation is fixed, real interest rates fall; (b) this causes investment to rise; (c) this causes a multiplied rise in national income; but (d) as national income rises, so the transactions demand for money rises, thus preventing quite such a large fall in interest rates.
3. The effect will be weak if the demand-for-money curve (L) is elastic and the investment demand curve is inelastic. The effects may also be unreliable because of an unstable and possibly inelastic investment demand.
4. The exchange rate transmission mechanism works as follows: (a) a rise in money supply causes interest rates to fall; (b) the rise in money supply plus the fall in interest rates causes an increased supply of domestic currency to come on to the foreign exchange market; this causes the exchange rate to fall; (c) this causes increased exports and reduced imports, and hence a multiplied rise in national income.
5. According to the theory of portfolio balance, if people have an increase in money in their portfolios, they will attempt to restore portfolio balance by purchasing assets, including goods. Thus an increase in money supply is transmitted directly into an increase in aggregate demand.
6. The demand for money is more stable in the long run than in the short run. This leads to a greater long-run stability in V (unless it changes as a result of other factors, such as institutional arrangements for the handling of money).

19.2 THE MONETARY EFFECTS OF CHANGES IN THE GOODS MARKET

If there is an expansion in one of the components of aggregate demand (C, I, G or $X - M$), what will be the monetary effects? Will the current level of money supply act as a constraint on the growth in national income? In other words, will an expansion of one component of aggregate demand, such as government expenditure, be at the expense of another component, such as investment?

The monetary effects of an increase in injections

Let us assume that business confidence grows and that, as a result, the level of investment increases. Let us also assume that there is a given quantity of real money balances in the economy and, further, that prices are constant in the short term. Will the rise in investment lead to a full multiplier effect on national income?

The effect of the rise in investment is illustrated in Figure 19.8. In Figure 19.8(a), the rise in investment leads to a rise in injections to J_2. Other things being equal, the real level of national income would rise to Y_2. But this increase in real national income also leads to a rise in the transactions demand for money. The rise in demand for real money balances leads to the demand-for-money curve in Figure 19.8(b) shifting from L to L'.

If the central bank does not wish to allow the real value of the economy's money supply to rise, the higher demand for money will force it to raise interest rates to r_2. The effect of higher real interest rates is to reduce the level of investment. The overall rise in injections will be smaller than the rise from J_1 to J_2. Also net saving (i.e. saving minus borrowing) will rise as the higher real interest rate acts as both an incentive for households to save and a disincentive for them to borrow. This causes an upward shift in the W curve. The result is that the real level of national income will not rise as far as Y_2. In the extreme case, there would be no rise in real national income at all.

If, however, the central bank responds to the increase in investment by expanding the real money supply to M_s', there will be no change in the real rate of interest and hence no dampening effect on either the volume of investment or consumption.

Assume that the government cuts its expenditure and thereby runs a public-sector surplus.

(a) What will this do initially to equilibrium national income?

(b) What will it do to the demand for money and initially to interest rates?

(c) Under what circumstances will it lead to

(i) a decrease in money supply;

(ii) no change in money supply?

(d) What effect will (i) and (ii) have on the rate of interest compared with its original level?

Crowding out

Another example of the monetary constraints on expansion in the goods market is the phenomenon known as ***financial crowding out***. This is where an increase in public-sector spending reduces private-sector spending (see Box 16.2 on page 506).

Definition

Financial crowding out Where an increase in government borrowing diverts money away from the private sector.

Figure 19.8 The monetary effects of a rise in injections

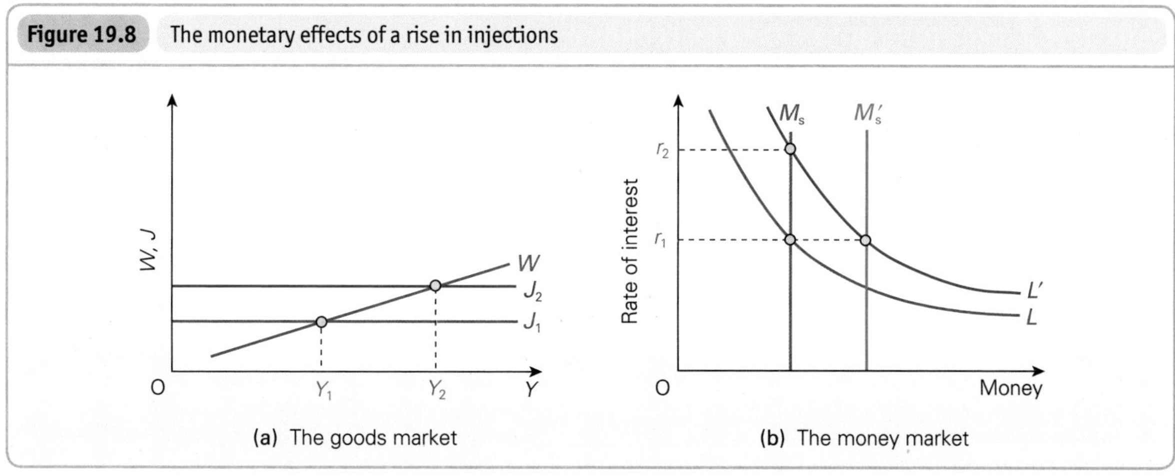

Figure 19.9 Different views on the demand for money

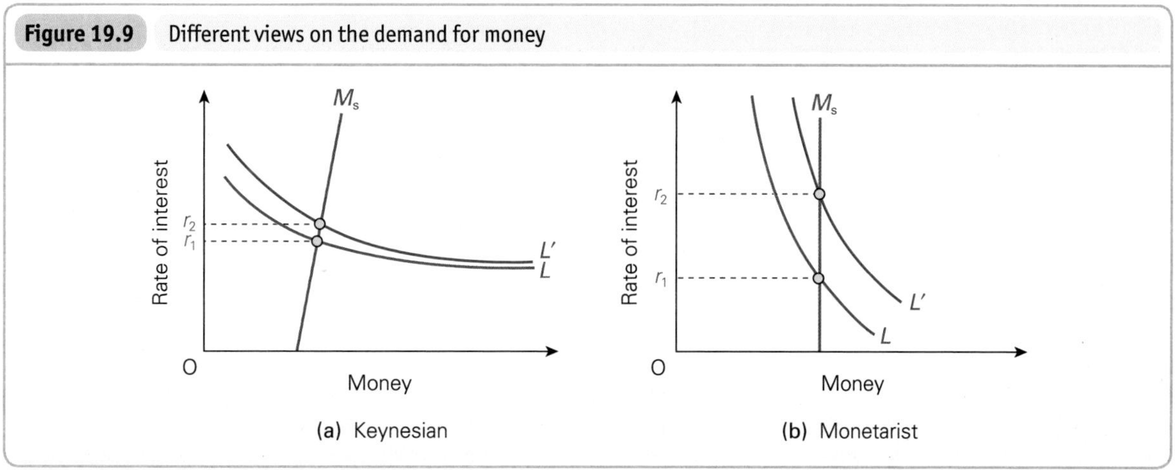

To illustrate the effects, assume that previously the government has had a balanced budget, but that now it chooses to expand the level of government expenditure without raising additional taxes. As a result, it runs a budget deficit ($G > T$). But this deficit will have to be financed by borrowing. This increased borrowing will lead to an increase in the money supply if it is financed by sales of government debt to financial institutions, especially debt with shorter maturity. Alternatively, if it is financed by selling bills or bonds outside the banking sector, there will be no increase in the money supply.

The effect can once more be shown in Figure 19.8. A rise in government spending on goods and services will cause injections to rise to J_2 and, other things being equal, real national income will rise to Y_2. But, as with the case of increased investment, this increase in real national income will lead to a rise in the demand for real money balances. In Figure 19.8(b), the demand-for-money curve shifts from L to L'.

If public-sector borrowing is financed in such a way as to allow the real money supply to expand to M_s' there will be no change in the real interest rate and no crowding-out effect. If, however, the real money supply is not allowed to expand, interest rates will rise to r_2. This in turn will reduce investment: crowding out will occur. Injections will fall back again below J_2. In the extreme case, injections could even fall back to J_1 and thus real national income return to Y_1. Here crowding out is total.

The extent of crowding out

Just how much crowding out will occur when there is an expansionary fiscal policy, but when the supply of real money balances is *not* allowed to expand, depends on two things.

The responsiveness (elasticity) of the demand for money to a change in interest rates. If the demand is relatively elastic (as in Figure 19.9(a)), the increase in demand, represented by a horizontal shift in the liquidity preference curve from L to L', will lead to only a small rise in real interest rates. If, however, the demand is relatively inelastic (as in Figure 19.9(b)), the same horizontal shift will lead to a bigger rise in real interest rates.

KI 9 p64

BOX 19.4 **CROWDING OUT IN AN OPEN ECONOMY** EXPLORING ECONOMICS

Taking exchange rate effects into account

Will fiscal policy be crowded out in an open economy with floating exchange rates? Assume that the government increases its expenditure but does not allow the money supply to expand: a case of pure fiscal policy. What will happen?

- The increased government expenditure will increase the demand for money (see Figure 19.8(b)).
- This will drive up interest rates – the amount depending on the elasticity of the liquidity preference curve.
- This will lead to an inflow of finance from abroad, which in turn will lead to an appreciation of the exchange rate.
- The higher exchange rate will reduce the level of exports (an injection) and increase the level of imports (a withdrawal). This will add to the degree of crowding out.

Thus in an open economy with floating exchange rates, an expansionary fiscal policy will be crowded out not only by higher interest rates, but also by a higher exchange rate.

We have argued that the short-term inflow of finance following a rise in the rate of interest will drive up the exchange rate. Are there any effects of expansionary fiscal policy on the demand for imports (and hence on the current account) that will go some way to offsetting this?

As we saw in section 19.1, Keynesians generally see the liquidity preference curve as being more elastic than do monetarists and new classical economists. They therefore argue that a rise in money demand normally leads to only a relatively modest rise in interest rates.

The responsiveness (elasticity) of investment to a change in interest rates. As we saw on page 603, Keynesians argue that investment is relatively unresponsive to changes in real interest rates. Businesspeople are much more likely to be affected by the state of the market for their product than by interest rates. Thus in Figure 19.10(a), there is only a small fall in the volume of investment. Monetarists and new classical economists, however, argue that investment is relatively responsive to changes in interest rates. Thus in Figure 19.10(b), there is a bigger fall in investment.

In the Keynesian case, therefore, the rise in demand for money arising from an expansionary fiscal policy will have only a small effect on interest rates and an even smaller effect on investment. Little or no crowding out takes place. In fact, the expansion of demand might cause an increase in investment through the accelerator effect (see pages 551–3). TC 15 p543

Monetarists and new classical economists argue that interest rates will rise significantly and that there will be a severe effect on investment. Crowding out is substantial. For this reason, they argue that, if money supply is to be kept under control to prevent inflation rising, it is vital for governments to reduce the size of their budget deficit. They argue that, in the long run, crowding out is total, given the long-run stability of the velocity of circulation.

Global crises and crowding out

Following the global financial crisis, the early 2010s witnessed a general tightening of fiscal policy around the world as governments sought to tackle the huge rises in public-sector debt that had resulted from bank bailouts and the fiscal stimulus packages that had been used to tackle the recession. Many governments, including the UK Coalition government, were unwilling to adopt a more expansionary

Figure 19.10 Different views on the demand for investment

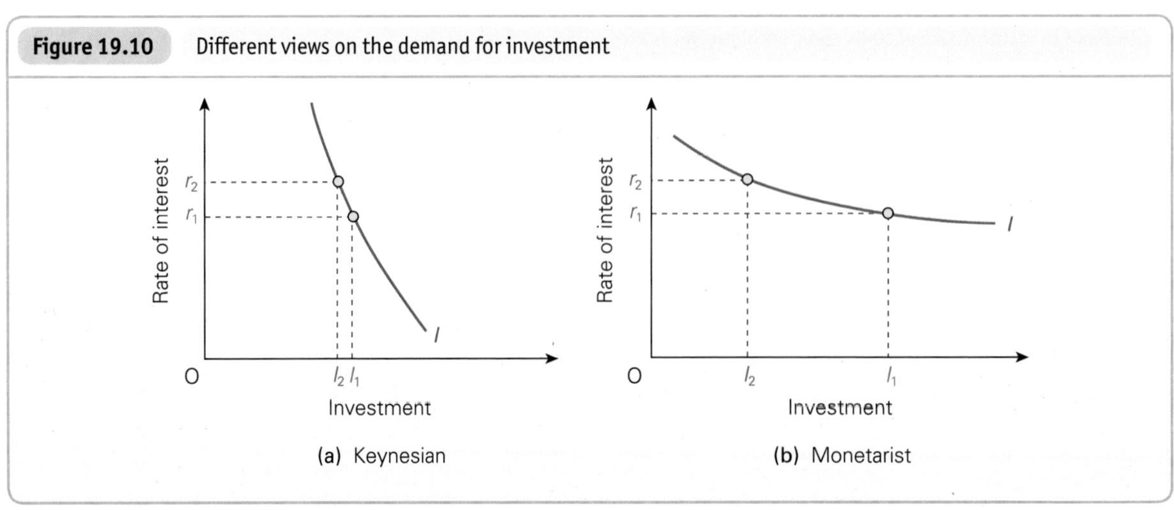

fiscal policy. They were afraid of crowding out private-sector investment and 'spooking' the markets, with people believing that they were not serious about deficit reductions.

The public finances were again placed under incredible strain in the early 2020s during the COVID-19 pandemic as governments once more became the 'shock absorber' of the economy. Borrowing rose in many countries to historically high levels as governments took a series of measures principally designed to safeguard jobs and incomes as they constrained economic activity to protect lives. Despite concerns once more about the sustainability of the public finances (see section 22.1), a widely held view was that governments should avoid pressing down too quickly and too hard on the fiscal brake pedal. Rather, governments could continue to take advantage of low borrowing costs.

In its World Economic Outlook Update in January 2021, the International Monetary Fund argued that:

> Advanced economies continue to enjoy extremely low borrowing costs and can use the opportunity to provide fiscal support as needed to ensure a lasting recovery. Moreover, with well-anchored inflation expectations and subdued inflation pressure across the group, monetary policy should remain accommodative until the recovery takes firm root.[1]

Is money supply exogenous or endogenous?

Money supply is *exogenous* (independently determined) if it can be fixed by the authorities and if it does not vary with aggregate demand and interest rates. The money supply 'curve' would be vertical, as in Figure 19.9(b). It would shift only if the government or central bank *chose* to alter the money supply.

Money supply is *endogenous* (determined within the model) if it is determined by aggregate demand and hence the demand for money: banks expanding or contracting credit in response to customer demand. In such a case, the money supply curve would be upward sloping or even horizontal. The more that money supply expands in response to an increase in aggregate demand, the more gently upward sloping the money supply curve would be.

The more elastic the money supply curve, the less will money act as a constraint on expansion in the goods market, and the less will a rise in government expenditure crowd out private expenditure. In other words, the less will real interest rates rise in response to a rise in the demand for real money balances.

The extreme monetarist position is that money supply is wholly exogenous. The extreme Keynesian position is that money supply is wholly endogenous: money simply passively expands to meet the demand for money.

In reality, money supply is partly exogenous and partly endogenous. The authorities are able to influence money supply, but banks and other financial institutions have considerable scope for creating credit in response to rises in demand. If control of the money supply is adopted as the basis for policy, the authorities must reduce the endogenous element to a minimum.

The authorities in many countries recognise the difficulties in controlling the money supply directly. They therefore influence the supply of money indirectly by controlling interest rates and hence the demand for money.

Sometimes, however, in extreme circumstances, the authorities may attempt to control money supply directly. As we saw in Chapter 18, central banks around the world injected large amounts of liquidity into their financial systems in response to the global financial crisis and the COVID-19 pandemic. The aim was to help stabilise their economies and ease credit conditions. This use of 'quantitative easing' is examined in section 22.2.

Section summary

1. Changes in injections or withdrawals will have monetary implications. If there is a rise in investment with no change in the supply of real money balances, the increased demand for money will drive up real interest rates and reduce both investment and consumption. The resulting rise in real income will be smaller.
2. Similarly, if there is a fiscal expansion and *no* change in the money supply, the increased demand for money will again drive up the real interest rate. This will to some extent crowd out private expenditure and thus reduce the effectiveness of the fiscal policy.
3. The extent of crowding out will depend on the shape of the liquidity preference curve and the investment demand curve. The less elastic the demand for money, and the more elastic the investment demand, the more crowding out will take place, and the less effective will fiscal policy be.
4. If there is a rise in aggregate demand, money supply may rise in response to this. The more elastic the supply of money curve, the less crowding out will take place.
5. Money supply is not totally exogenous. This makes it hard for the authorities to control it precisely. Generally, therefore, central banks try to control *interest rates* and attempt to alter liquidity to back this up. Sometimes, however, they may take more deliberate steps to inject extra liquidity into the financial system.

1 World Economic Outlook Update, IMF (January 2021), p. 10, www.imf.org/en/Publications/WEO/Issues/2021/01/26/2021-world-economic-outlook-update

19.3 MODELLING THE INTERACTION OF MONETARY POLICY AND THE GOODS MARKET

The goods and money markets

In this chapter, we have shown that there are two key markets in the economy at macroeconomic level, and that these two markets interact. The first is the goods market; the second is the money market. Each of these two markets has been analysed by using a model.

In the case of the goods market, the model is the simple Keynesian model (see section 17.2). Any change in injections (J) or withdrawals (W) will cause national income to change. For example, a rise in government purchases (an injection) increases aggregate expenditure (E) which causes a *multiplied* rise in equilibrium real national income (assuming that there are sufficient idle resources).

In the case of the money market, the model is the one showing the real demand for money (L) and the real supply of money (M) and their effect on the rate of interest. A change in the supply or demand for money will cause the equilibrium rate of interest to change. Monetary policy operates directly in this market, either by affecting the supply of money or by operating on interest rates.

What we have shown in this chapter is that the two markets *interact*: that changes in one market cause changes in the other. Therefore, we need a model which allows us to *combine* the goods and money markets. The traditional approach has been through a model known as the *IS/LM* model. The *IS* curve is based on equilibrium in the goods market; the *LM* curve is based on equilibrium in the money market. By examining the interaction of both markets we can see the implication for interest rates *and* output.

In many countries, including the UK, interest rates have become the key tool of monetary policy, with money supply controlled directly only in extreme circumstances. A (nominal) interest rate is announced by the central bank and then it supplies a given level of reserves to banks (central bank money), taking into account the real demand for money, so that the announced interest rate is the equilibrium one. Central banks do this principally to affect aggregate demand so as to meet an inflation rate target (normally set by the government). In most developed countries, including the UK, the USA and the eurozone, the target inflation rate is 2 per cent.

Under inflation targeting the authorities use monetary policy to affect equilibrium in the goods market. Therefore, the modern approach to modelling the interaction between the goods and money markets retains the *IS* curve as the *IS* curve relates to equilibrium in the goods market. However, the *LM* curve is replaced with a 'monetary policy curve' – the *MP* curve. The *MP* curve captures the interest rate choices of central bank.

The traditional *IS/LM* model can be found in the Appendix to this chapter. We now develop the *IS/MP* model.

To keep the analysis simple, in both models we assume a closed economy: i.e. one with no international trade or international financial flows. We drop this assumption in an extended version of the *IS/LM* model in the appendix to Chapter 25.

The *IS* curve

Deriving the IS curve

The *IS* curve is derived from the simple Keynesian model. Here we are using the injections/withdrawals version.

The top part of Figure 19.11 shows the injections and withdrawals diagram, only in this case, for simplicity, we are assuming that saving is the only withdrawal from the circular flow of income, and investment the only injection. The levels of saving (S) and investment (I) are *real* levels, and in equilibrium $I = S$ (i.e. $J = W$). The bottom part of Figure 19.11 shows the *IS* curve. This shows all the various combinations of real interest rates (r) and real national income (Y) at which $I = S$. (Case 19.3 on the student website shows how the *IS* curve can be derived using the income–expenditure approach – the 'Keynesian cross' diagram).

Assume initially that the real interest rate is r_1. Both investment and saving are affected by the level of real interest rates, and thus, other things being equal, an interest rate of r_1 will give particular investment and saving schedules. Let us say that, in the top part of Figure 19.11, these are shown by the curves I_1 and S_1. The equilibrium level of real national income will be where $I = S$, i.e. at Y_1. Thus in the lower part of Figure 19.11, an interest rate of r_1 will give a level of output Y_1. Thus point *a* is one point on the *IS* curve. At an interest rate of r_1 the goods market will be in equilibrium at output Y_1.

Now what will happen if the real rate of interest changes? Let us assume that it falls to r_2. This will cause a rise in investment and a fall in saving. A rise in investment is shown in the top part of Figure 19.11 by a shift in the investment line to I_2. Likewise a fall in saving is shown by a shift in the saving curve to S_2. This will lead to a multiplied rise in income to Y_2 (where $I_2 = S_2$). This corresponds to point *b* in the lower diagram, which therefore gives a second point on the *IS* curve.

Thus *lower* real interest rates are associated with *higher* real national income if equilibrium is to be maintained in the goods market ($I = S$).

The elasticity of the IS curve

The elasticity of the *IS* curve (i.e. the responsiveness of real national income to changes in real interest rates) depends on two main factors.[2]

The responsiveness of investment and saving to interest rate changes. The more investment and saving respond to a change in the real rate of interest, the bigger will be the vertical

2 Note that, as with demand and supply curves, the elasticity of the *IS* curve will vary along its length. Therefore, we should really talk about the elasticity at a particular point on the curve, or between two points.

Figure 19.11 Goods market equilibrium: deriving the *IS* curve

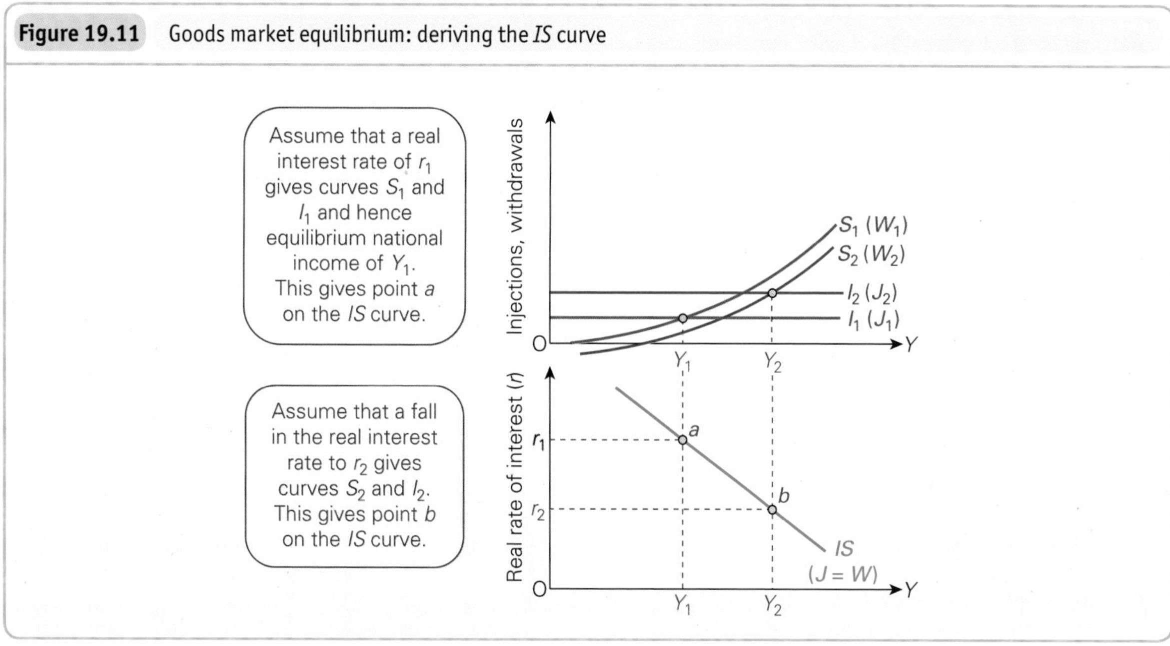

shift in the *I* and *S* curves in the top part of Figure 19.11, and thus the bigger will be the effect on national income. Therefore, the more interest-rate responsive is aggregate expenditure (*E*), the bigger is the impact of a change in interest rates on national income and the more elastic (flatter) is the *IS* curve.

KI 9 p64

The size of the multiplier. This is given by 1/*mps* (i.e. 1/*mpw* in the full model). The *mps* is given by the slope of the *S* curve. The flatter the curve, the bigger the multiplier. The larger the value of the multiplier, the bigger will be the effect on real national income of any rise in investment and fall in saving, and the more elastic therefore will be the *IS* curve. Thus the flatter the *S* curve in the top part of Figure 19.11, the flatter the *IS* curve in the bottom part.

TC 15 p543

In fact the multiplier process, whereby changes in expenditure generate further changes in expenditure because of their impact on national income, will interact with a series of ***amplifiers***. Commonly identified amplifiers are confidence, uncertainty and credit and financial market conditions. These affect the size of the change in spending that occurs as national income changes. The more powerful these amplifiers are, the flatter the *IS* curve. We discuss in section 19.4 the role of the financial sector as an amplifier.

In a complete model where there were three injections (I, G and X) and three withdrawals (S, T and M), what else would determine the shape of the 'JW' curve?

Keynesians argue that the *IS* curve is likely to be fairly inelastic (steep). The reason they give is that investment is not very responsive to changes in real interest rates: the demand-for-investment curve in Figure 19.2(b) on page 601 is relatively inelastic. Saving also, claim Keynesians, is unresponsive to real interest rate changes. The effect of this is that there will only be a relatively small shift in the *I* and *S* curves in response to a change in interest rates, and thus only a relatively small change in national income.

Monetarists, by contrast, argue that investment and saving are relatively responsive to changes in real interest rates and that therefore the *IS* curve is relatively elastic (relatively flat).

Shifts in the IS curve

A change in real interest rates will cause a movement *along* the *IS* curve. As we saw in Figure 19.11, a reduction in interest rates from r_1 to r_2 causes a movement *along* the *IS* curve from point *a* to point *b*. Hence as real interest rates fall, real aggregate demand increases.

A change in any *other* determinant of investment or saving, however, will *shift* the whole curve. The reason is that it will change the equilibrium level of real national income at any given real rate of interest.

An increase in investment, other than as a result of a fall in real interest rates, will shift the *IS* curve to the *right.* This could happen, for example, if there were a general increase in business confidence: a positive confidence shock.

A rise in business confidence *at the current real interest rate* will cause an upward shift of the *I* curve in the top part of Figure 19.11, which will cause a multiplied rise in real income. Thus, in the lower part of Figure 19.11, a higher equilibrium real income is now associated with each level of the real interest rate: the *IS* curve has shifted to the right. Likewise, for any given real interest rate, a fall in saving, and hence a rise in consumption, would also shift the *IS* curve to the right.

How does a confidence shock differ from the idea of confidence as an amplifier?

Definition

Amplifiers Mechanisms, such as confidence, uncertainty, and credit and financial market conditions, that amplify the magnitude of changes in spending.

In a complete model (with three injections and three withdrawals), where the *IS* curve was a '$J = W$' curve rather than a simple '$I = S$' curve, similar shifts would result from changes in other injections or withdrawals. Thus an expansionary fiscal policy that increased government expenditure on goods and services (*G*), or cut taxes (*T*), would also shift the '*IS*' curve (i.e. the *JW* curve) to the right. In each case, the rightward shift of the *IS* curve will be larger, the bigger the multiplier and the more powerful are amplifiers with which it interacts.

In a complete JW model, what else would cause the JW curve (a) to shift to the right; (b) to shift to the left?

The *MP* curve

Deriving the MP curve

To help analyse the monetary policy (*MP*) curve consider Figure 19.12. Unlike the *IS* curve, which was developed as part of the *IS/LM* model (see Appendix to this chapter) in the 1930s, the *MP* curve is a relatively new model, developed in the context of inflation targeting by central banks.[3]

We begin by assuming that the central bank has a *single mandate*: to target a given rate of inflation, π^*. In controlling inflation, the central bank adjusts the nominal policy rate. This is the rate of interest at which it is prepared to supply liquidity to financial institutions and which affects other interest rates in the economy. For ease of exposition we assume a single representative nominal interest rate (*i*).

As we saw earlier (see page 600), it is the *real* rate of interest that is key in affecting aggregate demand. We assume that people use the current rate of inflation (π) in forming expectations of the real interest rate. Hence, the real rate of interest (*r*) is simply the nominal interest rate (*i*) less the current rate of inflation (π).

The central bank raises *real* interest rates when inflation rises above the target (π^*) and lowers them when inflation falls below the target. To raise the real rate of interest (*r*), the nominal rate of interest (*i*) must rise *relative* to the current rate of inflation. Similarly, for the real rate of interest to fall the nominal interest rate must fall relative to the current rate of inflation.

An upward-sloping MP curve. The *MP* curve is drawn as upward sloping. To understand why, assume that the economy represented in Figure 19.12 is at point *a* with real national income Y_1 and real interest rates r_1. Assume too that inflation is currently at the target rate (π^*) and that Y_1 is the economy's potential output level, which in the short term is fixed.

Now assume that there is a positive demand-side shock. This (as we shall see later in Figure 19.14) is reflected in a rightward shift of the *IS* curve. This results in an increase in

Figure 19.12 Deriving the *MP* curve

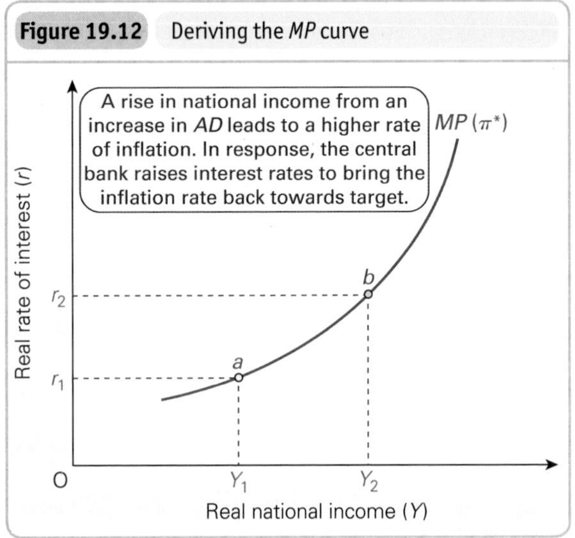

real national income, say to Y_2, but generates demand-pull inflation as spare capacity in the economy falls. This mirrors a movement along an expectations-augmented Phillips curve (see Figure 16.4) whereby as output rises (relative to its potential level), and unemployment falls (relative to its natural rate), the rate of inflation rises. Consequently the rate of inflation (π) rises above the target (π^*).

The central bank will respond by raising the real rate of interest, say to r_2. This gives a second point on the *MP* curve at point *b*.

The slope of the MP curve. The *extent* which the central bank raises real interest rates as national income rises depends on three key factors.

- First, is the increase in the rate of inflation. The more inflation increases, the more will the central bank raise interest rates and hence the steeper will be the *MP* curve. This is captured by the expectations-augmented Phillips curve (*EAPC*), its slope is reflected in the *MP* curve.
- Second, is the weight the central bank places on stabilising inflation. The more important this is, the larger the increase in real interest rates and hence the steeper the *MP* curve.
- Third, is the central bank's forecasts of how the transmission mechanisms of monetary policy identified in section 19.1 will affect inflation. Therefore, the *MP* curve represents the *short-term* response of the central bank. The more it believes that inflation will respond to a rise in real interest rates, the flatter will be the *MP* curve.

A movement along the curve. The short-term response of the central bank to a positive demand-side shock is to raise real interest rates: a move up the *MP* curve. But what if the economy had experienced a negative shock to aggregate demand? Because the fall in real national income causes the rate of inflation to fall below the target rate, the central bank responds by lowering the real rate of interest.

3 In fact, there are different versions of the *MP* curve. One version focuses on an interest rate target, rather than an inflation target. Another focuses on a complex target that is a combination of both inflation and national income or inflation and unemployment. The version we develop here is the most useful in the context of a specific inflation target and where the interest rate set by the central bank is only an intermediate variable determined by the actual rate of inflation relative to the target rate.

The relationship underpinning the *MP* curve can be summarised as follows:

$$Y\uparrow \rightarrow \pi > \pi^* \rightarrow r\uparrow$$
$$Y\downarrow \rightarrow \pi < \pi^* \rightarrow r\downarrow$$

The elasticity of the MP curve

KI 9 p64

The elasticity of the *MP* curve, i.e. the responsiveness of interest rates to changes in national income, will depend on the degree of slack in the economy.

If the economy is operating well below potential national income – a large negative output gap – a rise in national income (*Y*) will have little effect on inflation and hence little effect on the desired real rate of interest (*r*). The *MP* curve will be relatively flat. This means that the curve is relatively *inelastic* as interest rates (the dependent variable) are relatively unresponsive to changes in national income (the independent variable).

If, however, there is a positive output gap, with firms operating close to full capacity, a rise in income will be reflected largely in a rise in inflation, causing the central bank to make a relatively large change to interest rates. The *MP* curve will be relatively steep (elastic) as interest rates are relatively sensitive to changes in national income.

This means that the curve is likely to get steeper as national income rises, as in Figure 19.12. The closer the economy gets to full employment – i.e. the smaller the negative output gap or the bigger the positive output gap – the less slack there is in the economy. The less the slack, the more firms are likely to respond to a rise in demand by raising real prices (i.e. raising their prices above the rate of inflation) and the greater the resulting rise in inflation and the rise in central bank interest rates.

Shifts in the MP curve

A particular *MP* curve assumes a particular central bank target, a given expected rate of inflation and a particular level of potential income. If any one of these changes, a new *MP* curve will have to be drawn.

Change in the target rate of inflation. If the central bank chooses to raise the target rate of inflation, the *MP* curve will shift downwards. Any given level of national income and hence inflation rate will result in a lower central bank interest rate.

Cost-push inflation. If there is a reduction in cost-push inflation, perhaps from an easing of commodity prices or a fall in inflationary expectations, the *MP* curve will shift downwards. For any given level of national income, there will be a lower rate of inflation and thus the central bank will choose a lower real interest rate.

Change in potential national income. An increase in potential output, perhaps as a result of technological progress or a surge in investment in new capacity, will reduce demand-pull inflation pressures. This will shift the *MP* curve downwards. The downward shift of the *MP* curve will be greater at higher levels of output where there was previously a lack of spare capacity (see Figure 19.14(b)).

Central bank mandates

If, instead of targeting just inflation, the central bank targets a combination of inflation and national income, known as a Taylor rule (we examine Taylor rules in section 21.5 on pages 683–4), then the *MP* curve will change shape.

For example, putting a greater emphasis on targeting a particular level of national income will make the *MP* curve steeper, as changes in national income will cause the central bank to make larger changes in interest rates than it would have done if it targeted inflation alone. In the extreme case of targeting just national income and not inflation at all, the curve would be vertical at the targeted level of national income.

Alternatively, the central bank may target unemployment alongside inflation. Again this will tend to make the curve steeper the more closely unemployment is aligned to national income. For example, the Fed in the USA has a dual mandate: it is required to target not only inflation but also to maximise employment.

Case Study 19.4 on the student website analyses the *MP* curve in more detail.

If the central bank targets real national income rather than inflation, what will be the shape of the MP curve?

Equilibrium

Equilibrium national income and the rate of interest are given by the intersection of the *IS* and *MP* curves. This is shown as point *a* in Figure 19.13, giving equilibrium national income of Y_e and an interest rate of r_e.

To demonstrate why this is an equilibrium, consider what would happen if national income were not at Y_e but at Y_1. According to the *MP* curve (point *b*), the higher inflation associated with this higher level of national income would lead the central bank to set an interest rate of r_1. But this higher interest rate of r_1 will dampen aggregate demand. According to point *c* on the *IS* curve, the goods market will be in equilibrium at a level of national income of Y_2. This will cause the inflation rate to fall and hence the central bank to lower the rate of interest. As it does so, there will be a movement down along the *IS* curve and a rise in national income until equilibrium is reached at Y_e.

In practice, if the two markets are not in equilibrium, the central bank will attempt to move straight to equilibrium by forecasting the likely movements in the economy and the results of its actions. The Bank of England, for example, at the meetings of the Monetary Policy Committee, examines forecasts of inflation and output contained in its quarterly *Inflation Report* and other models of the economy.

The next step in the analysis is to consider how shifts in either curve affect national income, inflation and interest rates.

Figure 19.13 Equilibrium in the goods and money markets

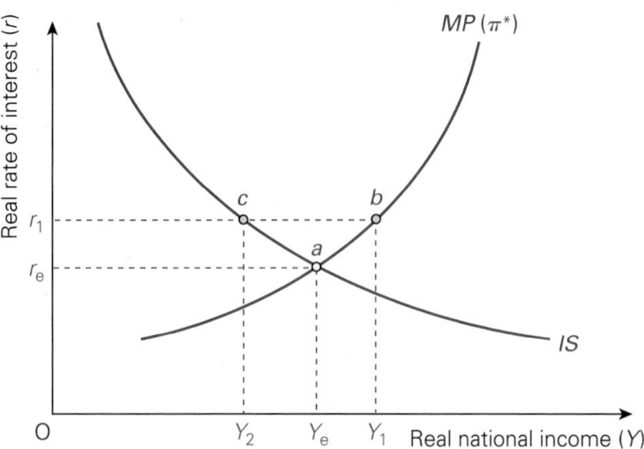

At Y_1, the central bank will set a real rate of interest of r_1. This will cause a fall in national income to Y_2 (a move along the *IS* curve). The central bank will then reduce the interest rate to r_e to achieve the target rate of inflation at Y_e.

*LOOKING AT THE MATHS

Equilibrium in the *IS/MP* model is where the two functions, *IS* and *MP*, are equal. The simplest mathematical representation of this is where both *IS* and *MP* are simple linear (i.e. straight-line) functions. The *IS* function could be expressed as

$$r = a - bY \qquad (1)$$

In other words, the higher the real rate of interest (r), the lower will be the level of aggregate demand and hence real national income (Y).[1] This is consistent with a downward-sloping *IS* curve.

The *MP* function can be written as

$$r = c + dY \qquad (2)$$

In other words, the higher the level of real national income (and hence the higher the rate of inflation), the higher will be the real rate of interest set by the central bank. This is consistent with an upward-sloping *MP* curve.

Equation (2) can be derived from the relationships between inflation (π) and national income and between inflation and the rate of interest. The relationship between inflation and national income is given by

$$\pi = e + f(Y - Y_p) \qquad (3)$$

where Y_p is potential national income. The greater the excess of actual (short-run) income over potential income (i.e. the bigger the positive output gap), the higher will be the rate of inflation.

The relationship between inflation and the rate of interest is given by the central bank response function, which, in its simplest form, is given by

$$r = g + h(\pi - \pi^*) \qquad (4)$$

where π^* is the target rate of inflation. The higher the actual inflation rate is relative to the target rate, the higher will be the rate of interest set by the central bank. Substituting equation (3) in equation (4) gives

$$r = g + h(e + f(Y - Y_p) - \pi^*) \qquad (5)$$

Assuming that Y_p and π^* are constant, equation (5) can be simplified as equation (2):

$$r = c + dY \qquad (2)$$

We can then solve for Y from equations (1) and (2) by setting the two equations equal. Thus

$$a - bY = c + dY$$

that is

$$bY + dY = a - c$$

giving

$$Y = \frac{a - c}{b + d}$$

Note that a change in any of the factors affecting Y, other than r, will shift the *IS* curve. Such factors include taxes, government expenditure, the exchange rate, expectations about income and prices, and so on.

Similarly, a change in any of the factors affecting r, other than Y, will shift the *MP* curve. Such factors include potential national income (Y_p), cost pressures, inflationary expectations and the inflation target (π^*).

The IS function can be written as

$$Y = IS(r, G, t, X, M, er, Y^e \ldots)$$

where G is government expenditure, t is the tax rate, X and M are the levels of exports and imports, er is the exchange rate, Y^e is the expected level of real national income and '. . .' represents other unspecified determinants.

Write an MP function in the form r = MP(– – – – –), identifying each of the determinants.

1 Note that although equation (1) shows r as a function of Y, the model in fact has Y as the dependent variable. In other words, r determines Y. We express equation (1) this way to make it consistent with equation (2), where r is the dependent variable.

Full effect of changes in the goods and money markets

Changes in goods market equilibrium resulting from changes to aggregate demand are illustrated by a shift in the *IS* curve. Changes to monetary policy or potential national income are illustrated by a shift in the *MP* curve.

Shifts in the IS curve

Assume in Figure 19.14(a) that equilibrium is at point *a*, at a level of national income of Y_1. Now assume that a positive demand shock occurs resulting in a *given* rightward shift in the *IS* curve from IS_1 to IS_2. This could arise, for example, because of a general increase in optimism over the future macroeconomic environment that leads economic agents to increase spending or because of a loosening of fiscal policy (e.g. an increase in government purchases). This causes national income and the inflation rate to rise. The central bank responds to the higher inflation by raising the real rate of interest. There is a movement up along the *MP* curve. Equilibrium is reached at point *b* at a level of national income of Y_2 and a rate of interest of r_2.

Shifts in the MP curve

As we noted earlier, many countries have adopted some form of inflation targeting. However, inflation targeting can take many different forms and the policy rule can be changed or adapted. For example, the Federal Reserve from 2008 and the Bank of England from 2013 supplemented their existing policy frameworks with forward guidance: statements about the likely path of future interest rates. By communicating that interest rates were likely to remain low for some time, the hope was that this would give economic agents confidence to bring forward spending.

To illustrate a change to the monetary policy rule using the *IS*/*MP* framework, consider the case where the central bank now sets a lower interest rate for any given level of output and rate of inflation. The effect of this looser monetary policy rule is to move the *MP* curve vertically downwards. This is illustrated by a move from MP_1 to MP_2 in Figure 19.14(b). The central bank reduces the nominal rate of interest so as to give a real rate of interest of r_3. As a result there is a movement along the *IS* curve to point *c* and national income rises to Y_3.

A reduction in cost-push inflation would have a similar effect. This may be the result of an easing of oil price inflation or a smaller percentage increase in the minimum wage. This again can be illustrated by a shift in the *MP* curve from MP_1 to MP_2 in Figure 19.14(b). An increase in potential national income would also shift the *MP* curve downwards, but as explained earlier, the reduction in the real rate of interest is larger at higher levels of national income. This is illustrated by a shift in the curve from MP_1 to MP'_2.

How would a central bank's aversion to inflation affect how much the MP curve moves vertically downwards in response to a reduction in cost-push inflation?

Shifts in both curves

If aggregate demand increases and, at the same time, either cost-push pressures ease or potential national income rises, actual income can rise without imposing extra inflationary pressures. This is illustrated in Figure 19.14(c). National income rises to Y_4. The central bank does not need to raise interest rates as there is no upward movement in inflation.

Size of the effect on national income of shifts in either or both curves

KI 9 p64

The magnitude of a change in income resulting from a shift in one or both curves depends not only on the size of the shift, but on the shape of the curves.

- The effect of a shift in the *IS* curve on national income (*Y*) will be larger, the *flatter* is the *MP* curve. When *MP* is relatively flat, either because of the central bank's monetary policy rule and/or because there is plenty of slack in the economy, a rightward shift in *IS* will lead to only a small

Figure 19.14 *IS*/*MP* analysis of changes in the goods and money markets

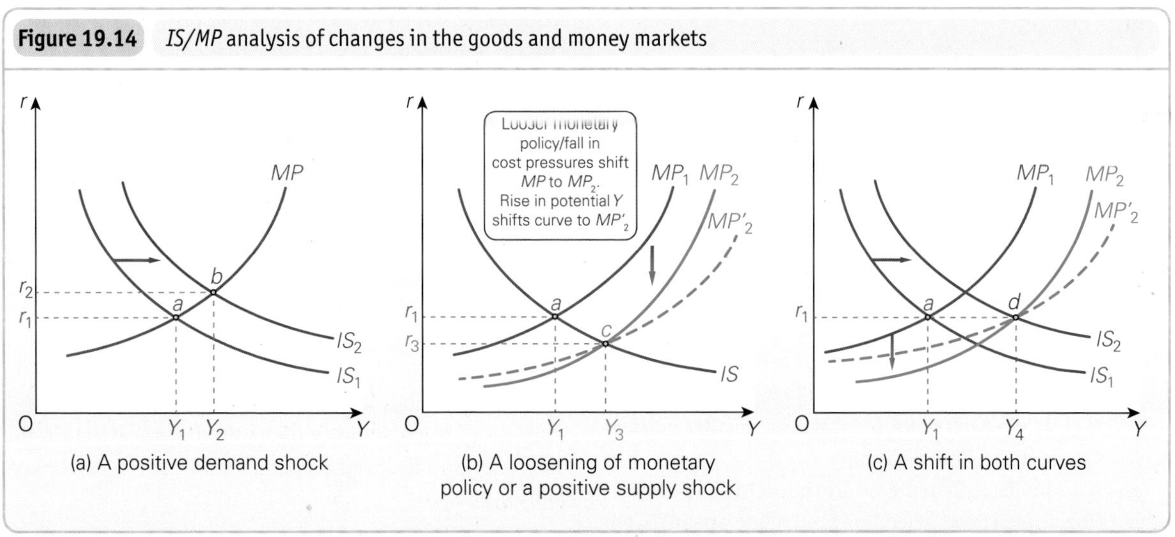

(a) A positive demand shock

(b) A loosening of monetary policy or a positive supply shock

(c) A shift in both curves

rise in the real rate of interest (r) by the central bank. This limits the extent to which interest rates offset the increase in aggregate demand.

- For a given value of the multiplier and strength of amplifiers, there will be a given rightward shift of the *IS* curve following an increase in aggregate demand. The less responsive is aggregate demand to changes in interest rates, the *steeper* will be the *IS* curve. Therefore, the rise in r that results from the rightward shift in the *IS* curve will lead to only a small curtailing of expenditures and the rise in national income will be greater.
- For a given interest-rate responsiveness of aggregate demand, there will be a given upward shift of the *IS* curve following a positive demand shock: more will be demanded at each rate of interest. The larger the value of the multiplier, and the more powerful the amplifiers with which it interacts, the *flatter* will be the *IS* curve and hence the larger its rightward shift for any given upward shift and the larger the resulting increase in national income (try drawing it).
- An increase in potential income will shift the *MP* curve to the right. This will have a larger effect on current real national income (Y) when the economy is operating near full capacity and the *MP* curve is steeper, as it will ease the capacity contraint and lead to a relatively large fall in r.
- For positive aggregate supply shocks in general (rightward shifts in the *MP* curve), when the *IS* curve is relatively flat, the fall in r will lead to a relatively large increase in expenditures and hence national income. Case 19.5 on the student website analyses supply shocks in more detail.
- The effect of a shift in either curve will be bigger if matched by a similar shift in the other curve.

Section summary

1. The *IS/MP* model shows the interaction between the goods and money markets. It allows us to examine the relationship between national income and interest rates where central bankers set interest rates.
2. Equilibrium in the goods market is shown by the *IS* curve. This shows all the combinations of the real rate of interest (r) and real national income (Y) where investment (I) equals saving (S) (or, in a complete Keynesian model, where injections equal withdrawals). As the rate of interest rises, so investment will fall and saving will rise: therefore equilibrium national income will fall. The *IS* curve is thus downward sloping.
3. The *MP* curve shows the real rate of interest that the central bank would choose at any particular level of national income. We assume that the rate of inflation rises with the level of national income. The central bank will thus raise the real rate of interest (i.e. the nominal rate plus the rate of inflation) as national income rises. This gives an upward-sloping *MP* curve. Supply shocks, a change in the inflation rate target or the central bank's monetary stance will lead to vertical shifts of the *MP* curve.
4. Equilibrium occurs where $IS = MP$. At this point the goods market is in equilibrium at the real interest rate chosen by the central bank.
5. A shift in either curve will lead to a new equilibrium. The resulting size of the change in real national income and real interest rates will depend on the size of the shift and the shape of the other curve.

19.4 CREDIT CYCLES AND THE GOODS MARKET

Credit cycles

The amount of credit extended to borrowers by financial institutions tends to go in cycles. These cycles reflect financial conditions. The term 'financial conditions' refers to the ease with which households and businesses can obtain credit. Financial conditions will fluctuate when the central bank implements changes in monetary policy. But other factors, including the confidence and financial well-being of investors and borrowers, matter too. Because of their potential impact on the macroeconomic environment, these conditions are closely monitored by central banks. Measures of financial conditions, such as the Bank of England's *Monetary and Financial Conditions Index*, are discussed further in Case Study 19.6 on the student website.

Fluctuations in credit in the UK are shown in Figure 19.15, which plots annual flows of lending from monetary financial institutions (MFIs) to households and private non-financial corporations from 1965. The flows are measured relative to GDP, allowing us to make better comparisons of the magnitude of credit flows over time.

As you can see, there were heightened flows of credit in the late 1980s and the early-to-mid-2000s. In each case, this was then followed by a period of significantly weaker credit growth and, for non-financial corporations, even net repayments of outstanding lending.

In analysing the interaction between the goods and money markets it is therefore important to understand how these cycles arise and what impact they have on aggregate demand and national output. We look at two theories of the instability of credit and the effect on the economy: the *financial accelerator* and the *financial instability hypothesis*.

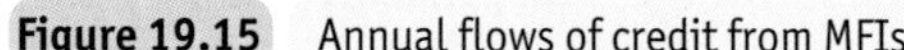

Figure 19.15 Annual flows of credit from MFIs

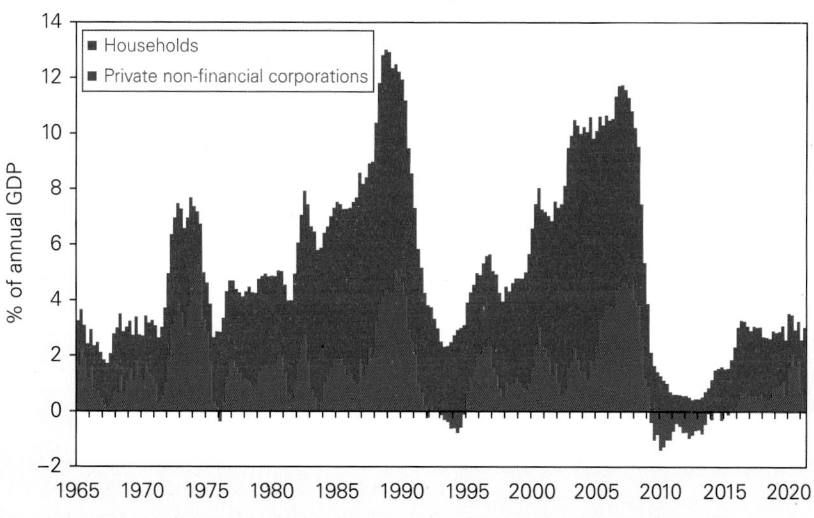

Note: The principal activity of Private Non-Financial Corporations (PNFCs) is the production of market goods or non-financial services
Sources: *Statistical Interactive Database*, series LPQVWNQ and LPQVWNV, Bank of England (data published 29 July 2021, seasonally adjusted), www.bankofengland.co.uk/boeapps/database/; and series YBHA, Office for National Statistics, www.ons.gov.uk/economy/grossdomesticproductgdp/

The financial accelerator

The ***financial accelerator*** explains how financial institutions can amplify the business cycle.[4] They tend to lend more when macroeconomic conditions are improving or already strong, but less when they are weak or deteriorate.

TC 12 p455

It is argued that large *pro-cyclical* credit cycles can occur if financial institutions use the macroeconomic environment as a basis for assessing the riskiness of their lending and the probability of default. A booming economy encourages banks to lend more; a recession makes them much more cautious. This is an example of the use of *heuristics* (see section 5.2, pages 141–2): banks using the macroeconomic situation to aid decision making.

KI 11 p72

This behaviour amplifies the effects of economic shocks. Positive economic shocks are magnified by increasing credit flows, while negative economic shocks are magnified by a weakening of credit flows.

TC 15 p543

4 We use the term 'financial accelerator' as this is the terminology used in the literature. However, a better name would be the 'financial amplifier', as it is not like the traditional (investment) accelerator which we examined in section 17.4 (see pages 551–3), which showed that the level of investment depended on the *rate of change* of national income as investment is used to *increase* capital for producing output and, with the exception of replacement investment, is thus only required when demand for output is increasing.

Definition

Financial accelerator The amplification of effects on the macroeconomy from economic shocks because of changes in the pricing and supply of credit by financial institutions.

Credit conditions as an amplifier of shocks

The financial accelerator is an example of an amplifier: a mechanism that amplifies the effects of economic shocks through its impact on expenditure. As with other amplifiers, such as confidence and uncertainty, the financial accelerator arises from a *positive* feedback loop. The effects on national income from economic shocks lead to a change in credit conditions which, in turn, affect aggregate demand. This then provides additional momentum to the change in national income.

One way in which credit conditions can vary with the macroeconomic environment is through its impact on *interest rate differentials*. While the financial system is characterised by a range of interest rates, we can think about the importance of interest rate differentials by considering a representative real borrowing rate (r_b) and a representative real interest rate on savings (r_s). The differential between the two rates ($r_b - r_s$) reflects the risks attached to lending to economic agents and the costs incurred by financial institutions in screening clients and then in arranging and managing loans. The bigger the risks and costs, the bigger the differential.

KI 11 p72

The differential typically falls in a boom and rises in a slowdown or recession. During a boom, for example, financial institutions may perceive the general riskiness of their lending to be lower. This allows them to reduce the differential of borrowing rates over saving rates. At the same time, with economic agents (consumers and firms) gaining more confidence, they may decide to spend more and reduce their level of savings. Banks may thus offer higher interest rates on savings, further reducing the differential between borrowing and saving rates. KI 34 p377

A second way in which credit conditions may vary across the business cycle is through changes in the *volume of credit* made available by financial institutions. Credit criteria are relaxed in a boom, as banks see rising output and incomes as a signal that lending is less risky. In a slowdown or recession, by contrast, lending is seen as more risky and hence credit criteria are tightened. KI 11 p72

Taken together, changes in interest rate differentials and credit constraints can lead to credit flows being strongly pro-cyclical – rising strongly in a boom; falling strongly in a recession. This is the financial accelerator.

The financial accelerator and national income

The financial accelerator affects the relationship between changes in national income and changes in aggregate expenditure. It does so by making aggregate demand more sensitive to changes in national income: changes in national income induce larger changes in spending. TC 15 p543

First, it *increases* the marginal propensity of households to consume domestically produced goods. To understand why, recall that the mpc_d is the proportion of the rise in national income which is spent on domestic goods and services. As national income rises, credit conditions ease and this allows C_d to rise further. However, when national income falls, credit conditions tighten causing C_d to fall further.

Second, credit conditions are important for investment (I). Here, the financial accelerator is amplifying the traditional investment accelerator (see page 551). When the economy expands, easier credit conditions for firms are likely to increase investment. When the economy contracts, credit conditions for firms are likely to tighten and cause investment to fall.

What effect does this have on the injections (J) line in the simple Keynesian model?

By affecting how spending responds to changes in national income, the financial accelerator interacts with the multiplier process. Since the marginal propensity of households and businesses to spend on domestic output is higher in the presence of the financial accelerator, the multiplier process is strengthened.

The financial accelerator and the IS/MP framework

Because the financial accelerator interacts with the multiplier, the *IS* curve is more *elastic*. Other amplifiers have the same effect. This is illustrated in Figure 19.16. Curve IS_1 shows the *IS* curve with no financial accelerator effects. With financial accelerator effects (or other amplifier effects), the curve becomes flatter, as captured by IS'_1. A change in interest rates (e.g. from r_1 to r_2) leads to a larger change in aggregate demand and national income (e.g. to Y_3 rather than Y_2).

When applying the *IS/MP* framework in the presence of interest rate differentials, we need to identify which interest rate is on the vertical axis. Since rates on saving typically track the central bank rate most closely, we now label the vertical axis the real interest rate on saving (r_S).

Effect of a negative demand shock. Consider now how a negative demand shock affects national income when there are financial accelerator effects. The process is illustrated in Figure 19.17.

Figure 19.16 *IS* curve with financial accelerator effects

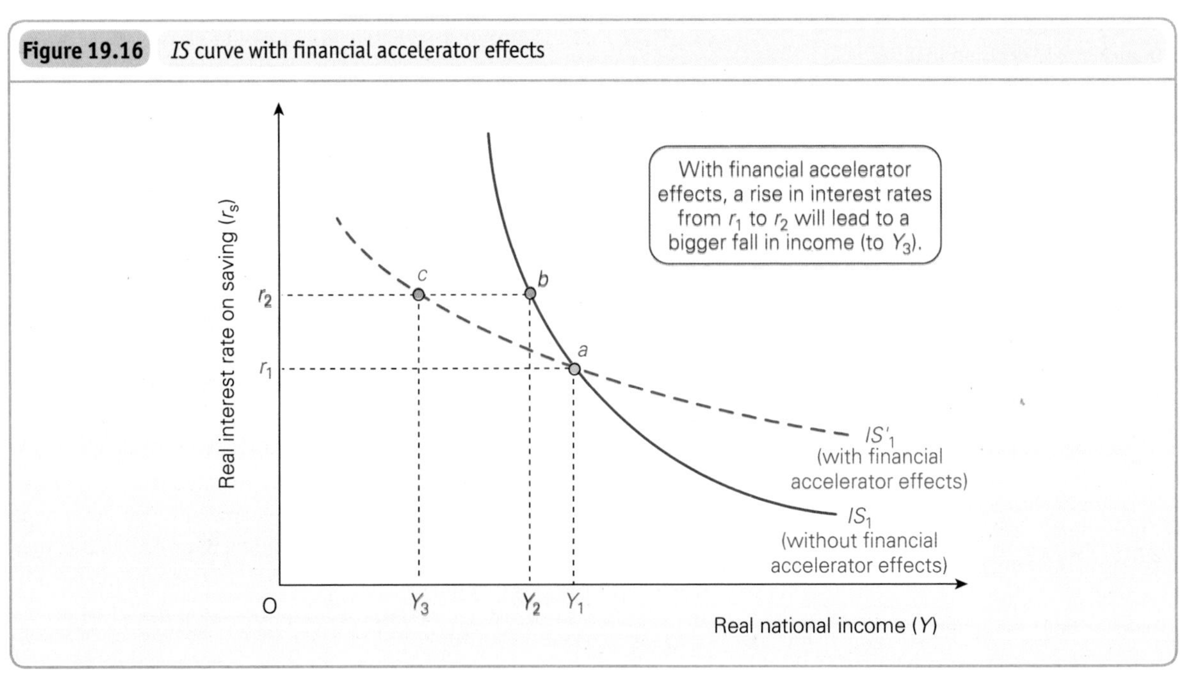

Figure 19.17 Financial accelerator: negative demand-side shock

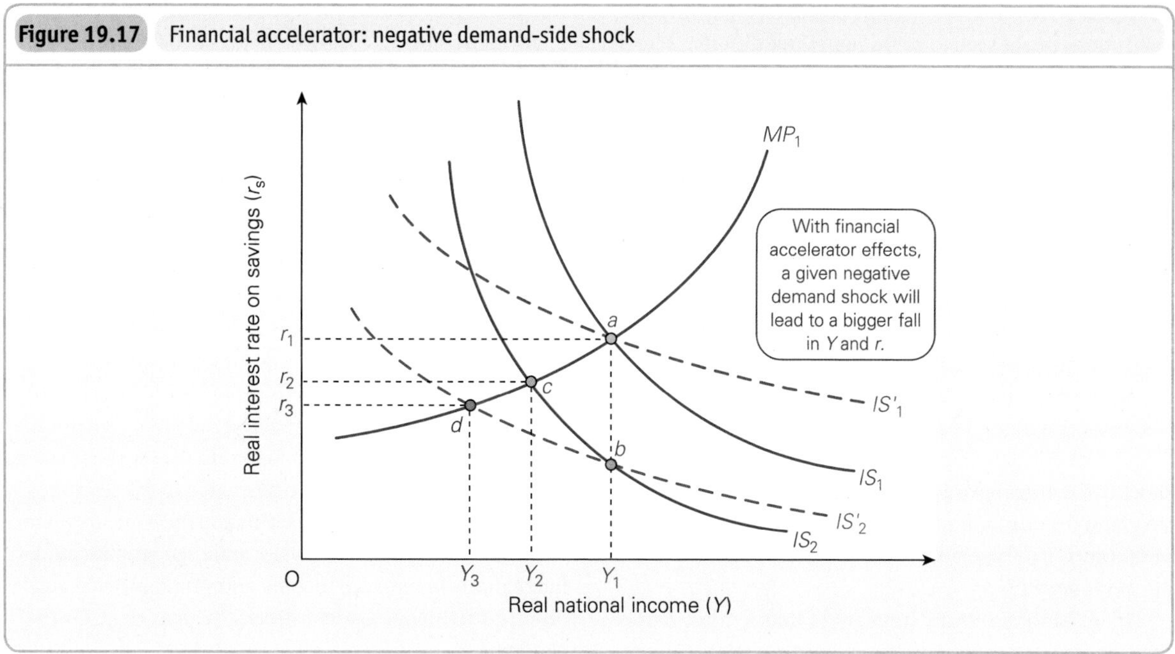

Assume the economy is at point *a* with the real interest on saving at r_1 and real national income at Y_1. Curve IS_1 represents the economy in the absence of financial accelerator effects. It is steeper than IS'_1, which illustrates the position with a given strength of financial accelerator effects.

The negative demand shock causes an equivalent downward movement of both *IS* curves. This is represented by the vertical distance *a–b* at the initial level of output, Y_1. In the absence of financial accelerator effects the *IS* curve moves to IS_2, while in the presence of financial accelerator effects the *IS* curve moves to IS'_2.

The new short-run equilibrium in the absence of the financial accelerator is at point *c*. Output has fallen from Y_1 to Y_2 and the rate of interest from r_1 to r_2. However, with financial accelerator effects, the fall in both output and the rate of interest is greater. There is a larger move down along the *MP* curve to point *d*, with output falling from Y_1 to Y_3 and the savings rate of interest falling from r_1 to r_3.

This larger decrease in the savings (and central bank) interest rate will put downward pressure on the interest rate on borrowing (r_b). However, the increase in the interest-rate differential ($r_b - r_s$) that occurs as output falls means that borrowing rates, while being expected to fall, will fall by less than they would in the absence of financial accelerator effects and thus offset the fall in aggregate demand less.

Why might borrowing rates sometimes rise following a negative demand shock?

The financial instability hypothesis

The second theory of credit cycles is the ***financial instability hypothesis (FIH)***. This theory argues that the volume of credit flows goes through stages which are ultimately destabilising for the economy. As flows of credit increase unsustainably as, it is argued, they inevitably do, they cause the health of the balance sheets of people and businesses to deteriorate. This then results in a period of consolidation during which spending growth is subdued.

KI 35 p459

The hypothesis argues that the financial system generates unsustainable growth in the goods market. Our appetite for goods and services is fed by increasing flows of credit which increasingly place greater strain on people's ability to meet their debt obligations. Eventually, the financial distress is too great and the growth in aggregate demand ends, perhaps very abruptly, as people take steps to improve their financial well-being.

The financial instability hypothesis is associated with American economist Hyman Minsky (1919–96). He argued that financial cycles are an inherent part of the economic cycle and are the primary source of fluctuations in national income. He believed that the accumulation of debt is not only pro-cyclical, but destabilising. While Minsky himself focused on the accumulation of debt by businesses, the role of the mortgage market in generating unsustainable stocks of household debt during the 2000s (see Box 18.2) has meant that his ideas are now frequently applied across the whole of the private sector.

KI 34 p453

Definition

Financial instability hypothesis The theory that the economy goes through stages of credit accumulation which initially fuel aggregate demand but because of increasing financial distress eventually see a collapse in aggregate demand.

Stages of the credit cycle. The extension of credit by financial institutions can be seen to go through three different stages: financial tranquillity, financial fragility and financial bust. During each of these stages both the credit criteria of banks and the ability of borrowers to afford their debts vary.

Minsky argued that credit flows will tend to increase after a period of sustained growth. The economy will move from a period of financial tranquillity to financial fragility, with banks and investors developing a heightened euphoria and confidence in the economy and in the returns of assets. Economists refer to this as ***irrational exuberance***, which results in people and businesses taking on bigger debts to acquire assets. These debts increasingly stretch their financial well-being.

A point is reached, perhaps triggered by an economic shock or a tightening of economic policy, when the euphoria stops and confidence is replaced with pessimism. A financial bust occurs. This moment is now commonly referred to as a ***Minsky moment***.

The result of a Minsky moment is that lenders reduce their lending, and economic agents look to increase their net worth (i.e. reduce debts or increase savings) to ensure their financial well-being. However, the result of these individual actions causes a decline in spending and in national income. The collapse in aggregate demand from financial distress can therefore lead to an economic downturn or recession – known as a *balance-sheet recession* (see page 521). This will be exacerbated if the selling of assets to improve financial well-being causes the value of assets falls. The paradoxical reduction of net worth is known as the paradox of debt (see page 524).

KI 35 p459

Minsky believed that credit cycles are inevitable in a free-market economy. Hence, the authorities will need to take action to moderate credit cycles.

The significance given to macro-prudential regulation by policy makers (see section 18.3) in response to the financial crisis is recognition of the dangers posed to the economy by credit cycles. It was hoped that this and the wider regulatory reforms would limit credit cycles and their amplification of fluctuations in national income and would provide greater financial resilience against shocks, such as the COVID-19 pandemic.

Definitions

Irrational exuberance Where banks and other economic agents are over-confident about the economy and/or financial markets and expect economic growth to remain stronger and/or asset prices to rise further than warranted by evidence. The term is associated with the economist Robert Shiller and his book *Irrational Exuberance* (2000) and with the former US Federal Reserve Chairman, Alan Greenspan.

Minsky moment A turning point in a credit cycle where a period of easy credit and rising debt is replaced by one of tight credit and debt consolidation.

BOX 19.5 AMPLIFIERS AND ECONOMIC SHOCKS

EXPLORING ECONOMICS

An application of the simple Keynesian model

Credit, confidence and uncertainty

The financial accelerator is an example of an amplifier: procyclical credit flows amplify the magnitude of changes in spending arising from fluctuations in national income. Other amplifiers have a similar impact on the responsiveness of aggregate expenditure to changes in national income.

Business and consumer confidence and uncertainty, for example, may positively respond to changes in national income in the way that credit and financial markets do. If a rise in national income were to cause confidence to rise and uncertainty to fall, such that people had a more optimistic outlook and felt more sure about future macroeconomic conditions, this would increase their willingness to spend. A fall in national income would have the opposite effect, reducing their willingness to spend.

The amplifiers interact with the multiplier process (we saw this in section 17.4 when we looked at the interaction of the multiplier and the (investment) accelerator: see page 553). The more powerful are the amplifiers, the larger are the changes in spending induced by changes in national income. They therefore strengthen the multiplier process. By acting as propagation mechanisms through which the effects of economic shocks are transmitted, they can accentuate the peaks and troughs of the business cycle and also contribute to the turning points.

KI 34 p453

Amplifiers and the 45° line diagram (Keynesian cross)

Amplifiers such as the financial accelerator make the aggregate expenditure line in the Keynesian cross diagram *steeper* (and therefore the *IS* curve flatter). This is because they increase the marginal propensity of households and business to spend on domestic output. A change in national income induces a larger change in spending on domestically produced goods and services than would otherwise be the case.[1]

The Keynesian cross diagram shows how we can apply the simple Keynesian model to analyse the amplification of fluctuations in output arising from demand shocks.

A negative demand shock with amplifiers

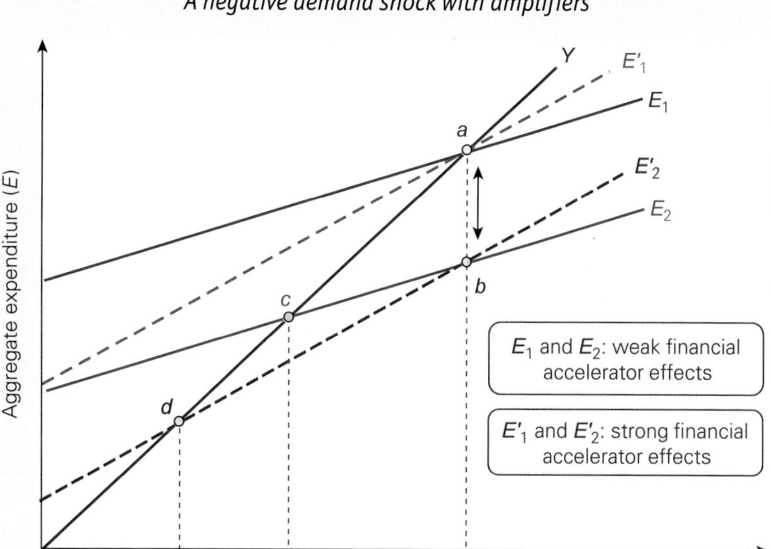

In the presence of 'weak' amplifier effects, the aggregate expenditure line is E_1, while in the presence of 'strong' amplifier effects it is E'_1. The two lines are drawn so that they intersect at Y_1, which we assume is the economy's potential level of national income: i.e. where there is a zero output gap. The E'_1 line would thus lie above the E_1 line in a boom, when the economy rises above Y_1, and below it in a recession, when output falls below Y_1.

Assume that the economy is initially at its potential national income level, Y_1. Consider now the effect of a given decrease in autonomous expenditure: i.e. expenditures unrelated to real national income. This could arise, for example, from a reduction in autonomous investment spending by firms, an increase in autonomous saving by households or from cuts to government purchases. This decrease in autonomous expenditure results in both of the E lines moving vertically downwards by the same distance.

From the diagram we can see that, in the presence of weak amplifiers, output falls from Y_1 to Y_2. However, in the presence of strong amplifiers, output falls from Y_1 to Y_3. The more power amplifiers lead to an additional decrease in output of $Y_2 - Y_3$. This captures how the amplifiers interact with the multiplier process to generate additional falls in expenditure. They increase the volatility of the economy in the face of economic shocks.

When amplifiers become shocks

Amplifiers propagate the effects of economic shocks. They can generate instability in the economy and enable the effects of shocks to persist through time. Yet amplifiers can themselves become the shocks that are then propagated, or that create the conditions for future shocks or events.

Confidence shocks, for example, are cited regularly as the source of economic shocks. A sudden change in the sentiment of people or businesses can lead to fluctuations in their willingness to spend. These effects are then subsequently propagated by amplifiers, including confidence itself.

The global financial crisis of the late 2000s illustrates how the financial system can be both a propagation mechanism and a cause of shocks. The unstainable growth of private-sector debt driven by investor exuberance was to culminate in a significant tightening of credit conditions known as a 'credit crunch'.

Therefore the financial system not only affects the slope of the aggregate curve in the Keynesian cross diagram but can cause the curve to shift. The credit market 'shock' associated with the global financial crisis can be captured by a downward shift of the aggregate expenditure curve similar to that illustrated in the diagram. Negative confidence or uncertainty shocks would be represented similarly.

1. *Is it possible for the aggregate expenditure line to be steeper than the 45° line in the presence of amplifier effects?*
2. *What has happened to the interest rate on borrowing and the interest rate on saving in the two scenarios shown in the diagram?*

Undertake desktop research to prepare a summary of literature exploring the ways by which uncertainty might affect the macroeconomy.

1 In terms of the injections and withdrawals diagram, the J line will now be upward sloping, showing that at higher levels of national income, banks will be more willing to finance investment. The W line will be less steep because a higher marginal propensity to consume domestic products will correspond to a lower marginal propensity to withdraw. Either way, there will be a bigger multiplier effect.

Section summary

1. The financial accelerator amplifies the impact on the economy of economic shocks. The lending behaviour of financial institutions is argued to be dependent on the state of the economy. Increasing output levels may weaken credit constraints and reduce the differential between interest rates on borrowing and on saving. Conversely, falling output levels increase credit constraints and the differential between interest rates on borrowing and saving.
2. The financial accelerator and other amplifiers such as confidence and uncertainty strengthen the multiplier process. This causes changes in national income, such as those caused by economic shocks, to induce larger changes in aggregate expenditure. The more powerful are amplifiers like the financial accelerator, the steeper is the aggregate expenditure curve and the flatter therefore the *IS* curve.
3. The financial instability hypothesis (FIH) characterises economies as progressing through stages. In the first stage people and businesses accumulate more debt. The accumulation of debt is driven by an overconfidence and euphoria and, hence, by an irrational exuberance.
4. The FIH predicts that debt accumulation will initially boost aggregate demand. However, as debt-servicing obligations progressively increase, the growth in aggregate demand will begin to weaken. A Minsky moment is reached when financial distress causes a collapse in aggregate demand. The result is a balance-sheet recession or slowdown.

*APPENDIX: THE *IS/LM* MODEL

In Section 19.3 we applied a framework known as the *IS/MP* model to analyse the interaction between monetary policy and the goods market. This framework recognises that many central bankers today attempt to achieve a target rate of inflation. They do this by seeking to influence the structure of interest rates in the economy and thereby to affect aggregate demand. We look at central bank objectives and their evolution in greater detail in Chapter 22.

The predecessor to the *IS/MP* model was the ***IS/LM* model**. As with the *IS/MP* model, *IS/LM* model allows us to examine the effects of changes originating in the money or goods markets on *both* national income *and* interest rates: it shows what the equilibrium will be in both the goods and the money markets simultaneously. The difference with the *IS/MP* model is that there is no inflation target. Instead, interest rates are purely market determined. The central bank is assumed to conduct monetary policy through changes in money supply.

As we saw earlier, the *IS* curve is based on equilibrium in the goods market. The *LM* curve is concerned with equilibrium in the money market. It shows all the various combinations of interest rates and national income at which the demand for money (*L*) equals the supply (*M*). The *LM* curve is different from the *MP* curve in that it analyses how the interest rate adjusts to help bring money demand into equilibrium with money supply. In other words, the interest rate equilibrates the money market at any given level of national income.

In constructing the *IS/LM* model we assume, for simplicity, that prices are constant, i.e. there is an absence of inflation. Therefore, there is no difference between the nominal interest rate (*i*) and real interest rate (*r*).

Definition

***IS/LM* model** A model showing simultaneous equilibrium in the goods market ($I = S$) and the money market ($L = M$).

The *IS* curve

We analysed the *IS* curve in depth in section 19.3, so only a brief overview is provided here. The curve shows combinations of national income and interest rates at which planned expenditure equals national income. This occurs when the flow of injections (*J*) is matched by the flow of withdrawals (*W*). Hence, when we consider all injections (*I, G* and *X*) and withdrawals (*S, T* and *M*), rather than just investment and saving, we may think of the curve as a *JW* curve.

When the real rate of interest (*r*) rises, there is a fall in investment and a rise in saving. This will lead to a multiplied fall in income. Thus *higher* interest rates are associated with *lower* national income, if equilibrium is to be maintained in the goods market ($J = W$). The *IS* curve is therefore drawn as downward sloping, as illustrated in Figure 19.11 on page 617.

A change in *interest rates* causes movements *along* the *IS* curve. Changes in any *other* determinant of injections and withdrawals *shift* the whole curve. The reason is that it will change the equilibrium level of national income at any given rate of interest. For example, if, in response to a decline in their net worth, firms reduce their investment at *the current interest rate* (resulting in a downward shift of the *I* curve in the top part of Figure 19.11), there is a multiplied fall in national income. Thus a lower equilibrium income is now associated with each level of the interest rate. The *IS* curve has shifted to the left.

The *LM* curve

Deriving the LM curve

To explain how the *LM* curve is derived consider Figure 19.18. The left-hand part of the diagram is the

Figure 19.18 Money market equilibrium: deriving the *LM* curve

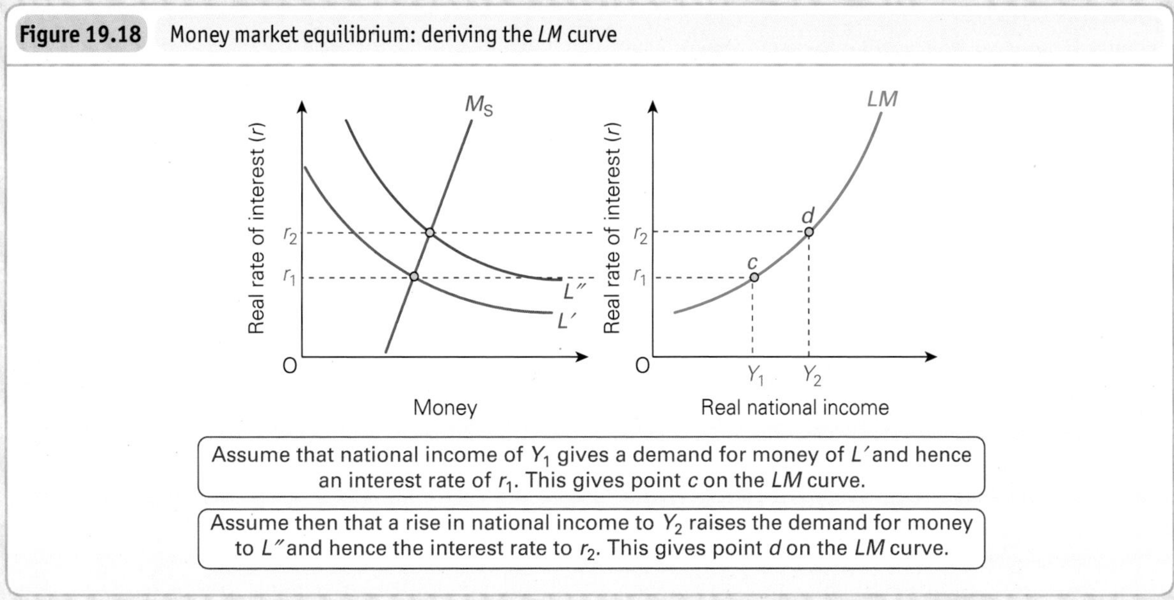

familiar money market diagram, showing a liquidity preference (demand for money) curve (L) and a supply of money curve (M).

At any given level of national income, there will be a particular level of transactions-plus-precautionary demand for money, and hence a given overall demand-for-money curve (L). Let us assume that, when national income is at a level of Y_1 in the right-hand part of Figure 19.18, the demand-for-money curve is L'. With the given money supply curve M_s, the equilibrium rate of interest will be r_1. Thus point *c* is one point on the *LM* curve. At a level of national income Y_1, the money market will be in equilibrium at a rate of interest of r_1. (Note that we are assuming that the money supply curve is not totally exogenous; in other words, the curve is upward sloping. In simple *IS/LM* models, the money supply curve is (unrealistically) assumed to be vertical.)

Now what will happen if the level of national income changes? Let us assume that national income rises to Y_2. The effect is to increase the transactions-plus-precautionary demand for money. The L curve shifts to the right: to, say, L''. This will cause the rate of interest to rise to the new equilibrium level of r_2. This therefore gives us a second point on the *LM* curve (point *d*).

Thus *higher* national income leads to a greater demand for money and hence *higher* interest rates if equilibrium is to be maintained in the money market. The *LM* curve is therefore upward sloping.

The elasticity of the LM curve

KI 9 p64

The elasticity of the *LM* curve (i.e. the responsiveness of interest rate changes to a change in national income) depends on two factors.[5]

5 Note that the rate of interest is the dependent variable and the level of national income is the independent variable. Thus the more elastic is the *LM* curve (i.e. the more responsive interest rates are to changes in national income), the *steeper* it will be.

The responsiveness of the demand for money to changes in national income. The greater the marginal propensity to consume, the more will the transactions demand for money rise as national income rises, and thus the more the L curve will shift to the right. Hence the more the equilibrium interest rate will rise, and the steeper will be the *LM* curve.

The endogeneity of money will lessen this effect. In the case of an upward-sloping money supply curve (as in Figure 19.18), the less steep it is, the more will money supply expand in response to a rise in the demand for money and the less will interest rates rise. Hence the flatter will be the *LM* curve. Where money supply simply expands passively to meet any rise in demand, the *LM* curve will be horizontal.

The responsiveness of the demand for money to changes in interest rates. The more the demand for money responds to a change in interest rates, the flatter will be the liquidity preference curve in the left-hand part of Figure 19.18. The flatter the L curve, the less will the equilibrium interest rate change for any given horizontal shift in the L curve (arising from a change in Y). The less the equilibrium interest rate changes, the flatter will be the *LM* curve.

The Keynesian and monetarist views on the shape of the *LM* curve reflect their respective views on the elasticity of the L curve. Keynesians argue that the L curve is likely to be relatively flat given the responsiveness of the speculative demand for money to changes in interest rates and the endogeneity of money. They thus argue that the *LM* curve is correspondingly relatively flat (depending, of course, on the scales of the axes). Monetarists, on the other hand, argue that the *LM* curve is relatively steep. This is because they see the demand for money as insensitive to changes in interest rates and the supply of money as being exogenous.

Shifts in the LM curve

A change in *national income* will cause a movement *along* the *LM* curve to a new equilibrating interest rate. Thus in Figure 19.18 a rise in national income from Y_1 to Y_2 leads to a movement along the *L* curve from point *c* to point *d* and hence a rise in the rate of interest from r_1 to r_2.

A change in any *other* determinant of the demand and supply of money will *shift* the whole curve. The reason is that it will change the equilibrium level of interest associated with any given level of national income.

An increase in the demand for money, other than as a result of a rise in income, will shift the *L* curve to the *right.* This could be due to people being paid less frequently, or a greater use of cash, or increased speculation that the price of securities will fall. This increased demand for money will raise the equilibrium rate of interest at the current level of national income. The *LM* curve will shift upwards.

An increased supply of money by the authorities will shift M_s the curve to the right. This will lower the rate of interest (in the left-hand part of Figure 19.18). This will shift the *LM* curve downwards: a lower rate of interest will be associated with any given level of national income.

Draw a diagram like Figure 19.18, only with just one L curve. Assume that the current level of national income is Y_1. Now assume that the supply of money decreases. Show the effect on
(a) the rate of interest;
(b) the position of the LM curve.

Equilibrium

The *IS* curve shows all the combinations of the rate of interest (*r*) and national income (*Y*) at which the *goods* market is in equilibrium. The *LM* curve shows all the combinations of *r* and *Y* at which the *money* market is in equilibrium. *Both* markets will be in equilibrium where the curves intersect. This is at r_e and Y_e in Figure 19.19.

KI 8 p44

But what would happen if both markets were not simultaneously in equilibrium? How would equilibrium be achieved?

KI 5 p21

Let us suppose that the current level of real national income is Y_1. This will create a demand for money that will lead to an equilibrium real interest rate of (point *a* on the *LM* curve). But at this low interest rate, the desired level of investment and saving would generate an income of Y_2 (point *b* on the *IS* curve). Thus national income will rise. But as national income rises, there will be a movement up along the *LM* curve from point *a*, since the higher income will generate a higher demand for money and hence push up interest rates. And as interest rates rise, so the desired level of investment will fall and the desired level of saving will rise so as to reduce the equilibrium level of national income below Y_2. There will be a movement back up along the *IS* curve from point *b*. Once the interest rate has risen to r_e, the actual level of income will be at the equilibrium level (i.e. *on* the *IS* curve). Both markets will now be in equilibrium.

Assume that national income is initially at Y_2 in Figure 19.19. Describe the process whereby equilibrium in both markets will be achieved.

Full effects of changes in the goods and money markets

IS/LM analysis can be used to examine the full effects of changes in the goods market. Such changes are illustrated by a shift in the *IS* curve. Likewise, the full effects of

Figure 19.19 Equilibrium in both the goods and money markets

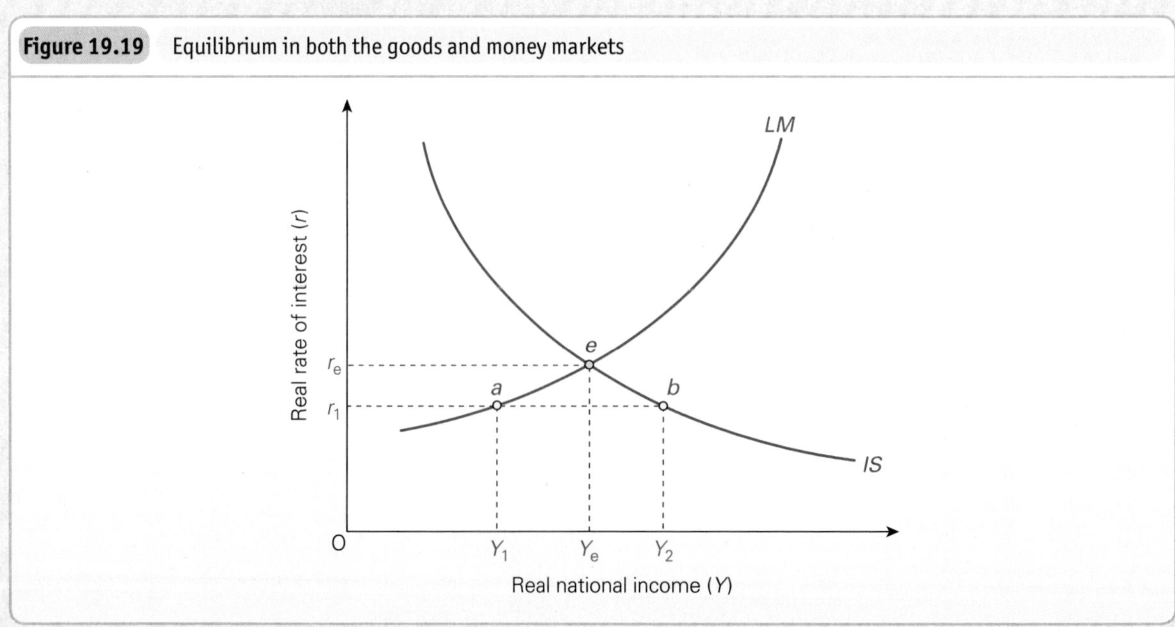

*LOOKING AT THE MATHS

Equilibrium in the *IS/LM* model is where the two functions, *IS* and *LM*, are equal. The simplest mathematical representation of this is where both *IS* and *LM* are simple linear (i.e. straight-line) functions. The *IS* function could be expressed as

$$r = a - bY \qquad \textbf{(1)}$$

In other words, the higher the rate of interest (r), the lower will be the level of aggregate demand and hence national income (Y).[1] This is consistent with a downward-sloping *IS* curve.

The *LM* function can be written as

$$r = g + hY \qquad \textbf{(2)}$$

In other words, the higher the level of real national income (and hence the higher the demand for money), the higher will be the real rate of interest. This is consistent with an upward-sloping *LM* curve.

We can then solve for Y by setting the two equations equal. Thus

$$a - bY = g + hY$$

that is

$$bY + hY = a - g$$

giving

$$Y = \frac{a - g}{h + b}$$

More complex IS and LM functions

In practice, neither function is likely to be linear. Both *IS* and *LM* are likely to be curves rather than straight lines. To understand why, we need to look at the other determinants of Y in the case of the *IS* curve and of r in the case of the *LM* curve. Let us first examine the *IS* function.

Real national income consists of five elements:

$$Y = C + I + G + X - M \qquad \textbf{(3)}$$

or

$$Y = C(Y, T, r, \pi^e) + I(r, \pi^e, \Delta Y) + G + X(er) - M(Y, T, r, \pi^e, er) \qquad \textbf{(3a)}$$

Equation (3a) is simply an expansion of equation (3) listing the key determinants of each of the variables in equation (3), where T is taxes, π^e is expected inflation and er is the exchange rate. Investment being a function of changes in national income (ΔY) is the accelerator effect. Thus an *IS* function could be expressed as

$$Y = IS\,(\underset{-}{r}, \underset{-}{T}, \underset{+}{\pi^e}, \underset{+}{\Delta Y}, \underset{+}{G}, \underset{-}{er}) \qquad \textbf{(4)}$$

All the variables in this function are contained in equation (3a). It is highly likely that the relationship between Y and most, if not all, these variables is non-linear (i.e. contains squared or higher power terms).

The sign under each of the variables indicates the direction in which Y changes when the variable changes. For example, the negative sign under the T term means that a rise in taxes would lead to a *fall* in Y. Put another way, the sign indicates the sign of the partial derivative of Y with respect to each variable. For example, the positive sign under the expected inflation term (π^e) means that when you differentiate Y with respect to π^e, you end up with a positive number. This simply means that a rise in π^e leads to a *rise* in Y.

Note that a change in r would lead to a movement along the *IS* curve. A change in any of the other determinants in equation (4) would shift the curve. A rise in any of the determinants with a positive sign would result in a rightward shift in the curve; a rise in any of the determinants with a negative sign would result in a leftward shift.

Turning to the *LM* function, this can be expressed as

$$r = LM\left(\underset{+}{Y}, \underset{-}{\frac{M_s}{P}}, \underset{+}{\pi^e}, \underset{+}{er^e}, \underset{-}{f}\right) \qquad \textbf{(5)}$$

where M_s/P is the real money supply, π^e is the expected rate of inflation, er^e is the expected exchange rate and f is the frequency with which people are paid. The *LM* curve assumes equilibrium in the money market. It therefore represents all the combinations of r and Y where the real demand for money is equal to the real supply. The real supply of money is given by the term M_s/P and the real demand for money depends on the other terms in equation (5) (see page 595). TC 13 p461

A rise in Y would cause a movement up along the *LM* curve. A rise in any of the other determinants would shift the curve: upwards in the case of the determinants with a positive sign; downwards in the case of those with a negative sign.

As with the *IS* function, it is highly likely that the relationship between r and most, if not all, the variables in the *LM* function is likely to be non-linear.

Maths Case 19.1 on the student website shows how equilibrium in the *IS/LM* model can be derived from specific *IS* and *LM* functions.

1 Note that although equation (1) shows r as a function of Y, the model in fact has Y as the dependent variable. In other words, r determines Y. We express equation (1) this way to make it consistent with equation (2), where r is the dependent variable.

changes in the money market can be illustrated by a shift in the *LM* curve.

Changes in the goods market

Consider a positive demand-side shock caused by a general increase in confidence. Assume that this 'confidence shock' leads firms to increase their investment and consumers to reduce their precautionary saving. The resulting increase in aggregate expenditure leads to a rightward shift in the *IS* curve. This is illustrated in Figure 19.20(a). It is assumed that there is no exogenous increase in the money supply and that, therefore, the *LM* curve does not shift. Income rises to Y_2, but interest rates also rise (to r_2).

The rise in the rate of interest to restricts the rise in real national income, since the higher real interest rate dampens both investment and consumption. The net rise in aggregate expenditure is less than the original increase. The steeper the *LM* curve, the less national income rises. The equilibrating

Figure 19.20 *IS/LM* analysis of changes in the goods and money markets

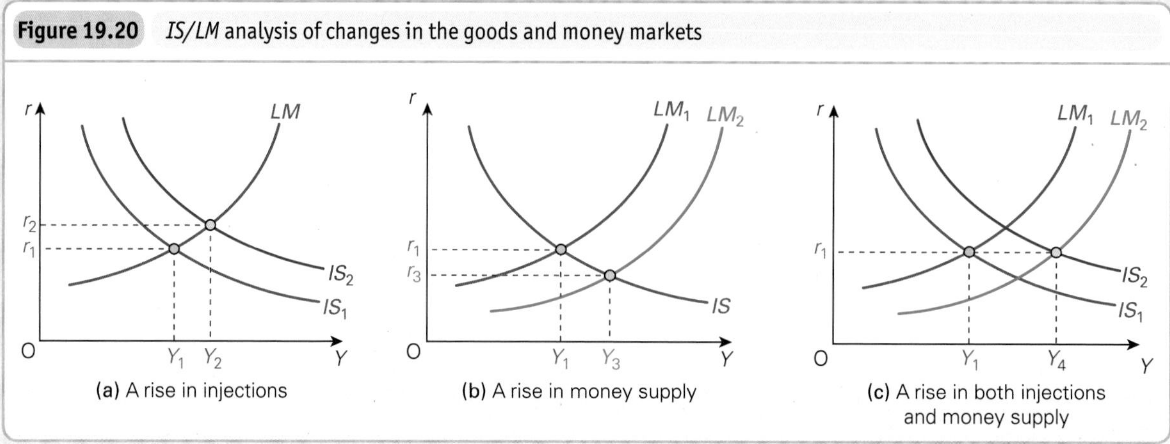

effect of interest rates in the money market therefore 'chokes off' some of the increase in national income originating from the positive demand-side shock.

The *IS/LM* framework allows us to see how monetary policy could accommodate the positive demand-side shock. If money supply is expanded to meet the extra demand for money, then interest rates will not have to rise. This is illustrated in Figure 19.20(c). The rightward shift in the *IS* curve is matched by a downward shift in the *LM* curve. The rate of interest remains at r_1 and there is a full multiplied rise in national income to Y_4.

In the context of the periods following the global financial crisis and the COVID-19 pandemic, central banks like the Federal Reserve and the Bank of England were keen that monetary policy should stimulate economic recovery. While remaining watchful of inflation, monetary policy was predominantly geared to stabilising and then supporting the economic recovery. This saw the authorities boost the money supply through asset purchases (see Box 22.10). One effect of this was to put downward pressure on the general structure of interest rates. As we saw in section 18.5, there is not a single interest rate. Rather, there is a series of interest rates on a range of financial instruments.

The *IS/LM* framework can be applied to analyse the policy dilemma that faces policy makers when aggregate demand is recovering from negative economic shocks: how quickly to put the brakes on quantitative easing. To do so too quickly runs the risk of stalling the recovery as general interest rates rise, even if the authorities maintain a low policy rate. As our analysis in section 19.4 showed, interest rate differentials tend to be greatest when output levels are relatively low. The authorities may therefore be wary of applying the monetary policy handbrake too quickly and too aggressively.

Changes in the money market

Now consider an increase in money supply. The *LM* curve shifts downwards. This is illustrated in Figure 19.20(b). Interest rates fall and this encourages an increase in borrowing and hence an increase in investment and consumption. This is shown by a movement down along the *IS* curve. National income rises. Equilibrium is reached at a rate of interest of r_3 and a national income of Y_3.

The fall in the rate of interest means that some of the extra money is absorbed in idle balances and is not all used to finance additional expenditure and this reduces the resulting increased national income. The effect on national income also depends on the elasticity of the *IS* curve. The steeper the *IS* curve, the less will national income rise. This will be the case when investment is relatively insensitive to cuts in interest rates.

If, however, the rise in money supply is accompanied by an autonomous rise in injections (for example, a rise in government expenditure), then the effect can be much bigger. If the downward shift in the *LM* curve is matched by a rightward shift in the *IS* curve, then the effect is once more illustrated in Figure 19.20(c).

To summarise: the effect on national income of a change in either market depends on the slope of the *IS* and *LM* curves.

- The flatter the *LM* curve and the steeper the *IS* curve, the bigger will be the effect of a given shift in the *IS* curve. When *LM* is relatively flat, a rightward shift in *IS* will lead to only a small rise in the rate of interest (r). If *IS* is steep, this rise in r will lead to only a small curtailing of investment because it is fairly unresponsive to changes in interest rates. In these two circumstances, the dampening effect on investment and consumption is limited. There will be a large increase in real national income (Y).
- The effect of a shift in the *LM* curve will be bigger when the liquidity preference curve (L) (e.g. in Figure 19.18(a)) is steep and the *IS* curve is relatively flat. When L is steep, there will be a relatively large downward shift in the *LM* curve for any given increase in the money supply and hence a relatively large fall in r. When *IS* is relatively flat, this fall in r will lead to a relatively large increase in investment and hence Y.
- The effect of a shift in either curve will be bigger if matched by a similar shift in the other curve.

On a diagram similar to Figure 19.19, trace through the effects of (a) a fall in investment and (b) a fall in the money supply. On what does the size of the fall in national income depend?

Appendix summary

1. The *IS/LM* model allows equilibrium to be shown in both goods and money markets simultaneously. The model shows the relationship between national income and interest rates.
2. Equilibrium in the goods market is shown by the *IS* curve. As the rate of interest rises, so investment will fall and saving will rise: thus equilibrium national income will fall. The *IS* curve is thus downward sloping.
3. A change in interest rates will cause a movement along the *IS* curve. A change in anything else that affects national income causes a shift in the *IS* curve.
4. Equilibrium in the money market is shown by the *LM* curve. This shows all the combinations of national income and the rate of interest where the demand for money (*L*) equals the supply (*M*). As national income rises, so the demand for money will rise: thus the equilibrium rate of interest in the money market will rise. The *LM* curve is therefore upward sloping.
5. A change in national income will cause a movement along the *LM* curve. A change in anything else that affects interest rates (i.e. a change in the demand or supply of money other than as a result of a change in national income) will shift the *LM* curve.
6. Simultaneous equilibrium in both goods and money markets (i.e. the equilibrium national income *and* the equilibrium rate of interest) is where $IS = LM$.
7. A change in injections or withdrawals will shift the *IS* curve. A rise in injections will shift it to the right. This will cause a rise in both national income and the rate of interest. The steeper the *IS* curve and the flatter the *LM* curve, the bigger will be the rise in income and the smaller the rise in the rate of interest.
8. A rise in money supply will shift the *LM* curve downwards. This will cause a fall in interest rates and a rise in national income. The rise in national income will be larger, the flatter is the *IS* curve and the steeper the liquidity preference curve (*L*) and hence the bigger the downward shift in the *LM* curve for any given increase in the money supply.

END OF CHAPTER QUESTIONS

1. Using one or more diagrams like Figures 19.2, 19.7, 19.8, 19.9 and 19.10, illustrate the following:
   (a) The effect of a contraction in the money supply on national income. Refer to both the interest rate and exchange rate transmission mechanisms and show how the shapes of the curves affect the outcome.
   (b) The effect of a fall in investment on national income. Again show how the shapes of the curves affect the outcome. Specify your assumptions about the effects on the supply of money.
2. Controlling the money supply is sometimes advocated as an appropriate policy for controlling inflation. What implications do different assumptions about the relationships between *M* and *V*, and *M* and *Y*, in the equation $MV = PY$ have for the effectiveness of this policy?
3. Why may an expansion of the money supply have a relatively small effect on national income? Why may any effect be hard to predict?
4. What impact might the balance sheets of economic agents have on the influence of interest rates in affecting aggregate expenditure?
5. Why does the exchange rate transmission mechanism strengthen the interest rate transmission mechanism?
6. Explain how the holding of a range of assets in people's portfolios may help to create a more direct link between changes in money supply and changes in aggregate demand.
7. Explain how financial crowding out can reduce the effectiveness of fiscal policy. What determines the magnitude of crowding out?
8. What determines the shape and position of the *IS* curve?
9. What determines the shape and position of the *MP* curve?
10. Using the *IS/MP* model analyse the possible effect of an increase in aggregate expenditure on output, the real interest rate and inflation.
11. Using the *IS/MP* model analyse how a lower bound on real interest rates might cause the economy to enter a deflationary spiral following a significant decrease in aggregate expenditure.
12. What impact does the financial accelerator have on the marginal propensity of households and businesses to consume domestic output? How does this affect the *IS* curve? What other amplifiers may have a similar effect?
13. Illustrate the impact on the *IS* curve of a general increase in interest rate differentials following a credit market disruption like that experienced during the financial crisis of the late 2000s.
14. Using the *IS/MP* framework illustrate how the financial accelerator affects the extent of the rise in output following a positive demand-side shock.
15. What implication does the financial instability hypothesis have for the balance sheets of different sectors of the economy?

*16. Using the *IS/LM* model analyse under what circumstances will (a) a rise in investment and (b) a rise in money supply cause a large rise in national income.

Online resources

Additional case studies on the student website

19.1 Crowding out. This case looks at a different version of crowding out from that analysed in section 19.2.

19.2 Sir John Hicks. A profile of the developer of *IS/LM* analysis.

19.3 The *IS* curve and the Keynesian Cross. A derivation of the *IS* curve using the income-expenditure approach.

19.4 Going behind the *MP* curve. A more formal analysis detailing the two relationships underpinning the *MP* curve: the *EAPC* and a monetary policy rule.

19.5 *IS/MP* and supply shocks. An application of the *IS/MP* framework to illustrate supply shocks.

19.6 Measuring financial conditions. An overview of measures of financial conditions.

Maths Case 19.1. Using *IS* and *LM* equations to find the equilibrium national income and interest rate. Using the algebra in a worked example.

Websites relevant to Chapters 18 and 19

Numbers and sections refer to websites listed in the Web Appendix and hotlinked from this book's website at **www.go.pearson.com/uk/sloman.**

- For news articles relevant to this and the previous chapter, see the *Economics News* section on the student website.
- For general news on money and banking, see websites in section A, and particularly A1–5, 7–9, 20–22, 25, 26, 31, 36.
- For monetary and financial data (including data for money supply and interest rates), see section F and particularly F2. Note that you can link to central banks worldwide from site F17. See also the links in B1.
- For monetary targeting in the UK, see F1 and E30. For monetary targeting in the eurozone, see F6 and 5.
- For student resources relevant to Chapters 18 and 19, see sites C1–10, 12, 19.

Aggregate Supply, Inflation and Unemployment

CHAPTER MAP

The focus so far of Part F has been to develop a better understanding of aggregate demand. We have looked at a variety of influences on aggregate demand and its components, including the effects of financial institutions and money markets. Now we consider in more detail the interaction of aggregate demand and aggregate supply. We will see that the effects of changes in aggregate demand on output, employment and prices depend crucially on the responsiveness of aggregate supply.

We begin this chapter by constructing the aggregate demand and supply (*AD/AS*) model. We then apply the model to analyse demand-pull and cost-push inflation, including the subsequent effects on prices and output that can result from these sources of inflation. In the next section (section 20.3) we extend this model to the modern context of inflation targeting by central banks. The *dynamic* aggregate demand and supply model, as it is called, can be used to analyse the response of economies to economic shocks by allowing for the impact of a central bank's monetary policy on the adjustment process.

The adjustment of economies to shocks is a theme we pursue further in the final two sections of the chapter. First, we focus on the role the labour market plays in determining the interaction between aggregate demand and supply. In doing so, we distinguish between classical and Keynesian perspectives on the labour market. Finally, we take a broader look at debates around output determination. We analyse the contrasting views of different macroeconomic schools on the behaviour of markets, the flexibility of aggregate supply and the role of expectations.

20.1 THE *AD/AS* MODEL

Our focus to this point has been on developing an understanding of aggregate demand. This is a sensible starting point since fluctuations in aggregate demand are generally argued to be the primary source of fluctuations in the economy's output path. However, to understand economic fluctuations more fully we need to analyse the interaction between aggregate demand and aggregate supply.

The problem with the circular flow model and the Keynesian multiplier model is that they take no account of just how firms make supply decisions: they assume that firms simply respond to demand. But supply decisions, as well as being influenced by current levels of demand, are also influenced by prices and costs. To be able to analyse the impact of changes in aggregate demand on national income *and* prices we make use of the aggregate demand–aggregate supply (*AD/AS*) model. This is illustrated in Figure 20.1. Note that the aggregate supply curve we shall be examining is the short-run curve (*SRAS*), as explained below.

As with demand and supply curves for individual goods, we plot quantity on the horizontal axis, except that now it is the *total quantity of national output,* (real) GDP; and we plot price on the vertical axis, except that now it is the *general* price level. Because the general price level relates to the prices of all domestically produced goods and services it is also known as the ***GDP deflator***.

We now examine each curve in turn.

Definition

GDP deflator The price index of all final domestically produced goods and services: i.e. all those items that contribute towards GDP.

The aggregate demand curve

In Chapter 15 we saw how aggregate demand consists of four elements: consumer spending (*C*), private investment (*I*), government expenditure on goods and services (*G*) and expenditure on exports (*X*) less expenditure on imports (*M*). Thus:

$$AD = C + I + G + X - M$$

The aggregate demand curve shows how much national output (GDP) will be demanded at each level of prices. But why does the *AD* curve slope downwards? Why will people demand less as prices rise? There are two effects that can cause this: income effects and substitution effects.

Income effects

KI 7 p44

For many people, when prices rise, their wages will not rise in line, at least not in the short run. There will therefore tend to be a redistribution of income away from wage earners (and hence consumers) to those charging the higher prices – namely, firms. Thus for consumers there has been an *income effect* of the higher prices. The rise in prices leads to a cut in real incomes and therefore people will spend less. Aggregate demand will fall. The *AD* curve will be downward sloping, as in Figure 20.1.

To some extent this will be offset by a rise in profits, but it is unlikely that much of the additional profits will be spent by firms on investment, especially if they see consumer expenditure falling; and any increase in dividends to shareholders will take a time before it is paid, and then may simply be saved rather than spent. To summarise: if prices rise more than wages, the redistribution from wages to profits is likely to lead to a fall in aggregate demand.

Figure 20.1 Aggregate demand and aggregate supply

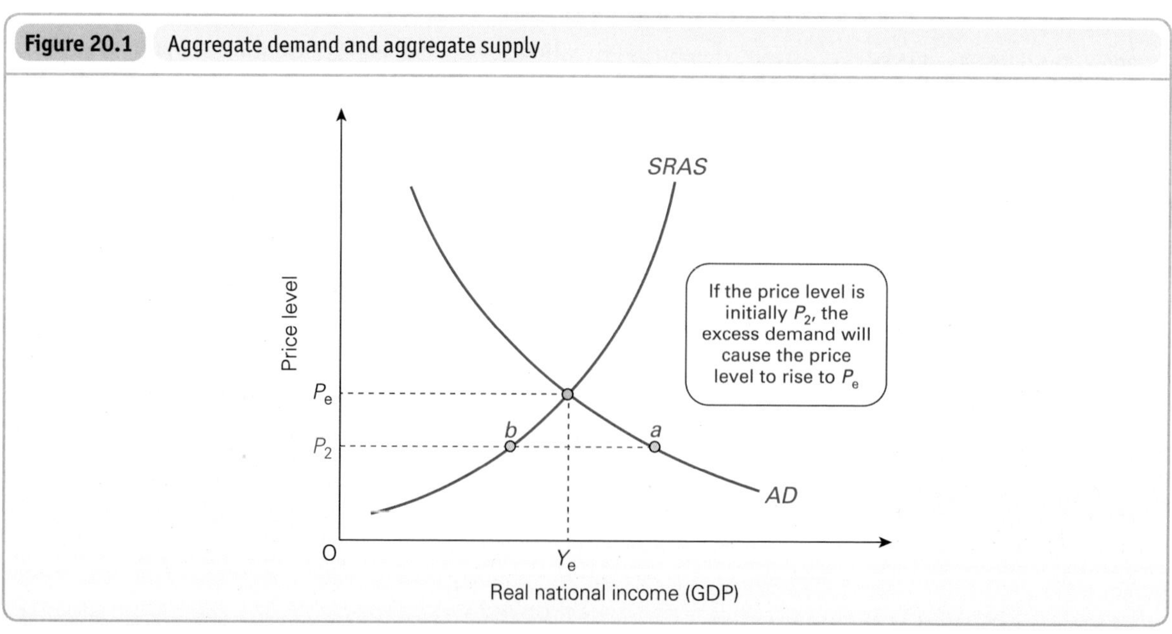

KI 33 p377

Clearly, this income effect will not operate if wages rise in line with prices. Real incomes of wage earners will be unaffected. In practice, as we shall see at several places in this book, in the short run wages do lag behind prices.

An income effect is also likely to occur as a result of progressive taxes. As prices and incomes rise, so people will find that they are paying a larger proportion of their incomes in taxes. As a result, they cannot afford to buy so much. This was a deliberate policy of the UK Chancellor in his 2021 Budget, where he announced that personal allowances would not rise with inflation from 2022/23 to 2025/26. The objective was for people to pay a higher proportion of their income in taxes as their incomes rose and thus contribute towards reducing public-sector net borrowing, which had soared during the COVID-19 pandemic. This automatic rise in the proportion of income paid in taxes as nominal incomes rise is known as *fiscal drag* – something we examine in section 22.2 (page 703).

Substitution effects

KI 7 p36

In the *micro*economic situation, if the price of one good rises, people will switch to alternative goods. This is the substitution effect of that price rise and helps to explain why the demand curve for a particular good will be downward sloping. At a *macro*economic level we can identify three main reasons why people will demand fewer products as prices rise.

- *An* ***international substitution effect***. If prices rise, people will be encouraged to buy fewer of the country's products and more imports instead (which are now relatively cheaper); the country will also sell fewer exports (which are now less competitive). Thus imports (a withdrawal) will rise and exports (an injection) will fall. Aggregate demand, therefore, will be lower.
- *An* ***inter-temporal substitution effect***. As prices rise, people will need more money to pay for their purchases. With a given supply of money in the economy, this will have the effect of driving up interest rates (see section 19.1). The effect of higher interest rates will be to discourage borrowing and encourage saving, with individuals postponing current consumption in favour of future consumption. The effect will be a reduction in spending and hence in aggregate demand.
- ***Real balance effect***. If prices rise, the value of people's savings will be eroded. They may thus save more (and spend less) to compensate.

The shape of the aggregate demand curve

We have seen that both the income and substitution effects of a rise in the general price level will cause the aggregate demand for goods and services to fall. Thus the *AD* curve is downward sloping. The bigger the income and substitution effects, the more elastic (flatter) will the curve be.

The slope of the aggregate demand curve is also dependent on the multiplier and its interaction with amplifier effects, such as expectations, confidence and credit conditions. This mirrors the analysis of the *IS* curve in sections 19.3 and 19.4. Changes in the general price level generate income and substitution effects whose impact on aggregate demand are then amplified. The stronger the multiplier/amplifier process the flatter is the *AD* curve. This is discussed further in Box 20.1, where we explore the relationship between the *AD* curve and the simple Keynesian model.

Shifts in the aggregate demand curve

The aggregate demand curve can shift inwards (to the left) or outwards (to the right), in exactly the same way as the demand curve for an individual good. A rightward shift represents an increase in aggregate demand, whatever the price level (a positive demand shock); a leftward shift represents a decrease in aggregate demand, whatever the price level (a negative demand shock).

A shift in the aggregate demand curve will occur if, for any given price level, there is a change in any of its components – consumption, investment, government expenditure or exports minus imports. Thus if the government decides to spend more, or if consumers spend more as a result of lower taxes, or if a general rise in business confidence causes firms to invest more, the *AD* curve will shift to the right.

Definitions

International substitution effect As prices rise, people at home and abroad buy less of this country's products and more products from abroad.

Inter-temporal substitution effect Higher prices may lead to higher interest rates and thus less borrowing and more saving. Current consumption falls; future consumption (from the higher savings) rises.

Real balance effect As the price level rises, so the value of people's money balances will fall. They will therefore spend less in order to increase their money balances and go some way to protecting their real value.

BOX 20.1 THE AGGREGATE DEMAND CURVE

Its relationship with the simple Keynesian model

In this box we look at the relationship between the aggregate demand and supply diagram, which we are developing in this section, and the national income and expenditure diagram (the Keynesian cross diagram), which we developed in section 17.2. This extends the initial analysis of Box 17.4 (see page 549).

The Keynesian cross and the *AD* curve

In the top half of diagram (a) is the Keynesian cross diagram. It shows the 45° line, along which real national income (Y) equals real $C_d + W$. It also shows three real planned aggregate expenditure (E) lines, each of which is drawn for a particular value of the GDP deflator (P). The higher the general price level, the lower is the level of real aggregate expenditure at any level of real national income.

With an initial price level (GDP deflator) of P_0, we assume that the aggregate expenditure line is E_0. This gives an equilibrium national income of Y_0. This corresponds to point *a* on the *AD* curve. If price now rises to P_1, the *E* line shifts downwards – say to E_1. Real national income falls to Y_1. This gives point *b* on the *AD* curve. Similarly, a further rise in the price level to P_2, gives point *c* on the *AD* curve.

Slope of the aggregate demand curve

The analysis shows that the slope of the *AD* curve is dependent on two factors.

Income and substitution effects. The bigger the income and substitution effects, the larger the vertical movements of the aggregate expenditure line and hence the flatter (more elastic) is the aggregate demand curve.

Multiplier-amplifier interaction. For a given change in spending (a given vertical shift in the *E* line) following a change in the price level, the impact on real national income will be larger the steeper the *E* line. The important point here is that the slope captures the strength of the interaction between the multiplier and amplifiers. The more powerful this interaction is, the steeper the *E* line and the flatter the *AD* curve.

Shifts of the aggregate demand curve

While each aggregate expenditure line is drawn for a given economy-wide price level, they are also subject to the impact of demand shocks. These shocks will affect the level of spending at any given level of national income and the general price level. Therefore, they affect the vertical position of the *E* line. This is shown in the top half of diagram (b).

Aggregate expenditure line E_0 is drawn for price level P_1 in the absence of demand shocks. If there is a positive demand shock, the aggregate expenditure line shifts upwards, say to E_1; if there is a negative demand shock, the aggregate expenditure line shifts downwards, say to E_2. The vertical

(a) *Deriving the AD curve from the simple Keynesian model*

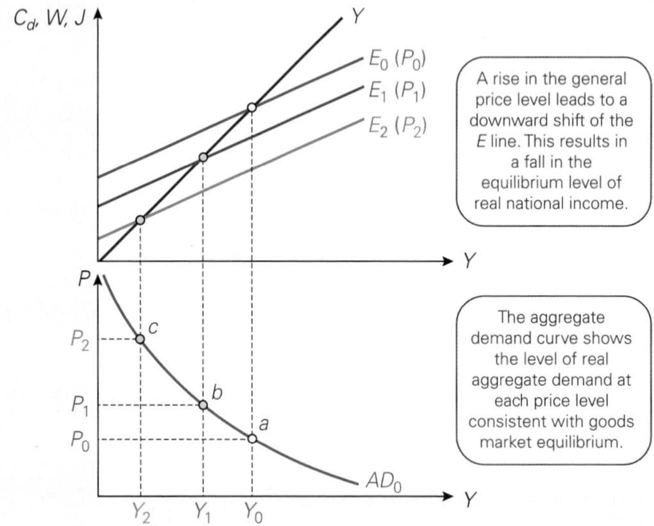

The aggregate supply curve

The aggregate supply (*AS*) curve shows the amount of goods and services that firms are able and willing to supply at each level of prices. We focus here on the *short-run AS* curve (*SRAS* curve).

When constructing this curve, we assume that various other things remain constant. These include technology and the total supply of factors of production (labour, land and capital).

The mainstream view is to also assume that wage rates and other input prices remain constant. The argument here is that wage rates are frequently determined by a process of collective bargaining and, once agreed, will typically be set for a whole year, if not two. Even if they are not determined by collective bargaining, wage rates often change relatively

EXPLORING ECONOMICS

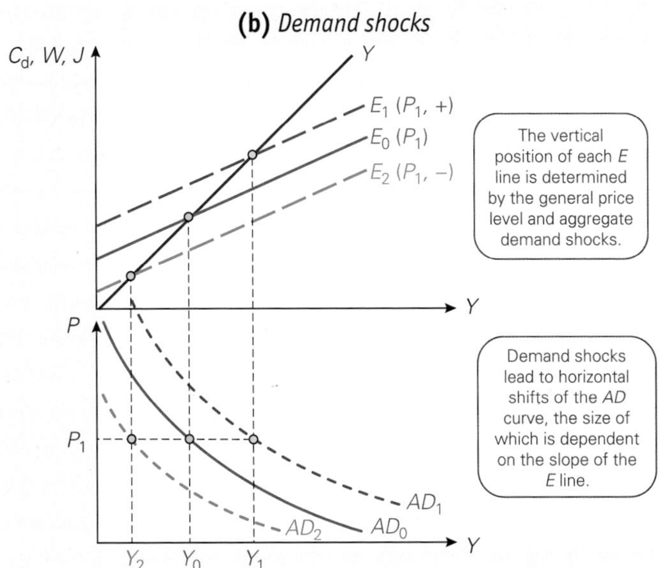

shifts of the *E* lines from demand shocks are then reflected by horizontal shifts in the *AD* curve in the bottom half of the diagram.

With a given price level P_1, we can identify a single point on an *AD* curve. In the absence of a demand shock, the equilibrium level of real aggregate expenditure is Y_0, while it is Y_1 and Y_2 for the illustrated positive and negative shocks, respectively. We can then repeat this for other price levels, thereby allowing us to sketch out a range of points along, AD_0 (no shock) AD_1 (positive shock) and AD_2 (negative shock).

The size of the shifts in the *AD* curve, for a given demand shock, is dependent on the slope of the aggregate expenditure curve. Therefore, the horizontal shift of the *AD* curve, at a given price level, reflects the transmission of the shock through the multiplier-amplifier process. The bigger the multiplier, and the more powerful the amplifiers with which it interacts, the larger is the impact on aggregate demand.

Equilibrium

As we have seen, a shift in the *E* line in the top diagram will shift the *AD* curve in the bottom diagram. The effect on prices and real national income of the shift in *AD* curve will depend on what happens to *aggregate supply*. There will be a movement along the *AS* curve. The outcome depends on its slope – something we explore in this chapter.

1. *Assume that a government increases its spending on goods and services (G). What role may expectations play in determining the size of the shifts of the aggregate expenditure (E) line and the aggregate demand (AD) curve?*
2. *Assume that there is a fall in aggregate expenditure/aggregate demand. Illustrate the effects on equilibrium real national income (Y) and the price level (P) using a double diagram as in this box. Include an AS curve so that equilibrium can be shown. You might want to refer back to Box 17.4 for help.*

Undertake desktop research to explore how confidence might affect aggregate expenditures. Summarise your findings.

infrequently. So too with the price of other inputs: except in perfect, or near perfect markets (such as the market for various raw materials), firms supplying capital equipment and other inputs tend to change their prices relatively infrequently. They do not immediately raise them when there is an increase in demand or lower them when demand falls.

The assumption of 'sticky' input prices turns out to be important in explaining why the *SRAS* curve is upward sloping, as shown in Figure 20.1. It is, however, not without criticism and we will revisit this in the final two sections of the chapter (see also sections 16.2 and 16.4).

So why does this 'stickiness' in input prices produce a short-run aggregate supply curve? The reason is simple. Because we are holding wages and other input prices constant, then as the prices of their products rise, firms' profitability at each level of output will be higher than before. This will encourage them to produce more.

But what *limits* the increase in aggregate supply in response to an increase in prices? In other words, why is the *SRAS* curve not horizontal? There are two main reasons:

- *Diminishing returns.* With some factors of production fixed in supply, notably capital equipment, firms experience a diminishing marginal physical product from their other factors, and hence have an upward-sloping marginal cost curve. In microeconomic analysis the upward-sloping cost curves of firms explain why the supply curves of individual goods and services slope upwards. Here in macroeconomics we are adding (horizontally) the supply curves of all goods and services and thus the aggregate supply curve also slopes upwards.

KI 19 p155

- *Growing shortages of certain variable factors.* As firms collectively produce more, even inputs that can be varied may increasingly become in short supply. Skilled labour may be harder to find, and certain raw materials may be harder to obtain.

Thus rising costs explain the upward-sloping short-run aggregate supply curve. The more steeply costs rise as production increases, the less elastic will the aggregate supply curve be. It is likely that, as the level of national output (i.e. national income) increases and firms reach full-capacity working, so marginal costs will rise faster. The *SRAS* curve will thus tend to get steeper (as shown in Figure 20.1).

Shifts in the short-run aggregate supply curve

The *SRAS* curve will shift if there is a change in any of the determinants that are held constant when we plot the curve. Several of these, notably technology, the labour force and the stock of capital, change only slowly – normally shifting the curve gradually to the right. This represents an increase in potential output.

However the growth of potential output is not smooth nor necessarily continuous. While this reflects, in part, the nature of technological progress, the COVID-19 pandemic illustrated how supply conditions can restrict the level of potential output, at least temporarily, and perhaps affect its subsequent growth.

Ordinarily, the major cause of shifts in the *SRAS* curve are changes in wage rates and other input prices. For example, a general rise in wage rates throughout the economy reduces the amount that firms wish to produce at any level of prices. The aggregate supply curve shifts to the left. A similar effect will occur if other costs, such as oil prices or indirect taxes, increase.

Equilibrium

Equilibrium in the macroeconomy occurs when aggregate demand and aggregate supply are equal. In Figure 20.1, this is at the price level P_e and national income (GDP) of Y_e. To demonstrate this, consider what would happen if aggregate demand exceeded aggregate supply: for example, at P_2 in Figure 20.1. The resulting shortages throughout the economy would drive up prices. This would encourage firms to produce more: there would be a movement up *along* the *SRAS* curve. At the same time, the increase in prices would reduce the level of aggregate demand: that is, there would also be a movement back up *along* the *AD* curve. The shortage would be eliminated when price had risen to P_e.

Shifts in the AD or SRAS curves

If the *AD* or *SRAS* curve shifts, there will be a movement along the other curve to the new point of equilibrium. For example, if there is a cut in income taxes and a corresponding increase in consumer demand, the *AD* curve will shift to the right. This will result in a movement up along the *SRAS* curve to the new equilibrium point: in other words, to a new higher level of national income and a higher price level. The more elastic the *SRAS* curve, the more will output rise relative to prices.

Section summary

1. An aggregate demand curve shows the relationship between aggregate demand ($C + I + G + X - M$) and the price level. The curve is downward sloping because of income and substitution effects. Its slope is dependent on the size of the effects as well as the size of the multiplier and the strength of the amplifiers with which the multiplier interacts.
2. If a rise in the price level causes wage rises to lag behind or causes a rise in the proportion of income paid in income tax, then consumers will respond to the resulting fall in their real incomes by cutting consumption. This is the income effect.
3. If a rise in the price level causes (a) imports to rise and exports to fall, (b) people to spend less and save more because of a rise in interest rates and possibly (c) people to spend less in order to maintain the value of their bank balances, these effects too will result in a fall in the level of aggregate demand. These are all substitution effects.
4. If the determinant of any component of aggregate demand (other than the price level) changes, the aggregate demand will shift.
5. The short-run aggregate supply (*SRAS*) curve is upward sloping. With sticky input prices, firms will find it profitable to supply more. The curve will be more elastic, the less rapidly diminishing returns set in and the more elastic the supply of variable factors.
6. The *SRAS* curve will shift to the left (upwards) if wage rates or other costs rise independently of a rise in aggregate demand.
7. Equilibrium in the economy occurs when aggregate demand equals aggregate supply. A rise in the price level will occur if there is a rightward shift in the aggregate demand curve or a leftward shift in the short-run aggregate supply curve.

20.2 *AD/AS* AND INFLATION

We first analysed inflation in section 15.6. There we identified two principal types of inflation: demand-pull and cost-push inflation. Demand-pull inflation is caused by continuing rises in aggregate demand while cost-push inflation is caused by continuing rises in costs, which occur *independently* of aggregate demand.

We can use our aggregate demand and supply framework to further our understanding of demand-pull and cost-push inflation. In particular, we can think about the possible subsequent effects on output and prices that might arise from these types of inflation. This illustrates the dynamic nature of economies: macroeconomic fluctuations or shocks frequently set in motion a chain of events.

TC 15 p543

Figure 20.2 Demand-pull inflation

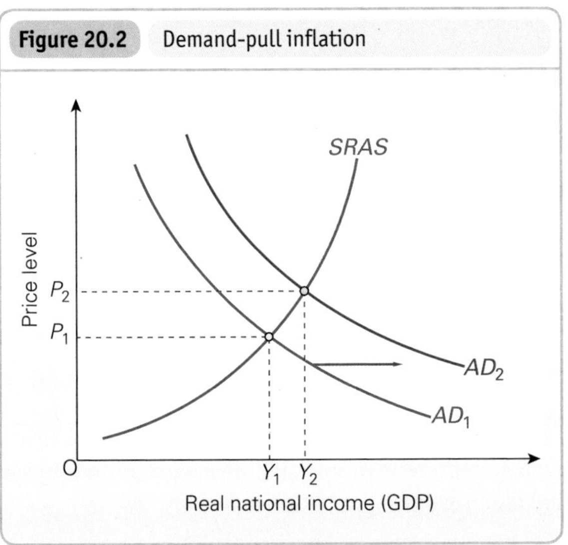

Demand-pull inflation

Demand-pull inflation can be represented by *continuous* shifts of the *AD* curve to the right. In Figure 20.2, the *AD* curve shifts to the right and continues doing so. A single increase in *AD* caused by a *positive* demand shock only causes inflation in short run. Once the price level has settled at its new higher level, the inflation rate falls back to zero. For demand-pull inflation to continue, the rightward shifts of the *AD* curve must also continue; for demand-pull inflation to rise, the rightward shifts must get faster.

Subsequent effects

In illustrating demand-pull inflation in Figure 20.2, we have analysed the short-term effects on output and the price level. Crucially, we have assumed that the factors taken as given in constructing the short-run aggregate *supply* curve remain constant. But eventually the *SRAS* curve will start shifting. In Figure 20.3 we analyse how this might happen and what this could mean subsequently for the economy's price level and output.[1]

As before, assume that aggregate demand rises. In Figure 20.3(a), there is some increase in output, and the price level rises from P_0 to P_1. If demand goes on rising, so that the *AD* curve goes on shifting to the right, the price level will go on rising and there will be demand-pull inflation. There will be a movement from point *a* to *b* to *c* in Figure 20.3(b).

1 In Figure 20.3 we have drawn the *AD* and *SRAS* 'curves' as straight lines. This simplification does not affect the argument but makes it easier to see what's going on.

Figure 20.3 Demand-pull inflation: initial and subsequent effects

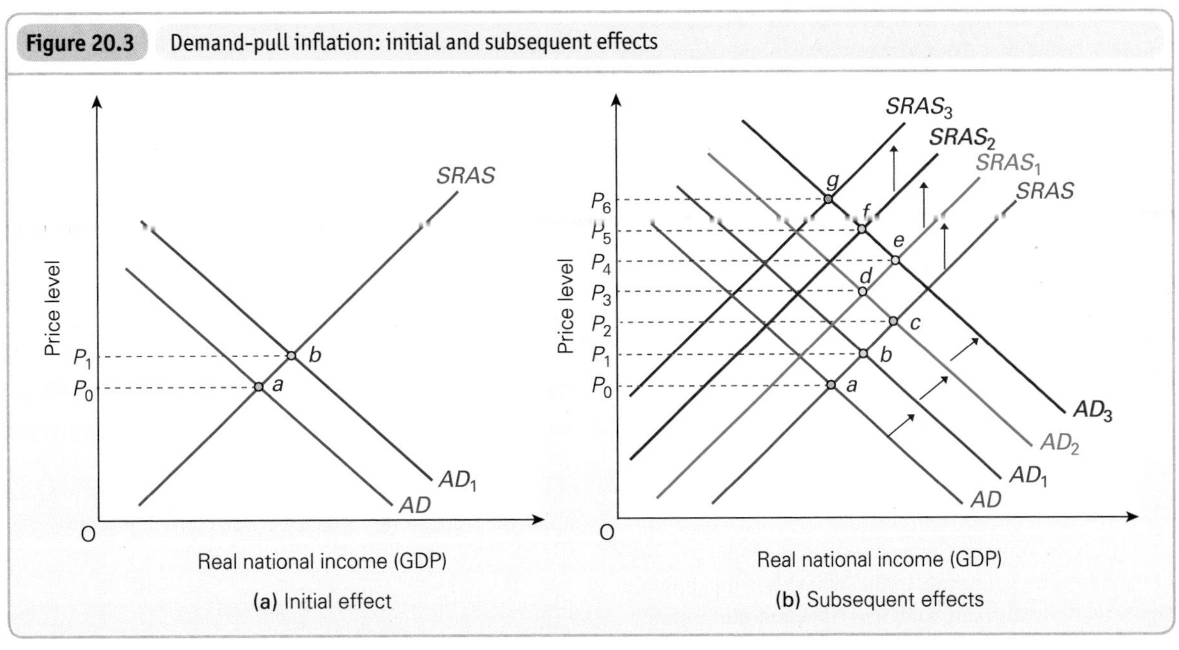

An important part of the subsequent adjustment process comes from the *interdependence of firms*. Rising aggregate demand will lead firms throughout the economy to raise their prices (in accordance with the short-run *AS* curve). But as raw material and intermediate good producers raise their prices, this will raise the costs of production further up the line. A rise in the price of steel will raise the costs of producing cars and washing machines. At the same time, workers, experiencing a rise in demand for labour, and seeing the prices of goods rising, will demand higher wages. Firms will be relatively willing to grant these wage demands since they are experiencing buoyant demand.

TC 10 p358

The effect of all this is to raise firms' costs, and hence their prices. As prices rise for any given level of output, the short-run *AS* curve shifts upwards.

All other things being equal, this will lead to a falling back of output but a further rise in prices as the economy moves to point *d*.

If there was to be a further rise in demand, we might perhaps observe a further outward movement of the *AD* curve, say to point *e*, but a further rise in prices. Then the *SRAS* curve will probably continue shifting upwards and the economy will move to point *f*.

If the source of the increase in demand was to cease or government now makes the control of inflation its main policy objective, this may stop further increases in aggregate demand. Aggregate supply may continue shifting upwards for a while as cost increases and expectations feed through. The economy moves to point *g*. In the extreme case, point *g* may be vertically above point *a*. The only effect of the shift in *AD* to AD_3 has been inflation.

Note that, although costs in Figure 20.3(b) have increased and hence the *AS* curves have shifted upwards, this is not *cost-push* inflation because the rise in costs is the result of the rise in *demand*.

Whatever the output and price paths that result from rising (or falling) demand, the analysis illustrates the dynamic nature of economies. The responses of economic agents, the interdependencies that exist between them and the workings of markets are important in determining the adjustment processes that take place following economic shocks. This is crucial too when thinking about cumulative causation: i.e. the ideas that economic effects can snowball. Multiple changes can result from an initial economic shock or set of events. In section 20.4 we focus on the role of the labour market in determining adjustment processes.

TC 15 p543

How would the shifts in the SRAS curve be affected if, in response to rising output levels, firms increased their investment expenditures?

Cost-push inflation

Cost-push inflation can be represented by *continuous* shifts of the *SRAS* curve upwards to the left. This is illustrated in Figure 20.4. As with our analysis of demand-pull inflation,

Figure 20.4 Cost-push inflation

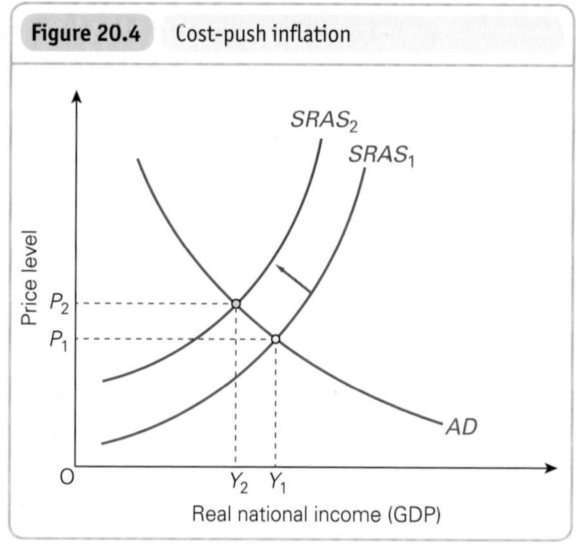

we need to distinguish between single shifts and continuous shifts of the *SRAS* curve when looking at cost-push inflation. A single *negative* supply shock will cause only temporary inflation. If cost-push inflation is to continue, the *SRAS* curve must keep shifting upwards to the left. Similarly, for the rate of cost-push inflation to rise, these shifts of the *SRAS* curve must get faster.

If we compare Figures 20.2 and 20.4, we can see that demand-pull and cost-push inflation have the opposite effect on output. This is because it is *positive* demand shocks but *negative* supply shocks that cause price levels to rise. Therefore, with demand-pull inflation, output and hence employment tend to rise. On the other hand, with cost-push inflation, output and employment tend to fall.

Subsequent effects

In illustrating cost-push inflation to this point, the aggregate demand curve has been unaffected by the shifts in the *SRAS* curve. After a time, this is unlikely to remain the case. We use Figure 20.5 to consider how the *AD* curve might be affected subsequently.[2]

Assume that there is some exogenous increase in costs: a sharp increase in world oil prices, or an increase in wages due to increased trade union activity, or firms raising prices to cover the costs of a rise in interest rates. In Figure 20.5(a), the *SRAS* curve shifts to $SRAS_1$. Prices rise to P_1 and there is a fall in national output.

If these increases in costs continue for some time, the *SRAS* curve will go on shifting upwards. Price rises will continue and there is cost-push inflation. The economy will move from point *a* to *b* to *c* in Figure 20.5(b). Continuous upward shifts in the *SRAS* curve are particularly likely if there is a continuing struggle between different groups (e.g.

2 Again, we simplify the diagrams by drawing the *AD* and *SRAS* 'curves' as straight lines.

Figure 20.5 Cost-push inflation: initial and subsequent effects

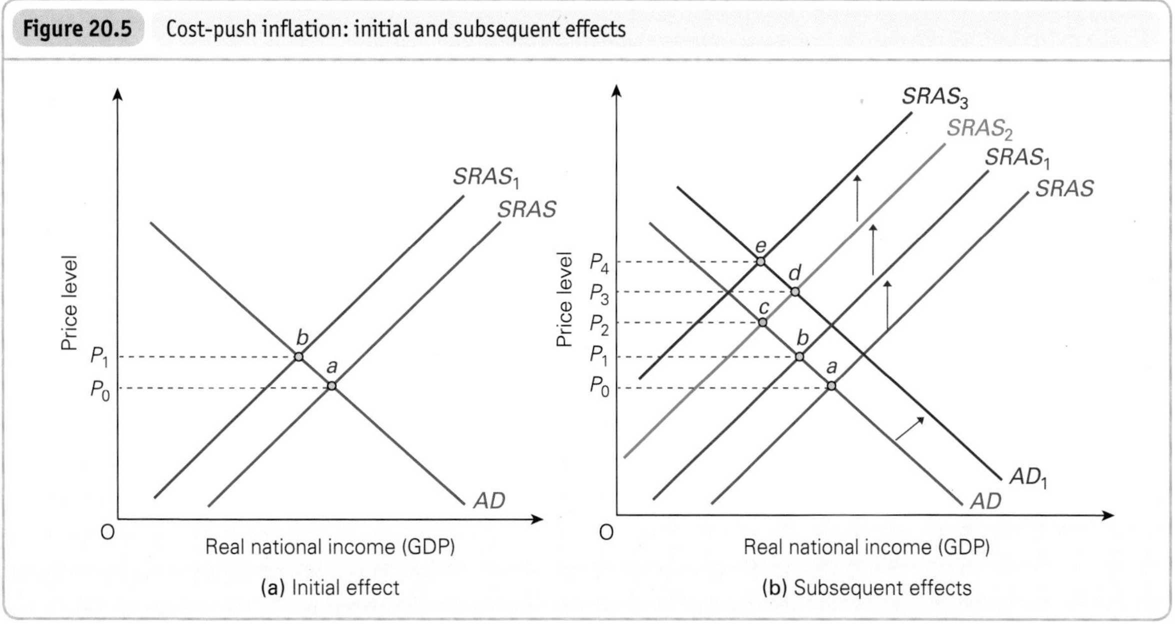

unions and employers' organisations) for a larger share of national income.

After a time, aggregate demand is likely to rise. This may be due to the government using expansionary fiscal and monetary policies to halt the falling output and employment. Aggregate demand shifts to AD_1 and there is a movement to point *d*. Alternatively, the central bank, pursing a policy of inflation targeting, may *tighten* monetary policy to combat the rise in prices. The *AD* curve will shift to the left.

There may be a further increase in costs and a movement to point *e*, and then a further increase in aggregate demand and so on. Again, the dynamics of the adjustment process following the initial effect in Figure 20.5(a) will shape the actual path that prices and national output take in Figure 20.5(b).

Note this time that, although demand has increased, this is not *demand-pull* inflation because the rise in demand is the result of the upward pressure on *costs*.

BOX 20.2 COST-PUSH INFLATION AND SUPPLY SHOCKS

EXPLORING ECONOMICS

It is important to distinguish a *single* supply shock, such as a rise in oil prices or an increase in VAT or excise duties, from a continuing upward pressure on costs, such as workers continually demanding increases in real wages above the level of labour productivity, or firms continually using their monopoly power to increase the real value of profits.

A single supply shock will give a *single* upward movement in the *SRAS* curve. Prices will move to a new higher equilibrium. An example occurred in the UK in January 2011 with the rise in VAT from 17.5 to 20 per cent. Cost-push inflation in this case is a *temporary* phenomenon. Once the new higher price level has been reached, the cost-push inflation disappears.

Periods of *continuous* upward pressure on costs result in *repeated* shifts of the *SRAS* curve. This can create a policy dilemma for central banks, such as the Bank of England, which are charged with meeting inflation-rate targets. Should they raise interest rates to slow the growth in aggregate demand, even if much of the cause of consumer price inflation is on the supply side?

An example of the dilemma from cost-push inflation is the periodic problem of rising world inflation resulting from rapidly developing economies, such as China, India and Brazil, demanding increased resources. Although the source is a rise in demand in these countries, the effect is a rise in costs for other countries as the resulting rise in food and commodity prices pushes up inflation rates around the world.

This was a problem from 2010 to 2012, just after the financial crisis. Several countries, including the UK, had only just emerged from recession but increasing commodity prices resulted in increased input prices for manufacturers (see chart). Many countries, including the UK, faced increasing inflationary pressures while, at the same time, experiencing often sizeable negative output gaps. Most central banks chose to keep interest rates at historic lows.

Give some examples of single shocks and continuing changes on the demand side. Does the existence of multiplier and accelerator effects make the distinction between single shocks and continuing effects more difficult to make on the demand side than on the supply side?

Conduct a search of news items over recent months to identify possible examples of 'genuine' cost-push inflation.

(continued)

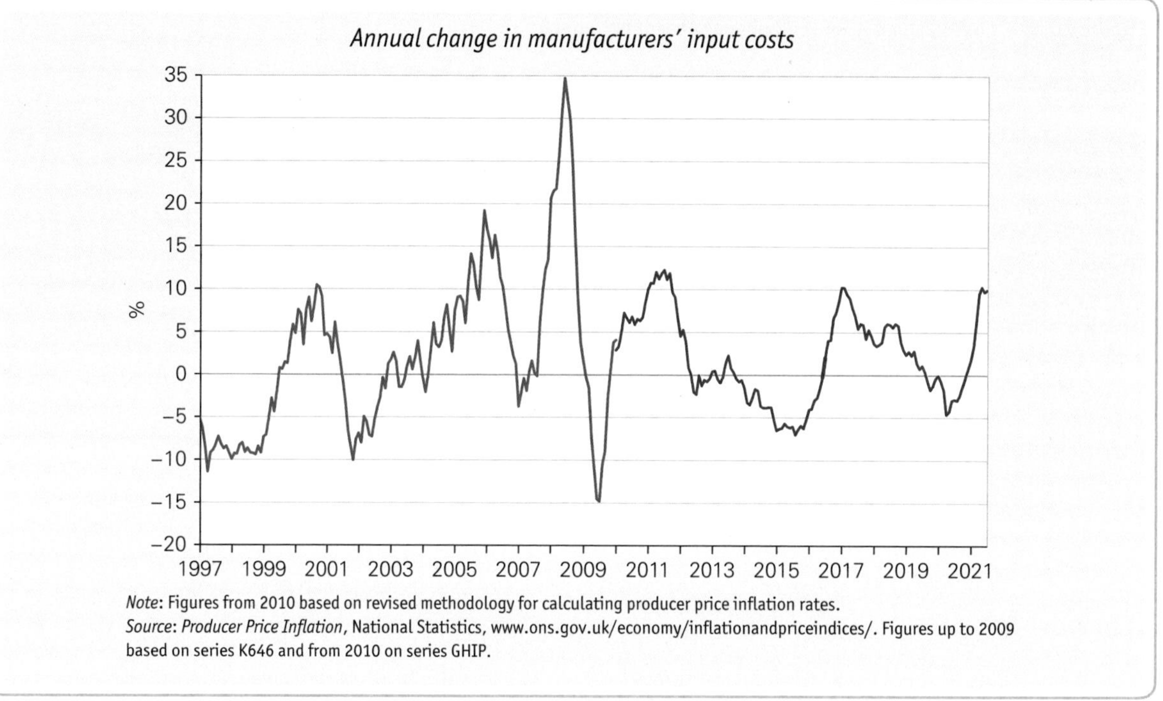

Note: Figures from 2010 based on revised methodology for calculating producer price inflation rates.
Source: *Producer Price Inflation*, National Statistics, www.ons.gov.uk/economy/inflationandpriceindices/. Figures up to 2009 based on series K646 and from 2010 on series GHIP.

Section summary

1. Demand-pull inflation occurs where there are continuous rightward shifts in the *AD* curve. Subsequently we would expect the *SRAS* curve to start shifting. This might occur as rising costs are passed from firm to firm, which then acts to shift the *SRAS* curve upwards.
2. Cost-push inflation occurs where there are continuous upward shifts in the *SRAS* curve. Subsequently we may expect to see *AD* start shifting rightwards. This might occur if the supply of money increases to meet the demand for more liquidity as transactions become increasingly costly.

20.3 AGGREGATE DEMAND AND SUPPLY WITH INFLATION TARGETING: THE *DAD/DAS* MODEL

A more modern version of the aggregate demand and supply model plots aggregate demand and supply, not against the level of prices, but against the *rate of inflation*. This model has become known as the *DAD/DAS* model, where *DAD* stands for 'dynamic aggregate demand' and *DAS* stands for 'dynamic aggregate supply'.

The *DAD/DAS* model shares common features with the *IS/MP* model, which we looked at in section 19.3. Both incorporate the interest rate choices of the central bank as it seeks to meet an inflation target (or a more complex target). Both models can, therefore, be used to analyse the effects of economic shocks on the macroeconomic environment via the central bank's response to these shocks.

The *DAD/DAS* model has three main advantages over the *IS/MP* model. First, we can observe the effects of economic shocks on inflation (as well as output). Second, we can directly model supply shocks. Third, we can more straightforwardly model the adjustment of macroeconomic outcomes across time periods and therefore the dynamic response of economies to demand and/or supply shocks.

In section 22.5, we show how the *DAD/DAS* and *IS/MP* models can be integrated to provide a comprehensive view of how economies adjust to economic shocks.

Aggregate demand and supply plotted against inflation

The *DAD/DAS* model is illustrated in Figures 20.6 and 20.7. As with the *AD/AS* model that we developed in section 20.2, the horizontal axis measures real national income (*Y*). The vertical axis, however, measures the *rate of inflation,* not the *level* of prices. The aggregate demand and supply curves are labelled *DAD* and *DAS* to distinguish them from the curves

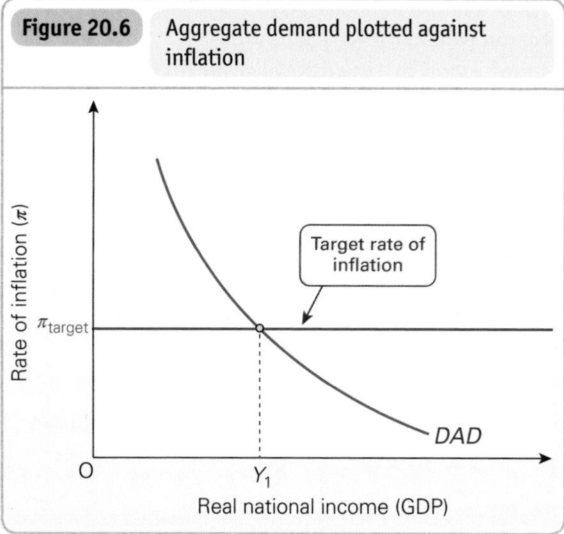

Figure 20.6 Aggregate demand plotted against inflation

in the normal aggregate demand and supply diagram. We also add a line showing the target rate of inflation (π_{target}).

Before we look at the properties of the model, let us examine each of the three lines in turn. The first two are illustrated in Figure 20.6.

The inflation target line

This is simply a horizontal line at the target rate of inflation (π_{target}). If the rate of inflation is above target, real interest rates will be raised by the central bank. If it is below target, real interest rates will be cut.[3]

If the government or central bank changes the target, the line will shift to the new target rate. The inflation target line is the anchor for the *vertical* position of the *DAD* curve. As we shall see, a change in the inflation target will be reflected by an equivalent vertical shift of the inflation target line and the *DAD* curve.

The dynamic aggregate demand curve

As with the normal *AD* curve, the *DAD* curve is downward sloping. In other words, a higher rate of inflation leads to a lower level of (real) aggregate demand. But why?

The reason is simple. It consists of a two-stage process.

1. If the rate of inflation (π) goes above the target level, the central bank will raise the *real* rate of interest (r). In other words it will raise the nominal rate *more* than the rise in the inflation rate. Thus if the rate of inflation goes up from a targeted 2 per cent to 3 per cent, the nominal interest rate (i) must rise by more than 1 percentage point in order to achieve a rise in the real interest rate.
2. The higher real rate of interest will then reduce (real) aggregate demand (*AD*), through both the interest rate and exchange rate mechanisms (see pages 600–7). This is equivalent to a movement leftwards up along an *IS* curve.

To summarise:

$$\pi\uparrow \rightarrow r\uparrow \rightarrow AD\downarrow$$

Similarly, a fall in the rate of inflation will cause the central bank to lower the real rate of interest (a movement rightwards down along an *IS* curve). This will reduce aggregate demand.

The slope of the DAD curve. The slope of the *DAD* curve depends on the strength of the two stages. The curve will be flatter:

- the more the central bank adjusts real interest rates in response to a change in inflation. The faster the central bank wants to get inflation back to its target level and the less concerned it is about cutting back on aggregate demand and hence output and employment, the larger will interest rate changes be;
- the more interest-rate sensitive is aggregate demand, and the stronger the interaction of the multiplier and amplifier process (the flatter the *IS* curve).

A movement along the DAD curve. This will be caused by changes in the rate of cost-push inflation (movements of the *DAS* curve). If the inflation rate rises, there will be a movement up the curve as the central bank raises the real rate of interest and this causes real national income to fall. When *inflation* begins to fall in response to the higher rate of interest, there will be a movement back down the curve again.

The position of the DAD curve. A given *DAD* curve represents a given monetary policy (the vertical position of the *MP* curve for a given inflation target). The particular *DAD* curve in Figure 20.6 intersects with the inflation target line at a real income of Y_1. This means that if inflation is on target, real national income will be Y_1. If Y_1 is the *potential* level of national output (the level of real national income with no output gap: see Box 15.3 on page 467), then the monetary policy the central bank has chosen is appropriate.

A shift in the DAD curve. Any factor that causes aggregate demand to change, other than the central bank responding to inflation being off-target, will cause the *DAD* curve to shift. A rightward shift represents an increase in aggregate demand (positive demand shock). A leftward shift represents a decrease (negative demand shock).

Causes of a rightward shift include tax cuts, increased government expenditure and a general rise in consumer or business confidence. These also cause the *IS* curve to shift rightwards.

The *DAD* curve will also shift to the right if the government or central bank sets a higher target rate of inflation. The reason is that this will lead to lower interest rates at every inflation rate. (This will be reflected in a downward shift in

3 Note that, in practice, although it is the nominal rate of interest (i) that the central bank changes, the objective is to affect the real rate of interest (r) in order to meet the inflation target.

the *MP* curve.) This can alternatively be viewed as a *vertical* shift of the *DAD* curve; the curve shifts upwards by the increase in the target rate of inflation.

The curve will also shift if the central bank *changes* its monetary policy, such that it no longer wants Y_1 to be the equilibrium level of national income. For example, if Y_1 in Figure 20.6 were below the potential level, and there was therefore demand-deficient unemployment, the central bank would reduce real interest rates to raise aggregate demand at the target inflation rate. This will shift the *DAD* curve to the right (and the *MP* curve vertically downwards). In other words, each rate of inflation along this new *DAD* curve would correspond to a lower real rate of interest (*r*) and hence a higher level of aggregate demand.

But what determines the actual level of *Y*? This is determined by the interaction of aggregate demand and aggregate supply. To show this we introduce a third line: the *DAS* curve.

The dynamic aggregate supply curve

The *DAS* curve, like the normal *AS* curve, is upward sloping. In the short run it will be relatively flat, mirroring the expectations-augmented Phillips curve (*EAPC*). In the long run it will be relatively steep, if not vertical at the potential level of national income, this time mirroring the long-run Phillips curve. The *DAS* curve is therefore an alternative presentation of the Phillips curve which analyses the relationship between inflation and *output* rather than inflation and *unemployment*.

The curve illustrated in Figure 20.7 is the short-run *DAS* curve. But why is it shaped this way? Why will a higher rate of inflation lead to higher real national income?

Assume that the economy is currently generating a real national income of Y_1 and that inflation is on target (π_{target}).

Figure 20.7 Aggregate demand and supply plotted against inflation

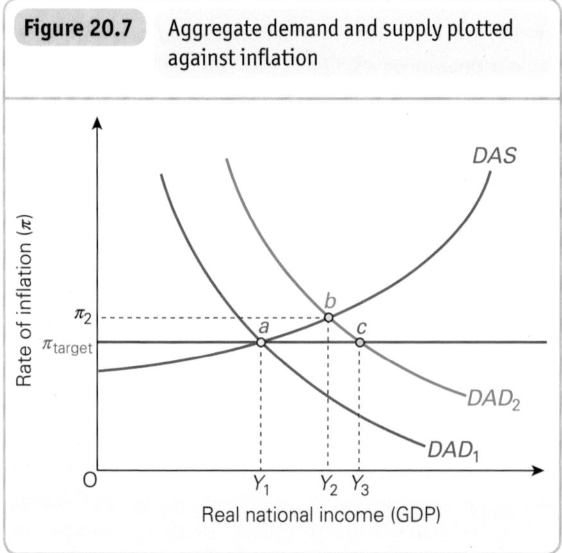

Equilibrium is at point *a*. Assume also that Y_1 represents the long-run potential level of output.

Now assume that there is general rise in confidence (a positive confidence shock) and that, as a result, the *DAD* curve shifts to DAD_2. Firms will respond to the higher aggregate demand partly by raising prices more than the current (i.e. target) rate of inflation and partly by increasing output: there is a movement along the *DAS* curve. Equilibrium moves to point *b*, where *DAD* = *DAS*.

TC 9 p132

But why will firms raise output as well as prices? The reason is the same as for the upward-sloping *AD* curve: 'sticky' input prices. Wage rises (and other input price rises) lag behind price rises. This is because it takes time to negotiate new wage rates. The higher prices now charged by firms will generate bigger profit margins for them, and thus they will supply more.

KI 33 p377

Over time, however, if the higher demand persists, wage rises would get higher. This would be the result of firms trying to obtain more labour to meet the higher demand and of unions seeking wage increases to compensate for the higher rate of inflation. Thus, assuming no increase in productivity, the *DAS* curve would shift upwards and continue doing so until real national income returned to the potential level Y_1. The long-run *DAS* curve would be vertical through point *a*.

Response to changes in aggregate demand and supply

A rise in aggregate demand

Assume, in Figure 20.7, that there has been a rise in real aggregate demand and that the *DAD* curve has shifted to DAD_2. Assume also that Y_1 is the potential level of national output. If inflation remained at its target rate, the economy would move to point *c*, with national income increasing to Y_3. But as firms respond partly by increasing prices more rapidly, equilibrium is reached at point *b*. In other words, there has been a movement up along the (short-run) *DAS* curve from point *a* to point *b* and back up along the new *DAD* curve from point *c* to point *b*. This movement along curve DAD_2 is the result of the higher interest rates imposed by the central bank in response to inflation rising to π_2.

But equilibrium at point *b* is above the target rate. This is unsustainable, even in the short run. One of two things must happen. The first option is for the central bank (or government) to accept a higher target rate of inflation: i.e. π_2. But if it does this, real income can only remain above its potential level in the short run. Soon, higher prices will feed through into higher wages and back into higher prices, and so on. The *DAS* curve will shift upwards.

The second option is for the central bank to reduce aggregate demand back to DAD_1. This will mean changing monetary policy, such that a higher real rate of interest is chosen for each rate of inflation. This tighter monetary policy shifts the *DAD* curve to the left.

In other words, if the central bank is adhering strictly to an inflation target, any rise in real aggregate demand can have only a temporary effect, since the higher inflation that results will force the central bank to bring aggregate demand back down again.

The one exception to this would be if the higher aggregate demand induced *positive* hysteresis effects, for example by encouraging firms to invest more and resulting in a higher potential level of national output. When the effects of this on aggregate supply began to be felt in terms of higher output, the short-term *DAS* curve itself would shift to the right, leading to a new equilibrium to the right of point *a*. In such a case, there would have been a long-term increase in output, even though the central bank was sticking to an inflation target.

TC 5 p48

Using a graph similar to Figure 20.7, trace through the effect of a reduction in aggregate demand.

A rise in aggregate supply

Assume now that aggregate supply rises. This could be a temporary 'supply shock', such as a cut in oil prices or a good harvest, or it could be a permanent increase caused, say, by technical progress. Let us take each in turn.

A temporary supply shock. In Figure 20.8, initial equilibrium is at point *a*, with curves DAD_1 and DAS_1 intersecting at point *a*, at the target rate of inflation. The rise in aggregate supply causes the *DAS* curve temporarily to shift from DAS_1 to DAS_2. Inflation thus falls below the target rate. As a result, the central bank reduces the real rate of interest (*r*). The effect is to increase aggregate demand. This is shown by a movement *along* curve DAD_1 from point *a* to point *d*. Inflation falls to π_3 and real national income rises to Y_4. Since this is only a temporary increase in aggregate supply, the central bank would not be expected to change its monetary policy. The *DAD* curve, therefore, will not shift.

As the supply shock subsides, aggregate supply will fall again. The *DAS* curve will shift back from DAS_2 to DAS_1, causing inflation to rise again. The result is a move back up the DAD_1 curve from point *d* to point *a*.

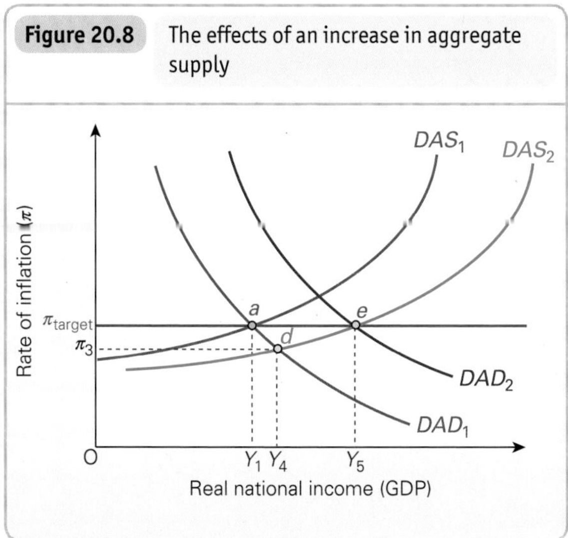

Figure 20.8 The effects of an increase in aggregate supply

1. *Trace through the effect of an adverse supply shock, such as a rise in oil prices.*
2. *What determines the amount that national income fluctuates when there is a temporary shift in the DAS curve?*

A permanent increase in aggregate supply. Now assume that DAS_2 represents a permanent increase in potential output. As before, the reduction in inflation causes the central bank to reduce interest rates. If there is no change in monetary policy, there would be simply be, once more, a movement from point *a* to point *d* with inflation now at π_3.

Once the central bank realises that the rise in aggregate supply is permanent, it will want to move to equilibrium at point *e*. To do this it will have to *change* its monetary policy and adopt a lower real interest rate at each rate of inflation (a shift downwards of the *MP* curve, as in the move to MP_2' in Figure 19.14(b) on page 621). This will shift the *DAD* curve to DAD_2. If it does this, equilibrium will be restored at the target rate of inflation. Y_5 will be the new sustainable level of real national income.

In other words, the central bank, by maintaining an inflation target, will allow aggregate demand to expand sufficiently to accommodate the full rise in aggregate supply.

The *AD/AS* and *DAD/DAS* models provide frameworks which can be used to analyse and debate the behaviour of the macroeconomy. We can, for example, use the models to consider the impact of economic shocks on key macroeconomic variables such as output and prices, or the effectiveness of changes to government spending in generating additional employment.

In the final two sections we begin our analysis of the alternative perspectives on how the macroeconomy behaves. First, we consider the crucial role played by the labour market before ending the chapter with an overview of some of the key controversies in macroeconomies.

The next chapter then builds on these sections to look at what this means for our understanding of the determination of output, employment and inflation. Throughout, you will see that the *AD/AS* and *DAD/DAS* models provide important frameworks through which to view these debates.

BOX 20.3 ANALYSING DEMAND-PULL AND COST-PUSH INFLATION USING THE *DAD/DAS* MODEL

EXPLORING ECONOMICS

Types of inflation under a policy of inflation targeting

We can use the *DAD/DAS* model to analyse the implications of demand-pull and cost-push pressures under a policy of inflation targeting.

The diagram below is similar to Figure 20.8. Assume that the central bank operates with an inflation target of π_{target} and that the economy is currently in equilibrium at point *a* with dynamic aggregate demand and supply given by DAD_1 and DAS_1, respectively. Real national income is at the potential (or 'natural') level of Y_1.

Demand-pull inflation

If there is a rise in aggregate demand to DAD_2, this will result in demand-pull pressures on inflation. The government or central bank could respond in either of two ways.

- Fiscal or monetary policy could be tightened to shift the *DAD* curve back to DAD_1, thereby maintaining inflation at the target level.
- A new higher inflation target could be adopted (e.g. π_2), allowing an equilibrium at point *b*. Note, however, that if the potential level of income remains at Y_1, Y_2 will not be sustainable. In the long run, the *DAS* curve will drift upwards, say to DAS_2, pushing inflation above the new higher target rate to π_3 (point *f*). A tighter monetary policy (DAD_3) would then be needed to bring national income back down to the potential level, Y_1.

Cost-push inflation

If costs rise faster than the rate of inflation (a *real* rise in costs), the *DAS* line will shift upwards (e.g. to DAS_2). Again, the government or central bank could respond in either of two ways.

- The central bank could stick to its target and adopt a tighter monetary policy. In this case the *DAD* curve will shift to the left to give an equilibrium at point c at the target rate of inflation. The potential level of output is now at the lower level of Y_3.
- The central bank could be given a higher target rate of inflation (π_2) to prevent real income falling. It will thus expand aggregate demand and the *DAD* line will shift to DAD_3. Equilibrium would now be at point *d*. The problem with this second approach is that if there has been a long-term reduction in potential output to Y_3 (as opposed to a one-off supply-side shock that is later reversed), there will be further upward pressure on inflation: the *DAS* curve will continue shifting upwards as long as real national income remains above Y_3. It will only be possible to keep to the target rate of inflation, at any level, if *DAD* is allowed to fall so that it intersects with *DAS* at Y_3.

If cost-push pressures reduce the potential level of real national income (e.g. from Y_1 to Y_3 in the diagram), why do demand-pull pressures not increase the potential level of real national income (e.g. from Y_1 to Y_2 in the diagram)?

Demand-pull and cost-push inflation

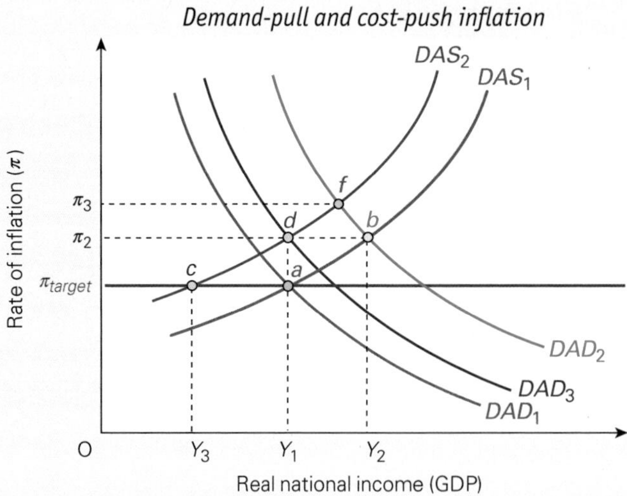

Section summary

1. The effects of adhering to an inflation target can be illustrated in a modified version of the aggregate demand and supply diagram. Inflation, rather than the price level, is plotted on the vertical axis. The aggregate demand curve in this diagram (labelled *DAD*) is downward sloping. This is because higher inflation encourages the central bank to raise interest rates and this leads to a fall in real national income.
2. The aggregate supply (*DAS*) curve in the short run is upward sloping. This can be explained by wage rises lagging behind price rises, which encourages firms to supply more in response to a rise in demand knowing that their profits will increase.
3. If aggregate demand rises, the *DAD* curve will shift to the right. The rate of inflation will rise above its target level. This is shown by a movement up the *DAS* curve and back up the new *DAD* curve to the new intersection point (as in Figure 20.7). The movement up the new *DAD* curve is in response to the higher interest rate now set by the central bank as it attempts to bring inflation back down to its target level.
4. Since the new equilibrium is above the target rate of inflation, the central bank must change to a tighter monetary policy and raise the real rate of interest. This shifts the *DAD* curve back to the left, and equilibrium is restored back at its original level. The rise in aggregate demand (unless accompanied by a rightward shift in aggregate supply) has had only a temporary effect on real national income.
5. A rise in aggregate supply (unless merely a temporary supply shock) will have a permanent effect on real national income. A rightward shift in aggregate supply will lead to an initial equilibrium at a rate of inflation below target and some rise in real national income as the rate of interest is reduced (as in Figure 20.8). The equilibrium is now below the target rate of inflation. The central bank must therefore change to a looser monetary policy and reduce the real rate of interest. This will shift the *DAD* curve to the right, causing a further rise in real national income that now fully reflects the rise in aggregate supply.

20.4 THE LABOUR MARKET AND AGGREGATE SUPPLY

Labour is a vital factor of production and so an important element of the aggregate supply relation we have considered in the previous sections of this chapter. The wage rate, quantity and quality of labour all, in one way or another, affect aggregate supply.

But the demand for labour is a derived demand: firms demand labour because of the goods and services workers help to produce. The level of aggregate demand for goods and services (*AD*) therefore affects the aggregate demand for labour in the economy (AD_L). Yet the aggregate demand for goods and services is itself affected by the price paid by firms for the labour it employs.

All of this illustrates the importance of the labour market to the behaviour of the economy. Therefore, we now take a closer look at how the labour market works.

Definitions

Aggregate demand for labour curve A curve showing the total demand for labour in the economy at different average real wage rates.

Aggregate supply of labour curve A curve showing the total number of people willing and able to work at different average real wage rates.

Modelling the labour market

Figure 20.9 shows the ***aggregate demand*** for labour and ***aggregate supply*** of labour: that is, the total demand and supply of labour in the whole economy. The *real* average wage rate is plotted on the vertical axis. As we saw in section 15.5, this is the average wage rate expressed in terms of its purchasing power to workers and the purchasing cost to employers. Therefore, the real wage is the nominal wage corrected for inflation.

Figure 20.9 Disequilibrium unemployment

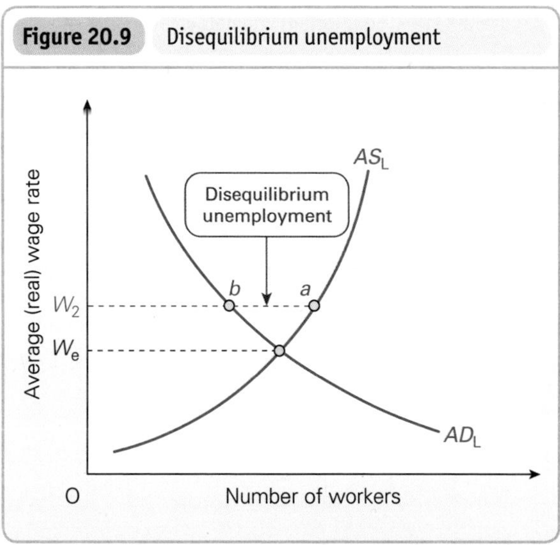

The aggregate supply of labour curve (AS_L) shows the number of workers *willing to accept jobs* at each real wage rate. This curve is relatively inelastic, since the size of the labour

KI 9 p64

force at any one time cannot change significantly. Nevertheless it is not totally inelastic because (a) a higher wage rate will encourage some people to enter the labour market (e.g. parents raising children), and (b) the unemployed will be more willing to accept job offers rather than continuing to search for a better-paid job.

The aggregate demand for labour curve (AD_L) slopes downwards. This is an extension of the microeconomic demand for labour curve (see section 10.1) and is based on the assumption of diminishing returns to labour. For a given capital stock, the more people are employed, the lower their marginal productivity. Thus firms take on more labour only if there is a fall in the real wage rate to compensate them for the lower output produced by the additional workers. On the other hand, the higher the real wage rate, the more will firms attempt to economise on labour and to substitute other factors of production for labour.

TC 13 p461

The labour market is in equilibrium at a real wage of W_e – where the demand for labour equals the supply.

If the wage rate were above W_e, the labour market would be in a state of disequilibrium. At a wage rate of W_1, there is an excess supply of labour of $a - b$. This is called ***disequilibrium unemployment***.

For disequilibrium unemployment to occur, two conditions must hold:

- The aggregate supply of labour must exceed the aggregate demand for labour.
- There must be a 'stickiness' in wages. In other words, the wage rate must not immediately fall to W_e, the market-clearing wage.

Even when the labour market *is* in equilibrium, however, not everyone looking for work will be employed. Some people will hold out, hoping to find a better job. This is illustrated in Figure 20.10.

The curve N shows the total number in the labour force. The horizontal difference between it and the aggregate supply of labour curve (AS_L) represents the excess of people looking for work over those actually willing to accept jobs at each wage rate. Q_e represents the equilibrium level of employment and the distance $d - e$ represents the ***equilibrium level of unemployment***. This is sometimes known as the ***natural level of unemployment***.

Figure 20.10 Equilibrium unemployment

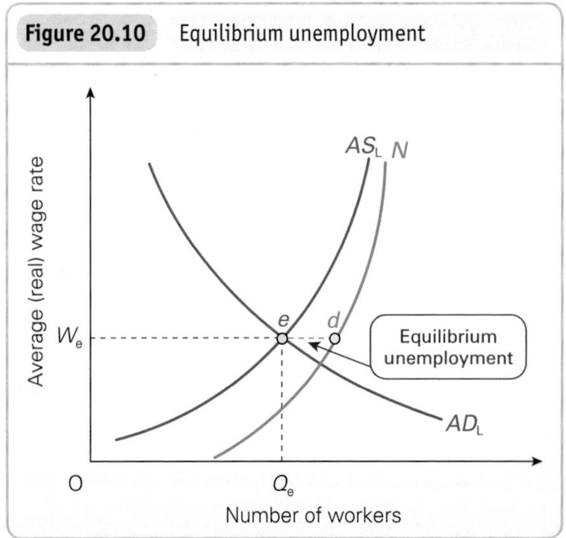

Figure 20.11 Equilibrium and disequilibrium unemployment

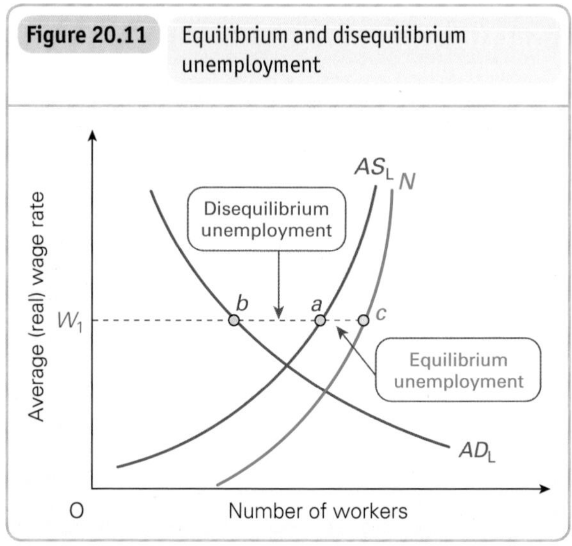

Note that the AS_L curve gets closer to the N curve at higher wages. The reason for this is that the higher the wages that are offered to the unemployed, the more willing they will be to accept jobs.

Figure 20.11 shows both equilibrium *and* disequilibrium unemployment. At a wage of W_1, disequilibrium unemployment is $a - b$; equilibrium unemployment is $c - a$; thus total unemployment is $c - b$.

We are now able to relate the concepts of equilibrium and disequilibrium unemployment to our discussion of the causes of unemployment in Chapter 15 (see pages 478–80). Real wage unemployment and demand-deficient unemployment are types of disequilibrium unemployment while structural, frictional and seasonal unemployment are types of equilibrium unemployment.

Disequilibrium unemployment

Real-wage unemployment is disequilibrium unemployment caused by real wages being driven up above the market-clearing level. In Figure 20.9, the wage rate is driven up

Definitions

Disequilibrium unemployment Unemployment resulting from real wage rates in the economy being above the equilibrium level.

Equilibrium ('natural') unemployment The unemployment that exists even when the labour market is in equilibrium. It is the difference between those who would like employment at the current wage and those who are willing and able to take a job.

above W_e. There are various possible reasons for this, as we saw in section 15.5. Some argue that it is the result of trade unions using their monopoly power to drive wages above the market-clearing level or, more generally, those in employment ('*insiders*') preventing the unemployed ('*outsiders*') from competing wages down. An alternative perspective is that firms may pay wage rates *above* market levels in order to provide an incentive for workers. This is the basis of the *efficiency wage hypothesis*.

TC 5 p48

Demand-deficient or cyclical unemployment is associated with fluctuations in aggregate demand. In the recessionary phase of a business cycle, demand-deficient unemployment is likely to rise; as the economy expands, it is likely to fall.

Demand-deficient unemployment is illustrated in Figure 20.12. Assume initially that the economy is at the peak of the business cycle. The aggregate demand for and supply of labour are equal at the current wage rate of W_1. There is no disequilibrium unemployment. Now assume that the economy moves into recession. Consumer demand falls and, as a result, firms demand less labour. The demand for labour shifts to AD_{L_2}. If there is a resistance to wage cuts, such that the real wage rate remains fixed at W_1, there will now be disequilibrium unemployment of $Q_1 - Q_2$.

Some Keynesians focus on the reluctance of real wage rates to fall from W_1 to W_2. Others, as we saw in Chapter 15, argue that the focus should be on the low level of aggregate demand. This, they argue, causes an equilibrium in the goods market at an output level that is too low to generate full employment. The disequilibrium in the labour market is the result of the low equilibrium output level in the goods market.

Equilibrium (or natural) unemployment

Although there may be overall *macro*economic equilibrium, with the *aggregate* demand for labour equal to the *aggregate* supply, and thus no disequilibrium unemployment, at a *micro*economic level supply and demand may not match. There may be excess demand for labour (vacancies) in some markets and excess supply (unemployment) in others.

Two commonly identified sources for these mismatches are skills and geography. There may be vacancies for computer technicians and unemployment in the steel industry, but unemployed steel workers cannot immediately become computer technicians. Even if the working population were relatively adaptable and, therefore, mobile between different sectors of the economy, there is still the potential problem that those unemployed may be in different geographical locations from where vacancies are located.

Then there is the problem of *imperfect information*. There is considerable turnover or 'churn' in the labour market, with some individuals being made redundant or quitting their jobs, while others are finding work. But employers are not fully informed about the labour available, and workers are not fully informed about what jobs are available and what they entail. The result is a process of search which sees employers searching for the right labour and workers for the right jobs.

The longer people search for a job, the better the wage offers they are likely to be made. This is illustrated in Figure 20.13 by the curve W_o. It shows the highest wage offer that the typical worker will have received since being unemployed.

When they first start looking for a job, people may have high expectations of getting a good wage. The longer they are unemployed, however, the more anxious they are likely to be to get a job, and therefore the lower will be the wage they are prepared to accept. The curve W_a shows the wage that is acceptable to the typical worker.

TC 9 p132

Why are W_o and W_a drawn as curves rather than straight lines?

The average duration of unemployment will be T_e. That is, workers will remain unemployed until they find a job at an acceptable wage.

Figure 20.12 Demand-deficient unemployment

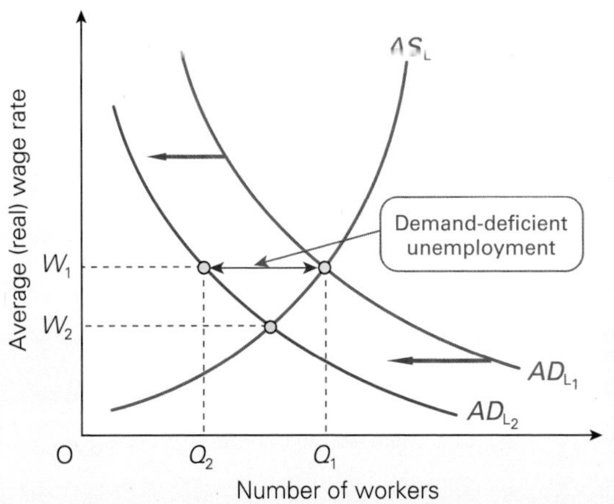

Figure 20.13 Average duration of unemployment

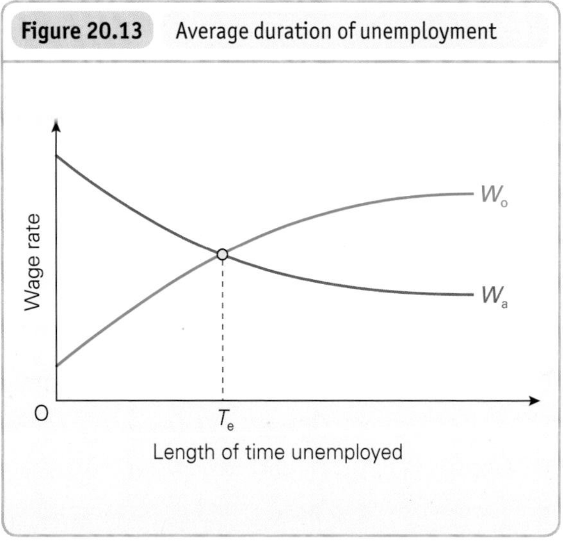

By improving the flow of job information, for example through government spending on job centres, the intention is to make the curve W_o reach its peak earlier. This has the effect of shifting the intersection of W_o and W_a to the left.

Other economists advocate reducing levels of unemployment benefit. The argument here is that this incentivises the unemployed to take work by making them more prepared to accept a lower wage. It will therefore have the effect of shifting the W_a curve downwards and again of shifting the intersection of W_o and W_a to the left.

KI5 p21

The classical model of labour markets and aggregate supply

The classical model is based on the 'classical' assumptions that real wage rates are flexible in the long run and that people are fully aware of price and wage changes, and hence do not believe that a given percentage pay increase will make them better off when prices are rising by the same percentage. In other words, people do not suffer from ***money illusion***.

Figure 20.14(a) shows again our aggregate demand and supply of labour diagram. The equilibrium real wage is W_e, where $AD_L = AS_L$, with Q_e workers employed. There is no disequilibrium unemployment at this real wage rate, but there is some equilibrium or natural unemployment. As we saw above, this is largely made up of frictional and structural unemployment. It is represented by the distance $(b - a)$.

With flexible prices and wage rates in the long run, *real* wage rates will also be flexible in the long run. This ensures that long-run employment is kept at Q_e.

The equilibrium in the labour market is matched by a corresponding equilibrium in the goods market, which is shown in Figure 20.14(b). The level of real national income corresponding to the natural level of employment is known as the ***natural level of income (or output)***. This is just another name for the *potential level of output* (Y_p): i.e. where there is no output gap (see Box 15.3, on page 467). The natural level of income is shown in the diagram as Y_p.

Now assume that aggregate demand for goods rises. This is shown by a rightward move of the aggregate demand curve from AD_1 to AD_2. It causes a movement up the short-run aggregate supply curve, $SRAS_1$, from point *e* to point *f*. The price level rises from P_1 to P_2. This causes the real wage to fall below W_e, say to W_1 in Figure 20.14(a). But at this real wage rate there is an excess demand for labour of $d - c$. This drives up the money (nominal) wage rate until the *real* wage rate has returned to W_e. Thus equilibrium employment is at Q_e and output is at its natural level irrespective of changes in aggregate demand.

In Figure 20.14(b), the rise in wage rates pushes up the *SRAS* curve to $SRAS_2$. Real national income falls back to Y_p and the price level rises to P_3. The long-run aggregate supply curve (*LRAS*) is thus vertical at Y_p.

Q_e would change only if there were some *exogenous* shift in the AD_L or AS_L curve (e.g. a growth in the working population would cause *N* and AS_L to shift to the right; a growth in

Definitions

Money illusion The belief that a *money* change in wages or prices represents a *real* change.

Natural level of real income (or output) The level of output consistent with the equilibrium or 'natural' level of employment.

Figure 20.14 Classical analysis of the labour market and output determination

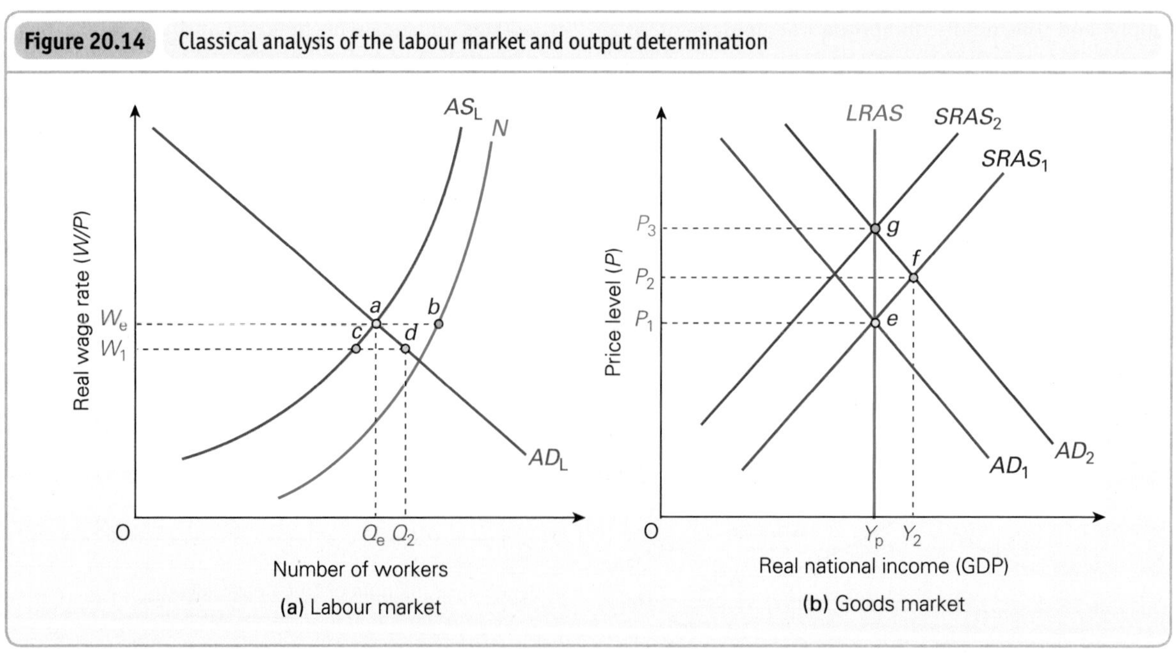

labour productivity would cause AD_L to shift to the right). In turn, this would affect the economy's natural level of output.

Assume that there is a fall in aggregate demand (for goods). Trace through the short-run and long-run effect on employment.

The time taken for national output and employment to return to their natural levels will depend on the speed with which money wages adjust. However, any disequilibrium experienced in the labour market will be temporary. Indeed, a group of economists known as new classical economists (see section 16.4) argue that wage and price flexibility is very great, especially with increased numbers of part-time and short-term jobs or people working in the gig economy. This flexibility is so great that both goods and labour markets clear virtually instantaneously. This is the assumption of *continuous market clearing* (see page 513).

KI 5 p21

Consequently, the speed of adjustment in the labour market to changes in aggregate demand means that there will be very little in the way of fluctuations in employment and output around their natural levels. Only if the change in aggregate demand were *unexpected* might there be any more significant effect on output and employment (see section 16.4, pages 513–4). For this reason, some economists refer to the short-run aggregate supply curve as the 'surprise aggregate supply curve'.

KI 10 p70

It is argued that once people recognise the impact that demand shocks have had on the prices of goods and services and, in turn, on their real wages, the labour market will readily adjust to equilibrium. As it does, the short-run (or surprise) aggregate supply curve moves readily to intersect the aggregate demand curve at the natural level of output.

Keynesian models of labour markets and aggregate supply

Keynesians take a very different view of labour markets, arguing that they are characterised by imperfections and frictions. In particular, they point to labour markets exhibiting considerable wage inflexibility. Employers often bargain with unions and usually set wage rates for a whole year. Even in non-unionised firms, wage rates are still often set for a year.

A negative output gap. The inflexibility of wages and of prices in goods markets is a concern when an economy experiences a fall in aggregate demand. This is because it can lead to significant falls in the *quantities* of output and employment. Compare this with the classical model, where the adjustment occurs through *prices* and *wages*. In the classical model, a fall in aggregate demand for goods (a leftward shift of the *AD* curve) causes prices in the goods market and wages in the labour market to fall. This eliminates the excess supply of goods in the goods market and disequilibrium unemployment in the labour market.

Keynesians argue that if there is a fall in consumer demand, firms usually respond *not* by cutting wages. Instead they lay off workers, cut hours, institute early retirement or do not replace workers when they leave. In the short run, therefore, wages in many sectors of the economy are insensitive to a fall in demand.

Consider an economy characterised by equilibrium in the labour and goods market. In Figure 20.15(a), employment is Q_e and the only unemployment is equilibrium unemployment of $b - a$. Meanwhile, real national income (output) is the natural level Y_1 and the economy's price level is P_1.

Assume now the case of a fall in aggregate demand, represented by a leftward shift of the aggregate demand curve

Figure 20.15 Keynesian analysis of the labour market and output determination

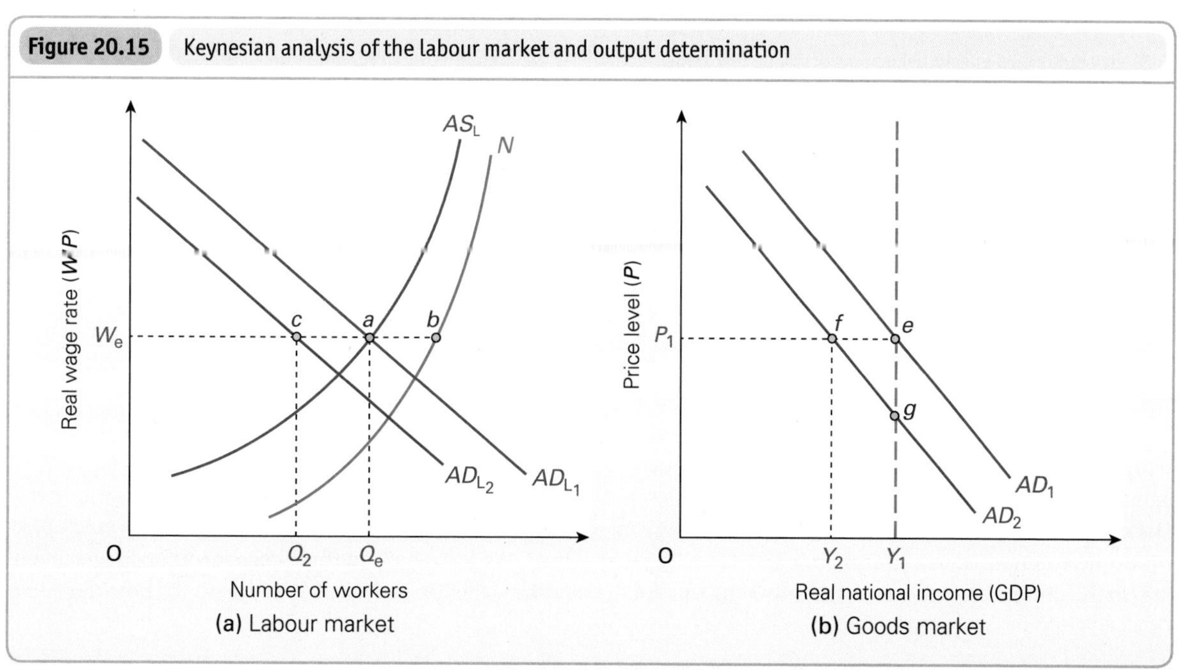

from AD_1 to AD_2 in Figure 20.15(b). In the Keynesian case, with sticky prices and wages, the aggregate price level does not fall. At P_1 firms find that they cannot sell all the goods they previously did. Hence, the adjustment to the fall in aggregate demand occurs solely through a fall in the quantity of output. The *SRAS* curve becomes a horizontal line at price level P_1 in Figure 20.15(b) and output falls from Y_1 to Y_2.

In the labour market, the stickiness of nominal wages means that, with nominal wages and prices not affected by the fall in demand, real wages are unaffected too. Hence, with a lower aggregate demand for goods but real wages still at their full-employment real wage rate, firms reduce their *effective* demand for labour. This is represented in Figure 20.15(a) by a fall in the aggregate demand for labour from AD_{L_1} to AD_{L_2}. Firms thus reduce employment from Q_e to Q_2. There is now demand-deficient unemployment of $a - c$. *Total* unemployment is $b - c$.

But what about the *long* run? Clearly it depends on how long the long run is. Many Keynesians argue that prices and especially wages exhibit a degree of inflexibility over quite a long period of time, and over this period of time, therefore, the aggregate supply curve would not be vertical. In other words, it could take some considerable time for the economy to move from point *f* in Figure 12.15(b) to point *g*.

The result could be an economy stuck at an output level below its potential. In such a scenario, Keynesians argue, governments can play an important role by helping to stimulate aggregate demand.

The possibility of a low-output equilibrium is a significant insight. But can the current analysis explain positive output gaps: i.e. output levels above potential output?

A positive output gap. Again, assume that the economy is characterised by equilibrium in both the goods and labour market. In the presence of sticky prices in the goods market, the increase in aggregate demand (a rightward shift of the *AD* curve) is reflected in full by an increase in output. There is no effect on the real wage. Hence, in the labour market, firms' effective demand for labour rises (a rightward shift of the AD_L curve). If we assume that workers choose to supply this additional demand, despite being off their AS_L curve, then employment rises to produce the additional goods.

A positive output gap can only persist for a time, however, before the pressure on prices and wages builds. In the long run, therefore, the aggregate supply curve will be upward sloping, but not vertical if higher demand stimulates firms to invest more and if, in turn, this investment leads to an increase in potential output.

Section summary

1. The goods and labour markets are interdependent. A rise in aggregate demand in the goods market will lead to a rise in the aggregate demand for labour.
2. Equilibrium in the labour market is where the aggregate demand and supply of labour are equal. However, even in equilibrium, there is likely to be some unemployment. This 'equilibrium unemployment' occurs when there are people unable or unwilling to fill job vacancies. This could be frictional or structural unemployment.
3. Disequilibrium unemployment occurs when real wage rates are above the level that will equate the aggregate demand and supply of labour. In the case of demand-deficient unemployment, the disequilibrium in the labour market may correspond to a low-output equilibrium in the goods market. A fall in real wage rates may be insufficient to remove the deficiency of demand in the labour market.
4. Classical economists argue that prices and wages respond quickly to changes in aggregate demand and supply. A fall in aggregate demand will quickly result in a fall in prices, with equilibrium remaining at the natural level of output. Likewise, nominal wages will quickly fall and there will be no disequilibrium unemployment.
5. Keynesian economists argue that, because of sticky prices and wages, a fall in demand in the goods market will lead to a fall in output and a fall in employment; disequilibrium unemployment will occur. The slower prices and wages are to adjust, the longer it is likely to persist.

20.5 *AD/AS* AND MACROECONOMIC CONTROVERSIES

In this chapter we have introduced the *AD/AS*, *DAD/DAS* and AD_L/AS_L models. These models allow us to analyse the interaction of aggregate demand and aggregate supply in determining the economy's output, price and employment levels. The nature of this interaction and, in particular, the way in which the economy adjusts to economic shocks highlights important differences between economists. In this final section of the chapter we discuss some of these differences and the implications they have for policy.

Most of the debate in macroeconomics has centred on the working of the market mechanism: just how well or how badly it achieves various macroeconomic objectives. We focus here on three major areas of disagreement: (a) how flexible are wages and prices; (b) how flexible is aggregate supply; (c) what is the role of expectations? We examine each in turn.

Controversy 1: the flexibility of prices and wages

Generally, the political right has tended to ally with those economists who argue that prices and wages are relatively flexible. Markets tend to clear, they say, and clear fairly quickly.

Disequilibrium unemployment is likely to be fairly small, according to their view, and normally only a temporary, short-run phenomenon. Any long-term unemployment, therefore, will be equilibrium (or 'natural') unemployment. To cure this, they argue, encouragement must be given to the free play of market forces: to a rapid response of both firms and labour to changes in market demand and supply, to a more rapid dissemination of information on job vacancies, and generally to greater labour mobility, both geographical and occupational.

There are some on the political right, however, who argue that in the short run wages may not be perfectly flexible. This occurs when unions attempt to keep wages above the equilibrium. In this case, disequilibrium unemployment may continue for a while. The solution here, they argue, is to curb the power of unions so that wage flexibility can be restored and disequilibrium unemployment cured.

The political centre and left have tended to ally with economists who reject the assumption of highly flexible wages and prices. There exist, they argue, frictions and market imperfections. If there is a deficiency of demand for labour in the economy, for example during a recession, there will be a resistance from unions to cuts in real wages and certainly to cuts in money wages. Any cuts that do occur will be insufficient to eliminate the disequilibrium, and will anyway serve only to reduce aggregate demand further, so that workers have less money to spend. The aggregate demand for labour curve in Figure 20.15 (see page 653) would shift further to the left.

The prices of goods may also be inflexible in response to changes in demand. As industry became more concentrated and more monopolistic over the years, firms, it is argued, became less likely to respond to a general fall in demand by cutting prices. Instead, they were likely to build up stocks if they thought the recession was temporary, or cut production and hence employment if they thought the recession would persist. It is also argued that many firms use cost-plus methods of pricing. If wages are inflexible downwards, and if they form a major element of costs, prices will also be inflexible downwards.

Thus, according to those who criticise the right, markets cannot be relied upon automatically to correct disequilibria and hence cure disequilibrium unemployment.

Why are real wages likely to be more flexible downwards than money wages?

The process of globalisation has helped to offset the growth in market power in many industries in recent years. Competition from China and India, for example, has made prices in many markets more flexible. In other markets, however, particularly in the service sector, international competition is less relevant and in others, global giants, such as Apple, Bayer, Boeing and GlaxoSmithKline, have considerable price-setting power.

Controversy 2: the flexibility of aggregate supply

The question here is, how responsive is national output (i.e. aggregate supply), and hence also employment, to a change in aggregate demand?

The arguments centre on the nature of the aggregate supply curve (*AS*). Three different *AS* curves are shown in Figure 20.16. In each of the three cases, it is assumed that the government raises aggregate demand through the use of fiscal and/or monetary policy. Aggregate demand shifts from AD_1 to AD_2. The effect on prices and output will depend on the shape of the *AS* curve.

Some economists, generally supported by the political right, argue that output is not determined by aggregate demand, except perhaps in the very short run. Instead, the rise in aggregate demand will simply lead to a rise in prices. They therefore envisage an *AS* curve like that in Figure 20.16(a).

If the government wants to expand aggregate supply and get more rapid economic growth, it is no good, they argue, concentrating on demand. Instead, governments should concentrate directly on supply by encouraging enterprise and competition, and generally by encouraging markets to operate more freely. For this reason, this approach is often labelled ***supply-side economics***.

Their critics, however, argue that a rise in aggregate demand will lead to a rise in output. In the extreme case where actual output is well below potential output, prices will not rise at all. In this case, the *AS* curve is like that in Figure 20.16(b). Output will rise to Y_2 with the price level remaining at *P*.

Others argue that both prices and output will rise. In this case, the short-term curve will be like that in Figure 20.16(c). If there is plenty of slack in the economy – idle machines, unemployed labour, etc. – output will rise a lot and prices only a little. But as slack is taken up, the *AS* curve becomes steeper. Firms, finding it increasingly difficult to raise output in the short run, simply respond to a rise in demand by

Definition

Supply-side economics An approach which focuses directly on aggregate supply and how to shift the aggregate supply curve outwards.

Figure 20.16 Contrasting views on the aggregate supply curve

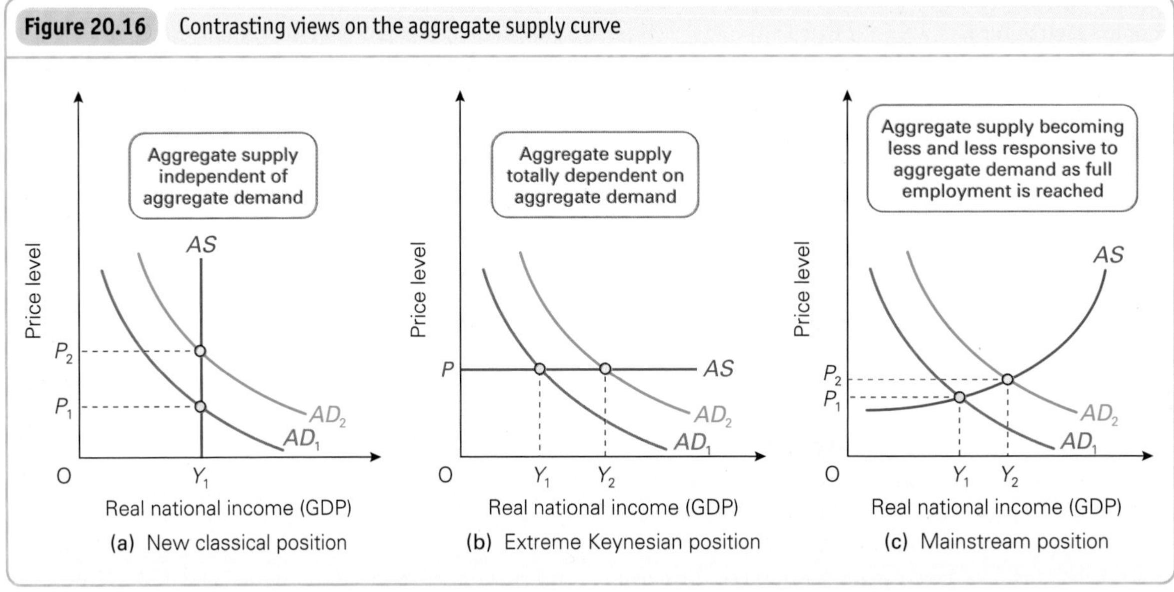

(a) New classical position

(b) Extreme Keynesian position

(c) Mainstream position

raising prices. This is the version of the *SRAS* curve we developed in section 20.1.

As we discussed in Chapter 16, a new macroeconomic consensus has emerged in recent times. It is generally agreed that the short-run *AS* curve is similar to that in Figure 20.16(c), but that in the long run, given time for prices and wages to adjust, the curve is much steeper, if not vertical. Any increase in aggregate demand will simply result in higher prices.

Aggregate demand and investment

There is not total agreement, however, that changes in aggregate demand have no long-term effect on output. One way in which changes in aggregate demand can have a lasting impact on output is if these affect firms' investment plans.

Assume there is a rise in aggregate demand. As a result, firms may be encouraged to invest in new plant and machinery (the accelerator effect). In so doing, they may well be able to increase output significantly in the long run with little or no increase in their prices. This would make their long-run *MC* curves much flatter than their short-run *MC* curves.

In Figure 20.17, the short-run *AS* curve (*SRAS*) shifts to the right. Equilibrium moves from point *a* to *b* to *d*. In this case, the long-run *AS* curve (*LRAS*) joining points *a* and *d* becomes more elastic. There is a relatively large increase in output and a relatively small increase in price.

KI 9 p64

The *LRAS* curve will be flatter and possibly even downward sloping if the investment involves the introduction of new cost-reducing technology, or if firms generally experience economies of scale. It will be steeper if the extra investment causes significant shortages of materials, machinery or labour. This is more likely when the economy is already operating near its full-capacity output.

1. *Will the shape of the LRAS curve here depend on just how the 'long' run is defined?*
2. *If a shift in the aggregate demand curve from AD to AD_1 in Figure 20.17 causes a movement from point a to point d in the long run, would a shift in aggregate demand from AD_1 to AD cause a movement from point d back to point a in the long run?*

The possibility that increases in aggregate demand can stimulate higher levels of investment, and so bring about higher capacity and a higher aggregate supply, has clear policy implications. For example, following the global financial crisis in the late 2000s and the COVID-19 pandemic in the early 2020s, there were calls from Keynesian economists for governments to expand and maintain their support for aggregate demand despite the pressures on the

Figure 20.17 Effect of investment on the long-run aggregate supply curve

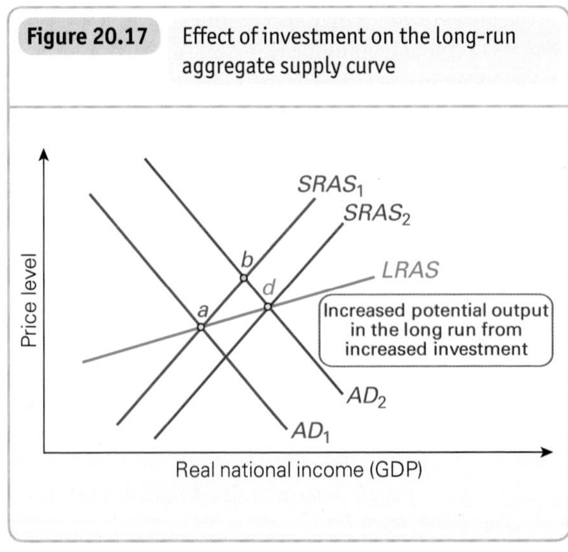

public finances. This would, they argued, give firms the confidence to invest, help boost the capacity of the economy, allow economic recovery to be sustained, and mitigate the potential for scarring effects (*hysteresis*) on future economic activity arising from the sharp economic contraction that had occurred.

Hysteresis

The possibility of economic hysteresis provides another means by which fluctuations in aggregate demand may generate long-term real effects on the economy. As you may have seen in sections 16.5 and 16.7, hysteresis refers to the lagging or persistence of an effect, even when the initial cause has been removed. In other words, an equilibrium position depends on the path taken to arrive there. In this context, hysteresis would be where long-run aggregate supply depends on what has been happening to aggregate demand and supply in the short run.

KI 33 p377

As we have just seen, hysteresis effects can affect potential output through the impact of economic shocks on firms' investment decisions. The labour market is another important channel through which hysteresis effects can arise. To illustrate this, we apply a Keynesian view of goods and labour markets, assuming that both prices and wages are sticky.

Now assume that the economy goes into recession, with a corresponding rise in demand-deficient unemployment and a fall in output. In Figure 20.18, the effective aggregate demand for labour curve has fallen from AD_{L_1} to AD_{L_2}. Demand-deficient unemployment is $a - b$ (the short-run effect).

As the recession persists, those previously laid off may not be readily re-employable, especially if they have been out of work for some time and have become deskilled and demoralised. The aggregate supply of labour curve shifts to the left, perhaps as far as AS_{L_2}. In such a case, there would now no longer be an excess supply of labour that firms regard as 'employable' ($AD_{L_2} = AS_{L_2}$). There is no downward pressure on real wages: a long-run equilibrium has been reached. The implication of this is that the long-run aggregate supply (of goods) curve is *not* vertical. A leftward shift in aggregate demand has led to a long-run fall in output.

Figure 20.18 The effect on wages and employment of a recovery from recession

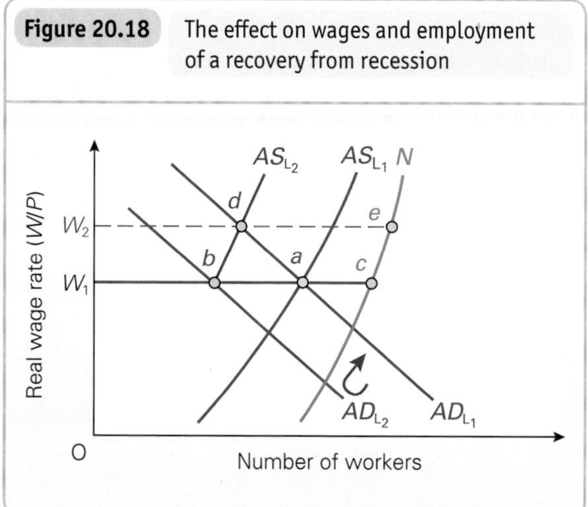

Assume now that the government pursues a reflationary policy, and that the aggregate demand for labour shifts back to AD_{L_1}. There will be a move up along AS_{L_2} to point *d*. Unemployment is now *e* – *d*, higher than the original level of *c* – *a*.

Hysteresis channels therefore propagate economic shocks and create persistent effects. As we saw in section 16.7, the effects may not only relate to future *levels* of economic activity but also to the rates of *growth*. The possibility of growth rate effects has led some to refer to the possibility of *super hysteresis* and has significant implications for longer-term living standards (see page 522).

What is 'learning by doing? Why is this a possible hysteresis channel?

Controversy 3: the role of expectations in the working of the market

How quickly and how fully will individuals and firms anticipate changes in prices and changes in output? How are their expectations formed, and how accurate are they? What effect do these expectations have? This has been the third major controversial topic.

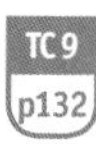

TC 9 p132

The political right tended to ally with those economists who argue that people's expectations adjust rapidly and fully to changing economic circumstances. They emphasise the role of expectations of *price* changes.

If aggregate demand expands, they argue, people will expect higher prices. Workers will realise that the apparently higher wages they are offered are an illusion. The higher wages are 'eaten up' by higher prices. Thus workers are not encouraged to work longer hours, and unemployed workers are not encouraged to take on employment more readily. Likewise, the higher prices that firms can charge are necessary to cover higher wages and other costs, and are not a reflection of higher real demand. Firms thus soon realise that any apparent increased demand for their products is an illusion. Their price rises will fully absorb the extra spending in money terms. There will be no increase in sales, and hence no increase in output and employment.

Therefore, they argue, increased aggregate demand merely fuels inflation and can do no more than give a very temporary boost to output and employment. If anything, the higher inflation could damage business confidence and thus worsen long-term output and employment growth by discouraging investment.

Those who criticise this view argue that the formation of expectations is more complex than this. Whether people expect an increase in demand to be fully matched by inflation depends on the current state of the economy and how any increase in demand is introduced.

If there is a lot of slack in the economy (if unemployment is very high and there are many idle resources) and if an increase in demand is in the form, say, of direct government spending on production (on roads, hospitals, sewers and other infrastructure) then output and employment may quickly rise. Here the effect of expectations may be beneficial. Rather than expecting inflation from the increased demand, firms may expect faster growth and an expansion of markets. As a result, they may choose to invest, and this in turn will produce further growth in output and employment.

Views on expectations, therefore, tend to parallel views on aggregate supply. The right argues that a boost to demand will not produce extra output and employment: aggregate supply is inelastic (as in Figure 20.16(a)) and therefore the higher demand will merely fuel expectations of inflation. Their critics argue that a boost to demand can increase aggregate supply and employment. If firms expect this, they will produce more.

If firms believe the aggregate supply curve to be moderately elastic, what effect will this belief have on the outcome of an increase in aggregate demand?

We examine the role of expectations in determining output and employment in the next chapter.

BOX 20.4 **COMMON GROUND BETWEEN ECONOMISTS?** EXPLORING ECONOMICS

Identifying areas of agreement

The financial crisis and the COVID-19 pandemic deeply impacted societies. They both shone lights on a series of important issues of relevance to economists. This would inevitably lead to differences of opinion among economists. Yet we can still identify areas of common ground between many economists over many issues. Hence, some degree of macroeconomic consensus may be argued to have survived the financial crisis. We summarise here three general areas of agreement first introduced in section 16.6 (see pages 525–6).

1. Fluctuations in aggregate demand can have significant effects on output and employment in the short term

With the exception of extreme new classical economists, most economists would accept that the short-run aggregate supply (*SRAS*) curve is *upward sloping,* albeit getting steeper as potential output is approached. There are two major implications of this analysis.

- Reductions in aggregate demand can cause reductions in output and increases in unemployment. In other words, too little spending will cause a recession.
- An expansion of aggregate demand by the government (whether achieved by fiscal or monetary policy, or both) will help to pull an economy out of a recession. There may be considerable time lags, however, before the economy fully responds to such expansionary policies.

2. Changes in aggregate demand will have much less effect on output and employment and much more effect on prices in the longer term

As we have seen, new classical economists and others argue that the long-run aggregate supply (*LRAS*) curve is vertical. Some Keynesian economists agree, but argue that the long run might be quite a long time. Others, while arguing that the *LRAS* curve is not vertical, would still see it as less elastic than the short-run aggregate supply curve.

Nevertheless, some Keynesians argue that changes in aggregate demand *will* have substantial effects on long-term output and employment via hysteresis channels, for example, because of changes in investment, spending on research and development and the growth of human capital. These effects impact on the level and growth of potential output.

3. Expectations have important effects on the economy

Virtually all economists argue that expectations are crucial in determining the success of government policy on unemployment and inflation. Whatever people expect to happen, their actions will tend to make it happen.

If people believe that an expansion of money supply will merely lead to inflation (the monetarist and new classical position), then it will. Firms and workers will adjust their prices and wage rates upwards. Firms will make no plans to expand output and will not take on any more labour. If, however, people believe that an expansion of demand will lead to higher output and employment (the Keynesian position), then, via the accelerator mechanism, it will.

Similarly, just how successful a deflationary policy is in curing inflation depends in large measure on people's expectations. If people believe that a deflationary policy will cause a recession, then firms will stop investing and will cut their workforce. If they believe that it will cure inflation and restore firms' competitiveness abroad, firms may increase investment.

To manage the economy successfully, therefore, the government must convince people that its policies will work. This is as much a job of public relations as of pulling the right economic levers. It is one of the reasons for making central banks independent. If people believe that the central bank will not be swayed from its task of keeping inflation on target, either by public opinion or by political pressure, then people will come to expect low inflation. It is also one of the reasons why central banks nowadays tend to issue 'forward guidance' – saying what they intend to do so that people can adjust their expectations and actions.

In Chapter 21 we will look further at the importance of expectations, particularly expectations of inflation and output. We will also consider the process by which people's expectations are formed.

1. *If constant criticism of governments in the media makes people highly cynical about any government's ability to manage the economy, what effect will this have on the performance of the economy?*
2. *Suppose that, as part of the national curriculum, everyone in the country had to study economics up to the age of 16. Suppose also that the reporting of economic events by the media became more thorough (and interesting!). What effects would these developments have on the government's ability to manage the economy? If you were a Keynesian, how would your answer differ from that of a new classicist?*

Undertake desktop research on a school of macroeconomic thought of your choice. This could, for example, be 'monetarist', 'new classical', 'new Keynesian' or 'post-Keynesian'. What are their core assumptions and analysis and their key policy recommendations? Write up your findings and prepare a presentation lasting for about 10 minutes that could be delivered to fellow students.

Section summary

1. Over the years there has been considerable debate among economists and politicians about how the market mechanism works at a macroeconomic level.
2. The right has tended to argue (a) that prices and wages are relatively flexible, (b) that aggregate supply is determined independently of aggregate demand and (c) that people's price and wage expectations adjust rapidly to shifts in aggregate demand so as to wipe out any output effect.
3. The centre and left to varying degrees have argued (a) that prices and wages are inflexible downwards, (b) that aggregate supply is relatively elastic when there is slack in the economy and (c) aggregate supply can be responsive to changes in aggregate demand in the longer term because of, for example, economic hysteresis or positive expectations of output and employment.

END OF CHAPTER QUESTIONS

1. For what reasons might the long-run aggregate supply curve be (a) vertical; (b) upward sloping; (c) downward sloping?
2. How would you attempt to assess whether a particular period of inflation was the result of cost-push or demand-pull pressures?
3. Repeat the analysis undertaken in Figure 20.5 to consider the possible subsequent effects following a period of demand-pull deflation.
4. What implications would a vertical short-run aggregate supply curve have for the effects of demand management policy?
5. What would cause (a) a steep *DAD* curve; (b) a gently sloping *DAD* curve? Compare the short-run and long-run effects of (i) a temporary adverse supply shock and (ii) a permanent supply reduction under each of (a) and (b).
6. Under what circumstances would a rightward shift in the *DAD* curve lead to a *permanent* increase in real national income?
7. What impact would an increase in potential output have on the *DAS* curve? How would the long-term rate of economic growth be reflected by the *DAS* curve?
8. For what reasons may the natural level of unemployment increase?
9. Assume that there is a positive technological shock. How would this impact on the equilibrium level of employment and the economy's potential output? Illustrate using diagrams of both the labour and goods markets.
10. How might fluctuations in aggregate demand lead to changes in output even under the assumption of continuous market clearing?
11. Given the Keynesian explanation for the persistence of high levels of unemployment after the recessions of the early 1980s and early 1990s, what policies would you advocate to reduce unemployment in the years following a recession?
12. What are the possible channels through which hysteresis effects can arise, such that demand shocks have persistent effects on the macroeconomy?

Online resources

Additional case studies on the student website

20.1 Micro-foundations of the *SRAS* curve. This case looks at the microeconomic foundations of the short-run aggregate supply curve and its shape.

20.2 The factors shaping the *LRAS*. This case looks at three important factors shaping the *AS* curve in the long run.

20.3 Going behind the *DAD* and *DAS* curves. This case provides further analysis of the *DAD* and *DAS* curves and their relationship with other macroeconomic models.

20.4 Do people volunteer to be unemployed? Is it useful to make the distinction, often made, between voluntary and involuntary unemployment?

20.5 Getting predictions wrong. How incorrect predictions can lead to a rise or fall in output in the new classical model.

Maths Case 20.1 Deriving the *DAD* curve. A mathematical demonstration of the derivation of the *DAD* curve from an *IS* curve and a Taylor rule.

Websites relevant to this chapter

See sites listed at the end of Chapter 22 on page 735.

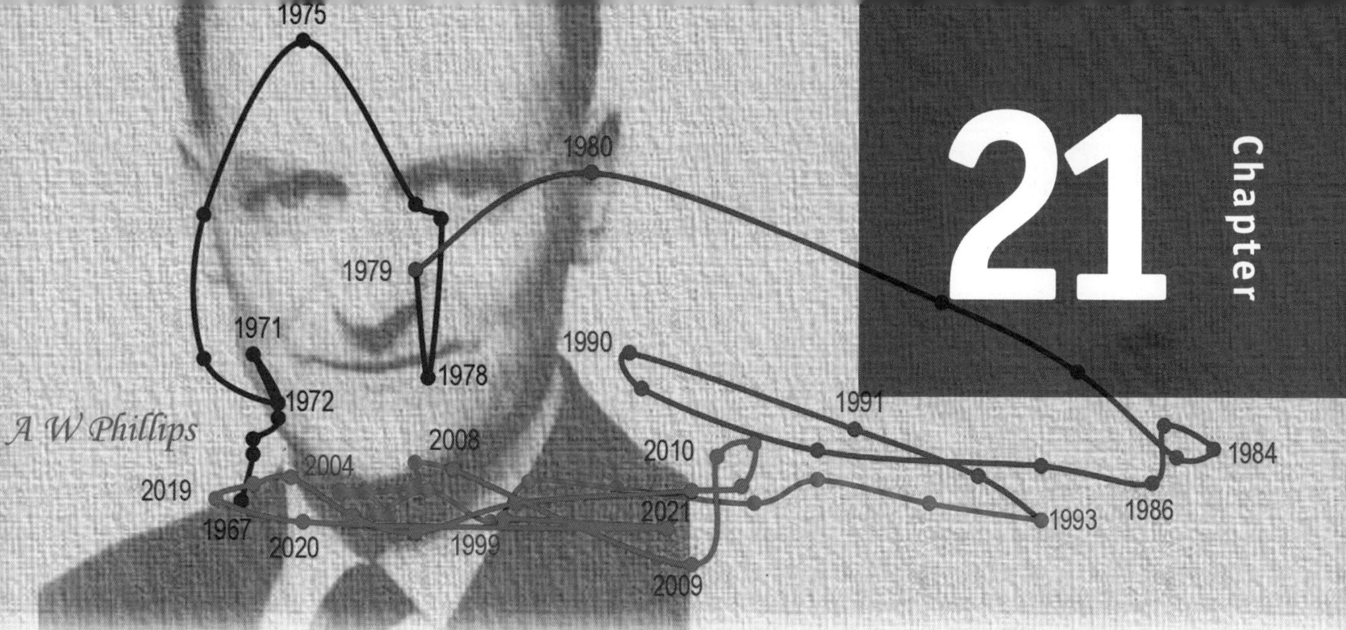

The Relationship between Inflation, Unemployment and Output

CHAPTER MAP

In this chapter we turn to the relationship between inflation and unemployment. We examine a range of alternative perspectives. Once more we shall see that a crucial element here is the response of aggregate supply to a change in aggregate demand, in this case reflected in the shape of the Phillips curve. If aggregate supply responds to changes in aggregate demand, then a rise in aggregate demand should lead to a fall in unemployment, but will probably lead to a rise in inflation.

We shall see that the behaviour of markets and the formation of expectations are especially important in affecting the unemployment/inflation relationship, both in the short run and in the long run.

Around the world, many central banks target inflation, often supplemented by other macroeconomic objectives. We therefore look at how the analysis of the inflation/unemployment relationship has led many governments to delegate monetary policy to their central banks. We consider some of the possible costs and benefits of delegation.

The chapter concludes by integrating the *IS/MP* model with the Phillips curve and *DAD/DAS* models to consider the adjustment paths of economies to economic shocks.

21.1 THE *EAPC* AND THE INFLATION–UNEMPLOYMENT RELATIONSHIP

The expectations-augmented Phillips curve (*EAPC*)

In Chapter 20 we discussed the interaction of aggregate demand and supply and the impact on output and prices from the frequent shocks that affect the economy. We saw how the adjustment process is affected, among other things, by the behaviour of product and labour markets and by expectations. In this section we look at the importance of inflationary expectations in affecting macroeconomic outcomes. To do so, we look more closely at the ***expectations-augmented Phillips curve (EAPC)*** that we introduced in Box 15.6 and section 16.4. It provides an alternative way of looking at the macroeconomy.

The *EAPC* was a major contribution to our understanding of the relationship between unemployment and inflation made by Milton Friedman (see Case Study 16.8 on the student website) and others in the late 1960s. They incorporated people's expectations about the future level of prices into the Phillips curve.

The original Phillips curve stems from the inverse relationship identified by Bill Phillips between wage inflation and unemployment for the UK from 1861 to 1957 (see Box 15.6). It appeared to offer a trade-off between inflation against unemployment. Lower unemployment could be bought at the cost of higher inflation, and vice versa, through changes in aggregate demand (relative to potential output).

KI 36 p459

Friedman argued that the theoretical trade-off implied by the simple Phillips curve relationship relied on permanent changes in the *real* wage. For the rate of unemployment to remain below its natural rate, i.e. the equilibrium rate, workers would need to supply labour at below the equilibrium real wage rate (e.g. W_e in Figure 20.10 on page 650). Friedman argued that this was implausible other than in the short term and that wage inflation would surely catch up with consumer price inflation to restore the real wage equilibrium.

Hence, Friedman believed that the theory underpinning the original Phillips curve relationship had failed to incorporate people's expectations of inflation. TC 9 p132

In its simplest form, this expectations-augmented Phillips curve may be expressed as

$$\pi = f(1/U) + \pi^e + k \qquad \textbf{(1)}$$

This states that the rate of price inflation (π) depends on three things.

- First, it is a function (f) of the inverse of unemployment ($1/U$). This is simply the original Phillips curve relationship. A rise in aggregate demand will lead to a fall in unemployment (a rise in $1/U$) and a rise in inflation: e.g. a movement from point *a* to point *b* in Figure 21.1.
- Second, the expected rate of inflation π^e must be added to the inflation that would result simply from the level of excess demand represented by ($1/U$).
- Third, if there are any exogenous cost pressures on inflation (k) (such as increases in international commodity prices), this must be added too.

Definition

Expectations-augmented Phillips curve A (short-run) Phillips curve whose position depends on the expected rate of inflation.

Figure 21.1 Expectations of inflation and the Phillips curve

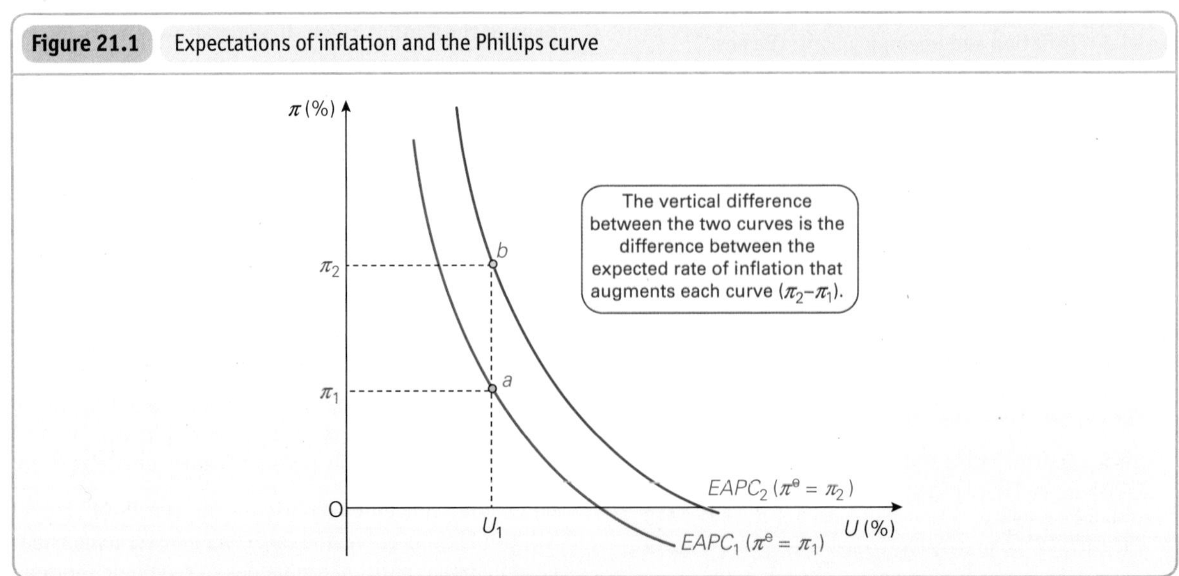

Thus if people expected a 3 per cent inflation rate ($\pi^e = 3\%$) and if excess demand were causing demand-pull inflation of 2 per cent ($f(1/U) = 2\%$) and exogenous increases in costs were adding another 1 per cent to inflation ($k = 1\%$), actual inflation would be $3 + 2 + 1 = 6$ per cent.

By augmenting the Phillips curve with expectations of inflation, we move from a single curve to a series of Phillips curves. The vertical position of each curve is determined by expectations of inflation (π^e) and any exogenous costs pressures (k). If we assume that on average $k = 0$, then we can simplify the *EAPC* framework so that each expectations-augmented Phillips curve is associated with a particular expected rate of inflation.

Figure 21.1 illustrates two hypothetical expectations-augmented Phillips curves. $EAPC_1$ is drawn for an expected inflation rate π_1, while $EAPC_2$ is drawn for an expected inflation rate π_2. Hence, for any given rate of unemployment, such as U_1, $EAPC_2$ is vertically higher than $EAPC_1$ by the difference ($\pi_2 - \pi_1$).

Assume the economy is represented by $EAPC_1$ in Figure 21.1. Illustrate the effects of positive and negative inflation shocks on the curve.

TC 9 p132

Expectations of inflation

But by what process do people form their inflationary expectations? We can identify two principal forms of expectations: adaptive and rational expectations. We examine each in turn. We will see that the response of inflation and unemployment to a rise in aggregate demand differs according to how expectations are formed.

Adaptive expectations

If we assume that people base their expectations of inflation on past inflation rates, then they form what are called ***adaptive expectations***. If, for example, last year people underpredicted the rate of inflation, then this year they will adapt by revising their expectations of inflation upwards.

The simplest form of adaptive expectations is to assume that people use last year's actual inflation rate (π_{t-1}) as their prediction for the rate of inflation this year (π_t^e):

$$\pi_t^e = \pi_{t-1}$$

Box 21.1 considers more sophisticated versions of adaptive expectations.

Rational expectations

The adaptive expectations hypothesis, it is argued, suffers from a serious flaw: it assumes that people base their expectations solely on the past. So if inflation is on an upward trend, the future of inflation will always be underestimated. Similarly, inflation will always be overestimated if it is on a downward trend. Thus people will normally be wrong.

But people will soon realise that it is not rational to base their expectations blindly on the past. They will look at the *current* situation and what is likely to affect inflation. Thus, it is argued, adaptive expectations cannot be a rational basis of behaviour.

Rational expectations are not based on past rates of inflation. Instead they are based on the current state of the economy and the current policies being pursued by the government. Workers and firms look at the information available to them – at the various forecasts that are published, at various economic indicators and the assessments of them by various commentators, at government pronouncements, and so on. From this information they predict the rate of inflation as well as they can. It is in this sense that the expectations are 'rational': people use their reason to assess the future on the basis of current information.

Definition

Adaptive expectations Where people adjust their expectations of inflation in the light of what has happened to inflation in the past.

***BOX 21.1 BASING EXPECTATIONS ON THE PAST** EXPLORING ECONOMICS

More sophisticated adaptive expectations models

More complex adaptive expectations models assume that π^e is a weighted average of past rates of inflation:

$$\pi_t^e = a\pi_{t-1} + b\pi_{t-2} + c\pi_{t-3} \ldots + m\pi_{t-n} \qquad (1)$$

where $a + b + c \ldots + m = 1$, and where $a > b > c$, etc.

In other words, people will base their expectations of inflation on the actual inflation rates over the last few time periods (e.g. months, quarters or years), but with the last period's inflation having a bigger influence on people's expectations than the previous period's and so on.

In times of rapidly *accelerating* inflation, people may adjust their expectations of inflation upward by the amount that inflation *rose* last period ($\Delta\pi_{t-1}$). This gives:

$$\Delta\pi_t^e = \Delta\pi_{t-1} \qquad (2)$$

Under what circumstances will term a in equation (1) be large relative to terms b, c, etc.?

But forecasters frequently get it wrong, and so do economic commentators! And the government does not always do what it says it will. Thus workers and firms base their expectations on *imperfect information*. Other versions assume that they may make very poor use of information. But, either way, people frequently forecast incorrectly. The crucial point about the rational expectations theory, however, is that these errors in prediction are *random*. People's predictions of inflation are just as likely to be too high as too low.[1]

TC 9 p132

KI 15 p132

Short-run and long-run perspectives

As we saw in Chapter 16, Friedman and other monetarists argued that there exists a long-run Phillips curve (*LRPC*) which is vertical at the natural (equilibrium) rate of unemployment. Only in the *short run* would higher aggregate demand reduce the unemployment rate below the natural rate (and raise output above its potential level). In the long run there would be no *real* increase in aggregate demand.

The idea that unemployment will return to its natural rate (and output to its potential level) following fluctuations in aggregate demand is commonly referred to as the ***natural rate hypothesis***. Although initially associated with monetarists, the hypothesis has become more widely incorporated into macroeconomic models.

How would the EAPCs and the LRPC be affected by an increase in the natural rate of unemployment?

However, not all economists accept that the natural rate of unemployment is unaffected by fluctuations in aggregate demand. As discussed in section 20.5, Keynesian economists, for example, have developed theories exploring how changes in aggregate demand can have effects on physical and human capital. These effects, they argue, can result in a non-vertical (downward-sloping) *LRPC* and, therefore, in non-vertical (upward-sloping) long-run *AS* and *DAS* curves.

[1] The rational expectations hypothesis can be stated as:

$$\pi_t = \pi_t^e + \left(\sum_{t=1}^{t=\infty} \varepsilon_t\right)(\varepsilon = 0)$$

In other words, the rate of inflation for any time period (π_t) will be the rate that people expected in that time period (π_t^e) plus an error term (e_t). This error term may be quite large but is equally likely to be positive or negative. Thus when you sum ($\sum$) the error terms over the years (strictly speaking, to infinity), the positive and negative values will cancel each other out and the sum will therefore be zero.

In understanding the long-run relationship between inflation and unemployment, it is important to analyse the adjustment of economies to economic shocks. Short-run adjustments to fluctuations in aggregate demand involve movements *along* expectation-augmented Phillips curves. Hence, the *EAPC* provides us with a framework to analyse the implications for inflation and the labour market from the frequent fluctuations in aggregate demand.

Whether people form adaptive or rational expectations is an important factor in determining how economies adjust to shocks. This is not only the case for their expectations of inflation but also for other macroeconomic variables, such as output.

Market clearing

Another important factor affecting the adjustment processes of economies is the speed with which markets clear through the adjustment of prices to equate demand and supply.

In models which assume market clearing, prices are deemed to be flexible and so adjust to bring about equilibrium between demand and supply. In the labour market, for example, wages are not sticky downwards, at least not in the long run. There can be no long-run disequilibrium unemployment: no long-run deficiency of demand.

The assumption made by new classical economists (see section 16.4) is that of *continuous* market clearing. This means that markets experience a very rapid adjustment of prices resulting in them clearing continuously. On the other hand, new Keynesian economists (see section 16.5) argue that there are frictions which impede and slow the adjustment of markets to economic shocks.

We now consider the effect of a range of views about both expectations and the degree of market clearing on the inflation/unemployment trade-off. We begin in section 21.2 with the original monetarist thinking, which combines adaptive expectations of inflation with the assumption that markets are relatively flexible.

Definition

Natural rate hypothesis The theory that, following fluctuations in aggregate demand, unemployment will return to a natural rate. This rate is determined by supply-side factors, such as labour mobility.

Section summary

1. A refinement of the simple Phillips curve involves the incorporation of people's expectations about the rate of inflation. This gives an expectations-augmented Phillips curve.
2. One explanation of how people form these expectations is given by the adaptive expectations hypothesis. In its simplest form, the hypothesis states that the expected rate of inflation this year is what it actually was last year: $\pi^e_t = \pi_{t-1}$.
3. An alternative process by which expectations are formed is known as rational expectations. This assumes that people base their expectations of inflation on a rational assessment of the current situation. People may predict wrongly, but they are equally likely to underpredict or to overpredict. On average, over the years, it is assumed that they will predict correctly.
4. Those who support the natural rate hypothesis argue that fluctuations in aggregate demand have no long-term effect on unemployment, which will adjust to its natural rate. Hence, the economy is characterised by an *LRPC* which is vertical at the natural rate of unemployment. The natural rate is determined by supply-side factors.
5. Though the natural rate hypothesis has become increasingly accepted by economists other than just monetarists, it is not universally accepted. The *EAPC* provides a framework to study the adjustment of economies to shocks and their longer-term impact on the inflation–unemployment relationship.
6. The formation of expectations and the flexibility of markets are two important factors in determining the long-term inflation–unemployment relationship.

21.2 INFLATION AND UNEMPLOYMENT: THE MONETARIST PERSPECTIVE

The 'fooling model'

As we have seen in the previous section, monetarists argued that the natural rate of unemployment is determined independently of aggregate demand. Consequently, the long-run Phillips curve is vertical. In the long run, it is supply-side policies that affect levels of structural and frictional unemployment. However, in the short run unemployment may deviate from its natural rate. To understand why, we develop a simple model of the economy known as the ***fooling model***.

The fooling model is based on three assumptions. First, prices and wages adjust relatively quickly to ensure equilibrium between demand and supply in goods and labour markets. Second, the actual rate of inflation can deviate from the expected rate since people have imperfect information. Third, people form adaptive expectations of inflation.

To make the analysis more straightforward, we assume that they use last year's actual inflation rate year (π_{t-1}) as their prediction for the expected rate of inflation this year (π^e_t):

$$\pi^e_t = \pi_{t-1} \qquad (2)$$

Also we assume that the economy's inflation rate last year was zero, no inflation is expected and there are no exogenous cost pressures on inflation ($k = 0$ in equation (1) on page 662).

In Figure 21.2 the economy is initially at point *a* with both actual and expected inflation of zero. The goods and labour markets are in equilibrium: $AD = AS$ and unemployment is at its natural rate, U_n.

Increase in aggregate demand. Assume that there is an increase in real aggregate demand. Firms respond partly by increasing prices by more than the current rate of inflation and partly by increasing output. The average nominal wage rates rises, but by less than consumer prices. Therefore the average *real* wage rate falls. This encourages firms to employ more people and raise output.

Figure 21.2 *EAPC* and the natural rate hypothesis

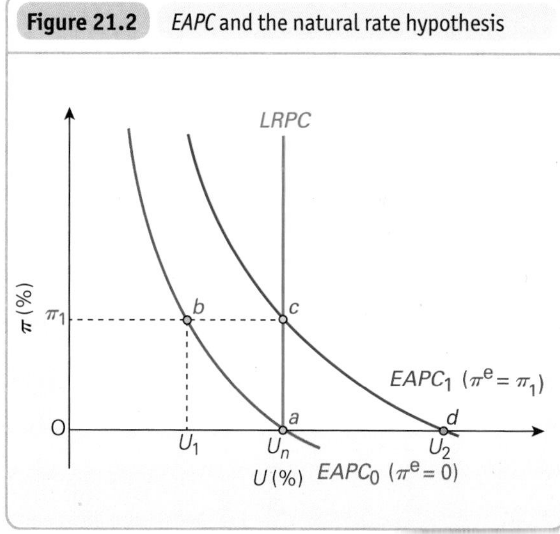

Definition

The fooling model Where workers, as a result of imperfect information, can be fooled into believing that a rise in *money* wages represents a rise in *real* wages.

Employment and labour hours will increase if workers are fooled into believing that their expected *real* wage rate is higher. The 'actual' labour supply curve (AS_{L_2}) is to the right of the 'true' labour supply curve (AS_L) as shown in Figure 21.3. This increase in economic activity is reflected in Figure 21.2 in the move *along* the expectations-augmented Phillips curve, $EAPC_0$ to, say, point *b*. The rate of inflation rises from zero to π_1.

If we now move ahead a year, people will have revised their expectations of inflation upwards to π_1. The result is that the Phillips curve has shifted up vertically by π_1 to $EAPC_1$. If *nominal* aggregate demand (i.e. demand purely in monetary terms, irrespective of the level of prices) continues to rise at the same rate, the whole of the increase will now be absorbed in higher prices. *Real* aggregate demand will fall back to its previous level and the economy will move to point *c* on the long-run Phillips curve. Unemployment will return to its natural rate, U_n, consistent with the natural rate hypothesis. There is no *demand-pull* inflation now ($f(1/U) = 0$), but inflation is π_1 per cent due to inflationary expectations.

TC 13 p461

Decrease in aggregate demand. Assume that the economy is at point *c* in Figure 21.2. It now experiences a decrease in the growth of nominal demand. Real aggregate demand falls. This time firms respond partly by reducing prices (or raising them by less than the rate of inflation) and partly by reducing output. Increases in the average nominal wage rate slow, but by less than consumer prices.

Employment and labour hours will decrease if workers believe that their *real* wage rate is lower. The 'actual' labour supply curve (AS_{L_1}) is to the left of the 'true' labour supply curve (AS_L) as shown in Figure 21.3. The economy moves down $EAPC_1$ to point *d*: the inflation rate falls to zero and unemployment rises above its natural rate (U_n) to U_2.

The following year the expected rate of inflation will fall to zero. The *EAPC* moves vertically down to $EAPC_0$. If the growth in nominal aggregate demand remains at its new lower rate, with inflation now at zero, the economy will again be at point *a* on the long-run Phillips curve. Unemployment is again at its natural rate.

The accelerationist hypothesis

The preceding analysis helps to show that when people form adaptive expectations of inflation, unemployment can deviate from its natural rate following changes in aggregate demand even if markets clear fairly quickly. This raises the theoretical possibility that governments could keep unemployment below the natural rate. But this would come at a cost since, to do so, it must raise nominal aggregate demand at ever-increasing rates.

Each time government is able to raise the nominal growth in aggregate demand there is a transitory period when real aggregate demand rises too. But inflationary expectations then rise to reflect higher inflation rates. This is mirrored in the labour market by real wages being driven back up to their equilibrium level. Hence, for the government to keep unemployment below its natural rate it needs to keep raising the growth in nominal aggregate demand – in other words, it must increase nominal aggregate demand faster and faster. This, of course, means that nominal aggregate demand needs to grow at more than the rate of inflation. However, the rate of inflation is itself getting progressively higher as people are continually raising their inflationary expectations.

The theory that unemployment can be reduced below the natural rate only at the cost of accelerating inflation is known as the ***accelerationist hypothesis***. Box 21.2 considers a numerical example of the hypothesis.

Definition

Accelerationist hypothesis The theory that unemployment can be reduced below the natural rate only at the cost of accelerating inflation.

Figure 21.3 The fooling model and the labour market

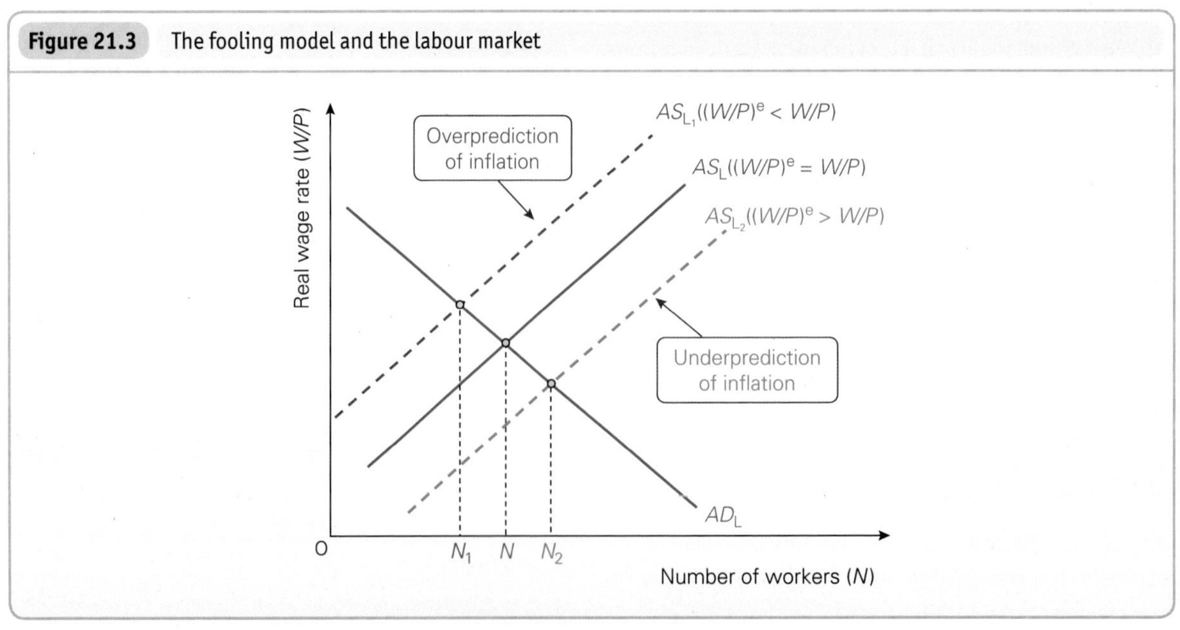

BOX 21.2 THE ACCELERATIONIST HYPOTHESIS EXPLORING ECONOMICS

The race to outpace inflationary expectations

Let us trace the course of inflation and expectations over a number of years in an imaginary economy. To keep the analysis simple, assume there is no growth in the economy and no exogenous cost pressures on inflation ($k = 0$ in equation (1) on page 662).

Year 1. Assume that at the outset, in year 1, there is no inflation of any sort; that none is expected; that $AD = AS$; and that equilibrium unemployment is 8 per cent. The economy is at point *a* in the diagram.

Year 2. Now assume that the government expands aggregate demand in order to reduce unemployment. Unemployment falls to 6 per cent. The economy moves to point *b* along $EAPC_1$. Inflation has risen to 4 per cent, but people, basing their expectations of inflation on year 1, still expect zero inflation. There is therefore no shift as yet in the Phillips curve. $EAPC_1$ corresponds to an expected rate of inflation of zero. (See Case Study 21.1 on the student website for an explanation of why the short-run Phillips curve slopes downwards.)

Year 3. People now revise their expectations of inflation to the level of year 2. The Phillips curve shifts up by 4 percentage points to $EAPC_2$. If *nominal* aggregate demand (i.e. demand purely in monetary terms, irrespective of the level of prices) continues to rise at the same rate, the whole of the increase will now be absorbed in higher prices. *Real* aggregate demand will fall back to its previous level and the economy will move to point *c*. Unemployment will return to 8 per cent. There is no *demand-pull* inflation now ($f(1/U) = 0$), but inflation is still 4 per cent due to expectations ($\pi^e = 4$ per cent).

Year 4. Assume now that the government expands real aggregate demand again so as to reduce unemployment once more to 6 per cent. This time it must expand nominal aggregate demand by more than it did in year 2, because this time, as well as reducing unemployment, it also has to validate the 4 per cent expected inflation. The economy moves to point *d* along $EAPC_2$. Inflation is now 8 per cent.

Year 5. Expected inflation is now 8 per cent (the level of actual inflation in year 4). The Phillips curve shifts up to $EAPC_3$. If at the same time the government tries to keep unemployment at 6 per cent, it must expand nominal aggregate demand 4 per cent faster in order to validate the 8 per cent expected inflation. The economy moves to point *e* along $EAPC_3$. Inflation is now 12 per cent.

Year 6 onwards. To keep unemployment at 6 per cent, the government must continue to increase nominal aggregate demand by 4 per cent more than the previous year. As the expected inflation rate goes on rising, the Phillips curve will go on shifting up each year.

What determines how rapidly the short-run Phillips curves in the diagram shift upwards?

Construct a table like the one in the diagram, only this time assume that the government wishes to reduce unemployment to 5 per cent. Assume that every year from year 1 onwards the government is prepared to expand aggregate demand by whatever it takes to do this. If this expansion of demand gives $f(1/U) = 7$ per cent, fill in the table for the first six years. Do you think that after a couple of years people might begin to base their expectations differently?

The accelerationist theory of inflation

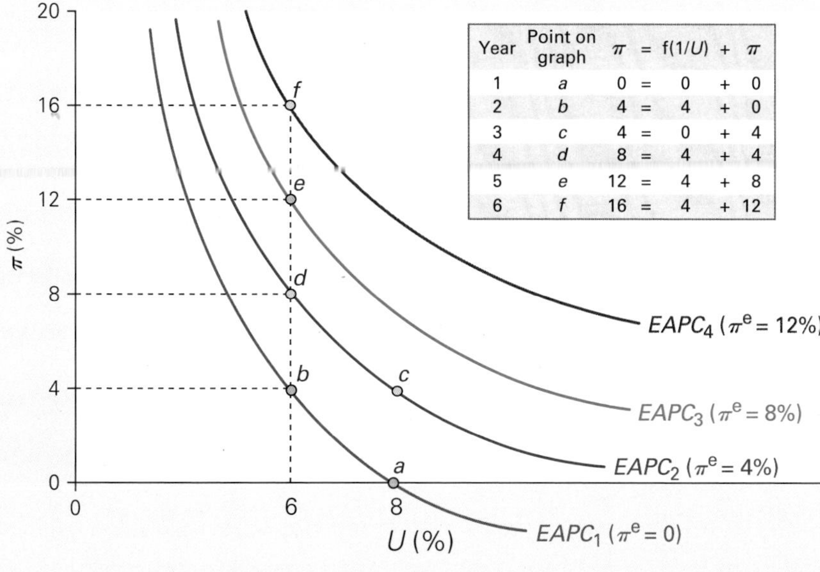

Year	Point on graph	π	=	f(1/U)	+	π
1	*a*	0	=	0	+	0
2	*b*	4	=	4	+	0
3	*c*	4	=	0	+	4
4	*d*	8	=	4	+	4
5	*e*	12	=	4	+	8
6	*f*	16	=	4	+	12

Stagflation and Phillips loops

In the 1970s, many countries experienced 'stagflation' – a simultaneous rise in unemployment and inflation. Monetarists used the adaptive expectations model to explain why this occurred. The explanation involved clockwise Phillips loops and rightward shifts in the long-run Phillips curve.

Clockwise Phillips loops

Consider a 10-year cycle. This is illustrated in Figure 21.4. The economy starts at position *a* in year 0. There is no inflation and the economy is at the natural rate of unemployment. The government pursues an expansionary policy over the next three years in order to reduce unemployment. The economy moves up through points *b*, *c* and *d*.

The government then starts worrying about inflation. It allows unemployment to rise somewhat, but as it is still below U_n there is still demand-pull inflation. The economy moves to point *e*. The government now allows unemployment to rise to U_n, but the Phillips curve still shifts up as expectations catch up with last year's inflation. The economy moves from point *e* to point *f*.

Thereafter the government allows unemployment to rise further, and the economy eventually returns to point *a*, via points *g*, *h*, *i* and *j*. The economy has thus moved through a clockwise loop.

Stagflation is easy to see. From points *d* to *f*, both unemployment *and* inflation are rising. What is more, several points are to the 'north-east' of other earlier points. For example, point *g* is north-east of point *c*. In other words, the rates of inflation *and* unemployment in year 6 (point *g*) are higher than in year 2 (point *c*).

?

Under what circumstances would a Phillips loop be (a) tall and thin; (b) short and wide?

Rightward shifts in the long-run Phillips curve

If frictional or structural unemployment rises (due, say, to increased unemployment benefits), U_n will increase. The long-run Phillips curve will shift to the right.

Figure 21.4 Clockwise Phillips loops

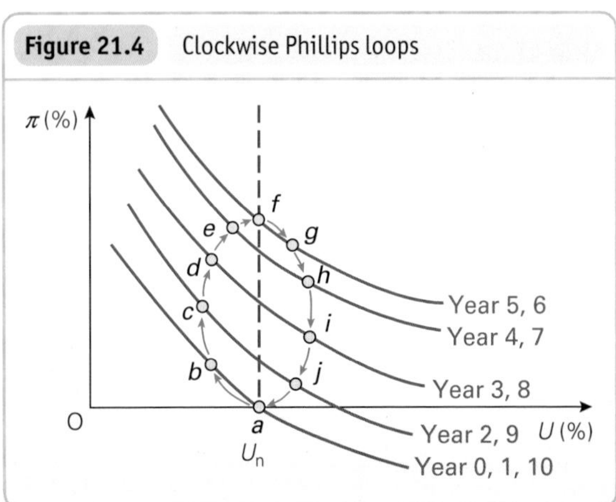

Assume that the economy was initially on the long-run Phillips curve with $U_n = 4$ per cent and a stable inflation rate of 2 per cent. Thanks to some supply-side shock, U_n now rises to 8 per cent. The government uses demand-management policy to keep the rise in unemployment to only 6 per cent. But this is now *below* U_n and thus inflation will increase. Thus both inflation *and* unemployment rates have risen.

Phillips loops and the political business cycle

The monetarist adaptive expectations model can also be applied to illustrate how the path of unemployment and inflation can follow a cycle mirroring the election cycle. In other words, policy makers may attempt to engineer a path for the macroeconomy that increases its probability of election. This path is known as the ***political business cycle***.

The theory suggests that the discretionary policy choices of government can purposefully destabilise the economy. Therefore, it is argued, governments should be made to adopt policy rules.

Imagine that a politically naïve government has been fulfilling election promises to reduce unemployment, cut taxes and increase welfare spending. In Figure 21.4 this is shown by a move from points *a* to *b* to *c*. However, by the time the next election comes, inflation is accelerating and unemployment is rising again. The economy is moving from point *d* to *e* to *f*. This is unlikely to be a successful strategy for a vote-maximising government.

What the political business cycle model suggests is that at the start of their electoral terms, governments will engineer a recession and begin to squeeze down inflationary expectations. Assuming the economy is already at point *f* as a result of previous political business cycles, the government will attempt to move the economy from point *f* to *g* to *h*.

But people are assumed to have short memories. Therefore, the government looks to engineer a pre-election boom and be rewarded for its economic management over the latter part of the election period. Unemployment falls, but inflation continues falling because of expectations adjusting downwards. The economy moves from point *h* to *i* to *j* to *a*.

How would the political business cycle be affected if governments were able to choose when to hold elections?

Policy implications

The implications of the monetarist application of the expectations-augmented Phillips curve are that monetary or

Definition

Political business cycle The theory that governments, after being elected, will engineer an economic contraction, designed to squeeze out inflation. They will then later engineer a pre-election boom to appeal to the electorate.

fiscal policy can have no *long-run* effect on unemployment. They can only be used to influence the inflation rate.

Ultimately, monetary and fiscal policies merely move the economy up or down the vertical long-run Phillips curve. An expansionary policy, for example, could only ever bring a *temporary* reduction in unemployment below U_n. Moreover, demand-side policy can be destabilising, especially if used by governments to court electoral popularity.

To reduce unemployment permanently, *supply-side* policies should be used. These could either be market-orientated policies of removing impediments to the working of the market (see section 23.5) or interventionist policies, such as improving education and training or the country's transport and communications infrastructure (see section 23.6). By reducing frictional and/or structural unemployment, such policies will shift the long-run Phillips curve back to the left.

Section summary

1. The monetarist model assumes that markets are relatively flexible. But the assumption of adaptive expectations allows unemployment to deviate from the natural rate in the short term. People can be fooled, allowing unemployment and output to fluctuate.
2. If there is excess demand in the economy, producing upward pressure on wages and prices, initially unemployment will fall. The reason is that workers and firms will believe that wage and price increases represent *real* wage and price increases respectively. Thus workers are prepared to take jobs more readily and firms choose to produce more. But as people's expectations adapt upwards to these higher wages and prices, so ever-increasing rises in nominal aggregate demand will be necessary to maintain unemployment below the natural rate. Price and wage rises will accelerate: i.e. the rate of inflation will rise.
3. The long-run Phillips curve, according to this analysis, is thus vertical at the natural rate of unemployment.
4. Stagflation can be explained in this model either by a movement from 9 o'clock to 12 o'clock round a clockwise Phillips loop, or by a rightward shift in the vertical Phillips curve combined with a mild expansionary policy.
5. The model also illustrates how governments can benefit electorally by generating a political business cycle.

21.3 INFLATION AND UNEMPLOYMENT: THE NEW CLASSICAL POSITION

New classical assumptions

Economists of the *new classical school* (see section 16.4) go further than the traditional monetarist theory described above. They argue that unless there are unexpected or 'surprise' events, there is not even a short-run trade-off between inflation and unemployment. The *EAPC* therefore represents a short-run trade-off between inflation and unemployment only in the presence of surprise events. It mirrors the surprise *SRAS* curve (see section 20.4).

The idea that output and employment only respond to unexpected price changes is frequently referred to as the 'Lucas surprise supply function'. This is associated with Robert Lucas, a leading figure in the development of new classical macroeconomics (see Box 21.3). The argument that there is normally *no* trade-off between unemployment and inflation, even in the short run, is based on two key assumptions:

- Prices and wages are flexible so that markets clear continuously.
- Expectations are 'rational', but are based on imperfect information.

TC 4 p45

TC 10 p358

Continuous market clearing. The new classical position is that markets clearly continuously. This is likely, they argue, in modern economies with flexible labour markets (see Box 10.8 on pages 302–3) and facing global competition. There is thus no disequilibrium unemployment, even in the short run. All unemployment, therefore, is *equilibrium* unemployment, or 'voluntary unemployment' as new classical economists tend to call it. Increases in unemployment are therefore due to an increase in the natural level of unemployment, as people choose not to take jobs because of a lack of incentives to do so.

TC 5 p48

Rational expectations. The monetarist analysis of the previous section was based on *adaptive* expectations. New classical analysis, by contrast, is based on *rational* expectations. As we saw above, these are assumed to diverge only randomly from the actual rate of inflation. On average they are assumed to be correct.

Anticipated fluctuations in aggregate demand

If markets continuously clear and if people are correct in their expectations, then fluctuations in aggregate demand will have no impact on unemployment either in the short run or long run. The only effect is on the rate of inflation.

In the new classical (rational expectations) model, unlike the adaptive expectations model, there is *no* lag in expectations. If their information is correct, people will rationally predict that output and employment will stay at the natural level. They predict that any change in *nominal* aggregate

demand will be reflected purely in terms of changes in prices, and that real aggregate demand will remain the same. If real aggregate demand remains the same, so will the demand for and supply of labour and the demand for and supply of goods. Thus, even in the *short* run, output and employment will stay at the natural level.

Is the assumption of rational expectations on its own sufficient for anticipated demand shocks to have no impact on economic activity even in the short run?

We can use Figure 21.5 to illustrate the adjustment of the economy under continuous market clearing, rational expectations and anticipated demand shocks.

Assume that the economy is at point *a* with unemployment at its natural rate, U_n, and an actual and expected inflation rate of zero. Now assume that government increases aggregate demand. With rational expectations and no surprises, people fully anticipate that the inflation rate will rise to π_1. $EAPC_0$, which is based on expectations of zero inflation, cannot be moved along. The moment that aggregate demand rises people correctly anticipate an inflation rate of π_1. Thus the whole *EAPC* moves vertically upwards to $EAPC_1$. As a result, the economy moves *directly* from point *a* to point *c*.

Surprise fluctuations in aggregate demand

Although over time people's expectations are assumed to be correct on average, it is more than likely that in any one period they will be wrong. Economic shocks which lead to unexpected changes in aggregate demand or supply mean that households and businesses are subject to 'surprises'.

To illustrate the economic effects of unexpected fluctuations in aggregate demand, assume again that the economy is

BOX 21.3 THE RATIONAL EXPECTATIONS REVOLUTION — EXPLORING ECONOMICS

Trying to 'unfool' the economics profession

The rational expectations revolution swept through the economics profession in the 1970s in a way that no other set of ideas had done since Keynes. Although largely associated with the free-market, non-interventionist wing of economics, the rational expectations revolution has been far more wide-reaching. Even economists implacably opposed to the free market nevertheless incorporated rational expectations into their models. Hence, rational expectations became part of the mainstream consensus that emerged up to the financial crisis of the late 2000s (see section 16.6).

The rational expectations revolution is founded on a very simple idea. People base their expectations of the future on the information they have available. They don't just look at the past, they also look at current information, including what the government is saying and doing and what various commentators have to say.

The new classical economists use rational expectations in the following context. If the *long-run* Phillips curve is vertical, so that an expansionary policy will in the end merely lead to inflation, it will be difficult for the government to fool people that this will not happen. If employers, unions, city financiers, economic advisers, journalists, etc., all expect this to happen, then it will: and it will happen in the *short run*. Why should firms produce more in response to a rise in demand if their costs are going to rise by just as much? Why should higher wages attract workers to move jobs, if wages everywhere are going up? Why should firms and unions not seek price and wage rises fully in line with the expected inflation?

But can the government not surprise people? The point here is that 'surprising' people really only means 'fooling' them – making them believe that an expansionary policy really *will* reduce unemployment. But why should the public be fooled? Why should people believe smooth-talking government ministers rather than the whole host of critics of the government, from the opposition, to economic commentators, to the next-door neighbour?

The rational expectations school revised the old saying 'You can't fool all the people all the time' to 'You can hardly fool the people at all'. And if that is so, argue the new classical economists, unemployment can only momentarily be brought below its natural level.

Two of the most famous rational expectations economists are Robert Lucas and Thomas Sargent. Robert Lucas, like Milton Friedman and many other famous conservative economists, has his academic base in the University of Chicago, where he has been a professor since 1974. In 1995, like Milton Friedman in 1976, Lucas was awarded the Nobel prize in economics. Tom Sargent is Professor of Economics at New York University and senior fellow at the Hoover Institution of Stanford University. He was Professor of Economics at Chicago in the 1990s.

In recent years, rational expectations have been incorporated into models characterised by market imperfections and frictions, such as those developed by new Keynesians (see section 16.5). In this context, government policy *can* be effective. For example, supply-side policies can be directed to removing market distortions.

How would less flexible input prices affect the adjustment of the economy to shocks?

Prepare a short PowerPoint presentation, lasting around 15 minutes, aimed at an audience with only a rudimentary level of economics. It should explain the new classical theory that attempts by policy makers to affect aggregate demand will have no long-term impact on economic activity. The presentation should explain the assumptions underpinning the theory and examine its applications. It should also look at criticisms of the theory.

Figure 21.5 Anticipated and unanticipated changes in aggregate demand

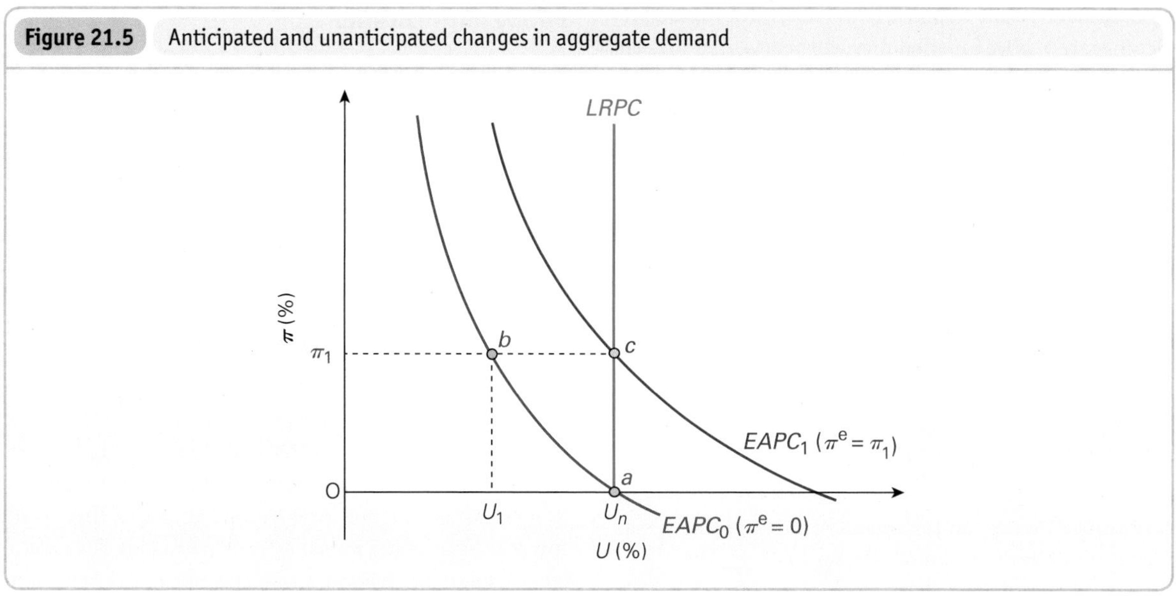

point *a* in Figure 21.5 above, with unemployment at its natural rate and zero inflation. The government now increases aggregate demand, but the size of the increase is unexpected. Prices and wages thus also rise more than people expect.

The response from firms and workers then depends on how they interpret the changes in prices and wages.

Consider first the response of firms. Robert Lucas likened the problem to one where the producers of different sectors comprised a series of islands. Each sector (island) would have to decide whether the rise in price was specific to them or to the chain of islands.

Assume that firms in a particular sector, which we will call sector *z*, believe that their price P_z has risen relative to the general price level, *P*. This leads them to believe that they are receiving a higher relative price than they really are, such that $(P_z/P)^e > P_z/P$. Hence their output and demand for labour increases.

If this behaviour is replicated across other sectors, there will be an increase in the economy's output and in the aggregate demand for labour. The impact on the labour market is shown in Figure 21.6.

An increase in the demand for labour, for example as shown by the shift in the aggregate demand for labour curve from AD_{L_2} to AD_{L_2}, leads to an increase in employment, say from N_1 to N_2. In doing so, employment rises above its equilibrium level N_1 (where expectations are correct), and output rises above its potential level.

Figure 21.6 The surprise inflation model and the labour market

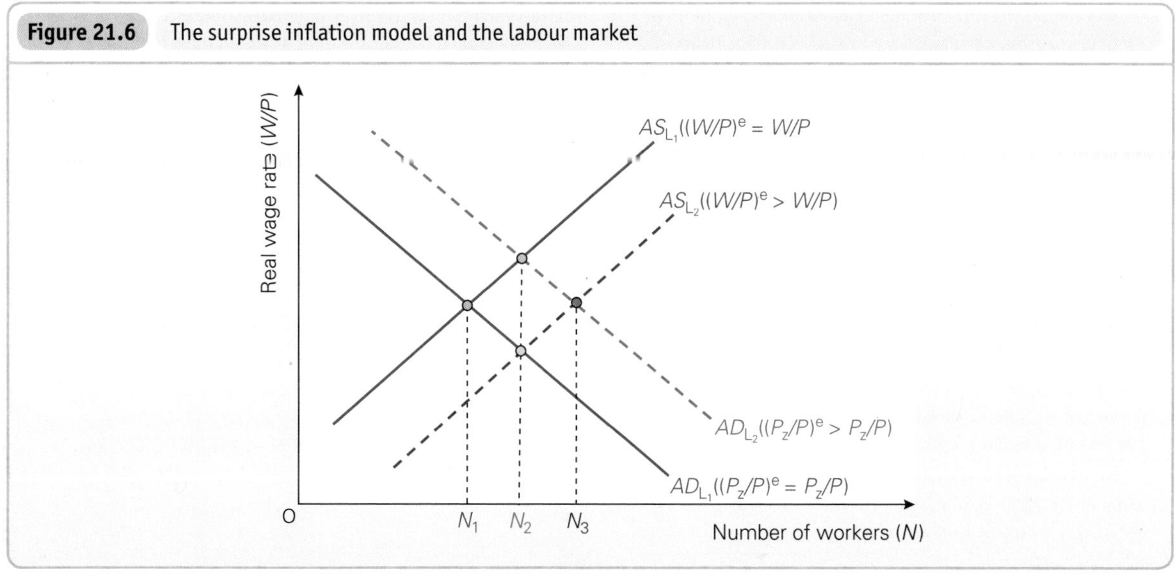

Consider now the response of workers. If they underpredict the rate of price inflation they will believe that they are getting a higher real wage (W/P) than they really are, such that $(W/P)^e > W/P$. They will supply more labour. This will be reflected by a rightward shift of the aggregate labour supply curve, such as that from AS_{L_1} to AS_{L_2} in Figure 21.6. In itself, this would be enough to increase employment, say to N_2. But if firms are underpredicting the rate of inflation too, then employment and output will increase further. For example, employment might rise to N_3.

The result of the surprise increase in aggregate demand is that workers or firms or both experience money illusion. This increases the employment of labour and output of goods. If we return to Figure 21.5, the surprise causes a move *along* an *EAPC*. If for simplicity we assume that the surprise occurred with people's expectations of inflation remaining at zero, then the increase in demand would cause unemployment to fall below the natural rate, say to U_1.

However, once the surprise becomes apparent, the *EAPC* shifts upwards, eventually reaching $EAPC_1$. Unemployment returns to its natural rate and national income to its potential level. If the growth of demand then remains at the same rate, long-run equilibrium is represented by point *c*.

What would the process of adjustment to the unanticipated size of the increase in aggregate demand look like if people had adjusted their inflationary expectation upwards from zero but to a rate less than π_1?

Policy implications

If the new classical 'surprise inflation model' is correct, anticipated changes in aggregate demand will have no effect on output and employment. *Unanticipated* changes in aggregate demand will have some effect, but only for as long as it takes people to realise their mistake and for their wages and prices to be corrected. Given rational expectations, people can be fooled in this way only by luck. There is no way that a government can *systematically* use demand management policy to keep output and employment above the natural level.

The new classical economists therefore totally reject Keynesian demand management policy, even in the short run. Monetary policy should be used to control inflation, but neither fiscal nor monetary policy can be used systematically to increase output and employment. Similarly, there is no fear of a deflationary monetary policy reducing output and employment and leading to a recession. The reduction in aggregate demand will simply lead to lower inflation. Output and unemployment will remain at the natural level.

Thus for new classicists, the problems of inflation and unemployment are totally separate. Inflation is caused by excessive growth in the money supply and should be controlled by monetary policy. Unemployment will be at the natural rate and should be reduced by supply-side policies designed to increase the incentives to work. In this respect, their views echo monetarist sentiments too.

BOX 21.4 FORECASTING THE WEATHER

CASE STUDIES AND APPLICATIONS

An example of rational expectations

KI 10 p70

'What's the weather going to be like tomorrow?' If you are thinking of having a picnic, you will want to know the answer before deciding.

So what do you do? You could base your assessment on past information. Yesterday was fine; so was the previous day. Today is glorious. So, you think to yourself, it's a good bet that tomorrow will be fine too. If, on the other hand, the weather has been very changeable recently, you may feel that it's wiser not to take the risk. These 'forecasts' are examples of *adaptive* expectations: your forecasts are based on the actual weather over the past few days.

But would you really base such a crucial decision as to whether or not to have a picnic on something so unreliable? Wouldn't you rather take on board more information to help you make up your mind?

The first thing that might come to mind is the old saying that a British summer is three fine days and a thunderstorm. We've just had the three fine days, you think to yourself, so perhaps we'd better stay at home tomorrow.

Or, being a bit more scientific about it, you look at the weather forecast. Seeing loads of sunshine symbols all over the map, you decide to take a chance.

Basing your expectations in this way on current information (including even seeing whether there is a red sky that night) is an example of *rational* expectations.

So you go on your picnic and, guess what, it rains! 'I bet if we had decided to stay at home, it would have been fine', you grumble, as you eat your soggy sandwiches.

What you are acknowledging is that your decision was made on *imperfect* information. But the decision was still rational. It was still the best decision you could have made on the information available to you.

Weather forecasters make mistakes. But they are probably just as likely to get it wrong in predicting a sunny day as in predicting a wet day. It is still rational to base your decisions on their forecasts provided they are reasonably accurate.

Under what circumstances might weather forecasters have a tendency to err on the side of pessimism or optimism? If you knew this tendency, how would this affect your decisions about picnics, hanging out the washing or watering the garden?

BOX 21.5 THE BOY WHO CRIED 'WOLF' | EXPLORING ECONOMICS

A government had better mean what it says

Do you remember the parable of the boy who cried 'Wolf!'?

There was once this little village on the edge of the forest. The villagers used to keep chickens, but when no one was around wolves would come out of the forest and carry off the chickens. So one of the boys in the village was given the job of keeping a lookout for wolves.

One day for a joke the boy called out 'Wolf, wolf! I see a wolf!' even though there was none. All the villagers came rushing out of their houses or back from the fields to catch the wolf. As you might expect, they were very angry to find that it was a false alarm.

The next day, thinking that this was great fun, the boy played the same trick again. Everyone came rushing out, and they were even more angry to find that they had been fooled again. But the boy just grinned.

The next day, when everyone was away in the fields, a wolf stalked into the village. The boy, spotting the animal, cried out 'Wolf, wolf! I see a wolf!' But the people in the fields said to each other 'We're not going to be fooled this time. We've had enough of his practical jokes.' And so they carried on working. Meanwhile, back in the village, the wolf was killing all the chickens.

You can probably guess what the villagers said when they returned in the evening to find just a large pile of feathers.

A government says, 'We will take tough action to bring the rate of inflation down to 2 per cent.' Now of course this might be a 'joke' in the sense that the government doesn't really expect to succeed or even seriously to try, but is merely attempting to persuade unions to curb their wage demands. But if unions *believe* in both the government's intentions and its ability to succeed, the 'joke' may pay off. Some unions may well moderate their pay demands.

But some may not. What is more, the government may decide to give tax cuts to boost its popularity and stimulate growth, knowing that union pay demands are generally quite moderate. As a result, inflation soars.

But can the government get away with it a second or third time? It's like the boy who cried 'Wolf!' After a time, people will simply not believe the government. If they see the government boosting aggregate demand, they will say to themselves, 'Here comes inflation. We'd better demand higher wages to compensate.'

Does this parable support the adaptive or the rational expectations hypothesis?

Examine the health and economic policies pursued during 2020–21 to tackle the coronavirus pandemic and its economic consequences. Are the lessons of this box relevant to public confidence in these policies and their success?

To prevent unanticipated changes in aggregate demand and thus to prevent unemployment deviating from its natural rate, new classical economists advocate the announcement of clear monetary rules and then sticking to them. The delegation of monetary policy to independent central banks with clear remits, such as inflation rate targets, can form part of this approach.

1. *If the government announced that it would, come what may, reduce the growth of money supply to zero next year, what (according to new classical economists) would happen? How might their answer be criticised?*
2. *For what reasons would a new classical economist support the policy of the Bank of England publishing its inflation forecasts and the minutes of the deliberations of the Monetary Policy Committee?*

Section summary

1. New classical theories assume continuous market clearing with flexible prices and wages in the short run as well as in the long run. It also assumes that people base their expectations of inflation on a rational assessment of the *current* situation.
2. People may predict wrongly, but they are equally likely to underpredict or to overpredict. On average, over the years, they will predict correctly.
3. The assumptions of continuous market clearing and rational expectations imply that only unexpected fluctuations in aggregate demand will cause unemployment to deviate from its natural rate. There can be no short-run trade-off between inflation and unemployment when changes in aggregate demand are anticipated.
4. If people correctly predict the rate of inflation, they will correctly predict that any increase in nominal aggregate demand will simply be reflected in higher prices. Total output and employment will remain the same: at the natural level.
5. If people underpredict the rate of inflation, they will believe that there has been a *real* increase in aggregate demand, and thus output and employment will increase. But they are just as likely to overpredict the rate of inflation, in which case they will believe that real aggregate demand has fallen. The result is that output and employment will fall.
6. When the government adopts fiscal and monetary policies, people will rationally predict their effects. Given that people's predictions are equally likely to err on either side, fiscal and monetary policies are useless as means of controlling output and employment.

21.4 INFLATION AND UNEMPLOYMENT: THE MODERN KEYNESIAN POSITION

Keynesians in the 1950s and early 1960s looked to aggregate demand to explain inflation and unemployment. Their approach was typically that of the inflationary/deflationary gap model (see pages 546–8). Although they recognised the existence of some cost-push inflation and some equilibrium unemployment, these factors were seen as relatively constant. As a result, there was thought to be a relatively stable inverse relationship between inflation and unemployment, as depicted by the Phillips curve. Governments could trade off inflation against unemployment by manipulating aggregate demand.

Modern developments of the Keynesian model

Keynesians still see aggregate demand as playing the crucial role in determining the rate of inflation and the levels of output and employment. They still argue that the free market works inefficiently: it frequently fails to clear; price signals are distorted by economic power; most wages and many prices are 'sticky'; and, most important, the free market is unlikely to settle at full employment.

They still argue, therefore, that it is vital for governments to intervene actively to prevent either a slump in demand or an overexpansion of demand.

Nevertheless, the Keynesian position has undergone some major modifications in recent years (see section 16.5). This has been in response to apparent shifts in the Phillips curve and the inability of the traditional Keynesian model to explain it.

The breakdown of the Phillips curve in the 1970s and the growing problem of 'stagflation' (see page 511) led many Keynesians to focus on cost-push causes of inflation. These causes included increased power and militancy of trade unions, a growing concentration of monopoly power in industry, and rising oil and other commodity prices. The effect was to push the short-run Phillips curve outwards.

Later, with a decline in industrial unrest in the 1990s and a growth of international competition keeping prices down, the Phillips curve apparently shifted inwards again. Keynesians attributed this partly to a *decline* in cost-push inflation. (These cost-push explanations are examined in Case Study 21.3 on the student website.)

More recently, Keynesian analysis has incorporated three major modifications:

- An increased importance attached to equilibrium unemployment.
- A rationale for the persistence of demand-deficient unemployment.
- The incorporation of the theory of expectations: either adaptive or rational.

Changes in equilibrium unemployment

Changes in structural unemployment

Most Keynesians include growth in equilibrium unemployment as part of the explanation of the apparent rightward shift in the Phillips curve in the 1970s and 1980s. As we noted in Chapter 16, rather than the natural rate, some Keynesians prefer to speak of the *non-accelerating-inflation rate of unemployment*, which is known more simply as the NAIRU. This acknowledges that there exist market imperfections. The NAIRU can be thought of as the rate of unemployment that is consistent with steady inflation in the near term.

Keynesians highlight the considerable structural rigidities that existed in the economy in a period of rapid industrial change. The changes include the following:

- Dramatic changes in technology. The microchip revolution, for example, made many traditional jobs obsolete.
- Competition from abroad. The introduction of new products from abroad, often of superior quality to domestic goods, or produced at lower costs, had led to the decline of many older industries: e.g. the textile industry.
- Shifts in demand away from the products of older labour-intensive industries to new 'high-tech' capital-intensive products.

Keynesians argue that the free market simply could not cope with these changes without a large rise in structural/technological unemployment. Labour was not sufficiently mobile – either geographically or occupationally – to move to areas where there were labour shortages or into jobs where there were skill shortages. A particular problem here was the lack of investment in education and training, with the result that the labour force was not sufficiently flexible to respond to changes in demand for labour.

1. *What effect did these developments have on (a) the Phillips curve; (b) the aggregate supply curve?*
2. *What policy implications follow from these arguments?*

From the mid-1980s up to the financial crisis of the late 2000s, structural unemployment was thought to have fallen as labour markets become more flexible and as various government supply-side policies took effect (see Chapter 23).

Hysteresis

If a recession causes a rise in unemployment which is not then fully reversed when the economy recovers, there is a problem of hysteresis (see pages 517–18 and 657). Recessions can lead to a growing number of people becoming both deskilled and demotivated. What is more, many firms, in an attempt to cut costs, cut down on training programmes.

In these circumstances, a rise in aggregate demand would not simply enable the long-term unemployed to be employed again. The effect is a rightward shift in the Phillips curve: a rise in the NAIRU. To reverse this, argue Keynesians, the government should embark on a radical programme of retraining.

Recessions also cause a lack of investment. The reduction in their capital stock means that many firms cannot respond to a recovery in demand by making significant increases in output and taking on many more workers. Instead they are more likely to raise prices. Unemployment may thus fall only modestly and yet inflation may rise substantially. The NAIRU increases: the Phillips curve shifts to the right.

These arguments hold in reverse. A period of sustained growth can reduce the NAIRU: the Phillips curve shifts to the left.

Are hysteresis effects likely to be asymmetrical (i.e. of different magnitude) following an economic boom rather than an economic slowdown?

The persistence of demand-deficient unemployment

Monetarists and new classical economists argue that markets, including the labour market, clear quickly, if not continuously. Keynesians point to frictions in the labour market which may prevent real wages from falling and helping to eliminate demand-deficient unemployment. Two major explanations for the persistence of real wage rates above equilibrium are efficiency wages and insider power. While we first came across these in Chapter 16 (see pages 516–17), we revisit them here in the context of the inflation–unemployment relationship.

- *Efficiency wages*. Wage rates work not only to balance the demand and supply of labour but also to motivate workers. If real wage rates are reduced when there is a surplus of labour (demand-deficient unemployment), then those workers already in employment may become dispirited and work less hard. If, on the other hand, firms keep wage rates up, then by maintaining a well-motivated workforce, by cutting down on labour turnover and by finding it easier to attract well-qualified labour, firms may find that their costs are reduced: a higher real wage rate is thus more profitable for them. The maximum-profit real wage rate (the *efficiency wage rate*: see page 297) is likely to be above the market-clearing real wage rate. Demand-deficient unemployment is likely to persist.

How might the possibility of labour shirking affect the real wage firms are willing to pay?

- *Insider power*. If those still in employment (the insiders) are members of unions while those out of work (the outsiders) are not, or if the insiders have special skills or knowledge that give them bargaining power with employers while the outsiders have no influence, then there is no mechanism whereby the surplus labour – the outsiders – can drive down the real wage rate and eliminate the demand-deficient unemployment.

These two features may help to explain why real wage rates did not fall during the recessions of the early 1980s and early 1990s.

However, with the more flexible labour markets of more recent years the dynamic response of output, employment, and real wages to demand shocks is likely to have changed. For example, real wages did fall consistently in the period following the financial crisis (see Figure 15.13 on page 483).

With more workers on flexible and zero-hour contracts or working in the gig economy, the effects of a recession may persist with people working fewer hours on such contracts. Also, with the dampening effect on purchasing power and with less pressure on firms to invest in labour-saving technology, recovery from recession may be slow.

The incorporation of expectations

Some Keynesians incorporate adaptive expectations into their models. Others incorporate rational expectations. Either way, their models differ from monetarist and new classical models in two important respects:

- Prices and wages are not perfectly flexible. Markets are characterised by various frictions and imperfections.
- Expectations influence *output* and *employment* decisions, not just pricing decisions.

KI 10 p70

Price and wage rigidities are likely to be greater *downwards* than upwards. It is thus necessary to separate the analysis of a decrease in aggregate demand from that of an increase.

Expansion of aggregate demand

Unless the economy is at full employment or very close to it, Keynesians argue that an expansion of demand *will* lead to an increase in output and employment, even in the long run after expectations have fully adjusted. This is a rejection of the natural rate hypothesis.

In Figure 21.7, assume that the economy has a fairly high rate of unemployment (U_1) but, at the same time, some cost inflation. Inflation is constant at a rate of π_1, with expectations of inflation at π_1 also. The economy is at point *a*.

Now assume that the economy begins to recover. Aggregate demand rises. As there is plenty of slack in the economy, output can rise and unemployment fall. The economy moves to point *b* on short-run Phillips curve, $SRPC_1$. The rise in inflation will feed through into expectations. The short-run Phillips curve will shift upwards. With adaptive expectations, it will initially shift up, say, to $SRPC_2$.

But will the short-run Phillips curve not go on shifting upwards as long as there is any upward pressure on inflation? Keynesians reject this argument for two reasons:

- If there is a gradual but sustained expansion of aggregate demand, firms, seeing the economy expanding

Figure 21.7 Modern Keynesian analysis of expansionary policies

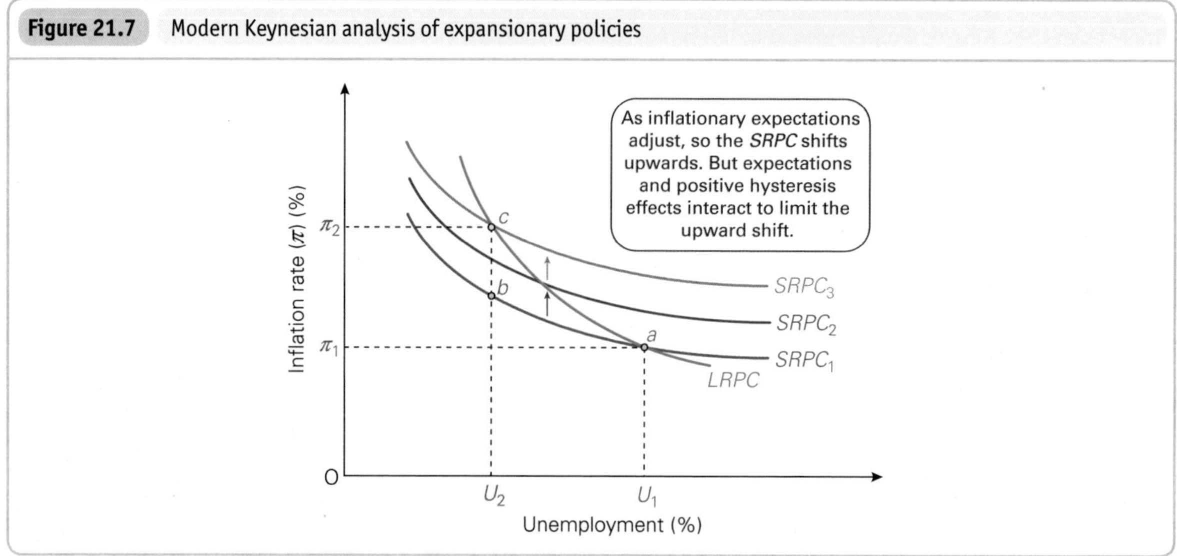

and seeing their orders growing, will start to invest more and make longer-term plans for expanding their labour force. People will generally *expect* a higher level of output, and this optimism will cause that higher level of output to be produced. In other words, expectations will affect output and employment as well as prices. The Phillips curve will shift downwards to the left, offsetting (partially, wholly or more than wholly) the upward shift from higher inflationary expectations. The NAIRU has fallen.

- If U_1 includes a considerable number of long-term unemployed, then the expansion of demand may be *initially* inflationary, since many of the newly employed will require some retraining (a costly exercise). But as these newly employed workers become more productive, their lower labour costs may offset any further upward pressure on wages from the expansion of demand. At the same time, the higher investment may embody new, more productive, techniques that will also help to prevent further acceleration in costs. This was the hope following the COVID-19 pandemic: the investment in technology and the adoption of new working practices mitigating the scarring effects from the deep economic contraction.

It is quite likely that these effects can prevent any further rises in inflation. Inflation can become stable at, say, π_2, with the economy operating at point *c*. The short-run Phillips curve settles at $SRPC_3$. There is thus a long-run downward-sloping Phillips curve (*LRPC*) passing through points *a* and *c*. What this analysis is assuming is that, in the medium to long run, the NAIRU itself is responsive to changes in real aggregate demand. In Figure 21.7, it falls to U_2.

Would it in theory be possible for this long-run Phillips curve to be horizontal or even upward sloping over part of its length?

If expectations are formed rationally rather than adaptively, there will merely be a quicker movement to this long-run equilibrium. If people rationally predict that the effect of government policy will be to move the economy to point *c*, then their predictions will bring this about. All rational expectations do is to bring the long run about much sooner! The theory of rational expectations on its own does not provide support specifically for either the new classical or the Keynesian position.

The lesson here for governments, however expectations are formed, is that a sustained, but moderate, increase in aggregate demand can lead to a sustained growth in aggregate supply. What should be avoided is an excessive and unsustainable expansion of aggregate demand, as occurred in the late 1980s in the UK and in the late 1990s in the USA. This will lead to a boom, only to be followed by a 'bust' and a consequent recession.

Contraction of aggregate demand

Many Keynesians argue that the short-run Phillips curve is kinked at the current level of real aggregate demand. A reduction in real aggregate demand will have only a slight effect on inflation since real wages are sticky downwards. Unions may well prefer to negotiate a reduction in employment levels, preferably by natural wastage (i.e. not replacing people when they leave), rather than accept a reduction in real wages. Even in non-unionised workplaces, real wage rates will not fall if they are already at the national

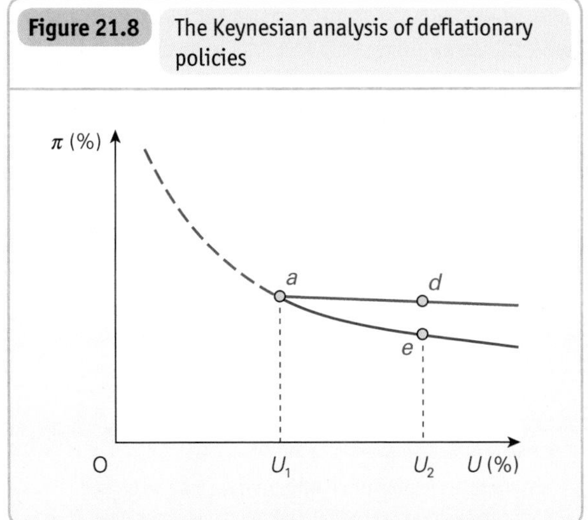

Figure 21.8 The Keynesian analysis of deflationary policies

minimum wage rate and the (nominal) national minimum wage rate rises each year with inflation. Thus in Figure 21.8, to the right of point *a*, the short-run Phillips curve is very shallow.

As long as this curve is not totally horizontal to the right of *a*, the introduction of expectations into the analysis will cause the short-run curve to shift downwards over time (if unemployment is kept above U_1) as people come to expect a lower rate of inflation.

With *adaptive* expectations, however, the curve could shift downwards very slowly indeed. If a movement from point *a* to point *d* represents only a 1 percentage point reduction in the rate of inflation, and if it takes, say, two years for this to be fully reflected in expectations, then if unemployment is kept at U_2, the inflation rate will fall (i.e. the curve shift downwards) by only 0.5 percentage points a year. This may be totally unacceptable politically if the inflation rate is already very high, and if U_2 is also very high.

Even with *rational* expectations the response may be too slow. If there is a resistance from unions to receiving increases in wages below the current rate of inflation and if national minimum wage rates are raised each year in line with inflation, then even if they rationally predict the correct amount by which inflation will fall, inflation will fall only slowly. People will rationally predict the downward stickiness of real wages, and sure enough, therefore, inflation will fall only slowly.

The worst scenario is when the government, in its attempt to eliminate inflation, keeps unemployment high for a number of years. As the core of long-term unemployed workers grows, an increasing number of workers become deskilled and therefore effectively unemployable. The effective labour supply is reduced, and firms find there is no longer a surplus of employable labour *despite* high unemployment. The NAIRU increases. A long-term equilibrium is reached at, say, point *e* with still substantial inflation. The *long*-run Phillips curve too may thus be relatively shallow to the right of point *a*.

Some economists argue that recessions generate unemployment 'scarring' (i.e. various negative outcomes for the people unemployed and possibly broader society too). What might these scarring effects be and what is likely to be their longer-term impact?

As we saw earlier, the downward stickiness of real wages was significantly less in the recession of 2008–9. This was partly because of a decline in union membership and power, partly because of a rise in part-time employment, the use of agency staff and the use of zero-hour contracts, and partly because of a willingness of people to accept lower wages rather than face the possibility of redundancy. This greater flexibility of labour markets gave a steeper Phillips curve to the right of point *a* than in previous recessions.

The Keynesian criticism of non-intervention

Keynesians are therefore highly critical of the new classical conclusion that governments should not intervene other than to restrain the growth of money supply. High unemployment may persist for many years and become deeply entrenched in the economy if there is no deliberate government policy of creating a steady expansion of demand.

Countries in the eurozone, such as Greece, Portugal and Spain, which had to seek bailouts in the early 2010s because of their high levels of debt, found themselves in this position. A condition of being granted bailouts was to reduce public-sector debt. This ruled out Keynesian expansionary fiscal policy. The very high rates of unemployment in these countries at the time, especially amongst the young (rates of over 50 per cent in Greece and Spain in the 15–24 age group), resulted in a problem of entrenchment and hysteresis that made reductions in unemployment slow and difficult to achieve.

Why is it important in the Keynesian analysis for there to be a steady expansion of demand?

Section summary

1. Modern Keynesians incorporate expectations into their analysis of inflation and unemployment. They also see an important role for cost-push factors and changes in equilibrium unemployment in explaining the position of the Phillips curve.
2. A growth in equilibrium unemployment in the 1970s and 1980s was caused by rapid changes in technology, greater competition from abroad and more rapid changes in demand patterns. It was also due to the persistence of unemployment beyond the recessions of the early 1980s and early 1990s and, to a lesser extent, the early 2010s, because of a deskilling of labour during the recessions (an example of hysteresis). The effect of increased equilibrium unemployment was to shift the Phillips curve to the right.
3. Demand-deficient unemployment may persist because real wage rates may be sticky downwards, even into the longer term. This stickiness may be the result of efficiency real wage rates being above market-clearing real wage rates and/or outsiders not being able to influence wage bargains struck between employers and insiders.
4. If expectations are incorporated into Keynesian analysis, the Phillips curve will become steeper in the long run (and steeper in the short run too in the case of rational expectations). It will not become vertical, however, since people will expect changes in aggregate demand to affect output and employment as well as prices.
5. If people expect a more rapid rise in aggregate demand to be sustained, firms will invest more, thereby reducing unemployment in the long run and not just increasing the rate of inflation. The NAIRU will fall. The long-run Phillips curve will be downward sloping.
6. The short- and long-run Phillips curves may be kinked. Reductions in real aggregate demand may have only a slight effect on inflation if real wage rates are sticky downwards.

21.5 CENTRAL BANKS AND INFLATION TARGETING

This chapter has examined alternative views on the relationships between unemployment and inflation. To do so we have used a Phillips curve (*EAPC/LRPC*) framework. In this section we examine these relationships in the modern context of central banks operating within targets.

We begin by considering why many governments have delegated the operation of monetary policy to central banks: i.e. giving them independence in setting interest rates and/or determining the money supply. We then show how the *EAPC/LRPC* and *DAD/DAS* frameworks can be used to analyse the determination of inflation, unemployment and output in the context of central banks operating with an inflation rate target.

The analysis illustrates how the dynamic response of economies to economic shocks can be affected by the mandate of the central bank. This, therefore, raises questions about the mandate chosen and the potential trade-offs between stabilising inflation and other macroeconomic objectives. We discuss these issues further in section 22.4.

Credibility and the delegation of monetary policy

If the natural rate hypothesis holds, then policy makers cannot use demand management policy to affect real GDP (output) or the rate of unemployment, except, perhaps, in the short run. The interest among economists since the 1960s in the natural rate hypothesis has been one of the key reasons for governments delegating monetary policy to central banks, sometimes through legal statute. In the UK, for example, the Bank of England was given operational independence over monetary policy in 1997.

This delegation is usually for the making of policy decisions, such as setting interest rates or whether to engage in quantitative easing. Normally, governments still decide what the policy objective(s) of the central bank should be – whether it is to achieve a target rate of inflation set by the government, or to do this while being mindful of other objectives, such as economic growth and lower unemployment.

Inflation bias

The case for delegating monetary policy was briefly presented in Chapter 16 (see page 520). As we saw there, the principal argument is that delegation can reduce the ***inflation bias*** arising from political interference in monetary policy. This is the extent to which the average rate of inflation is above the desirable rate for the efficient functioning of the economy.

So what is the cause of inflation bias? If society's preference is for a rate of unemployment below the natural rate, governments may be tempted to boost aggregate demand to

Definition

Inflation bias Excessive inflation that results from the government pursuing expansionary policy for short-term political gain. This may drive inflationary expectations and encourage the government to loosen policy even further.

try to reduce unemployment and increase their popularity. This temptation exists even though in the longer run it leads to higher inflation.

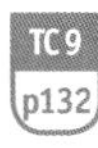

Because the public are aware of a government's temptation to reduce unemployment and the impact of this on inflation, they form *high* expectations of inflation. This then leads to governments delivering looser monetary policies simply to validate the high expectations of inflation.

Credibility of policy

To reduce expectations of inflation, the government could try to establish a reputation for maintaining low inflation. It could adopt an inflation rate target to help achieve this. Its success is likely to depend on the ***credibility*** of the target and hence the public's perception as to whether the government will stick to it. If the target lacks credibility, people's expectations of inflation may be higher and thus tougher deflationary policies may be required to bring inflation down, resulting in protracted periods of high unemployment.

The public may be reluctant to set their inflation expectations in accordance with low-inflation announcements made by the government. This can occur if they are perceived to be ***time-inconsistent policies***: policies that the government has an incentive to renege on at a future date. The problem is that the incentive for the government to boost demand and generate surprise inflation is particularly strong when actual and expected rates of inflation are low. Low inflation rate announcements are therefore more likely to be (or perceived to be) time inconsistent and lack credibility.

It is argued that low-inflation policies will only be credible, and hence ***time consistent***, if monetary policy is delegated to an independent authority, such as a central bank. Delegation provides people with the confidence to maintain low inflation expectations.

TC 9 p132

We look at a model of inflation bias in Box 21.6.

The *EAPC/LRPC* and *DAD/DAS* frameworks

Box 21.7 provides an indication of the number of central banks targeting, to one degree or another, the rate of inflation. To understand the relationship between inflation and unemployment, it is therefore important to do so within the context of delegated monetary policy. To do this, we combine the dynamic aggregate demand and supply (*DAD*/*DAS*) analysis, which we looked at in section 20.3, with the Phillips curve analysis of this chapter. Figure 21.9 illustrates the two models.

Central banks and the DAD curve

The *DAD* curve in Figure 21.9(b) shows a *negative* relationship between real aggregate demand and the rate of inflation. This is explained by central banks responding to higher inflation by raising nominal and real interest rates. The extent to which they do raise interest rates will reflect the weights attributed to inflation and output (or unemployment) in their monetary policy rule consistent with their mandate. The impact of higher interest rates on aggregate demand will then depend on the transmission mechanisms through which changes in real interest rates operate (see section 19.1).

The *slope* of the *DAD* curve therefore reflects the mandate of the central bank and the transmission mechanisms of monetary policy. The curve will be flatter the more emphasis that the central bank's monetary policy places on fluctuations in the rate of inflation *relative* to those in output or unemployment. It will also be flatter the more interest-rate responsive is aggregate demand and the more powerful the multiplier-amplifier process (see page 617).

Meanwhile, *shifts* in the *DAD* curve will be caused by exogenous shocks to aggregate demand – in other words, changes to aggregate demand brought about by factors other than the rate of inflation causing the central bank to adjust interest rates. Figure 21.9(b) shows the case of a positive demand shock: a rightward shift of the *DAD* curve from DAD_1 to DAD_2.

How would financial accelerator effects (see section 19.4) affect the DAD curve?

DAS and EAPC curves

The *DAS* curve in Figure 21.9(b) shows a *positive* relationship between output and inflation. Therefore a rise in aggregate demand (rightward shift of the *DAD* curve) will result in a movement up along the curve (e.g. from point a' to point b'): there will be higher output but at the cost of higher inflation.

Now consider how this is captured by the Phillips curve framework. The downward-sloping *EAPC* illustrates the short-run trade-off between unemployment and inflation. A rise in aggregate demand (e.g. from point *a* to point *b*) will result in a movement up along the curve: there will be lower unemployment but at the cost of higher inflation.

The slopes of both the *DAS* curve and the *EAPC* therefore capture the potential short-run trade-off between inflation and economic activity. The latter is represented by unemployment in the case of the *EAPC* curve and by output (real national income) in the case of the *DAS* curve.

The behaviour of the central bank may impact on the slope of the *EAPC* and the *DAS* curve. The more inflation

Definitions

Credibility (of policies) Policies that people believe the government will carry out once they have been announced.

Time-inconsistent policy announcement A policy announcement where there is an incentive for the policy maker to renege on it at a future date.

Time-consistent policy announcement A policy announcement where there is an incentive for the policy maker to stick to it over time.

*BOX 21.6 A MODEL OF INFLATION BIAS

The relationship between credibility and inflation

We can apply a new classical 'surprise inflation' model to examine how excessive inflation arises. People are assumed to form rational expectations, markets clear rapidly and the natural rate hypothesis holds. The model is based on the work of Fynn Kydland and Ed Prescott (1977)[1] who are often cited as having provided the theoretical foundations for central bank independence. It contributed to them winning the Nobel Prize in Economics in 2004.

The diagram includes a series of government indifference curves. Each one depicts a particular level of satisfaction (or happiness) of the government. We can think of these as reflecting the general preferences of society. At any point along a particular indifference curve the government derives a given level of satisfaction from the various combinations of unemployment and inflation shown.

The optimal rates of inflation and unemployment are assumed to be zero. Therefore the government's satisfaction is higher on those indifference curves that are closer to the origin. For example, satisfaction is higher on I_1 than it is on I_2, and so on. Note also that because we are measuring *undesirable* things on each axis, the curves slope differently from the traditional indifference curves which we examined in section 4.3: the ones here are bowed out, rather than bowed in.

The constraint on government's satisfaction is the trade-off between inflation and unemployment. The diagram shows how this is captured in the short run by the expectations-augmented Phillips curves (*EAPCs*) and in the long-run by a vertical Philips curve at the natural rate of unemployment (U_n). Each *EAPC* reflects only differences in the expected inflation rate (π^e): the higher the expected rate, the vertically higher the *EAPC*.

The incentive for the government to stimulate the economy

In this model, the government, not the central bank, has control of monetary policy. Assume that the economy is currently at point *a* with both the goods and labour markets in equilibrium. People's expectations of inflation are zero. Given this, the government's optimal inflation–unemployment choice is at point *b*, with lower

A model of inflation bias

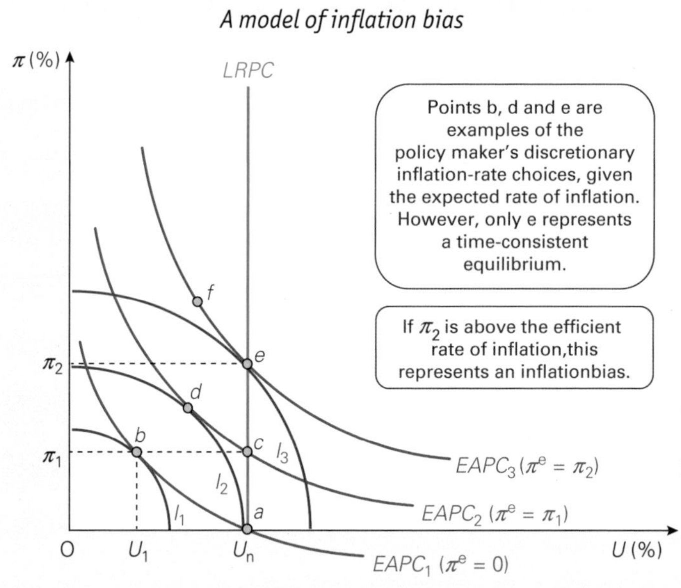

averse the central bank, and the more that people believe that it will be successful in keeping inflation close to the target rate, the flatter the *EAPC* and *DAS* curve will be. People's expectations will be anchored at the target rate and this will affect price-setting behaviour. If, however, the central bank's remit was also to be mindful of output and employment and, as a result, it was prepared to accept some fluctuations in inflation, the *EAPC* and *DAS* curve will be steeper.

Meanwhile, the vertical position of both curves is determined by inflationary expectations (π^e) and exogenous inflationary shocks (k). Higher inflationary expectations or adverse inflationary shocks result in both curves moving vertically upwards.

How would a change in the natural rate of unemployment or the level of potential national income affect the EAPC and DAS curve?

EXPLORING ECONOMICS

unemployment of U_1 but inflation of π_1. Since the preferred rate of unemployment is *below* the natural rate, people are prepared to put up with some inflation (π_1).

To get to point *b*, the government needs to surprise the public by relaxing monetary policy, for example by providing greater liquidity to the financial system and so putting downward pressure on real interest rates (see section 19.1). The loosening of monetary policy then raises aggregate demand.

However, point *b* is not sustainable. People will revise their inflationary expectations upwards. Consequently, real aggregate demand will fall back to the economy's potential national income level and unemployment will rise again to its natural rate. If nominal aggregate demand were to continue to grow at the new rate, the economy would settle at point *c*, with higher inflation (π_1) than before.

The response of the public: the issue of the government's credibility

But of course the public knows that any gain is likely to be temporary. Workers, for instance, know that any temporary increase in economic activity would be followed by a period where inflation rises and their real wages fall. Therefore, one possibility is that people keep their inflationary expectations sufficiently high that the government no longer benefits from generating further inflation and creating a surprise economic boom.

Consider point *e* in the diagram. Again, the economy is in equilibrium with unemployment at its natural rate. But, unlike the situation when the economy is at point *a* (or point *c*), the government no longer benefits from a surprise loosening of monetary policy. In simple terms, the now much higher inflation rate acts as a disincentive to government to generate surprise inflation. People would react badly to even higher inflation rates. The additional satisfaction to the government, therefore, from moving to say point *f* and reducing unemployment is outweighed by the dissatisfaction generated by the higher rate of inflation.

Point *e* is described as a 'consistent equilibrium'. The reason is that if the government says that it wants to target an inflation rate of π_2, this will be a time-consistent policy announcement. This means that there is no incentive, once people have set their inflationary expectations, for the government to generate surprise inflation and conduct monetary policy inconsistent with validating this high inflation rate. An inflation announcement of π_2 is therefore a *credible* policy. People believe that the government will stick to it.

By contrast, the government stating that it wants to target point *a*, with zero inflation, is a time-inconsistent policy announcement. Once people have set their inflationary expectations at zero, the government then has an incentive to generate surprise inflation. In other words, it conducts monetary policy which generates a positive inflation rate. A zero-inflation rate announcement by the government thus lacks credibility: government has an incentive to renege on it.

In the diagram, the credible inflation rate is π_2. At any point on the *LRPC* with an inflation rate below π_2 (i.e. below point *e*) there is an incentive for government to create surprise inflation.

If π_2 is above the rate that could be seen as desirable for the efficient functioning of the economy (generally thought by central banks to be around 2 per cent: see table in Box 21.7), then the government could be said to exhibit *inflationary bias*. If, for example, π_2 were 5 per cent and the efficient rate of inflation were 2 per cent, the government would be exhibiting an inflationary bias of 3 per cent (i.e. 5% – 2%).

1. ***Referring to the diagram, why is π_1 not a time consistent inflation rate policy?***
2. ***How would the delegation of monetary policy to a central bank whose mandate gives no weight to unemployment (or output) be reflected in its indifference curves? How does this affect its incentive to generate surprise inflation?***

Undertake desktop research to conduct a literature review on the arguments for and against central bank independence. Prepare a 10-minute PowerPoint presentation summarising these arguments.

1 Finn Kydland and Edward Prescott, 'Rules rather than discretion: the inconsistency of optimal plans', *Journal of Political Economy*, vol. 85, no. 3, pp. 473–92 (June 1977), www.jstor.org/stable/1830193

Okun's law

The link between the *DAS* curve and the *EAPC* can be understood by reference to ***Okun's law***. The law is named after Arthur Okun who, in a 1962 paper, investigated the relationship between unemployment and output in the USA. His work suggested that for every 1 percentage point that US unemployment was above its natural rate, US output would be 3 per cent below its potential output.

Definition

Okun's law The name given to the negative statistical relationship between the unemployment rate and deviations of output from potential output.

Figure 21.9 *EAPC/LRPC* and *DAD/DAS* frameworks

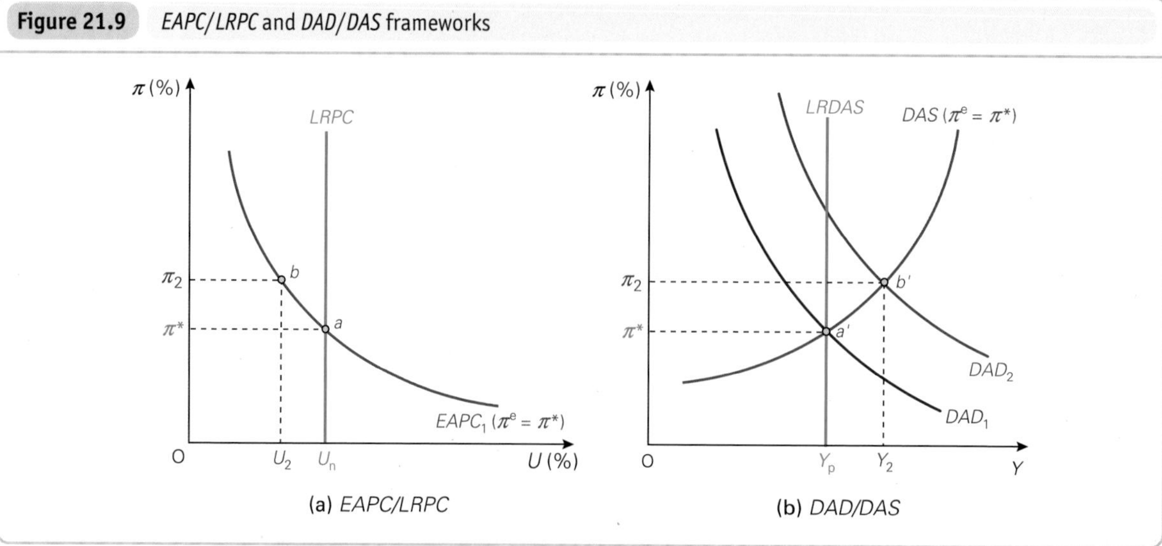

BOX 21.7 INFLATION TARGETING

CASE STUDIES AND APPLICATIONS

The fashion of the age

Many countries have turned to inflation targeting as their main macroeconomic policy. The table gives the targets for a selection of countries (as of 2021).

Part of the reason is the apparent failure of discretionary macroeconomic policies. Discretionary fiscal and monetary policies suffer from time lags, from being used for short-term political purposes and from failing to straighten out the business cycle. But if discretionary policies have seemed not to work, why choose an inflation target rather than a target for the money supply or the exchange rate?

Money supply targets were adopted by many countries in the 1980s, including the UK, and this policy too was largely a failure. Money supply targets proved very difficult to achieve. As we have seen, money supply depends on the amount of credit banks create, and this is not easy for the authorities to control. Then, even if money supply is controlled, this does not necessarily mean that aggregate demand will be controlled: the velocity of circulation may change. Nevertheless, many countries do still target the money supply, although in most cases it is not the main target.

Exchange rate targets, as we shall see in Chapter 25, may have serious disadvantages if the equilibrium exchange rate is not the one that is being targeted. The main instrument for keeping the exchange rate on target is the rate of interest. But, as we shall see in Box 22.9 (on page 728), if the rate of interest is being used to achieve an exchange rate target, it cannot be used for other purposes, such as controlling aggregate demand or inflation. Raising interest rates to achieve an exchange rate target may lead to a recession.

Inflation targets have proved relatively easy to achieve. There may be problems at first, if the actual rate of inflation is way above the target level. The high rates of interest necessary to bring inflation down may cause a recession. But once inflation has been brought down and the objective is then simply to maintain it at the target level, most countries have been relatively successful. And the more successful they are, the more people will expect this success to be maintained, which in turn will help to ensure this success.

So, have there been any problems with inflation targeting? Ironically, one of the main problems lay in its success. With worldwide inflation having fallen, and with global trade and competition helping to keep prices down, there was now less of a link between inflation and the business cycle. Booms no longer seemed to generate the inflation they once did. Gearing interest rate policy to maintaining low inflation could still see economies experiencing unsustainable booms, followed by recessions. Inflation may be controlled, but the business cycle may not be.

KI 34 p453

Some argue that the low interest rates seen in many countries during the first half of the 2000s helped to fuel unsustainable flows of lending. These boosted asset prices, including housing, which generated even higher levels of confidence among borrowers and lenders alike. However, by encouraging further investments that increasingly stretched the financial well-being of economic agents, the point was reached when a significant retrenchment by banks, business and people became inevitable.

KI 35 p459

Then there is the periodic problem of rising world inflation resulting from rapidly developing economies, such as China, India and Brazil. The resulting rise in food and commodity prices pushes up inflation rates around the world. Too strict an adherence to an inflation target could see higher interest rates and slow economic growth. This was a problem in many countries just after the financial crisis in 2010–12. Several countries, including the UK, had only just emerged from recession. Central banks faced a policy conundrum with the macroeconomic environment characterised on the one hand by increasing inflationary pressures but on the other by often sizeable negative output gaps. In fact, most central banks were to keep interest rates at historic lows.

KI 36 p459

Why may there be problems in targeting (a) both inflation and money supply; (b) both inflation and the exchange rate?

Country	Inflation target (%) (2021)	Details
Australia	2–3	Average over the medium term
Brazil	3.75	Tolerance band of ± 1.5 percentage points
Canada	2	Tolerance band of ± 1 percentage points
Chile	3	Tolerance band of ± 1 percentage point
Czech Republic	2	Tolerance band of ± 1 percentage point
Eurozone	2	Average for eurozone as a whole; over medium term
Hungary	3	Tolerance band of ± 1 percentage point
Iceland	2.5	
Israel	1–3	
Japan	2	
Mexico	3	Tolerance band of ± 1 percentage point
New Zealand	2	Tolerance band of ± 1 percentage point
Norway	2	Close to 2 per cent over time
Peru	2	Tolerance band of ± 1 percentage point
Poland	2.5	Tolerance band of ± 1 percentage point
South Africa	3–6	
South Korea	2	2 per cent over the medium term
Sweden	2	
Switzerland	< 2	
Thailand	1–3	
UK	2	Forward-looking inflation target; tolerance band of ± 1 percentage point
USA	2	Consistent with dual mandate: stable prices and maximum employment

Source: Various central bank websites (see BIS central bank hub, www.bis.org/cbanks.htm; see also Central Bank News, www.centralbanknews.info/p/inflation-targets.html).

Since Okun's law shows a close relationship between unemployment and output, movements along either *EAPCs* or short-run *DAS* curves capture cyclical volatility: a boom would be represented by a movement up both curves (e.g. from *a* to *b* in Figure 21.9(a) and from *a′* to *b′* in Figure 21.9(b); a recession would be represented by a movement down both curves.

KI 34 p453

Because of the close relationship between changes in unemployment and output, much of the earlier analysis in this chapter using the Phillips curve framework could readily have been undertaken through the lens of the *DAS* curve alongside the *DAD* curve.

Why might changes in the unemployment rate not match one-for-one changes in the output gap?

Central banks and a Taylor rule

If a central bank has the single objective of controlling inflation, it will try to prevent inflation deviating much from the target. This will give a relatively flat *DAD* curve.

Economic shocks will shift the *DAS* and/or *DAD* curves. With a relatively flat *DAD* curve, this could lead to large fluctuations in output and employment, which may be politically unacceptable. Given this, many economists have advocated the use of a ***Taylor rule***.[2] A Taylor rule takes *two* objectives into account – (1) inflation and (2) either real national income or unemployment – and seeks to get the optimum degree of stability of the two. The degree of importance attached to each of the two objectives can be decided by the government or central bank.

By adopting a Taylor rule the central bank adjusts interest rates when either the rate of inflation diverges from its target or the level of real national income (or unemployment) diverges from its potential (or natural) level.

A general form of the Taylor rule can be written as follows:

$$r = r^* + w_\pi(\pi - \pi^*) + w_Y(Y - Y_p)$$

where r is the real rate of interest set by the central bank; r^* is the real rate of interest consistent with long-run equilibrium in the economy, also known as 'the natural real interest rate'; π is the current rate of inflation; π^* is the target rate of

Definition

Taylor rule A rule adopted by a central bank for setting the rate of interest. It will raise the interest rate if (a) inflation is above target or (b) real national income is above the potential level (or unemployment is below the natural rate). The rule states how much interest rates will be changed in each case.

2 Named after John Taylor, from Stanford University, who in a 1993 paper, 'Discretion versus policy rules in practice', *Carnegie-Rochester Conference Series on Public Policy 39* (North-Holland, 1993), www.sciencedirect.com/science/article/abs/pii/016722319390009L, proposed a representative monetary policy rule based on the rate of inflation over the past four quarters and the percentage deviation of real GDP from a target.

inflation, Y is the current level of real national income and Y_P the potential level of real national income.

What this equation says is that if inflation goes above its target, or if real national income rises above its potential level, the central bank will raise the real rate of interest, the amount depending on the values of w_π and w_Y respectively. John Taylor proposed that for every 1 per cent that inflation rises above its target level, real interest rates should be raised by 0.5 percentage points (i.e. nominal rates should be raised by 1.5 percentage points), and that for every 1 per cent that real national income rises above its potential level, real interest rates should be raised by 0.5 percentage points (i.e. nominal rates should also be raised by 0.5 percentage points).

The terms 'doves' and 'hawks' are frequently used to describe central banks. How do these terms relate to the Taylor rule?

The weights attached to stabilising inflation and output (or unemployment) will therefore affect the slope of the *DAD* curve and, in turn, the extent of a possible trade-off between stabilising inflation and stabilising output (see below). By placing more weight on stabilising real national income around its potential level, for example, the curve will be relatively steep, such as those captured by dashed *DAD* curves in Figures 21.10(b) and 21.11(b).

The central bank and economic shocks

The response of the economy to economic shocks, whether on the supply side or the demand side, will depend on the mandate of the central bank. Shocks will affect both inflation and output. The interest-rate response of the central bank, however, may make one objective better but the other worse. For example, a supply-side shock may raise inflation and reduce output (and raise unemployment). If the central bank focuses solely on controlling inflation, it will raise the real rate of interest. But this will reduce output further. In other words, there may exist an ***inflation-output stabilisation trade-off*** which becomes an important consideration when deciding on the mandate for the central bank. Should it adopt a simple inflation rule or some version of a Taylor rule?

KI 36 p459

The idea of an inflation–output stabilisation trade-off relates to the *variability* of inflation and output (or unemployment). To illustrate the trade-off, we will apply the combined *EAPC/LRPC* and *DAD/DAS* frameworks. We do this for both demand and supply shocks under different assumptions about the central bank's mandate and therefore the monetary policy rule it adopts.

We will look at the case where the central bank follows a simple inflation target rule and changes interest rates as inflation diverges from the target. But we will also look at the case where it adjusts interest rates in response to changes in the level of national output relative to a given potential level (or in unemployment relative to a given natural rate): in other words, where it follows some form of Taylor rule.

The effect of stabilising output in *addition* to stabilising inflation is to make the *DAD* curve steeper.

Definition

Inflation-output stabilisation trade-off The possibility that there exists a trade-off between the variability of inflation and that of output or unemployment: i.e. more stable rates of inflation may be at the cost of more unstable economic activity.

Figure 21.10 Inflation shock

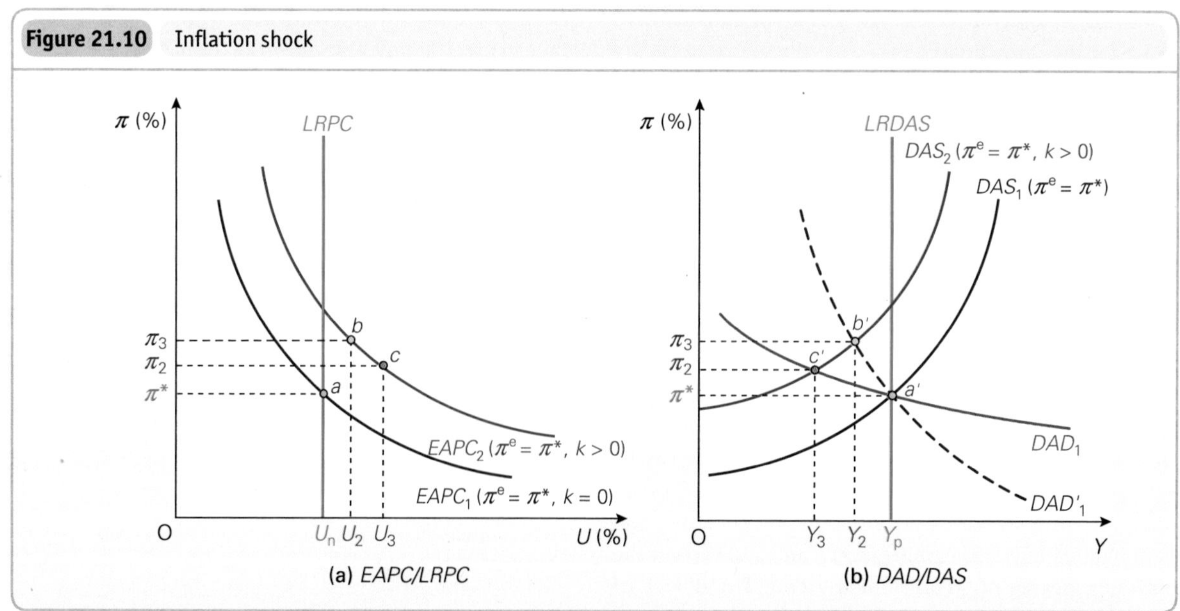

Supply shocks

Consider first a supply shock. Assume that this takes the form of a temporary period of higher commodity price inflation. This affects the vertical position of the *EAPC* in Figure 21.10(a) and the *DAS* curve in Figure 21.10(b). With a given expected rate of inflation (π^e), the inflation shock shifts each upwards by the increase in exogenous cost pressures (k).

Assume that an economy is initially in an equilibrium where both unemployment and output are at their long-run equilibrium values, U_n and Y_p, and inflation is at its target rate, π^*. This is shown by points *a* and *a'* in Figure 21.10. When the central bank adjusts interest rates to stabilise only inflation, the *DAD* curve is captured by DAD_1. However, when it follows a Taylor rule and additionally uses interest rates to stabilise output (or unemployment), the *DAD* curve is captured by DAD'_1.

Consider the short-term dynamic response of the economy when the central bank focuses solely on stabilising inflation. Assume that the adverse supply shock shifts the *DAS* curve to DAS_2 in Figure 21.10(b) and inflation rises. The central bank responds by raising the real rate of interest. This leads to a fall in output to Y_3, traced by the move along DAD_1 from point *a'* to *c'*. The fall in output is mirrored in Figure 21.10(a) by a rise in unemployment. There is a movement from point *a* on $EAPC_1$ to point *c* on $EAPC_2$. The rate of inflation can be seen from both models to have risen to π_2.

The adjustment of the economy is however different if the central bank is also mindful of output deviations. This is because it raises nominal and real interest rates by *less* in response to the inflation shock. The decline in economic activity therefore offsets some of the upward pressure on interest rates from higher inflation. This leads to a smaller reduction in economic activity but a larger rise in inflation. The fall in output is now traced by the move along DAD'_1 from point *a'* to *b'* and in unemployment by the move from point *a* on $EAPC_1$ to *b* on $EAPC_2$ in Figure 21.10(a). The rate of inflation can be seen from both models to have risen to π_3.

Demand shocks

Consider now the adjustment of the economy to a negative demand shock. This could, for example, be the result of a general decline in confidence or a reduction in government purchases. We will look at the effect of this decline in demand when a central bank adjusts interest rates to stabilise (a) inflation alone and (b) both inflation and output (a Taylor rule).

A negative demand shock shifts the *DAD* curve downwards. The effect of this shift on output and inflation will depend on the rule followed by the central bank. The central bank's actions will reduce the dampening effect of the shift. This reduction in the dampening effect will be greater if the central bank follows a Taylor rule than if it follows just a simple inflation target, assuming that the weight attached to stabilising inflation is the same in both cases.[3] We illustrate the effect in Figure 21.11.

Assume again that the economy is initially in equilibrium with output and unemployment at their long-run equilibrium values and inflation on target. When the central bank adjusts interest rates to stabilise only inflation the *DAD* curve is at DAD_1 before the demand shock and DAD_2 afterwards. However, when it additionally adjusts interest rates to stabilise output (or unemployment) the *DAD* curve is at DAD'_1 before the shock and DAD'_2 afterwards.

3 Note that the size of the vertical shift of the *DAD* curve is the same, whichever rule is followed, providing that the weight attached to stabilising inflation is the same. This is because the size of the shift depends only on the interest-rate responsiveness of aggregate demand and the weight that the central bank places on inflation.

Figure 21.11 Demand shock

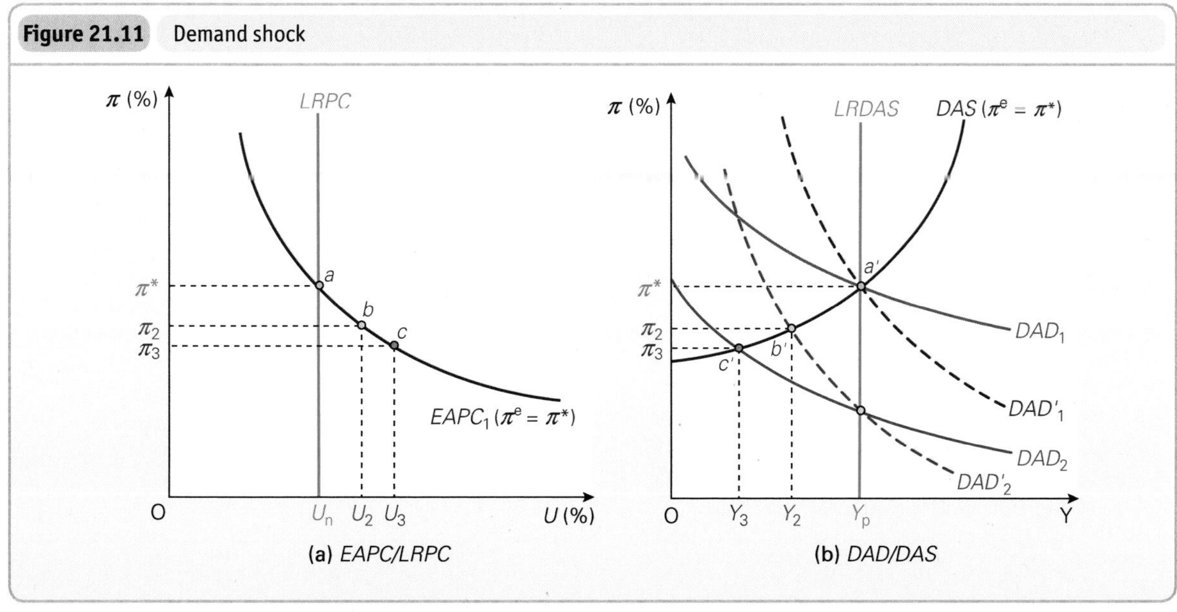

When the central bank focuses only on inflation, the economy slides down the dynamic aggregate supply curve from point a' to c' in Figure 21.11(b) and this is mirrored in unemployment by the move from point a to c on $EAPC_1$ in Figure 21.11(a). The rate of inflation can be seen from both models to fall to π_3.

If the central bank's adjustment of interest rates *also* reflects changes in output, then, in contrast to the supply shock, it adjusts nominal and real interest rates by *more*. This is because prices and output move in the same direction following a demand shock. Following a negative demand shock, the central bank will therefore wish to reduce nominal and real interest rates in response to both the decline in the rate of inflation and output. This implies a larger fall in nominal and real interest rates. In Figure 21.11(b), because interest rates are cut by more, the economy moves along DAD'_2 to point b'. There is a smaller fall in both national income and inflation from the negative shock because of the stronger actions of the central bank. In other words, the shock is less deflationary.

Draw a diagram similar to Figure 21.11 and illustrate the effect of a positive demand shock, showing how the effect differs according to whether a simple inflation rule is followed or a Taylor rule. Again assume that the weight attached to controlling inflation is the same with the simple rule and the Taylor rule.

Some economists argue that the inflation–output stabilisation trade-off is more significant with supply shocks than with demand shocks. This is because of the so-called ***divine coincidence*** in monetary policy when the economy experiences demand-side shocks. As we have seen, in response to a negative (positive) demand shock a central bank would decrease (increase) nominal and real interest rates to stabilise *both* inflation *and* output. In contrast, supply shocks result in output and prices moving in opposite directions. A negative (positive) supply shock tends to reduce (increase) output but cause the rate of inflation to rise (fall). Therefore, the mandate of the central bank may be more crucial in determining the monetary policy response.

In the final section of the chapter we go one step further in analysing the dynamic response of economies to shocks by incorporating the *IS/MP* alongside the *EAPC/LRPC* and *DAD/DAS* models. This allows us to view the adjustment of interest rates alongside that of output, unemployment and inflation. We also consider the longer-term adjustment of economies to shocks.

Definition

Divine coincidence in monetary policy The argument that the objective of stabilising inflation requires the same monetary policy response as stabilising output when the economy is faced with a demand shock (but not when faced with a supply shock).

Section summary

1. Many governments around the world have delegated monetary policy to their central banks. Consequently, many central banks are charged with targeting inflation, though their remits are often supplemented by other macroeconomic objectives.
2. New classical and monetarist ideas have helped provide the theoretical justifications for central bank independence. Delegating monetary policy, it is argued, can eliminate the inflation bias that would otherwise arise from monetary policies lacking credibility.
3. Policy announcements lack credibility and are time inconsistent when there is an incentive for policy makers to renege on them. By depoliticising monetary policy, it is argued that low inflation target announcements become more credible. This allows people to reduce their inflationary expectations thereby reducing actual inflation.
4. The dynamic aggregate supply curve is an alternative representation of the expectations-augmented Phillips curve, but with real national income rather than unemployment on the horizontal axis. We can view the behaviour of the economy and the relationship between inflation and economic activity through either the *EAPC* or the *DAD/DAS* frameworks.
5. The incorporation of the dynamic aggregate demand curve allows us to consider more formally the role of inflation-targeting central banks in affecting the behaviour of economies that are frequently hit by economic shocks, such as fluctuations in aggregate demand.
6. While the delegation of monetary policy can eliminate inflation bias, an inflation–output stabilisation trade-off may arise. This can be a serious problem with adjusting to supply shocks. It may be less problematic, however, with demand shocks, where prices and output movements require a similar adjustment of interest rates.
7. Some economists therefore advocate the use of a Taylor rule, whereby monetary policy targets the control of fluctuations in real national income or unemployment alongside those in inflation.

21.6 CENTRAL BANKS, ECONOMIC SHOCKS AND THE MACROECONOMY: AN INTEGRATED MODEL

The purpose of this section is to develop an integrated model of an economy bringing together the *IS/MP, DAD/DAS* and *EAPC/LRPC* frameworks. We model the possible response of a series of endogenous macroeconomic variables – output, unemployment, inflation and interest rates – to exogenous economic shocks. We pay particular attention to the role played by the expectations of inflation in affecting the dynamic response of economies. We consider first a demand shock and then a supply shock.

Demand-side shocks

Constant expectations of inflation

Figure 21.12 combines the three principal models that we have used to analyse the macroeconomy. Diagrams (a) and (b) combine the *EAPC/LRPC* and *DAD/DAS* models, as shown previously in section 21.5. The economy is assumed to be in long-run equilibrium. From these two models, we can see that unemployment is at the natural rate (U_n) (point a'), real national income at potential level (Y_p) (point a), the rate of inflation is at the target rate (π^*) and the expected rate of inflation is equal to the target rate ($\pi^e = \pi^*$).

From the *IS/MP* model in diagram (c), we can see that the central bank is setting a real rate of interest r^* (point a''). With the economy in long-run equilibrium at Y_p this interest rate is referred to as the economy's equilibrium or 'natural' real interest.

Short-run adjustment to a rise in aggregate demand. Now assume that there is a rise in aggregate demand from, say, a rise in consumer confidence. The *DAD* and *IS* curves shift to the right, to DAD_2 and IS_2 respectively. The rise in aggregate demand causes a rise in real national income, but also a rise in inflation. This is shown by a movement upwards along the short-run *DAS* curve to point b in diagram (b), which corresponds to movement upwards along the expectations-augmented Phillips curve to point b' in diagram (a).

In response to the higher rate of inflation of π_1, the central bank raises the nominal rate of interest (i) more than the rise in inflation (π), thereby raising the *real* rate of interest (r). The extent to which the real interest rate rises depends on the monetary policy rule of the central bank. Consequently, there is a movement upwards along a short-run *MP* curve in diagram (c). A new short-run equilibrium is reached at point b'', with a real interest rate of r_1.

Figure 21.12 Increase in real aggregate demand with constant inflationary expectations

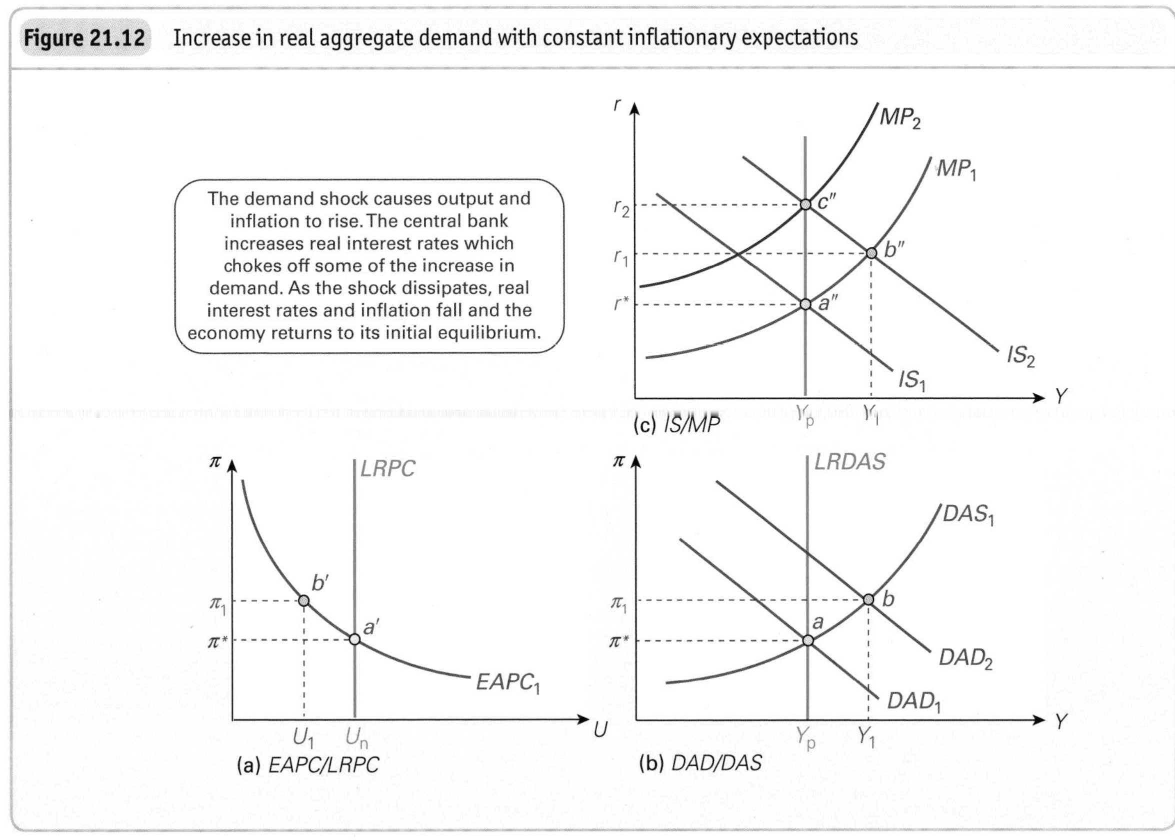

With the economy's real national income above its potential level and the unemployment rate below its natural rate, inflation rises to π_1 – above the target rate (π^*).

Long-term adjustment. The analysis now turns to the longer-term adjustment path of the economy (assuming expectations of inflation remain constant).

KI 34 p453

A likely scenario, given the volatility of economies, is that the positive demand-side shock will gradually subside. If so, the *DAD* will move leftwards in diagram (b). As aggregate demand falls, we slide back down the short-run *DAS* curve and the rate of inflation falls. This movement is mirrored by a corresponding movement down the *EAPC* in diagram (a). As the inflation rate falls the central bank reduces real interest rates. The nominal interest rate falls by more than the fall in the rate of inflation. Eventually, the economy returns to the original long-run equilibrium.

Another possibility is that the positive demand-shock may persist for some time – or that the central bank may forecast that it will. In this case, if the central bank is to return the economy to point *a* in diagram (b) with inflation on target and real national income at the potential level, it must shift the *DAD* curve back again. It does this by adopting a tighter monetary policy (i.e. a higher real interest rate for each rate of inflation). It thus raises the real interest rate above r_1, initially to r_2, as shown in diagram (c). In other words, the *MP* curve will shift upwards to MP_2.

The effect of the tighter monetary policy will be to shift the DAD_2 curve back towards DAD_1 and equilibrium will be restored at point *a*. This is matched in diagram (a) by a move from *b′* to *a′*. In diagram (c), the tighter monetary policy is represented by a movement up *along* curve IS_2 to point *c″*.

How will the composition of aggregate demand at points c″ and a″ in Figure 21.12(c) differ?

Adaptive expectations of inflation

Up to this point we have assumed that expectations of inflation are constant. We now consider how the economy's adjustment to a demand shock is affected if people's expectations of inflation *adjust* during this process. We assume that people's expectations of inflation in the current period are based on the actual rate of inflation in the previous period.

KI 33 p377

KI 10 p70

Each *EAPC*, short-run *DAS* curve and short-run *MP* curve is based on a given expected rate of inflation, which will directly impact on the actual rate of inflation. But what happens in the next time period when expectations adjust? The answer is that each short-run curve shifts upwards *if* the expected rate of inflation rises, and shifts downwards *if* it falls. This is illustrated in Figure 21.13.

Again we assume that at the initial equilibrium real national income is at its potential level (Y_p), unemployment is at the natural rate (U_n) and that expected inflation is the actual (targeted) inflation) ($\pi^e = \pi^*$).). Finally, the natural real rate of interest is r^*.

Figure 21.13 Increase in real aggregate demand with adaptive inflationary expectations

The demand shock causes output and inflation to rise. The central bank raises real interest rates and output weakens. An increase in inflationary expectations and then the disappearance of the shock cause economic activity to fall further. Real interest rates and inflationary expectations fall and the economy gradually returns to its initial equilibrium.

(c) IS/MP

(a) EAPC/LRPC

(b) DAD/DAS

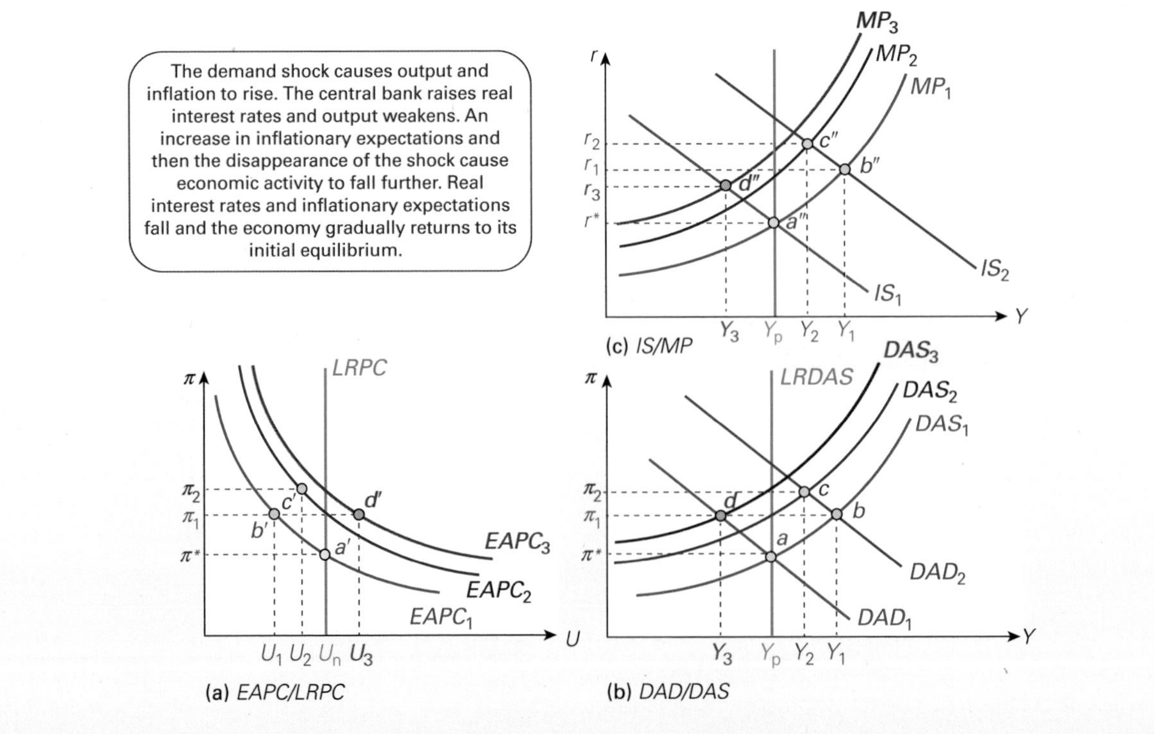

An initial positive demand shock. Now, as before, assume there is a positive demand shock with a rise in consumer confidence. To make the analysis more straightforward we will assume that the shock lasts two periods, at which point demand conditions return to their previous state. This rise in aggregate demand shifts the *DAD* curve to DAD_2 and the *IS* curve to IS_2. In the short run there is a movement along the DAS_1 and MP_1 curves to point *b* and *b″* respectively.

The rise in real aggregate demand and in economic activity is mirrored by the move along $EAPC_1$ from point *a′* to *b′* In the process, the rate of inflation rises from π^* to π_1. The central bank raises nominal and real interest rates, which chokes off some of the increase in aggregate demand. The extent to which it raises rates again depends on the monetary policy rule (and hence the shape of the *MP* and *DAD* curves).

Adjustment of expectations of inflation. We now assume that in the second period people raise their inflationary expectations to the now higher rate of inflation π_1, which, in turn, drives up the actual rate of inflation. This causes an upward shift in the *EAPC* and the *DAS* and *MP* curves, say to $EAPC_2$, DAS_2 and MP_2.

TC 9 p132

The central bank responds to the further rise in the rate of inflation by increasing real interest rates, which rise to r_2. The new short-run equilibrium in the second period sees the inflation rate at π_2, real national income fall from Y_1 to Y_2 and unemployment rise from U_1 to U_2. Thus, while the inflation rate is higher, economic activity falls back following its initial increase.

We now move into the third period. Expectations of inflation rise further to π_2. This is in response to the higher inflation rate experienced in the second period. Consequently, the *EAPC* and the *DAS* and *MP* curves shift upwards again, say to $EAPC_3$, DAS_3 and MP_3 respectively. But the aggregate demand shock is assumed now to disappear so that the *DAD* curve shifts leftwards back to its original position DAD_1. Therefore, the economy moves from point *c* to *d* in the *DAD/DAS* model and point *c′* to *d′* in the *EAPC* model. As it does, output falls below its potential level and unemployment rises above its natural rate. The central bank now reduces real interest rates in response, but because inflation is still above its target rate, the real interest rate r_3 is still above its natural level r^*.

Over the following periods, economic activity recovers as inflation and expected inflation fall. As it does so, the *EAPC* and the *DAS* and *MP* curves shift downwards. The economy therefore returns to its initial long-run equilibrium. The quicker expectations adjust, the sooner the economy will return to its long-run equilibrium.

If expectations were formed rationally with no time lags, what would be the implications for short-run DAS curves and for the response to a rise in aggregate demand?

Impulse response functions. The adjustment path of key macroeconomic variables to economic shocks can be represented in diagrams known as ***impulse response functions***. In Figure 21.14 we show the impulse response functions for output (real national income) and real interest rates consistent with the analysis in Figure 21.13. These time paths illustrate how both output and real interest rates adjust following the shock in period 1. For example, we can see clearly how output falls below its potential level during period 3. Both variables are assumed to gradually return to their original equilibrium levels.

Figure 21.14 Impulse response functions for a positive demand shock

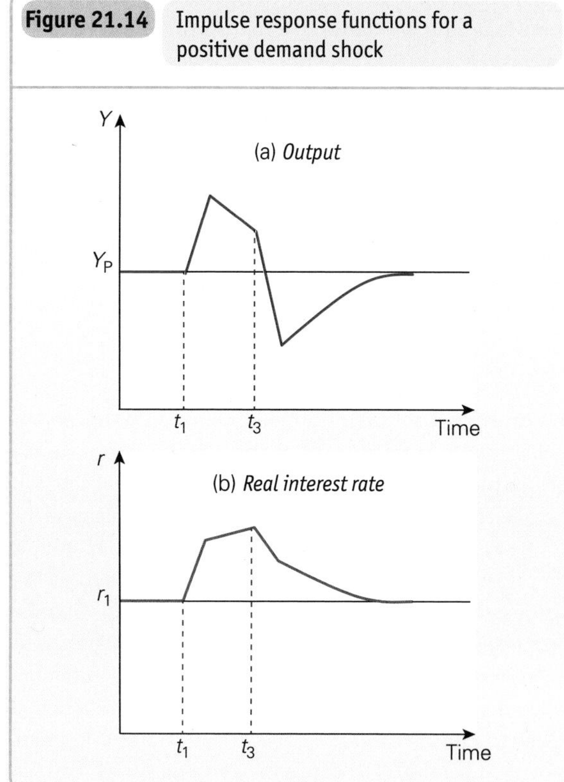

Based on the analysis in Figure 21.13, what would an impulse response function look like for the rate of inflation?

Assumptions about potential national income

The actual adjustment path of the economy to demand shocks is dependent on many factors. In the analysis above, the demand shock had no impact on potential national income. But, some Keynesians argue that potential national income depends to some extent on aggregate demand. If the economy experiences high aggregate demand and high output, this may encourage investment, both domestic and inward, and lead to an expansion of capacity and hence in

Definition

Impulse response functions The time paths of key macroeconomic variables following economic shocks.

potential national income. A rightward shift in the *DAD* curve may thus also result in a rightward shift in both the short-run and vertical long-run *DAS* curves.

If the increase in potential national income also corresponds to a lower natural rate of unemployment or lower NAIRU, the vertical long-run Phillips curve will also shift – in this case to the left.

Under what circumstances would a rise in potential real income not result in a fall in the NAIRU?

Supply-side shocks

We finish by considering a temporary supply-side shock. We will look at permanent changes in aggregate supply within the context of our integrated framework at the start Chapter 23, which focuses on long-term economic growth.

We assume that there is a one-period adverse economic shock, say caused by higher commodity price inflation. We again assume that people form their expectations of inflation adaptively, based on the previous period's inflation rate.

In Figure 21.15 the economy is at its long-run equilibrium when the inflationary shock occurs. There is now a higher inflation rate at any of level of economic output or unemployment because of the exogenous cost pressures. This has the effect of causing the *EAPC* and the *DAS* and *MP* curves to shift vertically upwards to $EAPC_2$, DAS_2 and MP_2 respectively. We can see from diagram (b) that we therefore move upwards along the *DAD* curve from point *a* to point *b*. The central bank raises real interest rates in response to the higher rate of inflation. In diagram (c) real interest rates rise from r^* to r_2. The extent of the rise again depends on the monetary policy rule. The more the central bank targets inflation stabilisation the more that the economy contracts (the flatter the *DAD* curve).

Despite the dampening effect on inflation from the fall in output, in the following period inflationary expectations rise. Hence, although the initial inflationary shock has now disappeared, the *EAPC* and the *DAS* and *MP* curves remain above their initial position. Thereafter, they gradually shift downwards as inflationary expectations fall, for example to $EAPC_3$, DAS_3 and MP_3. As they do, real interest rates fall and economic activity increases: real national income increases and the rate of unemployment falls. Eventually, the economy returns to its initial long-run equilibrium.

Based on the analysis in Figure 21.15 what would the impulse response functions look like for output, unemployment, inflation and real and nominal interest rates?

Figure 21.15 Adverse supply shock with adaptive inflationary expectations

The supply shock causes the inflation rate to rise. The central bank raises real interest rates which limits the rise in inflation but dampens economic activity. Despite the shock disappearing, inflationary expectations remain high and the economy only gradually returns to its initial equilibrium.

(a) EAPC/LRPC

(b) DAD/DAS

(c) IS/MP

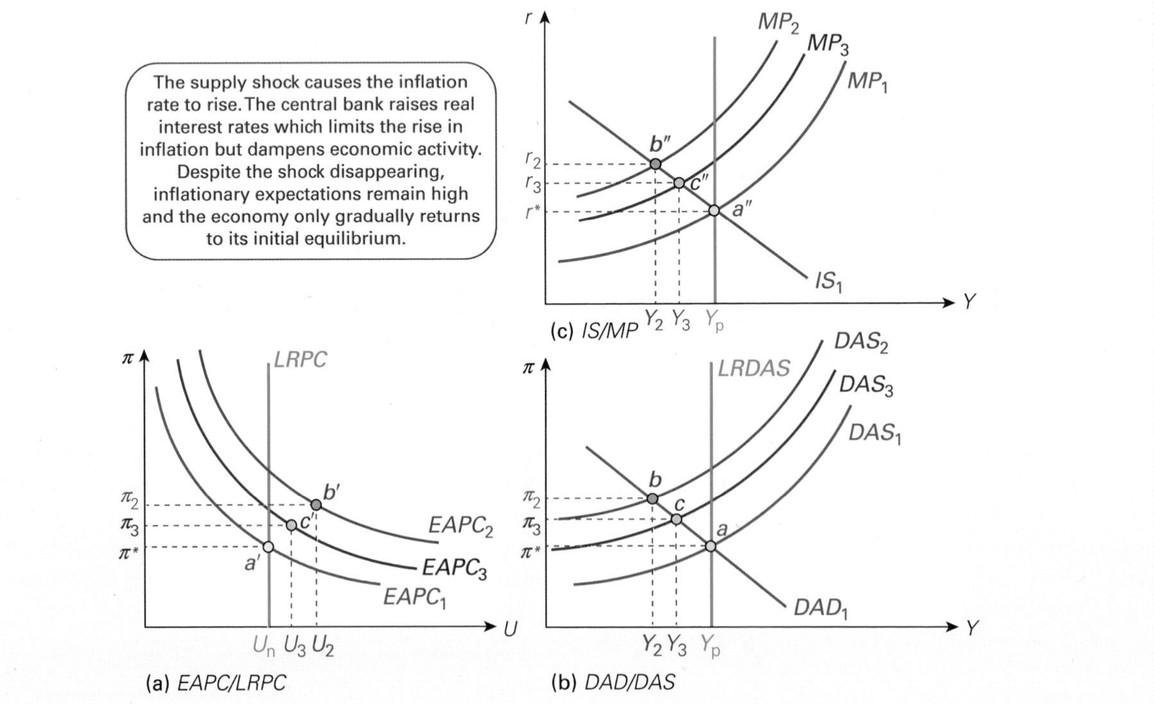

Section summary

1. Many central banks nowadays are tasked with using monetary policy to help deliver pre-defined macroeconomic objectives. This frequently involves targeting inflation.
2. By combining the *EAPC/LRPC, DAD/DAS* and *IS/MP* models it is possible to analyse the relationships between output, unemployment, inflation and interest rates in a contemporary policy-making context.
3. The combined frameworks can be used to analyse the effects of demand and supply shocks. Different adjustment paths for the economy result from different assumptions about the workings of the economy.
4. We can plot the adjustment paths for key macroeconomic variables following demand or supply shocks. The time plots are known as impulse response functions.

END OF CHAPTER QUESTIONS

1. Assume that inflation depends on two things: the level of aggregate demand, indicated by the inverse of unemployment ($1/U$), and the expected rate of inflation (π^e_t) Assume that the rate of inflation (π_t) is given by the equation

   $$\pi_t = (48/U - 6) + \pi^e_t$$

   Assume initially (year 0) that the actual and expected rate of inflation is zero.

   (a) What is the current (natural) rate of unemployment?

   (b) Now assume in year 1 that the government wishes to reduce unemployment to 4 per cent and continues to expand aggregate demand by as much as is necessary to achieve this. Fill in the rows for years 0 to 4 in the following table. It is assumed for simplicity that the expected rate of inflation in a given year (π^e_t) is equal to the actual rate of inflation in the previous year (π_{t-1}).

Year	U	$48/U–6$	+	π^e	=	π
0	...	...	+	...	=	...
1	...	...	+	...	=	...
2	...	...	+	...	=	...
3	...	...	+	...	=	...
4	...	...	+	...	=	...
5	...	...	+	...	=	...
6	...	...	+	...	=	...
7	...	...	+	...	=	...

   (c) Now assume in year 5 that the government, worried about rising inflation, reduces aggregate demand sufficiently to reduce inflation by 3 per cent in that year. What must the rate of unemployment be raised to in that year?

   (d) Assuming that unemployment stays at this high level, continue the table for years 5 to 7.

2. In the accelerationist model, if the government tries to maintain unemployment below the natural rate, what will determine the speed at which inflation accelerates?
3. What is the difference between adaptive expectations and rational expectations?
4. How can adaptive expectations of inflation result in clockwise Phillips loops? Why would these loops not be completely regular?
5. For what reasons may the NAIRU increase?
6. What is meant by inflation bias? What factors affect the potential magnitude of inflation bias?
7. Using the integrated *DAD/DAS* and *EAPC/LRPC* framework, analyse the effect of an unexpected increase in aggregate demand assuming that markets adjust relatively rapidly. Compare the adjustment path of the economy when inflationary expectations remain anchored with that when expectations are based on actual inflation in the previous period.
8. In what sense is it true to say that the Phillips curve is horizontal today?
9. Assume that the economy is at potential output and the natural rate of unemployment and that inflation is at the target rate set for the central bank by the government. In each of the following scenarios apply the integrated *EAPC, DAD/DAS* and *IS/MP* framework to analyse the economy's adjustment path.

   (a) A temporary fall in aggregate demand under the assumption that inflationary expectations remain anchored.

   (b) A temporary fall in aggregate demand where inflationary expectations are based on the rate of inflation in the previous period.

   (c) A temporary positive supply shock where inflationary expectations are based on the rate of inflation in the previous period.

Online resources

Additional case studies on the student website

21.1 Explaining the shape of the short-run Phillips curve. This shows how money illusion on the part of workers can explain why the Phillips curve is downward sloping.

21.2 The quantity theory of money restated. An examination of how the vertical long-run *AS* curve in the adaptive expectations model can be used to justify the quantity theory of money.

21.3 Cost-push factors in Keynesian analysis. How Keynesians incorporated cost-push inflation into their analysis of shifts in the Phillips curve.

21.4 Should central banks be independent of government? An examination of the arguments for and against independent central banks.

21.5 The Bank of England and Taylor rules. A comparison of the Bank of England's monetary policy rule with a simple Taylor rule.

Websites relevant to this chapter

See sites listed at the end of Chapter 22 on page 735.

Fiscal and Monetary Policy

CHAPTER MAP

Both fiscal and monetary policy can be used to control aggregate demand. Excessive growth in aggregate demand can cause unsustainable short-term growth and higher rates of inflation. Too little aggregate demand can result in a recession, with negative growth and rising unemployment.

Fiscal policy seeks to control aggregate demand by altering the balance between government expenditures and taxation. Monetary policy seeks to control aggregate demand by directly controlling money supply or by altering the rate of interest and then backing this up by any necessary changes in money supply.

In the first three sections of this chapter we examine fiscal and monetary work; how effective they are likely to be in controlling aggregate demand; and what are the potential pitfalls in their use.

We then turn to consider the arguments as to how much discretion or control policy makers should have over fiscal and monetary policy. Should governments adopt fixed targets for policy (e.g. inflation targets) or should they adjust policies according to circumstances? This is a debate reinvigorated by the global financial crisis and the COVID-19 pandemic and their impact on economies and wider society.

22.1 FISCAL POLICY AND THE PUBLIC FINANCES

Fiscal policy involves the government manipulating the level of government expenditure and/or rates of tax. An *expansionary* fiscal policy will involve raising government expenditure (an injection into the circular flow of income) or reducing taxes (a withdrawal from the circular flow). A *deflationary* (i.e. a contractionary) fiscal policy will involve cutting government expenditure and/or raising taxes.

But why might government wish to change its fiscal position? In other words, what are the roles for fiscal policy?

Roles for fiscal policy

Aggregate demand

Fiscal policy may be used to affect aggregate demand. There are two principal reasons for this.

To prevent the occurrence of fundamental disequilibrium in the economy. The government may wish to remove any severe deflationary or inflationary gaps. Hence, expansionary fiscal policy could be used to prevent an economy experiencing a severe or prolonged recession, such as that experienced in the Great Depression of the 1930s, the global financial crisis of the late 2000s and the COVID-19 pandemic of the early 2020s, when substantial tax cuts and increased government expenditure were used by many countries, including the UK and the USA, to help combat the collapse in aggregate demand. Likewise, deflationary fiscal policy could be used to prevent rampant inflation, such as that experienced in the 1970s.

TC 15 p543

Stabilisation policies. The government may wish to smooth out the fluctuations in the economy associated with the business cycle. This involves reducing government expenditure or raising taxes when the economy begins to boom. This will dampen down the expansion and prevent 'overheating' of the economy, with its attendant problems of rising inflation and a deteriorating current account balance of payments. Conversely if a recession looms, the government should cut taxes or raise government expenditure in order to boost the economy.

If these stabilisation policies are successful, they will amount merely to 'fine-tuning'. Problems of excess or deficient demand will never be allowed to get severe. Any movement of aggregate demand away from a steady growth path would be quickly 'nipped in the bud'.

Aggregate supply

Fiscal policy can also be used to influence aggregate supply. For example, government can increase its expenditure on education, training and infrastructure, or give tax incentives for investment and research and development. Such initiatives are ordinarily intended to increase the rate of growth of the economy's *potential* output and reduce the natural rate of unemployment. In the case of the COVID-19 pandemic, policies aimed at protecting businesses and jobs can be seen as attempts to mitigate the scarring effects on future economic activity by allowing economies to 'reboot' more seamlessly when health intervention measures were able to be relaxed. Supply-side policies are considered in more detail in Chapter 23.

Many governments around the world during the COVID-19 pandemic introduced job retention schemes allowing workers to be furloughed. Is this a use of fiscal policy to affect aggregate demand or aggregate supply?

In section 22.2 we look at how fiscal policy can be used. But first it is important to understand some of the terminology of government spending and taxation and some of the key fiscal indicators.

Government finances: some terminology

Government

When analysing government finances, the term 'government' is often used interchangeably with that of 'general government'. It is important to note that general government includes both *central* and *local* government. Separate balance sheets can be presented for each. An analysis of both may be particularly important in countries where local government has considerable autonomy from central government, such as varying tax rates or raising money by issuing debt instruments.

The terms ***budget deficit*** and ***budget surplus*** are frequently used in the context of government, and especially central government. In fact, these terms can be applied to any organisation to assess its financial well-being by comparing expenditure with revenues.

If general government's expenditure (including benefits) exceeds its revenue from taxation it would be running a budget deficit, sometimes known simply at the ***general government deficit***. Conversely, when general government's revenues exceed its expenditure there is a ***general government surplus***.

For most of the past 60 years, governments around the world have run budget deficits. The situation improved in many countries from the late 1990s due to a mix of strong economic growth and fiscal consolidation. The position was

> **Definitions**
>
> **Fiscal policy** Changing government expenditure and/or taxation for the purposes of influencing the macroeconomy.
>
> **Budget deficit** The excess of an organisation's spending over its revenues. When applied to government it is the excess of its spending over its tax receipts.
>
> **Budget surplus** The excess of an organisation's revenues over its expenditures. When applied to government it is the excess of its tax receipts over its spending.
>
> **General government deficit (or surplus)** The combined deficit (or surplus) of central and local government.

Figure 22.1 General government spending and receipts in advanced economies

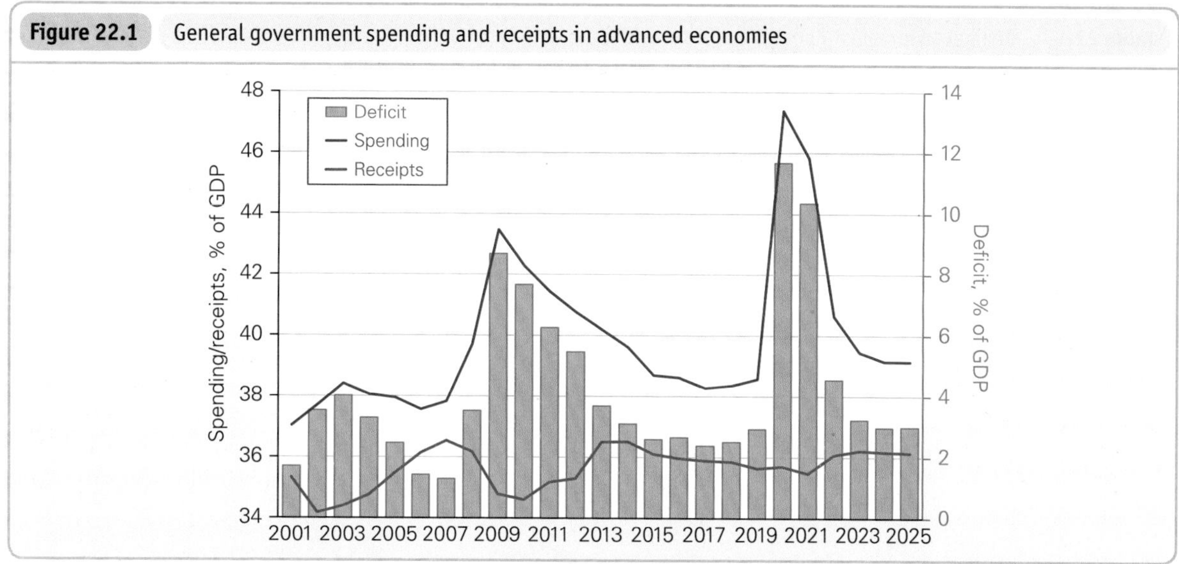

Notes: Data are for calendar years and from 2021 are forecasts; 39 economies based on IMF country classification.
Source: *World Economic Outlook*, IMF (April 2021), https://www.imf.org/en/Publications/WEO/weo-database/2021/April

to change dramatically, however, following first the global financial crisis of 2007–8 and later the COVID-19 pandemic of 2020–21 as governments around the world increased expenditure and cut taxes in an attempt to stave off recession. Government deficits soared.

The deterioration in the budgetary position of governments around the world is captured in Figure 22.1. It shows the 'gap' between general government expenditures and receipts across 39 advanced economies widening to over 8 per cent of national income following the financial crisis and 12 per cent in 2020.

Deficits, debt and borrowing. To finance their deficits, governments will have to borrow (e.g. through the issue of bonds (gilts) or Treasury bills). As we saw in section 18.3, this will lead to an increase in the money supply to the extent that the borrowing is from the banking sector. The purchase of bonds or Treasury bills by the (non-bank) private sector, however, will not lead to an increase in the money supply.

KI 26 p309

Deficits represent *annual* borrowing: a flow concept. The accumulated deficits over the years (minus any surpluses) gives total *debt*: a stock concept. It is the total amount owed by the government. Central and general government debt are known as ***national debt*** and ***general government debt*** respectively.

Note that the national debt is not the same thing as the country's overseas debt. In the case of the UK, only around one-quarter of national debt is owed overseas. The remainder is owed to UK residents. In other words, the government finances its budget deficits largely by borrowing at home and not from abroad.

Table 22.1 shows general government deficits/surpluses and debt for selected countries. They are expressed as a proportion of GDP.

Why are historical and international comparisons of deficit and debt measures best presented as proportions of GDP?

As you can see, in the period from 1995 to 2007, all the countries, with the exception of Ireland, Norway and Sweden, ran an average deficit. In the period from 2008 following the global financial crisis average deficits increased for most countries. The pressures on the public finances, however, then rose markedly with fiscal measures taken in response to the COVID-19 pandemic. And the bigger the deficit, the faster debt increases.

Public sector

To get a more complete view of public finances, we would need to look at the entire public sector: namely, central government, local government and public corporations.

There is one important caveat to this: corporations can transfer between the public and private sectors (a result of privatisation or nationalisation). These movements can distort public finance statistics.

Although the longer-term trend in many countries has been to privatise major industries, such as transport, energy and telecommunications, the financial crisis and the pandemic meant that large-scale government support was needed for such industries. This involved either a transfer of ownership or government taking on the financial liabilities of operations.

Definitions

National debt The accumulated deficits of central government. It is the total amount owed by central government, both domestically and internationally.

General government debt The accumulated deficits of central plus local government. It is the total amount owed by general government, both domestically and internationally.

Table 22.1 General government deficits/surpluses and gross debt, % of GDP

	General government deficits (−) or surpluses (+)			Gross general government debt		
	1995–2007	2008–19	2020–22	1995–2007	2008–19	2020–22
Austria	−2.8	−1.9	−6.6	66.3	79.3	84.9
Belgium	−1.3	−2.8	−8.2	108.9	102.0	118.0
France	−3.0	−4.2	−8.3	61.8	91.0	117.7
Germany	−3.1	−0.1	−4.2	61.1	72.0	70.1
Greece	−6.7	−6.2	−5.5	102.4	165.3	200.9
Ireland	1.3	−7.2	−5.0	41.5	81.9	65.0
Italy	−3.5	−3.0	−8.2	110.4	127.4	159.4
Japan	−5.7	−5.8	−7.7	142.9	224.1	264.1
Netherlands	−1.5	−1.8	−5.6	55.4	59.9	63.1
Norway	10.1	9.6	6.5	39.8	36.6	43.4
Portugal	−4.4	−5.1	−4.9	62.8	116.6	130.9
Spain	−1.3	−6.4	−10.1	52.9	83.0	122.1
Sweden	0.0	0.1	−2.6	54.7	39.7	40.2
UK	−2.0	−5.5	−10.0	39.5	79.3	109.7
USA	−3.3	−7.7	−9.0	62.0	100.0	128.4
Eurozone	−2.7	−2.8	−6.6	70.0	88.0	102.2

Note: Data for 2021 and 2022 are based on forecasts,
Source: Based on data from *AMECO database*, Tables 16.3 and 18.1 (European Commission, DG ECFIN).

The financial crisis of the late 2000s saw various banking corporations transferred wholly or partly to the public sector (nationalisation) in order to ensure their survival and the stability of the financial system. In the UK, this included banking groups such as Lloyds, Northern Rock and the Royal Bank of Scotland. The hope was to return these institutions to the private sector in due course. Meanwhile the pandemic saw the UK government suspend the normal operating arrangements of the country's train franchises and take on the train operators' deficits. This led to the Office for National Statistics moving their debts on to the government's balance sheet.

Total spending and receipts. In 2020/21, during the COVID-19 pandemic, UK public-sector total spending rose to almost £1.1 trillion, a 16 per cent real-terms increase in spending on the previous financial year (i.e. after adjusting for inflation). Meanwhile, receipts from public-sector activity in 2020/21, mainly from taxation, were worth around £800 billion, a 10 per cent real-terms decrease.

To understand better both the scale of public-sector spending and receipts and how they have evolved over time, we can present them as a proportion of national income (GDP). Figure 22.2 shows how the relative size of UK public-sector spending and receipts increased significantly over the first half of the last century with significant upward displacements after both world wars. Thereafter, their size as a share of national income tended to fluctuate around the 40 per cent mark, dependent on the effect of the business cycle on spending and receipts.

However, the global financial crisis and global health emergency were to have a significant effect on the public finances and, in particular, on the scale of public-sector spending. Spending would rise to 52 per cent of national income in 2020/21 – its highest level since the Second World War. Box 22.1 considers the impact that the world wars may have had on the public's attitude towards public-sector spending and whether the COVID-19 pandemic may similarly affect future fiscal choices of government.

Public-sector borrowing and debt. Figure 22.2 also shows that spending by the public sector typically exceeds its receipts. If the public sector spends more than it earns, it will have to finance the deficit through borrowing, known as ***public-sector net borrowing (PSNB)***. The principal form of borrowing is through the sale of gilts (government bonds).

The scale of public-sector net borrowing can be seen even more clearly in Figure 22.3. Since 1900, public-sector net borrowing has averaged over $4^{1}/_{4}$ per cent of national income. During each of the two world wars, public-sector net borrowing peaked at close to 28 per cent of GDP. In 2009/10, following the global financial crisis, it reached 10 per cent of GDP and then in 2020/21, during the COVID-19 pandemic, 17 per cent of GDP.

The precise amount of money the public sector needs to borrow in any one year is known as the ***public-sector net cash requirement (PSNCR)***. It differs slightly from the

Definitions

Public-sector net borrowing (PSNB) The difference between the expenditures of the public sector and its receipts from taxation and the revenues from public corporations.

Public-sector net cash requirement (PSNCR) A UK-based measure of what the public sector must borrow. It is based on when cash is actually paid or received (rather than when it is recorded) and takes into account financial transactions by the public sector.

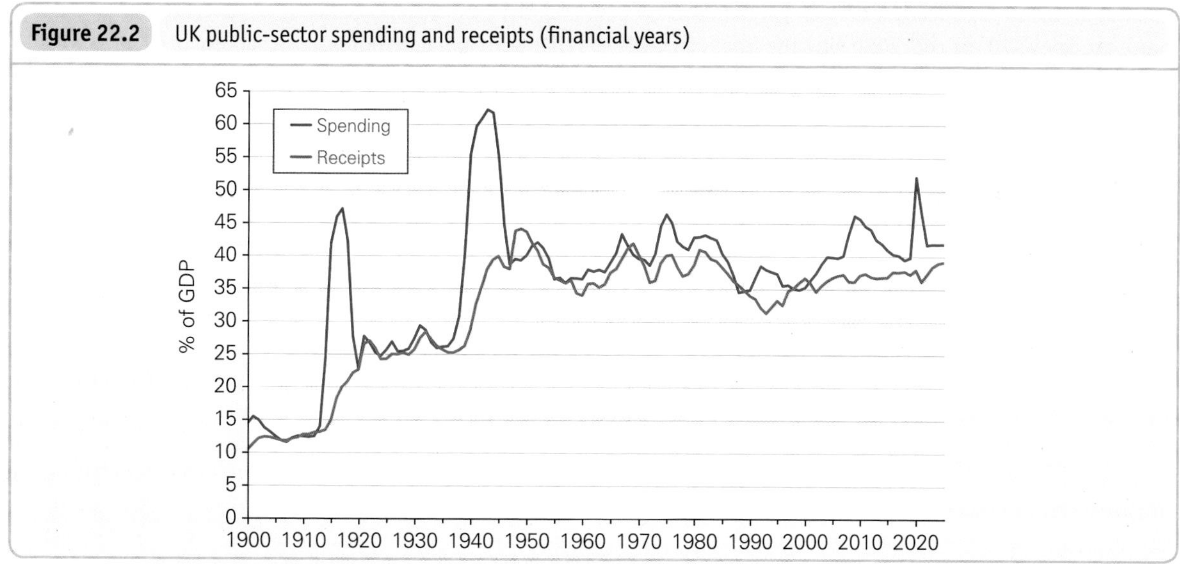

Figure 22.2 UK public-sector spending and receipts (financial years)

Note: OBR forecasts from 2021/22; figures exclude public banks.
Source: *Public Finances Databank*, Office for Budget Responsibility (July 2021), https://obr.uk/data/

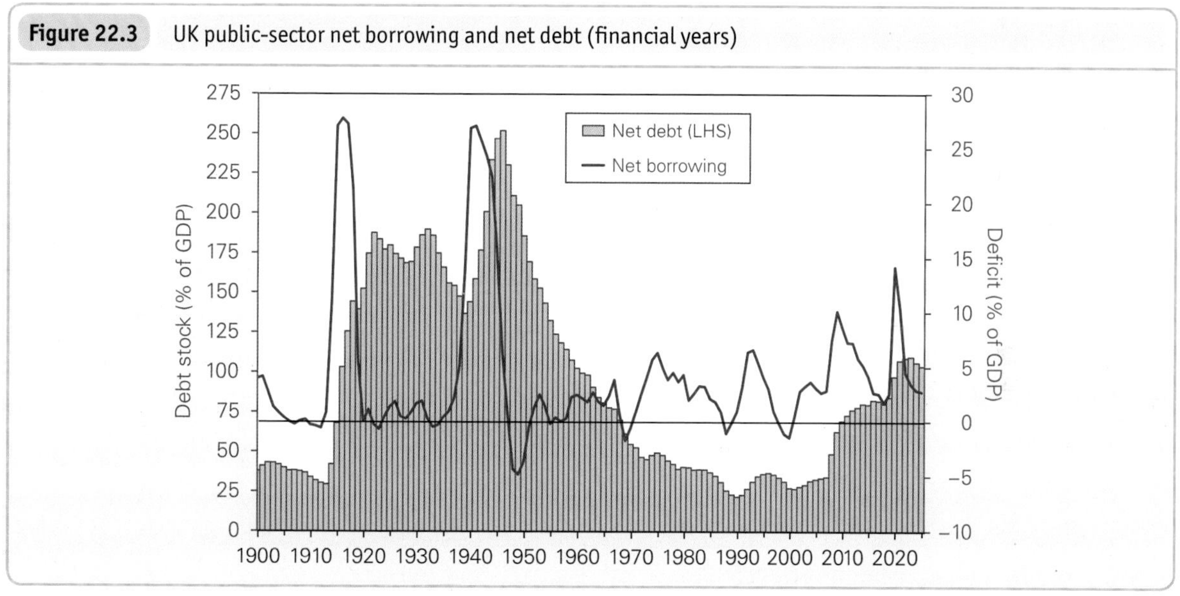

Figure 22.3 UK public-sector net borrowing and net debt (financial years)

Notes: OBR forecasts from 2021/22; figures exclude public banks.
Source: *Public Finances Databank*, Office for Budget Responsibility (July 2021), https://obr.uk/data/

PSNB for two main reasons. First, the net cash requirement reflects when cash is actually paid or received as opposed to when expenditures and receipts are recorded. Second, it also reflects financial transactions, such as loans to the private sector, which do not materially affect the long-term financial position of the public sector.

As with central and general government debt, public-sector debt is the current stock of the accumulated deficits over the years. In assessing the sustainability of this stock of debt – a theme we return to shortly – it is usual to focus on ***public-sector net debt***. This is the sector's gross debt less its liquid assets, which comprise official reserves and deposits held with financial institutions.

Figure 22.3 shows the relationship between *flows* of public-sector net borrowing and the amassed *stocks* of public-sector net debt. The public-sector net debt-to-GDP ratio rose to 252 per cent in 1946 following the large deficits associated with the Second World War. Despite running deficits almost continuously, economic growth meant that the debt-to-GDP

KI 26 p309

Definition

Public-sector (or general government) net debt Gross public-sector (or general government) debt minus liquid financial assets.

ratio was to fall below 22 per cent in 1990. The ratio then rose sharply to above 70 per cent following the financial crisis and the interventions to safeguard the financial system and the economy. It then rose above 100 per cent following the COVID-19 pandemic.

Current and capital expenditures. In presenting the public finances, it has become the custom to distinguish between ***current*** and ***capital expenditures***. Current expenditures involve the operational expenditures of the public sector, including the wages and salaries of public-sector staff, and the payments of welfare benefits. Capital expenditures are public-sector investment. Examples include expenditure on roads, hospitals and schools. Like all types of investment, they give rise to a stream of benefits over time.

So why might we wish to distinguish between current and capital expenditures? One reason is that capital expenditures generate long-term economic benefits which can be enjoyed into the future. In other words, by benefiting more than just the current generation, capital expenditure may help to promote intergenerational fairness. KI 4 p13

Another reason is that capital expenditures can increase potential output and thereby positively affect future growth rates. This, in turn, could increase future tax revenues and help to provide more sustainable foundations for the public finances over the longer term. TC 14 p468

However, the distinction between current and capital expenditures and the associated reasons for it is not without issues. Teachers and doctors, for instance, whose wages form part of public-sector current expenditure, would reasonably argue that their work generates benefits for future generations.

Since 1960, during which time total public-sector spending in the UK has averaged 40 per cent of GDP (see Figure 22.2), current spending has averaged 34 per cent of GDP and capital spending just 6 per cent of GDP. As we shall see in section 23.6, the UK's comparatively low share of public and private investment in GDP is argued to have contributed to a typically lower rate of growth in labour productivity than in competitor countries.

From the late 1960s through to 2000 the share of capital spending in total public-sector spending in the UK fell. What could have driven this change and does the composition of public spending matter?

Final expenditure and transfers. We can also distinguish between ***final expenditure*** on goods and services, and ***transfers***. This distinction recognises that the public sector directly adds to the economy's aggregate demand through its spending on goods and services, including the wages of public-sector workers, but also that it redistributes incomes between individuals and firms. Transfers include subsidies and benefit payments, such as payments to the unemployed.

Definitions

Current expenditure Recurrent spending on goods and factor payments.

Capital expenditure Investment expenditure; expenditure on assets.

Final expenditure Expenditure on goods and services. This is included in GDP and is part of aggregate demand.

Transfers Transfers of money from taxpayers to recipients of benefits and subsidies. They are not an injection into the circular flow but are the equivalent of a negative tax (i.e. a negative withdrawal).

BOX 22.1 COVID, CRISES AND PUBLIC-SECTOR SPENDING

CASE STUDIES AND APPLICATIONS

Will there by a displacement effect?

COVID-related public-sector spending

By the time of the UK Budget in March 2021, the cumulative cost of pandemic-related policy announcements was estimated at £344 billion. This comprised business support of £75 billion, support for households of £111 billion and support for public services, including health, education, and transport, of £158 billion.

Among the measures to support business were a series of loans and grants. These included a package of business interruption loan schemes, grants focused on the hospitality and leisure sectors and local restriction grants where COVID restrictions reduced demand or meant closure. Further sector-specific support included business rate holidays, reduced VAT rates and the Eat Out to Help Out Scheme, whereby pubs and restaurants were subsidised to allow customers to eat for half price from Mondays to Wednesdays (on food and soft drinks bills under £20).

Among the support for individuals were the Coronavirus Job Retention Scheme, which allowed firms to furlough workers and apply for a grant to cover some of their wages, the Self-Employed Income Support Scheme, self-assessment tax deferrals and mortgage payment holidays.

These measures contributed to public-sector spending as a share of national income (GDP) rise to 52 per cent in the financial year 2020/21 (up 12 percentage points on the financial year).

Peacock and Wiseman's Analysis

The chart shows the rise in public spending due to the pandemic in a historic perspective. It plots the total level of public-sector spending and its major components as a share of national income for each calendar year since 1900. Perhaps one of the most outstanding features of the chart is the impact of the two world wars on the relative size of public

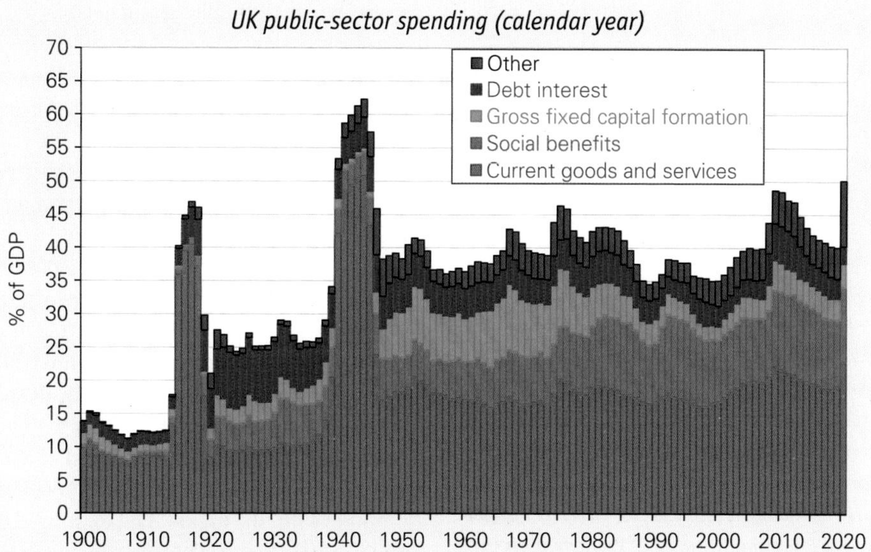

Sources: Based on data from *Millennium of Macroeconomic Data* (Bank of England) for 1900–1945, www.bankofengland.co.uk/statistics/research-datasets; and time series GZSN, ANSQ, ANLY, ANLO, EBFT and YBHA (ONS) from 1946 onwards, www.ons.gov.uk/economy/governmentpublicsectorandtaxes/publicsectorfinance/

spending. In particular, not only does the spending-to-GDP ratio rise during each war, but the size afterwards, even a few years later, returns to the pre-war level.

The upward displacement in the public spending-to-GDP ratio led to Alan Peacock and Jack Wiseman proposing two key ideas.[1]

Tolerable tax burden. This can be thought of as the tax burden that an average voter might be willing to tolerate. It is important because it acts as a constraint on public spending, at least over the longer term. The higher taxes paid to help fund the war may have resulted in an upward shift in the tolerable tax burden, therefore allowing public spending to rise relative to national income after the war.

Inspection effect. This is the effect of the wars 'shining a light' on issues where society believes that more government intervention may be needed. An inspection effect can therefore increase the tolerable tax burden.

The idea of an inspection effect may be particularly relevant in the aftermath of the global financial crisis and, perhaps even more so, the COVID-19 pandemic. This is because major changes in the role of the state and, in particular, the introduction of major social reforms occurred in the aftermath of the wars.

Examples of such reforms include the 1920 Unemployment Insurance Act which saw the introduction of the 'dole system' of payments to unemployed workers, the 1946 National Insurance Act which established a comprehensive system of social security and the 1946 National Health Service Act which led to the introduction of the NHS in 1948. The two Parliamentary Acts of 1946 were the result of the Beveridge Report, published in November 1942. Sir William Beveridge, a British economist and Liberal politician, led a report commissioned by the UK government in 1941 to consider reforms to social insurance, social security and social policy.

In terms of a purely statistical impact, the Beveridge reforms have contributed to a significant increase in the relative size of public-sector spending and, in particular, in expenditures on social benefits. Since 1950, total spending has been around 40 per cent of GDP, while that on social benefits has been just under 9 per cent of GDP. However, perhaps more importantly, these post-war reforms have had a lasting impact on British society and continue to shape public debates around the role of the state.

It is of course too early to draw any conclusions about the legacy of the pandemic for public spending or, more generally, for government intervention. Nonetheless, the pandemic has shone its own light brightly on many social issues, such as social care, health care, inequality, discrimination, poor transport infrastructure, educational opportunities and inter-generational issues. It is to be seen whether a displacement effect, in whatever form that takes, will arise as a result of the pandemic and its effects on the economy and society.

1. *Can the tolerable tax fall as well as rise?*
2. *In what ways other than in the size of total public-spending might an inspection effect influence government policy?*

Undertake desktop research into the Beveridge Report. Write a briefing note highlighting the key outcomes of the report and the impact that the Report has subsequently had on British economic and social policy.

1 Alan Peacock and Jack Wiseman, *The Growth in Public Expenditure in the United Kingdom*, Princeton University Press (1961), www.nber.org/books-and-chapters/growth-public-expenditure-united-kingdom

Key fiscal indicators

Sustainability of the public finances

We can use a range of fiscal indicators to assess the financial position of government and the whole public sector. The most commonly used indicators are those that convey information about the prudence or sustainability of the public sector's finances.

We can identify four measures which, in one way or another, allow us to say something about prudence or sustainability.

First is *net borrowing* by the government or the broader public sector (or its close counterpart in the net cash requirement); second is *net debt*. As we have seen, the first captures the relative flow receipts in comparison to its total expenditure, while the second measures the accumulated debt stock that has arisen from deficits.

A third indicator of sustainability is the ***current budget deficit***. If revenues are less than the sum of its *current* expenditures, then government or the broader public sector runs a deficit on the current budget. This means that the public sector, by not even meeting the full cost of its current expenditures out of its receipts, is also unable to meet any of the cost of its capital expenditures. As well as implications for the immediate sustainability of public finances, the constraints that a current budget deficit can place on capital expenditures could, as we discussed above, have implications for future economic growth and for the well-being of future generations. TC 14 p468

The fourth indicator of sustainability is the ***primary surplus (or deficit)***. This occurs when receipts are greater (or less) than expenditures *excluding* interest payments. The primary surplus is important for analysing the path of the debt-to-GDP ratio. The higher the real rate of interest on government debt and the higher the ratio of government debt to GDP, the higher must be the primary surplus to prevent the debt-to-GDP ratio from rising. The mathematics of this is demonstrated in the next section.

**The relationship between the primary surplus and the debt-to-GDP ratio*

KI 26 p309 For the debt-to-GDP ratio to fall requires that the public sector operates a given primary surplus-to-GDP ratio.

To see why this is so, we can use a rule of thumb that connects the primary surplus-to-GDP (PS/Y) ratio and the debt-to-GDP (D/Y) ratio. Then, to calculate the required primary surplus-to-GDP ratio to maintain the current value of the debt-to-GDP ratio, we multiply the current debt-to-GDP ratio (D/Y) by the sum of the *real* rate of interest (r) minus the *real* economic growth rate (g). This gives us what is referred to as the 'debt sustainability rule':

$$\frac{PS}{Y} = \frac{D}{Y} \times (r - g) \quad (1)$$

To illustrate the sustainability arithmetic, consider a country where the public-sector net debt-to-GDP ratio (D/Y) is currently 0.5 (i.e. 50 per cent). Assume that the real interest rate on borrowing (r) is 3 per cent and the annual real rate of economic growth (g) is 1 per cent. For the debt-to-GDP ratio (D/Y) to remain at its current level, the country will need to run a primary surplus equivalent to 1 per cent of GDP ($0.5 \times (3 - 1)$). If, however, the current debt-to-GDP ratio were currently 1 (i.e. 100 per cent), then it would need to run a primary surplus-to-GDP ratio of 2 per cent ($1 \times (3 - 1)$). 

Thus a country where the average real interest rate on public debt instruments (r) is greater than the real economic growth rate (g) will have to run primary surpluses for its debt-to-GDP ratio to fall. Furthermore, the required primary surplus-to-GDP ratio will be higher if the country has an already high debt-to-GDP ratio. In other words, the sustainability arithmetic tends to get more difficult for governments to comply with, the higher their existing debt-to-GDP ratio. This analysis is explored further, along with data from a number of countries, in Case Study 22.4 on the student website.

? *What primary balance-to-GDP ratio would a country need to run to sustain a debt-to-GDP ratio of 60 per cent if the real interest rate is 2 per cent and economic growth is 4 per cent?*

Figure 22.4 shows net borrowing, the primary deficit and net debt of general governments across 39 advanced economies since 2001. During this time, net borrowing has averaged 4.2 per cent and the primary deficit 2.7 per cent of GDP. We can also clearly see the deterioration in the deficit balances with the interventions following the global financial crisis and the COVID-19 pandemic. These led to a marked increase in the public-sector net debt-to-GDP ratio.

The business cycle and the public finances

When analysing the fiscal indicators, it is important to recognise that their values are affected by the state of the economy. In other words, there is both a structural and a cyclical component determining the path of our fiscal measures.

If the economy is booming, with people earning high incomes, the amount paid in taxes will be high. In a booming economy the level of unemployment will be low. Thus the amount paid out in unemployment benefits will also be low. The combined effect of increased tax revenues and

Definitions

Current budget deficit The amount by which government or public-sector expenditures classified as current expenditures exceed public-sector receipts.

Primary surplus (or deficit) The situation when the sum of government or public-sector expenditures excluding interest payments on its debt is less than (greater than) the sector's receipts.

Figure 22.4 General government deficits and debt in advanced economies

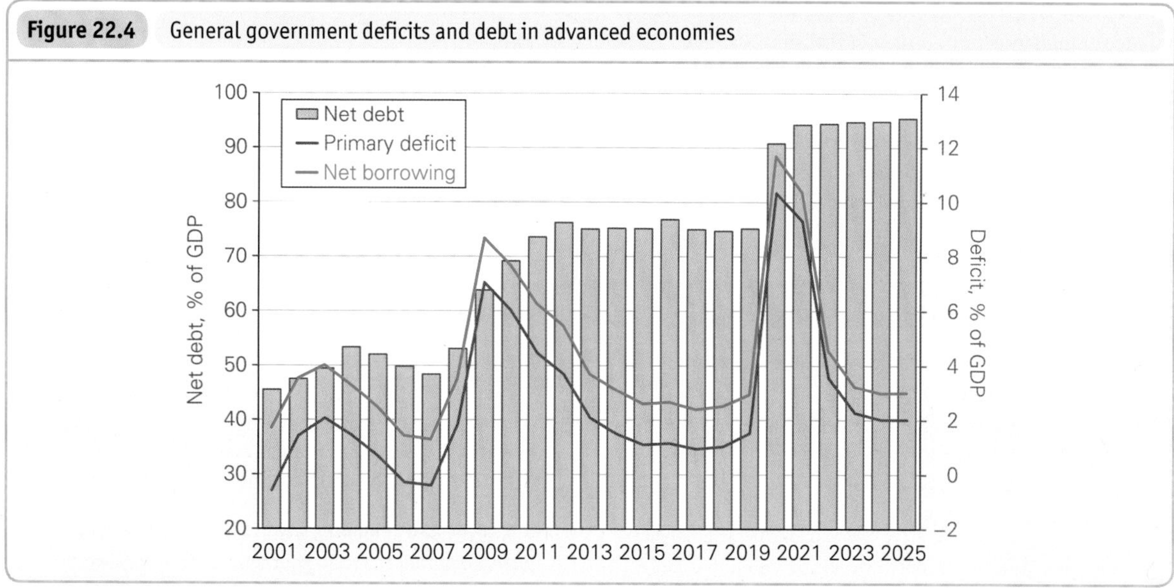

Notes: Data are for calendar years and from 2021 are forecasts; 39 economies based on IMF country classification.
Source: *World Economic Outlook*, IMF (April 2021), https://www.imf.org/en/Publications/WEO/weo-database/2021/April

reduced benefits is to improve public-sector balances, such as public-sector net borrowing. Indeed, rather than a reduced deficit there could be public-sector surplus. By contrast, if the economy were depressed, tax revenues would be low and the amount paid in benefits would be high. The public-sector deficit would thus be high.

How is the public-sector debt-to-GDP ratio likely to be affected by the state of the economy?

Since, therefore, the values of fiscal indicators are not entirely due to deliberate government policy, they may not give a very good guide to government intentions or to the longer-term financial well-being of government. By cyclically-adjusting measures of public-sector deficits or surpluses we remove their cyclical component. The deficit or surplus that would arise if the economy were producing at the potential level of national income is termed the ***structural deficit or surplus***. Remember that the potential level of national income is where there is no excess or deficiency of aggregate demand: where the output gap is zero (see page 466 and Box 15.3).

This relationship between the public-sector deficit or surplus and the state of the economy is illustrated in Figure 22.5. The tax revenue function is upward sloping. Its slope depends on tax rates. The government expenditure function (which in this diagram includes transfer payments, such as unemployment benefits) is drawn as downward sloping, showing that at higher levels of income and employment less is paid out in benefits. As can be clearly seen, there is only one level of income (Y_1) where there is a public-sector financial balance. Below this level of income there will be a public-sector deficit. Above this level there will be a surplus. The further income is from Y_1, the bigger will be the deficit or surplus.

Figure 22.5 National income and the size of the public-sector deficit or surplus

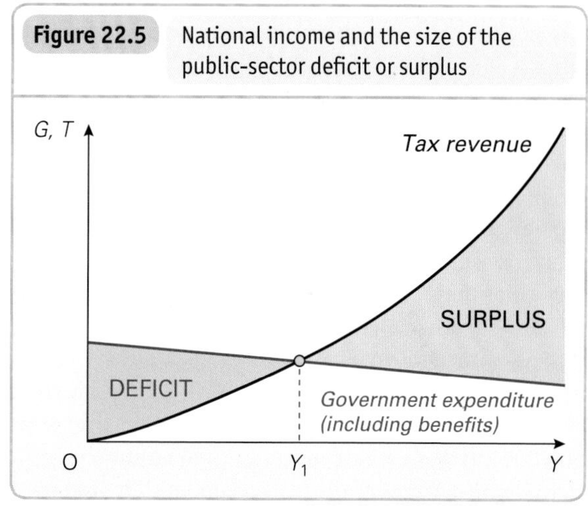

The fiscal stance

The government's ***fiscal stance*** refers to whether it is pursuing an expansionary or contractionary fiscal policy. Does the fact that countries such as the UK in most years run public sector deficits mean that their government's fiscal stance is mainly expansionary? Would the mere existence of a surplus mean that the stance was contractionary? The answer is no.

Definitions

Structural deficit (or surplus) The public-sector deficit (or surplus) that would occur if the economy were operating at the potential level of national income: i.e. one where there is a zero output gap.

Fiscal stance How expansionary or contractionary the Budget is.

Whether the economy expands or contracts depends on the balance of *total* injections and *total* withdrawals.

What we need to focus on is *changes* in the size of the deficit or surplus. If the deficit this year is lower than last year, then (*ceteris paribus*) aggregate demand will be lower this year than last. The reason is that either government expenditure (an injection) must have fallen, or tax revenues (a withdrawal) must have increased, or a combination of the two.

To conclude, the size of the deficit or surplus is a poor guide to the stance of fiscal policy. A large deficit *may* be due to a deliberate policy of increasing aggregate demand, but it may be due simply to the fact that the economy is depressed.

Section summary

1. The public sector comprises general government and public corporations. There exist a range of fiscal indicators that allow us to analyse the fiscal position and well-being of the public sector or its component sectors.
2. Key fiscal indicators include those that assess the sustainability of the public sector's finances. We can estimate a required primary surplus-to-GDP ratio needed to prevent the ratio of public-sector debt to GDP from rising. Countries with higher existing debt-to-GDP ratios, higher real interest costs and lower real rates of economic growth will need to operate larger primary surpluses (or smaller deficits) to prevent the ratio from rising further.
3. The government's fiscal policy influences the size of its budget deficit or surplus. Its size alone, however, is a poor guide to the government's fiscal stance. A large deficit, for example, may simply be due to the fact that the economy is in recession and therefore tax receipts are low. A better guide is whether the change in the deficit or surplus will be expansionary or contractionary.

22.2 THE USE OF FISCAL POLICY

The fiscal choices of government relate to decisions about public expenditures and taxation. These choices can shape future government receipts or expenditures. For example, the design of a country's income tax or benefits system evolves over time. As governments make policy changes, they shape the tax and benefit systems, including their relationship with macroeconomic variables such as national income or unemployment.

More generally, today's choices by government can commit future governments to certain expenditure and taxation flows. Indeed, some expenditure and taxation receipts *automatically* change as the macroeconomic environment changes. For example, income tax receipts automatically increase as nominal national income increases. The design of the income tax system and the rates and bands determine just how much receipts will change as nominal national income changes.

However, governments also make *discretionary* choices which deliberately manipulate taxes or levels of spending to affect current levels of aggregate demand, regardless of the automatic effects that occur across the business cycle. These decisions may then be reversed as economic conditions change.

For example, following the global financial crisis and the COVID-19 pandemic, governments around the world introduced a series of measures that were designed to support the economy. In other words, there was a significant net injection by the government into the economy. However, as the policy focus shifted to reducing the burgeoning public-sector deficit, fiscal policy was tightened.

In this section we begin by considering how expenditure and taxation flows automatically change across the business cycle and, in so doing, help to stabilise the economy. We then move on to discuss why governments might make deliberate changes to taxation and government expenditures and how effective they may be in managing the economy.

Automatic fiscal stabilisers

We saw from Figure 22.5 that the size of the public-sector surplus or deficit will automatically vary according to the level of national income. The effect of this will be to reduce the level of fluctuations in national income without the government having to take any deliberate action.

Taxes whose revenues rise as national income rises and benefits that fall as national income rises are called ***automatic stabilisers***. They have the effect of reducing the size of the multiplier, reducing both upward and downward movements of national income. Thus, in theory, the business cycle should be dampened by such built-in stabilisers. The more taxes rise or benefits fall, the bigger will be the *mpt* (the net marginal tax propensity). Remember that we defined this

Definition

Automatic fiscal stabilisers Tax revenues that rise and government expenditure that falls as national income rises. The more they change with income, the bigger the stabilising effect on national income.

as the proportion of any rise in income going in taxes and reduced benefits. The bigger the *mpt*, the smaller will be the multiplier and the greater will be the stabilising effect.

Draw an injections and withdrawals diagram, with a fairly flat W curve. Mark the equilibrium level of national income. Now draw a second steeper W curve passing through the same point. This second W curve would correspond to the case where tax rates were higher. Assuming now that there has been an increase in injections, draw a second J line above the first. Mark the new equilibrium level of national income with each of the two W curves. You can see that national income rises less with the steeper W curve. The higher tax rates are having a dampening effect on the multiplier.

The effectiveness of automatic stabilisers

Automatic stabilisers have the obvious advantage that they act instantly as soon as aggregate demand fluctuates. By contrast, it may take some time before the government can institute discretionary changes in taxes or government expenditure, especially if forecasting is unreliable.

Nevertheless, automatic stabilisers can never be the complete answer to the problem of fluctuations. Their effect is merely to reduce the multiplier – to reduce the severity of fluctuations, not to eliminate them altogether.

In addition, they tend to suffer two specific drawbacks: adverse effects on aggregate supply and the problem of 'fiscal drag'. Let us examine each in turn.

Adverse supply-side effects

High tax rates may discourage effort and initiative. The higher the marginal tax rate (*mpt*), the greater the stability provided by the tax system. But the higher tax rates are, the more likely they are to create a disincentive to work and to invest. For example, steeply progressive income taxes may discourage workers from doing overtime or seeking promotion. A higher marginal rate of income tax is equivalent to a higher marginal cost of working. People may prefer to work less and substitute leisure for income. The substitution effect of more progressive taxes may thus outweigh the income effect. These issues were examined in detail in section 11.2 (see pages 344–6).

KI 7 p36

High unemployment benefits may increase equilibrium unemployment. High unemployment benefits, by reducing the hardship of being unemployed, may encourage people to spend longer looking for the 'right' job rather than taking the first job offered. This has the effect of increasing unemployment and thus of shifting the Phillips curve to the right. This is because a longer average period of job search represents a higher level of friction in the economy and thus a higher natural (or equilibrium) level of unemployment.

High income-related benefits may create a poverty trap. The higher the level of income-related benefits and the more steeply they taper off, the greater will be the problem of the 'poverty trap'. What is the point in unemployed people seeking jobs, or people in very low-paid jobs seeking better ones, if as a result they lose their benefits and end up being little or no better off than before? The more that people are discouraged in this way, the lower will be the level of aggregate supply. (The question of the poverty trap was also examined in Chapter 11 (see pages 350–1).)

The problem of fiscal drag

Automatic stabilisers help to reduce upward and downward movements in national income. This is fine if the current level of income is the *desirable* level. But suppose that there is currently a deep recession in the economy, with mass unemployment. Who would want to stabilise the economy at this level?

In these circumstances, if the economy began to recover, the automatic stabilisers would act as a drag on the expansion. This is known as ***fiscal drag***. By reducing the size of the multiplier, the automatic stabilisers reduce the magnitude of the recovery. Similarly, they act as a drag on discretionary policy: the more powerful the automatic stabilisers are, the bigger the change in *G* or *T* that would be necessary to achieve a given change in national income.

Discretionary fiscal policy

Automatic stabilisers cannot prevent fluctuations. They merely reduce their magnitude. If there is a fundamental disequilibrium in the economy or substantial fluctuations in other injections and withdrawals, the government may choose to *alter* the level of government expenditure or the rates of taxation. This is known as ***discretionary fiscal policy***. It involves *shifting* the *J* and *W* lines.

In the UK, changes in taxation and some changes in government expenditure are announced by the Chancellor of the Exchequer in the Budget. Some of these changes apply to the coming financial year; some apply to the next financial year or even the one after that.

Since Budgets are normally held only once per year, 'fine-tuning' aggregate demand on a week-by-week or month-by-month basis is left to monetary policy – to changes in interest rates (see section 22.3). Occasionally, however, changes are made between Budgets. The global financial crisis and, in particular, the COVID-19 pandemic were to see a series of fiscal measures introduced, some of which required their own fine-tuning as events unfolded.

Note that discretionary changes in taxation or government expenditure, as well as being used to alter the level of

Definitions

Fiscal drag The tendency of automatic fiscal stabilisers to reduce the recovery of an economy from recession.

Discretionary fiscal policy Deliberate changes in tax rates or the level of government expenditure in order to influence the level of aggregate demand.

aggregate demand (fiscal policy), are also used for other purposes, including the following:

- *Altering aggregate supply*. Examples include tax incentives to encourage people to work more, or increased government expenditure on training or on transport infrastructure (e.g. roads and railways). We look at such 'supply-side policies' in Chapter 23.
- *Altering the distribution of income*. As Chapter 11 explained, taxation and benefits are the government's major means of redistributing incomes from the rich to the poor.

Fiscal impulse

The size of changes in discretionary policy can be measured by the ***fiscal impulse***. This attempts to identify non-cyclical policy responses and then determine whether the fiscal stance has tightened, loosened, or remained unchanged.

Definition

Fiscal impulse A measure of the change in the fiscal stance arising from discretionary fiscal policy changes.

BOX 22.2 THE FISCAL IMPULSE

Measuring changes in the fiscal stance

There are two principal ways in which we can measure the extent to which discretionary fiscal measures are supporting the economy: a bottom-up or top-down approach. Both approaches attempt to capture the size and direction of impulses on the economy arising from fiscal policy changes. In other words, they measure fiscal impulses.

Bottom-up approach: based on the cost of fiscal measures

This simply involves listing individual fiscal measures and then calculating their cost. These can be separated into 'above the line measures', which are measures that directly affect spending and revenues, and 'liquidity measures' which include loans, equity injections, and loan guarantees.

To illustrate the 'bottom-up approach', consider the following table which is a summary of the fiscal measures recorded by the IMF as of 5 June 2021 in response to the COVID-19 pandemic. The global discretionary fiscal policy response to the COVID-19 pandemic was estimated at this point to have involved additional spending and forgone revenues equivalent to 9.7 per cent of (2020) global GDP. When equity loans and guarantees are taken into consideration this figure rises to 15.9 per cent.

COVID-19 fiscal measures (as of 5 June 2021)

	US $ billions		% of 2020 GDP	
	Additional spending and forgone revenues	**Equity loans and guarantees**	**Additional spending and forgone revenues**	**Equity loans and guarantees**
India	93.3	138.6	3.5	5.2
China	710.6	192.7	4.8	1.3
France	251.9	399.8	9.6	15.2
Ireland	43.1	13.7	10.3	3.3
Italy	205.4	664.5	10.9	35.3
Germany	519.3	1058.0	13.6	27.8
UK	440.1	452.9	16.2	16.7
Japan	830.7	1429.2	16.5	28.3
USA	5328.3	510.0	25.4	2.4
Global	**10417.0**	**6132.0**	**9.7**	**6.2**

Source: *Fiscal Monitor: Database of Country Fiscal Measures in Response to the COVID-19 Pandemic*, IMF, www.imf.org/en/Topics/imf-and-covid19/Fiscal-Policies-Database-in-Response-to-COVID-19

Top-down approach: based on cyclically-adjusted budget balance

This assesses the fiscal stance by looking at the *level*, or more usually the *change*, of budget balance measures. One such example is the year-on-year change in the cyclically-adjusted general government deficit (CAGD) as a percentage of potential GDP.

By adjusting for the position of the economy in the business cycle and by excluding debt interest payments, the CAGD allows us to isolate more accurately the effect of discretionary policy changes. A larger deficit or a smaller surplus indicates a fiscal loosening, while a smaller deficit or a larger surplus indicates a fiscal tightening.

It is therefore commonly measured by *changes* in cyclically-adjusted budget balances: i.e. structural balances. A deterioration in a structural balance (a rise in the structural deficit or fall in the structural surplus) indicates a loosening of the fiscal stance, whereas an improvement indicates a tightening. Box 22.2 analyses the fiscal impulse for several countries over recent years.

The fiscal impulse should not be confused with fiscal multipliers. The fiscal impulse is measuring the magnitude of change in discretionary fiscal policy whereas multipliers, such as the government purchases multiplier, measure the impact of these changes on real national income. As with any economic impulse (shock) their impact will depend on the propagation mechanisms that transmit the impulse through the economy.

Let us now compare the relative effects of changing government expenditure and changing taxes. Will a £100 million increase in government expenditure have the same effect as a £100 million cut in taxes? Will the multiplier be the same in each case?

EXPLORING ECONOMICS

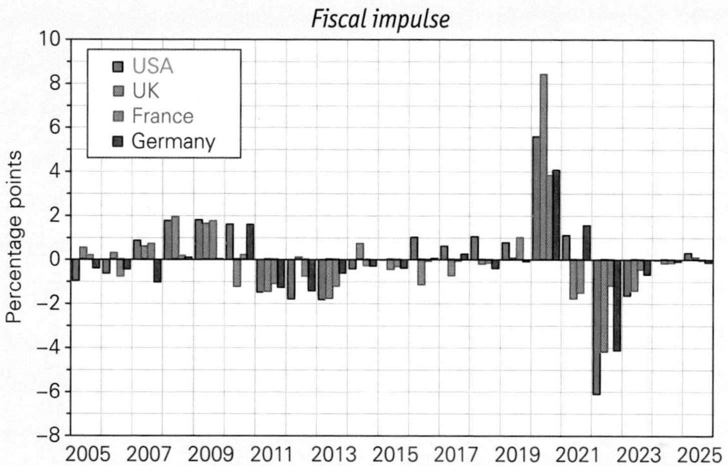

Note: Data are the annual percentage point change in the cyclically-adjusted general government deficit as a percentage of potential GDP.
Source: Based on data from *IMF World Economic Outlook Database* and *Fiscal Monitor*, Table A3, IMF (April 2021), www.imf.org/en/Publications/

The chart shows the fiscal impulse for a sample of countries from 2005 based on the percentage point change in the CAGD-to-potential-GDP ratio. Positive values indicate a fiscal loosening (rise in the CAGD-to-potential-GDP ratio) and negative values a fiscal tightening (fall in the CAGD-to-potential-GDP ratio).

The chart shows the extent of the *loosening* of countries' fiscal stance in 2020 in response to the COVID-19 pandemic. In the UK, for example, the CAGD-to-potential-GDP ratio rose by over 8.5 percentage points to 11 per cent. This represents a fiscal impulse of 8.5 per cent of GDP. Although the budget deficit was to remain high across our sample of countries, a *tightening* of fiscal policy followed the waning of the pandemic, particularly so in the UK and the USA.

The scale of the fiscal loosening in response to the pandemic is seen to dwarf that in response to the global financial crisis. The fiscal response in the UK and the USA, which were particularly badly affected by the financial crisis, led to a cumulative increase in the CAGD-to-potential-GDP ratio in 2008 and 2009 of around 3.5 percentage points. However, as in the aftermath of the pandemic, concerns about the size of deficits led governments to tighten policy quite quickly. This meant that over the period from 2008 to 2014 the cumulative fiscal impulse in both countries was close to zero.

How is the concept of the fiscal impulse different from that of a fiscal multiplier?

Undertake desktop research into the fiscal policy interventions of a country of your choice that followed the global financial crisis. Prepare a 'bottom-up' schedule of these interventions to capture the scale of support for the economy.

Discretionary fiscal policy: changing G

If government expenditure on goods and services (roads, health care, education, etc.) is raised, this will create a full multiplied rise in national income. The reason is that all the money gets spent and thus all of it goes to boosting aggregate demand.

Show the effect of an increase in government expenditure by using (a) the injections and withdrawals diagram; (b) the income/expenditure diagram (see Figures 17.8 and 17.10 on pages 542 and 544).

Discretionary fiscal policy: changing T

Cutting taxes by £1 million will have a smaller effect on national income than raising government expenditure on goods and services by £1 million. The reason is that cutting taxes increases people's *disposable* incomes, of which only *part* will be spent. Part will be withdrawn into extra savings, imports and other taxes. In other words, not all the tax cuts will be passed on round the circular flow of income as extra expenditure.

The proportion of the cut in taxes that will be withdrawn is given by the *mpw*, and the proportion that will circulate round the flow is given by the mpc_d. Thus if the mpc_d were 4/5, the tax multiplier would only be 4/5 of the normal multiplier.[1] If the mpc_d were 2/3, the tax multiplier would only be 2/3 of the normal multiplier, and so on. The formula for the tax multiplier (k_t) becomes

$$k_t = mpc_d \times k$$

Thus if the normal multiplier were 5 (given an mpc_d of 4/5), the tax multiplier would be $4/5 \times 5 = 4$. If the normal multiplier were 4 (given an mpc_d of 3/4), the tax multiplier would be $3/4 \times 4 = 3$, and so on. It should be obvious from this that the tax multiplier is always 1 less than the normal multiplier:

$$k_t = k - 1$$

Since the tax multiplier is smaller than the government expenditure multiplier, to achieve a given rise in income through tax cuts would therefore require a bigger budget deficit than if it were achieved through increased government expenditure. In other words, the required tax cut would be bigger than the required government expenditure increase.

Why will the multiplier effect of government transfer payments such as child benefit, pensions and social security be less than the full multiplier effect given by government expenditure on goods and services? Will this 'transfer payments multiplier' be the same as the tax multiplier? (Clue: will the recipients of such benefits have the same mpc_d as the average person?)

1 Strictly speaking, the tax multiplier is negative, since a *rise* in taxes causes a *fall* in national income.

The effectiveness of discretionary fiscal policy

How successful will discretionary fiscal policy be? Can it 'fine-tune' demand? Can it achieve the level of national income that the government would like it to achieve?

There are two main problem areas with discretionary fiscal policy. The first concerns the *magnitude* of the effects. If *G* or *T* is changed, how much will *total* injections and withdrawals change? What will be the size of the multiplier? How much will a change in aggregate demand affect output and employment, and how much will it affect prices?

TC 15 p543

The second concerns the *timing* of the effects. How quickly can policy be changed and how quickly will the changes affect the economy?

KI 33 p377

Problems of magnitude

Before changing government expenditure or taxation, the government will need to calculate the effect of any such change on national income, employment and inflation. Predicting these effects, however, is often very unreliable for a number of reasons.

TC 15 p543

Predicting the effect of changes in government expenditure

A rise in government expenditure of £*x* may lead to a rise in total injections (relative to withdrawals) that is smaller than £*x*. This will occur if the rise in government expenditure *replaces* a certain amount of private expenditure. For example, a rise in expenditure on state education may dissuade some parents from sending their children to private schools. Similarly, an improvement in the National Health Service may lead to fewer people paying for private treatment.

Crowding out. If the government relies on ***pure fiscal policy*** – that is, if it does not finance an increase in the budget deficit by increasing the money supply – it will have to borrow the money from the non-bank private sector. It will thus be competing with the private sector for finance and will have to offer higher interest rates. This will force the private sector also to offer higher interest rates, which may discourage firms from investing and individuals from buying on credit. Thus government borrowing *crowds out* private borrowing. In the extreme case, the fall in consumption and investment may completely offset the rise in government expenditure, with the result that aggregate demand does not rise at all.

Figure 22.6 illustrates the extent of crowding out. (It is the same as Figure 19.8 on page 613.) The rise in government expenditure shifts the injections line from J_1 to J_2

Definition

Pure fiscal policy Fiscal policy that does not involve any change in money supply.

Figure 22.6 The monetary effects of a rise in injections

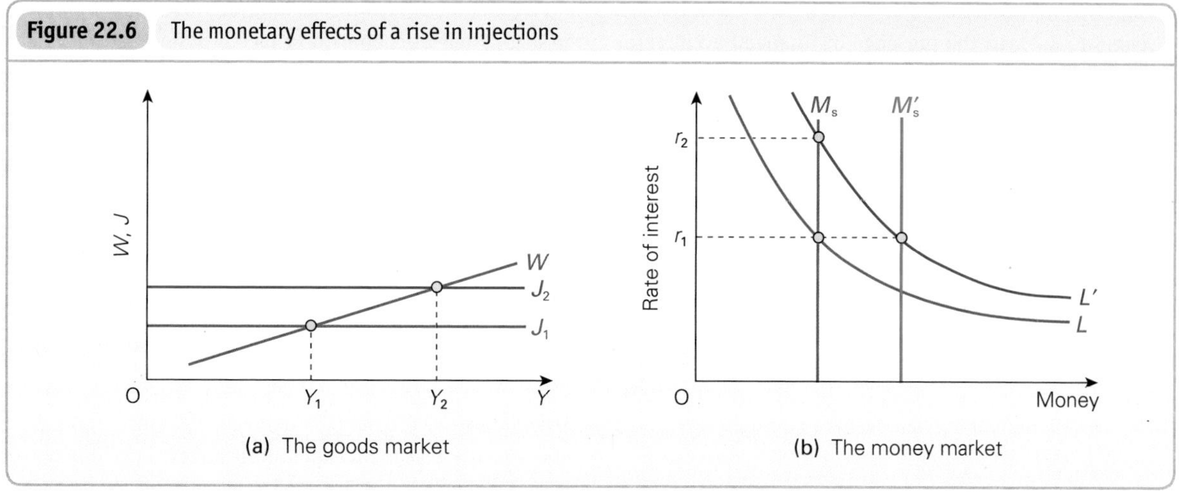

in Figure 22.6(a). The full multiplier effect of this would be a rise in national income to Y_2. However, the increased government expenditure leads to an increased demand for money. In Figure 22.6(b), the liquidity preference curve shifts to L'. This raises the real interest rate to r_2. Note that we are assuming that the money supply is purely *exogenous* – i.e. does not vary with the demand for money – and that, therefore, the money supply 'curve' is a vertical straight line (M_s).

The higher real rate of interest reduces investment. The injections line falls below J_2, and, as a result, national income does not rise as far as Y_2. The amount by which actual income falls short of Y_2 measures the extent of crowding out.

The amount of crowding out from pure fiscal policy depends on three things:

- The shape of the L curve. The flatter the curve, the less will interest rates rise. A greater amount of liquidity will be released from idle balances and there will be a bigger increase in the velocity of circulation.
- Whether money supply is exogenous. If the extra demand for money leads to banks creating extra credit, the money supply curve will be upward sloping, not vertical. The more money is created, the flatter will be the M_s curve, the less interest rates will rise and the less will be the crowding out.
- The responsiveness of investment (and consumption) to a change in real interest rates. The more responsive investment is to a rise in real interest rates, the more will the J curve shift downwards and the bigger will be the crowding-out effect.

If the fiscal policy is not *pure* fiscal policy, if the extra government borrowing is financed by borrowing from the banking sector, then the supply of money curve will shift to the right. If it were to shift as far as M'_s, the real rate of interest would remain at r_1 and there would be no crowding out.

How do people's expectations influence the extent of crowding out?

Predicting the effect of changes in taxes

A cut in taxes, by raising people's real disposable income, increases not only the amount they spend but also the amount they save. The problem is that it is not easy to predict the relative size of these two increases. In part it depends on whether people feel that the cut in tax is only temporary, in which case they may simply save the extra disposable income, or permanent, in which case they may adjust their consumption upwards.

Do theories of the long-run and short-run consumption function help us to understand consumer reactions to a change in taxes? (See section 17.1 and Case Studies 17.1–17.4 on the student website.)

Predicting the resulting multiplied effect on national income

Even if the government *could* predict the net initial effect on injections and withdrawals, the extent to which national income will change is still hard to predict for the following reasons:

- The size of the *multiplier* may be difficult to predict. This is because the mpc_d and mpw may fluctuate. For example, the amount of a rise in income that households save or consume will depend on their expectations about future price and income changes.
- Induced investment through the *accelerator* (see pages 551–3) is also extremely difficult to predict. It may be that a relatively small fiscal stimulus will be all that is necessary to restore business confidence, and that induced investment will rise substantially. In such a case, fiscal policy can be seen as a 'pump primer'. It is used to *start* the process of recovery, and then the *continuation* of the recovery is left to the market. But for pump priming to work, businesspeople must *believe* that it will work. Business confidence can change very rapidly and in ways that could not have been foreseen a few months earlier.
- The behaviour of commercial banks may also be hard to predict. Credit conditions may be pro-cyclical, perhaps

significantly so, resulting in a financial accelerator (see pages 623–5). In the presence of financial accelerator effects small changes in fiscal policy can have amplified effects on national income.

- Multiplier-accelerator interactions. If the initial multiplier and accelerator effects are difficult to estimate, their interaction will be virtually impossible to estimate. Small divergences in investment from what was initially predicted will become magnified as time progresses.

Random shocks

Forecasts cannot take into account the unpredictable, such as the attack on the World Trade Center in September 2001, or COVID-19 in 2020–1. Even events that might have been predicted, such as the banking crisis of 2007–9, often are not. Unfortunately, unpredictable or unpredicted events do occur and may seriously undermine the government's fiscal policy.

Give some examples of these random shocks.

Problems of timing

KI 33 p377

Fiscal policy can involve considerable time lags. If these are long enough, fiscal policy could even be *de*stabilising. Expansionary policies taken to cure a recession may not come into effect until the economy has *already* recovered and is experiencing a boom. Under these circumstances, expansionary policies are quite inappropriate: they simply worsen the problems of overheating. Similarly, contractionary policies taken to prevent excessive expansion may not take effect until the economy has already peaked and is plunging into recession. The contractionary policies only deepen the recession.

This problem is illustrated in Figure 22.7. Path (a) shows the course of the business cycle without government intervention. Ideally, with no time lags, the economy should be dampened in stage 2 and stimulated in stage 4. This would make the resulting course of the business cycle more like path (b), or even, if the policy were perfectly stabilising, a straight line.

With time lags, however, contractionary policies taken in stage 2 may not come into effect until stage 4, and expansionary policies taken in stage 4 may not come into effect until stage 2. In this case, the resulting course of the business cycle will be more like path (c). Quite obviously, in these circumstances 'stabilising' fiscal policy actually makes the economy less stable.

There are five possible lags associated with fiscal policy.

Time lag to recognition. Since the business cycle can be irregular and forecasting unreliable, governments may be unwilling to take action until they are convinced that the problem is serious.

Time lag between recognition and action. Most significant changes in government expenditure have to be planned well in advance. The government cannot increase spending on motorways overnight or suddenly start building new hospitals. As far as taxes are concerned, these can normally be changed only at the time of the Budget, and will not be instituted until the new financial year or at some other point in the future. As Budgets normally occur annually, there could be a considerable time lag if the problems are recognised a long time before the Budget.

Time lag between action and changes taking effect. A change in tax rates may not immediately affect tax payments, as some taxes are paid in arrears and new rates may take a time to apply.

Time lag between changes in government expenditure and taxation and the resulting change in national income, prices and employment. The multiplier round takes time. Accelerator effects take time. The multiplier and accelerator go on interacting. It all takes time.

Consumption may respond slowly to changes in taxation. The short-run consumption function tends to be flatter than the long-run function.

If the fluctuations in aggregate demand can be forecast, and if the lengths of the time lags are known, then all is not lost. At least the fiscal measures can be taken early and their delayed effects can be taken into account.

Figure 22.7 Fiscal policy: stabilising or destabilising?

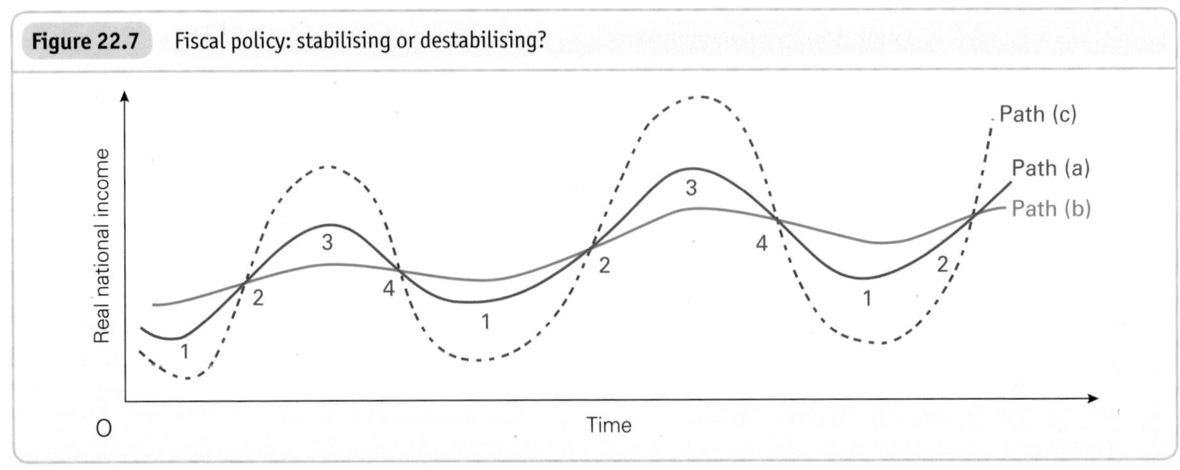

BOX 22.3 **RIDING A SWITCHBACK** EXPLORING ECONOMICS

A parable for finance ministers

Imagine that you are driving a car along a straight but undulating road. These undulations are not regular: some of the hills are steep, some are gentle; some are long, some are short.

You are given the instruction that you must keep the car going at a constant speed. To do this, you will need to accelerate going up the hills and brake going down them.

There is a serious problem, however. The car is no ordinary car. It has the following distinctly unusual features:

- The front windscreen and side windows are blacked out, so you cannot see where you are going! All you can see is where you have been by looking in your rear-view mirror.
- The brake and accelerator pedals both work with a considerable and unpredictable delay.
- The car's suspension is so good that you cannot feel whether you are going up or downhill. You can only judge this by looking in your mirror.
- Finally (you are relieved to know), the car has a special sensor and automatic steering that keep it in the correct lane.

As you are going along, you see that the road behind you is higher, and you realise that you are going downhill. The car gets faster and faster. You brake – but nothing happens. In your zeal to slow the car down, you put your foot down on the brake as hard as you can.

When the brake eventually does come on, it comes on very strongly. By this time, the car has already reached the bottom of the hill. As yet, however, you do not realise this and are still braking. But now the car is going up the next hill with the brakes still on. Looking in your mirror, you eventually realise this. You take your foot off the brake and start accelerating. But the pedals do not respond. The car is still slowing down rapidly, and you only just manage to reach the top of the hill.

Then, as you start going down the other side, the brakes eventually come off and the accelerator comes on . . .

This famous parable – first told by Frank Paish, Professor of Economics at the LSE, some 40 years ago – demonstrates how 'stabilising' activity can in fact be destabilising. When applied to fiscal policy, long and uncertain time lags can mean that the government can end up stimulating the economy in a boom and contracting it in a slump.

So what should be done? One alternative, of course, would be to try to reduce the time lags and to improve forecasting. But failing this, the best policy may be to do nothing: to take a 'steady as you go' or 'fixed throttle' approach to running the economy. Going back to the car analogy, a fixed throttle will not prevent the car from going faster downhill and slower uphill, but at least it will not make the speed even more irregular.

A recent version of the parable

In an article in the *New Statesman* on what Keynes' response would have been to the recovery and getting the public-sector deficit down, Vince Cable, the then UK Business Secretary, wrote:

> As in many economic policy disputes, much of the ideological rhetoric conceals different forecasting assumptions – in respect of the cyclical, as opposed to structural, deficit; the influence of asset prices on consumer behaviour; the impact of the unorthodox monetary policy of quantitative easing (QE) and its interaction with the velocity of circulation of money; and the weight to be attached to business confidence and sentiment in financial markets. Amid such uncertainty, economic policymaking is like driving a car with an opaque windscreen, a large rear-view mirror and poor brakes.[1]

So what are the policy implications of this uncertainty and the time lags in response to government policy initiatives? The Coalition government saw the answer in a fiscal rule of getting the deficit down and thereby restoring long-term confidence in financial markets and encouraging private investment.

Critics of the government argued that policy needed to be flexible and responsive to current circumstances. Even with the time lags associated with fiscal policy, it was probably better to ease back on cutting the deficit so quickly if demand appeared to falter rather than just sticking with the planned government expenditure cuts.

But at least there were the automatic fiscal stabilisers – the car's accelerator would automatically come on and the brake would be eased if the economy slowed down.

What would a fixed throttle approach to fiscal policy involve?

1 Vince Cable, 'Keynes would be on our side', *New Statesman* (12 January 2011).

Fiscal rules

Given the problems of pursuing active fiscal policy, many governments in recent years took a much more passive approach. Instead of the policy being changed as the economy changes, countries applied a set of fiscal rules.

The IMF in 2018[2] identified 96 countries using fiscal rules. These rules place some form of control on budgetary aggregates and can be categorised as either budget balance rules, debt rules, expenditure rules or revenue rules. These can differ according to whether they apply to central or general government (see pages 694–5) or to the whole public sector, their legal basis and the monitoring and enforcement procedures.

Designing rules for fiscal policy can be problematic. Economies are regularly hit by shocks. Some shocks may require more discretion than the current rules allow for. Hence, how flexible should any rules be?

2 'Second-Generation Fiscal Rules: Balancing Simplicity, Flexibility, and Enforceability', *Staff Discussion Notes*, IMF (13 April 2018), www.imf.org/en/Publications/Staff-Discussion-Notes/Issues/2018/04/12/Second-Generation-Fiscal-Rules-Balancing-Simplicity-Flexibility-and-Enforceability-45131

Following the severe disruption to the global economy that occurred with the credit crunch of 2008, countries resorted to discretionary fiscal policy to boost aggregate demand. Many abandoned fiscal rules – at least temporarily. However, rules were generally reinstated as the global economy pulled out of recession. In many cases, this heralded a 'second generation' of fiscal rules. These were often more flexible, for example allowing for more public investment or accounting for the impact of the business cycle. Many contained 'escape clauses' detailing those

BOX 22.4 THE EVOLUTION OF THE STABILITY AND GROWTH PACT

A supranational fiscal framework

Preparing for the euro

In signing the Maastricht Treaty in 1992, the EU countries agreed that to be eligible to join the single currency (i.e. the euro), they should have sustainable deficits and debts. This was interpreted as follows: the general government deficit should be no more than 3 per cent of GDP and general government debt should be no more than 60 per cent of GDP, or should at least be falling towards that level at a satisfactory pace.

But in the mid-1990s, several of the countries that were subsequently to join the euro had deficits and debts substantially above these levels (see chart). Getting them down proved a painful business. Government expenditure had to be cut and taxes increased. These fiscal measures, unfortunately, proved to be powerful! Unemployment rose and growth remained low.

The EU Stability and Growth Pact (SGP)

In June 1997, at the European Council meeting in Amsterdam, the EU countries agreed a Stability and Growth Pact (SGP). Under the SGP, governments adopting the euro should seek to balance their budgets (or even aim for a surplus) averaged over the course of the business cycle, and deficits should not exceed 3 per cent of GDP in any one year. A country's deficit was permitted to exceed 3 per cent only if its GDP declined by at least 2 per cent (or 0.75 per cent with special permission from the Council of Ministers). Otherwise, countries with deficits exceeding 3 per cent were required to make deposits of money with the European Central Bank. These would then become fines if the excessive budget deficit were not eliminated within two years.

There were two main aims of targeting a zero budget deficit over the business cycle. The first was to allow automatic stabilisers to work without 'bumping into' the 3 per cent deficit ceiling in years when economies were slowing. The second was to allow a reduction in government debts as a proportion of GDP (assuming that GDP grows on average at around 2–3 per cent per year).

From 2002, with slowing growth, Germany, France and Italy breached the 3 per cent ceiling (see chart). By 2007, however, after two years of relatively strong growth, deficits had been reduced well below the ceiling.

But then the global financial crisis hit. As the EU economies slowed, so deficits rose. To combat the recession, in November 2008 the European Commission announced a €200 billion fiscal stimulus plan, mainly in the form of increased public expenditure; €170 billion of the money would come from member governments and €30 billion from the EU, amounting to a total of 1.2 per cent of EU GDP. Most member governments quickly followed in announcing how their specific plans would accord with the overall plan.

The combination of the recession and the fiscal measures pushed most eurozone countries' budget deficits well above the 3 per cent ceiling, as the chart shows. The recession in EU countries deepened markedly in 2009, with GDP declining by 4.5 per cent in the eurozone as a whole.

In some cases, countries' public finances deteriorated unsustainably. Following high-profile rescue packages to Greece, Ireland and Portugal involving the International Monetary Fund and EU, the EU established a funding mechanism for eurozone countries in financial difficulties, known as the European Stability Mechanism (ESM). The ESM can provide loans to such countries or purchase the countries' bonds in the primary market. It became operational in October 2012. As well as taking on the management of existing rescue packages, financial assistance was granted subsequently to Spain and Cyprus.

The Fiscal Compact

With many countries experiencing burgeoning deficits and some countries requiring financial assistance, the SGP was no longer seen as a credible vehicle for constraining deficits: it needed reform. The result was an intense period of negotiation that culminated in early 2012 with a new intergovernmental treaty on limiting spending and borrowing. The treaty, known as the Fiscal Compact, requires that from January 2013 national governments not only abide by the excessive deficit procedure of the SGP but also keep structural deficits no higher than 0.5 per cent of GDP.

Structural deficits are that part of a deficit not directly related to the economic cycle and so would exist even if the economy were operating at its potential output. In the cases of countries with a debt-to-GDP ratio significantly below 60 per cent, the structural deficit is permitted to reach 1 per cent of GDP. Finally, where the debt-to-GDP ratio exceeds 60 per cent, countries should, on average, reduce it by one-twentieth per year.

Where a national government is found by the European Court of Justice not to comply with the Fiscal Compact, it has the power to fine that country up to 0.1 per cent of GDP payable to the European Stability Mechanism (ESM).

The average structural deficit across the eurozone fell from 4.3 per cent of GDP in 2010 to 1.3 per cent in 2019.

circumstances that would trigger a suspension of rules. Box 22.4 details the evolution of the Stability and Growth Pact: the EU's supranational fiscal framework.

The COVID-19 pandemic of the early 2020s saw the adoption of extraordinary fiscal measures. This meant that rules were again suspended, allowing governments to adopt a series of discretionary fiscal measures including the payment of retained staff's wages, tax deferrals and grants for business.

In section 22.4 we review the debate concerning constraints on a government's discretion over both its fiscal and its monetary policies.

CASE STUDIES AND APPLICATIONS

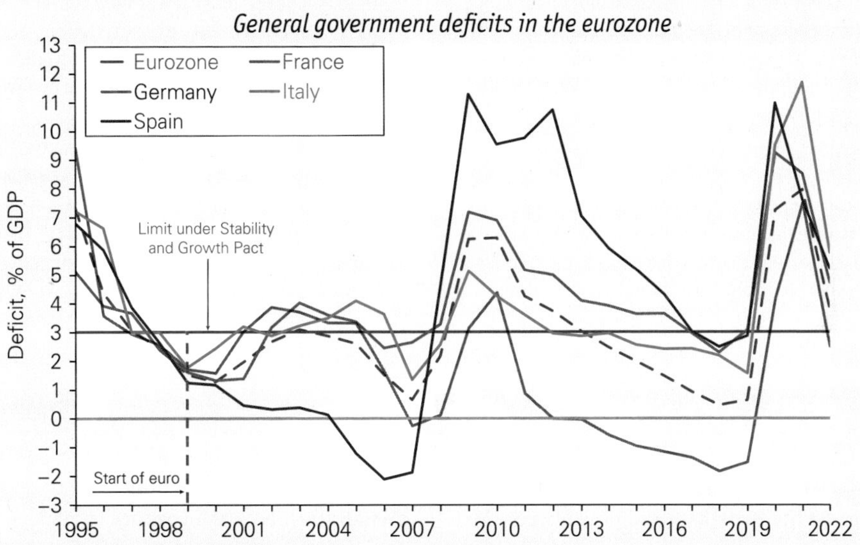

Note: Data from 2021 based on forecasts.
Source: Based on data in *AMECO Database*, European Commission (May 2021).

This improvement was mirrored in most individual eurozone countries, but, nonetheless, most countries still had structural deficits in excess of the target levels of the Fiscal Compact.

Activating the escape clause

In March 2020, the European Commission announced that it was activating the 'escape clause' introduced in 2011 as part of the reforms of the SGP following the global financial crisis. This allows member states to deviate from their medium-term budgetary objectives in periods of severe economic downturn.

The fiscal impulse in EU countries was immense. By November 2020, discretionary fiscal measures in Germany were 39.9 per cent of GDP. In Italy the figure was 48.7 per cent, in France 28.0 per cent, in Spain 16.9 and in the Netherlands 15.0 per cent. (In the UK it was 25.7 per cent and in the USA 14.3 per cent.)[1] These figures include the direct fiscal impulse of increased discretionary government expenditure and reduced taxes, plus deferrals of tax and other payments to government and various government loans and guarantees. These figures increased further in subsequent months.

In February 2021, the Recovery and Resilience Facility came into force, making €672.5 billion in loans and grants available to support reforms and investments undertaken by member governments. To access funds governments submitted national plans aligned to four dimensions: environmental sustainability, productivity, fairness and macroeconomic stability.

In March 2021, one year after the initial suspension of the SGP, the Commission announced that the escape clause would continue until at least 2023.

If there is a danger of recession, should governments loosen the straitjacket of fiscal policy targets?

Using the AMECO online database reproduce the chart in this Box for the structural balances of general government (see Table 17.1 in the database).

1 Julia Anderson et al., 'The fiscal response to the economic fallout from the coronavirus', *Bruegel Datasets*, Bruegel (24 November 2020), www.bruegel.org/publications/datasets/covid-national-dataset/

Section summary

1. Automatic fiscal stabilisers are tax revenues that rise, and benefits that fall, as national income rises. They have the effect of reducing the size of the multiplier and thus reducing cyclical upswings and downswings.
2. Automatic stabilisers take effect as soon as aggregate demand fluctuates, but they can never remove fluctuations completely. They also create disincentives and act as a drag on recovery from recession.
3. Discretionary fiscal policy is where the government deliberately changes taxes or government expenditure in order to alter the level of aggregate demand. Changes in government expenditure on goods and services have a full multiplier effect. Changes in taxes and benefits, however, have a smaller multiplier effect. The tax multiplier has a value 1 less than the full multiplier.
4. There are problems in predicting the magnitude of the effects of discretionary fiscal policy. Expansionary fiscal policy can act as a pump primer and stimulate increased private expenditure, or it can crowd out private expenditure. The extent to which it acts as a pump primer depends crucially on business confidence – something that is very difficult to predict beyond a few weeks or months. The extent of crowding out depends on monetary conditions and the government's monetary policy.
5. There are five possible time lags involved with fiscal policy: the time lag before the problem is diagnosed, the lag between diagnosis and new measures being announced, the lag between announcement and implementation, the lag while the multiplier and accelerator work themselves out, and the lag before consumption fully responds to new economic circumstances.
6. In recent years, many governments preferred a more passive approach towards fiscal policy. This has seen the adoption of fiscal rules based on fiscal indicators, such as the size of budget deficits and levels of debt.
7. However, the application of rules has been affected by the exceptional circumstances arising from the global financial crisis and the COVID-19 pandemic. This has meant their suspension or abandonment to allow governments to give a fiscal stimulus to their economies. The size of the stimulus can be measured by the fiscal impulse.

22.3 MONETARY POLICY

The Bank of England's Monetary Policy Committee (MPC) regularly meets to set the Bank Rate and possibly consider whether or not to alter the money supply directly through quantitative easing (see Box 22.7). The event often gets considerable media coverage, especially when a change is expected.

The fact is that changes in interest rates have gained a central significance in macroeconomic policy. And it is not just in the UK. Whether it is the European Central Bank setting interest rates for the eurozone countries, or the Federal Reserve Bank setting US interest rates, or any other central bank around the world choosing what the level of interest rates should be, monetary policy is seen as having a major influence on a whole range of macroeconomic indicators.

But is setting interest rates simply a question of making an announcement? In reality, it involves the central bank intervening in the money market to ensure that the interest rate announced is also the *equilibrium* interest rate.

The policy setting

In framing its monetary policy, the government must decide on what the goals of the policy are. Is the aim simply to control inflation, or does the government wish also to affect output and employment, or does it want to control the exchange rate?

The government also has to decide the role of the central bank in carrying out monetary policy. There are three possible approaches.

In the first, the government both sets the policy and decides the measures necessary to achieve it. Here the government would set the interest rate, with the central bank simply influencing money markets to achieve this rate. This first approach was used in the UK before 1997.

The second approach is for the government to set the policy *targets,* but for the central bank to be given independence in deciding interest rates. This is the approach adopted in the UK today. The government has set a target rate of CPI inflation of 2 per cent, but then the MPC is free to choose the rate of interest.

The third approach is for the central bank to be given independence not only in carrying out policy, but in setting the policy target itself. The ECB, within the statutory objective of maintaining price stability over the medium term, has decided on the target of keeping inflation below, but close to, 2 per cent over the medium term.

Finally, there is the question of whether the government or central bank should take a long-term or short-term perspective. Should it adopt a target for inflation or money supply growth and stick to it come what may? Or should it adjust its policy as circumstances change and attempt to 'fine-tune' the economy?

We will be looking primarily at *short-term* monetary policy: that is, policy used to keep to a set target for inflation or money supply growth, or policy used to smooth out fluctuations in the business cycle.

It is important first, however, to take a longer-term perspective. Governments generally want to prevent an excessive growth in the money supply over the longer term. Likewise they want to ensure that money supply grows enough and that there is not a shortage of credit, such as that during the credit crunch. If money supply grows too rapidly over the longer term, then high inflation is likely to become embedded in the economy, which will feed inflationary expectations; if money supply grows too slowly, or even falls, then recession is likely to result, investment may fall and long-term growth may be subdued.

Control of the money supply over the medium and long term

There are two major sources of monetary growth: (a) banks choosing to hold a lower liquidity ratio (probably in response to an increase in the demand for loans); (b) public-sector borrowing financed by borrowing from the banking sector. If the government wishes to restrict monetary growth over the longer term, it could attempt to control either or both of these.

Banks' liquidity ratio

The central bank could impose a statutory ***minimum reserve ratio*** on the banks, *above* the level that banks would otherwise choose to hold. Such ratios come in various forms. The simplest is where the banks are required to hold a given minimum percentage of deposits in the form of cash or deposits with the central bank. Other versions are where they are required to hold a given minimum percentage of certain specified types of deposit in the form of various liquid assets. This was the system used in the UK up to 1981. Various types of liquid asset had to add up to at least 12.5 per cent of certain 'eligible liabilities'.

The effect of a minimum reserve ratio is to prevent banks choosing to reduce their cash or liquidity ratio and creating more credit. This was a popular approach of governments in many countries in the past. Some countries imposed very high ratios indeed in their attempt to slow down the growth in the money supply.

Minimum reserve ratios also have the effect of reducing the bank deposits multiplier, since, for any expansion of the monetary base, *less* credit can be created. For example, if banks would otherwise choose a 10 per cent cash ratio, and if the central bank imposes a 20 per cent cash ratio, the bank deposits multiplier is reduced from $10 (= 1/{}^{1}/_{10})$ to $5 (= 1/{}^{1}/_{5})$.

A major problem with imposing restrictions of this kind is that banks may find ways of getting round them. After all, normally banks would like to lend and customers would like to borrow. It is very difficult to regulate and police every single part of countries' complex financial systems.

Nevertheless, attitudes changed substantially after the excessive lending of the mid-2000s. The expansion of credit had been based on 'liquidity' achieved through secondary marketing between financial institutions and the growth of securitised assets containing sub-prime debt (see pages 571–4). After the credit crunch and the need for central banks or governments to rescue ailing banks, such as Northern Rock and later the Royal Bank of Scotland in the UK and many other banks around the world, there were calls for greater regulation of banks to ensure that they had sufficient capital and operated with sufficient liquidity and that they were not exposed to excessive risk of default. As we saw in section 18.2, a number of measures were taken.

Public-sector deficits

In section 18.3, we showed how government borrowing tends to lead to an increase in money supply. To prevent this, deficits must be financed by selling *bonds* (as opposed to bills, which could well be taken up by the banking sector, thereby increasing money supply). However, to sell extra bonds the government will have to offer higher interest rates. This will have a knock-on effect on private-sector interest rates. The government borrowing will thus crowd out private-sector borrowing and investment.

If governments wish to reduce monetary growth and yet avoid financial crowding out, they must therefore reduce deficits. It is partly for this reason that many governments have constrained fiscal policy choices by applying fiscal rules or agreements, such as the Stability and Growth Pact in the eurozone (see Box 22.4).

How could long-term monetary growth come about if the government persistently ran a public-sector surplus?

Long-term monetary control and inflation

Although there are issues with achieving long-term control of the money supply, there is widespread agreement that it is important to do so. The argument is that *increasing* the money supply cannot increase output in the long run; all that will happen is an increase in prices.

It is argued that in the long run – after all adjustments in the economy have worked through – a change in the quantity of money in the economy will be reflected in a change in the general level of prices. But it will not induce permanent changes in real variables such as real output or unemployment.

This general principle, referred to as the ***long-run neutrality of money***, underlies much macroeconomic thinking. Real income or the level of employment are, in the long term, essentially determined by real factors, such as

Definitions

Minimum reserve ratio A minimum ratio of cash (or other specified liquid assets) to deposits (either total or selected) that the central bank requires banks to hold.

Long-run neutrality of money Changes in money supply over the long run will only affect prices and not real output or employment.

Figure 22.8 The demand for and supply of money

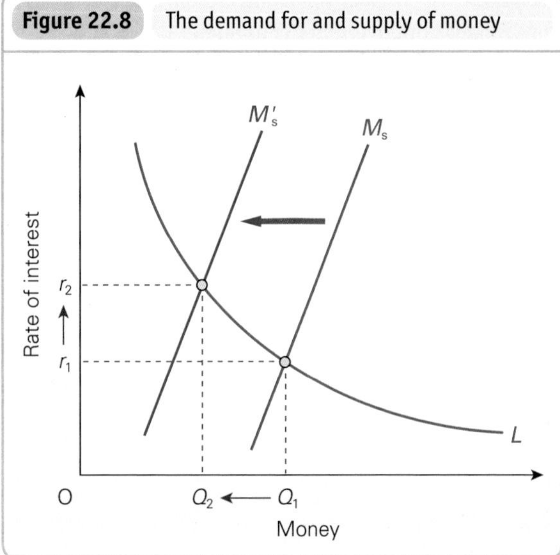

technology, population growth or the preferences of economic agents.[3]

If inflation is to be kept under control, therefore, it is important to control the supply of money. And if long-term control is to be achieved, it is also important not to allow excessive expansion (or contraction) of the money supply in the short term too. But what instruments does a central bank have at its disposal? We examine these next.

The operation of monetary policy in the short term

Assume that inflation is above its target rate and that the central bank wishes to operate a tighter monetary policy in order to reduce aggregate demand and so the rate of inflation. What can it do?

Aggregate demand is dependent on real interest rates (r). Assuming that in the short term the central bank is able to take the expected rate of inflation (π^e) as given, any change in the nominal rate of interest (i) will be matched by an equivalent change in the real rate of interest (r).

For any given supply of money (M_s) there will be a particular equilibrium real rate of interest at any one time: where the supply of money (M_s) equals the demand for money (L). This is shown as r_1 in Figure 22.8.

Thus to operate a tighter monetary policy, the authorities can do one of the following:

- Reduce money supply and accept whatever equilibrium interest rate results. Thus if money supply is reduced to Q_2 in Figure 22.8, a new higher rate of interest, r_2, will result.
- First raise interest rates to r_2 and then manipulate the money supply to reduce it to Q_2. The more endogenous the money supply is, the more this will occur automatically through banks adjusting credit to match the lower demand at the higher rate of interest and the less the central bank will have to take deliberate action to reduce liquidity.

3 See European Central Bank, www.ecb.int/mopo/intro/role/html/index.en.html

There is another possibility. This is to keep interest rates low (at r_1), but also reduce money supply to a level of Q_2. The trouble here is that the authorities cannot both control the money supply *and* keep interest rates down without running into the problem of disequilibrium. Since the demand for money now exceeds the supply by $Q_1 - Q_2$, some form of credit rationing would have to be applied.

Credit rationing was widely used in the past, especially during the 1960s. The aim was to keep interest rates low, so as not to discourage investment, but to restrict credit to more risky business customers and/or to consumers. In the UK, the Bank of England could order banks to abide by such a policy, although in practice it always relied on persuasion. The government also, from time to time, imposed restrictions on hire-purchase credit, by specifying minimum deposits or maximum repayment periods.

Such policies were progressively abandoned around the world from the early 1980s. They were seen to stifle competition and prevent efficient banks from expanding. Hire-purchase controls could badly hit certain industries (e.g. cars and other consumer durables), whose products are bought largely on hire-purchase credit. What is more, with the deregulation and globalisation of financial markets up to 2007, it had become very difficult to ration credit. If one financial institution were controlled, borrowers could simply go elsewhere.

With the excessive lending in sub-prime markets that had triggered the credit crunch of 2007–9, however, there were calls around the world for tighter controls over bank lending. But this was different from credit rationing as we have defined it. In other words, tighter controls, such as applying counter-cyclical buffers of capital to all banks as part of a strategy of macro prudential regulation (see pages 575–80), would be used to prevent reckless behaviour by banks, rather than to achieve a particular level of money at a lower rate of interest.

We thus focus on the two major approaches to monetary policy: (a) controlling the money supply and (b) controlling interest rates.

Techniques to control the money supply

There are two broad approaches to controlling the money supply.

The first is alter the level of liquidity in the banking system, on which credit is created. Suppose, for example, that banks operate a rigid 10 per cent cash ratio and have just two types of asset: cash and advances. Suppose also that the authorities are able to reduce cash in banks by £1 million. With a bank multiplier of 10 (= 1/cash ratio), advances must be reduced by £9 million, and hence (broad) money supply by £10 million (see Table 22.2). TC 15 p543

Table 22.2 Reducing the money supply

Change in liabilities		Change in assets	
Deposits	£10m ↓	Cash	£1m ↓
		Advances	£9m ↓

If banks operated a rigid 5 per cent cash ratio and the government reduced cash in banks by £1 million, how much must credit contract? What is the bank deposits multiplier?

The second approach is to alter the size of the bank deposits multiplier, by altering the ratio of reserves to deposits. Thus if the bank deposits multiplier can be reduced, credit will have to be reduced for any given reserve base.

Before they can apply techniques of monetary control, the authorities must make two preliminary decisions:

- Should a statutory minimum reserve or a minimum liquidity ratio be imposed on the banks, or should the banks be allowed to choose whatever ratios they consider to be prudent?
- Should the authorities attempt to control a range of liquid assets, or should they focus on controlling just the monetary base?

There are four techniques that a central bank could use to control the money supply. Assume in each case that the central bank wishes to *reduce* money supply.

Open-market operations

Open-market operations (OMOs) are the most widely used of the four techniques around the world. They alter the monetary base (cash in circulation outside the central bank). This then affects the amount of credit that banks can create and hence the level of broad money (M4 in the UK; M3 in the eurozone).

Open-market operations have historically involved the sale or purchase by the central bank of government securities (bonds or bills) in the open market. These sales or purchases are *not* in response to changes in the level of government deficits/surpluses. Rather, they are being conducted to implement monetary policy. Hence, they are best understood in the context of an unchanged deficit.

Alternatively open-market operations can involve repurchase agreements (repos) or reverse repurchase agreements.

KI 5 p21

Repos allow the central bank to increase the money supply by lending reserves to financial institutions with government securities (or other eligible securities) as collateral. The financial institution agrees to buy the securities back at a later date. If however the central bank wanted to reduce the money supply it will use reverse repos, which involve temporarily selling government securities, with an agreement to buy them back later.

OMOs are therefore designed to affect the reserve balances of financial institutions at the central bank. Where they reduce banks' reserves below their prudent ratio (or statutory ratio, if one is in force), banks will reduce advances. There will be a multiple contraction of credit and hence of (broad) money supply.

The effect will be limited if the extra securities are bills (as opposed to bonds) and if some are purchased by banks. The reduction in one liquid asset (balances with the central bank) will be offset to some extent by an increase in another liquid asset (bills). Open-market operations are more likely to be effective in reducing the money supply, therefore, when conducted in the bond market.

Why would it be difficult for a central bank to predict the precise effect on money supply of open-market operations?

Adjusting central bank lending to the banks

In most countries, the central bank is prepared to provide extra money to banks (through rediscounting bills, repo operations or straight loans). If banks obtain less money in this way, they will have to cut back on lending. Less credit will be created and broad money supply will thereby be reduced.

Whether or not banks *choose* to obtain extra money from the central bank depends on (a) the rate of interest charged by the central bank (i.e. its discount rate, repo rate or lending rate); and (b) its willingness to lend (or repurchase securities).

In some countries, it is the policy of the central bank to keep its interest rate to banks *below* market rates, thereby encouraging banks to borrow (or sell back securities) whenever such facilities are available. By controlling the amount of money it is willing to provide at these low rates, the central bank can control the monetary base and hence the amount of credit that banks can create.

In other countries, such as the UK and the eurozone countries, it is not so much the amount of money made available that is controlled, but rather the rate of interest (or discount). The higher this rate is relative to other market rates, the less willing will banks be to borrow and, hence, the lower will be the monetary base. Raising the central bank's interest rate, therefore, has the effect of reducing the money supply.

In some countries, central banks operate two rates: a main repo rate (or 'refinancing rate') on a set amount of money that the central bank wants to be made available, and a higher rate (a penal rate) used for 'last-resort' lending to banks short of liquidity. The European Central Bank operates such a system (see Box 22.8). Its higher rate is known as the 'marginal lending facility rate'.

Some central banks, including the ECB, have a third, lower rate. This is the rate they are willing to pay banks for short-term deposits of surplus money in the central bank.

Definition

Open-market operations The sale (or purchase) by the authorities of government securities in the open market in order to reduce (or increase) money supply.

BOX 22.5 **THE OPERATION OF MONETARY POLICY IN THE UK**

Managing the reserves

The Bank of England (the 'Bank') does not normally attempt to control money supply directly. Instead it seeks to control interest rates. The main way in which it does this is by paying interest at the Bank Rate on deposits placed overnight with the Bank: i.e. on the reserve accounts of financial institutions.

Asset purchases

Ordinarily the Bank of England would use *regular* open market operations (OMOs) to keep short-term interest rates close to the Bank Rate through their impact on overall liquidity. However, from March 2009 the Bank of England began deliberately injecting narrow money in a process known as 'quantitative easing' to meet its inflation rate target. This involves large-scale asset purchases, mainly government bonds, from financial institutions (see Box 22.7). The purchases are made with newly created (electronic) money which is credited to banks as reserve assets.

Between March 2009 and July 2012 the Bank of England injected £375 billion through the purchase of gilts. Then, following the EU referendum, the Bank purchased £60 billion of additional government bonds and £10 billion of corporate bonds between August 2016 and April 2017. Then, between March 2020 and December 2021, in response to the COVID-19 pandemic, the Bank increased its holdings of government and corporate bonds by a further £450 billion, taking its asset purchases to £895 billion.

The floor

The effect of quantitative easing has meant that the aggregate level of banks' reserves has become determined by the quantity of asset purchases. Given the abundance of reserves that are therefore available and which can be deposited with the Bank and earn Bank Rate, wholesale interest rates have settled close to Bank Rate. If market rates were to fall significantly below Bank Rate, then banks could borrow money in the market and then deposit it overnight and earn Bank Rate.

Pressure can also be exerted on interest rates through the 'operational standing facilities' that allow individual banks to borrow overnight at a spread of 25 basis points (0.25 percentage points) above Bank Rate. This is intended to create a ceiling on short-term interest rates by providing an alternative source of borrowing from financial institutions. However, the abundance of reserves means that the current

In some countries this rate became negative (a charge on banks) in the mid-2010s to encourage banks to lend money rather than merely keeping it on deposit at the central bank.

In response to the credit crunch of the late 2000s, central banks in several countries extended their willingness to lend to banks. The pressure on central banks to act as the 'liquidity backstop' grew as the inter-bank market ceased to function effectively in distributing reserves and, hence, liquidity between financial institutions. As a result, inter-bank rates rose sharply relative to the central bank's main rate. Increasingly, the focus of central banks was on providing the necessary liquidity to ensure the stability of the financial system. Yet, at the same time, by providing more liquidity, central banks were ensuring that monetary policy was not being compromised. The additional liquidity was needed to alleviate the upward pressure on market interest rates.

Changing the method of funding the national debt

Rather than focusing on controlling the monetary base (as in the case of the above two techniques), an alternative is for the authorities to attempt to alter the overall liquidity position of the banks. An example of this approach is a change by the authorities (the Debt Management Office in the UK) in the balance of ***funding*** the national debt. To reduce money supply the authorities issue more bonds and fewer bills. Banks' balances with the central bank will be little affected, but to the extent that banks hold fewer bills, there will be a reduction in their liquidity and hence a reduction in the amount of credit created. Funding is thus the conversion of one type of government debt (liquid) into another (illiquid).

One problem with this approach is that bonds are likely to command a higher interest rate than bills. By switching from bills to bonds, the government will be committing itself to these interest rates for the life of the bond.

If the Bank of England issues £1 million of extra bonds and buys back £1 million of Treasury bills, will there automatically be a reduction in credit by a set multiple of £1 million?

Variable minimum reserve ratios

If banks are required to maintain a statutory minimum reserve ratio and if the central bank is free to alter this ratio, it can use it as a means of controlling the money supply. It does this by affecting not the monetary base, but the size of the bank multiplier.

Assume that there are just two types of asset: cash and advances, and that banks are required to maintain a

Definition

Funding (in monetary policy) Where the authorities alter the balance of bills and bonds for any given level of government borrowing.

CASE STUDIES AND APPLICATIONS

monetary policy framework is best described as the 'floor system'.

The Bank stands ready to adapt its monetary policy framework as necessary. At some point in the future, banks' reserves are likely to fall below the levels demanded. At this point the Bank of England would be ready to lend reserves through regular OMOs, as had been the case before the financial crisis. Case 22.10 on the student website details the monetary policy framework that operated previously.

Term Funding Scheme

In March 2020 in response to the COVID-19 pandemic, the Bank of England cut Bank Rate from 0.75 per cent to 0.1 per cent. However, with such low interest rates it feared that banks and building societies might find it difficult to reduce their rates on savings accounts much further, thus making it difficult to reduce lending rates.

To help ensure that the cut in Bank Rate was passed on to borrowers, financial institutions could borrow from the Bank of England to grant four-year loans at rates 'at or very close to Bank Rate'. The quantity of funds made available to banks under this 'Term Funding Scheme' was at least 10 per cent of banks' total real economy lending. This percentage could be higher for banks that increased lending, especially to small and medium-sized enterprises (SMEs). The scheme was known as 'TFSME' (term funding for small and medium-sized enterprises).

The drawdown period for TFSME loans was initially intended to run until 31 October 2020. But, with further health-intervention measures imposed, it was decided to extend the drawdown period to 30 April 2021.

The TFSME was to mirror a Term Funding Scheme introduced in August 2016 following the outcome of the EU-referendum vote. That scheme, which closed to new lending in February 2018, made £127 billion of loans. By the end of August 2021 the TFSME has made close to £88 billion of loans.

Assume that the Bank of England wants to raise interest rates. Trace through the process by which it achieves this.

Using the Bank of England Statistical Interactive Database, download the Bank Rate paid on reserves (series YWMB47D). Create a chart of the series in Excel and then write a short summary explaining both what Bank Rate is and what your chart shows.

minimum 10 per cent cash ratio (a ratio above that which the banks would have chosen for reasons of prudence). The bank multiplier is thus 10 ($= 1/^1/_{10}$). Assume that banks' total assets are £100 billion, of which £10 billion are cash reserves and £90 billion are advances. This is illustrated in the left-hand side of Table 22.3.

Now assume that the central bank raises the minimum reserve ratio to 20 per cent. Banks still have £10 billion cash reserves, and so they have to reduce their advances to £40 billion (giving total assets of £50 billion, of which the £10 million cash is the required 20 per cent). This is shown in the right-hand side of Table 22.3. The bank multiplier has been reduced to 5 ($= 1/_{1/5}$).

In the past, central banks that imposed minimum reserve ratios on the banks tended to vary them in this way as a means of altering the money supply for any given monetary base. For example, several of the EU countries used this technique before joining the euro. Increasingly, countries that still have minimum reserve ratios are relying on open-market operations or direct lending to banks, rather than on varying the ratio. This is the case with the ECB, which has a fixed reserve ratio. Until January 2012 this ratio was 2 per cent. Since then it has been 1 per cent. The USA had for many years used variable minimum reserve ratios as a monetary policy tool. However, from March 2020 reserve requirement ratios were reduced to zero per cent with no plans to reimpose them (see Box 22.6).[4]

4 In one sense, it could be argued that the imposition of a minimum reserve ratio is a *form* of credit rationing. It restricts the ability of banks to expand credit as much as they would like for the amount of reserves they hold. In Figure 22.8, however, higher minimum reserves would still shift the *supply* curve, given that this curve measures broad money and not the monetary base. It is for this reason that we considered minimum reserve ratios under the heading of 'techniques to control the money supply'.

Table 22.3 Effect of raising the minimum reserve ratio from 10% to 20%

Initial position: 10% reserve ratio				**New position: 20% reserve ratio**			
Liabilities		**Assets**		**Liabilities**		**Assets**	
Deposits	£100bn	Reserve assets	£10bn	Deposits	£50bn	Reserve assets	£10bn
		Advances, etc.	£90bn			Advances, etc.	£40bn
Total	£100bn	Total	£100bn	Total	£50bn	Total	£50bn

BOX 22.6 CENTRAL BANKING AND MONETARY POLICY IN THE USA

How the 'Fed' works

The central bank in the USA is called the Federal Reserve System (or 'Fed'). It was set up in 1913 and consists of 12 regional Federal Reserve Banks, each of which is responsible for distributing currency and regulating banks in its region. But despite its apparent regional nature, it is still a national system. The Federal Reserve Board, based in Washington, decides on monetary policy and then the Federal Open Market Committee (FOMC) decides how to carry it out. The FOMC meets eight times a year. The Fed is independent of both the President and the Congress, and its chairman is generally regarded as having great power in determining the country's economic policy.

Since 1977 the Fed's statutory mandate has been to promote the goals of maximum employment, stable prices, and moderate long-term interest rates. Because of the reference to both prices and employment, the mandate is commonly referred to as a 'dual mandate'. Of course, these objectives may well conflict from time to time. In such a case, an assessment has to be made of which is the most pressing problem.

Since 2012 the FOMC has issued an annual statement on its long-run goals and monetary policy strategy. This has seen it consistently reaffirm that its long-run goal for inflation is for a consumer price inflation rate of 2 per cent. Significantly this means that the inflation rate should average 2 per cent over time and therefore if inflation has been running persistently below 2 per cent, monetary policy should aim for inflation to run moderately above 2 per cent for some time.

The Fed's policy instruments

To carry out its objectives, the FOMC has three main policy instruments.

Open-market operations. The most important one is *open-market operations.* These are conducted through the Federal Reserve Bank of New York, which buys and sells Treasury bills and government bonds. For example, if the FOMC wishes to increase money supply, the New York Fed will buy more of these securities. The purchasers, whether they be banks, corporations or individuals, will have their bank accounts duly credited. In other words, the Fed credits the accounts of sellers with a deposit and this enables a multiple increase in credit.

The discount rate. The second policy instrument is the *discount rate.* Known as the 'federal funds rate', this is the rate of interest at which the Fed is willing to lend to banks, thereby providing them with liquidity on which they can create credit. This is known as 'lending through the discount window'. If this rate is raised, banks are discouraged from borrowing, and credit is thereby squeezed. Since 1995, the FOMC has published its target federal funds rate. Sometimes this rate merely mirrors other market rates and is not, therefore, an active instrument of policy. On other occasions, however, the Fed changes it ahead of other market rates in order to signal its intentions to tighten (or loosen) monetary policy.[1]

Interest on excess reserves. Before March 2020, banks had been legally required to hold a certain minimum percentage of eligible deposit liabilities, primarily sight and time deposits, as reserves. The percentage was dependent on the size of the deposit liabilities. Interest was paid on these reserves, with the rate known as the IOR (interest on reserves). Reserves held in excess of requirements were paid an interest rate known as IOER (interest on excess reserves).

However, from March 2020 reserve requirement ratios were reduced to zero per cent. As well as helping to free up liquidity and support lending, large-scale asset purchases meant that the Fed was supplying 'ample reserves' (see below). Therefore, banks can choose to hold any reserves at the Fed as excess reserves thereby earning the IOER rate.

Federal Reserve Balance Sheet: Total Assets

Note: Asset position on first day of month.
Source: Based on data in *Federal Reserve Economic Data*, Federal Reserve Bank of St Louis, https://fred.stlouisfed.org/

Since no bank would want to lend surplus reserves below the IOER, the IOER acts as a floor in determining the rate at which banks engage in overnight borrowing or lending. The IOER stood at 0.1 per cent in April 2021.

Asset purchases

From 2008 to 2014 the Fed massively expanded its holding of longer-term securities through open-market purchases of assets, known as quantitative easing (QE). There were three rounds of QE over this period, which saw the balance sheet of the Federal Reserve increase from $900 billion at the start of 2008 to $4.5 trillion by the end of 2014 (see chart).

QE1. In November 2008 the Fed announced its intention to purchase $100 billion of corporate debt issued by government-sponsored financial enterprises and $500 billion of mortgage-backed securities (MBSs), including MBSs guaranteed by the two main mortgage lenders Fannie Mae and Freddie Mac, which had recently been nationalised to save them from collapse.

In March 2009, the Fed announced that it would increase its purchases of debt issued by government-sponsored financial enterprises by a further $100 billion and its purchases of MBSs by a further $750 billion. The hope was to stimulate bank lending and revive the collapsed housing market. It also announced that it would purchase $300 billion of longer-term Treasury securities

QE2. In November 2010, a second round of quantitative easing was announced as the economy struggled to recover from the financial crisis. Between November 2010 and June 2011, the Fed expanded its holding of longer-term Treasury securities by $600 billion.

In September 2011, the Fed announced that in the period up to June 2012 it would buy up to $400 billion of long-term government bonds in the market and sell an equal amount of shorter-dated ones (of less than three years). The plan became known as 'Operation Twist'. It was a way of altering the *funding* of national debt, rather than directly altering the monetary base. The hope was to stimulate investment and longer-term borrowing by driving down longer-term interest rates. The plan was expanded in June 2012 with the sale of a further $267 billion in Treasury securities by the end of the year.

QE3. In September 2012, the Fed launched a third round of quantitative easing. The Fed would buy mortgage-backed securities of $40 billion per month, extended to $85 billion per month in December 2012. And this would go on for as long as it took for the employment market to show significant improvement. It was this open-ended commitment which made QE3 different from QE1 and QE2. Under QE1 and QE2, the Fed purchased $2.3 trillion of assets.

In December 2013, the Federal Reserve announced the start of a tapering of its quantitative easing programme. In other words, monthly purchases of MBSs and longer-term Treasury securities were reduced. The conclusion of QE3 was formally announced in October 2014 after accumulating assets of $2.5 trillion.

Normalisation to pandemic

December 2015 marked the beginning of what the Fed termed the policy normalisation process. This saw the recommencement of reverse repurchase agreements to help control the Fed Funds Range. The Fed raised the federal funds rate by 0.25 percentage points (the first increase since June 2006).

Rates rose a further eight times up to December 2018. In the period January 2018 to August 2019, the Fed sold nearly $645 billion of assets it had purchased during periods of QE. This reverse QE has been dubbed 'quantitative tightening (QT).

But then, in August 2019, with a weakening global economy, the Fed began lowering rates (see Figure 22.10 on page 721) and ceased QT.

QE4. The COVID-19 pandemic, however, induced a dramatic loosening of policy. In March 2020, the target rate was reduced to 0–0.25 per cent and the Fed announced that over the coming months it would increase its holding of Treasury securities by $500 billion and mortgage-backed securities by $200 billion. QE4 had begun. Subsequently, it committed itself to unlimited purchases of Treasury securities and mortgage-backed securities as well as, for the first time, purchases of corporate bonds.

In April 2020, the Fed announced that it was providing $2.3 trillion of loans to support lending to households and business. This included the Main Street New Loan Facility providing four-year loans to lenders that would then be made available to businesses of up to 10 000 employees or a turnover of up to $2.5 billion in 2019.

In December 2020, the Fed announced that it would, for the foreseeable future, make asset purchases at a rate of $120 billion per month, comprising $80 billion of Treasury securities and $40 billion of mortgage-backed securities.

The monetary policy responses to COVID again led to a massive expansion of the Fed's balance sheet with its total assets doubling from $4.2 trillion to $8.4 trillion between March 2020 and September 2021 (see chart).

1. ***In what ways is the Fed's operation of monetary policy (a) similar to and (b) different from the Bank of England's?***
2. ***Could there be a potential moral hazard problem arising out of the actions taken by the Fed and the US government in response to the financial crisis?***

Using the Federal Reserve Economic Data (FRED) database recreate the chart in the Box on the total assets of the Federal Reserve incorporating the latest available data.

1 For details of the Fed's interest rate policy, see www.federalreserve.gov/fomc/fundsrate.htm

Difficulties in controlling money supply

The authorities may experience considerable difficulties in controlling broad money supply. Difficulties occur whether they focus on doing this via control of narrow money – the 'monetary base' – or whether they attempt to control a wider range of liquid assets.

Problems with monetary base control

Assume that the authorities seek to control narrow money: i.e. notes and coin. This could be done by imposing a statutory cash ratio on banks. Assume that a statutory ratio of 10 per cent is imposed. Then provided the authorities control the supply of cash by, say, open-market operations, it would seem that they can thereby control the creation of credit and hence deposits. There would be a bank multiplier of 10. For every £1 million decrease in cash held by the banks, money supply would fall by £10 million. There are serious problems, however, with this form of ***monetary base control***:

- Banks could hold cash in excess of the statutory minimum. For a time, therefore, they could respond to any restriction of cash by the authorities by simply reducing their cash ratio towards the minimum, rather than having to reduce credit.
- Unless cash ratios were imposed on every single financial institution, the control of certain institutions' lending would merely shift business to other uncontrolled institutions, including overseas ones. Banks operate in a global market. Thus UK banks can do business with UK borrowers using money markets abroad, thereby diverting potentially profitable business away from London. This is an example of Goodhart's law (see Box 22.9 on page 728).

KI 37 p728

- Alternatively, if those banks subject to statutory cash requirements were short of cash, they could attract cash away from the uncontrolled institutions.

The switching of business away from controlled banks is known as ***disintermediation***. To avoid this problem and to allow the greatest freedom of competition between financial institutions, the alternative is to use monetary base control with no *statutory* cash ratio.

But two major problems with monetary base control, with or without a statutory cash ratio, are the most serious of all. The first is that central banks *are always prepared to increase the monetary base, through repos or rediscounting, if it is demanded.* This makes it virtually impossible to have a precise control of the monetary base.

The second is the size and variability of the money multiplier. As we saw in section 18.3 (pages 586–7), the money multiplier is the number of times greater the rise in (broad) money supply is than the rise in the monetary base. As Figure 18.5 (see page 586) demonstrates, the broad money multiplier can be highly variable. In other words, controlling the monetary base would have a highly unpredictable effect on the money supply.

TC 15 p543

For these reasons, the support for monetary base control has waned in recent years.

1. *Trace through the effects of a squeeze on the monetary base from an initial reduction in cash to banks' liquidity being restored through gilt repos. Will this restoration of liquidity by the central bank totally nullify the initial effect of reducing the supply of cash? (Clue: what is likely to happen to the rate of interest?)*
2. *Given the difficulties of monetary base control, would you expect cash in circulation and broader measures of the money supply, such as M4, to rise and fall by the same percentage as each other?*

Problems with controlling broad money supply

One solution to the problems of monetary base control would be for the authorities to attempt to control broader money supply directly. In the UK, targets for the growth in broad money were an important part of monetary policy from 1976 to 1985. The UK has not targeted money supply growth since the 1980s, however. Similarly, until 2003 the European Central Bank adopted a 'reference value' of 4.5 per cent for M3 growth of the euro (see Box 18.4 on page 584 for a definition of M3). While a 'pillar' of its monetary policy, the ECB only used this as a guideline and not as a strict target.

How would such a policy work? Assume that the authorities want to operate a tight monetary policy. They sell bonds on the open market. Banks, now short of cash, obtain money from the central bank through rediscounting bills or through repos. Thus although the central bank has been obliged to restore the amount of cash it had withdrawn from the system, there has been a decrease in bills and short-term bonds held by the banks. Banks' *overall* liquidity has thus been reduced. Such measures could be backed up by changing the funding methods.

But as with monetary base control, there are problems with attempting to control broad money supply. Banks may be prepared to reduce their liquidity ratio. This is likely if they already have surplus liquidity, or if their customers are prepared to switch from sight to time accounts (for which banks require fewer cash reserves). This will involve offering higher interest rates on time accounts, and hence charging higher interest rates on bank loans. But if the demand for loans is relatively insensitive to interest rate changes, this will have little effect on credit or on overall deposits.

The use of open-market operations or funding to reduce money supply involves selling more bonds. But if potential purchasers believe interest rates will rise in the future

Definitions

Monetary base control Monetary policy that focuses on controlling the monetary base (as opposed to broad liquidity).

Disintermediation The diversion of business away from financial institutions that are subject to controls.

(highly likely when the government is attempting to operate a tighter monetary policy), they will hold off buying bonds now and may even attempt to sell bonds before bond prices fall. Thus the authorities may be forced into a large immediate increase in bond interest rates.

In circumstances where the central bank wants to *increase* broad money, the problem can be even more serious. Purchasing bonds may increase liquidity in the banking sector, but (a) people may not want to borrow if the economy is going into recession and people are trying to cut back on spending; (b) banks may be reluctant to lend, preferring to keep the extra liquidity in reserve as a precaution against people defaulting on debts. These were the problems facing various central banks around the world which were to engage in quantitative easing (see Box 22.7) following the financial crisis of the late 2000s and the subsequent economic slowdown.

Perhaps the biggest problem is the effect on interest rates.

The effect on interest rates

A policy of controlling money supply can lead to severe fluctuations in real interest rates. This can cause great uncertainty for business and can be very damaging to long-term investment and growth.

TC 9 p132

The problem is more acute if the overall demand for money is inelastic and is subject to fluctuations. In Figure 22.9, with money supply controlled at M_s, even a fairly moderate increase in demand from L to L' leads to a large rise in real interest rates from r to r_1.

And yet, if the authorities are committed to controlling money supply, they will have to accept that equilibrium interest rates may well fluctuate in this way.

Because of the above difficulties in controlling the money supply directly, countries have become increasingly reliant on controlling interest rates (backed up, normally, by open-market operations).

Figure 22.9 The effect on interest rates of a change in demand for money when money supply is kept under control

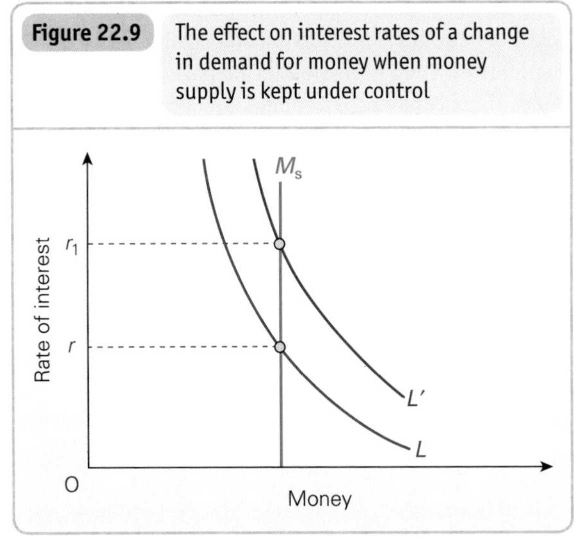

Techniques to control interest rates

The approach to monetary control today in many countries is to focus directly on interest rates. Normally an interest rate change will be announced, and then open-market operations will be conducted by the central bank to ensure that the money supply is adjusted so as to make the announced interest rate the *equilibrium* one. Figure 22.10 shows central bank (nominal) interest rates in the UK, USA and the eurozone since 2005.

Central banks look to affect *real* interest rates through their monetary operations that affect nominal interest rates. Assuming inflationary expectations are constant in

Figure 22.10 Central bank interest rates

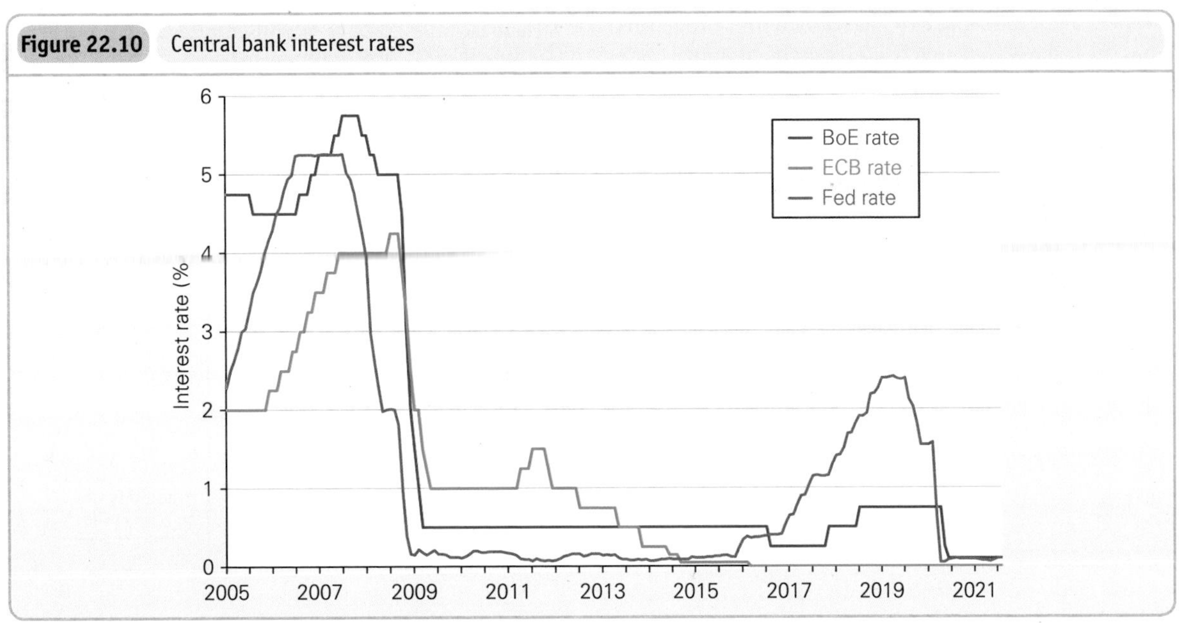

Note: Federal reserve rate is the federal funds effective rate.
Sources: Federal Reserve Bank, European Central Bank and Bank of England.

the short term, then, by announcing a particular change in nominal rates, this results in an equivalent change in real interest rates. Thus, in Figure 22.8 (on page 714), the central bank announces a rise in nominal interest rates which corresponds to an equivalent rise in real interest rates from r_1 to r_2 and then conducts open-market operations to ensure that the money supply is reduced from Q_1 to Q_2.

Let us assume that the central bank decides to raise interest rates. What does it do? In general, it will seek to keep banks short of liquidity. This will happen automatically on any day when tax payments by banks' customers exceed the money they receive from government expenditure. This excess is effectively withdrawn from banks and ends up in the government's account at the central bank. Even when this does not occur, issues of government debt will effectively keep the banking system short of liquidity.

This 'shortage' can then be used as a way of forcing through interest rate changes. Banks will obtain the necessary liquidity from the central bank through gilt repos or by selling it back (rediscounting) bills. The central bank can *choose the rate of interest to charge* (i.e. the gilt repo rate or the bill rediscount rate). This will then have a knock-on effect on other interest rates throughout the banking system.

The effects can be illustrated in Figure 22.11, both parts of which assume that the central bank wishes to raise the real interest rate (the real repo or discount rate) from r_1 to r_2.

KI 5 p21

In Figure 22.11(a), it is assumed that banks are short of liquidity and are seeking to sell gilts to the central bank on a repo basis. It is assumed that the central bank will supply as much cash (i.e. demand as many gilts through repos) as banks choose, but only at the central bank's chosen repo rate. The demand for gilts is thus perfectly elastic at the central bank's repo rate. The supply curve of gilts by the banks represents their demand for cash from the central bank, and hence is *downward* sloping: the lower the real repo rate, the cheaper it is for the banks to obtain cash. If the central bank raises the real repo rate to r_2 (via a rise in the nominal rate), banks will supply fewer gilts (i.e. demand less cash from the central bank). If there is less liquidity in the banking system, the money supply will fall.

In the event of banks having a surplus of liquidity, Figure 22.11(b) applies. Here banks are seeking to use their surplus liquidity to *buy* bills from the central bank. Their demand curve is *upward* sloping: the higher the rate of discount (i.e. the lower the price that banks have to pay for bills), the more the banks will demand. In this case, the central bank can raise the rate of discount by offering more bills for sale. By increasing the supply of bills from S_1 to S_2, it can increase the equilibrium real rate from r_1 to r_2.

In both cases, the central bank will first decide on the repo rate (or discount rate) and then adjust the supply or demand of gilts or bills to ensure that the chosen rate is the equilibrium rate.

Large-scale asset purchases

Following the financial crisis, and again during the COVID-19 pandemic, many central banks adopted a more aggressive form of OMOs. This involved large-scale asset purchases by central banks, primarily securitised mortgage debt and long-term government bonds.

The effect was to pump large amounts of additional cash directly into the economy in a process known as ***quantitative easing*** – or QE for short. The hope was to stimulate demand and, through the process of credit creation, to boost broad money too. Quantitative easing is discussed further in Box 22.7. (See Boxes 22.5, 22.6 and 22.8 for details of how the Bank of England, the Fed and the ECB do this in practice.)

> **Definition**
>
> **Quantitative easing** A deliberate attempt by the central bank to increase the money supply by buying large quantities of securities through open-market operations. These securities could be securitised mortgage and other private-sector debt or government bonds.

Figure 22.11 Central bank operations in the gilt repo and bill markets to affect interest rates

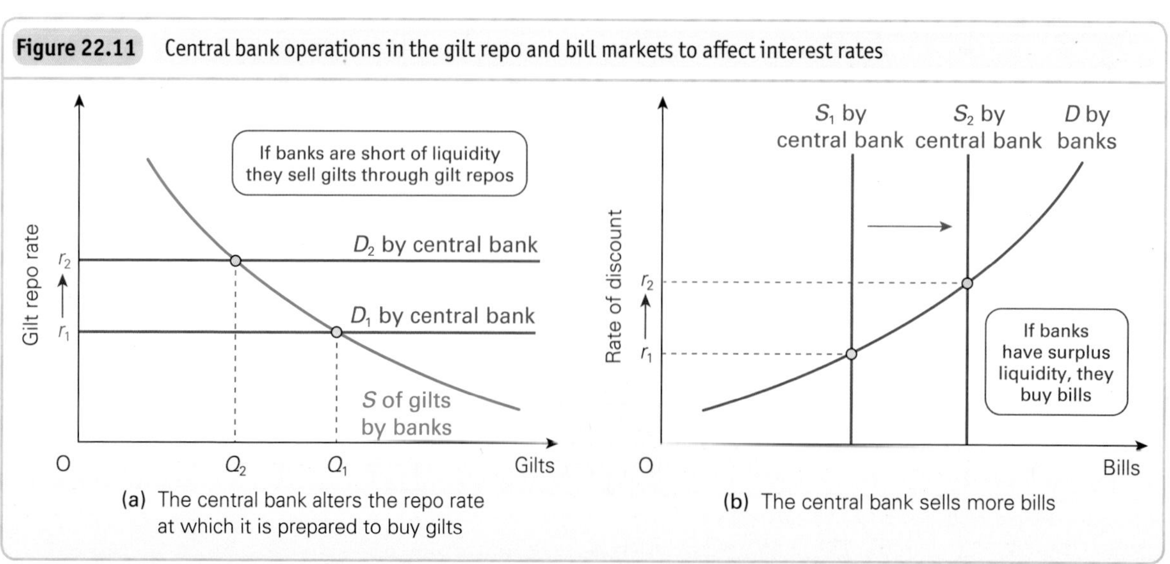

(a) The central bank alters the repo rate at which it is prepared to buy gilts

(b) The central bank sells more bills

BOX 22.7 QUANTITATIVE EASING

CASE STUDIES AND APPLICATIONS

Rethinking monetary policy in hard times

Increasing the money supply

As the economies of the world slid into recession in 2008, central banks became more and more worried that the traditional instrument of monetary policy – controlling interest rates – was insufficient to ward off a slump in demand.

Interest rates had been cut at an unprecedented rate and central banks were reaching the end of the road for further interest rate cuts. Despite nominal interest rates being at close to zero, they were having little effect on aggregate demand. The problem was that there was an acute lack of willingness of banks to lend and firms and consumers to borrow.

So what were central banks to do? The answer was to increase money supply directly, in a process known as *quantitative easing (QE)*. This involves an aggressive version of open-market operations, where the central bank buys up a range of assets, such as securitised mortgage debt and long-term government bonds. The effect is to pump large amounts of additional cash into the economy in the hope of stimulating demand and, through the process of credit creation, to boost broad money too.

QE in the USA

In the USA, in December 2008, at the same time as the federal funds rate was cut to a range of 0 to 0.25 per cent, the Fed was already embarking on large-scale quantitative easing. As we saw in Box 22.6, the Fed began buying hundreds of billions of dollars' worth of mortgage-backed securities on the open market and planned also to buy large quantities of long-term government debt.

The Federal Open Market Committee said that, 'The focus of the committee's policy going forward will be to support the functioning of financial markets and stimulate the economy through open-market operations and other measures that sustain the size of the Federal Reserve's balance sheet at a high level.' The result was that considerable quantities of new money were injected into the system. By October 2014, after three rounds of QE, it had purchased assets of $2.5 trillion.

QE resumed in March 2020 (QE4) in response to COVID-19 with an open-ended commitment by the Fed. Over the first 12 months of the response, its portfolio of securities held outright grew by over $3 trillion to $7.1 trillion, so massively expanding the Fed's balance sheet (see chart in Box 22.6).

QE in the UK

A similar approach was adopted in the UK. In January 2009, the Bank of England was given powers by the Treasury to buy on the open market up to £50 billion of existing government bonds (gilts) and high-quality private-sector assets, such as corporate bonds and commercial paper. The purchases from non-bank financial institutions were with newly created electronic money. But this was only the start.

In March 2009, as the recession deepened, the Chancellor agreed to increase the scale of purchases, so beginning the second and substantive phase of quantitative easing (see chart). These purchases, mainly government bonds, resulted in a substantial increase in banks' reserves at the Bank of England and hence in the Bank's balance sheet (see Table 18.2 on page 577). By July 2012, asset purchases totalled £375 billion. In August 2016, following the vote to leave the European Union, the Bank of England increased asset purchases by a further £70 billion.

Bank of England sterling reserve liabilities created for asset purchases

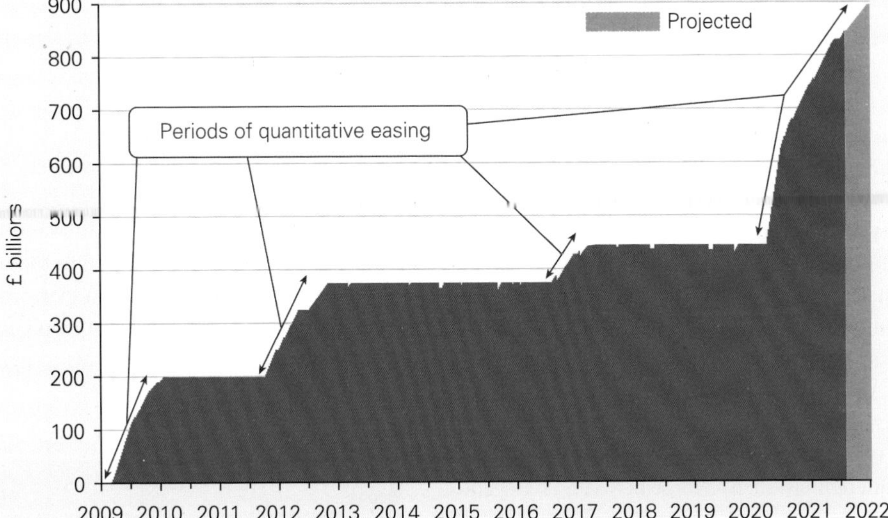

Source: Based on data from *Statistical Interactive Database*, series YWWB9R9, Bank of England (13 August 2021), www.bankofengland.co.uk/boeapps/iadb/

(continued)

Then between March 2020 and December 2021, in response to the COVID-19 pandemic, the Bank increased asset purchases by a further £450 billion, taking its asset purchases to £895 billion.

QE in the eurozone

As we shall see in Box 22.8, the ECB was more reticent about adopting quantitative easing. But with the risk of deflation becoming established, QE began in March 2015 at a rate of €60 billion per month. Initially, the scheme was to run to September 2016 with total purchases of up to €1.08 trillion. However, the end of QE was delayed several times as inflation rates remained stubbornly low. Monthly purchases rose in March 2016 to €80 billion, before falling back to €60 billion per month from April 2017 and to €30 billion per month in January 2018.

The first round of QE finally came to an end in December 2018, by which point asset purchases had reached €2.6 trillion. However, a second round of QE began in November 2019 at a rate of €20 billion per month. This was then supplemented from March 2020 by the Pandemic Emergency Purchase Programme (PEPP). Total asset purchases under PEPP were initially set at €750 billion but by December 2020 this had been raised to €1850 billion.

The transmission mechanism of asset purchases

By financing asset purchases through the creation of central bank reserves, quantitative easing involves increasing the amount of narrow money. It can also, indirectly, increase broad money. There are two principal ways in which this can happen.

Asset prices and yields. When non-bank financial intermediaries, including insurance companies and pension funds, sell assets to the central bank they can use the money to purchase other assets. In doing so, this will drive up their prices. This, in turn, reduces the yields on these assets (at a higher price there is less dividend or interest per pound spent on them), which should help to reduce interest rates thereby boosting aggregate demand.

Also, for those holding these now more expensive assets there is a positive wealth effect. For instance, households with longer-term saving plans involving securities will now have greater financial wealth. Again, this will boost spending.

Bank lending. Banks will find their reserve balances increase as those selling assets deposit the proceeds in their bank accounts. This will increase the liquidity ratio of banks, which could encourage them to grant more credit.

However, it is all very well increasing the monetary base, but a central bank cannot force banks to lend or people to borrow. That requires confidence. We observed in Figure 19.15 the continued weakness of bank lending to the non-bank private sector through the late 2000s and into the early 2010s.

This is not to say that quantitative easing failed in the UK and elsewhere: growth in credit and broad money could have been weaker still. However, it does illustrate the potential danger of this approach if, in the short run, little credit creation takes place. In the equation $MV = PY$, the rise in (narrow) money supply (M) may be largely offset by a fall in the velocity of circulation (V) (see pages 607–11).

On the other hand, there is also the danger that if this policy is conducted for too long, the growth in money supply could prove to be excessive, resulting in inflation rising above the target level. It is therefore important for central banks to foresee this and turn the monetary 'tap' off in time. This would involve 'quantitative tightening' – selling assets that the central bank had purchased, thereby driving down asset prices and driving up interest rates.

Would it be appropriate to define the policy of quantitative easing as 'monetarist'?

Using the ideas in this Box along with additional desktop research, prepare a briefing document for non-economists explaining what quantitative easing is, why it has been deployed and how it is intended to work.

Pass-through effect

A change in the central bank's interest rate will have a knock-on effect on other interest rates: the ***pass-through effect***. For example, in the UK, banks normally automatically adjust their base rates (to which they gear their other rates) when the Bank of England announces a change in the Bank Rate (i.e. the nominal repo rate). Thus a 0.25 percentage point rise in Bank Rate will normally mean a 0.25 percentage point rise in banks' deposit rates, overdraft rates, etc.

Changes in central bank interest rates, however, will not necessarily have an *identical* effect on other interest rates.

In section 19.4 we saw how some economists argue that interest rate differentials, such as those between saving and borrowing products, can be dependent on the macroeconomic environment. Economic growth may help to reduce the cost of borrowing relative to the return on saving, which further fuels spending and aggregate demand.

While interest rate differentials may vary across the business cycle, they can also be affected by disruptions in the functioning of financial markets. The financial crisis of the late 2000s can be seen in this light, with interest rate differentials between borrowing and saving or deposit rates rising sharply. This is illustrated in Figure 22.12, which shows the UK's Bank Rate alongside the average mortgage rate. As can be seen, the higher spread between Bank Rate and the average mortgage rate was to persist throughout the 2010s.

Definition

Pass-through effect (on interest rates) The effect on other interest rates in the economy when the central bank changes its rate(s).

Figure 22.12 Mortgage rate and Bank Rate

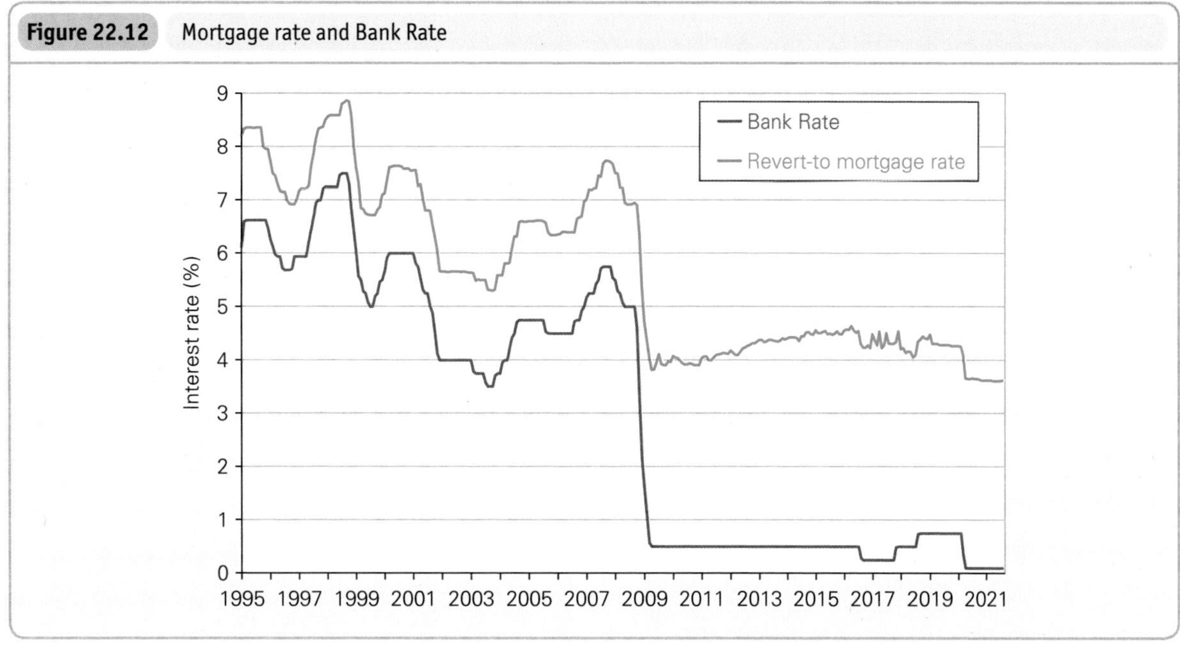

Source: Based on series IUMABEDR (Bank Rate) and IUMTLMV (mortgage rate) from *Statistical Interactive Database*, Bank of England (6 August 2021), www.bankofengland.co.uk/boeapps/iadb/

The mortgage rate is significant in the transmission mechanism of monetary policy in many countries. But for countries like the UK, with high rates of home ownership and/or large amounts of outstanding mortgage debt, changes in mortgage rates can have particularly powerful effects on consumer spending. Therefore, how closely the mortgage rate tracks the central bank policy rate is important.

How could we model a credit market disruption and its impact on interest rate differentials using the Keynesian cross (Keynesian 45° line) diagram?

The pass-through effect may therefore depend on the confidence of lenders and borrowers. But it may also be dependent on the *level* of nominal interest rates. As nominal interest rates on savings and deposit accounts get close to zero, as they did during the financial crisis and the COVID-19 pandemic, banks may be reluctant or unable to reduce rates further. This, in turn, can then limit the easing of credit conditions from further monetary policy loosening.

As Boxes 22.5, 22.6 and 22.8 show, many central banks have attempted to mitigate the problem of a limited pass-through effect of low interest rates by making use of *targeted* long-term repo operations. These are essentially long-term loans linked to the lending of commercial banks. The more credit these institutions extend to the non-bank private sector the more favourable are the terms of the repo operations.

BOX 22.8 **MONETARY POLICY IN THE EUROZONE** CASE STUDIES AND APPLICATIONS

The role of the ECB

The European Central Bank (ECB) is based in Frankfurt and is charged with operating the monetary policy of those EU countries that have adopted the euro. Although the ECB has the overall responsibility for the eurozone's monetary policy, the central banks of the individual eurozone countries, such as the Bank of France and Germany's Bundesbank, were not abolished. They are responsible for distributing euros and for carrying out the ECB's policy with respect to institutions in their own countries.

In operating the monetary policy of a 'euro economy' roughly the size of the USA, and in being independent from national governments, the ECB's power is enormous and is equivalent to that of the Fed (see Box 22.6). So what is the structure of this giant on the European stage, and how does it operate?

The structure of the ECB

The ECB has two major decision-making bodies: the Governing Council and the Executive Board.[1]

The Governing Council consists of the members of the Executive Board and the governors of the central banks of each of the eurozone countries. The Council's role is to set the main targets of monetary policy and to oversee the success (or otherwise) of that policy. It also sets interest rates at six-weekly meetings. Decisions are by simple majority. In the event of a tie, the president has the casting vote.

The Executive Board consists of a president, a vice-president and four other members. Each serves for an eight-year, non-renewable term. The Executive Board is responsible for implementing the decisions of the Governing Council and for preparing policies for the Council's consideration. Each

(continued)

member of the Executive Board has a responsibility for some particular aspect of monetary policy.

ECB independence

The ECB is one of the most independent central banks in the world. It has very little formal accountability to elected politicians. Although its president can be called before the European Parliament, the Parliament has virtually no powers to influence the ECB's actions. Until its January 2015 meeting, its deliberations were secret and no minutes of Council meetings were published. Subsequently, an account of meetings is published (usually with a lag of around two weeks) with an explanation of the policy stance. However, the minutes do not include details of how Council members voted or of future policy intentions, unlike the minutes published by the Bank of England which, from 2015, are available at the time of the policy announcement.

There is one area, however, where the ECB's power is limited by politicians and this concerns the exchange rate of the euro. Under the Maastricht Treaty, EU finance ministers have the responsibility for deciding on exchange rate policy (even though the ECB is charged with carrying it out). If the finance ministers want to stop the exchange rate of the euro rising, in order to prevent putting EU exporters at a competitive disadvantage, this will put pressure on the ECB to lower interest rates, which might run directly counter to its desire to meet its inflation and money supply targets. This is an example of the principle of 'targets and instruments'. If you have only one instrument (the rate of interest), it cannot be used to achieve two targets (the exchange rate and inflation) if these two targets are in conflict (see Box 22.9).

The target of monetary policy

The overall responsibility of the ECB is to achieve price stability in the eurozone. Since July 2021 the ECB has adopted a symmetric medium-term 2 per cent inflation rate target. This replaces the former target rate of below, but close to, 2 per cent over the medium. It is a weighted average rate for all the members of the eurozone, not a rate that has to be met by every member individually.

The ECB attempts to 'steer' short-term interest rates to influence economic activity to maintain price stability in the euro area in the medium term. Interest rates are set by the Governing Council by simple majority. In the event of a tie, the president has the casting vote.

From September 2019, the rates were as follows: 0.00 per cent for the main 'refinancing operations' of the ECB (i.e. the minimum rate of interest at which liquidity is offered once per week to 'monetary financial institutions' (MFIs) by the ECB and national central banks in the eurozone); a 'marginal lending' rate of 0.25 per cent (for providing overnight support to MFIs); and a 'deposit rate' of −0.50 per cent (the rate paid to MFIs for depositing overnight surplus liquidity with the ECB and national central banks in the eurozone).

The negative deposit rate meant that banks were being charged for 'parking' money with the ECB rather than lending it. This was intended to stimulate lending and hence economic activity.

The operation of monetary policy

The main instrument for keeping the ECB's desired interest rate as the equilibrium rate is open-market operations in government bonds and other recognised assets, mainly in the form of repos. These repo operations are conducted by the national central banks, which must ensure that the repo rate does not rise above the marginal overnight lending rate or below the deposit rate.

The normal operation of monetary policy involves two principal types of open-market operations:

Main refinancing operations (MROs). These are short-term repos normally with a maturity of one week. They take place weekly and are used to maintain liquidity consistent with the chosen ECB interest rate.

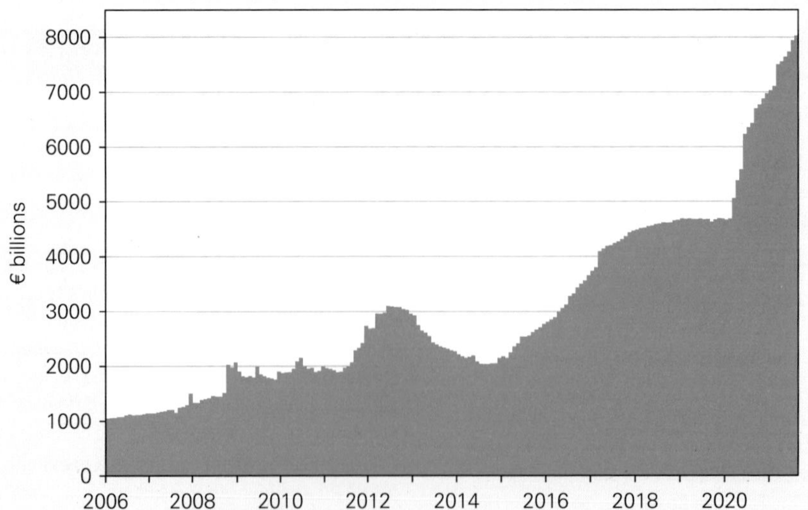

Source: Based on data in *Statistical Data Warehouse*, ECB, https://sdw.ecb.europa.eu/browse.do?node=9691294

Longer-term refinancing operations (LTROs). These take place monthly and typically have a maturity of three months. Longer maturities are available, but such operations are conducted more irregularly. They are to provide additional longer-term liquidity to banks as required at rates determined by the market, not the ECB.

The ECB sets a minimum reserve ratio. The ratio is designed primarily to prevent excessive lending and hence the need for excessive borrowing from the central bank or from other financial institutions.[2] From 1 January 1999 to 17 January 2012 the ratio was 2 per cent of key liquid and relatively liquid liabilities. It was then reduced to 1 per cent in an attempt to help stimulate bank lending. In other words, it was being used for the first time as part of an active monetary policy. However, it has not been used for this purpose since.

Non-standard policy measures

The financial crisis put incredible strains on commercial banks in the eurozone and, hence, on the ECB's monetary framework. Consequently, monetary operations were gradually modified, which, as we shall see, significantly expanded the size of the balance sheet of the ECB and central banks in the eurozone.

Securities Market Programme (SMP). In May 2010, the ECB began purchases of central government debt in the secondary market (i.e. not directly from governments) as well as purchases in both primary and secondary markets of private-sector debt instruments. This was designed to supply liquidity to the ailing banking system and by June 2012, €214 billion of purchases had been made of sovereign debt originating in Ireland, Greece, Spain, Italy and Portugal.

However, purchases under the SMP were offset by *selling* securities elsewhere. This offsetting process, known as ***sterilisation***, was designed to leave the overall money supply unchanged.

Three-year LTROs. In December 2011 and February 2012, the ECB conducted three-year refinancing operations (LTROs) aimed at alleviating liquidity pressures and stimulating lending. This saw €1 trillion drawn on by around 800 banks at a fixed interest rate of 1 per cent.

Targeted long-term refinancing operations (TLTROs). The aim of TLTROs was to provide long-term loans to commercial banks to stimulate bank lending to the non-financial private sector. The loans were said to be 'targeted' since the amounts that could be borrowed were to be tied to the size of eligible outstanding loans, while the interest rate charged was dependent on the lending history of each bank.

The first series of TLTROs was announced in June 2014, a second series in March 2016 (TLTRO-II) and a third series in July 2019 (TLTRO-III). The third TLTRO programme began in September 2019 with loans of up to three years. Rates were cut to as low as –1 per cent. By April 2021 banks had drawn in excess of €1 trillion.

Quantitative easing. In September 2014, the ECB finally announced that it would be commencing quantitative easing by purchasing marketable debt instruments, including public-sector bonds and asset-backed private-sector securities (see section 18.2 and Box 22.7). Between March 2015 and December 2019, the ECB made purchases worth €2.6 trillion.

Although purchases halted in December 2018 this proved to be only a temporary pause. With the annual rates of economic growth and price inflation at only around 1 per cent, the ECB announced in September 2019 that asset purchases would restart in November. The new round of QE was branded by some as 'QE Infinity' as the ECB committed itself to asset purchases of €20 billion per month for as long as was necessary for inflation and growth rates to return to satisfactory levels.

However, this was insufficient alone to mitigate the economic impact of the COVID-19 pandemic. In March 2020, an *additional* programme of asset purchases was announced. Known as the Pandemic Emergency Purchase Programme (PEPP), it was intended to have an initial 'envelope' of €750 billion. This was expanded by a further €600 billion in June 2020 and by another €500 billion in December 2020, taking the envelope up to €1850 billion.

What are the arguments for and against publishing the minutes of the meetings of the ECB's Governing Council and Executive Board?

Undertake desktop research to help prepare a briefing note summarising the responses of the ECB, the Fed and the Bank of England to the COVID-19 pandemic.

Definition

Sterilisation Actions taken by a central bank to offset the effects of foreign exchange flows or its own bond transactions so as to leave money supply unchanged.

1 See www.ecb.int/ecb/orga/decisions/govc/html/index.en.html
2 'The use of a minimum reserve system by the European System of Central Banks in Stage Three', www.ecb.europa.eu/press/pr/date/1998/html/pr981013_3.en.html

Problems with controlling interest rates

Even though central bank adjustment of the repo rate is the current preferred method of monetary control in most countries, it is not without its difficulties. The problems centre on the nature of the demand for loans. If this demand is (a) unresponsive to interest rate changes or (b) unstable because it can be significantly affected by other determinants (e.g. anticipated income or foreign interest rates), it will be very difficult to control by controlling the rate of interest.

Problem of an inelastic demand for loans

TC 6 p66

If the demand for loans is inelastic, as in Figure 22.13, any attempt to reduce demand (e.g. from Q_1 to Q_2) will involve large rises in real interest rates (r_1 to r_2). The problem will be compounded if the demand curve shifts to the right, due, say, to a consumer spending boom. High interest rates lead to the following problems:

Figure 22.13 An inelastic demand for loans

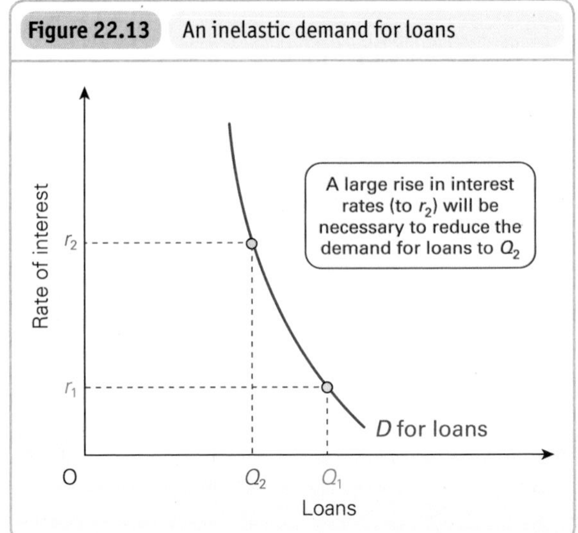

- They may discourage long-term investment (as opposed to current consumption) and hence long-term growth.
- They add to the costs of production, to the costs of house purchase and generally to the cost of living. They are thus cost inflationary.
- They are politically unpopular, since the general public do not like paying higher interest rates on overdrafts, credit cards and mortgages.
- The authorities may need to ensure a sufficient supply of longer-term securities so that liquidity can be constrained. This could commit the government to paying high rates on these bonds for some time.
- High interest rates encourage inflows of money from abroad. This makes it even more difficult to restrain bank lending. This drives up the exchange rate. A higher exchange rate makes domestic goods expensive relative to goods made abroad. This can be very damaging for export industries and industries competing with imports. Many firms in the UK suffered badly between 1997 and 2007

BOX 22.9 GOODHART'S LAW

'To control is to distort'

'If you want to tackle a problem, it's best to get to the root of it.'

This is a message that economists are constantly preaching. If you merely treat the symptoms of a problem rather than its underlying causes, the problem may simply manifest itself in some other form. What is more, the symptoms (or lack of them, if the treatment makes them go away) will now be a poor indicator of the problem. Let us illustrate this with a medical example.

Assume that you suffer from deteriorating eyesight. As a result, you get increasingly bad headaches. The worse the headaches become, the worse it suggests your eyesight is getting. The headaches are thus a symptom of the problem and an indicator of the problem's magnitude. So what do you do? One approach is to treat the symptoms. You regularly take painkillers and the headaches go away. But you have not treated the underlying problem – by getting stronger glasses, or perhaps even having eye surgery – all you have done is to treat the symptoms. As a result, headaches (or rather the lack of them) are now a poor indicator of your eyesight.

If you control the indicator rather than the underlying problem, the indicator ceases to be a good indicator. 'To control [the indicator] is to distort [its use as an indicator].' This is ***Goodhart's law*** and it has many applications in economics, especially when targets are set by the government. Let us take the example of a money supply target.

***Goodhart's law*: Controlling a symptom (i.e. an indicator) of a problem will not cure the problem. Instead, the indicator will merely cease to be a good indicator of the problem.**

Definition

Goodhart's law Controlling a symptom of a problem or only one part of the problem will not cure the problem: it will simply mean that the part that is being controlled now becomes a poor indicator of the problem.

from a high exchange rate, caused partly by higher interest rates in the UK than in the eurozone and the USA.

Evidence suggests that the demand for loans may indeed be quite inelastic, especially in the short run. Although investment plans may be curtailed by high interest rates, borrowing to finance current expenditure by many firms cannot easily be curtailed. Similarly, while householders may be discouraged from taking on new mortgages, they may find it difficult to reduce current expenditure as a means of reducing their credit card debt. What is more, although high interest rates may discourage many firms from taking out long-term fixed-interest loans, some firms may merely switch to shorter-term variable-interest loans.

Problem of an unstable demand

KI 34 p453

Accurate monetary control requires the authorities to be able to predict the demand curve for money. Only then can they set the appropriate level of interest rates. Unfortunately, the demand curve may shift unpredictably, making control very difficult. The major reason is *speculation*:

- If people think interest rates will rise and bond prices fall, in the meantime they will want to hold their assets in liquid form. The demand for money will rise.
- If people think exchange rates will rise, they will demand sterling while it is still relatively cheap. The demand for money will rise.
- If people think inflation will rise, the transactions demand for money may rise. People spend now while prices are still relatively low.
- If people think the economy is going to grow faster, the demand for loans will increase as firms seek to increase their investment.

It is very difficult for the authorities to predict what people's expectations, and hence speculation, will be. Speculation depends largely on world political events, rumour and 'random shocks'.

If the demand curve shifts very much, and if it is inelastic, monetary control will be very difficult. Furthermore, the central bank will have to make frequent and sizeable adjustments to interest rates. These fluctuations can be very damaging to business confidence and may discourage long-term investment.

Why does an unstable demand for money make it difficult to control the supply of money?

The net result of an inelastic and unstable demand for money is that substantial interest rate changes may be necessary to bring about the required change in aggregate demand. For example, central banks had to cut interest rates to virtually zero in their attempt to tackle the global recession of the late 2000s. Indeed, as we saw in Box 22.7, central banks took to other methods, and in particular quantitative easing, as the room for interest rate cuts simply disappeared.

EXPLORING ECONOMICS

Money as an indicator of aggregate demand

Monetarists from the 1960s argued that the level of money supply determines the level of nominal aggregate demand and prices. They therefore argued in favour of setting targets for the growth of money supply. Critics, however, argued that the level of money supply is only an indicator of the level of nominal aggregate demand (and a poor one at that). As soon as you start to control money supply, they said, the relationship between them breaks down. If, for example, you restrict the amount of money and yet people still want to borrow, money will simply circulate faster (the velocity of circulation (V) will rise), and hence aggregate demand may not decline.

The choice of money supply target

If targets for the growth of money supply are to be set, which measure of money supply should be chosen? Goodhart's law suggests that whichever measure is chosen it will, by virtue of its choice, become a poor indicator. If the government targets cash in circulation and directs its policy to reducing the amount of notes and coin in the economy, banks may try to reduce their customers' demand for cash by, say, increasing the charges for cash advances on credit cards. As a result, cash may well be constrained, but M4 may well go on rising.

The choice of institutions

If bank advances are a good indicator of aggregate demand, the government may choose to control bank lending. But as soon as it does so, bank lending will become a poor indicator. If people's demand for loans is still high and bank loans are becoming difficult to obtain, people will simply go elsewhere to borrow money. If you regulate part of the financial system, you are likely to end up merely diverting business to other parts which are unregulated.

How may the use of targets in the health service (such as getting waiting lists down) provide an example of Goodhart's law?

Prepare a short PowerPoint presentation, say of about 10 minutes, giving some everyday examples of Goodhart's law.

BOX 22.10 **USING INTEREST RATES TO CONTROL BOTH AGGREGATE DEMAND AND THE EXCHANGE RATE**

EXPLORING ECONOMICS

A problem of one instrument and two targets

Assume that the central bank is worried about excessive growth in the money supply and rising inflation. It thus decides to raise interest rates. One effect of these higher interest rates is to attract deposits into the country (causing a financial account surplus) and thus drive up the exchange rate. This makes imports cheaper and exports less competitive. This will result in a current account deficit, which will match the financial (plus capital) account surplus.

Now let us assume that the central bank becomes worried about the damaging effect on exports and wants to reduce the exchange rate. If it uses interest rates as the means of achieving this, it will have to lower them: lower interest rates will cause deposits to flow out of the country, and this will cause the rate of exchange to depreciate.

But there is a dilemma here. The central bank wants high interest rates to contain inflation, but low interest rates to help exporters. If interest rates are the only policy instrument, one objective will have to be sacrificed for the other.

Another example, but this time the reverse case, was when the UK voted to leave the EU in June 2016. Worried about the possible dampening effect on investment and economic growth from worries about trade relationships, the Bank of England *lowered* Bank Rate from 0.5 to 0.25 per cent and backed this up with another round of quantitative easing. However, the worries about UK trade also drove down the exchange rate, which increased the price of imports and increased inflation – at least temporarily. If the Bank of England had wanted to dampen this inflation, it would have to have *raised* Bank Rate. Clearly, it could not both lower and raise Bank Rate at the same time.

These examples illustrate a rule in economic policy: you must have at least as many instruments as targets. If you have two targets (e.g. low inflation and a low exchange rate), you must have at least two policy instruments (e.g. interest rates and one other).

If the central bank wanted to achieve a lower rate of inflation and also a higher exchange rate, could it under these circumstances rely simply on the one policy instrument of interest rates?

Prepare a short PowerPoint presentation, say of about 10 minutes, giving some other examples of the impossibility of using one policy instrument to achieve two policy objectives simultaneously.

Using monetary policy

It is impossible to use monetary policy as a precise means of controlling aggregate demand. It is especially weak when it is pulling against the expectations of firms and consumers, and when it is implemented too late. However, if the authorities operate a tight monetary policy firmly enough and long enough, they should eventually be able to reduce lending and aggregate demand. But there will inevitably be time lags and imprecision in the process.

An expansionary monetary policy is even less reliable. If the economy is in recession, no matter how low interest rates are driven, people cannot be forced to borrow if they do not wish to. Firms will not borrow to invest if they predict a continuing recession.

A particular difficulty in using interest rate reductions to expand the economy arises if the repo rate is nearly zero. First, as we saw earlier, there is the problem of a limited pass-through effect: the loosening of monetary policy may not be mirrored by the easing of credit conditions. Second, even if credit conditions do ease, they may not stimulate the economy. The problem is that (nominal) market interest rates cannot be negative (except in the case for overnight deposits by banks in the central bank), for clearly nobody would be willing to lend in these circumstances.

The UK and many eurozone countries were in this position in the early 2010s. They found themselves caught in the 'liquidity trap' (see page 602). Despite record low interest rates and high levels of liquidity, borrowing and lending remained low given worries about fiscal austerity and its dampening effects on economic growth.

One way in which central banks, like the Federal Reserve, the Bank of England and the ECB, attempted to encourage spending following the financial crisis of the late 2000s was by publicly indicating the expected path of future interest rates. By stating that interest rates were likely to remain low for some time, central banks hoped that *forward guidance* would give economic agents confidence to bring forward their spending.

Despite these problems, changing interest rates can be quite effective in the medium term. After all, they can be changed very rapidly. There are not the time lags of implementation that there are with various forms of fiscal policy. Indeed, since the early 1990s, most governments or central banks have used interest rate changes as the major means of keeping inflation and/or aggregate demand under control.

As we have seen, in the UK, the eurozone, the USA and many other countries, the government or central bank sets a target for the rate of inflation for the medium term, typically 2 per cent (see table in Box 21.7 on page 683). If forecasts suggest that inflation is going to be off-target, interest rate changes are announced, and then appropriate open-market operations are conducted to support the new interest rate. The use of such targets is examined in section 22.4.

One important effect of changing interest rates in this very public way is that it sends a clear message to people that inflation *will* be kept under control. People will therefore be more likely to adjust their expectations accordingly and keep their borrowing in check.

Section summary

1. Control of the growth in the money supply over the longer term will normally involve governments attempting to restrict the size of their deficits. Whilst this is relatively easy once inflation has been brought under control, it can lead to serious problems if inflation is initially high. Increases in taxes and cuts in government expenditure are not only politically unpopular, but could also result in a recession.
2. In the short term, the authorities can use monetary policy to restrict the growth in aggregate demand in one of two major ways: (a) reducing money supply directly; (b) reducing the demand for money by raising interest rates.
3. The money supply can be reduced directly by using open-market operations. This involves the central bank selling more government securities and thereby reducing banks' reserves when their customers pay for them from their bank accounts. Alternatively, the central bank can reduce the amount of lending or rediscounting it is prepared to do (other than as a last-resort measure). Rather than controlling the monetary base in either of these two ways, the central bank could adjust its funding of the national debt. This would involve increasing the sale of bonds relative to bills, thereby reducing banks' liquid assets. Finally, it could operate a system of variable minimum reserve ratios. Increasing these would force banks to cut back the amount of credit they create.
4. Controlling either the monetary base or broad liquidity in the short term, however, is difficult given that central banks are always prepared to provide liquidity to the banks on demand. Even if the authorities are successful in controlling the money supply, there then arises the problem of severe fluctuations in interest rates if the demand for money fluctuates and is relatively inelastic.
5. The normal method of control in the UK and many other countries involves the central bank influencing interest rates by its operations in the gilt repo and discount markets. The central bank keeps banks short of liquidity and then supplies them with liquidity, largely through gilt repos, at its chosen interest rate (gilt repo rate). This then has a knock-on effect on interest rates throughout the economy.
6. After the global financial crisis and then again in response to the COVID-19 pandemic, many central banks engaged in large-scale asset purchases. This meant that there was an abundant supply of reserves. Thus the interest rate paid by central bank on reserves deposited by commercial banks often provided a 'floor' for short-term market interest rates.
7. With an interest-inelastic demand for loans changes in interest rates may have to be very large to bring the required changes in monetary growth. High interest rates are politically unpopular and discriminate against those with high borrowing commitments. They also drive up the exchange rate, which can damage exports. Controlling aggregate demand through interest rates is made even more difficult by fluctuations in the demand for money. These fluctuations are made more severe by speculation against changes in interest rates, exchange rates, the rate of inflation, etc.
8. It is impossible to use monetary policy as a precise means of controlling aggregate demand in the short term. Nevertheless, controlling interest rates is a rapid way of responding to changing forecasts, and can be an important signal to markets that inflation will be kept under control, especially when, as in the UK and the eurozone, there is a firm target for the rate of inflation.

22.4 THE POLICY-MAKING ENVIRONMENT

Debates over the control of demand have shifted ground somewhat in recent years. There is now less debate over the relative effectiveness of fiscal and monetary policy in influencing aggregate demand. There is general agreement that a *combination* of fiscal and monetary policies will have a more powerful effect on demand than either used separately.

Economists have become increasingly interested in the environment within which policy is made. In this section we analyse debates around the extent to which governments ought to pursue active demand management policies or adhere to a set of policy rules.

KI 34 453

Those in the Keynesian tradition prefer discretionary policy – changing policy as circumstances change. Those in the monetarist and new classical tradition prefer to set firm rules (e.g. targets for inflation, public deficits or growth in the money supply) and then stick to them.

The case for rules

There are two important arguments against discretionary policy and for rules: the political incentives of governments and time lags.

Political behaviour

Politicians may attempt to manipulate the economy for their own political purposes – such as the desire to be re-elected. As we saw in section 21.2 when discussing the *political business cycle* (see page 668), the government, if not constrained by rules, may overstimulate the economy some time before an election so that growth is strong at election time. After the election, the government strongly dampens the economy to deal with the accelerating inflation rate, and to create enough slack for another boost in time for the next election.

A less extreme version is where governments from time to time use monetary and fiscal policy to try to boost their popularity. The manipulation of policy instruments is not necessarily systematic or regular in the way that the political business cycle model implies. Nonetheless, the manipulation is intended to court short-term favour with the public and may store up problems for the economy and, in the case of fiscal policy, for the public finances.

It is argued that when politicians behave in this way, fiscal policy may exhibit a ***deficit bias***. Because governments are more willing to use their discretion to loosen fiscal policy than they are to tighten fiscal policy, persistent deficits and a rising debt-to-GDP ratio can result. Table 22.1 (on page 696) provides some support for this. Therefore, fiscal rules may be needed to ensure the long-term sustainability of public finances and to provide *credibility* for fiscal policy and sound economic management.

As we saw in section 21.5, the importance of credibility in the conduct of monetary policy has provided the theoretical foundations for the delegation of monetary policy to central banks. The monetary policy counterpart to deficit bias is *inflation bias* (see page 678). If monetary policy is not delegated to the central bank, the government will have an incentive to loosen monetary policy to boost the economy and its popularity. However, this can lead to higher expectations of inflation with actual rates of inflation typically higher than it would otherwise be, but, it is argued, with unemployment no lower.

Time lags with discretionary policy

Both fiscal and monetary policies can involve long and variable time lags. These can make policy at best ineffective and at worst destabilising (see Figure 22.7 on page 708). Taking the measures *before* the problem arises, and thus lessening KI 33 p377 the problem of lags, is usually not an option since forecasting tends to be unreliable.

In contrast, by setting and sticking to rules, and then not interfering further, the government can provide a sound fiscal and monetary framework in which there is maximum freedom for individual initiative and enterprise, and in which firms are not cushioned from market forces and are therefore encouraged to be efficient. By the government setting a target for a steady reduction in the growth of money supply, or a target for the rate of inflation, and then resolutely sticking to it, people's expectations of inflation will be reduced, thereby making the target easier to achieve.

This sound and stable monetary environment, with no likelihood of sudden contractionary or expansionary fiscal or monetary policy, will encourage firms to take a longer-

term perspective and to plan ahead. This could then lead to increased capital investment and long-term growth.

The optimum situation is for all the major countries to adhere to mutually consistent rules, so that their economies do not get out of line. This will create more stable exchange rates and provide the climate for world growth (we explore this issue in section 26.1).

Advocates of this point of view in the 1970s and 1980s were monetarists and new classical macroeconomists, but support for the setting of targets was to become widespread. As we have seen, targets are set for both inflation and fiscal indicators, such as public-sector deficits.

Would it be desirable for all countries to stick to the same targets?

The case for discretion

Keynesians typically reject the argument that rules provide the environment for high and stable growth. Demand, argue KI 34 p453
Keynesians, is subject to many and sometimes violent exogenous shocks: e.g. changes in expectations, domestic political events (such as an impending election), financial market effects (such as the credit crunch), world economic factors (such as the global economic recession of 2008–9), world political events (such as a war) and global health emergencies (such as the COVID-19 pandemic). The resulting shifts in injections or withdrawals cause the economy to deviate from a stable full-employment growth path.

Any change in injections or withdrawals will lead to a TC 15 p543
cumulative effect on national income via the multiplier and accelerator and via changing expectations. These endogenous effects take time and interact with each other, and so a process of expansion or contraction can last many months before a turning point is eventually reached.

Since the exogenous changes in demand occur at irregular intervals and are of different magnitudes, the economy is likely to experience cycles of irregular duration and of varying intensity.

Given that the economy is inherently unstable and is buffeted around by various exogenous shocks, Keynesians argue

that the government needs actively to intervene to stabilise the economy. Otherwise, the uncertainty caused by unpredictable fluctuations will be very damaging to investment and hence to long-term growth in potential output (quite apart from the short-term effects of recessions on actual output and employment).

If demand fluctuates in the way Keynesians claim, and if the policy of having a money supply or inflation rule is adhered to, interest rates must fluctuate. But excessive fluctuations in interest rates will discourage long-term business planning and investment. What is more, the government may find it difficult to keep to its targets. This too may cause uncertainty and instability.

Definition

Deficit bias The tendency for frequent fiscal deficits and rising debt-to-GDP ratios because of the reluctance of policy makers to tighten fiscal policy.

Problems with rules and targets

The global financial crisis meant many countries that had adopted fiscal rules had to suspend their operation. While they were generally reintroduced, they often needed to be adapted, leading to a more flexible second generation of rules (see pages 709–10).

This was the case in the UK, which adopted a looser set of fiscal rules, known as a 'fiscal mandate', focused on cyclically-adjusted public-sector net borrowing and public-sector net debt (see Case 22.7 on the student website). However, with the UK government already committed to reviewing the rules following the 2019 election, the pandemic meant that the focus again was on discretionary fiscal measures. The hope was that a new set of rules could then be introduced.

The widespread suspension of fiscal rules (or the activation of 'escape clauses') following the pandemic was the second in a little over a decade. This highlights important questions about the degree of flexibility that can be designed into any rules and the need to revisit rules and targets from time to time.

Even if a target or policy framework has been in force for some time, it may cease to be the appropriate one. Economic circumstances might change. For example, an extended period of relatively low inflation may warrant a lower inflation target.

If an inflation target is chosen, then again, the problem of Goodhart's law is likely to apply. If people believe that their central bank will be successful in achieving its inflation target, then those expectations will feed into their inflationary expectations, and not surprisingly the target will be met.

The problem with inflation targets, therefore, is that they can become consistent with both a buoyant and a depressed economy. In other words, the Phillips curve may become *horizontal*. Consequently, as we explained in section 21.5, the *DAS* curve too becomes horizontal (at least up to near full capacity in the economy). Shifts in the *DAD* curve will simply lead to changes in real national income. Thus achieving an inflation target may not tackle the much more serious problem of creating stable economic growth and an environment which will encourage long-term investment.

In extreme cases, as occurred in 2008, the economy may slow down rapidly and yet cost-push factors may cause inflation to rise. Strictly adhering to an inflation rate target in these circumstances would demand *higher* interest rates, which could further restrict growth. A similar argument applied to the UK after the Brexit vote. The fall in the pound threatened to push up inflation and yet the Bank of England decided to cut Bank Rate. The aim was to ward off a downswing in the economy.

But if rules should not be stuck to religiously, does this mean that policy makers can engage in fine-tuning? Keynesians today recognise that fine-tuning may not be possible; nevertheless, significant and persistent excess or deficient demand *can* be corrected by demand management policy. For example, the decision taken following the global financial crisis and the COVID-19 pandemic by several central banks to cut interest rates and engage in quantitative easing, and by governments to increase expenditures and to cut taxes, helped to stave off even deeper recessions.

Improvements in forecasting, a willingness of governments to act quickly and the use of quick-acting policies can all help to increase the effectiveness of discretionary demand management.

Under what circumstances would adherence to money supply targets lead to (a) more stable interest rates and (b) less stable interest rates than pursuing discretionary demand management policy?

Conclusions

The following factors provide us with a framework to help analyse the relative merits of rules or discretion.

- The confidence of people in the effectiveness of either discretionary policies or rules: the greater the confidence, the more successful is either policy likely to be.
- The degree of self-stabilisation of the economy (in the case of rules), or conversely the degree of inherent instability of the economy (in the case of discretion).
- The size and frequency of exogenous shocks to demand: the greater they are, the greater the case for discretionary policy.
- In the case of rules, the ability and determination of governments to stick to the rules and the belief by the public that they will be effective.
- In the case of discretionary policy, the ability of governments to adopt and execute policies of the correct magnitude, the speed with which such policies can be effected and the accuracy of forecasting.

Section summary

1. The case against discretionary policy is that it involves unpredictable time lags that can make the policy destabilising. Also, the government may ignore the long-run adverse consequences of policies designed for short-run political gain.
2. The case in favour of rules is that they help to reduce deficit bias and inflationary bias and help create a stable environment for investment and growth.
3. The case against sticking to money supply or inflation rules is that they may cause severe fluctuations in interest rates and thus create a less stable economic environment for business planning. Given the changing economic environment in which we live, rules adopted in the past may no longer be suitable for the present.
4. Although perfect fine-tuning may not be possible, Keynesians argue that the government must have the discretion to change its policy as circumstances demand.

END OF CHAPTER QUESTIONS

1. What are the problems of relying on automatic fiscal stabilisers to ensure a stable economy at full employment?
2. Does it matter if a country has a large national debt as a proportion of its national income?
3. If the government is running a budget deficit, does this mean that national income will increase?
4. Of what significance are primary deficits or surpluses for the dynamics of a government's debt-to-GDP ratio?
5. What factors determine the effectiveness of discretionary fiscal policy?
6. Why is it difficult to use fiscal policy to 'fine-tune' the economy?
7. Assume that a bank has the following simplified balance sheet, and is operating at its desired liquidity ratio:

Liabilities	(£m)	Assets	(£m)
Deposits	100	Balances with central bank	10
		Advances	90
	100		100

Now assume that the central bank repurchases £5 million of government bonds on the open market. Assume that the people who sell the bonds all have their accounts with this bank and keep a constant amount of cash outside the bank.

(a) Draw up the new balance sheet directly after the purchase of the bonds.
(b) Now draw up the eventual balance sheet after all credit creation has taken place.
(c) Would there be a similar effect if the central bank rediscounted £5 billion of Treasury bills?
(d) How would such open-market operations affect the rate of interest?

8. Is it possible for the government to target the money supply over the longer term without targeting the level of public-sector net borrowing?
9. What are the mechanics whereby the central bank raises the rate of interest?
10. What is Goodhart's law? How is it relevant to (a) monetary policy; (b) using assignment grades to assess a student's ability; (c) paying workers according to the amount of output they produce; (d) awarding local authority contracts to cleaning or refuse disposal companies on the basis of tendered prices?
11. 'It is easier to control the monetary base than broader money, but it is less relevant to do so.' Do you agree with this statement?
12. Compare the relative merits of targeting (a) the money supply; (b) the exchange rate; (c) the rate of inflation.
13. Is there a compromise between purely discretionary policy and adhering to strict targets?

Online resources

Additional case studies on the student website

22.1 Banks, taxes and the fiscal costs of the financial crisis. A discussion of the government's financial interventions during the financial crisis and their impact on the public finances.

22.2 The national debt. This explores the question of whether it matters if a country has a high national debt.

22.3 Trends in public expenditure. This case examines attempts to control public expenditure in the UK and relates them to the crowding-out debate.

22.4 Fiscal arithmetic. Applying the relationship between the primary balance and government debt to analyse the sustainability of the public finances in a sample of advanced economies.

22.5 Injections against the contagion. The use of discretionary fiscal policy in the late 1990s.

22.6 Any more G and T? An analysis of the UK public finances using a series of fiscal indicators.

22.7 Fiscal rules in the UK. A summary of the changes to the fiscal rules that have been adopted in the UK since the late 1990s.

22.8 Discretionary policy in Japan. Attempts by successive Japanese governments since 1992 to bring the economy out of recession through expansionary fiscal policy.

22.9 Credit and the business cycle. This case traces cycles in the growth of credit and relates them to the business cycle. It also looks at some of the implications of the growth in credit.

22.10 From the corridor to the floor. An examination of the Bank of England's monetary policy framework before and after the global financial crisis.

22.11 Effective monetary policy versus banking efficiency and stability. This case examines potential conflicts between banking stability, efficiency and the effective operation of monetary policy.

22.12 *IS/MP*, policy and the aftermath of the banking crisis. Using the *IS/MP* framework we analyse the banking crisis and the subsequent recession and slow recovery.

22.13 Fiscal and monetary policy in the UK. An historical overview of UK fiscal and monetary policy.

22.14 *IS/LM* analysis of fiscal and monetary policy. An illustration of how we can use the *IS/LM* framework to examine the effects of fiscal and monetary policy taking into account both the goods and money markets.

Websites relevant to this chapter and Chapters 20 and 21

Numbers and sections refer to websites listed in the Web Appendix and hotlinked from this book's website at **www.go.pearson.com/uk/sloman**.

- For news articles relevant to this and the previous two chapters, see the *Economics News* section on the student website.
- For general news on fiscal and monetary policies, see websites in section A, and particularly A1–5. See also links to newspapers worldwide in A38, 39, 42, 43 and 44, and the news search feature in Google at A41. See also links to economics news in A42.
- For information on UK fiscal policy and government borrowing, see sites E30, 36; F2. See also sites A1–8 at Budget time.
- For a model of the economy (based on the Treasury model), see *The Virtual Chancellor* (site D1). In the model you can devise your own Budget.
- For monetary policy in the UK, see F1, C21 and E30. For monetary policy in the eurozone, see F6 and 5. For monetary policy in the USA, see F8. For monetary policy in other countries, see the respective central bank site in section F or in site F17.
- For demand-side policy in the UK, see the latest Budget Report (e.g. section on maintaining macroeconomic stability) at site E30.
- For inflation targeting in the UK and eurozone, see sites F1 and 6.
- For student resources relevant to this chapter, see sites C1–10, 12, 19, 21. Also see site D1 (*The Virtual Chancellor*).

Long-term Economic Growth and Supply-side Policies

CHAPTER MAP

In this chapter we turn our attention to the determinants of long-run economic growth. All developed countries have experienced economic growth over the past 60 years or so, but rates have differed significantly from one country to another. We look at some of these differences in section 23.1.

If an economy is to achieve sustained economic growth over the longer term, there must be a sustained increase in potential output. An important ingredient for long-term economic growth is the growth in labour productivity. This, in turn, depends on two major factors: a growth in the amount of capital that workers use, and technological progress. We can see these two elements if we look around us. Take a modern car factory, with its high-tech robot-driven equipment: it is no surprise that workers' productivity is much higher than it was, say, 30 years ago. Take a modern office, with powerful computers: again it is no surprise that today's office staff are much more productive than their counterparts of past years.

In section 23.2 we look at the effects of an increase in the rate of capital investment when there is no change in technology. As we shall see, the effect will simply be growth to a new higher level of national income, not a permanently higher rate of economic growth. If economic growth is to

be higher over the long term, therefore, there must be an increase in the rate of technological progress. We look at how this affects economic growth in section 23.3.

In the final three sections we look at various policy options to increase aggregate supply. Supply-side policies can be put into two broad categories: market orientated and interventionist. Market-orientated policies focus on 'freeing up' markets and improving market incentives. They involve policies such as tax cuts, privatisation and deregulation. Interventionist policies, by contrast, focus on ways of countering the inadequacies of markets through direct government provision of transport infrastructure, training or R&D, or financial support for private provision.

23.1 INTRODUCTION TO LONG-TERM ECONOMIC GROWTH

Twin characteristics of growth

Our focus so far in Part F has been on economic volatility. This is not surprising given that economies are inherently volatile and often experience significant fluctuations in economic activity. Yet when we step back and look at the longer span of history, these short-term fluctuations take on less significance. What we see is that economies tend to experience long-term economic growth.

These twin characteristics of growth are captured in Figure 23.1, which plots for the UK both the *level* of real GDP and annual percentage *changes* in real GDP. It shows that while the rate of economic growth is volatile, the volume of output grows over time.

The rate of long-term economic growth in developed nations, such as the UK, has meant that average living standards have improved markedly. When measured in terms of real GDP per head, all developed nations are considerably richer today than they were, say, 50 or 60 years ago.

The picture, however, is not one of universal improvement. People are not necessarily happier; there are many stresses in modern living; the environment is in many respects more polluted; inequality has increased in many countries; for many people work is more demanding and the working day is longer than in the past; there is more crime and more insecurity. Hence, 'more' is not always 'better'.

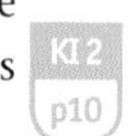
KI 2 p10

Nevertheless, most people *want* more consumer goods; they want higher incomes. In this chapter, we examine what causes long-term economic growth, and how it can be increased. We leave you to judge whether a materially richer society is a better society.

Long-run growth and the *DAD/DAS* and *IS/MP* models

Sustained economic growth over the longer term requires a sustained increase in *potential output*. This means that there has to be a continuous rightward shift in aggregate supply. When viewed through the *DAD/DAS* model, long-run growth therefore means a continuous rightward shift of the

Figure 23.1 Output and economic growth in the UK since 1700

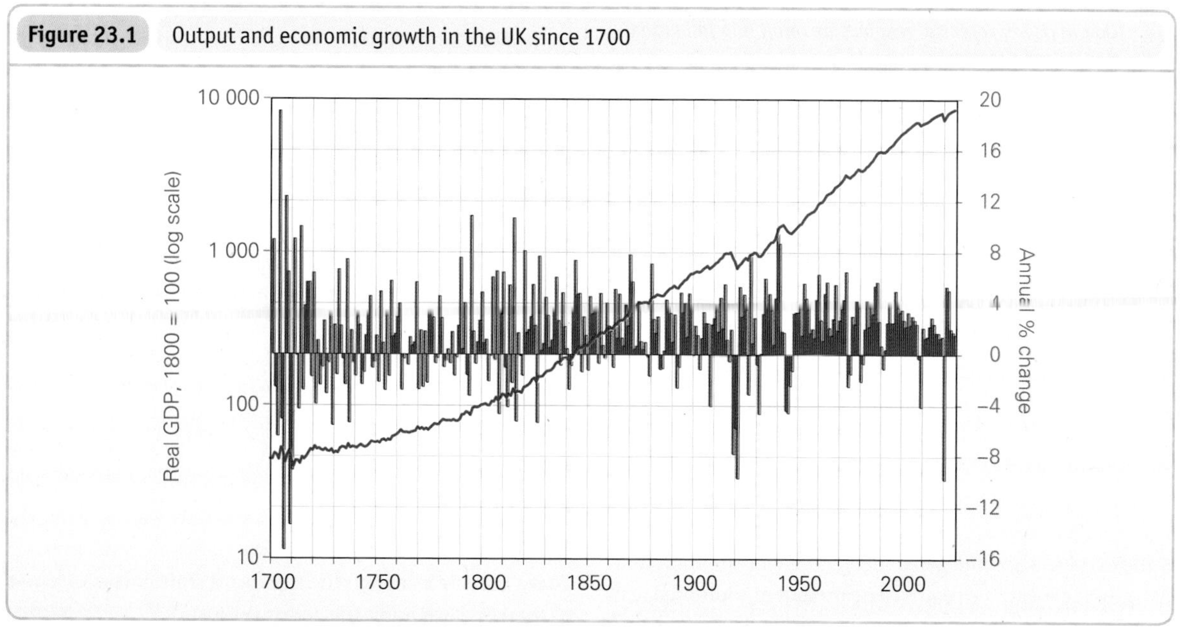

Note: Growth is the annual growth in constant-price GDP.
Sources: 1700–1948 based on data from *A Millennium of Macroeconomic Data*, Bank of England, www.bankofengland.co.uk/statistics/research-datasets; from 1949 to 2020 based on series ABMI and IHYP, National Statistics, www.ons.gov.uk/economy/grossdomesticproductgdp/; from 2021 based on *World Economic Outlook*, IMF (April 2021), www.imf.org/en/Publications/WEO/Issues/2021/03/23/world-economic-outlook-april-2021

Figure 23.2 Long-term growth in integrated *DAD/DAS* and *IS/MP* framework

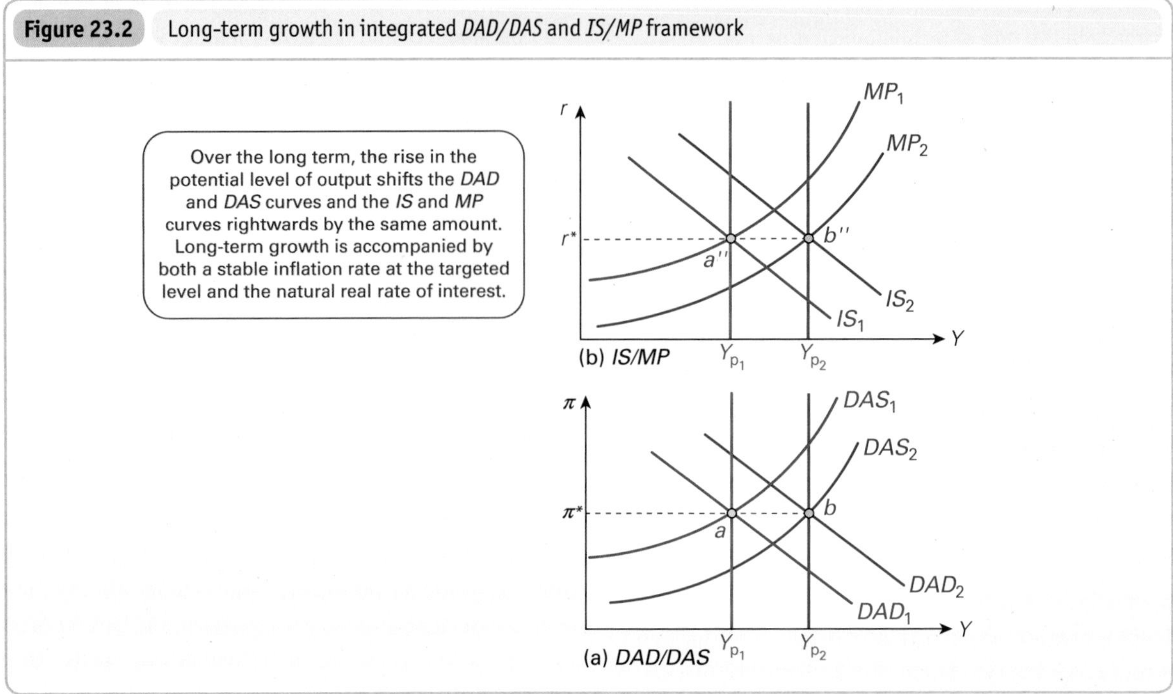

DAS curve. The rate of growth in potential output is then the rate at which the curve shifts rightwards.

We can use Figure 23.2 to illustrate the process of long-run growth through a simplified version of our integrated macroeconomic framework introduced in the previous chapter. It combines the *DAD/DAS* and *IS/MP* models. The relationship between the labour market and long-term growth is discussed as we go through the chapter.

Does a rise in potential real income result in a fall in the natural rate of unemployment?

Assume initially that the economy is at equilibrium characterised by output (real national income) at the potential level (Y_{P_1}), inflation at the target rate (π^*) and the interest rate at the natural rate (r^*). Now assume that potential output rises from Y_{P_1} to Y_{P_2}. We will look at how this might happen later in the chapter.

The DAD/DAS model

In Figure 23.2(a) the *DAS* curve moves rightwards – say to DAS_2. The size of the shift reflects the increase in the economy's productive capabilities. If the extra capacity is used, this also has the effect of increasing the real national income of the country; people are now able to make more purchases. There is also likely to be a rightward shift in the *DAD* curve. If the extra real income generated by the increase in potential output generates an equivalent amount of additional real spending, the *DAD* curve will shift to DAD_2. (This would be when Say's law is operative: see page 503.) In such a case, actual output would increase by the same amount as potential output: i.e. $Y_{P_2} - Y_{P_1}$.

If, however, the rise in potential output did not translate into sufficient extra spending, the *DAD* curve would not shift sufficiently to the right to give a new equilibrium at Y_{P_2} – a negative output gap would emerge. In such a case, discretionary fiscal and/or monetary policy may be required to shift the *DAD* curve to DAD_2.

Generally, however, over a time span of several years, periods of deficient demand are likely to be matched by periods of excess demand. In the long run, therefore, rightward shifts in the *DAS* curve would be matched by equivalent rightward shifts in the *DAD* curve. In other words, in the long run, economies tend towards equilibrium at the potential level of national income as markets and expectations adjust.

The IS/MP model

In Figure 23.2(b), the *MP* curve also shifts rightwards from the increase in potential output (i.e. from MP_1 to MP_2). This occurs because, with more productive capacity, the rate of inflation is now lower at any level of output. Hence, the central bank can now set a lower real rate of interest at any particular level of output than previously.

Meanwhile, if the extra capacity generates extra demand, the *IS* curve will shift to the right too. In periods of negative or positive output gaps, however, the shift in the *IS* curve is likely to fall short of or exceed the rightward shift in the *MP* curve. Over time, however, the rightward shift in the *IS* curve is likely to match the rightward shift in the *MP* curve as markets clear and expectations adjust.

Explain the mechanisms whereby the DAD and IS curves will shift by the same amount as the DAS and MP curves in the long run.

Figure 23.3 Long-term output growth (real GDP, 1960 = 100)

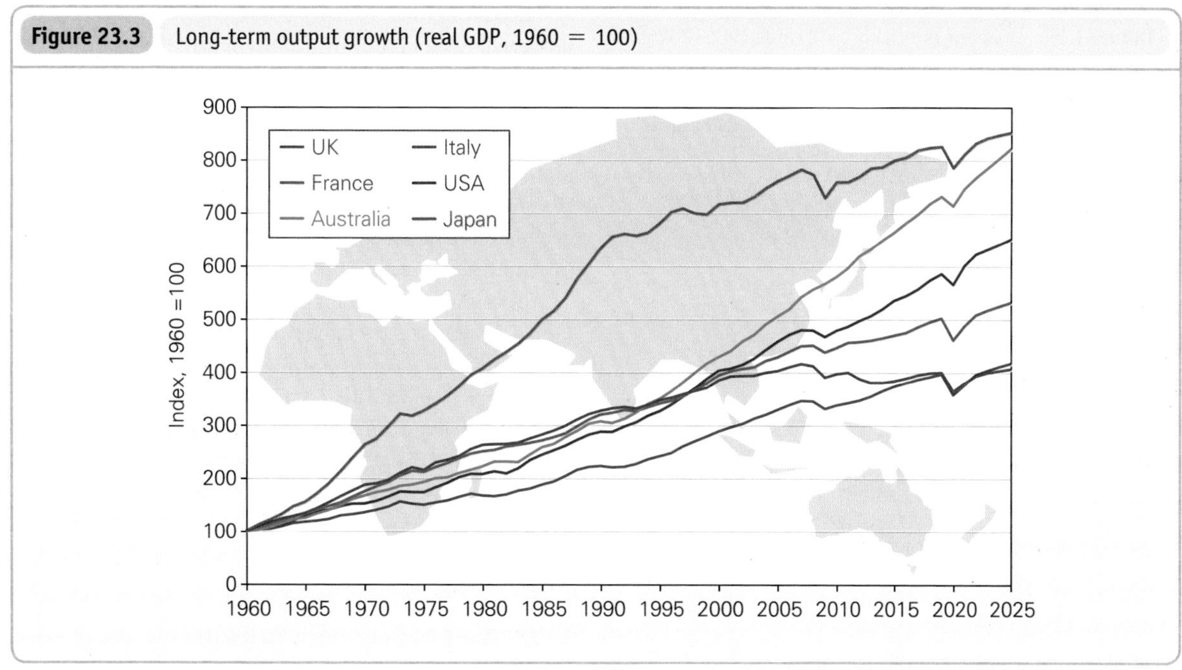

Notes: Data from 2021 based on forecasts.
Sources: Based on data in *AMECO Database*, European Commission, https://ec.europa.eu/info/business-economy-euro/indicators-statistics/economic-databases/macro-economic-database-ameco/ameco-database_en; and from 1980 *World Economic Outlook*, IMF (April 2021), www.imf.org/en/Publications/SPROLLS/world-economic-outlook-databases

Growth over the decades

Despite economic volatility, including the financial crisis and during the COVID-19 pandemic, most countries have experienced long-term economic growth. Figure 23.3 shows the path of real GDP (national output) in six developed economies, including the UK, from 1960. The fluctuations in output appear relatively minor compared with the long-term growth in output.

Such growth cannot be explained by a closing of the gap between actual and potential output: by an expansion of aggregate demand leading to a fuller use of resources. Instead, the explanation lies on the supply side. Countries' economic *capacity* has increased.

Comparing the growth performance of different countries

An increase in economic capacity is reflected in a growth in the average output per head of the population (per capita). Table 23.1 shows the average *annual* rate of growth in output per capita and output per employed person for several *developed* countries since the 1960s, alongside that for output (real GDP). The effect of even very small differences can have a significant effect when looked at over many years.

As you can see from Table 23.1, there has been a considerable difference in the rates of growth experienced by the different countries. Such differences have implications for the longer-term living standards of countries' populations. However, if economic growth is to give an indication of an increase in living standards, it has to be measured per head of the population.

Table 23.1 Average annual percentage growth rates, 1961–2022

	Real GDP	Real GDP per capita	Real GDP per worker
Japan	3.5	3.0	2.9
Portugal	3.0	2.8	2.8
Spain	3.2	2.4	2.5
Norway	3.0	2.3	1.9
Austria	2.6	2.2	2.1
Belgium	2.5	2.1	2.0
France	2.6	2.0	2.1
Germany	2.3	2.0	1.7
Italy	2.2	1.9	2.0
Sweden	2.5	1.9	1.9
USA	2.9	1.9	1.6
Netherlands	2.6	1.9	1.7
UK	2.2	1.8	1.7
Australia	3.3	1.7	1.4

Notes: (i) Figures from 2021 based on forecasts; (ii) German figures based on West Germany only up to 1991.
Source: Based on data from *AMECO database*, European Commission, DGECFIN.

Table 23.2 considers the average annual growth rates since 1980, both overall and per capita, for a wider range of countries than we have so far considered. Countries such as Canada, New Zealand and The Gambia had faster absolute growth rates than the UK, but with their more rapid population growth, experienced a lower per capita growth rate. Only South Korea experienced per capita growth rates greater than its absolute growth rate.

Table 23.2 Average annual growth rates 1980–2025 at constant prices: total and per capita

	Real GDP	Real GDP per capita
China	8.9	8.0
South Korea	3.8	5.0
India	6.2	4.5
Ireland	4.7	3.7
Singapore	5.7	3.5
Malaysia	5.5	3.4
Egypt	4.6	2.3
USA	2.6	1.7
UK	2.1	1.6
Spain	2.2	1.6
Australia	3.0	1.6
Japan	1.7	1.6
Netherlands	2.0	1.5
Germany	1.6	1.4
New Zealand	2.6	1.3
France	1.7	1.2
Canada	2.3	1.2
Italy	1.0	0.9
Jamaica	1.4	0.8
Brazil	2.1	0.7
Argentina	1.7	0.5
South Africa	1.9	0.1
The Gambia	3.5	0.0
Sierra Leone	2.0	−0.1

Note: Figures from 2021 based on forecasts.
Source: Authors' calculations based on data from *World Economic Outlook Database*, International Monetary Fund (April 2021).

In general, GDP per capita in the richer developed countries has grown at a slower rate than in the less rich ones. The result has been a narrowing of the gap. For example, in 1950 GDP per head in the USA (in purchasing-power standard terms) was 2.5 times that in West Germany and 20 times that in Japan. By 2023, GDP per head in the USA was estimated to be only 15 per cent higher than that in Germany and 35 per cent higher than that in Japan.

This ***convergence in GDP per head***, however, has not been universal. Although countries like Brazil, China, India and many other Asian countries have grown very rapidly, and in recent years some of the poorer African countries too, there remain others, often blighted by war or corruption or rapid population growth rates, where real GDP per capita has grown at pitifully slow rates, and in some cases has even declined. We examine the causes of low growth in developing countries in sections 26.3 to 26.5.

Although recent generations have come to expect economic growth, it is a relatively new phenomenon. For most of the last 2000 years, countries have experienced virtually static output per head over the long term. Economic growth has become significant only once countries have undergone an industrial revolution, and it is only with the technological advances of the twentieth and now the twenty-first centuries that long-term growth rates of 2 per cent or more have been achieved.

The causes of economic growth

If we look back at Table 23.1, we can see the importance of the growth in real GDP (output) per worker on the growth in real GDP per capita and hence for a country's living standards. Over the long term, the rate of growth of the workforce generally reflects population growth – although, with an ageing population, it tends to lag behind somewhat. Therefore, the growth in output per capita is principally the result of increases in output per worker.

Definition

Convergence in GDP per head The tendency for less rich developed countries to catch up with richer ones. Convergence does not apply to many of the poorer developing countries, however; the gap between them and richer countries has tended to widen.

***LOOKING AT THE MATHS**

Since 1961, the UK economy has grown on average by 2.2 per cent per annum. This means that it has doubled in size roughly every 32 years. Over the same period, the Australian economy has grown by an average of 3.3 per cent per annum. As a result, its economy has doubled in size roughly every 21 years.

But how do we work out these numbers of years? To do this we use logarithms. To find the number of years, n, that it takes an economy to grow by a factor x (e.g. 2 in the case of a doubling), we divide the log of x by the log of the factor by which the economy is growing each year, g (so $g = 1.022$ for 2.2% and $g = 1.033$ for 3.3%):

$$n = \frac{\log x}{\log g}$$

We can use our calculators to find the logs. Thus, in the case of the UK:

$$n = \frac{\log x}{\log g} = \frac{\log 2}{\log 1.022} = 31.9$$

and in the case of Australia:

$$n = \frac{\log x}{\log g} = \frac{\log 2}{\log 1.033} = 21.3$$

In practice, these figures are only approximate as the two countries' growth rates varied from year to year.

How long would it take an economy, like China, growing at an annual rate of close to 10 per cent to (a) double in size; (b) triple in size?

BOX 23.1 LABOUR PRODUCTIVITY

CASE STUDIES AND APPLICATIONS

How effective is UK labour?

KI 18 p154

A country's potential output depends on the productivity of its factors of production. There are two common ways of measuring labour productivity. The first is *output per worker*. This is the most straightforward measure to calculate. All that is required is a measure of total output and employment.

A second measure is *output per hour worked*. This has the advantage that it is not influenced by the *number* of hours worked. So for an economy like the UK, with a very high percentage of part-time workers on the one hand, and long average hours worked by full-time employees on the other, such a measure would be more accurate in gauging worker efficiency.

Both measures focus solely on the productivity of labour. In order to account directly for the productivity of capital we need to consider the growth in *total* factor productivity (*TFP*). This measure analyses output relative to the amount of factors used. Changes in total factor productivity over time provide a good indicator of technical progress.

International comparisons of labour productivity

Charts (a) and (b) show productivity levels of various economies using GDP per hour worked. Chart (a) shows countries' productivity relative to the UK. GDP per hour worked has been consistently lower in the UK than in France, Germany, the USA and, more recently, in the eurozone. In 2020, output per hour was higher than in the UK by 3 per cent in the eurozone, 14 per cent in Germany, 15 per cent in France and 22 per cent in the USA. Japan is the exception having seen consistently lower GDP per hour worked than the UK. In 2019 it was 26 per cent less than in the UK.

A major explanation of lower productivity in the UK is the fact that for decades it has invested a smaller proportion of its national income than most other industrialised nations. Nevertheless, until 2006 the gap had been narrowing. This was because UK productivity, although lower than in many other countries, was growing faster. This can be seen in chart (b). Part of the reason for this was the inflow of investment from abroad.

However, from 2006 to 2019 the gap generally widened again. This is in part due to the more flexible labour markets in the UK than in many other countries, with increased numbers of workers employed on zero-hour contracts or in the gig economy. The resulting lower wages reduces the pressure on employers to invest in more efficient technology.

Chart (c) compares labour productivity across both measures. Workers in the USA and the UK work longer hours than those in France and Germany. Thus whereas output *per hour worked* in the USA is on par with that in France and Germany, output *per person employed* in the USA is about 15 per cent higher than in France and 30 per cent higher than in Germany.

The evidence points to UK labour productivity being *lower* than that in the USA, France, Germany and the eurozone generally on both measures but higher than that in Japan.

In understanding the growth in labour productivity it is generally agreed that we need to focus on three issues: physical capital (see Box 23.2), human capital (see Box 23.3) and innovation and technological progress. The significance of these for the UK productivity gap is considered further in Case Study 23.2 on the student website.

(a) *Productivity in selected economies relative to the UK (GDP per hour worked)*

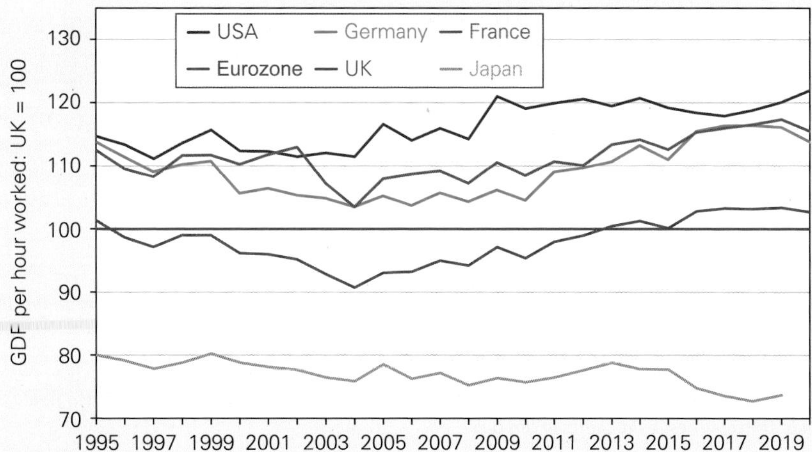

Note: Figures are current-price GDP per hour worked.
Source: Based on data in *OECDStat*, OECD (2021), https://stats.oecd.org/viewhtml.aspx?datasetcode=PDB_GR&&lang=en

(continued)

(b) *Productivity in selected economies (GDP per hour worked, 1995 = 100)*

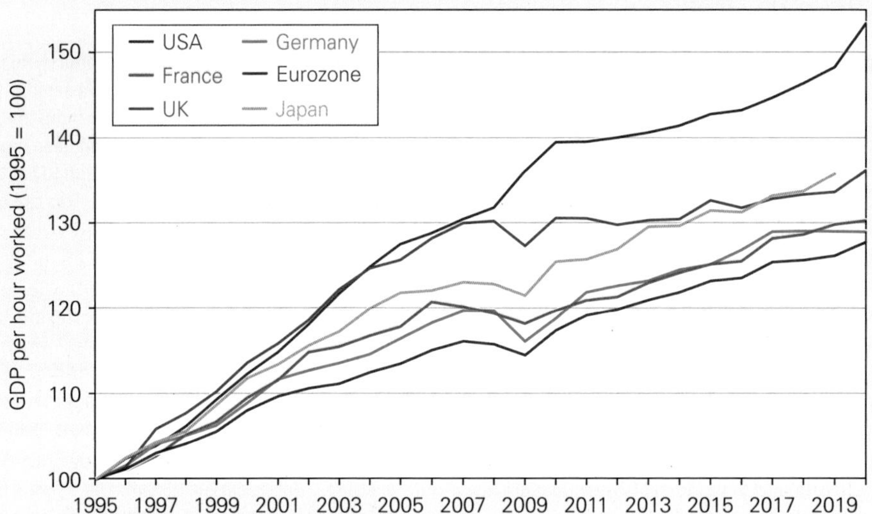

Note: Figures are constant-price GDP per hour worked.
Source: Based on data in *OECDStat*, OECD (2021), https://stats.oecd.org/viewhtml.aspx?datasetcode=PDB_GR&&lang=en

(c) *Productivity in selected economies, 2019 (UK = 100)*

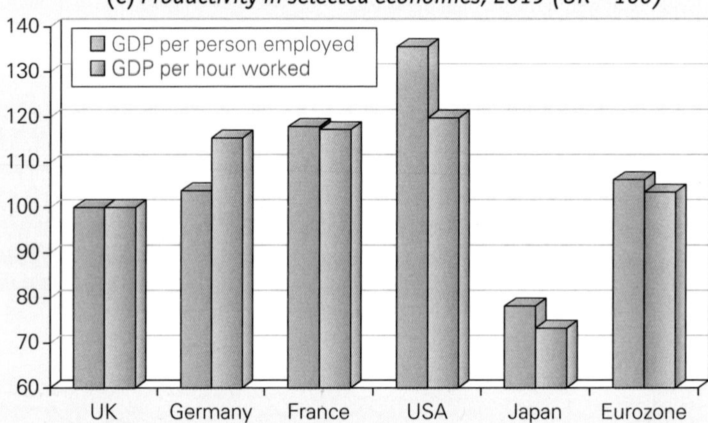

Note: Figures are current-price GDP per hour worked/person employed.
Source: Based on data in *OECDStat*, OECD (2021),
https://stats.oecd.org/viewhtml.aspx?datasetcode=PDB_GR&&lang=en

What could explain the differences in productivity between the five economies in chart (c), and why do the differences vary according to which of the two measures is used?

Do a search to find productivity levels and growth rates in two other developed countries. Explain your findings in comparison to the countries in the charts in this Box.

Output per worker is a measure of ***labour productivity***: it is an indicator of how effective workers are in the production process. Since the growth in output per worker is the key to understanding the growth in output per capita, it then follows that the growth of labour productivity is crucial in determining a country's long-run economic growth.

But what explains the growth in labour productivity? In fact, there are three key sources of growth in labour productivity:

- An increase in the quantity of *physical capital (K)*. Here we are referring to the accumulation of capital, such as machinery/equipment and office/factory space, that arises through investment. The better equipped workers are, the more productive they will be.

KI 26 p309

- An increase in ***human capital***. Here we are referring to the knowledge, skills, competencies and other attributes of individuals that impact on their ability to produce goods and services and to generate ideas.
- ***Technological progress***. Developments of computer technology, of new techniques in engineering, of lighter, stronger and cheaper materials, of digital technology in communications and of more efficient motors have all contributed to a massive increase in the productivity of capital. Machines today can produce much more output than machines in the past that cost the same to manufacture. Therefore workers are able to produce considerably more today, even allowing for the increases that have taken place in physical and human capital.

In the next two sections we will examine these sources of growth, beginning with the accumulation of physical capital.

Definitions

Labour productivity Output per unit of labour: for example, output per worker or output per hour worked.

Human capital The qualifications, skills, expertise and well-being that contribute to a worker's productivity.

Technological progress New and improved methods of production that can lead to increased productivity of labour and other factors of production.

Section summary

1. Economies are inherently volatile in the short run. But most countries experience growth over the long term. The determinants of long-term economic growth lie primarily on the supply side. Long-term growth is therefore consistent with continuous rightwards shifts of the *AS* or *DAS* curves.
2. Most developed countries have experienced average annual rates of economic growth of 2 per cent or more over the last 50 years, but there have been considerable differences between countries.
3. The income gap between developed countries has tended to narrow as the less rich ones have grown faster than the richer ones. Some of the poorest countries of the world, however, have experienced very low rates of growth, with the result that the gap between them and richer countries has widened.
4. When analysing the long-term rate of economic growth, we focus on the growth in real national income per capita (per head of the population). This is because it provides a better indicator of patterns in living standards than does the growth in total real national income.
5. A key determinant of the growth in real national income per capita is the growth in real national income per worker (labour productivity). There are three principal determinants of labour productivity: the quantity of physical capital, the quantity of human capital and technological progress.

23.2 ECONOMIC GROWTH WITHOUT TECHNOLOGICAL PROGRESS

Capital accumulation and capital deepening

The ratio of an economy's capital stock to the size of its labour force (K/L) is a measure of its ***capital intensity***. As countries accumulate capital, they have more manufactured equipment to help in production. This is referred to as ***capital accumulation***.

When the rate of capital accumulation is greater than the growth of the workforce, then each worker has more capital to work with. This is known as ***capital deepening***. However, if the rate of capital accumulation is less that the growth rate of the workforce, then ***capital shallowing*** occurs. The capital to

Definitions

Capital intensity The amount of physical capital that workers have to operate with and which can be measured by the amount of capital per worker (K/L).

Capital accumulation An increase in the amount of capital that an economy has for production.

Capital deepening An increase in the amount of capital per worker (K/L): i.e. an increase in capital intensity.

Capital shallowing A decrease in the amount of capital per worker (K/L): i.e. a fall in capital intensity.

labour ratio (K/L) rises with capital deepening but falls with capital shallowing.

Capital deepening and the resulting increase in capital per worker will generally increase output. In other words, the more equipment that is used by people at work, the more they are likely to produce. But to increase capital requires investment, and that investment requires resources – resources that could have been used for producing consumer goods. Thus more investment means diverting resources away from producing finished goods into producing machines, buildings and other capital equipment. This is the opportunity cost of investment.

The growth of a country's capital stock is therefore closely related to levels of investment. Figure 23.4 illustrates this point for the UK. For example, it shows the marked slowdown in the growth of the country's real *net* capital stock (the market value of the capital stock after accounting for the depreciation of assets) following the financial crisis and subsequent economic slowdown of the late 2000s. This is mirrored by a fall in the levels of investment relative to the size of the net capital stock.

Box 23.2 considers the different types of physical capital as recorded in countries' national accounts. It also looks at the extent to which rates of capital accumulation vary across developed economies.

A simple model of economic growth

A country's percentage rate of economic growth (g) depends crucially on two factors:

- The amount of extra capital that is required to produce an extra unit of output per year: i.e. the marginal capital/output ratio (k). The greater the marginal capital/output ratio, the lower will be the output per year that results from a given amount of investment.
- The percentage of national income that a country saves (s). The higher this percentage, the greater the amount of investment that can be financed.

There is a simple formula that relates the rate of economic growth to these two factors. It is known as the ***Harrod–Domar model*** (after the two economists, Sir Roy Harrod and Evsey Domar, who independently developed the model). The formula is:

$$g = s/k$$

Thus if a country saved 10 per cent of its national income (s = 10%), and if £4 of additional capital were required to produce £1 of extra output per annum (k = 4), then the rate of economic growth would be 10%/4 = 2.5 per cent.

What would be the rate of economic growth if 20 per cent of national income was saved and invested and the marginal capital/output ratio was $^5/_2$?

However, we need to make three qualifications to this simple model.

Declining marginal efficiency of capital. The first relates to the marginal capital/output ratio (k). Since the ratio measures how much additional capital is needed to produce one more

Definition

Harrod–Domar model A model that relates a country's rate of economic growth to the proportion of national income saved and the ratio of capital to output.

Figure 23.4 UK net capital stock and investment

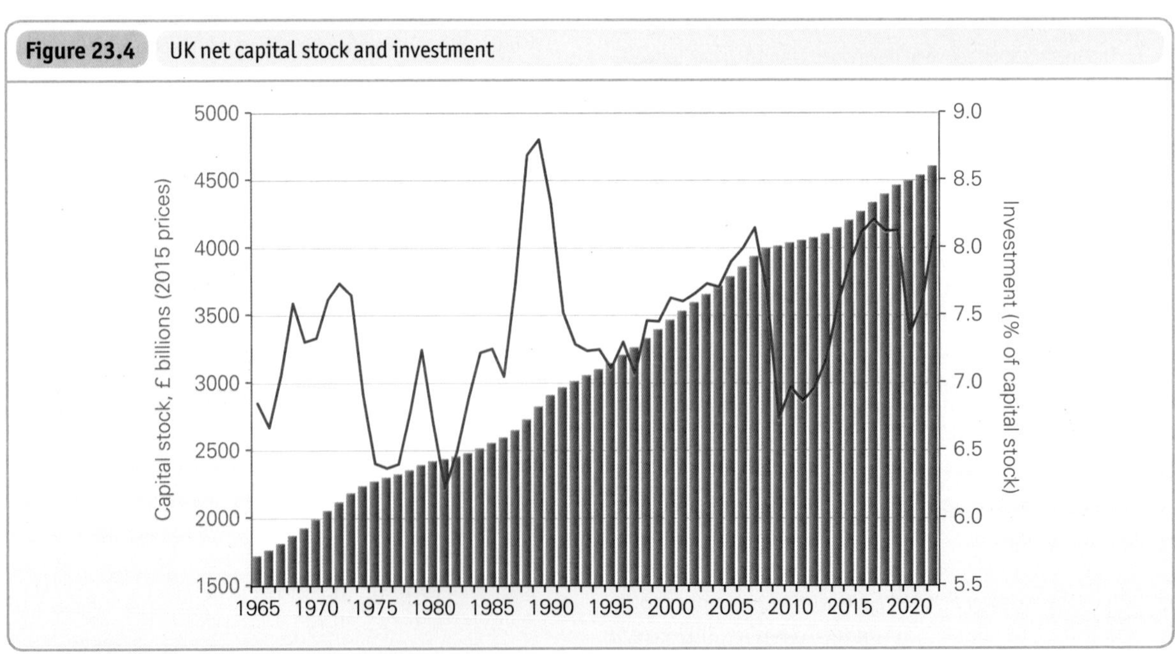

Notes: Investment is Gross Fixed Capital Formation (whole economy) at constant 2015 prices; data from 2021 are forecasts.
Source: Based on data in *AMECO Database*, European Commission (May 2021), https://ec.europa.eu/info/business-economy-euro/indicators-statistics/economic-databases/macro-economic-database-ameco/ameco-database_en

unit of output it reflects the effectiveness of additional capital. In fact, the ratio is the inverse of the *marginal efficiency of capital* (see page 311).

We can define the nation's marginal efficiency of capital (MEC) as the annual extra output (ΔY) yielded by an increase in the capital stock, relative to the cost of that extra capital (ΔK).

$$MEC = \frac{\Delta Y}{\Delta K} = \frac{\Delta Y}{I}$$

Thus if £4 of extra capital yielded an additional annual income of £1, the marginal efficiency of capital would be $^1/_4$. Since the marginal capital/output ratio (k) is $1/MEC$, then k must equal 4.

Thus, for a given workforce, as the capital stock increases the marginal efficiency of capital is likely to decline (and the marginal capital/output ratio to increase). This is because of diminishing returns to capital. KI 19 p156

KI 26 p309 *Required investment for replacement purposes.* The second qualification is that the larger the capital stock, the greater the amount of investment that will be required for replacement purposes. This means that a smaller proportion of a given amount of investment is available for increasing the size of the capital stock at higher capital stock levels. Instead, more and more replacement investment is needed simply to maintain existing stock levels.

KI 26 p309 *Required investment for new workers.* The third qualification is to allow for changes in the size of the workforce. For capital deepening to occur (an increase in the capital to labour ratio), capital must increase by a larger percentage than any increase in workers.

The neoclassical growth model

Constructing the neoclassical growth diagram

KI 8 p44 Let us now incorporate these three qualifications into a model of growth. This is known as the neoclassical or ***'Solow' growth model***, after the MIT economics professor and Nobel Prize winner, Robert Solow. The model is illustrated in Figure 23.5. The size of the capital stock per worker (K/L) is measured on the horizontal axis; the level of output per worker (Y/L), i.e. labour productivity, is measured on the vertical axis.

So how have we taken the three qualifications into account?

KI 19 p155 First, consider the assumption of diminishing returns to capital. The Y/L curve shows that as the capital stock per worker increases, so output per worker increases. The curve is commonly referred to as the ***economy's production function*** or the ***aggregate production function***. But, because of diminishing returns to capital the economy's production function gets less and less steep.

What will be the effect on investment per worker? Increased output per worker will mean increased saving and hence increased investment per worker. This is shown by the *actual* investment per worker curve (the I/L curve), which has the same general shape as the Y/L curve because saving is assumed to be a given proportion of GDP. The higher the share of saving and investment in GDP, the steeper will be this line. In this simple model, the vertical distance between the Y/L and I/L curves represents consumption per worker ($C/L = Y/L - I/L$).

Second, we consider the amount of investment required to replace existing capital that is wearing out or becoming obsolete. For a given annual rate of depreciation of capital (d), the bigger the capital stock, the larger the amount of replacement investment that will be required. The *required* investment per worker line (the I_r/L line) incorporates this required level of replacement investment. It is upward sloping because replacement investment will increase, the greater the capital stock per worker. The greater the rate of depreciation, the steeper this line will be. KI 26 p309

Third, we take into account the growth in the workforce. It is assumed that the number of workers grows at a constant rate per annum (n). To maintain a given capital/labour ratio, new workers will need to be equipped with capital. The required investment to do this is also incorporated in the required investment per worker curve (I_r/L). The higher the rate of growth in the workforce, the more investment will be required to maintain a given capital/labour ratio and hence the steeper the I_r/L line.

The I_r/L line will rotate upwards around the origin if either the rate of depreciation or the rate of growth of the workforce increases. This is because at any level of capital per worker more investment would be required for either greater amounts of depreciation or for equipping larger numbers of additional workers.

? *In the absence of growth in the workforce what does the required investment per worker curve capture?*

Definitions

Solow growth model A model which explains economic growth in terms of the effects on the capital stock and output of a change in investment.

Economy's production function (or aggregate production function) The relationship between the economy's capital per worker and output per worker (labour productivity), holding the level of human capital and the state of technology constant.

BOX 23.2 GETTING INTENSIVE WITH CAPITAL

How quickly does it grow?

In this box we take a look at two issues relating to capital. First, we consider what counts as capital in a country's national accounts. Second, we compare the growth of the capital stock in a sample of developed economies and then see how this compares with their rates of economic growth.

What is capital?

In a country's national accounts, capital consists of non-financial *fixed assets*. It does not include goods and services transformed or used up in the course of production; these are known as *intermediate goods and services*. Furthermore, it does not relate directly to the stock of human capital: the skills and attributes embodied in individuals that affect production (see Box 23.3).

A country's stock of fixed assets can be valued at its replacement cost, regardless of its age: this is its gross value. It can also be valued at its written-down value known as its net value. The net value takes into account the *consumption of capital* which occurs through wear and tear (depreciation) or when capital becomes naturally obsolescent.

The table shows that the estimated net capital stock of the UK in 2019 was £4.6 trillion or just over twice the value of (annual) GDP. This is considerably less than the estimate of human capital of £21.4 trillion in 2018, which was 10.1 times GDP (see Box 23.3).

The table shows that there are seven broad categories of fixed assets. The largest of these by value is *dwellings*, which includes houses, bungalows and flats. Residential housing yields rental incomes for landlords and, more generally, provides all of us with important consumption services, most notably shelter.

The second largest component by value is *other buildings and structures*. This includes buildings, other than residential dwellings, and most civil engineering and construction work. It includes structures such as factories, schools and hospitals and the country's railway track.

The third largest component is *ICT, other machinery and equipment*. It includes telecommunications equipment, computer hardware, office machinery and hardware as well as weapon systems equipment.

The fourth largest is *intellectual property products*. These include intangible fixed assets such as R&D, software and databases, and original literary and artistic works. The fifth largest is *land improvements*. This includes things such as land clearance and excavation which increase its value. The sixth largest by value is *transport equipment*. This includes items such as lorries, buses, railway rolling stock and civil aircraft. The smallest component is *cultivated biological resources*. This includes livestock for breeding, vineyards, orchards and forests.

UK net capital stock

Type	2019			Average real annual change, %	
	£ billions	% of fixed assets	% of GDP	1996–2019	2009–2019
Dwellings (excluding land)	1893	41.0	85.3	1.1	−0.1
Other buildings and structures	1515	32.8	68.3	2.0	1.9
ICT, other machinery and equipment	489	10.6	22.0	0.9	−0.9
Intellectual property products	321	6.9	14.5	3.6	2.8
Land improvements	258	5.6	11.6	5.4	2.9
Transport equipment	138	3.0	6.2	2.9	2.5
Cultivated biological resources	8	0.2	0.4	1.9	−0.3
All fixed assets	**4622**	**100.0**	**208.3**	**1.8**	**0.8**

Source: Based on data from *Capital stocks and fixed capital consumption, 2020* and series YBHA, National Statistics.

The final two columns of the table look at the annual growth in the stock of capital. The first of these shows that, on average, from 1996 to 2019 the volume of the UK capital stock increased by 1.8 per cent per year. From 1996 to 2008 the overall annual growth rate in the capital stock was 2.6 per cent compared to only 0.8 per cent from 2009 to 2019.

How quickly does capital grow? An international comparison

In models of economic growth, an important measure of how much capital is being used is the amount of capital per person employed (per worker). As we have seen, this is also known as

The movement to a steady-state equilibrium

Where is the economy's long-run equilibrium point in the model?

Assume initially that the size of the capital stock per worker is $(K/L)_0$ in Figure 23.5. This will generate an output per worker of $(Y/L)_0$ (point *a*). This output, in turn, will generate saving and investment per worker of $(I/L)_0$, but of this, $(I_r/L)_0$ will have to be used for replacement purposes and for equipping additional workers. The difference $(b - c)$ will be available for capital deepening: to increase the size of the capital stock.

The capital stock per worker will thus increase up to $(K/L)_1$ (point *g*). At this point, all investment will be required to replace depreciating capital and for equipping new workers. When this occurs, the level of investment is no longer sufficient for capital deepening. Instead, it is consistent merely with ***capital widening*** and therefore with the capital stock growing at the rate of the workforce plus the rate of depreciation $(n + d)$.

EXPLORING ECONOMICS

capital intensity. In the chart we plot the average annual rate of growth of capital per worker since 1961 (x-axis) against the average annual rate of growth of output (real GDP) per worker since 1961 (y-axis) in a selection of developed countries.

For each country we observe an increase in capital intensity, although the rates of capital deepening differ quite significantly. The data show that the UK ranks relatively low in terms of capital deepening. In the UK the capital stock per worker has grown at an average annual real rate of 1.2 per cent. This compares with, for example, Japan and Ireland, where the rate is 2.9 per cent, or France, where it is 2.2 per cent.

We would expect that the more rapid is the rate of capital accumulation, the faster is the growth of output per worker. This is largely borne out in the chart. However, while there is a strong statistical association between capital accumulation and economic growth, there are other factors that impact on long-term growth. Three of these are technological progress, *human* capital and the efficiency with which capital is deployed. We examine these later in this chapter.

1. *How does human capital (the skills and expertise of the workforce) fit into a national account's definition of capital?*
2. *Does the composition of a country's capital affect its long-run economic growth?*

From the AMECO database (https://ec.europa.eu/info/business-economy-euro/indicators-statistics/economic-databases/macro-economic-database-ameco/ameco-database_en#database) download data on the net capital stock at constant prices per person employed. Then, for a sample of up to three countries of your choice, plot a time series chart showing the year-to-year rates of growth across time. Finally, compose a short briefing note summarising the patterns in your chart.

Growth in capital and output per worker, 1961–2022

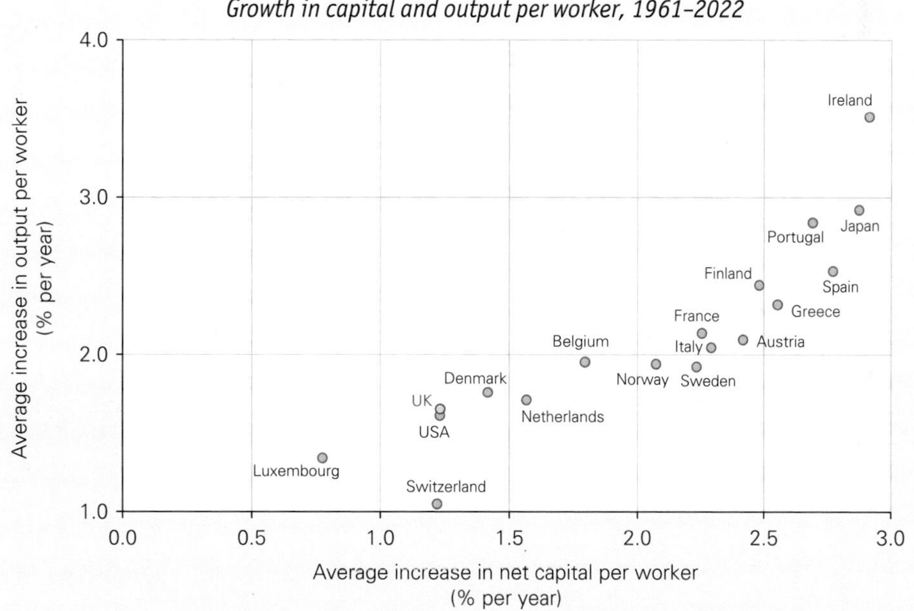

Note: Data from 2020 are forecasts; output and net capital are measured at constant prices.
Source: Based on data from *AMECO Database*, European Commission, https://ec.europa.eu/info/business-economy-euro/indicators-statistics/economic-databases/macro-economic-database-ameco/ameco-database_en

When the economy experiences capital widening, capital *per worker* (K/L) and output *per worker* (Y/L), and hence labour productivity, will cease growing. If we look at Figure 23.5, $(Y/L)_1$ represents the ***steady-state level of national income per worker***. However, at the steady state, the levels of capital (K) and output (Y) are growing, but only at the rate at which the labour force (L) is growing. This must be the case for the capital per worker (K/L) and labour per worker (Y/L) ratios to be constant.

Definitions

Capital widening The situation where the capital stock grows at the rate of growth of the workforce plus the rate of depreciation ($n + d$). Investment is merely equipping new workers and replacing worn out or obsolete capital.

Steady-state level of national income per worker The long-run equilibrium level of national income per worker. The level at which all investment is used to maintain the existing capital stock per worker at its current level.

Figure 23.5 Steady-state output per worker

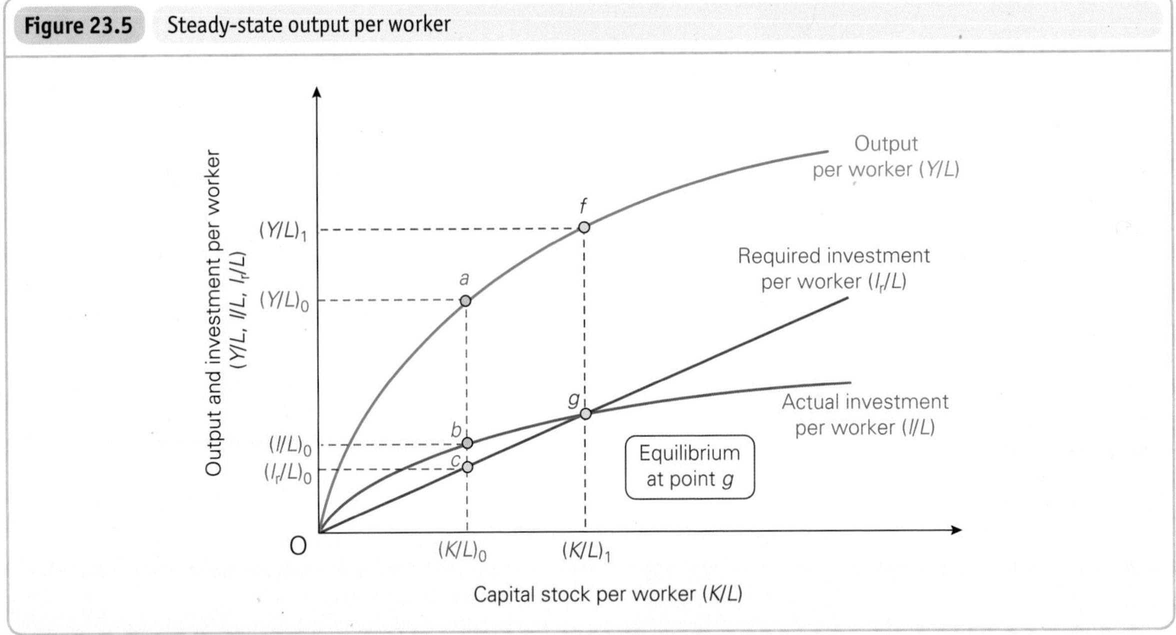

The neoclassical growth model and the saving rate

Effect of an increase in the saving rate

In the simple model, $g = s/k$ (or $g = s \times MEC$), an increase in the saving rate (s) will increase the growth rate (g). When we take into account diminishing returns to capital, depreciation and the growth in the number of workers, however, an increase in the saving rate will lead to only a *temporary* increase in output per worker. Therefore, there is no long-term growth in output per worker at all!

This is illustrated in Figure 23.6. If the saving rate increases, the investment curve will shift upwards. This is shown by a shift from $(I/L)_1$ to $(I/L)_2$. Investment is now above that which is necessary to maintain the capital stock at $(K/L)_1$. Capital intensity will rise, therefore, and so will national income per worker.

Figure 23.6 Effect of an increase in the rate of saving and investment

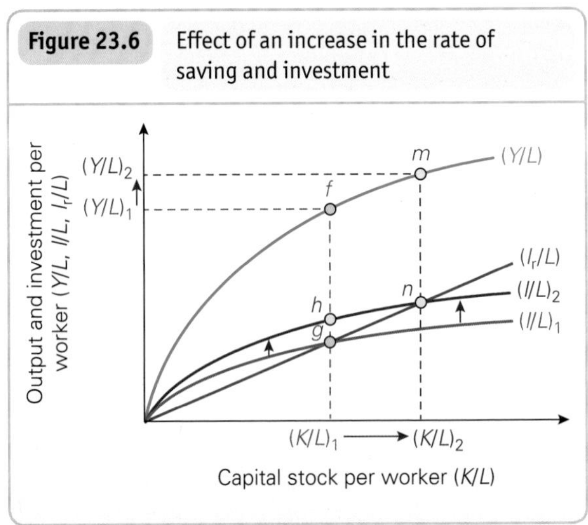

*LOOKING AT THE MATHS

Steady-state equilibrium in the Solow growth model is achieved where *actual* investment per worker (I/L) equals *required* investment per worker (I_r/L).

Actual investment per worker is assumed to be a given fraction (s) of the level of national income per worker Y/L, where national income per worker is a function of the total capital stock per worker (K/L): $Y/L = f(K/L)$. Thus

$$I/L = s(Y/L) = s \times f(K/L) \quad (1)$$

The required amount of investment (I_r) is dependent on the rate of depreciation of the capital stock (d) and the rate of growth of the working population (n). Each period a given proportion d of the capital stock (K) needs replacing. Additionally, the capital stock (K) must grow by a given proportion n to keep each worker equipped with the same amount of capital. Thus:

$$I_r = (d + n)K \quad (2)$$

We can write the required investment *per worker* (I_r/L) as:

$$I_r/L = (d + n)(K/L) \quad (3)$$

In steady-state equilibrium, given that $I/L = I_r/L$, from equations (1) and (3) we can write:

$$s \times f(K/L) = (d + n)(K/L)$$

Thus

$$K/L = \frac{s \times f(K/L)}{(d + n)}$$

Thus if we know the production function ($Y/L = f(K/L)$), the saving rate (s), the depreciation rate (d) and the rate of growth of the working population (n), we can solve for the steady-state equilibrium value of K/L and hence also for Y. Maths Case 23.1 on the student website gives a worked example of this.

But this growth is only temporary. Once the capital stock has risen to $(K/L)_2$, all the new higher level of investment will be absorbed in replacing capital and equipping additional workers ($I/L = I_r/L$ at point n). At this point, capital deepening ceases and capital widening occurs. Therefore real national income per worker stops rising. $(Y/L)_2$ represents the new steady-state national income.

Does this mean, therefore, that there is no long-term gain from an increase in the saving rate? There *is* a gain, to the extent that real national income per worker is now higher, and this higher average income will be received not just once, but every year from now on as long as the saving rate remains at the new higher level. There is no sustained growth in national income per worker, however. To achieve that, we would have to look to the other determinants of growth.

If there were a gradual increase in the saving rate over time, would this lead to sustained economic growth?

An optimum saving rate?

If an increase in the saving rate does at least lead to a higher level of output per head, is there an *optimum* level of saving? Clearly, we would need to define 'optimum'. One definition would be where consumption per worker is maximised.

KI 6 p29

An increase in the saving rate will do two things. First, for any level of national income per worker (Y/L) it will directly decrease consumption per worker (C/L) since what is saved is not directly spent. Second, as we have seen, it will lead to higher output per worker and hence higher income per worker. So, with a higher saving rate, consumption will be a smaller proportion, but of a higher income. This implies that there will be some optimum saving rate at which consumption per worker is maximised. This is illustrated in Figure 23.7.

If the saving rate is zero, the capital stock will be zero. Output and consumption per worker will thus be zero (point a). As saving rises above zero, so capital intensity (K/L) rises, as will both output and consumption per worker. At the other extreme, if the saving rate were 100 per cent, although the capital stock per worker would be high, all of the nation's income would go on maintaining that capital stock: there would be no consumption per worker (point b).

A saving rate somewhere between 0 and 100 per cent, therefore, will give the maximum consumption per worker. In Figure 23.7, this is a rate of s^*, giving a level of consumption per worker of $(C/L)^*$ (point m). This is sometimes known as the ***golden-rule saving rate***.

Evidence suggests that all countries have saving rates below the golden-rule level. Thus increases in saving rates would result in increases in consumption per worker.

If this is true, why do people not increase their rate of saving?

The neoclassical growth model and the growth of the workforce

An increase in the growth of the workforce (n) will have the effect of pivoting the required investment per worker curve (the I_r/L curve) upwards and making the curve steeper. Each period the capital stock must now grow by a higher given proportion than before to maintain a given capital/labour ratio. In other words, more investment is needed for capital widening. This is illustrated in Figure 23.8.

Initially the growth of the workforce is a rate n_1. Each period the capital stock must grow by a proportion n_1 to provide the necessary capital to match the growth in the workforce. Investment is also required to replace worn out or obsolete capital, which is determined by the rate of depreciation (d). The required investment curve is shown by $(I_r/L)_1$. The steady-state levels of capital and output per worker are $(K/L)_1$ and $(Y/L)_1$ respectively.

Definition

Golden-rule saving rate The rate of saving that maximises the level of long-run consumption per worker.

Figure 23.7 An optimum saving rate

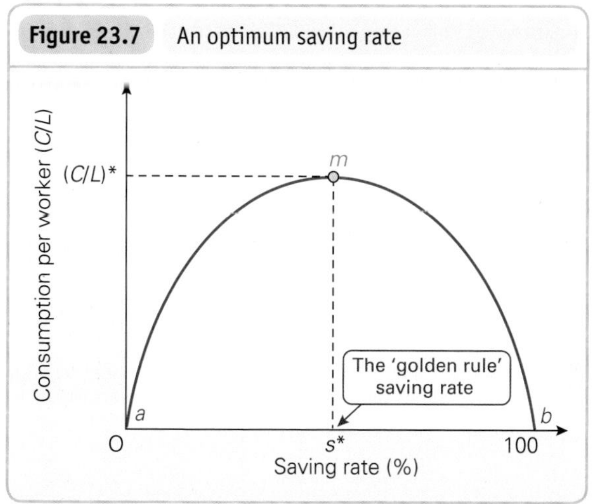

Figure 23.8 Effect of an increase in the growth rate of the workforce

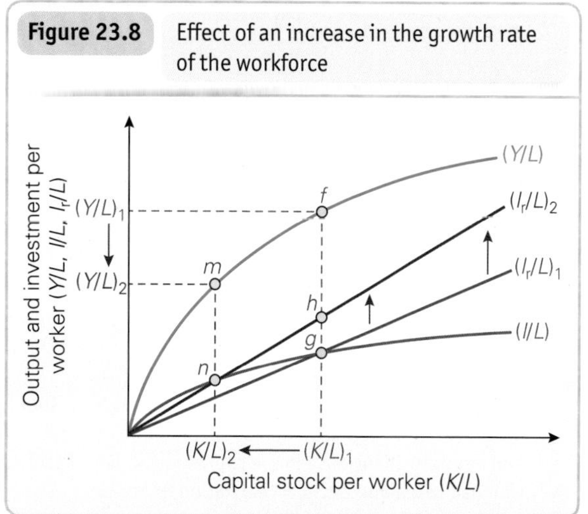

Following an increase in the rate of growth of the workforce to n_2, the required investment line becomes the steeper $(I_r/L)_2$ line. At the initial level of capital per worker $(K/L)_1$, there is now insufficient investment to maintain this capital intensity. In other words, because the labour input is growing more quickly, it is harder to accumulate capital. Capital per worker therefore falls. This is illustrated in Figure 23.8 by the fall in the steady-state capital per worker to $(K/L)_2$ and output per worker to $(Y/L)_2$. Capital shallowing occurs and labour productivity falls.

At the new steady state, output and hence national income are growing at the higher rate of n_2. However, although national income is now growing more quickly, national income *per worker* has ceased growing and is *lower* than at the initial steady state. Therefore aggregate living standards as measured in per-worker terms are lower.

But does this mean that *GDP* per head is lower? The answer depends on what has caused the growth of workforce. The workforce is the employed labour force. Therefore its size will depend on the size of the population, the labour force ***participation rate*** (i.e. the proportion of the population wishing to work), and the employment rate (i.e. the proportion of the labour force in employment).

Definition

Participation rate The percentage of the working-age population that is part of the workforce.

If the growth in the workforce is the result of growth in the population, then both GDP per worker and GDP per capita fall. However, if the growth in the workforce is the result of an increased participation rate or a higher employment rate, then GDP per capita will be *higher*. With a higher proportion of the population in work, GDP per capita is higher even though output per worker is lower.

1. *If there was a growth in the total number of worker hours because people worked longer hours, what would happen to GDP per hour worked and GDP per capita?*
2. *If people worked longer hours, how would you assess whether the country was better or worse off?*

Human capital

The analysis of Figures 23.5 and 23.6 need not be confined to the stock of *physical* capital: machines, buildings, tools, etc. It can also apply to *human capital*. Human capital, as we saw in section 23.1, refers to the skills and expertise of workers that have, in part, been acquired through education and training. If part of saving is used for investment in education and training, then the productivity of workers will rise, and so will output per worker.

In Figures 23.5 and 23.6, therefore, the horizontal axis measures both physical and human capital. An increase in either has the effect of increasing the steady-state level of national income per worker. In Boxes 23.2 and 23.3 we consider both how physical and human capital respectively are treated in countries' national accounts and at their rates of accumulation.

*LOOKING AT THE MATHS

The level of output (real GDP) per worker is calculated by dividing output (Y) by the size of the workforce (W_f):

$$Y/W_f \qquad (1)$$

The workforce is the employed labour force. This is determined by the size of the population (N), the labour force participation rate (L_{Fp}) and the unemployment rate (u):

$$W_f = N \times L_{Fp} \times (1 - u) \qquad (2)$$

The final term of equation (2) is therefore capturing the employment rate. We can therefore write the output per worker as:

$$Y/W_f = \frac{Y}{N \times L_{Fp} \times (1 - u)}$$

Thus for given rates of employment and labour force participation, the rate of growth of the workforce will tend to approximate the growth in the population, particularly over the longer term. In turn, changes in output in GDP per worker would be mirrored by similar changes in GDP per head.

Section summary

1. Capital deepening occurs when the economy's capital intensity (K/L) rises. This is important for long-term economic growth as it enables output per worker (Y/L) to rise. The rate of capital deepening is crucial in determining the long-term rate of growth of labour productivity and hence in living standards.
2. The Harrod–Domar model of economic growth shows that an increased saving rate will lead to higher investment and hence to an increase in the capital stock. This, in turn, will lead to a higher level of real national income.
3. The neoclassical growth model analyses the process of capital accumulation. It makes three important qualifications. First, the economy's production function is characterised by diminishing returns to capital; second, as the capital per worker ratio rises, more investment is needed for replacement purposes; and third, more investment will be needed to equip any new workers with the same level of capital as existing workers.

4. The neoclassical model shows how capital deepening eventually ceases if actual levels of investment are absorbed by all the extra investment required to maintain existing levels of capital intensity. Hence, national income per worker and capital per worker stop rising. A steady-state level of real national income per worker has been achieved.
5. At the steady-state, output per worker (Y/L) is constant. Therefore, an economy's output level (Y) is growing only at the rate at which the labour force is growing. In the absence of any growth in the labour force, output growth is also zero.
6. An increased saving rate will therefore lead only to a rise in output per worker, not to sustained higher growth. A new, higher steady-state level of real national income per worker is reached but growth has again ceased.
7. An optimum rate of saving could be defined as one where consumption per worker is maximised. This is sometimes known as the 'golden-rule saving rate'.
8. An increase in the workforce will lead to higher total output but, with a given saving rate, will lead to a reduction in output per worker.

23.3 ECONOMIC GROWTH WITH TECHNOLOGICAL PROGRESS

The effect of technological progress on output

What should be clear from the above analysis is that, without technological progress or some other means of increasing output from a given quantity of inputs, long-term growth *per worker* cannot be sustained.

TC 14 p468 Technological progress has the effect of increasing the output from a given amount of investment. This is shown in Figure 23.9. The initial investment and output per worker curves are $(I/L)_1$ and $(Y/L)_1$; steady-state income is at a level of $(Y/L)_1$ (point f). A technological advance has the effect of shifting the (Y/L) line upwards, say to $(Y/L)_2$. This higher aggregate production function leads to a higher investment per worker curve (for a given rate of saving). This is shown by curve $(I/L)_2$. The new long-term equilibrium capital stock is thus $(K/L)_2$, and the new steady-state level of income is $(Y/L)_2$ (point p).

If there is a 'one-off' technological advance, the effect is the one we have just illustrated. Real national income per worker rises to a higher level, but does not go on rising once the new steady-state level has been reached. But technological progress marches on over time. New inventions are made; new processes are discovered; old ones are improved. In terms of Figure 23.9, the aggregate production function (Y/L) *goes on* shifting upwards over time as does the (I/L) curve too.

Figure 23.9 Effect of a technological advance

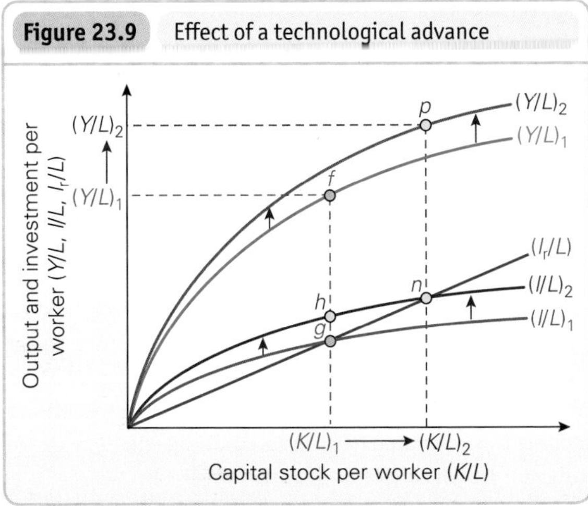

The faster the rate of technological progress, the faster will the aggregate production function shift upwards and the higher will be the rate of economic growth. This is illustrated in Figure 23.10, which shows the increase in output per worker over time. The faster the rate of technological progress, the higher the rate of growth of output per worker.

Maths Case 23.2 on the student website explores the algebra of technological progress.

The effect of an increase in the saving rate with a given rate of technological progress

Figure 23.11 shows the combined effects of an increased saving rate and continuing technological progress. The rate of technological progress gives the slope of the ***steady-state growth path***. This is the growth path of output per worker for

Definition

Steady-state (per-worker) growth path The growth path of output per worker for a given saving rate (where growth results from technological progress).

Figure 23.10 Effect of technological progress on output per worker

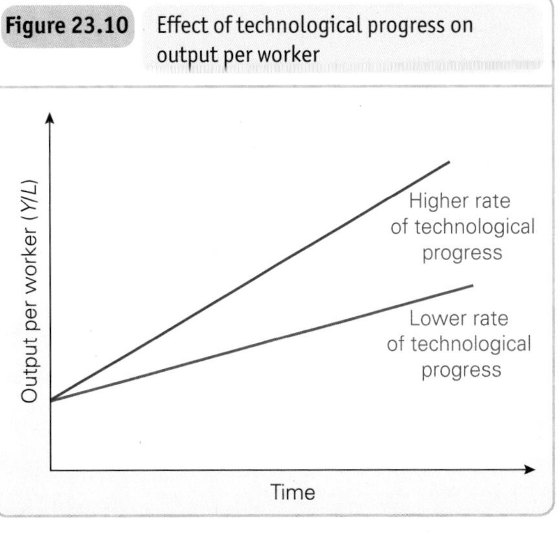

Figure 23.11 Effect of an increase in the saving rate, with a given rate of technological progress

Steady-state growth path 2
Steady-state growth path 1
Actual growth path
Output per worker
t_1
Time

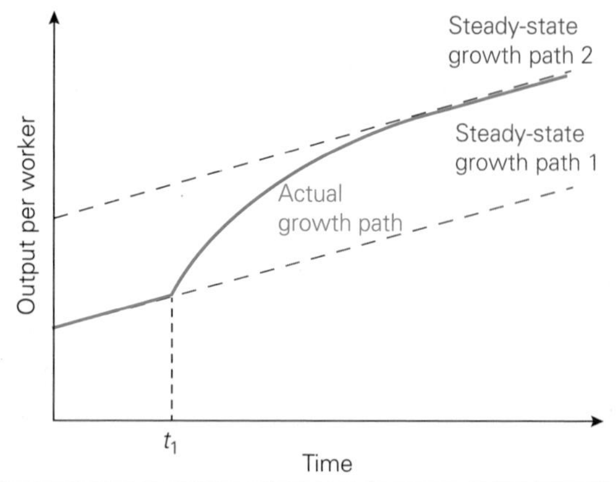

any given saving rate. The saving rate determines the *position* (as opposed to slope) of the curve.

Assume that the economy is on steady-state growth path 1. Then, at time t_1, there is an increase in the saving rate. This has the effect of increasing output per worker and the economy will move to wards steady-state growth path 2. But the full effect does not take place immediately, since new capital equipment takes time to plan and install and then to generate additional income, part of which will be used for more investment. Thus the actual growth path will follow the green line, gradually converging on steady-state growth path 2.

Endogenous growth theory

Continual technological advance is essential to sustaining capital deepening and growth in output per worker and labour productivity. Hence, an increase in technological progress is essential if a country wants to achieve faster rates of growth in the long term. But is this purely in the lap of the scientists and engineers? TC 14 p468

In the Solow growth model that we have been considering up to now, this is indeed the type of assumption made. In other words, technological progress is simply a 'given': it is exogenously determined.

Whilst the neoclassical model identifies the importance of technological progress for enduring growth, it does not offer governments actual policy prescriptions. What can be done to speed up the rate of innovation? Can governments adopt policies that encourage scientific breakthroughs and technological developments? ***Endogenous growth models*** attempt to answer such questions by incorporating technological advancement *within* the model.

> **Definition**
>
> **Endogenous growth models** Models where the rate of growth depends on the rate of technological progress and diffusion, both of which depend on institutions, incentives and the role of government.

What is endogenous about endogenous growth theory?

Endogenous growth models stress the importance of research and development, education and training and fostering innovation. Hence, policy makers are interested in appropriate policies that might, for example, make their country a world leader in innovation and technological advancement, especially if this helps to sustain higher long-run rates of economic growth, and so higher standards of living.

KI 24 p259
TC 5 p48

In such models, a major determinant of technological progress is the size and composition of the capital stock. As economies accumulate capital, they are likely to devote more resources to the development and maintenance of capital goods industries. In other words, they are likely to have a larger sector devoted to producing and developing capital goods. This, in turn, can raise the rate of technological progress and enable further capital accumulation. A virtuous circle is created. Consequently, rather than looking at capital accumulation and technological progress as separate sources of long-term economic growth, the two are arguably interdependent.

Investment in research and development can be encouraged through the use of patents and copyrights. These provide some protection to firms, enabling them to capture more of the benefits from their own ideas and thus providing them with an incentive to create and innovate. Furthermore, the striving for profit or the pursuit of competitive advantage over rival firms, through the design of either innovative products and services or the most cost-efficient production processes, are incentives that can drive this innovation and creativity. TC 5 p48

But there are limits to the ability of firms to exclude other firms from prospering from their own ideas, such as the development of products, processes and people. The virtuous circle is thus reinforced by externalities: the spill-over of ideas from one firm to another. New ideas cannot be put back into the metaphorical bottle once its lid is off.

A model of endogenous technological progress

Endogenous growth models argue two things. The first is that technological progress is *dependent* on various economic factors such as the rate of investment in research and development. This could be included as an element in the investment (I) term, i.e.

$$I = I_n + I_c$$

where I_n is investment in research and development of new technology (it could also include investment in training) and I_c is investment in capital that uses current technology. The greater the value of I_n/I_c the faster will the (Y/L) curve shift upwards in Figure 23.5 (see page 748) and the steeper will be the steady-state growth path in Figure 23.11. Any policy, then, that increases the proportion of national income being devoted to R&D and training will increase the long-run rate of economic growth.

The second factor is the responsiveness of national income to new technologies ($\Delta Y/I_n$). This will depend in part on the extent to which innovations spill over to other firms, which duplicate or adapt them, thereby adding to the increase in national income (ΔY). The greater the value of Δ/I_n, the greater will be the rate of economic growth: the steeper will be the steady-state growth path.

The values of I_n and $\Delta Y/I_n$ are thought to depend on structural and institutional factors within the economy and on the role of government. These include:

- attitudes of business, such as their inclination to take risk;
- the willingness of financial institutions to lend support to investment opportunities;
- tax incentives and government grants, for instance support for R&D;
- a research infrastructure (e.g. laboratories and the number and skills of researchers);
- the degree of competition within industies;
- incentives to develop new products and processes and/or to reduce costs;
- the magnitude of external spillovers from the generation of new products, processes and techniques;
- the stock of human capital.

The aggregate production function

As we have seen, endogenous growth models try to explain how the economy's production function shifts upwards over time. The process of capital accumulation creates the conditions for technological progress.

In some cases, then, the production function may also become steeper. In other words, a given rise in the capital stock will cause a larger rise in national income. The reason is that the benefits of the output from investment are not confined just to the firms doing the investing. Rather, some benefits spill over to other firms. For example, firms may be able to duplicate or develop other firms' ideas. Consequently, these spillovers may positively impact on the overall marginal product of capital.

Do all investment projects generate significant spillovers?

LOOKING AT THE MATHS

The above endogenous growth model can be expressed algebraically as follows:

$$\Delta Y/Y = v(I_n/Y)$$

This states that the rate of economic growth ($\Delta Y/Y$) depends on the proportion of national income devoted to R&D and training (I_n/Y) by an amount v.

The higher the value of I_n/Y and the higher the value of v, the steeper will be the steady-state growth path.

Policy implications

If there is a virtuous circle arising from firms investing and innovating, how can governments encourage this? Many economists argue that this requires supply-side policies. Examples include policies to influence research and development, education and training, industrial organisation and work practices – in other words, policies to affect aggregate supply directly.

There is less agreement, however, as to whether these policies should focus on delivering market solutions or involve greater state intervention. We look at this debate in the final sections of this chapter.

But encouraging investment does not just depend on effective supply-side policies. It also depends on the stability of the macroeconomic environment. It is not easy to plan ahead in times of great economic uncertainty. In the years following the financial crisis of 2007–8, uncertainty led to lower levels of investment and innovation in many countries. The result was that productivity and potential income grew at a slower rate.

In the decade following the financial crisis, annual productivity growth in advanced economies dropped to 0.3 per cent – down from around 1 per cent in the years before the crisis. If productivity growth had continued at 1 per cent, overall GDP in advanced economies would be some 5 per cent higher than it is today.[1] It remains to be seen whether the uncertainty following the COVID-19 pandemic will have a lasting dampening effect on investment and productivity.

By contrast, the less the volatility in output (real GDP), the greater will be the confidence of business to innovate and invest and the higher will be the growth in potential income.

Understanding the dynamic responses of economies to economic shocks was naturally important following the global financial crisis and the COVID-19 pandemic. Yet while these shocks are notable for their severity, it is nonetheless important that we understand the mechanisms by which economic shocks more generally are propagated. In particular, it is important to understand their effect on the level and growth of labour productivity.

Some economists argue that, given the inherent volatility of economies, governments should be more proactive. For example, imperfections in the financial system which result in credit cycles can have marked effects on flows of investment, including spending on research and development. They argue that governments have a role to play in helping to stabilise aggregate demand so as to support and encourage firms to invest and increase potential output.

1 See Christine Lagarde (Managing Director, International Monetary Fund), 'Reinvigorating productivity growth', *IMF Speeches* (3 April 2017), www.imf.org/en/News/Articles/2017/04/03/sp040317-reinvigorating-productivity-growth

BOX 23.3 UK HUMAN CAPITAL

Estimating the capabilities of the labour force

The OECD (2001) defines human capital as the 'knowledge, skills, competencies and attributes embodied in individuals that facilitate the creation of personal, social and economic well-being'.[1] Hence, trends in human capital have implications for a range of economic-related issues, including economic growth, unemployment, life satisfaction, the inequality of income, wealth and opportunity and also for social cohesiveness. But how we do we go about measuring human capital?

Measuring human capital

In estimating an individual's human capital, a common approach is to estimate the present value of an individual's *remaining lifetime labour income.* This can be done for representative individuals in categories defined by gender, age and educational attainment. An assumption is then made about the working life of individuals. In compiling the UK estimates it is assumed that the remaining lifetime labour income of individuals aged 65 and over is zero. Then an approach known as backwards recursion is applied.

Backwards recursion involves first estimating the remaining lifetime labour income of someone aged 64 with a particular gender, age and educational level. The remaining lifetime income in this case is simply their current labour income. For someone aged 63 it is their current labour income plus the present value of the remaining lifetime income of someone aged 64 with the same gender, age and educational level. This continues back to someone aged 16. In calculating the remaining lifetime labour income of representative individuals account is also taken of the probability that their level of educational attainment may rise and with it their expected future earnings.

Further working assumptions are necessary to complete the calculations. Two of the most important are: the rate of labour productivity growth is 2 per cent per annum and the discount rate is 3.5 per cent per annum, as recommended by HM Treasury's *Green Book* (2003) when undertaking appraisal and evaluation studies in central government.

Two measures of the stock of human capital are estimated. The first is for *employed human capital.* It is based on estimating the lifetime labour income of those in employment. The second is *full human capital.* It includes the human capital of the unemployed. This assumes that the human capital of those currently unemployed should be valued at the remaining lifetime labour income of employed individuals with the same characteristics (gender, age and educational attainment). It ignores any so-called scarring effects from being unemployed, such as the depreciation of job-specific or transferable skills. Such effects are likely to increase with the duration of unemployment.

Estimates of human capital

Between 2004 and 2011, the stock of human capital in the UK increased by an average of 1.4 per cent per annum (see chart). However, there was then a marked slowdown: between 2012 and 2018 it grew by only 0.6 per cent per annum.

Changes in the stock of human capital can be decomposed into several factors, including changes in educational attainment and population, changes in the gender balance and the impact of the age structure of society. Over the period since 2004, population growth and rising educational attainment, particularly the growth in numbers with degree-equivalent qualifications, have had the most significantly positive effects on human capital. In recent times, however, their impact has lessened, while, at the same time, an ageing population has reduced the growth in the stock of human capital.

In 2018 the constant-price estimate of human capital grew by only 0.2 per cent. Nonetheless, this meant that the value

Section summary

1. A higher long-term rate of growth in output per worker will normally require a faster rate of technological progress.
2. The rate of technological progress determines the slope of the steady-state growth path (i.e. the rate of steady-state growth). If there is a rise in the saving rate, this will shift the steady-state growth path upwards (parallel) and the actual growth path will gradually move from the lower to the higher path.
3. Endogenous growth models show how capital accumulation and technological progress interact. Hence, capital accumulation and technological progress are interdependent sources of long-term growth.
4. Endogenous growth theory argues that the rate of technological progress and its rate of diffusion depend on economic institutions and incentives. Supply-side policy could be used to alter these.

EXPLORING ECONOMICS

of the full human capital stock reached £21.4 trillion (10.1 times GDP) and employed human capital £20.8 trillion (9.9 times GDP).

In Box 23.2 we saw that the net value of the UK's physical capital in 2019 was a little over twice that of annual GDP. Therefore, the value of the stock of human capital is estimated to be around five times higher than the stock of physical capital.

We can also analyse the *distribution* of human capital by particular characteristics, such as occupation, age, educational attainment and place of residency. For example, in 2018, it was estimated that 38.8 per cent of UK employed human capital was embodied in those who had a degree (or equivalent), 62.6 per cent in males and 19.8 per cent in residents of London.

1. *In what ways are human capital and physical capital complementary?*
2. *Other than by educational attainment, in what ways might we wish to analyse the distribution of human capital?*

Using the human capital estimates dataset from the ONS (www.ons.gov.uk/peoplepopulationandcommunity/wellbeing/datasets/humancapitalestimates supplementarytables), calculate the percentage shares of human capital originating from the different regions and countries of the UK. Summarise your findings in a short briefing note.

1 *The Well-Being of Nations: The Role of Human and Social Capital*, Centre for Educational Research and Innovation, OECD (2001).

Employed and full human capital (2018 prices)

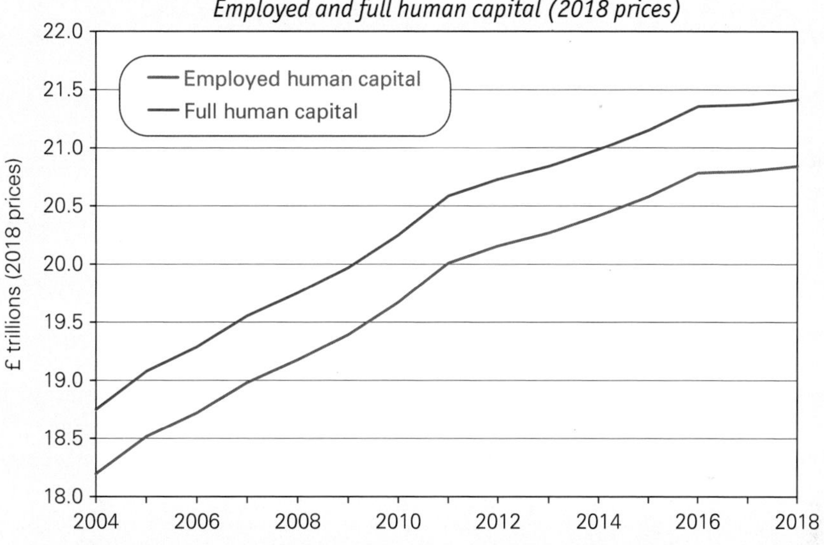

Source: Based on data in *Human Capital Estimates*, Office for National Statistics (October 2019). https://www.ons.gov.uk/peoplepopulationandcommunity/wellbeing/articles/humancapitalestimates/2004to2018

23.4 APPROACHES TO SUPPLY-SIDE POLICY

Macroeconomic objectives and supply-side policies

Long-term growth

Supply-side policies are policies designed to increase the quantity and/or productivity of the inputs used in production. If effective, such policies will increase potential output and thus, as we saw in section 23.1, shift the *AS* or *DAS* curves to the right. The more effective these policies are, the faster will potential output grow over time and the faster will the *AS* and *DAS* curves shift rightwards.

As we have seen throughout this chapter, technological progress is fundamental to long-term growth. Supply-side policies may therefore be directed at encouraging research and development. Specific measures might include increasing incentives for firms to take advantage of new ideas and innovations by investing in new capital, new production processes and perhaps organisational structures. But they will also need workers and managers with the tools, skills and flexibility to take full advantage of these innovations.

Thus supply-side policies to encourage economic growth are likely to focus not just on research and development, but also on education and training, infrastructure, industrial organisation, work practices and the whole range of incentives that may be necessary to make the best use of new ideas and techniques.

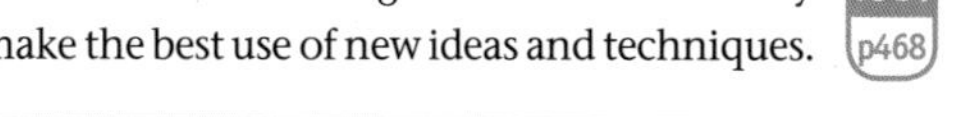

Supply-side policies Government policies that attempt to influence aggregate supply directly, rather than through aggregate demand.

Why do Keynesians argue that, even in the long run, demand-side policies will still be required if faster growth in aggregate supply is to be achieved?

Employment and unemployment

The cure for demand-deficient unemployment may lie on the demand side, but other types of unemployment require supply-side solutions.

Equilibrium unemployment – frictional, structural, etc. – is caused by rigidities or imperfections in the market. There is a mismatching of aggregate supply and demand, and vacancies are not filled despite the existence of unemployment. The problem is that labour is not sufficiently mobile, either occupationally or geographically, to respond to changes in the job market. Labour supply for particular jobs is too inelastic.

Supply-side policies aim to influence labour supply by helping workers to be more responsive to changes in job opportunities. They may also aim to make employers more adaptable and willing to operate within existing labour constraints. Alternatively, they may seek to reduce the monopoly power of unions to drive real wages above the equilibrium.

Successful supply-side policies that reduce equilibrium unemployment and increase employment and human capital also increase potential output. A rising stock of employed human capital (see Box 23.3) can contribute to the development of new products, processes and techniques and hence to the development of higher-quality capital. As we saw in the analysis of endogenous growth theories, there is also the potential that knowledge spillovers hasten progress. These spillovers are a form of externality with some of the benefits captured or consumed by others. In other words, these new ideas can then be developed by others.

KI 31 p364

Inflation

If inflation is caused by cost-push pressures, supply-side policy can help to reduce it in three ways:

- By reducing the power of unions and/or firms (for example, by the use of anti-monopoly legislation) and thereby encouraging more competition in the supply of labour and/or goods.
- By preventing people from exercising that power by some form of prices and incomes policy. (Such policies were used in the 1970s: see Case Study 23.7 on the student website.)
- By encouraging increases in productivity through retraining, or by investment grants to firms, or by tax incentives, etc.

KI 22 p195

The new classical approach

New classical economists argue that demand-side policy (by which they mean monetary policy) can only control inflation; it cannot affect growth and employment. Supply-side policy is the appropriate policy to increase output and reduce the level of unemployment.

New classical economists advocate policies to 'free up' the market: policies that encourage private enterprise, or provide incentives and reward initiative. Section 23.5 examines these ***market-orientated supply-side policies***.

TC 5 p48

This part of the new classical agenda has much in common with the ***neo-Austrian/libertarian school*** (see Box 12.7). The argument here is that a free market, with the absolute minimum of government interference, will provide the dynamic environment where entrepreneurs will be willing to take risks and develop new products and new techniques.

The neo-Austrians go further. They also argue that the prospect of monopoly profits is often what provides a major motivation for firms to take risks. The search to achieve market advantages through new products and new techniques is just as important a part of competition, they argue, as competition in the market for existing goods. Thus private property rights are a key element in neo-Austrian thought: the right to keep the fruits of innovation and investment, with minimum taxation.

The Keynesian approach

Modern Keynesians do not just advocate the management of demand. They also advocate supply-side policies, but generally of a more ***interventionist*** nature (e.g. training schemes, or policies to encourage firms to set up in areas of high unemployment).

The appropriate balance between demand and supply-side policies depends on the degree of slack in the economy. In a recession, the immediate policy requirement is to increase aggregate *demand* rather than aggregate supply. Over the long term, however, supply-side policies will be needed to increase potential output and to reduce equilibrium (structural and frictional) unemployment.

Does this mean that Keynesians would advocate using supply-side policies only at times of full employment?

'Third Way' supply-side policies

During the early years of the Labour government in the UK from 1997 under Tony Blair, there was much discussion of a 'Third Way' between the unfettered market system advocated by many of those on the right and the interventionist approach advocated by those on the left. The Third Way borrows from the right in advocating incentives, low taxes and free movements of capital. It also borrows from the left

Definitions

Market-orientated supply-side policies Policies to increase aggregate supply by freeing up the market.

Neo-Austrian/libertarian school A school of thought that advocates maximum liberty for economic agents to pursue their own interests and to own property.

Interventionist supply-side policies Policies to increase aggregate supply by government intervention to counteract the deficiencies of the market.

in advocating means whereby governments can provide support for individuals in need while improving economic performance by investing in the country's infrastructure, such as its transport and telecommunication systems, and in its social capital, such as schools, libraries and hospitals.

Its main thrust is the concept of helping people to help themselves. Thus unemployment policies should be focused on helping the unemployed become employable, with unemployment benefits linked to the obligation actively to look for work. Growth policies should be a mixture of strengthening market incentives and keeping taxes low, regulation to encourage more competition and prevent monopoly abuse, and providing improved infrastructure and improved education and training.

The COVID-19 pandemic was then to blur further the traditional dividing lines across the political spectrum and between economists on the relative merits of market-orientated versus interventionist supply-side policies. The result was that governments around the world, fearful of future scarring effects from the restrictions on economic activity, engaged in a series of interventionist measures, including job retention schemes and grants and loans to business. These measures, as we saw in sections 22.1 and 22.2, would have a significant impact on countries' public finances.

The link between demand-side and supply-side policies

Policies can have both demand-side and supply-side effects. For example, many supply-side policies involve increased government expenditure, whether on retraining schemes, on research and development projects, or on industrial relocation. They will therefore cause a rise in aggregate demand (unless accompanied by a rise in taxes). Similarly, supply-side policies of tax cuts designed to increase incentives will increase aggregate demand (unless accompanied by a cut in government expenditure). It is thus important to consider the consequences for demand when planning various supply-side policies.

Likewise, demand management policies often have supply-side effects. If a cut in interest rates boosts investment, there will be a multiplied rise in national income: a demand-side effect. But that rise in investment will also create increased productive capacity: a supply-side effect.

Section summary

1. Supply-side policies, if successful, will shift the *AS* and *DAS* curves to the right, and possibly shift the Phillips curve downwards/to the left.
2. An important role for supply-side policies is to help increase productivity and, in particular, promote more rapid technological progress and its adoption by business. By doing so, this can raise the long-term rate of economic growth.
3. Demand-side policies (fiscal and monetary) may be suitable for controlling demand-pull inflation or demand-deficient unemployment, but supply-side policies will be needed to control the other types of inflation and unemployment.
4. New classical and neo-Austrian economists favour market-orientated supply-side policies. Keynesians tend to favour interventionist supply-side policies. The Third Way advocates carefully targeted government intervention, regulation, welfare and education programmes to encourage people better to help themselves and markets to work more effectively.
5. Supply-side policies often have demand-side effects, and demand-side policies often have supply-side effects. It is important for governments to take these secondary effects into account when working out their economic strategy.

23.5 SUPPLY-SIDE POLICIES IN PRACTICE: MARKET-ORIENTATED POLICIES

Market-orientated policies in the 1980s

Radical market-orientated supply-side policies were first adopted in the early 1980s by the Thatcher government in the UK and the Reagan administration in the USA. The essence of these policies was to encourage and reward individual enterprise and initiative, and to reduce the role of

government; to put more reliance on market forces and competition, and less on government intervention and regulation. The policies were thus associated with the following:

- Reducing government expenditure so as to release more resources for the private sector.
- Reducing taxes so as to increase incentives.
- Reducing the monopoly power of trade unions so as to encourage greater flexibility in both wages and working practices and to allow labour markets to clear.
- Reducing the automatic entitlement to certain welfare benefits so as to encourage greater self-reliance.
- Reducing red tape and other impediments to investment and risk-taking.
- Encouraging competition through policies of deregulation and privatisation.
- Abolishing exchange controls and other impediments to the free movement of capital.

Such policies were increasingly copied by other governments around the world. Today most countries have adopted some or all of the above measures.

BOX 23.4 **THE SUPPLY-SIDE REVOLUTION IN THE USA** CASE STUDIES AND APPLICATIONS

'Reaganomics' and beyond

In both the UK and the USA, the 1980s proved to be years of radical political and economic change. Traditional economic and political practices were replaced by new and often controversial policies, although in theory many of the ideas advocated were based on old principles of laissez-faire capitalism.

In the USA, the era of 'Reaganomics' began in January 1981 when Ronald Reagan became President. With this new administration came a radical shift in policy aimed at directly tackling the supply side of the economy. This policy strategy involved four key strands:

- A reduction in the growth of Federal (central government) spending.
- A reduction in individual and corporate tax rates.
- A reduction in Federal regulations over private enterprise.
- A reduction in inflation through tight monetary policy.

On all four points, President Reagan achieved a degree of success. Federal spending growth was reduced, even though military spending rocketed. Tax rates fell dramatically. Deregulation was speeded up. Inflation at first was stabilised and then fell sharply.

These supply-side measures were hailed as a great success by Republicans, and followers in both the UK and the USA were quick to advocate an even bigger reduction in the government's role.

Critics remained sceptical and pointed to the costs of Reaganomics. Huge budget deficits plagued the Reagan administration and the Bush Snr, Clinton and Bush Jnr administrations that followed. The massive tax cuts were not matched by an equivalent cut in public expenditure; nor did they produce a sufficiently high rate of economic growth, through which additional tax revenues were to balance the budget. In the 1980s, 'civilian' or welfare spending was cut repeatedly in preference to the huge military budget. This led to increasing social hardship.

And such hardship still existed under George W. Bush. Indeed, with the onset of the credit crunch, things were to get worse as many poor people lost their houses. The emphasis had remained on cutting welfare and tightening requirements to receive state assistance. Critics claim that, even though the numbers on welfare might have fallen over the years, individuals and families remained in poverty, being forced to work for poverty wages as welfare support dwindled. The revolution was far from complete and its benefits to all social groups have been far from even.

The financial crisis of the late 2000s and the subsequent need for fiscal consolidation led to much debate, not only in the USA, about the form the fiscal consolidation should take and, more generally, about the role the state should play in modern economies. Whether, in such circumstances, current or future administrations will succeed in providing greater support for the poor without jeopardising the 'supply-side revolution' remains to be seen.

The preference for President Trump was to cut taxes. The corporate tax rate was cut from 35 to 21 per cent in 2017. This was partially reversed by President Biden who, when coming to office in 2021, planned to raise it to 28 per cent and engage in a multi-trillion dollar policy of welfare spending and public investment.

Are market-orientated supply-side policies incompatible with policies to redistribute national income more equally?

Research the economic policies pursued by Donald Trump in the USA between 2016 and 2020 and assess whether these could be described as a modern version of Reaganomics.

Government spending

The desire by many governments to limit the growth of government expenditure is not just to reduce the size of deficits and hence reduce the growth of money supply; it is also an essential ingredient of their supply-side strategy.

The public sector is portrayed as more bureaucratic and less efficient than the private sector. What is more, it is claimed that a growing proportion of public money has been spent on administration and other 'non-productive' activities, rather than on the direct provision of goods and services.

Two things are needed, it is argued: (a) a more efficient use of resources within the public sector and (b) a reduction in the relative size of the public sector. This would allow private investment to increase with no overall rise in aggregate demand. Thus the supply-side benefits of higher investment could be achieved without the demand-side costs of higher inflation.

In practice governments have found it very difficult to cut their share of expenditure in GDP (see Figure 23.12). This can arise when fiscal measures are used to alleviate the economic impact of crises, such as the global financial crisis and the COVID-19 pandemic. The deteriorating financial position of governments that follows can then require difficult fiscal choices to be made.

Why might a recovering economy (and hence a fall in government expenditure on social security benefits) make the government feel even more concerned to make discretionary cuts in government expenditure?

Taxes and the labour market

Over time, governments in many countries have cut the marginal rate of income tax. Here we consider the case of the UK.

In 1979, the standard marginal rate of income tax was 33 per cent, with higher rates rising to 83 per cent. By 2008

Figure 23.12 General government expenditure (% of GDP)

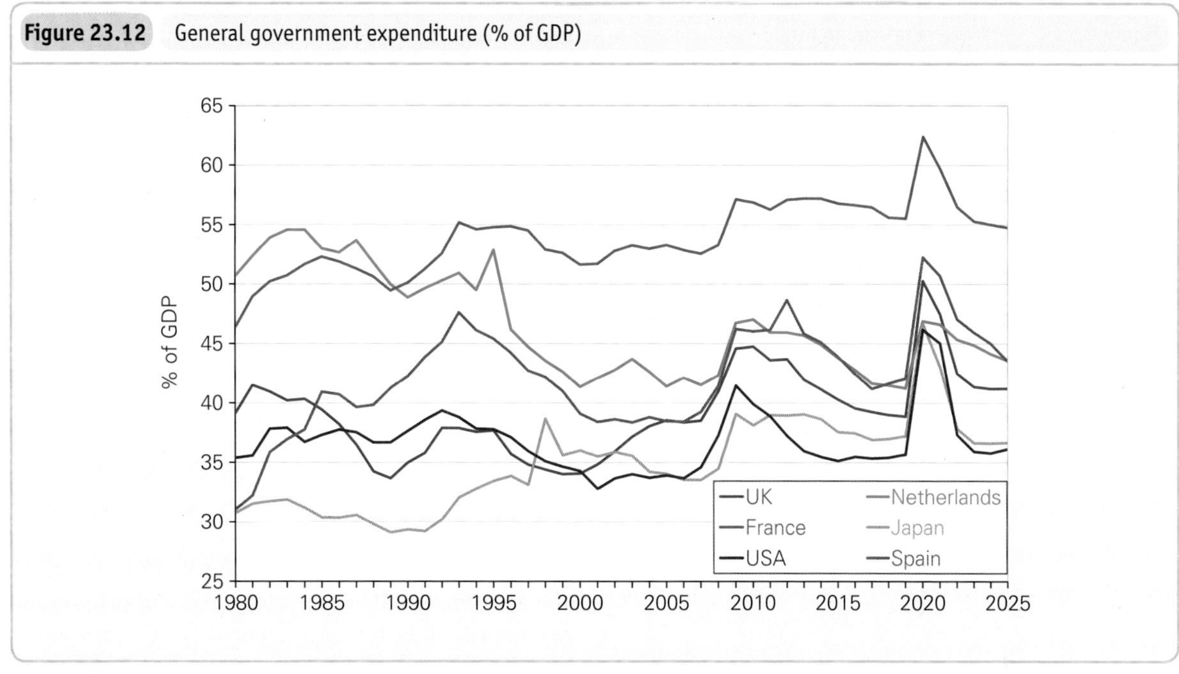

Notes: Data from 2021 based on forecasts.
Source: Based on data from *World Economic Outlook Database*, IMF, www.imf.org/external/ns/cs.aspx?id=28; and *AMECO Database*, European Commission, https://ec.europa.eu/info/business-economy-euro/indicators-statistics/economic-databases/macro-economic-database-ameco/ameco-database_en

the standard rate was 20 per cent and the higher rate was 40 per cent. From 2010, an additional 50 per cent tax rate was implemented for incomes in excess of £150 000, largely as a means of plugging the deficit in the public finances. This was subsequently reduced to 45 per cent from 2013.

Cuts in the marginal rate of income tax are claimed to have five beneficial effects: people work longer hours; more people wish to work; people work more enthusiastically; employment rises; unemployment falls. These are big claims. Are they true?

People work longer hours

A cut in the marginal rate of income tax has a *substitution effect* inducing people to work more and also an *income effect* causing people to work less. (At this point, you should review the arguments about the incentive effects of tax cuts: see pages 344–8.) Evidence suggests that the two effects will roughly cancel each other out. Anyway, for many people there is no such choice in the short run. There is no chance of doing overtime or working a shorter week. In the long run, there may be some flexibility in that people can change jobs.

More people wish to work

This applies largely to second income earners in a family, mainly women. A rise in after-tax wages may encourage more women to look for jobs. It may now be worth the cost in terms of transport, childcare, family disruption, etc. The effects of a 1 or 2 per cent cut in income tax rates, however, are likely to be negligible. A more significant effect may be achieved by raising tax allowances. Part-time workers, especially, could end up paying no taxes. Of course, if unemployment is already high, the government will not want to increase the labour force.

People work more enthusiastically

There is little evidence to test this claim. The argument, however, is that people will be more conscientious and will work harder if they can keep more of their pay.

Employment rises

If wages are flexible, total employment will rise. This is illustrated in Figure 23.13. The *N* curve shows the total labour force. The AS_L curve shows the number of people who are actually qualified and willing to do the specific jobs they are offered at each (after-tax) wage rate. Equilibrium is where the aggregate demand for labour (AD_L) is equal to the labour cost to the employer (i.e. the pre-tax wage rate). Assume an initial income tax per worker of $a - b$. The equilibrium employment will be Q_1. Workers receive an after-tax wage W_1 and thus supply Q_1 labour. Employers' labour cost is the pre-tax wage lc_1. At this wage, they demand Q_1 labour.

If the income tax per worker now falls to $c - d$, equilibrium employment will rise to Q_2. Firms will employ more workers because their labour costs have fallen to lc_2. More workers will take up jobs because their after-tax wages have risen to W_2.

Unemployment falls

One of the causes of natural (equilibrium) unemployment highlighted by new classical economists is the cushioning provided by unemployment benefit. If income tax rates are cut, there will be a bigger difference between after-tax wage

Figure 23.13 Effect of a tax cut on total unemployment

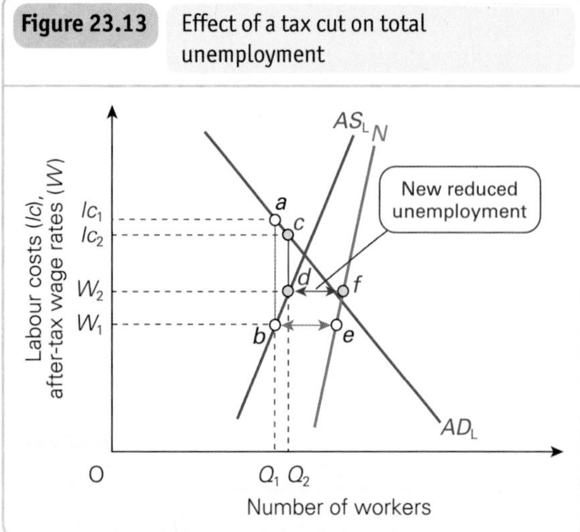

rates and unemployment benefit. More people will be motivated to 'get on their bikes' and look for work.

In Figure 23.13, the horizontal gap between N and AS_L represents equilibrium unemployment. With a cut in income tax per worker from $a - b$ to $c - d$, equilibrium unemployment will fall from $e - b$ to $f - d$.

What would happen to the AS_L curve and the level of unemployment if unemployment benefits were increased?

Despite the cuts in marginal rates of income tax in many countries, it has been commonplace for these to be offset by significant increases in other taxes. For example, in the UK, VAT was raised from 8 to 15 per cent per cent in 1979, to 17.5 per cent in 1992 and to 20 per cent in 2011.[2] The marginal rate of national insurance contributions for employees was 6.5 per cent in 1979; by 2011 it had risen to 12 per cent. The net effect was that government's receipts as a proportion of GDP were largely unchanged at just under 40 per cent.

Does this mean that there were no positive incentive effects from the 1979–97 Conservative government's tax measures?

To the extent that tax cuts do succeed in increasing take-home pay, there is a danger of 'sucking in' imports. In the UK, there is a high income elasticity of demand for imports. Extra consumer incomes may be spent on foreign-made electronic goods, foreign cars, holidays abroad and so on. Tax cuts can therefore have a serious effect on the current account of the balance of payments.

Taxes, business and investment

TC 5 p48

A number of financial incentives can be given to encourage investment. Selective intervention in the form of grants for specific industries or firms is best classified as an interventionist policy and will be examined in section 23.6. Market-orientated policies seek to reduce the general level of taxation on profits, or to give greater tax relief to investment.

A cut in taxes on business profits. A cut in corporation tax (the tax on business profits) will increase after-tax profits. This will leave more funds for ploughing back into investment. Also, the higher after-tax return on investment will encourage more investment to take place. In 1983, the main rate of corporation tax in the UK stood at 52 per cent. A series of reductions have taken place since then. By 2011 the main rate had been halved to 26 per cent; by 2017 it had fallen to 19 per cent.

Many countries were to follow a similar trend, hoping that low corporation tax rates would make their country an attractive destination for business investment. However, the danger of countries cutting taxes to make them more internationally competitive is that it is a prisoners' dilemma game. Countries cannot all have lower taxes than each other! You may simply end up with global taxes being lower and governments receiving less tax revenue. Governments thus have to make a judgement as to whether or not cutting taxes will stimulate other countries to do the same.

KI 23 p228

The pandemic, however, may have brought to an end further corporate tax cuts in many countries, at least for now. With the deterioration in the public finances from the measures taken by governments in response to COVID-19, following on from measures in response to the global financial crisis, the scope for further cuts appears more limited.

In March 2021, the UK government announced that, from 2023, the main corporation tax rate would increase to 25 per cent for companies with profits of £250 000 or higher. Then in April 2021, speaking ahead of the spring meeting of the International Monetary Fund, Janet Yellen, US Treasury Secretary, made the case for a minimum tax rate and an end to a 'race to the bottom'. The hope was that an international agreement could be found, building on the work by the OECD, for a global framework for taxation. Amongst other things, this would include increasing taxes on giant companies, such as Google, Amazon and Apple, and a fair international distribution of national tax revenues from such multinationals.

Tax relief or other incentives for investment. Another approach to increase investment is through the use of allowances or R&D expenditure credits. Investment allowances enable firms to offset the cost of investment against their pre-tax profit, thereby reducing their tax liability. R&D expenditure credits operate by providing firms with cash payments for a proportion of their R&D expenditure which, although subject to tax, nonetheless increase their net profit.

Successive governments have applied such R&D incentives. For example, in the UK small and medium-sized enterprises (SMEs) can offset multiple research and development costs against corporation tax. Since April 2015, the rate of relief for small and medium-sized enterprises was 230 per cent: taxable profits are reduced by £230 for every £100 of R&D

2 The rate was cut to 15 per cent in December 2008 for 13 months as part of the government's fiscal stimulus package.

expenditure. Meanwhile, larger companies can claim a R&D expenditure credit (RDEC) which, since April 2020, is worth 13 per cent of R&D expenditures.

Since April 2013, firms have been subject to a lower rate of corporation tax on profits earned from their patented inventions and certain other innovations. The idea is that firms will be provided with financial support to innovate where this results in their acquiring patents. Patents provide protection for intellectual property rights. Firms are liable to corporation tax on the profits attributable to qualifying patents at a reduced rate of 10 per cent.

In its Budget of March 2021, the UK government introduced a 2-year 'super-deduction' tax break. Operational for the period before the increase in the main corporation tax came into effect in 2023, firms could reduce their corporation tax bills by 130 per cent on eligible plant and machinery. The hope was that this would encourage firms to bring forward investment.

TC 3 p26

Reducing the power of labour

In Figure 23.14, if the power of unions to push wage rates up to W_1 were removed, then (assuming no change in the demand curve for labour) wage rates would fall to W_e. Disequilibrium unemployment ($Q_2 - Q_1$) would disappear. Employment would rise from Q_1 to Q_e.

Equilibrium unemployment, however, will rise somewhat as the gap between gross and effective labour supply widens. With the reduction in wage rates, some people may now prefer to remain on unemployment benefits.

If labour costs to employers are reduced, their profits will probably rise. This could encourage and enable more investment and hence economic growth. If the monopoly power of labour is reduced, then cost-push inflation will also be reduced.

The Thatcher government took a number of measures to weaken the power of labour. These included restrictions on union closed shops, restrictions on secondary picketing, financial assistance for union ballots, and enforced secret ballots on strike proposals (see section 10.2). It also set a lead in resisting strikes in the public sector.

As labour markets have become more flexible, with increased part-time working and short-term and zero-hour contracts, and as the process of globalisation has exposed more companies to international competition, so this has further eroded the power of labour in many sectors of the economy.

Is the number of working days lost through disputes a good indication of (a) union power; (b) union militancy?

A danger in driving down wages through increased competition in the labour market is that it reduces the incentive for firms to increase labour productivity. One cause of the UK's significantly lower output per hour than its major competitors (see chart (c) in Box 23.1) is that hourly wages are lower in many industries.

Reducing welfare

New classical economists claim that a major cause of unemployment is the small difference between the welfare benefits of the unemployed and the take-home pay of the employed. This causes voluntary unemployment (i.e. frictional unemployment). People are caught in a 'poverty trap': if they take a job, they lose their benefits (see pages 350–1).

A dramatic solution to this problem would be to cut unemployment benefits. Unlike policies to encourage investment, this supply-side policy would have a very rapid effect. It would shift the effective labour supply curve to the right. In Figure 23.15, equilibrium unemployment would fall from $a - b$ to $c - d$ if real wage rates were flexible downwards; or from $a - b$ to $a - e$ if they were not flexible. In the case of non-flexible real wage rates, the reduction in equilibrium unemployment would be offset by a rise in disequilibrium unemployment ($e - b$).

Figure 23.14 Effect of reducing the power of labour

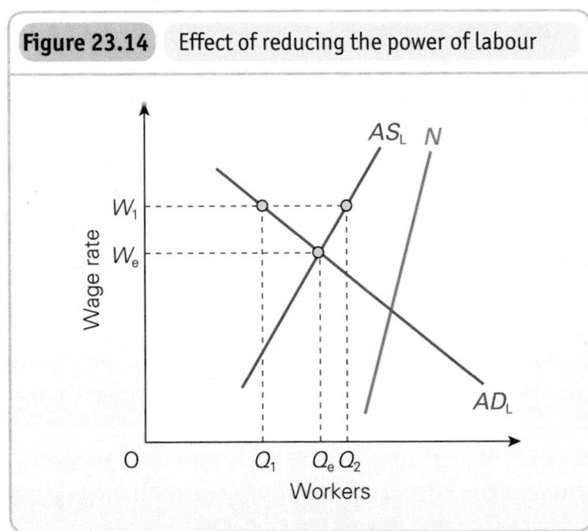

Figure 23.15 The effects of a cut in benefits on the number unemployed

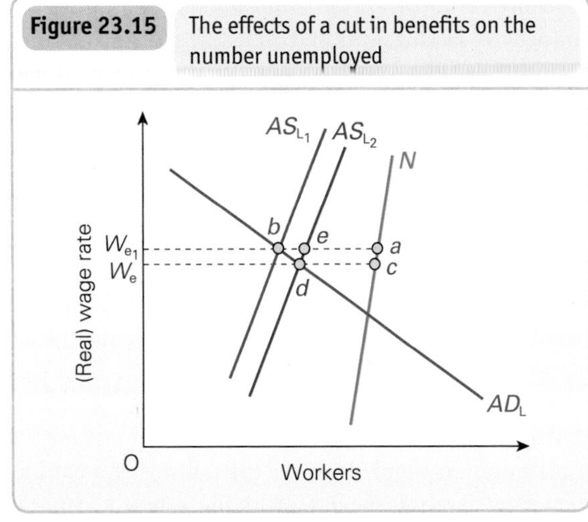

Figure 23.16 The effects of a cut in benefits on the average duration of unemployment

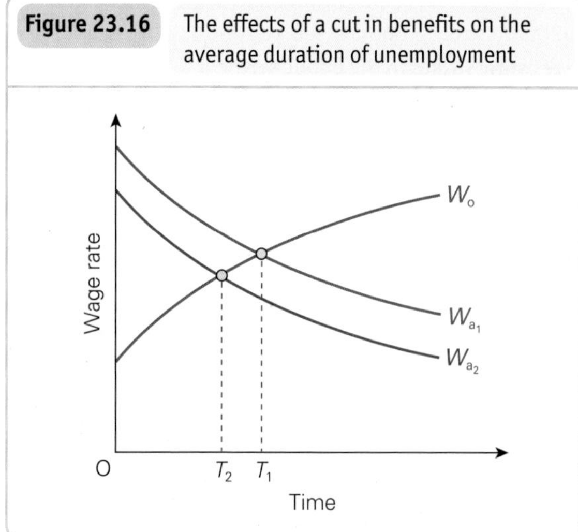

Because workers would now be prepared to accept a lower wage, the average length of job search by the unemployed would be reduced. In Figure 23.16, the average duration of unemployment would fall from T_1 to T_2.

Would a cut in benefits affect the W_o curve? If so, with what effect?

A major problem is that with changing requirements for labour skills, many of the redundant workers from the older industries are simply not qualified for new jobs that are created. What is more, the longer people are unemployed, the more demoralised they become. Employers would probably be prepared to pay only very low wage rates to such workers. To persuade these unemployed people to take these low-paid jobs, the welfare benefits would have to be slashed. A 'market' solution to the problem, therefore, may be a very cruel solution. A fairer solution would be an interventionist policy: a policy of retraining labour.

Another alternative is to make the payment of unemployment benefits conditional on the recipient making a concerted effort to find a job. In the jobseeker's allowance scheme introduced in the UK in 1996, claimants must be available for, and actively seeking, work and must sign a 'Claimant Commitment', which sets out the types of work the person is willing to do, and their plan to find work. Payment can be refused if the claimant refuses to accept the offer of a job.

Policies to encourage competition

If the government can encourage more competition, this should have the effect of increasing national output and reducing inflation. Five major types of policy have been pursued under this heading.

Privatisation

If privatisation simply involves the transfer of a natural monopoly to private hands (as with the water companies), the scope for increased competition is limited. However, where there is genuine scope for competition (e.g. in the supply of gas and electricity), privatisation can lead to increased efficiency, more consumer choice and lower prices (but see Box 14.4 on pages 444–6).

Alternatively, privatisation can involve the introduction of private services into the public sector (e.g. private contractors providing cleaning services in hospitals, or refuse collection for local authorities). Private contractors may compete against each other for the franchise. This may well lower the cost of provision of these services, but the quality of provision may also suffer unless closely monitored. The effects on unemployment are uncertain. Private contractors may offer lower wages and thus may use more labour. But if they are trying to supply the service at minimum cost, they may employ less labour.

KI 25 p274

Deregulation

This involves the removal of monopoly rights. In 1979, the UK's National Bus Corporation lost its monopoly of long-distance coach haulage. Private operators were now allowed to compete. This substantially reduced coach fares on a number of routes. In 1986, competition was allowed in providing local bus services (see Case Study 23.5 on the student website).

An example in the private sector was the so-called 'Big Bang' on the Stock Exchange in 1986. Under this, the monopoly power of 'jobbers' to deal in stocks and shares on the Stock Exchange was abolished. In addition, stockbrokers now compete with each other in the commission rates that they charge, and online share dealing has become commonplace.

Introducing market relationships into the public sector

This is where the government tries to get different departments or elements within a particular part of the public sector to 'trade' with each other, so as to encourage competition and efficiency. The best-known examples are within health and education.

KI 24 p259

One example is the UK's National Health Service. In 2003, the government introduced a system of 'foundation trusts' in England. Hospitals can apply for foundation trust status. If successful, they are given much greater financial autonomy in terms of purchasing, employment and investment decisions. NHS Improvement and NHS England are responsible for overseeing foundation trusts and NHS trusts. Critics argue that funds have been diverted to foundation hospitals away from the less well-performing hospitals where greater funding could help that performance.

As far as general practice is concerned, groups of GP practices are formed into Clinical Commissioning Groups (CCGs). These are responsible for arranging most of the NHS services within their boundaries. A key principle of the system is to give GPs a choice of 'providers' with the hope of reducing costs and driving up standards.

Public–private partnerships

Public–private partnerships (PPPs) are a way of funding public expenditure with private capital (see Case Study 23.4 on the student website). In the UK, the *Private Finance Initiative* (PFI), as it was known, began in 1992. The PFI meant that a private company, after a competitive tender, would be contracted by a government department or local authority to finance and build a project, such as a new road or a prison. The government then pays the company to maintain and/or run it, or simply rents the assets from the company. The public sector thus becomes a purchaser of services rather than a direct provider itself.

Critics claim that PFI projects have resulted in low quality of provision and that cost control has often been poor, resulting in a higher burden for the taxpayer in the long term. What is more, many of the projects have turned out to be highly profitable, suggesting that the terms of the original contracts were too lax.

In 2012, the UK government published reforms to the PFI process following concerns about the quality of provision and the costs being incurred. The reforms included the public sector taking a stake of up to 49 per cent in new private finance projects (PF2 projects). Despite the reforms, the collapse of Carillion, a British company heavily involved with PPPs in the UK and Canada through construction and support services, brought an end to new PPPs in the UK. In October 2018, the Chancellor announced that it would no longer use PF2, although existing agreements would be honoured.

Free trade and free capital movements

The opening up of international trade and investment is central to a market-orientated supply-side policy. One of the first measures of the Thatcher government (in October 1979) was to remove all exchange controls, thereby permitting the free inflow and outflow of capital, both long term and short term. Most other industrialised countries also removed or relaxed exchange controls during the 1980s and early 1990s.

The Single European Act of 1987, which came into force in 1993, was another example of international liberalisation. As we shall see in section 24.4, it created a 'single market' in the EU: a market without barriers to the movement of goods, services, capital and labour.

The greater openness of economies, it is argued, can help to raise an economy's longer-term rate of growth. This can occur through a series of mechanisms that positively affect labour productivity and therefore, as we have seen in this chapter, raise aggregate living standards. These include the incentives to adopt new ideas and methods in order to compete and the potential to increase the scale of production by serving wider markets.

The transfer of knowledge is often identified as a key benefit of greater openness. ***Knowledge transfer*** can occur, for example, through the exposure to new ideas, products or processes. A greater mobility of goods, finance and people across international borders may therefore facilitate knowledge transfer. This was an important argument on the Remain side in the Brexit debate prior to the referendum in 2016.

The opening up of trade and investment is not without its issues and its critics. For example, some have claimed that in the short term, industries may be forced to close by the competition from cheaper imported products, which can have a major impact on employment in the areas affected. A major plank of the Trump presidency was 'putting America first'. This involved a move away from free trade, and giving specific protection to US industries, such as vehicles and steel.

We examine the arguments for and against protection in section 24.2, while in section 24.5 we analyse the issue of openness further in respect of the UK's departure from the European Union.

> **Definition**
>
> **Knowledge transfer** The sharing and diffusion of knowledge between individuals, organisations and countries.

Section summary

1. Market-orientated supply-side policies aim to increase the rate of growth of aggregate supply by encouraging private enterprise and the freer play of market forces.
2. Reducing government expenditure as a proportion of GDP is a major element of such policies.
3. Tax cuts can be used to encourage more people to take up jobs, and to encourage people to work longer hours and more enthusiastically. They can be used to reduce equilibrium unemployment and encourage employers to take on more workers. Likewise, tax cuts for businesses or increased investment allowances may encourage higher investment. The effects of tax cuts depend on how people respond to incentives. For example, people will work longer hours only if the substitution effect outweighs the income effect.
4. Reducing the power of trade unions by legislation could reduce disequilibrium unemployment and cost-push inflation. It could also lead to a redistribution of income to profits, which could increase investment and growth (but possibly lead to greater inequality).
5. A reduction in welfare benefits, especially those related to unemployment, will encourage workers to accept jobs at lower wages and thus decrease equilibrium unemployment.
6. Various policies can be introduced to increase competition. These include privatisation, deregulation, introducing market relationships into the public sector, public–private partnerships and freer international trade and capital movements.

23.6 SUPPLY-SIDE POLICIES IN PRACTICE: INTERVENTIONIST POLICIES

The case for intervention

Many interventionist policies come under the general heading of ***industrial policy***: the government taking an active role to support investment in industry and to halt the decline of the manufacturing sector (see Box 23.5). The basis of the case for government intervention is that the free market is likely to provide too little research and development, training and investment.

TC 7 p79

TC 3 p26

As we saw in section 23.3, there are potentially large external benefits from research and development. Hence, the social rate of return on investment may be much higher than the private rate of return. Investment that is privately unprofitable for a firm may therefore still be economically desirable for the nation.

KI 31 p364

Similarly, investment in training may continue yielding benefits to society that are lost to the firms providing the training when the workers leave.

Investment often involves risks. Firms may be unwilling to take those risks, since the costs of possible failure may be too high. When looked at nationally, however, the benefits of investment might well have substantially outweighed the costs, and thus it would have been socially desirable for firms to have taken the risk. Successes would have outweighed failures.

KI 11 p72

For decades, the UK has had a lower level of investment relative to GDP than other industrialised countries. This is illustrated in Table 23.3. It could be argued, therefore, that there is a particularly strong case in the UK for government intervention to encourage investment.

Table 23.3 Gross fixed capital formation (investment), % of GDP

	1960–79	1980–99	2000–22	1960–2022
Japan	28.4	30.0	24.5	27.5
Austria	25.5	24.7	23.5	24.5
Norway	28.0	22.0	23.3	24.4
Switzerland	23.0	24.0	25.4	24.2
Ireland	23.3	21.1	25.4	23.4
France	23.8	21.4	22.4	22.6
Belgium	24.5	20.4	22.6	22.5
Italy	26.0	20.4	19.3	21.8
Australia	17.8	20.1	25.3	21.2
Netherlands	22.4	19.3	20.3	20.7
Canada	19.0	19.8	23.0	20.7
Germany	21.7	20.1	20.3	20.6
Spain	19.1	19.1	20.9	19.8
USA	17.1	18.2	20.4	18.7
UK	19.4	19.0	17.1	18.4
Denmark	16.7	16.5	20.2	17.9

Note: Data from 2021 based on forecasts.
Source: Based on data from *AMECO database*, European Commission (2021).

Imperfections in the capital market

Imperfections in the capital market may result in investment not being financed, even though it is privately profitable. Banks in the UK, unlike banks in France, Germany and Japan, have not traditionally been a source of finance for long-term investment by firms.

Similarly, if firms rely on raising finance by the issue of new shares, this makes them very dependent on the stock market performance of their shares, which depends on current profitability and expected profitability in the near future, not on long-term profitability.

Shareholders, who are mainly financial institutions, tend to demand too high a dividend rate from the companies in which they invest. This, in part, is due to competition between financial institutions to attract savers to buy their savings packages. The result is that there is less profit left over for ploughing back into investment. The fear of takeovers (the competition for corporate control) again makes managers overconcerned to keep shareholders happy. Finally, floating successful companies on the Stock Exchange provides a large windfall gain to the original owners. This encourages entrepreneurs to *set up* companies, but discourages them from making *long-term* commitments to them.

KI 25 p274

This has all led to the UK disease of 'short-termism': the obsession with short-term profits and the neglect of investment that yields profits only after a number of years.

Finally, in the case of ailing firms, if the government does not help finance a rescue investment programme, there may be substantial social costs from job losses. The avoidance of these social costs may make the investment socially, if not privately, profitable.

How would the radical right reply to these arguments?

Examples of interventionist supply-side policy

Nationalisation

This is the most extreme form of intervention, and one that most countries have in the past rejected, given the worldwide trend of privatisation. Nevertheless, many countries have stopped short of privatising certain key transport and power industries, such as the railways and electricity generation. Having these industries under public ownership may result in higher investment than if they were under private ownership. Thus French governments

Definition

Industrial policies Policies to encourage industrial investment and greater industrial efficiency.

have invested heavily in the state-owned railway system. This has resulted in fast, efficient rail services, with obvious benefits to rail users and the economy generally.

Nationalisation may also be a suitable solution for rescuing vital industries suffering extreme market turbulence. This was the case in 2008 with many banks. With the credit crunch, overexposure to risky investments in securitised sub-prime debt, inadequate levels of capital, declining confidence and plummeting share prices, many banks were taken into full or partial public ownership. In the UK, Northern Rock and Bradford & Bingley were fully nationalised, while the government took a temporary majority shareholding in the Royal Bank of Scotland and Lloyds Banking Group.

Direct provision

Improvements in infrastructure, such as a country's transport system, can be of direct benefit to industry. Alternatively, the government could provide factories or equipment to specific firms. The financial crisis and the COVID-19 pandemic raised the spectre of scarring effects: a collapse in current economic activity having adverse consequences for future economic outcomes. The IMF, OECD and other international organisations began calling for greater international expenditure on infrastructure as a way of increasing not only aggregate demand but potential output too. There were also growing calls on governments to gear such investments to reducing carbon emissions and improving biodiversity (see Box 13.1).

Funding research and development (R&D)

To increase a country's research and development, the government could fund universities or other research institutes through various grants, perhaps allocated by research councils. Alternatively, it could provide grants or tax relief to private firms to carry out R&D.

As we saw in section 23.5, the UK uses the tax system to encourage research and development (R&D). TC 5 p48

Despite this, UK gross expenditure on R&D as a percentage of GDP has been significantly lower than that of its main economic rivals (see Figure 23.17). This has contributed to a productivity gap between the UK and other G7 countries (see Box 23.1).

The UK's poor R&D record has occurred even though a sizeable number of UK-based companies are among the world's largest R&D spending companies, albeit within a narrow range of industries, such as pharmaceuticals, finance and aerospace. In part, this reflects the limited R&D expenditure by government; but it also reflects the low R&D intensity across the private sector. In other words, total R&D expenditure by British firms has often been low *relative* to the income generated by sales.

Training and education

It is generally recognised by economists and politicians alike that improvements in training and education can yield significant supply-side gains. Indeed, the UK's failure to invest as much in training as many of its major competitors is seen as a key explanation for the persistent productivity gap with many other advanced countries.

The government may set up training schemes, or encourage educational institutions to make their courses more vocationally relevant or introduce new vocational qualifications. Alternatively, the government can provide grants or tax relief to firms which themselves provide training schemes.

Education and training in the UK. From April 2017 in England, the Education and Skills Funding Agency (ESFA) took over responsibility for funding education and training for children, young people and adults. Hence, as well as the funding

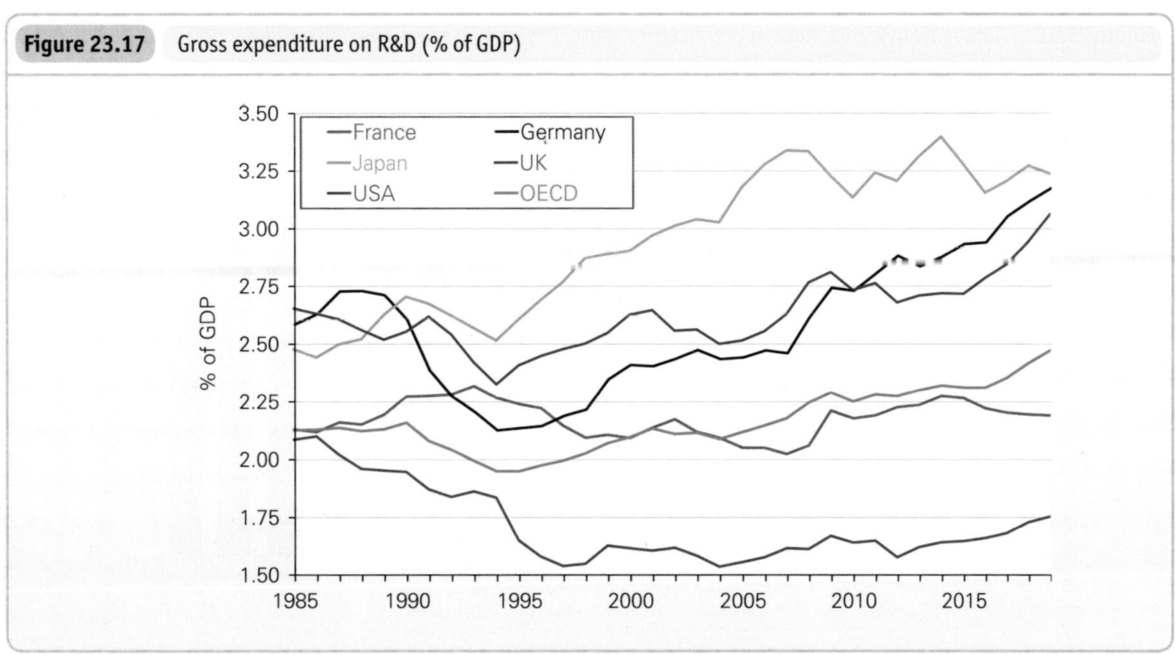

Note: OECD = 37 members (as of April 2021) of the Organisation for Economic Co-operation and Development.
Source: *Gross Domestic Spending on R&D*, OECD (2021), https://data.oecd.org/rd/gross-domestic-spending-on-r-d.htm

of education for pupils aged 5 to 16 it has responsibility for overseeing education and training for those aged 16 to 19 and apprenticeships and adult education.

As part of the government's strategy to support apprenticeships, the Apprenticeship Levy was introduced from April 2017. This saw employers with an annual wage bill of £3 million or more having to pay a levy of 0.5 per cent towards the funding of apprenticeships. Employers in England can then use funds in their apprenticeship accounts to pay for apprenticeship training and assessment with the payment dependent, in part, on the level of the apprenticeship: i.e. the equivalent educational level. For smaller employers, the government will pay up to 90 per cent of their training and assessment costs, although in the case of companies with fewer than 50 employees 100 per cent of these costs are paid for if the apprentices are aged between 16 and 18.

Figure 23.18 shows the steady expansion in the number of starts on government-funded apprenticeships in England between 2006/7 and 2009/10, followed by a more significant expansion in the early 2010s before then levelling off at around 500 000 per annum. While each age group has seen an increase in the number of apprenticeships, the growth in the number of learners aged 25 and over starting apprenticeships has been particularly rapid.

However, following the introduction of the Apprenticeship Levy, apprenticeship numbers fell. In 2018/19 there were 393 400 apprenticeship starts compared to 509 400 in 2015/16. In 2019/20 the number had fallen again to 322 500. Some have argued that the levy is too complex, that it can be difficult for employers to access funds and that it is merely seen by employers as another tax.

With concerns about the impact of the COVID-19 pandemic on human capital, particularly of younger people, the government introduced incentive payments for hiring apprentices in England. These were initially payments of £2000 for the hiring of apprentices aged 16 to 24 and £1500 for 25 and over between August 2020 and March 2021. This period was subsequently extended until September 2021, with employers receiving an incentive payment of £3000 for hiring apprentices of any age.

The government also introduced across England, Scotland and Wales a Kickstart grant designed to create new job placements for those aged 16 to 24 on Universal Credit who might otherwise be at risk of long-term unemployment. The grant of £1500 per job on placements up to the end of March 2022 was to be spent on setup costs and providing training and employability support.

The availability and take up of apprenticeships has, however, been a longstanding issue in the UK with numbers often considerably lower than in many competitor countries, such as Germany and Australia.

Alternative approaches to training in the UK, Germany, France and the USA are examined in Case 23.10 on the student website.

Advice, information and collaboration

The government may engage in discussions with private firms in order to find ways to improve efficiency and innovation. It may bring firms together to exchange information and create a climate of greater certainty, or it may bring firms and unions together to try to create greater industrial harmony. It can provide various information services to firms: technical assistance, the results of public research, information on markets, etc. KI 15 p132

Local Enterprise Partnerships (LEPs) are an example of partnerships created between local government and

Figure 23.18 Total government-funded apprenticeship starts, England (academic years August to July)

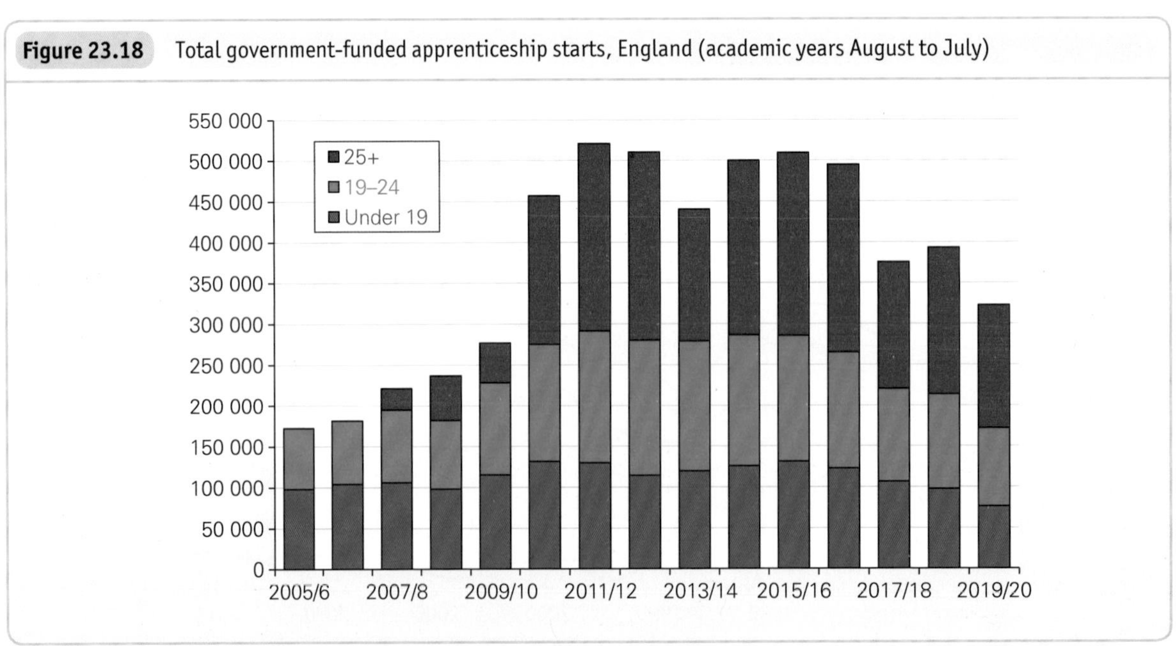

Source: Based on data from *Apprenticeships and traineeships*, Department for Education (6 April 2021), https://explore-education-statistics.service.gov.uk/find-statistics/apprenticeships-and-traineeships

BOX 23.5 **A MODERN APPROACH TO INDUSTRIAL POLICY** EXPLORING ECONOMICS

Framework conditions for the creation and growth of firms

Industrial policy attempts to increase investment and halt or slow the shrinking of the industrial sector. As with many other areas of economic policy, industrial policy throughout most of the world has undergone a radical reorientation in recent years. The government's role has generally shifted from one of direct intervention in the form of subsidies and protecting industry from competition, to one of focusing upon the external business environment and the conditions that influence its competitiveness.

The modern approach to industrial policy began to take shape in the 1980s reflecting both philosophical and structural forces:

- The rise of the political right from the 1980s led to a shift away from interventionist and towards market-based supply-side policy.
- Growing government debt, and a desire to curb public expenditure, acted as a key incentive to reduce the state's role in industrial affairs. This was argued to be one of the driving forces behind the European privatisation process since the 1980s.
- Industry, during the 1980s, became progressively more global in its outlook. As such, its investment decisions were increasingly being determined by external environmental factors, especially the technology, productivity and labour costs of its international competitors.

The modern approach to industrial policy that is widely adopted in many countries is to focus on improving those factors that shape a nation's competitiveness. This involves shifting away from particular sectors to targeting what are referred to as 'framework conditions for industry'. Policies can then be designed that are favourable for the creation and growth of firms. Examples include the following:

- The promotion of investment in physical and human capital. Human capital in particular, and the existence of a sound skills base, are seen as crucial for attracting global business and ensuring long-run economic growth.
- A reduction in non-wage employment costs, such as employers' social security and pension contributions. Many governments see these costs as too high and as a severe limitation on competitiveness and employment creation.
- The promotion of innovation and the encouragement of greater levels of R&D.
- Support for small and medium-sized enterprises. SMEs have received particular attention due to their crucial role in enhancing innovation, creating employment and contributing to skills development, especially in high-tech areas.
- The improvement of infrastructure. This includes both physical transport, such as roads and railways, and information highways.
- The protection of intellectual property by more effective use of patents and copyright. By reinforcing the law in these areas it is hoped to encourage firms to develop new products and commit themselves to research.

These policies, if they are to be truly effective, are likely to require co-ordination and integration, since they represent a radical departure from traditional industrial policy.

1. *In what senses could these industrial policies be described as (a) non-interventionist; (b) interventionist?*
2. *Does globalisation, and in particular the global perspective of multinational corporations, make industrial policy in the form of selective subsidies and tax relief more or less likely?*

Undertake an analysis of recent government policy initiatives in a country of your choice designed to create the framework conditions for the creation and growth of firms.

businesses in England. LEPs began in 2011 with the aim of promoting local economic development. These partnerships were designed to facilitate the flow of information between public and private organisations and help determine local strategic economic objectives.

What are the advantages and disadvantages of local collaborations, such as LEPs, as compared to geographically larger collaborations?

Regional and urban policy

Causes of regional imbalance

In addition to adopting supply-side measures that focus on the economy as a whole, governments may decide to target specific regions of the economy. Certain parts of the country suffer from lower economic growth and higher unemployment than others. These can be broad regions, such as the North East of England or Calabria in southern Italy, or much smaller areas, such as parts of inner cities. These regional and urban problems normally result from structural problems – the main one being the decline of certain industries, such as mining or heavy manufacturing industry, which had previously been concentrated in those areas.

When an area declines, there will be a downward ***regional multiplier effect***. The decline in demand and loss of jobs lead

Definition

Regional multiplier effects When a change in injections into or withdrawals from a particular region causes a multiplied change in income in that region. The regional multiplier (k_r) is given by $1/mpw_r$, where the import component of mpw_r consists of imports into that region either from abroad or from other regions of the economy.

TC 15 p543

to less money being spent in the local community; transport and other service industries lose custom. The whole region becomes more depressed.

In addition, labour may be geographically immobile. The regional pattern of industrial location may change more rapidly than the labour market can adjust to it. Thus jobs may be lost in the depressed areas more rapidly than people can migrate from them. Unemployment rises. Even when people do leave the area, this can compound the downward multiplier effect as spending further declines.

If the capital market functioned well, this could help to arrest the decline. If wages were lower and land were cheaper in the depressed areas, capital would be attracted there. In practice, capital, like labour, is often relatively immobile. *Existing* capital stock is highly immobile. Buildings and most machinery cannot be moved to where the unemployed are! *New* capital is much more mobile. But there may be insufficient new investment, especially during a recession, to halt regional decline, and investors may be put off by the depressed and run-down nature of the area, the lack of suitably qualified labour and lack of infrastructure.

Policy approaches

Policies targeted at specific regions (or sectors) tend to be more interventionist in nature. Interventionist policies involve encouraging firms to move. Such policies include the following.

TC 7 p79

Subsidies and tax concessions in the depressed regions. Businesses could be given general subsidies, such as grants to move, or reduced rates of corporation tax. Alternatively, grants or subsidies could be specifically targeted at increasing employment (e.g. reduced employers' national insurance contributions) or at encouraging investment (e.g. investment grants or other measures to reduce the costs of capital).

The provision of facilities in depressed regions. The government or local authorities could provide facilities, such as land and buildings at concessionary, or even zero, rents to incoming firms; or spend money on improving the infrastructure of the area (roads and communications, technical colleges, etc.).

The siting of government offices in the depressed regions. The government could move some of its own departments out of the capital and locate them in areas of high unemployment.

Recent regional policy for England had drawn heavily on these. This has included the establishment of Enterprise Zones, where firms can benefit from reduced planning restrictions, tax breaks and improved infrastructure, including access to superfast broadband. The government initially created 24 enterprise zones in 2012 before adding a further 24 in 2016/17.

Many of the Enterprise Zones encourage clustering: businesses in the same sector grouping together. The hope is that they can mutually benefit from external economies of scale (see page 169), such as co-operation and technological developments. However, the danger of such an approach, particularly given the relatively small geographic areas of Enterprise Zones, is that they may merely divert investment away from other areas rather than resulting in *additional* investment.

This was a criticism of a more recent policy: the establishment of eight 'freeports' in England, announced in the March 2021 Budget. Others were due to be announced in Scotland, Wales and Northern Ireland (see the blog *Freeports: boosting trade and investment or diverting it?* on the Sloman Economics News site). There are around 3500 freeports worldwide. They are treated as 'offshore' areas, with goods being allowed into the areas tariff free. This enables raw materials and parts to be imported and made into finished or semi-finished products within the freeport area and then either exported or 'imported' into the country after applying appropriate tariffs. The idea is to encourage new investment. But, as with Enterprise Zones, critics argue that freeports can divert investment from areas without such status. What is more, if this happens, it will reduce tax revenue to the government.

How might clustering effects be incorporated into endogenous growth theories?

Following the UK election of 2019 the 'levelling up' agenda would become an important focus of government economic policy, applying across the whole of the UK. Underpinning the agenda would be the goals of regenerating towns, helping 'city regions' become globally competitive, and making local growth policies more co-ordinated and coherent.

The Budget of 2021 saw a series of initiatives intended to deliver on these goals. These included announcements of a national infrastructure bank to be set up in Leeds, helping to support regional and local growth; of a second Treasury HQ in Darlington, County Durham; and the aim of relocating 22 000 civil servants outside of London and the South East by 2030. Various 'levelling-up' and community investment programmes were also announced. The largest of these was the £4.8 billion 'Levelling Up Fund' intended for investment in local infrastructure, including transport schemes and urban regeneration projects.

Case Study 23.14 on the student website is an extended case study of regional and urban policy in both the UK and the EU.

Section summary

1. Those in favour of interventionist industrial policy point to failings of the market, such as the externalities involved in investment and training, the imperfections in the capital market and the short-term perspective of decision makers.
2. Interventionist supply-side policy can take the form of grants for investment and research and development, advice and persuasion, the direct provision of infrastructure and the provision, funding or encouragement of various training schemes.
3. Regional and local disparities arise from a changing pattern of industrial production. With many of the older industries concentrated in certain parts of the country and especially in the inner cities, and with an acceleration in the rate of industrial change, so the gap between rich and poor areas has widened.
4. Regional disparities may persist because of capital and labour immobility and regional multiplier effects.
5. Policies targeted at specific regions or sectors tend to be interventionist in their approach. These include subsidies, tax concessions and the provision of facilities in depressed regions.

END OF CHAPTER QUESTIONS

1. For what reasons do countries experience very different long-run rates of economic growth from each other?
2. Why do developed countries experience a degree of convergence over time? Would you expect there to be total convergence of GDP per head?
3. If increased investment (using current technology) does not lead to increased long-run economic growth, does it bring any benefits?
4. What determines the rate of depreciation of capital? What would happen if the rate of depreciation fell?
5. What is meant by the 'steady-state economic growth path'? What determines its slope?
6. What is the significance of the term 'endogenous' in endogenous growth theory? What, according to this theory, determines the long-run rate of economic growth?
7. Under what circumstances would a higher rate of investment lead to a higher rate of economic growth?
8. What determines the rate of growth in total factor productivity?
9. What policy prescriptions do the neoclassical and endogenous growth theories offer policy makers who are looking to raise their country's long-run growth rate?
10. For what possible reasons may a country experience a persistently faster rate of economic growth than another?
11. What is the relationship between 'successful' supply-side policies and unemployment in (i) the short run and (ii) the long run, according to (a) Keynesian and (b) monetarist assumptions?
12. Why might market-orientated supply-side policies have undesirable side effects on aggregate demand?
13. What type of tax cuts are likely to create the greatest (a) incentives, (b) disincentives to effort?
14. Is deindustrialisation necessarily undesirable?
15. In what ways can interventionist industrial policy work *with* the market, rather than against it? What are the arguments for and against such policy?
16. What are the arguments for and against relying entirely on *discretionary* regional and urban policy?
17. Select a European country other than the UK and compare its regional and urban policy with that of the UK.

Online resources

Additional case studies on the student website

23.1 Growth accounting. This case study identifies various factors that contribute to economic growth and shows how their contribution can be measured.

23.2 Productivity performance and the UK economy. A detailed examination of how the UK's productivity compares with that in other countries.

23.3 The USA: is it a 'new economy'? An examination of whether US productivity increases are likely to be sustained.

23.4 Assessing PFI. An analysis of this 'third way' approach to funding public sector projects.

23.5 Deregulating the UK bus industry. Has this led to greater competition and improved services?

23.6 The R&D Scoreboard. An international comparison of spending by companies on R&D.

23.7 Controlling inflation in the past. This case study looks at the history of prices and incomes policies in the UK.

(continued)

23.8 UK industrial performance. This examines why the UK has had a poorer investment record than many other industrial countries and why it has suffered a process of 'deindustrialisation'.

23.9 Technology and economic change. How to get the benefits from technological advance.

23.10 Alternative approaches to training and education. This compares approaches to training and education in the UK with those in other countries.

23.11 Assistance to small firms in the UK. An examination of current government measures to assist small firms.

23.12 Small-firm policy in the EU. This looks at the range of support available to small and medium-sized firms in the EU.

23.13 Welfare to work. An examination of the UK Labour government's policy of providing support to people looking for work.

23.14 Regional and urban policy. This case looks at the causes of regional imbalance and urban decay and at the approaches to regional and urban policy in the UK and EU.

23.15 Unemployment and supply-side policies. This case looks at the classification by the OECD in 2006 of countries by their policies towards labour markets.

Maths Case 23.1 Finding the steady-state equilibrium in the Solow model. Using the algebra in a worked example.

Maths Case 23.2 The effect of technological progress in the Solow model. Using the algebra in a worked example.

Websites relevant to this chapter

Numbers and sections refer to websites listed in the Web Appendix and hotlinked from this book's website at **www.go.pearson.com/uk/sloman.**

- For news articles relevant to this chapter, see the *Economics News* section on the student website.
- For general news on unemployment, inflation, economic growth and supply-side policy, see websites in section A, and particularly A1–13, 18, 19, 21, 35, 37. See also links to newspapers worldwide in A38, 39, 42, 43 and 44, and the news search feature in Google at A41.
- For data on unemployment, inflation and growth, see links in B1; also see B4. For UK data, see B3 and 34. For EU data, see B38 and 47. For US data, see the data section of B17. For international data, see B15, 21, 24, 31, 33, 43 and 46. For links to datasets, see B28.
- For specific data on UK unemployment, search site B3. For international data on unemployment, see G1; H3 and 5.
- For information on the development of ideas, including information on classical, Keynesian, monetarist, new classical and new Keynesian thought, see C18.
- For the current approach to UK supply-side policy, see the latest Budget Report (e.g. sections on productivity and training) at site E30. See also sites E5, 9, 10, 18, 36 and 40.
- For support for a market-orientated approach to supply-side policy, see C17 and E34.
- For information on training in the UK and Europe, see sites E5; G5, 14.
- For information on the support for small business in the UK, see site E38.
- For information on regional policy in the UK, see site E2; and in the EU, see site G12.
- For student resources relevant to these three chapters, see sites C1–10, 19.

The World Economy

'Globalisation' is a word frequently used nowadays. It captures one of the key features of economics today: that it is global in nature. International trade and international financial flows have often grown at exceedingly rapid rates in recent decades. The result is that economies around the globe are highly interconnected so that what happens in one country can have profound effects on others.

In Chapter 24 we focus on international trade, looking at the benefits it brings, but also at the costs that can be incurred. This is important when analysing the calls, by some, for greater protectionism. Are people right to fear international competition? The chapter concludes by reflecting on the potential longer-term implications for the UK from its departure from the European Union.

With the growth in international trade and financial flows Chapter 25 focuses on the potential for countries to be more vulnerable to balance of payments problems and exchange rate fluctuations. It analyses the relationships between a country's balance of payments and its exchange rate.

Chapter 26 looks at particular aspects of global and regional interdependence. In this context, it analyses the euro and how economic and monetary union (EMU) operates. It considers whether the adoption of the euro by 19 EU countries has been of benefit to them and reflects on the future of the euro. Chapter 26 concludes by looking at the poorest countries of the world, whose development depends so much on the economic policies of the rich.

International Trade

CHAPTER MAP

Without international trade we would all be much poorer. There would be some items like pineapples, coffee, cotton clothes, foreign holidays and uranium that we would simply have to go without. Then there would be other items like wine and spacecraft that we could produce only very inefficiently. International trade has the potential to benefit all participating countries. This chapter explains why.

Totally free trade, however, may bring problems to countries or to groups of people within those countries. Many people argue strongly for restrictions on trade. Textile workers see their jobs threatened by cheap imported cloth. Car manufacturers worry about falling sales as customers switch to Japanese or other East Asian models. But are people justified in fearing international competition, or are they merely trying to protect some vested interest at the expense of everyone else? Section 24.2 examines these arguments and also looks at world attitudes towards trade restrictions.

A step on the road to freer trade is for countries to enter free trade agreements with just a limited number of other countries. Examples include the EU and the United States–Mexico–Canada Agreement (USMCA) (formerly the North America Free Trade Agreement). We consider such 'preferential trading systems' in section 24.3. Then, in section 24.4, we look in more detail at the EU and the development of the 'single European market'.

We finish by considering some of the possible economic implications for the UK following its departure from the European Union culminating with the EU–UK Trade and Cooperation Agreement which took effect from 1 January 2021. The focus here is on the supply-side effects from the UK's future trading relationships with the EU and the rest of the world.

This chapter may be studied directly after Chapter 12 or Chapter 14 if you prefer.

24.1 THE ADVANTAGES OF TRADE

The growth of world trade

Trade values

In 1960 the (nominal) *value* of world merchandise exports (i.e. the exports of goods) was US$130 billion. By 2018 this had grown to over $19.5 trillion. But as the COVID-19 pandemic disrupted economic activity and trade, the value of merchandise exports had slipped back to $17.6 trillion in 2020.

Figure 24.1 helps to put this into perspective by showing both the value of world merchandise exports and their value as a percentage of GDP. From just under 10 per cent in 1960, by 2008 they had grown to 25 per cent of GDP. Over this period, the value of world trade typically grew at more than twice the rate of the value of world output. However, since the financial crisis of the late 2000s, this trend has halted. In 2020, world merchandise exports were 21 per cent of world GDP, the same value as in 2009 and 2016.

Another way of looking at world trade is through the sum of both exports *and* imports. This is commonly used to capture the openness of economies. Table 24.1 shows total merchandise trade as a percentage of GDP for various countries. As you can see, in all cases the proportion was higher in the 2010s than in 1960s, and in some cases considerably higher. But, in some cases, it was lower in the 2010s than in the 2000s.

Which countries' merchandise trade had fallen as a percentage of GDP between the 2000s and the 2010s? Explain why.

So far, our focus has been on the trade of goods. But countries trade services too. Commercial services include manufacturing services on physical inputs (e.g. oil refining, assembly of electronics and packing), maintenance and repair, transport, construction, insurance and financial services, telecommunications and private health and education services. In 2020 the global value of exports of commercial services was $4.9 trillion, the equivalent of around 6 per cent of GDP. This was an increase from just $191 billion or 3 per cent of GDP in 1976.

Table 24.1 Merchandise trade, percentage of GDP

	1960s	1970s	1980s	1990s	2000s	2010s
USA	6.8	11.7	14.5	16.8	19.7	21.7
Japan	18.1	19.8	20.2	15.4	22.6	28.2
Australia	25.0	24.6	27.0	29.3	34.3	33.6
India	8.8	9.1	11.3	16.5	27.4	34.6
China	6.8	9.1	24.5	36.2	51.6	39.4
New Zealand	32.2	39.9	43.7	43.3	44.6	40.8
UK	30.5	38.7	39.3	36.8	36.6	41.1
France	20.7	30.0	35.7	37.3	44.5	44.6
Italy	22.1	31.9	34.5	33.0	41.4	47.5
Canada	31.8	39.9	45.0	55.0	59.0	51.9
Germany	n.a.	33.5	42.5	41.0	60.3	70.6
Ireland	57.2	75.0	89.7	104.0	92.6	74.7
Netherlands	77.5	79.7	81.9	85.2	110.1	142.6
High income	16.5	26.1	30.0	31.6	42.0	48.5
Low and middle income	18.3	23.2	29.5	34.2	48.1	42.8
World	**16.8**	**25.6**	**29.9**	**32.1**	**43.2**	**46.5**

Note: Merchandise trade as a share of GDP is the sum of merchandise exports and imports divided by the value of GDP, all in current US dollars.
Source: World Bank, series TG.VAL.TOTL.GD.ZS (2021), https://data.worldbank.org/indicator/TG.VAL.TOTL.GD.ZS

Figure 24.1 World merchandise exports, $ billions and % of world GDP

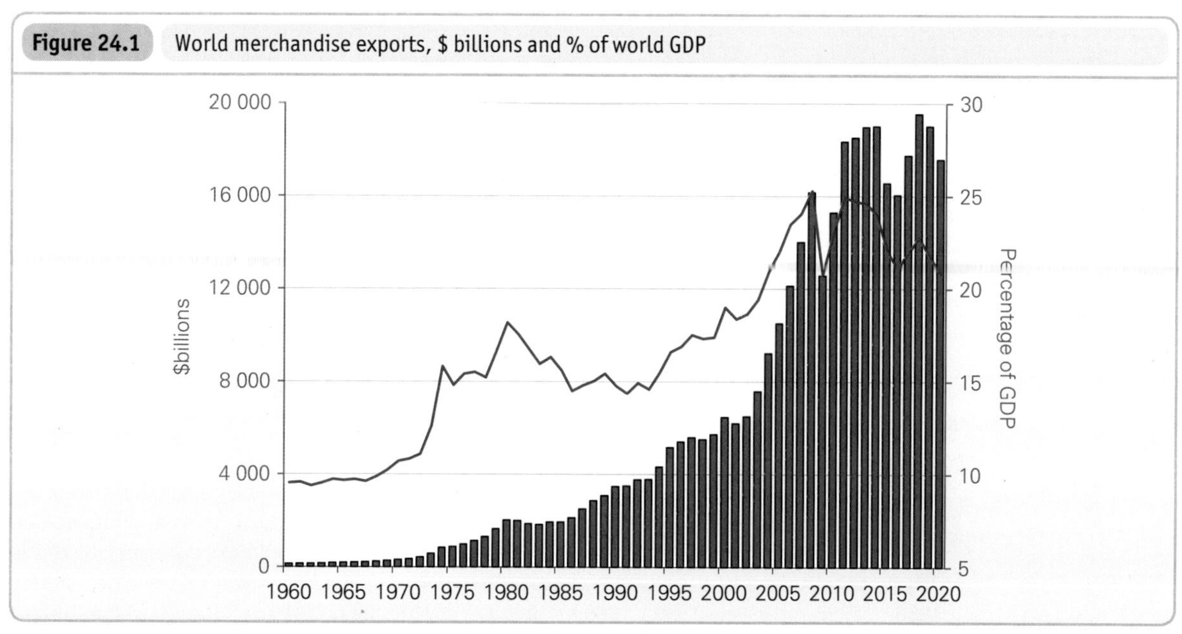

Sources: Merchandise exports data, *WTO Data Portal*, WTO (2021) https://data.wto.org/; World GDP data, series NY.GDP.MKTP.CD, World Bank (2021), http://data.worldbank.org/indicator/NY.GDP.MKTP.CD; and *World Economic Outlook*, IMF (April 2021), www.imf.org/en/Publications/WEO/Issues/2021/03/23/world-economic-outlook-april-2021

Table 24.2 Trade in services, percentage of GDP

	1980s	1990s	2000s	2010s
China	2.2	5.9	7.7	5.6
USA	3.5	4.7	5.5	7.0
Italy	6.7	8.6	10.2	11.0
India	3.1	4.8	10.5	11.8
Canada	6.9	9.4	10.9	11.9
Germany	8.6	8.6	12.8	16.8
France	10.9	11.2	13.5	18.3
UK	10.7	11.1	16.8	21.4
Netherlands	19.0	21.3	26.9	37.7
High income	7.5	8.3	11.2	15.0
Low and middle income	5.9	7.9	9.4	8.3
World	**7.3**	**8.4**	**10.7**	**12.5**

Note: Trade in services (as a share of GDP) is the sum of exports and imports in services divided by the value of GDP, all in current US dollars.
Source: World Bank, series BG.GSR.NFSV.GD.ZS (2021), https://data.worldbank.org/indicator/BG.GSR.NFSV.GD.ZS

Table 24.2 shows the sum of exports and imports of commercial services as a percentage of GDP in various countries since the 1980s. Though the flows are much smaller than those of merchandise goods, we still observe a significant increase in international flows of commercial services over the whole period, particularly in high-income economies.

Trade volumes

The dollar value of recorded global trade is affected by changes in prices and exchange rates as well as the volumes traded. Therefore, by adjusting the dollar value of trade flows for changes in export and import prices we are able to estimate the change in the *volumes* of goods being traded.

Figure 24.2 shows the growth in the value and volume of world merchandise exports from 1980. Over the period as a whole the value of merchandise exports grew at annual rate of 6.4 per cent. After accounting for changes in the prices of countries' exports, the volume of exports is estimated to have grown by 4.2 per cent per year.

The chart also shows the actual year-to-year changes in the values and volumes of merchandise exports. There are some significant differences between the changes in values and volumes. Take, for example, 2015 when the value of merchandise exports fell by 13 per cent. In contrast, the volume of exports rose by 2 per cent. The difference was largely attributable to the large fall in commodity prices in 2015 with, for example, global energy prices falling by as much as 45 per cent. TC 13 p461

From Figure 24.2 we can see the significant negative impact of the global financial crisis at the end of the 2000s on the volume of merchandise exports. In 2009, the volume of worldwide merchandise exports fell by approximately 12 per cent (while their value declined by 22 per cent). This was the biggest contraction in global trade since the Second World War.

Despite the initial rebound in 2010 the average rate of growth in the volume of exports from 2011 to 2019 was only $2^3/_4$ per cent compared to the 5.3 per cent average experienced from 1981 to 2007. This was partly attributable to weaker global economic growth, including in developing economies, such as China. Indeed, in some cases, such as Brazil, economies went into recession. But it was also partly attributable to the rise of protectionism evidenced perhaps most starkly by the 'tariff wars' between China and the USA.

Then, in 2020 as the world struggled with the COVID-19 pandemic, the volume of exports fell by over 5 per cent. The recovery in global trade would then depend, in part, on the extent of pandemic-related disruptions to economic activity, the success of vaccine rollouts and government policies to mitigate scarring effects.

Figure 24.2 Growth in world merchandise exports by value and volume

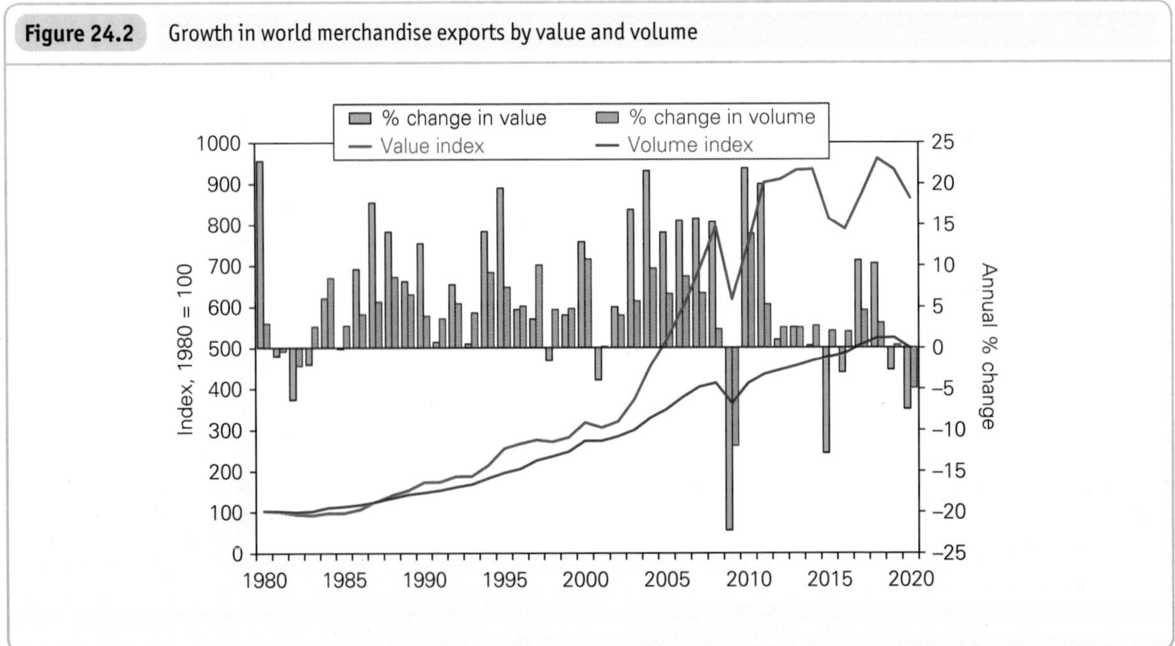

Source: Based on data from *WTO Data Portal*, WTO (2021), https://data.wto.org/

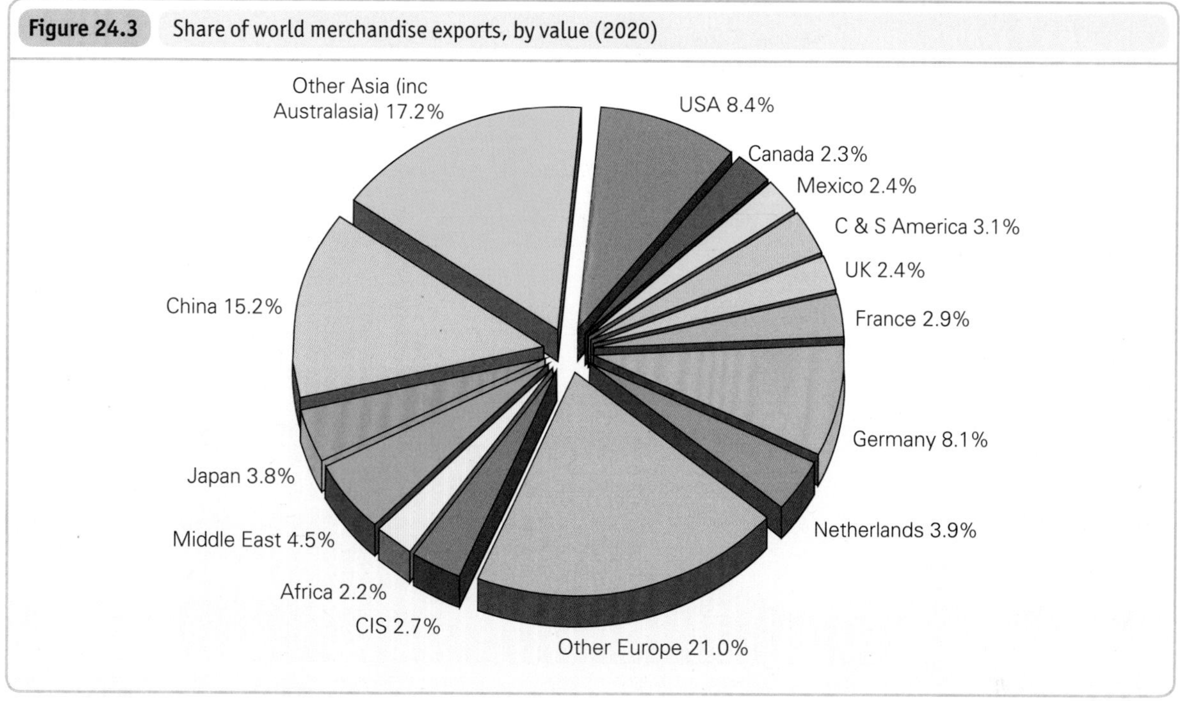

Figure 24.3 Share of world merchandise exports, by value (2020)

Source: Based on data in *World Trade Statistical Review 2021*, WTO (2021), Statistical Table A4, Chapter V, www.wto.org/english/res_e/statis_e/wts2021_e/wts21_toc_e.htm

If the volume of merchandise exports falls by less than their value, what can be inferred about what has happened to the prices of merchandise exports?

Trading nations

Developed economies have until recently dominated world trade. In 2018, they accounted (by value) for 52 per cent of world merchandise exports and 57 per cent of world merchandise imports (see Figure 24.3). Their share of world trade, however, has tended to decline over time. Thirty years earlier, they accounted for over 70 per cent of merchandise exports and imports (see Box 24.1). The reason for this changing global pattern in trade is that many of the countries with the most rapid *growth* in exports can now be found in the developing world.

The growth in merchandise exports from the group of developing nations collectively known as the BRICS[1] (Brazil, Russia, India, China and South Africa) has been especially rapid. Between them they accounted for just 5.5 per cent of the value of world exports in 1994. In 2020 they accounted for 19.9 per cent of world exports (see Figure 24.4). More recently, other countries, such as Mexico, Turkey, Cambodia and Vietnam, have joined the ranks of rapidly growing 'newly industrialised' developing countries.

Box 24.1 looks in more detail at the leading trading nations and at the countries with which they trade.

Figure 24.4 Share of world merchandise exports of BRICS, by value (%)

Source: Based on data from *WTO Data Portal*, WTO (2021), https://data.wto.org/

1 Sometimes the term is used to refer to just the first four countries. When South Africa is excluded, the term is written BRICs rather than BRICS.

BOX 24.1 TRADING PLACES

Patterns and trends in world trade

(a) *World merchandise exports by value*

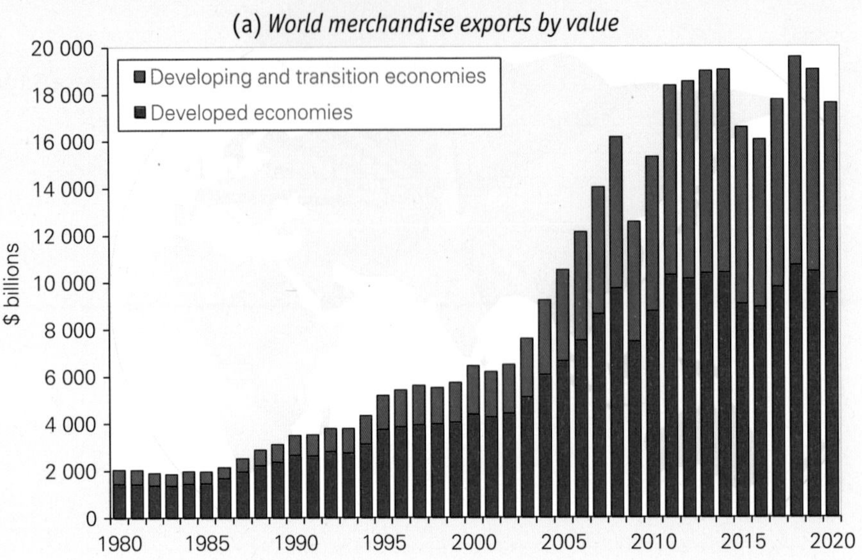

(b) *Annual growth in value of merchandise exports*

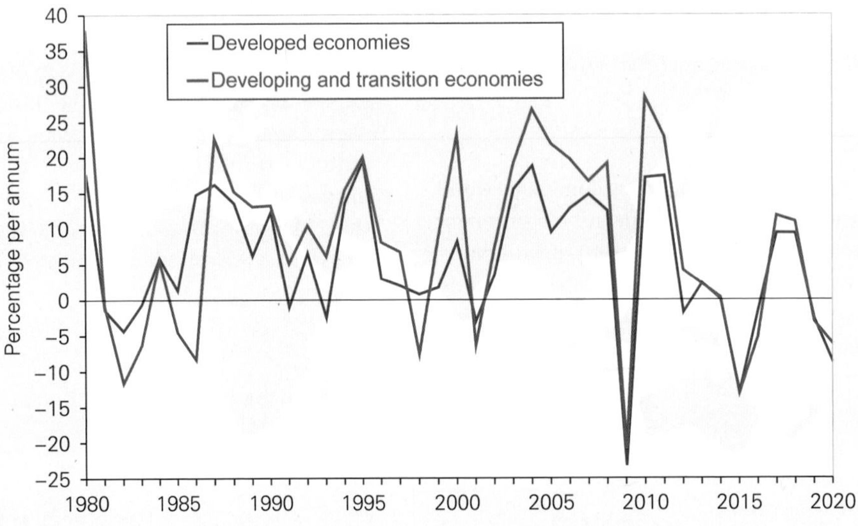

Source: Based on data from *UNCTADStat*, UNCTAD (2021) https://unctadstat.unctad.org/wds.

The past three decades have seen rapid changes in the composition of world trade flows. We have seen, for example, the rising importance of the BRICS and, in particular, of China (see Figure 24.4). More generally, the dominance of world trade by the developed nations has weakened. The charts show the growth in the value of world exports since 1980 originating from developed countries and from developing and transition (former communist) countries.

In 1980 the percentage of world merchandise exports originating from developed countries was 70 per cent. It remained above 70 per cent until 2000, since when it has fallen back to just above 50 per cent. In 2020, the percentage stood at 54 per cent.

Specialisation as the basis for trade

TC 1 p10 Why do countries trade with each other, and what do they gain from it? The reasons for international trade are really only an extension of the reasons for trade *within* a nation. Rather than people trying to be self-sufficient and do everything for themselves, it makes sense to specialise.

Firms specialise in producing certain goods. This allows them to gain economies of scale and to exploit their entrepreneurial and management skills and the skills of their labour force.

CASE STUDIES AND APPLICATIONS

Table (a) shows the world's leading merchandise exporters and importers by value for 2019. The UK is the tenth largest exporter of goods by value and the fifth largest importer.

Trade partners

But who do countries trade with? Table (b) looks at the trading partners of the world's leading trading countries. The table shows that trading blocs (see section 24.3) and geography matter. For instance, in the case of Germany over one-half of its trade is with other EU countries. Similarly, one-third of the value of the USA's exports and one-quarter of its imports can be attributed to Canada and Mexico, members of the United States–Mexico-Canada Agreement (USMCA), the successor to the North American Free Trade Association (NAFTA) (see page 800).

(a) *Top trading countries by value and world share, 2019*

Rank	Exporters	$ billion	Share	Rank	Importers	$ billion	Share
1	China	2499	13.2	1	USA	2568	13.4
2	USA	1646	8.7	2	China	2077	10.8
3	Germany	1489	7.9	3	Germany	1234	6.4
4	Netherlands	709	3.8	4	Japan	721	3.7
5	Japan	706	3.7	5	UK	692	3.6
6	France	570	3.0	6	France	651	3.4
10	UK	469	2.5	7	Netherlands	636	3.3

Source: *World Trade Statistical Review 2020*, Table A6, (WTO).

(b) *Merchandise trade by destination and origin, 2019*

China		USA		Germany		Japan		UK	
Export destinations	**%**	**Export destinations**	**%**	**Export destinations**	**%**	**Export destinations**	**%**	**Export destinations**	**%**
USA	19.3	Canada	17.8	EU 26	51.5	USA	19.8	EU 27	46.0
EU 27	16.5	EU 27	16.4	USA	9.0	China	19.1	USA	15.7
Hong Kong	12.2	Mexico	15.6	China	7.2	EU 27	9.7	China	6.4
Japan	5.9	China	6.5	UK	5.9	S Korea	6.6	Switzerland	3.3
S Korea	4.4	Japan	4.6	Switzerland	4.3	Taiwan	6.1	Hong Kong	2.4
Other	44.1	Other	39.2	Other	22.0	Other	38.7	Other	26.1
Import origins	**%**	**Import origins**	**%**	**Import origins**	**%**	**Import origins**	**%**	**Import origins**	**%**
EU 27	11.7	China	18.4	EU 26	52.1	China	23.4	EU 27	49.5
S Korea	9.6	EU 27	18.0	China	10.0	USA	11.3	China	9.7
Japan	8.5	Mexico	14.0	USA	6.6	EU 27	11.2	USA	9.5
Taiwan	8.3	Canada	12.7	Switzerland	4.3	Australia	6.3	Switzerland	3.4
USA	7.3	Japan	5.7	UK	3.4	S Korea	4.1	Norway	2.9
Other	54.6	Other	31.1	Other	23.6	Other	43.6	Other	25.1

Note: EU 27 = 27 members of the EU, and excludes the UK.
Source: Trade Profiles, WTO, www.wto.org/english/res_e/statis_e/trade_profiles_list_e.htm

Does the fact that world trade has increased at a much faster rate than world GDP (at least up until the financial crisis) highlight the limitations of trade as a driver of economic growth?

Download the latest Trade Profiles from the WTO. Compile a short briefing paper detailing the exports and imports of each country by the types of commodities.

It also allows them to benefit from their particular location and from the ownership of any particular capital equipment or other assets they might possess. With the revenues firms earn, they buy in the inputs they need from other firms and the labour they require. Firms thus trade with each other.

Countries also specialise. They produce more than they need of certain goods. What is not consumed domestically is exported. The revenues earned from the exports are used to import goods that are not produced in sufficient amounts at home.

Why does the USA not specialise as much as General Motors or Texaco? Why does the UK not specialise as much as Tesco? Is the answer to these questions similar to the answer to the questions 'Why does the USA not specialise as much as Luxembourg?' and 'Why does Tesco or Unilever not specialise as much as the local butcher?'?

But which goods should a country specialise in? What should it export and what should it import? The answer is that it should specialise in those goods in which it has a *comparative advantage*. Let us examine what this means.

The law of comparative advantage

Countries have different endowments of factors of production. They differ in population density, labour skills, climate, raw materials, capital equipment, etc. These differences tend to persist because factors are relatively immobile between countries. Obviously, land and climate are totally immobile, but even with labour and capital there are more restrictions on their international movement than on their movement within countries. Thus the ability to supply goods differs between countries.

KI 2 p10

What this means is that the relative cost of producing goods varies from country to country. For example, one country may be able to produce one fridge for the same cost as 6 tonnes of wheat or 3 MP4 players, whereas another country may be able to produce one fridge for the same cost as only 3 tonnes of wheat but 4 MP4 players. It is these differences in relative costs that form the basis of trade.

At this stage, we need to distinguish between *absolute advantage* and *comparative advantage*.

Absolute advantage

When one country can produce a good with less resources than another country, it is said to have an ***absolute advantage*** in that good. If France can produce grapes with less resources than the UK, and the UK can produce barley with less resources than France, then France has an absolute advantage in grapes and the UK an absolute advantage in barley. Production of both grapes and barley will be maximised by each country specialising and then trading with the other country. Both will gain.

Comparative advantage

The above seems obvious, but trade between two countries can still be beneficial even if one country could produce *all* goods with less resources than the other, providing the *relative* efficiency with which goods can be produced differs between the two countries.

Take the case of a developed country (DC) that is absolutely more efficient than a less developed country at producing both wheat and cloth. Assume that with a given amount of resources (labour, land and capital) the alternatives shown in Table 24.3 can be produced in each country.

Table 24.3 Production possibilities for two countries

		Kilos of wheat		Square metres of cloth
Less developed country	Either	2	or	1
Developed country	Either	4	or	8

Despite the developed country having an absolute advantage in both wheat and cloth, the less developed country (LDC) has a ***comparative advantage*** in wheat, and the developed country has a comparative advantage in cloth.

This is because wheat is relatively cheaper in the LDC: only 1 square metre of cloth has to be sacrificed to produce 2 kilos of wheat, whereas 8 square metres of cloth would have to be sacrificed in the developed country to produce 4 kilos of wheat (i.e. 2 square metres of cloth for every 1 kilo of wheat). In other words, the opportunity cost of wheat is four times higher in the developed country (8/4 compared with 1/2).

On the other hand, cloth is relatively cheaper in the developed country. Here the opportunity cost of producing 8 square metres of cloth is only 4 kilos of wheat, whereas in the LDC 1 square metre of cloth costs 2 kilos of wheat. Thus the opportunity cost of cloth is four times higher in the LDC (2/1 compared with 4/8).

Draw up a similar table to Table 24.3, only this time assume that the figures are: LDC 6 wheat or 2 cloth; DC 8 wheat or 20 cloth. What are the opportunity cost ratios now?

To summarise: countries have a comparative advantage in those goods that can be produced at a lower opportunity cost than in other countries.

If countries are to gain from trade, they should export those goods in which they have a comparative advantage and import

The law of comparative advantage. **Provided opportunity costs of various goods differ in two countries, both of them can gain from mutual trade if they specialise in producing (and exporting) those goods that have relatively low opportunity costs compared with the other country.**

Definitions

Absolute advantage A country has an absolute advantage over another in the production of a good if it can produce it with less resources than the other country.

Comparative advantage A country has a comparative advantage over another in the production of a good if it can produce it at a lower opportunity cost: i.e. if it has to forgo less of other goods in order to produce it.

those goods in which they have a comparative disadvantage. From this we can state a ***law of comparative advantage***.

See Case Study 24.1 on the student website for Ricardo's original statement of the law in 1817.

But why do they gain if they specialise according to this law? And just what will that gain be? We will consider these questions next.

The gains from trade based on comparative advantage

Before trade, unless markets are very imperfect, the prices of the two goods are likely to reflect their opportunity costs. For example, in Table 24.3, since the less developed country can produce 2 kilos of wheat for 1 square metre of cloth, the *price* of 2 kilos of wheat will roughly equal the price of 1 square metre of cloth.

Assume, then, that the pre-trade exchange ratios of wheat for cloth are as follows:

LDC : 2 wheat for 1 cloth
Developed country : 1 wheat for 2 cloth (i.e. 4 for 8)

> **Definition**
>
> **Law of comparative advantage** Trade can benefit all countries if they specialise in the goods in which they have a comparative advantage.

TC 2 p26

Both countries will now gain from trade, provided the exchange ratio is somewhere between 2:1 and 1:2. Assume, for the sake of argument, that it is 1:1, that 1 wheat trades internationally for 1 cloth. How will each country gain?

The LDC gains by exporting wheat and importing cloth. At an exchange ratio of 1:1, it now only has to give up 1 kilo of wheat to obtain a square metre of cloth, whereas before trade it had to give up 2 kilos of wheat.

The developed country gains by exporting cloth and importing wheat. Again at an exchange ratio of 1:1, it now has to give up only 1 square metre of cloth to obtain 1 kilo of wheat, whereas before it had to give up 2 square metres of cloth.

Thus both countries have gained from trade.

The actual exchange ratios will depend on the relative prices of wheat and cloth after trade takes place. These prices will depend on total demand for and supply of the two goods. It may be that the trade exchange ratio is nearer to the pre-trade exchange ratio of one country than the other. Thus the gains to the two countries need not be equal. (We will examine these issues below.)

1. *Show how each country could gain from trade if the LDC could produce (before trade) 3 wheat for 1 cloth and the developed country could produce (before trade) 2 wheat for 5 cloth, and if the exchange ratio (with trade) was 1 wheat for 2 cloth. Would they both still gain if the exchange ratio were (a) 1 wheat for 1 cloth; (b) 1 wheat for 3 cloth?*
2. *In question 1, which country gained the most from a trade exchange ratio of 1 wheat for 2 cloth?*

BOX 24.2 SHARING OUT THE JOBS

CASE STUDIES AND APPLICATIONS

A parable of comparative advantage

Imagine that you and a group of friends are fed up with the rat race and decide to set up a self-sufficient community. So you club together and use all your savings to buy an old run-down farmhouse with 30 acres of land and a few farm animals.

You decide to produce all your own food, make your own clothes, renovate the farmhouse, make all the furniture, provide all your own entertainment and set up a little shop to sell the things you make. This should bring in enough income to buy the few items you cannot make yourselves.

The day comes to move in, and that evening everyone gathers to decide how all the jobs are going to be allocated. You quickly decide that it would be foolish for all of you to try to do all the jobs. Obviously, it will be more efficient to specialise. This does not necessarily mean that everyone is confined to doing only one job, but it does mean that each of you can concentrate on just a few tasks.

But who is to do which job? The answer would seem to be obvious: you pick the best person for the job. So you go down the list of tasks. Who is to take charge of the renovations? Pat has already renovated a cottage, and is brilliant at bricklaying, plastering, wiring and plumbing. So Pat would seem to be the ideal person. Who is to do the cooking? Everyone agrees on this. Pat makes the best cakes, the best quiches and the best Irish stew. So Pat is everyone's choice for cook. And what about milking the sheep? 'Pat used to keep sheep', says Tarquin, 'and made wonderful feta cheese.' 'Good old Pat!' exclaims everyone.

It doesn't take long before it becomes obvious that 'clever-clogs' Pat is simply brilliant at everything, from planting winter wheat, to unblocking drains, to doing the accounts, to tie-dyeing. But it is soon realised that, if Pat has to do everything, nothing will get done. Even Chris, who has never done anything except market research, would be better employed milking the sheep than doing nothing at all.

So what's the best way of allocating the jobs so that the work gets done in the most efficient way? Sharon comes up with the solution. 'Everyone should make a list of all the jobs they could possibly do, and then put them in order from the one they are best at to the one they are worst at.'

So this is what everyone does. And then people are allocated the jobs they are *relatively* best at doing. Chris escapes milking the sheep and keeps the accounts instead. And Pat escapes with an eight-hour day!

If Pat took two minutes to milk the sheep and Tarquin took six, how could it ever be more efficient for Tarquin to do it?

Figure 24.5 Effect of trade on consumption possibilities

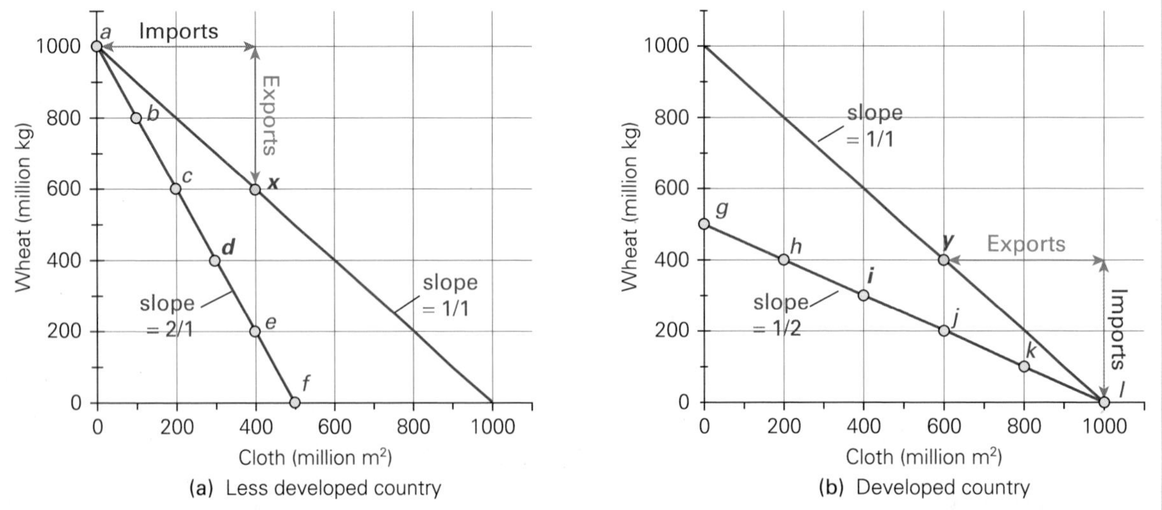

(a) Less developed country

(b) Developed country

Simple graphical analysis of comparative advantage and the gains from trade: constant opportunity cost

The gains from trade can be shown graphically using production possibility curves. Let us continue with the example of the developed and less developed countries that we looked at in Table 24.3, where both countries produce just two goods: wheat and cloth.

For simplicity, assume that the pre-trade opportunity costs of cloth in terms of wheat in the two countries do not vary with output: i.e. there are *constant opportunity costs* of

cloth in terms of wheat of 2/1 in the LDC and 1/2 in the developed country. Let us assume that the pre-trade production possibilities are as shown in Table 24.4.[2]

For each 100 extra square metres of cloth that the LDC produces, it has to sacrifice 200 kilos of wheat. For each extra 100 kilos of wheat that the developed country produces, it has to sacrifice 200 square metres of cloth. Straight-line pre-trade production possibility 'curves' can thus be drawn for the two countries with slopes of (minus) 2/1 and (minus) 1/2 respectively. These lines illustrate the various total combinations of the two goods that can be produced and hence consumed. They are shown as the blue lines in Figure 24.5.

Table 24.4 Pre-trade production possibilities

	Less developed country			Developed country	
	Wheat (million kg)	**Cloth (million m²)**		**Wheat (million kg)**	**Cloth (million m²)**
A	1000	0	*G*	500	0
B	800	100	*H*	400	200
C	600	200	*I*	300	400
D	400	300	*J*	200	600
E	200	400	*K*	100	800
F	0	500	*L*	0	1000

Assume that before trade the LDC produces (and consumes) at point *d*: namely, 400 million kilos of wheat and 300 million square metres of cloth; and that the developed country produces at point *i*: namely, 300 million kilos of wheat and 400 million square metres of cloth.

If they now trade, the LDC, having a comparative advantage in wheat, will specialise in it and produce at point *a*. It will produce 1000 million kilos of wheat and no cloth. The developed country will specialise in cloth and produce at point *l*. It will produce 1000 million square metres of cloth and no wheat.

For simplicity, let us assume that trade between the two countries takes place at an exchange ratio of 1:1 (i.e. 1 kilo of wheat for 1 square metre of cloth). This means that the two countries can now *consume* along the red lines in Figure 24.5: at, say, points *x* and *y*, respectively. At point *x* the LDC consumes 600 million kilos of wheat (a gain of 200 million kilos over the pre-trade position) and 400 million square metres of cloth (a gain of 100 million square metres over the pre-trade position). At point *y* the developed country consumes 400 million kilos of wheat (a gain of 100 million kilos over the pre-trade position) and 600 million square metres of cloth (a gain of 200 million square metres over the pre-trade position). Thus trade has allowed both countries to increase their consumption of both goods.

To summarise: before trade, the countries could only consume along their production possibility curves (the blue lines); after trade, they can consume along the higher red lines.

Note that in this simple two-country model total production and consumption of the two countries for each of the two goods must be the same, since one country's exports are the other's imports. Thus if the LDC produces at point *a* and consumes at point *x*, the developed country, producing at point *l*, must consume at point *y*. The effects on trade of the two countries consuming at points *x* and *y* are shown in Table 24.5.

2 Note that, for simplicity, it is assumed that the size of the two economies is similar. The LDC can still have an *absolute* disadvantage in both goods, however, because it may take many more resources to produce these goods. For example, it may have a very much larger population than the developed country and hence a very much lower output per person.

Table 24.5 The production and consumption gains from trade

	Less developed country			Developed country			Total	
	Production	Consumption	Imports (−) / Exports (+)	Production	Consumption	Imports (−) / Exports (+)	Production	Consumption
No trade								
Wheat (million kg)	400	400	0	300	300	0	700	700
Cloth (million m²)	300	300	0	400	400	0	700	700
With trade								
Wheat (million kg)	1000	600	+400	0	400	−400	1000	1000
Cloth (million m²)	0	400	−400	1000	600	+400	1000	1000

As complete specialisation has taken place in our example, the LDC now has to import all its cloth and the developed country has to import all its wheat. Thus, given the exchange ratio of 1:1, the LDC exports 400 million kilos of wheat in exchange for imports of 400 million square metres of cloth. (These imports and exports are also shown in Figure 24.5.)

The final two columns of Table 24.5 show that trade has increased the total production and consumption of the two countries.

1. *Draw a diagram with the same two countries and with the same production possibilities and exchange ratio as in Figure 24.5. But this time show how much would be imported and exported for each country if, after trade, the LDC consumes 500 million kilos of wheat. Fill the figures in on a table like Table 24.5.*
2. *If the opportunity cost ratio of wheat for cloth is 1/2 in the LDC, why is the slope of the production possibility curve 2/1? Is the slope of the production possibility curve always the reciprocal of the opportunity cost ratio?*
3. *Show (graphically) that, if the (pre-trade) opportunity cost ratios of the two countries were the same, there would be no gain from trade – assuming that the production possibility curves were straight lines and did not shift as a result of trade.*

International trade and its effect on factor prices

Countries tend to have a comparative advantage in goods that are *intensive in their abundant factor*. Canada has abundant land and hence it is cheap. Therefore Canada specialises in grain production since grains are land-intensive. South Asian countries have abundant supplies of labour with low wage rates, and hence specialise in clothing and other labour-intensive goods. Europe, Japan and the USA have relatively abundant and cheap capital, and hence specialise in capital-intensive manufactured goods.

Trade between such countries will tend to lead to greater equality in factor prices. For example, the demand for labour will rise in labour-abundant countries like India if they specialise in labour-intensive goods. This will push up wage rates in these low-wage countries, thereby helping to close the gap between their wage rates and those of the developed world. Without trade, wage rates would tend to be even lower.

Increasing opportunity costs and the limits to specialisation and trade

In practice, countries are likely to experience increasing opportunity costs (and hence have bowed-out production possibility curves). The reason for this is that, as a country increasingly specialises in one good, it has to use resources that are less and less suited to its production and which were more suited to other goods. Thus ever-increasing amounts of the other goods have to be sacrificed. For example, as a country specialises more and more in grain production, it has to use land that is less and less suited to growing grain. KI 2 p10

These increasing costs as a country becomes more and more specialised lead to the disappearance of its comparative cost advantage. When this happens, there will be no point in further specialisation. Thus whereas a country like Germany has a comparative advantage in capital-intensive manufactures, it does not produce only manufactures. It would make no sense not to use its fertile lands to produce food or its forests to produce timber. The opportunity costs of diverting all agricultural labour to industry would be very high.

Thus increasing opportunity costs limit the amount of a country's specialisation and hence the amount of its trade. There are also other limits to trade:

- Transport costs may outweigh any comparative advantage. A country may be able to produce bricks more cheaply than other countries, but their weight may make them too expensive to export.
- It may be the factors of production, rather than the goods, that move from country to country. Thus developed countries, rather than exporting finished goods to LDCs, may invest capital in LDCs to enable manufactures to be produced there. Also, labour may migrate from low-wage to high-wage countries.
- Governments may restrict trade (see section 24.2).

BOX 24.3 **TRADE AS EXPLOITATION?** EXPLORING ECONOMICS

Does free trade exploit cheap labour abroad?

People sometimes question the morality of buying imports from countries where workers are paid 'pittance' wages. 'Is it right', they ask, 'for us to support a system where workers are so exploited?' As is often the case with emotive issues, there is some truth and some misunderstanding in a point of view like this.

First the truth. If a country like the UK trades with a regime that denies human rights, and treats its workers very badly, we may thereby be helping to sustain a corrupt system. We might also be seen to be lending it moral support. In this sense, therefore, trade may not help the cause of the workers in these countries. It is arguments like these that were used to support the imposition of trade sanctions against South Africa in the days of apartheid.

Now the misunderstanding. If we buy goods from countries that pay low wages, we are *not* as a result contributing to their low-wage problem. Quite the reverse. If countries like India export textiles to the West, this will help to *increase* the wages of Indian workers. If India has a comparative advantage in labour-intensive goods, these goods will earn a better price by being exported than by being sold entirely in the domestic Indian market. Provided *some* of the extra revenues go to the workers, they will gain from trade. KI 4 p13

Under what circumstances would a gain in revenues by exporting firms not lead to an increase in wage rates?

The terms of trade

What price will our exports fetch abroad? What will we have to pay for imports? The answer to these questions is given by the ***terms of trade***.

To simplify matters, suppose there is only one exported good and only one imported good. In this case, the terms of trade are defined as P_x/P_m, where P_x is the price of the exported good and P_m is the price of the imported good. This is the reciprocal of the exchange ratio: for example, if 2x exchange for 1m (an exchange ratio of 2/1), the price of x will be half the price of m. The terms of trade will be 1/2.

1. *If 4x exchange for 3m, what are the terms of trade?*
2. *If the terms of trade are 3, how many units of the imported good could I buy for the money earned by the sale of 1 unit of the exported good? What is the exchange ratio?*

In the real world, where countries have *many* exports and imports, the terms of trade are given by

$$\frac{\text{Average price of exports}}{\text{Average price of imports}}$$

expressed as an index, where price changes are measured against a base year in which the terms of trade are assumed to be 100. Thus if the average price of exports relative to the average price of imports has risen by 20 per cent since the base year, the terms of trade will now be 120. The terms of trade for selected countries are shown in Figure 24.6 (with 2015 as the base year).

If the terms of trade rise (export prices rising relative to import prices), they are said to have 'improved', since fewer

Definition

Terms of trade The price index of exports divided by the price index of imports and then expressed as a percentage. This means that the terms of trade will be 100 in the base year. (Note that the price index for both exports and imports is expressed in terms of the domestic currency.)

Figure 24.6 Terms of trade for goods and services (2015 = 100)

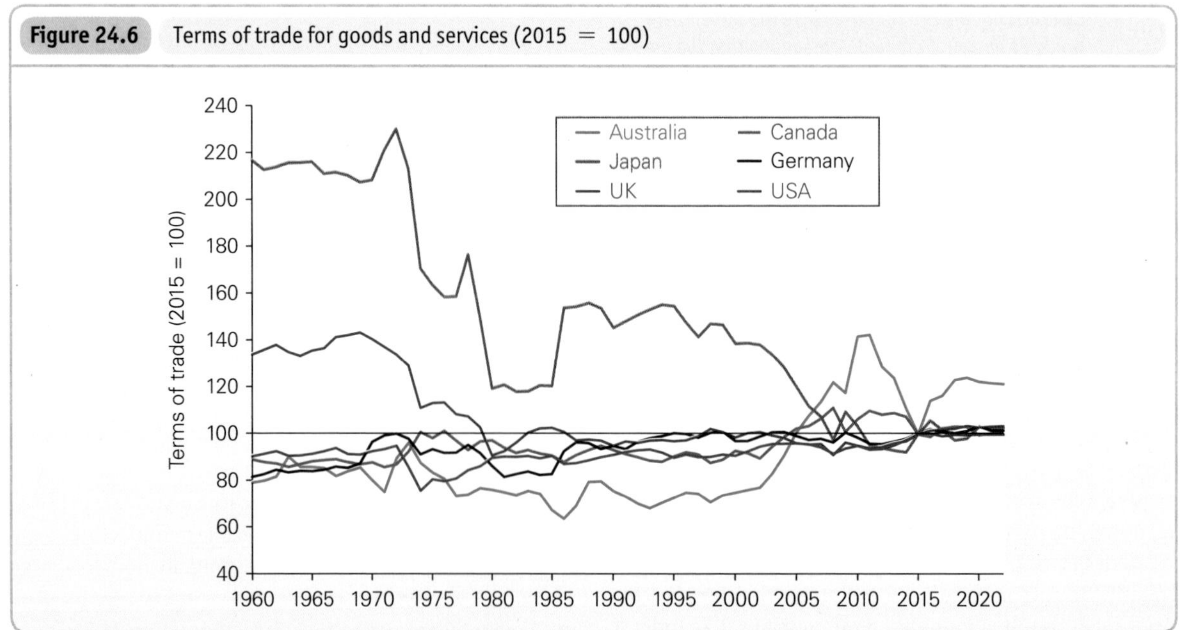

Note: Data from 2021 are based on forecasts.
Source: Based on data in *AMECO Database*, European Commission, DGECFIN (May 2021), https://ec.europa.eu/economy_finance/ameco/user/serie/SelectSerie.cfm

Figure 24.7 Determination of the price of an individual traded good

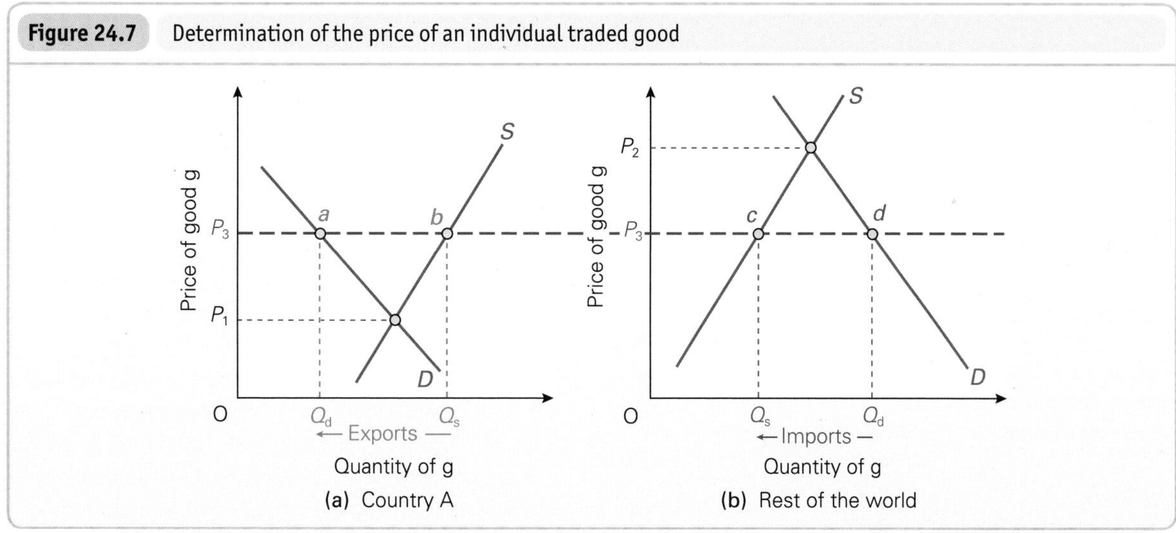

exports now have to be sold to purchase any given quantity of imports. Changes in the terms of trade are caused by changes in the demand for and supply of imports and exports, and by changes in the exchange rate.

In Figure 24.6, which countries' terms of trade improved in the 2000s?

The terms of trade and comparative advantage

Assuming there are two goods, x and m, trade can be advantageous to a country as long as the terms of trade P_x/P_m are different from the opportunity cost ratios of the two goods, given by MC_x/MC_m. For example, if the terms of trade were greater than the opportunity cost ratio ($P_x/P_m > MC_x/MC_m$), it would benefit the country to produce more x for export in return for imports of m, since the relative value of producing x (P_x/P_m) is greater than the relative cost (MC_x/MC_m).

With increasing opportunity costs, however, increasing specialisation in x will lead to MC_x rising (and MC_m falling), until $P_x/P_m = MC_x/MC_m$. At this point, there can be no more gain from further specialisation and trade: the maximum gain has been achieved and comparative cost advantages have been exhausted.

The determination of the terms of trade

When countries import and export many goods, the terms of trade will depend on the prices of all the various exports and imports. These prices will depend on the demand and supply of each traded good and their elasticities in the respective countries. Take the case of good g in which country A has a comparative advantage with respect to the rest of the world. This is illustrated in Figure 24.7.

Demand and supply curves of good g can be drawn for both country A and the rest of the world. (The upward-sloping supply curves imply increasing opportunity costs of production.) Before trade, country A has a low equilibrium price of P_1 and the rest of the world a high equilibrium price of P_2. After trade, price will settle at P_3 in both countries (assuming no transport costs), where total demand by both country A and the rest of the world together eqvuals total supply, and thus where the imports of g into the rest of the world ($d - c$) equal the exports from country A ($b - a$). The position of P_3 relative to P_1 and P_2 will depend on the elasticities of demand and supply.

KI 8
p44

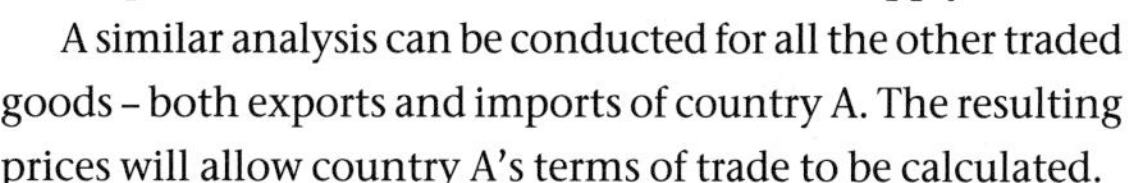

A similar analysis can be conducted for all the other traded goods – both exports and imports of country A. The resulting prices will allow country A's terms of trade to be calculated.

Draw a similar diagram to Figure 24.7 showing how the price of an individual good imported into country A is determined.

The analysis is complicated somewhat if different national currencies are involved, since the prices in each country will be expressed in its own currency. Thus to convert one country's prices to another currency will require knowledge of the rate of exchange: e.g. for the USA and the UK it might be \$1.50 = £1. But under a floating exchange rate system, the rate of exchange will depend in part on the demand for and supply of imports and exports. If the rate of exchange depreciates – say, from \$1.50 = £1 to \$1.25 = £1 – the UK's terms of trade will worsen. Exports will earn less foreign currency per pound: e.g. £1 worth of exports will now be worth only \$1.25 rather than \$1.50. Imports, on the other hand, will be more expensive: e.g. \$6 worth of imports previously cost £4; they now cost £4.80.

Why will exporters probably welcome a 'deterioration' in the terms of trade?

In a world of many countries and many goods, an individual country's imports and exports may have little effect on world prices. In the extreme case, the country may face prices totally dictated by the external world demand and supply. The country in this case is similar to an individual firm under perfect competition. The country is too small to influence world prices, and thus faces a horizontal demand curve for its exports and a horizontal supply curve for its imports. In foreign currency terms, therefore, the terms of trade are outside its control. Nevertheless, these terms of trade will probably be to its benefit, in the sense that the gains from trade will be virtually entirely received by this small country rather than the rest of the world. It is too small for its trade to depress the world price of its exports or drive up the price of its imports.

In general, a country's gains from trade will be greater the less elastic its own domestic demand and supply of tradable goods are, and the more elastic the demand and supply of other countries. You can see this by examining Figure 24.7. The less elastic the domestic demand and supply, the bigger will be the effect of trade on prices faced by that country. The more the trade price differs from the pre-trade price, the bigger the gain.

*Intermediate analysis of gains from trade

The analysis of section 12.1 (pages 361–3) can be used to demonstrate the welfare gains from trade and the limits to specialisation under conditions of increasing opportunity cost. A simple two-good model is used, and the pre-trade position is compared with the position with trade.

Pre-trade

Let us make the following simplifying assumptions:

- There are two goods, x and m.
- Country A has a comparative advantage in the production of good x.
- There are increasing opportunity costs in the production of both x and m. Thus the production possibility curve is bowed out.
- Social indifference curves can be drawn, each one showing the various combinations of x and m that give society in country A particular level of utility.

Figure 24.8 shows the pre-trade position in country A. Production and consumption at P_1C_1 will give the highest possible utility. (All other points on the production possibility curve intersect with lower indifference curves.)

If there is perfect competition, production will indeed be at P_1C_1 There are four steps in establishing this:

- The slope of the production possibility curve ($-\Delta m/\Delta x$) is the marginal rate of transformation (*MRT*), and equals MC_x/MC_m (see pages 362–3). For example, if the opportunity cost of producing 1 extra unit of x (Δx) was a sacrifice of 2 units of m ($-\Delta m$) then an extra unit of x would cost twice as much as an extra unit of m: i.e. $MC_x/MC_m = 2/1$, which is the slope of the production possibility curve, $-\Delta m/\Delta x$.
- The slope of each indifference curve ($-\Delta m/\Delta x$) is the marginal rate of substitution in consumption (*MRS*), and equals MU_x/MU_m. For example, if x had three times the marginal utility of m ($MU_x/MU_m = 3$), consumers would be willing to give up 3m for 1x ($-\Delta m/\Delta x = 3$).
- Under perfect competition,

$$\frac{MC_x}{MC_m} = \frac{P_x}{P_m} = \frac{MU_x}{MU_m}$$

- Thus the domestic pre-trade price ratio P_x/P_m under perfect competition must equal the slope of the production possibility curve (MC_x/MC_m) and the slope of the social indifference curve (MU_x/MU_m) This is the case at P_1C_1 in Figure 24.8.

1. *If production were at point a in Figure 24.8, describe the process whereby equilibrium at point P_1C_1 would be restored under perfect competition.*
2. *Why would production be unlikely to take place at P_1C_1 if competition were not perfect?*

With trade

If country A has a comparative advantage in good x, the price of x relative to m is likely to be higher in the rest of the world than in country A: i.e. world P_x/P_m > pre-trade domestic P_x/P_m. This is shown in Figure 24.9. The world price ratio is given by the slope of the line *WW*. With this new steeper world price ratio, the optimum production point will be P_2 where MRT (the slope of the production possibility curve) = world P_x/P_m (the slope of WW).

With production at P_2 the country can by trading consume *anywhere* along this line *WW*. The optimum consumption point will be C_2 where *MRS* (the slope of the indifference curve) = world P_x/P_m (the slope of WW). Thus trade has allowed consumption to move from point C_1 on the lower indifference curve I_1 to point C_2 on the higher indifference curve I_2. There has thus been a gain from trade. Perfect competition will ensure that this gain is realised, since production at P_2 and consumption at C_2 meet the equilibrium condition that

$$\frac{MC_x}{MC_m} = \frac{P_x}{P_m} = \frac{MU_x}{MU_m}$$

KI 14 p111

How much will be imported and how much will be exported? With production at P_2 and consumption at C_2

Figure 24.8 Equilibrium before trade

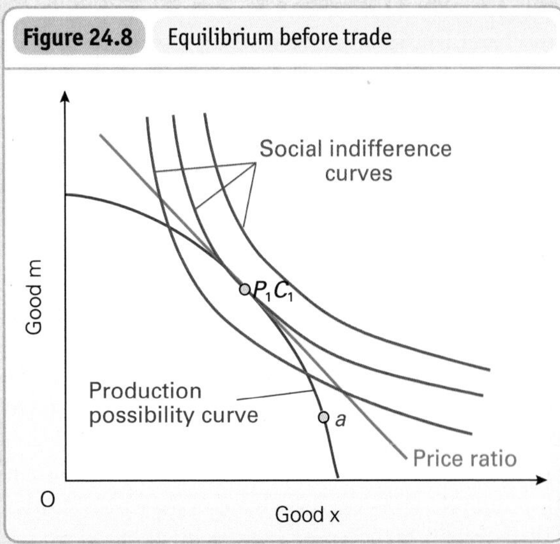

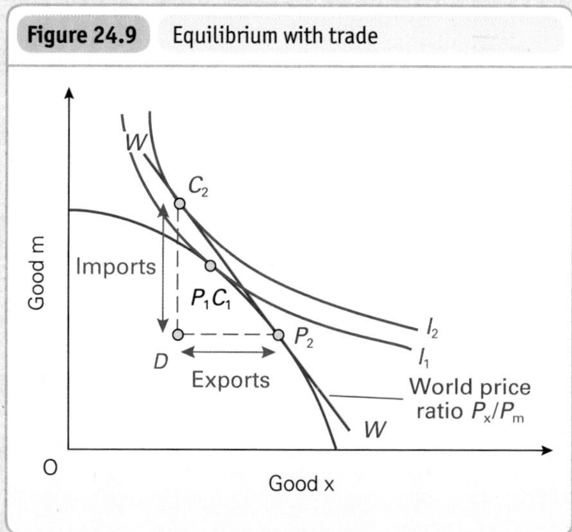

country A will import $C_2 - D$ of good m in exchange for exports of $P_2 - D$ of good x.

Similar diagrams to Figure 24.9 can be drawn for other countries. Since they show equilibrium for both imports and exports on the *one* diagram, economists refer to them as ***general equilibrium diagrams*** (see page 363 for another example).

1. *Draw a similar diagram to Figure 24.9, only this time assume that the two goods are good a measured on the vertical axis and good b measured on the horizontal axis. Assume that the country has a comparative advantage in good a. (Note that the world price ratio this time will be shallower than the domestic pre-trade price ratio.) Mark the level of exports of a and imports of b.*
2. *Is it possible to gain from trade if competition is not perfect?*

Other reasons for gains from trade

Decreasing costs

Even if there are no initial comparative cost differences between two countries, it will still benefit both to specialise in industries where economies of scale (either internal or external) can be gained, and then to trade. Once the economies of scale begin to appear, comparative cost differences will also appear, and thus the countries will have gained a comparative advantage in these industries.

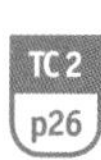

A similar argument applies to different models of the same product (e.g. different models of cars or electrical goods). Several countries, by specialising in just one or two models each, can gain the full economies of scale and hence a comparative advantage in their particular model(s). Then, through trade, consumers can gain from having a wider range from which to choose. Much of the specialisation that international trade permits is of this nature.

The decreasing cost reason for trade is particularly relevant for small countries where the domestic market is not large enough to support large-scale industries. Thus exports form a much higher percentage of GDP in small countries such as Singapore than in large countries such as the USA.

Would it be possible for a country with a comparative disadvantage in a given product at pre-trade levels of output to obtain a comparative advantage in it by specialising in its production and exporting it?

Differences in demand

Even with no comparative cost differences and no potential economies of scale, trade can benefit both countries if demand conditions differ.

If people in country A like beef more than lamb, and people in country B like lamb more than beef, then rather than A using resources better suited for lamb to produce beef and B using resources better suited for producing beef to produce lamb, it will benefit both to produce beef *and* lamb and to export the one they like less in return for the one they like more.

Increased competition

If a country trades, the competition from imports may stimulate greater efficiency at home. This extra competition may prevent domestic monopolies/oligopolies from charging high prices. It may stimulate greater research and development and the more rapid adoption of new technology, thereby increasing the economy's longer-term growth rate. It may lead to a greater variety of products being made available to consumers.

Trade as an 'engine of growth'

In a growing world economy, the demand for a country's exports is likely to grow, especially when these exports have a high income elasticity of demand. This provides a stimulus to growth in the exporting country.

Non-economic advantages

There may be political, social and cultural advantages to be gained by fostering trading links between countries.

The competitive advantage of nations

The theory of comparative advantage shows how countries can gain from trade, but why do countries have a comparative advantage in some goods rather than others?

One explanation is that it depends on the resources that countries have. If a country has plenty of land, then it makes sense to specialise in products that make use of this abundant resource. Thus Canada produces and exports wheat. If a country has a highly skilled workforce and an established research

Definition

General equilibrium diagrams (in trade theory) Indifference curve/production possibility curve diagrams that show a country's production and consumption of both imports and exports.

base, then it makes sense to specialise in high-tech products and export these. Thus Germany exports many highly sophisticated manufactured products. By contrast, many developing countries with plentiful but relatively low-skilled workers specialise in primary products or simple manufactured products.

In other words, countries should specialise in goods which make intensive use of their abundant resources. But this still does not give enough detail as to why countries specialise in the precise range of products that they do. Also, why do countries both export and import the *same* products? Why do many countries produce and export cars, but also import many cars?

According to Porter,[3] there are four key determinants of why nations are highly competitive in certain products but less so in others.

Available resources. These include 'given' resources, such as raw materials, population and climate, but also specialised resources that have been developed by humans, such as the skills of the labour force, the amount and type of capital, the transport and communications infrastructure, and the science and technology base. These specialised resources vary in detail from one country to another and give them a competitive advantage in very specific products. Once an industry has started to develop, this may attract further research and development, capital investment and training, all of which are very specific to that industry. This then further builds the country's competitive advantage in that industry. Thus the highly developed engineering skills and equipment in Germany give it a competitive advantage in producing well-engineered cars.

Demand conditions in the home market. The more discerning customers are within the country, the more this will drive the development of each firm's products and the more competitive the firm will then become in international markets. The demand for IT solutions within the USA drove the development of the software industry and gave companies such as Microsoft, Intel and Google an international advantage.

Strategy, structure and rivalry of firms. Competition between firms is not just in terms of price. Competitive rivalry extends to all aspects of business strategy, from product design, to marketing, to internal organisation, to production efficiency, to logistics. The very particular competitive conditions within each industry can have a profound effect on the development of firms within that industry and determine whether or not they gain an international competitive advantage. Strategic investments and rivalry gave Japanese electronics companies an international competitive advantage.

Related and supporting industries. Firms are more likely to be successful internationally if there are well-developed supporting industries within the home economy. These may be industries providing specialist equipment or specialist consultancy, or they may simply be other parts of the main value chain, from suppliers of inputs to distributors of the firms' output. The more efficient this value chain, the greater the competitive advantage of firms within the industry.

***The competitive advantage of nations* is the ability of countries to compete in the market for exports and with potential importers to their country. The competitiveness of any one industry depends on the availability and quality of resources, demand conditions at home in that industry, the strategies and rivalry of firms within the industry and the quality of supporting industries and infrastructure. It also depends on government policies, and there is also an element of chance.**

The above four determinants of competitive advantage are interlinked and influence each other. For example, the nature of related and supporting industries can influence a firm's strategic decision about whether to embark on a process of vertical integration or de-integration. Similarly, the nature of related and supporting industries depends on demand conditions in these industries and the availability of resources.

With each of the four determinants, competitive advantage can be stimulated by appropriate government supply-side policies, such as a supportive tax regime, investment in transport and communications infrastructure, investment in education and training, competition policy and sound macroeconomic management of the economy. Also, chance often has a large part to play. For example, any pharmaceutical company which discovers a cure for AIDS or for various types of cancer will give a significant competitive advantage to the country in which it is based.

Section summary

1. Countries can gain from trade if they specialise in producing those goods in which they have a comparative advantage: i.e. those goods that can be produced at relatively low opportunity costs. This is merely an extension of the argument that gains can be made from the specialisation and division of labour.
2. If two countries trade, then, provided that the trade price ratio of exports and imports is between the pre-trade price ratios of these goods in the two countries, both countries can gain. They can both consume *beyond* their production possibility curves.
3. With increasing opportunity costs there will be a limit to specialisation and trade. As a country increasingly specialises, its (marginal) comparative advantage will eventually disappear. Trade can also be limited by transport costs, factor movements and government intervention.
4. The terms of trade give the price of exports relative to the price of imports. Additional trade can be beneficial if the terms of trade (P_x/P_m) are greater than the relative marginal costs of exports and imports (MC_x/MC_m).

3 Michael E. Porter, *The Competitive Advantage of Nations*, The Free Press (1998).

5. A country's terms of trade are determined by the demand and supply of imports and exports and their respective elasticities. This will determine the prices at which goods are traded and affect the rate of exchange. A country's gains from trade will be greater the less elastic its own domestic demand and supply of tradable goods, and the more elastic the demand and supply of other countries.
6. Trade allows countries to achieve a higher level of utility by consuming on a higher social indifference curve. The maximum gain from trade is achieved by consuming at the point where the world price ratio is tangential to both the production possibility curve and a social indifference curve. This would be achieved under perfect competition.
7. Gains from trade also arise from decreasing costs (economies of scale), differences in demand between countries, increased competition from trade and the transmission of growth from one country to another. There may also be non-economic advantages from trade.
8. Comparative advantage is related to competitive advantage. Countries tend to have a competitive advantage in those industries where specialist resources have been developed, where products have been developed in response to changing consumer demands, where business strategy is conducive and where there is a network of supporting industries and infrastructure.

24.2 ARGUMENTS FOR RESTRICTING TRADE

Most countries have not pursued a policy of totally free trade. Their politicians know that trade involves costs as well as benefits. In this section, we will attempt to identify what these costs are, and whether they are genuine reasons for restricting trade.

Although countries may sometimes contemplate having completely free trade, they usually limit their trade. However, they certainly do not ban it altogether. The sorts of questions that governments pose are (a) should they have freer or more restricted trade and (b) in which sectors should restrictions be tightened or relaxed? Ideally, countries should weigh up the marginal benefits against the marginal costs of altering restrictions, although just *what* benefits and costs should be considered, and what weighting should be attached to them, may be highly contentious. For example, should external costs and benefits be considered and should these include *global* externalities?

Methods of restricting trade

Tariffs (customs duties). These are taxes on imports and are usually ***ad valorem tariffs***: i.e. a percentage of the price of the import. Tariffs that are used to restrict imports are most effective if demand is elastic (e.g. when there are close domestically produced substitutes). Tariffs can also be used as a means of raising revenue, but in this case, they are more effective if demand is inelastic. They can in addition be used to raise the price of imported goods to prevent 'unfair' competition for domestic producers.

Quotas. These are limits imposed on the quantity of a good that can be imported. Quotas can be imposed by the government, or negotiated with other countries which agree 'voluntarily' to restrict the amount of exports to the first country.

Exchange controls. These include limits on how much foreign exchange can be made available to importers (financial quotas), or to citizens travelling abroad, or for investment. Alternatively, they may take the form of charges for the purchase of foreign currencies.

Import licensing. The imposition of exchange controls or quotas often involves requiring importers to obtain licences. This makes it easier for the government to enforce its restrictions.

Embargoes. These are total government bans on certain imports (e.g. drugs) or exports to certain countries (e.g. to enemies during war).

Administrative barriers. Regulations may be designed to exclude imports: examples include customs delays and excessive paperwork.

Procurement policies. This is where governments favour domestic producers when purchasing equipment (e.g. defence equipment).

Dumping. Alternatively, governments may favour domestic producers by subsidising their exports in a process known as ***dumping***. The goods are 'dumped' at artificially low prices in the foreign market.

Arguments in favour of restricting trade

Economic arguments having some general validity

The infant industry argument. Some industries in a country may be in their infancy, but have a potential comparative advantage. This is particularly likely in developing countries. Such industries are too small yet to have gained economies of scale; their workers are inexperienced; they lack back-up

Definitions

***Ad valorem* tariffs** Tariffs levied as a percentage of the price of the import.

Dumping Where exports are sold at prices below marginal cost – often as a result of government subsidy.

BOX 24.4 **FREE TRADE AND THE ENVIRONMENT** CASE STUDIES AND APPLICATIONS

Do whales, rainforests and the atmosphere gain from free trade?

International trade provides an outlet for hardwood from the rainforests, for tiger parts for medicines, for chemicals and other industrial products produced with little regard for safety or environmental standards, and for products produced using electricity generated from low-cost, high-sulphur, highly polluting coal.

KI 31 p364

The problem is that countries are likely to export goods that they can produce at a relatively low opportunity cost. But these opportunity costs are *private* costs. They do not account of externalities. This is a powerful argument against free trade based on free-market prices.

Surely, though, the developed countries use taxes, legislation and other means to prevent the abuse of the environment? They may do, but this does not stop them importing products from countries that do not.

In reply, the advocates of free trade argue that it is up to each country to decide its own environmental standards. If a poor country produces a product in a cheap polluting way, the gains from exporting it may more than offset the environmental damage done.

There is some strength in this argument provided (a) the government of that country has done a proper study of the costs and benefits involved, including the external costs; and (b) the externalities are confined to within the country's borders. Unfortunately, in many cases neither of these conditions holds. Much of the pollution generated from industrial production has global effects (e.g. global warming).

As countries such as China and India take an increasingly large share of world exports of industrial products (see Figure 24.4), so these problems are likely to grow. Both countries have much lower environmental protection standards than those in Europe and North America.

Should the world community welcome the use of tariffs and other forms of protection by the rich countries against imports of goods from developing countries that have little regard for the environment?

Search for cases of disputes that have been lodged with the WTO or its predecessor, the GATT, concerning trade restrictions for environmental reasons. What were the arguments used by the countries for imposing the restrictions? What were the arguments used by the countries that were complaining? What were the arguments used by the WTO/GATT in making its judgment? Assess these arguments.

facilities, such as communications networks and specialist suppliers. They may have only limited access to finance for expansion. Without protection, these ***infant industries*** will not survive competition from abroad.

Protection from foreign competition, however, will allow them to expand and become more efficient. Once they have achieved a comparative advantage, the protection can then be removed to enable them to compete internationally.

The senile industry argument. This is similar to the infant industry argument. It is where industries with a potential comparative advantage have been allowed to run down and can no longer compete effectively. They may have considerable potential, but be simply unable to make enough profit to afford the necessary investment without some temporary protection. This is one of the most powerful arguments used to justify the use of special protection for the automobile and steel industries in the USA.

How would you set about judging whether an industry had a genuine case for infant/senile industry protection?

Definition

Infant industry An industry that has a potential comparative advantage, but which is as yet too underdeveloped to be able to realise this potential.

To reduce reliance on goods with little dynamic potential. Many developing countries have traditionally exported primaries: foodstuffs and raw materials. The world demand for these, however, is fairly income inelastic, and thus grows relatively slowly. In such cases, free trade is not an engine of growth. Instead, if it encourages countries' economies to become locked into a pattern of primary production, it may prevent them from expanding in sectors like manufacturing that have a higher income elasticity of demand. In recent years, for example, the value of exports of manufactures has typically been around two-thirds of the value of all merchandise exports. There may thus be a valid argument for protecting or promoting manufacturing industry. (We explore these arguments in section 26.4.)

To prevent dumping and other unfair trade practices. A country may engage in dumping by subsidising its exports. The result is that prices may no longer reflect comparative costs. Thus the world would benefit from tariffs being imposed to counteract such practices.

Does the consumer in the importing country gain or lose from dumping?

It can also be argued that there is a case for retaliating against countries that impose restrictions on your exports. In the *short* run, both countries are likely to be made worse off by a contraction in trade. But if the retaliation persuades the other country to remove its restrictions, it may have a longer-term benefit. In some cases, the mere threat of retaliation may be enough to get another country to remove its protection.

To prevent the establishment of a foreign-based monopoly. Competition from abroad, especially when it involves dumping or predatory pricing (see pages 254 and 429), could drive domestic producers out of business. The foreign company, now having a monopoly of the market, could charge high prices with a resulting misallocation of resources.

KI 22 p195

All of the above arguments suggest that governments should adopt a 'strategic' approach to trade. ***Strategic trade theory*** (see Box 24.5) argues that protecting certain industries allows a net gain *in the long run* from increased competition in the market. This argument has been used to justify the huge financial support given to the aircraft manufacturer Airbus, a consortium based in four European countries. The subsidies have allowed it to compete with Boeing, which would otherwise have a monopoly in many types of passenger aircraft. Airlines and their passengers worldwide, it is argued, have benefited from the increased competition.

KI 38 p778

To spread the risks of fluctuating markets. A highly specialised economy – Zambia with copper, Cuba with sugar – is highly susceptible to world market fluctuations. Greater diversity and greater self-sufficiency can reduce these risks.

To reduce the influence of trade on consumer tastes. It is a mistake to assume that fixed consumer tastes dictate the pattern of production through trade. Multinational companies through their advertising and other forms of sales promotion may influence consumer tastes. Thus some restriction on trade may be justified in order to reduce this 'producer sovereignty'.

In what ways may free trade have harmful cultural effects on developing countries?

Definition

Strategic trade theory The theory that protecting/supporting certain industries can enable them to compete more effectively with large monopolistic rivals abroad. The effect of the protection is to increase long-run competition and may enable the protected firms to exploit a comparative advantage that they could not have done otherwise.

BOX 24.5 STRATEGIC TRADE THEORY

EXPLORING ECONOMICS

An argument for protection?

Lester Thurow is professor of management and economics and former dean in the Sloan School of Management at the Massachusetts Institute of Technology (MIT), and an economics journalist and editor. He is also one of the USA's best-known and most articulate advocates of 'managed trade'.

Thurow (and others) have been worried by the growing penetration of US markets by imports from Japan and Europe and also from China and many other developing countries. Their response is to call for a carefully worked-out strategy of protection for US industries.

The *strategic trade theory* that they support argues that the real world is complex. It is wrong, they claim, to rely on free trade and existing comparative advantage. Particular industries will require particular policies of protection or promotion tailored to their particular needs:

- Some industries will require protection against unfair competition from abroad – not just to protect the industries themselves, but also to protect the consumer from the oligopolistic power that the foreign companies will gain if they succeed in driving the domestic producers out of business.
- Other industries will need special support in the form of subsidies to enable them to modernise and compete effectively with imports.
- New industries may require protection to enable them to get established – to achieve economies of scale and build a comparative advantage.
- If a particular foreign country protects or promotes its *own* industries, it may be desirable to retaliate in order to persuade the country to change its mind.

The arguments of strategic trade theorists are criticised by economic liberals. If the USA is protected from cheap imports from Asia, they claim, all that will be achieved is a huge increase in consumer prices. The car, steel, telecommunications and electrical goods industries might find their profits bolstered, but this is hardly likely to encourage them to be more efficient.

Another criticism of managed trade is the difficulty of identifying just which industries need protection, and how much and for how long. Governments do not have perfect knowledge. What is more, the political lobbyists from various interested groups are likely to use all sorts of tactics – legal or illegal – to persuade the government to look favourably on them. In the face of such pressure, will the government remain 'objective'? No, say the liberals.

So how do the strategic trade theorists reply? If it works for China and Japan, they say, it can work for the USA. What is needed is a change in attitudes. Rather than industry looking on the government as either an enemy to be outwitted or a potential benefactor to be wooed, and government looking on industry as a source of votes or tax revenues, both sides should try to develop a partnership – a partnership from which the whole country can gain.

But whether sensible, constructive managed trade is possible is a highly debatable point given the political context in which decisions would need to be made. 'Sensible' managed trade, say the liberals, is just pie in the sky. Under the presidency of Donald Trump, who vowed to 'put America first', calls for specific protection of certain industries in the USA received a more sympathetic hearing than from previous administrations. But whether increased protection, such as that in the steel and aluminium sectors, will have helped them to increase efficiency and regain comparative advantage remains to be seen.

(continued)

Airbus, a consortium based in four European countries, has received massive support from the four governments, in order to enable it to compete with Boeing, which until the rise of Airbus had dominated the world market for aircraft. To what extent are (a) air travellers; (b) citizens of the four countries likely to have gained or lost from this protection? (See Case Study 24.8 on the student website.)

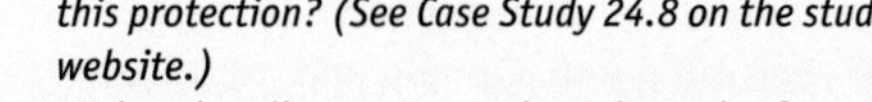

Undertake a literature search on the topic of strategic trade theory. Construct a short PowerPoint presentation summarising for a non-specialist the key ideas from this literature.

To prevent the importation of harmful goods. A country may want to ban or severely curtail the importation of things such as drugs, pornographic literature and live animals.

To take account of externalities. Free trade will tend to reflect private costs. Both imports and exports, however, can involve externalities. The mining of many minerals for export may damage the health of miners; the production of chemicals for export may involve pollution; the importation of juggernaut lorries may lead to structural damage to houses; shipping involves large amounts of CO_2 emissions (some 3 to 5 per cent of total world emissions) (see Box 24.4). KI 31 p364

In recent years, some politicians and green groups have called for the imposition of 'carbon tariffs'. The rate of tariff would reflect the amount of carbon emitted in the production of the good being imported. Such tariffs would be hard to implement, however. Assessing and valuing the carbon emitted would be very difficult and could lead to arbitrary tariff rates. Also, domestic goods would have to be subject to similar taxes.

Economic arguments having some validity for specific groups or countries

The arguments considered so far are of general validity: restricting trade for such reasons could be of net benefit to the world. There are other arguments, however, that are used by individual governments for restricting trade, where their country will gain, but at the *expense* of other countries, such that there will be a net loss to the world. Such arguments include the following.

The exploitation of market power. If a country, or a group of countries, has market power in the supply of exports (e.g. South Africa with diamonds, OPEC with oil) or market power in the demand for imports (e.g. the USA or other large, wealthy countries), it can exploit this power by intervening in trade. KI 22 p195

Let us first take the case of a country, or a group of countries acting as a cartel, which has monopoly power in the sale of a particular export: for example, West African countries in the sale of cocoa. But let us assume that there are many individual producers that are therefore price takers and are thus not in a position to exploit the country's overall market power. In Figure 24.10, these price-taking firms will collectively produce at point *a* where $P = MC$. Market equilibrium is at a trade price of P_1 and an output of Q_1.

The country's profit, however, would be maximised at point *b* where $MC = MR$, with output at the lower level of Q_2. By imposing an export tax of $P_2 - P_3$, therefore, the country can maximise its gain from this export. Producers will receive P_3 and will therefore supply Q_2 Market price will be P_2.

Figure 24.10 A country with a monopoly supply of an export

1. *How much would be the total tax revenue for the government?*
2. *Will the individual producers gain from the export tax?*

Now let us take the case of a country that has *monopsony* power in the demand for an import. This is illustrated in Figure 24.11. Without intervention, equilibrium will be at point *d* where demand equals supply. Q_1 would be purchased at a price of P_1.

But the marginal cost of imports curve will be *above* the supply curve because, given the country's size, the purchase of additional imports would drive up their price. This means that the cost of additional imports would be the new higher price (given by the supply curve) *plus* the rise in expenditure on the imports that would previously have been purchased at a lower price. The country will

Figure 24.11 A country with a monopsony demand for an import

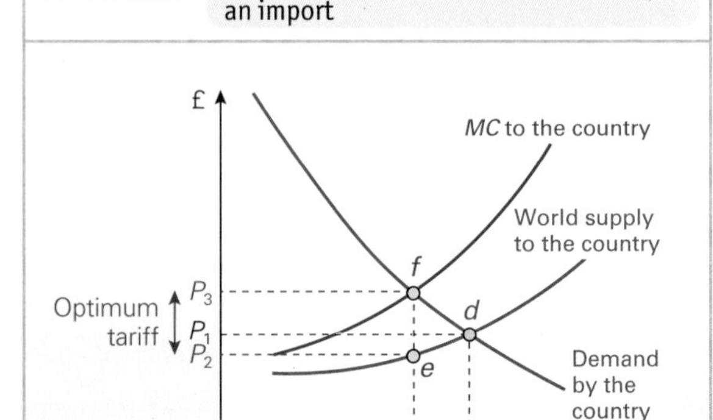

maximise its gain from trade at point f by importing Q_2, where demand equals marginal cost. Consumption can be reduced to Q_2 if the government imposes a tariff of $P_3 - P_2$. This is known as the ***optimum tariff***. The country now only pays P_2 to importers. Consumers have to pay P_3 (i.e. P_2 plus the tariff).

The country gains from such intervention, but only at the expense of the other countries with which it trades.

To protect declining industries. The human costs of sudden industrial closures can be very high. In areas heavily reliant on a declining industry, such as coal mining areas, or 'rust belt' towns in the USA or cities like Detroit, there can be huge costs to the individuals losing their jobs. Their lack of transferable skills may make them occupationally highly immobile. What is more, regional multiplier effects can compound the direct loss of income and consumption. In such circumstances, temporary protection may be warranted to allow industries that have lost comparative advantage to decline more slowly, or even to encourage inward investment in new more efficient technology (making senile industries new 'infants'). Such policies will be at the expense of the consumer, who will be denied access to cheaper foreign imports. Nevertheless, such arguments have gained huge support from populist movements in the USA and elsewhere and protection for such industries formed part of President Trump's 'America first' policies.

Definition

Optimum tariff A tariff that reduces the level of imports to the point where marginal social cost equals marginal social benefit.

To improve the balance of payments. Under certain special circumstances, when other methods of balance of payments correction are unsuitable, there may be a case for resorting to tariffs (see Chapter 25).

'Non-economic' arguments

A country may be prepared to forgo the direct economic advantages of free trade – consumption at a lower

***BOX 24.6 THE OPTIMUM TARIFF OR EXPORT TAX** — EXPLORING ECONOMICS

Using calculus

The size of the optimum export tax depends on the price elasticity of demand ($P\epsilon_d$). You can see this if you imagine rotating the demand and *MR* curves in Figure 24.10. The less elastic the demand curve, the bigger will be the optimum export tax. The formula for the optimum export tax rate is

$$t = 1/P\epsilon_d$$

The proof of this is as follows.

In Figure 24.10, the optimum tax rate is

$$(P_2 - P_3) \div P_2 \quad (1)$$

From the point of view of the country (as opposed to individual producers) this is simply

$$(P - MR) \div P \quad (2)$$

Remember from Box 2.5 on page 62 that price elasticity of demand is given by

$$P\epsilon_d = \frac{-dQ}{dP} \times \frac{P}{Q} \quad (3)$$

Remember also, from Box 6.10 (on page 188), that

$$MR = \frac{dTR}{dQ} = \frac{d(P \cdot Q)}{dQ} \quad (4)$$

From the rules of calculus:

$$\frac{d(P \cdot Q)}{dQ} = \frac{dP \cdot Q + dQ \cdot P}{dQ} \quad (5)$$

$$\therefore P - MR = P - \frac{dP \cdot Q + dQ \cdot P}{dQ} \quad (6)$$

$$\frac{P}{P - MR} = \frac{P}{P - \dfrac{dP \cdot Q + dQ \cdot P}{dQ}} \quad (7)$$

$$= 1 - \frac{P}{P - \dfrac{dP \cdot Q + dQ \cdot P}{dQ}} \quad (8)$$

Again from the rules of calculus:

$$= 1 - \left(\frac{dQ \cdot P}{dP \cdot Q} + \frac{dQ \cdot P}{dQ \cdot P}\right) \quad (9)$$

$$= 1 - \frac{dQ \cdot P}{dP \cdot Q} - 1 \quad (10)$$

$$= \frac{-dQ \cdot P}{dP \cdot Q} = P\epsilon_d \quad (11)$$

$\therefore$ from equations (2) and (11):

$$\frac{P - MR}{P} = \textit{optimum tax rate} = \frac{1}{P\epsilon_d}$$

See if you can devise a similar proof to show that the optimal import tariff, where a country has monopsony power, is $1/P\epsilon_s$ (where $P\epsilon_s$ is the price elasticity of supply of the import).

opportunity cost – in order to achieve objectives that are often described as 'non-economic':

- It may wish to maintain a degree of self-sufficiency in case trade is cut off in times of war. This may apply particularly to the production of food and armaments.
- It may decide not to trade with certain countries with which it disagrees politically.
- It may wish to preserve traditional ways of life. Rural communities or communities based on old traditional industries may be destroyed by foreign competition.
- It may prefer to retain as diverse a society as possible, rather than one too narrowly based on certain industries.

Pursuing such objectives, however, involves costs. Preserving a traditional way of life, for example, may mean that consumers are denied access to cheaper goods from abroad. Society must therefore weigh up the benefits against the costs of such policies.

If economics is the study of choices of how to use scarce resources, can these other objectives be legitimately described as 'non-economic'?

Problems with protection

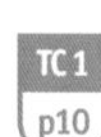

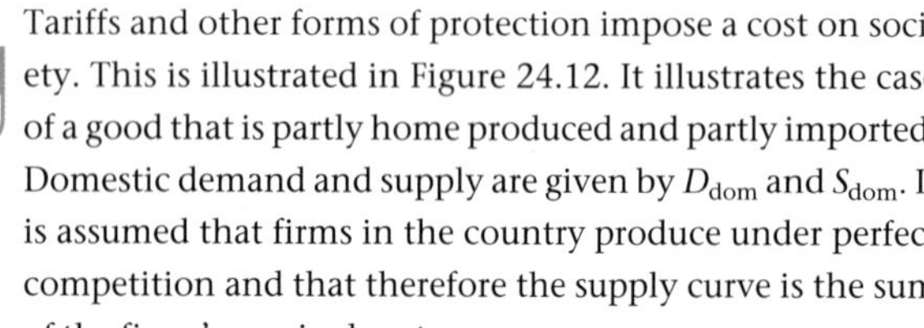

Tariffs and other forms of protection impose a cost on society. This is illustrated in Figure 24.12. It illustrates the case of a good that is partly home produced and partly imported. Domestic demand and supply are given by D_{dom} and S_{dom}. It is assumed that firms in the country produce under perfect competition and that therefore the supply curve is the sum of the firms' marginal cost curves.

Let us assume that the country is too small to affect world prices: it is a price taker. The world price is given, at P_w and world supply to the country (S_{world}) is perfectly elastic. At P_w, Q_2 is demanded, Q_1 is supplied by domestic suppliers and hence $Q_2 - Q_1$ is imported.

Now a tariff is imposed. This shifts up the world supply curve to the country by the amount of the tariff. Price rises to $P_w + t$. Domestic production increases to Q_3 consumption falls to Q_4, and hence imports fall to $Q_4 - Q_3$.

What are the costs of this tariff to the country? Consumers are having to pay a higher price, and hence consumer surplus falls from *ABC* to *ADE*. The cost to consumers in lost consumer surplus is thus *EDBC* (i.e. areas 1 + 2 + 3 + 4). *Part* of this cost, however, is redistributed as a *benefit* to other sections in society. *Firms* face a higher price, and thus gain extra profits (area 1): where profit is given by the area between the price and the *MC* curve. The *government* receives extra revenue from the tariff payments (area 3): i.e. $Q_4 - Q_3 \times$ tariff. These revenues can be used, for example, to reduce taxes.

But *part* of this cost is not recouped elsewhere. It is a net cost to society (areas 2 and 4).

Figure 24.12 The cost of protection

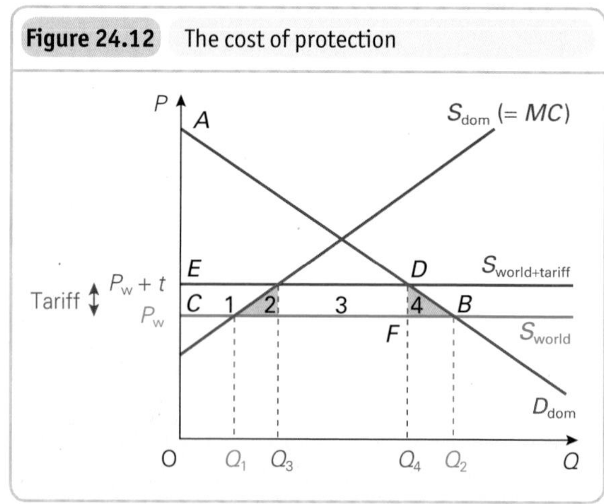

Area 2 represents the extra costs of producing $Q_3 - Q_1$ at home, rather than importing it. If $Q_3 - Q_1$ were still imported, the country would only be paying S_{world}. By producing it at home, however, the costs are given by the domestic supply curve (= *MC*). The difference between *MC* and S_{world} (area 2) is thus the efficiency loss on the production side.

Area 4 represents the loss of consumer surplus by the reduction in consumption from Q_2 to Q_4. Consumers have saved area FBQ_2Q_4 of expenditure, but have sacrificed area DBQ_2Q_4 of utility in so doing – a net loss of area 4.

The government should ideally weigh up such costs against any benefits that are gained from protection.

In this model, where the country is a price taker and faces a horizontal supply curve (the small country assumption), is any of the cost of the tariff borne by the overseas suppliers?

Apart from these direct costs to the consumer, there are several other problems with protection. Some are direct effects of the protection; others follow from the reactions of other nations.

Protection as 'second best'. Many of the arguments for protection amount merely to arguments for some type of government intervention in the economy. Protection, however, may not be the best way of dealing with the problem, since protection may have undesirable side effects. There may be a more direct form of intervention that has no side effects. In such a case, protection will be no more than a second-best solution.

For example, using tariffs to protect old, inefficient industries from foreign competition may help prevent unemployment in those parts of the economy, but the consumer will suffer from higher prices. A better solution would be to subsidise retraining and investment in those areas of the country in *new, efficient* industries – industries with a comparative advantage. In this way, unemployment is avoided, but the consumer does not suffer.

BOX 24.7 GIVING TRADE A BAD NAME

EXPLORING ECONOMICS

Arguments that don't add up

'Why buy goods from abroad and deny jobs to workers in this country?'

This is typical of the concerns that many people have about an open trade policy. However, these concerns are often based on arguments that do not stand up to close inspection. Here are four of them.

'Imports should be reduced since they lower the standard of living.'

'The money goes abroad rather than into the domestic economy.' Imports are consumed and thus add directly to consumer welfare. Also, provided they are matched by exports, there is no net outflow of money. Trade, because of the law of comparative advantage, allows countries to increase their standard of living: to consume beyond their production possibility curve (see Figures 24.5 and 24.9).

'Protection is needed from cheap foreign labour.'

Importing cheap goods from, say, Indonesia, allows more goods to be consumed. The UK uses less resources by buying these goods through the production and sale of exports than by producing them at home. However, there will be a cost to certain UK workers whose jobs are lost through foreign competition.

'Protection reduces unemployment.'

At a microeconomic level, protecting industries from foreign competition may allow workers in those industries to retain their jobs. But if foreigners sell fewer goods to the UK, they will not be able to buy so many UK exports. Thus unemployment will rise in UK export industries. Overall unemployment, therefore, is little affected, and in the meantime the benefits from trade to consumers are reduced. Temporary protection given to declining industries, however, may help to reduce structural unemployment.

'Dumping is always a bad thing, and thus a country should restrict subsidised imports.'

Dumping may well reduce world economic welfare: it goes against the law of comparative advantage. The importing country, however, may well gain from dumping. Provided the dumping is not used to drive domestic producers out of business and establish a foreign monopoly, the consumer gains from lower prices. The losers are the taxpayers in the foreign country and the workers in competing industries in the home country.

Are distributional arguments valid economic reasons for trade restrictions?

Go through each of these five arguments and provide a reply to the criticisms of them.

Even if the *existing* industries were to be supported, it would still be better to do this by paying them subsidies than by putting tariffs on imports. This argument can be expressed in terms of Figure 24.12. As we have seen, a tariff imposes costs on the consumer of areas 1 + 2 + 3 + 4. In the current example, area 2 may be a cost worth paying in order to increase domestic output to Q_3, (and hence reduce unemployment). Areas 1 and 3, as argued above, are merely *redistributed* elsewhere (to firms and the government respectively). But this still leaves area 4. This is a side-effect cost not recouped elsewhere.

A *subsidy*, on the other hand, would not have involved this side-effect cost. In order to raise output to Q_3, a rate of subsidy the same as the tariff rate would have to be given to producers. This would raise the amount they receive per unit to $P_w + t$. They would choose to supply Q_3 The price to the consumer, however, would *remain at the world price* P_w. There would thus be no cost to the consumer. The cost of the subsidy to the taxpayer would be areas 1 + 2. Area 1 would be redistributed to firms as extra profit. Area 2, as argued above, may be worth paying to achieve the desirable output and employment consequences.

If the aim is to increase output, a *production* subsidy is the best policy. If the aim is to increase employment, an *employment* subsidy is the best policy. In either case, to use *protection* instead would be no more than second best since it would involve side effects.

To conclude: the best policy is to tackle the problem directly. Unless the aim is specifically to reduce imports (rather than help domestic industry), protection is an indirect policy, and hence never more than second best.

1. *What would be the 'first-best' solution to the problem of an infant industry not being able to compete with imports?*
2. *Protection to allow the exploitation of monopoly/monopsony power can be seen as a 'first-best' policy for the country concerned. Similarly, the use of tariffs to counteract externalities directly involved in the trade process (e.g. the environmental costs of an oil tanker disaster) could be seen to be a first-best policy. Explain why.*

World multiplier effects. If the UK imposes tariffs or other restrictions, imports will be reduced. But these imports are other countries' exports. A reduction in their exports will reduce the level of injections into the 'rest-of-the-world' economy, and thus lead to a multiplied fall in rest-of-the-world income. Which in turn will lead to a reduction in demand for UK exports. This, therefore, tends to undo the benefits of the tariffs.

What determines the size of this world multiplier effect?

Retaliation. If the USA imposes restrictions on, say, imports from the EU, then the EU may impose restrictions on imports from the USA. Any gain to US firms competing with EU imports is offset by a loss to US exporters. What is more, US consumers suffer since the benefits from comparative advantage have been lost.

The increased use of tariffs and other restrictions can lead to a trade war: each country cutting back on imports from other countries. In the end, everyone loses.

Protection may allow firms to remain inefficient. By removing or reducing foreign competition, protection may reduce firms' incentive to reduce costs. Thus if protection is being given to an infant industry, the government must ensure that the lack of competition does not prevent it 'growing up'. Protection should not be excessive and should be removed as soon as possible.

Bureaucracy. If a government is to avoid giving excessive protection to firms, it should examine each case carefully. This can lead to large administrative costs.

Corruption. Some countries that have an extensive programme of protection suffer from corruption. Home producers want as much protection as possible. Importers want as much freedom as possible. It is very tempting for both groups to bribe officials to give them favourable treatment.

The World Trade Organization

After the Wall Street crash of 1929 (when prices on the US stock exchange plummeted), the world plunged into the Great Depression (see pages 504–5). Countries found their exports falling dramatically, and many suffered severe balance of payments difficulties. The response of many countries was to restrict imports by the use of tariffs and quotas. Of course, this reduced other countries' exports, which encouraged them to resort to even greater protectionism.

BOX 24.8 THE DOHA DEVELOPMENT AGENDA

A new direction for the WTO?

> Globalisation, based on the free play of comparative advantage, economies of scale and innovation, has produced a genuinely radical force, in the true sense of the word.
> It essentially amplifies and reinforces the strengths, but also the weaknesses, of market capitalism: its efficiency, its instability, and its inequality. If we want globalisation not only to be efficiency-boosting but also fair, we need more international rules and stronger multilateral institutions.[1]

In November 1999, the members of the World Trade Organization met in Seattle in the USA. What ensued became known as the 'Battle of Seattle' (see Case Study 24.4 on the student website). Anti-globalisation protesters fought with police; the world's developing economies fell out with the world's developed economies; and the very future of the WTO was called into question. The WTO was accused of being a free trader's charter, in which the objective of free trade was allowed to ride roughshod over anything that might stand in its way. Whatever the issue – the environment, the plight of developing countries, the dominance of trade by multinationals – free trade was king.

At Seattle, both the protesters and developing countries argued that things had gone far enough. The WTO must redefine its role, they argued, to respect *all* stakeholders. More radical voices called for the organisation to be scrapped. As Pascal Lamy, the EU Trade Commissioner, made clear in the speech quoted above, rules had to be strengthened, and the WTO had to ensure that the gains from trade were fairer and more sustainable.

The rebuilding process of the WTO began in Doha, Qatar, in 2001. The meeting between the then 142 members of the WTO concluded with the decision to launch a new round of WTO trade talks, to be called the Doha Development Agenda (DDA). As with previous trade rounds, the talks were designed to increase the liberalisation of trade. However, this time such a goal was to be tempered by a policy of strengthening assistance to developing economies.

At Doha it was agreed that the new trade talks would address questions such as:

- *Sustainable development and the environment.* In the past, international trade agreements always seemed to take precedence over international environmental agreements, even though they are legally equivalent. The hope this time was to achieve greater coherence between various areas of international policy making.
- *Trade and development.* The Doha round would attempt to address a number of issues of concern to developing countries as they become more integrated into the world's trading system. These included improving access to markets in developed countries and strengthening the special treatment that developing countries received, such as the ability to maintain higher rates of tariff protection.

Other areas identified for discussion include: greater liberalisation of agriculture; rules to govern foreign direct investment; the co-ordination of countries' competition policies; the use and abuse of patents on medicines; and the needs of developing countries.

The talks were originally scheduled for completion by January 2005, but this deadline was extended several times as new talks were arranged and failed to reach agreement. A particular sticking point was the unwillingness of rich countries, and the USA and the EU in particular, to make sufficient reductions in agricultural protection, given the pressure from their domestic farmers. The USA was unwilling to make substantial cuts in agricultural subsidies and the EU in agricultural tariffs.

There was also unwillingness on the part of large developing countries, such as India and Brazil, to reduce protection to their industrial and service sectors. What is more, there were large divergences in opinion between developing countries on how much they should reduce their own agricultural protection.

Breakdown of the talks

The talks seemed finally to have broken down at a meeting in Geneva in July 2008. Despite the willingness of developing countries to reduce industrial tariffs by more than 50 per cent, and that of the USA and the EU to make deep cuts in agricultural subsidies and tariffs, the talks foundered over the question of

The net effect of the Depression and the rise in protectionism was a dramatic fall in world trade. The volume of world trade in manufactures fell by more than a third in the three years following the Wall Street crash. Clearly there was a net economic loss to the world from this decline in trade.

After the Second World War there was a general desire to reduce trade restrictions, so that all countries could gain the maximum benefits from trade. There was no desire to return to the beggar-my-neighbour policies of the 1930s.

In 1947, 23 countries got together and signed the General Agreement on Tariffs and Trade (GATT). By 2021, there were 164 members of its successor organisation, the World Trade Organization (WTO), which was formed in 1995. Between them, the members of the WTO account for around 98 per cent of world trade. The aims of GATT, and now the WTO, have been to liberalise trade.

WTO rules

The WTO requires its members to operate according to various rules. These include the following:

- *Non-discrimination.* Under the 'most favoured nations clause', any trade concession that a country makes to one member must be granted to all signatories. The only exception is with free trade areas and customs unions (such as the EU). Here countries are permitted to abolish tariffs between themselves while still maintaining them with the rest of the world.
- *Reciprocity.* Any nation benefiting from a tariff reduction made by another country must reciprocate by making similar tariff reductions itself.
- *The general prohibition of quotas.*

CASE STUDIES AND APPLICATIONS

agricultural protection for developing countries. This was item 18 on a 'to-do' list of 20 items; items 1 to 17 had already been agreed. China and India wanted to protect poor farmers by retaining the ability to impose temporary tariffs on food imports in the event of a drop in food prices or a surge in imports. The USA objected. When neither side would budge, the talks collapsed.

Many commentators, however, argued that failure was no catastrophe. The gain from total liberalisation of trade would have boosted developing countries' GDP by no more than 1 per cent. And anyway, tariffs were already at an all-time low, demonstrating the extent to which progress had already been made. But with the global economic downturn of 2008–9, there were worries that protectionism would begin to rise again. This was a classic prisoners' dilemma (see pages 242–4 and 413). Policies that seemed to be in the interests of countries separately would be to the overall determinant of the world. The Nash equilibrium of such a 'game', therefore, is one where countries are generally worse off. As it turned out, the worries were largely unfounded – at least in the short term.

The Bali and Nairobi Packages

In December 2013, agreement was reached on a range of issues at the WTO's Bali Ministerial Conference and these were adopted in November 2014 by the General Council. The agreement means a streamlining of trade to make it 'easier, faster and cheaper', with particular focus on the promotion of development, boosting the trade of the least developed countries and allowing developing countries more options for providing food security, as long as this does not distort international trade.

This was the first significant agreement of the round and goes some way to achieving around 25 per cent of the goals set for the Doha round.

Then in December 2015, at the Ministerial Conference in Nairobi, another historic agreement was made on various trade initiatives that should provide particular benefits to the WTO's poorest members. This 'Nairobi Package' contains six Ministerial Decisions on agriculture, cotton and issues related to least developed countries, including a commitment to abolish export subsidies for farm exports. Such subsidies had been widely used by developed countries as a means of protecting their agricultural sector.

Despite some progress, this could well be the end of the road for the Doha round.

First, the Trump presidency was seen to reflect a new wave of protectionism around the world, with populist movements blaming free trade for the decline of many traditional sectors, with a loss of jobs and increased social deprivation.

Second, many governments, including the US, have pushed ahead with bilateral or ***plurilateral trade agreements*** (i.e. multi-country agreements). This has raised concern that, in contrast to multilateral WTO agreements, where all members are signed up, we will increasingly see a global patchwork of trading rules, regulations and standards. We discuss preferential trading arrangements in section 24.3.

Definition

Plurilateral trade agreement A trade agreement between more than two countries.

Does the process of globalisation mean that the role of the WTO is becoming less and less important?

Conduct a literature search around the topic of international trade and inequality. Summarise your findings in a PowerPoint presentation that could be presented to an audience of non-specialists in this area, and which would last for around 10–15 minutes.

1 'Global policy without democracy' (speech by Pascal Lamy, EU Trade Commissioner, given in 2001).

- *Fair competition.* If unfair barriers are erected against a particular country, the WTO can sanction retaliatory action by that country. The country is not allowed, however, to take such action without permission.
- *Binding tariffs.* Countries cannot raise existing tariffs without negotiating with their trading partners.

Unlike the GATT, the WTO has the power to impose sanctions on countries breaking trade agreements. If there are disputes between member nations, these will be settled by the WTO, and if an offending country continues to impose trade restrictions, permission will be granted for other countries to retaliate.

For example, in March 2002, the Bush administration imposed tariffs on steel imports into the USA in order to protect the ailing US steel industry (see Case Study 24.6 on the student website). The EU and other countries referred the case to the WTO, which in December 2003 ruled that they were illegal. This ruling made it legitimate for the EU and other countries to impose retaliatory tariffs on US products. President Bush consequently announced that the steel tariffs would be abolished.

Could US action to protect its steel industry from foreign competition be justified in terms of the interests of the USA as a whole (as opposed to the steel industry in particular)?

The greater power of the WTO has persuaded many countries to bring their disputes to it. From January 1995 to January 2021 the WTO had considered, or was considering, 600 disputes (compared with 300 by GATT over the whole of its 48 years).

Trade rounds

Periodically, member countries have met to negotiate reductions in tariffs and other trade restrictions. There have been eight 'rounds' of such negotiations since the signing of GATT in 1947. The last major round to be completed was the Uruguay round, which began in Uruguay in 1986, continued at meetings around the world and culminated in a deal being signed in April 1994. By that time, the average tariff on manufactured products was 4 per cent and falling. In 1947 the figure was nearly 40 per cent. The Uruguay round agreement also involved a programme of phasing in substantial reductions in tariffs and other restrictions up to the year 2002 (see Case Study 24.2 on the student website).

Despite the reduction in tariffs, many countries have still tried to restrict trade by various other means, such as quotas and administrative barriers. Also, barriers have been particularly high on certain non-manufactures. Agricultural protection in particular has come in for sustained criticism by developing countries. High fixed prices and subsidies given to farmers in the EU, the USA and other advanced countries mean that the industrialised world continues to export food to many developing countries that have a comparative advantage in food production! Farmers in developing countries often find it impossible to compete with subsidised food imports from the rich countries.

The most recent round of trade negotiations began in Doha, Qatar, in 2001 (see Box 24.8). The negotiations have focused on both trade liberalisation and measures to encourage development of poorer countries. In particular, the Doha Development Agenda, as it is called, is concerned with measures to make trade fairer so that its benefits are spread more evenly around the world. This would involve improved access for developing countries to markets in the rich world. The Agenda is also concerned with the environmental impacts of trade and development.

The negotiations were originally due to be completed in 2005, but, as Box 24.8 explains, deadlines continued to be missed. However, some progress was made at Ministerial Conferences in 2013 and 2015.

The Bali Package agreed in 2013 made commitments to streamline trade, boost trade among least developed countries and provide 'food security' for developing countries. The deal was proclaimed as the first substantial agreement since the WTO was formed in 1995.

This was followed in 2015 by the 'Nairobi Package' which built on the Bali Package by agreeing on actions in the areas of agriculture, cotton with particular relevance to the least developed countries. This included a commitment to begin to abolish export subsidies for farm exports. Nonetheless, considerable work remained in meeting the goals set in Doha. And with the rise in populist anti-globalisation movements, some argue that the Nairobi Package may be the high point of freer trade for some time to come.

Section summary

1. Countries use various methods to restrict trade, including tariffs, quotas, exchange controls, import licensing, export taxes, and legal and administrative barriers. Countries may also promote their own industries by subsidies.
2. Reasons for restricting trade that have some validity in a world context include the infant industry argument; the inflexibility of markets in responding to changing comparative advantage, dumping and other unfair trade practices; the danger of the establishment of a foreign-based monopoly; the problems of relying on exporting goods whose market is growing slowly or even declining; the need to spread the risks of fluctuating export prices; and the problems that free trade may adversely affect consumer tastes, may allow the importation of harmful goods and may not take account of externalities.
3. Often, however, the arguments for restricting trade are in the context of one country benefiting even though other countries may lose more. Countries may intervene in trade in order to exploit their monopoly/monopsony power. In the case of imports, the optimum tariff would be that which would reduce consumption to the level where price was equal to the country's marginal cost. In the case of exports, the optimum export tax would be that which reduced production to the level where the country's marginal revenue

was equal to marginal cost. Other 'beggar-my-neighbour' arguments include the protection of declining industries and improving the balance of payments.

4. Finally, a country may have other objectives in restricting trade, such as remaining self-sufficient in certain strategic products, not trading with certain countries of which it disapproves, protecting traditional ways of life or simply retaining a non-specialised economy.
5. In general, trade brings benefits to countries, and protection to achieve one objective may be at a very high opportunity cost. Other things being equal, there will be a net loss in welfare from restricting trade, with any gain in government revenue or profits to firms being outweighed by a loss in consumer surplus. Even if government intervention to protect certain parts of the economy is desirable, restricting trade is unlikely to be a first-best solution to the problem, since it involves side-effect costs. What is more, restricting trade may have adverse world multiplier effects; it may encourage retaliation; it may allow inefficient firms to remain inefficient; it may involve considerable bureaucracy and possibly even corruption.
6. Most countries of the world are members of the WTO and in theory are in favour of moves towards freer trade. The Uruguay round brought significant reductions in trade restrictions, both tariff and non-tariff.
7. The latest, the Doha round, focuses on trade liberalisation and aims to spread the benefits of trade across developing countries. It has yet to be concluded, but progress was made at the Bali and Nairobi ministerial conferences of 2013 and 2015. There is some doubt, however, as to whether any further progress will be made and whether the round, therefore, is effectively over. Many countries have moved to form bilateral or multi-country (plurilateral) trading agreements.

24.3 PREFERENTIAL TRADING

The world economy has, over time, seen the formation of a series of trade blocs. These are often based upon regional groupings of countries, such as the European Union (EU) or the United States–Mexico–Canada Agreement (USMCA). Such trade blocs are examples of ***preferential trading arrangements***. These arrangements involve trade restrictions with the rest of the world, and lower or zero restrictions between the members.

Although trade blocs clearly encourage trade between their members, many countries outside the blocs complain that they benefit the members at the expense of the rest of the world. For many developing economies, in need of access to the most prosperous nations in the world, this represents a significant check on their ability to grow and develop.

Types of preferential trading arrangement

There are three possible forms of such arrangements.

Free trade areas

A ***free trade area (FTA)*** is where member countries remove tariffs and quotas between themselves, but retain whatever restrictions *each member chooses* with non-member countries. Some provision will have to be made to prevent imports from outside coming into the area via the country with the lowest external tariff. The EU–UK Trade and Cooperation Agreement, which became effective in January 20201, is an example of an FTA (see section 24.5).

Customs unions

A ***customs union*** is like a free trade area, but in addition members must adopt *common* external tariffs and quotas with non-member countries.

Common markets

A ***common market*** is where member countries operate as a *single* market. As with a customs union, there are no tariffs and quotas between member countries and there are common external tariffs and quotas. But a common market goes further than this. A full common market includes the following features:

- *A common system of taxation.* In the case of a *perfect* common market, this will involve identical rates of tax in all member countries.
- *A common system of laws and regulations governing production, employment and trade.* For example, in a perfect common market, there would be a *single* set of laws governing issues such as product specification (e.g. permissible artificial additives to foods, or levels of exhaust emissions from cars), the employment and dismissal of labour, mergers and takeovers, and monopolies and restrictive practices.

Definitions

Preferential trading arrangements A trade agreement whereby trade between the signatories is freer than trade with the rest of the world.

Free trade area (FTA) A group of countries with few or no trade barriers between themselves.

Customs union A free trade area with common external tariffs and quotas.

Common market A customs union where the member countries act as a single market with free movement of labour and capital, common taxes and common trade laws.

- *Free movement of labour, capital and materials, and of goods and services.* In a perfect common market, this will involve a total absence of border controls between member states, the freedom of workers to work in any member country and the freedom of firms to expand into any member state.
- *The absence of special treatment by member governments of their own domestic industries.* Governments are large purchasers of goods and services. In a perfect common market, they should buy from whichever companies within the market offer the most competitive deal and not show favouritism towards domestic suppliers: they should operate a *common procurement policy*.

The definition of a common market is sometimes extended to include the following two features of *economic and monetary union*:

- *A fixed exchange rate between the member countries' currencies.* In the extreme case, this would involve a single currency for the whole market.
- *Common macroeconomic policies.* To some extent, this must follow from a fixed exchange rate, but in the extreme case it will involve a single macroeconomic management of the whole market, and hence the abolition of separate fiscal or monetary intervention by individual member states.

We will examine European economic and monetary union in section 26.2.

The direct effects of a customs union: trade creation and trade diversion

By joining a customs union (or free trade area), a country will find that its trade patterns change. Two such changes can be distinguished: trade creation and trade diversion.

Trade creation

Trade creation is where consumption shifts from a high-cost producer to a low-cost producer. The removal of trade barriers allows greater specialisation according to comparative advantage. Instead of consumers having to pay high prices for domestically produced goods in which the country has a comparative disadvantage, the goods can now be obtained more cheaply from other members of the customs union. In return, the country can export to them goods in which it has a comparative advantage.

KI 38 p778

For example, suppose that the most efficient producer in the world of good x is France. Assume that, before it joined the EU in 2004, Poland had to pay tariffs on good x from France. After joining the EU, however, it was then able to import good x from France without paying tariffs. There was a gain to Polish consumers. This gain is illustrated in Figure 24.13. Curves S_{Pol} and D_{Pol} show the domestic supply and demand curves in Poland. The diagram assumes for simplicity that Poland is a price taker as an importer of good x from France: the EU price is given.

The diagram shows that, before joining the EU, Poland had to pay the EU price *plus* the tariff (i.e. P_1). At P_1 Poland

Figure 24.13 Trade creation

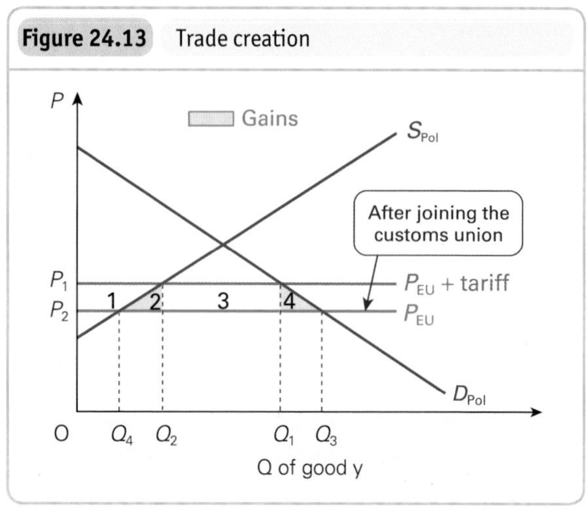

produced Q_2, consumed Q_1 and thus imported $Q_1 - Q_2$. With the removal of tariffs, the price fell to P_2. Consumption increased to Q_3 and production fell to Q_4. Imports thus increased to $Q_3 - Q_4$. Trade had been created.

The gain in welfare from the removal of the tariff is also illustrated in Figure 24.13. A reduction in price from P_1 to P_2 leads to an increase in Polish consumer surplus of areas 1 + 2 + 3 + 4. On the other hand, there is a loss in profits to domestic producers of good x of area 1 and a loss in tariff revenue to the government of area 3. There is still a net gain, however, of areas 2 + 4.

Trade diversion

Trade diversion is where consumption shifts from a lower-cost producer outside the customs union to a higher-cost producer within the union.

Assume that the most efficient producer of good y in the world was Russia – outside the EU. Assume that, before membership, Poland paid a similar tariff on good y from any country, and thus imported the product from Russia rather than the EU.

After joining the EU, however, the removal of the tariff made the EU product cheaper, since the tariff remained on the Russian product. Consumption thus switched to a higher-cost producer. There was thus a net loss in world efficiency. As far as Poland was concerned, consumers still gained, since they were paying a lower price than before, but this time the loss in profits to Polish producers plus the loss

Definitions

Trade creation Where a customs union leads to greater specialisation according to comparative advantage and thus a shift in production from higher-cost to lower-cost sources.

Trade diversion Where a customs union diverts consumption from goods produced at a lower cost outside the union to goods produced at a higher cost (but tariff-free) within the union.

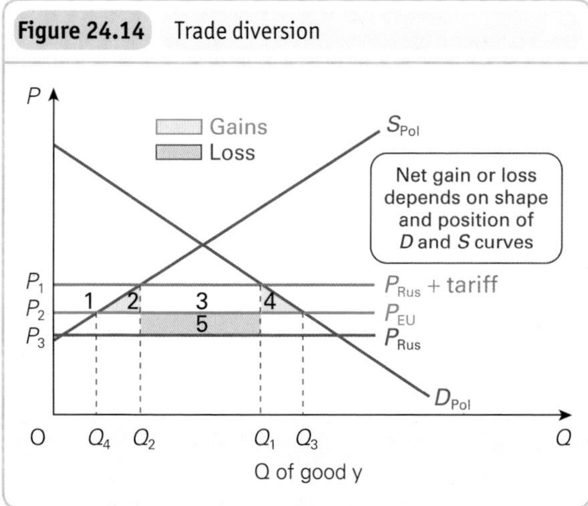

Figure 24.14 Trade diversion

in tariff revenue to the Polish government might have outweighed these gains, giving a net loss.

These benefits and costs are shown in Figure 24.14. For simplicity it assumes a constant Russian and EU price (i.e. that their supply curves to Poland are infinitely elastic). The domestic supply curve (S_{Pol}) is upward sloping, and is assumed to be equal to marginal cost.

Before joining the EU, Poland was importing good y from Russia at a price P_1 (i.e. the Russian price plus the tariff). Poland thus consumed Q_1, produced Q_2 domestically and imported the remainder, $Q_1 - Q_2$ On joining the EU, it was now able to consume at the EU (tariff-free) price of P_2. (Note that this is above the tariff-free Russian price, P_3.) What are the gains and losses to Poland?

- Consumers' gain: Polish consumer surplus rises by areas 1 + 2 + 3 + 4.
- Producers' loss: Polish producer surplus (profit) falls by area 1.
- Government's loss: previously tariffs of areas 3 + 5 were paid. Now no tariffs are paid. The Polish government thus loses this revenue.

There is thus a net gain of areas 1 + 2 + 3 + 4 minus areas 1 + 3 + 5, i.e. areas 2 + 4 minus area 5. If, however, area 5 is bigger than area 2 + 4, there is a net loss.

When trade *diversion* takes place, therefore, there may still be a net gain, but there may be a net loss. It depends on circumstances.

Under which of the following circumstances is there likely to be a net gain from trade diversion (refer to Figure 24.14): (a) a small difference between the EU price and the Russian pre-tariff price, and a large difference between the EU price and the Russian price with the tariff, or vice versa; (b) elastic or inelastic Polish demand and supply curves; (c) the Polish demand and supply curves close together or far apart?

A customs union is more likely to lead to trade diversion rather than trade creation:

- When the union's external tariff is very high. Under these circumstances, the abolition of the tariff within the union is likely to lead to a large reduction in the price of goods imported from other members of the union.
- When there is a relatively small cost difference between goods produced within and outside the union. Here the abolition of even relatively low tariffs within the union will lead to internally produced goods becoming cheaper than externally produced goods.

Longer-term effects of a customs union

The problem with the above analysis is that it assumes *static* demand and supply curves: in other words, supply and demand curves that are unaffected by changes in trading patterns. In reality, if a country joins a customs union, the curves are likely to shift. Membership itself affects demand and supply – perhaps beneficially, perhaps adversely.

Longer-term advantages (economic) include the following:

- Increased market size may allow a country's firms to exploit (*internal*) *economies of scale*. This argument is more important for small countries, which have therefore more to gain from an enlargement of their markets.
- *External economies of scale*. Increased trade may lead to improvements in the infrastructure of the members of the customs union (better roads, railways, financial services, etc.). This in turn could bring bigger long-term benefits from trade between members, and from external trade too, by making the transport and handling of imports and exports cheaper.
- The bargaining power of the whole customs union with the rest of the world may allow member countries to gain *better terms of trade*. This, of course, will necessarily involve a degree of political co-operation between the members.
- *Increased competition* between member countries may stimulate efficiency, encourage investment and reduce monopoly power. Of course, a similar advantage could be gained by the simple removal of tariffs with any competing country.
- Integration may encourage a *more rapid spread of technology*.

Longer-term disadvantages (economic) include the following:

- *Resources may flow from a country* to more efficient members of the customs union, or to the geographical centre of the union (so as to minimise transport costs). This can be a major problem for a *common market* (where there is free movement of labour and capital). The country could become a depressed 'region' of the community, with adverse regional multiplier effects.
- If integration encourages greater co-operation between firms in member countries, it may also encourage *greater oligopolistic collusion*, thus keeping prices to the consumer higher. It may also encourage mergers and takeovers which would increase monopoly power.

- *Diseconomies of scale.* If the union leads to the development of very large companies, they may become bureaucratic and inefficient.
- The *costs of administering* the customs union may be high. This problem is likely to be worse, the greater the intervention in the affairs of individual members.

It is extremely difficult to assess these arguments. To decide whether membership has been beneficial to a country requires a prediction of what things would have been like if it had not joined. No *accurate* predictions of this sort can be made, and they can never be tested. Also, many of the advantages and disadvantages are very long term, and depend on future attitudes, institutions, policies and world events, which again cannot be predicted.

In addition, some of the advantages and disadvantages are distinctly political, such as 'greater political power' or 'loss of sovereignty'.

How would you set about assessing whether or not a country had made a net long-term gain by joining a customs union? What sort of evidence would you look for?

Preferential trading in practice

Preferential trading has the greatest potential to benefit countries whose domestic market is too small, taken on its own, to enable them to benefit from economies of scale, and where they face substantial barriers to their exports. Most developing countries fall into this category, and as a result many have attempted to form preferential trading arrangements.

Examples in Latin America and the Caribbean are the Latin American Integration Association (ALADI), the Andean Community, the Central American Integration System (SICA) and the Caribbean Community (CARICOM). In 1991, a Southern Common Market (MerCoSur) was formed, consisting of Argentina, Brazil, Paraguay and Uruguay. Venezuela joined in 2012 but its membership has been suspended since 2016. It has a common external tariff and most of its internal trade is free of tariffs.

The Association of South-East Asian Nations (ASEAN) was formed in 1967 when six nations (Brunei, Indonesia, Malaysia, the Philippines, Singapore and Thailand) agreed to work towards an ASEAN Free Trade Area (AFTA). ASEAN now has 10 members (the new countries being Vietnam, Laos, Myanmar and Cambodia) with a population of over 660 million people and is dedicated to increased economic co-operation within the region.

By 2010, virtually all tariffs between the six original members had been eliminated and both tariff and non-tariff barriers are falling quickly for both original and new members. The ASEAN Economic Community (AEC) was established in 2015, ahead of schedule.

In Africa, the Economic Community of West African States (ECOWAS) has been attempting to create a common market between its 15 members which has a combined population of around 350 million. The West African franc has been used in eight of the countries and the plan is to introduce a common currency, the eco, for all members. However, the launch of this has been delayed several times because of disagreements and lack of convergence between members' economies and it is now not expected until the mid-2020s.

The African Continental Free Trade Area (AfCFTA) was agreed in 2018 and came into effect in January 2021. At that date, of the 55 African nations, only Eritrea was not a member, but was expected subsequently to join. AfCFTA is the world's largest free-trade area by number of countries and population (1.3 billion people). It has a combined GDP of $3.4 trillion.

While the longer-term ambition of AfCFTA is to create a continental single market and customs union, the hope is that the preferential trading arrangements across the continent will boost growth and reduce poverty. Its impact, however, will depend on progress in facilitating trade beyond mere tariff reductions, for example by reducing red tape and simplifying customs procedures.

United States–Mexico–Canada Agreement (USMCA)

The USMCA is a free-trade agreement between the USA, Mexico and Canada. It is the successor to NAFTA and, alongside the EU, is one of the two most powerful trading blocs in the world. NAFTA came into force in 1994 when the three countries agreed to abolish tariffs between themselves in the hope that increased trade and co-operation would follow. Tariffs between the USA and Canada were phased out by 1999, and tariffs between all three countries were eliminated as of 1 January 2008. Many non-tariff restrictions remain, although new ones are not permitted.

Shortly after coming to office, President Trump committed to renegotiating NAFTA. After difficult negotiations, a deal was eventually reached in September 2018 with the new USMCA being implemented from April 2020 following ratification by the three countries.

There were three main changes. First is greater rules-of-origin requirements for motor vehicles. To qualify for zero tariffs, 75 per cent of their components need to have been made within USMCA (not the previous 62.5 per cent) with at least 40 to 45 per cent of a vehicle's components being made by workers earning at least $16 per hour (by 2023). Second, Canada agreed to give US dairy farmers access to 3.6 per cent of Canada's dairy market. Third, was a strengthening of various standards inadequately covered in NAFTA such as in digital trade and financial services.

While USMCA has a market similar in size to the EU, it is at most only a free-trade area and not a common market. Unlike the EU, it does not seek to harmonise laws and regulations, except in very specific areas such as environmental management and labour standards. Member countries are permitted total legal independence, subject to the one proviso that they must treat firms of other member countries equally with their own firms – the principle of 'fair competition'. Nevertheless, NAFTA and then USMCA have encouraged a growth in trade between the members, most of which is trade creation rather than trade diversion.

Asia-Pacific Economic Co-operation forum (APEC)

The most significant move towards establishing a more widespread regional economic organisation in East Asia appeared with the creation of the Asia-Pacific Economic Co-operation (APEC) in 1989. APEC links 21 economies of the Pacific rim, including Asian, Australasian and North and South American countries (19 countries, plus Hong Kong and Taiwan). These countries account for over half of global GDP and almost half of the world's trade. At the 1994 meeting of APEC leaders, it resolved to create a free trade area across the Pacific by 2010 for the developed industrial countries, and by 2020 for the rest.

This preferential trading area is by no means as advanced as NAFTA and is unlikely to move beyond a free trade area. Within the region there exists a wide disparity across a range of economic and social indicators. Such disparities create a wide range of national interests and goals. Countries are unlikely to share common economic problems or concerns. In addition, political differences and conflicts within the region are widespread, reducing the likelihood that any organisational agreement beyond a simple economic one would succeed. Nevertheless, freer trade has brought economic benefits to the countries involved.

The longest established and most comprehensive of preferential trading arrangements is the European Union. The next section is devoted to examining its evolution from a rather imperfect customs union to a common market (though still not perfect).

The Trans-Pacific Partnership

The Trans-Pacific Trade Partnership (TPP) was an agreement between 12 Pacific-rim countries – Australia, Brunei, Canada, Chile, Japan, Malaysia, Mexico, New Zealand, Peru, Singapore, the USA and Vietnam, but not China. It was signed by the 12 countries in February 2016, but on coming into office in January 2017, Donald Trump withdrew the USA from the agreement.

The other 11 TPP countries signed up to a revised, though largely unchanged, version of the agreement in March 2018 known as the Comprehensive and Progressive Agreement for Trans-Pacific Partnership (CPTPP) or TPP-11. Each of these countries then began the process of officially ratifying the deal. The CPTPP came into force on 30 December 2018 with six initial members (Mexico, Japan, Singapore, New Zealand, Canada, Australia) with Vietnam joining in 2019.

China, South Korea, Indonesia, the Philippines, Thailand and Colombia have expressed an interest in joining. In January 2021, the UK began the process of formally applying to join the CPTPP.

The CPTPP is more than a simple free-trade agreement. In terms of trade it involves the removal of many non-tariff barriers as well as most tariff barriers. It also has elements of a single market. For example, it contains many robust and enforceable environmental protection, human rights and labour standards measures. It also allows for the free transfer of capital by investors in most circumstances.

However, it also establishes an 'investor–state dispute settlement' (ISDS) mechanism. This allows companies from any of the TPP countries to sue governments of any other countries in the agreement for treaty violations, such as giving favourable treatment to domestic companies, the seizing of companies' assets or controls over the movement of capital. Critics of ISDS claim that it gives too much power to companies and may prevent governments from protecting their national environment or domestic workers and companies.

Section summary

1. Countries may make a partial movement towards free trade by the adoption of a preferential trading system. This involves free trade between the members, but restrictions on trade with the rest of the world. Such a system can be either a simple free trade area, or a customs union (where there are common restrictions with the rest of the world), or a common market (where in addition there is free movement of capital and labour, and common taxes and trade laws).
2. A preferential trading area can lead to trade creation where production shifts to low-cost producers within the area, or to trade diversion where trade shifts away from lower-cost producers outside the area to higher-cost producers within the area.
3. There is a net welfare gain from trade creation: the gain in consumer surplus outweighs the loss of tariff revenue and the loss of profit to domestic producers. With trade diversion, however, these two losses may outweigh the gains to consumers: whether they do depends on the size of the tariffs and on the demand for and supply of the traded goods.
4. Preferential trading may bring dynamic advantages of increased external economies of scale, improved terms of trade from increased bargaining power with the rest of the world, increased efficiency from greater competition between member countries, and a more rapid spread of technology. On the other hand, it can lead to increased regional problems for members, greater oligopolistic collusion and various diseconomies of scale. There may also be large costs of administering the system.
5. There have been several attempts around the world to form preferential trading systems. The two most powerful are the European Union and the United States–Mexico–Canada Agreement (USMCA).

24.4 THE EUROPEAN UNION

Historical background

The European Economic Community (EEC) was formed by the signing of the Treaty of Rome in 1957 and came into operation on 1 January 1958.

The original six member countries of the EEC (Belgium, France, Italy, Luxembourg, the Netherlands and West Germany) had already made a move towards integration with the formation of the European Coal and Steel Community in 1952. This had removed all restrictions on trade in coal, steel and iron ore between the six countries. The aim had been to gain economies of scale and allow more effective competition with the USA and other foreign producers.

The EEC extended this principle and aimed eventually to be a full common market with completely free trade between members in all products, and with completely free movement of labour, enterprise and capital.

All internal tariffs between the six members had been abolished and common external tariffs established by 1968. But this still only made the EEC a *customs union*, since a number of restrictions on internal trade remained (legal, administrative, fiscal, etc.). Nevertheless the aim was eventually to create a full common market.

In 1973 the UK, Denmark and Ireland became members. Greece joined in 1981, Spain and Portugal in 1986, and Sweden, Austria and Finland in 1995. In May 2004, a further 10 countries joined: Cyprus, the Czech Republic, Estonia, Hungary, Latvia, Lithuania, Malta, Poland, Slovakia and Slovenia. Bulgaria and Romania joined in 2007. The last new member is Croatia, which joined in 2013. When the UK left the EU in 2020 (see section 24.5), there were then 27 members.

In March 2020, the General Affairs Council of the EU agreed to open accession talks with Albania and North Macedonia to join the EU. By doing so they moved from the second to the third of four stages (candidate status to negotiations) that culminate in accession to the EU. They therefore joined Montenegro, Serbia and Turkey at this stage. Bosnia and Herzegovina is currently at the first stage (application).

From customs union to common market

The EU is clearly a customs union. It has common external tariffs and no internal tariffs. But is it also a common market? For many years, there have been *certain* common economic policies.

Common Agricultural Policy (CAP). The Union has traditionally set common high prices for farm products. This has involved charging variable import duties to bring foreign food imports up to EU prices and intervention to buy up surpluses of food produced within the EU at these above-equilibrium prices (see section 3.4). Although the main method of support has shifted to providing subsidies (or 'income support') unrelated to current output, this still represents a *common* economic policy.

Regional policy. EU regional policy provides grants to firms and local authorities in relatively deprived regions of the Union (see Case Study 23.14 on the student website).

Competition policy. EU policy here has applied primarily to companies operating in more than one member state (see section 14.1). For example, Article 101 of the Treaty of Lisbon prohibits agreements between firms operating in more than one EU country (e.g. over pricing or sharing out markets) which adversely affect competition in trade between member states (see pages 431–2).

Harmonisation of taxation. VAT is the standard form of indirect tax throughout the EU. However, there are substantial differences in VAT rates between member states, as there are with other tax rates.

What would be the economic effects of (a) different rates of VAT, (b) different rates of personal income tax and (c) different rates of company taxation between member states if there were no other barriers to trade or factor movements?

Social policy. In 1989 the European Commission presented a *social charter* to the heads of state. This spelt out a series of worker and social rights that should apply in all member states (see Case Study 24.9 on the student website). These rights were grouped under 12 headings covering areas such as the guarantee of decent levels of income for both the employed and the non-employed, freedom of movement of labour between member countries, freedom to belong to a trade union and equal treatment of men and women in the labour market. However, the charter was only a recommendation and each element had to be approved separately by the European Council of Ministers.

The social chapter of the Maastricht Treaty (1991) attempted to move the Community forward in implementing the details of the social charter in areas such as maximum hours, minimum working conditions, health and safety protection, information and consultation of workers, and equal opportunities.

Would the adoption of improved working conditions necessarily lead to higher labour costs per unit of output?

Despite these various common policies, in other respects the Community of the 1970s and 1980s was far from a true common market: there were all sorts of non-tariff barriers such as high taxes on wine by non-wine-producing countries, special regulations designed to favour domestic producers, governments giving contracts to domestic producers (e.g. for defence equipment), and so on.

The category often cited by businesses as being the most important single barrier was that of regulations and norms. In some cases, the regulations merely added to the costs of imports. But in the cases of many mechanical engineering and telecommunications products, technical and health and safety regulations sometimes ruled out foreign imports altogether.

Moves towards a single market

The Single European Act of 1986, which came into force in July 1987, sought to remove these barriers and to form a genuine common market by the end of 1992 (see Box 24.10).

One of the most crucial aspects of the Act was its acceptance of the principle of ***mutual recognition***. This is the principle whereby if a firm or individual is permitted to do something under the rules and regulations of *one* EU country, it must also be permitted to do it in all other EU countries. This means that firms and individuals can choose the country's rules that are least constraining.

Mutual recognition also means that individual governments can no longer devise special rules and regulations that keep out competitors from other EU countries (see Box 24.9). Here was the answer to the dilemma of how to get all EU countries to agree to common sets of rules and regulations. All that was required was that they recognised the rules and regulations applying in each other's countries. However, there was a danger that governments would end up competing against each other to provide the lightest set of regulations in order to attract firms to invest in their country. This could be to the detriment of consumers and workers.

Thus *some* common sets of rules and regulations were still required. One other feature of the Single European Act helped here. This was the institution of *majority* voting in questions of harmonisation of rules and regulations. Previously, unanimous approval had been necessary. This had meant that an individual country could veto the dismantling of barriers. This new system of majority voting, however, does not currently apply to the harmonisation of taxes, although the European Commission continues to propose that majority voting be extended to taxation while recognising that 'there is no need for across the board harmonisation' of taxes.

> **Definition**
>
> **Mutual recognition** The EU principle that one country's rules and regulations must apply throughout the EU. If they conflict with those of another country, individuals and firms should be able to choose which to obey.

The benefits and costs of the single market

It is difficult to quantify the benefits and costs of the single market, given that many occur over a long period, and it is hard to know to what extent the changes that are taking place are the direct result of the single market.

One study conducted in 1998 did, nevertheless, estimate the benefits in terms of increased consumption (see Table 24.6). This found that the benefits to the smaller, lower-income countries, such as Portugal and Greece, were the greatest. Such estimates, however, do depend crucially on the assumptions made and are thus open to substantial error.

Then in 2012, the European Commission published *20 Years of the European Single Market*. This stated that, 'The GDP

BOX 24.9 MUTUAL RECOGNITION: THE CASSIS DE DIJON CASE

CASE STUDIES AND APPLICATIONS

Or when is a liqueur not a liqueur?

Crème de Cassis is an alcoholic blackcurrant drink made by the French firm Cassis de Dijon. Added to white wine, it makes the drink kir. It is not just the French who like drinking kir; it is also, among others, the Germans. In this seemingly innocent fact lay the seeds for the dismantling of some of the most serious trade barriers in Europe!

The story starts back in 1978. The West German company Rewe Zentral AG wanted to import Cassis, but found that under West German law it could not. The problem was that Cassis does not contain enough alcohol to be classed as a liqueur, and it also fell outside any other category of alcoholic drink that was permitted by West German law.

But Rewe was not to be put off. It started legal proceedings in Europe to challenge the German law. The basis of Rewe's case was that this law discriminated against non-German companies. After much legal wrangling, the European Court of Justice in Luxembourg ruled that Germany had no right to prevent the importation of a product that was legitimately on sale in another member country (i.e. France). The only exceptions to this ruling would be if the product were barred for reasons of consumer protection, health or fair trade. None of these applied to Cassis, so the Germans can now drink kir to their hearts' content without having to become smugglers.

But what of the implications of the case? These are enormous and were spelt out in the Single European Act: 'the Council may decide that provisions in force in a member state must be recognised as being equivalent to those applied by another'. In other words, individuals and firms can choose which country's sets of regulations suit them the best and then insist that they be applied in *all* member states.

'Mutual recognition' of each other's laws tends to lead to deregulation, as people choose those countries' laws that give them the greatest freedom. This appeals to economic and political liberals. Equally, it worries those who argue that regulations and laws on industrial standards have been instituted for a purpose, and should not be undone just because some other member country has not been wise enough to institute them itself.

How has the Cassis de Dijon ruling affected the balance of power in the EU between (a) individual states and the EU as a whole; (b) governments and the courts?

Undertake desktop research to investigate the role played by Mutual Recognition Agreements in facilitating trade between the European Union and 'third countries'.

of the EU27 was 2.13% – or €233 billion – higher in 2008 than it would have been without the Single Market. This can be equated to around €500 extra in income per EU citizen. Between 1992 and 2008, the Single Market helped to create 2.77 million new jobs.'

Even though the precise magnitude of the benefits is difficult to estimate, it is possible to identify the *types* of benefit that have resulted, many of which have been substantial.

Trade creation. The expansion of trade within the EU has reduced both prices and costs, as countries have been able to exploit their comparative advantage. Member countries have specialised further in those goods and services that they can produce at a comparatively low opportunity cost.

Reduction in the direct costs of barriers. This category includes administrative costs, border delays and technical regulations.

BOX 24.10 FEATURES OF THE SINGLE MARKET

CASE STUDIES AND APPLICATIONS

Since 1 January 1993 trade within the EU has operated very much like trade within a country. In theory, it should be no more difficult for a firm in Marseilles to sell its goods in Berlin than in Paris. At the same time, the single market allows free movement of labour and involves the use of common technical standards.

The features of the single market are summed up in two European Commission publications.[1] They are:

- Elimination of border controls on goods within the EU: no more long waits.
- Free movement of people across borders.
- Common security arrangements.
- No import taxes on goods bought in other member states for personal use.
- The right for everyone to live in another member state.
- Recognition of vocational qualifications in other member states: engineers, accountants, medical practitioners, teachers and other professionals able to practise throughout Europe.
- Technical standards brought into line, and product tests and certification agreed across the whole EU.
- Common commercial laws – making it attractive to form Europe-wide companies and to start joint ventures.
- Public contracts to supply equipment and services to state organisations now open to tenders across the EU.

So what does the single market mean for individuals and for businesses?

Individuals

Before 1993, if you were travelling in Europe, you had a 'duty-free allowance'. This meant that you could only take goods up to the value of €600 across borders within the EU without having to pay VAT in the country into which you were importing them. Now you can take as many goods as you like from one EU country to another, provided they are for your own consumption. But to prevent fraud, member states may ask for evidence that the goods have been purchased for the traveller's own consumption if they exceed specified amounts.

Individuals have the right to live and work in any other member state. Qualifications obtained in one member state must be recognised by other member states.

Firms

Before 1993 all goods traded in the EU were subject to VAT at every internal border. This involved some 60 million customs clearance documents at a cost of some €70 per consignment.[2]

This has all now disappeared. Goods can cross from one member state to another without any border controls: in fact, the concepts of 'importing' and 'exporting' within the EU no longer officially exist. All goods sent from one EU country to another will be charged VAT only in the country of destination. They are exempt from VAT in the country where they are produced.

One of the important requirements for fair competition in the single market is the convergence of tax rates. Although income tax rates, corporate tax rates and excise duties still differ between member states, there has been some narrowing in the range of VAT rates. Higher rates of VAT on luxury goods were abolished and countries are allowed to have no more than two lower rates of at least 5 per cent on 'socially necessary' goods, such as food and water supply.

There is a lower limit of 15 per cent on the standard rate of VAT. Actual rates as of 1 January 2021 nonetheless varied from 17 per cent in Luxembourg to 27 per cent in Hungary. However, during the early 2010s several countries, including Ireland, Greece and Portugal increased their standard rate of VAT as a means of reducing their budget deficits (see section 22.1). One effect of this is that the vast majority of EU countries now have a standard rate of VAT between 20 and 25 per cent.

In what ways would competition be 'unfair' if VAT rates differed widely between member states?

Using the Public Finances Databank from the Office for Budget Responsibility (http://obr.uk/) create a chart showing for the UK the percentage of public-sector current receipts collected from VAT (net of refunds) over time. Briefly summarise the findings of your chart.

1 *A Single Market for Goods*, Commission of the European Communities (1993); *10 Key Points about the Single European Market*, Commission of the European Communities (1992).

2 *A Single Market for Goods*, Commission of the European Communities (1993).

Table 24.6 Gains from the single market

Countries	Extra consumption as % of GDP
France, Germany, UK, Italy	2–3
Denmark	2–5
Netherlands, Spain	3–4
Belgium, Luxembourg	4–5
Ireland	4–10
Greece	5–16
Portugal	19–20

Source: C. Allen, M. Gasiorek and A. Smith, 'The competition effects of the single market in Europe', *Economic Policy* (1998).

Their abolition or harmonisation has led to substantial cost savings, shorter delivery times and a larger choice of suppliers.

Economies of scale. With industries based on a Europe-wide scale, many firms can now be large enough, and their plants large enough, to gain the full potential economies of scale (see Box 6.9 on pages 179–80). Yet the whole European market is large enough for there still to be adequate competition. Such gains have varied from industry to industry depending on the minimum efficient scale of a plant or firm. Economies of scale have also been gained from mergers and other forms of industrial restructuring.

Greater competition. Increased competition between firms has led to lower costs, lower prices and a wider range of products available to consumers. This has been particularly so in newly liberalised service sectors such as transport, financial services, telecommunications and broadcasting. In the long run, greater competition can stimulate greater innovation, a greater flow of technical information and the reorganisation ('rationalisation') of production to increase efficiency.

Despite these gains, the single market has not received universal welcome within the EU. Its critics argue that, in a Europe of oligopolies, unequal ownership of resources, rapidly changing technologies and industrial practices, and factor immobility, the removal of internal barriers to trade has merely exaggerated the problems of inequality and economic power. More specifically, the following criticisms are made.

Radical economic change is costly. Substantial economic change is necessary to achieve the full economies of scale and efficiency gains from a single European market. These changes necessarily involve redundancies – from bankruptcies, takeovers, rationalisation and the introduction of new technology. The severity of this structural and technological unemployment depends on (a) the pace of economic change and (b) the mobility of labour – both occupational and geographical. Clearly, the more integrated markets become across the EU, the less the costs of *future* change.

Adverse regional multiplier effects. Firms are likely to locate as near as possible to the 'centre of gravity' of their markets and sources of supply. The geographical expansion of firms' markets potentially to encompass the whole of the EU can tend to attract capital and jobs away from the edges of the Union to its geographical centre. TC 15 p543

In an ideal market situation, areas like the south of Italy or Portugal, should attract resources from other parts of the Union. Since they are relatively depressed areas, wage rates and land prices are lower. The resulting lower industrial costs should encourage firms to move into the areas. In practice, regional multiplier effects may worsen the problem (see pages 767–8). As capital and labour (and especially young and skilled workers) leave the extremities of the Union, so these regions are likely to become more depressed. If, as a result, their infrastructure is neglected, they then become even less attractive to new investment.

Has the problem of adverse regional multiplier effects been made better or worse by the adoption of a single European currency? (This issue is explored in section 26.3.) (Clue: without a single currency, how would the devaluation of the drachma (the former Greek currency) have affected a depressed Greek economy?)

The development of monopoly/oligopoly power. The free movement of capital can encourage the development of giant 'Euro-firms' with substantial economic power. Indeed, recent years have seen some very large European mergers (see Box 9.5 on pages 269–71). This can lead to higher, not lower, prices and less choice for the consumer. It all depends on just how effective competition is, and how effective EU competition policy is in preventing monopolistic and collusive practices.

Trade diversion. Just as increased trade creation has been a potential advantage from completing the internal market, so trade diversion has been a possibility too. This is more likely if *external* barriers remain high (or are even increased) and internal barriers are *completely* abolished.

Is trade diversion more likely or less likely in the following cases: (a) European producers gain monopoly power in world trade; (b) modern developments in technology and communications reduce the differences in production costs associated with different locations; (c) the development of the internal market produces substantial economies of scale in many industries?

Perhaps the biggest objection raised against the single European market is a political one: the loss of national sovereignty. Governments find it much more difficult to intervene at a microeconomic level in their own economies. This was one of the key arguments in the debate over the Britain's future within Europe in the run-up to the EU referendum in 2016 (see section 24.5).

Why may the newer members of the Union have the most to gain from the single market, but also the most to lose?

Completing the internal market

Despite the reduction in barriers, the internal market is still not 'complete'. In other words, various barriers to trade between member states still remain. Thus, in June 1997, an Action Plan was adopted by the European Council. Its aim was to ensure that all barriers were dismantled by the launch of the euro in January 1999.

In 1997, what is now known as Single Market Scoreboard was established to monitor the progress in dismantling trade barriers. This is now published annually and shows progress towards the total abandonment of any forms of internal trade restrictions (see Case Study 24.11 on the student website). It shows the percentage of EU Single Market Directives still to be transposed into national law. To counteract new barriers, the EU periodically issues new Directives. If this process is more rapid than that of the transposition of existing Directives into national law, the transposition deficit increases.

In addition to giving each country's 'transposition deficit', the Scoreboard identifies the number of infringements of the internal market that have taken place. The hope is that the 'naming and shaming' of countries will encourage them to make more rapid progress towards totally free trade within the EU.

In 1997, the average transposition deficit of member countries was 6.3 per cent. By 1999, this had fallen to 3.5 per cent and since 2012 has been generally stable at between 0.5 and 0.7 per cent. The exception was in 2016 when the deficit doubled to 1.5 per cent. But this was largely due to an exceptional number of new directives waiting to be transposed. Subsequently, the transposition deficit returned to normal levels.

Despite this success, national governments have continued to introduce *new* technical standards, several of which have had the effect of erecting new barriers to trade. Also, infringements of single market rules by governments have not always been dealt with. The net result is that, although trade is much freer today than in the early 1990s, especially given the transparency of pricing with the euro, there still do exist various barriers, especially to the free movement of goods.

If there have been clear benefits from the single market programme, why do individual member governments still try to erect barriers, such as new technical standards?

The effect of the new member states

Given the very different nature of the economies of many of the new entrants to the EU, and their lower levels of GDP per head, their potential gain from membership has been substantial. The gains come through trade creation, increased competition, technological transfer and inward investment, both from other EU countries and from outside the EU.

KI 38 p778

A study in 2004 concluded that Poland's GDP would rise by 3.4 per cent and Hungary's by almost 7 per cent.[4] Real wages would rise, with those of unskilled workers rising faster than those of skilled workers, in accordance with these countries' comparative advantage. There would also be benefits for the existing 15 EU countries from increased trade and investment, as well as cheaper inputs, but these would be relatively minor in comparison to the gains to the new members.

A European Commission Report produced in April 2009, five years after the enlargement,[5] found that the expansion had been a win–win situation for both old and new members. There had been significant improvements in the standard of living in new member states and they had benefited from modernisation of their economies and more stabilised institutions and laws. In addition, enterprises in old member states had enjoyed opportunities for new investment and exports, and there had been an overall increase in trade and competition between the member states.

When Lithuania adopted the euro in 2015 the number of countries using the euro had reached 19. Hence, in future years, with the possibility of other member states adopting the euro, trade within the EU is likely to continue to grow as a proportion of GDP. We examine the benefits and costs of the single currency and the whole process of economic and monetary union in the EU in section 26.2.

4 M. Maliszewska, 'Benefits of the single market expansion for current and new member states', *Studia i Analizy*, Centrum Analiz Spoleczno – Ekonomicznych (2004).

5 'Five years of an enlarged EU – economic achievements and challenges', *European Economy 1 2009*, Commission of the European Communities.

Section summary

1. The European Union is a customs union in that it has common external tariffs and no internal ones. But virtually from the outset it has also had elements of a common market, particularly in the areas of agricultural policy, regional policy, monopoly and restrictive practice policy, and to some extent in the areas of tax harmonisation and social policy.
2. Nevertheless, there have been substantial non-tariff barriers to trade within the EU, such as different tax rates, various regulations over product quality, licensing, state procurement policies, educational qualification requirements, financial barriers, various regulations and norms, and subsidies or tax relief to domestic producers.
3. The Single European Act of 1987 sought to sweep away these restrictions and to establish a genuine free market within the EU: to establish a full common market. Benefits from completing the internal market have included trade creation, cost savings from no longer having to administer barriers, economies of scale for firms now able to operate on a Europe-wide scale, and greater competition leading to reduced costs and prices, greater flows of technical information and more innovation.
4. Critics of the single market point to various changes in industrial structure that have resulted, bringing problems of redundancies and closures. They also point to adverse

regional multiplier effects as resources are attracted to the geographical centre of the EU, to possible problems of market power with the development of giant 'Euro-firms', and to the possibilities of trade diversion.

5. The actual costs and benefits of EU membership to the various countries vary with their particular economic circumstances – for example, the extent to which they gain from trade creation, or lose from adverse regional multiplier effects – and with their contributions to and receipts from the EU budget.
6. These cost and benefits in the future will depend on just how completely the barriers to trade are removed, on the extent of monetary union and on any further enlargements to the Union.

24.5 THE UK AND BREXIT

On 23 June 2016, the UK held a referendum on whether to remain a member of the EU. By a majority of 51.9 per cent to 48.1 per cent of the 72.1 per cent of the electorate who voted, Britain voted to leave the EU.

Alternative trading arrangements

The focus then turned to the alternative trading arrangements that could be agreed by the UK and EU. Table 24.7 helps to understand the options.

One possibility was 'The Norwegian model', which would have seen the UK join the European Economic Area (EEA), giving it access to the single market, but removing regulation in some key areas, such as fisheries and home affairs. This option was ruled out in favour of a bilateral trade agreement. There were three main possible types:

- 'The Canadian model' where the UK would form a comprehensive trade agreement with the EU to lower customs tariffs and other barriers to trade.
- 'The Swiss model' where the UK would negotiate a series of bilateral agreements with the EU, including selective or general access to the single market.
- 'The Turkish model' where the UK would form a customs union with the EU. In Turkey's case the agreement relates principally to manufactured goods.

At time passed, it became clearer that the government's preference was for a comprehensive trade agreement. On 31 January 2020, after several delays, the UK left the EU. At this point the European Union Withdrawal Agreement Act 2020, which had received Royal Assent on 23 January 2020, came into force. There then followed a transition period up to 31 December 2020, during which the UK remained in the single market and the customs union, while negotiations on a trade agreement took place.

In February 2020 both sides published their mandates for the negotiations. The UK reaffirmed its preference for a comprehensive bilateral free-trade agreement along the lines of that agreed with Canada. Failing that, the UK would make a complete break from the EU and simply use its membership of the WTO to make trade agreements. Meanwhile, the EU's mandate set out its objective for a 'close as possible' partnership with the UK, while preserving the integrity of the single market and the customs union.

On 24 December 2020, EU and UK negotiators reached an agreement on the text of a new EU–UK Trade and Cooperation Agreement (TCA). This took effect on 1 January 2021, when the UK became a 'third country': a non-EU country, where its citizens no longer enjoyed the rights to free movement across EU member states.

Overview of the Trade and Cooperation Agreement (TCA)

The EU–UK Trade and Cooperation Agreement is a variant of the Canadian model by providing for zero tariffs and zero quotas on all goods. 'Quota free' means that trade will not be restricted in quantity by the authorities on either side. 'Tariff free' means that customs duties will not be collected by the UK authorities on imports from the EU nor by the EU authorities on imports from the UK. However, to ensure that it is EU and UK business that benefit from these 'trade preferences', businesses must show that their products fulfil *rules of origin* requirements.

Trade preferences and rules of origin

Under rules of origin requirements, when a good is imported into the UK from outside the EU and then has value added to it by processing, packaging, cleaning, remixing, preserving, refashioning, etc., it can only count as a UK good if sufficient value or weight is added. The proportions vary by product, but generally goods must have approximately 50 per cent UK content (or 80 per cent of the weight of foodstuffs) to qualify for tariff-free access to the EU. For example, in the case of a petrol car, 55 per cent of its value must have been created in either the EU or UK.

In other cases, it is simply the question of whether the processing is deemed 'sufficient', rather than the imported inputs having a specific weight or value. For example, in the case of many garments produced in the UK and then sold in retail chains, many of which have branches in both the UK and EU, generally both the weaving and cutting of fabric to make garments, as well as the sewing, must take place in the UK/EU for the garments to be tariff free when exported from the UK to the EU and *vice versa*.

Table 24.7 Alternative trading relationships with the EU

Trading arrangement		Tariffs	Customs union and external trade	Non-tariff barriers/other policy and regulatory issues
EU membership		Full tariff-free trade	Common external tariffs No customs costs Access to EU free-trade agreements (FTAs)	Alignment of regulations, standards and specifications Non-discriminatory access for markets for services
EEA (Norway)		Some tariffs on agriculture and fisheries	Custom costs apply No access to EU free-trade agreements (FTAs)	Limited coverage of agricultural and fisheries Compliance with most EU rules and standards, including free movement of people and social policy
Bilateral agreements	UK	Zero tariffs and zero quotas on all goods	Custom costs apply No access to EU free-trade agreements (FTAs)	No financial services passport or mutual recognition for service suppliers (e.g. of personal qualifications) Compliance with EU standards for UK exports to EU
	Canada	Some tariffs on agriculture Tariffs for transitional period on manufactured goods	Custom costs apply No access to EU free-trade agreements (FTAs)	No financial services passport Compliance with EU standards for firms importing into EU
	Switzerland	Some tariffs on agriculture	Custom costs apply No access to EU free-trade agreements (FTAs)	Minimises non-tariff barriers in areas covered by agreements Limited coverage of services No financial services passport Complies with EU rules in sector covered by agreements, including free movements of people and social policy
	Turkey	Tariff exemptions apply only to manufactured goods and processed agricultural goods	No custom costs for manufactured goods Aligns external trade policy with EU	No financial services passport No special access for services Adopts EU product standards Compliance with environmental standards linked to goods and to rules on competition and state aid
WTO membership		EU external tariffs apply	Custom costs apply No access to EU free trade agreements (FTAs)	No financial services passport Compliance with EU standards for firms importing into EU

Source: Adapted from *EU Referendum: HM Treasury analysis key facts*, HM Treasury (18 April 2016) (available at https://www.gov.uk/government/news/eu-referendum-treasury-analysis-key-facts)

Figure 24.15 UK trade in goods and services as a % of GDP

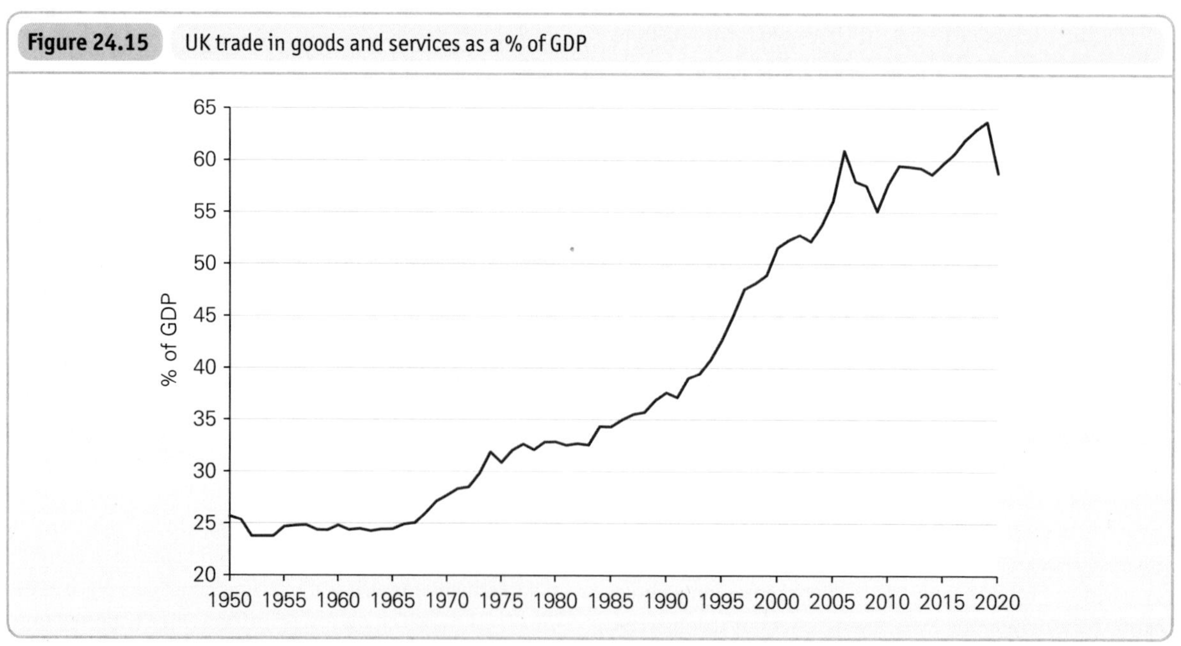

Note: Exports plus imports as a percentage of GDP.
Source: Based on data from ONS *Time Series Data*, series IKBK, IKBL, ABMI, www.ons.gov.uk/economy/grossdomesticproductgdp/timeseries/ikbk/ukea

Services

However, the TCA does not include free trade in services. The UK is a major exporter of services, including legal, financial, accounting, IT and engineering. It has a positive trade in services balance with the EU, unlike its negative trade in goods balance (see Box 25.2). Although some of the barriers which apply to other non-EU countries have been reduced for the UK in the TCA, UK service providers still face new barriers which impose costs. For example, some EU countries limit the time that businesspeople providing services can stay in their countries to six months in any twelve.

Mutual recognition for service providers no longer automatically applies. Therefore some EU countries will not recognise UK qualifications, unlike when the UK was a member of the single market. Authorities responsible for professional qualifications have had to submit recommendations to the EU–UK Partnership Council, which oversees the implementation of the TCA, for approval.

The financial services supplied by City of London firms are a major source of export revenue, with about 40 per cent of these revenues coming from the EU. Now outside the single market, these firms have lost their *passporting rights*. These allowed such firms to sell their services into the EU without the need for additional regulatory clearance.

The alternative now is for financial services firms to be granted 'equivalence' by the EU. A step in this process was the memorandum of understanding agreed by the EU and UK in 2021 that would create a joint regulatory forum overseeing regulatory co-operation. Nonetheless, equivalence would not cover the full range of financial services, excluding, for example, banking services such as lending and deposit taking.

VAT

Previously, goods could be imported into the UK from the rest of the EU without paying VAT in the UK on value added up to that point as VAT had already been collected in the EU. Similarly, goods exported from the UK to the rest of the EU would already have had VAT paid and hence would only be subject to the tax on additional value added. The UK was part of the EU VAT system and did not have to register for VAT in each EU country.

Now, VAT has to be paid on the goods as they are imported or released from a customs warehouse – similar to a customs duty. This is therefore likely to involve additional administration costs – the same as those with non-EU imports.

Ireland/Northern Ireland Protocol

The Protocol on Ireland and Northern Ireland means that Northern Ireland is subject to some EU rules related to the Single Market for goods and the Customs Union. The Protocol is intended to keep the land border between Northern Ireland and the Republic of Ireland open, while respecting the rules of the EU's internal market and customs union. This requires that checks and controls take place at 'Points of Entry on goods' entering Northern Ireland from the rest of the United Kingdom and that EU customs duties then apply to those goods deemed at risk of moving on to the EU.

Long-term growth, trade and Brexit

The effects of Brexit will take many years to become clear, including its impact on the UK's long-term rate of growth. In Chapter 23 we saw that long-term growth requires continuous increases in potential output. Therefore, a longer-term analysis of Brexit focuses on its impact on the economy's productive potential and crucially on labour productivity.

Much will depend on the UK's openness to world trade. Since the UK joined the EU in 1973 the openness of the UK economy has increased rapidly. Figure 24.15 shows the ratio of the total flow of imports and exports of goods and services to GDP since the 1950s. Over this period the ratio has risen from around 25 per cent to over 60 per cent.

Adverse effects of Brexit

In its 2016 analysis of the possible long-term implications of Brexit, the UK Treasury argued that the country's openness to trade and investment had been a key factor behind the growth in the economy's potential output.[6] Hence, maintaining this openness, it argued, would be important for long-term growth and so for raising living standards. Positive supply-side effects from openness might include:

- *Increasing market opportunities*. By serving wider markets, firms are able to exploit internal economies of scale (see pages 167–8 and 785) allowing them to reduce unit costs faster than non-exporting competitors.
- *Increasing competition*. Openness encourages firms to improve their productivity to maintain their market share and so encourages the adoption of new technologies and processes.
- *Knowledge transfer*. Openness enables the sharing and diffusion of knowledge. For example, technological know-how can be passed between firms in international supply chains, through internationally mobile workers or new international entrants. Openness increases access to foreign knowledge and exposure to alternative technologies, working practices and customer preferences.
- *Finance and investment*. The globalisation of finance and business provides greater access to credit and funding for investment, including through foreign direct investment (FDI).

The Treasury's analysis estimated the average impact of Brexit on households by modelling the adverse impacts on the supply side of the economy from lower levels of openness. To do so, it estimated the impact 15 years after leaving the EU of the three new types of trading arrangement shown in Table 24.7: Norway (EEA) model, Bilateral agreements, and WTO membership. It found that tax receipts would be lower, and that GDP would be between 3.4 per cent and 9.5 per cent lower, depending on the exact 'new deal'.

6 *EU Referendum: HM Treasury analysis key facts*, HM Treasury (18 April 2016), www.gov.uk/government/news/eu-referendum-treasury-analysis-key-facts

The Treasury estimated that with a Norwegian-type deal, households would be between £2400 and £2900 worse off each year at 2015 prices after 15 years. With a negotiated bilateral trade agreement they would be between £3200 and £5400 worse off, while no deal and reversion to WTO trading terms would create a household loss per annum of between £3700 and £6600 at 2015 prices.

The OECD suggested that Brexit would be like a tax, pushing up the costs and weakening the economy. Its analysis indicated that by 2030, GDP would be at least 5 per cent lower than it would otherwise have been, making households £3200 worse off (at 2016 prices). It continued that:

> In the longer term, structural impacts would take hold through the channels of capital, immigration and lower technical progress. In particular, labour productivity would be held back by a drop in foreign direct investment and a smaller pool of skills. The extent of forgone GDP would increase over time . . . The effects would be even larger in a more pessimistic scenario and remain negative even in the optimistic scenario.[7]

The OECD analysis points to the *structural change* the UK economy can expect to experience following its departure from the EU. The growth in openness experienced by the UK economy has occurred within the context of EU membership. Membership has influenced the patterns of trade and investment. It has provided the framework in which businesses have operated – for example, the development of supply chains across EU member countries. Structural changes accompanying Brexit, the OECD argues, will necessarily involve negative supply-side effects.

Can we incorporate trade effects into endogenous growth models?

Opportunities from Brexit

Despite the pessimistic forecasts from the vast majority of economists about the UK's departure from the EU, there was a group of eight economists in favour of Brexit.[8] They claimed that leaving the EU would lead to a stronger economy, with higher GDP, a faster growth in real wages, lower unemployment and a smaller gap between imports and exports. The main argument to support the claims was that the UK would be more able to pursue trade creation freed from various EU rules and regulations. In other words, there would be positive supply-side effects.

While disagreement about the impact on the UK's exit from the EU is to be expected, there is agreement that these effects will work primarily through their impact on the supply side of the economy.

However, perhaps less clear are the likely *distributional* effects of the UK's exit. Trade can impact on different sectors differently. Some expand; others decline. Consequently, a more complete analysis of Brexit, or of trading relationships more generally, must take account of distributional effects.

What particular sectors might a distributional analysis of the impact of trade consider?

7 *The Economic Consequences of Brexit: A Taxing Decision*, OECD (25 April 2016), www.oecd.org/economy/the-economic-consequences-of-brexit-a-taxing-decision.htm

8 Economists for Brexit (now Economists for Free Trade: www.economistsforfreetrade.com/)

Section summary

1. Following a referendum in June 2016 the UK voted to leave the European Union. On 31 January 2020, the UK left the EU, at which point the Withdrawal Agreement negotiated with the EU came into force. This allowed for a transition period up to the 31 December 2020, during which time the UK and EU entered into negotiations about their future relationship.
2. On 24 December 2020, EU and UK negotiators reached an agreement on a new EU–UK Trade and Cooperation Agreement (TCA). This provides for zero tariffs and zero quotas on all goods. However to benefit from these 'trade preferences', businesses must fulfil rules of origin requirements. The agreement does not include free trade in services, and financial institutions no longer have passporting rights to sell their services into the EU without the need for additional regulatory clearance.
3. Economic theory gives us a framework through which we can analyse the possible supply-side effects of Brexit and the EU–UK TCA and their implications for long-term growth and wellbeing.
4. Economists have overwhelmingly argued that the UK's decision to leave the EU will result in negative supply-side effects. Brexit, they argue, will impede cross-border trade with its EU partners and so reduce the UK's openness to trade and investment. This then adversely affects productivity growth and so living standards.
5. Some economists, however, have argued that outside of the EU the UK will be free of EU rules and regulations and able to create trade. The supply-side benefits will help to raise long-term growth and living standards.
6. Trade and the openness of economies have distributional effects. A more complete economic assessment of Brexit therefore requires that we consider such effects.

END OF CHAPTER QUESTIONS

1. Imagine that two countries, Richland and Poorland, can produce just two goods, computers and coal. Assume that for a given amount of land and capital, the output of these two products requires the following constant amounts of labour:

	Richland	Poorland
1 computer	2	4
100 tonnes of coal	4	5

Assume that each country has 20 million workers.

(a) Draw the production possibility curves for the two countries (on two separate diagrams).
(b) If there is no trade, and in each country 12 million workers produce computers and 8 million workers produce coal, how many computers and tonnes of coal will each country produce? What will be the total production of each product?
(c) What is the opportunity cost of a computer in (i) Richland; (ii) Poorland?
(d) What is the opportunity cost of 100 tonnes of coal in (i) Richland; (ii) Poorland?
(e) Which country has a comparative advantage in which product?
(f) Assuming that price equals marginal cost, which of the following would represent possible exchange ratios?
   (i) 1 computer for 40 tonnes of coal;
   (ii) 2 computers for 140 tonnes of coal;
   (iii) 1 computer for 100 tonnes of coal;
   (iv) 1 computer for 60 tonnes of coal;
   (v) 4 computers for 360 tonnes of coal.
(g) Assume that trade now takes place and that a computer exchanges for 65 tonnes of coal. Both countries specialise completely in the product in which they have a comparative advantage. How much does each country produce of its respective product?
(h) The country producing computers sells 6 million domestically. How many does it export to the other country?
(i) How much coal does the other country consume?
(j) Construct a table like Table 24.4 to show the no-trade and with-trade positions of each country.

2. If capital moves from developed to less developed countries, and labour moves from less developed to developed countries, what effects will these factor movements have on wage rates and the return on capital in the two types of country?
3. What factors determine a country's terms of trade?
4. Go through each of the arguments for restricting trade (both those of general validity and those having some validity for specific countries) and provide a counter-argument for not restricting trade.
5. If countries are so keen to reduce the barriers to trade, why do many countries frequently attempt to erect barriers?
6. What factors will determine whether a country's joining a customs union will lead to trade creation or trade diversion?
7. Why is it difficult to estimate the magnitude of the benefits of completing the internal market of the EU?
8. Look through the costs and benefits that we identified from the completion of the internal market. Do the same costs and benefits arise from the enlarged EU of 27 members?
9. Was a 'hard Brexit' (reverting to WTO rules and negotiating bilateral trade deals) necessarily an inferior alternative for the UK to remaining in the European single market or, at least, in the customs union?
10. What is meant by the concept of 'learning by exporting'?

Online resources

Additional case studies on the student website

24.1 David Ricardo and the law of comparative advantage. The original statement of the law of comparative advantage by David Ricardo back in 1817.

24.2 The Uruguay round. An examination of the negotiations that led to substantial cuts in trade barriers.

24.3 The World Trade Organization. This looks at the various opportunities and threats posed by this major international organisation.

24.4 The Battle of Seattle. This looks at the protests against the WTO at Seattle in November 1999 and considers the arguments for and against the free trade policies of the WTO.

24.5 Banana, banana. The dispute between the USA and the EU over banana imports.

24.6 Steel barriers. This examines the use of tariffs by the George W. Bush administration in 2002 to protect the ailing US steel industry.

24.7 Assessing NAFTA. Who are the winners and losers from NAFTA?

24.8 Strategic trade theory. The case of Airbus.

24.9 The social dimension of the EU. The principles of the social charter.

24.10 The benefits of the single market. Evidence of achievements and the Single Market Action Plan of 1997.

24.11 The Single Market Scoreboard. Keeping a tally on progress to a true single market.

(continued)

Websites relevant to this chapter

Numbers and sections refer to websites listed in the Web Appendix and hotlinked from this book's website at **www.go.pearson.com/uk/sloman.**

- For news articles relevant to this chapter, see the *Economics News* section on the student website.
- For general news on international trade, see websites in section A, and particularly A1–5, 7–9, 21, 23, 24, 25, 31. See also links to newspapers worldwide in A38, 39, 42, 43 and 44, and the news search feature in Google at A41.
- For international data on imports and exports, see site *H16 > Documents, data and resources > Statistics.* See also *World Economic Outlook* in B31. The ESDS International site (B35) has links to World Bank, IMF, OECD, UN and Eurostat datasets (but you will need to register, which is free to all UK higher education students).
- For UK data, see site B1 (site 1). See also B34. For EU data, see B38; see also B47 (Ameco online) sections 9–11.
- For discussion papers on trade, see H4 and 7.
- For trade disputes, see H16.
- For various pressure groups critical of the effects of free trade and globalisation, see H13, 14.
- For information on various preferential trading arrangements, see H20–23.
- For EU sites relating to trade, see G7, 8, 13, 20, 21, 22.
- For student resources relevant to this chapter, see sites C1–10, 19.

Chapter 25

The Balance of Payments and Exchange Rates

CHAPTER MAP

We live in a world in which events in one country or group of countries can have profound effects on other countries. Consider the late 2000s. Excessive sub-prime mortgage lending in the USA led to huge losses for many financial institutions. With such debt securitised into bonds held by financial institutions across the world, the credit crunch rapidly became global.

The COVID-19 pandemic of the early 2020s also illustrated how countries are interconnected in a multitude of ways. This global health emergency would have profound implications for the people of the world and saw significant economic policy interventions, some of which would have been previously hard to imagine.

As globalisation has increased, with trade and international financial movements having grown much more rapidly than countries' GDP, and, in general, having become much freer, so countries' vulnerability to balance of payments problems and exchange rate fluctuations has increased.

This chapter explores the relationships between a country's balance of payments and its exchange rate. We ask whether a country should allow its exchange rate to be determined entirely by market forces, with the possible instability that this brings, or whether it should attempt to fix its exchange rate to another currency, or at the very least attempt to reduce exchange rate fluctuations through central bank intervention in the foreign exchange market. We also consider the experience of countries in operating different types of exchange rate system.

25.1 ALTERNATIVE EXCHANGE RATE REGIMES

Policy objectives: internal and external

A country is likely to have various ***internal*** and ***external policy objectives***. *Internal* objectives include such things as economic growth and low rates of unemployment and inflation. *External* objectives include such things as avoiding current account balance of payments deficits, encouraging international trade and preventing excessive exchange rate fluctuations. Internal and external objectives may come into conflict, however.

KI 36 p459

A simple illustration of potential conflict is with the objectives of ***internal balance*** and ***external balance***.

Internal balance. This is where the economy is at the potential level of national income: i.e. where the output gap is zero (see Box 15.3 on page 467). This can be expressed in various ways, depending on the model of the economy and the policy objectives being pursued.

Thus, in the simple Keynesian model, internal balance is where the economy is at the *full-employment* level of national income: i.e. where Y_e (equilibrium national income) $= Y_f$ (full-employment national income) (see Chapter 17). In the monetarist and new classical models, it would be where the economy is on the vertical Phillips curve with stable inflation. In the context of inflation targeting, it would be where meeting the inflation target is consistent with achieving potential national income: i.e. where the *DAD* crosses the *DAS* curve at the targeted inflation rate (see Figure 20.7 on page 646).

If there is initially internal balance and then aggregate demand falls, in the short run output will fall below the potential level and disequilibrium unemployment will occur. Internal balance will be destroyed. The stickier wages and prices are, the longer it will take for internal balance to be restored.

External balance. This is the term for a *balance of payments* equilibrium. In the context of floating exchange rates, it is normally used in the narrow sense of a current account balance, and therefore also a capital plus financial account balance.

In the context of a fixed exchange rate, or an exchange rate target, it is often used more loosely to refer merely to a *total currency flow balance*. This is where the total demand and supply of the currency are equal at the targeted exchange rate with *no need for intervention from the reserves*: in other words, where any current account deficit is matched by a surplus on the other two accounts, and *vice versa*.

Conflicts between internal and external balance

It may, however, be difficult to achieve internal and external balance simultaneously. This is illustrated in Figure 25.1. Assume in Figure 25.1(b) that the exchange rate is er_1. Currency demand and supply curves are given by D and S_1 and there is no central bank intervention. Thus er_1 is the *equilibrium* exchange rate and there is external balance in the loose sense. Assume also that there is external balance in the narrow sense: i.e. a current account balance.

Let us also assume, however, that there is a recession. This is illustrated in Figure 25.1(a). Equilibrium national income is Y_{e_1}, where W_1 equals J_1. There is a deflationary gap: Y_{e_1} is below the full-employment level, Y_F. There is no *internal* balance.

Now assume that the government expands aggregate demand through fiscal policy in order to close the deflationary gap and restore internal balance. It raises injections to J_2 and reduces withdrawals to W_2. National income rises to Y_{e_2}. But this higher national income leads to an increased demand for imports. The supply of sterling will shift to S_2 in Figure 25.1(b). There is now a current account deficit, which destroys external balance in the narrow sense. If the government maintains the exchange rate at er_1 (by buying sterling from the reserves), external balance will be destroyed in the loose sense too.

External balance in the loose sense could be restored by allowing the exchange rate to depreciate to er_2, so that the demand and supply of sterling are equated at the new lower exchange rate.

But will this also correct the current account deficit and restore external balance in the narrow sense? It will go *some* way to correcting the deficit, as the lower exchange rate will make imports relatively more expensive and exports relatively cheaper. The amount that imports fall and exports rise will depend on their price elasticity of demand.

But there may also be an effect on the financial account. The higher aggregate demand will lead to a higher demand for money. This will drive up interest rates unless money supply is allowed to expand to offset the higher demand for money. If interest rates rise, this will lead to an inflow of finance (a financial account surplus). In Figure 25.1(b), the supply curve of sterling would shift to the left and the

Definitions

Internal policy objectives Objectives relating solely to the domestic economy.

External policy objectives Objectives relating to the economy's international economic relationships.

Internal balance Where the equilibrium level of national income is at the desired level.

External balance Narrow definition: where the current account of the balance of payments is in balance (and thus also the capital plus financial accounts). Loose definition: where there is a total currency flow balance at a given exchange rate.

Figure 25.1 Internal and external balance

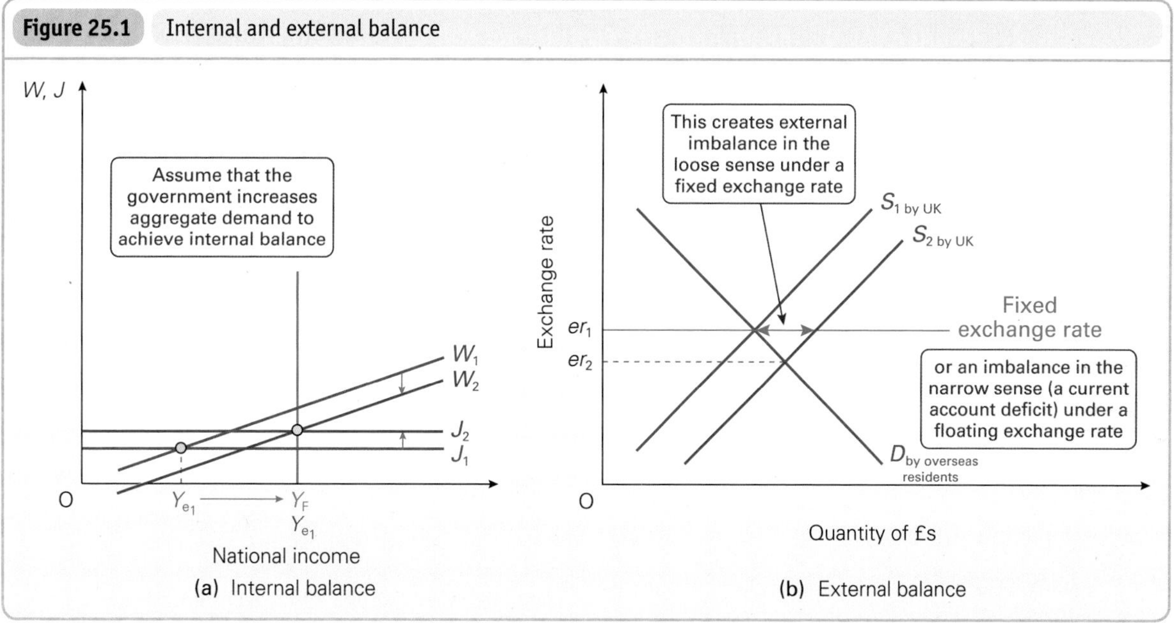

(a) Internal balance

(b) External balance

demand curve to the right. The exchange rate would not therefore fall as far as er_2. If the positive effect of higher interest rates on the financial account was bigger than the negative effect of higher imports on the current account, the exchange rate would actually *appreciate*.

Either way, there will be a current account deficit and an equal and opposite financial plus capital account surplus. Narrow external balance has not been restored in the short term. (We explore the long-term current account balance under floating exchange rates in section 25.3.)

Figure 25.2 shows the effect of various 'shocks' that can affect both internal and narrow external balance.

1. *Assume that there is both internal and narrow external balance. Now assume that as a result of inflation being below target, the central bank cuts interest rates. Into which of the four quadrants in Figure 25.2 will the economy move?*
2. *Imagine that there is an inflationary gap, but a current account equilibrium. Describe what will happen if the government raises interest rates in order to close the inflationary gap. Assume first that there is a fixed exchange rate; then assume that there is a floating exchange rate.*

The ability of the economy to correct these imbalances depends on the ***exchange rate regime***. We examine alternative exchange rate regimes in the final part of this section,

Definition

Exchange rate regime The system under which the government allows the exchange rate to be determined.

Figure 25.2 Effects on internal and (narrow) external balance

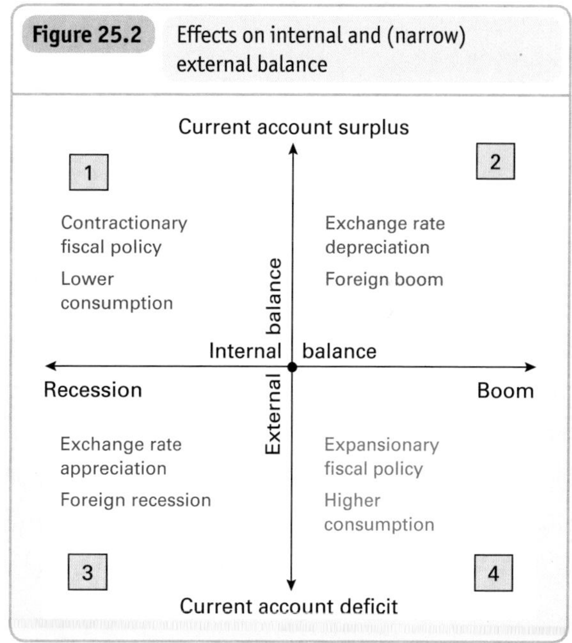

but first we must distinguish between nominal and real exchange rates.

Nominal and real exchange rates

A nominal exchange rate is simply the rate at which one currency exchanges for another. All exchange rates that you see quoted in the newspapers, on television or the Internet, or at travel agents, banks or airports, are nominal rates. Up to this point we have solely considered nominal rates.

TC 13 p461

BOX 25.1 THE BALANCE OF TRADE AND THE PUBLIC-SECTOR BUDGET BALANCE

EXPLORING ECONOMICS

A case of twin deficits?

We have seen that the external situation can affect the ability of an economy to achieve internal balance (where actual income is at the potential level). But it also impacts on the *composition* of aggregate demand. This is most readily demonstrated by observing the relationship between the *public sector's budget balance* and *the balance of trade*.

Consider the circular flow of income model that we introduced in Chapter 15. There we saw that actual (as opposed to planned) withdrawals from the circular flow (net saving (S) plus net taxes (T) plus imports (M)) must equal injections (investment (I) plus government expenditure (G) plus exports (X)):

$$S + T + M = I + G + X \quad (1)$$

The public sector's budget balance is simply the difference between its receipts (taxation and operating receipts, net of transfer expenditures) and its spending on goods and services, or $T - G$. The balance of trade is the difference between expenditure on exports and imports, or $X - M$. If we rearrange equation (1) slightly we find:

$$(T - G) = (X - M) + (I - S) \quad (2)$$

This tells us that if the public sector runs a budget surplus ($T - G$ is positive), there is a likelihood that the trade balance will be in surplus too. We can see from equation (2) that this will depend on the extent to which investment (I) and saving (S) differ from each other. In the case where investment and saving are equal, then a budget surplus would be exactly matched by a trade surplus, or a budget deficit by an identical trade deficit. The latter gives rise to the term 'the *twin deficits*'.

The chart plots the UK's public-sector budget balance as measured by public-sector net borrowing (see section 22.1) and its balance of trade. Each is presented as a percentage of GDP.

First, we see that from 1950 to 2020 the public sector typically ran a deficit with public-sector net borrowing averaging 2.8 per cent of GDP. Consequently, the public sector has been acting as a net injector of income. Second, we see that the balance of trade has more often than not been negative, with an average deficit of 0.8 per cent of GDP.

The size of the net withdrawal resulting from the trade deficit does not quite match the net injection from the public sector. This means that private-sector investment expenditure has been *less* than private saving ($I < S$). It also reinforces the arguments that we examined in Chapters 16 and 22 that public-sector deficits can reduce private investment. This, as we have seen, is known as *crowding out*. In the UK, public-sector borrowing has been financed partly through foreign borrowing from running a trade deficit and partly from the private saving that is not used for private investment.

If the exchange rate depreciated, how would this affect the trade and budget balances?

Using the IMF World Economic Outlook Database (www.imf.org/external/ns/cs.aspx?id=28), download for any other economy of your choice general government net lending/borrowing (per cent of GDP) and current account balance (per cent of GDP). Construct a line chart of the data, like the one in this Box, then briefly summarise your findings referring to whether they mirror those for the UK.

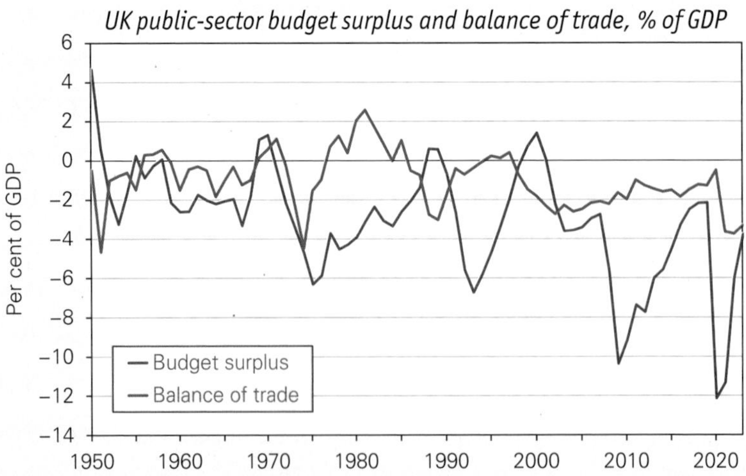

Source: Based on data from ONS, series J5II, KTMY and YBHA, www.ons.gov.uk/economy/; and forecasts for 2021–2023 from OBR Databank, https://obr.uk/efo/economic-and-fiscal-outlook-march-2021/

The ***real exchange rate*** is the exchange rate index adjusted for changes in the prices of imports (measured in foreign currencies) and exports (measured in domestic prices). Thus if a country has a higher rate of inflation for its exports than the weighted average inflation of the imports it buys from other countries, its real exchange rate index (RERI) will rise relative to its nominal exchange rate index (NERI).

The real exchange rate index can be defined as:

$$RERI = NERI \times P_X/P_M$$

where P_X is the domestic currency price index of exports and P_M is the foreign currencies weighted price index of imports. Thus if (a) a country's inflation is 5 per cent higher than the trade-weighted average of its trading partners (P_X/P_M rises by 5 per cent per year) and (b) its nominal exchange rate depreciates by 5 per cent per year (NERI falls by 5 per cent per year), its real exchange rate index will stay the same.

Take another example: if a country's export prices rise faster than the foreign currency prices of its imports (P_X/P_M rises), its real exchange rate will appreciate relative to its nominal exchange rate.

The real exchange rate thus gives us a better idea of the *quantity* of imports a country can obtain from selling a given quantity of exports. If the real exchange rate rises, the country can get more imports for a given volume of exports.

Definition

Real exchange rate A country's exchange rate adjusted for changes in the domestic currency prices of its exports relative to the foreign currency prices of its imports. If a country's prices rise (fall) relative to those of its trading partners, its real exchange rate will rise (fall) relative to the nominal exchange rate.

Figure 25.3 shows the nominal and real exchange rate indices of sterling. As you can see, the real exchange rate has tended to rise over time *relative* to the nominal exchange rate. This is because the UK has often experienced higher rates of inflation than the weighted average of its trading partners.

Table 25.1 shows that the size of the UK's *inflation rate differential* with the eurozone since the 1970s. During this period, the UK rate of inflation has typically been 1 percentage point higher than the weighted average of the eurozone economies.

Table 25.1 Inflation rate differential and annual rate of change in sterling exchange rate indices

	Inflation rate differential	Nominal exchange rate index	Real exchange rate index
1970–74	1.0	−3.2	−1.6
1975–79	5.8	−4.0	0.3
1980–84	0.1	−0.8	−0.8
1985–89	1.8	−1.3	−0.8
1990–94	0.7	−2.5	−1.5
1995–99	1.0	3.2	3.5
2000–04	−1.0	0.1	−0.6
2005–09	0.3	−4.5	−4.0
2010–14	0.6	1.5	2.7
2015–19	0.4	−2.1	−1.7
2020	−0.3	−0.9	−0.4
1970–2020	1.0	−1.4	−0.4

Note: Inflation rate differential is the difference between the annual % change in GDP deflator in the UK and the weighted average across the eurozone.
Source: Based on data from *Effective exchange rate indices*, Bank for International Settlements, www.bis.org/statistics/eer.htm; and series NY.GDP.DEFL.KD.ZG, World Bank, https://data.worldbank.org/indicator/NY.GDP.DEFL.KD.ZG

Figure 25.3 Sterling nominal and real exchange rate indices (Jan 1970 = 100)

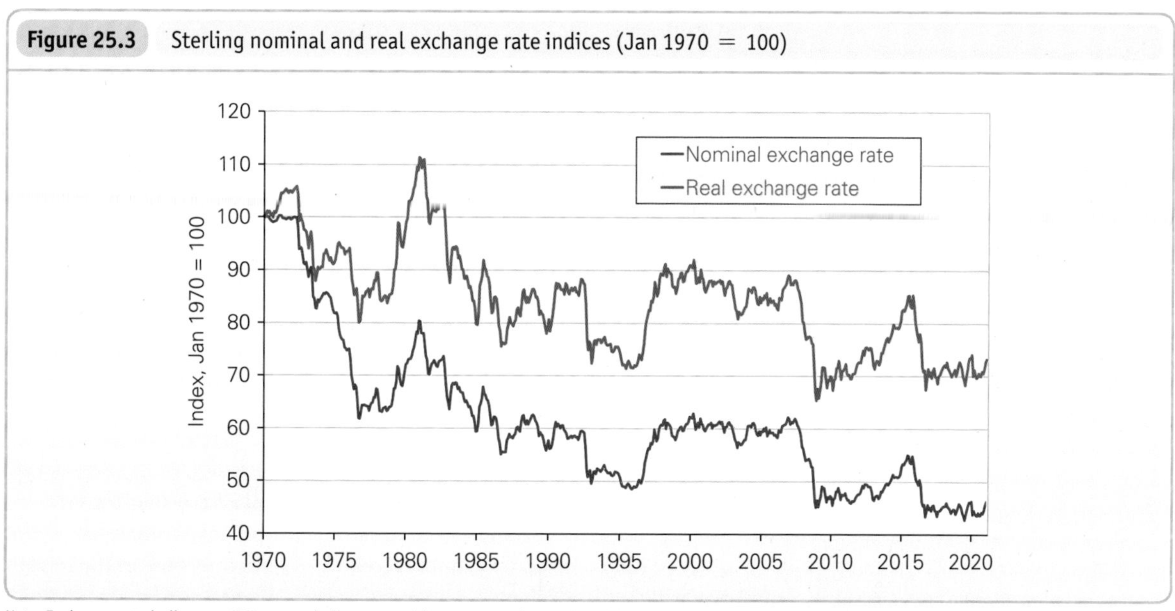

Note: Exchange rate indices are BIS narrow indices comprising 27 countries, re-based by the authors, Jan 1970 = 100.
Source: Based on data from *Effective exchange rate indices*, Bank for International Settlements, www.bis.org/statistics/eer.htm

BOX 25.2 **THE UK'S BALANCE OF PAYMENTS DEFICIT**

A cyclical problem or a long-term trend?

In the late 1980s, the UK current account balance of payments moved sharply into deficit, as the chart shows. In 1989, the current account deficit was 4.1 per cent of GDP – then a historic high. Opinions differed dramatically, however, as to how seriously we should have taken these figures. Not surprisingly, the government claimed that the problem was merely temporary and was not something to cause serious concern. The opposition parties (also not surprisingly) saw the figures as disastrous and a sign that the economy was badly off-course.

So who was correct? In fact there was an element of truth in both these claims.

The government was correct to the extent that the severity of the deficit partly reflected the unprecedented boom of the late 1980s. An average growth rate of real GDP of 4.5 per cent between 1985 and 1988 had led to a huge increase in imports. Since the boom could not be sustained, the growth in imports was bound to slow down. Another factor contributing to the deficit was the fall in oil revenues caused by a fall in oil prices. Oil exports fell from £16 billion in 1985 to £6 billion in 1989. Again, this fall in oil revenues was unlikely to continue once oil prices began to rise again.

The current account deficit was also a mirror image of the financial account surplus. This had been caused by a rise in interest rates, used to slow the economy down. As short-term finance flowed into the country to take advantage of the higher interest rate, so this drove the exchange rate up: the real exchange rate index rose by 4.25 per cent in 1988 (see Figure 25.3). The higher exchange rate contributed to the fall in exports and the rise in imports.

But the opposition parties were also correct. The severity of the deficit reflected an underlying weakness of the UK's trading position. If the deficit had been merely a cyclical problem associated with the boom phase of the business cycle, the current account should have gone into *surplus* in the early 1990s as the economy moved into recession. But even in the depths of the recession in 1991 (the economy shrank by over 1 per cent), the current account deficit was still 1.3 per cent of GDP.

The government, however, sought to place a large portion of the blame on a falling demand for exports as the rest of the world began to move into recession.

Subsequent events appeared to support the Conservative government's interpretation. The world economy was recovering in 1994 and the current account deficit virtually disappeared. But then, with a large appreciation of sterling from 1996, and an even larger appreciation of the real exchange rate (see Figure 25.3), the current account started to deteriorate again, as the diagram shows. Optimists claimed that this was, once more, simply a temporary situation, caused by a high exchange rate and low growth in demand in the eurozone.

By 2007, the current account deficit had reached 3.3 per cent of GDP. Optimists claimed that this was, once more, simply a temporary situation, caused by a high exchange rate and a relatively slower rate of growth in demand in the eurozone. Pessimists once more pointed to underlying supply-side weaknesses, with a deterioration in exports of goods not being matched by a rise in services exports.

With the financial crisis of 2007–8 and the subsequent recession hitting the UK economy particularly badly, the fall in confidence led to a depreciation in the exchange rate. Between October 2007 and October 2013 the sterling effective exchange rate fell in nominal terms by 20 per cent and in real terms by 13.5 per cent.

But this was not enough to prevent a further deterioration in the current account from 2011. Therefore when the *real* sterling effective exchange rate fell by 14 per cent between June and November 2016 following the Brexit vote there were fears that the lower exchange rates, if they persisted, would do little to improve the trade and current account deficits.

Table 25.1 also shows the average percentage change in the nominal and real sterling exchange rate indices since the 1970s. Over this period the nominal sterling exchange rate index has on average fallen by 1.4 per cent per year. However, after adjusting for the domestic price of exports and the foreign currency price of imports, the real sterling exchange rate index has fallen by 0.4 per cent per year. Hence, since 1970 the UK has experienced a small *real* depreciation of sterling.

By looking at the nominal and real exchange rate changes in Table 25.1 can we identify periods during which the UK's terms of trade rose?

The real exchange rate also gives a better idea than the nominal exchange rate of how competitive a country is. The lower the real exchange rate, the more competitive will the country's exports be. For example, Figure 25.3 shows that the UK became less competitive during the second half of the 1990s, and remained at similarly uncompetitive levels until 2008, thanks not only to a rise in the nominal exchange rate index, but also to higher inflation than its trading partners. Again, it became less competitive during the first part of the 2010s until the exchange rate fell following the Brexit referendum in 2016.

Alternative exchange rate regimes

There are a number of possible exchange rate regimes. They all lie somewhere between two extremes. These two extreme regimes are a ***totally fixed rate*** and a ***freely floating rate***.

In the case of a *fixed rate,* the government or central bank will almost certainly have to intervene in the foreign exchange market in order to maintain that rate, and will probably have to take internal policy measures too.

KI 15 p132

CASE STUDIES AND APPLICATIONS

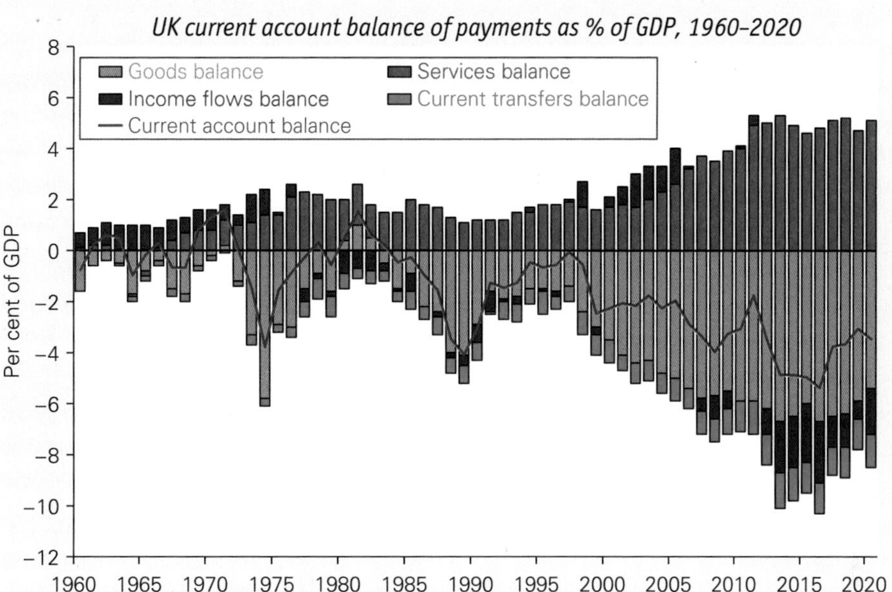

Source: Based on data from ONS series D28J, D28K, D28M, D28N and AA6H, www.ons.gov.uk/economy/nationalaccounts/balanceofpayments/

Pessimists again pointed to a much deeper malaise in the UK exporting sector and claimed that successive supply-side reforms had made too little difference.

The issue gained greater urgency with the UK's exit from the EU. British industry found itself operating in a new trading environment, including that with the EU, which was now governed by the Trade and Cooperation Agreement that came into effect from January 2021 (see section 24.6). Would this new environment enable or inhibit improvements to Britain's trading position?

1. *What options are open to UK exporters when faced with a high and rising value of sterling?*
2. *If the exchange rate depreciated, how would this affect the trade and budget balances?*

Look up data on the current account balances for two other major developed countries (G7 countries). Compare the fluctuations in the UK current account balances with your other two countries. Explain why the magnitude of the fluctuations (as a percentage of GDP) differs between the countries.

In the case of a *freely floating rate*, there is no government intervention in the foreign exchange market. Exchange rates fluctuate according to market forces – according to changes in the demand for and supply of currencies on the foreign exchange market. Changes in the exchange rate may well affect internal policy objectives, however, and thus cause the government to take various internal policy measures.

KI 5 p21

What adverse internal effects may follow from (a) a depreciation of the exchange rate; (b) an appreciation of the exchange rate?

Between these extremes there are a number of ***intermediate regimes***, where exchange rates are partly left to the market, but where the government intervenes to influence the rate. These intermediate regimes differ according to how much the government intervenes, and thus according to how much flexibility of the exchange rate it is prepared to allow.

Definitions

Totally fixed exchange rate Where the government takes whatever measures are necessary to maintain the exchange rate at some stated level.

Freely floating exchange rate Where the exchange rate is determined entirely by the forces of demand and supply in the foreign exchange market with no government intervention whatsoever.

Intermediate exchange rate regimes Where the government intervenes to influence movements in the exchange rate.

Correction under fixed exchange rates

Foreign exchange intervention

Unless the demand for and supply of the domestic currency on the foreign exchange markets are equal at the fixed rate – unless, in other words, there is a total currency flow balance – the central bank will have to intervene in the market and buy or sell the domestic currency to make up the difference. This is illustrated in Figure 25.4, which looks at the case of the UK.

Figure 25.4(a) shows the case of a currency flow deficit (an excess of pounds) of an amount *a* – *b*. The Bank of England thus has to purchase these excess pounds by drawing on its foreign exchange reserves, or by borrowing foreign currency from foreign banks.

In Figure 25.4(b), there is a currency flow surplus of *c* – *d*. In this case, the Bank of England has to supply *c* – *d* additional pounds to the market, and will acquire foreign currencies in exchange. It can use these to build up reserves or to pay back foreign loans.

Foreign exchange market intervention and the money supply. Maintaining a fixed exchange rate causes changes in the money supply. If the rate is maintained above the equilibrium (Figure 25.4(a)), there is a total currency flow deficit. The Bank of England buys pounds. It thereby withdraws them from circulation and reduces the money supply.

The effect of this reduction in money supply is to raise the equilibrium rate of interest. This attracts financial inflows and improves the financial account. It also dampens aggregate demand, and thus reduces imports and improves the current account. The net effect is to reduce the overall -currency flow deficit and thus reduce the gap *a* – *b* in Figure 25.4(a).

TC 15 p543

The problem here, of course, is that the lower aggregate demand may well result in a recession.

If the rate is maintained *below* equilibrium (Figure 25.4(b)), there is a total currency flow surplus. The Bank of England supplies additional pounds (which are spent by people abroad on UK exports, etc., and are thus injected into the UK economy). It thereby increases the money supply.

The effect of the increased money supply is to reduce interest rates. This worsens the financial account and, by boosting aggregate demand, increases imports. The currency flow surplus is reduced. The gap *d* – *c* narrows.

Sterilisation. If the Bank of England did not want the money supply to alter, it would have to counter these effects with other monetary measures: e.g. open-market operations. Thus when there is a deficit and money supply falls, the Bank of England could buy back government bonds from the general public, thereby restoring the money supply to its previous level. This will prevent the economy moving into recession.

This process of countering the effects on money supply of a balance of payments deficit or surplus is known as ***sterilisation***.

Describe the open-market operations necessary to sterilise the monetary effects of a balance of payments surplus. Would this in turn have any effect on the current or financial accounts of the balance of payments?

There is a problem with sterilisation, however. If the money supply is not allowed to change, the currency flow deficit or surplus will persist. In the case of a deficit, a recession may be avoided, but the central bank will have to continue using reserves to support the exchange rate. But reserves are not infinite. Sooner or later they will run out! A recession may be inevitable.

Correcting the disequilibrium

If a balance of payments deficit persists, and reserves continue to dwindle or foreign debts mount, the government will have to tackle the underlying disequilibrium. If the exchange rate

Definition

Sterilisation Where the government uses open-market operations or other monetary measures to neutralise the effects of balance of payments deficits or surpluses on the money supply.

Figure 25.4 Central bank intervention to maintain a fixed exchange rate

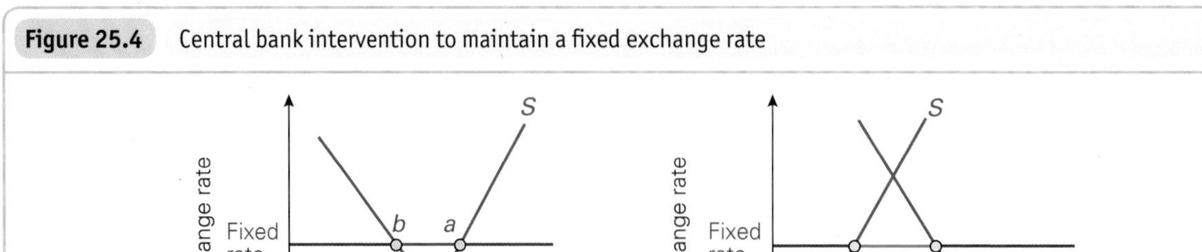

(a) Total currency flow deficit

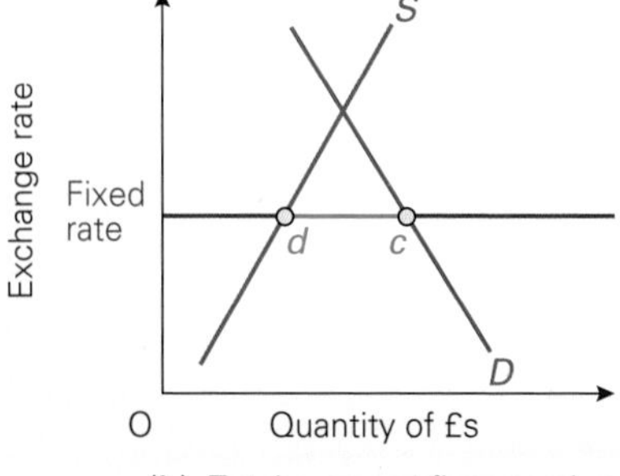

(b) Total currency flow surplus

is to remain fixed, it must shift the demand and supply curves so that they intersect at the fixed exchange rate.

It can use contractionary fiscal and monetary policies for this purpose. Such policies have two main effects on the current account: an income effect (***expenditure reducing***) and a substitution effect between home and foreign goods (***expenditure switching***).

KI 7 p36

Expenditure reducing. Contractionary policy reduces national income. This in turn reduces expenditure, including expenditure on imports, shifting the supply of sterling curve to the left in Figure 25.4(a). The bigger the marginal propensity to import, the larger the shift.

There is a possible conflict here, however, between external and internal objectives. The balance of payments may improve, but unemployment is likely to rise and the rate of growth to fall.

KI 36 p459

Under what circumstances would (a) contractionary and (b) expansionary policies cause no conflict between internal and external objectives?

Expenditure switching. If contractionary policies reduce the rate of inflation below that of foreign competitors, exports will become relatively cheaper compared with foreign competing goods and imports will become relatively more expensive compared with home-produced alternatives. Some foreign consumers will switch to UK exports. The more elastic the demand, the bigger the switch. Some UK consumers will switch from imports to home-produced goods. Again, the more elastic the demand, the bigger the switch. Demand in both cases will be more elastic the closer UK goods are as substitutes for foreign goods.

TC 6 p66

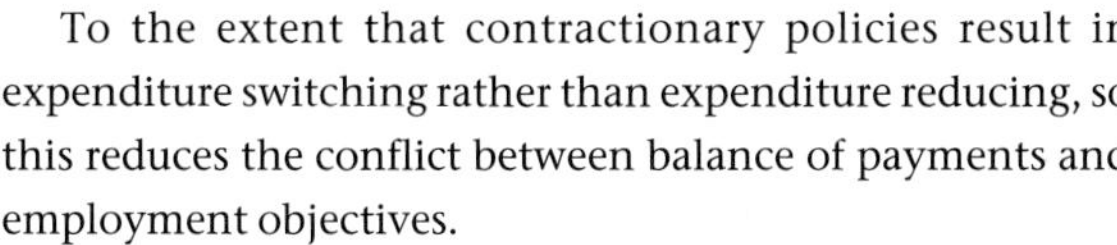

To the extent that contractionary policies result in expenditure switching rather than expenditure reducing, so this reduces the conflict between balance of payments and employment objectives.

Expenditure switching can also be achieved by placing restrictions on imports (tariffs and/or quotas) or the subsidising of exports. But this would conflict with the objective of free trade.

To the extent that fiscal and monetary policies affect interest rates, so this will affect the financial account of the balance of payments. Higher interest rates will increase the demand for sterling and will thus lead to an improvement on the financial account. (The implications of this are explored in section 25.2.)

Correction under free-floating exchange rates

Freely floating exchange rates should automatically and immediately correct any balance of payments deficit or surplus: by depreciation and appreciation, respectively. Foreign exchange dealers simply adjust the exchange rate so as to balance their books – in line with demand and supply.

KI 5 p21

As with fixed rates, an income effect and a substitution effect of the correction process can be distinguished. But the nature of the income and substitution effects of depreciation/appreciation is quite different from that of deflation. It is only the substitution effect that corrects the disequilibrium. The income effect makes the problem *worse*! First the substitution effect: ***expenditure switching***.

Figure 25.5 Adjustment of the exchange rate to a shift in demand and supply

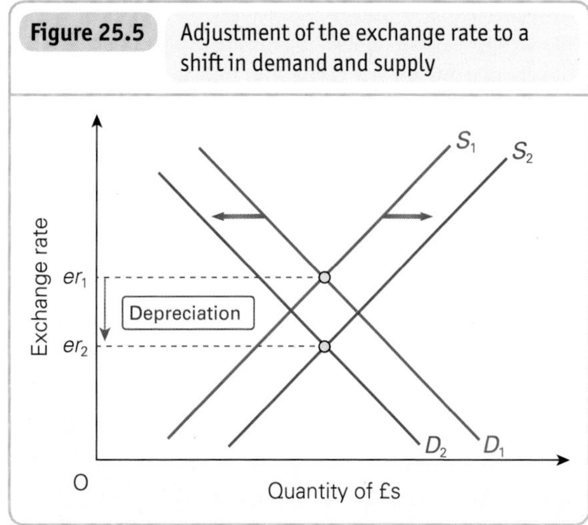

Expenditure switching (the substitution effect)

The process of adjustment. Assume a higher rate of inflation in the UK than abroad. As domestic prices rise relative to the price of imports, more imports will be purchased. The supply of pounds curve will shift to the right (to S_2 in Figure 25.5). UK exports will now be relatively more expensive for foreigners. Less will be sold. The demand for pounds curve will shift to the left (to D_2).

KI 7 p36

Foreign exchange dealers will now find themselves with a glut of unsold pounds. They will therefore lower the exchange rate (to er_2 in Figure 25.5). The amount that the exchange rate has to change depends on:

- The amount that the curves shift. Thus large differences in international inflation rates or large differences in international interest rates will cause large shifts in the demand for and supply of currencies, and hence large movements in exchange rates.

Definitions

Expenditure changing (reducing) from a contraction: the income effect Where contractionary policies lead to a reduction in national income and hence a reduction in the demand for imports.

Expenditure switching from a contraction: the substitution effect Where contractionary policies lead to a reduction in inflation and thus cause a switch in expenditure away from imports and towards exports.

Expenditure switching from depreciation: the substitution effect Where a lower exchange rate reduces the price of exports and increases the price of imports. This will increase the sale of exports and reduce the sale of imports.

- The elasticity of the curves. The less elastic the demand and supply curves of sterling, the greater the change in the exchange rate for any given shift in demand and supply.

But what determines the elasticity of the demand and supply curves? This is examined in Case Study 25.1 on the student website.

Expenditure changing (the income effect)

KI 7 p36

Depreciation, as well as affecting relative prices, will affect national income. This will cause ***expenditure changing***.

We have already established that, as the exchange rate falls, so more exports will be sold and less imports purchased: this was the substitution effect. But this is only an initial effect.

Exports are an injection into, and imports a withdrawal from, the circular flow of income. There will thus be a multiplied rise in national income. This income effect (expenditure *increasing*) reduces the effectiveness of the depreciation. Two situations can be examined.

A rise in national income and employment, but no change in prices. Assume that there are substantial unemployed resources, so that an increase in aggregate demand will raise output and employment but not prices. As national income rises, so imports rise (thereby tending to offset the initial fall), but exports are unaffected.

This is illustrated by the line $(X–M)_1$ in Figure 25.6. At low levels of national income, spending on imports is low; thus exports (X) exceed imports (M). $X–M$ is positive. As national income and hence imports rise, $X–M$ falls, and after a point becomes negative. Thus the $X–M$ line is downward sloping.

Assume an initial equilibrium national income at Y_1, where national income (Y) equals national expenditure (E_1), but with imports exceeding exports by an amount $a - b$. The exchange rate thus depreciates.

Figure 25.6 The income effect (stable prices)

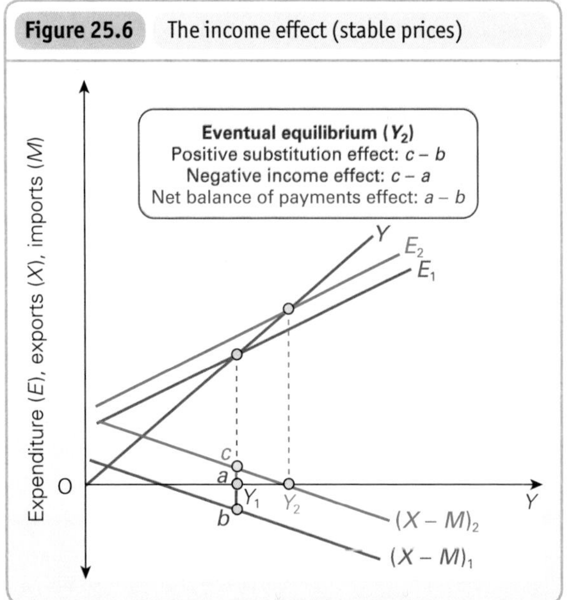

This will cause a substitution effect: exports rise and imports fall. The $X–M$ line therefore shifts upwards. But this in turn causes an income effect. Aggregate demand rises, and the E line shifts upwards.

An eventual internal and external equilibrium is reached at Y_2, where $Y = E_2$ and $(X–M)_2 = 0$.

The positive substitution effect of this depreciation is $c - b$. The negative income effect is $c - a$. The net effect is thus only $a - b$, which is the size of the initial deficit. Had it not been for this negative income effect, a smaller depreciation would have been needed.

At least in this case, the income effect is having a desirable *internal* consequence: reducing unemployment.

A rise in prices. If the economy is near full employment, the rise in aggregate demand from depreciation will make that depreciation even less effective. Not only will the higher demand lead directly to more imports, but it will also lead to higher inflation. There will thus be an adverse substitution effect too. This will partially offset the beneficial substitution effect of the depreciation. The higher inflation will have the effect of shifting the $X–M$ line back down again somewhat.

In the extreme case, where money supply expands to accommodate the rise in aggregate demand, $X–M$ may simply return to its original position. The depreciation will fail to correct the balance of payments disequilibrium. In Figure 25.5, the fall in the exchange rate to er_2 will simply lead to a further rightward shift in supply and a leftward shift in demand, until the gap between them is the same as it was at er_1.

To offset the income effect, a government may feel it necessary to back up a currency depreciation with deflationary demand management policies.

Intermediate exchange rate regimes

There are a number of possible intermediate systems between the two extremes of totally fixed and completely free-floating exchange rates.

Adjustable peg. The ***adjustable peg*** system is towards the fixed end of the spectrum. Exchange rates are fixed (or 'pegged') for a period of time – perhaps several years.

Definitions

Expenditure changing (increasing) from depreciation: the income effect Where depreciation, via the substitution effect, will alter the demand for imports and exports, and this, via the multiplier, will affect the level of national income and hence the demand for imports.

Adjustable peg A system whereby exchange rates are fixed for a period of time, but may be devalued (or revalued) if a deficit (or surplus) becomes substantial.

In the short and medium term, therefore, correction is the same as with a totally fixed system. Central banks have to intervene in the foreign exchange market to maintain the rate. If a deficit persists, then deflationary or other policies must be adopted to *shift* the currency demand and supply curves. This will be a problem, however, if there already exist substantial unemployed resources.

In the long term, if a fundamental disequilibrium occurs, the currency can be repegged at a lower or higher rate. Adjusting the peg downwards is known as ***devaluation***. Adjusting it upwards is known as ***revaluation***.

Alternatively, more frequent smaller adjustments could be made, thus moving the system away from the fixed end of the spectrum.

Managed floating. The ***managed floating*** system is towards the free-floating end of the spectrum. Exchange rates are not pegged: they are allowed to float. But the central bank intervenes from time to time to prevent excessive exchange rate fluctuations. It is thus a form of 'managed flexibility'.

Under such a system, the central bank does not seek to maintain a long-term or even medium-term disequilibrium rate. Rather it tries to allow an 'orderly' exchange rate -adjustment to major changes in demand and supply, while preventing the violent short-term swings that can occur with a totally free float (swings arising from currency speculation).

To back up the central bank's use of reserves, it may also alter interest rates to prevent exchange rate fluctuations. If, for example, there were a large-scale selling of the domestic currency, the central bank could raise interest rates to counter this effect and prevent the exchange rate from falling.

How would raising interest rates in this way affect the balance between the current and financial accounts of the balance of payments?

The degree of currency stability sought, and hence the degree of intervention required, will vary from country to country and from government to government. At one extreme, the government may intervene only if exchange rate fluctuations become very severe; at the other extreme, the government may try to maintain the exchange rate at some unofficial target level.

Crawling peg. The ***crawling peg*** system is midway between managed floating and the adjustable peg system. Instead of making large and infrequent devaluations (or revaluations), the government adjusts the peg by small amounts, but frequently – say, once a month, as the equilibrium exchange rate changes.

Joint float. Under a ***joint float*** a group of countries have a fixed or adjustable peg system between their own currencies, but jointly float against all other currencies.

Exchange rate band. With an ***exchange rate band*** the government sets a lower and an upper limit to the exchange rate: say, £ = \$1.60 and £1 = \$1.80. It then allows the exchange rate to fluctuate freely within these limits. It will intervene, however, if the rate hits the floor or the ceiling. Exchange rate bands could be narrow (say ± 1 per cent) or wide (say ± 15 per cent).

Exchange rate bands can be incorporated in other - systems – the band could be adjustable, crawling or fixed. For example, Figure 25.7 illustrates a crawling peg system with an exchange rate band.

The exchange rate mechanism (ERM) of the European Monetary System (EMS), which pre-dated the euro, was an example of a joint float against non-member currencies and an adjustably pegged exchange rate band with member currencies (see section 26.2). The ERM II system for Bulgaria, Croatia and Denmark (and potentially for other members of the EU in preparation to join the euro) is similar.

All these intermediate systems are attempts to achieve as many as possible of the advantages of both fixed and flexible exchange rates, with as few as possible of the attendant disadvantages. To assess any of these compromise systems, therefore, we must examine the advantages and disadvantages of fixed and flexible exchange rates. We do this in the next two sections.

Definitions

Devaluation Where the government repegs the exchange rate at a lower level.

Revaluation Where the government repegs the exchange rate at a higher level.

Managed floating A system of flexible exchange rates, but where the government intervenes to prevent excessive fluctuations or even to achieve an unofficial target exchange rate.

Crawling peg A system whereby the government allows a gradual adjustment of the exchange rate.

Joint float Where a group of currencies pegged to each other jointly float against other currencies.

Exchange rate band Where a currency is allowed to float between an upper and lower exchange rate, but is not allowed to move outside this band.

Figure 25.7 The crawling peg within exchange rate bands

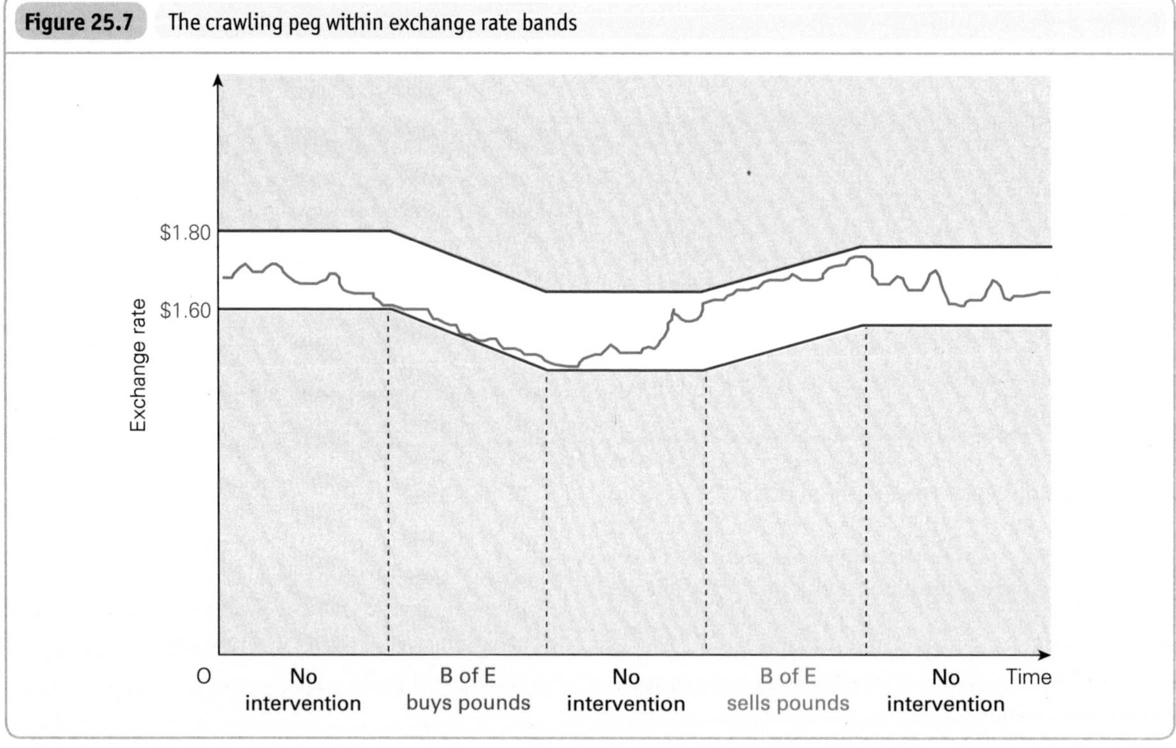

Section summary

1. There may be a conflict in achieving both internal and external balance simultaneously. The nature of the conflict depends on the exchange rate regime that the country adopts.
2. Nominal exchange rates are simply the rates at which one currency exchanges for another. Real exchange rates take account of differences in inflation rates between import and export prices and are a measure of the competitiveness of a country's exports.
3. Under a fixed exchange rate system, the government will have to intervene whenever the equilibrium exchange rate ceases to coincide with the fixed rate. If the equilibrium rate falls below the fixed rate, the government will have to buy in the domestic currency on the foreign exchange market. This will have the effect of reducing the money supply. Likewise, selling the domestic currency in order to prevent an appreciation will increase money supply. The government can prevent these changes in money supply by the use of appropriate open-market operations or other monetary measures. This is known as 'sterilisation'. Sterilisation, however, means that the disequilibrium is likely to go uncorrected.
4. If a deficit (or surplus) persists under a fixed rate, the government can attempt to shift the currency demand and supply curves. To cure a deficit, it can use contractionary fiscal or monetary policies. These have two effects. Deflation leads to a fall in national income (the income effect) and hence a fall in the demand for imports. It also leads to a fall in inflation and hence a switch in demand from foreign goods to home-produced goods (the substitution effect).
5. Correction under free-floating exchange rates also involves an income and a substitution effect. If there is a deficit, the exchange rate will depreciate. This will make imports more expensive and exports cheaper, and hence there will be a substitution effect as imports fall and exports rise.
6. The income effect of a depreciation, however, reduces its effectiveness. The rise in exports and fall in imports (i.e. the substitution effect of a depreciation) will lead to a multiplied rise in national income, which will cause imports to rise back again somewhat. The bigger this income effect, the bigger will be the depreciation necessary to achieve equilibrium in the foreign exchange market. Correction is made more difficult if any depreciation leads to increases in domestic prices and hence to a second substitution effect – only this time an adverse one.
7. There are intermediate exchange rate regimes between the extremes of fixed rates and free-floating rates. The exchange rate may be fixed for a period of time (the adjustable peg); or it may be allowed to change gradually (the crawling peg); or the government may merely intervene to dampen exchange rate fluctuations (managed floating); or the exchange rate may be allowed to fluctuate within a band, where the band in turn may be fixed, adjustable or crawling.

25.2 FIXED EXCHANGE RATES

In this section we examine the causes of balance of payments problems under fixed nominal exchange rates, in both the short run and the long run. First, in an optional section, we look at short-run causes and whether balance will be restored. We then look at longer-run, more fundamental causes of balance of payments problems. Finally, we assess the desirability of fixed exchange rates.

*Effects of shocks under fixed exchange rates

Under fixed exchange rates, it is unlikely that internal and external balance can persist for long without government intervention. Various macroeconomic 'shocks', such as changes in injections or withdrawals, or changes in international interest rates, are constantly occurring. These are likely to destroy either internal or external balance or both. Even with government intervention, it may still be very difficult, if not impossible, to restore both balances. Correction of balance of payments disequilibria will come into conflict with the other macroeconomic goals of growth, full employment and stable prices.

How the economy responds to shocks under fixed exchange rates, and which policy measures are most effective in dealing with the resultant disequilibria, depend on two things: (a) whether the shocks are internal or external; (b) the flexibility of wages and prices, which, in turn, depends on the time period under consideration.

Response to an internal shock

Let us assume that there is a fall in aggregate demand, caused by a fall in consumer demand or investment, or by a rise in saving.

Short-run effect. In the short run, prices and especially wages tend to be relatively inflexible (this is a central assumption of Keynesian analysis). The fall in aggregate demand will lead to a recession. Internal balance will be destroyed. In a closed economy, the central bank would probably reduce interest rates to boost the economy, either to tackle the recession directly or because forecast inflation had fallen below its target level.

In an open economy under fixed exchange rates, however, this is not possible. But why?

The lower aggregate demand will lead to a fall in imports, resulting in a *current account* surplus. There is an opposite effect on the *financial account,* however. The reduced aggregate demand will lead to a fall in the demand for money and hence downward pressure on interest rates. If interest rates were allowed to fall, there would be a resulting financial outflow and hence a financial account deficit.

But which would be the larger effect: the current account surplus or the financial account deficit? This depends on the marginal propensity to import (*mpm*) and the mobility of international finance. The higher the *mpm,* the bigger the current account surplus. The higher the international mobility of finance, the bigger the financial outflow and hence the bigger the financial account deficit. In today's world of massive financial flows across the foreign exchanges, international finance is highly, if not perfectly, mobile. If the central bank allows interest rates to fall, the financial account deficit will therefore exceed the current account surplus.

To prevent this happening, interest rates must not be allowed to fall or, at least, must fall only very slightly – just enough for the resulting financial account deficit to match the current account surplus. With hardly any fall in interest rates, money supply must thus be allowed to contract to match the fall in the demand for money.

Thus to maintain the fixed exchange rate (without massively draining reserves) interest rates will be determined by the balance of payments. They cannot be used for domestic purposes, such as targeting inflation, targeting real national income or some combination (e.g. a Taylor rule: see pages 683–6). Internal imbalance will persist in the short run.

Long-run effect. In the long run, there will be much greater, if not perfect, price and wage flexibility. Under new classical assumptions, such flexibility will exist in the short run too. This flexibility will ensure that internal balance is restored. The Phillips curve is vertical at the natural rate of unemployment.

But, with a fixed exchange rate, will it also ensure external balance? Again, let us assume that people decide to spend less and save more. As in the short run, this will lead to a *current account* surplus. This time, however, the effect is much bigger. In the short run, there was little or no price effect (i.e. no substitution effect) since there was little change in inflation. There was only an income effect from reduced imports caused by the recession. In the long run, however, the lower real aggregate demand reduces inflation. Assuming that inflation falls below that of trading partners, the *real* exchange rate falls. This makes exports relatively cheaper and imports relatively more expensive. This causes exports to rise and imports to fall.

The resulting rise in aggregate demand not only helps to eliminate the recession, but also helps to reduce the current account surplus.

Thus, despite a fixed *nominal* exchange rate, wage and price flexibility cause the *real* exchange rate to be flexible. This helps restore overall external balance. Nevertheless, a current account surplus may persist. Indeed, as the surplus is used to buy foreign assets, so, over time, these will yield an income, further crediting the current account.

But what is clear is that, although interest rates are determined by the need to maintain a fixed nominal exchange rate, wage and price flexibility in the long run will eventually restore internal balance. The question is, how long will the long run be? How long will the recession persist? If it is too long, and if interest rates cannot be cut, then can expansionary fiscal policy be used? We examine this in Box 25.3.

Response to an external shock

Assume now that there is a fall in demand for exports.

Short-run effect. The fall in exports causes the current account to go into deficit. It also reduces aggregate demand, causing a multiplied fall in national income. This reduces the demand for imports: the larger the *mpm*, the bigger the reduction in imports. Aggregate demand will go on falling until the lower injections are matched by lower withdrawals. But the current account deficit will not be eliminated, since the fall in withdrawals to match the fall in exports consists only partly of lower imports; part will consist of lower saving and lower tax receipts.

TC 15 p543

The reduction in aggregate demand reduces the transactions demand for money, putting downward pressure on interest rates. This would result in a financial outflow and hence a *financial account* deficit, making the overall currency flow deficit worse. To prevent this happening, the central bank must prevent interest rates from falling by reducing the money supply (through open-market operations). Indeed, given the current account deficit, interest rates may have to be slightly higher than they were originally in order to create a financial account surplus sufficient to offset the current account deficit. This will make the recession worse.

Long-run effect. The reduction in aggregate demand will put downward pressure on domestic inflation. This will help to reduce the real exchange rate and hence correct the current account deficit. It will also restore internal balance. Again, however, without fiscal policy, the long run may be some time in coming. The recession may persist.

Trace through the short-run and long-run internal and external effects (under a fixed exchange rate) of (a) a fall in domestic saving; (b) a rise in the demand for exports.

BOX 25.3 THE EFFECTIVENESS OF FISCAL AND MONETARY POLICIES UNDER FIXED EXCHANGE RATES

EXPLORING ECONOMICS

Monetary policy

Monetary policy is not very effective under fixed exchange rates.

Assume that the central bank, worried by rising inflation, wishes to reduce the growth in nominal aggregate demand. It thus reduces the rate of growth in money supply. This drives up interest rates and causes a fall in real national income.

What effect will this have on the balance of payments? The lower national income reduces expenditure on imports and hence leads to a surplus on the current account. Also, the higher interest rates encourage an inflow of finance and hence a surplus on the financial account too. This balance of payments surplus will *increase* money supply again and reduce interest rates back towards the original level. Aggregate demand will rise back towards its original level. Monetary policy has been ineffective.

But rather than changing the *supply* of money, can the government not directly alter interest rates? The problem here is that, in order to maintain the rate of exchange at the fixed level, the government's room for manoeuvre is very limited. For example, if it raises interest rates, the resulting inflow of finance will cause a balance of payments surplus. The government could, for a period of time, simply build up reserves, but it may not want to do this indefinitely.

The problem is more serious if the economy is in recession and the central bank wants to increase aggregate demand by *reducing* interest rates. The financial outflow will force the central bank to buy in the domestic currency by using its reserves. But it can do this for only so long. Eventually, it will be forced to raise interest rates again in order to stem the drain on the reserves. In today's world, with little in the way of exchange controls and with massive amounts of short-term international liquidity, such flows can be enormous. This gives the central bank virtually no discretion over changing interest rates. Interest rates will have to be kept at a level so as to maintain the exchange rate. In the case of *perfect* mobility of international finance, interest rates must be kept at world rates. Monetary policy will be totally ineffective.

Fiscal policy

Fiscal policy is much more effective.

Assume that there is a recession and the government wishes to increase aggregate demand. It thus cuts taxes and/or raises government expenditure. This raises national income and increases expenditure on imports. Also, higher inflation raises the real exchange rate. This makes exports less competitive and imports relatively cheaper. The current account moves into deficit.

The increase in aggregate demand will raise the demand for money and hence put upward pressure on interest rates. This will lead to an inflow of finance and a financial account surplus. To prevent this swamping the current account deficit, the central bank must prevent interest rates from rising very much. In the case of an infinitely elastic supply of finance, interest rates must not be allowed to rise at all.

Thus money supply must be allowed to expand to keep interest rates down. This expansion of the money supply thus reinforces the expansionary fiscal policy and prevents crowding out.

Thus a high level of international financial mobility enhances the effectiveness of fiscal policy.

Suppose that under a managed floating system the central bank is worried about high inflation and wants to keep the exchange rate up in order to prevent import prices rising. To tackle the problem of inflation, it raises interest rates. What will happen to the current and financial accounts of the balance of payments?

Causes of longer-term balance of payments problems under fixed exchange rates

With moderately flexible prices, current account balance may eventually be restored after 'one-off' shocks. However, long-term continuing shifts in the demand and supply of imports and exports can make balance of payments problems persist. We will examine four causes of these long-term shifts.

Different rates of inflation between countries. If a country has persistently higher rates of inflation than the countries with which it trades, it will have a growing current account deficit. Exports and import substitutes will become less and less competitive as its real exchange rate appreciates.

Different rates of growth between countries. If a country grows faster than the countries with which it trades, its imports will tend to grow faster than its exports.

Income elasticity of demand for imports higher than for exports. If the income elasticity of demand for imports is relatively high, and the income elasticity of demand for exports is relatively low, then as world incomes grow, the country's imports will grow faster than its exports. This has been a particular problem for many developing countries: they import manufactured goods and capital equipment, whose demand grows rapidly, and export primary products – food and raw materials – whose demand, until recent years, has grown relatively slowly (see section 26.4).

Long-term structural changes

- Trading blocs may emerge, putting up tariff barriers to other countries. Australian and New Zealand exports were adversely affected when the UK joined the EEC.
- Countries may exercise monopoly power to a greater extent than previously. The OPEC oil price increases of 1973/4 and 1978/9 are examples.
- Countries may develop import substitutes. Thus plastics and other synthetics have in many cases substituted for rubber and metals, worsening the balance of payments of traditional primary exporters.
- The nature and quality of a country's products may change. Thus Japan has shifted from producing low-quality simple manufactured goods in the 1950s to producing high-quality sophisticated manufactured goods today. This helped increase its exports.

To maintain a fixed exchange rate under such circumstances, governments have to take measures to correct the disequilibria. They can use demand-side policies (fiscal and monetary: see Box 25.3), supply-side policies or protectionist policies.

Advantages of fixed exchange rates

Many economists are opposed to fixed exchange rates, for reasons to be examined shortly. Nevertheless, many businesspeople are in favour of relatively rigid exchange rates. The following arguments are used.

Certainty. With fixed exchange rates, international trade and investment become much less risky, since profits are not affected by movements in the exchange rate.

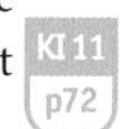

Little or no speculation. Provided the rate is absolutely fixed – and people believe that it will remain so – there is no point in speculating. For example, between 1999 and 2001, when the old currencies of the eurozone countries were still used, but were totally fixed to the euro, there was no speculation that the German mark, say, would change in value against the French franc or the Dutch guilder.

When the UK joined the ERM in 1990, it was hoped that this would make speculation pointless. As it turned out, speculation forced the UK to leave the ERM in 1992. Can you reconcile this with the argument that fixed rates discourage speculation?

Automatic correction of monetary errors. If the central bank allows the money supply to expand too fast, the resulting extra demand and lower interest rates will lead to a balance of payments deficit. This will force the central bank to intervene to support the exchange rate. Either it must buy the domestic currency on the foreign exchange market, thereby causing money supply to fall again (unless it sterilises the effect), or it must raise interest rates. Either way this will have the effect of correcting the error.

Preventing governments pursuing 'irresponsible' macroeconomic policies. If a government deliberately and excessively expands aggregate demand – perhaps in an attempt to gain short-term popularity with the electorate – the resulting balance of payments deficit will force it to constrain demand again (unless it resorts to import controls).

Disadvantages of fixed exchange rates

The new classical view

New classicists make two crucial criticisms of fixed rates.

Fixed exchange rates make monetary policy ineffective. Interest rates must be used to ensure that the overall balance of payments balances. As a result, money supply must be allowed to vary with the demand for money in order to keep interest rates at the necessary level. Thus monetary policy cannot be used for domestic purposes (see Box 25.3). Inflation depends on world rates, which may be high and domestically unacceptable. If the central bank tries to reduce inflation by attempting to reduce money supply and raise interest rates, the current and financial accounts will go into surplus. Money supply will thus increase until domestic inflation rises back to world levels.

Fixed rates contradict the objective of having free markets. Why fix the exchange rate, when a simple depreciation or appreciation can correct a disequilibrium? In the new classical world where markets clear, and supply and demand are relatively elastic, why not treat the foreign exchange market like any other, and simply leave it to supply and demand?

The Keynesian view

In the Keynesian world, wages and prices are relatively 'sticky', and demand-deficient unemployment and cost-push inflation may persist. As such, there is no guarantee of achieving both internal and external balance simultaneously when exchange rates are fixed. This leads to the following problems.

KI 34 p453

Balance of payments deficits can lead to a recession. A balance of payments deficit can occur even if there is no excess demand. As we saw above, this could be caused by different rates of growth or different rates of inflation from trading partners, a higher income elasticity of demand for imports than for exports, and so on. If protectionism is to be avoided, and if supply-side policies work only over the long run, the government will be forced to reduce the rate of growth of aggregate demand. This will lead to higher unemployment and possibly a recession.

If wages and prices are sticky downwards, the contraction may have to be severe if a significant improvement in the *current* account is to be made. Here, reliance would have to be placed largely on lower *incomes* reducing the demand for imports. If the deflation is achieved through higher interest rates, however, an improvement on the *financial* account may remove the need for a severe deflation, especially given the high degree of financial mobility that exists nowadays. Nevertheless, the rate of interest may still be higher than that desired for purely internal purposes.

If a country has a *persistent* current account deficit, it may need to have persistently higher interest rates than its competitors and suffer persistently lower growth rates as a result. It will also tend to build up short-term debts, as money is put on deposit in the country to take advantage of the higher interest rates. This can make the problem of speculation much more acute if people come to believe that the fixed rate cannot be maintained (see below).

TC 15 p543

Competitive deflations leading to world depression. If deficit countries deflated, but surplus countries reflated, there would be no overall world deflation or reflation. Countries may be quite happy, however, to run a balance of payments surplus and build up reserves. Countries may thus competitively deflate – all trying to achieve a balance of payments surplus. But this is beggar-my-neighbour policy. Not all countries can have a surplus! Overall, the world must be in balance. Such policies lead to general world deflation and a restriction in growth.

Problems of international liquidity. If trade is to expand, there must be an expansion in the supply of currencies acceptable for world trade (dollars, euros, gold, etc.): there must be adequate ***international liquidity***. Countries' reserves of these currencies must grow if they are to be sufficient to maintain a fixed rate at times of balance of payments disequilibrium. Conversely, there must not be excessive international liquidity. Otherwise the extra demand that would result would lead to world inflation. It is important under fixed exchange rates, therefore, to avoid too much or too little international liquidity.

The problem is how to maintain adequate control of international liquidity. The supply of dollars, for example, depends largely on US policy, which may be dominated by the US internal economic situation rather than by any concern for the well-being of the international community. Similarly, the supply of euros depends on the policy of the European Central Bank, which is governed by the internal situation in the eurozone countries.

Why will excessive international liquidity lead to international inflation?

Speculation. If speculators believe that a fixed rate simply cannot be maintained, speculation is likely to be massive. If there is a huge deficit, there is no chance whatsoever of a revaluation. Either the rate will be devalued or it will remain the same. Speculators will thus sell the domestic currency. After all, it is a pretty good gamble: heads they win (devaluation); tails they do not lose (no devaluation). This speculative selling will worsen the deficit, and may itself force the devaluation. Speculation of this sort had disastrous effects on some South East Asian currencies in 1997 (see Case Study 25.3 on the student website) and on the Argentinean peso in 2002 (see Case Study 26.10).

To what extent do Keynesians and new classicists agree about the role of fixed exchange rates?

Postscript

An argument used in favour of fixed rates is that they prevent governments from pursuing inflationary policies. But if getting inflation down is desirable, why do governments not pursue an anti-inflationary policy directly? Today, many governments make inflation targeting the goal of monetary policy and many do so by delegating monetary policy to the central bank to enhance the credibility of inflation targeting. Most, however, have floating exchange rates.

Definition

International liquidity The supply of currencies in the world acceptable for financing international trade and investment.

Section summary

*1. Macroeconomic shocks are constantly occurring. Whether internal and external balance will be restored under a fixed exchange rate, following a shock, depends on price and wage flexibility and on the time period.

*2. In the short run there is a degree of wage and price inflexibility. If there is a fall in aggregate demand, the resulting fall in national income will reduce the demand for imports. This will cause a current account surplus. The fall in aggregate demand will also reduce the demand for money and put downward pressure on interest rates. This will cause a financial account deficit. This effect can be large, given the high mobility of international finance. Interest rates are thus constrained by the need for the financial account to balance the current account.

*3. In the long run, with wage and price flexibility, the real exchange rate can change. This will help to restore both internal and external balance.

4. Over the longer term, balance of payments disequilibria under fixed exchange rates can arise from different rates of inflation and growth between countries, different income elasticities of demand for imports and exports, and long-term structural changes.

5. Under fixed exchange rates, monetary policy will not be very effective, but fiscal policy will be much more effective.

6. Fixed exchange rates bring the advantage of certainty for the business community, which encourages trade and foreign investment. They also help to prevent governments from pursuing irresponsible macroeconomic policies.

7. Both new classical and Keynesian economists, however, see important disadvantages in fixed exchange rates. New classical economists argue that they make monetary policy totally ineffective, and that they run counter to the efficiency objective of having free markets. Keynesians argue that fixed rates can lead to serious internal imbalance with perhaps a persistent recession; that with competitive deflations a recession can be worldwide; that there may be problems of excessive or insufficient international liquidity; and that speculation could be very severe if people came to believe that a fixed rate was about to break down.

25.3 FREE-FLOATING EXCHANGE RATES

Floating exchange rates and the freeing of domestic policy

With a freely floating exchange rate there can be no overall balance of payments disequilibrium. Foreign exchange dealers will constantly adjust the exchange rate to balance their books, so that the demand for and supply of any currency are equal.

TC 4 p45

This, therefore, removes the balance of payments constraint on domestic policy that exists under a fixed exchange rate. No reserves are required since there is no central bank intervention to support the exchange rate. The government would seem free to pursue whatever domestic policy it likes. Any resulting effects on the balance of payments are simply and automatically corrected by a depreciation or appreciation of the exchange rate.

In reality, however, things are not quite so simple. Even under a totally free-floating exchange rate, some constraints on domestic policy may be imposed by the effects of these exchange rate movements. For example, a depreciation of the exchange rate increases the price of imports. If the demand for imports is relatively inelastic, this may lead to a higher rate of inflation.

Response to shocks under a floating exchange rate

Internal shocks

Let us assume that there is a rise in aggregate demand that causes inflation. For the moment, however, let us also assume that monetary policy maintains real interest rates at international levels. For simplicity, let us assume that there is no inflation abroad. How will a floating exchange rate system cope with this internal shock of a rise in aggregate demand? The exchange rate will simply depreciate to maintain the competitiveness of exports and import substitutes.

For example, assume an initial exchange rate of £1 = $2. A UK product costing $2 in the USA will earn £1 for the UK exporter. If UK inflation now causes prices to double, the exchange rate will roughly halve. If it falls to £1 = $1, then the same product costing $2 in the USA will now earn £2 for the UK exporter, which in *real* terms is the same amount as before. This is the ***purchasing-power parity theory***. This states that domestic price changes will be offset by (nominal) exchange rate changes, thereby maintaining the same relative prices between countries as before.

If this is the case, need firms worry about losing competitiveness in world markets if domestic inflation is higher than world inflation?

Definition

Purchasing-power parity theory The theory that the exchange rate will adjust so as to offset differences in countries' inflation rates, with the result that the same quantity of internationally traded goods can be bought at home as abroad with a given amount of the domestic currency.

BOX 25.4 THE PRICE OF A BIG MAC

The Economist's guide to purchasing-power parity rates

At least once a year *The Economist* publishes its 'Big Mac index'. It is a light-hearted attempt to see if currencies are exchanging at their purchasing-power parity (PPP) rates. The test is the price at which a 'Big Mac' McDonald's hamburger sells in different countries! According to this simplified version of the purchasing-power parity theory, exchange rates should adjust so that a Big Mac costs the same in dollars everywhere.

If a Big Mac is taken as representative of all goods and services, then in January 2021, with a Big Mac selling for $5.66 in the USA, but only the equivalent of $1.81 in Russia, this implies that the Russian rouble was undervalued by 68 per cent.

In China a Big Mac cost 22.4 yuan. With an exchange rate of 6.45 yuan to the dollar this means that the equivalent dollar price was $3.46. This implies that the yuan was undervalued by 39 per cent. it was not the only Asian currency to be undervalued in Big Mac PPP terms. The Malaysian ringgit and the Indonesian rupiah, for instance, were also substantially undervalued. In Malaysia, a Big Mac cost 9.99 ringgits, while in Indonesia it cost 34 000 rupiah. With, at the time, exchange rates of 4.052 ringgits and 14 125 rupiahs to the dollar, this meant that in Malaysia a Big Mac cost $2.47, while in Indonesia it cost $2.41. This implied that the Malaysian ringgit was undervalued in Big Mac PPP terms by 56 per cent, while the Indonesian rupiah was undervalued by 57 per cent.

In India, the nearest product is a 'Maharajah Mac', which uses chicken rather than beef. Given that the meat accounts for less than 10 per cent of a burger's cost, it is a fair approximation to use this rather than a Big Mac. In January 2021 with a price of $2.59 at the dollar–rupee exchange rate, this implied that the rupee was undervalued by 54 per cent.

While Asia was often found to be the cheapest place to eat a burger, Europe tended to be more expensive. The most expensive was Switzerland, with the Swiss franc estimated to be 29 per cent overvalued. At the prevailing exchange rate of 0.89 Swiss francs to the dollar, a Big Mac in Switzerland cost the equivalent of $7.29. For a Big Mac to cost the same in

The hamburger standard, January 2021

Country	Big Mac price in dollars at current exchange rate	Under (−) or over (+) valuation against the dollar (%)
Russia	1.81	−68.0
Turkey	2.01	−64.5
South Africa	2.16	−61.9
Indonesia	2.41	−57.5
Malaysia	2.47	−56.4
Romania	2.47	−56.4
India	2.59	−54.3
Hong Kong	2.64	−53.3
Mexico	2.68	−52.6
Egypt	2.72	−52.0
Vietnam	2.86	−49.4
China	3.46	−38.9
Poland	3.51	−37.9
Saudi Arabia	3.73	−34.1
Japan	3.74	−33.9
Argentina	3.75	−33.8
Brazil	3.98	−29.7
South Korea	4.10	−27.5
Thailand	4.25	−24.9
Singapore	4.43	−21.7
UK	4.44	−21.6
New Zealand	4.87	−13.9
Denmark	4.90	−13.4
Australia	4.98	−11.9
Euro area[a]	5.16	−8.8
Canada	5.29	−6.6
USA[b]	5.66	0.0
Norway	6.09	7.5
Sweden	6.37	12.6
Switzerland	7.29	28.8

[a] Weighted average of member countries.
[b] Average of New York, Chicago, San Francisco and Atlanta.

If we now drop the assumption that real interest rates are maintained at the same level as abroad, the purchasing-power parity theory will break down. Let us assume that the rise in aggregate demand causes a rise in UK real interest rates. This could be either the effect of the higher demand for money pushing up interest rates, or a deliberate act of the central bank to bring the inflation rate back down to the target level.

There are now two effects on the exchange rate. The higher aggregate demand and higher inflation rate will cause the current account to move into deficit, thereby putting downward pressure on the exchange rate. The higher real interest rates, however, will cause the financial account to move into surplus as depositors choose to hold their money in pounds. This will put upward pressure on the exchange rate. Whether the exchange rate actually falls or rises depends on which of the two effects is the bigger. In today's world of huge international financial flows, the effect on the financial account is likely to be the larger one: the exchange rate will thus *appreciate*. The greater the interest elasticity of supply of such flows, the greater the appreciation.

TC 6 p66

But either way, because of the financial account effect, the new equilibrium exchange rate will be above the purchasing-power parity rate. This will adversely affect export industries, since the exchange rate has not fallen sufficiently (if at all) to compensate for their higher sterling price. It will also adversely affect domestic industries that compete with imports, since again the exchange rate has not fallen sufficiently to retain their competitiveness with imports. The current account thus remains in deficit, matched by an equal and opposite financial plus capital account surplus.

This is a position that has often characterised the UK. As we saw in Table 25.1, the rate of inflation has frequently been above that of major trading partners, while the current account has been persistently in deficit (see Box 25.2) and the capital plus financial account persistently in surplus (see Figure 15.15 on page 490).

CASE STUDIES AND APPLICATIONS

Switzerland as in America, the exchange rate would have had to be 1.15 francs to the dollar.

Across the euro area a Big Mac in January 2021 cost on average €4.25. With an exchange rate of €1 = $1.22, the euro area Big Mac cost $5.16, implying an undervaluation of the euro of 9 per cent.

So what of the UK? A Big Mac in January 2021 cost an average of £3.29. At the exchange rate at the time of £1 = $1.35, this meant a Big Mac cost $4.44 in the UK. This implies an *undervaluation* of 22 per cent. Yet, as recently as July 2014 the Big Mac index was indicating an overvaluation of sterling, albeit a small overvaluation of 3 per cent. The change, in part, reflects a Brexit effect: concerns around the UK's future trading relationships and the expectation that long-term growth could be adversely affected (see section 24.5).

International patterns

Generally, richer, developed countries' currencies seem to be overvalued and poorer ones' undervalued. The explanation lies in differences in local costs, such as rents and wages. These are higher in rich countries. According to David Parsley, of Vanderbilt University, and Shang-Jin Wei, of the International Monetary Fund, non-traded inputs, such as labour, rent and electricity, account for between 55 and 64 per cent of the price of a Big Mac.[1]

With lower rents and wages, you would expect average prices to be cheaper in poor countries than in rich ones because labour costs are lower. This is the basis of the so-called 'Balassa-Samuelson effect'. Rich countries have much higher productivity and hence higher wages in the traded-goods sector than poor countries do. Because firms compete for workers, this also pushes up wages in non-tradable goods and services, where rich countries' productivity advantage is smaller.[2]

A Big Mac index is now also produced adjusting for GDP per capita. In January 2021, it still suggested that the Russian rouble, Malaysian ringgit, Indonesian rupiah and Indian rupee were undervalued, but now by only 47, 28, 23 and 15 per cent, respectively. On the other hand, the Chinese yuan and the euro, which were found to be undervalued by 39 and 9 per cent in the unadjusted index, were now overvalued in the index adjusted for GDP per capita by 3 and 13 per cent respectively. While this adjustment may capture some of the differences between countries, such as in labour costs, it cannot capture differences attributable to transportation costs, or to consumer tastes which affect the amount consumers are willing to pay.

Also, exchange rates can diverge from their PPP values because of factors influencing the *financial account* of the balance of payments: factors such as actual and expected interest rate differentials, investment prospects and speculation about exchange rate movements.

Nevertheless, despite the limitation of the original Big Mac index, it does give some indication of whether a currency is above or below its long-term equilibrium rate.

1. ***If the Chinese yuan is undervalued by 39 per cent in PPP terms against the US dollar and the Swiss franc overvalued by 29 per cent, what implications does this have for the interpretation of Chinese, Swiss and US GDP statistics?***
2. ***Why do developing countries' currencies tend to be undervalued relative to those of developed countries (see table)?***
3. ***At the time the table was compiled, the Big Mac PPP rate for the Norwegian krone was $1 = kr9.19. What was the market exchange rate?***

1 David C. Parsley and Shang-Jin Wei, 'A prism into the PPP puzzles: the microfoundations of Big Mac real exchange rates', *NBER Working Paper No. 10074*, National Bureau of Economic Research (November 2003), www.nber.org/papers/w10074

2 *The Economist*, 30 July 2011.

The positive inflation rate differential between the UK and its major trading partners (see Table 25.1) has often meant higher UK interest rates. This was the case following the delegation of monetary policy to the Bank of England in 1997 with its remit to meet an inflation rate target. The resulting interest rate differential contributed to an appreciating real exchange rate in the late 1990s, which remained persistently high up to the onset of the financial crisis (see Figure 25.3).

The carry trade. The problem for current account deficit countries has often been made worse by the ***carry trade***, especially in the period running up to the financial crisis. This involves international investors taking advantage of nominal interest rate differences between countries.

Prior to the financial crisis of 2008, current account deficit countries, such as the UK, Australia and New Zealand, typically had relatively high interest rates, while current account surplus countries such as Japan and Switzerland had relatively low ones. It was thus profitable to borrow, say, yen at the low interest rate that obtained in Japan, exchange it into sterling and deposit the money at the higher interest rate available in the UK. If there was no change in the exchange rate between the pound and the yen, the investor made a profit equal to the difference in the interest rates.

Definition

Carry trade Borrowing at low interest rates and then using it to buy assets that earn higher rates. In foreign exchange markets, the carry trade involves borrowing money in a currency of a country where interest rates are low and exchanging it for another currency where the country pays higher interest rates.

BOX 25.5 THE EURO/DOLLAR SEESAW

Ups and downs in the currency market

For periods of time, world currency markets can be quite peaceful, with only modest changes in exchange rates. But with the ability to move vast sums of money very rapidly from one part of the world to another and from one currency to another, speculators can suddenly turn this relatively peaceful world into one of extreme turmoil – a turmoil that can be very damaging for business.

In this box we examine the huge swings of the euro against the dollar since the euro's launch in 1999.

First the down . . .

On 1 January 1999, the euro was launched and exchanged for $1.16. By October 2000, the euro had fallen to $0.85. The main cause of this 27 per cent depreciation was the growing fear that inflationary pressures were increasing in the USA and that, therefore, the Federal Reserve Bank would have to raise interest rates. At the same time, the eurozone economy was growing only slowly and inflation was well below the 2 per cent ceiling set by the ECB. There was thus pressure on the ECB to cut interest rates.

The speculators were not wrong. As the diagram shows, US interest rates rose, and ECB interest rates initially fell, and when eventually they did rise (in October 1999), the gap between US and ECB interest rates soon widened again.

In addition to the differences in interest rates, a lack of confidence in the recovery of the eurozone economy and a continuing confidence in the US economy encouraged investment to flow to the USA. This inflow of finance (and lack of inflow to the eurozone) further pushed up the dollar relative to the euro.

The low value of the euro meant a high value of the pound and other currencies relative to the euro. This made it very difficult for companies outside of the eurozone to export to eurozone countries and also for those competing with imports from the eurozone (which had been made cheaper by the fall in the euro).

In October 2000, with the euro trading at around 85¢, the ECB plus the US Federal Reserve Bank (America's central bank), the Bank of England and the Japanese central bank all intervened on the foreign exchange market to buy euros. This arrested the fall and helped to restore confidence in the euro.

. . . Then the up

The position completely changed in 2001. With the US economy slowing rapidly and fears of an impending recession, the Federal Reserve Bank reduced interest rates 11 times during the year: from 6.5 per cent at the beginning of the year to 1.75 per cent at the end (see the chart). Although the ECB also cut interest rates, the cuts were relatively modest: from 4.75 at the beginning of the year to 3.25 at the end. With eurozone interest rates now considerably above US rates, the euro began to rise.

Fluctuations between the euro and the dollar

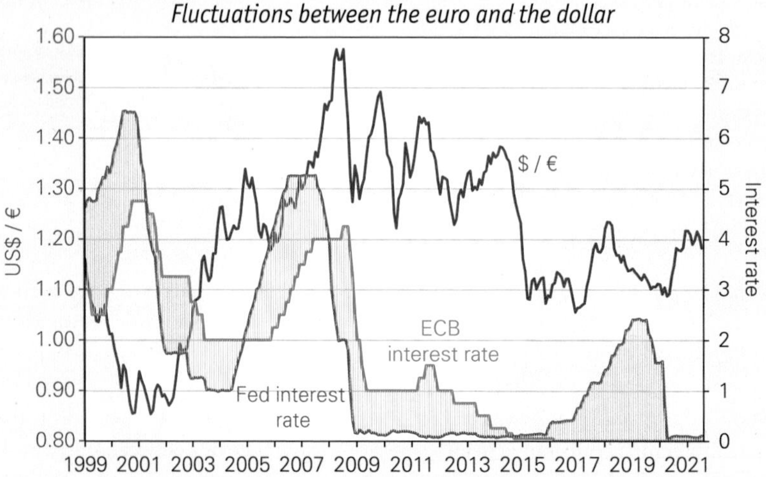

Notes: Federal reserve rate is the federal funds effective rate; ECB interest rate is the main refinancing operations rate.

Sources: $/€ based on data from *Statistical Interactive Database*, Bank of England, series XUMAERD (2 August 2021), www.bankofengland.co.uk/boeapps/iadb/; interest rate data from Federal Reserve Bank and European Central Bank.

If, however, the higher interest rates in the UK and other deficit countries were simply to compensate investors for the risk of currency depreciation, then there would be no excessive inflow of finance. The benefit of the higher interest rate would be offset by a depreciating currency. But the carry trade had the effect of making deficit currencies *appreciate*, thereby further boosting the carry trade by speculation of further exchange rate rises.

Thus the currencies of deficit countries appreciated, making their goods less competitive and worsening their current account deficit. Between 1996 and 2006, the average current account deficits as a percentage of GDP for Australia,

CASE STUDIES AND APPLICATIONS

In addition, a massive deficit on the US balance of payments current account, and a budget deficit nearing 4 per cent of GDP, made foreign investors reluctant to invest in the American economy. In fact, investors were pulling out of the USA. One estimate suggests that European investors alone sold $70 billion of US assets during 2002. The result of all this was a massive depreciation of the dollar and appreciation of the euro, so that by December 2004 the exchange rate had risen to $1.36: a 60 per cent appreciation since June 2001!

In 2004–5, with the US economy growing strongly again, the Fed raised interest rates several times, from 1 per cent in early 2004 to 5.25 by June 2006. The ECB kept interest rates constant at 2 per cent until early 2006. The result was that the euro depreciated against the dollar in 2005. But then the rise of the euro began again as the US growth slowed and eurozone growth rose and people anticipated a narrowing of the gap between US and eurozone interest rates.

In 2007 and 2008, worries about the credit crunch in the USA led the Fed to cut interest rates to stave off recession. In August 2007, the US federal funds rate was 5.25 per cent. It was then reduced on several occasions to stand at between 0 and 0.25 per cent by December 2008. The ECB, in contrast, kept the eurozone rate at 4 per cent for the first part of this period and even raised it to 4.25 per cent temporarily in the face of rapidly rising commodity prices. As a result, short-term finance flooded into the eurozone and the euro appreciated again, from $1.37 in mid-2007 to $1.58 in mid-2008.

. . . Then the steps down

Eventually, in September 2008, with the eurozone on the edge of recession and predictions that the ECB would cut interest rates, the euro at last began to fall. It continued to do so as the ECB cut rates. However, with monetary policy in the eurozone remaining tighter than in the USA, the euro began to rise again, only falling once more at the end of 2009 and into 2010 as US growth accelerated and speculators anticipated a tightening of US monetary policy.

Growing worries in 2010 about the level of government deficits and debt in various eurozone countries, such as Greece, Portugal, Spain, Italy and Ireland, contributed to speculation and thus growing volatility of the euro. Throughout the first part of 2010 investors became increasingly reluctant to hold the euro, as fears of debt default mounted. As such, the euro fell substantially from $1.44 in January 2010 to $1.19 in June – a 17 per cent depreciation.

Then, as support was promised by the ECB and IMF to Greece in return for deficit reduction policies, and similar support could be made available to other eurozone countries with severe deficits, fears subsided and the euro rose again. By the end of October 2010, the euro was trading at $1.39. In April 2011, the euro increased to a high of $1.44.

Then began a dramatic fall in the euro as concerns grew over the eurozone's sluggish recovery and continuing high debt levels. Speculators thus believed that eurozone interest rates would have to continue falling. The ECB cut the main interest rate from 1.5 per cent in October 2011 in a series of steps to 0.05 per cent by September 2014.

With the ECB reducing interest rates and people increasingly predicting the introduction of quantitative easing (QE), the euro depreciated during 2014. Between March and December 2014 it depreciated by 11 per cent against the dollar, while the euro exchange rate index depreciated by 4 per cent. With the announced programme of QE being somewhat larger than markets expected, in the week following the announcement in January 2015, the euro fell a further 2.3 per cent against the dollar, and the euro exchange rate index also fell by 2.3 per cent. The result was that the euro was trading at its lowest level against the US dollar since April 2003.

The euro strengthened against the dollar in 2017/18 as economic growth in the eurozone picked up. But this economic respite was to prove only temporary with the growth rate falling from 2.5 per cent in 2017 to only 1 per cent in 2019. After a pause from December 2018 (see Box 22.7), the ECB's programme of quantitative easing resumed in November 2019. The euro was on the slide again.

Then, with the COVID-19 pandemic, investors initially saw the dollar as a 'haven of last resort'. The euro therefore maintained its weakness against the dollar. But during 2020 as the US struggled to control the number of coronavirus cases and uncertainty grew around the outcome of the US presidential election, the dollar eased.

The path of the euro shows that the monetary policy decisions of the ECB and the Fed have been a major factor in the exchange rate volatility between the euro and the dollar – itself a cause of uncertainty in international trade and finance. However, other factors, such as the wellbeing of the public finances and the control in the spread of COVID-19, have also contributed to the euro–dollar seesaw.

How important are relative interest rates in the long run in the determination of bilateral exchange rates, such as that between the dollar and the euro?

Find out what has happened to the euro–dollar exchange rate over the past 12 months. (You can find the data from the Bank of England's Statistical Interactive Database at www.bankofengland.co.uk/boeapps/iadb/newintermed.asp.) Explain why the exchange rate has moved the way it has.

the USA and the UK were close to 4.5, 4 and 2, respectively. Between January 1996 and December 2006, the broad-based *real* exchange rate index of the Australian dollar appreciated by 17 per cent, of the US dollar by 4 per cent and of sterling by some 23 per cent.

Currencies of surplus countries depreciated, making their goods more competitive and further boosting their current account surpluses. For example, between 2004 and 2006 the average current account surpluses as a percentage of GDP for Japan and Switzerland were 3.5 and 13, respectively.

Their short-term interest rates averaged a mere 0.1 and 1.0 per cent respectively (compared with 3.4, 4.7 and 5.7 per cent for the USA, the UK and Australia). Yet between January 2004 and December 2006, the *real* exchange rate index of the yen depreciated by 21 per cent while that of the Swiss franc depreciated by 6 per cent.

With the credit crunch of 2007/8, however, short-term flows of finance declined significantly. This had the effect of reducing the carry trade and its effect on exchange rates. Hence, the current account became relatively more significant in determining exchange rates. The currencies of deficit countries, such as the UK and USA, began to depreciate and those of surplus countries, such as Japan and Switzerland, began to appreciate. Between September 2007 and September 2008, the *real* exchange rate indices of the US dollar and sterling depreciated by 2 and 13 per cent respectively; the yen and the Swiss franc appreciated by 3 and 2.75 per cent.

External shocks

Now let us assume that the rest of the world goes into recession (but with no change in international interest rates). The demand for UK exports will fall. This will lead to a depreciation of the exchange rate. This in turn will boost the demand for UK exports and domestic substitutes for imports. This boost to demand again will help to offset the dampening effect of the world recession.

Floating exchange rates thus help to insulate the domestic economy from world economic fluctuations.

Will there be any cost to the UK economy from a decline in the demand for exports resulting from a world recession?

The path to long-run equilibrium

If there is a single shock, and if there is initially both internal balance and also external balance in the narrow sense (i.e. a current account balance), eventually both internal balance and current account balance will be restored. Current account balance will be restored by a change in the exchange rate that restores purchasing-power parity. This is illustrated in Figure 25.8.

Figure 25.8 Exchange rate path to long-run equilibrium after a shock at time t^1

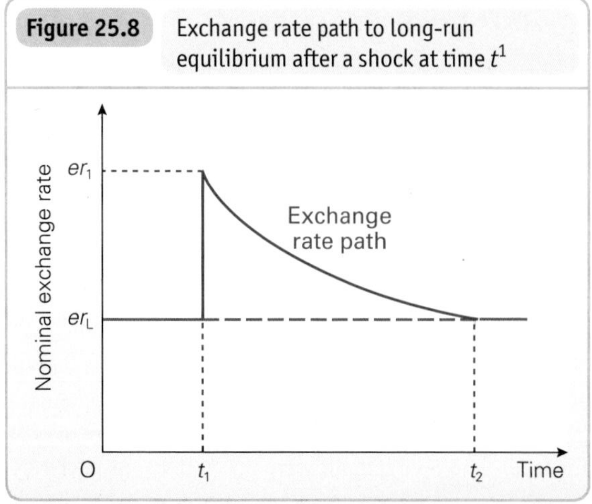

Assume that the country experiences the same long-term rate of inflation as its trading partners and that, therefore, the nominal exchange rate follows the same path as the real exchange rate. Assume also that there are no *long-term* changes to cause an appreciation or depreciation and that, therefore, the long-term equilibrium exchange rate is constant over time. This is shown by the horizontal line at er_L.

Now assume, as before, that there is a rise in aggregate demand and a resulting rise in interest rates. This occurs at time t_1. As the demand for imports rises, the current account goes into deficit. Higher interest rates, however, lead to a financial inflow and an immediate appreciation of the exchange rate to er_1. But then the exchange rate will gradually fall back to its long-run rate as the higher interest rates curb demand and interest rates can thus come back down.

What determines the level of er_1? This exchange rate must be high enough to balance the gain from the higher interest rate against the fact that the exchange rate will be expected to depreciate again back to its long-run equilibrium level er_L. For example, if the interest rate rises by 1 per cent, the exchange rate must rise to the level where people anticipate that it will fall by 1 per cent per year. Only that way will finance stop flowing into the country.

Describe the exchange rate path if there were a single shock that caused interest rates to fall. What determines the magnitude and speed of changes in the exchange rate in such a scenario?

Speculation

In the real world, shocks are occurring all the time. Also, there is considerable uncertainty over the future course of the exchange rate path. What is more, things are made more complicated by the activities of speculators. As soon as any exchange rate change is anticipated, speculators will buy or sell the currency.

KI 34 p453

Assume, for example, that there is a rise in UK inflation above international rates, but no change in interest rates. This causes a fall in the demand for exports and hence a fall in the demand for sterling (assuming a price elasticity of demand greater than 1), and a rise in imports and hence a rise in the supply of sterling. This is illustrated in Figures 25.9 and 25.10. The exchange rate depreciates from er_1 to er_2. Speculators seeing the exchange rate falling can react in one of two ways. The first is called *stabilising speculation*; the second is called *destabilising speculation* (see section 3.2).

Stabilising speculation

This occurs when speculators believe that any exchange rate change will soon be reversed.

In our example, speculators may anticipate that the central bank will raise interest rates or take some other measure to reduce inflation. They thus believe that the exchange rate will appreciate again. As a result, they buy more pounds and sell fewer. But this very act of speculation causes the appreciation they had anticipated.

Figure 25.9 Stabilising speculation

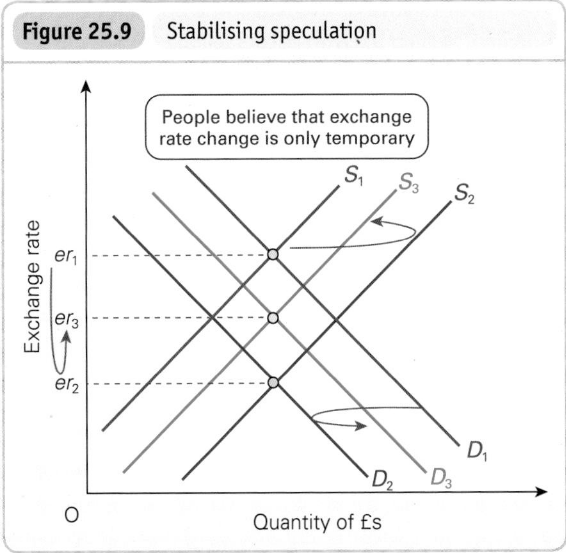

Figure 25.10 Destabilising speculation

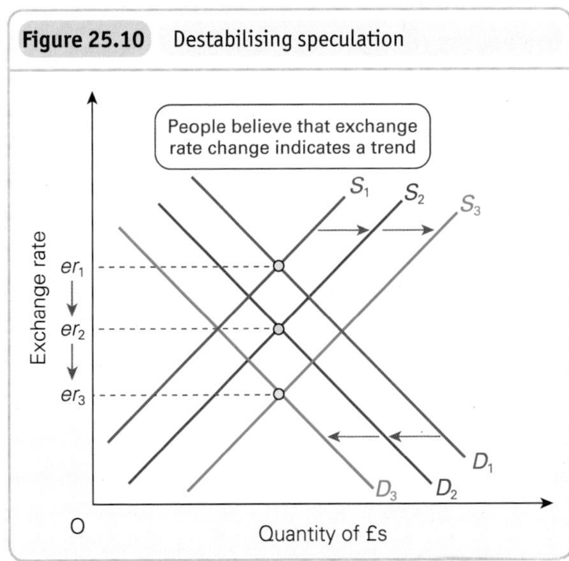

This is illustrated in Figure 25.9. Inflation has caused the demand for and supply of pounds to shift from D_1 to S_1 and D_2 and S_2, the exchange rate to fall from er_1 to er_2. Stabilising speculation then shifts the curves back again, to D_3 and S_3, and the exchange rate rises again to er_3.

The action of speculators in this case, therefore, prevents excessively large exchange rate changes. In general, stabilising speculation occurs whenever speculators believe that the exchange rate has 'overreacted' to the current economic situation.

Draw a similar diagram to Figure 25.9, showing how an initial appreciation of the exchange rate would similarly be reduced by stabilising speculation.

Destabilising speculation

KI 34 p453

This occurs when speculators believe that exchange rate movements will continue in the same direction.

In our example, speculators may believe that inflation will not be brought under control. They anticipate a continuing fall in the exchange rate and thus sell *now* before the exchange rate falls any further. In Figure 25.10, this speculation causes the demand and supply curves to shift further, to D_3 and S_3, and causes the exchange rate to fall further, to er_3.

Eventually, however, this destabilising speculation could cause ***overshooting***, with the exchange rate falling well below the purchasing-power parity rate. At this point speculators, believing that the rate will rise again, will start buying pounds again. This causes the exchange rate to rise.

Obviously, governments prefer stabilising to destabilising speculation. Destabilising speculation can cause severe exchange rate fluctuations. The resulting uncertainty is very damaging to trade. It is very important, therefore, that governments create a climate of confidence. People must believe that the government can prevent economic crises from occurring.

Conclusion

Whatever speculators anticipate will happen to the exchange rate, their actions will help to bring it about. If they think the sterling exchange rate will fall, they will sell pounds, hence causing it to fall. Thus speculators as a whole will gain. This applies to both stabilising and destabilising speculation.

If speculators on average gain from their speculation, who loses?

Advantages of a free-floating exchange rate

The advantages and disadvantages of free-floating rates are to a large extent the opposite of those of fixed rates.

Automatic correction. The government simply lets the exchange rate move freely to the equilibrium. In this way, balance of payments disequilibria are automatically and instantaneously corrected without the need for specific government policies – policies that under other systems can be mishandled.

TC 4 p45

No problem of international liquidity and reserves. Since there is no central bank intervention in the foreign exchange market, there is no need to hold reserves. A currency is automatically convertible at the current market exchange rate. International trade is thereby financed.

Insulation from external economic events. A country is not tied to a possibly unacceptably high world inflation rate, as it is

> **Definition**
>
> **Exchange rate overshooting** Where a fall (or rise) in the long-run equilibrium exchange rate causes the actual exchange rate to fall (or rise) by a greater amount before eventually moving back to the new long-run equilibrium level.

under a fixed exchange rate. It can choose its own inflation target. It is also to some extent protected against world economic fluctuations and shocks (see pages 829–34).

Governments are free to choose their domestic policy. Under a fixed rate, a government may have to deflate the economy even when there is high unemployment. Under a floating rate, the government can choose whatever level of domestic demand it considers appropriate, and simply leave exchange rate movements to take care of any balance of payments effect. This is a major advantage, especially when the effectiveness of deflation is reduced by downward wage and price rigidity, and when competitive deflation between countries may end up causing a world recession.

Disadvantages of a free-floating exchange rate

Despite these advantages, there are still some serious problems with free-floating exchange rates.

Speculation. Short-run instability can be lessened by stabilising speculation, thus making speculation advantageous. If, due to short-run inelasticity of demand, a deficit causes a very large depreciation, speculators will buy pounds, knowing that in the long run the exchange rate will appreciate KI 10 p70 again. Their action therefore helps to lessen the short-run fall in the exchange rate.

Nevertheless, in an uncertain world where there are few KI 34 p453 restrictions on currency speculation, where the fortunes and policies of governments can change rapidly, and where large amounts of short-term deposits are internationally 'footloose', speculation can be highly destabilising in the short run. Considerable exchange rate overshooting can occur.

An example of such overshooting occurred between August 2008 and March 2009 when the pound depreciated 14 per cent against the euro, 25 per cent against the US dollar and 33 per cent against the yen. The nominal sterling exchange rate index fell 16 per cent and the real index by 15 per cent (see Figure 25.3). Speculators were predicting that interest rates in the UK would fall further than in other countries and stay lower for longer. This was because the recessionary implications of a highly financialised economy such as the UK following the financial crisis were expected to be deeper. Consequently, inflation was expected to undershoot the Bank of England's 2 per cent target and perhaps even become negative. But the fall in the exchange rate represented considerable overshooting and both the nominal and real exchange rate indices rose by 9 per cent between March and June 2009.

This is just one example of the violent swings in exchange rates that have occurred in recent years. They even occur under managed floating exchange rate systems where governments have attempted to dampen such fluctuations!

The continuance of exchange rate fluctuations over a number of years is likely to encourage the growth of speculative holdings of currency. This can then cause even larger and more rapid swings in exchange rates.

Uncertainty for traders and investors. The uncertainty caused  by currency fluctuations can discourage international trade and investment. To some extent, the problem can be overcome by using the ***forward exchange market***. Here traders agree with a bank today the rate of exchange for some point in the future (say, in six months' time). This allows traders to plan future purchases of imports or sales of exports at a known rate of exchange. Of course, banks charge for this service since they are taking upon themselves the risks of adverse exchange rate fluctuations.

This will not help long-term investment, however, where decisions are made based on anticipated costs and revenue flows for many years to come. The possibility of exchange rate appreciation may well discourage firms from investing abroad.

Why would banks not be prepared to offer a forward exchange rate to a firm for, say, five years from now?

Lack of discipline on the domestic economy. Governments may pursue irresponsibly inflationary policies. Also, unions and firms may well drive up wages and prices, without the same fear of losing overseas markets or of the government imposing deflationary policies. The depreciation resulting from this inflation will itself fuel the inflation by raising the price of imports.

Conclusion

Neither fixed nor free-floating exchange rates are free from problems. For this reason, governments have sought a compromise between the two, the hope being that some intermediate system will gain the benefits of both, while avoiding most of their disadvantages.

One compromise was tried after the Second World War. This was the *adjustable peg*. Another is the system that replaced the adjustable peg in the early 1970s and continues for much of the world today. This is the system of *managed floating*. We examine these systems in the next section.

Definition

Forward exchange market Where contracts are made today for the price at which a currency will be exchanged at some specified future date.

BOX 25.6

THE EFFECTIVENESS OF MONETARY AND FISCAL POLICIES UNDER FLOATING EXCHANGE RATES

EXPLORING ECONOMICS

With a floating exchange rate, monetary policy is strong and fiscal policy is weak (the reverse of the case with fixed exchange rates).

Monetary policy

Assume that the economy is in recession and the central bank wishes to increase aggregate demand. It thus reduces interest rates. Three effects follow, each contributing to the effectiveness of the monetary policy.

1. *The expansionary monetary policy directly increases aggregate demand.* The size of the effect here depends on the amount that interest rates change and the elasticity of aggregate demand in response to the changes in interest rates.
2. *The exchange rate depreciates.* Higher aggregate demand increases imports and (via higher prices) reduces exports. This and the lower interest rates reduce the demand for and increase the supply of domestic currency on the foreign exchange market. The exchange rate thus depreciates.

   This reinforces the increase in domestic demand. A lower exchange rate makes exports less expensive again and therefore increases their demand (an injection). Imports become more expensive again and therefore their demand falls (a withdrawal). There is thus a *further* multiplied rise in income.
3. *Speculation may cause initial exchange rate overshooting.* Lower interest rates cause speculative financial outflows in anticipation of the depreciation. This causes the exchange rate to fall below its eventual rate – to overshoot, thus causing a further rise in aggregate demand.

This is only a short-term effect, however, since speculators will stop selling the domestic currency when the rate has gone so low that they feel it must rise again (back towards the purchasing-power parity level) sufficiently fast to offset the lower interest rates they are now getting. The greater the mobility of international finance and the better the information of the speculators, the shorter will the short run be.

Fiscal policy

Fiscal policy is relatively weak under a floating rate. Again, let us assume that the objective is to raise aggregate demand to combat a recession. The government thus reduces taxes and/or increases its expenditure. The rise in aggregate demand raises imports and (via higher prices) reduces exports. This effect on the current account of the balance of payments puts downward pressure on the exchange rate.

The higher aggregate demand, however, increases the transactions demand for money and hence *raises* interest rates. These higher interest rates will lead to financial inflows. This will put upward pressure on the exchange rate, which is likely to swamp the downward pressure from the current account deficit. There will therefore be an *appreciation* of the exchange rate. This will increase imports and reduce exports, thus reducing aggregate demand again, and reducing the effectiveness of the fiscal expansion.

Compare the relative effectiveness of fiscal and monetary policies as means of reducing aggregate demand under a system of floating exchange rates.

Section summary

1. Under a free-floating exchange rate, the balance of payments will automatically be kept in balance by movements in the exchange rate. This removes the *balance of payments* constraint on domestic policy. It does not, however, remove external constraints entirely.
2. According to the purchasing-power parity theory, any changes in domestic prices will simply lead to equivalent changes in the exchange rate, leaving the international competitiveness of home-produced goods unaffected. If, however, internal shocks cause changes in interest rates, there will be a change in the *financial* account balance. This will influence exchange rates and destroy the purchasing-power parity theory. The current account will go out of balance (in an equal and opposite way to the financial account).
3. This problem is made more acute by the carry trade, whereby people borrow money in low interest rate (current account surplus) countries and deposit them in high interest rate (current account deficit) countries. This causes deficit countries' exchange rates to appreciate, thereby worsening their current account deficit.
4. External shocks will be reflected in changes in exchange rates and will help to insulate the domestic economy from international economic fluctuations.
5. Exchange rate movements are highly influenced by speculation. If speculators believe that an appreciation or depreciation is merely temporary, their activities will help to stabilise the exchange rate. If, however, they believe that an exchange rate movement in either direction will continue, their activities will be destabilising and cause a bigger movement in the exchange rate.
6. The advantages of free-floating exchange rates are that they automatically correct balance of payments disequilibria; they eliminate the need for reserves; and they give governments a greater independence to pursue their chosen domestic policy.
7. On the other hand, a completely free exchange rate can be highly unstable, made worse by destabilising speculation. This may discourage firms from trading and investing abroad. What is more, a flexible exchange rate, by removing the balance of payments constraint on domestic policy, may encourage governments to pursue irresponsible domestic policies for short-term political gain.

25.4 EXCHANGE RATE SYSTEMS IN PRACTICE

The adjustable peg system: 1945–73

After the collapse in 1931 of the fixed exchange rate system of the gold standard (see section 16.2), the huge scale of the initial disequilibria caused wild swings in exchange rates. Many countries resorted to protectionism, given the great uncertainties associated with free trade under fluctuating exchange rates.

The Bretton Woods system

In 1944, the allied countries met at Bretton Woods in the USA to hammer out a new exchange rate system: one that would avoid the chaos of the 1930s and encourage free trade, but that would avoid the rigidity of the gold standard. The compromise they worked out was an adjustable peg system that lasted until 1971.

Under the ***Bretton Woods system*** there was a totally fixed dollar/gold exchange rate ($35 per ounce of gold). The USA guaranteed that it would freely convert dollars into gold. It was hoped that this would encourage countries to hold dollars as their major reserve currency. After all, if dollars were freely convertible into gold, they were as good as gold. All other countries pegged their exchange rate to the dollar.

To prevent temporary, short-term fluctuations in the exchange rate, central banks *intervened* on the foreign exchange markets using their foreign reserves. This enabled them to maintain the pegged rate within a 1 per cent band.

If the disequilibrium became more serious, governments were supposed to pursue policies of *deflation* or *reflation*. In the meantime, in the case of a deficit, the central bank might have insufficient reserves to maintain the exchange rate. The International Monetary Fund was set up to provide such liquidity. All countries were required to deposit a quota of funds with the IMF, depending on the size of their trade. The IMF would then lend to countries in balance of payments deficit to enable them to maintain their exchange rate. The more a country had to borrow from the IMF, the more the IMF would insist that it pursued appropriate deflationary policies to correct the disequilibrium.

If the deficit became severe, countries could *devalue*: the pegged rate could be adjusted (in consultation with the IMF).

Under this system, how would you expect countries to respond to a balance of payments surplus? Would a revaluation benefit such countries?

Advocates of an adjustable peg system argue that the Bretton Woods arrangement made a significant contribution to the long boom of the 1950s and 1960s.

- Since rates were fixed for a long period of time – perhaps many years – uncertainty was reduced and trade was encouraged.
- Pegged rates, plus the overseeing role of the IMF, prevented governments from pursuing irresponsible policies, and helped to bring about an international harmonisation of policies. They kept world inflation in check.
- If a deficit became severe, countries could devalue. This prevented them being forced into a depression or into adopting protectionist policies. The IMF ensured an orderly process of devaluation.

However, there were two serious weaknesses with the system. These became more and more apparent during the 1960s, and eventually led to the system's downfall.

Problems of adjustment to balance of payments disequilibria

To avoid internal policy being governed by the balance of payments, and to avoid being forced into a depression, countries with a fundamental deficit were supposed to devalue. There were several difficulties here, however.

- Identifying whether a deficit was fundamental. Governments were frequently overoptimistic about the future balance of payments position.
- If devaluation did take place, it could be very disruptive to firms. A devaluation suddenly alters the costs and revenues of importers and exporters by a substantial amount. If a devaluation is felt to be imminent, it can cause great uncertainty and may make them reluctant to take on new trade commitments.

Would this uncertainty have a similar or a different effect on exporting companies and companies using imported inputs?

- At first a devaluation might make a current account deficit *worse*: the ***J-curve effect***. The price elasticities of demand for imports and exports may be low in the short run (see Case Study 25.1 on the student website).

Definitions

Bretton Woods system An adjustable peg system whereby currencies were pegged to the US dollar. The USA maintained convertibility of the dollar into gold at the rate of $35 to an ounce.

J-curve effect Where a devaluation causes the balance of payments first to deteriorate and then to improve. The graph of the balance of payments over time thus looks like a letter J.

Directly after devaluation, few extra exports may be sold, and more will have to be paid for imports that do not have immediate substitutes. There is thus an initial deterioration in the balance of trade before it eventually improves. In Figure 25.11, devaluation takes place at time t_1. As you can see, the diagram has a J shape.

For these reasons, countries in deficit tended to put off devaluing until they were forced to by a crisis. The reluctance of countries to devalue caused other problems.

Stop-go policies. Countries had to rely much more on deflation as a means of curing deficits. The UK in particular found that, whenever the economy started to grow, the balance of payments went into deficit. This forced the government to curb demand again through fiscal and/or monetary policies.

KI 34 p453

Speculation. If countries delayed devaluing until a deficit became really severe, an eventual large devaluation became inevitable. This provided a field day for speculators: they could not lose, and there was a high probability of a substantial gain.

Large-scale disruption. The delay in devaluing plus the build-up of speculative pressure could cause the devaluation to be very large when it eventually came. This could be highly disruptive.

Countries' balance of payments deficits could be reduced and adjustment made easier if surplus countries were willing to revalue. There was a reluctance to do this, however, by countries such as Japan. Revaluation was strongly opposed by exporters (and producers of import substitutes), who would find it suddenly more difficult to compete. What is more, there were not the same pressures for surplus countries to revalue as there were for deficit countries to devalue. A lack of reserves can force deficit countries to devalue. Surplus countries, however, may be quite happy to carry on building up reserves.

The USA was not allowed to devalue when in deficit. The onus was on other countries to revalue, which they were reluctant to do. Hence large US deficits persisted. The problem of these deficits was linked to the second major problem area: that of international liquidity.

Figure 25.11 The J-curve effect

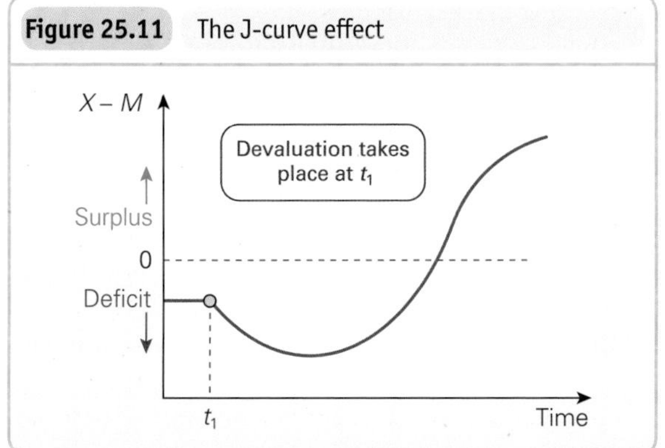

Problems of international liquidity and the collapse of the system

With an adjustable peg system, there have to be sufficient stocks of internationally acceptable currencies or other liquid assets. This 'international liquidity' is necessary both to finance trade and to provide enough reserves for central banks to support their currencies whenever there is a currency flow deficit. Under the Bretton Woods system, there were three main sources of liquidity: gold, dollars and IMF quotas. But since IMF quotas were only in existing currencies, they were not a source of *additional* liquidity.

As world trade expanded (see section 24.1), so deficits (and surpluses) were likely to be larger, and therefore more reserves were required. But the supply of gold was not expanding fast enough, so countries increasingly held dollars. After all, dollars earned interest. The willingness to hold dollars enabled the USA to run large balance of payments deficits. All the USA needed to do to pay for the deficits was to 'print' more dollars, which other countries were prepared to accept as reserves.

US balance of payments deficits in the 1960s got steadily worse. The financing of the Vietnam War, in particular, deepened the deficit. Dollars flooded out of the USA. World liquidity thus expanded rapidly, fuelling world inflation. Furthermore, the rapid growth in overseas dollar holdings meant that US gold reserves were increasingly inadequate to guarantee convertibility. Some countries, fearful that the USA might eventually be forced to suspend convertibility, chose to exchange dollars for gold. US gold reserves fell, creating a further imbalance and a deepening of the crises.

Despite various attempts to rescue the system, with its overreliance on the dollar, it eventually collapsed. The dollar was devalued against gold by 8 per cent in December 1971. In June 1972, the pound was floated. Over the following year, other countries followed suit, and despite a further dollar devaluation the system was finally abandoned in 1973. By mid-1973 gold was trading at $120 per ounce.

Why would the adjustable peg system have been less suitable in the world of the mid-1970s than it was back in the 1950s?

Managed floating

The world has been on a floating exchange rate system since the breakdown of the Bretton Woods system in the early 1970s. This allows adjustment to be made to the inevitable shifts in demand and supply, shifts that got more extreme in the early 1970s with a quadrupling of oil prices in 1973–4 and rapid changes in world trading patterns. Domestic policy has been largely freed from balance of payments constraints. At the same time, *managed* floating was claimed to allow adjustment to be gentler, ideally avoiding wild swings in the exchange rate aggravated by speculation.

Some minor currencies remain pegged (but adjustable) to a major currency such as the dollar, but float along with it against other currencies. Other currencies are pegged to each other, but jointly float against the rest of the world. The most notable examples of this have been the currencies of the exchange rate mechanism (ERM) of the European Monetary System (see section 26.2) and now the members of ERM II (see page 861).

Some countries allow their currencies to float freely. Most countries, however, from time to time have attempted to stabilise their exchange rate, and have thus been operating a system of 'managed flexibility'.

If the country decides to adopt a managed floating system, how could the central bank prevent the exchange rate from falling? There are two main methods:

- Using reserves or foreign loans to purchase domestic currency on the foreign exchange market.
- Raising interest rates to attract short-term financial inflows.

Problems with managed floating since 1972

Managing the exchange rate involved problems, however. Governments needed to know when to intervene, what exchange rate level they should aim to maintain, and how persistently they should try to maintain that rate in the face of speculative pressure.

Predicting the long-term equilibrium exchange rate

Differing inflation rates between countries will require exchange rate adjustments to maintain purchasing-power parity. It is not correct, however, for governments to assume that this will be the *only* cause of shifts in the long-term equilibrium exchange rate. For example, the 1973–4 and 1979–80 oil crises caused fundamental and unpredictable changes in currency demand and supply. So too did other factors, such as the dismantling of trade barriers within the EU, protectionist measures adopted in different parts of the world, structural economic change, changes in technology and changes in tastes.

It is therefore very difficult for the government to predict what the long-term equilibrium will be, and what proportion of any exchange rate movement is therefore due to *long-term* and what proportion merely to *short-term* phenomena.

The growth in speculative financial flows

The OPEC oil price increase in 1973–4 caused huge balance of payments deficits for oil importers. The OPEC countries could not spend all of these surpluses on additional imports since (a) they did not have the capacity to consume such a huge increase in imports and (b) the oil-importing countries did not have the capacity to supply such a huge increase in exports. The surpluses were thus largely invested in short-term dollar (and, to a lesser extent, other major currency) assets. This created a large capacity for short-term loans by Western banks. These moneys could be rapidly shifted from one world financial centre to another, depending on which country had the most favourable interest rates and exchange rates. This created a massive capacity for speculation, and thus made it difficult for countries to control exchange rates by currency sales alone. KI 10 p70

Over the years, the scale of speculative flows has continued to increase. Foreign exchange market data from the Bank for International Settlements show that in 2016 some $5 trillion was passing across the international exchanges every day. Reserves and access to foreign loans are simply inadequate to prevent concerted speculative selling.

To manage the exchange rate, therefore, central banks would have to rely much more on using interest rates.

Conflicts with internal policy

Using interest rates to support the exchange rate has become more and more unpopular as countries have preferred to use interest rates to keep inflation at or below a target level.

As a result of these problems, countries have increasingly opted for a system of freely floating exchange rates. The UK experience is considered in Box 25.7.

Would any of these problems be lessened by the world returning to an adjustable peg system? If so, what sort of adjustable peg system would you recommend?

The volatility of exchange rates

Exchange rates have become extremely volatile. We continue to observe this volatility when we adjust for changes in the prices of exports (measured in domestic prices) relative to the prices of imports (measured in foreign currencies). In other words, the *real* exchange rate is volatile too (see Figure 25.12). This means that nominal exchange rates have typically moved more than the relative prices of exported and imported goods and services. KI 34 p453

As a result of exchange rate volatility, currencies can gain or lose several percentage points in the space of a few days. These changes can then make all the difference between profit and loss for trading companies. There are a number of reasons for this volatility:

- Inflation or money supply targets. Central banks may have to make considerable changes to interest rates in order to keep to their targets. These in turn cause exchange rate fluctuations.
- A huge growth in international financial markets. This has encouraged the international transfer of money and capital.
- The abolition of exchange controls in most industrialised countries.
- The growth in information technology. The simple use of a computer can transfer capital and finance internationally in a matter of seconds.
- The preference for liquidity. With the danger of currency fluctuations, companies prefer to keep their financial capital as liquid as possible. They do not want to be locked into assets denominated in a declining currency.

Figure 25.12 Real exchange rate indices (2010 = 100)

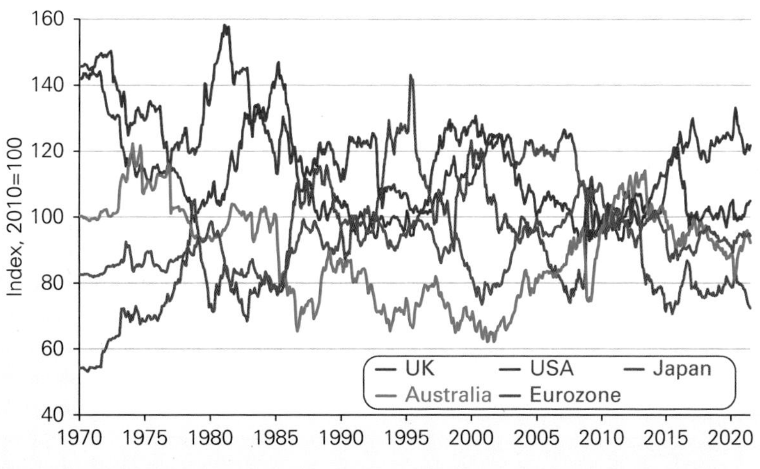

Note: Exchange rate indices are BIS narrow indices comprising 27 countries; prior to the introduction of the euro in 1999, eurozone figures are weighted average exchange rates of currencies that made up the euro.
Source: Based on data *Effective exchange rate indices*, Bank for International Settlements, www.bis.org/statistics/eer.htm

BOX 25.7 **STERLING SINCE THE 1990S** CASE STUDIES AND APPLICATIONS

The sterling seesaw

Between October 1990 and September 1992, sterling was in the ERM, at a central rate of £1 = 2.95 German marks, with permitted fluctuations of ± 6 per cent against any other ERM currency. However, this exchange rate proved unsustainably high and the UK was forced out of the ERM by a massive wave of speculation. Within two months of this, sterling had depreciated by some 15 per cent.

Since 1992, the UK has adopted a virtually free-floating exchange rate. Between 1992 and 1996, fluctuations in the exchange rate were relatively minor. The government was now targeting inflation, and with inflation coming down, it was at first able to reduce interest rates. But this mirrored reductions in inflation and interest rates in other countries, and thus there was little need for exchange rate changes.

A rise in sterling

By the beginning of 1996, however, speculators began buying pounds, believing that the exchange rate would appreciate. They saw that the economy was now beginning to grow quite rapidly, and was likely to continue doing so, given that an election was coming up. Inflation was thus likely to rise and this would force the government to raise interest rates. Indeed, by mid-1996 interest rates bottomed out and began to rise.

When the new Labour government was elected in 1997, the Bank of England was made independent. Over the following months, the Bank raised interest rates several times in order to bring the inflation down to the target level. The effect was to further fuel a large-scale appreciation of sterling. Between January 1996 and April 1998, the nominal exchange rate index rose by 27 per cent (see chart). This made it more difficult for UK exporters and industries competing with imports.

From 1998 to 2007 the pound was well above its purchasing-power parity rate. This was largely the result of UK interest rates being higher than eurozone and Japanese rates, and frequently above US rates too.

With the growth of the carry trade (see page 831), this had helped keep the exchange rate above the PPP rate. The overvaluation of the pound continued to put both the export and import competing sectors in the UK under great competitive pressure. The current account remained in deficit and in most years deteriorated (see the chart in Box 25.2 on page 819).

A fall in sterling

In late 2007, at last the pound began depreciating. With the effects of speculation, this became rapid. Worries about recession suggested that the Bank of England would reduce interest rates – as indeed it did: Bank Rate fell from 5 per cent in October 2008 to 0.5 per cent in March 2009.

But other central banks were reducing their rates too, so why did the pound depreciate while other currencies, including the Japanese yen and Australian dollar, appreciated. There were various reasons for this:

- The cut in the Bank Rate was greater than in the eurozone.
- There were worries that the recession would be deeper and more prolonged in the UK than elsewhere and that low interest rates would therefore persist for longer than in other countries.

(continued)

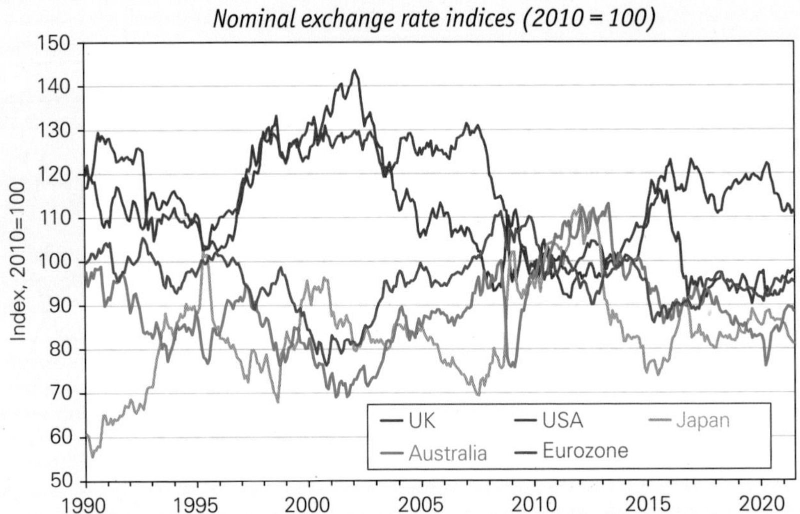

Note: Exchange rate indices are BIS narrow indices comprising 27 countries; prior to the introduction of the euro in 1999, eurozone figures are weighted average exchange rates of currencies that made up to the euro.

Source: Based on data from Bank for International Settlements, www.bis.org/statistics/eer.htm

- Investment in the UK was seen as riskier than in other countries, given the importance of the financial services sector in the UK (a sector badly hit by the credit crunch) and the more rapid rise in government borrowing than in many other countries.
- Commodity prices were rising, which pushed up the exchange rates for commodity exporting countries, such as Australia.

Significantly, the carry trade began to unwind. With the onset of recession, the UK's high current account deficit was no longer seen as a reason to expect relatively high interest rates. Many who had borrowed in yen or other low interest rate currencies to purchase sterling, now began selling sterling and returning to the original currencies, causing such currencies to appreciate substantially.

Between September 2008 and September 2010 the nominal sterling exchange rate depreciated by 9 per cent while the nominal exchange rate of the Japanese yen appreciated by 29 per cent. This appreciation of the yen prompted the Japanese central bank in September 2010 to begin intervening in the foreign exchange markets by selling yen and buying dollars.

Rising again

Eventually, in mid-2013, sterling began to rise. With recovery gaining momentum more rapidly in the UK than in the eurozone, speculators were predicting that the Bank of England would raise rates before the ECB and that this would cause the pound to appreciate. The actions of speculators ensured that this occurred.

The Brexit fall

On 23 June 2016, the UK held a referendum on whether to remain a member of the EU. As soon as it became clear that the UK had voted to leave the EU the pound began to fall sharply. Investor concern about the UK's future trading relationships and its likely negative impact on long-term growth, coupled with the Bank of England's reduction in Bank Rate from 0.5 to 0.25 per cent, a further round of quantitative easing (see Box 22.10) and the potential for further monetary loosening helped to fuel a marked fall in sterling.

Six weeks after the vote, sterling had depreciated by 11 per cent against the dollar and 9 per cent against the euro compared with directly before the referendum. When the UK left the European Union at the end of January 2020, the nominal sterling exchange rate index was some 14 per cent lower than at the end of 2015 compared with a 3 per cent fall in the US dollar index and a rise of 4 per cent of the euro index.

1. *Identify two factors in the UK economy which help to explain the appreciation of the real exchange rate after 1996.*
2. *What longer-term determinants are there of the sterling exchange rate index?*

Find out what has happened to the sterling–euro and sterling–dollar exchange rate over the past 12 months. You can access the data from the Bank of England's Statistical Interactive Database (www.bankofengland.co.uk/boeapps/iadb/). Explain why the exchange rates have moved the way they have.

BOX 25.8 **DO INFLATION RATES EXPLAIN LONGER-TERM EXCHANGE RATE MOVEMENTS?** EXPLORING ECONOMICS

Does PPP hold in the long run?

As we have seen in section 25.4, exchange rates have become extremely volatile. We can see from Figure 25.1 (page 815) that the trade-weighted *real* exchange rate of sterling exhibits considerable volatility. The real exchange rate adjusts for the terms of trade. The significance of movements in the real exchange rate is that it demonstrates that purchasing-power parity (PPP) fails to hold in the short run.

But does PPP hold in the long run? If so, differences in countries' inflation rates need to be reflected in changes in exchange rates. In this box, we consider whether long-term inflation rate differentials between the UK and the other countries have been reflected in long-term movements in the foreign currency price of sterling, i.e. in the number of foreign currency units per £.

Consider the chart. On the horizontal axis is plotted the average annual percentage change in the number of foreign currency units per £1 from 1981 to 2020. Positive values indicate that sterling appreciated against that currency; negative values that it depreciated. For instance, sterling appreciated by 0.8 per cent per annum against the Swedish krona, but depreciated by 2.4 per cent per annum against the Japanese yen.

On the vertical axis is plotted the inflation differential; this measures the difference between the average annual rate of inflation in the UK and that in each of the other nine countries. For instance, the average annual UK inflation rate was 3.2 percentage points *higher* than in Japan, but 0.9 percentage points *lower* than in New Zealand.

If inflation differentials are to be reflected in exchange rate changes, we would expect to see the observations for the ten countries lying along the downward-sloping blue line – the long-run PPP line. This line links positive values of the inflation differential with the equivalent percentage depreciation; this would be consistent with PPP holding in the long run.

Several of the observations are seen to lie close to the long-run PPP line. This is the case with the US dollar. A 1 per cent higher inflation rate in the UK than in the USA corresponds to a 1 per cent depreciation in sterling against the dollar.

It would appear therefore that long-term inflation differentials do affect movements in bilateral exchange rates. However, the chart also illustrates the need to consider more than just inflation-rate differentials.

Consider first Japan and Sweden which lie *above* the long-run PPP line. This is consistent with a real-terms *appreciation* of sterling.

As we have seen, the UK has experienced a positive inflation-rate differential with Japan of 3.2 percentage points per annum. Therefore the exchange rate would have needed to depreciate by 3.2 per cent per annum to compensate. Although sterling has typically depreciated against the yen, it has done so by only 2.4 per cent per annum. Meanwhile, the Swedish inflation rate has typically been 0.2 percentage points per

Inflation rate differentials and appreciation of sterling, 1981–2020

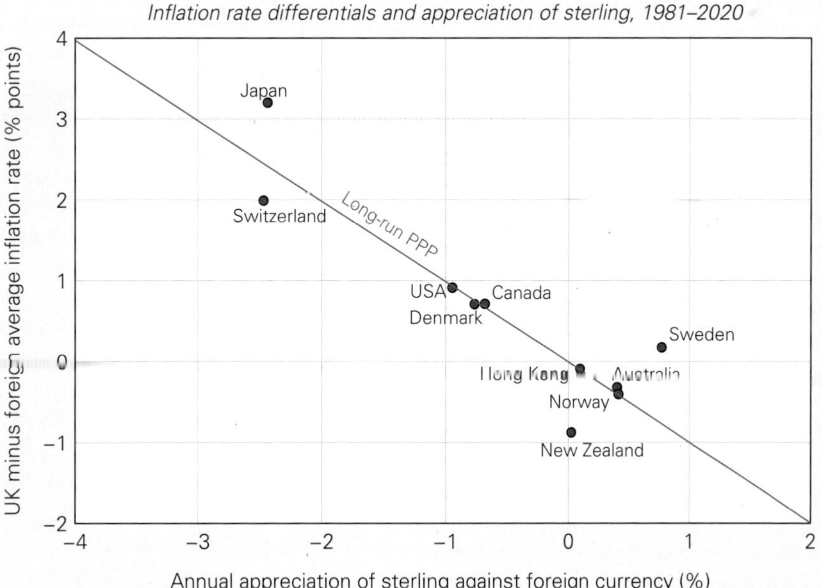

Sources: Exchange rate calculations based on bilateral sterling exchange rates from *Statistical Interactive Database*, Bank of England, https://www.bankofengland.co.uk/boeapps/iadb/; Inflation rate calculations based on GDP deflator data from *World Economic Outlook Database*, IMF (April 2021), www.imf.org/en/Publications/SPROLLs/world-economic-outlook-databases

(continued)

annum lower than in the UK. However, sterling has actually appreciated by 0.8 per cent per annum against the krona.

Consider now New Zealand and Switzerland which lie *below* the long-run PPP line. This is consistent with a real-terms *depreciation* of sterling.

The UK has experienced a negative inflation-rate differential of 0.9 percentage point per annum with New Zealand. However, there has been no equivalent nominal appreciation of sterling against the New Zealand dollar. Meanwhile, the Swiss inflation rate has typically been 2 percentage points per annum lower than in the UK. Although sterling has depreciated against the Swiss franc it has done so by 2.5 per cent per annum.

The analysis suggests that as well as inflation-rate differentials we therefore need to consider other causes of exchange rate movements. These include changes in relative interest rates, speculation, economic shocks, discovery of new resources, rate of productivity growth, and longer-term shifts in demand and supply for imports and exports.

Has the remit of the Bank of England's Monetary Policy Committee affected inflation rate differentials with other countries over the years?

Undertake a literature search of evidence relating to purchasing power parity. Write a short briefing paper on what this evidence shows.

- The growing speculative activities of trading companies. Many large companies have a team of dealers to help manage their liquid assets: to switch them from currency to currency in order to take advantage of market movements.
- The growing speculative activities of banks and other financial institutions.
- The growing belief that rumour and 'jumping on the bandwagon' are more important determinants of currency buying or selling than cool long-term appraisal. If people *believe* that speculation is likely to be destabilising, their actions will ensure that it is. Many companies involved in international trade and finance have developed a 'speculative mentality'.
- The growing belief that governments are powerless to prevent currency movements. As short-term capital (or 'hot money') grows relative to official reserves, it is increasingly difficult for central banks to stabilise currencies through exchange market intervention.

Although most governments and firms dislike highly volatile exchange rates, few today advocate a return to fixed exchange rates, or a system like the Bretton Woods one. In fact, apart from the Gulf states, very few countries still peg their currencies to the dollar. Even China, which from 1997 to 2005 was pegged to the dollar at $1 = 8.27 yuan, has moved to a managed float based round the weighted average of a basket of currencies. In April 2021, the yuan was trading at 6.50 to the dollar – an appreciation of over 20 per cent since 2005.

Despite the preference of most countries for floating exchange rates, suggestions have been made for reducing volatility. We examine some of these in Chapter 26.

Section summary

1. Under the Bretton Woods system (1945–71), currencies were pegged to the US dollar. The rate was supported from countries' reserves and if necessary, with loans from the IMF. If there was a moderate disequilibrium, countries were supposed to use deflationary/reflationary policies. If the disequilibrium became severe, they were supposed to devalue/revalue.
2. The system was claimed to bring certainty for business and a constraint on governments pursuing irresponsible fiscal and monetary policies, while avoiding the problem of a recession if a balance of payments deficit became severe.
3. However, it was sometimes difficult to identify whether a deficit was severe enough to warrant a devaluation; a devaluation itself could be very disruptive for firms; and devaluation at first could make the deficit worse (the J-curve effect). If a country were reluctant to devalue, it would have to rely on deflation and a possible recession to tackle a balance of payments deficit.
4. Problems for deficit countries were made worse by an unwillingness of surplus countries to revalue or reflate.
5. Dollars were the main source of international liquidity under the Bretton Woods system. The USA, by creating dollars to pay for balance of payments deficits, caused excessive liquidity. This caused worldwide inflation, a lack of confidence in the USA and an eventual collapse of the system.
6. Since the early 1970s the world has largely been on a managed floating exchange rate system. The degree of intervention varies from country to country and from time to time.
7. In theory, managed floating can give the necessary degree of exchange rate flexibility in a world where shifts in currency demand and supply have become much larger. It can also release domestic policy from being dominated by balance of payments considerations. At the same time, the intervention could (in theory) prevent violent exchange rate fluctuations and allow a more orderly adjustment to new equilibrium exchange rates.

8. Nevertheless, there are problems under managed floating of predicting long-term equilibrium exchange rates. What is more, with the massive growth in 'hot money' since the early 1970s, it has become increasingly difficult for countries on their own to counteract speculation. The main instrument of intervention has become the rate of interest. There may be a conflict, however, in using interest rates both to control exchange rates *and* to control the domestic economy.
9. Sterling exchange rates have shown considerable volatility over the years, with large divergences from the purchasing-power parity rate. For example, the rise in UK interest rates in 1997–8 caused a large appreciation of sterling, much to the consternation of exporters. The cut in interest rates in 2008 was accompanied by an equally large depreciation.
10. The volatility of exchange rates around the world has grown. Reasons include: a growth in international financial markets and a liberalisation of international financial movements combined with easier computer transfer of funds, a growth in speculative activities and a growing belief in the impotence of governments acting on their own to stabilise rates.

*APPENDIX: THE OPEN ECONOMY AND *IS/LM* ANALYSIS

In this appendix, we show how the *IS/LM* analysis that we examined in the appendix to Chapter 19 can be extended to incorporate the open economy. We will first assume a fixed rate of exchange and then later a free-floating rate.

Analysis under a fixed exchange rate

The BP curve

We start by introducing a third curve, the *BP* (balance of payments) curve. This curve, like the *IS* and *LM* curves, plots a relationship between the rate of interest (*r*) and the level of national income (*Y*). All points along the *BP* curve represent a position of *balance of payments equilibrium.*

We assume that prices are fixed in the short run; hence a change in the real interest rate (*r*) corresponds to an equivalent change in the nominal rate of interest (*i*). The *BP* curve slopes upwards from left to right (see Figure 25.13). Increases in the rate of interest (*r*) will cause the financial account to move into surplus as finance is attracted into the country. Increases in real national income (*Y*), in contrast, will cause the current account to move into deficit as more imports are purchased. If the overall balance of payments is to stay in equilibrium, current account deficits must be matched by financial (plus capital) account surpluses and vice versa. Thus a rise in *Y* must be accompanied by a rise in *r*, and reductions in *Y* must be accompanied by reductions in *r*. The *BP* curve therefore slopes upwards. Any point below the *BP* line represents a position of overall deficit; any point above the line, a position of surplus.

Figure 25.13 The *BP* curve

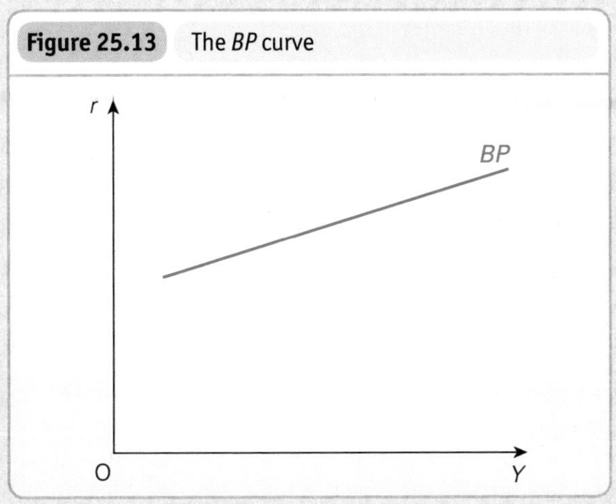

The slope of the *BP* curve depends on two factors.

The marginal propensity to import ($mpm = \Delta M/\Delta Y$). The higher the *mpm*, the steeper will be the *BP* curve. The reason is that with a high *mpm* there will be a correspondingly large rise in imports for any given rise in national income. This will cause a large current account deficit. To maintain an overall balance of payments equilibrium, this will require a correspondingly large financial account surplus. This in turn will require a large rise in interest rates. Thus the bigger the *mpm*, the larger the rise in interest rates that will be necessary to restore balance of payments equilibrium, and hence the steeper will be the BP curve.

The elasticity of supply of international finance. The greater the elasticity of supply of international finance, the less will be the rise in interest rates necessary to attract an inflow of finance and thereby restore balance of payments equilibrium after a rise in national income, and hence the flatter will be the *BP* curve. In the case of a perfectly elastic supply of international finance, the BP curve will be horizontal at the world rate of interest.

KI 9 p64

Equilibrium in the model

If we now put the *BP* curve on an *IS/LM* diagram, we have the position shown in Figure 25.14. Point *a* represents full equilibrium. At r_1 and Y_1, investment equals saving (point *a* is on the *IS* curve), the demand for money equals the supply (point *a* is also on the *LM* curve), and finally the balance of payments is in balance (point *a* is also on the *BP* curve). KI 8 p44

But what is the mechanism that ensures that all three curves intersect at the same point? To answer this question, let us assume that the three curves just happen to intersect at the same point, and then let us examine the effects of changes in fiscal and monetary policies, which shift the *IS* and *LM* curves respectively. Will equilibrium be restored? The answer is yes, via a change in the money supply. Let us examine fiscal and monetary policy changes in turn.

Fiscal policy under fixed exchange rates

An expansionary fiscal policy, i.e. a rise in government spending and/or a reduction in tax, will have the effect of shifting the *IS* curve to the right (e.g. to IS_2 in Figure 25.15). The reason is that for any given rate of interest there will be a higher equilibrium level of national income than before.

This will increase national income, but the extra demand for money that results will drive up interest rates. In a *closed* economy, equilibrium would now be at point *b* (r_2, Y_2), where $IS_2 = LM_1$. But in our open economy model, this equilibrium is *above the BP curve*. There is a balance of payments surplus. The reason for this is that the higher interest rates have caused a financial account surplus that is bigger than the current account deficit that results from the higher national income.

Such a surplus will cause the money supply to rise as funds flow into the country. This will in turn cause the *LM* curve to shift to the right. Equilibrium will finally be achieved at point *c* (r_3, Y_3), where $IS_2 = LM_2 = BP$. Thus under these conditions, the monetary effect of the change in the balance of payments will *reinforce* the fiscal policy and lead to a bigger rise in national income.

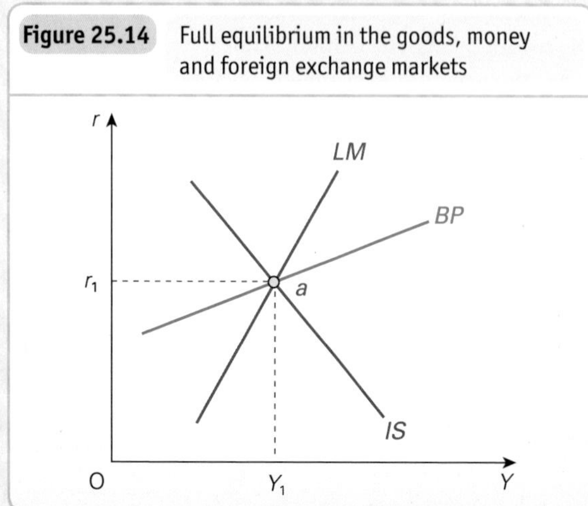

Figure 25.14 Full equilibrium in the goods, money and foreign exchange markets

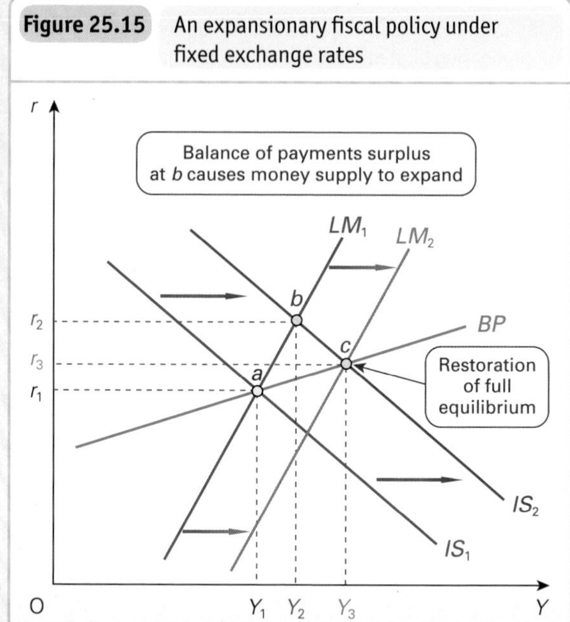

Figure 25.15 An expansionary fiscal policy under fixed exchange rates

What will be the effect of an expansionary fiscal policy on interest rates and national income if there is a perfectly elastic supply of international finance?

If the *BP* curve were steeper than the *LM* curve, the effect would be somewhat different. (Remember the *BP* curve will be steep if there is a high *mpm* and an inelastic supply of international finance.) This is illustrated in Figure 25.16.

TC 6 p66

Under these circumstances, an initial rise in national income to Y_2 (where $IS_2 = LM_1$) will cause a balance of payments *deficit* (point *b* is *below the BP curve*). The reason is that this time the current account deficit is bigger than the financial account surplus (due to a large *mpm* and a small inflow of finance). This will reduce the money supply and cause the *LM* curve to shift to the left. Equilibrium will be achieved at point *c*, where $LM_2 = IS_2 = BP$.

When the *BP* curve is steeper than the *LM* curve, therefore, the monetary effect of the change in the balance of payments will *dampen* the effect of the fiscal policy and lead to a smaller rise in national income.

Monetary policy under fixed exchange rates

An expansionary monetary policy will cause the *LM* curve to shift to the right (e.g. to LM_2 in Figure 25.17). The increased supply of money will drive down the rate of interest and increase national income. In a closed economy, equilibrium would now be at point *b* (r_2, Y_2), where $LM_2 = IS$. But in an open economy, this extra demand will have sucked in extra imports, and the lower interest rate will have led to net financial outflows. There will be a balance of payments deficit: point *b* is below the *BP* curve.

The balance of payments deficit will cause the money stock to fall as money flows abroad. This will cause the *LM* curve to shift back again to its original position. The economy will return to its initial equilibrium at point *a*.

Figure 25.16 An expansionary fiscal policy under fixed exchange rates: a steep BP curve

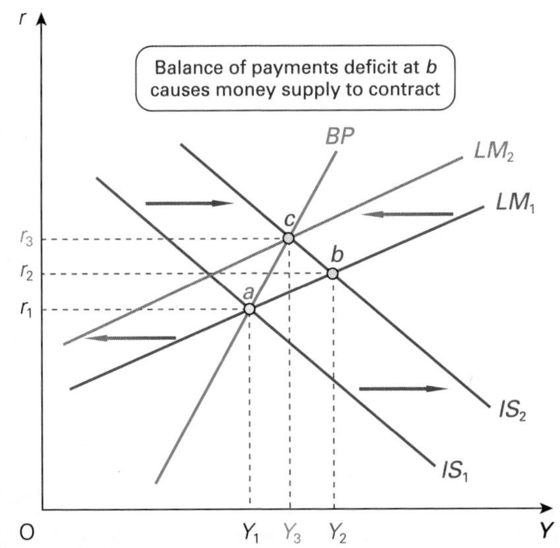

Figure 25.17 An expansionary monetary policy under fixed exchange rates

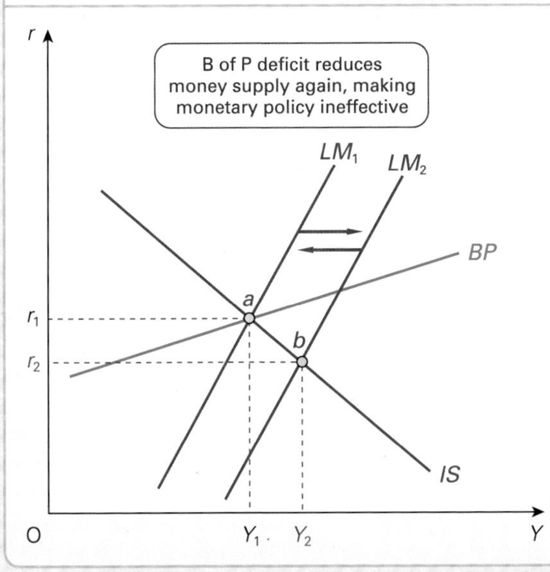

Thus under a fixed exchange rate regime, monetary policy alone will have *no long-term effect* on national income and employment. Only when accompanied by an expansion in aggregate demand (either through fiscal policy or through an autonomous rise in investment or a fall in savings) will an expansion of money supply lead to higher national income.

1. *Why does this conclusion remain the same if the BP curve is steeper than the LM curve?*
2. *Trace through the effects of a fall in exports (thereby shifting the BP curve).*
3. *Show what will happen if there is (a) a rise in business confidence and a resulting increase in investment; (b) a rise in the demand for money balance (say, for precautionary purposes).*

Analysis under free-floating exchange rates

As the exchange rate changes, the *BP* curve will shift (see Figure 25.18). If the *IS* and *LM* curves intersect *above* the *BP* curve, there will be a balance of payments surplus. This will cause the exchange rate to appreciate. The appreciation will cause the surplus to disappear. This in turn will cause the *BP* curve to shift upwards.

Similarly, if the *IS* and *LM* curves intersect *below* the *BP* curve, the resulting balance of payments deficit will cause a depreciation and a downward shift of the *BP* curve. Thus the *BP* curve will always shift so that it intersects where the *IS* and *LM* curves intersect.

Fiscal policy under floating exchange rates

Assume that the government pursues a reflationary fiscal policy. The *IS* curve shifts to IS_2 in Figure 25.19.

Figure 25.18 Movements of the BP curve under floating exchange rates

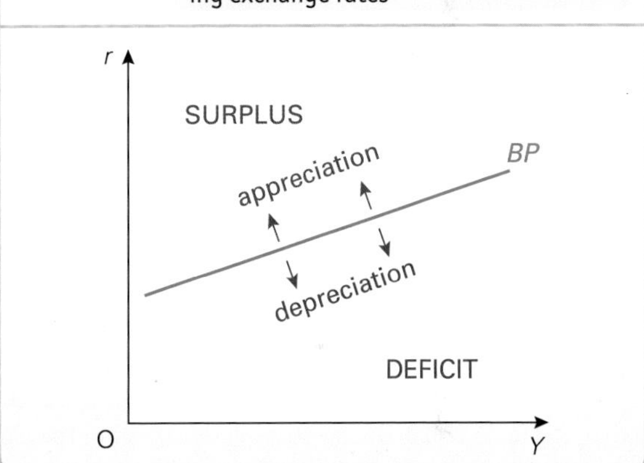

Figure 25.19 An expansionary fiscal policy under floating exchange rates

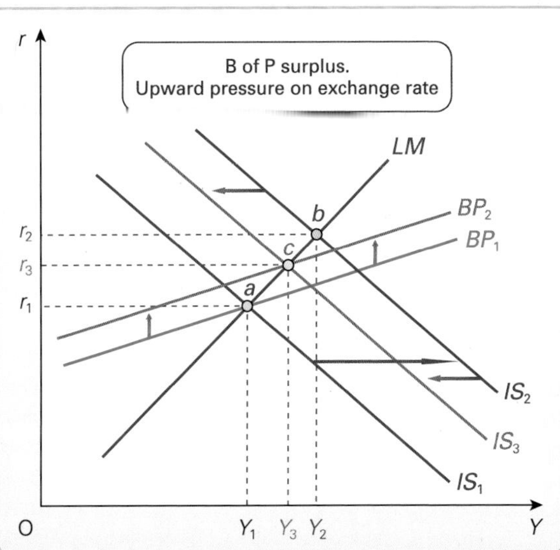

Figure 25.20 An expansionary fiscal policy under floating exchange rates: steep *BP* curve

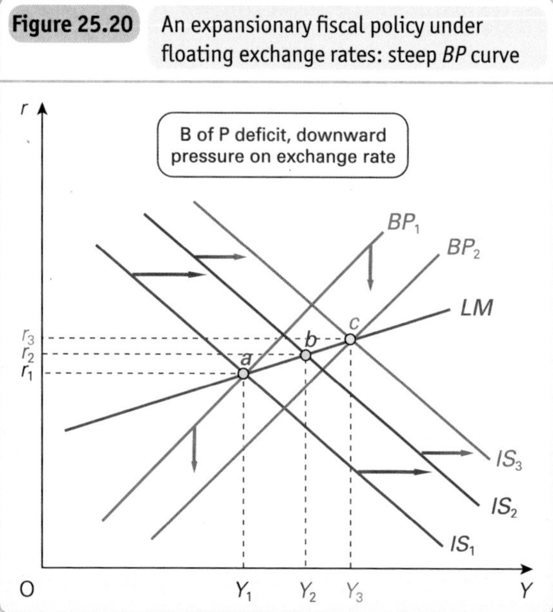

Figure 25.21 An expansionary monetary policy under floating exchange rates

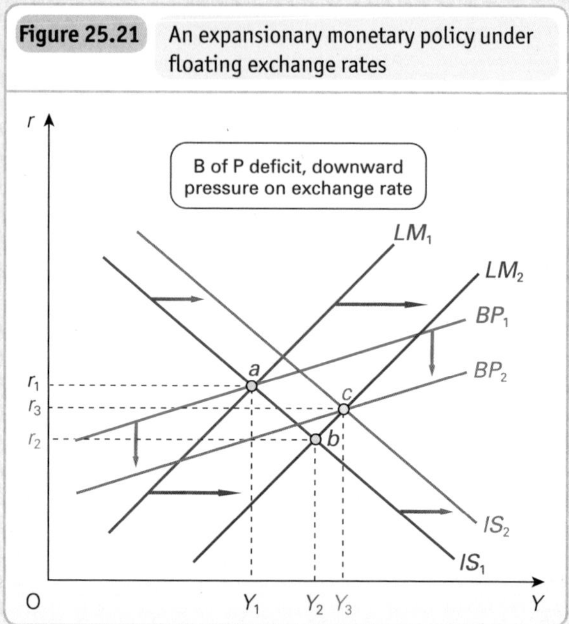

At point *b*, where the *LM* curve and the new *IS* curve intersect, there is a balance of payments surplus (due to higher financial inflows attracted by the higher rate of interest). This causes the exchange rate to appreciate and the *BP* curve to shift upwards.

But the higher exchange rate will cause a fall in exports and a rise in imports. This fall in aggregate demand will cause the *IS* curve to shift back towards the left. The new equilibrium will be at a point such as *c*. This represents only a modest change from point *a*. Thus under a floating exchange rate the effects of fiscal policy may be rather limited.

The effect will be stronger, however, the steeper the *BP* curve. In Figure 25.20, the *BP* curve is steeper than the *LM* curve. This time a rise in the *IS* curve from S_1 to IS_2 will lead to a balance of payments *deficit* and hence a *depreciation* of the exchange rate. The *BP* curve will shift *downwards*. The depreciation will cause a rise in exports and a fall in imports. This *rise* in aggregate demand will cause the *IS* curve to shift to the *right*. The new equilibrium will be at point *c*, which is at a higher level of national income, Y_3. Under these circumstances, the balance of payments effect makes fiscal policy stronger.

Under what circumstances would an expansionary fiscal policy have no effect at all on national income?

Monetary policy under floating exchange rates

An expansionary monetary policy will shift the *LM* curve to the right, to LM_2 in Figure 25.21. In a closed economy, equilibrium would now be at point *b*.

In an open economy under a floating exchange rate, the fall in the rate of interest will cause the exchange rate to depreciate and the *BP* curve to shift downwards. The depreciation will cause exports to rise and imports to fall. This increase in aggregate demand will shift the *IS* curve to the right. The new equilibrium will thus be at point *c*, where $LM_2 = IS_2 = BP_2$. This represents a large change from the initial point *a*.

Thus monetary policy can have a substantial effect on the level of national income under a system of floating exchange rates.

What will determine the size of the shift in the BP curve in each case?

Appendix summary

1. A *BP* curve can be added to an *IS/LM* diagram. It shows all the combinations of national income and interest rates at which the balance of payments is in equilibrium. The curve is upward sloping, showing that a rise in national income (causing a current account deficit) will require a rise in interest rates to give a counterbalancing financial account surplus.
2. The lower the *mpm* and the more elastic the supply of international finance, the flatter will be the *BP* curve.
3. Under a fixed exchange rate, the flatter the *BP* curve, the larger will be the effect on national income of an expansionary fiscal policy. Provided the *BP* curve is flatter than the *LM* curve, an expansionary fiscal policy

will cause a balance of payments surplus (via its effect of increasing interest rates). The resulting increase in money supply will strengthen the initial effect of the fiscal policy.

4. Monetary policy under fixed exchange rates will have no effect on national income. Any expansion of money supply will, by depressing interest rates, simply lead to a balance of payments deficit and thus a reduction in the money supply again.
5. Under a floating exchange rate an appreciation will shift the *BP* curve upwards and a depreciation will shift it downwards.
6. If the *BP* curve is flatter than the *LM* curve, fiscal policy under a floating exchange rate will be dampened by the resulting changes in the exchange rate. An expansionary fiscal policy will lead to an appreciation (due to the effects of higher interest rates), which in turn will dampen the rise in aggregate demand.
7. Monetary policy will have a relatively large effect on aggregate demand under floating rates. A rise in money supply will reduce interest rates and raise aggregate demand. This will cause a balance of payments deficit and thus a depreciation. This in turn will lead to a further expansion of aggregate demand.

END OF CHAPTER QUESTIONS

1. Assume a free-floating exchange rate. Draw a diagram like Figure 25.6 (on page 822), only this time show an initial equilibrium national income with a balance of payments surplus.
   (a) Mark the size of the surplus.
   (b) Show the resulting shifts in the $(X-M)$ and the E curves.
   (c) Mark the eventual equilibrium.
   (d) Show the size of the income and substitution effects (of the change in the exchange rate).
   (e) Under what circumstances will the income effect be (i) 'desirable'; (ii) 'undesirable'?
   (f) Could the income effect of the change in the exchange rate ever be larger than the substitution effect?
2. Compare the relative effectiveness of fiscal and monetary policy under (a) fixed; (b) free-floating exchange rates. How is the effectiveness influenced by the elasticity of supply of international finance?
3. What will be the effects on the domestic economy under free-floating exchange rates if there is a rapid expansion in world economic activity? What will determine the size of these effects?
4. The following table shows a selection of nominal exchange rate indices (effective exchange rates) for the years 2011 to 2020, based on 2011 = 100.
   (a) Explain what is meant by an exchange rate index (also known as an effective exchange rate).
   (b) Calculate the annual rate of appreciation or depreciation for each currency for each year from 2012. It is suggested that you use an Excel spreadsheet.
   (c) Calculate the percentage appreciation or depreciation of each currency when comparing 2020 with 2011.
5. For what reasons might the exchange rate diverge from the purchasing-power parity rate over the longer term?
6. Why does exchange rate overshooting occur? What determines its magnitude?
7. Consider the argument that in the modern world of large-scale, short-term international capital movements, the ability of individual countries to affect their exchange rate is very limited.
8. If speculators had better information about future exchange rates, would their actions be more or less stabilising than at present?

*9. Using *IS/LM/BP* analysis, trace through the effect of (a) a deflationary fiscal policy and (b) a deflationary monetary policy under (i) a fixed exchange rate; (ii) a free-floating exchange rate.

	2011	2012	2013	2014	2015	2016	2017	2018	2019	2020
Australian $	100.00	102.92	98.18	92.39	85.21	84.03	86.31	82.54	78.82	77.43
US $	100.00	103.33	106.20	109.11	125.17	125.97	124.84	121.94	126.12	124.89
Japanese yen	100.00	102.54	83.08	76.60	72.43	81.74	78.12	77.94	81.31	82.30
Sterling	100.00	104.38	101.83	108.00	115.04	102.05	95.67	96.12	95.70	94.77
Euro	100.00	93.97	99.03	99.26	89.19	91.08	93.65	96.77	94.08	94.79
S Korean won	100.00	100.53	108.53	115.72	118.84	114.17	116.96	118.01	113.58	110.79

Source: Based on data from *Monthly Effective Exchange Rate Indices (narrow)*, Bank for International Settlements (April 2021).

Online resources

Additional case studies on the student website

25.1 The Marshall–Lerner condition. An analysis of the determinants of the elasticities of demand and supply of a currency.

25.2 The gold standard. A historical example of fixed exchange rates.

25.3 Currency turmoil in the 1990s. Two examples of speculative attacks on currencies: first on the Mexican peso in 1995; then on the Thai baht in 1997.

25.4 The euro, the US dollar and world currency markets. An analysis of the relationship between the euro and the dollar.

Websites relevant to this chapter

See sites listed at the end of Chapter 26 on page 892.

Economies in an Interdependent World

CHAPTER MAP

With the growth in globalisation, countries have become increasingly dependent on each other. In the first section, we explore the nature of the interdependence of economies and why countries are so vulnerable to international fluctuations. We then look at what can be done to create a greater co-ordination of international economic policies and consider the role of the G7 and G20 countries in this process.

The extreme solution to currency instability is for countries to adopt a common currency. In section 26.2, we look at the euro and how economic and monetary union (EMU) operates. Has the adoption of a single currency by 19 EU countries been of benefit to them? How have the members sought to tackle the problems of some of the member states?

Then we turn to the economic problems of the poorer countries of the world. These include all the countries of Africa and Latin America and most of the countries of Asia. More than three-quarters of the world's population lives in these countries. As Theodore Schultz said when accepting the Nobel Prize in Economics in 1979:

> Most of the people of the world are poor, so if we knew the economics of being poor, we would know much of the economics that really matters.

In section 26.3 we look at the nature and extent of their poverty and the means by which it can be measured. Then, in section 26.4, we look at the trade relations between the poorer countries and the advanced industrialised world. As we shall see, most developing countries are highly dependent for their development, or lack of it, on their relationships with the rich world.

The final section looks at one of the most serious problems facing poorer countries: the problem of huge international debts. We look at various measures to reschedule debts so as to reduce repayments. We also look at various moves to cancel some of the debts, especially of the poorest countries.

26.1 GLOBALISATION AND THE PROBLEM OF INSTABILITY

We live in an interdependent world. Countries are affected by the economic health of other countries and by their governments' policies. Problems in one part of the world can spread like a contagion to other parts, with perhaps no country immune.

There are two major ways in which this process of 'globalisation' affects individual economies. The first is through trade. The second is through financial markets.

Interdependence through trade

So long as nations trade with one another, the domestic economic actions of one nation will have implications for those which trade with it. For example, if the US administration feels that the US economy is growing too fast, it might adopt various contractionary fiscal and monetary measures, such as higher tax rates or interest rates. US consumers will not only consume fewer domestically produced goods, but also reduce their consumption of imported products. But US imports are other countries' exports. A fall in these other countries' exports will lead to a multiplier effect in these countries. Output and employment will fall.

Changes in aggregate demand in one country thus send ripples throughout the global economy. The process whereby changes in aggregate demand in country A affect national income in country B via changes in country A's imports, and hence the exports of country B, is known as the ***international trade multiplier***.

Assume that the US economy expands. What will determine the size of the multiplier effect on other countries?

KI 34 p453

The more open an economy, the more vulnerable it will be to changes in the level of economic activity in the rest of the world. This problem will be particularly acute if a nation is heavily dependent on trade with one other nation (e.g. Canada on the USA) or one other region (e.g. Switzerland on the EU).

Until very recently, international trade had been growing as a proportion of countries' national income for many years. This is illustrated in Figure 26.1, which shows the ratio of the sum of global exports and imports of goods and services to global GDP since 1970. This is the measure of openness we introduced in Chapter 24 (see page 773). Over the period, the ratio has risen from just over 25 per cent to around 60 per cent.

The growth of trade flows relative to GDP reflects the greater openness of nations to trade. It also means that countries are more interdependent and more vulnerable to world trade fluctuations, such as the global recession of the late 2000s. World output fell by 2 per cent in 2009 (at market exchange rates), while the volume of goods and services (imports and exports) fell by 10 per cent. This was the biggest contraction in global trade since the Second World War. After modest growth in both GDP and trade from 2010 to 2019, global output fell by over 3.5 per cent in 2020 in response to the COVID-19 pandemic, with trade volumes falling by 8 per cent.

Definition

International trade multiplier The effect on national income in country B of a change in national income in country A.

Figure 26.1 World trade in goods and services (imports plus exports) as a % of GDP

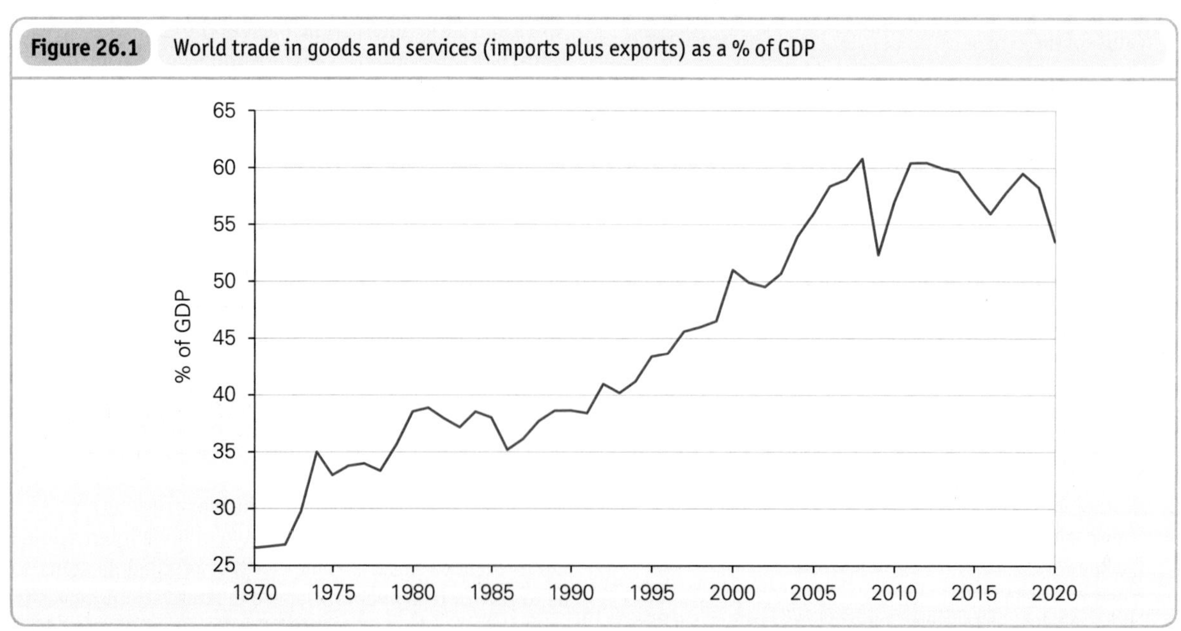

Note: 2020 figure is based on various forecasts
Source: Series NE.TRD.GNFS.ZS, World Bank, http://data.worldbank.org/indicator/NE.TRD.GNFS.ZS

There is some doubt, however, over world attitudes towards free trade. With the growth in protectionist rhetoric, such as that under the Trump administration, as well the disruption to trade from the COVID-19 pandemic, it is possible that world trade may have peaked as a proportion of GDP – at least for the time being.

Are exports likely to continue growing faster than GDP indefinitely? What will determine the outcome?

Financial interdependence

International trade has grown rapidly over the past 30 years, but international financial flows have grown much more rapidly. Trillions of dollars are traded across the foreign exchanges each day. Many of the transactions are short-term financial flows, moving to where interest rates are most favourable or to currencies where the exchange rate is likely to appreciate. This has meant that non-deposit financial institutions like pension funds, insurance companies and investment trusts have become important players on foreign exchange markets.

KI 35 p459

In Chapter 18 we identified a variety of financial instruments. The global nature of financial systems means that these financial instruments readily cross national borders. It also means that financial institutions operating in one country will have liabilities to foreign residents (individuals and institutions).

Figure 26.2 shows the growth in the claims of foreign residents on banks operating in the UK which take the form of sterling-denominated sight deposits, time deposits and repos. Holdings by foreign residents of these three financial instruments rose from £135 billion at the beginning of 1998 (11 per cent of sterling liabilities) to £627 billion in April 2008 (21 per cent of sterling liabilities). By June 2021, following the consolidation by banks of their balance sheets in response to the global financial crisis of 2007–8, the value of these liabilities was £479 billion (12 per cent of sterling liabilities), but this was still above the 1998 values, even after taking inflation into account.

Another demonstration of global financial interdependence is the foreign holdings of government securities. Figure 26.3 shows the importance of foreign demand for British gilts: i.e. for long-term British government securities. At the start of 1987, about £15 billion worth of gilts were held overseas, the equivalent to 11 per cent of holdings of gilts. By 2008, the total had risen to £191 billion or 36 per cent of all holdings. Then, with government borrowing rising rapidly in the aftermath of the financial crisis, foreign holdings rose rapidly, but not as rapidly as domestic holdings. This pattern was repeated following the COVID-19 pandemic, so that by 2021 although foreign holdings had risen to over £700 billion, the percentage had fallen to 28 per cent of holdings.[1] In Box 26.1 we consider the significance of foreign purchases of American government debt.

A stark example of global financial interdependence was the collapse of the sub-prime credit markets in the USA in the late 2000s, which spread like a contagion to cause a global recession. Household debt in many advanced economies, including the UK and USA, had grown markedly as a

1 Note that this still means that the bulk of national debt is held by residents in the UK. In other words, most of what the government owes is in the form of the savings by UK individuals and companies.

Figure 26.2 Sterling liabilities of UK banks to non-domestic residents

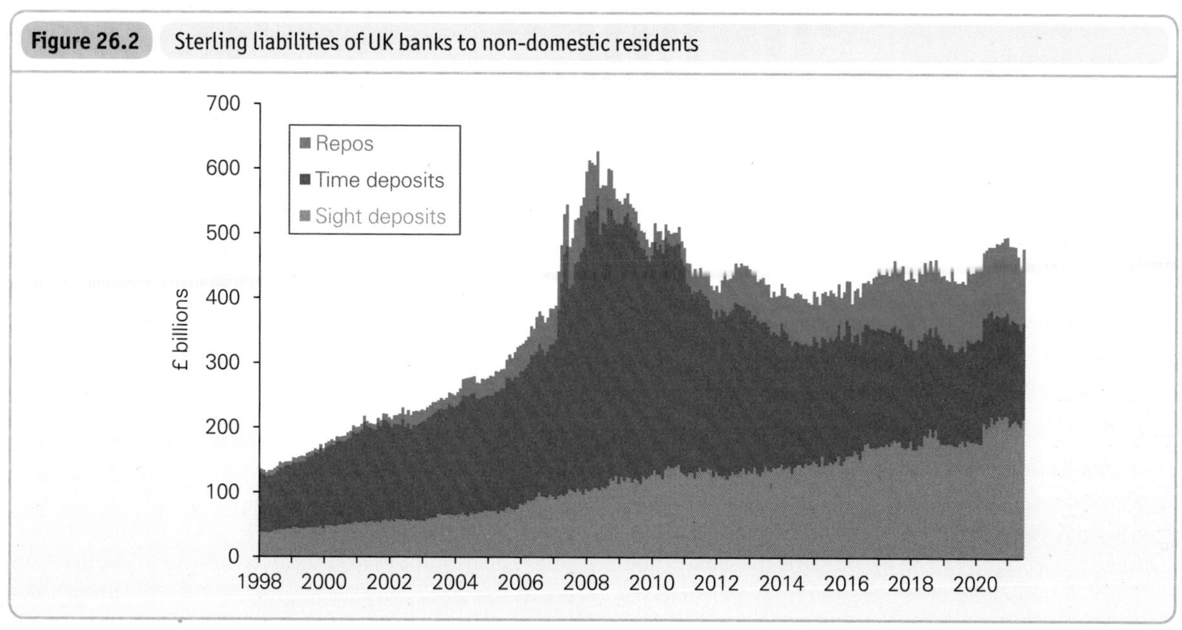

Note: Data include building societies from 2010; data are not seasonally adjusted.
Source: Based on series RPMTBFF, RPMTBFM, RPMTBFT (up to end of 2009) and RPMB3OM, RPMB3TM and RPMB3WM (from 2010) from *Statistical Interactive Database*, Bank of England (data published 29 July 2021), www.bankofengland.co.uk/boeapps/iadb/

BOX 26.1 ECONOMIC AND FINANCIAL INTERDEPENDENCIES: TRADE IMBALANCE IN THE USA AND CHINA

Is the world paying for excessive American expenditure?

America's current account deficit

In 2020, the USA had a current account deficit of close to \$650 billion – the equivalent of 3 per cent of GDP (see chart). American current account deficits are not new. In the period from 1997 to 2020, the, the US current account deficit averaged 3.3 per cent of GDP, reaching almost 6 per cent in 2006. It is forecast to remain at between 2 to 3 per cent during the first half of the 2020s.

The current account deficit is offset by an equal and opposite capital-plus-financial account surplus, much of which consists of the purchase of US government bonds and Treasury bills. These massive inflows to the USA are thought to represent some three-quarters of all the savings which the rest of the world invests abroad. These financial inflows have permitted the persistence of sizeable US current account deficits.

To attract such large inflows, it might be expected that US interest rates would have to be high. Yet US interest rates have been consistently low over the past couple of decades and, of course, exceptionally low during the global financial crisis and the COVID-19 pandemic. How is it, then, that with such low interest rates, the USA has managed to attract such vast inflows of finance and thereby maintain such a large financial account surplus?

China's appetite for dollars

Several Asian currencies, including the Chinese yuan (or 'renminbi'), were pegged to the dollar and had been running large current account surpluses. For instance, the Chinese current account surplus was typically around 5 to 10 per cent of GDP during the mid- to late 2000s (see chart). Instead of letting the yuan appreciate against the dollar, the Chinese central bank used the surpluses to buy dollars.

US and Chinese current account (% of GDP)

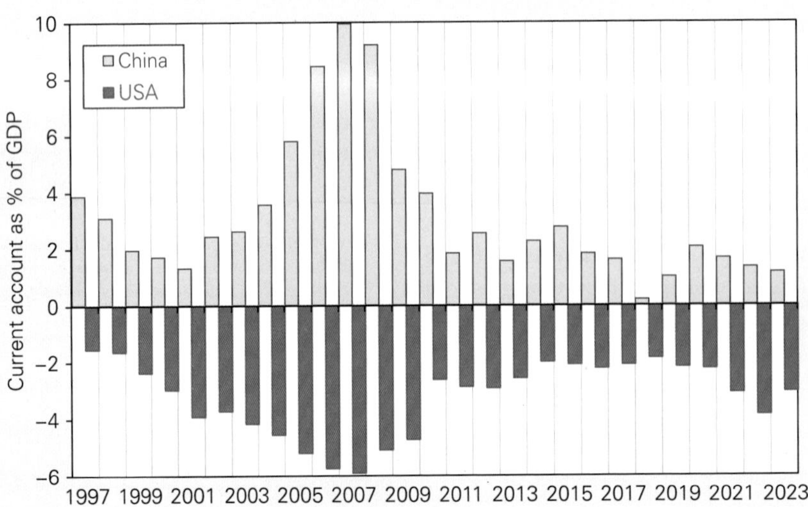

Note: Figures from 2020 are forecasts.
Source: Based on data from *World Economic Outlook Database*, IMF (April 2021), https://www.imf.org/en/Publications/SPROLLs/world-economic-outlook-databases

proportion of household disposable income. Between 1995 and 2007, the stock of debt held by UK households increased from around 100 per cent to 170 per cent of annual disposable income (see Box 17.2). In the USA over the same period, the stock of household debt increased from 95 to 145 per cent of annual disposable income.

As we discussed in section 18.2, the growth of domestic credit has been facilitated both by financial deregulation, including the removal of capital controls, and the greater use by financial institutions of wholesale funding. The process of securitisation (see pages 571–4), for instance, enabled financial institutions to raise capital from financial investors across the globe in order to provide domestic households with both mortgages and short-term credit. In other words, the aggressive expansion of domestic banks' balance sheets was funded by international financial flows.

CASE STUDIES AND APPLICATIONS

There were three perceived advantages in doing this. First, it allowed China to *build up reserves* and thereby bolster its ability to resist any future speculative attacks on its currency. Chinese foreign exchange reserves rose from around $170 billion in 2000 to $4 trillion in 2014 – a staggering 24-fold increase. The effect was a huge increase in global liquidity and hence money supply.

Second, and more important, it *kept their exchange rates low* and thereby helped to keep their exports competitive. This helped to sustain their rapid rates of economic growth. Third, it helped to *keep US interest rates down* and therefore boost US spending on Asian exports.

In 2005, the Chinese, after much international pressure, agreed to revalue the yuan and would then peg it against a basket of currencies with subsequent further revaluations. Between July 2005 and July 2008 the yuan was allowed to appreciate by around 18 per cent against the US dollar while the exchange rate index rose by 7 per cent (the exchange rate index of the US dollar fell by 15 per cent).

But, with the global economic downturn biting in 2008 and concerns about slowing Chinese export growth, the Chinese authorities effectively fixed the yuan once again.

This remained the case until June 2010 when again the yuan was revalued. Between June 2010 and January 2014 the yuan appreciated a further 12 per cent against the US dollar. Therefore, over the period from July 2005 to January 2014 the yuan had appreciated by around 33 per cent against the US dollar.

China's economic slowdown

The managed appreciation of the yuan, coupled with the slowdown of the global economy, saw China's current account surplus begin to wane, falling from 9 per cent of GDP in 2008 to 1.5 per cent by 2013. Meanwhile, though still sizeable, the USA's current account deficit had shrunk. By 2013 the deficit had fallen to 2.2 per cent of GDP – less than half the level of the mid-2000s.

China's economic growth rate, which had been as high as 14 per cent in 2007, fell back to between 6 and 8 per cent from 2012 (see figure in Box 1.5 on page 23). This reflected a sharp decline in the growth of the volume of China's exports of goods and services as the economic fallout from the financial crisis continued to affect global growth. China's export growth, which had averaged 26 per cent from 2002 to 2007, stood at 8 per cent in 2012. The growth of export volumes would then halve to 4 per cent in 2013 and again to 2 per cent in 2014, before contracting by 2 per cent in 2015.

China's central bank responded by cutting interest rates in late 2014 with the 1-year Loan Prime Rate (LRP) falling from 5.8 per cent to 4.3 per cent a year later. In August 2015, China also took steps to devalue the yuan against the US dollar. However, this raised expectations of further devaluations and loosening of monetary policy. Hence, the yuan began falling more sharply, forcing the central bank to sell dollars to reduce the rate of depreciation.

Although the yuan rose against the dollar through 2017, it then began to slide again later in 2018. Growth was easing as export growth weakened and now there was a threat of a trade war with the USA. In response to the country's persistent trade deficits with China, the Trump administration imposed tariffs on a range of Chinese imports with threats of more to come. With China responding with tariffs of its own, fears grew that the USA and China were embarked on a 'tit-for-tat' trade war.

By August 2019, the yuan had fallen below what many saw as the important threshold of 7 to the dollar. This was the first time it had done so in over a decade. This led the USA to declare China a 'currency manipulator'.

The USA and China signed a 'Phase 1' trade deal in 2020. This included a commitment from China not to engage in competitive devaluations. From May 2020 through to the end of the year, the yuan appreciated by around 9 per cent against the dollar.

Going forward, some argue that China may be more willing to allow the yuan to be determined by market forces and more widely traded on the international exchanges.

Examine the merits for the Chinese of (a) floating the yuan freely; (b) pegging it to a trade-weighted basket of currencies.

Using the IMF World Economic Outlook Database (www.imf.org/external/ns/cs.aspx?id=28), download for China data on output growth and the rates of inflation and unemployment from the early 1990s. Use the data, and any other you feel relevant, to construct a short note on the macroeconomic environment in China over the past three decades.

Financial deregulation and innovation has therefore created a complex chain of interdependencies between financial institutions, financial systems and economies. But this chain is only as strong as its weakest link. In the financial crisis of the late 2000s overly aggressive lending practices by banks in one part of the world impacted on financial investors worldwide. As US interest rates rose from 2004 to 2007 (see figure in Box 25.5), the income flows from American households to banks began to dry up; US households began to fall in arrears and, worse still, default on their loans. But these income flows were the source of the return for global financial investors who had purchased collateralised debt obligations (see page 572). Hence, the new financial order meant the contagion went international.

Global financial interdependence also means that changes in interest rates in one country can affect the economies of

Figure 26.3 Overseas holdings of UK government gilts

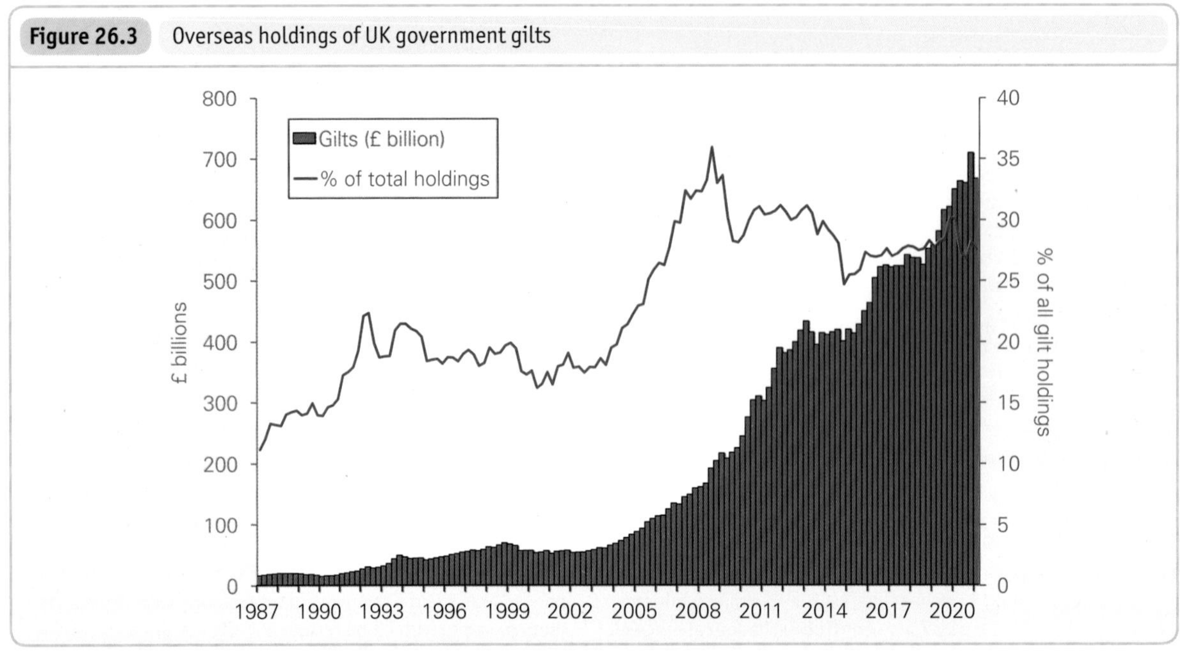

Source: Based on data from ONS, series NIJI and NLDU, www.ons.gov.uk/economy/governmentpublicsectorandtaxes/publicspending/

other countries. Assume that the Federal Reserve Bank in the USA, worried about rising inflation, decides to raise interest rates. What will be the effect on business in America's trading partners? There are three major effects.

- If aggregate demand in America falls, so will its expenditure on imports from firms abroad, thus directly affecting businesses exporting to the USA. With a decline in their exports, aggregate demand in these other countries falls.
- The higher interest rate in the USA will tend to drive up interest rates in other countries. This will depress investment. Again, aggregate demand will tend to fall in these countries.
- The higher interest rate will attract an inflow of funds to the USA from other countries. This will cause the dollar to appreciate relative to other currencies, which will make these other countries' exports to the USA more competitive and imports from the USA relatively more expensive. This will result in an improvement in the current account of the USA's trading partners: their exports rise and imports fall. This represents a rise in aggregate demand in these countries – the opposite from the first two effects.

What will be the effect on the UK economy if the European Central Bank cuts interest rates?

International business cycles

Major economic shocks in one part of the world, such as the USA or China, can reverberate around the globe. The credit crunch of 2007/8 resulting from defaults on US sub-prime debt was a dramatic example of this. As a consequence of both trade and financial interdependence, the world economy, like the economy of any individual country, tends to experience periodic fluctuations in economic activity – an *international* business cycle. The implication of this is that countries will tend to share common problems and concerns at the same time. At one time, the most pressing problem may be world inflationary pressures; at another time, it may be a world recession. TC 12 p455

In order to avoid 'beggar-my-neighbour' policies, it is better to seek *common* solutions to these common problems: i.e. solutions that are international in scope and design rather than narrowly based on national self-interest. For example, during a world recession, countries are likely to suffer from rising unemployment. Policies that lead to a depreciation of the exchange rate (such as cutting interest rates) will help to stimulate demand by making exports cheaper and imports more expensive. But this will then only worsen the trade balance of other countries, whose aggregate demand will thus fall. The first country is thus tackling its own unemployment at the expense of rising unemployment in other countries.

However, if other nations (which will also be experiencing higher unemployment) can be convinced to co-ordinate their policy actions, an expansionary *international* economic policy will benefit all. In addition to the resulting rise in their imports, all nations will also experience rising export sales.

Even if national policies are not in the strictest sense co-ordinated, discussions between nations regarding the nature and magnitude of the problems they face may help to improve the policy-making process.

Give some examples of beggar-my-neighbour policies.

The need for international policy co-ordination

Global economic interdependence and an international business cycle can aid the process of international co-operation between countries. For instance, in response to the financial crisis of the late 2000s world leaders were seriously worried that the whole world would plunge into recession. What was needed was a co-ordinated policy response from governments and central banks. This came in October 2008 when governments in Britain, Europe, North America and other parts of the world injected some $2 trillion of extra capital into banks.

Countries frequently meet in various groupings – from the narrow group of the world's seven richest countries (the G7) to broader groups such as the G20, which, in addition to the G7 and other rich countries, also includes larger developing countries, such as China, India, Brazil and Indonesia.

Today the G20 is considered to be the principal economic forum for discussing global economic and other concerns and for considering policy responses. In effect, the emergence of the G20 as the premier global forum recognises two important developments:

- First, there has been a remarkable growth seen in emerging economies such as India and China (see sections 24.1 and 26.4).
- Second, the increasing scale of interdependency through trade and finance and the impact of two recent global shocks – the global financial crisis and the COVID-19 pandemic – has demonstrated the need for a co-ordinated response from a larger representation of the international community.

Global interdependence also raises questions about the role that international organisations like the World Trade Organization (WTO) and the International Monetary Fund (IMF) should play. The WTO's role is to encourage freer trade. We considered its role in section 24.2. The IMF's remit is to promote global growth and stability, to help countries through economic difficulty and to help developing economies achieve macroeconomic stability and reduce poverty. In response to the global economic and financial crisis of the late 2000s, the IMF's budget was substantially increased. Then, in 2021 during the COVID-19 pandemic, member countries and central banks agreed to double the amount they stood ready to lend to the IMF.

International harmonisation of economic policies

The five main underlying causes of exchange rate movements are divergences in *interest rates, growth rates, inflation rates, current account balance of payments* and *government deficits*. Table 26.1 shows the variation in the levels of these and related indicators for a sample of nine countries. These divergences still remain considerable.

KI 35 p459

An important issue for G7 and G20 meetings is how to generate world economic growth without major currency fluctuations. To achieve this it is important that there is a ***harmonisation*** of economic policies between nations. In other words, it is important that all the major countries are pursuing consistent policies aiming at common international goals.

But how can policy harmonisation be achieved? As long as there are significant domestic differences between the major economies, there is likely to be conflict, not harmony. For example, if one country, say the USA, is worried about the size of its budget deficit, it may be unwilling to respond to world demands for a stimulus to aggregate demand to pull the world economy out of recession. What is more, speculators, seeing differences between countries, are likely to exaggerate them by their actions, causing large changes in exchange rates. The G7 countries have therefore sought to achieve greater ***convergence*** of their economies. But whilst convergence may be a goal of policy, in practice it has proved more elusive.

KI 34 p453

Referring to Table 26.1, in what respects was there greater convergence between these countries from the 2010s than previously?

Because of a lack of convergence, there are serious difficulties in achieving international policy harmonisation:

- Countries' budget deficits and national debt may differ substantially as a proportion of their national income. This puts very different pressures on the interest rates necessary to service these debts. In 2020, the UK had a general government gross debt to GDP ratio of just over 100 per cent. This compared with under 50 per cent for South Korea and over 250 per cent for Japan (see Table 26.1).
- Harmonising rates of monetary growth or inflation targets would involve letting interest rates fluctuate with the demand for money. Without convergence in the demand for money, interest rate fluctuations could be severe.
- Harmonising interest rates would involve abandoning monetary, inflation and exchange rate targets (unless interest rate 'harmonisation' meant adjusting interest rates so as to maintain monetary or inflation targets or a fixed exchange rate).

Definitions

International harmonisation of economic policies Where countries attempt to co-ordinate their macroeconomic policies so as to achieve common goals.

Convergence of economies When countries achieve similar levels of growth, inflation, budget deficits as a percentage of GDP, balance of payments, etc.

Table 26.1 International macroeconomic indicators

		Australia	China	France	Germany	Ireland	Japan	S Korea	UK	USA
Nominal exchange rate index (annual % change)	2000–07	2.16	3.10	0.85	1.04	1.29	−1.48	2.45	0.68	−1.35
	2008–10	3.10	3.19	−0.40	−0.57	0.19	10.24	−7.83	−8.01	−0.39
	2011–19	−1.66	3.09	0.11	0.19	−0.20	−0.81	1.51	−0.07	2.42
	2020	−0.72	2.90	1.54	2.03	1.59	2.51	−0.85	0.49	1.86
Short-term (3-month) nominal interest rates (%)	2000–07	5.56	2.57	3.24	3.24	3.24	0.20	4.82	4.91	3.56
	2008–09	5.03	2.75	2.22	2.22	2.22	0.60	3.60	2.47	1.28
	2010–19	2.59	5.46	0.12	0.12	0.12	0.17	2.23	0.64	0.81
	2020	0.26	6.98	−0.43	−0.43	−0.43	−0.04	0.92	0.30	0.53
Annual growth in real GDP, %	2000–07	3.35	10.55	2.15	1.55	5.79	1.45	5.67	2.75	2.72
	2008–09	2.30	9.94	−0.22	−0.18	−2.69	−0.94	3.54	−0.77	−0.04
	2010–19	2.62	7.32	1.32	1.68	6.90	0.95	2.92	1.81	2.27
	2020	−2.44	2.27	−8.23	−4.90	2.48	−4.83	−0.96	−9.92	−3.51
Unemployment rate (% of labour force)	2000–07	5.62	3.94	8.62	9.25	4.67	4.69	3.67	5.14	5.04
	2008–10	5.01	4.21	8.60	7.34	11.35	4.71	3.51	7.08	8.23
	2011–19	5.53	3.97	9.65	4.50	10.27	3.40	3.53	5.83	5.84
	2020	6.51	3.80	8.18	4.18	5.63	2.79	3.94	4.50	8.11
Consumer price inflation (% change in CPI)	2000–07	3.19	1.69	1.93	1.68	3.51	−0.32	2.97	1.59	2.78
	2008–10	2.99	2.83	1.67	1.37	−0.06	−0.23	3.46	3.02	1.71
	2011–19	2.03	2.52	1.23	1.45	0.62	0.60	1.59	2.11	1.79
	2020	0.87	2.39	0.53	0.37	−0.46	−0.02	0.54	0.85	1.25
Current account balance (% of GDP)	2000–07	−5.05	4.46	0.68	2.88	−1.75	3.25	1.31	−2.37	−4.79
	2008–10	−4.35	5.97	−0.63	5.76	−4.03	3.13	2.04	−3.47	−3.41
	2011–19	−2.86	1.71	−0.68	7.39	−0.79	2.55	4.76	−4.01	−2.25
	2020	2.49	2.03	−2.34	7.09	4.61	3.28	4.62	−3.93	−3.09
General government surplus (% of GDP)	2000–07	1.10	−1.84	−2.74	−2.53	1.45	−6.03	2.71	−1.87	−3.05
	2008–10	−3.60	−0.71	−5.78	−2.55	−17.63	−8.02	0.35	−8.13	−10.28
	2011–19	−2.86	−2.61	−3.73	0.73	−3.67	−5.39	0.83	−4.54	−5.55
	2020	−9.95	−11.39	−9.90	−4.19	−5.28	−12.62	−3.31	−13.43	−15.84
General government gross debt (% of GDP)	2000–07	13.44	25.96	63.05	62.88	29.07	160.68	21.83	37.55	61.10
	2008–10	16.27	31.88	79.02	73.61	63.31	195.04	28.81	62.26	85.32
	2011–19	36.06	44.17	94.96	71.47	88.20	229.78	38.87	84.91	104.92
	2020	63.13	66.83	113.46	68.93	59.80	256.22	48.68	103.66	127.11

Sources: a) Exchange rates: Bank for International Settlements, www.bis.org/statistics/eer.htm; b) Interest rates: OECD Data, OECD, https://data.oecd.org/; and *Federal Reserve Economic Data*, Federal Reserve Bank, St. Louis, https://fred.stlouisfed.org/; c) Other indicators: *World Economic Outlook database*, IMF, www.imf.org/en/Publications/SPROLLs/world-economic-outlook-databases

- Countries have different internal structural relationships. A lack of convergence here means that countries with higher endemic cost inflation would require higher interest rates and higher unemployment if international inflation rates were to be harmonised, or higher inflation if interest rates were to be harmonised.
- Countries have different rates of productivity increase, product development, investment and market penetration. A lack of convergence here means that the growth in exports (relative to imports) will differ for any given level of inflation or growth.
- Countries may be very unwilling to change their domestic policies to fall in line with other countries. They may prefer the other countries to fall in line with them!

If any one of the five – interest rates, growth rates, inflation rates, current account balance of payments or government deficits – could be harmonised across countries, it is likely that the other four would then not be harmonised.

Total convergence and thus total harmonisation may not be possible. Nevertheless, most governments favour some movement in that direction: some is better than none. To achieve this, co-operation is necessary.

Although co-operation is the ideal, in practice discord often tends to dominate international economic relations. The reason is that governments are normally concerned with the economic interests of other countries only if they coincide with those of their own country. This, however, can create a prisoners' dilemma problem (see pages 242–4 and 413). With each country looking solely after its own interests, the world economy suffers and everyone is worse off.

If total convergence were achieved, would harmonisation of policies follow automatically?

Section summary

1. Changes in aggregate demand in one country will affect the amount of imports purchased and thus the amount of exports sold by other countries and hence their national income. There is thus an international trade multiplier effect.
2. Changes in interest rates in one country will affect financial flows to and from other countries, and hence their exchange rates, interest rates and national income.
3. To prevent problems in one country spilling over to other countries and to stabilise the international business cycle will require co-ordinated policies between nations.
4. Currency fluctuations can be lessened if countries harmonise their economic policies. Ideally this will involve achieving compatible growth rates, inflation rates, balance of payments and government deficits (as percentages of GDP) and interest rates. The attempt to harmonise one of these goals, however, may bring conflicts with one of the other goals.
5. Leaders of the G7 and G20 countries meet at least annually to discuss ways of harmonising their policies. Usually, however, domestic issues are more important to the leaders than international ones, and frequently they pursue policies that are not in the interests of the other countries.

26.2 EUROPEAN ECONOMIC AND MONETARY UNION (EMU)

The ultimate way for a group of countries to achieve greater currency stability between themselves is to adopt a single currency and, therefore, to have a common central bank and a common monetary policy – to form an ***economic and monetary union (EMU)***. This is what has happened in the EU, with countries coming together to adopt a single currency – the euro. The euro began in 1999, with notes and coins circulating from 2002. Initially 11 countries joined; by 2015 there were 19 members.

The ERM (exchange rate mechanism)

The forerunner to EMU was the ***exchange rate mechanism (ERM)***. This was an adjustable peg system, where members pegged their exchange rates to each other while floating against the rest of the world. This encouraged trade between the members and enabled the combined reserves of all member countries to prevent excessive fluctuations of their currencies with the rest of the world.

Under the system, each currency was given a central exchange rate with each of the other ERM currencies in a grid. However, fluctuations were allowed from the central rate within specified bands, typically of up to 0.25 per cent. The central rates were adjusted from time to time by agreement. All the currencies floated jointly with currencies outside the ERM.

If a currency approached the upper or lower limit against *any* other ERM currency, intervention would take place to maintain the currencies within the band. This would take the form of central banks in the ERM selling the strong currency and buying the weak one. It could also involve the weak currency countries raising interest rates and the strong currency countries lowering them.

The ERM in practice

The ERM came into existence in March 1979 and the majority of the EU countries were members. The UK, however, initially chose not to join. Spain joined in 1989, the UK in 1990 and Portugal in April 1992.

Definitions

Economic and monetary union (EMU) The adoption by a group of countries of a single currency with a single central bank and a single monetary policy. In the EU, the term applies to the countries that have adopted the euro.

Exchange rate mechanism A semi-fixed system whereby participating EU countries allow fluctuations against each other's currencies only within agreed bands. Collectively they float freely against all other currencies.

Sterling entered the ERM at a central rate of £1 = 2.95 German marks with permitted fluctuations of ±6 against any other ERM currency. This rate proved unsustainable. German interest rates were rising to dampen inflationary pressures partly fuelled by substantial public expenditures following the reunification of Germany. US interest rates by contrast were falling to help stimulate economic growth in the face of recession. The result was a large outflow of capital from the USA, much of it going to Germany. The effect was to push up the value of the German mark. Consequently, currencies like sterling and the Italian lira were repeatedly at the bottom of their permitted exchange rate band with the mark. This was despite high and rising interest rates and, in the case of the UK, despite the economy sliding rapidly into recession.

In September 1992, things reached a crisis point. On 16 September – known thereafter as 'Black Wednesday' – the UK and Italy were forced to suspend their membership of the ERM. Both currencies were floated and depreciated substantially.

Turmoil returned in the summer of 1993, with pressure this time on the French franc. In response, EU finance ministers agreed to adopt very wide ±15 bands, though with bands this wide it hardly seemed like a 'pegged' system at all. Within months, however, the crisis passed and exchange rate fluctuations began to fall within a very narrow range and for most of the time within ±2.25 per cent.

Italy rejoined the ERM in November 1996 as part of its bid to join the single European currency. Austria joined in 1995, Finland in 1996 and Greece in 1998. By the time the ERM was replaced by the single currency in 1999, only Sweden and the UK were outside the ERM.

The Maastricht Treaty and the road to the single currency

The ERM was conceived as a stage on the road to complete economic and monetary union (EMU) of member states. Details of the path towards EMU were finalised in the Maastricht Treaty, which was signed in February 1992. The timetable for EMU involved the adoption of a single currency by 1999 at the latest.

Before they could join the single currency, member states were obliged to achieve convergence of their economies. Each country had to meet five convergence criteria:

- Inflation: should be no more than 1.5 per cent above the average inflation rate of the three countries in the EU with the lowest inflation.
- Interest rates: the rate on long-term government bonds should be no more than 2 per cent above the average of the three countries with the lowest inflation rates.
- Budget deficit: should be no more than 3 per cent of GDP at market prices.
- National debt: should be no more than 60 per cent of GDP at market prices.
- Exchange rates: the currency should have been within the normal ERM bands for at least two years with no realignments or excessive intervention.

Before the launch of the single currency, the Council of Ministers had to decide which countries had met the convergence criteria and would thus be eligible to form a ***currency union*** by fixing their currencies permanently to the euro. Their national currencies would effectively disappear.

At the same time, a European System of Central Banks (ESCB) would be created, consisting of a European Central Bank (ECB) and the central banks of the member states. The ECB would be independent, both from governments and from EU political institutions. It would operate the monetary policy on behalf of the countries that had adopted the single currency.

The birth of the euro

In March 1998, the European Commission ruled that 11 of the 15 member states were eligible to proceed to EMU in January 1999. The UK and Denmark were to exercise their opt-out, and Sweden and Greece failed to meet one or more of the convergence criteria. (Greece joined the euro in 2001.)

All 11 countries unambiguously met the interest rate and inflation criteria, but doubts were expressed by many 'Eurosceptics' as to whether they all genuinely met the other three criteria.

- *Exchange rates.* Neither Finland nor Italy had been in the ERM for two years and the Irish punt was revalued by 3 per cent on 16 March 1998. However, the Commission regarded these three countries as being sufficiently close to the reference value.
- *Government deficits.* All 11 countries met this criterion, but some countries only managed to achieve a deficit of 3 per cent or below by taking one-off measures, such as a special tax in Italy and counting privatisation receipts in Germany. Yet, under the Stability and Growth Pact, eurozone countries would be required to keep their deficits within the 3 per cent limit (see Box 22.4). The concern was that countries that only just met this criterion at time of entry would find it difficult to keep within the limit in times of recession or slow growth. This proved to be the case with France and Germany from 2002 to 2005.
- *Government debt.* Only four countries had debts that did not exceed 60 per cent (France, Finland, Luxembourg and the UK). However, the Maastricht Treaty allowed countries to exceed this value as long as the debt was

Definition

Currency union A group of countries (or regions) using a common currency.

'sufficiently diminishing and approaching the reference value at a satisfactory pace'. Critics argued that this phrase was interpreted too loosely.

The euro came into being on 1 January 1999, but euro banknotes and coins were not introduced until 1 January 2002. In the meantime, national currencies continued to exist alongside the euro, but at irrevocably fixed rates. The old notes and coins were withdrawn a few weeks after the introduction of euro notes and coins.

Ten new members joined the EU in May 2004, and another two in January 2007. Under the Maastricht Treaty, they were all required to make preparations for joining the euro by meeting the convergence criteria and being in a new version of the exchange rate mechanism with a wide exchange rate band. Under ERM II, euro candidate countries must keep their exchange rates within ±15 per cent of a central rate against the euro. Estonia, Lithuania and Slovenia were the first to join ERM II in June 2004 with Latvia, Cyprus, Malta and Slovakia following in 2005. Slovenia adopted the euro in 2007, Malta and Cyprus in 2008, Slovakia in 2009, Estonia in 2011, Latvia in 2014 and Lithuania in 2015, making a total of 19 countries using the euro.

Advantages of the single currency

EMU has several major advantages for its members.

Elimination of the costs of converting currencies. With separate currencies in each of the EU countries, costs were incurred each time one currency was exchanged into another. The elimination of these costs, however, was probably the least important benefit from the single currency. The European Commission estimated that the effect was to increase the GDP of the countries concerned by an average of only 0.4 per cent and perhaps less so for those countries with well-developed financial markets.

Increased competition and efficiency. Not only does the single currency eliminate the need to convert one currency into another (a barrier to competition), but it has brought more transparency in pricing, and has put greater downward pressure on prices in high-cost firms and countries. This, of course, does not necessarily favour business, which might find its profits squeezed, but it generally benefits consumers. Although there has been some price convergence across the eurozone, it has not been as extensive as many thought it would be.

KI 11 p72

Elimination of exchange rate uncertainty (between the members). Removal of exchange rate uncertainty has helped to encourage trade between the eurozone countries. Perhaps more importantly, it has encouraged investment by firms that trade between these countries, given the greater certainty in calculating costs and revenues from such trade.

In times of economic uncertainty, such as the credit crunch of 2008, exchange rate volatility between countries can be high. By adopting the euro, the uncertainty that would otherwise be created, is eliminated for trade between eurozone countries.

Increased inward investment. Investment from the rest of the world is attracted to a eurozone of over 340 million inhabitants, where there is no fear of internal currency movements. As well as potentially increasing its global share of FDI, by removing the uncertainty arising from possible exchange rate volatility between its 19 members, the eurozone countries may experience less volatility in FDI flows than would otherwise be the case.

Lower inflation and interest rates. A single monetary policy forces convergence in inflation rates (just as inflation rates are very similar between the different regions within a country). With the ECB being independent from short-term political manipulation, this has resulted in a low average inflation rate in the eurozone countries. This, in turn, has helped to convince markets that the euro will be strong relative to other currencies. The result is lower long-term rates of interest. This, in turn, further encourages investment in the eurozone countries, both by member states and by the rest of the world.

Opposition to EMU

European monetary union has, however, attracted considerable criticism. Many 'Eurosceptics' see within it a surrender of national political and economic sovereignty. Their arguments are essentially ones of principle.

Others, including those more sympathetic to monetary union in principle, raise concerns about the design of the monetary and fiscal systems within which monetary union operates – a design that, in principle, can be amended (see Boxes 22.4 and 22.7).

Arguments against EMU in principle

The lack of national currencies. This is a serious problem if an economy is at all out of harmony with the rest of the Union. For example, if countries such as Greece and Spain have higher rates of inflation (due, say, to greater cost-push pressures), then how are they to make their goods competitive with the rest of the Union? With separate currencies these countries could allow their currencies to depreciate. With a single currency, however, they could become depressed 'regions' of Europe, with rising unemployment and all the other problems of depressed regions within a country. This might then require significant regional policies – policies that might not be in place or, if they were, would be seen as too interventionist by the political right.

How might multiplier effects (the principle of cumulative causation) lead to prosperous regions becoming more prosperous and less prosperous regions falling even further behind?

TC 15 p543

Proponents of EMU argue that it is better to tackle the problem of high inflation in such countries by the disciplines of competition from other EU countries, than merely to feed that inflation by keeping separate currencies and allowing repeated depreciation, with all the uncertainty that they bring.

What is more, the high-inflation countries tend to be the poorer ones with lower wage levels (albeit faster wage *increases*). With the increased mobility of labour and capital as the single market deepens, resources are likely to be attracted to such countries. This could help to narrow the gap between the richer and poorer member states.

The critics of EMU counter this by arguing that labour is relatively immobile, given cultural and language barriers. Thus an unemployed worker in Dublin could not easily move to a job in Turin or Helsinki. What the critics are arguing here is that the EU is not an ***optimal currency area*** (see Box 26.2).

Loss of separate monetary policies. Perhaps the most serious criticism is that the same rate of interest must apply to all eurozone countries: the 'one-size-fits-all' problem. The trouble is that while one country might require a lower rate of interest in order to ward off recession (such as Portugal, Ireland and Greece in 2010–11), others might require a

Definition

Optimal currency area The optimal size of a currency area is the one that maximises the benefits from having a single currency relative to the costs. If the area were increased or decreased in size, the costs would rise relative to the benefits.

BOX 26.2 OPTIMAL CURRENCY AREAS

EXPLORING ECONOMICS

When it pays to pay in the same currency

Imagine that each town and village used a different currency. Think how inconvenient it would be having to keep exchanging one currency into another, and how difficult it would be working out the relative value of items in different parts of the country.

Clearly, there are benefits to using a common currency, not only within a country but across different countries. The benefits include greater transparency in pricing, more open competition, greater certainty for investors and the avoidance of having to pay commission when you change one currency into another. There are also the benefits from having a single monetary policy if that is delivered in a more consistent and effective way than by individual countries.

So why not have a single currency for the whole world? The problem is that the bigger a single currency area gets, the more likely the conditions are to diverge in the different parts of the area. Some parts may have high unemployment and require expansionary policies. Others may have low unemployment and suffer from inflationary pressures. They may require *contractionary* policies.

What is more, different members of the currency area may experience quite different shocks to their economies, whether from outside the union (e.g. a fall in the price of one of their major exports) or from inside (e.g. a prolonged strike). These 'asymmetric shocks' would imply that different parts of the currency area should adopt different policies. But with a common monetary policy and hence common interest rates, and with no possibility of devaluation/revaluation of the currency of individual members, the scope for separate economic policies is reduced.

The costs of asymmetric shocks (and hence the costs of a single currency area) will be greater, the less the mobility of labour and capital, the less the flexibility of prices and wage rates, and the fewer the alternative policies there are that can be turned to (such as fiscal and regional policies).

So is the eurozone an optimal currency area? Certainly, strong doubts have been raised by many economists.

- Labour is relatively immobile.
- There are structural differences between the member states.
- The transmission effects of interest rate changes are different between the member countries, given that countries have different proportions of borrowing at variable interest rates and different proportions of consumer debt to GDP.
- Exports to countries outside the eurozone account for different proportions of the members' GDP, and thus their economies are affected differently by a change in the rate of exchange of the euro against other currencies.
- Wage rates are relatively inflexible.
- Under the Stability and Growth Pact and the Fiscal Compact (see Box 22.4), the scope for using discretionary fiscal policy is curtailed except in times of severe economic difficulty, such as that during the COVID-19 pandemic, when an escape clause can be activated.

This does not necessarily mean, however, that the costs of having a single European currency outweigh the benefits. Also, the problems outlined above should decline over time as the single market develops. Finally, the problem of asymmetric shocks can be exaggerated. European economies are highly diversified; there are often more differences *within* economies than between them. Thus shocks are more likely to affect different industries or localities, rather than whole countries. Changing the exchange rate, if that were still possible, would hardly be an appropriate policy in these circumstances.

Why is a single currency area likely to move towards becoming an optimal currency area over time?

Undertake a literature search on work looking at whether the eurozone is an optimal currency area. Write a short review of the relevant literature you discover.

higher one to prevent inflation. Furthermore, some countries may be more sensitive to interest changes than others, hence the optimal change in interest rates for one country may represent too much or too little of a change in another.

The greater the convergence between economies within the eurozone, the less serious this problem is. Consequently, it was hoped that, with common fiscal rules and free trade, these divergences would diminish over time. Eurosceptics, however, argue that there has been increasing divergence between members especially in terms of the size of government deficits and debt and the confidence of the financial markets in countries' ability to tackle these deficits.

Asymmetric shocks. A third and related problem for members of a single currency occurs in adjusting to a shock when that shock affects members to different degrees. Such occurrences are known as ***asymmetric shocks***. For example, the banking crisis affected the UK more severely than other countries, given that London is a global financial centre. This problem is more serious, the less the factor mobility between member countries and the less the price flexibility within member countries.

This problem, however, should not be overstated. Divergences between economies are often the result of a lack of harmony between countries in their demand-management policies. This is impossible in the eurozone in the case of monetary policy, and more difficult in the case of fiscal policy, due in part, to the constraints of the Growth and Stability Pact and Fiscal Compact (see Box 22.4). Also, many of the shocks that face economies today are global and have similar (albeit not identical) effects on all countries. Adjustment to such shocks would often be better with a single co-ordinated policy, something that is much easier with a single currency and a single central bank.

Even when shocks are uniformly felt in the member states, however, there is still the problem that policies adopted centrally will have different effects on each country. This is because the transmission mechanisms of economic policy (i.e. the way in which policy changes impact on economic variables like growth and inflation) vary across countries.

Criticisms of the current design of EMU

Others, who are currently critical of the design of EMU, argue that with appropriate changes, the problems could be significantly reduced.

Monetary policy. In the case of monetary policy, it is argued that the ECB's remit had made it especially inflation-averse. Hence, it tended to be more 'hawkish' and less proactive in response to economic downturns in the eurozone, particularly if the downturn is accompanied by a persistence in inflation or by rising rates of inflation.

Some argue that the hawkishness of the ECB was most clearly seen when comparing its monetary stance with other central banks in the aftermath of the financial crisis (see Box 22.8). Concerned by the above-target consumer price inflation rates that had resulted from the rising rates of global commodity inflation before the financial crisis, the ECB was cautious in relaxing monetary policy. In comparison, central banks such as the US Federal Reserve, the Bank of England and the Bank of Japan were more 'dovish' and aggressively relaxed monetary policy (see Boxes 22.5 and 22.6). Indeed, it was not until late in 2014 that the ECB announced that it would be starting a programme of quantitative easing, around the very time that the Federal Reserve's programme was winding down. From July 2021 the ECB announced it would operate a symmetric 2 per cent inflation rate target. This may result in less hawkish responses going forward.

Critics also point to the underlying weakness of a single currency operating alongside separate *national* government debt issues. The greater the divergence of the eurozone countries, in terms of growth, inflation, deficits, debt and the proportions of debt securities maturing in the short term, the greater this problem becomes. 

Fiscal policy. Under the Stability and Growth Pact (SGP), countries were supposed to keep public-sector deficits below 3 per cent of GDP and their stocks of debt below 60 per cent of GDP (see Box 22.4 on pages 710–11). However, the Pact was not rigidly enforced. Furthermore, because the rules allowed for discretion in times of recession, deficits and debt rose sharply in the late 2000s (see Table 22.1 on page 696).

Subsequently, efforts have been made to change the framework within which national governments make their fiscal choices. The result is the Fiscal Compact, signed in March 2012 (see Box 22.4). This reaffirmed the Stability and Growth Pact rules, but added other requirements. For example, eurozone countries would now be required to keep *structural deficits* at or below 0.5 per cent of GDP and tougher penalties would be imposed on countries breaking the rules.

There are those who argue that, for eurozone members to benefit fully from monetary union, tighter fiscal rules alone are insufficient. Instead, they advocate greater fiscal harmonisation. In other words, the problem, they say, is one of incomplete integration.

By what means would a depressed country in an economic union with a single currency be able to recover? Would the market provide a satisfactory solution to its problems or would (union) government intervention be necessary, and if so, what form could that intervention take?

Future of the euro

When Lithuania adopted the euro on 1 January 2015 it became the nineteenth country to do so. Yet debates around the advantages and disadvantages of EMU intensified as the

Definition

Asymmetric shocks Shocks (such as an oil price increase or a recession in another part of the world) that have different-sized effects on different industries, regions or countries.

ongoing Greek debt crisis raised the prospect of Greece's exit from the euro (Grexit).

The Greek crisis

The perilous state of Greece's public finances had already seen two international bailouts agreed. These involved the IMF, the European Commission and the ECB – the so-called 'Troika' – and were worth €240 billion. However, these loans were contingent on the Greek government undertaking a series of economic measures, including significant fiscal tightening. However, the fiscal austerity measures contributed to a deterioration of the macroeconomic environment.

Matters came to a head at the end of 2014 when the final tranches of the Greek bailout programme were suspended by the Troika. This followed the formation in December 2014 of a Syriza-led Greek government which had fought the election on an anti-austerity platform.

What followed was a drawn-out set of negotiations between Greece and its international creditors. With no agreement on further aid to Greece yet reached, Greece was unable to meet a €1.55 billion repayment to the IMF on 30 June 2015. This made Greece the first developed country to have defaulted on a loan from the IMF. Meanwhile, conditions for Greek citizens continued to deteriorate. In July, the ECB announced that it would maintain its emergency liquidity assurance for the Greek financial system at levels agreed at the end of June. Without further credit for an already financially distressed banking system, capital controls were imposed with strict limits on withdrawals from bank accounts.

KI 35 p459

In August 2015, the Greek government and its international creditors reached an agreement on the terms of a third bailout worth €85 billion over three years. Further austerity measures continued. These were required in order for the periodic release of funds, but they were to place further strains on an already weak economy.

Greece exited its bailout programmes in August 2018 and some progress has been made in easing repayment terms. However, there remain concerns that these terms are still damaging for the Greek economy. Some, including the IMF, argue that although Greece was permitted in 2019 to re-enter debt markets, Greece's public finances may still not be sustainable in the long term, particularly given the additional pressures arising from the COVID-19 pandemic.

For the time being at least, Grexit has been avoided. However, the Greek debt crisis raises important questions about the conditions under which it would be beneficial for other EU member states to join the euro or for existing members to exit.

The single currency and gains from trade

The benefits from a country being a member of a single currency are greater the more it leads to trade with other members of the single currency. Table 26.2 shows for the 19 member states of the European Union that are also part of the single currency, the proportion of their exports, imports and total trade (i.e. exports and imports) to and from other EU member states. From the table we can see that about 60 per cent of trade in the EU is between member states. However, there are considerable differences in the importance of intra-EU trade for member states.

On the basis of intra-industry trade, it might be argued that countries like Greece and Ireland have least to gain from being part of a single currency with other EU nations. But we need to consider other factors too. The theory of optimal currency areas (see Box 26.2) suggests, for example, that the degree of convergence between economies and the flexibility of labour markets are important considerations for countries considering the costs of relinquishing their national currency.

Convergence or divergence?

The more similar economies are, the more likely it is that they will face similar or symmetric shocks which can be accommodated by a common monetary policy. Furthermore, greater wage flexibility and mobility of labour provide mechanisms for countries within a single currency to remain internationally competitive.

However, there remain considerable differences in the macroeconomic performance of these countries, reflecting continuing differences in the structures of their economies. Some of these were exacerbated by the financial crisis of the late 2000s and the COVID-19 pandemic.

Among the differences are the contrasting trade positions of eurozone economies. This is illustrated in Figure 26.4 which shows the current account balances of selected eurozone economies since 2001. In the ten-year period from 2001 to 2010, Portugal, Greece, and Spain ran large current account deficits, averaging 10, 9, and 6 per cent of GDP, respectively. By contrast, Germany ran a current account surplus of around 4 per cent of its GDP. In more recent years, however, the divergences in current account balances have narrowed.

In the absence of nominal exchange rate adjustments, countries like Greece and Spain, looking to a fall in the *real* exchange rate to boost competitiveness, need to have relatively lower rates of price inflation (see pages 815–18 and Box 25.8 on pages 843–4 on nominal and real exchange rates). Therefore, with a single currency, productivity growth and wage inflation take on even greater importance in determining a country's competitiveness. The competitive position of

Table 26.2 Intra-European Union trade, % of total trade

	Exports		Imports		Exports and Imports	
	2002–11	2012–21	2002–11	2012–21	2002–11	2012–21
EU-27	61.1	58.3	59.9	60.2	60.5	59.2
Eurozone	59.3	55.1	57.7	56.9	58.5	56.0
Luxembourg	79.2	79.1	73.9	80.0	76.3	79.6
Slovakia	83.2	79.9	73.1	77.1	78.0	78.5
Estonia	70.3	68.8	72.8	76.9	71.5	73.1
Austria	70.0	67.8	78.2	75.6	74.2	71.8
Portugal	70.5	67.9	73.0	72.5	72.0	70.5
Slovenia	74.9	72.9	77.1	66.3	76.0	69.7
Latvia	64.7	61.8	74.3	75.4	70.5	69.2
Belgium	67.8	63.6	64.7	59.8	66.3	61.8
Finland	50.9	52.7	61.0	66.5	55.6	59.7
Lithuania	58.3	54.4	57.4	64.0	57.8	59.4
France	56.0	51.9	62.9	63.9	59.7	58.4
Spain	63.6	58.6	57.8	54.0	60.2	56.2
Germany	56.1	51.5	59.1	61.7	57.4	56.0
Malta	37.2	47.0	61.6	58.3	51.7	54.3
Netherlands	69.9	66.3	43.8	40.1	57.5	54.0
Italy	54.6	50.0	55.1	55.6	54.8	52.6
Cyprus	53.7	37.1	58.7	58.5	58.0	52.6
Greece	55.8	48.8	54.9	49.4	55.1	49.2
Ireland	44.2	38.9	29.8	35.9	38.8	37.7

Source: Based on data from *AMECO database* (European Commission, DGECFIN).

countries will deteriorate if wage growth *exceeds* productivity growth. If this happens, unit labour costs (labour costs per unit of output) will increase.

Figure 26.5 shows how in the period from 2001 to 2008 labour costs increased at an average of between 3 and 4 per cent per annum in Greece, Portugal and Italy compared with

Figure 26.4 Current account balance of selected eurozone economies

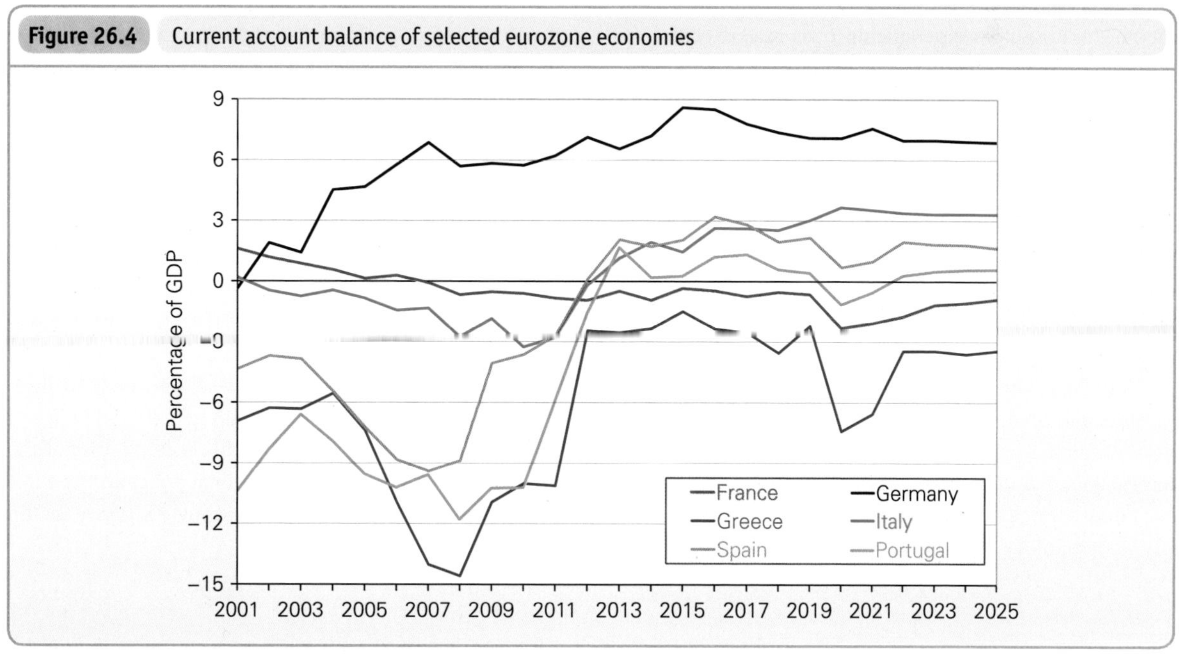

Notes: Figures from 2021 based on forecasts.
Source: Based on data in *World Economic Outlook Database*, IMF (April 2021), www.imf.org/en/Publications/SPROLLs/world-economic-outlook-databases

Figure 26.5 Growth in unit labour costs of selected eurozone economies

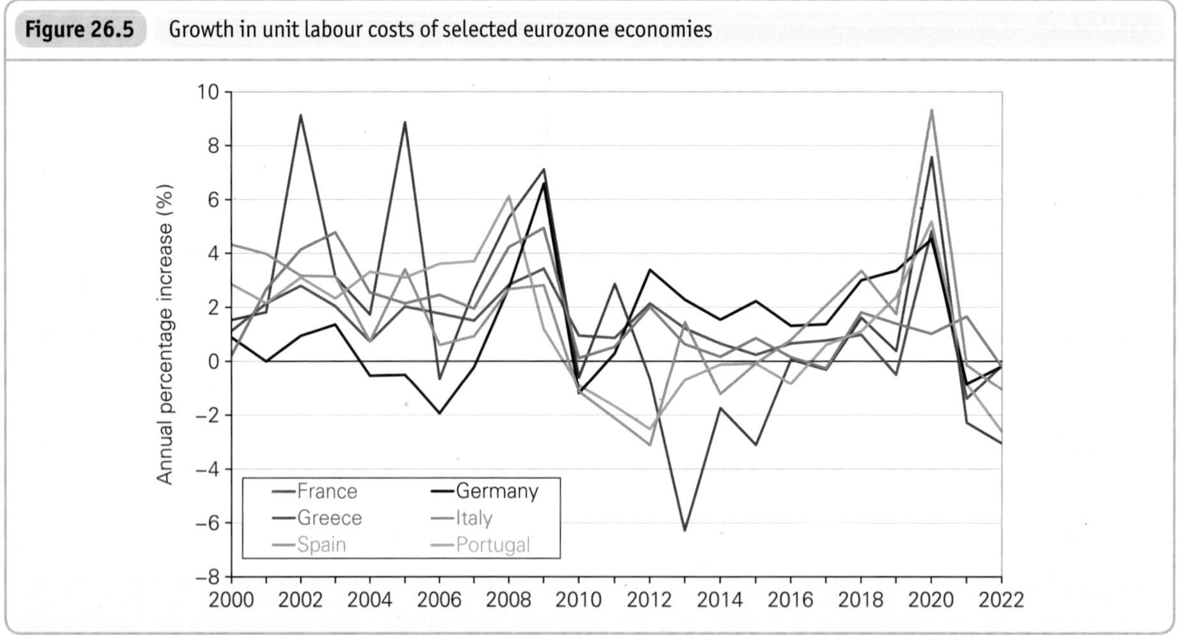

Notes: Unit labour costs are the ratio of compensation per employee to real GDP per person employed; Figures for 2021 and 2022 based on forecasts.
Source: Based on data in *AMECO Database*, European Commission, DGECFIN (May 2021), http://ec.europa.eu/economy_finance/db_indicators/ameco/index_en.htm

close to zero in Germany. This, other things being equal, put these countries at a competitive disadvantage.

The euro and the fiscal framework

The discussion so far highlights the importance of economic convergence in affecting the benefits and costs of being a member of the euro. Fiscal policy can provide some buffer against asymmetric shocks by enabling transfers of income to those areas experiencing lower rates of economic growth. Therefore, the fiscal framework within which the euro operates is important when considering the future of the euro.

To date, the eurozone has resisted a centralisation of national budgets. In a more centralised (or federal) system we would see automatic income transfers between different regions and countries. A country, say Greece, affected by a negative economic shock would pay less tax revenues and receive more expenditures from a central eurozone budget, while in a country, say Germany, experiencing a positive shock the opposite would be the case.

Since national budgets in the eurozone remain largely decentralised, fiscal transfers are principally determined by national fiscal frameworks. But the ability of these to offset the effects of negative economic shocks is constrained by the sustainability of national budgets. This is important because it places limits on the ability of national governments to use fiscal policy to offset the effects of negative economic shocks.

To provide maximum flexibility to use fiscal policy, it is important for countries to reduce the stock of public-sector debt as a percentage of annual GDP in times when the economy is growing. It is easier to do this if the economy runs a primary surplus. This is when public-sector receipts are greater than public-sector expenditures *excluding* interest payments: the bigger the surplus, the quicker the debt-to-GDP ratio can be reduced (see page 700). Also, the faster the rate of economic growth and the lower the real rate of interest, the quicker the ratio can be reduced.

KI 26 p309

Table 26.3 shows the public-sector debt-to-GDP ratios in a sample of eurozone economies in 2000, 2010 and 2020, alongside the factors that affect the path of the ratio. The table illustrates considerable differences between countries in the state of their public finances. Therefore, where fiscal policy is left to individual countries, those with an already high debt-to-GDP ratio, such as Greece, Italy and Portugal, will find it considerably more difficult to use fiscal policy to tackle a recession. Consequently, the sustainability of the current decentralised approach to fiscal policy in the eurozone is likely to be crucial in determining the future for the euro and those countries using it.

KI 35 p459

Table 26.3 Public-sector debt in selected eurozone countries

	General government gross debt-to-GDP, %			2010–20 averages		
	2000	2010	2020	Primary surplus-to-GDP, %	Real long-term interest rates, %	Economic growth, % p.a.
EU-27	66.2	80.7	92.4	−0.6	0.7	0.9
Eurozone	69.0	86.0	100.0	−0.6	0.7	0.7
Estonia	5.1	6.6	18.2	−0.4	2.2	3.1
Luxembourg	7.5	19.0	24.9	1.2	0.0	0.5
Lithuania	23.5	36.2	43.5	−1.1	0.7	2.0
Latvia	12.1	47.9	47.3	−1.2	0.0	3.2
Malta	60.7	65.3	54.3	0.7	0.0	4.4
Ireland	36.1	86.0	59.5	−3.7	1.5	6.0
Slovakia	50.5	40.9	69.2	−1.8	1.0	2.3
Finland	42.5	46.9	69.2	−1.0	−0.4	0.9
Germany	59.1	82.4	69.8	1.3	−0.6	1.3
Slovenia	25.9	38.3	80.8	−2.1	1.6	1.2
Austria	66.1	82.7	83.9	−0.1	−0.3	0.8
Netherlands	52.1	59.2	83.9	−0.6	−0.1	1.0
France	58.9	85.3	88.7	−2.5	0.4	0.5
Cyprus	55.7	56.4	114.1	−0.5	0.0	0.9
Belgium	109.6	100.3	118.2	−0.7	3.8	0.8
Spain	57.8	60.5	120.0	−3.8	2.2	0.0
Portugal	54.2	100.2	133.6	−0.9	3.1	0.1
Italy	109.0	119.2	155.8	0.8	2.0	−0.6
Greece	104.9	147.5	205.6	−1.3	9.3	−2.7

Source: *AMECO database*, European Commission, DGECFIN (May 2021), http://ec.europa.eu/economy_finance/ameco/user/serie/SelectSerie.cfm

Section summary

1. One means of achieving greater currency stability is for a group of countries to peg their exchange rates with each other and yet float jointly with the rest of the world. The exchange rate mechanism of the EU (ERM) was an example. Members' currencies were allowed to fluctuate against other member currencies within a band. The band was ± 2.25 per cent for the majority of the ERM countries until 1993.
2. The need for realignments seemed to have diminished in the late 1980s as greater convergence was achieved between the members' economies. Growing strains in the system, however, in the early 1990s led to a crisis in September 1992. The UK and Italy left the ERM. The bands were widened in 1993 to ± 15 per cent, although in practice fluctuations were kept within ± 2.25 per cent for most of the time from 1993 to the start of the euro in 1999.
3. The ERM was seen as an important first stage on the road to complete economic and monetary union.
4. The euro was born on 1 January 1999. Twelve countries adopted it, having at least nominally met the Maastricht convergence criteria. Euro notes and coins were introduced on 1 January 2002, with the notes and coins of the old currencies withdrawn a few weeks later.
5. The advantages claimed for EMU are that it eliminates the costs of converting currencies and the uncertainties associated with possible changes in inter-EU exchange rates. This encourages more investment, both inward and by domestic firms. What is more, a common central bank, independent from domestic governments, provides the stable monetary environment necessary for a convergence of the EU economies and the encouragement of investment and inter-Union trade.
6. Critics claim, however, that it makes adjustment to domestic economic problems more difficult. The loss of independence in policy making is seen by such people to be a major issue, not only because of the loss of political sovereignty, but also because domestic economic concerns may be at variance with those of the Union as a whole. A single monetary policy is claimed to be inappropriate for dealing with asymmetric shocks. What is more, countries and regions at the periphery of the Union may become depressed unless there is an effective regional policy.
7. The Greek sovereign debt crisis raised concerns about the future of the euro. Considerable differences remain in key macroeconomic indicators. This includes differences in the growth of labour productivity and unit labour costs, which are especially significant in the absence of nominal exchange rate adjustments.
8. There are also considerable differences in the financial health of the public finances of eurozone governments. This is significant because it affects the ability of national governments to use fiscal policy to absorb the adverse economic effects of negative shocks.

26.3 GLOBAL INEQUALITY

The gulf between rich and poor countries

The typical family in North America, western Europe, Japan and Australasia has many material comforts: plentiful food to eat; a house or apartment with electricity and running hot and cold water; an inside toilet connected to an underground sewerage system; access to free or affordable health care and education; numerous consumer durables; holidays away from home; visits to the cinema, concerts, sports events, etc. There are some people, it is true, who are very poor and, indeed, the problem of poverty in many developed countries has worsened in recent years. But it is only a small minority that cannot afford the basics of life, such as adequate food, shelter and clothing.

In most of Africa and large parts of Asia and Latin America, the picture is quite different. The majority of people live in poverty. For them life is a daily struggle for survival. Affluence does exist in these countries, but here it is the fortunate few who can afford good food, good housing and the various luxury items that typify life in the industrialised world.

A large proportion of the inhabitants live in the countryside. For many, this means living in a family with many children and working on a small amount of land with too little income to buy adequate agricultural machinery, fertilisers or pesticides. With a rapid growth in population there is less and less land to go round. As land is passed on from generation to generation, it is divided up between the offspring into smaller and smaller plots. Many who cannot make ends meet are forced to sell their land to the local landlords. Then as landless labourers they have to accept very low-paid jobs on the large farms or plantations. Others try to survive by borrowing, hoping to be able to pay off their debts with future crop sales. But often the only source of finance is again the local landlord who charges exorbitant rates of interest. As a result, they end up in a state of 'debt bondage' where they can never pay off their debts, but year in year out have to give part of their crops to the landlord as interest.

Others come to the rapidly growing cities. In the cities, at least there are some jobs. But typically more people migrate to the cities than there are jobs available. Thus the number of unemployed in the cities has grown inexorably. People are forced to do anything to earn a living: selling wares on street corners, or working as casual labourers, domestic servants or shoe shiners; some resort to prostitution and crime, others merely beg.

All round the outskirts of cities throughout the developing world, shanty towns mushroom as the poor flock in from the countryside. Families crowd into one- or two-roomed shacks, often with no electricity, no water and no sanitation. There are schools in these towns, but often parents cannot afford to allow their children to attend. Instead they have to send them out to work to supplement the family's meagre income. In some emerging countries, programmes to provide work and education in the shanty towns have helped reduce the problem somewhat; in other countries, the problem continues to worsen.

Statistics cannot give the complete picture, but they can give us some indication of the gulf between rich and poor countries. Table 26.4 gives some details.

In 2020, around 85 per cent of the world's population lived in developing countries (low- and middle-income countries), but these people earn only a little over a half of global GNY[2] (in purchasing-power parity terms). In fact, as Figure 26.6 shows, this share has been rising over time. In

2 GNY (gross national income): see appendix to Chapter 15.

Figure 26.6 World GNY in PPP terms (2017 prices)

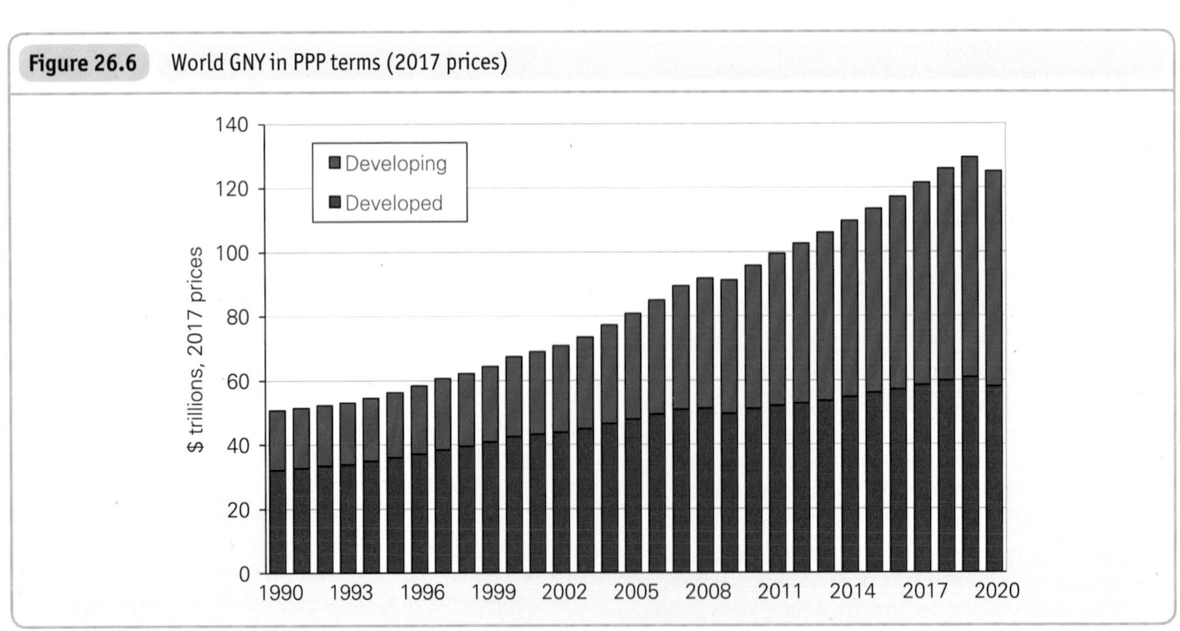

Note: Developing countries are classified as low-, lower-middle- and upper-middle-income economies; developed economies are high-income economies.
Source: Based on data from World Bank, series NY.GNP.MKTP.PP. KD, https://data.worldbank.org/indicator/DT.DOD.DECT.GN.ZS

Table 26.4 Selected development indicators

		Low-income economies	Lower-middle-income economies	Upper-middle-income economies	High-income economies	World
Economy	Population (millions), 2020	665	3 331	2 514	1 215	7 753
	Population growth (% p.a.), 2010–19	2.6	1.4	0.8	0.5	1.2
	GNY ($ trillions), 2019	1.6	19.7	49.3	65.6	136.0
	GNY per capita (PPP, $), 2019	2 450	6 761	17 264	52 629	17 718
	Growth in real GNY per capita (% p.a.), 2010–19	1.9	3.6	4.1	1.5	1.8
Poverty and quality of life	Under 5 mortality rate (per 1000 births), 2019	67.6	48.9	13.3	5.0	37.7
	Primary school completion rate (%), 2019	64.9	89.6	96.7	98.2	89.5
	Growth in output per person employed (%), 2010–19	2.2	4.0	4.3	1.0	2.4
Promoting sustainability	Mortality rate due to inadequate water, sanitation and hygiene (per 100 000), 2016	39.7	20.5	1.7	0.3	11.8
	Population with access to electricity (%), 2018	41.9	86.3	99.4	100.0	89.6
	Population using the internet (%), 2017	16.3	31.9	56.4	85.4	49.0
Gender development	Male life expectancy (years), 2015–18	61.0	66.4	72.4	78.0	70.1
	Female life expectancy (years), 2015–18	64.8	69.8	77.7	83.3	74.6
	Private firms with female top manager (%), 2019	11.9	20.1	19.8	19.3	18.5
	Seats in parliament held by women (%), 2020	22.7	21.4	25.7	29.6	25.2

Note: Low-income economies are those with GNY per capita of $1036 or less in 2020; lower-middle-income, $1036–$4045; upper-middle-income, $4046–$12 535; and high-income, $12 535 or more.
Source: Based on data from *Databank*, World Bank.

1990, developing countries' share of GNY was only 44 per cent. Despite this overall increase across developing countries, the poorest economies have experienced relatively little change in their share of global income.

In high-income countries, the average GNY per head in 2019 was $45 348. In low-income countries it was a mere $820. Even in purchasing-power parity (PPP) terms, the figures were $52 629 and $2450, respectively. The gulf between rich and poor countries can also be seen in other basic indicators, including health, life expectancy and literacy. This is illustrated in Table 26.4, which shows a series of indicators under one of four categories: size of the economy, poverty and quality of life, promoting sustainability and gender development.

The table shows how during the 2010s, growth in GNY per capita was faster in developing countries than in rich countries, especially in middle-income countries. This helped to further narrow the income gap between the developed and developing world. However, the rate at which extreme poverty was falling was already beginning to slow when the COVID-19 pandemic hit. As we saw in section 1.1, according to the World Bank in 2020 alone the pandemic may have pushed around 100 million people into extreme poverty – the first rise since 1998.[3]

The meaning of 'development'

Countries want to develop. But just what do we mean by 'development'? Clearly it is a normative concept. Its definition will depend on the goals that the economist assumes societies want to achieve. So how do economists define and measure development?

The basic needs approach

A starting point is to identify the basic needs that people have if they are to be able to realise their potential as human beings. Different economists have identified various lists of requirements, including the following items:

- Adequate food, shelter, warmth and clothing.
- Universal access to education.
- Availability of adequate health care.
- Availability of non-demeaning jobs.

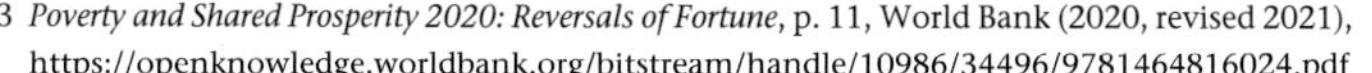

3 *Poverty and Shared Prosperity 2020: Reversals of Fortune*, p. 11, World Bank (2020, revised 2021), https://openknowledge.worldbank.org/bitstream/handle/10986/34496/9781464816024.pdf

- Sufficient free time to be able to enjoy social interaction.
- Freedom to make one's own economic decisions.
- Freedom to participate in the decisions of government and other bodies that affect one's life.

What other items might be included as basic needs?

There are four major problems with defining development in terms of a basic list of requirements.

The first is in deciding *what to include*. Any definition of *economic* development would clearly include people's *material* standard of living. But should development include social and political factors such as 'self-esteem', freedom from servitude and freedom of religion?

The second problem is in *measuring each of the items*. It is possible to measure such things as income per head, literacy rates and mortality rates. It is much more difficult, however, to measure the achievement of social and political objectives such as self-esteem.

The third problem is in arriving at a *single measure* of the level of development. You cannot add the average calorific intake to the number of doctors and nurses to the percentage of homes having various basic amenities such as running water. You can meaningfully add things up only if they are expressed in the same units, or if appropriate *weights* are attached to each of the items. Clearly, the assigning of any such weights would be highly controversial.

The fourth problem is in deciding the importance of the *distribution* of the various items. If, say, the average calorific intake increases, but the poorest sections of the population have less to eat, has the country really experienced an increase in the level of development?

However, many economists argue that the basic needs approach does provide a useful 'checklist' to see whether a country's development is broadly based or confined to just one or two indicators.

Would it be possible with this basic needs approach to say (a) that one country was more developed than another; (b) that one country was developing faster than another?

Using GNY to measure development

The desire to have a single measure for development and thus to be able to make simple comparisons between countries has led to the universal use of real gross national income (GNY) per capita as the main indicator. It has some major advantages:

- It takes into account virtually all the goods and services produced in a country, and converts them into a single measure by the use of market prices.
- Although markets are by no means perfect, they do reflect the strength of demand and the opportunity costs of supply.
- The rules for the measurement of GNY are universally agreed.
- Virtually all countries compile GNY statistics.
- Although not every item that affects human welfare is included in GNY, a sustained rise in GNY is generally agreed to be a necessary condition for a sustained rise in welfare.
- There is a fairly close correlation between the level of per capita GNY and other indicators such as mortality rates, literacy rates, and calorific and protein intake.

However, there are four fundamental criticisms of relying on simple GNY per capita as an indicator of development.

Many items are excluded. Much of production that does not get bought and sold will escape being recorded. This is a particular problem with rural societies that are largely subsistence-based. People grow their own food, build their own houses, make their own clothes and provide their own entertainment. GNY statistics are therefore likely to *understate* the level of production in these societies.

On the other hand, as these societies 'develop', the size of the market sector is likely to grow. A larger proportion of people's consumption will be of items they have purchased and which therefore do enter into GNY statistics. Thus GNY figures will *overstate* the rate of growth of production and consumption.

As an economy becomes more urbanised, there is likely to be a growth in *external* costs of production and consumption, such as pollution and crime. Traditional ways of life will be destroyed; people may find themselves increasingly in a competitive, uncaring environment. Again the growth in GNY is likely to *overstate* the growth in human welfare. KI 31 p364

Market prices may be highly distorted. GNY is based on market prices, but these prices may be distorted. Markets are often highly fragmented, and there is little competition to ensure that prices reflect undistorted marginal costs. Companies often have considerable monopoly power to push up prices of manufactured goods; landlords often have power to push up rents; governments may impose price controls on food; employers with monopsony power may be able to pay very low wages.

How would a redistribution of income to the powerful be likely to affect GNY?

Exchange rates may not reflect local purchasing power. GNY statistics are initially compiled in terms of the domestic currency. For purposes of international comparison they then have to be converted into a common currency – usually the US dollar – at the current exchange rate. But exchange rates reflect demand and supply of *traded* goods; they do not reflect the prices of *non-traded* goods. Generally, the price of non-traded goods and services in developing countries will be lower than the price of similar goods and services in advanced countries. The *level* of GNY is therefore likely to *understate* the level of production in poor countries. If, on the other hand, the proportion of traded goods increases over time, the *growth* of GNY will again *overstate* the growth in production.

It is much better, therefore, to estimate GNY using purchasing-power parity (PPP) exchange rates. Even if this is done, however, massive differences remain in GNY per head between rich and poor countries. This is illustrated in Figure 26.7, which shows GNY per head at PPP exchange rates as a percentage of the estimated world GNY per head.

Figure 26.7 GNY per person employed as a percentage of world GNY per head, 2019 (using purchasing power parity exchange rates)

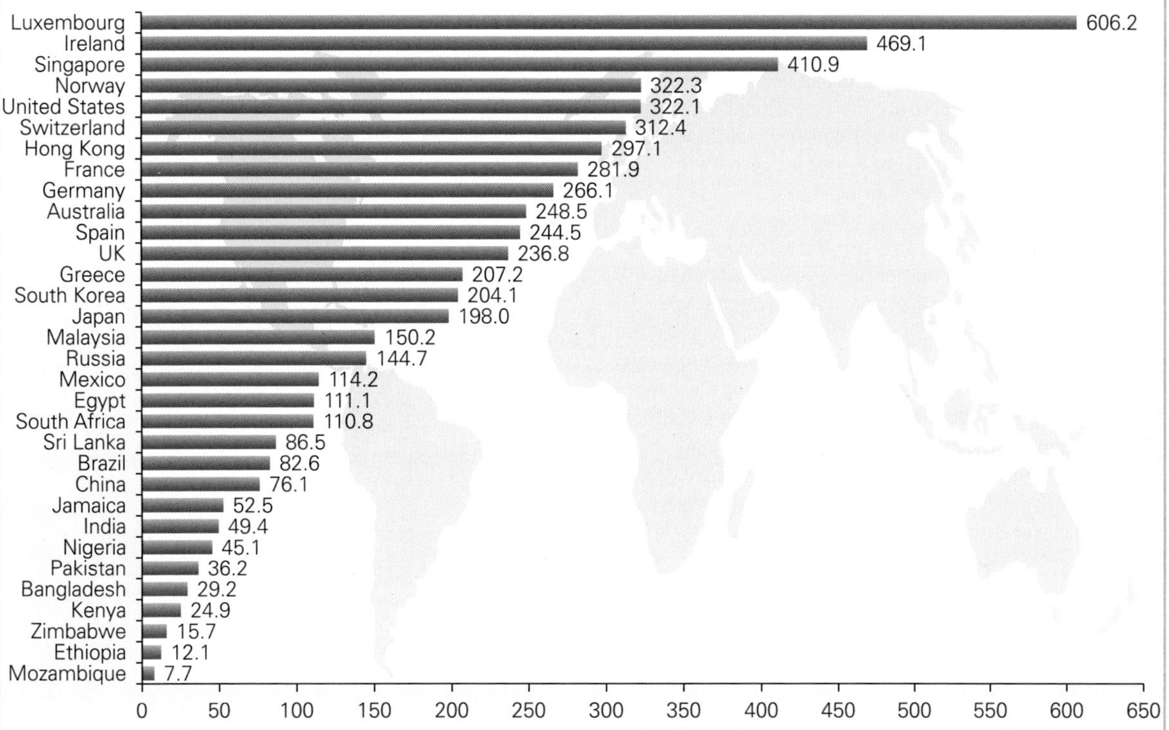

Luxembourg	606.2
Ireland	469.1
Singapore	410.9
Norway	322.3
United States	322.1
Switzerland	312.4
Hong Kong	297.1
France	281.9
Germany	266.1
Australia	248.5
Spain	244.5
UK	236.8
Greece	207.2
South Korea	204.1
Japan	198.0
Malaysia	150.2
Russia	144.7
Mexico	114.2
Egypt	111.1
South Africa	110.8
Sri Lanka	86.5
Brazil	82.6
China	76.1
Jamaica	52.5
India	49.4
Nigeria	45.1
Pakistan	36.2
Bangladesh	29.2
Kenya	24.9
Zimbabwe	15.7
Ethiopia	12.1
Mozambique	7.7

0 50 100 150 200 250 300 350 400 450 500 550 600 650

Source: Based on data from *Databank* series NY.GNP.PCAP.PP.CD, World Bank, http://databank.worldbank.org/data/home.aspx

Simple GNY per head ignores the distribution of income. Since the early 1980s, many developing countries have achieved relatively rapid growth in per capita GNY as they have sought overseas investment, privatised their industries and cut the levels of public provision. But with a deepening of poverty, a growing inequality in the distribution of income and an increase in unemployment, few would argue that this constitutes genuine 'development'.

Many who have advocated the concentration on GNY and its rate of growth have argued that, while the rich may be the first to benefit from prosperity, gradually the benefits will 'trickle down' to the poor. In practice, the wealth has failed to trickle down in many countries. The rich have got richer while the poor have got poorer. Given the weaknesses of GNY, but given the desirability of having a single measure of development, various composite indicators have been constructed. The most widely used is the ***Human Development Index (HDI)***, which is a combined measure of life expectancy, education and GDP per head at PPP exchange rates. This index is examined in Box 26.3.

Definition

Human Development Index (HDI) A composite index made up of three elements: an index for life expectancy, an index for school enrolment and adult literacy, and an index for GDP per capita (in PPP$).

Section summary

1. There are a number of ways of categorising countries according to their level of development.
2. The level of development of a country can be defined in terms of the extent to which it meets basic needs for human life. There is no universal agreement, however, about which items should be measured or about how to measure and weight them. Nevertheless, the approach provides a useful indicator of whether development is broadly based and how rapidly the most serious problems of poverty are being tackled.
3. The most widely used measure of development is GNY per head at PPP exchange rates. However, there are serious problems with using GNY: many items may be excluded, especially for a more subsistence-based society; prices may be highly distorted; and the statistics ignore the question of the distribution of income. Another widely used measure is the Human Development Index.

BOX 26.3 THE HUMAN DEVELOPMENT INDEX (HDI)

A measure of human welfare?

Since 1990, the United Nations Development Programme (UNDP) has published an annual Human Development Index (HDI). This is an attempt to provide a more broadly based measure of development than GDP or GNY. The HDI for each of the 189 countries (in 2019) has a value between 0 and 1. It is the average of three indices based on three sets of variables: (i) life expectancy at birth, (ii) education (a weighted average of (a) the mean years that a 25-year-old person or older has spent in school and (b) the number of years of schooling that a 5-year-old child is expected to have over their lifetime) and (iii) real GNY per capita, measured in US dollars at purchasing-power parity exchange rates. The aim is to give a measure of the extent to which people live a long and healthy life, are knowledgeable and have a decent standard of living.

The countries are then placed in one of four groups according to their HDI: very high human development (0.800 and above), high human development (0.700 to 0.799), medium human development (0.550 to 0.699) and low human development (below 0.550).

For each of the three indices making up the HDI, a sophisticated formula is used. In terms of GNY, the index attempts to measure material well-being by building in the assumption of a rapidly diminishing marginal utility of income above average world levels. The scores for each of the three HDI dimension indices are then aggregated into a single composite index using the geometric mean[1] of each.

The table is based on the 2020 Human Development Report. The first columns of the table show the HDIs for selected countries in 2019 and, for comparison, 2010. Adjacent to these values are the levels of GNY per capita in purchasing power terms for 2019 and the difference between the HDI and GNY per capita rankings in 2019. A positive difference means that a country has a higher ranking for HDI than GNY per capita.

As can be seen, the rankings differ substantially in some cases between the two measures. For some countries, such as Norway (which was the highest ranked country by HDI in 2019), Iceland, Sweden, Australia, the UK, Cuba and Sri Lanka, GNY *understates* their relative level of human development, whereas for others, such as the United Arab Emirates, Saudi Arabia, Nigeria, Pakistan and South Africa, GNY per capita *overstates* their relative level of human development. Thus South Africa (PPP) GNY per capita is over 40 per cent higher than that of Cuba and yet its HDI is lower.

The point is that countries with similar levels of national income may use that income quite differently.

Inequality-adjusted HDI

Recently, work has been done to adjust HDI figures for various other factors. The Inequality-adjusted Human Development Index (IHDI) adjusts the Human Development Index (HDI) for inequality in the distribution of life expectancy, mean years of schooling and disposable income or consumption per capita. The table shows the inequality-adjusted HDIs for each country and the difference between the inequality-adjusted HDI and the unadjusted HDI values.

Positive differences mean that a country has a higher ranking for the adjusted HDI than for the unadjusted (original) HDI. For example, the Czech Republic moves 14 places up the ranking after the adjustment. On the other hand, Brazil, South Africa, Hong Kong and Singapore move 20,18, 17 and 16 places respectively down the HDI rankings after the inequality adjustment.

Planetary pressures-adjusted HDI

The Planetary pressures-adjusted Human Development Index (PHDI) discounts the HDI for pressures on the planet. It adjusts for carbon dioxide emissions per person and the 'material footprint' per capita of domestic consumption: i.e. the value of raw materials extracted in domestic consumption. It therefore captures some of the pressures that humans place on the planet.

As with the Inequality-adjusted HDI, positive differences mean that a country has a higher ranking when adjusting for the planetary effects of the country's consumption. From the final column of the table we can see that the planetary-adjustment moves Sri Lanka and Cuba up the HDI ranking by 24 and 27 places, respectively. However, countries such as Singapore, the United Arab Emirates, Australia and the USA move down by 92, 87, 72 and 45 places, respectively.

1. *For what reasons are HDI and per capita GNY rankings likely to diverge?*
2. *Why do countries like the UAE, Saudi Arabia and South Africa have such a large difference between their HDI and per capita GNY rankings?*

Download the latest UN Human Development report. Prepare a PowerPoint presentation explaining the purpose of the Human Development Index and presenting an overview of the latest results.

26.4 TRADE AND DEVELOPING COUNTRIES

The role of international trade is one of the most contentious issues in development economics. Should countries adopt an open trading policy with few if any barriers to imports? Should governments actively promote trade by subsidising their export sector? Or should they restrict trade and pursue a policy of greater self-sufficiency? These are issues that we will be looking at in this section.

EXPLORING ECONOMICS

Human Development Index for selected countries (2019)

		Human Development Index (HDI)		Gross national income (GNY) per capita		Inequality-adjusted HDI (IHDI)		Planetary pressures-adjusted HDI (PHDI)	
		Value		(2017 PPP $)	GNY rank minus HDI rank	Value	HDI rank minus IHDI rank	Value	HDI rank minus PHDI rank
		2019	2010	2019		2019		2019	
	Very high human development								
1	Norway	0.957	0.940	66 494	7	0.899	0	0.781	−15
2	Ireland	0.955	0.901	68 371	4	0.885	−3	0.833	1
2	Switzerland	0.955	0.941	69 394	3	0.889	−1	0.825	0
4	Hong Kong	0.949	0.904	62 985	7	0.824	−17	n/a	n/a
4	Iceland	0.949	0.898	54 682	14	0.894	2	0.768	−26
6	Germany	0.947	0.927	55 314	11	0.869	−4	0.814	−1
7	Sweden	0.945	0.911	54 508	12	0.882	0	0.817	1
8	Australia	0.944	0.930	48 085	15	0.867	−3	0.696	−72
11	Singapore	0.938	0.909	88 155	−8	0.813	−15	0.656	−92
13	UK	0.932	0.912	46 071	13	0.856	−3	0.825	10
17	USA	0.926	0.916	63 826	−7	0.808	−11	0.718	−45
19	Japan	0.919	0.887	42 932	9	0.843	1	0.781	2
25	Spain	0.904	0.872	40 975	6	0.783	−10	0.795	11
26	France	0.901	0.879	47 173	−1	0.820	2	0.801	16
27	Czech Republic	0.900	0.870	38 109	9	0.860	14	0.768	−5
29	Italy	0.892	0.879	42 776	0	0.783	−6	0.792	12
31	United Arab Emirates	0.890	0.820	67 462	−24	n/a	n/a	0.609	−87
40	Saudi Arabia	0.854	0.809	47 495	−16	n/a	n/a	0.707	−33
52	Russia	0.824	0.781	26 157	2	0.740	2	0.728	−4
	High human development								
70	Cuba	0.783	0.781	8 621	45	n/a	n/a	0.749	27
72	Sri Lanka	0.782	0.754	12 707	23	0.673	−1	0.765	34
84	Brazil	0.765	0.727	14 263	1	0.570	−20	0.710	10
85	China	0.761	0.699	16 057	−11	0.639	2	0.671	−16
114	South Africa	0.709	0.664	12 129	−14	0.468	−18	0.648	−1
	Medium human development								
131	India	0.645	0.579	6 681	−5	0.475	−1	0.626	8
150	Zimbabwe	0.571	0.482	2 666	14	0.441	7	0.562	2
154	Pakistan	0.557	0.512	5 005	−15	0.384	−4	0.547	2
	Low human development								
161	Nigeria	0.539	0.482	4 910	−19	0.348	−2	0.532	0
173	Ethiopia	0.485	0.421	2 207	3	0.348	8	0.483	0
189	Niger	0.394	0.331	1 201	−4	0.284	3	0.390	0

[1] The geometric mean of n numbers is found by multiplying the n numbers together and then taking the nth root of the total.

Whether it is desirable that developing countries should adopt policies of more trade or less, trade is still vital. Certain raw materials, capital equipment and intermediate products that are necessary for development can be obtained only from abroad. Others *could* be produced domestically, but only at much higher cost.

The relationship between trade and development

What makes the issue of trade so contentious is the absence of a simple relationship between trade and development. Instead the relationship is complex and determined by a series of interactions between variables affecting both trade and development. Furthermore, while some countries have managed to use trade as an engine for economic growth and wider human development, others, despite trade liberalisation, have seen relatively little improvement in either their export performance or in human development.

In constructing a trade and development index, the UN[4] identified three broad groups of influences or dimensions which interact and affect a country's trade and development performance. Within these broad groups are various indicators which themselves interact. We consider briefly these three dimensions and some of the indicators within each dimension.

Structural and institutional dimension

Human capital. This relates to the skills and expertise of the workforce which affect a country's performance and its productivity. Education and health are key influences here. As well as affecting the economic growth of a country, higher educational attainment and better health conditions positively impact on social and human development.

Physical infrastructure. Infrastructure affects a country's productive capacity and so its potential output. Poor transport infrastructure, for example, is thought to be a major impediment to a country's export performance.

Financial environment. Credit is important to producers and consumers alike in helping to finance both short-term and longer-term commitments. For instance, it enables firms to finance day-to-day operational purchases but also longer-term investments in fixed assets such as buildings and machinery.

Institutional quality. This relates to issues of governance not just of firms themselves, but also to institutions, largely governmental.

Environment sustainability. The argument here is that excessive activity, particularly at the early stages of development, can result in environmental degradation. This can adversely affect human development and, in turn, economic development.

Trade policies and process dimension

Openness to trade. In the absence of market failures and externalities, trade liberalisation is argued to be a driver of development. However, there can be significant human costs in the transition process.

Effective access to foreign markets. The success of a country's export performance is crucially dependent on its effective access to markets. Barriers to access include tariffs and non-tariff barriers, such as regulatory standards in the markets of recipient countries. A wider definition of 'effective' access recognises other factors too. These might include the size of foreign markets, transport links, the characteristics of the goods being exported – for example how differentiated they are – as well as the cost of the exported goods.

Levels of development dimension

The third series of factors affecting both trade and human development relate to existing levels of development. In section 26.3 we discussed some of the issues in defining and measuring development. But, in general terms, we can think of the relevant development issues here as encompassing three components: economic development, social development and gender development.

Trade strategies

Despite the complexity of the relationship between trade and development, countries' policies towards trade typically go through various stages as they develop.

Primary outward-looking stage. Traditionally, developing countries have exported primaries – minerals such as copper, cash crops such as coffee and non-foodstuffs such as cotton – in exchange for manufactured consumer goods. Having little in the way of an industrial base, if they want to consume manufactured goods, they have to import them.

Secondary inward-looking stage. In seeking rapid economic development, most developing countries drew lessons from the experience of the advanced countries. The main conclusion was that industrialisation was the key to economic success.

But industrialisation required foreign exchange to purchase capital equipment. This led to a policy of ***import-substituting industrialisation***, which involved cutting back on non-essential imports and thereby releasing foreign exchange. Tariffs and other restrictions were imposed on those imports for which a domestic substitute existed or which were regarded as unimportant.

Secondary outward-looking stage. Once an industry had satisfied domestic demand, it had to seek markets abroad if expansion were to continue. What is more, as we shall see, import substitution brought a number of serious problems for developing countries. The answer seemed to be to look outward again, this time to the export of manufactured goods. Many of the most economically successful developing countries (especially Hong Kong, Singapore, South Korea, Taiwan and, more recently, China, India and Indonesia) have owed their high growth rates to a rapid expansion of manufactured exports.

We will now examine the three stages in more detail.

Definition

Import-substituting industrialisation A strategy of restricting imports of manufactured goods and using the foreign exchange saved to build up domestic substitute industries.

4 *Developing Countries in International Trade 2005: Trade and Development Index*, United Nations (2005).

Approach 1: Exporting primaries – exploiting comparative advantage

The justification for exporting primaries

Despite moves towards import substitution and secondary export promotion, many developing countries still rely heavily on primary exports. Three major arguments have traditionally been used for pursuing a policy of exporting primaries. In each case the arguments have also been used to justify a policy of free or virtually free trade.

Exporting primaries exploits comparative advantage. Traditional trade theory implies that countries should specialise in producing those items in which they have a comparative advantage: i.e. those goods that can be produced at relatively low opportunity costs. For most developing countries, this means that a large proportion of their exports should be primaries. KI 38 p778

The reasons for differences in comparative costs were examined by two Swedish economists, Eli Heckscher and Bertil Ohlin. They believed that comparative cost differences arise from differences in factor endowments. The ***Heckscher–Ohlin theory*** states that *a country should specialise in those goods that are intensive in the country's abundant factor.* The more abundant a factor, the relatively cheaper it is likely to be, and thus the lower will be the opportunity cost of producing goods that are intensive in its use. Thus labour-abundant developing countries should specialise in labour-intensive products. By exporting these products, which will typically be primaries, they can earn the foreign exchange to import goods that use large amounts of capital and other resources that are in short supply.

According to this theory, international trade would lead not only to higher consumption, but also to ***factor price equalisation***: i.e. the erosion of income inequalities between trading nations. For example, if wage rates are low in developing countries, trade will increase the demand for their labour-intensive products and thereby push up wage rates. International trade will also erode income differentials *within* countries. The demand for exports will increase the demand for the relatively cheap factors, and imports will reduce the demand for the relatively expensive ones. Thus the cheap factors will go up in price and the expensive ones will come down.

1. ***What effect will trade have on the price of capital in developing and developed countries?***
2. ***It is sometimes claimed that trade with developing countries is unjust because it leads to the importation of goods produced at pitifully low wages. How can the Heckscher–Ohlin theory be used to refute this claim? Is there any validity in the claim? (See Box 24.3.)***

Exporting primaries provides a 'vent for surplus'. Trade offers a ***vent for surplus***: i.e. a means of putting to use resources that would otherwise not be used. These surpluses occur where the domestic market is simply not big enough to consume all the available output of a particular good. There is far too little demand within Zambia to consume its potential output of copper. The same applies to Namibian uranium and Peruvian tin.

Exporting primaries provides an 'engine for economic growth'. According to this argument, developing countries benefit from the growth of the economies of the developed world. As industrial expansion takes place in the rich North, this creates additional demand for primaries from the poor South. In more recent years, the rapid growth in China, India and other industrialising developing countries saw a rapid growth in demand for commodities, many produced in the least developed countries. This drove up commodity prices in the first decade of the 2000s and benefited primary exporters (see Figure 26.8 on page 877). However, as we shall see, commodity prices can be very volatile; indeed, they generally fell across the 2010s.

Traditional trade theory in the context of development

There are several reasons for questioning whether the above arguments justify a policy of relying on primary exports as the means to development.

Comparative costs change over time. Over time, with the acquisition of new skills and an increase in the capital stock, a developing country that once had a comparative advantage in primaries may find that it now has a comparative advantage in certain *manufactured* products, especially those that are more labour-intensive and use raw materials of which the country has a plentiful supply. The market, however, cannot necessarily be relied upon to bring about a smooth transition to producing such products. 

Concentrating on primary production may hinder growth. The theory of comparative advantage shows how trade allows a country to consume beyond its production possibility curve (see pages 780–1). As its economy grows, however, this production possibility curve will *shift outwards.* By concentrating on primaries, the curve may shift outwards more slowly than if the country had pursued a policy of industrialisation. In other words, economic growth may be slower from a policy of exporting primaries than from a policy of industrialisation. KI 38 p778

Heckscher–Ohlin version of comparative advantage A country has a comparative advantage in those goods that are intensive in the country's relatively abundant factor.

Factor price equalisation The tendency for international trade to reduce factor price inequalities both between and within countries.

Vent for surplus Where international trade enables a country to exploit resources that would otherwise be unused.

The benefits from trade may not accrue to the nationals of the country. If a mine or plantation is owned by a foreign company, it will be the foreign shareholders who get the profits from the sale of exports. In addition, these companies may bring in their own capital and skilled labour from abroad. The benefits gained by the local people will probably be confined to the additional wages they earn. With these companies being in a position of monopsony power, the wages are often very low.

In recent years, the Fair Trade movement has focused attention on the low incomes received by many primary producers and their lack of market power. Only a tiny fraction of the price you pay for coffee, tea or bananas goes to local growers.

Why does this argument make GNY a better indicator of development than GDP? (See the appendix to Chapter 15.)

Trade may lead to less equality. Trade shifts income distribution in favour of those factors of production employed intensively in the export sector. If exports are labour intensive, greater equality will tend to result. But if they are land or raw material intensive, trade will redistribute income in favour of large landowners or mine owners.

KI 4 p13

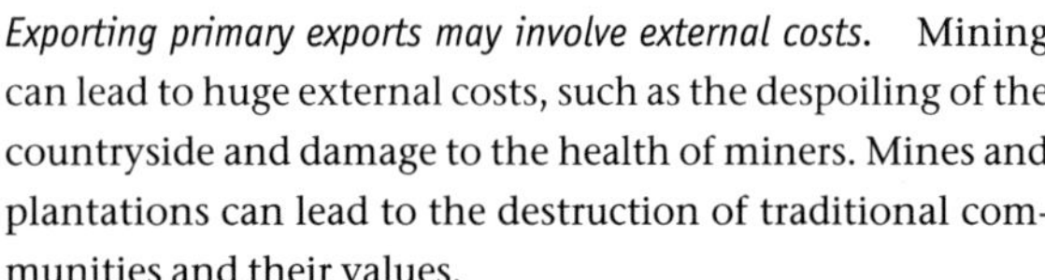

Exporting primary exports may involve external costs. Mining can lead to huge external costs, such as the despoiling of the countryside and damage to the health of miners. Mines and plantations can lead to the destruction of traditional communities and their values.

KI 31 p364

These arguments cast doubt on whether a policy of relying on free trade in primary exports is the best way of achieving economic development. Various trends in the international economy have also worked against primary exporters, causing them serious balance of payments problems.

Balance of payments problems: long term

Long-term trends in international trade have caused problems for primary exporting countries in various ways.

KI 9 p64

Low income elasticity of demand for primary products. As world incomes grow, so a smaller proportion of these incomes is spent on primaries. Since food is a necessity, consumers, especially in rich countries, already consume virtually all they require. A rise in incomes, therefore, tends to be spent more on luxury goods and services, and only slightly more on basic foodstuffs. The exceptions are certain 'luxury' imported foodstuffs such as exotic fruits. In the case of raw materials, as people's incomes grow, they tend to buy more and more expensive products. The extra value of these products, however, arises not from the extra raw materials they might contain, but from their greater sophistication.

This argument, however, has not always applied in recent years. The rapid growth of countries such as China and India, where people spend a relatively large proportion of any increase in their income on food, has led to periods of rapidly rising world food prices (see Figure 26.8). This has been aggravated by poor harvests in many parts of the world and by switching land to growing crops for biofuels instead of food. This has raised concerns among developing countries about 'food security' and hence the ability of people to afford foodstuffs. There has also been a rapid growth in demand by such countries for raw materials as inputs into the construction industry and the expanding industrial sector.

Agricultural protection in advanced countries. Faced with the problem of a slowly growing demand for food produced by their own farmers, advanced countries increasingly imposed restrictions on imported food. Reducing these restrictions has been one of the main aims of the Doha Development Agenda (the latest round of WTO trade negotiations: see Box 24.8 on pages 794–5).

Technological developments. Synthetic substitutes have in many cases replaced primaries in the making of consumer durables, industrial equipment and clothing. Also, the process of miniaturisation, as microchips have replaced machines, has meant that less and less raw materials have been required to produce any given amount of output.

Rapid growth in imports. There tends to be a high income elasticity of demand for imported manufactures. This is the result partly of better-off people in developing countries being able to afford luxury goods, and partly of the development of new tastes as people are exposed to the products of the developed world – products such as Coca-Cola®, Levi® jeans, mobile phones and iPods®. In fact, the whole process has been dubbed 'Coca-Colanisation'. Because of a lack of domestic substitutes, the price elasticity of demand for manufactured imports is low. This gives market power to the overseas suppliers of these imports, which tends to raise their price relative to exports.

The terms of trade. Between 1980 and 2000, the prices of many primary products declined. For instance, the nominal price index in the early 2000s for beverages (coffee and tea) was only one-quarter of its level in the late 1970s – and even less than that in real terms. This reflected the slow growth in demand for primaries and led to a *decline* in the terms of trade for primary exporters. This is because they were having to export more and more in order to buy any given quantity of imports, such as manufactured goods.

As Figure 26.8 shows, a quite different picture emerged in the 2000s. As the demand for food and raw materials grew rapidly, reflecting the rapid growth of China and various other emerging economies, so primary commodity prices rose sharply.

This came to an abrupt halt with the world recession of 2008–9, when primary product prices fell sharply. But the resumption of global growth saw primary commodity prices climb once more and in many cases to levels considerably higher than before the world recession. Thereafter, global growth rates fluctuated as economies, such as the eurozone, struggled to sustain prolonged periods of growth and commodity prices fell. During

Figure 26.8 World primary commodity prices (2010 = 100)

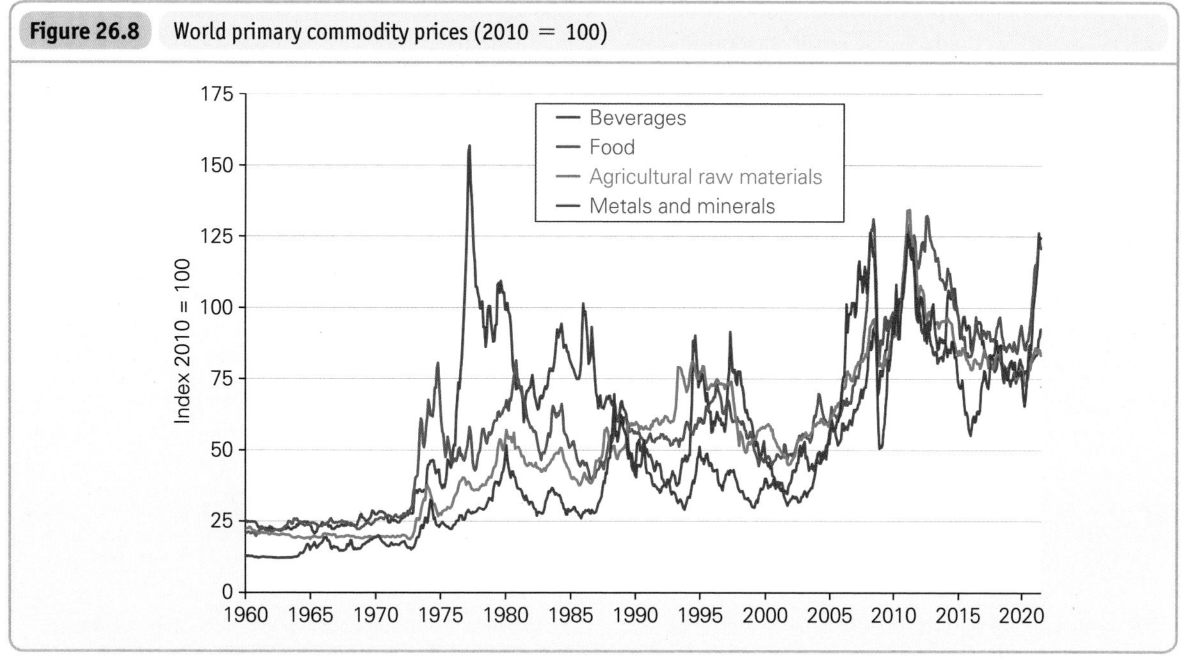

Source: Based on data from *World Bank Commodity Price Data (The Pink Sheet)*, Commodity Markets, World Bank, www.worldbank.org/en/research/commodity-markets

the COVID-19 pandemic in 2020, the aggregate commodity price index temporarily fell to levels seen during the financial crisis. Nevertheless, this was still some 75 per cent higher than in January 2000 (in nominal terms).

Balance of payments problems: short term

There are also problems for primary exporting countries in the *short term.*

As we have just seen, the prices of primary products can be subject to large fluctuations. This causes great uncertainty for primary exporters. The current account of the balance of payments fluctuates wildly, which tends to cause large swings in exchange rates or requires massive government intervention to stabilise them.

Price fluctuations are caused partly by the low price elasticity of demand and supply of primaries, but also by substantial *shifts* in their demand and supply.

The demand for *food* tends to be relatively stable, but that for minerals varies with the business cycle and tends to vary more than the demand for consumer goods. The reason is the *accelerator principle* (see section 17.4). Since the *level* of investment demand depends on the size of *changes* in consumer demand, investment will fluctuate much more than consumer demand. But since many minerals are inputs into *capital* equipment, their demand is also likely to fluctuate more than consumer demand. For example, with the boom in construction in emerging economies in the mid-2000s and again in 2010–11, the prices of iron ore, copper, nickel and lead shot up.

The supply of minerals is relatively stable. The supply of cash crops, however, varies with the harvest. Many developing countries are subject to drought or flood, which can virtually wipe out their export earnings from the relevant crop.

If a disastrous harvest of rice were confined to a particular country, would (a) the world price and (b) its own domestic price of rice fluctuate significantly? What would happen to the country's export earnings and the earnings of individual farmers?

With a price-inelastic world demand and supply for primaries, shifts in either curve will lead to substantial fluctuations in world prices. Figure 26.8 illustrates the extent of these fluctuations. The problem is most serious for countries that rely on just one or two primary products, such as Ghana, which relies on cocoa, and the Democratic Republic of Congo, which relies on copper and cobalt. Diversification into other primaries would help to reduce their exposure.

Approach 2: Import-substituting industrialisation (ISI)

Dissatisfaction with relying on primary exporting has led most countries to embark on a process of *industrialisation.* The newly industrialised countries (NICs), such as China, Malaysia, Brazil and India, are already well advanced along the industrialisation road. Other developing countries have not yet progressed very far, especially the poorest African countries.

TC 7 p79

The most obvious way for countries to industrialise was to cut back on the imports of manufactures and substitute them with home-produced manufactures. This could not be done overnight: it had to be done in stages, beginning with assembly, then making some of the components, and finally making all, or nearly all, of the inputs into production. Most developing countries have at least started on the first stage. Several of the more advanced developing countries have component-manufacturing industries. Only a few of the larger NICs, such as China, India, Brazil and South Korea, have built extensive capital goods industries.

The method most favoured by policy makers was ***tariff escalation***. Here tariff rates (or other restrictions) increased as one moved from the raw materials to the intermediate product to the finished product stage. Thus finished goods had higher tariffs than intermediate products. This encouraged assembly plants, which were protected by high tariffs from imported finished products, and were able to obtain components at a lower tariff rate.

One of the problems with ISI was that countries were desperately short of resources to invest in industry. As a result, a policy of ISI usually involved encouraging investment by multinational companies. But even without specific 'perks' (e.g. tax concessions, cheap sites, the cutting of red tape), multinationals would still probably be attracted by the protection afforded by the tariffs or quotas.

Definition

Tariff escalation The system whereby tariff rates increase the closer a product is to the finished stage of production.

BOX 26.4 WHEN DRIVING AND ALCOHOL DO MIX — CASE STUDIES AND APPLICATIONS

A case of import substitution in Brazil

Two major changes in world trade hit Brazil in the 1970s. The first was the fourfold increase in world oil prices. Brazil has very little oil of its own. The second was the slump in the world sugar cane market as a result of northern countries' protection of their sugar beet industries. Brazil was a major cane sugar exporter.

Faced with a resulting large increase in its import bill and a slump in its sugar exports, the Brazilian government came up with an ingenious solution. It could use surplus sugar cane to make alcohol, which could then be used instead of petrol for cars. Farmers were given subsidies to grown sugar cane.

Large distilleries were set up to convert the sugar cane into alcohol. At the same time, cars were produced (e.g. VW Beetles) that could run on alcohol (ethanol) rather than petrol.

Thus by one measure two problems were alleviated. By 1985, more than 90 per cent of cars produced in Brazil were designed to burn alcohol.

Then, with the decline in oil prices from the mid-1980s, the relative cost efficiency of alcohol-powered cars declined: at times it was cheaper to import oil than to produce alcohol. The government cut subsidies and by 1997 less than 1 per cent of cars produced in Brazil were alcohol-powered.

The dual-fuel solution

A more flexible solution was found in 2003 with the introduction of dual-fuel cars that could run on either alcohol or petrol or a mixture of the two. This gave consumers the chance of using whichever fuel was the cheapest at the time. The popularity of these 'flexi-fuel' cars gave a welcome boost to the sugar cane and ethanol industries.

However, despite the number of dual-fuel cars and vans in Brazil reaching over 80 per cent of the total in the early 2010s, the industry began to experience difficulties. The deteriorating macroeconomic climate depressed car usage and the purchase of new cars. Furthermore, in looking to control inflation the government was subsidising petrol prices and, with the price of oil falling from 2014, the effect was to make the use of ethanol less competitive compared with petrol. Again, the effect was to dampen the demand for ethanol.

The government subsequently took steps to revive the biofuel sector. It terminated its subsidies of petrol and also increased the proportion of ethanol in petrol from 25 per cent to 27 per cent.

The story illustrates the danger of basing major schemes on terms of trade existing at a particular time. If these terms of trade subsequently change, the schemes could prove to be uneconomical.

A new era for the biofuels industry

Brazil has also increased its support for another import-substituting drive: to displace diesel fuel with fuel produced from soybeans and other vegetable oils. The plan was for the percentage of vegetable oil blended with diesel to rise from 11 per cent in 2019 to 15 per cent in 2023 and then to 20 per cent in 2028. However, a surge in the price of soybeans from the second half of 2020 saw biodiesel prices rise sharply. In response the government temporarily reduced the required percentage of vegetable oil blended with diesel once more, illustrating the problems when designing and implementing policy.

Perhaps this long-term support for biodiesel will help to revive the vehicle industry in Brazil. But soya-based biodiesel can have very damaging effects on the environment. It is far less energy-efficient than sugar cane as a source of fuel and it absorbs less carbon per hectare as it grows. In fact, given that rainforest is being cleared to grow soya, the net effect is to reduce carbon capture substantially.

Could a case be made out for a flexible tax on oil imports to ensure that it was always profitable to produce alcohol?

Undertake desktop research to construct a short briefing note on the trends in renewable energy generation and capacity. You might find it helpful to look at evidence from The International Renewable Energy Agency (IRENA): an intergovernmental organisation that supports countries in their transition to a sustainable energy future.

Adverse effects of import substitution

Some countries, such as South Korea and Taiwan, pursued an inward-looking ISI policy for only a few years. For them it was merely a stage in development, rapidly to be followed by a secondary outward-looking policy. Infant industries were initially given protection, but when they had achieved sufficient economies of scale, the barriers to imports were gradually removed.

The countries that continued to pursue protectionist ISI policies generally had a poorer growth record. They also tended to suffer from other problems, such as a deepening of inequality. The development of the modern industrial sector was often to the detriment of the traditional sectors and also to the export sector.

The criticisms of ISI are numerous and include the following.

It ran directly counter to the principle of comparative advantage. Rather than confining ISI to genuine infant industries and then gradually removing the protection, ISI was applied indiscriminately to a whole range of industries. Countries ended up producing goods in which they had a comparative *disadvantage.*

If a country specialises in a good in which it has a comparative disadvantage, where will it be consuming with respect to its production possibility curve?

It cushioned inefficient practices and encouraged the establishment of monopolies. Without competition from imports, many of the industries were highly inefficient and wasteful of resources. What is more, in all but the largest or most developed of the developing countries the domestic market for many manufactures is small. If a newly established industry is to be large enough to gain the full potential economies of scale, it must be large relative to the market. This means that it will have considerable monopoly power.

It involved artificially low real interest rates. To encourage capital investment in the import-substituting industries, governments often intervened to keep interest rates low. This encouraged the use of capital-intensive technology with a consequent lack of jobs. It also starved other sectors (such as agriculture) of much-needed finance, and it discouraged saving.

It led to urban wages above the market-clearing level. Wage rates in the industrial sector, although still low compared with advanced countries, are often considerably higher than in the traditional sectors.

- They are pushed up by firms seeking to retain labour in which they have invested training. Governments, seeking to appease the politically powerful urban industrial working class, have often passed minimum wage laws.
- Trade unions, although less widespread in developing than in advanced countries, are mainly confined to the new industries.

Higher industrial wages again encourage firms to use capital-intensive techniques.

It involved overvalued exchange rates. Restricting imports tends to lead to an appreciation of the exchange rate. This makes non-restricted imports cheaper. This then discourages the production of domestic goods, such as food and component parts, which compete with those imports. Also, a higher exchange rate discourages exports. Exports tend to be priced in dollars. If the exchange rate appreciates, domestic currency will buy more dollars; or put another way, a dollar will exchange for less domestic currency. Thus exporters will earn less domestic currency as the exchange rate appreciates.

Why is an overvalued exchange rate likely to encourage the use of capital-intensive technology?

It did not necessarily save on foreign exchange. Many of the new industries were highly dependent on the importation of raw materials, capital equipment and component parts. These imported inputs, unlike imports of finished goods, were often supplied by a single firm, which could thus charge monopoly prices. What is more, a large proportion of the extra incomes generated by these industries tended to be spent on imports by the new urban elites.

Protection was not applied evenly. Many different tariff rates were used in one country: in fact, a policy of tariff escalation demands this. In addition, governments often used a whole range of other protectionist instruments, such as the licensing of importers, physical and value quotas, and foreign exchange rationing. These were often applied in a haphazard way. The result was that protection was highly uneven.

Income distribution was made less equal. Additional incomes generated by the modern sector tended to be spent on modern-sector goods and imported goods. Thus there was a multiplier effect *within* the modern sector, but virtually none between the sectors. Also, as we saw above, an overvalued exchange rate leads to a bias against agriculture, and thus further deepens the divide between rich and poor. Finally, the relatively high wages of the modern sector encourage workers to migrate to the towns, where many, failing to get a job, live in dire poverty.

Social, cultural and environmental costs. A policy of ISI often involved imposing an alien set of values. Urban life can be harsh, competitive and materialistic. Moreover, a drive for industrialisation may involve major costs to the environment, as a result of waste products from new industries and a lack of sewage systems in poor areas.

Finally, import substitution is necessarily limited by the size of the domestic market. Once that is saturated, ISI can come to an abrupt halt. At that stage, further expansion can come only from exporting; but if these industries have been overprotected, they will be unable to compete in world markets.

This has been a long list of problems and different economists put different emphases on them. Neoclassical economists stress the problems of market distortions, arguing that ISI leads to great inefficiency. Neo-Marxist economists, on the other hand, stress the problems of ***dependency***. Many of the new industries will be owned by multinational companies, which import unsuitable technologies. The countries will then become dependent on imported inputs and foreign sources of capital. (See Case Study 26.6 on the student website.)

Approach 3: Exporting manufactures – a possible way forward?

The countries with the highest rates of economic growth are those that have successfully made the transition to being exporters of manufactures. Table 26.5 gives some examples.

The transition from inward-looking to outward-looking industrialisation

How is a country to move from import substituting to being outward-looking? One approach is to take it industry by industry. When an industry has saturated the home market and there is no further scope for import substitution, it should then be encouraged to seek markets overseas. The trouble with this approach is that, if the country is still protecting other industries, there will probably still be an overvalued exchange rate. Thus specific subsidies, tax concessions or other 'perks' would have to be given to this industry to enable it to compete. The country would still be highly interventionist, with all the distortions and misallocation of resources that this tends to bring.

The alternative is to wean the whole economy off protection. Three major things will need doing:

- A devaluation of the currency in order to restore the potential profitability of the export sector.
- A dismantling of the various protective measures that had biased production towards the home market.
- A removal or relaxing of price controls.

But these are things that cannot be done 'at a stroke'. Firms may have to be introduced gradually to the greater forces of competition that an outward-looking trade policy brings. Otherwise there may be massive bankruptcies and a corresponding massive rise in unemployment.

The benefits from a secondary outward-looking policy

The advocates of outward-looking industrialisation make a number of points in its favour.

KI 38 p778

It conforms more closely to comparative advantage. Countries pursuing an open trade regime will be able to export only goods in which they have a comparative advantage. The resources used in earning a unit of foreign exchange from exports will be less than those used in saving a unit of foreign exchange by replacing imports with home-produced goods. In other words, resources will be used more efficiently.

Economies of scale. If the home market is too small to allow a firm to gain all the potential economies of scale, these can be gained by expanding into the export market.

Increased competition. By having to compete with foreign companies, exporters will be under a greater competitive pressure than industries shielded behind protective barriers. This will encourage (a) resource saving in the short run, both through their better *allocation* and through reductions in X inefficiency (see Box 7.5), and (b) innovation and investment, as firms attempt to adopt the latest technology, often obtained from developed countries.

KI 3 p13

Increased investment. To the extent that outward-looking policies lead to a greater potential for economic growth, they may attract more foreign capital. To the extent that they lead to increased incomes, additional saving will be generated, especially given that the *marginal* propensity to save may be quite high. The extra savings can be used to finance extra investment.

KI 4 p13

It can lead to more employment and a more equal distribution of income. According to the Heckscher–Ohlin theory, the manufactured goods in which a country will have a comparative advantage are those produced by labour-intensive techniques. Export expansion will thus increase the demand for labour relative to capital, and create more employment. The increased demand for labour will tend to lead to a rise in wages relative to profits.

Will the adoption of labour-intensive techniques necessarily lead to a more equal distribution of income?

It removes many of the costs associated with ISI. Under a policy of ISI, managers may spend a lot of their time lobbying politicians and officials, seeking licences (and sometimes paying bribes to obtain them), adhering to norms and regulations or trying to find ways around them. If an outward-looking policy involves removing all this, managers can turn their attention to producing goods more efficiently.

TC 5 p48

Definition

Dependency Where the development of a developing country is hampered by its relationships with the industrialised world.

Table 26.5 Growth rates and export performance of selected secondary outward-looking countries

	Average 1985–2019				2019	
	Annual growth in real GDP (%)	Annual growth in real GDP per capita (%)	Exports (% of GDP)	Manufactures exports (% of merchandise exports)	GDP per capita, PPP, $	GNI per capita, PPP, $
Brazil	2.7	1.3	11	48	15 300	14 890
China	9.7	8.7	21	84	16 804	16 760
Hong Kong	4.3	3.3	151	70	62 496	65 730
India	6.2	4.4	15	69	6 997	6 920
Malaysia	5.7	3.4	89	65	29 620	28 830
Singapore	6.2	3.9	25	73	101 649	92 270
South Korea	6.2	5.4	35	90	44 011	44 390
Low-income economies	3.5	0.7	22	9	2 497	2 450
Middle-income economies	4.4	2.9	23	61	12 148	11 968
Low- and middle-income economies	4.4	2.8	23	60	11 133	10 967
High-income economies	2.4	1.7	25	72	52 785	53 066
World	3.0	1.5	25	68	17 811	17 718

Source: Based on data from *Databank* (World Bank).

Drawbacks of an export-orientated industrialisation strategy

The export of manufactures is seen by many developed countries as very threatening to their own industries. Their response has often been to erect trade barriers. These barriers have tended to be highest in the very industries (such as textiles, footwear and processed food) where developing countries have the greatest comparative advantage. Even if the barriers are *currently* low, developing countries may feel that it is too risky to expand their exports of these products for fear of a future rise in barriers. Recognising this problem, the World Trade Organization is very keen to ensure fair access for developing countries to the markets of the rich world. This has been a core focus of the Doha Round of trade negotiations (see Box 24.8 on pages 794–5).

Consider the arguments from the perspective of an advanced country for and against protecting its industries from imports of manufactures from developing countries.

The successes of developing countries such as China, Malaysia and South Korea in exporting manufactures (see Table 26.5) do not imply that other developing countries will have similar success. As additional developing countries attempt to export their manufactures, they will be facing more and more competition from each other.

Another problem is that, if a more open trade policy involves removing or reducing exchange and capital controls, the country may become more vulnerable to speculative attack. This was one of the major contributing factors to the East Asian crisis of the late 1990s (see Case Study 26.2 on the student website). Gripped by currency and stock market speculation, and by banking and company insolvency, many countries of the region found that economic growth had turned into a major recession. The 'miracle' seemed to be over. Nevertheless, the countries with the fewest distortions fared the best during the crisis. Thus Singapore and Taiwan, which are open and relatively flexible, experienced only a slowdown, rather than a recession.

Exporting manufactures may thus be a very risky strategy for the least developed countries, such as many in Africa. Perhaps the best hope for the future may be for a growth in manufacturing trade *between* such developing countries. That way they can gain the benefits of specialisation and economies of scale that trade brings, while at the same time producing for a growing market. The feasibility of this approach depends on whether developing countries can agree to free trade areas or even customs unions between themselves (see section 24.3).

There does, however, seem to be a strong movement in this direction. The share of trade between developing countries (so-called South–South trade) in total world exports has doubled over the past 20 years, to over 25 per cent. Manufactured goods now account for nearly 60 per cent of South–South trade, respectively.

BOX 26.5 THE EVOLVING COMPARATIVE ADVANTAGE OF CHINA

Riding the dragon

Comparative advantage enables specialisation and trade and this can be one of the key factors that helps a country to grow and develop. During the 1990s and 2000s, China experienced an average rate of growth of just over 10 per cent per year. Its emergence as an economic power is due to many things, but its ability to exploit its *comparative advantage* is certainly one such factor.

A country's comparative advantage often derives from its abundant resources and China used its abundance of cheap labour. With labour costs estimated to be between 60 and 90 per cent lower than in the USA, it was this that attracted many manufacturing companies to China, making a range of products using moderately and low-skilled jobs.

According to UNCTAD's 2021 World Investment Report, China (excluding Hong Kong) was the world's second largest *recipient* of foreign direct investment (FDI) in 2020, with investment of just over $149 billion or 2.3 per cent of the country's gross fixed capital formation. This meant China was the recipient of around 15 per cent of global FDI. (The USA's FDI inflow was $156 billion in 2020 or 3.6 per cent of the country's gross fixed capital formation.)

Lu Zheng, the Director of the Institute of Industrial Economics under the Chinese Academy of Social Sciences, said that 'it [China's comparative advantage] will last at least two decades and play an important role in promoting China's economic growth'.

However, it is not just the quantity of labour that explained China's dominance in manufacturing. While many of its workers are low-skilled, many are educated. Furthermore, Paul Krugman notes another key factor:

> China's dominant role in the export of many labor-intensive manufactured goods surely reflects its combination of relatively abundant labor and relatively high manufacturing competence.[1]

It is unsurprising that companies would take advantage of lower costs of production and locate factories in China. But while China has benefited from this, many developed nations have seen a decline in their manufactured exports. Countries like the UK and USA gradually adjusted and moved to exploit their comparative advantage in the services sector. They saw a comparative disadvantage emerge in manufactured items. This changing comparative advantage as a country develops is well-documented and could it be that China will soon begin to see its own comparative advantage change?

Rising labour costs

China's low labour costs are crucial, but these have been rising, as workers demand higher wages, shorter hours and greater benefits. Data suggest that labour costs have been growing at some 20 per cent per year.

The first effect of this has been for some labour-intensive businesses to migrate towards inland China, where labour costs are lower.

Section summary

1. Trade is of vital importance for the vast majority of developing countries, and yet most developing countries suffer from chronic balance of trade deficits.
2. Developing countries have traditionally been primary exporters. This has allowed them to exploit their comparative advantage in labour-intensive goods and has provided a market for certain goods that would otherwise have no market at home.
3. There are reasons for questioning the wisdom of relying on traditional primary exports, however. With a low world income elasticity of demand for many primary products, with the development of synthetic substitutes for minerals and with the protection of agriculture in developed countries, the demand for primary exports from the developing world has grown only slowly. At the same time, the demand for manufactured imports into developing countries has grown rapidly. Until recently, the result was a decline in the terms of trade. The rapid growth in demand for primary products from China and India has, to some extent, reversed this trend and the terms of trade have improved for many primary exporters.
4. Import-substituting industrialisation (ISI) was seen to be the answer to the problems of primary exporting. ISI was normally achieved in stages, beginning with the finished goods stage and then working back towards the capital goods stage. ISI, it was hoped, would allow countries to benefit from the various long-term advantages associated with manufacturing.

CASE STUDIES AND APPLICATIONS

However, in other cases the move has been more significant. With a comparative advantage in low-cost labour disappearing, some labour-intensive businesses have left China, moving to other nations which can boast cheap labour, such as Bangladesh, Cambodia, Indonesia and Vietnam. This is especially the case for companies specialising in the production of clothes and shoes.

But the story will not stop there. These industries require labour and as long as this remains the case, when a country begins to grow this will lead to higher wage demands, which in turn will raise costs. Production will shift once more.

Moving up the value chain

So, what does this mean for China? When the USA and Europe lost their comparative advantage in the production of manufactured products, they had to look elsewhere. They developed a comparative advantage in the production of products requiring highly skilled labour and increasingly specialised in the services sector. However, with rising costs in emerging economies, more manufacturing, especially of high-value products, is being returned to these developed nations.

China will need to follow the pattern of the Western economies; its companies and workers will need to move up the value chain to find products that they can specialise in, which are not easily transferable to lower-wage countries.[2] This is no easy task, as moving up the value chain will involve entering into direct competition with countries that have had time to develop their comparative advantage.

In recent years, China has invested heavily in high-tech sectors, especially those, such as solar energy, where demand is expected to grow rapidly. Since 2020, it has seen growth rates in excess of 100 per cent per year in products such as new-energy vehicles, industrial robots, excavation machinery, transportation and microcomputer equipment. With a huge domestic market, a large R&D sector to support such developments and a large planned sector to provide predictable demand, China faces far less risk than smaller market economies heavily reliant on the export sector.

Why are countries likely to see their comparative advantage change as they develop?

Using the UNCTADStat Data Center download data on inward flows of FDI into China as a percentage of total FDI flows. Plot the data in a line chart and then briefly summarise the findings of your chart.

1 Paul Krugman, 'Increasing returns in a comparative advantage world', in Robert M. Stern, *Comparative Advantage, Growth, and the Gains from Trade and Globalization*, World Scientific (2011), Chapter 7, p. 45.

2 Mohan Kompella, 'China, comparative advantage and moving up the value chain', *The Story of Business blog* (25 November 2012).

5. For many countries, however, ISI brought as many problems, if not more, than it solved. It often led to the establishment of inefficient industries, protected from foreign competition and facing little or no competition at home either. It led to considerable market distortions, with tariffs and other forms of protection haphazardly applied; to overvalued exchange rates, with a resulting bias against exports and the agricultural sector generally; to a deepening of inequalities and to large-scale social problems as the cities expanded, as poverty and unemployment grew and as traditional values were undermined; to increased dependency on imported inputs; and to growing environmental problems.
6. The most rapidly growing of the developing countries are those that have pursued a policy of export-orientated industrialisation. This has allowed them to achieve the benefits of economies of scale and foreign competition, and to specialise in goods in which they have a comparative advantage (i.e. labour-intensive goods) and yet which have a relatively high income elasticity of demand. Whether countries that have pursued ISI can successfully turn to an open, export-orientated approach will depend to a large extent on the degree of competition they face not only from advanced countries but also from other developing countries.

26.5 THE PROBLEM OF DEBT

Perhaps the most serious of all balance of payments problems in the world today is that faced by some of the poorest developing countries. Many of them experience massive financial outflows year after year as a result of having to 'service' debt (i.e. pay interest and make the necessary repayments). Much of this debt has been incurred in their attempts to finance development. Figure 26.9 shows the growth of external debt (as a proportion of national income) that began in the early 1970s.

KI 35 p459

The oil shocks of the 1970s

In 1973–4, oil prices quadrupled and the world went into recession. Oil imports cost much more and export demand was sluggish. The current account deficit of oil-importing developing countries rose from 1.1 per cent of GNY in 1973 to 4.3 per cent in 1975.

It was not difficult to finance these deficits, however. The oil surpluses deposited in commercial banks in the industrialised world provided an important additional source of finance. The banks, flush with money and faced with slack demand in the industrialised world, were very willing to lend. Bank loans to developing countries rose from \$3 billion in 1970 to \$12 billion in 1975. These flows enabled developing countries to continue with policies of growth.

The world recession was short-lived, and with a recovery in the demand for their exports and with their debts being eroded by high world inflation, developing countries found it relatively easy to service these increased debts (i.e. pay interest and make the necessary capital repayments).

In 1979–80 world oil prices rose again (from \$15 to \$38 per barrel). This second oil shock, like the first one, caused a large increase in the import bills of developing countries. But the full effects on their economies this time were very much worse (see Figure 26.9), given the debts that had been accumulated in the 1970s and given the policies adopted by the industrialised world after 1979.

But why were things so much worse this time?

- The world recession was deeper and lasted longer (1980–83), and when recovery came, it came very slowly. Developing countries' current account balance of payments deteriorated sharply caused by a marked slowing down in the growth of their exports and to a fall in their export prices.
- The tight monetary policies pursued by the industrialised countries led to a sharp increase in interest rates, and the resulting fall in inflation meant, therefore, that there was a very sharp increase in real interest rates. This greatly increased developing countries' costs of servicing their debts, as can be seen in Figure 26.10.

Figure 26.9 External debt as a % of gross national income (GNY)

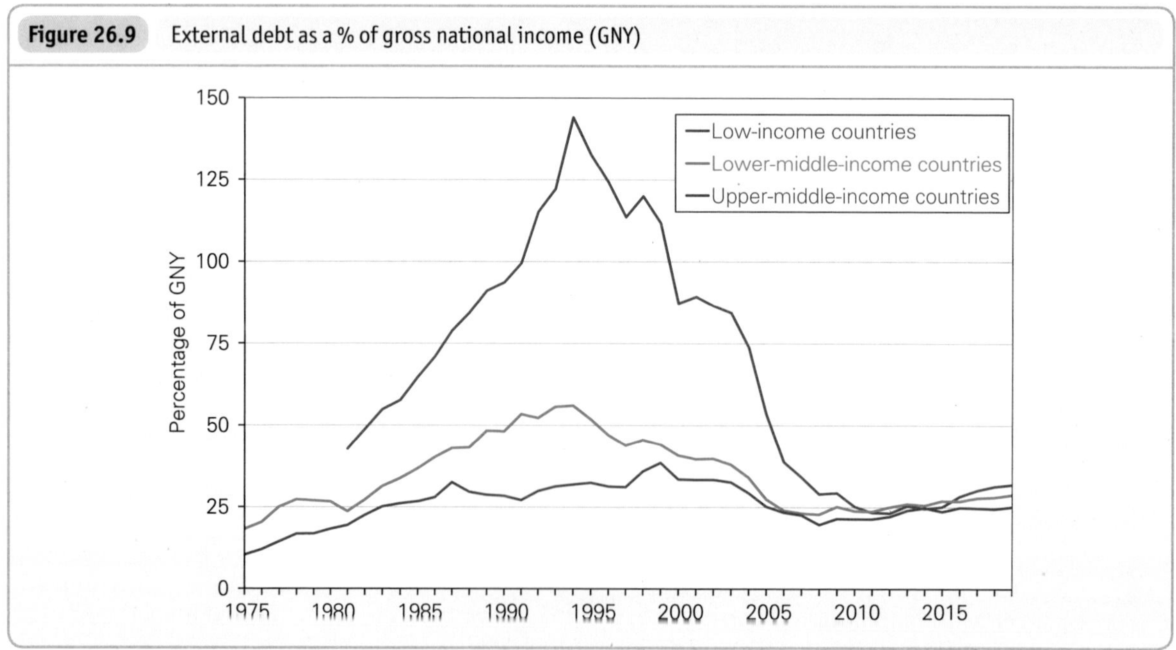

Source: Based on data from *Databank*, series DT.DOD.DECT.GN.ZS, World Bank, https://data.worldbank.org/indicator/DT.DOD.DECT.GN.ZS

Figure 26.10 Debt servicing costs as a percentage of gross national income (GNY)

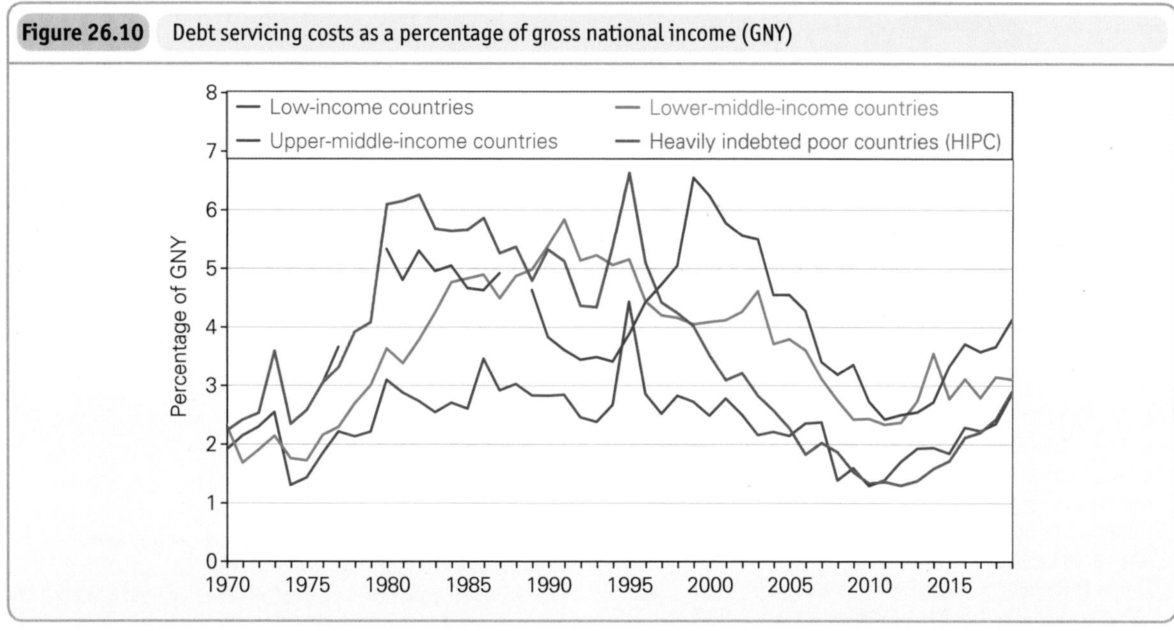

Source: Based on data from *Databank*, series DT.TDS.DECT.GN.ZS, World Bank, https://data.worldbank.org/indicator/DT.TDS.DECT.GN.ZS

- The problem was made worse by the growing proportion of debt that was at variable interest rates. This was largely due to the increasing proportion of debt that was in the form of loans from commercial banks.

Figure 26.10 shows how after 1979 debt servicing costs as a proportion of national income rose across developing countries, making it increasingly difficult for them to service their debts. Then in 1982 Mexico, followed by several other countries such as Brazil, Bolivia, Zaire and Sudan, declared that it would have to suspend payments. There was now a debt crisis, which threatened not only the debtor countries, but also the world banking system.

Coping with debt: rescheduling

There have been two dimensions to tackling the debt problems of developing countries. The first is to cope with difficulties in servicing their debt. This usually involves some form of rescheduling of the repayments. The second dimension is to deal with the causes of the problem. Here we will focus on rescheduling.

Rescheduling official loans

Official loans are renegotiated through the Paris Club. Industrialised countries are members of the club, which arranges terms for the rescheduling of their loans to developing countries. Agreements normally involve delaying the date for repayment of loans currently maturing, or spreading the repayments over a longer period of time. Paris Club agreements are often made in consultation with the IMF, which works out a programme with the debtor country for tackling its underlying economic problems.

Several attempts have been made since the mid-1980s to make rescheduling terms more generous, with longer periods before repayments start, longer to repay when they do start, and lower interest rates. In return, the developing countries have had to undertake various 'structural adjustment programmes' supervised by the IMF (see below).

But despite the apparent advances made by the Paris Club in making its terms more generous, the majority of low-income countries failed to meet the required IMF conditions, and thus failed to have their debts reduced. What is more, individual Paris Club members were often reluctant to reduce debts unless they were first convinced that other members were 'paying their share'. Nevertheless, some creditor countries unilaterally introduced more generous terms and even cancelled some debts.

The net effect of rescheduling, but only very modest debt forgiveness, can be seen in Figures 26.9 and 26.10. By the mid-1990s average debt service ratios had fallen from the levels of the mid-1980s and yet the ratio of total debt to GNY was higher. There were thus growing calls for the cancellation of debts (see below).

Rescheduling commercial bank loans

After the declarations by Mexico and other countries of their inability to service their debts, there was fear of an imminent collapse of the world banking system. Banks realised that disaster could be averted only by collective action of the banks to reschedule debts. Banks were prepared to reschedule some of the debts and to provide some additional loans in return for debtor countries undertaking structural adjustment (as described below). Additional loans, however, fell well short of the amount that was needed. Nevertheless, banks were

BOX 26.6 A DEBT TO THE PLANET

Developing an agenda for sustainable development

Ecocide

Faced with mounting debts and the need to service them, many developing countries have attempted to increase their export earnings. One way of achieving this is through the intensified extraction of minerals and ores or intensified farming, often by multinational corporations. But a consequence of this may be massive environmental damage.

Brazil. An example of a country forced into what has been called 'ecocide' in response to its huge debt burden is Brazil. One of the most environmentally damaging of all Brazilian projects has been the Grande Carajas iron ore project. Proposed in 1980, the Carajas scheme cost some $62 billion and has involved massive deforestation of an area larger than France and Britain combined. The Brazilian government has been willing to allow this environmental damage because Carajas is seen as a 'national export project'. Indeed, various plans have been approved for further mining activity in the area. In July 2013, for example, the Carajas Serra Sul S11D Iron Project, the largest iron ore mine project in the world, was approved and production began in December 2016, with supply expected to reach 90 million metric tonnes by 2018.

Venezuela. Another example of ecocide has occurred in Venezuela. The country has huge gold reserves – some 12 per cent of the world total. With the fall in oil prices in the 1990s, and hence a fall in revenues for Venezuela, one of the world's leading oil exporters, the Venezuelan authorities sought to exploit the country's gold reserves more aggressively. By 1994, the state had contracted out some 436 sites, covering 12 839 km^2. By 2000, this had risen to 30 000 km^2 (an area the size of Belgium), earning revenue of some $250 million per year.

The extraction of gold, however, has wrought great environmental damage. The richest gold reserves are in the Guayana region of Venezuela, which makes up part of the Amazon river basin. It is an area rich, and in many respects unique, in its biodiversity. The environmental impact of open-cast mining within the region is already being felt. One of the most serious consequences has been the poisoning of rivers with mercury (used to separate gold from other minerals). In addition to the destruction of the forests and rivers, there are many cases where indigenous peoples have had their human rights violated and have even been murdered to make way for the mines.

Indonesia. The misuse and destruction of rainforests caused dramatic effects in 1997. In large parts of Indonesia (another highly indebted country), it is normal practice to burn land after forests have been felled, either to clear it for crops or for replanting. In 1997, the El Niño effect on ocean currents had caused a major drought and the forest fires got out of hand. As a result, air pollution on a massive scale affected many countries in South East Asia. Most of Indonesia, Malaysia and Singapore became covered with a haze of dense smoke. The international air pollutant index has a scale on which readings above 500 are considered extremely hazardous. In parts of Malaysia readings of 1200 were recorded – equivalent to smoking a couple of packs of cigarettes a day. Schools and airports were closed, and income from tourism was lost throughout the region.

Biodiesel. A recent case of ecocide is the production of palm oil as a biofuel. The environmental justification was that the carbon dioxide given off by burning the fuel is offset by the carbon absorbed by growing the oil palm trees. But this has turned out to be only part of the story. The production of the additional palm oil has involved either cutting down rainforest, which, apart from being a much more efficient carbon absorber than oil palm trees, is habitat for many endangered species, or the draining and burning of peat lands, which sends huge amounts of carbon dioxide into the atmosphere.

increasingly setting aside funds to cover bad debt, and thus the crisis for the banks began to recede.

As banks felt less exposed to default, so they became less worried about it and less concerned to negotiate deals with debtor countries. Many of the more severely indebted countries, however, found their position still deteriorating rapidly. What is more, many of them were finding that the IMF adjustment programmes were too painful (often involving deep cuts in government expenditure) and were therefore abandoning them. Thus, in 1989, US Treasury Secretary Nicholas Brady proposed measures to *reduce* debt.

The *Brady Plan* involved the IMF and the World Bank lending funds to debtor countries to enable them to repay debts to banks. In return for this instant source of liquidity, the banks would have to be prepared to accept repayment of less than the full sum (i.e. they would sell the debt back to the country at a discount). To benefit from such deals, the debtor countries would have to agree to structural adjustment programmes. Several such agreements were negotiated; much of the debt reduction has involved debt swaps of one sort or another (see Case Study 26.16 on the student website).

What are the relative advantages and disadvantages to a developing country of rescheduling its debts compared with simply defaulting on them (either temporarily or permanently)?

CASE STUDIES AND APPLICATIONS

The Rio Declaration

In recent years, there has been growing international awareness of the scale of the environmental destruction that is taking place. In particular, the rich countries have begun to realise that they too might suffer from this destruction, with its consequences for global warming and the loss of many unique species of plants and animals. Increasingly, international agencies such as the IMF and the World Bank are taking ecological issues into account when considering appropriate development and adjustment programmes.

Many in the developed world now realise that development must be sustainable. It is no good trying to secure 'development' for the current generation if, in the process, the environment is damaged and future generations suffer. This is a message that has been well understood by indigenous peoples for countless generations, especially those living on marginal lands: from the Aborigines of the Australian outback to the tribes of the African bush. It is seen as a moral imperative that the land bequeathed by one's ancestors should be passed on in just as good a state to one's descendants (see page 403).

In 1992 in Rio de Janeiro, the United Nations Conference on Environment and Development (UNCED) put forward a programme for environmentally responsible development. In Agenda 21 it set out various policies that could be carried out by the international community. The policies, which were approved by 178 countries, included: targeting aid to projects that helped improve the environment (such as providing clean water); research into environmentally friendly farming methods; and programmes that help reduce population growth (such as family planning and education).

The test of such sentiments, however, is action. To monitor this, a Commission on Sustainable Development (CSD) was established in December 1992. In 2003, it set out a programme until 2015. Every two years from 2004 there was a particular focus for action, including themes around water, sanitation, sustainable development, climate change, forestry and biodiversity.

2030 Agenda for Sustainable Development

In September 2015, the UN adopted the 2030 Agenda for Sustainable Development. This saw a commitment to 17 Sustainable Development Goals (SDGs) and 169 targets, building on the Millennium Development Goals. The aim, the UN argued, is to end poverty, protect the planet and ensure prosperity for all. The overseer of the progress in meeting the goals and targets is a body known as the High Level Political Forum (HLPF).

The significance of the SDGs is the recognition that there exist intrinsically linked dimensions to sustainable development. The SDGs formally recognise three important dimensions: economic, social and environmental.

1. *If reductions in developing countries' debt are in the environmental interests of the whole world, then why have developed countries not gone much further in reducing or cancelling the debts owed to them?*
2. *Would it be possible to devise a scheme of debt repayments that would both be acceptable to debtor and creditor countries and not damage the environment?*

From the SDG indicators database (https://unstats.un.org/sdgs/indicators/database/) of the UN Statistics Division, access the global database to download the indicators from one of the 17 SDGs of your choice. Summarise your finding, noting the extent to which the indicators vary across countries and over time.

Dealing with debt: structural reform within the developing countries

The IMF has typically demanded that debtor countries pursue severe structural adjustment programmes before it has been prepared to sanction the rescheduling of debts. Such programmes have included:

- Tight fiscal and monetary policies to reduce government deficits, reduce interest rates and reduce inflation.
- Supply-side reforms to encourage greater use of the market mechanism and greater incentives for investment.
- A more open trade policy and devaluation of the currency in order to encourage more exports and more competition.

These policies, however, often brought extreme hardship as countries were forced to deflate. Unemployment and poverty increased and growth slowed down or became negative. Even though in the long run some developing countries emerged as more efficient and better able to compete in international trade, in the short run the suffering for many was too great to bear. Popular unrest and resentment against the IMF and the country's government led to riots in many countries and a breakdown of law and order.

A more 'complete' structural adjustment would extend beyond simple market liberalisation and tough monetary policies to much more open access to the markets of the rich countries (the subject of much of the Doha Round negotiations: see Box 24.8), to more aid and debt relief being channelled into health and education, and to greater research and development in areas that will benefit poor people: e.g. into efficient labour-intensive technology and into new strains of crops that are suitable for countries' specific climate and soil conditions, and which do not require large amounts of chemicals.

Dealing with debt: debt forgiveness

By the end of the 1990s, the debt burden of many of the poorest countries had become intolerable. Despite portions of their debt being written off under Paris Club terms, the debts of many countries were still rising. Between 1980 and 2000, the debt of sub-Saharan Africa had increased some 3.5 times, from $61 billion to $212 billion. Some countries, such as Ethiopia and Mozambique, were spending nearly half their export earnings on merely servicing their debt.

Even with substantial debt rescheduling and some debt cancellation, highly indebted countries were being forced to make savage cuts in government expenditure, much of it on health, education and transport. The consequence was a growth in poverty, hunger, disease and illiteracy. African countries on average were paying four times more to rich countries in debt servicing than they were spending on health and education: it was like a patient giving a blood transfusion to a doctor! The majority of these countries had no chance of 'growing their way out of debt'. The only solution for them was for a more substantial proportion of their debt to be written off.

The heavily indebted poor countries (HIPC) initiative

In 1996, the World Bank and the IMF launched the HIPC initiative. A total of 42 countries, mainly in Africa, were identified as needing substantial debt relief. This number was subsequently reduced to 39, of which 33 are in Africa. The object of the initiative has been to reduce the debts of such countries to 'sustainable' levels by cancelling debts above 200–250 per cent of GDP (this was reduced to 150 per cent in 1999 and to a lower level still for five countries).

The HIPC process has involved countries passing through two stages. In the first stage, eligible countries have had to demonstrate a track record of 'good performance'. This means that they have had to satisfy the IMF, the World Bank and the Paris Club that they have been undertaking adjustment measures, such as cutting government expenditure and liberalising their markets. It has also involved the countries preparing a Poverty Reduction Strategy Paper (PRSP) to show how they would use debt relief to tackle poverty, and especially how they would improve health and education. Once the IMF and the World Bank were satisfied that the country was making sufficient progress, the 'decision point' was reached and the level of debt relief would be determined. The country would then enter the second stage.

During this second stage, some interim debt relief has been provided. Meanwhile the country has had to establish a 'sound track record' by implementing policies established at the decision point and based on the PRSP. The length of this stage depends on how long it takes the country to implement the policies. At the end of the second stage, the country reaches the 'completion point' and debts are cancelled (as agreed at the decision point) by the various creditors, on a pro rata basis, to bring the debt to the sustainable threshold.

In 2006, debt relief for the HIPCs that reached the completion point was extended under the Multilateral Debt Relief Initiative (MDRI). This involved cancelling multilateral debt incurred before 2004.

By 2020, 37 of the HICPs had reached the completion point and were receiving MRDI relief, while two were at the pre-decision point. It is estimated that by the end of 2017 $76.2 billion had been cancelled under the HIPC programme and a further $43.3 billion under MDRI. The debt stocks of the post-decision-point HIPCs had been reduced by over 97 per cent, while poverty-reducing expenditure as a share of government revenue had increased from 42 per cent in 1999 to 46 per cent in 2017.

Despite this substantial relief, the programme has been heavily criticised. First, is the length of the process. For all the gains, debt-servicing costs as a share of national income had begun rising across the 39 HIPCs during the second half of the 2010s (see Figure 26.10). Second, are the excessively harsh conditions imposed on the HIPC countries. The required reductions in government expenditure had led to deep cuts in basic health and education, and deflationary policies had led to reductions in investment.

According to many charities, such as Oxfam, a much better approach would be to target debt relief directly at poverty reduction, with the resources released being used for investment in fields such as health, education, rural development and basic infrastructure. The focus, they argue, should be on what countries can afford to pay *after* essential spending on poverty relief and human development.

Then there are the non-HIPCs. Many of these countries have seen debts which divert a large percentage of their income from poverty relief. Furthermore, these countries too experienced a rise in their debt serving costs during the 2010s.

A new debt 'pandemic'

The situation deteriorated significantly in the early 2020s as the COVID-19 pandemic unfolded. A World Bank report published in October 2020 estimated that the pandemic may have increased the number of people suffering from extreme poverty, defined as those earning less than $1.90 a day, by up to 115 million with the figure rising to 150 million in 2021.[5]

5 *Poverty and Shared Prosperity 2020: Reversals of Fortune*, World Bank (2020, revised 2021), https://openknowledge.worldbank.org/bitstream/handle/10986/34496/9781464816024.pdf

Incomes fell in most developing countries with illness, lockdowns and business failures. This was compounded by a fall in their exports as the world economy contracted and by a 19 per cent fall in aid in 2020. The fall in incomes led to a decline in tax revenues. At the same time there were demands for increased government expenditure on healthcare and social support. Public-sector deficits thus rose steeply. And with slow vaccination rollouts, the pandemic persisted, holding back recovery.

This put developing countries in a 'trilemma', as the IMF called it.[6] Governments had to balance the objectives of:

- meeting increased spending needs from the emergency and its aftermath;
- limiting the substantial increase in public debt;
- trying to contain rises in taxes.

Developing countries were faced with a difficult trade-off between these objectives, as addressing one objective was likely to come at the expense of the other two. For example, higher spending would require higher deficits and debt or higher taxes.

The poorest countries had little scope for increased domestic borrowing and were being forced to borrow on international markets. But such debt is costly. Although international interest rates were generally low, many developing countries had to take on increasing levels of borrowing from private lenders at much higher rates of interest, substantially adding to the servicing costs of their debt.

Additional debt relief

International agencies and groups, such as the IMF, the World Bank, the United Nations and the G20, all advocated increased help to tackle this new debt crisis. In 2020–21, the IMF allocated $100 billion in lending through the Rapid Financing Instrument (RFI) and the Rapid Credit Facility (RCF) and nearly $500 million in debt service relief grants through the Catastrophe Containment and Relief Trust (CCRT). The World Bank also increased operations to $160 billion.

The IMF also increased special drawing rights (SDRs) from the current level of 204.2 billion ($293.3 billion) to 452.6 billion ($650 billion) – a rise of 121.6 per cent. SDRs are reserves created by the IMF whose value is a weighted average of five currencies – the US dollar (41.73 per cent), the euro (30.93 per cent), the Chinese yuan (10.92 per cent), the Japanese yen (8.33 per cent) and the pound sterling (8.09 per cent). This was the first such expansion since 2009 and had the support of both the G7 and the G20.

Normally an increase in SDRs would be allocated to countries according to their IMF quotas, which largely depend on the size of their GDP and their openness. Any new allocation under this formula would therefore go largely to developed countries, with developing economies getting only around $60 billion of the extra $357 billion. It was thus proposed that developed countries give much of their allocation to developing countries. These could then be used to cancel debts. This proposal was backed by Janet Yellen, the US Secretary of the Treasury who said she would 'strongly encourage G20 members to channel excess SDRs in support of recovery efforts in low-income countries, alongside continued bilateral financing'.

The G20 countries, with the support of the IMF and World Bank, also committed to suspend debt-service payments by eligible countries which requested to participate in its Debt Service Suspension Initiative (DSSI). There were 73 eligible countries. The scheme, extended to 31 December 2021, provided a suspension of debt-service payments owed to official bilateral creditors. In return, borrowers had to commit to use freed-up resources to increase social, health or economic spending in response to the crisis. As of April 2021, 45 countries had requested to participate, with savings totalling more than $10 billion.

Despite these initiatives, the scale of debt relief (as opposed to extra lending) was small in comparison to earlier initiatives. Under HIPC and MDRI, more than $100 billion of debt had been cancelled.

Imagine that you are an ambassador of a developing country at an international conference. What would you try to persuade the rich countries to do in order to help you and other poor countries overcome the debt problem? How would you set about persuading them that it was in their own interests to help you?

Should all debt be cancelled and aid increased?

In recent years there have been growing calls for the cancellation of debts and a significant increase in aid, especially for the poorest developing countries, many ravaged by war, drought, AIDS or COVID-19. The United Nations has for many years called on wealthy countries to give 0.7 per cent of their GDP in aid.

In 2020 the net flow of official government aid[7] amounted to $157 billion – a rise of 3.5 per cent on 2019, but still only a mere 0.32 per cent of gross national income (GNY). As Figure 26.11 shows, many countries fail to meet the UN target.

The UK had met the target from 2013. In 2015 the UK parliament passed legislation requiring government to meet the 0.7 per cent foreign aid target. However, in 2020 the government announced that, in response to the financial pressures from the COVID-19 pandemic, it would be cutting the aid target to 0.5 per cent. The government stated that it hoped to restore the target when the UK's finances allowed.

The argument against debt cancellation and a substantial increase in aid is that this could represent a 'moral

6 Abebe Aemro Selassie and Andrew Tiffin, 'The Policymaker's Trilemma', *IMF blog* (12 May 2021), https://blogs.imf.org/2021/05/12/the-policymakers-trilemma/

7 Official development assistance (ODA) from the 29 donor countries plus European Union institutions which comprise the OECD's Development Assistance Committee (DAC).

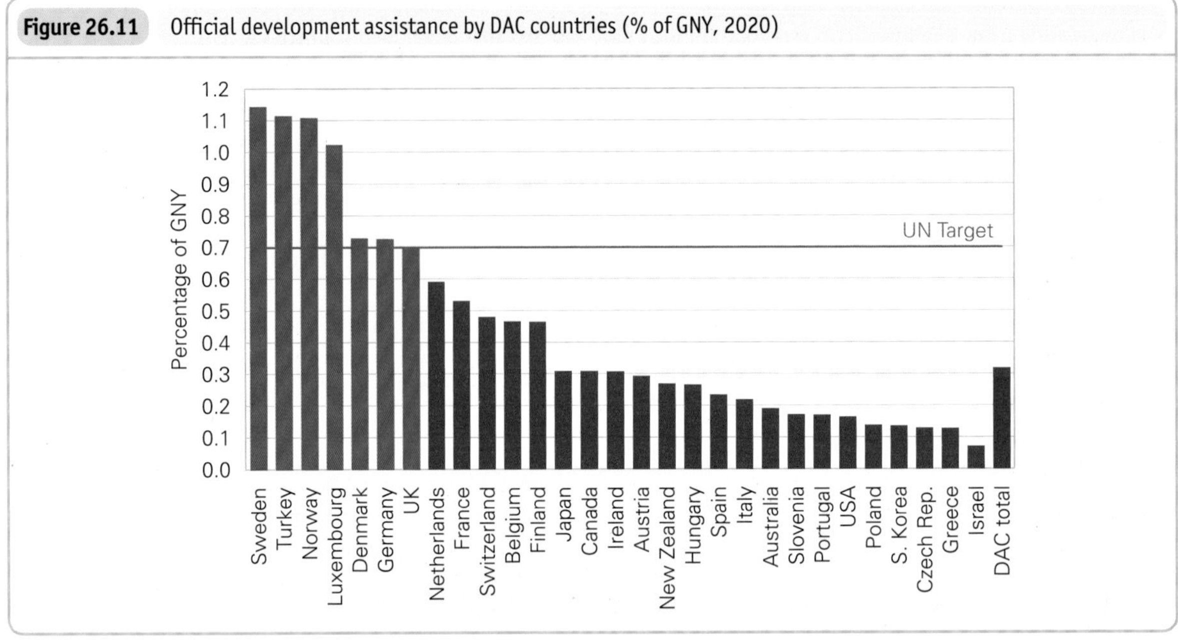

Figure 26.11 Official development assistance by DAC countries (% of GNY, 2020)

Source: Based on data from *Net ODA, OECD Data*, OECD (2021), https://data.oecd.org/oda/net-oda.htm

KI 17 p138

hazard' (see page 138). Once the burden of debt had been lifted and aid had been increased, countries might be tempted to squander the money. It might also encourage them to seek further loans, which might again be squandered.

For this reason, much of the disbursement of funds by donor countries, the IMF and other agencies has been conditional on countries pursuing policies of fiscal restraint and supply-side reform. But also, in recent years, conditionality has required recipient countries to pursue key poverty-reducing projects, such as health, education, clean water and other basic infrastructure projects. (Case Study 26.15 on the student website examines some of the issues surrounding aid.)

Section summary

1. After the 1973 oil crisis, many developing countries borrowed heavily in order to finance their balance of trade deficits and to maintain a programme of investment. After the 1979 oil price rises the debt problem became much more serious. There was a world recession and real interest rates were much higher. Debt increased dramatically, and much of it at variable interest rates.
2. Rescheduling can help developing countries to cope with increased debt in the short run and various schemes have been adopted by creditor countries and the banks.
3. If the problem is to be tackled, however, then either debts have to be written off – something that banks have been increasingly forced to do – or the developing countries themselves must take harsh corrective measures. The IMF has traditionally favoured 'structural adjustment' policies of deflation and market-orientated supply-side policies. An alternative is to use debt relief and aid to invest in health, education, roads and other infrastructure.
4. In 1996, the World Bank and the IMF launched the HIPC initiative to help reduce the debts of heavily indebted poor countries to sustainable levels. HIPC relief has been criticised, however, for being made conditional on the debtor countries pursuing excessively tough IMF adjustment programmes, for having an excessively long qualifying period and debt sustainability thresholds that are too high, and for delays in its implementation. A better approach might be to target debt relief directly at programmes to help the poor.
5. The COVID-19 pandemic had a severe effect on the economies of many poor counties and caused a surge in their debts. The IMF and other international institutions increased support, although the amount of debt cancellation was small compared to HIPC relief.

END OF CHAPTER QUESTIONS

1. Under what circumstances does a growth in financial flows make exchange rates less stable?
2. Assume that countries in the eurozone decide to pursue a deflationary fiscal policy. What effect is this likely to have on the UK economy?
3. It is often argued that international convergence of economic indicators is a desirable objective. Does this mean that countries should all seek to achieve the same rate of economic growth, monetary growth, interest rates and budget deficits as a percentage of their GDP, etc.?
4. Did the exchange rate difficulties experienced by countries under the ERM strengthen or weaken the arguments for progressing to a single European currency?
5. Assume that just some of the members of a common market like the EU adopt full economic and monetary union, including a common currency. What are the advantages and disadvantages to those members joining the full EMU and to those not?
6. Is the eurozone an optimal currency area? Explain your answer.
7. How are asymmetric shocks dealt with within a country? To what extent can this process be mirrored within the eurozone?
8. Would the world benefit from the general imposition of controls on the movement of international finance?
9. Compare the relative merits of using GNY statistics with those of various basic needs indicators when assessing both the level and the rate of a country's economic development.
10. If a developing country has a comparative advantage in primary products, should the government allow market forces to dictate the pattern of trade?
11. What are the advantages and disadvantages for a developing country of pursuing a policy of ISI?
12. Should all developing countries aim over the long term to become *exporters* of manufactured products?
13. How would you attempt to assess whether the technology used by an industry in a developing country was 'inappropriate'?
14. To what extent was the debt crisis of the early 1980s caused by inappropriate policies that had been pursued by the debtor countries?
15. Assess the operation and success of the HIPC programme.

Online resources

Additional case studies on the student website

26.1 **High oil prices.** What is their effect on the world economy?

26.2 **Crisis in South East Asia.** Causes of the severe recession in many South East Asian countries in 1997/8.

26.3 **The 1997/8 crisis in Asia: the role played by the IMF.**

26.4 **The Tobin tax.** An examination of the proposed tax, named after the economist James Tobin, imposed at a very small rate (of 0.05 to 0.5 per cent) on all foreign exchange transactions, or on just capital and financial account transactions.

26.5 **Converging on the euro.** Did the 11 countries that adopted the euro in 1999 genuinely meet the convergence criteria?

26.6 **Theories of development.** This looks at different approaches to the analysis of poverty and development.

26.7 **Multinational corporations and developing countries.** This examines whether multinational investment is a net benefit to developing countries.

26.8 **A miracle gone wrong.** Lessons from East Asia.

26.9 **Ethical business.** An examination of the likelihood of success of companies which trade fairly with developing countries.

26.10 **Argentina in crisis.** An examination of the collapse of the Argentinean economy in 2001/2, the default on its debts and the subsequent recovery.

26.11 **Structural problems within developing countries.** An analysis of problems around the neglect of agriculture, inappropriate technology and unemployment in developing countries.

26.12 **Unemployment in developing countries.** This looks at three models that have been developed to explain Third World unemployment.

26.13 **The Building BRICS of development.** A look at the importance of development for emerging economies.

26.14 **The great escape.** This case examines the problem of capital flight from developing countries to rich countries.

26.15 **Economic aid.** Does aid provide a solution to the debt problem?

26.16 **Swapping debt.** Schemes to convert a developing country's debt into other forms, such as shares in its industries.

(continued)

Websites relevant to Chapters 25 and 26

Numbers and sections refer to websites listed in the web appendix and hotlinked from this book's website at **go.pearson.com/uk/sloman.**

- For news articles relevant to this and the previous chapter, see the *Economics News* section on the student website.
- For general news on countries' balance of payments and exchange rates, see websites in section A, and particularly A1–5, 7–9, 20–25, 31, 35, 36. For articles on various aspects of economic development, see A27, 28; I9. See also links to newspapers worldwide in A38, 39, 42, 43 and 44, and the news search feature in Google at A41.
- For international data on balance of payments and exchange rates, see *World Economic Outlook* in B31 and *OECD Economic Outlook* in B21 (also in sections 11 and 9 of B1). See also I14. The International macrodata section of the UK Data Service site (B35) has links to World Bank, IMF, OECD, UN and Eurostat datasets (but you will need to register first, a service free to all UK higher education students).
- For UK data on balance of payments, search site B3 for 'Balance of Payments' or the 'Pink Book'. See also B34. For EU data, see B38; see also B47 (Ameco online) sections 9–11.
- For exchange rates, see A1, 3; B5, 34; F2, 6, 8. For real and nominal exchange rate indices, see B45.
- For discussion papers on balance of payments and exchange rates, see H4 and 7.
- For various pressure groups critical of the effects of free trade and globalisation, see H13 and 14.
- For information on EMU, see sites G1, 2, 3 and 6; F3–6 and 9.
- For the United Nations Development Programme and also its Human Development Reports, see site H17.
- For data on debt, search for 'International debt statistics' in DataBank on site B24.
- For student resources relevant to these two chapters, see sites C1–10, 19.

Postscript: *Reality Island*

Five handsome girls and five beautiful boys,
Descending by helicopter on Paradise Island.
All palm trees, white sand and lagoons.

Just them and Chris with his camera and Mel with her sound.
There for a year: to survive and thrive.

Hunting and gathering was easy at first,
Using sticks to get fruit, fish and coconuts.
Aisha the chef made wonderful fish and fruit stew with coconut shavings;
Ate it for breakfast, lunch and dinner.

Ollie the carpenter built straw huts,
Which kept them cool in the day and warm at night.
But nights were troublesome:
Those mysterious lights from behind the hill.

Lily said they were messages from God
And founded the Church of Good Lights.
Preached there on Sunday.
But no-one came.

Bill thought they were the fires of a fearsome tribe on the far side of the island.
Set up an army armed with spears to defend from attack.
Made himself General.
Gave himself watermelon pips.

Ishan, the clever one, with his first in Finance
Became central banker.
Created money from shells –
One conch worth 1000 mussels.
Quantitatively eased in a load more shells he found in a remote bay.
Island GDP soared – at least nominally.

Katja the make-up artist turned her hand to tattooing,
Using squid ink to etch beautiful pictures

Of turtles and birds of paradise on beautiful bodies.
But she worried about the lights.
Were they an omen?

Aisha was voted leader
And made everyone a lovely supper to celebrate.
Gave everyone lots of holidays.

Jack opened a chip shack,
Frying papaya chips in coconut oil,
Serving them in banana leaves.

Mia the chemist made plastic from palm resin and fish scales;
Used it to make containers for the fish and fruit in the deli.
Nicely disposable – chucked them into the sea,
Which took them far out of sight.

Ella the estate agent turned property tycoon;
Set up a casino, a nail bar and a bowling alley.
Used coconuts as bowling balls.
Everyone admired her – and Lily worried about her soul.

But the joys of paradise were waning.
Everyone wanted new thrills.
Sandy set up a surf school
And Pradeep made kite surfs from palm leaves.
Mia was put in charge of thrills,
Driving up the ante.

Lily was made poet in residence.
Wrote meaningful poems
Until the metre petered out.
But she still watched those lights;
Waiting for redemption,
Searching for meaning.

As she wandered through the village,
Past the beautiful bodies made more beautiful,
Past the shops and cafés,
Past the chippy,
Past the surf school and the barracks,
Past the plastic factory,
Past the landfill,
She longed for the helicopter's second coming.

John Sloman

1. *Had the contestants reduced their problem of scarcity by the end of the poem?*
2. *Did it matter if the plastic waste disappeared out to sea?*

Appendix 1: Some Techniques of Economic Analysis

As you will see if you flick back through the pages, there are many diagrams and tables and several equations. But this does not mean that there are many mathematical techniques that you will have to master in order to study this book. In fact there are relatively few techniques, but they are ones which we use many times in many different contexts. You will find that if you are new to the subject, you will very quickly become familiar with these techniques. If you are not new to the subject, perhaps you could reassure your colleagues who are!

On some university courses, however, you will take mathematics to a higher level. To meet your needs there are a number of optional 'Looking at the Maths' sections scattered throughout the book. These use maths to express arguments that have just been covered in words or diagrams. Most of these 'Looking at the Maths' sections also refer to 'Maths Cases' on the student website. These cases consist of worked examples and also have one or more questions at the end for you to test your understanding of the relevant technique. The answers to these questions are also given on the student website.

But please note that the 'Looking at the Maths' sections are purely optional and will not be suitable for many courses. In such cases you can simply ignore them.

Diagrams as pictures

On many occasions, we use diagrams simply to provide a picture of a relationship. Just as a photograph in a newspaper can often depict an event much more vividly than any verbal account, so too a diagram in economics can often picture a relationship with a vividness and clarity that could never be achieved by words alone.

For example, we may observe that as people's incomes rise, they spend a lot more on entertainment and only a little more on food. We can picture this relationship very nicely by the use of a simple graph.

In Figure A1.1, an individual's income is measured along the horizontal axis and expenditure on food and entertainment is measured up the vertical axis. There are just two lines on this diagram: one showing how the expenditure on entertainment rises as income rises, the other how the expenditure on food rises as income rises. Now we could use a diagram like this to plot actual data. But we may simply be using it as a sketch – as a picture. In this case we do not necessarily need to put figures on the two axes. We are simply showing the relative *shapes* of the two curves. These shapes tell us that the person's expenditure on entertainment rises more quickly than that on food, and that above a certain level of income the expenditure on entertainment becomes greater than that on food.

What else is the diagram telling us?

Figure A1.1 Effect of a rise in an individual's income on his or her expenditure on food and entertainment

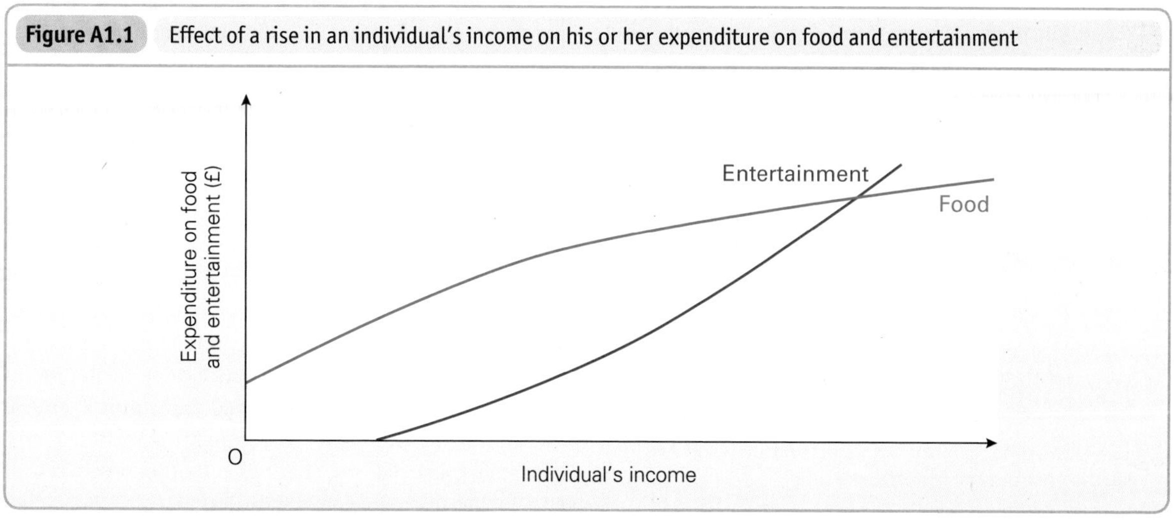

Table A1.1 UK unemployment, 2011 Q1–2020 Q4

	2011				2012				2013				2014				2015			
	Q1	Q2	Q3	Q4	Q1	Q1	Q1	Q1	Q1	Q2	Q3	Q4	Q1	Q2	Q3	Q4	Q1	Q2	Q3	Q4
Unemployment (millions)	2.48	2.54	2.66	2.69	1.83	1.83	1.83	1.83	2.54	2.52	2.40	2.36	2.21	2.06	1.96	1.87	1.83	1.85	1.76	1.69

	2016				2017				2018				2019				2020			
	Q1	Q2	Q3	Q4	Q1	Q2	Q3	Q4	Q1	Q2	Q3	Q4	Q1	Q2	Q3	Q4	Q1	Q2	Q3	Q4
Unemployment (millions)	1.69	1.64	1.62	1.59	1.53	1.49	1.43	1.46	1.42	1.36	1.38	1.36	1.30	1.33	1.31	1.29	1.37	1.38	1.62	1.74

Source: Based on *Time Series Data*, series MGSC, ONS (2021), www.ons.gov.uk/employmentandlabourmarket/peoplenotinwork/unemployment/timeseries/mgsc/

Representing real-life statistics

In many cases, we will want to depict real-world data. We may want to show, for example, how unemployment has changed over the years in a particular country, or how income is distributed between different groups in the population. In the first we will need to look at *time-series* data. In the second we will look at *cross-section* data.

Time-series data

Table A1.1 shows the level of UK unemployment between the first quarter of 2011 and the fourth quarter of 2020. A table like this is a common way of representing ***time-series data***. It has the advantage of giving the precise figures, and is thus a useful reference if we want to test any theory and see if it predicts accurately.

Notice that in this particular table the figures are given quarterly. Depending on the period of time over which we want to see the movement of a variable, it may be more appropriate to use a different interval of time. For example, if we wanted to see how unemployment had changed over the past 50 years, we might use annual figures or even average figures for longer periods of time. If, however, we wanted to see how unemployment had changed over the course of a year, we would probably use monthly or even weekly figures.

The table in Box 1.2 on page 9 shows time-series data for four different variables for four different countries. Would there have been any advantage in giving the figures for each separate year? Would there have been any disadvantage?

Time-series data can also be shown graphically. In fact the data from a table can be plotted directly on to a graph. Figure A1.2 plots the data from Table A1.1. Each dot on the graph corresponds to one figure from the table. The dots are then joined up to form a single line. Thus if you wanted to find the level of unemployment at any time between 2011 Q1 and 2020 Q4, you would simply find the appropriate date on the horizontal axis, read vertically upward to the line you have drawn, then read across to find the level of unemployment.

Definition

Time-series data Information depicting how a variable (e.g. the price of eggs) changes over time.

Although a graph like this cannot give you quite such an accurate measurement of each point as a table does, it gives a much more obvious picture of how the figures have moved over time and whether the changes are getting bigger (the curve getting steeper) or smaller (the curve getting shallower). We can also read off what the likely figure would be for some point *between* two observations.

What was the level of unemployment midway between quarter 2 and quarter 3 of 2020?

It is also possible to combine *two* sets of time-series data on one graph to show their relative movements over time. Table A1.2 shows the figures for UK economic growth for the same time period. Figure A1.3 plots these data along with those from Table A1.1. This enables us to get a clear picture of how unemployment and the rate of economic growth moved in relation to each other over the period in question. Note that we use a different vertical scale for the two variables. This is inevitable given that they are measured in different units.

How would it be possible to show three different lines on the same diagram?

All developed countries publish time-series data for the major macroeconomic variables such as national income, prices, employment and unemployment, interest rates, and imports and exports. Microeconomic data on the distribution of income, the performance of particular industries, the distribution of household expenditure, and so on, appear in the official government statistics. Firms, consumers' associations, charities and other organisations also publish microeconomic statistics.

Figure A1.2 UK Unemployment: 2011 Q1–2020 Q4

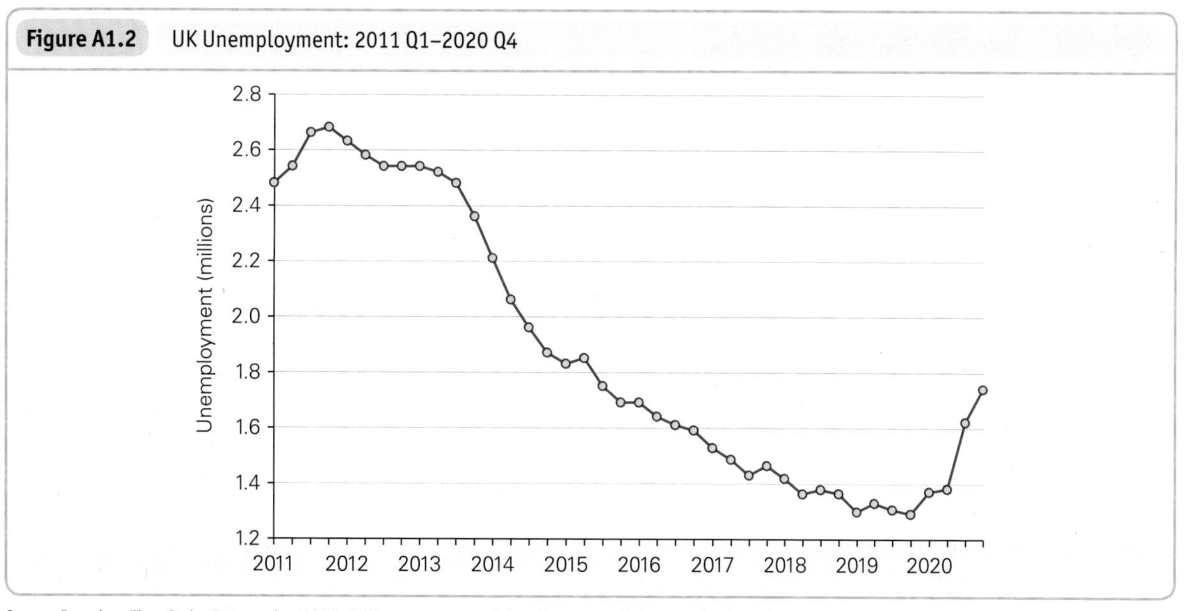

Source: Based on *Time Series Data*, series MGSC, ONS, www.ons.gov.uk/employmentandlabourmarket/peoplenotinwork/unemployment/timeseries/mgsc/unem

Table A1.2 UK economic growth, 2011 Q1–2020 Q4 (% increase over equivalent quarter in previous year)

	2011				2012				2013				2014				2015			
	Q1	**Q2**	**Q3**	**Q4**	**Q1**	**Q1**	**Q1**	**Q1**	**Q1**	**Q2**	**Q3**	**Q4**	**Q1**	**Q2**	**Q3**	**Q4**	**Q1**	**Q2**	**Q3**	**Q4**
Economic growth (%)	2.11	1.28	0.81	0.92	1.26	1.03	1.83	1.60	1.36	2.27	2.13	2.92	3.24	3.10	2.63	2.62	2.38	2.47	2.25	2.34

	2016				2017				2018				2019				2020			
	Q1	**Q2**	**Q3**	**Q4**	**Q1**	**Q2**	**Q3**	**Q4**	**Q1**	**Q2**	**Q3**	**Q4**	**Q1**	**Q2**	**Q3**	**Q4**	**Q1**	**Q2**	**Q3**	**Q4**
Economic growth (%)	2.01	1.68	1.67	1.56	1.87	1.65	1.85	1.53	1.12	1.32	1.41	1.21	1.71	1.40	1.29	1.19	−2.27	−21.34	−8.46	−7.28

Source: Based on *Time Series Data*, series YBEZ, ONS (2021), www.ons.gov.uk/economy/grossdomesticproductgdp/timeseries/ybez/

Figure A1.3 UK unemployment and four-quarter economic growth rate 2011 Q1–2020 Q4

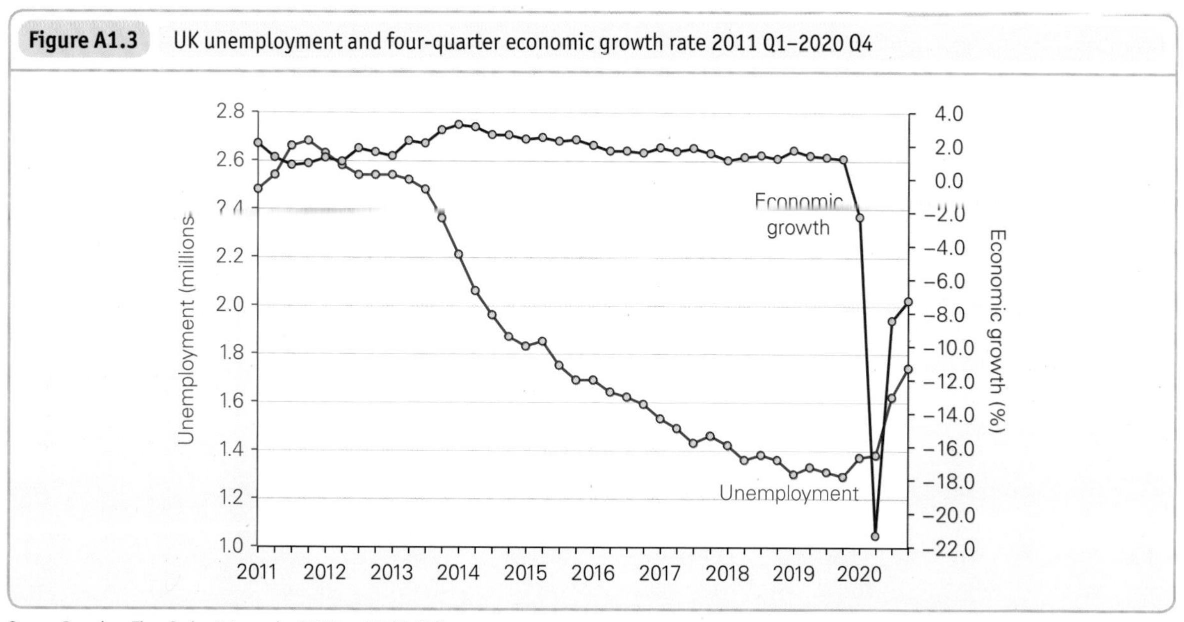

Source: Based on *Time Series Data*, series MGSC and YBEZ, ONS

Table A1.3 Income before taxes and benefits

	Quintile groups of households					
	Bottom 20%	**Next 20%**	**Middle 20%**	**Next 20%**	**Top 20%**	**Total**
1977	3	10	18	26	42	100
2019/20	4	8	14	23	51	100

Source: Household Disposable Income and Inequality, UK, 2019/20 – Reference Tables, Table 13, ONS (2021).

There are also several sources of data freely available on the Internet. Section B of Appendix 2 gives a number of websites containing datasets. These websites can be accessed directly from the hotlinks section of this book's own website (www.pearsoned.co.uk/sloman).

Cross-section data

Cross-section data show different observations made at the same point in time. For example, they could show the quantities of food and clothing purchased at various levels of household income, or the costs to a firm or industry of producing various quantities of a product.

Table A1.3 gives an example of cross-section data. It shows the distribution of household income in the UK before the deduction of taxes and the addition of benefits. It puts households into five equal-sized groups (or 'quintiles') according to their income. Thus the poorest 20 per cent of households are in one group, the next poorest 20 per cent are in the next and so on. Looking just at the 2019/20 figures, they show that the poorest 20 per cent earned just 4 per cent of total household incomes, whereas the richest 20 per cent earned 51 per cent.

Definition

Cross-section data Information showing how a variable (e.g. the consumption of eggs) differs between different groups or different individuals at a given time.

Cross-section data like these are often represented in the form of a chart. Figure A1.4 shows the data as a *bar chart,* and Figure A1.5 as two *pie charts.*

It is possible to represent cross-section data at two or more different points in time, thereby presenting the figures as a time series. In Table A1.3, figures are given for just two time periods. With a more complete time series we could graph the movement of the shares of each of the five groups over time.

Could bar charts or pie charts be used for representing time-series data?

Getting a true picture from the statistics

'There are lies, damned lies and statistics.' This well-known saying highlights the abuse of statistics – abuse, unfortunately, that is commonplace. Have you noticed how politicians always seem to be able to produce statistics to 'prove' that they are right and that their opponents are wrong? And it's not just politicians. Newspapers frequently present statistics in the most 'newsworthy' way; companies try to show their performance in the most flattering way; pressure groups fighting for a cause (such as the protection of the environment) again present statistics in the way that best supports their case.

It is not difficult to present data in such a way as to give a grossly distorted picture of a situation. Let us have a look at some of the most common examples.

Figure A1.4 The distribution of UK pre-tax income: the use of a bar chart

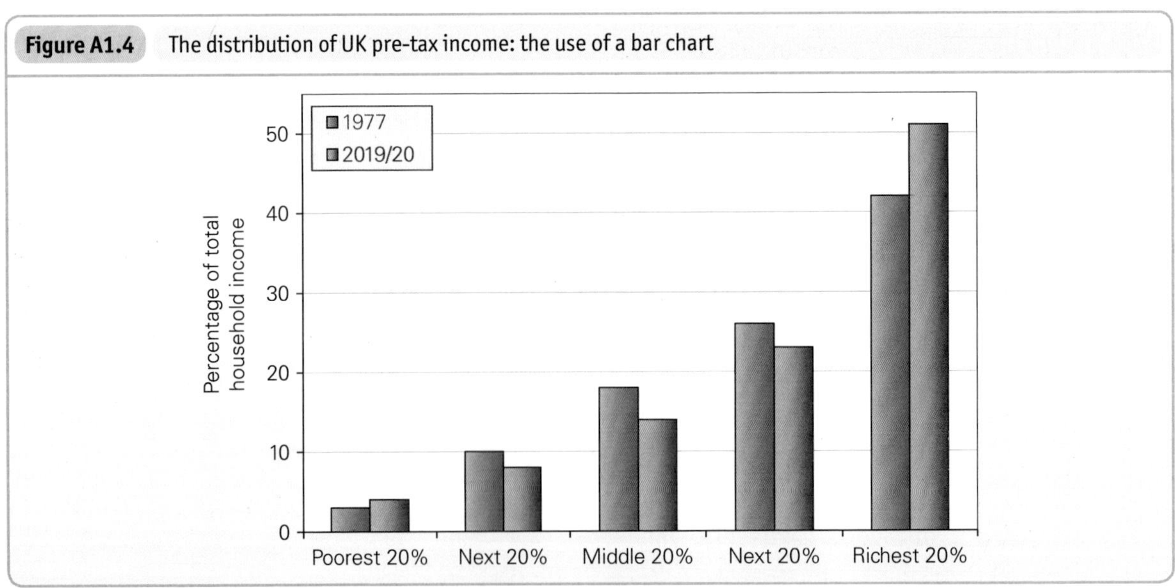

Source: Household Disposable Income and Inequality, UK, 2019/20 – Reference Tables, Table 13, ONS (2021).

Figure A1.5 The distribution of UK pre-tax income: the use of a pie chart

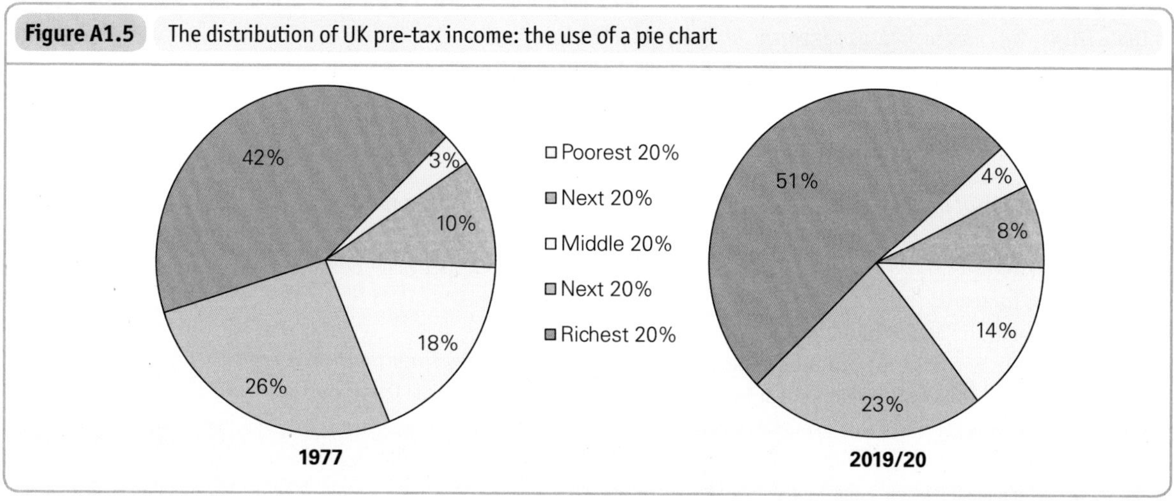

Source: *Household Disposable Income and Inequality, UK, 2019/20 – Reference Tables*, Table 13, ONS, (2021).

Selective use of data

This is where people select only those statistics that support their case and ignore those that do not. For example, assume that unemployment has risen but inflation has fallen. The government highlights the inflation statistics to show how successful its policies have been. The opposition parties do the opposite: they concentrate on the unemployment statistics to demonstrate the failure of government policy.

Graphical presentation of data

Two graphs may present exactly the same data and yet convey a quite different impression about them. Figure A1.6 shows how the amount that people buy of a particular foodstuff varies with their income. It is based on the imaginary data given in Table A1.4.

Diagram (a) shows *exactly the same* information as diagram (b), and yet at a glance it would seem from diagram (a) that people buy a lot more as their incomes rise, whereas from diagram (b) it would seem that people only buy a little more.

Clearly the choice of *scales* for the two axes will determine the shape of the graph.

1. *If the vertical scale for Figure A1.2 ran from 0 to 5 million, how would this alter your impression of the degree to which unemployment had changed?*
2. *What are the advantages and disadvantages of presenting data graphically with the axes starting from zero?*

Use of absolute or proportionate values

'People are paying more taxes now than they did when the government came to office', claims the opposition.

'Since coming into office we have cut taxes substantially', claims the government.

So who is right? Do we pay more or less tax? Quite possibly they are both right. If incomes have risen, we probably do pay more tax in total. After all, the more we earn, the greater the sum of money we will be paying in income tax; and the more we spend, the more we will be paying out in VAT. Thus in *absolute* terms we probably are paying more in taxes.

On the other hand, if the government has cut the rates of tax, we may be paying a smaller *proportion* of our income. In other words, a smaller proportion of a larger total can still represent an absolute increase.

Figure A1.6 The relationship between consumer income and the consumption of a particular foodstuff, using graphs with different scales

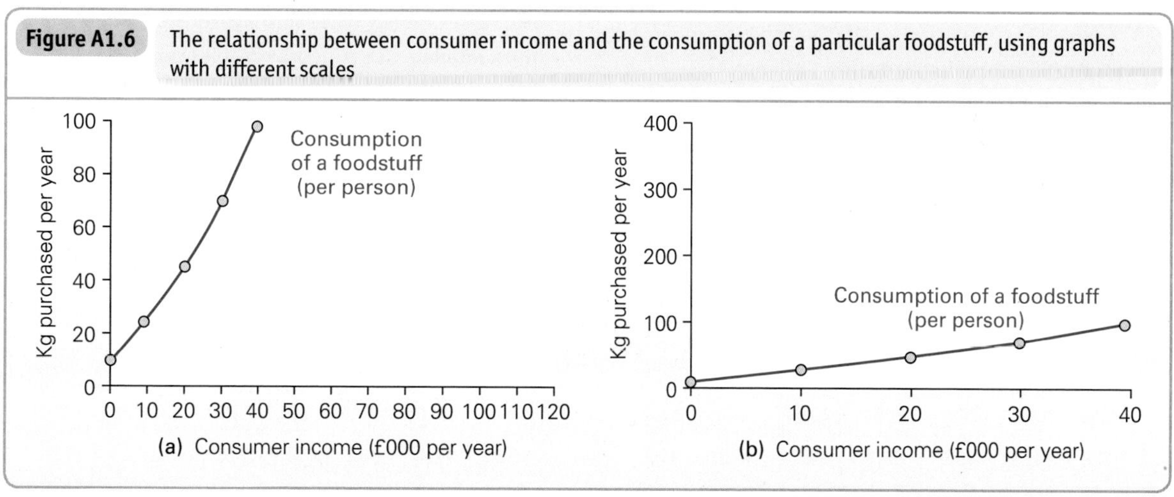

Table A1.4 Annual purchases per person of a particular foodstuff

Consumer income (£ per year)	0	10 000	20 000	30 000	40 000
Foodstuff purchased per person (kg per year)	10	25	45	70	100

Ignoring questions of distribution

'The average person has become better off under this government', claims a minister.

'Poverty has increased steeply under this government', claims the opposition. 'More than half the population are worse off now than when the government came to office.'

Surely, this time one of the claims must be wrong? But again, both could be right. The term 'average' normally refers to the ***mean***. The mean income is simply the total national income divided by the number in the population: i.e. income *per head*. If this is what is meant by the average, then the government may well be correct. Income per head may have risen.

If, however, a small number of people have got a lot richer and the rest have got a little poorer, the ***median*** income will have fallen. The median income is the income of the *middle* person. For example, if the population were 50 million, the median income would be the income of the 25 millionth richest person. This person's income may have fallen.

Real or nominal values

'Incomes have risen by 2 per cent this last year', claims the government.

'The standard of living has fallen', claims the opposition.

One of the most common abuses of statistics is deliberately switching between real and nominal figures, depending on what message you want to give your audience. ***Nominal*** figures are the simple monetary values at the prices ruling at the time. For example, if you earned a wage of £500 per week last year and are earning £510 per week this year, then in nominal terms your wage has risen by 2 per cent.

But what if prices have risen by 3 per cent? Your 2 per cent increase in wages will in fact buy you 1 per cent *less*. Your ***real*** wages have gone down by 1 per cent. In other words, to show how much better or worse off a person or nation is, the nominal figure must be corrected for inflation.

Thus:

Real growth = Nominal growth − Inflation

1. *If a bank paid its depositors 3 per cent interest and inflation was 5 per cent, what would be the real rate of interest?*
2. *Has your real income gone up or down this last year?*

The time chosen for comparison

'Between 1982 and 1990, Britain's real growth rate averaged 3.5 per cent per year', boasted the Conservative government of the time.

The distinction between nominal and real figures
Nominal figures are those using current prices, interest rates, etc. Real figures are figures corrected for inflation.

'Between 1979 and 1993, Britain could only manage a real growth rate of 1.6 per cent per year', chided the opposition.

Again, both were correct, but they had chosen either to include or to ignore the periods from 1979 to 1982 and from 1990 to 1993 when the real growth rate was negative.

Index numbers

Time-series data are often expressed in terms of ***index numbers***. Consider the data in Table A1.5. It shows index numbers of manufacturing output in the UK from 1991 to 2020.

One year is selected as the ***base year*** and this is given the value of 100. In our example this is 2018. The output for other years is then shown by their percentage variation from 100. For 1991 the index number is 89.0. This means that manufacturing output was 11 per cent lower in 1991

Definitions

Mean (or arithmetic mean) The sum of the values of each of the members of the sample divided by the total number in the sample.

Median The value of the middle member of the sample.

Nominal values Money values measured at *current* prices.

Real values Money values corrected for inflation.

Index number The value of a variable expressed as 100 plus or minus its percentage deviation from a base year.

Base year (for index numbers) The year whose index number is set at 100.

Table A1.5 UK manufacturing output (2018 = 100)

1991	**1992**	**1993**	**1994**	**1995**	**1996**	**1997**	**1998**	**1999**	**2000**	**2001**	**2002**	**2003**	**2004**	**2005**
89.0	88.9	90.2	94.5	95.9	96.6	98.3	98.6	99.0	100.7	99.3	96.8	96.5	98.3	98.4
2006	**2007**	**2008**	**2009**	**2010**	**2011**	**2012**	**2013**	**2014**	**2015**	**2016**	**2017**	**2018**	**2019**	**2020**
100.8	101.3	98.5	90.0	94.2	96.3	95.2	94.2	96.8	96.4	96.6	98.9	100.0	98.2	88.9

Source: Time Series data, series K22A (ONS, 2021), www.ons.gov.uk/economy/economicoutputandproductivity/output/timeseries/k22a/diop?

than in 2018. The index number for 2007 is 101.3. This means that manufacturing output was 1.3 per cent higher in 2007 than in 2018.

Does this mean that the value of manufacturing output in 2007 was 1.3 per cent higher than 2018 in money terms?

The use of index numbers allows us to see clearly any upward and downward movements and to make an easy comparison of one year with another. For example, Table A1.5 shows quite clearly that manufacturing output fell from 1991 to 1992 and from 2000 to 2003. It fell again from 2007 to 2009, from 2011 to 2013, 2014 to 2015 and dramatically from 2018 to 2020 with the onset of the coronavirus pandemic in 2020.

Using index numbers to measure percentage changes

To find the annual percentage growth rate in any one year we simply look at the percentage change in the index from the previous year. To work this out we use the following formula:

$$\left(\frac{I_t - I_{t-1}}{I_{t-1}}\right) \times 100$$

where I_t is the index in the year in question and I_{t-1} is the index in the previous year.

Thus to find the growth rate in manufacturing output from 2013 to 2014 we first see how much the index has risen ($I_t - I_{t-1}$). The answer is $96.8 - 94.2 = 2.6$. But this does *not* mean that the growth rate is 2.6 per cent. According to our formula, the growth rate is equal to

$$\frac{96.8 - 94.2}{94.2} \times 100$$
$$= 2.6/94.2 \times 100$$
$$= 2.76$$

What was the growth rate in manufacturing output from (a) 2005 to 2006; (b) 2008 to 2009; (c) 2019 to 2020?

The price index

Perhaps the best known of all price indices is the ***consumer prices index (CPI)***. It is an index of the prices of goods and services purchased by the average household. Movements in this index, therefore, show how the cost of living has changed. Annual percentage increases in the CPI are the commonest definition of the rate of inflation. Thus if the CPI went up from 100 to 110 over a 12 month period, we would say that the rate of inflation was 10 per cent.

If the CPI went up from 150 to 162 over 12 months, what would be the rate of inflation?

The use of weighted averages

The CPI is a ***weighted average*** of the prices of many items. The index of manufacturing output that we looked at previously was also a weighted average, an average of the output of many individual products.

To illustrate how a weighted average works, consider the case of a weighted average of the output of just three industries, A, B and C. Let us assume that in the base year (year 1) the output of A was £7 million, of B £2 million and of C £1 million, giving a total output of the three industries of £10 million. We now attach weights to the output of each industry to reflect its proportion of total output. Industry A is given a weight of 0.7 because it produces seven-tenths of total output. Industry B is given a weight of 0.2 and industry C a weight of 0.1. We then simply multiply each industry's index by its weight and add up all these figures to give the overall industry index.

The index for each industry in year 1 (the base year) is 100. This means that the weighted average index is also 100. Table A1.6 shows what happens to output in year 2. Industry A's output falls by 10 per cent, giving it an index of 90 in year 2. Industry B's output rises by 10 per cent and industry C's output rises by 30 per cent, giving indices of 110 and 130, respectively. But as you can see from the table, despite the fact that two of the three industries have had a rise in output, the total industry index has *fallen* from 100 to 98. The reason is that industry A is so much larger than the other two that its decline in output outweighs their increase.

The consumer prices index is a little more complicated. This is because it is calculated in two stages. First, products are grouped into categories such as food, clothing and services. A weighted average index is worked out for each group. Thus the index for food would be the weighted average of the indices for bread, potatoes, cooking oil, etc. Second, a weight is attached to each of the groups in order to work out an overall index.

Definitions

Consumer prices index (CPI) An index of the prices of goods bought by a typical household.

Weighted average The average of several items where each item is ascribed a weight according to its importance. The weights must add up to 1.

Table A1.6 Constructing a weighted average index

		Year 1		Year 2	
Industry	**Weight**	**Index**	**Index times weight**	**Index**	**Index times weight**
A	0.7	100	70	90	63
B	0.2	100	20	110	22
C	0.1	100	10	130	13
Total	1.0		100		98

Functional relationships

Throughout economics we examine how one economic variable affects another: how the purchases of cars are affected by their price; how consumer expenditure is affected by taxes, or by incomes; how the cost of producing washing machines is affected by the price of steel; how the rate of unemployment is affected by the level of government expenditure. These relationships are called ***functional relationships***. We will need to express these relationships in a precise way, preferably in the form of a table or a graph or an equation.

Simple linear functions

These are relationships which produce a straight line when plotted on a graph. Let us take an imaginary example of the relationship between total value added tax receipts in an economy (V) and the level of consumer expenditure (C). This functional relationship can be written as:

$$V = f(C)$$

This is simply shorthand for saying that VAT receipts are a function of (i.e. depend on) the level of consumer expenditure.

If we want to know just *how much* VAT revenue will be at any given level of consumer expenditure, we will need to spell out this functional relationship. Let us do this in each of the three ways.

As a table. Table A1.7 gives a selection of values of C and the corresponding level of V. It is easy to read off from the table the level of VAT receipts at one of the levels of consumer expenditure listed. It is clearly more difficult to work out the level of VAT receipts if consumer expenditure is £23.4 billion or £47.6 billion.

As a graph. Figure A1.7 plots the data from Table A1.7. Each of the dots corresponds to one of the points in the table. By joining the dots up into a single line we can easily read off the value for VAT receipts at some level of consumption other than those listed in the table. A graph also has the advantage of allowing us to see the relationship at a glance.

Definition

Functional relationships The mathematical relationships showing how one variable is affected by one or more others.

Table A1.7 A VAT function

Consumer expenditure (£bn per year)	VAT receipts (£bn per year)
0	0
10	2
20	4
30	6
40	8
50	10

Figure A1.7 A graph of the VAT function: $V = 0.2C$

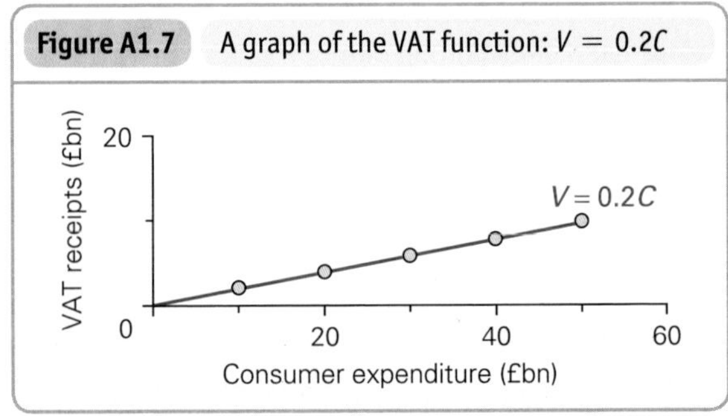

It is usual to plot the *independent variable* (i.e. the one that does not depend on the other) on the horizontal or x-axis, and the *dependent variable* on the vertical or y-axis. In our example, VAT receipts *depend* on consumer expenditure. Thus VAT receipts are the dependent variable and consumer expenditure is the independent variable.

As an equation. The data in the table can be expressed in the equation

$$V = 0.2C$$

This would be the equation if the VAT rate were 20 per cent on all goods and services.

An equation has the major advantage of being precise. We could work out *exactly* how much would be paid in VAT at any given level of consumption.

This particular function starts at the origin of the graph (i.e. the bottom left-hand corner). This means that when the value of the independent variable is zero, so too is the value of the dependent variable.

When a graph does not pass through the origin its equation will have the form

$$y = a + bx$$

where y stands for the dependent variable and x for the independent variable, and a and b will have numbers assigned in an actual equation. For example, the equation might be

$$y = 4 + 2x$$

This would give Table A1.8 and Figure A1.8.

Notice two things about the relationship between the equation and the graph:

- The point where the line crosses the vertical axis (at a value of 4) is given by the constant (a) term. If the a term

Table A1.8 $y = 4 + 2x$

x	y
0	4
1	6
2	8
3	10
4	12
5	14

Figure A1.8 $y = 4 + 2x$

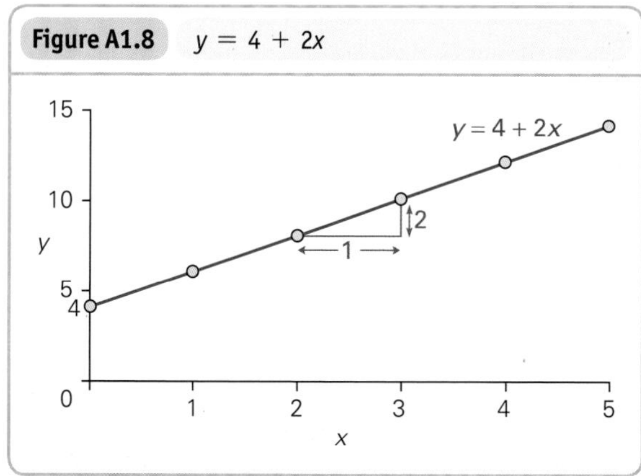

Figure A1.9 $y = 4 + 10x - x^2$

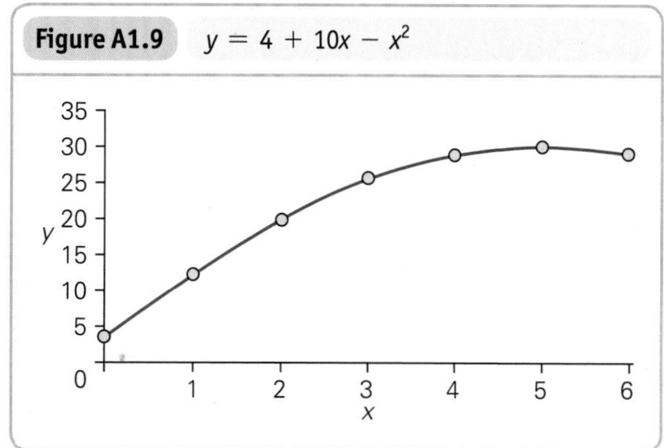

is negative, the line will cross the vertical axis *below* the horizontal axis.

- The slope of the line is given by the *b* term. The slope is 2/1: for every 1 unit increase in *x* there is a 2 unit increase in *y*.

On a diagram like Figure A1.8 draw the graphs for the following equations: $y = -3 + 4x$; $y = 15 - 3x$.

Note that in the second equation of the question, the *x* term is negative. This means that *y* and *x* are *inversely related*. As *x* increases, *y* decreases.

Non-linear functions

With these functions the equation involves a squared term (or other power terms). Such functions will give a curved line when plotted on a graph. As an example, consider the following equation:

$$y = 4 + 10x - x^2$$

Table A1.9 and Figure A1.9 are based on it.

As you can see, *y* rises at a decelerating rate and eventually begins to fall. This is because the negative x^2 term is becoming more and more influential as *x* rises and eventually begins to outweigh the 10*x* term.

What shaped graph would you get from the equations $y = -6 + 3x + 2x^2$ *and* $y = 10 - 4x + x^2$*?*

(If you cannot work out the answer, construct a table like Table A1.9 and then plot the figures on a graph.)

Table A1.9 $y = 4 + 10x - x^2$

x	y
0	4
1	13
2	20
3	25
4	28
5	29
6	28
7	25

*Elementary differentiation

In several starred boxes and *Looking at the Maths* sections we use some elementary calculus. The part of calculus we use is called ***differentiation***. This is a technique to enable us to calculate the rate of change of a variable. The purpose of this section is not to explain why differentiation involves the procedures it does, but simply to state the rules that are necessary for our purposes. You will need to consult a maths book if you want to know how these rules are derived.

First, let us see when we would be interested in looking at the rate of change of a variable. Take the case of a firm thinking of expanding. It will want to know how much its costs will increase as its output increases. It will want to know the rate of change of costs with respect to changes in output.

Let us assume that it faces a cost function of the form

$$C = 20 + 5Q + Q^2 \quad (1)$$

where *C* is the total cost of production and *Q* is the quantity produced. Table A1.10 and Figure A1.10 are derived from this equation.

The rate of increase in its costs with respect to increases in output is given by the *slope* of the cost curve in Figure A1.10. The steeper the slope, the more rapidly costs increase. At point *a* the slope of the curve is 11. This is found by drawing the tangent to the curve and measuring the slope of the tangent. At this point on the curve, what we are saying is that for each one unit increase in output there is an £11 increase in costs. (Obviously as the graph is curved, this rate of increase will vary at different outputs.)

This rate of increase in costs is known as the ***marginal cost***. It is the same with other variables that increase with

Definitions

Differentiation A mathematical technique to find the rate of change of one variable with respect to another.

Marginal cost The rate of increase in costs with respect to output.

quantity: their rate of increase is known as *marginal*. For example, *marginal revenue* is the rate of increase of sales revenue with respect to output.

We can use the technique of differentiation to derive a marginal from a total equation: in other words, to derive the slope of the total curve. Let us assume that we have an equation:

$$y = 10 + 6x - 4x^2 + 2x^3 \qquad (2)$$

When we differentiate it, we call the new equation dy/dx: this stands for the rate of increase in y (dy) with respect to the increase in x (dx).

The rules for differentiating a simple equation like equation (2) are very straightforward.

1. You delete the constant term (10). The reason for this is that, being constant, by definition it will not cause an increase in y as x increases, and it is the *increase* in y that we are trying to discover.
2. You delete the x from the x term which has no power attached, and just leave the number. Thus the term $6x$ becomes simply 6.
3. For any term with a power in it (a square, a cube, etc.), its value should be *multiplied* by the power term and the power term reduced by one. Thus in the term $4x^2$, the 4 would be multiplied by 2 (the power term), and the power term would be reduced from 2 to 1 (but x to the power of 1 is simply x). After differentiation, therefore, the term becomes $8x$. In the term $2x^3$, the 2 would be multiplied by 3 (the power term), and the power term would be reduced from 3 to 2. After differentiation, therefore, the term becomes $6x^2$.

Applying these three rules to the equation

$$y = 10 + 6x - 4x^2 + 2x^3 \qquad (2)$$

Gives

$$dy/dx = 6 - 8x + 6x^2 \qquad (3)$$

To find the rate of change of y with respect to x at any given value of x, therefore, you simply substitute that value of x into equation (3).

Thus when $x = 4$,

$$dy/dx = 6 - (8 \times 4) + (6 \times 16) = 70.$$

In other words, when $x = 4$, for every 1 unit increase in x, y will increase by 70.

Returning to our cost function in equation (1), what is the marginal cost equation? Applying the three rules to the equation

$$C = 20 + 5Q + Q^2 \qquad (1)$$

gives

$$dC/dQ = 5 + 2Q \qquad (4)$$

Thus at an output of 3, the marginal cost (dC/dQ) is $5 + (2 \times 3) = 11$, which is the slope of the tangent to point *a*.

Table A1.10 $C = 20 + 5Q + Q^2$

x	y
0	20
1	26
2	34
3	44
4	56
5	70
6	86
7	104
8	124

Figure A1.10 A total cost function: $C = 20 + 5Q + Q^2$

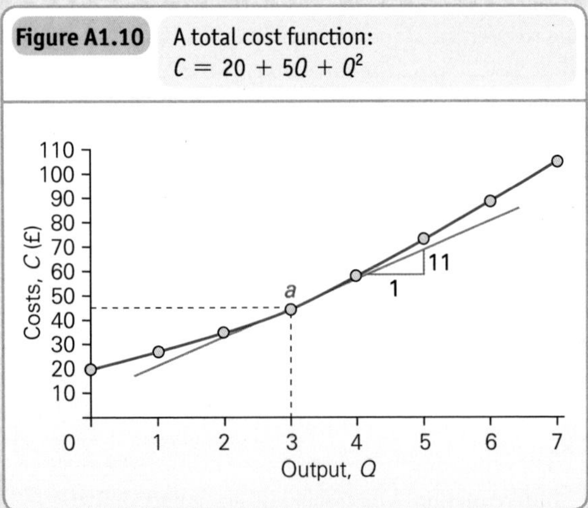

What would be the marginal cost equation if the total cost equation were

$$C = 15 + 20Q - 5Q^2 + Q^3?$$

What would be the marginal cost at an output of 8?

Finding the maximum or minimum point of a curve

The other important use we can make of calculus is to find the maximum or minimum point of a curve. This has a number of important applications. For example, a firm may want to know the minimum point on its average cost curve (a curve which shows how costs per unit of output vary as output increases). Also it is likely to want to know the output at which it will earn maximum profit. Let us examine this particular case.

Assume that the equation for total profit (Π) is:

$$\Pi = -20 + 12Q - Q^2 \qquad (5)$$

*BOX A1.1 WHEN IS GOOD NEWS REALLY GOOD?

CASE STUDIES AND APPLICATIONS

Are things getting better or merely getting worse more slowly?

Up to 2020, UK unemployment had fallen in most quarters since 2012 (see Figure A1.2). But then, with the onset of the coronavirus pandemic, unemployment rose and dramatically so in 2020 quarter 3 (see the diagram below). It continued to rise in 2020 quarter 4. What good news could the government possibly draw from this?

Governments, always in search of any glimmer of good economic news, proclaimed that unemployment was rising more slowly (in other words, that the rate of increase in unemployment was *falling*). This was perfectly correct.

To show this, let us assume that N is the number of people out of work. The rate of change of unemployment is therefore given by dN/dt (where t is time). A positive figure for dN/dt represents a rise in unemployment, a negative figure a fall. Its value is given by the slope of the blue line in the diagram. From the first quarter of 2020 this figure was positive. Bad news!

But the government sought a rosier interpretation. By using a second-order derivative, d^2N/dt^2, it could show that the rate of increase in unemployment in 2020 quarter 4 was falling. The value of this is given by the *slope* of the red line in the diagram and by the level of the blue line. The government proclaimed that this was evidence that the labour market was beginning to recover. Good news!

The use of calculus in this manner is a two-edged sword and such statistical sophistry is open to the political opposition, who could at a later date, if they so wished, claim that a fall in unemployment was bad economic news. Dare they? (What was happening in 2021 Q2?)

If the opposition were indeed to claim that a fall in unemployment was bad news, what would have to be the value of d^2N/dt^2: positive or negative?

Using the ONS series in the diagram, plot the level and rate of change of unemployment from 2020 Q1 to the latest quarter available. Describe the pattern in the diagram as (a) a 'good news' story and (b) a 'bad news' story.

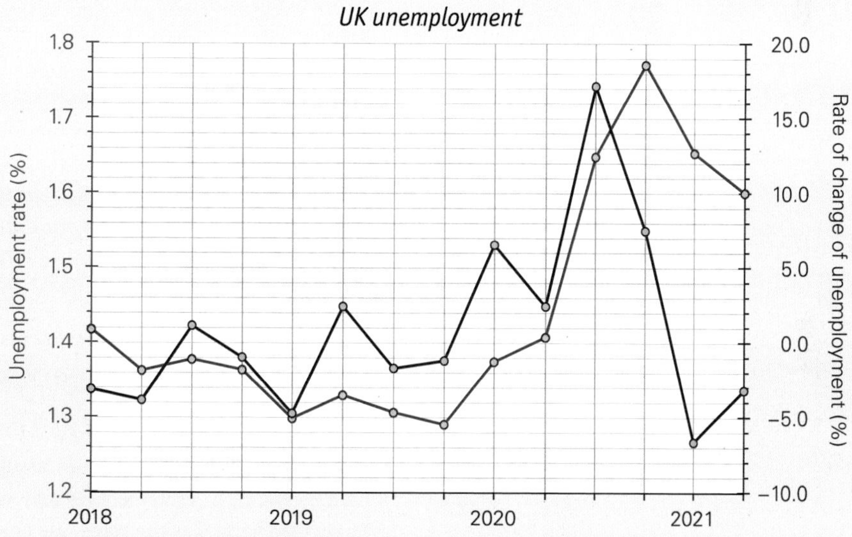

Source: Based on *Time Series Data*, series MGSC, ONS, www.ons.gov.uk/employmentandlabourmarket/peoplenotinwork/unemployment/timeseries/mgsc/unem

This gives profit at various outputs as shown in Table A1.11. The corresponding graph is plotted in Figure A1.11.

What is the meaning of a negative profit?

It can be seen at a glance that profits are maximised at an output of 6 units. But we could have worked this out directly from the profit equation without having to draw up a table or graph. How is this done?

Remember that when we differentiate a curve, the equation we get (known as 'the first derivative') gives us the slope of the curve. You can see that at the point of maximum profit (the top of the curve) its slope is zero: the tangent is horizontal. So all we have to do to find the top of the curve is to differentiate its equation and set it equal to zero.

Given that

$$\Pi = -20 + 12Q - Q^2 \quad (5)$$

then:

$$d\Pi/dQ = 12 - 2Q \quad (6)$$

Setting this equal to zero gives:

$$12 - 2Q = 0$$
$$\therefore \; 2Q = 12$$
$$\therefore \; Q = 6$$

Thus profits are maximised at an output of 6 units: the result we obtained from the table and graph.

The second derivative test

There is a problem with this technique, however. How can we tell from equation (6) that we have found the *maximum* rather than the *minimum?* The problem is that *both* the maximum *and* the minimum points of a curve have a zero slope.

The answer is to conduct a ***second derivative test***. This involves differentiating the equation a second time. This gives the rate of change of the *slope* of the original curve. If you look at Figure A1.11, as output increases, the tangent moves from being upward sloping, to horizontal, to downward sloping. In other words, the slope is getting less and less. Its rate of change is *negative.* Thus if we differentiate the equation for the slope (i.e. the first derivative), we should get a negative figure.

When we differentiate a second time, we get what is called the ***second derivative***. It is written d^2y/dx^2.

If we differentiate equation (6):

$$d\Pi/dQ = 12 - 2Q \qquad (6)$$

we get:

$$d^2\Pi/dQ^2 = -2 \qquad (7)$$

Table A1.11 $\Pi = -20 + 12Q - Q^2$

Q	Π
0	−20
1	−9
2	0
3	7
4	12
5	15
6	16
7	15
8	12
9	7
10	0

Figure A1.11 A total profit function: $\Pi = -20 + 12Q - Q^2$

(Note that the rules for differentiating a second time are the same as for the first time.) Given that the second derivative in this case is negative, we have demonstrated that we have indeed found the maximum profit point (at $Q = 6$), and not the minimum.

Given the following equation for a firm's average cost (AC), i.e. the cost per unit of output (Q):

$$AC = 60 - 16Q + 2Q^2$$

(a) At what output is AC at a minimum?
(b) Use the second derivative test to prove that this is a minimum and not a maximum.

Partial differentiation

Many relationships in economics involve more than two variables. For example, the demand for a product depends not just on its price, but also on income, the price of substitutes, the price of complements, etc. Similarly, a firm's cost of production depends not just on the quantity of output it produces, but also on wage rates, the prices of the various materials it uses, the productivity of its workers and machinery, and so on.

Such relationships can be expressed as a function as follows:

$$y = f(x_1, x_2, x_3, \ldots x_n)$$

where x_1, x_2, etc. are the various determinants of y.

Let us take a simple example where a firm's total cost (TC) depends on just two things: the quantity produced (Q) and the wage rate (W). The cost function will be of the form

$$TC = f(Q,W)$$

Assume that in the case of a particular firm the function is

$$TC = 20 + 10Q - 4Q^2 + 2Q^3 + 6W \qquad (8)$$

What we are likely to want to know is how this firm's total cost changes as quantity changes, assuming the wage rate is held constant. Alternatively we may wish to know how its total cost changes as the wage rate changes, assuming that output is held constant. To do this we use the technique of ***partial differentiation***. This involves the same technique as

Definitions

Second derivative test If on differentiating an equation a second time the answer is negative (positive), the point is a maximum (minimum).

Second derivative The rate of change of the first derivative, found by differentiating the first derivative.

Partial differentiation A mathematical technique used with functions containing two or more independent variables. The technique is used to find the rate of change of the dependent variable with respect to a single independent variable assuming that the other independent variables are held constant.

simple differentiation but applied to just the one variable that is not held constant.

Thus to find the rate of change of costs with respect to quantity in equation (8), we differentiate the equation with respect to Q and ignore the W term. We ignore it as it is held constant and is thus treated like the constant (20) term in the equation. Using the rules of differentiation, the ***partial derivative*** is thus

$$\frac{\partial TC}{\partial Q} = 10 - 8Q + 6Q^2 \qquad (9)$$

Note that instead of using the symbol 'd' that we used in simple differentiation, we now use the symbol "∂'.' Apart from that, the rules for partial differentiation are exactly the same as with simple differentiation.

If we now wanted to see how this firm's costs vary with the wage rate for any given output, then we would partially differentiate equation (8) with respect to W, giving

$$\frac{\partial TC}{\partial W} = 6$$

In other words, for each £1 rise in the wage rate, total cost would rise by £6.

Assume that the demand for a product is given by the following function:

$$Q_D = 1000 - 50P + 2P^2 + 10P_S + P_S^2$$

where Q_D is the quantity demanded, P is the price of the good and P_S is the price of a substitute good. What is the partial derivative of this demand function with respect to (a) the price of the good; (b) the price of the substitute good? Interpret the meaning of each partial derivative.

Definition

Partial derivative The partial derivative of a function of two or more independent variables is the derivative with respect to just one of those variables, while holding the others constant.

Appendix summary

1. Diagrams in economics can be used as pictures: to sketch a relationship so that its essentials can be perceived at a glance.
2. Tables, graphs and charts are also used to portray real-life data. These can be time-series data or cross-section data or both.
3. In order to get a true picture from economic data it is important to be aware of various ways that statistics can be abused: these include a selective use of data, a choice of axes on a graph to make trends seem more or less exaggerated or to make a curve more or less steep, confusing absolute and relative values, ignoring questions of distribution, confusing nominal and real values, and selecting the time period to make the statistics look the most favourable or unfavourable.
4. Presenting time-series data as index numbers gives a clear impression of trends and is a good way of comparing how two or more series (perhaps originally measured in different units) have changed over the same time period. A base year is chosen and the index for that year is set at 100. The percentage change in the value of a variable is given by the percentage change in the index (I). The formula is

$$\left(\frac{I_t - I_{t-1}}{I_{t-1}}\right) \times 100$$

Several items can be included in one index by using a weighted value for each of the items. The weights must add up to 1, and each weight will reflect the relative importance of that particular item in the index.

5. Functional relationships can be expressed as an equation, a table or a graph. In the linear (straight-line) equation $y = a + bx$, the a term gives the vertical intercept (the point where the graph crosses the vertical axis) and the b term gives the slope. When there is a power term (e.g. $y = a + bx + cx^2$), the graph will be a curve.

*6. Differentiation can be used to obtain the rate of change of one variable with respect to another. The rules of differentiation require that in an equation of the form

$$y = a + bx + cx^2 + dx^3$$

the a term disappears, the bx term simply becomes b, the cx^2 term becomes $2cx$, the dx^3 becomes $3dx^2$ and so on, with each extra term being multiplied by its power term and its power term being reduced by 1.

*7. To find the value of the x term at which the y term is at a maximum or minimum, the equation should be differentiated and set equal to zero. To check which it is – maximum or minimum – the second derivative should be calculated. If it is negative, then setting the first derivative equal to zero has yielded a maximum. If the second derivative is positive, then setting the first derivative to zero has yielded a minimum value.

Appendix 2: Websites

All the following websites can be accessed from this book's own website (http://www.pearsoned.co.uk/sloman). When you enter the site, click on **Hot Links.** You will find all the following sites listed. Click on the one you want and the 'hot link' will take you straight to it.

The sections and numbers below refer to the ones used in the websites listed at the end of each chapter. Thus if the list contained the number A21, this would refer to the *Conversation* site.

(A) General news sources

As the title of this section implies, the websites here can be used for finding material on current news issues or tapping into news archives. Most archives are offered free of charge. However, some do require you to register. As well as key UK and American news sources, you will also notice some slightly different places from where you can get your news, such as *The Moscow Times* and *The Japan Times*. Check out site numbers 38. *Refdesk,* 43. *Guardian World News Guide* and 44. *Online newspapers* for links to newspapers across the world. Try searching for an article on a particular topic by using site number 41. *Google News Search.*

1. BBC news
2. The Economist
3. The Financial Times
4. The Guardian
5. The Independent
6. ITN
7. The Observer
8. The Telegraph
9. Aljazeera
10. The New York Times
11. Fortune
12. Time Magazine
13. The Washington Post
14. The Moscow Times (English)
15. Pravda (English)
16. Straits Times (Singapore)
17. New Straits Times (Malaysia)
18. The Scotsman
19. The Herald
20. Euromoney
21. The Conversation
22. Market News International
23. Bloomberg Businessweek
24. International Business Times
25. CNN Money
26. Vox^{EU} (economic analysis and commentary)
27. Asia News Network
28. allAfrica.com
29. Greek News Sources (English)
30. France 24 (English)
31. Euronews
32. Australian Financial Review
33. Sydney Morning Herald
34. The Japan Times
35. Reuters
36. Bloomberg
37. David Smith's EconomicsUK.com
38. Refdesk (links to a whole range of news sources)
39. Newspapers and Magazines on World Wide Web
40. Yahoo News Search
41. Google News Search
42. ABYZ news links
43. Guardian World News Guide
44. Online newspapers

(B) Sources of economic and business data

Using websites to find up-to-date data is of immense value to the economist. The data sources below offer you a range of specialist and non-specialist data information. Universities have free access to the *UK Data Service* site (site 35 in this set), which is a huge database of statistics. Site 3, the *Office for National Statistics*, is the UK's main official data site and datasets can be downloaded as Excel files. The Economics Network's *Economic data freely available online* (site 1) gives links to various sections in over 40 UK and international sites.

1. Economics Network gateway to economic data
2. Office for Budget Responsibility
3. Office for National Statistics
4. Data Archive (Essex)
5. Bank of England Statistical Interactive Database
6. UK Official Statistics (GOV.UK)
7. Nationwide House Prices Site
8. House Web (data on housing market)
9. Economist global house price data
10. Halifax House Price Index
11. House prices indices from ONS)

12. Penn World Table
13. Economist economic and financial indicators
14. FT market data
15. Economagic
16. Groningen Growth and Development Centre
17. AEAweb: Resources for economists on the Internet (RFE): data
18. Joseph Rowntree Foundation
19. OECD iLibrary statistics
20. Energy Information Administration
21. OECDStat
22. CIA world statistics site (World Factbook)
23. Millennium Development Goal Indicators Database
24. World Bank Data
25. Federal Reserve Bank of St Louis, US Economic Datasets (FRED)
26. Ministry of Economy, Trade and Industry (Japan)
27. Financial data from Yahoo
28. DataMarket
29. Index Mundi
30. Knoema: Economics
31. World Economic Outlook Database (IMF)
32. Telegraph shares and markets
33. Key Indicators (KI) for Asia and the Pacific Series (Asia Development Bank)
34. Open data from data.gov.uk (Business and Economy)
35. UK Data Service (incorporating ESDS)
36. BBC News, market data
37. NationMaster
38. Economic Forecasts (European Commission)
39. Business and Consumer Surveys (all EU countries)
40. Gapminder
41. Trading Economics
42. WTO International Trade Statistics database
43. UNCTAD trade, investment and development statistics (UNCTADstat)
44. London Metal Exchange
45. Bank for International Settlements, global nominal and real effective exchange rate indices
46. United Nations: Monthly Bulletin of Statistics
47. AMECO database
48. The Conference Board data
49. Institute for Fiscal Studies: tools and resources
50. European Central Bank (ECB): statistics

(C) Sites for students and teachers of economics

The following websites offer useful ideas and resources to those who are studying or teaching economics. It is worth browsing through some just to see what is on offer. Try out the first four sites, for starters. The *Internet for Economics* (site 8) is a very helpful tutorial for economics students on using the Internet.

1. The Economics Network
2. Teaching Resources for Undergraduate Economics (TRUE)
3. EconEdLink
4. Studying Economics
5. Economics and Business Education Association
6. Tutor2U
7. Council for Economic Education
8. Dollars and Sense
9. Econoclass: Resources for economics teachers
10. Teaching resources for economists (RFE)
11. METAL – Mathematics for Economics: enhancing Teaching And Learning
12. Federal Reserve Bank of San Francisco: Economics Education
13. Excel in Economics Teaching (from the Economics Network)
14. Economics Online
15. Dr. T's EconLinks: Teaching Resources
16. Online Opinion (Economics)
17. Free to Choose TV from the Idea Channel
18. History of Economic Thought
19. Resources For Economists on the Internet (RFE)
20. Games Economists Play (non-computerised classroom games)
21. Bank of England education resources
22. Why Study Economics?
23. Economic Classroom Experiments
24. Veconlab: Charles Holt's classroom experiments
25. Experiments, games and role play from the Economics Network
26. MIT Open Courseware in Economics
27. EconPort
28. ThoughtCo. – Economics

(D) Economic models, simulations and classroom experiments

Economic modelling is an important aspect of economic analysis. There are several sites that offer access to a model or simulation for you to use, e.g. *Virtual Chancellor* (where you can play being Chancellor of the Exchequer). Using such models can be a useful way of finding out how economic theory works within a specific environment. Other sites link to games and experiments, where you can play a particular role, perhaps competing with other students.

1. Virtual Chancellor
2. Virtual Factory
3. Interactive simulation models (Economics Web Institute)
4. Classroom Experiments in Economics (Pedagogy in Action)
5. MobLab
6. Economics Network Handbook, Chapter on Simulations, Games and Role-play
7. Experimental Economics Class Material (David J Cooper)

8. Simulations
9. Experimental economics: Wikipedia
10. Software available on the Economics Network site
11. RFE Software
12. Virtual Worlds
13. Veconlab: Charles Holt's classroom experiments
14. EconPort Experiments
15. Denise Hazlett's Classroom Experiments in Macroeconomics
16. Games Economists Play
17. Finance and Economics Experimental Laboratory at Exeter (FEELE)
18. Classroom Expernomics
19. The Economics Network's Guide to Classroom Experiments and Games
20. Economic Classroom Experiments (Wikiversity)

(E) UK government and UK organisations' sites

If you want to see what a government department is up to, then look no further than the list below. Government departments' websites are an excellent source of information and data. They are particularly good at offering information on current legislation and policy initiatives.

1. Gateway site (GOV.UK)
2. Department for Communities and Local Government
3. Prime Minister's Office
4. Competition & Markets Authority
5. Department for Education
6. Foreign, Commonwealth & Development Office
7. Department for Transport
8. Department of Health
9. Department for Work and Pensions
10. Department for Business, Energy & Industrial Strategy
11. Environment Agency
12. Former Department of Energy and Climate Change
13. Low Pay Commission
14. Department for Environment, Food & Rural Affairs (Defra)
15. Office of Communications (Ofcom)
16. Office of Gas and Electricity Markets (Ofgem)
17. Official Documents OnLine
18. Office for Budget Responsibility
19. Office of Rail and Road (ORR)
20. The Takeover Panel
21. Sustainable Development Commission
22. Ofwat
23. National Statistics (ONS)
24. List of ONS releases from UK Data Explorer
25. HM Revenue & Customs
26. UK Intellectual Property Office
27. Parliament website
28. Scottish Government
29. Scottish Environment Protection Agency
30. HM Treasury
31. Equality and Human Rights Commission
32. Trades Union Congress (TUC)
33. Confederation of British Industry (CBI)
34. Adam Smith Institute
35. Chatham House
36. Institute for Fiscal Studies
37. Advertising Standards Authority
38. Businesses and Self-employed
39. Campaign for Better Transport
40. New Economics Foundation
41. Financial Conduct Authority
42. Prudential Regulation Authority

(F) Sources of monetary and financial data

As the title suggests, here are listed useful websites for finding information on financial matters. You will see that the list comprises mainly central banks, both within Europe and further afield. The links will take you to English language versions of non-English speaking countries' sites.

1. Bank of England
2. Bank of England Monetary and Financial Statistics
3. Banque de France (in English)
4. Bundesbank (German central bank)
5. Central Bank of Ireland
6. European Central Bank
7. Eurostat
8. US Federal Reserve Bank
9. Netherlands Central Bank (in English)
10. Bank of Japan (in English)
11. Reserve Bank of Australia
12. Bank Negara Malaysia (in English)
13. Monetary Authority of Singapore
14. Bank of Canada
15. National Bank of Denmark (in English)
16. Reserve Bank of India
17. Links to central bank websites from the Bank for International Settlements
18. The London Stock Exchange

(G) European Union and related sources

For information on European issues, the following is a wide range of useful sites. The sites maintained by the European Union are an excellent source of information.

1. Business, Economy, Euro (EC DG)
2. European Central Bank
3. EU official website
4. Eurostat
5. Employment, Social Affairs and Inclusion (EC DG)
6. Reports, Studies and Booklets on the EU

7. Internal Market, Industry, Entrepreneurship and SMEs (EC DG)
8. Competition (EC DG)
9. Agriculture and Rural Development (EC DG)
10. Energy (EC DG)
11. Environment (EC DG)
12. Regional and Urban Policy (EC DG)
13. Taxation and Customs Union (EC DG)
14. Education and Training (EC DG)
15. European Patent Office
16. European Commission
17. European Parliament
18. European Council
19. Mobility and Transport (EC DG)
20. Trade (EC DG)
21. Maritime Affairs and Fisheries (EC DG)
22. International Cooperation and Development (EC DG)
23. Financial Stability, Financial Services and Capital Markets Union (EC DG)

(H) International organisations

This section casts its net beyond Europe and lists the Web addresses of the main international organisations in the global economy. You will notice that some sites are run by charities, such as Oxfam, while others represent organisations set up to manage international affairs, such as the International Monetary Fund and the United Nations.

1. UN Food and Agriculture Organization (FAO)
2. United Nations Conference on Trade and Development (UNCTAD)
3. International Labour Organization (ILO)
4. International Monetary Fund (IMF)
5. Organisation for Economic Co-operation and Development (OECD)
6. OPEC
7. World Bank
8. World Health Organization (WHO)
9. United Nations (UN)
10. United Nations Industrial Development Organization (UNIDO)
11. Friends of the Earth
12. Institute of International Finance
13. Oxfam
14. Christian Aid (reports on development issues)
15. European Bank for Reconstruction and Development (EBRD)
16. World Trade Organization (WTO)
17. United Nations Development Programme
18. UNICEF
19. EURODAD – European Network on Debt and Development
20. NAFTA
21. South American Free Trade Areas
22. ASEAN
23. APEC

(I) Economics search and link sites

If you are having difficulty finding what you want from the list of sites above, the following sites offer links to other sites and are a very useful resource when you are looking for something a little bit more specialist. Once again, it is worth having a look at what these sites have to offer in order to judge their usefulness.

1. Gateway for UK official sites
2. Alta Plana
3. Data Archive Search
4. Inomics (information on economics courses and jobs)
5. Ideas: RePEc bibliographic database
6. Wikidata
7. Portal site with links to other sites (Economics Network)
8. Economic Articles for Investors, Students and Educators (Value Stock Guide)
9. Global goals 2030 (link to economic development resources)
10. Development Initiatives: resources
11. Top 100 Economics Blogs & Websites
12. Web links for economists from the Economics Network
13. EconData
14. Yale university: 75 Sources of Economic Data, Statistics, Reports, and Commentary
15. Excite Economics Links
16. Resources for Economists
17. Trade Map (trade statistics)
18. Resources for Economists on the Internet
19. UK University Economics Departments
20. Research in Economics Education
21. Development Gateway
22. Data.gov
23. WikiProject: Economics
24. National Bureau of Economic Research links to data sources

(J) Internet search engines

The following search engines have been found to be useful.

1. Google
2. Bing
3. Whoosh UK
4. Excite
5. Search.com
6. MSN
7. DuckDuckGo
8. Yahoo
9. Ask
10. Lycos
11. Webcrawler
12. Metacrawler: searches several search engines

Threshold Concepts and Key Ideas

THRESHOLD CONCEPTS

KEY IDEAS

10. **People's actions are influenced by their expectations**. People respond not just to what is happening now (such as a change in price), but to what they anticipate will happen in the future. 70
11. **People's actions are influenced by their attitudes towards risk**. Many decisions are taken under conditions of risk or uncertainty. Generally, the lower the probability of (or the more uncertain) the desired outcome of an action, the less likely people will be to undertake the action. 72
12. **The fallacy of composition**. What applies in one case will not necessarily apply when repeated in all cases. 96
13. **The principle of diminishing marginal utility**. The more of a product a person consumes, the less will be the additional utility gained from one more unit. 105
14. **The equi-marginal principle**. The optimum amount of two alternatives consumed (or produced) will be where the marginal benefit ratios of the two alternatives are equal to their marginal cost ratios:
$$\frac{MU_A}{MU_B} = \frac{P_A}{P_B}$$ 111
15. **Good decision making requires good information**. Where information is poor, decisions and their outcomes may be poor. 132
16. **Adverse selection**. A market process whereby buyers, sellers or products with certain unobservable characteristics (e.g. high risk or low quality) are more likely to enter the market at the current market price. This process can have a negative impact on economic efficiency and cause some potentially profitable markets to collapse. 137
17. **Moral hazard**. Following a deal, the actions/behaviour of one party to a transaction may change in a way that reduces the pay-off to the other party. In the context of insurance, it refers to customers taking more risks when they have insurance than when they do not have insurance. 138
18. **Output depends on the amount of resources and how they are used**. Different amounts and combinations of inputs will lead to different amounts of output. If output is to be produced efficiently, then inputs should be combined in the optimum proportions. 154
19. **The law of diminishing marginal returns** states that when increasing amounts of a variable factor are used with a given amount of a fixed factor, there will come a point when each extra unit of the variable factor will produce less extra output than the previous unit. 155
20. The **'bygones' principle** states that sunk (fixed) costs should be ignored when deciding whether to produce or sell more or less of a product. Only variable costs should be taken into account. 161
21. **Fixed costs and the time period**. Fixed costs occur only in the short run, since in the long run all inputs can be varied. 177
22. **Market power**. When firms have market power over prices, they can use this to raise prices and profits above the perfectly competitive level. Other things being equal, the firm will gain at the expense of the consumer. Similarly, if consumers or workers have market power, they can use this to their own benefit. 195
23. **People often think and behave strategically**. How you think others will respond to your actions is likely to influence your own behaviour. Firms, for example, when considering a price or product change will often take into account the likely reactions of their rivals. 228
24. **The nature of institutions and organisations is likely to influence behaviour**. There are various forces influencing people's decisions in complex organisations. Assumptions that an organisation will follow one simple objective (e.g. short-run profit maximisation) is thus too simplistic in many cases. 259
25. **The principal–agent problem**. Where people (principals), as a result of a lack of knowledge, cannot ensure that their best interests are served by their agents. Agents may take advantage of this situation to the disadvantage of the principals. 274
26. **Stocks and flows**. A stock is a quantity of something at a given point in time. A flow is an increase or decrease in something over a specified period of time. This is an important distinction and a common cause of confusion. 309
27. **The principle of discounting**. People generally prefer to have benefits today rather than in the future. Thus future benefits have to be reduced (discounted) to give them a present value. 310
28. **Allocative efficiency (simple formulation) in any activity** is achieved where marginal benefit equals marginal cost. Private efficiency is achieved where marginal private benefit equals marginal private cost ($MB = MC$). Social efficiency is achieved where marginal social benefit equals marginal social cost ($MSB = MSC$). 356
29. **Social efficiency (equi-marginal formulation)** is achieved where the marginal social benefit ratios are equal to the marginal social cost ratios for any two alternatives. In the case of two alternatives X and Y, this will be where:
$$\frac{MSB_x}{MSB_y} = \frac{MSC_x}{MSC_y}$$ 361
30. **Markets generally fail to achieve social efficiency**. There are various types of market failure. Market failures provide one of the major justifications for government intervention in the economy. 364
31. **Externalities are spillover costs or benefits**. Where these exist, even an otherwise perfect market will fail to achieve social efficiency. 364

32. **The free-rider problem**. People are often unwilling to pay for things if they can make use of things other people have bought. This problem can lead to people not purchasing things that would be to the benefit of them and other members of society to have. 373
33. **The problem of time lags**. Many economic actions can take a long time to take effect. This can cause problems of instability and an inability of the economy to achieve social efficiency. 377
34. **Economies suffer from inherent instability**. As a result, economic growth and other macroeconomic indicators tend to fluctuate. 453
35. **Balance sheets affect people's behaviour**. The size and structure of governments', institutions' and individuals' liabilities (and assets too) affect economic well-being and can have significant effects on behaviour and economic activity. 459
36. **Societies face trade-offs between economic objectives**. For example, the goal of faster growth may conflict with that of greater equality; the goal of lower unemployment may conflict with that of lower inflation (at least in the short run). This is an example of opportunity cost: the cost of achieving one objective may be achieving less of another. The existence of trade-offs means that policy makers must make choices. 459
37. **Goodhart's law**. Controlling a symptom (i.e. an indicator) of a problem will not cure the problem. Instead, the indicator will merely cease to be a good indicator of the problem. 728
38. **The law of comparative advantage**. Provided opportunity costs of various goods differ in two countries, both of them can gain from mutual trade if they specialise in producing (and exporting) those goods that have relatively low opportunity costs compared with the other country. 778
39. **The competitive advantage of nations**. The ability of countries to compete in the market for exports and with potential importers to their country. The competitiveness of any one industry depends on the availability and quality of resources, demand conditions at home in that industry, the strategies and rivalry of firms within the industry and the quality of supporting industries and infrastructure. It also depends on government policies and there is also an element of chance. 786
40. **The distinction between nominal and real figures**. Nominal figures are those using current prices, interest rates, etc. Real figures are figures corrected for inflation. A:6

Glossary

Abduction Using pieces of evidence to develop a plausible explanation. This can then be tested by gathering more evidence.

Absolute advantage A country has an absolute advantage over another in the production of a good if it can produce it with less resources than the other country can.

Accelerationist hypothesis/theory The theory that unemployment can only be reduced below the natural rate at the cost of accelerating inflation.

Accelerator coefficient The level of induced investment as a proportion of a rise in national income: $\alpha = I_i/\Delta Y$.

Accelerator theory The *level* of investment depends on the *rate of change* of national income, and as result tends to be subject to substantial fluctuations.

Active balances Money held for transactions and precautionary purposes.

Actual growth The percentage increase in national output actually produced.

***Ad valorem* tariffs** Tariffs levied as a percentage of the price of the import.

***Ad valorem* tax** A tax on a good levied as a percentage of its value. It can be a single-stage tax or a multi-stage tax (such as VAT).

Adaptive expectations hypothesis The theory that people base their expectations of inflation on past inflation rates.

Adjustable peg A system whereby exchange rates are fixed for a period of time, but may be devalued (or revalued) if a deficit (or surplus) becomes substantial.

Adverse selection (in general) A market process whereby either buyers, sellers or products with certain unobservable characteristics (e.g. high risk or low quality) are more likely to enter the market at the current market price. This process can have a negative impact on economic efficiency and cause some potentially profitable markets to collapse.

Adverse selection in the insurance market Where customers with the least desirable characteristics from the sellers' point of view are more likely to purchase an insurance policy at a price based on the average risk of all the potential customers.

Aggregate demand Total spending on goods and services made in the economy. It consists of four elements, consumer spending (C), investment (I), government spending (G) and the expenditure on exports (X), less any expenditure on imports of goods and services $AD = C + I + G + X - M$.

Aggregate demand for labour curve A curve showing the total demand for labour in the economy at different levels of real wage rates.

Aggregate expenditure (E) Aggregate demand in the Keynesian model: i.e. $C_d + J$.

Aggregate production function The relationship between the economy's capital per worker and output per worker (labour productivity), holding the level of human capital and the state of technology constant.

Aggregate supply The total amount of output in the economy.

Aggregate supply of labour curve A curve showing the total number of people willing and able to work at different average real wage rates.

Allocative efficiency A situation where the current combination of goods produced and sold gives the maximum satisfaction for each consumer at their current levels of income: where marginal benefit equals marginal cost for all goods. Note that a redistribution of income would lead to a different combination of goods that was allocatively efficient.

Alternative theories of the firm Theories of the firm based on the assumption that firms have aims other than profit maximisation.

Altruism (in economics) Positively valuing the pay-offs to others.

Ambient-based standards Pollution control that requires firms to meet minimum standards for the environment (e.g. air or water quality).

Amplifiers Mechanisms, such as confidence, uncertainty, and credit and financial market conditions, that amplify the magnitude of changes in spending.

Appreciation (of a currency) A rise in the free-market exchange rate of the domestic currency with foreign currencies.

Arbitrage The practice of taking advantage of price differentials in markets by buying in the low-priced markets and selling in the high-priced ones. The practice of buying and selling will tend to eliminate the price differentials. Interest rate arbitrage involves borrowing at low interest rates and lending at high rates. This will tend to eliminate the interest rate differentials.

Arc elasticity The measurement of elasticity between two points on a curve.

Assets Possessions of an individual or institution, or claims held on others.

Asymmetric information Where one party in an economic relationship has some information that is relevant to the value of the transaction that the other party does not have.

Asymmetric shocks Shocks (such as an oil price increase or a recession in another part of the world) that have different-sized effects on different industries, regions or countries.

Automatic fiscal stabilisers Tax revenues that rise and government expenditure that falls as national income rises. The more they change with income, the bigger the stabilising effect on national income.

Average (total) cost Total cost (fixed plus variable) per unit of output: $AC = TC/Q = AFC + AVC$.

Average cost pricing or **mark-up pricing** Where firms set the price by adding a profit mark-up to average cost.

Average fixed cost Total fixed cost per unit of output: $AFC = TFC/Q$.

Average physical product Total output (*TPP*) per unit of the variable factor in question: $APP = TPP/Q_v$.

Average rate of income tax Income taxes as a proportion of a person's total (gross) income: T/Y.

Average revenue Total revenue per unit of output. When all output is sold at the same price average revenue will be the same as price: $AR = TR/Q = P$.

Average variable cost Total variable cost per unit of output: $AVC = TVC/Q$.

Backwards induction A process by which firms think through the most likely outcome in the last period of competition and then work backwards step by step, thinking through the most likely outcomes in earlier periods of competition.

Balance of payments account The record of all the economic transactions between the residents of a specific country with the rest of the world for a specific time period, typically a year or a quarter. It records all the inflows and outflows of money under various headings. Inflows are recorded as credits; outflows are recorded as debits.

Balance of payments on current account The balance on trade in goods and services plus net investment income and current transfers.

Balance on trade in goods or **balance of visible trade** or **merchandise balance** Exports of goods minus imports of goods.

Balance on trade in goods and services (or balance of trade) Exports of goods and services minus imports of goods and services.

Balance on trade in services Exports of services minus imports of services.

Balance sheet A record of the stock of assets and liabilities of an individual or institution.

Balance-sheet recession A recession or economic slowdown caused by a collapse in aggregate demand arising from the actions of financially distressed people and businesses.

Bank bills Bills that have been accepted by another institution and hence insured against default.

Bank (or deposits) multiplier The number of times greater the expansion of bank deposits is than the additional liquidity in banks that causes it: $1/L$ (the inverse of the liquidity ratio).

Barometric firm price leadership Where the price leader is the one whose prices are believed to reflect market conditions in the most satisfactory way.

Barriers to entry Anything that prevents or impedes the entry of firms into an industry and thereby limits the amount of competition faced by existing firms.

Barter economy An economy where people exchange goods and services directly with one another without any payment of money. Workers would be paid with bundles of goods.

Base year (for index numbers) The year whose index number is set at 100.

Basic needs approach The attempt to measure development in terms of a country's ability to meet the basic requirements for life.

Basic rate of tax The main marginal rate of tax, applying to most people's incomes.

Behavioural theories of the firm Theories that attempt to predict the actions of firms by studying the behaviour of various groups of people within the firm and their interactions under conditions of potentially conflicting interests.

Benefit principle of taxation The principle that people ought to pay taxes in proportion to the amount they use government services.

Benefits in kind Goods or services which the state provides directly to the recipient at no charge or at a subsidised price. Alternatively, the state can subsidise the private sector to provide them.

Bid rigging Where two or more firms secretly agree on the prices they will tender for a contract. These prices will be above those that would have been submitted under a genuinely competitive tendering process.

Bilateral monopoly Where a monopsony buyer faces a monopoly seller.

Bill of exchange A certificate promising to repay a stated amount on a certain date, typically three months from the issue of the bill. Bills pay no interest as such, but are sold at a discount and redeemed at face value, thereby earning a rate of discount for the purchaser.

Bounded rationality When the ability to make rational decisions is limited by lack of information or the time necessary to obtain such information or by a lack of understanding of complex situations.

Bretton Woods system An adjustable peg system whereby currencies were pegged to the US dollar. The USA maintained convertibility of the dollar into gold at the rate of $35 to an ounce.

Broad money in UK (M4) Cash in circulation plus retail and wholesale bank and building society deposits.

Budget deficit The excess of central government's spending over its tax receipts.

Budget line A graph showing all the possible combinations of two goods that can be purchased at given prices and for a given budget.

Budget surplus The excess of central government's tax receipts over its spending.

Buffer stocks Stocks of a product used to stabilise its price. In years of abundance, the stocks are built up. In years of low supply, stocks are released on to the market.

Business cycle or **trade cycle** The periodic fluctuations of national output round its long-term trend.

Capital All inputs into production that have themselves been produced: e.g. factories, machines and tools.

Capital account of the balance of payments The record of the transfers of capital to and from abroad.

Capital accumulation An increase in the amount of capital that an economy has for production.

Capital adequacy ratio (CAR) The ratio of a bank's capital (reserves and shares) to its risk-weighted assets.

Capital expenditure Investment expenditure; expenditure on assets.

Capital intensity The amount of physical capital that workers have to operate with and which can be measured by the amount of capital per worker (K/L).

Capital market A financial market where longer-term debt instruments, like government bonds (gilts), can be bought and sold.

Capital widening The situation where the capital stock grows at the rate of growth of the workforce plus the rate of depreciation ($n + d$). Investment is merely equipping new workers and replacing worn out or obsolete capital

Carry trade Borrowing at low interest rates and then using it to buy assets that earn higher rates. In foreign exchange markets, the carry trade involves borrowing money in a currency of a country where interest rates are low and exchanging it for another currency where the country pays higher interest rates.

Cartel A formal collusive agreement.

Central bank Banker to the banks and the government. It oversees the banking system, implements monetary policy and issues currency.

Centrally planned or command economy An economy where all economic decisions are taken by the central authorities.

Certainty equivalent The guaranteed amount of money that an individual would view as equally desirable as the expected value of a gamble. Where a person is risk averse, the certainty equivalent is less than the expected value.

Certificates of deposit (CDs) Certificates issued by banks for fixed-term interest-bearing deposits. They can be resold by the owner to another party.

Ceteris paribus Latin for 'other things being equal'. This assumption has to be made when making deductions from theories.

Change in demand This is the term used for a shift in the demand curve. It occurs when a determinant of demand *other* than price changes.

Change in supply The term used for a shift in the supply curve. It occurs when a determinant *other* than price changes.

Change in the quantity demanded The term used for a movement along the demand curve to a new point. It occurs when there is a change in price.

Change in the quantity supplied The term used for a movement along the supply curve to a new point. It occurs when there is a change in price.

Claimant unemployment Those in receipt of unemployment-related benefits.

Classical model A macroeconomic model that assumes prices and wages are fully flexible.

Clearing system A system whereby inter-bank debts are settled.

Closed shop Where a firm agrees to employ only union members.

Club good A good which has a low degree of rivalry but is easily excludable.

Coase theorem When there are well-defined property rights and zero bargaining costs, then negotiations between the party creating the externality and the party affected by the externality can bring about the socially efficient market quantity.

Cobb–Douglas production function Like other production functions, this shows how output (TPP) varies with inputs of various factors (F_1, F_2, F_3, etc.). In the simple two-factor case it takes the following form:

$$TPP = f(F_1, F_2) = aF_1^{\alpha}F_2^{\beta}$$

If $\alpha + \beta = 1$, there are constant returns to scale; if $\alpha + \beta > 1$, there are increasing returns to scale; if $\alpha + \beta < 1$, there are decreasing returns to scale.

Collateralised debt obligations (CDOs) These are a type of security consisting of a bundle of fixed-income assets, such as corporate bonds, mortgage debt and credit card debt.

Collusive oligopoly Where oligopolists agree (formally or informally) to limit competition between themselves. They may set output quotas, fix prices, limit product promotion or development, or agree not to 'poach' each other's markets.

Collusive tendering Where two or more firms secretly agree on the prices they will tender for a contract. These prices will be above those which would be put in under a genuinely competitive tendering process.

Command-and-control (CAC) systems The use of laws or regulations backed up by inspections and penalties (such as fines) for non-compliance.

Command economy An economy where all economic decisions are made by a central planning process.

Commercial bills Bills of exchange issued by firms.

Common good or resource A good or resource that has a high degree of rivalry but the exclusion of non-payers is difficult.

Common market A customs union where the member countries act as a single market with free movement of labour and capital, common taxes and common trade laws.

Comparative advantage A country has a comparative advantage over another in the production of a good if it can produce it at a lower opportunity cost: i.e. if it has to forgo less of other goods in order to produce it.

Competition for corporate control The competition for the control of companies through takeovers.

Complementary goods A pair of goods consumed together. As the price of one goes up, the demand for both goods will fall.

Compounding The process of adding interest each year to an initial capital sum.

Compromise strategy A strategy whose worst outcome is better than under a high-risk strategy and whose best outcome is better than under a low-risk strategy.

Conglomerate merger When two firms in different industries merge.

Consortium Where two or more firms work together on a specific project and create a separate company to run the project.

Constant-cost industry An industry where average costs stay constant as the size of the industry expands.

Constrained discretion A set of principles or rules within which economic policy operates. These can be informal or enshrined in law.

Consumer durable A consumer good that lasts a period of time, during which the consumer can continue gaining utility from it.

Consumer prices index (CPI) An index of the weighted average of the prices of goods and services bought by a typical household. Its annual rate of change gives CPI inflation and is the measure used by most countries, including the UK, for their inflation target.

Consumer sovereignty A situation where firms respond to changes in consumer demand without being in a position in the long run to charge a price above average cost.

Consumer surplus The excess of what a person would have been prepared to pay for a good (i.e. the utility) over what that person actually pays.

Consumers' share of a tax on a good The proportion of the revenue from a tax on a good that arises from an increase in the price of the good.

Consumption The act of using goods and services to satisfy wants. This will normally involve purchasing the goods and services.

Consumption function The relationship between consumption and national income. It can be expressed algebraically or graphically.

Consumption of domestically produced goods and services (C_d) The direct flow of money payments from households to firms.

Consumption smoothing The act by households of smoothing their levels of consumption over time despite facing volatile incomes.

Contingent convertible debt instruments (Co-Cos) Debt instruments, like corporate bonds, which may be converted into equity capital when a trigger point, such as the level of financial distress of a corporation, is reached.

Continuous market clearing The new classical assumption that all markets in the economy continuously clear so that the economy is permanently in equilibrium.

Convergence in GDP per head The tendency for less rich developed countries to catch up the richer ones. Convergence does not apply to many of the poorer developing countries, however, where the gap between them and richer countries has tended to widen.

Convergence of economies When countries achieve similar levels of growth, inflation, budget deficits as a percentage of GDP, balance of payments, etc.

Co-ordination failure When a group of firms (e.g. banks) acting independently could have achieved a more desirable outcome if they had co-ordinated their decision making.

Core workers Workers, normally with specific skills, who are employed on a permanent or long-term basis.

Cost–benefit analysis The identification, measurement and weighing up of the costs and benefits of a project in order to decide whether or not it should go ahead.

Cost-plus pricing (full-cost pricing) (another name for mark-up pricing) When firms price their product by adding a certain profit 'mark-up' to average cost.

Cost-push inflation Inflation caused by persistent rises in costs of production (independently of demand).

Countervailing power When the power of a monopolistic/oligopolistic seller is offset by powerful buyers who can prevent the price from being pushed up.

Cournot equilibrium Where each of two firm's actual output is the same as what the other firm predicted it would produce: where the two firms' reaction curves cross.

Cournot model of duopoly A model where each firm makes its price and output decisions on the assumption that its rival will produce a particular quantity.

Crawling peg A system whereby the government allows a gradual adjustment of the exchange rate.

Credibility (of policies) Policies that people believe the government will carry out once they have been announced.

Credible threat (or promise) One that is believable to rivals because it is in the threatener's interests to carry it out.

Credit-constrained households Households which are limited in their ability to borrow against expected future incomes.

Credit crunch A sudden reduction in the availability of loans or credit from banks and other financial institutions.

Cross-price elasticity of demand The percentage (or proportionate) change in quantity demanded of one good divided by the percentage (or proportionate) change in the price of another.

Cross-price elasticity of demand (arc formula) $\Delta Q_{D_A}/\text{average } Q_{D_A} \div \Delta P_B/\text{average } PB$.

Cross-section data Information showing how a variable (e.g. the consumption of eggs) differs between different groups or different individuals at a given time.

Cross-subsidise To use profits in one market to subsidise prices in another.

Crowding out Where increased public expenditure diverts money or resources away from the private sector.

Cumulative causation (principle of) When an initial change causes an eventual change that is larger.

Currency union A group of countries (or regions) using a common currency.

Current account balance of payments Exports of goods and services minus imports of goods and services plus net incomes and current transfers from abroad. If inflows of money (from the sale of exports, etc.) exceed outflows of money (from the purchase of imports, etc.) there is a 'current account surplus' (a positive figure). If outflows exceed inflows there is a 'current account deficit' (a negative figure).

Current budget deficit The amount by which government or public-sector expenditures classified as current expenditures exceed public-sector receipts.

Current expenditure (by the government) Recurrent spending on goods and factor payments.

Customs union A free trade area with common external tariffs and quotas.

Deadweight loss of an indirect tax The loss of consumers' plus producers' surplus from the imposition of an indirect tax.

Deadweight welfare loss from externalities The loss of social surplus at the competitive market equilibrium compared with the social optimum where $MSC = MSB$.

Deadweight welfare loss of monopoly The loss of consumers' plus producers' surplus in monopoly or other imperfect markets (when compared with perfect competition).

Debentures (company bonds) Fixed-interest loans to firms. These assets can be traded on the stock market and their market price is determined by demand and supply.

Debt servicing Paying the interest and capital repayments on debt.

Debt-servicing costs The costs incurred when repaying debt, including debt interest payments.

Deciles Divisions of the population into ten equal-sized groups (an example of a quantile).

Decision tree (or game tree) A diagram showing the sequence of possible decisions by competitor firms and the outcome of each combination of decisions.

Decreasing-cost industry An industry where average costs decrease as the size of the industry expands.

Deduction Using a theory to draw conclusions about specific circumstances.

Deficit bias The tendency for frequent fiscal deficits and rising debt-to-GDP ratios because of the reluctance of policy makers to tighten fiscal policy.

Deflationary (or recessionary) gap The shortfall of national expenditure below national income (and injections below withdrawals) at the full-employment level of national income.

Deflationary policy Fiscal or monetary policy designed to reduce the rate of growth of aggregate demand.

Demand curve A graph showing the relationship between the price of a good and the quantity of the good demanded over a given time period. Price is measured on the vertical axis; quantity demanded is measured on the horizontal axis. A demand curve can be for an individual consumer or group of consumers, or more usually for the whole market.

Demand function An equation which shows the mathematical relationship between the quantity demanded of a good and the values of the various determinants of demand.

Demand-management policies Demand-side policies (fiscal and/or monetary) designed to smooth out the fluctuations in the business cycle.

Demand schedule (market) A table showing the different total quantities of a good that consumers are willing and able to buy at various prices over a given period of time.

Demand schedule for an individual A table showing the different quantities of a good that a person is willing and able to buy at various prices over a given period of time.

Demand-deficient or **cyclical unemployment** Disequilibrium unemployment caused by a fall in aggregate demand with no corresponding fall in the real wage rate.

Demand-pull inflation Inflation caused by persistent rises in aggregate demand.

Demand-side policies Policies designed to affect aggregate demand: fiscal policy and monetary policy.

Demand-side policy Government policy designed to alter the level of aggregate demand, and thereby the level of output, employment and prices.

Dependency Where the development of a developing country is hampered by its relationships with the industrialised world.

Depreciation (of a currency) A fall in the free-market exchange rate of the domestic currency with foreign currencies.

Depreciation (of capital) The decline in value of capital equipment due to age, or wear and tear.

Deregulation Where the government removes official barriers to competition (e.g. licences and minimum quality standards).

Derived demand The demand for a factor of production depends on the demand for the good which uses it.

Destabilising speculation Where the actions of speculators tend to make price movements larger.

Devaluation Where the government re-pegs the exchange rate at a lower level.

Differentiation A mathematical technique to find the rate of change of one variable with respect to another.

Diminishing marginal rate of substitution The more a person consumes of good X and the less of good Y, the less additional Y will that person be prepared to give up in order to obtain an extra unit of X: i.e. $\Delta Y/\Delta X$ diminishes.

Diminishing marginal returns When one or more factors are held fixed, there will come a point beyond which the extra output from additional units of the variable factor will diminish.

Diminishing marginal utility As more units of a good are consumed, additional units will provide less additional satisfaction than previous units.

Diminishing marginal utility of income Where each additional pound earned yields less additional utility than the previous pound.

Direct income support or direct aid A fixed grant to farmers that does not vary with current output. It may be based on acreage, number of livestock or past output.

Direct monetary transmission mechanism A change in money supply having a direct effect on aggregate demand.

Direct taxes Taxes on income and wealth. Paid directly to the tax authorities on that income or wealth.

Dirty floating (managed flexibility) A system of flexible exchange rates but where the government intervenes to prevent excessive fluctuations or even to achieve an unofficial target exchange rate.

Discount factor The value today of deciding to consume a good one period in the future as a proportion of the value when it is actually consumed.

Discount market An example of a money market in which new or existing bills, such as Treasury bills or commercial bills, are bought and sold at a discount below their face value: i.e. the value at which they will be redeemed on maturity.

Discounting The process of reducing the value of future flows to give them a present valuation.

Discounting: exponential A method of reducing future benefits and costs to a present value. The discount rate depends on just how much less, from the consumer's perspective, *future* utility and costs (from a decision made today) are than gaining the utility/incurring the costs *today*.

Discretionary fiscal policy Deliberate changes in tax rates or the level of government expenditure in order to influence the level of aggregate demand.

Diseconomies of scale Where costs per unit of output increase as the scale of production increases.

Disequilibrium unemployment Unemployment resulting from real wage rates in the economy being above the equilibrium level.

Disguised unemployment Where the same work could be done by fewer people.

Disintermediation The diversion of business away from financial institutions which are subject to controls.

Disposable income Household income after the deduction of taxes and the addition of benefits.

Distribution of income by class of recipient Measurement of the distribution of income between the classes of person who receive it (e.g. homeowners and non-homeowners or those in the North and those in the South).

Diversification This is where a firm expands into new types of business.

Divine coincidence in monetary policy The argument that the inflation–output stabilisation trade-off is less significant in the presence of demand shocks.

Dominant firm price leadership When firms (the followers) choose the same price as that set by a dominant firm in the industry (the leader).

Dominant strategy game Where the firm's optimal strategy remains the same irrespective of what it assumes its rivals are going to do.

Downward causation The name given to the impact on individual behaviour or well-being of aggregate or group effects. This is an example of cumulative causation (Threshold Concept 15).

Dumping When exports are sold at prices below marginal cost – often as a result of government subsidy.

Duopoly An oligopoly where there are just two firms in the market.

Dynamic stochastic general equilibrium (DSGE) models) Models that seek to explain macroeconomic phenomena by examining the microeconomic behaviour of rational forward-looking individual economic agents acting in a variety of market conditions. The microeconomic equilibria are subject to random shocks, such as technological change, political events or changes in the supply of natural resources.

Econometrics The science of applying statistical techniques to economic data in order to identify and test economic relationships.

Economic agents People or institutions making economic decisions. These could be individuals as consumers, workers, borrowers or savers, or firms, governments or other public institutions.

Economic and monetary union (EMU) The adoption by a group of countries of a single currency with a single central bank and a single monetary policy. In the EU the term applies to the countries that have adopted the euro.

Economic discrimination When workers of identical *ability* are paid different wages or are otherwise discriminated against because of race, age, sex, etc.

Economic efficiency A situation where each good is produced at the minimum cost and where individual people and firms get the maximum benefit from their resources.

Economic model A formal presentation of an economic theory.

Economic rent The excess that a factor is paid over the amount necessary to keep it in its current employment.

Economies of scale When increasing the scale of production leads to a lower long-run cost per unit of output.

Economies of scope When increasing the range of products produced by a firm reduces the cost of producing each one.

ECU (European Currency Unit) The predecessor to the euro: a weighted average of EU currencies. It was used as a reserve currency and for the operation of the exchange rate mechanism (ERM).

Effective rate of protection The percentage increase in an industry's domestic value added resulting from protection given to that industry.

Efficient (capital) market hypothesis The hypothesis that new information about a company's current or future performance will be quickly and accurately reflected in its share price.

Efficiency (technical) The firm is producing as much output as is technologically possible given the quantity of factor inputs it is using.

Efficiency wage hypothesis The hypothesis that the productivity of workers is affected by the wage rate that they receive.

Efficiency wage rate The profit-maximising wage rate for the firm after taking into account the effects of wage rates on worker motivation, turnover and recruitment.

Elastic demand (with respect to price) Where quantity demanded changes by a larger percentage than price. Ignoring the negative sign, it will have a value greater than 1.

Elasticity A measure of the responsiveness of a variable (e.g. quantity demanded or quantity supplied) to a change in one of its determinants (e.g. price or income).

EMS (The European Monetary System, mark 1) A system, prior to the euro, whereby EU countries co-operated to achieve greater exchange rate stability. It involved use of the exchange rate mechanism (the ERM).

Endogenous growth models Models which demonstrate that the rate of economic growth depends on the rate of technological progress and diffusion, both of which depend on institutions, incentives and the role of government.

Endogenous money supply Money supply that is determined (at least in part) by the demand for money.

Endogenous variable A variable whose value is determined by the model of which it is part.

Endowment effect (or divestiture aversion) The hypothesis that people ascribe more value to things when they own them than when they are merely considering purchasing or acquiring them – in other words, when the reference point is one of ownership rather than non-ownership.

Engel curve A line derived from indifference analysis showing how much of a good people will demand at different levels of income.

Entrepreneurship The initiating and organising of the production of new goods, or the introduction of new techniques, and the risk taking associated with it.

Envelope curve A long-run average cost curve drawn as the tangency points of a series of short-run average cost curves.

Environmental charges Charges for using natural resources (e.g. water or national parks), or for using the environment as a dump for waste (e.g. factory emissions or sewage).

Envy (in economics) Negatively valuing the pay-offs to others.

Equation of exchange $MV = PY$. The total level of spending on GDP (MV) equals the total value of goods and services produced (PY) that go to make up GDP.

Equilibrium A position of balance. A position from which there is no inherent tendency to move away.

Equilibrium price The price where the quantity demanded equals the quantity supplied: the price where there is no shortage or surplus.

Equilibrium ('natural') unemployment The difference between those who would like employment at the current wage rate and those willing and able to take a job.

Equi-marginal principle Consumers will maximise total utility from their incomes by consuming that combination of goods where $MU_a/P_a = MU_b/P_b = MU_c/P_c = MU_n/P_n$.

Equities Company shares. Holders of equities are owners of the company and share in its profits by receiving dividends.

Equity A distribution of income that is considered to be fair or just. Note that an equitable distribution is not the same as an equal distribution and that different people have different views on what is equitable.

ERM (the exchange rate mechanism) A system of semi-fixed exchange rates used by most of the EU countries prior to adoption of the euro. Members' currencies were allowed to fluctuate against each other only within agreed bands. Collectively they floated against all other currencies.

Excess burden (of a tax on a good) The amount by which the loss in consumer plus producer surplus exceeds the government surplus.

Excess capacity (under monopolistic competition) In the long run, firms under monopolistic competition will produce at an output below their minimum-cost point.

Exchange equalisation account The gold and foreign exchange reserves account in the Bank of England.

Exchange rate The rate at which one national currency exchanges for another. The rate is expressed as the amount of one currency that is necessary to purchase *one unit* of another currency (e.g. €1.20 = £1).

Exchange rate band Where a currency is allowed to float between an upper and lower exchange rate, but is not allowed to move outside this band.

Exchange rate index A weighted average exchange rate expressed as an index where the value of the index is 100 in a given base year. The weights of the different currencies in the index add up to 1.

Exchange rate mechanism See *ERM*.

Exchange rate overshooting Where a fall (or rise) in the long-run equilibrium exchange rate causes the actual exchange rate to fall (or rise) by a greater amount before eventually moving back to the new long-run equilibrium level.

Exchange rate: real A country's exchange rate adjusted for changes in the domestic currency prices of its exports relative to the foreign currency prices of its imports. If a country's prices rise (fall) relative to those of its trading partners, its real exchange rate will rise (fall) relative to the nominal exchange rate.

Exchange rate regime The system under which the government allows the exchange rate to be determined.

Exchange rate transmission mechanism How a change in money supply affects aggregate demand via a change in exchange rates.

Exclusionary abuses (in business) Business practices that limit or prevent effective competition from either actual or potential rivals.

Exogenous money supply Money supply that does not depend on the demand for money but is set by the authorities.

Exogenous variable A variable whose value is determined independently of the model of which it is part.

Expansion path The line on an isoquant map that traces the minimum-cost combinations of two factors as output increases. It is drawn on the assumption that both factors can be varied. It is thus a long-run path.

Expected value The long-run average value of a random variable. It is calculated by taking the sum of each possible value of the random variable multiplied by the probability it will occur.

Expectations-augmented Phillips curve A (short-run) Phillips curve whose position depends on the expected rate of inflation.

Expenditure changing (increasing) from depreciation: the income effect Where depreciation, via the substitution effect, will alter the demand for imports and exports, and this will, via the multiplier, affect the level of national income and hence the demand for imports.

Expenditure changing (reducing) from deflation: the income effect Where deflationary policies lead to a reduction in national income and hence a reduction in the demand for imports.

Expenditure switching from deflation: the substitution effect Where deflationary policies lead to a reduction in inflation and thus cause a switch in expenditure away from imports and also towards exports.

Expenditure switching from depreciation: the substitution effect Where a lower exchange rate reduces the price of exports and increases the price of imports. This will increase the sale of exports and reduce the sale of imports.

Explicit costs Costs where an actual transfer of money takes place between parties.

Exploitative abuse (in business) A business practice that directly harms the customer. Examples include high prices and poor quality.

Exponential discounting A method of reducing future benefits and costs to a present value. The discount rate depends on the level of impatience and remains constant in exponential discounting.

External balance (in the economy) Narrow definition: where the current account of the balance of payments is in balance (and thus also the capital plus financial accounts). Loose definition: where there is a total currency flow balance at a given exchange rate.

External benefits Benefits from production (or consumption) experienced by people *other* than the producer (or consumer) directly involved in the transaction.

External costs Costs of production (or consumption) borne by people *other* than the producer (or consumer) directly involved in the transaction.

External diseconomies of scale Where a firm's costs per unit of output increase as the size of the whole *industry* increases.

External economies of scale Where a firm's costs per unit of output decrease as the size of the whole *industry* grows.

External policy objectives Objectives relating to the economy's international economic relationships.

Externalities Costs or benefits of production or consumption experienced by people *other* than the producers and consumers directly involved in the transaction. They are sometimes referred to as 'spillover' or 'third-party' costs or benefits.

Factor price equalisation The tendency for international trade to reduce factor price inequalities both between and within countries.

Factors of production (or resources) The inputs into the production of goods and services: labour, land and raw materials, and capital.

Fallacy of composition What applies to the individual does not necessarily apply to the whole.

Final expenditure Expenditure on goods and services. This is included in GDP and is part of aggregate demand.

Financial accelerator The amplification of effects on the macroeconomy from economic shocks because of changes in the pricing and supply of credit by financial institutions.

Financial account of the balance of payments The record of the flows of money into and out of the country for the purposes of investment or as deposits in banks and other financial institutions.

Financial crowding out When an increase in government borrowing diverts money away from the private sector.

Financial deregulation The removal of or reduction in legal rules and regulations governing the activities of financial institutions.

Financial flexibility Where employers can vary their wage costs by changing the composition of their workforce or the terms on which workers are employed.

Financial instability hypothesis During periods of economic growth, economic agents (firms and individuals) tend to borrow more and MFIs are more willing to lend. This fuels the boom. In a period of recession, economic agents tend to cut spending in order to reduce debts and MFIs are less willing to lend. This deepens the recession. Behaviour in financial markets thus tends to amplify the business cycle.

Financial instruments Financial products resulting in a financial claim by one party over another.

Financial intermediaries The general name for financial institutions (banks, building societies, etc.) which act as a means of channelling funds from depositors to borrowers.

Financialisation A term used to describe the process by which financial markets, institutions and instruments becoming increasing significant in economies.

Fine-tuning The use of demand management policy (fiscal or monetary) to smooth out cyclical fluctuations in the economy.

First-best solution The solution of correcting a specific market distortion by ensuring that the whole economy operates under conditions of social efficiency (Pareto optimality).

First-degree price discrimination Where the seller of the product charges each consumer the maximum price he or she is prepared to pay for each unit.

First-mover advantage When a firm gains from being the first one to take action.

Fiscal drag The tendency of automatic fiscal stabilisers to reduce the recovery of an economy from recession.

Fiscal impulse A measure of the change in the fiscal stance arising from discretionary fiscal policy changes.

Fiscal policy Changing government expenditure and/or taxation for the purposes of influencing the macroeconomy.

Fiscal stance How deflationary or reflationary the Budget is.

Fixed costs Total costs that do not vary with the amount of output produced.

Fixed exchange rate (totally) Where the government takes whatever measures are necessary to maintain the exchange rate at some stated level.

Fixed factor An input that cannot be increased in supply within a given time period.

Flat organisation Where the senior management communicate directly with those lower in the organisational structure, bypassing middle management.

Flexible firm A firm that has the flexibility to respond to changing market conditions by changing the composition of its workforce.

Floating exchange rate When the government does not intervene in the foreign exchange markets, but simply allows the exchange rate to be freely determined by demand and supply.

Flow An amount of something occurring over a *period of time*: e.g. production per week, income per year, demand per week. (Contrasts with *stock*.)

Flow-of-funds equation The various items making up an increase (or decrease) in money supply.

Forward exchange market Where contracts are made today for the price at which currency will be exchanged at some specified future date.

Forward guidance Announcements from central banks about the likely path of policy designed to influence the decisions of households and businesses.

Framing The way in which a choice is presented or understood. A person may make different decisions depending on whether a choice is presented optimistically or pessimistically.

Franchising Where a firm is given the licence to operate a given part of an industry for a specified length of time.

Free trade area A group of countries with few or no trade barriers between themselves.

Freely floating exchange rate Where the exchange rate is determined entirely by the forces of demand and supply in the foreign exchange market with no government intervention whatsoever.

Free-market economy An economy where all economic decisions are taken by individual households and firms and with no government intervention.

Free-rider problem When it is not possible to exclude other people from consuming a good that someone has bought.

Frictional (search) unemployment Equilibrium unemployment which occurs as a result of imperfect information in the labour market. It often takes time for workers to find jobs (even though there are vacancies) and in the meantime they are unemployed.

Full-employment level of national income The level of national income at which there is no deficiency of demand.

Functional distribution of income Measurement of the distribution of income according to the source of income (e.g. from employment, from profit, from rent, etc.).

Functional flexibility Where employers can switch workers from job to job as requirements change.

Functional relationships The mathematical relationship showing how one variable is affected by one or more others.

Functional separation (banking) The separation of investment and retail banking designed to insulate core financial activities from other riskier activities.

Funding (in monetary policy) Where the authorities alter the balance of bills and bonds for any given level of government borrowing.

Future price A price agreed today at which an item (e.g. commodities) will be exchanged at some set date in the future.

Futures or forward market A market in which contracts are made to buy or sell at some future date at a price agreed today.

Gaia philosophy The respect for the rights of the environment to remain unharmed by human activity.

Humans should live in harmony with the planet and other species. We have a duty to be stewards of the natural environment, so that it can continue to be a self-maintaining and self-regulating system.

Game theory (or the theory of games) A mathematical method of decision making in which alternative strategies are analysed to determine the optimal course of action for the interested party, depending on assumptions about rivals' behaviour. Widely used in economics, game theory is also used as a tool in biology, psychology and politics.

GDP (gross domestic product at market prices) The value of output (or income or expenditure) in terms of the prices actually paid. GDP = GVA + taxes on products − subsidies on products.

GDP deflator The price index of all final domestically produced goods and services: i.e. all those items that contribute towards GDP.

Gearing or **leverage** (US term) The ratio of debt capital to equity capital: in other words, the ratio of borrowed capital (e.g. bonds) to shares.

General equilibrium A situation where all the millions of markets throughout the economy are in a simultaneous state of equilibrium.

General equilibrium diagrams (in trade theory) Indifference curve/production possibility curve diagrams that show a country's production and consumption of both imports and exports.

General government debt The accumulated deficits of central plus local government. It is the total amount owed by general government, both domestically and internationally.

General government deficit (or surplus) The combined deficit (or surplus) of central and local government.

Geographical immobility The lack of ability or willingness of people to move to jobs in other parts of the country.

Giffen good An inferior good whose demand increases as its price increases as a result of a positive income effect larger than the normal negative substitution effect.

Gini coefficient The area between the Lorenz curve and the 45° line divided by the total area under the 45° line.

Global systemically important banks (SIBs) Banks identified by a series of indicators as being significant players in the global financial system.

GNY (gross national income) GDP plus net income from abroad.

Gold standard The system whereby countries' exchange rates were fixed in terms of a certain amount of gold and whereby balance of payments deficits were paid in gold.

Golden-rule saving rate The rate of saving that maximises the level of long-run consumption per worker.

Goodhart's law Controlling a symptom of a problem or only one part of the problem will not *cure* the problem: it will simply mean that the part that is being controlled now becomes a poor indicator of the problem.

Government bonds or **'gilt-edged securities'** A government security paying a fixed sum of money each year. It is redeemed by the government on its maturity date at its face value.

Government surplus (from a tax on a good) The total tax revenue earned by the government from sales of a good.

Grandfathering Where the number of emission permits allocated to a firm is based on its *current* levels of emission (e.g. permitted levels for all firms could be 80 per cent of their current levels).

Green tax A tax on output designed to charge for the adverse effects of production on the environment. The socially efficient level of a green tax is equal to the marginal environmental cost of production.

Gross domestic product (GDP) The value of output produced within the country over a 12-month period.

Gross national income (GNY) GDP plus net income from abroad.

Gross value added at basic prices (GVA) The sum of all the values added by all industries in the economy over a year. The figures exclude taxes on products (such as VAT) and include subsidies on products.

Growth maximisation An alternative theory that assumes that managers seek to maximise the growth in sales revenue (or the capital value of the firm) over time.

Harrod–Domar model A model that relates a country's rate of economic growth to the proportion of national income saved and the ratio of capital to output.

Heckscher–Ohlin version of comparative advantage A country has a comparative advantage in those goods that are intensive in the country's relatively abundant factor.

Heterodox economists Economists who reject the assumptions of neoclassical economics, in particular the assumptions of rational optimising behaviour. They highlight the importance of institutional behaviour and factors influencing human behaviour.

Heuristics Mental short-cuts or rules of thumb that people use when trying to make complicated choices. They reduce the computational and/or research effort required but sometimes lead to systematic errors.

H-form organisation (holding company) Where the parent company holds interests in a number of subsidiary companies.

Historic costs The original amount the firm paid for factors it now owns.

Hit-and-run competition A strategy whereby a firm is willing to enter a market and make short-run profits and then leave again when the existing firm(s) cut prices. Costless exit makes hit-and-run behaviour more likely.

Horizontal equity The equal treatment of people in the same situation.

Horizontal merger When two firms in the same industry at the same stage in the production process merge.

Households' disposable income The income available for households to spend: i.e. personal incomes after deducting taxes on incomes and adding benefits.

Human capital The qualifications, skills and expertise that contribute to a worker's productivity.

Human Development Index (HDI) A composite index made up of three elements: an index for life expectancy, an index for school enrolment and adult literacy, and an index for GDP per capita (in PPP$).

Hyperbolic discounting The discount factor falls more quickly when comparing immediate pay-offs with those that occur at some point in the future than it does when comparing the same pay-offs but which all occur in the future.

Hysteresis The persistence of an effect even when the initial cause has ceased to operate. In economics, it refers to the persistence of unemployment even when the demand deficiency that caused it no longer exists.

Identification problem The problem of identifying the relationship between two variables (e.g. price and quantity demanded) from the evidence when it is not known whether or how the variables have been affected by *other* determinants. For example, it is difficult to identify the shape of a demand curve simply by observing price and quantity when it is not known whether changes in other determinants have *shifted* the demand curve.

Idle balances Money held for speculative purposes: money held in anticipation of a fall in asset prices.

Illegal (or shadow or underground) markets Where people ignore the government's price and/or quantity controls and sell illegally at whatever price equates illegal demand and supply.

Imperfect competition The collective name for monopolistic competition and oligopoly.

Implicit costs Costs which do not involve a direct payment of money to a third party, but which nevertheless involve a sacrifice of some alternative.

Import-substituting industrialisation (ISI) A strategy of restricting imports of manufactured goods and using the foreign exchange saved to build up domestic substitute industries.

Impulse response functions The time paths of key macroeconomic variables following economic shocks.

Impure public good A good that is partially non-rivalrous and non-excludable.

Incidence of tax The distribution of the burden of tax between sellers and buyers.

Income and expenditure account or profit and loss account A record of the flows of incomes, expenditure and saving of an individual or institution.

Income effect (of a price change) The effect of a change in price on quantity demanded arising from the consumer becoming better or worse off as a result of the price change.

Income effect of a rise in wage rates Workers get a higher income for a given number of hours worked and may thus feel they need to work *fewer* hours as wage rates rise.

Income effect of a tax rise Tax increases reduce people's incomes and thus encourage people to work more.

Income elasticity of demand The percentage (or proportionate) change in quantity demanded divided by the percentage (or proportionate) change in income.

Income elasticity of demand (arc formula) ΔQ_D/average $Q_D \Delta Y$/average Y.

Income–consumption curve A line showing how a person's optimum level of consumption of two goods changes as income changes (assuming the price of the goods remains constant).

Increasing-cost industry An industry where average costs increase as the size of the industry expands.

Increasing opportunity costs of production When additional production of one good involves ever increasing sacrifices of another.

Independence (of firms in a market) Where the decisions of one firm in a market will not have any significant effect on the demand curves of its rivals.

Independent risks Where two risky events are unconnected. The occurrence of one will not affect the likelihood of the occurrence of the other.

Index number The value of a variable expressed as 100 plus or minus its percentage deviation from a base year.

Indifference curve A line showing all those combinations of two goods between which a consumer is indifferent: i.e. those combinations that give the same level of utility.

Indifference map A graph showing a whole set of indifference curves. The further away a particular curve is from the origin, the higher the level of satisfaction it represents.

Indifference set A table showing the same information as an indifference curve.

Indirect monetary transmission mechanism A change in money supply affecting aggregate demand indirectly via some other variable.

Indirect taxes Taxes on expenditure (e.g. VAT). They are paid to the tax authorities, not by the consumer, but indirectly by the suppliers of the goods or services.

Indivisibilities The impossibility of dividing a factor into smaller units.

Induced investment Investment that firms make to enable them to meet extra consumer demand.

Induction Constructing general theories on the basis of specific observations.

Industrial policies Policies to encourage industrial investment and greater industrial efficiency.

Industry's infrastructure The network of supply agents, communications, skills, training facilities, distribution channels, specialised financial services, etc., that supports a particular industry.

Inelastic demand (with respect to price) Where quantity demanded changes by a smaller percentage than price. Ignoring the negative sign, it will have a value less than 1.

Infant industry An industry that has a potential comparative advantage, but which is as yet too underdeveloped to be able to realise this potential.

Inferior goods Goods whose demand *decreases* as consumer incomes increase. Such goods have a negative income elasticity of demand.

Inflation A general rise in the level of prices throughout the economy.

Inflation bias Excessive inflation that results from people raising their expectations of the inflation rate following expansionary demand management policy, encouraging government to loosen policy even further.

Inflation rate (annual) The percentage increase in prices over a 12-month period.

Inflation–output stabilisation trade-off The possibility that there exists a trade-off between the variability of inflation and that of output or unemployment: i.e. more stable rates of inflation may be at the cost of more unstable economic activity.

Inflationary gap The excess of national expenditure over income (and injections over withdrawals) at the full-employment level of national income.

Informal sector The parts of the economy that involve production and/or exchange, but where there are no money payments.

Infrastructure (industry's) The network of supply agents, communications, skills, training facilities, distribution channels, specialised financial services, etc. that supports a particular industry.

Injections (*J*) Expenditure on the production of domestic firms coming from outside the inner flow of the circular flow of income. Injections equal investment (*I*) plus government expenditure (*G*) plus expenditure on exports (*X*).

(Injections) multiplier The number of times by which a rise in income exceeds the rise in injections that caused it: $k = \Delta Y/\Delta J$.

(Injections) multiplier formula The formula for the multiplier: $k = 1/mpw$ or $1/(1-mpc_d)$.

Input–output analysis This involves dividing the economy into sectors where each sector is a user of inputs from and a supplier of outputs to other sectors. The technique examines how these inputs and outputs can be matched to the total resources available in the economy.

Insiders Those in employment who can use their privileged position (either as members of unions or because of specific skills) to secure pay rises despite an excess supply of labour (unemployment).

Interdependence (under oligopoly) One of the two key features of oligopoly. Each firm will be affected by its rivals' decisions. Likewise its decisions will affect its rivals. Firms recognise this interdependence. This recognition will affect their decisions.

Interest rate transmission mechanism How a change in money supply affects aggregate demand via a change in interest rates.

Intermediate exchange rate regimes Where the government intervenes to influence movements in the exchange rate.

Internal balance (of an economy) Where the equilibrium level of national income is at the desired level.

Internal policy objectives (national) Objectives relating solely to the domestic economy.

Internal rate of return The rate of return of an investment: the discount rate that makes the net present value of an investment equal to zero.

International harmonisation of economic policies Where countries attempt to co-ordinate their macroeconomic policies so as to achieve common goals.

International liquidity The supply of currencies in the world acceptable for financing international trade and investment.

International substitution effect As prices rise, people at home and abroad buy less of this country's products and more of products from abroad.

International trade multiplier The effect on national income in country B of a change in national income in country A.

Inter-temporal substitution effect Higher prices may lead to higher interest rates and thus less borrowing and more saving. Current consumption falls; future consumption (from the higher savings) rises.

Intervention price (in the CAP) The price at which the EU is prepared to buy a foodstuff if the market price were to be below it.

Interventionist supply-side policies Policies to increase aggregate supply by government intervention to counteract the deficiencies of the market.

Investment The production of items that are not for immediate consumption. This can include investment in plant and equipment; such investment builds the stock of firms' capital and yields a flow of future output. Investment also includes adding to stocks of goods or resources which are not sold or used in the current period, but will be in the future.

Irrational exuberance Where banks and other economic agents are over-confident about the economy and/or financial markets and expect economic growth to remain stronger and/or asset prices to rise further than warranted by evidence.

***IS/LM* model** A model showing simultaneous equilibrium in the goods market ($I = S$) and the money market ($L = M$).

Isocost A line showing all the combinations of two factors that cost the same to employ.

Isoquant A line showing all the alternative combinations of two factors that can produce a given level of output.

J-curve effect Where a devaluation causes the balance of trade first to deteriorate and then to improve. The graph of the balance of trade over time thus looks like a letter J.

Joint float Where a group of currencies pegged to each other jointly float against other currencies.

Joint supply Where the production of more of one good leads to the production of more of another.

Joint venture Where two or more firms set up and jointly own a new independent firm.

Just-in-time methods Where a firm purchases supplies and produces both components and finished products as they are required. This minimises stock holding and its associated costs. It does, however, put pressure on the supply chain and increases the probability that on occasion firms may not be able to meet demand – for example in times of bad weather.

Kinked demand theory The theory that oligopolists face a demand curve that is kinked at the current price, demand being significantly more elastic above the current price than below. The effect of this is to create a situation of price stability.

Knowledge transfer The sharing and diffusion of knowledge.

Labour All forms of human input, both physical and mental, into current production.

Labour force The number employed plus the number unemployed.

Labour productivity Output per unit of labour: for example, output per worker or output per hour worked.

Land (and raw materials) Inputs into production that are provided by nature: e.g. unimproved land and mineral deposits in the ground.

Law of comparative advantage Trade can benefit all countries if they specialise in the goods in which they have a comparative advantage.

Law of demand The quantity of a good demanded per period of time will fall as price rises and will rise as price falls, other things being equal (*ceteris paribus*).

Law of diminishing (marginal) returns When one or more factors are held fixed, there will come a point beyond which the extra output from additional units of the variable factor will diminish.

Law of large numbers The larger the number of events of a particular type, the more predictable will be their average outcome.

Lender of last resort The role of the Bank of England as the guarantor of sufficient liquidity in the monetary system.

Leverage (US term) or gearing The ratio of debt capital to equity capital: in other words, the ratio of borrowed capital (e.g. bonds) to shares.

Liabilities All legal claims for payment that outsiders have on an institution.

Liability Claim by others on an individual or institution; debt of that individual or institution.

Libertarian school A school of thought that advocates maximum liberty for economic agents to pursue their own interests and to own property.

Limit pricing Where a monopolist (or oligopolist) charges a price below the short-run profit-maximising level in order to deter new entrants.

Liquidity The ease with which an asset can be converted into cash without loss.

Liquidity preference The demand for holding assets in the form of money.

Liquidity ratio The proportion of a bank's total assets held in liquid form.

Liquidity trap The absorption of any additional money supply into idle balances at very low rates of interest, leaving aggregate demand unchanged.

Lock-outs Union members are temporarily laid off until they are prepared to agree to the firm's conditions.

Long run The period of time long enough for *all* factors to be varied.

Long run under perfect competition The period of time that is long enough for new firms to enter the industry.

Long-run average cost curve A curve that shows how average cost varies with output on the assumption that *all* factors are variable. (It is assumed that the least-cost method of production will be chosen for each output.)

Long-run marginal cost The extra cost of producing one more unit of output assuming that all factors are variable. (It is assumed that the least-cost method of production will be chosen for this extra output.)

Long-run neutrality of money Changes in money supply over the long run will only affect prices and not real output or employment

Long-run profit maximisation An alternative theory of the firm which assumes that managers aim to *shift* cost and revenue curves so as to maximise profits over some longer time period.

Long-run shut-down point This is where the *AR* curve is tangential to the *LRAC* curve. The firm can just make normal profits. Any fall in revenue below this level will cause a profit-maximising firm to shut down once all costs have become variable.

Lorenz curve A curve showing the proportion of national income earned by any given percentage of the population (measured from the poorest upwards).

Loss aversion Where the negative value placed on a loss is greater than the positive value placed on an equivalent sized gain. This dislike of losses is far greater than that predicted by standard economic theory.

Macro-prudential regulation Regulation which focuses not on a single financial institution but on the financial system as a whole and which monitors its overall stability, its resilience to shocks and its impact on the wider economy.

Macroeconomics The branch of economics that studies economic aggregates (grand totals): e.g. the overall level of prices, output and employment in the economy.

Managed flexibility (dirty floating) A system of flexible exchange rates but where the government intervenes to prevent excessive fluctuations or even to achieve an unofficial target exchange rate.

Margin squeeze Where a vertically integrated firm with a dominant position in an upstream market deliberately charges high prices for an input required by firms in a downstream market to drive them out of business.

Marginal benefit The additional benefit of doing a little bit more (or 1 unit more if a unit can be measured) of an activity.

Marginal capital/output ratio The amount of extra capital (in money terms) required to produce a £1 increase in national output. Since $I_i = \Delta K$, the marginal capital/output ratio $\Delta K/\Delta Y$ equals the accelerator coefficient α.

Marginal consumer surplus The excess of utility from the consumption of one more unit of a good (*MU*) over the price paid: $MCS = MU - P$.

Marginal cost (of an activity) The additional cost of doing a little bit more (or 1 unit more if a unit can be measured) of an activity.

Marginal cost (of production) The cost of producing one more unit of output: $MC = \Delta TC/\Delta Q$.

Marginal disutility of work The extra sacrifice/hardship to a worker of working an extra unit of time in any given time period (e.g. an extra hour per day).

Marginal efficiency of capital or **internal rate of return** The rate of return of an investment: the discount rate that makes the net present value of an investment equal to zero.

Marginal physical product The extra output gained by the employment of one more unit of the variable factor: $MPP = \Delta TPP/\Delta Q_V$.

Marginal productivity theory The theory that the demand for a factor depends on its marginal revenue product.

Marginal propensity to consume The proportion of a rise in national income that goes on consumption: $mpc = \Delta C/\Delta Y$.

Marginal propensity to import The proportion of an increase in national income that is spent on imports: $mpm = \Delta M/\Delta Y$.

Marginal propensity to save The proportion of an increase in national income saved: $mps = \Delta S/\Delta Y$.

Marginal propensity to withdraw The proportion of an increase in national income that is withdrawn from the circular flow: $mpw = \Delta W/\Delta Y$, where $mpw = mps + mpt + mpm$.

Marginal rate of factor substitution The rate at which one factor can be substituted by another while holding the level of output constant: $MRS = \Delta F_1/\Delta F_2 = MPP_{F2}/MPP_{F1}$.

Marginal rate of income tax The income tax rate. The rate paid on each *additional* pound earned: $\Delta T/\Delta Y$.

Marginal rate of substitution (between two goods in consumption) The amount of one good (Y) that a consumer is prepared to give up in order to obtain one extra unit of another good (X): i.e. $\Delta Y/\Delta X$.

Marginal revenue The extra revenue gained by selling one more unit per time period: $MR = \Delta TR/\Delta Q$.

Marginal revenue product (of a factor) The extra revenue a firm earns from employing one more unit of a variable factor: $MRP_{factor} = MPP_{factor} \times MR_{good}$.

Marginal tax propensity The proportion of an increase in national income paid in tax: $mpt = \Delta T/\Delta Y$.

Marginal utility The extra satisfaction gained from consuming one extra unit of a good within a given time period.

Market The interaction between buyers and sellers.

Market clearing A market clears when supply matches demand, leaving no shortage or surplus.

Market demand schedule A table showing the different total quantities of a good that consumers are willing and able to buy at various prices over a given period of time.

Market for loanable funds The market for loans from and deposits into the banking system.

Market loans Short-term loans (e.g. money at call and short notice).

Market-orientated supply-side policies Policies to increase aggregate supply by freeing up the market.

Mark-up A profit margin added to average cost to arrive at price.

Marshall–Lerner condition Depreciation will improve the balance of payments only if the sum of the price elasticities of demand for imports and exports is greater than 1.

Maturity gap The difference in the average maturity of loans and deposits.

Maturity transformation The transformation of deposits into loans of a longer maturity.

Maximax The strategy of choosing the policy that has the best possible outcome. Maximax is usually a high-risk strategy.

Maximin The strategy of choosing the policy whose worst possible outcome is the least bad. Maximin is usually a low-risk strategy.

Maximum price A price ceiling set by the government or some other agency. The price is not allowed to rise above this level (although it is allowed to fall below it).

Mean (or arithmetic mean) The sum of the values of each of the members of the sample divided by the total number in the sample.

Means-tested benefits Benefits whose amount depends on the recipient's income or assets.

Median The value of the middle member of the sample.

Medium of exchange Something that is acceptable in exchange for goods and services.

Menu costs of inflation The costs associated with having to adjust price lists or labels.

Merchandise balance See *Balance of trade in goods*.

Merit goods Goods which the government feels that people will underconsume and which therefore ought to be subsidised or provided free.

M-form (multi-divisional form) of corporate organisation Where the firm is split into a number of separate divisions (e.g. different products or countries), with each division then split into a number of departments.

Microeconomics The branch of economics that studies individual units: e.g. households, firms and industries. It studies the interrelationships between these units in determining the pattern of production and distribution of goods and services.

Minimum price A price floor set by the government or some other agency. The price is not allowed to fall below this level (although it is allowed to rise above it).

Minimum reserve ratio A minimum ratio of cash (or other specified liquid assets) to deposits (either total or selected) that the central bank requires banks to hold.

Minsky moment A turning point in a credit cycle where a period of easy credit and rising debt is replaced by one of tight credit and debt consolidation.

Misperceptions theory The theory that changes in economic activity are caused by people confusing changes in general prices with changes in relative prices.

Mixed command economy A planned economy that nevertheless makes some use of markets.

Mixed economy An economy where economic decisions are made partly by the government and partly through the market. In practice all economies are mixed.

Mixed market economy A market economy where there is some government intervention.

Mobility of labour The willingness and ability of labour to move to another job.

Monetarists Those who attribute inflation solely to rises in money supply.

Monetary base Notes and coin outside the central bank.

Monetary base control Monetary policy that focuses on controlling the monetary base (as opposed to broad liquidity).

Monetary financial institutions (MFIs) Deposit-taking institutions including banks, building societies and the Bank of England.

Monetary policy Where the central bank alters the supply of money in the economy and/or manipulates interest rates.

Money illusion When people believe that a *money* change in wages or prices represents a *real* change: in other words, they ignore or underestimate inflation.

Money market The market for short-term debt instruments, such as government bills (Treasury bills), in which financial institutions are active participants.

Money multiplier The number of times greater the expansion of money supply is than the expansion of the monetary base that caused it: $\Delta Ms/\Delta Mb$.

Monopolistic competition A market structure where, like perfect competition, there are many firms and freedom of entry into the industry, but where each firm produces a differentiated product and thus has some control over its price.

Monopoly A market structure where there is only one firm in the industry.

Monopsony A market with a single buyer or employer.

Moral hazard Where one party to a transaction has an incentive to behave in a way which reduces the pay-off to the other party: for example, the temptation to take more risks when you know that someone else will cover the risks if you get into difficulties. In the case of banks taking risks, the 'someone else' may be another bank, the central bank or the government.

Moral hazard (in insurance) Customers taking more risks when they have insurance than when they don't have insurance.

Multiplier (injections multiplier) The number of times a rise in income exceeds the rise in injections that caused it. $k = \Delta Y/\Delta J$.

Multiplier effect An initial increase in aggregate demand of £*x* million leads to an eventual rise in national income that is greater than £*x* million.

Multiplier formula (injections multiplier) The formula for the multiplier is $k = 1/mpw$ or $1/(1-mpc_d)$.

Mutual recognition The EU principle that one country's rules and regulations must apply throughout the EU. If they conflict with those of another country, individuals and firms should be able to choose which to obey.

Nash equilibrium The position resulting from everyone making their optimal decision based on their assumptions about their rivals' decisions. Without collusion, there is no incentive for any firm to move from this position.

National debt The accumulated deficits of central government. It is the total amount owed by central government, both domestically and internationally.

National expenditure on domestic product (*E*) Aggregate demand in the Keynesian model: i.e. $C_d + J$.

Nationalised industries State-owned industries that produce goods or services that are sold in the market.

Natural level of real income or output The level of output in monetarist analysis where the vertical long-run aggregate supply curve cuts the horizontal axis.

Natural level of unemployment The level of equilibrium unemployment in monetarist and new classical analysis measured as the difference between the (vertical) long-run gross labour supply curve (N) and the (vertical) long-run effective labour supply curve (AS_L).

Natural monopoly A situation where long-run average costs would be lower if an industry were under monopoly than if it were shared between two or more competitors.

Natural rate hypothesis The theory that, following fluctuations in aggregate demand, unemployment will return to a natural rate. This rate is determined by supply-side factors, such as labour mobility.

Natural rate of unemployment The rate of unemployment at which there is no excess or deficiency of demand for labour. The rate of unemployment consistent, therefore, with a constant rate of inflation: the rate of unemployment at which the vertical long-run Phillips curve cuts the horizontal axis.

Natural wastage When a firm wishing to reduce its work force does so by not replacing those who leave or retire.

Near money Highly liquid assets (other than cash).

Negative income tax A combined system of tax and benefits. As people earn more they gradually lose their benefits until beyond a certain level they begin paying taxes.

Neo-Austrian/libertarian school A school of thought that advocates maximum liberty for economic agents to pursue their own interests and to own property.

Net investment Total investment minus depreciation.

Net national income (NNY) GNY minus depreciation.

Net present value of an investment The discounted benefits of an investment minus the cost of the investment.

Net worth A sector's or country's stock of financial and non-financial assets minus its financial liabilities.

Network (business) An informal arrangement between businesses to work together towards some common goal.

Network economies (or network externalities) The benefits a consumer obtains from consuming a good or service increase with the number of other people who use the same good or service.

Neutrality of money (long run) Changes in money supply over the long run will only affect prices and not real output or employment.

New classical school The school of economists which believes that markets clear virtually instantaneously and that expectations are formed 'rationally'. Any expansion of demand will feed through virtually instantaneously into higher prices, giving a vertical short-run as well as a vertical long-run Phillips curve.

New Keynesians Economists who seek to explain how market imperfections and frictions can result in fluctuations in real GDP and the persistence of unemployment. They argue that governments may have to expand aggregate demand when demand-deficient unemployment is persistent.

Nominal GDP GDP measured at current prices.

Nominal national income National income measured at current prices.

Nominal values Money values measured at *current* prices.

Non-accelerating-inflation rate of unemployment (NAIRU) The rate of unemployment consistent with steady inflation in the near term, say, over the next 12 months.

Non-bank private sector Households and non-bank firms: in other words, everyone in the country other than banks and the government (central and local).

Non-collusive oligopoly Where oligopolists have no agreement between themselves either formal, informal or tacit.

Non-excludability Where it is not possible to provide a good or service to one person without it thereby being available free for others to enjoy.

Non-price competition Competition in terms of product promotion (advertising, packaging, etc.) or product development.

Non-rivalry Where the consumption of a good or service by one person will not prevent others from enjoying it.

Normal goods Goods whose demand increases as consumer incomes increase. They have a positive income elasticity of demand. Luxury goods will have a higher income elasticity of demand than more basic goods.

Normal profit The opportunity cost of being in business: the profit that could have been earned in the next best alternative business. It is counted as a cost of production.

Normal rate of return The rate of return (after taking risks into account) that could be earned elsewhere.

Normal-form game Where the possible pay-offs from different strategies or decisions are presented as a matrix.

Normative statement A value judgement.

Nudge theory Small changes in the way the same policy is presented that help some people make much better decisions for themselves, while imposing very little or no cost on those who are already making choices that maximise their wellbeing.

Numerical flexibility Where employers can change the size of their workforce as their labour requirements change.

Occupational immobility The lack of ability or willingness of people to move to other jobs irrespective of location.

Okun's law The name given to the negative statistical relationship between the unemployment rate and deviations of output from potential output.

Oligopoly A market structure where there are few enough firms to enable barriers to be erected against the entry of new firms.

Oligopsony A market with just a few buyers or employers.

Open economy One that trades with and has financial dealings with other countries.

Open-market operations The sale (or purchase) by the authorities of government securities in the open market in order to reduce (or increase) money supply or influence interest rates.

Operational standing facilities Central bank facilities by which individual banks can deposit reserves or borrow reserves.

Opportunity cost Cost measured in terms of the value of the best alternative forgone.

Optimal currency area The optimal size of a currency area is the one that maximises the benefits from having a single currency relative to the costs. If the area were increased or decreased in size, the costs would rise relative to the benefits.

Optimum tariff A tariff that reduces the level of imports to the point where the country's marginal social cost equals marginal social benefit.

Organisational slack Where managers allow spare capacity to exist, thereby enabling them to respond more easily to changed circumstances.

Output gap The difference between actual and potential output. When actual output exceeds potential output, the gap is positive. When actual output is less than potential output, the gap is negative.

Outsiders Those out of work or employed on a casual, part-time or short-term basis, who have little or no power to influence wages or employment.

Overheads Costs arising from the general running of an organisation, and only indirectly related to the level of output.

Paradox of debt (or paradox of deleveraging) The paradox that one individual can increase his or her net worth by selling assets, but if this is undertaken by a large number of people aggregate net worth declines because asset prices fall.

Paradox of thrift If society saves more, this may *reduce* its future income and consumption. The reason is that as people save more, they will spend less. Firms will thus produce less. There will thus be a multiplied *fall* in income.

Pareto improvement Where changes in production or consumption can make at least one person better off without making anyone worse off.

Pareto optimality Where all possible Pareto improvements have been made: where, therefore, it is impossible to make anyone better off without making someone else worse off.

Partial derivative The partial derivative of a function of two or more independent variables is the derivative with respect to just one of those variables, while holding the others constant.

Partial differentiation A mathematical technique used with functions containing two or more independent variables. The technique is used to find the rate of change of the dependent variable with respect to a single independent variable assuming that the other independent variables are held constant.

Participation rate The percentage of the working-age population that is part of the workforce.

Partnership A firm owned by two or more people. They each have unlimited liability for the firm's debts.

Peak-load pricing Price discrimination (second or third degree) where a higher price is charged in peak periods and a lower price in off-peak periods.

Perfect competition A market structure where there are many firms, none of which is large; where there is freedom of entry into the industry; where all firms produce an identical product; and where all firms are price takers.

Perfectly contestable market A market where there is free and costless entry and exit and the monopolist cannot immediately respond to entry.

Phillips curve A curve showing the relationship between (price) inflation and unemployment. The original Phillips curve plotted *wage* inflation against unemployment for the years 1861–1957.

Picketing When people on strike gather at the entrance to the firm and attempt to persuade workers or delivery vehicles from entering.

Pigouvian tax (or subsidy) A tax (or subsidy) designed to 'internalise' an externality. The marginal rate of a Pigouvian tax (or subsidy) should be equal to the marginal external cost (or benefit).

Plant economies of scale Economies of scale that arise because of the large size of the factory.

Plurilateral trade agreement A trade agreement between more than two countries.

Point elasticity The measurement of elasticity at a point on a curve. The formula for price elasticity of demand using the point elasticity method is: $dQ/dP \times P/Q$, where dQ/dP is the inverse of the slope of the tangent to the demand curve at the point in question.

Policy ineffectiveness proposition The conclusion drawn from new classical models that when economic agents anticipate changes in economic policy, output and employment remain at their equilibrium (or natural) levels.

Political business cycle The theory that governments, after being elected, will engineer an economic contraction, designed to squeeze out inflation. They will then later engineer a pre-election boom to appeal to the electorate.

Poll tax A lump-sum tax per head of the population. Since it is a fixed *amount*, it has a marginal rate of zero with respect to both income and wealth.

Polluter pays principle The principle that polluters ought to be charged (e.g. through green taxes) for the external environmental costs that they generate.

Pooling risks (for an insurance company) The more policies and insurance company issues and the more independent the risks of claims from these policies are, the more predictable will be the number of claims.

Portfolio balance The balance of assets, according to their liquidity, that people choose to hold in their portfolios.

Positive statement A value-free statement which can be tested by an appeal to the facts.

Post-Keynesians Economists who stress the importance of institutional and behavioural factors, and the role of business confidence in explaining the state of the economy. They argue that firms are more likely to respond to changes in demand by changing output rather than prices.

Potential growth The percentage increase in the capacity of the economy to produce.

Potential output The sustainable level output that could be produced in the economy: i.e. one that involves a 'normal' level of capacity utilisation and does not result in rising inflation.

Poverty trap (for developing countries) When countries are too poor to save and invest enough to achieve real per capita growth.

Poverty trap (for individuals) Where poor people are discouraged from working or getting a better job because any extra income they earn will be largely taken away in taxes and lost benefits.

Predatory pricing Where a firm charges a price below its short-run profit-maximising price in order to drive one or more competitors out of the market. This would normally involve setting a price below the average variable cost of a competitor.

Preferential trading arrangements A trade agreement whereby trade between the signatories is freer than trade with the rest of the world.

Present bias Where the relative weight people place on immediate costs and benefits versus those that occur in the future is far greater than predicted by the standard theory of exponential discounting. This can lead to time inconsistent behaviour.

Present value approach to appraising investment This involves estimating the value *now* of a flow of future benefits (or costs).

Present value (in consumption) The value a person places today on a good that will not be consumed until some point in the future.

Price benchmark A price which is typically used. Firms, when raising prices will usually raise it from one benchmark to another.

Price discrimination Where a firm sells the same product at different prices.

Price elasticity of demand (arc formula) ΔQ/average $Q \div \Delta P$/average P. The average in each case is the average between the two points being measured.

Price elasticity of demand ($P\epsilon_D$) The percentage (or proportionate) change in quantity demanded divided by the percentage (or proportionate) change in price: $\%\Delta Q_D \div \%\Delta P$.

Price elasticity of supply (arc formula) ΔQ_S/average $Q_S \div \Delta P$/average P.

Price elasticity of supply ($P\epsilon_S$) The percentage (or proportionate) change in quantity supplied divided by the percentage (or proportionate) change in price: $\%\Delta Q_S \div \%\Delta P$.

Price mechanism The system in a market economy whereby changes in price in response to changes in demand and supply have the effect of making demand equal to supply.

Price taker A person or firm with no power to be able to influence the market price.

Price-cap regulation Where the regulator puts a ceiling on the amount by which a firm can raise its price.

Price–consumption curve A line showing how a person's optimum level of consumption of two goods changes as the price of one of the two goods changes (assuming that income and the price of the other good remain constant).

Prices and incomes policy When the government seeks to restrain price and wage increases. This may be in the form of a voluntary agreement with firms and/or unions, or there may be statutory limits imposed.

Primary labour market The market for permanent full-time core workers.

Primary market in capital Where shares are sold by the issuer of the shares (i.e. the firm) and where, therefore, finance is channelled directly from the purchasers (i.e. the shareholders) to the firm.

Primary surplus (or deficit) The situation when the sum of government expenditures excluding interest payments on its debt is less than (greater than) its receipts.

Principal–agent problem Where people (principals), as a result of lack of knowledge, cannot ensure that their best interests are served by their agents.

Principle of cumulative causation An initial event can cause an ultimate effect that is much larger.

Prisoners' dilemma Where two or more firms (or people), by attempting independently to choose the best strategy for whatever the other(s) are likely to do, end up in a worse position than if they had co-operated in the first place.

Private efficiency Where a person's marginal benefit from a given activity equals the marginal cost.

Private limited company A company owned by its shareholders. Shareholders' liability is limited to the value of their shares. Shares can only be bought and sold privately.

Producers' share of a tax on a good The proportion of the revenue from a tax on a good that arises from a reduction in the price to the producer (after the payment of the tax).

Product differentiation When one firm's product is sufficiently different from its rivals' to allow it to raise the price of the product without customers all switching to the rivals' products. A situation where a firm faces a downward-sloping demand curve.

Production The transformation of inputs into outputs by firms in order to earn profit (or meet some other objective).

Production function The mathematical relationship between the output of a good and the inputs used to produce it. It shows how output will be affected by changes in the quantity of one or more of the inputs used in production, holding the level of technology constant.

Production function (economy's) (or aggregate production function) The relationship between the economy's capital per worker and output per worker (labour productivity), holding the level of human capital and the state of technology constant.

Production possibility curve A curve showing all the possible combinations of two goods that a country can produce within a specified time period with all its resources fully and efficiently employed.

Productive efficiency A situation where firms are producing the maximum output for a given amount of inputs, or producing a given output at the least cost. The least-cost combination of factors for a given output.

Productivity deal When, in return for a wage increase, a union agrees to changes in working practices that will increase output per worker.

Profit (rate of) Total profit ($T\Pi$) as a proportion of the total capital employed (K): $r = T\Pi/K$.

Profit and loss account or **income and expenditure account** A record of the flows of incomes, expenditure and saving of an individual or institution.

Profit satisficing Where decision makers in a firm aim for a target level of profit rather than the absolute maximum level.

Profit-maximising rule Profit is maximised where marginal revenue equals marginal cost.

Progressive tax A tax whose average rate with respect to income rises as income rises.

Propagation mechanisms The means by which economic shocks are transmitted through the economy.

Proportional tax A tax whose average rate with respect to income stays the same as income rises.

Prudential control The insistence by the Bank of England that recognised banks maintain adequate liquidity.

Public good A good or service that has the features of non-rivalry and non-excludability and as a result would not be provided by the free market.

Public limited company A company owned by its shareholders. Shareholders' liability is limited to the value of their shares. Shares may be bought and sold publicly – on the Stock Exchange.

Public-sector current budget deficit The amount by which public-sector expenditures classified as current expenditures exceed public-sector receipts

Public-sector net borrowing (PSNB) The difference between the expenditures of the public sector and its receipts from taxation and the revenues from public corporations.

Public-sector net cash requirement (PSNCR) A UK-based measure of what the public sector must borrow. It is based on when cash is actually paid or received (rather than when it is recorded) and takes into account financial transactions by the public sector.

Public-sector (or general government) net debt Gross public-sector (or general government) debt minus liquid financial assets.

Public-sector surplus or **public-sector debt repayment (PSDR)** The (annual) surplus of the public sector, and thus the amount of debt that can be repaid when public-sector income exceeds public-sector expenditures.

Purchasing-power parity (PPP) exchange rate An exchange rate corrected to take into account the purchasing power of a currency. $1 would buy the same in each country after conversion into its currency at the PPP rate.

Purchasing-power parity theory The theory that the exchange rate will adjust so as to offset differences in countries' inflation rates, with the result that the same quantity of internationally traded goods can be bought at home as abroad with a given amount of the domestic currency.

Purchasing-power standard (PPS) GDP GDP measured as a country's PPP exchange rate.

Pure fiscal policy Fiscal policy which does not involve any change in money supply.

Pure public good A good or service that has the characteristics of being perfectly non-rivalrous and completely non-excludable and as a result, would not be provided by the free market.

Quantiles Divisions of the population into equal-sized groups.

Quantitative easing (QE) A deliberate attempt by the central bank to increase the money supply by buying large quantities of securities through open-market operations. These securities could be securitised mortgage and other private sector debt or government bonds. When banks and other financial institutions lend the money, broad money expands by a multiple of this through the process of credit creation.

Quantity demanded The amount of a good a consumer is willing and able to buy at a given price over a given period of time.

Quantity theory of money The price level (P) is directly related to the quantity of money in the economy (M).

Quasi-rent Temporary economic rent arising from short-run supply inelasticity.

Quintiles Divisions of the population into five equal-sized groups (an example of a quantile).

Quota (set by a cartel) The output that a given member of a cartel is allowed to produce (production quota) or sell (sales quota).

Random walk Where fluctuations in the value of a share away from its 'correct' value are random: i.e. have no systematic pattern. When charted over time, these share price movements would appear like a 'random walk': like the path of someone staggering along drunk!

Rate of discount The rate that is used to reduce future values to present values.

Rate of economic growth The percentage increase in output, normally expressed over a 12-month or 3-month period.

Rate of inflation (annual) The percentage increase in the level of prices over a 12-month period.

Rate of profit Total profit (T) as a proportion of the capital employed (K): $r = T/K$.

Rational choices Choices that involve weighing up the benefit of any activity against its opportunity cost so that the decision maker successfully maximises his or her objective: e.g. happiness or profits.

Rational consumer A person who weighs up the costs and benefits to themself of each additional unit of a good purchased.

Rational consumer behaviour The attempt to maximise total consumer surplus.

Rational economic behaviour Doing more of activities whose marginal benefit exceeds their marginal cost and doing less of those activities whose marginal cost exceeds their marginal benefit.

Rational expectations Expectations based on the *current* situation. These expectations are based on the information people have to hand. Whilst this information may be imperfect and therefore people will make errors, these errors will be random.

Rational producer behaviour When a firm weighs up the costs and benefits of alternative courses of action and then seeks to maximise its net benefit.

Rationalisation The reorganising of production (often after a merger) so as to cut out waste and duplication and generally to reduce costs.

Rationing Where the government restricts the amount of a good that people are allowed to buy.

Reaction function (or curve) This shows how a firm's optimal output varies according to the output chosen by its rival (or rivals).

Real balance effect As the price level rises, so the value of people's money balances will fall. They will therefore *spend* less in order to increase their money balances and go some way to protecting their real value.

Real business cycle theory The new classical theory which explains cyclical fluctuations in terms of shifts in aggregate supply, rather than aggregate demand.

Real exchange rate A country's exchange rate adjusted for changes in the domestic currency prices of its exports relative to the foreign currency prices of its imports. If a country's prices rise (fall) relative to those of its trading partners, its real exchange rate will rise (fall) relative to the nominal exchange rate.

Real GDP GDP after allowing for inflation: i.e. GDP measured in *constant* prices, in other words in terms of the prices ruling in some base year.

Real income Income measured in terms of how much it can buy. If your *money* income rises by 10 per cent, but prices rise by 8 per cent, you can only buy 2 per cent more goods than before. Your *real* income has risen by 2 per cent.

Real national income National income after allowing for inflation: i.e. national income measured in constant prices: i.e. in terms of the prices ruling in some base year.

Real values Money values corrected for inflation.

Real-wage unemployment Disequilibrium unemployment caused by real wages being driven up above the market-clearing level.

Recession A period where national output falls for two successive quarters or more.

Recessionary (or deflationary) gap The shortfall of national expenditure below national income (and injections below withdrawals) at the full-employment level of national income.

Reciprocity (in economics) Where people's behaviour is influenced by the effects it will have on others.

Recognised banks Banks licensed by the Bank of England. All financial institutions using the word 'bank' in their title have to be recognised by the Bank of England. This requires them to have paid-up capital of at least £5 million and to meet other requirements about their asset structure and range of services.

Rediscounting bills of exchange Buying bills before they reach maturity.

Reference dependent loss aversion Where people value (or 'code') outcomes as either losses or gains in relation to a reference point such that losses are disliked more than would be predicted by standard diminishing marginal utility.

Reference dependent preferences Where people value (or 'code') outcomes as either gains or losses in relation to a reference point.

Reflationary policy Fiscal or monetary policy designed to increase the rate of growth of aggregate demand.

Regional Development Agencies (RDAs) Nine agencies, based in English regions, which initiate and administer regional policy within their area.

Regional multiplier effects When a change in injections into or withdrawals from a particular region causes a multiplied change in income in that region. The regional multiplier (k_r) is given by $1/mpw_r$, where the import component of *mpw*, consists of imports into that region either from abroad or from other regions of the economy.

Regional unemployment Structural unemployment occurring in specific regions of the country.

Regression analysis A statistical technique which allows a functional relationship between two or more variables to be estimated.

Regressive tax A tax whose average rate with respect to income falls as income rises.

Regulatory capture Where the regulator is persuaded to operate in the industry's interests rather than those of the consumer.

Relative price The price of one good compared with another (e.g. good X is twice the price of good Y).

Replacement costs What the firm would have to pay to replace factors it currently owns.

Resale (or retail) price maintenance Where the manufacturer of a product (legally) insists that the product should be sold at a specified retail price.

Reserve averaging The process whereby individual banks manage their average level of overnight reserves between MPC meetings using the Bank of England's operational standing facilities and/or the inter-bank market.

Residual demand curve A firm's residual demand curve illustrates the relationship between the output it produces and the market price for the product, holding constant the output produced by other firms.

Restrictive practice Where two or more firms agree to adopt common practices to restrict competition.

Retail banks 'High street banks'. Banks operating extensive branch networks and dealing directly with the general public, with published interest rates and charges.

Retail deposits and loans Deposits and loans made through bank/building society branches at published interest rates.

Retail price index (RPI) An index of the prices of goods bought by a typical household.

Revaluation Where the government re-pegs the exchange rate at a higher level.

Reverse repos When gilts or other assets are *purchased* under a sale and repurchase agreement. They become an asset to the purchaser.

Risk When a (desirable) outcome of an action may or may not occur, but the probability of its occurring is known. The lower the probability, the greater the risk involved in taking the action.

Risk averse Where a person is not prepared to take a gamble even if the odds of gaining are favourable.

Risk loving Where a person is willing to take a gamble even if the odds of gaining are unfavourable.

Risk neutral Where a person is willing to take a gamble if the odds are favourable and is unwilling if the odds are unfavourable.

Risk premium The expected value of a gamble minus a person's certainty equivalent.

Risk transformation The process whereby banks can spread the risks of lending by having a large number of borrowers.

Sale and repurchase agreement (repos) An agreement between two financial institutions whereby one in effect borrows from another by selling it assets, agreeing to buy them back (repurchase them) at a fixed price and on a fixed date.

Sales revenue maximisation An alternative theory of the firm based on the assumption that managers aim to maximise the firm's short-run total revenue.

Say's law Supply creates its own demand. In other words, the production of goods will generate sufficient demand to ensure that they are sold.

Scarcity The excess of human wants over what can actually be produced to fulfil these wants.

Scarring effects The idea that an economic downturn can result in long-lasting damage to the economy and to individuals' economic situations.

Search theory This examines people's behaviour under conditions of ignorance where it takes time to search for information.

Seasonal unemployment Unemployment associated with industries or regions where the demand for labour is lower at certain times of the year.

Second best (problem of) The difficulty of working out the best way of correcting a specific market distortion if distortions in other parts of the market continue to exist.

Second derivative The rate of change of the first derivative: found by differentiating the first derivative.

Second derivative test If on differentiating an equation a second time the answer is negative (positive), the point is a maximum (minimum).

Secondary action Industrial action taken against a company not directly involved in a dispute (e.g. a supplier of raw materials to a firm whose employees are on strike).

Secondary labour market The market for peripheral workers, usually employed on a temporary or part-time basis, or a less secure 'permanent' basis.

Secondary market in capital Where shareholders sell shares to others. This is thus a market in 'second-hand' shares.

Secondary marketing Where assets are sold before maturity to another institution or individual. The possibility of secondary marketing encourages people or institutions to buy assets/grant loans in the primary market, knowing that they can sell them if necessary in the secondary market. The sale of existing shares and bonds on the stock market is an example of secondary marketing.

Second-best solution The solution to a specific market distortion that recognises distortions elsewhere and seeks to minimise the overall distortionary effects to the economy of tackling this specific distortion.

Second-degree price discrimination Where a firm offers consumers a range of different pricing options for the same or similar product. Consumers are then free to choose whichever option they wish but the price is often dependent on some factor such as the quantity purchased.

Securitisation Where future cash flows (e.g. from interest rate or mortgage payments) are turned into marketable securities, such as bonds. The sellers (e.g. banks) get cash now rather than having to wait and can use it to fund loans to customers. The buyers make a profit by buying below the discounted value of the future income. Such bonds can be very risky, however, as the future cash flows may be less than anticipated.

Self-fulfilling speculation The actions of speculators tend to cause the very effect that they had anticipated.

Semi-strong efficiency (of share markets) Where share prices adjust quickly, fully and accurately to publicly available information.

Sensitivity analysis Where a range of possible values of uncertain costs and benefits are given to see whether the project's desirability is sensitive to these different values.

Sequential move game One firm (the first mover) makes and implements a decision. Rival firms (second movers) can observe the actions taken by the first mover before making their own decisions.

Set-aside A system in the EU of paying farmers not to use a certain proportion of their land.

Shadow (or illegal or underground) markets Where people ignore the government's price and/or quantity controls and sell illegally at whatever price equates illegal demand and supply.

Shares (equities) A part ownership of a company. Companies' distributed profits are paid to shareholders in the form of dividends according to the number of shares held.

Short run (in production) The period of time over which at least one factor is fixed.

Short run under perfect competition The period during which there is insufficient time for new firms to enter the industry.

Short selling The practice of borrowing an asset (for a fee) and selling it, hoping that the price will fall so that it can then be purchased and returned to the lender. The difference between the sale and purchase price (minus the fee) is thus profit to the short seller.

Short-run shut-down point This is where the *AR* curve is tangential to the *AVC* curve. The firm can only just cover its variable costs. Any fall in revenue below this level will cause a profit-maximising firm to shut down immediately.

Short-termism Where firms and investors take decisions based on the likely short-term performance of a company, rather than on its long-term prospects. Firms may thus sacrifice long-term profits and growth for the sake of a quick return.

Sight deposits Deposits that can be withdrawn on demand without penalty.

Simultaneous single-move game A game where each player has just one move, where each player plays at the same time and acts without knowledge of the actions chosen by other players.

Size distribution of income Measurement of the distribution of income according to the levels of income received by individuals (irrespective of source).

Social benefit Private benefit plus externalities in consumption.

Social capital (OECD definition) Networks, together with shared norms, values and understandings, that facilitate co-operation within or among groups.

Social cost Private cost plus externalities in production.

Social efficiency A situation of Pareto optimality: where all possible Pareto improvements have been made: where, therefore, it is impossible to make anyone better off without making someone else worse off.

Social efficiency (improvement in) A Pareto improvement: where changes in production or consumption can make at least one person better off without making anyone worse off.

Social rate of discount A rate of discount that reflects *society's* preferences for present benefits over future ones.

Social surplus Total social benefits minus total social costs.

Social-impact standards Pollution control that focuses on the effects on people (e.g. on health or happiness).

Socially optimal or **socially efficient output** The output where $MSC = MSB$: the output where total social surplus is maximised.

Sole proprietorship A firm owned by one person. That person has unlimited liability.

Solow growth model A model which explains economic growth in terms of the effects on the capital stock and output of a change in investment.

Sovereign debt crisis The financial and economic problems caused by excessive public-sector debt and by the fear that governments will be unable to raise sufficient finance to repay maturing debt.

Special drawing rights (SDRs) Additional liquidity created by the IMF. SDRs give countries the right to borrow a certain amount of additional funds from the IMF, with no requirement for extra deposits (quotas).

Special purpose vehicle (SPV) Legal entities created by financial institutions for conducting specific financial functions, such as bundling assets together into fixed interest bonds and selling them.

Specialisation and division of labour Where production is broken down into a number of simpler, more specialised tasks, thus allowing workers to acquire a high degree of efficiency.

Specific tax A tax on a good levied at a fixed amount per unit of the good, irrespective of the price of that unit.

Speculation Where people make buying or selling decisions based on their anticipations of future prices.

Speculators People who buy (or sell) commodities or financial assets with the intention of profiting by selling them (or buying them back) at a later date at a higher (lower) price.

Spot price The current market price.

Spreading risks (for an insurance company) The more policies an insurance company issues and the more independent the risks of claims from these policies are, the more predictable will be the number of claims.

Stabilising speculation Where the actions of speculators tend to reduce the magnitude of price fluctuations.

Stagflation A term used to refer to the combination of stagnation (low growth and high unemployment) and high inflation.

Stakeholders (in a company) People who are affected by a company's activities and/or performance (customers, employees, owners, creditors, people living in the neighbourhood, etc.). They may or may not be in a position to take decisions, or influence decision taking, in the firm.

Standardised unemployment rate The measure of the unemployment rate used by the ILO and OECD. The unemployed are defined as persons of working age who are without work, available to start work within two weeks and either have actively looked for work in the last four weeks or are waiting to take up an appointment.

Steady-state (per worker) growth path The growth path of output per worker for a given saving rate (where growth results from technological progress).

Steady-state level of national income The long-run equilibrium level of national income. The level at which all investment is used to maintain the existing capital stock at its current level.

Sterilisation Actions (e.g. open-market operations) taken by a central bank to offset the effects of foreign exchange flows or its own bond transactions so as to leave money supply unchanged.

Stochastic shocks Shocks that are random and hence unpredictable, or predicable only as occurring within a range of values.

Stock An amount of something (inputs, goods, money, etc.) existing at a point of time. (Contrasts with *flow*.)

Stock (or inventory) appreciation The increase in monetary value of stocks due to increased prices. Since this does not represent increased output, it is not included in GDP.

Stop–go policies Alternate deflationary and reflationary policies to tackle the currently most pressing of the four problems which fluctuate with the business cycle.

Strategic alliance Where two firms work together, formally or informally, to achieve a mutually desirable goal.

Strategic trade theory The theory that protecting/supporting certain industries can enable them to compete more effectively with large monopolistic rivals abroad. The effect of the protection is to increase long-run competition and may enable the protected firms to exploit a comparative advantage that they could not have done otherwise.

Strong efficiency (of share markets) Where share prices adjust quickly, fully and accurately to all available information, both public and that only available to insiders.

Structural public-sector deficit (or surplus) The public-sector deficit (or surplus) that would occur if the economy were operating at the potential level of national income: i.e. one where there is a zero output gap.

Structural unemployment Equilibrium unemployment that arises from changes in the pattern of demand or supply in the economy. People made redundant in one part of the economy cannot immediately take up jobs in other parts (even though there are vacancies).

Structuralists Economists who focus on specific barriers to development and how to overcome them.

Subcontracting Where a firm employs another firm to produce part of its output or some of its input(s).

Sub-prime debt Debt where there is a high risk of default by the borrower (e.g. mortgage holders who are on low incomes facing higher interest rates and falling house prices).

Subsistence production Where people produce things for their own consumption.

Substitute goods A pair of goods which are considered by consumers to be alternatives to each other. As the price of one goes up, the demand for the other rises.

Substitutes in supply These are two goods where an increased production of one means diverting resources away from producing the other.

Substitution effect of a price change The effect of a change in price on quantity demanded arising from the consumer switching to or from alternative (substitute) products.

Substitution effect of a rise in wage rates Workers will tend to substitute income for leisure as leisure now has a higher opportunity cost. This effect leads to *more* hours being worked as wage rates rise.

Substitution effect of a tax rise Tax increases reduce the opportunity cost of leisure and thus encourage people to work less.

Substitution effect – international As prices rise, people at home and abroad buy less of this country's products and more of products from abroad.

Sunk costs Costs that cannot be recouped (e.g. by transferring assets to other uses). Examples include specialised machinery or the costs of an advertising campaign.

Super hysteresis The situation where a recession not only affects subsequent levels of national output but also subsequent rates of growth.

Supernormal profit (also known as **pure profit, economic profit, abnormal profit**, or simply **profit**) The excess of total profit above normal profit.

Supply curve A graph showing the relationship between the price of a good and the quantity of the good supplied over a given period of time.

Supply schedule A table showing the different quantities of a good that producers are willing and able to supply at various prices over a given time period. A supply schedule can be for an individual producer or group of producers, or for all producers (the market supply schedule).

Supply-side economics An approach which focuses directly on aggregate supply and how to shift the aggregate supply curve outwards.

Supply-side policies Government policies that attempt to alter the level of aggregate supply directly (rather than through changes in aggregate demand). Such policies aim to increase *potential* output. They focus on increasing the quantity and/or productivity of resources.

Surplus on the current budget The amount by which public-sector receipts exceed those expenditures classified as current expenditures.

Sustainability (environmental) The ability of the environment to survive its use for economic activity.

Sustainable output The level of national output corresponding to no excess or deficiency of aggregate demand.

Switching costs The costs to a consumer of switching to an alternative supplier.

Systemically important banks (SIBs) Banks identified by a series of indicators as being significant players in the global financial system.

Tacit collusion Where oligopolists take care not to engage in price cutting, excessive advertising or other forms of competition. There may be unwritten 'rules' of collusive behaviour such as price leadership.

Takeover bid Where one firm attempts to purchase another by offering to buy the shares of that company from its shareholders.

Takeover constraint The effect that the fear of being taken over has on a firm's willingness to undertake projects that reduce distributed profits.

Target real wage theory The theory that unions bargain for target real wage increases each year irrespective of the level of real growth in the economy.

Tariff escalation The system whereby tariff rates increase the closer a product is to the finished stage of production.

Tariffs (or import levies) Taxes on imported products: i.e. customs duties.

Tax allowance An amount of income that can be earned tax-free. Tax allowances vary according to a person's circumstances.

Tax avoidance The rearrangement of one's affairs so as to reduce one's tax liability.

Tax evasion The illegal non-payment of taxes (e.g. by not declaring income earned).

Taylor rule A rule adopted by a central bank for setting the rate of interest. It will raise the interest rate if (a) inflation is above target or (b) real national income is above the sustainable level (or unemployment is below the natural rate). The rule states how much interest rates will be changed in each case.

Technical efficiency The firm is producing as much output as is technologically possible given the quantity of factor inputs it is using.

Technological unemployment Structural unemployment that occurs as a result of the introduction of labour-saving technology.

Technology-based standards Pollution control that requires firms' emissions to reflect the levels that could be achieved from using the best available pollution control technology.

Terms of trade The price index of exports divided by the price index of imports and then expressed as a percentage. This means that the terms of trade will be 100 in the base year

Theory of the firm (traditional) The analysis of pricing and output decisions of the firm under various market conditions, assuming that the firm wishes to maximise profit.

Third-degree price discrimination Where a firm divides consumers into different groups based on some characteristic that is relatively easy to observe and informative about how much consumers are willing to pay. The firm then charges a different price to consumers in different groups, but the same price to all the consumers within a group.

Tie-in sales Where a firm is only prepared to sell a first product on the condition that its customers by a second product from it.

Time consistency Where a person's preferences remain the same over time. For example, it is time consistent if you plan to buy a book when your student loan arrives and then actually do so when it does.

Time deposits Deposits that require notice of withdrawal or where a penalty is charged for withdrawals on demand.

Time-consistent policy announcement A policy announcement where there is an incentive for the policy maker to stick to it over time.

Time-inconsistent policy announcement A policy announcement where there is an incentive for the policy maker to renege on it at a future date.

Time-series data Information depicting how a variable (e.g. the price of eggs) changes over time.

Total consumer expenditure on a product (*TE*) (per period of time) The price of the product multiplied by the quantity purchased: $TE = PQ$.

Total consumer surplus The excess of a person's total utility from the consumption of a good (TU) over the amount that person spends on it over the amount that person spends on it (TE): $TCS = TU - TE$.

Total cost The sum of total fixed costs and total variable costs: $TC = TFC + TVC$.

Total currency flow on the balance of payments The current plus capital plus financial account balance but excluding the reserves.

Total physical product The total output of a product per period of time that is obtained from a given amount of inputs.

Total (private) surplus Total consumer surplus ($TU - TE$) plus total producer surplus ($TR - TVC$).

Total producer surplus (*TPS*) Total revenue minus total variable cost ($TR - TVC$): in other words, total profit plus total fixed cost ($T\Pi + TFC$).

Total revenue A firm's total earnings from a specified level of sales within a specified period: $TR = P \times Q$.

Total revenue (*TR*) (per period of time) The total amount received by firms from the sale of a product, before the deduction of taxes or any other costs. The price multiplied by the quantity sold. $TR = P \times Q$.

Total social surplus Total benefits to society from consuming a good minus total costs to society from producing it. In the absence of externalities, total social surplus is the same as total (private) surplus.

Total utility The total satisfaction a consumer gets from the consumption of all the units of a good consumed within a given time period.

Tradable permits Firms are issued or sold permits by the authorities that give them the right to produce a given level of pollution. Firms that do not have sufficient permits to match their pollution levels can purchase additional permits to cover the difference, while those that reduce their pollution levels can sell any surplus permits for a profit.

Trade creation Where a customs union leads to greater specialisation according to comparative advantage and thus a shift in production from higher-cost to lower-cost sources.

Trade cycle or **business cycle** The periodic fluctuations of national output round its long-term trend.

Trade diversion Where a customs union diverts consumption from goods produced at a lower cost outside the union to goods produced at a higher cost (but tariff free) within the union.

Traditional theory of the firm The analysis of pricing and output decisions of the firm under various market conditions, assuming that the firm wishes to maximise profit.

Tragedy of the commons When resources are commonly available at no charge people are likely to overexploit them.

Transfer payments Moneys transferred from one person or group to another (e.g. from the government to individuals) without production taking place.

Transfers (by the government) Transfers of money from taxpayers to recipients of benefits and subsidies. They are not an injection into the circular flow but are the equivalent of a negative tax (i.e. a negative withdrawal).

Treasury bills Bills of exchange issued by the Bank of England on behalf of the government. They are a means whereby the government raises short-term finance.

Trigger strategy Once a firm observes that its rival has broken some agreed behaviour it never co-operates with them again.

Tying Where a firm is only prepared to sell a first product (the tying good) on the condition that its consumers buy a second product from it (the tied good).

U-form (unitary form) of corporate organisation Where the managers of the various departments of a firm are directly responsible to head office, normally to a chief executive.

Uncertainty When an outcome may or may not occur and its probability of occurring is not known.

Underemployment Where people who want full-time work are only able to find part-time work.

Underground (or illegal or shadow) markets Where people ignore the government's price and/or quantity controls and sell illegally at whatever price equates illegal demand and supply.

Unemployment The number of people of working age who are actively looking for work but are currently without a job. (Note that there is much debate as to who should officially be counted as unemployed.)

Unemployment rate The number unemployed expressed as a percentage of the labour force.

Unit elastic demand Where quantity demanded changes by the same percentage as price. Ignoring the negative sign, it will have a value equal to 1.

Universal benefits Benefits paid to everyone in a certain category irrespective of their income or assets.

Util An imaginary unit of satisfaction from the consumption of a good.

Value added tax (VAT) A tax on goods and services, charged at each stage of production as a percentage of the value added at that stage.

Variable costs Total costs that vary with the amount of output produced.

Variable factor An input that can be increased in supply within a given time period.

Velocity of circulation The number of times annually that money on average is spent on goods and services that make up GDP.

Vent for surplus When international trade enables a country to exploit resources that would otherwise be unused.

Vertical equity The redistribution from the better off to the worse off. In the case of taxes, this means the rich paying proportionately more taxes than the poor.

Vertical merger When two firms in the same industry at different stages in the production process merge.

Vertical restraints Conditions imposed by one firm on another which is either its supplier or its customer.

Wage taker An employer or employee who has no power to influence the market wage rate.

Wage–price spiral Wages and prices chasing each other as the aggregate demand curve continually shifts to the right and the aggregate supply curve continually shifts upwards.

Weak efficiency (of share markets) Where share dealing prevents cyclical movements in shares.

Weighted average The average of several items where each item is ascribed a weight according to its importance. The weights must add up to 1.

Wholesale banks Banks specialising in large-scale deposits and loans and dealing mainly with companies.

Wholesale deposits and loans Large-scale deposits and loans made by and to firms at negotiated interest rates.

Withdrawals (*W*) (or leakages) Incomes of households or firms that are not passed on round the inner flow. Withdrawals equal net saving (S) plus net taxes (T) plus expenditure on imports (M): $W = S + T + M$.

Working to rule Workers do the bare minimum they have to, as set out in their job descriptions.

X inefficiency When a firm fails to be technically efficient because of a lack of competitive pressures to cut costs.

Yield on a share The dividend received per share expressed as a percentage of the current market price of the share.

Publisher's Acknowledgements

Image credits:

FM, 5, 1, 2, 33, 34, 77, 103, 104, 131, 153, 194, 223, 257, 283, 323, 324, 355, 400, 428, 451, 452, 500, 529, 530, 561, 599, 635, 693, 736, 771, 772, 813, 851, 893, 894 John Sloman: Courtesy of John Sloman; **FM Dr Dean Garratt:** Courtesy of Dr Dean Garratt; **FM Jon Guest:** Courtesy of Jon Guest; **530 Central Intelligence Agency:** Political World Map, CIA World Factbook; **661 Alamy Images:** History collection 2016/Alamy Stock Photo.

Text credits:

9 European Commission: Statistical Annex of the European Economy (Commission of the European Communities, various tables and years); **9 International Monetary Fund:** World Economic Outlook (IMF, April 2021).; **23 International Monetary Fund:** Data drawn from World Economic Outlook Database (IMF, April 2021), www.imf.org/external/pubs/ft/weo/2019/02/weodata/index.aspx; **24 Strahan publisher:** Adam Smith, An Inquiry into the Nature and Causes of the Wealth of Nations, Volume 1, chapter 2, Page 17, 1776.; **24 University Press:** Adam Smith, An Inquiry into the Nature and Causes of the Wealth of Nations, Volume 4, chapter 2, 1827.; **25 Strahan publisher:** Adam Smith, An Inquiry into the Nature and Causes of the Wealth of Nations, Volume 1, chapter 7, Page 75, 1776.; **49 Lloyds Banking Group plc:** Based on data in Halifax House Price Index (Lloyds Banking Group), www.halifax.co.uk/assets/pdf/march-2021-house-price-index-pdf; **52 Office for National Statistics:** Based on data from RPI All Items Index (ONS), www.ons.gov.uk/economy/inflationandpriceindices/timeseries/chaw/mm23; and various, 2021; **82 The Home Office:** Next steps following the consultation on delivering the government's alcohol strategy, p. 3, Home Office (July 2013), https://assets.publishing.service.gov.uk/government/uploads/system/uploads/attachment_data/file/223773/Alcohol_consultation_response_report_v3.pdf; **83 Parallel Parliament:** Written questions, answers and Statements, UK Parliament (24 February 2020), https://questions-statements.parliament.uk/written-questions/detail/2020-02-24/HL1749; **85 IGM Forum:** 'Prices of medical supplies', IGM Forum (26 May 2020), www.igmchicago.org/surveys/prices-of-medical-supplies-2/; **95 University of Reading:** JS in Richard Tiffin, Kelvin Balcombe, Matthew Salois and Ariane Kehlbacher Estimating Food and Drink Elasticities (University of Reading, 2011); **95 Office for National Statistics:** Income elasticity data: National Food Survey 2000 (National Statistics, 2001), extracted by JS from Tables 6.3 and 6.5; **111 Adam Smith:** Quoted by Adam Smith; **120 Department for Education:** Free School Meals: Voucher Schemes, Department for Education; **120 BBC:** Coronavirus: Call for cash to replace school meal vouchers', BBC News (14 April 2020); **126 American Economic Association:** Robert T Jensen and Nolan H Miller, 'Giffen behaviour and subsistence consumption', American Economic Review, Vol. 98, No. 4 (2008), pp. 1553–77; **155 Macmillan Publishers:** T. R. Malthus, First Essay on Population (Macmillan, 1798), pp. 13–14; **155 United Nations:** World Population Prospects: The 2019 Revision (United Nations, Department of Economic and Social Affairs), https://population.un.org/wpp/ (Medium variant for predictions); **179 European Commission:** C. F. Pratten, 'A survey of the economies of scale', in Research into the 'Costs of Non-Europe', Volume 2 (Commission of the European Communities, Luxembourg, 1988).; **180 European Commission:** European Commission/Economists Advisory Group Ltd, 'Economies of scale', The Single Market Review, Sub-series V, Volume 4 (Commission of the European Communities, Luxembourg, 1997).; **196 The Resolution Foundation:** Based on data in Is everybody concentrating? Resolution Foundation; **201 The Economist Newspaper Limited:** 'A thinkers' guide', The Economist (30 March 2000), www.economist.com/business-special/2000/03/30/a-thinkers-guide; **204 Office for National Statistics:** Based on series J4MC from Time Series Data (National Statistics), www.ons.gov.uk/businessindustryandtrade/retailindustry/timeseries/j4mc/drsi; **205 Office for National Statistics:** How our internet activity has influenced the way we shop: October 2019, ONS (November 2019), www.ons.gov.uk/businessindustryandtrade/retailindustry/articles/howourinternetactivityhasinfluencedthewayweshop/october2019; **228 Department for Business, Energy and Industrial Strategy:** The State of UK Competition, November 2020, Competition and Markets Authority (30 November 2020); **233 The World Bank Group:** Nominal oil price data from World Commodity Price Data (The Pink Sheet), Commodity Markets (World Bank); **233 Organisation for Economic**

Co-operation and Development: Price Index from Data Extracts (OECD); **263 Elsevier:** Robert Piron and Luis Fernandez, 'Are fairness constraints on profit seeking important?' Journal of Economic Psychology, Vol. 16, (March 1995), pp. 73–96, www.sciencedirect.com/science/article/abs/pii/016748709400037B; **263 Bloomberg L.P:** Tyler Cowen, 'Price gouging can be a type of hurricane aid', Bloomberg Opinion (5 September 2017), www.bloomberg.com/opinion/articles/2017-09-05/price-gouging-can-be-a-type-of-hurricane-aid; **263 John Wiley & Sons, Inc:** Luis Cabral and Lei Xu. 'Seller reputation and price gouging: Evidence from the COVID-19 pandemic', Economic In?uiry, (7 March 2021); **263 American Economic Association:** Daniel Kahneman, Jack L Knetch and Richard Thaler, 'Fairness as a constraint of profit seeking: Entitlement in the market'. American Economic Review, Vol. 76 (4) (September 1986) ; **270 The United Nations Conference on Trade and Development:** 'Cross Border Mergers & Acquisitions', World Investment Report Annex Tables (UNCTAD, June 2021), Tables 5 and 7, http://unctad.org/en/Pages/DIAE/World_Investment_Report/Annex-Tables.aspx; **271 The United Nations Conference on Trade and Development:** 'Cross Border Mergers & Acquisitions' World Investment Report Annex Tables (UNCTAD, June 2021), Tables 7 and 5, http://unctad.org/en/Pages/DIAE/World_Investment_Report/Annex-Tables.aspx; **278 John Wiley & Sons, Inc:** Jennifer Greenslade and Miles Parker 'New insights into price-setting behaviour in the UK: Introduction and survey results' The Economic Journal, Vol. 122, Issue 558 (February 2012), https://onlinelibrary.wiley.com/doi/abs/10.1111/j.1468-0297.2011.02492.x; **279 John Wiley & Sons, Inc:** Jennifer Greenslade and Miles Parker 'New insights into price-setting behaviour in the UK: Introduction and survey results' The Economic Journal, Vol. 122, Issue 558 (February 2012), https://onlinelibrary.wiley.com/doi/abs/10.1111/j.1468-0297.2011.02492.x; **279 European Central Bank:** Richard Morris and Rupert de Vincent-Humphreys, 'Price-setting behaviour: insights from a survey of large firms', European Central Bank Economic Bulletin Boxes (November 2019), www.ecb.europa.eu/pub/economic-bulletin/focus/2019/html/ecb.ebbox201907_04~1d48c6bf77.en.html; **288 The Home Office:** Ciaran Devlin, Olivia Bolt, Dhiren Patel, David Harding and Ishtiaq Hussain. Impacts of migration on UK native employment: An analytical review of the evidence, Home Office and Department for Business, Innovation and Skills (March 2014), https://assets.publishing.service.gov.uk/government/uploads/system/uploads/attachment_data/file/287287/occ109.pdf; **294 John Wiley & Sons, Inc:** F. Engels, The Condition of the Working Class in England, translated by W. O. Henderson and W. H. Chaloner (Basil Blackwell, 1971), pp. 199–200; **299 Department for Business, Energy and Industrial Strategy:** Based on Trade union statistics 2019, Table 1.2b (BEIS and ONS), www.gov.uk/government/statistics/trade-union-statistics-2019; **300 Office for National Statistics:** Annual Survey of Hours and Earnings (National Statistics, 2019).; **300 Office for National Statistics:** Annual Survey of Hours and Earnings (ONS, 2019).; **303 Department for Business, Energy and Industrial Strategy:** The characteristics of those in the gig economy, Department for Business, Energy & Industrial Strategy (February 2018), https://assets.publishing.service.gov.uk/government/uploads/system/uploads/attachment_data/file/687553/The_characteristics_of_those_in_the_gig_economy.pdf; **303 The Supreme court:** Uber BV and others (Appellants) v Aslam and others (Respondents) [2021] UKSC 5 On appeal from: [2018] EWCA Civ 2748' Press Summary, The Supreme Court (19 February 2021), www.supremecourt.uk/presssummary/uksc-2019-0029.html; **326 Office for National Statistics:** Based on data from Household Disposable Income and Inequality, UK, 2019/20 – Reference Tables, Table 12, ONS (January 2021), www.ons.gov.uk/peoplepopulationandcommunity/personalandhouseholdfinances/incomeandwealth/datasets/householddisposableincomeandinequality; **328 Office for National Statistics:** Based on data from Household Disposable Income and Inequality, UK, 2019/20 – Reference Tables, Table 9, ONS (January 2021), www.ons.gov.uk/peoplepopulationandcommunity/personalandhouseholdfinances/incomeandwealth/datasets/householddisposableincomeandinequality; **328 Organisation for Economic Co-operation and Development:** Based on data in Income Inequality, OECD dataset (accessed 21 April 2021), https://data.oecd.org/inequality/income-inequality.htm; **328 The World Bank Group:** World Bank Gini Index (2021), https://data.worldbank.org/indicator/SI.POV.GINI; **329 The World Bank Group:** World Development Indicators: Distribution of income or consumption, Table 1.3, The World Bank (various years), http://wdi.worldbank.org/tables; **330 Office for National Statistics:** Based on data from Household Disposable Income and Inequality, UK, 2019/20 – Reference Tables, Table 28, ONS (January 2021), www.ons.gov.uk/peoplepopulationandcommunity/personalandhouseholdfinances/incomeandwealth/datasets/householddisposableincomeandinequality; **331 Office for National Statistics:** The effects of taxes and benefits on household income, disposable income estimate: 2020, Table 13, ONS (January 2021), www.ons.gov.uk/peoplepopulationandcommunity/personalandhouseholdfinances/incomeandwealth/datasets/householddisposableincomeandinequality; **331 Office for National Statistics:** Based on data in the Annual Survey of Hours and Earnings, Table 14.2a, National Statistics (October 2020), www.ons.gov.uk/employmentandlabourmarket/peopleinwork/earningsandworkinghours/datasets/occupation4digitsoc2010ashetable14; **332 Office for National Statistics:** Based on data in The Effects of Taxes and Benefits on UK Household Income, Table 12, National Statistics (2020), www.ons.gov.uk/peoplepopulationandcommunity/personalandhouseholdfinances/incomeandwealth/bulletins/theeffectsoftaxesandbenefitsonhouseholdincome/financialyearending2018/relateddata; **333 Office for National Statistics:** Based on data in

The Effects of Taxes and Benefits on UK Household Income, Table 17, ONS (2020), www.ons.gov.uk/peoplepopulationandcommunity/personalandhouseholdfinances/incomeandwealth/datasets/theeffectsoftaxesandbenefitsonhouseholdincomefinancialyearending2014; **333 Office for National Statistics:** Based on Total Wealth: Wealth in Great Britain: April 2016 to March 2018, National Statistics (5 December 2019), www.ons.gov.uk/peoplepopulationandcommunity/personalandhouseholdfinances/incomeandwealth/bulletins/totalwealthingreatbritain/latest; **334 Progress Publishers:** F. Engels, The Condition of the Working Class in England (Progress Publishers, 1973), pp. 166–7; **341 Organisation for Economic Co-operation and Development:** Extracted from Revenue statistics tables in StatExtracts, OECD, https://data.oecd.org/tax/tax-revenue.htm#indicator-chart; **347 Economic Review:** This box is based on D. Ulph, 'Tax cuts: will they work?', Economic Review (March 1987); **349 European Commission:** Based on data in Social Protection tables, Eurostat (2021), https://ec.europa.eu/eurostat/databrowser/view/tps00098/default/table?lang=en; **391 Department of Transport:** Economic Case for HS2 – the Y Network and London–West Midlands, Department for Transport (February 2011), https://webarchive.nationalarchives.gov.uk/20110720164411/http://highspeedrail.dft.gov.uk/sites/highspeedrail.dft.gov.uk/files/hs2-economiccase.pdf; **391 Department of Transport:** Full Business Case: High Speed Two, Table 2.9, Department for Transport (April 2020), https://assets.publishing.service.gov.uk/government/uploads/system/uploads/attachment_data/file/939905/full-business-case-hs2-phase-one.pdf; **392 House of commons:**'Public Accounts Committee Oral evidence: Department for Transport Recall', Public Accounts Committee, House of Commons (15 October 2020), https://committees.parliament.uk/oralevidence/1038/default/; **393 Department of Transport:** Based on Department for Transport; **397 American Economic Association:** F. von Hayek, 'The use of knowledge in society', American Economic Review (September 1945), p. 519, www.econlib.org/library/Essays/hykKnw.html; **397 Penguin Random House Group:** L. von Mises, Socialism: An Economic and Sociological Analysis (Jonathan Cape, 1936), p. 138, https://mises.org/library/socialism-economic-and-sociological-analysis; **410 Office for National Statistics:** Environmental Taxes, Table 1 (ONS, 3 June 2020), www.ons.gov.uk/economy/environmentalaccounts/datasets/ukenvironmentalaccountsenvironmentaltaxes; **411 Organisation for Economic Co-operation and Development:** Based on data in Environmental Taxation (OECD, 2021), www.oecd.org/environment/tools-evaluation/environmentaltaxation.htm; **418 Department of Transport:** Based on data from Table TSGB0101, Transport Statistics of Great Britain Database 2020 (Department for Transport, December 2020), www.gov.uk/government/statistical-data-sets/tsgb01-modal-comparisons; **419 Office for National Statistics:** Based on data in Family spending workbook 1: detailed expenditure and trends (National Statistics, March 2021), www.ons.gov.uk/peoplepopulationandcommunity/personalandhouseholdfinances/expenditure/datasets/familyspendingworkbook1detailedexpenditureandtrends; **419 European Commission:** Passenger cars per 1000 inhabitants (Eurostat, 2021), https://ec.europa.eu/eurostat/web/products-datasets/-/ROAD_EQS_CARHAB; **431 European Commission:** Cartel Statistics, Competition DG, European Commission (December 2020), https://ec.europa.eu/competition/cartels/statistics/statistics.pdf; **433 European Commission:** 'Antitrust: Commission on fines five envelope producers over 19.4 million in cartel settlement'. Press release (European Commission, 11 December 2014), https://ec.europa.eu/commission/presscorner/api/files/document/print/en/ip_14_2583/IP_14_2583_EN.pdf; **438 Home Department by Command of Her Majesty:** 'Decision on relevant merger situation and substantial lessening of competition', Phase 1 Full text decision, CMA (17 July 2020), https://assets.publishing.service.gov.uk/media/5f11717ed3bf7f5bb2fd2752/VSH_Decision_on_SLC.pdf; **454 International Monetary Fund:** Based on data in World Economic Outlook, IMF (April 2021), www.imf.org/en/Publications/SPROLLS/world-economic-outlook-databases; **463 European Commission:** AMECO database, Table 6.2, European Commission, DGECFIN; **465 Office for National Statistics:** Personal Well-being across the UK, 2015/16 (Office for National Statistics, July 2016).; **465 Office for National Statistics:** Personal well-being in the UK, quarterly: April 2011 to September 2020, Office for National Statistics (February 2021), www.ons.gov.uk/peoplepopulationandcommunity/wellbeing/bulletins/personalwellbeingintheukquarterly/april2011toseptember2020; **469 International Monetary Fund:** Based on data in World Economic Outlook Database, IMF (April 2021), www.imf.org/external/ns/cs.aspx?id=28; **470 Office for National Statistics:** Based on data in Quarterly National Accounts, series KGZ7, KG7T and IHYR, ONS, www.ons.gov.uk/economy/grossdomesticproductgdp/; **475 European Commission:** Based on data from Eurostat Database, Eurostat, European Commission; **477 Office for National Statistics:** Based on data in Labour Force Survey, series YBWF, YBWG and YBWH, National Statistics, www.ons.gov.uk/employmentandlabourmarket/peoplenotinwork/unemployment/; **479 European Commission:** Based on data in AMECO Database, European Commission (to 1980), https://ec.europa.eu/info/business-economy-euro/indicators-statistics/economic-databases/macro-economic-database-ameco/ameco-database_en; **479 International Monetary Fund:** World Economic Outlook, IMF (April 2021), www.imf.org/en/Publications/SPROLLs/world-economic-outlook-databases; **483 Office for National Statistics:** Based on Time Series Data, series D7G7 and K8IA, ONS, www.ons.gov.uk/economy/inflationandpriceindices/; **488 Office for National Statistics:** Based on data from Office for National Statistics; **490 Office for National Statistics:** Based on data from Balance of Payments time series and series YBHA, ONS, www.ons.gov.uk/economy/nationalaccounts/balance

ofpayments/datasets/balanceofpayments; www.ons.gov.uk/economy/grossdomesticproductgdp/timeseries/ybha/ukea; **491 Bank of England:** Based on data in Statistical Interactive Database, Bank of England, www.bankofengland.co.uk/boeapps/iadb/; **497 Office for National Statistics:** UK National Accounts, The Blue Book: 2020, ONS, www.ons.gov.uk/economy/grossdomesticproductgdp/compendium/unitedkingdomnationalaccountsthebluebook/2020; **497 Office for National Statistics:** UK National Accounts, The Blue Book: 2020, ONS, www.ons.gov.uk/economy/grossdomesticproductgdp/compendium/unitedkingdomnationalaccountsthebluebook/2020; and series QWND, ONS; **501 Bank of England:** Based on data from Millennium of Macroeconomic Data, Bank of England, www.bankofengland.co.uk/statistics/research-datasets; **501 Office for National Statistics:** ONS time series explorer, ONS), www.ons.gov.uk/timeseriestool; **501 International Monetary Fund:** World Economic Outlook Database, IMF (April 2021), www.imf.org/en/Publications/SPROLLS/world-economic-outlookdatabases#sort=%40imfdate%20descending. Data from 2021 based on forecasts; **508 Macmillan Publishers:** J. M. Keynes, The General Theory of Employment, Interest and Money, Macmillan (1967), p. 9; **521 International Monetary Fund:** World Economic Outlook Database, IMF (April 2021) www.imf.org/en/Publications/SPROLLS/world-economic-outlook-databases; data from 2021 based on forecasts; **523 Oxford University Press:** Adapted from Dosi G, Pereira M C, Roventini A and Virgillito M E, Causes and consequences of hysteresis: aggregate demand, productivity, and employment. Industrial and Corporate Change, Volume 27, Issue 6 (December 2018), pp. 1015–44, https://doi.org/10.1093/icc/dty010; **525 Macmillan Publishers:** J. M. Keynes, The General Theory of Employment, Interest and Money, Macmillan (1967), pp. 358–9; **538 European Commission:** Based on data from Business and Consumer Surveys, European Commission, DGECFIN, http://ec.europa.eu/economy_finance/db_indicators/surveys/time_series/index_en.htm; **539 European Commission:** Based on data in AMECO Database, European Commission, DGECFIN (May 2021), http://ec.europa.eu/economy_finance/ameco/user/serie/SelectSerie.cfm; **551 European Commission:** Based on data in AMECO Database, European Commission, DGECFIN (May 2021), http://ec.europa.eu/economy_finance/db_indicators/ameco/index_en.htm; figures from 2021 based on forecasts; **554 Office for National Statistics:** Based on data in Quarterly National Accounts, series IHYR and KG7T, ONS, www.ons.gov.uk/economy/grossdomesticproductgdp/; **555 Office for National Statistics:** Based on data from National Balance Sheet and series YBHA and HABN, National Statistics, www.ons.gov.uk/economy/nationalaccounts/uksectoraccounts/datasets/thenationalbalancesheetestimates; www.ons.gov.uk/economy/grossdomesticproductgdp/; **556 Office for National Statistics:** Based on data from Preliminary UK National Balance Sheet Estimates and series HABN, National Statistics, www.ons.gov.uk/economy/nationalaccounts/uksectoraccounts/datasets/preliminaryuknationalbalancesheetestimates; www.ons.gov.uk/economy/grossdomesticproductgdp/timeseries/habn/ukea?referrer=search&searchTerm=habn; **566 Bank of England:** Based on data in Bankstats, Table B1.4, Bank of England (29 March 2021), www.bankofengland.co.uk/statistics/tables; **569 Bank of England:** (i) Data showing liabilities of banks and building societies based on series LPMALOA and RPMTBJF (up to the end of 2009) and RPMB3UQ (from 2010) from Statistical Interactive Database, Bank of England (data published 2 June 2021, not seasonally adjusted), www.bankofengland.co.uk/boeapps/iadb/; **569 Office for National Statistics:** GDP data from Quarterly National Accounts series YBHA, Office for National Statistics (GDP figures are the sum of the latest four quarters), www.ons.gov.uk/economy/grossdomesticproductgdp/timeseries/ybha/qna; **573 Bank of England:** Based on data from Statistical Interactive Database, Bank of England series LPMVUJD (up to 2010) and LPMB8GO (data published 29 March 2021), www.bankofengland.co.uk/boeapps/iadb/; **573 Office for National Statistics:** Series YBHA, National Statistics, www.ons.gov.uk/economy/grossdomesticproductgdp/timeseries/ybha/; **577 Bank of England:** Bankstats Table B1.1.3, Bank of England (6 April 2021), www.bankofengland.co.uk/statistics/tables; **579 Bank of England:** Based on data from Statistical Interactive Database, series LPMBL22, Bank of England (9 April 2021), www.bankofengland.co.uk/boeapps/iadb/; **582 Bank of England:** Based on data from Statistical Interactive Database, series IUMABEDR and IUMASOIA, Bank of England (9 April 2021), www.bankofengland.co.uk/boeapps/iadb/; **584 Bank of England:** Based on data in Bankstats, Tables A1.1.1 and A2.2.1, Bank of England (29 March 2021), www.bankofengland.co.uk/statistics/tables; **584 Bank of England:** Based on data in Bankstats, Table A2.3, Bank of England (29 March 2021), www.bankofengland.co.uk/statistics/tables; **586 Bank of England:** Based on series LPMBL22 (reserves), LPMAVAB (notes and coin) and LPMAUYN (M4) from Statistical Interactive Database, Bank of England (29 March 2021, seasonally adjusted except for reserves), www.bankofengland.co.uk/boeapps/iadb/; **588 Bank of England:** Statistical Interactive Database, Series LPMVQJW, Bank of England (29 March 2021, seasonally adjusted), www.bankofengland.co.uk/boeapps/iadb/; **590 Bank of England:** Based on data in Bankstats, Table A3.2, Bank of England (29 March 2021); **596 Bank of England:** Based on data from Statistical Interactive Database, series IUMABEDR, IUMASOIA, IUMZID2, IUMALNZC, IUMTLMV, Bank of England (9 April 2021), http://www.bankofengland.co.uk/boeapps/iadb/; **608 Bank of England:** Statistical Interactive Database, series LPQVQJW, Bank of England (2 June 2021), www.bankofengland.co.uk/boeapps/iadb/; **608 Office for National Statistics:** Quarterly National Accounts, series IHYO, Office for National Statistics, www.ons.gov.uk/economy/grossdomesticproductgdp/; **609 Bank of England:** Statistical Interactive Database, series

LPQVVHK, LPQVVHQ, LPQVVHW and LPQVQJW, Bank of England, (2 June 2021) www.bankofengland.co.uk/boeapps/iadb/; **609 Office for National Statistics:** Quarterly National Accounts, series IHYO, Office for National Statistics, www.ons.gov.uk/economy/grossdomesticproductgdp/; **610 Bank of England:** Statistical Interactive Database, series LPMAVAB and LPQAUYN, Bank of England (February 2021), www.bankofengland.co.uk/boeapps/iadb/; **610 Office for National Statistics:** Quarterly National Accounts, series YBHA, Office for National Statistics, www.ons.gov.uk/economy/grossdomesticproductgdp/; **615 International Monetary Fund:** World Economic Outlook Update, IMF (January 2021), p. 10, www.imf.org/en/Publications/WEO/Issues/2021/01/26/2021-world-economic-outlook-update; **623 Bank of England:** Statistical Interactive Database, series LPQVWNQ and LPQVWNV, Bank of England (data published 2 June 2021, seasonally adjusted), www.bankofengland.co.uk/boeapps/iadb; **623 Office for National Statistics:** Series YBHA, Office for National Statistics, www.ons.gov.uk/economy/grossdomesticproductgdp/; **644 Office for National Statistics:** Producer Price Inflation, National Statistics, www.ons.gov.uk/economy/inflationandpriceindices/. Figures up to 2009 based on series K646 and from 2010 on series GHIP; **695 International Monetary Fund:** World Economic Outlook, IMF (April 2021), www.imf.org/external/pubs/ft/weo/2020/02/weodata/groups.htm; **696 European Commission:** Based on data from AMECO database, Tables 16.3 and 18.1 (European Commission, DG ECFIN); **697 The National Archives:** Public Finances Databank, Office for Budget Responsibility (March 2021), https://obr.uk/data/; **697 The National Archives:** Public Finances Databank, Office for Budget Responsibility (March 2021), https://obr.uk/data/; **699 Bank of England:** Based on data from Millennium of Macroeconomic Data (Bank of England) for 1900–1945, www.bankofengland.co.uk/statistics/research-datasets; **699 Office for National Statistics:** GZSN, ANSQ, ANLY, ANLO, EBFT and YBHA (ONS) from 1946 onwards, www.ons.gov.uk/economy/governmentpublicsectorand taxes/publicsectorfinance/; **701 International Monetary Fund:** World Economic Outlook, IMF (April 2021), www.imf.org/external/pubs/ft/weo/2020/02/weodata/groups.htm; **704 International Monetary Fund:** Fiscal Monitor: Database of Country Fiscal Measures in Response to the COVID-19 Pandemic, IMF, www.imf.org/en/Topics/imf-and-covid19/Fiscal-Policies-Database-in-Response-to-COVID-19; **705 International Monetary Fund:** Based on data from IMF World Economic Outlook Database and Fiscal Monitor, Table A3, IMF (April 2021), www.imf.org/en/Publications/; **709 The New Statesman:** Vince Cable, 'Keynes would be on our side', New Statesman (12 January 2011), www.newstatesman.com/economy/2011/01/investment-keynesessay; **711 European Commission:** Based on data in AMECO Database, European Commission (May 2021), https://ec.europa.eu/info/business-economy-euro/indicators-statistics/economic-databases/macro-economic-database-ameco/ameco-database_en; **718 Federal Reserve Bank of St. Louis:** Based on data in Federal Reserve Economic Data, Federal Reserve Bank of St Louis, https://fred.stlouisfed.org/; **721 Federal Reserve Bank of St. Louis:** Based on Federal Reserve Bank; **721 European Central Bank:** Based on European Central Bank; **721 Bank of England:** Based on Bank of England; **723 Bank of England:** Based on data from Statistical Interactive Database, series YWWB9R9, Bank of England (18 June 2021), www.bankofengland.co.uk/boeapps/iadb/; **725 Bank of England:** Based on series IUMABEDR (Bank Rate) and IUMTLMV (mortgage rate) from Statistical Interactive Database, Bank of England (7 June 2021), www.bankofengland.co.uk/boeapps/iadb/; **726 European Central Bank:** Based on data in Statistical Data Warehouse, ECB, https://sdw.ecb.europa.eu/browse.do?node=9691294; **737 Bank of England:** Based on data from A Millennium of Macroeconomic Data (Bank of England) 1700–1948 available at https://www.bankofengland.co.uk/statistics/research-datasets; **737 Office for National Statistics:** Based on series ABMI and IHYP, National Statistics, 1949 to 2020 www.ons.gov.uk/economy/grossdomesticproductgdp/; **737 International Monetary Fund:** Based on World Economic Outlook, IMF (April 2021), 2021 www.imf.org/en/Publications/WEO/Issues/2021/03/23/world-economic-outlook-april-2021; **739 European Commission:** Based on data in AMECO Database, European Commission, https://ec.europa.eu/info/business-economy-euro/indicators-statistics/economic-databases/macro-economic-database-ameco/ameco-database_en; **739 International Monetary Fund:** World Economic Outlook, IMF (April 2021), 1980 www.imf.org/en/Publications/SPROLLS/world-economic-outlook-databases; **739 European Commission:** Based on data from AMECO database, European Commission, DGECFIN; **740 International Monetary Fund:** Authors' calculations based on data from World Economic Outlook Database, International Monetary Fund (April 2021); **741 Organisation for Economic Co-operation and Development:** Based on data in OECDStat, OECD (2021), https://stats.oecd.org/viewhtml.aspx?datasetcode=PDB_GR&&lang=en; **742 Organisation for Economic Co-operation and Development:** Based on data in OECDStat, OECD (2021), https://stats.oecd.org/viewhtml.aspx?datasetcode=PDB_GR&&lang=en; **742 Organisation for Economic Co-operation and Development:** Based on data in OECDStat, OECD (2021), https://stats.oecd.org/viewhtml.aspx?datasetcode=PDB_GR&&lang=en; **744 European Commission:** Based on data in AMECO Database, European Commission (May 2021), https://ec.europa.eu/info/business-economy-euro/indicators-statistics/economic-databases/macro-economic-database-ameco/ameco-database_en; **746 Office for National Statistics:** Based on data from Capital stocks, consumption of fixed capital, 2020 and series YBHA, National Statistics, www.ons.gov.uk/economy/nationalaccounts/uksectoraccounts/bulletins/capitalstocks consumptionoffixedcapital/2020; https://www.ons.gov.

uk/economy/grossdomesticproductgdp/; **747 European Commission:** Based on data from AMECO Database, European Commission, https://ec.europa.eu/info/business-economy-euro/indicators-statistics/economic-databases/macro-economic-database-ameco/ameco-database_en; **755 Office for National Statistics:** Based on data in Human Capital Estimates, Office for National Statistics (October 2019); **759 International Monetary Fund:** Based on data from World Economic Outlook Database, IMF, www.imf.org/external/ns/cs.aspx?id=28; **759 European Commission:** AMECO Database, European Commission, https://ec.europa.eu/info/business-economy-euro/indicators-statistics/economic-databases/macro-economic-database-ameco/ameco-database_en; **764 European Commission:** Based on data from AMECO database, European Commission (2021); **765 Organisation for Economic Co-operation and Development:** Gross Domestic Spending on R&D, OECD (2021), https://data.oecd.org/rd/gross-domestic-spending-on-r-d.htm; **766 Department for Education:** Based on data from Apprenticeships and traineeships, Department for Education (6 April 2021), https://explore-education-statistics.service.gov.uk/find-statistics/apprenticeships-and-traineeships; **773 World Trade Organization:** Merchandise exports data, WTO Data Portal, WTO (2021) https://data.wto.org/; **773 The World Bank Group:** World GDP data, series NY.GDP.MKTP.CD, World Bank (2021), http://data.worldbank.org/indicator/NY.GDP.MKTP.CD; **773 International Monetary Fund:** World Economic Outlook, IMF (April 2021), www.imf.org/en/Publications/WEO/Issues/2021/03/23/world-economic-outlook-april-2021; **773 The World Bank Group:** World Bank, series TG.VAL.TOTL.GD.ZS (2021), https://data.worldbank.org/indicator/TG.VAL.TOTL.GD.ZS; **774 The World Bank Group:** World Bank, series BG.GSR.NFSV.GD.ZS (2021), https://data.worldbank.org/indicator/BG.GSR.NFSV.GD.ZS; **774 World Trade Organization:** Based on data from WTO Data Portal, WTO (2021), https://data.wto.org/; **775 World Trade Organization:** Based on data in World Trade Statistical Review 2020, WTO (2020), Statistical Table A4, Chapter VI, www.wto.org/english/res_e/statis_e/wts2020_e/wts20_toc_e.htm; **775 World Trade Organization:** Based on data from WTO Data Portal, WTO (2021), https://data.wto.org/; **776 United Nations Conference on Trade and Development:** Based on data from UNCTADStat, UNCTAD (2021); **777 World Trade Organization:** World Trade Statistical Review 2020, Table A6, (WTO); **777 World Trade Organization:** Trade Profiles, WTO, www.wto.org/english/res_e/statis_e/trade_profiles_list_e.htm; **782 European Commission:** Based on data in AMECO Database, European Commission, DGECFIN, (May 2021), https://ec.europa.eu/economy_finance/ameco/user/serie/SelectSerie.cfm; **794 World Trade Organization:** 'Global policy without democracy' (speech by Pascal Lamy, EU Trade Commissioner, given in 2001); **805 Oxford University Press:** C. Allen, M. Gasiorek and A. Smith, 'The competition effects of the single market in Europe', Economic Policy (1998); **808 The National Archives:** Adapted from EU Referendum: HM Treasury analysis key facts, HM Treasury (18 April 2016) (available at https://www.gov.uk/government/news/eu-referendum-treasury-analysis-key-facts); **808 Office for National Statistics:** Based on data from ONS Time Series Data, series IKBK, IKBL, ABMI, www.ons.gov.uk/economy/grossdomesticproduct-gdp/timeseries/ikbk/ukea; **810 Organisation for Economic Co-operation and Development:** The Economic Consequences of Brexit: A taxing decision, OECD (25 April 2016), www.oecd.org/economy/the-economic-consequences-of-brexit-a-taxingdecision.htm; **816 Office for National Statistics:** Based on data from ONS, series J5II, KTMY and YBHA, www.ons.gov.uk/economy/grossdomesticproduct-gdp/timeseries/ybha/edp4; and forecasts for 2021 and 2022 from OBR Databank; **817 Bank for International Settlements:** Based on data from Effective exchange rate indices, Bank for International Settlements, www.bis.org/statistics/eer.htm?m=6%7C187; **817 Bank for International Settlements:** Based on data from Effective exchange rate indices, Bank for International Settlements, www.bis.org/statistics/eer.htm; **817 The World Bank Group:** Series NY.GDP.DEFL.KD.ZG, World Bank, https://data.worldbank.org/indicator/NY.GDP.DEFL.KD.ZG; **819 Office for National Statistics:** Based on data from ONS series D28J, D28K, D28M, D28N and AA6H, www.ons.gov.uk/economy/nationalaccounts/balanceofpayments/; **832 Bank of England:** Based on data from Statistical Interactive Database, Bank of England, series XUMAERD (1 April 2021), www.bankofengland.co.uk/boeapps/iadb/; **832 European Central Bank:** Data from Federal Reserve Bank and European Central Bank; **841 Bank for International Settlements:** Based on data Effective Exchange Rate Indices, Bank for International Settlements; **842 Bank for International Settlements:** Based on data from Bank for International Settlements; **843 Bank of England:** Exchange rate calculations based on bilateral sterling exchange rates from Statistical Interactive Database, Bank of England, https://www.bankofengland.co.uk/boeapps/iadb/; **843 International Monetary Fund:** Inflation rate calculations based on GDP deflator data from World Economic Outlook Database, IMF (April 2021), www.imf.org/en/Publications/SPROLLs/world-economic-outlook-databases#sort=%40imfdate%20descending; **849 Bank for International Settlements:** Based on data from Monthly Effective Exchange Rate Indices (narrow), Bank for International Settlements (April 2021); **851 Theodore William Schultz:** Quoted by Theodore Schultz(1979); **852 The World Bank Group:** Series NE.TRD.GNFS.ZS, World Bank, http://data.worldbank.org/indicator/NE.TRD.GNFS.ZS; **853 Bank of England:** Based on series RPMTBFF, RPMTBFM, RPMTBFT (up to end of 2009) and RPMB3OM, RPMB3TM and RPMB3WM (from 2010) from Statistical Interactive Database, Bank of England (data published 2 June 2021), www.bankofengland.co.uk/boeapps/iadb/; **856 Office for National Statistics:** Based on data from ONS, series NIJI and NLDU, www.ons.gov.uk/

economy/governmentpublicsectorandtaxes/publicspending/; **854 International Monetary Fund:** Based on data from World Economic Outlook Database, IMF (April 2021), www.imf.org/external/pubs/ft/weo/2019/02/weodata/weorept.aspx?pr.x=70&pr.y=11&sy=1995&ey=2022&scsm=1&ssd=1&sort=country&ds=&br=1&c=924%2C111&s=BCA_NGDPD&grp=0&a=; **858 Bank for International Settlements:** Bank for International Settlements, www.bis.org/statistics/eer.htm?m=6%7C381%7C676; **858 Organisation for Economic Co-operation and Development:** OECD Data, OECD, https://data.oecd.org/; and Federal Reserve Economic Data, Federal Reserve Bank, St. Louis, https://fred.stlouisfed.org/; **858 International Monetary Fund:** World Economic Outlook database, IMF, www.imf.org/en/Publications/SPROLLs/world-economic-outlook-databases#sort=%40imfdate%20descending; **865 European Commission:** Based on data from AMECO database (European Commission, DGECFIN); **865 International Monetary Fund:** Based on data in World Economic Outlook Database, IMF (April 2021), www.imf.org/en/Publications/SPROLLs/world-economic-outlook-databases#sort=%40imfdate%20descending; **866 International Monetary Fund:** Based on data in AMECO Database, European Commission, DGECFIN (May 2021), http://ec.europa.eu/economy_finance/db_indicators/ameco/index_en.htm; **867 European Commission:** AMECO database, European Commission, DGECFIN (May 2021), http://ec.europa.eu/economy_finance/ameco/user/serie/SelectSerie.cfm; **868 The World Bank Group:** Based on data from World Bank, series NY.GNP.MKTP.PP. KD, http://data.worldbank.org/indicator/NY.GDP.MKTP.PP.KD; **869 The World Bank Group:** Based on data from Databank (World Bank); **871 The World Bank Group:** Based on data from Databank series NY.GNP.PCAP.PP.CD, World Bank, http://databank.worldbank.org/data/home.aspx; **877 The World Bank Group:** Based on data from World Bank Commodity Price Data (The Pink Sheet), Commodity Markets, World Bank, www.worldbank.org/en/research/commodity-markets; **881 The World Bank Group:** Based on data from Databank (World Bank); **882 World Scientific:** Paul Krugman, 'Increasing returns in a comparative advantage world', in Robert M. Stern, Comparative Advantage, Growth, and the Gains from Trade and Globalization (World Scientific, 2011), Chapter 7, p. 45; **884 The World Bank Group:** Based on data from Databank, series DT.DOD.DECT.GN.ZS, World Bank, http://databank.worldbank.org/data/home.aspx; **885 The World Bank Group:** Based on data from Databank, series DT.TDS.DECT.GN.ZS, World Bank, http://databank.worldbank.org/data/home.aspx; **890 Organisation for Economic Co-operation and Development:** Based on data from Net ODA, OECD Data, OECD (2021), https://data.oecd.org/oda/net-oda.htm; **Appendix 1 2 Office for National Statistics:** Based on Time Series Data, series MGSC, ONS (2021), www.ons.gov.uk/employmentandlabourmarket/peoplenotinwork/unemployment/timeseries/mgsc/unem?referrer=search&searchTerm=mgsc; **Appendix 1 3 Office for National Statistics:** Based on Time Series Data, series MGSC, ONS, www.ons.gov.uk/employmentandlabourmarket/peoplenotinwork/unemployment/timeseries/mgsc/unem; **Appendix 1 3 Office for National Statistics:** Based on Time Series Data, series MGSC and YBEZ, ONS, www.ons.gov.uk/employmentandlabourmarket/peoplenotinwork/unemployment/; **Appendix 1 3 Office for National Statistics:** Based on Time Series Data, series YBEZ, ONS (2021), www.ons.gov.uk/economy/grossdomesticproductgdp/timeseries/ybez/ukea?referrer=search&searchTerm=ybez; **Appendix 1 4 Office for National Statistics:** Household Disposable Income and Inequality, UK, 2019/20 – Reference Tables, Table 13, ONS (2021); **Appendix 1 4 Office for National Statistics:** Household Disposable Income and Inequality, UK, 2019/20, Reference Tables, Table 13, ONS (2021); **Appendix 1 4 Office for National Statistics:** The Effects of Taxes and Benefits on Household Income: Financial Year Ending 2019, Table 2, ONS (2020), www.ons.gov.uk/peoplepopulationandcommunity/personalandhouseholdfinances/incomeandwealth/datasets/theeffectsoftaxesandbenefitsonhouseholdincomefinancialyearending2014; **Appendix 1 6 Office for National Statistics:** Time Series data, series K22A (ONS, 2021), www.ons.gov.uk/economy/economicoutputandproductivity/output/timeseries/k22a/diop?referrer=search&searchTerm=k22a; **Appendix 1 11 Office for National Statistics:** Based on Time Series Data, series MGSC, ONS, www.ons.gov.uk/employmentandlabourmarket/peoplenotinwork/unemployment/timeseries/mgsc/unem; **894 John Sloman:** Courtesy of John Sloman.

Index

Note: emboldened page numbers refer to pages containing definitions